The 1989 Dow Jones-Irwin Business and Investment Almanac

The 1989 DOW JONES-IRWIN Business and Investment Almanac

Edited by

Sumner N. Levine
State University of New York
at Stony Brook
and Editor
Financial Analyst's Handbook
and
The Investment Manager's Handbook

Executive Editor
Caroline Levine

DOW JONES-IRWIN
Homewood, Illinois 60430

Sponsoring editor: Richard A. Luecke
Project editor: Jean Roberts
Production manager: Carma W. Fazio
Compositor: Arcata Graphics/Kingsport
Typeface: 8/9 Caledonia
Printer: Arcata Graphics/Kingsport

"The Library of Congress has catalogued this serial publication as follows:"

The . . . Dow Jones-Irwin business and investment almanac. —
1982- — Homewood, Ill. : Dow Jones-Irwin, c1982-

v. : ill. ; 24 cm.

Annual.
Editor: Sumner N. Levine.
Continues: Dow Jones-Irwin business almanac.
ISSN 0733-2610 = The Dow Jones-Irwin business and investment almanac

1. Business—Periodicals. 2. Investments—United States—Periodicals. 3. Corporations—United States—Finance—Periodicals. 4. United States—Economic conditions—1971- —Periodicals. I. Levine, Sumner N. II. Dow Jones-Irwin. III. Title: Dow Jones Irwin business and investment almanac. IV. Title: Business and investment almanac.
HF5003.D68a 330.9'005 82-643830
AACR 2 MARC-S

Library of Congress [8711]

Printed in the United States of America

1 2 3 4 5 6 7 8 9 0 K 5 4 3 2 1 0 9 8

Preface

This 13th edition of the annual *Dow Jones-Irwin Business and Investment Almanac* contains a number of new features in response to the rapidly changing business and investment scene as well as updates on our standard features.

The editor and publisher are, of course, pleased with the acceptance of the *Dow Jones-Irwin Business and Investment Almanac* as a standard and unique reference for the business and investment community. As always, we continue to invite suggestions from our readers. All suggestions should be sent to: *Dow Jones-Irwin Business and Investment Almanac,* P.O. Box D, Setauket, New York 11733.

Sumner N. Levine
Editor

References to companies, securities, and other investment information do not constitute a recommendation or endorsement.

Contents

The 1989 Dow Jones-Irwin Business and Investment Almanac

Business in Review

September 1987—September 1988

September 1987*

8 Interest rates are expected to climb further following Friday's rise in the discount and prime rates. Analysts say the Fed, which raised its discount rate to 6% from 5½%, will push rates higher before year end to show Chairman Greenspan's resolve to fight inflation. But some investors fear a tighter Fed policy may spell the end of the bull stock market.

OPEC's fragile stability is being threatened by the growing political rift between Saudi Arabia and Iran, the two largest producers. As a result, some analysts say, oil prices may fall to about $16 a barrel in the coming months from about $19.30 currently.

The Hunt brothers are proposing to sell major parts of their two main energy firms to settle a multibillion-dollar legal battle with bank creditors. It is the Hunts' first attempt in months to reach an out-of-court pact.

Brazil's finance minister plans to hold talks soon with Mexico and Argentina on his radical new debt proposal. The meeting revives creditors' fears of a joint moratorium, or even default, by big debtor nations.

Allegis agreed to sell Hilton International to Ladbroke Group of Britain for $1.07 billion, the first step in a divestiture program. Allegis is expected to post only a modest gain on Hilton, but analysts said other non-airline assets may bring big returns.

The jobless rate stayed at 6% in August, indicating the economy continued to grow modestly. A survey of purchasing agents also said the economy expanded last month.

Bond-rating agencies are preparing to give the coveted triple-A rating to securities backed by junk bonds.

9 Financial markets were roiled by fears the Fed has begun a long period of rising interest rates. The Dow Jones industrials skidded as much as 62 points before rallying to close at 2545.12, off 16.26. Long-term bond prices finished down 1¾ points, fueling speculation the Fed will need to calm inflation worries. The dollar was relatively stable, aided by central bank intervention.

Brazil's finance minister dropped his radical foreign-debt proposal after Treasury Secretary Baker rejected it as a "nonstarter." Meanwhile, Argentina may take a tougher stance on its foreign debt following the Peronist victory in Sunday's election.

The Big Three auto makers are making another push into Europe, aided by the weaker dollar. Ford and Chrysler separately announced plans to resume car exports next year.

10 Banking regulators agreed to pump $970 million into First City Bancorp. of Texas and turn over management to a group led by ex-Chicago banker A. Robert Abboud. The federal bailout could be the second-biggest in U.S. history, after Continental Illinois. The Abboud group plans to raise at least $500 million in added capital through stock offers.

Ford recalled 4.3 million vehicles to correct fuel-system defects that have caused 230 engine fires and injured 16 people. The move, though not costly, is a major embarrassment for the nation's No. 2 auto maker.

Digital Equipment unveiled a series of minicomputers and workstations that analysts said will further the company's strong growth.

Toshiba announced steps to prevent illegal technology sales to the Soviet bloc. The move, plus tougher Japanese export controls, may induce Congress to ease proposed sanctions against Toshiba, Senate aides said.

Stock and bond prices recovered slightly, helped by a stronger dollar. The Dow Jones industrials closed up 4.15, at 2549.27, after moving in a fairly narrow range. Some long-term Treasury bonds rose nearly ¼ point. Oil surged on Mideast tensions.

U.S. auto makers have trimmed third-quarter production estimates only slightly from a month ago. But fore-

---

*The cut-off date for Business in Review is usually Labor Day because of our production schedule. Since the last entry in the previous *Almanac* was September 4, 1987, the current entry commences September 8, 1987.

casts for the fourth quarter indicate that sharper reductions may be needed unless sales pick up.

11 The Drexel inquiry appears to have expanded far beyond last year's insider-trading case involving Ivan Boesky. Federal investigators are now focusing on a number of transactions involving the investment bank and the head of its junk bond operations, Michael Milken.

First City Bancorp. of Texas faces major uncertainties despite new management and a $970 million federal bailout. The main issues are Texas's ailing economy and questions about whether the bailout is big enough.

Mortgage rates are surging again, with fixed-rate loans jumping an average ½ point, to nearly 11%, in the past two weeks. Some economists expect rates to increase further.

An OPEC committee acknowledged that members are exceeding their oil-production quotas. But the panel, meeting in Vienna, adopted a low-key strategy for the problem.

U.S. businesses plan to spend 2.5% more on plant and equipment this year, less than the 3.1% increase they expected three months before. Still, economists remain fairly bullish on the outlook for capital spending.

14 The trade deficit grew to a record $16.47 billion in July, though analysts said the figure isn't as gloomy as it looks. Much of the gain resulted from a surge in oil imports as Mideast tensions grew. Still, the gap indicates that a turnaround in trade is a long way off.

The dollar rallied despite Friday's trade report, making some traders more bullish. The currency's rise also boosted bond and stock prices.

Saudi Arabia's oil minister said the kingdom wouldn't resume its role as OPEC's "swing producer" to curb overproduction. He also ruled out pressing Persian Gulf neighbors to stick to their oil quotas.

Ford has tentatively accepted the UAW's request to guarantee a fixed number of jobs at every U.S. plant, sources said, though differences remain. Meanwhile, Chrysler is trying to avoid a strike in Canada.

15 Chrysler's Canadian unit braced for a strike after the Canadian Auto Workers union rejected a new contract offer. Meanwhile, Ford and the UAW continued contract talks as a midnight strike deadline loomed.

16 Bond prices tumbled amid renewed weakness in the dollar, deepening a bond market slump that analysts say could last for years. Some 30-year Treasury bonds slid more than 1½ points, erasing all of last week's gains. Stock prices also skidded, as the Dow Jones industrials fell 46.46 points, to 2566.58.

Honda Motor is expected to announce tomorrow that it will build a second U.S. assembly plant in Ohio, escalating its already aggressive expansion strategy in the U.S.

Retail sales surged 1.3% in August, led by a jump in auto purchases. Industrial production rose just 0.3%. Auto sales in early September slid 51.9% from a strong year earlier.

17 Stock prices skidded in the final hour of trading, taking their cue from a volatile bond market. The Dow Jones industrials closed down 36.39, at 2530.19. Treasury bonds swung sharply, though most interest rates wound up little changed. The dollar firmed despite continued bearishness about the currency.

Honda Motor plans to build cars in the U.S. and export them, sources said. Such a move would be another first by a Japanese auto maker.

The industrial operating rate rose to 81% of capacity in August, the highest level since November 1984.

18 Ford and the UAW reached a tentative contract agreement that includes sweeping job guarantees. The union now will try to win similar terms from ailing GM, which may indicate if job security becomes a major issue in other industries. Meanwhile, a strike at Chrysler's Canada unit appeared over as both sides agreed on a new contract.

PepsiCo signed an accord to open two Pizza Hut restaurants in Moscow, making it the first U.S. company to form a joint venture with the Soviets. It also would be the first U.S. restaurant to operate in the country.

21 The Ford-UAW job security plan negotiated last week is less sweeping than initially thought and doesn't fully protect all workers from layoffs, an analysis shows. Still, GM will have difficulty accepting such a program.

Chrysler's Canadian workers accepted a new three-year contract, ending a six-day strike.

Second-quarter GNP growth was revised upward to a 2.5% rate. Meanwhile, White House chief economist Beryl Sprinkel, who announced he would resign in November, said that interest rates are "much higher than can be justified by inflation."

The Fed's policy panel is expected to leave its credit strategy unchanged at tomorrow's meeting. But analysts say rates may rise soon anyway.

An oil-import fee is being urged by a new Harvard study to counteract growing U.S. dependence on foreign supplies. The report, to be released today, lashes Reagan's energy policies and is likely to revive national debate over the import-fee issue.

Japan's GNP showed no growth in the quarter ended June 30, though economists remain optimistic that the Japanese economy will strengthen led by rising domestic demand.

22 Stock prices fell below the 2500 level amid inflation worries, tumbling 31.82 points to close at 2492.82. Bond prices reversed field after a strong start, winding up with modest declines. The dollar fell sharply from its morning highs.

Greenspan said there is "very little" evidence that inflation is accelerating. The Federal Reserve Board's policy arm meets today to set monetary policy for the coming weeks.

Consumer spending rose a brisk 1.5% in August, the biggest increase in six months, reflecting strong car sales. But many economists expect spending to slow in the fourth quarter as consumers rebuild their savings. The nation's savings rate last month fell to 1.8% of after-tax income.

The FSLIC has incurred operating losses totaling $1.3 billion by taking control of failing thrifts and allowing them to stay open, a General Accounting Office study concluded.

23 Stocks rebounded sharply, pushing the Dow Jones industrials up a record 75.23 points, to 2568.05. The rally, fueled by a stronger dollar and bond market, snapped a five-day decline in which the industrials lost over 120 points. The dollar rose 0.9% against the yen, while some long-term Treasury bonds reached the highest level in a week.

24 Consumer prices rose 0.5% in August, or at a 5.8% annual rate, due to a surge in energy and housing costs. The increase, the sharpest since January, renewed worries about inflation. Meanwhile, durable goods orders fell 3.1% last month, the first decline since January.

Bond prices and the dollar weakened in reaction to the economic reports, though stocks finished higher. The Dow Jones Industrial Average rose 17.62 points, to 2585.67.

Treasury Secretary Baker said the U.S. would back a major boost in the World Bank's capital and lending. But any increase, which would bolster Baker's Third World debt strategy, faces opposition in Congress.

Brazil plans to present a more accommodating debt proposal to foreign banks tomorrow, though major differences remain. Brazil's new plan is said to suggest that a large amount of debt be converted to exit bonds.

West Germany is expected to come under further pressure to stimulate its economy when finance ministers from the Group of Seven meet Saturday. Officials hinted they don't plan any significant action on the dollar.

U.S. auto sales slid 38.3% in mid-September despite generous buyer-incentive programs. The decline reinforced worries that the 1987 car market may be weaker than expected.

25 Bond prices skidded after a report that Japan is tightening credit sparked worries about higher U.S. interest rates. Some actively traded 30-year Treasury bonds declined over 1¼ points. The Japan report also pushed the dollar lower in quiet trading. Stock prices eased as well, as the Dow Jones industrials closed down 19.25 points, at 2566.42.

Reagan came under pressure to sign a budget and debt bill approved by Congress this week. But the president indicated he may still veto the measure, saying it would force him to choose between defense cuts and tax increases, both of which he opposes.

London share prices tumbled after Britain reported an unexpectedly wide merchandise trade deficit for July. The report heightened fears of higher U.K. interest rates.

28 Japan assured other members of the Group of Seven that it hasn't begun a major credit tightening. The group, which met in Washington, also reaffirmed its dollar exchange-rate targets. Confusion about Japan's policy may help push up U.S. interest rates, analysts say, while the dollar pact is being blamed partly for recent swings in interest rates.

General Motors unveiled aggressively big price increases on 1988-model cars, apparently in a bid to bolster revenue and earnings.

OPEC production has plunged recently in response to a sharp drop in global oil demand. If the lower output continues, some OPEC members may try to seek an increase in the group's benchmark price of $18 a barrel.

29 Revlon offered to buy the stake that Salomon plans to sell to investor Warren Buffett. The cosmetics giant said if Salomon turns it down, Revlon might seek to buy up to 25% of the investment firm in the open market. Sources said Salomon's accord to sell stock to Buffett was designed to block Revlon from becoming a big shareholder in the firm.

Avis was sold for the fifth time in four years, this time to its employees. Avis's ESOP bought the nation's No. 2 car rental firm from a Wesray Capital group for $750 million plus assumption of $1 billion in debt.

30 Bond prices tumbled as yields on long-term Treasury issues surged above 9¾%, the highest level in nearly two years. A heavy slate of government borrowing was cited for the slump, which came despite a sharp rise in the dollar. Stocks also fell on worries about the bond market, with the Dow Jones industrials off 10.93 points to 2590.57.

Henry Ford II died of complications from pneumonia. The death of the 70-year-old former Ford Motor chief won't affect the ownership structure of the No. 2 auto maker.

Victor Posner pleaded no contest to income tax evasion, ending a bitter, eight-year fight. The move by the financier, who could face up to 40 years in prison, may lead to the breakup of his business empire.

October 1987

1 Baker suggested that gold play a role in setting currency rates. The Treasury Secretary, speaking at the World Bank and IMF annual meetings, proposed that economic planning be based partly on "a basket of commodities." If accepted, the plan would help ensure that nations don't follow monetary policies that encourage inflation or discourage growth. The U.S. dollar firmed.

The secretary also called for a new IMF facility to help cushion debtor nations against higher interest rates. Separately, Japan is taking a role in helping resolve the debt crisis.

The index of leading indicators rose 0.6% in August, the seventh consecutive monthly increase. But some economists suggested the gain may overstate future growth. Separately, home sales rose 2.7% in August after increasing a strong 4% in July.

2 Stock prices plunged on interest rate worries, though computerized sell programs exaggerated the fall. The Dow Jones industrials plummeted a record 91.55 points, to 2548.63, though the percentage drop was only 3.47%. Sell signals from two influential forecasters helped knock the slack market off balance.

SEC Chairman Ruder suggested steps to reduce market volatility caused by program trading, including halts in trading in all markets.

Interest-rate fears grew in the U.S. as Bonn boosted an important rate and pressure continued in Tokyo for higher rates. Treasury bond prices staged a late rally despite concern short-term U.S. rates will soon rise, including banks' prime rates.

Saudi Arabia is considering a proposal to again link its oil prices to spot markets. A report of the possible Saudi move, which could undermine OPEC's fixed-price system, sent oil futures lower in feverish selling.

Several foreign car makers are raising prices on their 1988 U.S. models, reflecting more-powerful engines or more luxury options.

5 Stocks rallied as investors focused on corporate profits rather than the weaker dollar and bond market. The Dow Jones industrials rose 42.92, to 2639.20. Bonds were hurt partly by a surge in commodity prices.

Factory orders fell 1.7% in August, the first drop since January. Construction spending rose 1.6%, led by robust nonresidential building. The figures run counter to trends many economists see in both sectors.

Associated British Foods plans a hostile $951.2 million takeover bid for S & W Berisford. Separately, a breakup of Hill Samuel is expected.

Japan's brokerage fees will be cut Monday, likely slashing the profits of U.S. and European firms with seats on the Tokyo Stock Exchange.

6 Gold-oriented mutual funds rose an average 19.4% in the third quarter, far outpacing the 5.7% average gain for all equity mutual funds tracked by Lipper Analytical Services. Fixed-income funds fell an estimated 2.1%.

Ford joined Hertz's management in agreeing to buy the car rental firm from Allegis for $1.3 billion. The purchase is aimed at keeping Hertz as Ford's biggest customer. Allegis, meanwhile, will lose its chairman.

The jobless rate fell to 5.9% in September, the lowest level since November 1979. Also, the latest survey of purchasing agents indicates the economy grew in September and is poised for a strong fourth quarter.

7 Bond prices skidded to near their lows for this year, deepening the market's long slump. Traders cited a weaker dollar, higher commodity prices and growing signs that the U.S. and Japan may tighten credit further. Among active issues, the latest 30-year Treasury bond fell one point and its yield surged to 9.8%. Stock prices showed little change.

Investment advisers averaged a 35.4% return on stock picks for the first nine months of 1987, slightly behind the S&P index, a survey says.

The economy is expected to continue growing moderately next year but fall into a recession in 1989, according to a consensus forecast by an economists' association.

8 The prime rate rose to 9¼% from 8¾% at major banks, bringing the rate to its highest level in over 1½ years. Bankers expect further increases in the coming months. Most other short-term rates held steady, though long-term Treasury bond prices slumped as yields rose to near their highs for the year.

Stocks recovered partially from Tuesday's record loss. The Dow Jones industrials closed up 2.45 points, at 2551.08. The dollar was lower.

BankAmerica reached an accord with Japanese investors that will boost its capital a modest $350 million, but on onerous terms. Separately, an audit of the bank's foreign exchange operations found $26 million in unreconciled trading accounts.

Oil prices rebounded in the U.S. amid skepticism that Saudi Arabia would link its oil prices to spot markets. The kingdom officially denied such plans. OPEC, meanwhile, faces a choice of changing either its oil-price policy or production quotas.

GE said profit rose 16% in the third quarter, bolstered by results in financial services, aircraft engines, plastics and medical systems.

9 Bond prices slumped to their lowest levels this year as a surge in short-term interest rates rattled financial markets. Rates on six-month Treasury bills jumped to about 7.3%, while yields on 30-year bonds rose to 9⅞%. Fears of even higher rates sparked a sell-off in stocks. The Dow Jones industrials slid 34.44, to 2516.64. The dollar also fell.

Top Fed officials indicated they don't see any need now for raising the discount rate. But they acknowledged the policy could change if inflation fears worsen in financial markets.

GM and the UAW reached tentative agreement on a new three-year contract, apparently averting a strike once thought inevitable. Sources said the union won a contract similar to the one negotiated with Ford, despite GM's demands for major changes.

Major retailers posted only slight sales gains for September, citing high consumer debt, increased clothing prices and the absence of a big fashion trend. The month was especially disappointing for specialty stores.

Demand for single-family homes is starting to be hurt by rising interest rates, real estate executives say. Higher rates also are slowing activity in commercial real estate, they say.

12 Interest rates are expected to rise further as central banks try to quell inflation fears with tighter monetary policies. Meanwhile, the stock market's record slide last week renewed fears that some computerized trading could push prices even lower.

A group of top executives said it believes the economy will continue to grow at a 2.5% to 3% rate in 1987 and 1988 without a big rise in inflation or interest rates. But some on the Business Council are less optimistic about the inflation and rate outlook.

13 Salomon announced a broad restructuring that will slash fourth-quarter profit by up to $70 million. As expected, the securities firm will lay off 800 people and pull out of the slumping municipal bonds and money markets businesses. Other firms are expected to scramble for Salomon's huge tax-exempt business.

Chemical Bank plans to cut its British staff nearly 18% and reduce its activity in the Euromarkets. Chemical is the third major U.S. bank to cut its London staff recently.

UAW officials approved the new three-year contract negotiated last week with GM. Though the rank and file is expected to ratify the accord, some provisions have displeased local leaders and prompted concern among some analysts and investors.

14 IBM posted a 12% rise in quarterly earnings, its first gain in 1½ years. But the increase mainly reflected the sale of Intel stock and other factors, prompting analysts to say that IBM's expected rebound has stalled amid stiff competition. IBM's stock fell $4 in heavy trading before closing at $148.75, down 75 cents.

Stock prices rebounded as bonds posted their first gains in a week and the dollar firmed. But trading in all three markets was slow as investors awaited today's U.S. trade report. The Dow Jones industrials closed up 36.72 points at 2508.16.

Fed Chairman Greenspan said inflation isn't accelerating and that the economy is doing better than most forecasters predicted. He also said he expects overall growth in 1987 to be "somewhat better" than 2.5%.

15 Financial markets were rocked by a smaller-than-expected improvement in the August U.S. trade deficit. The dismal trade news sent short-term interest rates up sharply and the dollar and bond prices plunging. Perhaps hardest hit was the stock market, where the Dow Jones industrials skidded a record 95.46 points to close at 2412.70.

U.S. car sales slid 39% in early October after the Big Three auto makers ended sales incentives.

16 Stocks and bonds slid further as Treasury Secretary Baker tried to calm the markets, saying the rise in interest rates isn't justified. The Dow Jones industrials plunged 57.61 points to 2355.09. Bond yields continued to rise and Chemical Bank boosted its prime rate to 9¾% from 9¼. The dollar eased slightly.

Takeover stocks are being battered by jitters about interest rates. Also, Wall Street firms are reexamining operations.

Retail sales slipped 0.4% in September, reflecting lower car sales. The drop further illustrates the shift from a consumer-driven economy. Meanwhile, auto makers are curbing October production plans.

OPEC output is rising, partly because Saudi Arabia's reported plan to link crude prices to the spot market has boosted demand for Saudi oil.

Tax-increase packages continued to be pushed by congressional Democrats despite a renewed threat of a presidential veto.

19 The record plunge by stocks Friday (October 16) left analysts guessing about the outlook for the market and the overall economy. The sell-off sent the Dow Jones industrials skidding a record 108.35 points, to 2246.74, while Big Board volume soared to a high of 338.5 million shares. Despite the tumult, bond prices edged higher and the dollar eased. Gold rose sharply.

Treasury Secretary Baker reiterated that the U.S. may let the dollar fall unless Bonn eases credit. But he denied the U.S. has acted already. Baker's warning was the latest sign that the February accord to stabilize exchange rates may be weakening.

Many big banks are reluctant to follow Chemical New York and raise their prime rate to 9¾% from 9¼%, though Marine Midland boosted its rate Friday. Bankers say they'll wait for more upward pressure on rates.

Producer prices rose only 0.3% in September, or at a 3.7% annual rate, suggesting inflation is still moderate. Energy prices plunged, but food costs rose sharply. Meanwhile, industrial output edged up 0.2% last month.

20 The stock market crashed (October 19) as panic selling swept the Dow Jones industrials down 508.00 points, or 22.6%, to 1738.74. The record decline far exceeded the drop on Oct. 28, 1929, when the average slid 12.8%. Most other market indicators also skidded to record lows, as Big Board volume soared to 604.3 million shares, well above the previous record.

Economists don't expect the market's debacle to usher in a depression, mainly due to safeguards in the banking and financial systems. But many small investors remain worried.

Treasury bond prices rallied from an early slide, winding up with huge gains in heavy trading. Some 30-year Treasury issues closed up more than three points. Gold surged to 4½-year highs, though a broad range of other commodity prices declined.

The plunge by London stocks could threaten a record $12.2 billion share offering by British Petroleum later this month. Meanwhile in France, the record drop on the Paris bourse could have political repercussions.

21 Blue-chip stocks rallied following Monday's crash, but many smaller issues continued to be pummeled by nervous investors. The Dow Jones industrials swung wildly before closing up a record 102.27 points, at 1841.01. Bond prices closed sharply higher and interest rates tumbled. Many commodities plunged.

Fed Chairman Greenspan tried to calm markets by signaling a switch from an anti-inflation to an anti-recession policy. Meanwhile, consumers are scaling back on spending.

Housing starts jumped 4.4% in September, but analysts called it an aberration and said they expect future declines. Some said fears about rising interest rates may have prompted a rush by home buyers and builders.

The dollar soared, aided by the stock market nervousness and signs of support among the major monetary powers. The new U.S.-West German economic cooperation helped stabilize the U.S. currency, though the agreement faces further tests.

22 Stocks rebounded broadly as the Dow Jones industrials rocketed 186.84 points, to 2027.85, far exceeding Tuesday's record gain. The average now has recovered over half the 508.00 points it lost Monday. Big Board volume was the third highest ever. Despite the recovery, there was disagreement over the market's prospects for today and tomorrow.

Most interest rates fell again, helping to boost stocks. But the rate declines were smaller, prompting fears that the bond rally is fizzling. The dollar and commodities gained.

Tokyo stocks bounced back, recovering more than half their loss from Tuesday's record drop. London share prices posted a record one-day gain in volatile trading. Other markets around the world also rebounded.

23 Stocks fell back in volatile trading, as the Dow Jones industrials skidded 77.42 points to 1950.43. Heavy selling by foreigners, and by U.S. investors meeting margin calls, helped fuel the drop. Still, there were signs of stability in the market. The Big Board and other stock exchanges will close early today, Monday and Tuesday due to the order backlog.

Interest rates tumbled further as major banks cut their prime rates to 9% from 9¼. Treasury bond prices continued to surge. The dollar recovered from an early decline.

The Chicago Merc said that it will impose daily price limits on stock-index futures and options contracts, starting today. The action is in response to the unprecedented market swings of the past several days.

Economists have turned bearish following the stock market's collapse. Though few are predicting a recession anytime soon, nearly all economists have scaled back their forecasts.

26 Financial markets face an overhaul following last week's crash. Possible changes may involve dealer capital, coordination among markets, and the role of options and futures in stock trading. Some stock-index exchanges already are taking steps, and the agency overseeing futures trading may be revamped.

Foreigners are pulling back from U.S. stocks, though a mass exodus is called unlikely. Most U.S. stocks fell Friday, but the market was calmer.

The economy remains healthy despite a wider trade deficit, latest data show. GNP grew at a 3.8% rate in the third quarter, while consumer prices rose only 0.2% in September. But analysts say the economy may be weakened by the stock market crash.

Interest rates may resume rising soon following last week's explosive bond rally, corporate treasurers say. Meanwhile, the gloom has deepened in the municipal bond business.

OPEC appears less likely to boost oil prices in December because the stock market crashes may slow demand for petroleum. The recovery in other commodity prices also may be hurt, some economists say.

Machine tool orders rose 35% in September and remain good despite the stock market slide, officials say.

27 Stock prices suffered another meltdown as heavy domestic and foreign selling sent the Dow Jones industrials plummeting 156.83 points, the second-biggest drop ever, to close at 1793.93. The 8.04% decline brought the average to near last Monday's close, when it slid 22.6%. Despite shortened hours, Big Board volume was the sixth highest.

Over-the-counter stocks collapsed below 1985 levels as dealers dumped shares they had bought last week from panicky customers. The Nasdaq Composite Index skidded 9%.

Interest rates tumbled as speculation grew that the Fed will ease credit further due to the stock market crash. But some executives fear a weaker dollar may dampen the bond rally and drive rates back up. The dollar was mixed in New York trading.

The British government is considering a proposal to scrap a planned share offering in British Petroleum. Underwriters of the record issue face possible losses of nearly $2.54 billion due to the plunge in stock prices.

Consumer spending fell 0.5% in September, led by a drop in car sales. Analysts expect further declines due to the stock-market crash. Personal income climbed 0.7% last month, the biggest gain since February.

Brazil and major creditor banks are discussing a plan to clear some of Brazil's more than $3 billion in overdue interest. Sources indicated that the proposal is being sponsored by the U.S. Treasury and Federal Reserve.

Hong Kong stocks plunged 33% as trading resumed after a four-day suspension. The crash came despite a government bailout of the stock futures exchange. Traders were worried stocks may head even lower.

Tokyo stocks nose-dived in moderate trading, surprising investors. The Nikkei index posted its third-biggest point drop ever. The sell-off in Asia drove stocks sharply lower in London and other European markets.

28 Stocks pulled out of a nose dive once again, helped partly by renewed foreign buying. The Dow Jones industrials gained 52.56 points, to 1846.49. Though other market indexes also rose, the advance wasn't overwhelmingly broad. Over-the-counter stocks continued to fall, as did smaller issues on the Amex.

Bond prices tumbled, pushing interest rates up sharply for the first time in over a week. The sell-off was prompted partly by a decline in the dollar. The currency skidded to a seven-year low against the mark.

Britain is expected to proceed with a record $12.1 billion share offering in British Petroleum, though underwriters face huge potential losses.

29 The dollar tumbled in heavy trading, though central bank intervened to slow its slide. The currency fell to a near eight-year low against the mark and a five-year low against the pound. Traders cited pessimism about U.S. efforts to cut its trade and budget deficits. The Fed, meanwhile, faces a choice of defending the dollar or the economy.

Stocks closed mixed following a rocky session, buffeted partly by the weaker dollar. The Dow Jones industrials swung sharply before ending up 0.33, at 1846.82. Over-the-counter stocks continued to slump.

Bond prices fell despite a decline in short-term interest rates and signs of further Fed credit easing. The drop was sparked by the dollar's fall.

30 Stocks rose sharply on speculation that the dollar's slide may benefit rather than hamper the economy. The Dow Jones industrials closed up 91.51 points, at 1938.33, the third biggest gain ever. The dollar slid to a 40-year low against the yen and a seven-year low against the mark before staging a rebound.

A new monetary accord among the U.S., West Germany and Japan is predicted by U.S. officials. They say the market crash and weaker dollar are helping to make a pact likely.

Britain will proceed with a record $12.33 billion share offering in British Petroleum, but it announced safeguards designed to prevent the stock price from collapsing. The sale has sparked concern in world markets.

First Chicago may rethink a $200 million investment in Wood Gundy, an underwriter in the BP offering.

Reagan's chief economist, Beryl Sprinkel, said the stock market's collapse likely will slow the economy. But Sprinkel, who agreed yesterday to remain head economic adviser, said he doesn't expect a recession.

Precious metals plunged amid speculation that central banks were selling gold to help buy dollars. On the New York Comex, gold tumbled $11.80, to $468.70 an ounce.

November 1987

2 Economic growth is expected to slow to a crawl due to the market crash, pulling down inflation and long-term interest rates, according to a consensus of 35 economists surveyed by The Wall Street Journal.

A slowdown is suggested by latest U.S. data. Leading indicators fell 0.1% in September, while home sales slid 5.2%. But purchasing agents said the economy was strong in October.

Stocks continued to rebound Friday, pushing up the Dow Jones industrials 55.20, to 1993.53. Bond prices eased, and the dollar was mixed. Analysts, meanwhile, are voicing doubts about a new dollar accord.

Losses on stock and index options from the market crash are believed to total several hundred million dollars, industry officials said. Meanwhile, the growth of stock-index futures is expected to slow for awhile.

3 Texaco lost an appeal of a $10.3 billion judgment awarded to Pennzoil nearly two years ago. The surprise decision by the Texas Supreme Court left only the U.S. Supreme Court for Texaco to press its case. Texaco immediately said it will seek a Supreme Court review.

The dollar slumped further as traders sensed the U.S. and major allies no longer intend to prop up the currency. The dollar fell to a 40-year low against the yen and nearly an eight-year low against the mark.

Factory orders rose 1.1% in September, while construction spending jumped 1.5%. The figures encouraged economists, though many believe the market crash may slow capital spending. Non-farm productivity surged at a 2.6% rate in the third quarter.

4 SEC Chairman Ruder plans to tell a Senate panel today that "serious consideration" was given to temporarily halting Big Board trading on Oct. 20 because heavy selling was straining the specialist system.

Texaco's failed appeal of a $10.3 billion legal judgment is expected to put more pressure on the firm to settle its dispute with Pennzoil or to file a Chapter 11 reorganization plan as quickly as possible, sources said.

Federal securities laws may provide Texaco with the best chance for winning a Supreme Court review.

Shares fell in London and on other European exchanges as the dollar's decline in overseas trading worried investors. The Japanese markets were closed for a holiday.

5 Baker said the Reagan administration's top priority is to avoid a recession caused by high interest rates, even at the risk of a weakening dollar. In an interview, the Treasury secretary said liquidity is crucial to calming the turbulent markets, adding that tight monetary policy and rising interest rates contributed to the market crash.

The dollar fell further amid bearishness about the currency's outlook. The drop was cushioned, however, by speculation that West Germany may lower interest rates today.

Bond prices rose further, boosted by speculation that the U.S. and West Germany may lower interest rates. Stock prices declined, but the drop wasn't as bad as many expected. The Dow Jones industrials fell 18.24, to 1945.29. OTC issues were flat.

U.S. oil prices plunged on an industry report of higher stockpiles and concerns about OPEC's December meeting. In hectic trading, prices fell briefly below $19 a barrel before closing at $19.07, down 42 cents.

British banks cut base rates to 9% from 9.5% after the government eased credit to aid tumbling London stocks. But the cut brought only a partial recovery by stocks. Other European and Asian shares posted declines.

U.S. car sales were flat in late October, indicating the stock market crash had little immediate impact. Still, the outlook remains uncertain. Sales of European luxury cars fell sharply during the month.

6 Interest rates fell in the U.S. and West Germany as bond prices continued their explosive rally. The rate cut by West Germany was a victory for the monetary policy of Treasury Secretary Baker. Major U.S. banks lowered their prime rates to 8¾% from 9%, and many expect further declines. The dollar's plunge steepened following the U.S. pledge to stress lower interest rates.

Stock prices climbed, boosted by the drop in interest rates. The Dow Jones industrials rose 40.12 to 1985.41. Over-the-counter also gained as the Nasdaq index added nearly 2%. London shares advanced but most other foreign markets declined.

Japanese and U.S. chip makers remain antagonistic despite the easing of Washington sanctions. Separately, MIT canceled plans to buy a supercomputer, citing U.S. pressure not to choose a Japanese machine.

Toyota is expected to announce plans to build an engine plant in Kentucky, broadly expanding its U.S. manufacturing operations.

Major retailers reported sluggish sales for October. There was some softening, particularly in big-ticket items, following the market crash.

Precious-metals prices plunged on concerns about a possible recession. Silver prices on the New York Comex hit their lowest price since March. Platinum came under particularly heavy selling pressure.

9 Corporate profits soared 33% in the third quarter but the outlook is less rosy. Analysts had been forecasting a slowdown for the current quarter and next year even before the Oct. 19 stock-market crash, and the event has reinforced their expectations. Canadian profits rose sharply, led by resource firms.

Unemployment inched up to 6% in October from 5.9% in September. Economists said the report shows an economy robust enough to withstand the stock market's blow. Separately, consumer credit rose sharply.

The Fed's easing of credit and the dollar's drop will help avert a recession, many economists say. But they add that inflation and interest rates will rise, hurting the bond market. Meanwhile, the Fed decided to tighten credit before the crash, minutes of a Sept. 22 meeting show.

The price of copper jumped to more than $1 a pound, its highest level in seven years, prompted by tight supplies of the metal.

10 The dollar slumped to new lows amid pessimism about efforts to cut the U.S. budget deficit. Traders said the deficit talks are now the top issue affecting the market. Worries about the dollar helped drive stocks sharply lower, though the resumption of program trading had little impact. The Dow Jones industrials closed down 58.85 points, at 1900.20. OTC stocks skidded 2%.

Reagan's stance in budget talks was clarified by the White House. Officials denied the president agreed to accept either a cap on Social Security increases or a new gasoline tax as part of a deficit-cutting plan.

Major oil companies plan to boost capital spending slightly next year, especially on foreign exploration and production. The forecast is based on expectations of stable oil prices. U.S. crude-oil futures fell yesterday.

11 The Fed doesn't plan to push interest rates lower unless it sees further weakness in the economy, Fed officials said. They added that the central bank is holding its discount rate at 6%, partly in an attempt to ease the dollar's fall. Reagan, meanwhile, caused the dollar to rebound sharply by saying he doesn't want the currency to drop further.

Southland postponed a $1.5 billion junk bond offering, prompting worries about other big takeover financings. The delay left Goldman Sachs and Salomon Brothers with $100 million each in loans to Southland. Also, Touche Ross may face a liability risk.

Saudi Arabia's oil minister pledged to keep OPEC's bench mark price at $18 a barrel for another year, calling it vital to market stability. He also ruled out any return by the Saudis to being OPEC's "swing" producer. U.S. crude-oil futures rose.

Home-buying appears to be slowing following the stock market crash. Many lenders say mortgage applications for new homes and resales have dropped sharply since Oct. 19.

12 Japan's trade surplus continued to shrink in October from a year earlier. The surplus with the U.S. grew, however, though only by 0.1%. Tokyo said its overall trade surplus should narrow the rest of this year.

U.S. heating oil prices rose, buoyed by a report of a major decline in U.S. stockpiles. It was the first oil contract to recover from last week's slide.

13 The trade gap shrank to $14.08 billion in September, reflecting lower oil imports and a jump in exports. The narrowing, from a $15.68 billion deficit in August, fueled optimism that the nation's trade woes may be easing. But analysts say shrinking the trade gap will be hard as long as the U.S. economy remains stronger than that of its allies.

West Germany appears less resistant to stimulating its economy following the recent plunge by the dollar and stock prices. But Bonn is linking any shift in policy to U.S. progress on reducing its budget deficit.

Ford Motor said it will buy up to $2 billion of its common stock, partly answering questions about what it will do with its huge cash hoard.

OPEC is renewing efforts to stop members from cheating on oil quotas. The group hopes to reach agreement soon on a output-monitoring system, though the oil industry is skeptical.

16 Producer prices fell 0.2% in October, suggesting fears of renewed inflation are largely unfounded. The unexpected drop in finished-goods prices was the first since July 1986. Meanwhile, retail sales fell only 0.1% last

month, indicating the stock market crash had little immediate impact on consumers.

U.S. car sales fell 10.1% in early November from a year ago. Though there was little evidence the stock market plunge had affected sales, the outlook remains uncertain. Chrysler reduced some prices on Friday.

17 The supreme court upheld the convictions of former Journal reporter Winans and two others, a major boost to the federal crackdown on Wall Street insider trading. In reinterpreting the law of mail and wire fraud, the court also gave prosecutors a powerful new weapon against the misuse of inside information.

Industrial output climbed 0.6% in October, mainly because of a rebound in auto production. The surge in car output isn't expected to last, but U.S. manufacturers appear to be having brisk export growth. Many firms, in fact, have big order backlogs.

Japanese investors have slashed purchases of U.S. debt securities, a trend that could undermine the outlook for lower U.S. interest rates, analysts say. Last month, Japanese were net sellers of foreign bonds.

The NASD moved to prevent OTC stock dealers from dropping out of the market when prices fall sharply. Some market makers are said to have withdrawn bid and ask quotations during last month's crash.

World oil prices are coming under further pressure due to continued high output and discounting by OPEC members, particularly Iran. Egypt yesterday became the latest non-OPEC producer to cut prices.

18 AT&T proposed an $800 million rate cut in long-distance service to put pressure on local Bell concerns to lower their connection charges. The long-distance cut, averaging 3.6% annually, would start January 1. But AT&T said the cuts would be much less if it doesn't win a dispute with the Bell companies over connection fees.

Major retailers appear to have had soft sales in the first half of November, indicating waning consumer confidence may be starting to affect buying. Four big retailers posted mixed quarterly results.

West Germany hinted it might be edging closer to more-stimulative economic measures. But it also indicated it didn't plan any strong steps, such as increasing planned tax cuts.

The dollar tumbled as optimism waned about a U.S. deficit accord. Stock and bond prices also sagged, but trading remained light as investors awaited news of the budget talks. The Dow Jones industrials finished down 26.85 points, at 1922.25.

U.S. crude-oil prices declined to less than $18.50 a barrel, or near three-month lows, amid continued reports of a world-wide oversupply.

19 Housing starts slid 8.2% in October to the lowest level in nearly 4½ years. The sharp decline was attributed to the stock market crash and the earlier surge by interest rates. But analysts said the recent easing of interest rates should prevent housing starts from falling further.

Greenspan gave Fed support to a Senate bill that would allow banks to affiliate with securities firms. A new version of the legislation may be introduced as soon as today.

20 Tokyo's property boom is cooling, partly due to new tax laws. But the Japanese don't appear to be slowing investment in overseas real estate.

Mexico tried to calm the panic caused by the peso's plunge Wednesday on the free-exchange market.

GM is cutting production further, reflecting growing uncertainty in the auto industry. The moves mean output will be slashed at nearly half of GM's 23 U.S. car-assembly plants until late January. Ford and Chrysler also are reviewing production.

Pennzoil offered terms for settling its huge legal battle with Texaco. Pennzoil said it would accept a nonrefundable $1.5 billion payment and a $5 billion cap on any court award.

The SEC embraced a definition of insider trading that includes the "misappropriation" theory. But the agency's support isn't unanimous.

23 The deficit accord reached Friday still faces tough going in Congress. Lawmakers from both sides are unhappy with the package, which claims $30.2 billion in savings this fiscal year and $45.8 billion the next. Though specific tax increases still need to be negotiated, corporations are sure to be hit the hardest.

Major industrial nations are likely to meet now that the U.S. has a deficit pact. But U.S. officials say preparations could take several weeks.

A new wave of retrenchment is starting to affect Wall Street following the stock market crash. Drexel Burnham, which confirmed it laid off 100 people, is one of several firms undergoing cost-cutting reviews.

Volkswagen plans to close or sell its only U.S. manufacturing plant, citing slow sales and financial losses. The pullout, the first by a foreign car maker, is viewed as an early sign of a shakeout among auto plants that is expected to last several years.

24 The Chicago Board of Trade will impose daily price limits on its two stock-index futures contracts because of rising volatility since the market crash. Other futures markets have imposed similar ceilings recently.

Most financial markets reacted coolly to Friday's (November 20) deficit agreement. The dollar and bond prices fell, while stocks edged higher in the final hour of trading. The Dow Jones industrials closed up 9.45 at 1923.08. Foreign stock markets generally gained.

Gold and silver prices have turned upward, and some analysts say it may be a belated response to last month's stock-market crash. On the New York Comex yesterday, gold rose $5.70, to $476 an ounce.

25 Third-quarter GNP growth was revised upward to a robust 4.1% rate from 3.8% estimated before. The revision, reflecting stronger exports and business investment, highlights the buoyancy of the economy as it approached the October 19 stock market crash. Also, after-tax corporate profits rose 5.2% in the quarter, the biggest increase in a year.

West Germany led a round of European interest-rate cuts to support the dollar, triggering rallies on most financial markets. But the dollar and U.S. bonds sank as a Bundesbank aide voiced disappointment with the U.S. deficit pact. The Dow Jones industrials rose 40.45 to 1963.53.

Car sales remained sluggish in mid-November, declining 12% from a year earlier. The latest results reinforced concerns that have led GM and Chrysler to reduce production and lay off workers. Truck sales continued to be relatively strong, however.

A new world oil glut is expected to depress prices again. Rising supplies and slowing demand may push prices to as low as $15 a barrel this spring from $18 now. But the decline could prompt OPEC to tighten output, making any price drop short-lived.

27 Consumer spending was flat in October, reflecting the end of auto incentives. Durable goods orders rose 0.3%, suggesting exports continued to aid manufacturers. The figures indicate the economy was behaving largely as expected before the stock crash.

West Germany reiterated that a planned economic-stimulus package won't have any major initiatives, such as expanding planned tax cuts.

30 Retailers reported mixed sales results for the first few days of the holiday shopping season. In most parts of the country, consumers appeared cautious because of worries about the economic outlook. The sales picture is further clouded by steep discounting at many stores, which helps boost sales figures but is likely to hurt profit margins.

The CFTC is investigating whether a few big securities firms manipulated a stock-index futures contract, the Major Market Index, the day after Black Monday. The contract surged just when the stock market was threatening to disintegrate.

Purchasing agents said the economy slowed in November, though they added it's too early to estimate the full impact of the stock market crash. Machine tool orders soared 48% in October and were said to remain relatively strong during November.

Inflation worries remain despite the stock crash, mainly due to higher commodity prices and the weak dollar, analysts say. Bonds slid Friday on inflation fears. The dollar and stocks also dropped. The Dow Jones industrials fell 36.47, to 1910.48.

West Germany plans to lower interest rates at a state-controlled lending institution to help stimulate the country's economy, officials said.

Eight Latin American debtor nations ended a summit by demanding relief from their nearly $400 billion in total debt. But they fell far short of inaugurating a so-called debtors' cartel, which creditor banks have feared.

Tokyo is preparing to remove import quotas on several farm products to quiet U.S. criticism of Japan's huge trade surplus. The action won't affect the trade imbalance much, but it is considered important symbolically.

December 1987

1 The dollar tumbled to record lows, depressing stock prices and speeding plans for a meeting of the Group of

Seven nations. Traders linked the slide to worries that U.S. economic policy is in disarray. The Dow Jones industrials closed off 76.93 points, at 1833.55, a 4% decline. OTC and foreign stocks also plunged, as did many commodity prices. U.S. Treasury securities rebounded.

PaineWebber agreed to sell an 18% voting stake to Tokyo-based Yasuda Mutual Life Insurance for $300 million. The move will boost PaineWebber's capital 26% and may help the securities firm stay independent.

The FASB proposed that companies disclose the credit risks of all financial instruments, including certain debt not carried on balance sheets.

2 The dollar rebounded, bolstered by central bank intervention and speculation the Bundesbank will cut its discount rate tomorrow as part of West Germany's economic-stimulus package. But the intervention did little to change overall bearishness about the U.S. currency. Japan's central bank appeared resigned to letting the dollar drift lower.

OPEC is growing more divided over oil pricing and output levels. Some analysts say the split may be serious enough to prevent the group from reaching a production-price pact at next week's Vienna meeting.

Texaco told creditors it would offer Pennzoil a non-refundable payment of less than $400,000 in exchange for a cap of over $2 billion on any court award in their $10.3 billion battle.

Leading indicators fell 0.2% in October, reflecting the stock crash. Some analysts said the drop doesn't suggest an economic downturn. Construction spending fell 0.5%.

The CFTC refused indefinitely to approve 11 new stock-index futures contracts, reflecting Black Monday jitters. The agency asked futures exchanges to revise the proposed contracts and add more safeguards.

3 Shearson's decision to buy E. F. Hutton Group for nearly $1 billion is an aggressive bid to dethrone Merrill Lynch as the top retail broker. The purchase will more than double Shearson's sales force, creating a powerful selling machine. But Shearson also is gambling on its ability to turn around an ailing firm, especially after the stock crash.

Retailers failed to achieve hoped-for sales gains at the start of the holiday shopping season despite deep discounting, independent surveys show. Analysts said sales last week were essentially flat with a year ago.

West Germany unveiled its economic-stimulus package, which was welcomed by Washington but widely viewed as too modest to boost the German economy or the dollar. The currency fell amid doubts the German discount rate will be cut today.

4 Stocks plunged as investors ignored cuts in European interest rates and dollar and bond rallies. Gloomy news about U.S. retail sales helped drive the Dow Jones industrials down 72.44 points, to 1776.53. Most OTC and foreign stocks also fell. Though the Bundesbank-led rate cuts pushed the dollar higher, traders remain bearish about the currency.

Consumer spending showed signs of weakening during November. U.S. car sales fell 6.4% last month, while retailers reported only slight sales gains. Though the results weren't as bad as feared, analysts said they still suggested an economic slowdown.

Factory orders rose a healthy 1.1% in October, largely due to a surge in orders for aircraft and other transportation items. Also, non-farm productivity strengthened in the third quarter, rising at a revised 3.6% rate.

7 The U.S. is shifting its international economic policy, putting more emphasis on supporting the dollar. The move, in reciprocation for recent European interest-rate cuts and West Germany's fiscal-stimulus package, comes at the request of European officials seeking help for firms whose exports to the U.S. have been hurt by the weak currency.

Citicorp will cut expenses at its investment banking unit in the wake of the market crash, the chairman said. Meanwhile, Kidder will lay off 1,000 to reduce costs; Charles Schwab is scaling back expansion plans.

GM and its finance unit face a possible downgrade on $54 billion of long-term debt by Moody's, which said it is concerned about GM's "ability to regain momentum."

The jobless rate fell to 5.9% in November from 6% in October, and employment grew, suggesting a strong economy after the market dive. Sales of heavy trucks, an indicator of spending intentions, fell 9.7% in October as order cancellations grew.

Japan's GNP grew at an 8.4% annual rate in the quarter ended September 30, driven by domestic demand.

8 Interest rates surged amid speculation the Fed may be tightening credit slightly to aid the dollar. The speculation intensified as the Fed refrained from intervening in credit markets, surprising analysts. The dollar continued to climb, helping to lift stocks. The Dow Jones industrials closed up 45.43 points, at 1812.17.

The stock crash hasn't slowed economic growth much so far, though it has created uncertainty, a new report from Fed district banks suggests.

The Big Board is investigating the performance of market makers in J. P. Morgan and Gould shares, which had huge price swings during the October market crash, sources said.

L. F. Rothschild will dismiss 700 employees, or about 40% of its work force, over the next six months. The securities firm has been reeling from massive losses and recent difficulties in selling part of its operations.

OPEC ministers were pessimistic about averting another oil-price collapse as they began arriving for their Vienna meeting. Several said it will depend on curbing runaway oil production, particularly by Iraq.

Texaco and Pennzoil's prospects for a quick settlement appeared to fade after their chief executives met twice with Texaco creditors and shareholders. Neither side budged from its previous proposals.

9 Several OPEC members supported an effort to maintain the group's $18-a-barrel benchmark for another year. But world oil prices fell as traders braced for a contentious OPEC meeting in Vienna, which starts today.

Purchasing managers expect economic growth to strengthen in 1988 with only a mild increase in inflation, according to a mid-November survey. The optimism is fueled by significant gains in U.S. export business.

10 Stocks rallied again, raising speculation that prices have successfully tested their October lows. The Dow Jones industrials rose 34.15, to 1902.52. OTC shares also climbed, though a power outage limited trading. The rally came despite worries about today's October trade report, which kept most currency and bond traders on the sidelines.

11 The trade gap swelled to a record $17.63 billion in October, sending the dollar and bond prices plunging. The deficit, reflecting a surge in imports, stunned Reagan economists but isn't expected to alter monetary or fiscal policy. Stocks skidded in late trading after ignoring the trade report initially. The Dow Jones industrials fell 47.08, to 1855.44.

Investors face many of the same factors this morning as they did October 19, when the stock market crashed.

Financial services firms are undergoing a retrenchment after five years of expanding profits and employment. Some have trimmed staff, others are freezing hiring, and many are seeking ways to cut costs.

OPEC appeared close to a production-price accord despite threats of a boycott by Iran. Most of the members agreed in principle to keep the benchmark at $18 a barrel and to defend that price by cutting back output to about 17.5 million barrels a day.

14 Pennzoil's agreement to accept $3 billion as settlement of its legal wrangle with Texaco illustrates Carl Icahn's ability as a negotiator. The plan—proposed by the corporate raider and other Texaco shareholders and which could be forced on Texaco—would give Pennzoil cash to acquire reserves and may lead to a big profit for Icahn.

OPEC failed to reach a 1988 accord due to Iran and Iraq. But the oil cartel—minus one or both of the warring nations—is ready to set a plan to hold prices and output unchanged.

A. H. Robins must set aside $2.48 billion for Dalkon Shield victims, a federal court ruled, stirring questions of how it will raise the funds to compensate some 200,000 women claiming injury from the IUD.

15 OPEC reached a weak price-production pact for 1988 that is unlikely to prevent a slide in oil prices. News of the accord sent world oil prices plunging and sparked rallies on U.S. stock and bond markets. The Dow Jones industrials soared 65.82 to 1932.86. Meanwhile, the dollar skidded to post-World War II lows against the yen and mark before rebounding.

Mexico devalued the controlled peso rate, used by most businesses in import and export transactions, by 18% against the dollar. The devaluation is aimed at stabilizing Mexico's volatile exchange-rate system.

Bank of Boston will take a $200 million charge on Third World loans, the first time a major U.S. bank has actually charged off such debt. It could increase pressure on other big banks to take similar action.

Industrial output rose 0.4% in November, another sign that the nation's industry continued to show strength following the stock market crash. Business inventories rose 0.8% in October, while sales dropped 0.1%.

16 Bond prices rallied following another plunge in oil, gold and other commodity prices. Oil skidded to below $17 a barrel in reaction to OPEC's weak accord, though the price slide isn't expected to last long enough to boost the economy significantly.

The dollar recovered slightly from new lows after the White House said it isn't seeking a weaker currency. An early stock rally fizzled, meanwhile, and the Dow Jones industrials closed up only 8.62, at 1941.48. OTC and most foreign stocks finished higher.

The U.S. current-account gap grew to a record $43.38 billion in the third quartor. For the first time in over 50 years, foreign investors earned more on their U.S. holdings than American investors earned abroad.

U.S. car sales eased 1.9% in early December from an unusually strong year-earlier period. The better-than-expected results suggest consumers were attracted by price cuts on many of the Big Three's models. Sales of light trucks continued to soar.

17 Oil prices tumbled in record trading to below $16 a barrel, the lowest level in a year. The continued slide, following OPEC's weak production-price pact this week, further eased inflation worries and helped fuel rallies on the bond and stock markets. The Dow Jones industrials closed up 32.99 points, at 1974.47. The dollar eased in light trading.

A compromise bailout plan for the Farm Credit System was worked out by House-Senate negotiators. The bill calls for $4 billion in federal aid and creates a secondary market for farm mortgages and rural housing loans.

Phillips Petroleum plans to lay off up to 10% of its work force and consolidate operations in a bid to save up to $200 million over two years. The cutbacks are the oil industry's first since this week's OPEC accord.

CBOE President Charles Henry said the SEC told him about noon on October 20 that the Big Board would close in minutes. It was the first official confirmation that the markets nearly closed on "Terrible Tuesday."

U.S. businesses plan to boost spending on plant and equipment 7.3% next year, a Commerce Department survey says. Separately, housing starts rose 7.5% in November, mainly reflecting lower interest rates.

18 The dollar tumbled below 126 yen for the first time since 1949 after Reagan's ex-economic adviser, Martin Feldstein, said it could fall to 100 yen in three or four years. The plunge in oil prices slowed, meanwhile, prompting new inflation worries. Stock and bond prices declined, with the Dow Jones industrials skidding 50.07 points, to 1924.40.

Texaco and Pennzoil representatives hinted they were close to a $3 billion settlement of the companies' four-year-old dispute. Texaco advisers said the firms were no more than $300 million apart, a relatively small amount in the $10.3 billion case.

Third-quarter GNP growth was revised upward again, to a 4.3% rate from 4.1% previously. The change was a further sign of the economy's strength before the stock crash.

21 Texaco and Pennzoil face new challenges after reaching a $3 billion settlement over the weekend. Texaco will lose about 20% of its net worth after paying Pennzoil, and its Chapter 11 reorganization plan still needs shareholder approval. Pennzoil will have to spend the settlement money quickly, and carefully, to avoid having a huge tax liability.

Ivan Boesky was sentenced to three years in prison, ending a chapter in Wall Street's biggest scandal. There were suggestions Friday that Boesky has implicated far more people and firms in the insider-trading case than have been suspected.

Fed Chairman Greenspan said October's record trade gap was "an aberration" that probably was reversed last month. Separately, the Fed decided November 3 to keep interest rates down because of the stock crash.

22 Manufacturers Hanover plans to slash about 2,500 jobs, or 8.5% of its work force, over the next three months, the latest financial institution to make cutbacks. The banking concern also may pull out of some businesses. Bank earnings have been under pressure this year due to Brazil's foreign-debt problems and the October stock market crash.

The New York Fed has decided to allow a fourth Japanese firm, a unit of Nikko Securities, to become a primary dealer in U.S. government securities, according to sources.

23 The group of seven industrial nations said the dollar has fallen enough and

implied they would intervene to keep it within a newly agreed-upon target range. The bottom of the range appears to be at or near the dollar's current level; the top of the range wasn't specified.

Oil prices surged on reports OPEC is cutting output, though analysts called the reports premature. On the New York Merc, crude rose $1.21, to $16.61 a barrel. Heating oil and gasoline prices also soared. The recovery helped push up oil company stocks.

IBM is backing Steve Chen's plan to design the world's most powerful computer. The partnership may help the U.S. effort to stay competitive with Japan in supercomputers, a field where IBM isn't a big player.

Retailers are more confident that Christmas sales will be up slightly this year. But the gain may be the slimmest since the 1982 recession.

The economic outlook has darkened due to the stock crash, and policy changes are needed to ease the risk of a recession, the OECD said.

24 Stocks and bonds rallied on the Group of Seven's statement supporting the dollar, though the currency itself gained slightly. The Dow Jones industrials rose 27.19 to 2005.64, while some long-term Treasury bonds jumped about 1⅜ points. Currency traders were disappointed with the Group of Seven move, putting its credibility at risk.

U.S. car sales fell 18% in mid-December from a year earlier, but the results were still stronger than some analysts had predicted. Sales of light trucks continued to be robust.

Japan's cabinet approved a draft budget for the coming fiscal year that boosts spending 4.8%.

The U.S. economy is expected to grow only 2.4% in 1988, according to the White House's latest forecast. But chief economist Sprinkel said even that pace depends on Fed actions.

The oil rally fizzled as traders reacted skeptically to various OPEC statements that members were cutting output. On the New York Merc, the February crude contract closed up three cents, at $16.64.

28 Machine tool orders in November rose 3.5% from a year ago but were down 49% from the previous month. Despite the relatively weak results, machine tool builders expect modestly higher sales in 1988.

Copper and nickel prices may surge further in the coming months due to tight supplies, analysts say. But prices may subside after that.

Christmas sales surged in the final days of the season, aided by unusually steep price cuts. Based on retailer reports, seasonal sales appeared to have increased 2% to 5%, though that represents no real gain if November's 3.5% inflation rate is considered. Still, fears that the stock market crash would cause sales to collapse proved unfounded.

29 The treasury plans to announce a financing scheme to help Mexico reduce its foreign bank debt, officials said. Under the proposal, which may be unveiled today, as much as $10 billion in existing Mexican debt could be swapped for new debt backed by the U.S.

The dollar ended sharply lower despite a renewed call by the White House to stabilize the currency. Traders and economists again said it will take more than words from the U.S. to restore the dollar's health.

Stocks and bonds tumbled as well, in part due to the dollar's weakness. The Dow Jones industrials skidded 56.70 points, to 1942.97. Over-the-counter shares fell sharply.

South Korea's economy grew 12.2% this year despite labor unrest during the summer, the Bank of Korea said. The growth, little changed from 12.5% in 1986, was due partly to stronger exports, officials said.

Poland plans to restructure income taxes and introduce a value-added tax next year. It also expects a $1 billion trade surplus but won't allocate more money for foreign debt payments.

The copper market is being "very closely" monitored by the CFTC because of the recent price surge caused by low supplies, officials said.

30 Mexico's debt-swap plan was unveiled, though bankers said the novel proposal likely wouldn't work for other big debtor countries. Under the plan, worked out with J. P. Morgan, Mexico will offer to swap up to $10 billion in new bonds backed by the U.S. for a portion of its foreign bank debt. Both banks and Mexico will share the costs of the plan.

The dollar edged lower despite reports of modest central bank intervention. Stocks also continued to fall, though Treasury bond prices rallied. The Dow Jones industrials declined 16.08, to 1926.89. London stocks posted their biggest drop in a month.

Pennzoil said it will reap over $2.6 billion before taxes from its Texaco settlement, putting it "in a strong position" for "major acquisitions." Most of the $400 million in expenses apparently are for legal costs.

The IMF announced an $8.4 billion special fund to provide low-cost loans to the world's poorest nations. The fund is viewed as a major shift from the IMF's traditional role as a short-term monetary institution focusing on balance-of-payments difficulties.

31 Leading indicators slid 1.7% in November, reflecting the plunge in stock prices and modest weakness in other areas. The drop, the first since January and the biggest in nearly 3½ years, is consistent with predictions that economic growth is likely to slow in coming months. Separately, sales of single-family homes declined 1.2% last month.

Regional banks appear willing to accept big losses under the Mexican debt plan, putting pressure on big banks. Also, two banks boosted foreign-loan loss reserves. Meanwhile, Mexico has done better than other big debtors in winning concessions.

Saudi Arabia plans to borrow as much as $8 billion to help finance its $37.7 billion budget for next year. The proposed borrowing, the first in the kingdom's modern history, reflects a sharp drop in Saudi oil revenues.

January 1988

4 Major central banks plan another round of intervention to counter an expected assault on the dollar, officials in Europe said. The central banks want currencies to stay within broad trading ranges that were generally agreed upon last month but weren't disclosed, one official said. The dollar fell in Tokyo early Monday despite Bank of Japan intervention.

Long-term interest rates will ease in the next six months, then rebound to end the year slightly higher, according to the average estimate of 36 economists surveyed by the Journal. Most predict an economic slowdown in 1988 but not a recession.

Texaco may sell assets at a loss as part of a broad restructuring plan that would allow the firm to emerge from Chapter 11 proceedings. Texaco said it would face years of depressed profits without the revamping.

Factory orders inched up 0.1% in November amid signs of sluggish growth ahead. One analyst said any slowdown depends on whether exports and U.S. capital spending can grow enough to offset expected weakness in consumer spending and construction.

The economy grew in December at a "much brisker pace" than the month before, according to the latest survey of purchasing agents. New orders and output rose sharply.

5 The dollar rebounded from postwar lows after central bank intervention, sparking stock and bond rallies but sending gold prices skidding. The Dow Jones industrials closed up 76.42 points, at 2015.25, the fourth biggest gain ever. The bond rally faded, however, on renewed inflation fears. OTC stocks surged, while foreign shares ended mixed.

Hoffmann-La Roche made an unsolicited offer to acquire Sterling Drug for $72 a share, or $4.2 billion. The proposal to combine the two major drug companies apparently augurs a resurgence in big-time takeovers, aided by lower stock prices.

6 The dollar soared 3.8% against the yen and 2.6% against the mark in one of its best showings in years. Aggressive central bank intervention triggered the rally, helping the currency rise to its pre-Christmas level. But analysts remain pessimistic about the dollar's long-term course.

Stock and bond prices followed the dollar higher. The Dow Jones industrials closed up 16.25, at 2031.50. OTC and foreign shares also gained.

Texaco's largest holder, Carl Icahn, sought permission to file a competing Chapter 11 reorganization plan. Icahn's proposal would keep most of the $3 billion Texaco-Pennzoil settlement intact but remove some of Texaco's takeover defenses.

The NASD is introducing a fully computerized trading system aimed at reducing the gridlock that paralyzed much of the OTC stock market during the October crash.

Sterling Drug will resist any takeover effort, according to Hoffmann-La Roche, which launched a $72-a-share, $4.2 billion offer for the drug firm. Sterling rose $17.25, to $74.125, on speculation of a higher bid.

Arbitragers hope the Hoffmann-La Roche offer is the end of over two months of sluggish takeover activity, which began with the market crash.

7 A new regulatory system for financial markets will be urged by the presidential task force on the October stock crash. In a report to be sent to Reagan tomorrow, the panel will recommend: setting daily price limits on all securities, setting consistent margin requirements, and creating a unified system of clearing and settling trades.

The dollar's rally continued, though major industrial nations are taking a big gamble with their costly intervention effort. Stocks also rose, with the Dow Jones industrials closing up 6.30 at 2037.80. Bonds tumbled.

A CFTC report appears to have deepened the mystery surrounding the sudden rise of the Major Market Index contract on October 20, which may have helped save the stock market from a total meltdown.

OPEC may be able to prop up oil prices a few weeks longer. New estimates, to be released today, will show that world oil demand has increased while OPEC output may have fallen. But analysts said conditions in the oil market continue to be bearish.

Citicorp is eliminating 400 jobs in its investment-banking unit, the latest cost cuts at a major bank. Merrill Lynch's job cuts could total several thousand by the end of the month.

8 Mexico's debt-swap plan is apparently drawing little support from the country's major U.S. lenders. Most either don't plan to participate in the swap or will submit bids that may be unacceptable to the Mexicans.

The CBOE is reducing its staff over 10% due to a steep drop in stock-index-option trading since the market crash. Separately, a $600 million skyscraper for New York's five commodity exchanges was scrapped.

11 The Brady report on the stock crash concludes that the financial system nearly collapsed on October 20 and that major changes are needed to guard against a reoccurrence. Traders said Friday's plunge by stocks and bonds suggests the markets are still vulnerable to the same factors that caused the crash.

The Dow Jones industrials plummeted 140.58 points, to 1911.31, the third biggest drop ever. The dollar also fell. Meanwhile, firms remain bearish about the currency.

The unemployment rate fell to 5.8% in December, the lowest level in nearly 8½ years. The drop, accompanied by a surge in non-farm payrolls, underscores the economy's strength after the October crash.

Texaco will take $4.9 billion in fourth-quarter charges as part of a restructuring following the Pennzoil settlement. The move won praise from analysts but not from Texaco's biggest shareholder, Carl Icahn.

Global oil consumption appears to be more than one million barrels a day higher than previously estimated, new figures by the IEA suggest.

12 Security Pacific boosted reserves for troubled Third World debt by $350 million, bringing total reserves to about 54% of all its non-trade loans. The move could lead to another round of loan-loss reserve increases at some of the nation's biggest banks.

Reagan said the October crash resulted from market factors and not from the U.S. trade or budget deficits or the sliding dollar. The president claimed, incorrectly, that the Brady report exonerated his policies.

Saudi Arabia expects the price of oil to drop to $15 a barrel soon and is quietly planning measures to preserve its oil revenue, sources said.

Portfolio insurance has shrunk two-thirds or more since the October crash. The strategy, which was criticized in the Brady report, faces an even more limited future if the panel's proposals are adopted.

13 The dollar and stocks fell while interest rates were mostly steady as investors worried about Friday's trade report. The Dow Jones industrials finished off 16.58 at 1928.55. Oil prices gyrated before ending lower.

14 Texaco was told by the IRS that it may owe $6.5 billion in back taxes, partly relating to purchases of Saudi oil from 1979 to 1981. The news stunned Texaco, which already faces payments of over $5 billion to emerge from Chapter 11, as well as Pennzoil and other parties. But analysts said Texaco likely won't have to pay such a large claim.

Morgan Stanley and Spear Leeds are being investigated by the SEC as part of a broad inquiry into possibly illegal stock parking, sources said. The investigation, which also includes Kidder Peabody, Jefferies & Co. and other firms, is an outgrowth of the Boesky case, the sources said.

The U.S. and Japan stepped up efforts to bolster the dollar by arranging to supply the Fed with more yen to buy dollars in currency markets. The move was announced in a joint statement by Reagan and visiting Prime Minister Noboru Takeshita.

U.S. car sales rose 17.1% in early January, but analysts called the figure disappointing because year-ago sales were unusually weak.

15 The big board said it is curbing the use of program trading on days when the Dow Jones Industrial Average moves over 75 points. The action inflamed the debate on Wall Street about computerized trading. Some major investors said the exchange's restrictions might make the market even more volatile.

Chemical New York became the first major bank to forgo recent reserve increases for Third World loans. The move signals a growing split between money-center and regional banks on the foreign-debt issue.

Retail sales climbed 0.7% in December, though the gain mainly reflected strong car sales. The results suggest consumer spending is sluggish but isn't as weak as analysts had expected after the stock crash.

The dollar fell sharply on the eve of today's U.S. trade report as dealers reacted to a bearish forecast about the currency. Stocks eased and bonds edged up as investors and traders awaited the November trade data.

18 Producer prices fell 0.3% in December, indicating inflation remains under control. For 1987, prices rose 2.2%. Industrial output gained 0.2% last month and 3.8% for the year.

Carl Icahn will try to block Texaco's Chapter 11 reorganization plan even if a shareholders' panel supports it, sources said. Representatives said holders won't back Icahn's attempt to file a rival reorganization plan.

New York City plans to shift a major part of its $30 billion pension fund into foreign bonds amid concern the dollar may be weak for years.

Oil prices are expected to drop in the near term, but they could surge on further signs that OPEC output is falling and world demand is rising.

Brazil said it won't resume full interest payments to banks until it gets new loans equal to at least two-thirds of the interest due this year.

The sharp narrowing of the November trade deficit triggered market rallies Friday and bolstered arguments that the nation's trade picture is improving. But analysts said the gap, which shrank to $13.22 billion in November, may not continue to improve so significantly. Investors, meanwhile, may soon focus on other economic indicators.

19 First Chicago added $240 million to reserves for troubled foreign loans, heightening pressure on other big U.S. banks to follow. But New York money-center banks as of yesterday hadn't joined the latest round of reserve increases. Regulators have been expecting five of the top 10 banks to boost reserves.

Debtor nations owed an estimated $1.19 trillion at the end of 1987 and could owe $1.245 trillion by the end of this year, the World Bank said.

Japan is expected to maintain restrictions on car exports to the U.S. for another year. The move is mainly to avoid a flare-up in trade tensions, because Japanese auto makers have been exporting less anyway.

20 IBM reported higher earnings for the fourth quarter and year, but the results disappointed analysts. Concern about soft revenue and fierce competition prompted many to cut their estimates of IBM's 1988 profit and to lower their ratings on its stock. Some even suggested the results bode ill for the entire computer industry. IBM's stock tumbled $6, to $111.75.

Stock prices closed lower, led by IBM. The Dow Jones industrials finished down 27.52, at 1936.34. Bond prices and the dollar also sank.

Italian financier Carlo De Benedetti appeared close to gaining effective control of Societe Generale de Belgique, the big holding company.

The industrial operating rate rose to 82.1% of capacity in December, the highest since March 1980. Consumer confidence rebounded last month.

OPEC's oil production is starting to plummet, in part due to new discipline by cartel members. The trend could limit further declines in oil prices, which are expected to bottom out at $14 to $15 a barrel soon.

21 Four technology firms reported strong earnings for the latest quarter, though their stocks all plunged on expectations that profits won't be as high for at least a year. Other technology stocks also skidded, helping to push the rest of the market lower. The Dow Jones industrials finished down 57.20, at 1879.14. The dollar tumbled, while bonds rallied.

Consumer prices edged up 0.1% in December as energy and apparel costs fell. But prices for all of 1987 rose 4.4%, led by higher oil prices. Housing starts slid 16.2% last month as apartment building nosedived.

Japanese investment in U.S. firms more than doubled last year, to a record $5.9 billion. Investment is expected to be brisk again this year, spurred by the strong yen.

22 Curbs on program trading will be extended to at least February 5 to help control volatility and promote investor confidence, the New York Stock Exchange said. Meanwhile, traders and analysts applauded a proposal by Big Board Chairman John Phelan to limit the daily price moves of individual stocks. But some speculators opposed the idea.

Bond prices rallied as the dollar firmed and stocks recovered from an early sell-off. Some long-term interest rates fell to a seven-month low.

Short interest skidded 23% on the Big Board for the month ended January 15. It fell 8.2% on the Amex.

25 Kodak agreed to buy Sterling Drug for $89.50 a share, or $5.1 billion, making it a major player in the pharmaceutical business. The friendly accord also ends Sterling's takeover troubles with Hoffmann-La Roche, which last week raised its bid to $81 a share. Analysts said Kodak is paying a big premium for Sterling.

Some big securities firms are voluntarily curbing program trading in an effort to restore investor confidence and avoid federal regulation. Shearson Lehman is ceasing program trading for its own account.

Texaco's bankruptcy judge blocked Carl Icahn's bid to file an alternate reorganization plan. The decision makes it more likely that Texaco's plan will win holder approval.

26 Drexel was notified by the SEC that the agency's staff will seek civil charges of major securities law violations against the firm and several employees, including junkbond chief Michael Milken, sources said. The SEC staff's decision indicates that the 15-month investigation of Drexel is nearing a climax.

U.S. car sales surged nearly 32% in mid-January from an unusually weak year-earlier period. Analysts cited growing confidence in the economy and a break in winter storms.

Japan is bracing for a new round of U.S. criticism following a report that foreign semiconductor makers have lost market share in Japan.

27 Durable-goods orders rose 6.7% in December, the biggest jump in over a year. But the gain largely resulted from a surge in aircraft orders, which move erratically. Economists expect growth in factory orders to slow in the first quarter.

Stocks and bonds slid as the orders report spurred speculation that interest rates aren't likely to ease soon. The Dow Jones industrials fell 25.86, to 1920.59. The dollar also weakened.

The increase in labor costs and wage settlements leveled off last year after narrowing for most of the decade, the Labor Department said.

28 The economy grew at a robust 4.2% rate in the fourth quarter, but there are signs of a slowdown ahead. The GNP increase, which brought 1987 growth to 2.9%, resulted mainly from heavy inventory buildup as consumer spending eased. Analysts contend that production is slowing in the current quarter as businesses work off excess stocks.

Most interest rates tumbled on the report's suggestions of slower growth. The bond rally came even as the Treasury announced a $27 billion debt sale. Stocks and the dollar fell.

IBM is expected to announce a restructuring of senior management in the next few days, sources said. The plans were interpreted as a sign that IBM's board believes the firm's turn-around is proceeding too slowly.

The Big Three auto makers' combined profits may have jumped as much as 68% in the fourth quarter, though sales fell, analysts said.

29 The Fed may ease its grip on credit amid new signs of sluggish economic growth, allowing interest rates to decline broadly. Long-term bond yields dropped sharply for the second day in a row, leaving them below 8½% for the first time in more than six months.

PS New Hampshire filed a Chapter 11 petition, making it the first major utility to seek bankruptcy-law protection in nearly 50 years. The company has been burdened by heavy debt from the Seabrook nuclear project.

Brazil is near a settlement with its foreign bank and government creditors, sources said. Although details aren't final, the plan calls for Brazil to immediately pay more than $300 million to its creditor banks.

Consumer spending rose 0.5% in December, spurred by higher car and truck sales. But first-quarter outlays are expected to be sluggish. Personal income last month increased 0.7%.

February 1988

1 American Brands reached an agreement to acquire its suitor, E-II Holdings, for $17.05 a share, or about $1.1 billion. The 'Pac Man' defense eliminates E-II as a predator and expands the tobacco firm's product lines. But analysts said American Brands is still vulnerable to takeovers and there isn't much immediate benefit for shareholders.

Bond market bullishness is growing, as many investment fears have dissipated. Bond prices surged Friday and stocks jumped on the prospect of lower interest rates. Meanwhile, gold prices sank to four-month lows.

The economy's growth rate slowed in January but strong new orders indicated a "respectable" first quarter, purchasing agents reported.

2 Brazil will pay $350 million to commercial banks today, a sign it is committed to reaching a full settlement with creditors in coming weeks. Further payments are planned as the debt negotiations progress.

Credit ratings were lowered on five major U.S. banks by S&P, which cited concern over loans to less-developed countries. Separately, bond investors are taking a grim view of the creditworthiness of money-center banks.

The CFTC issued its final report on the market's crash, calling for better coordination among regulators and exchange officials, including action against a trading practice known as intermarket "front-running."

3 The prime rate fell to 8½% from 8¾% amid growing speculation that the economy and inflation are slowing. Leading indicators fell 0.2% in December, the third decline in a row, though few expect a recession. Bond prices surged and long-term Treasury yields slid to nine-month lows. The dollar skidded, while stocks recovered from an early sell-off.

The Fed is being encouraged by Reagan officials in its move toward an easier monetary policy.

The SEC's report on the October crash called for better market surveillance and tougher rules for specialists and broker-dealers. But the report ignored the Brady panel's recommendation for a new regulatory body to oversee the markets.

Big Board directors are expected to vote tomorrow on a proposed two-tier limit on program trading, sources said. One proposal would reinforce present curbs on index arbitrage.

4 Factory orders rose 2.5% in December, countering predictions of a major economic slowdown. Still, a Commerce official cautioned that other data suggest "there will be some slowdown in growth." Most of the December gain came in transportation-equipment orders, which vary widely from month to month.

Bond prices slumped as investors reacted coolly to the Treasury's $9 billion note sale. The drop helped push stocks lower. The Dow Jones industrials closed off 28.34, at 1924.57. The dollar, meanwhile, surged on rumors of a Soviet nuclear accident.

U.S. car sales jumped 34.2% in late January, contradicting the dire predictions that followed the stock crash. Still, the gain partly reflected a weak year-earlier period. Meanwhile, auto makers have cut first-quarter car output schedules to a five-year low.

5 Major retailers posted modest sales gains for January, though promotions helped some stores register sharper rises. Analysts said the sales figures weren't that meaningful because of post-holiday belt-tightening, volatile weather and other factors.

Chrysler posted an 8% rise in quarterly profit and adopted "poison pill" anti-takeover measures. Chairman Iacocca said Chrysler hadn't been approached by a potential buyer but was concerned about recent foreign attempts to acquire U.S. firms.

The Big Board voted to curb use of index arbitrage in an effort to limit stock-price volatility. The move, which had been expected, strengthens the exchange's voluntary restraints on program trading passed Jan. 14.

Nonfarm productivity fell at an annual rate of 0.2% in the fourth quarter. The decline trimmed the gain in productivity for all of 1987 to a 0.8% rate, the lowest in five years.

8 The Fed's policy arm meets this week to decide whether to bolster the slowing economy with lower interest rates. One economist called it "one of the most critical" Fed sessions in recent memory. The Fed appears to have loosened credit slightly, but Fed officials worry that easing too much could hurt the dollar and worsen the U.S. trade deficit.

The jobless rate remained at 5.8%

in January, but a sluggish rise in jobs signaled slower growth ahead. Interest rates plunged Friday in reaction. The dollar rallied, but stocks fell.

Post-crash legislation appears unlikely, at least for this year. Senate Banking panel members indicated that financial markets would be given time to implement their own reforms before Congress takes any action.

Ford employees in Britain were set to strike at midnight, in what would be the biggest walkout by U.K. manufacturing workers in recent years. Contract talks broke off Friday and no new negotiations were scheduled.

9 CBOE floor traders plan to refund up to $2 million to as many as 200 clients who traded certain stock-index options on Oct. 20, the day after Black Monday, industry officials said. But the unprecedented action isn't likely to restore investor confidence anytime soon in stock-index options, the officials said.

Nomura Securities' U.S. unit has laid off about 6% of its staff, showing that even Japanese firms aren't immune from the slump on Wall Street. The layoffs reverse Nomura's rapid expansion in foreign operations.

10 Carlo de Benedetti appeared close to reaching an accord with a group led by Belgian businessman Andre Leysen to share control of Generale de Belgique, the giant Belgian holding concern. Such a pact between the Italian financier and the largely Belgian group would bring sweeping changes to the company.

Some short-term interest rates fell sharply amid growing speculation the Fed is easing credit slightly. Bond prices gained, and a late rally pushed the Dow Jones industrials up 18.74, to 1914.46. The dollar drifted lower.

11 Stocks and bonds rallied amid continued speculation that the Fed is easing credit. The Dow Jones industrials closed up 47.58 points, at 1962.04, the biggest gain since January 4. Short-term interest rates declined further, while some active Treasury issues climbed half a point. The dollar was narrowly mixed.

Any growth in banks' power to trade securities should be slow and include greater supervision, the GAO said. The recommendation is a blow to banks' efforts to get broad underwriting authority from Congress.

New York banks are mounting a drive to soften state prohibitions on banks underwriting securities.

Insurance companies are making major cuts in costs and personnel due to falling revenue and rising competition. The biggest retrenchment so far has been at Met Life, where about 1,000 accepted early retirement.

12 Retail sales rose 0.5% in January, mainly due to a surge in auto sales. The gain, following a revised 1.2% increase in December, suggests consumers haven't retrenched greatly. Meanwhile, state jobless claims fell for the second week in a row.

The Generale de Belgique battle took another turn as Suez of France and Andre Leysen formed an alliance that would exclude Carlo De Benedetti from control of the company. But the alliance is tentative.

16 Federated's board is expected to decide today whether to sell the company, accept a management-led buy-out, or restructure. The retailer agreed over the weekend to open talks with potential suitors, including Campeau, which plans to sweeten its proposed bid to over $65 a share, or $5.75 billion. Another expected bidder is Kohlberg Kravis.

Carlo De Benedetti launched a bid for an added 15% of Generale de Belgique. But he was undercut as the Belgian firm's stock soared well above his offer price. A French-Belgian alliance that was seeking control of the company collapsed Friday.

The U.S. trade deficit shrank by about $1 billion in December, to $12.2 billion, another sign that the nation's trade problems are easing. But imports remained stubbornly strong at a level about 50% higher than exports.

Japan's trade surplus in January was down 29% from a year earlier but was 22% higher than in December.

Producer prices rose 0.4% in January, reflecting a jump in food costs. But the increase, the first since September, doesn't suggest a broad resurgence in inflation. Business inventories climbed 0.8% in December.

U.S. car sales edged up 0.3% during early February as consumers shrugged off winter weather and worries about a recession.

17 Firestone agreed to form a joint venture with Bridgestone of Japan that would own and manage Firestone's global tire business. Under the plan, Firestone would get over $1 billion, much of which would go to holders, while Bridgestone would own 75% of the new venture. Analysts say a possible

Firestone bid by Italy's Pirelli likely prompted the pact.

Federated Department Stores rejected a sweetened takeover bid by Campeau of $66 a share, or $6.14 billion. The retailer is weighing a major restructuring plan that will give it time to consider other offers.

First Boston agreed to provide about $1.1 billion in financing for Campeau, trying to reassert itself after losing top merger specialists.

The World Bank is expected to vote this week to ask member nations for a $75 billion increase in capital. But the request, which would cost the U.S. about $416 million over several years, faces opposition in Congress.

A Bank of Tokyo unit agreed to buy Union Bank of Los Angeles from Standard Chartered for $750 million, reflecting the shifting balance of power in global banking. It would be one of the largest Japanese investments ever in a U.S. financial firm.

18 Housing starts fell 1.9% in January, offering no sign of a rebound in an industry expecting its worst year since the recession of 1982. The decline follows a revised drop of 15.5% in December. Separately, output at the nation's factories, mines and utilities continued to climb, growing a modest 0.2% last month after gaining a revised 0.4% in December.

Campeau boosted its hostile offer for Federated to $5.47 billion amid signs of a possible bidding war for the retailer. Potential suitors are said to include Kolhberg Kravis, Dillard Department Stores and developers Alfred Taubman and Melvin Simon.

Firestone's chief said the accord selling 75% of the company's tire business to Bridgestone of Japan will allow Firestone to reach its goal of becoming a retail-oriented concern.

Bridgestone's major aim in gaining control of Firestone's tire operations is to tap the business of other Japanese manufacturers in the U.S.

19 Reagan's final budget was sent to Congress and projects a $129.5 billion deficit for fiscal 1989 that even aides concede is optimistic. The budget, which is expected to generate little controversy, marks the final failure of Reagan's effort to cut the deficit and outlines the dimensions of the problem that his successor faces.

Ford Motor's profit rose 19% in the fourth quarter, but the results were below analysts' expectations, causing its stock to skid $2.50, to $42. Earnings were hurt by troubles in Latin America and higher marketing costs.

Foreign oil producers are heightening efforts to buy interests in U.S. refining and marketing operations. Saudi Arabia is said to be seeking a 50% stake in certain Texaco refineries, while Nigeria is holding talks with at least four U.S. oil companies.

22 Corporate profits surged 51% in the fourth quarter, though the gain was exaggerated by one-time charges and credits. Still, there were strong sales in a variety of industries. Most analysts expect a slowdown in earnings this year.

World oil markets are weakening further, and many oilmen say prices could fall by $1 to $2 a barrel soon. That could pose a new test for OPEC, whose output is beginning to rise again after plunging in January.

The Fed likely won't cut short-term interest rates right now because the economy appears to be perking up, analysts say. But several predict slower growth in the next few months will prompt the Fed to ease credit.

The central bank was criticized by Reagan and his economic advisers, who said the Fed pursued an overly tight monetary policy last year.

23 Nissan plans to follow its main Japanese rivals by building major auto components in the U.S., including engines. It also is considering expanding its U.S. assembly capacity. Separately, Nissan said it is closer to a joint vehicle venture with Ford.

Shortages of semifinished steel are worsening in the U.S., prompting mounting criticism of steel import quotas and claims of price-gouging within the steel industry itself.

Campeau extended the deadline for its friendly $66-a-share bid for Federated Department Stores amid signs of a slowdown in bank financing talks. Some sources said Campeau is balking at added banks fees, but others cited logistical problems.

24 Greenspan confirmed that the Fed recently eased credit, allowing interest rates to decline. But the Fed chairman told Congress there are "very few signs" of a recession, suggesting the central bank won't ease further unless there are new hints of weakness in the economy.

Bond prices rallied on Greenspan's testimony, while precious metals and other commodities tumbled. Stocks were mixed, while the dollar fell.

Durable-goods orders fell 2.8% in January, mainly because of a drop in the volatile transportation-equipment sector. Some economists viewed the report bullishly, and Greenspan described it as "quite strong."

Texaco agreed to pay $1.25 billion to settle an oil-pricing dispute with the U.S. government. The pact brings to $6.75 billion the amount Texaco has agreed to pay to settle various claims, including the one from Pennzoil.

25 Northrop is being investigated by the military over employee claims of widespread fraudulent billing on the secret Stealth bomber program. Also, one current and three former Northrop employees filed a civil suit, claiming Northrop destroyed internal audit documents identifying false labor charges.

Fed Chairman Greenspan harshly criticized a top Treasury official's attempt to influence Fed policy. He warned that further attempts could be dangerously counterproductive.

U.S. car sales rose 11.9% in mid-February, but analysts said the results may not justify plans by the Big Three makers to boost production.

GM plans to rehire 8,600 workers at four U.S. and Canadian assembly plants, citing rising consumer demand and declining inventory.

26 Fourth-quarter GNP growth was revised upward to a 4.5% rate, reflecting less-severe drops in consumer spending and equipment purchases. The revision, from a 4.2% rate, bolsters the view the stock crash didn't immediately hurt the economy.

Campeau intensified its quest for Federated Department Stores by reinforcing its financing and increasing its hostile tender offer to $66 a share, or $5.84 billion. Federated's directors met to consider various options.

Mexico's debt-swap plan appears to be a success, mainly because of European and Japanese banks and regional U.S. institutions, bankers said. But the plan may cut Mexico's foreign debt far less than expected.

World oil prices slumped to two-month lows, hurt by increased OPEC production and a reported buildup in U.S. supplies. On the New York Merc, crude closed at $15.92 a barrel.

Stocks and bonds ended lower after early rallies reversed course. The Dow Jones industrials closed off 22.38, at 2017.57. The dollar also fell.

Nearly half of all U.S. patents issued last year went to foreigners, many of them Japanese. The U.S. Patent Office warned that the trend poses a threat to U.S. dominance in some leading technologies.

29 Campeau is expected to present to Federated's board today a definitive takeover accord of $68 a share, or $6.02 billion. Both firms have been negotiating since Thursday night, when Federated agreed to open talks. If the pact is accepted, Campeau is expected to sell many of Federated's retail chains to help pay off the huge debt from the acquisition.

Consumer prices rose 0.3% in January, or at a 4.2% compound annual rate, suggesting inflation may be worsening even though consumer spending is sluggish. The sharpest price increases were in services.

Confidence in the economy outweighs pessimism for the first time since the October stock crash, a survey of American consumers found.

A Third World debt plan will be unveiled today by American Express Chairman James Robinson. Under the proposal, a new agency would offer to buy shaky loans from banks at a discount and help devise economic programs for debtor nations.

March 1988

1 Stock prices rallied, pushing the Dow Jones industrials up 48.41, to 2071.62, its highest level since the October crash. The active session was dominated by takeover-related trades and issues with high dividends. Bonds were little changed, while oil and precious-metals prices surged. The dollar generally eased.

Takeover activity reached a recent peak with the announcement of six transactions totaling $5.4 billion. The flurry, fueled by low stock prices, isn't expected to slow soon. But hostile bank mergers may be rare.

Federated Department Stores is said to have received a takeover bid from R. H. Macy, derailing Campeau's hopes for a quick agreement on its $6.02 billion proposal. Federated's directors were deliberating on both takeover bids as of late yesterday.

2 Leading indicators slid 0.6% in January, portending slow growth. But December's index was revised to a 0.3% rise rather than a 0.2% drop, and few analysts foresee a recession. Construction

outlays fell 2.9% in January but were up 0.4% in December.

Oil prices tumbled to 10-week lows on reports that Arabian Oil, 20%-owned by Saudi Arabia and Kuwait, offered discounts from official OPEC prices. The report was denied.

3 Federated agreed to be acquired by R. H. Macy for cash and securities that some Wall Street analysts valued at about $6.1 billion. But Campeau immediately raised its hostile tender offer to an estimated $68 a share in cash, or $6.18 billion. Traders reacted coolly to the Macy agreement, though Campeau's efforts face a number of obstacles.

Factory orders fell 0.6% in January, indicating slower growth in the quarter. But the report probably overstates the weakness, and orders are expected to be fairly strong in coming months. Separately, home sales fell 9% in January to a five-year low.

4 Car sales surged 24% in late February, surprising analysts and even auto makers. Combined sales of autos and light trucks jumped 25.5%. Incentive programs apparently fueled the increase, though the results were striking because of sluggishness in other consumer sectors.

Major retailers posted weak sales for February, renewing recession fears. Sears posted a 1.1% gain, but many others reported declines.

Texaco will emerge from Chapter 11 later this year as a smaller firm, focused on exploration and production rather than on refining and marketing, and increasingly involved in joint ventures, company executives said.

7 The jobless rate fell to 5.7% in February as job creation surged. The figure—down from 5.8% and the lowest since 1979—suggests the economy is growing faster than estimated. But the bond market reacted negatively to the news, which led to worries of higher interest rates and inflation. Prices of long-term Treasury bonds fell steeply.

Purchasing agents say U.S. economic growth is slowing and that output is likely to slow this month.

Reagan advisers are expected to decide soon whether to urge sanctions against Japan for not giving more construction work to U.S. firms.

Findings by a GATT panel could invalidate part of the 1986 U.S.-Japan semiconductor trade pact.

Some OPEC members are curbing output and others are calling for the group's pricing panel to meet in efforts to stem the oil-price drop.

Campeau agreed to sell two Federated Department Store chains to May Department Stores for $1.5 billion if its hostile bid succeeds.

8 Mobil agreed to sell its Montgomery Ward unit to a management-led group for $1.5 billion and the assumption of $2.3 billion in debt. The sale, which ends an unsuccessful expansion into retailing, will result in neither a gain nor a loss, Mobil said. Analysts began speculating that a debt-lightened Mobil will be out shopping for acquisitions.

Copper-futures prices rose for the fifth consecutive session on renewed supply concerns and better-than-expected economic prospects.

9 Stock prices rallied on continued takeover activity, pushing the Dow Jones industrials up 24.70 points, to 2081.07, a post-crash high. Trading was active. Traders and analysts cited a growing bullish sentiment and the approaching end of the first quarter, which is persuading money managers to buy more stocks. Bond prices rebounded from an early slump and closed nearly unchanged.

A bill defining insider trading won't be enacted by Congress, Rep. Dingell predicted. But the Energy and Commerce panel chairman said he is sure lawmakers will move to improve ways of detecting that crime.

Major oil-producing nations may be considering further cuts in output to halt the slide in prices. Venezuela called for an emergency OPEC meeting, while non-OPEC producers will meet in London today to discuss steps to firm up the world oil market.

10 An oil-price rebound is now being predicted by some industry officials, who cite increased capital spending by many oil firms this year. But a key question is OPEC, which may meet soon to counter falling prices by cutting output further.

Bridgestone of Japan hasn't indicated whether it will continue to seek Firestone's tire operations following Pirelli of Italy's $1.85 billion bid to acquire all of Firestone.

Fixed mortgage rates continue to hover just below 10%, and analysts now are expecting that level to hold through the second quarter.

11 Stock prices plunged in the afternoon, fueled by program selling. The Dow Jones industrials closed off 48.24, at

2026.03. The sell-off was sparked by several factors, including a weaker dollar, higher gold and oil prices, and apparently unfounded rumors of new indictments on Wall Street. Bonds drifted lower.

Futures experts said almost nothing has been done to prevent another stock market crash. They added that the few changes already made could worsen future market downturns.

Japan's trade surplus fell 26.5% in February from a year ago, the 10th drop in a row. The surplus with the U.S. also narrowed as imports from America surged in a variety of areas, including manufactured goods.

14 Macy is expected today to sweeten its estimated $6.1 billion merger accord with Federated, acknowledging the pact is threatened by Campeau's $6.18 billion tender bid. Meanwhile, a federal judge is scheduled to hear arguments this afternoon on lawsuits relating to the takeover battle. His ruling on several matters could decide the fate of Federated.

Retail sales rose 0.6% in February, mainly due to strong auto sales. Economists expect consumer spending to remain modest in coming months. Producer prices fell 0.2%, reflecting drops in food and energy prices.

U.S. farm exports are expected to surge further in the fiscal year ending Sept. 30, but analysts say the upswing may not last much beyond that.

15 Reagan will seek a consensus among regulators on ways to prevent another market crash, officials said. The president, under pressure from Congress, intends to set up an inter-agency panel, headed by Treasury Secretary Baker, to thrash out a policy on market reforms. Some regulatory heads disagree on the changes needed.

The CBOE was named a defendant in the first class-action lawsuit brought since the October crash.

Macy raised its bid for control of Federated to an estimated $6.35 billion and secured an option to buy two of its best-known divisions. But investors appeared disappointed by the new bid. Also, Campeau extended its $6.18 billion offer until Friday.

Business inventories rose 0.4% in January, less than half December's pace. Economists were divided on whether it was a positive sign. Manufacturing and wholesale inventories rose, but retail stocks declined.

First RepublicBank will consider today whether to seek federal aid to avoid the possible failure of its flagship Dallas bank and perhaps other banks. It could be one of the largest federal bank rescues in history.

16 First RepublicBank said it has approached federal regulators about an FDIC-assisted bailout to prevent the collapse of some of its banks. The Texas banking firm also rescinded preferred dividend payments.

Car sales rose 3.5% in early March, a slowdown from the rapid growth last month. The smaller gain mainly resulted from lower sales at GM after incentive programs ended.

The U.S. current-account deficit shrank to $38.99 billion in the fourth quarter, helped by the weak dollar. But the deficit for all of 1987 in the broad trade measure hit a record.

17 Industrial output gained a modest 0.2% in February, aided by rising exports. Increased production of business equipment and construction supplies were the main factors. Also, housing starts jumped 8.9% last month, rebounding from sharp declines the previous two months.

Bond prices slumped as the economic reports renewed inflation worries. But stocks rallied, partly due to easing concern about today's report on U.S. trade. The dollar firmed.

OPEC production has plunged to the lowest level this year, putting less downward pressure on oil prices. The sudden drop was attributed mainly to lower output by Saudi Arabia. Meanwhile, world oil prices soared, mostly in reaction to turmoil in Panama.

An investment newsletter publisher, Edwin Fishbaine, was charged by the SEC with failing to tell readers that he was paid to tout the securities of several Canadian companies.

18 The trade gap grew slightly in January to $12.44 billion, though imports fell 6% to a nine-month low. Exports dropped 10%, partly due to seasonal factors, though they stayed far ahead of year-earlier levels. Still, some analysts said the figures suggest the U.S. export boom may be slowing. Exports of manufactured goods fell 7.6% in the month.

Investors responded favorably to the report, sparking rallies in the dollar and stock and bond markets. The Dow Jones industrials climbed 21.72, to 2086.04, a post-crash high.

First RepublicBank received a $1 billion loan from the FDIC to help stem the loss of depositors and customers while the firm seeks investors. The FDIC said it hopes to find a permanent solution within six months.

The bailout of Texas banks and thrifts could swell the federal deficit and force new cuts before the fall election, some Reagan aides said.

The industrial operating rate remained at 82.4% of capacity in February, the highest in about eight years.

British Chancellor of the Exchequer Nigel Lawson regained the upper hand over monetary policy by pushing key U.K. interest rates lower.

Saudi Arabia offered price incentives to lure back oil customers and revive its crude output, which has plunged recently. OPEC's president plans to announce steps on Tuesday to stabilize oil markets.

21 Bridgestone of Japan defended its accord to pay $80 a share, or $2.6 billion, for Firestone as necessary to expand in the U.S. tire market. Meanwhile, Pirelli of Italy, which had offered $58 a share, dropped its bid.

Campeau is considering several major changes in its $6.18 billion offer for Federated Department Stores after losing a key court ruling Friday. The court refused to invalidate Federated's "poison pill" defense.

22 Oil prices swung sharply before closing lower in one of the most volatile sessions in six months. The gyrations, fueled by OPEC statements, caused equal turbulence in the bond markets, where prices also finished down. Stocks skidded, but trading was very light. The Dow Jones industrials fell 20.23, to 2067.14.

Indonesia's oil minister Subroto was ousted in a cabinet shake-up in Jakarta. As a result, war-torn OPEC loses an important peacemaker.

Texaco shareholders gave "overwhelming support" to the company's bankruptcy-reorganization plan, a source said. Approval would move Texaco one step closer to emerging from Chapter 11 proceedings.

23 Four major insurers were accused of creating a liability crisis by conspiring to manipulate the availability and cost of commercial coverage. The antitrust suits name Hartford Fire, Allstate, Aetna Life and Cigna.

Oil prices tumbled further in jittery trading. The drop was attributed to the cancellation of an OPEC news conference and continued reaction to Saudi Arabia's confirmation of selling oil at a discount. Stocks, bonds and the dollar ended little-changed.

24 The Texaco-Pennzoil battle officially ended as a bankruptcy court approved Texaco's reorganization plan, allowing it to emerge from Chapter 11 on April 7. Despite the end of the four-year struggle, Texaco still faces major hurdles, including huge debt and a possible proxy fight by its largest shareholder, Carl Icahn.

OPEC's price-monitoring panel revived plans to meet, which sent oil prices surging. Though the session may accomplish little, sources said merely scheduling it may help OPEC weather the current price crunch.

Interest rates rose slightly as the gain in oil prices heightened worries about inflation. Stocks drifted again, while the dollar edged lower.

Consumer prices edged up 0.2% in February, suggesting inflation remains under control. Meanwhile, the estimate for fourth-quarter GNP growth was revised upward to a 4.8% annual rate from 4.5% previously.

U.S. car sales fell 2.3% in mid-March, the first year-to-year decline in any 10-day period since the beginning of the year. The drop wasn't severe, but it signaled a slowdown.

25 The dollar plunged, triggering a sharp slide in the stock market. Dealers said the currency was hurt by reports of strong U.S. personal income and consumer spending, which stirred fears of a bigger U.S. trade deficit. The Dow Jones industrials closed off 43.77, at 2023.87. Bonds finished little changed.

Consumer spending rose 0.7% in February, while income grew 0.9%. Though spending appears to be rebounding from a drop in the fourth quarter, economists expect only modest increases in coming months.

Du Pont plans to phase out production of chlorofluorocarbons, which have been linked to the depletion of the ozone layer. Du Pont estimates it produces 25% of all CFCs.

Federated's suitors are showing few signs of weakening their resolve. Macy is reopening talks to revise its merger accord with Federated so it tops Campeau's latest bid. But Federated agreed to meet with Campeau, which also may raise its bid.

28 The White House said it will accept a measure authorizing the president to block foreign takeovers of U.S. firms on national security grounds. As a re-

sult of the compromise, a more controversial provision requiring foreigners to disclose U.S. investments could be dropped, improving prospects that Reagan will sign the sweeping trade bill.

Bond prices rallied Friday as stocks fell further. The stock market's weakness heightened fears about a replay of the October crash, prompting investors to switch into government-backed bonds, traders said. The Dow Jones industrials shed 108.42 points last week to close at 1978.95.

The Fed's credit policy panel probably will vote to leave its recent strategy unchanged, despite worries about inflation, surveyed economists said.

The dollar declined amid growing bearish sentiment, despite renewed central bank intervention. Traders in New York estimated the Fed bought up to $70 million Friday.

Operating losses at the most insolvent thrifts have grown to the point where the FSLIC will have trouble reducing its huge liability for failures even if no more thrifts go broke.

29 The dollar fell sharply, taking bond prices with it. The currency's slump—to its lowest levels since January—renewed concern that foreign investors may cut back purchases of dollar-denominated investments and stirred fears of inflation and higher interest rates. Although the Dow Jones industrials edged up, losers outnumbered gainers.

House-Senate conferees are expected today to approve a controversial provision requiring advance notice of plant closings, despite renewed threats of a Reagan veto. The move could jeopardize business support for the sweeping trade package.

Mulroney said he expects Canada's trade pact with the U.S. to be approved by both nations.

Top bank executives received large 1987 bonuses, despite presiding over record losses last year.

30 Kohlberg Kravis said it will seek clearance to buy up to 15% of Texaco, increasing pressure for a restructuring of the oil giant. The investment partnership said it already holds 4.92%. Texaco stock jumped $3.25 to $48, its highest level since March 1984, raising the company's market value by $789 million.

The index of leading indicators rose 0.9% last month after a revised 1.1% drop in January, heralding neither a recession nor a boom. Single-family home sales surged 20.3% after a 10.3% plunge.

Japan agreed to give U.S. construction companies the right to bid on 14 major public-works projects, averting likely trade sanctions.

House-Senate conferees approved a provision requiring advance notice of plant closings, a move that could lead Reagan to veto the trade bill.

The dollar recovered much of its Monday loss, thanks to continued intervention by the Bank of Japan and the Fed as well as short-covering. Bond prices rebounded in response, and stocks staged a broad advance.

31 First RepublicBank's financial condition continues to worsen and casts increasing doubt on the cost projections for a federal bailout or a rescue by a buyer. The Texas concern, in a draft of its shareholder report, painted a picture of troubles out of control. And its auditors said the company "may be unable to continue in its present form."

The Big Three auto makers accused their Japanese rivals of dumping compact pickup trucks in the U.S., but stopped short of filing formal dumping charges in Washington.

The three U.S. makers raised second-quarter production plans above year-ago levels, reflecting near-term optimism for the auto market.

A robust Tokyo Stock Exchange is entering the new Japanese fiscal year poised to break its pre-crash record high. Corporate profits and liquidity have drawn money to the market.

Orders for factory goods fell 0.8% last month as businesses continued to trim built-up inventories. But many economists say the outlook for manufacturing is fairly bright.

April 1988

1 Macy outbid Campeau in the battle for Federated. But as Federated directors prepared to meet today to weigh the latest offers, no one would call the contest closed. Speculation was that Campeau would go higher.

Merrill Lynch overtook Salomon Brothers as top U.S. underwriter in the first quarter, and appears set to hold its lead for the year.

4 Campeau won the battle for Federated

Department Stores, agreeing to sell two prime Federated divisions to rival suitor R. H. Macy. The $6.6 billion takeover, ending a 10-week struggle, will make Toronto-based Campeau the largest department-store retailer in America. But it also leaves Campeau heavily indebted in a sluggish retail environment.

The jobless rate fell to 5.6% in March, a nine-year low, amid an unexpectedly big gain in jobs. The report suggests the economy grew moderately in the first quarter. Construction spending fell 0.3% in February.

The economy's continued strength along with moderate inflation continues to surprise analysts. But some fear that financial markets are headed for rough times because of efforts to enact a major trade bill.

Japan's current-account surplus narrowed further in February as imports of manufactured goods surged a record 77.5%. Separately, Japan's unemployment rate was 2.7% during February, unchanged from January.

5 Bond prices tumbled amid signs that the Fed is nudging up interest rates because of surprising strength in the economy. The catalyst was Friday's report of a drop in the jobless rate. The Fed apparently is reversing its credit policy in order to fight possible inflationary pressures. Stocks also sank, as the Dow Jones industrials declined 7.46, to 1980.60. The dollar was narrowly mixed.

The Big Board plans to prohibit intermarket front-running in futures, or trading futures in order to profit on knowledge of impending orders in the stock market. The practice came under scrutiny after the October crash.

6 Aramco named Saudi Arabia's oil minister Hisham Nazer as chairman, further diminishing the role of four major U.S. oil companies in the firm and the Saudi oil industry. Saudi Arabia took over Aramco during the 1970s from a partnership of Exxon, Texaco, Chevron and Mobil. Aramco remains the world's biggest crude-oil producing company.

Interest rates eased, helped by a stronger dollar and a Fed official's comment that the central bank is determined to restrain inflation. The dollar's rise also helped spur a late rally in the stock market.

Energy prices weakened, mainly on rumors about Saturday's meeting of OPEC's price-monitoring panel.

Standard & Poor's plans to move its international department to London from New York, part of a big expansion of its European business.

Campeau expects to sell about $4.4 billion in Federated assets to help finance its purchase of the big retailer.

7 Stocks and bonds surged in reaction to a stronger dollar, which rallied on a report the Group of Seven will agree next week to stabilize the currency at 125 yen. The Dow Jones industrials soared 64.16 points, to 2061.67, the sharpest gain in over three months. But most short-term interest rates climbed, and speculation is growing that the prime rate may go up soon. Gold hit a two-week low.

U.S. car sales jumped 6.1% in late March, surprising auto makers and giving them their best first quarter since 1985. The surge mainly resulted from consumers taking advantage of continuing broad price discounts. Truck sales also were strong.

Most top executives on Wall Street took cuts in salary last year as their companies saw earnings plunge. Morgan Stanley was the only major publicly held securities firm to post higher 1987 profit and the only one to boost the pay of top executives.

Mortgage rates continued to fall in March, but analysts suggested the bottom is near. Fixed-rate mortgages in early March had an average effective interest rate of 10.34%, down from 10.48% in early February and the lowest in nearly a year.

8 The big board voted to sharply increase capital requirements for its 52 specialist firms. The move, which officials called largely symbolic, indicates the October crash is likely to result in major changes in the New York exchange's market-making system. The Big Board is under pressure to revamp the specialist system, whose performance has been criticized in studies of the crash.

Major retailers posted moderate sales gains for March, an improvement from February's weak results. But an early Easter shopping season accounted for much of the gain. Analysts expect retailers to report flat or lower profit for the first quarter.

The dollar drifted lower as the British pound surged against the West German mark despite intervention. Stocks rose, though profit-taking limited the gains by blue chips. Bonds inched lower in sluggish trading.

Japanese investors were the largest net buyers of foreign equities last year, surpassing the British, who had held the top spot for several years, Salomon Brothers' London unit said. Most of the Japanese purchases have been directed to the U.S. market.

Brazil suspended cost-of-living wage increases for state workers in a bid to curb the government deficit. The move came as Brazil's top economic officials prepared to travel to Washington for talks with the IMF.

The IMF is expected to make it easier for debtor nations to qualify for aid, in part by giving them more time to implement economic reforms.

11 Stocks and bonds surged on Friday as interest rates declined. The Dow Jones industrials closed up 28.02, at 2090.19, a post-crash high. Meanwhile, the stock market has become cautious, and dull, since the crash.

The pound rose further despite a cut in the U.K. base rate to 8% from 8½%. The dollar was little changed.

OPEC will try again to form an alliance with nonmember oil producers to jointly reduce output. The latest effort, aimed at bolstering sagging oil prices, appears to have a better chance than in the past because the initiative came from eight non-OPEC nations. OPEC representatives plan to hold talks with as many as 10 nonmembers later this month.

12 Oil prices surged to four-month highs in reaction to OPEC's plan to discuss output cuts with nonmember producers. The April 23 session may not succeed, but it showed again that OPEC can cause prices to jump merely by scheduling a meeting. Oil prices are expected to remain relatively firm until the results of the April talks are known.

Bond prices plunged, partly due to the rise in oil prices. Stocks rebounded from an early slump to close higher. The dollar also climbed.

Japan's trade surplus fell 7.4% in March from a year earlier, the 11th consecutive monthly decline. But the surplus rose slightly from February.

Index arbitrage may have worsened the stock market's January 8 slide, when the industrial average plunged 140 points, an SEC study says.

13 The big board is discussing halting all program trading when the Dow Jones Industrial Average moves over 150 points, and closing the market entirely if the average moves over 300 points. The proposals, introduced at a briefing for big institutional traders, amount to additional "circuit breakers" aimed at preventing another stock crash.

Stocks gained further, pushing the Dow Jones industrials up 14.09 points to a post-crash high of 2110.08. Most interest rates drifted lower, while the dollar edged up. Many investors continued to stay on the sidelines.

U.S. crude-oil prices rose above $18 a barrel, though analysts warned that the markets may be too optimistic.

Nissan Motor plans to cut exports to the U.S. at least through September because of slow sales. The No. 2 Japanese auto maker has been hurt by an old product line and muddled image.

Middle South Utilities said it may be difficult to avoid a bankruptcy filing for one or more of its units because of adverse rate decisions.

14 Texas Air's fitness to run an airline is being investigated by federal regulators. The FAA also proposed fining the company's Eastern Airlines unit $823,000 for alleged safety violations. The inquiry is aimed at pressuring Texas Air into complying with safety rules, but there is an implicit threat that regulators could ground the company's planes.

A dollar-stabilization pact was reaffirmed by the Group of Seven industrial nations, as expected. The dollar rose against most European currencies but weakened against the yen. Stocks ended mixed, snapping a six-day rally. Bonds closed up slightly.

Retail sales surged 0.8% in March, indicating consumer spending has rebounded from a post-crash slump. For the first quarter, sales were up 1.7% from a depressed fourth quarter and 6.7% higher than a year earlier.

U.S. car sales slid 15.6% in early April, partly due to holidays and the vagaries of sales incentives.

Several big U.S. companies have formed a consortium to try to break into the Soviet market. The group, which includes Kodak, RJR Nabisco and Ford, will attempt to negotiate a trade agreement with Moscow.

15 A trade-bill provision requiring advance notice of factory closings was retained by congressional leaders after protests by labor and Democrats. The action makes it all but certain Reagan will veto the bill.

Carlo de Benedetti failed to win a seat on Generale de Belgique's board, frustrating for now his bid for control. But many observers believe the Italian financier eventually could get a major role in the Belgian company.

Financial markets were rattled by an unexpected swelling of the February U.S. trade deficit. News of the $13.83 billion gap sent the Dow Jones industrials skidding 101.46 points, or 4.82%, to 2005.64, its fifth-biggest drop ever. Most interest rates surged as Treasury bonds fell 1½ points. The dollar plunged despite intervention. Precious metals soared.

The markets' slide may have been worsened by the "circuit breakers" set up to avoid another crash, many traders said. Meanwhile, exchange heads expect to agree on cross-market circuit breakers within 30 days.

U.S. auto makers boosted second-quarter output plans again, mainly to replenish inventories depleted by strong first-quarter sales.

Brazil will soon announce further spending cuts, part of a program to slash the government's deficit and help "stabilize" the economy.

18 The safety investigation of Texas Air is being sharply broadened as the Transportation Department today begins a full inspection of Continental Airlines. Regulators decided to place the unit in the widespread inspection program because the FAA has almost $1 million in fines pending against Continental.

Producer prices rose 0.6% in March, renewing fears of higher inflation and interest rates. Industrial output increased 0.1%, and U.S. businesses said they plan to increase capital spending 8.8% this year.

U.S. government bonds again could be the worst performers this year among the world's major bond markets, according to some analysts.

Bond prices fell further on news of the rise in producer prices, and short-term rates rose. Stock prices rebounded slightly, helped by a firmer dollar and some bargain-hunting.

The three television networks lost millions of viewers this past TV season as watchers defected to cable TV, independent stations and VCRs.

The Big Three auto makers' profits in the first quarter may have fallen as much as 15%, due to lower output and costly buyer incentives, analysts say. The earnings outlook for the current quarter is more upbeat, though.

GM is giving top officials short-term bonuses, even though the auto maker had said it would stress long-term incentives when it overhauled its bonus program a year ago.

Fixed-rate mortgages are rising again after months of decline, but bigger increases would be needed to damp the strong sales of homes.

19 World oil prices surged after the U.S. attack on Iranian oil platforms, but the gains were pared later in New York. Stocks and bonds closed lower. The dollar was mixed, while the British pound hit a six-year high.

20 The trade bill was completed by House-Senate conferees amid a renewed threat of a Reagan veto. The panel dropped a requirement that foreigners disclose U.S. investment but kept a measure requiring advance notice of factory closings. Congressional leaders said this may be the last chance to pass a major trade bill in this Congress, but they ruled out the idea of revising the legislation.

Housing starts rose 1.9% in March following a revised 9.6% gain in February. Analysts were cheered by the results, but they still expect 1988 starts to be the lowest in six years.

21 Municipal bond interest can be taxed by Congress, the Supreme Court ruled. The decision rattled the bond markets, though Congress isn't likely to rush to raise revenue by taxing state and local bonds. In the same ruling, the justices upheld a 1982 law that states keep records of who buys municipal bonds.

Consumer prices climbed 0.5% in March, led by a record surge in apparel costs. The rise, equal to a 6.4% annual rate, was another sign that inflation is heating up. Economists are expecting more bad inflation news.

Program trading is facing renewed public criticism following last week's plunge by the Dow Jones industrials. The SEC approved a Big Board curb on such trading.

Major U.S. steelmakers are expected to report their best quarterly earnings since 1979. Analysts say the industry's growth should continue.

Japan's big steel firms are preparing to report solid operating earnings for the latest fiscal year.

22 Energy prices are expected to be volatile next week during OPEC's historic meeting with non-member oil producers. But many are skeptical that any lasting changes will emerge from the talks, which are aimed at jointly restraining production.

GM's earnings climbed 18% in the first

quarter but would have fallen 6% without an accounting change.

25 The U.S. is trying to derail OPEC's attempt to form an alliance with nonmember oil producers. Energy Secretary Herrington has visited six Asian nations to lobby against the OPEC effort, which is aimed at reducing oil output to prop up prices. It isn't clear yet if the U.S. campaign will affect this week's talks between OPEC and nonmember producers.

GM plans major cutbacks over five years that will reduce car-production capacity to match current sales. The retrenchment is a big about-face for GM, which has insisted its market-share losses were only temporary.

Firestone will be dropped as a tire supplier for GM's North American vehicles. The decision is a major blow, but Firestone said it won't affect the merger with Bridgestone.

Durable goods orders were nearly unchanged in March from the previous month, when they edged up 0.1%. The February figure was sharply revised from an initial 1.8% drop.

Machine-tool orders rose 55% last month from a year ago, boosting the quarterly total to a seven-year high.

Major central banks are prepared to intervene again to prop up the dollar, senior Japanese officials said. The banks intervened heavily nearly two weeks ago after the U.S. trade report sent the dollar skidding.

Chrysler plans to shift production of its K-cars to Mexico from the U.S. The decision has riled union officials and could create a ticklish public relations problem for the auto maker.

26 The trade bill picked up more support in the Senate, though Democrats didn't claim to have the two-thirds necessary to override an anticipated Reagan veto. The Senate is expected to vote on the bill today.

U.S. car sales edged up 1.2% in mid-April, recovering from a sharp drop earlier in the month. The slight rebound had been expected because many analysts called the early April plunge an aberration. But sales still lagged the strong March results.

27 Four big steelmakers had strong first-quarter results as the long-beleaguered industry notched its best quarter since 1979. USX, National Steel and Wheeling-Pittsburgh returned to profitability, while Bethlehem Steel's earnings more than tripled.

More big oil companies reported major gains in first-quarter earnings, aided by stronger refining and petro-chemical results. Texaco's profit more than doubled, Chevron's surged 81% and Sun's jumped 58%. Phillips Petroleum returned to profitability.

World oil demand is expected to grow much more sharply this year than many in the industry originally projected. The anticipated surge may bail out oil-producing nations even if they don't agree to restrain output at their meetings this week in Vienna.

GNP grew at a 2.3% annual rate in the first quarter, a languid pace that quieted fears of a recession and higher inflation. The growth reflected a rebound in consumer spending—particularly on durable goods—strong business investment and a smaller trade deficit.

28 OPEC and nonmember producers moved closer to coordinating output, though higher projections for world oil demand lessened the urgency to cut production. OPEC will further study a plan to trim exports 5%.

Crude-oil futures closed sharply lower after swinging widely on rumors about the talks in Vienna.

Consumer spending rose 0.7% in March, showing signs of continued strength. The increase followed a revised 0.8% gain in February. Personal income climbed 0.8% last month.

Chrysler's earnings fell 32% in the first quarter, mainly due to a write-off for plant closings. Also, Chrysler delayed until year end two car-production moves that have fueled tensions at the UAW contract talks.

29 Ford's profit rose 9% in the first quarter, to $1.62 billion, an auto industry record for any quarter. The results, which surprised analysts and topped GM's and Chrysler's combined earnings, were boosted by unexpectedly strong overseas profit. But Ford's U.S. earnings fell 11%, partly because of higher labor costs and heavy use of buyer incentives.

Duke Power agreed in principle to manage a troubled nuclear plant in California, though Duke is based in North Carolina. It would be the first time a utility has taken over another's management of a nuclear facility.

May 1988

2 A huge jet order is pitting Boeing against both McDonnell Douglas and Airbus

Industrie. The buyer, International Lease Finance, plans to order at least 100 jets next week, and expects to give it either to Boeing alone or to split it between the other two. The more than $4 billion order could be an industry record.

OPEC ministers tried last night to reach a compromise on proposals for joining nonmember producers in an effort to boost oil prices. Despite last week's unprecedented talks, prospects for a world OPEC seem slim.

Banks and the U.S. Treasury are engaged in an increasingly bitter argument over each other's handling of the world debt problem. The quarrel could complicate and prolong debt negotiations with Brazil and Argentina.

Leading indicators rose 0.8% in March, another sign of the economy's strength. The gain followed a revised 1.3% increase in February and a 0.7% drop in January. Separately, purchasing agents said the economy picked up steam in April, but so did prices.

The Fed probably will raise short-term interest rates slightly in the next few weeks in an attempt to keep inflation in check, economists say.

3 OPEC renewed contact with nonmember oil producers, hoping to keep alive a possible alliance. OPEC's failure over the weekend to agree on joint production cuts with nonmembers sent oil prices plunging on spot and futures markets. The ministers decided to delay any action until OPEC's next meeting June 8.

Blue-chip stocks gained in reaction to oil's slide, but the broad market remained in a slump. Precious metals futures fell, while the dollar was mixed. Most interest rates edged up.

Factory orders climbed 1.6% in March, led by strong bookings for transportation equipment and military gear. Meanwhile, construction outlays rose 1.5%, helped by a jump in spending on public buildings.

Non-farm productivity increased at a modest 0.9% rate in the first quarter, continuing a recent slowdown.

A manufacturer's decision to stop supplying retailers for discounting prices isn't automatically illegal unless there is an effort to fix prices, the Supreme Court ruled. But the decision isn't expected to have a big impact.

4 The Continental Illinois bank fraud case ended as the jury acquitted one defendant, an Oklahoma oil man, but was unable to reach a verdict on two former bankers. The case is perhaps the biggest bank fraud trial ever.

The NASD said it will provide more information to investors about disciplinary actions taken against member firms and their employees.

5 U.S. car sales fell 6.7% in late April from a strong year-ago period. Analysts said the decline was smaller than expected, indicating auto makers might maintain aggressive output plans for the second period.

Kuwait's 22% stake in BP is being investigated by Britain, which cited concerns about the Arab oil producer's influence over the firm.

6 The SEC moved to limit third-market trading by allowing the NASD to halt over-the-counter trading in a stock pending a corporate announcement. The 3–2 decision, giving the NASD the same power as the Big Board and Amex, makes it possible for the first time to ban trading in a stock in all domestic markets. Trading among institutions and in foreign markets would still be possible.

Major retailers posted lower sales for April, continuing a sluggish trend. Analysts cited persistent weakness in women's apparel and unusually cool weather in the Northeast and West. Variety stores and discounters performed better than apparel stores.

Energy futures prices rose following an explosion at a major U.S. refining plant. Stocks fell in nervous trading, while bonds were narrowly mixed. The dollar strengthened.

9 Corporate profits rose 24% in the first quarter, but economists see a slowdown ahead. The increase, though smaller than the 51% and 33% in the previous two quarters, was spread across a range of industries, a Wall Street Journal survey shows. Many sectors were aided by a weaker dollar and lower tax rates. Canadian profits also were higher.

The jobless rate fell to 5.4% in April, a 14-year low. The decline, along with a modest increase in jobs, suggests healthy growth in the economy but is likely to fuel worries about a worsening of the inflation rate.

Campeau's choice to head its Allied-Federated retail operations quit unexpectedly, intensifying management disarray. Robert Morosky resigned following a feud with Chairman Robert Campeau, sources said.

Boeing is finding in its oldest jets still in service a "general incidence of corrosion damage" that requires extensive repair work. The discovery is the main finding so far in a 17-month internal study, researchers said.

Texas Air sued its pilots and machinists unions, accusing them of conspiring to destroy its Eastern Air unit. The suit, which seeks $1.5 billion in damages, came as Texas Air reported a widened loss for the first quarter.

Fixed-rate mortgages rose in April to an average 10.48%, ending five months of declines. Analysts indicated rates may continue climbing.

10 Top Fed officials have decided to nudge up short-term interest rates to head off inflation, and there are signs the process may already have begun. Several Fed policymakers said that the economy may be at a turning point, and that action is needed now to keep inflation in check. Though the federal funds rate rose yesterday, an increase in the discount rate isn't expected soon.

Bond prices were little changed despite the apparent Fed action, which analysts said was anticipated. Stocks fell in moderate trading.

The British pound surged 1.1% against the dollar following a bullish forecast by a Goldman Sachs economist in London. The rally prompted central bank intervention, but the pound is expected to remain strong.

Daiwa Securities launched a $2.5 billion mutual fund that will buy U.S. government and corporate bonds. It is the biggest new fund ever to invest in the U.S. and signals renewed Japanese interest in those markets.

11 The prime rate is expected to rise soon, reflecting recent increases in banks' own borrowing costs and signs the Fed is tightening credit. Bankers predict the prime will climb to at least 8¾% or possibly 9% from the current rate of 8½%. It would be the first increase since last October, just before the stock market crash.

White House chief economist Beryl Sprinkel said he isn't bothered by Fed efforts to boost short-term rates.

Five big securities firms temporarily halted the most popular form of program trading, stock-index arbitrage, for their own accounts. But analysts said the move, in response to pressure from clients and regulators, won't end volatility in the market.

Investors showed little reaction to the news, as stocks inched higher. Bonds drifted slightly lower.

12 Stocks tumbled around the world on fears of rising interest rates. The Dow Jones industrials slid 37.80 points, to 1965.85, following big declines in London and Tokyo. Analysts cited a higher U.S. prime rate and expectations that other rates will soon move up. But they attributed the sell-off largely to pessimism about inflation and the market. Bond prices and precious metals closed lower.

The U.S. prime rate climbed to 9% from 8½%, and bankers predict further increases this summer. Yesterday's increase, the first since October, had been widely expected.

Financial markets are "rigged," former Treasury chief Donald Regan told a congressional panel. He added that trading in stock-index futures should be suspended or banned.

The curb on program trading by several big Wall Street firms isn't likely to cure the stock market's ills, as yesterday's decline showed.

The Treasury and major banks are near a compromise that could help clear the way for a $67.2 billion settlement of Brazilian debt. The preliminary pact eventually will bring Brazil current on bank interest payments.

13 The Treasury completed its quarterly financing with the sale of new 30-year bonds at an average yield of 9.17%, the highest in over two years. Though the bond sale results were largely expected, analysts still fear higher interest rates lie ahead.

A change in phone regulation was proposed by the FCC. The plan would give telephone companies the choice of having either rate increases or profits subject to federal control.

Retail sales eased 0.6% in April, but analysts said a revised 1.7% surge in March indicates consumer spending continues to grow moderately. The Fed recently has been anxious to hold down the rise in consumer spending to help keep inflation in check.

Boeing appears to have won the lion's share of a more than $4 billion jet order that International Lease Finance expects to announce next week. The huge order has been the object of intense competition among Boeing, McDonnell Douglas and Airbus.

Fed Chairman Greenspan said that U.S. banks are being forced to make higher-risk loans and must increase rates to remain profitable.

14 Inflation remains moderate at the wholesale level but could heat up in the months ahead, the April producer-

price figures indicate. Prices for finished goods rose a mild 0.4% last month, but the prices manufacturers paid for raw and semifinished materials went up sharply. Analysts say this could prompt producers to increase their prices eventually.

The Fed's credit tightening last week helped calm inflation fears, but some economists say further tightening may be needed this summer.

Japan's trade surplus shrank in April from a year earlier, the 12th decline in a row. Exports to the U.S. fell, led by lower auto shipments.

Japanese corporate profits were up sharply in the latest fiscal year, analysts say, aided by a surge in domestic demand and the strong yen.

U.S. car sales climbed further in early May, giving auto makers more confidence that 1988 results will stay even with last year's healthy market.

Auto production plans have been boosted again for the second quarter, and forecasts for the third quarter indicate a 9.6% increase in output.

17 Texaco is holding secret talks with Carl Icahn in an attempt to end a threatened proxy fight by its biggest shareholder. The meetings, held during the past week, have focused on ways Texaco can mollify the profit-minded Icahn by restructuring itself, sources said. Meanwhile, Texaco expects to complete soon the first of $5 billion in asset sales.

Irving Bank won a proxy fight for control of its board, dealing a major setback to Bank of New York's hostile takeover bid. Preliminary results from the May 6 vote indicate Irving's board was reelected by 52% to 48%.

An administration panel on the October crash proposed only one major change: imposing market "circuit breakers" to interrupt trading during big price drops. The group rejected calls to curtail program trading or attempt to damp market volatility.

Soybean futures rocketed to four-year highs amid signs that some small investors are jumping into commodity speculation because they are disenchanted with the stock market. Bond prices eased as the surge in commodities fueled inflation fears.

Stock prices rallied on speculation the U.S. trade deficit narrowed in March. The Dow Jones industrials closed up 17.08 points, at 2007.63.

Industrial output surged 0.7% in April, led by a pick-up in manufacturing. The increase reflected a big gain in auto production, with output of manufacturing equipment and home appliances also rising strongly.

Investment bankers led by Drexel are planning to repackage junk bonds into investment-grade securities following a new rating policy by S&P.

The junk bond market is rebounding as recession fears ease. About $2 billion of new corporate junk bond issues are expected within 30 days.

18 The trade deficit shrank to a three-year low of $9.75 billion in March, as exports increased 23%. The sharp narrowing, from $13.83 billion in February, isn't likely to be repeated in coming months, though it shows the trade picture is improving. Separately, the U.S. industrial sector operated at 82.7% of capacity in April, the highest level in eight years.

Purchasing agents expect the economy to keep growing and prices to keep rising for the rest of the year, signaling a swelling of inflation.

Stock and bond prices plunged as investors worried that robust exports and economic growth will lead to higher inflation and interest rates. The Dow Jones industrials finished down 21.22 points, at 1986.41. Bond yields surged to five-month highs.

The dollar soared 1% against the mark and reached three-month highs against other European currencies. But analysts remain bearish about the dollar. Precious metals fluctuated sharply before closing lower.

19 Stocks and bonds fell further as investors continued to worry about rising inflation and interest rates. The Dow Jones industrials sank 35.32 points, to 1951.09, while Treasury bond prices dropped over ¾ of a point. The dollar also slumped, while precious metals prices firmed.

The U.S. was urged by European officials to curb its domestic demand to ease world-wide trade imbalances and to keep inflation in check.

Housing starts edged up 0.5% in April despite a sharp drop in single-family construction. The single-family sector is expected to weaken further as interest rates continue rising.

The U.S. threatened to file a trade complaint against Tokyo if it attempts to stall a GATT review of a dispute over beef and citrus imports.

20 Investors must learn to live with volatility in the financial markets, a Reagan panel on the October crash told Con-

gress. The leader of the group, Treasury Undersecretary George Gould, asserted that it is the active trader, not the long-term investor, who is hurt by volatility and whose recent withdrawal from the market has concerned Wall Street.

Chrysler expects profit in the second quarter will fall short of the $2 a share posted a year earlier.

Union Carbide has angered many on Wall Street by slashing its dividend 46%. The firm's stock has plunged 19% in two days, and prospects for a major rebound appear remote.

23 Consumer prices rose 0.4% in April, or at a 5.3% annual rate, led by a surge in clothing, food and beverage costs and the first increase in energy prices since November. The April rise, though smaller than the 0.5% gain in March, is likely to heighten fears about inflation.

Some investment managers say investors are overly worried about inflation and that long-term bonds will soon look attractive. Separately, the Fed tightened credit in late March, newly released minutes show.

The outlook for oil prices is being muddied by the possibility of a new petroleum glut. Though prices are still expected to firm later this year, they first may plunge to a 1988 low this summer, many analysts believe.

24 Stock prices eased in the slowest session since late November, and analysts don't expect the listless trading pace to improve soon. The Dow Jones industrials closed off 11.11, at 1941.48. Stocks of rumored takeover targets, which helped lift the market to a post-crash high last month, are now leading it lower.

Bonds and the dollar edged down. Soybean, corn and wheat futures prices tumbled as Midwest rains squelched fears of a drought.

Fuji Bank of Japan gained a toehold in the U.S. government securities market by agreeing to acquire 24.9% of the Chicago-based primary dealer owned by Kleinwort Benson.

American International has acquired 5.3% of Kleinwort, but the U.S. insurer said it doesn't plan a bid.

25 The trade bill was vetoed by Reagan, effectively dooming the legislation. The House immediately voted to override, but the Senate isn't likely to follow. Though Reagan said he is willing to sign a modified version of the trade bill, Democrats plan to use the veto as a campaign issue this fall, making the prospect for new legislation this year uncertain.

The free-trade accord between the U.S. and Canada faces major obstacles in the Canadian Parliament. But both countries hope to have the pact implemented this summer.

SEC Chairman Ruder and Fed Chairman Greenspan offered sharply different views to the Senate Banking panel on the health of the markets and the need for government action.

26 Carl Icahn proposed to acquire Texaco for $60 a share, or $14.5 billion, after truce talks between the two sides collapsed. But the offer depends on several factors, including Texaco's willingness to present the bid to holders and Icahn's ability to obtain financing. Texaco officials were skeptical that such an offer, which could lead to history's biggest takeover, would ever be completed.

The trade deficit shrank to $35.95 billion in the first quarter, helped by strong exports of machinery. Overall exports climbed 9.8%, while imports rose 1.3%. Both hit record levels.

Reagan may propose his own, narrow trade bill if Congress doesn't pass a revised measure, U.S. Trade Representative Clayton Yeutter said.

27 First-quarter GNP growth was revised upward to a brisk 3.9% annual rate, reflecting a jump in exports during March. The revision, from 2.3% estimated earlier, indicates that the economy is far stronger than many had predicted. But it also is likely to worsen inflation fears.

Short-term interest rates surged to their highest levels since the October stock crash. The threat of rising inflation apparently prompted the Fed to tighten credit a bit further. Stocks and the dollar moved higher.

Long Island Lighting reached a final agreement with New York state to scrap its Shoreham nuclear plant. The move is a blow to the industry, but officials said the heavy cost to utility customers could make shutting other plants more difficult politically.

31 Carl Icahn is expected to unveil a plan Thursday to finance his $12.4 billion bid for Texaco. The proposal, similar to a leveraged buy-out, calls for Icahn to sell the company's Canadian and Far East interests, which some analysts say could fetch up to $7 billion. The re-

maining $5.4 billion could come from Texaco's huge cash flow, Icahn said. His bid was rejected Friday.

Nissan Motor returned to an operating profit in its latest fiscal year and said net income tripled.

Japan's major banks posted record profits for the year, boosted by loans to individuals and small firms.

Rising U.S. interest rates are expected to push up rates in other countries this year, with the difference between domestic and foreign bond yields widening, analysts say.

The economy may be slowing after a robust first quarter, the April consumer spending report suggests. Consumer outlays were practically unchanged last month, while personal income grew only 0.1%. The weakness could help calm inflation worries.

Machine-tool orders surged 94% in April as manufacturers bought more factory machinery to meet strong foreign and domestic demand.

Iraq may agree to join other oil exporters in cutting output, even if it remains outside OPEC's quota system, Iraq's oil minister said. The development renews the possibility OPEC may reach an accord with nonmember producers to limit output.

June 1988

1 Stock prices surged as investors shrugged off inflation worries and jumped back into the market, raising hopes of an early summer rally. The Dow Jones industrials closed up 74.68, at 2031.12, the biggest one-day gain since a post-crash rebound on January 4. The rise was fueled by a strong bond market, which gained despite a jump in commodity prices. The dollar also rose.

The Fed is trying to avoid raising its discount rate because of worries about jolting the still-jittery financial markets, according to Fed officials.

Retail food prices could soar this year if dry weather in the Farm Belt continues, as is expected. The Commodity Research Bureau's futures price index rose 2.3% yesterday, the largest one-day gain since 1979.

"Gray-market" importers won a major victory in the Supreme Court. The justices upheld Customs Service rules allowing discount retailers to import most brand-name goods without using authorized dealers.

New-home sales climbed 4% during April, but rising mortgage rates are expected to weaken demand soon. Meanwhile, a recent rebound in home sales around the country has become a buying panic in California.

2 Stocks and bonds continued to rally, as long-term Treasury issues surged 1⅝ points, the biggest gain in four months. The Dow Jones industrials closed up 32.89 points, at 2064.01, in heavy trading, while retail buying in the OTC market picked up. Many commodity prices also climbed, with platinum leading precious metals higher. The dollar was mixed.

Carl Icahn said he will sell his $1.8 billion stake in Texaco if he loses his proxy fight against its management. Icahn denied any attempt to threaten other Texaco holders, whose shares could fall if he sells his position.

Koppers agreed to be acquired by a Beazer-led group for $61 a share, or $1.71 billion. The accord ends one of the bitterest takeover battles ever.

Factory orders climbed 1.2% in April, while leading indicators rose 0.2%, the third monthly gain in a row. Both reports signal continued health in the economy. Also, construction spending rose 0.1% in the month.

West German GNP grew 1.5% in the first quarter, likely quieting suggestions from trading partners that Bonn further stimulate the economy.

3 The stock and bond rally fizzled on profit-taking and renewed inflation fears. The Dow Jones industrials closed off 11.56 at 2052.45, but the moderate fall fueled hopes of a rebound. Long-term interest rates rose amid a surge in commodity prices.

The British pound skidded despite London's scramble to bolster the currency with higher interest rates and intervention. The dollar was mixed.

Few Wall Street firms expect to imitate Shearson anytime soon and take an equity position in a client's hostile takeover bid. Shearson's image was bruised by its participation in the recent battle for Koppers.

Major retailers reported slight sales gains for May, raising concern that the recent sluggishness may slow the overall economy. Analysts said many retailers are cutting back on fall and winter merchandise orders.

General Motors' Class E stock plunged

in heavy trading on news that H. Ross Perot, the former chairman of the EDS unit, had lured away eight managers to form a new company.

6 Computer chip makers said they may ask Reagan for further trade sanctions against Japan. The warning from the U.S. semiconductor industry came after negotiations to boost foreign access to Japan's chip market collapsed Friday. The standoff casts doubts on Japan's pledge to buy more U.S.-made chips.

The jobless rate rose to 5.6% in May from 5.4% in April, but the level of hiring suggests the economy is still growing moderately. A big employment survey says third-quarter hiring plans will reach a four-year high.

Purchasing agents said the economy continued to expand modestly last month, aided by new orders.

Foreign brokerage firms are involved in over a third of the suspected insider-trading cases that stock exchanges referred to the SEC in 1986 and 1987, a federal study says.

Long-term interest rates could ease a bit further before starting to rise again, many analysts say. Rates tumbled almost a third of a point last week, helped by a stable dollar and signs the economy isn't overheating.

7 The SEC has investigated suspicious trading in the securities of Textron, Sperry, IBM and several other companies, according to congressional subcommittee aides reviewing the agency's pursuit of foreign-based insider trading. The aides were critical of the SEC and of delays by stock exchanges in referring suspicious transactions to the agency.

A takeover lawyer for Sullivan & Cromwell, George Kern, was accused by the SEC of "grossly unreasonable judgment" in a 1986 takeover battle.

Non-farm productivity climbed at a 3.6% annual rate in the first quarter, far above the previous estimate and reflecting a robust economy.

Major British banks raised their base rates another half point, to 8.5%, to try to halt the pound's recent fall.

Thrift regulators liquidated two insolvent California S&Ls for a record $1.35 billion. But industry officials doubt the move will sharply cut the rates thrifts pay to lure deposits.

Union workers have the right to sue employers over a dismissal, even if their contract allows for arbitration procedures, the Supreme Court ruled. The justices said federal law doesn't bar such suits if state laws permit.

8 Mortgage rates are edging up, according to two recent surveys. The average rate last week on a 30-year fixed-rate mortgage was 10.58%, up from 10.32% a month earlier.

U.S. banks earned $5 billion in the first quarter, missing a record quarterly profit only because of the $1.5 billion loss at First RepublicBank of Dallas. The FDIC expects an accord soon on recapitalizing the bank.

9 Stocks and bonds rallied as a drop in commodity prices eased inflation worries. The Dow Jones industrials jumped 48.36 points, or 2.4%, to 2102.95, just below the post-crash high. Big Board volume hit a high for 1988. Long-term Treasury bonds gained about a point, while the dollar also rose. The fall by commodities came as rain in the Midwest Farm Belt reduced fears of a drought.

Fed Chairman Greenspan said that further declines by the dollar could actually start hurting efforts to narrow the U.S. trade deficit.

Reagan's trade-bill veto was sustained by the Senate, and Democratic leaders began exploring whether Congress can pass a compromise version. The president vetoed the bill mainly because of a provision requiring advance notice of factory closings.

10 Businesses plan to boost spending 10.7% on new plant and equipment this year, another sign of economic strength. The Commerce Department survey, taken in April and May, found that spending plans were well above the 8.8% increase projected earlier in the year.

New U.S. trade figures indicate that the nation's trade deficit is shrinking, but not as sharply as previously reported.

Japan's trade surplus declined 21% in May, as booming imports continued to outpace export growth.

The OECD revised upward its growth projections for industrialized countries to 3% this year and 2.5% in 1989, but expressed concern over the U.S. trade deficit and inflation.

13 Interest rates should hold steady in the near term, analysts say, despite jitters about tomorrow's trade report. Meanwhile, central banks are expected to refrain from policy shifts before the Toronto summit.

Tighter U.S. fiscal policy and more West German expansion are being sought by the Bank for International Settlements to ensure global financial stability and noninflationary growth.

West Germany's trade surplus narrowed 14.9% in March as imports again grew faster than exports.

GM's financing arm named Nomura Securities sales agent for a $5 billion medium-term note program.

14 Liggett group breached an implied warranty, made in ads, that smoking was safe, a federal jury ruled. The Newark, N.J., jury awarded $400,000 to the widower of a heavy smoker who died of lung cancer but said the woman was 80% responsible for her death. Jurors held Liggett was aware of the dangers and should have warned customers.

The Supreme Court, in a victory of banks over securities firms, let stand the Fed's approval for commercial bank affiliates to underwrite certain securities in limited volume. Most big banking firms said they would waste no time entering the new lines.

15 The U.S. trade deficit narrowed in April to its lowest level in more than three years. Imports fell a steep 6.4% from March, indicating the weak dollar is helping with a turnaround. Bonds and stocks rallied in response. The $9.89 billion gap, far smaller than expected, came despite a 2.5% drop in exports. Imports are expected to rise in coming months but to be outpaced by export gains.

Agriculture Secretary Lyng warned lawmakers that the worsening drought could turn into a national disaster if farm regions don't get rain soon. But he advised them against a hasty drought-relief package.

OPEC ministers reached a weak compromise pact that leaves oil output quotas unchanged for six months, ending the cartel's deadlock.

Sales of cars made in North America fell 4.8% in early June. Analysts downplayed the drop, saying demand is strong despite incentive cuts.

Occidental Petroleum completed an offering of 51.8 million shares for $1.37 billion, the biggest equity issue ever by a U.S. industrial firm.

16 Prices of corn, wheat and soybean futures soared past landmark levels as speculation grew that the Midwest drought would cause some crop prices to soon rise higher than during the 1983 drought. Prices climbed as much as allowed in one day's trading. Rising grain prices panicked livestock traders and some hog and cattle futures plummeted.

The federal investigation into alleged bribery and price-fixing in defense contracts is focusing on as many as 50 consultants paid by more than a dozen contractors, officials said.

House Democrats decided to push a revived trade bill stripped of the provisions that led to Reagan's veto. The decision increases the chances Congress this year will enact a bill designed to open foreign markets.

Wells Fargo has begun to place its $125 million in loans to Argentina on a nonaccrual basis, bankers say. Such an action would pressure other banks to follow suit and would aggravate concerns about Third World debt.

Industrial output grew 0.4% in May, but retail sales edged up just 0.1%. The reports indicate economic growth is being led more by exports and less by consumer demand, a shift needed to shrink the trade deficit.

The current-account deficit widened in the first quarter, due largely to changes in valuation of U.S. assets because of the fluctuating dollar.

17 The fragile recovery of agriculture-related businesses could be undone by the Midwest drought. Bankers, farm-equipment makers and rural realtors all are becoming jittery about a year that had started off appearing strong. Mississippi River barge traffic may halt if the dry spell keeps up.

While grain and soybean futures continued their rally, stocks and bond prices tumbled from their recent highs due to concerns about the drought's inflationary pressures.

The export boom is straining manufacturers, two Fed reports suggest. U.S. industries operated at a high 82.9% of capacity in May, one said.

Business inventories grew 0.5% in April and sales by manufacturers, retailers and wholesalers fell 0.2%, the Commerce Department reported.

The battle for Texaco culminating at today's annual meeting could be decided by the 4.9% block that Kohlberg Kravis was holding in April.

Texaco is selling to Saudi Arabia a refinery stake along with gasoline market access for $1.2 billion.

Japan's GNP grew 2.7% in the latest quarter—the fastest rate in a decade—on strong consumer spending and capital outlays. But the current-quarter rate is expected to slow.

18 Housing starts fell 12.2% in May, the largest drop in five months, leaving many industry economists pessimistic. The drop resulted mainly from the recent rise in interest rates.

Japanese superconductor developers are far ahead of their U.S. rivals in plans for commercialization, according to a government report.

Interest rates could rise further this summer, some analysts fear, pointing to pressures on major central banks to tighten credit policy. But the dollar is expected to hold firm.

21 Carl Icahn conceded defeat in his proxy fight for five seats on Texaco's board. Icahn's move came after Kohlberg Kravis said it had voted its 4.9% stake for the incumbent directors, erasing doubts about the victor.

The Fed increasingly appears to be tightening credit slightly to try to restrain inflation, and other central banks may follow. The apparent tightening helped Treasury bonds rebound, but stocks fell in slow trading.

The dollar rose to a 7½-month high against the mark and gained against most other major currencies.

Corn and soybean futures prices rose to the upper limit of their daily trading ranges as drought fears dominated the Chicago futures market.

22 Consumer prices rose 0.3% in May, the smallest gain in three months, as clothing prices leveled off after a recent surge. Though inflation is expected to worsen later this year, the May report suggests consumer prices may stay moderate for the next few months, except for an anticipated jump in food prices.

Bond prices rallied briefly after the report but ended little changed. Stocks swung widely before closing higher. The dollar was mixed.

Brazil said it reached agreement with a creditor bank committee to reschedule $62 billion of foreign debt and receive $5.2 billion in new loans.

Mexico said its foreign debt shrank in the first quarter, the first significant narrowing in three years.

The economic summit ended in Toronto as the seven leaders expressed broad satisfaction with the economy and their policies. But the summit was marked by a shift of influence from the U.S. to Japan and the EC.

23 The dollar soared to its highest level in months, sparking stock and bond market rallies. The Dow Jones industrials closed up 43.03, to a post-crash high of 2152.20, while Treasury bonds rose 1¾ points. The dollar, which surged 2% against the yen and 1.5% against the mark, was aided by heavy Japanese buying and signs central banks wouldn't intervene. Precious metals slumped.

Durable goods orders slid 2.2% in May, the biggest drop in nine months. Though the decline resulted solely from lower aircraft orders, the report indicated that manufacturers in general may be facing slower growth.

The Pentagon bribery scandal involves as many as 100 contracts valued at tens of billions of dollars, Rep. Dingell said. The chief prosecutor in the inquiry said indictments could be returned by the end of the year.

The defense industry already is in turmoil because of the scandal, and major changes are possible in U.S. military procurement practices.

The drought threatens to deal a severe blow to the U.S. on world agricultural markets, just as it was beginning to regain some of the business lost to other nations earlier in the decade. The farm-export program has been a major contributor to the nation's trade balance.

24 The economy will grow at a 3% pace in 1988 rather than 2.4% as it had forecast earlier, the administration said. But it said higher-than-expected interest rates will mean little help toward reducing the budget deficit.

27 IBM is planning another redeployment of its work force in a renewed bid to cut costs, sources said. The plan, which has yet to get final approval, is said to call for thousands of workers to change jobs and many to be relocated. A major aim is to move more people into sales, though IBM also hopes many will quit rather than relocate, the sources said.

The government is selling corn at an unprecedented rate to counter the rise in feed grain prices, which have surged due to the drought. The move is aimed at helping livestock owners.

Drought-related dust storms are damaging more farms and ranches than at any time since 1955.

Consumer spending rose 0.5% in May, another sign the economy is slowing after a brisk first quarter. But economists say sluggish spending will allow export-driven economic growth to continue without fueling inflation. Personal income rose 0.3%.

Machine tool orders jumped 72% in May to a seven-year high. Orders remain brisk in June, executives say.

The Fed is expected to leave credit conditions unchanged when its policy committee meets this week. But the panel also may authorize credit-tightening moves to be implemented at the first sign inflation is heating up.

The dollar's rally is likely to continue until central banks intervene, dealers say. Also, U.S. officials confirmed that the Group of Seven hasn't changed its policy on the dollar.

Oil prices are expected to fall another $1 to $3 a barrel, reflecting slowing demand, OPEC quota cheating and a buildup of inventories.

28 The SEC charged a Morgan Stanley analyst and a Taiwanese businessman in a $19 million insider-trading scheme, the second biggest after Boesky. The agency said analyst Stephen Wang Jr. passed confidential data gleaned from his job at Morgan to Fred Lee, who traded in securities of at least 25 companies. The investigation is continuing, and Morgan itself is said to be under SEC scrutiny.

The U.S. intervened in currency markets to slow the dollar's rise, but officials indicated the move was largely symbolic and didn't reflect a commitment to stop further gains.

Bond prices fell in the U.S. and overseas, partly on speculation that central banks may soon raise interest rates to bolster their currencies. Stocks also plunged on rate fears.

Grain prices continued to surge amid predictions that little rain will fall in the drought-stricken Farm Belt for at least the next week or two. Meanwhile, cattlemen appear to be the first victims of the drought.

29 The dollar rebounded after an early slide as traders shrugged off heavy dollar-selling by European central banks. The stronger currency, which reached a six-month high against the yen but ended generally mixed, fueled stock and bond rallies. The Dow Jones industrials closed up 22.41, at 2130.87, while active Treasury issues gained about a point.

Grain and soybean futures plunged as a shift in the weather increased the chances of rain in the Farm Belt. The sell-off cooled inflation fears, but farm futures prices are now expected to be volatile. Meanwhile, the U.S. is facing a severe forest-fire threat.

The surge in food prices isn't expected to prompt the Fed to tighten credit, though it probably will cause the central bank to react more swiftly to other inflationary signs.

American Brands was sued by four big junk-bond investors over its plan to sell part of E-II Holdings to a less credit-worthy concern. The suit is a rare display of institutional pique.

30 A break in the drought led to the biggest one-day drop in soybean futures prices since 1973. Heavy rain in the Farm Belt, and forecasts of more rain, also deflated corn, wheat and oat futures for the second day. The CRB index, a closely watched inflation gauge, fell 6.49, to 260.71, its third-biggest drop ever.

IBM announced a revamping that is likely to cut its U.S. work force by 3,000 to 4,000 and result in a $600 million pretax charge for the second quarter. The move indicates IBM's resolve to cut costs and staffing.

Leading indicators fell 0.1% in May, the first drop since January and a sign the economy may be slowing. The decline partly reflected lower stock prices and a drop in plant and equipment orders. Separately, new home sales fell 0.3% last month.

The dollar was narrowly mixed despite continued dollar-selling by West European central banks. Bond prices swung widely before closing lower, and stocks also sank. The Dow Jones industrials fell 8.89, at 2121.98.

Oil prices declined amid uncertainty about OPEC production, but gasoline prices remained strong.

July 1988

1 Oil prices plunged again as OPEC production continued to outpace demand. The drop in crude prices and a steadier dollar helped fuel stock and bond market rallies. The Dow Jones industrials closed up 19.73, at 2141.71, while the transportation average hit a post-crash high.

Grain futures prices rose sharply amid forecasts for a return of dry weather to the Midwest in July, the most critical month for corn and soybeans. Some corn-growing states may see the biggest percentage drop in output since the Dust Bowl years.

Mutual-fund sales skidded 21% in May to the lowest level in more than three years. Both stock and bond mutual funds had net outflows for the first time since the October crash.

Takeover targets led the stock market to a post-crash high in the second quarter. Murray Ohio was the biggest gainer, rising 106.5%.

The U.S.'s net debtor position worsened last year due to increased foreign investment in the country.

5 The economy will expand for at least another year, despite higher inflation and interest rates, according to a Wall Street Journal survey of 38 economists. Most expect unemployment to fall further and marveled at the rebound from the October market crash. In June the economy grew at its fastest pace since December, purchasing agents said.

The Pentagon's decision to halt payments on $1 billion in Navy contracts foreshadows a much wider cut-off on projects tainted by the unfolding defense procurement scandal.

Food-exporting competitors of the U.S. and Canada will have plenty of crops to "buffer" the market effect of the North American drought, a Reagan administration report says.

Housing starts fell 9% in May, despite the recent recovery in home sales. Some industry officials said they expect a rebound for June starts. Meanwhile, overall construction spending edged up 1.1% in May.

6 The Big Board plans to drop a major post-crash reform that barred automated index arbitrage whenever the Dow Jones industrials moved 50 or more points in a session, sources said. The plan is one more sign that efforts to revamp the nation's stock and futures markets after the crash are proceeding slowly.

Soybean futures prices plunged after the government forecast above-normal moisture for some parts of the Midwest. But some corn futures closed higher because little of the rain was expected to fall in major corn-growing areas, analysts said.

"Junk" bonds had an average 8.2% return in the first half of 1988, the highest of any U.S. fixed-income security. In the world's major bond markets, Australian and Canadian government bonds had higher returns, with 17% and 14.1%, respectively.

Mexico plans to reduce its foreign bank debt by as much as $10 billion with a series of programs it hopes to present to banks this fall, Finance Minister Gustavo Petricioli said.

7 A plant-closings bill cleared the Senate, in a maneuver to revive the trade bill. The legislation would require employers to give advance notice of layoffs and plant closings.

Auto sales surged 13.6% in late June, continuing the healthy pace of recent months. Ford's domestic car sales jumped 27%, while GM's grew 18% and Chrysler's rose 8.4%.

The drought is dashing the hopes of some troubled Farm Credit System banks for a turnaround this year. They also may be forced to seek far more federal aid, an official said.

The outlook for food prices worsened amid growing evidence of serious drought damage to U.S. crops. Soybean and wheat futures soared, while corn fell in volatile trading. Sugar futures hit a six-year high.

Stocks and bonds skidded as the surge by commodity prices revived inflation fears. The Dow Jones industrials closed down 28.45, at 2130.16. Long-term Treasury bonds fell about 1¼ points. The dollar weakened.

Talk of a special OPEC meeting surfaced as quota cheating by some members appeared to worsen. Speculation about an emergency session boosted oil prices, but OPEC sources said the talk was premature.

8 Bailing out thrifts is likely to cost far more than expected, the Bank Board said, shaking Congress's confidence in the agency. Chairman Danny Wall said aiding insolvent Texas thrifts would cost $15.2 billion, more than double his previous estimate. He also said $42.5 billion needs to be raised to deal with the thrift crisis over the next decade.

Drexel Burnham's settlement talks with the SEC have foundered, and the investment firm is bracing for an array of charges soon. The charges are expected to include misuse of inside data and stock "parking."

The SEC adopted a narrow "one share, one vote" rule aimed at ending only extreme cases of unequal voting rights. The rule includes a broad exemption for state takeover laws.

The Big Board and Chicago Merc have agreed on a series of far-reaching trading limits and halts designed to curb sharp declines in stock and stock-index futures markets.

World oil markets were swept by a buying panic following the North Sea disaster. Prices of everything from gasoline to home-heating oil surged up to $1 a barrel, sparking fears of worsening U.S. inflation this year.

Stock prices fell in reaction to the inflation worries, but bonds were little changed. The dollar was mixed.

11 The economy continues to grow briskly, fueling worries about higher interest

rates and inflation. The latest sign of economic strength came with Friday's report that the unemployment rate fell to 5.3% in June, the lowest level since 1974. Some analysts say the economic expansion could last for years.

The Fed likely will tighten credit shortly to counter inflation fears, analysts say. And even if the Fed doesn't act quickly, banks are expected to increase their prime rates soon.

12 Central banks agreeed for the first time on uniform capital requirements for banks from the 12 leading industrial nations. The new standard calls for internationally active banks to have capital equal to 8% of their assets by the end of 1992. The agreement came after West Germany reluctantly made concessions.

International bankers are worried that the new capital rules will further hinder their competitiveness against other financial institutions, particularly investment banks and insurers.

A huge drought-relief bill is expected to win congressional approval and be signed by Reagan as early as this month. The package, which may be introduced in Congress today, could cost up to $5.5 billion in the current fiscal year, economists say.

Soybean and corn futures plunged following weekend rains in the Midwest and forecasts for more rain this week. Still, the expected rainfall isn't expected to break the drought.

13 OPEC's oil production has surged to the highest level in a year, swelling the market glut. Despite falling prices and talk about curbing excess output, OPEC's daily production may have grown to 20 million barrels a day, up about 1.5 million barrels from June. Reasons for the surge aren't clear, though it is being led by Middle East members.

U.S. corn output is expected to plunge 26% this year to a five-year low, based on the effects of the drought so far, the Agriculture Department said. Soybean output is expected to fall 14%, and wheat 13%. Grain futures rose in reaction.

Merrill Lynch's profit fell 36% in the second quarter as sluggish stock trading cut commission revenue.

14 The revised trade bill was passed by the House, 376 to 45, and is expected to win Senate approval later this summer. The bill, which is stripped of a plant-closings provision that prompted a Reagan veto in May, is now considered to have a good chance of winning the president's signature. The measure is aimed at further opening foreign markets and aiding domestic industries.

Fed Chairman Greenspan indicated the central bank likely will push up short-term interest rates in the weeks ahead to head off inflation. The Fed apparently hopes to slow economic growth to a 2% to 2.5% rate from 3.6% in the first quarter.

Stocks and the dollar were buoyed initially by Greenspan's remarks, while bonds swung widely and ended lower. The Dow Jones industrials closed up 11.73 points, at 2104.37.

U.S. car sales fell 2.1% in early July from a year earlier as buying eased after an unusually strong June.

Domestic auto makers are sticking with their cautiously optimistic production plans for the third quarter.

15 The prime rate rose to 9½% from 9%, the third increase this year and the highest rate in about three years. Banks are expected to boost their prime rates further in the next few months as continued economic growth fuels inflation fears and prompts the Fed to tighten credit.

Stock and bond markets had little reaction to the prime-rate increase, which had been expected. The dollar surged despite Fed intervention.

Retail sales climbed 0.5% in June, led by a healthy rise in auto buying. Though the increase was smaller than expected, many economists said that modest sales gains will help the U.S. shift to more export-led growth.

More money-center banks posted earnings gains for the second quarter. Chemical Bank, Security Pacific and Bank of New York all rebounded from big losses in the year-ago quarter.

16 The trade deficit grew to $10.93 billion in May, but analysts said the long-term improvement in the gap appears on track. The dollar soared on the report. Despite sales by the Fed and other central banks, the U.S. currency rose 1.7% against the yen and 1.6% against the West German mark to its highest point in months. Imports rose 3.4%, outpacing a 2.3% increase in exports.

The Fed has tightened credit apparently a bit more than thought, analysts say, adding that they expect further rate boosts this summer. The dollar's surge is pressuring foreign central banks to raise their rates.

Producer prices and industrial output

rose moderately in June, suggesting the economy is still growing steadily without a rapid speed-up of inflation. Business inventories rose 0.6% in May while sales rose 0.9%.

Memory-chip prices have begun to fall, leading computer makers and semiconductor firms to hope that the shortage will ease toward year end.

19 Oil prices surged by about $1 a barrel on speculation an Iran-Iraq cease-fire would help restore unity to OPEC. But many traders and analysts were skeptical the rally would last, saying peace between Iran and Iraq would only increase the flow of oil into a glutted world market.

Bond and stock prices fell as the oil rally revived inflation worries. The Dow Jones industrials closed off 11.56 at 2117.89. The dollar was mixed.

Grain futures plunged as forecasts for rain prompted speculation that there may be a turn in the drought. Soybean futures took the biggest slide in 15 years. Corn, wheat and oat futures also ended sharply lower.

Atlantic Richfield said the IRS demanded over $1 billion in back taxes and interest in a long-running dispute related to the company's Alaskan oil production from 1980 to 1983. Arco is attempting to settle the claim.

20 Oil company profits surged in the second quarter, analysts say, further evidence that the industry has adjusted to lower energy prices.

Crude prices remain weak despite the recent growth in demand because OPEC members have been trying to sell as much oil as they can.

The dollar plunged amid apparent central bank intervention against the currency. Stocks also skidded despite a retreat by oil prices that helped bolster bonds. The Dow Jones industrials closed off 20.63, at 2097.26.

Housing starts climbed 5.1% in June, led by a big increase in single-family homes. But the prospects for further growth are uncertain.

22 General Motors' profit jumped 54% in the second quarter, helped by higher sales and an accounting change. The results were slightly above analysts' expectations.

BankAmerica reported a $162 million profit for the second quarter, in contrast to a huge year-earlier loss. The results reflect a broad-based, gradual improvement at the bank.

Stock prices skidded on interest rate worries and disappointment over the earnings of high-tech companies. Bonds and the dollar also fell.

The plunge by soybean futures began to slow amid bargain buying and forecasts for renewed hot weather.

25 Eastern Airlines is ending service to 14 cities and slashing 4,000 jobs, citing growing losses, new competitive pressures and recent setbacks in cost-cutting labor talks. The 12% cuts in flights and jobs, the most severe in the carrier's efforts to shrink its way to profitability, signal the Texas Air unit is backing away from recent attempts to appear more conciliatory toward its unions.

The dollar is being allowed to trade in a much broader range than had been previously thought, traders said. The conclusion follows a week in which major central banks put a halt to the dollar's recent surge.

Inflation remained moderate in June as consumer prices rose a mild 0.3% despite surging food costs. But economists still expect a pickup in inflation in the second half. For the first half, consumer prices rose at a 4.4% rate, the same as for 1987.

Machine tool orders soared 89% in June, indicating durable-goods manufacturers are buying new equipment to meet strong demand for their products. Machine tool makers expect good sales at least through 1988.

The drought is speeding the decline of the nation's cattle herd to the lowest level in about 25 years, the government is expected to report this week. The census is likely to fuel speculation of higher beef prices.

26 Thrift liquidations may be stepped up through payouts to depositors, Bank Board Chairman Danny Wall said. But the board would have to increase bond sales to fund the payouts, reversing a recent decision.

U.S. car sales rose 3.4% in mid-July, showing that consumer demand remains strong despite cutbacks in buyer-incentive programs.

27 Food-inflation forecasts were cut by some economists as more rain in the Farm Belt helped send commodity prices plunging. The Commodity Research Bureau's widely watched futures index fell 8.11 points, to 245.52, its second-biggest drop ever. Though the rain hasn't ended the drought, food prices are expected to climb 6% or less next year.

A $5.5 billion drought-relief measure was approved by a House panel, though Reagan warned that such measures may be too costly.

Durable goods orders rose 8.8% in June because of strong bookings for commercial aircraft and military equipment. Though orders were about flat if those categories are excluded, many economists contend the factory-goods sector remains healthy.

The dollar's rally continued, aided by the durable goods report. Both stock prices and interest rates edged higher, but trading was sluggish.

28 The economy grew at a 3.1% annual rate in the second quarter, reflecting strong capital spending and an improving trade balance. The latest GNP growth, following a revised 3.4% rate in the first quarter, was reduced half a point by lower farm output due to the drought. Meanwhile, a GNP-based inflation measure shows prices rose at a 4.1% rate, the fastest pace in over four years.

Interest rates surged amid speculation the Fed may be tightening credit to head off inflation. Stocks and the dollar finished lower.

Ford Motor's profit rose 11% in the second quarter, reflecting strong overseas operations. Domestic earnings fell about 8% even though the auto maker won its biggest share of the U.S. car market since 1979.

29 Fed credit policy hasn't changed in recent weeks, Chairman Alan Greenspan indicated, saying "there have been fewer surprises than normal" in the latest economic statistics. But Greenspan, testifying before a House subcommittee, reiterated that the Fed should "err more on the side of restrictiveness."

Stock prices rebounded on his remarks, as the Dow Jones industrials surged 28.63, to 2082.33, the biggest gain in over a month. Most interest rates rose, as did the dollar.

Merrill Lynch is investigating whether trading in advance of Business Week articles can be traced to a recent series of Thursday morning breakfasts between one of its stockbrokers and printing plant workers.

The drought is easing in many regions of the country, though the cut in grain and livestock supplies will still lead to higher food prices.

Drought-relief legislation was approved by the House and Senate, but lawmakers plan to trim the bills later because of the budget deficit.

Consumer spending surged 1% in June, indicating that consumers continue to fuel economic growth but that inflation may heat up.

August 1988

1 First RepublicBank's major operations will be taken over by NCNB in the second-largest rescue ever. NCNB, in a major gamble, will put up $210 million for a 20% stake in the new Texas bank while the FDIC will put in $4 billion. The takeover could hurt future capital-raising efforts of many banks and accelerate a battle between First RepublicBank debt holders and federal regulators.

Stocks soared in heavy trading, with the Dow Jones Industrials climbing 46.40 points to 2128.73, its biggest rise since June 8. The dollar rose despite central bank intervention.

Farm prices rose 3.6% in July to the highest level in four years as the drought cut into grain supplies. Since April, farm prices have soared 9%.

The Business Week trading probe has expanded to include Paine Webber and Integrated Resources, for a total of eight Wall Street firms. Evidence indicates improper trading in advance of one of the magazine's columns may be wider than first thought.

Federal regulators hope to reach a pact soon for Bass Group to rescue the troubled thrift unit of Financial Corp. of America with as much as $2.2 billion in government aid.

The Bank Board closed three insolvent Oklahoma thrifts. Accounts at two will be transferred while depositors at the third will get payouts.

2 Argentina was expected to announce a series of measures to battle its growing budget deficit, inflation and foreign-debt troubles. The moves probably will begin with a currency devaluation of as much as 10%.

Construction activity grew in June, led by nonresidential building, two surveys show. The Commerce Department said construction spending inched up 0.1%, with nonresidential outlays up 2.5%, reflecting strength in capital spending.

3 The plant closings bill will become law without Reagan's signature. The president, succumbing to election-year politics, said he won't veto the measure, which requires employers to give 60 days notice of plant closings and layoffs. Despite Reagan's strong opposition,

many firms don't expect the law to cause big problems, saying they already give workers at least that much notice.

Texaco put its 78% stake in Texaco Canada up for sale, a move that could spark a bidding war for the giant oil and gas unit. The proposed sale, which could fetch up to $3.3 billion, was one of the major demands Carl Icahn made in his proxy battle.

Economic growth appeared robust in June, latest statistics indicate. Leading indicators surged 1.4%, the biggest rise in 1½ years, though they fell a revised 0.8% in May. Factory orders climbed 5.5%, the strongest in 18 years. Home sales rose 8.4%.

A manufacturing boom is straining the capacity of the nation's factories despite some slowing in the overall economy, a new Fed report says.

A new type of stock trading could begin by this fall. The Big Board and three other exchanges are competing to develop a new trading method that could handle large stock orders without jolting the rest of the market.

4 The trade bill cleared the Senate 85-11 and was sent to Reagan, who is expected to sign it. The measure, which is designed to open foreign markets to more U.S. goods and boost domestic industries, was finally embraced by both Democrats and Republicans. The revised legislation is largely stripped of the protectionism it first contained.

Argentina may soon get an emergency $500 million loan from the U.S. to pay overdue interest on its foreign debt, sources said. But delays in negotiating the loan may still force U.S. banks to classify the debt as nonperforming, hurting their profits.

U.S. car sales jumped 6.9% in late July, continuing a recent boom. The strong showing by domestic makers offset disappointing results for importers. For the full month, sales were even with the year-ago period.

5 The drought appears to be intensifying at the worst possible time for the soybean crop. Soybean futures soared yesterday on renewed forecasts of unseasonably hot and dry weather in the Farm Belt, ending a brief period of rains. Corn and wheat contracts also rose.

Congressional conferees agreed to extend special relief to dairy farmers as they sought to reconcile major differences in the House and Senate drought-assistance bills.

Retail sales edged up only slightly in July, due to the slump in women's apparel and the hot weather. Analysts said retailers are likely to post lower earnings for the second quarter but may show an improvement later.

Brazil is having trouble getting full commitments for a $5.2 billion loan, part of its debt restructuring. Some bankers say the Oct. 31 restructuring deadline won't be met unless ways are found to complete the loan.

8 Rupert Murdoch agreed to acquire closely held Triangle Publications for $3 billion. The purchase, to be made through News Corp., adds TV Guide, Seventeen magazine and the Daily Racing Form to the media magnate's empire. Previously, analysts have valued Triangle at about $1 billion.

A drought-damage survey by the Agriculture Department is expected to predict a decline in the U.S. soybean crop that could be so sharp as to force food companies to seek imports. Severe damage is also likely to be reported for the corn harvest.

Unemployment inched up to 5.4% in July from a 14-year low in June. But the report suggests the economy is still growing vigorously and probably won't allay inflation fears.

Profits more than doubled at major U.S. companies in the second quarter as large banks rebounded from year-ago losses and the strong economy buoyed basic industries.

Canadian corporate earnings rose 30%, propelled by growth at mining and forest-products companies.

9 The dollar climbed further against the mark, but U.S. and West German intervention checked the advance and the U.S. currency ended mixed. The dollar's strength was aided by Friday's U.S. employment report, which suggested a vigorous economy. The mark's slide is reflecting the Bundesbank's inability to defend its currency.

The bond market was stable due to the firming dollar as pressure grew for the Fed to push up short-term interest rates, economists said. Stocks extended their latest slump.

Britain's major banks raised their base rates half a point, to 11%. The surprise move reflected the government's renewed attack on inflation.

Brazil and creditor banks are moving swiftly to complete a new debt restructuring, which includes a $5.2 billion loan. Despite some bankers' gloom last week, banks have committed to over 90% of the loan.

10 The Fed boosted its discount rate to 6.5% from 6%, putting the battle against inflation ahead of election-year pressures and a rising dollar. Fed officials made clear they plan to push up other short-term interest rates, likely forcing bank prime rates and mortgage rates higher. The rise in rates could cause the dollar to surge above the trading range established by major industrial nations.

Stocks and bonds slumped and the dollar soared in reaction to the Fed move. The Dow Jones industrials slid 28.27, to 2079.13. Rates on Treasury bills, bank CDs and commercial paper reached post-crash highs.

11 Stocks and bonds slid further amid rising interest rates, while the dollar's rally fizzled. The Dow Jones industrials fell 44.99, to 2034.14, or a total of 3.4% since the Fed boosted its discount rate on Tuesday. The Treasury's latest 30-year bond declined 1¾ points, pushing the yield to 9.37%, the highest since December. The dollar's retreat was blamed partly on profit-taking.

Consumer savings rates aren't expected to rise immediately despite the jump in other interest rates. Big banks will be "playing the spread" on consumer CD rates for a week or two, according to one banking expert.

Japan's central bank may face renewed pressure to boost its discount rate following Tuesday's increase by the Fed. The U.S. rate rise sent Japanese stock prices skidding Wednesday in their biggest decline this year.

Japan's trade surplus rose 3.5% in July, the first increase in 15 months. But the closely watched surplus with the U.S. continued to decline.

12 The prime rate rose half a point, to a three-year high of 10%, as the Fed continued to tighten credit. Major banks are expected to boost their prime rates further this year as a result of the Fed's effort to damp inflation pressures. Americans with variable-rate home-equity loans will be among the first and hardest hit by the higher prime rates.

Mortgage rates soared to the highest level this year in reaction to Tuesday's rise in the Fed's discount rate. But the housing industry is still expected to turn in a strong year.

The drought is expected to slash the nation's corn crop 37% this year. The Agriculture Department, in its most comprehensive survey yet, also predicts a 23% drop in soybean output and even sharper declines for spring wheat and other grains.

Retail sales rose 0.5% in July, mainly because of strong auto buying. The moderate gain shows consumer spending continues to grow slowly, which is having a moderating influence on the economy, analysts say.

15 Drexel's Michael Milken and 26 other employees owned a stake in Ivan Boesky's arbitrage firm beginning in 1984. The Drexel group tripled its money in two years from Boesky's speculation in takeover stocks.

Inflation may rise sharply in coming months, the 0.5% increase in July producer prices suggests. Excluding food and energy, finished goods prices surged 0.6% last month, the biggest gain in nearly two years. Business inventories rose 0.7% in June.

Interest rates will keep rising the rest of this year and into 1989 without provoking a downturn in the economy, corporate treasurers predict.

Mortgage rates were continuing to move higher even before the recent increases in the discount and prime rates, recent surveys suggest.

16 Industrial output rose 0.8% in July, fueling concern that a robust economy will worsen inflation and lead to higher interest rates. The production surge at factories, mines and utilities was the strongest since October and reflected big gains by business equipment and materials.

Stock prices skidded, partly in reaction to the economic report. The Dow Jones industrials fell 33.25, to 2004.27, its lowest level since May. Bonds leveled off after last week's plunge. The dollar was mixed.

U.S. car sales were unexpectedly strong in early August despite the lack of major incentives. Though the daily selling rate fell 7.6%, it was less than analysts predicted. Dealers cited anticipation of higher prices.

General Electric agreed to sell its semiconductor business to Harris Corp. for an undisclosed amount. GE had been trying to sell the operations, which include certain assets acquired with RCA in 1986, for two years.

17 The trade gap worsened in June as a strong U.S. economy pushed imports up to a record level. The $12.54 billion deficit, far wider than May's revised

$9.76 billion gap, underscores the difficulty of improving the trade balance. The 5.7% rise in imports stemmed from increased American purchases of foreign capital goods, consumer products and autos. U.S. exports fell 2.4%.

Stocks and bonds closed higher after investors shook off worries about the big trade deficit. The Dow Jones industrials ended up 17.24 points, at 2021.51. The dollar also rebounded.

The nation's industry operated at 83.5% of capacity in July, up from 83.1% in June and reflecting across-the-board increases in production.

18 Upjohn received final approval from the FDA to sell its anti-baldness drug, minoxidil, in the U.S. The decision, which was expected, makes the drug the nation's first prescription treatment for certain types of baldness. Upjohn now must make the drug a commercial success amid claims that its safety and effectiveness are exaggerated.

Housing starts edged up a modest 2.4% in July, and economists expect the industry to weaken further as interest rates continue to climb. Starts of single-family homes eased last month, while multifamily units rose for the first time in three months.

19 Whirlpool agreed to a joint venture with N. V. Philips of the Netherlands, creating one of the world's largest appliance businesses. The U.S. company will pay about $470 million for a 53% stake in the venture. Whirlpool's strategy is aimed partly at gaining a major foothold in Europe before 1992, when trade barriers are lifted within the EC and penetration by U.S. firms would be harder.

22 The Hunt brothers conspired to corner the silver market in 1979–80, a federal jury ruled, awarding more than $130 million to a Peruvian minerals firm that claimed investment losses due to artificially inflated prices. The verdict may be a boon for thousands of investors who have sued the Hunts and other defendants. The Hunts' lawyer vowed an appeal.

Eight more Texas thrifts will be bailed out with $5.5 billion in government aid, the most costly multiple rescue ever. The Bank Board estimates that it may cost $15.2 billion to mop up the state's S&L crisis.

The Fed's policy committee voted in June to tighten its grip on credit "slightly" because of inflationary pressures, meeting minutes show.

Toyota is expected to regain its position as Japan's most profitable company this week by posting its first earnings increase in three years.

24 Consumer prices rose 0.4% in July as the drought pushed grocery store prices up 1.4%, the biggest gain since 1984. Fruit and vegetable prices soared, but meat prices fell because of a drop in the cost of pork. The rise, which some economists called modest, joins other indicators that show clear increases in the inflation rate last month. Orders for durable goods dropped 7% on a slump in orders for transport equipment.

Interest rates fell following release of the better-than-expected inflation report. Stock prices remained flat.

West Germany's trade surplus in June grew 71% from a year ago to a record $7.45 billion, pushed by higher exports. The report increases chances of a record full-year surplus despite Bonn's efforts to narrow the gap.

The dollar rose slightly, although selloffs by central banks kept traders in check. Traders said it appeared that 1.90 German marks is the level governments have agreed to target.

25 OPEC oil output is surging again, led by the United Arab Emirates. Total production hit 20 million barrels a day last week, a record for the year. Projected levels for August appear well over the production ceiling set by the 13-nation group. Most analysts expect prices to weaken further in the weeks ahead but many still see some recovery later in the year due to seasonal factors.

Sales of U.S. cars and trucks were stronger than expected in mid-August, although they fell 13.4% from year-earlier levels that had been pushed up by incentives. Despite higher interest rates, Detroit is optimistic.

The dollar declined as traders rushed to buy marks ahead of a news conference that the West German Bundesbank called for today. Higher interest rates are expected to be announced. Bond prices slipped.

Soybean futures prices rose on speculation that the Agriculture Department may subsidize sales of U.S. soybean oil to China.

26 The economy is growing faster than thought and inflation is accelerating, the latest government statistics indicate. GNP grew at a revised 3.3% annual rate in the second quarter, with the underlying growth masked by the severe impact of the drought. Corporate profits grew 11.5%. Prices increased at a revised annual rate of 5.1%, up sharply from the first quarter's 1.7% pace.

Bond yields surged on the inflation report. The yield on 30-year Treasury bonds jumped to nearly 9½%, the highest level this year. Stock prices, meanwhile, fell in quiet trading.

Interest rates were raised across Europe in an orchestrated anti-inflation effort, kicked off by the Bundesbank. Further increases are expected this year. The dollar was pushed down on the news as West Germany vowed that it would defend the mark.

Britain's current-account deficit widened sharply in July. News of the record $3.64 billion gap, about twice as big as expected, set off a rise in interest rates, a nose dive for shares and fears of higher inflation.

29 Consumer spending rose 0.5% in July, less than half the 1.1% pace in June but quick enough to prompt inflation worries. Personal income grew 0.6%, the same as in June, while wages and salaries jumped 1%.

Ten insolvent thrifts were taken over by five healthier institutions as the pace of regulator-assisted rescues continued to accelerate. In the past two weeks, 31 thrifts have been closed or merged by the Bank Board.

The Bank Board is cracking down on risky growth by insolvent and undercapitalized thrifts in the face of heavy pressure from Congress.

30 Bond prices climbed as the stronger dollar, lower oil prices and a drop in new home sales helped ease inflation fears. It was the biggest rally in nearly a month, but many traders expect it to be short-lived. The dollar rebounded. Stock prices also gained, but trading remained thin.

31 Nomura Securities of Japan appears to be maneuvering to get a foothold in the Chicago futures and options business. The big securities firm is said to be negotiating for 51% of closely held GNP Commodities.

The index of leading indicators fell 0.8% and factory orders slid 3.5% in July. Economists still expect strong growth for at least the next several months.

September 1988

1 The dollar rallied to a nine-month high of 136.53 yen in New York following statements by Bank of Japan officials that they wouldn't raise interest rates along with other nations. Japanese stocks and bonds sank along with the yen in international markets. The severe reaction could force the Japanese central bank to reverse itself.

Another 14 thrifts will be rescued, using $1.9 billion in FSLIC aid and lifting to $10.2 billion the commitment to mergers in the past two weeks. The latest, in Oklahoma, will be shuffled into six regional institutions.

Japanese life insurers are curtailing their heavy "dividend-capture" trading of U.S. stocks, a move likely to decrease Big Board volume.

Washington Public Power agreed to settle litigation over the system's 1983 $2.25 billion bond default just a week before trial was to begin. As part of the settlement, WPPSS will agree to a judgment against it.

2 U.S. stocks retreated, partly due to concern that today's unemployment report could lead to higher interest rates. The Dow Jones industrials slipped 29.34 points to 2002.31.

Tokyo share prices plunged as the yen's weakness and signs of tighter credit in Japan unnerved investors. The Nikkei index sank 431.69 points, the second-biggest drop of the year. Bonds slipped to 1988 lows. Stocks in London and Frankfurt also fell.

Retail sales remained weak in August as the slump in women's apparel continued. Sales edged up only 1.6% from a year earlier and fell 1% from July, according to one analyst's figures. Stores blamed hot weather for hampering sales of fall clothes. While some analysts see a rebound with cooler weather, others are trimming profit estimates.

Productivity fell at a revised 1.4% annual pace in the second quarter, slower than an earlier estimate of 1.7%. Construction spending grew 1.2% in July, but was offset by a revised June drop of 1.5%.

Industry Surveys*

The following provides information about a number of industries as well as financial data on companies in each industry. Financial Ratios are defined in the section *Investment and Financial Terms* (page 386).

EXPLANATIONS OF FINANCIAL AND STOCK MARKET INFORMATION

Revenue and Earnings

It should be noted that 12-month figures are trailing ones, calculated from figures shown in the latest interim reports and latest fiscal year reports, when appropriate. Fiscal figures are as reported by the company. Interim figures are based on cumulative data. All earnings per share figures are primary, and are reflected in all calculations. Earnings per share and total earnings figures show earnings from total operations. Earnings are before extraordinary items, but when this is not possible, special earnings footnotes are shown immediately to the right of the company name in the stock tables and these special footnotes are explained as follows:

◇—includes extraordinary gains
◆—includes extraordinary losses
□—excludes extraordinary gains
■—excludes extraordinary losses

5-Year Earnings Growth Rate The annual compound growth rate in primary earnings per share over the last five years computed by the least squares method using logarithms of the earnings per share data, brought up to date through the latest 12 months' earning per share by weighting the first and last points. The five-year earnings growth rate is calculated only for those companies which have all positive earnings per share data for each of the periods used in the calculation. An NC footnote will appear for all companies which do not have a positive earnings per share record for the five-year period. An NC footnote will appear for all companies which have an incomplete record of earnings per share for the five-year period.
Par Growth Rate Retained latest 12 months' earnings per share multiplied by latest 12 months return on common equity, as a percent of latest 12 months' earnings per share. Extra growth rate in EPS can be derived by subtracting par growth rate from 5-year EPS growth rate.

Dividends

Dividends are the latest indicated rate, and the yield is based on that amount and the latest close.
5-Year Growth Rate The figure is arrived at by the least squares method, using dividends actually paid for the first five years and the indicated rate for the sixth point.

Ratios

Profit Margin The profit margin of the company based on latest 12 months' revenue and earnings.
Asset Turnover The latest 12 months' return on total assets divided by the latest 12 months' profit margin.
Return on Common Equity The latest 12 months' earnings divided by stockholder equity from the latest balance sheet.
Return on Total Assets Based on the latest 12 months total earnings and the total asset as reported in the company's latest fiscal year balance sheet.
Leverage Ratio The latest 12 months' return on common equity divided by the latest 12 months' return on total assets.
Debt to Equity The total long-term debt of the company as a percentage of the total common equity of the company, both from the latest annual balance sheet.

Shareholdings

Market Value Latest reported shares outstanding times latest closing price per share of the common stock.
Latest Shares Outstanding Latest reported shares outstanding, adjusted for any subsequent stock splits or dividends.
Held by Banks-Funds The single figure here represents shares held by institutions with equity assets exceeding $100 million—banks, insurance companies, investment companies and managers, independent investment advisors and others. Shares held are adjusted for any stock splits or stock dividends that occur subsequent to the quarterly reporting date of the institutions covered. The data is furnished by Computer Directions Advisers, Inc.
Insider Net Trading Net change in insider holdings—purchases vs. sales—based on the latest SEC report in thousands of shares. 0 means there were no transactions or transactions netted to 0; +0 means transactions net-

* The financial data on companies in each industry come from the Media General *IndustriScope*, 301 East Grace Street, Richmond, VA 23219; June 30, 1988.

ted to purchases of fewer than 500 shares, and −0 means transactions netted to sales of fewer than 500 shares.

The most recent monthly period for insider transactions is January 12, 1988, to February 10, 1988.

Short Interest Ratio Short interest for the latest month reported, divided by average daily volume for the month corresponding to the report. The figure shows the number of days it would take to cover the short interest if the trading rate continued at the rate of the month covered by the report.

Short interest for the current issue is for the period January 15, 1988, through February 15, 1988.

GENERAL FOOTNOTES

*—As applied to beta figures, an asterisk denotes a co-efficient at least as large as its probable error (i.e., .6745 times the standard error of its mean).

G—Value calculated greater than allowed range.

L—Value calculated less than allowed range.

a—Under current dividend yield, an "a" indicates a stock dividend.

b—Indicates cash plus stock dividend when applied to dividend yield column.

NA—Item not applicable to this stock.

NE—Negative earnings invalidate calculation.

NC—Data required for calculation not available.

NS—Negative stockholder equity invalidates calculations.

NM—No meaningful figure

q—Based on first quarter information.

s—Based on second quarter information.

n—Based on third quarter information.

f—Based on fiscal year information.

*—When applied to 12-month earnings, an asterisk indicates an actual amount for an interim period, other than a quarterly multiple, resulting from a fiscal year change.

Trends and Forecasts: Aerospace (SIC 372,376)

(in millions of dollars except as noted)

ITEM	1984	1985	1986[1]	1987[2]	1988[3]	Percent Change: Compound Annual 1972-85	Compound Annual 1980-85	Annual 1985-86	Annual 1986-87	Annual 1987-88
Industry Data										
Value of shipments[4]	77,826	90,795	97,064	102,863	110,371	11.9	9.2	6.9	6.0	7.3
Value of shipments (1982$)	71,276	82,298	86,675	90,255	93,190	3.8	2.5	5.3	4.1	3.3
Total employment (000)	693	746	786	814	836	1.7	0.7	5.4	3.6	2.7
Production workers (000)	344	372	393	409	420	1.1	−0.8	5.6	4.1	2.7
Average hourly earnings ($)	13.24	13.88	14.34	14.84	—	7.9	7.0	3.3	3.5	—
Product Data										
Value of shipments[5]	70,200	80,625	86,858	91,801	98,140	11.6	8.6	7.7	5.7	6.9
Value of shipments (1982$)	64,076	72,896	77,224	80,394	82,690	3.5	1.9	5.9	4.1	2.9
Shipments price index[6] (1982=100)	109.5	110.4	112.0	114.0	118.5	7.7	6.6	1.4	1.8	3.9

[1]Estimated except for exports and imports.
[2]Estimated.
[3]Forecast.
[4]Value of all products and services sold by the Aerospace industry.
[5]Value of products classified in the Aerospace industry produced by all industries.
[6]Developed by the Office of Aerospace Policy and Analysis, ITA.
SOURCE: U.S. Department of Commerce: Bureau of the Census, Bureau of Economic Analysis, International Trade Administration (ITA). Estimates and forecasts by ITA.

Source: *U.S. Industrial Outlook 1988*, U.S. Department of Commerce.

Aerospace Manufacturing

Company	Revenue: Pct. Change Last Qtr	Revenue: Pct. Change FY to Date	Revenue: Pct. Change Last 12 Mos	Earnings: Last 12 Mos	Earnings: Per Share Last 12 Mos	Per Share Pct. Change Last Qtr	Per Share Pct. Change FY to Date	Per Share Pct. Change Last 12 Mos	5-Year Growth Rate	Par Growth Rate	Date of Report
-	%	%	%	$Mil	$	%	%	%	%	%	-
Ind. Group	3.0	3.2	1.9	3,513.7	3.53	35.0	35.7	61.3	5	11	- - -
Boeing Co	-4.0	-4.0	-8.2	498.0q	3.23	17.1	17.1	-21.0	8	5	03-88
Curtiss-Wright □	17.8	17.8	2.9	27.4q	5.59	-12.2	-12.2	21.0	NC	9	03-88
Fairchild Ind	-7.5	-7.5	-30.0	12.0q	.20	NE	NE	NE	NC	0	03-88
Gen Dynamics	6.7	6.7	4.6	437.6q	10.33	2.9	2.9	NE	NC	25	03-88
Gen Motors H	NA	NA	NA	NA	NA	NA	NA	NA	NA	NC	00-00
Grumman Corp	6.5	6.5	-2.4	.7q	-.12	1.7	1.7	-100.0	NC	1	03-88
Lockheed Corp	.0	.0	6.4	449.0q	6.95	41.5	41.5	12.8	12	17	03-88
Martin Marietta	13.8	13.8	10.7	237.5q	4.41	20.0	20.0	21.5	NC	20	03-88
McDonnel Doug	7.7	7.7	5.7	321.2q	8.02	25.5	25.5	25.1	4	7	03-88
Northrop Corp	-2.1	-2.1	5.5	193.2q	4.11	241.4	241.4	351.6	31	14	03-88
Rockwell Intl	-4.2	-5.3	-5.4	721.4s	2.64	26.6	32.2	18.4	16	16	03-88
Utd Technol	9.8	9.8	9.0	615.7q	4.71	25.3	25.3	5133.3	-14	9	03-88

Company	Dividends: Current Rate Amt	Current Rate Yield	5-Year Growth Rate	Payout Last FY	Payout Last 5 Yrs.	Last X-Dvd Date
-	$	%	%	%	%	-
Ind. Group	1.12	3.1	1	30	28	- - - -
Boeing Co	1.60	2.7	9	45	29	05-09-88
Curtiss-Wright □	1.60	3.1	7	28	117	07-05-88
Fairchild Ind	.20	1.8	-26	NE	NE	06-21-88
Gen Dynamics	1.00	1.9	5	10	16	07-13-88
Gen Motors H	.40	1.3	NA	NA	NA	05-06-88
Grumman Corp	1.00	4.6	6	NE	39	05-04-88
Lockheed Corp	1.60	3.6	0	20	12	05-18-88
Martin Marietta	1.10	2.5	5	25	43	05-31-88
McDonnel Doug	2.56	4.0	14	29	24	05-27-88
Northrop Corp	1.20	4.0	18	60	38	05-24-88
Rockwell Intl	.72	3.4	9	29	27	05-10-88
Utd Technol	1.60	4.2	3	31	43	05-16-88

Company	Ratio Analysis: Profit Margin	Asset Turnover	Return on Total Assets	Leverage Ratio	Return on Equity	Debt to Equity	Current Ratio
-	π/r x	r/a =	π/a x	a/e =	π/e	%	-
Ind. Group	3.7	1.54	5.7	2.79	15.9	27	1.3
Boeing Co	3.3	1.21	4.0	2.50	10.0	5	1.3
Curtiss-Wright □	15.9	.53	8.5	1.46	12.4	21	4.8
Fairchild Ind	2.7	.93	2.5	10.32	25.8	239	2.5
Gen Dynamics	4.6	1.89	8.7	3.14	27.3	27	1.4
Gen Motors H	NA	NC	NA	NC	NA	NA	NA
Grumman Corp	.0	NC	NC	NC	.1	88	2.3
Lockheed Corp	4.0	1.78	7.1	3.03	21.5	42	.9
Martin Marietta	4.5	1.89	8.5	3.08	26.2	31	1.4
McDonnel Doug	2.4	1.58	3.8	2.84	10.8	25	1.1
Northrop Corp	3.2	1.94	6.2	3.29	20.4	3	.8
Rockwell Intl	6.1	1.36	8.3	2.63	21.8	23	1.2
Utd Technol	3.5	1.49	5.2	2.75	14.3	43	1.6

Company	Shareholdings: Market Value	Latest Shares Outstndg.	Held by Banks-Funds	Insider Net Trading	Short Interest Ratio	Fiscal Year Ends
-	$Mil	000	000	000	Days	Mo
Ind. Group	36,231	986,180	394,911	+ 2	5.4	- -
Boeing Co	8,946	152,273	75,180	+1	1.8	12
Curtiss-Wright □	253	4,871	3,621	0	0.0	12
Fairchild Ind	154	14,126	5,594	0	1.4	12
Gen Dynamics	2,222	41,925	17,495	+7	6.9	12
Gen Motors H	3,948	130,496	4,002	+6	NA	NA
Grumman Corp	710	32,662	10,417	0	3.8	12
Lockheed Corp	2,919	65,972	43,372	0	2.5	12
Martin Marietta	2,367	52,905	24,105	-43	2.2	12
McDonnel Doug	2,483	38,716	13,988	0	8.5	12
Northrop Corp	1,399	46,821	21,454	+31	12.2	12
Rockwell Intl	5,809	275,000	102,014	0	2.7	09
Utd Technol	5,021	130,413	73,669	0	1.5	12

Trends and Forecasts: Airlines (SIC 451)

ITEM	1984	1985	1986	1987[1]	1988[2]	Percent Change: Compound Annual 1972-85	Compound Annual 1980-85	Annual 1984-85	Annual 1985-86	Annual 1986-87	Annual 1987-88
Total operating revenue (billions $)	43.8	46.7	50.5[3]	55.6	60.6	11.6	6.7	6.6	8.1	10.0	9.0
Employment (000)	345	355	422	435	454	1.3	−0.3	2.9	18.9	3.1	4.4
Revenue passenger miles (billions)	305	336	366	420	462	6.3	5.7	10.2	8.9	14.8	10.0

[1]Estimate.
[2]Forecast.
[3]Includes Federal Express for the first time.

SOURCE: U.S. Department of Commerce, International Trade Administration (ITA); Air Transport Association of America. Estimates and forecasts by ITA.

Source: ***U.S. Industrial Outlook 1988,*** **U.S. Department of Commerce.**

Evolution of Major U.S. Passenger Carriers Since Deregulation (Status as of August 1987)

Rank	Parent	Formed from establishment, merger, or acquisition (in approximate order) of:
1	Texas Air	New York Air, Continental, Eastern, People Express (Frontier-Provincetown-Britt), Rocky Mountain
2	United	United
3	American	American, Air Cal
4	Delta	Delta, Atlantic Southeast, Comair, Western
5	Northwest	Northwest, Republic (Southern-North Central), Hughes Air West
6	TWA	TWA, Ozark
7	Pan Am	Pan Am, National, Ransome
8	USAir	USAir, Suburban (PSA approved)
9	Piedmont	Piedmont, Empire, Jet Stream

SOURCE: U.S. Department of Transportation.

Source: ***U.S. Industrial Outlook 1988,*** **U.S. Department of Commerce.**

Airlines

Company	Revenue: Pct. Change: Last Qtr	Revenue: Pct. Change: FY to Date	Revenue: Pct. Change: Last 12 Mos	Earnings: Last 12 Mos	Earnings: Per Share: Last 12 Mos	Earnings: Per Share: Pct. Change: Last Qtr	Earnings: Per Share: Pct. Change: FY to Date	Earnings: Per Share: Pct. Change: Last 12 Mos	Earnings: 5-Year Growth Rate	Earnings: Par Growth Rate	Earnings: Date of Report	Dividends: Current Rate: Amt	Dividends: Current Rate: Yield	Dividends: 5-Year Growth Rate	Dividends: Payout: Last FY	Dividends: Payout: Last 5 Yrs.	Dividends: Last X-Dvd Date
-	%	%	%	$Mil	$	%	%	%	%	%	-	$	%	%	%	%	-
Ind. Group	24.3	28.2	27.7	1,611.2	1.37	NE	NE	351.6	NC	8	- - -	.37	1.5	0	10	10	- - - -
Air Midwest	-9.5	-9.5	10.8	-2.4q	-.63	NE	NE	NE	NC	-13	03-88	.00	.0	0	0	NE	12-10-85
Air Wisconsin □	48.4	48.4	32.5	8.3q	1.11	NE	NE	117.6	1	12	03-88	.00	.0	0	0	0	04-02-84
Airlease Ltd	25.0	25.0	100.0	8.8q	1.90	12.5	12.5	140.5	NC	-2	03-88	2.23	11.7	0	115	94	06-24-88
Alaska AirGrp	22.6	22.6	45.2	18.9q	1.26	NE	NE	-3.8	-7	6	03-88	.16	.8	0	19	10	07-11-88
Am West Airlns ◇	44.4	44.4	67.9	-56.0q	-4.40	NE	NE	NE	NC	0	03-88	.00	.0	0	0	0	00-00-00
AMR Corp	30.2	30.2	26.0	246.9q	4.06	229.4	229.4	-17.6	NC	9	03-88	.00	.0	0	0	0	01-28-80
Atlantic SE Air	24.7	24.7	30.2	10.5q	.79	-40.0	-40.0	-9.2	39	12	03-88	.00	.0	0	0	0	08-26-85
British Airways	65.9	36.3	69.5	387.8n	5.40	39.8	85.0	NC	NC	29	12-87	1.44	5.5	0	0	0	06-10-88
Comair Inc	53.0	43.6	44.2	5.1f	.55	NE	NE	NE	NC	4	03-88	.32	3.8	0	29	8	05-04-88
Command Airways □	38.5	30.2	33.3	1.4n	.94	NE	957.1	NE	NC	20	02-88	.00	.0	0	0	0	00-00-00
Delta Air Lines ◇	17.7	34.4	38.4	262.3n	5.36	228.6	-11.4	1.7	NC	10	03-88	1.20	2.2	1	17	27	05-05-88
HAL Inc	24.3	24.3	30.1	-11.4q	-5.95	-100.0	-100.0	-100.0	NC	-86	03-88	.00	.0	0	NE	NE	03-10-87
KLM Airlines	9.9	11.0	12.9	165.4s	3.26	-8.2	16.2	76.2	39	13	09-87	.75	4.1	0	24	13	08-14-87
Metro Airlines	41.0	43.0	40.8	1.1n	.18	NE	-90.2	-71.9	NC	4	01-88	.00	.0	0	0	0	01-16-87
Midway Arlns	27.1	27.1	35.0	5.2q	.41	-100.0	-100.0	-52.9	NC	7	03-88	.00	.0	0	0	0	00-00-00
NWA Inc ◇	6.0	6.0	26.5	94.5q	3.44	NE	NE	26.9	40	5	03-88	.90	2.0	3	25	27	06-09-88
Pan Am Corp ◇	8.6	18.2	18.2	-265.3f	-1.91	NE	NE	NE	NC	0	12-87	.00	.0	0	0	0	00-00-00
Pres Airways	12.5	-9.9	-10.8	-33.8f	-4.95	NE	NE	NE	NC	0	12-87	.00	.0	0	0	0	00-00-00
PS Group	-21.5	-21.5	-53.5	73.0q	9.52	NE	NE	NE	NC	27	03-88	.60	2.0	0	8	56	04-19-88
Simmons Airlines	15.1	22.7	21.8	5.6n	1.19	15.4	7.5	-11.2	NC	14	04-88	.00	.0	0	0	0	00-00-00
SkyWest Inc	29.3	23.0	23.2	-2.3f	-.55	NC	-100.0	-100.0	NC	-12	03-88	.04	.7	0	NE	6	01-13-88
SW Airlines	.1	.1	.5	30.2q	.94	NE	NE	-19.7	-10	5	03-88	.13	.7	0	21	10	06-07-88
Texas Air	4.2	4.2	44.3	-489.7q	-13.02	NE	NE	NE	NC	-98	03-88	.00	.0	0	0	NE	07-06-83
Trans Wrld Air	11.7	11.7	25.3	47.6q	-.30	NE	NE	NE	NC	25	03-88	.00	.0	0	0	0	00-00-00
UAL Cp ◇	13.2	13.2	-6.0	941.9q	18.64	NE	NE	775.1	NC	32	03-88	.00	.0	0	12	22	08-10-87
USAir Grp	168.3	168.3	99.8	148.5q	4.04	-100.0	-100.0	-9.8	5	8	03-88	.12	.3	0	2	3	07-11-88
Wings West Arlns	74.7	60.0	57.1	1.4n	.36	-100.0	NE	NE	NC	26	01-88	.00	.0	0	0	0	00-00-00
WorldCorp	-4.2	-4.2	23.4	7.7q	.24	-84.6	-84.6	NE	NC	0	03-88	.00	.0	0	0	0	00-00-00

Company	Ratio Analysis: Profit Margin	Ratio Analysis: Asset Turnover	Ratio Analysis: Return on Total Assets	Ratio Analysis: Leverage Ratio	Ratio Analysis: Return on Equity	Ratio Analysis: Debt to Equity	Ratio Analysis: Current Ratio	Shareholdings: Market Value	Shareholdings: Latest Shares Outstndng.	Shareholdings: Held by Banks-Funds	Shareholdings: Insider Net Trading	Shareholdings: Short Interest Ratio	Shareholdings: Fiscal Year Ends
-	π/r x	r/a =	π/a x	a/e =	π/e	%	-	$Mil	000	000	000	Days	Mo
Ind. Group	2.6	1.08	2.8	3.86	10.8	131	1.0	17,699	695,797	289,016	+ 37	1.8	- -
Air Midwest	-2.9	1.10	-3.2	4.00	-12.8	197	.7	14	3,873	890	+39	0.0	12
Air Wisconsin □	5.2	.81	4.2	2.79	11.7	104	1.4	115	7,399	2,274	0	0.0	12
Airlease Ltd	55.0	.13	6.9	1.48	10.2	40	NA	88	4,625	33	0	0.0	12
Alaska AirGrp	2.5	1.08	2.7	2.59	7.0	75	1.2	308	16,126	9,749	-3	0.6	12
Am West Airlns ◇	-8.9	1.10	-9.8	.00	NM	806	1.0	102	14,626	750	0	0.0	12
AMR Corp	3.2	.91	2.9	3.17	9.2	104	1.0	2,992	58,810	46,950	0	2.2	12
Atlantic SE Air	8.4	.60	5.0	2.46	12.3	96	2.8	132	12,681	4,901	0	0.0	12
British Airways	5.8	2.00	11.6	3.44	39.9	37	.7	1,891	72,020	1,633	0	1.6	03
Comair Inc	5.8	1.09	6.3	1.54	9.7	34	4.5	75	9,005	2,639	0	0.0	03
Command Airways □	5.0	1.00	5.0	3.94	19.7	186	.5	23	1,420	177	0	0.0	05
Delta Air Lines ◇	4.0	1.23	4.9	2.76	13.5	53	1.0	2,676	48,652	31,281	0	4.7	06
HAL Inc	-3.6	2.17	-7.8	10.99	-85.7	415	.7	53	1,905	291	0	0.2	12
KLM Airlines	6.0	.82	4.9	3.39	16.6	115	1.6	941	50,849	7,209	0	0.3	03
Metro Airlines	.8	1.88	1.5	2.87	4.3	118	1.2	41	6,177	1,352	0	0.0	04
Midway Arlns	1.4	1.50	2.1	3.29	6.9	103	.9	121	10,290	3,600	0	0.0	12
NWA Inc ◇	1.8	1.22	2.2	2.82	6.2	62	.6	1,385	30,110	25,244	0	3.6	12
Pan Am Corp ◇	-7.4	1.62	-12.0	.00	NS	-405	.7	348	139,308	19,263	0	10.1	12
Pres Airways	-51.2	3.25	-66.5	.00	NS	-29	.3	13	8,532	446	0	0.0	12
PS Group	20.6	.52	10.7	2.67	28.6	106	.9	246	8,074	3,945	0	0.9	12
Simmons Airlines	5.3	1.28	6.8	2.07	14.1	59	2.5	76	4,410	582	0	0.0	07
SkyWest Inc	-3.3	1.42	-4.7	2.30	-10.8	63	2.0	23	4,115	1,279	0	0.0	03
SW Airlines	3.9	.74	2.9	2.03	5.9	49	1.8	613	32,254	22,263	0	1.3	12
Texas Air	-5.7	1.02	-5.8	16.88	-97.9	995	.9	626	42,115	27,235	0	3.2	12
Trans Wrld Air	1.1	1.00	1.1	22.45	24.7	1217	1.5	1,037	30,503	2,502	0	0.5	12
UAL Cp ◇	11.0	1.04	11.4	2.82	32.2	49	1.0	2,075	21,200	37,193	0	0.5	12
USAir Grp	3.9	.72	2.8	2.79	7.8	95	.9	1,593	42,918	34,637	+1	1.7	12
Wings West Arlns	3.2	2.06	6.6	4.00	26.4	108	2.1	39	3,906	90	0	0.0	04
WorldCorp	5.4	1.26	6.8	.00	NS	-148	1.7	52	9,894	608	0	17.6	12

Trends and Forecasts: Apparel and Other Mill Products (SIC 23)

(in millions of dollars except as noted)

ITEM	1984	1985	1986[1]	1987[2]	Percent Change: Compound Annual 1972-85	Percent Change: Compound Annual 1980-85	Percent Change: Annual 1985-86	Percent Change: Annual 1986-87
Industry Data								
Value of shipments[3]	57,578	56,993	58,147	60,942	5.7	4.5	2.0	4.8
Value of shipments (1982$)	55,674	54,509	55,208	56,360	0.7	0.9	1.3	2.1
Total employment (000)	1,147	1,059	1,046	1,042	−2.0	−4.1	−1.2	−0.4
Production workers (000)	977	904	889	889	−2.1	−4.4	−1.7	0.0
Average hourly earnings ($)	5.35	5.70	—	—	6.4	6.0	—	—
Product Data								
Value of shipments[4]	50,672	50,047	51,089	53,239	5.8	4.4	2.1	4.2
Value of shipments (1982$)	49,223	48,212	48,831	49,695	1.0	1.1	1.3	1.8
Trade Data								
Value of imports	14,002	15,711	18,171	22,114	17.3	19.2	15.7	21.7
Value of exports	1,026	991	1,178	1,442	9.6	−9.2	18.9	22.4

[1]Estimated except for exports and imports.
[2]Estimated.
[3]Value of all products and services sold by the Apparel and Other Mill Products industry.
[4]Value of products classified in the Apparel and Other Mill Products industry produced by all industries.

SOURCE: U.S. Department of Commerce: Bureau of the Census, Bureau of Economic Analysis, International Trade Administration (ITA). Estimates and forecasts by ITA.

Source: *U.S. Industrial Outlook 1988*, U.S. Department of Commerce.

Trends and Forecasts: Men's and Boys' Outerwear (SIC 231,2321,2327,2328)

(in millions of dollars except as noted)

					Percent Change			
					Compound Annual		Annual	
ITEM	1984	1985	1986[1]	1987[2]	1972-85	1980-85	1985-86	1986-87
Industry Data								
Value of shipments[3]	14,401	14,316	14,656	15,595	4.6	2.6	2.4	6.4
2311 Men/Boys' Suits/Coats	3,209	3,321	3,404	3,411	2.5	3.4	2.5	0.2
2321 Men's Shirts/Nightwear	3,689	3,674	3,560	3,838	4.4	1.1	−3.1	7.8
2327 Men's & Boys' Trousers	2,373	2,235	2,275	2,437	1.9	2.2	1.8	7.1
2328 Men/Boys' Work Clothes	5,130	5,086	5,417	5,909	8.6	3.5	6.5	9.1
Value of shipments (1982$)	13,783	13,465	13,417	13,680	−1.1	−0.4	−0.4	2.0
2311 Men/Boys' Suits/Coats	3,032	3,057	3,067	3,011	−3.1	−1.5	0.3	−1.8
2321 Men's Shirts/Nightwear	3,568	3,457	3,340	3,499	−1.0	−1.2	−3.4	4.8
2327 Men's & Boys' Trousers	2,261	2,109	2,122	2,155	−3.1	−1.0	0.6	1.6
2328 Men/Boys' Work Clothes	4,922	4,842	4,889	5,016	1.9	1.2	1.0	2.6
Total employment (000)	309	279	272	269	−3.1	−5.6	−2.5	−1.1
2311 Men/Boys' Suits/Coats	73.9	64.9	61.1	58.9	−4.9	−4.4	−5.9	−3.6
2321 Men's Shirts/Nightwear	90.9	80.1	80.8	80.5	−2.6	−7.1	0.9	−0.4
2327 Men's & Boys' Trousers	54.8	49.7	48.4	46.6	−4.6	−5.0	−2.6	−3.7
2328 Men/Boys' Work Clothes	89.6	84.7	82.0	83.1	−0.4	−5.3	−3.2	1.3
Production workers (000)	269	245	240	238	−3.2	−5.7	−2.0	−0.8
2311 Men/Boys' Suits/Coats	63.9	57.4	54.4	52.6	−4.7	−4.0	−5.2	−3.3
2321 Men's Shirts/Nightwear	78.5	69.1	70.0	70.1	−3.0	−7.9	1.3	0.1
2327 Men's & Boys' Trousers	48.1	42.5	41.4	39.6	−4.9	−5.3	−2.6	−4.3
2328 Men/Boys' Work Clothes	78.1	75.8	73.9	75.5	−0.5	−5.3	−2.5	2.2
Average hourly earnings ($)	5.21	5.60	—	—	6.5	5.4	—	—
2311 Men/Boys' Suits/Coats	5.82	6.49	6.40	6.47	5.8	5.5	−1.4	1.1
2321 Men's Shirts/Nightwear	5.00	5.08	5.14	5.22	6.6	4.6	1.2	1.6
2327 Men's & Boys' Trousers	5.19	5.59	5.50	5.56	7.0	6.1	−1.6	1.1
2328 Men/Boys' Work Clothes	4.94	5.37	5.58	5.67	7.2	5.2	3.9	1.6

Product Data								
Value of shipments[4]	11,198	11,106	11,323	12,030	4.5	1.9	2.0	6.2
2311 Men/Boys' Suits/Coats	2,578	2,562	2,579	2,585	2.8	2.5	0.7	0.2
2321 Men's Shirts/Nightwear	2,781	2,999	2,894	3,099	4.8	1.4	−3.5	7.1
2327 Men's & Boys' Trousers	1,776	1,630	1,661	1,789	1.0	2.1	1.9	7.7
2328 Men/Boys' Work Clothes	4,064	3,915	4,189	4,557	8.0	1.7	7.0	8.8
Value of shipments (1982$)	10,794	10,562	10,469	10,695	−0.9	−0.4	−0.9	2.2
2311 Men/Boys' Suits/Coats	2,450	2,380	2,345	2,298	−2.1	−1.1	−1.5	−2.0
2321 Men's Shirts/Nightwear	2,698	2,838	2,728	2,848	−0.6	−0.6	−3.9	4.4
2327 Men's & Boys' Trousers	1,762	1,637	1,627	1,674	−3.2	0.3	−0.6	2.9
2328 Men/Boys' Work Clothes	3,884	3,707	3,770	3,875	1.1	−0.3	1.7	2.8
Trade Data								
Value of imports	4,196	4,407	4,938	—	16.6	14.6	12.0	—
2311 Men/Boys' Suits/Coats	940	945	931	1,099	16.0	17.5	−1.5	18.0
2321 Men's Shirts/Nightwear	2,455	2,568	2,948	3,921	16.6	13.1	14.8	33.0
2327 Men's & Boys' Trousers	0.0	0.0	0.0	—	—	—	—	—
2328 Men/Boys' Work Clothes	801	894	1,059	1,663	17.2	16.2	18.5	57.0
Value of exports	203	192	246	372	6.5	−15.8	28.1	51.2
2311 Men/Boys' Suits/Coats	18.7	44.5	56.0	81.1	18.3	2.4	25.8	44.8
2321 Men's Shirts/Nightwear	81.1	80.2	101	147	10.5	−19.4	25.9	45.5
2327 Men's & Boys' Trousers	59.5	63.7	86.8	142	8.7	−0.0	36.3	63.6
2328 Men/Boys' Work Clothes	43.4	4.0	2.2	1.7	−15.6	−48.9	−45.0	−22.7

[1]Estimated except for exports and imports.
[2]Estimated.
[3]Value of all products and services sold by the Men's and Boys' Outerwear industry.
[4]Value of products classified in the Men's and Boys' Outerwear industry produced by all industries.

SOURCE: U.S. Department of Commerce: Bureau of the Census, Bureau of Economic Analysis, International Trade Administration (ITA). Estimates and forecasts by ITA.

Source: *U.S. Industrial Outlook 1988*, U.S. Department of Commerce.

Trends and Forecasts: Children's and Infants' Outerwear (SIC 2361,2363)

(in millions of dollars except as noted)

					Percent Change			
					Compound Annual		Annual	
ITEM	1984	1985	1986[1]	1987[2]	1972-85	1980-85	1985-86	1986-87
Industry Data								
Value of shipments[3]	1,505	1,413	1,451	1,509	4.0	4.3	2.7	4.0
2361 Child's Dresses/Blouses	1,332	1,269	1,334	1,401	5.2	5.5	5.1	5.0
2363 Childrens Coats/Suits	173	145	117	108	−2.0	−3.9	−19.3	−7.7
Value of shipments (1982$)	1,503	1,406	1,431	1,453	0.7	2.2	1.8	1.5
2361 Child's Dresses/Blouses	1,349	1,288	1,338	1,367	1.9	4.0	3.9	2.2
2363 Childrens Coats/Suits	154	118	92.5	86.1	−6.2	−9.7	−21.6	−6.9
Total employment (000)	36.2	30.3	29.2	28.7	−2.9	−6.9	−3.6	−1.7
2361 Child's Dresses/Blouses	31.4	26.7	26.2	25.9	−2.1	−6.3	−1.9	−1.1
2363 Childrens Coats/Suits	4.8	3.6	3.0	2.8	−7.0	−10.6	−16.7	−6.7
Production workers (000)	30.9	25.6	25.7	24.4	−3.2	−7.1	0.4	−5.1
2361 Child's Dresses/Blouses	26.4	22.3	23.0	21.9	−2.5	−6.8	3.1	−4.8
2363 Childrens Coats/Suits	4.5	3.3	2.7	2.5	−6.7	−9.0	−18.2	−7.4
Average hourly earnings ($)	5.07	5.47	—	—	6.3	7.6	—	—
2361 Child's Dresses/Blouses	5.07	5.52	5.59	5.80	6.4	8.0	1.3	3.8
2363 Childrens Coats/Suits	5.06	5.16	5.20	5.21	5.7	5.0	0.8	0.2

Product Data								
Value of shipments[4]	1,339	1,275	1,334	1,371	4.5	3.9	4.6	2.8
2361 Child's Dresses/Blouses	1,173	1,135	1,224	1,270	5.7	5.6	7.7	3.8
2363 Childrens Coats/Suits	166	139	110	101	−1.7	−5.9	−20.9	−8.2
Value of shipments (1982$)	1,345	1,275	1,323	1,328	1.4	2.1	3.8	0.4
2361 Child's Dresses/Blouses	1,197	1,161	1,236	1,248	2.8	4.3	6.5	1.0
2363 Childrens Coats/Suits	148	114	86.9	80.6	−5.9	−11.4	−23.8	−7.2
Shipments price index[5] (1982=100)	99.8	100.9	102.5	104.8	3.2	2.0	1.6	2.2
2361 Child's Dresses/Blouses	98.0	97.8	99.0	101.8	3.0	1.3	1.2	2.8
2363 Childrens Coats/Suits	112.1	122.2	126.5	125.5	4.5	6.4	3.5	−0.8
Trade Data								
Value of exports	14.5	12.5	12.4	13.7	14.3	−11.5	−0.8	10.5
2361 Child's Dresses/Blouses	10.6	9.7	11.7	11.1	13.8	−14.1	20.6	−5.1
2363 Childrens Coats/Suits	3.9	2.8	0.7	2.6	16.1	4.9	−75.0	271.4
Export/shipments ratio	0.015	0.014	0.014	0.015	10.1	−13.6	0.0	7.1
2361 Child's Dresses/Blouses	0.013	0.013	0.015	0.014	9.5	−17.5	15.4	−6.7
2363 Childrens Coats/Suits	0.023	0.020	0.006	0.026	19.4	10.8	−70.0	333.3

[1]Estimated except for exports and imports.

[2]Estimated.

[3]Value of all products and services sold by the Children's and Infants' Outerwear industry.

[4]Value of products classified in the Children's and Infants' Outerwear industry produced by all industries.

[5]Developed by the Office of Industry Assessment, ITA.

SOURCE: U.S. Department of Commerce: Bureau of the Census, Bureau of Economic Analysis, International Trade Administration (ITA). Estimates and forecasts by ITA.

Source: *U.S. Industrial Outlook 1988*, U.S. Department of Commerce.

Apparel

Company	Revenue Pct. Change Last Qtr %	Revenue Pct. Change FY to Date %	Revenue Pct. Change Last 12 Mos %	Earnings Last 12 Mos $Mil	Per Share Last 12 Mos $	Per Share Pct. Change Last Qtr %	Per Share Pct. Change FY to Date %	Per Share Pct. Change Last 12 Mos %	5-Year Growth Rate %	Par Growth Rate %	Date of Report -	Dividends Current Rate Amt $	Current Rate Yield %	5-Year Growth Rate %	Payout Last FY %	Payout Last 5 Yrs. %	Last X-Dvd Date -
Ind. Group	8.2	12.0	8.8	235.1	.65	- 37.0	- 43.3	- 27.5	13	9	- - -	.17	1.5	1	16	18	- - - -
Angelica	9.3	9.3	5.7	17.3q	1.87	4.3	4.3	.5	4	8	04-88	.72	2.7	10	37	32	06-09-88
Bobbie Brooks	.0	.0	-42.8	.4q	.05	NE	NE	-79.2	NC	4	03-88	.00	.0	0	0	0	00-00-00
Champ Prods	16.3	16.3	22.0	7.7q	2.27	84.6	84.6	37.6	49	13	03-88	.40	1.0	1	19	35	04-26-88
Chaus Bernard	-34.7	-7.7	2.2	-3.0n	-.16	-100.0	-100.0	-100.0	NC	-5	03-88	.00	.0	0	0	0	00-00-00
Coated Sales	39.5	40.1	40.0	10.9f	.55	17.6	37.5	37.5	NC	27	02-88	.00	.0	0	0	0	00-00-00
Eagle Clothes □	-12.6	-8.1	-4.2	-1.7n	-.22	NE	-100.0	-100.0	NC	-8	04-88	.00	.0	0	0	0	00-00-00
Farah Inc	-2.8	-5.2	-11.3	.4s	.07	-42.4	2800.0	-77.4	NC	1	04-88	.00	.0	0	NE	41	10-28-86
Forstmann&Co	21.7	21.7	4.9	-2.8q	-1.41	-60.5	-60.5	-100.0	NC	-7	04-88	.00	.0	0	0	0	00-00-00
Garan Inc	36.9	36.1	21.1	4.5s	1.71	145.7	360.0	87.9	-22	4	03-88	.80	3.6	-9	74	46	05-18-88
Genesco Inc	9.9	9.9	-13.3	8.6q	.40	NE	NE	-37.5	NC	15	04-88	.00	.0	0	0	0	00-00-00
Hampton Ind	10.6	10.6	4.3	3.9q	1.07	11.1	11.1	-21.3	10	8	03-88	.00	.0	0	0	0	06-10-87
Johnston Ind	9.5	11.7	12.1	7.5n	2.29	-38.6	-15.3	-10.5	73	18	03-88	.00	.0	0	0	0	00-00-00
Judys Inc ◇	-4.9	-2.0	-1.6	.0f	.00	NE	-100.0	-100.0	NC	NC	01-88	.06	2.4	0	NE	33	01-20-88
Kellwood Co	19.5	22.1	22.0	30.2f	2.61	18.0	18.6	18.6	19	14	04-88	.72	2.7	28	24	23	06-06-88
Lakeland Ind	76.2	43.8	43.7	.3n	.11	NE	-52.2	-56.0	NC	5	10-87	.00	.0	0	0	0	00-00-00
Littlefield Adam	-55.4	-46.1	-23.8	-3.2s	-2.99	NE	NE	-100.0	NC	-76	06-87	.00	.0	0	0	NE	05-24-83
Liz Claiborne	19.1	19.1	24.9	116.0q	1.34	5.4	5.4	21.8	48	28	03-88	.18	1.0	0	12	11	05-04-88
Mayfair Inds	75.0	75.0	42.3	2.6q	.68	-10.5	-10.5	-5.6	NC	17	03-88	.00	.0	0	0	0	00-00-00
Nutmeg Inds	53.8	53.8	146.1	2.8q	.63	300.0	300.0	293.8	NC	41	04-88	.00	.0	0	0	0	01-22-87
Oak Hill Sptswr	-6.7	-6.7	11.3	1.2q	.34	-95.8	-95.8	-65.7	-1	6	03-88	.00	.0	0	0	0	00-00-00
Oxford Inds	2.6	8.1	9.1	-2.0n	-.20	-100.0	-100.0	-100.0	NC	-5	02-88	.50	4.7	16	49	30	05-09-88
Pannill Knit	-29.3	-29.3	9.6	14.5q	.96	NE	NE	-7.7	NC	37	03-88	.00	.0	0	0	0	00-00-00
Phil-Van Heu	6.8	6.8	-3.2	22.0q	.78	-72.6	-72.6	-55.7	8	9	04-88	.28	2.7	15	21	15	08-16-88
Pope Evan Rob	152.6	129.0	93.4	-32.7n	-4.69	NE	NE	NE	NC	0	03-88	.00	.0	0	0	0	02-01-83
Quiksilver Inc	79.3	77.5	78.2	3.1s	.51	50.0	38.5	18.6	NC	30	04-88	.00	.0	0	0	0	11-20-87
Rocky Mtn Under	13.6	13.6	.0	-1.6q	-.52	-83.3	-83.3	NE	NC	-21	03-88	.00	.0	0	0	0	00-00-00
Russ Togs	-7.1	-7.1	-6.0	7.7q	1.00	-50.0	-50.0	-45.1	-1	3	04-88	.60	4.3	0	36	34	06-27-88
Salant Corp	26.6	26.6	10.9	4.4q	1.25	100.0	100.0	86.6	NC	18	02-88	.00	.0	0	0	NE	07-30-84
Sanmark Star	55.8	39.8	25.8	1.2s	.15	-57.1	-52.6	-57.1	6	9	12-87	.00	.0	0	0	0	01-04-88
State o Maine	-21.1	52.3	52.7	4.1f	1.70	-77.8	77.1	77.1	NC	25	02-88	.00	.0	0	0	0	08-07-87
Sup Surgical	8.7	8.7	8.1	5.2q	2.14	38.9	38.9	38.1	14	10	03-88	.50	1.8	14	22	23	05-20-88
Thackeray Cp	20.5	20.5	10.2	.1q	.03	NE	NE	NE	NC	1	03-88	.00	.0	0	0	NE	00-00-00
Tultex Cp	-15.0	-16.7	.9	24.2s	.88	-50.0	-63.0	6.0	18	11	05-88	.36	3.8	21	25	25	09-02-88
Winjak Inc	-49.1	-49.1	-25.0	-18.6q	-5.12	-100.0	-100.0	NE	NC	0	03-88	.00	.0	0	NE	NE	09-25-87
Wolf, Howard	-5.0	-8.1	.0	-.1n	-.12	-50.0	40.0	NE	NC	-2	02-88	.00	.0	0	0	0	08-09-84

Company	Ratio Analysis Profit Margin π/r	Asset Turnover r/a	Return on Total Assets π/a	Leverage Ratio a/e	Return on Equity π/e	Debt to Equity %	Current Ratio -	Shareholdings Market Value $Mil	Latest Shares Outstndg. 000	Held by Banks-Funds 000	Insider Net Trading 000	Short Interest Ratio Days	Fiscal Year Ends Mo
Ind. Group	3.3	1.79	5.9	2.07	12.2	40	2.9	3,848	330,071	98,651	- 652	1.8	- -
Angelica	5.5	1.45	8.0	1.56	12.5	16	3.1	247	9,307	5,047	+2	0.0	01
Bobbie Brooks	2.5	.76	1.9	1.84	3.5	0	1.9	8	7,333	362	0	0.0	12
Champ Prods	4.2	1.74	7.3	2.11	15.4	68	4.2	133	3,421	1,337	0	0.8	12
Chaus Bernard	-.9	2.78	-2.5	1.88	-4.7	16	2.4	98	18,678	1,614	0	0.6	06
Coated Sales	8.7	1.89	16.4	1.63	26.7	18	3.3	18	20,130	4,626	-150	0.0	02
Eagle Clothes □	-1.5	1.87	-2.8	2.75	-7.7	23	2.1	7	7,714	1,472	0	1.3	07
Farah Inc	.1	2.00	.2	2.50	.5	49	1.6	53	5,906	2,410	+2	1.4	10
Forstmann&Co	-1.3	1.23	-1.6	4.13	-6.6	250	5.5	34	5,058	1,407	0	0.5	01
Garan Inc	3.6	1.47	5.3	1.49	7.9	14	3.6	59	2,611	1,228	0	0.0	09
Genesco Inc	2.1	1.57	3.3	4.64	15.3	123	4.6	66	15,174	4,107	0	2.1	01
Hampton Ind	2.3	1.74	4.0	2.03	8.1	59	3.8	36	3,788	548	0	0.0	12
Johnston Ind	6.3	1.38	8.7	2.05	17.8	44	2.8	54	3,229	776	0	0.0	06
Judys Inc ◇	.0	NC	NC	NC	.0	7	1.8	11	4,526	67	0	0.0	01
Kellwood Co	4.3	2.09	9.0	2.12	19.1	43	2.3	298	11,251	7,064	+4	0.1	04
Lakeland Ind	1.3	2.62	3.4	1.35	4.6	0	4.1	10	2,462	301	0	0.0	01
Littlefield Adam	-20.0	1.29	-25.8	2.95	-76.2	14	1.3	1	1,074	53	0	0.0	12
Liz Claiborne	10.5	2.29	24.0	1.35	32.5	4	4.1	1,642	87,006	38,230	-145	0.0	12
Mayfair Inds	7.0	1.84	12.9	1.35	17.4	2	3.1	31	3,750	136	-374	0.0	12
Nutmeg Inds	8.8	1.64	14.4	2.86	41.2	29	1.6	49	4,273	122	0	0.0	01
Oak Hill Sptswr	1.0	3.50	3.5	1.57	5.5	5	2.6	17	3,304	789	0	0.0	12
Oxford Inds	-.3	3.00	-.9	1.67	-1.5	12	2.3	107	9,974	5,485	0	1.7	05
Pannill Knit	5.8	.93	5.4	6.83	36.9	453	4.7	146	15,000	1,834	0	10.5	12
Phil-Van Heu	4.3	2.09	9.0	1.49	13.4	5	3.2	93	9,039	3,257	0	0.0	01
Pope Evan Rob	-27.7	1.94	-53.7	.00	NM	432	1.5	2	6,725	1,179	0	0.0	06
Quiksilver Inc	7.6	2.32	17.6	1.68	29.5	0	2.0	35	6,000	1,028	0	0.0	10
Rocky Mtn Under	-3.9	3.26	-12.7	1.66	-21.1	9	2.1	6	2,948	277	+9	0.0	12
Russ Togs	2.9	1.76	5.1	1.47	7.5	1	2.9	100	7,216	4,592	0	0.0	01
Salant Corp	3.1	1.77	5.5	3.25	17.9	115	3.1	44	3,655	1,127	0	0.4	11
Sanmark Star	1.6	1.38	2.2	4.00	8.8	24	3.5	33	7,191	854	0	0.0	06
State o Maine	7.5	1.89	14.2	1.78	25.3	9	2.0	40	2,476	89	0	0.0	02
Sup Surgical	4.9	1.80	8.8	1.45	12.8	10	3.7	67	2,465	1,144	0	0.6	12
Thackeray Cp	.1	2.00	.2	3.50	.7	283	4.4	36	5,107	478	0	10.1	12
Tultex Cp	7.4	1.45	10.7	1.78	19.0	23	2.7	259	27,578	4,474	+1	29.9	11
Winjak Inc	-51.7	2.97	-53.7	.00	NM	29	.7	5	3,646	1,130	0	3.1	12
Wolf, Howard	-1.3	1.31	-1.7	1.35	-2.3	0	3.4	2	1,056	7	0	0.0	05

Trends and Forecasts: Savings Institutions (SIC 603 and 612)

(in billions of dollars except as noted)

Item	1984	1985	1986	1987[1]	1988[2]	Percent Change: Compound Annual 1972-1985	Compound Annual 1980-1985	Annual 1985-1986	Annual 1986-1987	Annual 1987-1988
Assets	1,184	1,286	1,402	1,486	1,575	10.9	10.2	9.0	6.0	6.0
Mortgages held	699	756	774	789	805	8.3	4.9	2.4	1.9	2.0
Mortgage-backed securities	132	135	184	212	233	—	26.9	36.3	15.2	9.9
Deposits	967	1,030	1,082	1,125	1,193	10.2	9.5	5.0	4.0	6.0
Net worth	48	59	71	74	80	7.9	6.0	20.3	4.2	8.1
Net new savings[3]	51	−13	−10	−20	15	—	—	—	—	—
Mortgages made	199	216	298	322	290	9.9	22.0	38.0	8.1	−9.9
Number of institutions	3,550	3,603	3,586	3,600	3,575	−2.0	−4.2	−0.5	0.4	−0.7
Number of offices	25,019	25,660	25,759	26,017	26,276	6.3	1.7	0.4	1.0	1.0
Employment (000)	391	428	476	499	529	7.7	5.9	11.2	4.8	6.0

[1]Estimated.
[2]Forecast.
[3]This series is extremely volatile, making percent changes unmeaningful.

SOURCE: Federal Home Loan Bank Board, National Council of Savings Institutions, Bureau of Labor Statistics.

Source: *U.S. Industrial Outlook 1988,* U.S. Department of Commerce.

Trends and Forecasts: Commercial Banking (SIC 602)

(in billions of dollars except as noted)

Item	1984	1985	1986	1987[1]	1988[2]	Percent Change: Compound Annual 1972-85	Compound Annual 1980-85	Annual 1985-86	Annual 1986-87	Annual 1987-88
Assets	2,265	2,484	2,800	3,080	3,419	9.8	10.1	12.7	10.0	11.0
Loans	1,465	1,617	1,801	1,963	2,159	11.0	13.7	11.4	9.0	10.0
Investments	378	420	475	547	618	6.6	5.2	13.1	15.2	13.0
Deposits	1,633	1,773	2,015	2,236	2,504	8.5	8.4	13.7	11.0	12.0
Employment (000)	1,518	1,544	1,565	1,580	1,596	3.2	1.5	1.4	1.0	1.0

[1]Estimated.
[2]Forecast.

SOURCE: Board of Governors of the Federal Reserve System and Bureau of Labor Statistics. Estimates and forecasts by U.S. Department of Commerce, International Trade Administration.

Source: *U.S. Industrial Outlook 1988,* U.S. Department of Commerce.

Company	Revenue: Pct. Change Last Qtr	Revenue: Pct. Change FY to Date	Revenue: Pct. Change Last 12 Mos	Earnings: Last 12 Mos	Earnings: Per Share Last 12 Mos	Earnings: Per Share Pct. Change Last Qtr	Earnings: Per Share Pct. Change FY to Date	Earnings: Per Share Pct. Change Last 12 Mos	Earnings: 5-Year Growth Rate	Earnings: Par Growth Rate	Earnings: Date of Report	Dividends: Current Rate Amt	Dividends: Current Rate Yield	Dividends: 5-Year Growth Rate	Dividends: Payout Last FY	Dividends: Payout Last 5 Yrs.	Dividends: Last X-Dvd Date	Ratio Analysis: Pro-fit Mar-gin	Ratio Analysis: Asset Turn-over	Ratio Analysis: Return on Total Assets	Ratio Analysis: Lever-age Ratio	Ratio Analysis: Return on Equity	Ratio Analysis: Debt to Eq-uity	Ratio Analysis: Curr-ent Ratio	Shareholdings: Mar-ket Value	Shareholdings: Latest Shares Out-stndng.	Shareholdings: Held by Banks-Funds	Shareholdings: Insider Net Trad-ing	Shareholdings: Short Int-erest Ratio	Shareholdings: Fiscal Year Ends
-	%	%	%	$Mil	$	%	%	%	%	%	-	$	%	%	%	%	-	π/r x	r/a =	π/a x	a/e =	π/e	%	-	$Mil	000	000	000	Days	Mo
New York Banks																														
Ind. Group	14.8	14.7	17.1	-3,070.6	-3.43	54.4	36.5	-100.0	NC	-15	---	1.51	5.3	1	258	39	----	-3.9	.10	-.4	26.50	-10.6	164	NC	31,112	1,093,703	595,425	+474	1.2	--
ApplBk	14.5	14.5	32.8	18.6q	4.06	-10.2	-10.2	12.5	NC	9	03-88	.00	.0	0	0	0	00-00-00	7.1	.08	.6	15.17	9.1	1	NA	158	4,587	1,558	0	0.4	12
Arrow Bk	10.7	6.0	6.6	4.2f	1.83	2.0	5.8	5.8	NC	10	12-87	.56	3.4b	0	30	26	04-18-88	13.1	.09	1.2	11.67	14.0	22	NA	37	2,290	152	0	0.0	12
Bank of NY Co	31.0	22.3	22.3	103.4f	2.97	9.8	-40.2	-40.2	0	4	12-87	1.80	5.2	10	58	35	04-18-88	4.8	.08	.4	23.25	9.3	65	NA	1,147	33,113	15,604	+32	16.5	12
Bankers Tr NY	6.5	6.5	17.6	3.0q	-.14	-9.0	-9.0	-100.0	NC	1	03-88	1.86	5.0	10	8300	34	06-29-88	.1	.00	.0	NC	.1	83	NA	2,926	79,079	53,124	+19	0.7	12
Beverly Sav Bk ...... ■	5.6	5.6	4.5	.9q	.33	-73.3	-73.3	-32.7	NC	2	03-88	.12	1.0	0	0	0	02-23-88	3.9	.08	.3	9.67	2.9	43	NA	36	2,875	558	0	0.0	12
BMJ Financial	25.0	25.0	23.0	5.6q	1.82	-7.3	-7.3	14.5	NC	12	03-88	.52	2.4	0	26	25	04-25-88	11.7	.09	1.1	15.73	17.3	18	NA	66	3,096	0	0	0.0	12
Boston Five Cent	22.0	18.0	4.5	12.1s	1.66	.0	-23.1	-24.5	NC	5	04-88	.72	4.1	0	19	13	07-01-88	5.8	.09	.5	17.00	8.5	143	NA	125	7,040	1,203	0	0.0	10
Cenvest Inc	42.0	42.0	32.3	2.9q	.75	-42.4	-42.4	-28.6	NC	2	03-88	.40	3.3	0	28	11	06-29-88	6.4	.09	.6	7.67	4.6	82	NA	43	3,578	712	0	0.0	12
Chase Manhttn	17.8	17.8	19.8	-722.0q	-9.59	175.9	175.9	-100.0	NC	-27	03-88	2.16	7.2	5	NE	85	04-25-88	-6.5	.11	-.7	31.71	-22.2	203	NA	2,540	85,025	57,399	+42	2.8	12
Chemical Bkg	37.1	37.1	34.3	-814.4q	-16.31	23.4	23.4	-100.0	NC	-41	03-88	2.72	8.9	7	NE	111	06-09-88	-11.2	.09	-1.0	35.40	-35.4	90	NA	1,722	56,227	34,247	+103	2.4	12
ChBk B	NA	NA	NA	NA	NA	NA	NA	NA	NA	NC	00-00	.76	18.4	NA	NA	NA	06-09-88	NA	NC	NA	NC	NA	NA	NA	139	33,668	17,425	0	NA	NA
Cheshire Fincl	5.6	3.3	7.1	4.5s	1.14	11.1	4.8	18.8	NC	1	09-87	.86	5.8	0	0	0	06-20-88	15.0	.09	1.3	4.54	5.9	4	NA	59	4,000	0	0	0.0	03
Citicorp	10.1	10.1	19.2	-1044.0q	-4.11	17.4	17.4	-100.0	NC	-20	03-88	1.48	5.9	9	NE	60	04-25-88	-3.6	.14	-.5	29.00	-14.5	278	NA	7,907	317,867	210,973	+503	2.5	12
Commun Bank	12.8	12.8	11.3	4.2q	1.64	-17.4	-17.4	-13.2	NC	5	03-88	.76	4.8	0	44	38	06-09-88	8.6	.10	.9	11.11	10.0	3	NA	41	2,554	528	0	0.0	12
Commun Natl B&T . □	.0	.5	5.2	.5f	.02	NC	-33.3	-33.3	NC	6	12-86	.00	.0	0	0	0	00-00-00	2.5	.12	.3	18.67	5.6	24	NA	16	24,830	11	0	0.0	12
Cornerstone Fincl ... □	10.0	13.4	16.6	1.6f	.81	-100.0	-42.6	-42.6	NC	5	12-87	.36	3.6	0	42	27	04-11-88	11.4	.10	1.1	8.00	8.8	66	NA	20	1,958	130	0	0.0	12
Dime Svg NY .... □	26.4	26.4	13.0	67.4q	2.98	-13.0	-13.0	-11.6	NC	10	03-88	.00	.0	0	0	0	00-00-00	6.9	.09	.6	16.67	10.0	101	NA	359	22,767	13,756	0	0.2	12
Empire of Amer	9.9	9.9	3.2	-10.9q	-1.14	-100.0	-100.0	-100.0	NC	-9	03-88	.26	9.5	0	183	8	03-25-88	-1.1	.09	-.1	74.00	-7.4	266	NA	41	15,000	400	0	3.1	12
Evergreen Bcp	24.4	51.5	.0	.0*	2.49	23.6	57.6	19.1	NC	0	12-87	.72	3.4	0	27	26	04-25-88	NC	NC	NC	NC	.0	8	NA	64	3,063	219	0	0.0	12
Fst Emp .... ◇	77.9	77.9	70.3	45.7q	5.13	29.2	29.2	5.6	31	10	03-88	1.00	2.0	13	17	18	05-31-88	8.7	.10	.9	13.33	12.0	6	NA	358	7,190	2,364	+1	0.3	12
FNB Rochester	32.4	20.6	14.2	1.6f	.93	.0	2.2	2.2	NC	15	12-87	.00	.0	0	0	0	02-24-88	10.0	.09	.9	16.78	15.1	0	NA	2	350	125	+0	0.0	12
Hamptons Bancshrs	69.0	69.0	36.3	1.1q	1.26	-66.7	-66.7	-30.0	NC	6	03-88	.44	2.5	0	22	6	03-09-88	7.3	.11	.8	11.75	9.4	1	NA	14	810	161	0	0.0	12
Home City S Bk	.5	.5	-1.3	5.1q	1.77	-3.5	-3.5	-23.4	NC	6	03-88	.12	.5	0	0	0	06-06-88	6.9	.09	.6	10.17	6.1	2	NA	67	2,875	650	0	0.0	12
Home Savings Bk	11.3	11.3	9.4	26.1q	2.17	.0	.0	7.4	NC	8	03-88	.60	3.8	0	12	6	06-27-88	17.4	.09	1.6	7.13	11.4	0	NA	191	12,025	6,941	0	0.0	12
Irving Bk Cp	10.6	10.6	14.4	-212.0q	-9.63	79.5	79.5	-100.0	NC	-35	03-88	2.42	3.4	6	NE	82	05-25-88	-9.6	.09	-.9	31.33	-28.2	85	NA	1,332	18,725	7,157	+4	0.4	12
KeyCorp	13.4	13.4	30.6	83.2q	2.22	-4.0	-4.0	-26.5	8	5	03-88	1.20	5.7	14	48	36	06-24-88	7.4	.09	.7	16.57	11.6	54	NA	614	29,073	6,339	0	0.0	12
Mfrs Hanover	9.3	9.3	1.9	-1109.1q	-26.73	18.5	18.5	-100.0	NC	-60	03-88	3.28	10.9	2	NE	283	06-27-88	-14.0	.11	-1.5	35.87	-53.8	411	NA	1,478	49,056	26,522	+12	12.4	12
Matthews Wght	-100.0	-99.6	-48.8	-.4n	.02	-100.0	-100.0	-99.1	NC	-1	09-87	.00	.0	0	0	0	00-00-00	-1.7	.12	-.2	5.50	-1.1	0	NA	4	6,241	134	0	0.0	12
Merchants Bk NY	19.4	19.1	18.9	9.2f	6.98	10.1	10.3	10.3	16	16	12-87	1.00	.4	8	14	15	06-07-88	20.9	.08	1.6	11.88	19.0	0	NA	317	1,322	30	0	0.0	12
Mid Hudson S B .... ◇	7.5	7.5	4.7	2.6q	2.41	-20.9	-20.9	-5.9	NC	9	03-88	.28	1.4	0	0	0	06-06-88	11.8	.09	1.1	9.09	10.0	0	NA	21	1,061	97	0	0.0	12
Morgan, J.P.	9.1	9.1	5.5	343.9q	1.82	1588.9	1588.9	-48.7	-18	1	03-88	1.50	3.9	10	359	38	06-14-88	4.9	.10	.5	14.40	7.2	58	NA	7,021	180,606	111,276	+18	2.0	12
Natl Svgs Bk	35.8	16.8	2.2	2.6s	2.31	NE	900.0	69.9	NC	7	03-88	.20	1.0	0	0	0	06-28-88	5.7	.11	.6	13.33	8.0	12	NA	24	1,153	88	0	0.0	09
N Side Sav Bk	15.3	1.5	1.9	4.6s	1.27	290.9	-42.1	13.4	NC	5	03-88	.00	.0	0	0	0	00-00-00	8.7	.08	.7	7.14	5.0	76	NA	59	3,680	1,801	0	0.0	09
Plymth 5 Cent SB	13.5	10.2	15.7	1.2n	.46	-30.4	18.8	9.5	NC	4	09-87	.00	.0	0	0	0	00-00-00	5.5	.11	.6	6.50	3.9	52	NA	23	2,300	88	0	0.0	12
Poughkeepsie S B	39.8	39.8	49.5	11.3q	3.00	117.0	117.0	44.2	NC	10	03-88	.40	2.0	0	8	4	04-12-88	7.2	.10	.7	16.29	11.4	310	NA	78	3,922	1,119	0	0.0	12

Rep NY	24.8	24.8	23.0	21.8q	.17	-29.9	-29.9	-96.8	-27	-13	03-88	1.20	2.8	4	180	32	06-09-88	1.2	.08	.1	22.00	2.2	155	NA	1,299	29,873	10,066	-278	0.7	12
Seamen's Cp	.0	119.5	.0	.0*	1.89	-64.0	-54.3	270.6	NC	0	06-87	.40	6.7	0	11	8	05-03-88	NC	NC	NC	NC	.0	29	NA	100	16,638	5,013	0	0.0	12
Southold Sav Bk	.0	.0	.0	7.5f	1.37	NC	NC	NC	NC	23	12-86	.00	.0	0	0	0	00-00-00	14.7	.10	1.4	16.36	22.9	31	NA	117	5,500	1,293	0	0.0	12
Sterling Bncp	33.3	1.3	.0	4.6f	.73	58.3	-29.8	-29.8	-4	-1	12-87	.80	6.5	3	110	73	06-09-88	8.5	.07	.6	12.17	7.3	68	NA	78	6,387	1,301	0	3.4	12
Trustco Bk	5.5	3.6	5.1	6.8f	2.70	21.7	17.4	17.4	19	11	12-87	1.00	3.7	18	34	33	03-07-88	11.1	.09	1.0	18.10	18.1	21	NA	66	2,462	291	+3	0.0	12
US Trust	7.7	9.8	9.7	34.4f	3.34	NE	11.0	11.0	17	12	12-87	1.16	2.8	10	30	33	07-01-88	10.2	.13	1.3	14.00	18.2	32	NA	403	9,837	4,570	+15	0.0	12

Middle Atlantic Banks

Ind. Group	12.9	20.7	26.3	1,938.9	1.97	- 16.7	- 38.8	- 32.6	13	4	- - -	1.10	3.5	1	48	34	- - - -	5.0	.10	.5	17.80	8.9	55	NC	29,776	945,101	173,558	- 68	.4	- -
Anchor Svgs Bk □	8.0	-.4	31.1	22.0n	.64	-97.4	-89.0	NC	NC	6	03-88	.00	.0	0	13	13	00-00-00	3.2	.09	.3	21.00	6.3	117	NA	95	17,595	1,422	0	0.0	06
Atlantic Bcp	17.2	11.5	18.1	1.0n	.81	-22.2	-34.1	-25.7	NC	6	09-87	.36	3.3b	0	14	7	06-23-88	7.7	.10	.8	13.75	11.0	40	NA	14	1,268	0	+2	0.0	12
Atlantic Fed S Bk	-64.6	7.7	11.1	1.2f	1.53	-9.1	13.3	13.3	NC	7	03-88	.10	1.1	0	3	2	03-25-88	6.0	.10	.6	13.00	7.8	58	NA	7	784	0	0	0.0	03
Baltimore Bcp	33.9	33.9	22.4	24.0q	1.92	33.3	33.3	134.1	NC	8	03-88	.50	3.0	0	21	19	06-13-88	9.0	.09	.8	13.25	10.6	41	NA	213	12,691	8,387	+9	0.0	12
Banco de Sant	NA	NA	NA	NA	NA	NA	NA	NA	NA	NC	00-00	.31	.5	NA	NA	NA	10-26-87	NA	NC	NA	NC	NA	NA	NA	5,581	94,600	261	0	NA	NA
Bank of Del	9.9	9.9	5.8	16.8q	2.23	5.9	5.9	12.1	14	9	03-88	.38	3.5	7	35	36	05-16-88	10.3	.10	1.0	15.20	15.2	0	NA	190	7,612	1,610	+27	0.0	12
Barclays PLC	37.5	37.5	37.5	349.1f	1.95	-62.9	-63.0	-63.0	NC	1	12-87	1.63	5.3	0	86	17	08-17-87	2.0	.10	.2	22.50	4.5	80	NA	5,175	184,000	1,825	0	0.1	12
Bell Svgs Bk	25.4	22.6	25.0	5.1n	2.05	-38.6	5.4	22.0	NC	11	03-88	.00	.0	0	0	0	00-00-00	8.5	.12	1.0	10.90	10.9	174	NA	25	2,501	573	0	0.0	06
Bryn Mawr Bank	8.1	8.1	8.6	3.3q	2.95	-8.1	-8.1	7.7	NC	9	03-88	1.32	4.6	0	40	40	07-01-88	13.2	.10	1.3	12.77	16.6	0	NA	31	1,084	171	+0	0.0	12
BT Fncl Cp	.0	.0	1.4	5.5q	1.77	.0	.0	-11.1	NC	6	03-88	.72	4.7	0	41	36	02-02-88	8.0	.09	.7	15.57	10.9	24	NA	47	3,087	66	0	0.0	12
Cayuga Svgs Bk	-19.1	1.6	.0	-.6f	-.62	44.0	-100.0	-100.0	NC	-7	12-87	.40	3.6	0	NE	113	04-26-88	-3.2	.06	-.2	22.50	-4.5	0	NA	10	897	11	0	0.0	12
Cent Jersey Bcp	20.1	20.1	14.1	16.3q	3.84	9.6	9.6	12.9	NC	9	03-88	1.60	3.9	0	37	40	03-03-88	15.5	.08	1.3	12.31	16.0	25	NA	173	4,249	358	0	0.0	12
Citzns Fst Bcp	23.9	23.9	16.2	27.4q	1.57	8.3	8.3	14.6	23	12	03-88	.60	3.8b	15	31	23	07-14-88	13.7	.09	1.2	16.25	19.5	15	NA	277	17,300	1,854	+2	12.0	12
Cmwlth Bcshs	38.3	38.3	47.0	8.5q	1.33	-17.1	-17.1	-22.2	-7	4	03-88	.80	4.7	-3	57	40	03-25-88	6.8	.10	.7	12.71	8.9	26	NA	109	6,358	105	+0	0.0	12
Constellation Bcp	19.6	19.6	17.4	18.9q	3.08	21.2	21.2	26.2	13	11	03-88	1.08	4.2	8	34	36	05-24-88	10.4	.09	.9	19.67	17.7	19	NA	159	6,173	1,166	+0	0.0	12
CoreStates Fnl	8.3	8.3	6.0	170.4q	4.07	17.8	17.8	14.0	10	11	03-88	1.50	3.6	12	35	34	05-27-88	11.5	.10	1.1	15.45	17.0	62	NA	1,619	39,245	18,010	+23	0.0	12
Dauphin Dep	9.0	9.0	6.7	35.7q	3.20	10.5	10.5	8.5	12	9	03-88	1.28	4.3	10	38	39	07-01-88	13.3	.09	1.2	13.00	15.6	21	NA	335	11,183	1,961	+5	0.0	12
Equimark Corp □	16.5	10.5	10.5	8.9f	.64	150.0	433.3	433.3	NC	5	12-87	.04	.3	0	0	0	06-06-88	3.3	.09	.3	18.33	5.5	58	NA	122	9,921	1,565	+12	1.2	12
Finl Trust	38.0	38.0	45.9	9.2q	4.26	-8.8	-8.8	-10.5	NC	10	03-88	1.76	4.4	0	38	35	01-26-88	17.0	.10	1.7	9.71	16.5	2	NA	79	1,982	107	0	0.0	12
Fst Am Savings ◇	12.3	7.3	6.8	6.7f	1.95	-7.7	7.1	7.1	NC	6	12-87	.32	2.6	0	13	5	01-25-88	14.3	.09	1.3	5.85	7.6	0	NA	43	3,450	1,044	0	0.0	12
Fst Eastern	14.2	14.2	11.4	21.0q	2.75	38.0	38.0	32.2	NC	10	03-88	.88	2.8	0	32	40	05-31-88	12.0	.10	1.2	12.17	14.6	16	NA	237	7,594	656	+2	0.0	12
Fst Fid Bcp	9.8	9.8	61.9	133.1q	2.12	296.7	296.7	-37.5	-12	1	03-88	1.64	4.5	8	137	46	05-24-88	5.4	.09	.5	19.60	9.8	32	NA	2,172	53,619	10,774	-2	0.7	12
Fst Natl Penn	13.0	13.0	8.5	6.0q	2.72	-27.6	-27.6	-18.1	NC	10	03-88	.00	.0	0	33	51	00-00-00	7.9	.09	.7	14.14	9.9	5	NA	63	2,222	437	+1	0.0	12
Fst Penn Cp	11.5	11.5	4.5	-60.7q	-1.79	1266.7	1266.7	-100.0	NC	-31	03-88	.00	.0	0	0	0	03-03-80	-11.0	.09	-1.0	30.50	-30.5	106	NA	414	38,033	11,452	0	0.0	12
Fst Peo Fn □	17.6	17.6	6.9	7.7q	2.29	28.0	28.0	48.7	NC	13	03-88	.00	.0	0	0	55	00-00-00	10.0	.09	.9	14.67	13.2	8	NA	87	3,346	317	0	0.0	12
Frankford Cp	9.1	9.1	4.8	5.8q	2.01	2.2	2.2	5.2	NC	7	03-88	1.08	5.1	0	48	41	06-02-88	13.5	.10	1.3	11.23	14.6	0	NA	61	2,892	339	-1	0.0	12
Fulton Fncl	15.2	15.2	4.7	15.8q	2.40	7.3	7.3	11.6	NC	11	03-88	.80	3.9	0	31	31	06-24-88	14.4	.10	1.4	12.21	17.1	12	NA	152	7,333	581	0	0.0	12
Germantown S Bk	-.7	-.7	293.3	5.6q	1.23	37.5	37.5	NC	NC	8	03-88	.00	.0	0	0	0	00-00-00	4.7	.09	.4	20.50	8.2	121	NA	40	4,025	540	0	0.0	12
Harleysville Natl	20.0	20.0	19.0	3.9q	4.06	-2.7	-2.7	-1.5	NC	13	03-88	1.16	2.8b	0	12	6	03-07-88	15.6	.10	1.5	12.07	18.1	0	NA	39	952	0	0	0.0	12
Home Unity S B	-8.3	-8.3	-20.1	-8.4q	-4.07	-100.0	-100.0	-100.0	NC	-44	03-88	.00	.0	0	0	0	04-24-87	-9.7	.08	-.8	55.25	-44.2	647	NA	8	2,117	110	0	0.0	12
Horizon Bncp	16.6	16.6	15.3	45.6q	5.02	10.1	10.1	28.4	15	13	03-88	1.60	2.4	9	30	34	07-11-88	11.9	.10	1.2	16.17	19.4	1	NA	576	8,777	2,067	+2	4.0	12
HUBCO Inc	4.8	1.9	27.2	5.1s	1.33	35.7	32.7	14.7	26	13	06-87	.40	2.3b	13	29	36	05-09-88	2.1	.09	1.1	16.36	18.0	4	NA	67	3,908	196	0	0.0	12
Independence Bcp	13.1	13.1	27.2	25.7q	2.64	-16.9	-16.9	-21.2	9	8	03-88	1.16	5.0	6	41	39	04-25-88	0.0	.09	.9	15.22	13.7	32	NA	223	9,676	1,825	+1	0.0	12
Interchange Fncl	4.3	4.3	5.5	2.4q	1.26	-23.5	-23.5	7.7	NC	14	03-88	.48	3.3	0	28	12	06-15-88	2.6	.10	1.2	18.83	22.6	11	NA	25	1,727	20	0	0.0	12
Johnstown Sav Bk	-6.0	-6.0	30.0	1.6n	.82	-21.1	12.5	NC	NC	3	09-87	.24	3.8	0	0	0	06-24-88	6.2	.10	.6	7.83	4.7	0	NA	12	1,940	125	0	0.0	12

Continued

Company	Revenue: Pct. Change Last Qtr	Revenue: Pct. Change FY to Date	Revenue: Pct. Change Last 12 Mos	Earnings: Last 12 Mos	Earnings Per Share: Last 12 Mos	Per Share Pct. Change: Last Qtr	Per Share Pct. Change: FY to Date	Per Share Pct. Change: Last 12 Mos	5-Year Growth Rate	Par Growth Rate	Date of Report	Dividends: Current Rate Amt	Current Rate Yield	5-Year Growth Rate	Payout Last FY	Payout Last 5 Yrs.	Last X-Dvd Date	Ratio Analysis: Profit Margin	Asset Turnover	Return on Total Assets	Leverage Ratio	Return on Equity	Debt to Equity	Current Ratio	Shareholdings: Market Value	Latest Shares Outstndng.	Held by Banks-Funds	Insider Net Trading	Short Interest Ratio	Fiscal Year Ends
-	%	%	%	$Mil	$	%	%	%	%	%	-	$	%	%	%	%	-	π/r	x r/a	= π/a	x a/e	= π/e	%	-	$Mil	000	000	000	Days	Mo
Middle Atlantic Banks (Continued)																														
Keystone Fncl	-45.9	2.4	2.4	24.3f	2.00	122.7	14.3	14.3	NC	8	12-87	.80	4.5	0	38	24	03-25-88	11.6	.09	1.1	11.73	12.9	2	NA	216	12,163	2,424	0	0.0	12
Keystone Heritage	14.1	14.1	9.6	4.2q	2.30	11.8	11.8	18.6	NC	8	03-88	.88	3.1b	0	34	30	04-25-88	12.4	.09	1.1	12.00	13.2	12	NA	46	1,647	188	0	0.0	12
LSB Bncshrs	19.6	19.6	8.6	3.6q	2.22	-3.6	-3.6	2.3	NC	9	03-88	.80	4.2	0	30	24	06-27-88	14.4	.08	1.2	11.17	13.4	0	NA	31	1,621	0	0	0.0	12
Mellon Bank	-10.2	-10.2	1.0	63.1q	1.76	-100.0	-100.0	-77.4	-6	1	03-87	1.40	4.7	6	45	38	04-25-88	1.9	.11	.2	18.00	3.6	101	NA	824	27,576	15,897	0	6.8	12
Meridian Bcp	23.3	23.3	24.6	81.0q	1.95	-20.0	-20.0	-26.1	7	6	03-88	1.10	5.5	23	48	40	06-09-88	8.8	.11	1.0	14.00	14.0	20	NA	726	36,533	10,475	0	0.0	12
Midlantic Cp	-44.3	4.5	4.4	161.5f	4.40	2375.0	7.3	7.3	3	9	12-87	1.48	3.4	5	24	25	06-27-88	10.5	.09	.9	15.44	13.9	22	NA	1,625	37,793	10,992	+1	0.0	12
Morsemere Fincl	7.2	9.9	11.3	4.3f	2.31	-21.7	-3.3	NC	NC	14	12-87	.00	.0	0	0	0	00-00-00	8.8	.13	1.1	12.27	13.5	113	NA	18	1,850	163	0	0.0	12
Natl Cm Bk NJ	28.6	28.6	23.2	35.9q	3.48	17.9	17.9	21.3	23	14	03-88	1.28	3.1	8	26	32	06-09-88	13.5	.08	1.1	20.00	22.0	0	NA	431	10,374	383	0	0.0	12
Natl Penn Bnshr	14.0	5.6	4.8	6.7f	2.85	19.6	19.2	19.2	NC	13	12-87	.96	2.5b	0	28	27	07-25-88	15.6	.10	1.6	11.88	19.0	8	NA	91	2,376	137	-0	0.0	12
Onondaga Savs Bk	2.7	2.7	296.6	5.6q	.67	NC	NC	NC	NC	7	03-88	.00	.0	0	0	0	00-00-00	4.7	.09	.4	17.00	6.8	0	NA	43	6,121	463	0	0.0	12
Pennbancorp	-47.0	-47.0	-11.0	34.0q	2.58	10.2	10.2	13.2	12	9	03-88	1.00	4.0	11	35	35	05-09-88	12.4	.09	1.1	12.73	14.0	17	NA	327	13,195	3,090	+5	0.0	12
Peo Sav Bk	12.8	12.8	5.2	2.5q	1.02	-17.9	-17.9	2450.0	NC	4	03-88	.43	3.9	0	0	0	05-27-88	12.5	.09	1.1	6.00	6.6	34	NA	27	2,444	387	0	0.0	12
Piedmont BkGrp	8.3	8.3	10.8	5.9q	2.06	-3.8	-3.8	13.2	24	13	03-88	.56	3.2	17	23	25	06-09-88	11.6	.10	1.2	15.00	18.0	30	NA	56	3,273	42	0	0.0	12
Pioneer Am Hld	10.3	3.2	.0	1.6f	2.55	23.1	10.9	10.9	-6	9	12-87	.00	.0	0	0	0	00-00-00	10.0	.09	.9	10.44	9.4	6	NA	27	686	0	0	0.0	12
PNC Fincl	5.7	5.7	36.8	331.0q	3.88	237.8	237.8	-4.2	7	8	03-88	1.88	4.2	13	53	36	05-27-88	10.3	.09	.9	17.11	15.4	41	NA	3,718	83,778	36,866	+3	0.8	12
Progress Fncl	20.3	14.6	16.6	2.2f	2.30	17.4	9.5	9.5	NC	13	12-87	.12	.9	0	0	0	06-27-88	7.9	.10	.8	16.50	13.2	141	NA	13	959	24	0	0.0	12
Ramapo Fncl	.0	3.4	8.6	2.0s	1.49	-50.0	-26.0	.7	4	8	06-87	.60	3.2	0	31	24	01-25-88	8.0	.10	.8	16.88	13.5	42	NA	22	1,198	83	+1	0.0	12
Seaboard S&L	4.3	8.8	11.1	.8f	.94	-21.4	-16.8	-16.8	NC	8	12-87	.15	1.8b	0	11	3	02-09-88	8.0	.09	.7	13.43	9.4	74	NA	7	890	0	0	0.0	12
SW Bancorp	-30.1	-30.1	-20.0	-5.1q	-1.08	-100.0	-100.0	-100.0	NC	-34	03-88	.00	.0	0	0	0	03-25-88	-9.8	.14	-1.4	24.14	-33.8	46	NA	11	5,282	204	-167	0.0	12
SW National	5.0	5.0	2.3	1.3q	1.67	11.1	11.1	-5.6	NC	2	03-88	.74	3.4	0	44	40	02-04-88	3.0	.10	.3	10.00	3.0	0	NA	60	2,735	62	0	0.0	12
Statewide Bcp NJ	9.1	9.1	13.1	20.4q	1.87	.0	.0	5.1	9	9	03-88	.80	4.0	16	42	35	06-14-88	11.3	.09	1.0	15.70	15.7	3	NA	184	9,188	1,933	+1	0.0	12
Suburban Bcp	30.7	30.7	28.5	7.4q	1.84	-14.6	-14.6	-3.7	NC	9	03-88	.26	1.4	0	12	2	02-24-88	13.7	.08	1.1	9.36	10.3	0	NA	78	4,293	726	0	0.0	12
Suffolk Bcp	13.9	10.8	10.7	5.1n	1.78	-25.0	-3.1	4.7	NC	14	09-87	.52	3.9	0	32	17	06-07-88	16.5	.09	1.5	13.27	19.9	0	NA	43	3,271	225	0	0.0	12
Susquehanna Bcsh	2.1	2.1	5.5	16.1q	2.02	16.7	16.7	29.5	3	8	03-88	.80	4.4	9	38	34	04-26-88	14.0	.09	1.3	10.62	13.8	5	NA	144	7,931	817	+0	0.0	12
Tompkins Cnty Tr	23.8	23.8	14.8	2.9q	1.68	-1.7	-1.7	-12.5	NC	6	03-88	.88	2.6	0	49	28	06-20-88	9.4	.10	.9	14.56	13.1	0	NA	61	1,780	65	0	0.0	12
Trustco Bcp	-47.3	-46.8	-22.9	7.3s	4.27	-73.4	-69.7	-39.2	NC	4	06-87	2.65	2.1	0	0	0	08-08-88	8.7	.07	.6	19.50	11.7	3	NA	308	2,461	33	0	0.0	12
Ultra Bcp	9.6	9.6	7.3	16.0q	3.31	4.8	4.8	7.8	23	13	03-88	1.16	3.5	0	30	164	05-27-88	15.7	.09	1.4	14.14	19.8	16	NA	153	4,562	460	+0	0.0	12
Union Natl Cp	8.1	8.1	3.8	30.4q	3.07	1.4	1.4	9.6	10	7	03-88	1.36	4.5	9	43	43	05-16-88	10.1	.09	.9	13.11	11.8	11	NA	300	9,908	3,519	0	0.0	12
Utd Jer Bk	35.0	35.0	26.9	111.4q	2.34	4.9	4.9	6.4	10	9	03-88	.96	4.4	12	39	35	03-31-88	11.7	.09	1.1	14.00	15.4	12	NA	930	42,753	9,474	+4	0.1	12
Utd Natl Bk NJ	1.6	1.6	4.1	7.1q	3.70	13.4	13.4	19.7	NC	13	03-88	.84	2.3	0	23	24	07-11-88	14.2	.10	1.4	12.29	17.2	45	NA	69	1,915	131	0	0.0	12
Unvrsty Natl B&T	-10.2	-10.2	50.0	1.9q	3.72	60.0	60.0	37.8	27	14	03-88	.40	1.2	0	12	8	07-27-87	9.0	.10	.9	18.00	16.2	0	NA	18	522	0	0	0.0	12
USBancp Inc Pa	.6	.6	-2.7	-13.4q	-5.81	-92.6	-92.6	-100.0	NC	-26	03-88	.00	.0	0	NE	105	06-01-87	-19.1	.09	-1.8	14.28	-25.7	15	NA	30	2,525	62	0	0.0	12
Valley Natl Bcp	3.4	3.4	1.5	30.7q	3.62	3.3	3.3	5.5	19	11	03-88	1.75	3.6	0	35	33	06-04-88	22.7	.09	2.0	11.10	22.2	0	NA	406	8,466	254	0	0.0	12
Washington Bcp	27.1	27.1	25.6	-24.6q	-3.92	30.3	30.3	-100.0	NC	-29	03-88	.28	1.6	0	NE	188	06-06-88	-12.6	.09	-1.1	24.55	-27.0	35	NA	125	7,029	873	0	0.0	12
Wash Bancorp	6.9	6.9	3.4	3.9q	1.73	51.7	51.7	12.3	NC	10	03-88	.05	.4	0	0	0	04-25-88	13.0	.09	1.2	8.42	10.1	67	NA	32	2,300	60	0	0.0	12
Webster Fincl	10.7	10.7	341.6	4.3q	1.15	-15.6	-15.6	NC	NC	6	03-88	.05	.5	0	8	8	08-17-87	8.1	.09	.7	9.14	6.4	23	NA	40	3,722	1,456	0	0.0	12
West Mass Bkshrs	3.4	3.4	71.4	1.3q	.93	-28.0	-28.0	NC	NC	7	03-88	.05	.6	0	0	0	02-02-88	10.8	.09	1.0	7.60	7.6	47	NA	12	1,301	156	0	0.0	12
Wilmington Sav	9.7	7.5	8.1	4.7f	1.04	355.6	181.1	181.1	NC	4	12-87	.20	2.1	0	0	0	05-27-88	3.9	.10	.4	12.75	5.1	0	NA	44	4,539	1,499	0	0.0	12

Company	Revenue: Pct. Change Last Qtr	Revenue: Pct. Change FY to Date	Revenue: Pct. Change Last 12 Mos	Earnings: Last 12 Mos	Earnings: Per Share Last 12 Mos	Earnings: Per Share Pct. Change Last Qtr	Earnings: Per Share Pct. Change FY to Date	Earnings: Per Share Pct. Change Last 12 Mos	Earnings: 5-Year Growth Rate	Earnings: Par Growth Rate	Earnings: Date of Report	Dividends: Current Rate Amt	Dividends: Current Rate Yield	Dividends: 5-Year Growth Rate	Dividends: Payout Last FY	Dividends: Payout Last 5 Yrs.	Dividends: Last X-Dvd Date	Ratio Analysis: Profit Margin	Ratio Analysis: Asset Turnover	Ratio Analysis: Return on Total Assets	Ratio Analysis: Leverage Ratio	Ratio Analysis: Return on Equity	Ratio Analysis: Debt to Equity	Ratio Analysis: Current Ratio	Shareholdings: Market Value	Shareholdings: Latest Shares Outstndng.	Shareholdings: Held by Banks-Funds	Shareholdings: Insider Net Trading	Shareholdings: Short Interest Ratio	Shareholdings: Fiscal Year Ends
-	%	%	%	$Mil	$	%	%	%	%	%	-	$	%	%	%	%	-	π/r x	r/a =	π/a x	a/e =	π/e	%	-	$Mil	000	000	000	Days	Mo
Pacific States Banks																														
Ind. Group	13.0	189.3	6.6	- 749.5	- 1.55	8.5	6.6	- 100.0	NC	- 9	- - -	.90	3.7	1	99	43	- - - -	- 2.2	.09	- .2	27.00	- 5.4	120	NC	16,285	680,795	245,465	+ 102	.8	- -
Alaska Bncp	-43.8	-40.6	-42.1	-6.7f	-5.41	-100.0	-100.0	-100.0	NC	0	12-87	.10	10.0	0	NE	NE	11-06-87	-60.9	.09	-5.4	.00	NM	41	NA	1	1,230	0	0	0.0	12
Alliance Bcp	NA	NA	NA	NA	NA	NA	NA	NA	NA	NC	00-00	.00	.0	NA	NA	NA	00-00-00	NA	NC	NA	NC	NA	NA	NA	55	9,767	1	0	NA	NA
Am Sav Fincl	6.2	-.2	-1.6	4.2n	1.94	-16.9	-37.4	-34.5	NC	8	03-88	.20	1.0	0	4	2	06-24-88	7.2	.10	.7	13.00	9.1	72	NA	42	2,182	166	+4	0.0	06
Bancorp Hawaii	19.7	19.7	10.5	55.9q	5.93	15.3	15.3	15.4	10	11	03-88	1.76	3.1	8	29	31	05-18-88	10.9	.09	1.0	16.10	16.1	16	NA	523	9,292	5,817	+0	0.0	12
BankAmerica ○	-28.3	-28.3	-21.5	-913.0q	-6.21	64.7	64.7	NE	NC	-37	03-88	.00	.0	0	0	NE	11-07-85	-9.7	.10	-1.0	36.90	-36.9	151	NA	2,231	165,284	38,881	+12	1.6	12
BSD Bancorp	4.8	4.8	4.7	2.1q	.59	100.0	100.0	883.3	NC	10	03-88	.00	.0	0	0	0	00-00-00	4.8	.13	.6	17.17	10.3	14	NA	17	3,496	84	0	0.0	12
Cal Rep Bancorp	18.2	18.2	11.4	5.2q	2.30	13.7	13.7	18.6	NC	18	03-88	.40	1.9	0	13	7	05-24-88	13.3	.11	1.4	15.36	21.5	0	NA	48	2,291	33	0	0.0	12
Calif Fincl	1.7	1.7	5.7	7.9q	1.99	-35.3	-35.3	-12.3	NC	13	03-88	.40	4.3	0	18	7	01-26-88	10.8	.10	1.1	15.09	16.6	283	NA	37	4,029	479	0	0.0	12
Calif Fst Bk	7.5	3.4	3.5	40.1f	3.01	41.3	27.0	27.0	21	7	12-87	1.08	3.2	1	33	45	06-06-88	6.9	.10	.7	16.43	11.5	62	NA	448	13,479	9,662	0	0.0	12
Cent Pacific	-9.7	-1.4	-1.4	-2.5f	-.44	NE	-100.0	-100.0	NC	-5	12-87	.00	.0	0	0	NE	12-23-83	-3.6	.08	-.3	18.00	-5.4	0	NA	36	5,561	808	+3	0.0	12
City Natl □	10.8	10.8	12.0	40.5q	2.00	-3.9	-3.9	20.5	21	14	03-88	.64	2.7b	12	27	31	06-24-88	12.8	.09	1.2	17.00	20.4	1	NA	487	20,292	3,775	+1	0.0	12
County Sav Bk	11.1	11.1	11.7	6.5q	.74	-88.1	-88.1	-51.6	NC	16	03-88	.00	.0	0	0	0	03-09-88	6.2	.08	.5	31.20	15.6	143	NA	32	7,006	726	0	0.0	12
Eldorado Bcp	7.8	7.8	4.7	2.3q	1.13	11.1	11.1	20.2	28	11	03-88	.20	1.5b	0	15	6	05-27-88	10.5	.11	1.2	11.58	13.9	1	NA	28	2,136	291	0	0.0	12
Fst Commer Bncp □	6.5	6.5	.0	1.1q	.33	300.0	300.0	NE	NC	7	03-88	.00	.0	0	0	0	00-00-00	5.5	.11	.6	11.17	6.7	13	NA	22	3,808	203	0	0.0	12
Fst Hawaiian	17.7	17.7	12.2	37.1q	2.76	18.0	18.0	16.9	13	11	03-88	1.10	3.6	11	36	37	05-25-88	10.7	.08	.9	19.56	17.6	30	NA	44	1,454	4,566	0	0.0	12
Fst Intst Bcp □	1049.4	1049.4	54.4	-467.4q	-12.72	-28.1	-28.1	-100.0	NC	-29	03-88	2.92	5.8	6	NE	89	06-16-88	-7.4	.12	-.9	25.78	-23.2	156	NA	2,302	45,359	32,532	+4	1.1	12
Fst Intst Bcp A	NA	NA	NA	NA	NA	NA	NA	NA	NA	NC	00-00	.00	.0	NA	NA	NA	00-00-00	NA	NC	NA	NC	NA	NA	NA	11	33,880	0	0	NA	NA
Fst Mutl Svg Bk	7.5	7.0	6.2	1.4f	1.29	54.5	48.3	48.3	NC	11	12-87	.09	.7b	0	0	0	06-15-88	8.2	.11	.9	13.11	11.8	0	NA	12	968	1	0	0.0	12
Fst Natl Cal	145.9	167.9	171.4	1.8f	.69	.0	43.8	43.8	NC	6	12-87	.10	1.1b	0	0	0	02-05-88	4.7	.11	.5	13.60	6.8	5	NA	24	2,574	18	+1	0.0	12
FstFed Fincl	19.7	19.7	.6	15.3q	2.14	-11.5	-11.5	-13.4	NC	16	03-88	.00	.0	0	0	0	10-30-87	9.2	.09	.8	19.63	15.7	477	NA	101	6,645	2,215	0	0.0	12
Grt Amer First	2.4	2.4	3.0	70.8q	2.99	-54.4	-54.4	-35.6	39	9	03-88	.60	5.6	0	16	11	05-04-88	4.9	.10	.5	23.00	11.5	313	NA	247	23,285	8,701	0	0.4	12
Guardian Bcp	NA	NA	NA	NA	NA	NA	NA	NA	NA	NC	00-00	.00	.0	NA	NA	NA	00-00-00	NA	NC	NA	NC	NA	NA	NA	19	1,295	0	+4	NA	NA
Imperial Bcp	-67.4	-67.4	-13.7	12.2q	1.16	35.0	35.0	45.0	49	9	03-88	.08	.7	0	0	0	04-11-88	10.8	.06	.7	14.00	9.8	12	NA	124	10,339	340	0	0.0	12
La Jolla Bcp	23.7	4.0	3.0	2.2f	.45	.0	18.4	18.4	NC	8	12-87	.05	.7	0	11	6	03-08-88	6.5	.11	.7	12.71	8.9	0	NA	36	5,002	80	+15	0.0	12
Lincoln Bancorp	59.5	30.6	26.6	2.1f	.82	.0	.0	.0	NC	10	12-87	.00	.0	0	0	0	05-13-88	11.1	.06	.7	14.86	10.4	0	NA	24	2,569	46	0	0.0	12
Merchants Bk Cal	6.7	6.7	-14.2	-2.3q	-.87	NE	NE	NE	NC	0	03-87	.00	.0	0	0	0	00-00-00	-38.3	.07	-2.5	.00	NM	0	NA	1	5,431	0	0	0.0	12
Metrobank	36.1	36.1	29.4	3.6q	1.00	.0	.0	33.3	NC	9	03-88	.10	1.1	0	10	4	05-18-88	8.2	.06	.5	20.20	10.1	0	NA	37	4,105	11	0	3.0	12
Mt Baker Bank	-4.2	-4.2	.0	1.6q	1.02	-62.8	-62.8	-44.6	NC	7	03-88	.30	1.9	0	23	6	12-28-87	8.4	.11	.9	11.11	10.0	5	NA	24	1,563	126	0	0.0	12
Napa Valley Bcp	-35.7	-35.7	3.7	2.9q	1.16	31.6	31.6	3.6	NC	10	03-88	.28	2.4b	0	25	6	07-11-88	10.4	.10	1.0	12.70	12.7	8	NA	29	2,558	347	0	0.0	12
Natl Bcp Alaska	6.4	-1.3	-.8	16.4f	2.74	-24.1	-9.3	-9.3	NC	8	12-87	.50	1.9	0	15	12	12-28-87	13.9	.06	.9	10.56	9.5	0	NA	155	5,977	431	+4	0.0	12
Pac Wstn Bncsh	203.1	100.0	48.0	-.8s	.04	-100.0	-100.0	-90.9	-17	5	06-87	.12	2.7	0	21	16	06-14-88	-1.0	.20	-.2	13.00	-2.6	5	NA	52	11,472	1,717	+11	0.0	12
Plaza Comm Bcp	23.8	23.8	20.0	4.2q	.76	20.0	20.0	22.6	17	14	03-88	.10	1.1b	0	12	14	07-26-88	14.0	.08	1.1	14.27	15.7	0	NA	47	5,326	54	+1	0.0	12
Puget Sound Bcp	9.0	9.0	-1.6	17.9q	1.11	-10.0	-10.0	-54.3	0	2	03-88	.80	4.2	13	65	33	05-31-88	4.9	.10	.5	14.60	7.3	145	NA	302	15,898	5,326	+5	0.0	12

Continued

Company	Revenue Pct. Change Last Qtr	Revenue Pct. Change FY to Date	Revenue Pct. Change Last 12 Mos	Earnings Last 12 Mos	Earnings Per Share Last 12 Mos	Per Share Pct. Change Last Qtr	Per Share Pct. Change FY to Date	Per Share Pct. Change Last 12 Mos	5-Year Growth Rate	Par Growth Rate	Date of Report	Dividends Current Rate Amt	Current Rate Yield	5-Year Growth Rate	Payout Last FY	Payout Last 5 Yrs.	Last X-Dvd Date	Profit Margin	Asset Turnover	Return on Total Assets	Leverage Ratio	Return on Equity	Debt to Equity	Current Ratio	Market Value	Latest Shares Outstndng.	Held by Banks-Funds	Insider Net Trading	Short Interest Ratio	Fiscal Year Ends
-	%	%	%	$Mil	$	%	%	%	%	%	-	$	%	%	%	%	-	π/r	x r/a	= π/a	x a/e	= π/e	%	-	$Mil	000	000	000	Days	Mo
Pacific States Banks (Continued)																														
Santa Monica Bank	14.7	7.6	7.8	8.5f	2.50	15.1	19.6	19.6	NC	14	12-87	.60	1.6b	0	0	0	06-09-88	20.7	.07	1.4	13.14	18.4	90	NA	123	3,377	66	0	0.0	12
SDNB Financl	-3.1	-3.1	18.1	.7q	.55	7.1	7.1	NC	NC	5	03-88	.08	.9b	0	0	0	04-18-88	5.4	.07	.4	13.25	5.3	22	NA	10	1,198	0	0	0.0	12
Sec Pacific	6.9	6.9	21.6	46.4q	.25	22.6	22.6	-94.8	-55	-10	03-88	1.96	5.4	11	7200	40	04-27-88	.6	.17	.1	15.00	1.5	55	NA	3,967	109,061	64,516	+3	4.7	12
Silicon Valley Bcsh . ◇	52.9	29.3	30.7	1.5f	1.51	182.4	122.1	NC	NC	13	12-87	.00	.0	0	0	0	05-12-88	8.8	.08	.7	18.86	13.2	0	NA	13	981	12	0	0.0	12
Sumitomo Bk	12.4	12.4	5.4	21.7q	3.09	26.6	26.6	34.3	11	8	03-88	1.16	4.9	-9	38	43	06-24-88	7.0	.09	.6	21.67	13.0	19	NA	165	7,009	162	0	0.0	12
Transwld Bncp	7.0	7.0	.0	1.2q	1.14	4.2	4.2	14.0	NC	10	03-88	.00	.0	0	0	0	03-22-88	6.7	.10	.7	14.71	10.3	12	NA	9	950	0	+7	0.0	12
US Bcp	54.8	38.6	38.7	99.6f	2.43	-33.3	-5.1	-5.1	8	7	12-87	1.00	4.0	6	33	31	05-27-88	8.6	.08	.7	16.57	11.6	55	NA	1,028	40,935	20,351	+28	0.0	12
Wash FSBk Ore	-54.6	-53.6	-53.4	1.5f	.97	-24.1	-11.8	NC	NC	5	12-87	.24	2.7	0	12	12	05-10-88	7.5	.11	.8	9.00	7.2	186	NA	14	1,575	36	0	0.0	12
Wells Fargo	9.7	9.7	12.1	92.9q	1.31	58.1	58.1	-75.1	-19	-3	03-88	2.40	4.0	11	300	38	06-24-88	2.0	.10	.2	20.50	4.1	170	NA	3,132	52,757	34,310	0	1.7	12
WestAmer Bcp	.3	.3	1.6	1.9q	.37	-36.7	-36.7	-79.9	-1	0	03-88	.40	2.7	0	69	36	07-11-88	1.5	.13	.2	15.50	3.1	31	NA	76	5,117	948	0	0.0	12
Westcorp	-23.6	41.1	41.7	9.7f	.59	-7.7	-23.4	-23.4	NC	9	12-87	.00	.0	0	0	0	00-00-00	6.0	.08	.5	17.80	8.9	415	NA	118	16,222	7,500	0	0.0	12
Wstn Bank	6.0	-1.8	-2.9	2.0f	1.09	25.6	43.4	137.0	NC	12	12-87	.00	.0	0	0	0	05-16-88	6.1	.10	.6	19.17	11.5	11	NA	18	1,770	110	0	0.0	12
Wstn Commercial	-13.2	-16.8	-17.6	.3f	.06	NE	NE	NE	NC	2	12-87	.00	.0	0	0	0	00-00-00	2.1	.10	.2	9.50	1.9	6	NA	10	4,290	17	0	0.0	12

Trends and Forecasts: Construction Materials (SIC 321,324,3251,-3,3271-3,-5,3296,3441,-8)

(in millions of dollars except as noted)

						Percent Change				
						Compound Annual		Annual		
ITEM	1984	1985	1986[1]	1987[1]	1988[2]	1972-85	1980-85	1985-86	1986-87	1987-88
Industry Data										
Value of shipments (1982$)	37,463	39,053	40,143	39,659	38,159	0.1	0.1	2.8	−1.2	−3.8
3211 Flat Glass	2,015	2,186	2,299	2,184	1,960	2.2	4.4	5.2	−5.0	−10.3
3241 Hydraulic Cement	4,018	3,979	4,055	3,922	3,815	−1.1	−1.6	1.9	−3.3	−2.7
3251 Brick & Structural Tile	907	994	1,077	1,033	1,002	−2.0	1.7	8.4	−4.1	−3.0
3253 Ceramic Wall/Floor Tile	518	505	648	681	660	4.1	2.9	28.3	5.1	−3.1
3271 Concrete Block & Brick	1,543	1,513	1,619	1,587	1,539	−1.8	−1.6	7.0	−2.0	−3.0
3272 Concrete Products, nec	4,083	4,252	4,250	4,080	3,919	−0.6	1.2	−0.0	−4.0	−3.9
3273 Ready-mixed Concrete	9,286	9,419	9,611	9,325	9,040	−0.2	−0.3	2.0	−3.0	−3.1
3275 Gypsum Products	1,606	1,900	1,998	1,958	1,910	2.3	7.4	5.2	−2.0	−2.5
3296 Mineral Wool	2,913	3,118	3,268	3,433	3,600	3.8	2.7	4.8	5.0	4.9
3441 Fabr Structural Metal	8,173	8,672	8,758	8,757	8,015	−0.9	−2.3	1.0	−0.0	−8.5
3448 Prefab Metal Buildings	2,402	2,516	2,559	2,700	2,700	3.3	0.3	1.7	5.5	0.0

[1]Estimated.
[2]Forecast.

SOURCE: U.S. Department of Commerce: Bureau of the Census, Bureau of Economic Analysis, International Trade Administration (ITA). Estimates and forecasts by ITA.

Source: *U.S. Industrial Outlook 1988,* U.S. Department of Commerce.

Trends and Forecasts: Hydraulic Cement (SIC 3241)

(in millions of dollars except as noted)

ITEM	1984	1985	1986[1]	1987[2]	1988[3]	Percent Change: Compound Annual 1972-85	Compound Annual 1980-85	Annual 1985-86	Annual 1986-87	Annual 1987-88
Industry Data										
Value of shipments[4]	4,183	4,222	4,233	4,012	—	6.8	1.3	0.3	−5.2	—
Value of shipments (1982$)	4,018	3,979	4,055	3,922	3,815	−1.1	−1.6	1.9	−3.3	−2.7
Total employment (000)	22.6	21.2	20.6	19.5	—	−2.6	−7.0	−2.8	−5.3	—
Production workers (000)	17.4	15.9	15.4	14.5	—	−3.2	−8.1	−3.1	−5.8	—
Average hourly earnings ($)	14.32	14.20	14.29	14.43	—	7.5	4.8	0.6	1.0	—
Product Data										
Value of shipments[5]	4,023	4,124	4,135	3,923	—	6.7	1.2	0.3	−5.1	—
Value of shipments (1982$)	3,864	3,887	3,961	3,835	3,727	−1.2	−1.7	1.9	−3.2	−2.8
Shipments price index[6] (1982=100)	104.1	106.1	104.4	102.3	—	8.0	2.9	−1.6	−2.0	—
Trade Data										
Value of imports	294	432	469	510	—	14.8	17.0	8.6	8.7	—
Import/new supply ratio[7]	0.068	0.095	0.102	0.115	—	7.1	14.6	7.4	12.7	—
Value of exports	23.9	31.5	17.8	17.0	—	17.9	0.1	−43.5	−4.5	—
Export/shipments ratio	0.006	0.008	0.004	0.004	—	11.3	0.0	−50.0	0.0	—

[1]Estimated except for exports and imports.
[2]Estimated.
[3]Forecast.
[4]Value of all products and services sold by the Hydraulic Cement industry.
[5]Value of products classified in the Hydraulic Cement industry produced by all industries.
[6]Developed by the Office of Industry Assessment, ITA.
[7]New supply is the sum of product shipments plus imports.
SOURCE: U.S. Department of Commerce: Bureau of the Census, Bureau of Economic Analysis, International Trade Administration (ITA). Estimates and forecasts by ITA.

Source: *U.S. Industrial Outlook 1988,* U.S. Department of Commerce.

Company	Revenue			Earnings								Dividends						Ratio Analysis							Shareholdings					
	Pct. Change: Last Qtr	Pct. Change: FY to Date	Pct. Change: Last 12 Mos	Last 12 Mos	Per Share: Last 12 Mos	Per Share Pct. Change: Last Qtr	Per Share Pct. Change: FY to Date	Per Share Pct. Change: Last 12 Mos	5-Year Growth Rate	Par Growth Rate	Date of Report	Current Rate: Amt	Current Rate: Yield	5-Year Growth Rate	Payout: Last FY	Payout: Last 5 Yrs.	Last X-Dvd Date	Profit Margin	Asset Turnover	Return on Total Assets	Leverage Ratio	Return on Equity	Debt to Equity	Current Ratio	Market Value	Latest Shares Outstndng.	Held by Banks-Funds	Insider Net Trading	Short Interest Ratio	Fiscal Year Ends
-	%	%	%	$Mil	$	%	%	%	%	%	-	$	%	%	%	%	-	π/r x	r/a =	π/a x	a/e =	π/e	%	-	$Mil	000	000	000	Days	Mo
Cement																														
Ind. Group	- 1.8	- 3.1	4.5	221.4	.72	NE	NE	180.4	NC	7	- - -	.23	1.8	0	28	44	- - - -	5.2	.87	4.5	2.22	10.0	56	1.9	3,900	295,727	41,879	+ 14	7.8	- -
Calmat Co	-8.8	-8.8	-13.0	59.3q	1.92	-57.0	-57.0	-19.3	102	10	03-88	.48	1.2	6	15	25	06-03-88	10.1	.88	8.9	1.53	13.6	13	2.2	1,169	30,363	8,534	+13	0.0	12
Devcon Intl ▫	15.3	15.3	2.1	8.7q	6.32	25.2	25.2	33.9	NC	29	03-88	.00	.0	0	0	0	00-00-00	18.1	1.03	18.7	1.53	28.7	14	2.1	44	1,308	32	0	0.0	12
Fla Rock Ind	50.8	37.1	26.6	24.4s	2.64	38.7	43.4	20.5	19	17	03-88	.50	1.7	29	22	16	06-13-88	7.6	1.83	13.9	1.50	20.9	13	3.1	274	9,208	3,309	0	0.2	09
For Bet Liv	9.8	9.8	16.9	2.2q	2.55	-54.5	-54.5	-2.7	NC	14	03-88	.10	1.0	0	4	6	05-09-88	2.7	1.63	4.4	3.20	14.1	117	2.5	9	873	0	0	0.0	12
Giant Grp	.7	.7	3.7	5.6q	1.19	700.0	700.0	-68.9	NC	9	03-88	.00	.0	0	0	0	00-00-00	6.7	.49	3.3	2.85	9.4	128	3.5	86	4,640	1,879	0	25.3	12
Ideal Basic	-1.9	-1.9	-2.9	-9.0q	-.05	NE	NE	NE	NC	-46	03-88	.00	.0	0	0	NE	05-31-84	-3.8	.74	-2.8	16.32	-45.7	957	1.6	506	176,029	9,525	0	51.2	12
Lafarge Cp	7.8	7.8	26.1	73.1q	1.68	NE	NE	223.1	NC	11	03-88	.24	1.4	0	13	49	05-10-88	5.9	1.17	6.9	1.88	13.0	38	1.7	775	43,634	4,943	0	0.3	12
Lone Star Ind	-50.4	-50.4	-17.5	36.3q	1.91	NE	NE	-72.4	NC	0	03-88	1.90	5.8	0	95	68	05-31-88	5.2	.46	2.4	2.33	5.6	48	1.6	543	16,505	9,275	+2	3.2	12
NWn St Port	-28.1	-28.1	766.6	.7q	.74	NE	NE	-22.9	NC	3	02-88	.00	.0	0	0	NE	03-11-88	2.7	.56	1.5	1.80	2.7	1	.6	16	994	9	0	0.0	11
Puerto Rican C	6.1	6.1	10.2	12.4q	6.29	88.1	88.1	56.1	NC	18	03-88	.75	1.9	0	5	3	07-08-88	16.5	.62	10.2	1.99	20.3	56	3.6	79	1,981	280	0	2.9	12
Slattery Grp	2.2	2.2	9.5	1.4q	.93	20.8	20.8	97.9	NC	3	03-88	.00	.0	0	0	18	02-11-85	.6	2.33	1.4	2.29	3.2	6	1.5	41	1,473	376	0	0.0	12
Tex Ind	12.5	7.2	6.1	6.3n	.44	NE	NE	-38.0	NC	-2	02-88	.77	1.9b	0	NE	36	05-02-88	1.0	.98	.9	3.67	3.3	172	2.3	359	8,719	3,717	0	10.9	05
Misc. Building Materials																														
Ind. Group	39.2	25.0	42.0	925.6	2.45	- 6.9	- 8.9	47.7	36	21	- - -	.52	2.1	1	18	25	- - - -	5.8	1.38	8.0	3.30	26.4	87	1.8	8,706	350,893	111,328	+ 41	1.8	- -
Am Woodmark ▫	14.3	11.8	12.0	5.3f	.70	-40.0	-23.9	-23.9	NC	19	04-88	.00	.0	0	0	0	05-24-88	4.1	2.02	8.3	2.30	19.1	59	1.7	63	7,532	1,175	0	0.0	04
Ameron Inc	12.3	12.3	1.2	17.3q	3.56	NE	NE	40.7	11	8	02-88	1.12	2.9	4	28	35	07-22-88	5.5	.98	5.4	2.04	11.0	34	2.3	191	4,863	1,011	+23	0.0	11
Armstrng Wrld	16.3	16.3	20.7	157.5q	3.35	25.4	25.4	22.7	35	12	03-88	1.00	2.7	10	28	31	05-02-88	6.4	1.53	9.8	1.80	17.6	8	1.5	1,717	46,247	29,233	+2	2.1	12
Bairnco Cp	13.9	13.9	7.5	29.3q	2.79	20.0	20.0	17.2	2	10	03-88	.80	2.2	20	28	23	05-31-88	4.5	1.47	6.6	2.08	13.7	31	1.9	373	10,428	5,206	0	1.7	12
Bird Inc ◇	-7.6	-7.6	-.5	-8.3q	-2.35	-100.0	-100.0	NE	NC	-19	03-88	.00	.0	0	0	0	12-14-81	-4.4	1.73	-7.6	2.54	-19.3	60	1.8	26	4,186	1,324	0	0.0	12
Butler Mfg	17.4	17.4	6.9	5.8q	1.23	NE	NE	16.0	NC	0	03-88	1.32	4.0	0	206	263	06-13-88	.9	2.33	2.1	2.38	5.0	28	1.7	148	4,524	994	+1	0.0	12
Ceradyne	-8.6	-8.6	13.6	-6.5q	-1.23	-100.0	-100.0	NE	NC	-26	03-88	.00	.0	0	0	0	00-00-00	-26.0	.62	-16.2	1.59	-25.8	23	2.2	33	5,608	469	0	0.0	12
Chem Fabrics ▫	20.3	24.1	22.2	1.8n	.40	366.7	NE	NE	NC	21	03-88	.00	.0	0	0	0	00-00-00	5.5	1.55	8.5	2.46	20.9	5	1.2	39	4,331	276	-0	0.0	06
Custom Energy ◇ ▫	29.1	193.6	-2200.0	1.1n	.02	-50.0	-62.5	NE	NC	25	03-88	.00	.0	0	0	0	00-00-00	2.6	1.92	5.0	5.00	25.0	259	2.0	30	30,470	416	0	0.0	06
Dallas Cp	5.6	5.6	3.5	5.3q	.71	NE	NE	NE	NC	0	03-88	.63	5.5	-5	129	80	06-17-88	1.3	1.77	2.3	2.30	5.3	56	2.3	89	7,407	4,381	0	2.0	12
Elcor Cp	8.6	6.3	3.3	1.4n	.20	-100.0	-100.0	-76.5	NC	0	03-88	.22	3.1	5	19	419	04-11-88	1.1	1.64	1.8	2.28	4.1	78	2.5	50	7,032	1,821	+1	8.6	06
Formica	13.7	13.7	12.9	13.5q	1.12	69.2	69.2	33.3	NC	14	03-88	.00	.0	0	0	0	00-00-00	3.2	1.28	4.1	3.49	14.3	94	2.0	147	12,804	6,037	0	0.0	12
Hauserman Inc	27.0	21.4	14.5	-12.0n	-5.09	NE	NE	NE	NC	-43	03-88	.00	.0	6	NE	276	03-14-88	-8.0	1.88	-15.0	2.84	-42.6	55	1.9	14	2,325	440	0	0.0	06
Ind Acoustics	1098.0	1098.0	311.8	3.1q	1.02	40.0	40.0	131.8	-6	9	03-88	.25	3.2	12	25	29	02-29-88	1.3	4.00	5.2	2.17	11.3	13	1.5	22	2,898	27	0	0.0	12
Insituform Grp	35.7	35.7	30.0	-3.1q	-.33	NC	NC	-100.0	NC	-21	03-88	.00	.0	0	0	0	09-02-86	-23.8	.75	-17.8	1.19	-21.2	0	5.1	77	8,967	1,412	0	0.0	12
Insituform Gulf	100.0	70.4	77.7	.9n	.33	NE	118.2	106.3	NC	16	03-88	.00	.0	0	0	0	00-00-00	5.6	2.11	11.8	1.36	16.1	0	3.1	9	3,000	199	0	0.0	06

Continued

Misc. Building Materials (Continued)

Company	Revenue: Pct. Change Last Qtr	Revenue: Pct. Change FY to Date	Revenue: Pct. Change Last 12 Mos	Earnings: Last 12 Mos	Earnings Per Share: Last 12 Mos	Earnings Per Share Pct. Change: Last Qtr	Earnings Per Share Pct. Change: FY to Date	Earnings Per Share Pct. Change: Last 12 Mos	Earnings: 5-Year Growth Rate	Earnings: Par Growth Rate	Earnings: Date of Report
-	%	%	%	$Mil	$	%	%	%	%	%	-
Insituform NA	32.3	32.3	28.5	-.7q	-.08	33.3	33.3	-100.0	NC	-4	03-88
Kerkhoff Inds	NA	NA	NA	NA	NA	NA	NA	NA	NA	NC	00-00
Knape & Vogt Mfg	5.5	21.1	19.5	4.8n	1.20	-15.8	11.6	4.3	10	5	03-88
Lawson Prods	15.1	15.1	10.8	19.9q	1.35	65.0	65.0	53.4	NC	20	03-88
Manville Cp	5.7	5.7	7.7	156.9q	5.50	-19.1	-19.1	51.9	NC	15	03-88
Modular Tech	27.5	11.9	9.6	-3.4n	-.83	NE	2400.0	-100.0	NC	-43	03-88
Nichols Homeshld	12.4	12.4	13.5	6.6q	1.22	-72.7	-72.7	1.7	NC	23	03-88
Novo Cp	-17.7	-17.7	8.5	-3.0q	-.44	NE	NE	-100.0	NC	-15	03-88
Owens Corn	.0	.0	.0	248.0q	5.30	NC	NC	NC	NC	0	03-88
Rep Gypsum	-5.6	-9.0	-14.5	2.2n	.21	-83.3	-60.6	-65.6	5	-5	03-88
Supradur Cos	41.7	41.7	33.3	2.1q	1.97	2.3	2.3	23.9	NC	21	03-88
Thermal Profile	2.6	-3.7	-11.7	-.7s	-.25	NE	NE	NE	NC	-7	09-87
US Intec	11.4	11.4	5.5	.9q	.29	-56.3	-56.3	-69.1	NC	5	03-88
USG Corp	3.2	3.2	4.4	159.1q	3.08	-53.3	-53.3	-29.7	35	17	03-88
Vulcan Matls	20.0	20.0	3.3	120.5q	11.36	38.9	38.9	28.1	18	14	03-88

Company	Dividends: Current Rate Amt	Dividends: Current Rate Yield	Dividends: 5-Year Growth Rate	Dividends: Payout Last FY	Dividends: Payout Last 5 Yrs.	Dividends: Last X-Dvd Date	Ratio Analysis: Profit Margin	Ratio Analysis: Asset Turnover	Ratio Analysis: Return on Total Assets	Ratio Analysis: Leverage Ratio	Ratio Analysis: Return on Equity	Ratio Analysis: Debt to Equity	Ratio Analysis: Current Ratio	Shareholdings: Market Value	Shareholdings: Latest Shares Outstndg.	Shareholdings: Held by Banks-Funds	Shareholdings: Insider Net Trading	Shareholdings: Short Interest Ratio	Shareholdings: Fiscal Year Ends
-	$	%	%	%	%	-	π/r x	r/a =	π/a x	a/e =	π/e	%	-	$Mil	000	000	000	Days	Mo
Insituform NA	.00	.0	0	0	0	00-00-00	-3.9	.79	-3.1	1.35	-4.2	9	4.1	67	7,131	1,001	0	0.0	12
Kerkhoff Inds	.00	.0	NA	NA	NA	00-00-00	NA	NC	NA	NC	NA	NA	NA	4	2,890	0	0	NA	NA
Knape & Vogt Mfg	.66	4.6	8	47	41	05-16-88	4.9	1.47	7.2	1.54	11.1	25	4.3	58	4,007	1,031	0	0.0	06
Lawson Prods	.24	.8	0	15	16	06-28-88	13.0	1.42	18.5	1.29	23.8	0	5.2	428	14,748	5,910	0	0.0	12
Manville Cp	.00	.0	0	0	0	05-20-82	7.5	.76	5.7	2.58	14.7	21	3.5	48	24,001	457	0	31.4	12
Modular Tech	.00	.0	0	0	0	00-00-00	-10.0	2.28	-22.8	1.89	-43.0	28	2.1	11	3,969	627	0	0.0	06
Nichols Homeshld	.00	.0	0	0	0	00-00-00	3.8	2.61	9.9	2.34	23.2	54	1.9	49	5,474	673	0	0.0	12
Novo Cp	.00	.0	0	0	0	00-00-00	-3.9	1.69	-6.6	2.27	-15.0	75	2.4	4	6,693	258	0	0.0	12
Owens Corn	.00	.0	0	0	0	00-00-00	7.0	2.23	15.6	.00	NS	-183	1.2	830	39,989	18,003	0	10.8	12
Rep Gypsum	.36	6.5	48	88	36	05-24-88	4.2	.93	3.9	1.69	6.6	40	3.5	55	10,075	2,663	+16	0.1	06
Supradur Cos	.00	.0	0	0	0	02-05-82	5.8	1.64	9.5	2.17	20.6	37	2.5	11	1,038	110	0	0.0	12
Thermal Profile	.00	.0	0	0	0	00-00-00	-4.7	.53	-2.5	2.76	-6.9	50	.9	2	3,068	399	0	0.0	03
US Intec	.00	.0	0	0	0	00-00-00	1.6	1.56	2.5	1.84	4.6	47	4.7	17	3,000	631	0	0.0	12
USG Corp	1.12	2.3	16	28	28	05-18-88	5.4	1.41	7.6	3.43	26.1	122	1.2	2,479	51,640	18,433	+0	0.4	12
Vulcan Matls	3.92	2.6	7	31	38	08-19-88	12.6	1.03	13.0	1.62	21.1	12	2.0	1,614	10,548	6,711	-1	0.0	12

Trends and Forecasts: Chemicals and Allied Products (SIC 28)

(in millions of dollars except as noted)

ITEM	1984	1985	1986[1]	1987[2]	1988[3]	Percent Change: Compound Annual 1972-85	Compound Annual 1980-85	Annual 1985-86	Annual 1986-87	Annual 1987-88
Industry Data										
Value of shipments[4]	198,233	197,311	204,240	210,400	—	10.0	4.0	3.5	3.1	—
Value of shipments (1982$)	193,297	189,473	192,843	196,061	—	1.8	0.8	1.6	2.0	—
Total employment (000)	843	826	814	805	—	−0.1	−1.9	−1.5	−1.2	—
Production workers (000)	490	476	472	467	—	−0.8	−2.7	−0.9	−1.1	—
Average hourly earnings ($)	11.69	12.26	12.87	13.50	—	8.0	6.9	5.0	4.9	—
Product Data										
Value of shipments[5]	185,784	185,167	191,650	197,450	—	10.1	4.0	3.5	3.1	—
Value of shipments (1982$)	180,748	177,334	180,250	183,850	—	1.8	0.8	1.6	2.0	—
Shipments price index[6] (1982 = 100)	103.4	105.1	—	—	—	7.8	3.1	—	—	—
Trade Data										
Value of imports	11,910	13,472	13,984	14,550	—	16.5	14.1	3.8	4.1	—
Import/new supply ratio[7]	0.061	0.065	—	—	—	5.6	8.1	—	—	—
Value of exports	22,626	21,797	22,562	24,750	—	13.5	0.2	3.5	9.7	—
Export/shipments ratio	0.121	0.116	—	—	—	3.3	−3.8	—	—	—

[1]Estimated except for exports and imports.
[2]Estimated.
[3]Forecast.
[4]Value of all products and services sold by the Chemicals and Allied Products industry.
[5]Value of products classified in the Chemicals and Allied Products industry produced by all industries.
[6]Developed by the Office of Industry Assessment, ITA.
[7]New supply is the sum of product shipments plus imports.

SOURCE: U.S. Department of Commerce: Bureau of the Census, Bureau of Economic Analysis, International Trade Administration (ITA). Estimates and forecasts by ITA.

Source: *U.S. Industrial Outlook 1988,* U.S. Department of Commerce.

Trends and Forecasts: Petrochemicals (SIC 2821,2822,2824,2843,2865,2869,2873,2895)

(in millions of dollars except as noted)

ITEM	1984	1985	1986[1]	1987[2]	1988[3]	Percent Change: Compound Annual 1972-85	Compound Annual 1980-85	Annual 1985-86	Annual 1986-87	Annual 1987-88
Industry Data										
Value of shipments[4]	84,505	80,377	83,190	85,770	—	10.5	1.6	3.5	3.1	—
Value of shipments (1982$)	83,443	80,711	82,000	83,640	—	1.7	0.7	1.6	2.0	—
Total employment (000)	265	256	253	252	—	−1.1	−3.6	−1.0	−0.4	—
Production workers (000)	166	159	157	154	—	−1.6	−4.1	−1.5	−1.5	—
Average hourly earnings ($)	13.55	14.22	14.80	15.45	—	8.5	7.2	5.0	5.0	—
Product Data										
Value of shipments[5]	81,097	76,862	79,550	82,020	—	10.8	2.0	3.5	3.1	—
Value of shipments (1982$)	79,509	76,740	77,970	79,530	—	1.7	1.1	1.6	2.0	—
Shipments price index[6] (1982 = 100)	102.0	100.2	—	—	—	8.7	0.6	—	—	—
Trade Data										
Value of imports	6,310	6,841	6,905	6,900	—	17.0	16.2	1.6	0.0	—
Import/new supply ratio[7]	0.065	0.074	—	—	—	5.5	13.1	—	—	—
Value of exports	11,470	10,975	11,544	13,000	—	14.1	−1.0	5.2	12.6	—
Export/shipments ratio	0.139	0.141	—	—	—	3.6	−3.1	—	—	—

[1]Estimated except for exports and imports.
[2]Estimated.
[3]Forecast.
[4]Value of all products and services sold by the Petrochemicals industry.
[5]Value of products classified in the Petrochemicals industry produced by all industries.
[6]Developed by the Office of Industry Assessment, ITA.
[7]New supply is the sum of product shipments plus imports.

SOURCE: U.S. Department of Commerce: Bureau of the Census, Bureau of Economic Analysis, International Trade Administration (ITA). Estimates and forecasts by ITA.

Source: *U.S. Industrial Outlook 1988*, U.S. Department of Commerce.

Trends and Forecasts: Plastics Materials and Resins (SIC 2821)

(in millions of dollars except as noted)

ITEM	1984	1985	1986[1]	1987[2]	1988[3]	Percent Change: Compound Annual 1972-85	Compound Annual 1980-85	Annual 1985-86	Annual 1986-87	Annual 1987-88
Industry Data										
Value of shipments[4]	20,776	20,262	20,659	23,854	—	12.3	6.3	2.0	15.5	—
Value of shipments (1982$)	19,167	19,045	19,807	20,797	21,837	2.6	4.5	4.0	5.0	5.0
Total employment (000)	54.2	55.4	55.1	55.5	—	0.1	−1.2	−0.5	0.7	—
Production workers (000)	33.2	34.4	34.4	34.2	—	−0.1	−1.2	0.0	−0.6	—
Average hourly earnings ($)	13.33	14.33	14.87	15.27	—	8.5	8.1	3.8	2.7	—
Product Data										
Value of shipments[5]	22,730	21,574	21,827	26,404	—	12.8	3.7	1.2	21.0	—
Value of shipments (1982$)	20,788	20,122	20,927	23,020	24,102	2.8	1.8	4.0	10.0	4.7
Shipments price index[6] (1982=100)	109.3	107.2	95.1	—	—	9.8	1.7	−11.3	—	—
Trade Data										
Value of imports (ITA)[7]	725	772	872	895	—	—	—	13.0	2.6	—
Import/new supply ratio[8]	0.031	0.032	0.035	0.033	—	—	—	9.4	−0.1	—
Value of exports	2,655	2,457	2,805	2,878	—	14.2	−1.9	14.2	2.6	—
Export/shipments ratio	0.117	0.114	0.125	0.121	—	1.2	−5.3	9.6	−3.2	—

[1]Estimated except for exports and imports.
[2]Estimated.
[3]Forecast.
[4]Value of all products and services sold by the Plastics Materials and Resins industry.
[5]Value of products classified in the Plastics Materials and Resins industry produced by all industries.
[6]Developed by the Office of Industry Assessment, ITA.
[7]Import data are developed by the chapter author.
[8]New supply is the sum of product shipments plus imports.
SOURCE: U.S. Department of Commerce: Bureau of the Census, Bureau of Economic Analysis, International Trade Administration (ITA). Estimates and forecasts by ITA.

Source: *U.S. Industrial Outlook 1988,* U.S. Department of Commerce.

Trends and Forecasts: Synthetic Rubber (SIC 2822)

(in millions of dollars except as noted)

ITEM	1984	1985	1986[1]	1987[2]	1988[3]	Percent Change: Compound Annual 1972-85	Compound Annual 1980-85	Annual 1985-86	Annual 1986-87	Annual 1987-88
Industry Data										
Value of shipments[4]	3,409	2,841	3,000	3,018	3,036	7.7	1.3	5.6	0.6	0.6
Value of shipments (1982$)	3,527	2,943	3,109	3,134	3,153	−0.8	−1.0	5.6	0.8	0.6
Total employment (000)	10.7	9.8	9.5	9.3	9.2	−1.4	−3.0	−3.1	−2.1	−1.1
Production workers (000)	7.0	6.3	6.1	6.0	5.9	−2.0	−3.2	−3.2	−1.6	−1.7
Average hourly earnings ($)	15.36	15.18	15.75	16.50	—	8.2	6.4	3.8	4.8	—
Product Data										
Value of shipments[5]	3,688	3,449	3,640	3,662	3,684	7.9	1.2	5.5	0.6	0.6
Value of shipments (1982$)	3,837	3,585	3,788	3,823	3,846	−0.6	−1.4	5.7	0.9	0.6
Shipments price index[6] (1982 = 100)	96.1	96.2	96.1	95.8	95.8	8.5	2.7	−0.1	−0.3	0.0
Trade Data										
Value of imports	335	382	350	350	340	16.2	17.2	−8.4	0.0	−2.9
Import/new supply ratio[7]	0.083	0.100	0.088	0.087	0.084	7.3	14.4	−12.0	−1.1	−3.4
Value of exports	674	628	711	819	900	10.5	−3.4	13.2	15.2	9.9
Export/shipments ratio	0.183	0.182	0.195	0.224	0.244	2.5	−4.6	7.1	14.9	8.9

[1]Estimated except for exports and imports.
[2]Estimated.
[3]Forecast.
[4]Value of all products and services sold by the Synthetic Rubber industry.
[5]Value of products classified in the Synthetic Rubber industry produced by all industries.
[6]Developed by the Office of Industry Assessment, ITA.
[7]New supply is the sum of product shipments plus imports.

SOURCE: U.S. Department of Commerce: Bureau of the Census, Bureau of Economic Analysis, International Trade Administration (ITA). Estimates and forecasts by ITA.

Source: *U.S. Industrial Outlook 1988,* U.S. Department of Commerce.

Trends and Forecasts: Tires and Inner Tubes (SIC 3011)

(in millions of dollars except as noted)

						Percent Change				
						Compound Annual		Annual		
ITEM	1984	1985	1986[1]	1987[2]	1988[3]	1972-85	1980-85	1985-86	1986-87	1987-88
Industry Data										
Value of shipments[4]	10,723	10,434	10,809	11,199	—	4.7	3.5	3.6	3.6	—
Value of shipments (1982$)	11,239	11,153	11,787	12,443	12,958	−1.4	3.1	5.7	5.6	4.1
Total employment (000)	70.4	70.3	66.0	63.6	—	−3.2	−4.2	−6.1	−3.6	—
Production workers (000)	56.3	55.9	54.8	54.1	—	−3.0	−3.3	−2.0	−1.3	—
Average hourly earnings ($)	14.18	14.70	15.23	15.59	—	8.0	6.7	3.6	2.4	—
Product Data										
Value of shipments[5]	10,281	10,069	10,421	10,796	—	5.7	3.8	3.5	3.6	—
Value of shipments (1982$)	10,777	10,763	11,495	12,276	—	−0.5	3.4	6.8	6.8	—
Shipments price index[6] (1982=100)	95.5	93.8	96.4	95.0	96.0	6.2	0.3	2.8	−1.5	1.1
Trade Data										
Value of imports	1,792	1,872	1,951	—	—	13.0	10.6	4.2	—	—
Import/new supply ratio[7]	0.154	0.162	—	—	—	6.1	5.2	—	—	—
Value of exports	419	369	339	—	—	10.5	−7.4	−8.1	—	—
Export/shipments ratio	0.041	0.037	0.033	—	—	4.5	−10.7	−10.8	—	—

[1]Estimated except for exports and imports.
[2]Estimated.
[3]Forecast.
[4]Value of all products and services sold by the Tires and Inner Tubes industry.
[5]Value of products classified in the Tires and Inner Tubes industry produced by all industries.
[6]Developed by the Office of Industry Assessment, ITA.
[7]New supply is the sum of product shipments plus imports.
SOURCE: U.S. Department of Commerce: Bureau of the Census, Bureau of Economic Analysis, International Trade Administration (ITA). Estimates and forecasts by ITA.

Source: *U.S. Industrial Outlook 1988,* U.S. Department of Commerce.

Company	Revenue Pct. Change Last Qtr	Revenue Pct. Change FY to Date	Revenue Pct. Change Last 12 Mos	Earnings Last 12 Mos	Earnings Per Share Last 12 Mos	Per Share Pct. Change Last Qtr	Per Share Pct. Change FY to Date	Per Share Pct. Change Last 12 Mos	5-Year Growth Rate	Par Growth Rate	Date of Report	Dividends Current Rate Amt	Current Rate Yield	5-Year Growth Rate	Payout Last FY	Payout Last 5 Yrs.	Last X-Dvd Date	Profit Margin	Asset Turnover	Return on Total Assets	Leverage Ratio	Return on Equity	Debt to Equity	Current Ratio	Market Value	Latest Shares Outstndng.	Held by Banks-Funds	Insider Net Trading	Short Interest Ratio	Fiscal Year Ends
-	%	%	%	$Mil	$	%	%	%	%	%	-	$	%	%	%	%	-	π/r	x r/a	= π/a	x a/e	= π/e	%	-	$Mil	000	000	000	Days	Mo
Chemicals and Synthetics																														
Ind. Group	17.3	18.0	20.1	8,054.4	4.60	60.9	60.5	40.8	20	11	---	1.71	3.2	1	38	46	----	7.0	1.11	7.8	2.31	18.0	47	1.7	92,716	1,713,462	755,793	- 275	.9	--
Aceto Cp	4.1	5.0	-7.3	4.2n	1.14	26.2	21.3	-8.8	4	-2	03-88	1.34	8.8b	0	7	5	06-07-88	4.2	1.50	6.3	1.51	9.5	17	4.3	55	3,606	802	0	0.0	06
Advd Polymer	200.0	200.0	.0	-3.4q	-.45	NE	NE	NC	NC	-20	03-88	.00	.0	0	0	0	00-00-00	NM	NC	NC	NC	-19.8	18	23.6	75	8,666	1,373	0	0.0	12
Air Pd & Chem	17.4	13.6	10.5	194.4s	3.51	39.7	50.4	1850.0	-7	11	03-88	1.20	2.4	16	30	34	06-28-88	8.5	.85	7.2	2.36	17.0	54	1.3	2,776	54,843	36,191	+18	1.7	09
Am Cyanamid	13.3	13.3	9.9	281.7q	3.10	31.3	31.3	33.6	13	9	03-88	1.20	2.2	4	36	45	05-23-88	6.5	1.05	6.8	2.21	15.0	30	1.5	4,835	89,741	51,215	0	1.6	12
Aristech/Chem □	24.7	24.7	25.6	108.8q	4.31	301.9	301.9	138.1	NC	24	03-88	.80	2.3	0	20	12	04-25-88	11.2	1.76	19.7	1.52	30.0	17	2.6	900	25,897	21,982	0	0.2	12
Ausimont Comp	5.2	5.2	16.5	68.7q	2.32	46.3	46.3	32.6	NC	13	03-88	.60	1.7	0	20	12	05-27-88	8.2	1.04	8.5	2.11	17.9	22	1.8	1,034	29,113	5,074	0	0.0	12
Borden Chem	NA	NA	NA	NA	NA	NA	NA	NA	NA	NC	00-00	.00	.0	NA	NA	NA	00-00-00	NA	NC	NA	NC	NA	NA	NA	590	32,100	4,383	0	NA	NA
Cabot Corp ■	40.7	34.9	32.1	35.6s	1.33	-2.9	-6.6	-45.3	-10	2	03-88	.92	2.3	0	65	42	05-24-88	2.2	1.09	2.4	2.50	6.0	37	1.3	1,076	26,981	16,592	0	0.3	09
Calgon Carbon	21.3	21.3	22.6	20.2q	2.13	52.4	52.4	53.2	NC	20	03-88	.20	.4	0	5	3	06-09-88	11.3	1.17	13.2	1.70	22.4	25	2.4	492	9,737	3,959	+0	0.0	12
Dow Chemical	32.0	32.0	25.8	1506.0q	7.89	108.6	108.6	86.5	28	18	03-88	2.40	2.6	2	32	62	06-24-88	10.5	1.00	10.5	2.49	26.1	66	1.7	17,474	192,284	89,837	-20	2.0	12
Dupont ◆	12.1	12.1	15.5	1985.0q	8.22	51.2	51.2	30.5	12	8	03-88	3.80	4.1	7	45	51	05-09-88	6.3	1.11	7.0	2.03	14.2	22	1.6	22,224	239,287	87,565	-0	5.4	12
Essex Chemical	38.3	38.3	13.0	-15.8q	-2.06	7.7	7.7	-100.0	NC	-47	03-88	.52	1.6	10	NE	134	07-06-88	-7.0	1.01	-7.1	5.24	-37.2	183	1.1	237	7,504	1,673	0	1.0	12
Ethyl Corp ○	23.4	23.4	13.8	200.0q	1.64	18.9	18.9	7.9	22	15	03-88	.44	2.0	16	25	26	06-09-88	11.0	.92	10.1	2.07	20.9	64	2.4	2,657	120,788	43,634	-406	2.8	12
Genex Cp	166.7	166.7	-33.3	-3.6q	-.25	NE	NE	NE	NC	0	03-88	.00	.0	0	0	0	00-00-00	NM	NC	NC	NC	NM	7	.8	9	13,680	641	0	0.0	12
Georgia Bonded	-3.3	-2.9	-5.8	-.4n	-.25	-100.0	-100.0	-100.0	NC	-5	03-88	.00	.0	0	45	4	08-25-86	-1.3	1.62	-2.1	2.29	-4.8	8	1.7	5	1,430	34	0	0.0	06
Georgia Gulf	44.2	44.2	31.1	119.8q	7.60	284.3	284.3	198.0	NC	74	03-88	.90	1.3	0	4	2	05-27-88	15.5	2.50	38.8	2.17	84.1	29	1.8	909	13,417	8,424	0	0.1	12
Grace W R ○	34.7	34.7	41.0	159.6q	1.87	-4.3	-4.3	NE	NC	3	03-88	1.40	5.3	1	74	547	04-29-88	3.3	1.09	3.6	3.06	11.0	84	1.5	2,247	84,400	53,779	+90	2.1	12
Henley Grp ○	-27.6	-27.6	-1.2	-92.0q	-.88	NE	NE	NE	NC	-5	03-88	.00	.0	0	0	0	00-00-00	-2.8	.61	-1.7	2.88	-4.9	92	1.4	2,425	103,211	51,416	0	0.0	12
Hercules Inc	-.4	-.4	2.4	728.4q	13.24	-64.7	-64.7	139.4	40	28	03-88	1.92	4.1	7	12	30	05-27-88	27.1	.77	20.9	1.59	33.3	22	3.6	2,312	48,797	29,014	0	3.9	12
Immucor Inc	23.5	24.5	14.2	.9n	.24	133.3	80.0	84.6	NC	11	02-88	.00	.0	0	0	0	04-16-87	11.3	.79	8.9	1.19	10.6	12	14.7	24	3,221	470	0	0.0	05
Imperial Chem	24.0	24.0	38.7	1518.0q	9.04	29.5	29.5	-37.2	37	20	03-88	2.41	3.2	20	40	33	03-07-88	6.9	1.71	11.8	2.36	27.9	44	1.8	12,442	164,250	14,071	0	1.3	12
Intl Flav Frag	25.1	25.1	21.3	115.3q	3.05	30.1	30.1	25.5	10	8	03-88	1.60	3.0	4	44	52	06-21-88	14.6	.90	13.2	1.33	17.5	0	4.3	2,016	37,776	19,531	0	2.8	12
Koppers Co	12.9	12.9	10.3	5.3q	.15	NE	NE	-92.7	NC	-8	03-88	1.20	2.0	-5	278	3500	02-12-88	.3	1.67	.5	2.40	1.2	40	1.8	1,632	27,198	17,345	-2	0.3	12
Monsanto Co	13.7	13.7	12.7	508.0q	6.73	62.5	62.5	16.2	NC	7	03-88	3.00	3.4	7	49	62	05-06-88	6.4	.94	6.0	2.17	13.0	40	1.7	6,465	74,098	46,204	+3	1.2	12
Oil Dri Cp	17.8	12.5	12.0	6.0n	1.08	20.0	7.4	-6.1	40	15	04-88	.20	1.0	38	17	16	06-20-88	9.2	1.35	12.4	1.48	18.4	16	3.3	109	5,444	911	0	0.0	07
Pacer Tech	35.7	28.9	20.0	.0n	.01	NC	.0	.0	NC	0	03-88	.00	.0	0	0	0	00-00-00	.0	NC	NC	NC	.0	0	1.5	5	9,371	120	0	0.0	06
Pennwalt Corp	-7.5	-7.5	-.4	53.0q	4.10	8.0	8.0	9.9	NC	5	03-88	2.40	3.0	0	56	94	06-27-88	4.7	1.09	5.1	2.20	11.2	46	2.0	910	11,214	8,099	0	0.8	12
Portage Ind	19.6	19.6	4.7	.5q	.19	-100.0	-100.0	-74.0	NC	19	03-88	.00	.0	0	0	0	00-00-00	2.3	1.78	4.1	4.68	19.2	4	.4	6	2,175	765	0	0.0	12
Publicker Ind	515.6	515.6	269.2	-3.4q	-.27	NE	NE	NE	NC	-23	03-88	.00	.0	0	0	0	00-00-00	-7.1	.87	-6.2	3.76	-23.3	195	7.8	25	12,556	1,210	+10	0.0	12
Regal Intl	156.3	90.7	100.0	-3.8f	-.32	NE	NE	NE	NC	-61	12-87	.00	.0	0	0	0	00-00-00	-38.0	1.04	-39.6	1.55	-61.3	2	2.4	6	14,484	1,078	0	0.0	12
Rohm & Haas	16.4	16.4	11.2	199.8q	2.95	12.0	12.0	29.4	16	13	03-88	.92	2.6	14	30	32	05-09-88	8.7	1.17	10.2	1.86	19.0	25	2.0	2,319	66,735	40,495	+19	1.3	12
Stepan Co	17.0	17.0	14.8	12.0q	4.06	43.3	43.3	48.7	19	15	03-88	.92	2.0	8	23	30	05-24-88	4.0	1.73	6.9	2.90	20.0	74	1.7	133	2,849	576	+15	0.0	12
Syntro Cp	-37.5	-55.0	-80.0	-5.2s	-.59	NE	NE	NE	NC	-28	03-88	.00	.0	0	0	0	00-00-00	NM	NC	NC	NC	-27.7	9	21.3	20	8,959	461	0	0.0	09
Union Carbide	15.8	15.8	15.6	267.0q	2.00	47.1	47.1	39.9	NC	7	03-88	1.50	6.7	38	85	1277	05-03-88	3.7	.95	3.5	7.60	26.6	356	1.3	2,950	131,089	76,374	0	1.0	12
Wellman Inc	24.9	24.9	38.5	26.9q	1.94	52.5	52.5	63.0	NC	23	03-88	.00	.0	0	0	0	00-00-00	9.7	1.36	13.2	1.76	23.2	40	3.6	526	14,215	6,677	0	0.0	12
Witco Cp	18.0	18.0	10.6	56.9q	2.46	-40.0	-40.0	-16.6	9	4	03-88	1.50	4.2	8	43	37	06-14-88	3.8	1.42	5.4	2.06	11.1	47	3.1	796	22,346	13,818	0	0.9	12

Company	Revenue Pct. Change Last Qtr	Revenue Pct. Change FY to Date	Revenue Pct. Change Last 12 Mos	Earnings Last 12 Mos	Earnings Per Share Last 12 Mos	Earnings Per Share Pct. Change Last Qtr	Earnings Per Share Pct. Change FY to Date	Earnings Per Share Pct. Change Last 12 Mos	Earnings 5-Year Growth Rate	Earnings Par Growth Rate	Earnings Date of Report	Dividends Current Rate Amt	Dividends Current Rate Yield	Dividends 5-Year Growth Rate	Dividends Payout Last FY	Dividends Payout Last 5 Yrs.	Dividends Last X-Dvd Date	Ratio Analysis Profit Margin	Ratio Analysis Asset Turnover	Ratio Analysis Return on Total Assets	Ratio Analysis Leverage Ratio	Ratio Analysis Return on Equity	Ratio Analysis Debt to Equity	Ratio Analysis Current Ratio	Shareholdings Market Value	Shareholdings Latest Shares Outstndng.	Shareholdings Held by Banks-Funds	Shareholdings Insider Net Trading	Shareholdings Short Interest Ratio	Shareholdings Fiscal Year Ends
-	%	%	%	$Mil	$	%	%	%	%	%	-	$	%	%	%	%	-	π/r	x r/a	= π/a	x a/e	= π/e	%	-	$Mil	000	000	000	Days	Mo
Specialty Chemicals																														
Ind. Group	19.0	18.4	22.2	897.0	1.35	29.7	35.3	29.1	10	10	- - -	.53	2.0	0	36	41	- - - -	6.5	1.35	8.8	1.86	16.4	23	2.0	17,270	648,769	216,392	+ 60	.3	- -
Airgas Inc ◦ •	17.9	21.7	22.4	4.2f	.80	10.5	33.3	33.3	NC	22	03-88	.00	.0	0	0	0	00-00-00	3.2	1.31	4.2	5.21	21.9	308	1.9	88	5,477	1,549	0	0.0	03
Am Colloid	35.5	35.5	23.3	3.7q	.73	33.3	33.3	NC	NC	-1	03-88	.79	4.9	0	14	6	05-17-88	3.9	.95	3.7	2.16	8.0	63	3.0	82	5,128	782	0	0.0	12
Balchem Cp	12.5	12.5	16.6	.4q	.28	-28.6	-28.6	21.7	NC	15	03-88	.03	.8	0	0	3	12-04-87	5.7	1.46	8.3	2.01	16.7	21	1.2	5	1,199	0	0	0.0	12
Betz Laboratories	19.4	19.4	15.4	42.1q	2.70	17.7	17.7	20.0	5	8	03-88	1.68	3.5	13	56	53	07-22-88	10.4	1.41	14.7	1.39	20.5	0	1.8	738	15,300	9,960	+3	0.0	12
Bio Rad Lab A	34.7	34.7	29.1	8.5q	1.13	36.7	36.7	27.0	94	17	03-88	.00	.0	0	0	0	00-00-00	4.9	1.31	6.4	2.66	17.0	64	1.9	125	5,638	681	0	0.2	12
Bio Rad Lab B	NA	NA	NA	NA	NA	NA	NA	NA	NA	NC	00-00	.00	.0	NA	NA	NA	06-11-86	NA	NA	NA	NC	NA	NA	NA	42	1,925	52	0	NA	NA
Cambrex	11.2	11.2	33.7	7.6q	1.61	-49.3	-49.3	NC	NC	10	03-88	.00	.0	0	0	0	00-00-00	6.8	1.10	7.5	1.32	9.9	9	3.9	104	5,596	2,888	0	0.0	12
Chemed Cp	9.3	9.3	8.4	20.6q	2.32	8.3	8.3	-43.8	8	5	03-88	1.72	5.2	5	70	56	05-16-88	5.2	1.50	7.8	2.33	18.2	41	1.6	293	8,812	6,769	+4	0.5	12
Crompt & Knwl	14.0	14.0	18.3	13.0q	2.16	53.8	53.8	1100.0	-1	10	03-88	.92	2.7	5	34	58	05-02-88	5.3	1.81	9.6	1.79	17.2	17	2.3	205	6,034	2,291	+22	1.6	12
Detrex Chemical	3.6	3.6	5.2	2.8q	1.78	19.6	19.6	32.8	-9	2	03-88	1.20	3.6	4	72	48	06-09-88	2.8	1.64	4.6	1.48	6.8	18	3.5	53	1,580	537	0	0.0	12
Dexter Cp ◦	14.1	14.1	20.2	45.5q	1.83	28.9	28.9	30.7	9	9	03-88	.80	3.1	6	35	40	06-09-88	5.6	1.34	7.5	2.07	15.5	36	2.4	649	24,836	15,821	0	0.0	12
Diam Crystal • □	-80.0	-79.3	-79.3	1.4f	.57	-100.0	11.8	11.8	-30	-1	03-88	.80	2.3	6	140	70	05-16-88	5.6	.23	1.3	1.31	1.7	1	3.7	90	2,567	1,170	0	0.0	03
Ecogen	183.3	183.3	66.6	-2.3q	-.16	NE	NE	NE	NC	-15	03-88	.00	.0	0	0	0	00-00-00	-46.0	.27	-12.2	1.26	-15.4	1	4.7	37	6,611	981	0	0.0	12
Ferro Corp	17.7	17.7	19.9	36.1q	2.63	67.3	67.3	37.0	16	10	03-88	.68	1.8	2	29	41	05-09-88	4.0	1.70	6.8	2.04	13.9	25	1.9	537	13,852	8,214	0	0.2	12
Flamemaster Cp	.0	-7.4	.0	.3s	.23	-16.7	-40.0	15.0	NC	15	03-88	.00	.0	0	0	0	00-00-00	6.0	1.52	9.1	1.65	15.0	0	7.3	9	2,496	0	+0	0.0	09
Fuller H B Co	14.2	13.4	12.5	25.6s	2.67	-17.8	-1.8	18.7	18	13	05-88	.56	2.1	9	15	18	04-27-88	4.0	1.95	7.8	2.04	15.9	20	1.9	248	9,460	4,731	0	0.0	11
Grt Lakes Ch	18.5	18.5	44.5	67.7q	3.94	76.9	76.9	77.5	17	14	03-88	.38	1.1	19	18	20	06-27-88	13.5	.87	11.7	1.47	17.2	11	1.9	1,112	17,377	12,009	-3	0.9	12
Hawkins Chem	29.7	26.6	19.3	2.2s	.60	45.5	55.0	39.5	14	13	03-88	.12	1.5b	0	18	11	04-04-88	5.9	2.02	11.9	1.38	16.4	1	2.6	27	3,268	101	0	0.0	09
Huntington Intl	42.2	47.7	47.4	13.0s	.97	-70.4	-71.2	4.3	NC	31	03-88	.00	.0	0	0	0	03-16-87	14.9	1.28	19.1	1.64	31.4	14	1.4	204	8,356	3,963	0	0.0	09
Hyponex Cp	-6.6	-6.6	10.0	-10.9q	-1.83	-95.1	-95.1	-100.0	NC	-49	03-88	.00	.0	0	0	0	00-00-00	-9.0	.51	-4.6	10.59	-48.7	877	2.7	74	5,919	1,184	0	0.0	12
Intl Genetic	120.0	68.4	50.0	-3.3f	-.42	NE	NE	NE	NC	-27	12-87	.00	.0	0	0	0	00-00-00	NM	NC	NC	NC	-27.3	0	16.4	42	7,737	1,277	0	0.0	12
Kinark Cp	8.1	8.1	.0	-3.9q	-1.14	66.7	66.7	NE	NC	-33	03-88	.00	.0	0	0	0	00-00-00	-13.4	.79	-10.6	3.12	-33.1	108	.8	15	3,483	381	-8	0.0	12
Lawter Int	16.1	16.1	10.4	17.8q	.76	31.3	31.3	28.8	NC	8	03-88	.52	3.9	3	59	88	05-09-88	15.3	1.06	16.2	1.58	25.6	7	4.4	318	23,520	6,759	+12	1.6	12
LeaRonal Inc	9.2	21.8	23.1	8.2n	.89	13.6	13.3	30.9	1	6	11-87	.48	2.9	9	42	35	05-24-88	5.5	1.93	10.6	1.30	13.8	5	5.4	156	9,318	4,034	0	0.1	02
Loctite Cp	21.3	26.8	27.9	38.5n	2.12	20.8	36.8	31.7	16	14	03-88	.72	2.1	11	27	29	05-27-88	9.6	1.32	12.7	1.67	21.2	6	1.9	618	17,969	7,708	+28	0.3	06
Lubrizol Corp	7.8	7.8	6.1	79.1q	2.02	-6.2	-6.2	5.8	9	5	03-88	1.28	3.5	0	58	62	05-04-88	7.6	1.11	8.4	1.51	12.7	9	3.0	1,432	38,961	27,161	0	0.7	12
MacDermid Inc	35.4	23.6	23.7	6.4f	1.76	10.0	18.1	18.1	5	12	03-88	.52	2.0	3	30	32	06-09-88	5.3	1.66	8.8	1.90	16.7	24	1.7	94	3,627	2,158	0	0.0	03
Melamine Chem	11.3	5.0	14.8	6.4n	1.24	121.4	41.3	NC	NC	0	03-88	.00	.0	0	0	0	00-00-00	20.6	1.53	31.5	.00	NM	0	.8	71	5,450	1,167	0	0.0	06
Montedison	NA	NA	NA	NA	NA	NA	NA	NA	NA	NC	00-00	.00	.0	NA	NA	NA	00-00-00	NA	NC	NA	NC	NA	NA	NA	2,582	196,699	1,292	0	NA	NA
Morton Thiokol	31.7	18.4	17.2	157.7n	3.30	14.5	18.7	19.1	15	13	03-88	.84	2.0	8	26	26	05-24-88	7.0	1.36	9.5	1.77	16.8	3	1.5	1,972	47,381	28,416	+9	1.7	06
Nalco Chem	23.2	23.2	18.2	87.2q	2.20	37.0	37.0	30.2	4	8	03-88	1.32	3.5	1	59	64	08-15-88	9.8	1.19	11.7	1.67	19.5	15	1.8	1,463	39,149	26,055	0	0.2	12
NCH Corp	16.3	17.4	17.3	30.0f	3.29	74.0	55.2	55.2	19	13	04-88	.92	2.1	0	22	36	05-25-88	6.0	1.62	9.7	1.85	17.9	13	2.7	408	9,211	2,536	0	3.3	04
Nuclear Metals	34.1	12.2	4.6	-1.8s	-.66	600.0	-32.0	-100.0	NC	-4	03-88	.00	.0	0	0	0	11-18-80	-4.0	.68	-2.7	1.63	-4.4	24	4.5	32	2,701	1,216	0	0.0	09
Oakite Products	4.6	4.6	1.2	4.3q	2.62	35.8	35.8	58.8	5	6	03-88	1.52	4.0	0	63	72	05-16-88	5.4	2.02	10.9	1.39	15.1	5	3.4	62	1,646	440	+1	0.0	12
Petrolite Corp	10.8	17.4	15.2	12.2s	1.07	-8.3	4.2	-12.3	-14	0	04-88	1.12	4.7	4	108	63	07-01-88	4.0	1.23	4.9	1.45	7.1	0	2.5	276	11,485	3,292	0	0.0	10

Continued

Company	Revenue Pct. Change Last Qtr	Revenue Pct. Change FY to Date	Revenue Pct. Change Last 12 Mos	Earnings Last 12 Mos	Earnings Per Share Last 12 Mos	Earnings Per Share Pct. Change Last Qtr	Earnings Per Share Pct. Change FY to Date	Earnings Per Share Pct. Change Last 12 Mos	Earnings 5-Year Growth Rate	Earnings Par Growth Rate	Earnings Date of Report	Dividends Current Rate Amt	Dividends Current Rate Yield	Dividends 5-Year Growth Rate	Dividends Payout Last FY	Dividends Payout Last 5 Yrs.	Dividends Last X-Dvd Date	Profit Margin	Asset Turnover	Return on Total Assets	Leverage Ratio	Return on Equity	Debt to Equity	Current Ratio	Market Value	Latest Shares Outstndng.	Held by Banks-Funds	Insider Net Trading	Short Interest Ratio	Fiscal Year Ends
-	%	%	%	$Mil	$	%	%	%	%	%	-	$	%	%	%	%	-	π/r x	r/a =	π/a x	a/e =	π/e	%	-	$Mil	000	000	000	Days	Mo
Specialty Chemicals (Continued)																														
Prods Research	1.7	1.5	1.0	8.0s	.91	25.0	17.9	11.0	17	13	03-88	.40	2.1	11	37	37	05-09-88	8.3	1.48	12.3	1.82	22.4	46	3.3	153	8,078	3,320	-6	0.0	09
Quaker Chemical	19.3	19.3	17.5	10.8q	1.65	17.9	17.9	25.0	7	9	03-88	.54	2.4	12	32	32	04-11-88	7.0	1.30	9.1	1.52	13.8	6	2.3	151	6,621	2,403	0	0.0	12
Sigma-Aldrich	27.2	27.2	22.6	46.0q	1.86	40.0	40.0	28.3	21	19	03-88	.32	.7	15	16	18	02-24-88	14.2	1.13	16.1	1.46	23.5	8	3.1	1,157	24,624	10,346	-1	0.0	12
Spec Comp	68.2	68.2	22.2	.5q	.50	666.7	666.7	61.3	NC	22	03-88	.00	.0	0	0	0	00-00-00	4.5	2.31	10.4	2.09	21.7	52	2.6	5	1,014	95	0	0.0	12
Univar Cp	17.8	17.8	39.6	12.5q	1.41	43.8	43.8	291.7	-16	11	05-88	.40	2.0	-21	16	34	05-10-88	1.1	3.27	3.6	4.08	14.7	121	1.4	176	8,679	1,596	+1	0.0	02
Vista Chem	42.0	39.9	28.2	38.2s	2.12	166.7	208.3	8.7	NC	18	03-88	.50	.9	0	NE	2	05-24-88	5.3	1.43	7.6	3.13	23.8	117	1.6	915	15,780	6,098	-4	0.3	09
WD Forty Co	17.0	12.7	6.8	14.9n	1.98	-24.6	52.0	32.0	9	8	05-88	1.65	5.2	15	101	75	04-05-88	19.1	1.99	38.1	1.19	45.4	0	6.0	239	7,523	1,815	0	0.0	08
Whittaker Corp	17.8	15.5	1107.8	40.2s	5.24	175.7	118.5	1441.2	NC	18	04-88	1.00	3.1	-20	15	44	07-11-88	8.8	1.06	9.3	2.41	22.4	23	1.2	214	6,682	3,144	+3	0.8	10
Tires and Inner Tubes																														
Ind. Group	35.4	17.3	6.3	1,226.0	7.80	- 37.8	- 32.9	142.6	35	49	- - -	.93	2.1	0	11	26	- - - -	8.9	1.27	11.3	4.94	55.8	193	1.5	6,112	136,991	70,766	+ 27	1.5	- -
Bandag Inc	16.5	16.5	14.6	63.1q	4.03	16.0	16.0	27.5	18	38	03-88	.80	1.2	10	18	22	06-14-88	14.4	1.51	21.7	2.17	47.1	7	1.6	1,009	15,284	6,880	0	0.2	12
Cooper Tire	8.6	8.6	12.6	31.1q	3.06	6.3	6.3	19.1	5	12	03-88	.52	1.4	8	15	17	05-27-88	4.6	1.63	7.5	1.87	14.0	32	2.6	383	10,183	4,586	+12	0.0	12
Danaher □	36.3	36.3	27.8	26.8q	1.19	207.1	207.1	133.3	NC	26	03-88	.00	.0	0	0	0	09-09-87	4.0	1.03	4.1	6.32	25.9	381	2.0	419	22,807	3,493	+6	3.9	12
GenCorp ◇	545.1	25.4	-27.0	523.0s	11.22	NE	NE	1093.6	63	0	05-88	.60	3.1	2	5	17	04-26-88	28.9	1.63	47.2	.00	NS	-488	.9	619	31,730	22,354	+10	0.6	11
Goodyear Tire	15.3	15.3	13.5	582.0q	10.41	-58.1	-58.1	82.6	16	27	03-88	1.60	2.5	3	13	31	05-10-88	5.7	1.21	6.9	4.59	31.7	179	1.5	3,683	56,987	33,453	-1	3.0	12
Rubber and Plastic Products																														
Ind. Group	34.3	56.0	46.6	779.3	1.89	52.3	23.9	310.8	48	15	- - -	.48	1.9	0	13	18	- - - -	8.5	1.13	9.6	2.15	20.6	39	2.0	10,266	409,716	89,054	+ 23	1.3	- -
Action Indus □	54.6	31.6	22.6	-4.8n	-.82	NE	500.0	-100.0	NC	-15	03-88	.00	.0	0	NE	11	05-26-87	-3.1	1.45	-4.5	3.33	-15.0	92	1.8	32	5,506	1,856	+1	0.0	06
AEP Inds	45.6	47.3	32.8	4.0s	1.31	59.1	56.1	36.5	NC	18	04-88	.00	.0	0	0	0	00-00-00	4.7	2.30	10.8	1.69	18.3	12	2.0	32	3,014	468	0	0.0	10
Alpine Grp	2.9	47.7	65.3	-2.4n	-.56	-100.0	-100.0	-100.0	NC	-40	01-88	.00	.0	0	0	0	00-00-00	-3.0	.97	-2.9	13.79	-40.0	965	2.6	25	3,914	169	0	11.9	04
Am Biltrite	17.9	17.9	21.8	3.8q	1.83	171.4	171.4	20.4	22	11	03-88	.15	.6	-9	11	14	06-20-88	2.6	1.88	4.9	2.53	12.4	55	2.1	51	1,985	401	0	0.6	12
Am Western Cp	36.6	36.6	13.4	1.8q	.39	30.0	30.0	-7.1	6	8	03-88	.00	.0	0	0	0	05-03-88	3.1	1.39	4.3	1.91	8.2	41	2.3	27	4,681	655	0	0.0	12
Arco Chem	29.8	29.8	29.9	306.0q	3.07	83.1	83.1	NC	NC	22	03-88	.60	1.7	0	8	5	05-02-88	14.7	.82	12.1	2.26	27.4	15	1.3	3,546	99,550	16,039	0	0.5	12

Atlantis Grp	33.5	33.5	400.0	4.1q	.64	185.7	185.7	NC	NC	37	03-88	.00	.0	0	0	0	00-00-00	4.6	.70	3.2	11.66	37.3	707	2.7	29	6,686	117	0	0.0	12
Bamberger Poly	57.1	57.1	50.0	2.9q	1.09	31.8	31.8	26.7	NC	88	03-88	.00	.0	0	0	0	09-24-87	1.9	4.42	8.4	10.46	87.9	318	1.6	25	2,625	197	0	0.1	12
Blasius Ind □	8.3	10.1	11.1	-3.3n	-.95	NE	-100.0	-100.0	NC	-29	02-88	.00	.0	0	0	0	00-00-00	-6.6	.53	-3.5	8.26	-28.9	547	4.3	8	3,955	428	0	0.0	05
Carlisle Cos	9.1	9.1	16.6	19.9q	2.39	29.8	29.8	12.2	-5	6	03-88	1.12	3.3	5	49	40	05-12-88	3.6	1.78	6.4	1.67	10.7	15	2.4	274	8,050	3,265	+0	0.4	12
Chariot Grp	2.7	2.7	51.6	.8q	.33	-94.4	-94.4	-17.5	NC	5	03-88	.24	4.8	0	44	19	06-27-88	1.7	1.65	2.8	7.14	20.0	360	1.7	13	2,588	42	0	0.0	12
Charter Crellin	52.0	52.0	55.5	3.0q	1.81	22.9	22.9	41.4	NC	20	03-88	.00	.0	0	0	0	00-00-00	5.4	1.13	6.1	3.34	20.4	137	2.6	25	1,950	161	0	0.0	12
Chelsea Indus	9.4	9.0	5.9	.8s	.32	-100.0	-100.0	-84.6	-21	-2	03-88	.72	4.5	4	97	34	05-27-88	.4	2.25	.9	2.11	1.9	40	2.6	34	2,087	703	0	0.4	09
Component Tech	50.0	50.0	26.6	1.1q	.67	85.7	85.7	116.1	NC	13	03-88	.00	.0	0	0	0	00-00-00	5.8	1.55	9.0	1.49	13.4	13	3.3	18	1,451	411	0	0.0	12
Costar Cp	17.6	17.6	26.3	.9q	.57	NE	NE	533.3	NC	5	02-88	.00	.0	0	0	0	00-00-00	3.8	.92	3.5	1.34	4.7	9	2.7	26	1,702	17	0	0.0	11
CPC Rexcel	95.2	95.2	87.8	4.9q	1.10	170.0	170.0	205.6	NC	35	03-88	.00	.0	0	0	0	00-00-00	7.9	1.27	10.0	3.53	35.3	148	1.6	61	4,400	247	0	0.0	12
ESSEF Cp	50.6	74.5	238.4	5.6s	1.21	-18.6	18.4	NC	NC	17	03-88	.00	.0	0	0	0	00-00-00	4.2	2.02	8.5	2.00	17.0	31	1.7	73	4,884	1,253	0	0.0	09
Fluorocarbon Co	120.8	120.8	108.0	6.2q	1.40	130.0	130.0	35.9	14	11	04-88	.30	1.4	14	28	19	07-11-88	3.0	2.53	7.6	1.87	14.2	58	4.5	93	4,320	1,759	0	0.0	01
Forward Inds	-9.1	-6.6	-7.1	.5f	.44	NE	NE	NE	NC	17	09-87	.00	.0	0	0	20	00-00-00	3.8	2.16	8.2	2.04	16.7	0	1.6	2	1,034	16	0	0.0	09
Himont	53.9	49.5	165.9	276.1s	4.22	68.4	21.8	NC	NC	18	04-88	1.20	2.9	0	9	9	05-04-88	19.3	.95	18.3	1.41	25.8	11	4.6	2,690	64,634	8,545	0	3.4	10
Jesup Grp	660.0	590.2	592.8	-24.4f	-2.01	-100.0	-100.0	-100.0	NC	0	09-87	.00	.0	0	0	0	00-00-00	-6.3	.86	-5.4	.00	NM	917	1.1	58	14,932	1,189	0	0.0	09
Kleer-Vu Ind	-6.5	-8.1	-57.1	-1.7s	-.19	NE	NE	-100.0	NC	-15	06-87	.00	.0	0	NE	38	12-16-85	-14.2	.56	-8.0	1.88	-15.0	35	1.0	4	7,896	480	0	0.1	12
Mark IV ◇	31.9	31.9	41.5	21.2q	2.01	75.0	75.0	48.9	59	23	05-88	.00	.0	0	0	0	02-02-87	4.9	.71	3.5	6.54	22.9	470	5.0	126	10,811	1,759	0	23.8	02
O'Sullivan	.4	.4	5.8	13.1q	1.22	31.8	31.8	82.1	15	15	03-88	.28	1.9b	23	26	26	06-09-88	7.3	1.81	13.2	1.52	20.1	10	2.2	192	13,242	1,621	0	0.0	12
Pantasote Inc	23.2	23.2	23.2	-1.7q	-.43	6.7	6.7	NE	NC	-9	03-88	.00	.0	0	0	0	11-02-81	-1.1	1.64	-1.8	4.72	-8.5	56	1.5	28	3,993	403	0	0.1	12
Plymouth A	-12.0	-12.0	-20.8	-4.7q	-2.52	NE	NE	NE	NC	0	02-88	.00	.0	0	0	0	00-00-00	-12.4	1.77	-21.9	.00	NM	1000	1.1	2	1,659	16	0	4.8	11
Plymouth B	NA	NA	NA	NA	NA	NA	NA	NA	NA	NC	00-00	.00	.0	NA	NA	NA	00-00-00	NA	NC	NA	NC	NA	NA	NA	1	839	14	0	NA	NA
Polymer Intl	-153.0	-19.9	-19.5	3.8f	1.01	-100.0	36.5	36.5	NC	15	03-88	.00	.0	0	0	0	09-03-87	11.5	.69	7.9	1.91	15.1	18	1.9	49	5,304	407	0	0.0	03
Rospatch Cp	-13.8	-13.8	20.8	2.2q	.86	NE	NE	NE	-30	5	03-88	.00	.0	-18	27	55	01-09-87	1.6	1.63	2.6	1.96	5.1	40	2.3	49	2,472	460	0	0.0	12
Rubbermaid	26.9	26.9	27.2	89.6q	1.22	25.0	25.0	19.6	19	15	03-88	.36	1.5	14	28	28	05-09-88	8.3	1.51	12.5	1.65	20.6	9	1.9	1,737	73,504	33,630	+19	3.5	12
SAY Indus	-22.7	-30.7	-34.6	-1.0n	-.75	-100.0	-100.0	-100.0	NC	-6	02-88	.00	.0	0	0	0	00-00-00	-5.9	.75	-4.4	1.30	-5.7	8	5.4	13	5,056	980	0	0.0	05
Schulman, A Inc	30.2	32.2	29.2	23.3s	2.60	7.8	41.1	36.1	18	15	02-88	.58	1.4	17	16	17	04-20-88	4.4	2.48	10.9	1.72	18.7	9	2.5	373	8,928	4,588	-8	0.0	08
Sealed Air	18.4	18.4	39.8	21.5q	2.70	14.9	14.9	17.4	24	12	03-88	.56	1.2	12	20	22	05-27-88	6.8	1.38	9.4	1.62	15.2	15	2.2	380	8,109	4,512	+10	0.0	12
Sun Coast Plastics	396.6	151.8	118.1	.0n	.00	NC	-100.0	-100.0	NC	NC	03-88	.00	.0	0	0	0	00-00-00	.0	NC	NC	NC	.0	127	1.3	16	14,423	207	0	0.0	06
Velcro Industries	16.5	12.0	8.8	3.4s	1.14	38.5	13.7	-30.1	NC	1	03-88	.92	6.3	0	88	46	02-24-88	4.0	.78	3.1	2.16	6.7	44	1.2	44	3,004	167	0	0.0	09
Versa Technol	1.9	10.7	12.1	5.8f	1.49	14.7	35.5	35.5	26	35	03-88	.40	1.6	32	28	18	01-25-88	12.6	1.38	24.9	1.92	47.9	38	2.4	94	3,886	1,367	0	0.0	03
Voplex Corp	-14.5	-14.5	-7.5	-3.0q	-1.11	-28.0	-28.0	NE	NC	-27	03-88	.40	5.8	9	NE	228	04-26-88	-4.1	2.22	-9.1	2.15	-19.6	28	1.7	18	2,642	505	0	0.1	12

Trends and Forecasts: Electronic Computing Equipment (SIC 3573)

(in millions of dollars except as noted)

ITEM	1984	1985	1986[1]	1987[2]	1988[3]	Percent Change: Compound Annual 1972-85	Compound Annual 1980-85	Annual 1985-86	Annual 1986-87	Annual 1987-88
Industry Data										
Value of shipments[4]	53,524	55,315	53,244	57,504	63,254	17.9	15.8	-3.7	8.0	10.0
Total employment (000)	374	356	329	316	332	7.2	3.1	-7.6	-4.0	5.1
Production workers (000)	158	133	115	105	105	5.7	-0.3	-13.5	-8.7	4.8
Average hourly earnings ($)	9.77	10.40	11.20	12.10	—	7.2	8.3	7.7	8.0	—
Product Data										
Value of shipments[5]	49,275	49,998	48,848	47,857	52,642	17.6	14.3	-2.3	-2.0	10.0
Trade Data										
Value of imports (ITA)[6]	7,834	8,285	11,128	13,977	18,170	—	47.7	34.3	25.6	30.0
Value of exports (ITA)[7]	13,511	13,964	14,670	17,443	20,930	19.7	12.9	5.1	18.9	20.0
Export/shipments ratio	0.270	0.237	0.300	0.331	0.361	0.6	-4.3	26.6	10.3	9.1

[1]Estimated except for exports and imports.
[2]Estimated.
[3]Forecast.
[4]Value of all products and services sold by the Electronic Computing Equipment industry.
[5]Value of products classified in the Electronic Computing Equipment industry produced by all industries.
[6]Import data, developed by the chapter author, are on a C.I.F. valuation basis.
[7]Export data are developed by the chapter author.
SOURCE: U.S. Department of Commerce: Bureau of the Census, Bureau of Economic Analysis, International Trade Administration (ITA). Estimates and forecasts by ITA.

Source: *U.S. Industrial Outlook 1988,* U.S. Department of Commerce.

Company	Revenue Pct. Change Last Qtr	Revenue Pct. Change FY to Date	Revenue Pct. Change Last 12 Mos	Earnings Last 12 Mos	Per Share Last 12 Mos	Per Share Pct. Change Last Qtr	Per Share Pct. Change FY to Date	Per Share Pct. Change Last 12 Mos	5-Year Growth Rate	Par Growth Rate	Date of Report	Dividends Current Rate Amt	Current Rate Yield	5-Year Growth Rate	Payout Last FY	Payout Last 5 Yrs.	Last X-Dvd Date	Profit Margin	Asset Turnover	Return on Total Assets	Leverage Ratio	Return on Equity	Debt to Equity	Current Ratio	Market Value	Latest Shares Outstndng.	Held by Banks-Funds	Insider Net Trading	Short Interest Ratio	Fiscal Year Ends
-	%	%	%	$Mil	$	%	%	%	%	%	-	$	%	%	%	%	-	π/r x	r/a =	π/a x	a/e =	π/e	%	-	$Mil	000	000	000	Days	Mo
Computers,Subsystems and Peripherals																														
Ind. Group	29.0	48.7	21.9	10,693.9	2.41	26.2	39.3	45.7	9	10	- - -	.76	2.0	1	11	14	- - - -	7.3	1.07	7.8	1.82	14.2	17	2.2	163,193	4,338,421	G	+1715	1.0	- -
Adaptec Inc	-6.0	2.6	3.5	3.8f	.50	-59.1	-36.7	-36.7	NC	12	03-88	.00	.0	0	0	0	00-00-00	6.4	1.58	10.1	1.20	12.1	0	5.8	42	7,531	2,735	0	0.0	03
Alliant Cptr Syst ▫	13.3	13.3	48.6	2.2q	.21	-86.7	-86.7	-44.7	NC	4	03-88	.00	.0	0	0	0	00-00-00	4.0	.50	2.0	2.05	4.1	84	9.3	62	9,796	866	0	0.0	12
Alloy Cptr	3.7	3.7	7.1	.7q	.14	-94.1	-94.1	-70.8	NC	4	03-88	.00	.0	0	0	0	00-00-00	1.6	1.81	2.9	1.34	3.9	0	3.4	11	4,689	609	0	0.0	12
Alpha Microsysts ▫	3.3	-1.3	-2.1	1.1f	.35	NE	NE	NE	NC	5	02-88	.00	.0	0	0	0	00-00-00	2.4	1.58	3.8	1.42	5.4	0	3.0	20	3,149	307	0	0.0	02
Alpharel Inc	17.3	-85.4	.0	.0*	-1.10	NE	-100.0	-100.0	NC	0	03-88	.00	.0	0	0	0	00-00-00	NC	NC	NC	NC	.0	3	6.6	15	8,990	1,361	0	0.0	12
Amdahl Corp	15.4	15.4	43.2	160.0q	3.04	58.8	58.8	139.4	48	20	03-88	.20	.4	0	7	17	05-10-88	10.3	1.03	10.6	1.97	20.9	13	2.2	2,826	52,336	21,059	-157	1.9	12
Am Magnetic	75.0	75.0	62.5	.9q	.17	NE	NE	NE	NC	4	03-88	.00	.0	0	0	0	00-00-00	6.9	.58	4.0	1.05	4.2	0	29.3	25	4,939	1,253	0	0.0	12
Anderson Jac	-2.0	1.4	.0	-6.6n	-2.44	NE	NE	NE	NC	0	12-87	.00	.0	0	0	0	11-25-83	-16.9	1.95	-33.0	.00	NM	0	.8	4	2,739	152	0	1.8	03
Apogee Robotics	133.3	140.0	50.0	.0n	.02	NE	NE	NE	NC	0	03-88	.00	.0	0	0	0	00-00-00	.0	NC	NC	NC	.0	0	1.3	7	3,277	0	0	0.0	06
Apollo Cptr	36.9	36.9	38.3	25.7q	.71	61.1	61.1	65.1	NC	11	03-88	.00	.0	0	0	0	03-01-84	4.3	1.33	5.7	2.00	11.4	52	3.1	555	36,406	20,796	+6	0.0	12
Apple Cptr	50.7	54.3	51.7	326.2s	2.47	134.6	115.5	104.1	30	34	03-88	.32	.7	0	7	3	05-16-88	9.8	2.26	22.1	1.76	39.0	0	2.7	5,759	124,521	81,607	-6	0.0	09
Appld Data Comm	85.7	21.7	16.6	-3.0n	-1.01	NE	NE	NE	NC	-49	12-87	.00	.0	0	0	0	00-00-00	-42.9	.94	-40.5	1.21	-49.2	0	3.8	3	2,980	966	0	0.0	03
Appld Magnet	26.2	43.5	57.8	18.8s	1.23	18.5	71.4	132.1	20	13	03-88	.00	.0	0	0	0	12-04-87	7.5	1.28	9.6	1.30	12.5	2	3.8	239	14,618	7,649	0	0.3	09
Archive Cp ▫	37.4	38.4	35.0	8.2s	.68	27.3	88.2	385.7	NC	13	03-88	.00	.0	0	0	0	00-00-00	7.9	1.27	10.0	1.27	12.7	1	4.4	78	12,876	5,518	0	0.0	09
AST Research	91.0	94.0	85.7	10.1n	.88	55.2	-28.4	-28.5	NC	10	03-88	.00	.0	0	0	0	00-00-00	3.0	2.33	7.0	1.46	10.2	0	3.3	187	11,695	2,384	0	0.0	06
Atari Cp	159.9	159.9	121.1	40.5q	.70	-37.5	-37.5	18.6	NC	24	03-88	.00	.0	0	0	0	06-22-87	6.8	1.15	7.8	3.10	24.2	80	1.9	456	57,951	6,393	0	10.5	12
Audiotronics Cp	.0	-9.1	-16.6	-1.1n	-.95	-100.0	-100.0	NE	NC	-55	03-88	.00	.0	0	0	NE	07-10-84	-22.0	.64	-14.1	3.90	-55.0	270	15.5	1	1,189	13	0	0.6	06
Automated Systs	12.5	1.1	.0	-1.5n	-.44	-100.0	-100.0	-100.0	NC	-12	03-88	.00	.0	0	0	0	00-00-00	-12.5	.81	-10.1	1.20	-12.1	8	9.0	13	3,159	817	0	0.0	06
BancTec Inc ▫	1.3	9.1	8.1	7.1f	1.24	93.3	72.2	72.2	NC	27	03-88	.00	.0	0	0	0	00-00-00	7.6	1.51	11.5	2.30	26.5	46	2.2	49	6,147	2,736	0	0.0	03
Barrister Inf	-.9	13.2	15.1	.2f	.06	-100.0	-81.3	-81.3	NC	1	03-88	.00	.0	0	0	0	05-21-86	.5	1.40	.7	1.71	1.2	7	2.7	9	3,058	1,086	+12	0.3	03
Barry Wright	6.2	6.2	5.5	6.2q	.76	-65.0	-65.0	-14.6	-11	1	03-88	.60	7.3	9	59	45	04-14-88	3.0	1.50	4.5	1.42	6.4	5	3.0	68	8,263	2,876	0	0.0	12
BGS Systs	25.8	25.8	33.3	1.9q	.64	NE	NE	NC	-3	-10	04-88	1.20	15.0	0	0	0	04-11-88	11.9	.61	7.3	1.49	10.9	1	3.0	23	2,844	686	0	0.0	01
Britton Lee	29.8	29.8	-10.0	-11.7q	-1.44	NE	NE	NE	NC	-98	03-88	.00	.0	0	0	0	00-00-00	-43.3	1.33	-57.4	1.71	-98.3	4	1.9	20	8,167	3,138	0	0.0	12
C 3 Inc	43.3	27.2	27.5	13.4f	1.34	-66.7	211.6	211.6	4	17	03-88	.00	.0	0	0	0	07-14-81	13.1	1.10	14.4	1.17	16.9	0	6.8	115	9,909	4,527	0	0.1	03
C COR Electronics	36.8	19.0	26.9	1.1n	.48	-100.0	34.6	33.3	NC	9	03-88	.00	.0	0	0	0	00-00-00	3.3	1.55	5.1	1.78	9.1	44	3.3	18	2,038	222	0	0.0	06
Check Tech ▫	16.1	24.1	50.0	-.6s	-.12	-100.0	-100.0	NE	NC	-14	03-88	.00	.0	0	0	0	00-00-00	-4.0	1.28	-5.1	2.80	-14.3	36	1.8	15	3,728	42	0	0.0	09
Chips&Technologies	58.3	86.1	110.0	19.8n	1.40	39.3	54.2	70.7	NC	75	03-88	.00	.0	0	0	0	00-00-00	15.7	2.49	39.1	1.92	75.0	4	2.1	259	13,835	1,803	0	0.0	06
Cipher Data	-2.6	-4.8	-8.0	6.4n	.44	88.9	60.9	-10.2	-8	5	03-88	.00	.0	0	0	0	05-25-83	3.7	1.05	3.9	1.18	4.6	2	6.1	144	14,396	8,519	0	0.0	06
Ciprico Inc	40.0	32.5	11.1	-.1s	-.04	NE	NC	-100.0	NC	-1	03-88	.00	.0	0	0	0	01-06-86	-1.0	1.00	-1.0	1.10	-1.1	0	7.7	11	1,969	417	0	0.0	09
CMS Enhancements	55.5	59.4	78.4	1.8n	.22	14.3	-5.0	-8.3	NC	31	03-88	.00	.0	0	0	0	00-00-00	1.3	4.46	5.8	5.26	30.5	0	1.2	29	7,357	48	0	0.0	06
Comdisco Inc	12.2	23.6	34.4	26.4s	.62	-14.3	-100.0	-66.3	11	3	03-88	.24	1.0	19	8	9	05-23-88	2.0	.45	.9	6.33	5.7	100	NA	1,004	41,179	13,866	-62	0.6	09
Comnet Cp	10.8	10.8	10.0	3.0n	1.18	66.7	89.3	145.8	NC	23	12-87	.00	.0	0	0	0	00-00-00	6.8	1.28	8.7	2.68	23.3	34	1.5	24	2,380	674	0	0.0	03
Compaq Cptr	108.3	108.3	109.9	162.9q	4.24	116.1	116.1	138.2	NC	41	03-88	.00	.0	0	0	0	00-00-00	11.2	1.62	18.1	2.25	40.8	37	2.0	2,599	39,905	21,254	-85	6.0	12
CompuScan ◦ •	-54.8	-36.5	-33.3	-6.0n	-1.05	NE	NE	NE	NC	0	02-88	.00	.0	0	0	0	00-00-00	-75.0	.90	-67.4	.00	NM	20	2.0	2	5,581	1,059	0	0.0	05
Comp Automation ▫	16.0	11.6	9.5	.3n	.12	-95.0	-54.3	-78.6	NC	4	03-88	.00	.0	0	0	0	00-00-00	1.3	1.69	2.2	1.86	4.1	1	1.7	16	2,264	69	0	0.0	06

Continued

Company	Revenue Pct. Change Last Qtr	Revenue Pct. Change FY to Date	Revenue Pct. Change Last 12 Mos	Earnings Last 12 Mos	Per Share Last 12 Mos	Per Share Pct. Change Last Qtr	Per Share Pct. Change FY to Date	Per Share Pct. Change Last 12 Mos	5-Year Growth Rate	Par Growth Rate	Date of Report	Dividends Current Rate Amt	Current Rate Yield	5-Year Growth Rate	Payout Last FY	Payout Last 5 Yrs.	Last X-Dvd Date	Profit Margin	Asset Turnover	Return on Total Assets	Leverage Ratio	Return on Equity	Debt to Equity	Current Ratio	Market Value	Latest Shares Outstndng.	Held by Banks-Funds	Insider Net Trading	Short Interest Ratio	Fiscal Year Ends
-	%	%	%	$Mil	$	%	%	%	%	%	-	$	%	%	%	%	-	π/r x	r/a =	π/a x	a/e =	π/e	%	-	$Mil	000	000	000	Days	Mo
Computers,Subsystems and Peripherals (Continued)																														
Comp Consoles ◻	10.1	10.1	5.5	10.7q	.81	133.3	133.3	179.3	NC	33	03-88	.00	.0	0	0	0	07-01-83	7.0	1.00	7.0	4.76	33.3	264	2.5	117	13,408	2,688	-18	0.0	12
Comp Designed	.0	.0	.0	.1s	.03	NC	.0	200.0	NC	3	02-88	.00	.0	0	0	0	00-00-00	3.3	.55	1.8	1.78	3.2	6	1.1	1	3,206	376	0	0.0	08
Comp Entry ◇	-1.1	-1.1	6.8	2.8q	.57	-93.8	-93.8	21.3	28	12	03-88	.00	.0	0	0	0	00-00-00	3.6	1.56	5.6	2.13	11.9	60	3.1	24	4,826	856	0	0.0	12
Comp Memories	-100.0	-97.8	-96.7	-9.6s	-.86	.0	-100.0	NE	NC	-46	09-87	.00	.0	0	0	0	06-01-83	NM	NC	NC	NC	-46.4	0	3.1	21	11,431	877	0	0.0	03
Comp Microfilm	33.3	33.3	30.0	1.0q	.40	180.0	180.0	110.5	NC	22	03-88	.00	.0	0	0	0	07-27-87	7.7	1.45	11.2	1.94	21.7	33	1.8	16	2,573	46	0	0.0	12
Comp Prods	8.8	8.8	2.7	-13.7q	-.69	NE	NE	NE	NC	-38	03-88	.00	.0	0	0	0	04-01-85	-12.3	.85	-10.5	3.63	-38.1	171	2.1	33	19,815	8,494	0	0.0	12
Concurrent Cptr	7.8	12.6	14.8	14.1n	1.23	47.6	131.7	141.2	NC	8	04-88	.00	.0	0	0	0	00-00-00	5.2	1.08	5.6	1.43	8.0	5	2.9	205	11,535	1,328	+2	0.0	07
Control Data ◻	9.8	9.8	2.2	23.2q	.55	-26.7	-26.7	NE	NC	2	03-88	.00	.0	0	0	NE	09-09-85	.7	1.29	.9	2.44	2.2	37	NA	1,104	41,275	25,488	-5	3.2	12
Convergent Inc	13.7	13.7	32.8	-25.7q	-.54	NE	NE	NE	NC	-13	03-88	.00	.0	0	0	0	00-00-00	-6.5	1.42	-9.2	1.45	-13.3	10	2.9	148	49,246	15,828	0	0.0	12
Convex Cptrs ◻	53.5	53.5	67.3	5.0q	.29	-28.6	-28.6	45.0	NC	9	03-88	.00	.0	0	0	0	00-00-00	6.5	.52	3.4	2.65	9.0	123	5.7	141	17,048	4,687	0	0.0	12
Corvus Systs ◻	-11.4	-25.2	-29.2	-7.1n	-.25	NE	NE	NE	NC	0	02-88	.00	.0	0	0	0	00-00-00	-24.5	1.76	-43.0	.00	NS	-100	.7	6	29,660	1,307	0	0.0	05
Cray Research	-31.9	-31.9	-7.4	116.3q	3.71	-52.5	-52.5	-22.4	47	19	03-88	.00	.0	0	0	0	08-19-85	18.8	.69	12.9	1.47	19.0	18	2.8	2,632	30,788	21,506	-35	3.0	12
CSP Inc	4.3	1.4	.0	.3n	.12	.0	-60.0	-14.3	-24	2	05-88	.00	.0	0	0	0	00-00-00	3.0	.50	1.5	1.13	1.7	0	19.9	16	2,743	563	0	0.0	08
Data General ◇◻	10.9	10.2	4.2	-36.5s	-1.42	NE	NE	NE	NC	-6	03-88	.00	.0	0	0	0	11-21-83	-2.7	1.26	-3.4	1.82	-6.2	14	1.6	652	27,594	19,487	-6	7.5	09
Data Measurement	52.2	52.2	20.0	.5q	.42	-60.0	-60.0	-45.5	NC	7	03-88	.00	.0	0	0	0	00-00-00	4.2	1.00	4.2	1.71	7.2	3	2.0	11	1,233	55	0	0.0	12
Data Switch Cp	11.1	11.1	75.4	2.9q	.26	NE	NE	225.0	NC	8	03-88	.00	.0	0	0	0	06-15-83	2.9	.83	2.4	3.17	7.6	123	1.9	87	10,888	2,838	-4	0.0	12
Datacopy	68.2	78.4	85.7	-1.3f	-.18	-100.0	-100.0	-100.0	NC	-13	12-87	.00	.0	0	0	0	00-00-00	-10.0	1.17	-11.7	1.11	-13.0	4	10.8	29	4,810	731	+1	0.0	12
Dataflex	102.6	52.6	53.3	.3f	.16	.0	-54.3	-54.3	NC	9	03-88	.00	.0	0	0	0	05-16-88	1.3	3.15	4.1	2.15	8.8	29	2.1	8	1,844	20	0	0.0	03
Datametrics Cp ◻	26.8	29.9	35.0	1.2s	.22	NC	220.0	69.2	NC	80	04-88	.00	.0	0	0	0	00-00-00	4.4	3.20	14.1	5.67	80.0	47	1.7	9	3,745	191	0	0.0	10
Datapoint Cp ◇	12.2	8.2	5.0	13.5n	-.14	NE	NE	NE	NC	8	04-88	.00	.0	0	0	0	02-09-81	4.1	.80	3.3	2.27	7.5	56	1.8	51	10,263	5,081	0	0.8	07
Dataproducts	12.9	1.9	1.7	-20.2f	-.98	-100.0	-100.0	-100.0	NC	-11	03-88	.16	1.5	1	NE	108	05-27-88	-5.9	1.05	-6.2	1.48	-9.2	7	3.1	210	19,785	11,173	0	0.2	03
Dataram Cp	5.6	-11.8	-6.6	.3f	.16	-100.0	-66.7	-66.7	NC	2	04-88	.00	.0	0	0	0	05-12-80	2.1	.90	1.9	1.16	2.2	0	10.5	14	1,863	296	0	0.1	04
Datarex Systs	38.9	38.9	65.5	1.1q	.61	.0	.0	52.5	NC	18	03-88	.00	.0	0	0	0	00-00-00	2.3	2.26	5.2	3.37	17.5	143	2.9	31	1,766	51	0	5.7	12
Datasouth Cmptr	-7.3	-7.3	-15.7	-.4q	-.07	NE	NE	-100.0	NC	-2	03-88	.00	.0	0	0	0	00-00-00	-2.5	.88	-2.2	1.09	-2.4	0	15.2	10	5,691	248	+0	0.0	12
Datum Inc	-1.5	-1.5	7.6	1.1q	.39	25.0	25.0	8.3	NC	7	03-88	.00	.0	0	0	0	00-00-00	3.9	1.23	4.8	1.44	6.9	12	4.9	13	2,729	734	0	0.0	12
Davox Corp	58.9	58.9	70.5	.3q	.00	-81.3	-81.3	-100.0	NC	NC	03-88	.00	.0	0	0	0	00-00-00	1.0	.90	.9	1.33	1.2	9	3.9	25	5,034	582	-5	0.0	12
Delta Data Systs ◻	26.5	-60.5	.0	.0*	-.25	NE	NE	NE	NC	0	03-88	.00	.0	0	0	0	00-00-00	NC	NC	NC	NC	.0	500	1.1	2	14,351	1,457	0	0.0	09
Dest Cp	8.9	52.6	57.8	-9.4f	-1.23	-100.0	NE	NE	NC	0	03-88	.00	.0	0	0	0	00-00-00	-31.3	1.16	-36.3	.00	NM	53	1.3	24	7,672	1,550	0	0.0	03
DH Tech Inc	-26.8	-26.8	-11.7	2.3q	.48	-71.4	-71.4	.0	NC	18	03-88	.00	.0	0	0	0	00-00-00	15.3	.99	15.2	1.19	18.1	0	5.5	26	4,820	798	0	0.0	12
Digital Equip	17.2	21.1	21.4	1281.8n	9.67	1.3	20.0	28.9	30	20	03-88	.00	.0	0	0	0	05-12-86	11.9	1.28	15.2	1.34	20.4	4	3.4	14,935	130,008	93,196	-23	1.7	06
Distributed Log	317.6	335.5	184.6	-.2s	-.08	NE	NE	NE	NC	-2	04-88	.00	.0	0	0	0	00-00-00	-.5	1.40	-.7	3.14	-2.2	76	1.9	10	2,505	435	0	0.0	10
Duquesne Systs	933.3	149.0	108.0	11.3s	1.05	1150.0	150.0	114.3	52	23	03-88	.00	.0	0	0	0	03-02-87	21.7	.95	20.6	1.14	23.4	0	5.2	201	10,448	3,197	0	0.0	09
ECC Intl Cp ◻	11.6	18.8	22.8	4.3n	.92	9.1	22.8	24.3	15	14	03-88	.20	2.1	0	20	15	06-13-88	10.0	.91	9.1	2.03	18.5	33	4.6	43	4,486	1,715	+0	0.0	06
Ekco Grp	.0	5800.0	.0	1.1f	.05	NE	NE	NE	NC	1	12-87	.00	.0	0	0	0	12-22-80	4.2	.21	.9	1.33	1.2	9	5.3	46	21,535	3,106	0	0.0	12
Elbit Cptr	5.9	6.2	7.1	14.6s	1.08	-56.0	-26.0	-9.2	NC	15	09-87	.14	3.5	0	62	29	04-04-88	8.1	1.12	9.1	1.96	17.8	17	1.9	56	14,020	154	0	0.0	03
Electron Assoc	25.3	25.3	16.6	.1q	.05	-66.7	-66.7	-77.3	NC	1	03-88	.00	.0	0	0	0	00-00-00	.3	1.67	.5	2.20	1.1	38	2.3	9	2,863	258	0	0.0	12
Elron Electronic	-250.0	-75.2	.0	.0*	-.43	NE	NE	NE	NC	0	03-88	.00	.0	0	0	0	01-18-83	NC	NC	NC	NC	.0	61	2.0	32	10,739	334	0	0.0	12

ELXSI Inc	8.1	8.1	18.1	.9q	.01	NC	NC	NE	NC	3	03-88	.00	.0	0	0	0	00-00-00	3.5	.66	2.3	1.48	3.4	3	2.8	25	87,541	7,077	-94	0.0	12
EMC Cp	56.8	56.8	85.5	23.4q	.99	-83.3	-83.3	17.9	NC	19	03-88	.00	.0	0	0	0	09-01-87	16.6	.90	14.9	1.28	19.0	5	6.0	143	23,363	4,759	0	0.4	12
Emulex Cp	22.9	18.8	13.4	6.7n	.54	122.2	116.7	31.7	-4	11	03-88	.00	.0	0	0	0	02-29-84	5.7	1.40	8.0	1.33	10.6	2	4.1	87	12,168	5,036	0	0.0	06
Encore Cptr □	157.1	189.5	180.0	-1.6s	-.08	NE	NE	NE	NC	-25	04-88	.00	.0	0	0	0	00-00-00	-5.7	1.75	-10.0	2.54	-25.4	65	2.4	55	22,531	3,429	0	0.0	10
Esprit Syst	35.7	16.9	10.5	-1.8n	-.25	NE	NE	NC	NC	-86	02-88	.00	.0	0	0	0	00-00-00	-8.6	2.05	-17.6	4.87	-85.7	19	1.2	4	7,629	0	0	0.0	05
Everex Systs	60.6	72.5	79.5	10.3n	.47	-21.4	-10.8	NC	NC	14	04-88	.00	.0	0	0	0	00-00-00	4.3	2.12	9.1	1.54	14.0	1	2.7	141	23,485	3,246	+2512	0.0	07
Filenet Cp	68.5	68.5	87.0	5.3q	.59	180.0	180.0	NC	NC	20	03-88	.00	.0	0	0	0	00-00-00	9.1	1.81	16.5	1.23	20.3	4	6.0	142	9,640	1,630	0	0.0	12
Fingermatrix	.0	.0	-100.0	-4.6q	-.55	NE	NE	NE	NC	0	08-87	.00	.0	0	0	0	00-00-00	NC	NC	NC	NC	NM	0	2.1	32	11,068	516	0	0.0	05
Franklin Cptr	52.2	84.9	83.3	2.8f	.58	87.0	NE	NE	NC	48	03-88	.00	.0	0	0	0	00-00-00	6.4	4.09	26.2	1.81	47.5	47	4.9	67	4,159	140	0	0.0	03
Gandalf Tech	33.9	26.2	22.0	7.8n	.66	12.5	8.9	13.8	6	13	04-88	.00	NA	0	0	0	00-00-00	5.0	1.56	7.8	1.62	12.6	21	2.7	88	12,140	1,929	-300	0.0	07
Gateway Comm	-12.2	-12.2	-14.2	-.1q	-.01	-85.7	-85.7	-100.0	NC	-2	03-88	.00	.0	0	0	0	00-00-00	-.8	1.75	-1.4	1.64	-2.3	0	2.8	13	4,220	487	0	0.0	12
Gen Automation	22.7	24.6	35.1	-2.3n	-.40	-100.0	NE	NE	NC	-21	03-88	.00	.0	0	0	0	00-00-00	-4.6	1.61	-7.4	2.82	-20.9	10	1.6	8	5,456	382	0	0.0	06
Genisco Tech	16.9	10.1	2.5	-6.2s	-2.19	NE	NE	NE	NC	-45	03-88	.00	.0	0	0	0	03-10-81	-15.1	1.40	-21.2	2.12	-44.9	2	1.6	6	2,672	587	0	0.0	09
Gould Inc	11.2	11.2	20.6	-93.1q	-2.07	38.5	38.5	NE	NC	-20	03-88	.00	.0	0	0	NE	06-09-86	-9.7	.81	-7.9	2.47	-19.5	64	2.1	741	44,591	25,157	0	1.2	12
Griffin Tech	12.5	12.5	9.0	-.6q	-.22	NE	NE	-100.0	NC	-15	04-88	.00	.0	0	0	0	00-00-00	-5.0	.96	-4.8	3.13	-15.0	93	1.7	8	2,188	484	0	0.0	01
Hetra Cptr&Comm	-16.7	-25.0	-28.5	-1.2f	-.73	-100.0	-100.0	-100.0	NC	-46	12-87	.00	.0	0	0	0	00-00-00	-24.0	.64	-15.4	3.00	-46.2	100	1.4	1	1,606	133	0	0.0	12
Hewlett-Pack	23.7	24.8	20.5	747.0s	2.95	30.2	41.7	35.3	8	14	04-88	.26	.5	13	9	10	06-16-88	8.3	1.11	9.2	1.62	14.9	2	2.0	14,342	257,251	117,785	-3	1.4	10
Honeywell Inc	17.1	17.1	29.3	267.7q	6.15	41.7	41.7	925.0	-17	8	03-88	2.10	3.0	3	35	41	05-23-88	3.9	1.31	5.1	2.33	11.9	30	1.2	3,014	42,528	29,088	+0	2.4	12
Hutchinson Tech	45.5	55.7	60.0	4.0s	1.01	-42.5	-30.6	-12.2	NC	16	03-88	.00	.0	0	0	0	00-00-00	4.2	2.10	8.8	1.86	16.4	43	2.1	53	3,812	839	+9	0.0	09
Info International ○	.0	-2.0	.0	1.9f	.79	.0	-23.3	-23.3	-7	5	04-88	.22	1.5	4	28	25	07-11-88	5.6	1.04	5.8	1.26	7.3	0	5.0	34	2,237	822	0	0.0	04
Info Science	-26.3	-24.3	-23.5	-4.6n	-.71	NE	NE	NE	NC	0	01-88	.00	.0	0	0	0	00-00-00	-35.4	1.20	-42.6	.00	NM	7	.7	5	4,862	1,216	+2	0.0	04
Infotron Syst	36.4	36.4	14.1	-6.9q	-1.37	NE	NE	NE	NC	-14	03-88	.00	.0	0	0	0	00-00-00	-7.8	1.05	-8.2	1.65	-13.5	0	1.7	66	5,107	2,630	0	0.0	12
Intelligent Electrns	56.2	34.6	45.3	3.3s	.81	58.8	29.4	88.4	NC	23	04-88	.00	.0	0	0	0	00-00-00	3.5	4.20	14.7	1.55	22.8	0	2.8	35	3,417	346	0	0.0	10
Intelligent Sys	-6.1	-6.1	177.5	8.4q	.85	-100.0	-100.0	25.0	NC	-7	03-88	1.15	36.8	0	97	40	12-24-87	5.2	1.71	8.9	2.28	20.3	5	1.8	30	9,658	1,911	0	0.2	12
Intergraph Cp	36.0	36.0	17.0	77.0q	1.35	66.7	66.7	20.5	27	14	03-88	.00	.0	0	0	0	06-17-85	11.2	.97	10.9	1.25	13.6	1	4.1	1,818	56,821	32,739	-67	0.0	12
Intermec Cp	35.7	35.2	34.9	5.2f	.85	61.1	30.8	30.8	5	14	03-88	.00	.0	0	0	0	03-09-83	6.1	1.66	10.1	1.41	14.2	0	3.0	113	6,117	2,377	-15	0.0	03
Intl Bus Mach	80.8	80.8	24.8	5386.0q	8.95	17.7	17.7	20.0	0	7	03-88	4.40	3.5	5	50	45	05-09-88	9.1	.93	8.5	1.66	14.1	10	2.3	76,049	597,052	281,411	+1	2.6	12
Intl Totalizator	-30.3	-30.3	53.3	.9q	.13	-100.0	-100.0	NE	NC	13	03-88	.00	.0	0	0	0	03-24-86	3.9	1.49	5.8	2.31	13.4	7	1.5	16	7,073	516	0	0.0	12
Interphase	53.1	37.1	25.0	1.1s	.40	23.1	-12.5	-27.3	15	12	04-88	.00	.0	0	0	0	00-00-00	7.3	1.22	8.9	1.36	12.1	8	3.6	25	2,653	279	0	0.0	10
Iomega Cp	81.3	81.3	-4.6	-16.2q	-1.09	NE	NE	NE	NC	-63	03-88	.00	.0	0	0	0	00-00-00	-15.7	1.82	-28.6	2.21	-63.3	28	1.7	65	15,252	1,660	+16	0.0	12
IPL Sytems	54.5	54.5	100.0	.8q	.17	-50.0	-50.0	41.7	NC	15	03-88	.00	.0	0	0	0	00-00-00	13.3	.94	12.5	1.21	15.1	0	5.5	11	5,008	95	0	0.0	12
ISC Systems	-2.8	8.2	7.8	9.0n	.58	100.0	68.0	13.7	7	9	03-88	.00	.0	0	0	0	06-18-81	5.1	1.16	5.9	1.53	9.0	20	4.3	100	14,794	4,807	-5	0.0	06
Iverson	132.3	132.3	108.0	4.4q	1.14	93.3	93.3	81.0	NC	47	03-88	.00	.0	0	0	0	03-10-87	8.5	1.76	15.0	3.15	47.3	114	1.6	60	3,781	1,329	0	0.0	12
Kaypro Cp	-32.3	-28.6	-12.7	-13.7s	-.39	-100.0	-100.0	-100.0	NC	-93	02-88	.00	.0	0	0	0	00-00-00	-15.4	2.14	-33.0	2.82	-93.2	50	1.7	23	36,166	599	0	0.0	08
Key Tronic	33.9	31.2	24.5	1.7n	.19	-100.0	NE	NE	-41	3	03-88	.00	.0	0	0	0	00-00-00	1.3	1.54	2.0	1.30	2.6	3	3.4	47	8,819	2,872	0	0.0	06
KNW Systs	29.7	17.5	20.0	.2n	.10	-100.0	-87.5	-77.8	-6	3	03-88	.00	.0	0	0	0	09-22-86	1.1	1.36	1.5	1.67	2.5	11	2.4	9	2,227	340	0	0.1	06
LDI Cp	59.1	59.1	74.3	4.8q	1.09	27.8	27.8	28.2	NC	14	04-88	.00	.0	0	0	0	00-00-00	3.4	.71	2.4	5.83	14.0	289	NA	60	4,667	466	0	0.0	01
Lee Data	-12.3	-11.4	-11.3	-5.1f	-.37	-90.0	-100.0	-100.0	NC	-5	03-88	.00	.0	0	0	0	00-00-00	-5.0	.80	-4.0	1.33	-5.3	10	5.0	40	12,318	3,279	0	0.0	03
Lexicon Cp	9.3	-1.0	-10.5	-2.8s	-.38	-100.0	-100.0	-100.0	NC	-19	02-88	.00	.0	0	0	0	02-10-86	-16.5	.63	-10.4	1.80	-18.7	1	1.6	7	7,491	2,558	0	0.0	08
LSI Logic	32.7	32.7	37.2	13.3q	.34	140.0	140.0	325.0	NC	5	03-88	.00	.0	0	0	0	03-17-86	4.8	.60	2.9	1.83	5.3	43	8.7	502	39,395	18,613	0	0.0	12
LTX	36.1	48.3	45.0	4.2n	.43	NE	NE	NE	NC	8	04-88	.00	.0	0	0	0	03-22-83	2.6	1.35	3.5	2.26	7.9	72	2.6	169	9,507	5,326	0	0.0	07
Mass Cmptr	-5.9	9.2	15.9	3.7n	.24	-85.7	.0	20.0	NC	7	03-88	.00	.0	0	0	0	00-00-00	4.6	1.09	5.0	1.30	6.5	5	4.1	57	14,735	5,592	+29	0.0	06
Masstor Sys	31.9	31.9	10.5	.1q	.05	.0	.0	-28.6	NC	0	03-88	.00	.0	0	0	0	00-00-00	.2	1.50	.3	1.33	.4	8	3.2	37	17,093	3,590	0	0.0	12
Maxtor Cp	59.0	54.7	54.8	14.1f	.72	-8.8	-39.0	-39.0	NC	14	03-88	.00	.0	0	0	0	06-13-86	5.2	1.08	5.6	2.48	13.9	104	5.1	224	19,055	5,457	-13	0.0	03
Megadata Cp	-22.9	-9.8	9.0	1.2s	.57	-33.3	-16.7	23.9	1	14	04-88	.00	.0	0	0	0	12-07-84	10.0	1.17	11.7	1.20	14.0	0	4.7	5	2,105	272	0	0.0	10

Continued

Company	Revenue: Pct. Change Last Qtr	Revenue: Pct. Change FY to Date	Revenue: Pct. Change Last 12 Mos	Earnings: Last 12 Mos	Earnings: Per Share Last 12 Mos	Earnings: Per Share Pct. Change Last Qtr	Earnings: Per Share Pct. Change FY to Date	Earnings: Per Share Pct. Change Last 12 Mos	Earnings: 5-Year Growth Rate	Earnings: Par Growth Rate	Earnings: Date of Report	Dividends: Current Rate Amt	Dividends: Current Rate Yield	Dividends: 5-Year Growth Rate	Dividends: Payout Last FY	Dividends: Payout Last 5 Yrs.	Dividends: Last X-Dvd Date	Ratio Analysis: Profit Margin	Ratio Analysis: Asset Turnover	Ratio Analysis: Return on Total Assets	Ratio Analysis: Leverage Ratio	Ratio Analysis: Return on Equity	Ratio Analysis: Debt to Equity	Ratio Analysis: Current Ratio	Shareholdings: Market Value	Shareholdings: Latest Shares Outstndng.	Shareholdings: Held by Banks-Funds	Shareholdings: Insider Net Trading	Shareholdings: Short Interest Ratio	Shareholdings: Fiscal Year Ends
-	%	%	%	$Mil	$	%	%	%	%	%	-	$	%	%	%	%	-	π/r x	r/a =	π/a x	a/e =	π/e	%	-	$Mil	000	000	000	Days	Mo
Computers,Subsystems and Peripherals (Continued)																														
Micom Syst	22.9	13.6	13.1	9.8f	.52	4.2	-25.7	-25.7	-15	6	03-88	.00	.0	0	0	0	03-14-83	4.4	1.07	4.7	1.21	5.7	3	4.3	290	18,552	8,052	0	0.0	03
Microage Inc	38.5	38.9	37.2	3.9s	.93	78.6	75.9	NE	NC	20	03-88	.00	.0	0	0	0	00-00-00	1.7	4.29	7.3	2.75	20.1	27	1.6	36	4,051	1,108	-39	0.0	09
Micropolis Cp	30.3	30.3	37.0	28.2q	2.48	14.5	14.5	32.6	134	20	03-88	.00	.0	0	0	0	00-00-00	9.2	1.16	10.7	1.89	20.2	54	5.0	206	11,428	8,041	+17	0.0	12
Miltope Grp	14.3	14.3	-5.9	-3.8q	-.64	-57.1	-57.1	-100.0	NC	-19	03-88	.00	.0	0	0	0	00-00-00	-6.0	1.23	-7.4	2.51	-18.6	77	3.1	43	5,961	936	+0	0.0	12
Miniscribe Cp	125.7	125.7	113.5	31.7q	.83	56.3	56.3	43.1	NC	31	03-88	.00	.0	0	0	0	00-00-00	7.2	1.61	11.6	2.70	31.3	97	2.6	349	28,456	15,599	-4	0.0	12
Moniterm	64.7	64.7	142.8	2.1q	.44	.0	.0	NE	NC	31	03-88	.00	.0	0	0	0	00-00-00	6.2	2.08	12.9	2.40	30.9	1	1.6	27	4,039	365	+4	0.0	12
MSI Data	13.3	27.6	26.7	4.9f	.99	64.7	191.2	191.2	NC	16	03-88	.00	.0	0	0	23	04-08-88	5.4	1.85	10.0	1.63	16.3	8	2.5	75	5,191	2,604	0	0.0	03
Natl Compt Sys	-13.0	-13.0	-23.2	18.1q	.99	14.3	14.3	26.9	23	13	04-88	.24	1.8	25	23	19	06-06-88	9.0	.99	8.9	1.96	17.4	45	2.3	236	17,500	7,418	-1	0.0	01
Natl Micronetics	3.0	8.0	.0	.1n	.03	-81.8	NE	NE	NC	1	03-88	.00	.0	0	0	0	07-01-83	.3	1.33	.4	2.75	1.1	90	1.4	23	9,394	635	0	0.0	06
NBI Inc	-53.4	-50.1	-39.2	-11.1n	-4.39	NE	NE	NE	NC	-12	03-88	.00	.0	0	0	0	03-10-81	-6.4	.83	-5.3	2.30	-12.2	59	2.3	39	8,937	4,027	0	5.4	06
NCR	14.3	14.3	15.0	431.9q	4.74	35.4	35.4	33.1	13	15	03-88	1.24	1.9	11	22	24	07-01-88	7.4	1.39	10.3	1.94	20.0	5	1.7	6,042	91,890	49,421	-22	1.7	12
Netwk Systems	48.3	48.3	23.8	19.2q	.66	150.0	150.0	20.0	18	10	03-88	.00	.0	0	0	0	04-16-85	14.8	.59	8.7	1.15	10.0	2	10.1	335	29,173	17,480	-99	0.0	12
Norsk Data	30.2	30.1	44.8	33.4s	.87	-100.0	-100.0	-61.0	NC	12	06-87	.35	NA	0	8	5	05-23-88	8.5	.66	5.6	3.71	20.8	86	1.7	163	18,672	8,692	0	0.0	12
Novell Inc	45.5	58.9	78.1	25.5s	.94	63.2	45.7	-11.3	NC	25	04-88	.00	.0	0	0	0	04-14-87	11.2	1.76	19.7	1.28	25.2	1	3.8	762	26,722	12,652	-300	0.0	10
Opus Computer	40.7	18.6	-7.1	.2s	.08	NE	NE	NE	NC	40	03-88	.00	.0	0	0	0	12-22-83	1.5	2.40	3.6	11.11	40.0	200	.7	2	3,927	22	0	0.0	09
Pacer Cp	-35.7	7.6	12.5	1.4f	.68	82.4	65.9	65.9	NC	22	03-88	.00	.0	0	0	0	00-00-00	15.6	.99	15.4	1.42	21.9	5	4.4	21	2,009	695	0	0.0	03
Par Tech	-14.9	-21.2	-21.9	-2.4f	-.31	-100.0	-100.0	-100.0	NC	-5	12-87	.00	.0	0	0	0	00-00-00	-4.2	.98	-4.1	1.27	-5.2	0	4.4	52	7,730	1,109	0	0.3	12
PDA Engineering	12.7	8.0	9.5	.5n	.12	175.0	19.0	-57.1	-25	4	03-88	.00	.0	0	0	0	00-00-00	2.2	1.09	2.4	1.71	4.1	7	2.1	15	3,841	1,303	0	0.0	06
Perceptronics	38.8	63.7	63.6	-.8n	-.24	11.1	58.3	-100.0	NC	-12	12-87	.00	.0	0	0	0	11-14-85	-1.5	2.13	-3.2	3.72	-11.9	155	2.8	17	3,452	885	0	0.0	03
Personal Cmptr	146.2	107.7	100.0	-.4n	-.14	NE	NE	NE	NC	0	03-88	.00	.0	0	0	0	01-14-88	-5.0	1.54	-7.7	.00	NS	0	9.8	18	3,475	20	0	0.0	06
Priam Cp	3.6	9.3	12.1	-3.6n	-.16	300.0	NE	NE	NC	-10	03-88	.00	.0	0	0	0	00-00-00	-2.6	1.54	-4.0	2.38	-9.5	10	1.3	40	24,311	5,971	0	0.0	06
Primages	-40.0	-34.0	-33.3	-1.2n	-.23	NE	NE	NE	NC	0	09-87	.00	.0	0	0	0	00-00-00	-30.0	.51	-15.4	.00	NM	222	1.6	10	4,517	0	0	0.0	12
Prime Computer	64.1	64.1	24.6	67.4q	1.38	25.0	25.0	35.3	8	15	03-88	.00	.0	0	0	0	06-13-83	6.1	1.61	9.8	1.57	15.4	3	2.9	745	48,075	33,031	-27	7.8	12
Printronix	21.6	1.1	.8	.9f	.20	NE	NE	NE	NC	2	03-88	.00	.0	0	0	0	00-00-00	.7	1.57	1.1	1.36	1.5	0	3.3	47	4,581	1,284	+5	0.0	03
Pyramid Tech	50.0	48.0	43.4	4.9s	.58	380.0	4500.0	NE	NC	10	03-88	.00	.0	0	0	0	00-00-00	7.4	1.07	7.9	1.24	9.8	2	4.9	120	7,986	1,471	0	0.0	09
Qantel Cp ◦	-7.5	-12.8	-12.5	9.1f	.56	22.2	86.7	86.7	NC	0	04-88	.00	.0	0	0	0	00-00-00	11.8	1.54	18.2	.00	NS	-123	NA	18	16,184	1,022	0	0.0	04
QMS Inc	84.5	65.1	60.0	7.7s	.82	31.6	-27.0	-4.7	24	14	03-88	.00	.0	0	0	0	09-17-84	5.1	1.33	6.8	2.03	13.8	25	2.2	81	9,489	2,730	0	23.9	09
Quantum Cp	32.0	56.0	56.1	-3.2f	-.35	-100.0	-100.0	-100.0	NC	-3	03-88	.00	.0	0	0	0	00-00-00	-1.7	1.35	-2.3	1.30	-3.0	0	6.3	103	9,171	4,853	0	0.0	03
Recog Equip	1.8	4.5	5.8	6.4s	.61	-100.0	-100.0	-41.9	NC	5	04-88	.00	.0	0	0	0	00-00-00	2.4	1.04	2.5	1.92	4.8	44	3.0	82	9,933	4,733	0	3.2	10
Rexon Inc	45.0	38.1	60.8	7.9s	.72	37.5	34.5	63.6	NC	15	03-88	.00	.0	0	0	0	00-00-00	6.6	1.36	9.0	1.63	14.7	17	2.5	71	10,163	2,195	+392	0.0	09
Rodime plc	.4	.4	-23.4	-9.4q	-1.20	NE	NE	NE	NC	-14	12-87	.00	.0	0	0	0	00-00-00	-13.1	.72	-9.4	1.45	-13.6	6	3.5	23	7,881	306	0	0.0	09
SBE Inc	55.0	47.5	37.5	.7s	.02	-100.0	-50.0	-50.0	NC	19	04-88	.00	.0	0	0	0	00-00-00	6.4	2.23	14.3	1.32	18.9	0	2.7	6	16,593	165	-55	0.0	10
Scan Optics	25.8	25.8	45.1	-1.5q	-.23	-75.0	-75.0	-100.0	NC	-4	03-88	.00	.0	0	0	0	00-00-00	-3.3	.88	-2.9	1.41	-4.1	6	3.4	29	6,295	1,744	+55	0.0	12

Sci Micro	17.7	17.7	67.1	-7.3q	-.83	-100.0	-100.0	-100.0	NC	-22	03-88	.00	.0	0	0	0	00-00-00	-5.7	1.53	-8.7	2.52	-21.9	0	1.4	16	8,898	1,490	+15	0.0	12
Seagate Tech	27.0	26.8	35.0	97.9n	1.96	-43.2	-41.1	-18.7	52	28	03-88	.00	.0	0	0	0	06-10-83	8.5	1.41	12.0	2.31	27.7	85	6.0	878	48,759	22,257	0	0.0	06
Selecterm Inc	6.8	6.8	-4.1	1.3q	.48	283.3	283.3	152.6	-18	7	03-88	.00	.0	0	0	0	00-00-00	5.7	1.12	6.4	1.09	7.0	0	NA	13	2,601	237	0	0.0	12
Sequent Cptr Systs	89.3	89.3	80.0	3.3q	.42	9.1	9.1	NE	NC	8	03-88	.00	.0	0	0	0	00-00-00	7.3	.88	6.4	1.20	7.7	2	5.4	132	7,711	1,076	0	0.0	12
Sigma Designs	42.2	42.2	45.7	6.1q	1.25	38.5	38.5	68.9	139	38	04-88	.00	.0	0	0	0	03-11-87	12.0	2.08	25.0	1.54	38.4	0	2.9	90	4,430	1,069	0	0.0	01
Star Technologies	-27.0	-19.0	-18.1	2.2f	.15	-33.3	50.0	50.0	NC	55	03-88	.00	.0	0	0	0	00-00-00	6.1	1.26	7.7	7.14	55.0	350	1.8	33	15,346	2,086	0	0.0	03
Storage Technl	3.1	3.1	4.7	31.2q	.16	.0	.0	-63.6	NC	0	03-88	.00	.0	0	0	0	00-00-00	4.1	.85	3.5	.00	NS	-2847	2.4	456	228,090	62,946	0	2.3	12
Stratus Cptr	44.9	44.9	48.8	21.6q	1.07	52.6	52.6	46.6	NC	21	03-88	.00	.0	0	0	0	00-00-00	10.7	1.39	14.9	1.42	21.1	6	3.1	556	19,166	10,860	+10	0.0	12
Symbol Tech	85.8	114.6	116.2	17.5n	.97	200.0	239.1	361.9	NC	20	03-88	.00	.0	0	0	0	06-01-88	21.9	.79	17.3	1.16	20.1	5	9.2	401	18,004	11,112	+15	0.7	06
Syntech Intl	-135.4	821.4	.0	.0*	.07	80.0	1500.0	NE	NC	0	03-88	.00	.0	0	0	NE	00-00-00	NC	NC	NC	NC	.0	11	2.8	35	9,286	1,513	0	0.0	12
System Indus	20.8	16.5	14.5	4.6n	.94	-6.9	-14.7	-6.9	NC	14	04-83	.00	.0	0	0	0	06-24-81	3.4	1.85	6.3	2.27	14.3	20	1.7	28	4,920	1,367	+32	0.0	07
Systems Integr	24.3	8.1	-8.9	4.5s	.37	120.0	14.3	-47.1	3	-15	03-88	1.20	15.7	0	0	0	06-27-88	7.4	.72	5.3	1.25	6.6	0	5.8	92	12,082	2,580	0	0.0	09
Tab Products	10.0	7.4	5.6	7.4n	1.11	22.2	15.5	12.1	9	11	02-88	.20	1.3	33	20	16	05-19-88	5.6	1.95	10.9	1.28	13.9	2	3.6	100	6,608	2,433	0	5.7	05
Tandem Cptr	27.6	23.2	27.1	103.1s	1.03	.0	-9.6	7.3	23	14	03-88	.00	.0	0	0	0	06-15-87	9.0	1.19	10.7	1.34	14.3	1	3.6	1,907	94,185	69,519	-85	2.1	09
Tandon Cp	-470.2	-62.5	.0	.0*	.38	NE	NE	NE	NC	0	03-88	.00	.0	0	0	0	04-13-83	NC	NC	NC	NC	.0	4	2.5	133	59,183	4,717	0	0.0	12
TEC Inc	-71.4	-51.7	-41.6	-1.0s	-1.06	NE	NE	NE	NC	-28	12-87	.00	.0	0	0	NE	09-08-86	-14.3	1.27	-18.2	1.53	-27.8	6	1.2	3	856	8	0	0.0	06
Tech Data	74.5	74.5	87.0	5.2q	1.09	100.0	100.0	87.9	NC	48	04-88	.00	.0	0	0	0	05-01-87	3.0	6.80	20.4	2.36	48.1	9	1.7	76	4,778	722	0	0.0	01
Teknowledge Inc	-20.0	-23.4	-5.5	-11.9n	-1.68	NE	-100.0	-100.0	NC	-26	03-88	.00	.0	0	0	0	00-00-00	-70.0	.35	-24.3	1.08	-26.2	0	12.1	31	7,188	286	0	0.0	06
Telematics Intl	40.0	40.0	70.3	7.3q	.45	100.0	100.0	114.3	NC	13	03-88	.00	.0	0	0	0	00-00-00	15.9	.73	11.6	1.13	13.1	0	8.1	196	15,840	4,194	0	0.0	12
TeleVideo Sys	22.5	12.1	11.8	-20.1s	-.43	-100.0	-100.0	NE	NC	-18	04-88	.00	.0	0	0	0	00-00-00	-19.3	.68	-13.1	1.35	-17.7	0	2.8	57	47,655	1,421	0	0.0	10
Telex Corp	7.8	8.9	11.2	75.4s	5.10	-22.7	-6.9	3.9	33	22	09-87	.00	.0	0	0	0	00-00-00	8.6	1.42	12.2	1.76	21.5	28	NA	719	14,675	5,074	0	4.0	03
Telxon Cp	34.4	22.9	22.7	13.9f	1.04	14.8	14.3	14.3	40	20	03-88	.00	.0	0	0	1	05-13-86	11.2	1.37	15.3	1.31	20.1	1	4.0	285	12,822	7,607	+19	0.0	03
Tempest Tech	26.1	40.1	36.8	4.5f	.61	75.0	60.5	NC	NC	87	03-88	.00	.0	0	0	0	00-00-00	17.3	3.72	64.3	1.35	86.5	0	3.6	42	8,000	1,225	0	0.0	03
Terminal Data	4.4	7.0	-10.3	-.1s	-.02	NE	-54.5	NE	NC	-1	03-88	.00	.0	0	0	0	01-22-85	-.4	1.00	-.4	1.75	-.7	35	4.6	11	4,492	660	0	0.0	09
Three Com	117.8	122.7	111.2	18.3n	.73	4.5	-5.4	2.8	NC	24	02-88	.00	.0	0	0	0	00-00-00	8.8	2.34	20.6	1.17	24.0	0	6.8	553	27,136	13,664	0	0.0	05
Tigera Grp	100.0	100.0	-96.4	-15.0q	-.72	NE	NE	NE	NC	-37	03-88	.00	.0	0	0	0	00-00-00	NM	NC	NC	NC	-37.1	1	4.2	30	20,920	2,609	0	0.0	12
Titan Cp	3.1	3.1	1.6	.2q	.00	-88.9	-88.9	-100.0	NC	NC	03-88	.00	.0	0	0	0	00-00-00	.2	1.00	.2	2.00	.4	19	3.2	40	12,794	2,387	0	0.0	12
TRW Inc	6.7	6.7	11.1	258.9q	4.27	31.3	31.3	24.9	NC	11	03-88	1.60	3.3	5	40	54	05-09-88	3.7	1.59	5.9	3.10	18.3	61	1.3	2,925	59,700	37,249	+93	3.0	12
Ultimate Cp	39.6	23.3	22.9	13.0f	1.32	-100.0	-7.7	-7.7	NC	15	04-88	.00	.0	0	0	0	09-16-83	6.2	1.18	7.3	2.00	14.6	6	2.1	130	9,839	4,803	0	30.8	04
Unisys Cp	-33.3	-33.3	2.2	617.1q	3.35	35.1	35.1	NE	NC	14	03-88	1.00	2.8	0	28	56	06-17-88	6.9	.90	6.2	3.19	19.8	62	1.3	5,683	158,964	104,858	+1	4.6	12
Valid Logic	84.5	84.5	31.0	-6.2q	-.02	NE	NE	NE	NC	-14	03-88	.00	.0	0	0	0	00-00-00	-8.2	1.11	-9.1	1.49	-13.6	8	2.7	108	17,654	4,323	0	0.0	12
Verdix Cp	57.1	18.5	20.0	.1f	.01	200.0	NE	NE	NC	5	03-88	.00	.0	0	0	0	00-00-00	1.7	.82	1.4	3.21	4.5	14	.4	11	7,739	813	0	0.0	03
Vermont Resch	8.3	-17.9	-20.0	-4.0s	-2.03	NE	NE	NE	NC	0	03-88	.00	.0	0	0	NE	12-02-82	NM	NC	NC	NC	NM	0	2.4	3	2,006	177	0	0.0	09
Wang Labs B	2.9	11.6	12.4	111.3n	.69	250.0	NE	NE	NC	6	03-88	.16	1.5	14	NE	26	06-21-88	3.6	1.11	4.0	1.88	7.5	45	1.9	1,787	162,464	73,927	+1	1.7	06
Wang Labs C	NA	NA	NA	NA	NA	NA	NA	NA	NA	NC	00-00	.11	1.0	NA	NA	NA	06-21-88	NA	NC	NA	NC	NA	NA	NA	565	50,776	78	0	NA	NA
Wells American	40.6	89.2	128.5	.5n	.11	.0	NE	NE	NC	8	12-87	.00	.0	0	0	0	00-00-00	3.1	1.94	6.0	1.27	7.6	5	4.5	7	4,956	337	0	40.2	03
Wespercorp	-42.9	-52.2	-50.0	-.1n	-.03	NE	NE	NE	NC	0	03-88	.00	.0	0	0	NE	01-26-83	-2.0	1.60	-3.2	.00	NS	-7	.5	1	3,586	34	0	1.6	06
Wicat Systs	9.3	40.0	39.2	-4.9f	-.23	NE	NE	NE	NC	-15	03-88	.00	.0	0	0	0	00-00-00	-12.6	.98	-12.4	1.23	-15.3	1	3.6	54	21,114	2,092	0	0.0	03
Wiland Services	22.6	22.6	.0	.3q	.09	NE	NE	NE	NC	6	03-88	.00	.0	0	0	0	00-00-00	1.9	1.11	2.1	2.81	5.9	110	1.4	6	3,564	426	0	0.0	12
Wyse Technology	83.7	72.9	75.4	25.3n	1.79	25.6	26.6	28.8	NC	27	12-87	.00	.0	0	0	0	00-00-00	6.4	1.72	11.0	2.49	27.4	93	4.6	283	14,339	8,381	0	0.0	03
Xebec	-72.4	-72.4	-57.3	-41.7q	-3.16	NE	NE	NE	NC	0	12-87	.00	.0	0	0	0	07-11-83	-85.1	1.40	-19.1	.00	NM	56	1.1	4	13,210	282	0	0.0	09
XL Datacomp	40.7	46.9	61.2	8.5s	1.11	20.0	163.0	50.0	NC	22	03-88	.00	.0	0	0	0	05-29-87	4.5	1.36	6.1	3.62	22.1	0	1.7	186	6,836	2,840	+1	0.0	09
Xylogics Inc	16.9	30.2	50.0	3.8s	1.21	17.4	43.9	65.8	NC	18	04-88	.00	.0	0	0	0	00-00-00	12.7	1.04	13.2	1.36	18.0	7	4.2	30	2,923	592	0	0.0	10
Zentec Corp	-29.4	-29.4	-10.0	-1.1q	-.36	-100.0	-100.0	-100.0	NC	-14	03-88	.00	.0	0	0	0	00-00-00	-4.1	1.39	-5.7	2.39	-13.6	2	5.5	4	3,515	397	0	0.0	12
Zitel Cp	38.9	68.3	18.7	1.0s	.20	NE	NE	NE	NC	13	03-88	.00	.0	0	0	0	00-00-00	5.3	1.57	8.3	1.54	12.8	9	2.9	12	4,933	663	0	0.0	09
Zycad Cp	10.8	10.8	21.4	2.9q	.19	33.3	33.3	NE	NC	9	03-88	.00	.0	0	0	0	00-00-00	8.5	.75	6.4	1.33	8.5	0	3.6	64	14,734	2,595	0	0.0	12

Value of New Construction Put in Place

(in billions of 1982 dollars except as noted)

TYPE OF CONSTRUCTION	1977	1982	1984	1985	1986	1987[1]	1988[2]	Percent Change 1986-87	Percent Change 1987-88
TOTAL	295.9	246.6	308.8	324.8	347.8	344.0	344.5	−1.1	0.2
Residential	148.3	84.7	144.4	145.8	168.6	171.9	174.2	2	1
Single-family	100.2	41.5	80.4	79.2	92.0	97.5	99.5	6	2
Multifamily	16.2	15.5	26.5	26.3	28.0	22.4	20.2	−20	−10
Home improvement	32.0	27.7	37.5	40.3	48.6	52.0	54.6	7	5
Private nonresidential	87.1	108.1	108.1	120.8	114.9	106.1	102.5	− 8	−3
Manufacturing facilities	12.2	17.3	12.7	14.1	12.0	10.5	11.0	−12	5
Office	8.4	23.0	23.9	28.3	25.0	20.5	17.4	−18	−15
Hotels & motels	1.5	4.1	6.2	6.6	6.5	6.0	5.4	−8	−10
Other Commercial	15.1	14.2	20.4	25.2	24.7	22.5	22.0	−9	−2
Religious	1.7	1.5	2.0	2.2	2.4	2.3	2.3	−4	0
Educational	1.1	1.5	1.5	1.7	2.0	2.7	2.8	35	5
Hospital & institutional	5.2	5.9	5.8	5.0	4.7	5.1	5.4	9	5
Misc. buildings	1.9	1.7	2.3	2.4	2.4	2.6	2.6	10	0
Telephone & telegraph	6.3	7.1	6.8	7.0	7.7	7.5	7.8	−3	5
Railroads	2.0	2.6	3.4	3.7	2.8	2.5	2.4	−10	−3
Electric utilities	17.1	18.3	14.8	14.9	15.7	14.9	14.2	−5	−5
Gas utilities	3.8	5.5	4.2	5.0	4.8	4.9	5.0	2	2
Petroleum pipelines	1.8	0.4	0.3	0.3	0.3	0.3	0.3	0	10
Farm structures	7.0	3.7	2.9	2.0	1.8	1.7	1.6	−8	−5
Misc. structures	2.0	1.3	1.9	2.5	2.1	2.1	2.1	0	0
Public works	60.5	53.8	55.3	58.2	64.4	66.0	67.8	2	3
Housing & redevelopment	1.5	1.7	1.5	1.4	1.3	1.4	1.4	8	0
Federal industrial	1.3	1.6	1.7	1.8	1.5	1.4	1.5	−5	5
Educational	8.7	5.9	5.1	6.0	7.4	7.4	7.8	0	5
Hospital	2.8	2.0	1.9	1.8	1.8	1.8	1.9	0	5
Other public buildings	5.8	5.8	6.3	7.1	8.7	9.7	10.1	11	5
Highways	16.6	16.3	18.4	19.0	20.2	19.6	20.2	−3	3
Military facilities	2.2	2.2	2.7	2.9	3.4	3.5	3.4	3	−4
Conservation & development	5.8	5.0	4.5	4.6	4.4	4.8	4.4	8	−8
Sewer systems	8.0	5.5	6.1	6.9	7.7	8.5	9.1	10	7
Water supplies	2.7	2.9	2.6	2.6	3.2	3.3	3.5	3	5
Misc. public structures	5.3	4.9	4.5	4.1	4.8	4.7	4.7	−2	0

[1]Estimated.
[2]Forecast.
Note: Detail may not sum to totals due to rounding.

SOURCE: U.S. Department of Commerce; Bureau of the Census and Internationl Trade Administration (ITA). Estimates and forecasts by ITA.

Source: *U.S. Industrial Outlook 1988,* U.S. Department of Commerce.

Company	Revenue Pct. Change Last Qtr	Revenue Pct. Change FY to Date	Revenue Pct. Change Last 12 Mos	Earnings Last 12 Mos	Per Share Last 12 Mos	Per Share Pct. Change Last Qtr	Per Share Pct. Change FY to Date	Per Share Pct. Change Last 12 Mos	5-Year Growth Rate	Par Growth Rate	Date of Report	Dividends Current Rate Amt	Current Rate Yield	5-Year Growth Rate	Payout Last FY	Payout Last 5 Yrs.	Last X-Dvd Date	Profit Margin	Asset Turnover	Return on Total Assets	Leverage Ratio	Return on Equity	Debt to Equity	Current Ratio	Market Value	Latest Shares Outstndng.	Held by Banks-Funds	Insider Net Trading	Short Interest Ratio	Fiscal Year Ends
-	%	%	%	$Mil	$	%	%	%	%	%	-	$	%	%	%	%	-	π/r	x r/a =	π/a	x a/e =	π/e	%	-	$Mil	000	000	000	Days	Mo
Residential Construction																														
Ind. Group	13.1	16.1	16.9	176.3	.45	- 100.0	- 64.5	- 19.1	14	3	- - -	.28	3.3	0	19	17	- - - -	2.0	.75	1.5	5.47	8.2	128	2.3	2,972	352,064	53,152	+ 45	6.1	- -
Am Continental □	-23.9	-23.9	-22.3	8.9q	.14	-92.6	-92.6	-89.9	-1	11	03-88	.00	.0	0	0	1	05-11-87	1.3	.15	.2	54.50	10.9	996	NA	123	17,547	682	-6	0.0	12
Anthony Ind	.9	.9	10.8	7.6q	1.67	20.0	20.0	288.4	16	11	03-88	.44	3.0	8	26	31	05-31-88	2.9	2.03	5.9	2.64	15.6	59	2.1	64	4,414	1,096	+58	36.5	12
BEI Holding	-19.4	-27.1	-46.4	2.7s	.27	-15.4	-95.0	NE	NC	1	04-88	.24	3.5	0	26	23	03-15-88	7.1	.72	5.1	1.25	6.4	11	NA	63	9,096	1,275	0	0.0	10
Calprop Cp	300.0	300.0	108.3	4.0q	1.05	1450.0	1450.0	54.4	5	12	03-88	.00	.0	0	0	0	11-13-87	5.3	1.28	6.8	1.79	12.2	11	NA	33	3,792	523	0	0.0	12
Calton Inc	46.5	46.5	16.5	24.6q	.66	125.0	125.0	61.0	NC	31	02-88	.00	.0	0	0	0	08-25-87	14.6	.82	11.9	2.63	31.3	98	NA	149	38,360	2,916	0	0.1	11
Cavalier Homes	-1.7	-1.7	171.4	1.1q	.52	-100.0	-100.0	26.8	NC	16	03-88	.00	.0	0	0	0	00-00-00	1.2	5.42	6.5	2.45	15.9	35	1.6	10	2,052	87	0	0.0	12
Centex Cp □	27.9	12.0	11.9	24.1f	1.50	-15.4	-39.3	-39.3	NC	6	03-88	.25	.9	0	17	11	06-09-88	1.7	1.35	2.3	2.87	6.6	49	NA	406	15,036	8,646	0	0.9	03
Comm & Cable	1000.0	1000.0	41.1	-1.1q	-.11	NE	NE	-100.0	NC	-15	01-88	.00	.0	0	0	0	00-00-00	-4.6	.50	-2.3	6.48	-14.9	436	NA	24	9,733	221	0	0.0	10
Contl Homes □	15.2	3.5	3.9	2.7f	.72	33.3	-54.4	-54.4	NC	12	05-88	.00	.0	0	0	0	00-00-00	2.0	1.30	2.6	4.69	12.2	150	NA	12	3,692	347	0	0.0	05
Gen Homes	-23.6	-15.5	-25.0	-119.0s	-7.93	NE	NE	-100.0	NC	-87	03-88	.00	.0	0	0	0	00-00-00	-39.4	.54	-21.3	4.08	-86.9	102	NA	23	15,009	873	0	12.7	09
Hovnanian Ent	3.6	5.0	4.8	26.2f	1.24	35.0	40.9	40.9	62	38	02-88	.00	.0	0	0	0	04-14-87	8.7	1.08	9.4	4.05	38.1	70	NA	196	20,938	2,627	0	0.0	02
Kauf Broad Ho	104.3	68.1	43.1	43.0s	1.59	75.0	65.9	31.4	NC	18	05-88	.30	2.6	0	15	6	05-10-88	5.1	1.55	7.9	2.87	22.7	83	NA	317	27,004	869	0	41.2	11
Key Co A	NA	NA	NA	NA	NA	NA	NA	NA	NA	NC	00-00	.00	.0	NA	NA	NA	00-00-00	NA	NC	NA	NC	NA	NA	NA	2	1,129	6	0	NA	NA
Key Co B	-33.7	-33.7	-8.5	-2.3q	-1.38	-100.0	-100.0	-100.0	NC	-30	01-88	.20	80.0	-8	NE	39	06-22-8[illegible]	-5.3	1.83	-9.7	2.66	-25.8	0	1.5	0	1,129	51	0	45.8	10
Lennar Corp	7.8	12.8	25.4	25.1s	2.57	-6.3	6.1	29.8	32	11	05-88	.24	1.2	2	9	15	08-01-8[illegible]	7.2	.65	4.7	2.60	12.2	85	NA	192	9,931	3,391	+5	0.7	11
Levitt Cp	-7.4	-7.4	7.2	1.9q	.58	-25.0	-25.0	-10.8	NC	7	03-88	.00	.0	0	0	0	00-00-00	1.8	1.00	1.8	3.94	7.1	249	NA	17	3,400	190	0	3.0	12
Linc Logs	-4.3	34.8	35.7	.7f	.50	NE	100.0	100.0	NC	13	01-88	.05	1.0b	0	0	0	05-09-88	3.7	2.08	7.7	1.90	14.6	17	1.3	7	1,328	0	0	0.0	01
Lindal Cedar	47.5	47.5	68.0	1.9q	1.07	100.0	100.0	50.7	74	23	03-88	.00	.0	0	0	0	02-17-88	4.5	2.53	11.4	2.04	23.2	16	1.5	19	1,901	76	0	0.0	12
M I Schottenstein	38.0	38.0	43.6	4.8q	.79	18.2	18.2	11.3	NC	45	03-88	.00	.0	0	0	0	00-00-00	3.0	3.13	9.4	4.82	45.3	253	NA	36	5,965	112	0	0.0	12
Natl Enterpr	-13.9	-13.9	2.3	-5.1q	-.83	NE	NE	-100.0	NC	-31	03-88	.00	.0	0	0	0	00-00-00	-5.8	1.43	-8.3	3.70	-30.7	104	1.5	12	7,138	557	0	0.0	12
NVRyan	17.6	17.6	136.8	26.3q	.95	633.3	633.3	20.3	NC	10	03-88	.64	8.8	0	62	23	03-25-88	2.9	1.41	4.1	7.80	32.0	364	2.3	176	24,213	315	0	0.0	12
Oriole Hms A	2.2	2.2	18.0	7.4q	1.89	166.7	166.7	145.5	35	12	03-88	.45	4.2	-18	23	51	03-07-88	6.3	.86	5.4	2.89	15.6	80	NA	21	1,956	210	0	0.0	12
Oriole Hms B	NA	NA	NA	NA	NA	NA	NA	NA	NA	NC	00-00	.50	4.5	NA	NA	NA	03-07-88	NA	NC	NA	NC	NA	NA	NA	22	1,984	70	0	NA	NA
Ryland Grp	-9.1	-9.1	15.3	31.7q	2.42	-8.5	-8.5	5.7	35	19	03-88	.50	3.0	17	16	21	07-11-88	3.8	2.18	8.3	2.86	23.7	74	3.2	214	12,682	8,536	0	0.2	12
Std Pacific	12.2	15.4	69.3	39.9n	1.52	73.9	55.4	NC	NC	6	09-87	1.20	12.0	0	22	22	02-02-88	11.8	1.08	12.8	2.20	28.1	72	3.5	269	26,908	7,896	0	0.2	12
Toll Bros	57.6	50.3	20.7	20.8s	.69	50.0	52.2	32.7	NC	43	04-88	.00	.0	0	0	0	04-21-87	12.8	.89	11.4	3.74	42.6	0	1.4	192	30,067	3,030	-12	0.0	10
US Home	-12.5	-12.5	-.3	-47.0q	-1.18	-80.0	-80.0	NE	NC	-27	03-88	.00	.0	0	0	NE	08-27-84	-6.2	1.05	-6.5	4.12	-26.8	142	NA	120	39,895	6,316	0	1.7	12
UDC Univ Dev	29.7	29.7	13.8	34.9q	3.22	5.0	5.0	16.7	53	9	03-88	2.40	12.7	0	69	64	06-09-88	14.1	.99	13.9	2.63	36.5	124	NA	176	9,327	1,432	0	1.1	12
Valley Forge	-19.2	-19.2	-15.1	1.7q	1.02	-14.6	-14.6	25.9	43	8	03-88	.22	2.5	0	17	18	05-27-88	6.1	1.00	6.1	1.69	10.3	47	4.1	15	1,697	15	0	0.0	12
Wash Homes	-8.0	7.1	9.3	8.8n	1.87	-5.6	5.0	13.3	NC	22	04-88	.16	1.2	0	0	0	05-31-88	9.4	1.05	9.9	2.44	24.2	67	NA	65	4,741	787	0	39.5	07
General Contractors																														
Ind. Group	- 4.4	.6	.9	109.9	.51	NE	NE	NE	NC	2	- - -	.31	1.6	0	67	64	- - - -	.9	1.78	1.6	3.25	5.2	38	1.4	4,088	206,778	68,578	- 12	.7	- -
Am Med Bldg	12.4	64.2	62.0	-3.5f	-.30	NE	NE	NE	NC	-88	12-87	.00	.0	0	0	0	07-20-83	-7.4	3.47	-25.7	3.40	-87.5	0	1.1	13	12,925	963	0	0.4	12
Black Ind	-14.3	-1.9	-8.3	.7s	.75	-100.0	53.8	-14.8	14	6	03-88	.20	1.9	15	51	28	12-18-87	6.4	1.25	8.0	1.10	8.8	0	9.3	9	831	63	0	0.0	09
Blount Inc A	25.1	25.1	1.7	5.9q	.49	-94.4	-94.4	-36.4	-22	0	05-88	.45	2.8	11	68	39	06-09-88	.5	2.00	1.0	4.10	4.1	108	1.2	118	7,312	3,624	0	1.3	02

Continued

Company	Revenue Pct. Change Last Qtr	Revenue Pct. Change FY to Date	Revenue Pct. Change Last 12 Mos	Earnings Last 12 Mos	Earnings Per Share Last 12 Mos	Earnings Per Share Pct. Change Last Qtr	Earnings Per Share Pct. Change FY to Date	Earnings Per Share Pct. Change Last 12 Mos	Earnings 5-Year Growth Rate	Earnings Par Growth Rate	Earnings Date of Report	Dividends Current Rate Amt	Dividends Current Rate Yield	Dividends 5-Year Growth Rate	Dividends Payout Last FY	Dividends Payout Last 5 Yrs.	Dividends Last X-Dvd Date	Ratio Analysis Pro-fit Mar-gin	Ratio Analysis Asset Turn-over	Ratio Analysis Return on Total Assets	Ratio Analysis Lever-age Ratio	Ratio Analysis Return on Equity	Ratio Analysis Debt to Eq-uity	Ratio Analysis Curr-ent Ratio	Shareholdings Mar-ket Value	Shareholdings Latest Shares Out-stndng.	Shareholdings Held by Banks-Funds	Shareholdings Insider Net Trad-ing	Shareholdings Short Int-erest Ratio	Shareholdings Fiscal Year Ends
-	%	%	%	$Mil	$	%	%	%	%	%	-	$	%	%	%	%	-	π/r x	r/a =	π/a x	a/e =	π/e	%	-	$Mil	000	000	000	Days	Mo
General Contractors (Continued)																														
Blount Inc B	NA	NA	NA	NA	NA	NA	NA	NA	NA	NC	00-00	.40	2.5	NA	NA	NA	06-09-88	NA	NC	NA	NC	NA	NA	NA	76	4,766	204	0	NA	NA
Dycom Ind	69.2	94.6	87.9	4.1n	.91	50.0	40.0	42.2	55	21	04-88	.00	.0	0	0	0	12-01-87	3.8	2.55	9.7	2.13	20.7	28	1.8	69	4,460	580	-30	0.0	07
DynCorp ♦	12.7	12.7	-24.0	-.8q	-.08	-100.0	-100.0	-100.0	NC	-3	03-88	.31	1.6	7	48	29	03-18-88	-.1	3.00	-.3	2.00	-.6	2	1.8	206	10,611	2,990	0	0.7	12
Fluor Corp	27.8	21.4	10.4	124.7s	1.56	NE	NE	NE	NC	24	04-88	.00	.0	-31	42	NE	12-18-86	2.9	2.07	6.0	3.92	23.5	44	1.7	1,694	78,810	37,729	0	1.7	10
Foster Wheeler	-10.1	-10.1	-4.2	1.4q	.04	-16.1	-16.1	-95.6	-41	-3	03-88	.44	2.6	0	489	55	05-10-88	.1	1.00	.1	3.00	.3	42	1.7	584	35,112	11,544	+10	0.9	12
Gen Magnaplate	83.3	28.9	33.3	.8n	.96	355.6	108.6	95.9	45	12	03-88	.10	.9	0	17	12	03-07-88	10.0	.91	9.1	1.52	13.8	36	7.0	9	795	59	0	0.0	06
Jacobs Eng	146.9	167.2	123.0	5.8s	1.20	220.0	219.0	344.4	NC	19	03-88	.00	.0	0	0	0	02-24-88	1.0	4.90	4.9	3.82	18.7	40	1.4	90	4,705	519	0	0.0	09
Morrison Knuds	-2.9	-2.9	-11.9	-58.4q	-5.41	20.0	20.0	-100.0	NC	-21	03-88	1.48	3.6	3	NE	71	05-12-88	-3.2	2.03	-6.5	2.52	-16.4	21	1.5	446	10,813	7,663	+4	0.5	12
Peter JM	NA	NA	NA	NA	NA	NA	NA	NA	NA	NC	00-00	.00	.0	NA	NA	NA	00-00-00	NA	NC	NA	NC	NA	NA	NA	134	13,750	356	0	NA	NA
Seligman&Assc	-57.1	-79.3	-68.7	1.2n	.66	-47.6	-37.7	-28.3	31	12	04-87	.00	.0	0	0	0	00-00-00	24.0	.30	7.3	1.67	12.2	41	NA	8	1,785	55	0	0.0	07
Stone & Web ◦	3.8	3.8	3.5	46.1q	6.14	-29.4	-29.4	24.8	3	8	03-88	2.40	3.6	-2	27	35	06-27-88	15.9	.52	8.3	1.61	13.4	9	1.9	513	7,622	1,440	0	0.8	12
Sutron Cp	50.0	39.5	33.3	-.7n	-.19	NE	-100.0	NC	NC	-21	09-87	.00	.0	0	0	0	00-00-00	-8.8	1.03	-9.1	2.33	-21.2	58	2.0	3	4,222	16	0	0.0	12
Turner Cp	-97.0	-97.0	-10.9	-21.9q	-5.01	47.1	47.1	-100.0	NC	-39	03-88	1.30	6.6	10	NE	89	05-16-88	-1.0	2.30	-2.3	13.30	-30.6	58	1.0	85	4,292	660	+5	5.2	12
Union Valley	8.7	8.7	56.1	4.5q	1.13	12.5	12.5	61.4	NC	40	03-88	.00	.0	0	0	0	00-00-00	3.9	1.38	5.4	7.37	39.8	527	NA	32	3,967	113	0	0.0	12
Other Building - Heavy																														
Ind. Group	3.6	9.0	- 5.3	- 701.7	- 2.91	NE	- 100.0	- 100.0	NC	- 38	- - -	.33	3.4	1	136	74	- - - -	- 8.7	1.06	- 9.2	3.68	-33.9	56	1.0	2,313	243,497	55,083	+ 147	1.9	- -
ACMAT Cp	-37.8	-37.8	-17.6	2.9q	.77	-83.7	-83.7	22.2	NC	10	03-88	.00	.0	0	0	0	00-00-00	20.7	.35	7.2	1.39	10.0	15	5.4	59	5,217	118	0	0.0	12
ACMAT Cp A	NA	NA	NA	NA	NA	NA	NA	NA	NA	NC	00-00	.00	.0	NA	NA	NA	00-00-00	NA	NC	NA	NC	NA	NA	NA	22	2,938	102	+100	NA	NA
Am Ship Bldg ◦	61.4	90.8	5.8	-8.5s	-1.16	NE	NE	NE	NC	-24	03-88	.00	.0	-13	NE	NE	05-04-87	-23.6	.44	-10.4	2.33	-24.2	49	2.4	32	6,013	1,337	+36	2.1	09
Atkinson Guy F	2.6	2.6	10.3	2.2q	.26	4.8	4.8	-74.0	NC	-2	03-88	.64	3.8	0	256	45	04-25-88	.2	2.50	.5	2.40	1.2	26	1.7	146	8,777	2,722	0	0.0	12
Banister Contl	231.0	231.0	82.7	.4q	.09	-100.0	-100.0	-94.7	NC	1	03-88	.00	NA	0	0	0	09-17-79	.2	1.50	.3	2.00	.6	4	1.4	44	5,932	618	+11	0.0	12
Bank Bldg Eq ◦	26.5	25.2	10.3	4.6s	3.02	NE	NE	NE	NC	67	04-88	.40	5.8	-11	19	71	05-10-88	5.4	2.69	14.5	5.29	76.7	17	1.1	10	1,476	154	0	0.0	10
Bonneville Pac	-6.5	118.7	109.0	8.5f	.73	-66.7	52.1	52.1	NC	35	04-88	.00	.0	0	0	0	00-00-00	37.0	.28	10.3	3.43	35.3	55	.3	81	12,702	1,847	0	0.0	04
Brand Cos	63.1	63.1	21.6	-3.9q	-.84	NE	NE	-100.0	NC	-20	03-88	.00	.0	0	0	1	00-00-00	-3.0	2.50	-7.5	2.61	-19.6	5	1.3	48	4,636	2,891	0	0.0	12
Burnup & Sims Inc	6.3	2.5	2.5	6.5n	.46	-44.4	-9.5	360.0	NC	6	01-88	.00	.0	0	0	69	08-03-81	3.2	1.09	3.5	1.83	6.4	49	3.0	233	15,961	1,740	0	0.0	04
Dravo Corp	5.3	5.3	-58.5	-130.6q	-9.09	NE	NE	NE	NC	0	03-88	.00	.0	-16	NE	NE	04-28-87	-52.0	.82	-42.4	.00	NM	45	1.4	226	14,681	7,849	0	0.8	12
Fischbach Cp	-21.3	-22.6	-27.0	-32.8s	-8.42	NE	NE	NE	NC	-32	03-88	.00	.0	0	0	NE	08-19-85	-3.4	1.94	-6.6	4.89	-32.3	33	1.2	37	3,911	1,140	0	13.0	09
Goldfield Cp	700.0	700.0	166.6	.9q	.03	NE	NE	NC	NC	17	03-88	.00	.0	0	0	0	00-00-00	11.3	.67	7.6	2.20	16.7	33	1.6	10	26,884	758	0	2.8	12
Insituform East	108.3	43.7	46.1	1.6n	.35	NE	450.0	NE	3	18	03-88	.00	.0	0	0	0	10-31-85	8.4	1.40	11.8	1.49	17.6	13	2.8	35	4,685	248	0	0.0	06
Kasler Cp	-5.6	.0	.0	1.9s	.40	225.0	257.1	NE	NC	15	04-88	.00	.0	0	0	NE	06-25-85	1.8	1.89	3.4	4.53	15.4	208	2.7	50	5,035	1,795	0	0.0	10
KDI Cp	4.2	4.2	5.6	19.0q	1.96	16.7	16.7	145.0	21	20	03-88	.30	1.8	0	16	21	06-01-88	6.0	1.73	10.4	2.23	23.2	59	2.2	164	9,697	1,775	0	1.9	12
Maxpharma	-87.5	-89.6	-78.3	-6.9s	-2.69	NE	NE	NE	NC	-93	06-87	.00	.0	0	0	0	08-31-81	-86.3	.49	-42.6	2.19	-93.2	7	.9	6	2,940	192	0	3.3	12
McDermott Intl	8.4	4.3	2.5	-510.1n	-13.78	NE	-100.0	-100.0	NC	-56	12-87	1.80	9.2	8	NE	283	06-14-88	-15.0	.77	-11.6	4.25	-49.3	75	.8	725	37,181	23,142	0	2.1	03
Myers LE Grp	-.7	-.7	11.1	-2.9q	-1.37	NE	NE	NE	NC	-25	03-88	.00	.0	0	0	0	03-08-82	-4.1	2.10	-8.6	2.88	-24.8	60	3.2	7	2,269	118	0	0.0	12
Std Shares	11.2	8.7	8.5	14.4f	5.47	-71.2	-49.8	-49.8	0	8	02-88	1.25	1.3	0	23	66	12-24-87	2.1	1.38	2.9	3.38	9.8	17	2.3	249	2,626	953	0	3.9	02
Tacoma Btbldg	51.8	51.8	-66.6	.0q	-.01	-100.0	-100.0	-100.0	NC	0	03-88	.00	.0	0	0	0	12-07-82	.0	NC	NC	NC	.0	377	1.6	83	60,690	3,127	0	11.6	12
Todd Shipyards	-34.0	-34.0	-15.7	-65.2q	-16.33	-100.0	-100.0	NE	NC	-99	06-87	.00	.0	7	NE	593	01-09-87	-17.4	.84	-14.7	6.74	-99.1	9	.7	12	4,194	1,160	0	3.2	03
Transnatl Inds	-17.8	-17.8	-13.3	-4.8q	-1.83	NE	NE	NE	NC	-44	04-88	.00	.0	0	0	0	00-00-00	-12.3	1.02	-12.6	3.49	-44.0	132	2.0	4	2,646	463	0	0.0	01
Williams Ind	8.6	2.1	13.9	1.1n	.43	25.0	-75.8	-44.9	9	6	04-88	.00	.0	0	0	0	08-06-84	1.2	1.42	1.7	3.47	5.9	150	NA	32	2,406	834	0	0.0	07

Data Processing and Computer Software

Company	Revenue Pct. Change Last Qtr	Revenue Pct. Change FY to Date	Revenue Pct. Change Last 12 Mos	Earnings Last 12 Mos	Earnings Per Share Last 12 Mos	Earnings Per Share Pct. Change Last Qtr	Earnings Per Share Pct. Change FY to Date	Earnings Per Share Pct. Change Last 12 Mos	Earnings 5-Year Growth Rate	Earnings Par Growth Rate	Earnings Date of Report	Dividends Current Rate Amt	Dividends Current Rate Yield	Dividends 5-Year Growth Rate	Dividends Payout Last FY	Dividends Payout Last 5 Yrs.	Dividends Last X-Dvd Date	Profit Margin	Asset Turnover	Return on Total Assets	Leverage Ratio	Return on Equity	Debt to Equity	Current Ratio	Market Value	Latest Shares Outstndng.	Held by Banks-Funds	Insider Net Trading	Short Interest Ratio	Fiscal Year Ends
-	%	%	%	$Mil	$	%	%	%	%	%	-	$	%	%	%	%	-	π/r x	r/a =	π/a x	a/e =	π/e	%	-	$Mil	000	000	000	Days	Mo
Computer Software, Data Processing																														
Ind. Group	30.8	42.9	28.5	1,051.1	.69	41.5	42.6	56.4	44	14	- - -	.10	.5	1	7	8	- - - -	7.3	1.21	8.8	1.81	15.9	26	2.5	27,784	1,503,392	488,135	- 422	.3	- -
Adobe Systs	95.8	100.0	107.4	13.1s	1.23	86.4	102.7	108.5	NC	56	05-88	.00	.0	0	0	0	03-12-87	23.4	1.74	40.6	1.37	55.7	0	3.2	411	10,201	4,143	0	0.0	11
Adv Comp Tech	-46.9	-46.9	-33.3	-.5q	-.26	-100.0	-100.0	-100.0	NC	-13	03-88	.00	.0	0	0	0	00-00-00	-5.0	1.16	-5.8	2.16	-12.5	30	1.6	2	1,797	200	0	0.0	12
AGS Cptr	31.9	31.9	28.7	16.5q	1.30	39.3	39.3	32.7	21	16	03-88	.00	.0	0	0	0	06-01-87	3.1	2.39	7.4	2.09	15.5	44	2.2	359	13,131	6,233	0	0.2	12
Aldus Cp	93.9	93.9	176.4	9.2q	.75	60.0	60.0	141.9	NC	21	03-88	.00	.0	0	0	0	00-00-00	19.6	.96	18.8	1.13	21.2	0	9.8	220	10,876	608	0	0.0	12
Algorex Cp	28.6	-24.3	-30.0	-2.0n	-.69	NE	NE	NE	NC	-48	03-88	.00	.0	0	0	0	00-00-00	-28.6	.63	-18.0	2.64	-47.6	140	2.6	7	2,783	515	0	0.0	06
Altai Inc	52.2	57.8	62.5	.6n	.29	250.0	200.0	141.7	NC	15	04-88	.00	.0	0	0	0	00-00-00	4.6	2.57	11.8	1.24	14.6	0	4.6	9	2,271	205	0	0.0	07
Altos Cptr Syst ◇	5.9	14.8	-18.5	12.2n	.95	-71.4	44.0	6.7	11	12	03-88	.00	.0	0	0	0	00-00-00	7.1	1.07	7.6	1.51	11.5	22	3.9	109	11,920	3,448	0	0.0	06
Am Managemnt	31.5	31.5	29.1	7.4q	.72	-10.0	-10.0	38.5	NC	21	03-88	.00	.0	0	0	0	06-11-87	4.0	2.23	8.9	2.40	21.4	10	1.6	157	9,642	3,486	0	0.0	12
Am Software	12.5	16.1	14.8	10.3f	1.00	30.0	17.6	17.6	20	16	04-88	.24	1.7	0	12	7	06-29-88	19.1	.80	15.2	1.36	20.6	0	3.4	145	10,193	3,486	0	0.0	04
Anacomp Inc □	219.1	244.0	275.0	29.6s	.75	185.7	233.3	400.0	NC	73	03-88	.00	.0	0	0	NE	07-14-83	7.0	1.44	10.1	7.22	72.9	403	2.1	385	35,409	9,701	+104	8.0	09
Analysts Intl	19.6	25.0	26.4	3.2n	.89	9.5	320.0	1680.0	NC	27	03-88	.15	1.9	0	0	NE	12-24-87	4.8	3.75	18.0	1.82	32.7	0	2.0	29	3,598	537	0	0.0	06
Ashton Tate	20.3	20.3	21.7	45.1q	1.77	19.4	19.4	28.3	69	25	04-88	.00	.0	0	0	0	01-13-87	16.1	1.12	18.1	1.39	25.2	3	3.0	681	25,938	16,784	+141	0.0	01
ASK Cptr Systs	45.7	43.5	35.1	9.3n	.72	53.8	23.8	26.3	13	11	03-88	.00	.0	0	0	0	00-00-00	7.3	1.07	7.8	1.45	11.3	1	3.0	197	12,887	9,673	0	0.0	06
Autodesk Inc	49.1	49.1	49.1	23.8q	1.01	66.7	66.7	62.9	NC	21	04-88	.00	.0	0	0	0	03-30-87	27.0	.70	19.0	1.09	20.7	0	12.8	691	23,824	13,227	0	0.0	01
Autolnfo Inc	60.0	64.7	50.0	-.7f	-.17	NE	NE	NE	NC	-29	05-87	.00	.0	0	0	0	00-00-00	-23.3	1.00	-23.3	1.25	-29.2	0	3.2	14	4,082	628	0	0.0	05
Automated Lang	-40.0	-21.6	-25.0	-7.1f	-.86	NC	-100.0	-100.0	NC	0	12-87	.00	.0	0	0	0	00-00-00	NM	NC	NC	NC	NM	63	.7	46	8,259	141	0	0.0	12
Automatic Data	11.9	12.3	12.0	161.7n	2.09	26.9	26.6	25.9	17	14	03-88	.52	1.3	11	22	24	06-14-88	10.7	1.05	11.2	1.65	18.5	24	2.6	3,122	77,076	49,566	-5	1.0	06
Avant Garde □	-24.0	.0	-5.5	-4.3n	-1.14	NE	NE	NE	NC	-47	01-88	.00	.0	0	0	0	00-00-00	-25.3	1.31	-33.1	1.43	-47.3	1	2.4	8	3,770	662	0	0.0	04
AW Cptr Systs	-61.5	-61.5	-40.0	-.9q	-.26	-100.0	-100.0	-100.0	NC	-50	03-88	.00	.0	0	0	0	00-00-00	-30.0	.77	-23.1	2.16	-50.0	11	1.5	1	3,285	46	0	0.0	12
Bio Logic Syst	44.4	22.5	28.5	.9f	.30	37.5	.0	.0	NC	13	02-88	.00	.0	0	0	0	00-00-00	10.0	.99	9.9	1.33	13.2	22	8.6	12	2,623	45	0	0.0	02
Blockbuster Ent	208.6	208.6	292.8	5.5q	1.22	142.9	142.9	NE	NC	13	03-88	.00	.0	0	0	0	03-30-88	10.0	.74	7.4	1.77	13.1	35	1.6	254	7,010	544	0	0.0	12
Boole & Babbage ◇	41.4	37.0	32.4	2.7s	.77	66.7	70.4	71.1	NC	36	03-88	.00	.0	0	0	0	00-00-00	5.5	1.95	10.7	3.32	35.5	0	1.1	28	3,168	520	0	0.0	09
CIS Technologies ◆	.0	-50.0	.0	-4.4f	-.33	NE	NE	NE	NC	-36	10-87	.00	.0	0	0	0	00-00-00	NC	NC	NC	NC	-36.1	4	19.8	19	17,567	0	0	0.0	10
Cadence Design	49.0	49.0	52.9	4.0q	.36	150.0	150.0	125.0	NC	16	03-88	.00	.0	0	0	0	05-24-88	15.4	.76	11.7	1.36	15.9	4	4.1	78	10,226	1,020	0	0.0	12
CCX Network	383.3	221.0	.0	.0‡	.82	400.0	256.5	36.7	NC	0	03-88	.00	.0	0	0	0	03-24-86	NC	NC	NC	NC	.0	71	1.4	66	4,123	663	0	0.0	03

Continued

Company	Revenue Pct. Change Last Qtr	Revenue Pct. Change FY to Date	Revenue Pct. Change Last 12 Mos	Earnings Last 12 Mos	Earnings Per Share Last 12 Mos	Per Share Pct. Change Last Qtr	Per Share Pct. Change FY to Date	Per Share Pct. Change Last 12 Mos	5-Year Growth Rate	Par Growth Rate	Date of Report	Dividends Current Rate Amt	Current Rate Yield	5-Year Growth Rate	Payout Last FY	Payout Last 5 Yrs.	Last X-Dvd Date	Ratio Analysis Profit Margin	Asset Turnover	Return on Total Assets	Leverage Ratio	Return on Equity	Debt to Equity	Current Ratio	Shareholdings Market Value	Latest Shares Outstndng.	Held by Banks-Funds	Insider Net Trading	Short Interest Ratio	Fiscal Year Ends
-	%	%	%	$Mil	$	%	%	%	%	%	-	$	%	%	%	%	-	π/r	x r/a	= π/a	x a/e	= π/e	%	-	$Mil	000	000	000	Days	Mo
Computer Software, Data Processing (Continued)																														
Cerner Cp	111.1	111.1	116.6	4.3q	1.15	38.9	38.9	105.4	NC	21	03-88	.00	.0	0	0	0	00-00-00	11.0	.98	10.8	1.94	20.9	4	2.1	87	3,580	1,495	0	0.0	12
Cheyenne Sftwre	.0	25.0	.0	-1.4f	-.20	NE	NE	NE	NC	-18	06-87	.00	.0	0	0	0	00-00-00	NM	NC	NC	NC	-17.9	0	24.3	30	7,756	316	0	0.0	06
CMX Cp	-9.7	8.4	18.1	.4n	.04	-100.0	-75.0	-50.0	NC	9	03-88	.00	.0	0	0	0	00-00-00	3.1	1.26	3.9	2.23	8.7	26	1.9	9	8,994	40	0	0.0	06
Cognos Inc	13.8	13.8	19.4	2.1q	.20	-70.6	-70.6	-76.7	NC	4	05-88	.00	.0	0	0	0	00-00-00	2.4	1.13	2.7	1.41	3.8	10	3.9	55	10,258	457	0	0.0	02
Comptek Rsch	45.1	39.7	37.1	1.2f	.54	-64.7	20.0	20.0	NC	7	03-88	.16	2.1	0	30	38	05-09-88	2.5	2.96	7.4	1.41	10.4	8	3.7	17	2,183	688	0	0.0	03
Comp Assoc	102.4	129.3	129.4	101.8f	1.29	82.6	74.3	74.3	50	46	03-88	.00	.0	0	0	0	05-08-87	14.4	1.61	23.2	1.99	46.2	48	2.9	2,335	79,138	43,571	-97	2.9	03
Comp Data Syst	23.3	29.7	25.4	3.1n	1.10	92.9	122.5	93.0	4	18	03-88	.12	1.0	18	16	10	01-25-88	4.8	1.27	6.1	3.33	20.3	73	2.0	34	2,683	669	0	0.0	06
Comp Factory	51.7	47.2	55.7	9.4s	1.12	36.8	25.4	33.3	59	12	03-88	.00	.0	0	0	0	03-04-87	4.1	2.15	8.8	1.40	12.3	0	3.3	148	8,100	4,896	0	0.2	09
Comp Horizons	23.2	18.0	.0	.0‡	.84	NE	47.1	1.2	NC	0	03-88	.00	.0	0	0	0	07-12-83	NC	NC	NC	NC	.0	7	3.8	29	2,696	982	0	0.0	12
Comp Language	24.9	24.9	18.2	-.7q	-.06	15.6	15.6	NE	NC	-5	03-88	.12	1.8	0	NE	37	06-13-88	-.6	1.67	-1.0	1.60	-1.6	6	2.0	92	13,647	729	0	0.0	12
Comp Sciences	6.4	11.7	11.6	43.5f	2.73	27.9	31.3	31.3	15	15	03-88	.00	.0	0	0	0	00-00-00	3.8	1.92	7.3	2.10	15.3	31	1.7	702	15,958	10,100	-1	1.1	03
Computrac	-30.0	-30.0	-30.0	-.3q	-.04	100.0	100.0	-100.0	NC	-7	04-88	.07	1.3	0	NE	11	12-29-87	-4.3	.42	-1.8	1.39	-2.5	11	2.7	32	5,958	1,684	+5	0.2	01
Comshare Inc ♦	12.1	13.4	11.5	1.9n	.68	87.5	-19.0	7.9	NC	8	03-88	.00	.0	0	0	0	00-00-00	2.5	1.52	3.8	2.13	8.1	9	1.3	51	2,551	247	-2	0.0	06
Continuum Co	-22.4	3.8	3.4	2.5f	.57	-100.0	-24.0	-24.0	NC	20	03-88	.00	.0	0	0	9	03-24-86	4.2	1.52	6.4	3.17	20.3	45	1.2	52	4,350	1,046	0	0.0	03
Corporate Sftwre	77.7	77.7	86.4	2.3q	.64	100.0	100.0	NC	NC	18	03-88	.00	.0	0	0	0	00-00-00	3.3	3.00	9.9	1.82	18.0	5	2.1	52	3,797	746	0	0.0	12
Cullinet Softwr ♦	-2.1	23.9	24.0	-47.0f	-1.45	NE	NE	NE	NC	-39	04-88	.00	.0	0	0	0	01-22-85	-21.7	1.11	-24.1	1.63	-39.4	0	1.5	278	32,286	10,963	0	0.7	04
Cybertek Cp	-9.4	-13.5	-15.3	.3f	.08	-66.7	-84.0	-84.0	NC	3	03-88	.00	.0	0	0	0	00-00-00	1.4	.64	.9	2.78	2.5	7	2.1	9	3,599	236	0	0.0	03
Cycare Systs	39.2	39.2	23.7	3.2q	.59	400.0	400.0	31.1	3	7	03-88	.00	.0	0	0	0	04-30-86	4.4	.95	4.2	1.74	7.3	23	2.4	55	5,549	1,164	+5	0.0	12
Daisy Syst	20.2	15.0	11.3	-7.8s	-.44	NE	NE	NE	NC	-6	03-88	.00	.0	0	0	0	00-00-00	-7.2	.67	-4.8	1.19	-5.7	0	6.1	190	17,901	6,749	0	0.0	09
Data I O	-12.6	-12.6	-4.4	-5.2q	-.52	-90.0	-90.0	-100.0	NC	-9	03-88	.00	.0	0	0	0	08-22-83	-8.1	.86	-7.0	1.26	-8.8	0	3.4	68	8,414	2,972	0	0.0	12
Datatab Inc	-11.1	-5.6	-25.0	.0s	.06	NE	NE	NE	NC	0	06-87	.00	.0	0	0	0	00-00-00	.0	NC	NC	NC	.0	0	.5	0	706	0	0	0.0	12
DBA Systs ◇□	-14.9	-21.7	-13.7	4.1n	1.43	37.0	35.4	26.5	6	17	03-88	.00	.0	0	0	0	06-27-83	5.9	.83	4.9	3.39	16.6	162	3.3	71	3,031	709	0	0.0	06
Decision Sys	-7.1	.0	-40.0	.0s	-.02	-100.0	-100.0	NE	NC	0	10-87	.00	.0	0	0	0	00-00-00	.0	NC	NC	NC	.0	0	.7	9	2,295	18	0	0.0	04
Digilog Inc	-20.9	-18.6	-16.6	.8s	.33	-93.8	-76.7	-35.3	NC	8	03-88	.00	.0	0	0	0	03-03-87	5.3	1.15	6.1	1.26	7.7	1	4.2	16	2,617	294	0	0.0	09
DST Syst Inc	6.0	6.0	37.6	20.5q	1.04	13.6	13.6	28.4	16	17	03-88	.16	.9	0	11	11	06-07-88	14.7	.67	9.8	2.09	20.5	26	1.3	345	19,446	964	0	0.0	12
Dyatron	14.5	14.5	11.7	3.8q	1.20	60.0	60.0	126.4	NC	38	03-88	.00	.0	0	0	0	03-16-81	10.0	1.97	19.7	1.91	37.6	22	1.7	63	4,818	392	0	0.0	12
Dynamics Research	10.9	10.9	23.6	3.7q	.75	7.7	7.7	44.2	37	23	03-88	.00	.0	0	0	2	11-04-87	3.9	2.62	10.2	2.26	23.1	0	1.5	40	5,029	1,124	-22	0.0	12
Epsilon Data	14.5	-.8	-9.6	.5n	.18	NE	100.0	NE	NC	4	02-88	.00	.0	0	0	0	00-00-00	1.1	2.55	2.8	1.43	4.0	1	2.5	30	2,801	529	0	0.0	05
Evans & Suth	4.0	4.0	20.3	13.2q	1.54	-60.0	-60.0	4.1	8	14	03-88	.00	.0	0	0	0	06-10-81	9.7	.68	6.6	2.12	14.0	66	3.7	130	8,369	5,330	0	0.0	12
FDP Cp	-15.0	-5.7	7.6	.8s	.21	-50.0	NC	600.0	-31	5	05-88	.00	.0	0	0	0	00-00-00	5.7	.68	3.9	1.18	4.6	0	8.3	16	3,631	845	0	0.0	11
Fidata Cp	-9.1	-9.1	-85.2	1.6q	.34	NE	NE	NE	NC	3	03-88	.00	.0	0	0	0	08-31-81	32.0	.07	2.3	1.35	3.1	0	NA	30	4,439	788	0	0.3	12
Finl Inds	-50.0	-14.3	.0	.6n	.69	-40.0	20.0	9.5	NC	6	09-87	.00	.0	0	0	0	00-00-00	60.0	.10	6.1	1.03	6.3	0	6.7	5	931	0	0	0.0	12
Fst Fncl Mgmt	221.1	221.1	187.5	15.0q	1.25	37.5	37.5	56.3	39	7	03-88	.00	.0	0	0	0	04-07-87	6.5	.63	4.1	1.63	6.7	12	NA	455	16,101	7,836	-0	0.0	12
Gen Computer	-28.9	-.9	.0	.7n	.43	-100.0	13.3	-15.7	NC	8	02-88	.00	.0	0	0	0	00-00-00	4.7	1.23	5.8	1.45	8.4	0	2.6	10	1,458	187	0	0.0	05

GME/ElDatSys	NA	NA	NA	NA	NA	NA	NA	NA	NA	NC	00-00	.60	1.6	NA	NA	NA	05-06-88	NA	NC	NA	NC	NA	NA	NA	2,415	63,774	17,578	+7	NA	NA
Gen Parametrics	8.8	3.5	.0	3.3s	.40	.0	-8.7	-14.9	NC	14	04-88	.00	.0	0	0	0	00-00-00	14.3	.87	12.4	1.13	14.0	0	8.2	32	7,947	1,000	0	0.0	10
Group 1 Sftwre	36.4	28.1	25.0	1.7n	.52	60.0	40.0	44.4	NC	36	12-87	.00	.0	0	0	0	00-00-00	17.0	1.16	19.8	1.83	36.2	0	2.3	32	3,311	160	0	0.0	03
GTECH Corp	66.4	9.0	9.3	4.8f	.50	-100.0	-38.3	-38.3	1	9	02-88	.00	.0	0	0	0	00-00-00	3.4	.74	2.5	3.68	9.2	150	1.1	100	9,611	3,716	-11	0.0	02
Hadron Inc	-11.3	7.7	8.3	.8n	.05	-33.3	.0	-28.6	NC	21	12-87	.00	.0	0	0	0	00-00-00	3.1	1.87	5.8	3.53	20.5	85	1.6	10	13,764	128	0	0.0	03
HBO Co	8.8	8.8	20.9	13.5q	.65	75.0	75.0	NE	NC	37	03-88	.30	3.3	39	32	24	06-24-88	7.5	1.77	13.3	5.20	69.2	98	.9	134	14,868	3,892	+10	0.0	12
Henry Jack Assoc	24.4	9.3	6.2	.7n	.17	466.7	8.3	-26.1	NC	7	03-88	.00	.0	0	0	0	00-00-00	4.1	.78	3.2	2.31	7.4	18	1.5	11	3,617	143	0	0.0	06
Hogan Systs	-4.5	5.9	6.8	1.0f	.07	-7.1	-81.1	-81.1	NC	3	03-88	.00	.0	0	0	0	12-05-83	2.1	.90	1.9	1.47	2.8	0	2.8	59	14,330	3,283	0	0.0	03
Ind Training Cp	-45.8	-19.4	-16.6	-.5f	-.63	-100.0	-100.0	-100.0	NC	-19	12-87	.00	.0	0	0	0	00-00-00	-10.0	.81	-8.1	2.28	-18.5	22	1.7	4	775	15	0	0.0	12
Infodata Systs	7.1	2.7	9.0	.7f	.31	600.0	520.0	520.0	NC	14	12-87	.00	.0	0	0	0	00-00-00	5.8	1.55	9.0	1.50	13.5	4	2.4	7	1,718	223	-3	0.0	12
Informix Cp	263.4	263.4	150.0	7.6q	.76	100.0	100.0	90.0	NC	17	03-88	.00	.0	0	0	0	00-00-00	12.7	1.09	13.9	1.22	17.0	0	5.5	272	11,576	3,514	-50	0.0	12
Inmac	34.0	38.8	37.4	9.1n	.99	12.0	20.3	30.3	NC	25	04-88	.09	.5	0	5	3	03-07-88	4.3	3.09	13.3	2.03	27.0	0	1.8	170	9,088	1,730	-20	0.0	07
IntelliCorp	-10.7	2.7	5.0	-4.6n	-.66	-100.0	NE	-100.0	NC	-17	03-88	.00	.0	0	0	0	00-00-00	-21.9	.60	-13.1	1.26	-16.5	0	3.6	20	7,136	2,251	0	0.0	06
Interleaf Inc	64.5	60.4	61.1	5.6f	.47	150.0	NE	NE	NC	16	03-88	.00	.0	0	0	0	00-00-00	9.7	1.29	12.5	1.27	15.9	4	4.5	142	11,334	6,420	0	0.0	03
Intermetrics Inc	13.3	13.3	4.2	1.6q	.47	87.5	87.5	261.5	NC	14	05-88	.00	.0	0	0	0	00-00-00	3.3	2.21	7.3	1.88	13.7	3	2.0	16	3,430	582	0	0.0	02
Irwin Magnetics	-17.1	-7.5	.0	2.1n	.40	-84.2	-51.7	-48.7	NC	8	03-88	.00	.0	0	0	0	00-00-00	4.3	1.51	6.5	1.26	8.2	0	4.4	34	4,893	887	0	0.0	06
ISI Systs	17.1	18.3	56.5	5.2n	.78	21.1	42.9	NC	NC	16	03-88	.24	1.6	0	8	8	07-01-88	14.4	1.28	18.4	1.24	22.9	8	4.1	100	6,683	793	0	2.1	06
Keane Assoc	35.6	35.6	14.6	1.2q	.90	130.0	130.0	462.5	9	15	03-88	.00	.0	0	0	25	05-06-86	2.6	3.31	8.6	1.79	15.4	19	2.1	16	1,379	160	0	0.0	12
Kenilworth Systs	300.0	300.0	-50.0	-1.3q	-.03	NE	NE	NE	NC	-30	03-88	.00	.0	0	0	0	00-00-00	NM	NC	NC	NC	-29.5	0	.1	18	35,300	97	0	0.0	12
LCS Ind	4.3	4.4	-2.7	-.4s	-.24	-79.2	-84.1	-100.0	NC	-7	03-88	.00	.0	0	0	0	00-00-00	-1.1	1.64	-1.8	3.61	-6.5	32	1.2	5	1,510	77	+4	0.0	09
Lodgistix	-3.5	23.1	4.5	-1.4n	-.25	NC	NE	NE	NC	-13	03-88	.00	.0	0	0	0	00-00-00	-6.1	1.57	-9.6	1.38	-13.2	2	2.9	8	5,609	1,188	+4	0.0	06
Lotus Development	38.3	38.3	43.6	76.6q	1.67	29.0	29.0	50.5	NC	38	03-88	.00	.0	0	0	0	02-24-87	17.9	1.35	24.1	1.57	37.9	15	2.6	1,037	43,673	32,476	-435	0.0	12
MacNeal Sch	24.4	24.4	24.1	9.3q	.76	12.5	12.5	26.7	32	17	04-88	.28	1.9	0	24	23	08-22-88	25.8	.84	21.7	1.24	27.0	6	4.4	176	12,213	7,087	0	1.1	01
Mai Basic Four	35.1	27.1	22.7	24.7s	1.65	16.7	19.4	27.9	NC	12	03-88	1.00	5.0	0	0	0	12-18-87	6.8	1.69	11.5	2.75	31.6	65	2.3	293	14,721	3,640	0	0.0	09
Mgmnt Sci Amer	35.3	35.3	30.3	7.4q	.43	NE	NE	-42.7	NC	11	03-88	.00	.0	0	0	0	12-20-82	2.7	1.33	3.6	3.11	11.2	5	.6	203	16,610	8,584	0	0.0	12
Manatron Inc	-17.4	-7.9	12.5	-.4n	-.24	-100.0	-100.0	-100.0	NC	-7	01-88	.00	.0	0	0	0	00-00-00	-4.4	.98	-4.3	1.58	-6.8	2	2.3	7	2,090	0	0	0.0	04
Medstat Sys	30.8	19.2	20.0	.7s	.30	33.3	23.1	36.4	NC	19	03-88	.00	.0	0	0	0	00-00-00	11.7	1.05	12.3	1.54	18.9	19	2.6	28	2,642	217	0	0.0	09
Mentor Graphics	33.9	33.9	27.8	23.0q	1.35	60.0	60.0	68.8	NC	12	03-88	.00	.0	0	0	0	00-00-00	9.6	1.04	10.0	1.23	12.3	0	5.0	580	16,443	11,322	-10	0.0	12
Micro Pro Intl	-11.4	4.8	7.5	-2.8n	-.23	-100.0	-100.0	-100.0	NC	-8	05-88	.00	.0	0	0	0	00-00-00	-6.5	1.06	-6.9	1.20	-8.3	0	5.3	35	13,290	2,853	+2	0.0	08
Microbilt Cp	76.9	76.9	33.3	3.3q	.79	107.7	107.7	58.0	NC	16	04-88	.06	.3	0	0	0	06-24-88	16.5	.71	11.7	1.44	16.8	25	9.6	70	4,046	788	0	0.0	01
Micros Syst	2.0	11.2	.0	-.2s	-.03	NE	NE	NE	NC	-3	12-87	.00	.0	0	0	0	00-00-00	-1.1	1.27	-1.4	1.86	-2.6	31	2.3	9	5,911	30	+2	0.0	06
Microsoft	64.7	70.8	68.8	111.2n	1.99	88.6	69.7	65.8	NC	47	03-88	.00	.0	0	0	0	09-21-87	21.4	1.80	38.6	1.20	46.5	1	4.6	3,567	53,239	7,003	-15	0.0	06
MPSI Systs	7.7	30.2	20.8	.1s	.01	-100.0	NC	-95.5	-35	1	03-88	.00	.0	0	0	0	02-27-84	.3	1.00	.3	2.00	.6	2	1.6	25	8,413	2,004	0	0.0	09
MTech Cp	25.1	25.1	21.7	15.6q	1.29	3.8	3.8	38.7	NC	19	03-88	.00	.0	0	0	0	00-00-00	6.3	1.06	6.7	2.85	19.1	126	3.5	348	11,700	1,584	0	0.0	12
Natl Business Sys	109.4	73.6	74.3	13.7f	.82	NE	60.8	60.8	NC	10	09-87	.00	.0	0	0	0	08-11-86	7.2	.54	3.9	2.46	9.6	78	2.7	33	16,713	962	0	0.0	09
Natl Data Cp	10.5	11.4	18.6	15.5n	1.35	19.4	16.9	-14.0	8	13	02-88	.44	1.9	9	37	39	05-16-88	9.0	1.10	9.9	2.00	19.8	18	1.8	266	11,444	5,538	+0	0.0	05
NEECO Inc	82.5	88.4	89.8	4.8f	1.08	73.7	54.3	54.3	NC	17	03-88	.00	.0	0	0	0	00-00-00	4.3	2.77	11.9	1.39	16.5	0	3.6	62	4,480	2,368	0	0.0	03
Networdd Inc	-100.0	-50.0	.0	-.3f	-.51	NE	NE	NE	NC	-25	01-88	.00	.0	0	0	0	05-01-87	NC	NC	NC	NC	-25.0	0	.0	1	536	0	0	0.0	01
On Line Sftwre	19.2	49.5	60.3	6.4n	.97	31.8	37.3	47.0	NC	30	02-88	.00	.0	0	0	0	05-28-87	7.5	.84	6.3	4.76	30.0	267	3.3	40	6,023	2,170	-31	23.4	05
Oracle Systs	118.6	119.9	123.5	31.4n	.49	200.0	184.6	188.2	NC	38	02-88	.00	.0	0	0	0	12-21-87	13.8	1.58	21.8	1.74	38.0	11	2.3	1,148	58,140	21,761	0	0.0	05

Continued

Company	Revenue: Pct. Change: Last Qtr	Revenue: Pct. Change: FY to Date	Revenue: Pct. Change: Last 12 Mos	Earnings: Last 12 Mos	Earnings: Per Share: Last 12 Mos	Earnings: Per Share: Pct. Change: Last Qtr	Earnings: Per Share: Pct. Change: FY to Date	Earnings: Per Share: Pct. Change: Last 12 Mos	Earnings: 5-Year Growth Rate	Earnings: Par Growth Rate	Earnings: Date of Report	Dividends: Current Rate: Amt	Dividends: Current Rate: Yield	Dividends: 5-Year Growth Rate	Dividends: Payout: Last FY	Dividends: Payout: Last 5 Yrs.	Dividends: Last X-Dvd Date	Ratio Analysis: Profit Margin	Ratio Analysis: Asset Turnover	Ratio Analysis: Return on Total Assets	Ratio Analysis: Leverage Ratio	Ratio Analysis: Return on Equity	Ratio Analysis: Debt to Equity	Ratio Analysis: Current Ratio	Shareholdings: Market Value	Shareholdings: Latest Shares Outstndng.	Shareholdings: Held by Banks-Funds	Shareholdings: Insider Net Trading	Shareholdings: Short Interest Ratio	Shareholdings: Fiscal Year Ends
-	%	%	%	$Mil	$	%	%	%	%	%	-	$	%	%	%	%	-	π/r x	r/a =	π/a x	a/e =	π/e	%	-	$Mil	000	000	000	Days	Mo
Computer Software, Data Processing (Continued)																														
Pansophic Sys	26.0	43.9	47.0	19.2n	1.04	17.1	13.0	11.8	22	15	01-88	.16	1.0	0	6	2	06-20-88	12.8	.97	12.4	1.40	17.4	1	2.9	279	17,995	10,280	0	0.2	04
Paychex Inc	24.1	23.5	22.9	6.7n	.53	50.0	44.8	32.5	39	28	02-88	.00	.0	0	0	0	11-16-87	8.9	2.31	20.6	1.35	27.9	10	3.6	229	12,926	6,265	0	0.0	05
Penta Sys Intl	15.7	1.9	.0	-1.4f	-.27	NE	-100.0	-100.0	NC	-33	12-87	.00	.0	0	0	0	00-00-00	-6.4	1.77	-11.3	2.95	-33.3	19	1.2	7	5,273	720	0	0.0	12
Perception Tech	6.7	-6.9	-40.0	-2.5s	-.70	NE	-100.0	-100.0	NC	-12	03-88	.00	.0	0	0	0	00-00-00	-27.8	.36	-10.1	1.22	-12.3	10	11.0	13	3,292	694	0	0.0	09
Phoenix Amer	.0	12.6	18.1	2.9n	.44	-87.5	52.4	63.0	-15	17	03-88	.00	.0	0	0	0	00-00-00	11.2	.61	6.8	2.54	17.3	41	NA	18	6,375	406	0	0.0	06
Policy Mgmt	20.5	20.5	18.1	18.0q	1.11	25.0	25.0	23.3	15	14	03-88	.00	.0	0	0	0	10-03-83	9.5	.68	6.5	2.11	13.7	82	6.1	400	16,001	10,777	-19	0.0	12
Quality Syst ♦	-4.3	.0	.0	-.1n	-.01	-100.0	-100.0	-100.0	NC	-1	12-87	.00	.0	0	0	0	05-11-83	-1.0	.90	-.9	1.44	-1.3	0	3.4	6	4,291	233	0	0.0	03
Rabbit Software	125.0	82.6	66.6	-2.4n	-.21	NE	NE	NE	NC	0	09-87	.00	.0	0	0	0	00-00-00	-48.0	1.47	-70.6	.00	NM	14	2.2	42	13,159	375	0	0.0	12
Sage Software	.0	.7	.0	1.5f	.30	-43.8	-30.2	-30.2	NC	7	04-88	.00	.0	0	0	0	00-00-00	10.0	.59	5.9	1.24	7.3	0	6.6	31	4,829	1,783	0	0.0	04
Samna Cp	16.7	16.7	50.0	1.7q	.72	8.3	8.3	71.4	NC	71	03-88	.00	.0	0	0	0	00-00-00	14.2	3.15	44.7	1.58	70.8	0	2.0	16	2,525	604	0	0.0	12
Scicom Data	21.2	17.1	14.2	1.0n	1.02	20.0	30.5	39.7	NC	26	03-88	.00	.0	0	0	37	03-13-86	6.3	1.89	11.9	2.15	25.6	56	2.1	7	1,043	174	0	0.0	06
Sci Software	-29.4	-29.4	.0	-1.4q	-.39	-100.0	-100.0	NE	NC	-6	03-88	.00	.0	0	0	0	00-00-00	-5.6	.66	-3.7	1.57	-5.8	7	2.0	12	3,562	1,597	+3	0.0	12
Scitex Cp	-9.0	-9.0	1.2	-1.0q	-.09	NE	NE	NE	NC	-1	03-88	.00	.0	0	0	0	03-29-83	-.6	.67	-.4	3.50	-1.4	28	1.3	56	10,948	1,323	0	0.0	12
SEI Corp	11.4	11.4	5.0	11.0q	.87	85.7	85.7	NE	NC	23	03-88	.05	.2	0	0	0	06-20-88	8.7	1.78	15.5	1.61	24.9	0	1.3	249	11,856	5,084	0	0.0	12
Shared Med Systs	-1.2	-1.2	1.5	43.0q	1.73	-13.7	-13.7	32.1	12	13	03-88	.80	3.7	19	40	35	03-25-88	11.0	1.27	14.0	1.67	23.4	5	2.7	548	25,205	14,438	+1	0.0	12
Silvar Lisco	3.3	.0	4.0	-1.1n	-.14	NE	NE	-100.0	NC	-7	01-88	.00	.0	0	0	0	00-00-00	-4.2	.90	-3.8	1.74	-6.6	12	1.9	17	7,404	1,271	+1	0.0	04
Softech Inc	25.3	14.5	6.8	1.3n	.35	NE	NE	NC	NC	7	02-88	.00	.0	0	0	0	05-09-83	2.8	1.68	4.7	1.40	6.6	12	4.1	16	3,624	1,394	0	0.0	05
Software Pub	39.4	49.0	54.8	7.8s	1.02	76.2	86.8	200.0	17	25	03-88	.00	.0	0	0	0	00-00-00	16.3	1.37	22.3	1.13	25.1	0	8.9	180	7,622	2,588	0	0.0	09
Springboard Sftwre	-75.0	-75.0	-44.4	-2.2q	-.98	-100.0	-100.0	-100.0	NC	-36	03-88	.00	.0	0	0	0	00-00-00	-44.0	.57	-25.0	1.44	-36.1	0	11.1	8	2,465	277	0	0.0	12
Step Saver Data	-39.1	-19.7	-11.1	-2.4n	-.41	NC	-100.0	-100.0	NC	-51	03-88	.00	.0	0	0	0	00-00-00	-30.0	1.43	-42.9	1.19	-51.1	0	5.0	0	5,681	18	+10	0.0	06
Sterling Sftwr	8.9	11.9	2.0	5.5s	.43	-25.0	-38.7	-47.6	8	7	03-88	.00	.0	0	0	0	06-12-85	2.7	.89	2.4	3.08	7.4	155	2.5	40	5,913	1,821	0	0.4	09
Stockholder Systs	20.8	42.9	42.8	3.4f	.83	4.2	23.9	23.9	18	21	03-88	.14	1.5	0	17	8	12-30-87	17.0	.99	16.8	1.50	25.2	1	4.4	38	4,014	326	-27	0.0	03
Summagraphics	26.8	21.6	22.2	2.3n	.77	141.7	85.7	NC	NC	37	02-88	.00	.0	0	0	0	00-00-00	7.0	2.49	17.4	2.10	36.5	2	1.7	50	3,508	706	0	0.0	05

SunGard Data	29.8	29.8	30.6	8.9q	.85	21.1	21.1	28.8	NC	13	03-88	.00	.0	0	0	0	00-00-00	9.1	.90	8.2	1.52	12.5	15	2.0	190	10,120	6,549	0	0.0	12
Symbolics	-29.3	-12.6	-40.5	-26.3n	-.99	NE	NE	NE	NC	-42	03-88	.00	.0	0	0	0	00-00-00	-28.0	.99	-27.6	1.51	-41.8	2	2.9	36	27,112	3,948	0	0.0	06
System Software	118.8	123.7	126.3	3.9s	.77	42.9	34.6	63.8	NC	20	04-88	.00	.0	0	0	0	00-00-00	9.1	1.32	12.0	1.64	19.7	1	2.0	100	5,051	1,133	0	0.0	10
Systs Cptr Tech	4.4	.0	-5.5	2.4s	.17	NE	NE	NE	NC	6	03-83	.00	.0	0	0	0	00-00-00	7.1	.69	4.9	1.20	5.9	7	7.0	38	13,845	2,949	0	0.0	09
Technalysis Cp	16.7	16.7	7.1	1.4q	.86	29.4	29.4	24.6	11	14	03-88	.25	2.5	13	25	23	01-15-88	9.3	1.86	17.3	1.17	20.3	0	6.2	16	1,635	213	+1	0.0	12
Technol Marketing	50.0	31.4	14.2	-.4n	-.16	-33.3	-100.0	-100.0	NC	-50	11-87	.00	.0	0	0	0	00-00-00	-5.0	3.08	-15.4	3.25	-50.0	25	1.1	2	2,776	21	0	0.0	02
Telos Cp	33.7	27.9	27.8	3.8f	1.00	-7.1	37.0	37.0	NC	29	03-88	.00	.0	0	0	0	00-00-00	3.8	3.97	15.1	1.92	29.0	0	1.7	37	3,693	836	0	0.0	03
Tenera	-13.3	-13.3	34.6	8.8q	.98	-8.0	-8.0	444.4	NC	8	03-88	.80	11.0	0	0	0	06-24-88	25.1	1.04	26.0	1.63	42.3	0	2.4	63	8,699	747	0	0.4	12
Teradata Cp	116.2	70.1	82.0	5.9n	.57	.0	-25.9	NC	NC	20	03-88	.00	.0	0	0	0	00-00-00	8.3	1.48	12.3	1.60	19.7	22	2.8	258	13,043	5,496	0	0.0	06
Three Cl Inc	-28.6	-21.1	-33.3	-1.2n	-.38	NC	-100.0	-100.0	NC	-13	12-87	.00	.0	0	0	0	00-00-00	-60.0	.20	-12.1	1.09	-13.2	0	10.9	25	19,046	80	0	0.0	03
Total Systs	36.1	36.1	31.5	7.7q	.48	33.3	33.3	37.1	34	25	03-88	.00	.0	0	0	0	05-02-86	15.4	1.42	21.8	1.13	24.7	0	5.2	302	15,916	283	+0	0.0	12
Triad System	14.8	11.8	6.8	6.8s	.87	72.7	54.5	70.6	NC	9	03-88	.00	.0	0	0	0	00-00-00	5.5	.80	4.4	2.09	9.2	1	2.8	92	7,369	4,759	-21	0.0	09
TSR Inc	227.8	28.9	45.0	.4n	.16	-61.1	-35.3	-38.5	-16	4	02-83	.00	.0	0	0	0	04-01-85	1.4	1.79	2.5	1.52	3.8	13	2.5	6	2,256	333	0	0.0	05
202 Data Sys	-50.0	-70.0	-33.3	.4s	.13	-100.0	-100.0	-18.8	NC	3	04-88	.00	.0	0	0	0	00-00-00	20.0	.12	2.4	1.33	3.2	14	5.0	10	3,351	164	0	0.0	10
Utd Educ & Soft	60.1	60.1	95.6	5.1q	.97	133.3	133.3	169.4	NC	37	04-88	.00	.0	0	0	0	04-15-88	5.7	1.07	6.1	6.07	37.0	109	2.4	48	4,616	669	+45	0.0	01
Utd Tote	18.0	23.1	25.0	1.3s	.85	50.0	75.0	9.0	NC	15	04-88	.00	.0	0	104	23	00-00-00	6.5	.83	5.4	2.83	15.3	120	1.8	18	1,630	339	0	0.0	10
VM Software	27.0	27.0	.0	3.2q	.51	-16.7	-16.7	-35.4	39	14	03-88	.00	.0	0	0	0	12-22-86	10.0	.98	9.8	1.42	13.9	0	4.3	104	6,406	2,407	0	0.0	12
Warner Cptr □	12.0	18.1	15.7	2.5s	.40	.0	17.6	37.9	NC	34	04-88	.00	.0	0	0	0	00-00-00	11.4	1.41	16.1	2.12	34.2	3	1.8	35	5,936	413	0	0.0	10
Worldwide Cptr	19.4	19.4	14.2	.4q	.22	40.0	40.0	69.2	NC	17	03-88	.00	.0	0	0	0	00-00-00	2.5	4.72	11.8	1.42	16.7	0	2.1	3	1,610	0	0	0.0	12
Xscribe Cp	2.7	7.4	6.6	.5f	.10	-100.0	-72.2	NC	NC	12	03-88	.00	.0	0	0	0	00-00-00	1.6	2.25	3.6	3.31	11.9	31	2.6	8	5,062	571	0	0.0	03

Trends and Forecasts: Drugs (SIC 283)

(in millions of dollars except as noted)

						Percent Change				
						Compound Annual		Annual		
ITEM	1984	1985	1986[1]	1987[2]	1988[3]	1972-85	1980-85	1985-86	1986-87	1987-88
Industry Data										
Value of shipments[4]	28,967	31,332	33,667	36,331	—	11.1	9.5	7.5	7.9	—
2831 Biological Products	2,669	2,713	2,945	3,190	—	16.8	13.8	8.6	8.3	—
2833 Medicinals & Botanicals	3,410	3,283	3,293	3,441	—	15.4	3.2	0.3	4.5	—
2834 Pharmaceutical Preps	22,888	25,335	27,429	29,700	—	10.2	10.1	8.3	8.3	—
Value of shipments (1982$)	25,757	25,820	26,124	26,536	27,007	3.7	1.7	1.2	1.6	1.8
2831 Biological Products	2,644	2,307	2,436	2,538	2,670	9.7	7.9	5.6	4.2	5.2
2833 Medicinals & Botanicals	3,611	3,583	3,667	3,752	3,837	9.5	2.9	2.3	2.3	2.3
2834 Pharmaceutical Preps	19,502	19,930	20,021	20,245	20,500	2.6	0.9	0.5	1.1	1.3
Total employment (000)	167	164	165	167	168	1.8	−1.1	0.6	1.2	0.6
2831 Biological Products	26.2	25.0	26.2	27.6	28.2	7.2	2.7	4.8	5.3	2.2
2833 Medicinals & Botanicals	17.3	15.7	15.8	16.2	16.6	5.5	0.3	0.6	2.5	2.5
2834 Pharmaceutical Preps	124	123	123	123	123	0.7	−1.8	0.0	0.0	0.0
Production workers (000)	81.8	78.8	80.9	81.5	82.3	1.3	−2.3	2.7	0.7	1.0
2831 Biological Products	12.6	11.8	12.1	12.5	12.8	6.4	1.0	2.5	3.3	2.4
2833 Medicinals & Botanicals	9.5	8.6	9.8	10.1	10.5	4.9	−1.1	14.0	3.1	4.0
2834 Pharmaceutical Preps	59.7	58.4	59.0	58.9	59.0	0.2	−3.1	1.0	−0.2	0.2
Average hourly earnings ($)	10.74	11.48	11.88	12.28	—	7.6	7.1	3.5	3.4	—
2831 Biological Products	8.44	9.20	9.27	9.96	—	6.9	9.5	0.8	7.4	—
2833 Medicinals & Botanicals	12.50	13.61	13.98	14.45	—	7.7	6.5	2.7	3.4	—
2834 Pharmaceutical Preps	10.96	11.60	12.03	12.45	—	7.7	7.0	3.7	3.5	—
Product Data										
Value of shipments[5]	26,877	29,532	31,653	34,048	—	11.0	10.7	7.2	7.6	—
2831 Biological Products	2,788	3,021	3,217	3,464	—	14.9	13.5	6.5	7.7	—
2833 Medicinals & Botanicals	3,398	3,347	3,357	3,509	—	11.7	1.2	0.3	4.5	—
2834 Pharmaceutical Preps	20,692	23,164	25,079	27,075	—	10.5	12.2	8.3	8.0	—

Value of shipments (1982$)	23,832	24,250	24,510	24,845	25,253	3.7	2.7	1.1	1.4	1.6
2831 Biological Products	2,761	2,569	2,661	2,756	2,864	8.0	7.7	3.6	3.6	3.9
2833 Medicinals & Botanicals	3,629	3,700	3,780	3,869	3,960	6.0	1.0	2.2	2.4	2.4
2834 Pharmaceutical Preps	17,442	17,981	18,068	18,220	18,429	2.9	2.4	0.5	0.8	1.1
Shipments price index[6] (1982=100)	112.8	121.5	128.8	136.8	—	6.8	7.7	6.0	6.2	—
2831 Biological Products	102.5	118.1	121.4	126.2	—	6.7	5.5	2.8	4.0	—
2833 Medicinals & Botanicals	93.6	90.4	88.7	90.6	—	3.9	0.1	−1.9	2.1	—
2834 Pharmaceutical Preps	118.5	128.9	138.9	148.7	—	7.4	9.7	7.8	7.1	—
Trade Data										
Value of imports	1,665	1,896	2,322	2,815	3,408	17.0	16.0	22.5	21.2	21.1
2831 Biological Products	76.8	163	158	180	200	27.0	60.5	−3.1	13.9	11.1
2833 Medicinals & Botanicals	1,341	1,517	2,007	2,479	3,050	15.9	12.9	32.3	23.5	23.0
2834 Pharmaceutical Preps	247	216	157	156	158	23.1	28.5	−27.3	−0.6	1.3
Import/new supply ratio[7]	0.058	0.060	0.068	0.076	—	5.2	4.6	13.3	11.8	—
2831 Biological Products	0.027	0.051	0.047	0.049	—	9.9	41.5	−7.8	4.3	—
2833 Medicinals & Botanicals	0.283	0.312	0.374	0.414	—	2.7	8.6	19.9	10.7	—
2834 Pharmaceutical Preps	0.012	0.009	0.006	0.006	—	12.3	12.5	−33.3	0.0	—
Value of exports	2,637	2,671	3,087	3,265	3,493	12.5	6.3	15.6	5.8	7.0
2831 Biological Products	456	516	623	598	600	18.2	5.9	20.7	−4.0	0.3
2833 Medicinals & Botanicals	1,497	1,465	1,815	2,006	2,220	11 9	4.8	23.9	10.5	10.7
2834 Pharmaceutical Preps	684	691	648	660	673	10.8	10.4	−6.2	1.9	2.0
Export/shipments ratio	0.098	0.090	0.098	0.096	—	1.2	−4.1	8.9	−2.0	—
2331 Biological Products	0.164	0.171	0.194	0.173	—	2.9	−6.7	13.5	−10.8	—
2833 Medicinals & Botanicals	0.441	0.438	0.541	0.572	—	0.1	3.7	23.5	5.7	—
2834 Pharmaceutical Preps	0.033	0.030	0.026	0.024	—	0.3	−1.3	−13.3	−7.7	—

[1]Estimated except for exports and imports.
[2]Estimated.
[3]Forecast.
[4]Value of all products and services sold by the Drugs industry.
[5]Value of products classified in the Drugs industry produced by all industries.
[6]Developed by the Office of Industry Assessment, ITA.
[7]New supply is the sum of product shipments plus imports.

SOURCE: U.S. Department of Commerce: Bureau of the Census, Bureau of Economic Analysis, International Trade Administration (ITA). Estimates and forecasts by ITA.

Source: *U.S. Industrial Outlook 1988,* U.S. Department of Commerce.

Trends and Forecasts: Soap, Cleaners, and Toilet Goods (SIC 284)

(in millions of dollars except as noted)

						Percent Change				
						Compound Annual		Annual		
ITEM	1984	1985	1986[1]	1987[2]	1988[3]	1972-85	1980-85	1985-86	1986-87	1987-88
Industry Data										
Value of shipments[4]	28,517	29,555	30,474	31,561	—	8.9	6.1	3.1	3.6	—
2841 Soap & Other Detergents	9,468	10,053	10,191	10,583	—	8.7	4.0	1.4	3.8	—
2842 Polishes/Sanitation Gds	4,902	4,541	4,665	4,734	—	7.1	1.9	2.7	1.5	—
2843 Surface Active Agents	2,482	2,534	2,568	2,594	—	14.0	7.9	1.3	1.0	—
2844 Toilet Preparations	11,665	12,427	13,050	13,650	—	9.0	9.6	5.0	4.6	—
Value of shipments (1982$)	25,984	26,124	26,471	27,067	27,685	1.4	0.2	1.3	2.3	2.3
2841 Soap & Other Detergents	9,031	9,348	9,533	9,727	9,920	1.4	−0.6	2.0	2.0	2.0
2842 Polishes/Sanitation Gds	4,665	4,232	4,296	4,355	4,420	−0.8	−2.4	1.5	1.4	1.5
2843 Surface Active Agents	2,462	2,425	2,455	2,485	2,515	7.3	4.1	1.2	1.2	1.2
2844 Toilet Preparations	9,826	10,119	10,187	10,500	10,830	1.5	1.5	0.7	3.1	3.1
Total employment (000)	125	123	123	120	—	0.7	0.2	0.0	−2.4	—
2841 Soap & Other Detergents	32.8	34.1	34.1	34.1	—	0.6	−0.6	0.0	0.0	—
2842 Polishes/Sanitation Gds	21.9	20.2	21.4	21.0	—	−1.7	−3.9	5.9	−1.9	—
2843 Surface Active Agents	9.3	9.3	9.7	10.1	—	2.3	4.7	4.3	4.1	—
2844 Toilet Preparations	60.9	59.8	57.4	55.2	55.0	1.7	1.7	−4.0	−3.8	−0.4
Production workers (000)	73.4	71.9	71.0	70.0	—	0.1	−0.8	−1.3	−1.4	—
2841 Soap & Other Detergents	19.2	20.0	20.0	20.1	—	−0.2	−2.2	0.0	0.5	—
2842 Polishes/Sanitation Gds	13.8	12.8	12.9	12.8	—	−1.1	−2.7	0.8	−0.8	—
2843 Surface Active Agents	4.5	4.4	4.5	4.6	—	1.1	4.1	2.3	2.2	—
2844 Toilet Preparations	35.9	34.7	33.6	32.5	32.2	0.7	0.4	−3.2	−3.3	−0.9
Average hourly earnings ($)	9.70	10.28	—	—	—	7.4	6.6	—	—	—
2841 Soap & Other Detergents	12.11	13.20	13.77	14.36	—	7.7	7.6	4.3	4.3	—
2842 Polishes/Sanitation Gds	8.94	9.04	9.36	9.40	—	7.5	6.7	3.5	0.4	—
2843 Surface Active Agents	11.03	11.55	11.96	12.47	—	8.1	8.7	3.5	4.3	—
2844 Toilet Preparations	8.38	8.83	9.26	9.71	—	7.1	5.9	4.9	4.9	—
Product Data										
Value of shipments[5]	27,096	27,938	28,755	29,706	—	8.7	6.2	2.9	3.3	—
2841 Soap & Other Detergents	8,265	8,512	8,535	8,825	—	8.8	3.7	0.3	3.4	—
2842 Polishes/Sanitation Gds	4,096	4,115	4,227	4,289	—	6.9	4.1	2.7	1.5	—
2843 Surface Active Agents	2,580	2,485	2,523	2,552	—	11.8	4.2	1.5	1.1	—
2844 Toilet Preparations	12,155	12,826	13,470	14,040	—	8.9	9.2	5.0	4.2	—

Value of shipments (1982$)	24,645	24,641	24,861	25,369	26,032	1.3	0.2	0.9	2.0	2.6
2841 Soap & Other Detergents	7,923	7,962	8,022	8,156	8,450	1.5	−0.7	0.8	1.7	3.6
2842 Polishes/Sanitation Gds	3,932	3,873	3,928	3,982	4,042	−0.9	−0.1	1.4	1.4	1.5
2843 Surface Active Agents	2,552	2,362	2,396	2,430	2,470	5.3	0.1	1.4	1.4	1.6
2844 Toilet Preparations	10,239	10,444	10,515	10,800	11,070	1.4	1.1	0.7	2.7	2.5
Shipments price index[6] (1982 = 100)	110.7	114.0	116.3	117.4	—	7.2	6.0	2.0	0.9	—
2841 Soap & Other Detergents	104.6	107.2	106.7	108.5	—	7.2	4.5	−0.5	1.7	—
2842 Polishes/Sanitation Gds	104.3	106.4	107.7	107.7	—	7.6	4.3	1.2	0.0	—
2843 Surface Active Agents	101.1	105.2	105.3	105.2	—	6.2	4.0	0.1	−0.1	—
2844 Toilet Preparations	120.1	124.1	129.4	130.7	—	7.3	8.2	4.3	1.0	—
Trade Data										
Value of imports	470	572	688	710	749	23.6	25.6	20.3	3.2	5.5
2841 Soap & Other Detergents	68.9	80.3	105	84.9	90.0	27.3	24.2	30.8	−19.1	6.0
2842 Polishes/Sanitation Gds	23.1	25.3	28.6	35.3	42.0	20.7	19.0	13.0	23.4	19.0
2843 Surface Active Agents	95.8	145	175	159	147	22.3	19.2	20.7	−9.1	−7.5
2844 Toilet Preparations	282	322	380	431	470	23.8	30.6	18.0	13.4	9.0
Import/new supply ratio[7]	0.017	0.020	—	—	—	13.2	17.3	—	—	—
2841 Soap & Other Detergents	0.006	0.007	—	—	—	16.1	18.5	—	—	—
2842 Polishes/Sanitation Gds	0.026	0.029	—	—	—	14.5	12.6	—	—	—
2843 Surface Active Agents	0.036	0.055	0.065	0.059	—	9.0	13.7	18.2	−9.2	—
2844 Toilet Preparations	0.024	0.025	—	—	—	13.2	20.1	—	—	—
Value of exports	715	670	689	779	884	11.6	−1.7	2.8	13.1	13.5
2841 Soap & Other Detergents	144	132	119	139	160	7.7	−3.7	−9.8	16.8	15.1
2842 Polishes/Sanitation Gds	85.7	76.3	75.0	81.6	90.0	9.5	−3.4	−1.7	8.8	10.3
2843 Surface Active Agents	155	149	175	199	224	12.5	−1.3	17.4	13.7	12.6
2844 Toilet Preparations	331	312	320	360	410	14.5	−0.6	2.6	12.5	13.9
Export/shipments ratio	0.026	0.024	0.024	0.026	—	2.7	−7.3	0.0	8.3	—
2841 Soap & Other Detergents	0.017	0.016	0.014	0.015	—	−0.9	−6.2	−12.5	7.1	—
2842 Polishes/Sanitation Gds	0.021	0.019	0.018	0.019	—	2.4	−6.8	−5.3	5.6	—
2843 Surface Active Agents	0.060	0.060	0.069	0.078	—	0.7	−5.1	15.0	13.0	—
2844 Toilet Preparations	0.027	0.024	0.024	0.025	—	4.8	−9.3	0.0	4.2	—

[1]Estimated except for exports and imports.
[2]Estimated.
[3]Forecast.
[4]Value of all products and services sold by the Soap, Cleaners, and Toilet Goods industry.
[5]Value of products classified in the Soap, Cleaners, and Toilet Goods industry produced by all industries.
[6]Developed by the Office of Industry Assessment, ITA.
[7]New supply is the sum of product shipments plus imports.
SOURCE: U.S. Department of Commerce: Bureau of the Census, Bureau of Economic Analysis, International Trade Administration (ITA). Estimates and forecasts by ITA.

Source: *U.S. Industrial Outlook 1988*, U.S. Department of Commerce.

Company	Revenue Pct. Change Last Qtr	Revenue Pct. Change FY to Date	Revenue Pct. Change Last 12 Mos	Earnings Last 12 Mos	Earnings Per Share Last 12 Mos	Earnings Per Share Pct. Change Last Qtr	Earnings Per Share Pct. Change FY to Date	Earnings Per Share Pct. Change Last 12 Mos	Earnings 5-Year Growth Rate	Earnings Par Growth Rate	Earnings Date of Report	Dividends Current Rate Amt	Dividends Current Rate Yield	Dividends 5-Year Growth Rate	Dividends Payout Last FY	Dividends Payout Last 5 Yrs.	Dividends Last X-Dvd Date	Ratio Analysis Profit Margin	Ratio Analysis Asset Turnover	Ratio Analysis Return on Total Assets	Ratio Analysis Leverage Ratio	Ratio Analysis Return on Equity	Ratio Analysis Debt to Equity	Ratio Analysis Current Ratio	Shareholdings Market Value	Shareholdings Latest Shares Outstndng.	Shareholdings Held by Banks-Funds	Shareholdings Insider Net Trading	Shareholdings Short Interest Ratio	Shareholdings Fiscal Year Ends
	%	%	%	$Mil	$	%	%	%	%	%	-	$	%	%	%	%	-	π/r	x r/a	= π/a	x a/e	= π/e	%	-	$Mil	000	000	000	Days	Mo
Ethical Drugs																														
Ind. Group	14.5	15.9	17.8	6,969.0	1.69	28.4	27.9	12.4	13	9	- - -	1.00	2.9	1	39	42	- - - -	11.3	.96	10.9	2.06	22.5	17	1.9	143,226	4,124,666	G	+ 28	2.5	- -
A L Labs	66.4	66.4	38.9	6.9q	.77	25.0	25.0	26.2	44	10	03-88	.12	1.0	0	16	12	06-14-88	3.8	.74	2.8	4.43	12.4	215	1.6	111	9,065	2,129	0	0.0	12
Abbott Labs	18.4	18.4	15.8	663.1q	2.92	22.6	22.6	20.7	18	19	03-88	1.20	2.7	19	35	35	04-11-88	14.5	1.04	15.1	2.10	31.7	13	1.4	10,178	226,169	109,651	+1	0.6	12
Adv Magnetics ♦	-30.8	9.1	33.3	.9s	.28	-100.0	-50.0	21.7	NC	7	03-88	.00	.0	0	0	0	00-00-00	22.5	.28	6.2	1.08	6.7	0	10.8	21	3,040	109	0	0.0	09
Alco Hlth	21.2	22.7	25.5	20.5s	1.61	38.7	33.8	27.8	NC	13	03-88	.12	.4	0	0	0	11-23-87	1.1	4.00	4.4	3.30	14.5	71	1.8	368	12,686	4,278	0	0.0	09
Alpha One Bio	-100.0	-90.0	.0	-.6n	-.18	-100.0	-100.0	NC	NC	-18	12-87	.00	.0	0	0	0	00-00-00	-60.0	.20	-11.8	1.54	-18.2	15	3.5	22	3,383	302	0	0.0	03
Alza Cp A	36.3	36.3	36.1	15.1q	.45	33.3	33.3	45.2	39	11	03-88	.00	.0	0	0	0	07-09-86	30.8	.20	6.2	1.76	10.9	56	7.4	752	31,152	15,037	0	4.1	12
Am Home Prod	9.6	9.6	4.0	865.7q	5.90	11.7	11.7	10.7	9	13	03-88	3.60	4.9	9	58	60	05-09-88	16.8	1.12	18.8	1.82	34.2	0	2.1	10,780	145,924	79,525	+32	1.7	12
Amgen □	-42.1	48.7	46.6	1.7f	.10	NE	100.0	100.0	NC	1	03-88	.00	.0	0	0	0	00-00-00	3.9	.23	.9	1.11	1.0	10	9.3	451	16,691	5,857	-3	0.0	03
Appld Bioscience	48.6	48.6	37.0	3.2q	.99	40.0	40.0	59.7	NC	14	03-88	.00	.0	0	0	0	00-00-00	8.6	.79	6.8	2.07	14.1	5	1.2	55	3,190	894	0	0.0	12
Barr Labs □	-11.3	-8.4	-5.0	2.5n	.34	-69.2	-54.5	-53.4	NC	8	03-88	.00	.0	0	0	0	00-00-00	4.5	1.07	4.8	1.60	7.7	26	3.2	61	7,562	596	-5	0.0	06
Beecham Grp	-11.4	-11.3	87.1	355.3s	.96	33.3	21.1	NC	NC	7	09-87	.59	3.7	0	44	44	06-14-88	8.6	1.06	9.1	1.92	17.5	29	2.2	6,088	377,548	8,250	0	0.0	03
Biocraft Labs	6.6	102.0	104.0	14.6f	1.05	-31.6	105.9	105.9	NC	22	03-88	.00	.0	0	0	0	01-16-86	14.6	1.23	18.0	1.23	22.1	5	5.7	216	13,962	2,194	0	43.1	03
Biomerica Inc	.0	-6.7	.0	-2.0n	-.33	-100.0	NE	NE	NC	-44	02-88	.00	.0	0	0	0	12-15-80	NM	NC	NC	NC	-43.5	0	3.8	4	5,888	310	0	0.0	05
Biopharmceutics	-14.3	-11.5	-33.3	-5.6s	-.70	NC	NE	-100.0	NC	-63	03-88	.00	.0	0	0	0	00-00-00	NM	NC	NC	NC	-62.9	1	25.7	7	7,986	189	0	3.6	09
Biotechnica Intl	287.5	287.5	42.8	-8.9q	-1.70	NE	NE	NE	NC	0	03-88	.00	.0	0	0	0	00-00-00	-89.0	.43	-38.2	.00	NS	-1278	10.2	18	5,177	159	0	0.0	12
Block Drugs Co	20.5	15.7	15.5	37.9f	2.29	20.0	16.2	16.2	11	12	03-88	.56	1.9b	4	23	27	06-07-88	10.6	1.12	11.9	1.36	16.2	10	2.8	470	16,076	2,897	-4	0.0	03
Bolar Pharm	92.0	92.0	89.6	21.6q	1.09	105.9	105.9	101.9	30	29	03-88	.03	.1	10	3	5	02-09-88	19.6	1.18	23.2	1.27	29.4	0	3.1	509	19,658	5,726	0	9.1	12
Bristol-Myers	12.8	12.8	11.7	746.3q	2.59	19.7	19.7	19.4	13	8	03-88	1.68	4.1	2≥	57	48	06-27-88	13.4	1.18	15.8	1.46	23.1	7	3.0	11,661	287,931	149,266	+148	2.0	12
Calif Biotech	88.9	88.9	.0	-8.6q	-.73	NE	NE	NE	NC	-11	03-88	.00	.0	0	0	0	00-00-00	-95.6	.10	-9.1	1.18	-10.7	0	1.9	77	11,674	2,027	0	0.0	12
Camb Bio Sci	50.0	50.0	200.0	-5.3q	-.67	NE	NE	NE	NC	-28	03-88	.00	.0	0	0	0	00-00-00	NM	NC	NC	NC	-27.7	5	9.3	105	7,832	630	0	0.0	12
Carter-Wallace	5.3	7.1	7.0	37.8f	2.50	10.6	16.8	16.8	20	13	03-88	.54	1.4	18	20	18	05-05-88	7.8	1.31	10.2	1.61	16.4	11	2.4	568	15,150	2,749	0	0.2	03
Centocor Inc	48.1	48.1	90.0	7.4q	.65	30.8	30.8	NE	NC	7	03-88	.00	.0	0	0	0	00-00-00	13.0	.38	5.0	1.30	6.5	6	3.6	303	11,216	4,188	+12	0.0	12
Collaborative Rsh	60.0	43.4	40.0	-.8n	-.07	NE	NE	NE	NC	-5	05-88	.00	.0	0	0	0	00-00-00	-5.7	.72	-4.1	1.10	-4.5	0	8.5	40	10,676	819	0	0.0	08
Cooper Develop	.0	1400.0	-98.5	-11.4s	-3.70	NE	-100.0	NE	NC	-19	04-88	.00	.0	0	0	0	07-28-87	NM	NC	NC	NC	-18.5	2	1.6	42	3,259	107	+100	0.0	10
Cytogen	-14.3	-14.3	60.0	-7.0q	-.59	NE	NE	NE	NC	-16	03-88	.00	.0	0	0	0	00-00-00	-87.5	.17	-14.9	1.05	-15.7	0	18.8	94	11,922	631	0	0.0	12
Diagnostic Prods	24.4	24.4	25.8	10.2q	1.63	39.4	39.4	40.5	25	20	03-88	.16	.4	0	0	0	07-14-88	26.2	.78	20.4	1.07	21.9	0	11.0	259	6,157	1,197	0	0.0	12
Duramed Phar	-6.3	-6.3	-5.2	-5.7q	-2.18	-100.0	-100.0	-100.0	NC	0	03-88	.00	.0	0	0	0	00-00-00	-31.7	.86	-27.4	.00	NM	629	.7	13	3,025	60	0	0.0	12
E Z EM Inc	27.2	22.6	21.2	6.7n	.84	23.1	39.5	33.3	NC	16	02-88	.00	.0	0	0	0	05-16-86	11.8	1.19	14.1	1.16	16.4	0	6.7	85	7,989	1,312	+0	0.0	05
Elan Cp	34.6	8.9	10.0	-3.6f	-.24	-100.0	-100.0	-100.0	NC	-7	03-88	.00	.0	0	0	25	06-15-87	-32.7	.19	-6.1	1.08	-6.6	0	18.0	134	15,319	4,328	0	0.0	03
Evergood Prods ◇	-4.8	5.6	6.2	-.3f	-.22	NE	NE	NE	NC	-4	12-87	.00	.0	0	0	0	00-00-00	-1.8	1.33	-2.4	1.79	-4.3	10	1.9	2	1,232	0	0	0.0	12
Forest Labs	46.3	32.8	32.8	16.8f	.96	22.7	24.7	24.7	34	17	03-88	.00	.0	0	0	0	05-16-86	19.8	.75	14.9	1.15	17.1	1	4.9	364	17,353	6,464	0	4.8	03
Genentech Inc	92.7	92.7	94.1	54.2q	.64	350.0	350.0	NE	NC	18	03-88	.00	.0	0	0	0	03-02-87	20.4	.71	14.4	1.28	18.4	11	3.6	2,123	78,644	13,226	-130	5.3	12
Glaxo Hldgs	32.6	32.6	33.8	952.9s	1.29	41.7	43.8	44.9	NC	37	12-87	.45	2.6	0	16	20	04-18-88	29.5	1.17	34.4	1.65	56.8	1	2.1	12,677	740,236	42,487	0	0.4	06
Greenwich Pharm	.0	100.0	.0	-7.0s	-.42	NE	NE	NE	NC	0	06-87	.00	.0	0	0	0	00-00-00	NC	NC	NC	NC	NM	0	5.1	159	17,457	286	0	0.0	12

Hickam Dow	.0	.0	.0	1.2q	.49	-23.1	-23.1	-38.8	12	10	03-88	.00	.0	0	0	0	00-00-00	10.0	.69	6.9	1.39	9.6	19	21.0	16	2,188	574	0	0.0	12
Hycor Biomed	17.6	17.6	16.6	.4q	.08	200.0	200.0	NE	NC	15	03-88	.00	.0	0	0	0	00-00-00	5.7	1.56	8.9	1.66	14.8	15	2.6	7	5,072	36	0	0.0	12
ICN Pharm	55.1	55.1	33.0	-31.3q	-1.69	7.1	7.1	-100.0	NC	-24	02-88	.00	.0	0	0	0	00-00-00	-23.5	.20	-4.6	5.26	-24.2	253	2.1	118	17,119	2,568	0	42.6	11
Immunex Cp	108.0	108.0	75.0	.7q	.09	NE	NE	NE	NC	3	03-88	.00	.0	0	0	0	00-00-00	5.0	.20	1.0	2.50	2.5	148	17.9	118	7,680	3,377	0	0.0	12
Incstar Cp	160.0	143.6	116.6	.8f	.26	1000.0	188.9	188.9	20	12	03-88	.00	.0	0	0	0	00-00-00	6.2	1.45	9.0	1.34	12.1	12	3.3	17	3,071	338	0	0.0	03
Integ Genetics	.0	.0	.0	-3.7q	-.37	-100.0	-100.0	NE	NC	-12	03-88	.00	.0	0	0	0	00-00-00	-33.6	.30	-10.1	1.19	-12.0	8	9.7	41	10,165	1,519	0	0.0	12
Invitron Cp	-334.4	-78.7	.0	.0*	-.57	NE	NE	NC	NC	0	03-88	.00	.0	0	0	0	00-00-00	NC	NC	NC	NC	.0	88	1.1	75	13,634	714	0	0.0	06
Jones Med Ind	26.7	26.7	16.6	1.0q	.30	28.6	28.6	7.1	NC	17	03-88	.00	.0	0	0	0	00-00-00	14.3	1.04	14.9	1.15	17.2	9	15.0	17	3,146	22	0	0.0	12
Leiner P Nutri	15.8	-1.6	-1.3	3.0f	.86	-17.1	-14.9	-14.9	8	13	03-88	.00	.0	0	0	0	00-00-00	4.2	1.90	8.0	1.61	12.9	0	2.3	33	3,473	502	+3	0.0	03
Life Tech ◇	15.0	15.0	22.5	12.5q	.92	62.5	62.5	170.6	NC	16	03-88	.00	.0	0	0	0	00-00-00	10.0	1.21	12.1	1.34	16.2	7	4.5	196	13,260	1,091	0	0.0	12
Lifecore Biomed	37.5	8.3	33.3	.1n	.01	NE	NE	NE	NC	2	03-88	.00	.0	0	0	0	00-00-00	2.5	.48	1.2	1.25	1.5	7	7.0	26	5,146	92	0	0.0	06
Lilly Eli Co	1.2	1.2	-3.5	671.7q	4.63	15.7	15.7	11.0	10	11	03-88	2.30	2.7	9	45	45	05-09-88	18.4	.70	12.8	1.73	22.1	12	1.9	11,672	139,369	91,937	+44	6.5	12
Liposome	100.0	100.0	150.0	-6.6q	-.49	NE	NE	NE	NC	-27	03-88	.00	.0	0	0	0	00-00-00	NM	NC	NC	NC	-26.5	1	14.3	48	13,628	2,583	0	0.0	12
Lyphomed Inc	9.7	9.7	27.3	19.8q	.66	-25.0	-25.0	13.8	57	13	03-88	.00	.0	0	0	0	06-23-86	11.2	.62	6.9	1.94	13.4	70	7.3	306	29,868	10,009	0	0.0	12
Marion Labs	23.9	33.0	38.6	139.0n	.88	56.3	62.8	69.2	54	31	03-88	.28	1.5	31	26	26	06-14-88	19.0	1.61	30.6	1.50	45.8	0	1.9	2,811	150,937	62,136	-64	1.8	06
MedCh Prods	95.0	54.1	66.6	2.2s	.55	7.1	8.0	57.1	NC	32	02-88	.00	.0	0	0	0	03-14-88	22.0	1.18	25.9	1.25	32.4	1	5.1	52	3,605	91	-300	0.1	08
Merck & Co	29.3	29.3	24.7	976.5q	2.42	40.8	40.8	39.9	19	22	03-88	1.28	2.3	11	37	41	05-26-88	18.1	.95	17.2	2.68	46.1	8	1.4	23,089	410,469	211,610	+10	2.2	12
Molecular Biosyst	-850.0	121.7	150.0	.9f	.11	NE	175.0	175.0	NC	7	03-88	.00	.0	0	0	0	00-00-00	18.0	.36	6.4	1.03	6.6	1	29.0	129	8,899	738	0	0.0	03
Mylan Labs	10.8	.9	1.0	25.2f	.70	16.7	7.7	7.7	54	24	03-88	.10	.8	0	14	13	06-29-88	26.3	.88	23.2	1.21	28.1	7	6.6	470	36,139	5,256	-4	25.8	03
Natures Sunshine	17.8	17.8	21.2	2.4q	1.00	94.4	94.4	127.3	6	25	03-88	.00	.0	0	0	0	05-16-88	6.0	2.73	16.4	1.54	25.3	2	1.8	29	2,423	409	-1	0.0	12
Newport Pharm	-437.0	-13.3	.0	.0*	-.23	NE	NE	NE	NC	0	03-88	.00	.0	0	0	0	00-00-00	NC	NC	NC	NC	.0	72	6.2	56	11,261	980	-1	0.0	12
Novo Industri	82.3	41.3	41.4	78.3f	3.07	44.6	9.3	9.3	3	12	12-87	.51	1.5	9	13	11	04-21-88	9.7	.73	7.1	1.99	14.1	23	2.0	860	25,487	6,778	0	1.0	12
Pfizer Inc	15.9	15.9	11.7	718.0q	4.26	15.9	15.9	5.7	13	10	03-88	2.00	3.9	14	44	43	07-25-88	14.1	.74	10.4	1.78	18.5	6	2.1	8,492	164,489	94,371	-6	1.3	12
Praxis Biol	-66.7	-66.7	-26.6	-2.8q	-.22	-100.0	-100.0	-100.0	NC	-12	03-88	.00	.0	0	0	0	00-00-00	-25.5	.38	-9.7	1.28	-12.4	6	6.5	52	13,503	403	0	0.0	12
Ribi Immuno	100.0	100.0	.0	-1.5q	-.16	NE	NE	NE	NC	-10	03-88	.00	.0	0	0	0	05-01-85	NM	NC	NC	NC	-10.0	0	19.3	39	8,623	949	0	0.0	12
Robins, AH	7.8	7.8	7.9	-1644.3q	-65.26	NE	NE	-100.0	NC	0	03-88	.00	.0	0	0	NE	11-19-84	NM	NC	NC	NC	NS	0	3.7	616	24,161	8,350	0	0.0	12
Rorer Group	9.0	9.0	8.3	55.4q	1.72	17.4	17.4	454.8	12	8	03-88	.80	2.3	3	46	39	02-29-88	5.9	.85	5.0	2.84	14.2	114	1.7	1,111	31,419	21,705	0	4.3	12
Scher Plough	9.6	9.6	11.8	333.0q	2.92	26.4	26.4	27.0	10	12	03-88	1.40	2.7	4	38	43	05-02-88	12.0	.88	10.5	2.20	23.1	13	1.3	5,736	111,914	68,667	-6	2.8	12
Smith Labs □	45.8	37.0	57.1	-4.9s	-.36	50.0	100.0	-100.0	NC	-11	04-88	.00	.0	0	0	0	00-00-00	-44.5	.20	-8.9	1.21	-10.8	11	8.9	29	13,210	1,124	-1	0.0	10
Smithkline Beck	15.8	15.8	15.4	590.2q	4.69	16.5	16.5	24.1	9	23	03-88	1.84	4.1	6	36	42	05-09-88	13.2	1.01	13.3	2.80	37.2	45	1.3	5,549	124,348	78,726	0	1.9	12
Squibb Corp	26.9	26.9	34.6	379.9q	3.65	34.8	34.8	33.7	17	14	03-88	1.60	2.5	13	35	38	05-16-88	16.6	.83	13.7	1.82	24.9	5	1.7	6,530	103,033	63,992	+128	2.0	12
Summa Med	150.0	329.4	350.0	-1.4n	-.15	NE	NE	NE	NC	0	12-87	.00	.0	0	0	0	00-00-00	-15.6	1.99	-31.1	.00	NS	-72	.4	15	9,911	564	0	0.0	03
Synbiotics □	53.8	51.1	40.0	.1f	.03	-100.0	200.0	200.0	NC	2	03-88	.00	.0	0	0	0	00-00-00	1.4	.71	1.0	1.80	1.8	5	2.4	37	4,583	704	0	0.0	03
Synergen	-26.1	-26.1	-25.0	-1.4q	-.14	-100.0	-100.0	-100.0	NC	-3	03-88	.00	.0	0	0	0	00-00-00	-23.3	.11	-2.5	1.12	-2.8	12	56.5	72	9,544	1,913	0	0.0	12
Syntex Corp	13.1	11.9	15.7	284.4n	2.41	19.2	21.3	23.6	19	22	04-88	1.30	3.1	25	41	38	05-09-88	23.1	1.07	24.8	1.90	47.1	21	1.5	4,957	118,367	57,169	+25	1.3	07
Unimed Inc	42.9	17.6	33.3	-.8s	-.27	NE	NE	NE	NC	-10	03-88	.00	.0	0	0	0	03-02-81	-20.0	.38	-7.5	1.32	-9.9	7	7.1	15	3,227	136	0	0.0	09
Utd Guardian	27.3	27.3	.0	-.5q	-.09	NC	NC	-100.0	NC	-15	05-87	.00	.0	0	0	NE	09-12-85	-10.0	.94	-9.4	1.56	-14.7	24	3.4	33	4,796	262	+3	0.0	02
Unvrsty Genetic	-28.6	-28.6	100.0	-3.3q	-.34	NE	NE	NE	NC	-83	10-87	.00	.0	0	0	0	00-00-00	-82.5	.62	-50.8	1.62	-82.5	8	1.9	3	12,208	658	-5	0.0	07
Upjohn Co	10.9	10.9	10.0	319.5q	1.71	18.6	18.6	18.8	17	11	03-88	.72	2.2	9	36	39	06-30-88	12.4	.85	10.5	1.82	19.1	26	2.1	6,108	187,941	103,616	+53	1.0	12
Ventrex Labs	18.5	8.6	.0	-5.3s	-.49	NE	NE	NE	NC	-48	03-88	.00	.0	0	0	0	00-00-00	-44.2	.81	-35.6	1.34	-47.7	17	4.7	15	10,727	1,832	0	0.0	09
Warner-Lambrt	12.9	12.9	12.9	305.9q	4.35	19.6	19.6	.5	NC	18	03-88	2.16	3.2	4	43	81	05-02-88	8.5	1.46	12.4	2.82	35.0	34	1.3	4,647	68,587	41,457	+1	0.7	12
XOMA Cp	1100.0	1100.0	.0	-3.4q	-.78	NE	NE	NE	NC	-9	03-88	.00	.0	0	0	0	00-00-00	-37.8	.13	-5.1	1.73	-8.8	64	18.8	140	10,602	2,907	0	0.0	12
Zenith Labs	-44.0	-44.0	-17.3	-16.4q	-.78	NE	NE	NE	NC	-51	03-88	.00	.0	0	0	20	11-25-86	-43.2	.51	-21.9	2.32	-50.8	24	1.3	27	21,205	1,593	0	26.0	12

Continued

Company	Revenue: Pct. Change Last Qtr	Revenue: Pct. Change FY to Date	Revenue: Pct. Change Last 12 Mos	Earnings: Last 12 Mos	Earnings: Per Share Last 12 Mos	Earnings: Per Share Pct. Change Last Qtr	Earnings: Per Share Pct. Change FY to Date	Earnings: Per Share Pct. Change Last 12 Mos	Earnings: 5-Year Growth Rate	Earnings: Par Growth Rate	Earnings: Date of Report	Dividends: Current Rate Amt	Dividends: Current Rate Yield	Dividends: 5-Year Growth Rate	Dividends: Payout Last FY	Dividends: Payout Last 5 Yrs.	Dividends: Last X-Dvd Date	Ratio Analysis: Profit Margin	Ratio Analysis: Asset Turnover	Ratio Analysis: Return on Total Assets	Ratio Analysis: Leverage Ratio	Ratio Analysis: Return on Equity	Ratio Analysis: Debt to Equity	Ratio Analysis: Current Ratio	Shareholdings: Market Value	Shareholdings: Latest Shares Outstndng.	Shareholdings: Held by Banks-Funds	Shareholdings: Insider Net Trading	Shareholdings: Short Interest Ratio	Shareholdings: Fiscal Year Ends
	%	%	%	$Mil	$	%	%	%	%	%	-	$	%	%	%	%	-	π/r x	r/a =	π/a x	a/e =	π/e	%	-	$Mil	000	000	000	Days	Mo
Proprietary Drugs																														
Ind. Group	22.6	10.9	10.7	143.1	.88	71.3	74.6	48.6	17	10	- - -	.25	1.6	1	24	25	- - - -	6.9	.65	4.5	3.04	13.7	58	1.0	2,411	155,938	21,785	- 70	4.1	- -
Carrington Labs	77.8	77.8	25.0	-4.8q	-.87	NE	NE	NE	NC	-76	02-88	.00	.0	0	0	0	00-00-00	-96.0	.53	-50.5	1.51	-76.2	0	6.8	66	5,618	1,781	0	0.0	11
Chattem Inc	15.2	-2.9	1.6	2.5n	1.47	657.1	-55.8	-18.3	-4	6	02-88	.56	2.9	4	33	25	02-08-88	4.2	.79	3.3	2.88	9.5	56	1.2	28	1,452	485	0	0.0	05
Erbamont	11.4	11.4	8.4	124.8q	2.82	121.1	121.1	77.4	28	15	03-88	.60	2.2	0	20	20	05-10-88	12.5	.44	5.5	3.53	19.4	69	.8	1,190	44,289	3,817	0	1.2	12
GNC Inc	-1.3	-1.3	1.1	1.2q	.04	42.9	42.9	-80.0	NC	-4	04-88	.16	3.3	19	1600	96	05-25-88	.3	2.67	.8	1.63	1.3	10	2.2	161	33,015	8,068	0	0.0	01
IGI	-18.4	-15.3	-11.1	.8n	.10	.0	80.0	NE	NC	10	09-87	.00	.0	0	0	0	00-00-00	5.0	.88	4.4	2.16	9.5	64	2.3	66	7,507	365	0	0.0	12
Inst Clin Pharm	.0	.0	.0	2.3n	.00	NC	NC	NC	NC	NC	03-87	.00	.0	0	0	0	00-00-00	20.9	NC	NC	NC	NC	0	.0	62	5,150	36	0	0.0	NA
Iroquois Brands	-11.6	-11.6	-1.3	-1.4q	-2.06	-30.8	-30.8	-100.0	NC	-17	03-88	.00	.0	0	0	0	12-04-81	-1.9	1.11	-2.1	7.86	-16.5	342	1.8	13	585	220	0	0.0	12
KV Pharma	33.3	20.7	12.5	1.0n	.11	NE	18.2	-38.9	NC	20	12-87	.00	.0	0	0	0	07-29-86	3.7	1.68	6.2	3.29	20.4	131	1.9	64	4,747	1,009	0	33.3	03
Natures Bounty	-147.2	80.3	.0	.0*	.18	-50.0	33.3	NE	NC	0	03-88	.00	.0	0	0	0	00-00-00	NC	NC	NC	NC	.0	30	1.2	6	3,933	174	0	0.0	09
Par Pharm	14.3	20.3	38.0	12.5s	1.11	20.8	31.8	54.2	49	28	03-88	.02	.1	0	0	0	06-06-88	14.4	1.11	16.0	1.78	28.5	35	2.8	201	11,004	1,385	-67	26.6	09
Pharmacontrol	118.2	113.9	100.0	-3.0f	-.68	NE	NE	NE	NC	-27	06-87	.00	.0	0	0	0	00-00-00	-37.5	.18	-6.7	4.00	-26.8	240	3.3	11	5,870	177	0	0.0	06
Scherer RP Cp	32.1	27.4	27.6	11.4f	1.04	29.4	30.0	30.0	NC	8	03-88	.36	1.3	2	32	229	06-14-88	3.9	1.18	4.6	2.50	11.5	40	2.7	250	9,100	1,963	-3	0.0	03
T Cell Sciences	25.0	90.0	100.0	-1.2n	-.15	NE	NE	NE	NC	-12	01-88	.00	.0	0	0	0	00-00-00	-30.0	.27	-8.2	1.40	-11.5	0	8.2	25	8,224	431	0	0.0	04
Thompson Med	7.4	7.4	15.2	9.8q	1.30	46.3	46.3	44.4	-8	14	02-88	.40	1.9	31	36	26	06-24-88	6.8	2.12	14.4	1.42	20.5	0	3.2	159	7,447	1,260	0	0.0	11
Viratek Inc	-50.0	-50.0	-87.5	-12.8q	-1.61	NE	NE	NE	NC	-99	02-88	.00	.0	0	0	0	08-19-86	NM	NC	NC	NC	-99.2	0	3.5	108	7,997	614	0	0.0	11

Cosmetics and Grooming Aids

Company	Revenue: Pct. Change Last Qtr	Revenue: Pct. Change FY to Date	Revenue: Pct. Change Last 12 Mos	Earnings: Last 12 Mos	Earnings: Per Share Last 12 Mos	Earnings: Per Share Pct. Change Last Qtr	Earnings: Per Share Pct. Change FY to Date	Earnings: Per Share Pct. Change Last 12 Mos	Earnings: 5-Year Growth Rate	Earnings: Par Growth Rate	Earnings: Date of Report	Dividends: Current Rate Amt	Dividends: Current Rate Yield	Dividends: 5-Year Growth Rate	Dividends: Payout Last FY	Dividends: Payout Last 5 Yrs.	Dividends: Last X-Dvd Date	Ratio Analysis: Profit Margin	Ratio Analysis: Asset Turnover	Ratio Analysis: Return on Total Assets	Ratio Analysis: Leverage Ratio	Ratio Analysis: Return on Equity	Ratio Analysis: Debt to Equity	Ratio Analysis: Current Ratio	Shareholdings: Market Value	Shareholdings: Latest Shares Outstndng.	Shareholdings: Held by Banks-Funds	Shareholdings: Insider Net Trading	Shareholdings: Short Interest Ratio	Shareholdings: Fiscal Year Ends
	%	%	%	$Mil	$	%	%	%	%	%	-	$	%	%	%	%	-	π/r ×	r/a =	π/a ×	a/e =	π/e	%	-	$Mil	000	000	000	Days	Mo
Ind. Group	18.0	19.0	8.8	576.5	1.66	16.0	17.8	101.9	10	13	- - -	.78	3.0	0	43	61	- - - -	6.6	1.26	8.3	3.05	25.3	80	1.6	8,715	341,255	127,216	+ 222	.9	- -
Alberto Cul A	NA	NA	NA	NA	NA	NA	NA	NA	NA	NC	00-00	.30	1.2	NA	NA	NA	04-29-88	NA	NC	NA	NC	NA	NA	NA	132	5,147	1,380	0	NA	NA
Alberto Cul B ◇	21.6	20.1	20.6	23.1s	1.64	44.0	75.0	107.6	NC	14	03-88	.30	.9	4	18	44	04-28-88	4.1	2.07	8.5	2.05	17.4	18	1.8	490	13,914	1,643	0	17.8	09
Alfin Inc	9.7	4.8	-21.7	-7.5n	-1.06	NE	NE	NE	NC	-74	04-83	.00	.0	0	0	0	02-28-86	-41.7	.79	-33.0	2.25	-74.3	10	1.9	26	6,696	484	0	2.0	07
Aloette Cosmetics	18.2	18.2	13.3	2.2q	.73	41.7	41.7	7.4	NC	16	03-88	.00	.0	0	0	0	00-00-00	12.9	1.03	13.3	1.19	15.8	5	8.3	20	2,936	28	0	0.0	12
Avon Products	20.6	20.6	1.7	171.3q	2.42	-63.0	-63.0	5.7	0	4	03-88	2.00	8.3	-3	77	89	05-13-88	6.0	1.12	6.7	3.37	22.6	108	1.2	1,700	70,840	44,482	0	0.5	12
Beauticontrol Cos	43.5	34.8	21.7	2.8s	.73	75.0	80.8	2.8	NC	19	05-88	.00	.0	0	0	0	00-00-00	10.0	1.59	15.9	1.18	18.8	0	4.9	58	3,941	198	0	0.0	11
Beauty Labs	142.9	104.9	150.0	.8n	.46	-68.2	-62.5	NC	NC	0	12-87	.00	.0	0	0	0	00-00-00	8.0	2.86	22.9	.00	NM	0	1.3	6	2,317	222	0	0.0	03
Butler John	14.7	13.3	9.5	5.1s	.79	15.8	22.6	12.9	NC	15	02-88	.16	.7	0	17	9	02-08-88	11.1	.94	10.4	1.78	18.5	30	3.1	149	6,477	799	+35	0.0	08
Carme Inc □	20.8	12.9	.0	.7n	.27	25.0	22.2	NE	NC	47	04-88	.00	.0	0	0	0	00-00-00	7.8	1.58	12.3	3.80	46.7	53	1.0	13	2,696	20	-4	0.0	07
CCA Inds	4.8	4.8	25.0	-.3q	-.04	-100.0	-100.0	-100.0	NC	-6	02-88	.00	.0	0	0	0	00-00-00	-3.0	1.33	-4.0	1.58	-6.3	33	5.2	5	6,948	733	0	0.0	11
Del Labs	7.4	7.4	1.8	3.4q	2.38	26.0	26.0	12.8	6	9	03-88	.40	1.2	4	18	17	05-09-88	3.1	1.32	4.1	2.61	10.7	93	2.7	42	1,289	188	0	0.2	12
DEP Cp	1.8	41.8	50.8	4.3n	.71	185.7	222.2	153.6	15	25	04-88	.00	.0	0	0	0	05-02-88	5.0	1.34	6.7	3.79	25.4	192	1.9	67	5,951	1,168	0	0.0	07
Genzyme	29.3	29.3	42.8	.3q	.03	.0	.0	-40.0	NC	1	03-88	.00	.0	0	0	0	00-00-00	1.5	.47	.7	1.29	.9	13	6.8	76	8,509	2,806	0	0.0	12
Gillette Co	18.5	18.5	13.0	250.2q	2.17	35.4	35.4	804.2	-5	25	03-88	.86	2.1	6	37	55	04-26-88	7.6	1.21	9.2	4.53	41.7	140	1.6	4,643	115,350	51,758	+46	0.9	12
Golden Oil	-33.3	-43.5	-50.0	-.4f	-.03	NC	NE	NE	NC	-8	06-87	.00	.0	0	0	0	00-00-00	-40.0	.14	-5.7	1.32	-7.5	21	.7	3	12,340	133	0	0.0	06
Goody Products	6.0	6.0	17.5	10.3q	1.59	-7.8	-7.8	32.5	12	10	03-88	.46	2.4	14	22	24	06-09-88	5.1	1.51	7.7	1.77	13.6	31	3.1	122	6,486	896	0	0.0	12
Guest Supply	74.7	74.4	27.7	-9.7s	-2.73	NE	NE	-100.0	NC	-35	03-88	.00	.0	0	0	0	00-00-00	-21.1	1.26	-26.6	1.30	-34.6	1	2.7	21	3,742	624	0	0.0	09
Helene Curtis	35.2	35.2	26.5	12.3q	3.34	1000.0	1000.0	9.9	20	13	05-88	.30	.7	0	10	4	07-26-88	2.3	2.26	5.2	2.67	13.9	36	1.5	165	3,937	1,064	0	0.0	02
Johnson Prdts	-15.5	-9.9	-9.3	-.5n	-.11	-100.0	-100.0	-100.0	NC	-4	05-88	.00	.0	0	0	0	04-30-80	-1.7	1.29	-2.2	1.82	-4.0	27	2.1	8	3,987	308	0	0.0	08
Lee Pharm	7.2	-8.4	-49.1	-2.8s	-.71	-100.0	-95.8	-100.0	NC	-30	03-88	.00	.0	0	0	0	10-27-86	-9.7	1.74	-16.9	1.75	-29.5	0	1.7	22	3,960	352	+145	0.0	09
MEM Co	19.7	19.7	5.8	2.2q	.81	NE	NE	-20.6	-5	1	03-88	.60	3.8	2	74	52	06-24-88	3.1	1.35	4.2	1.26	5.3	0	3.9	42	2,658	718	0	0.0	12
Minnetonka	-19.6	-19.6	-21.3	58.1q	3.30	-18.2	-18.2	459.3	NC	63	03-88	.00	.0	0	0	0	05-27-87	40.3	1.09	44.1	1.42	62.5	0	2.7	295	19,527	3,806	0	0.0	12
Noxell Cp	8.9	8.9	8.9	46.0q	1.14	18.2	18.2	16.3	17	14	03-88	.40	2.1	19	33	32	03-14-88	9.2	1.70	15.6	1.38	21.6	0	3.0	508	26,722	13,081	0	0.0	12
Redken Labs	11.2	3.8	5.1	4.4n	1.49	16.7	-11.8	23.1	-12	6	04-88	.20	.5	-7	12	21	04-04-88	3.6	1.33	4.8	1.56	7.5	15	2.8	95	2,741	325	0	0.0	07
Ross Cosmetics	42.9	50.0	22.2	.2s	.08	-100.0	-50.0	NE	NC	5	02-88	.00	.0	0	0	0	00-00-00	1.8	1.50	2.7	2.00	5.4	22	2.1	7	2,144	0	0	0.0	08

Trends and Forecasts: Electronic Components and Accessories (SIC 367)

(in millions of dollars except as noted)

ITEM	1984	1985	1986[1]	1987[2]	1988[3]	Percent Change: Compound Annual 1972-85	Compound Annual 1980-85	Annual 1985-86	Annual 1986-87	Annual 1987-88
Industry Data										
Value of shipments[4]	47,983	42,920	43,893	47,549	51,427	12.9	9.2	2.3	8.3	8.2
Value of shipments (1982$)	48,290	50,263	54,282	61,020	68,512	11.5	13.9	8.0	12.4	12.3
Total employment (000)	582	558	531	529	563	4.0	2.3	−4.8	−0.4	6.4
Production workers (000)	375	345	319	321	342	3.0	0.5	−7.5	0.6	6.5
Average hourly earnings ($)	8.17	8.71	8.92	8.85	—	7.6	6.9	2.4	−0.8	—
Product Data										
Value of shipments[5]	45,489	42,487	41,692	45,120	48,782	13.1	10.2	−1.9	8.2	8.1
Value of shipments (1982$)	45,769	50,185	52,569	59,140	66,460	11.2	15.1	4.8	12.5	12.4
Shipments price index[6] (1982=100)	100.7	92.7	92.3	92.2	92.5	−5.9	−4.1	−0.4	−0.1	0.3
Trade Data										
Value of imports (ITA)[7]	10,351	8,545	9,329	10,422	11,568	24.0	13.6	9.2	11.7	11.0
Value of exports (ITA)[8]	7,410	6,190	7,126	8,551	9,577	15.4	4.4	15.1	20.0	12.0

[1]Estimated except for exports and imports.

[2]Estimated.

[3]Forecast.

[4]Value of all products and services sold by the Electronic Components and Accessories industry.

[5]Value of products classified in the Electronic Components and Accessories industry produced by all industries.

[6]Developed by the Office of Microelectronics and Instrumentation, ITA.

[7]Import data are developed by the chapter author.

[8]Export data are developed by the chapter author.

SOURCE: U.S. Department of Commerce: Bureau of the Census, Bureau of Economic Analysis, International Trade Administration (ITA). Estimates and forecasts by ITA.

Source: *U.S. Industrial Outlook 1988,* U.S. Department of Commerce.

Trends and Forecasts: Radio and TV Communication Equipment (SIC 3662)

(in millions of dollars except as noted)

ITEM	1984	1985	1986[1]	1987[2]	1988[3]	Percent Change: Compound Annual 1972-85	Compound Annual 1980-85	Annual 1985-86	Annual 1986-87	Annual 1987-88
Industry Data										
Value of shipments[4]	40,919	47,618	49,618	54,600	60,422	13.5	14.9	4.2	10.0	10.7
Value of shipments (1982$)	37,311	42,726	43,709	45,894	48,648	8.1	8.5	2.3	5.0	6.0
Total employment (000)	505	542	538	534	535	4.2	5.6	−0.7	−0.7	0.2
Production workers (000)	242	258	247	247	250	3.6	4.0	−4.3	0.0	1.2
Average hourly earnings ($)	10.69	11.53	11.53	11.89	—	7.5	7.4	0.0	3.1	—
Product Data										
Value of shipments[5]	39,924	45,725	47,646	52,429	58,020	13.9	14.6	4.2	10.0	10.7
Value of shipments (1982$)	36,403	41,027	41,971	44,069	46,713	8.5	8.3	2.3	5.0	6.0
Shipments price index[6] (1982=100)	109.7	111.5	—	—	—	5.0	5.9	—	—	—
Trade Data										
Value of imports (ITA)[7]	2,881	3,707	3,939	4,075	4,197	22.8	26.6	6.3	3.5	3.0
Import/new supply ratio[8]	0.067	0.075	0.076	0.072	0.068	7.3	9.8	1.3	−5.3	−5.6
Value of exports (ITA)[9]	2,768	2,897	3,144	3,325	3,525	12.7	8.0	8.5	5.8	6.0
Export/shipments ratio	0.069	0.063	0.066	0.063	0.061	−1.1	−5.8	4.8	−4.5	−3.1

[1]Estimated except for exports and imports.
[2]Estimated.
[3]Forecast.
[4]Value of all products and services sold by the Radio and TV Communication Equipment industry.
[5]Value of products classified in the Radio and TV Communication Equipment industry produced by all industries.
[6]Developed by the Office of Industry Assessment, ITA.
[7]Import data are developed by the chapter author.
[8]New supply is the sum of product shipments plus imports.
[9]Export data are developed by the chapter author.

SOURCE: U.S. Department of Commerce: Bureau of the Census, Bureau of Economic Analysis, International Trade Administration (ITA). Estimates and forecasts by ITA.

Source: *U.S. Industrial Outlook 1988*, U.S. Department of Commerce.

Company	Revenue: Pct. Change Last Qtr	Revenue: Pct. Change FY to Date	Revenue: Pct. Change Last 12 Mos	Earnings: Last 12 Mos	Earnings: Per Share Last 12 Mos	Earnings: Per Share Pct. Change Last Qtr	Earnings: Per Share Pct. Change FY to Date	Earnings: Per Share Pct. Change Last 12 Mos	Earnings: 5-Year Growth Rate	Earnings: Par Growth Rate	Earnings: Date of Report	Dividends: Current Rate Amt	Dividends: Current Rate Yield	Dividends: 5-Year Growth Rate	Dividends: Payout Last FY	Dividends: Payout Last 5 Yrs.	Dividends: Last X-Dvd Date	Ratio Analysis: Profit Margin	Ratio Analysis: Asset Turnover	Ratio Analysis: Return on Total Assets	Ratio Analysis: Leverage Ratio	Ratio Analysis: Return on Equity	Ratio Analysis: Debt to Equity	Ratio Analysis: Current Ratio	Shareholdings: Market Value	Shareholdings: Latest Shares Outstndng.	Shareholdings: Held by Banks-Funds	Shareholdings: Insider Net Trading	Shareholdings: Short Interest Ratio	Shareholdings: Fiscal Year Ends
-	%	%	%	$Mil	$	%	%	%	%	%	-	$	%	%	%	%	-	π/r x	r/a =	π/a x	a/e =	π/e	%	-	$Mil	000	000	000	Days	Mo
Electronic Devices																														
Ind. Group	8.2	13.1	11.1	732.9	.83	- 9.4	- 9.1	34.1	4	6	- - -	.22	1.2	0	21	23	- - - -	3.7	1.19	4.4	2.00	8.8	19	2.0	14,693	830,337	265,936	- 513	1.3	- -
Anaren Micrwve	-15.3	-11.2	-10.0	1.3n	.32	-81.8	-35.5	-40.7	3	5	03-88	.00	.0	0	0	0	03-30-81	4.8	.79	3.8	1.26	4.8	12	7.7	28	4,209	1,210	0	0.0	06
Andersen Grp	16.9	16.9	8.5	-8.0q	-4.51	NE	NE	NE	NC	0	05-88	.00	.0	0	0	0	07-01-83	-15.7	1.51	-23.7	.00	NM	224	1.8	12	1,789	243	0	0.0	02
Anthem Elects	-401.4	-57.4	.0	.0*	.50	-100.0	-36.8	31.6	NC	0	03-88	.00	.0	0	0	4	07-16-87	NC	NC	NC	NC	.0	6	4.3	158	11,275	8,329	-6	0.8	12
Avnet Inc	23.3	19.7	17.7	45.8n	1.28	171.4	145.5	161.2	-15	4	03-88	.50	2.0	0	78	38	05-27-88	2.6	1.65	4.3	1.63	7.0	34	5.0	908	35,622	24,824	+2	0.4	06
AVX Corp	75.2	75.2	51.6	18.1q	1.37	65.4	65.4	495.7	NC	9	03-88	.06	.3	0	0	35	07-05-88	5.7	.75	4.3	2.26	9.7	75	2.6	245	13,062	8,520	0	3.6	12
Base Ten Systs	NA	NA	NA	NA	NA	NA	NA	NA	NA	NC	00-00	.00	.0	NA	NA	NA	01-16-84	NA	NC	NA	NC	NA	NA	NA	17	2,798	561	0	NA	NA
Base Ten	23.5	39.3	18.9	-.4s	-.10	NE	NE	NE	NC	-3	04-88	.00	.0	0	0	0	01-16-84	-.9	1.11	-1.0	3.20	-3.2	80	1.6	4	642	51	0	0.0	10
Burr-Brown	37.0	37.0	27.5	6.5q	.67	1150.0	1150.0	123.3	3	10	03-88	.00	.0	0	0	0	12-15-86	4.2	1.26	5.3	1.87	9.9	30	2.2	150	9,498	2,866	-20	0.0	12
Cetec Corp	-4.7	-4.7	3.1	.5q	.31	-30.0	-30.0	34.8	NC	2	03-88	.20	1.8	5	59	66	05-02-88	1.5	1.67	2.5	1.72	4.3	19	2.5	19	1,767	525	0	0.0	12
Comdial Cp	-6.3	-6.3	10.1	-9.2q	-.51	-100.0	-100.0	NE	NC	0	03-88	.00	.0	0	0	0	00-00-00	-10.6	1.46	-15.5	.00	NM	19	.8	17	17,975	1,005	+10	0.0	12
Cosmo Commun	.0	.0	50.0	-1.5q	-.30	NE	NE	-100.0	NC	-6	03-88	.00	.0	0	0	0	00-00-00	-3.1	1.03	-3.2	2.00	-6.4	3	1.9	14	5,060	734	+60	0.0	12
Datamarine	22.7	23.8	11.7	.8s	.71	81.8	42.3	-20.2	20	15	03-88	.00	.0	0	0	0	00-00-00	4.2	2.17	9.1	1.63	14.8	11	2.6	8	1,082	92	+3	0.0	09
Decom Sys	-8.3	-30.2	-33.3	.1s	.02	-87.5	-100.0	-94.1	NC	3	03-88	.00	.0	0	0	0	00-00-00	1.3	1.23	1.6	2.06	3.3	60	4.0	4	2,714	11	0	0.0	09
Dewey Electrns	-27.6	2.6	.0	.0n	.02	-100.0	-100.0	NC	NC	0	03-88	.00	.0	0	0	0	00-00-00	.0	NC	NC	NC	.0	79	1.7	3	1,339	60	0	0.0	06
Di-An-Controls	-66.7	-66.7	.0	.7q	.80	-100.0	-100.0	NE	NC	54	03-88	.00	.0	0	0	0	00-00-00	70.0	.63	43.8	1.23	53.8	0	7.5	1	826	0	-2	0.0	12
Dotronix Inc	132.6	167.5	192.3	1.8n	.65	-100.0	4.7	38.3	NC	32	03-88	.00	.0	0	0	0	00-00-00	4.7	2.19	10.3	3.07	31.6	58	1.5	17	3,242	392	0	0.0	06
Dyansen Cp	15.4	15.4	35.0	.8q	.17	-100.0	-100.0	-5.6	NC	15	03-88	.00	.0	0	0	0	00-00-00	3.0	2.33	7.0	2.20	15.4	35	1.7	10	4,995	940	0	0.0	12
E Systems	-2.8	-2.8	1.2	59.2q	1.92	-5.7	-5.7	-6.8	7	10	03-88	.50	1.7	10	26	26	06-13-88	4.9	1.82	8.9	1.55	13.8	12	2.9	886	30,803	14,805	-21	2.7	12
EDO Cp	9.0	9.0	9.2	6.6q	.98	-13.0	-13.0	16.7	NC	9	03-88	.28	1.6	15	28	22	06-03-88	5.1	.84	4.3	3.05	13.1	75	1.9	112	6,314	2,425	0	41.0	12
Electron Missiles □	-42.9	-32.5	-33.3	-.7n	-.15	NE	NE	NC	NC	0	12-87	.00	.0	0	0	0	00-00-00	-17.5	1.05	-18.4	.00	NM	229	3.0	2	4,108	176	-0	0.0	03
Eng Measure	13.0	.0	-10.0	-.3n	-.11	-100.0	-100.0	-100.0	NC	-6	01-88	.00	.0	0	0	0	00-00-00	-3.3	.88	-2.9	1.97	-5.7	23	2.5	7	2,821	77	0	0.0	04
Flextronics Inc	135.4	102.2	102.7	5.2f	.59	22.2	59.5	NC	NC	52	03-88	.00	.0	0	0	0	00-00-00	3.6	2.22	8.0	6.50	52.0	148	1.6	63	9,030	910	0	0.0	03
GenRad	1.9	1.9	-4.4	-34.8q	-2.12	NE	NE	NE	NC	-48	03-88	.00	.0	0	0	NE	09-25-85	-17.8	.97	-17.2	2.77	-47.7	81	2.1	198	16,516	11,058	0	5.2	12
Gentex Cp	-2.7	-2.7	.0	1.0q	.17	-42.9	-42.9	-15.0	NC	14	03-88	.00	.0	0	0	0	00-00-00	7.1	1.58	11.2	1.26	14.1	3	4.5	23	5,843	253	0	0.0	12
HEI Inc	12.5	16.7	.0	.3s	.21	NE	NE	NE	NC	12	02-88	.00	.0	0	0	0	00-00-00	4.3	1.37	5.9	2.03	12.0	68	3.0	4	1,423	18	0	0.0	08
IFR Systs	10.0	15.5	8.8	5.6n	.92	6.3	48.9	35.3	NC	24	03-88	.23	2.6	0	0	0	05-09-88	15.1	1.58	23.9	1.35	32.2	11	5.3	54	6,175	677	0	0.0	06
ILC Tech	11.3	11.2	10.0	1.4s	.65	NE	NE	NE	NC	17	03-88	.00	.0	0	0	0	00-00-00	4.2	1.81	7.6	2.25	17.1	22	2.2	13	2,176	491	0	0.0	09
Interactive Tech	82.9	82.9	83.3	2.3q	.57	88.9	88.9	54.1	NC	21	01-88	.00	.0	0	0	0	00-00-00	10.5	.73	7.7	2.71	20.9	0	1.4	48	3,859	53	0	0.0	10
Jetronic Ind	6.0	6.0	8.6	-5.1q	-2.10	NE	NE	-100.0	NC	-41	04-88	.00	.0	0	0	0	08-11-86	-8.1	1.47	-11.9	3.45	-41.1	62	1.6	5	2,457	202	0	0.0	01
KLA Instruments	37.6	20.7	14.6	6.4n	.35	7.7	-17.1	-36.4	16	7	03-88	.00	.0	0	0	0	12-17-84	6.3	.87	5.5	1.35	7.4	0	3.2	329	17,556	10,108	+30	0.0	06
Knogo Cp	-46.7	-4.7	-4.0	1.1f	.16	-100.0	-87.2	-87.2	-4	-1	02-88	.30	2.2	0	144	6	04-14-88	2.3	.39	.9	1.22	1.1	0	NA	89	6,507	1,459	0	1.3	02
Lowrance Elect	1.4	2.6	.0	-1.0n	-.32	-100.0	-100.0	-100.0	NC	-8	04-88	.00	.0	0	0	0	00-00-00	-2.3	1.65	-3.8	2.21	-8.4	7	1.6	6	3,484	570	0	0.0	07
Marlton	-80.0	-80.0	-70.0	-4.7q	-1.42	NE	NE	NE	NC	-43	03-88	.00	.0	0	0	0	10-30-79	-78.3	.24	-18.8	2.27	-42.7	0	1.4	3	3,338	0	0	0.0	12
Merrimac Ind	32.4	32.4	6.2	1.1q	.57	NE	NE	338.5	-11	9	03-88	.00	.0	0	0	0	04-18-88	6.5	1.17	7.6	1.17	8.9	1	6.5	14	1,999	650	0	0.0	12
Mitel Cp	-1.3	-7.5	-7.5	-32.6f	-.41	NE	NE	NE	NC	-12	03-88	.00	NA	0	0	0	00-00-00	-7.8	.63	-4.9	2.45	-12.0	7	1.7	197	78,951	8,064	-225	6.6	03

New Century Ent	33.3	149.7	157.1	-8.6f	-.58	NE	NE	NE	NC	-65	02-88	.00	.0	0	0	0	00-00-00	-23.9	.66	-15.7	4.15	-65.2	155	NA	10	14,958	90	-400	0.0	02
N Atlantic Ind	-11.1	-11.1	-11.1	-5.3q	-1.54	NE	NE	-100.0	NC	-29	03-88	.00	.0	0	0	0	04-04-84	-16.6	.96	-16.0	1.82	-29.1	21	2.2	11	3,488	650	0	0.0	12
Northn Telecom	5.1	5.1	7.7	344.7q	1.39	.0	.0	9.4	12	12	03-88	.24	NA	5	17	16	06-06-88	7.0	1.01	7.1	2.08	14.8	10	1.4	4,493	236,491	30,881	0	0.0	12
Pac Scientific	136.5	82.3	82.5	4.4f	.80	266.7	53.8	53.8	-20	4	12-87	.40	2.9	3	50	35	06-13-88	2.8	1.14	3.2	2.25	7.2	49	2.0	76	5,552	2,482	+0	0.0	12
Plantronics	5.3	7.3	5.4	10.0n	1.63	10.0	16.8	31.5	17	14	03-88	.16	.8	0	11	16	04-28-88	8.5	1.13	9.6	1.56	15.0	17	3.3	122	6,009	4,712	+38	0.0	06
Regency Electro	-25.9	-1.3	-1.3	.4n	.03	-100.0	-100.0	NE	NC	1	03-88	.00	.0	-6	182	89	11-09-87	.5	1.00	.5	2.00	1.0	15	2.7	60	10,732	3,063	0	0.0	06
Ripley Co Inc	.0	.0	20.0	.3q	.57	-21.1	-21.1	72.7	-2	6	05-88	.20	3.5	0	33	36	03-24-88	5.0	1.18	5.9	1.54	9.1	12	3.1	3	589	99	0	0.0	02
Robotic Vision	2.4	2.5	-11.7	.1s	.02	-100.0	NE	NE	NC	2	03-88	.00	.0	0	0	0	00-00-00	.7	1.86	1.3	1.62	2.1	0	2.0	26	5,106	684	0	0.0	09
Sci-Atlanta	6.1	7.3	6.7	30.4n	1.29	32.0	37.9	NE	NC	14	03-88	.12	.9	1	12	32	05-19-83	5.8	1.83	10.6	1.42	15.1	2	3.9	325	23,449	11,972	0	1.2	06
Sec Tag Sys	16.7	47.2	60.0	.5f	.04	NE	NE	NE	NC	7	03-88	.00	.0	0	0	0	00-00-00	6.3	.94	5.9	1.15	6.8	8	10.4	31	14,462	1,192	0	0.0	03
Semtech Cp	42.9	42.9	41.6	1.1q	.36	233.3	233.3	157.1	NC	15	04-88	.00	.0	0	0	0	03-14-83	6.5	1.35	8.8	1.72	15.1	38	4.0	14	2,891	473	0	0.8	01
Servo Cp Am	-2.6	-19.3	-16.6	-.8s	-1.18	-100.0	-100.0	-100.0	NC	-11	04-88	.00	.0	0	0	0	00-00-00	-5.3	1.32	-7.0	1.54	-10.8	4	2.3	9	697	16	0	0.0	10
Solitron Device	-49.2	-22.6	-24.0	-4.7f	-1.06	-100.0	-100.0	-100.0	NC	-18	02-88	.00	.0	0	0	0	00-00-00	-12.4	.62	-7.7	2.27	-17.5	52	1.7	21	4,392	878	0	0.0	02
Sooner Defense	38.5	16.9	.0	-2.5n	-.50	.0	-33.3	-100.0	NC	-29	03-88	.00	.0	0	0	0	00-00-00	-11.9	.77	-9.2	3.20	-29.4	132	1.2	9	5,364	495	0	0.0	06
Stanford Telec	3.9	3.2	3.6	.7f	.15	-12.5	-75.0	-75.0	-5	3	03-88	.00	.0	0	0	0	06-17-86	1.2	1.67	2.0	1.45	2.9	0	2.5	52	4,528	1,268	-4	0.0	03
Sun Electric	-7.1	-7.1	7.5	3.4q	.47	11.1	11.1	NC	NC	4	03-88	.00	.0	0	0	0	02-22-82	1.7	1.24	2.1	2.00	4.2	47	2.9	121	7,010	3,232	0	5.7	10
Tech Ops Sev	48.1	37.0	18.1	.7s	.34	57.1	50.0	NC	NC	0	03-88	.00	.0	0	0	0	00-00-00	5.4	NC	NC	NC	NC	0	1.9	8	2,118	0	0	0.1	09
Technic Commun	-11.1	-36.8	-25.0	-.2s	-.18	NE	-100.0	NE	NC	-8	03-88	.00	.0	0	0	0	08-02-83	-6.7	.94	-6.3	1.32	-8.3	0	5.4	11	1,205	80	+1	0.0	09
Tektronix Inc	4.1	1.0	1.6	.9n	.03	-100.0	-99.2	-98.0	-40	-2	02-88	.60	2.4	2	41	29	07-11-88	.1	.00	.1	1.00	.1	6	2.8	707	27,732	20,115	0	8.3	05
TeleConcepts	-11.5	-11.5	41.6	.3q	.08	NE	NE	NE	NC	5	03-88	.00	.0	0	0	0	02-15-83	1.8	.22	2.2	2.05	4.5	55	3.5	7	3,458	230	0	0.9	12
Telemation	.0	2.7	.0	.4f	.09	NE	NC	NC	NC	6	12-87	.00	.0	0	0	0	10-27-86	3.6	.86	3.1	1.97	6.1	52	2.1	9	4,679	10	0	0.0	12
Tex Inst	15.4	15.4	13.5	267.7q	2.99	3.3	3.3	102.0	NC	12	03-88	.72	1.5	0	23	83	06-24-88	4.6	1.37	6.3	2.46	15.5	28	2.1	3,823	78,618	58,927	-6	1.8	12
Torotel Inc	.0	-4.1	.0	-2.1n	-.88	33.3	-85.7	NE	NC	0	01-88	.00	.0	0	0	0	04-24-85	-19.1	1.55	-29.6	.00	NM	100	.9	3	2,548	144	0	0.0	04
Varian Assoc	24.8	24.1	21.4	1.4s	.05	138.9	-100.0	NE	NC	-1	03-88	.26	.8	-2	27	20	07-18-88	.1	2.00	.2	1.50	.3	9	1.6	674	21,841	14,041	0	0.4	09
Varo Inc	7.4	18.8	18.9	4.4f	.98	45.5	19.5	21.0	NC	5	04-88	.40	1.9	0	41	66	02-25-88	3.9	1.31	5.1	1.75	8.9	6	2.1	92	4,419	1,168	+28	0.2	04
Vishay Inter	128.8	72.1	54.2	13.8n	1.76	50.0	36.3	25.7	20	18	03-88	.00	.0	0	0	0	12-15-87	15.2	.89	13.6	1.31	17.8	9	4.4	241	7,918	1,994	0	0.0	06
Wavetek	21.8	16.2	17.1	3.2s	.36	25.0	21.4	9.1	NC	5	03-88	.00	.0	0	0	0	03-25-83	3.6	.97	3.5	1.34	4.7	4	3.1	64	8,888	4,681	0	0.0	09

Electronic Systems

Ind. Group	7.9	12.3	9.3	387.3	.46	- 16.8	- 2.4	- 28.1	- 12	3	- - -	26	.6	2	41	20	- - - -	1.7	.94	1.6	4.13	6.6	71	1.3	26,298	626,173	83,883	- 92	2.6	- -
Adage Inc	-34.5	-10.4	-11.6	-27.9f	-3.50	NE	NE	NE	NC	-68	03-88	.00	.0	0	0	0	09-16-83	-73.4	.70	-51.5	1.32	-68.2	4	3.2	14	8,375	1,983	0	0.0	03
AEL Inds	26.4	26.4	15.4	1.9q	.46	-50.0	-50.0	-42.5	21	4	05-88	.00	.0	0	0	0	08-09-85	1.5	1.13	1.7	2.12	3.6	23	1.3	42	4,377	1,703	0	0.0	02
Andover Controls	6.1	1.8	-4.3	2.8n	.75	12.5	13.2	10.3	19	19	03-88	.00	.0	0	0	0	00-00-00	12.7	1.23	15.6	1.19	18.5	0	5.5	35	3,484	1,241	-5	0.0	06
Astro Med	44.1	44.1	38.4	1.7q	.78	133.3	133.3	122.9	46	15	04-88	.00	.0	0	0	0	00-00-00	9.4	1.03	9.7	1.54	14.9	21	3.2	30	2,120	383	0	0.0	01
Circon Inc	-5.8	-5.8	36.6	-2.4q	-.46	NE	NE	NE	NC	-12	03-88	.00	.0	0	0	0	00-00-00	-5.9	1.03	-6.1	2.03	-12.4	55	2.4	19	5,189	707	0	0.0	12
Cohu Inc	15.7	15.7	10.7	2.2q	1.14	57.9	57.9	208.1	8	11	03-88	.24	2.1	6	19	26	06-01-88	7.1	1.54	10.9	1.27	13.8	0	4.2	21	1,821	246	0	0.0	12
Cubic Corp □	4.6	1.9	3.7	7.3s	.97	11.1	-11.7	79.6	-24	4	03-88	.42	2.7	3	38	27	03-14-88	2.0	1.40	2.8	2.32	6.5	65	2.7	120	7,649	2,328	0	0.5	09
DSC Commun	7.3	7.3	4.2	16.2q	.39	66.7	66.7	39.3	NC	8	03-88	.00	.0	0	0	0	05-24-88	5.1	.86	4.4	1.75	7.7	28	2.2	351	41,283	17,585	0	0.0	12
EECO Inc	46.8	46.8	32.8	2.3q	.58	NE	NE	75.8	NC	5	03-88	.24	3.1	5	63	54	05-12-84	2.7	1.22	3.3	2.82	9.3	45	1.5	30	3,972	638	0	0.0	12
Electron Telecom	25.0	25.0	-40.0	.1q	.07	-16.7	-16.7	-84.4	NC	0	03-88	.08	1.9	0	100	11	08-30-85	3.3	.54	1.9	1.05	2.0	0	23.0	8	1,795	67	0	0.0	12
Epsco Inc	9.8	9.8	44.4	.8q	.54	8.3	8.3	.0	NC	7	03-88	.00	.0	0	0	0	00-00-00	3.1	1.10	3.4	1.97	6.7	53	3.8	20	1,454	191	0	0.0	12
Fibronics	.0	.0	9.3	-3.9q	-.64	-100.0	-100.0	NE	NC	-23	03-88	.00	.0	0	0	0	06-13-85	-11.1	.95	-10.6	2.14	-22.7	23	1.7	23	6,031	513	0	0.0	12
Gen Datacomm	-6.8	-11.1	-5.0	-13.4s	-.85	-100.0	-100.0	-100.0	NC	-16	03-88	.00	.0	0	0	0	05-25-84	-7.1	1.17	-8.3	1.95	-16.2	10	3.6	48	14,324	3,372	0	1.0	09
IEC Electronics	55.2	38.5	52.6	2.0s	.73	43.8	24.2	62.2	24	10	03-88	.20	1.8	0	15	3	03-21-88	6.9	1.33	9.2	1.51	13.9	13	2.7	29	2,651	247	0	0.0	09
Intech Inc	-12.2	-10.9	-12.5	-.3f	-.11	-100.0	-100.0	-100.0	NC	-5	03-88	.00	.0	0	0	0	07-20-87	-2.1	2.00	-4.2	1.19	-5.0	0	5.1	6	3,147	45	0	0.0	03

Continued

Electronic Systems (Continued)

Revenue and Earnings

Company	Revenue Pct. Change Last Qtr	Revenue Pct. Change FY to Date	Revenue Pct. Change Last 12 Mos	Earnings Last 12 Mos	Per Share Last 12 Mos	Per Share Pct. Change Last Qtr	Per Share Pct. Change FY to Date	Per Share Pct. Change Last 12 Mos	5-Year Growth Rate	Par Growth Rate	Date of Report
-	%	%	%	$Mil	$	%	%	%	%	%	-
Keptel	-8.2	.0	31.5	2.0s	.52	-40.0	-30.0	NC	NC	33	03-88
Lifeline Sys	2.3	2.3	11.7	.6q	.17	-42.9	-42.9	88.9	NC	5	03-88
Logicon Inc	-10.1	.6	.4	9.1f	1.93	NE	52.0	52.0	10	13	03-88
Metro-Tel Cp	-31.6	14.6	.0	.0n	-.03	NE	NC	-100.0	NC	0	03-88
Napco Sec	28.9	22.7	18.5	3.8n	.87	22.7	16.9	16.0	38	27	03-88
NEC Cp	12.1	12.1	8.7	127.6s	.08	50.0	25.0	-82.6	-33	4	09-87
Novar Electrns	-17.5	-17.5	-5.8	-1.7q	-.57	NE	NE	NE	NC	-20	03-88
Old Dominion	-27.3	6.5	-20.0	-.8s	-.29	.0	NE	-100.0	NC	-12	04-88
Plessey Co Ltd	-22.7	6.8	6.8	224.4f	3.03	-18.5	16.1	16.1	11	10	03-88
Porta Syst	9.9	9.9	20.9	-2.9q	-.54	23.1	23.1	-100.0	NC	-12	03-88
Radionics Inc	14.8	14.8	20.0	3.3q	.79	31.3	31.3	49.1	10	15	03-88
Ramtek Corp	1.1	4.8	9.3	.7s	.17	-50.0	NE	NE	NC	5	12-87
SCI Systs Inc	75.0	40.0	37.7	17.4n	.84	10.5	13.5	13.5	17	13	03-88
Science Dynamics	-28.6	-28.6	-16.6	.2q	.09	-83.3	-83.3	-64.0	NC	4	03-88
Sensormatic Elec	27.4	17.4	7.7	14.0n	.49	-18.2	2.9	19.5	NC	6	02-88
SHL Systemhouse	45.6	41.0	44.8	11.4s	.42	-40.6	-17.1	-30.0	NC	7	02-88
Silicon Gen	38.1	18.4	15.7	-1.4n	-.11	NC	-100.0	-100.0	NC	-4	03-88
Sunair Electrns	-94.4	-66.7	.0	.0*	.36	-83.3	-65.0	16.1	NC	0	03-88
TCI Intl	47.7	34.8	25.5	4.5s	1.47	6.1	9.6	32.4	5	19	03-88
Tech Ops Land	9.3	9.3	20.0	4.2q	2.03	14.3	14.3	NC	NC	54	12-87
Trans-Inds	12.5	12.5	15.7	.0q	.01	.0	.0	NE	NC	0	03-88
Trans-Lux Cp	6.3	6.3	11.1	-.6q	-.31	-25.0	-25.0	NE	NC	-3	03-88
Univ Sec Inst	-22.2	-15.4	-12.0	-.5f	-.14	-100.0	-100.0	-100.0	NC	-5	03-88
UTL Cp	35.2	17.7	-15.3	-6.9n	-1.60	-100.0	-100.0	-100.0	NC	-23	03-88
Vicon Ind	18.8	21.7	19.4	.7s	.29	550.0	NE	NE	NC	4	03-88
VMX Inc	-61.3	-30.5	-23.3	-11.2n	-.54	NE	NE	NE	NC	-35	03-88

Dividends

Company	Current Rate Amt	Current Rate Yield	5-Year Growth Rate	Payout Last FY	Payout Last 5 Yrs.	Last X-Dvd Date
-	$	%	%	%	%	-
Keptel	.00	.0	0	0	0	00-00-00
Lifeline Sys	.00	.0	0	0	0	00-00-00
Logicon Inc	.32	1.6	19	15	13	06-21-88
Metro-Tel Cp	.00	.0	0	0	15	08-29-86
Napco Sec	.00	.0	0	0	0	08-21-85
NEC Cp	.00	.0	0	86	10	03-24-87
Novar Electrns	.00	.0	0	NE	NE	12-10-85
Old Dominion	.00	.0	0	0	0	00-00-00
Plessey Co Ltd	1.94	6.8	27	53	40	06-02-88
Porta Syst	.00	.0	0	0	0	07-01-83
Radionics Inc	.00	.0	0	0	0	00-00-00
Ramtek Corp	.00	.0	0	0	0	00-00-00
SCI Systs Inc	.00	.0	0	0	0	06-16-87
Science Dynamics	.00	.0	0	0	0	00-00-00
Sensormatic Elec	.05	.6	5	10	12	05-27-88
SHL Systemhouse	.00	.0	0	0	0	12-15-86
Silicon Gen	.00	.0	0	0	0	06-15-83
Sunair Electrns	1.87	40.4	0	0	39	05-10-88
TCI Intl	.00	.0	0	0	0	00-00-00
Tech Ops Land	.00	.0	0	0	0	00-00-00
Trans-Inds	.00	.0	0	0	0	07-13-87
Trans-Lux Cp	.08	.9b	0	NE	34	06-14-88
Univ Sec Inst	.00	.0	0	0	0	07-10-81
UTL Cp	.00	.0	0	0	0	08-22-83
Vicon Ind	.00	.0	0	0	0	07-05-83
VMX Inc	.00	.0	0	0	0	00-00-00

Ratio Analysis and Shareholdings

Company	Profit Margin	Asset Turnover	Return on Total Assets	Leverage Ratio	Return on Equity	Debt to Equity	Current Ratio	Market Value	Latest Shares Outstndng.	Held by Banks-Funds	Insider Net Trading	Short Interest Ratio	Fiscal Year Ends
-	π/r x	r/a =	π/a x	a/e =	π/e	%	-	$Mil	000	000	000	Days	Mo
Keptel	8.0	1.35	10.8	3.04	32.8	82	1.6	21	4,324	759	0	0.0	09
Lifeline Sys	3.2	1.19	3.8	1.32	5.0	5	3.8	12	3,310	621	0	0.0	12
Logicon Inc	4.4	2.48	10.9	1.44	15.7	0	3.0	91	4,497	1,787	-1	30.2	03
Metro-Tel Cp	.0	NC	NC	NC	.0	100	3.7	3	2,000	13	0	0.0	06
Napco Sec	11.9	1.57	18.7	1.45	27.1	26	5.7	53	4,353	860	0	0.0	06
NEC Cp	.7	1.00	.7	5.14	3.6	102	1.2	22,070	281,597	434	0	0.0	03
Novar Electrns	-10.6	.86	-9.1	2.22	-20.2	1	1.4	9	2,738	430	0	0.0	12
Old Dominion	-10.0	.74	-7.4	1.59	-11.8	31	4.5	8	2,575	101	+0	0.0	10
Plessey Co Ltd	9.1	1.30	11.8	2.45	28.9	5	1.8	2,108	73,970	0	0	0.0	03
Porta Syst	-5.6	1.05	-5.9	2.03	-12.0	83	7.4	59	5,451	1,031	0	14.4	12
Radionics Inc	9.2	1.32	12.1	1.22	14.8	1	5.4	56	4,210	744	0	0.0	12
Ramtek Corp	2.0	1.05	2.1	2.24	4.7	17	1.5	4	3,994	735	0	0.0	06
SCI Systs Inc	2.5	1.60	4.0	3.28	13.1	136	3.0	281	20,849	8,293	0	0.0	06
Science Dynamics	4.0	.83	3.3	1.09	3.6	0	11.6	7	3,036	59	-50	0.0	12
Sensormatic Elec	12.6	.45	5.7	1.23	7.0	5	NA	241	28,324	14,802	-1	0.0	05
SHL Systemhouse	5.8	.90	5.2	1.27	6.6	2	4.4	202	24,060	12,414	0	0.0	08
Silicon Gen	-3.2	.72	-2.3	1.61	-3.7	22	1.9	44	12,171	2,671	0	0.0	06
Sunair Electrns	NC	NC	NC	NC	.0	0	17.0	20	4,429	417	0	0.0	09
TCI Intl	8.3	.93	7.7	2.42	18.6	4	.8	43	2,910	624	-46	0.0	09
Tech Ops Land	23.3	1.42	33.1	1.63	53.8	4	1.0	69	2,118	0	0	0.3	09
Trans-Inds	.0	NC	NC	NC	.0	74	1.4	10	2,710	51	0	0.0	12
Trans-Lux Cp	-3.0	.43	-1.3	1.85	-2.4	64	4.2	13	1,371	371	0	61.7	12
Univ Sec Inst	-2.3	1.30	-3.0	1.70	-5.1	11	2.6	7	3,684	556	0	0.0	03
UTL Cp	-31.4	.24	-7.5	3.00	-22.5	155	5.7	29	4,124	988	+10	0.0	06
Vicon Ind	1.6	1.06	1.7	2.47	4.2	82	3.2	16	2,643	803	0	0.3	09
VMX Inc	-48.7	.63	-30.9	1.14	-35.2	0	6.7	29	13,053	3,070	0	0.0	06

Company	Revenue: Pct. Change: Last Qtr	Revenue: Pct. Change: FY to Date	Revenue: Pct. Change: Last 12 Mos	Earnings: Last 12 Mos	Earnings: Per Share: Last 12 Mos	Earnings: Per Share: Pct. Change: Last Qtr	Earnings: Per Share: Pct. Change: FY to Date	Earnings: Per Share: Pct. Change: Last 12 Mos	Earnings: 5-Year Growth Rate	Earnings: Par Growth Rate	Earnings: Date of Report	Dividends: Current Rate: Amt	Dividends: Current Rate: Yield	Dividends: 5-Year Growth Rate	Dividends: Payout: Last FY	Dividends: Payout: Last 5 Yrs.	Dividends: Last X-Dvd Date	Ratio Analysis: Profit Margin	Ratio Analysis: Asset Turnover	Ratio Analysis: Return on Total Assets	Ratio Analysis: Leverage Ratio	Ratio Analysis: Return on Equity	Ratio Analysis: Debt to Equity	Ratio Analysis: Current Ratio	Shareholdings: Market Value	Shareholdings: Latest Shares Outstndng.	Shareholdings: Held by Banks-Funds	Shareholdings: Insider Net Trading	Shareholdings: Short Interest Ratio	Shareholdings: Fiscal Year Ends
	%	%	%	$Mil	$	%	%	%	%	%	-	$	%	%	%	%	-	π/r x	r/a =	π/a x	a/e =	π/e	%	-	$Mil	000	000	000	Days	Mo
Radio - TV Manufacture																														
Ind. Group	34.8	90.7	13.1	13.8	.54	124.3	- 30.3	- 37.4	2	0	- - -	.17	.5	1	20	16	- - - -	.2	.50	.1	3.00	.3	29	1.7	14,387	448,948	32,429	0	1.6	- -
Andrea Radio	11.1	11.1	.0	.3q	.53	-33.3	-33.3	3.9	-11	-3	03-88	.72	7.7	-7	120	110	05-25-88	7.5	1.05	7.9	1.11	8.8	0	11.0	5	508	3	0	0.0	12
Andrews Group	696.3	929.1	1097.2	-16.9n	-2.64	NC	NE	NC	NC	-59	09-87	.00	.0	0	0	0	00-00-00	-3.8	1.66	-6.3	9.41	-59.3	561	2.0	31	6,602	0	0	0.0	12
Armatron Intl	87.2	63.6	44.4	-.7s	-.28	NE	NE	NE	NC	-17	03-88	.00	.0	0	0	0	00-00-00	-2.7	2.04	-5.5	3.04	-16.7	26	1.1	6	2,541	227	0	0.3	09
Carver Cp	-15.7	-15.7	9.0	-.1q	-.01	-100.0	-100.0	-100.0	NC	-1	03-88	.00	.0	0	0	0	00-00-00	-.4	1.00	-.4	1.25	-.5	0	12.2	15	3,414	297	0	0.0	12
Craig Corp	8.6	-26.3	.0	.0‡	1.45	-7.0	4.1	184.3	NC	0	03-88	.00	.0	0	0	0	12-21-79	NC	NC	NC	NC	.0	376	1.2	30	2,135	300	0	0.0	06
Digitech Inc	-36.8	-36.8	16.6	-5.2q	-.40	-100.0	-100.0	-100.0	NC	0	01-88	.00	.0	0	0	0	00-00-00	-74.3	.44	-32.7	.00	NM	128	1.0	27	13,504	355	0	0.0	10
Elexis Cp	65.0	65.0	12.5	-2.8q	-1.31	-100.0	-100.0	-100.0	NC	-72	03-88	.00	.0	0	0	0	00-00-00	-31.1	.79	-24.6	2.92	-71.8	3	1.3	4	2,247	205	0	0.0	12
Emerson Radio	-33.0	-10.0	-10.0	-16.7f	-.46	-100.0	-100.0	-100.0	NC	-17	03-88	.00	.0	0	0	0	10-17-86	-2.3	1.26	-5.2	3.35	-17.4	82	2.3	136	36,306	8,562	0	0.6	03
Esquire Radio	150.6	150.6	239.1	2.1q	4.28	535.0	535.0	613.3	NC	7	03-88	.99	2.4	-2	22	36	04-04-88	2.7	.85	5.0	1.78	8.9	0	2.3	20	483	146	0	9.6	12
Inrad Inc	28.6	28.6	.0	.1q	.06	.0	.0	-71.4	-17	2	03-88	.00	.0	0	0	0	00-00-00	3.3	.39	1.3	1.15	1.5	0	6.8	6	1,396	20	0	0.0	12
Kustom Elect	7.1	7.1	9.0	.1s	.09	300.0	150.0	-60.9	NC	2	03-88	.00	.0	0	0	0	11-13-85	.8	1.88	1.5	1.27	1.9	0	4.1	9	1,949	12	0	0.0	09
Microdyne	-1.8	7.5	-4.7	-1.6s	-.39	NC	NE	NE	NC	-7	04-88	.00	.0	0	NE	NE	11-06-87	-8.0	.74	-5.9	1.12	-6.6	3	11.3	14	4,093	696	0	0.0	10
Pioneer Elec	52.5	52.5	-3.5	65.7q	.58	244.4	244.4	61.1	NC	5	12-87	.12	.3b	-12	36	66	09-23-87	3.1	1.19	3.7	1.73	6.4	4	1.8	3,535	75,624	133	0	5.7	09
Polk Audio	5.3	19.0	.0	1.6n	.65	4.3	15.6	-9.7	NC	17	12-87	.00	.0	0	0	0	01-14-87	8.4	1.73	14.5	1.16	16.8	0	6.5	18	2,443	242	0	0.0	03
Recoton Cp	22.7	22.7	13.7	-.8q	-.30	80.0	80.0	-100.0	NC	-7	03-88	.00	.0	0	0	0	00-00-00	-2.4	1.17	-2.8	2.50	-7.0	101	5.4	14	2,558	575	0	0.0	12
Repco Inc	23.8	15.1	12.5	.0s	.04	100.0	-57.1	NE	NC	0	06-87	.00	.0	0	0	0	00-00-00	.0	NC	NC	NC	.0	82	6.3	1	1,260	94	0	0.0	12
Sony Corp	42.6	34.3	.0	.0‡	1.11	144.4	-20.3	-25.5	NC	0	12-87	.29	.7	8	19	16	03-24-88	NC	NC	NC	NC	.0	24	1.6	9,105	231,236	1,964	0	9.7	03
Sound Advice	52.3	56.0	57.5	2.1n	.70	62.5	67.6	66.7	NC	27	03-88	.00	.0	0	0	0	00-00-00	4.0	4.15	17.8	1.49	26.6	1	2.5	16	3,021	188	0	0.0	06
Tele Comm	NA	NA	NA	NA	NA	NA	NA	NA	NA	NC	00-00	.00	.0	NA	NA	NA	08-03-87	NA	NC	NA	NC	NA	NA	NA	657	27,967	891	0	NA	NA
Wells Gard El	-7.5	-7.5	26.0	.6q	.15	-75.0	-75.0	114.3	NC	5	03-88	.00	.0	0	0	NE	08-26-83	2.1	1.86	3.9	1.23	4.8	0	4.9	29	3,741	572	0	7.1	12
Zenith Eltrns	5.0	5.0	17.2	-14.0q	-.81	-75.0	-75.0	NE	NC	-3	03-88	.00	.0	0	0	0	06-07-82	-.6	1.67	-1.0	2.90	-2.9	66	2.0	710	25,920	16,947	0	1.6	12

Trends and Forecasts: Measuring and Controlling Instruments (SIC 3822,3823,3824,3829)

(in millions of dollars except as noted)

						Percent Change				
						Compound Annual		Annual		
ITEM	1984	1985	1986[1]	1987[2]	1988[3]	1972-85	1980-85	1985-86	1986-87	1987-88
Industry Data										
Value of shipments[4]	9,367	9,775	9,771	9,966	—	11.1	6.5	-0.0	2.0	—
3822 Environmental Controls	1,966	1,989	2,228	2,272	—	8.0	5.2	12.0	2.0	—
3823 Process Controls	4,308	4,610	4,287	4,373	—	13.3	9.0	-7.0	2.0	—
3824 Fluid Meters & Devices	811	865	943	915	—	8.9	-0.4	9.0	-3.0	—
3829 Instruments, nec	2,283	2,311	2,313	2,406	—	11.2	6.0	0.1	4.0	—
Value of shipments (1982$)	8,257	8,640	8,333	8,214	8,478	4.4	-0.4	-3.6	-1.4	3.2
3822 Environmental Controls	1,814	1,775	1,924	1,887	1,962	2.2	0.1	8.4	-1.9	4.0
3823 Process Controls	3,590	3,981	3,502	3,416	3,518	5.3	-0.3	-12.0	-2.5	3.0
3824 Fluid Meters & Devices	748	736	850	813	837	3.1	-5.0	8.1	-4.4	3.0
3829 Instruments, nec	2,106	2,099	2,056	2,098	2,161	5.4	1.1	-2.0	2.0	3.0
Total employment (000)	131	125	126	124	—	1.7	-1.8	0.8	-1.6	—
Production workers (000)	75.8	71.9	71.8	70.6	—	1.3	-2.2	-0.1	-1.7	—
Average hourly earnings ($)	9.34	9.81	9.92	10.07	—	7.4	7.3	1.1	1.5	—
Product Data										
Value of shipments[5]	9,055	9,710	9,781	9,970	—	11.5	6.8	0.7	1.9	—
3822 Environmental Controls	2,030	2,046	2,292	2,337	—	9.1	7.5	12.0	2.0	—
3823 Process Controls	4,115	4,454	4,142	4,225	—	14.2	7.4	-7.0	2.0	—
3824 Fluid Meters & Devices	860	958	1,044	1,013	—	8.6	0.9	9.0	-3.0	—
3829 Instruments, nec	2,051	2,253	2,303	2,395	—	10.9	8.3	2.2	4.0	—

Value of shipments (1982$)	7,987	8,587	8,352	8,230	8,496	4.8	-0.1	-2.7	-1.5	3.2
3822 Environmental Controls	1,872	1,825	1,979	1,941	2,019	3.2	2.2	8.4	-1.9	4.0
3823 Process Controls	3,429	3,846	3,384	3,301	—	6.1	-1.8	-12.0	-2.5	—
3824 Fluid Meters & Devices	794	870	941	900	927	2.9	-3.8	8.2	-4.4	3.0
3829 Instruments, nec	1,892	2,046	2,047	2,088	2,151	5.0	3.3	0.0	2.0	3.0
Shipments price index[6] (1982=100)	113.9	113.2	117.6	121.8	—	6.5	6.9	3.9	3.6	—
3822 Environmental Controls	108.4	112.1	115.8	120.4	—	5.7	5.2	3.3	4.0	—
3823 Process Controls	120.0	115.8	122.4	128.0	—	7.5	9.3	5.7	4.6	—
3824 Fluid Meters & Devices	108.4	110.1	110.9	112.5	—	5.5	4.8	0.7	1.4	—
3829 Instruments, nec	108.4	110.1	112.5	114.7	—	5.5	4.8	2.2	2.0	—
Trade Data										
Value of imports (ITA)[7]	496	570	782	895	—	15.7	14.6	37.2	14.5	—
Import/new supply ratio[8]	0.052	0.055	0.074	0.082	—	3.5	6.6	34.5	10.8	—
Value of exports (ITA)[9]	1,526	1,562	1,534	1,662	—	10.0	1.9	-1.8	8.3	—
Export/shipments ratio	0.169	0.161	0.157	0.167	—	-1.3	-4.6	-2.5	6.4	—

[1]Estimated except for exports and imports.

[2]Estimated.

[3]Forecast.

[4]Value of all products and services sold by the Measuring and Controlling Instruments industry.

[5]Value of products classified in the Measuring and Controlling Instruments industry produced by all industries.

[6]Developed by the Office of Industry Assessment, ITA.

[7]Import data are developed by the chapter author on a C.I.F. valuation basis.

[8]New supply is the sum of product shipments plus imports.

[9]Export data are developed by the chapter author.

SOURCE: U.S. Department of Commerce: Bureau of the Census, Bureau of Economic Analysis, International Trade Administration (ITA). Estimates and forecasts by ITA.

Source: *U.S. Industrial Outlook 1988,* U.S. Department of Commerce.

Electronic Controls and Instruments

Company	Revenue: Pct. Change Last Qtr	Revenue: Pct. Change FY to Date	Revenue: Pct. Change Last 12 Mos	Earnings: Last 12 Mos	Earnings Per Share: Last 12 Mos	Per Share Pct. Change: Last Qtr	Per Share Pct. Change: FY to Date	Per Share Pct. Change: Last 12 Mos	5-Year Growth Rate	Par Growth Rate	Date of Report	Dividends: Current Rate Amt	Current Rate Yield	5-Year Growth Rate	Payout Last FY	Payout Last 5 Yrs.	Last X-Dvd Date
-	%	%	%	$Mil	$	%	%	%	%	%	-	$	%	%	%	%	-
Ind. Group	22.1	127.1	17.8	216.3	.53	68.7	49.9	102.7	- 4	4	- - -	.23	1.6	1	33	28	- - - -
Adams Rus El	-2.4	7.0	9.7	-.3s	-.04	-100.0	-61.5	-100.0	NC	0	03-88	.00	.0	0	0	0	00-00-00
Ametek Inc □	23.0	23.0	14.3	42.0q	.96	9.1	9.1	14.3	6	6	03-88	.60	3.8	12	56	52	06-10-88
Andros Analyzers	-6.5	12.8	21.4	2.0n	.72	6.3	21.1	38.5	NC	17	04-88	.00	.0	0	0	0	00-00-00
Aritech	28.7	28.7	18.6	3.6q	1.23	12.0	12.0	9.8	NC	9	03-88	.00	.0	0	0	0	00-00-00
Austron Inc	-18.5	7.0	28.5	.8n	.20	-10.0	333.3	NE	NC	12	03-88	.00	.0	0	0	0	00-00-00
Bear Auto Svc	19.6	19.6	13.0	-1.6q	-.27	16.7	16.7	-100.0	NC	-6	03-88	.00	.0	0	0	0	00-00-00
Boonton Electr	20.0	20.0	40.0	.8s	.52	50.0	66.7	116.7	-12	10	03-88	.00	.0	0	0	0	00-00-00
Bowmar Instr	-18.3	-6.9	-20.8	-4.1s	-.69	NC	NC	-100.0	NC	-71	03-88	.00	.0	0	0	0	00-00-00
Brajdas	51.8	40.1	41.1	1.9f	.64	700.0	276.5	276.5	NC	40	02-88	.00	.0	0	0	0	00-00-00
CEM Cp	25.9	33.8	33.3	1.8n	.77	37.5	53.8	48.1	NC	19	03-88	.00	.0	0	0	0	00-00-00
Chronar Cp	650.0	650.0	166.6	-7.3q	-.67	NE	NE	NE	NC	-53	03-88	.00	.0	0	0	0	06-29-87
Compucom Systs	1700.0	1700.0	3200.0	1.3q	.10	NE	NE	NE	NC	14	03-88	.00	.0	0	0	0	00-00-00
CompuDyne	-7400.0	-46.5	.0	.0*	-.15	-100.0	-100.0	-100.0	NC	0	03-88	.00	.0	0	0	0	00-00-00
Daniel Inds ♦	17.3	15.9	17.3	-7.3s	-.71	NE	NE	NE	NC	-11	03-88	.18	2.3	4	NE	NE	05-31-88
Data Translation	21.2	21.2	28.0	2.8q	.90	-5.6	-5.6	20.0	NC	17	02-88	.00	.0	0	0	0	01-09-87
Diagnostic Rt A	6.9	15.4	16.9	3.7f	.66	-19.2	8.2	8.2	1	13	03-88	.00	.0	0	0	0	07-18-83
Diagnostic Rt B	NA	NA	NA	NA	NA	NA	NA	NA	NA	NC	00-00	.00	.0	NA	NA	NA	00-00-00
Dranetz Tech	34.5	34.5	20.8	2.6q	.55	.0	.0	19.6	-4	6	03-88	.24	2.8	55	44	22	06-20-88
ECI Telecom	29.3	29.3	30.0	1.4q	.26	900.0	900.0	NE	NC	9	03-88	.00	.0	0	0	0	00-00-00
Edison Control	-87.5	-71.1	-75.0	.0f	.02	-100.0	-95.9	-95.9	NC	0	12-87	.00	.0	0	0	0	00-00-00
EIL Instruments	32.6	25.3	15.6	.5s	.30	42.9	62.5	-41.2	0	5	04-88	.00	.0	0	0	0	01-13-87
EIP Microwave	-45.8	-51.0	-33.3	-1.0s	-.45	-100.0	-100.0	-100.0	NC	-20	03-88	.12	2.7	15	86	26	06-27-88
Electro Sensors	30.0	30.0	25.0	.7q	.35	66.7	66.7	12.9	NC	13	03-88	.10	3.3	0	23	11	04-26-88
Electromag Science	25.4	25.4	32.6	7.1q	.98	25.0	25.0	24.1	27	24	03-88	.00	.0	0	0	0	05-27-86
Energy Conv Dev	-55.2	-24.1	23.0	-18.8n	-3.22	NE	NE	NE	NC	0	03-88	.00	.0	0	0	0	00-00-00
Entronics Cp	-78.6	-81.7	-50.0	.6n	.18	-100.0	-97.9	NC	NC	22	02-88	.00	.0	0	0	0	00-00-00

Company	Ratio Analysis: Profit Margin	Asset Turnover	Return on Total Assets	Leverage Ratio	Return on Equity	Debt to Equity	Current Ratio	Shareholdings: Market Value	Latest Shares Outstndng.	Held by Banks-Funds	Insider Net Trading	Short Interest Ratio	Fiscal Year Ends
-	π/r x	r/a =	π/a x	a/e =	π/e	%	-	$Mil	000	000	000	Days	Mo
Ind. Group	2.8	1.29	3.6	2.00	7.2	33	2.1	5,580	395,745	133,987	+ 24	.7	- -
Adams Rus El	-.2	1.00	-.2	1.50	-.3	32	5.5	48	5,673	2,182	0	0.2	09
Ametek Inc □	6.4	1.22	7.8	2.13	16.6	61	4.0	692	43,956	17,892	+1	0.0	12
Andros Analyzers	11.8	1.11	13.1	1.29	16.9	7	4.2	30	3,363	1,303	0	0.0	07
Aritech	2.8	1.25	3.5	2.69	9.4	19	1.1	45	2,964	1,087	0	0.0	12
Austron Inc	8.9	.98	8.7	1.41	12.3	17	5.8	11	3,600	324	0	0.0	06
Bear Auto Svc	-1.7	1.35	-2.3	2.74	-6.3	66	2.3	64	5,962	1,332	0	0.0	12
Boonton Electr	5.7	1.26	7.2	1.40	10.1	14	4.1	9	1,428	179	+30	0.0	09
Bowmar Instr	-10.8	1.27	-13.7	5.16	-70.7	178	1.2	8	6,006	412	0	0.7	09
Brajdas	4.0	2.05	8.2	4.83	39.6	52	1.2	22	2,795	7	0	0.0	02
CEM Cp	15.0	1.13	17.0	1.12	19.1	0	8.0	38	2,217	394	0	0.0	06
Chronar Cp	-30.4	.60	-18.3	2.91	-53.3	75	2.3	81	10,637	709	0	0.0	12
Compucom Systs	2.0	2.00	4.0	3.38	13.5	145	3.4	43	23,112	475	0	0.0	12
CompuDyne	NC	NC	NC	NC	.0	107	2.4	12	1,027	154	0	3.0	12
Daniel Inds ♦	-5.1	1.06	-5.4	1.61	-8.7	13	2.0	80	10,200	2,434	0	0.0	09
Data Translation	8.8	1.38	12.1	1.37	16.6	0	3.1	23	3,103	1,141	0	0.0	11
Diagnostic Rt A	6.0	.88	5.3	2.51	13.3	92	3.5	30	3,604	645	0	0.0	03
Diagnostic Rt B	NA	NC	NA	NC	NA	NA	NA	15	2,033	469	0	NA	NA
Dranetz Tech	9.0	1.11	10.0	1.10	11.0	0	10.2	41	4,779	1,078	0	0.0	12
ECI Telecom	5.4	.67	3.6	2.56	9.2	20	1.7	17	5,041	0	0	0.0	12
Edison Control	.0	NC	NC	NC	.0	0	33.5	5	2,100	482	0	0.0	12
EIL Instruments	.8	2.63	2.1	2.43	5.1	77	2.9	10	1,538	140	0	0.0	10
EIP Microwave	-7.1	1.35	-9.6	1.66	-15.9	22	3.4	10	2,191	223	0	0.0	09
Electro Sensors	14.0	1.25	17.5	1.05	18.4	0	18.5	5	1,811	12	0	0.0	12
Electromag Science	10.3	1.45	14.9	1.58	23.5	27	3.5	91	7,131	3,185	+4	0.0	12
Energy Conv Dev	NM	NC	NC	NC	NM	64	1.9	43	5,945	917	-6	0.0	06
Entronics Cp	15.0	.79	11.8	1.88	22.2	0	2.0	12	4,206	171	0	0.0	05

Environ Tectonics	28.1	17.9	25.0	.0f	.00	NE	-100.0	-100.0	NC	NC	02-88	.00	.0	0	0	0	12-23-85	.0	NC	NC	NC	.0	15	1.3	7	2,791	0	0	0.0	02
Fischer & Port	17.8	17.8	18.1	3.2q	.62	NE	NE	520.0	34	4	03-88	.00	.0	0	0	0	03-04-88	1.5	1.40	2.1	1.90	4.0	7	2.5	63	4,607	2,120	0	0.2	12
Fluke, John	5.2	2.9	.4	2.7s	.28	10.0	8.5	-76.5	-23	3	03-88	.00	.0	0	0	0	03-09-88	1.3	1.23	1.6	1.56	2.5	1	2.2	145	8,459	4,192	0	1.5	09
Frequency Elec	65.0	56.0	34.2	4.5n	.74	-57.1	-22.0	-45.2	5	7	01-88	.00	.0	0	0	0	05-27-86	8.8	.60	5.3	1.28	6.8	8	6.7	62	5,642	2,255	0	0.0	04
Galileo Elec	-13.3	-11.9	6.0	1.3s	.22	-100.0	-100.0	-72.5	NC	3	03-88	.00	.0	0	0	0	05-18-87	3.7	.62	2.3	1.13	2.6	0	8.2	55	6,232	2,407	+2	0.0	09
Gen Kinetics	10.5	-33.8	-27.2	-.4n	-.48	-100.0	-100.0	-100.0	NC	-12	02-88	.00	.0	0	0	0	00-00-00	-5.0	1.34	-6.7	1.76	-11.8	29	3.2	3	912	22	0	0.0	05
Geodynamics Cp	13.8	13.3	17.6	2.9n	1.00	19.0	24.6	22.0	NC	17	02-88	.00	.0	0	0	0	05-26-87	7.3	1.59	11.6	1.45	16.8	0	2.8	32	2,759	528	0	0.0	05
HDR Power Syst	31.6	12.9	12.5	.7n	.40	300.0	-13.5	-20.0	NC	24	03-88	.00	.0	0	0	0	00-00-00	7.8	2.29	17.9	1.35	24.1	0	3.8	7	1,985	28	0	0.0	06
Howe Rich	7.1	11.1	11.4	1.6f	.84	NE	NE	NE	NC	0	12-87	.00	.0	0	0	0	02-07-84	2.1	1.48	3.1	.00	NS	-2317	2.0	17	1,904	0	0	5.0	12
Imo Delaval	79.3	79.3	19.0	19.7q	1.40	28.6	28.6	NE	NC	7	03-88	.32	1.5	0	16	9	06-20-88	4.5	.73	3.3	2.88	9.5	120	2.9	299	14,240	6,702	0	1.7	12
Impact Systs	48.3	29.5	30.4	2.6f	.27	133.3	107.7	107.7	NC	0	03-88	.00	.0	0	0	0	00-00-00	8.7	1.95	17.0	.00	NS	-9	2.5	36	9,010	1,071	0	0.0	03
Instron Corp	20.0	20.0	13.6	3.5q	.57	30.0	30.0	-18.6	75	8	03-88	.12	.8	11	22	21	06-10-88	3.5	1.26	4.4	2.34	10.3	1	1.4	90	6,022	1,963	0	0.0	12
Interspec Inc	43.1	43.1	105.8	2.5q	.57	7.1	7.1	159.1	NC	12	02-88	.00	.0	0	0	0	00-00-00	7.1	1.21	8.6	1.37	11.8	8	4.1	49	4,456	1,557	0	0.0	11
Johnson Contr	23.6	22.6	17.3	103.5s	2.70	85.7	60.2	26.8	3	8	03-88	1.10	3.1	9	48	40	06-06-88	3.5	1.71	6.0	2.23	13.4	26	1.2	1,310	36,903	18,799	0	8.3	09
Kollmorgen Cp	18.2	18.2	2.2	4.4q	.42	NE	NE	NE	NC	1	03-88	.32	2.2	-4	800	NE	05-17-88	1.4	1.57	2.2	2.59	5.7	81	2.3	148	10,395	3,646	0	1.2	12
Measurex Corp	14.2	17.6	18.1	31.0s	1.62	51.6	35.4	31.7	NC	15	05-88	.28	.8	0	17	14	06-23-88	12.6	.95	12.0	1.52	18.2	3	3.2	649	18,416	12,669	-89	1.1	11
Medar Inc	27.9	25.5	.0	.0*	-.71	NE	NE	NE	NC	0	03-88	.00	.0	0	0	0	00-00-00	NC	NC	NC	NC	.0	23	4.1	15	5,387	459	0	0.0	12
MTS Systems Cp	15.1	11.0	7.2	3.4s	.76	178.9	150.0	-44.9	0	4	03-88	.28	1.1	3	75	21	06-06-88	2.9	1.21	3.5	1.89	6.6	23	2.2	110	4,407	2,148	+1	0.0	09
Nanometrics Inc	103.8	103.8	23.0	-1.6q	-.22	NE	NE	NE	NC	-9	03-88	.00	.0	0	0	0	00-00-00	-10.0	.65	-6.5	1.40	-9.1	21	6.3	16	7,624	1,479	0	0.0	12
Nellcor	7.4	19.7	27.3	10.6n	.74	-10.5	12.5	13.8	NC	20	03-88	.00	.0	0	0	0	00-00-00	11.4	1.36	15.5	1.27	19.7	0	4.1	142	13,654	3,641	0	0.0	06
Newport Electrncs	18.4	18.4	14.2	.6q	.55	4.3	4.3	34.1	NC	10	03-88	.00	.0	0	0	0	00-00-00	3.8	1.74	6.6	1.56	10.3	2	2.3	6	1,182	66	0	0.0	12
Nichols Rsch	12.0	10.1	17.1	2.3n	.66	46.2	25.0	22.2	NC	18	05-88	.00	.0	0	0	0	00-00-00	5.6	2.23	12.5	1.45	18.1	0	2.9	24	3,131	231	0	0.0	08
Nicolet Instr	23.4	17.4	17.2	-4.7f	-.72	-100.0	-100.0	-100.0	NC	-6	03-88	.00	.0	0	0	11	10-31-86	-3.3	1.15	-3.8	1.55	-5.9	5	2.2	85	6,623	4,121	+75	0.6	03
Nuclear Data	6.6	14.1	13.3	-6.6f	-3.01	NE	NE	NE	NC	0	02-88	.00	.0	0	0	0	04-13-81	-12.9	1.63	-21.0	.00	NM	8	.9	2	1,710	144	0	0.0	02
Resdel Ind	69.6	46.0	43.7	-.1n	.00	NE	-100.0	-100.0	NC	NC	03-88	.00	.0	0	0	0	01-28-87	-.4	3.00	-1.2	3.58	-4.3	139	2.5	18	6,030	37	+6	0.0	06
Rheometrics NC	22.7	33.3	50.0	.3n	.10	NE	NE	NE	NC	2	03-88	.00	.0	0	0	0	00-00-00	1.3	.77	1.0	2.30	2.3	64	2.0	14	2,805	488	0	0.0	06
Sym Tek Systs	1.6	-6.7	-4.1	-.1s	-.13	-26.7	-100.0	-100.0	NC	-1	09-87	.00	.0	0	0	0	00-00-00	-.4	1.25	-.5	2.40	-1.2	7	1.7	20	1,302	255	0	0.0	03
Tenney Engr	22.9	22.9	-4.7	-.9q	-.26	.0	.0	-100.0	NC	-11	03-88	.00	.0	0	0	3	05-25-84	-4.5	1.09	-4.9	2.31	-11.3	76	3.5	6	3,513	675	0	0.0	12
Teradyne Inc	37.3	37.3	31.2	-16.0q	-.54	NE	NE	NE	NC	-6	03-88	.00	.0	0	0	0	08-01-83	-3.9	1.23	-4.8	1.27	-6.1	5	3.8	426	24,162	19,619	0	3.6	12
Veeco Instrs	47.3	43.9	29.4	10.6s	1.01	40.0	39.4	910.0	-18	6	03-88	.40	2.0	17	45	39	05-03-88	4.5	1.16	5.2	2.02	10.5	43	3.1	217	10,580	5,020	0	0.5	09
Wash Scientific	2.8	-3.0	2.9	1.6s	.66	-38.5	-9.7	112.9	18	8	02-88	.15	1.8	16	22	20	12-17-87	4.6	1.24	5.7	1.72	9.8	41	4.5	20	2,480	298	0	0.0	08

Energy: Coal, Oil, and Gas

CONSUMPTION BY FUEL TYPE AND SECTOR 1973–1987 [Quadrillon (10^{15}) BTU]

Residential and Commercial*				Transportation*			
Total	Coal	Natural Gas[1]	Petroleum	Total	Coal	Natural Gas[4]	Petroleum
1973	0.254	7.626	4.391	1973	0.003	0.743	17.821
1974	0.257	7.518	3.996	1974	0.002	0.685	17.396
1975	0.209	7.581	3.805	1975	0.001	0.595	17.610
1976	0.203	7.866	4.181	1976	(2)	0.559	18.499
1977	0.205	7.461	4.206	1977	(2)	0.543	19.230
1978	0.214	7.624	4.070	1978	(3)	0.539	20.019
1979	0.187	7.891	3.448	1979	(3)	0.612	19.817
1980	0.145	7.539	3.035	1980	(3)	0.650	19.009
1981	R0.167	7.242	2.634	1981	(3)	0.058	18.800
1982	R0.187	7.433	2.449	1982	(3)	0.612	R18.418
1983	R0.192	7.025	R2.498	1983	(3)	0.505	R18.592
1984	R0.192	7.292	R2.585	1984	(3)	0.545	19.295
1985	R0.176	7.079	2.573	1985	(3)	0.519	19.558
1986	R0.176	R6.825	R2.576	1986		0.499	R20.235
1987	0.167	6.853	6.606	1987	(3)	0.513	20.606

* Geographic coverage: the 50 United States and District of Columbia.

The Residential and Commercial Sector consists of housing units, non-manufacturing business establishments (e.g., wholesale and retail businesses), health and educational institutions, and government office buildings.

R = Revised data.

· Totals may not equal sum of components due to independent rounding.

The Transportation Sector consists of both private and public passenger and freight transportation, as well as government transportation, including military operations.

[1] Includes supplemental gaseous fuels.

[2] Less than 0.5 trillion BTU.

[3] Since 1978, the small amounts of coal consumed for transportation have been reported as industrial sector consumption.

[4] Pipeline fuel only, including supplemental gaseous fuels.

Industrial*				Electric Utilities*			
Total	Coal	Natural Gas[1]	Petroleum	Total	Coal	Natural Gas[1]	Petroleum[2]
1973	4.057	10.388	9.113	1973	8.658	3.748	3.515
1974	3.868	10.003	8.698	1974	8.534	3.519	3.365
1975	3.666	8.532	8.151	1975	8.786	3.240	3.166
1976	3.660	8.761	9.018	1976	9.720	3.152	3.477
1977	3.453	8.636	9.786	1977	10.262	3.284	4.901
1978	3.314	8.539	9.890	1978	10.238	3.297	3.987
1979	3.593	8.549	10.576	1979	11.260	3.613	3.283
1980	3.155	8.394	9.524	1980	12.123	3.810	2.634
1981	3.157	8.257	8.295	1981	12.583	3.768	2.202
1982	2.552	7.116	R7.797	1982	12.582	3.342	1.568
1983	2.490	6.821	7.420	1983	13.213	2.998	1.544
1984	2.842	7.449	7.885	1984	14.020	3.220	1.286
1985	2.776	7.080	7.702	1985	14.542	3.160	1.090
1986	2.643	6.693	R7.934	1986	14.444	2.691	1.452
1987	2.610	6.873	8.156		15.190	2.940	1.250

* Geographic coverage: the 50 United States and District of Columbia.

The Industrial Sector is made up of construction, manufacturing, agriculture, and mining establishments.

R = Revised data.

· Totals may not equal sum of components due to independent rounding.

[1] Includes supplemental gaseous fuels.

[2] Includes petroleum products reported as "oil consumed at steam units" through 1979 and "heavy oil" from 1980 forward, which are assumed to be residual fuel oil; petroleum products reported as "oil consumed by gas turbine and internal combustion units" through 1979 and "light oil" from 1980 forward, which are assumed to be distillate fuel oil and kerosene; and petroleum coke.

Source: *Monthly Energy Review,* U.S. Department of Energy, Energy Information Administration, March 1988.

PETROLEUM—CRUDE OIL[1] SUPPLY AND DISPOSITION*

		Supply				
		Field Production		Imports		
		Total Domestic	Alaskan	Total	SPR[2]	Other
		Thousand barrels per day				
1973	AVERAGE	9,208	198	3,244		3,244
1974	AVERAGE	8,774	193	3,477		3,477
1975	AVERAGE	8,375	191	4,105		4,105
1976	AVERAGE	8,132	173	5,287		5,287
1977	AVERAGE	8,245	464	6,615	21	6,594
1978	AVERAGE	8,707	1,229	6,356	162	6,195
1979	AVERAGE	8,552	1,401	6,519	67	6,452
1980	AVERAGE	8,597	1,617	5,263	44	5,219
1981	AVERAGE	8,572	1,609	4,396	256	4,141
1982	AVERAGE	8,649	1,696	3,488	165	3,323
1983	AVERAGE	8,688	1,714	3,329	234	3,096
1984	AVERAGE	8,879	1,722	3,426	197	3,229
1985	AVERAGE	8,971	1,825	3,201	118	3,083
1986	AVERAGE	8,680	1,867	4,178	48	4,130
1987	AVERAGE	E8,311	E1,961	4,639	73	4,567

* Geographic coverage: the 50 United States and the District of Columbia.
· Totals may not equal sum of components due to independent rounding.
[1] Includes lease condensate.
[2] Strategic Petroleum Reserve.
Source: *Monthly Energy Review*, U.S. Department of Energy, Energy Information Administration.

Oil, Natural Gas Producers

Company	Revenue Pct. Change Last Qtr %	Revenue Pct. Change FY to Date %	Revenue Pct. Change Last 12 Mos %	Earnings Last 12 Mos $Mil	Earnings Per Share Last 12 Mos $	Earnings Per Share Pct. Change Last Qtr %	Earnings Per Share Pct. Change FY to Date %	Earnings Per Share Pct. Change Last 12 Mos %	Earnings 5-Year Growth Rate %	Earnings Par Growth Rate %	Earnings Date of Report	Dividends Current Rate Amt $	Dividends Current Rate Yield %	Dividends 5-Year Growth Rate %	Dividends Payout Last FY %	Dividends Payout Last 5 Yrs. %	Dividends Last X-Dvd Date	Profit Margin π/r	Asset Turnover r/a	Return on Total Assets π/a	Leverage Ratio a/e	Return on Equity π/e	Debt to Equity %	Current Ratio	Market Value $Mil	Latest Shares Outstndng. 000	Held by Banks-Funds 000	Insider Net Trading 000	Short Interest Ratio Days	Fiscal Year Ends Mo
Ind. Group	11.1	11.6	8.2	- 423.8	- .26	- 42.7	- 32.3	NE	NC	- 13	- - -	.76	6.9	0	203	121	- - - -	- 1.2	.67	- .8	4.25	- 3.4	172	1.1	22,511	2,061,546	287,572	- 30	1.7	- -
Allegheny & Wstrn	-15.0	-20.8	-19.1	5.9n	.72	-40.4	-72.5	-68.6	43	4	03-88	.30	4.0	0	12	8	05-10-88	3.3	.88	2.9	2.41	7.0	73	2.1	60	8,058	2,449	0	0.0	06
Asamera Inc	-.3	-.3	-46.0	27.6q	.85	850.0	850.0	NE	NC	13	03-88	.20	2.1	10	29	NE	03-25-88	24.0	.46	11.1	1.48	16.4	8	4.8	376	38,613	7,041	+1	0.0	12
Barnwell Indus	10.0	16.4	30.0	1.9s	1.40	38.5	69.6	109.0	NC	0	03-88	.00	.0	0	0	NE	03-10-86	14.6	.58	8.4	.00	NS	-201	1.3	17	1,392	58	0	0.0	09
Baruch-Foster	-13.6	-13.6	.0	-1.2q	-.42	NE	NE	NE	NC	-10	03-88	.00	.0	0	0	0	07-08-85	-15.0	.38	-5.7	1.70	-9.7	52	1.8	15	2,718	372	0	1.4	12
Basic Res Intl	80.6	28.0	7.6	1.3n	.01	NC	NE	NE	NC	1	09-87	.00	.0	0	0	0	00-00-00	9.3	.12	1.1	1.09	1.2	0	4.9	29	101,777	1,160	0	0.0	12
Cdn Occid Pet □	-.1	-.1	14.5	55.2q	.83	-18.2	-18.2	22.1	-2	4	03-88	.40	NA	16	39	24	05-27-88	9.4	.39	3.7	2.16	8.0	36	1.7	993	66,723	1,082	0	0.0	12
Coastal Corp	22.1	22.1	17.5	115.5q	2.12	2.4	2.4	-30.3	2	11	03-88	.40	1.4	11	16	15	05-24-88	1.5	.93	1.4	9.64	13.5	409	.9	1,288	44,594	20,481	0	3.4	12
Consol O & G	-6.7	-6.7	.0	-3.0q	-.52	NE	NE	NE	NC	0	02-88	.00	.0	0	0	0	05-28-80	-18.8	.19	-3.5	.00	NS	-289	.2	21	7,152	1,071	+12	5.5	11
Damson Oil	3.3	-7.0	-4.1	-29.9s	-.31	NE	NE	NE	NC	0	03-88	.00	.0	0	0	0	00-00-00	NM	NC	NC	NC	NM	2479	1.2	6	96,025	2,760	0	1.2	09
Devon Resourc	115.0	115.0	25.0	-1.7q	-.27	NE	NE	NE	NC	-22	03-88	.50	25.0	0	NE	NE	02-09-88	-17.0	.29	-4.9	1.55	-7.6	38	1.8	13	6,281	0	0	0.0	12
Diam Sham Off	4.2	4.2	11.7	-5.2q	-.11	110.0	110.0	NE	NC	-42	03-88	2.80	18.1	0	NE	NE	02-02-88	-4.6	.30	-1.4	1.14	-1.6	0	2.3	828	53,443	203	0	3.3	12
Dome Petrol •	4.6	4.6	3.5	-589.0q	-1.74	-100.0	-100.0	NE	NC	0	03-88	.00	NA	0	0	0	06-03-81	-39.1	.36	-14.2	.00	NS	-211	.9	404	358,988	16,244	0	0.2	12
Dorchester Hugoton	75.0	75.0	33.3	2.0q	.38	220.0	220.0	153.3	30	6	03-88	.28	2.2	35	63	75	06-24-88	50.0	.37	18.7	1.18	22.0	7	1.7	68	5,372	732	0	0.0	12
Ensource Inc	-16.5	-16.5	-12.1	-4.6q	-1.71	-100.0	-100.0	-100.0	NC	-20	03-88	.00	.0	0	0	0	05-15-86	-15.9	.26	-4.1	4.78	-19.6	186	1.3	25	3,359	345	0	0.0	12
Equity Oil	19.2	19.2	55.5	.8q	.07	NC	NC	NE	NC	1	03-88	.05	1.0	0	71	54	11-06-87	5.7	.25	1.4	1.43	2.0	0	4.5	63	12,245	3,981	0	0.0	12
Forest Oil	36.4	36.4	29.7	7.7q	.21	NE	NE	NE	NC	9	03-88	.00	.0	0	0	124	04-29-88	7.1	.23	1.6	5.75	9.2	252	.8	102	7,427	1,333	0	0.0	12
Fortune Natl	-34.3	-31.2	-28.5	-.2f	-.13	NE	NE	NE	NC	-2	12-87	.00	.0	0	0	0	00-00-00	-2.0	.20	-.4	6.00	-2.4	0	NA	1	2,667	10	0	0.0	12
Free Mc Egy	56.5	56.5	28.2	19.2q	.27	100.0	100.0	-51.8	NC	-16	03-88	2.20	15.9	0	1048	NE	04-25-88	11.4	.15	1.7	1.35	2.3	21	.7	809	58,280	650	0	0.0	12
Gulf Appld Tech	-70.0	-70.0	-47.6	-3.2q	-1.02	-100.0	-100.0	-100.0	NC	-11	03-88	.00	.0	0	0	NE	06-29-84	-29.1	.29	-8.4	1.26	-10.6	1	3.1	22	3,315	393	+2	0.0	12
Hamilton Oil	1.8	1.8	20.0	25.7q	.92	35.7	35.7	135.9	5	7	03-88	.10	.4	0	4	8	06-09-88	8.0	.34	2.7	2.74	7.4	83	1.6	691	25,586	5,565	+3	0.0	12
Harken Oil Gas	18.2	18.2	316.1	1.8q	.04	-40.0	-40.0	-33.3	NC	6	03-88	.00	.0	0	0	0	00-00-00	.4	3.50	1.4	4.14	5.8	89	.9	93	22,589	4,419	0	0.0	12
Howell Corp	78.0	78.0	102.8	2.2q	.45	180.0	180.0	NE	NC	1	03-88	.32	2.5	-2	108	NE	05-25-88	1.0	1.50	1.5	2.73	4.1	64	1.1	62	4,794	769	-26	0.0	12
MAPCO	20.1	20.1	13.0	74.6q	3.67	113.6	113.6	1.1	6	11	03-88	1.00	1.7	-11	36	31	05-18-88	4.4	1.25	5.5	2.65	14.6	62	1.3	1,226	21,086	14,903	0	0.4	12
Maxus Engy	7.0	7.0	-66.7	-499.6q	-5.91	NE	NE	NE	NC	0	03-88	.00	.0	-39	NE	NE	05-19-87	-77.7	.34	-26.3	.00	NM	413	.9	717	89,580	41,683	+7	3.7	12
May Petrol	.0	.0	-18.7	-8.3q	-.56	1100.0	1100.0	NE	NC	-21	03-88	.00	.0	0	0	0	10-22-80	-63.8	.20	-12.9	1.59	-20.5	22	1.5	18	14,646	1,193	0	0.0	12
Maynard Oil	48.3	48.3	45.4	1.7q	.28	NE	NE	NE	NC	6	03-88	.00	.0	0	0	0	00-00-00	10.6	.41	4.3	1.33	5.7	12	4.5	22	5,364	541	0	0.0	12
MCO Holding	-45.1	-45.1	-54.2	2.0q	.31	157.1	157.1	NE	NC	3	03-88	.00	.0	0	0	0	00-00-00	4.2	.10	.4	8.00	3.2	200	.8	66	5,606	1,537	0	6.4	12
MFG Oil	NA	NA	NA	NA	NA	NA	NA	NA	NA	NC	00-00	.00	.0	NA	NA	NA	00-00-00	NA	NC	NA	NC	NA	NA	NA	341	32,853	0	0	NA	NA
Mission Rscs	NA	NA	NA	NA	NA	NA	NA	NA	NA	NC	00-00	.00	.0	NA	NA	NA	00-00-00	NA	NC	NA	NC	NA	NA	NA	30	4,239	0	0	NA	NA
Mitchell Energy	7.0	7.0	1.7	12.1q	.26	233.3	233.3	116.7	-37	-1	04-88	.34	3.4	0	126	33	06-13-88	2.1	.29	.6	3.50	2.1	160	1.0	473	47,330	12,436	0	0.1	01
N Cdn Oils	18.5	18.5	16.6	28.1q	.64	17.6	17.6	1180.0	-25	5	03-88	.20	NA	0	0	0	06-09-88	30.9	.11	3.5	2.14	7.5	35	6.5	439	27,212	1,827	0	0.2	12
Numac O & G	32.3	32.3	38.7	7.3q	.29	-10.0	-10.0	38.1	-3	4	03-88	.00	NA	0	0	0	12-12-83	17.0	.14	2.4	1.75	4.2	22	1.1	223	25,535	2,868	0	2.0	12
Occid Petrol	7.7	7.7	9.7	218.0q	.91	34.2	34.2	56.9	-6	-8	03-88	2.50	9.4	0	321	160	06-20-88	1.3	1.00	1.3	3.31	4.3	125	1.1	5,639	212,776	107,430	+63	1.2	12
Pauley Petro	-10.1	-16.6	-14.7	2.9s	-.22	NE	-30.8	NC	NC	11	03-88	.00	.0	0	0	0	00-00-00	2.4	2.00	4.8	2.19	10.5	34	1.3	187	12,910	323	-60	0.5	08
Petrol Ind Inc	-25.0	-25.0	100.0	.1q	.06	-100.0	-100.0	NE	NC	5	03-88	.00	.0	0	0	0	00-00-00	5.0	1.00	5.0	1.06	5.3	0	14.0	3	1,836	31	0	0.0	12

Petro Devlp	-3.1	-3.1	.0	-.3q	-.04	NC	NC	-100.0	NC	-3	03-88	.00	.0	0	0	0	00-00-00	-2.5	.40	-1.0	3.20	-3.2	134	1.2	7	7,525	83	0	0.0	12
Petromineral	-27.3	-27.3	-12.5	-1.0q	-.12	NC	NC	NE	NC	-13	03-88	.00	.0	0	0	NE	00-00-00	-14.3	.55	-7.8	1.63	-12.7	18	1.6	6	7,963	455	0	0.0	12
Plains Petrol	38.3	38.3	-80.0	9.2q	1.01	192.3	192.3	134.9	NC	34	03-88	.10	.4	0	13	10	06-06-88	34.1	.82	27.8	1.35	37.6	6	1.7	234	9,094	4,193	0	0.0	12
Prairie Oil Roy	2.4	2.4	54.5	6.4q	.82	-31.8	-31.8	192.9	-5	12	03-88	.00	NA	0	0	0	01-10-85	37.6	.20	7.7	1.57	12.1	0	4.2	52	7,846	494	0	0.0	12
Ranger Oil	21.1	21.1	8.2	15.0q	.18	-22.2	-22.2	125.0	NC	8	03-88	.00	.0	0	0	0	11-25-80	19.0	.17	3.2	2.50	8.0	46	4.6	419	74,532	5,666	-60	45.2	12
Samson Energy	69.6	69.6	22.2	1.0q	.34	550.0	550.0	54.5	NC	-16	03-88	1.60	11.7	0	609	NE	05-24-88	9.1	.29	2.6	1.65	4.3	56	8.4	47	3,452	43	0	0.4	12
Santa Fe Engy	18.7	18.7	35.6	-14.0q	-.49	.0	.0	NE	NC	-32	03-88	2.88	16.7	0	NE	NE	06-24-88	-10.2	.34	-3.5	1.34	-4.7	0	.3	493	28,604	30	0	0.1	12
Saxon Oil	-3.3	-3.3	200.0	.9q	.01	NC	NC	NE	NC	8	03-88	.00	.0	0	0	0	00-00-00	7.5	.88	6.6	1.18	7.8	10	4.0	1	3,388	2,907	0	0.0	12
Saxon Oil Dev	-3.6	-3.6	.0	2.0q	.08	NC	NC	NE	NC	0	03-88	.08	11.6	0	133	NE	06-24-88	16.7	.41	6.9	1.25	8.6	20	3.9	18	25,703	832	0	0.0	12
Sceptre Rscs	78.2	78.2	48.3	8.3q	.12	-60.0	-60.0	140.0	NC	5	03-88	.00	.0	0	0	0	00-00-00	9.0	.20	1.8	2.94	5.3	116	1.2	145	40,110	178	+32	0.0	12
Scurry Rainbow	.5	.5	17.3	21.9q	1.65	-16.3	-16.3	103.7	4	1	03-88	1.50	9.0	0	29	11	05-27-88	27.0	.26	7.0	1.67	11.7	2	3.7	224	13,462	251	0	15.8	12
Snyder Oil	35.7	35.7	70.9	5.2q	.22	-33.3	-33.3	NE	NC	-17	03-88	1.20	15.0	0	480	NE	04-11-88	9.8	.32	3.1	1.23	3.8	15	1.2	138	17,234	2,483	0	0.6	12
SEstn Mich Gas	87.0	87.0	64.9	7.7q	1.61	23.4	23.4	40.0	10	8	03-88	1.04	5.2b	5	71	74	08-01-88	4.1	1.41	5.8	3.84	22.3	130	1.1	92	4,594	191	0	0.0	12
Summit En ♦	-11.1	-6.3	.0	-2.1s	-.79	-100.0	NE	NE	NC	-47	01-88	.00	.0	0	0	0	03-11-82	-70.0	.31	-21.6	2.16	-46.7	71	1.5	4	3,936	465	0	0.0	07
Sun Engy Prt	-.8	-.8	15.4	143.0q	.47	-75.0	-75.0	NE	NC	-13	03-88	1.59	10.6	0	270	570	05-04-88	9.1	.37	3.4	1.56	5.3	39	.7	4,499	299,925	627	0	0.0	12
Tex Am Energy	-19.0	-19.0	-30.4	-12.6q	-1.71	90.9	90.9	NE	NC	0	03-87	.00	.0	0	0	0	08-28-85	-11.3	.90	-10.2	.00	NS	-5	.4	16	8,315	679	0	0.0	12
Tex Pacific	-13.3	-13.3	-16.6	2.6q	.71	-9.5	-9.5	-13.4	-19	7	03-88	.40	1.3	5	55	28	03-01-88	52.0	.24	12.4	1.30	16.1	0	NA	114	3,729	676	0	0.0	12
Total Petro NA	3.7	3.7	15.8	-31.7q	-1.55	NE	NE	-100.0	NC	-21	03-88	.40	2.7	7	NE	117	05-18-88	-1.8	1.72	-3.1	5.32	-16.5	196	1.2	358	24,297	4,670	0	0.6	12
Unimar Co	.9	1.5	35.3	-46.1n	-.59	NE	NE	NC	NC	-63	09-87	1.17	18.7	0	NE	NE	05-10-88	-26.2	.25	-6.6	3.20	-21.1	136	.7	66	10,547	2,503	0	0.4	12
Walker Energy	-12.5	-12.5	-25.0	-9.0q	-1.03	NE	NE	NE	NC	-68	03-88	.00	.0	0	0	NE	00-00-00	NM	NC	NC	NC	-68.2	5	.2	3	8,762	100	0	5.0	12
Whiting Petro	50.0	50.0	100.0	.4q	.05	NC	NC	66.7	NC	8	03-88	.00	.0	0	0	0	00-00-00	20.0	.34	6.7	1.12	7.5	0	6.1	7	8,288	51	0	0.0	12
Wichita River	14.3	14.3	-250.0	.9q	8.01	-85.6	-85.6	NE	NC	0	03-88	.00	.0	0	0	0	03-21-88	30.0	1.20	36.0	.00	NM	60	.7	3	449	5	0	0.7	12
Wilshire Oil	5.3	5.3	33.3	.6q	.08	.0	.0	NE	NC	6	03-88	.00	.0	0	0	NE	06-20-88	7.5	.15	1.1	5.00	5.5	245	1.9	55	8,387	895	0	0.0	12
Wiser Oil	25.4	25.4	29.1	.2q	.03	-13.3	-13.3	-70.0	-49	-2	03-88	.40	2.5	-16	800	98	05-16-88	.6	.33	.2	1.00	.2	1	4.2	142	9,033	3,205	-2	0.0	12

Oil Refining and Marketing

Ind. Group	- 14.0	7.3	- 4.6	19,838.1	2.35	3.8	- 3.6	- 15.3	- 7	- 1	---	2.52	5.2	0	35	32	----	5.4	.87	4.7	2.47	11.6	35	1.3	257,933	5,300,762	G	- 691	3.9	--
Adam Rsc En	.6	.6	8.0	3.0q	.37	900.0	900.0	236.4	NC	0	03-88	.00	.0	0	0	0	00-00-00	4.5	4.91	22.1	.00	NS	-93	1.0	17	6,958	486	0	2.1	12
Adobe Rscs □	84.6	84.6	24.2	17.4q	.64	83.3	83.3	NE	NC	9	03-88	.00	.0	0	0	0	00-00-00	14.7	.25	3.7	2.49	9.2	23	1.2	227	29,833	5,707	0	0.0	12
Amerada Hess ◇	3.2	3.2	24.6	114.5q	1.38	-62.8	-62.8	-61.3	NC	3	03-38	.60	2.3	-26	11	260	06-07-88	2.4	.92	2.2	2.41	5.3	49	1.1	2,175	84,066	41,792	+1	2.5	12
Am Petrofina	12.1	12.1	27.7	93.9q	7.13	54.0	54.0	156.5	NC	9	03-88	2.00	2.9	0	8	72	05-26-88	3.7	1.38	5.1	2.51	12.8	51	1.1	914	13,193	285	+0	0.6	12
Amoco Cp	10.5	10.5	18.2	1569.0q	6.11	78.4	78.4	130.6	-8	6	03-88	3.50	4.8	4	62	53	05-05-88	7.6	.83	6.3	2.06	13.0	25	1.1	18,727	257,413	105,260	0	3.4	12
Ashland Oil □	19.1	24.1	20.1	166.1s	5.56	2366.7	150.0	24.4	NC	10	03-88	2.00	2.8	-6	42	95	05-24-88	2.2	1.86	4.1	3.80	15.6	74	1.2	2,249	31,027	11,198	+4	1.7	09
Atlantic Rchfld	27.4	27.4	23.9	1386.0q	7.57	67.9	67.9	143.4	NC	11	03-88	4.00	5.0	13	60	99	05-16-88	8.0	.76	6.1	3.87	23.6	107	1.4	14,675	182,300	92,601	0	3.6	12
Brit Petrol	97.9	29.1	29.1	2624.8f	5.64	144.8	112.8	112.8	13	8	12-87	3.05	5.8	12	51	54	02-29-88	5.0	1.24	6.2	2.87	17.8	39	1.5	24,045	457,993	16,831	0	1.4	12
British Petro	NA	NA	NA	NA	NA	NA	NA	NA	NA	NC	00-00	.00	.0	NA	NA	NA	00-00-00	NA	NC	NA	NC	NA	NA	NA	27	2,100	4,498	0	NA	NA
Buckeye Prtnr	-4.9	-4.9	-.6	35.0q	2.87	16.1	16.1	25.9	NC	3	03-88	2.20	10.5	0	60	33	02-02-88	23.2	.26	6.0	2.28	13.7	115	2.1	255	12,121	2,021	0	0.0	12
Calumet Ind	-6.8	-12.0	-7.5	-2.5s	-1.06	NE	NE	-100.0	NC	-15	03-88	.00	.0	0	NE	39	11-24-87	-6.8	.69	-4.7	3.21	-15.1	158	1.7	16	2,450	279	+5	0.0	09
Challenger Intl	1.6	-15.6	-8.6	-2.1s	-.49	100.0	-93.8	NE	NC	-17	04-88	.00	.0	0	0	NE	01-13-86	-.4	8.50	-3.4	5.03	-17.1	0	1.2	7	4,316	80	0	0.0	10
Charter Co □	.1	.1	-5.6	33.3q	.70	300.0	300.0	-58.1	NC	39	03-88	.02	.5	0	0	NE	12-21-87	3.2	3.41	10.9	3.65	39.8	86	1.9	184	47,416	26,327	0	0.7	12
Chevron Cp	9.5	9.5	18.9	1462.0q	4.27	229.3	229.3	172.0	-9	4	03-88	2.60	5.7	0	82	64	05-04-88	5.5	.76	4.2	2.21	9.3	40	1.3	15,523	342,109	131,735	0	5.0	12
Crown Ctrl A	11.2	11.2	12.1	47.4q	6.06	NE	NE	NE	NC	24	03-88	.00	.0	0	0	188	04-03-84	4.3	2.63	11.3	2.15	24.3	2	1.8	90	4,818	504	0	0.4	12
Crown Ctrl B	NA	NA	NA	NA	NA	NA	NA	NA	NA	NC	00-00	.00	.0	NA	NA	NA	04-03-84	NA	NC	NA	NC	NA	NA	NA	25	1,434	209	0	NA	NA
Diam Sham RM	10.7	10.7	10.8	3.4q	.15	-100.0	-100.0	NE	NC	-2	03-88	.40	2.6	0	64	NE	05-16-88	.2	2.00	.4	3.50	1.4	149	1.6	370	23,896	11,090	0	0.7	12
Exxon Cp	2.0	2.0	14.0	4840.0q	3.13	-40.0	-40.0	-4.6	6	4	03-88	2.20	4.8	5	55	52	05-09-88	6.3	1.03	6.5	2.22	14.4	15	1.0	64,718	1,426,300	475,493	-81	7.9	12
Getty Petro	-15.5	-15.5	30.6	21.1q	1.92	560.0	560.0	143.0	NC	23	04-88	.20	1.1	6	12	17	06-29-88	1.6	4.56	7.3	3.52	25.7	118	1.3	199	11,079	1,123	0	0.3	01
Gulf Cda Rsc	NA	NA	NA	NA	NA	NA	NA	NA	NA	NC	00-00	.40	2.7	NA	NA	NA	05-24-88	NA	NC	NA	NC	NA	NA	NA	2,224	149,480	9,308	0	NA	NA

Continued

Company	Revenue: Pct. Change Last Qtr	Revenue: Pct. Change FY to Date	Revenue: Pct. Change Last 12 Mos	Earnings: Last 12 Mos	Earnings Per Share: Last 12 Mos	Per Share Pct. Change: Last Qtr	Per Share Pct. Change: FY to Date	Per Share Pct. Change: Last 12 Mos	5-Year Growth Rate	Par Growth Rate	Date of Report	Dividends Current Rate: Amt	Current Rate: Yield	5-Year Growth Rate	Payout: Last FY	Payout: Last 5 Yrs.	Last X-Dvd Date	Profit Margin	Asset Turnover	Return on Total Assets	Leverage Ratio	Return on Equity	Debt to Equity	Current Ratio	Market Value	Latest Shares Outstndng.	Held by Banks-Funds	Insider Net Trading	Short Interest Ratio	Fiscal Year Ends
-	%	%	%	$Mil	$	%	%	%	%	%	-	$	%	%	%	%	-	π/r x	r/a =	π/a x	a/e =	π/e	%	-	$Mil	000	000	000	Days	Mo
Oil Refining and Marketing (Continued)																														
Holly Corp	47.0	44.6	35.5	16.4n	3.98	472.0	3108.3	138.3	9	72	04-88	.00	.0	0	0	9	09-24-85	4.4	2.68	11.8	6.09	71.9	110	1.3	125	4,127	2,522	0	0.4	07
Imperial Oil	4.9	4.9	10.0	689.0q	4.21	-16.7	-16.7	37.6	15	7	03-88	1.80	NA	3	37	44	05-25-88	9.7	.75	7.3	1.70	12.4	22	2.3	7,488	163,674	5,273	0	0.0	12
Intl Recovery	469.6	346.7	355.5	1.0f	.30	800.0	400.0	400.0	NC	26	03-88	.00	.0	0	0	0	00-00-00	2.4	6.13	14.7	1.79	26.3	37	2.7	25	3,000	0	0	0.0	03
Ivax Cp	200.0	187.2	180.0	.5f	.03	-75.0	-83.3	-83.3	NC	7	10-87	.00	.0	0	0	0	05-08-87	3.6	.78	2.8	2.46	6.9	6	.8	145	13,690	39	0	35.1	10
Kerr-McGee	21.4	21.4	15.3	74.1q	1.52	-50.0	-50.0	NE	NC	1	03-88	1.10	3.1	0	64	306	05-27-88	2.7	.89	2.4	2.25	5.4	39	1.2	1,689	48,252	30,921	+10	3.1	12
Mobil Corp	8.9	8.9	9.0	1511.0q	3.67	98.4	98.4	22.7	0	3	03-88	2.40	5.5	2	72	68	05-03-88	2.9	1.28	3.7	2.43	9.0	44	1.0	17,894	411,359	185,006	+3	4.3	12
Murphy Oil	7.0	7.0	13.7	-53.1q	-1.57	-100.0	-100.0	NE	NC	-12	03-88	1.00	3.2	0	NE	588	05-10-88	-3.5	.74	-2.6	2.73	-7.1	45	1.3	1,047	33,626	12,921	-5	8.9	12
Pac Resources	-2.3	-2.3	18.2	5.4q	.10	70.0	70.0	-92.9	NC	-3	03-88	.20	1.6	0	500	11	05-25-88	.6	1.67	1.0	3.30	3.3	93	2.4	221	17,187	3,674	+2	0.0	12
Pennzoil Co	8.9	8.9	6.4	46.0q	.73	20.0	20.0	-62.9	-27	-15	03-88	2.20	2.9	0	319	117	05-24-88	2.5	.56	1.4	5.29	7.4	232	2.3	3,124	41,044	18,440	0	0.7	12
Petro Heat Pwr	50.8	50.8	43.6	6.6q	.38	50.0	50.0	NE	NC	-71	03-88	1.33	7.8	0	0000	62	06-09-88	1.6	1.94	3.1	9.13	28.3	488	1.1	51	3,000	544	0	0.3	12
Phillips Petrol	16.4	16.4	21.4	197.0q	.77	NE	NE	113.9	-37	3	03-88	.60	3.8	-3	1000	66	04-28-88	1.8	.89	1.6	7.63	12.2	335	1.2	3,596	228,334	120,740	-646	1.3	12
Quaker St Cp	-9.1	-9.1	-7.5	-50.6q	-1.91	-42.9	-42.9	-100.0	NC	-22	03-88	.80	3.8	0	NE	80	05-09-88	-6.1	1.36	-8.3	1.90	-15.8	33	1.9	560	26,353	10,560	0	1.4	12
Royal Dutch	-88.0	-80.4	-80.4	5769.1f	4.02	-71.5	-58.8	-58.8	-10	-17	12-87	6.62	6.0	5	67	42	05-17-88	59.6	.21	12.6	2.06	25.9	17	1.4	30,418	276,209	61,076	0	2.7	12
Shell Transport	-90.2	-84.1	-84.0	3175.3f	2.22	-59.0	-54.3	-54.3	-11	-23	12-87	4.64	6.5	3	67	41	03-18-88	60.5	.17	10.4	2.06	21.4	17	1.4	19,749	276,209	4,825	0	1.1	12
Sun Co Inc	7.2	7.2	13.3	248.0q	3.43	62.9	62.9	34.5	-8	1	03-88	3.00	5.5	6	93	60	05-04-88	2.6	.81	2.1	2.24	4.7	29	1.4	5,904	107,843	48,730	0	6.3	12
Tesoro Petrol	-3.1	4.8	7.9	-5.1s	-.70	NE	NE	NE	NC	-3	03-88	.00	.0	0	0	NE	08-05-86	-.4	2.25	-.9	3.11	-2.8	72	1.4	140	14,017	4,212	+2	9.1	09
Texaco Canada	-99.9	-99.9	-19.9	246.1q	2.72	11.5	11.5	20.9	0	5	03-88	1.20	NA	3	45	41	05-16-88	12.3	.52	6.4	1.48	9.5	3	2.8	3,397	120,768	1,939	0	0.0	12
Texaco	5.2	5.2	13.8	-4283.0q	-17.64	104.1	104.1	-100.0	NC	-55	03-88	3.00	6.4	-18	NE	NE	04-27-88	-12.3	1.02	-12.6	3.71	-46.7	6	1.9	11,384	242,852	85,553	0	2.5	12
Tosco Corp	7.9	7.9	45.9	29.0q	.15	66.7	66.7	-92.4	NC	0	03-88	.00	.0	0	0	0	07-06-82	2.4	2.17	5.2	.00	NS	-1072	2.0	109	36,478	3,524	0	11.3	12
Unocal Cp	13.4	13.4	26.7	-157.0q	-1.07	-100.0	-100.0	-100.0	NC	-17	03-88	1.00	2.9	1	64	40	04-05-88	-1.7	.94	-1.6	5.56	-8.9	261	1.4	3,992	116,562	72,975	0	3.4	12
Valero Energy	74.3	74.3	-49.4	-39.9q	3.24	NE	NE	NE	NC	-8	03-88	.00	.0	0	0	NE	08-07-84	-5.5	.75	-4.1	1.98	-8.1	43	1.7	207	25,876	7,941	+14	3.7	12

Trends and Forecasts: Health Care Expenditures

(in billions of dollars except as noted)

Item	1984	1985	1986	1987[1]	1988[2]	Percent Change: Compound Annual 1972-85	Percent Change: Compound Annual 1980-85	Percent Change: Annual 1985-86	Percent Change: Annual 1986-87	Percent Change: Annual 1987-88
TOTAL	391.1	422.6	458.2	498.9	544.0	12.3	11.3	8.4	8.9	9.0
Health services and supplies	375.4	407.2	442.0	481.6	525.6	12.6	11.5	8.5	9.0	9.1
Personal health care	341.9	371.3	404.1	441.2	481.8	12.5	11.1	8.8	9.2	9.2
Hospital care	156.3	167.2	179.6	193.5	211.1	12.7	10.5	7.4	7.7	9.1
Physicians' services	75.4	82.8	92.0	102.1	111.4	12.9	12.1	11.1	11.0	9.1
Dentists' services	24.6	27.1	29.6	32.7	35.5	12.9	11.9	9.2	10.5	8.6
Other professional services	11.0	12.4	14.1	16.2	18.3	16.0	16.9	13.7	14.9	13.0
Consumer nondurables[3]	26.5	28.7	30.6	32.7	35.5	9.0	8.8	6.6	6.9	8.6
Consumer durables	7.0	7.5	8.2	8.8	9.5	9.5	8.1	9.3	7.3	8.0
Nursing home care	31.7	35.0	38.1	42.0	46.0	13.8	11.4	8.9	10.2	9.5
Other health services	9.5	11.0	11.9	13.1	14.5	11.7	12.9	8.2	10.1	10.7
Program administration and net cost of insurance	22.6	23.6	24.5	25.9	28.0	13.0	21.0	3.8	5.7	8.1
Government public health activities	11.0	12.3	13.4	14.5	15.8	14.6	11.0	8.9	8.2	9.0
Research and construction of medical facilities	15.6	15.4	16.3	17.3	18.4	6.7	5.3	5.8	6.1	6.4
Research[4]	6.8	7.4	8.2	9.0	9.8	9.1	6.5	10.8	9.8	8.9
Construction	8.9	8.1	8.1	8.3	8.6	5.2	4.5	0.0	2.5	3.6

[1]Estimated.

[2]Forecast.

[3]Includes only expenditures for prescription drugs, over-the-counter drugs, and medical sundries dispensed through retail channels. Spending for drugs dispensed in hospitals and by physicians is reported within those cost categories.

[4]Research expenditures of drug companies and other manufacturers and providers of medical equipment and supplies are included in the expenditure class in which the product falls.

NOTE: Totals may differ from sum of constituent figures because of rounding.

SOURCE: Bureau of Data Management and Strategy, Office of National Cost Estimates, Health Care Financing Administration; and U.S. Department of Commerce: Bureau of the Census, and International Trade Administration (ITA). Estimates and forecasts by ITA.

Source: *U.S. Industrial Outlook 1987,* U.S. Department of Commerce.

Trends and Forecasts: X-ray and Electromedical Apparatus (SIC 3693)

(in millions of dollars except as noted)

ITEM	1984	1985	1986[1]	1987[2]	1988[3]	Percent Change: Compound Annual 1972-85	Compound Annual 1980-85	Annual 1985-86	Annual 1986-87	Annual 1987-88
Industry Data										
Value of shipments[4]	5,175	5,001	5,201	5,576	6,022	20.5	14.6	4.0	7.2	8.0
Value of shipments (1982$)	4,882	4,648	5,222	5,570	5,887	11.8	9.1	12.3	6.7	5.7
Total employment (000)	46.4	46.3	45.9	45.4	—	10.9	3.6	−0.9	−1.1	—
Production workers (000)	21.7	21.3	20.7	20.5	—	9.1	2.7	−2.8	−1.0	—
Average hourly earnings ($)	8.75	9.17	—	—	—	6.7	6.6	—	—	—
Product Data										
Value of shipments[5]	4,782	4,594	4,778	5,122	5,532	21.1	13.7	4.0	7.2	8.0
Value of shipments (1982$)	4,511	4,269	4,797	5,117	5,408	12.3	8.3	12.4	6.7	5.7
Shipments price index[6] (1982 = 100)	106.0	107.6	99.6	100.1	102.3	7.8	5.1	−7.4	0.5	2.2
Trade Data										
Value of imports (ITA)[7]	840	1,053	1,294	1,298	1,330	23.7	27.5	22.9	0.3	2.5
Import/new supply ratio[8]	0.149	0.186	0.213	0.202	0.194	1.8	10.3	14.5	−5.2	−4.0
Value of exports (ITA)[9]	1,099	1,161	1,330	1,481	1,678	22.7	6.7	14.6	11.4	13.3
Export/shipments ratio	0.230	0.253	0.278	0.289	0.303	1.4	−6.1	9.9	4.0	4.8

[1]Estimated except for exports and imports.
[2]Estimated.
[3]Forecast.
[4]Value of all products and services sold by the X-ray and Electromedical Apparatus industry.
[5]Value of products classified in the X-ray and Electromedical Apparatus industry produced by all industries.
[6]Developed by the Office of Industry Assessment, ITA.
[7]Import data are developed by the chapter author on a C.I.F. valuation basis.
[8]New supply is the sum of product shipments plus imports.
[9]Export data are developed by the chapter author.
SOURCE: U.S. Department of Commerce: Bureau of the Census, Bureau of Economic Analysis, International Trade Administration (ITA). Estimates and forecasts by ITA.

Source: *U.S. Industrial Outlook 1988*, U.S. Department of Commerce.

Trends and Forecasts: Surgical Appliances and Supplies (SIC 3842)

(in millions of dollars except as noted)

ITEM	1984	1985	1986[1]	1987[2]	1988[3]	Percent Change: Compound Annual 1972-85	Compound Annual 1980-85	Annual 1985-86	Annual 1986-87	Annual 1987-88
Industry Data										
Value of shipments[4]	7,117	7,865	8,769	9,524	10,229	13.9	15.3	11.5	8.6	7.4
Value of shipments (1982$)	6,544	7,028	8,440	9,167	9,931	6.9	11.5	20.1	8.6	8.3
Total employment (000)	73.8	76.3	83.9	83.7	—	4.3	4.3	10.0	−0.2	—
Production workers (000)	49.5	49.2	53.7	52.7	—	3.9	3.3	9.1	−1.9	—
Average hourly earnings ($)	7.79	8.34	—	—	—	7.1	6.3	—	—	—
Product Data										
Value of shipments[5]	6,015	6,911	7,706	8,368	8,987	14.9	15.1	11.5	8.6	7.4
Value of shipments (1982$)	5,525	6,158	7,417	8,054	8,725	7.8	11.4	20.4	8.6	8.3
Shipments price index[6] (1982=100)	108.9	112.3	103.9	103.9	103.0	6.5	3.4	−7.5	0.0	−0.9
Trade Data										
Value of imports (ITA)[7]	141	163	227	258	281	21.4	11.5	39.3	13.7	8.9
Import/new supply ratio[8]	0.023	0.023	0.029	0.030	0.030	5.8	−3.2	26.1	3.4	0.0
Value of exports (ITA)[9]	442	480	524	590	658	15.2	17.6	9.2	12.6	11.5
Export/shipments ratio	0.073	0.069	0.068	0.071	0.073	0.2	2.2	−1.4	4.4	2.8

[1]Estimated except for exports and imports.
[2]Estimated.
[3]Forecast.
[4]Value of all products and services sold by the Surgical Appliances and Supplies industry.
[5]Value of products classified in the Surgical Appliances and Supplies industry produced by all industries.
[6]Developed by the Office of Industry Assessment, ITA.
[7]Import data are developed by the chapter author on a C.I.F. valuation basis.
[8]New supply is the sum of product shipments plus imports.
[9]Export data are developed by the chapter author.

SOURCE: U.S. Department of Commerce: Bureau of the Census, Bureau of Economic Analysis, International Trade Administration (ITA). Estimates and forecasts by ITA.

Source: *U.S. Industrial Outlook 1988,* U.S. Department of Commerce.

Trends and Forecasts: Dental Equipment and Supplies (SIC 3843)

(in millions of dollars except as noted)

ITEM	1984	1985	1986[1]	1987[2]	1988[3]	Percent Change: Compound Annual 1972-85	Compound Annual 1980-85	Annual 1985-86	Annual 1986-87	Annual 1987-88
Industry Data										
Value of shipments[4]	1,213	1,257	1,307	1,438	1,531	9.0	0.1	4.0	10.0	6.5
Value of shipments (1982$)	1,130	1,146	1,256	1,410	1,475	2.3	−4.4	9.6	12.3	4.6
Total employment (000)	14.4	14.4	14.7	14.2	—	1.2	−2.9	2.1	−3.4	—
Production workers (000)	9.3	9.2	9.0	8.7	—	0.6	−3.5	−2.2	−3.3	—
Average hourly earnings ($)	7.96	9.11	—	—	—	7.6	8.9	—	—	—
Product Data										
Value of shipments[5]	1,023	1,042	1,084	1,192	1,269	8.7	−0.8	4.0	10.0	6.5
Value of shipments (1982$)	953	950	1,041	1,169	1,223	2.0	−5.2	9.6	12.3	4.6
Shipments price index[6] (1982 = 100)	107.4	109.6	104.1	102.0	103.8	6.6	4.7	−5.0	−2.0	1.8
Trade Data										
Value of imports (ITA)[7]	66.3	75.0	91.0	97.0	102	14.6	12.8	21.3	6.6	5.2
Import/new supply ratio[8]	0.061	0.067	0.077	0.075	0.074	5.1	12.6	14.9	−2.6	−1.3
Value of exports (ITA)[9]	137	132	155	175	200	10.9	0.8	17.4	12.9	14.3
Export/shipments ratio	0.134	0.127	0.143	0.147	0.158	2.1	1.7	12.6	2.8	7.5

[1]Estimated except for exports and imports.
[2]Estimated.
[3]Forecast.
[4]Value of all products and services sold by the Dental Equipment and Supplies industry.
[5]Value of products classified in the Dental Equipment and Supplies industry produced by all industries.
[6]Developed by the Office of Industry Assessment, ITA.
[7]Import data are developed by the chapter author on a C.I.F. valuation basis.
[8]New supply is the sum of product shipments plus imports.
[9]Export data are developed by the chapter author.
SOURCE: U.S. Department of Commerce: Bureau of the Census, Bureau of Economic Analysis, International Trade Administration (ITA). Estimates and forecasts by ITA.

Source: *U.S. Industrial Outlook 1987*, U.S. Department of Commerce.

Hospital and Laboratory Instruments

Company	Revenue Pct. Change Last Qtr %	Revenue Pct. Change FY to Date %	Revenue Pct. Change Last 12 Mos %	Earnings Last 12 Mos $Mil	Per Share Last 12 Mos $	Per Share Pct. Change Last Qtr %	Per Share Pct. Change FY to Date %	Per Share Pct. Change Last 12 Mos %	5-Year Growth Rate %	Par Growth Rate %	Date of Report -	Dividends Current Rate Amt $	Current Rate Yield %	5-Year Growth Rate %	Payout Last FY %	Payout Last 5 Yrs. %	Last X-Dvd Date -
Ind. Group	30.7	33.1	23.3	146.0	.31	101.0	103.7	NE	NC	6	- - -	.06	.5	1	9	9	- - - -
Abiomed Inc	33.3	4.3	.0	-.6f	-.13	-100.0	-100.0	NC	NC	-25	03-88	.00	.0	0	0	0	00-00-00
ADAC Labs	27.4	25.1	28.3	4.3s	.11	100.0	250.0	NE	NC	0	03-88	.00	.0	0	0	0	11-22-82
Aequitron Med	36.2	29.1	31.2	-.3n	-.06	NE	166.7	-100.0	NC	-4	01-88	.00	.0	0	0	0	00-00-00
Alliance Imaging	74.3	68.5	81.8	1.4n	.50	18.2	45.5	NC	NC	88	01-88	.00	.0	0	0	0	00-00-00
Amserv Inc	.0	.0	.0	-3.6n	-1.52	NE	NE	NE	NC	0	03-88	.00	.0	0	0	0	00-00-00
Biogen NV	78.1	78.1	57.1	-17.9q	-.81	NE	NE	NE	NC	-26	03-88	.00	.0	0	0	0	00-00-00
Biomet	107.8	67.3	59.6	11.6n	.96	61.1	55.1	52.4	63	19	02-88	.00	.0	0	0	0	05-01-86
Birtcher Cp	33.3	-4.3	-14.2	-.4n	-.32	NE	NE	NE	NC	-57	03-88	.00	.0	0	0	0	00-00-00
Cabot Medical	63.6	55.2	50.0	1.1s	.17	25.0	25.0	54.5	NC	17	04-88	.00	.0	0	0	0	00-00-00
Camb Med Tech	14.3	14.3	.0	-.3q	-.16	NE	NE	NE	NC	-16	09-87	.00	.0	0	0	0	02-01-83
Circadian	-9.1	-5.6	.0	-1.1n	-.26	-100.0	-100.0	-100.0	NC	-8	03-88	.00	.0	0	0	0	00-00-00
Clini-Therm	-20.0	-20.0	-16.6	-2.3q	-.32	NC	NC	-100.0	NC	0	09-87	.00	.0	0	0	0	00-00-00
Cobe Labs	24.4	24.4	15.8	11.4q	1.71	68.8	68.8	22.1	16	13	03-88	.00	.0	0	0	0	01-23-86
Coherent Inc	17.9	26.4	23.6	1.2s	.14	NE	NE	NE	NC	1	03-88	.00	.0	0	0	0	10-01-84
Cordis Cp □	-242.2	26.0	.7	-49.7n	-3.76	NE	NE	NE	NC	-88	03-88	.00	.0	0	0	0	07-21-83
Crop Genetics	-100.0	-28.0	-33.3	-3.0f	-.65	NE	NE	NE	NC	-13	03-88	.00	.0	0	0	0	00-00-00
Damon Corp	21.0	23.0	21.8	4.6s	.47	100.0	2700.0	NE	NC	4	02-88	.20	.8	0	65	NE	04-28-88
Datascope Cp	20.1	21.7	23.1	8.4n	1.94	62.5	76.9	27.6	34	20	03-88	.00	.0	0	0	0	09-23-86
Diasonics Inc	7.4	7.4	20.3	12.9q	.18	-100.0	-100.0	NE	NC	12	03-88	.00	.0	0	0	0	00-00-00
Dynatech Cp	16.6	20.7	20.6	24.5f	2.08	27.9	-1.0	-1.0	18	16	03-88	.00	.0	0	0	0	03-02-84
Elscint Ltd □	22.4	14.9	14.7	-21.6n	-.98	NE	NE	NE	NC	0	12-87	.00	.0	0	0	0	00-00-00
EMPI Inc	11.5	11.5	10.0	.3q	.18	40.0	40.0	NE	NC	9	03-88	.00	.0	0	0	0	00-00-00
Exovir	.0	.0	.0	-1.9f	-.61	NE	NE	NE	NC	-86	12-87	.00	.0	0	0	0	00-00-00
FONAR Cp	41.9	39.2	31.7	2.2n	.10	33.3	80.0	66.7	NC	25	03-88	.00	.0	0	0	0	08-25-87
Gelman Sci	20.4	16.1	13.4	.7n	.33	70.0	114.3	-28.3	NC	4	04-88	.00	.0	0	0	0	12-31-80
Hlthdyne	36.4	36.4	-5.7	-6.7q	-.45	-100.0	-100.0	NE	NC	-9	03-88	.00	.0	0	0	0	05-26-83
Hemotec Inc	27.3	27.3	25.0	-.8q	-.35	-50.0	-50.0	-100.0	NC	-15	03-88	.00	.0	0	0	0	06-08-82
Imatron	2400.0	175.0	150.0	-9.4f	-.38	NE	NE	NE	NC	-90	12-87	.00	.0	0	0	0	00-00-00
Intermedics Inc	20.8	20.4	19.1	27.6s	1.61	50.0	79.6	3925.0	NC	24	04-88	.03	.1	0	0	0	02-01-88
Laser Indus	-322.7	-72.8	.0	.0*	1.05	-100.0	-100.0	8.2	NC	0	03-88	.00	.0	0	0	0	00-00-00
MDT Cp	667.7	491.6	483.3	3.3f	.75	225.0	188.5	188.5	NC	15	03-88	.00	.0	0	0	0	00-00-00
Medical Dynamics	.0	.0	.0	-.2s	.00	NC	NC	NE	NC	NC	03-88	.00	.0	0	0	0	00-00-00
Med Graphics	26.3	26.3	.0	-1.0q	-.51	NE	NE	-100.0	NC	-17	03-88	.00	.0	0	0	0	00-00-00
Medtronic Inc	31.5	30.1	30.0	86.5f	6.32	20.3	20.4	20.4	14	18	04-88	1.20	1.5	9	16	20	07-05-88
Micron Prods	12.5	12.5	33.3	.4q	.22	.0	.0	-37.1	NC	10	09-87	.00	.0	0	0	0	00-00-00
Minntech Cp	17.6	22.4	18.1	-.5f	-.39	NC	-100.0	-100.0	NC	-6	03-88	.00	.0	0	0	0	00-00-00
Modern Controls	25.0	25.0	33.3	1.4q	.67	50.0	50.0	81.1	27	19	03-88	.10	.9	0	16	7	05-02-88

Company	Ratio Analysis Profit Margin π/r	Asset Turnover r/a	Return on Total Assets π/a	Leverage Ratio a/e	Return on Equity π/e	Debt to Equity %	Current Ratio -	Shareholdings Market Value $Mil	Latest Shares Outstndng. 000	Held by Banks-Funds 000	Insider Net Trading 000	Short Interest Ratio Days	Fiscal Year Ends Mo
Ind. Group	3.9	1.10	4.3	1.81	7.8	25	2.5	5,709	488,847	97,186	- 85	.6	- -
Abiomed Inc	-12.0	1.35	-16.2	1.54	-25.0	0	2.4	40	4,651	100	0	0.3	03
ADAC Labs	6.3	1.90	12.0	.00	NS	-10	1.1	75	24,967	1,564	0	0.0	09
Aequitron Med	-1.4	1.36	-1.9	2.16	-4.1	26	1.5	16	4,631	590	+1	0.0	04
Alliance Imaging	7.0	.97	6.8	12.87	87.5	744	NA	21	3,517	135	0	0.0	04
Amserv Inc	-60.0	1.50	-90.0	.00	NM	567	1.1	8	2,529	23	0	0.0	06
Biogen NV	NM	NC	NC	NC	-26.4	8	7.6	150	22,228	3,126	0	0.0	12
Biomet	14.0	1.19	16.6	1.14	18.9	0	7.9	307	12,151	4,655	0	0.0	05
Birtcher Cp	-6.7	1.01	-6.8	8.40	-57.1	14	3.6	6	2,073	15	0	0.0	06
Cabot Medical	6.1	1.74	10.6	1.58	16.7	5	2.5	18	6,649	22	0	0.0	10
Camb Med Tech	-10.0	.61	-6.1	2.59	-15.8	126	4.5	4	2,500	77	0	0.0	06
Circadian	-5.5	1.15	-6.3	1.30	-8.2	0	3.3	7	4,490	743	+5	0.0	06
Clini-Therm	-46.0	.70	-32.4	.00	NM	189	3.3	5	7,233	45	0	0.0	06
Cobe Labs	5.6	1.46	8.2	1.52	12.5	18	3.3	189	6,623	2,407	-11	0.0	12
Coherent Inc	.7	1.14	.8	1.75	1.4	5	1.9	99	8,295	3,528	+27	0.0	09
Cordis Cp □	-39.1	.89	-34.9	2.51	-87.7	61	1.9	237	13,370	8,284	0	0.0	06
Crop Genetics	NM	NC	NC	NC	-13.0	0	29.7	49	4,659	1,092	0	0.0	03
Damon Corp	2.4	1.50	3.6	2.14	7.7	33	2.6	254	9,540	3,019	+37	0.2	08
Datascope Cp	8.3	1.22	10.1	1.98	20.0	47	3.6	206	4,438	2,423	-5	0.0	06
Diasonics Inc	4.7	1.17	5.5	2.22	12.2	28	1.8	161	69,603	12,831	-132	0.0	12
Dynatech Cp	6.7	1.45	9.7	1.66	16.1	29	3.3	263	11,800	5,561	0	0.0	03
Elscint Ltd □	-14.6	.78	-11.4	.00	NS	-226	1.0	21	16,626	133	0	0.0	03
EMPI Inc	2.7	1.48	4.0	2.35	9.4	100	5.9	5	1,753	24	0	0.0	12
Exovir	NC	NC	NC	NC	-86.4	0	5.5	30	3,109	105	0	0.0	12
FONAR Cp	4.1	1.54	6.3	3.97	25.0	56	.9	40	21,876	1,092	0	0.0	06
Gelman Sci	1.2	1.33	1.6	2.38	3.8	76	2.5	26	2,338	481	0	7.4	07
Hlthdyne	-8.2	.84	-6.9	1.32	-9.1	5	4.7	66	14,665	4,221	+5	0.0	12
Hemotec Inc	-16.0	.62	-9.9	1.56	-15.4	38	4.4	6	2,461	306	0	0.0	12
Imatron	-94.0	.54	-50.3	1.80	-90.4	5	2.1	15	24,973	947	0	0.0	12
Intermedics Inc	13.0	1.14	14.8	1.65	24.4	10	2.1	659	15,503	6,431	-2	0.3	10
Laser Indus	NC	NC	NC	NC	.0	59	2.7	18	4,565	320	0	17.2	12
MDT Cp	4.7	1.28	6.0	2.50	15.0	75	2.6	63	4,897	799	0	0.0	03
Medical Dynamics	-6.7	1.19	-8.0	1.14	-9.1	0	7.3	5	41,718	0	0	0.0	09
Med Graphics	-11.1	1.25	-13.9	1.24	-17.2	0	5.1	10	1,986	198	0	0.0	12
Medtronic Inc	13.2	1.17	15.5	1.45	22.4	1	2.9	1,083	13,690	8,338	+2	0.7	04
Micron Prods	10.0	.89	8.9	1.07	9.5	0	4.7	5	2,013	35	0	0.1	06
Minntech Cp	-3.8	1.18	-4.5	1.36	-6.1	13	4.6	12	1,424	64	0	0.0	03
Modern Controls	17.5	1.08	18.9	1.17	22.2	0	6.9	23	2,134	113	0	0.0	12

Ratio Analysis: π/r x r/a = π/a x a/e = π/e

Continued

Hospital and Laboratory Instruments (Continued)

Company	Revenue Pct. Change Last Qtr	Revenue Pct. Change FY to Date	Revenue Pct. Change Last 12 Mos	Earnings Last 12 Mos	Earnings Per Share Last 12 Mos	Earnings Per Share Pct. Change Last Qtr	Earnings Per Share Pct. Change FY to Date	Earnings Per Share Pct. Change Last 12 Mos	5-Year Growth Rate	Par Growth Rate	Date of Report	Dividends Current Rate Amt	Dividends Current Rate Yield	Dividends 5-Year Growth Rate	Payout Last FY	Payout Last 5 Yrs.	Last X-Dvd Date	Profit Margin	Asset Turnover	Return on Total Assets	Leverage Ratio	Return on Equity	Debt to Equity	Current Ratio	Market Value	Latest Shares Outstndng.	Held by Banks-Funds	Insider Net Trading	Short Interest Ratio	Fiscal Year Ends
-	%	%	%	$Mil	$	%	%	%	%	%	-	$	%	%	%	%	-	π/r	x r/a	= π/a	x a/e	= π/e	%	-	$Mil	000	000	000	Days	Mo
Mtn Med Equip	11.0	-.7	.0	.6f	.19	NE	NE	NE	NC	7	03-88	.00	.0	0	0	0	02-28-83	2.2	.86	1.9	3.53	6.7	110	1.8	18	3,069	554	0	0.0	03
Newport Cp	29.0	21.0	18.6	6.4n	.72	91.7	56.8	30.9	1	8	04-88	.12	.8	4	12	9	05-19-88	12.5	.66	8.2	1.13	9.3	0	6.5	130	8,428	4,317	0	0.0	07
Novametrix Med	32.5	31.0	33.3	.6n	.14	100.0	-20.0	NC	NC	4	01-88	.00	.0	0	0	0	00-00-00	3.0	.97	2.9	1.41	4.1	16	4.1	31	3,553	666	0	0.0	03
OCG Technology	.0	100.0	.0	-1.4s	-.16	NE	NE	NE	NC	0	12-87	.00	.0	0	0	0	00-00-00	NC	NC	NC	NC	NM	0	2.3	11	9,143	428	0	0.0	06
Oncogene Science	-44.4	35.9	25.0	.1f	.01	-100.0	-75.0	-75.0	NC	0	09-87	.00	.0	0	0	0	00-00-00	2.0	.20	.4	1.00	.4	0	23.6	33	9,100	507	0	0.0	09
St Jude Med	43.2	43.2	26.9	20.7q	1.86	57.1	57.1	40.9	NC	22	03-88	.00	.0	0	0	0	10-01-86	25.9	.79	20.4	1.10	22.4	1	11.9	411	11,269	6,064	+10	0.0	12
Staodynam Inc	.0	10.0	12.5	.5f	.20	NE	150.0	150.0	NC	15	02-88	.00	.0	0	0	0	00-00-00	5.6	1.59	8.9	1.65	14.7	29	3.1	6	2,064	14	-20	0.0	02
Stryker Cp	14.8	14.8	20.3	13.4q	.87	22.7	22.7	24.3	20	18	03-88	.00	.0	0	0	0	06-12-87	8.7	1.47	12.8	1.39	17.8	5	3.3	359	15,595	4,492	-1	0.0	12
Survival Tech	-41.9	3.2	16.6	.8n	.29	-100.0	NE	NE	NC	13	04-88	.00	.0	0	0	0	00-00-00	2.9	1.24	3.6	3.53	12.7	70	1.2	14	2,815	51	0	0.0	07
US Surgical	17.2	17.2	21.8	21.0q	1.73	28.6	28.6	34.1	NC	11	03-88	.60	1.8	0	28	28	05-26-88	8.0	1.08	8.6	2.05	17.6	75	2.9	388	11,683	5,711	0	3.2	12
Vicon Fiber	-20.6	32.5	37.5	-2.0f	-.38	-100.0	NE	NE	NC	-77	12-86	.00	.0	0	0	0	00-00-00	-18.2	1.41	-25.6	3.00	-76.9	46	1.1	8	3,521	1	0	0.0	12
Vipont Pharm	50.9	54.0	64.7	2.5s	.42	28.6	58.3	110.0	NC	19	03-88	.00	.0	0	0	0	00-00-00	8.9	1.26	11.2	1.67	18.7	27	3.3	97	5,605	470	0	0.0	09
Waters Instrument	-6.5	-6.5	.0	.3q	.17	-100.0	-100.0	54.5	NC	3	04-88	.08	2.4	-7	20	36	04-04-88	2.5	1.68	4.2	1.43	6.0	10	3.4	4	1,324	64	0	0.0	01

Hospital and Laboratory Supplies

Company	Revenue Pct. Change Last Qtr	Revenue Pct. Change FY to Date	Revenue Pct. Change Last 12 Mos	Earnings Last 12 Mos	Earnings Per Share Last 12 Mos	Earnings Per Share Pct. Change Last Qtr	Earnings Per Share Pct. Change FY to Date	Earnings Per Share Pct. Change Last 12 Mos	5-Year Growth Rate	Par Growth Rate	Date of Report	Dividends Current Rate Amt	Dividends Current Rate Yield	Dividends 5-Year Growth Rate	Payout Last FY	Payout Last 5 Yrs.	Last X-Dvd Date	Profit Margin	Asset Turnover	Return on Total Assets	Leverage Ratio	Return on Equity	Debt to Equity	Current Ratio	Market Value	Latest Shares Outstndng.	Held by Banks-Funds	Insider Net Trading	Short Interest Ratio	Fiscal Year Ends
Ind. Group	15.3	18.0	19.0	1,702.5	1.66	21.3	- 5.3	26.4	12	10	- - -	.65	2.2	1	31	38	- - - -	7.1	1.03	7.3	2.23	16.3	42	1.8	29,455	983,896	397,462	-1930	.7	- -
Acme United	12.7	12.7	8.5	.6q	.20	NE	NE	NE	NC	1	03-88	.16	2.2	-12	75	67	05-10-88	1.6	1.19	1.9	1.58	3.0	35	7.4	23	3,173	1,467	0	0.0	12
Ballard Med Prods	45.5	45.5	83.3	1.2q	.33	137.5	137.5	230.0	NC	21	12-87	.00	.0	0	0	0	00-00-00	10.9	1.50	16.4	1.29	21.1	0	3.8	53	3,651	266	0	0.0	09
Bard C R	19.1	19.1	17.3	65.6q	2.26	23.5	23.5	23.5	18	17	03-88	.48	1.3	20	21	19	04-26-88	9.8	1.38	13.5	1.61	21.8	15	2.1	1,105	28,803	18,405	+13	2.1	12
Bausch&Lomb	13.0	13.0	17.3	87.7q	2.89	17.0	17.0	14.2	13	10	03-88	1.00	2.1	1	30	36	05-25-88	10.1	.89	9.0	1.69	15.2	28	3.1	1,400	29,948	17,529	+1	3.3	12
Baxter Intl	12.2	12.2	13.6	348.0q	1.19	40.9	40.9	38.4	-1	7	03-88	.50	2.5	14	39	39	06-07-88	5.4	.85	4.6	2.67	12.3	61	1.5	4,897	240,352	120,391	-6	1.3	12
Becton, Dick ◻	18.8	17.4	16.9	140.9s	3.45	20.0	2.0	15.0	25	12	03-88	.86	1.7	6	22	30	06-07-88	8.2	.90	7.4	2.22	16.4	56	1.7	2,076	40,416	23,383	+7	0.0	09
Bio Medicus	24.1	27.7	33.3	1.0f	.18	NE	-10.0	-10.0	NC	10	03-88	.00	.0	0	0	0	00-00-00	8.3	1.06	8.8	1.13	9.9	0	6.9	43	5,799	313	0	0.0	03
Bioplasty Inc ◇ ◆	20.0	8.1	.0	.2f	.10	NE	NE	NE	NC	13	07-87	.00	.0	0	0	0	00-00-00	5.0	1.34	6.7	1.87	12.5	19	2.7	3	2,048	0	0	0.0	07
Biosearch Med ◻	8.5	8.5	5.5	-.5q	-.07	NE	NE	NE	NC	0	03-88	.00	.0	0	0	0	00-00-00	-2.6	1.54	-4.0	.00	NM	1760	2.2	12	5,964	163	0	0.0	12
Collagen Cp	60.0	23.6	18.1	-1.4n	-.18	-100.0	-100.0	-100.0	NC	-4	03-88	.00	.0	0	0	0	07-28-86	-5.4	.74	-4.0	1.08	-4.3	1	8.3	68	7,527	1,617	0	0.0	06
Concept Inc	15.2	13.6	13.8	4.1n	.55	41.7	33.3	34.1	59	16	05-88	.00	.0	0	0	0	02-23-88	10.0	1.22	12.2	1.27	15.5	7	5.4	102	7,541	3,366	+78	0.0	08
Conmed Cp	28.6	28.6	18.1	1.2q	.44	-16.7	-16.7	NC	NC	12	03-88	.00	.0	0	0	0	00-00-00	9.2	1.00	9.2	1.29	11.9	6	5.3	17	2,835	7	0	0.0	12
Cooper Cos ◻	94.9	115.9	80.5	-44.1s	-2.20	NE	-100.0	-100.0	NC	-20	04-88	.40	4.0	0	14	28	12-28-87	-5.0	.64	-3.2	5.34	-17.1	144	1.0	231	23,095	4,158	0	16.9	10
Criticare Systs	70.0	77.1	120.0	1.8s	.34	42.9	28.6	88.9	NC	19	12-87	.00	.0	0	0	0	00-00-00	16.4	.94	15.4	1.24	19.1	0	5.3	40	6,270	257	0	0.0	06
Dahlberg	17.6	17.6	30.9	.9q	.29	-61.5	-61.5	81.3	NC	5	03-88	.00	.0	0	0	0	00-00-00	1.6	2.25	3.6	1.50	5.4	2	2.5	31	2,846	435	+8	0.0	12
Delmed Inc	-16.2	-16.2	-14.8	-7.5q	-.16	-100.0	-100.0	NE	NC	-39	03-88	.00	.0	0	0	0	00-00-00	-32.6	.55	-17.9	2.20	-39.3	76	3.2	43	43,058	1,520	0	0.2	12
Dento Med	.0	.0	.0	-.9f	-.07	NE	NE	NE	NC	-12	12-87	.00	.0	0	0	0	07-07-83	NC	NC	NC	NC	-11.7	0	27.0	18	13,679	196	0	0.0	12
Durr Fillauer	15.4	15.4	11.2	7.1q	.93	30.0	30.0	12.0	8	10	03-88	.18	1.3	12	20	18	05-16-88	1.3	3.54	4.6	2.61	12.0	64	2.4	110	7,900	3,029	+0	0.0	12
Electro Catheter	20.0	24.3	28.5	-.9s	-.25	NE	NE	NE	NC	-23	02-88	.00	.0	0	0	0	12-20-84	-10.0	1.58	-15.8	1.46	-23.1	3	2.4	12	3,397	142	-5	0.0	08
Everest&Jen A	NA	NA	NA	NA	NA	NA	NA	NA	NA	NC	00-00	.20	1.7	NA	NA	NA	05-18-88	NA	NC	NA	NC	NA	NA	NA	67	5,755	966	-0	NA	NA

Everest&Jen B	-3.2	-3.2	-6.6	-.1q	-.02	NE	NE	-100.0	NC	-1	03-88	.10	.7	0	NE	54	05-18-88	-.1	1.00	-.1	1.00	-.1	63	2.6	34	2,355	119	0	0.0	12
Fisher Sci Grp	4.2	4.2	317.2	35.4q	.97	100.0	100.0	NC	NC	12	03-88	.00	.0	0	0	0	00-00-00	3.9	1.64	6.4	1.88	12.0	14	2.0	736	36,824	30,059	0	0.0	12
Gamma Biologic	6.3	2.2	.0	-.1f	-.02	-100.0	NE	NE	NC	-1	03-88	.00	.0	0	0	NE	12-20-85	-.6	.67	-.4	1.50	-.6	17	1.7	29	4,615	517	0	0.0	03
Gen Probe	.0	.0	33.3	-7.8q	-.58	NE	NE	NC	NC	-37	03-88	.00	.0	0	0	0	00-00-00	NM	NC	NC	NC	-37.0	5	7.2	93	15,565	901	0	0.0	12
Hana Biologics	-36.8	-1.9	.0	-3.3n	-.49	NE	NE	NE	NC	-24	03-88	.00	.0	0	0	0	00-00-00	-47.1	.37	-17.2	1.41	-24.3	13	5.4	64	6,575	367	0	0.0	06
Hlth-Chem	-8.0	-8.0	6.2	.5q	.06	-100.0	-100.0	-75.0	NC	2	03-88	.00	.0	0	0	0	10-16-80	1.5	.47	.7	2.86	2.0	81	4.1	33	7,322	1,073	0	0.4	12
Hillenbrand Ind	20.8	23.0	19.0	68.3s	1.81	28.9	43.5	31.2	15	17	05-88	.40	1.1	17	23	30	04-18-88	8.5	1.21	10.3	2.13	21.9	40	2.0	1,322	37,769	12,736	-79	0.3	11
Invacare Corp	34.1	34.1	22.8	2.6q	.47	57.1	57.1	-24.2	NC	11	03-88	.00	.0	0	0	3	00-00-00	1.9	1.74	3.3	3.21	10.6	122	2.6	48	5,569	525	-1704	0.0	12
IPCO Corp	-1.4	4.1	3.3	1.3n	.22	-75.0	NE	NE	NC	-1	03-88	.36	4.0	14	NE	40	07-08-88	.6	1.50	.9	2.33	2.1	55	1.8	47	5,228	1,729	-15	0.0	06
Johnsn & John	16.7	16.7	15.2	876.5q	5.09	19.1	19.1	28.5	8	15	03-88	2.00	2.5	10	33	43	05-18-88	10.5	1.28	13.4	1.88	25.2	21	1.9	13,701	172,617	103,989	+1	2.3	12
Kirschner Medical	108.7	108.7	185.7	1.3q	.72	220.0	220.0	928.6	NC	6	03-88	.00	.0	0	0	0	00-00-00	6.5	.60	3.9	1.44	5.6	28	6.7	58	2,154	714	0	0.0	12
Lumex	5.2	5.2	1.3	-.7q	-.16	-100.0	-100.0	-100.0	NC	-3	03-88	.08	.6	4	200	11	07-14-88	-.9	1.33	-1.2	1.67	-2.0	26	3.0	53	4,207	1,399	0	0.0	12
Marquest Med	43.2	39.2	34.2	-2.8n	-.69	-100.0	-100.0	-100.0	NC	-15	12-87	.07	1.2	0	0	0	06-30-87	-6.0	.90	-5.4	2.59	-14.0	98	2.4	22	3,900	738	0	0.0	03
Medex Inc	16.7	17.3	18.1	2.5n	.64	35.7	28.9	23.1	12	14	03-88	.08	.8b	16	11	11	02-05-88	9.6	1.24	11.9	1.32	15.7	9	7.0	39	3,935	687	+2	0.0	06
Med Sterilization	.0	23.1	.0	-1.6f	-.97	-100.0	NE	NE	NC	-70	12-87	.00	.0	0	0	0	00-00-00	-53.3	.45	-24.2	2.88	-69.6	78	.5	6	1,636	15	0	0.0	12
Mediq Inc	-21.2	-6.0	6.0	8.0s	.32	-30.0	-21.1	39.1	-8	7	03-88	.12	2.9	0	31	20	06-09-88	3.3	.76	2.5	4.32	10.8	203	1.4	67	16,267	2,003	0	4.7	09
Mentor Cp Minn ◇	16.7	20.7	21.2	6.4f	.57	55.6	54.1	54.1	47	14	03-88	.16	1.4	0	28	10	04-04-88	16.0	.61	9.8	2.05	20.1	85	8.7	128	10,858	1,490	0	0.0	03
Monoclonal Antibod ♦	20.0	-18.7	-25.0	-7.3f	-2.05	NE	NE	NE	NC	-83	03-88	.00	.0	0	0	0	00-00-00	NM	NC	NC	NC	-83.0	7	2.3	15	3,558	249	0	0.0	03
Natl Patent	-24.9	-24.9	-13.0	12.1q	1.01	NE	NE	NE	NC	15	03-88	.10	1.3	0	13	NE	03-28-88	5.9	.66	3.9	4.18	16.3	233	4.3	88	11,792	1,482	0	0.7	12
Nova Pharm	44.4	.0	25.0	-9.4n	-.43	NE	NE	NE	NC	-36	09-87	.00	.0	0	0	0	00-00-00	NM	NC	NC	NC	-36.3	1	2.6	168	22,444	2,049	-215	0.0	12
Phoenix Med	34.5	34.5	25.0	1.2q	.66	.0	.0	NE	NC	15	03-88	.00	.0	0	0	0	00-00-00	8.0	1.14	9.1	1.63	14.8	38	3.5	20	1,927	194	0	0.0	12
Puritan Bennett	17.1	17.1	14.6	12.0q	1.08	36.4	36.4	.0	NC	16	03-88	.11	.4	1	11	23	01-11-88	6.7	1.55	10.4	1.66	17.3	9	2.3	305	11,093	8,181	-2	0.0	12
Q Med	-46.7	-46.7	44.4	-4.0q	-.66	-100.0	-100.0	-100.0	NC	-74	02-88	.00	.0	0	0	0	05-12-87	-30.8	1.34	-41.2	1.80	-74.1	0	2.0	14	6,041	528	-10	0.0	11
Quest Med	-45.7	-45.7	-28.5	1.8q	.24	NC	NC	NE	NC	12	03-88	.00	.0	0	0	0	00-00-00	18.0	.57	10.2	1.16	11.8	0	5.8	18	6,620	724	0	0.0	12
Sci-Med Life	12.9	34.6	40.0	-.3f	-.13	-100.0	-100.0	-100.0	NC	-5	02-88	.00	.0	0	0	0	12-31-86	-2.1	1.29	-2.7	1.78	-4.8	52	3.3	42	2,555	574	0	0.0	02
Span Amer Med	50.0	43.9	50.0	.7s	.20	NE	400.0	42.9	-5	11	03-88	.00	.0	0	0	0	02-21-86	3.9	1.28	5.0	2.12	10.6	77	3.3	10	3,267	212	0	0.0	09
Spectran Cp	-33.3	-33.3	-25.0	-.9q	-.21	NE	NE	NE	NC	-10	03-88	.00	.0	0	0	0	00-00-00	-30.0	.26	-7.7	1.29	-9.9	18	5.4	5	4,592	303	0	0.0	12
Symbion Inc	8.3	8.3	-14.2	-1.7q	-.22	NE	NE	NE	NC	-13	03-88	.00	.0	0	0	0	00-00-00	-28.3	.42	-12.0	1.12	-13.4	0	8.6	14	7,461	257	0	0.0	12
Tambrands Inc	10.3	10.3	11.7	79.2q	3.57	14.6	14.6	12.3	11	12	03-88	1.92	3.6	7	53	57	06-01-88	14.4	1.35	19.4	1.30	25.2	0	3.1	1,190	22,252	14,560	-3	0.7	12
Thermedics	27.1	27.1	10.5	1.0q	.06	.0	.0	NE	NC	3	03-88	.00	.0	0	0	0	11-03-86	4.8	.38	1.8	1.50	2.7	39	9.0	160	16,186	882	-2	5.0	12
Trimedyne Inc	200.0	186.0	150.0	2.9s	.45	NE	NE	NE	NC	31	03-88	.00	.0	0	0	0	00-00-00	14.5	1.52	22.0	1.42	31.2	5	3.6	77	5,857	779	0	0.0	09
Utd Industrial	13.0	13.0	8.8	15.2q	1.14	36.8	36.8	NE	NC	7	03-88	.64	4.1	22	59	55	08-01-88	5.0	1.30	6.5	2.40	15.6	14	1.1	206	13,204	3,139	0	0.3	12
Vestar Inc	100.0	100.0	200.0	-4.1q	-.68	NE	NE	NE	NC	-32	03-88	.00	.0	0	0	0	00-00-00	NM	NC	NC	NC	-31.5	0	15.5	49	6,266	1,005	0	0.0	12
Wendt Bristol	11.9	7.4	4.3	.5n	.43	20.0	-8.9	-14.0	NC	12	12-87	.00	.0	0	0	0	00-00-00	2.1	1.71	3.6	3.22	11.6	140	2.9	8	1,110	1	+1	0.0	03
West Co	12.0	12.0	6.9	12.2q	.76	-33.3	-33.3	-29.6	1	5	03-88	.30	2.1	9	32	24	07-14-88	4.7	.94	4.4	1.77	7.8	33	2.0	233	16,218	5,672	0	1.2	12

Hospitals and Laboratories

Ind. Group	5.5	3.4	3.5	132.0	.14	58.8	38.1	- 59.0	NC	- 3	- - -	.35	2.1	2	49	30	- - - -	.6	1.00	.6	3.33	2.0	134	1.4	13,769	840,895	316,390	- 312	.6	- -
Am Hlth Cos	4.2	9.7	9.7	8.9f	1.27	34.5	13.4	13.4	NC	4	03-88	1.00	6.1b	0	46	17	05-25-88	19.8	.84	16.6	1.17	19.4	0	1.6	115	6,949	3,580	0	0.0	03
Am Hlthcare ♦	35.3	33.0	32.7	-47.2f	-3.94	NE	NE	NE	NC	0	12-87	.00	.0	0	0	0	00-00-00	-9.6	.95	-9.1	.00	NM	406	.3	8	11,962	42	0	0.5	12
Am Med Intl ◇ □	10.3	7.8	16.2	103.3n	1.23	13.9	-3.0	373.1	NC	4	05-88	.72	4.0	14	57	58	07-08-88	3.6	.78	2.8	3.86	10.8	190	1.3	1,453	81,290	28,636	0	1.4	08
Basic Amer Med □	22.8	22.8	-9.0	-16.1q	-2.05	NE	NE	NE	NC	-80	03-88	.00	.0	0	0	0	05-05-87	-7.3	1.33	-9.7	8.22	-79.7	314	.6	41	7,863	476	0	0.0	12
Bio Tech Genl	15.4	38.5	33.3	-5.4f	-.93	NE	NE	NE	NC	0	12-87	.00	.0	0	0	0	00-00-00	NM	NC	NC	NC	NS	-200	7.8	26	5,840	760	0	0.0	12

Continued

Company	Revenue: Pct. Change Last Qtr	Revenue: Pct. Change FY to Date	Revenue: Pct. Change Last 12 Mos	Earnings: Last 12 Mos	Earnings Per Share: Last 12 Mos	Earnings Per Share Pct. Change: Last Qtr	Earnings Per Share Pct. Change: FY to Date	Earnings Per Share Pct. Change: Last 12 Mos	Earnings: 5-Year Growth Rate	Earnings: Par Growth Rate	Earnings: Date of Report	Dividends Current Rate: Amt	Dividends Current Rate: Yield	Dividends: 5-Year Growth Rate	Dividends Payout: Last FY	Dividends Payout: Last 5 Yrs.	Dividends: Last X-Dvd Date	Ratio Analysis: Profit Margin	Ratio Analysis: Asset Turnover	Ratio Analysis: Return on Total Assets	Ratio Analysis: Leverage Ratio	Ratio Analysis: Return on Equity	Ratio Analysis: Debt to Equity	Ratio Analysis: Current Ratio	Shareholdings: Market Value	Shareholdings: Latest Shares Outstndng.	Shareholdings: Held by Banks-Funds	Shareholdings: Insider Net Trading	Shareholdings: Short Interest Ratio	Shareholdings: Fiscal Year Ends
-	%	%	%	$Mil	$	%	%	%	%	%	-	$	%	%	%	%	-	π/r x	r/a =	π/a x	a/e =	π/e	%	-	$Mil	000	000	000	Days	Mo
Hospitals and Laboratories (Continued)																														
Biotech Rsch Lab	100.0	100.0	100.0	1.6q	.27	1100.0	1100.0	NE	NC	16	03-88	.00	.0	0	0	0	12-13-82	11.4	1.08	12.3	1.30	16.0	9	4.7	52	6,176	1,325	0	0.0	12
CDC Life Sci	-6.4	-6.4	6.8	27.7q	1.27	47.6	47.6	30.9	NC	18	03-88	.00	.0	0	0	0	00-00-00	12.6	.53	6.7	2.70	18.1	67	2.1	556	21,816	3,386	0	0.0	12
Cel Sci	.0	.0	.0	-1.7f	-.08	NE	NE	NE	NC	0	09-87	.00	.0	0	0	0	00-00-00	NC	NC	NC	NC	NM	0	2.5	23	23,246	0	0	0.0	09
Celgene	400.0	400.0	.0	-4.5q	-.95	NE	NE	NC	NC	-15	03-88	.00	.0	0	0	0	00-00-00	NM	NC	NC	NC	-15.3	0	33.3	52	5,225	219	0	0.0	12
Cetus Corp	18.3	18.4	18.4	-15.3n	-.58	NE	NE	NE	NC	-9	03-88	.00	.0	0	0	0	00-00-00	-34.0	.15	-5.1	1.75	-8.9	62	8.3	347	26,688	7,111	0	0.0	06
Charter Med A ♦	28.4	29.1	27.6	50.5s	1.64	-19.6	-6.4	2.5	17	16	03-88	.24	.7	0	11	11	06-10-88	4.4	1.02	4.5	4.27	19.2	213	1.9	713	21,368	13,994	0	1.0	09
Charter Med B	NA	NA	NA	NA	NA	NA	NA	NA	NA	NC	00-00	.24	.7	NA	NA	NA	06-10-88	NA	NC	NA	NC	NA	NA	NA	327	9,764	1,724	0	NA	NA
Chemex Pharma	.0	.0	.0	.0‡	-.32	NE	NE	NE	NC	0	09-87	.00	.0	0	0	0	00-00-00	NC	NC	NC	NC	.0	0	17.3	36	9,937	1,458	-1	0.0	12
Commun Psych	22.0	22.0	26.5	62.1q	1.37	15.6	15.6	17.1	21	14	02-88	.36	1.4	29	22	19	06-06-88	20.7	.73	15.2	1.26	19.1	12	4.4	1,154	45,946	30,711	-55	2.2	11
Comprhen Care	14.9	9.4	6.8	9.4n	.89	17.6	-1.5	27.1	2	6	02-88	.40	3.6	24	41	30	04-25-88	4.6	.96	4.4	2.50	11.0	112	2.4	112	10,143	3,919	0	0.0	05
DDI Pharm	.0	.0	-33.3	.3q	.07	33.3	33.3	NE	NC	10	03-88	.00	.0	0	0	0	00-00-00	15.0	.61	9.1	1.07	9.7	0	14.0	16	4,983	292	0	0.0	12
Diagnostek ♦	505.6	365.6	400.0	.4f	.03	200.0	-40.0	-40.0	NC	3	03-88	.00	.0	0	0	0	00-00-00	2.7	1.07	2.9	1.10	3.2	0	9.0	42	12,034	173	0	0.0	03
Enzo Biochem □	45.5	41.5	22.2	-4.5n	-.40	-100.0	-100.0	-100.0	NC	-19	04-88	.00	.0	0	0	0	06-30-86	-40.9	.14	-5.9	3.22	-19.0	208	20.3	48	11,359	819	0	0.0	07
Enzon Inc ♦	.0	.0	.0	-3.6n	-.36	NE	NE	NE	NC	-25	03-88	.00	.0	0	0	0	00-00-00	NC	NC	NC	NC	-24.8	0	46.0	75	10,770	297	0	0.0	06
Gateway Med	-9.7	33.3	.0	-4.1n	-.49	NC	-100.0	-100.0	NC	0	01-88	.00	.0	0	0	0	07-01-86	-8.2	.45	-3.7	.00	NM	507	.9	2	8,975	98	0	0.0	04
Genetic Eng □	-100.0	.0	.0	-.1n	-.06	NE	NE	NE	NC	-25	05-87	.00	.0	0	0	0	00-00-00	NC	NC	NC	NC	-25.0	0	.7	2	2,390	0	0	0.0	08
Hlth Mgmt	90.8	84.9	113.3	4.7s	.87	42.3	38.5	47.5	NC	16	03-88	.00	.0	0	0	0	00-00-00	2.9	1.31	3.8	4.32	16.4	264	1.7	51	4,786	1,042	0	0.0	09
Hlthcare Intl	33.6	27.7	25.3	2.8n	.26	-100.0	-97.6	-59.4	NC	7	03-88	.00	.0	0	0	0	00-00-00	1.0	.80	.8	8.75	7.0	538	1.5	39	8,939	1,162	+5	0.1	06
Hlthcare Svc Am	4.0	4.0	39.5	-26.1q	-3.00	NC	NC	NE	NC	-99	03-88	.00	.0	0	0	0	00-00-00	-19.5	.74	-14.5	6.82	-98.9	4	.2	33	11,977	1,340	0	0.0	12
Hlthways Systs	80.9	48.3	34.6	-6.5n	-3.44	NE	NE	NE	NC	0	03-88	.00	.0	0	0	0	00-00-00	-9.8	3.29	-32.2	.00	NM	9	NA	7	1,896	4	0	0.0	06
HMO Amer	6.3	6.3	19.2	-.8q	-.11	-100.0	-100.0	NE	NC	-7	03-88	.00	.0	0	0	0	00-00-00	-.8	4.38	-3.5	1.91	-6.7	0	1.4	15	6,968	364	0	0.0	12
Horizon Hlthcre	NA	NA	NA	NA	NA	NA	NA	NA	NA	NC	00-00	.00	.0	NA	NA	NA	00-00-00	NA	NC	NA	NC	NA	NA	NA	14	6,690	888	0	NA	NA
Hosp Cp Am	-19.1	-19.1	-6.2	-57.5q	-.56	15.3	15.3	-100.0	NC	-7	03-88	.72	1.9	18	NE	26	06-27-88	-1.3	.69	-.9	3.33	-3.0	114	2.1	2,630	70,376	47,835	-282	0.9	12
Humana Inc	-12.3	-13.5	-6.1	216.2n	2.19	20.8	23.9	630.0	-1	12	05-88	.92	3.4	16	41	40	06-27-88	6.0	1.12	6.7	3.19	21.4	122	1.5	2,638	97,686	55,098	+4	3.1	08
Imreg Inc	-50.0	-44.4	.0	-3.2f	-.31	NE	NE	NE	NC	-56	12-87	.00	.0	0	0	0	00-00-00	NM	NC	NC	NC	-56.1	0	11.7	109	6,751	788	0	0.0	12
Maxicare Hlth	10.2	10.2	60.0	-263.3q	-7.87	NE	NE	NE	NC	0	03-88	.00	.0	0	0	0	07-09-85	-14.2	1.87	-26.5	.00	NS	-1008	.5	50	33,466	23,241	0	0.0	12
Medical Care	76.2	76.2	50.0	.7q	.04	233.3	233.3	-42.9	NC	1	03-88	.00	.0	0	0	0	00-00-00	1.0	.60	.6	2.17	1.3	89	2.7	87	9,705	2,003	+0	0.0	12
Medicore Inc	25.6	25.6	25.0	1.0q	.23	.0	.0	2200.0	NC	8	03-88	.00	.0	0	0	0	10-24-85	5.0	.90	4.5	1.76	7.9	8	2.3	14	4,796	224	0	0.0	12
Natl Med Ent	69.3	-6.5	-21.9	91.0n	1.26	33.3	33.3	21.2	-8	5	02-88	.64	2.8	14	70	33	05-16-88	3.3	.79	2.6	3.77	9.8	161	1.5	1,695	74,933	38,668	-4	3.5	05
Nichols Institute	53.2	68.8	.0	.0‡	.33	-100.0	700.0	NE	NC	0	03-88	.00	.0	0	0	0	03-29-88	NC	NC	NC	NC	.0	130	1.5	55	4,072	791	0	0.1	12
Oranogenesis	NA	NA	NA	NA	NA	NA	NA	NA	NA	NC	00-00	.00	.0	NA	NA	NA	09-14-87	NA	NC	NA	NC	NA	NA	NA	118	6,357	403	0	NA	NA
PCS Inc	32.9	40.7	40.0	11.6f	.80	52.9	50.9	50.9	NC	87	03-88	.00	.0	0	0	0	00-00-00	15.1	.73	11.0	7.93	87.2	0	1.0	377	14,507	1,192	0	0.0	03
Psicor Inc	32.9	35.6	32.0	1.4s	.37	62.5	76.9	12.1	NC	12	03-88	.00	.0	0	0	0	00-00-00	4.2	1.90	8.0	1.50	12.0	3	1.9	21	3,703	435	0	0.0	09
RediCare Inc	21.1	40.9	35.7	1.6f	.18	100.0	200.0	200.0	NC	9	02-88	.00	.0	0	0	0	06-07-83	8.4	.80	6.7	1.31	8.8	13	1.7	25	8,973	1,710	0	0.0	02
Repligen Cp	66.7	216.2	200.0	.3f	.03	NE	NE	NE	NC	1	03-88	.00	.0	0	0	0	00-00-00	2.5	.52	1.3	1.08	1.4	1	12.0	55	7,297	291	0	0.0	03
Safeguard Hlth	1.8	1.8	10.9	3.1q	.44	71.4	71.4	NE	NC	13	03-88	.00	.0	0	0	0	10-16-85	4.4	2.23	9.8	1.33	13.0	5	2.7	35	6,673	2,530	0	0.0	12
Summit Hlth	-98.0	-33.8	-33.4	1.3n	.04	-60.0	-63.6	-63.6	-25	0	03-88	.04	2.1	0	48	16	06-14-88	.3	1.00	.3	5.00	1.5	149	1.2	59	31,250	5,302	+20	0.0	06
T 2 Medical	NA	NA	NA	NA	NA	NA	NA	NA	NA	NC	00-00	.00	.0	NA	NA	NA	00-00-00	NA	NC	NA	NC	NA	NA	NA	65	6,223	0	0	NA	NA
Total Health	800.0	800.0	.0	-9.8q	-1.72	NE	NE	NE	NC	-96	09-87	.00	.0	0	0	0	07-22-87	NM	NC	NC	NC	-96.1	2	8.8	5	4,928	179	0	0.0	06
US Hlthcare	17.7	17.7	19.1	-2.3q	-.04	-33.3	-33.3	-100.0	NC	-9	03-88	.16	2.9	0	600	12	06-13-88	-.4	2.25	-.9	1.89	-1.7	0	1.6	254	46,099	25,429	0	0.0	12
Univ Health	78.6	78.6	39.2	4.1q	.27	2500.0	2500.0	.0	-40	3	03-88	.00	.0	0	0	0	07-05-83	.5	1.40	.7	3.86	2.7	166	1.1	116	17,120	6,451	0	0.0	12

Health Maintenance Organizations' Revenues

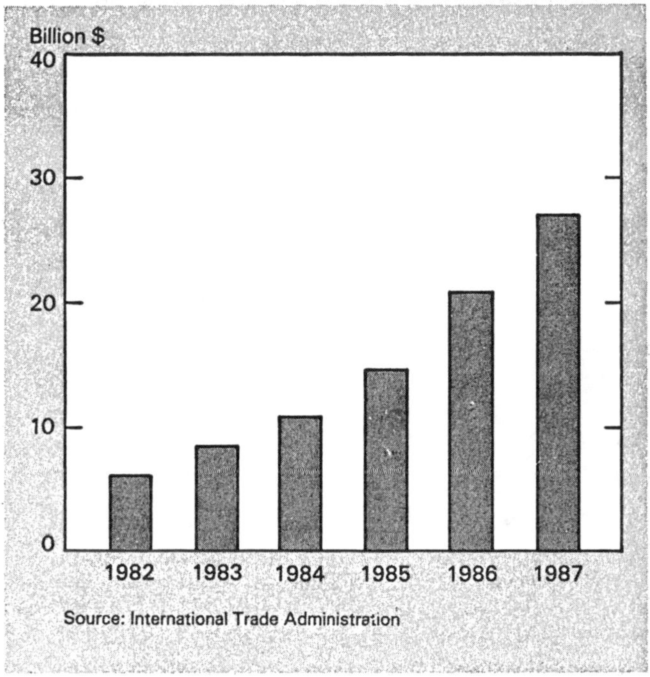

Source: *U.S. Industrial Outlook 1988*, U.S. Department of Commerce.

GROWTH OF HEALTH MAINTENANCE ORGANIZATIONS, 1980-87

Date	Number of Prepaid Plans	Enrollment (millions)	Percent of U.S. population enrolled
June 1980	236	9.1	4.0
June 1981	243	10.2	4.4
June 1982	265	10.8	4.7
June 1983	280	12.5	5.3
June 1984	306	15.1	6.4
December 1984	337	16.7	7.1
December 1985	480	21.0	8.8
December 1986	593	25.0[1]	10.4[1]
December 1987	NA	30.0[1]	12.2[1]

[1]Estimated.

SOURCE: U.S. Department of Health and Human Services; and U.S. Department of Commerce.

Source: *U.S. Industrial Outlook 1988*, U.S. Department of Commerce.

Trends and Forecasts: Household Appliances (SIC 363)

(in millions of dollars except as noted)

ITEM	1984	1985	1986[1]	1987[2]	1988[3]	Percent Change: Compound Annual 1972-85	Compound Annual 1980-85	Annual 1985-86	Annual 1986-87	Annual 1987-88
Industry Data										
Value of shipments[4]	16,249	16,230	16,766	17,723	—	6.8	4.6	3.3	5.7	—
3631 Household Cooking Equip	3,579	3,297	3,270	3,462	—	10.1	6.0	−0.8	5.9	—
3632 Household Refrigerators	3,088	3,341	3,594	3,799	—	5.2	6.3	7.6	5.7	—
3633 Household Laundry Equip	2,716	2,838	3,097	3,429	—	5.8	5.8	9.1	10.7	—
3634 Elect Housewares & Fans	3,239	3,100	2,932	2,951	—	5.1	−1.2	−5.4	0.6	—
3635 Household Vacuums	1,307	1,302	1,431	1,455	—	8.2	11.5	9.9	1.7	—
3636 Sewing Machines	170	178	186	193	—	0.8	−15.1	4.5	3.8	—
3639 Home Appliances, nec	2,151	2,175	2,256	2,434	—	9.3	9.0	3.7	7.9	—
Value of shipments (1982$)	15,299	15,105	15,692	16,617	16,885	1.3	0.6	3.9	5.9	1.6
3631 Household Cooking Equip	3,254	2,964	3,085	3,225	3,200	4.1	1.7	4.1	4.5	−0.8
3632 Household Refrigerators	2,902	3,088	3,245	3,469	3,565	−0.6	1.0	5.1	6.9	2.8
3633 Household Laundry Equip	2,617	2,725	2,988	3,299	3,430	0.3	2.1	9.7	10.4	4.0
3634 Elect Housewares & Fans	3,081	2,950	2,805	2,840	2,775	0.6	−4.2	−4.9	1.2	−2.3
3635 Household Vacuums	1,268	1,228	1,350	1,415	1,465	4.0	9.0	9.9	4.8	3.5
3636 Sewing Machines	164	171	178	185	185	−5.6	−18.7	4.1	3.9	0.0
3639 Home Appliances, nec	2,013	1,977	2,041	2,184	2,265	3.4	4.3	3.2	7.0	3.7
Total employment (000)	132	124	124	127	125	−2.1	−4.4	0.0	2.4	−1.6
Production workers (000)	105	97.2	96.8	100	98.0	−2.3	−4.3	−0.4	3.3	−2.0
Average hourly earnings ($)	9.38	9.82	10.19	10.37	—	7.5	6.7	3.8	1.8	—

Product Data										
Value of shipments[5]	15,359	15,215	15,701	16,578	—	6.6	4.6	3.2	5.6	—
3631 Household Cooking Equip	3,404	3,219	3,192	3,382	—	9.2	6.7	−0.8	6.0	—
3632 Household Refrigerators	2,990	2,998	3,226	3,410	—	5.9	6.4	7.6	5.7	—
3633 Household Laundry Equip	2,459	2,580	2,815	3,116	—	5.5	7.5	9.1	10.7	—
3634 Elect Housewares & Fans	2,998	2,836	2,682	2,678	—	5.3	−1.7	−5.4	−0.1	—
3635 Household Vacuums	1,173	1,160	1,272	1,290	—	7.8	7.3	9.7	1.4	—
3636 Sewing Machines	178	190	198	203	—	1.7	−10.3	4.2	2.5	—
3639 Home Appliances, nec	2,157	2,233	2,316	2,499	—	8.0	6.8	3.7	7.9	—
Value of shipments (1982$)	14,455	14,148	14,664	15,524	15,765	1.2	0.5	3.6	5.9	1.6
3631 Household Cooking Equip	3,096	2,894	3,011	3,150	3,125	3.2	2.3	4.0	4.6	−0.8
3632 Household Refrigerators	2,810	2,771	2,913	3,114	3,200	0.1	1.0	5.1	6.9	2.8
3633 Household Laundry Equip	2,370	2,477	2,716	2,998	3,120	−0.0	3.7	9.6	10.4	4.1
3634 Elect Housewares & Fans	2,851	2,699	2,539	2,570	2,500	0.8	−4.7	−5.9	1.2	−2.7
3635 Household Vacuums	1,138	1,094	1,200	1,255	1,300	3.6	4.8	9.7	4.6	3.6
3636 Sewing Machines	173	183	190	195	195	−4.8	−14.2	3.8	2.6	0.0
3639 Home Appliances, nec	2,018	2,029	2,095	2,242	2,325	2.2	2.1	3.3	7.0	3.7
Shipments price index[6] (1982=100)	106.1	107.3	106.3	106.0	—	5.3	3.9	−0.9	−0.3	—
Trade Data										
Value of imports	2,068	2,387	2,733	2,945	—	13.9	19.1	14.5	7.8	—
Import/new supply ratio[7]	0.128	0.146	—	—	—	5.5	12.2	—	—	—
Value of exports	1,067	945	938	1,200	—	9.1	−6.6	−0.7	27.9	—
Export/shipments ratio	0.060	0.053	—	—	—	2.0	−10.8	—	—	—

[1]Estimated except for exports and imports.
[2]Estimated.
[3]Forecast.
[4]Value of all products and services sold by the Household Appliances industry.
[5]Value of products classified in the Household Appliances industry produced by all industries.
[6]Developed by the Office of Industry Assessment, ITA.
[7]New supply is the sum of product shipments plus imports.
SOURCE: U.S. Department of Commerce: Bureau of the Census, Bureau of Economic Analysis, International Trade Administration (ITA). Estimates and forecasts by ITA.

Source: *U.S. Industrial Outlook 1988,* U.S. Department of Commerce.

Trends and Forecasts: Household Furniture (SIC 251)

(in millions of dollars except as noted)

						Percent Change				
						Compound Annual		Annual		
ITEM	1984	1985	1986[1]	1987[2]	1988[3]	1972-85	1980-85	1985-86	1986-87	1987-88
Industry Data										
Value of shipments[4]	15,545	15,838	16,692	17,855	—	6.0	4.3	5.4	7.0	—
2511 Wood Furniture, House	6,613	6,728	7,117	7,675	—	6.8	6.1	5.8	7.8	—
2512 Upholstered Furn, House	4,363	4,551	4,758	5,067	—	6.1	4.1	4.5	6.5	—
2514 Metal Furniture, House	1,796	1,829	1,945	2,088	—	5.7	4.5	6.3	7.4	—
2515 Mattresses & Bedsprings	1,956	1,921	2,043	2,176	—	4.8	−0.1	6.4	6.5	—
Value of shipments (1982$)	14,675	14,526	15,051	15,729	15,889	0.0	0.1	3.6	4.5	1.0
2511 Wood Furniture, House	6,042	5,965	6,173	6,482	6,546	−0.0	1.0	3.5	5.0	1.0
2512 Upholstered Furn, House	4,181	4,197	4,337	4,532	4,600	0.8	0.1	3.3	4.5	1.5
2514 Metal Furniture, House	1,790	1,811	1,901	1,974	1,984	0.4	3.1	5.0	3.8	0.5
2515 Mattresses & Bedsprings	1,897	1,815	1,886	1,962	1,972	−0.5	−4.1	3.9	4.0	0.5
Total employment (000)	279	272	271	278	—	−1.2	−2.1	−0.4	2.6	—
Production workers (000)	237	230	231	238	—	−1.3	−2.1	0.4	3.0	—
Average hourly earnings ($)	6.16	6.53	6.83	7.07	—	6.6	5.9	4.6	3.5	—

Product Data										
Value of shipments[5]	14,941	15,251	16,078	17,198	—	6.0	4.2	5.4	7.0	—
2511 Wood Furniture, House	6,166	6,263	6,626	7,144	—	6.6	5.1	5.8	7.8	—
2512 Upholstered Furn, House	4,104	4,287	4,482	4,774	—	6.1	5.2	4.5	6.5	—
2514 Metal Furniture, House	1,796	1,770	1,882	2,021	—	5.7	4.3	6.3	7.4	—
2515 Mattresses & Bedsprings	2,071	2,170	2,308	2,459	—	5.5	1.2	6.4	6.5	—
Value of shipments (1982$)	14,119	14,000	14,505	15,155	15,307	0.1	0.1	3.6	4.5	1.0
2511 Wood Furniture, House	5,633	5,554	5,747	6,034	6,095	−0.1	0.1	3.5	5.0	1.0
2512 Upholstered Furn, House	3,935	3,952	4,082	4,266	4,330	0.8	1.1	3.3	4.5	1.5
2514 Metal Furniture, House	1,790	1,753	1,840	1,910	1,919	0.4	2.9	5.0	3.8	0.5
2515 Mattresses & Bedsprings	2,008	2,050	2,131	2,217	2,228	0.1	−2.8	4.0	4.0	0.5
Shipments price index[6] (1982=100)	105.8	108.9	110.8	113.5	—	5.9	4.1	1.7	2.4	—
2511 Wood Furniture, House	109.5	112.8	115.3	118.4	—	6.8	5.0	2.2	2.7	—
2512 Upholstered Furn, House	104.3	108.5	109.8	111.9	—	5.3	4.0	1.2	1.9	—
2514 Metal Furniture, House	100.4	101.0	102.3	105.8	—	5.3	1.4	1.3	3.4	—
2515 Mattresses & Bedsprings	103.3	106.0	108.5	111.1	—	5.4	4.1	2.4	2.4	—
Trade Data										
Value of imports (ITA)[7]	2,010	2,646	3,236	3,721	—	21.8	25.5	22.3	15.0	—
Import/new supply ratio[8]	0.119	0.148	0.168	0.178	—	13.7	18.3	13.5	6.0	—
Value of exports (ITA)[9]	208	165	159	183	—	13.4	−3.9	−3.6	15.1	—
Export/shipments ratio	0.014	0.011	0.010	0.011	—	6.3	−7.2	−9.1	10.0	—

[1]Estimated except for exports and imports.
[2]Estimated.
[3]Forecast.
[4]Value of all products and services sold by the Household Furniture industry.
[5]Value of products classified in the Household Furniture industry produced by all industries.
[6]Developed by the Office of Industry Assessment, ITA.
[7]Import data, developed by the chapter author, includes an indeterminate amount of office furniture.
[8]New supply is the sum of product shipments plus imports.
[9]Export data are developed by the chapter author.
SOURCE: U.S. Department of Commerce: Bureau of the Census, Bureau of Economic Analysis, International Trade Administration (ITA). Estimates and forecasts by ITA.

Source: *U.S. Industrial Outlook 1988*, U.S. Department of Commerce.

Company	Revenue Pct. Change Last Qtr	Revenue Pct. Change FY to Date	Revenue Pct. Change Last 12 Mos	Last 12 Mos	Earnings Per Share Last 12 Mos	Per Share Pct. Change Last Qtr	Per Share Pct. Change FY to Date	Per Share Pct. Change Last 12 Mos	5-Year Growth Rate	Par Growth Rate	Date of Report	Dividends Current Rate Amt	Current Rate Yield	5-Year Growth Rate	Payout Last FY	Payout Last 5 Yrs.	Last X-Dvd Date	Ratio Analysis Pro-fit Mar-gin	Asset Turn-over	Return on Total Assets	Lever-age Ratio	Return on Equity	Debt to Eq-uity	Curr-ent Ratio	Shareholdings Mar-ket Value	Latest Shares Out-stndng.	Held by Banks-Funds	Insider Net Trad-ing	Short Int-erest Ratio	Fiscal Year Ends
-	%	%	%	$Mil	$	%	%	%	%	%	-	$	%	%	%	%	-	π/r x	r/a =	π/a x	a/e =	π/e	%	-	$Mil	000	000	000	Days	Mo
Furniture, Home Furnishings																														
Ind. Group	16.2	17.4	20.0	196.1	1.19	4.8	8.9	21.4	14	10	- - -	.32	2.0	1	23	25	- - - -	4.6	1.59	7.3	1.84	13.4	37	2.6	2,631	166,600	49,602	+ 401	.0	- -
AA Importing	-16.9	-16.9	-5.2	-1.0q	-.40	-100.0	-100.0	-100.0	NC	-13	04-88	.00	.0	0	0	0	00-00-00	-2.8	2.25	-6.3	2.10	-13.2	72	4.9	10	2,683	217	+11	0.0	01
Bassett Furniture	9.7	12.7	12.5	22.3f	2.65	-6.6	14.2	14.2	-5	5	11-87	1.00	2.9	-2	40	42	05-11-88	4.7	1.66	7.8	1.10	8.6	0	7.1	288	8,280	2,302	-0	0.0	11
Berkline Corp	-1.9	-2.9	-2.3	.1n	.04	350.0	-40.5	-94.3	-23	-6	03-88	.50	3.7	0	238	74	06-28-88	.1	3.00	.3	1.67	.5	8	2.1	21	1,523	312	+493	0.0	06
Bush Industries	6.5	6.5	25.0	5.8q	1.27	13.8	13.8	62.8	NC	32	03-88	.00	.0	0	0	0	04-19-88	6.1	1.79	10.9	2.89	31.5	54	1.5	53	4,553	708	0	0.1	12
Chartwell Grp	40.4	40.4	160.0	2.3q	.36	-64.3	-64.3	-16.3	NC	8	03-88	.00	.0	0	0	0	03-19-87	2.9	.69	2.0	4.00	8.0	221	2.4	44	6,160	1,821	0	0.0	12
Classic Cp ■	-21.2	-21.3	-15.6	-1.4s	-.89	-100.0	-100.0	NE	NC	-17	12-87	.00	.0	0	0	0	00-00-00	-5.2	1.65	-8.6	1.94	-16.7	0	1.9	1	1,627	278	0	0.0	06
CraftmaticContour	-36.7	-22.4	-8.0	-3.3s	-.83	-57.1	-50.0	-100.0	NC	-37	03-88	.00	.0	0	0	0	00-00-00	-7.2	2.26	-16.3	2.25	-36.7	41	1.9	9	4,000	386	0	0.0	09
DMI Furniture □	11.9	10.7	2.5	1.0s	.18	50.0	42.9	NE	NC	0	02-88	.00	.0	0	0	0	00-00-00	2.5	2.40	6.0	.00	NS	-216	2.0	6	2,657	515	0	0.0	08
Dresher Inc	81.1	34.8	24.4	2.8n	.63	.0	2.2	3.3	34	16	03-88	.16	2.6	0	23	13	05-04-88	5.0	2.82	14.1	1.50	21.2	0	2.6	28	4,523	1,616	0	0.0	06
Falcon Prod	-6.4	-6.4	.0	.6q	.37	.0	.0	76.2	NC	35	01-88	.00	.0	0	0	0	02-07-80	1.9	1.84	3.5	10.09	35.3	524	1.8	6	1,620	11	0	0.0	10
Flexsteel Ind	4.9	6.9	6.4	8.5n	1.18	20.0	39.1	31.1	5	9	03-88	.48	3.8	8	34	35	05-19-88	5.2	2.12	11.0	1.34	14.7	11	4.8	89	7,136	1,913	0	0.0	06
Huffman Koos	-1.1	-1.1	5.4	-1.5q	-.37	-100.0	-100.0	-100.0	NC	-9	04-88	.00	.0	0	0	0	00-00-00	-1.9	1.58	-3.0	2.83	-8.5	38	1.7	17	4,000	584	0	0.0	01
La Z Boy	27.9	15.9	15.9	25.4f	1.39	6.8	3.7	3.7	11	11	04-88	.40	2.7	15	29	26	05-13-88	5.2	1.81	9.4	1.64	15.4	14	2.6	268	18,040	2,671	0	0.0	04
Ladd Furniture	-2.9	-2.9	16.7	27.1q	1.43	-2.8	-2.8	13.5	35	21	03-88	.25	1.5	0	15	14	04-26-88	7.1	2.10	14.9	1.74	26.0	41	4.1	323	19,290	8,411	0	0.0	12
Leggett Platt	15.6	15.6	10.4	38.4q	2.32	7.3	7.3	7.4	19	13	03-88	.64	2.1	14	18	19	05-23-88	5.7	1.75	10.0	1.83	18.3	40	2.7	501	16,373	6,647	+8	0.5	12
Ohio Mattress	14.9	17.1	51.2	28.1s	1.30	42.9	34.9	52.9	16	7	05-88	.48	2.6	12	37	49	04-11-88	4.4	1.20	5.3	2.23	11.8	78	2.9	404	21,998	11,549	0	0.0	11
Pulaski Furn	3.3	10.8	13.8	5.4s	1.86	35.1	16.7	21.6	15	12	04-88	.40	2.5	23	21	19	05-25-88	4.7	1.53	7.2	2.08	15.0	57	3.0	47	2,913	345	0	0.0	10
Rowe Furniture ◇	-.5	10.8	10.9	2.2f	1.15	-94.1	21.1	21.1	36	9	11-87	.32	2.8	32	23	17	06-20-88	2.4	2.04	4.9	2.49	12.2	53	1.7	20	1,768	266	0	0.0	11
Shelby Wms	8.8	8.8	18.9	9.6q	.94	6.3	6.3	4.4	18	12	03-88	.24	1.8	0	26	16	04-26-88	5.9	1.59	9.4	1.72	16.2	36	3.3	134	10,301	2,982	-118	0.0	12
Sierra Hlth	1.7	1.7	11.0	-.2q	-.02	-71.4	-71.4	NE	NC	-2	03-88	.00	.0	0	0	0	00-00-00	-.1	4.00	-.4	4.25	-1.7	43	.8	11	5,697	430	+8	0.0	12
Univ Furniture	105.6	105.6	49.2	22.6q	1.24	24.0	24.0	24.0	NC	12	03-88	.12	.7	0	5	2	02-01-88	7.7	.96	7.4	1.82	13.5	12	1.6	336	19,495	5,264	0	0.0	12
Winston Furn	1.5	1.5	32.0	1.3q	1.08	500.0	500.0	NC	NC	8	03-88	.00	.0	0	0	0	00-00-00	3.9	.97	3.8	2.18	8.3	61	1.9	16	1,963	374	0	0.1	12
Appliances																														
Ind. Group	5.6	6.0	1.2	349.5	1.94	- 13.9	- 13.1	4.1	4	8	- - -	.93	3.7	1	45	44	- - - -	5.0	1.72	8.6	1.77	15.2	15	1.9	4,412	177,249	95,033	+ 37	.7	- -
Dynamics Amer ◇	10.9	10.9	-6.0	8.5q	2.08	NE	NE	NE	-16	9	03-88	.20	.9	5	22	12	02-08-88	6.9	.81	5.6	1.70	9.5	21	2.0	95	4,037	2,001	0	0.2	12
Hlth-Mor	60.3	60.3	25.0	.4q	.15	55.6	55.6	-84.7	-36	-5	03-88	.68	6.8	11	1360	58	06-02-88	1.3	.85	1.1	1.27	1.4	7	2.7	22	2,219	428	+26	2.7	12
Linc Foodsvc	6.8	6.8	-2.0	2.3q	.64	-30.0	-30.0	-13.5	NC	15	03-88	.00	.0	0	0	0	00-00-00	4.9	1.67	8.2	1.83	15.0	42	2.9	20	3,524	403	0	0.0	12
Maytag Cp	-4.1	-4.1	-5.7	144.0q	1.85	-12.2	-12.2	27.6	17	12	03-88	1.00	4.2	11	50	59	05-25-88	7.6	2.16	16.4	1.60	26.2	8	2.5	1,807	76,486	34,812	+0	0.8	12
Mor-Flo Inds	-.2	-.2	3.0	-4.3q	-1.74	-100.0	-100.0	-100.0	NC	-11	03-88	.01	.2	0	0	1	12-01-87	-2.1	1.67	-3.5	3.23	-11.3	86	2.1	15	2,491	176	-0	0.0	12
Natl Presto	.6	.6	-6.4	17.0q	2.29	2.4	2.4	.4	-5	4	03-88	1.27	4.3	7	51	46	05-27-88	16.7	.48	8.0	1.19	9.5	3	7.8	216	7,371	3,129	0	0.2	12
Rangaire	-.5	-4.1	-6.0	2.4n	.56	-60.0	50.0	180.0	15	13	04-88	.00	.0	-16	9	37	02-06-87	3.1	1.42	4.4	2.98	13.1	120	2.0	22	3,855	939	+11	0.0	07
Welbilt Cp	19.7	19.7	16.9	13.6q	1.66	25.7	25.7	19.4	NC	17	03-88	.00	.0	0	0	0	07-27-87	5.6	1.50	8.4	2.00	16.8	44	3.2	225	8,034	2,023	0	0.0	12
Whirlpool Cp	9.7	9.7	4.2	165.6q	2.35	-27.3	-27.3	-12.6	4	7	03-88	1.10	3.8	5	43	40	05-18-88	3.9	1.77	6.9	1.84	12.7	13	1.4	1,990	69,232	51,122	0	2.6	12

Trends And Forecasts: Life Insurance (SIC 6311)

(in billions of dollars except as noted)

Item	1984	1985	1986[1]	1987[2]	1988[2]	Percent Change: Compound Annual 1972-85	Compound Annual 1979-85	Annual 1985-86	Annual 1986-87	Annual 1987-88
Premium receipts	134.8	155.9	194.1	223.2	245.5	10.1	10.7	24.5	15.0	10.0
New life insurance purchases[3]	1,114.8	1,231.2	1,308.8	1,413.5	1,526.6	14.5	16.5	6.3	8.0	8.0
Life insurance in force[3]	5,550.0	6,053.1	6,720.2	7,325.0	7,984.3	10.5	11.1	11.0	9.0	9.0
Total benefits paid	60.4	66.5	68.3	72.4	76.7	10.3	9.8	2.7	6.0	6.0
Life insurance assets	723.0	825.9	937.6	1,073.4	1,127.1	10.0	11.4	13.5	14.5	5.0
Total employment (000)[4]	536.7	552.6	578.9	580.0	580.0	0.4	1.0	4.8	0.2	0.0

[1]Estimated.
[2]Forecast.
[3]Excludes foreign business.
[4]Home office personnel only.
SOURCE: American Council of Life Insurance. U.S. Department of Commerce: International Trade Administration (ITA). Estimates and forecasts by ITA.

Source: *U.S. Industrial Outlook 1988*, U.S. Department of Commerce.

Trends and Forecasts: Property/Casualty Insurance (SIC 6331)

(in billions of dollars except as noted)

Industry data	1984	1985	1986[1]	1987[2]	1988[2]	Percent Change: Compound Annual 1972-85	Compound Annual 1979-85	Annual 1985-86	Annual 1986-87	Annual 1987-88
Net premiums written	118.2	144.2	175.3	193.4	210.8	10.5	8.2	21.6	10.3	9.0
Underwriting gain(loss)	(19.4)	(22.6)	(13.7)	(7.0)	(7.0)	—	—	39.4	48.9	—
Net investment income	17.7	19.5	28.3	30.0	25.0	18.7	11.8	45.1	6.0	(16.7)
Operating earnings after taxes	(2.2)	(3.3)	12.7	21.0	16.0	—	—	—	65.4	(23.8)

[1]Estimated.
[2]Forecast.
SOURCE: Insurance Information Institute; U.S. Department of Commerce, International Trade Administration (ITA). Estimates and forecasts by ITA.

Source: *U.S. Industrial Outlook 1988*, U.S. Department of Commerce.

LIFE INSURANCE COMPANY ASSETS, 1985 AND 1986

Type of Asset	1985 Billions of Dollars	1985 Percent of Total	1986 Billions of Dollars	1986 Percent of Total	Percent Change 1985-86
Corporate securities					
Bonds	296.8	36.0	342.0	36.5	15.2
Stocks	77.5	9.4	90.9	9.7	17.3
Mortgages	171.8	20.8	193.8	20.6	12.8
Policy loans	54.4	6.6	54.1	5.8	−0.6
Government securities	124.6	15.0	144.6	15.4	16.1
Real estate	28.8	3.5	31.6	3.4	9.7
Miscellaneous	72.0	8.7	80.6	8.6	11.9
Total	825.9	100.0	937.6	100.0	13.5

SOURCE: The American Council of Life Insurance.

Source: *U.S. Industrial Outlook 1988*, U.S. Department of Commerce.

Company	Revenue Pct. Change Last Qtr	Revenue Pct. Change FY to Date	Revenue Pct. Change Last 12 Mos	Earnings Last 12 Mos	Per Share Last 12 Mos	Per Share Pct. Change Last Qtr	Per Share Pct. Change FY to Date	Per Share Pct. Change Last 12 Mos	5-Year Growth Rate	Par Growth Rate	Date of Report	Dividends Current Rate Amt	Current Rate Yield	5-Year Growth Rate	Payout Last FY	Payout Last 5 Yrs.	Last X-Dvd Date	Profit Margin	Asset Turnover	Return on Total Assets	Leverage Ratio	Return on Equity	Debt to Equity	Current Ratio	Market Value	Latest Shares Outstndng.	Held by Banks-Funds	Insider Net Trading	Short Interest Ratio	Fiscal Year Ends
-	%	%	%	$Mil	$	%	%	%	%	%	-	$	%	%	%	%	-	π/r x	r/a =	π/a x	a/e =	π/e	%	-	$Mil	000	000	000	Days	Mo

Life, Accid., Health Ins.

Company	Rev. Last Qtr	Rev. FY to Date	Rev. Last 12 Mos	Last 12 Mos $Mil	EPS Last 12 Mos	EPS Last Qtr	EPS FY to Date	EPS Last 12 Mos	5-Yr Growth	Par Growth	Date of Report	Div. Amt	Yield	5-Yr Growth	Payout Last FY	Payout Last 5 Yrs.	Last X-Dvd Date	Profit Margin	Asset Turnover	Return on Total Assets	Leverage Ratio	Return on Equity	Debt to Equity	Current Ratio	Market Value	Latest Shares Outstndng.	Held by Banks-Funds	Insider Net Trading	Short Int. Ratio	Fiscal Year Ends
Ind. Group	4.3	10.6	9.6	4,325.8	2.50	- 4.4	- 4.0	2.8	14	7	- - -	.92	4.0	1	32	39	- - - -	3.8	.32	1.2	9.17	11.0	32	NC	37,088	1,602,128	564,078	+ 482	.7	- -
Academy Ins Grp ... □	-2.0	-2.0	-3.4	3.7q	.05	100.0	100.0	NE	NC	5	03-88	.00	.0	0	0	NE	06-24-85	3.3	.33	1.1	4.09	4.5	1	NA	99	71,861	2,150	0	0.0	12
Acap Cp	-32.3	-32.1	-30.7	-.9f	-.39	NE	NE	NE	NC	-13	12-87	.00	.0	0	0	0	00-00-00	-10.0	.18	-1.8	6.94	-12.5	40	NA	1	2,697	0	0	0.0	12
Accel Intl Cp .... □	-4.0	-4.0	-1.5	3.9q	.77	130.8	130.8	30.5	5	9	03-88	.00	.0	0	0	0	04-25-88	6.2	.32	2.0	4.50	9.0	42	NA	37	4,628	683	-1	0.0	12
Aegon	-99.9	-99.9	-13.0	151.6q	5.47	15.5	15.5	26.3	NC	12	03-88	.54	1.3b	0	10	11	08-28-87	4.0	.15	.6	21.33	12.8	362	NA	1,481	35,696	1	0	0.0	12
Aetna Life Cas .... □	16.4	16.4	10.7	812.9q	7.03	-28.8	-28.8	7.7	23	8	03-88	2.76	6.1	2	36	60	07-25-88	3.5	.31	1.1	12.18	13.4	12	NA	5,128	113,632	75,645	+2	1.2	12
Alfa Cp .... □	230.7	230.7	164.1	15.8q	.94	80.0	80.0	40.3	10	13	03-88	.30	2.3	15	32	29	05-09-88	11.3	.42	4.8	4.10	19.7	38	NA	219	16,846	284	0	0.0	12
AllCity Insur ....□ ■	14.3	11.4	12.0	6.0f	.85	325.0	84.8	84.8	NC	29	12-87	.00	.0	0	0	0	00-00-00	10.7	.45	4.8	5.96	28.6	42	NA	20	7,000	0	0	0.0	12
Alleghany Cp	-17.6	-17.6	28.4	55.1q	8.63	-55.8	-55.8	-31.6	NC	11	03-88	.00	.0	0	0	0	03-28-83	5.3	.66	3.5	3.11	10.9	32	NA	441	6,268	3,076	0	2.3	12
Am Bankers Insur ... □	22.7	22.7	6.7	-35.0q	-2.74	-18.2	-18.2	-100.0	NC	-34	03-88	.50	4.3	2	NE	110	06-06-83	-5.1	.51	-2.6	11.00	-28.6	97	NA	147	12,812	6,520	+0	0.0	12
Am Family Cp .... □	28.1	28.1	29.7	97.3q	1.21	20.0	20.0	18.6	32	14	03-88	.24	1.8	16	20	23	05-09-88	4.9	.39	1.9	9.32	17.7	7	NA	1,083	80,956	18,391	+0	0.3	12
Am Fst Cp Okla	-79.5	-79.5	-85.5	-13.0q	-2.39	NE	NE	NE	NC	0	03-88	.00	.0	0	0	0	12-03-85	NM	NC	NC	NC	NM	234	NA	3	5,570	200	0	0.0	12
Am Guaranty	.0	100.0	.0	.4n	.09	NC	NE	NE	NC	11	09-87	.00	.0	0	0	NE	04-28-83	40.0	.26	10.3	1.02	10.5	0	NA	3	4,131	113	0	0.0	12
Am Heritage Lf ...... ■	21.7	21.7	12.5	10.1q	2.21	13.2	13.2	11.6	6	5	03-88	1.08	4.2	11	43	39	07-05-88	4.7	.49	2.3	4.61	10.6	2	NA	117	4,542	565	0	0.0	12
Am Income Life ...... ■	5.9	5.9	4.9	20.5q	1.67	61.3	61.3	24.6	1	9	03-88	.40	2.8	0	27	24	06-09-88	16.0	.29	4.7	2.62	12.3	0	NA	179	12,461	4,566	0	0.0	12
Am Integrity	-19.2	-19.2	-6.5	1.8q	.27	-81.8	-81.8	-56.5	7	4	03-88	.00	.0	0	0	0	00-00-00	2.5	.68	1.7	2.29	3.9	0	NA	15	6,719	547	0	0.0	12
Am Natl Ins .... □	7.9	7.9	8.1	89.3q	3.12	-6.6	-6.6	8.7	3	3	03-88	1.40	4.2	12	42	36	06-10-88	9.7	.23	2.2	2.73	6.0	0	NA	947	28,267	4,523	0	0.0	12
Am Reliance Grp	10.0	10.0	23.4	4.0q	1.54	-34.0	-34.0	-29.7	NC	11	03-88	.20	2.6	0	4	1	05-12-88	6.9	.52	3.6	3.67	13.2	13	NA	20	2,568	139	0	0.0	12
Am Travellers	39.6	39.6	43.7	3.0q	1.00	-8.0	-8.0	19.0	NC	14	03-88	.00	.0	0	0	0	00-00-00	13.0	.63	8.2	1.72	14.1	0	NA	25	3,526	1,353	0	0.0	12
AmVestors Fnl .... □	21.9	21.9	50.0	4.8q	.48	60.0	60.0	26.3	NC	6	03-88	.20	2.4	10	43	77	07-11-88	1.7	.41	.7	14.86	10.4	23	NA	51	6,234	1,198	0	0.0	12
Aneco Reinsur ....□ :	17.9	16.9	62.5	2.3n	.99	166.7	338.9	NC	NC	59	09-87	.00	.0	0	0	0	00-00-00	17.7	.44	7.7	7.66	59.0	3	NA	7	2,661	306	0	0.0	12
Aon cp .... □	23.7	23.7	30.0	187.0q	2.85	7.7	7.7	.7	10	9	03-88	1.28	4.9	5	42	43	04-27-88	7.2	.36	2.6	6.35	16.5	39	NA	1,705	64,650	30,449	0	0.5	12
Argonaut Grp .... □	25.8	4.9	6.2	57.0n	4.87	NE	509.1	98.0	NC	24	09-87	.00	.0	0	0	0	00-00-00	13.5	.24	3.3	7.21	23.8	0	NA	503	11,709	2,607	0	0.0	12
Assoc Companies ... □	26.1	28.4	25.0	.9f	.65	73.7	22.6	22.6	NC	8	12-87	.00	.0	0	0	5	00-00-00	9.0	.26	2.3	3.57	8.2	0	NA	8	1,425	0	0	0.0	12
Atlantic Amer	-13.0	-13.0	-1.9	-7.3q	-.76	-100.0	-100.0	-100.0	NC	-14	03-88	.08	1.8	17	NE	33	06-24-88	-4.9	.55	-2.7	4.59	-12.4	129	NA	44	9,789	938	+2	0.0	12
BMA Cp	20.1	20.1	12.3	5.6q	.55	NE	NE	NE	NC	-2	03-88	1.20	3.5	6	297	75	05-09-88	1.2	.42	.5	3.80	1.9	9	NA	338	9,805	3,300	0	0.0	12
Cap Holding .... □	2.7	2.7	29.5	172.1q	3.42	12.0	12.0	11.8	11	11	03-88	.94	2.9	6	26	29	08-26-88	5.1	.33	1.7	8.88	15.1	25	NA	1,482	46,318	28,803	-31	3.3	12
Celina Fnl .... □	-17.4	-17.4	-48.3	-.2q	-.11	-87.5	-87.5	-100.0	NC	-5	03-88	.00	.0	0	0	0	05-28-82	-1.3	.16	-.6	8.33	-5.0	3	NA	2	1,573	68	0	0.0	12
Cent Res Life .... ◇	8.4	4.7	4.1	-1.5f	-.37	-100.0	-100.0	-100.0	NC	-15	12-87	.24	4.8	0	NE	18	11-08-88	-2.0	1.75	-3.5	2.57	-9.0	0	NA	20	3,902	135	0	0.0	12
CIGNA Cp .... □	8.1	8.1	1.4	587.9q	6.94	-62.6	-62.6	-5.8	NC	7	03-88	2.96	6.3	14	34	176	06-06-88	3.4	.32	1.1	10.73	11.8	6	NA	3,682	78,550	60,009	0	0.8	12
Citzns Ins Co	10.5	9.5	14.2	-.3f	-.33	NE	NE	NE	NC	-8	12-87	.00	.0	0	0	0	00-00-00	-3.8	.26	-1.0	7.90	-7.9	0	NA	19	836	0	0	0.0	12
CNL Financial .... □	2.9	1.5	.0	.6s	.30	12.5	-7.1	-30.2	-9	2	06-87	.22	5.2	6	71	43	02-26-88	4.3	.51	2.2	3.32	7.3	0	NA	8	1,782	1	0	0.0	12
Colonial Lf & Ac .... □	10.9	10.9	9.3	23.5q	3.06	13.9	13.9	12.1	9	8	03-88	1.00	3.4	11	29	26	07-11-88	10.6	.58	6.1	2.05	12.5	2	NA	220	7,471	3,153	0	0.0	12
Conseco	461.2	461.2	293.6	24.3q	3.31	62.1	62.1	105.6	NC	62	03-88	.00	.0	0	0	0	00-00-00	5.6	.13	.7	88.71	62.1	902	NA	58	5,280	1,223	0	18.4	12
Consumers Fncl ..... □	185.0	185.0	60.0	1.6q	.38	NE	NE	65.2	15	6	03-88	.12	2.2	15	23	20	04-11-88	4.0	.33	1.3	6.62	8.6	19	NA	15	2,806	26	+8	0.0	12
Contl Genl .... ■	16.7	16.7	10.0	1.4q	.35	-33.3	-33.3	-52.7	NC	5	03-88	.10	1.7	0	25	10	05-23-88	4.2	.48	2.0	3.25	6.5	0	NA	24	4,181	146	0	0.0	12

Continued

Company	Revenue: Pct. Change Last Qtr	Revenue: Pct. Change FY to Date	Revenue: Pct. Change Last 12 Mos	Earnings: Last 12 Mos	Earnings Per Share: Last 12 Mos	Per Share Pct. Change: Last Qtr	Per Share Pct. Change: FY to Date	Per Share Pct. Change: Last 12 Mos	5-Year Growth Rate	Par Growth Rate	Date of Report	Dividends: Current Rate Amt	Current Rate Yield	5-Year Growth Rate	Payout Last FY	Payout Last 5 Yrs.	Last X-Dvd Date	Profit Margin	Asset Turnover	Return on Total Assets	Leverage Ratio	Return on Equity	Debt to Equity	Current Ratio	Market Value	Latest Shares Outstndng.	Held by Banks-Funds	Insider Net Trading	Short Interest Ratio	Fiscal Year Ends
-	%	%	%	$Mil	$	%	%	%	%	%	-	$	%	%	%	%	-	π/r x	r/a =	π/a x	a/e =	π/e	%	-	$Mil	000	000	000	Days	Mo
Life, Accid., Health Ins. (Continued)																														
Cotton St Lf □	-4.1	-4.1	5.0	1.1q	.39	-100.0	-100.0	-33.9	10	2	03-88	.24	4.4	6	44	41	06-13-88	5.2	.29	1.5	3.27	4.9	0	NA	15	2,748	43	0	0.0	12
Donegal Grp □	388.2	370.8	342.8	1.3f	.45	800.0	1400.0	1400.0	NC	4	12-87	.20	3.3	0	11	10	06-03-88	4.2	.86	3.6	1.83	6.6	0	NA	18	2,933	75	0	0.0	12
Durham Cp □	26.0	26.0	20.0	8.1q	.97	-100.0	-100.0	-42.9	-7	0	03-88	.92	3.1	4	79	38	05-18-88	2.5	.48	1.2	3.08	3.7	0	NA	247	8,430	1,850	0	0.0	12
Empire State	.0	7.1	.0	-.3s	-.15	NE	NE	-100.0	NC	-6	06-87	.00	.0	0	0	0	00-00-00	-10.0	.14	-1.4	4.14	-5.8	0	NA	3	1,663	0	0	0.0	12
Equitable of Iowa □	4.7	4.7	19.4	17.3q	1.97	-83.3	-83.3	15.2	7	3	03-88	1.00	4.9	1	42	50	05-13-88	3.2	.31	1.0	6.90	6.9	22	NA	173	8,443	3,288	0	0.0	12
Equitable Iowa	NA	NA	NA	NA	NA	NA	NA	NA	NA	NC	00-00	1.00	4.8	NA	NA	NA	05-13-88	NA	NC	NA	NC	NA	NA	NA	25	1,207	78	0	NA	NA
Fst Cap Hold	51.1	51.1	93.8	35.9q	1.40	48.4	48.4	28.4	NC	19	03-88	.00	.0	0	0	0	00-00-00	7.2	.10	.7	26.43	18.5	0	NA	144	19,886	7,007	0	15.3	12
Fst Executive □	-21.9	-3.9	-3.9	177.8f	1.74	125.0	13.7	13.7	23	12	12-87	.00	.0	0	0	0	09-29-86	5.1	.22	1.1	11.09	12.2	0	NA	865	72,839	32,359	0	0.0	12
Fst Farwest	45.4	45.4	35.8	-.1q	-.06	-100.0	-100.0	NE	NC	0	03-88	.00	.0	0	0	0	07-26-82	.0	NC	NC	NC	-.4	77	NA	16	1,307	56	0	0.0	12
Frontier Insur	17.0	17.0	26.6	6.5q	1.73	84.6	84.6	74.7	NC	30	03-88	.00	.0	0	0	0	00-00-00	17.1	.42	7.2	4.10	29.5	0	NA	36	3,664	240	0	0.0	12
Geneve Cap Grp □	-15.0	-16.8	-16.8	2.3f	.67	-100.0	-85.7	-85.7	NC	2	12-87	.10	.1	0	15	3	06-29-87	2.2	.18	.4	5.50	2.2	100	NA	135	1,471	66	0	0.0	12
Home Beneficial	.0	.0	-1.0	37.9q	3.47	6.0	6.0	-3.6	5	7	03-88	1.12	4.0	10	30	25	05-16-88	20.5	.18	3.7	2.81	10.4	0	NA	301	10,766	1,781	0	0.0	12
Home Group	17.3	13.8	13.7	172.2f	3.34	NE	943.8	943.8	NC	18	12-87	.20	1.5	0	4	NE	05-25-88	6.9	.39	2.7	7.07	19.1	60	NA	449	34,512	14,517	0	0.7	12
ICH Corp □	10.4	10.4	52.3	15.8q	-.10	-100.0	-100.0	-100.0	NC	3	03-88	.00	.0	0	0	2	05-20-86	.6	.33	.2	16.50	3.3	300	NA	379	52,266	10,884	0	1.8	12
Independent Ins ◆	6.7	6.7	4.9	28.4q	3.99	-11.4	-11.4	22.0	1	6	03-88	1.52	4.6	3	37	31	02-03-88	6.1	.39	2.4	4.17	10.0	11	NA	220	6,715	836	0	0.0	12
Integon Cp	55.3	55.3	98.6	30.5q	.96	-37.0	-37.0	20.0	NC	14	03-88	.16	2.5	0	6	3	04-29-88	5.1	.47	2.4	7.13	17.1	105	NA	190	29,285	452	+0	0.0	12
Intercontinental Lf □	132.9	129.4	59.3	1.6s	1.09	73.7	97.3	17.2	NC	8	06-87	.00	.0	0	0	0	00-00-00	3.1	.23	.7	11.71	8.2	68	NA	18	1,482	2	0	0.0	12
Investors Herit □	-1.7	-.9	.0	1.5f	1.58	-53.0	-52.7	-52.7	4	5	12-87	.00	.0	7	41	25	00-00-00	3.3	.33	1.1	4.27	4.7	0	NA	24	937	0	0	0.0	12
Jefferson Pilot ■	16.4	16.4	7.3	147.2q	2.30	.0	.0	-17.3	5	5	03-88	1.28	4.0	12	54	38	05-09-88	13.0	.29	3.8	3.11	11.8	0	NA	1,269	39,203	18,731	0	2.2	12
John Adams Lf □	-15.8	-15.8	-25.0	-2.6q	-.87	NC	NC	NE	NC	-22	03-88	.00	.0	0	0	0	00-00-00	-28.9	.17	-4.8	4.63	-22.2	0	NA	8	2,845	294	0	0.0	12
Kansas City Life □	2.3	2.3	2.6	24.7q	3.29	29.3	29.3	25.6	3	6	03-88	1.04	3.4	3	31	33	02-02-88	8.9	.17	1.5	5.53	8.3	3	NA	228	7,397	1,076	0	0.0	12
Kauf Broad Inc	40.0	40.0	30.8	58.3q	1.87	14.8	14.8	14.7	NC	14	02-88	.32	2.3	17	14	16	04-26-88	3.6	.31	1.1	15.55	17.1	205	NA	439	31,090	15,057	+83	2.9	11
Kent Cent Life □	10.1	10.1	25.4	31.3q	2.62	235.7	235.7	78.2	22	10	03-88	.40	3.1	13	17	16	03-11-88	5.7	.40	2.3	5.22	12.0	41	NA	175	13,424	4,458	0	0.0	12
Lamar Life □	-6.1	-4.5	-4.2	10.0f	5.47	-77.8	-18.6	-18.6	6	4	12-87	1.78	1.8	0	16	13	02-24-88	11.0	.22	2.4	2.63	6.3	0	NA	178	1,818	67	-1	0.0	12
Laurentain Cap ◇	-37.8	26.1	26.0	.1f	.01	-71.4	NE	NE	NC	0	12-97	.00	.0	0	0	0	00-00-00	.1	.00	.0	NC	.1	3	NA	57	16,181	609	0	0.0	12
Lawrence Ins	30.7	30.7	17.8	7.0q	.97	-5.3	-5.3	16.9	NC	15	03-88	.32	1.9	0	0	0	06-28-88	10.6	.58	6.1	3.61	22.0	0	NA	123	7,309	30	0	4.7	12
Lib Cp	2.1	2.1	-.2	25.2q	2.71	25.0	25.0	-1.1	13	7	03-88	.80	2.1	0	28	30	06-09-88	6.6	.29	1.9	5.37	10.2	62	NA	327	8,583	1,960	+12	0.6	12
LifeSurance	-13.6	-13.6	-10.0	.8q	1.01	-5.9	-5.9	2.0	NC	9	03-87	.00	.0	0	0	0	00-00-00	8.9	.21	1.9	4.53	8.6	0	NA	6	755	0	0	0.0	12
Linc Natl Cp ■	-11.7	-11.7	4.5	236.0q	5.20	2.4	2.4	9.7	10	6	03-88	2.36	5.0	8	42	43	07-01-88	3.5	.37	1.3	9.08	11.8	20	NA	1,978	42,088	24,128	0	1.8	12
Manhattan Natl ■	-8.4	-15.6	-15.9	-3.9f	-.46	NE	NE	NE	NC	-5	12-87	.00	.0	0	0	148	04-29-86	-2.0	.20	-.4	12.25	-4.9	0	NA	50	8,534	960	0	0.0	12
Mid South Insur	58.2	58.2	77.7	-4.0q	-1.53	-100.0	-100.0	-100.0	NC	-15	03-88	.24	3.1	0	44	5	08-01-88	-5.0	1.30	-6.5	1.94	-12.6	0	NA	20	2,602	329	0	0.0	12
Midland Co	19.8	19.8	9.8	11.0q	3.24	15.4	15.4	23.2	27	14	03-88	.30	1.4	2	7	12	06-14-88	8.2	.62	5.1	2.98	15.2	17	NA	72	3,365	443	0	0.0	12
Milwaukee Insur ■	8.6	8.6	50.0	4.4q	1.51	-44.9	-44.9	-15.2	NC	11	03-88	.00	.0	0	0	0	00-00-00	6.7	.58	3.9	2.92	11.4	0	NA	29	3,067	362	0	0.0	12
Monarch Cap □	-42.4	38.6	38.6	45.0f	5.63	-47.2	11.3	11.3	15	10	12-87	.00	.0	0	0	16	05-24-85	2.2	.41	.9	10.67	9.6	13	NA	325	7,205	4,145	0	0.3	12
Natl Insur Grp	51.7	51.7	66.6	2.4q	.78	16.7	16.7	NC	NC	12	03-88	.00	.0	0	0	0	00-00-00	16.0	.48	7.6	1.63	12.4	0	NA	76	4,164	573	0	0.0	12
Natl Western Life □	-7.3	27.4	27.4	6.7f	1.93	NE	-31.3	-31.3	3	8	12-87	.00	.0	0	0	0	00-00-00	1.6	.38	.6	12.50	7.5	0	NA	37	3,278	744	0	0.0	12
Nobel Insur	31.4	31.4	52.6	-6.3q	-1.23	-100.0	-100.0	-100.0	NC	-22	03-88	.44	8.2	0	NE	311	06-10-88	-10.9	.47	-5.1	3.12	-15.9	0	NA	29	5,353	1,811	+3	0.0	12

N Am Natl ◇	.0	-3.1	-7.1	2.5n	.92	11.1	-16.4	48.4	18	11	12-87	.02	.3b	-9	1	2	06-2[illegible]-88	19.2	.19	3.7	2.95	10.9	0	NA	22	2,778	175	0	0.0	03
NWn Natl Life	-25.5	-25.5	12.3	43.3q	3.89	21.5	21.5	10.8	25	8	03-88	1.12	3.8	5	25	27	04-2[illegible]-88	2.3	.26	.6	18.50	11.1	40	NA	327	11,180	7,605	+0	0.0	12
Old Rep Intl □	-9.9	-4.2	-4.2	93.2f	4.38	3066.7	111.6	111.6	1	15	12-87	.74	3.1b	3	17	21	03-3[illegible]-88	8.5	.39	3.3	5.45	18.0	26	NA	409	17,039	9,112	0	0.0	12
Orion Cap Cp	15.3	15.3	20.4	24.4q	2.92	-22.1	-22.1	NE	NC	18	03-88	.76	4.4	5	24	NE	06-0[illegible]-88	4.4	.61	2.7	9.00	24.3	100	NA	113	6,502	3,566	+1	6.9	12
PHLCORP Inc	-1.1	21.2	54.3	-7.5n	.70	-100.0	-100.0	NC	NC	0	09-87	.00	.0	0	0	0	00-0[illegible]-00	-2.5	.68	-1.7	.00	NS	-131	NA	138	13,510	320	0	5.4	12
Pioneer Financial	48.7	48.7	88.7	6.5q	1.18	36.4	36.4	21.6	NC	12	03-88	.00	.0	0	0	0	10-0[illegible]-87	3.5	.66	2.3	5.09	11.7	0	NA	49	6,151	1,644	0	0.0	12
Preferred Risk	-1.3	-1.3	3.3	6.2n	3.32	24.0	5.2	4.7	6	8	09-87	1.00	3.7	11	27	25	03-3[illegible]-88	20.0	.26	5.2	2.29	11.9	0	NA	51	1,919	554	0	0.0	12
Pres Life	20.3	14.5	14.3	20.7f	.97	66.7	29.3	29.3	NC	17	12-87	.08	.6	0	4	5	06-1[illegible]-88	5.6	.25	1.4	13.29	18.6	48	NA	273	21,383	1,640	0	0.0	12
Prof Inv Ins	-16.3	45.9	42.3	-2.8f	-.98	-100.0	-100.0	-100.0	NC	-33	12-87	.00	.0	0	0	0	00-0[illegible]-00	-7.6	.61	-4.6	7.24	-33.3	46	NA	14	2,879	0	0	0.0	12
Protective Life	12.1	12.1	13.5	15.0q	1.05	33.3	33.3	-14.6	-11	2	03-88	.70	5.1	6	69	35	02-12-88	4.3	.30	1.3	4.77	6.2	0	NA	199	14,494	4,707	+404	0.0	12
Provident Lf Acc	25.8	25.8	25.6	5.8q	.15	-86.7	-86.7	-91.7	-27	-3	03-88	.84	4.1	4	154	32	05-24-88	.2	.50	.1	6.00	.6	21	NA	757	37,378	0	0	0.0	12
Re Capital	370.0	370.0	525.0	1.1q	.16	1400.0	1400.0	NE	NC	1	03-88	.00	.0	0	0	NE	08-26-86	2.2	.36	.8	1.63	1.3	0	NA	76	7,558	2,637	0	0.0	12
Rockwood Hldg	-10.3	-10.3	-2.5	-18.2q	-4.58	-100.0	-100.0	-100.0	NC	-72	03-88	.00	.0	0	0	NE	02-08-85	-12.1	.57	-6.9	10.42	-71.9	0	NA	9	3,959	298	0	0.0	12
Sec Am Fin	1.0	1.0	5.1	2.7q	.71	.0	.0	-16.5	NC	10	03-88	.07	1.0b	0	7	6	05-11-88	6.6	.52	3.4	3.32	11.3	0	NA	24	3,528	216	0	0.0	12
So Sec Life	-4.2	-4.5	.0	.2n	.19	50.0	27.3	35.7	NC	3	09-87	.00	.0	0	0	0	00-00-00	2.2	.36	.8	3.13	2.5	0	NA	5	1,537	0	0	0.0	12
Southlife Hldg	101.5	101.5	70.3	3.5q	.65	13.3	13.3	22.6	NC	11	03-88	.00	.0	0	0	0	00-00-00	7.6	.16	1.2	9.00	10.8	0	NA	26	4,983	799	0	0.0	12
Stamford Cap □	-39.9	-31.4	-31.1	-5.2f	-.62	NE	NE	NE	NC	-6	12-87	.02	.3	0	0	7	01-04-[illegible]8	-9.8	.15	-1.5	3.73	-5.6	58	NA	117	18,020	2,801	0	0.0	12
Torchmark Cp	5.6	5.6	2.8	201.1q	3.12	20.3	20.3	11.4	24	13	03-88	1.20	3.7	22	34	30	07-11-[illegible]8	12.5	.38	4.7	4.64	21.8	33	NA	1,837	55,867	21,749	-0	0.6	12
Travelers Cp	17.7	17.7	2.6	350.7q	3.36	-19.0	-19.0	-20.4	-1	2	03-88	2.40	6.5	7	64	50	04-25-88	1.9	.37	.7	10.86	7.6	6	NA	3,729	101,475	74,402	0	3.5	12
UniCARE Fncl	10.7	10.7	21.4	4.7q	1.21	89.5	89.5	101.7	NC	19	03-88	.00	.0	0	0	0	00-00-00	9.2	.50	4.6	4.11	18.9	0	NA	42	4,000	191	0	0.0	12
Utd Cos Fncl	64.8	64.8	47.6	8.9q	2.41	-33.8	-33.8	-19.9	8	10	03-88	.60	3.4	2	19	18	06-09-88	3.1	.35	1.1	12.45	13.7	154	NA	65	3,671	1,098	0	0.0	12
Utd Home Life	-4.8	-4.8	.0	.4q	.22	-100.0	-100.0	-29.0	15	-1	03-88	.30	5.0	5	94	71	04-26-88	4.4	.18	.8	4.38	3.5	0	NA	11	1,794	696	0	0.0	12
Utd Insurance	9.9	9.9	50.6	7.7q	2.22	6.7	6.7	52.1	NC	23	03-88	.00	.0	0	0	0	00-00-00	6.5	.58	3.8	6.00	22.8	85	NA	48	3,458	767	0	0.0	12
Utd Investors Mgmt □	9.8	12.1	11.8	34.6f	.92	26.3	19.5	19.5	NC	12	12-87	.20	2.3	0	22	102	12-15-8[illegible]	15.2	.55	8.3	1.80	14.9	0	NA	325	37,735	2,292	0	0.0	12
Univ Holding	-33.3	-33.3	-17.6	-.8q	-.36	-100.0	-100.0	-100.0	NC	-10	03-88	.00	.0	0	0	0	00-00-0[illegible]	-5.7	.32	-1.8	5.33	-9.6	0	NA	5	2,340	14	0	0.0	12
USLICO Cp	-13.0	-13.0	-14.3	28.9q	2.58	16.4	16.4	14.2	1	7	03-88	.96	4.2	0	36	26	05-16-8[illegible]	6.2	.24	1.5	7.27	10.9	24	NA	256	11,057	2,556	0	0.0	12
USLIFE Cp	-.1	-.1	-.3	71.9q	3.87	-8.4	-8.4	-.8	1	5	03-88	1.28	3.4	8	31	27	05-04-88	6.0	.33	2.0	4.00	8.0	28	NA	682	18,074	9,672	0	2.1	12
Wash Natl Cp	12.2	12.2	27.6	-23.4q	-2.27	-13.8	-13.8	-100.0	NC	-9	03-88	1.08	3.9	0	NE	72	06-08-88	-2.7	.37	-1.0	5.90	-5.9	1	NA	303	11,022	5,816	0	0.3	12
Westbridge Cap	-12.5	-12.5	-13.8	-8.6q	-2.08	-100.0	-100.0	NE	NC	-41	03-88	.00	.0	0	0	0	08-24-83	-13.9	.57	-7.9	5.20	-41.1	89	NA	8	4,148	149	0	0.0	12
Williams A L	9.3	9.3	28.5	41.0q	1.66	21.6	21.6	36.1	48	35	03-88	.00	.0	0	0	0	09-16-83	14.4	.87	12.5	2.78	34.7	34	NA	328	24,722	8,173	0	0.0	12

Trends and Forecasts: Sawmills and Planing Mills - General (SIC 2421)

(in millions of dollars except as noted)

						Percent Change				
						Compound Annual		Annual		
ITEM	1984	1985	1986[1]	1987[2]	1988[3]	1972-85	1980-85	1985-86	1986-87	1987-88
Industry Data										
Value of shipments[4]	13,118	12,974	14,938	16,978	—	5.5	0.6	15.1	13.7	—
Value of shipments (1982$)	11,512	11,731	13,196	14,712	15,244	−0.3	−0.5	12.5	11.5	3.6
Total employment (000)	143	136	145	147	—	−1.6	−4.9	6.6	1.4	—
Production workers (000)	125	120	128	129	—	−1.7	−4.6	6.7	0.8	—
Average hourly earnings ($)	8.08	8.22	8.57	8.90	—	6.7	5.3	4.3	3.9	—
Product Data										
Value of shipments[5]	13,122	12,922	14,639	16,723	—	6.0	1.0	13.3	14.2	—
Value of shipments (1982$)	11,499	11,682	12,978	14,554	15,080	0.3	−0.1	11.1	12.1	3.6
Shipments price index[6] (1982=100)	114.1	110.7	112.6	114.9	—	5.8	1.1	1.7	2.0	—
Quantity shipped (Million Board Feet)	36,765	37,200	—	—	—	−0.1	2.6	—	—	—
Trade Data										
Value of imports	2,866	3,073	3,123	3,000	2,900	7.8	7.4	1.6	−3.9	−3.3
Import/new supply ratio[7]	0.179	0.192	0.176	0.152	—	1.4	5.2	−8.3	−13.6	—
Value of exports	983	916	1,149	1,232	1,311	8.7	−8.3	25.4	7.2	6.4
Export/shipments ratio	0.075	0.071	0.078	0.074	—	2.6	−9.2	9.9	−5.1	—

[1]Estimated except for exports and imports.
[2]Estimated.
[3]Forecast.
[4]Value of all products and services sold by the Sawmills and Planing Mills - General industry.
[5]Value of products classified in the Sawmills and Planing Mills - General industry produced by all industries.
[6]Developed by the Office of Industry Assessment, ITA.
[7]New supply is the sum of product shipments plus imports.
SOURCE: U.S. Department of Commerce: Bureau of the Census, Bureau of Economic Analysis, International Trade Administration (ITA). Estimates and forecasts by ITA.

Source: *U.S. Industrial Outlook 1988*, U.S. Department of Commerce.

Company	Revenue Pct. Change Last Qtr	Revenue Pct. Change FY to Date	Revenue Pct. Change Last 12 Mos	Earnings Last 12 Mos	Per Share Last 12 Mos	Per Share Pct. Change Last Qtr	Per Share Pct. Change FY to Date	Per Share Pct. Change Last 12 Mos	5-Year Growth Rate	Par Growth Rate	Date of Report	Dividends Current Rate Amt	Current Rate Yield	5-Year Growth Rate	Payout Last FY	Payout Last 5 Yrs.	Last X-Dvd Date	Profit Margin	Asset Turnover	Return on Total Assets	Leverage Ratio	Return on Equity	Debt to Equity	Current Ratio	Market Value	Latest Shares Outstndng.	Held by Banks-Funds	Insider Net Trading	Short Interest Ratio	Fiscal Year Ends
-	%	%	%	$Mil	$	%	%	%	%	%	-	$	%	%	%	%	-	r/r x	r/a =	r/a x	a/e =	r/e	%	-	$Mil	000	000	000	Days	Mo
Lumber and Wood Products																														
Ind. Group	13.8	14.6	16.4	2,537.3	3.01	29.4	29.6	49.7	40	10	- - -	1.15	3.9	0	34	51	- - - -	7.2	1.11	8.0	2.05	16.4	49	1.9	25,940	874,867	332,979	- 711	.9	- -
Alpine Intl ◇	12.5	12.5	-63.6	-.6s	-.17	NE	NE	NE	NC	-86	12-87	.00	.0	0	0	0	11-12-87	-15.0	.37	-5.5	15.58	-85.7	43	1.0	1	3,181	84	0	0.0	06
Baltek Cp	30.4	30.4	30.7	3.0q	1.17	29.2	29.2	3.5	NC	15	03-88	.14	1.6b	0	9	5	12-30-87	8.8	1.34	11.8	1.48	17.5	11	2.1	23	2,545	168	0	0.0	12
Bohemia Inc	15.4	17.2	17.0	-11.9f	-2.51	-100.0	-100.0	-100.0	NC	-13	04-88	.20	.9b	0	NE	NE	05-26-88	-4.6	1.15	-5.3	2.25	-11.9	37	1.8	104	4,742	2,053	0	0.0	04
Boise Cascade	11.4	11.4	4.8	211.3q	4.38	86.1	86.1	92.1	58	10	03-88	1.20	2.6	0	31	56	06-09-88	5.4	1.17	6.3	2.29	14.4	64	1.5	2,095	45,047	29,355	-6	3.1	12
Champ Intl	15.4	15.4	9.6	428.5q	4.51	81.4	81.4	82.6	NC	13	03-88	1.00	2.8	-3	16	28	06-10-88	9.0	.79	7.1	2.32	16.5	81	1.1	3,433	95,033	60,355	0	1.4	12
Etz Lavud Ltd	20.2	21.1	20.8	1.8f	1.06	-45.5	20.5	19.1	-23	13	03-87	.00	.0	0	0	9	09-17-85	3.1	1.48	4.6	2.78	12.8	23	1.3	8	1,744	7	0	0.0	03
Georgia Pacific	14.0	14.0	18.5	484.0q	4.54	43.7	43.7	44.1	49	13	03-88	1.20	2.9	3	25	39	05-16-88	5.5	1.49	8.2	2.21	18.1	48	1.7	4,440	106,023	63,968	+1	1.7	12
Hines Ed Lum □	NA	NA	NA	NA	NA	NA	NA	NA	NA	NC	00-00	.00	.0	NA	NA	NA	06-14-85	NA	NA	NA	NC	NA	NA	NA	4	1,470	591	0	NA	NA
IP Timberlands	50.0	50.0	31.7	130.0q	2.63	19.6	19.6	15.9	NC	-1	03-88	2.72	12.0	0	108	100	06-24-88	58.0	.25	14.7	1.10	16.1	0	3.5	1,026	45,332	688	0	0.0	12
Kamenstein	18.5	17.5	6.2	-.1s	-.04	NE	NE	NE	NC	-2	06-87	.00	.0	0	0	0	00-00-00	-.6	1.33	-1.1	1.36	-1.5	0	3.4	5	2,429	239	0	0.0	12
La Pacific	14.2	14.2	23.3	155.2q	4.05	181.4	181.4	87.5	NC	12	03-88	.92	2.7	3	24	50	05-12-88	7.8	1.01	7.9	1.89	14.9	50	1.5	1,284	38,334	13,043	0	2.7	12
Macmillan Bloedel	10.7	10.7	22.6	311.8q	2.87	57.4	57.4	108.0	NC	18	03-88	.85	NA	0	32	30	05-09-88	9.7	1.46	14.2	1.84	26.1	15	32.4	1,729	102,447	16,959	+8	0.0	12
Morgan Prods	2.9	2.9	-.2	16.4q	2.02	13.3	13.3	45.3	NC	20	03-88	.00	.0	0	0	0	00-00-00	3.9	2.87	11.2	1.81	20.3	35	3.0	193	8,392	5,129	0	2.9	12
Paxton Frank	8.7	10.6	9.6	3.5f	1.16	-4.5	28.9	28.9	-7	4	03-88	.59	4.2	9	50	36	06-14-88	3.4	1.82	6.2	1.18	7.3	7	6.0	41	2,937	738	0	0.0	03
Ply-Gem	26.6	26.6	34.9	7.6q	.67	3.4	3.4	-29.5	17	7	03-88	.12	.8	7	18	15	05-16-88	2.3	1.70	3.9	2.18	8.5	72	3.5	170	11,173	3,208	-740	0.5	12
Pope & Talbot	15.4	15.4	31.5	29.4q	2.45	21.8	21.8	27.6	NC	17	03-88	.50	2.7	1	19	40	07-26-88	6.7	1.75	11.7	1.83	21.4	36	1.9	224	11,956	6,311	+20	2.5	12
Potlatch Cp	3.9	3.9	1.0	96.3q	3.45	50.8	50.8	30.7	39	12	03-88	.92	3.0	3	27	43	05-10-88	9.6	.77	7.4	2.22	16.4	62	2.1	825	26,710	9,816	+1	1.8	12
Rayonier Timb	10.8	10.8	1.4	49.0q	2.53	28.8	28.8	7.7	NC	-1	03-88	2.60	13.0	0	111	115	05-24-88	69.0	.29	19.9	1.15	22.8	8	.6	400	20,000	1,428	0	0.0	12
Trus Joist Cp	24.3	24.3	37.9	13.5q	1.93	13.0	13.0	55.6	21	18	03-88	.36	1.5	14	15	19	06-20-88	5.0	2.14	10.7	2.07	22.2	41	2.2	168	6,859	2,766	0	0.0	12
Weyerhaeuser	14.7	14.7	21.2	458.9q	1.98	-28.0	-28.0	26.9	22	5	03-88	1.20	4.4	0	42	71	06-03-88	6.3	1.02	6.4	1.92	12.3	43	2.0	8,399	306,803	100,088	+6	2.8	12
Willamette Inc	25.3	25.3	20.9	138.8q	5.47	76.7	76.7	54.5	64	18	03-88	1.20	2.4	0	17	34	05-23-88	9.2	1.28	11.8	1.91	22.5	48	1.9	1,289	25,408	13,472	0	0.0	12
WTD Inds	39.5	66.7	67.0	8.4f	1.31	27.6	52.3	52.3	NC	37	04-88	.00	.0	0	0	0	00-00-00	2.9	2.79	8.1	4.51	36.5	190	1.6	79	6,302	2,513	0	0.0	04

Trends and Forecasts: Metal-Cutting Machine Tools (SIC 3541)

(in millions of dollars except as noted)

ITEM	1984	1985	1986[1]	1987[2]	1988[3]	Percent Change: Compound Annual 1972-85	Compound Annual 1980-85	Annual 1985-86	Annual 1986-87	Annual 1987-88
Industry Data										
Value of shipments[4]	3,212	3,377	3,450	3,105	3,450	6.9	−8.4	2.2	−10.0	11.1
Value of shipments (1982$)	3,073	3,066	3,194	2,849	3,136	−2.5	−12.7	4.2	−10.8	10.1
Total employment (000)	42.4	42.8	—	—	—	−1.6	−10.1	—	—	—
Production workers (000)	24.7	24.9	—	—	—	−2.2	−12.2	—	—	—
Average hourly earnings ($)	11.65	12.42	—	—	—	7.6	6.7	—	—	—
Product Data										
Value of shipments[5]	2,815	2,921	3,000	2,700	3,000	6.7	−10.0	2.7	−10.0	11.1
Value of shipments (1982$)	2,692	2,646	2,778	2,477	2,727	−2.7	−14.3	5.0	−10.8	10.1
Shipments price index[6] (1982=100)	103.9	109.8	—	—	—	8.9	4.8	—	—	—
Trade Data										
Value of imports	1,322	1,690	2,018	2,200	2,300	23.8	6.4	19.4	9.0	4.5
Import/new supply ratio[7]	0.319	0.367	0.402	0.449	0.434	12.8	12.9	9.5	11.7	−3.3
Value of exports	455	500	571	582	600	7.7	−6.0	14.2	1.9	3.1
Export/shipments ratio	0.162	0.171	0.190	0.216	0.200	1.0	4.5	11.1	13.7	−7.4

[1]Estimated except for exports and imports.
[2]Estimated.
[3]Forecast.
[4]Value of all products and services sold by the Metal-Cutting Machine Tools industry.
[5]Value of products classified in the Metal-Cutting Machine Tools industry produced by all industries.
[6]Developed by the Office of Industry Assessment, ITA.
[7]New supply is the sum of product shipments plus imports.

SOURCE: U.S. Department of Commerce: Bureau of the Census, Bureau of Economic Analysis, International Trade Administration (ITA). Estimates and forecasts by ITA.

Source: ***U.S. Industrial Outlook 1988,*** **U.S. Department of Commerce.**

Trends and Forecasts: Metal-Forming Machine Tools (SIC 3542)

(in millions of dollars except as noted)

ITEM	1984	1985	1986[1]	1987[2]	1988[3]	Percent Change: Compound Annual 1972-85	Compound Annual 1980-85	Annual 1985-86	Annual 1986-87	Annual 1987-88
Industry Data										
Value of shipments[4]	1,309	1,413	1,380	1,281	1,429	5.6	−4.2	−2.3	−7.2	11.6
Value of shipments (1982$)	1,264	1,336	1,302	1,197	1,323	−3.9	−8.4	−2.5	−8.1	10.5
Total employment (000)	16.1	17.7	—	—	—	−2.3	−8.0	—	—	—
Production workers (000)	10.5	11.5	—	—	—	−2.8	−8.8	—	—	—
Average hourly earnings ($)	11.72	11.97	—	—	—	7.4	6.1	—	—	—
Product Data										
Value of shipments[5]	1,363	1,433	1,400	1,300	1,450	6.0	−3.9	−2.3	−7.1	11.5
Value of shipments (1982$)	1,316	1,354	1,321	1,215	1,343	−3.5	−8.1	−2.4	−8.0	10.5
Shipments price index[6] (1982=100)	103.2	105.3	—	—	—	9.7	4.5	—	—	—
Trade Data										
Value of imports	341	427	675	450	470	21.2	9.4	58.1	−33.3	4.4
Import/new supply ratio[7]	0.138	0.157	0.227	0.164	0.170	11.1	10.1	44.6	−27.8	3.7
Value of exports	289	278	343	286	319	6.4	−8.1	23.4	−16.6	11.5
Export/shipments ratio	0.212	0.194	0.245	0.220	0.220	0.4	−4.4	26.3	−10.2	0.0

[1]Estimated except for exports and imports.
[2]Estimated.
[3]Forecast.
[4]Value of all products and services sold by the Metal-Forming Machine Tools industry.
[5]Value of products classified in the Metal-Forming Machine Tools industry produced by all industries.
[6]Developed by the Office of Industry Assessment, ITA.
[7]New supply is the sum of product shipments plus imports.

SOURCE: U.S. Department of Commerce: Bureau of the Census, Bureau of Economic Analysis, International Trade Administration (ITA). Estimates and forecasts by ITA.

Source: *U.S. Industrial Outlook 1988*, U.S. Department of Commerce.

Company	Revenue Pct. Change Last Qtr	Revenue Pct. Change FY to Date	Revenue Pct. Change Last 12 Mos	Earnings Last 12 Mos	Per Share Last 12 Mos	Per Share Pct. Change Last Qtr	Per Share Pct. Change FY to Date	Per Share Pct. Change Last 12 Mos	5-Year Growth Rate	Par Growth Rate	Date of Report	Current Rate Amt	Current Rate Yield	Dividends 5-Year Growth Rate	Payout Last FY	Payout Last 5 Yrs.	Last X-Dvd Date	Profit Margin	Asset Turnover	Return on Total Assets	Leverage Ratio	Return on Equity	Debt to Equity	Current Ratio	Market Value	Latest Shares Outstndng.	Held by Banks-Funds	Insider Net Trading	Short Interest Ratio	Fiscal Year Ends
-	%	%	%	$Mil	$	%	%	%	%	%	-	$	%	%	%	%	-	π/r x	r/a =	π/a x	a/e =	π/e	%	-	$Mil	000	000	000	Days	Mo
Machine Tools and Accessories																														
Ind. Group	14.1	15.4	16.3	9.9	.10	655.2	174.4	NE	NC	- 2	- - -	.59	2.3	0	78	96	- - - -	.2	1.00	.2	2.00	.4	33	2.0	4,146	163,348	66,989	+ 5	1.0	- -
Acme-Clevelnd	-.9	-1.8	2.6	-6.5s	-1.07	NE	-100.0	-100.0	NC	-9	03-88	.40	3.5	-22	56	NE	04-25-88	-3.4	1.12	-3.8	1.79	-6.8	10	1.8	71	6,280	3,797	+1	1.0	09
Barden Cp	6.1	6.5	3.8	4.2s	2.65	13.5	28.1	19.4	-4	5	04-88	1.00	2.5	0	44	41	05-26-88	5.2	1.23	6.4	1.27	8.1	1	4.3	64	1,600	475	0	0.0	10
Brenco Inc	29.8	29.8	33.3	.5q	.05	166.7	166.7	.0	NC	-2	03-88	.12	1.4	-21	NE	NE	06-13-88	1.4	.86	1.2	1.08	1.3	0	4.8	84	9,691	3,749	0	0.0	12
Brown & Shrpe	5.9	5.9	6.9	-1.1q	-.30	150.0	150.0	NE	NC	-3	03-88	.40	2.5	-7	NE	43	05-16-88	-.7	.86	-.6	2.00	-1.2	21	2.4	55	3,494	1,956	0	0.0	12
Cinn Milacron ◻	-1.1	-1.1	-3.7	-79.8q	-3.34	5.3	5.3	-100.0	NC	-46	03-88	.72	2.8	0	NE	NE	05-16-88	-9.7	1.16	-11.3	3.38	-38.2	84	1.9	609	23,773	13,845	+5	8.0	12
Cross Trecker	-8.4	-2.4	-1.8	-25.2s	-2.04	NE	NE	NE	NC	-13	03-88	.00	.0	0	0	NE	08-18-86	-6.0	1.10	-6.6	2.03	-13.4	20	2.0	221	12,384	8,832	0	0.0	09
Fedl Mogul	13.4	13.4	15.1	41.9q	3.32	12.5	12.5	876.5	-7	6	03-88	1.72	4.2	5	49	56	05-23-88	3.8	1.37	5.2	2.37	12.3	39	1.7	515	12,519	6,824	0	0.0	12
Gleason Cp	-4.8	-4.8	-8.0	-3.2q	-.55	NE	NE	NE	NC	-3	03-88	.00	.0	0	0	0	08-02-82	-1.4	1.36	-1.9	1.74	-3.3	17	1.8	68	5,648	1,765	+0	0.0	12
Hein-Werner	124.0	124.0	130.4	2.5q	1.24	31.0	31.0	26.5	80	8	03-88	.25	1.6	0	22	23	12-21-87	2.4	1.79	4.3	2.35	10.1	36	2.2	35	2,281	91	0	0.0	12
Kaydon Cp	-3.3	-3.3	5.6	17.9q	2.10	20.8	20.8	53.3	NC	32	03-88	.20	.7	0	3	2	06-14-88	13.6	1.10	14.9	2.39	35.6	70	1.8	255	8,354	2,842	0	0.0	12
Kennametal	21.8	18.5	15.1	22.8n	2.23	44.4	47.0	243.1	NC	7	03-88	1.08	2.9	2	57	126	05-04-88	5.7	1.23	7.0	1.96	13.7	43	2.6	377	10,258	6,537	-1	0.0	06
Latshaw Entprs	8.1	4.2	4.7	1.2s	2.08	18.8	16.7	15.6	NC	7	04-88	.50	2.4	0	27	25	06-14-88	5.5	1.27	7.0	1.33	9.3	2	5.4	12	569	159	0	0.0	10
Monarch Mach	19.4	19.4	16.6	.7q	.16	400.0	400.0	-42.9	-24	-4	03-88	.80	3.9	0	667	212	05-12-88	.9	.89	.8	1.38	1.1	0	3.0	75	3,674	1,470	0	6.8	12
Newcor	10.6	-9.7	-30.7	1.4s	.48	-64.7	-57.1	2300.0	NC	3	04-88	.32	4.6	4	53	194	07-11-88	1.9	1.58	3.0	2.77	8.3	83	2.2	20	2,816	472	0	0.0	10
NS Group	NA	NA	NA	NA	NA	NA	NA	NA	NA	NC	00-00	.00	.0	NA	NA	NA	00-00-00	NA	NC	NA	NC	NA	NA	NA	192	13,246	0	0	NA	NA
Ransburg Corp	16.1	16.1	-5.1	-13.9q	-1.73	NE	NE	NE	NC	-19	02-88	.00	.0	-9	NE	NE	06-19-87	-6.9	1.07	-7.4	2.51	-18.6	16	1.3	93	8,063	3,572	0	0.8	11
Regal-Beloit	54.4	54.4	43.2	8.8q	1.56	147.4	147.4	113.7	36	15	03-88	.40	2.2	13	33	41	06-24-88	7.6	1.53	11.6	1.76	20.4	43	4.5	165	8,909	2,405	0	0.1	12
Shopsmith ◊	20.6	-1.3	.0	.5f	.31	NE	NE	NE	NC	10	03-88	.00	.0	0	0	6	12-04-84	1.3	3.38	4.4	2.23	9.8	0	1.3	5	1,436	169	0	0.0	03
Sun Dist ◆	9.9	9.9	336.0	4.0q	.35	NE	NE	NC	NC	-13	03-88	1.10	12.2	0	NE	NE	06-27-88	.9	1.89	1.7	3.53	6.0	171	2.7	100	11,100	277	0	0.0	12
Timken Co	32.1	32.1	24.9	30.0q	2.23	NE	NE	NE	NC	1	03-88	1.20	1.5	-19	128	NE	05-16-88	2.3	.87	2.0	1.60	3.2	17	2.1	1,097	13,995	7,569	0	3.5	12
Wedco Tech	75.7	29.3	29.4	3.2f	.98	-65.5	42.0	42.0	NC	40	03-88	.15	1.5	0	5	44	03-31-88	14.5	.88	12.8	3.73	47.8	142	1.6	33	3,258	183	0	0.8	03

Trends and Forecasts: Steel Mill Products (SIC 3312, 3315, 3316, 3317)

(in millions of net tons unless otherwise indicated)

Item	1977	1982	1983	1984	1985	1986	1987	1988[2]	Percent Change: Compound Annual 1977-87	Percent Change: Annual 1987-88
Raw steel production	125.0	74.6	84.6	92.5	88.3	81.6	83.0	83.5	−4.0	0.6
Continuous casting (percent)	12.5	29.0	32.1	39.6	44.4	53.0	61.0	—	17.2	—
Steel mill product shipments	91.1	61.6	67.6	73.7	73.0	70.3	71.0	71.6	−2.5	0.7
Exports	2.0	1.8	1.2	1.0	0.9	0.9	1.1	1.2	−5.8	9.1
Exports/shipments ratio	0.022	0.029	0.013	0.013	0.012	0.013	0.015	0.017	−3.4	8.3
Apparent domestic consumption	108.5	76.4	83.5	98.9	96.4	90.1	89.6	90.3	−1.9	0.5
Imports	19.3	16.7	17.1	26.2	24.3	20.7	19.7	19.9	0.2	0.5
Imports as a percent of apparent consumption	17.8	21.8	20.5	26.4	25.2	23.0	22.0	22.0	2.1	0.2

[1]Estimated.
[2]Forecast.

SOURCE: American Iron and Steel Institute, U.S. Department of Commerce: Bureau of the Census, International Trade Administration (ITA). Estimates and forecasts by ITA.

Trends and Forecasts: Titanium

(in short tons except as noted)

	1981	1982	1983	1984	1985	1986	1987[1]	1988[2]	1992[2]
Sponge Metal									
Production	26,400	15,600	13,966	24,326	23,257	17,402	18,400	19,200	26,500
Consumption	31,559	17,328	15,100	24,713	21,606	19,489	19,200	21,500	27,000
Imports for consumption	6,490	1,355	1,199	2,267	1,717	1,626	1,000	900	1,000
Imports as a percent of consumption	21	8	7	9	8	8	5	4	4
Industry stocks (Dec. 31)	3,719	3,353	3,136	3,147	4,755	3,180	2,650	2,500	3,000
Government stocks	32,331	32,331	32,331	32,470	36,331	36,831	36,831	36,831	36,831
Producer price (Dec 31, $/lb)	7.65	5.55	3.50-4.00	3.50-4.00	3.75-4.00	3.75-4.25	3.80-4.25	—	—
Scrap Metal									
Consumption	14,795	8,528	10,467	15,549	14,720	16,487	18,900	19,000	19,500
Stocks	10,484	11,073	12,635	12,489	11,686	11,558	10,200	10,000	10,000
Imports	3,787	1,277	1,572	1,850	2,134	2,374	1,800	2,000	2,500
Exports	3,280	4,286	5,379	4,109	6,760	6,403	7,600	7,800	8,000
Ingot									
Production	45,923	25,326	26,411	39,530	35,387	35,093	35,900	36,500	42,000
Consumption	43,525	26,727	25,495	39,062	35,020	33,801	36,900	36,000	40,000
Stocks (Dec. 31)	3,592	2,488	3,242	4,526	4,000	4,100	3,500	4,500	5,000
Mill Products									
Net Shipments	25,493	18,263	15,933	22,690	23,253	20,842	22,500	23,000	26,000
Imports	1,116	870	953	843	1,449	1,345	900	1,000	1,200
Exports	6,049	3,600	2,154	2,849	3,355	3,251	4,200	4,500	5,000

[1]Estimated.
[2]Forecast.

SOURCE: U.S. Department of Commerce: International Trade Administration (ITA); U.S. Bureau of Mines. Estimates and forecasts by ITA.

Source: *U.S. Industrial Outlook 1988,* U.S. Department of Commerce.

Trends and Forecasts: Aluminum, Copper and Zinc (SIC 3331,3333,3334)

(in millions of dollars except as noted)

ITEM	1984	1985	1986[1]	1987[2]	1988[3]	Percent Change: Compound Annual 1972-85	Compound Annual 1980-85	Annual 1985-86	Annual 1986-87	Annual 1987-88
Industry Data										
Value of shipments[4]	9,121	7,089	6,968	8,026	8,605	2.6	−11.3	−1.7	15.2	7.2
3331 Primary Copper	2,753	2,239	2,247	2,805	3,100	−1.6	−16.5	0.4	24.8	10.5
3333 Primary Zinc	356	362	367	372	378	−0.3	−2.6	1.4	1.4	1.6
3334 Primary Aluminum	6,011	4,488	4,355	4,849	5,127	6.6	−8.5	−3.0	11.3	5.7
Value of shipments (1982$)	9,103	7,305	6,420	7,310	7,582	−3.1	−9.1	−12.1	13.9	3.7
3331 Primary Copper	2,967	2,405	2,450	2,750	3,100	−3.6	−9.9	1.9	12.2	12.7
3333 Primary Zinc	333	378	359	362	360	−5.8	−2.8	−5.0	0.8	−0.6
3334 Primary Aluminum	5,804	4,522	3,611	4,198	4,121	−2.5	−9.1	−20.1	16.3	−1.8
Total employment (000)	30.3	26.1	27.2	29.3	29.6	−4.7	−10.9	4.2	7.7	1.0
3331 Primary Copper	6.0	4.6	4.0	4.3	4.5	−9.6	−14.9	−13.0	7.5	4.7
3333 Primary Zinc	1.8	1.8	1.5	1.5	1.5	−9.2	−11.4	−16.7	0.0	0.0
3334 Primary Aluminum	22.5	19.7	21.7	23.5	23.6	−2.0	−9.7	10.2	8.3	0.4
Production workers (000)	23.7	20.0	19.0	20.4	20.6	−5.1	−11.3	−5.0	7.4	1.0
3331 Primary Copper	4.6	3.4	3.1	3.4	3.6	−10.5	−15.9	−8.8	9.7	5.9
3333 Primary Zinc	1.3	1.3	1.1	1.0	1.0	−10.1	−12.9	−15.4	−9.1	0.0
3334 Primary Aluminum	17.8	15.3	14.8	16.0	16.0	−2.0	−9.9	−3.3	8.1	0.0
Average hourly earnings ($)	15.64	16.13	—	—	—	9.2	5.1	—	—	—
3331 Primary Copper	14.34	16.13	15.84	14.76	—	9.7	7.8	−1.8	−6.8	—
3333 Primary Zinc	12.29	12.72	12.49	11.46	—	8.7	4.4	−1.8	−8.2	—
3334 Primary Aluminum	16.20	16.41	14.07	13.59	—	8.6	4.4	−14.3	−3.4	—
Product Data										
Value of shipments[5]	12,505	10,176	9,123	10,298	10,884	4.6	−7.6	−10.3	12.9	5.7
3331 Primary Copper	3,880	3,369	3,393	3,978	4,300	1.2	−9.4	0.7	17.2	8.1
3333 Primary Zinc	667	632	640	650	661	2.5	1.6	1.3	1.6	1.7
3334 Primary Aluminum	7,958	6,175	5,090	5,670	5,923	7.8	−7.3	−17.6	11.4	4.5

Value of shipments (1982$)	12,028	10,374	8,451	9,332	9,583	−1.3	−5.1	−18.5	10.4	2.7
3331 Primary Copper	4,125	3,637	3,700	3,900	4,300	−1.1	−2.3	1.7	5.4	10.3
3333 Primary Zinc	602	633	610	615	612	−3.6	0.3	−3.6	0.8	−0.5
3334 Primary Aluminum	7,302	6,104	4,142	4,817	4,671	−1.2	−7.0	−32.1	16.3	−3.0
Shipments price index[6] (1982=100)	104.1	98.0	110.7	111.4	116.0	5.8	−3.2	13.0	0.6	4.1
3331 Primary Copper	94.0	92.7	91.7	102.0	100.0	2.2	−7.3	−1.1	11.2	−2.0
3333 Primary Zinc	110.9	99.7	105.0	105.8	108.0	6.4	1.4	5.3	0.8	2.1
3334 Primary Aluminum	109.8	101.2	122.9	117.7	126.6	8.9	−0.7	21.4	−4.2	7.6
Trade Data										
Value of imports	2,651	2,066	2,940	3,407	3,239	8.3	−0.6	42.3	15.9	−4.9
3331 Primary Copper	710	528	759	880	780	6.0	−12.5	43.8	15.9	−11.4
3333 Primary Zinc	649	521	498	547	550	8.5	9.8	−4.4	9.8	0.5
3334 Primary Aluminum	1,293	1,018	1,683	1,980	1,909	9.7	5.5	65.3	17.6	−3.6
Import/new supply ratio[7]	0.175	0.169	—	—	—	3.1	6.4	—	—	—
3331 Primary Copper	0.155	0.135	—	—	—	4.3	−3.0	—	—	—
3333 Primary Zinc	0.493	0.452	0.438	0.457	0.454	3.6	4.7	−3.1	4.3	−0.7
3334 Primary Aluminum	0.140	0.141	0.248	0.259	0.244	1.6	12.0	75.9	4.4	−5.8
Value of exports	556	540	334	415	424	6.3	−14.2	−38.1	24.3	2.2
3331 Primary Copper	158	95.6	46.0	34.0	60.0	−5.2	13.6	−51.9	−26.1	76.5
3333 Primary Zinc	1.7	2.9	5.1	5.5	4.9	2.5	14.1	75.9	7.8	−10.9
3334 Primary Aluminum	397	442	283	375	359	17.9	−16.8	−36.0	32.5	−4.3
Export/shipments ratio	0.045	0.053	—	—	—	1.6	−7.2	—	—	—
3331 Primary Copper	0.041	0.028	—	—	—	−6.4	25.5	—	—	—
3333 Primary Zinc	0.003	0.005	0.008	0.008	0.007	0.0	10.8	60.0	0.0	−12.5
3334 Primary Aluminum	0.050	0.072	0.056	0.066	0.061	9.5	−10.2	−22.2	17.9	−7.6

[1]Estimated except for exports and imports.
[2]Estimated.
[3]Forecast.
[4]Value of all products and services sold by the Aluminum, Copper and Zinc industry.
[5]Value of products classified in the Aluminum, Copper and Zinc industry produced by all industries.
[6]Developed by the Office of Industry Assessment, ITA.
[7]New supply is the sum of product shipments plus imports.
SOURCE: U.S. Department of Commerce: Bureau of the Census, Bureau of Economic Analysis, International Trade Administration (ITA). Estimates and forecasts by ITA.

Source: *U.S. Industrial Outlook 1988,* U.S. Department of Commerce.

Company	Revenue Pct. Change Last Qtr	Revenue Pct. Change FY to Date	Revenue Pct. Change Last 12 Mos	Earnings Last 12 Mos	Earnings Per Share Last 12 Mos	Earnings Per Share Pct. Change Last Qtr	Earnings Per Share Pct. Change FY to Date	Earnings Per Share Pct. Change Last 12 Mos	Earnings 5-Year Growth Rate	Earnings Par Growth Rate	Earnings Date of Report	Dividends Current Rate Amt	Dividends Current Rate Yield	Dividends 5-Year Growth Rate	Dividends Payout Last FY	Dividends Payout Last 5 Yrs.	Dividends Last X-Dvd Date	Ratio Analysis Profit Margin	Ratio Analysis Asset Turnover	Ratio Analysis Return on Total Assets	Ratio Analysis Leverage Ratio	Ratio Analysis Return on Equity	Ratio Analysis Debt to Equity	Ratio Analysis Current Ratio	Shareholdings Market Value	Shareholdings Latest Shares Outstndng.	Shareholdings Held by Banks-Funds	Shareholdings Insider Net Trading	Shareholdings Short Interest Ratio	Shareholdings Fiscal Year Ends
-	%	%	%	$Mil	$	%	%	%	%	%	-	$	%	%	%	%	-	π/r x	r/a =	π/a x	a/e =	π/e	%	-	$Mil	000	000	000	Days	Mo
Iron and Steel Mills																														
Ind. Group	7.0	14.1	11.0	1,768.8	1.31	158.0	247.4	NE	NC	5	- - -	.70	2.9	0	44	63	- - - -	3.8	.84	3.2	3.38	10.8	88	1.3	27,364	1,141,973	325,470	+ 12	3.9	- -
Acme Steel .... □	25.8	25.8	39.7	8.2q	1.42	82.1	82.1	NE	NC	7	03-88	.00	.0	0	0	0	00-00-00	2.3	1.78	4.1	1.61	6.6	8	1.5	116	5,822	1,907	-4	0.0	12
Amcast	22.0	17.6	16.3	4.6n	.63	109.1	61.7	-36.4	NC	2	05-88	.44	3.1	3	169	80	06-03-88	1.5	1.67	2.5	2.20	5.5	56	1.9	102	7,185	3,451	0	0.0	08
Ampco-Pitts	-4.6	-4.6	-21.5	.5q	.05	-100.0	-100.0	NE	NC	-2	03-88	.30	2.3	-9	81	NE	04-04-88	.2	1.00	.2	1.50	.3	37	1.8	126	9,576	6,398	0	5.4	12
Armco Inc .... □	2.9	2.9	9.7	81.0q	.83	-100.0	-100.0	NE	NC	12	03-88	.00	.0	0	0	NE	05-07-84	2.7	1.07	2.9	4.10	11.9	86	1.6	891	86,961	53,339	+2	2.2	12
Athlone Indus .... □	14.9	14.9	11.3	-3.6q	-1.80	14.3	14.3	-100.0	NC	-75	03-88	1.60	9.0	0	NE	NE	04-19-88	-1.7	1.12	-1.9	20.84	-39.6	1081	1.7	47	2,642	622	0	2.0	12
Bethlehem Stl	17.5	17.5	12.2	163.7q	2.33	223.7	223.7	NE	NC	17	03-88	.00	.0	0	0	NE	08-06-85	3.4	1.00	3.4	5.09	17.3	118	1.3	1,775	74,343	42,604	0	2.3	12
Birmingham St	46.4	71.4	70.3	20.3n	2.86	165.6	120.2	107.2	NC	27	03-88	.30	.9	0	0	0	07-27-88	6.3	1.65	10.4	2.94	30.6	119	2.0	218	6,847	3,420	+4	0.3	06
Broken Hill	17.4	12.2	45.5	648.7n	1.37	366.7	374.1	NC	NC	4	02-88	.91	3.7	0	0	0	04-22-88	9.5	.55	5.2	2.25	11.7	55	1.2	9,750	391,942	2,013	0	0.1	05
Carpenter Tech	17.6	10.0	5.3	15.6n	1.72	NE	488.0	72.0	-21	-1	03-88	2.10	4.3	0	420	104	05-19-88	3.0	.87	2.6	2.00	5.2	43	2.6	451	9,132	6,035	0	0.4	06
CCX Inc .... ■	-23.6	-26.4	-12.7	-15.6s	-4.06	NE	NE	NE	NC	0	12-87	.00	.0	0	0	0	09-09-81	-38.0	1.29	-48.9	.00	NM	6	1.6	14	3,913	1,057	+10	0.4	06
Clevel-Cliffs	-29.0	-29.0	13.8	25.1q	1.48	NE	NE	NE	NC	7	03-88	.00	.0	-43	9	NE	08-20-86	7.5	.51	3.8	1.92	7.3	35	3.8	372	16,537	6,335	+37	0.1	12
Copperweld Cp	44.2	44.2	23.6	13.9q	1.31	400.0	400.0	NE	NC	15	03-88	.05	.3	0	0	NE	05-16-88	5.7	1.05	6.0	2.52	15.1	63	2.4	135	8,649	1,273	0	8.1	12
CSC Inds	18.4	18.4	22.6	-18.7q	-2.16	-100.0	-100.0	NE	NC	-68	03-88	.00	.0	0	0	0	00-00-00	-9.4	1.60	-15.0	4.55	-68.2	63	1.0	16	8,632	913	0	0.0	12
Foster L B	9.7	9.7	-54.1	11.7q	1.07	-34.5	-34.5	NE	NC	34	03-88	.00	.0	0	0	NE	01-07-86	5.4	2.33	12.6	2.67	33.6	17	1.7	66	9,714	2,643	0	0.0	12
Friedman Ind	16.2	26.2	25.5	3.4f	.85	-6.3	77.1	77.1	36	-51	03-88	5.16	108.6b	63	620	204	07-01-88	5.8	1.52	8.8	1.15	10.1	5	12.0	18	3,842	413	0	0.1	03
Grt N Iron Ore	4.5	-12.0	-12.5	3.8f	2.56	-17.0	-17.7	-17.7	9	-5	12-87	3.00	10.8	0	53	77	01-04-88	54.3	.43	23.6	1.25	29.5	0	2.3	42	1,500	101	0	53.3	12
Hanna M A Co	384.3	384.3	314.0	44.5q	2.94	156.7	156.7	NE	NC	13	03-88	.40	1.3	-19	16	NE	05-17-88	6.8	.65	4.4	3.39	14.9	77	1.4	443	14,303	6,759	0	1.1	12
Hofmann Indus	-33.3	-7.9	-6.2	-.9n	-.42	NE	-100.0	-100.0	NC	-7	01-88	.00	.0	0	0	0	09-29-80	-2.0	1.50	-3.0	2.23	-6.7	34	2.1	13	1,907	185	0	0.0	04
Inland Steel	14.7	14.7	9.6	151.4q	4.19	379.3	379.3	132.8	NC	21	03-88	.25	.7	0	0	NE	05-04-88	4.2	1.71	7.2	3.04	21.9	113	1.5	1,228	33,293	0	0	2.2	12
Interlake Cp	9.8	9.8	20.8	52.8q	4.61	-9.5	-9.5	52.6	36	13	03-88	1.40	3.1	1	29	43	06-07-88	6.3	1.21	7.6	2.47	18.8	29	1.8	534	11,736	5,735	0	1.1	12
Keystone Cons	3.3	9.9	11.4	-5.9n	-3.08	-100.0	-100.0	NE	NC	-29	03-88	.00	.0	0	0	0	00-00-00	-2.3	1.91	-4.4	6.55	-28.8	79	1.1	22	1,895	111	+0	4.0	06
Laclede Steel	15.7	15.7	13.9	8.5q	3.11	331.4	331.4	78.7	NC	7	03-88	.70	1.9	0	15	9	05-12-88	3.1	1.39	4.3	2.14	9.2	42	2.5	99	2,704	428	0	0.0	12
Lindberg Corp	8.9	8.9	2.7	-.8q	-.17	40.0	40.0	-100.0	NC	-10	03-88	.25	2.8	-11	NE	341	05-04-88	-1.1	1.55	-1.7	2.47	-4.2	66	2.1	42	4,702	591	-51	0.0	12
Lukens Inc	25.7	25.7	25.5	25.5q	4.52	122.6	122.6	109.3	NC	14	03-88	.88	2.1	1	18	69	05-03-88	4.8	1.65	7.9	2.14	16.9	35	1.8	235	5,640	3,327	+2	0.2	12
LVI Grp	3.0	3.0	48.7	3.8q	.12	-50.0	-50.0	-7.7	NC	19	03-88	.00	.0	0	0	0	00-00-00	.7	3.86	2.7	6.85	18.5	167	1.2	59	19,753	4,575	0	12.1	12
Natl Intergrp	-46.6	-26.1	-26.1	24.6f	-1.33	NE	NE	NE	NC	3	03-88	.00	.0	-22	NE	NE	03-25-88	.7	1.71	1.2	2.75	3.3	59	1.5	353	21,549	11,288	0	2.0	03
Natl-Standard .... ◇	8.7	13.4	10.8	2.2s	.54	NE	NE	NE	NC	3	03-88	.00	.0	0	NE	NE	02-27-87	.8	1.75	1.4	2.29	3.2	42	1.5	41	4,464	1,460	0	0.0	09
NWn Stl & Wr	27.2	25.6	22.5	14.4n	1.92	151.4	190.5	149.4	NC	4	04-88	1.00	4.2	0	28	NE	06-21-88	3.1	1.68	5.2	1.65	8.6	36	2.1	177	7,506	2,446	0	0.0	07
Oregon Steel	NA	NA	NA	NA	NA	NA	NA	NA	NA	NC	00-00	.00	.0	NA	NA	NA	00-00-00	NA	NC	NA	NC	NA	NA	NA	186	7,309	0	0	NA	NA
Proler Intl	40.3	40.3	39.5	15.4q	9.82	490.2	490.2	1509.8	NC	18	04-88	1.40	2.2	0	19	67	06-28-88	13.6	1.21	16.4	1.29	21.2	7	3.9	100	1,569	930	0	1.3	01

Quanex Cp	42.2	38.2	28.7	18.3s	1.11	NE	NE	NE	NC	19	04-88	.02	.1	0	0	NE	07-11-88	4.5	1.47	6.6	2.89	19.1	100	1.7	172	12,259	4,454	0	0.8	10
Tubos Mexico	12.3	12.3	-29.9	6.3q	.36	-100.0	-100.0	-77.6	-23	2	03-86	.00	.0	0	0	0	09-21-83	3.2	.22	.7	2.43	1.7	120	3.0	68	21,000	10	0	0.7	12
UNR Inds	34.2	34.2	20.8	18.4q	5.01	3825.0	3825.0	381.7	NC	31	03-88	.00	.0	0	0	0	01-27-81	5.0	1.68	8.4	3.73	31.3	18	4.4	12	3,687	211	0	0.0	12
USX Cp	7.8	7.8	8.0	311.5q	.89	333.3	333.3	NE	NC	-2	03-88	1.20	3.8	-3	245	NE	05-02-88	2.1	.67	1.4	4.71	6.6	120	1.0	8,404	264,701	133,469	0	2.9	12
Valley Inds	50.7	50.7	21.9	1.3q	.15	NE	NE	NE	NC	8	02-88	.00	.0	0	0	0	06-28-82	1.5	2.20	3.3	2.48	8.2	56	1.3	27	9,070	776	0	0.0	11
Wheel-Pitts St	3.1	3.1	4.0	63.5q	10.65	63.8	63.8	NE	NC	0	03-88	.00	.0	0	0	0	12-31-73	6.3	1.11	7.0	.00	NS	-322	2.8	73	5,115	797	0	39.3	12
Worthington Ind	11.9	8.9	8.4	51.4n	1.25	54.2	34.8	25.0	17	13	02-88	.44	1.9	10	31	31	05-26-83	5.9	1.92	11.3	1.74	19.7	20	2.5	933	40,574	15,394	+12	0.0	05

Copper Mining and Refining

Ind. Group	45.1	47.9	58.9	821.7	2.67	404.0	354.0	538.3	NC	10	---	1.97	11.0	1	10	23	----	17.2	.58	9.9	3.95	39.1	162	1.5	5,760	320,895	67,065	-4	2.5	--
ASARCO Inc	63.2	63.2	47.0	275.9q	7.41	NE	NE	NE	NC	20	03-88	.80	3.2	0	2	NE	05-03-88	18.1	.73	13.3	1.71	22.8	21	2.1	1,053	42,101	20,724	+5	14.0	12
Atlas Consol B	57.5	57.5	67.5	2.4q	.08	NE	NE	NE	NC	0	03-88	.00	.0	0	0	0	04-06-8	1.2	.50	.6	.00	NM	4513	.3	94	83,611	833	0	2.7	12
Avery Inc	47.0	47.0	24.1	-65.7q	-5.43	NE	NE	NE	NC	-94	12-87	.00	.0	0	0	0	00-00-00	-10.2	.48	-4.9	19.10	-93.6	1408	3.5	20	12,100	420	0	0.0	09
Campbell Rsc	-5.6	-5.6	-366.6	-.8q	-.02	-100.0	-100.0	-100.0	NC	-1	03-88	.00	NA	0	0	0	05-21-84	-2.0	.25	-.5	1.40	-.7	18	1.2	60	43,623	1,227	+3	0.0	12
Free Mc Cop	NA	NA	NA	NA	NA	NA	NA	NA	NA	NC	00-00	.00	.0	NA	NA	NA	00-00-00	NA	NC	NA	NC	NA	NA	NA	422	21,345	0	0	NA	NA
Newmont Mng	-17.7	-17.7	55.8	367.6q	5.64	29.8	29.8	145.2	NC	0	03-88	8.85	21.6	7	17	41	05-20-88	74.9	.25	18.7	.00	NS	-356	.9	2,723	66,403	20,880	0	2.3	12
O'Okiep Copp	59.4	60.0	57.1	5.4f	.35	-60.9	-62.8	-62.8	NC	1	12-86	.31	3.7	0	0	0	06-20-88	12.3	.64	7.9	1.27	10.0	14	1.4	59	7,000	0	0	0.0	12
Phelps Dodge	52.6	52.6	82.9	231.4q	7.20	860.0	860.0	526.1	NC	20	03-88	.30	.7	0	3	NE	02-12-88	12.8	.80	10.3	2.07	21.3	37	1.9	1,272	30,747	22,311	-12	3.3	12
Silver King Mns	126.3	84.2	100.0	5.5n	.40	400.0	333.3	566.7	NC	29	12-87	.00	.0	0	0	0	00-00-00	45.8	.47	21.7	1.33	28.9	9	.9	58	13,965	670	0	0.0	03

Aluminum Refining

Ind. Group	20.3	21.3	25.7	828.7	2.03	314.2	304.0	7.0	NC	6	---	.67	2.0	-1	27	50	----	3.8	.89	3.4	2.47	8.4	61	2.0	13,456	391,324	190,890	+341	.9	--
Alcan Alum	28.0	28.0	19.4	537.0q	3.18	169.2	169.2	86.0	NC	12	03-88	.72	2.2	-7	23	73	05-04-88	7.4	.95	7.0	2.16	15.1	37	2.8	5,119	158,116	62,670	+32	1.4	12
Alum Co Am	18.2	18.2	53.6	353.2q	3.98	260.7	260.7	9.6	NC	6	03-88	1.20	2.3	-4	48	57	05-02-88	4.4	.82	3.6	2.56	9.2	64	1.6	4,695	88,162	65,587	+303	1.8	12
Div Industries ◇ □	124.7	124.7	15.2	-2.1q	-.40	100.0	100.0	NE	NC	-6	01-88	.00	.0	0	0	0	00-00-00	-1.1	2.09	-2.3	2.70	-6.2	68	1.3	20	5,227	656	0	0.0	10
KaiserTech	-4.8	-4.8	-12.3	-299.8q	-6.80	NE	NE	NE	NC	-37	03-88	.00	.0	0	0	NE	02-04-85	-15.3	.76	-11.6	3.20	-37.1	110	1.6	782	45,309	25,617	+6	0.7	12
Matrix Sci	-21.7	-5.5	-10.5	-1.5n	-.19	-61.8	-70.5	NC	NC	-3	03-88	.00	.0	0	33	10	00-00-00	-2.2	1.09	-2.4	1.29	-3.1	0	4.4	121	7,983	0	0	0.0	06
Reynolds Metal	23.6	23.6	20.3	246.5q	4.79	175.0	175.0	11.1	NC	13	03-88	.80	1.6	-9	14	139	06-02-88	5.5	1.04	5.7	2.70	15.4	86	1.9	2,694	53,873	36,093	0	2.3	12
Toth Alum ♦	.0	.0	.0	-4.6f	-.18	NE	NE	NE	NC	-31	08-87	.00	.0	0	0	0	00-00-00	NC	NC	NC	NC	-30.7	1	.6	27	32,654	267	0	0.0	08

Lead, Nck, Tn, Zn Mining & Refining

Ind. Group	51.4	60.0	25.5	355.3	1.65	839.9	839.9	NE	NC	12	---	.51	2.1	0	18	41	----	9.7	.69	6.7	2.67	17.9	62	2.1	4,821	195,155	46,284	0	7.2	--
Cominco Ltd	46.0	46.0	10.3	107.1q	1.23	3400.0	3400.0	NE	NC	12	03-88	.21	NA	0	24	NE	12-04-87	7.5	.75	5.6	2.68	15.0	46	2.4	1,232	68,417	1,682	0	0.1	12
Gulf Res & Ch	-61.0	-61.0	-16.3	-1.7q	-.18	-100.0	-100.0	-100.0	NC	-1	03-88	.00	.0	0	0	0	00-00-00	-1.4	.36	-.5	2.20	-1.1	68	2.7	138	9,293	2,537	0	8.6	12
Inco Ltd	77.4	77.4	43.5	250.0q	2.29	NE	NE	NE	NC	15	03-88	.80	2.5	0	18	NE	04-26-88	12.0	.69	8.3	2.78	23.1	75	1.9	3,408	104,867	41,337	0	1.0	12
Utd Park City	100.0	100.0	.0	-1.6q	-.15	NE	NE	NE	NC	-12	03-88	.00	.0	0	0	0	00-00-00	NM	NC	NC	NC	-12.0	0	2.5	20	10,801	597	0	0.0	12
Zemex Cp	1.1	1.1	2.7	1.5q	.79	12.5	12.5	-51.2	NC	3	03-88	.40	3.2	-8	38	475	06-02-88	4.1	1.05	4.3	1.33	5.7	0	3.1	22	1,777	131	0	26.3	12

Historical Performance: Metal and Mineral Mining, Except Fuels (SIC 10,14)

(in millions of dollars except as noted)

ITEM	1972	1973	1974	1975	1976	1977	1978	1979	1980	1981	1982	1983	1984
Industry Data													
Value of shipments[1]	10,124	11,838	14,187	14,761	16,702	16,930	19,823	23,974	25,134	25,288	19,667	21,120	23,150
Value of shipments (1982$)	20,995	23,216	25,567	24,334	26,175	25,070	27,331	30,424	29,215	26,811	19,667	20,335	21,458
Total employment (000)	198	206	217	210	209	206	212	225	221	222	183	161	164
Production workers (000)	160	165	173	165	163	160	166	176	170	169	136	120	123
Average hourly earnings ($)	4.17	4.48	4.91	5.47	5.98	6.45	7.16	7.95	8.73	9.79	10.23	10.43	10.91
Trade Data													
Value of imports (BuM)[2]	1,634	1,849	2,916	2,833	2,844	2,966	3,734	4,518	4,916	4,619	3,475	3,181	3,810
Import/new supply ratio[3]	0.139	0.135	0.170	0.161	0.146	0.149	0.165	0.159	0.164	0.155	0.150	0.131	0.141
Value of exports (BuM)[4]	399	533	876	1,117	1,022	1,126	1,874	2,797	3,625	3,177	2,592	2,378	2,216
Export/shipments ratio	0.039	0.045	0.062	0.076	0.061	0.067	0.095	0.117	0.144	0.126	0.132	0.113	0.096

[1]Value of all products and services sold by the Metal and Mineral Mining, Except Fuels industry.

[2]Import data are developed by the chapter author.

[3]New supply is the sum of product shipments plus imports.

[4]Export data are developed by the chapter author.

SOURCE: U.S. Department of Interior, Bureau of Mines; U.S. Department of Commerce: Bureau of the Census, Bureau of Economic Analysis, International Trade Administration (ITA).

Source: *U.S. Industrial Outlook 1988,* U.S. Department of Commerce.

Trends and Forecasts: Motor Vehicles and Car Bodies (SIC 3711)

(in millions of dollars except as noted)

ITEM	1984	1985	1986[1]	1987[2]	1988[3]	Percent Change: Compound Annual 1972-85	Compound Annual 1980-85	Annual 1985-86	Annual 1986-87	Annual 1987-88
Industry Data										
Value of shipments[4]	118,066	122,327	132,547	120,003	126,459	8.4	13.0	8.4	−9.5	5.4
Value of shipments (1982$)	112,404	114,151	123,025	110,827	116,209	2.5	8.4	7.8	−9.9	4.9
Total employment (000)	296	296	275	270	265	−1.0	1.6	−7.1	−1.8	−1.9
Production workers (000)	248	250	240	230	225	−1.0	2.5	−4.0	−4.2	−2.2
Average hourly earnings ($)	14.46	16.70	—	—	—	8.5	5.7	—	—	—
Product Data										
Value of shipments[5]	112,358	119,632	125,400	114,069	120,909	8.6	14.3	4.8	−9.0	6.0
Value of shipments (1982$)	106,970	111,635	116,391	105,346	111,109	2.6	9.5	4.3	−9.5	5.5
Shipments price index[6] (1982 = 100)	104.9	107.1	—	—	—	5.8	4.3	—	—	—
Trade Data										
Value of imports (ITA)[7]	21,400	26,600	33,450	40,000	—	17.2	11.5	25.8	19.6	—
Import/new supply ratio[8]	0.171	0.206	0.255	—	—	8.0	0.5	23.8	—	—
Value of exports (ITA)[9]	1,700	2,043	2,350	2,700	—	8.2	−6.7	15.0	14.9	—
Export/shipments ratio	0.017	0.020	0.023	—	—	0.8	−15.7	15.0	—	—

[1]Estimated except for exports and imports.
[2]Estimated.
[3]Forecast.
[4]Value of all products and services sold by the Motor Vehicles and Car Bodies industry.
[5]Value of products classified in the Motor Vehicles and Car Bodies industry produced by all industries.
[6]Developed by the Office of Industry Assessment, ITA.
[7]Import data are developed by the chapter author.
[8]New supply is the sum of product shipments plus imports.
[9]Export data are developed by the chapter author.
SOURCE: U.S. Department of Commerce: Bureau of the Census, Bureau of Economic Analysis, International Trade Administration (ITA). Estimates and forecasts by ITA.

Source: *U.S. Industrial Outlook 1988,* U.S. Department of Commerce.

Trends and Forecasts: Motor Vehicle Parts & Stampings (SIC 3465,3592,3647,3691,3694,3714)

(in millions of dollars except as noted)

ITEM	1984	1985	1986[1]	1987[2]	1988[3]	Percent Change: Compound Annual 1972-85	Compound Annual 1980-85	Annual 1985-86	Annual 1986-87	Annual 1987-88
Industry Data										
Value of shipments[4]	80,123	86,236	90,958	94,650	97,098	9.1	11.4	5.5	4.1	2.6
3465 Automotive Stampings	14,137	15,038	15,790	16,422	16,914	8.4	12.1	5.0	4.0	3.0
3592 Pistons, Rings, Etc.	3,096	3,092	3,090	3,090	3,090	11.6	11.0	−0.1	0.0	0.0
3647 Vehicle Lighting Equip	1,419	1,453	1,482	1,497	1,500	8.6	10.7	2.0	1.0	0.2
3691 Storage Batteries	2,916	2,797	2,685	2,631	2,631	8.5	1.7	−4.0	−2.0	0.0
3694 Engine Electrical Equip	5,971	5,925	5,925	5,925	5,925	8.6	10.0	0.0	0.0	0.0
3714 Parts & Accessories	52,583	57,931	61,986	65,085	67,038	9.3	12.0	7.0	5.0	3.0
Value of shipments (1982$)	78,300	83,223	87,374	90,459	92,333	0.7	5.2	5.0	3.5	2.1
3465 Automotive Stampings	13,548	13,718	14,342	14,835	15,197	1.2	8.3	4.5	3.4	2.4
3592 Pistons, Rings, Etc.	2,931	2,888	2,872	2,856	2,843	1.4	4.9	−0.6	−0.6	−0.5
3647 Vehicle Lighting Equip	1,363	1,385	1,406	1,412	1,408	0.9	3.4	1.5	0.4	−0.3
3691 Storage Batteries	3,198	3,085	2,947	2,872	2,857	3.7	3.5	−4.5	−2.5	−0.5
3694 Engine Electrical Equip	5,751	5,654	5,627	5,600	5,569	1.3	5.3	−0.5	−0.5	−0.6
3714 Parts & Accessories	51,509	56,493	60,181	62,884	64,460	0.4	4.7	6.5	4.5	2.5
Total employment (000)	619	625	651	670	680	−0.2	1.0	4.2	2.9	1.5
Production workers (000)	500	503	524	539	547	−0.4	1.5	4.2	2.9	1.5
Average hourly earnings ($)	12.54	13.58	—	—	—	7.8	5.6	—	—	—

Product Data										
Value of shipments[5]	82,074	85,961	90,751	94,499	96,989	3.9	10.7	5.6	4.1	2.6
3465 Automotive Stampings	14,696	15,835	16,627	17,292	17,811	3.0	13.7	5.0	4.0	3.0
3592 Pistons, Rings, Etc.	2,565	2,562	2,560	2,560	2,560	3.4	9.0	−0.1	0.0	0.0
3647 Vehicle Lighting Equip	935	1,016	1,036	1,047	1,050	3.4	11.4	2.0	1.1	0.3
3691 Storage Batteries	2,794	2,671	2,564	2,513	2,513	3.3	1.5	−4.0	−2.0	0.0
3694 Engine Electrical Equip	5,280	5,493	5,493	5,493	5,493	9.1	12.6	0.0	0.0	0.0
3714 Parts & Accessories	55,805	58,384	62,471	65,594	67,562	3.8	10.4	7.0	5.0	3.0
Value of shipments (1982$)	80,231	82,908	87,146	90,285	92,198	0.5	4.5	5.1	3.6	2.1
3465 Automotive Stampings	14,090	14,422	15,102	15,621	16,003	1.8	9.9	4.7	3.4	2.4
3592 Pistons, Rings, Etc.	2,428	2,393	2,379	2,366	2,355	−0.5	3.0	−0.6	−0.5	−0.5
3647 Vehicle Lighting Equip	898	968	983	988	986	0.7	4.1	1.5	0.5	−0.2
3691 Storage Batteries	3,064	2,946	2,814	2,743	2,729	3.5	3.2	−4.5	−2.5	−0.5
3694 Engine Electrical Equip	5,087	5,245	5,217	5,192	5,163	1.9	8.1	−0.5	−0.5	−0.6
3714 Parts & Accessories	54,664	56,935	60,651	63,376	64,963	0.0	3.2	6.5	4.5	2.5
Shipments price index[6] (1982 = 100)	102.3	103.6	104.0	104.6	105.1	8.2	5.6	0.4	0.6	0.5
Trade Data										
Value of imports	12,125	13,729	15,370	18,583	20,442	15.6	21.8	12.0	20.9	10.0
Import/new supply ratio[7]	0.113	0.121	—	—	—	5.3	9.5	—	—	—
Value of exports	11,149	11,734	10,658	11,393	12,190	11.4	10.1	−9.2	6.9	7.0
Export/shipments ratio	0.133	0.134	—	—	—	2.1	−0.6	—	—	—

[1]Estimated except for exports and imports.
[2]Estimated.
[3]Forecast.
[4]Value of all products and services sold by the Motor Vehicle Parts & Stampings industry.
[5]Value of products classified in the Motor Vehicle Parts & Stampings industry produced by all industries.
[6]Developed by the Office of Industry Assessment, ITA.
[7]New supply is the sum of product shipments plus imports.
SOURCE: U.S. Department of Commerce: Bureau of the Census, Bureau of Economic Analysis, International Trade Administration (ITA). Estimates and forecasts by ITA.

Source: *U.S. Industrial Outlook 1988,* U.S. Department of Commerce.

Company	Revenue			Earnings								Dividends						Ratio Analysis							Shareholdings					
	Pct. Change				Per Share							Current Rate			Payout															
						Pct. Change																								
Company	Last Qtr	FY to Date	Last 12 Mos	Last 12 Mos	Last 12 Mos	Last Qtr	FY to Date	Last 12 Mos	5-Year Growth Rate	Par Growth Rate	Date of Report	Amt	Yield	5-Year Growth Rate	Last FY	Last 5 Yrs.	Last X-Dvd Date	Profit Margin	Asset Turnover	Return on Total Assets	Leverage Ratio	Return on Equity	Debt to Equity	Current Ratio	Market Value	Latest Shares Outstndng.	Held by Banks-Funds	Insider Net Trading	Short Interest Ratio	Fiscal Year Ends
-	%	%	%	$Mil	$	%	%	%	%	%	-	$	%	%	%	%	-	π/r x	r/a =	π/a x	a/e =	π/e	%	-	$Mil	000	000	000	Days	Mo
Auto Manufacture																														
Ind. Group	12.7	11.2	6.5	10,609.3	6.70	17.6	14.5	25.9	9	11	- - -	2.12	4.4	3	28	25	- - - -	4.3	1.44	6.2	2.61	16.2	18	1.3	73,442	1,516,765	603,135	+ 104	2.0	- -
Amertek	60.4	52.6	68.7	1.4s	.35	66.7	400.0	600.0	NC	15	06-87	.00	.0	0	0	0	00-00-00	5.2	1.81	9.4	1.64	15.4	0	2.1	6	3,517	0	0	0.0	12
Athey Prods	6.3	6.3	7.8	4.0q	1.13	23.8	23.8	43.0	NC	18	03-88	.00	.0	0	0	0	12-21-87	9.8	1.50	14.7	1.24	18.2	3	5.3	47	3,519	361	0	0.0	12
Chrysler Cp	29.1	16.3	16.3	1289.7f	5.90	5.4	-6.6	-6.5	70	16	12-87	1.00	4.1	0	17	10	06-09-88	4.9	1.33	6.5	3.05	19.8	51	.9	5,392	221,217	124,400	+45	1.4	12
ESI Ind	19.2	19.2	105.5	2.5q	.53	-61.5	-61.5	82.8	NC	14	03-88	.00	.0	0	0	0	10-09-87	2.3	1.78	4.1	3.37	13.8	144	1.9	14	4,235	1,330	0	0.0	12
Ford Motor Co	14.3	14.3	12.3	4756.8q	9.49	15.3	15.3	25.2	NC	19	03-88	2.40	4.5	63	17	16	04-26-88	6.4	1.66	10.6	2.42	25.7	9	1.2	28,084	527,400	280,138	+5	2.9	12
Ford of Can	13.4	13.4	.4	117.4q	14.17	-8.6	-8.6	-29.9	NC	7	03-88	4.00	NA	0	40	38	03-07-88	.8	4.00	3.2	3.22	10.3	20	1.1	893	8,291	96	0	2.8	12
Fruehauf Cp	-21.4	-21.4	-29.6	-52.2q	-6.47	NE	NE	NE	NC	0	03-88	.00	.0	0	0	NE	00-00-00	-3.1	.97	-3.0	.00	NS	-2757	1.8	29	12,058	493	0	8.7	12
Gen Motors	1.3	1.3	.0	3720.5q	10.55	18.7	18.7	36.7	10	6	03-88	5.00	6.2	17	50	40	05-06-88	3.6	1.19	4.3	2.63	11.3	12	1.6	25,051	312,654	118,947	+34	3.7	12
Honda Motor	52.5	35.9	15.6	673.5n	.68	72.7	28.6	NC	-29	-4	12-87	.86	.7	13	109	10	03-24-88	2.8	2.18	6.1	2.25	13.7	27	1.2	11,625	91,532	3,458	0	13.6	02
Jaguar PLC	96.9	53.6	53.4	115.7f	2.55	413.3	275.0	454.3	NC	30	12-87	.22	4.5	0	8	11	04-04-88	6.1	1.95	11.9	2.80	33.3	4	1.2	888	180,900	24,122	0	0.0	12
Larizza Inds	19.0	19.0	34.6	11.0q	.85	.0	.0	NC	NC	42	03-88	.00	.0	0	0	0	00-00-00	10.5	1.60	16.8	2.51	42.1	81	2.6	193	13,800	721	0	0.2	12
Mack Trucks	9.9	9.9	8.3	5.9q	.19	66.7	66.7	NE	NC	1	03-88	.00	.0	0	0	0	00-00-00	.3	2.00	.6	2.00	1.2	14	1.8	417	29,507	12,480	+19	0.0	12
Oshkosh Truck	-13.7	-13.8	-18.0	19.9s	2.22	-44.7	-46.4	-26.0	NC	16	03-88	.40	2.7	0	10	6	07-11-88	5.3	2.00	10.6	1.82	19.3	0	2.2	133	9,008	3,346	0	0.0	09
Pullman Co	64.6	65.7	55.7	16.2s	.38	-20.0	-20.0	-5.0	NC	6	03-88	.12	1.5	0	29	14	06-14-88	2.1	1.10	2.3	3.96	9.1	146	1.3	324	41,150	25,086	+0	1.5	09
Rawson Koenig	110.0	36.7	33.3	-1.4f	-.37	NE	NE	NE	NC	-61	09-87	.00	.0	0	0	0	00-00-00	-11.7	1.76	-20.6	2.96	-60.9	109	3.0	2	3,902	69	0	0.0	09
Spartan Motors	48.8	63.2	61.5	1.4n	.24	60.0	120.0	118.2	21	31	09-87	.05	1.0	0	0	0	06-20-88	6.7	2.82	18.9	2.06	38.9	31	2.3	29	5,554	31	0	0.0	12
Subaru of Amer	-12.7	-9.6	-16.2	-73.0s	-1.51	-100.0	-100.0	-100.0	NC	-27	04-88	.00	.0	38	NE	23	11-17-87	-4.3	2.63	-11.3	2.42	-27.3	24	1.9	315	48,521	8,057	0	0.0	10
Auto Parts and Accessories (Suppliers)																														
Ind. Group	13.5	15.1	10.7	734.6	1.43	- 12.3	- 14.6	24.4	8	7	- - -	.56	2.5	1	33	32	- - - -	3.4	1.38	4.7	2.43	11.4	59	2.0	10,944	480,859	181,011	- 308	1.0	- -
Allen Group	2.5	2.5	-12.7	-20.4q	-3.00	NE	NE	NE	NC	-18	03-88	.00	.0	3	NE	1350	09-22-87	-5.8	1.16	-6.7	2.70	-18.1	59	2.2	89	8,199	3,631	0	5.6	12
Appld Pwr □	39.8	37.2	95.2	4.3n	.40	91.2	83.7	NC	NC	6	05-88	.10	.3	0	NE	11	05-10-88	2.6	1.62	4.2	1.79	7.5	9	2.0	225	6,241	1,952	0	0.0	08
Armtek Cp ◇	5.0	12.4	31.0	25.7s	2.60	121.4	75.4	NE	NC	10	03-88	.48	1.5	6	23	47	05-27-88	2.0	1.65	3.3	3.85	12.7	146	1.9	305	9,751	7,322	-346	9.7	09
Arvin Indus	-9.8	-9.8	16.0	20.7q	.92	-100.0	-100.0	-62.9	19	1	03-88	.68	3.1	4	28	30	06-06-88	1.5	1.73	2.6	2.12	5.5	54	2.8	411	18,791	9,327	0	0.5	12
Audiovox	38.5	38.5	37.3	6.7q	.83	14.3	14.3	48.2	NC	11	02-88	.00	.0	0	0	0	00-00-00	2.2	2.27	5.0	2.14	10.7	4	1.9	51	9,007	1,386	0	0.1	11
Autodie Cp □	44.5	12.2	-12.5	-2.3s	-.45	26.7	-98.0	-100.0	NC	-7	02-88	.00	.0	0	0	0	00-00-00	-3.7	.41	-1.5	4.80	-7.2	285	1.6	77	5,151	563	0	0.0	08
Barnes Group	10.3	10.3	5.8	19.2q	3.02	55.0	55.0	24.3	59	12	03-88	1.20	3.7	12	41	40	05-25-88	4.1	1.56	6.4	3.09	19.8	76	2.0	177	5,417	2,478	0	0.0	12
Buell Indus	2.4	8.1	6.8	4.1s	1.70	-30.4	10.5	4.3	13	7	04-88	.40	2.1	10	20	15	05-09-88	5.3	1.32	7.0	1.37	9.6	5	4.8	47	2,422	429	0	0.0	10
Champion Parts □	26.4	26.4	13.6	1.4q	.44	NE	NE	109.5	NC	7	03-88	.00	.0	0	0	12	09-19-86	1.1	1.64	1.8	3.94	7.1	151	2.4	25	3,204	188	0	0.0	12
Champ Spark	4.7	4.7	-14.6	24.0q	.64	11.1	11.1	NE	NC	5	03-88	.15	1.2	-37	8	73	05-19-88	3.3	1.12	3.7	1.68	6.2	5	2.3	469	37,553	16,877	0	1.7	12
Dana Corp	22.9	22.9	16.9	144.7q	3.38	24.6	24.6	96.5	14	9	03-88	1.52	4.0	6	44	47	05-27-88	3.3	1.58	5.2	3.17	16.5	78	1.5	1,562	40,700	20,879	-2	2.2	12
Defiance Precision	4.7	100.0	126.9	-6.9n	-1.54	-100.0	NE	NE	NC	-38	03-88	.00	.0	0	0	0	00-00-00	-11.7	.91	-10.6	3.61	-38.3	133	.7	6	4,639	694	0	0.0	06
Donaldson □	20.4	24.1	20.9	15.4n	1.54	52.9	57.3	37.5	NC	10	04-88	.38	1.6	0	31	40	05-24-88	4.4	1.75	7.7	1.81	13.9	32	2.9	230	9,748	4,520	+24	2.1	07
Durakon Ind	40.6	40.6	32.9	5.8q	.94	9.1	9.1	20.5	NC	17	03-88	.00	.0	0	0	0	02-03-86	5.0	1.36	6.8	2.43	16.5	95	2.7	84	6,167	1,383	0	0.0	12
Eaton Corp	11.9	11.9	-12.7	201.3q	7.55	19.3	19.3	57.6	NC	14	03-88	2.00	2.4	8	27	23	05-03-88	6.2	1.08	6.7	2.79	18.7	74	1.8	2,072	24,931	13,615	+0	1.3	12

Echlin Inc	17.5	17.6	19.4	52.8n	.95	45.5	10.0	-10.4	4	3	05-88	.62	3.6	15	60	42	06-29-88	4.3	1.42	6.1	1.43	8.7	12	3.1	950	55,469	39,187	0	1.9	08
Equion Cp □	-3.6	16.5	20.0	3.4n	.66	-21.4	32.5	26.9	NC	15	04-88	.00	.0	0	0	0	00-00-00	4.0	1.85	7.4	1.97	14.6	41	2.3	28	4,194	435	0	0.0	07
Excel Ind	24.2	24.2	22.8	5.7q	.97	28.6	28.6	12.8	NC	9	03-88	.40	3.3	0	40	25	04-04-88	2.9	2.31	6.7	2.34	15.7	69	2.6	70	5,800	581	0	0.0	12
Hastings Mfg	5.1	5.1	4.7	1.5q	3.43	-9.6	-9.6	-25.1	2	6	03-88	.60	1.9	-5	16	16	05-18-88	2.3	1.52	3.5	2.20	7.7	58	2.7	13	420	51	0	3.4	12
Intermet Cp	4.8	4.8	8.8	19.3q	.90	-34.5	-34.5	-2.2	NC	16	03-88	.20	1.5	0	18	11	02-11-88	6.0	1.82	10.9	1.88	20.5	39	1.9	237	18,043	1,558	0	0.0	12
Jason Inc	-2.0	-2.0	4.1	2.1q	.63	-46.4	-46.4	6.8	NC	22	03-88	.00	.0	0	0	0	04-26-88	2.8	1.50	4.2	5.26	22.1	158	1.3	19	2,658	334	0	0.0	12
Jiffy Lube Intl	66.9	76.9	77.2	6.9f	.44	62.5	46.7	57.1	NC	18	03-88	.00	.0	0	0	0	03-23-87	8.8	.74	6.5	2.69	17.5	116	2.1	160	14,231	2,680	0	0.0	03
Kysor Ind	15.4	15.4	30.1	12.8q	1.87	12.8	12.8	24.7	NC	14	03-88	.56	2.6	20	27	24	07-07-88	5.5	1.87	10.3	1.97	20.3	33	2.3	144	6,568	2,279	+9	0.6	12
Magna Intl	24.9	17.5	12.2	23.2n	.83	-58.8	-54.9	-53.4	NC	2	04-88	.48	4.5	0	31	23	08-09-88	1.8	1.00	1.8	2.89	5.2	105	1.2	296	27,819	9,362	0	0.0	07
Modine Mfg	12.6	13.2	13.1	25.0f	1.67	41.7	27.5	27.5	NC	11	03-88	.52	2.9	0	26	25	05-25-88	6.3	1.46	9.2	1.76	16.2	29	2.5	262	14,763	4,402	+6	0.0	03
Mr Gasket	-5.8	-5.8	-1411.1	1.4q	.12	-85.7	-85.7	NE	NC	3	03-88	.00	.0	0	0	1	00-00-00	1.2	.92	1.1	2.73	3.0	134	4.5	54	10,629	1,484	0	0.0	12
NEOAX Inc	52.0	52.0	40.6	7.7q	.18	-100.0	-100.0	NE	NC	37	03-88	.00	.0	0	0	0	00-00-00	3.2	1.03	3.3	11.12	36.7	429	2.2	87	8,616	2,102	0	0.0	12
Premier Ind	16.9	13.9	12.4	59.6n	1.36	34.6	35.1	34.7	12	16	02-88	.40	1.2	11	26	26	06-20-88	11.8	1.55	18.3	1.22	22.3	3	7.5	1,435	43,495	8,331	0	0.0	05
Raytech Cp	14.7	14.7	20.1	.5q	-.01	-100.0	-100.0	-100.0	NC	19	03-88	.05	.9	0	0	0	02-22-88	.4	1.50	.6	5.33	3.2	115	1.2	17	3,127	592	0	0.0	12
Seaport Cp	5.3	5.3	.0	.4q	.16	NE	NE	NE	NC	0	03-88	.00	.0	0	0	0	00-00-00	2.4	2.08	5.0	.00	NM	350	1.0	2	2,072	31	0	3.0	12
Simpson Indust	3.3	3.3	74.1	6.0q	.95	57.9	57.9	50.8	35	5	03-88	.56	3.4	0	67	58	05-26-88	4.1	1.34	5.5	2.20	12.1	51	1.7	103	6,321	3,105	0	0.0	12
Smith AO A	-4.1	-4.1	1.6	11.4q	1.01	-48.7	-48.7	-64.3	NC	1	03-88	.80	4.4	86	58	66	04-25-88	1.2	1.42	1.7	2.29	3.9	42	1.6	155	8,481	1,524	0	4.9	12
Smith AO B	NA	NA	NA	NA	NA	NA	NA	NA	NA	NC	00-00	.80	5.1	NA	NA	NA	04-25-88	NA	NC	NA	NC	NA	NA	NA	55	3,497	1,758	0	NA	NA
Sparton Corp	-19.2	-10.9	-19.8	8.1n	1.03	-58.3	-27.3	-35.6	NC	6	03-88	.52	4.5	13	41	51	06-09-88	3.9	1.95	7.6	1.67	12.7	1	1.9	91	7,914	1,802	0	0.0	06
SPX Cp	19.2	19.2	18.9	29.1q	2.36	34.3	34.3	-4.8	0	5	03-88	1.20	3.2	10	52	38	08-15-88	3.6	1.44	5.2	1.94	10.1	45	2.6	460	12,308	6,734	0	1.2	12
Std Motor Prd	19.4	19.4	22.7	15.0q	1.14	-29.0	-29.0	-19.1	-3	7	03-88	.32	2.4	6	26	24	05-10-88	4.0	1.35	5.4	1.91	10.3	37	3.2	179	13,229	4,662	0	0.0	12
Sudbury Inc	39.0	58.5	61.0	12.8n	1.10	-21.4	-6.7	19.6	NC	25	02-88	.00	.0	0	0	0	00-00-00	2.7	1.67	4.5	5.62	25.3	210	2.0	94	12,729	758	0	0.0	05
Trico Prods	-.2	-.9	-1.2	-16.0f	-8.67	-100.0	-100.0	-100.0	NC	-19	12-87	1.00	1.6	0	NE	303	05-27-88	-10.3	1.16	-11.9	1.41	-16.8	0	1.9	115	1,847	173	0	0.0	12
Venturian Cp	-6.8	-6.8	220.0	.7q	.74	-100.0	-100.0	NE	NC	4	03-88	.00	.0	0	0	39	03-11-85	2.2	1.14	2.5	1.44	3.6	2	4.0	12	958	284	0	0.0	12
Wynn's Intl	2.6	2.6	6.0	1.5q	.40	-100.0	-100.0	-71.2	NC	-1	03-88	.60	3.0	0	128	49	05-26-88	.5	1.60	.8	2.38	1.9	54	2.4	75	3,750	1,558	0	0.1	12

Auto Parts & Accessories (Retailers)

Ind. Group	15.1	14.1	13.8	270.8	1.27	31.7	23.7	26.6	13	11	- - -	.51	2.2	1	34	38	- - - -	4.9	2.14	10.5	1.70	17.9	21	2.6	4,903	209,287	87,476	+ 18	.7	- -
Action Auto Str □	45.7	50.9	50.0	1.4n	.50	350.0	90.0	66.7	NC	14	03-88	.00	.0	0	0	0	00-00-00	1.8	2.11	3.8	3.66	13.9	163	1.5	22	2,963	179	+2	0.0	06
Armor All Prods	59.3	18.1	17.7	22.3f	1.07	70.8	30.5	30.5	NC	18	03-88	.52	2.4	0	38	20	05-27-88	17.7	1.47	26.1	1.33	34.7	0	2.4	450	20,908	2,433	0	0.0	03
Coast Dist	14.6	6.8	6.7	2.5f	.58	NE	1833.3	1833.3	NC	15	12-87	.00	.0	0	0	0	00-00-00	2.3	2.61	6.0	2.52	15.1	96	3.5	26	3,843	1,089	-2	5.9	12
Genuine Parts	14.9	14.9	10.6	156.8q	2.00	30.0	30.0	26.6	8	10	03-88	1.04	2.7	12	48	51	05-31-88	5.8	2.64	15.3	1.35	20.6	3	3.9	2,945	77,244	45,337	+5	1.9	12
Mid Am Indus	6.3	6.3	-1.1	-3.3q	-1.82	NE	NE	NE	NC	-18	03-88	.00	.0	0	0	NE	03-10-86	-3.8	1.89	-7.2	2.51	-18.1	54	2.1	13	1,837	465	+3	0.0	12
Pep Boys	15.4	15.4	13.9	33.7q	.61	-9.1	-9.1	10.9	16	12	04-88	.10	.8	14	13	14	06-27-88	5.9	1.22	7.2	1.97	14.2	58	1.6	709	54,519	21,076	0	0.3	01
Ragan, Brad	23.0	23.0	636.0	2.6q	1.18	NE	NE	NC	9	5	03-88	.12	.5	0	12	18	05-06-88	1.4	1.86	2.6	2.04	5.3	11	1.9	49	2,191	422	0	0.0	12
Rep Auto	.9	.9	-9.0	-2.6q	-.88	NE	NE	NE	NC	-11	03-88	.00	.0	0	0	NE	12-26-85	-2.9	1.69	-4.9	2.24	-11.0	72	3.6	15	2,824	1,667	0	0.0	12
Std Products	5.6	4.3	3.0	30.4n	2.77	10.3	.0	-1.8	22	17	03-88	.80	2.7	55	19	18	04-05-88	6.3	2.14	13.5	1.77	23.9	14	2.1	313	10,619	4,512	+10	0.0	06
Steego Corp ○ ♦	7.1	5.6	9.2	-1.0n	-.11	NE	NE	NE	NC	-2	01-88	.00	.0	0	0	NE	12-16-87	-.4	1.75	-.7	3.43	-2.4	78	1.8	55	10,056	1,144	+0	1.5	04
Sup Ind Intl	8.2	8.2	12.3	9.9q	1.58	29.3	29.3	16.2	29	16	03-88	.25	1.5b	0	16	11	06-27-88	5.7	1.40	8.0	2.31	18.5	52	2.4	95	5,813	2,163	0	0.0	12
TBC Corp	19.3	19.3	17.3	13.6q	1.28	81.3	81.3	106.5	NC	25	03-88	.00	.0	0	0	0	09-09-87	2.9	3.83	11.1	2.24	24.9	0	1.7	150	10,600	6,016	0	0.0	12
Trak Auto	14.4	14.4	6.8	4.5q	.76	-11.1	-11.1	137.5	-13	8	04-88	.00	.0	0	0	0	00-00-00	2.1	2.00	4.2	1.93	8.1	29	2.3	62	5,870	973	0	0.0	01

Trends and Forecasts: Selected Retail Establishments (SICs 52-59, 5311, 5812, 5813)

Type of Retailer	Sales (in billions) 1984	1985	1986	1987[1]	1988[2]	Percent Change: Compound Annual 1972-85	1980-85	Annual 1985-86	1986-87	1987-88
Total retailing	1,293	1,374	1,454	1,541	1,633	9.1	7.5	5.8	6.0	6.0
Department stores (SIC 5311)	129	135	143	152	161	7.2	7.8	5.9	6.3	5.9
Eating and drinking places (SIC 5812, 5813)	125	131	145	158	172	10.7	7.8	10.7	9.0	9.0
Apparel and accessory stores (SIC 56)	65	74	81	86.7	92.8	8.5	7.1	9.5	7.0	7.0

[1]Estimated.
[2]Forecast.

SOURCE: U.S. Department of Commerce, Bureau of the Census, and International Trade Administration (ITA). Estimates and forecast by ITA.

Source: *U.S. Industrial Outlook 1988*, U.S. Department of Commerce.

Trends and Forecasts: Food Retailing (SIC 54)

(in millions of dollars except where noted)

Sales	Industry Data 1983	1984	1985	1986	1987[1]	1988[2]	Percent Change 1983-4	1984-5	1985-6	1986-7[1]	1987-8[2]
All food-grocery stores	255,678	271,278	283,987	296,040	307,586	322,965	6.1	6.3	4.2	3.9	5.0
Chainstore groups[3]	142,377	150,488	158,217	164,634	171,549	180,298	5.7	5.1	4.1	4.2	5.1
Grocery stores	239,629	254,854	267,004	278,483	290,458	305,656	6.4	4.8	4.3	4.1	5.2
Chainstore groups[3]	139,947	148,126	155,649	161,812	168,770	177,884	5.8	5.1	4.0	4.3	5.4
Retail Bakeries	3,964	4,228	4,240	4,802	5,229	5,360	6.7	0.3	13.3	8.9	2.5
Other food grocery stores[4]	12,085	12,196	12,743	12,755	11,899	11,949	5.4	4.5	0.1	−6.7	0.4
Employment and Earnings											
Total employment (000)	2,556	2,654	2,775	2,873	2,971	3,069	3.8	4.6	3.5	3.4	3.3
Non-supervisor employment (000)	2,374	2,442	2,567	2,657	2,742	2,824	2.9	5.1	3.5	3.2	3.0
Average hourly earnings, non-supervisory employment ($)	7.51	7.64	7.35	7.08	6.99	—	1.7	−3.8	−3.7	−1.3	—

[1]Estimate
[2]Forecast
[3]Companies which had 11 or more retail establishments.
[4]Meat/seafood, produce, confectionery, dairy, and miscellaneous food-grocery retailers.

SOURCE: U.S. Department of Commerce, Bureau of the Census and International Trade Administration (ITA). Estimates and forecasts by ITA.

Source: *U.S. Industrial Outlook 1988*, U.S. Department of Commerce.

Company	Revenue Pct. Change Last Qtr	Revenue Pct. Change FY to Date	Revenue Pct. Change Last 12 Mos	Earnings Last 12 Mos	Earnings Per Share Last 12 Mos	Per Share Pct. Change Last Qtr	Per Share Pct. Change FY to Date	Per Share Pct. Change Last 12 Mos	5-Year Growth Rate	Par Growth Rate	Date of Report	Dividends Current Rate Amt	Current Rate Yield	5-Year Growth Rate	Payout Last FY	Payout Last 5 Yrs.	Last X-Dvd Date	Ratio Analysis Profit Margin	Asset Turnover	Return on Total Assets	Leverage Ratio	Return on Equity	Debt to Equity	Current Ratio	Shareholdings Market Value	Latest Shares Outstndng.	Held by Banks-Funds	Insider Net Trading	Short Interest Ratio	Fiscal Year Ends
-	%	%	%	$Mil	$	%	%	%	%	%	-	$	%	%	%	%	-	π/r x	r/a =	π/a x	a/e =	π/e	%	-	$Mil	000	000	000	Days	Mo
Food Chain Stores																														
Ind. Group	- 18.6	11.8	15.4	1,345.3	1.02	9.1	16.0	60.6	14	12	- - -	.31	1.6	1	29	34	- - - -	1.7	3.47	5.9	2.90	17.1	61	1.3	23,057	1,183,272	251,285	- 116	.8	- -
Albertson's Inc	11.1	11.1	9.5	131.7q	1.97	20.5	20.5	26.3	13	14	04-88	.36	1.7	13	25	27	08-01-88	2.2	4.27	9.4	2.11	19.8	28	1.4	2,225	66,419	28,442	-33	1.9	01
Arden Group Inc ◆	.4	.4	-6.7	8.4q	4.47	116.4	116.4	106.9	38	31	03-88	.30	.7	0	8	3	08-11-87	2.3	2.70	6.2	5.42	33.6	175	1.7	66	1,513	700	0	0.0	12
Atlantic Grp	3.8	6.3	23.0	.7n	.40	-38.5	-41.2	NE	NC	39	02-88	.00	.0	0	0	0	00-00-00	2.2	3.77	8.3	4.69	38.9	139	1.8	21	2,597	0	0	0.0	05
Big Bear	4.7	4.1	2.8	15.5s	1.72	30.0	28.9	3.0	11	17	02-88	.00	.0	0	0	0	01-25-88	1.7	4.29	7.3	2.30	16.8	30	1.5	237	9,013	5,739	-74	0.0	08
Bildner & Sons	64.6	67.6	69.2	-9.8n	-1.73	-100.0	-100.0	-100.0	NC	-48	10-87	.00	.0	0	0	0	00-00-00	-22.3	1.25	-27.8	1.74	-48.3	30	1.2	6	5,618	596	0	0.0	01
Borman's Inc	-2.5	-2.5	-4.5	-31.1q	-11.09	-100.0	-100.0	NC	NC	0	05-88	.00	.0	0	NE	NE	02-09-88	-3.0	4.53	-13.6	.00	NM	875	1.1	34	2,808	707	0	0.3	01
Bruno's Inc	24.8	20.3	19.1	38.5n	.50	44.4	34.5	28.2	16	15	03-88	.10	.9	17	23	21	04-25-88	2.9	4.41	12.8	1.49	19.1	6	1.6	879	78,987	19,568	0	0.0	06
Casey's Gen St	22.6	19.0	19.0	10.6f	.90	23.1	23.3	23.3	31	19	04-88	.00	.0	0	0	0	08-05-86	3.1	2.90	9.0	2.07	18.6	75	3.2	153	11,787	3,767	0	0.0	04
Circle K Cp	17.2	16.0	16.0	54.9f	1.04	52.6	11.8	11.8	17	13	04-88	.28	1.8	3	27	31	06-06-88	2.1	2.29	4.8	3.69	17.7	173	2.1	675	43,877	25,980	0	5.4	04
Convenient Food	73.1	73.1	162.9	2.8q	.90	47.4	47.4	13.9	21	30	03-88	.00	.0	0	0	9	08-31-87	3.9	1.36	5.3	5.57	29.5	233	1.5	32	3,031	352	0	0.0	12
Cullum Companies ▫	25.7	20.6	16.3	17.4n	1.06	-18.5	-4.8	-3.6	7	9	03-88	.36	1.8	7	30	30	06-24-88	1.5	3.93	5.9	2.24	13.2	62	1.6	332	16,411	6,246	0	0.0	06
Dairy Mart	NA	NA	NA	NA	NA	NA	NA	NA	NA	NC	00-00	.00	.0	NA	NA	NA	07-16-86	NA	NC	NA	NC	NA	NA	NA	18	2,184	1,903	0	NA	NA
Dairy Mart Conv	29.5	29.5	24.8	4.4q	.97	425.0	425.0	NE	NC	15	04-88	.00	.0	0	0	0	07-16-86	.8	3.88	3.1	4.87	15.1	246	1.1	19	2,347	152	0	0.0	01
Dee Cp	12.1	12.2	112.1	208.0s	1.18	-40.5	-39.2	NC	NC	19	10-87	.00	.0	0	17	17	00-00-00	2.4	3.08	7.4	2.50	18.5	11	.8	2,917	176,760	0	0	0.0	04
Delchamps Inc	5.4	9.5	11.4	7.3n	1.11	33.3	25.0	16.8	-3	8	03-88	.38	1.5	0	29	16	10-29-87	.9	5.11	4.6	2.39	11.0	50	1.5	128	6,994	2,295	-2	0.0	06
Farm Fresh	-.5	-.5	-8.3	-3.7q	-.28	-100.0	-100.0	-100.0	NC	-3	03-88	.00	.0	0	0	0	07-13-84	-.5	2.40	-1.2	2.67	-3.2	77	2.1	148	13,412	3,348	0	0.0	12
Food Lion	26.2	26.2	23.2	91.5q	.29	40.0	40.0	38.1	30	20	03-88	.07	.7	0	15	11	07-15-88	2.9	3.93	11.4	2.37	27.0	36	1.4	1,700	161,920	10,421	0	0.0	12
Food Lion	NA	NA	NA	NA	NA	NA	NA	NA	NA	NC	00-00	.06	.5	NA	NA	NA	07-15-88	NA	NA	NA	NC	NA	NA	NA	1,823	158,490	7,430	0	NA	NA
Foodarama	1.1	1.1	2.5	4.0q	3.21	81.0	81.0	143.2	64	14	01-88	.00	.0	0	0	0	09-17-79	.8	5.38	4.3	3.28	14.1	94	1.1	36	1,287	190	0	0.0	10
Gen Host	-67.7	-38.9	-38.8	56.8f	2.40	NC	727.6	727.6	17	25	01-88	.28	2.5	13	10	18	06-09-88	14.3	.81	11.6	2.46	28.5	74	1.9	227	19,938	6,085	0	0.1	01
Giant Food A	8.8	8.8	7.2	80.7q	1.34	30.8	30.8	65.4	12	16	05-88	.40	2.0	24	26	28	06-06-88	2.9	3.14	9.1	2.49	22.7	66	1.5	1,231	60,054	16,138	0	1.9	02
Grt A & P Tea	-4.7	21.7	21.6	103.4f	2.71	20.0	48.9	48.9	34	11	02-88	.50	1.3	0	18	6	04-11-88	1.1	4.55	5.0	2.74	13.7	56	1.1	1,482	38,126	10,891	+3	1.2	02
Hannaford Bros	15.0	15.0	14.2	25.1q	2.70	15.4	15.4	17.4	13	14	03-88	.64	1.5	6	22	25	06-13-88	2.3	3.57	8.2	2.18	17.9	51	1.4	396	9,289	2,605	0	0.0	12
Ingles Markets	19.7	17.5	16.0	10.9s	.68	66.7	16.7	NC	NC	8	03-88	.20	2.0	0	32	28	12-15-87	1.5	2.73	4.1	2.63	10.8	90	2.2	180	17,548	258	0	0.0	09
Kroger	9.1	9.1	6.5	189.5q	2.28	20.0	20.0	293.1	-3	10	03-88	1.12	3.1	3	48	63	05-04-88	1.1	3.82	4.2	4.48	18.8	75	1.1	2,837	79,370	28,073	0	2.9	12
Marsh Supermkt	15.9	9.8	9.8	7.8f	1.53	-7.7	15.9	15.9	25	11	03-88	.44	2.1	5	27	34	07-11-88	.9	5.00	4.5	3.42	15.4	111	1.3	104	5,095	2,041	-4	0.0	03
Mayfair Supermkt	17.9	14.6	12.9	11.4s	1.45	29.0	34.5	43.6	40	38	02-88	.00	.0	0	1	2	08-25-87	2.2	5.32	11.7	3.22	37.7	106	.8	182	7,840	971	-5	0.0	08
Mott's Super	-14.3	-14.3	-98.5	-1.4q	-.51	NE	NE	NE	NC	-6	03-88	.00	.0	0	0	NE	02-04-86	-46.7	.06	-2.9	2.10	-6.1	8	1.1	27	2,786	608	0	0.0	12
Munford Inc	2.4	2.4	1.9	-7.5q	-1.94	NE	NE	-100.0	NC	-20	03-88	.54	3.2	-6	NE	53	12-22-87	-1.6	2.63	-4.2	3.64	-15.3	85	1.3	66	3,907	1,647	0	0.3	12
Natl Conv Str	13.2	9.7	10.9	.0n	.00	NE	NE	NE	NC	NC	03-88	.36	3.7	8	NE	71	06-20-88	.0	NC	NC	NC	.0	373	1.1	215	22,355	12,038	0	0.2	06

Continued

Company	Revenue Pct. Change Last Qtr	Revenue Pct. Change FY to Date	Revenue Pct. Change Last 12 Mos	Earnings Last 12 Mos	Per Share Last 12 Mos	Per Share Pct. Change Last Qtr	Per Share Pct. Change FY to Date	Per Share Pct. Change Last 12 Mos	5-Year Growth Rate	Par Growth Rate	Date of Report	Dividends Current Rate Amt	Current Rate Yield	5-Year Growth Rate	Payout Last FY	Payout Last 5 Yrs.	Last X-Dvd Date	Profit Margin	Asset Turnover	Return on Total Assets	Leverage Ratio	Return on Equity	Debt to Equity	Current Ratio	Market Value	Latest Shares Outstndng.	Held by Banks-Funds	Insider Net Trading	Short Interest Ratio	Fiscal Year Ends
-	%	%	%	$Mil	$	%	%	%	%	%	-	$	%	%	%	%	-	π/r x	r/a =	π/a x	a/e =	π/e	%	-	$Mil	000	000	000	Days	Mo
Food Chain Stores (Continued)																														
Penn Traffic	NA	NA	NA	NA	NA	NA	NA	NA	NA	NC	00-00	.00	.0	NA	NA	NA	00-00-00	NA	NC	NA	NC	NA	NA	NA	13	959	0	0	NA	NA
Seaway Food Town ◇	6.8	7.2	10.4	9.2s	8.58	76.5	803.6	517.3	17	36	03-88	.68	2.1	2	36	47	02-09-88	1.9	4.47	8.5	4.56	38.8	150	1.2	40	1,237	166	0	0.0	09
Stop & Shop	-66.3	12.2	12.1	55.7f	2.01	139.1	45.7	45.7	-4	9	01-88	.64	1.5	15	31	28	02-22-88	1.3	3.69	4.8	2.69	12.9	81	1.7	1,224	27,900	16,153	0	0.0	01
Sunshine-Jr	-.8	-.8	8.5	1.6q	.92	442.9	442.9	-39.5	-4	3	03-88	.48	2.7	0	79	39	05-19-88	.9	4.00	3.6	1.94	7.0	38	1.0	30	1,702	531	0	0.0	12
Uni Marts Inc	16.1	18.8	23.5	2.3s	.36	60.0	42.9	24.1	NC	9	03-88	.08	1.0b	0	23	7	06-15-88	1.8	3.39	6.1	1.90	11.6	36	1.3	49	6,290	543	0	0.0	09
Vons Cons	-585.6	-3.3	.0	.0*	-.14	NE	NE	-100.0	NC	0	03-88	.00	.0	0	0	0	00-00-00	NC	NC	NC	NC	.0	353	.7	281	27,050	5,901	0	0.4	12
Weis Markets	1.6	1.6	2.2	77.0q	1.69	7.7	7.7	15.0	11	12	03-88	.50	1.6	7	25	22	04-28-88	6.8	2.10	14.3	1.19	17.0	0	5.2	1,384	45,559	20,378	0	1.0	12
Winn Dixie	.2	.3	1.4	109.9n	2.68	-12.3	-2.2	2.3	0	5	03-88	1.86	4.6	7	66	60	06-09-88	1.2	6.50	7.8	1.91	14.9	14	1.6	1,643	40,812	8,422	0	13.9	06
Department Stores																														
Ind. Group	26.6	10.4	8.0	3,662.4	2.59	- 12.0	- 41.3	- 8.3	0	5	- - -	1.54	4.1	0	39	39	- - - -	3.2	.94	3.0	4.17	12.5	76	2.0	44,992	1,203,356	598,847	- 785	3.6	- -
Alexander's Inc	-5.2	-.2	-.3	-2.8n	-.59	NC	-100.0	-100.0	NC	-3	04-88	.00	.0	0	0	0	08-20-80	-.5	3.00	-1.5	2.00	-3.0	53	2.0	252	4,976	1,792	+14	38.0	07
Ames Dept St	14.8	14.8	11.1	31.9q	.85	-15.8	-15.8	11.8	6	7	04-88	.10	.7	7	11	11	07-27-88	1.5	2.53	3.8	1.97	7.5	29	2.1	552	37,453	20,758	-2	0.5	01
Bankers Note	-9.7	-9.7	5.4	-1.4q	-.45	10.0	10.0	-100.0	NC	-22	04-88	.00	.0	0	0	0	06-02-86	-3.6	4.06	-14.6	1.50	-21.9	0	2.4	10	3,178	260	-10	0.0	01
Campeau Cp ◇ ◆	-42.7	160.9	.0	.0*	-7.26	NE	-100.0	NC	NC	0	01-88	.24	1.6	0	NE	NE	06-09-88	NC	NC	NC	NC	NS	-1300	.8	613	40,845	23	0	0.0	01
Carter Hawley □	-115.5	255.0	.0	.0*	-9.21	NE	42.6	-100.0	NC	0	04-88	17.31	184.6	-9	NE	NE	09-11-87	NC	NC	NC	NC	.0	482	1.6	212	22,586	7,330	-81	25.7	07
Crowley Milner	-11.6	-11.6	-5.1	-2.1q	-4.13	NE	NE	-100.0	NC	-14	04-88	1.00	3.6	14	NE	43	04-11-88	-1.9	2.32	-4.4	2.50	-11.0	77	2.2	14	509	53	0	0.0	01
Dayton Hudson	18.1	18.1	16.1	221.0q	2.38	-7.7	-7.7	-9.5	2	6	04-88	1.02	2.9	11	38	29	05-16-88	2.0	1.80	3.6	3.08	11.1	92	1.5	3,261	91,866	55,821	+32	1.5	01
Dillard Dept	24.2	24.2	21.5	92.7q	2.88	11.1	11.1	19.5	21	14	04-88	.16	.4	21	5	5	07-26-88	4.0	1.55	6.2	2.32	14.4	69	2.1	1,332	32,202	9,999	0	3.6	01
Fedrtd Dep Str	3.2	5.8	5.7	313.0f	3.40	9.0	9.0	9.0	4	12	01-88	.00	.0	7	42	39	00-00-00	2.8	1.96	5.5	2.15	11.8	30	1.9	6,522	89,651	61,184	0	2.5	01
Gottschalks	24.1	24.1	25.1	5.1q	.62	12.5	12.5	3.3	NC	10	04-88	.00	.0	0	0	0	04-13-87	3.1	1.45	4.5	2.29	10.3	51	2.0	100	8,520	2,558	0	0.0	01
Hills Dept St	11.4	11.4	12.1	20.4q	1.10	NE	NE	NC	NC	0	04-88	.00	.0	0	0	0	00-00-00	1.3	2.08	2.7	.00	NS	-2281	1.0	203	19,144	2,960	0	3.0	01
Holmes, D.H.	-1.4	-1.4	1.1	-4.8q	-.91	NE	NE	-100.0	NC	-7	04-88	.00	.0	-13	NE	77	06-15-87	-1.8	1.39	-2.5	2.84	-7.1	75	1.5	61	3,563	716	+22	0.0	01
INTERCO Inc	-.4	-.4	18.5	149.2q	3.68	29.0	29.0	11.9	4	7	05-88	1.72	3.8	2	46	50	06-17-88	4.5	1.67	7.5	1.67	12.5	25	3.6	1,676	37,446	24,129	0	1.4	02
JG Industries	3.5	3.5	-5.2	-.5q	-.08	NE	NE	-100.0	NC	-3	04-88	.00	.0	0	0	0	00-00-00	-.2	2.00	-.4	6.25	-2.5	124	1.5	24	5,948	48	0	0.0	01
May Dept Strs	-1.1	-1.1	-1.9	442.0q	2.90	.0	.0	13.3	9	9	04-88	1.28	3.8	14	39	37	05-25-88	4.3	1.65	7.1	2.39	17.0	44	2.2	5,168	152,574	90,759	0	0.8	01
Mays J W	7.4	-3.0	-4.0	-.2n	-.31	NE	-100.0	-100.0	NC	-1	04-88	.00	.0	0	0	0	00-00-00	-.3	2.00	-.6	2.33	-1.4	37	1.0	48	2,178	121	0	0.0	07
Mercantile Strs	4.6	4.6	5.7	130.2q	3.53	1.4	1.4	11.0	12	12	04-88	.80	1.9	15	19	19	08-25-88	6.0	1.60	9.6	1.55	14.9	24	4.9	1,543	36,844	14,789	-794	2.2	01
Nordstrom	17.0	17.0	16.8	96.7q	1.18	26.3	26.3	21.6	21	15	04-88	.22	.8	24	16	16	05-24-88	4.9	1.59	7.8	2.32	18.1	45	1.9	2,378	81,287	26,398	+38	0.0	01
Penney, JC	-1.6	-1.6	2.4	603.0q	4.16	5.5	5.5	7.8	7	8	04-88	2.00	4.1	6	35	37	04-05-88	3.9	1.44	5.6	2.59	14.5	62	2.7	6,790	139,645	81,375	-22	2.9	01
Proffitt's Inc	21.3	21.3	14.2	1.8q	.48	-21.4	-21.4	-4.0	NC	10	04-88	.00	.0	0	0	0	00-00-00	3.8	1.18	4.5	2.29	10.3	76	3.1	21	2,747	518	0	0.0	01
Sears, Roebuck	16.0	16.0	9.3	1541.0q	4.07	-37.3	-37.3	5.7	6	6	03-88	2.00	5.4	7	45	45	05-27-88	3.1	.68	2.1	5.38	11.3	70	NA	13,958	378,517	194,892	+18	0.9	12
Strawbrid & Cloth	8.8	8.8	9.5	26.1q	3.34	-28.9	-28.9	21.0	14	9	04-88	1.03	3.1b	25	24	21	04-06-88	3.1	1.61	5.0	2.74	13.7	101	3.0	240	7,281	1,739	0	0.0	01
Stuarts Dept	-.4	-.4	1.5	.1q	.01	NE	NE	-94.4	NC	1	04-88	.00	.0	0	0	0	09-03-85	.1	3.00	.3	2.00	.6	68	2.5	15	4,396	625	0	0.0	01

Company	Revenue Pct. Change Last Qtr	Revenue Pct. Change FY to Date	Revenue Pct. Change Last 12 Mos	Earnings Last 12 Mos	Per Share Last 12 Mos	Per Share Pct. Change Last Qtr	Per Share Pct. Change FY to Date	Per Share Pct. Change Last 12 Mos	5-Year Growth Rate	Par Growth Rate	Date of Report	Current Rate Amt	Current Rate Yield	5-Year Growth Rate	Payout Last FY	Payout Last 5 Yrs.	Last X-Dvd Date	Profit Margin	Asset Turnover	Return on Total Assets	Leverage Ratio	Return on Equity	Debt to Equity	Current Ratio	Market Value	Latest Shares Outstndng.	Held by Banks-Funds	Insider Net Trading	Short Interest Ratio	Fiscal Year Ends
-	%	%	%	$Mil	$	%	%	%	%	%	-	$	%	%	%	%	-	s/r x	r/a =	s/a x	a/e =	s/e	%	-	$Mil	000	000	000	Days	Mo
Discount and Variety Stores																														
Ind. Group	- 8.6	- 5.2	10.8	2,167.7	1.35	9.5	6.6	24.7	16	13	- - -	.32	1.3	1	17	21	- - - -	2.7	2.48	6.7	2.46	16.5	59	1.9	41,817	1,686,347	643,339	+ 693	4.2	- -
Allison's Place	-27.8	-27.8	-2.7	-7.3q	-2.61	-100.0	-100.0	-100.0	NC	0	04-88	.00	.0	0	0	0	00-00-00	-20.9	3.09	-64.6	.00	NM	33	.9	1	2,788	169	0	0.0	01
Best Products	-4.3	-4.3	-2.1	23.0q	.84	NE	NE	NE	NC	6	04-88	.00	.0	0	0	40	05-23-86	1.1	1.73	1.9	3.00	5.7	98	1.9	359	26,809	13,859	0	0.1	01
Brendle's Inc	32.9	32.9	14.3	3.4q	.41	NE	NE	-41.4	NC	5	04-88	.00	.0	0	0	0	00-00-00	1.4	2.00	2.8	1.86	5.2	· 20	1.8	63	8,080	2,512	0	0.0	01
Carson Pirie	25.7	25.7	28.2	-32.7q	-2.94	NC	NC	NC	NC	-23	04-88	.10	.8	0	NE	141	08-22-88	-3.3	1.52	-5.0	4.40	-22.0	162	1.5	170	12,989	6,977	+121	12.6	01
Child World	14.8	14.8	17.3	9.9q	.86	NE	NE	-8.5	NC	5	04-88	.00	.0	0	0	0	00-00-00	1.3	1.77	2.3	2.17	5.0	14	1.4	175	11,501	1,615	0	0.0	01
Consol Store	8.7	8.7	46.2	12.2q	.28	-25.0	-25.0	-24.3	NC	10	04-88	.00	.0	0	0	0	06-17-86	2.0	2.45	4.9	1.94	9.5	43	2.4	231	45,099	14,375	0	1.5	01
Costco Wholesale ...♦ □	31.2	50.5	61.5	9.3n	.37	.0	383.3	184.6	NC	11	05-88	.00	.0	0	0	0	00-00-00	.5	5.00	2.5	4.20	10.5	153	1.2	350	24,378	3,710	-75	0.0	08
CVN Cos	-247.3	711.3	.0	.0*	.29	-34.8	500.0	NE	NC	0	02-88	.00	.0	0	0	0	06-30-86	NC	NC	NC	NC	.0	8	2.4	250	17,378	5,835	+44	0.0	08
Dollar General Cp	7.1	7.1	4.3	7.0q	.37	NE	NE	NC	-18	3	04-88	.20	2.3	14	57	26	04-15-88	1.2	2.58	3.1	2.06	6.4	45	3.1	159	18,489	4,096	0	0.0	12
Family Dollar	21.9	19.2	18.1	25.0s	.88	17.9	4.2	-12.9	13	10	02-88	.32	2.5	32	30	20	06-09-88	4.1	2.51	10.3	1.52	15.7	0	2.1	362	28,129	10,011	0	1.2	08
Hecks Inc	-24.4	-27.1	-27.0	-61.3f	-6.91	NE	NE	NE	NC	-86	12-87	.00	.0	0	0	NE	08-04-87	-14.8	1.58	-23.4	3.67	-85.9	96	1.3	16	8,876	1,874	0	0.0	12
Home Shop	19.4	33.0	51.4	18.0n	.21	-12.5	-41.4	-41.7	NC	15	05-88	.00	.0	0	0	0	01-20-87	2.5	1.32	3.3	4.61	15.2	284	2.4	425	87,175	2,115	0	74.0	08
Jamesway Corp	6.6	6.6	12.5	10.7q	.76	-66.7	-66.7	-13.6	0	9	04-88	.08	.9	17	10	7	07-01-88	1.5	2.87	4.3	2.28	9.8	60	2.9	124	13,613	6,270	0	0.3	01
K mart Cp	4.4	4.4	6.9	697.3q	3.43	5.3	5.3	11.4	12	10	04-88	1.32	3.8	11	33	36	05-13-88	2.7	2.33	6.3	2.51	15.8	62	1.9	7,078	201,496	148,345	0	1.9	01
Lillian Vernon	.3	9.4	9.5	8.0f	1.43	-4.3	60.7	NC	NC	22	02-88	.00	.0	0	0	0	00-00-00	6.3	1.63	10.3	2.13	21.9	40	2.3	66	6,140	1,080	0	3.2	02
Lionel Cp	28.6	25.0	26.0	7.1n	.56	NE	NE	-66.5	NC	9	10-87	.00	.0	0	0	0	00-00-00	2.2	1.95	4.3	2.16	9.3	45	2.4	58	13,153	4,336	0	1.3	01
Marcade Grp	99.4	99.4	129.5	4.4q	.13	25.0	25.0	NE	NC	0	04-88	.00	.0	0	0	0	00-00-00	2.2	5.59	12.3	.00	NM	654	1.8	31	11,331	1,117	0	23.4	01
Mars Stores	-14.7	-14.7	-4.5	-8.2q	-3.75	NE	NE	NE	NC	0	04-88	.00	.0	0	0	0	00-00-00	-7.9	4.05	-32.0	.00	NM	251	1.5	2	2,180	197	0	0.0	01
Michaels Str	71.6	71.6	51.6	4.9q	.49	-25.0	-25.0	36.1	NC	17	04-88	.00	.0	0	0	0	00-00-00	2.6	3.12	8.1	2.15	17.4	71	3.4	56	9,522	1,725	0	13.1	01
Nichols, SE	3.2	3.2	7.8	-1.3q	-.28	NE	NE	-100.0	NC	-3	04-88	.00	.0	0	0	0	12-31-80	-.4	2.25	-.9	2.78	-2.5	95	2.9	27	4,675	1,506	0	0.0	01
Pace Membership	43.8	43.8	57.9	4.6q	.36	NE	NE	NE	NC	5	04-88	.00	.0	0	0	0	00-00-00	.4	5.00	2.0	2.35	4.7	45	2.1	109	12,850	2,500	-2	0.0	01
Pic 'n Save	18.4	18.4	19.1	47.3q	1.20	.0	.0	16.5	13	25	03-88	.00	.0	0	0	0	06-11-86	12.7	1.56	19.8	1.24	24.6	1	3.7	623	39,580	26,441	0	0.0	12
Pier 1 Imports	21.8	21.8	21.9	17.2q	.55	21.4	21.4	22.2	5	16	05-88	.08	.7	0	12	3	08-04-88	5.0	1.34	6.7	2.78	18.6	104	2.3	356	29,968	9,951	0	18.0	02
Price Co	27.5	25.2	24.6	89.8n	1.83	26.7	29.7	28.0	41	24	05-88	.00	.0	0	0	0	02-04-86	2.3	4.70	10.8	2.19	23.7	52	1.9	1,875	49,020	24,301	-8	0.0	08
Rose's Stores	3.9	3.9	8.7	16.9q	.83	-13.5	-13.5	-32.0	2	6	04-88	.21	2.2	23	34	20	03-07-88	1.3	3.15	4.1	2.12	8.7	47	2.7	195	20,570	2,030	0	0.0	01
Rose's Stores	NA	NA	NA	NA	NA	NA	NA	NA	NA	NC	00-00	.21	2.3	NA	NA	NA	03-07-88	NA	NC	NA	NC	NA	NA	NA	100	11,166	3,355	0	NA	NA
Svc Merchandise	16.9	16.9	8.0	29.3q	.88	NE	NE	NE	NC	9	03-88	.08	.8	-2	11	15	05-17-88	1.0	1.90	1.9	5.05	9.6	203	1.6	333	33,315	13,485	+18	0.0	12
Sharper Image	27.9	27.9	366.6	4.5q	.57	NE	NE	90.0	NC	55	04-88	.00	.0	0	0	0	00-00-00	2.7	5.56	15.0	3.66	54.9	2	1.1	43	7,105	401	0	0.0	01
Spiegel Inc	5.8	5.8	8.3	42.5q	1.03	7.1	7.1	NC	NC	27	03-88	.18	2.0	0	0	0	03-24-88	3.9	1.46	5.7	5.75	32.8	320	3.5	399	45,000	1,978	0	0.0	12
Three D Dp A	NA	NA	NA	NA	NA	NA	NA	NA	NA	NC	00-00	.10	2.9	NA	NA	NA	04-25-88	NA	NA	NA	NC	NA	NA	NA	6	1,710	83	0	NA	NA
Three D Dp B	-11.7	-11.7	-17.0	.8q	.27	62.5	62.5	8.0	-17	4	10-87	.06	1.6	0	27	19	04-25-88	2.4	1.75	4.2	1.31	5.5	0	3.9	8	2,111	190	0	4.4	07
TJX Cos	8.7	8.7	18.7	71.4q	1.39	13.3	13.3	31.1	NC	23	04-88	.50	2.6	0	6	3	08-05-88	4.3	3.28	14.1	2.52	35.5	15	1.9	1,010	53,136	6,949	0	0.3	01
Toys R Us	36.5	36.5	29.7	225.4q	1.62	54.5	54.5	35.0	21	20	04-88	.00	.0	0	0	0	06-30-86	6.8	1.63	11.1	1.79	19.9	16	1.3	4,846	125,068	73,151	+228	5.7	01
Tuesday Morning	13.0	13.0	15.6	3.4q	.85	NE	NE	-15.0	NC	13	03-88	.00	.0	0	0	0	05-18-87	4.6	1.91	8.8	1.51	13.3	31	5.9	31	3,876	832	0	0.0	12
Wal-Mart Strs	-99.9	-99.9	-.1	517.4q	1.18	35.0	35.0	35.6	33	26	04-88	.16	.5	18	5	9	06-13-88	4.1	3.12	12.8	2.39	30.6	56	1.8	17,287	564,474	176,455	+366	3.2	01
Warehouse Club	7.8	6.2	17.4	1.8s	.26	NE	NE	NE	NC	13	03-88	.00	.0	0	0	0	00-00-00	.8	4.00	3.2	4.03	12.9	109	1.0	13	7,051	378	0	0.0	09
Weisfields Inc	15.6	15.6	11.7	1.6q	1.46	350.0	350.0	20.7	-1	5	04-88	.50	2.0	5	38	34	06-27-88	2.8	1.18	3.3	2.27	7.5	12	1.7	27	1,092	296	0	0.0	01
Wholesale Club	39.4	39.4	52.3	.3q	.07	NE	NE	NE	NC	1	04-88	.00	.0	0	0	0	00-00-00	.1	5.00	.5	2.00	1.0	34	2.3	25	4,499	653	0	0.0	01
Woolworth FW	12.4	12.4	9.8	257.0q	3.92	25.6	25.6	12.6	NC	10	04-88	1.64	3.1	7	33	37	04-26-88	3.5	2.57	9.0	1.92	17.3	24	1.9	3,349	64,255	37,273	+2	0.7	01
Zayre Corp	12.0	12.0	13.2	106.2q	1.82	-77.8	-77.8	11.7	15	11	04-88	.40	1.9	42	18	14	08-05-88	1.7	2.88	4.9	2.96	14.5	65	1.8	1,177	56,700	30,913	-0	1.1	01

Trends and Forecasts: Telephone and Telegraph Apparatus (SIC 3661)

(in millions of dollars except as noted)

ITEM	1984	1985	1986[1]	1987[2]	1988[3]	Percent Change: Compound Annual 1972-85	Compound Annual 1980-85	Annual 1985-86	Annual 1986-87	Annual 1987-88
Industry Data										
Value of shipments[4]	15,783	17,775	—	—	—	11.1	7.7	—	—	—
Value of shipments (1982$)	15,183	16,689	—	—	—	5.0	4.7	—	—	—
Total employment (000)	133	131	—	—	—	−0.2	−3.1	—	—	—
Production workers (000)	82.3	75.6	—	—	—	−1.7	−5.6	—	—	—
Average hourly earnings ($)	12.09	12.08	—	—	—	7.6	7.1	—	—	—
Product Data										
Value of shipments[5]	14,481	16,267	—	—	—	11.5	7.8	—	—	—
Value of shipments (1982$)	13,930	15,273	—	—	—	5.4	4.9	—	—	—
Shipments price index[6] (1982 = 100)	104.1	106.6	—	—	—	5.6	2.7	—	—	—
Trade Data										
Value of imports (ITA)[7]	1,817	2,028	2,185	2,320	—	27.5	36.9	7.7	6.2	—
Import/new supply ratio[8]	0.126	—	—	—	—	—	—	—	—	—
Value of exports (ITA)[9]	777	832	850	870	—	20.2	8.4	2.2	2.4	—
Export/shipments ratio	0.061	—	—	—	—	—	—	—	—	—

[1]Estimated except for exports and imports.
[2]Estimated.
[3]Forecast.
[4]Value of all products and services sold by the Telephone and Telegraph Apparatus industry.
[5]Value of products classified in the Telephone and Telegraph Apparatus industry produced by all industries.
[6]Developed by the Office of Industry Assessment, ITA.
[7]Import data are developed by the chapter author.
[8]New supply is the sum of product shipments plus imports.
[9]Export data are developed by the chapter author.
SOURCE: U.S. Department of Commerce: Bureau of the Census, Bureau of Economic Analysis, International Trade Administration (ITA). Estimates and forecasts by ITA.

Source: *U.S. Industrial Outlook 1988,* U.S. Department of Commerce.

Company	Revenue: Pct. Change: Last Qtr	Revenue: Pct. Change: FY to Date	Revenue: Pct. Change: Last 12 Mos	Earnings: Last 12 Mos	Earnings: Per Share: Last 12 Mos	Earnings: Per Share: Pct. Change: Last Qtr	Earnings: Per Share: Pct. Change: FY to Date	Earnings: Per Share: Pct. Change: Last 12 Mos	Earnings: 5-Year Growth Rate	Earnings: Par Growth Rate	Earnings: Date of Report	Dividends: Current Rate: Amt	Dividends: Current Rate: Yield	Dividends: 5-Year Growth Rate	Dividends: Payout: Last FY	Dividends: Payout: Last 5 Yrs.	Dividends: Last X-Dvd Date	Ratio Analysis: Profit Margin	Ratio Analysis: Asset Turnover	Ratio Analysis: Return on Total Assets	Ratio Analysis: Leverage Ratio	Ratio Analysis: Return on Equity	Ratio Analysis: Debt to Equity	Ratio Analysis: Current Ratio	Shareholdings: Market Value	Shareholdings: Latest Shares Outstndng.	Shareholdings: Held by Banks-Funds	Shareholdings: Insider Net Trading	Shareholdings: Short Interest Ratio	Fiscal Year Ends
-	%	%	%	$Mil	$	%	%	%	%	%	-	$	%	%	%	%	-	π/r x	r/a =	π/a x	a/e =	π/e	%	-	$Mil	000	000	000	Days	Mo
Broadcasting																														
Ind. Group	35.6	42.6	11.5	1,026.9	1.10	78.7	67.5	58.5	34	14	- - -	.27	.9	0	18	19	- - - -	6.9	.59	4.1	4.41	18.1	209	1.9	52,048	1,794,792	332,871	+ 105	3.5	- -
Acton Cp □	10.7	10.7	-15.3	7.0q	3.84	-96.8	-96.8	NE	NC	0	03-88	.00	.0	0	0	0	06-26-87	63.6	.47	30.0	.00	NM	0	.3	17	1,183	105	0	0.0	12
Am Comm & TV	-42.9	.0	.0	-2.0f	-.03	NE	NE	NE	NC	0	09-87	.00	.0	0	0	0	00-00-00	-66.7	.37	-24.7	.00	NS	-667	.1	7	76,769	0	0	0.0	09
Am Tel & Com	13.9	13.9	23.0	55.6q	.51	60.0	60.0	59.4	NC	29	03-88	.00	.0	0	0	0	00-00-00	7.5	.61	4.6	6.33	29.1	264	NA	2,750	108,909	16,211	0	0.0	12
Assocd Comm A	25.0	25.0	80.0	28.1q	1.28	NE	NE	NE	NC	85	03-88	.00	.0	0	0	0	04-13-88	NM	NC	NC	NC	84.6	40	4.4	136	6,046	2,207	+19	0.0	12
Assocd Comm B	NA	NA	NA	NA	NA	NA	NA	NA	NA	NC	00-00	.00	.0	NA	NA	NA	04-13-88	NA	NC	NA	NC	NA	NA	NA	143	6,205	1,874	+49	NA	NA
Cablevi Syst	72.8	72.8	93.8	-84.0q	-4.04	NE	NE	NE	NC	0	03-88	.00	.0	0	0	0	00-00-00	-24.3	.50	-12.2	.00	NS	-593	NA	743	21,777	5,096	0	0.3	12
Cap Cities/ABC	34.4	34.4	14.3	325.5q	19.19	190.9	190.9	53.4	16	14	03-88	.20	.1	0	1	2	06-24-88	6.8	.90	6.1	2.39	14.6	76	1.7	5,370	16,900	12,980	+3	22.1	12
CBS Inc □	-4.6	-4.6	-35.5	448.8q	17.55	-10.4	-10.4	2.7	25	31	03-88	3.00	1.9	2	17	31	05-19-88	16.4	.70	11.5	3.25	37.4	80	3.4	3,784	23,630	16,572	0	3.9	12
Century Comm	26.6	74.6	87.0	-9.1n	-.30	NC	-100.0	-100.0	NC	0	02-88	.00	.0	0	0	0	05-19-87	-5.7	.28	-1.6	.00	NM	898	1.0	521	28,939	11,847	0	0.0	05
Chris-Craft	6.4	6.4	6.9	16.7q	.75	NE	NE	17.2	NC	23	03-88	.00	.0	0	0	0	03-25-88	6.8	.28	1.9	12.21	23.2	313	1.3	482	22,159	6,682	-71	3.2	12
Clear Channel	29.0	29.0	30.7	2.1q	.54	-50.0	-50.0	45.9	NC	16	03-88	.00	.0	0	0	0	04-22-88	6.2	.65	4.0	4.00	16.0	290	5.0	57	3,883	349	0	0.0	12
Comcast Cp	38.5	38.5	97.0	-6.2q	-.10	NE	NE	NE	NC	-5	03-88	.12	.7	39	NE	41	05-26-88	-1.8	.33	-.6	4.00	-2.4	238	1.9	834	50,178	27,616	+106	0.0	12
Falcon Cable	19.1	19.1	37.5	.2q	.02	-100.0	-100.0	NE	NC	-75	03-88	2.15	10.3	0	1006	NE	06-24-88	.9	.33	.3	2.33	.7	126	NA	134	6,399	732	0	0.1	12
Finl News Net	52.4	68.5	104.3	2.9s	.23	16.7	11.8	21.1	NC	26	02-88	.00	.0	0	0	0	00-00-00	6.2	2.61	16.2	1.59	25.7	0	1.1	93	12,061	1,445	0	0.0	08
Fst AmeriCable	.0	.0	-50.0	-.1q	.00	NC	NC	-100.0	NC	NC	11-87	.00	.0	0	0	0	00-00-00	-10.0	.14	-1.4	2.00	-2.8	33	.8	14	35,026	0	0	0.0	08
Galaxy Cablvsn	733.3	733.3	85.7	.5q	.27	NE	NE	NE	NC	-6	03-88	1.40	8.5	0	60	NE	06-24-88	3.8	.37	1.4	1.07	1.5	0	NA	35	2,142	0	0	6.4	12
Infinity Broadcast	25.7	25.7	47.1	2.1q	.23	NE	NE	-67.6	NC	10	03-88	.00	.0	0	0	0	00-00-00	2.7	.33	.9	11.11	10.0	919	1.2	248	8,331	2,738	0	0.0	12
Intl Brdcst	14.1	55.8	84.6	-.4s	.35	-59.7	-71.1	-89.9	NC	-3	03-88	.00	.0	0	0	0	00-00-00	-.8	1.50	-1.2	2.58	-3.1	79	1.1	16	1,642	188	0	0.0	09
Jacor Comm	72.0	72.0	81.4	-4.0q	-.44	NE	NE	NE	NC	-19	03-88	.00	.0	0	0	0	00-00-00	-8.2	.38	-3.1	6.19	-19.2	441	3.0	59	9,831	1,501	0	0.0	12
Jones Intercable □	38.7	22.8	25.8	10.8n	.87	820.0	215.8	171.9	29	16	02-88	.00	.0	0	0	0	04-01-85	27.7	.15	4.2	3.83	16.1	253	NA	144	12,252	879	0	0.0	05
Jones Intercable	NA	NA	NA	NA	NA	NA	NA	NA	NA	NC	00-00	.00	.0	NA	NA	NA	04-01-85	NA	NC	NA	NC	NA	NA	NA	90	7,545	4,756	+3	NA	NA
Jones Int Inv	NA	NA	NA	NA	NA	NA	NA	NA	NA	NC	00-00	1.60	10.8	NA	NA	NA	05-25-88	NA	NC	NA	NC	NA	NA	NA	117	7,926	66	0	NA	NA
Jones Spacelink A ◇	13.7	-27.0	8.0	10.5n	.19	550.0	325.0	NC	NC	61	02-88	.00	.0	0	0	0	00-00-00	19.4	.20	3.8	15.97	60.7	0	NA	144	54,770	109	0	0.0	05
Lin Broadcasting	24.1	24.1	25.7	91.3q	1.64	47.1	47.1	32.3	27	25	03-88	.00	.0	0	0	0	04-01-87	36.7	.46	17.0	1.44	24.5	13	3.7	3,301	51,672	38,325	-4	0.0	12
Malrite Com Grp	NA	NA	NA	NA	NA	NA	NA	NA	NA	NC	00-00	.00	.0	NA	NA	NA	00-00-00	NA	NC	NA	NC	NA	NA	NA	35	4,231	1,038	0	NA	NA
Malrite Commun	16.4	16.4	31.5	-6.1q	-.73	NE	NE	NE	NC	-16	03-88	.00	.0	0	NE	3	00-00-00	-5.0	.44	-2.2	7.18	-15.8	484	1.0	119	13,628	651	0	0.0	12
Midwest Comm	27.0	19.9	21.1	1.2n	.40	-66.7	-45.5	NC	NC	10	03-88	.00	.0	0	0	0	00-00-00	1.1	2.64	2.9	3.34	9.7	13	1.4	14	2,986	771	0	0.0	06
Park Commun	12.1	12.1	9.2	18.1q	1.31	46.7	46.7	20.2	10	12	03-88	.00	.0	0	0	0	09-03-85	11.8	.62	7.3	1.67	12.2	42	2.8	397	13,800	1,247	0	0.0	12
Price Comm	-8.6	9.6	9.2	-14.0f	-1.19	NE	NE	NE	NC	0	12-87	.00	.0	0	0	0	01-20-88	-13.2	.30	-4.0	.00	NS	-376	2.2	87	9,681	2,000	0	44.5	12
QVC Network	240.2	240.2	1058.3	2.5q	.21	NE	NE	NE	NC	11	04-88	.00	.0	0	0	0	00-00-00	1.8	3.11	5.6	1.93	10.8	29	1.3	91	10,117	496	0	0.0	01
Reuters Hldg	114.4	77.9	77.8	207.1f	1.48	104.5	70.1	70.1	NC	55	12-87	.44	1.5	0	24	23	03-25-88	12.6	2.20	27.7	2.80	77.6	0	1.0	23,767	830,296	32,306	0	0.0	12
Satellite Netwk	-22.2	-22.2	27.2	-.5q	-.06	NE	NE	NE	NC	-7	03-88	.00	.0	0	0	0	00-00-00	-3.6	1.23	-4.6	1.41	-6.5	1	2.9	48	8,964	360	0	0.0	12
Scripps Howard	20.6	20.6	12.9	-8.0q	-.78	-95.7	-95.7	-100.0	NC	-13	03-88	.80	1.0	0	65	49	05-23-88	-3.3	.42	-1.4	4.43	-6.2	221	1.2	857	10,328	1,049	0	0.0	12

Continued

Company	Revenue: Pct. Change Last Qtr	Revenue: Pct. Change FY to Date	Revenue: Pct. Change Last 12 Mos	Earnings: Last 12 Mos	Earnings: Per Share Last 12 Mos	Per Share Pct. Change Last Qtr	Per Share Pct. Change FY to Date	Per Share Pct. Change Last 12 Mos	5-Year Growth Rate	Par Growth Rate	Date of Report	Dividends: Current Rate Amt	Current Rate Yield	5-Year Growth Rate	Payout Last FY	Payout Last 5 Yrs.	Last X-Dvd Date	Ratio Analysis: Profit Margin	Asset Turnover	Return on Total Assets	Leverage Ratio	Return on Equity	Debt to Equity	Current Ratio	Shareholdings: Market Value	Latest Shares Outstndng.	Held by Banks-Funds	Insider Net Trading	Short Interest Ratio	Fiscal Year Ends
-	%	%	%	$Mil	$	%	%	%	%	%	-	$	%	%	%	%	-	π/r	x r/a =	π/a	x a/e =	π/e	%	-	$Mil	000	000	000	Days	Mo
Broadcasting (Continued)																														
TCA Cable TV	13.3	14.5	20.3	6.6s	.56	41.7	43.5	9.8	7	5	04-88	.32	.9	30	52	29	04-05-88	10.2	.47	4.8	2.56	12.3	140	NA	413	12,059	3,383	0	0.0	10
Tele Commun A ◇	144.1	146.9	80.9	84.0s	.52	-54.5	-25.7	26.8	45	12	06-87	.00	.0	0	0	0	08-03-87	7.6	.28	2.1	5.57	11.7	401	NA	3,656	146,972	96,631	0	0.0	12
Telecrafter	60.9	97.8	55.5	.5s	.08	-100.0	100.0	NE	NC	6	02-88	.00	.0	0	0	0	00-00-00	3.6	.83	3.0	1.90	5.7	48	2.4	41	7,451	53	0	0.0	08
Telemundo Grp	39.3	39.3	500.0	-40.4q	-4.81	NE	NE	NC	NC	-80	03-88	.00	.0	0	0	0	00-00-00	-44.9	.24	-10.8	7.44	-80.3	479	1.0	119	13,643	9,836	0	0.0	12
Turner Bdct B	NA	NA	NA	NA	NA	NA	NA	NA	NA	NC	00-00	.00	.0	NA	NA	NA	00-00-00	NA	NC	NA	NC	NA	NA	NA	324	21,775	1,790	0	NA	NA
Turner Bdct A	25.2	25.2	12.9	-105.6q	-3.65	NE	NE	NE	NC	0	03-88	.00	.0	0	0	0	07-13-81	-15.4	.37	-5.7	.00	NS	-525	1.5	305	21,775	1,992	0	39.1	12
TVX Broadcast Grp	670.2	438.3	276.4	-19.7s	-3.36	NE	NE	NE	NC	0	06-87	.00	.0	0	0	0	00-00-00	-30.8	.61	-18.7	.00	NM	1285	.9	15	5,949	718	0	0.0	12
Utd Cable TV	18.4	17.7	16.7	-2.7n	-.07	NE	NE	NE	NC	-9	02-88	.06	.2	5	NE	NE	06-27-88	-1.1	.45	-.5	9.80	-4.9	798	NA	1,267	37,275	17,752	0	9.9	05
Utd Television	14.7	14.7	10.0	7.6q	.70	NE	NE	9.4	NC	14	03-88	.00	.0	0	0	0	00-00-00	7.7	.52	4.0	3.50	14.0	94	1.1	349	10,963	3,504	0	0.0	12
Viacom Inc	NA	NA	NA	NA	NA	NA	NA	NA	NA	NC	00-00	.00	.0	NA	NA	NA	00-00-00	NA	NC	NA	NC	NA	NA	NA	904	36,724	5,016	0	NA	NA
Telephone Utility																														
Ind. Group	9.4	9.8	7.1	16,332.3	2.63	12.1	14.4	24.6	29	4	- - -	1.88	5.3	0	61	57	- - - -	9.2	.58	5.3	2.70	14.3	68	1.1	216,948	6,130,344	G	+ 115	1.2	- -
ACC Corp	15.3	15.3	6.0	.8q	.22	NE	NE	37.5	NC	9	03-88	.00	.0	0	0	0	00-00-00	2.3	1.39	3.2	2.78	8.9	78	1.0	10	3,448	26	0	0.0	12
ADC Telecomm	4.9	16.5	18.4	17.8s	1.37	15.4	42.2	48.9	76	24	04-88	.00	.0	0	0	0	10-28-87	9.9	1.72	17.0	1.38	23.5	4	3.2	210	13,035	5,467	0	0.0	10
Adv Telecom	-20.0	23.1	23.8	9.5f	1.18	-3.1	35.6	35.6	NC	26	03-88	.00	.0	0	0	0	00-00-00	11.4	1.39	15.8	1.66	26.2	26	2.1	143	7,855	2,194	0	0.0	03
Advantage Cos	146.2	146.2	150.0	.4q	.12	300.0	300.0	NE	NC	5	03-88	.00	.0	0	0	0	00-00-00	2.0	.85	1.7	3.12	5.3	134	1.1	17	4,088	0	0	0.0	12
AIM Telephone □	2.8	18.5	20.0	.7f	.15	-100.0	-44.4	-44.4	NC	11	02-88	.00	.0	0	0	0	00-00-00	2.3	1.61	3.7	3.05	11.3	77	1.9	20	3,705	47	0	0.0	02
ALC Comm	-3.3	-3.3	-10.3	-8.5q	-1.01	-100.0	-100.0	NE	NC	0	03-88	.00	.0	0	0	0	00-00-00	-2.2	1.91	-4.2	.00	NS	-245	.7	28	13,613	1,579	0	0.0	12
ALLTEL Cp	14.2	14.2	8.0	109.2q	3.21	21.9	21.9	89.9	8	10	03-88	1.52	4.3	4	44	58	06-10-88	14.3	.45	6.5	2.94	19.1	97	.8	1,171	33,092	7,299	-9	0.7	12
Am Tel & T	2.8	2.8	.9	2091.0q	1.94	15.0	15.0	1285.7	NC	6	03-88	1.20	4.5	0	64	124	06-24-88	6.2	.87	5.4	2.69	14.5	50	1.4	28,721	1,073,692	236,093	+1	2.7	12
Ameritech Cp	5.0	5.0	2.9	1194.2q	8.59	5.9	5.9	8.1	NC	6	03-88	5.40	5.9	0	59	56	06-24-88	12.4	.52	6.4	2.45	15.7	58	.7	12,468	137,006	43,722	+1	4.4	12
Artel Comm Cp	25.0	25.0	25.0	-1.7q	-.50	NE	NE	NE	NC	-40	03-88	.00	.0	0	0	0	00-00-00	-34.0	.93	-31.5	1.25	-39.5	0	4.1	10	3,533	149	0	0.0	12
BCE Inc	3.3	3.3	3.8	1092.0q	3.90	-1.1	-1.1	2.6	4	5	03-88	2.44	NA	4	61	58	06-09-88	7.4	.57	4.2	2.88	12.1	79	1.0	8,555	278,200	0	0	0.0	12
Bell Atlantic	1.4	1.4	3.0	1262.0q	6.36	7.8	7.8	7.1	NC	5	03-88	4.08	5.7	0	61	58	06-24-88	12.2	.48	5.9	2.44	14.4	59	.9	14,244	198,176	64,633	+0	6.6	12
BellSouth	19.2	19.2	10.8	1623.9q	3.37	-9.6	-9.6	-1.2	NC	4	03-88	2.36	5.5	0	62	57	04-05-88	12.7	.46	5.9	2.31	13.6	53	1.0	20,695	481,269	128,259	+5	6.9	12
Brit Telecom	36.0	28.1	28.3	2618.4n	4.21	43.9	35.0	38.0	NC	12	12-87	1.94	4.4	0	41	34	07-29-88	14.3	.73	10.4	2.22	23.1	42	.9	26,595	601,025	2,975	0	0.0	03
C TEC	NA	NA	NA	NA	NA	NA	NA	NA	NA	NC	00-00	.00	.0	NA	NA	NA	00-00-00	NA	NC	NA	NC	NA	NA	NA	107	3,112	132	0	NA	NA
CTEC Cp	4.2	4.2	7.1	13.1q	2.38	-18.6	-18.6	30.8	9	10	03-88	.92	2.6	9	37	44	05-03-88	9.7	.48	4.7	3.34	15.7	124	1.5	193	5,541	466	0	0.0	12
Cellular Comm □	146.8	146.8	281.8	-17.0q	-.94	NE	NE	NE	NC	-34	03-88	.00	.0	0	0	0	10-07-87	-40.5	.19	-7.5	4.56	-34.2	270	2.4	568	20,467	12,179	0	0.0	12
Centel Cp	7.2	7.2	8.1	158.6q	3.63	5.6	5.6	41.2	5	8	03-88	1.72	3.7	3	47	53	07-01-88	10.6	.50	5.3	2.91	15.4	86	1.1	2,011	43,357	19,418	+11	0.2	12
Centex Telemgmt	104.8	104.8	133.3	-.3q	-.05	NE	NE	NC	NC	-2	03-88	.00	.0	0	0	0	00-00-00	-.7	1.71	-1.2	1.42	-1.7	1	3.1	122	8,748	2,150	0	0.0	12
Century Tel	13.5	13.5	9.4	24.0q	2.01	13.2	13.2	33.1	9	9	03-88	.88	2.5	3	44	55	05-31-88	14.8	.34	5.1	3.25	16.6	126	.8	404	11,407	4,665	-6	0.1	12
Checkpoint Sys	22.7	22.7	5.7	1.1q	.11	NE	NE	-78.8	NC	5	03-88	.00	.0	0	0	0	05-28-86	3.0	1.10	3.3	1.42	4.7	12	3.0	75	8,725	2,678	0	0.0	12
Cinn Bell	19.9	19.9	29.2	68.3q	2.15	28.0	28.0	17.5	12	7	03-88	1.12	3.7	7	47	50	06-29-88	10.3	.58	6.0	2.53	15.2	71	1.1	949	31,496	8,145	+2	0.1	12

Comcoa Inc ◻	85.2	85.2	112.5	.3q	.01	33.3	33.3	NE	NC	14	04-88	.00	.0	0	0	0	00-00-00	1.8	1.72	3.1	4.61	14.3	214	.7	53	3,753	75	0	0.0	01
Comm Transmiss	16.1	21.0	54.1	5.2n	.21	-33.3	125.0	NC	NC	0	02-88	.00	.0	0	0	0	00-00-00	7.0	.36	2.5	.00	NM	2183	.2	69	10,653	1,358	0	0.0	05
Contel Cp	9.6	9.6	-2.7	46.9q	.59	5.6	5.6	-81.0	-19	-8	03-88	2.08	6.0	5	358	75	05-10-88	1.6	.56	.9	3.67	3.3	129	.6	2,697	78,188	40,853	+13	2.1	12
Digital Microwave	61.1	93.6	95.0	7.1f	.60	100.0	150.0	150.0	NC	91	03-88	.00	.0	0	0	0	00-00-00	18.2	2.87	52.2	1.74	91.0	14	2.5	186	11,266	1,516	-30	0.0	03
Eagle Telephonics	-57.5	-57.5	-26.3	.5q	.02	-100.0	-100.0	-83.3	NC	5	01-88	.00	.0	0	0	0	00-00-00	1.8	1.11	2.0	2.30	4.6	6	3.6	10	15,240	215	0	0.0	10
Elcotel Inc	122.2	135.5	136.3	2.2f	.39	-100.0	-22.0	-22.0	NC	26	03-88	.00	.0	0	0	0	05-15-87	8.5	2.31	19.6	1.32	25.9	0	3.6	25	5,387	369	0	0.0	03
Ericsson LM Tel	-17.4	-1.7	36.5	62.5n	1.82	-100.0	-42.0	NC	NC	6	09-87	.00	.0	0	41	41	00-00-00	1.3	.92	1.2	4.83	5.8	38	1.9	1,597	41,891	3,440	0	0.0	12
Graphic Scanning ◇	7.7	-1.5	4.5	42.5n	1.21	NE	4.7	75.4	NC	89	03-88	.00	.0	0	0	0	11-01-83	37.3	.56	21.0	4.24	89.1	179	1.4	284	36,051	9,848	0	0.0	06
GTE Cp	6.7	6.7	2.7	1140.4q	3.35	7.7	7.7	-2.9	NC	4	03-88	2.52	6.4	8	75	89	05-17-88	7.3	.58	4.2	3.55	14.9	116	.9	12,737	325,550	163,792	0	1.1	12
Inter Tel	25.1	63.3	.0	.0*	.23	NE	133.3	360.0	NC	0	03-88	.00	.0	0	0	0	08-17-81	NC	NC	NC	NC	.0	47	1.6	27	7,907	162	0	0.0	12
Intl Mobile Mach	100.0	100.0	50.0	-12.5q	-1.20	NE	NE	NE	NC	-60	03-88	.00	.0	0	0	0	00-00-00	NM	NC	NC	NC	-59.8	1	4.1	94	11,745	769	-5	0.0	12
Intl Telechrg	1461.9	1461.9	2133.3	2.2q	.12	NE	NE	NE	NC	13	03-88	.00	.0	0	0	0	00-00-00	3.3	1.48	4.9	2.59	12.7	88	2.0	160	14,357	257	-6	17.2	12
Linc Telecom	9.3	9.3	6.7	23.6q	2.66	44.9	44.9	17.2	10	8	03-88	1.36	4.1	3	46	54	06-24-88	13.6	.60	8.2	2.05	16.8	44	NA	286	8,668	2,359	0	0.0	12
MCI Communicatn	18.4	18.4	10.3	119.0q	.42	171.4	171.4	NE	NC	9	03-88	.00	.0	0	0	0	08-22-83	2.9	.79	2.3	4.09	9.4	212	1.2	4,001	285,795	128,816	+12	0.0	12
Millicom Inc ◇	777.8	777.8	-80.1	-5.2q	-.66	-100.0	-100.0	-100.0	NC	-7	03-88	.00	.0	0	0	0	00-00-00	-23.6	.14	-3.4	2.00	-6.8	25	5.4	152	7,491	574	0	0.0	12
NW Telecom	4.3	4.3	41.6	3.1q	.97	-29.5	-29.5	-12.6	12	4	03-88	.66	2.8	7	54	61	07-06-88	6.1	.43	2.6	5.00	13.0	250	1.1	76	3,220	273	0	0.0	12
NYNEX Cp	6.2	6.2	6.0	1288.4q	6.34	5.4	5.4	-5.9	NC	5	03-88	4.04	6.1	0	59	55	06-24-88	10.5	.54	5.7	2.46	14.0	66	1.3	13,611	203,915	66,337	+12	4.0	12
Pac Telecom	4.7	4.7	7.7	51.3q	1.33	94.4	94.4	19.8	-6	3	03-88	.96	6.7	8	76	69	05-16-88	9.7	.45	4.4	2.68	11.8	75	.9	546	38,328	2,305	0	0.0	12
Pac Telesis	8.2	8.2	4.6	1016.0q	2.37	29.1	29.1	-2.1	NC	3	03-88	1.76	5.9	0	73	61	04-04-88	10.9	.44	4.8	2.69	12.9	67	.8	12,909	432,100	180,761	+0	4.4	12
Philipp LD Tel	5.5	7.9	7.7	65.6f	.64	-55.3	-66.8	-66.8	32	26	12-87	.15	1.7	-19	11	14	03-09-88	20.6	.34	7.1	4.86	34.5	261	1.0	393	43,721	2,776	0	0.1	12
Phonemate Inc	-1.3	-1.3	10.8	.7q	.25	-100.0	-100.0	-3.8	NC	70	03-88	.00	.0	0	0	0	00-00-00	.6	2.00	1.2	58.33	70.0	450	1.1	7	2,172	0	0	0.0	12
Roch Tele	-.5	-.5	-28.6	38.2q	3.39	23.5	23.5	-4.2	0	2	03-88	2.72	5.8	5	83	63	07-26-88	13.1	.35	4.6	2.67	12.3	82	1.1	506	10,878	3,564	+0	0.0	12
So N Eng Tel	3.6	3.6	2.4	140.9q	4.56	1.7	1.7	.4	6	4	03-88	3.00	5.8	4	63	65	06-14-88	9.5	.54	5.1	2.55	13.0	60	.7	1,610	30,966	7,911	0	0.4	12
SouthernNet Inc	97.8	97.8	73.8	9.2q	.72	200.0	200.0	NE	NC	19	03-88	.00	.0	0	0	0	00-00-00	4.2	2.60	10.9	1.75	19.1	27	.7	255	13,763	1,034	0	0.0	12
Swtrn Bell	6.6	6.6	3.3	1028.1q	3.42	-7.6	-7.6	-1.2	NC	4	03-88	2.48	6.3	0	65	58	07-01-88	12.7	.40	5.1	2.59	13.2	63	.9	11,893	300,127	116,162	+78	3.8	12
Teleconnect	NA	NA	NA	NA	NA	NA	NA	NA	NA	NC	00-00	.00	.0	NA	NA	NA	00-00-00	NA	NC	NA	NC	NA	NA	NA	181	12,097	0	0	NA	NA
Telefonica	NA	NA	NA	NA	NA	NA	NA	NA	NA	NC	00-00	1.50	5.9	NA	NA	NA	06-28-88	NA	NC	NA	NC	NA	NA	NA	20,465	802,562	16,132	0	NA	NA
Telephone Data	13.1	13.1	11.1	11.9q	.73	-29.4	-29.4	-25.5	7	4	03-88	.36	1.2	10	44	42	06-06-88	6.6	.36	2.4	3.63	8.7	160	.9	466	15,084	7,457	-0	3.1	12
TeleQuest	-76.1	-76.1	-53.5	-7.5q	-1.98	NE	NE	NE	NC	0	03-88	.00	.0	0	0	0	00-00-00	-57.7	1.17	-67.6	.00	NM	2	2.2	3	3,801	282	0	0.0	12
TIE Comm	-1.6	-1.6	-10.7	-11.1q	-.36	NE	NE	NE	NC	-8	03-88	.00	.0	0	0	0	07-19-83	-4.5	.84	-3.8	2.11	-8.0	6	2.4	86	34,470	4,657	+0	1.2	12
TPI Enterprises	42.9	42.9	33.3	-5.8q	-.20	NE	NE	NE	NC	-3	03-88	.00	.0	0	0	0	08-01-83	NM	NC	NC	NC	-3.4	0	4.2	136	25,979	3,267	0	0.0	12
US West	5.6	5.6	2.8	1041.8q	5.53	20.4	20.4	10.8	NC	5	03-88	3.52	6.2	0	61	56	04-14-88	12.2	.45	5.5	2.55	14.0	66	.9	10,462	185,579	70,973	+16	3.9	12
US Cellular	NA	NA	NA	NA	NA	NA	NA	NA	NA	NC	00-00	.00	.0	NA	NA	NA	00-00-00	NA	NC	NA	NC	NA	NA	NA	406	20,407	0	0	NA	NA
Utd Telcom	31.8	31.8	33.9	-30.5q	-.31	153.8	153.8	-100.0	NC	-13	03-88	1.92	6.0	2	NE	141	06-06-88	-1.0	.50	-.5	3.60	-1.8	156	1.1	3,243	100,547	51,922	0	2.9	12
Vicom Inc	-23.5	-23.5	.0	-.2q	-.10	NE	NE	NE	NC	-7	03-87	.00	.0	0	0	0	00-00-00	-2.9	.55	-1.6	4.44	-7.1	289	NA	1	2,096	0	+20	0.0	12

Trends and Forecasts: Textile Mill Products (SIC 22)

(in millions of dollars except as noted)

ITEM	1984	1985	1986[1]	1987[2]	Percent Change: Compound Annual 1972-85	Percent Change: Compound Annual 1980-85	Percent Change: Annual 1985-86	Percent Change: Annual 1986-87
Industry Data								
Value of shipments[3]	55,489	53,276	55,247	57,456	5.1	2.5	3.7	4.0
Value of shipments (1982$)	53,177	51,333	52,969	54,306	0.2	−0.3	3.2	2.5
Total employment (000)	710	658	661	683	−2.8	−4.2	0.5	3.3
Production workers (000)	611	565	569	590	−3.0	−4.3	0.7	3.7
Average hourly earnings ($)	6.56	6.91	7.14	7.40	7.3	5.9	3.3	3.6
Product Data								
Value of shipments[4]	52,258	50,132	52,087	54,051	5.2	2.3	3.9	3.8
Value of shipments (1982$)	50,052	48,270	49,892	51,040	0.4	−0.5	3.4	2.3
Shipments price index[5] (1982=100)	104.8	104.4	—	—	4.7	2.8	—	—
Trade Data								
Value of imports	3,539	3,697	4,225	4,630	8.1	12.7	14.3	9.6
Value of exports	1,541	1,462	1,653	1,898	7.1	−10.1	13.1	14.8

[1]Estimated except for exports and imports.
[2]Estimated.
[3]Value of all products and services sold by the Textile Mill Products industry.
[4]Value of products classified in the Textile Mill Products industry produced by all industries.
[5]Developed by the Office of Industry Assessment, ITA.

SOURCE: U.S. Department of Commerce: Bureau of the Census, Bureau of Economic Analysis, International Trade Administration (ITA). Estimates and forecasts by ITA.

Source: *U.S. Industrial Outlook 1988,* U.S. Department of Commerce.

Company	Revenue: Pct. Change Last Qtr	Revenue: Pct. Change FY to Date	Revenue: Pct. Change Last 12 Mos	Earnings: Last 12 Mos	Earnings: Per Share Last 12 Mos	Earnings: Per Share Pct. Change Last Qtr	Earnings: Per Share Pct. Change FY to Date	Earnings: Per Share Pct. Change Last 12 Mos	Earnings: 5-Year Growth Rate	Earnings: Par Growth Rate	Earnings: Date of Report	Dividends: Current Rate Amt	Dividends: Current Rate Yield	Dividends: 5-Year Growth Rate	Dividends: Payout Last FY	Dividends: Payout Last 5 Yrs.	Dividends: Last X-Dvd Date	Ratio Analysis: Profit Margin	Ratio Analysis: Asset Turnover	Ratio Analysis: Return on Total Assets	Ratio Analysis: Leverage Ratio	Ratio Analysis: Return on Equity	Ratio Analysis: Debt to Equity	Ratio Analysis: Current Ratio	Shareholdings: Market Value	Shareholdings: Latest Shares Outstndng.	Shareholdings: Held by Banks-Funds	Shareholdings: Insider Net Trading	Shareholdings: Short Interest Ratio	Shareholdings: Fiscal Year Ends
-	%	%	%	$Mil	$	%	%	%	%	%	-	$	%	%	%	%	-	π/r	x r/a =	π/a	x a/e =	π/e	%	-	$Mil	000	000	000	Days	Mo
Textile Mills																														
Ind. Group	- 1.9	.9	7.4	735.1	1.05	2.8	- 1.3	3.7	13	9	- - -	.37	2.6	1	24	29	- - - -	3.9	1.51	5.9	2.27	13.4	54	2.4	9,824	702,643	143,491	+ 18	1.3	- -
Adams-Millis	8.7	8.7	3.5	5.8q	1.22	-18.2	-18.2	-9.0	19	8	03-88	.24	1.5	19	19	16	05-11-88	2.9	1.62	4.7	2.17	10.2	64	2.9	73	4,689	3,028	0	0.3	12
Aileen Inc	9.0	7.4	12.5	-5.3s	-1.03	1000.0	NE	NE	NC	-23	04-88	.00	.0	0	0	0	00-00-00	-9.8	1.65	-16.2	1.43	-23.1	3	2.1	17	5,148	676	0	0.0	10
Alba-Waldens	-5.7	-5.7	4.3	-.7q	-.34	-66.7	-66.7	-100.0	NC	-3	03-88	.00	.0	0	0	28	09-07-84	-1.5	1.33	-2.0	1.55	-3.1	7	2.5	14	1,862	392	0	0.0	12
Bayly Cp	-40.3	-38.4	-23.8	-20.0s	-8.41	-100.0	-100.0	-100.0	NC	0	04-88	.12	4.2	0	NE	NE	09-09-87	-13.3	1.89	-25.2	.00	NM	370	1.3	7	2,276	347	0	0.0	10
Belding Hemin	9.1	9.1	19.0	5.7q	2.52	85.7	85.7	60.5	13	10	03-88	.62	1.6	2	18	23	05-25-88	3.8	1.61	6.1	2.25	13.7	75	4.0	87	2,251	466	0	1.6	12
Burke Mills □	3.8	3.8	5.0	.3q	.12	150.0	150.0	-40.0	-11	4	03-88	.00	.0	0	0	0	00-00-00	1.4	1.86	2.6	1.35	3.5	12	4.4	4	2,741	0	0	0.0	12
Concord Fab B	NA	NA	NA	NA	NA	NA	NA	NA	NA	NC	00-00	.00	.0	NA	NA	NA	00-00-00	NA	NC	NA	NC	NA	NA	NA	6	1,783	0	0	NA	NA
Courtaulds Ltd	3.7	3.7	4.0	231.8s	.63	6.7	6.7	12.5	33	14	09-87	.23	3.8	17	18	22	06-15-88	6.3	1.48	9.3	2.37	22.0	29	1.7	2,276	379,400	683	0	0.0	03
Crown Crafts	37.0	34.2	33.3	5.4f	1.74	61.5	91.2	91.2	NC	50	03-88	.00	.0	0	0	0	09-15-87	7.5	2.84	21.3	2.35	50.0	51	2.5	43	3,104	176	0	5.9	03
CrownAmerica □	7.9	14.4	12.7	.9s	.76	650.0	17.2	-29.6	NC	3	02-88	.40	4.6	27	62	34	04-04-88	.9	2.44	2.2	2.59	5.7	43	1.5	10	1,150	9	0	0.0	08
Culp Inc ◇	-9.6	-3.9	-3.8	2.7f	.61	-89.7	-48.3	-48.3	-7	6	04-88	.08	1.0	0	13	7	07-06-88	1.6	1.69	2.7	2.37	6.4	77	3.1	34	4,426	1,098	+4	0.0	04
Damon Creat	-16.3	-16.3	-17.9	-3.4q	-3.03	NE	NE	NE	NC	-32	03-88	.00	.0	0	0	0	00-00-00	-10.6	1.62	-17.2	1.85	-31.8	14	2.2	6	1,100	0	0	0.0	12
Delta Woodside	11.7	14.0	33.7	25.3n	1.46	10.8	15.6	35.2	NC	44	03-88	.00	.0	0	0	0	00-00-00	5.5	3.11	17.1	2.54	43.5	67	2.1	200	17,395	1,391	0	0.0	06
Dixie Yarns	80.9	80.9	100.9	29.4q	2.54	28.6	28.6	8.5	NC	11	03-88	.58	3.1	0	21	30	02-23-88	4.5	1.84	8.3	1.72	14.3	36	2.6	218	11,806	4,320	0	0.0	12
Fab Indus	15.2	15.2	18.3	9.9q	2.76	-26.1	-26.1	-7.1	9	9	02-88	.60	2.1	16	20	17	12-08-87	7.0	1.20	8.4	1.36	11.4	1	4.5	104	3,632	1,437	0	0.0	11
Fieldcrest Mill	2.6	2.6	19.5	-8.4q	-.82	-100.0	-100.0	-100.0	NC	-6	03-88	.68	3.6	-11	NE	67	06-14-88	-.6	1.67	-1.0	3.20	-3.2	160	3.4	193	10,216	3,765	+0	3.3	12
Goldtex Inc	-33.3	-6.4	27.2	.7n	.32	115.4	-68.3	NC	NC	32	04-88	.00	.0	0	0	0	00-00-00	2.5	2.84	7.1	4.48	31.8	209	1.1	8	2,227	629	0	0.0	07
Guilford Mills	.6	5.8	11.7	25.5n	2.48	13.2	19.7	18.1	5	9	03-88	.80	3.3	11	27	24	04-29-88	4.5	1.49	6.7	2.00	13.4	57	4.1	254	10,536	5,098	0	9.1	06
Hancock Fab	2.0	2.0	2.0	21.1q	1.55	5.4	5.4	4.0	NC	18	04-88	.40	2.2	0	20	10	06-14-88	7.8	1.79	12.5	1.90	23.7	47	4.1	235	12,860	7,948	0	0.0	01
Quaker Fabric	-17.1	-17.1	-5.6	.8q	.86	-100.0	-100.0	-44.5	NC	6	05-88	.00	.0	0	0	10	10-30-84	.8	2.25	1.8	3.11	5.6	122	2.6	13	1,730	340	0	1.5	02
Ruddick Corp	23.3	9.0	9.2	16.8s	1.73	35.3	36.5	13.8	4	10	03-88	.45	2.1	0	30	25	06-06-88	1.7	3.24	5.5	2.35	12.9	46	1.6	198	9,336	1,441	+1	4.0	09
Russell Cp	8.2	8.2	8.9	47.9q	1.22	20.8	20.8	14.0	15	14	03-88	.24	1.4	7	16	18	05-02-88	9.8	1.10	10.8	1.58	17.1	26	3.9	660	39,092	13,125	+19	2.1	12
Savoy Ind	42.2	56.3	42.1	-6.6n	-.67	NE	NE	NE	NC	0	09-87	.00	.0	0	0	0	00-00-00	-8.1	1.46	-11.8	.00	NM	655	1.9	1	9,873	103	0	0.0	12
Springs Indus	12.0	12.0	12.6	57.1q	3.21	15.7	15.7	55.1	5	8	03-88	1.00	3.1	-4	26	37	06-06-88	3.3	1.61	5.3	2.13	11.3	51	3.0	576	17,737	4,114	0	1.7	12
Stanley Interiors	15.4	15.4	13.6	2.4q	.58	100.0	100.0	-32.6	NC	8	03-88	.00	.0	0	0	0	00-00-00	1.3	1.46	1.9	3.95	7.5	188	2.6	33	4,013	735	0	0.0	12
Stanwood Cp	-27.6	-27.6	-16.5	-4.1q	-2.61	17.9	17.9	NE	NC	-17	03-88	.00	.0	0	0	0	00-00-00	-4.1	1.32	-5.4	3.06	-16.5	150	5.5	11	1,563	265	0	0.1	12
Stevens JP	-63.6	-63.6	-16.3	56.9q	3.41	17.1	17.1	8.9	NC	8	01-88	.95	1.4	0	36	78	05-25-88	4.1	1.44	5.9	1.93	11.4	33	3.1	1,066	15,595	8,403	0	0.7	10
Texfi Ind	-44.2	-25.1	-17.7	5.0s	.55	-38.7	-7.5	31.0	NC	24	04-88	.00	.0	0	0	0	07-24-87	3.7	2.05	7.6	3.13	23.8	112	1.8	51	8,064	1,625	-7	8.3	10
Unifi Inc	13.9	6.7	2.1	23.2n	2.19	50.0	152.2	151.7	10	26	03-88	.00	.0	0	0	0	02-24-86	8.0	1.98	15.8	1.65	26.1	33	3.2	224	9,542	8,150	0	0.0	06
Utd Mer Mfrs	-8.7	-13.2	-8.6	-46.3n	-5.08	NE	-100.0	NE	NC	-46	03-88	.00	.0	0	0	0	00-00-00	-6.8	1.25	-8.5	5.42	-46.1	330	3.2	36	9,101	5,583	0	1.3	06
V.F. Corp	2.5	2.5	43.0	179.5q	2.64	12.5	12.5	24.5	10	15	03-88	.84	2.8	17	29	28	06-06-88	6.9	1.42	9.8	2.22	21.8	53	2.1	2,004	67,940	49,275	0	1.3	12
West Point-P	-7.7	-5.7	-19.4	75.8s	2.47	-3.8	7.2	5.6	0	5	02-88	1.20	3.2	0	36	43	05-19-88	4.6	1.04	4.8	2.00	9.6	39	2.7	1,157	30,455	18,869	0	0.3	08

Financial Statement Ratios by Industry

Many quantitative indicators are used to assess the financial strength of an enterprise and the success of its operations. The simplest is to assemble related financial items, such as sales and profits, and express the relationship in the form of a ratio. Using these ratios, various aspects of corporate operations may be compared with the performance of other corporations or groups of corporations of similar size or in a similar industry.

The Quarterly Financial Report's (QFR) ratio formatted income statement and selected balance sheet ratios are expressed as a percent of net sales and total assets, respectively. The operating and financial characteristics of the respective industries and asset size groups are thus reduced to a common denominator to facilitate analysis.

The ratio tables include the following additional basic operating ratios:

1. *Annual rate of profit on stockholders' equity at end of the period.* This ratio is obtained by multiplying income for the quarter before or after domestic taxes [including branch income (loss) and equity in the earnings of nonconsolidated subsidiaries net of foreign taxes] by four, to put it on an annual basis, and then dividing by stockholders' equity at the end of the quarter. It measures the rate of return which accrues to stockholders on their investment.

2. *Annual rate of profit on total assets.* This ratio is obtained by multiplying income, as defined in deriving the rate of profit on stockholders' equity, both before and after taxes, by four and then dividing by total assets at the end of the quarter. This ratio measures the productivity of assets in terms of producing income.

3. *Total current assets to total current liabilities.* This ratio is obtained by dividing total current assets by total current liabilities. It measures the ability to discharge current maturing obligations from existing current assets.

4. *Total cash, U.S. government and other securities to current liabilities.* This ratio is obtained by dividing total cash, U.S. government and other securities by total current liabilities. It measures the ability to discharge current liabilities from liquid assets.

5. *Total stockholders' equity to total debt.* This ratio is obtained by dividing total stockholders' equity by the total of short-term loans, current installments on long-term debt, and long-term debt due in more than one year. It indicates the extent of leverage financing used.

DESCRIPTION OF THE SAMPLE

The frame from which the major portion of the sample continues to be selected consists of the Internal Revenue Service (IRS) file of those corporate entities which are required to file Form 1120 or 1120S and which also have as their principal industrial activity manufacturing, mining, or wholesale or retail trade. The IRS file is sampled once each year. At the time the sample is selected, the file does not contain those corporate entities whose first income tax return has not been processed. In addition, several months elapse between the selection of this sample and its introduction into the QFR program. To keep the QFR sample of corporations with assets over $25 million as up to date as possible, a separate sample is drawn each calendar quarter from a frame comprising applications for a Federal Social Security Employer's Identification Number filed with the Social Security Administration (SSA) during the previous quarter by new corporations. In processing the composite list of sample companies, a screening technique is used to insure that corporations drawn from the SSA frame could not have been drawn from the IRS frame.

Stratification is used in the sample selection process. In sampling from the IRS frame, stratification by industry and size is employed. In sampling from the SSA frame, stratification is by division and size alone. The measures of size used in the IRS frame are total assets and gross receipts while the measure of size used in the SSA frame is number of employees. From the third quarter 1977, through the fourth quarter 1986 the strata composed of manufacturing firms with assets of less than $250,000 and the strata which contained corporations in the SSA frame are estimated by multivariate techniques. Beginning in the first quarter 1987, the QFR universe of corporations was redefined to exclude these strata. The sampling fractions applied to the other various industry-size strata vary according to both industry and size. They range from approximately one out of 850 to one out of one.

Nearly all corporations whose operations

Source: *Quarterly Financial Report*, Bureau of the Census. The exhibits in this section are from the same publication.

are within the scope of the QFR and which have total assets greater than $50 million are included in the sample. Corporations whose total assets are between $10 million and $50 million and whose receipts exceed the estimated average value for a corporation with $25 million in assets in its industry are also in the sample. Thus, for the most part, corporations with assets over $25 million are permanent sample members with a one out of one sampling fraction.

In those industry-size strata for which the sampling fraction is less than one out of one, a replacement scheme is utilized which provides that one eighth of the sample is replaced each quarter. Corporations removed are those that have been in the reporting group longest (usually eight quarters). Therefore, samples of small corporations for adjacent quarters are seven-eighths identical; for quarters ending nine months apart they are five-eighths identical; etc.

Notice of Change

Beginning in the first quarter 1987, the universe of manufacturing corporations was redefined to exclude corporations with less than $250,000 in assets at the time of sample selection.

Beginning in the fourth quarter of 1987, the mining, wholesale, and retail trade tables only include estimates for corporations with assets of $25 million or over at the time of sample selection, fall 1987. To provide comparability, mining and trade data for the first three quarters of 1987 have been restated to reflect this change.

Industry Contents

Ratios for Firms with Assets $25 Million and Under

Ratios for Firms with Assets $25 Million and Over

TABLE 1—INCOME STATEMENT
FOR CORPORATIONS INCLUDED IN ESIC MAJOR GROUPS 20 AND 21

(See NOTE below.)

	Food and Kindred Products[1]				
	1Q 1987	2Q 1987	3Q 1987	4Q 1987	1Q 1988
	(percent of net sales)				
INCOME STATEMENT IN RATIO FORMAT					
Net sales, receipts, and operating revenues	100.0	100.0	100.0	100.0	100.0
Less: Depreciation, depletion, and amortization of property, plant and equipment	2.6	2.4	2.4	2.6	2.5
Less: All other operating costs and expenses	90.8	90.2	90.2	89.8	90.7
Income (or loss) from operations	6.7	7.4	7.4	7.6	6.8
Non-operating income (expense)	-0.8	-0.1	-0.6	0.6	0.4
Income (or loss) before income taxes	5.9	7.3	6.8	8.2	7.2
Less: Provision for current and deferred domestic income taxes	2.2	2.8	2.4	2.5	1.9
Income (or loss) after income taxes	3.7	4.5	4.4	5.7	5.3
	(percent)				
OPERATING RATIOS (see explanatory notes)					
Annual rate of profit on stockholders' equity at end of period:					
Before income taxes	21.61	28.17	26.27	31.03	26.40
After taxes	13.58	17.42	17.03	21.56	19.27
Annual rate of profit on total assets:					
Before income taxes	8.17	10.85	10.31	12.17	10.37
After taxes	5.13	6.71	6.68	8.46	7.57
BALANCE SHEET RATIOS (based on succeeding table)					
Total current assets to total current liabilities	1.34	1.38	1.37	1.38	1.46
Total cash, U.S. Government and other securities to total current liabilities	0.22	0.23	0.25	0.22	0.22
Total stockholders' equity to total debt	1.03	1.07	1.14	1.13	1.10

NOTE: Beginning in the first quarter 1987, the universe of corporations represented by these estimates was redefined to exclude corporations with less than $250,000 in assets at the time of sample selection.

[1]In the first quarter 1988, a number of corporations were reclassified by industry. To provide comparability, the four quarters of 1987 have been restated to reflect these reclassifications.

[2]Tobacco industry data have been collapsed into food industry data. Major merger and acquisition activity in recent years resulted in the reclassification of a significant portion of gross receipts and assets from tobacco to food. The remainder, comprised of data from highly specialized tobacco manufacturers, is to small to be considered publishable as a separate industry.

TABLE 2—BALANCE SHEET
FOR CORPORATIONS INCLUDED IN ESIC MAJOR GROUPS 20 AND 21

(See NOTE below.)

	Food and Kindred Products[1]				
	1Q 1987	2Q 1987	3Q 1987	4Q 1987	1Q 1988
	(percent of total assets)				
SELECTED BALANCE SHEET RATIOS					
Total cash, U.S. Government and other securities	5.7	5.9	6.3	5.7	5.4
Trade accounts and trade notes receivable	11.1	11.3	11.6	11.2	11.5
Inventories	14.9	14.4	14.6	15.4	15.4
Total current assets	35.5	35.1	35.1	35.3	35.6
Net property, plant and equipment	34.1	34.0	34.0	34.5	34.3
Short-term debt including installments on long-term debt	9.3	8.2	7.5	7.5	7.0
Total current liabilities	26.5	25.4	25.6	25.7	24.3
Long-term debt	27.5	27.9	27.0	27.2	28.6
Total liabilities	62.2	61.5	60.8	60.8	60.7
Stockholders' equity	37.8	38.5	39.2	39.2	39.3

NOTE: Beginning in the first quarter 1987, the universe of corporations represented by these estimates was redefined to exclude corporations with less than $250,000 in assets at the time of sample selection.

[1]In the first quarter 1988, a number of corporations were reclassified by industry. To provide comparability, the four quarters of 1987 have been restated to reflect these reclassifications.

[2]Tobacco industry data have been collapsed into food industry data. Major merger and acquisition activity in recent years resulted in the reclassification of a significant portion of gross receipts and assets from tobacco to food. The remainder, comprised of data from highly specialized tobacco manufacturers, is to small to be considered publishable as a separate industry.

Food and Kindred Products Assets Under $25 Million					Tobacco Manufactures[2]					Tobacco Manufactures[2] Assets Under $25 Million				
1Q 1987	2Q 1987	3Q 1987	4Q 1987	1Q 1988	1Q 1987	2Q 1987	3Q 1987	4Q 1987	1Q 1988	1Q 1987	2Q 1987	3Q 1987	4Q 1987	1Q 1988
(percent of net sales)					(percent of net sales)					(percent of net sales)				
100.0	100.0	100.0	100.0	100.0										
2.2	2.1	1.9	1.9	1.8										
95.0	94.5	95.1	95.0	94.9										
2.8	3.4	3.0	3.1	3.3										
-0.3	0.0	-0.1	0.0	0.0										
2.5	3.5	2.9	3.1	3.2										
1.1	1.4	1.0	0.9	0.9										
1.5	2.1	2.0	2.2	2.3										
(percent)					(percent)					(percent)				
16.50	22.25	19.26	20.66	20.97										
9.54	13.47	12.93	14.57	15.03										
7.31	10.60	9.35	9.87	10.76										
4.22	6.42	6.28	6.96	7.72										
1.94	1.96	1.98	1.89	1.95										
0.31	0.36	0.42	0.35	0.40										
1.36	1.59	1.68	1.62	1.95										

Food and Kindred Products Assets Under $25 Million					Tobacco Manufactures[2]					Tobacco Manufactures[2] Assets Under $25 Million				
1Q 1987	2Q 1987	3Q 1987	4Q 1987	1Q 1988	1Q 1987	2Q 1987	3Q 1987	4Q 1987	1Q 1988	1Q 1987	2Q 1987	3Q 1987	4Q 1987	1Q 1988
(percent of total assets)					(percent of total assets)					(percent of total assets)				
9.2	11.0	13.2	10.8	12.3										
21.6	22.3	23.1	22.3	22.0										
22.1	22.1	21.7	22.3	21.6										
57.3	59.0	62.1	58.8	59.6										
35.9	35.6	31.9	34.3	33.6										
9.7	9.8	10.2	10.2	9.9										
29.6	30.1	31.4	31.2	30.6										
22.9	20.1	18.7	19.3	16.5										
55.7	52.3	51.5	52.2	48.7										
44.3	47.7	48.5	47.8	51.3										

TABLE 3—INCOME STATEMENT
FOR CORPORATIONS INCLUDED IN ESIC MAJOR GROUPS 22 AND 26

(See NOTE below.)

	Textile Mill Products[1]				
	1Q 1987	2Q 1987	3Q 1987	4Q 1987	1Q 1988
	(percent of net sales)				
INCOME STATEMENT IN RATIO FORMAT					
Net sales, receipts, and operating revenues	100.0	100.0	100.0	100.0	100.0
Less: Depreciation, depletion, and amortization of property, plant and equipment	3.1	3.0	2.9	2.7	3.1
Less: All other operating costs and expenses	89.6	89.7	88.3	89.5	90.5
Income (or loss) from operations	7.3	7.3	8.7	7.7	6.4
Non-operating income (expense)	-1.0	-1.9	-2.1	-1.4	-1.4
Income (or loss) before income taxes	6.3	5.4	6.7	6.4	5.0
Less: Provision for current and deferred domestic income taxes	2.4	2.3	2.2	2.2	1.8
Income (or loss) after income taxes	3.9	3.1	4.4	4.2	3.3
	(percent)				
OPERATING RATIOS (see explanatory notes)					
Annual rate of profit on stockholders' equity at end of period:					
Before income taxes	22.92	20.21	26.15	25.71	18.37
After taxes	14.11	11.69	17.37	16.94	11.92
Annual rate of profit on total assets:					
Before income taxes	10.08	9.17	10.68	10.38	7.51
After taxes	6.20	5.30	7.09	6.84	4.87
BALANCE SHEET RATIOS (based on succeeding table)					
Total current assets to total current liabilities	2.39	2.42	2.37	2.25	2.33
Total cash, U.S. Government and other securities to total current liabilities	0.25	0.25	0.28	0.26	0.27
Total stockholders' equity to total debt	1.37	1.45	1.08	1.08	1.10

NOTE: Beginning in the first quarter 1987, the universe of corporations represented by these estimates was redefined to exclude corporations with less than $250,000 in assets at the time of sample selection.

[1] 1987 data are revised.

[2] In the first quarter 1988, a number of corporations were reclassified by industry. To provide comparability, the four quarters of 1987 have been restated to reflect these reclassifications.

TABLE 4—BALANCE SHEET
FOR CORPORATIONS INCLUDED IN ESIC MAJOR GROUPS 22 AND 26

(See NOTE below.)

	Textile Mill Products[1]				
	1Q 1987	2Q 1987	3Q 1987	4Q 1987	1Q 1988
	(percent of total assets)				
SELECTED BALANCE SHEET RATIOS					
Total cash, U.S. Government and other securities	5.9	5.8	6.5	6.3	6.2
Trade accounts and trade notes receivable	23.1	22.7	22.7	22.3	21.1
Inventories	24.6	25.2	23.5	23.2	23.7
Total current assets	55.4	55.8	54.8	53.8	53.4
Net property, plant and equipment	32.5	32.3	30.8	31.4	31.5
Short-term debt including installments on long-term debt	6.8	6.9	8.1	7.5	6.8
Total current liabilities	23.2	23.1	23.2	24.0	22.9
Long-term debt	25.4	24.4	29.8	29.9	30.5
Total liabilities	56.0	54.6	59.2	59.6	59.1
Stockholders' equity	44.0	45.4	40.8	40.4	40.9

NOTE: Beginning in the first quarter 1987, the universe of corporations represented by these estimates was redefined to exclude corporations with less than $250,000 in assets at the time of sample selection.

[1] 1987 data are revised.

[2] In the first quarter 1988, a number of corporations were reclassified by industry. To provide comparability, the four quarters of 1987 have been restated to reflect these reclassifications.

Textile Mill Products Assets Under $25 Million					Paper and Allied Products[2]					Paper and Allied Products Assets Under $25 Million				
1Q 1987	2Q 1987	3Q 1987	4Q 1987	1Q 1988	1Q 1987	2Q 1987	3Q 1987	4Q 1987	1Q 1988	1Q 1987	2Q 1987	3Q 1987	4Q 1987	1Q 1988
(percent of net sales)					(percent of net sales)					(percent of net sales)				
100.0	100.0	100.0	100.0	100.0	100.0	100.0	100.0	100.0	100.0	100.0	100.0	100.0	100.0	100.0
2.3	2.1	2.4	2.0	2.2	4.8	4.4	4.5	4.2	4.6	3.0	2.3	2.1	2.1	2.5
91.8	92.9	89.4	92.7	93.5	86.0	86.0	85.3	85.6	83.7	91.3	93.5	91.6	92.9	91.1
5.9	5.0	8.2	5.3	4.3	9.2	9.6	10.2	10.2	11.7	5.7	4.2	6.4	5.0	6.4
-0.5	-1.3	-0.1	-0.1	-0.1	-0.8	-0.5	0.0	-0.9	-1.1	-0.3	-1.0	-1.1	-0.5	-1.2
5.4	3.7	8.2	5.2	4.2	8.4	9.1	10.2	9.2	10.6	5.4	3.2	5.2	4.5	5.2
2.1	1.7	1.8	1.5	0.8	3.4	3.6	3.8	3.3	3.8	1.7	1.1	1.1	1.6	1.7
3.3	1.9	6.4	3.6	3.4	5.1	5.6	6.4	6.0	6.8	3.7	2.1	4.1	2.9	3.5
(percent)					(percent)					(percent)				
24.47	19.79	32.24	23.30	16.33	20.66	23.56	26.48	23.66	26.92	31.93	22.64	30.82	25.05	26.92
14.75	10.40	25.20	16.45	13.16	12.45	14.36	16.68	15.25	17.35	21.99	14.77	24.05	16.16	18.01
11.47	9.13	17.75	11.63	8.99	9.37	10.74	12.16	10.88	12.46	12.49	8.59	13.95	11.37	12.18
6.91	4.80	13.87	8.21	7.24	5.65	6.55	7.66	7.01	8.03	8.60	5.60	10.88	7.33	8.15
2.04	1.95	2.45	2.07	2.16	1.70	1.66	1.68	1.71	1.76	1.71	1.60	1.81	1.88	1.96
0.24	0.27	0.41	0.30	0.35	0.18	0.16	0.17	0.17	0.13	0.26	0.20	0.21	0.24	0.19
1.55	1.62	2.26	1.98	2.47	1.46	1.49	1.52	1.53	1.54	1.19	1.12	1.51	1.46	1.44

Textile Mill Products Assets Under $25 Million					Paper and Allied Products[2]					Paper and Allied Products Assets Under $25 Million				
1Q 1987	2Q 1987	3Q 1987	4Q 1987	1Q 1988	1Q 1987	2Q 1987	3Q 1987	4Q 1987	1Q 1988	1Q 1987	2Q 1987	3Q 1987	4Q 1987	1Q 1988
(percent of total assets)					(percent of total assets)					(percent of total assets)				
7.7	9.5	11.1	9.9	10.7	3.2	3.0	3.1	3.0	2.3	9.7	8.2	7.7	7.8	5.7
29.7	28.0	27.6	28.6	28.1	11.3	12.0	12.3	12.0	12.6	25.4	28.0	28.9	26.5	26.2
26.9	29.0	25.4	25.2	22.3	11.7	11.7	11.3	11.5	11.7	25.8	26.4	26.5	24.8	24.1
65.8	68.1	66.2	67.8	65.0	30.0	30.1	30.1	29.8	29.7	64.4	65.8	66.4	62.0	58.4
29.3	28.2	29.5	27.3	28.4	59.7	59.5	59.3	59.4	59.2	30.3	29.7	29.7	32.4	36.5
11.1	11.5	8.6	9.9	9.1	4.2	4.5	4.5	3.8	3.5	10.9	14.1	12.9	10.9	8.8
32.3	34.9	27.0	32.7	30.1	17.6	18.1	17.9	17.4	16.9	37.5	41.2	36.6	33.0	29.8
19.2	16.9	15.8	15.3	13.2	26.7	26.1	25.9	26.3	26.4	21.9	19.9	17.1	20.1	22.8
53.1	53.9	44.9	50.1	45.0	54.6	54.4	54.1	54.0	53.7	60.9	62.1	54.7	54.6	54.8
46.9	46.1	55.1	49.9	55.0	45.4	45.6	45.9	46.0	46.3	39.1	37.9	45.3	45.4	45.2

TABLE 5—INCOME STATEMENT
FOR CORPORATIONS INCLUDED IN ESIC MAJOR GROUPS 27 AND 28

(See NOTE below.)

	Printing and Publishing[1]				
	1Q 1987	2Q 1987	3Q 1987	4Q 1987	1Q 1988
	(percent of net sales)				
INCOME STATEMENT IN RATIO FORMAT					
Net sales, receipts, and operating revenues	100.0	100.0	100.0	100.0	100.0
Less: Depreciation, depletion, and amortization of property, plant and equipment	3.8	3.7	3.6	3.4	3.8
Less: All other operating costs and expenses	87.0	85.2	84.3	85.0	87.4
Income (or loss) from operations	9.2	11.1	12.2	11.6	8.8
Non-operating income (expense)	-0.9	-0.6	-0.1	-1.4	1.5
Income (or loss) before income taxes	8.3	10.5	12.1	10.2	10.3
Less: Provision for current and deferred domestic income taxes	3.5	4.4	4.7	4.1	3.5
Income (or loss) after income taxes	4.8	6.2	7.4	6.1	6.8
	(percent)				
OPERATING RATIOS (see explanatory notes)					
Annual rate of profit on stockholders' equity at end of period:					
Before income taxes	22.59	30.22	34.13	31.46	28.45
After taxes	13.10	17.70	20.91	18.78	18.72
Annual rate of profit on total assets:					
Before income taxes	9.80	12.65	14.40	13.00	11.93
After taxes	5.69	7.41	8.82	7.76	7.85
BALANCE SHEET RATIOS (based on succeeding table)					
Total current assets to total current liabilities	1.69	1.58	1.69	1.59	1.64
Total cash, U.S. Government and other securities to total current liabilities	0.33	0.30	0.29	0.31	0.29
Total stockholders' equity to total debt	1.48	1.40	1.33	1.34	1.33

NOTE: Beginning in the first quarter 1987, the universe of corporations represented by these estimates was redefined to exclude corporations with less than $250,000 in assets at the time of sample selection.

[1]1987 data are revised.

[2]During the first quarter of 1988, a number of companies were reclassified by industry. Data for the four quarters of 1987 have been revised to reflect these reclassifications, as well as respondent(s) corrections of submitted data subsequent to original publication.

TABLE 6—BALANCE SHEET
FOR CORPORATIONS INCLUDED IN ESIC MAJOR GROUPS 27 AND 28

(See NOTE below.)

	Printing and Publishing[1]				
	1Q 1987	2Q 1987	3Q 1987	4Q 1987	1Q 1988
	(percent of total assets)				
SELECTED BALANCE SHEET RATIOS					
Total cash, U.S. Government and other securities	7.3	6.9	6.5	7.2	6.4
Trade accounts and trade notes receivable	17.6	17.2	18.4	18.3	17.0
Inventories	8.5	8.5	8.3	7.7	8.1
Total current assets	37.5	36.9	37.1	37.6	36.1
Net property, plant and equipment	30.7	30.1	29.3	28.5	28.7
Short-term debt including installments on long-term debt	4.1	4.6	4.6	5.2	4.6
Total current liabilities	22.2	23.3	22.0	23.6	22.0
Long-term debt	25.2	25.3	27.1	25.6	27.0
Total liabilities	56.6	58.1	57.8	58.7	58.1
Stockholders' equity	43.4	41.9	42.2	41.3	41.9

NOTE: Beginning in the first quarter 1987, the universe of corporations represented by these estimates was redefined to exclude corporations with less than $250,000 in assets at the time of sample selection.

[1]1987 data are revised.

[2]During the first quarter of 1988, a number of companies were reclassified by industry. Data for the four quarters of 1987 have been revised to reflect these reclassifications, as well as respondent(s) corrections of submitted data subsequent to original publication.

Printing and Publishing [1] Assets Under $25 Million					Chemicals and Allied Products [2]					Chemicals and Allied Products Assets Under $25 Million				
1Q 1987	2Q 1987	3Q 1987	4Q 1987	1Q 1988	1Q 1987	2Q 1987	3Q 1987	4Q 1987	1Q 1988	1Q 1987	2Q 1987	3Q 1987	4Q 1987	1Q 1988
(percent of net sales)					(percent of net sales)					(percent of net sales)				
100.0	100.0	100.0	100.0	100.0	100.0	100.0	100.0	100.0	100.0	100.0	100.0	100.0	100.0	100.0
3.3	3.2	3.1	3.1	3.3	4.4	4.3	4.3	4.6	4.4	2.1	2.0	2.1	2.2	2.6
91.1	89.5	90.2	91.0	91.0	86.1	87.6	85.8	88.5	85.5	93.5	92.3	92.8	94.3	90.8
5.5	7.3	6.6	5.9	5.7	9.5	8.1	9.9	6.9	10.1	4.4	5.7	5.1	3.5	6.6
-1.0	-0.6	-1.2	-0.7	-0.6	2.7	2.5	5.3	0.7	4.4	-1.2	-0.9	-0.6	-1.2	-1.0
4.5	6.6	5.4	5.2	5.1	12.3	10.6	15.2	7.6	14.5	3.1	4.8	4.5	2.2	5.6
1.7	2.1	1.4	1.7	1.0	4.2	3.5	5.3	3.1	4.1	1.3	2.4	1.1	1.4	1.6
2.9	4.5	4.1	3.5	4.1	8.1	7.1	9.9	4.5	10.4	1.9	2.4	3.4	0.8	3.9
(percent)					(percent)					(percent)				
22.68	34.23	26.34	27.80	25.90	25.22	22.41	31.75	16.80	32.25	14.23	23.46	19.45	10.56	28.49
14.33	23.27	19.69	18.74	20.86	16.62	15.06	20.65	9.98	23.14	8.47	11.76	14.74	3.96	20.14
8.71	13.51	10.81	11.18	10.29	11.48	10.32	14.56	7.34	14.27	6.01	9.83	8.86	4.40	11.26
5.50	9.19	8.08	7.54	8.29	7.56	6.94	9.47	4.36	10.24	3.58	4.93	6.71	1.65	7.96
1.75	1.79	1.80	1.72	1.73	1.51	1.53	1.49	1.42	1.47	1.79	1.87	2.08	1.86	2.01
0.36	0.42	0.40	0.40	0.38	0.20	0.21	0.23	0.19	0.18	0.27	0.32	0.38	0.30	0.29
1.16	1.22	1.24	1.27	1.14	1.64	1.71	1.71	1.58	1.60	1.44	1.47	1.61	1.26	1.25

Printing and Publishing [1] Assets Under $25 Million					Chemicals and Allied Products [1,2]					Chemicals and Allied Products Assets Under $25 Million				
1Q 1987	2Q 1987	3Q 1987	4Q 1987	1Q 1988	1Q 1987	2Q 1987	3Q 1987	4Q 1987	1Q 1988	1Q 1987	2Q 1987	3Q 1987	4Q 1987	1Q 1988
(percent of total assets)					(percent of total assets)					(percent of total assets)				
11.7	13.7	13.2	13.7	12.7	4.5	4.9	5.5	4.7	4.3	10.0	12.1	12.7	11.2	9.8
27.9	27.6	29.4	29.8	28.7	13.6	13.7	14.0	13.5	14.2	27.5	29.6	26.8	27.1	28.4
13.6	13.2	13.8	11.9	12.3	12.9	12.5	12.3	12.8	12.7	26.9	25.5	26.0	26.8	26.3
56.5	58.3	59.4	59.1	57.3	34.9	34.9	35.6	35.1	35.3	67.4	70.6	68.7	68.3	68.3
36.5	34.6	34.4	33.0	34.0	34.8	34.5	34.0	33.9	33.5	26.2	24.2	24.6	26.2	26.9
8.7	9.8	10.5	10.1	10.2	5.3	5.0	5.5	5.6	5.8	11.5	12.7	9.6	13.0	10.2
32.3	32.5	33.0	34.4	33.0	23.0	22.9	23.9	24.7	23.9	37.6	37.8	33.0	36.7	34.0
24.6	22.5	22.5	21.5	24.5	22.5	22.0	21.4	21.9	21.9	17.9	15.8	18.7	19.9	21.6
61.6	60.5	59.0	59.8	60.3	54.5	53.9	54.2	56.3	55.8	57.8	58.1	54.5	58.4	60.5
38.4	39.5	41.0	40.2	39.7	45.5	46.1	45.8	43.7	44.2	42.2	41.9	45.5	41.6	39.5

TABLE 7—INCOME STATEMENT
FOR CORPORATIONS INCLUDED IN ESIC MAJOR GROUPS 28.1 AND 28.3

(See NOTE below.)

	Industrial Chemicals and Synthetics[1,2]				
	1Q 1987	2Q 1987	3Q 1987	4Q 1987	1Q 1988
	(percent of net sales)				
INCOME STATEMENT IN RATIO FORMAT					
Net sales, receipts, and operating revenues	100.0	100.0	100.0	100.0	100.0
Less: Depreciation, depletion, and amortization of property, plant and equipment	6.1	5.8	5.8	6.2	5.7
Less: All other operating costs and expenses	84.6	84.2	85.0	85.9	83.0
Income (or loss) from operations	9.3	9.9	9.3	7.9	11.3
Non-operating income (expense)	1.0	1.7	8.2	0.4	1.4
Income (or loss) before income taxes	10.3	11.6	17.5	8.3	12.7
Less: Provision for current and deferred domestic income taxes	3.5	3.9	6.8	3.4	4.0
Income (or loss) after income taxes	6.8	7.7	10.7	5.0	8.7
	(percent)				
OPERATING RATIOS (see explanatory notes)					
Annual rate of profit on stockholders' equity at end of period:					
Before income taxes	21.66	25.54	36.88	18.99	29.05
After taxes	14.33	16.92	22.50	11.32	19.96
Annual rate of profit on total assets:					
Before income taxes	9.12	10.99	15.82	7.83	12.17
After taxes	6.03	7.28	9.65	4.67	8.36
BALANCE SHEET RATIOS (based on succeeding table)					
Total current assets to total current liabilities	1.45	1.46	1.39	1.35	1.45
Total cash, U.S. Government and other securities to total current liabilities	0.11	0.15	0.19	0.14	0.14
Total stockholders' equity to total debt	1.33	1.44	1.46	1.34	1.39

NOTE: Beginning in the first quarter 1987, the universe of corporations represented by these estimates was redefined to exclude corporations with less than $250,000 in assets at the time of sample selection.

[1]Included in Chemicals and Allied Products.

[2]In the first quarter 1988, a number of corporations were reclassified by industry. To provide comparability, the four quarters of 1987 have been restated to reflect these reclassifications.

[3]1987 data are revised.

TABLE 8—BALANCE SHEET
FOR CORPORATIONS INCLUDED IN ESIC MAJOR GROUPS 28.1 AND 28.3

(See NOTE below.)

	Industrial Chemicals and Synthetics[1,2]				
	1Q 1987	2Q 1987	3Q 1987	4Q 1987	1Q 1988
	(percent of total assets)				
SELECTED BALANCE SHEET RATIOS					
Total cash, U.S. Government and other securities	2.3	3.4	4.5	3.3	3.2
Trade accounts and trade notes receivable	13.7	13.7	13.7	13.7	14.7
Inventories	12.1	11.3	11.3	11.8	11.8
Total current assets	31.5	32.0	33.0	32.3	33.1
Net property, plant and equipment	41.4	40.9	39.9	39.5	38.5
Short-term debt including installments on long-term debt	4.9	4.4	5.4	5.0	4.5
Total current liabilities	21.8	21.9	23.8	23.9	22.9
Long-term debt	26.7	25.6	24.1	25.7	25.6
Total liabilities	57.9	57.0	57.1	58.8	58.1
Stockholders' equity	42.1	43.0	42.9	41.2	41.9

NOTE: Beginning in the first quarter 1987, the universe of corporations represented by these estimates was redefined to exclude corporations with less than $250,000 in assets at the time of sample selection.

[1]Included in Chemicals and Allied Products.

[2]In the first quarter 1988, a number of corporations were reclassified by industry. To provide comparability, the four quarters of 1987 have been restated to reflect these reclassifications.

[3]1987 data are revised.

Industrial Chemicals and Synthetics[1] Assets Under $25 Million					Drugs[1,3]					Drugs[1] Assets Under $25 Million				
1Q 1987	2Q 1987	3Q 1987	4Q 1987	1Q 1988	1Q 1987	2Q 1987	3Q 1987	4Q 1987	1Q 1988	1Q 1987	2Q 1987	3Q 1987	4Q 1987	1Q 1988
(percent of net sales)					(percent of net sales)					(percent of net sales)				
100.0	100.0	100.0	100.0	100.0	100.0	100.0	100.0	100.0	100.0	100.0	100.0	100.0	100.0	100.0
2.4	3.0	2.7	3.4	2.9	3.1	3.6	3.5	3.5	3.3	3.1	3.4	4.0	3.0	3.4
93.6	95.1	91.5	99.2	88.5	83.7	85.9	84.0	88.8	85.4	94.6	96.6	93.8	90.0	88.7
3.9	1.9	5.8	-2.6	8.6	13.2	10.5	12.4	7.7	11.3	2.3	0.0	2.2	7.0	7.9
-2.7	-2.2	-0.5	-2.8	-1.8	7.4	7.4	5.9	-1.4	14.7	-1.1	-0.8	-0.5	0.5	-2.4
1.2	-0.2	5.3	-5.3	6.8	20.6	17.9	18.4	6.2	26.0	1.2	-0.8	1.7	7.5	5.5
1.0	1.1	1.7	0.4	2.2	6.2	5.3	5.6	4.2	6.2	3.7	4.5	-0.6	1.1	0.8
0.1	-1.3	3.5	-5.8	4.6	14.4	12.6	12.7	2.0	19.8	-2.5	-5.3	2.3	6.4	4.7
(percent)					(percent)					(percent)				
8.84	-2.00	30.78	-34.62	50.29	34.69	28.96	31.33	11.91	51.51	3.50	-1.74	4.99	27.40	34.37
1.09	-10.81	20.65	-37.46	34.18	24.28	20.42	21.74	3.80	39.18	-7.26	-11.33	6.58	23.55	29.37
2.14	-0.48	8.34	-9.45	14.69	17.63	15.02	15.80	5.31	23.45	1.75	-1.06	2.46	12.72	10.52
0.26	-2.60	5.60	-10.23	9.99	12.34	10.59	10.96	1.69	17.83	-3.63	-6.91	3.25	10.94	8.99
1.73	1.96	1.98	1.59	2.17	1.49	1.43	1.34	1.25	1.26	1.91	2.77	2.02	1.77	2.10
0.28	0.37	0.42	0.27	0.32	0.29	0.23	0.23	0.20	0.16	0.62	1.11	0.74	0.57	0.40
0.46	0.62	0.58	0.55	0.64	2.41	2.47	2.33	1.99	2.00	2.09	3.41	1.61	1.43	1.11

Industrial Chemicals and Synthetics[1] Assets Under $25 Million					Drugs[1,3]					Drugs[1] Assets Under $25 Million				
1Q 1987	2Q 1987	3Q 1987	4Q 1987	1Q 1988	1Q 1987	2Q 1987	3Q 1987	4Q 1987	1Q 1988	1Q 1987	2Q 1987	3Q 1987	4Q 1987	1Q 1988
(percent of total assets)					(percent of total assets)					(percent of total assets)				
9.6	12.2	13.2	10.6	9.9	6.8	5.6	6.1	5.9	4.2	19.7	26.9	23.3	21.0	11.2
22.4	24.7	22.8	21.1	24.8	12.2	12.3	12.7	12.1	12.6	17.7	17.9	22.2	23.2	22.3
24.0	23.6	22.8	26.0	26.1	11.7	11.9	11.7	12.7	12.6	19.8	19.4	15.3	18.3	22.1
58.6	65.0	62.4	62.9	66.7	35.4	34.1	35.1	36.3	34.4	60.3	67.0	63.6	65.5	59.3
31.5	31.3	31.6	30.8	28.3	27.6	27.5	26.8	26.8	27.5	33.7	26.4	25.8	26.6	32.1
13.1	9.3	8.1	17.7	7.0	4.7	5.9	7.1	8.7	8.8	6.2	6.4	13.8	18.6	9.1
33.9	33.2	31.5	39.5	30.7	23.7	23.8	26.1	29.0	27.3	31.5	24.1	31.6	37.0	28.3
39.1	29.1	38.4	32.0	38.6	16.4	15.2	14.5	13.8	13.9	17.7	11.5	16.9	13.9	18.6
75.8	76.0	72.9	72.7	70.8	49.2	48.1	49.6	55.4	54.5	50.0	39.0	50.6	53.6	69.4
24.2	24.0	27.1	27.3	29.2	50.8	51.9	50.4	44.6	45.5	50.0	61.0	49.4	46.4	30.6

TABLE 9—INCOME STATEMENT
FOR CORPORATIONS INCLUDED IN ESIC MAJOR GROUPS 29 AND 30
(See NOTE below.)

	Petroleum and Coal Products[1]				
	1Q 1987	2Q 1987	3Q 1987	4Q 1987	1Q 1988
	(percent of net sales)				
INCOME STATEMENT IN RATIO FORMAT					
Net sales, receipts, and operating revenues	100.0	100.0	100.0	100.0	100.0
Less: Depreciation, depletion, and amortization of property, plant and equipment	9.2	7.9	7.8	7.9	7.9
Less: All other operating costs and expenses	87.2	86.0	85.3	86.2	85.0
Income (or loss) from operations	3.6	6.1	6.9	5.9	7.0
Non-operating income (expense)	2.6	2.9	1.3	-6.1	3.2
Income (or loss) before income taxes	6.2	9.0	8.2	-0.2	10.2
Less: Provision for current and deferred domestic income taxes	1.1	1.9	2.3	0.1	2.2
Income (or loss) after income taxes	5.2	7.1	5.9	-0.3	8.0
	(percent)				
OPERATING RATIOS (see explanatory notes)					
Annual rate of profit on stockholders' equity at end of period:					
Before income taxes	9.50	16.30	14.84	-0.32	18.00
After taxes	7.89	12.89	10.64	-0.52	14.12
Annual rate of profit on total assets:					
Before income taxes	4.11	6.77	6.38	-0.13	7.63
After taxes	3.41	5.35	4.57	-0.22	5.99
BALANCE SHEET RATIOS (based on succeeding table)					
Total current assets to total current liabilities	1.14	1.17	1.09	1.01	0.97
Total cash, U.S. Government and other securities to total current liabilities	0.29	0.34	0.27	0.26	0.25
Total stockholders' equity to total debt	1.66	1.49	1.70	1.60	1.58

NOTE: Beginning in the first quarter 1987, the universe of corporations represented by these estimates was redefined to exclude corporations with less than $250,000 in assets at the time of sample selection.
[1]1987 data are revised.
[2]In the first quarter 1988, a number of corporations were reclassified by industry. To provide comparability, the four quarters of 1987 have been restated to reflect these reclassifications.
[3]Revised.

TABLE 10—BALANCE SHEET
FOR CORPORATIONS INCLUDED IN ESIC MAJOR GROUPS 29 AND 30
(See NOTE below.)

	Petroleum and Coal Products[1]				
	1Q 1987	2Q 1987	3Q 1987	4Q 1987	1Q 1988
	(percent of total assets)				
SELECTED BALANCE SHEET RATIOS					
Total cash, U.S. Government and other securities	4.9	5.6	4.6	5.0	5.1
Trade accounts and trade notes receivable	6.6	6.8	6.8	6.7	6.7
Inventories	5.3	5.5	5.8	5.5	5.6
Total current assets	19.0	19.5	18.7	19.0	19.3
Net property, plant and equipment	57.1	56.7	57.0	55.8	55.9
Short-term debt including installments on long-term debt	4.0	3.7	4.0	5.0	6.4
Total current liabilities	16.7	16.6	17.1	18.9	20.0
Long-term debt	22.1	24.1	21.4	21.1	20.5
Total liabilities	56.8	58.5	57.0	58.3	57.6
Stockholders' equity	43.2	41.5	43.0	41.7	42.4

NOTE: Beginning in the first quarter 1987, the universe of corporations represented by these estimates was redefined to exclude corporations with less than $250,000 in assets at the time of sample selection.
[1]1987 data are revised.
[2]In the first quarter 1988, a number of corporations were reclassified by industry. To provide comparability, the four quarters of 1987 have been restated to reflect these reclassifications.

Petroleum and Coal Products Assets Under $25 Million					Rubber and Misc. Plastics Products[2]					Rubber and Misc. Plastics Products Assets Under $25 Million				
1Q 1987	2Q 1987	3Q 1987	4Q 1987	1Q 1988	1Q[3] 1987	2Q 1987	3Q 1987	4Q 1987	1Q 1988	1Q 1987	2Q 1987	3Q 1987	4Q 1987	1Q 1988
(percent of net sales)					(percent of net sales)					(percent of net sales)				
100.0	100.0	100.0	100.0	100.0	100.0	100.0	100.0	100.0	100.0	100.0	100.0	100.0	100.0	100.0
2.7	1.9	2.7	3.2	3.5	3.6	3.3	3.2	3.3	3.3	3.2	3.1	3.6	3.0	3.0
101.7	91.6	90.1	93.0	100.6	89.9	90.1	90.4	90.9	89.5	90.9	90.4	90.5	92.0	90.1
-4.3	6.5	7.3	3.8	-4.0	6.5	6.7	6.3	5.8	7.2	5.9	6.5	5.9	5.0	6.9
0.2	0.7	-0.1	-1.4	-1.1	1.0	0.9	0.5	1.8	-0.1	-0.4	-0.3	-0.8	-0.2	0.8
-4.2	7.2	7.2	2.4	-5.1	7.5	7.6	6.9	7.7	7.1	5.5	6.2	5.1	4.9	7.8
0.4	2.0	1.7	0.6	0.3	2.1	2.1	2.1	2.5	1.8	1.8	1.9	1.3	1.6	1.4
-4.6	5.2	5.4	1.8	-5.4	5.4	5.5	4.7	5.2	5.4	3.7	4.3	3.8	3.2	6.4
(percent)					(percent)					(percent)				
-17.81	28.52	42.71	10.82	-22.64	27.56	33.46	29.52	32.19	28.26	24.88	31.11	24.64	25.32	38.91
-19.57	20.59	32.39	8.22	-23.80	19.95	24.05	20.29	21.62	21.22	16.85	21.49	18.34	16.83	31.87
-7.93	15.40	16.61	4.88	-10.30	10.46	11.72	10.49	11.79	10.60	11.12	13.81	10.77	10.41	16.53
-8.71	11.17	12.75	3.71	-10.83	7.58	8.43	7.21	7.92	7.96	7.53	9.54	8.01	6.92	13.54
2.09	2.23	1.40	1.40	1.84	1.61	1.52	1.53	1.59	1.57	1.86	1.82	1.84	1.74	1.76
0.76	0.81	0.21	0.34	0.55	0.18	0.16	0.17	0.16	0.14	0.27	0.25	0.28	0.27	0.24
1.94	2.15	1.66	1.87	2.30	1.09	0.94	0.95	1.05	1.05	1.48	1.47	1.41	1.21	1.28

Petrolum and Coal Products Assets Under $25 Million					Rubber and Misc. Plastics Products[2]					Rubber and Misc. Plastics Products Assets Under $25 Million				
1Q 1987	2Q 1987	3Q 1987	4Q 1987	1Q 1988	1Q 1987	2Q 1987	3Q 1987	4Q 1987	1Q 1988	1Q 1987	2Q 1987	3Q 1987	4Q 1987	1Q 1988
(percent of total assets)					(percent of total assets)					(percent of total assets)				
20.8	21.2	7.7	12.4	17.0	5.4	4.9	5.1	5.0	4.2	9.1	8.5	9.3	9.3	8.2
20.0	19.1	24.2	23.2	19.2	21.3	21.3	21.3	21.7	21.9	27.4	28.3	27.9	26.0	26.8
13.3	14.6	14.4	11.2	14.1	18.4	17.8	17.4	18.2	18.5	21.8	21.0	20.4	21.5	21.6
57.2	58.1	51.3	50.6	56.5	48.4	47.3	46.6	48.4	47.2	61.9	60.8	60.3	60.5	59.7
34.2	32.6	39.8	41.1	34.5	35.9	35.7	35.8	34.1	34.5	33.8	33.7	34.3	32.3	34.3
6.4	11.0	10.1	13.0	6.4	8.5	9.8	8.9	8.2	9.1	10.6	11.1	10.2	12 8	11.7
27.3	26.1	36.6	36.2	30.7	30.0	31.1	30.4	30.5	30.1	33.3	33.5	32.8	34.7	33.9
16.5	14.2	13.6	11.1	13.4	26.3	27.6	28.4	26.7	26.6	19.6	19.2	21.0	21.1	21.5
55.5	45.8	60.6	54.9	54.5	62.0	65.0	64.5	63.4	62.5	55.3	55.6	56.3	58.9	57.5
44.5	54.2	39.4	45.1	45.5	38.0	35.0	35.5	36.6	37.5	44.7	44.4	43.7	41.1	42.5

TABLE 11—INCOME STATEMENT
FOR CORPORATIONS INCLUDED IN ESIC MAJOR GROUPS 32 AND 33

(See NOTE below.)

	Stone, Clay and Glass Products[1]				
	1Q[2] 1987	2Q 1987	3Q 1987	4Q 1987	1Q 1988
	(percent of net sales)				
INCOME STATEMENT IN RATIO FORMAT					
Net sales, receipts, and operating revenues	100.0	100.0	100.0	100.0	100.0
Less: Depreciation, depletion, and amortization of property, plant and equipment	4.9	4.4	4.0	4.6	4.9
Less: All other operating costs and expenses	90.2	85.7	85.1	88.6	92.0
Income (or loss) from operations	4.9	9.9	10.9	6.8	3.1
Non-operating income (expense)	3.2	-0.6	-1.1	-2.4	-1.3
Income (or loss) before income taxes	8.1	9.3	9.8	4.5	1.9
Less: Provision for current and deferred domestic income taxes	2.7	3.2	3.0	1.3	1.1
Income (or loss) after income taxes	5.4	6.1	6.7	3.1	0.8
	(percent)				
OPERATING RATIOS (see explanatory notes)					
Annual rate of profit on stockholders' equity at end of period:					
Before income taxes	20.44	28.49	29.33	12.71	4.54
After taxes	13.68	18.61	20.18	8.98	1.88
Annual rate of profit on total assets:					
Before income taxes	8.84	10.68	11.50	5.12	1.79
After taxes	5.92	6.98	7.92	3.62	0.74
BALANCE SHEET RATIOS (based on succeeding table)					
Total current assets to total current liabilities	1.79	1.60	1.64	1.77	1.68
Total cash, U.S. Government and other securities to total current liabilities	0.32	0.27	0.31	0.38	0.30
Total stockholders' equity to total debt	1.33	0.95	1.08	1.15	1.07

NOTE: Beginning in the first quarter 1987, the universe of corporations represented by these estimates was redefined to exclude corporations with less than $250,000 in assets at the time of sample selection.

[1] In the first quarter 1988, a number of corporations were reclassified by industry. To provide comparability, the four quarters of 1987 have been restated to reflect these reclassifications.

[2] Revised.

TABLE 12—BALANCE SHEET
FOR CORPORATIONS INCLUDED IN ESIC MAJOR GROUPS 32 AND 33

(See NOTE below.)

	Stone, Clay and Glass Products[1]				
	1Q 1987	2Q 1987	3Q 1987	4Q 1987	1Q 1988
	(percent of total assets)				
SELECTED BALANCE SHEET RATIOS					
Total cash, U.S. Government and other securities	6.7	6.1	7.0	7.9	6.3
Trade accounts and trade notes receivable	15.9	16.0	16.3	15.2	14.6
Inventories	12.2	11.7	10.9	11.1	11.9
Total current assets	38.2	36.6	36.8	37.0	35.6
Net property, plant and equipment	43.8	41.3	40.4	41.7	40.6
Short-term debt including installments on long-term debt	5.9	7.7	5.9	5.3	6.0
Total current liabilities	21.3	22.8	22.5	21.0	21.2
Long-term debt	26.7	31.7	30.5	29.7	30.9
Total liabilities	56.7	62.5	60.8	59.7	60.6
Stockholders' equity	43.3	37.5	39.2	40.3	39.4

NOTE: Beginning in the first quarter 1987, the universe of corporations represented by these estimates was redefined to exclude corporations with less than $250,000 in assets at the time of sample selection.

[1] In the first quarter 1988, a number of corporations were reclassified by industry. To provide comparability, the four quarters of 1987 have been restated to reflect these reclassifications.

Stone, Clay and Glass Products Assets Under $25 Million					Primary Metal Industries[1]					Primary Metal Industries Assets Under $25 Million				
1Q[2] 1987	2Q 1987	3Q 1987	4Q 1987	1Q 1988	1Q 1987	2Q 1987	3Q 1987	4Q 1987	1Q 1988	1Q 1987	2Q 1987	3Q 1987	4Q 1987	1Q 1988
(percent of net sales)					(percent of net sales)					(percent of net sales)				
100.0	100.0	100.0	100.0	100.0	100.0	100.0	100.0	100.0	100.0	100.0	100.0	100.0	100.0	100.0
4.1	3.4	3.1	3.3	3.4	4.0	3.8	3.6	3.6	3.6	3.1	3.0	2.8	2.8	2.8
97.2	88.4	87.6	91.5	99.9	91.4	90.7	91.4	91.3	89.1	92.5	93.8	94.0	93.5	91.7
-1.2	8.2	9.4	5.2	-3.3	4.6	5.5	5.0	5.1	7.3	4.4	3.2	3.2	3.7	5.5
0.0	-0.1	0.6	0.1	-0.4	-0.4	-1.5	0.6	-2.6	-0.5	-0.3	-0.5	-0.5	0.5	-0.5
-1.3	8.0	10.0	5.3	-3.7	4.2	4.0	5.6	2.5	6.8	4.1	2.7	2.7	4.2	5.0
1.1	2.1	2.8	1.9	0.0	1.3	1.9	1.8	0.7	2.1	1.8	1.4	1.1	1.7	1.5
-2.4	5.9	7.2	3.4	-3.7	2.9	2.0	3.8	1.8	4.7	2.3	1.3	1.6	2.5	3.5
(percent)					(percent)					(percent)				
-4.52	37.81	45.29	21.66	-13.00	14.31	13.72	19.84	9.32	25.37	18.17	12.21	11.69	19.21	23.13
-8.53	27.81	32.51	13.96	-13.17	9.90	7.01	13.37	6.78	17.48	10.05	5.80	6.84	11.34	16.08
-2.30	16.75	22.58	11.47	-6.73	4.76	4.77	6.48	3.16	8.36	7.98	5.44	5.40	9.03	11.85
-4.34	12.32	16.21	7.39	-6.82	3.29	2.44	4.37	2.30	5.76	4.41	2.59	3.16	5.33	8.24
1.94	2.06	2.16	2.28	2.31	1.60	1.67	1.63	1.70	1.73	1.78	1.78	1.88	1.87	2.07
0.39	0.37	0.52	0.59	0.53	0.22	0.27	0.34	0.26	0.23	0.26	0.23	0.26	0.29	0.33
1.97	1.39	2.05	2.16	2.10	1.05	1.14	1.04	1.13	1.02	1.42	1.47	1.58	1.66	2.04

Stone, Clay and Glass Products Assets Under $25 Million					Primary Metal Industries[1]					Primary Metal Industries Assets Under $25 Million				
1Q 1987	2Q 1987	3Q 1987	4Q 1987	1Q 1988	1Q 1987	2Q 1987	3Q 1987	4Q 1987	1Q 1988	1Q 1987	2Q 1987	3Q 1987	4Q 1987	1Q 1988
(percent of total assets)					(percent of total assets)					(percent of total assets)				
11.6	10.6	15.3	16.5	14.5	5.7	7.0	9.2	6.6	5.6	8.8	7.7	8.4	9.7	10.3
28.0	29.4	30.1	27.8	27.3	16.5	16.4	16.1	16.6	17.3	26.4	26.7	27.9	27.0	30.3
15.1	15.4	15.6	15.2	18.6	17.4	16.8	16.3	17.3	17.4	23.2	21.8	23.3	23.2	21.7
58.4	58.9	63.8	63.9	63.6	41.6	42.8	44.1	43.2	42.5	60.8	59.7	62.2	62.9	65.4
35.4	35.0	30.5	31.3	32.1	43.7	42.3	41.0	42.5	41.2	32.3	33.7	31.4	31.8	29.1
8.6	7.9	6.3	7.7	5.8	6.2	6.0	5.3	5.2	5.1	13.1	12.6	12.0	12.0	10.5
30.1	28.6	29.5	28.1	27.5	26.0	25.6	27.0	25.4	24.5	34.1	33.5	33.1	33.7	31.6
17.3	24.0	18.0	16.9	18.8	25.3	24.4	26.0	24.8	27.2	17.9	17.8	17.2	16.2	14.7
49.1	55.7	50.1	47.0	48.2	66.7	65.2	67.3	66.0	67.1	56.1	55.4	53.8	53.0	48.8
50.9	44.3	49.9	53.0	51.8	33.3	34.8	32.7	34.0	32.9	43.9	44.6	46.2	47.0	51.2

TABLE 13—INCOME STATEMENT
FOR CORPORATIONS INCLUDED IN ESIC MAJOR GROUPS 33.1-2 AND 33.5-6
(See NOTE below.)

	Iron and Steel[1 2]				
	1Q 1987	2Q 1987	3Q 1987	4Q 1987	1Q 1988
	(percent of net sales)				
INCOME STATEMENT IN RATIO FORMAT					
Net sales, receipts, and operating revenues	100.0	100.0	100.0	100.0	100.0
Less: Depreciation, depletion, and amortization of property, plant and equipment	4.0	3.8	3.7	3.6	3.6
Less: All other operating costs and expenses	91.4	90.6	91.1	91.4	90.3
Income (or loss) from operations	4.6	5.6	5.1	5.1	6.1
Non-operating income (expense)	-0.9	-0.7	-1.0	-2.3	-2.2
Income (or loss) before income taxes	3.7	4.9	4.2	2.8	4.0
Less: Provision for current and deferred domestic income taxes	0.9	1.7	1.3	0.9	1.1
Income (or loss) after income taxes	2.9	3.2	2.9	1.9	2.8
	(percent)				
OPERATING RATIOS (see explanatory notes)					
Annual rate of profit on stockholders' equity at end of period:					
Before income taxes	23.16	28.26	23.49	15.67	24.06
After taxes	17.83	18.26	16.17	10.68	17.19
Annual rate of profit on total assets:					
Before income taxes	4.65	6.35	5.31	3.69	4.99
After taxes	3.58	4.10	3.66	2.51	3.56
BALANCE SHEET RATIOS (based on succeeding table)					
Total current assets to total current liabilities	1.48	1.53	1.57	1.59	1.64
Total cash, U.S. Government and other securities to total current liabilities	0.22	0.26	0.24	0.27	0.26
Total stockholders' equity to total debt	0.59	0.69	0.70	0.78	0.60

NOTE: Beginning in the first quarter 1987, the universe of corporations represented by these estimates was redefined to exclude corporations with less than $250,000 in assets at the time of sample selection.
[1]Included in Primary Metal Industries.
[2]In the first quarter 1988, a number of corporations were reclassified by industry. To provide comparability, the four quarters of 1987 have been restated to reflect these reclassifications.

TABLE 14—BALANCE SHEET
FOR CORPORATIONS INCLUDED IN ESIC MAJOR GROUPS 33.1-2 AND 33.5-6
(See NOTE below.)

	Iron and Steel[1 2]				
	1Q 1987	2Q 1987	3Q 1987	4Q 1987	1Q 1988
	(percent of total assets)				
SELECTED BALANCE SHEET RATIOS					
Total cash, U.S. Government and other securities	7.0	7.7	7.1	7.9	7.4
Trade accounts and trade notes receivable	18.0	17.8	18.2	17.7	17.9
Inventories	19.0	18.3	18.3	18.6	18.7
Total current assets	45.9	46.0	46.0	46.8	46.0
Net property, plant and equipment	45.6	44.8	44.9	44.0	42.0
Short-term debt including installments on long-term debt	6.1	5.9	5.5	5.3	4.6
Total current liabilities	31.0	30.1	29.2	29.4	28.0
Long-term debt	28.0	26.6	27.1	24.9	30.0
Total liabilities	79.9	77.5	77.4	76.5	79.3
Stockholders' equity	20.1	22.5	22.6	23.5	20.7

NOTE: Beginning in the first quarter 1987, the universe of corporations represented by these estimates was redefined to exclude corporations with less than $250,000 in assets at the time of sample selection.
[1]Included in Primary Metal Industries.
[2]In the first quarter 1988, a number of corporations were reclassified by industry. To provide comparability, the four quarters of 1987 have been restated to reflect these reclassifications.

Iron and Steel[1] Assets Under $25 Million					Nonferrous Metals[1,2]					Nonferrous Metals[1] Assets Under $25 Million				
1Q 1987	2Q 1987	3Q 1987	4Q 1987	1Q 1988	1Q 1987	2Q 1987	3Q 1987	4Q 1987	1Q 1988	1Q 1987	2Q 1987	3Q 1987	4Q 1987	1Q 1988
(percent of net sales)					(percent of net sales)					(percent of net sales)				
100.0	100.0	100.0	100.0	100.0	100.0	100.0	100.0	100.0	100.0	100.0	100.0	100.0	100.0	100.0
3.1	3.3	3.0	2.7	2.9	4.1	3.8	3.5	3.7	3.6	3.1	2.9	2.7	2.8	2.7
91.6	92.6	92.8	93.9	94.2	91.3	90.9	91.7	91.3	87.9	93.0	94.3	94.5	93.3	91.0
5.3	4.1	4.1	3.3	2.9	4.5	5.3	4.8	5.0	8.5	3.9	2.8	2.8	3.9	6.3
0.1	-0.9	-1.5	0.6	-0.9	0.2	-2.4	2.4	-3.0	1.3	-0.5	-0.3	-0.1	0.4	-0.5
5.4	3.2	2.6	4.0	2.0	4.7	2.8	7.2	2.1	9.8	3.5	2.5	2.7	4.4	5.8
2.2	1.5	1.4	1.9	1.2	1.8	2.2	2.4	0.4	3.2	1.7	1.4	1.0	1.7	1.6
3.2	1.8	1.2	2.0	0.8	2.9	0.7	4.8	1.7	6.6	1.8	1.1	1.7	2.7	4.2
(percent)					(percent)					(percent)				
19.65	9.58	8.82	14.45	6.61	10.36	6.62	18.01	5.88	25.99	17.08	14.51	13.67	21.90	30.65
11.72	5.23	4.21	7.42	2.65	6.37	1.52	11.97	4.67	17.62	8.82	6.30	8.64	13.55	22.20
9.42	5.52	4.68	7.52	3.92	4.87	3.14	7.57	2.63	11.84	7.06	5.40	5.80	9.76	14.80
5.62	3.02	2.23	3.86	1.57	2.99	0.72	5.03	2.09	8.03	3.64	2.35	3.66	6.04	10.72
1.88	2.17	2.00	2.03	2.33	1.79	1.87	1.70	1.86	1.85	1.73	1.63	1.83	1.80	1.99
0.28	0.29	0.27	0.32	0.48	0.21	0.30	0.44	0.25	0.18	0.25	0.21	0.25	0.28	0.28
1.51	2.54	2.07	1.95	3.40	1.61	1.68	1.39	1.50	1.53	1.35	1.07	1.36	1.54	1.73

Iron and Steel[1] Assets Under $25 Million					Nonferrous Metals[1,2]					Nonferrous Metals[1] Assets Under $25 Million				
1Q 1987	2Q 1987	3Q 1987	4Q 1987	1Q 1988	1Q 1987	2Q 1987	3Q 1987	4Q 1987	1Q 1988	1Q 1987	2Q 1987	3Q 1987	4Q 1987	1Q 1988
(percent of total assets)					(percent of total assets)					(percent of total assets)				
9.0	7.6	7.8	9.4	12.7	4.4	6.3	11.1	5.3	3.9	8.7	7.8	8.8	9.8	9.5
25.1	24.0	26.1	25.9	25.9	14.9	15.0	14.3	15.5	16.7	27.3	28.2	29.0	27.6	32.0
25.0	21.6	20.2	21.5	20.5	15.7	15.2	14.6	16.0	15.9	22.0	21.9	25.0	24.0	22.1
61.1	56.0	57.3	60.6	61.5	37.2	39.5	42.4	39.5	38.8	60.7	61.8	65.0	64.1	66.8
33.7	36.4	36.4	33.4	31.9	41.6	39.8	37.4	41.0	40.4	31.5	32.2	28.7	31.0	28.1
14.2	9.3	10.4	13.2	7.1	6.4	6.1	5.3	5.1	5.5	12.5	14.4	12.8	11.6	11.6
32.5	25.8	28.6	29.8	26.4	20.8	21.1	25.0	21.2	21.0	35.1	37.8	35.5	35.6	33.5
17.5	13.5	15.2	13.4	10.3	22.7	22.1	24.9	24.7	24.2	18.0	20.2	18.2	17.4	16.3
52.1	42.3	47.0	48.0	40.8	53.0	52.6	58.0	55.3	54.4	58.7	62.8	57.6	55.4	51.7
47.9	57.7	53.0	52.0	59.2	47.0	47.4	42.0	44.7	45.6	41.3	37.2	42.4	44.6	48.3

TABLE 15—INCOME STATEMENT
FOR CORPORATIONS INCLUDED IN ESIC MAJOR GROUPS 34 AND 35

(See NOTE below.)

	Fabricated Metal Products[1]				
	1Q 1987	2Q 1987	3Q 1987	4Q. 1987	1Q 1988
	(percent of net sales)				
INCOME STATEMENT IN RATIO FORMAT					
Net sales, receipts, and operating revenues	100.0	100.0	100.0	100.0	100.0
Less: Depreciation, depletion, and amortization of property, plant and equipment	3.2	3.0	3.0	3.0	3.0
Less: All other operating costs and expenses	90.4	90.0	90.0	90.4	90.5
Income (or loss) from operations	6.4	7.0	7.0	6.6	6.5
Non-operating income (expense)	-2.7	-0.5	-0.5	-1.1	-0.2
Income (or loss) before income taxes	3.7	6.4	6.5	5.5	6.3
Less: Provision for current and deferred domestic income taxes	2.0	2.4	2.0	1.6	1.8
Income (or loss) after income taxes	1.8	4.0	4.5	3.9	4.5
	(percent)				
OPERATING RATIOS (see explanatory notes)					
Annual rate of profit on stockholders' equity at end of period:					
Before income taxes	12.04	21.33	21.68	18.26	21.19
After taxes	5.68	13.26	14.95	13.00	15.24
Annual rate of profit on total assets:					
Before income taxes	5.25	9.34	9.55	8.18	9.02
After taxes	2.48	5.81	6.59	5.82	6.49
BALANCE SHEET RATIOS (based on succeeding table)					
Total current assets to total current liabilities	1.95	1.94	2.03	2.04	1.96
Total cash, U.S. Government and other securities to total current liabilities	0.33	0.31	0.33	0.32	0.25
Total stockholders' equity to total debt	1.49	1.52	1.52	1.56	1.36

NOTE: Beginning in the first quarter 1987, the universe of corporations represented by these estimates was redefined to exclude corporations with less than $250,000 in assets at the time of sample selection.

[1] In the first quarter 1988, a number of corporations were reclassified by industry. To provide comparability, the four quarters of 1987 have been restated to reflect these reclassifications.

[2] Revised.

TABLE 16—BALANCE SHEET
FOR CORPORATIONS INCLUDED IN ESIC MAJOR GROUPS 34 AND 35

(See NOTE below.)

	Fabricated Metal Products[1]				
	1Q[2] 1987	2Q 1987	3Q 1987	4Q 1987	1Q 1988
	(percent of total assets)				
SELECTED BALANCE SHEET RATIOS					
Total cash, U.S. Government and other securities	9.2	8.6	9.0	8.6	7.0
Trade accounts and trade notes receivable	21.3	22.0	22.2	21.1	21.5
Inventories	20.5	20.3	20.6	21.4	22.6
Total current assets	53.8	53.8	54.5	54.3	54.2
Net property, plant and equipment	29.5	29.0	28.2	28.5	28.2
Short-term debt including installments on long-term debt	6.9	6.7	6.4	5.9	7.1
Total current liabilities	27.6	27.8	26.9	26.5	27.7
Long-term debt	22.4	22.1	22.6	22.7	24.1
Total liabilities	56.4	56.2	55.9	55.2	57.4
Stockholders' equity	43.6	43.8	44.1	44.8	42.6

NOTE: Beginning in the first quarter 1987, the universe of corporations represented by these estimates was redefined to exclude corporations with less than $250,000 in assets at the time of sample selection.

[1] In the first quarter 1988, a number of corporations were reclassified by industry. To provide comparability, the four quarters of 1987 have been restated to reflect these reclassifications.

[2] Revised.

Fabricated Metal Products Assets Under $25 Million					Machinery, Except Electrical[1]					Machinery, Except Electrical Assets Under $25 Million				
1Q 1987	2Q 1987	3Q 1987	4Q 1987	1Q 1988	1Q[2] 1987	2Q 1987	3Q 1987	4Q 1987	1Q 1988	1Q 1987	2Q 1987	3Q 1987	4Q 1987	1Q 1988
(percent of net sales)					(percent of net sales)					(percent of net sales)				
100.0	100.0	100.0	100.0	100.0	100.0	100.0	100.0	100.0	100.0	100.0	100.0	100.0	100.0	100.0
3.1	2.9	2.8	2.9	2.8	4.6	4.3	4.4	4.1	4.3	3.5	3.2	3.5	3.3	3.1
91.7	91.1	91.4	92.1	91.6	91.2	89.6	89.9	91.0	90.5	94.0	94.1	92.3	94.7	92.4
5.2	5.9	5.8	5.0	5.6	4.1	6.1	5.7	4.9	5.2	2.5	2.7	4.3	2.0	4.5
-1.3	-0.6	-0.3	-1.0	-0.8	-0.6	2.3	2.1	3.4	2.6	-0.8	-1.2	-0.4	-1.2	-0.3
3.9	5.3	5.5	4.0	4.8	3.5	8.5	7.8	8.3	7.8	1.7	1.4	3.9	0.7	4.2
1.8	2.0	1.2	1.1	1.5	2.1	2.5	2.4	1.8	2.1	1.5	1.3	1.8	1.1	1.6
2.1	3.3	4.3	2.9	3.3	1.5	6.0	5.4	6.5	5.6	0.2	0.1	2.1	-0.3	2.6
(percent)					(percent)					(percent)				
15.20	20.65	22.02	15.93	19.99	6.25	15.95	14.69	16.41	14.65	5.65	4.84	13.30	2.71	14.58
8.05	12.85	17.02	11.43	13.81	2.61	11.21	10.20	12.93	10.63	0.55	0.43	7.05	-1.18	8.94
7.18	10.12	11.10	8.01	9.41	3.30	8.55	7.76	8.59	7.63	2.60	2.31	6.26	1.24	6.89
3.80	6.30	8.58	5.74	6.50	1.38	6.00	5.39	6.76	5.54	0.25	0.20	3.32	-0.54	4.22
2.03	2.12	2.19	2.18	2.02	1.84	1.98	1.99	1.81	1.80	2.08	2.06	2.15	2.11	2.13
0.40	0.38	0.37	0.37	0.29	0.29	0.32	0.31	0.27	0.22	0.36	0.37	0.40	0.39	0.33
1.67	1.82	1.87	1.82	1.58	2.43	2.40	2.24	2.27	2.24	1.49	1.66	1.53	1.52	1.67

Fabricated Metal Products Assets Under $25 Million					Machinery, Except Electrical[1]					Machinery, Except Electrical Assets Under $25 Million				
1Q 1987	2Q 1987	3Q 1987	4Q 1987	1Q 1988	1Q[2] 1987	2Q 1987	3Q 1987	4Q 1987	1Q 1988	1Q 1987	2Q 1987	3Q 1987	4Q 1987	1Q 1988
(percent of total assets)					(percent of total assets)					(percent of total assets)				
12.8	11.6	11.0	11.3	9.5	7.4	7.6	7.1	6.7	5.7	12.0	12.4	12.5	12.7	10.9
25.5	26.4	27.2	26.0	26.5	18.3	18.3	18.1	18.3	18.8	24.3	24.9	24.5	26.0	27.2
23.2	24.0	24.4	24.9	26.5	17.9	17.7	17.3	17.5	18.1	29.0	27.7	26.6	27.1	28.2
64.5	65.5	66.0	66.0	66.0	46.8	47.1	45.9	45.4	45.6	69.4	68.8	66.9	69.1	70.0
29.7	28.7	28.3	28.3	27.5	24.8	24.4	24.2	23.7	23.5	24.8	23.9	26.2	24.4	23.7
9.8	9.0	9.6	9.5	11.3	5.5	5.1	4.9	5.8	6.2	12.7	11.4	10.4	10.2	10.2
31.8	30.9	30.1	30.2	32.7	25.5	23.8	23.1	25.0	25.3	33.4	33.5	31.1	32.8	32.9
18.6	18.0	17.3	18.1	18.6	16.2	17.2	18.6	17.3	17.1	18.2	17.1	20.2	19.8	18.0
52.8	51.0	49.6	49.7	52.9	47.2	46.4	47.2	47.7	47.9	53.9	52.4	53.0	54.3	52.8
47.2	49.0	50.4	50.3	47.1	52.8	53.6	52.8	52.3	52.1	46.1	47.6	47.0	45.7	47.2

TABLE 17—INCOME STATEMENT
FOR CORPORATIONS INCLUDED IN ESIC MAJOR GROUPS 36 AND 37

(See NOTE below.)

	Electrical and Electronic Equipment[1]				
	1Q 1987	2Q 1987	3Q 1987	4Q 1987	1Q 1988
	(percent of net sales)				
INCOME STATEMENT IN RATIO FORMAT					
Net sales, receipts, and operating revenues	100.0	100.0	100.0	100.0	100.0
Less: Depreciation, depletion, and amortization of property, plant and equipment	4.0	3.7	3.6	3.6	3.8
Less: All other operating costs and expenses	91.0	90.5	90.2	91.3	89.8
Income (or loss) from operations	4.9	5.8	6.2	5.1	6.4
Non-operating income (expense)	2.7	1.6	1.2	0.0	0.9
Income (or loss) before income taxes	7.6	7.4	7.3	5.1	7.3
Less: Provision for current and deferred domestic income taxes	2.3	2.6	2.6	1.6	2.0
Income (or loss) after income taxes	5.3	4.7	4.8	3.5	5.2
	(percent)				
OPERATING RATIOS (see explanatory notes)					
Annual rate of profit on stockholders' equity at end of period:					
Before income taxes	17.05	17.06	17.37	13.12	16.83
After taxes	11.91	10.96	11.28	8.91	12.08
Annual rate of profit on total assets:					
Before income taxes	8.23	8.20	8.28	6.10	7.93
After taxes	5.74	5.27	5.38	4.14	5.69
BALANCE SHEET RATIOS (based on succeeding table)					
Total current assets to total current liabilities	1.64	1.67	1.64	1.61	1.62
Total cash, U.S. Government and other securities to total current liabilities	0.25	0.26	0.24	0.23	0.23
Total stockholders' equity to total debt	2.46	2.35	2.28	2.27	2.25

NOTE: Beginning in the first quarter 1987, the universe of corporations represented by these estimates was redefined to exclude corporations with less than $250,000 in assets at the time of sample selection.

[1]During the first quarter of 1988, a number of companies were reclassified by industry. Data for the four quarters of 1987 have been revised to reflect these reclassifications, as well as respondent(s) corrections of submitted data subsequent to original publication.

[2]In the first quarter 1988, a number of corporations were reclassified by industry. To provide comparability, the four quarters of 1987 have been restated to reflect these reclassifications.

TABLE 18—BALANCE SHEET
FOR CORPORATIONS INCLUDED IN ESIC MAJOR GROUPS 36 AND 37

(See NOTE below.)

	Electrical and Electronic Equipment[1]				
	1Q 1987	2Q 1987	3Q 1987	4Q 1987	1Q 1988
	(percent of total assets)				
SELECTED BALANCE SHEET RATIOS					
Total cash, U.S. Government and other securities	7.6	7.8	7.3	7.2	7.0
Trade accounts and trade notes receivable	18.0	18.1	18.5	18.3	17.6
Inventories	21.0	21.7	21.4	20.8	21.2
Total current assets	50.3	51.1	50.9	50.3	49.8
Net property, plant and equipment	24.4	24.0	23.7	23.8	23.4
Short-term debt including installments on long-term debt	5.0	5.5	5.8	5.1	5.5
Total current liabilities	30.6	30.7	31.1	31.3	30.7
Long-term debt	14.6	14.9	15.1	15.3	15.4
Total liabilities	51.8	51.9	52.3	53.5	52.9
Stockholders' equity	48.2	48.1	47.7	46.5	47.1

NOTE: Beginning in the first quarter 1987, the universe of corporations represented by these estimates was redefined to exclude corporations with less than $250,000 in assets at the time of sample selection.

[1]During the first quarter of 1988, a number of companies were reclassified by industry. Data for the four quarters of 1987 have been revised to reflect these reclassifications, as well as respondent(s) corrections of submitted data subsequent to original publication.

[2]In the first quarter 1988, a number of corporations were reclassified by industry. To provide comparability, the four quarters of 1987 have been restated to reflect these reclassifications.

Electrical and Electronic Equipment Assets Under $25 Million					Transportation Equipment [2]					Transportation Equipment Assets Under $25 Million				
1Q 1987	2Q 1987	3Q 1987	4Q 1987	1Q 1988	1Q 1987	2Q 1987	3Q 1987	4Q 1987	1Q 1988	1Q 1987	2Q 1987	3Q 1987	4Q 1987	1Q 1988
(percent of net sales)					(percent of net sales)					(percent of net sales)				
100.0	100.0	100.0	100.0	100.0	100.0	100.0	100.0	100.0	100.0	100.0	100.0	100.0	100.0	100.0
2.9	2.8	2.6	2.8	2.7	4.0	4.3	3.3	3.7	3.7	2.5	2.6	2.7	2.1	2.2
93.1	95.4	91.7	92.4	92.9	90.5	89.8	92.7	91.9	91.7	91.1	90.5	93.3	93.2	93.2
4.0	1.8	5.7	4.8	4.4	5.5	5.8	4.1	4.4	4.6	6.4	7.0	4.0	4.7	4.6
-1.0	-0.9	-0.8	-1.9	-0.5	1.8	2.0	1.6	1.1	2.5	-0.5	-0.8	-0.6	-0.6	-0.5
3.0	0.9	4.9	3.0	3.9	7.3	7.8	5.7	5.5	7.2	6.0	6.2	3.4	4.1	4.1
2.2	2.3	2.5	2.2	1.6	2.4	2.4	1.2	1.4	1.7	2.0	2.4	1.2	0.9	1.3
0.8	-1.4	2.4	0.8	2.2	4.9	5.4	4.5	4.2	5.5	3.9	3.8	2.2	3.2	2.8
(percent)					(percent)					(percent)				
10.84	3.46	20.87	12.74	15.76	24.98	26.71	16.52	18.55	23.09	29.36	35.83	15.93	19.96	23.46
2.84	-5.39	10.29	3.47	9.14	16.69	18.40	13.00	14.00	17.73	19.46	21.71	10.42	15.66	16.00
4.92	1.51	8.43	5.26	6.92	9.21	10.05	6.21	6.77	8.41	12.09	14.67	6.79	8.97	9.11
1.29	-2.35	4.16	1.43	4.01	6.16	6.92	4.89	5.11	6.46	8.01	8.88	4.44	7.04	6.21
1.92	1.94	1.75	1.82	1.94	1.26	1.30	1.29	1.30	1.28	1.81	1.70	1.70	1.79	1.77
0.35	0.35	0.29	0.30	0.34	0.18	0.18	0.16	0.17	0.16	0.24	0.24	0.30	0.33	0.26
1.75	1.51	1.37	1.41	1.48	2.19	2.13	2.12	2.02	2.09	1.18	1.23	1.37	1.61	1.24

Electrical and Electronic Equipment Assets Under $25 Million					Transportation Equipment [2]					Transportation Equipment Assets Under $25 Million				
1Q 1987	2Q 1987	3Q 1987	4Q 1987	1Q 1988	1Q 1987	2Q 1987	3Q 1987	4Q 1987	1Q 1988	1Q 1987	2Q 1987	3Q 1987	4Q 1987	1Q 1988
(percent of total assets)					(percent of total assets)					(percent of total assets)				
12.7	12.7	11.8	11.8	12.8	7.3	6.9	6.2	6.6	6.3	8.7	9.1	11.1	12.8	10.3
24.6	25.8	25.7	27.1	26.8	16.8	17.6	17.3	17.7	18.1	23.3	23.3	24.1	23.2	25.0
30.3	29.1	30.8	29.5	29.5	23.4	23.1	23.4	22.7	22.9	29.7	29.6	25.6	30.0	30.9
70.7	70.7	71.8	71.5	72.9	51.0	50.6	50.0	50.8	50.5	64.8	64.6	63.2	68.9	69.7
21.5	21.9	21.0	21.5	21.7	27.1	26.7	26.3	25.6	25.2	30.6	32.0	33.1	25.5	23.5
10.5	12.4	14.1	13.3	13.7	2.4	2.4	2.5	2.4	2.3	12.7	13.4	12.1	13.7	13.2
36.8	36.5	41.1	39.3	37.7	40.6	39.0	38.7	39.1	39.5	35.7	37.9	37.2	38.6	39.3
15.5	16.5	15.3	15.9	16.1	14.4	15.4	15.3	15.7	15.2	22.2	19.8	19.0	14.2	18.0
54.6	56.3	59.6	58.7	56.1	63.1	62.4	62.4	63.5	63.6	58.8	59.1	57.4	55.1	61.2
45.4	43.7	40.4	41.3	43.9	36.9	37.6	37.6	36.5	36.4	41.2	40.9	42.6	44.9	38.8

TABLE 19—INCOME STATEMENT
FOR CORPORATIONS INCLUDED IN ESIC MAJOR GROUPS 37.1 AND 37.7

(See NOTE below.)

	Motor Vehicles and Equipment [1,2]				
	1Q 1987	2Q 1987	3Q 1987	4Q 1987	1Q 1988
	(percent of net sales)				
INCOME STATEMENT IN RATIO FORMAT					
Net sales, receipts, and operating revenues	100.0	100.0	100.0	100.0	100.0
Less: Depreciation, depletion, and amortization of property, plant and equipment	4.4	5.0	3.3	3.9	3.9
Less: All other operating costs and expenses	90.1	89.1	93.9	92.3	91.7
Income (or loss) from operations	5.4	5.9	2.9	3.8	4.4
Non-operating income (expense)	2.7	2.9	2.4	2.1	3.7
Income (or loss) before income taxes	8.1	8.8	5.2	5.9	8.1
Less: Provision for current and deferred domestic income taxes	2.5	2.6	0.6	1.3	1.9
Income (or loss) after income taxes	5.6	6.2	4.7	4.6	6.2
	(percent)				
OPERATING RATIOS (see explanatory notes)					
Annual rate of profit on stockholders' equity at end of period:					
Before income taxes	26.81	29.14	13.69	18.28	24.90
After taxes	18.40	20.46	12.24	14.14	19.21
Annual rate of profit on total assets:					
Before income taxes	11.82	13.12	6.14	7.94	10.80
After taxes	8.11	9.21	5.49	6.15	8.33
BALANCE SHEET RATIOS (based on succeeding table)					
Total current assets to total current liabilities	1.39	1.49	1.50	1.53	1.44
Total cash, U.S. Government and other securities to total current liabilities	0.27	0.27	0.23	0.27	0.24
Total stockholders' equity to total debt	2.47	2.32	2.27	2.11	2.32

NOTE: Beginning in the first quarter 1987, the universe of corporations represented by these estimates was redefined to exclude corporations with less than $250,000 in assets at the time of sample selection.

[1]Included in Transportation Equipment.

[2]In the first quarter 1988, a number of corporations were reclassified by industry. To provide comparability, the four quarters of 1987 have been restated to reflect these reclassifications.

TABLE 20—BALANCE SHEET
FOR CORPORATIONS INCLUDED IN ESIC MAJOR GROUPS 37.1 AND 37.7

(See NOTE below.)

	Motor Vehicles and Equipment [1,2]				
	1Q[3] 1987	2Q 1987	3Q 1987	4Q 1987	1Q 1988
	(percent of total assets)				
SELECTED BALANCE SHEET RATIOS					
Total cash, U.S. Government and other securities	8.2	7.3	6.1	7.1	6.8
Trade accounts and trade notes receivable	17.6	19.1	18.5	18.2	19.4
Inventories	10.7	10.3	10.7	10.1	10.1
Total current assets	41.7	40.4	39.8	40.9	40.5
Net property, plant and equipment	31.1	30.8	30.3	29.1	28.5
Short-term debt including installments on long-term debt	2.3	2.1	2.0	1.9	1.7
Total current liabilities	29.9	27.2	26.5	26.7	28.1
Long-term debt	15.5	17.3	17.7	18.6	17.0
Total liabilities	55.9	55.0	55.1	56.5	56.6
Stockholders' equity	44.1	45.0	44.9	43.5	43.4

NOTE: Beginning in the first quarter 1987, the universe of corporations represented by these estimates was redefined to exclude corporations with less than $250,000 in assets at the time of sample selection.

[1]Included in Transportation Equipment.

[2]In the first quarter 1988, a number of corporations were reclassified by industry. To provide comparability, the four quarters of 1987 have been restated to reflect these reclassifications.

[3]Revised.

Motor Vehicles and Equipment [1,2] Assets Under $25 Million					Aircraft, Guided Missiles and Parts [1,2]					Aircraft, Guided Missiles and Parts [1] Assets Under $25 Million				
1Q 1987	2Q 1987	3Q 1987	4Q 1987	1Q 1988	1Q 1987	2Q 1987	3Q 1987	4Q 1987	1Q 1988	1Q 1987	2Q 1987	3Q 1987	4Q 1987	1Q 1988
(percent of net sales)					(percent of net sales)					(percent of net sales)				
100.0	100.0	100.0	100.0	100.0	100.0	100.0	100.0	100.0	100.0	100.0	100.0	100.0	100.0	100.0
2.2	2.0	2.4	1.5	1.7	3.3	3.2	3.3	3.3	3.4	3.8	5.4	4.0	3.3	5.0
91.4	90.4	93.2	93.6	94.3	90.8	91.1	90.8	91.4	91.7	85.4	87.7	87.8	85.4	86.7
6.4	7.6	4.4	4.9	4.0	5.9	5.7	5.9	5.3	4.9	10.9	7.0	8.2	11.3	8.3
-0.8	-0.8	-0.6	-0.5	-0.3	0.5	0.7	0.7	0.0	1.0	-1.2	-1.1	-0.4	-0.8	-1.2
5.6	6.8	3.8	4.5	3.7	6.5	6.3	6.6	5.3	5.9	9.7	5.8	7.8	10.6	7.1
1.6	2.2	1.2	1.0	1.1	2.3	2.1	2.2	1.5	1.3	2.4	1.6	1.9	1.9	1.6
4.0	4.5	2.7	3.4	2.6	4.2	4.3	4.3	3.8	4.6	7.2	4.2	5.9	8.6	5.5
(percent)					(percent)					(percent)				
30.42	44.84	20.31	27.34	22.67	22.84	22.21	22.19	19.75	19.63	32.39	19.08	27.94	29.57	19.63
21.83	30.19	14.13	21.05	15.89	14.81	14.91	14.68	14.18	15.15	24.29	13.78	20.96	24.18	15.19
13.09	17.99	8.48	12.16	9.02	6.84	6.80	6.74	5.86	5.80	16.70	9.70	14.21	17.20	10.06
9.39	12.11	5.90	9.36	6.32	4.43	4.56	4.45	4.21	4.48	12.52	7.01	10.66	14.07	7.79
1.88	1.69	1.69	1.88	1.86	1.17	1.19	1.17	1.16	1.18	2.13	1.94	2.13	2.15	2.41
0.22	0.22	0.26	0.32	0.29	0.12	0.12	0.12	0.10	0.10	0.47	0.38	0.55	0.59	0.49
1.24	1.15	1.29	1.62	1.21	2.29	2.35	2.37	2.35	2.19	2.22	2.07	1.99	2.85	2.78

Motor Vehicles and Equipment [1,2] Assets Under $25 Million					Aircraft, Guided Missiles and Parts [1,2]					Aircraft, Guided Missiles and Parts [1] Assets Under $25 Million				
1Q 1987	2Q 1987	3Q 1987	4Q 1987	1Q 1988	1Q 1987	2Q 1987	3Q 1987	4Q 1987	1Q 1988	1Q 1987	2Q 1987	3Q 1987	4Q 1987	1Q 1988
(percent of total assets)					(percent of total assets)					(percent of total assets)				
7.5	8.9	10.1	13.2	11.3	6.4	6.5	6.3	5.6	5.5	14.8	12.1	17.0	18.6	13.3
23.0	23.5	25.2	26.7	28.6	12.9	12.9	13.0	14.6	13.7	22.8	21.3	21.6	17.1	17.5
32.9	33.0	27.4	33.5	31.4	42.4	42.0	42.3	41.9	42.5	27.2	25.5	23.7	30.0	32.7
65.8	67.5	64.8	76.4	73.7	62.8	63.5	62.9	63.6	63.3	67.2	60.9	65.5	67.3	65.2
29.9	29.8	31.7	21.0	21.3	21.3	20.9	20.5	20.6	20.2	30.6	35.2	30.2	25.0	26.3
13.1	15.6	13.4	14.0	13.6	2.1	2.0	2.3	2.6	2.6	7.8	8.4	8.5	11.0	7.8
35.0	39.9	38.4	40.5	39.7	53.9	53.3	53.8	54.7	53.7	31.5	31.4	30.8	31.3	27.1
21.6	19.3	18.8	13.4	19.3	10.9	11.0	10.3	10.2	10.9	15.4	16.2	17.1	9.5	10.5
57.0	59.9	58.3	55.5	60.2	70.1	69.4	69.6	70.3	70.4	48.5	49.1	49.1	41.8	48.7
43.0	40.1	41.7	44.5	39.8	29.9	30.6	30.4	29.7	29.6	51.5	50.9	50.9	58.2	51.3

TABLE 21—INCOME STATEMENT
FOR CORPORATIONS INCLUDED IN ESIC MAJOR GROUP 38 AND OTHER DURABLE MANUFACTURING INDUSTRIES

(See NOTE below.)

	Instruments and Related Products [1]				
	1Q 1987	2Q 1987	3Q 1987	4Q 1987	1Q 1988
	(percent of net sales)				
INCOME STATEMENT IN RATIO FORMAT					
Net sales, receipts, and operating revenues	100.0	100.0	100.0	100.0	100.0
Less: Depreciation, depletion, and amortization of property, plant and equipment	5.0	4.8	4.7	4.2	4.6
Less: All other operating costs and expenses	89.4	88.5	88.0	90.7	88.9
Income (or loss) from operations	5.[illegible]	6.7	7.3	5.1	6.5
Non-operating income (expense)	3.1	2.2	2.9	3.1	4.4
Income (or loss) before income taxes	8.6	8.9	10.2	8.2	10.9
Less: Provision for current and deferred domestic income taxes	3.1	3.0	3.2	2.0	2.5
Income (or loss) after income taxes	5.5	5.9	7.1	6.2	8.3
	(percent)				
OPERATING RATIOS (see explanatory notes)					
Annual rate of profit on stockholders' equity at end of period:					
Before income taxes	15.12	16.02	19.13	15.89	20.41
After taxes	9.63	10.60	13.22	11.96	15.62
Annual rate of profit on total assets:					
Before income taxes	8.15	8.68	10.17	8.04	9.68
After taxes	5.19	5.75	7.03	6.06	7.41
BALANCE SHEET RATIOS (based on succeeding table)					
Total current assets to total current liabilities	1.64	1.75	1.73	1.72	1.71
Total cash, U.S. Government and other securities to total current liabilities	0.21	0.23	0.21	0.23	0.21
Total stockholders' equity to total debt	2.59	2.66	2.47	2.19	1.74

NOTE: Beginning in the first quarter 1987, the universe of corporations represented by these estimates was redefined to exclude corporations with less than $250,000 in assets at the time of sample selection.

[1] In the first quarter 1988, a number of corporations were reclassified by industry. To provide comparability, the four quarters of 1987 have been restated to reflect these reclassifications.

TABLE 22—BALANCE SHEET
FOR CORPORATIONS INCLUDED IN ESIC MAJOR GROUP 38 AND OTHER DURABLE MANUFACTURING INDUSTRIES

(See NOTE below.)

	Instruments and Related Products [1]				
	1Q 1987	2Q 1987	3Q 1987	4Q 1987	1Q 1988
	(percent of total assets)				
SELECTED BALANCE SHEET RATIOS					
Total cash, U.S. Government and other securities	5.6	5.8	5.3	5.6	4.8
Trade accounts and trade notes receivable	16.0	16.5	17.0	16.5	15.5
Inventories	17.6	17.3	16.8	16.2	15.6
Total current assets	43.7	43.8	43.5	42.8	39.7
Net property, plant and equipment	27.0	26.6	26.5	25.8	24.7
Short-term debt including installments on long-term debt	7.4	5.7	6.2	5.3	4.6
Total current liabilities	26.7	25.0	25.2	24.9	23.1
Long-term debt	13.3	14.7	15.4	17.9	22.5
Total liabilities	46.1	45.8	46.8	49.4	52.6
Stockholders' equity	53.9	54.2	53.2	50.6	47.4

NOTE: Beginning in the first quarter 1987, the universe of corporations represented by these estimates was redefined to exclude corporations with less than $250,000 in assets at the time of sample selection.

[1] In the first quarter 1988, a number of corporations were reclassified by industry. To provide comparability, the four quarters of 1987 have been restated to reflect these reclassifications.

Instruments and Related Products Assets Under $25 Million					Other Durable Mfg. Industries					Other Durable Mfg. Industries Assets Under $25 Million				
1Q 1987	2Q 1987	3Q 1987	4Q 1987	1Q 1988	1Q 1987	2Q 1987	3Q 1987	4Q 1987	1Q 1988	1Q 1987	2Q 1987	3Q 1987	4Q 1987	1Q 1988
(percent of net sales)					(percent of net sales)					(percent of net sales)				
100.0	100.0	100.0	100.0	100.0	100.0	100.0	100.0	100.0	100.0	100.0	100.0	100.0	100.0	100.0
3.1	2.6	2.8	2.9	2.7	3.0	2.7	2.6	2.6	3.0	2.5	2.2	2.1	1.9	2.5
92.1	91.6	86.8	94.3	93.7	91.6	89.2	89.6	90.9	90.9	94.2	91.6	91.8	93.7	93.4
4.7	5.8	10.4	2.8	3.6	5.5	8.1	7.8	6.5	6.0	3.2	6.2	6.1	4.4	4.1
-0.8	-1.1	-0.8	-1.0	-0.2	-0.6	-0.2	-0.6	-0.6	-0.6	0.1	-0.3	-0.4	-0.4	-0.2
3.9	4.7	9.6	1.8	3.5	4.9	7.9	7.2	5.9	5.4	3.3	5.9	5.7	3.9	4.0
2.8	2.5	3.7	1.9	2.4	2.3	3.2	2.6	2.1	1.9	1.8	2.2	1.6	1.0	1.1
1.2	2.2	5.8	0.0	1.1	2.6	4.7	4.6	3.7	3.5	1.5	3.8	4.0	3.0	2.9
(percent)					(percent)					(percent)				
11.85	15.43	31.98	6.68	11.75	16.40	30.48	29.50	24.18	18.65	13.94	30.87	30.76	22.03	16.98
3.57	7.08	19.50	-0.14	3.69	8.65	18.28	18.87	15.37	12.14	6.46	19.56	21.88	16.52	12.38
6.17	7.73	16.19	3.02	5.62	7.92	14.25	13.81	11.24	8.81	6.71	13.77	14.20	10.36	8.46
1.86	3.54	9.87	-0.06	1.76	4.18	8.55	8.84	7.14	5.74	3.11	8.73	10.10	7.77	6.17
2.59	2.45	2.79	2.57	2.43	2.01	1.97	2.00	1.98	2.05	1.98	1.86	1.89	1.91	2.04
0.48	0.44	0.51	0.48	0.42	0.27	0.26	0.27	0.29	0.26	0.26	0.25	0.27	0.27	0.28
1.91	1.77	1.74	1.39	1.63	1.68	1.57	1.56	1.48	1.51	1.63	1.39	1.48	1.47	1.62

Instruments and Related Products Assets Under $25 Million					Other Durable Mfg. Industries[1]					Other Durable Mfg. Industries Assets Under $25 Million				
1Q 1987	2Q 1987	3Q 1987	4Q 1987	1Q 1988	1Q 1987	2Q 1987	3Q 1987	4Q 1987	1Q 1988	1Q 1987	2Q 1987	3Q 1987	4Q 1987	1Q 1988
(percent of total assets)					(percent of total assets)					(percent of total assets)				
14.0	13.8	13.5	14.2	13.2	7.3	7.2	7.4	7.7	6.8	8.8	8.8	9.4	9.2	8.9
28.2	27.7	27.1	27.6	29.8	21.3	22.0	21.5	19.5	19.6	25.3	26.7	25.0	23.0	22.5
30.7	31.8	30.9	30.9	30.7	22.9	22.1	22.7	23.2	23.4	28.7	27.3	28.3	30.2	30.2
75.9	76.3	74.5	75.9	77.1	55.4	54.3	54.6	53.5	54.0	67.4	66.4	66.2	66.0	65.3
18.4	18.3	19.3	19.5	18.7	34.4	34.6	35.4	35.2	35.6	26.4	26.5	27.2	27.4	27.9
9.9	10.7	8.0	9.2	10.1	9.7	9.8	9.2	10.0	9.7	13.1	14.9	13.9	15.6	13.7
29.3	31.1	26.7	29.6	31.8	27.5	27.5	27.3	27.0	26.4	34.1	35.8	34.9	34.6	32.0
17.4	17.6	21.2	23.4	19.3	19.0	20.0	20.8	21.3	21.6	16.4	17.3	17.3	16.4	17.0
47.9	49.9	49.4	54.7	52.2	51.7	53.2	53.2	53.5	52.7	51.9	55.4	53.8	53.0	50.2
52.1	50.1	50.6	45.3	47.8	48.3	46.8	46.8	46.5	47.3	48.1	44.6	46.2	47.0	49.8

TABLE 23—INCOME STATEMENT
FOR CORPORATIONS INCLUDED IN ESIC MAJOR GROUP 20, ASSETS $25 MILLION AND OVER

	Food and Kindred Products[1]				
	1Q 1987	2Q 1987	3Q 1987	4Q 1987	1Q 1988
INCOME STATEMENT IN RATIO FORMAT	(percent of net sales)				
Net sales, receipts, and operating revenues	100.0	100.0	100.0	100.0	100.0
Less: Depreciation, depletion, and amortization of property, plant and equipment	2.7	2.5	2.5	2.7	2.6
Less: All other operating costs and expenses	89.9	89.4	89.2	88.8	89.9
Income (or loss) from operations	7.5	8.1	8.3	8.5	7.4
Non-operating income (expense)	-2.0	-1.4	-1.8	-0.4	-0.3
Income (or loss) before income taxes	5.5	6.7	6.5	8.0	7.1
Net income (or loss) of foreign branches and equity in earnings (losses) of non-consolidated subsidiaries (net of foreign taxes)	1.1	1.3	1.1	1.1	0.9
Less: Provision for current and deferred domestic income taxes	2.5	3.1	2.7	2.8	2.2
Income (or loss) after income taxes	4.2	5.0	4.9	6.3	5.8
OPERATING RATIOS (see explanatory notes)	(percent)				
Annual rate of profit on stockholders' equity at end of period:					
Before income taxes	22.16	28.82	27.03	32.09	26.96
After taxes	14.01	17.86	17.47	22.27	19.71
Annual rate of profit on total assets:					
Before income taxes	8.25	10.87	10.39	12.36	10.34
After taxes	5.22	6.73	6.72	8.58	7.56

[1]In the first quarter 1988, a number of corporations were reclassified by industry. To provide comparability, the four quarters of 1987 have been restated to reflect these reclassifications.

TABLE 24—INCOME STATEMENT
FOR CORPORATIONS INCLUDED IN ESIC MAJOR GROUP 22, ASSETS $25 MILLION AND OVER

	Textile Mill Products[1]				
	1Q 1987	2Q 1987	3Q 1987	4Q 1987	1Q 1988
INCOME STATEMENT IN RATIO FORMAT	(percent of net sales)				
Net sales, receipts, and operating revenues	100.0	100.0	100.0	100.0	100.0
Less: Depreciation, depletion, and amortization of property, plant and equipment	3.5	3.4	3.1	3.0	3.4
Less: All other operating costs and expenses	88.5	88.4	87.9	88.4	89.4
Income (or loss) from operations	8.0	8.3	8.9	8.6	7.1
Non-operating income (expense)	-1.3	-2.2	-2.9	-2.0	-1.9
Income (or loss) before income taxes	6.7	6.0	6.0	6.7	5.2
Net income (or loss) of foreign branches and equity in earnings (losses) of non-consolidated subsidiaries (net of foreign taxes)	0.1	0.1	0.1	0.1	0.1
Less: Provision for current and deferred domestic income taxes	2.5	2.5	2.4	2.4	2.1
Income (or loss) after income taxes	4.2	3.6	3.7	4.4	3.2
OPERATING RATIOS (see explanatory notes)	(percent)				
Annual rate of profit on stockholders' equity at end of period:					
Before income taxes	22.40	20.32	23.99	26.45	19.02
After taxes	13.89	12.02	14.60	17.08	11.53
Annual rate of profit on total assets:					
Before income taxes	9.65	9.18	8.98	10.09	7.19
After taxes	5.98	5.43	5.46	6.52	4.36

[1]1987 data are revised.

TABLE 25—INCOME STATEMENT
FOR CORPORATIONS INCLUDED IN ESIC MAJOR GROUP 26, ASSETS $25 MILLION AND OVER

	Paper and Allied Products[1]				
	1Q 1987	2Q 1987	3Q 1987	4Q 1987	1Q 1988
INCOME STATEMENT IN RATIO FORMAT	(percent of net sales)				
Net sales, receipts, and operating revenues	100.0	100.0	100.0	100.0	100.0
Less: Depreciation, depletion, and amortization of property, plant and equipment	5.2	4.9	4.9	4.6	4.9
Less: All other operating costs and expenses	85.0	84.6	84.1	84.3	82.4
Income (or loss) from operations	9.8	10.6	10.9	11.1	12.7
Non-operating income (expense)	-1.5	-1.3	-0.5	-1.8	-1.7
Income (or loss) before income taxes	8.3	9.4	10.4	9.3	11.0
Net income (or loss) of foreign branches and equity in earnings (losses) of non-consolidated subsidiaries (net of foreign taxes)	0.6	0.8	0.7	0.8	0.6
Less: Provision for current and deferred domestic income taxes	3.7	4.0	4.3	3.6	4.1
Income (or loss) after income taxes	5.3	6.2	6.9	6.5	7.4
OPERATING RATIOS (see explanatory notes)	(percent)				
Annual rate of profit on stockholders' equity at end of period:					
Before income taxes	19.90	21.61	26.14	23.56	26.92
After taxes	11.81	14.34	16.12	15.18	17.29
Annual rate of profit on total assets:					
Before income taxes	9.13	10.90	12.02	10.84	12.49
After taxes	5.42	6.62	7.41	6.99	8.02

[1] In the first quarter 1988, a number of corporations were reclassified by industry. To provide comparability, the four quarters of 1987 have been restated to reflect these reclassifications.

TABLE 26—INCOME STATEMENT
FOR CORPORATIONS INCLUDED IN ESIC MAJOR GROUP 27, ASSETS $25 MILLION AND OVER

	Printing and Publishing[1]				
	1Q 1987	2Q 1987	3Q 1987	4Q 1987	1Q 1988
INCOME STATEMENT IN RATIO FORMAT	(percent of net sales)				
Net sales, receipts, and operating revenues	100.0	100.0	100.0	100.0	100.0
Less: Depreciation, depletion, and amortization of property, plant and equipment	4.0	3.9	3.8	3.5	4.1
Less: All other operating costs and expenses	84.9	82.9	81.4	82.1	85.6
Income (or loss) from operations	11.1	13.1	14.9	14.4	10.4
Non-operating income (expense)	-1.6	-2.0	-1.2	-2.8	1.5
Income (or loss) before income taxes	9.5	11.1	13.6	11.6	11.8
Net income (or loss) of foreign branches and equity in earnings (losses) of non-consolidated subsidiaries (net of foreign taxes)	0.7	1.4	1.7	1.1	1.1
Less: Provision for current and deferred domestic income taxes	4.4	5.5	6.3	5.3	4.8
Income (or loss) after income taxes	5.8	7.0	9.0	7.4	8.1
OPERATING RATIOS (see explanatory notes)	(percent)				
Annual rate of profit on stockholders' equity at end of period:					
Before income taxes	22.57	29.28	35.98	32.32	29.03
After taxes	12.82	16.40	21.20	18.79	18.23
Annual rate of profit on total assets:					
Before income taxes	10.10	12.43	15.29	13.45	12.34
After taxes	5.74	6.96	9.01	7.82	7.75

[1] 1987 data are revised.

TABLE 27—INCOME STATEMENT
FOR CORPORATIONS INCLUDED IN ESIC MAJOR GROUP 28, ASSETS $25 MILLION AND OVER

	Chemicals and Allied Products[1]				
	1Q[2] 1987	2Q 1987	3Q 1987	4Q 1987	1Q 1988
INCOME STATEMENT IN RATIO FORMAT	(percent of net sales)				
Net sales, receipts, and operating revenues	100.0	100.0	100.0	100.0	100.0
Less: Depreciation, depletion, and amortization of property, plant and equipment	4.6	4.5	4.5	4.8	4.5
Less: All other operating costs and expenses	85.5	87.1	85.2	87.9	85.0
Income (or loss) from operations	10.0	8.3	10.3	7.3	10.5
Non-operating income (expense)	0.1	0.0	2.5	-1.3	1.5
Income (or loss) before income taxes	10.1	8.3	12.8	5.9	12.0
Net income (or loss) of foreign branches and equity in earnings (losses) of non-consolidated subsidiaries (net of foreign taxes)	3.0	2.9	3.4	2.2	3.4
Less: Provision for current and deferred domestic income taxes	4.4	3.6	5.7	3.3	4.4
Income (or loss) after income taxes	8.6	7.6	10.4	4.9	11.0
OPERATING RATIOS (see explanatory notes)	(percent)				
Annual rate of profit on stockholders' equity at end of period:					
Before income taxes	25.63	22.36	32.27	17.07	32.40
After taxes	16.92	15.20	20.90	10.24	23.25
Annual rate of profit on total assets:					
Before income taxes	11.69	10.35	14.80	7.48	14.40
After taxes	7.72	7.03	9.59	4.49	10.33

[1]In the first quarter 1988, a number of corporations were reclassified by industry. To provide comparability, the four quarters of 1987 have been restated to reflect these reclassifications.
[2]Revised.

TABLE 28—INCOME STATEMENT
FOR CORPORATIONS INCLUDED IN ESIC MAJOR GROUP 28.1, ASSETS $25 MILLION AND OVER

	Industrial Chemicals and Synthetics[1]				
	1Q 1987	2Q 1987	3Q 1987	4Q 1987	1Q 1988
INCOME STATEMENT IN RATIO FORMAT	(percent of net sales)				
Net sales, receipts, and operating revenues	100.0	100.0	100.0	100.0	100.0
Less: Depreciation, depletion, and amortization of property, plant and equipment	6.2	6.0	5.9	6.3	5.8
Less: All other operating costs and expenses	84.3	83.7	84.7	85.3	82.7
Income (or loss) from operations	9.5	10.3	9.4	8.4	11.5
Non-operating income (expense)	-1.2	0.0	6.1	-1.3	-1.0
Income (or loss) before income taxes	8.3	10.3	15.5	7.1	10.4
Net income (or loss) of foreign branches and equity in earnings (losses) of non-consolidated subsidiaries (net of foreign taxes)	2.2	1.8	2.4	1.8	2.6
Less: Provision for current and deferred domestic income taxes	3.6	4.0	7.0	3.5	4.0
Income (or loss) after income taxes	7.0	8.1	10.9	5.4	8.9
OPERATING RATIOS (see explanatory notes)	(percent)				
Annual rate of profit on stockholders' equity at end of period:					
Before income taxes	21.77	25.87	36.96	19.77	28.69
After taxes	14.44	17.25	22.53	12.03	19.72
Annual rate of profit on total assets:					
Before income taxes	9.22	11.24	15.97	8.22	12.11
After taxes	6.12	7.50	9.73	5.00	8.32

[1]In the first quarter 1988, a number of corporations were reclassified by industry. To provide comparability, the four quarters of 1987 have been restated to reflect these reclassifications.

TABLE 29—INCOME STATEMENT
FOR CORPORATIONS INCLUDED IN ESIC MAJOR GROUP 28.3, ASSETS $25 MILLION AND OVER

	Drugs[1]				
	1Q 1987	2Q 1987	3Q 1987	4Q 1987	1Q 1988
INCOME STATEMENT IN RATIO FORMAT	(percent of net sales)				
Net sales, receipts, and operating revenues	100.0	100.0	100.0	100.0	100.0
Less: Depreciation, depletion, and amortization of property, plant and equipment	3.1	3.6	3.5	3.5	3.3
Less: All other operating costs and expenses	83.3	85.6	83.6	88.7	85.2
Income (or loss) from operations	13.6	10.8	12.9	7.7	11.5
Non-operating income (expense)	1.3	0.0	-1.1	-6.0	8.6
Income (or loss) before income taxes	14.9	10.8	11.8	1.7	20.1
Net income (or loss) of foreign branches and equity in earnings (losses) of non-consolidated subsidiaries (net of foreign taxes)	6.4	7.7	7.3	4.5	7.2
Less: Provision for current and deferred domestic income taxes	6.3	5.3	6.0	4.4	6.6
Income (or loss) after income taxes	15.0	13.2	13.2	1.8	20.7
OPERATING RATIOS (see explanatory notes)	(percent)				
Annual rate of profit on stockholders' equity at end of period:					
Before income taxes	35.31	29.74	32.04	11.54	51.86
After taxes	24.90	21.23	22.15	3.33	39.37
Annual rate of profit on total assets:					
Before income taxes	17.95	15.36	16.16	5.14	23.84
After taxes	12.66	10.97	11.17	1.48	18.10

[1] 1987 data are revised.

TABLE 30—INCOME STATEMENT
FOR CORPORATIONS INCLUDED IN ESIC MAJOR GROUP 29, ASSETS $25 MILLION AND OVER

	Petroleum and Coal Products[1]				
	1Q 1987	2Q 1987	3Q 1987	4Q 1987	1Q 1988
INCOME STATEMENT IN RATIO FORMAT	(percent of net sales)				
Net sales, receipts, and operating revenues	100.0	100.0	100.0	100.0	100.0
Less: Depreciation, depletion, and amortization of property, plant and equipment	9.2	8.0	7.9	7.9	8.0
Less: All other operating costs and expenses	87.1	85.9	85.2	86.1	84.9
Income (or loss) from operations	3.7	6.1	6.9	5.9	7.1
Non-operating income (expense)	0.6	0.9	-0.2	-7.4	0.7
Income (or loss) before income taxes	4.3	7.0	6.7	-1.5	7.8
Net income (or loss) of foreign branches and equity in earnings (losses) of non-consolidated subsidiaries (net of foreign taxes)	2.0	2.0	1.6	1.3	2.5
Less: Provision for current and deferred domestic income taxes	1.0	1.9	2.3	0.1	2.3
Income (or loss) after income taxes	5.3	7.1	5.9	-0.3	8.1
OPERATING RATIOS (see explanatory notes)	(percent)				
Annual rate of profit on stockholders' equity at end of period:					
Before income taxes	9.59	16.25	14.78	-0.36	18.12
After taxes	7.98	12.85	10.59	-0.55	14.24
Annual rate of profit on total assets:					
Before income taxes	4.15	6.74	6.36	-0.15	7.68
After taxes	3.45	5.33	4.55	-0.23	6.04

[1] 1987 data are revised.

TABLE 31—INCOME STATEMENT
FOR CORPORATIONS INCLUDED IN ESIC MAJOR GROUP 30, ASSETS $25 MILLION AND OVER

	Rubber and Misc. Plastics Products [1]				
	1Q[2] 1987	2Q 1987	3Q 1987	4Q 1987	1Q 1988
INCOME STATEMENT IN RATIO FORMAT	(percent of net sales)				
Net sales, receipts, and operating revenues	100.0	100.0	100.0	100.0	100.0
Less: Depreciation, depletion, and amortization of property, plant and equipment	3.9	3.4	3.0	3.4	3.4
Less: All other operating costs and expenses	89.2	89.8	90.4	90.2	89.2
Income (or loss) from operations	6.9	6.8	6.6	6.4	7.3
Non-operating income (expense)	0.6	0.4	0.0	2.0	-1.9
Income (or loss) before income taxes	7.5	7.3	6.6	8.3	5.4
Net income (or loss) of foreign branches and equity in earnings (losses) of non-consolidated subsidiaries (net of foreign taxes)	1.5	1.4	1.5	1.2	1.4
Less: Provision for current and deferred domestic income taxes	2.3	2.3	2.8	3.1	2.0
Income (or loss) after income taxes	6.7	6.4	5.3	6.4	4.8
OPERATING RATIOS (see explanatory notes)	(percent)				
Annual rate of profit on stockholders' equity at end of period:					
Before income taxes	29.01	34.88	32.27	35.37	24.06
After taxes	21.64	25.60	21.39	23.84	17.02
Annual rate of profit on total assets:					
Before income taxes	10.18	10.84	10.37	12.34	8.63
After taxes	7.59	7.95	6.87	8.32	6.10

[1]In the first quarter 1988, a number of corporations were reclassified by industry. To provide comparability, the four quarters of 1987 have been restated to reflect these reclassifications.
[2]Revised.

TABLE 32—INCOME STATEMENT
FOR CORPORATIONS INCLUDED IN ESIC MAJOR GROUP 32, ASSETS $25 MILLION AND OVER

	Stone, Clay and Glass Products[1]				
	1Q 1987	2Q 1987	3Q 1987	4Q 1987	1Q 1988
INCOME STATEMENT IN RATIO FORMAT	(percent of net sales)				
Net sales, receipts, and operating revenues	100.0	100.0	100.0	100.0	100.0
Less: Depreciation, depletion, and amortization of property, plant and equipment	5.2	4.8	4.4	5.3	5.6
Less: All other operating costs and expenses	87.6	84.6	84.0	87.1	88.4
Income (or loss) from operations	7.3	10.6	11.6	7.6	6.0
Non-operating income (expense)	3.6	-1.9	-3.1	-4.2	-2.8
Income (or loss) before income taxes	10.9	8.7	8.5	3.4	3.2
Net income (or loss) of foreign branches and equity in earnings (losses) of non-consolidated subsidiaries (net of foreign taxes)	0.8	1.1	1.2	0.6	1.1
Less: Provision for current and deferred domestic income taxes	3.3	3.7	3.2	1.0	1.5
Income (or loss) after income taxes	8.4	6.1	6.5	3.0	2.8
OPERATING RATIOS (see explanatory notes)	(percent)				
Annual rate of profit on stockholders' equity at end of period:					
Before income taxes	26.38	26.23	25.22	10.04	9.29
After taxes	18.96	16.38	17.00	7.50	5.96
Annual rate of profit on total assets:					
Before income taxes	11.02	9.48	9.38	3.77	3.44
After taxes	7.92	5.92	6.32	2.82	2.21

[1]In the first quarter 1988, a number of corporations were reclassified by industry. To provide comparability, the four quarters of 1987 have been restated to reflect these reclassifications.

TABLE 33—INCOME STATEMENT
FOR CORPORATIONS INCLUDED IN ESIC MAJOR GROUP 33, ASSETS $25 MILLION AND OVER

	Primary Metal Industries[1]				
	1Q 1987	2Q 1987	3Q 1987	4Q 1987	1Q 1988
INCOME STATEMENT IN RATIO FORMAT	(percent of net sales)				
Net sales, receipts, and operating revenues	100.0	100.0	100.0	100.0	100.0
Less: Depreciation, depletion, and amortization of property, plant and equipment	4.2	4.0	3.8	3.8	3.7
Less: All other operating costs and expenses	91.2	90.2	91.0	91.0	88.7
Income (or loss) from operations	4.6	5.9	5.2	5.3	7.6
Non-operating income (expense)	-1.1	-3.3	-0.2	-4.4	-1.1
Income (or loss) before income taxes	3.5	2.6	5.0	0.9	6.5
Net income (or loss) of foreign branches and equity in earnings (losses) of non-consolidated subsidiaries (net of foreign taxes)	0.7	1.6	1.1	1.3	0.6
Less: Provision for current and deferred domestic income taxes	1.2	2.1	2.0	0.5	2.2
Income (or loss) after income taxes	3.0	2.2	4.1	1.7	4.9
OPERATING RATIOS (see explanatory notes)	(percent)				
Annual rate of profit on stockholders' equity at end of period:					
Before income taxes	13.83	13.90	20.92	7.92	25.66
After taxes	9.89	7.16	14.24	6.14	17.66
Annual rate of profit on total assets:					
Before income taxes	4.46	4.70	6.58	2.59	8.08
After taxes	3.19	2.42	4.48	2.01	5.56

[1]In the first quarter 1988, a number of corporations were reclassified by industry. To provide comparability, the four quarters of 1987 have been restated to reflect these reclassifications.

TABLE 34—INCOME STATEMENT
FOR CORPORATIONS INCLUDED IN ESIC MAJOR GROUPS 33.1-2, ASSETS $25 MILLION AND OVER

	Iron and Steel[1]				
	1Q 1987	2Q 1987	3Q 1987	4Q 1987	1Q 1988
INCOME STATEMENT IN RATIO FORMAT	(percent of net sales)				
Net sales, receipts, and operating revenues	100.0	100.0	100.0	100.0	100.0
Less: Depreciation, depletion, and amortization of property, plant and equipment	4.1	3.8	3.8	3.6	3.6
Less: All other operating costs and expenses	91.4	90.4	91.0	91.1	90.0
Income (or loss) from operations	4.6	5.8	5.2	5.2	6.3
Non-operating income (expense)	-1.1	-1.0	-1.3	-2.9	-2.0
Income (or loss) before income taxes	3.4	4.8	4.0	2.4	4.3
Net income (or loss) of foreign branches and equity in earnings (losses) of non-consolidated subsidiaries (net of foreign taxes)	0.2	0.3	0.3	0.3	-0.2
Less: Provision for current and deferred domestic income taxes	0.7	1.8	1.3	0.8	1.1
Income (or loss) after income taxes	2.8	3.3	3.0	1.9	3.0
OPERATING RATIOS (see explanatory notes)	(percent)				
Annual rate of profit on stockholders' equity at end of period:					
Before income taxes	23.79	31.71	25.94	15.85	26.22
After taxes	18.93	20.67	18.16	11.15	19.00
Annual rate of profit on total assets:					
Before income taxes	4.33	6.40	5.35	3.45	5.03
After taxes	3.44	4.17	3.75	2.43	3.64

[1]In the first quarter 1988, a number of corporations were reclassified by industry. To provide comparability, the four quarters of 1987 have been restated to reflect these reclassifications.

TABLE 35—INCOME STATEMENT
FOR CORPORATIONS INCLUDED IN ESIC MAJOR GROUPS 33.5-6, ASSETS $25 MILLION AND OVER

	Nonferrous Metals[1]				
	1Q 1987	2Q 1987	3Q 1987	4Q 1987	1Q 1988
INCOME STATEMENT IN RATIO FORMAT	(percent of net sales)				
Net sales, receipts, and operating revenues	100.0	100.0	100.0	100.0	100.0
Less: Depreciation, depletion, and amortization of property, plant and equipment	4.4	4.1	3.7	3.9	3.8
Less: All other operating costs and expenses	90.9	89.9	91.0	90.7	87.0
Income (or loss) from operations	4.7	6.0	5.3	5.4	9.2
Non-operating income (expense)	-1.0	-6.5	1.0	-6.4	0.1
Income (or loss) before income taxes	3.7	-0.5	6.3	-1.0	9.3
Net income (or loss) of foreign branches and equity in earnings (losses) of non-consolidated subsidiaries (net of foreign taxes)	1.4	3.4	2.1	2.5	1.6
Less: Provision for current and deferred domestic income taxes	1.8	2.4	2.8	0.1	3.6
Income (or loss) after income taxes	3.2	0.5	5.6	1.4	7.3
OPERATING RATIOS (see explanatory notes)	(percent)				
Annual rate of profit on stockholders' equity at end of period:					
Before income taxes	9.68	5.87	18.52	3.67	25.39
After taxes	6.12	1.07	12.36	3.45	17.03
Annual rate of profit on total assets:					
Before income taxes	4.61	2.86	7.78	1.64	11.49
After taxes	2.92	0.52	5.19	1.54	7.71

[1]In the first quarter 1988, a number of corporations were reclassified by industry. To provide comparability, the four quarters of 1987 have been restated to reflect these reclassifications.

TABLE 36—INCOME STATEMENT
FOR CORPORATIONS INCLUDED IN ESIC MAJOR GROUP 34, ASSETS $25 MILLION AND OVER

	Fabricated Metal Products[1]				
	1Q 1987	2Q 1987	3Q 1987	4Q 1987	1Q 1988
INCOME STATEMENT IN RATIO FORMAT	(percent of net sales)				
Net sales, receipts, and operating revenues	100.0	100.0	100.0	100.0	100.0
Less: Depreciation, depletion, and amortization of property, plant and equipment	3.2	3.1	3.2	3.1	3.1
Less: All other operating costs and expenses	89.4	89.1	88.7	88.9	89.5
Income (or loss) from operations	7.4	7.8	8.1	8.0	7.4
Non-operating income (expense)	-4.3	-1.3	-1.4	-1.8	-0.3
Income (or loss) before income taxes	3.1	6.5	6.7	6.2	7.0
Net income (or loss) of foreign branches and equity in earnings (losses) of non-consolidated subsidiaries (net of foreign taxes)	0.5	0.8	0.7	0.7	0.7
Less: Provision for current and deferred domestic income taxes	2.1	2.7	2.7	2.0	2.0
Income (or loss) after income taxes	1.5	4.5	4.6	4.9	5.7
OPERATING RATIOS (see explanatory notes)	(percent)				
Annual rate of profit on stockholders' equity at end of period:					
Before income taxes	10.06	21.75	21.46	19.78	21.97
After taxes	4.20	13.52	13.62	14.02	16.17
Annual rate of profit on total assets:					
Before income taxes	4.19	8.93	8.75	8.27	8.81
After taxes	1.75	5.55	5.55	5.86	6.49

[1]In the first quarter 1988, a number of corporations were reclassified by industry. To provide comparability, the four quarters of 1987 have been restated to reflect these reclassifications.

TABLE 37—INCOME STATEMENT
FOR CORPORATIONS INCLUDED IN ESIC MAJOR GROUP 35, ASSETS $25 MILLION AND OVER

	Machinery, Except Electrical[1]				
	1Q[2] 1987	2Q 1987	3Q 1987	4Q 1987	1Q 1988
INCOME STATEMENT IN RATIO FORMAT	(percent of net sales)				
Net sales, receipts, and operating revenues	100.0	100.0	100.0	100.0	100.0
Less: Depreciation, depletion, and amortization of property, plant and equipment	4.9	4.5	4.7	4.3	4.7
Less: All other operating costs and expenses	90.5	88.4	89.2	90.1	90.0
Income (or loss) from operations	4.6	7.1	6.1	5.6	5.4
Non-operating income (expense)	-3.0	0.6	-0.2	-1.2	0.0
Income (or loss) before income taxes	1.7	7.7	5.9	4.4	5.4
Net income (or loss) of foreign branches and equity in earnings (losses) of non-consolidated subsidiaries (net of foreign taxes)	2.4	2.6	3.1	5.8	3.4
Less: Provision for current and deferred domestic income taxes	2.2	2.8	2.6	2.0	2.3
Income (or loss) after income taxes	1.8	7.5	6.4	8.3	6.5
OPERATING RATIOS (see explanatory notes)	(percent)				
Annual rate of profit on stockholders' equity at end of period:					
Before income taxes	6.33	17.44	14.88	18.18	14.66
After taxes	2.87	12.64	10.63	14.75	10.86
Annual rate of profit on total assets:					
Before income taxes	3.40	9.50	7.99	9.69	7.74
After taxes	1.54	6.89	5.71	7.87	5.74

[1]In the first quarter 1988, a number of corporations were reclassified by industry. To provide comparability, the four quarters of 1987 have been restated to reflect these reclassifications.
[2]Revised.

TABLE 38—INCOME STATEMENT
FOR CORPORATIONS INCLUDED IN ESIC MAJOR GROUP 36, ASSETS $25 MILLION AND OVER

	Electrical and Electronic Equipment[1]				
	1Q 1987	2Q 1987	3Q 1987	4Q 1987	1Q 1988
INCOME STATEMENT IN RATIO FORMAT	(percent of net sales)				
Net sales, receipts, and operating revenues	100.0	100.0	100.0	100.0	100.0
Less: Depreciation, depletion, and amortization of property, plant and equipment	4.2	3.9	3.8	3.8	4.0
Less: All other operating costs and expenses	90.7	89.7	89.9	91.1	89.3
Income (or loss) from operations	5.1	6.5	6.3	5.1	6.7
Non-operating income (expense)	0.6	0.2	-0.2	-1.0	-0.4
Income (or loss) before income taxes	5.6	6.7	6.1	4.1	6.4
Net income (or loss) of foreign branches and equity in earnings (losses) of non-consolidated subsidiaries (net of foreign taxes)	2.7	1.7	1.7	1.4	1.5
Less: Provision for current and deferred domestic income taxes	2.3	2.7	2.6	1.5	2.1
Income (or loss) after income taxes	6.0	5.7	5.1	3.9	5.7
OPERATING RATIOS (see explanatory notes)	(percent)				
Annual rate of profit on stockholders' equity at end of period:					
Before income taxes	17.65	18.26	17.08	13.16	16.93
After taxes	12.78	12.40	11.36	9.42	12.36
Annual rate of profit on total assets:					
Before income taxes	8.57	8.85	8.27	6.19	8.03
After taxes	6.20	6.01	5.50	4.43	5.86

[1]During the first quarter of 1988, a number of companies were reclassified by industry. Data for the four quarters of 1987 have been revised to reflect these reclassifications, as well as respondent(s) corrections of submitted data subsequent to original publication.

TABLE 39—INCOME STATEMENT
FOR CORPORATIONS INCLUDED IN ESIC MAJOR GROUP 37, ASSETS $25 MILLION AND OVER

	Transportation Equipment[1]				
	1Q 1987	2Q 1987	3Q 1987	4Q 1987	1Q 1988
INCOME STATEMENT IN RATIO FORMAT	(percent of net sales)				
Net sales, receipts, and operating revenues	100.0	100.0	100.0	100.0	100.0
Less: Depreciation, depletion, and amortization of property, plant and equipment	4.1	4.4	3.3	3.7	3.8
Less: All other operating costs and expenses	90.4	89.8	92.6	91.9	91.6
Income (or loss) from operations	5.5	5.8	4.1	4.4	4.6
Non operating income (expense)	-0.6	-0.7	-0.6	-1.2	-0.3
Income (or loss) before income taxes	4.9	5.1	3.5	3.3	4.3
Net income (or loss) of foreign branches and equity in earnings (losses) of non-consolidated subsidiaries (net of foreign taxes)	2.4	2.7	2.3	2.3	3.0
Less: Provision for current and deferred domestic income taxes	2.4	2.4	1.2	1.4	1.7
Income (or loss) after income taxes	4.9	5.5	4.6	4.2	5.6
OPERATING RATIOS (see explanatory notes)	(percent)				
Annual rate of profit on stockholders' equity at end of period:					
Before income taxes	24.84	26.45	16.53	18.51	23.08
After taxes	16.61	18.31	13.07	13.96	17.77
Annual rate of profit on total assets:					
Before income taxes	9.14	9.93	6.19	6.73	8.40
After taxes	6.11	6.87	4.90	5.08	6.46

[1] In the first quarter 1988, a number of corporations were reclassified by industry. To provide comparability, the four quarters of 1987 have been restated to reflect these reclassifications.

TABLE 40—INCOME STATEMENT
FOR CORPORATIONS INCLUDED IN ESIC MAJOR GROUP 37.1, ASSETS $25 MILLION AND OVER

	Motor Vehicles and Equipment[1]				
	1Q 1987	2Q 1987	3Q 1987	4Q 1987	1Q 1988
INCOME STATEMENT IN RATIO FORMAT	(percent of net sales)				
Net sales, receipts, and operating revenues	100.0	100.0	100.0	100.0	100.0
Less: Depreciation, depletion, and amortization of property, plant and equipment	4.5	5.1	3.3	3.9	3.9
Less: All other operating costs and expenses	90.1	89.0	93.9	92.3	91.7
Income (or loss) from operations	5.4	5.8	2.8	3.8	4.4
Non-operating income (expense)	-0.7	-0.7	-0.8	-1.2	-0.4
Income (or loss) before income taxes	4.7	5.1	2.0	2.5	3.9
Net income (or loss) of foreign branches and equity in earnings (losses) of non-consolidated subsidiaries (net of foreign taxes)	3.5	3.8	3.3	3.5	4.3
Less: Provision for current and deferred domestic income taxes	2.6	2.7	0.5	1.3	1.9
Income (or loss) after income taxes	5.6	6.3	4.8	4.6	6.3
OPERATING RATIOS (see explanatory notes)	(percent)				
Annual rate of profit on stockholders' equity at end of period:					
Before income taxes	26.73	28.83	13.56	18.15	24.93
After taxes	18.32	20.26	12.20	14.05	19.25
Annual rate of profit on total assets:					
Before income taxes	11.79	13.01	6.10	7.89	10.83
After taxes	8.08	9.14	5.49	6.10	8.36

[1] In the first quarter 1988, a number of corporations were reclassified by industry. To provide comparability, the four quarters of 1987 have been restated to reflect these reclassifications.

TABLE 41—INCOME STATEMENT
FOR CORPORATIONS INCLUDED IN ESIC MAJOR GROUP 37.7, ASSETS $25 MILLION AND OVER

	Aircraft, Guided Missiles and Parts[1]				
	1Q 1987	2Q 1987	3Q 1987	4Q 1987	1Q 1988
INCOME STATEMENT IN RATIO FORMAT	(percent of net sales)				
Net sales, receipts, and operating revenues	100.0	100.0	100.0	100.0	100.0
Less: Depreciation, depletion, and amortization of property, plant and equipment	3.2	3.1	3.3	3.3	3.4
Less: All other operating costs and expenses	90.9	91.2	90.8	91.5	91.8
Income (or loss) from operations	5.8	5.7	5.8	5.2	4.8
Non-operating income (expense)	-0.1	-0.2	0.0	-0.5	0.2
Income (or loss) before income taxes	5.8	5.4	5.8	4.7	5.1
Net income (or loss) of foreign branches and equity in earnings (losses) of non-consolidated subsidiaries (net of foreign taxes)	0.6	0.9	0.7	0.5	0.8
Less: Provision for current and deferred domestic income taxes	2.3	2.1	2.2	1.5	1.3
Income (or loss) after income taxes	4.1	4.3	4.3	3.7	4.5
OPERATING RATIOS (see explanatory notes)	(percent)				
Annual rate of profit on stockholders' equity at end of period:					
Before income taxes	22.63	22.28	22.08	19.54	19.63
After taxes	14.60	14.93	14.55	13.96	15.15
Annual rate of profit on total assets:					
Before income taxes	6.71	6.75	6.65	5.73	5.76
After taxes	4.33	4.53	4.38	4.10	4.45

[1]In the first quarter 1988, a number of corporations were reclassified by industry. To provide comparability, the four quarters of 1987 have been restated to reflect these reclassifications.

TABLE 42—INCOME STATEMENT
FOR CORPORATIONS INCLUDED IN ESIC MAJOR GROUP 38, ASSETS $25 MILLION AND OVER

	Instruments and Related Products[1]				
	1Q 1987	2Q 1987	3Q 1987	4Q 1987	1Q 1988
INCOME STATEMENT IN RATIO FORMAT	(percent of net sales)				
Net sales, receipts, and operating revenues	100.0	100.0	100.0	100.0	100.0
Less: Depreciation, depletion, and amortization of property, plant and equipment	5.4	5.1	5.0	4.4	4.9
Less: All other operating costs and expenses	88.9	88.0	88.2	90.1	88.2
Income (or loss) from operations	5.7	6.9	6.8	5.5	6.9
Non-operating income (expense)	1.0	-0.5	0.3	0.9	1.7
Income (or loss) before income taxes	6.7	6.4	7.1	6.4	8.6
Net income (or loss) of foreign branches and equity in earnings (losses) of non-consolidated subsidiaries (net of foreign taxes)	2.7	3.2	3.2	2.8	3.5
Less: Provision for current and deferred domestic income taxes	3.2	3.1	3.1	2.1	2.5
Income (or loss) after income taxes	6.2	6.5	7.3	7.1	9.4
OPERATING RATIOS (see explanatory notes)	(percent)				
Annual rate of profit on stockholders' equity at end of period:					
Before income taxes	15.42	16.07	18.02	16.58	21.12
After taxes	10.18	10.89	12.69	12.86	16.59
Annual rate of profit on total assets:					
Before income taxes	8.34	8.77	9.63	8.47	10.01
After taxes	5.51	5.94	6.78	6.57	7.86

[1]In the first quarter 1988, a number of corporations were reclassified by industry. To provide comparability, the four quarters of 1987 have been restated to reflect these reclassifications.

TABLE 43—INCOME STATEMENT
FOR CORPORATIONS INCLUDED IN MINING, ALL WHOLESALE TRADE AND ESIC MAJOR GROUPS 50, 51, ASSETS $25 MILLION AND OVER[1]

	All Mining[2]				
	1Q[3] 1987	2Q 1987	3Q 1987	4Q 1987	1Q 1988
	(percent of net sales)				
INCOME STATEMENT IN RATIO FORMAT					
Net sales, receipts, and operating revenues	100.0	100.0	100.0	100.0	100.0
Less: Depreciation, depletion, and amortization of property, plant and equipment	15.4	14.3	13.9	13.5	13.8
Less: All other operating costs and expenses	84.1	83.5	82.3	84.2	81.1
Income (or loss) from operations	0.5	2.2	3.8	2.4	5.1
Non-operating income (expense)	-3.5	-5.7	-1.8	-2.1	0.9
Income (or loss) before income taxes	-3.0	-3.4	2.0	0.2	5.9
Less: Provision for current and deferred domestic income taxes	1.2	2.5	1.9	1.6	2.3
Income (or loss) after income taxes	-4.2	-5.9	0.1	-1.3	3.6
	(percent)				
OPERATING RATIOS (see explanatory notes)					
Annual rate of profit on stockholders' equity at end of period:					
Before income taxes	-3.82	-4.55	2.63	0.34	8.17
After taxes	-5.36	-7.86	0.08	-1.94	4.96
Annual rate of profit on total assets:					
Before income taxes	-1.30	-1.61	0.96	0.12	2.99
After taxes	-1.82	-2.77	0.03	-0.70	1.82
BALANCE SHEET RATIOS (based on succeeding table)					
Total current assets to total current liabilities	1.34	1.43	1.36	1.36	1.38
Total cash, U.S. Government and other securities to total current liabilities	0.46	0.49	0.47	0.45	0.47
Total stockholders' equity to total debt	0.89	0.97	1.05	1.01	1.04

[1]Beginning in the fourth quarter 1987, these tables only include estimates for corporations with assets of $25 million or over at the time of sample selection, fall 1987. 1987 data have been restated to reflect this definitional change.
[2]In the first quarter 1988, a number of corporations were reclassified by industry. To provide comparability, the four quarters of 1987 have been restated to reflect these reclassifications.
[3]Revised.

TABLE 44—BALANCE SHEET
FOR CORPORATIONS INCLUDED IN MINING, ALL WHOLESALE TRADE AND ESIC MAJOR GROUPS 50, 51, ASSETS $25 MILLION AND OVER[1]

	All Mining[2]				
	1Q 1987	2Q 1987	3Q 1987	4Q 1987	1Q 1988
	(percent of total assets)				
SELECTED BALANCE SHEET RATIOS					
Total cash, U.S. Government and other securities	7.4	7.4	7.4	7.4	7.6
Trade accounts and trade notes receivable	8.2	8.0	8.5	8.7	8.7
Inventories	3.9	3.8	3.8	3.8	4.0
Total current assets	21.5	21.5	21.7	22.3	22.6
Net property, plant and equipment	60.1	59.3	59.5	59.0	58.8
Short-term debt including installments on long-term debt	4.3	3.4	3.4	3.5	3.4
Total current liabilities	16.1	15.0	15.9	16.5	16.3
Long-term debt	33.6	33.0	31.3	31.9	31.8
Total liabilities	66.1	64.7	63.4	64.0	63.4
Stockholders' equity	33.9	35.3	36.6	36.0	36.6

[1]Beginning in the fourth quarter 1987, these tables only include estimates for corporations with assets of $25 million or over at the time of sample selection, fall 1987. 1987 data have been restated to reflect this definitional change.
[2]In the first quarter 1988, a number of corporations were reclassified by industry. To provide comparability, the four quarters of 1987 have been restated to reflect these reclassifications.
[3]Revised.

All Wholesale Trade [2]					Wholesale Trade, Durable Goods [2]					Wholesale Trade, Nondurable Goods [2]				
1Q[3] 1987	2Q 1987	3Q 1987	4Q 1987	1Q 1988	1Q[3] 1987	2Q 1987	3Q 1987	4Q 1987	1Q 1988	1Q 1987	2Q 1987	3Q 1987	4Q 1987	1Q 1988
(percent of net sales)					(percent of net sales)					(percent of net sales)				
100.0	100.0	100.0	100.0	100.0	100.0	100.0	100.0	100.0	100.0	100.0	100.0	100.0	100.0	100.0
1.0	0.9	0.9	1.0	0.9	1.1	1.1	1.0	1.3	1.0	0.9	0.8	0.8	0.8	0.8
97.3	97.2	97.0	97.3	97.1	97.3	97.0	96.7	96.7	96.6	97.3	97.4	97.3	97.8	97.5
1.7	1.8	2.0	1.7	2.0	1.6	1.9	2.3	2.0	2.4	1.8	1.8	1.9	1.4	1.7
0.0	-0.2	0.0	-0.1	-0.3	0.0	-0.2	0.2	0.0	-0.3	0.0	-0.2	-0.2	-0.2	-0.3
1.7	1.6	2.0	1.5	1.7	1.6	1.7	2.5	2.0	2.1	1.8	1.5	1.7	1.1	1.4
0.6	0.7	0.7	0.8	0.6	0.8	0.9	0.9	1.1	0.9	0.6	0.5	0.6	0.5	0.4
1.1	0.9	1.3	0.8	1.1	0.9	0.8	1.6	0.9	1.3	1.2	1.0	1.0	0.7	1.0
(percent)					(percent)					(percent)				
13.64	13.26	16.68	13.33	14.36	10.70	12.02	17.21	14.86	14.05	16.73	14.59	16.12	11.64	14.71
8.56	7.69	10.62	6.64	9.28	5.77	5.74	11.07	6.56	8.24	11.49	9.77	10.14	6.73	10.47
4.69	4.47	5.60	4.45	4.88	3.79	4.08	5.81	5.10	4.90	5.58	4.87	5.38	3.77	4.85
2.94	2.59	3.57	2.22	3.15	2.04	1.95	3.74	2.25	2.87	3.83	3.26	3.38	2.18	3.46
1.40	1.38	1.37	1.36	1.37	1.52	1.48	1.45	1.46	1.47	1.27	1.26	1.27	1.24	1.26
0.18	0.19	0.18	0.18	0.16	0.20	0.19	0.16	0.18	0.17	0.16	0.20	0.20	0.18	0.15
1.03	1.00	1.00	1.01	1.02	1.10	1.04	1.02	1.09	1.13	0.96	0.97	0.98	0.93	0.92

All Wholesale Trade [2]					Wholdsale Trade, Durable Goods [2]					Wholesale Trade, Nondurable Goods [2]				
1Q[3] 1987	2Q 1987	3Q 1987	4Q 1987	1Q 1988	1Q[3] 1987	2Q 1987	3Q 1987	4Q 1987	1Q 1988	1Q 1987	2Q 1987	3Q 1987	4Q 1987	1Q 1988
(percent of total assets)					(percent of total assets)					(percent of total assets)				
8.1	9.0	8.5	8.6	7.3	9.3	9.3	8.0	8.8	8.0	6.9	8.7	8.9	8.4	6.6
25.5	25.6	26.5	26.1	25.9	26.1	26.4	28.5	27.7	27.0	24.9	24.7	24.4	24.4	24.6
24.4	24.7	24.7	25.7	26.2	29.5	29.8	29.3	29.7	30.2	19.4	19.4	19.9	21.5	21.8
62.9	64.0	64.6	64.6	63.8	70.9	71.2	71.5	71.1	70.3	55.0	56.5	57.2	57.8	56.8
20.4	19.5	19.0	19.0	19.2	16.7	16.1	15.7	16.1	16.1	24.2	23.0	22.6	21.9	22.5
17.2	18.3	18.5	18.4	18.1	18.8	19.5	20.1	18.8	17.7	15.7	17.1	16.8	18.1	18.5
45.0	46.5	47.2	47.6	46.4	46.8	48.2	49.2	48.7	47.8	43.2	44.7	45.1	46.5	44.9
16.1	15.3	14.9	14.7	15.3	13.3	13.2	12.8	12.7	13.0	19.0	17.5	17.2	16.8	17.6
65.6	66.3	66.4	66.6	66.0	64.6	66.0	66.2	65.7	65.1	66.6	66.6	66.6	67.6	67.0
34.4	33.7	33.6	33.4	34.0	35.4	34.0	33.8	34.3	34.9	33.4	33.4	33.4	32.4	33.0

TABLE 45—INCOME STATEMENT
FOR CORPORATIONS INCLUDED IN RETAIL TRADE, ESIC MAJOR GROUPS 53, 54, AND ALL OTHER RETAIL TRADE, ASSETS $25 MILLION AND OVER[1]

	All Retail Trade[2]				
	1Q 1987	2Q 1987	3Q 1987	4Q 1987	1Q 1988
	(percent)				
OPERATING RATIOS (see explanatory notes)					
Annual rate of profit on stockholders' equity at end of period:					
Before income taxes	14.08	18.76	17.23	31.47	
After taxes	8.02	11.27	10.22	20.30	
Annual rate of profit on total assets:					
Before income taxes	5.25	6.94	5.93	10.85	
After taxes	2.99	4.17	3.52	7.00	
BALANCE SHEET RATIOS (based on succeeding table)					
Total current assets to total current liabilities	1.72	1.68	1.56	1.64	
Total cash, U.S. Government and other securities to total current liabilities	0.15	0.15	0.12	0.13	
Total stockholders' equity to total debt	1.20	1.16	1.03	1.00	

[1]Beginning in the fourth quarter 1987, these tables only include estimates for corporations with assets of $25 million or over at the time of sample selection, fall 1987. 1987 data have been restated to reflect this definitional change.
[2]In the first quarter 1988, a number of corporations were reclassified by industry. To provide comparability, the four quarters of 1987 have been restated to reflect these reclassifications.
[3]Revised.

TABLE 46—BALANCE SHEET
FOR CORPORATIONS INCLUDED IN RETAIL TRADE, ESIC MAJOR GROUPS 53, 54, AND ALL OTHER RETAIL TRADE, ASSETS $25 MILLION AND OVER[1]

	All Retail Trade				
	1Q 1987	2Q 1987	3Q 1987	4Q 1987	1Q 1988
	(percent of total assets)				
SELECTED BALANCE SHEET RATIOS					
Total cash, U.S. Government and other securities	4.3	4.4	3.7	3.9	
Trade accounts and trade notes receivable	14.3	13.9	13.9	15.0	
Inventories	27.7	27.9	29.5	26.5	
Total current assets	48.7	48.6	49.4	48.2	
Net property, plant and equipment	36.3	36.0	35.2	35.6	
Short-term debt including installments on long-term debt	4.9	6.0	7.5	6.2	
Total current liabilities	28.3	28.9	31.7	29.5	
Long-term debt	26.2	25.9	26.0	28.3	
Total liabilities	62.7	63.0	65.6	65.5	
Stockholders' equity	37.3	37.0	34.4	34.5	

[1]Beginning in the fourth quarter 1987, these tables only include estimates for corporations with assets of $25 million or over at the time of sample selection, fall 1987. 1987 data have been restated to reflect this definitional change.
[2]In the first quarter 1988, a number of corporations were reclassified by industry. To provide comparability, the four quarters of 1987 have been restated to reflect these reclassifications.

General Merchandise Stores[2]					Retail Food Stores					All Other Retail Trade[2]				
1Q 1987	2Q 1987	3Q 1987	4Q 1987	1Q 1988	1Q 1987	2Q 1987	3Q 1987	4Q 1987	1Q 1988	1Q 1987	2Q 1987	3Q 1987	4Q[3] 1987	1Q 1988
(percent of net sales)					(percent of net sales)					(percent of net sales)				
100.0	100.0	100.0	100.0		100.0	100.0	100.0	100.0		100.0	100.0	100.0	100.0	
1.9	1.9	1.9	1.5		1.4	1.5	1.5	1.5		2.3	2.2	2.2	2.1	
93.6	93.7	93.0	90.1		96.3	96.0	96.2	96.0		93.6	92.9	93.2	92.4	
4.5	4.5	5.2	8.4		2.3	2.5	2.3	2.5		4.0	4.9	4.6	5.5	
-1.4	-0.7	-1.2	-1.0		-0.5	-0.5	-0.6	-0.9		-0.7	-0.5	-1.2	-0.7	
3.0	3.8	4.0	7.4		1.7	2.0	1.7	1.6		3.3	4.4	3.3	4.8	
0.9	1.3	1.4	2.6		0.8	0.8	0.7	0.5		1.7	1.9	1.5	1.8	
2.1	2.4	2.5	4.9		0.9	1.2	0.9	1.0		1.6	2.5	1.9	3.0	
(percent)					(percent)					(percent)				
10.94	14.64	16.55	39.51		20.30	23.86	20.39	20.95		15.33	21.52	16.70	25.94	
7.57	9.43	10.49	25.87		10.54	14.17	11.57	13.87		7.49	12.22	9.31	16.15	
4.27	5.64	5.74	14.35		6.30	7.46	6.01	5.36		5.89	8.21	6.13	9.63	
2.96	3.63	3.64	9.40		3.27	4.43	3.41	3.55		2.88	4.66	3.42	6.00	
1.97	1.89	1.66	1.82		1.23	1.24	1.20	1.23		1.70	1.69	1.61	1.64	
0.09	0.09	0.06	0.08		0.20	0.20	0.17	0.16		0.20	0.21	0.17	0.19	
1.37	1.30	1.08	1.15		0.99	1.00	0.88	0.65		1.12	1.10	1.04	1.05	

General Merchandise Stores[2]					Retail Food Stores					All Other Retail Trade[2]				
1Q 1987	2Q 1987	3Q 1987	4Q 1987	1Q 1988	1Q 1987	2Q 1987	3Q 1987	4Q 1987	1Q 1988	1Q 1987	2Q 1987	3Q 1987	4Q 1987	1Q 1988
(percent of total assets)					(percent of total assets)					(percent of total assets)				
2.6	2.6	2.1	2.4		6.5	6.2	5.4	4.9		5.3	5.5	4.7	5.1	
22.5	22.0	21.4	23.8		3.7	3.7	3.7	3.7		9.8	9.8	9.8	10.5	
29.1	29.3	31.8	27.2		26.1	25.8	25.6	24.5		26.7	27.2	28.7	26.8	
56.0	55.9	57.1	55.4		39.5	38.8	38.2	38.7		44.5	45.0	45.6	44.9	
29.8	28.9	28.5	29.8		49.2	49.7	48.0	45.0		37.5	37.1	36.9	37.3	
4.9	6.9	9.6	7.1		3.7	3.5	3.7	4.9		5.3	6.0	6.9	6.0	
28.4	29.6	34.4	30.4		32.0	31.3	31.8	31.4		26.2	26.6	28.4	27.3	
23.6	22.7	22.5	24.5		27.6	27.9	29.6	34.3		28.4	28.7	28.4	29.5	
60.9	61.5	65.3	63.7		69.0	68.7	70.5	74.4		61.6	61.8	63.3	62.9	
39.1	38.5	34.7	36.3		31.0	31.3	29.5	25.6		38.4	38.2	36.7	37.1	

General Business and Economic Indicators

SELECTED BUSINESS STATISTICS

SEASONALLY ADJUSTED WHERE APPLICABLE

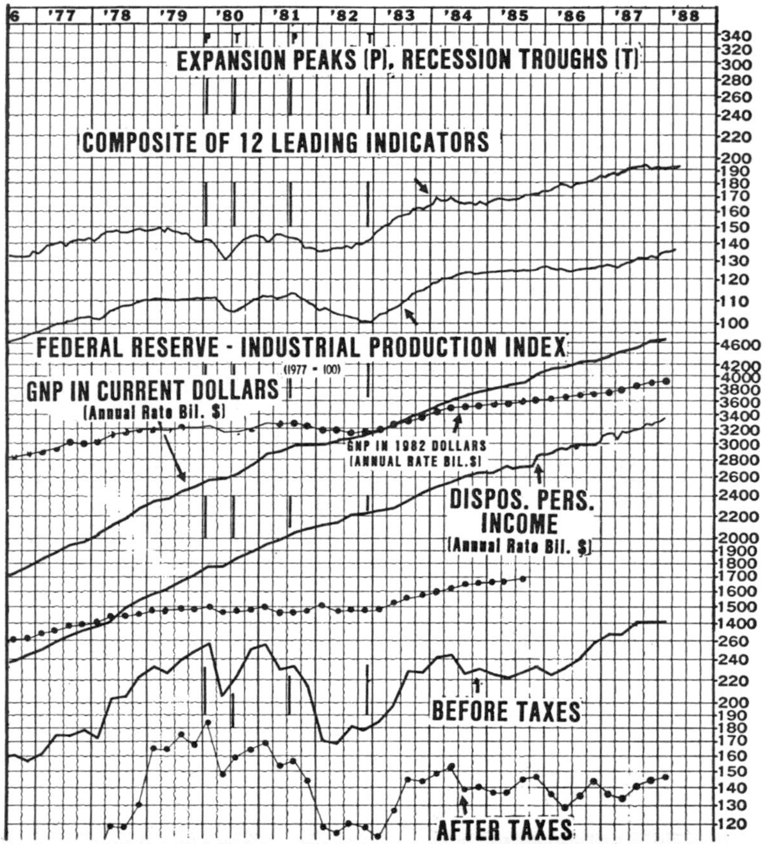

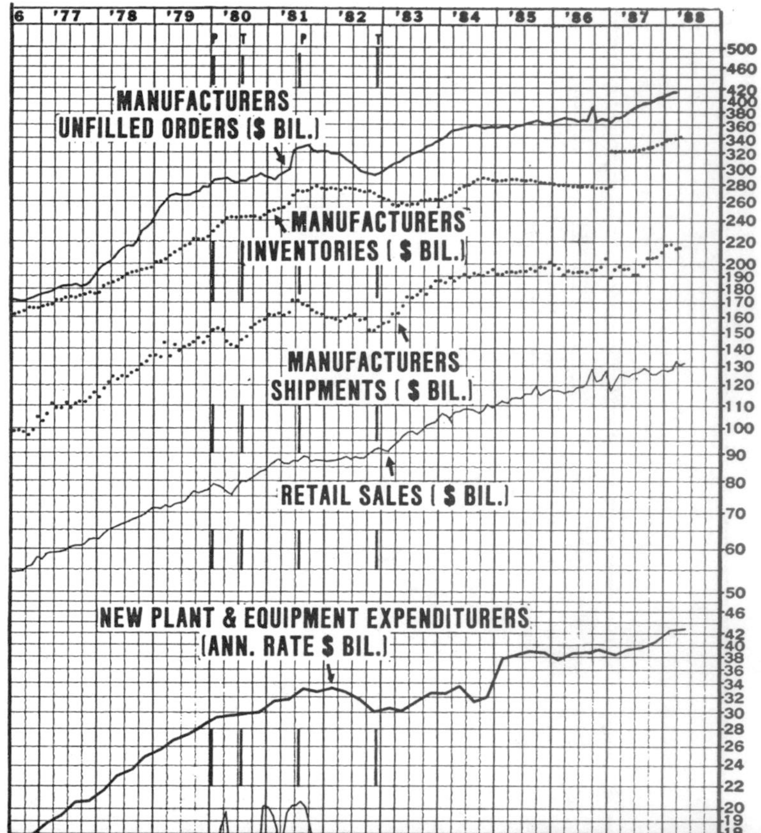

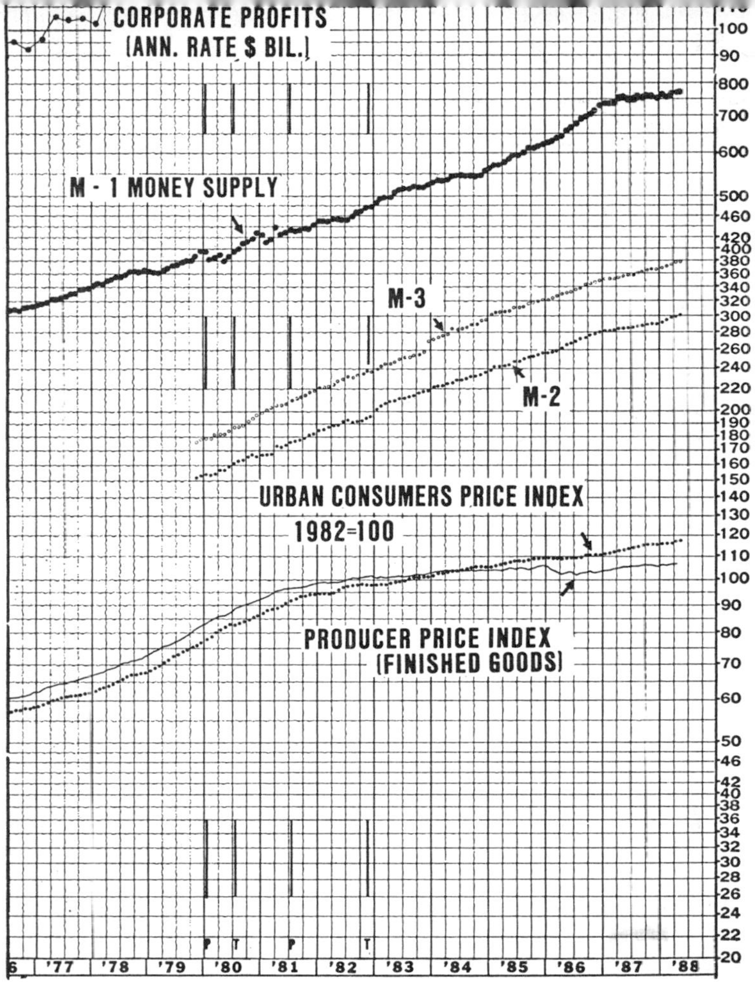

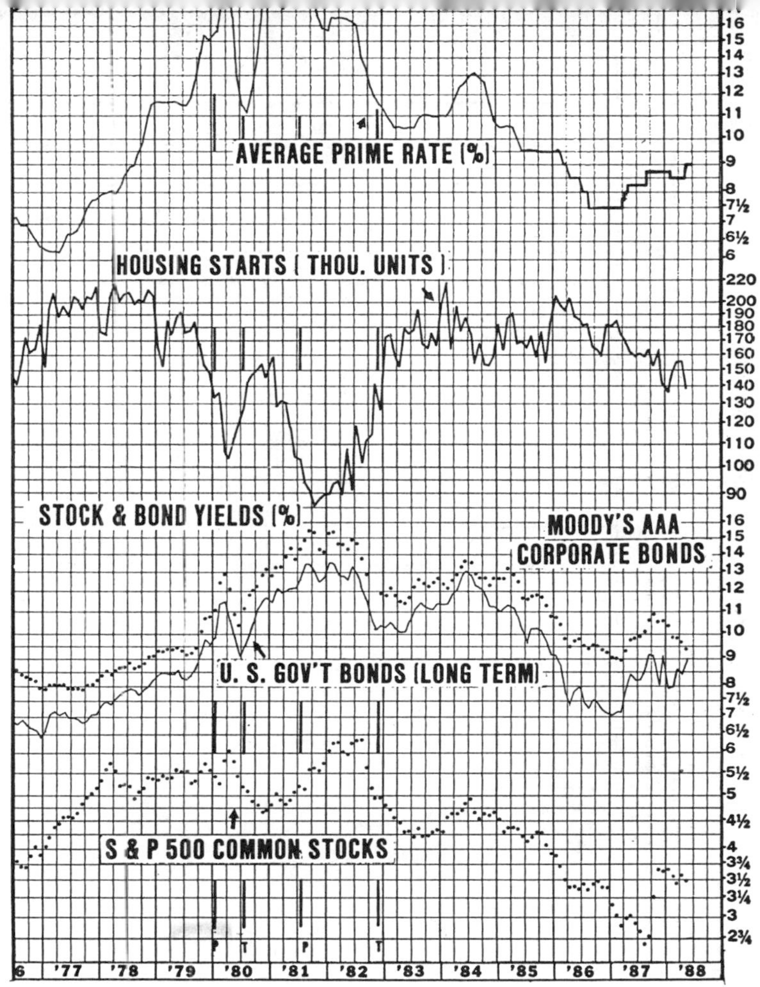

Source: *5-Trend CYCLI-GRAPHS*. The charts are courtesy of Securities Research Company, a Division of Babson-United Investment Advisors, Inc., 208 Newbury Street, Boston, MA 02116, July quarterly edition, 1988.

COMPOSITE INDEXES AND THEIR COMPONENTS

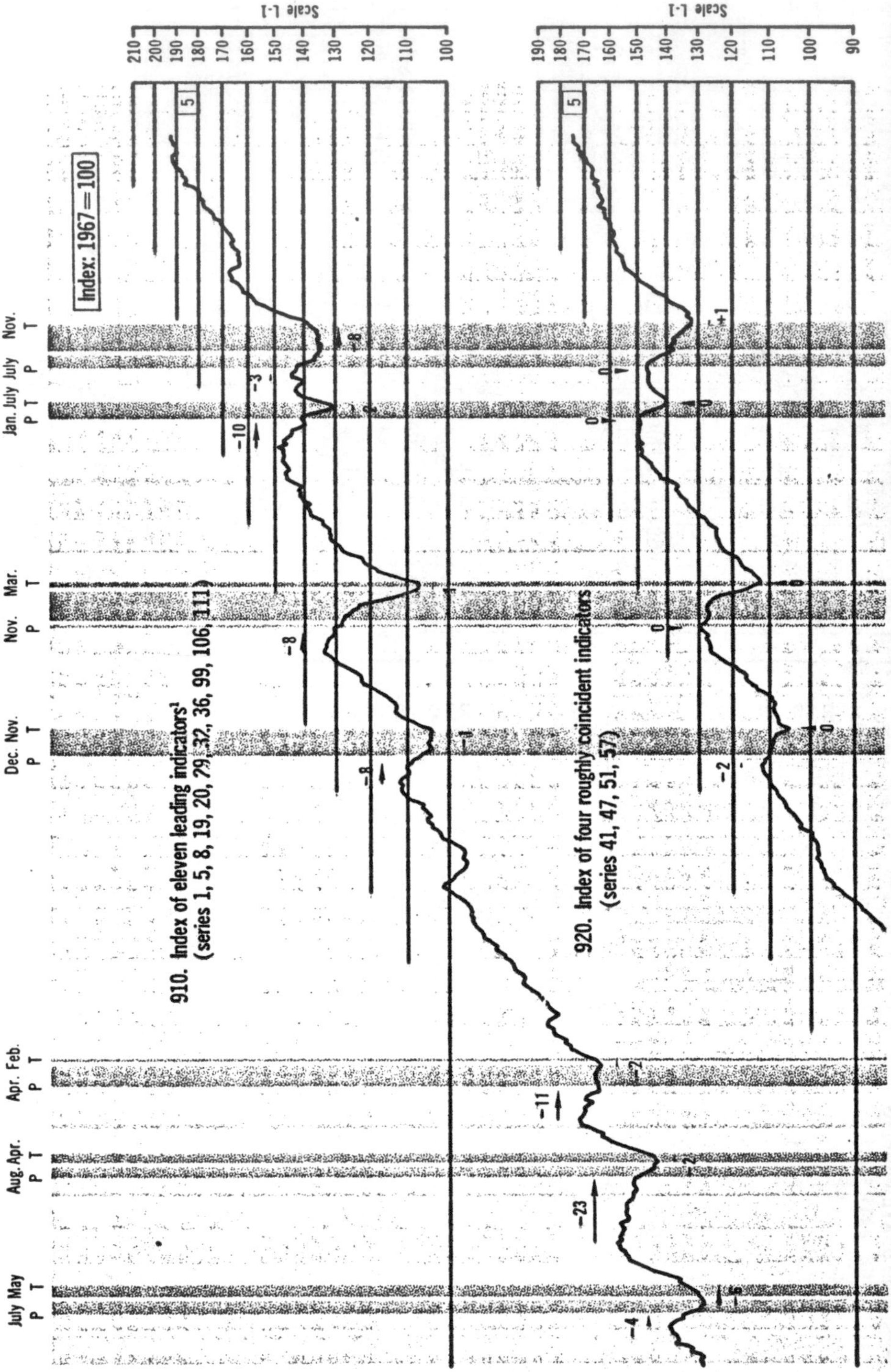

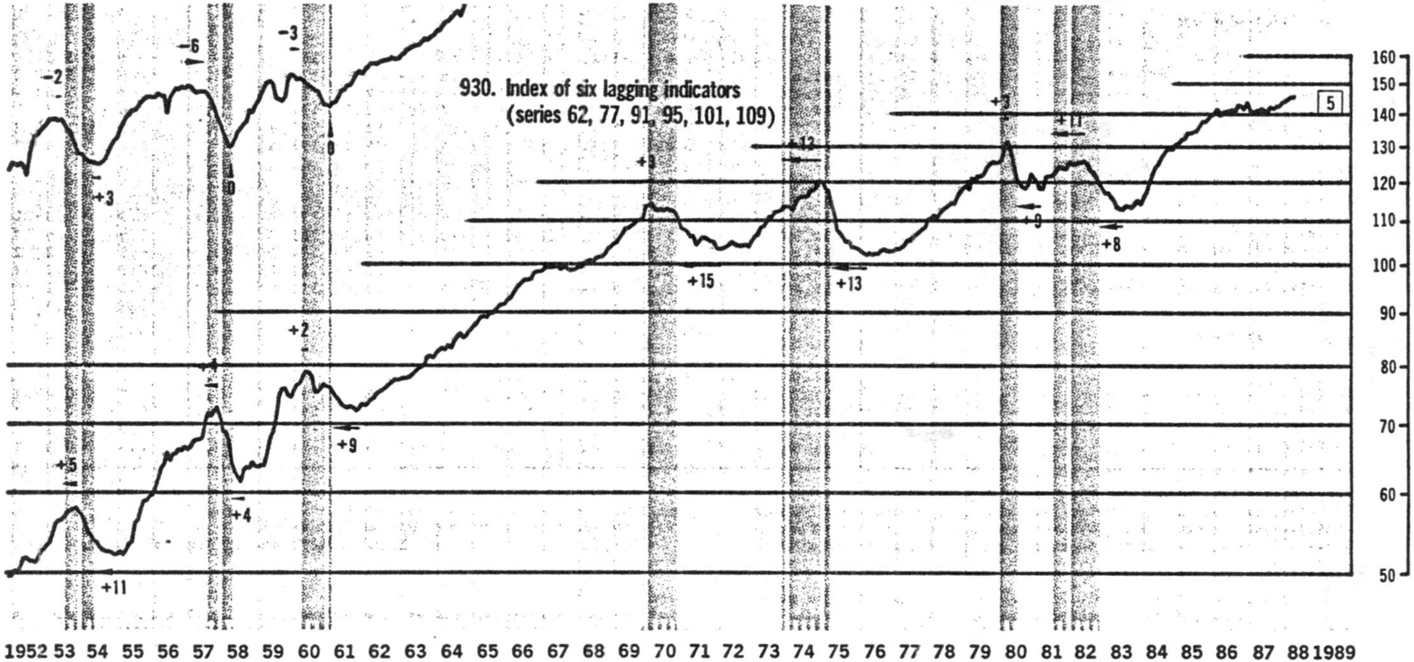

NOTE: Numbers entered on the chart indicate length of leads (−) and lags (+) in months from reference turning dates.
[1]Values of this index prior to January 1984 include a twelfth component, series 12, which has been suspended from the current index.

Source: *Business Conditions Digest,* U.S. Department of Commerce, Bureau of Economic Analysis, June 1988.

Composition of Leading, Coincident, and Lagging Indicators

I. THE TWELVE LEADING INDICATORS

1. Average weekly hours paid to production or non-supervisory workers in manufacturing.
5. Average weekly claims for Unemployment Insurance (inversely related).
8. New orders for consumer goods and materials in 1982 dollars.
12. Monthly estimate of net formation of new businesses incorporated.
19. Index of 500 common stock prices.
20. Contracts and orders for new plant and equipment in 1982 dollars.
29. Index of new private housing starts.
32. Percentage of purchasing agents in greater Chicago area who experience slower deliveries in current month.
36. Change in manufacturing and trade inventories on hand and on order in 1982 dollars.
99. Change in index of 28 sensitive materials prices.
106. Money supply (M2 in 1982 dollars).
111. Change in business and consumer credit (consumer installment credit, business and real estate loans, etc.).

II. THE FOUR COINCIDENT INDICATORS

41. Employees on non-agricultural payrolls.
47. Index of industrial production, including all stages in manufacturing, mining, gas and electrical utilities.
51. Personal income less transfer payments in 1982 dollars.
57. Monthly volume of sales in manufacturing, wholesale, and retail in 1982 dollars.

III. THE SIX LAGGING INDICATORS

62. Index of labor costs per unit of manufacturing output.
77. Ratio of manufacturing and trade inventories to sales in 1982 dollars.
91. Average duration of unemployment in weeks (inversely related).
95. Ratio of consumer installment credit to personal income.
101. Commercial and industrial loans outstanding in 1982 dollars.
109. Average prime rate charged by banks.

NATIONAL INCOME

[Billions of dollars; quarterly data at seasonally adjusted annual rates]

Period	National income	Compensation of employees[1]	Proprietors' income with inventory valuation and capital consumption adjustments		Rental income of persons with capital consumption adjustment	Corporate profits with inventory valuation and capital consumption adjustments					Net interest
						Total	Profits with inventory valuation adjustment and without capital consumption adjustment			Capital consumption adjustment	
			Farm	Nonfarm			Total	Profits before tax	Inventory valuation adjustment		
1982	2,518.4	1,907.0	24.6	150.9	13.6	150.0	159.2	169.6	−10.4	−9.2	272.3
1983	2,719.5	2,020.7	12.4	178.4	13.2	213.7	196.7	207.6	−10.9	17.0	281.0
1984	3,028.6	2,213.9	30.5	204.0	8.5	266.9	234.2	240.0	−5.8	32.7	304.8
1985 r	3,234.0	2,367.5	30.2	225.6	9.2	282.3	222.6	224.3	−1.7	59.7	319.0
1986 r	3,437.1	2,507.1	36.4	250.3	12.4	298.9	244.7	236.4	8.3	54.2	331.9
1987 r	3,678.7	2,683.4	43.0	270.0	18.4	310.4	258.7	276.7	−18.0	51.7	353.6
1982: IV	2,548.2	1,931.1	28.5	159.8	15.8	146.1	150.7	164.1	−13.4	−4.5	266.9
1983: IV	2,851.5	2,092.7	19.3	188.6	12.4	248.5	223.4	231.5	−8.1	25.1	290.2
1984: IV	3,096.1	2,272.7	28.1	209.7	5.6	266.9	224.6	226.1	−1.6	42.3	313.1
1985: IV r	3,312.8	2,426.7	29.2	235.0	7.8	291.4	228.4	235.0	−6.6	63.0	322.7
1986: I r	3,378.9	2,461.0	27.6	245.5	10.6	303.2	243.4	222.5	21.0	59.8	331.1
II r	3,421.8	2,483.4	46.4	248.3	12.5	297.1	242.1	230.3	11.8	55.0	334.1
III r	3,450.9	2,518.2	33.3	251.7	13.1	301.2	249.2	240.5	8.7	52.0	333.3
IV r	3,496.6	2,565.8	38.4	255.8	13.4	293.9	244.1	252.1	−8.1	49.8	329.3
1987: I r	3,573.0	2,608.9	46.7	263.5	17.4	298.3	247.5	261.8	−14.4	50.8	338.3
II r	3,631.8	2,652.0	43.0	265.9	17.8	305.2	253.6	273.7	−20.0	51.5	348.1
III r	3,708.0	2,702.8	35.2	271.5	18.1	322.0	269.9	289.4	−19.5	52.1	358.3
IV r	3,802.0	2,769.9	47.0	279.0	20.5	316.1	263.7	281.9	−18.2	52.4	369.5
1988: I r	3,850.8	2,816.4	44.7	279.2	20.5	316.2	266.8	286.2	−19.4	49.4	373.9
II p	....	2,872.6	38.0	284.6	17.9	....	....	....	−29.8	47.9	382.1

[1] Includes employer contributions for social insurance.

Source: Department of Commerce, Bureau of Economic Analysis.

Note.—Series revised beginning 1985. See *Survey of Current Business, July 1988.*

Source: *Economic Indicators,* Council of Economic Advisers.

GROSS NATIONAL PRODUCT

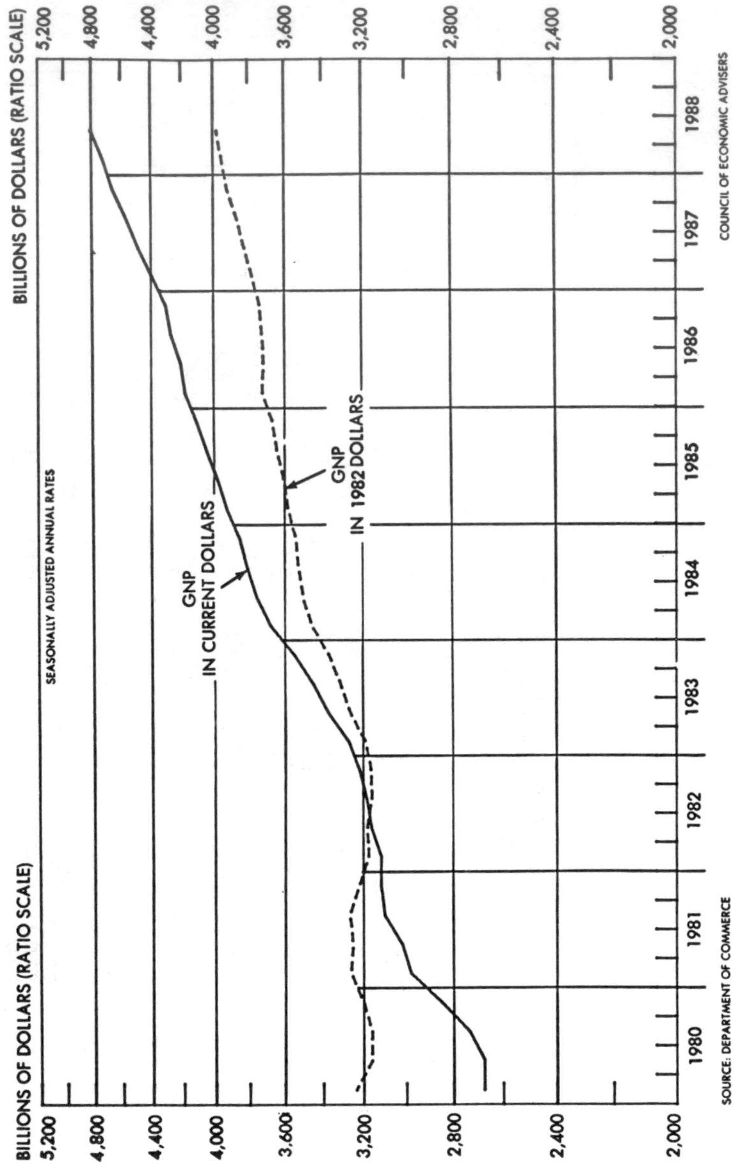
BILLIONS OF DOLLARS (RATIO SCALE)
SEASONALLY ADJUSTED ANNUAL RATES
5,200
4,800
4,400
4,000
3,600
3,200
2,800
2,400
2,000
GNP IN CURRENT DOLLARS
GNP IN 1982 DOLLARS
1980
1981
1982
1983
1984
1985
1986
1987
1988
SOURCE: DEPARTMENT OF COMMERCE
COUNCIL OF ECONOMIC ADVISERS

[Billions of current dollars; quarterly data at seasonally adjusted annual rates]

Period	Gross national product	Personal consumption expenditures	Gross private domestic investment	Exports and imports of goods and services: Net exports	Exports	Imports	Government purchases of goods and services: Total	Federal: Total	Federal: National defense	Federal: Nondefense	State and local	Final sales	Gross domestic purchases [1]
1980	2,732.0	1,732.6	437.0	32.1	351.0	318.9	530.3	208.1	142.7	65.4	322.2	2,740.3	2,699.8
1981	3,052.6	1,915.1	515.5	33.9	382.8	348.9	588.1	242.2	167.5	74.8	345.9	3,028.6	3,018.7
1982	3,166.0	2,050.7	447.3	26.3	361.9	335.6	641.7	272.7	193.8	78.9	369.0	3,190.5	3,139.7
1983	3,405.7	2,234.5	502.3	−6.1	352.5	358.7	675.0	283.5	214.4	69.1	391.5	3,412.8	3,411.8
1984	3,772.2	2,430.5	664.8	−58.9	383.5	442.4	735.9	310.5	234.3	76.2	425.3	3,704.5	3,831.1
1985 r	4,014.9	2,629.0	643.1	−78.0	370.9	448.9	820.8	355.2	259.1	96.0	465.6	4,003.6	4,092.8
1986 r	4,240.3	2,807.5	665.9	−104.4	378.4	482.8	871.2	366.2	277.5	88.7	505.0	4,224.7	4,344.7
1987 r	4,526.7	3,012.1	712.9	−123.0	428.0	551.1	924.7	382.0	295.3	86.7	542.8	4,487.5	4,649.7
1982: IV	3,212.5	2,117.0	409.6	14.1	335.9	321.9	671.8	293.2	205.4	87.7	378.7	3,272.4	3,198.5
1983: IV	3,545.8	2,315.8	579.8	−25.8	364.7	390.5	676.1	276.1	221.5	54.6	400.0	3,514.8	3,571.6
1984: IV	3,851.8	2,493.4	661.8	−67.9	385.7	453.6	764.5	326.0	244.1	81.9	438.5	3,806.8	3,919.7
1985: V r	4,107.9	2,700.4	654.1	−103.2	369.2	472.4	856.7	376.6	268.6	108.0	480.1	4,100.7	4,211.2
1986: I r	4,180.4	2,739.0	686.6	−93.0	376.9	469.9	847.8	356.6	266.8	89.9	491.2	4,136.5	4,273.4
II r	4,207.6	2,772.1	667.8	−101.2	373.9	475.1	868.8	368.7	277.2	91.5	500.2	4,188.1	4,308.7
III r	4,268.4	2,842.8	653.0	−109.1	377.8	486.9	881.8	372.7	288.0	84.7	509.1	4,267.7	4,377.6
IV r	4,304.6	2,876.0	656.4	−114.3	385.2	499.4	886.5	366.7	278.1	88.7	519.7	4,306.6	4,418.9
1987: I r	4,391.8	2,921.7	685.5	−119.1	395.3	514.4	903.8	372.7	287.3	85.4	531.1	4,354.1	4,510.9
II r	4,484.2	2,992.2	698.5	−122.2	416.8	539.0	915.7	377.5	294.8	82.6	538.2	4,451.5	4,606.3
III r	4,568.0	3,058.2	702.8	−125.2	440.4	565.6	932.2	386.3	299.8	86.4	546.0	4,553.5	4,693.2
IV r	4,662.8	3,076.3	764.9	−125.7	459.7	585.4	947.3	391.4	299.2	92.2	555.9	4,590.7	4,788.4
1988: I r	4,724.5	3,128.1	763.4	−112.1	487.8	599.9	945.2	377.7	298.4	79.3	567.5	4,659.2	4,836.6
II p	4,806.9	3,186.8	756.5	−90.6	501.1	591.7	954.2	375.2	295.7	79.5	579.0	4,763.9	4,897.5

[1] GNP less exports of goods and services plus imports of goods and services.

Note.—Series revised beginning 1985. See *Survey of Current Business*, July 1988.

Source: Department of Commerce, Bureau of Economic Analysis.

Source: *Economic Indicators*, Council of Economic Advisers.

GROSS NATIONAL PRODUCT IN 1982 DOLLARS

[Billions of 1982 dollars; quarterly data at seasonally adjusted annual rates]

Period	Gross national product	Personal consumption expenditures	Gross private domestic investment			Exports and imports of goods and services			Government purchases of goods and services					Final sales	Gross domestic purchases [1]
			Nonresidential fixed	Residential fixed	Change in business inventories	Net exports	Exports	Imports	Total	Federal			State and local		
										Total	National defense	Nondefense			
1980	3,187.1	2,000.4	379.2	137.0	−6.9	57.0	388.9	332.0	620.5	246.9	171.2	75.7	373.6	3,194.0	3,130.1
1981	3,248.8	2,024.2	395.2	126.5	23.9	49.4	392.7	343.4	629.7	259.6	180.3	79.3	370.1	3,225.0	3,199.4
1982	3,166.0	2,050.7	366.7	105.1	−24.5	26.3	361.9	335.6	641.7	272.7	193.8	78.9	369.0	3,190.5	3,139.7
1983	3,279.1	2,146.0	361.2	149.3	−6.4	−19.9	348.1	368.1	649.0	275.1	206.9	68.2	373.9	3,285.5	3,299.1
1984	3,501.4	2,249.3	425.2	170.9	62.3	−84.0	371.8	455.8	677.7	290.8	218.5	72.3	387.0	3,439.1	3,585.4
1985 r	3,618.7	2,354.8	453.5	174.4	9.1	−104.3	367.2	471.4	731.2	326.0	237.2	88.8	405.2	3,609.6	3,723.0
1986 r	3,721.7	2,455.2	433.1	195.0	15.4	−137.5	378.4	515.9	760.5	333.4	251.4	82.0	427.1	3,706.3	3,859.3
1987 r	3,847.0	2,521.0	445.1	195.2	34.4	−128.9	427.8	556.7	780.2	339.0	264.9	74.1	441.2	3,812.6	3,975.9
1982: IV	3,159.3	2,078.7	352.3	115.8	−59.3	11.7	336.0	324.3	660.1	289.5	201.4	88.2	370.6	3,218.6	3,147.6
1983: IV	3,365.1	2,191.9	390.4	159.9	27.0	−46.2	355.5	401.6	642.2	266.0	211.6	54.4	376.2	3,338.1	3,411.3
1984: IV	3,535.2	2,281.1	444.4	169.6	41.7	−94.8	376.6	471.4	693.2	300.5	225.3	75.2	392.7	3,493.5	3,630.0
1985: IV r	3,662.4	2,386.9	460.9	179.4	7.7	−125.3	367.4	492.6	752.7	340.6	241.4	99.2	412.1	3,654.7	3,787.6
1986: I r	3,719.3	2,415.1	446.8	185.5	45.7	−115.7	374.5	490.2	741.8	322.7	241.1	81.6	419.1	3,673.6	3,834.9
II r	3,711.6	2,440.9	432.8	195.7	23.6	−140.2	372.1	512.4	758.8	333.6	250.8	82.8	425.2	3,688.0	3,851.8
III r	3,721.3	2,478.6	425.6	199.0	3.0	−151.8	379.1	530.9	766.9	336.7	260.7	76.0	430.2	3,718.3	3,873.0
IV r	3,734.7	2,486.2	427.3	199.7	−10.5	−142.4	387.8	530.2	774.5	340.5	253.1	87.4	434.0	3,745.2	3,877.2
1987: I r	3,776.7	2,490.2	418.2	198.4	29.8	−132.8	394.9	527.7	772.9	334.0	257.0	77.0	438.9	3,746.9	3,909.5
II r	3,823.0	2,516.6	434.8	197.6	27.8	−126.0	416.4	542.3	772.2	332.1	264.8	67.3	440.1	3,795.2	3,949.0
III r	3,865.3	2,545.2	462.8	192.1	13.0	−130.7	440.9	571.6	782.9	342.1	269.5	72.6	440.8	3,852.2	3,996.0
IV r	3,923.0	2,531.7	464.8	192.7	67.1	−126.0	459.2	585.2	792.6	347.7	268.2	79.5	444.9	3,855.9	4,049.0
1988: I r	3,956.1	2,559.8	473.4	189.5	66.0	−109.0	486.2	595.1	776.4	327.8	264.6	63.2	448.7	3,890.1	4,065.1
II p	3,986.3	2,574.2	489.2	190.8	45.0	−90.1	495.6	585.7	777.2	325.3	260.9	64.4	451.9	3,941.3	4,076.4

[1] GNP less exports of goods and services plus imports of goods and services.

NOTE.—Series revised beginning 1985. See *Survey of Current Business*, July 1988.

Source: Department of Commerce, Bureau of Economic Analysis.

Source: *Economic Indicators*, Council of Economic Advisers.

PERSONAL CONSUMPTION EXPENDITURES

[Billions of dollars, except as noted; quarterly data at seasonally adjusted annual rates]

Period	Total personal consumption expenditures	Durable goods				Nondurable goods					Services	Retail sales of new passenger cars (millions of units)	
		Total durable goods	Motor vehicles and parts	Furniture and household equipment	Other	Total nondurable goods	Food	Clothing and shoes	Gasoline and oil	Other		Domestics	Imports
1982	2,050.7	252.7	108.9	95.7	48.1	771.0	398.8	124.4	89.1	158.7	1,027.0	5.8	2.2
1983	2,234.5	289.1	130.4	107.1	51.6	816.7	421.9	135.1	90.2	169.5	1,128.7	6.8	2.4
1984	2,430.5	335.5	157.4	118.8	59.3	867.3	448.5	146.7	90.0	182.1	1,227.6	8.0	2.4
1985 r	2,629.0	372.2	179.1	129.9	63.2	911.2	471.6	156.4	90.6	192.6	1,345.6	8.2	2.8
1986 r	2,807.5	406.5	196.4	140.0	70.1	943.6	501.0	167.0	73.3	202.2	1,457.3	8.2	3.2
1987 r	3,012.1	421.9	195.8	148.3	77.8	997.9	526.4	178.2	77.0	216.3	1,592.3	7.1	3.2
1982: IV	2,117.0	263.8	115.7	99.1	49.0	786.6	407.0	126.5	89.8	163.4	1,066.5	6.0	2.5
1983: IV	2,315.8	310.0	144.4	112.4	53.2	837.9	430.8	141.1	91.9	174.0	1,167.9	7.4	2.6
1984: IV	2,493.4	346.7	162.3	122.7	61.8	879.6	456.1	149.8	89.0	184.7	1,267.1	7.7	2.6
1985: IV r	2,700.4	373.2	173.8	134.7	64.7	932.7	482.5	160.6	91.0	198.5	1,394.5	7.0	3.1
1986: I r	2,739.0	381.4	179.4	135.9	66.0	938.4	490.3	163.0	86.3	198.8	1,419.2	7.7	3.0
II r	2,772.1	393.0	187.7	138.8	66.5	937.2	498.0	167.0	71.7	200.5	1,441.9	8.0	3.1
III r	2,842.8	429.9	217.5	142.0	70.5	944.7	503.2	168.7	68.9	203.9	1,468.2	9.5	3.4
IV r	2,876.0	421.8	201.0	143.3	77.5	954.1	512.6	169.4	66.3	205.8	1,500.1	7.7	3.4
1987: I r	2,921.7	403.5	181.7	145.9	75.9	977.5	521.0	174.5	72.1	209.9	1,540.7	6.7	2.9
II r	2,992.2	420.5	194.5	147.8	78.3	995.3	525.3	176.8	77.4	215.8	1,576.4	7.1	3.1
III r	3,058.2	441.4	212.9	150.2	78.3	1,006.6	528.4	180.4	79.3	218.5	1,610.2	8.0	3.5
IV r	3,076.3	422.0	194.0	149.4	78.6	1,012.4	530.9	181.2	79.3	220.9	1,641.9	6.6	3.3
1988: I r	3,128.1	437.8	202.2	154.7	81.0	1,016.2	535.9	180.5	76.3	223.5	1,674.1	7.6	3.2
II p	3,186.8	446.9	206.8	159.0	81.2	1,030.3	542.4	182.5	78.5	226.9	1,709.6	7.5	3.1

Note.—Series revised beginning 1985. See *Survey of Current Business*, July 1988.

Source: Department of Commerce, Bureau of Economic Analysis.

Source: *Economic Indicators*, Council of Economic Advisers.

CORPORATE PROFITS

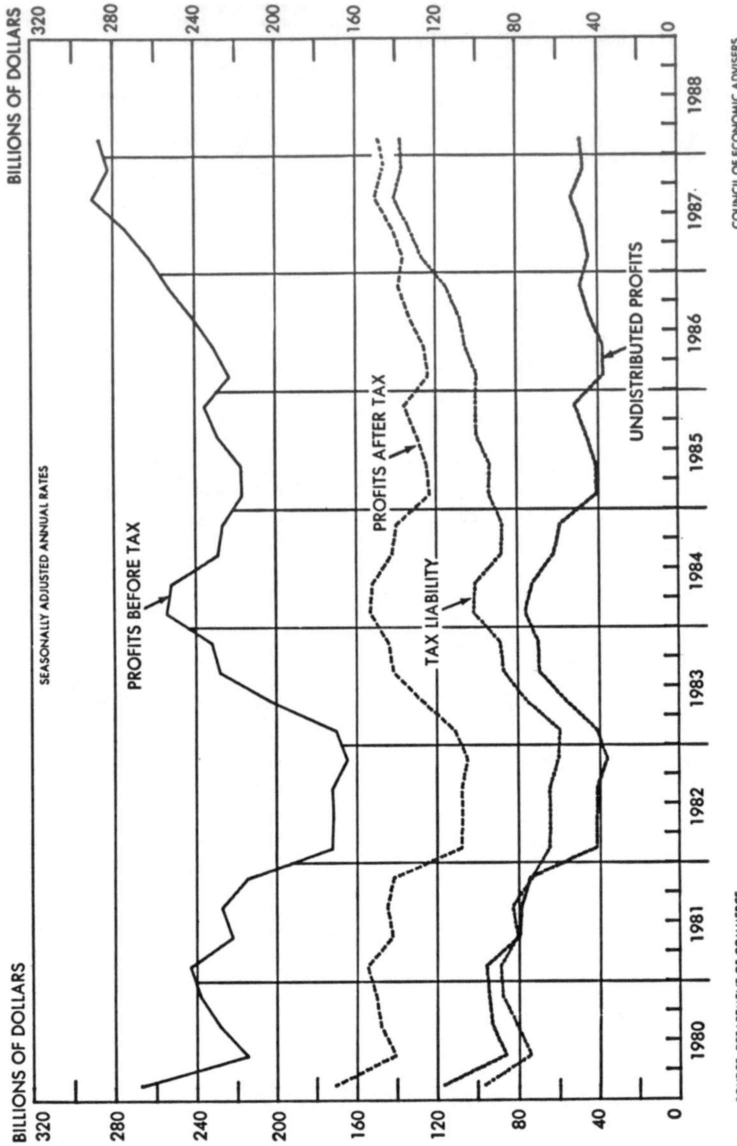
BILLIONS OF DOLLARS
SEASONALLY ADJUSTED ANNUAL RATES
PROFITS BEFORE TAX
PROFITS AFTER TAX
TAX LIABILITY
UNDISTRIBUTED PROFITS
320
280
240
200
160
120
80
40
0
1980
1981
1982
1983
1984
1985
1986
1987
1988
SOURCE: DEPARTMENT OF COMMERCE
COUNCIL OF ECONOMIC ADVISERS

[Billions of dollars; quarterly data at seasonally adjusted annual rates]

Period	Profits (before tax) with inventory valuation adjustment [1]						Profits before tax	Tax liability	Profits after tax			Inventory valuation adjustment
	Total [2]	Domestic industries							Total	Dividends	Undistributed profits	
		Total	Financial	Nonfinancial								
				Total [3]	Manufacturing	Wholesale and retail trade						
1980	194.0	159.6	21.0	138.6	77.1	21.6	237.1	84.8	152.3	54.7	97.6	−43.1
1981	202.3	173.8	16.5	157.3	88.5	32.5	226.5	81.1	145.4	63.6	81.8	−24.2
1982	159.2	131.2	11.8	119.4	58.0	34.6	169.6	63.1	106.5	66.9	39.6	−10.4
1983	196.7	166.6	18.1	148.5	70.1	38.9	207.6	77.2	130.4	71.5	58.9	−10.9
1984	234.2	203.3	13.0	190.3	88.8	51.2	240.0	93.9	146.1	79.0	67.0	−5.8
1985 r	222.6	191.4	22.8	168.6	79.7	44.1	224.3	96.4	127.8	83.3	44.6	−1.7
1986 r	244.7	212.8	31.8	180.9	79.4	46.1	236.4	106.6	129.8	88.2	41.6	8.3
1987 r	258.7	222.3	30.1	192.1	96.8	42.8	276.7	133.8	142.9	95.5	47.4	−18.0
1982: IV	150.7	121.6	18.7	102.9	46.8	33.6	164.1	59.8	104.3	68.5	35.8	−13.4
1983: IV	223.4	190.7	15.5	175.2	88.6	43.1	231.5	88.1	143.4	73.9	69.5	−8.1
1984: IV	224.6	193.9	13.6	180.3	79.8	51.8	226.1	87.0	139.2	80.8	58.4	−1.6
1985: IV r	228.4	193.6	26.0	167.6	83.8	38.5	235.0	99.8	135.2	84.0	51.2	−6.6
1986: I r	243.4	208.5	31.6	176.9	75.4	48.5	222.5	99.2	123.2	86.2	37.0	21.0
II r	242.1	213.5	34.5	179.0	80.5	43.4	230.3	104.9	125.4	88.0	37.4	11.8
III r	249.2	217.2	32.4	184.9	73.8	49.9	240.5	107.9	132.6	88.9	43.7	8.7
IV r	244.1	211.9	28.9	183.0	87.7	42.5	252.1	114.3	137.9	89.8	48.1	−8.1
1987: I r	247.5	213.0	30.7	182.3	84.8	46.5	261.8	126.3	135.5	91.7	43.8	−14.4
II r	253.6	219.2	31.4	187.8	93.8	37.8	273.7	132.6	141.1	94.0	47.0	−20.0
III r	269.9	234.6	29.5	205.1	107.0	44.1	289.4	140.0	149.5	97.0	52.4	−19.5
IV	263.7	222.2	28.8	193.4	101.7	43.0	281.9	136.2	145.7	99.3	46.4	−18.2
1988: I r	266.8	236.6	27.6	209.0	110.6	43.9	286.2	136.9	149.4	101.3	48.1	−19.4
II p	....	....	....	....	....	....	....	....	....	103.1	....	−29.8

[1] See p. 157 for profits with inventory valuation and capital consumption adjustments.
[2] Includes rest of the world, not shown separately.
[3] Includes industries not shown separately.

Note.—Series revised beginning 1985. See *Survey of Current Business*, July 1988.

Source: Department of Commerce, Bureau of Economic Analysis.

Source: *Economic Indicators*, Council of Economic Advisers.

Price Data

Definitions are applicable to the exhibits on pages 165–173.

Price data are gathered by the Bureau of Labor Statistics from retail and primary markets in the United States. Price indexes are given in relation to a base period (1967 = 100, unless otherwise noted).

DEFINITIONS

The **Consumer Price Index** (CPI) is a measure of the average change in the prices paid by urban consumers for a fixed market basket of goods and services. The CPI is calculated monthly for two population groups, one consisting only of urban households whose primary source of income is derived from the employment of wage earners and clerical workers, and the other consisting of all urban households. The wage earner index (CPI–W) is a continuation of the historic index that was introduced well over a half-century ago for use in wage negotiations. As new uses were developed for the CPI in recent years, the need for a broader and more representative index became apparent. The all urban consumer index (CPI–U) introduced in 1978 is representative of the 1982–84 buying habits of about 80 percent of the noninstitutional population of the United States at that time, compared with 32 percent represented in the CPI–W. In addition to wage earners and clerical workers, the CPI–U covers professional, managerial, and technical workers, the self-employed, short-term workers, the unemployed, retirees, and others not in the labor force.

The CPI is based on prices of food, clothing, shelter, fuel, drugs, transportation fares, doctor's and dentist's fees, and other goods and services that people buy for day-to-day living. The quantity and quality of these items are kept essentially unchanged between major revisions so that only price changes will be measured. All taxes directly associated with the purchase and use of items are included in the index.

Data are collected from more than 21,000 retail establishments and 60,000 tenants in 91 urban areas across the country are used to develop the "U.S. city average."

NOTES ON THE DATA

In January 1983, the Bureau changed the way in which homeownership costs are measured for the CPI–U. A rental equivalence method replaced the asset-price approach to homeownership costs for that series. In January 1985, the same change was made in the CPI–W. The central purpose of the change was to separate shelter costs from the investment component of homeownership so that the index would reflect only the cost of shelter services provided by owner-occupied homes. An updated CP-U and CPI-W were introduced with release of the January 1987 data.

Additional Sources of Information

For a discussion of the general method for computing the CPI, see *BLS Handbook of Methods, Volume II, The Consumer Price Index*, Bulletin 2134–2 (Bureau of Labor Statistics, 1984). The recent change in the measurement of homeownership costs is discussed in Robert Gillingham and Walter Lane, "Changing the treatment of shelter costs for homeowners in the CPI," *Monthly Labor Review*, June 1982, pp. 9–14. An overview of the recently introduced revised CPI, reflecting 1982–84 expenditure patterns, is contained in *The Consumer Price Index: 1987 Revision*, Report 736 (Bureau of Labor Statistics, 1987).

Additional detailed CPI data and regular analyses of consumer price changes are provided in the *CPI Detailed Report*, a monthly publication of the Bureau. Historical data for the overall CPI and for selected groupings may be found in the *Handbook of Labor Statistics*, Bulletin 2217 (Bureau of Labor Statistics, 1985).

Source: *Monthly Labor Review*, U.S. Department of Labor, Bureau of Labor Statistics, June 1988.

CONSUMER PRICE INDEX FOR ALL URBAN CONSUMERS AND FOR URBAN WAGE EARNERS AND CLERICAL WORKERS: U.S. CITY AVERAGE, BY EXPENDITURE CATEGORY AND COMMODITY OR SERVICE GROUP

(1982-84=100, unless otherwise indicated)

Series	Annual average		1987									1988			
	1986	1987	Apr.	May	June	July	Aug.	Sept.	Oct.	Nov.	Dec.	Jan.	Feb.	Mar.	Apr.
CONSUMER PRICE INDEX FOR ALL URBAN CONSUMERS:															
All items	109.6	113.6	112.7	113.1	113.5	113.8	114.4	115.0	115.3	115.4	115.4	115.7	116.0	116.5	117.1
All items (1967=100)	328.4	340.4	337.7	338.7	340.1	340.8	342.7	344.4	345.3	345.8	345.7	346.7	347.4	349.0	350.8
Food and beverages	109.1	113.5	112.8	113.3	113.8	113.7	113.8	114.2	114.3	114.3	114.8	115.7	115.8	116.0	116.7
Food	109.0	113.5	112.8	113.3	113.8	113.7	113.8	114.1	114.3	114.2	114.7	115.7	115.7	115.9	116.6
Food at home	107.3	111.9	111.3	112.0	112.6	112.1	112.1	112.4	112.4	112.1	112.8	114.1	113.9	113.9	114.6
Cereals and bakery products	110.9	114.8	114.3	114.6	114.7	115.2	115.3	115.4	115.6	116.2	116.8	118.1	118.7	118.9	119.8
Meats, poultry, fish, and eggs	104.5	110.5	108.6	109.6	110.4	111.4	111.9	112.7	112.0	111.2	110.3	111.0	110.6	111.2	111.5
Dairy products	103.3	105.9	105.3	105.7	105.5	105.3	105.7	106.4	106.9	106.9	106.7	107.4	107.3	107.2	107.1
Fruits and vegetables	109.4	119.1	120.1	121.8	124.1	119.6	117.4	117.4	117.8	117.4	123.4	126.4	124.7	123.0	126.0
Other foods at home	109.4	110.5	110.6	110.5	110.2	110.0	110.4	110.3	110.6	110.2	110.0	111.3	111.8	112.0	112.1
Sugar and sweets	109.0	111.0	110.7	110.8	111.2	111.1	111.3	111.6	111.6	111.4	111.0	112.2	112.2	112.6	112.3
Fats and oils	106.5	108.1	108.0	108.5	107.8	108.4	108.3	107.8	107.4	108.0	107.7	108.5	109.5	110.3	110.3
Nonalcoholic beverages	110.4	107.5	108.5	108.0	106.8	105.9	105.9	105.8	106.7	105.0	104.8	106.9	107.7	107.7	107.8
Other prepared foods	109.2	113.8	113.3	113.4	113.7	114.1	114.8	114.6	114.7	115.1	115.0	115.9	116.1	116.3	116.6
Food away from home	112.5	117.0	116.1	116.4	116.8	117.2	117.5	118.0	118.3	118.6	118.9	119.3	119.7	120.2	120.7
Alcoholic beverages	111.1	114.1	113.3	113.6	114.0	114.4	114.7	114.9	115.2	115.4	115.4	115.8	116.8	117.4	118.0
Housing	110.9	114.2	113.2	113.6	114.3	114.7	115.4	115.6	115.5	115.5	115.6	116.2	116.6	117.0	117.3
Shelter	115.8	121.3	120.2	120.5	120.8	121.3	122.2	122.5	123.2	123.4	123.7	124.6	125.0	125.6	125.8
Renters' costs (12/82=100)	121.9	128.1	127.1	127.3	127.9	129.3	130.1	129.8	129.4	129.2	129.1	130.8	131.3	132.9	132.9
Rent, residential	118.3	123.1	122.0	122.3	122.3	123.0	123.8	124.4	124.8	124.8	125.6	126.0	126.3	126.4	126.6
Other renters' costs	118.6	127.4	127.1	127.1	129.1	132.8	133.3	130.5	127.7	126.7	124.1	129.4	130.4	136.6	136.0
Homeowners' costs (12/82=100)	119.4	124.8	123.6	124.0	124.2	124.4	125.4	126.0	127.1	127.4	128.0	128.5	129.0	129.2	129.4
Owners' equivalent rent (12/82=100)	119.4	124.8	123.6	124.1	124.2	124.4	125.4	126.0	127.2	127.5	128.0	128.6	129.0	129.2	129.5
Household insurance (12/82=100)	119.2	124.0	122.4	123.0	123.6	124.5	125.1	125.5	125.8	125.9	126.2	126.9	127.1	127.8	128.2
Maintenance and repairs	107.9	111.8	110.3	110.2	111.1	113.2	112.9	112.7	112.8	113.5	113.3	113.7	114.3	113.3	115.3
Maintenance and repair services	111.2	114.8	112.8	112.3	113.7	116.8	116.5	116.3	116.4	116.9	116.6	117.4	117.9	116.4	119.4
Maintenance and repair commodities	103.7	107.8	107.2	107.5	107.8	108.4	108.2	107.8	108.1	108.9	109.1	108.7	109.5	109.2	109.7
Fuel and other utilities	104.1	103.0	101.3	102.2	104.9	105.0	105.9	105.5	103.2	102.4	102.0	102.4	102.8	102.7	102.8
Fuels	99.2	97.3	94.7	96.1	100.8	100.4	101.4	101.0	96.9	95.5	95.1	95.6	96.0	95.8	95.7
Fuel oil, coal, and bottled gas	77.6	77.9	77.5	77.1	77.2	77.1	77.8	77.6	78.5	80.3	80.5	80.8	80.9	80.5	80.2
Gas (piped) and electricity	105.7	103.8	100.8	102.5	108.1	107.6	108.7	108.2	103.3	101.4	100.9	101.5	101.9	101.7	101.6
Other utilities and public services	117.9	120.1	119.7	119.8	119.4	120.5	121.1	120.8	121.2	121.3	120.9	121.3	121.8	121.7	122.3
Household furnishings and operations	105.2	107.1	107.2	107.1	107.1	107.2	107.3	107.5	107.4	107.4	107.3	107.5	107.7	108.3	109.1
Housefurnishings	102.2	103.6	104.0	103.5	103.5	103.6	103.8	103.9	103.6	103.6	103.3	103.5	103.7	104.7	104.9
Housekeeping supplies	108.2	111.5	111.1	111.7	111.9	111.7	111.5	111.8	112.3	112.4	112.5	113.1	113.2	112.9	113.8
Housekeeping services	108.5	110.6	110.3	110.6	110.5	110.8	110.9	111.0	111.2	111.2	111.4	111.5	111.6	111.7	114.7

Continued

CONSUMER PRICE INDEX FOR ALL URBAN CONSUMERS AND FOR URBAN WAGE EARNERS AND CLERICAL WORKERS: U.S. CITY AVERAGE, BY EXPENDITURE CATEGORY AND COMMODITY OR SERVICE GROUP *(continued)*

(1982-84=100, unless otherwise indicated)

Series	Annual average		1987									1988			
	1986	1987	Apr.	May	June	July	Aug.	Sept.	Oct.	Nov.	Dec.	Jan.	Feb.	Mar.	Apr.
Apparel and upkeep	105.9	110.6	111.5	111.1	109.3	107.3	109.4	113.3	115.4	115.4	112.7	110.4	110.2	114.3	117.0
Apparel commodities	104.2	108.9	110.0	109.5	107.6	105.3	107.6	111.8	114.0	114.0	111.0	108.6	108.3	112.7	115.5
Men's and boys' apparel	106.2	109.1	109.2	109.9	109.0	107.8	108.3	110.6	112.0	112.5	110.7	109.0	109.1	111.6	112.9
Women's and girls' apparel	104.0	110.4	112.8	111.2	107.6	104.2	108.4	115.3	118.3	117.7	112.6	108.2	107.8	115.3	119.6
Infants' and toddlers' apparel	111.8	112.1	114.1	113.1	110.1	107.7	109.0	112.1	116.2	116.7	114.5	113.6	111.4	114.0	117.1
Footwear	101.9	105.1	105.8	106.5	105.6	103.4	104.2	105.7	107.3	108.0	107.2	106.1	105.8	107.3	109.4
Other apparel commodities	101.7	108.0	105.9	105.8	107.6	108.2	109.3	110.3	110.7	110.7	111.3	112.9	113.1	113.6	114.6
Apparel services	115.1	119.6	118.6	119.3	119.5	120.0	119.8	119.9	120.8	121.1	121.4	121.6	122.0	122.2	122.6
Transportation	102.3	105.4	104.2	104.7	105.4	106.0	106.5	106.6	107.1	107.8	107.6	107.1	106.8	106.5	107.2
Private transportation	101.2	104.2	103.0	103.5	104.3	104.9	105.4	105.4	106.0	106.8	106.5	106.0	105.7	105.4	106.0
New vehicles	110.6	114.4	113.5	113.8	114.1	114.4	114.0	113.8	115.0	116.3	116.4	116.1	116.0	115.7	115.6
New cars	110.6	114.6	113.6	114.0	114.3	114.7	114.4	114.1	115.2	116.6	116.6	116.2	116.2	116.0	115.9
Used cars	108.8	113.1	111.3	113.4	114.7	115.4	115.5	116.0	116.2	116.5	116.3	116.0	116.0	116.1	116.6
Motor fuel	77.1	80.2	78.5	79.1	80.8	82.2	84.3	84.0	83.2	83.2	82.0	79.7	78.3	77.5	79.4
Gasoline	77.0	80.1	78.4	79.0	80.7	82.1	84.3	84.0	83.1	83.1	81.8	79.5	78.1	77.3	79.2
Maintenance and repair	110.3	114.8	114.3	114.3	114.4	114.5	115.1	115.7	116.1	116.5	116.9	117.2	117.7	118.5	118.8
Other private transportation	115.1	120.8	119.4	119.7	120.3	120.8	120.7	121.1	122.8	123.8	123.8	124.7	125.0	124.9	125.0
Other private transportation commodities	96.3	96.9	96.0	96.7	96.7	96.3	96.8	97.6	98.0	97.6	97.5	98.2	98.1	98.3	98.2
Other private transportation services	118.8	125.6	124.0	124.2	125.0	125.7	125.5	125.8	127.8	129.2	129.2	130.1	130.6	130.3	130.5
Public transportation	117.0	121.1	120.9	120.6	120.2	120.2	121.5	122.1	121.2	122.0	122.1	121.8	120.8	121.4	122.4
Medical care	122.0	130.1	128.7	129.2	129.9	130.7	131.2	131.7	132.3	132.8	133.1	134.4	135.5	136.3	136.9
Medical care commodities	122.8	131.0	129.0	129.9	130.8	131.6	132.2	132.7	133.5	134.2	134.9	135.4	136.1	137.0	138.1
Medical care services	121.9	130.0	128.7	129.0	129.6	130.4	131.0	131.5	132.0	132.5	132.7	134.1	135.3	136.1	136.6
Professional services	120.8	128.8	127.5	127.9	128.8	129.5	130.0	130.7	131.2	131.5	131.8	133.2	134.5	135.4	136.0
Hospital and related services	123.1	131.6	129.7	130.1	130.6	132.0	133.0	133.3	134.2	135.4	135.9	137.6	139.0	140.0	140.7
Entertainment	111.6	115.3	114.5	114.8	114.9	115.4	115.6	116.1	116.9	117.3	117.4	118.1	118.3	119.0	119.6
Entertainment commodities	107.9	110.5	109.9	110.3	110.3	110.7	110.6	110.7	111.2	112.2	112.6	112.9	112.9	113.4	114.2
Entertainment services	116.8	122.0	121.0	121.2	121.4	122.0	122.5	123.5	124.5	124.3	124.3	125.4	125.7	126.5	127.0
Other goods and services	121.4	128.5	126.6	126.9	127.2	128.0	128.5	131.1	131.6	131.8	132.1	133.4	134.2	134.6	134.8
Tobacco products	124.7	133.6	131.6	131.8	132.4	135.0	135.3	135.9	136.3	136.5	137.0	140.8	142.2	142.8	142.9
Personal care	111.9	115.1	114.2	114.9	114.9	115.3	115.6	116.0	116.2	116.3	116.5	117.3	117.8	118.1	118.5
Toilet goods and personal care appliances	111.3	113.9	113.2	113.7	113.7	114.3	114.3	114.7	114.9	115.0	115.0	116.1	116.4	116.8	117.4
Personal care services	112.5	116.2	115.1	116.0	116.1	116.2	116.8	117.2	117.4	117.5	117.9	118.4	119.1	119.2	119.5
Personal and educational expenses	128.6	138.5	136.1	136.3	136.7	136.9	137.7	142.1	142.8	143.1	143.4	143.9	144.7	145.0	145.2
School books and supplies	128.1	138.1	136.2	136.4	136.5	136.5	136.7	141.3	142.3	142.3	142.4	144.6	146.3	146.2	146.3
Personal and educational services	128.7	138.7	136.3	136.5	136.8	137.2	137.9	142.3	143.1	143.4	143.6	144.0	144.8	145.1	145.3

All items	109.6	113.6	112.7	113.1	113.5	113.8	114.4	115.0	115.3	115.4	115.4	115.7	116.0	116.5	117.1
Commodities	104.4	107.7	107.2	107.5	107.7	107.6	108.2	108.9	109.3	109.5	109.3	109.2	109.1	109.8	110.7
Food and beverages	109.1	113.5	112.8	113.3	113.8	113.7	113.8	114.2	114.3	114.3	114.8	115.7	115.8	116.0	116.7
Commodities less food and beverages	101.4	104.0	103.6	103.7	103.8	103.8	104.6	105.5	106.1	106.5	105.7	105.1	105.0	105.9	106.9
Nondurables less food and beverages	97.8	101.1	100.7	100.9	100.7	100.6	102.0	103.5	104.2	104.3	103.1	102.1	101.9	103.4	105.0
Apparel commodities	104.2	108.9	110.0	109.5	107.6	105.3	107.6	111.8	114.0	114.0	111.0	108.6	108.3	112.7	115.5
Nondurables less food, beverages, and apparel	95.9	99.5	98.3	98.7	99.6	100.5	101.5	101.6	101.5	101.8	101.5	101.2	101.0	101.0	102.0
Durables	106.6	108.2	107.7	107.9	108.2	108.4	108.3	108.3	108.8	109.6	109.5	109.4	109.4	109.5	109.7
Services	115.4	120.2	118.9	119.3	120.1	120.5	121.2	121.7	121.9	122.0	122.2	122.9	123.4	123.8	124.1
Rent of shelter (12/82=100)	120.2	125.9	124.8	125.1	125.4	126.0	126.9	127.2	128.0	128.1	128.5	129.4	129.8	130.4	130.6
Household services less rent of' shelter (12/82=100)	112.8	113.1	111.4	112.3	114.8	115.1	115.8	115.5	113.5	112.6	112.3	112.7	113.1	113.0	113.7
Transportation services	116.3	121.9	120.9	120.9	121.3	121.7	122.0	122.5	123.4	124.5	124.6	125.1	125.2	125.4	125.8
Medical care services	121.9	130.0	128.7	129.0	129.6	130.4	131.0	131.5	132.0	132.5	132.7	134.1	135.3	136.1	136.6
Other services	119.4	125.7	124.1	124.4	124.7	125.1	125.6	127.9	128.7	128.8	129.0	129.6	130.2	130.7	131.0
Special indexes:															
All items less food	109.3	113.6	112.7	113.0	113.5	113.8	114.5	115.1	115.5	115.7	115.5	115.7	116.0	116.6	117.2
All items less shelter	108.0	111.6	110.8	111.1	111.7	111.8	112.3	113.0	113.2	113.3	113.2	113.3	113.5	114.0	114.7
All items less homeowners' costs (12/82=100)	111.2	115.1	114.2	114.6	115.1	115.3	115.9	116.5	116.6	116.8	116.6	116.9	117.1	117.7	118.4
All items less medical care	108.8	112.6	111.7	112.1	112.5	112.7	113.3	113.9	114.2	114.4	114.3	114.6	114.8	115.3	115.9
Commodities less food	101.7	104.3	103.9	104.0	104.1	104.1	104.9	105.7	106.3	106.7	106.0	105.5	105.4	106.3	107.3
Nondurables less food	98.5	101.8	101.3	101.4	101.4	101.3	102.6	104.0	104.6	104.8	103.7	102.8	102.7	104.1	105.6
Nondurables less food and apparel	96.9	100.3	99.1	99.5	100.3	101.1	102.0	102.2	102.1	102.4	102.1	101.9	101.9	101.9	102.9
Nondurables	103.5	107.5	106.9	107.2	107.4	107.3	108.1	109.0	109.4	109.5	109.1	109.1	109.0	109.8	111.0
Services less rent of' shelter (12/82=100)	118.7	123.1	121.6	122.1	123.2	123.7	124.2	124.9	124.6	124.6	124.6	125.3	125.8	126.0	126.5
Services less medical care	114.6	119.1	117.8	118.2	119.0	119.4	120.1	120.6	120.8	120.8	121.0	121.7	122.1	122.4	122.8
Energy	88.2	88.6	86.4	87.4	90.7	91.1	92.7	92.3	89.8	89.0	88.3	87.4	87.0	86.5	87.3
All items less energy	112.6	117.2	116.4	116.7	116.9	117.1	117.6	118.3	118.9	119.2	119.2	119.7	120.0	120.6	121.2
All items less food and energy	113.5	118.2	117.4	117.6	117.7	118.0	118.6	119.4	120.1	120.5	120.4	120.8	121.1	121.9	122.4
Commodities less food and energy	108.6	111.8	111.5	111.7	111.4	111.2	111.6	112.9	113.7	114.1	113.5	113.2	113.3	114.6	115.5
Energy commodities	77.2	80.2	78.5	79.1	80.6	81.8	83.8	83.5	82.9	83.1	82.0	80.0	78.8	78.0	79.7
Services less energy	116.5	122.0	120.9	121.2	121.4	122.0	122.7	123.2	123.9	124.2	124.4	125.2	125.7	126.1	126.5
Purchasing power of the consumer dollar:															
1982-84=$1.00	91.3	88.0	88.6	88.4	88.0	87.8	87.3	86.9	86.7	86.5	86.6	86.4	86.2	85.8	85.4
1967=$1.00	30.5	29.4	29.6	29.5	29.4	29.3	29.2	29.0	29.0	28.9	28.9	28.8	28.8	28.7	28.5

Continued

CONSUMER PRICE INDEX FOR ALL URBAN CONSUMERS AND FOR URBAN WAGE EARNERS AND CLERICAL WORKERS: U.S. CITY AVERAGE, BY EXPENDITURE CATEGORY AND COMMODITY OR SERVICE GROUP *(continued)*

(1982-84 = 100, unless otherwise indicated)

Series	Annual average		1987									1988			
	1986	1987	Apr.	May	June	July	Aug.	Sept.	Oct.	Nov.	Dec.	Jan.	Feb.	Mar.	Apr.
CONSUMER PRICE INDEX FOR URBAN WAGE EARNERS AND CLERICAL WORKERS:															
All items	108.6	112.5	111.6	111.9	112.4	112.7	113.3	113.8	114.1	114.3	114.2	114.5	114.7	115.1	115.7
All items (1967=100)	323.4	335.0	332.3	333.4	334.9	335.6	337.4	339.1	340.0	340.4	340.2	341.0	341.6	343.0	344.7
Food and beverages	108.9	113.3	112.6	113.1	113.6	113.5	113.6	114.0	114.1	114.1	114.5	115.4	115.5	115.7	116.3
Food	108.8	113.3	112.5	113.1	113.6	113.5	113.6	114.0	114.1	114.0	114.5	115.4	115.4	115.6	116.2
Food at home	107.1	111.7	111.0	111.7	112.3	111.9	111.9	112.2	112.2	111.9	112.5	113.7	113.5	113.5	114.2
Cereals and bakery products	110.9	114.8	114.3	114.5	114.8	115.2	115.3	115.4	115.7	116.2	116.9	118.1	118.8	118.9	119.9
Meats, poultry, fish, and eggs	104.4	110.4	108.5	109.5	110.4	111.3	111.8	112.7	112.0	111.2	110.1	110.8	110.5	111.1	111.4
Dairy products	103.2	105.7	105.1	105.6	105.3	105.1	105.5	106.2	106.7	106.7	106.4	107.1	107.0	106.9	106.9
Fruits and vegetables	109.4	118.8	119.5	121.1	123.9	119.6	117.3	117.1	117.5	117.4	123.0	125.7	124.0	122.2	125.2
Other foods at home	109.1	110.4	110.4	110.4	110.1	109.9	110.3	110.2	110.5	110.1	109.8	111.3	111.7	111.9	112.0
Sugar and sweets	109.0	110.9	110.5	110.7	111.1	111.0	111.3	111.5	111.6	111.2	110.9	112.1	112.1	112.4	112.2
Fats and oils	106.4	107.9	107.9	108.3	107.6	108.2	108.1	107.6	107.3	107.9	107.6	108.4	109.5	110.3	110.2
Nonalcoholic beverages	110.0	107.5	108.4	108.1	106.8	105.9	106.0	106.0	106.9	105.2	104.9	107.2	107.9	108.0	107.9
Other prepared foods	109.0	113.6	113.1	113.2	113.5	113.9	114.6	114.4	114.5	114.9	114.8	115.7	115.8	116.0	116.4
Food away from home	112.5	116.9	116.0	116.2	116.7	117.0	117.4	117.9	118.2	118.5	118.8	119.1	119.6	120.0	120.6
Alcoholic beverages	111.1	113.9	113.2	113.5	113.9	114.2	114.4	114.6	114.9	115.2	115.1	115.6	116.6	117.3	117.9
Housing	109.7	112.8	111.8	112.2	112.9	113.2	114.0	114.1	114.0	113.9	114.1	114.6	115.0	115.4	115.6
Shelter	113.5	118.8	117.7	118.1	118.2	118.8	119.6	120.0	120.7	120.9	121.2	121.9	122.4	122.9	123.0
Renters' costs (12/84=100)	109.5	114.6	113.8	114.0	114.2	115.3	116.0	116.2	116.0	115.9	115.9	116.9	117.3	118.4	118.4
Rent, residential	118.2	122.9	121.9	122.1	122.2	122.8	123.6	124.2	124.5	124.6	125.3	125.7	126.1	126.2	126.3
Other renters' costs	119.1	128.2	128.3	128.6	129.7	133.6	134.2	132.2	129.3	128.1	124.5	129.2	130.0	136.9	136.1
Homeowners' costs (12/84=100)	108.8	113.8	112.7	113.1	113.2	113.4	114.3	114.8	115.9	116.2	116.6	117.1	117.6	117.8	118.0
Owners' equivalent rent (12/84=100)	108.8	113.7	112.7	113.1	113.2	113.4	114.3	114.8	115.9	116.2	116.6	117.1	117.6	117.8	118.0
Household insurance (12/84=100)	109.4	114.1	112.5	113.1	113.8	114.6	115.1	115.5	115.8	115.9	116.1	116.7	116.7	117.2	117.3
Maintenance and repairs	107.7	111.3	110.2	110.2	111.0	112.6	112.4	112.1	112.2	112.7	112.5	113.0	113.6	112.8	114.7
Maintenance and repair services	110.5	114.7	113.2	112.5	113.9	116.9	116.6	116.4	116.0	116.5	115.9	117.1	117.6	116.6	119.8
Maintenance and repair commodities	103.1	106.0	105.2	106.0	106.3	106.3	106.2	105.8	106.3	106.9	107.1	106.9	107.5	107.1	107.5
Fuel and other utilities	103.9	102.7	101.0	101.8	104.6	104.7	105.6	105.2	102.8	102.0	101.7	102.0	102.5	102.3	102.5
Fuels	99.2	97.1	94.4	95.8	100.7	100.2	101.3	100.8	96.5	95.1	94.8	95.2	95.6	95.4	95.4
Fuel oil, coal, and bottled gas	77.8	77.6	77.3	76.8	77.0	76.9	77.5	77.3	78.2	80.1	80.2	80.4	80.6	80.2	79.9
Gas (piped) and electricity	105.7	103.6	100.6	102.2	108.0	107.4	108.6	108.1	103.0	101.1	100.7	101.2	101.6	101.4	101.4
Other utilities and public services	117.7	120.1	119.6	119.7	119.4	120.4	121.0	120.7	121.1	121.2	120.9	121.2	121.8	121.7	122.3
Household furnishings and operations	105.0	106.7	106.9	106.7	106.7	106.8	106.9	107.1	107.0	107.0	106.9	107.1	107.2	107.8	108.7
Housefurnishings	101.9	103.1	103.4	103.0	102.9	103.1	103.3	103.4	103.1	103.1	102.9	103.0	103.1	104.1	104.2
Housekeeping supplies	108.5	111.8	111.5	112.0	112.1	112.1	111.9	112.2	112.7	112.8	112.9	113.5	113.6	113.4	114.3
Housekeeping services	109.1	110.9	110.7	110.9	110.9	111.1	111.2	111.3	111.4	111.4	111.6	111.7	111.8	111.9	115.6
Apparel and upkeep	105.8	110.4	111.4	110.9	109.1	107.1	109.1	112.9	115.2	115.2	112.6	110.3	110.0	113.9	116.3

Apparel commodities	104.2	108.8	109.9	109.4	107.4	105.3	107.4	111.5	113.9	113.9	111.1	108.6	108.3	112.4	114.9
Men's and boys' apparel	105.9	103.5	108.3	109.0	108.2	106.9	107.7	109.8	111.5	112.0	110.4	108.6	108.7	111.1	112.2
Women's and girls' apparel	103.8	110.3	113.0	111.4	107.7	104.4	108.2	115.2	118.2	117.6	112.6	108.2	107.9	114.9	118.8
Infants' and toddlers' apparel	113.5	114.0	115.9	115.3	111.7	109.7	110.6	113.9	118.6	118.7	116.4	115.2	113.3	116.0	119.1
Footwear	102.1	105.5	106.1	106.7	105.8	103.9	104.7	106.0	107.9	108.6	108.0	106.8	106.4	107.7	109.6
Other apparel commodities	101.6	107.4	105.5	105.1	107.0	107.3	108.2	109.8	110.4	110.5	110.6	112.2	112.0	112.8	113.9
Apparel services	115.0	119.2	118.4	118.9	119.1	119.5	119.3	119.4	120.3	120.7	120.9	121.1	121.5	121.6	122.0
Transportation	101.7	105.1	103.8	104.4	105.1	105.8	106.3	106.4	106.9	107.6	107.3	106.8	106.4	106.2	106.8
Private transportation	100.9	104.1	102.8	103.4	104.3	104.9	105.5	105.5	106.1	106.7	106.4	105.9	105.6	105.3	105.9
New vehicles	110.4	114.0	113.2	113.5	113.7	113.9	113.5	113.3	114.5	115.9	116.1	115.8	115.7	115.3	115.3
New cars	110.4	114.3	113.3	113.7	114.0	114.4	114.0	113.8	114.9	116.2	116.3	115.9	116.0	115.7	115.7
Used cars	108.8	113.1	111.3	113.4	114.7	115.4	115.5	115.9	116.1	116.4	116.2	115.9	116.0	116.1	116.6
Motor fuel	77.1	80.3	78.5	79.2	80.9	82.3	84.5	84.1	83.3	83.3	82.0	79.7	78.3	77.5	79.4
Gasoline	76.9	80.2	78.5	79.1	80.8	82.2	84.4	84.1	83.2	83.2	81.9	79.5	78.1	77.3	79.2
Maintenance and repair	110.6	115.1	114.6	114.6	114.7	114.9	115.4	116.0	116.3	116.7	117.0	117.4	117.8	118.6	118.9
Other private transportation	113.8	119.0	117.5	117.8	118.5	118.9	118.7	119.1	121.0	122.0	122.0	122.9	123.2	123.1	123.0
Other private transportation commodities	96.3	96.7	95.7	96.4	96.6	96.3	96.7	97.3	97.7	97.2	97.4	98.1	98.0	98.1	97.9
Other private transportation services	117.1	123.4	121.8	122.0	122.8	123.4	123.1	123.4	125.8	127.1	127.1	128.0	128.5	128.2	128.3
Public transportation	116.8	120.4	120.3	120.3	119.7	119.7	120.8	121.4	120.7	121.2	121.3	121.2	120.4	120.8	121.7
Medical care	122.0	130.2	128.8	129.3	130.0	130.8	131.4	132.0	132.6	133.0	133.4	134.6	135.8	136.5	137.1
Medical care commodities	122.2	130.2	128.2	129.1	130.1	130.9	131.3	131.9	132.6	133.4	134.1	134.7	135.4	136.1	137.2
Medical care services	122.0	130.3	128.9	129.3	130.0	130.8	131.4	132.0	132.6	133.0	133.2	134.6	135.8	136.6	137.1
Professional services	120.9	129.0	127.6	128.1	128.9	129.6	130.2	130.9	131.4	131.7	132.0	133.4	134.7	135.5	136.1
Hospital and related services	122.6	131.1	129.1	129.5	130.0	131.4	132.4	132.8	133.7	134.9	135.4	136.9	138.4	139.3	140.1
Entertainment	111.0	114.8	114.0	114.4	114.5	115.0	115.1	115.6	116.3	116.7	116.9	117.4	117.6	118.2	118.9
Entertainment commodities	107.8	110.6	110.0	110.5	110.5	110.9	110.8	110.9	111.3	112.2	112.6	112.8	112.9	113.5	114.2
Entertainment services	116.5	121.8	120.8	121.1	121.2	121.8	122.2	123.2	124.3	124.1	124.0	124.9	125.2	126.0	126.5
Other goods and services	120.9	127.8	125.9	126.2	126.6	127.5	128.0	130.3	130.8	131.0	131.3	132.7	133.6	134.0	134.2
Tobacco products	124.8	133.7	131.7	131.8	132.5	135.1	135.4	136.0	136.5	136.7	137.2	141.0	142.3	143.0	143.1
Personal care	111.9	115.0	114.1	114.7	114.8	115.1	115.4	115.8	116.1	116.2	116.4	117.1	117.5	117.7	118.1
Toilet goods and personal care appliances	111.2	113.9	113.1	113.6	113.6	114.1	114.3	114.6	115.0	115.0	115.1	116.0	116.2	116.5	117.0
Personal care services	112.6	116.1	115.0	115.9	116.0	116.2	116.7	117.1	117.3	117.4	117.8	118.3	118.9	119.0	119.3
Personal and educational expenses	128.5	138.2	135.9	136.1	136.4	136.7	137.4	141.8	142.4	142.8	143.0	143.4	144.3	144.6	144.7
School books and supplies	127.8	137.9	136.2	136.3	136.4	136.4	136.6	140.7	141.8	141.8	141.9	143.9	145.3	145.2	145.4
Personal and educational services	128.6	138.4	136.1	136.3	136.7	137.0	137.7	142.1	142.7	143.1	143.3	143.6	144.5	144.8	144.9
All items	108.6	112.5	111.6	111.9	112.4	112.7	113.3	113.8	114.1	114.3	114.2	114.5	114.7	115.1	115.7
Commodities	103.9	107.3	106.7	107.0	107.3	107.3	107.9	108.5	108.9	109.1	108.9	108.8	108.7	109.3	110.1
Food and beverages	108.9	113.3	112.6	113.1	113.6	113.5	113.6	114.0	114.1	114.1	114.5	115.4	115.5	115.7	116.3
Commodities less food and beverages	100.3	103.6	103.0	103.3	103.4	103.5	104.3	105.1	105.7	106.0	105.4	104.7	104.5	105.3	106.3
Nondurables less food and beverages	97.3	100.8	100.2	100.4	100.4	100.4	101.8	103.1	103.8	104.0	102.8	101.7	101.4	102.7	104.3
Apparel commodities	104.2	108.8	109.9	109.4	107.4	105.3	107.4	111.5	113.9	113.9	111.1	108.6	108.3	112.4	114.9
Nondurables less food, beverages, and apparel	95.3	99.2	97.9	98.4	99.3	100.3	101.4	101.5	101.3	101.6	101.2	100.8	100.5	100.4	101.6
Durables	104.9	106.6	106.0	106.4	106.6	106.9	106.8	106.9	107.4	108.0	108.0	107.9	107.9	108.0	108.1

Continued

CONSUMER PRICE INDEX FOR ALL URBAN CONSUMERS AND FOR URBAN WAGE EARNERS AND CLERICAL WORKERS: U.S. CITY AVERAGE, BY EXPENDITURE CATEGORY AND COMMODITY OR SERVICE GROUP *(concluded)*

(1982-84=100, unless otherwise indicated)

Series	Annual average		1987									1988			
	1986	1987	Apr.	May	June	July	Aug.	Sept.	Oct.	Nov.	Dec.	Jan.	Feb.	Mar.	Apr.
Services	114.7	119.4	118.1	118.5	119.3	119.7	120.4	120.9	121.1	121.2	121.3	122.0	122.5	122.8	123.1
Rent of shelter (12/84=100)	109.0	114.0	113.0	113.4	113.5	114.0	114.9	115.2	115.9	116.1	116.4	117.1	117.5	118.0	118.2
Household services less rent of shelter (12/84=100)	103.9	104.0	102.4	103.2	105.7	105.9	106.6	106.3	104.2	103.4	103.1	103.5	103.9	103.8	104.4
Transportation services	115.4	120.8	119.7	119.8	120.2	120.6	120.7	121.2	122.5	123.5	123.6	124.1	124.4	124.5	124.8
Medical care services	122.0	130.3	128.9	129.3	130.0	130.8	131.4	132.0	132.6	133.0	133.2	134.6	135.8	136.6	137.1
Other services	118.7	124.7	123.2	123.5	123.7	124.1	124.6	126.9	127.7	127.8	127.9	128.5	129.0	129.5	129.8
Special indexes:															
All items less food	108.5	112.2	111.3	111.6	112.1	112.4	113.1	113.7	114.0	114.3	114.1	114.2	114.4	115.0	115.5
All items less shelter	107.4	111.0	110.1	110.5	111.1	111.2	111.8	112.4	112.6	112.7	112.5	112.7	112.8	113.2	113.9
All items less homeowners' costs (12/84=100)	102.8	106.4	105.5	105.9	106.4	106.6	107.1	107.7	107.8	108.0	107.8	108.0	108.1	108.6	109.2
All items less medical care	107.8	111.5	110.6	111.0	111.5	111.7	112.3	112.9	113.1	113.3	113.2	113.4	113.6	114.0	114.6
Commodities less food	101.2	103.9	103.3	103.6	103.7	103.8	104.6	105.4	105.9	106.3	105.6	105.0	104.9	105.7	106.6
Nondurables less food	98.0	101.4	100.8	101.0	101.0	101.1	102.4	103.6	104.2	104.4	103.3	102.4	102.2	103.4	104.9
Nondurables less food and apparel	96.4	100.0	98.7	99.2	100.0	101.0	101.9	102.0	101.9	102.2	101.8	101.5	101.4	101.4	102.5
Nondurables	103.3	107.2	106.6	106.9	107.2	107.2	107.9	108.8	109.2	109.2	108.8	108.8	108.7	109.4	110.5
Services less rent of shelter (12/84=100)	107.1	110.8	109.5	109.9	111.1	111.5	112.0	112.5	112.2	112.2	112.2	112.8	113.2	113.4	113.9
Services less medical care	113.9	118.2	116.9	117.4	118.1	118.5	119.2	119.7	119.9	119.9	120.1	120.7	121.1	121.4	121.7
Energy	87.4	88.0	85.8	86.8	90.1	90.5	92.2	91.8	89.3	88.6	87.8	86.8	86.3	85.8	86.7
All items less energy	111.5	116.0	115.3	115.6	115.7	115.9	116.4	117.1	117.7	118.0	118.0	118.5	118.7	119.3	119.9
All items less food and energy	112.3	116.8	116.0	116.3	116.3	116.6	117.2	117.9	118.7	119.1	119.0	119.3	119.6	120.3	120.8
Commodities less food and energy	107.6	110.8	110.5	110.7	110.5	110.3	110.8	111.8	112.7	113.1	112.6	112.3	112.4	113.5	114.3
Energy commodities	77.2	80.3	78.6	79.2	80.7	82.0	84.1	83.8	83.0	83.2	82.1	80.0	78.7	77.9	79.7
Services less energy	115.8	121.2	120.1	120.4	120.6	121.1	121.8	122.4	123.1	123.4	123.7	124.3	124.8	125.2	125.6
Purchasing power of the consumer dollar:															
1982-84=$1.00	92.0	89.0	89.6	89.3	88.9	88.7	88.2	87.8	87.6	87.4	87.5	87.3	87.2	86.8	86.4
1967=$1.00	30.9	29.9	30.1	30.0	29.9	29.8	29.6	29.5	29.4	29.4	29.4	29.3	29.3	29.2	29.0

Source: *Monthly Labor Review,* U.S. Department of Labor, Bureau of Labor Statistics, June, 1988.

CONSUMER PRICE INDEX—U.S. CITY AVERAGE AND AVAILABLE LOCAL AREA DATA: ALL ITEMS

(1982-84=100, unless otherwise indicated)

Area[1]	Pricing schedule[2]	Other index base	All Urban Consumers							Urban Wage Earners						
			1987			1988				1987			1988			
			Apr.	May	Dec.	Jan.	Feb.	Mar.	Apr.	Apr.	May	Dec.	Jan.	Feb.	Mar.	Apr.
U.S. city average	M	-	112.7	113.1	115.4	115.7	116.0	116.5	117.1	111.6	111.9	114.2	114.5	114.7	115.1	115.7
Region and area size[3]																
Northeast urban	M	-	115.0	115.4	118.3	118.9	119.2	119.6	120.4	114.1	114.5	117.4	117.9	118.1	118.4	119.2
Size A - More than 1,200,000	M	-	115.7	116.2	119.4	120.0	119.9	120.4	121.3	114.1	114.7	117.8	118.1	118.0	118.5	119.3
Size B - 500,000 to 1,200,000	M	-	113.3	113.6	115.6	116.2	117.0	117.5	118.2	112.3	112.6	114.5	115.1	116.0	116.4	117.0
Size C - 50,000 to 500,000	M	-	113.8	113.8	116.2	117.1	117.2	117.2	118.2	116.1	116.3	118.8	119.6	119.8	119.8	120.7
North Central urban	M	-	110.9	111.1	113.3	113.4	113.7	114.3	114.9	109.0	109.3	111.4	111.5	111.8	112.3	113.0
Size A - More than 1,200,000	M	-	111.5	111.7	113.9	114.1	114.7	115.1	115.7	109.1	109.3	111.4	111.6	112.1	112.5	113.1
Size B - 360,000 to 1,200,000	M	-	111.1	111.1	113.0	113.3	113.5	114.2	115.0	108.4	108.5	110.7	110.9	111.1	111.8	112.6
Size C - 50,000 to 360,000	M	-	110.6	111.1	113.6	113.4	113.4	114.6	115.2	109.5	110.0	112.6	112.4	112.3	113.4	114.0
Size D - Nonmetropolitan (less than 50,0000	M	-	108.9	109.1	110.9	110.6	110.5	111.1	111.8	108.5	108.7	110.7	110.4	110.2	110.6	111.3
South urban	M	-	111.5	111.8	114.0	114.1	114.4	114.8	115.4	110.9	111.3	113.5	113.6	113.8	114.2	114.7
Size A - More than 1,200,000	M	-	112.4	112.8	114.9	114.9	115.2	115.5	116.0	111.6	112.0	114.2	114.1	114.4	114.7	115.1
Size B - 450,000 to 1,200,000	M	-	112.1	112.2	114.5	114.8	115.1	115.8	116.3	110.3	110.5	112.7	112.9	113.0	113.6	114.1
Size C - 50,000 to 450,000	M	-	110.7	111.1	112.8	113.3	113.4	114.0	114.5	111.1	111.5	113.3	113.6	113.8	114.3	114.9
Size D - Nonmetropolitan (less than 50,000)	M	-	109.6	110.2	112.6	112.8	112.7	112.7	113.6	110.3	110.9	113.3	113.5	113.4	113.4	114.2
West urban	M	-	113.7	114.1	116.2	116.7	116.9	117.5	117.9	112.6	113.0	115.0	115.5	115.6	116.2	116.6
Size A - More than 1,250,000	M	-	114.8	115.3	117.2	117.9	118.2	118.9	119.2	112.5	113.0	114.8	115.3	115.6	116.2	116.6
Size B - 330,000 to 1,250,000	M	-	112.3	112.6	115.0	115.8	115.6	115.9	-	112.5	112.9	115.2	116.0	115.7	116.0	-
Size C - 50,000 to 330,000	M	-	113.3	112.9	116.0	116.0	115.9	116.2	116.8	112.7	112.3	115.4	115.3	115.3	115.6	116.2

(continued)

CONSUMER PRICE INDEX—U.S. CITY AVERAGE AND AVAILABLE LOCAL AREA DATA: ALL ITEMS *(concluded)*

(1982-84=100, unless otherwise indicated)

Area[1]	Pricing schedule[2]	Other index base	All Urban Consumers							Urban Wage Earners						
			1987			1988				1987			1988			
			Apr.	May	Dec.	Jan.	Feb.	Mar.	Apr.	Apr.	May	Dec.	Jan.	Feb.	Mar.	Apr.
Size classes:																
A	M	12/86	102.2	102.5	104.7	105.0	105.3	105.7	106.3	102.2	102.6	104.7	105.0	105.2	105.6	106.1
B	M	-	112.2	112.3	114.5	115.0	115.2	115.8	116.4	110.8	111.1	113.2	113.6	113.8	114.3	114.9
C	M	-	111.7	111.9	114.2	114.5	114.6	115.1	115.8	112.0	112.2	114.6	114.8	114.9	115.4	116.1
D	M	-	110.0	110.5	112.7	112.9	113.1	113.5	114.1	110.2	110.7	113.1	113.2	113.4	113.7	114.3
Selected local areas																
Chicago, IL-Northwestern IN	M	-	112.8	113.3	115.7	115.3	116.6	116.9	117.1	109.5	109.9	112.2	111.9	112.9	113.2	113.3
Los Angeles-Long Beach, Anaheim, CA	M	-	116.0	116.8	118.5	118.9	119.7	120.6	121.1	113.3	114.1	115.7	115.9	116.6	117.5	118.0
New York, NY-Northeastern NJ	M	-	116.6	117.3	120.6	121.3	121.1	121.5	122.6	115.3	116.0	119.1	119.6	119.3	119.7	120.6
Philadelphia, PA-NJ	M	-	115.5	116.4	118.9	119.3	119.3	119.6	120.0	115.3	116.2	119.0	119.3	119.0	119.5	119.8
San Francisco-Oakland, CA	M	-	114.8	115.0	117.4	118.4	117.9	119.1	118.7	113.9	113.9	116.4	117.5	117.0	117.9	117.8
Baltimore, MD	1	-	-	113.7	-	116.8	-	117.7	-	-	113.2	-	116.2	-	117.3	-
Boston, MA	1	-	-	115.3	-	120.1	-	122.1	-	-	115.2	-	120.2	-	121.8	-
Cleveland, OH	1	-	-	111.6	-	113.9	-	115.1	-	-	107.0	-	109.3	-	110.2	-
Miami, FL	1	-	-	111.1	-	114.5	-	115.1	-	-	110.3	-	113.8	-	114.3	-
St. Louis, MO-IL	1	-	-	111.3	-	113.4	-	114.2	-	-	110.9	-	113.0	-	113.8	-
Washington, DC-MD-VA	1	-	-	115.3	-	118.3	-	119.2	-	-	114.6	-	117.6	-	118.5	-
Dallas-Ft. Worth, TX	2	-	112.2	-	113.9	-	114.0	-	115.4	111.7	-	113.8	-	113.8	-	114.8
Detroit, MI	2	-	111.2	-	112.6	-	113.7	-	114.4	108.6	-	109.8	-	110.9	-	111.9
Houston, TX	2	-	106.4	-	107.3	-	108.0	-	108.2	106.1	-	107.4	-	108.1	-	108.1
Pittsburgh, PA	2	-	110.8	-	113.0	-	113.3	-	114.5	106.4	-	108.6	-	108.9	-	110.1

[1] Area is the Consolidated Metropolitan Statistical Area (CMSA), exclusive of farms and military. Area definitions are those established by the Office of Management and Budget in 1983, except for Boston-Lawrence-Salem, MA-NH Area (excludes Monroe County); and Milwaukee, WI Area (includes only the Milwaukee MSA). Definitions do not include revisions made since 1983.

[2] Foods, fuels, and several other items priced every month in all areas; most other goods and services priced as indicated:.

M - Every month.

1 - January, March, May, July, September, and November.

2 - February, April, June, August, October, and December.

[3] Regions are defined as the four Census regions.

- Data not available.

NOTE: Local area CPI indexes are byproducts of the national CPI program. Because each local index is a small subset of the national index, it has a smaller sample size and is, therefore, subject to substantially more sampling and other measurement error than the national index. As a result, local area indexes show greater volatility than the national index, although their long-term trends are quite similar. Therefore, the Bureau of Labor Statistics strongly urges users to consider adopting the national average CPI for use in escalator clauses.

Source: *Monthly Labor Review*, U.S. Department of Labor, Bureau of Labor Statistics.

ANNUAL DATA: CONSUMER PRICE INDEX, U.S. CITY AVERAGE, ALL ITEMS AND MAJOR GROUPS

(1982-84=100)

Series	1979	1980	1981	1982	1983	1984	1985	1986	1987
Consumer Price Index for All Urban Consumers:									
All items:									
Index	72.6	82.4	90.9	96.5	99.6	103.9	107.6	109.6	113.6
Percent change	11.3	13.5	10.3	6.2	3.2	4.3	3.6	1.9	3.6
Food and beverages:									
Index	79.9	86.7	93.5	97.3	99.5	103.2	105.6	109.1	113.5
Percent change	10.7	8.5	7.8	4.1	2.3	3.7	2.3	3.3	4.0
Housing:									
Index	70.1	81.1	90.4	96.9	99.5	103.6	107.7	110.9	114.2
Percent change	12.3	15.7	11.5	7.2	2.7	4.1	4.0	3.0	3.0
Apparel and upkeep:									
Index	84.9	90.9	95.3	97.8	100.2	102.1	105.0	105.9	110.6
Percent change	4.3	7.1	4.8	2.6	2.5	1.9	2.8	.9	4.4
Transportation:									
Index	70.5	83.1	93.2	97.0	99.3	103.7	106.4	102.3	105.4
Percent change	14.3	17.9	12.2	4.1	2.4	4.4	2.6	-3.9	3.0
Medical care:									
Index	67.5	74.9	82.9	92.5	100.6	106.8	113.5	122.0	130.1
Percent change	9.2	11.0	10.7	11.6	8.8	6.2	6.3	7.5	6.6
Entertainment:									
Index	76.7	83.6	90.1	96.0	100.1	103.8	107.9	111.6	115.3
Percent change	6.7	9.0	7.8	6.5	4.3	3.7	3.9	3.4	3.3
Other goods and services:									
Index	68.9	75.2	82.6	91.1	101.1	107.9	114.5	121.4	128.5
Percent change	7.2	9.1	9.8	10.3	11.0	6.7	6.1	6.0	5.8
Consumer Price Index for Urban Wage Earners and Clerical Workers:									
All items:									
Index	73.1	82.9	91.4	96.9	99.8	103.3	106.9	108.6	112.5
Percent change	11.4	13.4	10.3	6.0	3.0	3.5	3.5	1.6	3.6

Source: *Monthly Labor Review*, U.S. Department of Labor, Bureau of Economic Analysis.

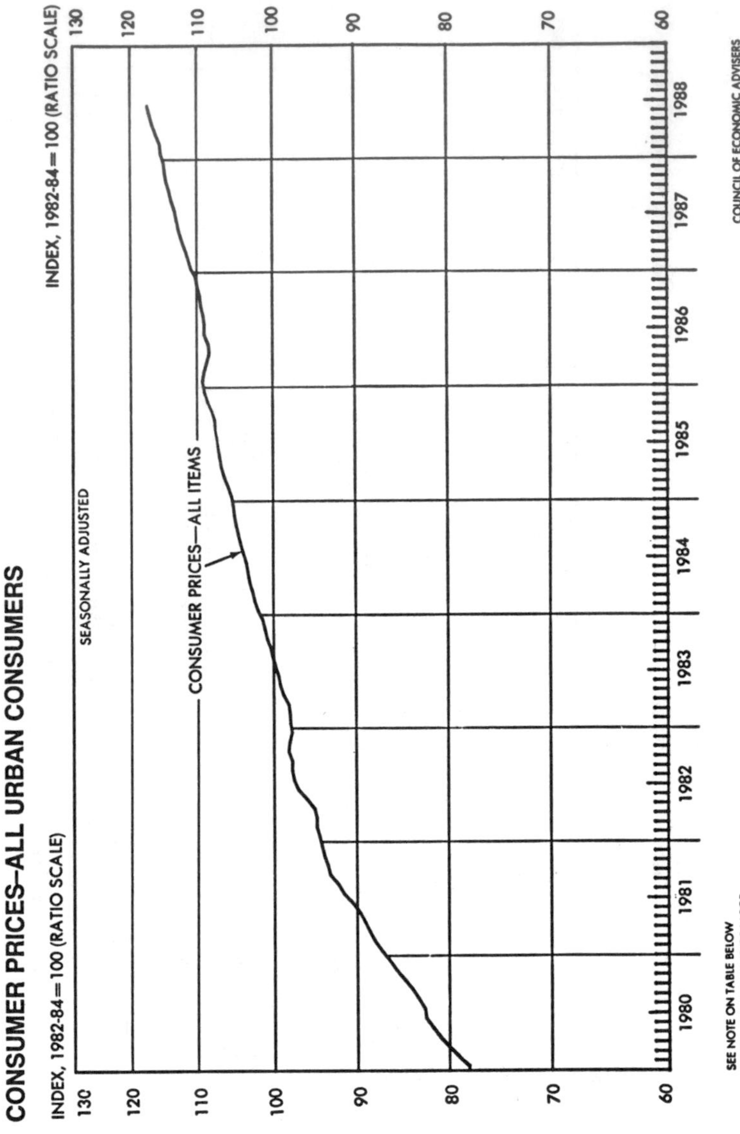
CONSUMER PRICES–ALL URBAN CONSUMERS
INDEX, 1982-84=100 (RATIO SCALE)
INDEX, 1982-84=100 (RATIO SCALE)
SEASONALLY ADJUSTED
CONSUMER PRICES—ALL ITEMS
130
120
110
100
90
80
70
60
1980
1981
1982
1983
1984
1985
1986
1987
1988
SEE NOTE ON TABLE BELOW
SOURCE: DEPARTMENT OF LABOR
COUNCIL OF ECONOMIC ADVISERS

[1982–84=100, except as noted; monthly data seasonally adjusted, except as noted]

Period	All items [1]		Food	Housing						Apparel and upkeep	Transportation			Medical care	Energy [2]	All items less food, shelter, and energy
					Shelter											
	Not seasonally adjusted (NSA)	Seasonally adjusted		Total [1]	Total	Renters' costs (Dec. 1982=100)	Homeowners' costs (Dec. 1982=100)	Maintenance and repairs (NSA)	Fuel and other utilities		Total [1]	New cars	Motor fuel			
Rel. imp. [3]	100.0	....	16.1	42.5	27.8	7.9	19.7	0.2	7.7	6.3	17.5	4.4	3.3	5.8	7.6	48.5
1980	82.4	....	86.8	81.1	81.0	....	....	82.4	75.4	90.9	83.1	88.4	97.4	74.9	86.0	80.6
1981	90.9	....	93.6	90.4	90.5	....	....	90.7	86.4	95.3	93.2	93.7	108.5	82.9	97.7	88.3
1982	96.5	....	97.4	96.9	96.9	....	....	96.4	94.9	97.8	97.0	97.4	102.8	92.5	99.2	95.1
1983	99.6	....	99.4	99.5	99.1	103.0	102.5	99.9	100.2	100.2	99.3	99.9	99.4	100.6	99.9	100.0
1984	103.9	....	103.2	103.6	104.0	108.6	107.3	103.7	104.8	102.1	103.7	102.8	97.9	106.8	100.9	105.0
1985	107.6	....	105.6	107.7	109.8	115.4	113.1	106.5	106.5	105.0	106.4	106.1	98.7	113.5	101.6	109.0
1986	109.6	....	109.0	110.9	115.8	121.9	119.4	107.9	104.1	105.9	102.3	110.6	77.1	122.0	88.2	112.7
1987	113.6	....	113.5	114.2	121.3	128.1	124.8	111.8	103.0	110.6	105.4	114.6	80.2	130.1	88.6	117.0
1987: June	113.5	113.5	113.9	114.0	120.8	127.5	124.4	111.1	103.0	110.8	105.3	114.4	80.1	130.0	88.5	116.9
July	113.8	113.8	113.8	114.2	121.2	128.5	124.5	113.2	103.1	109.9	105.9	114.8	81.1	130.7	88.7	117.3
Aug	114.4	114.3	113.9	114.8	121.9	128.9	125.4	112.9	103.6	110.3	106.7	115.0	83.8	131.3	90.2	117.6
Sept	115.0	114.6	114.5	115.0	122.2	128.8	125.9	112.7	103.3	111.3	106.8	115.2	83.2	131.9	89.8	117.9
Oct	115.3	115.0	114.7	115.3	122.8	128.6	126.9	112.8	103.0	112.7	107.2	115.5	83.0	132.4	89.3	118.5
Nov	115.4	115.3	114.8	115.5	123.1	128.8	127.2	113.5	103.4	113.1	107.7	115.7	83.0	133.0	89.6	118.9
Dec	115.4	115.5	115.3	115.9	123.8	129.5	127.9	113.3	103.3	112.2	107.4	115.7	81.6	133.5	88.9	118.9
1988: Jan	115.7	115.9	115.6	116.4	124.5	130.9	128.4	113.7	103.2	112.3	107.3	115.5	80.4	134.6	88.3	119.5
Feb	116.0	116.1	115.3	116.8	125.1	131.5	129.0	114.3	103.7	112.0	107.1	115.8	78.9	135.4	87.8	119.8
Mar	116.5	116.7	115.7	117.2	125.7	133.0	129.3	113.3	103.5	114.2	107.2	116.2	79.2	136.0	87.8	120.4
Apr.	117.1	117.2	116.5	117.5	125.8	132.6	129.6	115.3	104.0	116.5	107.5	116.2	80.1	136.8	88.5	121.1
May	117.5	117.6	117.0	117.8	126.2	132.8	130.0	114.3	103.9	116.5	108.2	116.4	81.5	137.7	88.9	121.5
June	118.0	118.0	117.7	118.2	126.7	133.3	130.6	114.7	104.0	116.1	108.4	116.6	80.8	138.3	88.7	121.8

[1] Includes items not shown separately.
[2] Household fuels—gas (piped), electricity, fuel oil, etc.—and motor fuel. Motor oil, coolant, etc. also included through 1982.
[3] Relative importance, December 1987.

NOTE.—Beginning with data for January 1988, the reference base was changed from 1967=100 to 1982–84=100.

Data beginning 1983 incorporate a rental equivalence measure for homeownership costs and therefore are not strictly comparable with figures for earlier periods.

Data beginning 1987 and 1988 calculated on a revised basis.

Source: Department of Labor, Bureau of Labor Statistics.

Source: *Economic Indicators*, Council of Economic Advisers.

Purchasing Power of the Dollar: 1940 to 1986

[**1967=$1.00.** Producer prices prior to 1961, and consumer prices prior to 1964, exclude Alaska and Hawaii. For 1940 and 1945, producer prices based on all commodities index; subsequent years based on finished goods index. Obtained by dividing the average price index for the 1967 base period (100.0) by the price index for a given period and expressing the result in dollars and cents. Annual figures are based on average of monthly data]

YEAR	ANNUAL AVERAGE AS MEASURED BY—		YEAR	ANNUAL AVERAGE AS MEASURED BY—		YEAR	ANNUAL AVERAGE AS MEASURED BY—	
	Producer prices	Consumer prices		Producer prices	Consumer prices		Producer prices	Consumer prices
1940	$2.469	$2.381	1960	$1.067	$1.127	1974	$.678	$.677
1945	1.832	1.855	1961	1.067	1.116	1975	.612	.620
1948	1.252	1.387	1962	1.064	1.104	1976	.586	.587
1949	1.289	1.401	1963	1.067	1.091	1977	.550	.551
1950	1.266	1.387	1964	1.063	1.076	1978	.510	.512
1951	1.156	1.285	1965	1.045	1.058	1979	.459	.460
1952	1.163	1.258	1966	1.012	1.029	1980	.405	.405
1953	1.175	1.248	1967	1.000	1.000	1981	.371	.367
1954	1.172	1.142	1968	.972	.960	1982	.356	.346
1955	1.170	1.247	1969	.938	.911	1983	.351	.335
1956	1.138	1.229	1970	.907	.860	1984	.343	.321
1957	1.098	1.186	1971	.880	.824	1985	.340	310
1958	1.073	1.155	1972	.853	.799	1986	.345	.304
1959	1.075	1.145	1973	.782	.751			

Source: U.S. Bureau of Labor Statistics. Monthly data in U.S. Bureau of Economic Analysis, *Survey of Current Business.*

Source: *Statistical Abstract of the United States,* 1988, U.S. Department of Commerce.

Federal Budget: Procedure and Timetable

Congressional Budget Timetable

CONGRESSIONAL BUDGET ACT OF 1974: THE NEW BUDGET PROCESS IN TEN STEPS

1. To give Congress an earlier and better start in reviewing and reshaping the budget, the Executive Branch must submit a "current services budget" by November 10th for the new fiscal year that starts the following October 1st. The current services budget should project the spending required to maintain ongoing programs throughout the following fiscal year at existing commitment levels, or at commitment levels specified by existing legislation based on current economic assumptions. The Joint Economic Committee should review and assess the current services budget and report to Congress by December 31st.

2. The President will continue to submit his new budget to Congress in late January or early February. In addition to the traditional budget totals and breakdowns, the budget document must include a list of existing "tax expenditures"—i.e., estimates of revenues lost to the Treasury through preferential tax treatment—as well as any proposed changes in tax expenditures. The budget must also contain estimates of expenditures for programs for which funds are appropriated one year in advance and five-year budget projections of all federal spending under existing programs.

3. Reports of all standing committees to the House and Senate Budget Committees of the spending plans of those committees on all matters under their jurisdiction, including spending under new legislation, are required by March 15th for the upcoming fiscal year.

4. An annual report of the Congressional Budget Office to the Budget Committees on alternative budget levels and national budget priorities is required on or before April 1st.

5. By April 15th, the Budget Committees must report concurrent resolutions to the House and Senate floors, and Congress will have to clear the initial budget resolution by May 15th. This initial budget resolution sets target totals for appropriations, outlays, taxes, the budget surplus or deficit, and the federal debt. Within these overall targets, the resolution will break down appropriations and outlays by the functional categories used in the President's budget document, as well as by classifications used by the appropriations subcommittees for the 13 appropriations bills. The resolution will include any recommended changes in tax revenues and in the level of the federal debt ceiling.

6. Committees report bills or resolutions authorizing new budget authority by May 15th.

7. The basic appropriations process proceeds within the Appropriations Committees, but is subject to targets of the budget resolution.

8. Scorekeeping reports will be issued periodically by the Congressional Budget Office on the status of budget authority, revenue, outlays and debt legislation, comparing the amounts and changes in such legislation with the First Congressional Budget Resolution.

9. Subject to prior authorization, all appropriations bills have to be cleared by the middle of September—no later than the seventh day after Labor Day. By September 15th, after finishing action on all appropriations and other spending bills, Congress must adopt a second, and final, budget resolution that may either affirm or revise the budget targets set by the initial resolution. This resolution must provide for a final budget reconciliation by changing either one or more of the following: (1) appropriations (both for the upcoming fiscal year or carried over from previous fiscal years) and/or entitlements; (2) revenues; and (3) the public debt. The final resolution will direct the committees that have jurisdiction over these matters to report the necessary legislative changes. The Budget Committees will then combine these changes and report them to the floor in the form of a reconciliation bill.

If Congress has withheld all appropriations and entitlement bills from the President until passage of the final reconciliation bill, then this bill becomes the final budget legislation, subject to Presidential signature (or veto). If, on the other hand, each individual appropriations bill has been signed by the President upon passage by the Congress, the final reconciliation bill—upon signature by the President—supersedes all the previously passed individual bills.

10. The new fiscal year begins on October 1st.

FEDERAL BUDGET: PROCEDURE AND TIMETABLE

Congressional Budget Timetable

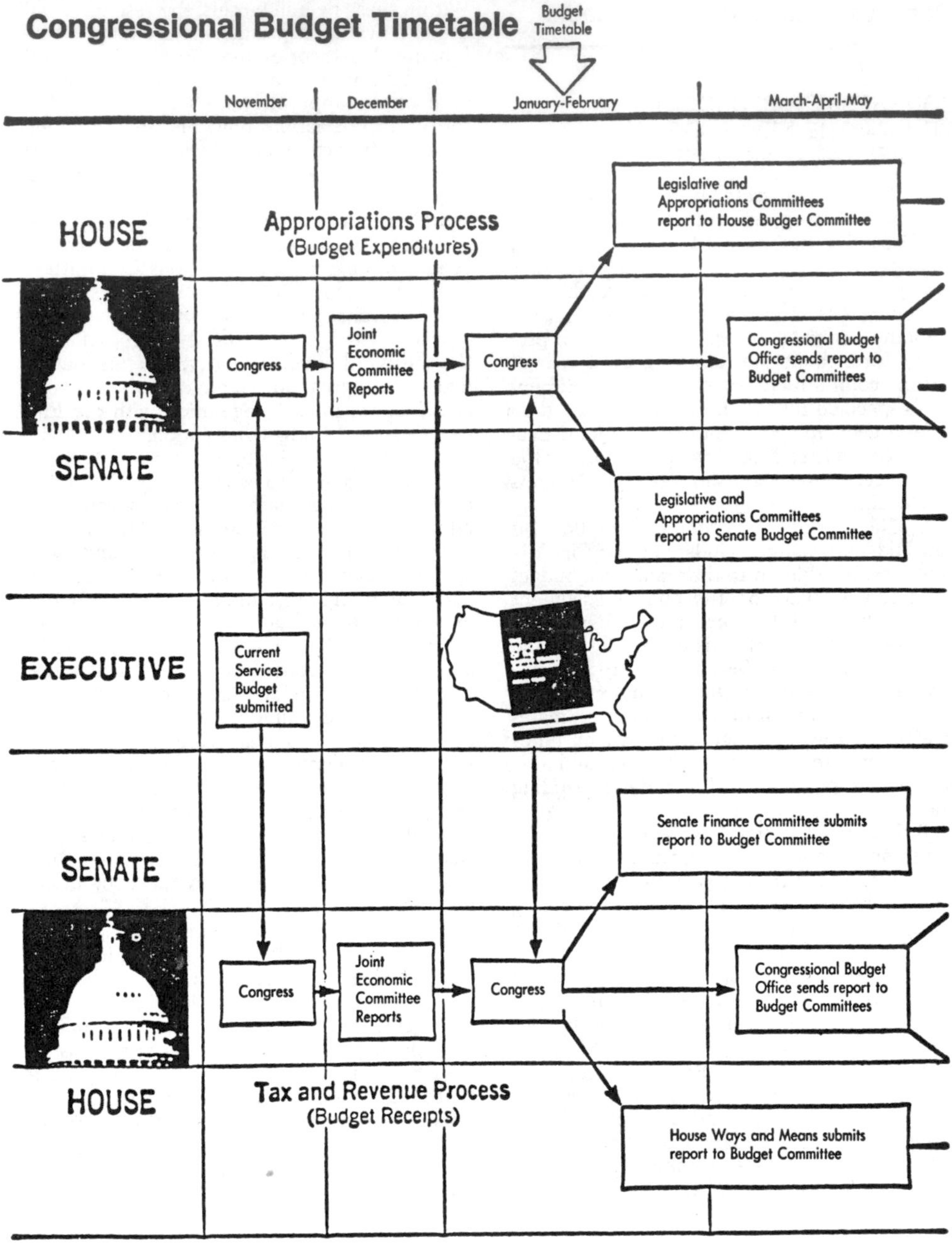

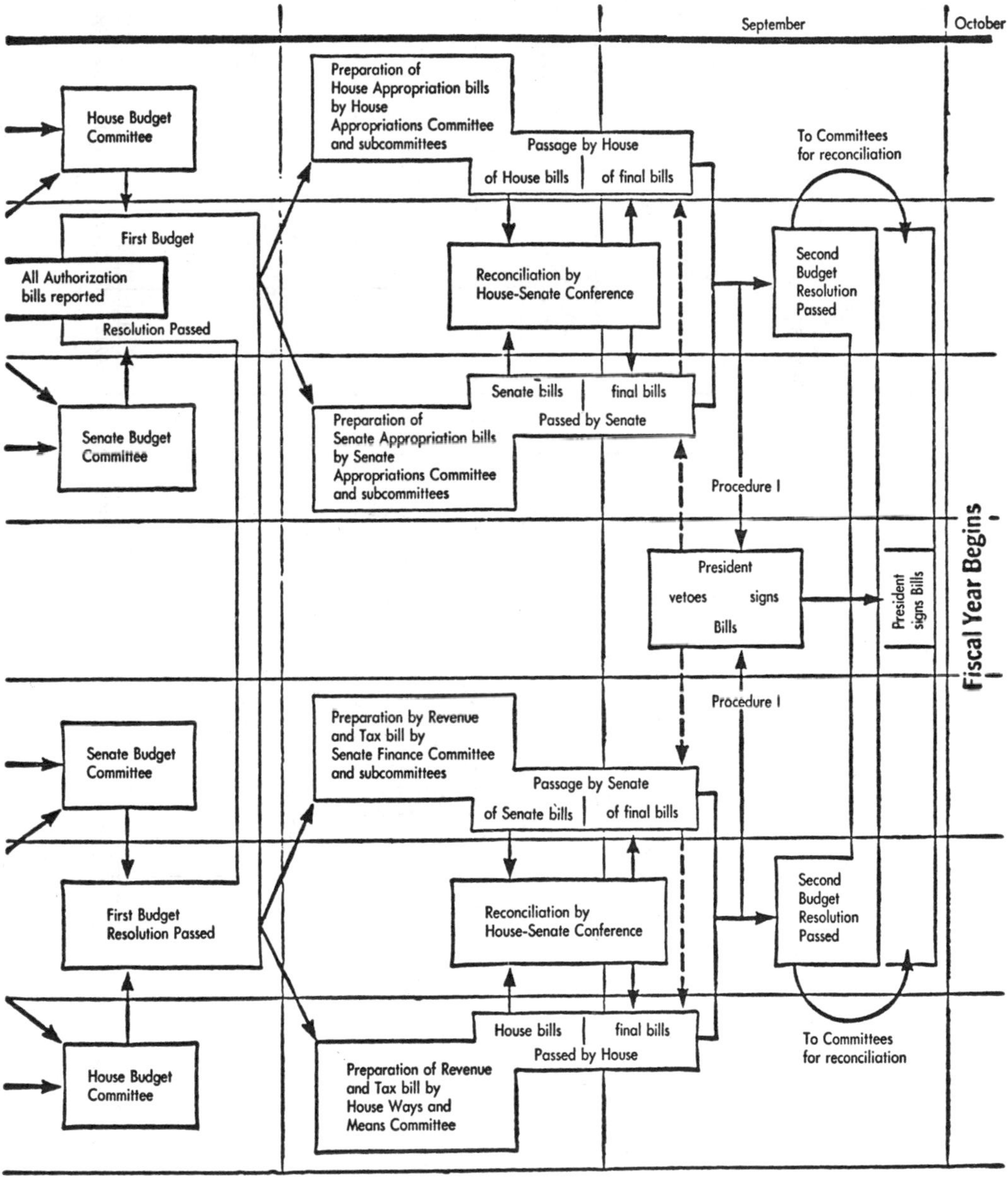

Source: The Conference Board, "The Federal Budget: Its Impact on the Economy," Michael E. Levy, assisted by Delos R. Smith.

SELECTED UNEMPLOYMENT RATES

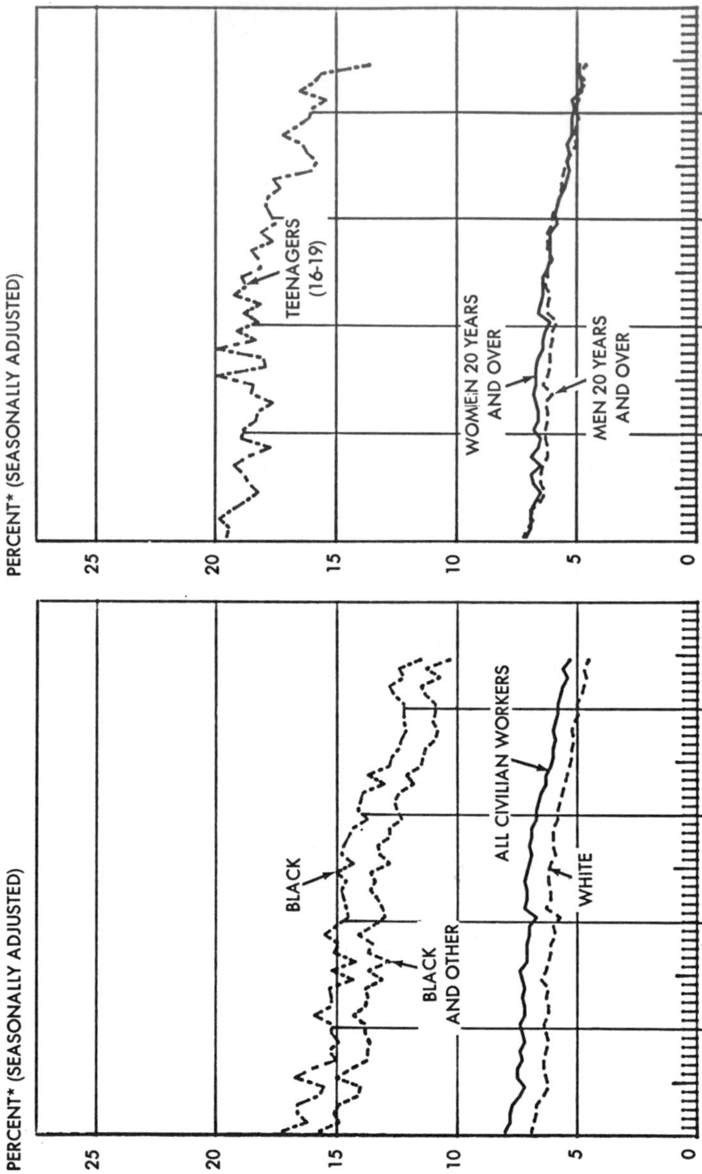

*UNEMPLOYMENT AS PERCENT OF CIVILIAN LABOR FORCE IN GROUP SPECIFIED.

SOURCE: DEPARTMENT OF LABOR

COUNCIL OF ECONOMIC ADVISERS

[Monthly data seasonally adjusted]

Period	Unemployment rate, all workers [1]	Unemployment rate (percent of civilian labor force in group): All civilian workers	By sex and age: Men 20 years and over	By sex and age: Women 20 years and over	By sex and age: Both sexes 16–19 years	By race: White	By race: Black and other	By race: Black	By selected groups: Experienced wage and salary workers	By selected groups: Married men, spouse present	By selected groups: Women who maintain families	By selected groups: Full-time workers	By selected groups: Part-time workers	Labor force time lost (percent) [2]
1980	7.0	7.1	5.9	6.4	17.8	6.3	13.1	14.3	6.9	4.2	9.2	6.9	8.8	7.9
1981	7.5	7.6	6.3	6.8	19.6	6.7	14.2	15.6	7.3	4.3	10.4	7.3	9.4	8.5
1982	9.5	9.7	8.8	8.3	23.2	8.6	17.3	18.9	9.3	6.5	11.7	9.6	10.5	11.0
1983	9.5	9.6	8.9	8.1	22.4	8.4	17.8	19.5	9.2	6.5	12.2	9.5	10.4	10.9
1984	7.4	7.5	6.6	6.8	18.9	6.5	14.4	15.9	7.1	4.6	10.3	7.2	9.3	8.6
1985	7.1	7.2	6.2	6.6	18.6	6.2	13.7	15.1	6.8	4.3	10.4	6.8	9.3	8.1
1986	6.9	7.0	6.1	6.2	18.3	6.0	13.1	14.5	6.6	4.4	9.8	6.6	9.1	7.9
1987	6.1	6.2	5.4	5.4	16.9	5.3	11.6	13.0	5.8	3.9	9.2	5.8	8.4	7.1
1987: June	6.0	6.1	5.5	5.3	16.0	5.3	11.5	12.8	5.8	4.0	9.5	5.9	7.3	7.1
July	6.0	6.0	5.4	5.4	15.8	5.2	11.4	12.7	5.8	3.8	9.3	5.7	8.1	6.9
Aug	5.9	6.0	5.2	5.3	16.2	5.2	11.3	12.4	5.7	3.7	9.0	5.6	8.2	6.9
Sept	5.8	5.9	5.0	5.4	16.4	5.1	10.9	12.3	5.5	3.7	8.8	5.5	8.4	6.8
Oct	5.9	6.0	5.1	5.2	17.2	5.2	10.8	12.1	5.5	3.7	8.9	5.6	8.3	6.8
Nov	5.8	5.9	5.0	5.2	16.6	5.1	11.0	12.2	5.5	3.5	8.5	5.5	8.2	6.8
Dec	5.7	5.8	4.9	5.2	16.1	4.9	10.9	12.2	5.4	3.4	8.4	5.4	8.0	6.6
1988: Jan	5.7	5.8	5.1	5.1	16.0	5.0	10.9	12.2	5.5	3.6	8.9	5.4	8.3	6.6
Feb	5.6	5.7	4.9	5.2	15.4	4.8	11.3	12.6	5.3	3.4	8.3	5.3	7.9	6.6
Mar	5.5	5.6	4.9	4.8	16.5	4.7	11.5	12.8	5.2	3.4	7.5	5.3	7.7	6.5
Apr	5.4	5.4	4.6	4.8	15.9	4.6	10.7	12.2	5.0	3.0	8.7	5.1	7.4	6.2
May	5.5	5.6	4.9	4.9	15.6	4.7	11.3	12.4	5.4	3.3	8.4	5.2	7.7	6.4
June	5.2	5.3	4.6	4.9	13.6	4.5	10.3	11.5	5.0	3.1	7.8	4.9	7.8	6.3

[1] Unemployed as percent of total labor force including resident Armed Forces.
[2] Aggregate hours lost by the unemployed and persons on part time for economic reasons as percent of potentially available labor force hours.

Source: Department of Labor, Bureau of Labor Statistics.

Source: *Economic Indicators*, Council of Economic Advisers.

MONEY STOCK, LIQUID ASSETS, AND DEBT MEASURES

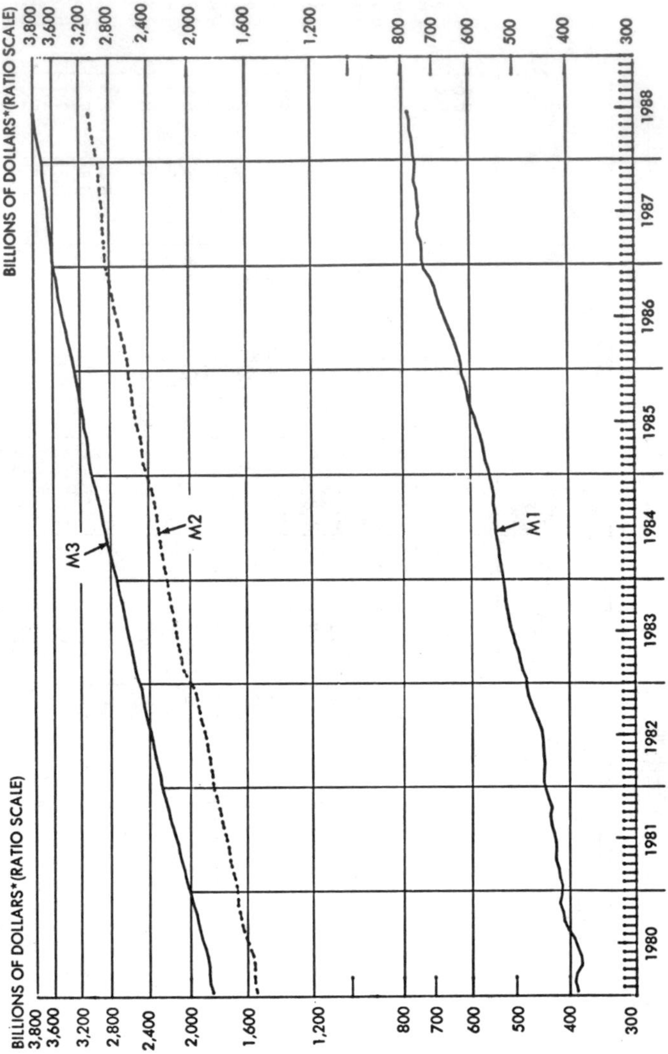

* AVERAGES OF DAILY FIGURES; SEASONALLY ADJUSTED
SOURCE: BOARD OF GOVERNORS OF THE FEDERAL RESERVE SYSTEM

COUNCIL OF ECONOMIC ADVISERS

[Averages of daily figures, except as noted; billions of dollars, seasonally adjusted]

Period	M1	M2	M3	L	Debt	Percent change from year or 6 months earlier [2]			
	Sum of currency, demand deposits, travelers' checks, and other checkable deposits (OCDs)	M1 plus overnight RPs and Eurodollars, MMMF balances (general purpose and broker/dealer), MMDAs, and savings and small time deposits	M2 plus large time deposits, term RPs, term Eurodollars, and institution-only MMMF balances	M3 plus other liquid assets	Debt of domestic nonfinancial sectors (monthly average) [1]	M1	M2	M3	Debt
1980: Dec	412.2	1,633.1	1,990.8	2,327.6	3,880.9	6.8	8.9	10.2	9.6
1981: Dec	439.1	1,795.5	2,236.5	2,599.0	4,262.1	6.5	9.9	12.3	9.8
1982: Dec	476.4	1,954.0	2,443.2	2,852.9	4,645.5	8.5	8.8	9.2	9.0
1983: Dec	522.1	2,185.2	2,693.2	3,154.4	5,181.7	9.6	11.8	10.2	11.5
1984: Dec	551.9	2,363.6	2,978.3	3,519.4	5,932.6	5.7	8.2	10.6	14.5
1985: Dec	620.1	2,562.6	3,196.0	3,825.4	6,749.4	12.4	8.4	7.3	13.8
1986: Dec	725.4	2,807.8	3,490.4	4,133.8	r7,607.7	17.0	9.6	9.2	12.7
1987: Dec	750.8	2,901.1	3,661.1	r4,323.9	r8,305.4	3.5	3.3	4.9	9.2
1987: June	742.1	2,851.7	3,580.1	4,232.3	7,939.3	4.7	3.2	5.2	8.9
July	743.6	2,858.2	3,587.6	4,235.1	7,980.7	3.4	2.2	4.2	8.2
Aug	746.5	2,869.5	3,605.5	4,257.8	8,031.0	4.2	2.9	4.7	8.5
Sept	747.5	2,880.9	3,620.5	4,283.5	r8,092.9	3.7	3.3	5.0	8.9
Oct	756.2	2,894.7	3,642.0	r4,312.2	r8,163.3	3.1	3.3	5.3	r9.1
Nov r	752.7	2,896.6	3,656.7	4,323.1	8,245.8	1.7	3.4	5.2	9.5
Dec r	750.8	2,901.1	3,661.1	4,323.9	8,305.4	2.4	3.5	4.6	9.4
1988: Jan r	758.8	2,925.0	3,686.8	4,360.7	8,352.3	4.1	4.7	5.6	9.5
Feb r	759.5	2,946.0	3,719.5	4,392.0	8,407.5	3.5	5.4	6.4	9.6
Mar r	762.9	2,967.5	3,744.4	4,418.6	8,468.8	4.2	6.1	7.0	9.5
Apr r	770.0	2,991.7	3,766.9	4,460.7	8,527.7	3.7	6.8	7.0	9.1
May r	770.0	3,003.1	3,780.3	4,488.9	8,584.7	4.6	7.5	6.9	8.4
June p	776.2	3,016.7	3,800.7	....	....	6.9	8.1	7.8	....

[1] Consists of outstanding credit market debt of the U.S. Government, State and local governments, and private nonfinancial sectors; data from flow of funds accounts.
[2] Annual changes are from December to December and monthly changes are from 6 months earlier at a seasonally adjusted annual rate.

NOTE.—See p. 27 for components.

Source: Board of Governors of the Federal Reserve System.

Source: *Economic Indicators*, Council of Economic Advisers.

Bank Failures

NUMBER AND DEPOSITS OF BANKS CLOSED BECAUSE OF FINANCIAL DIFFICULTIES, 1934–1987

Year	Number					Deposits (in thousands of dollars)					Assets[4]
			Insured					Insured			
	Total	Non-Insured[1]	Total	Without disbursements by FDIC[2]	With disbursements by FDIC[3]	Total	Non-Insured[1]	Total	Without disbursements by FDIC[2]	With disbursements by FDIC[3]	(in Thousands Dollars)
Total	**1,333**	**136**	**1,197**	**8**	**1,189**	**49,280,025**	**143,501**	**49,136,524**	**41,147**	**49,095,377**	**58,850,328**
1934	61	52	9	...	9	37,333	35,365	1,968	...	1,968	2,661
1935	32	6	26	1	25	13,988	583	13,405	85	13,320	17,242
1936	72	3	69	...	69	28,100	592	27,508	...	27,508	31,941
1937	84	7	77	2	75	34,205	528	33,677	328	33,349	40,370
1938	81	7	74	...	74	60,722	1,038	59,684	...	59,684	69,513
1939	72	12	60	...	60	160,211	2,439	157,722	...	157,772	181,514
1940	48	5	43	...	43	142,788	358	142,430	...	142,430	161,898
1941	17	2	15	...	15	29,796	79	29,717	...	29,717	34,804
1942	23	3	20	...	20	19,540	355	19,185	...	19,185	22,254
1943	5	...	5	...	5	12,525	...	12,525	...	12,525	14,058
1944	2	...	2	...	2	1,915	...	1,915	...	1,915	2,098
1945	1	...	1	...	1	5,695	...	5,695	...	5,695	6,392
1946	2	1	1	...	1	494	147	347	...	347	351
1947	6	1	5	...	5	7,207	167	7,040	...	7,040	6,798
1948	3	...	3	...	3	10,674	...	10,674	...	10,674	10,360
1949	9	4	5	1	4	9,217	2,552	6,665	1,190	5,475	4,886
1950	5	1	4	...	4	5,555	42	5,513	...	5,513	4,005
1951	5	3	2	...	2	6,464	3,056	3,408	...	3,408	3,050
1952	4	1	3	...	3	3,313	143	3,170	...	3,170	2,388
1953	5	1	4	2	2	45,101	390	44,711	26,449	18,262	18,811
1954	4	2	2	...	2	2,948	1,950	998	...	998	1,138
1955	5	...	5	...	5	11,953	...	11,953	...	11,953	11,985
1956	3	1	2	...	2	11,690	360	11,330	...	11,330	12,914
1957	3	1	2	1	1	12,502	1,255	11,247	10,084	1,163	1,253
1958	9	5	4	...	4	10,413	2,173	8,240	...	8,240	8,905
1959	3	...	3	...	3	2,593	...	2,593	...	2,593	2,858
1960	2	1	1	...	1	7,965	1,035	6,930	...	6,930	7,506

1961	9	4	5	...	5	10,611	1,675	8,936	...	8,936	9,820
1962	3	2	1	1	...	4,231	1,220	3,011	3,011	...	...[5]
1963	2	...	2	...	2	23,444	...	23,444	...	23,444	26,179
1964	8	1	7	...	7	23,867	429	23,438	...	23,438	25,849
1965	9	4	5	...	5	45,256	1,395	43,861	...	43,861	58,750
1966	8	1	7	...	7	106,171	2,648	103,523	...	103,523	120,647
1967	4	...	4	...	4	10,878	...	10,878	...	10,878	11,993
1968	3	...	3	...	3	22,524	...	22,524	...	22,524	25,154
1969	9	...	9	...	9	40,134	...	40,134	...	40,134	43,572
1970	8	1	7	...	7	55,229	423	54,806	...	54,806	62,147
1971	6	...	6	...	6	132,058	...	132,058	...	132,058	196,520
1972	3	2	1	...	1	99,784	79,304	20,480	...	20,480	22,054
1973	6	...	6	...	6	971,296	...	971,296	...	971,296	1,309,675
1974	4	...	4	...	4	1,575,832	...	1,575,832	...	1,575,832	3,822,596
1975	14	1	13	...	13	340,574	1,000	339,574	...	339,574	419,950
1976	17	1	16	...	16	865,659	800	864,859	...	864,859	1,039,293
1977	6	...	6	...	6	205,208	...	205,208	...	205,208	232,612
1978	7	...	7	...	7	854,154	...	854,154	...	854,154	994,035
1979	10	...	10	...	10	110,696	...	110,696	...	110,696	132,988
1980	10	...	10	...	10	216,300	...	216,300	...	216,300	236,164
1981	10	...	10	...	10	3,826,022	...	3,826,022	...	3,826,022	4,859,060
1982	42	...	42	...	42	9,908,379	...	9,908,379	...	9,908,379	11,632,415
1983	48	...	48	...	48	5,441,608	...	5,441,608	...	5,441,608	7,026,923
1984	79	...	79	...	79	2,883,162	...	2,883,162	...	2,883,162	3,276,411
1985[6]	120	...	120	...	120	8,059,441	...	8,059,441	...	8,059,441	8,741,268
1986[7]	138	...	138	...	138	6,471,100	...	6,471,100	...	6,471,100	6,991,600
1987[7]	184	...	184	...	184	6,281,500	...	6,281,500	...	6,281,500	6,850,700

[1]For information regarding each of these banks, see table 22 in the 1963 *Annual Report* (1963 and prior years), and explanatory notes to tables regarding banks closed because of financial difficulties in subsequent annual reports. One noninsured bank placed in receivership in 1934, with no deposits at time of closing, is omitted (see table 22 note 9). Deposits are unavailable for seven banks.

[2]For information regarding these cases, see table 23 of the *Annual Report* for 1963.

[3]For information regarding each bank, see the *Annual Report* for 1958, pp. 48-83 and pp. 98-127, and tables regarding deposit insurance disbursements in subsequent annual reports. Deposits are adjusted as of December 31, 1982.

[4]Insured banks only.

[5]Not available.

[6]Includes data for one bank granted financial assistance although no disbursement was required until January, 1986.

[7]Excludes data for banks granted financial assistance under Section 13(c)(1) of the Federal Deposit Insurance Act to prevent failure.

Source: Federal Deposit Insurance Corporation *1987 Annual Report*

TEN LARGEST BANK FAILURES (By Asset Size)

	Assets	Deposits	Date
Franklin National Bank New York, New York	$3,655,662,000	$1,444,981,606	October 8, 1974
First National Bank and Trust Company, Oklahoma City, Oklahoma	1,419,445,375	1,006,657,507	July 14, 1986
The First National Bank of Midland, Midland, Texas	1,404,092,000	1,076,217,000	October 14, 1983
United States National Bank San Diego, California	1,265,868,099	931,954,458	October 18, 1973
United American Bank in Knoxville, Knoxville, Tennessee	778,434,000	584,619,000	February 14, 1983
Banco Credito y Ahorro Ponceno, Ponce, Puerto Rico	712,540,000	607,610,000	March 31, 1978
Park Bank of Florida St. Petersburg, Florida	592,900,000	543,900,000	February 14, 1986
Yankee Bank for Finance and Savings, FSB, Boston, Massachusetts	521,700,000	474,800,000	October 16, 1987
Penn Square Bank, N.A. Oklahoma City, Oklahoma	516,799,000	470,445,000	July 6, 1982
The Hamilton National Bank of Chattanooga, Chattanooga, Tennessee	412,107,000	336,292,000	February 16, 1974

Source: Federal Deposit Insurance Corporation *1987 Annual Report*

Government Budget, Receipts, and Deficits: Historical Data

Federal Government Receipts as Percentages of GNP

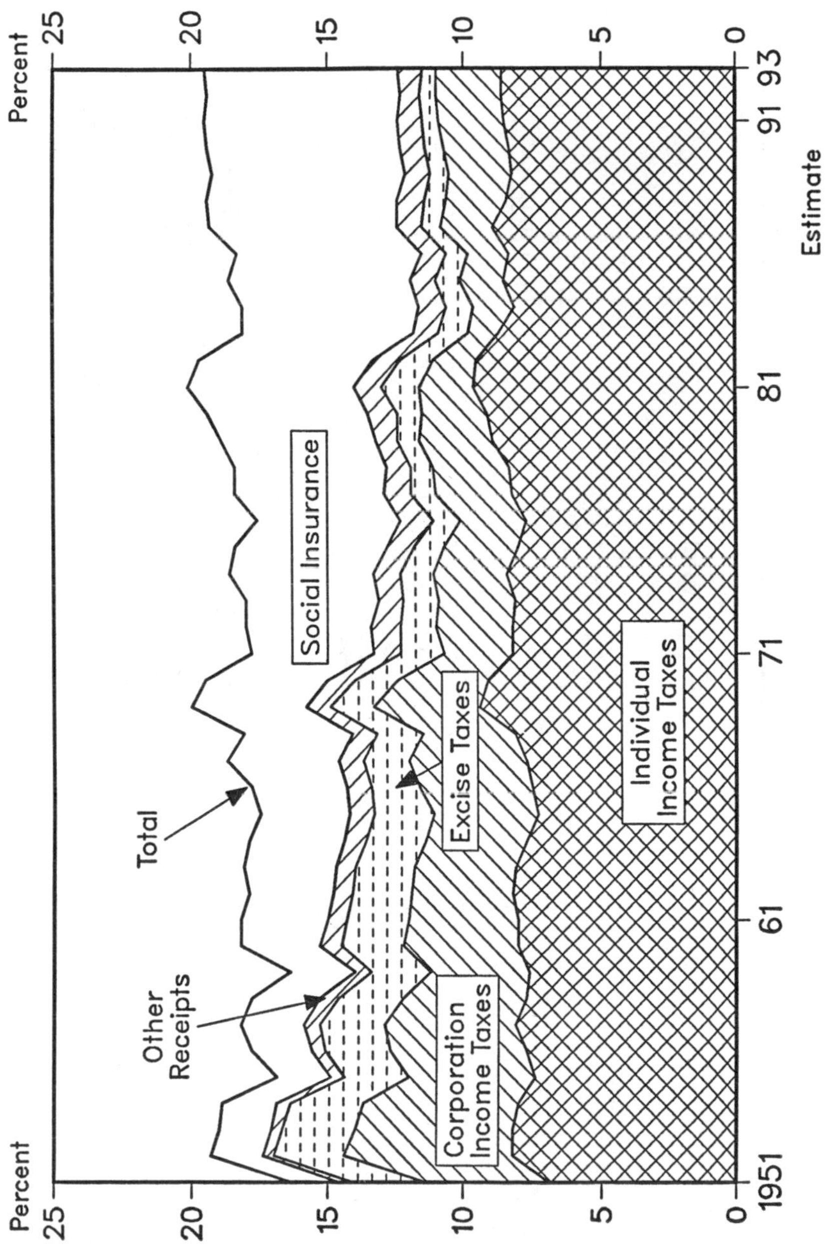

Source: *Historical Tables*, Budget of the United States Government, Fiscal 1989, Executive Office of the President, Office of Management and Budget.

Federal Government Outlays as Percentages of GNP

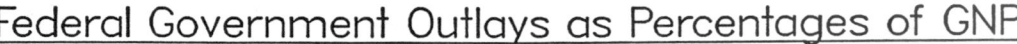

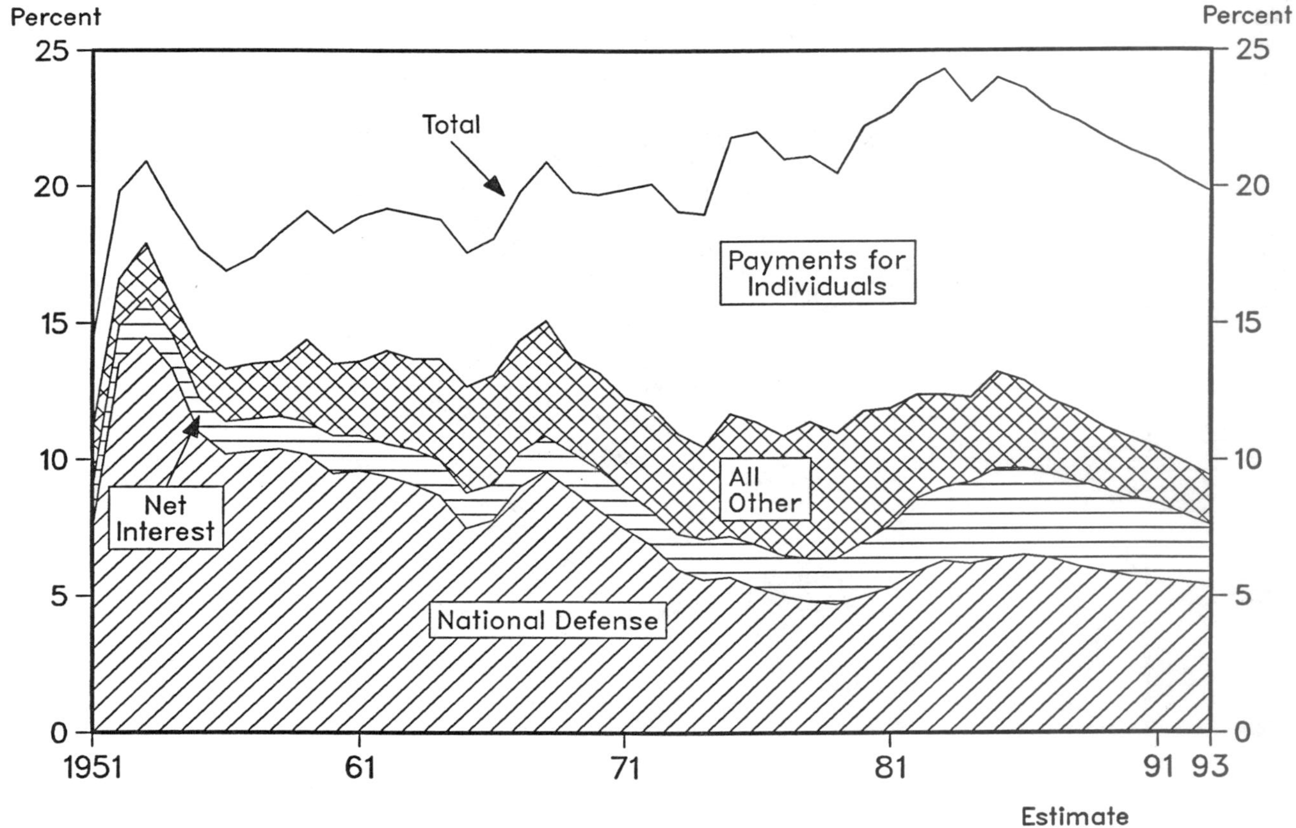

Source: *Historical Tables,* Budget of the United States Government, Fiscal 1989, Executive Office of the President, Office of Management and Budget.

Percentage Composition of Federal Government Receipts

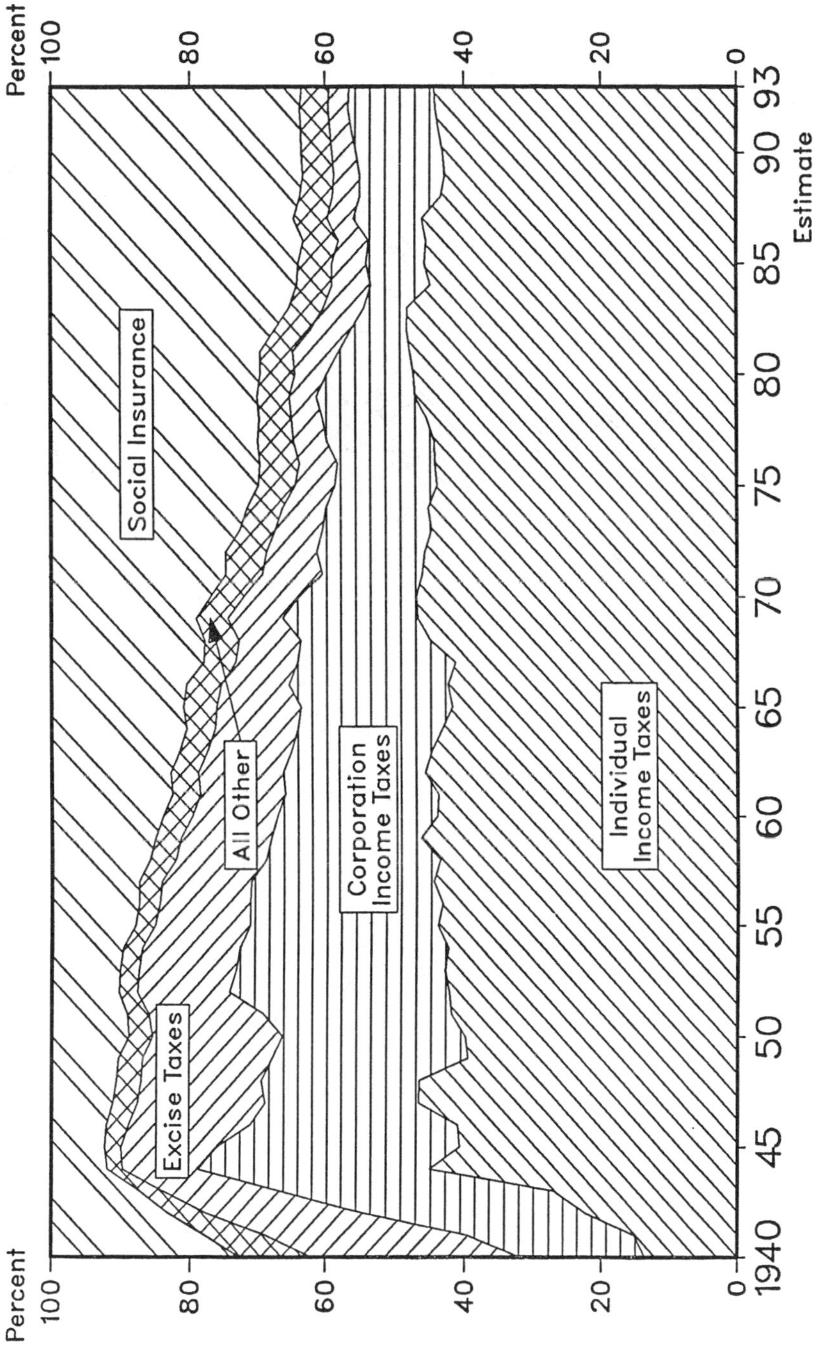

Source: *Historical Tables*, Budget of the United States Government, Fiscal 1989, Executive Office of the President, Office of Management and Budget.

Percentage Composition of Federal Government Outlays

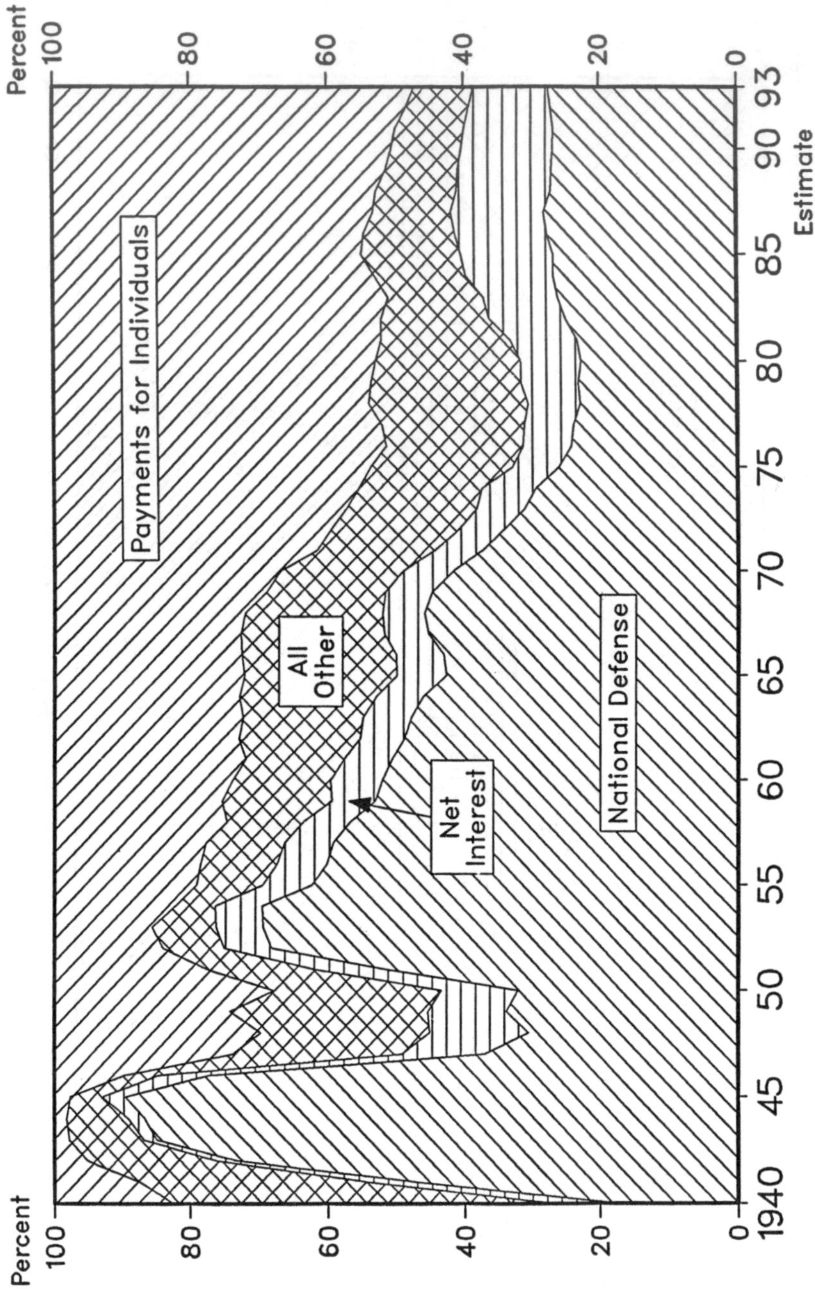

Source: *Historical Tables*, Budget of the United States Government, Fiscal 1989, Executive Office of the President, Office of Management and Budget.

TOTAL GOVERNMENT EXPENDITURES AS PERCENTAGES OF GNP: 1947-1987
(percent)

	Federal outlays			Addendum:	State and Local Government	
	On-budget	Off-Budget	Total Federal	Federal Grants-in-Aid, NIPA Basis	Expenditures From Own Sources Net of Nontax Receipts (NIPA Basis)	Total Government Expenditures
1947	15.3%	0.1%	15.4%	(0.7)%	4.6%	20.1%
1948	11.9	0.1	12.0	(0.7)	5.3	17.3
1949	14.6	0.2	14.7	(0.8)	5.8	20.6
1950	15.8	0.2	16.0	(0.9)	6.7	22.7
1951	14.0	0.4	14.4	(0.8)	6.1	20.5
1952	19.3	0.5	19.8	(0.7)	6.0	25.8
1953	20.2	0.6	20.8	(0.8)	5.9	26.8
1954	18.4	0.8	19.2	(0.8)	6.4	25.6
1955	16.7	1.0	17.7	(0.8)	6.9	24.6
1956	15.7	1.2	16.9	(0.8)	6.9	23.8
1957	16.0	1.4	17.4	(0.8)	7.1	24.5
1958	16.6	1.7	18.3	(1.0)	7.6	25.9
1959	17.3	1.9	19.1	(1.3)	7.7	26.8
1960	16.1	2.1	18.2	(1.4)	7.6	25.8
1961	16.6	2.3	18.9	(1.3)	8.1	27.0
1962	16.7	2.4	19.2	(1.4)	8.1	27.2
1963	16.4	2.5	18.9	(1.4)	8.2	27.1
1964	16.3	2.5	18.8	(1.6)	8.2	27.1
1965	15.1	2.5	17.6	(1.6)	8.3	25.9
1966	15.5	2.7	18.2	(1.7)	8.4	26.6
1967	17.2	2.6	19.8	(1.9)	8.6	28.4
1968	18.3	2.6	21.0	(2.1)	8.9	29.9
1969	17.0	2.7	19.8	(2.1)	9.2	29.0
1970	17.0	2.8	19.8	(2.3)	9.4	29.2
1971	16.8	3.1	19.9	(2.5)	10.0	29.9
1972	16.8	3.2	20.0	(2.8)	9.8	29.8
1973	15.6	3.6	19.2	(3.2)	9.3	28.5
1974	15.3	3.7	19.0	(2.9)	9.5	28.5
1975	17.9	4.0	21.8	(3.2)	10.0	31.8
1976	17.8	4.1	21.9	(3.4)	9.9	31.8
TQ	17.1	4.3	21.4	(3.4)	9.9	31.3
1977	17.0	4.2	21.2	(3.4)	9.1	30.3
1978	17.0	4.1	21.1	(3.4)	8.8	29.9
1979	16.5	4.1	20.6	(3.2)	8.5	29.1
1980	17.8%	4.3%	22.1%	(3.2)%	8.6%	30.7%
1981	18.2	4.5	22.7	(3.0)	8.3	31.0
1982	18.9	4.8	23.8	(2.7)	8.6	32.4
1983	19.9	4.4	24.3	(2.6)	8.7	33.0
1984	18.6	4.5	23.1	(2.5)	8.3	31.4
1985	19.5	4.5	24.0	(2.5)	8.5	32.5
1986	19.2	4.4	23.6	(2.6)	8.6	32.2
1987	18.4	4.4	22.8	(2.3)	9.3	32.1

* 0.05 percent or less.

TOTAL GOVERNMENT EXPENDITURES BY MAJOR CATEGORY OF EXPENDITURE AS PERCENTAGES OF GNP: 1947-1987
(in billions of dollars)

	Defense and International	Net Interest	Federal Payments for Individuals: Social Security and Medicare	Federal Payments for Individuals: Other	Other Federal	State and Local From Own Sources (Except Net Interest)	Total Government
1947	8.3%	1.9%	0.2%	3.9%	1.2%	4.6%	20.1%
1948	5.5	1.8	0.2	3.4	1.1	5.3	17.3
1949	7.3	1.7	0.2	3.6	1.9	5.8	20.6
1950	6.9	1.8	0.3	4.8	2.1	6.7	22.7
1951	8.6	1.5	0.5	2.8	1.1	6.1	20.5
1952	14.2	1.4	0.6	2.6	1.0	6.0	25.8
1953	15.0	1.4	0.7	2.3	1.4	5.9	26.8
1954	13.8	1.3	0.9	2.5	0.7	6.4	25.6
1955	11.6	1.3	1.1	2.6	1.1	6.9	24.6
1956	10.7	1.2	1.3	2.4	1.3	6.8	23.8
1957	11.0	1.2	1.5	2.4	1.3	7.1	24.5
1958	11.1	1.3	1.8	2.9	1.3	7.6	25.9
1959	10.8	1.2	2.0	2.8	2.4	7.7	26.8
1960	10.1	1.4	2.2	2.5	2.0	7.5	25.8
1961	10.2	1.3	2.4	3.0	2.1	8.1	27.0
1962	10.4	1.3	2.5	2.7	2.3	8.1	27.2
1963	10.0	1.3	2.6	2.6	2.4	8.1	27.1
1964	9.5	1.3	2.6	2.5	2.9	8.2	27.1
1965	8.3	1.2	2.5	2.4	3.1	8.3	25.9
1966	8.6	1.2	2.7	2.3	3.3	8.4	26.6
1967	9.7	1.2	3.1	2.4	3.4	8.7	28.4
1968	10.3	1.2	3.3	2.5	3.5	9.1	29.9
1969	9.4	1.3	3.6	2.6	2.9	9.4	29.0
1970	8.7	1.3	3.7	2.9	3.1	9.6	29.2
1971	7.9	1.3	4.0	3.6	3.0	10.1	29.9
1972	7.3	1.2	4.1	3.9	3.3	9.9	29.8
1973	6.3	1.2	4.5	3.7	3.4	9.5	28.5
1974	6.0	1.3	4.6	3.8	3.0	9.8	28.5
1975	6.1	1.2	5.1	5.0	4.1	10.2	31.8
1976	5.7	1.3	5.3	5.3	4.1	10.1	31.8
TQ	5.5	1.4	5.4	4.8	4.2	10.1	31.3
1977	5.4	1.4	5.4	4.8	4.1	9.3	30.3
1978	5.2	1.4	5.4	4.3	4.6	9.0	29.9
1979	5.1	1.3	5.3	4.2	4.3	8.9	29.1
1980	5.5%	1.4%	5.7%	4.7%	4.3%	9.2%	30.7%
1981	5.7	1.6	6.0	4.8	3.9	9.0	31.0
1982	6.3	2.0	6.5	4.9	3.4	9.4	32.4
1983	6.7	1.9	6.7	5.2	3.1	9.4	33.0
1984	6.6	2.3	6.4	4.4	2.6	9.1	31.4
1985	6.8	2.5	6.5	4.3	3.1	9.3	32.5
1986	6.9	2.5	6.5	4.3	2.8	9.3	32.2
1987	6.7	2.4	6.5	4.2	2.3	10.0	32.1

TOTAL GOVERNMENT EXPENDITURES BY MAJOR CATEGORY OF EXPENDITURE: 1947-1987
(in billions of dollars)

			Federal Payments for Individuals				
	Defense and International	Net Interest	Social Security and Medicare	Other	Other Federal	State and Local From Own Sources (Except Net Interest)	Total Government
1947	18.6	4.3	0.4	8.6	2.6	10.2	44.9
1948	13.7	4.4	0.5	8.5	2.7	13.1	43.0
1949	19.2	4.6	0.6	9.5	5.0	15.3	54.3
1950	18.4	4.9	0.7	12.9	5.7	17.8	60.5
1951	27.2	4.7	1.5	8.8	3.4	19.1	64.7
1952	48.8	4.7	2.0	8.9	3.4	20.6	88.4
1953	54.9	5.2	2.6	8.3	5.1	21.7	97.8
1954	50.9	4.8	3.3	9.3	2.6	23.6	94.5
1955	45.0	4.9	4.3	10.0	4.3	26.5	95.1
1956	44.9	5.2	5.4	9.8	5.4	28.6	99.4
1957	48.6	5.4	6.5	10.5	5.6	31.4	108.0
1958	50.2	5.7	8.0	12.9	5.7	34.3	116.8
1959	52.2	5.9	9.5	13.2	11.4	36.9	129.2
1960	51.1	7.1	11.4	12.8	10.0	38.2	130.5
1961	52.8	6.8	12.2	15.3	10.7	42.0	139.9
1962	58.0	7.0	14.0	14.9	13.0	45.0	151.9
1963	58.7	7.9	15.5	15.5	13.9	47.9	159.3
1964	59.7	8.2	16.2	16.0	18.4	51.8	170.4
1965	55.9	8.4	17.1	16.0	20.7	55.9	173.9
1966	63.7	9.0	20.3	16.8	24.4	62.2	196.3
1967	77.0	9.5	24.5	18.7	27.1	69.3	226.0
1968	87.2	10.1	28.4	21.3	30.0	76.9	254.1
1969	87.1	11.7	33.0	24.1	26.7	86.9	269.5
1970	86.0	12.8	36.4	28.3	30.6	94.8	288.9
1971	83.0	13.2	42.6	37.8	31.9	106.9	315.5
1972	84.0	14.2	47.7	45.2	38.4	113.9	343.2
1973	80.8	15.3	57.2	47.3	43.0	121.4	365.1
1974	85.1	17.9	65.7	54.5	42.7	138.2	403.9
1975	93.6	18.9	77.7	75.8	62.0	155.9	483.9
1976	96.1	22.8	89.6	90.5	68.9	172.4	540.3
TQ	24.7	6.1	24.0	21.3	18.9	45.4	140.6
1977	103.6	26.2	104.5	91.8	79.4	180.3	585.8
1978	112.0	29.5	116.7	94.3	100.3	196.4	649.2
1979	123.8	32.0	130.8	102.1	104.2	218.6	711.4
1980	146.7	36.9	151.0	126.5	114.2	244.9	820.2
1981	170.6	49.0	179.1	144.3	115.4	268.7	927.2
1982	197.6	61.9	203.1	153.7	106.4	294.0	1,016.5
1983	221.8	63.8	224.0	171.3	101.5	313.4	1,095.7
1984	243.3	83.3	237.0	162.8	97.6	335.3	1,159.3
1985	268.9	99.4	256.1	169.6	122.3	365.9	1,282.2
1986	287.5	104.7	270.7	178.7	117.3	392.0	1,350.9
1987	293.6	106.1	285.0	184.4	102.9	441.1	1,413.2

TOTAL GOVERNMENT SURPLUSES OR DEFICITS (-) IN ABSOLUTE AMOUNTS AND AS PERCENTAGES OF GNP: 1947-1987
(dollar amounts in billions)

	Federal Government					*As Percentages of GNP*		
	On-Budget	*Off-Budget*	*Total Federal*	*State and Local (NIPA Basis)*	*Total Government*	*Total Federal*	*State and Local*	*Total Government*
1947....	2.9	1.2	4.0	1.6	5.6	1.8%	0.7%	2.5%
1948....	10.5	1.2	11.8	0.6	12.4	4.8	0.2	5.0
1949....	-.7	1.3	0.6	-.2	0.4	0.2	-.1	0.2
1950....	-4.7	1.6	-3.1	-1.3	-4.4	-1.2	-.5	-1.7
1951....	4.3	1.8	6.1	-.5	5.6	1.9	-.2	1.8
1952....	-3.4	1.9	-1.5	-.4	-2.0	-.4	-.1	-.6
1953....	-8.3	1.8	-6.5	0.3	-6.2	-1.8	0.1	-1.7
1954....	-2.8	1.7	-1.2	-.3	-1.4	-.3	-.1	-.4
1955....	-4.1	1.1	-3.0	-1.6	-4.6	-.8	-.4	-1.2
1956....	2.5	1.5	3.9	-.8	3.2	0.9	-.2	0.8
1957....	2.6	0.8	3.4	-.9	2.5	0.8	-.2	0.6
1958....	-3.3	0.5	-2.8	-2.0	-4.8	-.6	-.4	-1.1
1959....	-12.1	-.7	-12.8	-1.8	-14.6	-2.7	-.4	-3.0
1960....	0.5	-.2	0.3	0.4	0.7	0.1	0.1	0.1
1961....	-3.8	0.4	-3.3	-.3	-3.6	-.6	-*	-.7
1962....	-5.9	-1.3	-7.1	*	-7.1	-1.3	*	-1.3
1963....	-4.0	-.8	-4.8	0.3	-4.4	-.8	0.1	-.8
1964....	-6.5	0.6	-5.9	0.6	-5.3	-.9	0.1	-.8
1965....	-1.6	0.2	-1.4	0.8	-.7	-.2	0.1	-.1
1966....	-3.1	-.6	-3.7	0.6	-3.1	-.5	0.1	-.4
1967....	-12.6	4.0	-8.6	-1.5	-10.1	-1.1	-.2	-1.3
1968....	-27.7	2.6	-25.2	0.4	-24.7	-3.0	0.1	-2.9
1969....	-.5	3.7	3.2	-.4	2.9	0.3	-*	0.3
1970....	-8.7	5.9	-2.8	3.7	0.8	-.3	0.4	0.1
1971....	-26.1	3.0	-23.0	-.5	-23.5	-2.2	-*	-2.2
1972....	-26.4	3.1	-23.4	8.2	-15.2	-2.0	0.7	-1.3
1973....	-15.4	0.5	-14.9	14.9	-*	-1.2	1.2	-*
1974....	-8.0	1.8	-6.1	10.6	4.5	-.4	0.8	0.3
1975....	-55.3	2.0	-53.2	5.8	-47.4	-3.5	0.4	-3.1
1976....	-70.5	-3.2	-73.7	6.8	-66.9	-4.3	0.4	-3.9
TQ	-13.3	-1.4	-14.7	-1.4	-16.2	-3.3	-.3	-3.6
1977....	-49.7	-3.9	-53.6	24.4	-29.3	-2.[illegible]	1.3	-1.5
1978....	-54.9	-4.3	-59.2	31.4	-27.8	-2.7	1.4	-1.3
1979....	-38.2	-2.0	-40.2	26.5	-13.7	-1.6	1.1	-.6
1980....	-72.7	-1.1	-73.8	25.7	-48.1	-2.8%	1.0%	-1.8%
1981....	-73.9	-5.0	-78.9	32.4	-46.5	-2.6	1.1	-1.6
1982....	-120.0	-7.9	-127.9	34.8	-93.1	-4.1	1.1	-3.0
1983....	-208.0	0.2	-207.8	42.6	-165.2	-6.3	1.3	-5.0
1984....	-185.6	0.3	-185.3	63.0	-122.3	-5.0	1.7	-3.3
1985....	-221.6	9.4	-212.3	60.4	-151.8	-5.4	1.5	-3.8
1986....	-237.9	16.7	-221.2	60.5	-160.7	-5.3	1.4	-3.8
1987....	-170.0	19.6	-150.4	47.2	-103.3	-3.4	1.1	-2.3

* If dollars, $50 million or less. If percent, 0.05 percent or less.

NOTES TO HISTORICAL TABLES AND CHARTS

Because of the numerous changes in the way budget data have been presented over time, there are inevitable difficulties in trying to produce comparable data to cover so many years. The general rule underlying all of these tables is to provide data in as meaningful and comparable a fashion as is possible. To the extent feasible, the data are presented on a basis consistent with current budget concepts. When a structural change is made, insofar as possible the data are adjusted for all years. For example, one major function in the 1988 Budget was entitled "general purpose fiscal assistance." The principal component of that function—indeed, the reason that function was of sufficient importance to be a separate major function—was the general revenue sharing program. General revenue sharing started in 1963 and its last significant outlays were in 1986. With the abolition of general revenue sharing, the general purpose fiscal assistance function has been converted from being a separate major function to being a subfunction in the general government function. The data base incorporates the general purpose fiscal activities as a subfunction of the general government function for all years—not just since the abolition of general revenue sharing.

NOTE ON THE FISCAL YEAR

The Federal fiscal year begins on October 1 and ends on the subsequent September 30. It is designated by the year in which it ends; for example, fiscal year 1987 began October 1, 1986 and ended on September 30, 1987. Prior to fiscal year 1977 the Federal fiscal years began on July 1 and ended on June 30. In calendar year 1976 the July–September period was a separate accounting period (known as the transition quarter or TQ) to bridge the period required to shift to the new fiscal years.

BUDGET SUMMARY

(In billions of dollars)

	1987	1988	1989	1990	1991	1992	1993
Receipts	854.1	909.2	964.7	1,044.1	1,124.4	1,189.9	1,258.1
Outlays	1,004.6	1,055.9	1,094.2	1,148.3	1,203.7	1,241.0	1,281.3
Surplus or deficit (–)	–150.4	–146.7	–129.5	–104.2	–79.3	–51.1	–23.3
Gramm-Rudman-Hollings deficit targets	–144.0	–144.0	–136.0	–100.0	–64.0	–28.0	0.0
Difference	6.4	2.7	–6.5	4.2	15.3	23.1	23.3

Note.—Totals include social security, which is off-budget.

Source: *The United States Budget in Brief,* Fiscal Year 1989, Executive Office of the President, Office of Management and Budget.

Note: The Balanced Budget and Emergency Deficit Control Act is commonly referred to as Gramm-Rudman-Hollings for its principal architects. The proposed budget has as its major objective, a balanced budget by 1991 to meet the deficit reduction targets set out in the Act.

OUTPUT, CAPACITY, AND CAPACITY UTILIZATION[1]

Seasonally adjusted

Series	1987			1988	1987			1988	1987			1988
	Q2	Q3	Q4	Q1	Q2	Q3	Q4	Q1	Q2	Q3	Q4	Q1^r
	Output (1977 = 100)				Capacity (percent of 1977 output)				Utilization rate (percent)			
1 **Total industry**	**128.2**	**130.9**	**133.0**	**134.5**	**160.4**	**161.3**	**162.2**	**163.1**	**79.9**	**81.2**	**82.1**	**82.4**
2 Mining	99.0	100.6	103.2	102.5	129.7	129.0	128.4	127.7	76.3	78.0	81.2	80.2
3 Utilities	108.3	111.6	112.5	115.1	138.3	138.8	139.4	139.8	78.3	80.5	80.6	82.3
4 **Manufacturing**	**133.2**	**135.7**	**137.9**	**139.6**	**165.6**	**166.7**	**167.7**	**168.9**	**80.5**	**81.4**	**82.3**	**82.7**
5 Primary processing	116.1	119.2	122.1	122.7	139.0	139.8	140.6	141.6	83.5	85.3	86.9	86.8
6 Advanced processing	143.5	145.8	147.5	149.6	181.6	182.9	184.1	185.6	79.0	79.7	80.1	80.7
7 **Materials**	**116.5**	**119.1**	**121.9**	**122.6**	**146.7**	**147.2**	**147.8**	**148.5**	**79.4**	**81.0**	**82.9**	**82.5**
8 Durable goods	122.9	125.5	129.6	131.3	163.1	163.9	164.7	165.7	75.4	76.7	79.1	79.4
9 Metal materials	77.0	83.6	91.1	86.6	110.0	109.4	108.8	108.8	70.0	76.5	84.0	79.0
10 Nondurable goods	124.0	128.2	129.3	130.3	143.8	144.7	145.6	146.8	86.2	88.6	89.3	88.0
11 Textile, paper, and chemical	125.1	130.5	132.3	133.1	143.4	144.4	145.4	146.7	87.2	90.4	91.5	89.6
12 Paper	137.7	144.5	......	......	143.9	145.1	......	......	95.7	99.6	99.2	98.8
13 Chemical	125.3	130.7	......	......	149.8	150.9	......	......	83.6	86.3	89.1	86.8
14 Energy materials	98.7	100.0	101.8	100.9	120.2	120.1	119.9	119.7	82.1	83.3	85.2	84.4

Series	Previous cycle[2]		Latest cycle[3]		1987	1987					1988			
	High	Low	High	Low	Apr.	Aug.	Sept.	Oct.	Nov.	Dec.	Jan.^r	Feb.^r	Mar.^r	Apr.
	Capacity utilization rate (percent)													
15 **Total industry**	**88.6**	**72.1**	**86.9**	**69.5**	**79.6**	**81.4**	**81.1**	**81.9**	**82.1**	**82.4**	**82.5**	**82.4**	**82.4**	**82.7**
16 Mining	92.8	87.8	95.2	76.9	75.9	78.2	79.1	80.6	81.5	81.5	80.7	79.6	80.3	81.5
17 Utilities	95.6	82.9	88.5	78.0	76.8	81.3	80.0	80.5	81.2	80.4	82.4	82.8	81.8	81.1
18 **Manufacturing**	**87.7**	**69.9**	**86.5**	**68.0**	**80.2**	**81.5**	**81.3**	**82.0**	**82.2**	**82.5**	**82.7**	**82.6**	**82.6**	**83.0**
19 Primary processing	91.9	68.3	89.1	65.1	83.5	85.3	85.1	86.2	87.0	87.8	87.1	86.6	86.6	87.1
20 Advanced processing	86.0	71.1	85.1	69.5	78.7	79.9	79.5	80.1	80.0	80.1	80.7	80.8	80.7	81.1
21 **Materials**	**92.0**	**70.5**	**89.1**	**68.5**	**79.1**	**81.1**	**81.2**	**82.1**	**82.9**	**83.7**	**83.0**	**82.2**	**82.4**	**82.9**
22 Durable goods	91.8	64.4	89.8	60.9	75.0	76.6	77.0	78.3	79.0	80.2	79.7	79.2	79.2	79.9
23 Metal materials	99.2	67.1	93.6	45.7	68.8	77.5	78.3	82.4	83.3	87.6	80.1	78.5	78.3	79.1
24 Nondurable goods	91.1	66.7	88.1	70.7	86.5	88.6	88.7	88.2	89.0	90.5	88.8	87.5	87.8	88.1
25 Textile, paper, and chemical	92.8	64.8	89.4	68.8	87.5	90.5	90.7	90.4	91.0	92.7	90.8	88.7	89.3	89.6
26 Paper	98.4	70.6	97.3	79.9	95.1	99.9	98.5	97.4	98.7	101.6	100.6	97.8	98.1	......
27 Chemical	92.5	64.4	87.9	63.5	83.9	86.4	87.4	88.0	88.6	90.8	87.8	86.1	86.7	......
28 Energy materials	94.6	86.9	94.0	82.3	81.3	84.0	83.5	84.9	85.7	85.1	84.7	84.1	84.4	**84.8**

1. These data also appear in the Board's G.3 (402) release. For address, see inside front cover.

2. Monthly high 1973; monthly low 1975.

3. Monthly highs 1978 through 1980; monthly lows 1982.

Source: *Federal Reserve Bulletin,* Board of Governors of the Federal Reserve System.

INDUSTRIAL PRODUCTION Indexes and Gross Value[1]

Monthly data are seasonally adjusted

Groups	1977 proportion	1987 avg.	1987 Apr.	May	June	July	Aug.	Sept.	Oct.	Nov.	Dec.	1988 Jan.[r]	Feb.	Mar.[p]	Apr.[e]
			Index (1977 = 100)												
MAJOR MARKET															
1 **Total index**	**100.00**	**129.8**	**127.4**	**128.4**	**129.1**	**130.6**	**131.2**	**131.0**	**132.5**	**133.2**	**133.9**	**134.4**	**134.4**	**134.7**	**135.6**
2 Products	57.72	138.3	137.2	137.2	137.8	139.5	139.9	139.4	140.9	141.0	141.3	142.7	143.5	143.6	144.3
3 Final products	44.77	136.8	134.5	135.8	136.2	137.9	138.4	137.8	139.3	139.2	139.8	141.1	141.7	141.9	142.6
4 Consumer goods	25.52	127.7	126.6	128.2	127.2	128.9	129.4	127.7	129.0	129.4	129.8	131.2	131.5	131.2	131.9
5 Equipment	19.25	148.8	144.9	145.8	148.1	149.7	150.2	151.2	153.0	152.2	153.1	154.3	155.3	156.1	156.9
6 Intermediate products	12.94	143.4	139.9	142.1	143.3	145.0	145.3	144.9	146.1	147.3	146.5	148.1	149.5	149.3	150.1
7 Materials	42.28	118.2	116.2	116.3	117.2	118.5	119.4	119.7	121.2	122.5	123.7	123.0	122.1	122.5	123.6
Consumer goods															
8 Durable consumer goods	6.89	120.2	118.1	120.2	117.4	120.4	121.2	118.6	124.3	123.9	120.3	121.7	120.8	120.8	122.3
9 Automotive products	2.98	118.5	115.7	118.0	114.9	117.5	118.0	114.2	124.3	121.3	115.4	118.7	117.6	121.0	122.3
10 Autos and trucks	1.79	115.1	111.5	113.1	107.9	112.3	112.4	107.2	122.2	118.7	110.2	112.8	111.8	116.4	118.0
11 Autos, consumer	1.16	90.7	91.8	91.0	87.4	86.4	76.8	79.1	94.7	91.9	83.7	77.5	79.5	86.3	91.0
12 Trucks, consumer	.63	160.5	148.1	154.2	146.0	160.4	178.4	159.4	173.2	168.5	159.5	178.3	171.6	172.2	....
13 Auto parts and allied goods	1.19	123.5	121.9	125.3	125.4	125.3	126.6	124.8	127.5	125.2	123.3	127.7	126.4	127.8	128.7
14 Home goods	3.91	121.6	119.9	121.8	119.3	122.5	123.6	121.9	124.3	125.8	123.9	124.0	123.2	120.6	122.4
15 Appliances, A/C and TV	1.24	141.5	137.7	142.2	133.4	141.7	147.1	141.8	145.7	150.1	142.7	142.2	140.6	133.1	137.0
16 Appliances and TV	1.19	142.1	139.2	142.3	133.4	142.6	145.5	140.6	146.1	150.5	142.6	140.9	141.4	133.0	....
17 Carpeting and furniture	.96	130.7	133.5	133.3	132.3	134.1	132.0	131.6	132.9	133.5	133.9	134.2	132.3	133.1	....
18 Miscellaneous home goods	1.71	102.0	99.4	100.7	101.8	102.2	102.0	102.2	104.1	103.9	104.8	105.2	105.5	104.6	....
19 Nondurable consumer goods	18.63	130.5	129.8	131.1	130.9	132.1	132.5	131.0	130.8	131.5	133.3	134.7	135.4	135.1	135.4
20 Consumer staples	15.29	137.3	136.4	137.7	137.6	138.9	139.2	137.8	137.4	138.3	140.7	142.3	143.0	142.5	142.8
21 Consumer foods and tobacco	7.80	136.2	134.4	135.6	136.0	137.2	137.4	137.0	137.5	137.3	139.2	140.3	140.7	139.7	....
22 Nonfood staples	7.49	138.5	138.5	139.9	139.2	140.6	141.2	138.6	137.2	139.4	142.2	144.3	145.4	145.4	145.7
23 Consumer chemical products	2.75	162.9	164.7	165.9	164.4	165.7	167.4	163.6	160.0	163.5	167.7	170.7	171.7	171.7	....
24 Consumer paper products	1.88	151.8	148.9	152.9	153.1	153.8	153.9	153.2	151.8	152.8	157.0	157.1	158.7	158.5	....
25 Consumer energy	2.86	106.3	106.5	106.4	105.9	108.0	107.7	105.0	105.8	107.4	108.0	110.6	111.6	111.5	....
26 Consumer fuel	1.44	93.1	94.5	92.1	91.9	92.7	91.4	91.6	92.4	93.2	95.4	95.4	97.0	98.5	....
27 Residential utilities	1.42	119.8	118.7	121.0	120.2	123.6	124.3	118.7	119.4	121.8	120.7	126.0	126.4	....	....
Equipment															
28 Business and defense equipment	18.01	153.6	150.0	150.8	153.2	154.4	154.5	155.2	157.2	156.6	157.8	159.2	160.3	160.9	161.9
29 Business equipment	14.34	144.5	140.8	141.7	144.2	145.6	145.6	146.3	148.7	148.3	149.8	151.2	152.3	153.2	154.5
30 Construction, mining, and farm	2.08	62.2	58.6	61.2	63.0	65.0	66.4	66.1	66.5	66.3	67.4	67.1	67.6	68.4	69.0
31 Manufacturing	3.27	117.9	111.1	111.5	117.2	120.4	120.9	122.0	120.5	120.6	122.2	125.4	124.9	125.8	127.6
32 Power	1.27	82.6	82.4	84.0	84.0	81.8	82.8	81.1	83.0	83.1	84.2	86.2	88.3	88.3	88.6
33 Commercial	5.22	226.5	220.9	222.0	226.7	227.9	227.7	229.1	232.4	232.1	235.5	238.0	240.4	240.8	242.1
34 Transit	2.49	108.4	110.4	110.1	105.4	106.1	104.7	105.1	112.5	111.2	109.1	106.5	107.6	109.9	111.7
35 Defense and space equipment	3.67	188.9	186.1	186.5	188.6	188.7	189.1	189.8	190.3	188.7	188.9	190.6	191.5	190.9	190.6
Intermediate products															
36 Construction supplies	5.95	131.5	127.3	128.3	131.5	133.1	132.5	132.3	133.3	134.2	133.8	136.8	137.7	136.6	137.2
37 Business supplies	6.99	153.5	150.5	153.8	153.4	155.2	156.3	155.6	157.1	158.4	157.4	157.8	159.6	160.1	....
38 General business supplies	5.67	158.6	155.5	158.2	158.5	160.5	161.0	160.9	162.3	164.3	163.3	163.1	165.2	165.7	....
39 Commercial energy products	1.31	131.1	129.0	135.0	131.1	132.3	135.8	132.7	134.6	132.9	131.8	135.0	135.5	135.7	....
Materials															
40 Durable goods materials	20.50	125.0	122.2	121.6	124.0	125.2	125.5	126.4	128.7	130.2	132.0	131.8	131.2	131.5	132.9
41 Durable consumer parts	4.92	100.9	96.2	95.2	99.2	98.5	99.6	99.0	102.3	103.1	104.6	104.7	104.2	104.0	105.7
42 Equipment parts	5.94	159.0	157.1	156.0	158.3	159.3	159.5	161.1	162.2	163.2	165.3	167.4	167.4	168.1	169.6
43 Durable materials n.e.c.	9.64	116.4	114.1	113.9	115.5	117.7	117.9	118.9	121.6	123.6	125.5	123.7	122.6	122.9	124.2
44 Basic metal materials	4.64	86.7	81.8	81.9	83.6	86.6	90.4	91.3	95.3	96.5	100.0	92.9	90.7	90.5	91.5
45 Nondurable goods materials	10.09	125.8	125.4	125.3	124.1	127.6	128.3	128.6	128.2	129.6	132.5	129.9	128.4	129.4	130.3
46 Textile, paper, and chemical materials	7.53	127.6	126.9	126.5	125.1	129.6	130.6	131.2	131.0	132.3	135.6	132.7	130.2	131.6	132.6
47 Textile materials	1.52	111.7	125.0	....	111.9	117.8	116.7	116.0	113.0	112.7	113.6	112.6	110.2	111.8	....
48 Pulp and paper materials	1.55	141.0	137.4	137.4	139.0	145.4	145.0	143.3	142.0	144.4	149.0	148.0	144.4	145.3	....
49 Chemical materials	4.46	128.4	125.0	125.0	124.9	128.1	130.4	132.2	133.4	134.7	138.4	134.2	132.1	133.6	....
50 Miscellaneous nondurable materials	2.57	120.4	121.1	122.0	120.9	122.0	121.4	120.9	119.7	121.7	123.3	121.8	123.2	....	....
51 Energy materials	11.69	99.8	97.5	99.3	99.4	99.0	100.9	100.2	101.8	102.8	101.7	101.4	100.7	100.9	101.4
52 Primary energy	7.57	105.0	102.3	103.6	104.0	102.5	104.6	104.6	106.8	108.4	107.7	107.3	105.0	104.8	....
53 Converted fuel materials	4.12	90.3	88.7	91.4	91.0	92.5	94.1	92.2	92.7	92.6	90.7	90.6	92.8	93.8	....

Continued

INDUSTRIAL PRODUCTION Indexes and Gross Value[1] (*concluded*)

Groups	SIC code	1977 proportion	1987 avg.	1987									1988			
				Apr.	May	June	July	Aug.	Sept.	Oct.	Nov.	Dec.	Jan.[r]	Feb.	Mar.[p]	Apr.[e]
				Index (1977 = 100)												
MAJOR INDUSTRY																
1 Mining and utilities	.....	15.79	104.3	101.4	103.1	103.0	103.7	105.4	105.4	106.8	107.9	107.3	107.8	107.0	106.9	107.4
2 Mining	.....	9.83	100.7	98.6	99.2	99.2	99.2	100.9	101.9	103.6	104.6	104.6	103.3	101.7	102.4	103.8
3 Utilities	.....	5.96	110.3	106.0	109.6	109.4	111.2	112.9	111.2	112.1	113.2	111.7	115.2	115.7	114.4	113.5
4 Manufacturing	.....	84.21	134.6	132.4	133.2	134.0	135.6	135.9	135.7	137.3	137.9	138.9	139.4	139.5	140.0	140.9
5 Nondurable	.....	35.11	136.7	134.6	135.7	136.9	138.5	138.8	138.6	138.1	139.6	141.3	141.4	141.2	141.5	142.0
6 Durable	.....	49.10	133.1	130.9	131.4	132.0	133.5	133.8	133.7	136.8	136.7	137.3	137.9	138.3	138.9	140.1
Mining																
7 Metal	10	.50	77.5	65.7	71.7	70.7	71.4	79.3	86.5	85.6	90.4	96.5	91.5	84.2	......	......
8 Coal	11.12	1.60	131.8	121.9	127.2	128.8	127.9	130.5	133.3	140.3	142.9	140.6	140.2	133.7	129.1	131.5
9 Oil and gas extraction	13	7.07	92.7	93.1	92.1	91.8	91.8	93.0	93.3	94.1	94.2	94.1	93.1	92.6	94.5	95.6
10 Stone and earth minerals	14	.66	128.2	125.4	127.6	128.5	130.7	130.3	130.0	131.0	134.1	135.6	132.1	134.5	135.1	......
Nondurable manufactures																
11 Foods	20	7.96	137.7	136.0	137.4	137.7	138.5	138.8	139.5	138.0	138.9	140.1	141.2	142.0	141.4	......
12 Tobacco products	21	.62	103.4	99.6	106.6	107.0	106.8	110.4	101.7	103.7	106.5	110.5	105.8	105.3	......	......
13 Textile mill products	22	2.29	115.8	116.6	115.7	117.2	118.3	119.8	118.2	116.8	117.3	118.2	116.2	115.3	116.0	......
14 Apparel products	23	2.79	107.4	105.3	106.4	107.7	109.7	108.4	107.6	108.0	109.4	107.8	108.7	108.0	......	......
15 Paper and products	26	3.15	144.4	140.5	141.3	142.6	148.8	148.9	147.4	146.0	148.3	150.6	149.9	148.0	149.6	......
16 Printing and publishing	27	4.54	172.0	169.2	171.4	174.1	174.0	174.7	174.9	175.2	175.7	176.9	177.5	179.6	179.5	179.7
17 Chemicals and products	28	8.05	140.1	137.3	138.1	139.3	140.8	142.3	142.4	141.5	144.4	147.9	147.9	145.8	146.2	......
18 Petroleum products	29	2.40	93.5	94.0	92.6	92.3	94.1	92.9	93.5	94.6	93.3	96.1	96.3	95.9	97.6	98.7
19 Rubber and plastic products	30	2.80	163.6	160.5	162.2	165.4	167.2	164.8	165.2	166.7	169.9	170.6	170.5	172.3	172.5	......
20 Leather and products	31	.53	60.0	60.2	61.4	60.8	59.2	61.3	60.7	59.6	60.7	57.5	58.3	59.7	59.9	......
Durable manufactures																
21 Lumber and products	24	2.30	130.3	127.8	130.3	131.1	132.8	131.1	126.9	129.8	134.0	133.6	136.3	139.4	137.1	......
22 Furniture and fixtures	25	1.27	152.8	148.2	150.5	153.9	156.2	155.2	155.9	156.0	158.5	159.4	158.0	158.5	159.2	......
23 Clay, glass, stone products	32	2.72	119.1	120.6	117.2	117.9	118.8	116.5	118.6	118.9	120.5	120.1	120.4	121.6	121.9	......
24 Primary metals	33	5.33	81.5	76.1	77.0	78.8	81.4	85.1	84.5	90.6	90.2	90.6	86.5	85.3	84.9	86.0
25 Iron and steel	331.2	3.49	70.8	65.0	65.7	68.3	70.9	76.0	74.6	82.0	79.7	81.9	77.8	75.6	74.3	......
26 Fabricated metal products	34	6.46	111.0	109.9	108.5	111.1	111.1	110.1	111.1	113.5	113.6	115.8	117.1	117.8	118.8	119.5
27 Nonelectrical machinery	35	9.54	152.7	150.4	149.7	151.8	155.3	154.3	156.6	158.0	157.2	161.0	162.9	163.5	164.6	166.2
28 Electrical machinery	36	7.15	172.3	168.4	171.1	170.5	172.5	174.3	173.4	175.5	175.6	175.9	177.4	177.6	177.0	179.3
29 Transportation equipment	37	9.13	129.2	127.8	129.4	126.5	127.6	128.1	125.5	132.0	130.4	128.1	128.6	128.4	130.0	131.3
30 Motor vehicles and parts	371	5.25	111.8	109.8	112.0	107.4	109.4	109.1	105.6	116.0	114.0	110.2	109.7	109.3	113.1	115.4
31 Aerospace and miscellaneous transportation equipment	372–6.9	3.87	152.8	152.3	153.1	152.4	152.3	153.9	152.5	153.7	152.7	152.4	154.2	154.5	153.0	153.0
32 Instruments	38	2.66	143.9	142.8	142.1	144.5	143.8	146.3	145.6	146.7	147.8	145.5	148.2	149.2	149.9	150.8
33 Miscellaneous manufactures	39	1.46	102.6	101.4	101.9	101.2	100.5	102.2	102.1	104.6	104.5	105.6	105.0	106.1	105.5	......
Utilities																
34 Electric	.....	4.17	126.6	122.3	128.8	128.8	131.0	132.0	127.5	126.8	127.5	125.6	130.3	130.7	129.2	......
		Gross value (billions of 1982 dollars, annual rates)														
MAJOR MARKET																
35 Products, total	.....	**517.5**	**1,735.8**	**1,710.0**	**1,723.0**	**1,720.4**	**1,732.5**	**1,741.7**	**1,735.9**	**1,774.1**	**1,772.4**	**1,778.8**	**1,790.6**	**1,798.7**	**1,808.9**	**1,818.2**
36 Final	.....	405.7	1,333.8	1,316.5	1,324.7	1,320.1	1,326.6	1,334.9	1,330.3	1,360.9	1,359.9	1,359.4	1,375.5	1,382.0	1,388.6	1,396.9
37 Consumer goods	.....	272.7	866.0	857.1	862.8	855.1	863.2	866.4	856.9	876.6	879.8	881.2	893.6	894.7	896.4	901.8
38 Equipment	.....	133.0	467.8	459.4	461.9	465.0	463.5	468.5	473.4	484.4	480.1	478.2	481.9	487.3	492.3	495.1
39 Intermediate	.....	111.9	402.0	393.6	398.4	400.3	405.9	406.8	405.6	413.2	412.5	419.4	415.1	416.7	420.3	421.3

1. These data also appear in the Board's G.12.3 (414) release. For address, see inside front cover.

A major revision of the industrial production index and the capacity utilization rates was released in July 1985. See "A Revision of the Index of Industrial Production" and accompanying tables that contain revised indexes (1977=100) through December 1984 in the FEDERAL RESERVE BULLETIN, vol. 71 (July 1985), pp. 487–501. The revised indexes for January through June 1985 were shown in the September BULLETIN.

Source: *Federal Reserve Bulletin*, Board of Governors of the Federal Reserve System.

U.S. BUDGET RECEIPTS AND OUTLAYS (millions of dollars)[1]

Source or type	Fiscal year 1986	Fiscal year 1987	Calendar year						
			1986		1987		1988		
			H1	H2	H1	H2	Feb.	Mar.	Apr.
RECEIPTS									
1 **All sources**	**769,091**	**854,143**	**394,345**	**387,524**	**447,282**	**421,712**	**60,355**	**65,730r**	**109,323**
2 Individual income taxes, net	348,959	392,557	169,444	183,156	205,157	192,575	25,651	20,637r	53,334
3 Withheld	314,803	322,463	153,919	164,071	156,760	170,203	28,046	33,296	24,913
4 Presidential Election Campaign Fund	36	33	31	4	30	4	4	7	7
5 Nonwithheld	105,994	142,957	78,981	27,733	112,421	31,223	1,179	4,315	50,477
6 Refunds	71,873	72,896	63,488	8,652	64,052	8,853	3,577	16,982r	22,062
Corporation income taxes									
7 Gross receipts	80,442	102,859	41,946	42,108	52,396	52,821	2,652	14,909	14,030
8 Refunds	17,298	18,933	9,557	8,230	10,881	7,119	1,677	2,203	2,004
9 Social insurance taxes and contributions, net	283,901	303,318	156,714	134,006	163,519	143,755	28,500	25,676	37,357
10 Employment taxes and contributions[2]	255,062	273,185	139,706	122,246	146,696	130,388	25,739	25,141	34,464
11 Self-employment taxes and contributions[3]	11,840	13,987	10,581	1,338	12,020	1,889	1,368	880	8,833
12 Unemployment insurance	24,098	25,418	14,674	9,328	14,514	10,977	2,399	179	2,477
13 Other net receipts[4]	4,742	4,715	2,333	2,429	2,310	2,390	362	356	416
14 Excise taxes	32,919	32,510	15,944	15,947	15,845	17,680	2,204	2,885	2,767
15 Customs deposits	13,327	15,032	6,369	7,282	7,129	7,993	1,296	1,444	1,204
16 Estate and gift taxes	6,958	7,493	3,487	3,649	3,818	3,610	566	622	749
17 Miscellaneous receipts[5]	19,884	19,307	10,002	9,605	10,299	10,399	1,164	1,760	1,886
OUTLAYS									
18 **All types**	**990,231**	**1,004,586**	**486,058**	**505,980**	**502,223**	**532,107**	**84,257**	**94,877r**	**95,433**
19 National defense	273,375	281,999	135,367	138,544	142,886	146,995	23,670	26,484	26,747
20 International affairs	14,152	11,649	5,384	8,938r	4,374	4,487	516	1,490	1,561
21 General science, space, and technology	8,976	9,216	4,191r	4,594	4,324	5,469	749	956	949
22 Energy	4,735	4,115	2,484	2,446r	2,335	1,468	−1,635	538	382
23 Natural resources and environment	13,639	13,363	6,245	7,141	6,175	7,590	969	1,082	1,037
24 Agriculture	31,449	27,356	14,482	15,660r	11,824	14,640	1,014	1,160	2,099
25 Commerce and housing credit	4,890	6,182	860	3,764r	4,893	3,852	−866	2,409	1,203
26 Transportation	28,117	26,228	12,658	14,745	12,113	14,096	1,995	1,838	2,053
27 Community and regional development	7,233	5,051	3,169	3,651r	3,108	2,075	459	535	555
28 Education, training, employment, and social services	30,585	29,724	14,712	16,209r	14,182	15,592	3,041	2,545	2,253
29 Health	35,935	39,968	17,872	18,795	20,318	20,750	3,650	3,765	3,791
30 Social security and medicare	268,921	282,473	135,214	138,299	142,864	158,469	24,585	26,145	24,920
31 Income security	119,796	123,250	60,786	59,979r	62,248	61,201	11,264	12,738r	12,916
32 Veterans benefits and services	26,356	26,782	12,193	14,190r	12,264	14,956	2,170	2,555	3,748
33 Administration of justice	6,603	7,548	3,352	3,413r	3,626	4,291	704	868	825
34 General government	6,104	5,948	3,566	1,860r	3,344	3,560	806	383	697
35 General-purpose fiscal assistance	6,431	1,621	2,179	2,886	337	1,175	45	0	0
36 Net interest[6]	136,008	138,570	68,054	66,226r	70,110	71,933	13,988	12,187	12,592
37 Undistributed offsetting receipts[7]	−33,007	−36,455	−17,183	−16,475r	−19,102	−17,684r	−2,868	−2,802	−2,895

1. Functional details do not add to total outlays for calendar year data because revisions to monthly totals have not been distributed among functions. Fiscal year total for outlays does not correspond to calendar year data because revisions from the *Budget* have not been fully distributed across months.
2. Old-age, disability, and hospital insurance, and railroad retirement accounts.
3. Old-age, disability, and hospital insurance.
4. Federal employee retirement contributions and civil service retirement and disability fund.
5. Deposits of earnings by Federal Reserve Banks and other miscellaneous receipts.
6. Net interest function includes interest received by trust funds.
7. Consists of rents and royalties on the outer continental shelf and U.S. government contributions for employee retirement.

SOURCES. U.S. Department of the Treasury, *Monthly Treasury Statement of Receipts and Outlays of the U.S. Government*, and the U.S. Office of Management and Budget, *Budget of the U.S. Government, Fiscal Year 1988*.

Source: *Federal Reserve Bulletin*, Board of Governors of the Federal Reserve System.

Largest Companies

The 100 Largest U.S. Industrial Corporations (ranked by sales)

Rank '87	Rank '86	Company	Sales ($000)	Sales % Change from '86	Profits ($000)	Profits Rank	Profits % Change from '86	Assets ($000)	Assets Rank	Stockholders' Equity ($000)	Stockholders' Equity Rank
1	1	General Motors (Detroit)	101,781,900	(1.0)	3,550,900	4	20.6	87,421,900	1	33,225,100	3
2	2	Exxon (New York)	76,416,000	9.3	4,840,000	2	(9.7)	74,042,000	2	33,626,000	2
3	3	Ford Motor (Dearborn, Mich.)	71,643,400	14.2	4,625,200	3	40.8	44,955,700	4	18,492,700	4
4	4	International Business Machines (Armonk, N.Y.)	54,217,000	5.8	5,258,000	1	9.8	63,688,000	3	38,263,000	1
5	5	Mobil (New York)	51,223,000*	14.2	1,258,000	11	(10.6)	41,140,000	5	16,783,000	5
6	6	General Electric (Fairfield, Conn.)	39,315,000	11.7	2,915,000	5	17.0	38,920,000	6	16,480,000	6
7	8	Texaco (White Plains, N.Y.)	34,372,000*	8.7	(4,407,000)	480	—	33,962,000	9	9,171,000	12
8	7	American Tel. & Tel (New York)	33,598,000	(1.4)	2,044,000	6	1,370.5	38,426,000	7	14,455,000	9
9	9	E. I. du Pont de Nemours (Wilmington, Del.)	30,468,000	(12.2)	1,786,000	8	16.1	28,209,000	10	14,244,000	10
10	11	Chrysler (Highland Park, Mich.)[1]	26,257,700	16.6	1,289,700	10	(8.1)	19,944,600	15	6,502,900	15
11	10	Chevron (San Francisco)	26,015,000*	6.8	1,007,000	19	40.8	34,465,000	8	15,780,000	7
12	12	Philip Morris (New York)	22,279,000*	7.7	1,842,000	7	24.6	19,145,000	17	6,823,000	14
13	15	Shell Oil (Houston)[2]	20,852,000*	23.9	1,230,000	13	39.3	26,937,000	11	14,842,000	8
14	13	Amoco (Chicago)	20,174,000*	10.4	1,360,000	9	82.1	24,827,000	12	12,107,000	11
15	17	United Technologies (Hartford)	17,170,200	9.6	591,700	37	713.6	11,928,600	28	4,292,600	31
16	19	Occidental Petroleum (Los Angeles)	17,096,000	11.4	240,000**	95	32.5	16,739,000	20	5,164,000	25
17	18	Procter & Gamble (Cincinnati)[3]	17,000,000	10.1	327,000	69	(53.9)	13,715,000	23	5,990,000	19
18	20	Atlantic Richfield (Los Angeles)	16,281,400	11.6	1,224,300	14	99.0	22,669,900	14	5,877,500	20
19	14	RJR Nabisco (Atlanta)	15,868,000	(6.6)	1,209,000	15	13.6	16,861,000	19	6,038,000	17
20	16	Boeing (Seattle)	15,355,000	(6.0)	480,000	46	(27.8)	12,566,000	26	4,987,000	29
21	21	Tenneco (Houston)	15,075,000	3.6	(218,000)	474	—	18,503,000	18	3,773,000	36
22	35	BP America (Cleveland)[4]	14,611,000*	58.5	(564,000	41	—	23,287,000	13	5,574,000	22
23	22	USX (Pittsburgh)	13,898,000*	(0.7)	219,000	106	—	19,557,000	16	5,529,000	23
24	27	Dow Chemical (Midland, Mich.)	13,377,000	20.4	1,240,000	12	69.4	14,356,000	22	5,769,000	21
25	26	Eastman Kodak (Rochester, N.Y.)	13,305,000	15.2	1,178,000	16	215.0	14,451,000	21	6,013,000	18
26	23	McDonnell Douglas (St. Louis)	13,146,100	3.8	313,000	73	12.8	8,535,600	38	2,969,900	50
27	24	Rockwell International (Pittsburgh)[5]	12,123,400	(1.4)	635,100	33	3.9	8,739,200	36	3,314,200	43
28	25	Allied-Signal (Morristown, N.J.)	11,597,000	(1.7)	656,000	30	8.4	10,226,000	30	3,129,000	46
29	34	Pepsico (Purchase, N.Y.)	11,500,200	23.8	594,800	36	30.0	9,022,700	35	2,508,600	57
30	30	Lockheed (Calabasas, Calif.)	11,370,000	10.7	421,000	54	3.2	6,301,000	56	2,087,000	67
31	37	Kraft (Glenview, Ill.)	11,010,500¶	25.9	489,400	45	18.5	5,486,700	61	1,898,400	71
32	31	Phillips Petroleum (Bartlesville, Okla.)[9]	10,721,000	9.6	35,000	324	(84.6)	12,111,000	27	1,617,000	81
33	28	Westinghouse Electric (Pittsburgh)	10,679,000	(0.5)	738,900	27	10.2	9,953,100	33	3,576,600	40
34	32	Xerox (Stamford, Conn.)[6]	10,320,000	10.1	578,000	39	24.3	11,598,000	29	5,105,000	26
35	29	Goodyear Tire & Rubber (Akron, Ohio)	10,123,200	(2.0)	770,900	26	521.2	8,395,900	41	1,834,400	75
36	46	Unisys (Blue Bell, Pa.)	9,712,900	30.7	578,000	38	—	9,958,000	32	4,544,700	30
37	39	Minnesota Mining & Manufacturing (St. Paul)	9,429,000	9.6	918,000	20	17.8	8,031,000	44	5,060,000	27
38	44	Digital Equipment (Maynard, Mass.)[3]	9,389,400	23.7	1,137,400	17	84.2	8,407,400	40	6,293,500	16
39	36	General Dynamics (St. Louis)	9,344,000	1.4	437,300	52	—	5,031,800	68	1,601,000	83
40	40	Sara Lee (Chicago)[3]	9,154,600	15.3	267,100	80	19.5	4,191,700	88	1,416,00	101

The definitions and concepts underlying the figures in this directory are explained on page 205.

Market Value		Profits as Percent of: Sales		Assets		Stockholders' Equity		Earnings per Share				Total Return to Investors: 1987		1977–87 Annual Average		Industry Table Number
									% Change from	Annual Growth Rate 1977–87						
($000)	Rank	%	Rank	%	Rank	%	Rank	'87/$	'86	%	Rank	%	Rank	%	Rank	
22,314,900	5	3.5	307	4.1	336	10.7	314	10.06	22.5	(1.4)	310	(0.6)	276	6.9	345	17
58,074,500	2	6.3	165	6.5	217	14.4	213	3.43	(7.5)	9.8	160	13.7	163	20.9	133	18
21,665,600	7	6.5	161	10.3	75	25.0	50	9.05	46.9	11.1	138	39.1	67	20.1	149	17
68,063,900	1	9.7	66	8.3	144	13.7	227	8.72	11.7	6.7	207	(0.7)	277	10.3	310	6
17,842,700	11	2.5	369	3.1	360	7.5	366	3.06	(11.3)	2.6	273	2.5	256	16.8	211	18
39,770,300	3	7.4	127	7.5	181	17.7	148	3.20	17.2	10.3	152	5.3	233	10.4	173	7
10,869,800	27	—		—		—		(10.15)	—	—		6.1	229	11.1	299	18
30,733,900	4	6.1	172	5.3	278	14.1§	221	1.88	3,660.0	(12.3)	344	12.9	168	5.0	361	7
20,626,300	9	5.9	181	6.3	229	12.5	261	7.39	16.4	7.2	201	7.4	217	14.3	245	5
5,353,900	56	4.9	224	6.5	219	19.8	102	5.90	(6.5)	17.2	47	(7.7)	315	17.1	204	17
15,779,800	14	3.9	284	2.9	365	6.4	376	2.94	40.7	(0.1)	300	(8.3)	320	13.8	255	18
21,998,400	6	8.3	100	9.6	100	27.0	42	7.75	25.0	18.7	37	22.8	120	23.4	84	25
N.A.		5.9	180	4.6	320	8.3	357	N.A.	—	—		—		—		18
19,322,600	10	6.7	147	5.5	270	11.2	298	5.31	82.5	4.4	243	10.4	187	16.9	208	18
5,314,300	57	3.4	317	5.0	303	13.8	226	4.52	1,574.1	4.8	239	(24.0)	386	11.2	298	1
5,769,300	49	1.4	401	1.4	403	4.6§	395	1.06**	47.2	(9.6)	336	(4.7)	299	9.1	327	8
13,691,400	21	1.9	382	2.4	381	5.5	384	1.87	(55.5)	(3.9)	326	15.2	156	11.7	290	23
13,815,200	20	7.5	122	5.4	275	20.8	84	6.68	97.6	8.8	174	21.0	128	16.5	218	18
12,615,200	22	7.6	117	7.2	192	20.0§	97	4.70	22.7	10.4	150	(5.6)	303	21.0	129	25
7,423,600	33	3.1	337	3.8	345	9.6	340	3.10	(27.6)	9.5	164	(25.4)	390	20.5	143	1
6,598,800	38	—		—		—		(1.81)	—	—		10.8	181	10.2	315	18
N.A.		3.9	285	2.4	380	10.1	331	N.A.	—	—		—		—		18
8,524,300	31	1.6	393	1.1	412	4.0§	399	0.54	—	(10.6)	338	44.0	54	5.3	359	18
16,026,300	13	9.3	77	8.6	130	21.5	76	6.47	69.4	8.0	185	58.0	28	18.8	168	5
13,936,300	19	8.9	86	8.2	150	19.6	106	3.62	227.1	7.4	198	10.4	186	13.2	266	22
2,414,900	123	2.4	371	3.7	347	10.5	316	7.75	13.0	9.2	166	(13.9)	353	11.3	297	1
5,289,200	59	5.2	210	7.3	188	19.2	116	2.27	10.2	15.8	65	(13.9)	352	22.7	92	1
4,798,400	65	5.7	192	6.4	222	21.0§	82	3.90	19.6	2.0	282	(26.2)	397	5.6	357	1
9,147,000	29	5.2	212	6.6	215	23.7	62	2.26	29.1	12.2	119	30.9	89	17.8	189	3
2,677,200	106	3.7	296	6.7	211	20.2	96	6.41	3.7	17.9	44	(29.4)	411	22.2	107	1
7,178,200	36	4.4	258	8.9	122	25.8	45	3.60	22.9	7.0	203	2.8	252	21.0	128	8
3,653,600	85	0.3	425	0.3	428	2.2§	412	0.06	(93.3)	(25.4)	358	24.4	115	9.9	318	18
7,231,200	35	6.9	143	7.4	184	20.7	88	5.12	15.8	13.6	94	(8.2)	317	24.0	75	7
5,655,400	52	5.6	194	5.0	299	11.3	295	5.35	25.0	0.6	294	(1.6)	286	7.9	337	22
3,574,200	86	7.6	118	9.2	114	42.0	10	12.73	997.4	16.1	59	47.1	45	20.5	142	21
5,248,000	61	6.0	177	5.8	249	12.7	256	3.15	—	5.9	215	29.2	98	7.9	336	6
14,189,900	18	9.7	63	11.4	59	18.1	140	4.02	18.2	8.5	179	13.5	164	15.1	236	22
15,113,400	15	12.1	34	13.5	31	18.1	141	8.53	77.3	19.9	30	28.9	99	19.3	163	6
2,263,900	130	4.7	237	8.7	127	27.3	41	10.26	—	18.4	40	(26.9)	401	20.4	145	1
4,636,600	67	2.9	347	6.4	226	18.9	124	2.35	16.3	12.4	115	6.6	221	25.4	62	8

The 100 Largest U.S. Industrial Corporations (ranked by sales) *(continued)*

Rank '87	Rank '86	Company	Sales ($000)	Sales % Change from '86	Profits ($000)	Profits Rank	Profits % Change from '86	Assets ($000)	Assets Rank	Stockholders' Equity ($000)	Stockholders' Equity Rank
41	59	Conagra (Omaha)[7,8]	9,001,600*	52.3	148,700	148	41.3	2,482,500	150	722,500	195
42	•	Beatrice (Chicago)[9]	8,926,000[10]	6.3	N.A.		—	7,903,000	46	308,000	332
43	33	Sun (Radnor, Pa.)	8,691,000	(7.3)	348,000	64	(9.6)	12,580,000	25	5,229,000	24
44	50	Georgia-Pacific (Atlanta)	8,603,000	19.1	458,000	49	54.7	5,870,000	58	2,680,000	55
45	41	ITT (New York)[6]	8,551,000	8.3	1,018,100	18	106.2	13,354,300	24	7,819,500	13
46	45	Unocal(Los Angeles)	8,466,000*	13.2	181,000	129	2.8	10,062,000	31	1,766,000	76
47	43	Anheuser-Busch (St. Louis)	8,258,400*	7.6	614,700	35	18.7	6,491,600	54	2,892,200	53
48	47	Caterpillar (Peoria, Ill.)	8,180,000	11.7	350,000	63	360.5	6,866,000	52	3,565,000	41
49	51	Hewlett-Packard (Palo Alto, Calif.)[11]	8,090,000	13.9	644,000	31	24.8	8,133,000	43	5,022,000	28
50	53	Johnson & Johnson (New Brunswick, N.J.)	8,012,000	14.4	833,000	24	152.8	6,546,000	53	3,485,000	42
51	79	Aluminum Co. of America (Pittsburgh)	7,767,000	66.4	200,100‡	120	(21.3)	9,901,900	34	3,910,700	33
52	66	International Paper (Purchase, N.Y.)	7,763,000	41.1	407,000	56	33.4	8,710,000	37	4,052,000	32
53	48	Raytheon (Lexington, Mass.)	7,659,400	4.8	445,100	51	13.2	4,062,200	92	1,849,100	73
54	38	Coca-Cola (Atlanta)	7,658,300	(11.7)	916,100	21	(1.9)	8,355,600	42	3,223,800	45
55	55	Monsanto (St. Louis)	7,639,000	11.0	436,000	53	0.7	8,455,000	39	3,901,000	34
56	49	LTV (Dallas)	7,581,800	4.3	502,600	44	—	5,706,100	59	(2,045,400)	493
57	57	Coastal (Houston)	7,413,900	11.2	113,100	78	58.0	7,989,300	45	859,800	166
58	62	Weyerhaeuser (Tacoma)	6,989,800	23.7	446,600	50	61.4	7,201,900	50	3,716,200	38
59	42	Union Carbide (Danbury, Conn.)	6,914,000	(11.7)	232,000	98	(53.2)	7,892,000	47	1,247,000	115
60	54	Ashland Oil (Russell, Ky.)[5]	6,870,900	(1.7)	133,400	166	(36.0)	4,058,000	93	1,065,400	136
61	58	TRW (Cleveland)	6,821,200	5.8	243,400	94	11.8	4,377,500	83	1,416,700	100
62	60	Motorola (Schaumburg, Ill.)	6,707,000	13.9	308,000	75	58.8	5,321,000	64	3,008,000	49
63	52	Honeywell (Minneapolis)	6,679,300	(5.7)	253,700	85	—	5,285,200	66	2,245,300	61
64	70	Borden (New York)	6,514,400	30.2	267,100	81	19.6	4,157,400	90	1,658,800	79
65	68	American Brands (Old Greenwich, Conn.)	6,323,400*,¶	20.2	522,700	43	43.1	7,343,100	49	2,966,400	51
66	63	Baxter Travenol Laboratories (Deerfield, Ill.)	6,223,000	10.5	331,000	68	(25.5)	7,638,000	48	3,713,000	39
67	73	Emerson Electric (St. Louis)[5]	6,170,300	24.6	467,200	48	14.3	4,867,800	73	2,702,500	54
68	61	Pillsbury (Minneapolis)[7]	6,127,800	4.8	181,900	128	(12.6)	3,853,000	98	1,378,900	104
69	64	Northrop (Los Angeles)	6,052,500	7.9	94,200	194	128.6	3,123,600	115	947,500	150
70	65	Ralston Purina (St. Louis)[5]	5,868,000	6.4	523,100	42	34.6	3,863,700	96	961,500	148
71	67	Archer Daniels Midland (Decatur, Ill.)[3]	5,774,600	8.2	265,400	83	15.2	3,862,100	97	2,367,700	58
72	69	Textron (Providence)[6]	5,661,400	8.3	256,300‡	84	7.1	5,343,600	63	2,307,200	59
73	71	Colgate-Palmolive (New York)	5,647,500	13.3	54,000	277	(69.6)	3,227,700	110	941,100	151
74	75	NCR (Dayton, Ohio)	5,640,700	15.5	419,300	55	24.6	4,187,500	89	2,161,500	63
75	72	Texas Instruments (Dallas)	5,594,500	12.5	308,500**	74	960.1	4,256,300	85	2,246,400	60
76	76	Bristol-Myers (New York)	5,401,200	11.7	709,600	28	20.4	4,732,000	76	3,229,300	44
77	80	General Mills (Minneapolis)[7]	5,208,300	13.6	222,000	104	21.0	2,280,400	157	730,400	192
78	78	PPG Industries (Pittsburgh)	5,182,600	10.6	377,100	60	19.2	4,987,900	69	2,043,500	68
79	77	Martin Marietta (Bethesda, Md.)	5,165,100	8.7	230,600	99	14.0	2,794,100	131	907,700	158
80	91	Merck (Rahway, N.J.)	5,061,300	22.6	906,400	22	34.1	5,680,000	60	2,116,700	65
81	56	W. R. Grace (New York)	5,046.300¶	(25.9)	173,100	134	—	4,473,600	79	1,463,300	96
82	74	American Home Products (New York)	5,028,300	2.1	845,100	23	8.5	4,608,400	77	2,529,700	56
83	84	Pfizer (New York)	4,919,800	9.9	690,200	29	4.6	6,922,600	51	3,882,400	35
84	81	CPC International (Englewood Cliffs, N.J.	4,903,000	7.8	354,800	62	61.9	3,260,500	108	1,086,500	130
85	90	Kimberly-Clark (Dallas)	4,884,700	13.5	325,200	70	20.7	3,885,700	95	1,571,900	89
86	82	North American Philips (New York)[12]	4,846,900	7.0	(18,100)	445	—	3,102,300	117	1,073,600	133
87	92	Amerada Hess (New York)	4,784,600	19.2	229,900	101	—	5,304,800	65	2,158,500	64
88	88	H. J. Heinz (Pittsburgh)[13]	4,639,500	6.3	338,500	66	12.2	3,364,200	106	1,392,900	102
89	89	Bethlehem Steel (Bethlehem, Pa.)	4,620,500	6.6	174,300**	132	—	4,774,800	74	1,208,400	121
90	86	Champion International (Stamford, Conn.)	4,614,700	5.2	382,000	58	90.2	6,103,300	57	2,936,300	52

Market Value ($000)	Rank	Profits as Percent of: Sales %	Sales Rank	Assets %	Assets Rank	Stockholders' Equity %	Stockholders' Equity Rank	Earnings per Share: '87/$	% Change from '86	Annual Growth Rate 1977–87 %	Annual Growth Rate 1977–87 Rank	Total Return to Investors: 1987 %	1987 Rank	1977–87 Annual Average %	1977–87 Annual Average Rank	Industry Table Number
1,947,600	148	1.7	391	6.0	241	20.6	90	1.85	21.3	16.6	54	(9.4)	324	33.4	12	8
N.A.		—		—		—		—	—	—		—		—		8
6,037,800	44	4.0	280	2.8	370	6.7	372	3.21	(9.3)	(1.2)	307	(0.3)	275	15.3	234	18
3,888,400	79	5.3	204	7.8	169	17.1§	164	4.23	57.2	5.2	230	(4.3)	298	5.8	354	9
6,316,300	40	11.9	38	7.6	174	13.0	246	6.76	109.3	5.2	231	40.7	62	15.8	226	7
4,225,400	76	2.1	376	1.8	394	10.2	327	1.56)	3.3	(2.3)	315	9.2	195	11.8	289	18
10,419,900	28	7.4	125	9.4	106	21.3	77	2.04	20.7	19.6	32	29.7	96	29.6	23	3
6,554,400	39	4.3	268	5.1	295	9.8	336	3.51	355.8	(3.8)	325	55.9	30	4.4	368	11
16,054,600	12	8.0	108	7.9	158	12.8	252	2.50	23.8	16.7	53	39.7	64	21.0	130	6
14,477,600	16	10.4	56	12.7	40	23.9	60	4.83	161.1	13.1	104	16.2	151	14.2	248	19
3,966,900	78	2.6	362	2.0	391	5.1	387	2.25‡	(24.0)	(2.1)	312	41.5	59	11.8	288	15
4,518,400	71	5.2	209	4.7	314	10.0§	332	3.68	27.1	4.0	251	15.4	153	12.0	283	9
4,561,200	69	5.8	183	11.0	63	24.1	57	6.12	20.0	12.8	109	1.5	264	18.1	178	7
14,335,700	17	12.0	36	11.0	62	28.4	37	2.43	0.4	10.6	147	3.5	216	17.5	191	3
5,900,800	48	5.7	188	5.2	287	11.2	300	5.63	1.4	4.2	247	12.2	174	17.1	203	5
364,100	372	6.6	152	8.8	124	—		4.24	—	—		53.8	32	(8.1)	393	15
1,287,400	195	1.5	397	1.4	404	13.2§	242	2.10	275.0	2.9	268	12.7	170	22.4	103	18
5,717,900	50	6.4	163	6.2	235	12.0§	280	3.18	66.5	3.3	264	5.7	232	7.6	341	9
3,244,300	93	3.4	326	2.9	363	18.6	128	1.76	(63.2)	(1.4)	309	2.6	254	15.7	227	5
1,905,100	152	1.9	381	3.3	357	12.5§	263	4.27	(30.6)	1.4	289	6.1	230	17.4	195	18
3,033,400	97	3.6	302	5.6	267	17.2	162	4.01	10.6	5.3	227	16.2	152	16.0	222	7
6,141,000	42	4.6	245	5.8	250	10.2	328	2.39	56.2	7.4	197	41.3	60	17.4	193	7
2,822,800	101	3.8	288	4.8	308	11.3	297	575	—	5.2	229	(6.2)	306	12.6	272	7
3,997,700	77	4.1	275	6.4	221	16.1	178	3.62	20.7	10.3	153	8.1	205	23.3	86	8
5,009,000	63	8.3	101	7.1	197	17.6§	152	4.60	44.7	12.1	123	9.6	193	23.4	81	25
6,000,000	45	5.3	205	4.3	330	8.9	350	1.14	(32.9)	7.2	200	20.4	130	10.8	306	19
7,749,800	32	7.6	120	9.6	101	17.3	158	2.00	6.8	9.3	165	27.6	104	16.3	219	7
3,285,500	92	3.0	344	4.7	312	13.2	240	2.10	(11.9)	8.9	172	6.5	224	18.0	181	8
1,393,600	189	1.6	396	3.0	361	9.9	333	2.01	125.8)	2.3	279	(33.0)	422	16.6	217	1
5,173,900	62	8.9	82	13.5	30	54.4	3	7.23	42.9	18.4	39	(8.3)	319	20.7	138	8
3,509,700	87	4.6	243	6.9	206	11.2	301	1.54	13.1	11.1	140	22.0	125	16.8	210	8
2,127,300	139	4.5	249	4.8	309	11.1	306	2.92‡	0.9	4.8	238	(26.0)	394	11.5	292	1
3,004,100	98	1.0	409	1.7	397	5.7	382	0.78	(69.0)	(9.3)	335	(0.9)	279	12.2	281	23
5,593,800	53	7.4	126	10.0	81	19.4	108	4.51	31.9	12.9	105	45.5	50	23.3	85	6
4,265,000	75	5.5	196	7.2	189	13.7	229	3.59**	1,416.7	7.7	191	43.4	55	10.6	308	7
12,584,000	23	13.1	29	15.0	23	22.0	73	2.47	19.6	13.8	91	3.8	244	21.3	124	19
4,422,600	73	4.3	270	9.7	96	30.4	33	2.50	21.7	7.8	189	18.4	140	18.6	169	8
4,312,800	74	7.3	131	7.6	177	18.5	134	3.19	19.9	15.9	64	(6.5)	308	23.0	89	4
2,423,700	121	4.5	254	8.3	145	25.4	48	4.25	15.8	12.8	108	11.2	180	24.3	71	1
20,783,300	8	17.9	10	16.0	18	42.8	7	6.68	37.7	13.2	100	29.9	95	22.5	99	19
2,310,800	128	3.4	319	3.9	342	11.8	286	2.03	—	0.9	291	3.5	247	12.4	274	5
11,617,600	24	16.8	12	18.3	9	33.4	25	5.73	10.6	11.4	133	(1.4)	284	15.8	225	19
8,936,200	30	14.0	27	10.0	85	17.8	147	4.08	4.6	12.6	113	(21.4)	378	16.8	212	19
3,784,100	81	7.2	134	10.9	65	32.7	27	4.34	88.7	12.0	125	5.1	234	19.3	165	8
4,601,500	68	6.7	150	8.4	138	20.7	86	3.73	27.1	10.3	154	28.6	101	22.7	93	9
N.A.		—		—		—		N.A.	—	—		—		—		7
2,411,400	124	4.8	232	4.3	331	10.6	315	2.73	—	2.5	275	6.8	219	10.2	311	18
5,456,800	55	7.3	130	10.1	79	24.3	54	2.47	12.3	15.4	72	2.1	258	26.1	54	8
1,390,500	190	3.8	292	3.7	349	14.4	211	2.77**	—	—		168.0	4	1.6	378	15
3,405,900	89	8.3	99	6.3	231	13.0	247	4.03	93.8	4.0	253	14.1	160	9.9	317	9

The 100 Largest U.S. Industrial Corporations (ranked by sales) *(concluded)*

Rank '87	Rank '86	Company	Sales ($000)	Sales % Change from '86	Profits ($000)	Profits Rank	Profits % Change from '86	Assets ($000)	Assets Rank	Stockholders' Equity ($000)	Stockholders' Equity Rank
91	210	Hoechst Celanese (Somerville, N.J.)[14]	4,596,000	178.6	169,000	136	347.1	5,388,000	62	3,103,000	47
92	85	IC Industries (Chicago)	4,581,200¶	3.2	251,700	86	—	4,871,400	72	1,573,000	88
93	104	Quaker Oats (Chicago)[3]	4,538,600	23.6	243,900	93	35.8	3,250,100	109	1,087,500	129
94	87	Cambell Soup (Camden, N.J.)[15]	4,490,400	2.6	247,300	92	10.8	3,090,000	118	1,736,100	77
95	149	James River Corp. of Virginia (Richmond)[13]	4,479,000	71.8	169,900	135	78.3	4,210,500	87	1,847,200	74
96	83	Litton Industries (Beverly Hills, Calif.)[15]	4,419,700	(2.2)	138,100	162	94.1	4,880,800	71	1,053,800	138
97	96	Abbott laboratories (North Chicago, Ill.)	4,387,900	15.2	632,600	34	17.0	4,385,700	82	2,093,500	66
98	144	Triangle Industries (New York)	4,336,100	62.5	52,200	281	304.1	3,771,900	100	423,200	278
99	106	BASF (Parsippany, N.J.)[16]	4,333,500	18.9	130,700‡	168	25.0	2,557,500	148	918,500	155
100	99	Smithkline Beckman (Philadelphia)	4,328,800	15.6	570,100	40	9.4	4,446,200	80	1,584,600	86

¶ Includes sales from discontinued operations of at least 10%; see explanations of sales on page 205.

N.A. Not available.

• Indicates that a corporation was not among the 500 in 1986.

* Does not include excise taxes; see the explanation of "sales" on page 205.

** Reflects an extraordinary credit of at least 10%; see the explanation of "net income" and "earnings per share" on page 205.

‡ Reflects an extraordinary charge of at least 10%; see the explanation of "net income" and "earnings per share" on page 205.

§ Dividends paid by company on its mandatory redeemable preferred stock were subtracted from net income in calculating this figure.

1 Figures include American Motors (1986 rank: 113) acquired August 5, 1987.

2 Owned by Royal Dutch/Shell Group (1986 International 500 rank: 1).

3 Figures are for fiscal year ended June 30, 1987.

4 Name changed from Standard Oil June 29, 1987. Owned by British Petroleum (1986 International 500 rank: 2)

5 Figures are for fiscal year ended September 30, 1987.

6 Financial subsidiaries would add 25% or more to sales if consolidated.

Market Value		Profits as Percent of: Sales		Assets		Stockholders' Equity		Earnings per Share				Total Return to Investors				Industry Table Number
									% Change from	Annual Growth Rate 1977–87		1987		1977–87 Annual Average		
($000)	Rank	%	Rank	%	Rank	%	Rank	'87/$	'86	%	Rank	%	Rank	%	Rank	
N.A.		3.7	298	3.1	359	5.4	385	N.A.	—	—		—		—		5
3,753,100	82	5.5	198	5.2	286	16.0	180	2.23	—	7.0	202	46.8	46	24.7	64	8
3,675,300	83	5.4	202	7.5	180	22.4	70	3.10	42.5	15.2	76	6.0	231	26.6	50	8
3,656,400	84	5.5	197	8.0	152	14.2	217	3.81	10.4	8.8	173	0.1	272	17.9	182	8
2,037,200	146	3.8	290	4.0	337	9.2§	344	2.03	14.7	20.2	28	(29.0)	409	27.1	44	9
2,172,800	136	3.1	338	2.8	367	13.1	244	5.16	104.8	15.6	66	(2.5)	292	20.8	137	7
11,024,800	26	14.4	23	14.4	27	30.2	35	2.78	19.8	18.8	35	7.6	213	24.1	74	19
771,200	281	1.2	405	1.4	405	12.3	268	1.79	297.8	—		6.3	224	35.2	9	14
N.A.		3.0	342	5.1	294	14.2	218	N.A.	—	—		—		—		5
7,354,000	34	13.2	28	12.8	37	36.0	17	4.50	32.7	19.7	31	5.0	236	18.6	170	19

[7] Figures are for fiscal year ended May 31, 1987.
[8] Figures include Monfort of Colorado (1986 rank: 216) acquired May 13, 1987.
[9] Figures are for fiscal year ended February 28, 1987.
[10] FORTUNE estimate.
[11] Figures are for fiscal year ended October 31, 1987.
[12] Owned by Philips' Gloeilampenfabrieken (1986 International 500 rank: 11).
[13] Figures are for fiscal year ended April 30, 1987.
[14] Company was formed by the merger of American Hoechst (1986 rank: 210) and Celanese (1986 rank: 134) February 27, 1987. Owned by Hoechst (1986 International 500 rank: 19).
[15] Figures are for fiscal year ended July 31, 1987.
[16] Owned by BASF (1986 International 500 rank: 17).

DEFINITIONS AND EXPLANATIONS

Sales All companies on the list must have derived more than 50% of their sales from manufacturing and/or mining. Sales include rental and other revenues but exclude dividends, interest, and other non-operating revenues. Sales of subsidiaries are included if they are consolidated. Sales from discontinued operations are included when these figures are published. When the sales are at least 10% higher for this reason, there is a symbol (¶) next to the sales figure. All figures are for the year ending December 31, 1987, unless otherwise noted. Sales figures do not include excise taxes collected by the manufacturer, and so the figures for some corporations—most of which sell gasoline, liquor, or tobacco—may be lower than those published by the corporations themselves. If they are at least 5% lower for this reason, there is an asterisk (*) next to the sales figures.

Assets are those shown at the company's fiscal year-end.

Net Income is shown after taxes and after extraordinary credits or charges if any are shown on the income statement. A double asterisk (**) signifies an extraordinary credit reflecting at least 10 percent of the net income shown, a double dagger (‡) an extraordinary charge of at least 10 percent. Cooperatives provide only "net margin" figures, which are not comparable with the net income figures in these listings, and therefore N.A. is shown in that column.

Stockholders' Equity is the sum of capital stock, surplus, and retained earnings at the company's year-end. Redeemable preferred stock is excluded if its redemption is either mandatory or outside the control of the company, except in the case of cooperatives. For purposes of calculating "net income as percent of stockholders' equity," any dividends paid on redeemable preferred stock, if that stock's redemption is either mandatory or outside the control of the company, have been subtracted from the net income figure.

Market Value The figure shown was arrived at by multiplying the number of common shares outstanding (at the latest date available) by the price per common share as of March 15, 1988.

Earnings per Share For all companies, the figures shown are the primary earnings per share that appear on the company's income statement. Per-share earnings for 1986 and 1977 are adjusted for stock splits and stock dividends. They are not restated for mergers, acquisitions, or accounting changes made after 1977. A double asterisk (**) signifies an extraordinary credit reflecting at least 10 percent of the net income shown, a double dagger (‡) an extraordinary charge of at least 10 percent. Results are listed as not available (N.A.) where the companies are cooperatives, joint ventures, or wholly owned subsidiaries of other companies, or if the figures were not published in 1977. The growth rate is the average annual growth, compounded. No growth rate is given if the company had a loss in either 1977 or 1987.

Total Return to Investors includes both price appreciation and dividend yield, to an investor in the company's stock. The figures shown assume sales at the end of 1987 of stock owned at the end of 1977 and 1986. It has been assumed that any proceeds from cash dividends, the sale of rights and warrant offerings, and stock received in spin-offs were reinvested at the end of the year in which they were paid. Returns are adjusted for stock splits, stock dividends, recapitalizations, and corporate reorganizations as they occur; however, no effort has been made to reflect the cost of brokerage commissions or of taxes. Results are listed as not available (N.A.) if shares are not publicly traded or traded on only a limited basis. If companies have more than one class of shares outstanding, only the more widely held and actively traded has been considered.

Total-return percentages shown are the returns received by the hypothetical investor described above. The ten-year figures are annual averages, compounded.

The 100 Largest International Industrial Corporations (ranked by sales)

Rank 1987	Rank 1986	Company	Country	Sales $ Millions	Net Income $ Millions	Net Income Rank	Assets $ Millions	Assets Rank	Stockholders' Equity $ Millions	Stockholders' Equity Rank	Employees Number	Employees Rank	Industry Code
1	1	Royal Dutch/Shell Group	Britain/Neth.	78,319.3	4,725.8	1	87,231.3	1	43,330.8	1	136,000	26	29
2	2	British Petroleum	Britain	45,205.9	2,280.1	2	50,363.7	2	20,295.2	3	126,020	34	29
3	4	Toyota Motor	Japan	41,455.0	1,699.6	5	33,180.1	7	20,743.1	2	84,207	53	40
4	3	IRI[2,3]	Italy	41,270.0	146.5	161	N.A.		N.A.		422,000	2	33
5	5	Daimler-Benz	W. Germany	37,535.5	970.2	13	29,626.9	11	5,983.6	26	326,288	5	40
6	8	Volkswagen[4]	W. Germany	30,392.7[2]	242.1	96	28,050.1	14	6,559.2	23	260,458	8	40
7	9	Hitachi[5]	Japan	30,332.2	617.3	32	36,573.5	5	12,534.1	7	161,325	17	36
8	15	Fiat	Italy	29,642.8	1,830.2	3	40,730.2	4	9,837.9	11	270,578	7	40
9	13	Siemens[12]	W. Germany	27,462.9	649.6	29	29,783.0	10	8,428.5	16	359,000	3	36
10	6	Matsushita Electric Industrial[5]	Japan	27,325.7[7]	862.4[7]	17	28,613.1	13	15,188.7	5	134,764	27	36
11	7	Unilever	Britain/Neth.	27,128.8	1,278.6	7	18,858.1	28	5,744.8	28	294,000	6	20
12	11	Philips' Gloeilampenfabrieken	Neth.	26,021.2	316.9	66	26,970.0	15	8,120.5	18	336,672	4	36
13	14	Nissan Motors[5]	Japan	25,650.5	123.9	178	25,629.4	16	9,328.8	13	105,443	41	40
14	18	Renault[2]	France	24,539.7	613.7	33	19,057.2	25	(1,074.7)	496	188,936	11	40
15	10	ENI[2,4]	Italy	24,242.5	483.6	42	43,716.4	3	8,534.5	15	119,152	38	29
16	12	Nestlé[4]	Switzerland	23,625.9	1,224.8	10	19,774.1	21	9,550.1	12	163,030	16	20
17	17	BASF	W. Germany	22,333.7[4]	584.7	34	18,965.6	27	7,541.6	20	133,759	28	28
18	36	CGE (Cie Générale d'Électricité)	France	21,204.3	304.8	69	32,107.0	9	3,106.4	65	219,460	9	36
19	20	Elf Aquitaine[2]	France	21,186.4	690.2	27	28,830.5	12	9,989.4	10	73,000	63	29
20	21	Samsung	South Korea	21,053.5	249.3	90	14,558.7	39	1,727.9	140	160,596	20	36
21	16	Bayer	W. Germany	20,662.2	833.3	18	20,469.2	20	8,629.4	14	164,400	14	28
22	19	Hoechst	W. Germany	20,558.1	766.6	22	18,418.0	29	5,537.3	29	167,781	13	28
23	24	Toshiba[5]	Japan	20,378.1	213.8	114	22,543.3	18	4,070.0	47	121,000	37	36
24	23	Peugeot[4]	France	19,658.2	1,116.1	12	14,462.7	40	3,852.9	52	160,600	19	40
25	25	Imperial Chemical Industries	Britain	18,232.8	1,245.8	8	16,572.3	32	6,497.3	25	127,800	32	28
26	34	Honda Motor[8]	Japan	17,237.7	516.2	39	11,055.6	59	4,912.7	34	57,130	80	40
27	26	Petrobrás (Petróleo Brasileiro)[2]	Brazil	15,640.5	171.5	143	15,460.3	36	7,640.1	19	67,909	68	29
28	42	NEC[5]	Japan	15,325.1	94.0	221	18,986.1	26	3,530.1	57	101,227	42	36
29	33	Nippon Steel[5]	Japan	14,639.8	(69.7)	473	24,707.1	17	4,510.7	40	69,269	66	33
30	35	Volvo	Sweden	14,576.0	730.4	25	13,756.0	44	4,117.3	46	75,340	59	40
31	28	Total	France	14,487.7	242.2	95	13,609.2	47	4,371.1	43	34,110	136	29
32	37	Lucky-Goldstar	South Korea	14,422.3	180.7	132	10,268.5	65	1,935.0	120	88,403	48	36
33	29	Thyssen[6]	W. Germany	14,177.3	151.3	157	8,752.2	79	1,876.4	128	121,533	36	33
34	45	Robert Bosch	W. Germany	14,110.0[4]	440.9[4]	49	11,574.6[4]	56	3,373.9[4]	60	160,783	18	40
35	39	Daewoo	South Korea	13,437.9	36.8	336	19,680.8	22	1,801.3	134	94,888	43	36
36	40	Pemex (Petróleos Mexicanos)[2,3,9]	Mexico	13,130.4	2.5	446	34,633.6	6	16,978.5	4	178,745	12	29
37	38	Saint-Gobain	France	13,123.7	461.2	46	14,902.3	37	2,774.1	77	131,000	30	32

The definitions and concepts underlying the figures in this directory are explained on page 210.

(continued)

The 100 Largest International Industrial Corporations *(concluded)*

Rank 1987	Rank 1986	Company	Country	Sales $ Millions	Net Income $ Millions	Net Income Rank	Assets $ Millions	Assets Rank	Stockholders' Equity $ Millions	Stockholders' Equity Rank	Employees Number	Employees Rank	Industry Code
38	48	Mitsubishi Electric[5]	Japan	12,980.5	66.3	268	13,342.8	48	3,476.8	58	73,536	62	36
39	•	INI[2]	Spain	12,734.5	(344.9)	492	32,329.6	8	8,341.9	17	163,821	15	33
40	31	General Motors of Canada[10]	Canada	12,732.4	3.8	445	4,550.5	166	1,874.5	129	44,749	103	40
41	32	Bat Industries	Britain	12,330.1	1,231.0	9	16,063.1	34	7,442.2	21	154,164	22	21
42	47	Ruhrkohle	W. Germany	11,274.1	10.5	434	11,841.1	54	925.3	232	127,213	33	10
43	58	Fujitsu[5]	Japan	11,194.2	132.3	171	13,716.3	45	4,670.5	37	89,293	47	44
44	118	Usinor-Sacilor[2,4,5]	France	11,165.0	(969.5)	496	13,657.8	46	(135.3)	493	90,082	46	33
45	22	Mitsubishi Heavy Industries[5]	Japan	11,157.3	170.2	145	19,370.5	23	3,659.4	55	58,200	78	45
46	46	Mazda Motor[12]	Japan	11,057.5	29.1	367	7,888.4	89	2,250.9	98	28,285	175	40
47	30	Nippon Oil[5]	Japan	11,041.0	68.1	260	9,552.8	70	2,628.8	82	11,140	352	29
48	52	Montedison	Italy	10,636.2	315.4	67	19,168.1	24	2,971.6	70	66,785	70	28
49	60	Electrolux	Sweden	10,623.2	288.8	75	8,484.7	82	1,956.9	116	140,500	24	36
50	51	Ciba-Geigy	Switzerland	10,568.3	737.4	24	17,426.6	31	11,158.5	8	86,109	50	28
51	43	Ford Motor of Canada[10]	Canada	10,539.8	63.0	277	2,786.0	270	880.3	249	27,200	183	40
52	67	BMW (Bayerische Motoren)	W. Germany	10,181.9	209.3	116	6,572.6	119	2,094.9	106	55,769	81	40
53	27	Kuwait Petroleum[1,2]	Kuwait	10,107.0	246.5	92	20,840.0	19	14,499.1	6	15,552	291	29
54	50	Thomson[2]	France	9,977.6	176.8	135	15,560.1	35	1,427.6	159	86,000	51	36
55	71	Adam Opel	W. Germany	9,561.1[10]	266.7	83	3,846.5	198	972.6	221	55,282	82	40
56	•	Mitsubishi Motors[5]	Japan	9,523.3[9]	90.2[9]	228	7,620.0[9]	92	979.4[9]	220	25,409	194	40
57	57	Ford-Werke	W. Germany	9,466.3[10]	450.5	48	4,805.1	157	1,228.3	180	47,104	96	40
58	59	Rhône-Poulenc[2]	France	9,342.6	366.8	59	11,274.2	58	3,173.6	64	82,500	54	28
59	54	Mannesmann	W. Germany	9,265.1	119.2	184	8,565.4	80	2,286.8	96	122,298	35	45
60	41	Canadian Pacific	Canada	9,206.5	623.1	31	13,844.6	43	4,969.6	33	85,400	52	33
61	79	Showa Shell Sekiyu	Japan	8,989.7	49.9	303	6,796.3	111	461.2	370	2,578	485	29
62	94	Hanson Trust[6]	Britain	8,890.4	891.1	15	10,358.1	64	3,053.0	67	88,000	49	20
63	53	Indian Oil[2,5]	India	8,629.0	335.6	63	3,179.9	237	1,043.0	209	32,604	144	29
64	55	Petrofina	Belgium	8,583.2	471.9	44	9,706.4	66	3,265.5	62	22,100	222	29
65	76	Ford Motor[10]	Britain	8,541.9	355.7	60	8,281.4	86	2,055.7	109	47,000	97	40
66	74	Statoil[2]	Norway	8,337.5	(277.5)	489	9,042.1	76	473.3	366	10,627	362	29
67	49	Petróleos de Venezuela[2]	Venezuela	8,290.5	1,511.7	6	12,336.7	51	10,096.1	9	44,203	105	29
68	75	ASEA	Sweden	8,235.0	193.9	122	11,396.2	57	1,835.4	132	72,868	64	45
69	63	Norsk Hydro[2]	Norway	8,083.5	271.4	81	10,755.5	62	1,856.6	130	39,139	123	28
70	70	Sanyo Electric[14]	Japan	7,983.7	(118.9)	482	11,735.4	55	4,718.1	36	40,590	118	36
71	61	Sony[5]	Japan	7,956.4[7]	156.5[7]	155	9,687.2	67	4,179.3	45	47,583	94	36
72	64	Fried. Krupp	W Germany	7,846.4	13.4	426	6,631.4	117	1,027.7	212	56,205	81	33
73	65	GEC (General Electric Co.)[5]	Britain	7,830.0	649.1	30	8,876.6	78	4,651.6	38	157,000	21	36
74	73	Michelin	France	7,808.2	405.1	55	10,497.5	63	2,231.2	100	117,000	39	30
75	72	Grand Metropolitan[4]	Britain	7,741.5	718.9	26	7,436.7	97	2,822.4	75	129,436	31	49

76	77	Akzo Group	Netherlands	7,668.4	465.0	45	6,686.0	116	2,157.1	103	67,400	69	28
77	69	Dalgety[4]	Britain	7,631.0	117.6	188	1,945.0	354	546.7	331	23,966	207	20
78	83	Barlow Rand[4]	South Africa	7,617.9	222.1	108	5,240.9	148	1,094.3	201	140,445	25	20
79	44	Idemitsu Kosan[9]	Japan	7,596.3[9]	5.2[9]	442	8,544.2[9]	81	280.1[9]	435	5,792[9]	434	29
80	111	Man[1]	W. Germany	7,438.2	68.2	258	6,611.7	118	1,175.9	188	52,229	85	45
81	100	IBM Japan	Japan	7,333.4[10]	513.6	40	5,357.7	144	2,389.9	89	20,210	234	44
82	81	Nippon Kokan[5,16]	Japan	7,325.2	(129.4)	483	17,719.1	30	1,609.5	147	35,146	130	33
83	78	Isuzu Motors[12]	Japan	7,179.9	46.7	311	6,125.6	129	903.9	239	24,609	203	40
84	•	Repsol[2,4]	Spain	7,146.2	383.5	57	7,000.8	105	2,871.4	72	18,910	246	29
85	137	Metallgesellschaft[6]	W. Germany	7,117.5	42.0	317	3,861.3	197	734.7	278	24,813	201	33
86	86	Nippondenso	Japan	7,102.2	215.9	113	7,382.9	98	3,825.5	54	45,572	100	40
87	93	Sharp[5]	Japan	6,994.4	128.8	174	9,612.5	68	2,677.8	79	29,346	164	36
88	56	Brown Boveri	Switzerland	6,951.5	112.6	192	11,927.6	53	3,418.8	59	93,900	44	36
89	85	BTR	Britain	6,801.4	785.0	20	6,163.1	127	2,431.8	87	81,800	55	45
90	82	Sunkyong	South Korea	6,781.6	91.0	227	3,521.1	212	784.6	266	17,985	258	29
91	98	Canon	Japan	6,753.1	91.6	225	9,351.6	71	3,061.4	66	37,521	126	44
92	62	British Coal[2,5]	Britain	6,737.2	(429.8)	495	10,819.9	60	(57.9)	492	141,529	23	10
93	88	Veba Oel	W. Germany	6,716.1[4]	(11.1)	455	2,937.4	255	640.3	307	17,028	266	29
94	128	British Aerospace	Britain	6,679.7	(180.3)	487	8,019.3	88	1,921.8	122	93,038	45	41
95	108	Japan Tobacco[2]	Japan	6,674.6[9]	303.3[9]	71	12,312.4[9]	52	6,502.9[9]	24	29,600[9]	162	21
96	90	Kobe Steel[5]	Japan	6,645.8	(74.6)	474	14,068.5	42	1,218.7	182	30,033	157	33
97	87	Alcan Aluminium	Canada	6,546.0	433.0	50	7,660.0	91	3,970.0	49	63,000	73	33
98	112	SAAB-Scania	Sweden	6,523.0	227.8	103	6,374.4	123	1,155.1	191	50,373	89	40
99	106	Pechiney[2]	France	6,479.1	121.3	181	6,972.9	106	1,392.9	162	46,200	98	33
100	91	IBM Deutschland	W. Germany	6,425.5[10]	303.4	70	5,672.2	139	2,240.9	99	30,544	155	44

The definitions and concepts underlying the figures in this directory are explained on page 210.

• Indicates that a corporation was not among the 500 in 1986.

N.A. Not available.

[1] Figures are for fiscal year ended June 30, 1987.

[2] Government-owned.

[3] Figure is a FORTUNE estimate.

[4] Figures include some significant subsidiaries owned 50% or less, either fully or on a prorated basis.

[5] Figures are for fiscal year ended March 31, 1987.

[6] Figures are for fiscal year ended September 30, 1987.

[7] Company's figures are unaudited due to change in fiscal year-end from November 20, 1986, to March 31, 1987.

[8] Figures are for fiscal year ended February 28, 1987.

[9] Figures are for parent company only.

[10] Revenues may include sales to the U.S. parent company or to ther affiliates also on this list.

[11] Merger of Usinor and Sacilor on December 30, 1987.

[12] Figures are for fiscal year ended October 31, 1987.

[13] Figures are for fiscal year ended October 20, 1987.

[14] Figures are for fiscal year ended November 30, 1987.

[15] Company's figures are unaudited due to change in fiscal year-end from October 31, 1986, to March 31, 1987.

[16] Company changed its name to NKK on June 8, 1988.

NOTES TO THE INTERNATIONAL 100*

Sales All companies on the list must have derived more than 50% of their sales from manufacturing and/or mining. Sales do not include excise taxes or customs duties levied according to either volume or value sales, and so the figures for some companies—most of which sell gasoline, liquor, or tobacco—may be lower than those published by the companies themselves. Unless otherwise noted, figures exclude intracompany transactions and include consolidated subsidiaries more than 50% owned, either fully or on a prorated basis. Figures have been converted to dollars using an exchange rate that consists of the official average rate during each company's fiscal year (ended December 31, 1987, unless otherwise noted).

Assets Totals shown at each company's year-end. Figures have been converted to dollars at the official exchange rate at each company's year-end.

Net Income is shown after taxes, minority interests, and extraordinary items. Figures have been converted to dollars using an exchange rate that consists of the official average rate during each company's fiscal year (ended December 31, 1987, unless otherwise noted).

Stockholders' Equity is shown at each company's year-end. Minority interest is not included. Figures have been converted to dollars at the official exchange rate at each company's year-end.

Employees The figure shown is either a year-end or yearly average number as published.

Industry Code Numbers used in the directory indicate which industry represents the greatest volume of industrial sales for each company. The numbers refer to the industry groups listed below, which are based on categories established by the U.S. Office of Management and Budget and issued by the Federal Statistical Policy and Standards Office. The median figures in the tables refer only to results of companies in the 500. No attempt has been made to calculate medians in groups or countries with fewer than four companies.

Code No.	Industry
10	Mining, crude-oil production
20	Food
21	Tobacco
22	Textiles
23	Apparel
25	Furniture
26	Forest products
27	Publishing, printing
28	Chemicals
29	Petroleum refining
30	Rubber products
31	Leather
32	Building materials
33	Metals
34	Metal products
36	Electronics
37	Transportation equipment
38	Scientific and photographic equipment
40	Motor vehicles and parts
41	Aerospace
42	Pharmaceuticals
43	Soaps, cosmetics
44	Computers
45	Industrial and farm equipment
46	Jewelry, silverware
47	Toys, sporting goods
49	Beverages

* Top 100 from the Fortune 500.

The 25 Largest Industrial Companies in the World (ranked by sales)

Rank '87	Rank '86	Company	Headquarters	Industry	Sales (000)	Profits (000)
1	1	General Motors	Detroit	Motor vehicles	101,781,900	3,550,900
2	3	Royal Dutch/Shell Group	London/The Hague	Petroleum refining	78,319,300	4,725,800
3	2	Exxon	New York	Petroleum refining	76,416,000	4,840,000
4	4	Ford Motor	Dearborn, Mich.	Motor vehicles	71,643,400	4,625,200
5	5	International Business Machines	Armonk, N.Y.	Computers	54,217,000	5,258,000
6	6	Mobil	New York	Petroleum refining	51,223,000	1,258,000
7	7	British Petroleum	London	Petroleum refining	45,205,900	2,280,100
8	12	Toyota Motor	Toyota City (Japan)	Motor vehicles	41,455,000	1,699,600
9	11	IRI	Rome	Metals	41,270,000	146,500
10	8	General Electric	Fairfield, Conn.	Electronics	39,315,000	2,915,000
11	13	Daimler-Benz	Stuttgart	Motor vehicles	37,535,500	970,200
12	10	Texaco	White Plains, N.Y.	Petroleum refining	34,372,000	(4,407,000)
13	9	American Tel. & Tel.	New York	Electronics	33,598,000	2,044,000
14	14	E.I. du Pont de Nemours	Wilmington, Del.	Chemicals	30,468,000	1,786,000
15	18	Volkswagen	Wolfsburg (W. Ger.)	Motor vehicles	30,392,700	242,100
16	19	Hitachi	Tokyo	Electronics	30,332,200	617,300
17	27	Fiat	Turin	Motor vehicle	29,642,800	1,830,200
18	25	Siemens	Munich	Electronics	27,462,900	649,600
19	15	Matsushita Electric Industrial	Osaka	Electronics	27,325,700	862,400
20	16	Unilever	London/Rotterdam	Food	27,128,800	1,278,600
21	21	Chrysler	Highland Park, Mich.	Motor vehicles	26,257,700	1,289,700
22	22	Philips' Gloeilampenfabrieken	Eindhoven (Netherlands)	Electronics	26,021,200	316,900
23	17	Chevron	San Francisco	Petroleum refining	26,015,000	1,007,000
24	26	Nissan Motor	Tokyo	Motor vehicles	25,650,500	123,900
25	31	Renault	Paris	Motor vehicles	24,539,700	613,700

Source: Reprinted by permission from *FORTUNE* Magazine;

The 25 Largest Diversified Service Companies (ranked by sales)

Rank '87	Rank '86	Company	Sales[1] ($000)	Assets ($000)	Assets Rank	Profits ($000)	Profits Rank	Stockholders' Equity ($000)	Stockholders' Equity Rank
1	6	Super Valu Stores (Eden Prairie, Minn.)[2]	9,317,700	2,016,200	33	111,800	18	677,400	27
2	2	Fleming Cos. (Oklahoma City)	8,608,100	1,342.100	41	49,500‡	37	522,100	39
3	3	McKesson (San Francisco)[3]	6,671,600	2,207,600	28	89,700	23	762,200	23
4	6	Hospital Corp. of America (Nashville)	4,675,900	6,182,600	1	(58,400)	90	1,945,700	6
5	12	Ryder System (Miami)	4,609,100	5,770,600	2	187,100	10	1,414,000	12
6	10	National Intergroup (Pittsburgh)[3]	4,541,300	2,098,600	30	(45,000)	88	745,700	25
7	11	Capital Cities Comm./ABC (New York)	4,440,300	5,378,400	4	279,100	9	2,224,900	3
8	8	Electronic Data Systems (Dallas)[4]	4,323,800	2,957,900	23	323,100	8	1,053,500	14
9	13	ARA Holding (Philadelphia)[5]	4,019,000	1,656,400	36	21,600	59	157,000	71
10	5	Fluor (Irvine, Calif.)[6]	3,924,500	2,061,200	32	26,600**	56	531,700	37
11	15	Wetterau (Hazelwood, Mo.)[3]	3,842,200	682,800	66	35,000	46	208,900	64
12	16	Sysco (Houston)[7]	3,655,900	860,300	59	61,800	28	456,000	41
13	7	Alco Standard (Valley Forge, Pa.)[5]	3,616,500	1,324,300	42	80,200	25	604,300	29
14	17	Henley Group (La Jolla, Calif.)	3,516,000	4,698,000	6	(278,000)	97	3,364,000	1
15	21	Warner Communications (New York)	3,403,600	3,897,000	9	328,100	5	1,541,700	11
16	19	Bergen Brunswig (Orange, Calif.)[8]	3,376,000	785,000	61	15,900	62	188,700	66
17	20	National Medical Enterprises (Los Angeles)[9]	3,370,000¶	3,434,000	15	63,000‡	27	925,000	18
18	14	Halliburton (Dallas)	3,368,000	3,270,600	20	48,100	39	2,081,500	5
19	18	Dun & Bradstreet (New York)	3,359,200	3,316,800	19	393,000	3	1,663,800	9
20	28	Walt Disney (Burbank, Calif.)[5]	3,140,000	3,806,300	10	444,700	2	1,845,400	8
21	31	Gulf & Western (New York)[6,10]	2,903,600	4,928,900	5	356,100	4	2,106,600	4
22	24	Humana (Louisville, Ky.)[8]	2,831,800	3,208,800	21	182,800	11	1,012,000	15
23	22	Enserch (Dallas)	2,796,100	3,336,500	18	30,500	51	783,200	21
24	27	Turner (New York)	2,789,900	981,800	52	(22,300)	84	49,800	93
25	4	CBS (New York)	2,762,000	3,910,200	8	452,500	1	1,201,600	13

The definitions and concepts underlying the figures in this directory are explained below.
¶ Includes sales from discontinued operations of at least 10%.
** Reflects an extraordinary credit of at least 10%; see the explanations of "profits" and "earnings per share" below.
‡ Reflects an extraordinary charge of at least 10%; see the explanations of "profits" and "earnings per share" below.
§ Dividends paid on mandatory redeemable preferred stock subtracted from net income.
N.A. Not available.
[1] Net sales include all operating revenues and revenues from discontinued operations when they are published. All figures are for the fiscal year ending December 31, 1987, unless otherwise noted. Sales of subsidiaries are included when they are consolidated. All companies on the list must have derived more than 50% of their revenues from non-manufacturing and/or non-mining businesses. Excluded (but eligible for the lists that follow) are companies deriving more than 50% of their revenues solely from banking, life insurance, finance, retailing, transportation, or utilities.

DEFINITIONS AND EXPLANATIONS TO THE SERVICE COMPANIES

Assets are those shown at the company's fiscal year-end.

Profits are shown after taxes and after extraordinary credits or charges if any are shown on the income statement. A double asterisk (**) signifies an extraordinary credit reflecting at least 10% of the net income shown, a double dagger (‡) an extraordinary charge of at least 10%. Figures in parentheses indicate a loss. Cooperatives provide only "net margin" figures, which are not comparable, therefore N.A. is shown.

Stockholders' equity is the sum of capital stock, surplus, and retained earnings at the company's year-end. Redeemable preferred stock is excluded if its redemption is either mandatory or outside the control of the company, except in the case of cooperatives. For purposes of calculating "net income as percent of stockholders' equity," any dividends paid on redeemable preferred stock, if that stock's redemption is either mandatory or outside the control of the company, have

Employees Number	Employees Rank	Profits as Percent of Sales %	Sales Rank	Stockholders' Equity %	Equity Rank	Earnings per Share '87($)	'86($)	'77($)	Annual Growth Rate 1977–87 %	Growth Rank	Total Return to Investors 1987 %	1987 Rank	1977–87 Annual Average %	Average Rank
33,595	15	1.2	56	16.5	27	1.50	1.23	0.31	17.2	16	(25.7)	70	19.0	34
18,620	26	0.6	73	9.5	55	1.86‡	1.80	1.14	5.0	43	(18.5)	66	16.6	44
17,000	31	1.3	54	11.8	46	2.07	1.98	1.31	4.7	44	(13.4)	59	18.0	38
63,000	5	—		—		(0.71)	2.08	0.65	—		4.5	33	18.1	37
41,213	11	4.1	32	13.2	36	2.29	2.09	0.73	12.0	25	(19.4)	69	23.5	21
7,492	56	—		—		(2.46)	(4.50)	3.12	—		(12.8)	58	—	
20,120	24	6.3	22	12.5	41	16.46	27.55**	3.13	1.80	13	28.8	10	27.9	14
43,433	10	7.5	15	30.7	4	N.A.	N.A.	N.A.	—		—		—	
119,000	2	0.5	74	13.8§	32	N.A.	N.A.	N.A.	—		—		—	
14,351	42	0.7	67	5.0	69	0.33**	(0.76)	1.49	(14.0)	56	20.4	18	3.8	68
11,500	47	0.9	63	16.7	25	2.82	2.90	1.41	7.2	40	(10.0)	53	14.1	53
12,000	45	1.7	50	13.6	34	1.40	1.34	0.28	17.3	15	(8.7)	49	30.0	13
16,400	36	2.2	45	13.3	35	1.81	1.33	1.03	5.7	41	0.1	37	18.4	35
16,500	35	—		—		(2.87)	(5.33)	N.A.	—		(5.0)	44	—	
8,900	54	8.8	12	21.3	14	2.09	1.26	0.75	10.9	27	24.3	15	21.5	28
4,000	73	0.5	75	8.4	58	1.19	1.54	(0.03)	—		(0.9)	39	27.9	15
75,000	4	1.9	48	6.8	65	0.83‡	1.08‡	0.37	8.4	36	(13.9)	60	24.2	20
48,600	7	1.4	53	2.3	75	0.45	(4.85)	3.03	(17.4)	59	4.6	32	1.1	72
60,000	6	11.7	7	23.6	10	2.58	2.23	0.53	17.2	17	6.6	30	25.6	17
30,000	19	14.2	3	24.1	9	3.23	1.82	0.63	17.7	14	38.1	6	21.5	30
19,300	25	12.3	4	16.9	24	5.76	4.28**	2.32	9.5	34	13.9	25	27.2	16
46,500	8	6.5	18	18.1	21	1.86	0.56	0.16	27.8	4	4.2	34	31.4	10
16,500	34	1.1	59	3.9	71	0.27	0.17	1.77	(17.1)	58	11.9)	26	9.5	63
3,373	75	—		—		(5.09)	2.41	0.75	—		(17.1)	65	15.5	51
16,900	32	16.4	2	37.7	3	17.74	5.42	6.50	10.6	28	25.8	13	17.0	41

[2] Figures are for fiscal year ended February 29, 1988.
[3] Figures are for fiscal year ended March 31, 1987.
[4] Wholly owned by General Motors (No. 1 on the FORTUNE 500 Industrials list).
[5] Figure are for fiscal year ended September 30, 1987.
[6] Figures are for fiscal year ended October 31, 1987.
[7] Figures are for fiscal year ended June 30, 1987.
[8] Figures are for fiscal year ended August 31, 1987.
[9] Figures are for fiscal year ended May 31, 1987.
[10] Financial subsidiaries would add 25% or more to sales if consolidated.
Source: "Reprinted by permission from *FORTUNE Magazine,* © 1988 Time Inc. All rights reserved."

been subtracted from the net income figure.

Employees The figure shown is a year-end total except when it is followed by a dagger (†), in which case it is an average.

Earnings per Share For all companies the figures shown are the primary earnings per share that appear on the company's income statement. Per-share earnings for 1986 and 1977 are adjusted for stock splits and stock dividends. They are not restated for mergers, acquisitions, or accounting changes made after 1977. A double asterisk (**) signifies an extraordinary credit reflecting at least 10% of the net income shown, a double dagger (‡) an extraordinary charge of at least 10%. Figures in parentheses indicate a loss. Results are listed as not available (N.A.) if the companies are cooperatives, joint ventures, or wholly owned subsidiaries of other companies. The growth rate is the average annual growth, compounded. No growth rate is given if the company had a loss in either 1977 or 1987.

Total Return to Investors Total return to investors includes both price appreciation and dividend yield to an investor in the com-

The 25 Largest Life Insurance Companies (ranked by assets)

Rank 1987	Rank 1986	Company	Assets[1] ($000)	Premium and Annuity Income[2] ($000)	Rank	Net Investment Income ($000)	Rank
1	1	Prudential of America (Newark, N.J.)*	108,815,200	14,049,400	1	6,805,700	2
2	2	Metropolitan Life (New York)*	88,140,100	13,963,800	2	6,897,800	1
3	3	Equitable Life Assurance (New York)*	49,288,200	5,501,800	5	2,741,700	5
4	4	Aetna Life (Hartford)[7]	45,684,600	7,964,100	3	3,170,800	3
5	6	Teachers Insurance & Annuity (New York)	33,210,400	3,059,700	11	3,134,100	4
6	5	New York Life (New York)*	31,843,700	5,596,000	4	2,474,900	6
7	8	Travelers (Hartford)[8]	28,595,500	3,826,600	8	2,276,300	7
8	7	John Hancock Mutual Life (Boston)*	27,354,900	4,403,100	6	2,089,700	8
9	9	Connecticut General Life (Bloomfield)[9]	26,785,500	2,761,000	13	1,622,600	9
10	10	Northwestern Mutual Life (Milwaukee)*	22,602,900	3,626,300	9	1,554,500	10
11	11	Massachusetts Mutual Life (Springfield)*	19,879,300	2,509,800	15	1,482,500	12
12	12	Principal Mutual Life (Des Moines)*	19,027,700	3,985,500	7	1,518,400	11
13	14	Mutual of New York (New York)*	14,757,800	3,126,900	10	1,071,400	14
14	13	New England Mutual Life (Boston)*	14,204,300	2,703,700	14	1,018,700	15
15	15	Executive Life (Los Angeles)	11,400,300	1,077,000	37	1,134,800	13
16	16	Mutual Benefit Life (Newark)*	10,096,000	2,020,700	18	891,000	16
17	17	Connecticut Mutual Life (Hartford)*	9,932,300	2,131,400	16	683,400	19
18	19	IDS Life (Minneapolis)[10]	8,963,400	1,536,900	26	650,600	20
19	18	State Farm Life (Bloomington, Ill.)	8,453,500	1,348,700	29	739,700	18
20	20	Variable Annuity Life (Houston)	7,770,700	885,900	38	645,200	21
21	21	Nationwide Life (Columbus, Ohio)	7,299,000	1,133,600	36	428,100	27
22	25	New York Life & Annuity (Wilmington, Del.)	7,123,100	1,759,500	22	571,800	22
23	24	Pacific Mutual Life (Newport Beach, Calif.)*	6,981,400	1,627,200	23	502,000	23
24	22	Aetna Life & Annuity (Hartford)	6,612,700	1,244,000	32	364,700	30
25	29	Equitable Variable Life (New York)	6,606,200	1,835,200	20	448,600	26

Data for all companies are on the statutory accounting basis required by state insurance regulatory authorities.
* Indicates a mutual company.
[1] As of December 31, 1987.
[2] Includes premium income from life, accident, and health policies, annuities, and from contributions to deposit administration funds.
[3] After dividends to policyholders and federal income taxes, excluding capital gains and losses. Figures in parentheses indicate a loss.
[4] Face value of all life policies, including variable life insurance, as of December 31, 1987.

pany's stock. The figures shown assume sales at the end of 1987 of stock owned at the end of 1977 and 1986. It has been assumed that any proceeds from cash dividends, the sale of rights and warrant offerings, and stock received in spinoffs were reinvested when they were paid. Returns are adjusted for stock splits, stock dividends, recapitalizations, and corporate reorganizations as they occur; however, no effort has been made to reflect the cost of brokerage commissions or of taxes. Results are listed as not available (N.A.) if shares are not publicly traded or are traded on only a limited basis. If companies have more than one class of shares outstanding, only the more widely held and actively traded has been considered.

Total return percentages shown are the returns received by the hypothetical investor described above. The ten-year figures are annual averages, compounded.

Net Gain from Operations[3]			Life Insurance in Force[4]		Increase in Life Insurance in Force[5]				Employees[6]	
	Rank									
($000)	Mutual	Stock	($000)	Rank	($000)	Rank	Percent	Rank	Number	Rank
930,200	1		644,896,700	1	42,502,900	2	7.1	28	66,167	1
359,900	2		569,446,200	2	50,031,600	1	9.6	21	36,200	2
147,700	4		313,217,500	3	22,019,100	5	7.6	26	26,000	4
197,900		4	221,008,600	4	7,889,300	13	3.7	31	17,235	10
206,000		3	19,217,800	31	1,951,800	27	11.3	16	3,065	34
137,100	5		209,647,500	5	22,851,100	4	11.0	17	20,270	7
62,800		7	161,200	39	10,000	35	—		33,373	3
165,800	3		177,400	38	10,900	34	—		16,435	11
232,000		1	131,536,400	7	10,687,300	11	8.8	23	12,187	13
20,100	11		157,594,200	6	20,515,500	6	15.0	10	8,303	18
22,300	10		86,200	43	9,600	36	—		11,405	14
66,100	6		79,535,600	12	7,340,200	14	10.2	19	10,184	15
32,800	8		68,070,100	16	7,018,300	15	12.2	15	9,337	17
(73,500)	24		62,600	45	2,700	37	—		7,332	20
13,400		18	53,370,900	18	7,917,300	12	17.4	7	850	43
35,400	7		58,000	47	2,200	38	—		4,594	24
13,500	14		51,645,600	19	3,906,700	20	8.2	24	23,198	5
46,400		11	18,746,100	32	2,823,500	22	15.2	9	6,626	21
99,700		6	119,968,400	8	14,004,200	10	13.2	12	18,698	8
21,000		14	2,900	49	(.300)	41	—		1,309	40
15,800		16	20,741,900	30	1,506,900	28	8.0	25	6,548	22
(42,500)		23	43,973,800	20	4,838,500	18	12.4	14	20,270	6
9,700	16		32,790,300	22	2,094,200	26	6.8	29	3,105	33
(42,700)		24	25,233,100	26	2,966,100	21	13.3	11	3,472	30
(17,200)		26	73,069,300	13	16,250,000	9	28,6	4	N.A.	

[5] Change between December 31, 1986, and December 31, 1987.
[6] Includes home office, field force, and full-time agents.
[7] Wholly owned by Aetna Life & Casualty (No. 4 on Diversified Financial list).
[8] Wholly owned by Travelers Corp. (No. 7 on Diversified Financial list).
[9] Wholly owned by CIGNA (No. 6 on Diversified Financial list).
[10] Wholly owned by American Express (No. 1 on the Diversified Financial list).

Source: "Reprinted by permission from *FORTUNE Magazine,*

The 25 Largest Commercial Banking Companies (ranked by assets)

Rank '87	Rank '86	Company	Assets[1] ($000)	Deposits ($000)	Deposits Rank	Loans[2] ($000)	Loans Rank	Profits ($000)	Profits Rank
1	1	Citicorp (New York)	203,607,000	119,561,000	1	133,467,000	1	(1,138,000)	99
2	3	Chase Manhattan Corp. (New York)	99,133,400	68,578,000	3	65,260,000	2	(894,800)	96
3	2	BankAmerica Corp. (San Francisco)	92,833,000	76,290,000	2	61,245,000	3	(955,000)	97
4	7	Chemical New York Corp. (New York)[5]	78,189,000	55,509,000	4	47,732,000	6	(853,700)‡	94
5	4	J. P. Morgan & Co. (New York)	75,414,000	43,987,000	7	28,923,000	9	83,300	22
6	6	Security Pacific Corp. (Los Angeles)	73,356,000	45,551,000	5	49,940,000	5	15,700	66
7	5	Manufacturers Hanover Corp (New York)	73,348,100	45,176,400	6	52,964,900	4	(1,140,200)	100
8	8	Bankers Trust New York Corp. (New York)	56,520,600	30,220,400	11	24,886,000	11	1,200‡	72
9	9	First Interstate Bancorp (Los Angeles)	50,926,600	37,569,700	8	31,556,700	8	(556,200)	90
10	11	First Chicago Corp. (Chicago)	44,209,300	31,537,700	10	26,464,600	10	(570,700)	91
11	10	Wells Fargo & Co. (San Francisco)	44,183,300	32,319,800	9	35,433,900	7	50,800	41
12	13	Bank of Boston Corp. (Boston)	34,116,600	22,471,600	15	24,024,300	12	19,700	63
13	26	First RepublicBank Corp. (Dallas)[6]	33,210,700	25,490,600	12	22,848,900	13	(656,800)	93
14	14	Continental Illinois Corp. (Chicago)	32,391,000	19,624,000	20	18,940,000	17	(609,500)	92
15	22	PNC Financial Corp. (Pittsburgh)	31,432,600	20,347,700	18	16,647,400	23	204,800	5
16	12	Mellon Bank Corp. (Pittsburgh)	30,525,000	21,548,000	16	19,069,000	16	(863,000)	95
17	21	Bank of New England Corp. (Boston)	29,474,800	22,767,400	13	21,578,200	14	140,500	15
18	16	NCNB Corp. (Charlotte, N.C.)	28,915,400	19,550,000	21	17,086,800	20	166,900	8
19	34	First Fidelity Bankcorp. (Newark, N.J.)[7]	28,850,300	20,938,000	17	17,402,000	19	86,300	21
20	17	First Union Corp. (Charlotte, N.C.)	27,629,500	17,425,300	23	15,125,100	25	283,100	1
21	18	Suntrust Banks (Atlanta)	27,187,900	22,493,300	14	18,120,100	18	282,800	2
22	15	First Bank System (Minneapolis)	26,850,000	15,799,000	29	12,888,000	30	49,600	42
23	48	Shawmut National Corp. (Boston)[8]	26,477,000	17,247,000	25	17,055,000	21	158,900	12
24	19	Marine Midland Banks (Buffalo and New York)	25,453,300	17,303,200	24	20,119,400	15	(408,800)	89
25	20	Irving Bank Corp (New York)	23,534,000	15,152,000	30	14,427,000	26	(193,300)	86

‡ Reflects an extraordinary charge of at least 10%; see the explanations of "profits" and "earnings per share" on pages 212–213.

** Reflects an extraordinary credit of at least 10%; see the explanations of "profits" and "earnings per share" on pages 212–213.

[1] As of December 31, 1987. All companies on the list must have more than 80% of their assets in chartered commercial banking institutions.

[2] Net of unearned discount and loan loss reserve. Figure includes lease financing.

[3] Figure is for Pittsburgh National.

[4] Figure is for CBT.

Stockholders' Equity ($000)	Rank	Employees Number	Rank	Net Profit as Percent of Equity %	Rank	Earnings per Share '87($)	'86($)	'77($)	Annual Growth Rate: 1977–87 %	Rank	Total Return to Investors 1987 %	Rank	1977–87 Annual Average %	Rank
8,810,000	1	90,000	1	—		(4.26)	3.57	1.49	—		(26.1)	71	10.9	74
3,852,300	3	42,390	4	—		(11.56)	6.63	1.91	—		(34.0)	80	11.3	72
3,259,000	5	65,151	2	—		(6.43)	(3.74)	2.72	—		(53.0)	88	(6.7)	83
3,003,000	6	28,597	7	—		(16.68)‡	7.57	3.03	—		(46.0)	85	9.0	76
5,036,000	2	15,731	15	1.7	67	0.39	4.74	1.33	(11.5)	61	(9.4)	41	18.7	44
3,368,000	4	43,260	3	0.5	71	0.01	4.86	1.63	(39.9)	69	(23.2)	67	15.5	57
2,704,100	8	29,125	6	—		(27.04)	7.99	5.15	—		(48.3)	86	3.6	81
2,899,100	7	12,292	27	0.0	74	0.02‡	6.01	1.26	(33.9)	68	(27.1)	73	20.5	32
2,165,700	10	36,253	5	—		(11.99)	7.19	3.29	—		(20.4)	62	11.9	69
1,801,800	12	15,108	17	—		(10.71)	4.70	2.88	—		(30.7)	77	6.4	79
2,247,600	9	20,100	10	2.3	66	0.52	5.03	2.01	(12.7)	62	(12.5)	47	18.6	46
1,748,000	14	20,200	9	1.1	70	0.10	3.69	0.85	(19.2)	65	(12.3)	46	22.1	16
1,157,500	31	15,239	16	—		(22.31)	1.65	3.46	—		(79.1)	91	(10.0)	84
1,364,000	22	9,624	34	—		(6.07)	0.60	4.02	—		(42.2)	84	(15.9)	88
1,840,600	11	11,814	28	11.1	38	2.96	4.44	1.25[2]	9.0	29	(6.5)	33	21.7	21
1,078,000	33	16,650	14	—		(31.17)	6.20	3.57	—		(49.2)	87	6.6	78
1,461,200	20	18,752	12	9.6	46	2.04	3.52	1.02[3]	7.2	39	(12.7)	48	21.3	23
1,510,200	17	12,334	26	11.0	41	2.03	2.53	0.70	11.2	21	(16.7)	58	16.8	53
1,585,400	16	13,900	21	5.4	59	1.23	3.95	1.33	(0.8)	55	(0.3)	16	14.4	55
1,794,400	13	20,284	8	15.8	5	2.55	2.53	0.53	16.9	5	(16.4)	57	21.9	18
1,673,700	15	20,047	11	16.9	2	2.17	1.86	0.47[4]	16.6	6	(6.2)	32	19.0	43
1,397,000	21	9,400	35	3.6	63	0.73	3.42	1.20	(4.9)	58	(11.9)	45	15.0	59
1,463,000	19	15,000	18	10.9	43	2.10	5.07	1.75**	1.8	52	(18.4)	59	21.0	25
981,900	35	13,900	20	—		N.A.	7.19	1.58	—		—		—	
827,000	40	10,400	32	—		(10.83)	6.83	2.58	—		(0.6)	17	19.4	40

[5] Figures reflect merger with Texas Commerce Banshares (No. 29 among last year's Commercial Banks) May 1, 1987.

[6] Formed by the merger of RepublicBank Corp. (No. 26 among last year's Commercial Banks) and Interfirst Corp. (No. 32 last year) June 8, 1987.

[7] Formed by the merger of Fidelcor (No. 43 among last year's Commercial Banks) and first Fidelity Bancorp. (No. 34 last year) February 29, 1988.

[8] Figures reflect acquisition of Hartford National Corp. (No. 38 among last year's Commercial Banks) February 29, 1988.

Source: "Reprinted by permission from *FORTUNE Magazine;* © 1988 Time Inc. All rights reserved."

The 50 Largest International Banks*

The top 50 bank holding companies in the world are listed according to the size of their assets. Also shown are each bank's total deposits and its respective ranking (in parentheses) as well as the total capital and pretax earnings, along with its ranking (in parentheses) in those categories. For any bank to be ranked in deposits, capital or earnings, the bank must first be among the top 50 in assets. Those cases where bank figures were not available or could not be confirmed for accuracy are indicated by dashes.**

Rank 1986	Rank 1987	Name of Bank	Assets (US$ millions) 1987	Assets (US$ millions) 1986	Deposits (US$ millions) 1987	Capital (US$ millions) 1987	Pretax Earnings (US$ millions) 1987
1	1	Dai-Ichi Kangyo Bank[1] Japan	$270,675	$192,380	$212,013(1)	$4,844(18)	$1,373(2)
4	2	Sumitomo Bank[1] Japan	250,483	164,892	194,973(2)	5,634(9)	877(16)
3	3	Fuji Bank[1,2] Japan	243,974	170,320	187,871(3)	5,507(10)	1,437(1)
7	4	Mitsubishi Bank[1] Japan	227,444	155,173	178,452(5)	5,191(14)	1,336(3)
9	5	Sanwa Bank[1] Japan	224,427	151,298	175,602(6)	4,697(20)	1,233(5)
6	6	Industrial Bank of Japan[2,3] Japan	215,323	161,604	183,064(4)	5,225(13)	780(22)
8	7	Credit Agricole[2,4] France	214,382	155,128	142,506(10)	8,741(3)	853(17)
2	8	Citicorp United States	198,388	191,355	119,561(20)	8,810(2)	−240(176)
5	9	Norinchukin Bank[2,3,4] Japan	186,290	162,343	170,876(7)	852(152)	—
10	10	Banque Nationale de Paris France	182,675	142,533	149,847(8)	5,379(12)	852(18)
11	11	Deutsche Bank West Germany	168,904	131,862	101,833(27)	6,860(6)	1,030(7)
12	12	Credit Lyonnais France	168,344	130,318	141,747(12)	4,601(21)	918(11)
13	13	Mitsubishi Trust and Banking Corp.[2,3,4] Japan	165,868	127,364	141,911(11)	3,883(28)	1,109(6)
15	14	Barclays United Kingdom	165,564	116,596	137,850(13)	7,767(4)	639(32)
14	15	National Westminster Bank United Kingdom	164,133	123,054	144,004(9)	9,236(1)	1,328(4)
21	16	Tokai Bank[1] Japan	161,698	110,827	129,056(14)	3,282(37)	694(26)

22	17	Mitsui Bank[1,2,4] Japan	154,071	106,592	120,620(19)	3,128(43)	928(10)
17	18	Mitsui Trust & Banking Co.[2,3] Japan	145,484	116,048	127,778(16)	3,025(44)	421(51)
20	19	Societe Generale France	144,951	111 126	125,430(17)	4,109(26)	701(24)
27	20	Sumitomo Trust & Banking Co.[1,2,4] Japan	144,623	99,200	128,187(15)	3,168(41)	945(9)
18	21	Long-Term Credit Bank of Japan[2,3,4] Japan	138,768	115,521	117,119(21)	3,284(35)	663(30)
16	22	Taiyo Kobe Bank[2,3,4] Japan	138,474	116,507	109,699(23)	2,309(59)	579(36)
19	23	Bank of Tokyo[3] Japan	136,378	111,988	109,149(25)	4,265(24)	675(29)
26	24	Dresdner Bank West Germany	130,463	101,227	122,357(18)	4,232(25)	622(34)
25	25	Yasuda Trust & Banking Co.[2,3,4] Japan	128,698	101,335	109,814(22)	2,592(52)	679(28)
23	26	Dawiwa Bank[2,3,4] Japan	126,104	102,828	109,546(24)	2,266(60)	474(45)
28	27	Union Bank of Switzerland[2,4] Switzerland	123,189	93,757	105,536(26)	7,497(5)	836(19)
29	28	Compagnie Financiere de Paribas France	122,275	93,180	74,933(42)	5,875(8)	894(12)
32	29	Swiss Bank Corp.[2] Switzerland	112,454	84,922	98,774(28)	6,739(7)	710(23)
33	30	Toyo Trust and Banking Co.[2,3,4] Japan	109,062	81,834	96,211(30)	1,991(70)	577(37)
31	31	Hongkong & Shanghai Banking Corp. Hongkong	105,902	90,735	95,818(31)	4,281(23)	—
37	32	Commerzbank West Germany	101,236	75,461	97,067(29)	3,172(40)	472(47)
30	33	Chase Manhattan Corp. United States	97,165	92,147	68,578(48)	3,852(30)	882(15)
36	34	Westdeutsche Landesbank West Germany	96,147	76,275	89,212(32)	2,568(53)	178(109)
40	35	Bayerische Vereinsbank West Germany	94,541	72,155	88,948(33)	2,237(64)	396(55)
35	36	Nippon Credit Bank[2,3,4] Japan	92,830	78,256	77,561(35)	1,713(85)	335(65)
44	37	Banca Nazionale de Lavoro Italy	92,374	70,704	81,227(34)	2,974(46)	198(100)
34	38	Midland Bank United Kingdom	91,377	78,520	75,234(41)	4,877(17)	964(8)
24	39	BankAmerica Corp. United States	90,896	102,204	76,290(39)	3,259(38)	−869(186)

Continued

The 50 Largest International Banks *(concluded)*

Rank 1986	Rank 1987	Name of Bank	Assets (US$ millions) 1987	Assets (US$ millions) 1986	Deposits (US$ millions) 1987	Capital (US$ millions) 1987	Pretax Earnings (US$ millions) 1987
41	40	Kyowa Bank[2,3,4] Japan	86,959	71,633	69,673(47)	1,948(71)	483(42)
48	41	Algemene Bank Nederland Netherlands	84,731	66,945	70,880(46)	3,283(36)	413(52)
45	42	Lloyds Bank United Kingdom	84,700	70,634	76,549(38)	4,513(22)	−468(179)
42	43	Shoko Chukin Bank[2,4,5] Japan	83,581	71,538	77,108(36)	1,787(79)	86(138)
52	44	Bayerische Landesbank[2] West Germany	83,036	62,594	71,707(45)	1,812(73)	442(49)
49	45	Credit Suisse Switzerland	82,492	63,919	73,372(44)	5,087(15)	573(38)
50	46	Rabobank Nederland Netherlands	81,743	63,762	77,034(37)	4,735(19)	567(39)
51	47	Amsterdam-Rotterdam Bank Netherlands	80,287	62,986	74,399(43)	2,868(49)	375(56)
58	48	Deutsche Genossenschaftsbank West Germany	80,117	57,466	48,235(65)	1,722(84)	297(70)
53	49	Hypo Banks[2] West Germany	79,800	61,997	76,014(40)	2,410(56)	403(54)
47	50	Banco do Brasil[2,4] Brazil	78,992	67,383	27,486(102)	5,398(11)	886(14)

* In order to compile the global banking rankings, *Institutional Investor* first asked more than 500 of the world's leading bank holding companies to report their assets, deposits, capital and pretax earnings in local currencies as of year-end 1986 and year-end 1987. Banks that reported figures for fiscal years are noted in the tables. For the sake of comparability, we then converted the local currencies into U.S. dollars at year-end rates for banks on calendar years. For those not on calendar years, the conversion rates used are those prevailing at the end of each bank's fiscal year. The conversion figures were provided by the money desk of a major U.S. bank.

It should be noted that the banks were asked to report consolidated figures for all other banks in which they have an interest of 50 percent or more. Those that chose not to provide consolidated figures are noted. The banks were also asked if their figures included recent mergers and acquisitions; those that said they did not are also noted. Figures reflect consolidated bank holding company interests only; industrial and other nonbank holdings are not included.

Banks were asked to report their figures published in these tables using the following definitions:

Total assets exclude contra accounts where contra accounts are defined as acceptances, bonds or other securities held for customers; letters of credit; guarantees; and similar instruments.

Capital includes funds supplied by shareholders, such as permanent preferred stock, share capital, retained earnings or undistributed profits and contingent type reserves. It excludes reserves for possible loan losses, subordinated debt and redeemable preferred stock.

Pretax earnings include earnings before taxes and extraordinary items.

** The table reproduced here includes only the top 50 of the top 200 banks in assets listed in the *Institutional Investor.*

1 As of March 31, 1987, 1986.

2 Figures do not include all subsidiaries owned 50 percent or more.

3 As of September 31, 1087, 1986.

4 Not adjusted for all mergers and acquisitions.

5 Asset and deposits as of September 30, 1987, 1986; capital and earnings as of March 31, 1987, 1986.

Source: *Institutional Investor,* June 1988.

The 100 Largest Brokerage Houses*

Rank 1987	Rank 1988	Name of Firm	Total Broker-Dealer Capital ($ millions)	Equity Capital ($ millions)	Subordinated Debt ($ millions)	"Excess" Net Capital ($ millions)
2	1	Shearson Lehman Brothers[1]	$4,071.2	$2,136.5	$1,934.7	$ 812.4
1	2	Salomon Brothers	3,133.2	2,029.1	1,104.1	1,190.2
3	3	Merrill Lynch, Pierce, Fenner & Smith	2,903.8	2,103.8	800.0	646.2
4	4	Goldman, Sachs & Co.[2]	2,402.0[3]	1,656.0	746.0	1,107.0
5	5	Drexel Burnham Lambert	1,740.0	1,218.0	522.0	987.0
8	6	Dean Witter Reynolds	1,344.0	761.0	583.0	418.0
13	7	Paine Webber	1,321.0	821.0	500.0	741.0
9	8	Bear, Stearns & Co.	1,320.5	934.0	386.5	579.7
7	9	Prudential-Bache Securities	1,263.6	953.0	310.6	246.1
—	10	First Boston Corp.	1,183.8	730.8	453.0	666.1
10	11	E. F. Hutton & Co.	1,114.0	661.0	453.0	243.0
11	12	Morgan Stanley & Co.	1,096.8	696.8	400.0	394.0
16	13	Smith Barney, Harris Upham & Co.	952.0	770.0	182.0	147.0
12	14	Donaldson, Lufkin & Jenrette Securities Corp.	849.0	239.0	610.0	157.0
14	15	Kidder, Peabody & Co.	676.0[4]	339.0	337.0	283.0
18	16	Allen & Co.	376.8	376.8	—	—
31	17	Charles Schwab & Co.	359.0	276.0	83.0	94.0
19	18	Thomson McKinnon Securities	305.0	200.0	105.0	105.2
17	19	Shelby Cullom Davis & Co.	299.4	299.4	—	201.0
24	20	Oppenheimer & Co.	247.0	163.0	84.0	99.5
23	21	A. G. Edwards & Sons	243.0	243.0	—	111.0
21	22	Van Kampen Merritt	241.0	241.0	—	59.0
22	23	Spear, Leeds & Kellogg	238.0	166.0	72.0	77.0
25	24	Dillon, Read & Co.	223.5	174.3	49.2	64.3
30	25	Nomura Securities International	222.7	122.7	100.0	94.9
20	26	L. F. Rothschild & Co.	219.7	104.5	115.2	37.2
26	27	John Nuveen & Co.	193.5	193.5	—	119.7
27	28	UBS Securities	189.0	14.0	175.0	142.0
41	29	Gruntal & Co.	160.3	118.8	41.5	44.2
36	30	Wetheim Schroder & Co.	140.1	109.7	30.4	70.1
37	31	Alex. Brown & Sons	137.0	117.0	20.0	73.0
32	32	Cowen & Co.	119.5	101.7	17.8	62.3
34	33	Jefferies & Co.	118.2	88.2	30.0	70.6
—	34	SBCI Swiss Bank Corp. Investment Banking	115.0	75.0	40.0	95.3
33	35	Daiwa Securities America	114.0	114.0	—	25.0
29	36	Neuberger & Berman	108.6	108.6	—	74.4
39	37	Prescott, Ball & Turben	108.0	98.0	10.0	16.7
28	38	Allen & Co. Inc.	104.1	100.6	3.5	20.4
57	39	Yamaichi International (America)	103.0	103.0	—	55.7
15	40	Stephens	102.9	102.9	—	78.5
51	41	Lazard Freres & Co.	100.0	100.0	—	77.4
43	42	Edward D. Jones & Co.	99.0	67.0	32.0	62.0
42	43	Brown Brothers Harriman & Co.	95.2	95.2	—	—
35	44	Nikko Securities Co. International	94.1	44.1	50.0	35.0
45	45	Fidelity Brokerage Services	92.3	92.3	—	24.1
47	46	Janney Montgomery Scott	83.0	83.0	—	32.9
—	47	S. G. Warburg Securities	81.0	81.0	—	54.3
40	48	M. A. Schapiro & Co.	78.5	78.5	—	56.1
48	49	Advest	78.0	78.0	—	17.0
45	50	Gruss Partners	77.1	77.1	—	65.8
49	51	Mabon, Nugent & Co.	76.1	76.1	—	32.1
58	52	Blunt Ellis & Loewi	75.0	37.5	37.5	17.8
—	53	Weiss, Peck & Greer	73.0	58.0	15.0	29.0
50	54	Interstate Securities Corp.	71.5	49.0	22.5	27.6
53	55	bateman Eichler, Hill Richards	68.0	51.0	17.0	18.0
44	56	Glickenhaus & Co.	64.4	64.4	—	20.4
60	57	McDonald & Co. Securities	64.1	64.1	—	31.1
56	58	Keefe, Bruyette & Woods	64.0	53.6	10.4	47.6

Continued

The 100 Largest Brokerage Houses *(concluded)*

Rank 1987	Rank 1988	Name of Firm	Total Broker-Dealer Capital ($ millions)	Equity Capital ($ millions)	Subordinated Debt ($ millions)	Excess Net Capital ($ millions)
61	59	Ryan, Beck & Co.	62.9	62.9	—	52.8
67	60	Arnhold & S. Bleichroeder	62.0	59.0	3.0	42.0
62	61	Piper, Jaffray & Hopwood	60.0	60.0	—	18.0
—	62	Legg Mason Wood Walker	59.3	45.4	13.9	22.2
65	63	Tucker, Anthony & R. L. Day	57.0	54.0	3.0	23.5
59	64	J. C. Bradford & Co.	55.6	55.6	—	23.1
63	65	Kaufmann, Alsberg & Co.	54.9[5]	54.9	—	19.0
54	66	S. D. Securities	54.2	54.2	—	30.7
70	67	Furman Seiz Mager Dietz & Birney	54.0	44.0	10.0	30.7
86		Herzog, Heine, Geduld	54.0	30.0	24.0	38.0
64		Ziegler Co.	54.0	54.0	—	29.4
73	70	McMahan & Co.	53.9	21.4	32.5	16.1
68	71	Dain Bosworth	53.0	53.0	—	19.0
77		Morgan Keegan & Co.	53.0	53.0	—	27.0
69	73	William Blair & Co.	50.0	50.0	—	29.4
74	74	Robert W. Baird & Co.	43.0	43.0	—	18.0
80	75	Bernard L. Madoff	41.8	41.8	—	32.4
71	76	Ohio Co.	41.6	41.6	—	17.0
—	77	ABD Securities Corp.	40.0	40.0	—	24.4
72	78	Montgomery Securities	39.5	32.0	7.5	25.3
78	79	Eppler, Guerin & Turner	39.3	39.3	—	29.3
79	80	Carl Marks & Co.	37.5	34.5	3.0	16.5
87	81	Rauscher Pierce Refsnes	37.1	32.9	4.2	11.3
75	82	Easton & Co.	36.0	35.4	0.6	29.5
98	83	Howard, Weil, Labouisse, Friedrichs	35.6	35.6	—	9.8
85	84	Hambrecht & Quist	35.4[5]	35.4	—	11.2
—	85	Quick & Reilly	35.3	35.3	—	30.1
82	86	Crowell, Weedon & Co.	35.1	35.1	—	10.7
84		Raymond, James & Assocates	35.1	35.1	—	12.8
89	88	Wedbush Securities	31.7	31.1	0.6	20.8
91	89	Wheat, First Securities	31.6	29.1	2.5	10.2
—	90	Eaton Vance Distributors	31.0	31.0	—	3.7
83		MKI Securities Corp.	31.0	20.0	11.0	14.0
96	92	J. J. B. Hilliard, W. L. Lyons	30.9	27.8	3.1	14.0
99	93	Chicago Corp.	30.8	24.4	6.4	15.6
81	94	Rothschild	29.0	20.0	9.0	11.0
—	95	Eberstadt Fleming	28.8	28.8	—	9.9
88		Johnson, Lane, Space, Smith & Co.	28.8	20.2	8.6	14.4
93	97	Ernst & Co.	27.2	24.2	3.0	8.1
—	98	C. J. Lawrence, Morgan Grenfell	27.0[6]	24.0	3.0	24.0
66	99	Moseley Securities Corp.	26.5	9.5	17.0	4.7
—	100	Asiel & Co.	26.1	26.1	—	18.5

[1] Now Shearson Lehman Hutton.

[2] The Goldman, Sachs & Co. entry is not exactly comparable with others because of the way the firm is structured. Its broker-dealer operation is the umbrella organization that includes the subsidiaries (and their capital). In other firms, the broker-dealer operation is normally just one of the subsidiaries under the parent company.

[3] As of 11/27/87. [4] As of 12/28/87. [5] As of 9/30/87. [6] As of 12/30/87.

Source: Ranking America's Biggest Brokers, *Institutional Investor,* April 1988.

America's Most and Least Admired Corporations*

AT THE TOP AND BOTTOM OF THE 306 COMPANIES

RANK	COMPANY	SCORE	RANK	COMPANY	SCORE
1	**Merck** Pharmaceuticals	9.00	306	**Financial Corp. of Amer.** Savings institutions	2.62
2	**Rubbermaid** Rubber products	8.29	305	**American Motors** Motor vehicles and parts	3.05
3	**Dow Jones** Publishing, printing	8.24	304	**BankAmerica** Commercial banking	3.21
4	**Procter & Gamble** Soaps, cosmetics	8.15	303	**LTV** Metals	3.24
5	**Liz Claiborne** Apparel	8.14	302	**Bethlehem Steel** Metals	3.69
6	**3M** Scientific/photographic equip.	8.10	301	**Texas Air** Transportation	4.00
7	**Philip Morris** Tobacco	8.07	300	**Manville** Glass, building materials	4.14
8	**J.P. Morgan & Co.** Commercial banking	8.03	299	**Kaiser Alum. & Chem.** Metals	4.19
9	**RJR Nabisco** Tobacco	7.90	298	**Control Data** Computers (and office equip.)	4.32
10	**Wal-Mart Stores** Retailing	7.90	297	**Coleco Industries** Toys, sporting goods	4.34

The most admired
An old friend is missing—IBM. For the first time it is out of the top ten. RJR Nabisco and Wal-Mart, both newcomers to the list, tied for ninth place.

The least admired
Perception may not square with reality in the case of Control Data and Bethelehem, but the other cellar dwellers have good reason for being in the dark.

Source: Ellen Schultz, *Fortune*,

* HOW IT WAS DONE. FORTUNE polled more than 8,000 top executives, outside directors, and financial analysts for the sixth annual Corporate Reputations Survey. They were asked to rate the ten largest companies in their own industry—analysts ranked concerns in the industry they follow—on eight key attributes: quality of management, quality of products or services, innovativeness, long-term investment value, financial soundness, community and environmental responsibility, use of corporate assets, and ability to attract, develop, and keep talented people. Ratings are on a scale of 0 (poor) to 10 (excellent). Some 3,480 people responded to the survey, and 90% of the returns were in hand before the stock market crashed on October 19.

The survey covers companies that appear in the annual FORTUNE 500 and FORTUNE Service 500 directories. Companies are assigned to one of 33 industries according to the business that contributed most to their 1986 sales (or, in the case of financial companies, the largest share of their assets). Some industries have fewer than ten companies, but to appear in the survey an industry group had to have at least four. A total of 306 companies were included in the survey.

America's Top 100 Growth Companies

Rank	COMPANY	Sales: 5 Year Annual % Growth	Sales: Latest 12-Month (mil.)	EPS: 5-Year Annual % Growth	EPS: Latest 12-Month	Return[1] on Equity	Debt/ Equity	Book Value/ Share	Recent Price	P/E
1	Reebok Int'l	239%	$1,561.4	157%	$ 1.55	68%	0%	$ 2.64	$ 16⅝	10.7
2	Autodesk	152	87.8	135	1.01	28	0	4.82	29	28.7
3	Wyse Technology	139	456.6	89	1.89	23	93	6.33	20½	10.8
4	TCBY Enterprises	134	81.0	95	0.56	30	18	1.42	12	21.4
5	Neeco	132	111.7	99	1.08	15	0	6.51	13½	12.5
6	Maxtor	126	271.2	118	0.72	29	104	5.33	11¾	16.3
7	Addington Resources	125	177.6	80	2.38	32	85	8.84	24	10.1
8	Sigma Designs	118	50.6	113	1.25	45	0	2.17	21	16.8
9	Informix	117	54.3	89	0.71	20	0	3.86	23¾	33.5
10	3 Com	115	252.0	100	0.79	17	2	4.49	19⅝	24.8
11	Consolidated Stores	114	600.9	37	0.28	11	43	2.84	5⅜	19.2
12	Envirodyne Inds	112	487.8	100	2.32	37	105	7.07	31⅞	13.7
13	CUC Int'l	111	212.1	82	1.01	19	14	5.83	25¼	25.0
14	Acuson	110	119.8	278	0.84	27	0	3.14	28¼	33.6
15	Ben & Jerry's Homemade	108	34.9	76	0.63	14	31	3.01	15¾	25.0
16	LA Gear	106	130.9	181	2.55	19	0	4.38	32⅜	12.7
17	Best Buy	106	439.0	71	0.34	22	11	6.78	7¾	22.8
18	Cinplex Odeon	105	542.1	65	0.82	12	137	6.94	9⅞	12.0
19	Tech Data	104	173.9	100	1.09	32	9	2.27	16	14.7
20	EMC Corp	103	140.7	122	0.99	30	5	5.25	6¾	6.8
21	Jepson	102	559.6	81	0.89	39	103	3.41	7	7.9
22	Mestek	101	140.1	99	0.72	26	32	3.40	5⅞	8.2
23	Mentor Graphics	96	238.9	41	1.35	12	0	11.40	35	25.9
24	Tempest Technologies	94	26.2	105	0.61	77	0	0.65	5⅛	8.4
25	V Band	93	51.8	94	1.37	29	0	3.80	15	10.9
26	Patten	91	116.4	73	0.79	37	115	2.13	5⅜	6.8
27	Impact Systems	89	30.3	122	0.27	12	2	1.14	4⅛	15.3
28	PAM Transport Svcs	88	73.3	45	0.25	25	67	4.00	3½	14.0
29	AMRE	87	138.9	128	0.83	35	1	2.03	20⅛	24.3
30	Integrated Device Tech	86	121.1	38	0.46	4	20	2.99	15½	33.7
31	Golden Valley Micro	85	113.1	NM	1.14	38	2	3.65	26⅜	23.1
32	Terex	81	225.2	96	1.98	20	0	1.19	16	8.1
33	Stratus Computer	81	201.0	65	1.07	22	6	5.34	28⅝	26.8
34	LyphoMed	80	176.5	60	0.66	15	70	4.94	10¾	16.3
35	Adaptec	79	58.8	66	0.50	27	0	4.19	5⅝	11.3
36	JWP	78	682.5	43	1.91	22	130	9.37	23¼	12.2
37	Groundwater Tech.	77	66.1	76	0.80	49	46	0.54	19	23.8
38	Westwood One	77	99.3	51	0.73	13	134	5.19	12⅝	17.3

39	Tekelec	77	20.1	26	0.45	17	0	3.80	18	40.0
40	Iverson Technology	75	52.3	83	1.14	28	95	4.68	15½	13.6
41	Advanced marketing Svc	74	110.0	91	0.76	73	9	0.61	15¼	20.1
42	Ryan's Family Stk Houses	72	165.3	58	0.33	22	0	1.64	5⅜	16.3
43	Sbarro	72	100.1	57	0.92	18	1	4.40	19¼	20.9
44	Eaton Financial	72	59.6	16	0.54	8	69	7.23	8	14.8
45	Interactive Technol	71	24.2	56	0.61	21	0	2.95	12¼	20.1
46	Jan Bell Marketing	70	79.3	77	0.81	31	0	3.54	21⅝	26.7
47	Computer Assoc Int'l	69	709.1	47	1.29	26	48	2.79	29	22.5
48	Durakon Inds	68	117.1	46	0.94	19	28	4.77	13½	14.4
49	Beauticontrol Costmetics	66	28.4	55	0.73	14	0	3.95	14½	19.9
50	Getty Petroleum	65	1,287.2	116	1.92	20	118	7.48	17⅞	9.3
51	VM Software	65	32.3	39	0.51	28	0	3.35	16½	32.4
52	Carolco Pictures	64	97.6	11	0.43	19	105	2.40	7½	17.4
53	Compaq Computer	63	1,452.6	93	4.24	47	37	11.69	65	15.3
54	Larizza Inds	63	106.4	75	0.66	79	81	1.89	14⅛	21.4
55	Federal Inds	63	1,713.8	56	1.70	13	74	13.28	13⅝	8.1
56	Actmedia	63	97.6	46	0.37	12	0	3.60	14½	39.2
57	Ashton-Tate	62	279.5	65	1.77	29	3	7.23	26	14.7
58	Cascades	62	549.7	32	0.47	15	105	3.27	5¼	11.1
59	Teleconnect	62	167.9	20	0.90	25	58	3.66	15	16.7
60	Riedel Environ tech	61	56.7	103	0.57	15	6	4.30	13⅜	23.5
61	CCX Network	61	56.4	31	0.82	14	71	4.16	15¾	19.2
62	Vanguard Technology	60	60.6	58	0.91	32	2	3.46	18¾	20.6
63	Genco Inds	60	47.8	32	0.33	1	116	6.05	7	21.2
64	Expeditors Int'l	59	147.8	42	1.06	25	9	4.90	17	16.0
65	Home Depot	59	1,566.3	39	1.22	22	16	6.52	28⅞	23.7
66	Capital Cities/ABC	59	4,769.9	15	19.19	13	76	137.40	317⅛	17.5
67	Valcom	58	178.5	103	0.96	14	2	3.94	9¾	10.2
68	Michaels Stores	58	185.6	88	0.49	16	139	3.48	5⅝	11.5
69	Flextronics	57	146.4	48	0.59	16	74	2.07	6¾	11.4
70	Trans World Music	56	196.8	83	1.23	39	16	2.95	23	18.7
71	Sage Software	56	14.6	55	0.30	14	0	4.27	6½	21.7
72	Quicksilver	54	40.8	90	0.51	40	0	1.76	5⅝	11.0
73	Group 1 Software	54	12.9	64	0.63	40	1	1.43	10½	16.7
74	First Financial Mngmt	54	233.7	42	1.25	9	9	13.84	29¼	23.4
75	Video Display	53	25.4	55	0.54	27	115	1.79	8½	15.7
76	Atlantic Southeast Air	53	125.7	49	0.79	14	96	6.59	10¼	13.0
77	Home Office Ref Lab	52	51.3	125	1.12	61	0	2.00	28⅞	25.8
78	Canonie Environmental	52	43.1	86	1.10	32	0	4.31	26¾	24.3
79	Lotus Development	50	428.1	61	1.67	38	26	2.61	23¾	14.2
80	Air Cargo Equipment	50	23.5	51	0.92	30	11	3.28	6⅞	7.5

America's Top 100 Growth Companies *(concluded)*

		Sales		EPS						
Rank	COMPANY	5-Year Annual % Growth	Latest 12-Month (mil.)	5-Year Annual % Growth	Latest 12-Month	Return[1] on Equity	Debt/ Equity	Book Value/ Share	Recent Price	P/E
81	Cruise America	50%	$ 44.0	39%	$ 0.49	12%	9%	$ 5.18	$ 7⅛	14.6
82	GTECH	50	143.4	37	1.10	21	142	5.44	10½	9.5
83	Computer Entry System	49	78.1	45	0.57	12	51	4.32	4⅞	8.6
84	Downey Designs Int'l	49	51.3	37	0.51	75	2	0.86	4½	8.7
85	Ohio Mattress	49	642.7	8	1.30	13	78	10.81	18¼	14.0
86	Liz Claiborne	47	1,105.8	48	1.34	42	0	2.84	18¾	14.0
87	JB Hunt Transport Svcs	47	310.7	31	0.95	20	51	5.15	19½	20.5
88	Intertans	46	114.9	28	0.55	15	0	3.73	11½	20.9
89	Healthcare Svcs Group	46	33.6	20	0.53	17	0	3.70	10½	19.8
90	Sodisco	45	326.2	39	0.71	32	98	2.78	5⅞	8.3
91	Genentech	44	266.3	62	0.62	13	47	4.51	27¼	44.0
92	Precision Castparts	44	414.5	51	2.27	28	88	5.48	32¾	14.4
93	Swift Energy	44	11.9	47	1.01	18	0	1.64	9¼	9.2
94	Mentor	44	39.6	43	0.57	14	2	2.91	11⅞	20.8
95	ERC Int'l	44	125.4	32	1.11	24	101	4.27	10⅜	9.4
96	Spartech	44	181.5	14	0.92	15	123	5.22	7½	8.2
97	Cambridge Shopping Ctr	44	197.4	10	0.56	4	24	25.45	23½	41.9
98	Merrill	43	58.7	65	0.48	9	17	5.16	7⅞	16.4
99	Meridian Technologies	43	51.9	58	0.27	3	13	1.69	3	11.1
100	Cray Research	43	619.1	53	3.71	28	18	19.85	84¼	22.7

Source: William O'Neil & Co. NM: Not Meaningful 1. Most recent fiscal year

Source: Reprinted by permission *Financial World*, 1988.

Largest Certified Public Accounting (CPA) Firms*

Altschuler, Melvoin & Glasser
69 West Washington Street
Chicago, IL 60602
312-236-9500

Arthur Andersen & Company[1]
69 West Washington Street
Chicago, IL 60602
312-346-6262

Arthur Young & Company[1]
277 Park Avenue
New York, NY 10017
212-922-2000

Baird, Kurtz & Dobson
928 Grand Avenue
Kansas City, MO 64106
816-221-7544

Cherry, Bekaert & Holland
1 NCNB Plaza
Charlotte, NC 28280
704-377-3741

Clifton, Gunderson & Co.
808 Commercial National Bank Building
Peoria, IL 61602
309-671-4511

Coopers & Lybrand[1]
1251 Avenue of the Americas
New York, NY 10020
212-536-2000

Crowe, Chizek & Co.
330 East Jefferson Boulevard
South Bend, IN 46624
219-232-3992

Deloitte Haskins & Sells[1]
1114 Avenue of the Americas
New York, NY 10036
219-790-0500

Ernst & Whinney[1]
2000 National City Center
Cleveland, OH 44114
216-861-5000

Grant Thornton
605 Third Avenue
New York, NY 10016
212-599-0100

Kenneth Leventhal & Company
2049 Century Park East
Los Angeles, CA 90067
213-277-0880

Laventhol & Horwath
1845 Walnut Street
Philadelphia, PA 19103
215-299-1700

McGladrey Hendrickson & Pullen
640 Capital Square
4th & Locust
Des Moines, IA 50309
515-284-8660

Moss Adams & Co.
2830 Bank of California Center
Seattle, WA 98164
206-223-1820

George S. Olive & Co.
320 North Meridian Street
Indianapolis, IN 46204
317-267-8400

Oppenheim, Appel, Dixon & Co.
One New York Plaza
New York, NY 10004
212-422-1000

Pannell, Kerr, Forster & Co.
420 Lexington Avenue
New York, NY 10017
212-867-8000

---

* Firms with the largest number of American Institute of Certified Public Accountants (AICPA) members.

[1] One of the "Big 8" accounting firms.

Source: American Institute of Certified Public Accountants.

Peat, Marwick, Main & Co.[1]
345 Park Avenue
New York, NY 10022
212-758-9700

Plante & Moran
26211 Central Park Boulevard
Southfield, MI 48037
313-352-2500

Price Waterhouse & Co.[1]
1251 Avenue of the Americas
New York, NY 10020
212-489-8900

Seidman & Seidman/BDO
15 Columbus Circle
New York, NY 10023
212-765-7500

Touche Ross & Company[1]
1633 Broadway
New York, NY 10019
212-489-1600

Capital Sources for Startup Companies and Small Businesses

Sources of Venture Capital

INTRODUCTION

What Is An SBIC?

Although individual investors have been providing venture capital for new and small business in the United States for many years, no institutional sources of such financing existed until 1958 when Congress passed the Small Business Investment Act.

Small business investment companies (SBICs) and minority enterprise small business investment companies (MESBICs) are financial institutions created to make equity capital and long-term credit (with maturities of at least 5 years) available to small, independent businesses. SBICs are licensed by the Federal Government's Small Business Administration, but they are privately-organized and privately-managed firms which set their own policies and make their own investment decisions. In return for pledging to finance only small businesses, SBICs may qualify for long-term loans from SBA. Although all SBICs will consider applications for funds from socially and economically disadvantaged entrepreneurs. MESBICs normally make all their investments in this area.

What Have SBICs Done?

To date, SBICs have disbursed over $7-billion to over 85,000 small businesses. The concerns they have financed have far out-performed all national averages as measured by increases in assets, sales, profits, and new employment.

Which SBIC Should You See?

This Directory of members of the National Association of Small Business Investment Companies (NASBIC) lists over 300 SBICs and MESBICs. They represent about 90% of the industry's resources and are located in all parts of the country.

In using this Directory, you should look at the following factors:

A. *Size of Financing:* Because they differ in size and investment policies, SBICs establish different dollar limits on the financings they make. Listed here are each SBIC's preferred maximum size of loan or investment.
B. *Investment Policy:* Even though most SBICs have both equity investments and straight loans in their portfolios, each has a policy on which type of financing it prefers. You should match your requirements with the SBIC's preference.
C. *Industry Preference:* SBICs differ widely. Because of the expertise of its officers and directors, an SBIC often specializes in making loans and investments in certain industries, as listed here.
D. *Geographical Preferences:* Generally speaking, SBICs are more likely to make loans and investments near their offices, even though many of them operate regionally or even nationally. Therefore, it would probably be wise to contact first those SBICs closest to your business.

Consider the information included in the directory only as a general guide. Every SBIC departs from its usual policies in special cases. Furthermore, SBICs often work together in making loans or investments in greater amounts than any of them could make separately. No SBIC should be ruled out as a possible source of financing, but this directory is designed to give you an idea about which ones are most likely to be interested in your plan.

Is Your Firm a Qualified Small Business?

A company qualifies as small if it has a net worth under $6 million and average after-tax earnings of less than $2 million during the past two years. If your firm does not meet these financial tests it may still qualify as small either under an employment standard or amount of annual sales. Both these standards vary from industry to industry. A phone call or a note to any NASBIC member will clear up the eligibility question quickly.

Source: *Venture Capital, Where to Find It,* published by the National Association of Small Business Investment Companies, 618 Washington Building, Washington, D.C. 20005.

How Do You Present Your Case To An SBIC?

There is nothing mysterious about asking an SBIC for money. You should prepare a report on your operations, financial condition, and requirements. Specifically, the report should include detailed information on key personnel, products, proposed new product lines, patent positions, market data and competitive position, distribution and sales methods, and other pertinent materials.

How Long Will It Take?

There are no hard and fast rules about the length of time it will take an SBIC to investigate and close a transaction. Ordinarily, an initial response, either positive or negative, is made quickly. On the other hand, the thorough study an SBIC must make before it can make a final decision could take several weeks.

Naturally, a well-documented presentation on your part will reduce the amount of time the SBIC will require.

How Are SBIC Financings Structured?

Every single SBIC financing is tailored individually to meet your needs and to make the best use of the SBIC's funds. You and the SBIC will negotiate the terms. The SBIC might buy shares of your stock or it might make a straight loan.

Usually, SBICs are interested in generating capital gains, so they will purchase stock in your company or advance funds through a note, or debenture, with conversion privileges or rights to buy stock at a predetermined later date.

How Can SBIC Money Provide Additional Credit Lines?

If the SBIC money is provided to you in a subordinated position, it will often do double or triple duty. Industry averages show that for every SBIC dollar placed with a small business concern, two additional senior dollars become available from commercial banks or other sources.

Are There Unique Advantages To SBIC Financing?

Yes. Before it receives its license, an SBIC must prove that its management and directors are experienced individuals with a broad range of business and professional talents.

This expertise will be applied to assist your business, supplementing the skills of your own management team. Here again, the actual pattern of management and financial counseling will be cut to fit each specific situation.

SBICs can make only long-term loans or equity investments; therefore, their interests and yours will coincide—both of you will want your firm to grow and prosper.

Will I Be Treated Fairly?

As mentioned above, SBICs are licensed by the Federal Government only after their officers and directors have been carefully screened. Furthermore, all the SBICs listed in this Directory are NASBIC members and all have voluntarily subscribed to the Association's Code of Ethics and Trade Practice Rules.

The Code provides, in part, that "the constant goal of each SBIC shall be to improve the welfare of the small business concerns which it serves. Each SBIC shall promote and maintain ethical standards of conduct and deal fairly and honestly with all small business concerns seeking its assistance."

What Is NASBIC?

The SBIC industry is represented in Washington by the National Association of Small Business Investment Companies (NASBIC). For 30 years, NASBIC has promoted the growth and vitality of the industry through effective representation and successful professional programs.

NASBIC is the voice of the SBIC industry before Congress and the Administration. Among other activities, the Association has successfully fought for government policies permitting SBICs to channel more venture capital and long-term loans to new and growing small businesses.

NASBIC also cooperates closely with other independent business associations in advancing the interests of small business at the federal level.

For More Information:

Contact any SBIC, MESBIC or Associate Member in this directory.

SBICs and MESBICs

ALABAMA

Alabama SBIC, Inc. [MESBIC]
500 First National
Southern National Bldg., 5th Ave. N. & 20th Street
Birmingham, AL 35203
(205) 324-5234
Contact
Mr. William Billingsley

First SBIC of Alabama
16 Midtown Park East
Mobile, AL 36606
(205) 476-0700
Contact
Mr. David C. DeLaney, President
Preferred Limit of Loans or Investments
Up to $500,000
Investment Policy
Will make loans and/or equity investments
Industry Preference
Diversified
Geographical Preference
South

Hickory Venture Capital Corp.
699 Gallatin Street, Suite A-2
Huntsville, AL 35801
(205) 539-1931
Contact
Mr. J. Thomas Noojin, Chairman/President
Mr. Jeffrey C. Atkinson, Vice President
Mr. Monro B. Lanier, Investment Manager
Preferred Limit of Loans or Investments
Above $1 Million
Investment Policy
Prefer equity-type investments
Industry Preference
Diversified
Geographical Preference
South/Midwest/Southwest

Remington Fund, Inc. (The)
P.O. Box 10686
Birmingham, AL 35202
(205) 326-3509
Contact
Ms. Lana Sellers, President
Preferred Limit of Loans or Investments
Up to $500,000
Investment Policy
Prefer equity-type investments
Industry Preference
Communications
Consumer Products
Industrial Products
Geographical Preference
South

Tuskegee Capital Corp. [MESBIC]
4453 Richardson Road
Montgomery, AL 36108
(205) 281-8059
Contact
Mr. A. G. Bartholomew, V. P. /Gen. Mgr.
Preferred Limit of Loans or Investments
Up to $100,000
Investment Policy
Prefer straight loans
Industry Preference
Diversified
Geographical Preference
Alabama

ALASKA

Alaska Business Investment Corp.
301 W. Northern Lights Boulevard
Anchorage, AK 99510
Contact
Mr. James L. Cloud, Vice President

Calista Business Investment Corp. [MESBIC]
503 E. 6th Avenue
Anchorage, AK 99501
(907) 277-0425
Contact
Mr. Matthew Nicolai, President
Preferred Limit of Loans or Investments
Up to $250,000
Investment Policy
Will make loans and/or equity investments
Industry Preference
Diversified

ARIZONA

Branch Office:
Norwest Growth Fund, Inc.
8777 East Via de Ventura, Suite 335
Scottsdale, AZ 85258
(602) 483-8940
(Main Office in Minnesota)
Contact
Mr. Robert F. Zicarelli, Chairman
Preferred Limit of Loans or Investments
Up To $100,000
Investment Policy
Will make loans and/or equity investments
Industry Preference
Diversified
Geographical Preference
Arizona

Rocky Mountain Equity Corp.
4530 N. Central Avenue, #3
Phoenix, AZ 85012
(602) 274-7558
Contact
Mr. Chris Wilson
Preferred Limit of Loans or Investments
Up to $100,000
Investment Policy
Prefer straight loans
Industry Preference
Diversified

Valley National Investors, Inc.
201 North Central, Suite 900
Phoenix, AZ 85004
(602) 261-1577
Contact
Mr. John M. Holliman, III, Managing Director
Preferred Limit of Loans or Investments
Above $1 Million
Investment Policy
Prefer equity-type investments
Industry Preference
Diversified
Geographical Preference
Southwest

ARKANSAS

Capital Management Services, Inc. [MESBIC]
1910 N. Grant, #200
Little Rock, AR 72207
(501) 664-8613
Contact
Mr. David L. Hale, President
Preferred Limit of Loans or Investments
Up to $250,000
Investment Policy
Will make loans and/or equity investments
Industry Preferences
Diversified
Geographical Preference
Arkansas

Independence Financial Services, Inc.
P.O. Box 3878
Batesville, AR 72503
(501) 793-4533
Contact
Mr. John C. Freeman, President
Preferred Limit of Loans or Investments
Up to $250,000
Investment Policy
Will make loans and/or equity investments
Industry Preference
Diversified

Kar-Mal Venture Capital, Inc.
2821 Kavanaugh Boulevard
Little Rock, AR 72205
(501) 661-0010
Contact
Ms. Amelia S. Karam, President
Preferred Limit of Loans or Investments
Up to $250,000
Investment Policy
Prefer equity-type investments
Industry Preference
Diversified

Power Ventures, Inc. [MESBIC]
P.O. Box 518
Highway 270 North
Malvern, AR 72104
(501) 332-3965
Contact
Mr. Dorsey D. Glover, President
Preferred Limit of Loans or Investments
Up to $100,000
Investment Policy
Prefer equity-type investments
Industry Preference
Diversified
Geographical Preference
Southwest

CALIFORNIA

BankAmerica Ventures, Inc.
555 California Street, #3908, 12th Floor
San Francisco, CA 94104
(415) 622-2230
Contact
Mr. Patrick J. Topolski, Vice President
Mr. Hugo Braun
Preferred Limit of Loans or Investments
Above $1 Million
Investment Policy
Prefer equity-type investments
Industry Preference
Communications
Computer Products
Electronics
Genetic Engineering
Medical-Health
Geographical Preference
West

Bay Venture Group
One Embarcadero Center, Suite 3303
San Francisco, CA 94111
(415) 989-7680
Contact
Mr. William R. Chandler, General Partner
Preferred Limit of Loans or Investments
Up to $250,000
Preferred Limit of Loans or Investments
Above $1 Million
Investment Policy
Prefer equity-type investments
Industry Preference
Diversified
Geographical Preference
California

Ivanhoe Venture Capital, Ltd.
737 Pearl Street, Suite 201
La Jolla, CA 92037
(619) 454-8882
Contact
Mr. Alan R. Toffler, Managing General Partner
Mr. P. Frederick Wulff
Preferred Limit of Loans or Investments
Up to $250,000
Investment Policy
Prefer equity-type investments
Industry Preference
Diversified
Geographical Preference
West

Letigo Capital Partners
1015 Gayley Avenue #202
Los Angeles, CA 90024
(213) 208-3892
Contact
Mr. Donald Peterson, General Partner
Preferred Limit of Loans or Investments
Up to $500,000
Investment Policy
Will make loans and/or equity investments
Industry Preference
Diversified

Magna Pacific Investments [MESBIC]
977 N. Broadway, Suite 301
Los Angeles, CA 90012
(213) 680-2525
Contact
Mr. David Wong, President
Preferred Limit of Loans or Investments
Up to $250,000

Investment Policy
Will make loans and/or equity investments
Industry Preference
Computer Products
Electronics
Diversified
Geographical Preference
National

Merrill, Pickard, Anderson & Eyre I
2 Palo Alto Square, Suite 425
Palo Alto, CA 94306
(415) 856-8880
Contact
Mr. Steven L. Merrill, Managing Partner
Preferred Limit of Loans or Investments
Above $1 Million
Investment Policy
Prefer equity-type investments
Industry Preference
Communications
Computer Products
Electronics
Genetic Engineering
Medical-Health
Geographical Preference
National

New Kukje Investment Co. [MESBIC]
958 S. Vermont Avenue, Suite C
Los Angeles, CA 90006
(213) 389-8679
Contact
Mr. George Chey, Chairman
Mr. Chung K. Noh, President
Mr. James Thorburn, General Manager
Preferred Limit of Loans or Investments
Up to $100,000
Investment Policy
Prefer straight loans
Industry Preference
Diversified
Geographical Preference
West

Opportunity Capital Corp. [MESBIC]
39650 Liberty Street, Suite 425
Fremont, CA 94538
(415) 651-4412
Contact
Mr. J. Peter Thompson, President
Preferred Limit of Loans or Investments
Up to $250,000
Investment Policy
Prefer equity-type investment
Industry Preference
Communications
Industrial Products
Transportation
Diversified
Geographical Preference
National

PBC Venture Capital Inc.
P.O. Box 6008
Bakersfield, CA 93386
(805) 395-3206
Contact
Mr. Henry Wheeler, President/Gen. Mgr.
Preferred Limit of Loans or Investments
Up to $100,000
Geographical Preference
Southwest/West

Draper Associates
3000 Sand Hill Road, IV-210
Menlo Park, CA 94025
(415) 854-7472
Contact
Mr. Tim Draper, Vice President, CFO

First American Capital Funding, Inc.
[MESBIC]
38 Corporate Park, Suite B
Irvine, CA 92714
(714) 660-9288
Contact
Dr. Luu Trankiem, President
Preferred Limit of Loans or Investments
Above $1 Million
Investment Policy
Prefer straight loans

Industry Preference
Communications
Consumer Products
Energy/Natural Resources
Geographical Preference
California

First Interstate Capital, Inc.
5000 Birch Street, Suite 10100
Newport Beach, CA 92660
(714) 253-4360
Contact
Mr. Ron Hall, Managing Director
Mr. Charles Fullerton, Managing Director
Mr. Roger Drufva, Director
Preferred Limit of Loans or Investments
Up to $1 Million
Investment Policy
Prefer equity-type investments
Industry Preference
Diversified
Geographical Preference
Southwest
West

First SBIC of California
650 Town Center Drive, 17th Floor
Costa Mesa, CA 92626
(714) 556-1964
Contact
Mr. Tim Hay, President
Mr. Brian Jones, Managing Partner
Mr. John Geer, Managing Partner
Branch Office
5 Palo Alto Square, Suite 1038
Palo Alto, CA 94306
(415) 424-8011
Contact
Mr. James B. McElwee, Managing Partner
Branch Office
155 N. Lake Avenue, Suite 1010
Pasadena, CA 91109
(818) 304-3451
Contact
Mr. John D. Padgett, Managing Partner
Mr. Tony Stevens, Managing Partner
(Information applies to all offices)
Preferred Limit of Loans or Investments
Above $1 Million
Investment Policy
Prefer equity-type investments
Industry Preference
Diversified
Geographical Preference
National

Hamco Capital Corp.
235 Montgomery Street
San Francisco, CA 94104
(415) 393-9813
Contact
Mr. William R. Hambrecht, President
Preferred Limit of Loans or Investments
Up to $500,000
Investment Policy
Will make loans and/or equity investments
Industry Preference
Diversified

Helio Capital, Inc. [MESBIC]
5900 S. Eastern Avenue, Suite 136
Commerce, CA 90040
(213) 627-6660
Contact
Mr. Frank R. Remski, General Manager
Mr. Chester Koo, President
Ms. Sung-Hyun Kim, Secretary
Preferred Limit of Loans or Investments
Up to $300,000
Investment Policy
Will make loans and/or equity investments
Industry Preference
Diversified
Geographical Preference
Southwest

Imperial Ventures, Inc.
9920 S. LaCienega Boulevard
Inglewood, CA 90301
(213) 417-5830
Contact
Mr. John Upshur, Sr. Vice President

Investment Policy
Prefer equity-type investments
Industry Preference
Communications
Computer Products
Electronics
Genetic Engineering
Medical-Health
Geographical Preference
California

Bentley Capital [MESBIC]
592 Vallejo Street, Suite 2
San Francisco, CA 94133
(415) 982-8073
Contact
Mr. John Hung, President
Mr. Lap-Chung Chan, Vice President
Mr. Louis Leong, Vice President
Preferred Limit of Loans or Investments
Up to $500,000
Investment Policy
Will make loans and/or equity investments
Industry Preferences
Computer Products
Consumer Products
Industrial Products
Medical-Health
Diversified
Geographical Preference
West

Business Equity & Development Corp.
[MESBIC]
1411 Olympic Boulevard, Suite 200
Los Angeles, CA 90015
(213) 385-0351
Contact
Mr. Leon M. N. Garcia, Interim Director
Preferred Limit of Loans or Investments
Up to $250,000
Investment Policy
Prefer equity-type investments
Industry Preference
Diversified
Geographical Preference
California

California Capital Investors, Ltd.
11812 San Vicente Boulevard
Los Angeles, CA 90049
(213) 820-7222
(Bancorp Venture Capital, Inc. under same management)
Contact
Mr. Arthur H. Bernstein, General Partner
Ms. Lynda S. Gibson, Investment Officer
Preferred Limit of Loans or Investments
Up to $500,000
Investment Policy
Will make loans and/or equity investments
Industry Preference
Communications
Consumer Products
Medical-Health
Transportation
Diversified
Geographical Preference
West

Charterway Investment Corp. [MESBIC]
222 S. Hill Street, Suite 800
Los Angeles, CA 90012
(213) 687-8534
Contact
Mr. Harold Chuang, President
Preferred Limit of Loans or Investments
Up to $250,000
Investment Policy
Will make loans and/or equity investment
Industry Preference
Diversified
Geographical Preference
West

Continental Investors, Inc. [MESBIC]
8781 Seaspray Drive
Huntington Beach, CA 92646
(714) 964-5207
Contact
Mr. Lac Thantrong, President
Mr. Marc Thantrong, Vice President

Preferred Limit of Loans or Investments
Up to $100,000
Investment Policy
Prefer straight loans
Industry Preference
Consumer Products
Diversified
Geographical Preference
California

<u>Crosspoint Investment Corp.</u>
1951 Landings Drive
Mountain View, CA 94043
(415) 964-3545
Contact
Mr. Max S. Simpson, President
Preferred Limit of Loans or Investments
Up to $250,000
Investment Policy
Will make loans and/or equity investments
Industry Preference
Communications
Electronics
Industrial Products
Medical-Health
Diversified
Investment Policy
Prefer equity-type investments
Industry Preference
Diversified
Geographical Preference
California

<u>Branch Office</u>
<u>Pyramid Ventures, Inc.</u>
600 Montgomery Street
San Francisco, CA 94111
(415) 986-0444
(Main office in New York)
Contact
Mr. Duane Kirkpatrick, President
Preferred Limit of Loans or Investments
Up to $1 Million
Investment Policy
Prefer equity-type investments
Industry Preference
Communications
Computer Products
Electronics
Genetic Engineering
Medical-Health
Geographical Preference
West

<u>San Joaquin Capital Corp.</u>
1415 18th Street, Suite 306
Bakersfield, CA 93301
Mailing Address: P.O. Box 2538
Bakersfield, CA 93303
(805) 323-7581
Contact
Mr. Chester W. Troudy, President
Preferred Limit of Loans or Investments
Up to $250,000
Investment Policy
Prefer equity-type investments
Industry Preference
Industrial Products
Diversified
Geographical Preference
West

<u>Seaport Ventures, Inc.</u>
525 B Street, Suite 630
San Diego, CA 92101
(619) 232-4069
Contact
Ms. Carole Rhoades, Vice President
Preferred Limit of Loans or Investments
Up to $500,000
Investment Policy
Will make loans and/or equity investments
Industry Preference
Diversified
Geographical Preference
West

<u>Union Venture Corp.</u>
445 S. Figueroa Street, 12th Floor
Los Angeles, CA 90071
(213) 236-4092
Contact
Mr. Jeffrey A. Watts, President
Preferred Limit of Loans or Investments
Above $1 Million
Investment Policy
Prefer equity-type investments
Industry Preference
Diversified
Geographical Preference
West

<u>Unity Capital Corp.</u> [MESBIC]
10055 Barnes Canyon Road, Suite A-4
San Diego, CA 92121
(619) 452-3180
Contact
Mr. Frank W. Owen, President
Ms. Sandra Hyde, Secretary
Preferred Limit of Loans or Investments
Up to $100,000
Investment Policy
Prefer straight loans
Industry Preference
Diversified
Geographical Preference
California

<u>VK Capital</u>
50 California Street, 24th Floor
San Francisco, CA 94111
(415) 391-5600
Contact
E. Payson Smith, General Partner
F. Van Kasper, General Partner
Karen J. Popp, Assistant
Preferred Limit of Loans or Investments
Up to $250,000
Investment Policy
Will make loans and/or equity investments
Industry Preference
Diversified
Geographical Preference
West

<u>Westamco Investment Co.</u>
8929 Wilshire Boulevard, Suite 400
Beverly Hills, CA 90211
(213) 652-8288
Contact
Mr. Leonard G. Muskin, President
Mr. Scott T. Van Evert, Vice President
Preferred Limit of Loans or Investments
Up to $500,000
Investment Policy
Will make loans and/or equity investments
Industry Preference
Construction/Real Estate
Diversified
Geographical Preference
West

CONNECTICUT

<u>Capital Impact Corp.</u>
961 Main Street
Bridgeport, CT 06601
(203) 384-5670
Contact
Mr. William D. Starbuck, President
Mr. Paul Larsen, A. Vice President
Ms. Olivia Daniels, Investment Officer
Preferred Limit of Loans or Investments
Up to $1 Million
Investment Policy
Will make loans and/or equity investments
Industry Preference
Diversified
Geographical Preference
Northeast

<u>Capital Resource Co. of Connecticut</u>
699 Bloomfield Avenue
Bloomfield, CT 06002
(203) 243-1114
Contact
Mr. I. Martin Fierberg, General Partner
Preferred Limit of Loans or Investments
Up to $100,000
Investment Policy
Will make loans and/or equity investments
Industry Preference
Diversified
Geographical Preference
Northeast

<u>First Connecticut SBIC (The)</u>
177 State Street
Bridgeport, CT 06604
(203) 366-4726
Contact
Mr. David Engelson, President
Preferred Limit of Loans or Investments
Up to $1 Million
Investment Policy
Will make loans and/or equity investments
Industry Preference
Diversified
Geographical Preference
Northeast

<u>First New England Capital Ltd., Ptnrs.</u>
255 Main Street
Hartford, CT 06106
(203) 249-4321
Contact
Mr. Richard C. Klaffky, President
Mr. John L. Ritter, Vice President
Mr. Paul F. Rumanelli, Treasurer
Preferred Limit of Loans or Investments
Up to $1 Million
Investment Policy
Will make loans and/or equity investments
Industry Preference
Diversified
Geographical Preference
Northeast

<u>Marcon Capital Corp.</u>
49 Riverside Avenue
Westport, CT 06880
(203) 226-6893
Contact
Mr. Martin A. Cohen, Chairman
Preferred Limit of Loans or Investments
Up to $1 Million
Investment Policy
Will make loans and/or equity investments
Industry Preference
Communications
Construction/Real Estate
Diversified
Geographical Preference
Northeast

<u>Northeastern Capital Corp.</u>
209 Church Street
New Haven, CT 06510
(203) 865-4500
Contact
Mr. Moshe Reiss, President
Preferred Limit of Loans or Investments
Up to $250,000
Investment Policy
Prefer straight loans
Industry Preference
Diversified
Geographical Preference
Northeast

<u>Regional Financial Enterprises</u>
36 Grove Street
New Canaan, CT 06840
(203) 966-2800
Contact
Mr. Knute C. Albrecht, General Partner
Preferred Limit of Loans or Investments
Above $1 Million
Investment Policy
Prefer equity-type investments
Industry Preference
Communications
Consumer Products
Industrial Products
Medical-Health
Diversified
Geographical Preference
National

<u>SBIC of Connecticut</u>
1115 Main Street, Suite 610
Bridgeport, CT 06604
(203) 367-3282
Contact
Mr. Kenneth F. Zarrilli, President
Mr. Sigmund L. Miller
Preferred Limit of Loans or Investments
Up to $100,000

Investment Policy
Prefer equity-type investments
Industry Preference
Construction/Real Estate
Geographical Preference
Northeast

DELAWARE

Morgan Investment Corp.
902 Market Street
Wilmington, DE 19801
(302) 651-3800
Contact
Mr. William E. Pike, President
Preferred Limit of Loans or Investments
Above $1 Million
Investment Policy
Will make loans and/or equity investments
Industry Preferences
Diversified
Geographical Preference
National

DISTRICT OF COLUMBIA

Allied Capital Corp.
1666 K Street NW, Suite 901
Washington, DC 20006
(202) 331-1112
Contact
Mr. Brooks Browne, Senior Vice President
Mr. Will Dunbar, Vice President
Mr. Fred Russell, Vice President
Preferred Limit of Loans or Investments
Up to $1 Million
Investment Policy
Will make loans and/or equity investments
Industry Preference
Communications
Computer Products
Industrial Products
Medical-Health
Diversified
Geographical Preference
Northeast/South/Midwest

American Security Capital Corp.
730 15th Street, NW
Washington, DC 20013
(202) 624-4843
Contact
Mr. Brian K. Mercer, Vice President
Ms. Trish Wojtaszek, A.T.
Preferred Limit of Loans or Investments
Up to $500,000
Investment Policy
Prefer equity-type investments
Industry Preference
Communications
Computer Products
Medical-Health
Diversified
Geographical Preference
Northeast

Broadcast Capital, Inc. [MESBIC]
1771 N Street, N.W., Suite 404
Washington, DC 20036
(202) 429-5393
Contact
Mr. John E. Oxedine, President
Preferred Limit of Loans or Investments
Up to $500,000
Investment Policy
Prefer straight loans
Industry Preference
Communications
Geographical Preference
National

D.C. Bancorp Venture Capital Co.
1801 K Street, N.W.
Washington, DC 20006
(202) 955-6970
Contact
Mr. Allan A. Weissburg, President
Preferred Limit of Loans or Investments
Up to $500,000
Investment Policy
Prefer equity-type investments
Industry Preference
Diversified
Geographical Preference
Northeast/South

Fulcrum Venture Capital Corp. [MESBIC]
1030 15th Street, N.W., Suite 203
Washington, DC 20005
(202) 785-4253
Contact
Ms. Renate Todd, Vice President
Preferred Limit of Loans or Investments
Up to $500,000
Investment Policy
Prefer equity-type investments
Industry Preference
Consumer Products
Electronics
Industrial Products
Transportation
Geographical Preference
National

Syncom Capital Corp. [MESBIC]
1030 - 15th Street N.W., Suite 203
Washington, DC 20005
(202) 293-9428
Contact
Mr. Herbert P. Wilkins, President
Preferred Limit of Loans or Investments
Up to $500,000
Investment Policy
Will make loans and/or equity investments
Industry Preference
Communications

Washington Ventures, Inc.
1320 18th Street, N.W.
Washington, DC 20036
(202) 895-2560
Contact
Mr. Kenneth A. Swain, President
Preferred Limit of Loans or Investments
Up to $500,000
Investment Policy
Prefer equity-type investments
Industry Preference
Diversified
Geographical Preference
National

FLORIDA

Caribank Capital Corp.
2400 East Commerical Boulevard, Suite 814
Ft. Lauderdale, FL 33308
(305) 776-1133
Contact
Mr. Michael E. Chaney, President
Ms. Elaine E. Healy, Investment Officer
Preferred Limit of Loans or Investments
Up to $500,000
Investment Policy
Prefer equity-type investments
Industry Preference
Communications
Electronics
Genetic Engineering
Industrial Products
Diversified
Geographical Preference
National

Ideal Financial Corp. [MESBIC]
780 N.W. 42nd Avenue, Suite 501
Miami, FL 33126
(305) 442-4665
Contact
Mr. Eclore T. Reynaldo, General Manager
Mr. Rafael Elortegui
Ms. Joaquin Membiela
Preferred Limit of Loans or Investments
Up to $100,000
Investment Policy
Will make loans and/or equity investments
Industry Preference
Diversified
Geographical Preference
Florida

J & D Capital Corp.
12747 Biscayne Boulevard
N. Miami, FL 33160
(305) 893-0303
Contact
Mr. Jack Carmel, President
Preferred Limit of Loans or Investments
Up to $1 Million
Investment Policy
Will make loans and/or equity investments
Industry Preference
Construction/Real Estate
Diversified
Retailing
Geographical Preference
National

Small Business Assistance Corp.
2612 W. 15th Street
Panama City, FL 32401
(904) 785-9577
Contact
Mr. Charles S. Smith, President
H. N. Tillman, Secretary
Preferred Limit of Loans or Investments
Up to $250,000
Investment Policy
Will make loans and/or equity investments
Industry Preference
Construction/Real Estate
Geographical Preference
South

Southeast Venture Capital, Ltd. I
One Southeast Financial Center
Miami, FL 33131
(305) 375-6470
Contact
Mr. James Fitzsimons, President
Mr. Frank Young, Vice President
Ms. Anne Cario, Treasurer
Preferred Limit of Loans or Investments
Up to $1 Million
Investment Policy
Prefer equity-type investments
Industry Preference
Communications
Computer Products
Electronics
Industrial Products
Medical-Health
Geographical Preference
South

Universal Financial Services, Inc. [MESBIC]
3550 Biscayne Boulevard, Suite 702
Miami, FL 33137
(305) 573-1496
Contact
Mr. Norman Zipkin, President
Preferred Limit of Loans or Investments
Up to $250,000
Investment Policy
Prefer equity-type investments
Industry Preference
Construction/Real Estate
Medical-Health
Transportation
Geographical Preference
Northeast/South

Venture Group, Inc.
5433 Buffalo Avenue
Jacksonville, FL 32208
(904) 355-6265
Contact
Mr. Ellis W. Hitzing, President
Preferred Limit of Loans or Investments
Up to $100,000
Investment Policy
Prefer straight loans
Industry Preference
Automotive
Geographical Preference
South

GEORGIA

North Riverside Capital Corp.
50 Technology Park/Atlanta
Norcross, GA 30092
(404) 252-1076
Contact
Mr. Thomas R. Barry, President
Preferred Limit of Loans or Investments
Up to $1 Million

Investment Policy
Prefer equity-type investments
Industry Preference
Diversified
Geographical Preference
South

HAWAII

Bancorp Hawaii SBIC, Inc.
P.O. Box 2900
Honolulu, HI 96846
(808) 521-6411
Contact
Mr. Thomas T. Triggs, Vice President/Gen. Mgr.
Preferred Limit of Loans or Investments
Up to $250,000
Investment Policy
Prefer equity-type investments
Industry Preference
Diversified
Geographical Preference
West

Pacific Venture Capital, Inc. [MESBIC]
222 South Vineyard Street, Suite PH-1
Honolulu, HI 96813
(808) 521-6502
Contact
Mr. Dexter J. Taniguchi
Preferred Limit of Loans or Investments
Up to $100,000
Investment Policy
Will make loans and/or equity investments
Industry Preference
Diversified
Geographical Preference
Hawaii

ILLINOIS

Alpha Capital Venture Partners
Three First National Plaza, Suite 1400
Chicago, IL 60602
(312) 372-1556
Contact
Mr. Andrew H. Kalnow, Managing Partner
Mr. Daniel W. O'Connell, General Partner
Preferred Limit of Loans or Investments
Up to $500,000
Investment Policy
Will make loans and/or equity investments
Industry Preference
Communications
Computer Products
Electronics
Industrial Products
Diversified
Geographical Preference
Midwest

Amoco Venture Capital Co. [MESBIC]
200 E. Randolph Drive
Chicago, IL 60601
(312) 856-6523
Contact
Mr. Gordon E. Stone, President
C. S. Carstens, Vice President
Preferred Limit of Loans or Investments
Up to $250,000
Investment Policy
Prefer equity-type investments
Industry Preference
Diversified
Geographical Preference
National

Business Ventures, Inc.
20 N. Wacker Drive, Suite 550
Chicago, IL 60606
(312) 346-1580
Contact
Mr. Milton Lefton, President
Preferred Limit of Loans or Investments
Up to $250,000
Investment Policy
Will make loans and/or equity investments
Industry Preference
Diversified
Geographical Preference
Midwest

Chicago Community Ventures, Inc. [MESBIC]
104 S. Michigan, Suite 215
Chicago, IL 60603
(312) 726-6084
Contact
Ms. Phyllis George, President
Preferred Limit of Loans or Investments
Up to $250,000
Investment Policy
Will make loans and/or equity investments
Industry Preference
Diversified
Geographical Preference
Midwest

Combined Fund (The) [MESBIC]
1525 E. 53rd Street, Suite 908
Chicago, IL 60615
(312) 363-0300
Contact
Mr. E. Patric Jones, President
Preferred Limit of Loans or Investments
Up to $250,000
Investment Policy
Will make loans and/or equity investments
Industry Preference
Diversified

Continental Illinois Venture Corp.
231 S. LaSalle Street
Chicago, IL 60697
(312) 828-8021
Contact
Mr. John L. Hines, President
Preferred Limit of Loans or Investments
Above $1 Million
Investment Policy
Prefer equity-type investments
Industry Preference
Communications
Consumer Products
Genetic Engineering
Industrial Products
Medical-Health
Geographical Preference
National

Enterprise Financial Capital Development Corp.
865 Busse Highway
Park Ridge, IL 60068
(312) 692-6050
Contact
Mr. Robert S. Russell, President
Mr. Donald J. Popernik
Preferred Limit of Loans or Investments
Up to $500,000
Investment Policy
Will make loans and/or equity investments
Industry Preference
Diversified
Geographical Preference
National

First Capital Corp. of Chicago
Three First National Plaza, Suite 1330
Chicago, IL 60670
(312) 732-5400
Contact
Mr. John A. Canning, Jr., President
Preferred Limit of Loans or Investments
Above $1 Million
Investment Policy
Prefer equity-type investments
Industry Preference
Diversified
Geographical Preference
National

Frontenac Capital Corp.
208 S. LaSalle Street, Suite 1900
Chicago, IL 60604
(312) 368-0044
Contact
Mr. David A. R. Dullum, President
Mr. Rodney L. Goldstein, Vice President
Mr. Martin J. Koldyke, Chairman
Preferred Limit of Loans or Investments
Up to $1 Million
Investment Policy
Prefer equity-type investments
Industry Preference
Communications
Computer Products
Electronics
Medical-Health
Geographical Preference
Midwest

Mesirow Capital Partners SBIC, Ltd.
135 S. LaSalle Street, Suite 3910
Chicago, IL 60603
(312) 670-6000
Contact
Mr. James C. Tyree, General Partner
Mr. William P. Sutter, Jr., Senior Vice President
Mr. Daniel P. Howell, Vice President
Preferred Limit of Loans or Investments
Above $1 Million
Investment Policy
Prefer equity-type investments
Industry Preference
Diversified
Geographical Preference
National

Tower Ventures [MESBIC]
Sears Tower, BSC 43-50
Chicago, IL 60684
(312) 875-0571
Contact
Mr. Robert T. Smith, President
Mr. Jose Victoria, Portfolio Manager
Mr. Dennis Schauer, Financial Analyst
Preferred Limit of Loans or Investments
Up to $250,000
Investment Policy
Will make loans and/or equity investments
Industry Preference
Diversified
Geographical Preference
National

Walnut Capital Corp.
208 S. LaSalle Street, 9th Floor, Suite 1043
Chicago, IL 60604
(312) 346-2033
Contact
Mr. Burton W. Kanter, Chairman
Preferred Limit of Loans or Investments
Up to $500,000
Investment Policy
Will make loans and/or equity investments
Industry Preference
Communications
Medical-Health
Geographical Preference
National

INDIANA

1st Source Capital Corp.
100 N. Michigan
South Bend, IN 46601
(219) 236-2180
Contact
Mr. Gene Cavanaugh, Vice President
Preferred Limit of Loans or Investments
Up to $250,000
Investment Policy
Prefer equity-type investments
Industry Preference
Diversified
Geographical Preference
Midwest

Circle Ventures, Inc.
2502 Roosevelt Avenue
Indianapolis, IN 46218
(317) 636-7242
Contact
Ms. Murray M. Welch
Preferred Limit of Loans or Investments
Up to $100,000
Investment Policy
Will make loans and/or equity investments
Industry Preference
Communications
Electronics
Energy/Natural Resources
Industrial Products
Diversified
Geographical Preference
Midwest

White River Capital Corp.
P.O. Box 929
Columbus, IN 47202
(812) 376-1759
Contact
Mr. Thomas Washburn, President
Mr. Bradley J. Kime, VP - Investments
Preferred Limit of Loans or Investments
Up to $250,000
Investment Policy
Will make loans and/or equity investments
Industry Preference
Communications
Diversified
Geographical Preference
Midwest

IOWA

MorAmerica Capital Corp.
800 American Building
Cedar Rapids, IA 52401
(319) 363-8249
Contact
Mr. David R. Schroder, President
Mr. Robert A. Comey, Executive Vice President
Preferred Limit of Loans or Investments
Up to $1 Million
Investment Policy
Will make loans and/or equity investments
Industry Preference
Diversified
Geographical Preference
Midwest
National

KANSAS

Kansas Venture Capital, Inc.
Bank IV Tower, Suite 1030
One Townsite Plaza
Topeka, KS 66603
(913) 233-1368
Contact
Mr. Larry High, Executive Vice President
Mr. Rex E. Wiggins
Preferred Limit of Loans or Investments
Up to $500,000
Investment Policy
Will make loans and/or equity investments
Industry Preference
Communications
Computer Products
Electronics
Industrial Products
Diversified
Geographical Preference
Kansas

KENTUCKY

Equal Opportunity Finance, Inc. [MESBIC]
420 Hurstbourne Lane, Suite 201
Louisville, KY 40222
(502) 423-1943
Contact
Mr. Frank P. Justice, President
Mr. David A. Sattich, Vice President
Mr. Donald L. Davis, Assistant Secretary
Preferred Limit of Loans or Investments
Up to $250,000
Investment Policy
Will make loans and/or equity investments
Industry Preference
Diversified
Geographical Preference
Kentucky/Indiana/Ohio/W. Virginia

Financial Opportunities, Inc.
P.O. Box 35710
Louisville, KY 40232-5710
(502) 451-3800
Contact
Mr. Gary F. Duerr, Investment Advisor
Mr. George Spalding, Jr., Investment Advisor
Preferred Limit of Loans or Investments
Up to $180,000
Investment Policy
Will make loans and/or equity investments
Industry Preference
Diversified
Geographical Preference
South

Mountain Ventures, Inc.
911 Main Street
P.O. Box 628
London, KY 40741
(606) 864-5175
Contact
Mr. Roger E. Whitehouse, President
Mr. Jerry Rickett
Preferred Limit of Loans or Investments
Up to $250,000
Investment Policy
Will make loans and/or equity investments
Industry Preference
Computer Products
Consumer Products
Electronics
Industrial Products
Diversified
Geographical Preference
Kentucky

LOUSIANA

Dixie Business Investment Co., Inc.
P.O. Box 588
Lake Providence, LA 71254
(318) 559-1558
Contact
Mr. L. Wayne Baker, President
Mr. George S. Lensing, Chairman of the Board
Ms. Evelyn S. LeBeau, Assistant Manager
Preferred Limit of Loans or Investments
Up to $100,000
Investment Policy
Prefer straight loans
Industry Preference
Construction/Real Estate
Industrial Products
Diversified
Geographical Preference
South

Louisiana Equity Capital Corp.
Louisiana National Bank
P.O. Box 1511
Baton Rouge, LA 70821
(504) 389-4421
Contact
Mr. Melvin L. Rambin, President
Mr. Thomas J. Adamek, Investment Officer
Preferred Limit of Loans or Investments
Up to $500,000
Investment Policy
Prefer equity-type investments
Industry Preference
Diversified
Geographical Preference
National

MAINE

Maine Capital Corp.
70 Center Street
Portland, ME 04101
(207) 772-1001
Contact
Mr. David Coit, President
Preferred Limit of Loans or Investments
Up to $250,000
Investment Policy
Prefer equity-type investments
Industry Preference
Diversified
Geographical Preference
Northeast

MARYLAND

First Maryland Capital, Inc.
107 W. Jefferson Street
Rockville, MD 20850
(301) 251-6630
Contact
Mr. Joseph A. Kenary, President
Preferred Limit of Loans or Investments
Up to $100,000
Investment Policy
Will make loans and/or equity investments
Industry Preference
Communications
Geographical Preference
Northeast/South

Greater Washington Investments, Inc.
5454 Wisconsin Avenue, Suite 1315
Chevy Chase, MD 20815
(301) 656-0626
Contact
Mr. Don A. Christensen, President
Mr. Cyril W. Draffin, Jr., Vice President
Mr. Jeffrey T. Griffin, Vice President
Preferred Limit of Loans or Investments
Up to $1 Million
Investment Policy
Will make loans and/or equity investments
Industry Preference
Communications
Computer Products
Consumer Products
Industrial Products
Medical-Health
Geographical Preference
South/Northeast/Midwest

Jiffy Lube Capital Corp.
7008 Security Boulevard
Baltimore, MD 21207
(301) 298-8200
Contact
Ms. Eleanor C. Harding, President
Preferred Limit of Loans or Investments
Up to $500,000
Investment Policy
Prefer straight loans
Industry Preference
Automotive Aftermarket
Geographical Preference
National

MASSACHUSETTS

BancBoston Ventures, Inc.
100 Federal Street
Boston, MA 02110
(617) 434-2442
Contact
Ms. Diana Frazier, Vice President
Mr. Charles C. Woodard, Vice President
Mr. Jeffrey W. Wilson, VP & Treasurer
Preferred Limit of Loans or Investments
Above $1 Million
Investment Policy
Prefer equity-type investments
Industry Preference
Communications
Computer Products
Electronics
Industrial Products
Medical-Health
Geographical Preference
National

Branch Office
First SBIC of California
50 Milk Street, 15th Floor
Boston, MA 02109
(617) 542-7601
(Main Office in California)
Contact
Mr. Michael Cronin, Managing Partner
Preferred Limit of Loans or Investments
Above $1 Million
Investment Policy
Prefer equity-type investments
Industry Preference
Diversified
Geographical Preference
National

Branch Office
Fleet Venture Resources, Inc.
1740 Massachusetts Avenue
Boxborough, MA 01719
(617) 263-0177
(Main Office in Rhode Island)
Contact
Mr. James A. Saalfield, Vice President
Preferred Limit of Loans or Investments
Above $1 Million
Investment Policy
Prefer equity-type investments
Industry Preference
Communications
Computer Products
Electronics
Industrial Products
Medical-Health

Geographical Preference
National

New England Capital Corp.
One Washington Mall, 7th Floor
Boston, MA 02108
(617) 722-6400
Contact
Mr. Z. David Patterson, Executive Vice President
Preferred Limit of Loans or Investments
Above $1 Million
Investment Policy
Prefer equity-type investments
Industry Preference
Communications
Computer Products
Electronics
Industrial Products
Medical-Health
Geographical Preference
National

Orange Nassau Capital Corp.
260 Franklin Street, Suite 1500
Boston, MA 02110
(617) 451-6220
(Atlantic Energy, Atlas II Capital, Vadus Capital all under Orange Nassau management)
Contact
Mr. Joost E. Tjaden, President
Ms. Janet L. Hennessy, VP /Treasurer
Preferred Limit of Loans or Investments
$200,000 - $400,000
Investment Policy
Will make loans and/or equity investments
Industry Preference
Diversified
Geographical Preference
National

Pioneer Ventures Ltd. Partnership
60 State Street
Boston, MA 02109
(617) 742-7825
Contact
Mr. Christopher W. Lynch, Partner
Mr. Frank M. Polestra, Partner
Preferred Limit of Loans or Investments
Up to $1 Million
Investment Policy
Will make loans and/or equity investments
Industry Preference
Diversified
Geographical Preference
Northeast

Shawmut National Ventures Corp.
1 Federal Street, 30th Floor
Boston, MA 02211
(617) 556-4700
Contact
Mr. Steven James Lee, President
Preferred Limit of Loans or Investments
Up to $1 Million
Investment Policy
Prefer equity-type investments
Industry Preference
Energy/Natural Resources
Genetic Engineering
Industrial Products
Medical-Health
Diversified
Geographical Preference
National

TA Associates
45 Milk Street
Boston, MA 02109
(617) 338-0800
(Advent Atlantic, Advent Industrial Capital, Advent IV, V, Chestnut Street Partners, Chestnut Capital Intl. II and Mezzanine Capital under TA management)
Contact
Mr. David D. Croll, Managing Partner
Mr. Richard H. Churchill, Partner
Mr. Stephen F. Gormley, Partner
Preferred Limit of Loans or Investments
Above $1 Million
Investment Policy
Prefer equity-type investments
Industry Preference
Communications
Geographical Preference
National

UST Capital Corp.
40 Court Street
Boston, MA 02108
(617) 726-7171
Contact
Mr. C. W. Dick, President
Mr. Arthur F. F. Snyder, Director
Preferred Limit of Loans or Investments
Up to $500,000
Investment Policy
Will make loans and/or equity investments
Industry Preference
Computer Products
Consumer Products
Energy/Natural Resources
Medical-Health
Diversified
Geographical Preference
Northeast

MICHIGAN

Doan Resources Limited Partnership
4251 Plymouth Road
P.O. Box 986
Ann Arbor, MI 48106
(313) 747-9401
Contact
Mr. Ian R.N. Bund, General Partner
Mr. Richard M. Goff
Preferred Limit of Loans or Investments
Above $1 Million
Investment Policy
Will make loans and/or equity investments
Industry Preference
Communications
Computer Products
Electronics
Medical-Health
Diversified
Geographical Preference
National

Metro-Detroit Investment Co. [MESBIC]
30777 Northwestern, Suite 300
Farmington Hills, MI 48018
(313) 851-6300
Contact
Mr. William J. Fowler, President
Mr. George Caracostas
Preferred Limit of Loans or Investments
Up to$250,000
Investment Policy
Will make loans and/or equity investments
Industry Preference
Communications
Industrial Products
Medical-Health
Transportation
Geographical Preference
Michigan

Motor Enterprises, Inc. [MESBIC]
3044 W. Grand Boulevard, Suite 13-152
Detroit, MI 48202
(313) 556-4273
Contact
Mr. James Kobus, President
Preferred Limit of Loans or Investments
Up to $250,000
Investment Policy
Prefer straight loans
Industry Preference
Transportation/Manufacturing
Geographical Preference
National

Mutual Investment Co. Inc. [MESBIC]
21415 Civic Center Drive, Suite 217
Southfield, MI 48076
(313) 357-2020
Contact:
Mr. Timothy Taylor, Treasurer
Preferred Limit of Loans or Investments
Up to $250,000
Investment Policy
Will make loans and/or equity investments
Industry Preference
Food Services

Branch Office
Regional Financial Enterprises
325 E. Eisenhower Parkway
Ann Arbor, MI 48104
(313) 769-0941
(Main Office in Connecticut)
Contact
Mr. James A. Parsons, General Partner
Preferred Limit of Loans or Investments
Above $1 Million
Investment Policy
Prefer equity-type investments
Industry Preference
Communications
Consumer Products
Industrial Products
Medical-Health
Diversified
Geographical Preference
National

MINNESOTA

FBS Small Business Investment Co.
120 S. 6th Street
First Bank Place East
Minneapolis, MN 55480
(612) 370-4764
Contact
Mr. John H. Bullion, Vice President
Mr. Richard J. Rinkoff, Vice President
Preferred Limit of Loans or Investments
Up to $500,000
Investment Policy
Prefer equity-type investments
Industry Preference
Communications
Computer Products
Electronics
Industrial Products
Medical-Health
Geographical Preference
Midwest

Northland Capital Venture Partnership
277 W. 1st Street
613 Missabe Building
Duluth, MN 55802
(218) 722-0545
Contact
Mr. George G. Barnum, Jr., General Partner
Preferred Limit of Loans or Investments
Up to $250,000
Investment Policy
Prefer equity-type investments
Industry Preference
Diversified
Geographical Preference
Midwest

North Star Ventures II, Inc.
100 S. Fifth Street, Suite 2200
Minneapolis, MN 55402
(612) 333-1133
Contact
Mr. Terrence W. Glarner, President
Preferred Limit of Loans or Investments
Up to $1 Million
Investment Policy
Prefer equity-type investments
Industry Preference
Communications
Consumer Products
Electronics
Medical-Health
Diversified
Geographical Preference
Midwest/National

Norwest Growth Fund, Inc.
222 S. Ninth Street, Suite 2800
Minneapolis, MN 55402
(612) 372-8770
Contact
Mr. Daniel J. Haggerty, President
Mr. Leonard J. Brandt, Vice President
Mr. Timothy A. Stepanek, Vice President
Preferred Limit of Loans or Investments
Above $1 Million

Investment Policy
Prefer equity-type investments
Industry Preference
Diversified
Geographical Preference
National

Shared Ventures, Inc.
6550 York Avenue S., Suite 419
Minneapolis, MN 55435
(612) 925-3411
Contact
Mr. Howard Weiner, President
Preferred Limit of Loans or Investments
Up to $250,000
Investment Policy
Prefer equity-type investments
Industry Preference
Consumer Products
Industrial Products
Medical-Health
Transportation
Diversified
Geographical Preference
Midwest

Threshold Ventures, Inc.
430 Oak Grove Street, Suite 200
Minneapolis, MN 55403
(612) 874-7199
Contact
Mr. John L. Shannon, President
Preferred Limit of Loans or Investments
Up to $250,000
Investment Policy
Prefer equity-type investments
Industry Preference
Communications
Consumer Products
Electronics
Industrial Products
Diversified
Geographical Preference
Midwest/Minnesota

MISSOURI

Bankers Capital Corp.
3100 Gilham Road
Kansas City, MO 64109
(816) 531-1600
Contact
Mr. Raymond E. Glasnapp, President
Preferred Limit of Loans or Investments
Up to $100,000
Investment Policy
Will make loans and/or equity investments
Industry Preference
Diversified

Capital for Business, Inc.
11 S. Meramec, Suite 800
St. Louis, MO 63105
(314) 854-7427
Contact
Mr. James F. O'Donnell, President
Mr. Bart Bergman, Executive Vice President
Mr. Timothy P. Nolan, Senior Investment Officer
Preferred Limit of Loans or Investments
Up to $1 Million
Investment Policy
Will make loans and/or equity investments
Industry Preference
Computer Products
Electronics
Industrial Products
Medical-Health
Transportation
Geographical Preference
National

Branch Office
MorAmerica Capital Corporation
Commerce Tower, Suite 2724
911 Main Street
Kansas City, MO 64105
(816) 842-0114
Contact
Mr. Kevin F. Mullane, Vice President
Preferred Limit of Loans or Investments
Up to $1 Million
Investment Policy
Will make loans and/or equity investments
Industry Preference
Communications
Computer Products
Electronics
Genetic Engineering
Industrial Products
Geographical Preference
Midwest/National

United Missouri Capital Corp.
1010 Grand Avenue, 2nd Floor
Kansas City, MO 64106
(816) 556-7333
Contact
Mr. Joe Kessinger, President
Preferred Limit of Loans or Investments
Up to $1 Million
Investment Policy
Will make loans and/or equity investments
Industry Preference
Communications
Computer Products
Consumer Products
Electronics
Diversified
Geographical Preference
Missouri /Kansas

NEW HAMPSHIRE

VenCap, Inc.
1155 Elm Street
Manchester, NH 03101
(603) 644-6100
Contact
Mr. Richard J. Ash, President
Preferred Limit of Loans or Investments
Up to $100,000
Investment Policy
Will make loans and/or equity investments
Industry Preference
Diversified

NEW JERSEY

Bishop Capital, L.P.
58 Park Place
Newark, NJ 07102
(201) 332-1051
Contact
Mr. Charles J. Irish, President
Ms. Susan M. Glynn, Executive Assistant
Preferred Limit of Loans or Investments
Up to $500,000
Investment Policy
Prefer equity-type investments
Industry Preference
Diversified
Geographical Preference
Northeast

Capital Circulation Corp. [MESBIC]
208 Main Street
Fort Lee, NJ 07024
(201) 947-8637
Contact
Ms. Judy Kao, General Manager
Preferred Limit of Loans or Investments
Up to $100,000
Investment Policy
Prefer straight loans
Industry Preference
Communications
Consumer Products
Medical-Health
Geographical Preference
Northeast

ESLO Capital Corp.
212 Wright Street
Newark, NJ 07114
(201) 242-4488
Contact
Mr. Leo Katz, President
Preferred Limit of Loans or Investments
Up to $500,000
Investment Policy
Will make loans and/or equity investments
Industry Preference
Construction/Real Estate
Transportation
Diversified
Geographical Preference
Northeast/South

First Princeton Capital Corp.
227 Hamburg Turnpike
Pompton Lakes, NJ 07442
(201) 831-0330
Contact
Mr. Michael Lytell, CEO/COO
Preferred Limit of Loans or Investments
Up to $250,000
Investment Policy
Will make loans and/or equity investments
Industry Preference
Construction/Real Estate
Consumer Products
Industrial Products
Diversified
Geographical Preference
Northeast

Monmouth Capital Corp.
P.O. Box 335
Eatontown, NJ 07724
(201) 542-4927
Contact
Mr. Eugene W. Landy, President
Mr. Ralph B. Patterson, Executive Vice President
Preferred Limit of Loans or Investments
Up to $500,000
Investment Policy
Will make loans and/or equity investments
Industry Preference
Diversified
Geographical Preference
Northeast

Rutgers Minority Investment Co. [MESBIC]
180 University Avenue, 3rd Floor
Newark, NJ 07102
(201) 648-5627
Contact
Mr. Oscar Figueroa, President
Preferred Limit of Loans or Investments
Up to $250,000
Investment Policy
Will make loans and/or equity investments
Industry Preference
Diversified
Geographical Preference
Northeast

Tappan Zee Capital Corp.
201 Lower Notch Road
Little Falls, NJ 07424
(201) 256-8280
Contact
Mr. Jack Birnberg, Chairman
Preferred Limit of Loans or Investments
Up to $500,000
Investment Policy
Will make loans and/or equity investments
Industry Preference
Diversified
Geographical Preference
Northeast

Unicorn Ventures II
14 Commerce Drive
Cranford, NJ 07016
(201) 276-7880
(Unicorn Ventures, Ltd. under same management)
Contact
Mr. Frank P. Diassi, General Partner
Preferred Limit of Loans or Investments
Up to $1 Million
Investment Policy
Will make loans and/or equity investments
Industry Preference
Diversified
Geographical Preference
National

NEW MEXICO

Albuquerque SBIC
P.O. Box 487
Albuquerque, NM 87103
(505) 247-0145
Contact
Mr. Albert T. Ussery, President
Preferred Limit of Loans or Investments
Up to $100,000
Investment Policy
Will make loans and/or equity investments

Industry Preference
Diversified
Geographical Preference
New Mexico

Associated Southwest Investors [MESBIC]
2400 Louisiana Street NE, Suite 4
Albuquerque, NM 87110
(505) 881-0066
Contact
Mr. John R. Rice, President
Preferred Limit of Loans or Investments
Up to $250,000
Investment Policy
Will make loans and/or equity investments
Industry Preference
Diversified

Equity Capital Corp.
110 E. Marcy Street, Suite 101
Sante Fe, NM 87501
(505) 988-4273
Contact
Mr. Jerry A. Henson, President
Preferred Limit of Loans or Investments
Up to $250,000
Investment Policy
Prefer to make equity-type investments
Industry Preference
Communications
Electronics
Industrial Products
Medical-Health
Diversified
Geographical Preference
South/Southwest/West

NEW YORK

AMEV Capital Corp.
One World Trade Center, Suite 5001
New York, NY 10048
(212) 323-9800
Contact
Mr. Martin S. Orland, President
Mr. Emmett Bonner, Vice President
Mr. Bruce Bromberg, Vice President
Preferred Limit of Loans or Investments
Up to $1 Million
Investment Policy
Will make loans and/or equity investments
Industry Preference
Diversified
Geographical Preference
National

American Commercial Capital Corp
310 Madison Avenue, Suite 1304
New York, NY 10017
(212) 986-3305
Contact
Mr. Gerald J. Grossman, President
Preferred Limit of Loans or Investments
Up to $1 Million
Investment Policy
Will make loans and/or equity investments
Industry Preference
Construction/Real Estate
Electronics
Industrial Products
Transportation
Geographical Preference
Northeast

BT Capital Corp.
280 Park Avenue
New York, NY 10017
(212) 850-1916
Contact
Mr. James G. Hellmuth, Vice-Chairman
Mr. Noel Urben, President
Ms. B. Martha Cassidy, Vice President
Preferred Limit of Loans or Investments
Above $1 Million
Investment Policy
Prefer equity-type investments
Industry Preference
Communications
Consumer Products
Industrial Products
Medical-Health
Diversified
Geographical Preference
National

Boston Hambro Capital Co.
17 East 71st Street
New York, NY 10021
(212) 288-7778
Contact
Mr. Edwin A. Goodman, President
Mr. Bob Bertoldi, CFO
Preferred Limit of Loans or Investments
Up to $1 Million
Investment Policy
Will make loans and/or equity investments
Industry Preference
Diversified
Geographical Preference
National

Bridger Capital Corp.
645 M adison Avenue
New York, NY 10022
(212) 758-8500
Contact
Mr. Seymour L. Wane, President
Preferred Limit of Loans or Investments
Up to $400,000
Investment Policy
Will make loans and/or equity investments
Industry Preference
Diversified
Geographical Preference
National

CMNY Capital L.P.
77 Water Street
New York, NY 10005
(212) 437-7078
Contact
Mr. Robert Davidoff, Vice President
Mr. Howard Davidoff, Vice President
Preferred Limit of Loans or Investments
Up to $500,000
Investment Policy
Prefer equity-type investments
Industry Preference
Diversified
Geographical Preference
National

Citicorp Venture Capital, Ltd.
153 E. 53rd Street, 28th Floor
New York, NY 10043
(212) 559-1127
Contact
Mr. Peter G. Gerry, President
Mr. David A. Wegmann
Ms. Diane Rivas, Assistant Manager
Preferred Limit of Loans or Investments
Above $1 Million
Investment Policy
Prefer equity-type investments
Industry Preference
Diversified
Geographical Preference
National

Clinton Capital Corp.
79 Madison Avenue, Suite 800
New York, NY 10016
(212) 696-4334
Contact
Mr. Mark Scharfman, President
Mr. Mitchell A. Rothken, Vice President
Mr. Peter Brennan, Vice President
Preferred Limit of Loans or Investments
Above $1 Million
Investment Policy
Prefer straight loans
Industry Preference
Diversified
Geographical Preference
National

Croyden Capital Corp.
45 Rockefeller Plaza, Suite 2168
New York, NY 10111
(212) 974-0184
Contact
Mr. Larry Gorfinkle, President
Ms. Rose Mayerson
Preferred Limit of Loans or Investments
Up to $250,000
Investment Policy
Prefer equity-type investments

Industry Preference
Consumer Products
Electronics
Industrial Products
Diversified
Geographical Preference
Northeast

Diamond Capital Corp.
805 3rd Avenue, Suite 1100
New York, NY 10022
(212) 838-1255
Contact
Ms. Diana Ortado, Executive Vice President
Preferred Limit of Loans or Investments
Up to $500,000
Investment Policy
Prefer straight loans
Industry Preference
Diversified
Geographical Preference
Northeast

ELK Associates Funding Corp. [MESBIC]
600 Third Avenue, Suite 3810
New York, NY 10016
(212) 972-8550
Contact
Mr. Gary C. Granoff, President
Ellen M. Walker, Vice President
Margaret Chance, Secretary
Preferred Limit of Loans or Investments
Up to $250,000
Investment Policy
Prefer straight loans
Industry Preference
Construction/Real Estate
Transportation
Diversified
Geographical Preference
Northeast

Edwards Capital Co.
215 Lexington Avenue, Suite 805
New York, NY 10016
(212) 686-2568
Contact
Mr. Edward H. Teitlebaum, Managing Partner
Preferred Limit of Loans or Investments
Up to $250,000
Investment Policy
Prefer straight loans
Industry Preference
Transportation
Geographical Preference
New York

Equico Capital Corp. [MESBIC]
1290 Avenue of the Americas, Suite 3400
New York, NY 10104
(212) 397-8660
Contact
Mr. Duane E. Hill, President
Mr. Divakar Kamath, Vice President
Preferred Limit of Loans or Investments
Up to $1 Million
Investment Policy
Will make loans and/or equity investments
Industry Preference
Diversified
Geographical Preference
National

Everlast Capital Corp. [MESBIC]
350 Fifth Avenue, Suite 2805
New York, NY 10118
(212) 695-3910
Contact
Mr. Frank J. Segreto, Vice President
Preferred Limit of Loans or Investments
Up to $250,000
Investment Policy
Will make loans and/or equity investments
Industry Preference
Construction/Real Estate
Consumer Products
Geographical Preference
Northeast

Fairfield Equity Corp.
200 E. 42nd Street
New York, NY 10017
(212) 867-0150

Contact
Mr. Matthew A. Berdon, President
Preferred Limit of Loans or Investments
Up to $250,000
Investment Policy
Will make loans and/or equity investments
Industry Preference
Communications
Consumer Products
Diversified
Geographical Preference
Northeast

Ferranti High Technology, Inc.
515 Madison Avenue, Suite 1225
New York, NY 10022
(212) 688-9828
Contact
Mr. Sanford R. Simon, President
Mr. Michael R. Simon, Vice President
Mr. Joseph J. Katz, Vice President
Preferred Limit of Loans or Investments
Up to $500,000
Investment Policy
Will make loans and/or equity investments
Industry Preference
Diversified
Geographical Preference
National

Fifty-Third St. Ventures, L.P.
155 Main Street
Cold Spring, NY 10516
(914) 265-4157
Contact
Mr. Daniel Tessler, General Partner
Preferred Limit of Loans or Investments
Above $1 Million
Investment Policy
Prefer equity-type investments
Industry Preference
Diversified
Geographical Preference
Northeast
National

Branch Office
Fleet Venture Resources, Inc.
666 Third Avenue 10017
New York, NY 10017
(212) 972-8126
(Main office in Rhode Island)
Contact
Mr. Habib Y. Gorgi, Vice President
Preferred Limit of Loans or Investments
Above $1 Million
Investment Policy
Prefer equity-type investments
Industry Preference
Communications
Computer Products
Electronics
Industrial Products
Medical-Health
Geographical Preference
National

Fundex Capital Corp.
525 Northern Boulevard
Great Neck, NY 11021
(516) 466-8550
Contact
Mr. Howard Sommer, President
Mr. Martin Albert, Vice President
Preferred Limit of Loans or Investments
Up to $1 Million
Investment Policy
Will make loans and/or equity investments
Industry Preference
Diversified
Geographical Preference
Northeast

GHW Capital Corp.
25 W. 45th Street, Suite 707
New York, NY 10036
(212) 687-1708
Contact
Ms. Nesta Stephens, President
Mr. Jack Graff
Preferred Limit of Loans or Investments
Up to $250,000
Investment Policy
Prefer straight loans
Industry Preference
Diversified
Geographical Preference
Northeast

Genesee Funding, Inc.
100 Corporate Woods
Rochester, NY 14623
(716) 262-4716
Contact
Mr. Keene Bolton, President
Preferred Limit of Loans or Investments
Up to $200,000
Investment Policy
Will make loans and/or equity investments
Industry Preference
Computer Products
Electronics
Industrial Products
Medical-Health
Diversified
Geographical Preference
Northeast

Hanover Capital Corp. (The)
150 E. 58th Street, Suite 2710
New York, NY 10155
(212) 980-9670
Contact
Mr. Robert Wilson, Vice President
Preferred Limit of Loans or Investments
Up to $500,000
Investment Policy
Will make loans and/or equity investments
Industry Preference
Computer Products
Construction/Real Estate
Electronics
Medical-Health
Geographical Preference
Northeast

Harvest Ventures
767 Third Avenue, 7th Floor
New York, NY 10017
(212) 838-7776
(ASEA-Harvest Partners II, Bohlen Capital, European Development Capital, WFG Harvest Partners, 767 L.P. under Harvest management)
Contact
Mr. Harvey J. Wertheim, Managing Director
Mr. Harvey Mallement, Managing Director
Preferred Limit of Loans or Investments
Above $1 Million
Investment Policy
Will make loans and/or equity investments
Industry Preference
Communications
Computer Products
Consumer Products
Industrial Products
Medical-Health
Geographical Preference
National

Ibero-American Investors Corp. [MESBIC]
38 Solo Street
Rochester, NY 14604
(716) 262-3440
Contact
Mr. Emilio Serrano, President
Ms. Lauren Burns, Chief Financial Executive
Preferred Limit of Loans or Investments
Up to $250,000
Investment Policy
Will make loans and/or equity investments
Industry Preference
Diversified
Geographical Preference
New York

Irving Capital Corp.
1290 Avenue of Americas, 29th Floor
New York, NY 10104
(212) 408-4800
Contact
Mr. J. Andrew McWethy, President
Ms. Kathleen Snyder
Mr. Steve Tuttle
Preferred Limit of Loans or Investments
Above $1 Million
Investment Policy
Prefer equity-type investments
Industry Preference
Diversified
Geographical Preference
National

Kwiat Capital Corp.
576 Fifth Avenue
New York, NY 10036
(212) 391-2461
Contact
Mr. Sheldon Kwiat, President
Preferred Limit of Loans or Investments
Up to $100,000
Investment Policy
Will make loans and/or equity investments
Industry Preference
Diversified
Geographical Preference
Northeast

M & T Capital Corp.
One M & T Plaza, 12th Floor
Buffalo, NY 14240
(716) 842-5881
Contact
Mr. William Randon, President
Ms. Norma Gracia, Treasurer
Preferred Limit of Loans or Investments
Up to $500,000
Investment Policy
Will make loans and/or equity investments
Industry Preference
Communications
Computer Products
Industrial Products
Medical-Health
Diversified
Geographical Preference
National

MH Capital Investors, Inc.
270 Park Avenue, 5th Floor
New York, NY 10017
(212) 808-0109
Contact
Mr. Thomas J. Sandleitner, Chairman
Mr. Kevin P. Falvey
Ms. Kathleen P. Prime
Preferred Limit of Loans or Investments
Above $1 Million
Investment Policy
Prefer equity-type investments
Industry Preference
Communications
Consumer Products
Industrial Products
Medical-Health
Diversified
Geographical Preference
National

Manhattan Central Capital Corp. [MESBIC]
38 West 32 Street
New York, NY 10001
(212) 684-6411
Contact
Mr. David Choi

Medallion Funding Corp. [MESBIC]
205 E. 42nd Street, Suite 2020
New York, NY 10017
(212) 682-3300
Contact
Mr. Alvin Murstein, President
Mr. Michael Fanger, Vice President
Preferred Limit of Loans or Investments
Up to $1 Million
Investment Policy
Will make loans and/or equity investments
Industry Preference
Construction/Real Estate
Transportation
Diversified
Geographical Preference
Northeast

Minority Equity Capital Co., Inc. [MESBIC]
275 Madison Avenue, Suite 1901
New York, NY 10016
(212) 686-9710

Contact
Mr. Donald F. Greene, President
Ms. Edith Best-McQueen, Sr. Administrator
Preferred Limit of Loans or Investments
Up to $500,000
Investment Policy
Will make loans and/or equity investments
Industry Preference
Diversified
Geographical Preference
Puerto Rico/National

NatWest USA Capital Corp.
175 Water Street
New York, NY 10038
(212) 602-1200
Contact
Mr. Orville G. Aarons, Sr. VP & Gen. Manager
Mr. Jeffrey S. Wilks, Vice President
Preferred Limit of Loans or Investments
Up to $1 Million
Investment Policy
Will make loans and/or equity investments
Industry Preference
Diversified
Geographical Preference
National

Norstar Capital Inc.
One Norstar Plaza
Albany, NY 12207
(518) 447-4492
Contact
Mr. Raymond A. Lancaster, President
Ms. Barbara S. Murphy, Vice President
Mr. Stephen Puricelli, Associate
Preferred Limit of Loans or Investments
Up to $1 Million
Investment Policy
Will make loans and/or equity investments
Industry Preference
Communications
Energy/Natural Resources
Industrial Products
Medical-Health
Diversified
Geographical Preference
Northeast

Norwood Venture Corp.
145 W. 45th Street, Suite 1211
New York, NY 10036
(212) 869-5075
Contact
Mr. Mark R. Littell, President
Preferred Limit of Loans or Investments
Up to $1 Million
Industry Preference
Diversified
Geographical Preference
National

North American Funding Corp. [MESBIC]
177 Canal Street
New York, NY 10013
(212) 226-0080
Contact
Mr. Franklin Wong, President
Preferred Limit of Loans or Investments
Up to $250,000
Investment Policy
Prefer straight loans
Industry Preference
Diversified
Geographical Preference
National

North Street Capital Corp. [MESBIC]
250 North Street, RA-6S
White Plains, NY 10625
(914) 335-7901
Contact
Mr. Ralph L. McNeal, Sr., President
Preferred Limit on Loans or Investments
Up to $250,000
Investment Policy
Prefer equity type investments
Industry Preference
Diversified

Onondaga Venture Capital Fund, Inc
327 State Tower Building.
Syracuse, NY 13202
(315) 478-0157
Contact
Mr. Irving W. Schwartz, Exec. Vice President
Preferred Limit of Loans or Investments
Up to $250,000
Investment Policy
Will make loans and/or equity investments
Industry Preference
Diversified
Geographical Preference
Northeast

Pan Pac Capital Corp. [MESBIC]
121 East Industry Court
Deer Park, NY 11729
(516) 586-7900
Contact
Dr. Ing-Ping J. Lee
Preferred Limit of Loans or Investments
Up to $100,000
Investment Policy
Will make loans and/or equity investments
Industry Preference
Diversified

Pyramid Ventures, Inc.
280 Park Avenue
New York, NY 10015
(212) 850-1934
Contact
Mr. Robert Barbanell, Chairman
Mr. John Popovitch, Treasurer
Preferred Limit of Loans or Investments
Up to $1 Million
Investment Policy
Prefer equity-type investments
Industry Preference
Communications
Computer Products
Electronics
Genetic Engineering
Medical-Health
Geographical Preference
West

Questech Capital Corporation
600 Madison Avenue, 21st Floor
New York, NY 10022
(212) 758-7722
Contact
Mr. John E. Koonce, President
Mr. James L. Arnold, Secretary
Mr. Gary A. Prince, Chief Financial Officer
Preferred Limit of Loans of Investments
Up to $1 Million
Investment Policy
Prefer equity-type investments
Industry Preference
Communications
Computer Products
Electronics
Genetic Engineering
Medical-Health
Geographical Preference
National

R & R Financial Corporation
1451 Broadway
New York, NY 10036
(212) 790-1400
Contact
Mr. Martin Eisenstadt, Vice President
Preferred Limit of Loans or Investments
Up to $250,000
Investment Policy
Prefer straight loans
Industry Preference
Communications
Consumer Products
Diversified
Geographical Preference
Northeast

Rand SBIC, Inc.
1300 Rand Building
Buffalo, NY 14203
(716) 853-0802
Contact
Mr. Donald A. Ross, President
Mr. Thomas J. Bernard, Vice President
Preferred Limit of Loans or Investments
Up to $250,000
Investment Policy
Will make loans and/or equity investments
Industry Preference
Diversified
Geographical Preference
Northeast

Small Business Electronics Inv. Corp
1220 Peninsula Boulevard
Hewlett, NY 11557
(516) 374-0743
Contact
Mr. Stanley Meisels, President
Preferred Limit of Loans or Investments
Up to $100,000
Investment Policy
Prefer straight loans
Industry Preference
Diversified
Geographical Preference
New York

Southern Tier Capital Corp.
55 S. Main Street
Liberty, NY 12754
(914) 292-3030
Contact
Mr. Milton Brizel, President
Preferred Limit of Loans or Investments
Up to $100,000
Investment Policy
Will make loans and/or equity investments
Industry Preference
Diversified
Geographical Preference
New York State

TLC Funding Corp.
141 S. Central Avenue
Hartsdale, NY 10530
(914) 683-1144
Contact
Mr. Philip G. Kass, President
Preferred Limit of Loans or Investments
Up to $500,000
Investment Policy
Prefer straight loans
Industry Preference
Retail Establishments
Diversified
Geographical Preference
Northeast

Transportation Capital Corp. [MESBIC]
60 E. 42nd Street, Suite 3115
New York, NY 10165
(212) 697-4885
Contact
Mr. Melvin L. Hirsch, President
Preferred Limit of Loans or Investments
Above $1 Million
Investment Policy
Prefer straight loans
Industry Preference
Medical-Health
Transportation
Diversified
Geographical Preference
National

Vega Capital Corp.
720 White Plains Road
Scarsdale, NY 10583
(914) 472-8550
Contact
Mr. Victor Harz, President
Mr. Ronald A. Linden, Vice President
Preferred Limit of Loans or Investments
Up to $1 Million
Investment Policy
Will make loans and/or equity investments
Industry Preference
Construction/Real Estate
Consumer Products
Industrial Products
Medical-Health
Diversified
Geographical Preference
National

Venture Opportunities Corp. [MESBIC]
110 E. 59th Streeet, 29th Floor
New York, NY 10022
(212) 832-3737

Contact
Mr. Fred March, President
Ms. Flora March, Vice President
Preferred Limit of Loans or Investments
Up to $250,000
Investment Policy
Will make loans and/or equity investments
Industry Preference
Diversified
Geographical Preference
Northeast/National

Venture SBIC, Inc.
249-12 Jericho Turnpike
Floral Park, NY 11001
(516) 352-0068
Contact
Mr. Arnold Feldman, President
Mr. Jerome Feldman, Secretary
Preferred Limit of Loans or Investments
Up to $250,000
Investment Policy
Will make loans and/or equity investments
Industry Preference
Construction/Real Estate
Consumer Products
Transportation
Diversified
Geographical Preference
New York

Winfield Capital Corp.
237 Mamaroneck Avenue
White Plains, NY 10605
(914) 949-2600
Contact
Mr. Stanley Pechman, President
Preferred Limit of Loans or Investment
Up to $500,000
Investment Policy
Will make loans and/or equity investments
Industry Preference
Diversified
Geographical Preference
Northeast

Wood River Capital Corp.
645 Madison Avenue
New York, NY 10022
(212) 750-9420
Contact
Mr. Thomas A. Barron, President
Preferred Limit of Loans or Investments
Up to $1 Million
Investment Policy
Will make loans and/or equity investments
Industry Preference
Diversified
Geographical Preference
National

NORTH CAROLINA

Delta Capital, Inc.
227 N. Tryon Street, Suite 201
Charlotte, NC 28202
(704) 372-1410
Contact
Mr. Alex B. Wilkins, Jr., President
Preferred Limit of Loans or Investments
Up to $500,000
Investment Policy
Will make loans and/or equity investments
Industry Preference
Diversified
Geographical Preference
South/National

Heritage Capital Corp.
2095 Two First Union Center
Charlotte, NC 28282
(704) 334-2867
Contact
Mr. William R. Starnes, President
Mr. G. Kinsey Roper, Executive Vice President
Mr. J. Wylie Fox, Vice President
Preferred Limit of Loans or Investments
Up to $500,000
Investment Policy
Prefer equity-type investments
Industry Preference
Diversified
Geographical Preference
South

Kitty Hawk Capital, Ltd.
1640 Independence Center
Charlotte, NC 28246
(704) 333-3777
Contact
Mr. Walter H. Wilkinson, Jr., General Partner
Mr. W. Chris Hegele, General Partner
Preferred Limit of Loans or Investments
Up to $250,000
Investment Policy
Prefer equity-type investments
Industry Preference
Communications
Computer Products
Consumer Products
Industrial Products
Medical-Health
Geographical Preference
South

NCNB Venture Co., L.P.
One NCNB Plaza, Suite T39
Charlotte, NC 28255
(704) 374-0435
Contact
Mr. Michael F. Elliott
Mr. S. Epes Robinson
Preferred Limit of Loans or Investments
Above $1 Million
Investment Policy
Prefer equity-type investments
Industry Preference
Communications
Computer Products
Electronics
Industrial Products
Medical-Health
Geographical Preference
Northeast/South/Southwest

OHIO

A. T. Capital Corp.
900 Euclid Avenue, T-18
Cleveland, OH 44101
(216) 687-4970
Contact
Mr. Robert Salipante, President
Ms. Lisa M. Simecek, Manager
Ms. Kathleen C. Braun, Associate
Preferred Limit of Loans or Investments
Up to $500,000
Investment Policy
Prefers equity-type investments
Industry Preference
Communications
Computer Products
Electronics
Medical-Health
Geographical Preference
National

Capital Funds Corp.
800 Superior Avenue, 10th Floor
Cleveland, OH 44114
(216) 622-8628
Contact
Mr. Carl G. Nelson, Vice President & Manager
Mr. David B. Chilcote, Vice President
Mr. Robert F. Williams, Associate
Preferred Limit of Loans or Invesments
Up to $1 Million
Investment Policy
Will make loans and/or equity investments
Industry Preference
Communications
Computer Products
Consumer Products
Electronics
Industrial Products
Geographical Preference
Midwest

Center City MESBIC, Inc. [MESBIC]
40 S. Main Street, Suite 762
Dayton, OH 45402
(513) 461-6164
Contact
Mr. Michael A. Robinson, President
Ms. Yyvette R. Beach, Office Manager
Preferred Limit of Loans or Investments
Up to $100,000
Investment Policy
Will make loans and/or equity investments
Industry Preference
Diversified
Geographical Preference
Ohio

Clarion Capital Corp.
35555 Curtis Boulevard
Eastlake, OH 44114
(216) 953-0555
Contact
Mr. Morton A. Cohen, Chairman/President
Mr. Michael Boeckman, Vice President
Mr. Douglas Elliott, Vice President
Preferred Limit of Loans or Invesments
Up to $500,000
Investment Policy
Prefers equity-type investments
Industry Preference
Communications
Genetic Engineering
Industrial Products
Medical-Health
Diversified
Geographical Preference
Northeast/Midwest/West

First Ohio Capital Corp.
606 Madison Avenue
Toledo, OH 43604
(419) 259-7151
Contact
Mr. Michael J. Aust, Vice President
Ms. Ann Sciarini, Investment Analyst
Mr. David McMacken, General Manager
Preferred Limit of Loans or Investments
Up to $250,000
Investment Policy
Will make loans and/or equity investments
Industry Preference
Diversified
Geographical Preference
Midwest

Gries Investment Co.
1500 Statler Office Tower
Cleveland, OH 44115
(216) 861-1146
Contact
Mr. Robert D. Gries, President
Mr. Richard F. Brezic, Vice President
Preferred Limit of Loans or Investments
Up to $500,000
Investment Policy
Prefer equity-type investments
Industry Preference
Diversified
Geographical Preference
National

National City Capital Corp.
629 Euclid Avenue
Cleveland, OH 44114
(216) 575-2491
Contact
Mr. John B. Naylor, President
Ms. Martha A. Barry, Vice President
Preferred Limit of Loans or Investments
Up to $500,000
Investment Policy
Prefer equity-type investments
Industry Preference
Diversified
Geographical Preference
Northeast/South/Midwest

Branch Office
River Capital Corp.
796 Huntington Building
Cleveland, OH 44115
(216) 781-3655
(Main Office in Virginia)
Contact
Mr. Peter D. Van Oosterhout, President
Preferred Limit of Loans or Investments
Up to $500,000
Investment Policy
Prefer equity-type investments
Industry Preference
Communications
Energy/Natural Resources
Industrial Products

Medical-Health
Diversified
Geographical Preference
National

__Seagate Venture Management Inc.__
245 Summit Street, Suite 1403
Toledo, OH 43603
(419) 259-8397
Contact
Mr. Charles A. Brown, Vice President
Mr. John A. Collins, VC Investment Officer
Preferred Limit of Loans or Investments
Up to $250,000
Investment Policy
Will make loans and/or equity investments
Industry Preference
Communications
Computer Products
Electronics
Industrial Products
Diversified
Geographical Preference
Midwest

OKLAHOMA

__Alliance Business Investment Co.__
One Williams Center, Suite 2000
Tulsa, OK 74172
(918) 584-3581
Contact
Mr. Barry M. Davis, President
Mr. Mark Blankenship, Vice President
Preferred Limit of Loans or Investments
Up to $500,000
Investment Policy
Prefer equity-type investments
Industry Preference
Energy/Natural Resources
Industrial Products
Medical-Health
Transportation
Diversified
Geographical Preference
Southwest

__Western Venture Capital Corp.__
4880 S. Lewis
Tulsa, OK 74105
(918) 749-7981
Contact
Mr. William B. Baker, President
Mr. John M. Lare, Vice President
Preferred Limit of Loans or Investments
Up to $500,000
Investment Policy
Will make loans and/or equity investments
Industry Preference
Communications
Electronics
Industrial Products
Transportation
Diversified
Geographical Preference
Southwest/National

OREGON

__Northern Pacific Capital Corp.__
P.O. Box 1658
Portland, OR 97207
(503) 241-1255
Contact
Mr. Joseph P. Tennant, President
Preferred Limit of Loans or Investments
Above $1 Million
Investment Policy
Will make loans and/or equity investments
Industry Preference
Consumer Products
Industrial Products
Transportation
Geographical Preference
West

__Branch Office__
__Norwest Growth Fund, Inc.__
1300 SW 5th Avenue, Suite 3018
Portland, OR 97201
(503) 223-6622
(Main office in Minnesota)
Contact
Mr. Anthony Miadich, Vice President
Mr. Dale J. Vogel, Vice President
Preferred Limit of Loans or Investments
Above $1 Million
Investment Policy
Prefer equity-type investments
Industry Preference
Diversified
Geographical Preference
National

PENNSYLVANIA

__Capital Corp. of America__
225 S. 15th Street, Suite 920
Philadelphia, PA 19102
(215) 732-1666
Contact
Mr. Martin M. Newman, President
Preferred Limit of Loans or Investments
Up to $250,000
Investment Policy
Will make loans and/or equity investments
Industry Preference
Computer Products
Medical-Health
Diversified
Geographical Preference
National

__Enterprise Venture Capital Corp. of PA__
227 Franklin Street, Suite 215
Johnstown, PA 15901
(814) 535-7597
Contact
Mr. Donald W. Cowie, Vice President
Preferred Limit of Loans or Investments
Up to $100,000
Investment Policy
Will make loans and/or equity investments
Industry Preference
Computer Products
Consumer Products
Electronics
Industrial Products
Diversified
Geographical Preference
Pennsylvania

__Fidelcor Capital Corp.__
123 S. Broad Street
Philadelphia, PA 19109
(215) 985-7287
Contact
Mr. Bruce H. Luehrs, President
Ms. Elizabeth T. Crawford, Vice President
Preferred Limit of Loans or Investmetns
Up to $1 Million
Investment Policy
Will make loans and/or equity investments
Industry Preference
Diversified
Geographical Preference
Northeast

__Branch Office__
__First SBIC of California__
P.O. Box 512
Washington, PA 15301
(412) 223-0707
(Main Office in California)
Contact
Mr. Daniel Dye
Preferred Limit of Loans or Investments
Above $1 Million
Investment Policy
Prefer equity-type investments
Industry Preference
Diversified
Geographical Preference
National

__First Valley Capital Corp.__
One Center Square, Suite 201
Allentown, PA 18101
(215) 776-6760
Contact
Mr. Matthew Thomas, President
Preferred Limit of Loans or Investments
Up to $100,000
Investment Policy
Will make loans and/or equity investments
Industry Preference
Diversified
Geographical Preference
Northeast

__Franklin Corp. SBIC (The)__
Plymouth Meeting Executive Campus
610 W. Germantown Pike, Suite 461
Plymouth Meeting, PA 19462
(215) 941-6746
Contact
Mr. Stephen L. Brown, Chairman
Mr. Norman S. Strobel, President
Mr. James S. Eisberg, Sec. & General Counsel
Preferred Limit of Loans or Investments
Up to $1 Million
Investment Policy
Will make loans and/or equity investments
Industry Preference
Construction/Real Estate
Energy/Natural Resources
Industrial Products
Medical-Helath
Diversified
Geographical Preference
Northeast/National

__Greater Philadelphia Venture Capital Corp., Inc.__
225 S. 15th Street, Suite 920
Philadelphia, PA 19102
(215) 732-1666
Contact
Mr. Martin M. Newman, General Manager
Preferred Limit of Loans or Investments
Up to $250,000
Investment Policy
Will make loans and/or equity investments
Industry Preference
Communications
Electronics
Geographical Preference
Northeast

__Meridian Capital Corp.__
222 Blue Bell West
Blue Bell, PA 19422
(203) 966-2800
Contact
Mr. Joseph E. Laky, President/CEO
Mr. Richard E. Meyers
Preferred Limit of Loans or Investments
Up to $500,000
Investment Policy
Will make loans and/or equity investments
Industry Preference
Consumer Products
Industrial Products
Diversified
Geographical Preference
Northeast

__Meridian Venture Partners__
259 Radnor-Chester Road, Suite 220
Radnor, PA 19087
(215) 254-2999
Contact
Mr. Raymond R. Rafferty, Jr.
Mr. Robert E. Brown, Jr.
Mr. George P. Keeley
Preferred Limit of Loans or Investments
Up to $1 Million
Investment Policy
Prefer equity-type investments
Industry Preference
Communications
Computer Products
Electronics
Medical-Health
Diversified
Geographical Preference
Northeast

__PNC Capital Corp.__
5th Avenue & Wood Street
Pittsburgh, PA 15222
(412) 762-2245
Contact
Mr. David M. Hillman, Executive Vice President
Mr. Peter V. Del Presto, Vice President
Mr. David J. Blair, Vice President

Preferred Limit of Loans or Investments
Up to $1 Million
Investment Policy
Will make loans and/or equity investments
Industry Preference
Communications
Computer Products
Electronics
Industrial Products
Medical-Health
Geographical Preference
Northeast/Midwest

PUERTO RICO

North America Investment Corp. [MESBIC]
Banco Popular Center, Suite 1710
Hato Rey, PR 00919
(809) 754-6177
Contact
Mr. S. Ruiz - Betancourt, President
Preferred Limit of Loans or Investments
Up to $250,000
Investment Policy
Will make loans and/or equity investments
Industry Preferences
Communications
Industrial Products
Medical-Health
Transportation
Diversified
Geographical Preference
Puerto Rico/Virgin Islands/Carribean

RHODE ISLAND

Domestic Capital Corp.
815 Reservoir Avenue
Cranston, RI 02910
(401) 946-3310
Contact
Mr. Nathaniel B. Baker, President
Mr. H. Jeffrey Baker
Mr. Daniel Rinaldi
Preferred Limit of Loans or Investments
Up to $500,000
Investment Policy
Prefer straight loans
Industry Preference
Diversified
Geographical Preference
Northeast

Fleet Venture Resources, Inc.
111 Westminster Street
Providence, RI 02920
(401) 278-6770
Contact
Mr. Robert Van Degna, President
Preferred Limit of Loans or Investments
Above $1 Million
Investment Policy
Prefer equity-type investments
Industry Preference
Communications
Computer Products
Electronics
Industrial Products
Medical-Health
Geographical Preference
National

Monarch Narragansett Ventures, Inc.
50 Kennedy Plaza
Providence, RI 02903
(401) 751-1000
Contact
Mr. Arthur D. Little, Chairman
Mr. Gregory P. Barber
Preferred Limit of Loans or Investments
Above $1 Million
Investment Policy
Prefer equity-type investments
Industry Preference
Communications
Consumer Products
Electronics
Industrial Products
Diversified
Geographical Preference
National

Old Stone Capital Corp.
One Old Stone Square, 11th Floor
Providence, RI 02901
(401) 278-2534
Contact
Mr. Stephen P. Higginbotham, President
Ms. Denise Massotti, Assistant Secretary
Preferred Limit of Loans or Investments
Up to $1 Million
Investment Policy
Prefer straight loans
Industry Preference
Construction/Real Estate
Geographical Preference
Northeast
Branch Office
River Capital Corp.
555 S. Main Street, Suite 321
Providence, RI 02903
(401) 861-7470
(Main Office in Virginia)
Contact
Mr. Peter D. Van Oosterhout, President
Mr. Robert E. Lee
Preferred Limit of Loans or Investments
Up to $500,000
Investment Policy
Prefer equity-type investments
Industry Preference
Communications
Energy/Natural Resources
Industrial Products
Medical-Health
Diversified
Geographical Preference
National

Wallace Capital Corp.
170 Westminster Street
Providence, RI 02903
(401) 273-9191
Contact
Mr. Lloyd W. Granoff, President
Preferred Limit of Loans or Investments
Up to $500,000
Investment Policy
Will make loans and/or equity investments
Industry Preference
Diversified
Geographical Preference
Northeast

SOUTH CAROLINA

Reedy River Ventures
P.O. Box 17526
Greenville, SC 29606
(803) 297-9198
Contact
Mr. John M. Sterling, Jr., General Partner
Mr. Tee Hooper, Jr.
Preferred Limit of Loans or Investments
Up to $500,000
Investment Policy
Prefer equity-type investments
Industry Preference
Computer Products
Electronics
Energy/Natural Resources
Industrial Products
Diversified
Geographical Preference
South

TENNESSEE

Chickasaw Capital Corp. [MESBIC]
P.O. Box 387
Memphis, TN 38147
(901) 523-6404
Contact
Mr. Thomas L. Moore, President
Mr. C. P. Sims, Jr., Vice President
Mr. James P. Farrell, Director
Preferred Limit of Loans or Investments
Up to $100,000
Investment Policy
Prefer straight loans
Industry Preference
Diversified
Geographical Preference
Tennessee

Financial Resources, Inc.
2800 Sterick Building
Memphis, TN 38103
(901) 527-9411
Contact
Mr. Milton C. Picard, Chairman
Preferred Limit of Loans or Investments
Up to $250,000
Investment Policy
Prefer equity-type investments
Industry Preference
Diversified
Geographical Preference
National

Leader Capital Corp.
P.O. Box 708
Memphis, TN 38101-0708
(901) 578-2405
Contact
Mr. Edward Pruitt, President
Preferred Limit of Loans or Investments
Up to $250,000
Investment Policy
Will make loans and/or equity investments
Industry Preference
Homeowner Services
Geographical Preference
South

Tennessee Equity Capital Corp. [MESBIC]
1102 Stonewall Jackson
Nashville, TN 37220
(615) 373-4502
Contact
Mr. Walter Cohen, President/CEO
Preferred Limit of Loans or Investments
Up to $500,000
Investment Policy
Prefer equity-type investments
Industry Preference
Communications
Computer Products
Electronics
Medical-Health
Diversified
Geographical Preference
South/National

Valley Capital Corp. [MESBIC]
100 W. Martin L. King Boulevard, Suite 806
Chattanooga, TN 37402
(615) 265-1557
Contact
Mr. Lamar Partridge, President
Ms. Faye Donato, Administrative Assistant
Preferred Limit of Loans or Investments
Up to $250,000
Investment Policy
Prefer straight loans
Industry Preference
Communications
Consumer Products
Medical-Health
Diversified
Geographical Preference
South

TEXAS

Americap Corp.
7575 San Felipe, Suite 160
Houston, TX 77063
(713) 780-8084
Contact
Mr. James L. Hurn, President
Preferred Limit of Loans or Investments
Up to $500,000
Investment Policy
Prefer equity-type investments
Industry Preference
Communications
Computer Products
Electronics
Medical-Health
Geographical Preference
Southwest

Brittany Capital Company
2424 LTV Tower
1525 Elm Street
Dallas, TX 75201
(214) 954-1515

Contact
Mr. Robert E. Clements, General Partner
Mr. Steven S. Peden, General Partner
Preferred Limit of Loans or Investments
Up to $100,000
Investment Policy
Will make loans and/or equity investments
Industry Preference
Diversified
Geographical Preference
National

Business Capital Corp.
4809 Cole Avenue, Suite 250
Dallas, TX 75205
(214) 522-3739
Contact
Mr. Keith Martin, President
Preferred Limit of Loans or Investments
Up to $100,000
Investment Policy
Will make loans and/or equity investments
Industry Preference
Communications
Industrial Products
Transportation
Geographical Preference
Southwest

Capital Marketing Corp.
P.O. Box 1000
Keller, TX 76248
(817) 656-7380
Contact
Mr. Ray Ballard, General Manager
Mr. Morris Whetstone, Operating Officer
Preferred Limit of Loans or Investments
Up to $1 Million
Investment Policy
Prefer straight loans
Industry Preference
Grocery
Geographical Preference
Texas

Capital Southwest Venture Corp.
12900 Preston Road, Suite 700
Dallas, TX 75230
(214) 233-8242
Contact
Mr. William R. Thomas, President
Mr. J. Bruce Duty, Vice President
Mr. Patrick F. Hamner, Vice President
Preferred Limit of Loans or Investments
Up to $1 Million
Investment Policy
Prefer equity-type investments
Industry Preference
Communications
Consumer Products
Industrial-Products
Diversified
Geographical Preference
National

Central Texas SBIC
514 Austin Avenue, P.O. Box 2600
Waco, TX 76702
(817) 753-6461
Contact
Mr. David G. Horner, President
Mr. Ross L. Miller, Secretary
Preferred Limit of Loans or Investments
Up to $100,000
Investment Policy
Will make loans and/or equity investments
Industry Preference
Construction/Real Estate
Consumer Products
Industrial Products
Transportation
Diversified
Geographical Preference
Texas

Energy Assets, Inc.
4900 Republic Bank Center
Houston, TX 77002
(713) 236-9999
Contact
Mr. Matthew R. Simmons, President
Preferred Limit of Loans or Investments
Up to $100,000
Investment Policy
Prefer equity-type investments
Industry Preference
Energy/Natural Resources
Geographical Preference
Southwest

Energy Capital Corp.
953 Esperson Building
Houston, TX 77002
(214) 236-0006
Contact
Mr. Herbert Poyner, Jr.
Preferred Limit of Loans or Investments
Up to $1 Million
Investment Policy
Prefer straight loans
Industry Preference
Energy/Natural Resources
Geographical Preference
Southwest

Enterprise Capital Corp.
4543 Post Oak Place Drive, Suite 130
Houston, TX 77027
(713) 621-9444
Contact
Mr. Fred S. Zeidman, President
Mr. Fiore P. Talarico, Jr., Vice President
Preferred Limit of Loans or Investments
Up to $1,000,000
Investment Policy
Will make loans and/or equity investments
Industry Preference
Diversified
Geographical Preference
National

FCA Investment Co.
3000 Post Oak Boulevard, Suite 1790
Houston, TX 77056
(713) 965-0061
Contact
Mr. R. S. Baker, Jr., Chairman
Preferred Limit of Loans or Investments
Up to $250,000
Investment Policy
Will make loans and/or equity investments
Industry Preference
Diversified
Geographical Preference
National

First Interstate Capital Corp. of Texas
P.O. Box 3326
Houston, TX 77253
(713) 226-1625
Contact
Mr. Richard Smith, President
Mr. David M. Miller, Vice President
Preferred Limit of Loans or Investments
Above $1 Million
Investment Policy
Prefer equity-type investments
Industry Preference
Communications
Energy/Natural Resources
Industrial Products
Medical-Health
Diversified
Geographical Preference
South/Midwest/Southwest

Livingston Capital Ltd.
P.O. Box 2507
Houston, TX 77252
(713) 872-3213
Contact
Mr. J. Livingston Kosberg, Partner
Mr. Mark J. Brookner
Ms. Glory S. Green
Preferred Limit of Loans or Investments
Up to $250,000
Investment Policy
Will make loans and/or equity investments
Industry Preference
Diversified
Geographical Preference
Southwest

MESBIC Financial Corp. of Dallas [MESBIC]
12655 N. Central Expressway, Suite 814
Dallas, TX 75243
(214) 991-1597
Contact
Mr. Donald R. Lawhorne, President
Mr. Thomas G. Gerron, VP /Controller
Mr. Ira D. Harrison, Vice President Bus. Dev.
Preferred Limit of Loans or Investments
Up to $250,000
Investment Policy
Will make loans and/or equity investments
Industry Preference
Diversified
Geographical Preference
Southwest

MESBIC Financial Corp. of Houston [MESBIC]
811 Rusk, Suite 201
Houston, TX 77002
(713) 228-8321
Contact
Mr. Lynn Miller, President
Preferred Limit of Loans or Investments
Up to $250,000
Investment Policy
Will make loans and/or equity investments
Industry Preference
Diversified
Geographical Preference
Texas

MVenture Corp
P.O. Box 662090
Dallas, TX 75266-2090
(214) 939-3131
Contact
Mr. J. Wayne Gaylord, President
Mr. Thomas F. Bartlett, Sr. Vice President
Preferred Limit of Loans or Investments
Up to $1 Million
Investment Policy
Prefer equity-type investments
Industry Preference
Communications
Industrial Products
Transportation
Diversified
Geographical Preference
Southwest/Midwest

Mapleleaf Capital Corp
55 Waugh Drive, Suite 710
Houston, TX 77007
(713) 880-4494
Contact
Mr. Edward M. Fink, President
Preferred Limit of Loans or Investments
Above $1 Million
Investment Policy
Prefer equity-type investments
Industry Preference
Diversified

Neptune Capital Corp.
5956 Sherry Lane, Suite 800
Dallas, TX 75225
(214) 739-1414
Contact
Mr. Richard C. Strauss, President
Mr. Richard L. McConn, Vice President
Preferred Limit of Loans or Investments
Up to $250,000
Investment Policy
Will make loans and/or equity investments
Industry Preference
Diversified
Geographical Preference
National

Branch Office
North Riverside Capital Corp.
400 N. St. Paul, Suite 1265
Dallas, TX 75201
(214) 220-2717
(Main Office in Georgia)
Contact
Mr. David G. Franklin
Preferred Limit of Loans or Investments
Up to $1 Million
Investment Policy
Prefer equity-type investments
Industry Preference
Diversified
Geographical Preference
South/Southwest

Omega Capital Corp.
755 S. 11th Street, Suite 250
Beaumont, TX 77701
(409) 832-0221
Contact
Mr. Ted E. Moor, Jr., President
Preferred Limit of Loans or Investments
Up to $100,000
Investment Policy
Will make loans and/or equity investments
Industry Preference
Communications
Computer Products
Consumer Products
Electronics
Diversified
Geographical Preference
Texas

Red River Ventures, Inc.
777 E. 15th Street
Plano, TX 75074
(214) 422-4999
Contact
Mr. Delwin Morton, President
Preferred Limit of Loans or Investments
Up to $250,000
Investment Policy
Will make loans and/or equity investments
Industry Preference
Diversified
Geographical Preference
National

Republic Venture Group, Inc.
P.O. Box 225961
Dallas, TX 75265
(214) 922-5078
Contact
Mr. Robert H. Wellborn, Chief Executive Officer
Mr. James A. O'Donnell, President
Mr. Mark C. Masur, Vice President
Preferred Limit of Loans or Investments
Above $1 Million
Investment Policy
Will make loans and/or equity investments
Industry Preference
Communications
Computer Products
Consumer Products
Diversified
Geographical Preference
National

Retzloff Capital Corp.
P.O. Box 41250
Houston, TX 77240
(713) 466-4633
Contact
Mr. Steven F. Retzloff, Presidentresident
Preferred Limit of Loans or Investments
Up to $500,000
Investment Policy
Will make loans and/or equity investments
Industry Preference
Communications
Electronics
Industrial Products
Medical-Health
Diversified
Geographical Preference
National

Revelation Resources
2929 Allen Parkway, Suite 1705
Houston, TX 77019
(713) 526-3603
Contact
Mr. Michael Walker, President
Mr. Chris Matthews
Mr. Bob Oliver
Preferred Limit of Loans or Investments
Up to $250,000
Investment Policy
Will make loans and/or equity investments
Industry Preference
Communications
Diversified
Geographical Preference
National

Rust Capital Ltd.
114 W. 7th Street, Suite 500
Austin, TX 78701
(512) 482-0806
Contact
Mr. Jack A. Morgan, Jr.
Preferred Limit of Loans or Investments
Up to $1 Million
Investment Policy
Will make loans and/or equity investments
Industry Preference
Communications
Industrial Products
Hotels, Restaurants
Medical-Health
Diversified
Geographical Preference
Southwest

SBI Capital Corp.
P.O. Box 570368
Houston, TX 77257
(713) 975-1188
Contact
Mr. William E. Wright, President
Preferred Limit of Loans or Investments
Above $1 Million
Investment Policy
Will make loans and/or equity investments
Industry Preference
Computer Products
Electronics
Industrial Products
Medical-Health
Diversified
Geographical Preference
Texas

San Antonio Venture Group, Inc.
2300 W. Commerce
San Antonio, TX 78207
(512) 223-3633
Contact
Mr. Tom Woodley, Investment Advisor
Geographical Preference
Southwest

Southwestern Venture Capital of Texas
P.O. Box 1719
Sequin, TX 78155
(512) 379-0380
Contact
Mr. J.A. Bettersworth President
Preferred Limit of Loans or Investments
Up to $250,000
Investment Policy
Will make loans and/or equity investments
Industry Preference
Diversified

Sunwestern Capital Corp.
12221 Merit Drive, Suite 1300
Dallas, TX 75251
(214) 239-5650
(Sunwestern Ventures Co. under same management)
Contact
Mr. Thomas W. Wright, President
Mr. James F. Leary, Exec. Vice President
Mr. Michael D. Brown
Preferred Limit of Loans or Investments
Up to $500,000
Investment Policy
Prefer equity-type investments
Industry Preference
Communications
Computer Products
Consumer Products
Electronics
Industrial Products
Geographical Preference
Southwest

Wesbanc Ventures, Ltd.
2401 Fountainview, Suite 950
Houston, TX 77057
(713) 977-7421
Contact
Mr. Stuart Schube, General Partner
E. H. Batey
Preferred Limit of Loans or Investments
Up to $500,000

Investment Policy
Will make loans and/or equity investments
Industry Preference
Diversified
Geographical Preference
National

VERMONT

Quesneska Capital Corp.
123 Church Street
Burlington, VT 05401
(802) 865-1806
Contact
Mr. Albert W. Coffrin, III, President
Preferred Limit of Loans or Investments
Up to $250,000
Investment Policy
Will make loans and/or equity investments
Industry Preference
Diversified
Geographical Preference
Vermont/New England

VIRGINIA

East West United Investment Co. [MESBIC]
815 W. Broad Street
Falls Church, VA 22046
(703) 237-7200
Contact
Mr. Doug Bui, President
Mr. Ha Bui, Vice President
Mr. Hung Bui, Secretary
Preferred Limit of Loans or Investments
Up to $100,000
Investment Policy
Prefer straight loans
Industry Preference
Diversified
Geographical Prefernce
Virginia/District of Columbia/Maryland

Hillcrest Group
P.O. Box 1776
Richmond, VA 23214
(804) 643-7358
(Crestar Capital, James River Capital, under Hillcrest Group management)
Contact
Mr. A. Hugh Ewing, III, General Partner
Mr. James B. Farinholt, Jr., General Partner
Mr. John P. Funkhouser, General Partner
Preferred Limit of Loans or Investments
Up to $1 Million
Investment Policy
Prefer equity-type investments
Industry Preference
Diversified
Geographical Preference
South

Metropolitan Capital Corp.
2550 Huntington Avenue
Alexandria, VA 22303
(703) 960-4698
Contact
Mr. J. B. Toomey, President
Mr. S. W. Austin, Vice President
Mrs. K. A. Idle, Administrator/Corp. Secretary
Preferred Limit of Loans or Investments
Up to $250,000
Investment Policy
Will make loans and/or equity investments
Industry Preference
Diversified
Geographical Preference
National

River Capital Corp.
1033 N. Fairfax, Suite 306
Alexandria, VA 22314
(703) 739-2100
Contact
Mr. Peter D. Van Oosterhout, President
Mr. Carl L. Schmitz, Jr., Vice President
Preferred Limit of Loans or Investments
Up to $500,000
Investment Policy
Prefer equity-type investments
Industry Preference
Communications

Energy/Natural Resources
Industrial Products
Medical-Health
Diversified
Geographical Preference
Northeast/South

<u>Sovran Funding Corp.</u>
Sovran Center, One Comm'l. Place, 6th Floor
Norfolk, VA 23510
(804) 441-4041
Contact
Mr. David A. King, Jr., President
Mr. A. Allen Kendle, Investment Officer
Preferred Limit of Loans or Investments
Up to $1 Million
Investment Policy
Prefer equity-type investments
Industry Preference
Communications
Consumer Products
Electronics
Industrial Products
Medical-Health
Geographical Preference
South

<u>Tidewater SBI Corp</u>
1214 First Virginia Bank Tower
Norfolk, VA 23510
(804) 627-2315
Contact
Mr. Gregory H. Wingfield, President
Ms. Diane Newell, Asst. Secy./Treas.
Preferred Limit of Loans or Investments
Up to $250,000
Investment Policy
Will make loans and/or equity investments
Industry Preference
Computer Products
Electronics
Industrial Products
Diversified
Manufacturing
Geographical Preference
Virginia

<u>Washington Finance & Inv. Corp.</u> [MESBIC]
100 E. Broad Street
Falls Church, VA 22046
(703) 534-7200
Contact
Mr. Chang H. Lie, President
Ms. Hae R. Yoon, Assistant Secretary
Preferred Limit of Loans or Investments
Up to $250,000
Investment Policy
Will make loans and/or equity investments
Industry Preference
Consumer Products
Geographical Preference
Northeast

WASHINGTON

<u>Peoples Capital Corp.</u>
2411 4th Avenue, Suite 400
Seattle, WA 98121
(206) 344-5463
Contact
Mr. R. W. Maider, President
Preferred Limit of Loans or Investments
Up to $250,000
Investment Policy
Will make loans and/or equity investments
Industry Preference
Communications
Medical-Health
Retailing

WISCONSIN

<u>Banc One Venture Corporation</u>
111 E. Wisconsin Avenue
Milwaukee, WI 53202
(414) 765-2274
Contact
Mr. H. Wayne Foreman, President
Ms. Colleen Henderson, Vice President
Preferred Limit of Loans or Investments
Up to $1 Million
Investment Policy
Prefer equity-type investments
Industry Preference
Diversified
Geographical Preference
National

<u>Bando McGlocklin Capital Corp.</u>
13555 Bishops Court, Suite 205
Brookfield, WI 53005
(414) 784-9010
Contact
Mr. George Schonath, CEO
Mr. Sal Bando, President
Mr. Jon McGlocklin, Executive VP
Preferred Limit of Loans or Investments
Up to $1 Million
Investment Policy
Prefer straight loans
Industry Preference
Construction/Real Estate
Consumer Products
Industrial Products
Medical-Health
Transportation
Geographical Preference
Wisconsin/Midwest

<u>Capital Investments, Inc.</u>
744 N. 4th Street
Milwaukee, WI 53203
(414) 273-6560
Contact
Mr. Robert L. Banner, Vice President
Mr. Steven C. Rippl, Treasurer
Preferred Limit of Loans or Investments
Up to $1 Million
Investment Policy
Will make loans and/or equity investments
Industry Preference
Communications
Electronics
Industrial Products
Medical-Health
Diversified
Geographical Preference
Midwest

<u>Future Value Ventures, Inc.</u> [MESBIC]
622 N. Water Street, Suite 500
Milwaukee, WI 53202
(414) 278-0377
Contact
Mr. William Beckett, President
Ms. Victoria Treul, Administrative Assistant
Preferred Limit of Loans or Investments
Up to $350,000
Investment Policy
Prefer equity-type investments
Industry Preference
Communications
Computer Products
Consumer Products
Diversified
Geographical Preference
National

<u>M & I Ventures Corp.</u>
770 N. Water Street
Milwaukee, WI 53202
(414) 765-7910
Contact
Mr. John T. Byrnes, President
Mr. Andrew E. Marein, Vice President
Preferred Limit of Loans or Investments
Up to $500,000
Investment Policy
Will make loans and/or equity investments
Industry Preference
Electronics
Industrial Products
Medical-Health
Transportation
Diversified
Geographical Preference
Midwest

<u>Branch Office</u>
<u>MorAmerica Capital Corp.</u>
600 East Mason Street
Milwaukee, WI 53202
(414) 276-3839
(Main Office in Iowa)
Contact
Mr. Steven J. Massey, Vice President
Preferred Limit of Loans or Investments
Up to $1 Million
Investment Policy
Will make loans and/or equity investments
Industry Preference
Diversified
Geographical Preference
Midwest
National

<u>Super Market Investors, Inc.</u>
P.O. Box 473
Milwaukee, WI 53201
(414) 547-7999
Contact
Mr. David H. Maass, President & Treasurer
Mr. Charles F. Benjamin, VP & Secretary
Preferred Limit of Loans or Investments
Up to $100,000
Investment Policy
Prefer straight loans
Industry Preference
Retail grocery
Geographical Preference
Midwest

ASSOCIATE MEMBERS

Some of these firms represent non-SBIC venture capitalists who also invest in small businesses. Others are firms which provide professional services to SBICs and to small business concerns. Companies are listed alphabetically.

Mr. Ellis Bagley
600 N. McClurg Center, Suite 4402-A
Chicago, IL 60611
(312) 664-3891

Mr. Robert B. Leisy
Consultant
P.O. Box 4405
Whittier, CA 90607
(213) 698-4862

<u>3i - Investors in Industry Corp.</u>
99 High Street, Suite 1530
Boston, MA 02110
(617) 542-8560
Contact
Mr. William Holm, Senior Vice President
Mr. Allan Ferguson, Manager
<u>Branch Office</u>
450 Newport Center Drive, Suite 250
Newport Beach, CA 92660
(714) 720-1421
Contact
Mr. John Ulrich, Sr. Vice President
Mr. Fred Haney, Manager
Preferred Limit of Loans or Investments
Up to $1 Million
Investment Policy
Prefer equity-type investments
Industry Preference
Communications
Computer Products
Electronics
Medical-Health
Diversified
Geographical Preference
National

<u>3 M</u>
3M Center, Building 220-13W-20
St. Paul, MN 55144
(612) 733-8317
Contact
Mr. George L. Hegg, Vice President

<u>Abbott Capital Corp.</u>
9933 Lawler Avenue, Suite 125
Skokie, IL 60077
(312) 982-0404
Contact
Mr. Richard Lassar, President

<u>Acorn Ventures, Inc.</u>
2401 Fountainview, Suite 950
Houston, TX 77057
(713) 977-7421
Contact
Mr. Stuart Schube, President
Mr. Walter Cunningham, Vice President

Alimansky Venture Group Inc.
605 Madison Avenue, Suite 300
New York, NY 10022
(212) 832-7300
Contact
Mr. Burt Alimansky, Managing Director
Mr. Philip Sussman
Preferred Limit of Loans or Investments
Above $1 Million
Investment Policy
Will make loans and/or equity investments
Industry Preference
Consumer Products
Electronics
Industrial Products
Medical-Health
Diversified
Geographical Preference
National

Allsop Venture Partners
2750 1st Avenue, N.E., Suite 210
Cedar Rapids, IA 52402
(319) 363-8971
Contact
Mr. Robert W. Allsop, General Partner
Mr. Paul D. Rhines, General Partner
Preferred Limit of Loans or Investments
Above $1 Million
Investment Policy
Prefer equity-type investments
Industry Preference
Communications
Industrial Products
Diversified
Geographical Preference
National

Allstate Insurance Company
VC Division
Allstate Plaza E-2
Northbrook, IL 60062
(312) 402-5681
Contact
Mr. Robert L. Lestina, Director
Mr. Paul J. Renze
Preferred Limit of Loans or Investments
Above $1 Million
Investment Policy
Prefer equity-type investments
Industry Preference
Communications
Computer Products
Consumer Products
Electronics
Genetic Engineering
Geographical Preference
National

Arthur Andersen & Co.
33 W. Monroe Street, Suite 600
Chicago, IL 60603
(312) 507-6150
Contact
Mr. Norman Carlson, Partner
Mr. Richard J. Strotman, Partner*
*(312) 580-0033

Arthur Andersen & Co.
5600 First Republic Bank Plaza
Dallas, TX 75202
(214) 741-8300
Contact
Mr. Robert Philip, Partner

Arthur Andersen & Co.
8251 Greensboro Drive, Suite 400
McLean, VA 22102
(703) 734-7300
Contact
Mr. John Cherin, Managing Partner

Arthur Young & Co.
1111 Summer Street
Stamford, CT 06905
(203) 356-1800
Contact
Mr. Robert J. Brennan, Partner

Arthur Young & Co.
2859 Paces Ferry Road, Suite 1400
Atlanta, GA 30339
(404) 431-3346
Contact
Mr. John Huntz, Jr., Director

Arthur Young & Co.
277 Park Avenue
New York, NY 10172
(212) 407-1611
Contact
Mr. Dennis Serlen, General Partner

Arthur Young & Co.
2121 San Jacinto, Suite 700
Dallas, TX 75201
(214) 969-8702
Contact
Mr. Ed B. Beanland, Partner
Mr. Stanley A. Thomas
Ms. Diane C. Hately

Arthur Young & Co. Entrepreneurial Services Group
1 Sansome Street, Suite 3300
San Francisco, CA 94104
(415) 393-2733
Contact
Mr. Jerome Engel, Partner & Director of E. S. G.
Mr. Marc Berger, Partner
Mr. Don Yee, Partner

Baker, Kirk & Bissex, P.C.
114 W. 7th Street
600 Norwood Tower
Austin, TX 78701
(713) 790-9316
Contact
Mr. Walter E. Bissex, Vice President
Preferred Limit of Loans or Investments
Up to $100,000
Investment Policy
Prefer equity-type investments
Industry Preference
Computer Products
Electronics
Genetic Engineering
Medical-Health
Environmental
Geographical Preference
Southwest

Battery Ventures
200 Portland Street, 5th Floor
Boston, MA 02110
(617) 367-1000
Contact
Mr. Richard D. Frisbie, General Partner
Mr. Robert G. Barrett, General Partner
Mr. Oliver D. Curme, General Partner
Preferred Limit of Loans or Investments
Above $1 Million
Investment Policy
Will make loans and/or equity investments
Industry Preference
Communications
Computer Products
Electronics
Geographical Preference
National

Beacon Partners/Hawthorne Partners
71 Strawberrry Hill Avenue, Suite 614
Stamford, CT 06902
(203) 348-8858
Contact
Mr. Leonard Vignola, Jr.
Ms. Barbara J. Hann
Preferred Limit of Loans or Investments
Up to $100,000
Investment Policy
Will make loans and/or equity investments
Industry Preference
Communications
Computer Products
Electronics
Industrial Products
Medical-Health
Geographical Preference
Northeast

Bercham & Moses, P.C.
81 Broad Street
Milford, CT 06460
(203) 783-1200
Contact
Bruce Peabody, Esq.

William Blair Venture Partners
135 S. LaSalle Street, 29th Floor
Chicago, IL 60603
(312) 853-8250
Contact
Mr. James E. Crawford, III, Partner
Mr. Samuel B. Guren, Partner
Mr. Scott F. Meadow, Partner
Preferred Limit of Loans or Investments
Above $1 Million
Investment Policy
Prefer equity-type investments
Industry Preference
Diversified
Geographical Preference
National

Brentwood Associates
11661 San Vicente Boulevard, Suite 707
Los Angeles, CA 90049
(213) 826-6581
Contact
Mrs. Leslie Shaw, Vice President of Finance
Preferred Limit of Loans or Investments
Above $1 Million
Investment Policy
Prefer equity-type investments
Industry Preference
Communications
Computer Products
Consumer Products
Electronics
Medical-Health
Geographical Preference
West

Burton & Co., Inc.
P.O. Box 7319
Philadelphia, PA 19101
(215) 751-0399
Contact
Mr. Reginald C. Burton

Capital Strategy Group, Inc. (The)
20 N. Wacker Drive
Chicago, IL 60606
(312) 444-1170
Contact
Mr. Eric E. von Bauer, President
Preferred Limit of Loans or Investments
Up to $500,000
Investment Policy
Will make loans and/or equity investments
Industry Preference
Communications
Computer Products
Consumer Products
Electronics
Industrial Products
Geographical Preference
Midwest

Cardinal Development Capital Fund I
40 S. 3rd Street
Columbus, OH 43215
(614) 464-5550
Contact
Mr. Daniel A. Fronk, Partner
Mr. Thomas Walker
Mr. Rick Fucht

Centennial Fund (The)
1999 Broadway, Suite 2100
P.O. Box 13977
Denver, CO 80202
(303) 298-9066
Contact
Mr. G. Jackson Tankersley, Jr., General Partner
Mr. Mark Dubovoy
Mr. David Bullwinkle
Preferred Limit of Loans or Investments
Above $1 Million
Investment Policy
Will make loans and/or equity investments
Industry Preference
Communications
Computer Products
Electronics
Medical-Health
Diversified

Geographical Preference
West

Cherry Tree Ventures
3800 W. 80th Street
Minneapolis, MN 55431
(612) 893-9012
Contact
Mr. John Bergstrom, Associate
Mr. Mark Derus, Associate
Preferred Limit of Loans or Investments
Up to $1 Million
Investment Policy
Prefer equity-type investments
Industry Preference
Communications
Computer Products
Consumer Products
Medical-Health
Transportation
Geographical Preference
Midwest

Columbine Venture Management, Inc.
5613 DTC Parkway, Suite 510
Englewood, CO 80111
(303) 694-3222
Contact
Mr. Mark Kimmel, President
Mr. Sherman J. Muller
Mr. Terry E. Winters
Preferred Limit of Loans or Investments
Above $1 Million
Investment Policy
Prefer equity-type investments
Industry Preference
Communications
Computer Products
Electronics
Genetic Engineering
Medical-Health
Geographical Preference
Rocky Mountain Region

Cooley Godward Castro Huddles & Tatum
One Maritime Plaza, 20th Floor
San Francisco, CA 94111
(415) 981-5252
Contact
Mr. James C. Gaither, General Partner

CoreStates Enterprise Fund
One Penn Center, Suite 1360
Philadelphia, PA 19103
(215) 568-4677
Contact
Mr. Paul A. Mitchell, President
Mr. Michael F. Donoghue, Vice President
Preferred Limit of Loans or Investments
Up to $1 Million
Investment Policy
Will make loans and/or equity investments
Industry Preference
Communications
Industrial Products
Diversified
Geographical Preference
Northeast

Corporation for Innovation Development
One N. Capitol Street, Suite 520
Indianapolis, IN 46204
(317) 635-7325
Contact
Mr. Marion C. Dietrich, President
Mr. M. Archie Leslie, Vice President
Mr. Donald K. Taylor, Vice President
Preferred Limit of Loans or Investments
Up to $500,000
Investment Policy
Will make loans and/or equity investments
Industry Preference
Communications
Computer Products
Consumer Products
Medical-Health
Diversified
Geographical Preference
Indiana

Criterion Venture Partners
1000 Louisiana
Houston, TX 77002
(713) 751-2400
Contact
Mr. David O. Wicks, Jr., Senior Partner
Mr. M. Scott Albert, Partner
Mr. David C. Hull, Jr., Partner
Preferred Limit of Loans or Investments
Up to $1 Million
Investment Policy
Prefer equity-type investments
Industry Preference
Communications
Computer Products
Electronics
Genetic Engineering
Medical-Health
Geographical Preference
Southwest

DFC Ventures Limited
100 Spear Street, Suite 1430
San Francisco, CA 94105
(415) 777-2847
Contact
Mr. Chris C. Ellison, North American Manager
Mr. Alan M. Bonny, Ventures Manager
Preferred Limit of Loans or Investments
Up to $1 Million
Investment Policy
Prefer equity-type investments
Industry Preference
Communications
Computer Products
Electronics
Genetic Engineering
Medical-Health
Geographical Preference
West

DnC Capital Corp
600 Fifth Avenue
New York, NY 10020
(212) 765-4800
Contact
Mr. Jack A. Prizzi, Managing Director
Preferred Limit of Loans or Investments
Up to $500,000
Industry Preference
Communications
Computer Products
Electronics
Industrial Products
Medical-Health
Geographical Preference
National

Deloitte, Haskins & Sells
155 E. Broad Street
Columbus, OH 43215
(614) 229-4700
Contact
Mr. David P. Lauer, Partner
Mr. Randy Lawson, Manager

Dominion Bankshares Corp.
P.O. Box 13327
Roanoke, VA 24040
(703) 563-7880
Contact
Mr. J. Richard Patterson, II, Asst. VP

Eaton & Van Winkle
600 Third Avenue
New York, NY 10016
(212) 867-0606
Contact
Mr. Arthur A. Lane, Partner

Edwards & Angell
P.O. Box 2621
Palm Beach, FL 33480
(305) 833-7700
Contact
Mr. Jonathon E. Cole, Managing Partner
Mr. John G. Igoe
Branch Office
265 Franklin Street
Boston, MA 02110
(617) 439-4444
Contact
Mr. Leonard Q. Slapp

El Dorado Ventures
2 N. Lake Avenue, Suite 480
Pasadena, CA 91101
(818) 793-1936
Contact
Mr. Brent T. Rider, General Partner
Mr. Gary W. Kalbach, General Partner
Preferred Limit of Loans or Investments
Above $1 Million
Investment Policy
Prefer equity-type investments
Industry Preference
Communications
Computer Products
Electronics
Genetic Engineering
Medical-Health
Geographical Preference
West

Ernst & Whinney
5941 Variel
Woodland Hills, CA 91367
(818) 888-0707
Contact
Mr. Larry Gray, Partner
Mr. Peter Griffith, Senior Manager

FAS/Bekhor International
701 B Street, Suite 1500
San Diego, CA 92101
(619) 544-1600
Contact
Mr. Ray W. McKewon, Managing Director
Mr. William J. Patton, Managing Director
Ms. Shelly D. Owen, Associate
Preferred Limit of Loans or Investments
Above $1 Million
Investment Policy
Prefer equity-type investments & other investment banking services and transactions
Industry Preference
Communications
Computer Products
Consumer Products
Electronics
Medical-Health
Geographical Preference
National

Fine & Ambrogne
Exchange Place
Boston, MA 02109
(617) 367-0100
Contact
Mr. Arnold M. Zaff, Partner

First Chicago Investment Advisors
Three First National Plaza, Suite 0140
Chicago, IL 60670
(312) 732-4919
Contact
Mr. Bon French, Vice President
Mr. David S. Timson, Vice President
Mr. Patrick McGiney, Vice President
Preferred Limit of Loans or Investments
Above $1 Million
Investment Policy
Prefer equity-type investments
Industry Preference
Diversified
Geographical Preference
National

First Interstate Equity Corporation
P.O. Box 29751
Phoenix, AZ 85038-9751
(602) 271-6071
Contact
Mr. Harry Bonsall, President

Fostin Capital Corp.
P.O. Box 67
Pittsburgh, PA 15230
(412) 928-8900
Contact
Mr. William F. Woods, President
Mr. Thomas M. Levine, Exec. Vice President
Mr. Joel P. Adams, Vice President
Preferred Limit of Loans or Investments
Up to $1 Million
Investment Policy
Prefer equity-type investments
Industry Preference
Communcations
Computer Products

Consumer Products
Electronics
Medical-Health
Geographical Preference
National/Pennsylvania

Founders Ventures
14016 Camino Barco
Saratoga, CA 95070
Contact
Mr. Glen McLaughlin, President
Preferred Limit of Loans or Investments
Up to $250,000
Investment Policy
Will make loans and/or equity investments
Industry Preference
Communications
Computer Products
Electronics
Industrial Products
Medical-Health
Geographical Preference
West/California

Fryberger, Buchanan, et al P.A.
700 Lonsdale Building
Duluth, MN 55802
(218) 722-0861
Contact
Mr. Nick Smith, President

Golder, Thoma & Cressey
120 S. LaSalle Street, Suite 630
Chicago, IL 60603
(312) 853-3322
Contact
Mr. Stanley C. Golder, General Partner
Preferred Limit of Loans or Investments
Above $1 Million
Investment Policy
Prefer equity-type investments
Industry Preference
Communications
Industrial Products
Medical-Health
Transportation
Diversified
Geographical Preference
National

Greyrock Shared Ventures Ltd.
150 King Street, West, Suite 1212
Toronto, Canada M5H 1J9
(416) 979-7677
Contact
Mr. D. P. Driscoll, Vice President
Mr. S. Inwentash, Vice President
Preferred Limit of Loans or Investments
Up to $1 Million
Investment Policy
Prefer equity-type investments
Industry Preference
Communications
Computer Products
Consumer Products
Genetic Engineering
Medical-Health
Geographical Preference
Northeast/Midwest/Southwest

Great American Investment Corp.
4209 San Mateo, NE
Albuquerque, NM 87110
(505) 883-6273
Contact
Mr. James A. Arias, President
Preferred Limit of Loans or Investments
Up to $500,000
Investment Policy
Will make loans and/or equity investments
Industry Preference
Diversified
Geographical Preference
National

Great Lakes Capital Management, Inc.
7001 Orchard Lake Road, Suite 330
W. Bloomfield, WI 48322
(313) 737-4545
Contact
Mr. John D. Berkaw, President
Mr. David P. Greeneisen
Ms. Debra A. Ball

Preferred Limit of Loans or Investments
Up to $1 Million
Investment Policy
Prefer equity-type investments
Industry Preference
Communications
Computer Products
Electronics
Industrial Products
Medical-Health
Geographical Preference
Midwest

Heizer Corp.
261 Bluff's Edge Drive
Lake Forest, IL 60045
(312) 234-3883
Contact
Mr. E. F. Heizer, Jr., (Ned), Chairman
Preferred Limit of Loans or Investments
Up to $1 Million
Investment Policy
Prefer equity-type investments

Houston Partners
401 Louisiana, 8th Floor
Houston, TX 77002
(713) 222-8600
Contact
Mr. Harvard H. Hill, Jr., Managing Partner
Mr. Roger A. Ramsey, General Partner
Preferred Limit of Loans or Investments
Up to $1 Million
Investment Policy
Prefer equity-type investments
Industry Preference
Computer Products
Electronics
Genetic Engineering
Industrial Products
Medical-Health
Geographical Preference
South/Southwest/West

Hunton & Williams
P.O. Box 1535
Richmond, VA 23212
(804) 788-8200
Contact
Mr. C. Porter Vaughan, III, Esq.

IEG Venture Management, Inc.
401 N. Michigan Avenue, Suite 2020
Chicago, IL 60611
(312) 644-0890
Contact
Mr. Francis I. Blair, President
Preferred Limit of Loans or Investments
Up to $500,000
Investment Policy
Prefer equity-type investments
Industry Preference
Communications
Computer Products
Electronics
Energy/Natural Resources
Industrial Products
Geographical Preference
Midwest

Intercoastal Capital Corp.
380 Madison Avenue, 18th Floor
New York, NY 10017
(212) 986-0482
Contact
Mr. Herbert Krasnow, President

InterVen Partners
333 S. Grand Avenue, Suite 4050
Los Angeles, CA 90071
(213) 622-1922
Contact
Mr. David B. Jones, President
Mr. Jonathan E. Funk
Mr. Kenneth M. Deemer
Branch Office
227 SW Pine, Suite 200
Portland, OR 97204
(503) 223-4334
Contact
Mr. Wayne Kingsley
Preferred Limit of Loans or Investments
Above $1 Million

Investment Policy
Prefer equity-type investments
Industry Preference
Diversified
Geographical Preference
West

Japan Associated Finance Co., Ltd.
Toshiba Building IOF 1-1-1 Shibaura
Minato-Ku Tokyo, Japan
(03) 456-5101
Contact
Mr. Kunio Takai, President
Mr. Takeshi Ogawa, General Manager
Preferred Limit of Loans or Investments
Up to $1 Million
Investment Policy
Prefer equity-type investments
Industry Preference
Computer Products
Consumer Products
Electronics
Industrial Products
Medical-Health
Geographical Preference
West/National

Jenkens & Gilchrist, P.C.
1445 Ross Avenue, Suite 3200
Dallas, TX 75202
(214) 855-4500
Contact
Mr. John R. Holzgraefe, Member
Mr. Mark D. Widger, Member
Mr. W. Alan Kailer, Member

Frank Hawkins Kenan Institute (The)
CB #3440 The Kenan Center
University of North Carolina
Chapel Hill, NC 27599-3440
(919) 962-8201
Contact
Mr. Rollie Tillman, Director

Kirk Organization (The)
101 S. Hanley Road, Suite 250
St. Louis, MO 63105
(314) 862-5475
Contact
Mr. Larry Kirchenbauer, President

Kirkland & Ellis
200 E. Randolph Drive
Chicago, IL 60601
(312) 861-2465
Contact
Mr. Edward T. Swan

Kleinwort, Benson (NA) Corp.
333 S. Grand Avenue, Suite 2900
Los Angeles, CA 90071
(213) 680-2297
Contact
Mr. Alan L. J. Bowen, Senior Vice President
Mr. Nicholas Marshi, Vice President
Mr. John Hooper, Vice President
Preferred Limit of Loans or Investments
Above $1 Million
Investment Policy
Will make loans and/or equity investments
Industry Preference
Communications
Construction/Real Estate
Consumer Products
Industrial Products
Diversified
Geographical Preference
West/National

Klotz Venture Capital Group
426 Essex Street, #J, P.O. Box 586
Hackensack, NJ 07601
(201) 489-2080
Contact
Mr. Sam Klotz
Preferred Limit of Loans or Investments
Up to $1 Million
Investment Policy
Will make loans and/or equity investments
Industry Preference
Communications
Construction/Real Estate

Electronics
Energy/Natural Resources
Diversified
Geographical Preference
Norheast/South/National

Kutak Rock & Campbell
1101 Connecticut Avenue, N.W.
Washington, DC 20036
(202) 828-2400
Contact
Mr. Thomas C. Evans
Mr. Steven E. Levy

Lord, Bissell & Brook
115 S. LaSalle Street, Suite 3500
Chicago, IL 60603
(312) 443-0265
Contact
Mr. John K. O'Connor, Partner
Mr. Leland E. Hutchinson
Mr. David B. Weinberg

Lubrizol Enterprises, Inc.
29400 Lakeland Boulevard
Wickliffe, OH 44092
(216) 943-4200
Contact
Mr. Donald L. Murfin, President
Mr. Gregory P. Lieb, Vice President, Finance
Preferred Limit of Loans or Investments
Up to $1 Million
Investment Policy
Will make loans and/or equity investments
Industry Preference
Genetic Engineering
Geographical Preference
National

McKee & Company
7031 E. Camelback Road, Suite 541
Scottsdale, AZ 85251
(602) 945-7403
Contact
Mr. William B. McKee

Mann Judd Landau
230 Park Avenue
New York, NY 10169
(212) 661-5500
Contact
Mr. Stanley Weinstein, Sr. Partner

Massachusetts Technology Develop. Corp.
131 State Street, Suite 215
Boston, MA 02109
(617) 723-4920
Contact
Mr. Robert J. Crowley, Vice President

Mayer, Brown & Platt
520 Madison Avenue
New York, NY 10022
(212) 437-7132
Contact
Mr. Herbert B. Max, Esq.

Med-Wick Associates
1902 Fleet National Bank Building
Providence, RI 02903
(401) 751-5270
Contact
Mr. A. A. T. Wickersham, Chmn./Pres.

Michael, Best & Friedrich
250 E. Wisconsin Ave.
Milwaukee, WI 53202
(414) 271-6560
Contact
Mr. Robert J. Johannes, Partner

Michigan Venture Capital Division
Treasury Department
P.O. Box 15128
Lansing, MI 48901
Contact
Mr. Paul E. Rice, Administrator

Mid America Resource Corp.
3200 Belmont Avenue
Youngstown, OH 44505
(216) 759-3668
Contact
Mr. Arnold J. Clebone

Miller Venture Partners
P. O. Box 808
Columbus, IN 47202
(812) 376-3331
Contact
Mr. William I. Miller, General Partner
Mr. Ira Peppercorn, Vice President
Preferred Limit of Loans or Investments
Up to $250,000
Investment Policy
Prefer equity-type investments
Industry Preference
Diversified
Geographical Preference
Midwest

Morgan, Holland Ventures Corp.
One Liberty Square
Boston, MA 02109
(617) 423-1765
Contact
Mr. James F. Morgan, Managing Partner

Morgan Stanley Venture Partners
1251 Avenue of the Americas, 28th Floor
New York, NY 10020
(212) 703-4000
Contact
Mr. William F. Murdy, General Partner
Mr. Guy L. de Chazal, General Partner
Mr. Robert L. Burr, General Partner*
*101 California Street, Suite 2400
San Francisco, CA 94111
(415) 576-2000
Preferred Limit of Loans or Investments
Above $1 Million
Investment Policy
Prefer equity-type investments
Industry Preference
Communications
Computer Products
Electronics
Medical-Health
Geographical Preference
National

Morgenthaler Ventures
700 National City Bank Building
Cleveland, OH 44114
(216) 621-3070
Contact
Mr. Robert D. Pavey, General Partner
Mr. Paul S. Brentlinger, General Partner
Mr. Robert C. Bellas, General Partner
Preferred Limit of Loans or Investments
Above $1 Million
Investment Policy
Prefer equity-type investments
Industry Preference
Communications
Computer Products
Electronics
Genetic Engineering
Medical-Health
Geographical Preference
National

NEPA Venture Fund, L.P.
125 Goodman Drive
Bethlehem, PA 18015
(215) 865-6550
Contact
Mr. Frederick J. Beste, III, President
Mr. Glen Bressner
Preferred Limit of Loans or Investments
Above $1 Million
Investment Policy
Prefer equity-type investments
Industry Preference
Diversified
Geographical Preference
Northeast

National Bank of Canada
535 Madison Avenue
New York, NY 10022
(212) 605-8801
Contact
Mr. Thomas R. Thompson
Preferred Limit of Loans or Investments
Above $1 Million
Investment Policy
Prefer equity-type investments
Industry Preference
Communications
Consumer Products
Industrial Products
Medical-Health
Diversified
Geographical Preference
National

New Enterprise Associates
1119 St. Paul Street
Baltimore, MD 21202
(301) 244-0115
Contact
Mr. Charles W. Newhall, III

Nippon Investment and Finance Co.
1-25-1 Nishi-Shinjuku
Shinjuku Ku, Tokyo 163 Japan
(03) 349-0961
Contact
Mr. Yoshio Fukuda, General Manager
Preferred Limit of Loans or Investments
Above $1 Million
Investment Policy
Will make loans and/or equity investments
Industry Preference
Diversified
Geographical Preference
National

Noro-Moseley Partners
4200 Northside Parkway NW, Building 9
Atlanta, GA 30327
(404) 233-1966
Contact
Mr. Charles Moseley, General Partner

North American Capital Corp.
510 Broad Hollow Road, Suite 205
Melville, NY 11747
(516) 752-9696
Contact
Mr. Don W. Fleischauer, Senior Vice President
Mr. Steven W. Roth, Vice President
Preferred Limit of Loans or Investments
Above $1 Million
Investment Policy
Prefer equity-type investments
Industry Preference
Consumer Products
Industrial Products
Geographical Preference
National

Northern Trust Company (The)
50 South LaSalle Street, Suite B-11
Chicago, IL 60675
(312) 630-4122
Contact
Mr. Michael R. Zook, Senior Vice President

Olwine, Connelly, Chase, et al
299 Park Avenue
New York, NY 10017
(212) 207-1231
Contact
Mr. Roger Mulvihill

Original Enterprises, Inc.
P.O. Box 671
Concord, CA 94522-0671
(415) 825-7017
Contact
Mr. Winn Parker, President
Preferred Limit of Loans or Investments
Above $1 Million
Investment Policy
Will make loans and/or equity investments
Industry Preference
Communications
Computer Products
Genetic Engineering
Industrial Products
Medical-Health
Geographical Preference
West/National

Oxford Partners
1266 Main Street
Stamford, CT 06902
(203) 964-0592
Contact
Mr. Kenneth W. Rind, General Partner
Branch Office
233 Wilshire Boulevard, Suite 830
Santa Monica, CA 90401
(213) 458-3135
Contact
Mr. Stevan A. Birnbaum, General Partner
Preferred Limit of Loans or Investments
Above $1 Million
Investment Policy
Prefer equity-type investments
Industry Preference
Communications
Computer Products
Electronics
Genetic Engineering
Medical-Health
Geographical Preference
National

Pacific Inland Venture Partnership, Ltd.
222 South Harbor Boulevard, Suite 700
Anaheim, CA 92805
(714) 758-1042
Contact
Mr. Eugene J. Anton, President
Preferred Limit of Loans or Investments
Above $1 Million
Industry Preference
Communications
Computer Products
Industrial Products
Medical-Health
Diversified
Geographical Preference
National

Pathfinder Venture Capital Fund
7300 Metro Bouelvard, Suite 585
Minneapolis, MN 55435
(612) 835-1121
Contact
Mr. Jack Ahrens, Investment Officer
Mr. A. J. Greenshields, Investment Officer
Mr. Brian P. Johnson, Investment Officer
Preferred Limit of Loans or Investments
Above $1 Million
Industry Preference
Computer Products
Electronics
Genetic Engineering
Medical-Health
Geographical Preference
National

Peat Marwick Main & Co.
300 Oceangate, Suite 530
Long Beach, CA 90802
(213) 972-4000
Contact
Mr. Jeremiah R. Kanaly, Partner
Mr. Robert A. Swan, Partner

Peat Marwick Main & Co.
303 E. Wacker Drive
Chicago, IL 60601
(312) 938-1000
Contact
Mr. Michael E. Lavin, Partner
Mr. Richard A. Reck

Peat Marwick Main & Co.
1700 IDS Center
Minneapolis, MN 55402
(612) 341-2222
Contact
Mr. Tim Flynn, Senior Manager
Mr. Don Bug, Partner
Mr. Pat Holliston, Manager

Peat Marwick Main & Co.
1601 Elm Street, Suite 1400
Dallas, TX 75201
(214) 754-2354
Contact
Mr. Keith L. Voigts, Partner

Pepper, Hamilton & Scheetz
100 Renaissance Center, Suite 3600
Detroit, MI 48243
(313) 259-7110
Contact
Mr. Michael B. Staebler, Partner

Peregrine Associates
1299 Ocean Avenue, Suite 306
Santa Monica, CA 90401
(213) 458-1441
Contact
Mr. Gene Miller, Partner
Preferred Limit of Loans or Investments
Above $1 Million
Investment Policy
Prefer equity-type investments
Industry Preference
Communications
Computer Products
Electronics
Genetic Engineering
Medical-Health
Geographical Preference
Northeast/Southwest/West

Piper, Jaffrey & Hopwood, Inc.
222 S. 9th Street
Minneapolis, MN 55402
(612) 342-6000
Contact
Mr. Hunt Greene, Managing Director
Mr. Frank Bennett, Vice President
Mr. Buzz Benson, Vice President
Preferred Limit of Loans or Investments
Up to $1 Million
Investment Policy
Will make loans and/or equity investments
Industry Preference
Communications
Computer Products
Consumer Products
Genetic Engineering
Medical-Health
Geographical Preference
National

Porter & Travers
445 Park Avenue, Suite 1500
New York, NY 10022-2606
(212) 832-6800
Contact
Mr. James J. Busuttil, Esq.
Mr. Gilbert D. Porter, Esq.
Mr. Gordon Travers, Esq.

Price Waterhouse
1251 Avenue of the Americas
New York, NY 10020
(212) 819-4819
Contact
Mr. James M. Coriston

Primus Capital Fund
One Cleveland Center, Suite 2140
Cleveland, OH 44114
(216) 621-2185
Contact
Mr. Loyal W. Wilson, Managing Partner
Mr. James T. Bartlett
Mr. William C. Mulligan
Preferred Limit of Loans or Investments
Above $1 Million
Investment Policy
Prefer equity-type investments
Industry Preference
Communications
Consumer Products
Industrial Products
Medical-Health
Diversified
Geographical Preference
Midwest

Procordia-Harvest Venture Partners
767 Third Avenue
New York, NY 10017
(212) 838-7776
Contact
Mr. Harvey Wertheim, Managing Director

QED Research
125 California Avenue
Palo Alto, CA 94306
(415) 321-9827
Contact
Dr. James Plummer, President

Railroad Aggregates
6435 S. Pontiac Court
Englewood, CO 80111
(303) 741-2556
Contact
Mr. Mitchell E. Albert, President
Preferred Limit of Loans or Investments
Up to $100,000
Investment Policy
Prefer equity-type investments
Industry Preference
Energy/Natural Resources
Transportation
Geographical Preference
National

Realty Growth Capital Corp.
271 Madison Avenue
New York, NY 10016
(212) 983-6880
Contact
Mr. Alan Levitt

Reprise Capital Corp.
585 Stewart Avenue
Garden City, NY 11530
(516) 222-2555
Contact
Mr. Irwin B. Nelson, President
Mr. Stanley Tulchin, Chairman
Mr. Norman Tulchin, Executive Vice President
Preferred Limit of Loans or Investment
Above $1 Million
Investment Policy
Turnaround situtations only. Debt and/or equity.
Industry Preference
Communications
Consumer Products
Electronics
Industrial Products
Diversified
Geographical Preference
National

Riordan & McKinzie
611 Anton Blvd.
Costa Mesa, CA 92626
(714) 549-4555
Contact
Mr. Michael P. Ridley, Esq.

Rothschild Ventures, Inc.
One Rockefeller Plaza
New York, NY 10020
(212) 757-6000
Contact
Mr. Jess L. Belser, President
Preferred Limit of Loans or Investments
Above $1 Million
Investment Policy
Prefer equity-type investments
Industry Preference
Communications
Computer Products
Electronics
Genetic Engineering
Medical-Health
Geographical Preference
National

SB Capital Corp.
2 Bloor Street East, Suite 3304
Toronto, Ontario M4W 1A7
(416) 967-5439
Contact
Mr. A. G. Fells, President

Salomon Brothers Venture Capital
Salomon Brothers, Inc.
Two New York Plaza, 14th Floor
New York, NY 10004
(212) 747-6293
Contact
Mr. Melvin W. Ellis, Vice President
Mr. John L. Cassis, Vice President
Ms. Robin F. Grossman, Vice President

Preferred Limit of Loans or Investments
Above $1Million
Investment Policy
Prefer equity-type investments
Industry Preference
Communications
Computer Products
Electronics
Genetic Enginerring
Medical-Health
Geographical Preference
National

Security Capital Corp.
6100 Baltimore National Pike
Baltimore, MD 21228
(301) 788-0600
Contact
Mr. William Hoffman, CPA, Vice President
Preferred Limit of Loans or Investments
Up to $1 Milion
Investment Policy
Prefer equity-type investments
Industry Preference
Communications
Construction/Real Estate
Medical-Health
Transportation
Diversified
Geographical Preference
Northeast/South/West

Smith, Helms, Mulliss & Moore
P.O. Box 31247
Charlotte, NC 28231
(704) 372-9510
Contact
Mr. B. Bernard Burns, Jr., Partner
Mr. Jeffrey S. Hay, Associate
Mr. Harrison L. Marshall, Associate

South Atlantic Capital Corp.
614 W. Bay Street, Suite 200
Tampa, FL 33606
(813) 229-7400
Contact
Mr. Don Burton, General Partner
Mr. Dick Brandewie
Ms. Sandi Barber
Investment Policy
Prefer equity-type investments
Industry Preference
Communications
Medical-Health
Diversified
Geographical Preference
South

Spensley, Horn, Jubas & Lubitz
1880 Century Park East, Suite 500
Los Angeles, CA 90067
(213) 553-5050
Contact
Mr. Bruce W. McRoy, Partner
Industry Preference
Communications
Computer Products
Electronics
Genetic Engineering
Medical-Health
Geographical Preference
Southwest

State Street Bank & Trust Co.
3414 Peachtree Road, NE, Suite 736
Atlanta, GA 30326
(404) 364-9500
Contact
Mr. Kent D. Mitchell, Vice President

Sussex Leasing
175 Great Neck Road
Great Neck, NY 11021
(516) 482-7373
Contact
Mr. Jack Kaufman

Taylor & Turner
220 Montgomery Street, Penthouse 10
San Francisco, CA 94104
(415) 398-6821
Contact
Mr. Marshall Turner, Financial Partner
Mr. Bill Taylor, Financial Partner
Preferred Limit of Loans or Investments
Above $1 Million
Investment Policy
Prefer equity-type investments
Industry Preference
Computer Products
Electronics
Genetic Engineering
Industrial Products
Medical-Health
Geographical Preference
West

Technology Funding, Inc. II
2000 Alameda, Suite 250
San Mateo, CA 94403
(415) 345-2200
Contact
Mr. Charles R. Kokesh

Texas Infinity Corp.
12221 Merit Drive, Suite 1305
Dallas, TX 75251
(214) 980-7070
Contact
Mr. C. Charles Bahr, III, CEO
Mr. Douglas R. Folkman, Senior Vice President

Texas Investment Fund, L.P.
6910 Fannin Street, Suite 100
Houston, TX 77030
(713) 790-9335
Contact
Mr. Philip A. Tuttle, General Partner
Mr. Terry K. Dorsey, General Partner
Preferred Limit of Loans or Investments
Above $1 Million
Investment Policy
Prefer equity type investments
Industry Preference
Diversified
Geographical Preference
Midwest/Southwest/West

UNC Ventures, Inc.
711 Atlantic Avenue, 3rd Floor
Boston, MA 02111
(617) 482-7070
Contact
Mr. Edward Dugger, III, President
Ms. Gabrielle Simms, Associate
Mr. Winston Lynch, Database Administrator
Preferred Limit of Loans or Investments
Up to $1 Million
Investment Policy
Prefer equity-type investments
Industry Preference
Diversified
Geographial Preference
National

University City Science Center
3624 Market Street, 1st Floor East
Philadelphia, PA 19104
(215) 387-2255
Contact
Mr. Mark M. Herrman

Vencap Equities Alberta, Ltd.
10180 101st Street, Suite 1980
Edmonton, Alberta
Canada T5J 3S4
(403) 420-1171
Contact
Mr. Derek Mather, CEO

Venture Capital Fund of New England
160 Federal Street, 23rd Floor
Boston, MA 02110
(617) 439-4646
Contact
Mr. Richard A. Farrell, Mng. Gen. Partner
Preferred Limit of Loans or Investments
Up to $1 Million
Investment Policy
Prefer equity-type investments
Industry Preference
Communications
Computer Products
Electronics
Genetic Engineering
Medical-Health
Geographical Preference
Northeast

Venture Economics, Inc.
16 Laurel Avenue
P.O. Box 348
Wellesley Hills, MA 02181
(617) 431-8100
Contact
Ms. Jane Morris, Vice President

Venture Investors of Wisconsin
102 State Street
Madison, WI 53703
(608) 256-8185
Contact
Mr. Roger H. Ganser
Mr. John Nels
Preferred Limit of Loans or Investments
Up to $500,000
Investment Policy
Prefer equity-type investments
Industry Preference
Computer Products
Consumer Products
Genetic Engineering
Industrial Products
Medical-Health
Geographical Preference
Midwest

Washington Resources Group, Inc.
1300 New York Ave., N.W., Suite 204E
Washington, DC 20005
(202) 789-8772
Contact
Mr. Wayne A. Mills, President

Wells Fargo Capital Markets Inc.
420 Montgomery Street, 9th Floor
San Francisco,CA 94163
(415) 396-5837
Contact
Mr. Charles Greenberg, President
Ms. Sandra J. Menichelli, Vice President
Preferred Limit of Loans or Investments
Above $1 Million
Investment Policy
Will make loans and/or equity investments
Industry Preference
Consumer Products
Industrial Products
Transportation
Diversified
Geographical Preference
West/National

Young, Smith & Peacock, Inc.
3343 N. Central Avenue, 16th Floor
Phoenix, AZ, 85012
(602) 264-8800
Contact
Mr. Mike Dinan, Vice President

Small Business Administration (SBA) Field Offices

Alabama
2121 8th Avenue North
Birmingham, Alabama 35203
205/254-1344

Alaska
8th and C Street
Anchorage, Alaska 99501
907/271-4022

Arizona
2005 North Central Avenue
Phoenix, Arizona 85004
602/241-2200

301 West Congress Street
Federal Bldg., Box 33
Tucson, Arizona 85701
602/792-6715

Arkansas
320 W. Capitol Avenue
Little Rock, Arkansas 72201
501/378-5871

California
2202 Monterey Street
Fresno, California 93721
209/487-5189

350 South Figueroa Street
Los Angeles, California 90071
213/688-2956

660 J Street
Sacramento, California
95814
916/551-1445

880 Front Street
San Diego, California 92188
619/293-5440

*450 Golden Gate Avenue
P.O. Box 36044
San Francisco, California
94102
415/556-7487

211 Main Street
San Francisco, California
94105
415/974-0642

901 W. Civic Center Drive
Santa Ana, California 92701
714/836-2494

Colorado
*999 18th Street
Denver, Colorado 80202
303/294-7001

721 19th Street
Denver, Colorado 80202
303/844-2607

Connecticut
330 Main Street
Hartford, Connecticut 06106
203/240-0700

Delaware
844 King Street
Wilmington, Delaware 19801
302/573-6294

District of Columbia
1111 18th St., N.W.
Washington, D.C. 20036
202/634-4950

Florida
400 West Bay Street
Jacksonville, Florida 32202
904/791-3782

1320 S. Dixie Highway
Coral Gables, Florida 33146
305/350-5521

700 Twiggs Street
Tampa, Florida 33602
813/228-2594

5601 Corporate Way S.
West Palm Beach, Florida
33407
305/689-3922

Georgia
*1375 Peachtree Street, N.E.
Atlanta, Georgia 30367
404/881-4999

1720 Peachtree Road, N.W.
Atlanta, Georgia 30309
404/347-2441

52 North Main Street
Statesboro, Georgia 30458
912/489-8719

Source: Small Business Administration.

* Regional Office

Guam
Pacific News Bldg.
238 O'Hara Street
Agana, Guam 96910
671/472-7277

Hawaii
300 Ala Moana
P.O. Box 2213
Honolulu, Hawaii 96850
808/541-2990

Idaho
1020 Main Street
Boise, Idaho 83702
208/334-1096

Illinois
*230 South Dearborn Street
Chicago, Illinois 60604
312/353-0359

219 South Dearborn Street
Chicago, Illinois 60604
312/353-4528

511 W. Capitol Street
Springfield, Illinois 62704
217/492-4416

Indiana
New Federal Bldg.
575 North Pennsylvania Street
Indianapolis, Indiana 46209
317/269-7272

Iowa
210 Walnut Street
Des Moines, Iowa 50309
515/284-4422

373 Collins Road, N.E.
Cedar Rapids, Iowa 52402
319/399-2571

Kansas
Main Place Bldg.
110 East Waterman Street
Wichita, Kansas 67202
316/269-6271

Kentucky
600 Federal Place
Louisville, Kentucky 40202
502/582-5976

Louisiana
1661 Canal Street
New Orleans, Louisiana
70112
504/589-6685

500 Fannin Street
Federal Bldg. & Courthouse
Shreveport, Louisiana 71101
318/226-5196

Maine
40 Western Avenue
Augusta, Maine 04330
207/622-8378

Maryland
10 N. Calvert Street
Baltimore, Maryland 21204
301/962-4392

Massachusetts
*60 Batterymarch Street
Boston, Massachusetts
02110
617/451-2030

150 Causeway Street
Boston, Massachusetts 02114
617/223-3224

1550 Main Street
Springfield, Massachusetts
01103
413/565-5590

Michigan
477 Michigan Avenue
McNamara Bldg.
Detroit, Michigan 48226
313/226-6075

300 S. Front Street
Marquette, Michigan 49885
906/225-1108

Minnesota
100 North 6th Street
Minneapolis, Minnesota
55403
612/370-2324

Mississippi
One Hancock Plaza
Gulfport, Mississippi 39501
601/863-4449

100 West Capitol Street
New Federal Bldg.
Jackson, Mississippi 39269
601/960-4378

Missouri
*911 Walnut Street
Kansas City, Missouri 64106
816/426-2989

* Regional Office

1103 Grand Avenue
Kansas City, Missouri 64106
816/374-3419

815 Olive Street
St. Louis, Missouri 63101
314/425-6600

620 S. Glenstone Street
Springfield, Missouri 65802
417/864-7670

Montana
2601 First Avenue North
Billings, Montana 59101
406/657-6047

301 South Park Avenue
Helena, Montana 59626
406/449-5381

Nebraska
11145 Mill Valley Road
Omaha, Nebraska 68134
402/221-4691

Nevada
301 East Stewart Street
Las Vegas, Nevada 89125
702/385-6611

50 South Virginia Street
Reno, Nevada 89505
702/784-5268

New Hampshire
55 Pleasant Street
Concord, New Hampshire
03301
603/225-1400

New Jersey
1800 East Davis Street
Camden, New Jersey 08104
609/757-5183

60 Park Place
Newark, New Jersey 07102
201/645-2434

New Mexico
Patio Plaza Building
5000 Marble Ave., N.E.
Albuquerque, N.M. 87110
505/766-3430

New York
*26 Federal Plaza
New York, New York 10278
212/264-7772

445 Broadway
Albany, New York 12207
518/472-6300

111 West Huron Street
Buffalo, New York 14202
716/846-4301

333 East Water Street
Elmira, New York 14901
607/734-8130

35 Pinelaw Road
Melville, New York 11747
516/454-0750

26 Federal Plaza
New York, New York 10278
212/264-4355

100 State Street
Rochester, New York 14614
716/263-6700

100 South Clinton St.
Syracuse, New York 13260
315/423-5383

North Carolina
222 S. Church Street
Charlotte, North Carolina
28202
704/371-6563

North Dakota
657 2nd Avenue
Fargo, North Dakota 58108
701/239-5131

Ohio
1240 East 9th St.
AJC Federal Bldg.
Cleveland, Ohio 44199
216/522-4180

85 Marconi Boulevard
Columbus, Ohio 43215
614/469-6860

550 Main Street
Cincinnati, Ohio 45202
513/684-2814

Oklahoma
200 N.W. 5th Street
Oklahoma City, Oklahoma
73102
405/231-4301

Oregon
1220 S.W. Third Avenue
Portland, Oregon 97204
503/221-2682

* Regional Office

Pennsylvania
*475 Allendale Road
King of Prussia, Pennsylvania
19406
215/962-3750

475 Allendale Road
King of Prussia, Pennsylvania
19406
215/962-3846

100 Chestnut Street
Harrisburg, Pennsylvania
17101
717/782-3840

960 Penn Avenue
Pittsburgh, Pennsylvania
15222
412/644-2780

Penn Place
20 North Pennsylvania Avenue
Wilkes-Barre, Pennsylvania
18701
717/826-6497

Puerto Rico
Federal Building
Carlos Chardon Avenue
Hato Rey, Puerto Rico 00919
809/753-4002

Rhode Island
380 Westminster Mall
Providence, Rhode Island
02903
401/528-4586

South Carolina
1835 Assembly Street
Columbia, South Carolina
29201
803/765-5376

South Dakota
101 South Main Avenue
Sioux Falls, South Dakota
57102
605/336-2980

Tennessee
404 James Robertson
Parkway
Nashville, Tennessee 37219
615/251-5881

Texas
Federal Building
300 East 8th Street
Austin, Texas 78701
512/482-5288

400 Mann Street
Corpus Christi, Texas 78408
512/888-3331

*8625 King George Drive
Bldg. C
Dallas, Texas 75235
214/767-7643

1100 Commerce Street
Dallas, Texas 75242
214/767-0605

10737 Gateway West
El Paso, Texas 79902
915/543-7586

221 West Lancaster Avenue
819 Taylor Street 76102
817/334-3613

222 East Van Buren Street
Harlingen, Texas 78550
512/427-8533

2525 Murthworth
Houston, Texas 77054
713/660-4401

1611 10th Street
Lubbock, Texas 79401
806/743-7462

100 East Travis
Marshall, Texas 75670
214/935-5257

7400 Blanco Road
San Antonio, Texas 78216
512/229-4535

Utah
125 South State Street
Salt Lake City, Utah 84138
801/524-5800

Vermont
87 State Street
Montpelier, Vermont 05602
802/828-4474

Virginia
400 North 8th Street
Richmond, Virginia 23240
804/771-2617

Virgin Islands
Veterans Drive
St. Thomas, Virgin Islands
00801
809/774-8530

* Regional Office

P.O. Box 4010
Christiansted, Virgin Islands
00820
809/773-3480

Washington
*2615 4th Avenue
Seattle, Washington 98121
206/442-5676

915 Second Avenue
Seattle, Washington 98174
206/442-5534

Washington, D.C.
1111 18th Street, N.W.
Washington, D.C. 20036
202/634-4950

W. 920 Riverside Avenue
Spokane, Washington 99210
509/456-3783

West Virginia
168 W. Main
Clarksburg, West Virginia
26301
304/623-5631

550 Eagan Street
Charleston, West Virginia
25301
304/347-5220

Wisconsin
500 South Barstow Street
Eau Claire, Wisconsin 54701
715/834-9012

212 East Washington Avenue
Madison, Wisconsin 53703
608/264-5261

310 West Wisconsin Avenue
Milwaukee, Wisconsin 53203
414/291-3941

Wyoming
100 East B Street
Casper, Wyoming 82602
307/261-5761

* Regional Office

Returns on Various Types of Investments*

R. S. Salomon, Jr.
Eric H. Sorensen
Caroline H. Davenport
Maria A. Fiore

Long-Term Returns and Asset Allocation Decisions

Some years ago, we began tracking the performance of several financial and tangible asset categories in an effort to better understand the impact of inflation on investment returns. The first report—published in 1977— took aim at what was then a well-established convention: Stocks are an effective hedge against inflation. In fact, stocks were the only asset that did not beat inflation in the 1968–77 period that was the subject of our inaugural study.

This year's study includes 20 years worth of data for the first time. The numbers reinforce our original finding, with stocks barely outpacing inflation over the past two decades. In the same period, stocks have trailed bonds, which gives us the opportunity to take a closer look at another widely accepted investment maxim: Stocks always perform better than bonds over long periods of time. We believe that the similarity of returns provided by stocks and bonds has important implications for asset allocation decisions.

This report monitors the performance of 14 asset categories relative to inflation as measured by the Consumer Price Index (CPI). The number of assets is somewhat overstated, however, since there are several tangible asset categories that are not legitimate alternatives for institutional investors. Broadly speaking, tangible assets fall into three categories: real estate, commodities and collectibles. Only two of these are realistic investment alternatives for institutions. Collectible markets are fun to monitor, but essentially impossible for institutions to participate in. Collectibles do not serve an economic purpose and thus have no economic value—this makes it very difficult to project returns.

WHEN THE STOCK/BOND DECISION MATTERS

In analyzing the 20-year returns presented in Figure 1, one remarkable fact stands out: Since 1968, bonds and stocks have provided similar returns, with bonds slightly outpacing equities. This contradicts the accepted theory that stocks will always provide better returns over long periods. It could be argued that the returns for the 1968–88 period are a fluke, or that they are irrelevant because of peculiarities of the beginning or ending periods. In fact, however, the returns for the S&P 500 and the Salomon Brothers index of high-grade corporate bonds—our measures of stock and bond performance—differ very little in the ten-year and five-year intervals. Looked at another way, stock and bond returns were also very close in the 1970s and in the 1980s—two distinctly different periods.

Portfolio managers devote a lot of resources to the stock/bond asset allocation decision. As the one-year stock/bond results demonstrate, the decision can be an extremely important one over relatively short periods. In our view, the decision would also be a critical one over a long period only if a manager had an *extreme* view about the likely course of inflation. The bond/stock asset allocation decision is most critical in times of hyperinflation or deflation. In between, as shown in the diagram below, there is a zone which we have called "normal times" where inflation may be high in one period and low in another, but it is not near extreme levels.

The 20-year return on Treasury bills, which surpassed both stocks and bonds, provides another surprise in the long term return figures. We believe that the high return on

* Although the information in this report has been obtained from sources which Salomon Brothers Inc. believes to be reliable, we do not guarantee its accuracy and such information may be incomplete or condensed. All opinions and estimates included in this report constitute our judgment as of this date and are subject to change without notice. This report is for information purposes only and is not intended as an offer or solicitation with respect to the purchase or sale of any security.

Editor's Note: Stock returns are for the S&P 500 and include appreciation plus dividends. Bond returns are for Salomon Brothers Index and include appreciation plus interest.

Source: *Long-Term Returns and Asset Allocation Decisions*, by R. S. Salomon, Jr., Eric H. Sorensen, Caroline H. Davenport, and Maria A. Fiore

Figure 1. Compound Annual Rates of Return

	20 Years	Rank	10 Years	Rank	5 Years	Rank	1 Years	Rank
Coins	15.1	1	13.4	1	10.1	4	14.0	3
U.S. Stamps	12.9	2	10.5	3	0.2	12	1.4	13
Gold	12.8	3	9.6	7	2.2	11	3.1	10
Chinese Ceramics[a]	12.0	4	9.2	8	5.5	8	10.5	5
Oil[b]	9.9	5	3.7	12	-10.7	14	19.5E	2
Diamonds[c]	9.9	6	9.6	6	7.5	7	24.9	1
Old Masters[a]	8.8	7	8.0	9	12.0	3	13.4	4
Treasury Bills	8.5	8	10.1	5	7.6	6	6.0	8
Bonds	8.1	9	10.3	4	13.4	2	6.2	7
Housing	7.7	10	6.2	10	5.0	9	2.0	12
Stocks	6.8	11	13.3	2	13.6	1	-4.9	14
CPI	**6.3**	**12**	**6.1**	**11**	**3.3**	**10**	**3.1**	**9**
Silver	5.9	13	2.8	14	-11.6	15	-7.4	15
U.S. Farmland	5.9	14	0.6	15	-6.5	13	3.1	11
Foreign Exchange	4.7	15	3.2	13	9.5	5	8.6	6

[a] Source: Sotheby's. 1988 index level for Chinese Ceramics does not reflect sales held May 17-19 in Hong Kong.
[b] Oil index figures have been revised to reflect refiners' acquisition cost of crude oil. Source: U.S. Department of Energy.
[c] Source: The Diamond Registry.
Note: All returns are for the period ended June 1, 1988, based on latest available data.
CPI Consumer Price Index.

cash is a function of the unprecedented expansion in debt that has taken place over the past 20 years. Practically speaking, the return on cash would have been extremely difficult to capture. To do so, an investor would have had to accurately forecast a debt buildup on a scale never previously experienced in this country.

The comparison between 20-year returns and returns in the latest 12-month period suggests that it has become increasingly difficult to beat inflation. Only eight assets provided real returns last year. Diamonds topped the list: Two price increases occurred during the 12-month period, breaking a pattern of flat to modestly increasing prices since 1980. Stocks ranked next to last, reflecting the effect of the collapse in prices last October.

THE EXPERIENCE OF TWO DECADES

The return data in Figure 1 raises questions about the value of stock/bond decisions over long periods. Analyzing returns for the past two decades suggests that there is another allocation decision that can meaningfully affect performance: The choice between tangible and financial assets. In the inflationary 1970s, Treasury bills, stocks and bonds significantly underperformed tangible assets, trailing the rate of inflation. In the lower inflation environment of the 1980s, stocks, bonds and bills have provided the best returns.

We expect the good relative performance of financial assets to persist. Inflation is likely to remain moderate: There will be some cyclical pickup in the months ahead, but the rate of gain will not reach the levels experienced in the 1970s. Having said this, we admit that certain assets have a contrarian appeal that could become compelling if their prices fall further or inflation exceeds our expectations. Farmland, for example, is showing signs of hitting a bottom: The year-to-year increase in 1988 is the first such rise since 1982. Conversely, the contrarian might find reason to

Figure 2. Bond/Stock Allocation in Different Inflation Environments

Deflation	"Normal Times"	Hyperinflation
Bonds Provide Best Return	Stock/Bond Returns Indistinguishable	Stocks Provide Best Return
100% Bonds	Indifferent	100% Stocks

Figure 3. 1980s — A Decade for Financial Assets
(Compound Annual Rate of Return, 1980-88)

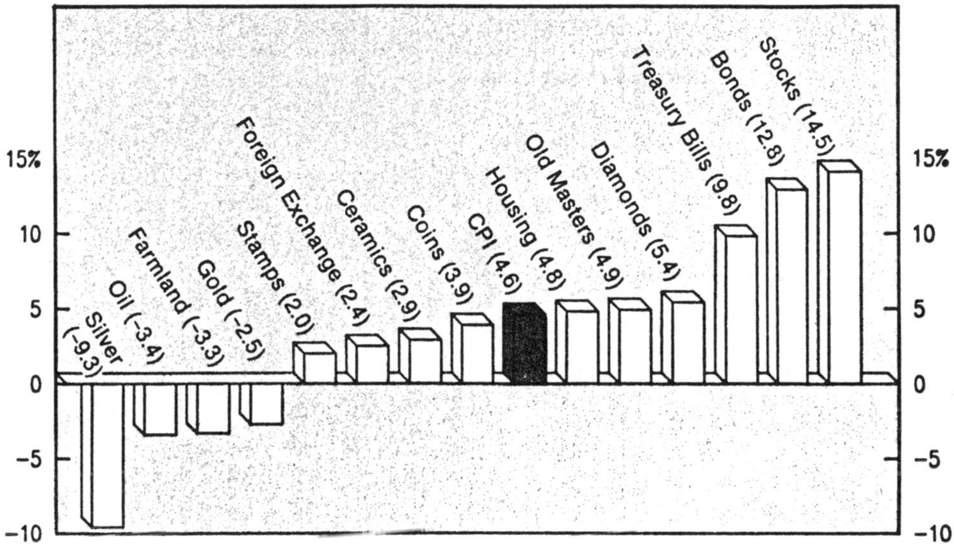

shy away from coins, given the consistently strong performance of this asset class. The tenant farmer who sells his coin collection today to buy the land he works might well be rewarded with extraordinary returns.

Figure 4. The 1970s — A Decade for Collectibles and Commodities
(Compound Annual Rate of Return, 1970-80)

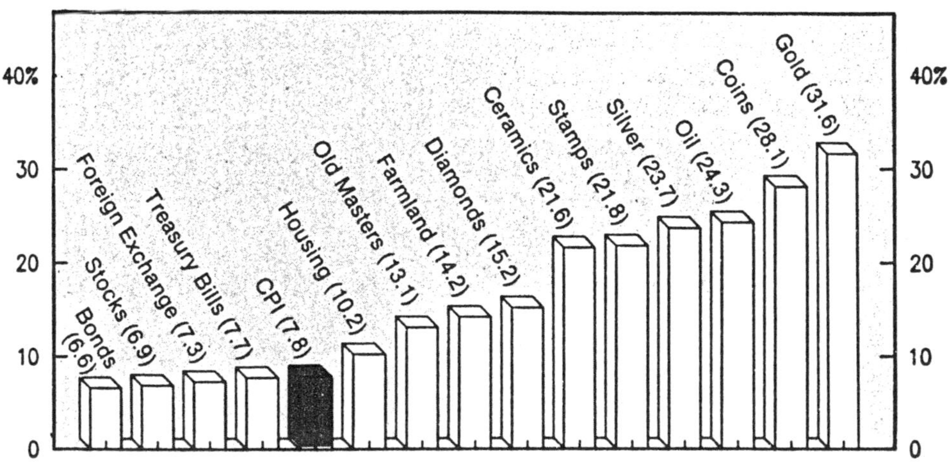

Stock Market: U.S. and Foreign

The Crash of 1987

During October 1987, the nation's securities markets experienced an extraordinary surge of volume and price volatility. The most widely followed indicator of the U.S. stock market's movements, the Dow Jones Industrial Average index of 30 NYSE stocks the ("DJIA"), had reached an intra-day high of 2746.65 on August 25, 1987. On October 2, the DJIA closed at 2640.99. During the week of October 5, the index declined by 158.78 points; during the week of October 12, by 235.48 points. On October 19, the DJIA declined 508.32 points, and by its low point mid-day on October 20 it had declined to 1708.70, or over 1,000 points (37%) below its August 25 high. Even with its erratic but substantial recovery over the next few trading sessions, by October 30, the DJIA stood at 1,994, down over 26% from its August high. Broader indexes also declined for the month of October. For example, the Standard & Poor's ("S&P") index of 500 stocks declined 21.8%, the composite indexes for the nation's three principal securities markets, the New York Stock Exchange ("NYSE"), American Stock Exchange ("Amex"), and the National Association of Securities Dealers Automated Quotation ("NASDAQ") system for over-the-counter ("OTC") stock trading, experienced declines in October of 21.9%, 27%, and 27.2%, respectively.

After October 19 and 20, the securities and futures markets did not return to a status even approaching "normalcy" until the end of the month. The final eight trading sessions in October included six sessions in which the DJIA moved (as measured by closing prices) more than 50 points, including the largest one-day rise in the index (186.84 points or 10.1% on October 21), and the second-largest point and sixth-largest percentage decline (156.83 points or 8% on October 26).[1] In addition, although six of these sessions were shortened to close at 2:00 P.M. (Eastern Time),[2] daily NYSE volume for the remainder of October exceeded 240 million shares (including a 449 million share day on October 21 and a 392 million share day on October 22). Finally, it was not until October 29 that the aberrational discount to cash in the SPZ futures abated.

The increased market volatility from the October market break receded only gradually by year-end. The implied volatility of the options on March expiration S&P 500 futures ("SPH"), which had skyrocketed from around 20 points prior to the break to over 65 points, was still around 30 to 35 points by December 31, 1987.[3] By some estimates, the 1987 volatility for S&P stocks is roughly equivalent to 35% of the stock prices—more than twice the annual level of volatility for 1983 through 1986.[4]

LONDON

The London securities market was transformed radically on October 27, 1986, generally referred to as "Big Bang Day." The Big Bang heralded a wholesale restructuring of London's capital markets, including changing the name of the stock exchange to the International Stock Exchange of the United Kingdom and the Republic of Ireland. Among the most significant changes was the introduction

Source: *The October 1987 Market Break*, Division of Market Regulation, U.S. Securities and Exchange Commission.

[1] On October 26, the S&P 500 index also fell 20.55 (8.28%). Total NYSE volume was 308.8 million shares, with 1,791 issues declining, 134 gaining, and 104 unchanged. The Amex and NASDAQ composite indexes declined 9.3% and 9.0%, respectively.

[2] After the 4:00 close on October 22, the NYSE announced that the exchange's trading hours would be temporarily reduced, with the close moved to 2:00, to permit members to process the enormous trading volume during the market break. All major securities and index futures similarly reduced trading hours. Starting on November 2, trading hours were gradually extended and returned to normal on November 12.

[3] There are several methods used to estimate the price volatility of an individual security or group of securities. Unlike the more familiar method which estimates volatility from empirical data, "implied volatility" is a measure of the volatility of the security or security index that is implicit in the actual prices which exist in the market for options in these securities. This method assumes that the actual trade price is representative of the fair price for the option, an assumption more likely to be true for actively traded option series. *See* L. McMillan, *Options as a Strategic Investment*, New York Institute of Finance (2nd ed. 1986) at 411.

[4] One firm has estimated that the representative bid-ask spread on the average S&P 500 stock, which had been 0.45% of market value on September 1, 1987, was still at approximately 0.77% on November 3 as a result of greater market risk from price volatility. Kidder, Peabody & Co., *The Impact of October 19 on Transaction Costs in the Equity and Stock Index Futures Markets. A Preliminary Update* (November 1987). *See also* Chapter Three.

of a new system of trading, referred to as "dealing,"—using the Stock Exchange Automated Quotations System ("SEAQ"). Under the new system, trading is very similar to over-the-counter ("OTC") trading in the United States. The screen-based system provides competitive market makers the ability to input "firm" quotations into SEAQ terminals.[5] Trades, referred to as "bargains," are negotiated and finalized over the phone between market makers or between a market maker and his customer. The ISE has not yet developed automatic routing or execution systems.

During the October market break, the ISE experienced many of the same problems as the U.S. OTC market. On Monday, October 19, the FT-SE 100 dropped 249.6 points, losing nearly 10.1% of its value.[6] Tuesday saw that record eclipsed with a 250.7 point drop in the index, or 11.6%.[7] More than 2,000 stocks declined while only 75 stocks rose on October 20. Volume of 798 million shares was 250% greater than a year earlier and 31% over the previous week's volume.[8]

TOKYO (TKE)

Like the U.S. exchange markets, the TKE experienced a lack of liquidity on October 20 and 21. On Tuesday, October 20, the Nikkei dropped 620 points to 25,745, a 2.4% decline. On Wednesday the Nikkei suffered an additional 14.9% loss in its value, by far the worst one-day drop in the TKE's history. By November 19, the Nikkei had fallen a total of 19% from its pre-market break high. On October 20, the sell orders so overwhelmed the buy orders that some 80 stocks never opened.[9] In addition, the TKE informed the staff that during the day trading in 700 stocks (nearly half the 1,500 that are listed on the exchange) was halted because prices in those stocks plunged at an unprecedented rate to their pre-set daily price limits.[10] The intense sell pressure on October 20, which caused prices to collapse, led the exchange to seek ways to attract buy interest and stabilize market conditions. Thus, the TKE lowered its initial margin collateral requirement to 50% from 70% and raised the collateral valuation rate to 70% from 60%. These eased margin requirements were intended to encourage purchases to offset the sell order imbalances.

It was not until the final two hours of trading that any buyers emerged at all. Although four major Japanese firms, Nomura, Daiwa, Nikko and Yamaichi, reportedly entered the market as buyers of industrial stocks, their activity was not enough to turn the tide on October 20 and the Nikkei closed down 14.9%.[11] By Wednesday, October 21, however, a dramatic change in sentiment had occurred. A torrent of buy orders flowed in, causing serious liquidity problems on the sell side. During the first half hour of trading, only three stocks were traded. During the course of the day, trading in 151 stocks was halted because their prices had risen to the level of their daily price limits. Firms reported that it was nearly impossible to find sellers on that Wednesday. The Nikkei closed up a record 2,037.32.

[5] The ISE generally requires that market makers deal at their posted quotes for at least the number of shares posted. Quotations subject to this requirement are referred to as "firm quotations."

[6] The London market effectively was closed on Friday, October 16 because of a severe wind storm that paralyzed the city. Thus, the greater than 200-point drop in the FT-SE 100 is partly explained as pent-up selling demand from Friday in response to the 109-point drop in the DJIA.

[7] This compares with an 11% drop in the value of the NASDAQ Composite Index (a broad-based index of U.S. OTC stock) on Monday, October 19, and a 9% drop on Tuesday, October 20.

[8] Despite the heavy processing burden the increased volume caused, ISE's settlement systems functioned well. *The New York Times* reported that settlements appeared to have been conducted normally and no significant liquidity problems appeared on November 2, the first settlement day since the October market break. The article also reported that approximately 85% of settlements are normally concluded on settlement day and that that level appeared to have been achieved. *See* Trades Settled in London, *N.Y.T.*, Nov. 3, 1987, at D22.

Source: Tokyo Stock Exchange
* Exchange Rate: U.S. $1.00 = 125 yen.

[9] *See Economist*, Nov. 14, 1987, at 85. The TKE's rules specify a maximum ratio between buy and sell orders. When that ratio is exceeded, trading is temporarily halted.

[10] Daily price limits are intended to check extreme volatility by stipulating the maximum a stock's price may change during a trading day. Once the limit is reached, trading is halted until the next trading day.

[11] *See Fin. Times*, Oct. 21, 1987, at 2, col. 1.

Stock Exchanges

Common Stocks (shares of ownership in a corporation) are traded on several exchanges. The best known are the New York Stock Exchange and the American Stock Exchange, both located in Manhattan's financial district. Generally, the stocks of the largest companies are traded on the New York Stock Exchange, while somewhat smaller companies are traded on the American Exchange. There are also a number of regional exchanges such as the Midwest Exchange in Chicago and the Pacific Exchange in San Francisco. These exchanges trade stocks of local corporations as well as stocks listed on the New York and American Exchanges.

In addition, there is the Over-The Counter-Market (OTC) which, unlike the exchanges previously mentioned, does not have a specific location but consists of a network of brokers and dealers linked by telephone and private wires. Smaller or relatively new companies are traded on the OTC. Trading information for many (but far from all) stocks on the OTC market is collected and displayed on a computerized system, the National Association of Security Dealers Automatic Quote System (NASDAQ).

Large institutional traders (mutual and pension funds, insurance companies, etc.) often trade blocks of stocks directly with one another. This information is collected and displayed on the Instinet System.

Major Stock Exchanges*

UNITED STATES

AMERICAN STOCK EXCHANGE, INC.
86 Trinity Place
New York, New York 10006

BOSTON STOCK EXCHANGE, INC.
One Boston Place
Boston, Massachusetts 02109

THE CINCINNATI STOCK EXCHANGE, INC.
205 Dixie Terminal Building
Cincinnati, Ohio 45202

MIDWEST STOCK EXCHANGE, INC.
120 South LaSalle Street
Chicago, Illinois 60603

NEW YORK STOCK EXCHANGE, INC.
11 Wall Street
New York, New York 10005

PACIFIC STOCK EXCHANGE, INC.
618 South Spring Street
Los Angeles, California 90014

301 Pine Street
San Francisco, California 94104

PHILADELPHIA STOCK EXCHANGE, INC.
1900 Market Street
Philadelphia, Pennsylvania 19103

SPOKANE STOCK EXCHANGE, INC.
206 Radio Central Building
Spokane, Washington 99201

FOREIGN

AUSTRALIA

SYDNEY STOCK EXCHANGE
Tower Building
Australia Square
P.O. Box H67
Sydney, New South Wales 2000

BELGIUM

BRUSSELS STOCK EXCHANGE
Palais de la Bourse
1000 Brussels

CANADA

ALBERTA STOCK EXCHANGE
300–5th Avenue S.W.
Calgary, Alberta T2P 3C4

BOURSE DE MONTRÉAL
The Stock Exchange Tower
800 Victoria Square
Montreal, Quebec H4Z 1A9

TORONTO STOCK EXCHANGE
2 First Canadian Place
Toronto, Ontario M5X 1J2

VANCOUVER STOCK EXCHANGE
Stock Exchange Tower
P.O. Box 10333
609 Granville Street
Vancouver, B.C. V7Y 1H1

WINNIPEG STOCK EXCHANGE
303–167 Lombard Avenue
Winnipeg, Manitoba R3B OT6

* See page 471 for a listing of futures and options exchanges.

FRANCE

BOURSE DE PARIS—PARIS STOCK EXCHANGE
Palais de la Bourse
75002 Paris

GERMANY

FRANKFURTER WERTPAPIERBORE—FRANKFORT EXCHANGE
Borsenplatz 6
6000 Frankfurt am Main 1

HONG KONG

STOCK EXCHANGE OF HONG KONG
One Exchange Square
Hong Kong

JAPAN

TOKYO STOCK EXCHANGE
1–1 Nihonbashi Kayaba-cho-z-chome
Cho-Ku, Tokyo 103

THE NETHERLANDS

AMSTERDAMSE EFFECTENBEURS—AMSTERDAM STOCK EXCHANGE
Beursplein 5
1012 JW Amsterdam

SWITZERLAND

GENEVA STOCK EXCHANGE
Ruedela Confédération 8
CH-1204 Geneva

ZÜRICH STOCK EXCHANGE
Boersenkommissariat, Bleicherweg 5
CH-8001 Zürich

UNITED KINGDOM

LONDON STOCK EXCHANGE
Old Broad Street
London, England EC 2N 1HP

Investment Returns on Stocks, Bonds, and Bills

Roger G. Ibbotson, Laurence B. Siegel,** Katie B. Weigel****

Our look at history consists of examining the returns of five capital market sectors. We measure total returns (capital gains plus income) on common stocks, long-term corporate bonds, long-term government bonds, U.S. Treasury bills, and rates of inflation on consumer goods. Comparing the returns from the various sectors gives us insights into the returns available from taking risk and the relationships between capital market returns and inflation.

THE RISKS AND REWARDS

We display graphically the rewards and risks available from the U.S. capital markets over the past 62 years. Exhibit 1 shows the growth of an investment in common stocks, long-term government bonds, and Treasury bills as well as the increase in the inflation index over the 62-year period. Each of the series is initiated at $1 at year-end 1925. The vertical scale is logarithmic so that equal distances represent equal percentage changes anywhere along the axis. The graph vividly portrays that despite setbacks such as that of October 1987, common stocks were the big winner over the entire period. If $1 were invested in stocks at year-end 1925 and all dividends reinvested, the dollar investment would have grown to $347.96 by year-end 1987. This phenomenal growth was not without substantial risk, especially during the earlier portion of the period. In contrast, long-term government bonds (with a constant 20-year maturity) exhibited much less risk, but grew to only $13.35.

A virtually riskless strategy (for those with short-term time horizons) has been to buy U.S. Treasury bills. However, Treasury bills have had a marked tendency to track inflation, with the result that their real (inflation adjusted) return is near zero for the entire 1926–1987 period. Note that the tracking is only prevalent over the latter portion of the period. During periods of deflation (such as the late 1920s and early 1930s) the Treasury bill returns were near zero, but not negative, since no one intentionally buys securities with negative yields. Beginning in the early 1940s, the yields (returns) on Treasury bills were pegged by the government at low rates while high inflation was experienced. The government pegging ended with the U.S. Treasury-Federal Reserve Accord in March 1951.

We summarize the investment returns in Exhibit 2 by presenting the average annual returns over the 1926–1987 period. Common stocks returned a compounded (geometric mean) total return of 9.9 percent per year. The annual compound return from capital appreciation alone was 4.9 percent. After adjusting for inflation, annual compounded total returns were 6.6 percent per year.

The average total return over any single year (arithmetic mean) for stocks was 12.1 percent, with positive returns recorded in more than two-thirds of the years (42 out of 62 years). The risk or degree of return fluctuation is measured by standard deviation as 21.2 percent. The frequency distribution (histogram) counts the number of years the returns fell in each 5 percent return increment. Note the wide variations in common stock returns relative to the other capital market sectors. Annual stock returns ranged from 54.0 percent in 1933 to −43.3 percent in 1931.

A simple example illustrates the difference between geometric and arithmetic means. Suppose $1 were invested in a common stock port-folio that experiences successive annual returns of +50 percent and −50 percent. At the end of the first year, the portfolio is worth $1.50. At the end of the second year, the portfolio is worth $0.75. The annual arithmetic mean is 0 percent, whereas the annual geometric mean (compounded return) is −13.4 percent. Naturally, it is the geometric mean that more directly measures the change in wealth over more than one period. On the other hand, the arithmetic mean is a better representation of typical performance over any single annual period.

The other capital market sectors also had returns commensurate with their risks. Long-term corporate bonds outperformed the default-free, long-term government bonds, which in turn outperformed the essentially riskless U.S. Treasury bills. Over the entire period the riskless U.S. Treasury bills had a return almost identical with the inflation rate. Thus, we again note that the real rate of interest (the inflation-adjusted riskless rate) has been on average very near 0 percent historically.

MEASUREMENT OF THE FIVE SERIES

The returns were computed by compounding monthly returns, with no adjustments made for transactions costs or taxes. We describe each of the five total return se-

* Professor, Yale School of Management, New Haven, Connecticut.

** Managing Director, Ibbotson Associates, Inc., Chicago, Illinois.

*** Senior Consultant, Ibbotson Associates, Inc.

EXHIBIT 1: WEALTH INDEXES OF INVESTMENTS IN THE U.S. CAPITAL MARKETS, 1926–1987 (assumed initial investment of $1.00 at year-end 1925, includes reinvestment income)

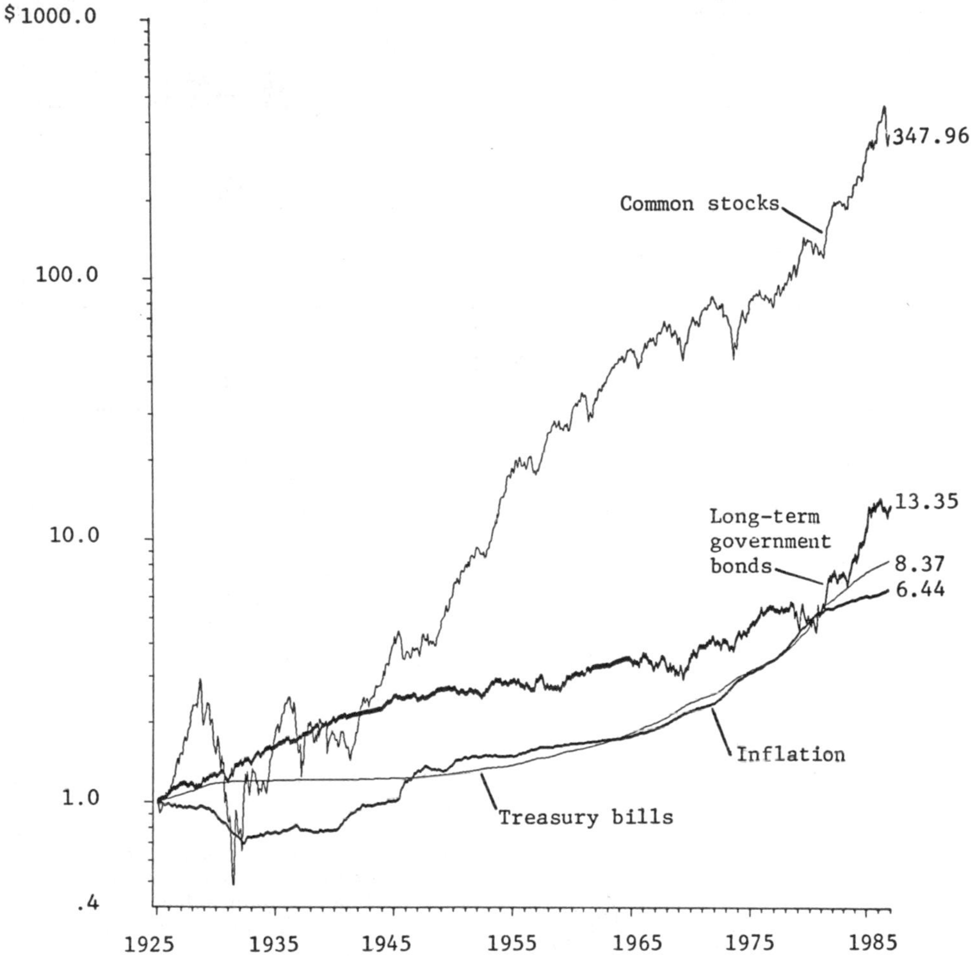

Source: *Stocks, Bonds, Bills, and Inflation: 1988 Yearbook,* published by Ibbotson Associates, Inc. [8 S. Michigan Avenue, Suite 707, Chicago, IL. 60603, phone 312-263-3434], 1988.

ries which are listed annually in Exhibit 3. The index numbers in Exhibit 3 are dollar values of a $1 investment made on December 31, 1925. They can be converted to yearly returns by taking the ratio of a given year-end index value to the previous year-end value, then subtracting one (1). For example, the return for common stocks for 1987 equals $(347.965 \div 330.668) - 1 = 0.052$, or 5.2 percent.

Common Stocks

The total return index is based upon Standard & Poor's (S&P) Composite Index with dividends reinvested monthly. To the extent that the 500 stocks currently included in the S&P Composite Index (prior to March 1957, there were 90 stocks) are representative of all stocks in the United States, the market value weighting scheme allows the returns of the index to correspond to the aggregate stock market returns in the U.S. economy.

Long-Term Corporate Bonds

We measure the total returns of a corporate bond index with approximately 20 years to maturity. We use Salomon Brothers' High-Grade Long-Term Corporate Bond Index from its beginning in 1969 through 1986. For the period 1946–68 we backdate Salomon Brothers' index using Salomon Brothers' monthly yield data and similar methodology.

EXHIBIT 2: BASIC SERIES: TOTAL ANNUAL RETURNS, 1926–1987

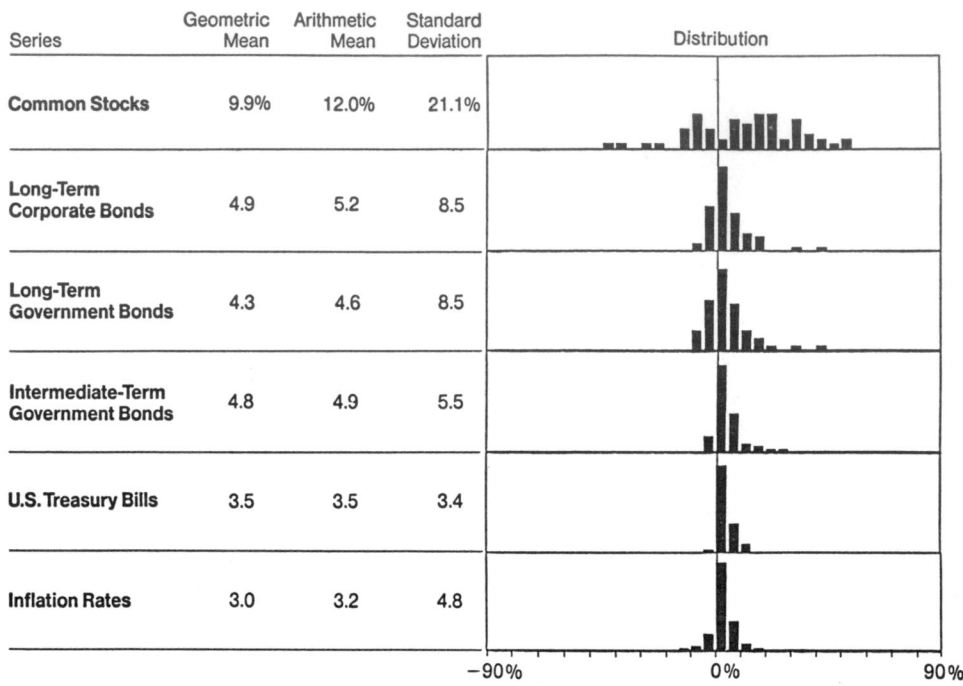

Series	Geometric Mean	Arithmetic Mean	Standard Deviation
Common Stocks	9.9%	12.0%	21.1%
Long-Term Corporate Bonds	4.9	5.2	8.5
Long-Term Government Bonds	4.3	4.6	8.5
Intermediate-Term Government Bonds	4.8	4.9	5.5
U.S. Treasury Bills	3.5	3.5	3.4
Inflation Rates	3.0	3.2	4.8

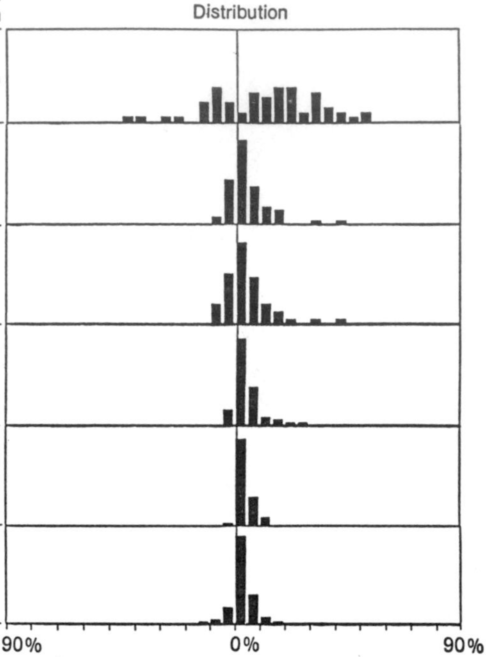

Source: *Stocks, Bonds, Bills and Inflation: 1988 Yearbook,* Ibbotson Associates, Inc., Chicago, 1988.

For the period 1926–45 we compute returns using Standard & Poor's monthly high-grade corporate composite bond yield data, assuming a 4 percent coupon and a 20-year maturity.

Long-Term Government Bonds

To measure the total returns of long-term U.S. government bonds, we use the bond data obtained from the U.S. Government Bond File (constructed by Lawrence Fisher) at the Center for Research in Security Prices (CRSP) at the University of Chicago. We attempt to maintain a 20-year bond portfolio whose returns do not reflect the potential tax benefits, impaired negotiability, or the special redemption or call privileges frequently characterizing government bond prices and yields.

U.S. Treasury Bills

For the U.S. Treasury bill index, we again use the data in the CRSP U.S. Government Bond File. We measure one-month holding period returns for the shortest-term bills not less than one month in maturity. Since U.S. Treasury bills were not initiated until 1929, we use short-term coupon bonds whenever bill quotes are unavailable.

Consumer Price Index

We utilize the Consumer Price Index for All Urban Consumers (CPI-U), not seasonally adjusted, to measure inflation. The CPI-U, and its predecessor, the CPI (which we use prior to January 1978) is constructed by the Bureau of Labor Statistics, U.S. Department of Labor, Washington, D.C.

EXHIBIT 3: BASIC SERIES, INDEXES OF YEAR-END CUMULATIVE WEALTH, 1925–1987 (year-end 1925 = 1.000)

	Common Stocks		Long-Term Government Bonds		Long-Term Corporate Bonds	U.S. Treasury Bills	Consumer Price Index
Year	Total Returns	Capital Appreciation Only	Total Returns	Capital Appreciation Only	Total Returns	Total Returns	Rates of Inflation
1925....	1.000	1.000	1.000	1.000	1.000	1.000	1.000
1926....	1.116	1.057	1.078	1.039	1.074	1.033	.985
1927....	1.535	1.384	1.174	1.095	1.154	1.065	.965
1928....	2.204	1.908	1.175	1.061	1.186	1.099	.955
1929....	2.018	1.681	1.215	1.059	1.225	1.152	.957
1930....	1.516	1.202	1.272	1.072	1.323	1.179	.899
1931....	.859	.636	1.204	.981	1.299	1.192	.814
1932....	.789	.540	1.407	1.108	1.439	1.204	.730
1933....	1.214	.792	1.406	1.073	1.588	1.207	.734
1934....	1.197	.745	1.547	1.146	1.808	1.209	.749
1935....	1.767	1.053	1.624	1.170	1.982	1.211	.771
1936....	2.367	1.346	1.746	1.225	2.116	1.213	.780
1937....	1.538	.827	1.750	1.194	2.174	1.217	.804
1938....	2.016	1.035	1.847	1.228	2.307	1.217	.782
1939....	2.008	.979	1.957	1.271	2.399	1.217	.778
1940....	1.812	.829	2.076	1.319	2.480	1.217	.786
1941....	1.602	.681	2.095	1.305	2.548	1.218	.862
1942....	1.927	.766	2.162	1.315	2.614	1.221	.942
1943....	2.427	.915	2.207	1.310	2.688	1.225	.972
1944....	2.906	1.041	2.270	1.314	2.815	1.229	.993
1945....	3.965	1.361	2.513	1.423	2.930	1.233	1.015
1946....	3.645	1.199	2.511	1.392	2.980	1.238	1.199
1947....	3.853	1.199	2.445	1.327	2.911	1.244	1.307
1948....	4.065	1.191	2.528	1.340	3.031	1.254	1.343
1949....	4.829	1.313	2.691	1.395	3.132	1.268	1.318
1950....	6.360	1.600	2.692	1.366	3.198	1.283	1.395
1951....	7.888	1.863	2.586	1.281	3.112	1.302	1.477
1952....	9.336	2.082	2.616	1.262	3.221	1.324	1.490
1953....	9.244	1.944	2.711	1.270	3.331	1.348	1.499
1954....	14.108	2.820	2.906	1.325	3.511	1.360	1.492
1955....	18.561	3.564	2.868	1.271	3.527	1.381	1.497
1956....	19.778	3.658	2.708	1.164	3.287	1.415	1.540
1957....	17.646	3.134	2.910	1.208	3.573	1.459	1.587
1958....	25.298	4.327	2.733	1.097	3.494	1.482	1.615
1959....	28.322	4.694	2.671	1.029	3.460	1.526	1.639
1960....	28.455	4.554	3.039	1.124	3.774	1.566	1.663
1961....	36.106	5.607	3.068	1.092	3.956	1.600	1.674
1962....	32.955	4.945	3.280	1.122	4.270	1.643	1.695
1963....	40.468	5.879	3.319	1.092	4.364	1.695	1.723
1964....	47.139	6.642	3.436	1.084	4.572	1.754	1.743
1965....	53.008	7.244	3.460	1.047	4.552	1.823	1.777
1966....	47.674	6.295	3.586	1.036	4.560	1.910	1.836
1967....	59.104	7.560	3.257	.895	4.335	1.991	1.892
1968....	65.641	8.139	3.248	.846	4.446	2.094	1.981
1969....	60.059	7.210	3.083	.754	4.086	2.232	2.102
1970....	62.465	7.222	3.457	.791	4.837	2.378	2.218
1971....	71.406	8.001	3.914	.843	5.370	2.482	2.292
1972....	84.956	9.252	4.136	.840	5.760	2.577	2.371
1973....	72.500	7.645	4.090	.775	5.825	2.756	2.579
1974....	53.311	5.373	4.268	.748	5.647	2.976	2.894
1975....	73.144	7.068	4.661	.754	6.474	3.149	3.097
1976....	90.584	8.422	5.441	.815	7.681	3.309	3.246
1977....	84.076	7.453	5.405	.750	7.813	3.479	3.466
1978....	89.592	7.532	5.342	.682	7.807	3.728	3.778
1979....	106.112	8.459	5.277	.615	7.481	4.115	4.281

Continued

EXHIBIT 3: (*Concluded*)

Year	Common Stocks		Long-Term Government Bonds		Long-Term Corporate Bonds Total Returns	U.S. Treasury Bills Total Returns	Consumer Price Index Rates of Inflation
	Total Returns	Capital Appreciation Only	Total Returns	Capital Appreciation Only			
1980	140.513	10.639	5.069	.530	7.285	4.578	4.812
1981	133.615	9.605	5.162	.475	7.215	5.251	5.242
1982	162.221	11.023	7.245	.589	10.374	5.805	5.445
1983	198.743	12.926	7.294	.530	10.862	6.315	5.652
1984	211.197	13.106	8.420	.542	12.642	6.937	5.875
1985	279.114	16.558	11.027	.639	16.549	7.473	6.097
1986	330.668	18.981	13.722	.735	19.833	7.934	6.166
1987	347.965	19.366	13.352	.657	19.780	8.367	6.438

Source: *Stocks, Bonds, Bills, and Inflation: 1988 Yearbook*, Ibbotson Associates, Inc., Chicago, 1988.

The Constant Dollar Dow

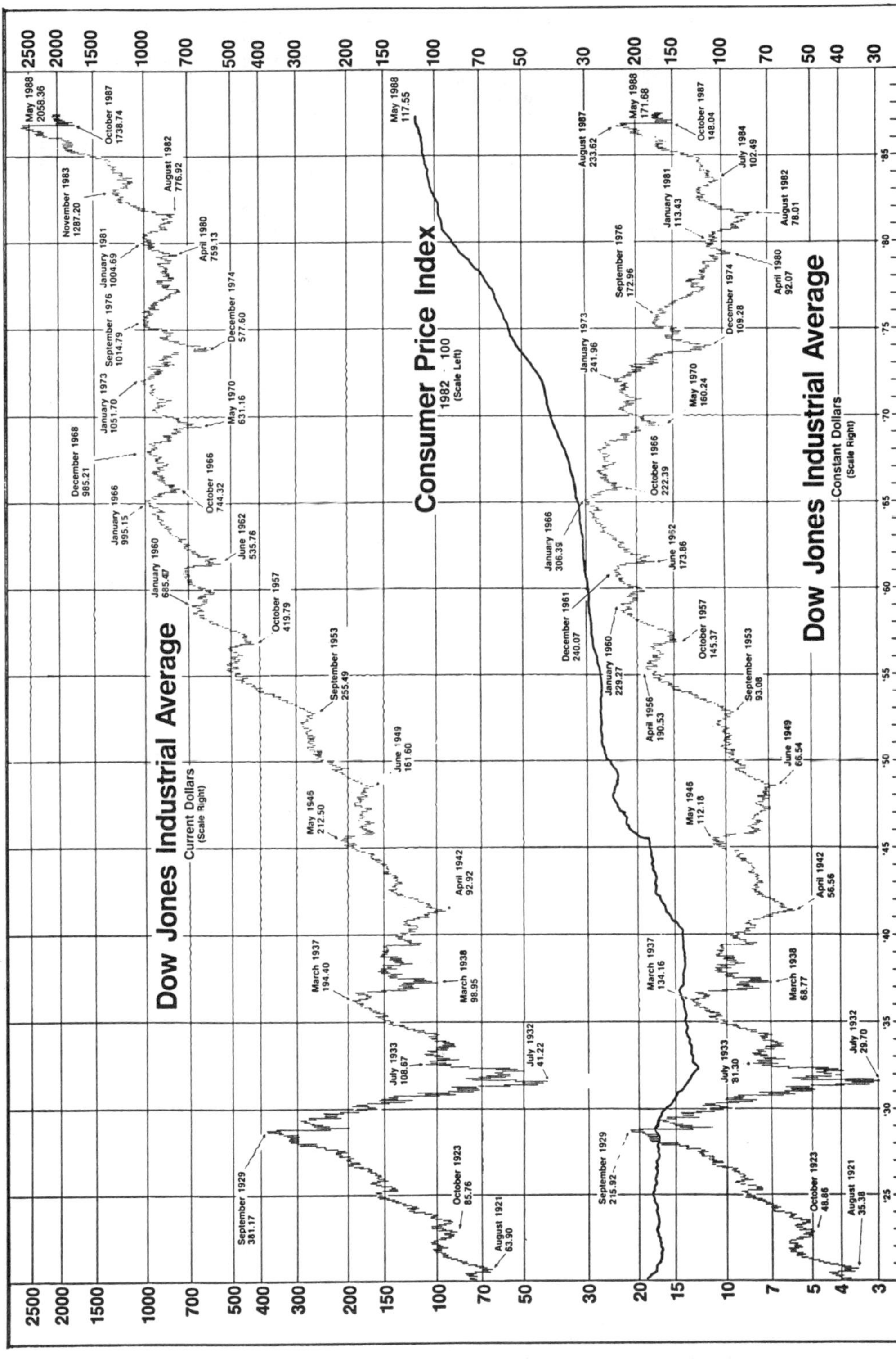

Source: *The Media General Financial Weekly*, Media General Financial Services, 301 East Grace Street, Richmond, VA 23261, June 27, 1988.

Cash Dividends on NYSE Listed Common Stocks

	Common stocks		
	Number of issues listed at year end	Number paying cash dividends during year	Estimated aggregate cash payments (millions)
1929	842	554	$ 2,711
1930	848	576	2,667
1935	776	387	1,336
1940	829	577	2,099
1941	834	627	2,281
1942	834	648	1,997
1943	845	687	2,063
1944	864	717	2,223
1945	881	746	2,275
1946	933	798	2,669
1947	964	851	3,255
1948	986	883	3,806
1949	1,017	887	4,235
1950	1,039	930	5,404
1951	1,054	961	5,467
1952	1,067	975	5,595
1953	1,069	964	5,874
1954	1,076	968	6,439
1955	1,076	982	7,488
1956	1,077	975	8,341
1957	1,098	991	8,807
1958	1,086	961	8,711
1959	1,092	953	9,337
1960	1,126	981	9,872
1961	1,145	981	10,430
1962	1,168	994	11,203
1963	1,194	1,032	12,096
1964	1,227	1,066	13,555
1965	1,254	1,111	15,302
1966	1,267	1,127	16,151
1967	1,255	1,116	16,866
1968	1,253	1,104	18,124
1969	1,290	1,121	19,404
1970	1,330	1,120	19,781
1971	1,399	1,132	20,256
1972	1,478	1,195	21,490
1973	1,536	1,276	23,627
1974	1,543	1,308	25,662
1975	1,531	1,273	26,901
1976	1,550	1,304	30,608
1977	1,549	1,360	36,270
1978	1,552	1,373	41,151
1979	1,536	1,359	46,937
1980	1,540	1,361	53,072
1981	1,534	1,337	60,628
1982	1,499	1,287	62,224
1983	1,518	1,259	67,102
1984	1,511	1,243	68,215
1985	1,503	1,206	74,237
1986	1,536	1,180	76,161
1987	1,606	1,219	84,377

Source: New York Stock Exchange *Fact Book 1988.*

NYSE Common Stock Index—Daily Closings, 1987 (December 31, 1965 = 50)

	Jan.	Feb.	Mar.	Apr.	May	June	July	Aug.	Sept.	Oct.	Nov.	Dec.
1	•	•	•	166.04	162.64	163.48	170.52	•	181.21	182.97	•	130.50
2	141.01	157.45	161.58	166.76	•	162.77	171.83	•	180.12	183.43	142.74	131.21
3	•	157.28	162.16	170.20	•	165.27	•	178.07	179.34	•	140.11	127.01
4	•	159.31	164.41	•	163.22	166.16	•	177.39	177.58	•	139.11	125.91
5	144.39	160.36	165.41	•	166.34	165.49	•	178.54	•	183.44	141.81	•
6	144.81	159.93	165.45	170.96	166.47	•	171.55	180.37	•	178.98	140.04	•
7	146.43	•	•	168.35	166.13	•	172.89	180.87	•	178.55	•	128.23
8	147.55	•	•	168.51	165.49	167.13	173.42	•	175.59	176.32	•	131.42
9	148.39	158.83	164.25	166.09	•	167.38	173.15	•	175.79	174.64	136.35	133.56
10	•	157.18	165.57	165.72	•	167.53	173.57	183.45	177.46	•	134.06	131.07
11	•	158.47	165.39	•	164.70	168.24	•	186.13	180.02	•	135.46	131.79
12	149.31	157.58	165.96	•	165.39	169.85	•	185.70	•	173.52	138.88	•
13	149.14	159.56	165.31	162.14	165.70	•	173.18	186.95	•	176.02	137.60	•
14	150.58	•	•	158.31	165.76	•	174.67	186.69	180.54	171.26	•	135.26
15	152.09	•	•	161.03	162.25	170.60	174.58	•	177.98	167.45	•	135.61
16	152.21	•	164.34	162.59	•	171.35	175.70	•	176.51	159.13	138.16	138.34
17	•	162.48	166.41	•	•	171.44	176.67	186.76	176.48	•	136.21	136.02
18	•	162.56	166.64	•	161.45	171.84	•	184.12	176.36	•	137.58	139.15
19	153.71	162.76	167.28	•	157.93	172.53	•	184.38	•	128.62	134.72	•
20	153.62	162.82	169.37	162.19	157.02	•	175.08	187.04	•	133.04	135.56	•
21	152.90	•	•	165.50	158.07	•	173.59	187.51	174.25	145.02	•	139.49
22	155.97	•	•	162.55	159.05	173.77	173.45	•	178.48	139.45	•	139.54
23	154.02	161.12	170.83	162.23	•	173.22	173.03	•	179.53	139.22	136.13	141.36
24	•	161.38	171.08	159.37	•	172.40	173.70	186.27	178.86	•	137.93	140.85
25	•	161.97	170.50	•	•	173.55	•	187.99	179.14	•	136.90	•
26	153.63	161.41	170.77	•	162.72	172.67	•	186.94	•	127.88	•	•
27	155.85	162.01	168.37	159.27	162.64	•	174.47	185.26	•	130.51	135.13	•
28	156.72	•	•	159.80	163.61	•	175.24	182.99	180.74	130.31	•	137.50
29	156.19		•	160.94	163.48	172.99	177.00	•	180.06	136.28	•	136.84
30	156.11		164.56	162.86	•	171.07	178.32	•	180.24	140.80	129.69	138.52
31	•		165.89		•		178.64	184.45		•		138.23
High	**156.72**	**162.82**	**171.08**	**170.96**	**166.47**	**173.77**	**178.64**	**187.99**	**181.21**	**183.44**	**142.74**	**141.36**
Low	**141.01**	**157.18**	**161.58**	**158.31**	**157.02**	**162.77**	**170.52**	**177.39**	**174.25**	**127.88**	**129.69**	**125.91**
Avg.	**151.17**	**160.23**	**166.43**	**163.88**	**163.00**	**169.58**	**174.28**	**184.18**	**178.39**	**157.13**	**137.21**	**134.88**

• Exchange closed.

Source: The New York Stock Exchange *Fact Book 1988.*

NYSE Common Stock Index—Yield and P/E Ratio

End of period	Yield•	Price/earnings ratio★	End of period	Yield•	Price/earnings ratio★
1987			**1979**		
December	3.4%	15.5	**December**	6.2%	10.1
September	2.9	22.0	**September**	6.0	9.9
June	2.7	21.1	**June**	6.4	9.9
March	2.8	20.2	**March**	5.7	10.5
1986			**1978**		
December	3.4	16.1	**December**	5.9	10.3
September	3.3	16.6	**September**	5.3	10.9
June	3.3	16.6	**June**	5.5	11.8
March	3.5	15.5	**March**	6.0	10.7
1985			**1977**		
December	3.6	13.5	**December**	5.7	11.6
September	4.2	10.7	**September**	5.5	11.3
June	4.2	12.6	**June**	5.3	12.7
March	4.4	11.3	**March**	5.2	12.6
1984			**1976**		
December	4.5	10.4	**December**	4.6	14.3
September	4.5	10.6	**September**	4.6	13.4
June	4.9	10.1	**June**	4.3	14.1
March	4.5	11.6	**March**	4.2	15.2
1983			**1975**		
December	4.4	13.0	**December**	4.6	13.8
September	4.2	13.9	**September**	5.0	13.8
June	4.1	13.9	**June**	4.3	17.9
March	4.9	14.7	**March**	5.0	13.3
1982			**1974**		
December	5.2	14.7	**December**	5.7	7.8
September	6.1	12.5	**September**	6.2	7.2
June	7.0	11.3	**June**	4.5	9.7
March	7.2	10.3	**March**	4.4	10.8
1981			**1973**		
December	6.7	11.3	**December**	4.1	12.1
September	7.1	9.9	**September**	3.5	13.6
June	6.0	11.9	**June**	3.8	12.8
March	5.7	12.5	**March**	3.4	13.8
1980			**1972**		
December	5.4	13.1	**December**	3.1	18.5
September	5.7	12.7	**September**	3.3	17.4
June	6.0	9.8	**June**	3.4	17.0
March	6.8	9.4	**March**	3.2	17.0

• Total dollar value of dividend payments during latest 12 months—through June 1983 and indicated dollar value through June 1985—divided by market value at end of period and multiplied by 100. Beginning in July 1985, latest quarterly dividend divided by closing price at end of period.

★ Latest closing price divided by trailing 12 months of earnings.

Source: The New York Stock Exchange *Fact Book 1988.*

Compounded Growth Rates in NYSE Index•

	Initial year															Index at year end
	'72	'73	'74	'75	'76	'77	'78	'79	'80	'81	'82	'83	'84	'85	'86	
'72																**64.48**
'73	−19.6															**51.82**
'74	−25.1	−30.3														**36.13**
'75	−9.6	−4.1	31.9													**47.64**
'76	−2.7	3.8	26.6	21.5												**57.88**
'77	−4.0	0.3	13.3	5.0	−9.3											**52.50**
'78	−3.0	0.7	10.4	4.0	−3.8	2.1										**53.62**
'79	−0.6	3.0	11.4	6.8	2.3	8.6	15.5									**61.95**
'80	2.4	6.0	13.7	10.3	7.7	14.0	20.5	25.7								**77.86**
'81	1.1	4.0	10.2	6.9	4.2	7.9	9.9	7.1	−8.7							**71.11**
'82	2.3	5.1	10.6	7.9	5.8	9.1	10.9	9.4	2.0	14.0						**81.03**
'83	3.6	6.3	11.4	9.0	7.4	10.4	12.2	11.3	6.9	15.7	17.5					**95.18**
'84	3.4	5.8	10.3	8.1	6.6	9.1	10.3	9.2	5.5	10.7	9.1	1.3				**96.38**
'85	5.0	7.4	11.7	9.8	8.6	11.1	12.4	11.9	9.3	14.3	14.5	13.0	26.1			**121.58**
'86	5.6	7.9	11.9	10.2	9.1	11.4	12.6	12.2	10.1	14.3	14.4	13.3	19.9	14.0		**138.58**
'87	5.2	7.3	10.9	9.3	8.2	10.2	11.1	10.6	8.5	11.7	11.3	9.8	12.8	6.6	−0.3	**138.23**

• **Index figures taken at year end.**

Source: The New York Stock Exchange *Fact Book 1988.*

THE MAJOR MARKET AVERAGES

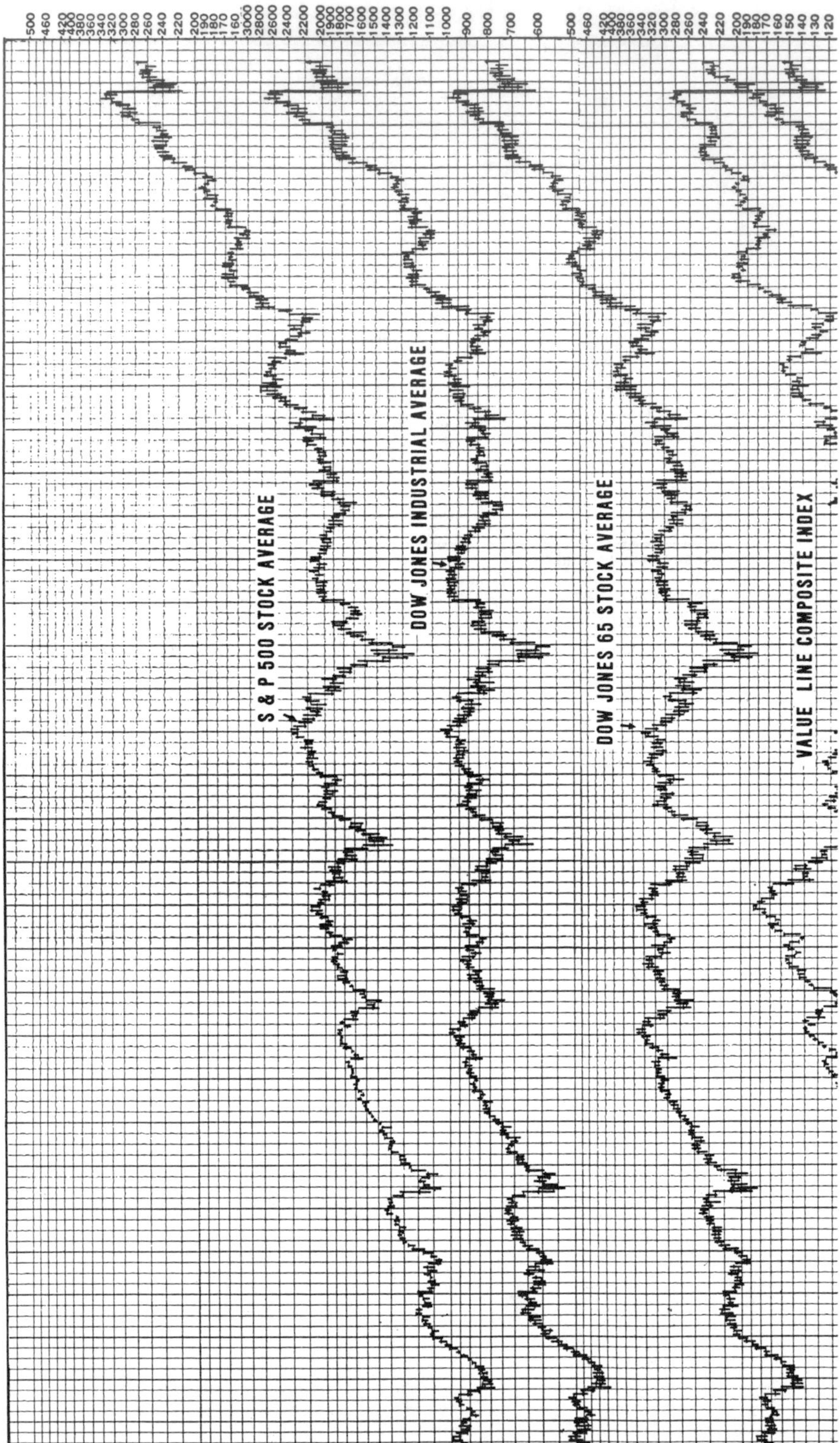

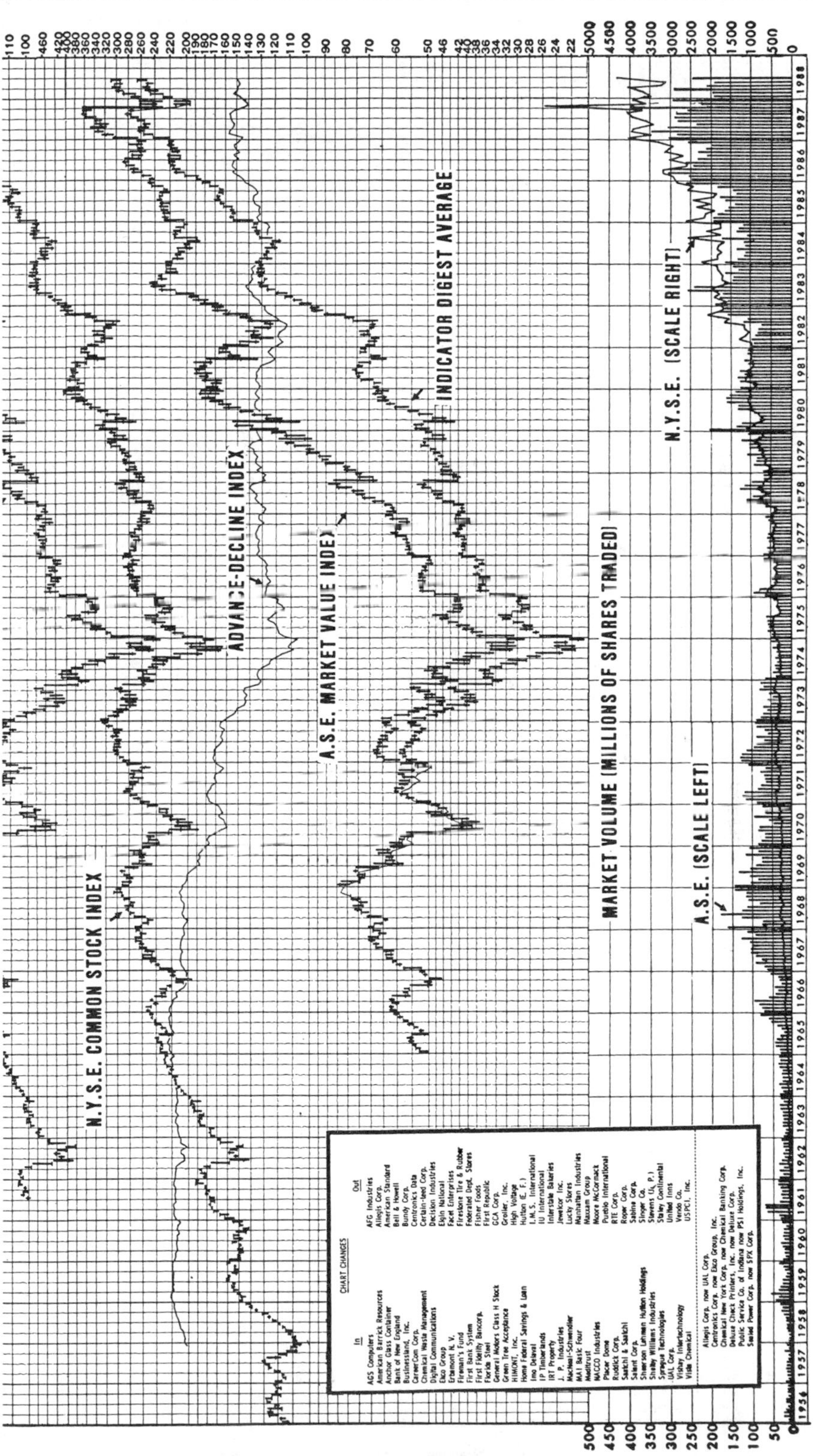

Source: *5-Trend CYCLI-GRAPHS.* The charts are courtesy of Securities Research Company, a Division of Babson-United Investment Advisors, Inc., 208 Newbury Street, Boston, MA 02116, July quarterly edition, 1988.

Quarterly Dow Jones Industrial Stock Average

The table below lists the earnings (losses) of the Dow Jones Industrial Average based on generally accepted accounting principles. The price-earnings ratio for the DJI correctly reflects deficit/negative earnings for the 1982 September and December quarters. The 1985 December quarter and year-end dividend reflects $2.00 GM dividend distribution value of one share of class H common for each 20 shares of common held. The 1984 December quarter and year-end dividend reflects $1.87½ GM dividend distribution value of one share of class E common for each 20 shares of common held. N.A.-Not available. d-Indicates deficit/negative earnings for the quarter.

Year	Quarter Ended	Clos. Avg.	Qtrly Chg.	% Chg.	Qtrly Earns	12-Mth Earns	P/E Ratio	Qtrly Divs	12-Mth Divs	Divs Yield	Payout Ratio
1988	June 30	2141.71	+ 153.65	+ 7.73	N.A.	N.A.	N.A.	20.18	73.92	3.45	N.A.
	Mar. 31	1988.06	+ 49.23	+ 2.54	47.03	144.45	13.8	18.02	71.85	3.61	.4974
1987	Dec. 31	1938.83	− 657.45	− 25.32	16.54	133.05	14.6	17.67	71.20	3.67	.5351
	Sept. 30	2596.28	+ 177.75	+ 7.34	44.77	137.99	18.8	18.05	70.62	2.72	.5117
	June 30	2418.53	+ 113.84	+ 4.94	36.11	126.23	19.2	18.11	69.36	2.87	.5494
	Mar. 31	2304.69	+ 408.74	+ 21.56	35.63	126.49	18.2	17.37	68.19	2.96	.5391
1986	Dec. 31	1895.95	+ 128.37	+ 7.26	21.48	115.59	16.4	17.09	67.04	3.54	.5800
	Sept. 30	1767.58	− 125.14	− 6.61	33.01	118.80	14.9	16.79	67.14	3.80	.5652
	June 30	1892.72	+ 74.11	+ 4.08	36.37	103.39	18.3	16.94	65.37	3.45	.6323
	Mar. 31	1818.61	+ 271.94	+ 17.58	24.73	96.43	18.9	16.22	63.38	3.49	.6573
1985	Dec. 31	1546.67	+ 218.04	+ 16.41	24.69	96.11	16.1	17.19	62.03	4.01	.6454
	Sept. 30	1328.63	− 6.83	− 0.51	17.60	90.78	14.6	15.02	61.83	4.65	.6811
	June 28	1335.46	+ 68.68	+ 5.14	29.41	102.26	13.1	14.95	61.53	4.61	.6017
	Mar. 29	1266.78	+ 55.21	+ 4.56	24.41	107.87	11.7	14.87	61.56	4.86	.5707
1984	Dec. 31	1211.57	+ 4.86	+ 0.40	19.36	113.58	10.7	16.99	60.63	5.00	.5338
	Sept. 28	1206.71	+ 74.31	+ 6.56	29.08	108.11	11.2	14.72	58.41	4.84	.5403
	June 29	1132.40	− 32.49	− 2.79	35.02	102.07	11.1	14.98	57.67	5.09	.5650
	Mar. 30	1164.89	− 93.75	− 7.45	30.12	87.38	13.3	13.94	56.39	4.84	.6453
1983	Dec. 30	1258.64	+ 25.51	+ 2.07	13.89	72.45	17.4	14.77	56.33	4.47	.7775
	Sept. 30	1233.13	+ 11.17	+ 0.91	23.04	56.12	22.0	13.98	54.59	4.43	.9727
	June 30	1221.96	+ 91.93	+ 8.13	20.33	11.59	105.4	13.70	54.05	4.42	4.6635
	Mar. 31	1130.03	+ 83.49	+ 7.98	15.19	9.52	118.7	13.88	54.10	4.79	5.6828
1982	Dec. 31	1046.54	+ 150.29	+ 16.77	d2.44	9.15	114.4	13.03	54.14	5.17	5.9169
	Sept. 30	896.25	+ 84.32	+ 10.38	d21.49	35.15	25.5	13.44	55.55	6.20	1.5804
	June 30	811.93	− 10.84	− 1.32	18.26	79.90	10.2	13.75	55.84	6.88	.6989
	Mar. 31	822.77	− 52.23	− 5.97	14.82	97.13	8.5	13.92	56.28	6.84	.5794
1981	Dec. 31	875.00	+ 25.02	+ 2.94	23.56	113.71	7.7	14.44	56.22	6.42	.4944
	Sept. 30	849.98	− 126.90	− 12.99	23.26	123.32	6.9	13.73	56.18	6.61	.4539
	June 30	976.88	− 26.99	− 2.69	35.49	128.91	7.6	14.19	55.98	5.73	.4266
	Mar. 31	1003.87	+ 39.88	+ 4.14	31.40	123.60	8.1	13.86	54.99	5.48	.4449
1980	Dec. 31	963.99	+ 31.57	+ 3.39	33.17	121.86	7.9	14.40	54.36	5.64	.4461
	Sept. 30	932.42	+ 64.50	+ 7.43	28.85	111.58	8.4	13.53	53.83	5.77	.4824
	June 30	867.92	+ 82.17	+ 10.46	30.18	116.40	7.5	13.20	52.81	6.08	.4537
	Mar. 31	785.75	− 52.99	− 6.32	29.66	120.77	6.5	13.23	52.10	6.63	.4314
1979	Dec. 31	838.74	− 39.93	− 4.54	22.89	124.46	6.7	13.87	50.98	6.08	.4096
	Sept. 28	878.67	+ 36.69	+ 4.36	33.67	136.26	6.4	12.51	51.45	5.85	.3776
	June 29	841.98	− 20.20	− 2.34	34.55	128.99	6.5	12.49	50.35	5.98	.3903
	Mar. 30	862.18	+ 57.17	+ 7.10	33.35	124.10	6.9	12.11	49.48	5.74	.3987
1978	Dec. 29	805.01	− 60.81	− 7.02	34.69	112.79	7.1	14.34	48.52	6.03	.4302
	Sept. 29	865.82	+ 46.87	+ 5.72	26.40	101.59	8.5	11.41	47.42	5.48	.4668
	June 30	818.95	+ 61.59	+ 8.13	29.66	91.37	9.0	11.62	46.74	5.71	.5115
	Mar. 31	757.36	− 73.81	− 8.88	22.04	89.23	8.5	11.15	46.53	6.14	.5215
1977	Dec. 30	831.17	− 15.94	− 1.88	23.49	89.10	9.3	13.24	45.84	5.51	.5145
	Sept. 30	847.11	− 69.19	− 7.55	16.18	89.86	9.4	10.73	44.73	5.28	.4978
	June 30	916.30	− 2.83	− 0.31	27.52	97.18	9.4	11.41	43.85	4.79	.4512
	Mar. 31	919.13	− 85.52	− 8.51	21.91	95.51	9.6	10.46	42.63	4.64	.4463
1976	Dec. 31	1004.65	+ 14.46	+ 1.46	24.25	96.72	10.4	12.13	41.40	4.12	.4280
	Sept. 30	990.19	− 12.59	− 1.27	23.50	95.81	10.3	9.85	38.90	3.93	.4060
	June 30	1002.78	+ 3.33	+ 0.33	25.85	90.68	11.1	10.19	38.10	3.80	.4202
	Mar. 31	999.45	+ 147.04	+ 17.25	23.12	81.87	12.2	9.23	36.88	3.69	.4505
1975	Dec. 31	852.41	+ 58.53	+ 7.37	23.34	75.66	11.3	9.63	37.46	4.39	.4951
	Sept. 30	793.88	− 85.11	− 10.72	18.37	75.47	10.5	9.05	38.28	4.82	.5072
	June 30	878.99	+ 110.84	+ 12.61	17.04	83.83	10.5	8.97	38.66	4.40	.4612
	Mar. 31	768.15	+ 151.91	+ 24.65	16.91	93.47	8.2	9.81	38.56	5.02	.4125
1974	Dec. 31	616.24	+ 8.37	+ 1.38	23.15	99.04	6.2	10.45	37.72	6.12	.3809
	Sept. 30	607.87	− 194.54	− 24.24	26.73	99.73	6.1	9.43	37.89	6.23	.3799
	June 28	802.41	− 44.27	− 5.23	26.68	93.26	8.6	8.87	36.82	4.59	.3948
	Mar. 29	846.68	− 4.18	− 0.49	22.48	89.46	9.5	8.97	36.22	4.28	.4049
1973	Dec. 31	850.86	− 96.24	− 11.31	23.84	86.17	9.9	10.62	35.33	4.15	.4100
	Sept. 28	947.10	+ 55.39	+ 6.21	20.26	82.09	11.5	8.36	33.70	3.56	.4105
	June 29	891.71	− 59.30	− 6.23	22.88	77.56	11.5	8.27	33.10	3.71	.4268
	Mar. 30	951.01	− 69.01	− 6.76	19.19	71.98	13.2	8.08	32.70	3.44	.4543
1972	Dec. 29	1020.02	+ 66.75	+ 7.00	19.76	67.11	15.2	8.99	32.27	3.16	.4808
	Sept. 29	953.27	+ 24.24	+ 2.61	15.73	62.15	15.3	7.76	31.13	3.27	.5009
	June 30	929.03	− 11.67	− 1.24	17.30	58.87	15.8	7.87	30.88	3.32	.5245
	Mar. 30	940.70	+ 50.50	+ 5.67	14.32	56.76	16.6	7.65	30.81	3.27	.5428

Source: Reprinted by courtesy of *Barron's National Business and Financial Weekly*, July 5, 1988.

Stock Market Averages by Industry Group

These definitions apply to pages 280–301.

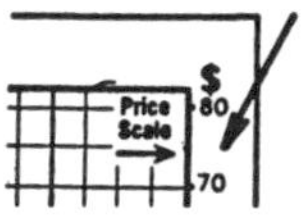

Price Scale — The price ranges are always read from the scale at the right-hand side of each chart. This scale is equal to 15 times the Earnings and Dividend scale at the left, so when the Price Range bars and the Earnings line coincide, it shows the price is at 15 times earnings. When the price is above the earnings line, the ratio of price to earnings is greater than 15 times earnings; when below, it is less.

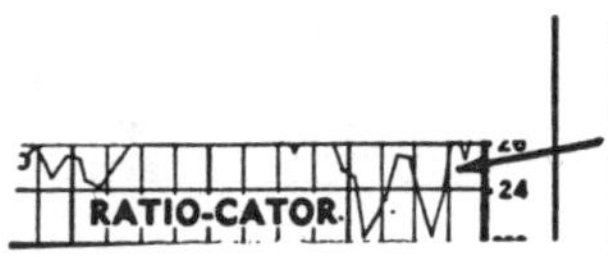

Monthly Ratio-Cator: The plottings for this line are obtained by dividing the closing price of the stock by the closing price of the Dow-Jones Industrial Average on the same day. The resulting percentage is multiplied by a factor of 4.5 (450) to bring the line closer to the price bars and is read from the right hand scale. The plotting indicates whether the stock has kept pace, outperformed, or lagged behind the general market as represented by the DJIA.

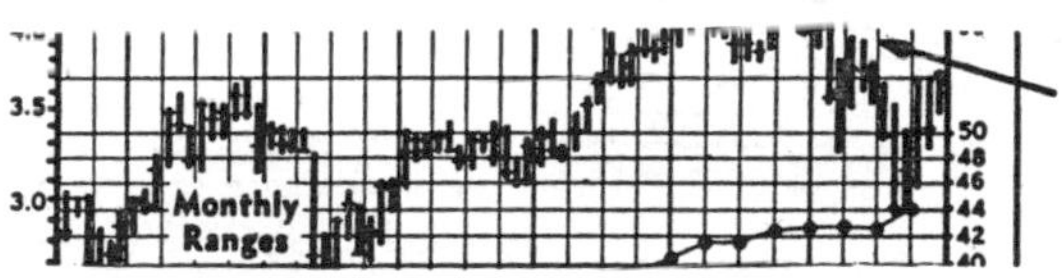

Monthly Price Ranges represented by the solid vertical bars show the highest and lowest point of each month's transactions. Crossbars indicate the month's closing price.

Source: *5-Trend CYCLI-GRAPHS.* The charts are courtesy of Securities Research Company, a Division of Babson-United Investment Advisors, Inc., 208 Newbury Street, Boston, MA 02116, July quarterly edition, 1988.

STOCK MARKET AVERAGES BY INDUSTRY GROUP

PRICES & EARNS. SOURCE: S&P RATIO-CATOR FACTOR: 7 (700)

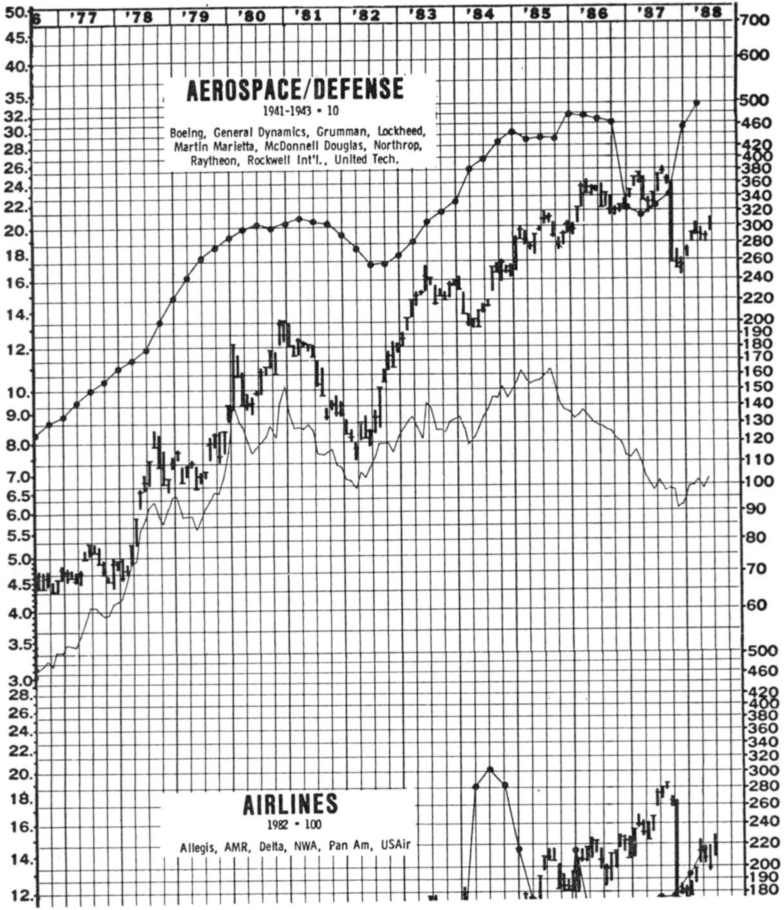

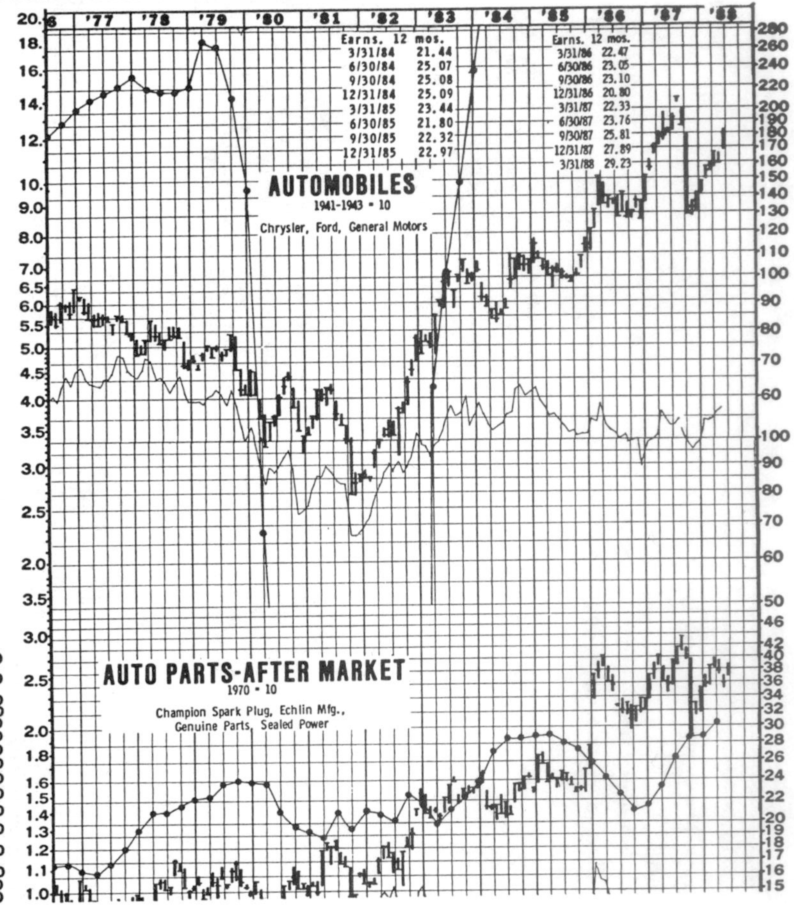

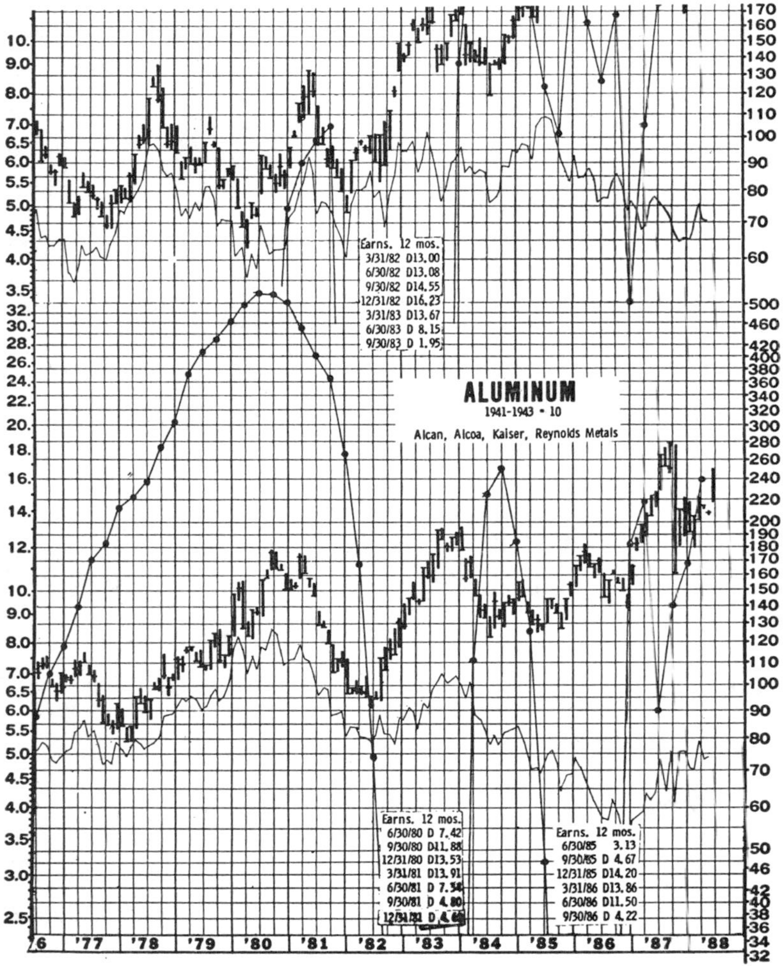
ALUMINUM
1941-1943 = 10
Alcan, Alcoa, Kaiser, Reynolds Metals
Earns. 12 mos.
3/31/82 D13.00
6/30/82 D13.08
9/30/82 D14.55
12/31/82 D16.23
3/31/83 D13.67
6/30/83 D 8.15
9/30/83 D 1.95
Earns. 12 mos.
6/30/80 D 7.42
9/30/80 D11.88
12/31/80 D13.53
3/31/81 D13.91
6/30/81 D 7.54
9/30/81 D 4.80
Earns. 12 mos.
6/30/85 3.13
9/30/85 D 4.67
12/31/85 D14.20
3/31/86 D13.86
6/30/86 D11.50
9/30/86 D 4.22
'77 '78 '79 '80 '81 '82 '83 '84 '85 '86 '87 '88

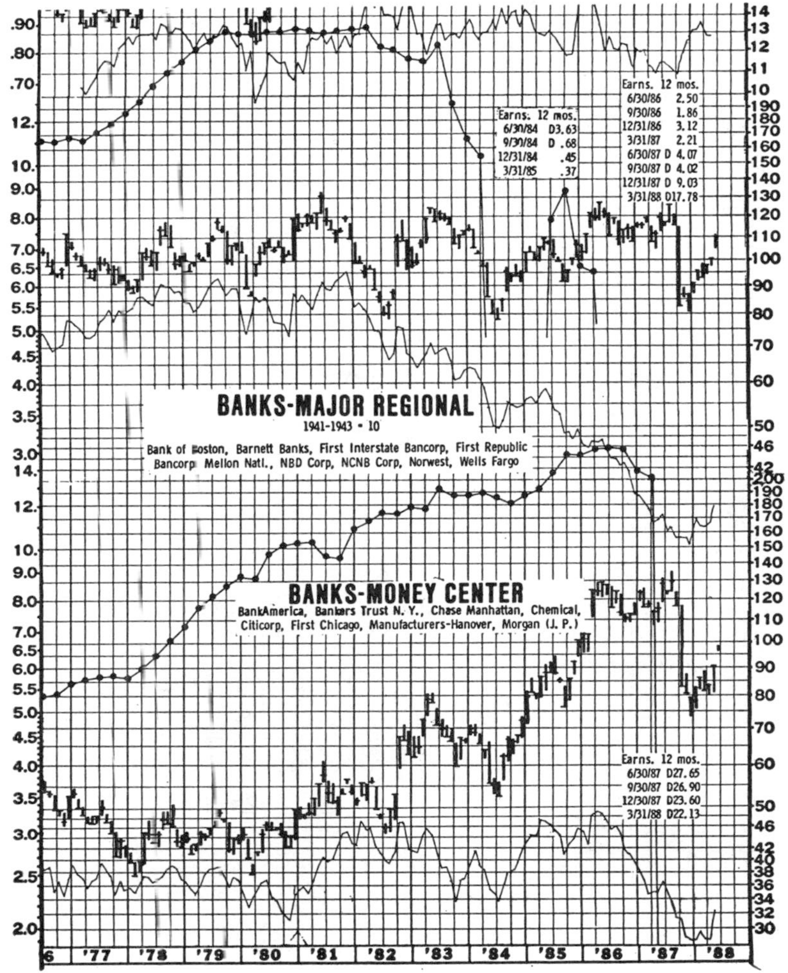
BANKS-MAJOR REGIONAL
1941-1943 = 10
Bank of Boston, Barnett Banks, First Interstate Bancorp, First Republic Bancorp, Mellon Natl., NBD Corp, NCNB Corp, Norwest, Wells Fargo
Earns. 12 mos.
6/30/84 D3.63
9/30/84 D .68
12/31/84 .45
3/31/85 .37
Earns. 12 mos.
6/30/86 2.50
9/30/86 1.86
12/31/86 3.12
3/31/87 2.21
6/30/87 D 4.07
9/30/87 D 4.02
12/31/87 D 9.03
3/31/88 D17.78
BANKS-MONEY CENTER
BankAmerica, Bankers Trust N.Y., Chase Manhattan, Chemical, Citicorp, First Chicago, Manufacturers-Hanover, Morgan (J.P.)
Earns. 12 mos.
6/30/87 D27.65
9/30/87 D26.90
12/30/87 D23.60
3/31/88 D22.13
'77 '78 '79 '80 '81 '82 '83 '84 '85 '86 '87 '88

STOCK MARKET AVERAGES BY INDUSTRY GROUP *(continued)*

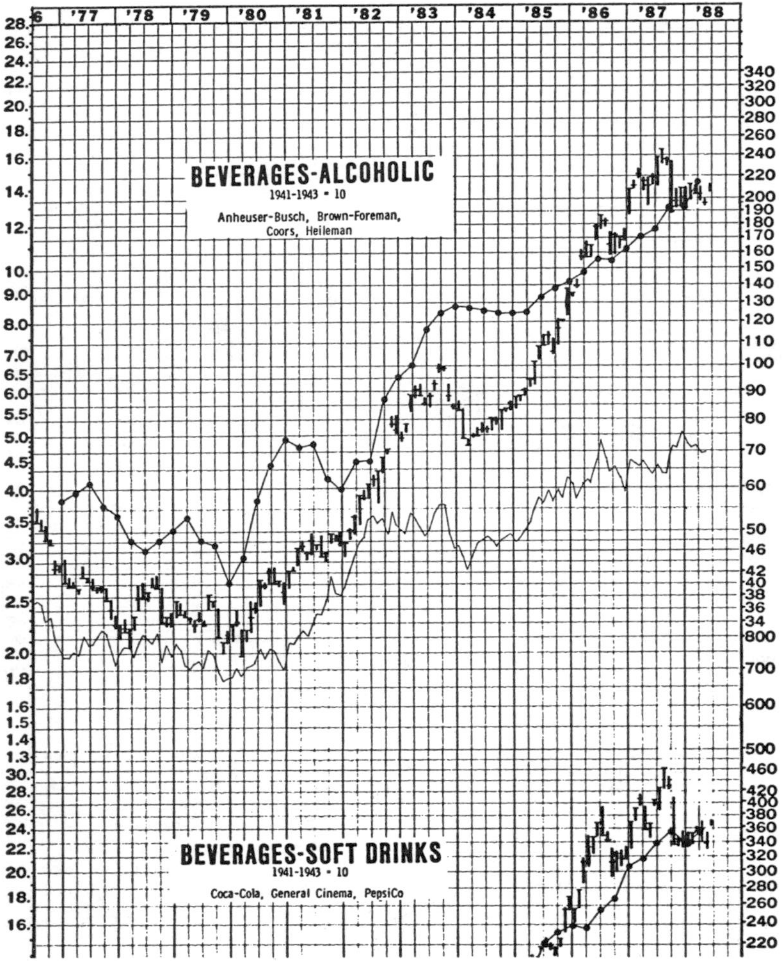

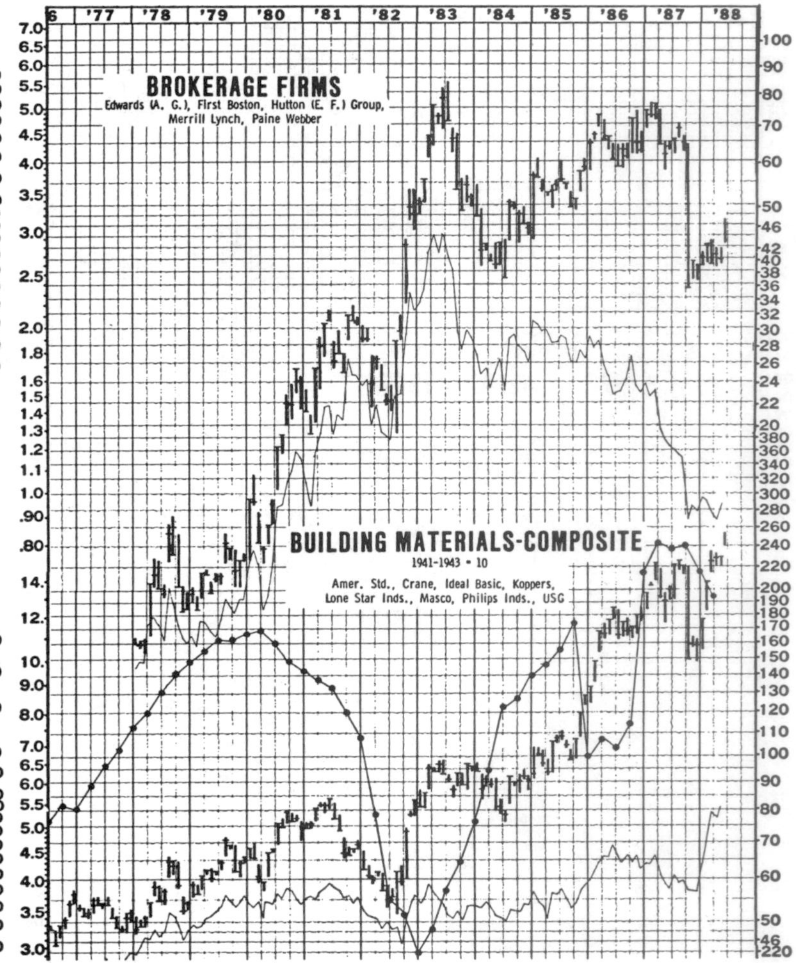

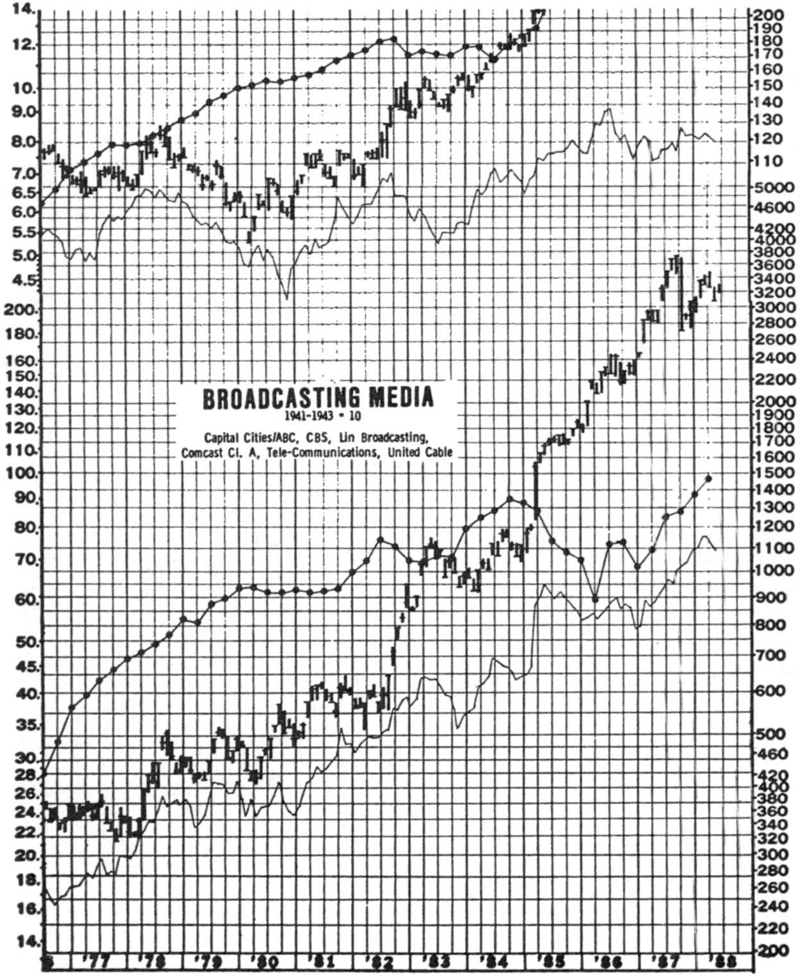
BROADCASTING MEDIA
1941-1943 = 10
Capital Cities/ABC, CBS, Lin Broadcasting, Comcast Cl. A, Tele-Communications, United Cable

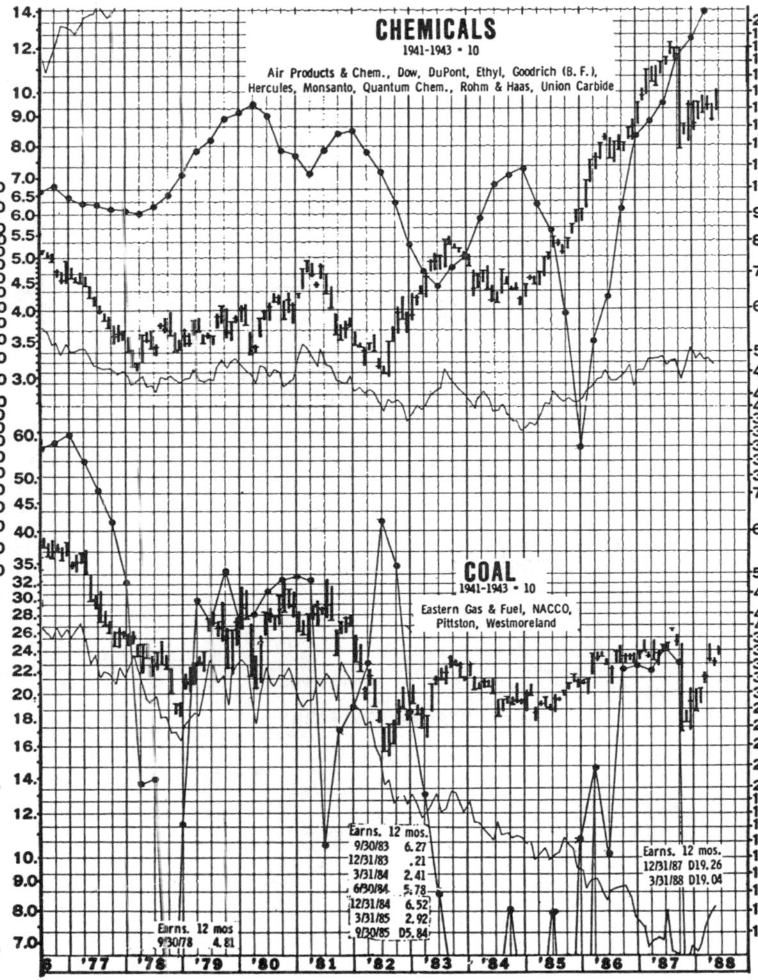
CHEMICALS
1941-1943 = 10
Air Products & Chem., Dow, DuPont, Ethyl, Goodrich (B. F.), Hercules, Monsanto, Quantum Chem., Rohm & Haas, Union Carbide
COAL
1941-1943 = 10
Eastern Gas & Fuel, NACCO, Pittston, Westmoreland
Earns. 12 mos 9/30/78 4.81
Earns. 12 mos. 9/30/83 6.27 12/31/83 .21 3/31/84 2.41 6/30/84 5.78 12/31/84 6.52 3/31/85 2.92 9/30/85 D5.84
Earns. 12 mos. 12/31/87 D19.26 3/31/88 D19.04

STOCK MARKET AVERAGES BY INDUSTRY GROUP *(continued)*

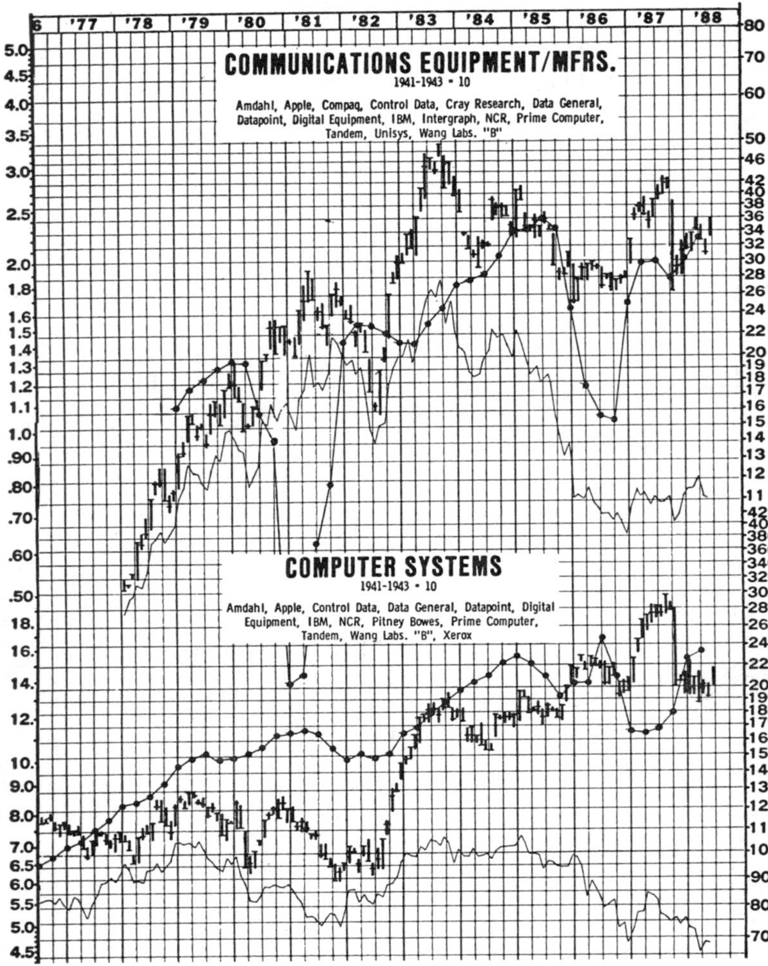
COMMUNICATIONS EQUIPMENT/MFRS.
1941-1943 = 10
Amdahl, Apple, Compaq, Control Data, Cray Research, Data General, Datapoint, Digital Equipment, IBM, Intergraph, NCR, Prime Computer, Tandem, Unisys, Wang Labs. "B"
COMPUTER SYSTEMS
1941-1943 = 10
Amdahl, Apple, Control Data, Data General, Datapoint, Digital Equipment, IBM, NCR, Pitney Bowes, Prime Computer, Tandem, Wang Labs. "B", Xerox

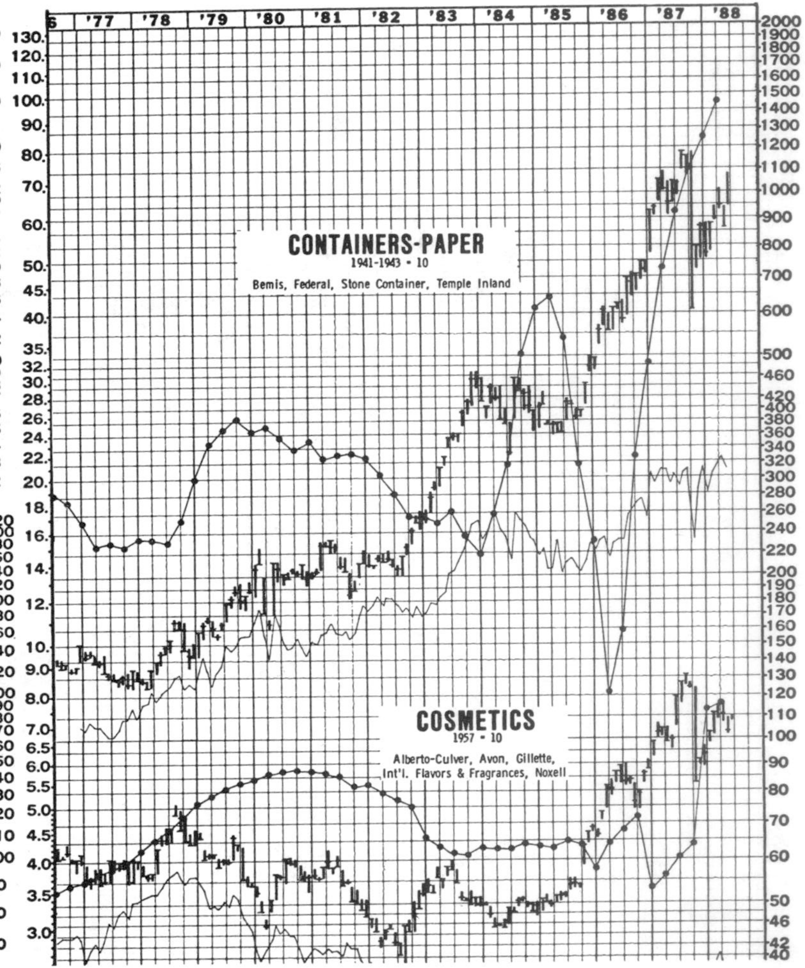
CONTAINERS-PAPER
1941-1943 = 10
Bemis, Federal, Stone Container, Temple Inland
COSMETICS
1957 = 10
Alberto-Culver, Avon, Gillette, Int'l. Flavors & Fragrances, Noxell

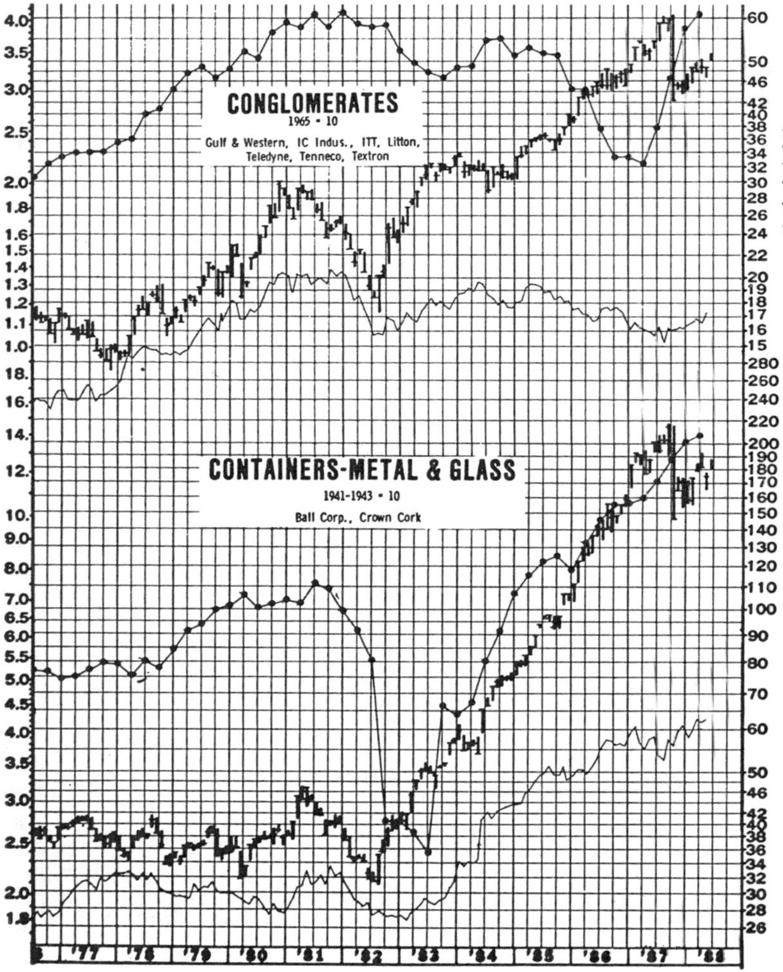
CONGLOMERATES
1965 = 10
Gulf & Western, IC Indus., ITT, Litton, Teledyne, Tenneco, Textron
CONTAINERS-METAL & GLASS
1941-1943 = 10
Ball Corp., Crown Cork
'77 '78 '79 '80 '81 '82 '83 '84 '85 '86 '87 '88

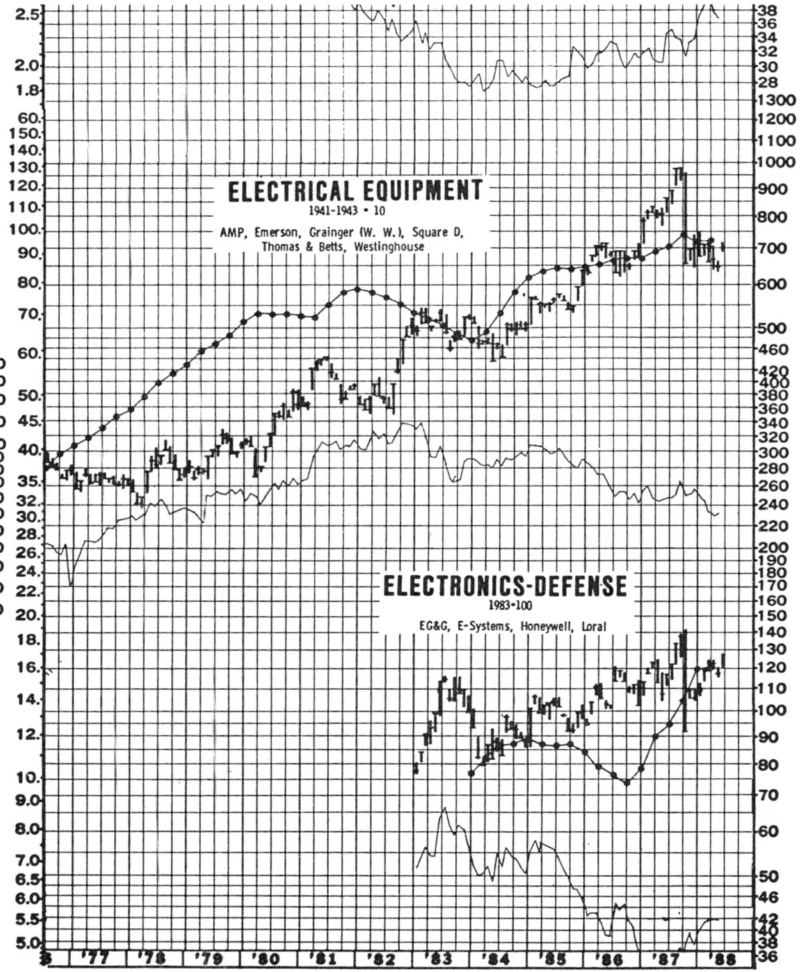
ELECTRICAL EQUIPMENT
1941-1943 = 10
AMP, Emerson, Grainger (W. W.), Square D, Thomas & Betts, Westinghouse
ELECTRONICS-DEFENSE
1983=100
EG&G, E-Systems, Honeywell, Loral
'77 '78 '79 '80 '81 '82 '83 '84 '85 '86 '87 '88

STOCK MARKET AVERAGES BY INDUSTRY GROUP *(continued)*

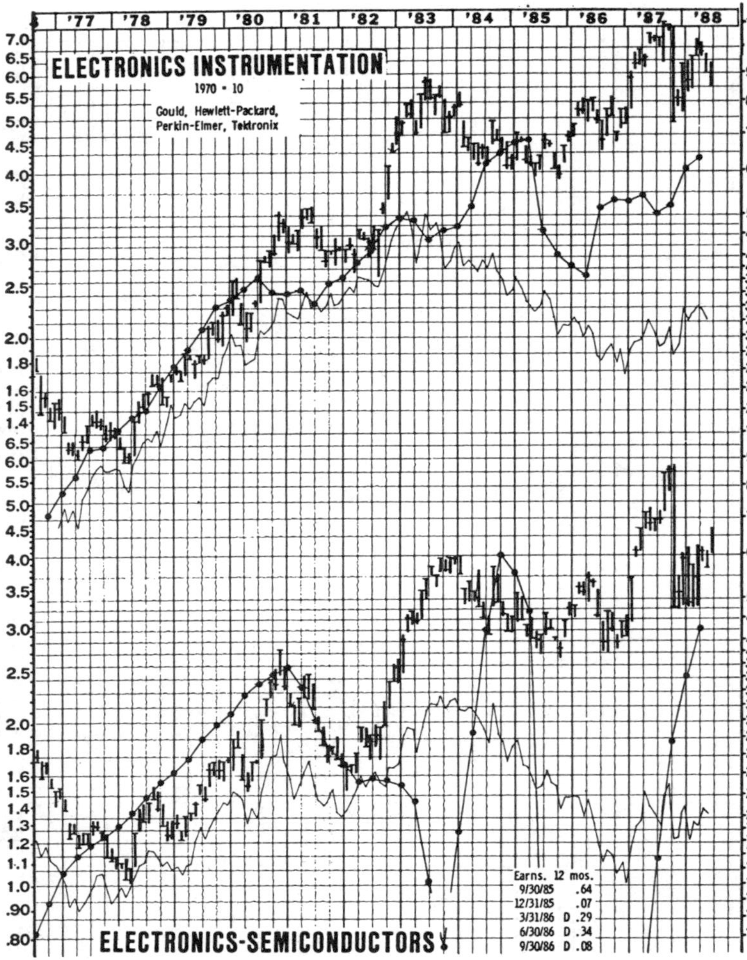

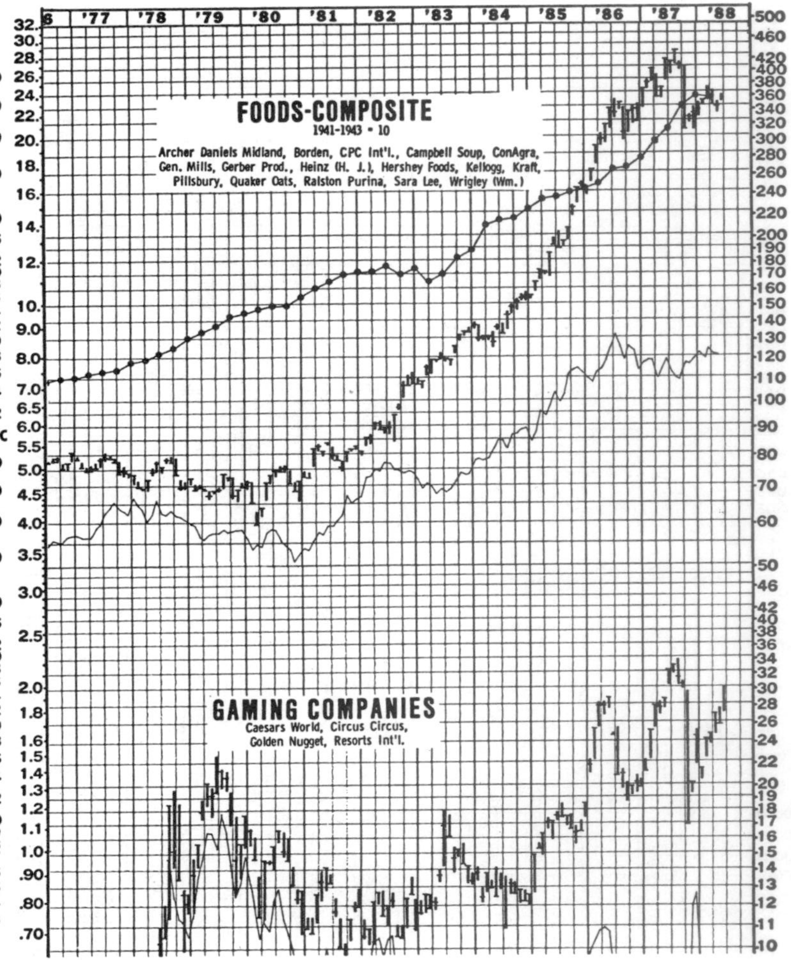

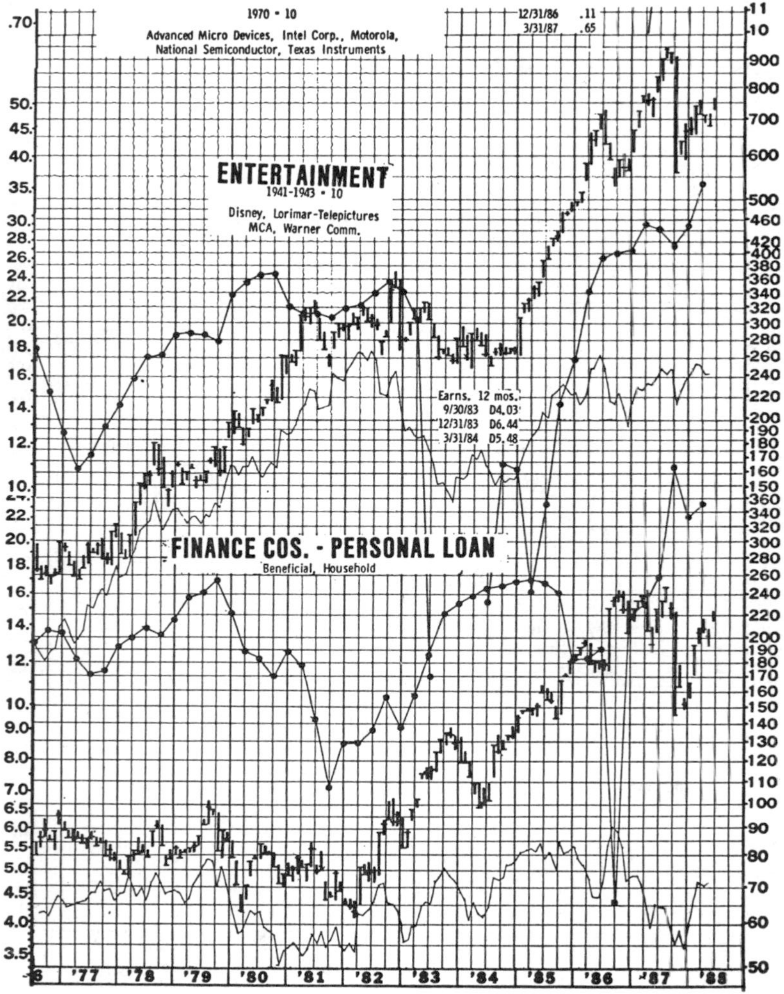
1970 = 10
Advanced Micro Devices, Intel Corp., Motorola, National Semiconductor, Texas Instruments
12/31/86 .11
3/31/87 .65
ENTERTAINMENT
1941-1943 = 10
Disney, Lorimar-Telepictures MCA, Warner Comm.
Earns. 12 mos.
9/30/83 D4.03
12/31/83 D6.44
3/31/84 D5.48
FINANCE COS. - PERSONAL LOAN
Beneficial, Household
'77 '78 '79 '80 '81 '82 '83 '84 '85 '86 '87 '88

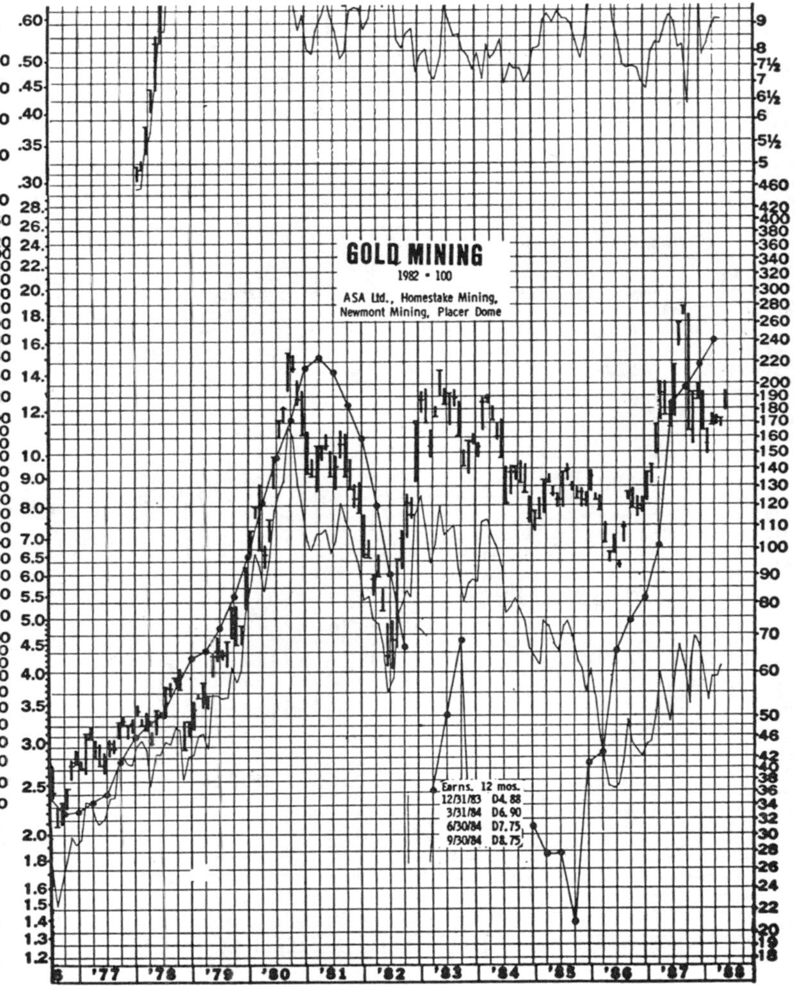
GOLD MINING
1982 = 100
ASA Ltd., Homestake Mining, Newmont Mining, Placer Dome
Earns. 12 mos.
12/31/83 D4.88
3/31/84 D6.90
6/30/84 D7.75
9/30/84 D8.75
'77 '78 '79 '80 '81 '82 '83 '84 '85 '86 '87 '88

STOCK MARKET AVERAGES BY INDUSTRY GROUP *(continued)*

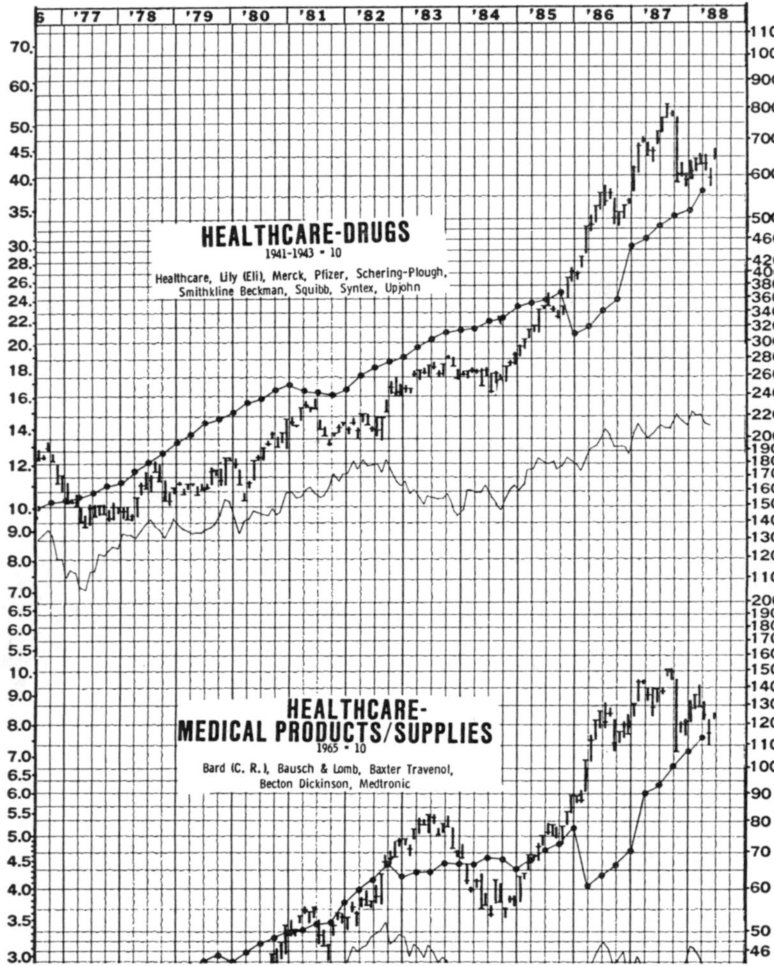

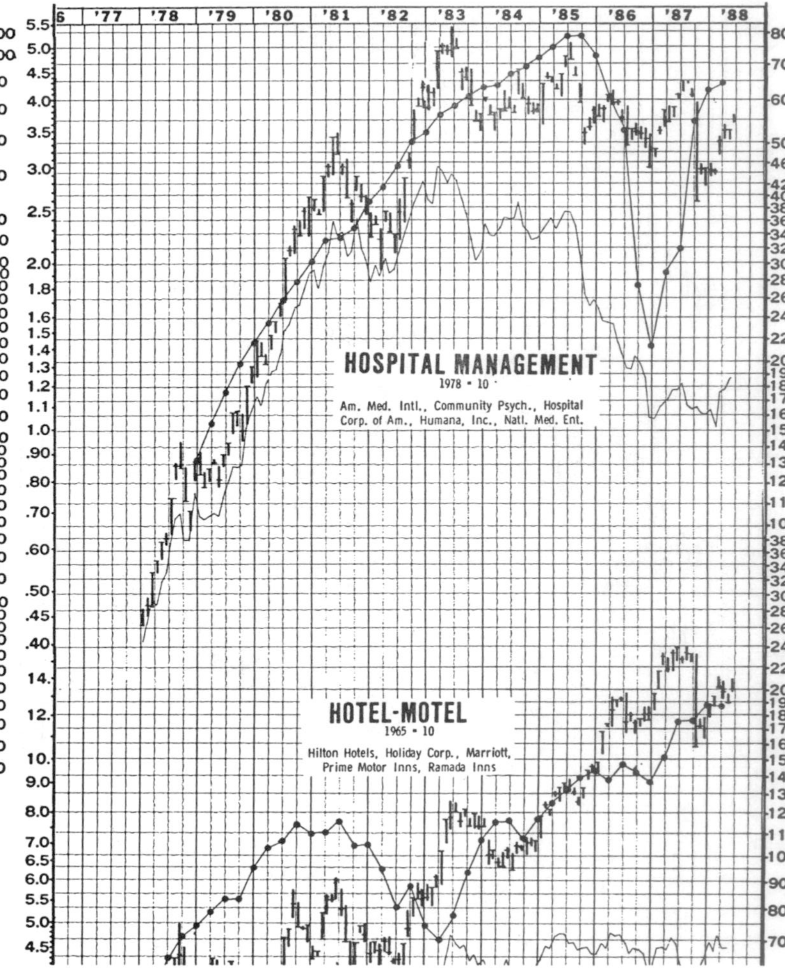

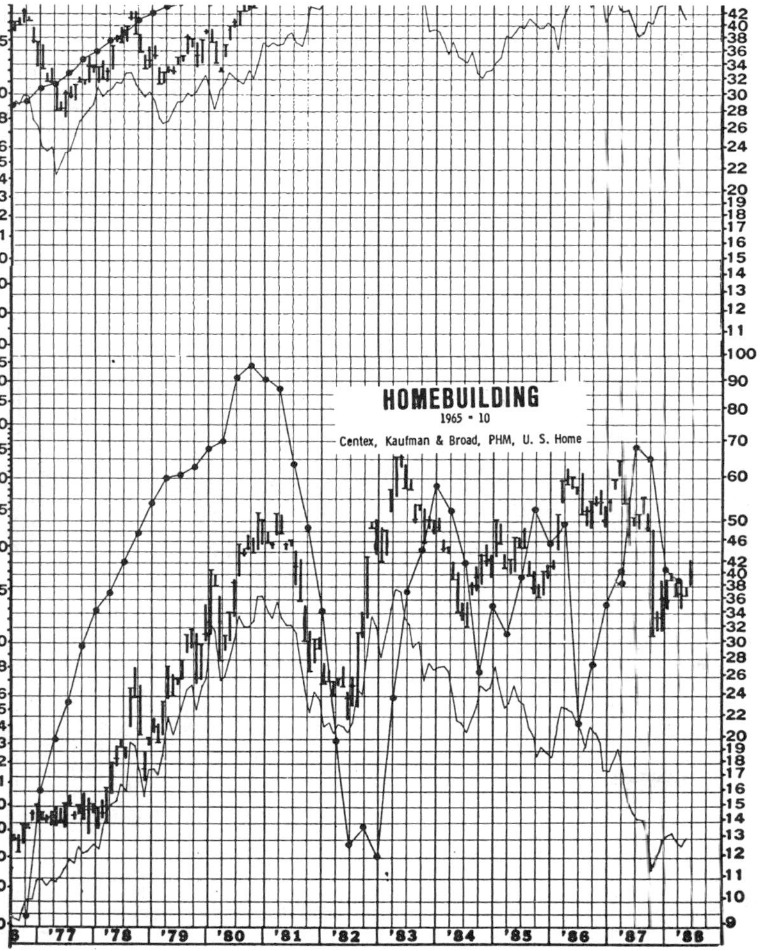
HOMEBUILDING
1965 = 10
Centex, Kaufman & Broad, PHM, U. S. Home
'77 '78 '79 '80 '81 '82 '83 '84 '85 '86 '87 '88

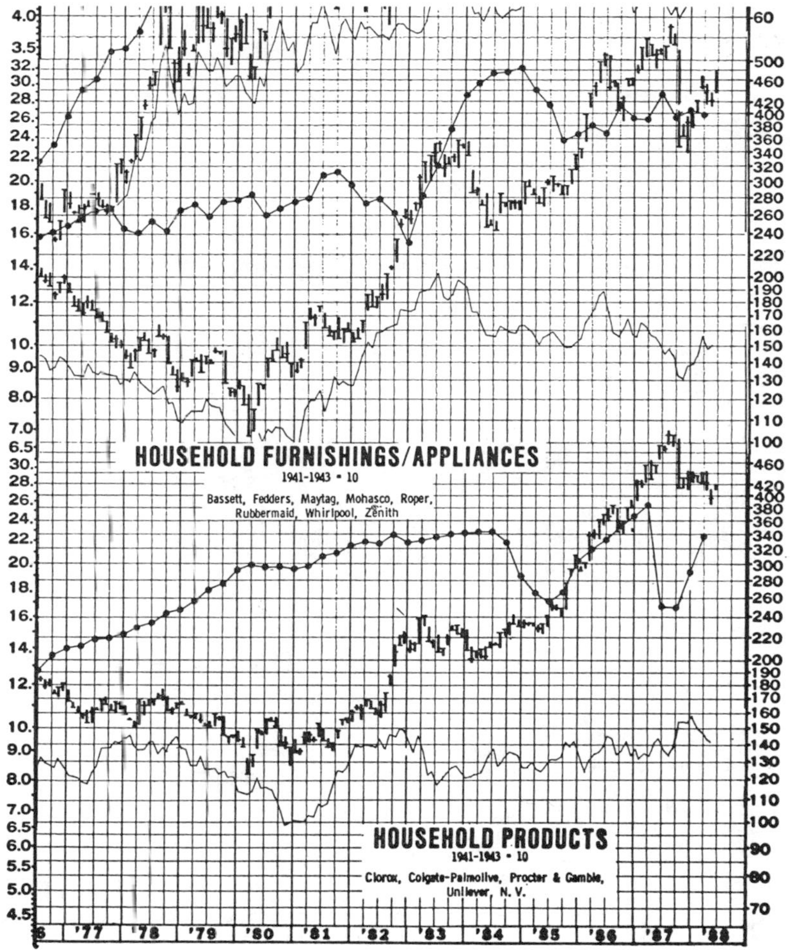
HOUSEHOLD FURNISHINGS/APPLIANCES
1941-1943 = 10
Bassett, Fedders, Maytag, Mohasco, Roper,
Rubbermaid, Whirlpool, Zenith
HOUSEHOLD PRODUCTS
1941-1943 = 10
Clorox, Colgate-Palmolive, Procter & Gamble,
Unilever, N. V.
'77 '78 '79 '80 '81 '82 '83 '84 '85 '86 '87 '88

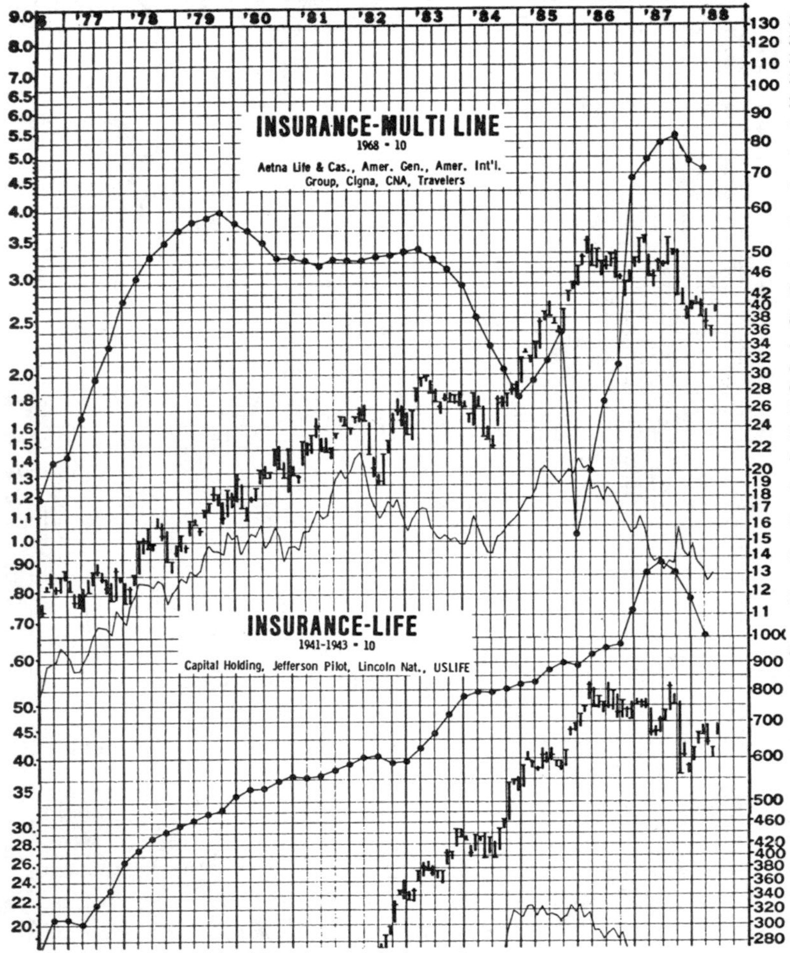
INSURANCE-MULTI LINE
1968 = 10
Aetna Life & Cas., Amer. Gen., Amer. Int'l. Group, Cigna, CNA, Travelers
INSURANCE-LIFE
1941-1943 = 10
Capital Holding, Jefferson Pilot, Lincoln Nat., USLIFE
'77
'78
'79
'80
'81
'82
'83
'84
'85
'86
'87
'88

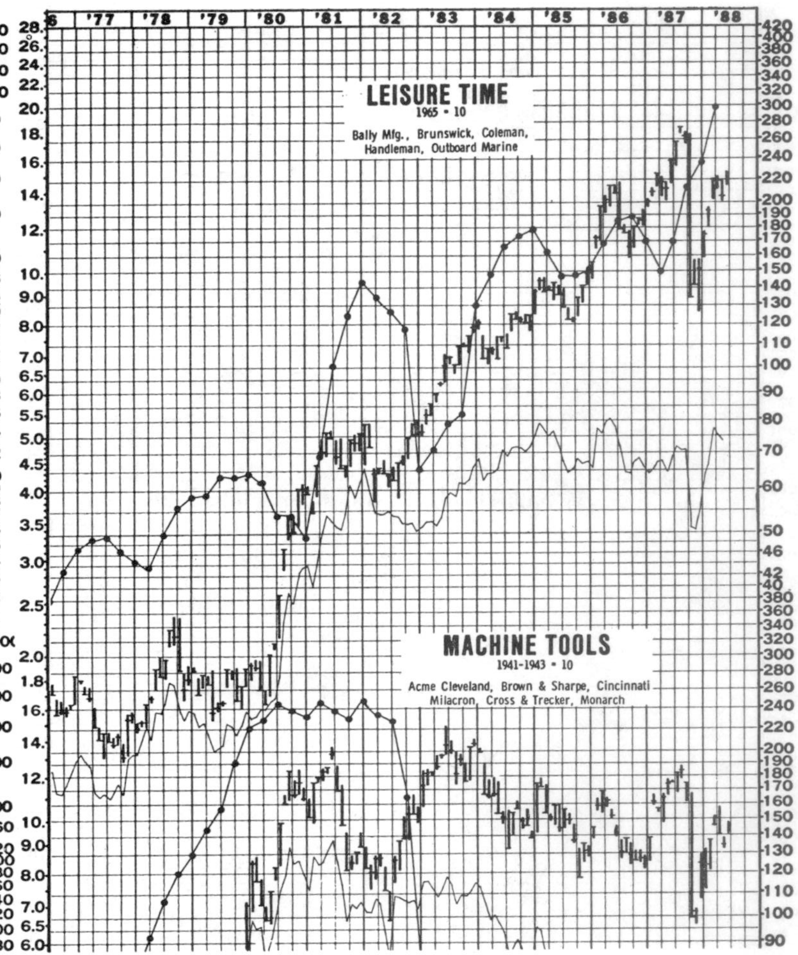
LEISURE TIME
1965 = 10
Bally Mfg., Brunswick, Coleman, Handleman, Outboard Marine
MACHINE TOOLS
1941-1943 = 10
Acme Cleveland, Brown & Sharpe, Cincinnati Milacron, Cross & Trecker, Monarch
'77
'78
'79
'80
'81
'82
'83
'84
'85
'86
'87
'88

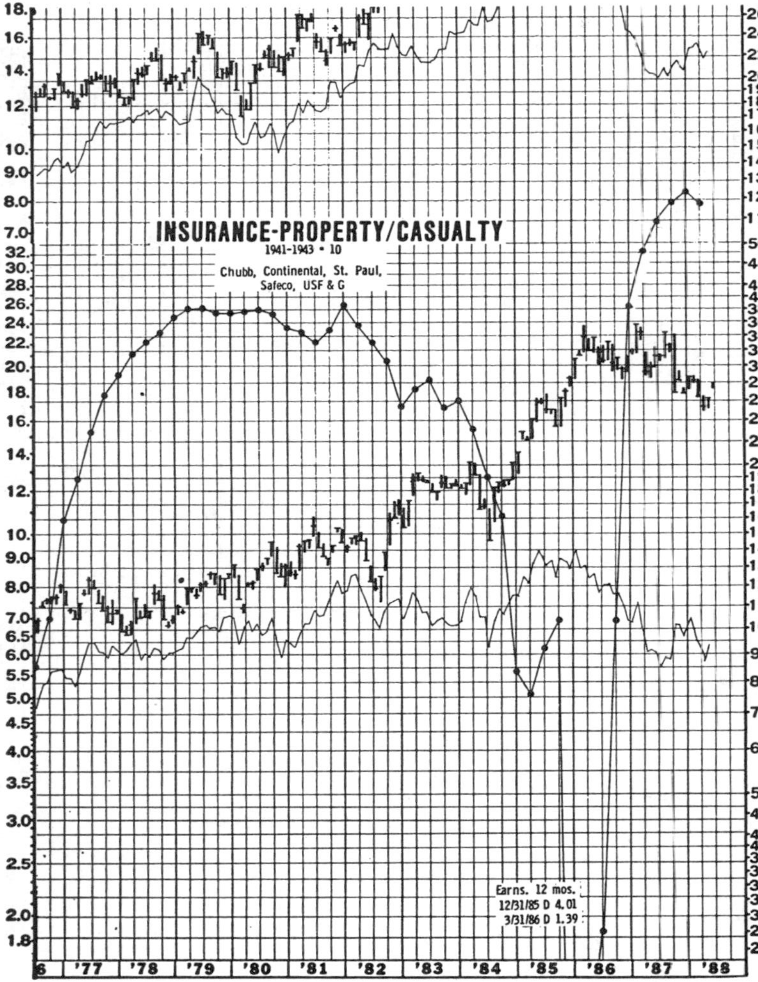
INSURANCE-PROPERTY/CASUALTY
1941-1943 = 10
Chubb, Continental, St. Paul, Safeco, USF & G
Earns. 12 mos.
12/31/85 D 4.01
3/31/86 D 1.39
'77 '78 '79 '80 '81 '82 '83 '84 '85 '86 '87 '88

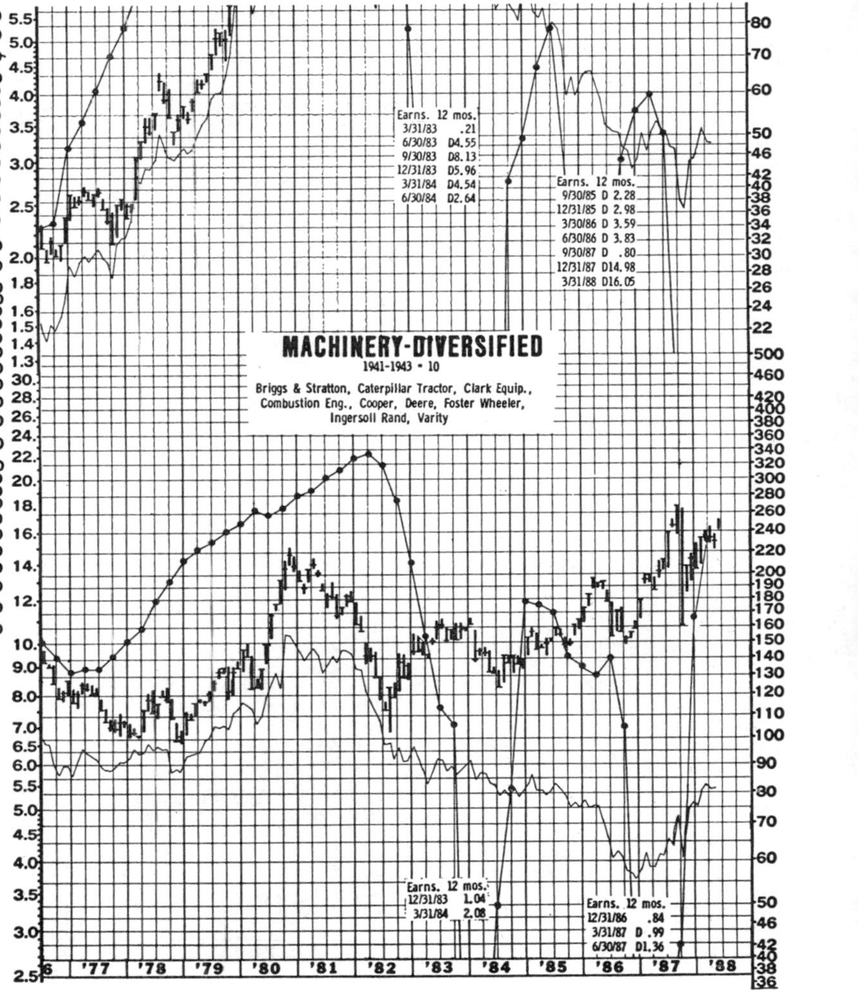
MACHINERY-DIVERSIFIED
1941-1943 = 10
Briggs & Stratton, Caterpillar Tractor, Clark Equip., Combustion Eng., Cooper, Deere, Foster Wheeler, Ingersoll Rand, Varity
Earns. 12 mos.
3/31/83 .21
6/30/83 D4.55
9/30/83 D8.13
12/31/83 D5.96
3/31/84 D4.54
6/30/84 D2.64
Earns. 12 mos.
9/30/85 D 2.28
12/31/85 D 2.98
3/30/86 D 3.59
6/30/86 D 3.83
9/30/87 D .80
12/31/87 D14.98
3/31/88 D16.05
Earns. 12 mos.
12/31/83 1.04
3/31/84 2.08
Earns. 12 mos.
12/31/86 .84
3/31/87 D .99
6/30/87 D1.36
'77 '78 '79 '80 '81 '82 '83 '84 '85 '86 '87 '88

STOCK MARKET AVERAGES BY INDUSTRY GROUP *(continued)*

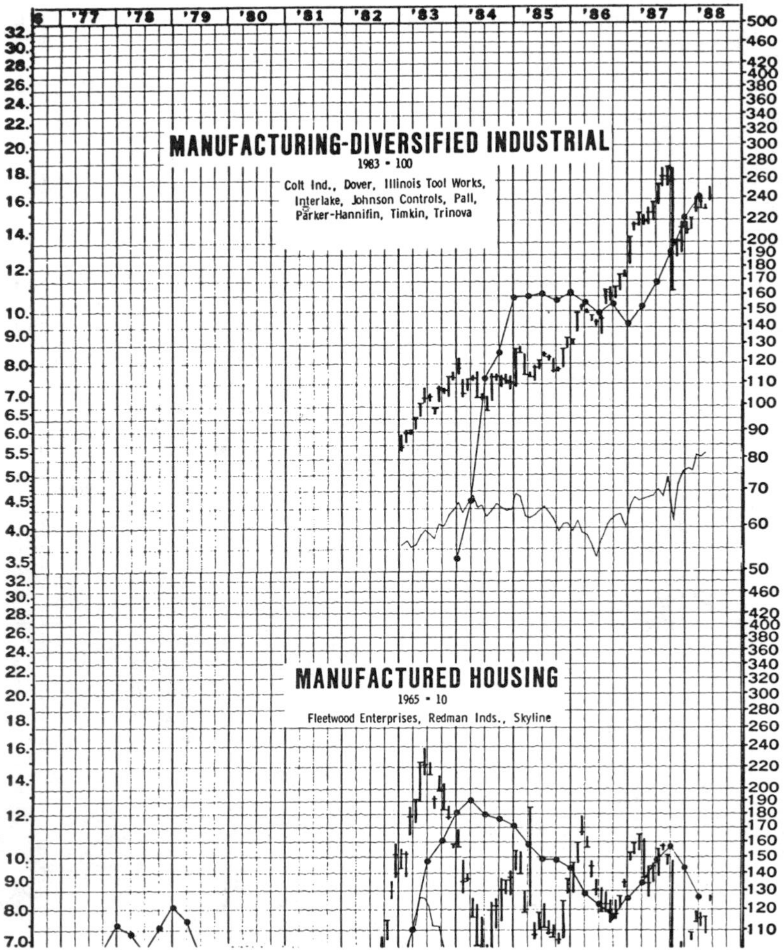
MANUFACTURING-DIVERSIFIED INDUSTRIAL
1983 = 100
Colt Ind., Dover, Illinois Tool Works, Interlake, Johnson Controls, Pall, Parker-Hannifin, Timkin, Trinova
MANUFACTURED HOUSING
1965 = 10
Fleetwood Enterprises, Redman Inds., Skyline

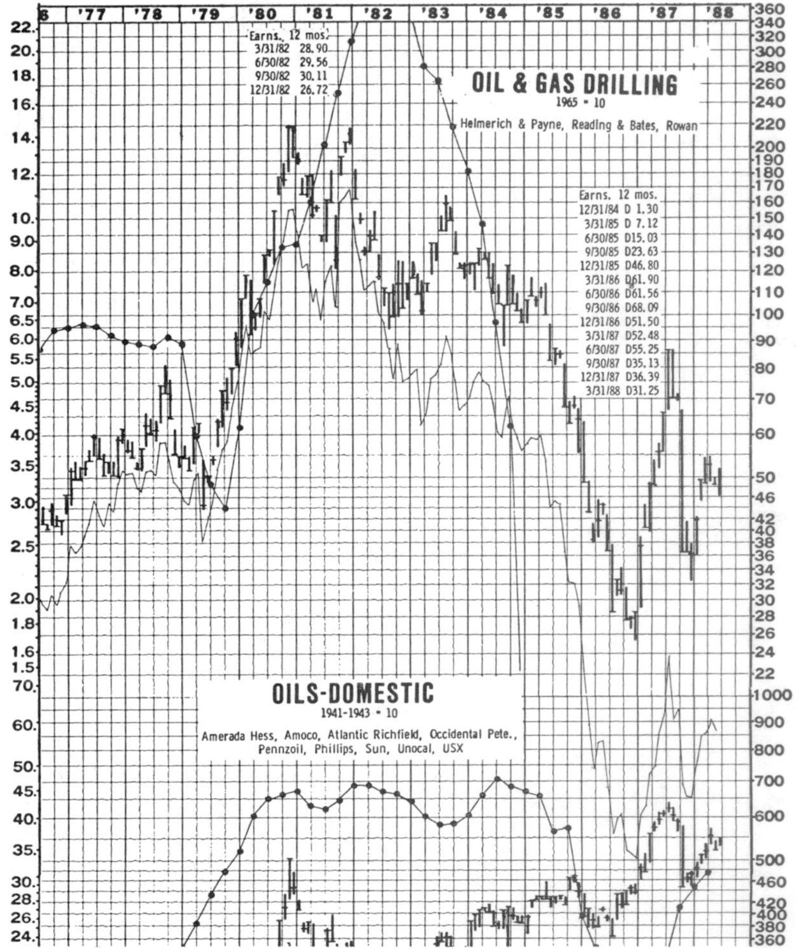
OIL & GAS DRILLING
1965 = 10
Helmerich & Payne, Reading & Bates, Rowan
Earns., 12 mos.
3/31/82 28.90
6/30/82 29.56
9/30/82 30.11
12/31/82 26.72
Earns. 12 mos.
12/31/84 D 1.30
3/31/85 D 7.12
6/30/85 D15.03
9/30/85 D23.63
12/31/85 D46.80
3/31/86 D61.90
6/30/86 D61.56
9/30/86 D68.09
12/31/86 D51.50
3/31/87 D52.48
6/30/87 D55.25
9/30/87 D35.13
12/31/87 D36.39
3/31/88 D31.25
OILS-DOMESTIC
1941-1943 = 10
Amerada Hess, Amoco, Atlantic Richfield, Occidental Pete., Pennzoil, Phillips, Sun, Unocal, USX

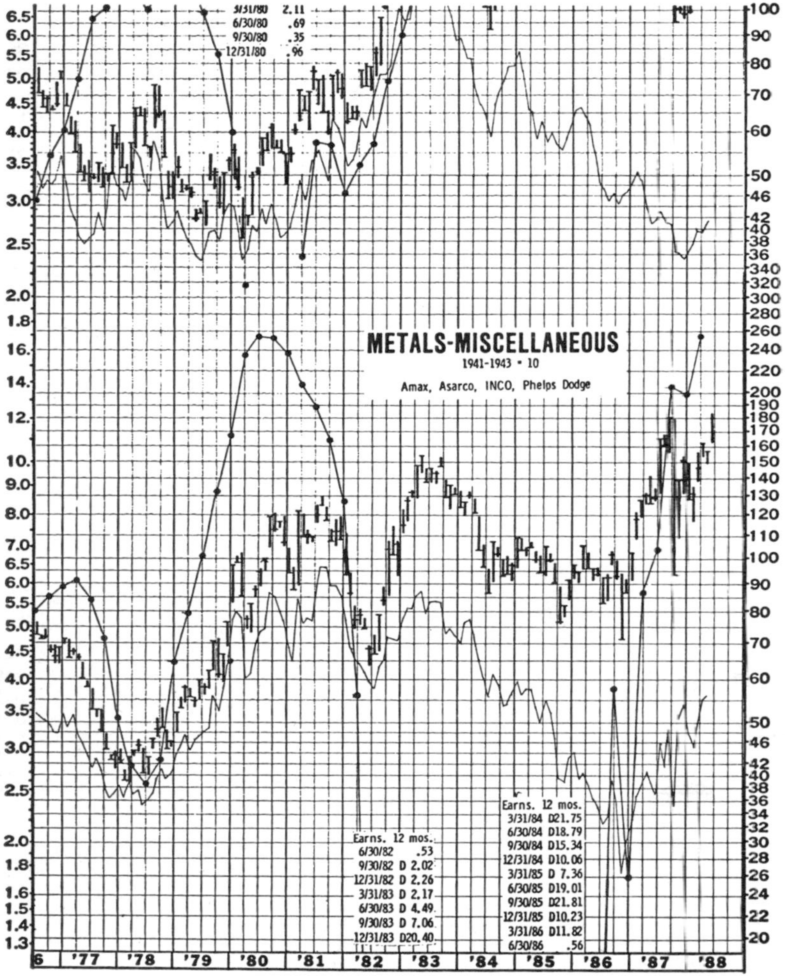
METALS-MISCELLANEOUS
1941-1943 = 10
Amax, Asarco, INCO, Phelps Dodge
3/31/80 2.11
6/30/80 .69
9/30/80 .35
12/31/80 .96
Earns. 12 mos.
6/30/82 .53
9/30/82 D 2.02
12/31/82 D 2.26
3/31/83 D 2.17
6/30/83 D 4.49
9/30/83 D 7.06
12/31/83 D20.40
Earns. 12 mos.
3/31/84 D21.75
6/30/84 D18.79
9/30/84 D15.34
12/31/84 D10.06
3/31/85 D 7.36
6/30/85 D19.01
9/30/85 D21.81
12/31/85 D10.23
3/31/86 D11.82
6/30/86 .56
'77 '78 '79 '80 '81 '82 '83 '84 '85 '86 '87 '88

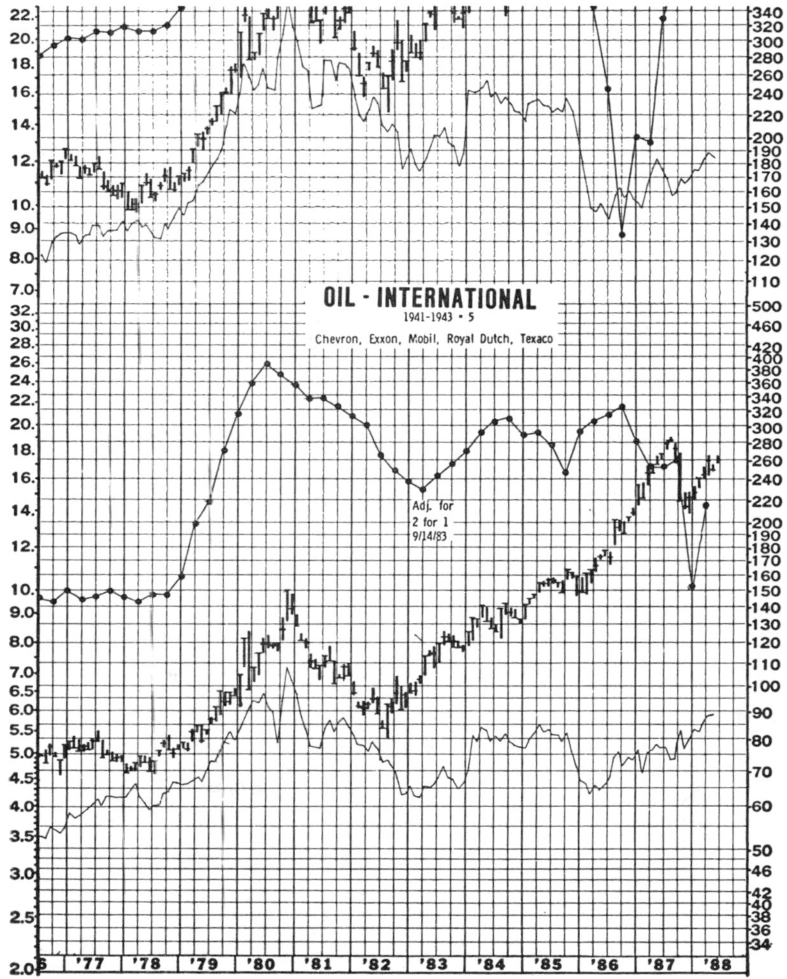
OIL - INTERNATIONAL
1941-1943 = 5
Chevron, Exxon, Mobil, Royal Dutch, Texaco
Adj. for
2 for 1
9/14/83
'77 '78 '79 '80 '81 '82 '83 '84 '85 '86 '87 '88

STOCK MARKET AVERAGES BY INDUSTRY GROUP *(continued)*

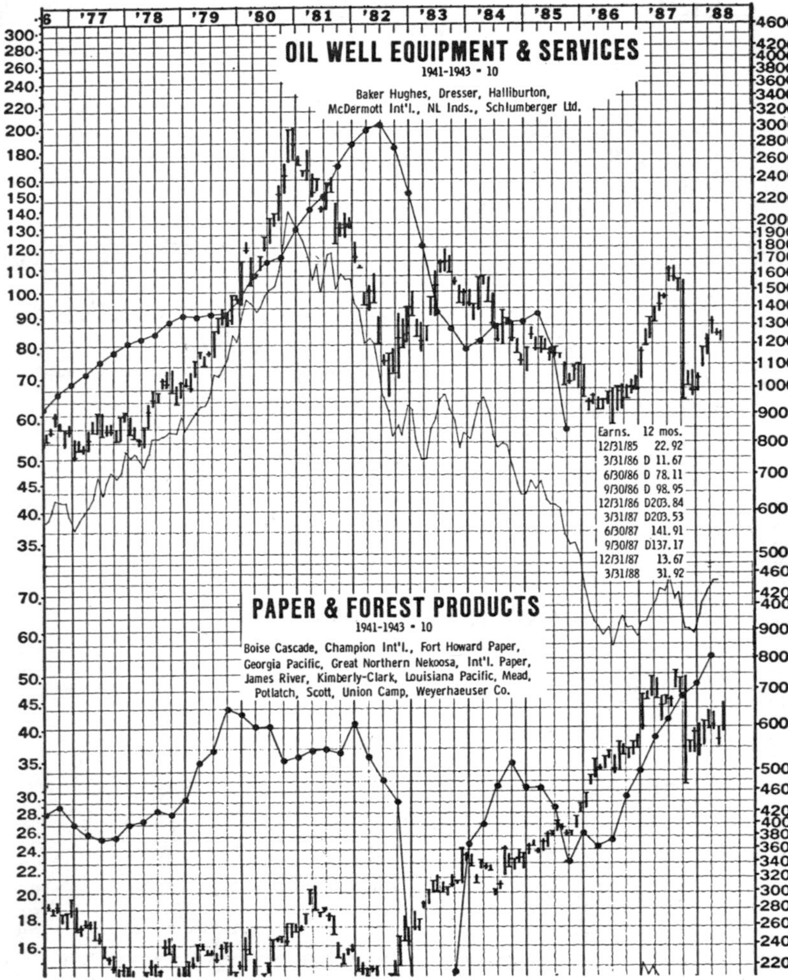
OIL WELL EQUIPMENT & SERVICES
1941-1943 = 10
Baker Hughes, Dresser, Halliburton, McDermott Int'l., NL Inds., Schlumberger Ltd.
Earns. 12 mos.
12/31/85 22.92
3/31/86 D 11.67
6/30/86 D 78.11
9/30/86 D 98.95
12/31/86 D203.84
3/31/87 D203.53
6/30/87 141.91
9/30/87 D137.17
12/31/87 13.67
3/31/88 31.92
PAPER & FOREST PRODUCTS
1941-1943 = 10
Boise Cascade, Champion Int'l., Fort Howard Paper, Georgia Pacific, Great Northern Nekoosa, Int'l. Paper, James River, Kimberly-Clark, Louisiana Pacific, Mead, Potlatch, Scott, Union Camp, Weyerhaeuser Co.
'77 '78 '79 '80 '81 '82 '83 '84 '85 '86 '87 '88

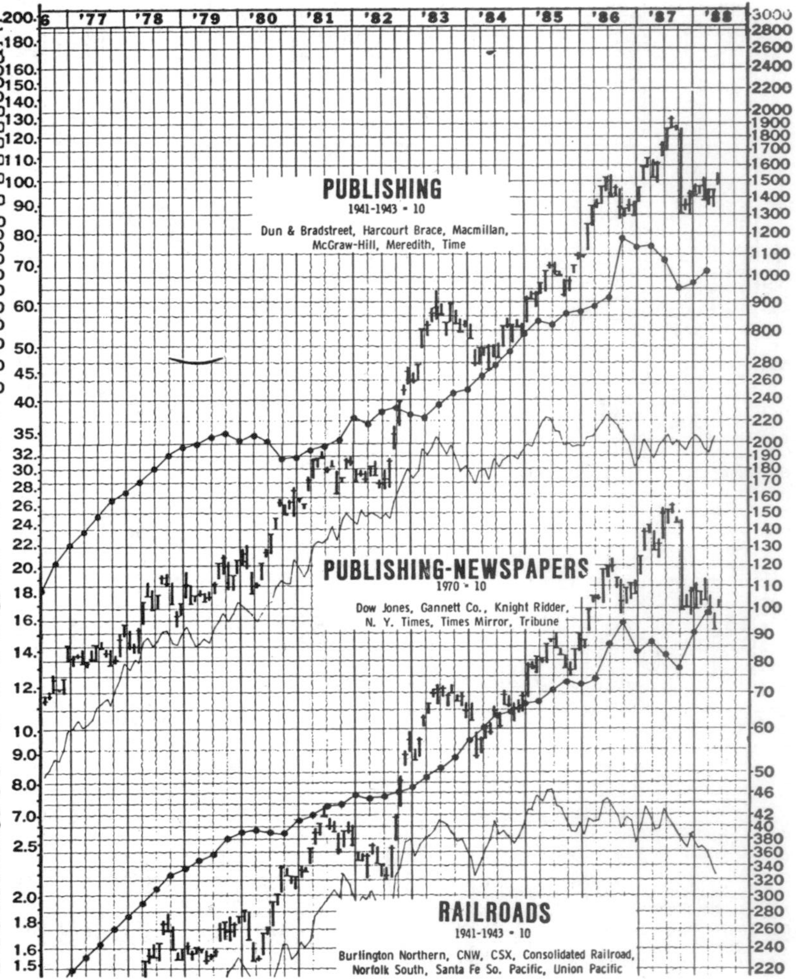
PUBLISHING
1941-1943 = 10
Dun & Bradstreet, Harcourt Brace, Macmillan, McGraw-Hill, Meredith, Time
PUBLISHING-NEWSPAPERS
1970 = 10
Dow Jones, Gannett Co., Knight Ridder, N. Y. Times, Times Mirror, Tribune
RAILROADS
1941-1943 = 10
Burlington Northern, CNW, CSX, Consolidated Railroad, Norfolk South, Santa Fe So. Pacific, Union Pacific
'77 '78 '79 '80 '81 '82 '83 '84 '85 '86 '87 '88

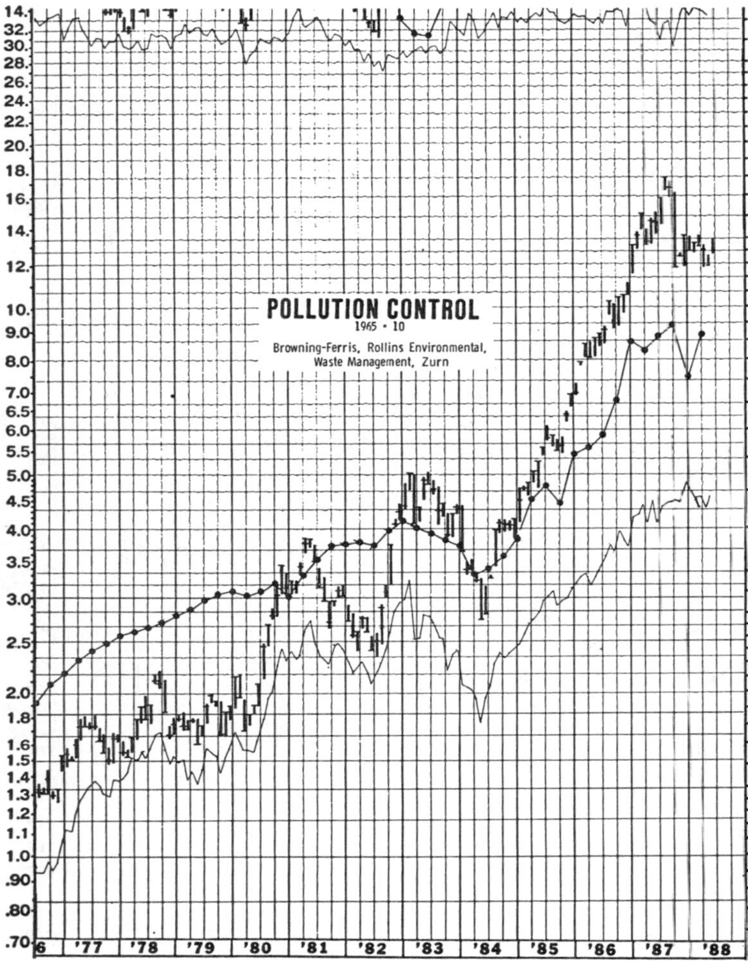
POLLUTION CONTROL
1965 • 10
Browning-Ferris, Rollins Environmental, Waste Management, Zurn
'77 '78 '79 '80 '81 '82 '83 '84 '85 '86 '87 '88

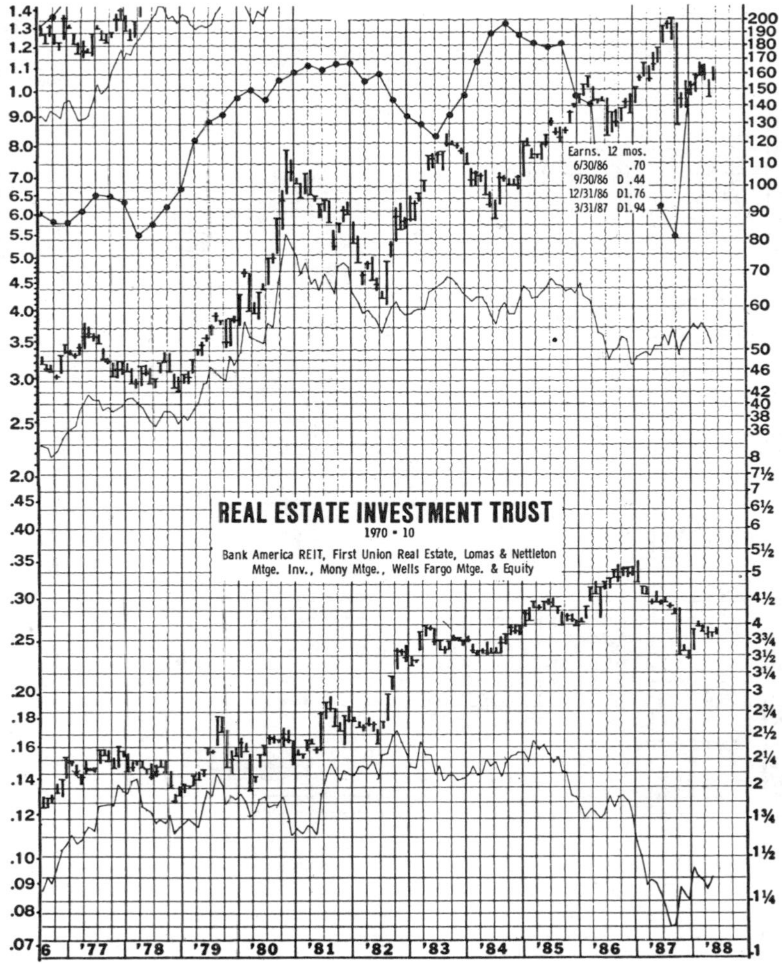
REAL ESTATE INVESTMENT TRUST
1970 • 10
Bank America REIT, First Union Real Estate, Lomas & Nettleton Mtge. Inv., Mony Mtge., Wells Fargo Mtge. & Equity
Earns. 12 mos.
6/30/86 .70
9/30/86 D .44
12/31/86 D1.76
3/31/87 D1.94
'77 '78 '79 '80 '81 '82 '83 '84 '85 '86 '87 '88

STOCK MARKET AVERAGES BY INDUSTRY GROUP *(continued)*

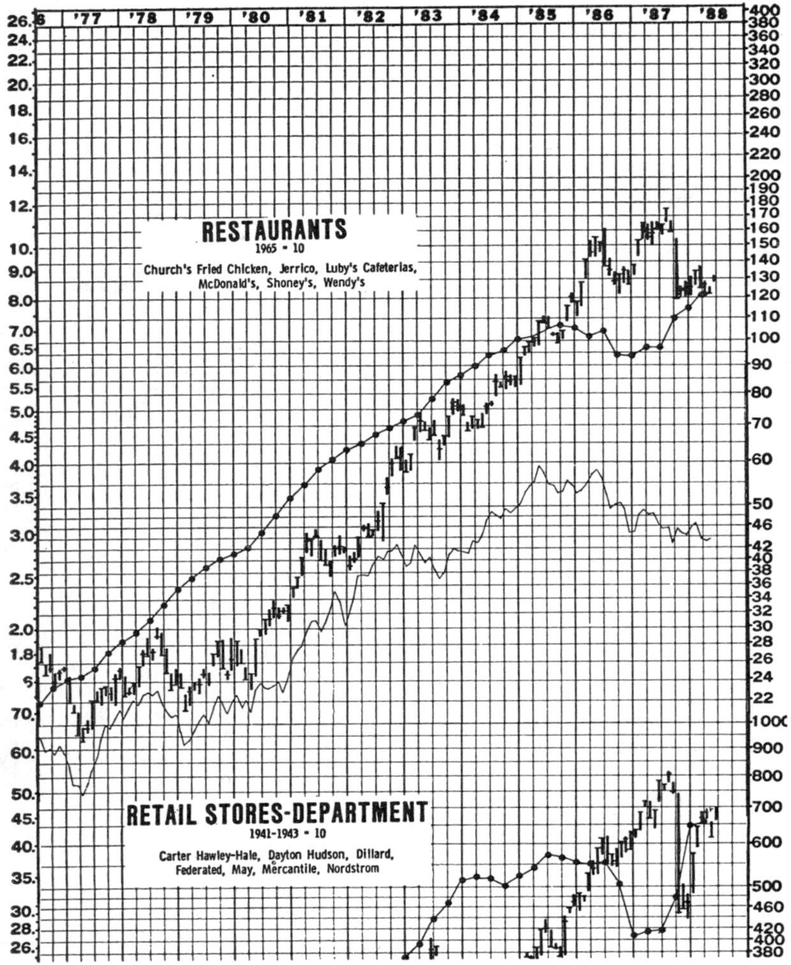
RESTAURANTS
1965 = 10
Church's Fried Chicken, Jerrico, Luby's Cafeterias, McDonald's, Shoney's, Wendy's
RETAIL STORES-DEPARTMENT
1941-1943 = 10
Carter Hawley-Hale, Dayton Hudson, Dillard, Federated, May, Mercantile, Nordstrom
'77 '78 '79 '80 '81 '82 '83 '84 '85 '86 '87 '88

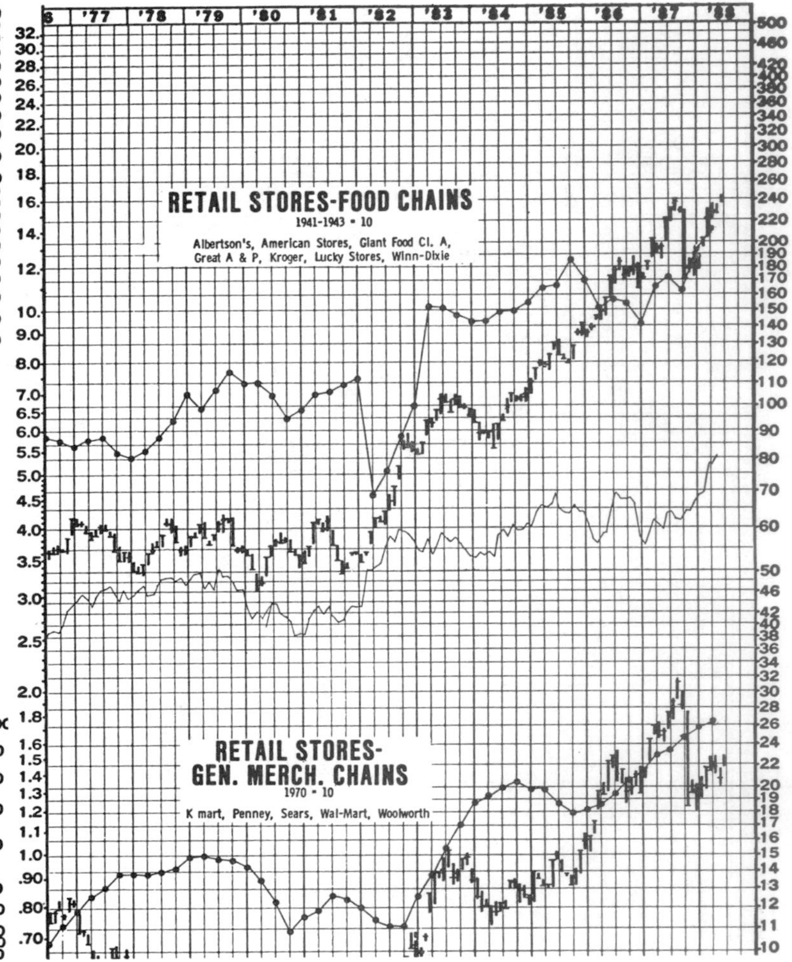
RETAIL STORES-FOOD CHAINS
1941-1943 = 10
Albertson's, American Stores, Giant Food Cl. A, Great A & P, Kroger, Lucky Stores, Winn-Dixie
RETAIL STORES-GEN. MERCH. CHAINS
1970 = 10
K mart, Penney, Sears, Wal-Mart, Woolworth
'77 '78 '79 '80 '81 '82 '83 '84 '85 '86 '87 '88

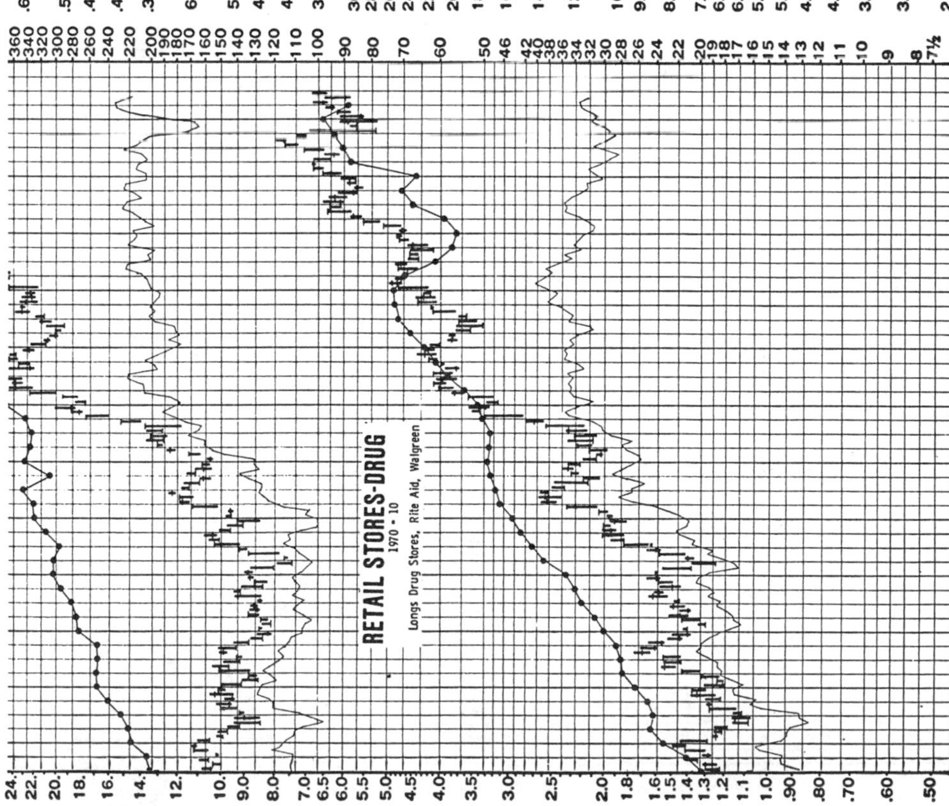
RETAIL STORES-DRUG
1970 - 10
Longs Drug Stores, Rite Aid, Walgreen

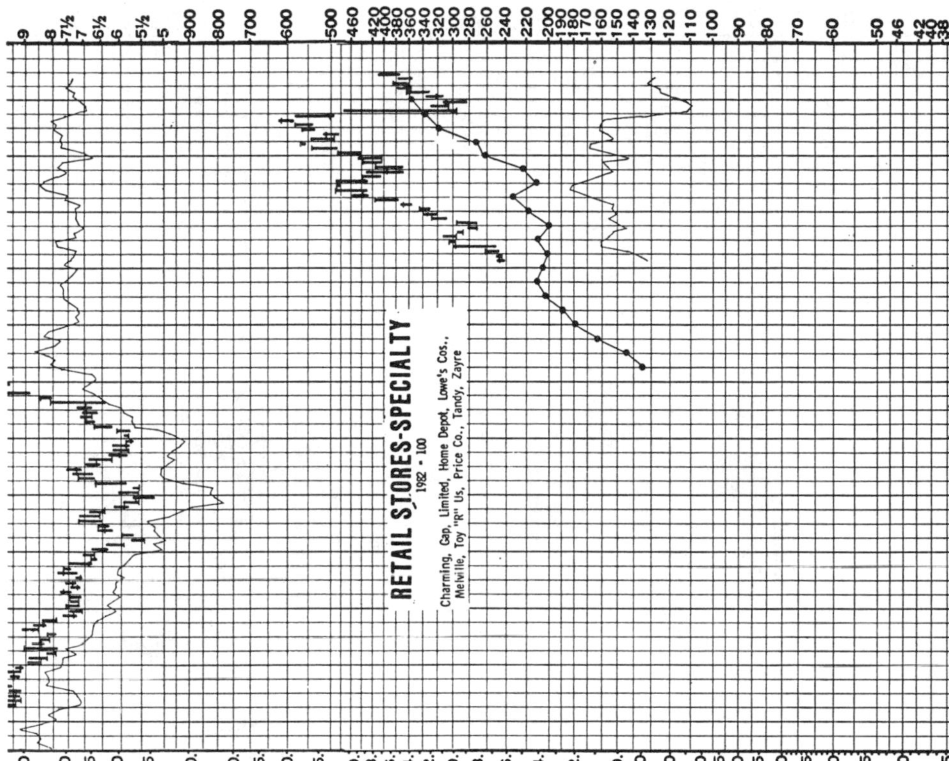
RETAIL STORES-SPECIALTY
1982 - 100
Charming, Gap, Limited, Home Depot, Lowe's Cos.,
Melville, Toy "R" Us, Price Co., Tandy, Zayre

STOCK MARKET AVERAGES BY INDUSTRY GROUP *(continued)*

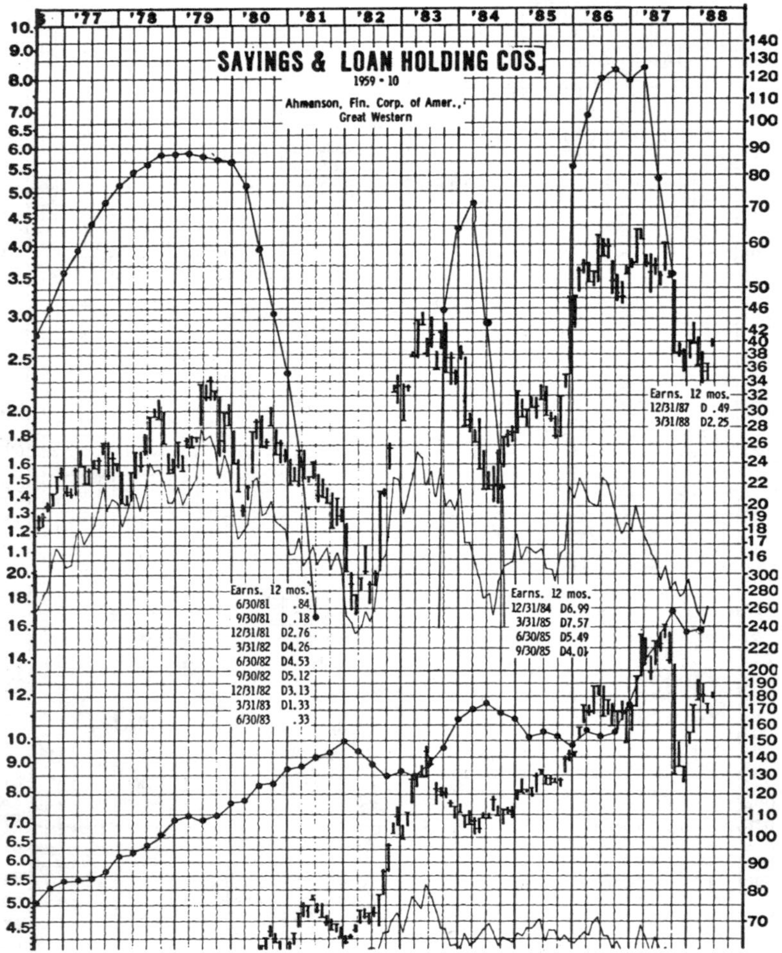

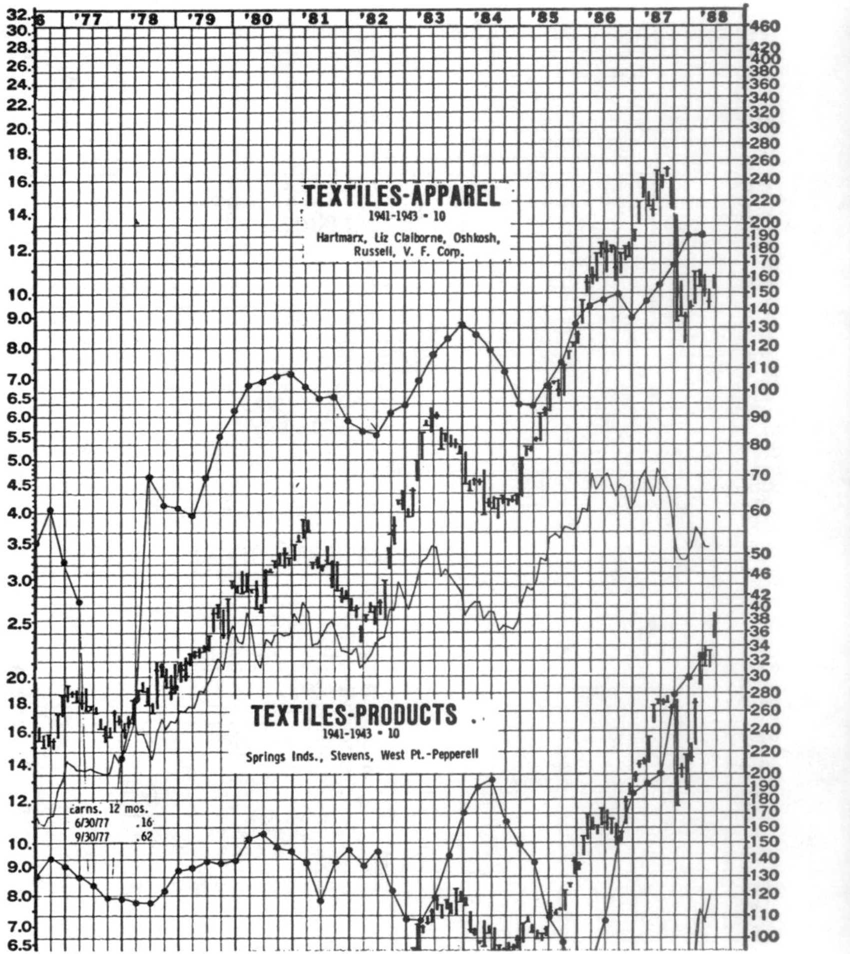

Components-Dow Jones 65 Stock Averages

INDUSTRIALS

Allied Sig.	Exxon	Philip Morris
Alum Co	Gen Electric	Primerica
Amer Exp	Gen Motors	Proc Gamb
AT&T	Goodyear	Sears
Beth Steel	IBM	Texaco
Boeing	Int'l Paper	Union Carbide
Chevron	McDonald's	USX Corp.
Coca-Cola	Merck	United Tech
Du Pont	Minn M&M	Westinghouse
Eastman	Navistar	Woolworth

TRANSPORTATION

AMR Corp.	CSX Corp.	Santa Fe
Amer Pres	Delta Air	Southwest Airl
Burlington	Fed Express	TWA
Canadian Pac	Norfolk So	UAL Corp.
Caro Freight	NWA Inc.	Union Pac
Cons Freight	Pan Am	USAir
Cons Rail	Ryder System	

UTILITIES

Am El Power	Cons N Gas	Panhandle
Centerior	Detroit Edis	Peoples En
Colum-Gas	Houston Ind	Phila Elec
Comwlth Edis	Niag Mohawk	Pub Serv E
Cons Edison	Pacific G&E	Sou Cal Edis

Source: Reprinted by courtesy of *Barron's National Business and Financial Weekly*, July 7, 1988.

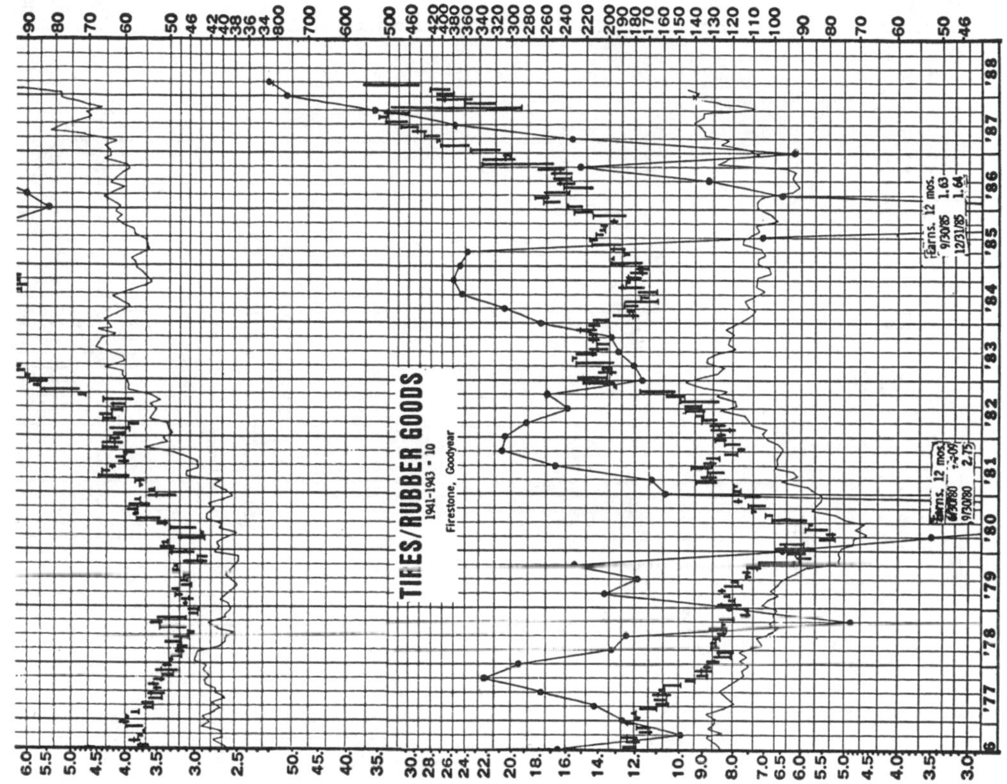

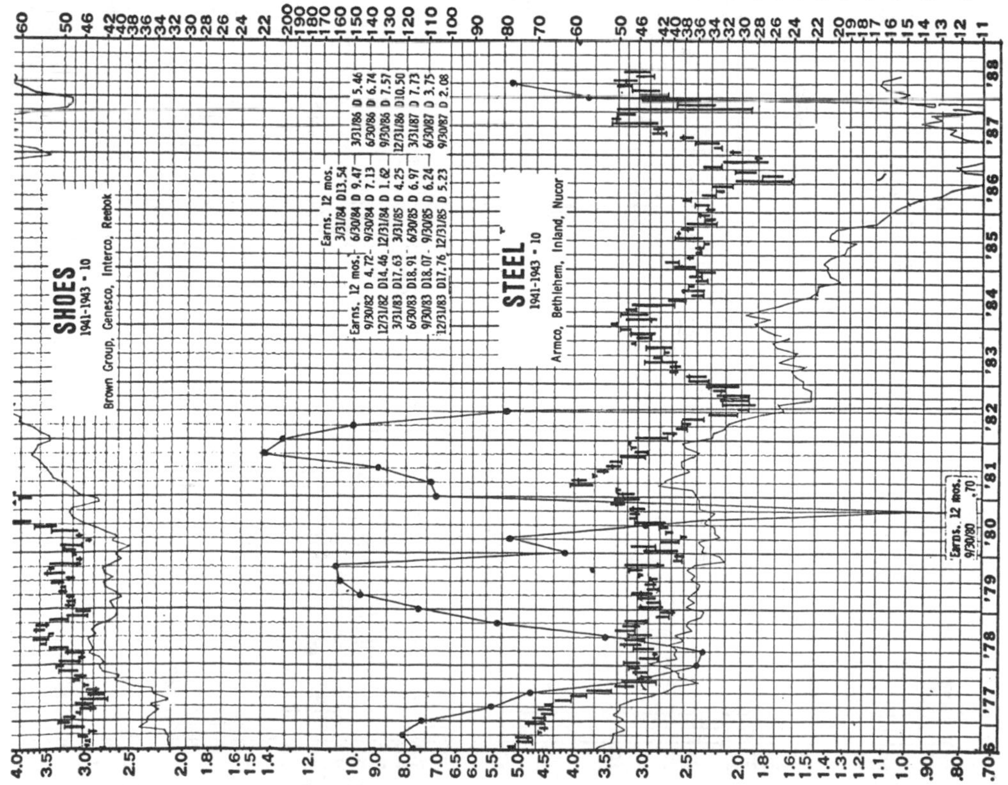

STOCK MARKET AVERAGES BY INDUSTRY GROUP *(concluded)*

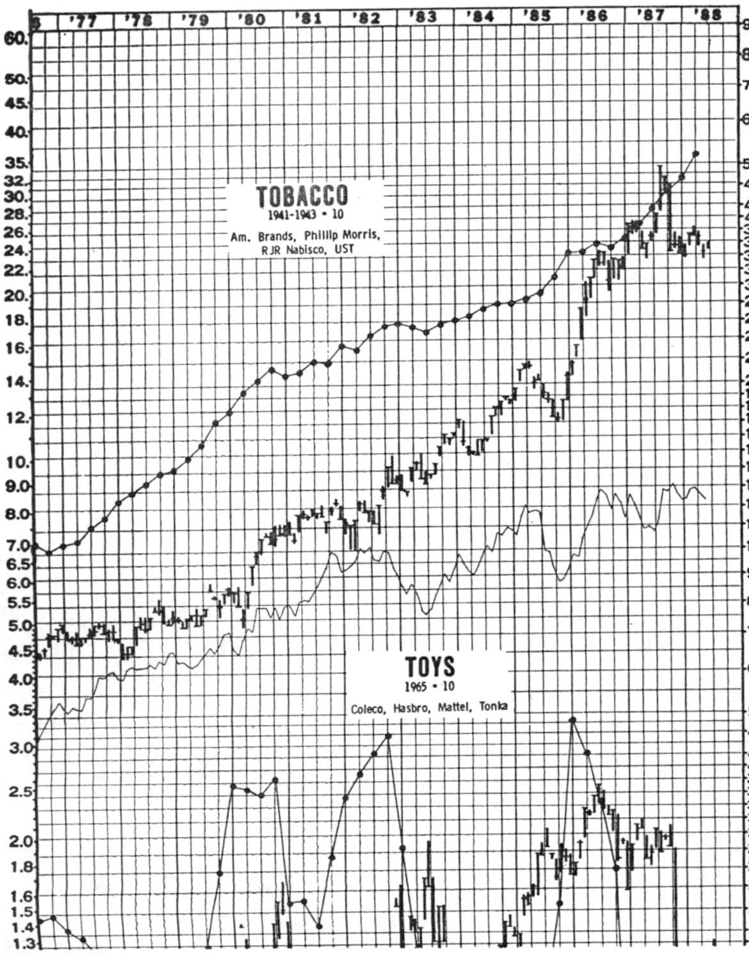

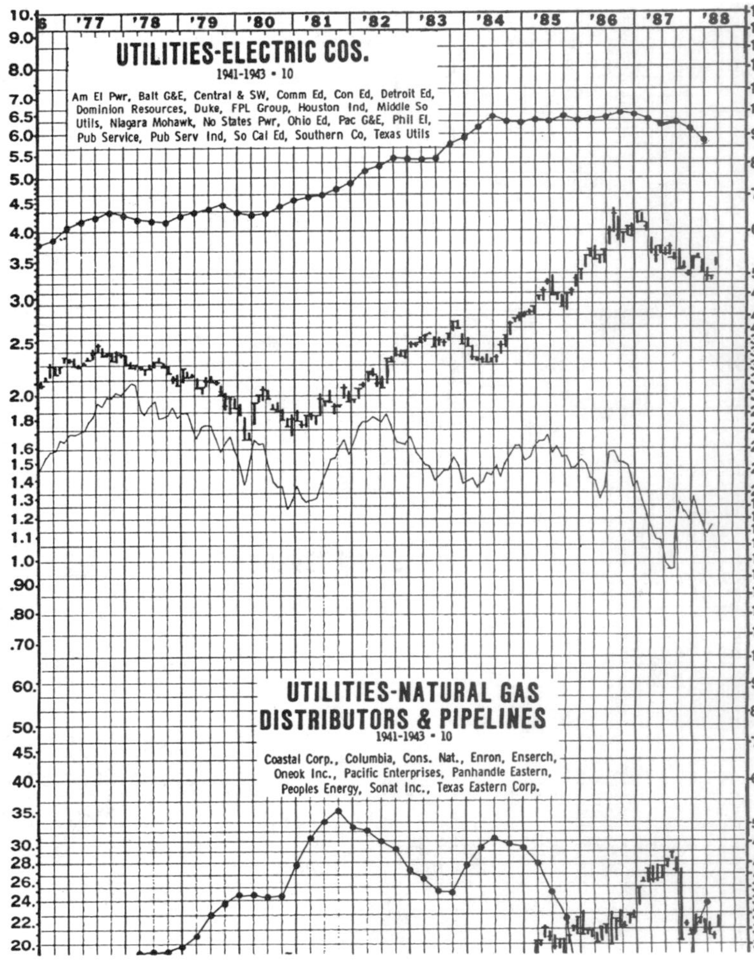

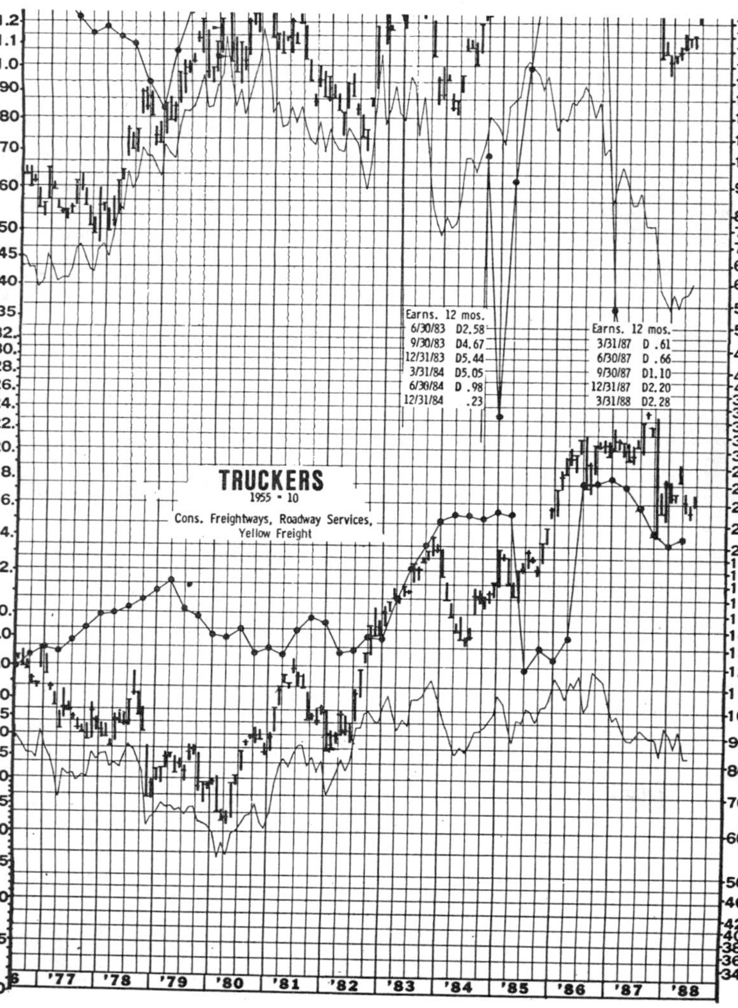

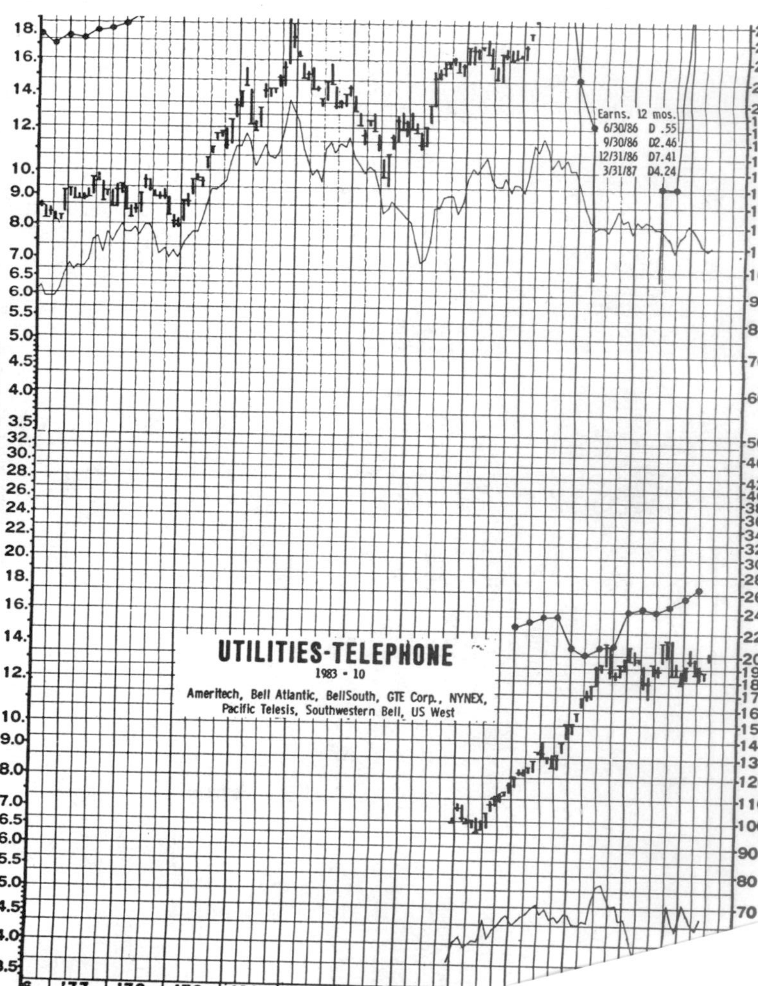

FINANCIAL DATA ON DOW JONES INDUSTRIALS

	This Week					History				Earnings			P/E Ratio			Dvds	
	Vol-ume	Close	Price Change	Market Value	Pct. of Total	52-Week High	52-Week Low	5-Year High	5-Year Low	Last 12Mos	% Ch	5-Yr. Growth	Today	5-Year Avg High	5-Year Avg Low	Indic. Amt	Yield
	00	$	$	$Mil	%	$	$	$	$	$	%	%	-	-	-	$	%
Dow Jones Ind. ...	995,455	2131.58	-11.38	475,398.0	100.00	2722.42	1738.74	2722.42	1027.04	136.34	18.06	52	15.6	43.2	14.8	75.28	3.5
Allied-Signal	14,513	35.00	.50	5,248.2	1.10	48.75	26.00	NC	NC	2.95	-6.65	NC	11.9	NC	NC	1.80	5.1
Alum Co Am	23,688	52.63	-.12	4,639.5	.98	64.75	33.75	64.75	29.25	3.98	9.64	NC	13.2	NC	NC	1.20	2.3
Am Express Co ...	36,135	27.00	-.12	11,423.2	2.40	39.88	20.75	40.63	12.50	1.11	-56.30	1	24.3	19.4	11.5	.76	2.8
Am Tel & T	74,567	26.50	-.25	28,452.8	5.99	35.88	20.00	35.88	14.88	1.94	1285.71	NC	13.7	NC	NC	1.20	4.5
Bethlehem Stl	50,051	24.13	2.50	1,793.5	.38	24.50	9.13	29.50	4.63	2.33	NE	NC	10.4	NC	NC	.00	.0
Boeing Co	43,376	59.00	1.25	8,984.1	1.89	59.13	28.75	64.88	21.25	3.23	-21.03	8	18.3	13.5	8.6	1.60	2.7
Chevron Cp	35,288	45.25	-3.12	15,480.4	3.26	64.63	32.00	64.63	29.25	4.27	171.97	-9	10.6	14.4	9.4	2.60	5.7
Coca Cola Co	23,479	38.63	.25	14,268.2	3.00	53.13	29.00	53.13	15.16	2.51	.80	15	15.4	16.9	10.9	1.20	3.1
Dupont .... •	21,529	92.25	.75	22,074.2	4.64	131.00	75.00	131.00	35.13	8.22	30.48	12	11.2	13.8	8.9	3.80	4.1
Eastman Kodak ...	33,780	45.50	-.12	14,758.9	3.10	70.69	39.13	70.69	26.81	3.79	154.36	1	12.0	27.9	19.4	1.80	4.0
Exxon Cp	79,116	44.63	-1.50	63,648.6	13.39	50.38	30.88	50.38	14.25	3.13	-4.57	6	14.3	9.4	6.5	2.20	4.9
Gen Electric	47,636	43.88	.13	40,160.9	8.45	66.38	38.38	66.38	22.69	2.75	9.13	4	16.0	16.8	11.9	1.40	3.2
Gen Motors	29,761	79.75	.50	24,934.2	5.24	94.13	50.00	94.13	50.00	10.55	36.66	10	7.6	7.9	5.4	5.00	6.3
Goodyear Tire	13,229	64.25	-1.37	3,661.4	.77	76.50	35.00	76.50	23.00	10.41	82.63	16	6.2	15.3	9.6	1.60	2.5
Intl Bus Mach	83,377	126.63	1.50	75,601.7	15.90	175.88	100.00	175.88	92.25	8.95	19.97	0	14.1	16.5	11.4	4.40	3.5
Intl Paper	15,585	48.50	.13	5,111.2	1.08	56.00	27.00	57.81	22.13	4.24	18.11	20	11.4	20.3	14.2	1.30	2.7
McDonald's Cp	19,712	45.75	.13	8,676.5	1.83	61.13	31.38	61.13	16.28	3.01	18.04	14	15.2	16.8	10.6	.56	1.2
Merck & Co	36,184	55.25	.00	22,678.4	4.77	74.25	47.94	74.25	13.03	2.42	39.88	19	22.8	22.0	13.9	1.28	2.3
Minn Mng Mfg	23,643	65.75	.38	14,957.3	3.15	83.50	45.00	83.50	34.63	4.31	21.75	8	15.3	16.7	12.1	2.12	3.2
Navistar Intl	34,704	6.63	.00	1,665.3	.35	8.38	3.00	14.75	3.00	.80	NE	NC	8.3	NC	NC	.00	.0
Philip Morris	26,786	83.38	-2.12	19,728.7	4.15	124.50	77.13	124.50	27.00	8.25	26.92	20	10.1	11.9	7.8	3.60	4.3
Primerica	59,824	27.25	.38	1,456.9	.31	49.75	21.75	53.50	15.06	3.28	.92	30	8.3	13.9	8.2	1.60	5.9
Proct & Gambl	13,384	77.00	-.75	13,041.8	2.74	103.50	48.00	103.50	45.63	3.19	-30.04	-14	24.1	23.4	14.5	2.80	3.6
Sears, Roebuck ...	22,082	36.63	-.62	13,863.2	2.92	59.50	26.00	59.50	26.00	4.07	5.71	6	9.0	12.3	7.8	2.00	5.5
Texaco .... ◦	49,754	46.63	-1.87	11,323.0	2.38	52.50	23.50	52.50	23.50	-17.64	-100.00	NC	NE	NC	NC	3.00	6.4
Union Carbide	28,556	22.75	-.62	2,982.3	.63	32.13	15.50	33.13	10.91	2.00	39.86	NC	11.4	NC	NC	1.50	6.6
Utd Technol	12,193	38.63	-.12	5,037.2	1.06	60.50	30.00	60.50	26.94	4.71	5133.33	-14	8.2	52.4	36.2	1.60	4.1
USX Cp	20,305	31.63	-1.12	8,371.2	1.76	39.38	21.00	39.38	14.50	.89	NE	NC	35.5	NC	NC	1.20	3.8
Westinghouse	13,355	56.13	.38	8,042.0	1.69	75.00	40.00	75.00	18.63	5.23	13.94	18	10.7	12.5	7.7	2.00	3.6
Woolworth FW	9,863	51.88	-2.37	3,333.2	.69	60.75	29.50	60.75	11.31	3.92	12.64	NC	13.2	12.3	7.2	1.64	3.2
Unweighted Avg. .	33,182	49.96	-.25	15,846.6	3.33	66.54	35.15	68.00	24.12	3.43	256.07	8	13.8	17.5	11.5	1.89	3.7

Source: *The Media General Financial Weekly*, Media General Financial Services, 301 East Grace Street, Richmond, VA 23219, July 4, 1988.

DOW JONES INDUSTRIAL, TRANSPORTATION AND UTILITY AVERAGES

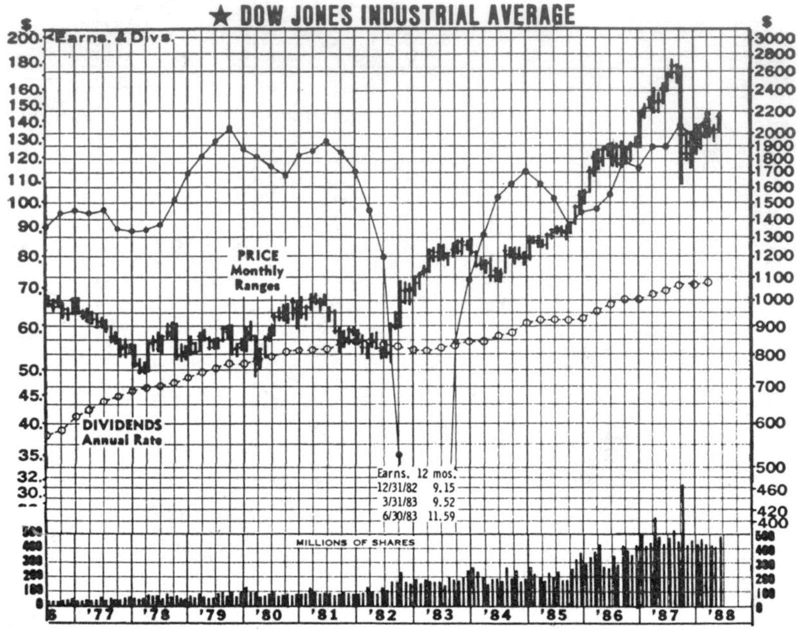

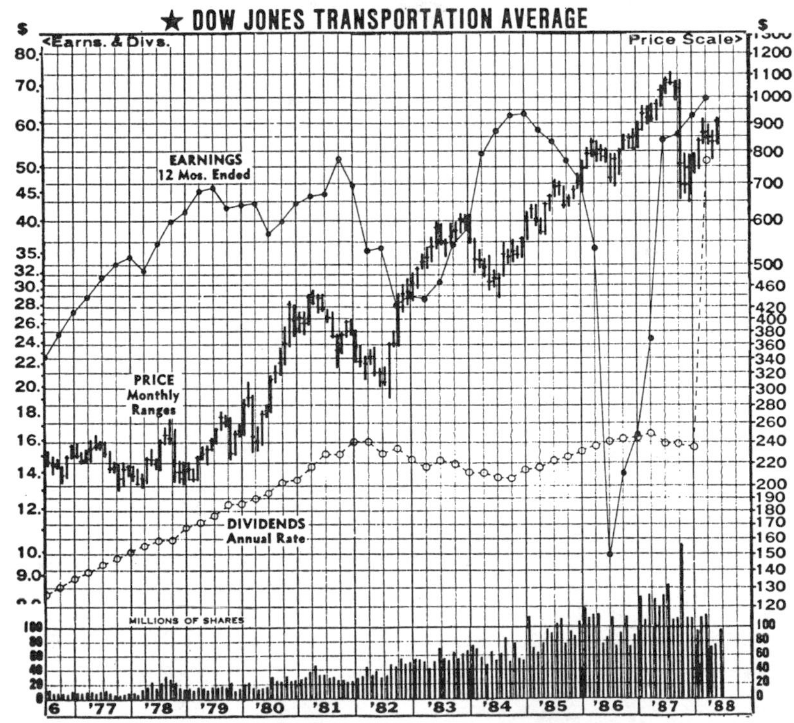

DOW JONES INDUSTRIAL, TRANSPORTATION AND UTILITY AVERAGES *(concluded)*

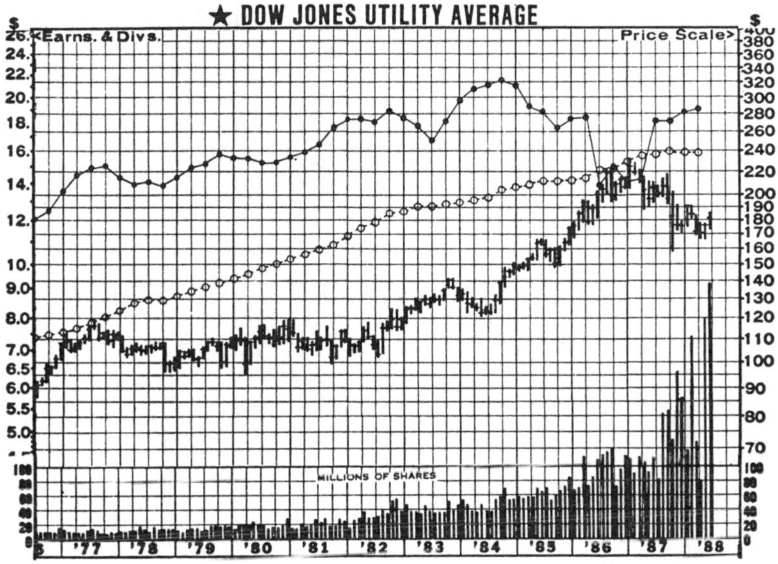

Source: *5-Trend CYCLI-GRAPHS.* The charts are courtesy of Securities Research Company, a Division of Babson-United Investment Advisors, Inc., 208 Newbury Street, Boston, MA 02116, July quarterly edition, 1988.

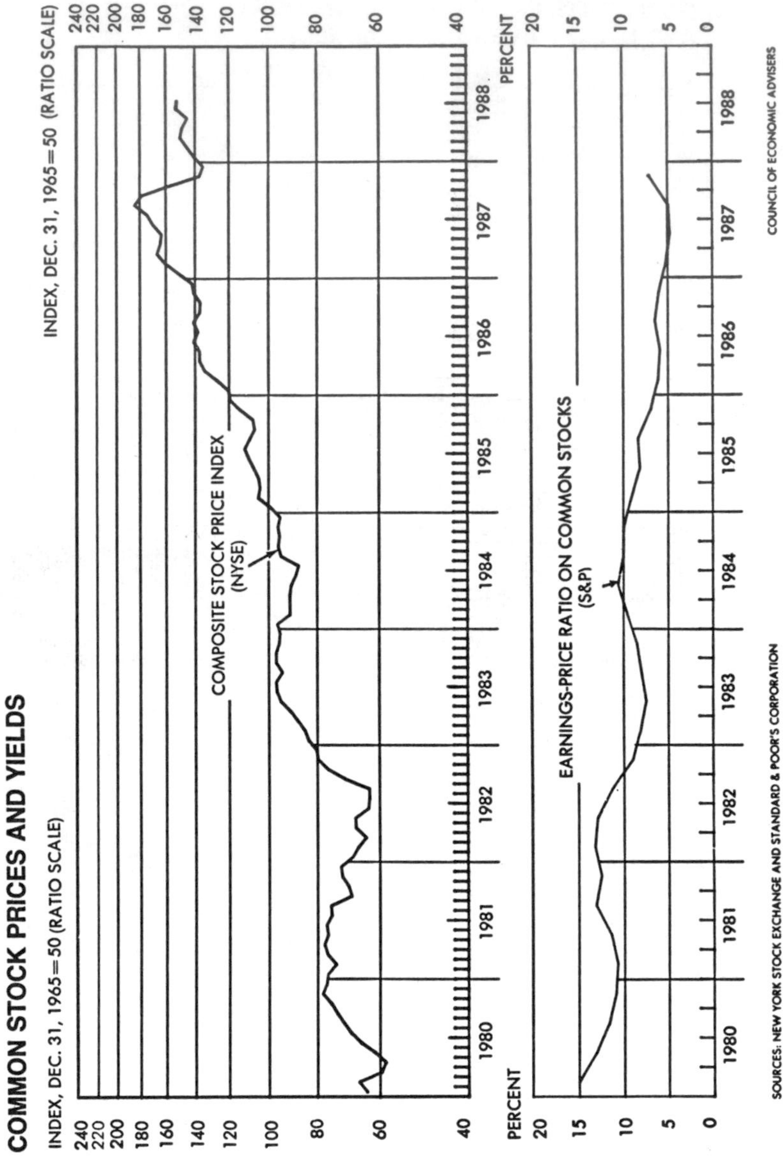
COMMON STOCK PRICES AND YIELDS
INDEX, DEC. 31, 1965=50 (RATIO SCALE)
240
220
200
180
160
140
120
100
80
60
40
COMPOSITE STOCK PRICE INDEX
(NYSE)
PERCENT
20
15
10
5
0
EARNINGS-PRICE RATIO ON COMMON STOCKS
(S&P)
1980
1981
1982
1983
1984
1985
1986
1987
1988
SOURCES: NEW YORK STOCK EXCHANGE AND STANDARD & POOR'S CORPORATION
COUNCIL OF ECONOMIC ADVISERS

Period	Common stock prices [1]							Common stock yields (percent) [5]	
	New York Stock Exchange indexes (Dec. 31, 1965=50) [2]					Dow-Jones industrial average [3]	Standard & Poor's composite index (1941–43=10) [4]	Dividend-price ratio	Earnings-price ratio
	Composite	Industrial	Transportation	Utility	Finance				
1981	74.02	85.44	72.61	38.91	73.52	932.92	128.05	5.20	11.96
1982	68.93	78.18	60.41	39.75	71.99	884.36	119.71	5.81	11.60
1983	92.63	107.45	89.36	47.00	95.34	1,190.34	160.41	4.40	8.03
1984	92.46	108.01	85.63	46.44	89.28	1,178.48	160.46	4.64	10.02
1985	108.09	123.79	104.11	56.75	114.21	1,328.23	186.84	4.25	8.12
1986	136.00	155.85	119.87	71.36	147.20	1,792.76	236.34	3.49	6.09
1987	161.70	195.31	140.39	74.30	146.48	2,275.99	c 286.83	3.08	5.49
1987: July	174.28	214.12	157.48	74.18	152.25	2,481.72	310.09	2.83	
Aug	184.18	226.49	164.02	78.20	160.94	2,655.01	329.36	2.69	
Sept	178.39	219.52	158.58	76.13	154.08	2,570.80	318.66	2.78	4.93
Oct	157.13	189.86	140.95	73.27	137.35	2,224.59	280.16	3.25	
Nov	137.21	163.42	117.57	69.86	118.30	1,931.86	245.01	3.66	
Dec	134.88	162.19	115.85	67.39	111.47	1,910.07	240.96	3.71	7.08
1988: Jan	140.55	168.47	121.20	70.01	119.40	1,947.35	250.48	3.66	
Feb	145.13	173.44	126.09	72.89	124.36	1,980.65	258.13	3.56	
Mar	149.88	181.57	135.15	71.16	125.27	2,044.31	265.74	3.48	
Apr	148.46	180.88	133.43	69.40	121.67	2,036.13	262.61	3.57	
May	144.99	176.02	127.63	68.66	120.35	1,988.91	256.12	3.80	
June	152.72	184.92	136.02	r 72.25	r 129.04	2,104.94	270.68	3.59	
July	152.12	184.09	136.49	71.50	129.99	2,104.22	269.05	3.65	
Week ended:									
1988: July 2 r	153.45	185.64	138.81	72.47	130.37	2,126.92	271.53	3.60	
9	153.94	186.39	139.46	72.18	131.27	2,129.40	272.41	3.59	
16	152.66	184.80	136.99	71.66	130.43	2,110.28	270.01	3.63	
23	151.47	183.28	135.46	71.22	129.55	2,094.67	267.83	3.63	
30	150.45	181.99	134.01	70.86	128.77	2,082.11	266.08	3.75	

1 Average of daily closing prices.
2 Includes all the stocks (more than 1,500) listed on the NYSE.
3 Includes 30 stocks.
4 Includes 500 stocks.
5 Standard & Poor's series. Dividend-price ratios based on Wednesday closing prices. Earnings-price ratios based on prices at end of quarter.

NOTE.—All data relate to stocks listed on the New York Stock Exchange (NYSE).

Sources: New York Stock Exchange, Dow-Jones & Company, Inc., and Standard & Poor's Corporation.

Source: *Economic Indicators*, Council of Economic Advisers.

NEW SECURITY ISSUES U.S. Corporations
Millions of dollars

Type of issue or issuer, or use	1985	1986	1987^r	1987 Aug.	1987 Sept.	1987 Oct.	1987 Nov.	1987 Dec.	1988 Jan.	1988 Feb.^{r}	1988 Mar.
1 **All issues**[1]	**239,015**	**423,726**	**391,154**	**21,888**	**29,363**	**20,710**	**14,322**	**11,872**	**22,175^r**	**22,364**	**25,787**
2 **Bonds**[2]	**203,500**	**355,293**	**324,646**	**17,685**	**23,705**	**17,631**	**13,624**	**11,098**	**19,485^r**	**18,474**	**20,815**
Type of offering											
3 Public, domestic	119,559	231,936	209,279	14,852	22,045	16,135	12,891	10,763	18,246^r	16,683	19,827
4 Private placement, domestic[3]	46,200	80,760	91,068	n.a.	n.a.	n.a.	n.a.	n.a.	n.a.	n.a.	n.a.
5. Sold abroad	37,781	42,596	24,299	2,833	1,660	1,496	733	335	1,239	1,791	988
Industry group											
6 Manufacturing	63,973	91,548	61,573	3,402^r	3,509^r	2,784^r	1,280	928^r	3,053^r	3,151	3,482
7 Commercial and miscellaneous	17,066	40,124	48,961	1,281	1,479	1,165	483	2,577	2,084	1,396	1,007
8 Transportation	6,020	9,971	11,974	296	25	263	0	226	0	200	1,017
9 Public utility	13,649	31,426	22,962	1,533	1,702	1,025	895	1,570	1,142	1,718	2,259
10 Communication	10,832	16,659	7,340	856	930	1,384	290	510	206	101	115
11 Real estate and financial	91,958	165,564	171,841	10,318^r	16,060^r	11,011^r	10,676	5,287^r	13,000^r	11,907	12,936
12 **Stocks**[3]	**35,515**	**68,433**	**66,508**	**4,203**	**5,658**	**3,079**	**698**	**774**	**2,690**	**3,890**	**4,972**
Type											
13 Preferred	6,505	11,514	10,123	906	1,112	236	162	61	1,388	376	625
14 Common	29,010	50,316	43,228	3,297	4,546	2,843	533	713	1,302	3,514	4,347
15 Private placement[3]	....	6,603	13,157	n.a.	n.a.	n.a.	n.a.	n.a.	n.a.	n.a.	n.a.
Industry group											
16 Manufacturing	5,700	15,027	13,880	370	858	703	237	76	268	296	258
17 Commercial and miscellaneous	9,149	10,617	12,888	996	807	656	86	14	360	44	99
18 Transportation	1,544	2,427	2,439	0	11	40	149	1	1	474	25
19 Public utility	1,966	4,020	4,322	85	529	75	25	0	100	142	93
20 Communication	978	1,825	1,458	277	75	107	1	11	60	0	63
21 Real estate and financial	16,178	34,517	31,521	2,475	3,378	1,498	200	672	1,901	2,933	4,434

1. Figures which represent gross proceeds of issues maturing in more than one year, are principal amount or number of units multiplied by offering price. Excludes secondary offerings, employee stock plans, investment companies other than closed-end, intracorporate transactions, equities sold abroad, and Yankee bonds. Stock data include ownership securities issued by limited partnerships.

2. Monthly data include only public offerings.

3. Data are not available on a monthly basis. Before 1987, annual totals include underwritten issues only.

SOURCES. IDD Information Services, Inc., U.S. Securities and Exchange Commission and the Board of Governors of the Federal Reserve System.

Source: *Federal Reserve Bulletin*, Board of Governors of the Federal Reserve System.

How to Understand and Analyze Financial Statements*

Fred B. Renwick†

Analyzing financial statements in corporate annual reports can be easy, fun, and rewarding, if you know what to look for. This short essay explains in a nutshell what to look for and how to analyze financial statements.

Only four statements are important to understand and analyze, namely:

- The *balance sheet*, which states the financial condition of the corporation as of one particular date: the date posted at the top of the statement.
- The *income statement*, which shows the amount of earnings for the year currently ending, and conveys information regarding the efficiency and profitability of the business.
- The *statement of retained earnings*, which gives further information regarding one of the lines on the balance sheet, and also shows the division of net income for the year between dividend payout to stockholders and earnings retained and reinvested in the business.
- The *statement of sources and uses of funds*, which gives further information regarding total current assets and total current liabilities as stated on the balance sheet; and shows the net changes during the year in working capital.

Additionally, corporate annual reports usually contain supplementary information which expands upon items in the four basic statements, and includes: (1) a letter or report of independent accountants and auditors addressed to stockholders and directors of the company certifying and validating the figures in the four statements, (2) notes which report material information regarding line items in each statement, (3) segment information which summarizes selected information by industry and geographic segments, (4) restatement pursuant to Financial Accounting Standards Board (FASB) *Statement of Financial Accounting Standards No. 33* to account for effects of inflation and changing prices on items in the four primary statements, and (5) a long-term (5 or 10-year) summary of selected items from the four primary statements.

The following section explains each statement in detail, Section II explains how to analyze the statements, Section III explains notes and supplementary information.

1. FOUR FINANCIAL STATEMENTS: WHAT TO LOOK FOR

BALANCE SHEETS

Exhibit 1 shows a balance sheet for Universal Manufacturing Corporation (UMC), a hypothetical company which produces and distributes goods and services in the health industry. Universal's single line of business is divided into two industry segments: human and animal health products, and environmental health products and services.

Observe the format of Universal's balance sheet, the *report form*, where total assets, $26 million, are itemized first and total financing (total liabilities and stockholders' equity), $26 million, are itemized below the asset section. Some corporations prefer to use the *account form*, where assets are listed on the left side of the form and liabilities and owners' equity sections are listed to the right of the asset section. UMC is using the *report form*.

The balance sheet shows the ownership of total corporate assets as of the date of the statement. For example, the following calculation implies that if UMC's tangible assets were liquidated as of the date posted at the top of the balance sheet, $17.8 million would be available for distribution among the preferred and common stockholders.

Total assets owned by UMC	$26,000,000
Less: Intangibles	200,000
Total tangible assets owned by UMC	$25,800,000
Amount required to pay total liabilities	8,000,000
Amount remaining for the stockholders	$17,800,000

Further, the above example illustrates a critical point: the difference between *current market value* (the amount UMC's assets would really bring if sold) versus the *accounting book value* (the $17.8 million). Relationships exist between market and book values, but accounting statements (except for FASB *No. 33*) are factual reports of *book*, not *market*, values of corporate assets.

The following paragraphs explain each line entry on balance sheets.

Starting at the top of the balance sheet, after the name of the corporation, title, and date of the statement, total assets are itemized, with current assets (total, $13.6 million) always first.

---

* See also the definition of financial terms, page 386.

† Fred B. Renwick is Professor of Finance at the Graduate School of Business Administration, New York University, New York, N.Y.

EXHIBIT 1

UNIVERSAL MANUFACTURING CORPORATION
Balance Sheet
December 31, 1983

Assets	**1983**	**1982**
Current assets		
Cash	$ 350,000	$ 250,000
Marketable securities at cost (market value: 1983, $2,980,000; 1982, $1,900,000)	2,850,000	1,830,000
Accounts receivable Less: Allowance for bad debt: 1983, $24,000; 1982, $21,000	4,800,000	4,370,000
Inventories	5,600,000	4,950,000
Total current assets	$13,600,000	$11,400,000
Fixed assets (property, plant, and equipment)		
Land	$ 734,000	$ 661,000
Building	5,762,000	5,258,000
Machinery	11,435,000	10,011,000
Office equipment	614,000	561,000
	18,545,000	16,491,000
Less: Accumulated depreciation	6,435,000	5,671,000
Net fixed assets	12,110,000	10,820,000
Prepayments and deferred charges	90,000	61,600
Intangibles (goodwill, patent, trademarks)	200,000	200,000
Total assets	$26,000,000	$22,481,600

Liabilities	**1983**	**1982**
Current liabilities		
Accounts payable	$ 2,910,000	$ 2,300,000
Notes payable	1,420,000	730,000
Accrued expenses payable	430,000	350,000
Federal income taxes payable	1,240,000	1,320,000
Total current liabilities	$ 6,000,000	$ 4,700,000
Long-term liabilities		
First mortgage bonds, 8% interest, due 2003	$ 2,000,000	$ 2,000,000
Total liabilities	$ 8,000,000	$ 6,700,000
Stockholders' Equity		
Capital stock		
Preferred stock, 6% cumulative, $100 par value each; authorized, issued, and outstanding 13,600 shares	1,360,000	1,360,000
Common stock, 30 cents par value each; authorized, issued, and outstanding 760,000 shares	228,000	228,000
Capital surplus	1,112,000	1,112,000
Accumulated retained earnings	15,300,000	13,081,600
Total stockholders' equity	$18,000,000	$15,781,600
Total liabilities and stockholders' equity	$26,000,000	$22,481,600

Current assets consist of:

1. *Cash*, $350,000, which is what you would expect, namely pocket-book currency and coins in the treasurer's office, plus demand deposits at a commercial bank. Cash is synonymous with liquidity,
2. *Marketable securities*, $2.85 million, which usually are cash equivalents or highly liquid securities such as Treasury Bills of the federal government or negotiable certificates of deposit (CDs), or demand notes issued by large corporations,
3. *Accounts receivable*, $4.8 million, which consist of payments due from customers who purchased UMC's goods and services on credit and have not paid yet but are scheduled to pay within the next few months. Since a small fraction of customers might never pay (because of death, financial disaster, flood, or other catastrophe), an allowance is made, $24,000, pursuant to good accounting practices for bad debts,
4. *Inventories*, $5.6 million, which consist of (*a*) finished goods in stock and ready for sale or shipment, (*b*) work and merchandise in process, and (*c*) supplies and raw materials inventories; and are priced on the balance sheet at the lower of cost or market on either a first-in-first-out (Fifo) or last-in-first-out (Lifo) basis. Pricing policy is usually stated in a note.

Total current assets, $13.6 million, are the sum of the four aforecited figures and usually are earmarked for use within the coming 12 months. In other words, *current* means within the next 12 months.

Fixed assets (property, plant and equipment) are the permanent tangible capital owned by the business, and are listed *at cost* (original purchase price) next on the balance sheet; and consists of:

1. *Land,* $734,000, or ground upon which buildings or other assets such as forests, air or water rights, and the like are built,
2. *Building,* $5.762 million, which are structures such as offices, warehouses, and the like where business is conducted,
3. *Machinery,* $11.435 million, which are mechanical apparatuses for increasing productivity and economic efficiency,
4. *Office equipment,* $614,000, which is what you would expect, namely desks, typewriters, copiers, and the like.

Accumulated depreciation, $6.435 million, is the total depreciation (deterioration of property, plant, and equipment due to physical wear and tear) accumulated to date for accounting purposes against UMC's assets. It is important to know about three concepts of depreciation, namely: (1) depreciation calculated for tax purposes which is figured pursuant to the Tax Code to benefit from allowable accelerated rates of depreciation, (2) accounting depreciation, which can be either straight-line or accelerated and is usually explained in a note, (3) economic depreciation, which comes from technological obsolescence and deterioration in ability to continue generating future income at current rates due to changes in demand and markets for the goods and services produced by UMC. The balance sheet states only number two, accounting depreciation.

Net fixed assets, $12,110,000, are the sum of the four above figures, minus accounting depreciation; and are used by the business to generate future (beyond the coming 12 months) income.

Prepayments and deferred charges, $90,000, state total amounts paid in advance for assets not yet obtained (such as paid-up premiums on a fire insurance policy covering the next five years, or rental paid on computers for the next three years); and for benefits to be received in future years for expenditures already made (such as for research and development, moving the business to a new location, or expenses incurred in bringing a new product to market).

Intangibles, $200,000, are assets such as goodwill, trademarks, franchises, patents, copyrights, and the like which have no physical existence; yet are valuable in producing business income.

Total assets, $26 million, are current, plus fixed, plus prepayments and deferred charges, plus intangibles; and state the size of the business and are the total property owned by the business.

Look next at the lower part of the balance sheet, which concerns the financing of the business. Financing must come from either borrowing (liabilities) or ownership equity.

Underneath the asset section of the balance sheet (or on the right side if the company uses the account form), total current liabilities, $6 million, always are itemized next, then long-term liabilities, $2 million, then finally stockholders' equity of $18 million.

Total current liabilities consist of bills due and payable by UMC within the next 12 months, all of which fall into one of four categories:

1. *Accounts payable,* $2.91 million, which are bills currently owed and due to creditors,
2. *Notes payable,* $1.42 million, which are current obligations owed to a bank or other short-term lender,
3. *Accrued expenses payable,* $430,000, include wages due employees, fees to attorneys, current pension or retirement obligations, and the like.
4. *Federal income taxes payable,* $1.24 million, is the current tax payable to the Internal Revenue Service, and is sufficiently important to merit a line of its own on the corporate balance sheet.

Long-term liabilities, $2 million for UMC, can include straight debt (like UMC's which pays 8 percent interest and matures in 2003), convertible bonds (bonds which pay interest like straight bonds but are convertible upon demand of the bond owner into a stated number of shares of common stock), or "other" long-term debt (like pollution control and industrial revenue bonds or sinking-fund debentures). UMC has only straight debt outstanding.

Total liabilities, $8 million, are the sum of current and long-term liabilities and constitute the total financing obtained from borrowings.

Stockholders' equity, $18 million consists of:

1. *Capital stock,* $1.588 million, which includes both preferred stock and common stock but no convertible preferred stock and no warrants or rights to purchase either bonds or common stock,
2. *Capital surplus,* $1.112 million, which is the amount paid in by shareholders over the par or legal value of 30 cents for each common share,
3. *Accumulated retained earnings,* $15.3 million, which are earnings not paid out in dividends but have been retained and reinvested in the business. Further information regarding accumulated retained earnings since inception of the business is set forth below in the *statement of retained earnings.*

Capital stock represents proprietary interest in the company, is represented by stock certificates authorized and issued by the company, and can belong to either of several classes, including:

1. *Preferred stock,* which has preference or takes priority over other shares regarding dividend payout (6 percent in UMC's case), and which can be cumulative, which means that if the company fails to pay dividends for whatever reason for any year, then the 6 percent of $100 or $6 per preferred share accumulates on the books and must be paid before common stockholders can receive future dividends. Total preferred stock authorized and issued by UMC is $100 per share times 13,600 shares or $1.36 million.
2. *Common stock,* which represents the remaining ownership of the company and is entitled to receive a dividend along with fluctuations in value of the stock. Par value is the legal stated value of each common share; so the par value (30 cents per share times 760,000 shares or $228,000) plus the additional amount or capital surplus ($1.112 million) together state the amount UMC received upon issuing 760,000 shares, namely $1.34 million divided by 760,000 or $1.76 per share.

The bottom line, *total liabilities and stockholders equity,* states the financing of the corporation, and shows where UMC obtained the $26 million to buy the total assets itemized at the top of the balance sheet.

We turn next to income statements.

INCOME STATEMENTS

Exhibit 2 shows UMC's income statement, where the important items to look for, after the name of the company, the title, and date of the statement at the heading, are:

1. *Net sales,* which is where most of the business revenue comes from for most businesses, except rental and leasing companies, $23,850,000.
2. *Net Operating Income* (NOI) or profit before interest and taxes, which states profit from business operations, without regard to financing, $5,878,000.
3. *Total Income* before interest and taxes, which states the return on total capital available to the business during the year, $6,220,000.
4. *Less:* provision for federal income tax, $2,240,000.
5. *Total Income,* after tax but before interest deduction, which states the after-tax profitability of the corporation and is widely used in computing cost of capital for a business enterprise, $3,980,000.

EXHIBIT 2

UNIVERSAL MANUFACTURING CORPORATION
Consolidated Income Statement
December 31, 1983 and 1982

	1983	1982
Net sales	$23,850,000	$19,810,000
Cost of sales and operating expenses		
Cost of goods sold	8,940,000	7,209,000
Depreciation	800,000	750,000
Selling and administrating expenses	8,232,000	6,814,000
Operating profit	$ 5,878,000	$ 5,037,000
Other income		
Dividends and interest	342,000	183,000
Total Income	$ 6,220,000	$ 5,220,000
Less: Interest on bonds	160,000	160,000
Income before provision for federal income tax	$ 6,060,000	$ 5,060,000
Provision for federal income tax	2,240,000	1,980,000
Net profit for year	$ 3,820,000	$ 3,080,000
Common shares outstanding	760,000	760,000
Net earnings per share	$ 4.92	$ 3.95

Statement of Accumulated Retained Earnings

	1983	1982
Balance January 1	$13,081,600	$11,413,200
Net profit for year	3,820,000	3,080,000
Total	$16,901,600	$14,493,200
Less: Dividends paid on		
Preferred stock	81,600	81,600
Common stock	1,520,000	1,330,000
Balance December 31	$15,300,000	$13,081,600

6. *Net income* (NI) or profit for the year, which states earnings after taxes and after all fixed charges. The net profit for the year is available for (a) dividend payout to preferred stockholders, (b) dividend payout to common stockholders, and (c) retention and reinvestment in the business, $3,820,000.
7. *Net earnings per share* (EPS), which equals total earnings available for distribution to common stockholders ($3.82 million minus 6% dividend owed on 13,600 shares of $100 par value preferred stock, or $3,738,400), divided by 760,000 common shares outstanding, $4.92.

$$\$3,820,000 - 0.06(13,600)(\$100) = \$3,738,400$$

$$\$3,738,400/760,000 = \$4.92 \text{ per share}$$

Cost of sales and operating expenses falls into one of three categories:

1. *Cost of goods sold,* which states the amount of labor, material, and other expenses in producing the items sold, $8,940,000.
2. *Depreciation expense,* which states the amount of capital (producer's durables) consumed in producing the goods and services sold and which must be replaced or restored to its original capacity, $800,000.
3. *Selling and administrating expenses,* which includes office expenses, executives salaries, salespersons salaries, advertising and promotion expenses and the like, $8,232,000.

Operating profit, also called net operating income, $5.878 million, is the income from business operations, and is an important indicator of how efficiently the fixed assets were employed during the year.

Other income, $342,000, is from UMC's marketable securities of $1.83 million at cost as of one year ago.

Total income, $6.22 million, is the sum of operating profit from the business and income from other sources.

Interest on bonds, $160,000, (8 percent of 2 million) is itemized next on the income statement, followed by:

Income after interest, before tax	$6,060,000
Provision for federal income tax	2,240,000
Net profit for the year	3,820,000
Net earnings per share	$4.92

We turn next to statements of accumulated retained earnings.

STATEMENTS OF ACCUMULATED RETAINED EARNINGS

The bottom part of Exhibit 2 contains the accumulated retained earnings statement for UMC, and shows at the beginning of the balance, since the starting date of the business to January 1 of the current year, $13,081,600—to which is added the net profit for the year, $3,820,000, to get total accumulated retained earnings of $16,901,600.

Dividends paid to stockholders are itemized next:

Preferred stock dividend: 6 percent of $1,360,000	$ 81,600
Common stock dividend: $2.00 per share declared times 760,000 shares	1,520,000
Total dividends paid	$1,601,600

Balance, December 31 (15.3 million) equals the difference between the total available ($16,901,600) and total dividends paid. Retained earnings are an important source of finance of corporate capital assets.

We turn next to statements of sources and uses of funds.

STATEMENT OF SOURCE AND APPLICATION OF FUNDS

Exhibit 3 is a statement of source and application or use of funds for UMC. Ordinarily, *funds* imply cash; but in a broader sense, *funds* include cash equivalents and substitutes for cash, such as short-term credit, notes, and account payable and accrued liabilities to meet the short-term financing needs of the business. So *funds* in the broader sense imply net *working capital,* which is the difference between current assets and current liabilities.

Sources of funds in general include transactions which increase the amount of working capital, such as:

1. Net profit from operations.
2. Sale or consumption of noncurrent assets.
3. Long-term borrowing.
4. Issuing additional shares of capital stock.
5. Annual depreciation.

Uses of funds in general include transactions which decrease working capital, such as:

1. Declaring cash dividends.
2. Repaying long-term debt.
3. Buying noncurrent assets.
4. Repurchasing outstanding capital stock.

In the case of UMC and Exhibit 3, funds were provided by net income, $3.82 million, and current depreciation expense, $800,000. Some analysts worry that depreciation is not cash, depreciation is a bookkeeping entry. But the capital was consumed in the process of producing the goods and services sold; so the business pays the cash to itself to ultimately replace the consumed capital. Depreciation expense is a source of funds.

Total funds provided for UMC are $4,620,000.

EXHIBIT 3

UNIVERSAL MANUFACTURING CORPORATION
Statement of Source and Application of Funds
December 31, 1983

	1983	
Funds were provided by		
Net income	$3,820,000	
Depreciation	800,000	
Total		$4,620,000
Funds were used for		
Dividends on preferred stock	$ 81,600	
Dividends on common stock	1,520,000	
Plant and equipment	1,720,300	
Sundry assets	398,100	
Total		$3,720,000
Increase in Working Capital		$ 900,000
Analysis of changes in working capital—1983		
Changes in current assets		
Cash	$ 100,000	
Marketable securities	1,020,000	
Accounts receivable	430,000	
Inventories	650,000	
Total		$2,200,000
Changes in current liabilities		
Accounts payable	$ 610,000	
Notes payable	690,000	
Accrued expenses payable	80,000	
Federal income tax payable	(80,000)	
Total		$1,300,000

Uses of funds are itemized next, where all uses fall into one of four categories:

Dividends on preferred stock	$ 81,600
Dividends on common stock	1,520,000
Plant and equipment	1,720,300
Sundry assets	398,100
Total uses or application of funds	$3,720,000

Increase in working capital, $900,000, is the difference between the total funds provided, $4.62 million, and the total funds used, $3.72 million.

An *analysis of changes in working capital* for the year is included in the statement of source and application of funds, and gives further information regarding the $900,000 increase in working capital, which is explained by analyzing changes in current assets together with changes in current liabilities.

Changes in current assets total $2.2 million, itemized as follows:

1. *Cash* increased from $250,000 to $350,000, giving a net change of $100,000,
2. *Marketable securities* increased from $1.83 million to $2.85 million, giving a net change of $1.02 million,
3. *Accounts receivable* increased from $4.37 million to $4.8 million, giving a net change of $430,000,
4. *Inventories* increased from $4.95 million to $5.6 million, giving a net change of $650,000.

Changes in current liabilities total $1.3 million, itemized as follows:

1. *Accounts payable* increased from $2.3 million to $2.91 million, giving a net change of $610,000,
2. *Notes payable* increased from $730,000 to $1.42 million, giving a net change of $690,000,
3. *Accrued expenses payable* increased from $350,000 to $430,000, giving a net change of $80,000,
4. *Federal income taxes payable* decreased from $1.32 million to $1.24 million, giving a net change of ($80,000).

The difference between the changes in current assets ($2.2 million) and changes in current liabilities ($1.3 million) equals the $900,000 increase in working capital.

We turn next to understanding more regarding how to analyze financial statements.

II. ANALYZING FINANCIAL STATEMENTS

The analysis of all four statements consists primarily of calculating ratios; but other methods including the time trend of the ratio, information theory, and flow-of-funds analysis are sometimes used. We shall limit our analysis to using ratios.[1]

In general, financial analysts, investors, creditors, and others look for two kinds of information regarding business enterprises:

1. *Risk,* including financial, business, market, and country or political risks,
2. *Return,* including productivity, efficiency, and profitability of corporate capital investments.

A third factor, *growth rate,* is important too, primarily because high steady growth is usually worth more than low or no growth.

BALANCE SHEET RATIOS

Balance sheet ratios belong to one of the three following categories:

1. *Liquidity and turnover ratios,* which indicate the ability of the corporation to pay current liabilities,
2. *Capitalization,* also called *leverage,* or *debt ratios,* which is the amount of borrowing relative to other factors such as total capitalization, total assets, or total equity,
3. *Net asset ratios,* which indicate the amount of assets backing each class of outstanding securities.

Liquidity ratios are calculated to judge whether the corporation owns sufficient cash and cash-equivalents or substitutes to comfortably pay short-term obligations, and include:

1. *Current liquidity,* the ability to pay current liabilities from current assets:

Current ratio:

$$\frac{\text{Current assets}}{\text{Current liabilities}} = \frac{\$13{,}600{,}000}{\$\ 6{,}000{,}000} = 2.3 \text{ to } 1$$

In total dollar amounts, the numerator in the current ratio, minus the denominator, states *net working capital,* where

Total current assets	$13,600,000
Less: Total current liabilities	6,000,000
Working capital	$ 7,600,000

2. *Quick asset* (sometimes called *acid test*) *ratio:*

$$\frac{\text{Quick assets}}{\text{Current liabilities}} = \frac{\$8{,}000{,}000}{\$6{,}000{,}000} = 1.33$$

Where quick assets are total current assets minus inventories, because inventories usually are less liquid than either cash, marketable securities, or accounts receivable:

Total current assets	$13,600,000	
Less: Inventories	5,600,000	
Quick assets		$8,000,000
Less: Total current liabilities		6,000,000
Net quick assets		$2,000,000

3. The *cash plus marketable securities ratio* indicates the firm's ability to pay current liabilities without relying on either inventories or accounts receivable:

$$\frac{\text{Cash plus marketable securities}}{\text{Total current liabilities}} = \frac{\$3{,}200{,}000}{\$6{,}000{,}000} = 0.53$$

Liquidity and turnover of inventories ratios indicate how close inventories approximate true liquidity through total sales, and are the three following figures:

1. *Inventory as a percent of total current assets:*

$$\frac{\text{Inventory}}{\text{Total current assets}} = \frac{\$5{,}600{,}000}{\$13{,}600{,}000} = 41.18 \text{ percent}$$

2. *Cost of goods sold,* including depreciation and capital consumption, *to average inventory ratio:*

$$\frac{\text{Cost of goods sold plus depreciation}}{\text{Inventory}} = \frac{\$9{,}740{,}000}{\$5{,}600{,}000} = 1.74$$

3. *Inventory turnover ratio:*

$$\frac{\text{Net sales}}{\text{Inventory}} = \frac{\$23{,}850{,}000}{\$5{,}600{,}000} = 4.26 \text{ times}$$

Liquidity of receivables ratios indicate how close accounts receivable approximate true liquidity through total sales, and are the two following figures:

1. Average collection period ratio, which indicates the number of day's sales in accounts receivables:

$$\frac{\text{Receivables} \times \text{Days in year}}{\text{Annual sales}} = \frac{\$4{,}800{,}000 \times 360}{\$23{,}850{,}000} = 72.45$$

2. Accounts receivable turnover ratio:

$$\frac{\text{Annual sales}}{\text{Accounts receivable}} = \frac{\$23{,}850{,}000}{\$4{,}800{,}000} = 4.97$$

Liquidity and turnover of tangible and fixed asset ratios indicate relationships between total sales and total assets, and are given by the following two figures:

1. Fixed asset turnover ratio:

$$\frac{\text{Sales}}{\text{Net fixed assets}} = \frac{\$23{,}850{,}000}{\$12{,}110{,}000} = 1.97$$

2. Total asset turnover ratio:

[1] Comparison of these ratios with those typical of the industry is very helpful. Typical values are given on page 114. More detailed tabulations are provided by Dun & Bradstreet and Robert Morris Associates.

$$\frac{\text{Net sales}}{\text{Average total tangible assets}} = \frac{\$23{,}850{,}000}{\$25{,}800{,}000} = 0.9244$$

Capitalization ratios include:

1. Debt ratio:

$$\frac{\text{Total liabilities}}{\text{Total assets}} = \frac{\$8{,}000{,}000}{\$26{,}000{,}000} = 30.77 \text{ percent}$$

2. Current liabilities as a percent of total liabilities:

$$\frac{\text{Current liabilities}}{\text{Total liabilities}} = \frac{\$6{,}000{,}000}{\$8{,}000{,}000} = 75 \text{ percent}$$

3. Debt-to-net-worth ratio:

$$\frac{\text{Total liabilities}}{\text{Net Worth}} = \frac{\$8{,}000{,}000}{\$18{,}000{,}000} = 0.4444$$

4. Long-term debt capitalization ratio:

$$\frac{\text{Long-term debt}}{\text{Total capitalization}} = \frac{\$2{,}000{,}000}{\$19{,}800{,}000} = 10.10 \text{ percent}$$

5. Preferred stock ratio:

$$\frac{\text{Preferred stock}}{\text{Total capitalization}} = \frac{\$1{,}360{,}000}{\$19{,}800{,}000} = 6.87 \text{ percent}$$

6. Common stock ratio:

$$\frac{\text{Common stock plus accumulated earnings}}{\text{Total capitalization}} = \frac{\$16{,}440{,}000}{\$19{,}800{,}000} = 83.03 \text{ percent}$$

7. Summary:

Total assets	$26,000,000	
Less: Intangibles	$ 200,000	
Less: Total current liabilities	$ 6,000,000	
Total capitalization	$19,800,000	100.00%
Bonds (long-term debt)	2,000,000	10.10
Preferred stock	1,360,000	6.87
Common stock (including capital surplus and retained earnings)	16,440,000	83.03

8. Long-term debt as a percent of total liabilities:

$$\frac{\text{Long-term debt}}{\text{Total liabilities}} = \frac{\$2{,}000{,}000}{\$8{,}000{,}000} = 25.00 \text{ percent}$$

Net asset value ratios include:

1. Net asset value per $1,000 bond; $9,900 per bond.

$$\frac{\text{Net tangible assets available to meet bondholders' claims}}{\text{Number of \$1,000 bonds outstanding}} = \frac{\$19{,}800{,}000}{2{,}000{,}000}$$

where the numerator is calculated as follows:

Total assets	$26,000,000
Less: Intangibles	200,000
Total tangible assets	$25,800,000
Less: Current liabilities	6,000,000
Net tangible assets available to meet bondholders' claims	$19,800,000

2. Net asset value per share of preferred stock: $1,308.82

$$\frac{\text{Net assets backing the preferred stock}}{\text{Number of shares of preferred stock outstanding}} = \frac{\$17{,}800{,}000}{13{,}600}$$

where the numerator is calculated as follows:

Total assets	$26,000,000
Less: Intangibles	200,000
Total tangible assets	$25,800,000
Less: Current liabilities	6,000,000
Less: Long-term liabilities	2,000,000
Net assets backing the preferred stock	$17,800,000

3. Net book value per share of common stock: $21.63

$$\frac{\text{Net assets available for the common stock}}{\text{Total number of shares outstanding}} = \frac{\$16{,}440{,}000}{760{,}000} = \$21.63$$

where the numerator is calculated as follows:

Total assets	$26,000,000
Less: Intangibles	200,000
Total tangible assets	$25,800,000
Less: Current liabilities	6,000,000
Less: Long-term liabilities	2,000,000
Less preferred stock	1,360,000
Net assets available for the common stock	$16,440,000

Finally, estimate the youngest average plant age by dividing the current (1983) depreciation expense accrual ($800,000 from the Statement of Source and Application of Funds) into accumulated depreciation ($6,435,000 from the Balance Sheet) to get 8.04 years. Because some plants and pieces of equipment may have been fully written off over time, we can say that UMC's Fixed Assets, on average, are over 8 years old.

INCOME STATEMENT RATIOS

Income statement ratios belong to one of the two following categories:

1. *Coverage*, which analyzes financial risk by relating the financial charges of a corporation to its ability to service them.
2. *Productivity* or *capital efficiency ratios*, which relate income to total sales and to investment.

Coverage ratios include:

1. Interest coverage ratio: 38.875

$$\frac{\text{Net operating income before interest and taxes}}{\text{Interest charges on bonds}} = \frac{\$6,220,000}{\$160,000} = 38.875$$

2. Cash flow coverage ratio, which indicates the firm's ability to service debt, which is related to both interest and principal payments and is not met out of earnings per se, but out of cash: 19.5 times.

$$\frac{\text{Annual cash flow before interest and taxes}}{\text{Interest on bonds plus principal repayments}/(1-T)} = \frac{\$7,020,000}{\$\ 360,000} = 19.5$$

where:

Net operating income before interest and taxes	$6,220,000	
Plus annual depreciation expense	800,000	
Annual cash flow before interest and taxes	$7,020,000	
Face value 20-year 8% bonds due 2003	$2,000,000	
Annual Repayment rate after taxes $2,000,000 divided by 20 years	100,000	
Before tax annual bond repayment rate $100,000 divided by 1 minus the effective tax rate, say 50 %		$200,000
Plus: 8% interest on $2,000,000		160,000
Interest plus principal repayments		$360,000

Since interest payments are made before taxes, the adjustment is necessary to convert principal repayments which are made after taxes to before-tax equivalents.

3. Preferred dividend coverage ratio: 46.81

$$\frac{\text{Income available for paying preferred dividends}}{\text{Total dividends to preferred shareholders}} = \frac{\$3,820,000}{\$81,600} = 46.81$$

4. Earnings per common share: $4.92

$$\frac{\text{Earnings available for distribution to common shareholders}}{\text{Total number of common shares outstanding}} = \frac{\$3,738,400}{760,000} = \$4.92$$

where:

Net profit for the year	$3,820,000
Less: Dividend requirements on preferred stock	81,600
Earnings available for common stock	$3,738,400

5. Primary earnings for the year: $4.94

$$\frac{\text{Earnings for the year}}{\text{Common stock plus stock equivalents}} = \frac{\$3,820,000}{773,500} = \$4.94$$

Assuming the 13,600 preferred shares had been convertible and converted, on a share-for-share basis, into common stock.

13,600 + 760,000 = 773,600 common shares after conversion

6. Fully diluted earnings per share: $4.79

$$\frac{\text{Adjusted earnings}}{\text{Adjusted shares outstanding}} = \frac{\$3,900,000}{813,600} = \$4.79$$

where:

Earnings for the year	$3,820,000
Plus: interest on convertible bonds	$ 160,000
Less: income tax applicable to interest deduction	80,000
Adjusted earnings for the year	$3,900,000
Common shares outstanding	760,000
Preferred convertible stock equivalent common shares	13,600
Twenty common shares per $1,000 convertible bond (2,000) outstanding ..	40,000
Adjusted shares outstanding	813,600

7. Summary:

Earnings per share	$4.92
Primary earnings	4.94
Fully diluted earnings	4.79

8. Price-earnings ratio: Approximately 15 times

$$\frac{\text{Market price of stock}}{\text{Earnings per share}} = \frac{\$72.25}{\$4.92} = 14.69$$

Productivity or capital efficiency ratios include:

1. Operating margin of profit: 24.65%.

$$\frac{\text{Operating profit}}{\text{Sales}} = \frac{\$5,878,000}{\$23,850,000} = 24.65\%$$

Previous year:

$$= \frac{\$5,037,000}{\$19,810,000} = 25.43\%$$

2. Operating cost ratio: 75.35%.

	Amount	Ratio
Net sales	$23,850,000	100.00%
Operating costs............	17,972,000	75.35
Operating profit	$ 5,878,000	24.65%

3. Net profit ratio: 16.02%.

$$\frac{\text{Net profit for the year}}{\text{Net sales}} = \frac{\$3,820,000}{\$23,850,000} = 16.02\%$$

Previous year: 15.55%

$$=\frac{\$3{,}080{,}000}{\$19{,}810{,}000}=15.55\%$$

RATIOS FROM STATEMENTS OF ACCUMULATED RETAINED EARNINGS

Retained earnings statements ratios belong to one of the two following categories:

1. Dividend payout ratio.
2. Earnings retention ratio.

The dividend payout ratio for UMC is: 40.66%.

$$\frac{\text{Dividends paid to common stockholders}}{\text{Income available for common stockholders}}=\frac{\$1{,}520{,}000}{\$3{,}738{,}400}=40.66\%$$

where:

Net profit for the year	$3,820,000
Dividends on preferred stock	81,600
Earnings available for common	$3,738,400

The earnings retention ratio for UMC is: 59.34%.

$$\frac{\text{Earnings retained}}{\text{Earnings available for payout}}=\frac{\$2{,}218{,}400}{\$3{,}738{,}400}=59.34\%$$

where:

Net profit for the year	$3,820,000
Less: Dividends paid on preferred stock	$ 81,600
Less: Dividends paid on common stock	1,520,000
Earnings retained	$2,218,400

Summary:

Dividend payout ratio	40.66%
Earnings retention ratio	59.34
Earnings available	100.00%

Dividends per share: $2.00.

$$\frac{\text{Total dividends paid to common shareholders}}{\text{Number of common shares outstanding}}=\frac{\$1{,}520{,}000}{760{,}000}=\$2.00$$

Balance December 31, $15,300,000.

RATIOS FROM STATEMENTS OF SOURCE AND APPLICATION OF FUNDS

Since an analysis was stated directly on the statement of source and use of funds in Exhibit 3, that part of the analysis is completed; however we still need to calculate profitability ratios which belong to one of the two following categories:

1. Return on assets.
2. Return on equity.

Return on assets ratios include:

Return on total assets: 27.67%.

$$\frac{\text{Total income}}{\text{Last year's total assets}}=\frac{\$6{,}220{,}000}{\$22{,}481{,}600}=27.67\%$$

After tax return on total assets: 17.70%.

$$\frac{\text{Total income after tax but before interest}}{\text{Last year's total assets}}=\frac{\$3{,}980{,}000}{\$22{,}481{,}600}=17.70\%$$

where:

Total income	$6,220,000
Less: Provision for total taxes	2,240,000
After tax total income	$3,980,000

Return on equity ratio: 25.92%.

$$\frac{\text{Income available for distribution to common stockholders}}{\text{Last year's total equity of common stockholders}}=\frac{\$3{,}738{,}400}{\$14{,}421{,}600}=25.92\%$$

where:

Last year's total stockholder equity	$15,781,600
Less: Preferred stock value	1,360,000
Last year's common stock equity	$14,421,600

We turn next to further discussion of notes and supplemental information.

III. NOTES AND SUPPLEMENTAL INFORMATION

As explained in the introduction, financial statements in corporate annual reports usually are accompanied by:

- A *report of independent accountants and auditors* certifying the statements conform to generally accepted accounting principles and that generally accepted auditing standards and procedures were used.
- *Notes* which further explain details and disclose relevant information regarding line items on all four statements.
- *Segment information*, which summarizes selected items by business, industry, and geographic segment.
- A *restatement* of almost everything in current (in contrast with the traditional historical original purchase) prices, and to account for the effects of inflation on items reported in the standard statements.
- *Long-term record* summarizing selected items over a five- or ten-year time span.

EXHIBIT 4
SEGMENT REPORTING AND FOREIGN OPERATIONS

	Industry Segments			Georgraphic Segments				
					Foreign			
	Segment No. 1	Segment No. 2	Consolidated	Domestic	OECD	Other	Eliminations	Consolidated
1983								
Sales, unaffiliated customers	$20,044,000	$3,806,000	$23,850,000	$12,647,000	$ 9,029,000	$2,175,000		$23,850,000
Sales, intersegment				2,171,000	346,000	21,000	($2,539,000)	
Total sales	$20,044,000	$3,806,000	$23,850,000	$14,818,000	$ 9,375,000	$2,196,000	($2,539,000)	$23,850,000
Pretax operating income	5,435,000	443,000	5,878,000	3,690,000	1,820,000	211,000	157,000	5,878,000
Identifiable assets at December 31	21,700,000	4,300,000	26,000,000	16,549,000	10,168,000	2,353,000	(3,070,000)	26,000,000
Depreciation expense	666,000	134,000	800,000					
Capital spending	1,884,300	234,100	2,118,400					
1982								
Sales, unaffiliated customers	$16,629,000	$3,181,000	$19,810,000	$10,519,000	$ 7,511,000	$1,780,000		$19,810,000
Sales, intersegment				2,614,000	246,000	14,000	($2,878,000)	
Total sales	$16,629,000	$3,181,000	$19,810,000	$13,133,000	$ 7,757,000	$1,794,000	($2,878,000)	$19,810,000
Pretax operating income	4,627,000	410,000	5,037,000	3,512,000	1,449,000	126,000	(50,000)	5,037,000
Identifiable assets at December 31	19,027,000	3,473,000	22,500,000	14,728,000	8,660,000	2,005,000	(2,893,000)	22,500,000
Depreciation expense	611,000	127,000	738,000					
Capital spending	1,751,000	190,000						
1981								
Sales, unaffiliated customers	$14,461,000	$2,779,000	$17,240,000	$ 9,504,000	$ 6,152,000	$1,584,000		$17,240,000
Sales, intersegment				2,677,000	155,000	3,000	($2,835,000)	
Total sales	$14,461,000	$2,779,000	$17,240,000	$12,181,000	$ 6,307,000	$1,587,000	($2,835,000)	$17,240,000
Pretax operating income	4,163,000	378,000	4,541,000	3,552,000	1,234,000	119,000	(364,000)	4,541,000
Identifiable assets at December 31	16,614,000	3,341,000	19,955,000	13,627,000	7,818,000	1,590,000	(3,179,000)	19,955,000
Depreciation expense	551,000	102,000	653,000					
Capital spending	1,969,000	238,000	2,207,000					

REPORT OF INDEPENDENT ACCOUNTANTS

A typical report of independent accountants is addressed to the stockholders and board of directors of the corporation and will read as follows:

"In our opinion, the accompanying consolidated financial statements, appearing on pages — through —, present fairly the financial position of Universal Manufacturing Corporation and its subsidiary companies at December 31, 1983 and 1982, and the results of their operations and changes in financial position for the years then ended, in conformity with generally accepted accounting principles consistently applied. Also, in our opinion, the five-year comparative consolidated summary of operations presents fairly the financial information included therein. Our examinations of these statements were made in accordance with generally accepted auditing standards and accordingly included such tests of the accounting records and such other auditing procedures as we considered necessary in the circumstances."

The report will be signed with the name and address of the accounting firm and dated.

EXHIBIT 5

UNIVERSAL MANUFACTURING CORPORATION
SCHEDULE OF INCOME FROM CONTINUING OPERATIONS
AND OTHER CHANGES IN SHAREHOLDERS' EQUITY
ADJUSTED FOR EFFECTS OF CHANGING PRICES
For the Year Ended December 31, 1983

			Adjusted for	
		As Reported (historical cost)	**General Inflation (constant 1983 $)**	**Specific (current) Costs**
Income from continuing operations				
Net sales	$23,850,000			
Other income	342,000			
Total revenue from continuing operations		$24,192,000	$24,192,000	$24,192,000
Costs and other deductions				
Depreciation expenses		800,000	1,076,000	1,115,000
Other costs and expenses		17,172,000	17,699,000	17,273,000
Interest expense		160,000	160,000	160,000
Federal and foreign income taxes		2,240,000	2,240,000	2,240,000
Total costs and other deductions		$20,372,000	$21,175,000	$20,788,000
Net income from continuing operations		$ 3,820,000	$ 3,017,000	$ 3,404,000
Purchasing power gain on net monetary liabilities (Net amounts owed)			1,000	1,000
Increase in current cost of inventories and property, plant and equipment during 1983				1,911,000
Less: effect of increase in general price level during 1983				2,788,000
Excess of increase in specific prices over increase in the general price level				($ 877,000)
Net income		$ 3,820,000		
Adjusted net income			$ 3,018,000	
Net change in shareholders' equity from above		$ 3,820,000	$ 3,018,000	$ 2,528,000

Summarized Balance Sheet
Adjusted for Changing Prices
At December 31, 1983

		Adjusted for	
	As reported	**General Inflation (constant 1983 $)**	**Specific (current) Costs**
Assets			
Inventories	$ 5,600,000	$ 6,175,000	$ 5,670,000
Property, plant and equipment	12,110,000	13,354,000	16,327,000
All other assets	8,290,000	9,141,000	7,506,000
Total assets	$26,000,000	$28,670,000	$29,503,000
Total liabilities	8,000,000	7,600,000	7,600,000
Shareholders' equity	$18,000,000	$21,070,000	$21,903,000

EXHIBIT 5 *(concluded)*

Supplementary financial data
Five-Year Comparison of Selected Data
Adjusted for Changing Prices

	Years Ended December 31				
	1979	**1980**	**1981**	**1982**	**1983**
Sales					
As reported	$14,020,000	$15,610,000	$17,240,000	$19,810,000	$23,850,000
1983 constant dollars	19,543,000	20,211,000	20,063,000	20,970,000	23,850,000
Net income					
As reported					$ 3,820,000
1983 constant dollars					3,017,000
Current costs					3,404,000
Earnings per share					
As reported					$4.92
1983 constant dollars					3.86
Current costs					4.37
Common stock dividends declared per share					
As reported	$1.40	$1.43	$1.55	$1.75	$2.00
1983 constant dollars	1.95	1.85	1.80	1.85	2.00
Net assets at year-end					
As reported					$18,000,000
1983 constant dollars					21,070,000
Current costs					21,903,000
Purchasing power gain on net monetary liabilities					1,000
Market price per common share at year-end					
Actual	$69.25	$68.13	$55.50	$67.63	$72.25
1983 constant dollars	90.50	84.95	64.00	72.45	68.50
Average consumer price index*	181.5	195.4	217.4	239.0	253.0

* Hypothetical, for illustrative purposes only.

NOTES TO FINANCIAL STATEMENTS

Notes disclose additional information regarding entries in all four primary statements, and usually are considered an integral part of the statements, included in and covered by the auditor's certification. Some corporations include the next three items to be discussed, segment information, effects of inflation, and long-term comparative summary of operations, in the notes. If included in some place other than the notes, then look for whether the statement was excluded from the auditor's audit.

SEGMENT INFORMATION

Notes disclosing geographic area and industry segment information usually summarize selected items such as net sales, operating income, total assets, depreciation and amortization, and capital expenditures for industry segments (business segments or product groups) and foreign operations.

Exhibit 4 shows the segment information for UMC's two segments.

As you can see from Exhibit 4, industry segment number one, Human and Animal Health Products, accounts for 84 percent ($20,044,000 divided by $23,850,000) of total sales, and 92 percent ($5,435,000 divided by $5,878,000) of UMC's operating income; all supported by 83.46 percent ($21,700,000 divided by $26,000,000) of total assets. Eleven percent ($234,100 divided by $2,118,400) of total capital expenditures were made in industry segment number two, Environmental Health Products and Services for the treatment of water and air pollution.

Exhibit 4 also shows, based on the following ratios, that UMC's business is roughly 60 percent domestic United States; 40 percent nondomestic:

Net Sales:

$$\frac{\text{United States}}{\text{Total company}} = \frac{\$14{,}818{,}000}{\$23{,}850{,}000} = 62.13\%$$

Operating income:

$$\frac{\text{United States}}{\text{Total company}} = \frac{\$3{,}690{,}000}{\$5{,}037{,}000} = 62.78\%$$

Total assets:

$$\frac{\text{United States}}{\text{Total company}} = \frac{\$16{,}549{,}000}{\$26{,}000{,}000} = 63.65\%$$

SUPPLEMENTAL INFORMATION ON INFLATION ACCOUNTING

Pursuant to Financial Accounting Standards Board (FASB) *Statement of Financial Accounting Standards No. 33*, public enterprises that have either (1) inventories and property, plant, and equipment (before deducting accumulated

EXHIBIT 6

TEN-YEAR FINANCIAL SUMMARY
UNIVERSAL MANUFACTURING CORPORATION

	1983	1982	1981	1980	1979	1978	1977	1976	1975	1974
Net sales	$23,850,000	$19,810,000	$17,240,000	$15,610,000	$14,020,000	$12,604,000	$11,040,000	$ 9,426,000	$ 8,324,000	$ 7,611,000
Total income before tax	6,060,000	5,060,000	4,535,000	4,164,000	3,783,000	3,619,000	3,195,000	2,747,000	2,521,000	2,286,000
Net profit for the year	3,820,000	3,080,000	2,775,000	2,555,000	2,288,000	2,105,000	1,827,000	1,512,000	1,314,000	1,179,000
Earnings per share	4.92	3.95	3.56	3.28	2.94	2.71	2.36	1.95	1.70	1.53
Dividends per share	2.00	1.75	1.55	1.43	1.40	1.40	1.24	1.12	1.10	1.03
Net working capital	7,600,000	6,700,000	6,300,000	5,500,000	5,023,000	3,596,000	3,424,000	2,964,000	2,604,000	2,261,000
Total assets	26,000,000	22,481,600	19,934,000	17,594,000	15,390,000	12,433,000	9,890,000	8,348,000	7,365,000	6,643,000
Net plant and equipment	12,110,000	10,820,000	9,918,000	8,747,000	6,743,000	4,740,000	3,635,000	3,150,000	2,830,000	2,479,000
Long term debt	2,000,000	2,000,000	2,000,000	2,000,000	2,000,000	2,000,000	2,000,000	1,000,000	1,000,000	1,000,000
Preferred stock	1,360,000	1,360,000	1,360,000	1,360,000	1,360,000	1,360,000	1,360,000	1,360,000	1,360,000	1,360,000
Common stock and surplus	1,340,000	1,340,000	1,340,000	1,340,000	1,340,000	1,340,000	1,340,000	1,340,000	1,340,000	1,340,000
Book value per share	21.63									

depreciation) amounting to more than $125 million or (2) total assets amounting to more than $1 billion (after deducting accumulated depreciation) are required to report supplementary information in addition to the primary financial statements. FASB *Standards No. 33* are:

For fiscal years ended on or after December 25, 1979, enterprises are required to report:

a. Income from continuing operations adjusted for the effects of general inflation.
b. The purchasing power gain or loss on net monetary items.

For fiscal years ended on or after December 25, 1979, enterprises are also required to report:

a. Income from continuing operations on a current cost basis.
b. The current cost amounts of inventory and property, plant, and equipment at the end of the fiscal year.
c. Increases or decreases in current cost amounts of inventory and property, plant, and equipment, net of inflation.

Enterprises are required to present a five-year summary of selected financial data, including information on income, sales and other operating revenues, net assets, dividends per common share, and market price per share. In the computation of net assets, only inventory and property, plant, and equipment need be adjusted for the effects of changing prices.

UMC, because of its "small company" asset size, would be exempt from FASB *No. 33*'s reporting requirement. However, Exhibit 5 restates UMC's statement of income from continuing operations, restated for changing prices, for the year ending December 31, 1983; and UMC's five-year comparison of selected data adjusted for changing prices.

A final note on Notes: Feel free to speak with your friendly auditor, or sleuth on your own, regarding additional information which might remain undisclosed and could pertain to:

a. Liabilities arising out of company pension plans (e.g., ERISA).
b. Contractual obligations (e.g., the capitalized value of lease payments).
c. Legal judgments currently enforceable.
d. Contingent liabilities (e.g., pending lawsuits or possible income tax assessment).

TEN-YEAR FINANCIAL SUMMARY

Long-term performance of UMC is summarized and reported on the ten-year financial summary statement, Exhibit 6.

The long-term view is used for detecting trends and changes in trends in important factors such as net sales, total assets, net operating income, earnings per share, and dividends per share. On balance, the trends for UMC look pretty good: upward.

A Guide to SEC Corporate Filings

The purpose of the Federal securities laws is to provide disclosure of material financial and other information on companies seeking to raise capital through the public offering of their securities, as well as companies whose securities are already publicly held. This aims enables investors to evaluate the securities of these companies on an informed and realistic basis.

The Securities Act of 1933 is a *disclosure* statute. It generally requires that, before securities may be offered to the public, a registration statement must be filed with the Commission disclosing prescribed categories of information. Before the sale of securities can begin, the registration statement must become "effective," and investors must be furnished a prospectus containing the most significant information in the registration statement.

The Securities Exchange Act of 1934 deals in large part with securities already outstanding and requires the registration of securities listed on a national securities exchange, as well as "Over-the-Counter" securities in which there is a substantial public interest. Issuers of registered securities must file annual and other periodic reports designed to provide a public file of current material information. The Exchange Act also requires disclosure of material information to holders of registered securities in solicitations of proxies for the election of directors or approval of corporate action at a stockholder's meeting, or in attempts to acquire control of a company through a tender offer or other planned stock acquisitions. It provides that insiders of companies whose equity securities are registered must report their holdings and transactions in all equity securities of their companies.

Form 10-K

This report provides a comprehensive overview of the registrant. The report must be filed within 90 days after close of company's fiscal year and contains the following items of disclosure:

Items Reported
Part I

1. **Business.** Identifies principal products and services of the company, principal markets and methods of distribution and, if "material," competitive factors, backlog and expectation of fulfillment, availability of raw materials, importance of patents, licenses, and franchises, estimated cost of research, number of employees, and effects of compliance with ecological laws.

   If there is more than one line of business, a statement is included for the last three years. The statement includes total sales and net income for each line which during either of the last two fiscal years accounted for 10 percent or more of total sales or pretax income.
2. **Properties.** Location and character of principal plants, mines, and other important properties and if held in fee or leased.
3. **Legal Proceedings.** Brief description of material legal proceedings pending.
4. **Submission of Matters to a Vote of Security Holders.** Information relating to the convening of a meeting of shareholders, whether annual or special, and the matters voted upon.

Part II

5. **Market for the Registrants' Common Stock and Related Security Holder Matters.** Includes principal market in which voting securities are traded with high and low sales prices (in the absence thereof, the range of bid and asked quotations for each quarterly period during the past two years) and the dividends paid during the past two years. In addition to the frequency and amount of dividends paid, this item contains a discussion concerning future dividends.
6. **Selected Financial Data.** These are five-year selected data including net sales and operating revenue; income or loss from continuing operations, both total and per common share; total assets; long-term obligations including redeemable preferred stock; cash dividend declared per common share. The data also includes additional items that could enhance understanding and trends in financial condition and results of operations. Further, the effects of inflation and changing prices should be reflected in the five-year summary.
7. **Management's Discussion and Analysis of Financial Condition and Results of Operations.** Under broad guidelines, this includes: liquidity, capital resources and results of operations; trends that are favorable or unfavorable as well as significant events or uncertainties; causes of any material changes in the financial state-

Source: A *Guide to SEC Corporate Filings,* Disclosure, Inc., 5161 River Road, Bethesda, MD 20816. Provided by Disclosure. To order copies of any SEC filings, call 800-638-8241.

ments as a whole; limited data concerning subsidiaries; discussion of effects of inflation and changing prices.

8. **Financial Statements and Supplementary Data.** Two-year audited balance sheets as well as three-year audited statements of income and changes in financial condition.
9. **Disagreements on Accounting and Financial Disclosure.**

Part III

10. **Directors and Executive Officers of the Registrant.** Name, office, term of office and specific background data on each.
11. **Remuneration of Directors and Officers.** List of each director and 3 highest paid officers with aggregate annual remuneration exceeding $40,000. Also includes total paid all officers and directors.
12. **Security Ownership of Beneficial Owners and Management.** Identification of owners of 5 percent or more of registrant's stock in addition to listing the amount and percent of each class of stock held by officers and directors.
13. **Certain Relationships and Related Transactions.**

Part IV

14. **Exhibits, Financial Statement Schedules and Reports on Form 8-K.** Complete, audited annual financial information and a list of exhibits filed. Also, any unscheduled material events or corporate changes filed in an 8-K during the year.

Form 10-K Schedules

- **I.** Investments other than investments in affiliates
- **II.** Receivables from related parties and underwriters, promoters and employees other than affiliates
- **III.** Condensed financial information
- **IV.** Indebtedness of affiliates (not current)
- **V.** Property, plant and equipment
- **VI.** Accumulated depreciation, depletion, and amortization of property, plant and equipment
- **VII.** Guarantees of securities of other issuers
- **VIII.** Valuation and qualifying accounts
- **IX.** Short-term borrowings
- **X.** Supplementary income statement information
- **XI.** Supplementary profit and loss information
- **XII.** Income from dividends (equity in net profit and loss of affiliates)

20-F

Annual Registration/statement filed by certain foreign issuers of securities trading in the United States. The 20-F report must be filed 6 months after close of fiscal year.

Part I

Item 1	Business
Item 2	Description of Property
Item 3	Material Legal Proceedings
Item 4	Control of Registrant
Item 5	Nature of Trading Market
Item 6	Exchange Controls and Other Limitations Affecting Security Holders
Item 7	Taxation
Item 8	Selected Financial Data
Item 9	Management Discussion and Analysis
Item 10	Directors and Officers
Item 11	Compensation
Item 12	Options to Purchase Securities from Registrant or Subsidiaries
Item 13	Interests of Management in Certain Transactions

Part II

Item 14	Description of Securities

Part III

Item 15	Defaults upon Senior Securities
Item 16	Changes in Securities and Changes in Security for Registered Securities

Part IV

Item 17	Financial Statements and Exhibits

10-Q

This is the quarterly financial report filed by most companies, which, although unaudited, provides a continuing view of a company's financial position during the year. The 10-Q report must be filed within 45 days of the close of a fiscal quarter.

Items Reported
Part I

FINANCIAL STATEMENTS

1. Financial Statements
2. Management Discussion
3. Statement of Source and Application of Funds

4. A narrative analysis of material changes in the amount of revenue and expense items in relation to previous quarters, including the effect of any changes in accounting principals.

Part II

1. **Legal Proceedings.** Brief description of material legal proceedings pending; when civil rights or ecological statutes are involved, proceedings must be disclosed.
2. **Changes in Securities.** Material changes in the rights of holders of any class of registered security.
3. **Defaults upon Senior Securities.** Material defaults in the payment if principal, interest, sinking fund or purchase fund installment, dividend, or other material default not cured within 30 days.
4. **Submission of Matters to a Vote of Security Holders.** Information relating to the convening of a meeting of shareholders, whether annual or special, and the matters voted upon, with particular emphasis on the election of directors.
5. **Other Materially Important Events.** Information on any other item of interest to shareholders not already provided for in this form.
6. **Exhibits and Reports on Form 8K.** Any unscheduled material events or corporate changes filed on an 8-K during the prior quarter.

8-K

This is a report of unscheduled material events or corporate changes deemed of importance to the shareholders or to the SEC. Corporate changes must be filed 15 days after the event, except for Other Materially Important Events which has no mandatory filing time.

1. Changes in Control of Registrant.
2. Acquisition or Disposition of Assets.
3. Bankruptcy or Receivership.
4. Changes in Registrant's Certifying Accountant.
5. Other Materially Important Events.
6. Resignations of Registrant's Directors.
7. Financial Statements and Exhibits.

10-C

"Over-the-counter" companies use this form to report changes in name and amount of NASDAQ-listed securities. It is similar in purpose to the 8-K and must be filed 10 days after change.

13-F

A quarterly report of equity holdings required of all institutions with equity assets of $100 million or more. This includes banks, insurance companies, investment companies, investment advisors and large internally managed endowments, foundations and pension funds. This report must be filed 45 days after close of fiscal quarter.

Proxy Statement

A proxy statement provides official notification to designated classes of stockholders of matters to be brought to a vote at a shareholders' meeting. Proxy votes may be solicited for changing the company name, transferring large blocks of stock, electing new officers, or many other matters. Disclosures normally made via a proxy statement may in some cases be made using Form 10-K (Part III).

Registration Statements

Registration statements are of two principal types: (1) "offering" registrations filed under the 1933 Securities Act, and (2) "trading" registrations filed under the 1934 Securities Exchange Act.

"Offering" registrations are used to register securities before they may be offered to investors. Part I of the registration, a preliminary prospectus or "red herring," is promotional in tone; it carries all the sales features that will be contained in the final prospectus. Part II of the registration contains detailed information about marketing agreements, expenses of issuance and distribution, relationship of the company with experts named in the registration, sales to special parties, recent sales of unregistered securities, subsidiaries of registrant, franchises and concessions, indemnification of directors and officers, treatment of proceeds from stock being registered, and financial statements and exhibits.

"Offering" registration statements vary in purpose and content according to the type of organization issuing stock:

S-1 Companies reporting under the 1934 Act for less than 3 years. Permits no incorporation by reference and requires complete disclosure in the prospectus.

S-2 Companies reporting under the

1934 Act for 3 years or more but do not meet the minimum voting stock requirement. Reference of 1934 Act reports permits incorporation and presentation of financial information in the prospectus or in an annual report to shareholders delivered with the prospectus.

S-3 Companies reporting under the 1934 Act for 3 or more years and having at least $150 million of voting stock held by non-affiliates, or as an alternative test, $100 million of voting stock coupled with an annual trading volume of 3 million shares. Allows minimal disclosure in the prospectus and allows maximum incorporation by reference of 1934 Act reports.

S-4 Registration used in certain busi-

Quick Reference Chart to Contents of SEC Filings

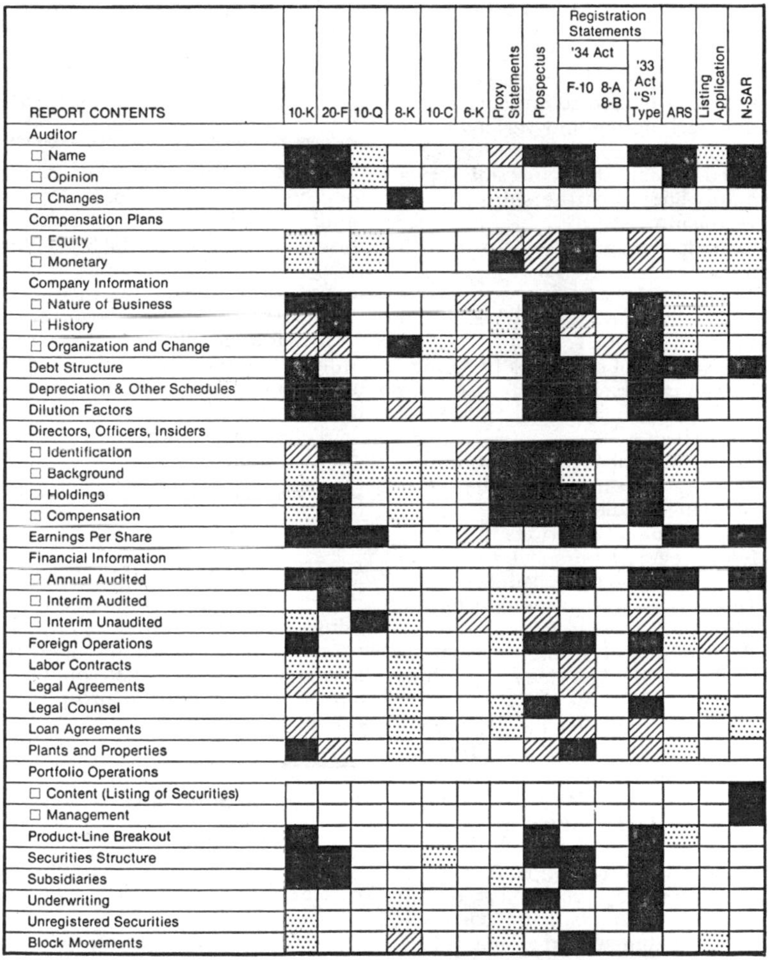

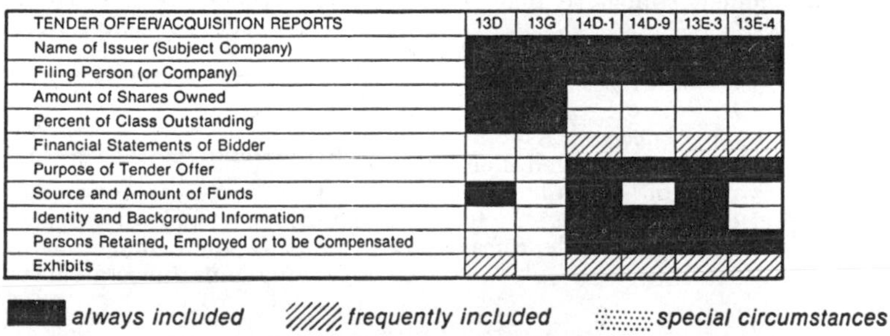

ness combinations or registrations. Replaces S-14, S-15, 7/85.

N-1A Filed by open-end management investment companies other than separate accounts of insurance companies.

N-2 Filed by closed-end investment companies.

N-5 Registration of small business investment companies.

N-SAR Annual statement of management investment companies.

S-6 Filed by unit investment trusts registered under the Investment Act of 1940 on Form N-8B-2.

S-8 Registration used to register securities to be offered to employees under stock option and various other benefit plans.

S-11 Filed by real estate companies, primarily limited partnerships and investment trusts.

S-18 Short form registration up to $7.5 million.

SE Non-electronically filed exhibits of registrants filing with the EDGAR PILOT PROJECT.

F-1 Registration of securities by foreign private issuers eligible to use form 20-F, for which no other form is prescribed.

F-2 Registration of securities of foreign private issuers meeting certain 1934 Act filing requirements.

F-3 Registration of securities of foreign issuers offered pursuant to certain types of transactions, subject to the 1934 Act filing requirements for the preceding three years.

F-6 Registration of depository shares evidenced by American depository receipts.

"Trading" registrations are filed to permit trading among investors on a securities exchange or in the over-the-counter market. Registration statements which serve to register securities for trading fall into three categories:

(1) **Form 10** is used by companies during the first two years they are subject to the 1934 Act filing requirements. It is a combination registration statement and annual report with information content similar to that of SEC-required 10-Ks.

(2) **Form 8-A** is used by 1934 Act registrants wishing to register *additional* securities or classes thereof.

(3) **Form 8-B** is used by "successor issuers" (usually companies which have changed their name or state of incorporation) as notification that previously registered securities are to be traded under a new corporate identification.

Prospectus

When the sale of securities as proposed in an "offering" registration statement is approved by the SEC, any changes required by the SEC are incorporated into the prospectus. This document must be made available to investors before the sale of the security is initiated. It also contains the actual offering price, which may have been changed after the registration statement was approved.

Annual Report to Shareholders

The Annual Report is the principal document used by most major companies to communicate directly with shareholders. Since it is not a required, official SEC filing, companies have considerable discretion in determining what types of information this report will contain and how it is to be presented.

In addition to financial information, the Annual Report to Shareholders often provides non-financial details of the business which are not reported elsewhere. These may include marketing plans and forecasts of future programs and plans.

Form 8 (Amendment)

Form 8 is used to amend or supplement filings previously submitted. 1933 Act registration statements are amended by filing an amended registration statement (pre-effective amendment) or by the prospectus itself, as previously noted.

Listing Application

Like the ARS, a listing application is not an official SEC filing. It is filed by the company with the NYSE, AMEX or other stock exchange to document proposed new listings. Usually a Form 8-A registration is filed with the SEC at about the same time.

N-SAR

This form serves as either the annual or semiannual report for every registered investment company and as the annual report form for registered unit investment trusts. It is filed 60 days after the end of the appropriate period.

Tender Offers/Acquisition Reports

13-G

An annual report which must be filed by all reporting persons (primarily institutions) meeting the 5% equity ownership rule within 45 days after the end of each calendar year.

1. Name of issuer
2. Name of person filing
3. 13D-1 or 13D-2 applicability
4. Amount of shares beneficially owned:
   Percent of class outstanding
   Sole or shared power to vote
   Sole or shared power to dispose
5. Ownership of 5% or less of a class of stock
6. Ownership of more than 5% on behalf of another person
7. Identification of subsidiary which acquired the security being reported on by the parent holding company (if applicable)
8. Identification and classification of members of the group (if applicable)
9. Notice of dissolution of the group (if applicable)
10. Certification

13-D

Filing required by 5% (or more) equity owners within ten days of acquisition event.

1. Security and issuer
2. Identity and background of person filing the statement
3. Source and amount of funds or other consideration
4. Purpose of the transaction
5. Interest in securities of the issuer
6. Contracts, arrangements or relationships with respect to securities of the issuer
7. Material to be filed as exhibits which may include but are not limited to:
   a. Letter agreements between the parties
   b. Formal offer to purchase

14D-1

Tender offer filing made with the SEC at time offer is made to holders of equity securities of target company, if acceptance of offer would give the offerer over 5% ownership of the subject securities:

1. Security and subject company
2. Identity and background information
3. Past contacts, transactions or negotiations with subject company
4. Source and amount of funds or other consideration
5. Purpose of the tender offer and plans or proposals of the bidder
6. Interest in securities of the subject company
7. Contracts, arrangements or relationships with respect to the subject company's securities
8. Persons retained, employed or to be compensated
9. Financial statements of certain bidders
10. Additional information
11. Material to be filed as exhibits which may include but are not limited to:
    a. The actual offer to purchase
    b. The letter to shareholders
    c. The letter of transmittal with notice of guaranteed delivery
    d. The press release
    e. The summary publication in business newspapers or magazines
    f. The summary advertisement to appear in business newspapers or magazines.

14D-9

A solicitation/recommendation statement that must be submitted to equity holders and filed at the SEC by the management of a firm subject to a tender offer within ten days of the making of the tender offer:

1. Security and subject company
2. Tender offer of the bidder
3. Identify and background
4. The solicitation or recommendation
5. Persons retained, employed or to be compensated
6. Recent transactions and intent with respect to securities
7. Certain negotiations and transactions by the subject company
8. Additional information
9. Material to be filed as exhibits

13E-4

Issuer tender offer statement pursuant to the Securities Exchange Act of 1934:

1. Security and issuer
2. Source and amount of funds

3. Purpose of the tender offer and plans or proposals of the issuer or affiliates
4. Interest in securities of the issuer
5. Contracts, arrangements or relationships with respect to the issuer's securities
6. Person retained, employed or to be compensated
7. Financial information
8. Additional information
9. Material to be filed as exhibits which may include but is not limited to the offer to purchase which is being sent to the shareholders to whom the tender offer is being made.

13E-3

Transaction statement pursuant to the Securities Exchange Act of 1934 with respect to a public company or affiliate going private

1. Issuer and class of security subject to the transaction
2. Identity and background of the individuals
3. Past contacts, transactions or negotiations
4. Terms of the transaction
5. Plans or proposals of the issuer or affiliate
6. Source and amount of funds or other considerations
7. Purpose, alternatives, reasons and effects
8. Fairness of the transaction
9. Reports, opinions, appraisals and certain negotiations
10. Interest in securities of the issuer
11. Contracts, arrangements or relationships with respect to the issuer's securities
12. Present intention and recommendation of certain persons with regard to the transaction
13. Other provisions of the transaction
14. Financial information
15. Persons and assets employed, retained or utilized
16. Additional information
17. Material to be filed as exhibits

How to Read the New York Stock Exchange and American Stock Exchange Quotations

(1)	(2)	(3)	(4)	(5)	(6)	(7)	(8)	(9)	(10)	(11)
52 Weeks				Yld	P-E	Sales				Net
High	Low	Stock	Div.	%	Ratio	100s	High	Low	Close	Chg.
					A A A					
14¾	9⅛	AAR	.44	4.3	7	26	10½	10¼	10¼	¼
52¼	32¼	ACF	2.76	6.0	10	51	46	45½	46	
27	12⅞	AMF	1.24	5.1	12	1453	24¼	23¾	24⅛ +	¼
24¾	10⅞	AM Intl				51	13⅞	13¾	13¾	
11⅜	6⅜	APL				51	6⅜ d	6¼	6¼	⅛

Source: Reprinted by permission of *The Wall Street Journal,* Dow Jones & Co., Inc., 1981.

The composite quotations take into account prices paid for a stock on the New York or American Exchanges, plus those prices paid on regional exchanges, Over-the-Counter (OTC) and elsewhere, as shown in the example from the Wall Street Journal. The stock market quotations are explained below:

(1) The highest price per share paid in the past 52 weeks in terms of ⅛ of a dollar, i.e., 10⅛ means $10.125.

(2) The lowest price paid per share in the last 52 weeks.

(3) The name of the company in abbreviated form.

(4) The regular annual dividend paid. Special or extra dividends are specified by letters given in the footnotes in the Explanatory Notes shown below.

(5) The yield, that is, the annual dividend divided by the current price of the stock expressed in percent. For example, a stock that sells for $20.00 per share and pays a dividend of $2.00 per share has a yield of 10 percent (2/20).

(6) The P/E ratio is the current price of the stock divided by the company's last reported annual earnings per share. The P/E ratio is generally high for companies which are thought to have a relatively large and persistent earning's growth rate. The average P/E ratio for the Dow Jones stocks varied from 7.7 to 10.2 during the last five years.

(7) The number of shares sold on the day reported in 100s of shares.
(8) The highest price paid per share on the day reported.
(9) The lowest price paid per share on the day reported.
(10) The last price paid per share on the day reported.
(11) The change in the closing price from the previous day's closing price.

EXPLANATORY NOTES
(For New York and American Exchange listed issues)

Sales figures are unofficial.

The 52-Week High and Low columns show the highest and the lowest price of the stock in consolidated trading during the preceding 52 weeks plus the current week, but not the current trading day.

u—Indicates a new 52-week high. d—Indicates a new 52-week low.

s—Split or stock dividend of 25 percent or more in the past 52 weeks. The high-low range is adjusted from the old stock. Dividend begins with the date of split or stock dividend.

n—New issue in the past 52 weeks. The high-low range begins with the start of trading in the new issue and does not cover the entire 52-week period.

g—Dividend or earnings in Canadian money. Stock trades in U.S. dollars. No yield or PE shown unless stated in U.S. money.

Unless otherwise noted, rates of dividends in the forogoing table are annual disbursements based on the last quarterly or semi-annual declaration. Special or extra dividends or payments not designated as regular are identified in the following footnotes.

a—Also extra or extras. b—Annual rate plus stock dividend. c—Liquidating dividend. e—Declared or paid in preceding 12 months. i—Declared or paid after stock dividend or split up. j—Paid this year, dividend omitted, deferred or no action taken at last dividend meeting. k—Declared or paid this year, an accumulative issue with dividends in arrears. r—Declared or paid in preceding 12 months plus stock dividend. t—Paid in stock in preceding 12 months, estimated cash value on ex-dividend or ex-distribution date.

x—Ex-dividend or ex-rights. v—Ex-dividend and sales in full. z—Sales in full.

wd—When distributed. wi—When issued. ww—With warrants. xw—Without warrants.

vi—In bankruptcy or receivership or being reorganized under the Bankruptcy Act, or securities assumed by such companies.

How to Read Over-the-Counter NASDAQ Listings

(1) (2) Stock & Div.	(3) Sales 100s	(4) Bid	(5) Asked	(6) Net Chg.
CentVtPS 1.92	8	13⅝	13¾ +	⅛
Centrn CP 2.56	4	23¼	23½	. . .
Centura Enrg	135	10½	10¾ −	½
CenturyBK .48	573	13	13⅛ −	⅛
CenturyOil Gs	49	7⅜	7⅝	. . .
Cetus Corptn	231	17⅛	17⅜ +	⅛
CFS Cont .40	18	13⅝	13⅞ +	⅛
CGA Assc Inc	155	10½	11 −	¼
Chalco Ind Inc	2	6	6½ −	¼

The over-the-counter quotations are explained below.

(1) The company's name, usually abbreviated.
(2) Annual regular dividend per share, unless accompanied by a notation which is explained in the OTC Explanatory Notes (below).
(3) Number of shares sold that day in hundreds, i.e., 2 means 200 shares.
(4) Bid price per share at closing time, i.e., the price at which broker-dealer will buy the stock from the investor. Prices do not include mark-up or commission.
(5) Ask price per share at closing time, i.e., the price at which the broker-dealer will sell the stock.*
(6) The change in the closing bid price from the previous day.

* Bid and ask prices are usually quoted in ⅛ (12.5 cents) of a dollar, i.e., 12⅛ means $12.125, 12½ means $12.50, etc. Very inexpensive stocks are quoted at 1/16 (6.25 cents) and 1/32 (3.125 cents) of a dollar.

OTC EXPLANATORY NOTES

z—Sales in full.

a—Annual rate plus cash extra. b—Paid so far in 1981, no regular rate. c—Payment of accumulated dividends. d—Paid in 1980. e—Cash plus stock paid in 1980. f—Cash plus stock paid in 1981. g—Annual rate plus stock dividend. h—Paid in 1981, latest dividend omitted. i—Percent paid in stock in 1980. j—Percent in stock paid in 1981, latest dividend omitted. k—Percent in stock paid in 1981. n—Asked price not applicable. p—Granted temporary exception from Nasdaq qualifications. q—In bankruptcy proceedings. ut—Units. wt—Warrants. x—Ex-dividend, ex-rights or ex-distribution. (z) No representative quote.

The Ex-dividend Explained

The ex-dividend status of a stock is indicated by an *x* in the newspaper quotation or *xd* on the ticker tape. This is an abbreviation for *without dividend.*

A stock that is purchased during the ex-dividend period will not pay a previously declared dividend to its new owner. The ex-dividend period spans four business days before the so-called record date—the date a dividend issuing corporation uses to tally its shareowners. An ex-dividend stock buyer is not entitled to a dividend because his name is not recorded with the dividend issuing corporation until after the record date.

The New York Stock Exchange requires that the buyer in every transaction be recorded with the issuing corporation on the fifth business day following a trade. A stock buyer, therefore, must purchase his shares at least five business days before the record date in order for the corporation to record his name in time for him to receive his dividend. A purchase one day later disqualifies a buyer from a dividend because the transfer of ownership cannot be completed by the record date. Therefore, on the fourth business day prior to the record date, a stock is sold ex-dividend.

In our example below, the corporation's Board has decided to pay a 50%o dividend to shareholders of record on Monday, the 10th. A person buying shares up to the close of business on Monday, the 3rd, would be eligible for the dividend because normal settlement (5 business days) will be made on Monday the 10th. On Tuesday, the 4th, however, the stock would begin selling ex-dividend because a stock purchaser as of that date could not settle till after the record date.

On the ex-dividend date, the Exchange specialist will reduce all open buy orders and open sell stop orders by the amount of the dividend. This is done to more equitably reflect the stock's value since purchasers of stock on or after the ex-dividend date are ineligible for a dividend.

EX-DIVIDEND EXPLANATION

Any Month Date	Calendar Day	Status
3	Monday	With/Dividend
4	Tuesday	Ex-Dividend (Without Dividend)
5	Wednesday	" "
6	Thursday	" "
7	Friday	" "
8	Saturday	Not a trading day
9	Sunday	Not a trading day
10	Monday	Record Date/Business Day
11	Tuesday	Business Day

Source: *Taking The Mystery Out of Ex-Dividend,* The New York Stock Exchange, Inc.

Margin Accounts Explained

Stocks may be purchased by paying the purchase price in full (plus commissions and taxes) or on a margin account. With the margin account, the investors put up part of the purchase price in cash or securities, and the broker lends the remainder. The margin investor must pay the usual commissions as well as interest on the broker's loan. The stocks purchased on margin are held by the broker as collateral on the loan. Dividends are applied to the margin account and help offset the interest payments.

Margin (M) is defined as the market value (V) of the securities less the broker's loan (L), divided by the market value of the securities. The ratio is expressed as a percentage:

$$M = \frac{V - L}{V} \times 100$$

Example: You buy 100 shares of a stock at \$20 per share at a total cost (V) of \$2,000. You put up \$1,200 in cash and borrow (L) \$800 from the broker. The margin at the time of purchase is

$$M = \frac{\$2,000 - \$800}{\$2,000} \times 100 = 60\%$$

The margin at the time of purchase is called *initial margin.* The smallest allowed value of initial margin (set by the Federal Reserve) is currently 50%. Thus, with the above stock, if you buy 100 shares at \$20 per share on 50% initial margin, you put up \$1,000 (.5 × \$2,000), and the broker's loan is \$1,000.

After the purchase there is a *maintenance margin* (set by the Exchange) below which the margin is not permitted to decrease. The maintenance margin on the New York Stock Exchange is 25%. Some brokers, however, require a higher maintenance margin of about 30%. Thus, if the 100 shares of stocks discussed above decrease in price from $20 to $13 per share, then the margin is

$$M = \left(\frac{\$1,300 - \$1,000}{\$1,300}\right) \times 100 = 23\%$$

The margin of 23% is now below the maintenance margin of 25% set by the Exchange. The securities are said to be *under margined*, and a call for additional cash (or securities) is issued by the broker in order to bring up the margin to 25%. If the investor does not meet the call for additional cash (margin call) within a specified time, the stocks in the margin account are immediately sold.

MARGIN REQUIREMENTS (percent of market value and effective date)

	Mar. 11, 1968	June 8, 1968	May 6, 1970	Dec. 6, 1971	Nov. 24, 1972	Jan. 3, 1974
Margin stocks	70	80	65	55	65	50
Convertible bonds	50	60	50	50	50	50
Short sales.............	70	80	65	55	65	50

Note: Regulations G, T, and U of the Federal Reserve Board of Governors, prescribed in accordance with the Securities Exchange Act of 1934, limit the amount of credit to purchase and carry margin stocks that may be extended on securities as collateral by prescribing a maximum loan value, which is a specified percentage of the market value of the collateral at the time the credit is extended. Margin requirements are the difference between the market value (100 percent) and the maximum loan value. The term "margin stocks" is defined in the corresponding regulation.

Source: *Federal Reserve Bulletin.*

Short Selling Explained

Short selling provides an opportunity to profit from a decline in the price of a stock. If you believe that a stock is due for a substantial decline, you arrange to have your broker borrow the stock from another investor who owns the shares. The borrowed stock is then sold. This cash is held as collateral against the borrowed shares. When (and if) the stock price declines, you purchase the stock at the market price and use it to replace the borrowed shares. The broker arranges the return of your cash collateral less the cost of the repurchased stock. Your profit per share is the price received on the sale of the stock less the purchase price.

There are certain cash outlays and costs associated with the short sale. Generally there is no charge for borrowing the stock, although occasionally stock lenders may charge a premium over the market price. You must deposit $2,000 or the required initial margin, whichever is the greater, at the time the stock is borrowed. Thus, if you borrow 100 shares of a stock priced at $50 per share and the margin required is 50%, you must put up $2,500 (.5 × $50 × 100) in cash or securities. The margin deposit is returned when you close out the short sale. You pay commission when the stock is sold and when it is repurchased. In addition, you must pay the stock lender any dividends which are declared during the period you are short the stock. It is well to remember that if cash is used for the deposit, there is a loss of the interest which you would have obtained if the cash had been invested.

The dividend payments and interest loss can be reduced or eliminated if you short stocks which pay little or no dividends and use interest-bearing securities (such as T-bills or negotiable certificates of deposit) as the margin deposit.

An increase in the price of the stock can result in substantial losses since you may be forced to repurchase at a higher price than you sold. If there are many short sellers seeking to purchase the stock in order to close out their position, prices may be driven to very high levels.

The short sale cannot be executed while the stock price is declining on the exchange. According to the rules of the SEC, the stock must undergo an increase in price prior to the execution of a short sale.

New Mutual Fund Reporting Regulations

The new SEC regulations concerning mutual fund reporting practices which went into effect May 1988 require that an easy-to-read table giving all fund charges must appear near the front of all prospectuses. Included must be such items as front end and back end loads, 12b–1 plans to recover marketing and distribution costs, and sales loads imposed on reinvested dividends applied everytime the find reinvest dividends. Typically, fund expense ratios (annual operating expenses to assets) range from .7% to 1%.

Advertisements that contain yields must calculate yields (capital gains plus dividends) on a consistent basis prescribed by the SEC, taking into account any front end sales charges. To put the yield figure into perspective, ads must provide one, five and ten year total return information.

Fund fees are now shown in the newspaper listing by means of the following letters after the fund's name:

r	indicates a back end load or redemption fee
p	indicates a 12b–1 plan is in effect
t	indicates both a back end and a 12b–1 fee
N.L.	indicates there is no front end or back end load

How to Read Mutual Fund Quotations

The following is an example of typical fund quotations as reported in the Wall Street Journal. The mutual fund quotations are explained in the adjacent column.

(1)	(2) NAV	(3) Offer Price	(4) NAV Chg.
Able Assoc	24.33	N.L.+	.80
Acorn Fnd	28.28	N.L.+	.03
ADV Fund	15.38	N.L.+	.02
Afuture Fd	15.59	N.L.+	.10
AIM funds			
Conv Yld	15.42	16.49+	.09
Edsn Gld	14.59	15.60+	.09
HiYld Sc	8.98	9.60+	.02
Alpha Fnd	17.82	N.L.+	.01
Am Birthrt	12.29	13.43−	.03
American Funds Group			
Am Bal	8.73	9.54	. . .
Amcap F	6.21	6.79+	.01
Am Mutl	12.46	13.62−	.01

Source: Reprinted by permission of *The Wall Street Journal*, Dow Jones & Co., Inc., 1981. All rights reserved.

(1) Name of fund in abbreviated form.

(2) NAV means "net asset value" per share of the stock. It is the price at which the fund will buy shares from investors.

The NAV is obtained from

$$NAV = \frac{M + C - L}{N}$$

M = market value of all stock in the fund's portfolio at the end of the trading day
C = fund's cash or cash equivalent position
L = fund's liabilities
N = number of shares issued by fund

(3) Offer price is the price per share at which the fund will sell shares to investors. With no load (NL, no sales charge) funds, the offer price and the NAV are the same. With load funds, a sales charge (load) is added to the NAV to arrive at the sales price.

(4) The NAV change is the change in net asset value (at the close of the stock market) from that of the previous day.

Top 50 Performing Mutual Funds for 5 Years

What $10,000 Grew to In 5 Years (1983–1987)**

1		Merrill Lynch Pacific Fund	$36,384
2		Alliance International Fund	32,928
3		Putnam International Equities Fund	31,646
4	*	T.Rowe Price International Stock Fund	30,636
5	*	Transatlantic Growth Fund	29,253
6	*	Scudder International Fund	27,866
7		Templeton Foreign Fund	27,492
8		Putnam OTC Emerging Growth Fund	27,392
9		United International Growth Fund	26,465
10		Kemper International Fund	25,924
11	*	Prudential-Bache Utility Fund	25,481
12		G.T. Pacific Growth Fund	25,421
13	+	Fidelity Magellan Fund	25,291
14	*	Vanguard High Yield Stock Fund	25,223
15		Phoenix Growth Fund Series	25,201
16	+	Strong Total Return Fund	24,902
17	*	Mutual Shares Corporation	24,814
18		United Income Fund	24,474
19	*	Mutual Qualified Income Fund	24,441
20	*	Dodge & Cox Stock Fund	24,300
21	*	Federated Stock Trust	24,258
22	*	Windsor Fund (c)	24,221
23		So Gen International Fund	24,093
24		New Perspective Fund	23,919
25		Princor Capital Accumulation Fund	23,784
26	*	Keystone International Fund	23,711
27	*	Sequoia Fund (c)	23,517
28		Guardian Park Avenue Fund	23,462
29		Fidelity Destiny Portfolio I	23,380
30		Phoenix Stock Fund Series	23,349
31	*	Loomis Sayles Capital Development	23,085
32	*	Lehman Opportunity Fund	22,801
33		Oppenheimer Equity Income Fund	22,770
34		Phoenix Balanced Fund	22,644
35		Weingarten Equity Fund	22,620
36		Washington Mutual Investors Fund	22,464
37		Templeton World Fund	22,414
38		Pilgrim MagnaCap Fund	22,371
39	*	Loomis Sayles Mutual Fund	22,360
40		American Leaders Fund	22,357
41	+	Strong Investment Fund	22,314
42		Merrill Lynch Basic Value Fund	22,167
43		Dreyfus Leverage Fund	22,157
44		Merrill Lynch Phoenix Fund	22,153
45		FPA Paramount Fund (c)	22,062
46	*	Boston Co Capital Appreciation Fund	22,040
47		Investment Company of America	21,946
48	+	Fidelity Select–Financial Services	21,891
49	*	T.Rowe Price New Era Fund	21,872
50	*	Selected American Shares	21,858

Top 50 Performing Mutual Funds for 10 Years

What $10,000 Grew To In 10 Years (1978–1987)**

1		Fidelity Magellan Fund	$148,029
2	*	Loomis Sayles Capital Development (c)	97,986
3	*	Twentieth Century Growth Investors	91,178
4		International Investors	90,060
5	*	Twentieth Century Select Investors	88,605
6		New England Growth Fund	87,357
7		Weingarten Equity Fund	81,695
8		Phoenix Stock Fund Series	80,726
9	+	Franklin Gold Fund	79,911
10	*	Lindner Fund	74,850
11		American Capital Pace Fund	74,435
12		AMEV Growth Fund	73,874
13		Lehman Capital Fund	71,898
14		United Vanguard Fund	70,813
15	*	Evergreen Fund	67,243
16		Fidelity Destiny Portfolio I	65,307
17		IDS New Dimensions Fund	65,117
18		IDS Growth Fund	65,000
19		Shearson Appreciation Fund	64,828
20		New York Venture Fund	64,534
21	*	Nicholas Fund	64,429
22		AMEV Capital Fund (c)	64,171
23		Phoenix Growth Fund Series	64,143
24		Putnam International Equities Fund	63,589
25	*	US Gold Shares Fund	63,296
26		United International Growth Fund	62,171
27	*	Partners Fund	61,357
28	*	AMEV Special Fund (c)	61,180
29		Growth Fund of America	61,013
30		AMCAP Fund	60,759
31	*	Tudor Fund	60,367
32	*	Janus Investment Fund	60,177
33		So Gen International Fund	59,949
34	*	Hartwell Growth Fund	59,550
35	*	SteinRoe Special Fund	59,421
36		Investors Research Fund	59,345
37	*	Vanguard High Yield Stock Fund	58,713
38		Constellation Growth Fund	58,681
39	*	Sequoia Fund (c)	58,605
40		Mass Financial Capital Development	57,873
41		Oppenheimer Global Fund	57,734
42		Fidelity Equity-Income Fund	56,967
43		New Perspective Fund	56,526
44	*	Windsor Fund (c)	56,203
45		Oppenheimer Time Fund	56,079
46	*	Columbia Growth Fund	55,911
47		Guardian Park Avenue Fund	55,889
48	*	Mutual Shares Corporation	55,465
49		Putnam Voyager Fund	55,377
50		Putnam Vista Basic Value	55,112

* No-load fund, + Low-load fund, (No symbol) Load fund, (c) fund closed to new investment

** Does not take into account sales commissions or income taxes that would have to be paid. Includes reinvestment of all dividends and capital gains.
Source: *Donoghue's Mutual Funds Almanac*, 1988–1989, $23, Box 540, Holliston, MA 01746.

BARRON'S / LIPPER GAUGE

Debt and Equity Funds

FUND NAME	OBJ.	LOAD	TOTAL NET ASTS (MIL) 6/30/88	NAV 6/30/88	PERFORMANCE (RETURN ON INITIAL $10,000 INVESTMENT) 12/31/87- 6/30/88	6/30/87- 6/30/88	6/30/83- 6/30/88	YIELD % 6/30/88	PER SHARE LATEST 12 MONTHS CAP GAINS	INC DIVS	LATEST AVAILABLE PRICE/ EARNINGS	ANNUAL % TURNOVER
AAL CAPITAL GROWTH	G	SC	$ 27.5	$ 8.80	$ 10,877.60	$ ☆	$ ☆	0.0	$ 0.00	$ 0.04	N/A	N/A
AAL INCOME	FI	SC	28.0	9.58	10,446.30	☆	☆	0.0	0.05	0.73	N/A	N/A
AARP CAPITAL GROWTH	G	NO	94.2	23.69	12,219.80	10,010.80	☆	2.4	1.35	0.57	N/A	54
AARP GENERAL BOND	FI	NO	123.3	14.80	10,453.60	10,660.80	☆	9.5	0.00	1.41	N/A	193
AARP GNMA	FI	NO	2,829.3	15.16	10,475.60	10,719.60	☆	9.1	0.00	1.37	N/A	51
AARP GROWTH AND INCOME	GI	NO	247.2	21.16	10,831.40	9,382.00	☆	4.2	0.77	0.89	N/A	43
ABT EMERGING GROWTH	CA	SC	26.3	8.75	12,376.20	8,492.90	14,265.20	0.0	0.25	0.00	22.4	65
ABT GROWTH & INCOME TR	GI	SC	114.8	10.54	12,009.30	9,976.90	17,249.60	3.1	2.55	0.37	17.3	94
ABT SECURITY INCOME	OI	SC	9.9	8.79	11,073.40	8,261.50	12,710.90	2.3	0.73	0.21	N/A	186
ABT UTILITY INCOME FD	UT	SC	118.0	13.57	11,096.50	10,552.30	16,803.30	6.4	0.75	0.89	12.0	85
ACORN FUND (R)	SG	NO	530.1	38.55	11,890.80	10,303.40	19,361.10	1.3	4.88	0.52	25.4	52
ADAM INVESTORS	CA	NO	6.4	11.60	10,720.90	9,410.90	☆	9.5	1.65	1.18	N/A	117
ADDISON CAPITAL	GI	LO	26.4	14.62	11,342.10	9,134.80	☆	1.8	0.01	0.16	N/A	25
ADTEK FUND	CA	NO	24.4	9.32	10,086.40	7,908.30	☆	3.3	0.00	0.31	N/A	107
ADVANCE AMER: CORP BD	FI	LO	0.9	9.92	10,481.90	☆	☆	0.0	0.00	0.67	N/A	N/A
ADVANCE AMER: GNMA MTG	FI	LO	0.7	10.03	10,535.30	☆	☆	0.0	0.00	0.56	N/A	N/A
ADVANCE AMER: US GOVT	FI	LO	0.9	10.11	10,524.20	☆	☆	0.0	0.00	0.52	N/A	N/A
ADVANTAGE TR US GOVT	FI	LO	178.7	9.50	10,477.50	10,713.70	☆	10.1	0.00	0.95	N/A	58
ADVEST ADVANTAGE GOVT (R)	FI	NO	217.9	8.68	10,315.20	10,111.80	☆	7.4	0.06	0.64	N/A	412
ADVEST ADVANTAGE GRO (R)	G	NO	27.3	11.47	11,052.40	9,028.80	☆	1.5	0.00	0.16	N/A	55
ADVEST ADVANTAGE INC (R)	I	NO	60.2	9.74	11,048.80	9,874.50	☆	6.1	0.07	0.59	N/A	46
ADVEST ADVANTAGE SPEC (R)	CA	NO	3.6	9.60	12,151.90	9,746.20	☆	0.0	0.00	0.00	N/A	57
AETNA INCOME SHARES	FI	NO	233.9	12.93	10,581.00	11,030.40	18,187.70	0.0	1.47	0.00	N/A	53
AFFILIATED FUND	GI	SC	3,420.9	9.79	11,179.40	9,408.70	20,652.70	4.8	1.34	0.50	14.8	43
AFUTURE FUND	G	NO	9.4	9.69	10,453.10	8,247.10	7,310.00	0.9	0.00	0.08	N/A	355
AGE HIGH INCOME	FI	LO	1,833.7	3.38	10,954.40	10,695.00	16,972.40	12.8	0.00	0.43	N/A	23
AIM CONVERTIBLE SEC	CV	SC	18.9	9.61	11,162.70	9,094.70	11,415.20	6.4	0.26	0.62	N/A	250
AIM GOV FDS: US GOV SEC	FI	SC	0.4	9.67	#9,971.80	☆	☆	0.0	0.00	0.30	N/A	N/A
ALGER FIXED INCOME (R)	FI	NO	2.8	9.13	10,359.90	10,509.50	☆	7.8	0.00	0.71	N/A	29
ALGER GROWTH (R)	G	NO	5.6	10.30	10,640.50	8,751.10	☆	0.0	0.00	0.00	N/A	136
ALGER HIGH YIELD (R)	FI	NO	3.5	9.28	10,801.30	10,824.20	☆	10.8	0.00	0.99	N/A	29
ALGER INCOME & GROWTH (R)	GI	NO	2.3	10.56	11,258.60	10,077.30	☆	3.6	0.08	0.38	N/A	36
ALGER SMALL CAPITAL (R)	SG	NO	3.6	11.28	11,799.20	9,178.20	☆	0.0	0.00	0.00	N/A	268
ALLEGRO GROWTH	G	NO	4.7	12.93	10,820.10	9,095.00	☆	0.5	0.17	0.06	N/A	20
ALLIANCE BALANCED FUND	B	SC	117.0	13.14	11,688.00	10,505.30	22,189.10	3.2	2.75	0.46	18.1	136
ALLIANCE BOND-HIGH YLD	FI	SC	354.8	8.58	10,816.00	10,231.00	☆	12.7	0.00	1.08	N/A	96
ALLIANCE BOND: MTY INCO	FI	SC	37.6	11.82	10,471.20	10,616.20	17,484.50	9.6	0.00	1.13	N/A	95
ALLIANCE BOND-US GOVT	FI	SC	520.9	8.51	10,393.70	10,640.70	☆	10.9	0.00	0.92	N/A	255
ALLIANCE CANADIAN FUND	IF	SC	27.2	7.02	12,017.40	10,599.30	15,871.00	0.8	2.00	0.06	15.3	72
ALLIANCE CONVERTIBLE	CV	SC	88.3	9.37	11,735.10	9,970.10	☆	6.1	0.20	0.58	N/A	96
ALLIANCE COUNTERPOINT	GI	SC	45.3	14.72	11,696.40	9,393.40	☆	2.0	0.95	0.31	15.9	24
ALLIANCE DIVIDEND SHARES	GI	SC	343.3	2.96	11,325.70	9,613.60	19,914.90	3.6	0.78	0.12	18.0	60
ALLIANCE FUND	G	SC	821.1	6.21	12,137.30	9,999.50	16,284.10	1.7	1.89	0.12	23.0	100
ALLIANCE INTERNATIONAL	IF	SC	132.3	16.09	11,387.10	9,580.30	26,272.80	1.2	6.34	0.21	N/A	58
ALLIANCE MORTGAGE INC	FI	SC	655.9	9.16	10,696.60	10,978.50	☆	10.8	0.00	0.98	N/A	211

ALLIANCE TECHNOLOGY	TK	SC	197.0	23.60	11,671.60	9,507.20	13,830.20	0.0	5.73	0.00	31.4	248
ALLIANCE WORLD EQUITY	GL	SC	2.4	6.20	10,915.50	9,382.10	☆	1.5	4.06	0.12	N/A	220
AMA CLASSIC GROWTH	G	NO	38.8	9.13	11,158.20	9,015.30	14,237.00	8.6	1.01	0.82	16.4	148
AMA GLOBAL GROWTH	GL	NO	119.2	19.81	11,499.60	9,566.30	☆	3.2	0.13	0.64	16.9	20
AMA GROWTH & INCOME	GI	NO	14.4	18.44	11,093.00	9,237.50	☆	3.1	0.00	0.58	N/A	46
AMA INC-CLASSIC INCOME	FI	NO	41.1	8.83	10,444.00	10,454.00	14,9[illegible]2.30	7.4	0.00	0.65	N/A	67
AMA INC-GLOBAL INCOME	WI	NO	14.7	20.04	10,199.00	10,557.50	☆	5.7	0.00	1.15	N/A	N/A
AMA INC-GLOBAL SHT TERM	WI	NO	28.4	10.15	10,270.20	10,643.30	☆	5.3	0.00	0.54	N/A	N/A
AMANA MUTUAL-INCOME	EI	NO	3.7	9.47	11,001.00	8,808.50	☆	2.9	0.00	0.27	N/A	55
AMCAP FUND	G	SC	1,726.3	10.56	10,942.00	9,668.50	17,010.80	2.0	0.39	0.22	21.0	17
AMERICAN ASSET YLD FD	EI	SC	0.1	0.20	4,132.20	2,401.00	☆	0.0	0.00	0.00	N/A	N/A
AMERICAN BALANCED FUND	B	SC	215.0	10.86	11,034.00	10,090.70	19,213.80	5.9	0.42	0.65	15.0	42
AMER CAPITAL COMSTOCK	CA	SC	929.9	13.53	11,437.00	8,967.80	15,859.80	2.6	1.70	0.37	14.6	69
AMER CAPITAL CORP BOND	FI	SC	208.9	7.14	10,896.50	11,153.10	18,16[illegible].90	11.1	0.00	0.79	N/A	28
AMER CAPITAL ENTERPRISE	G	SC	547.2	10.57	11,185.20	8,875.80	14,19[illegible].00	2.0	2.39	0.23	21.7	56
AMER CAPITAL FED MORT	FI	SC	56.8	12.93	10,512.50	10,660.40	☆	8.2	0.00	1.06	N/A	254
AMER CAPITAL GOVT	FI	SC	6,065.2	10.28	10,472.80	10,489.30	☆	9.8	0.03	1.01	N/A	277
AMER CAPITAL GROWTH	G	NO	12.8	16.15	11,373.20	6,947.20	8,422.50	0.0	2.40	0.00	N/A	139
AMER CAPITAL HARBOR	CV	SC	371.9	12.50	11,261.80	9,484.60	15,377.50	6.6	0.58	0.84	19.1	83
AMER CAPITAL HIGH YIELD	FI	SC	599.7	9.15	11,032.20	10,640.00	17,205.90	13.9	0.00	1.26	N/A	66
AMER CAPITAL LIFE GOVT	FI	NO	103.5	8.68	10,406.00	10,494.60	☆	9.5	0.02	0.82	N/A	65
AMER CAPITAL LIFE STOCK	G	NO	26.4	8.65	10,853.20	7,827.80	☆	1.8	0.08	0.16	N/A	75
AMER CAPITAL OTC	SG	SC	45.6	6.44	10,860.00	6,566.60	☆	0.0	0.23	0.00	27.4	61
AMER CAPITAL PACE	CA	SC	2,488.4	22.38	11,134.30	8,808.30	15,847.20	3.7	2.52	0.85	20.7	36
AMER CAPITAL VENTURE	CA	SC	228.1	12.08	10,404.80	8,679.70	11,034.30	2.8	3.14	0.38	20.9	132
AMERICAN GROWTH	G	SC	65.7	6.79	10,743.70	9,055.70	13,272.30	2.2	1.27	0.16	15.2	197
AMERICAN HERITAGE FUND (S)	CA	NO	0.8	1.17	11,142.90	7,769.70	3,688.30	0.0	0.09	0.00	N/A	N/A
AMERICAN INV GROWTH	G	NO	59.6	6.43	11,669.70	9,285.60	8,160.40	0.7	0.75	0.05	34.2	158
AMERICAN INV INCOME	FI	NO	22.2	8.46	11,005.10	10,978.50	14,013.[illegible]0	13.5	0.00	1.14	N/A	72
AMERICAN INV OPTION	OG	SC	0.7	8.89	9,877.80	9,115.30	☆	0.2	1.74	0.02	N/A	182
AMERICAN LEADERS	GI	LO	160.3	13.03	11,045.80	9,792.80	20,751.70	3.2	0.50	0.43	13.8	28
AMERICAN MUTUAL	GI	SC	2,615.7	18.81	11,151.30	10,111.80	19,942.10	4.5	0.71	0.87	14.2	13
AMERICAN NATIONAL GROWTH	G	SC	102.3	4.58	10,817.30	9,211.10	13,452.30	2.0	0.78	0.09	16.5	45
AMERICAN NATIONAL INCOME	EI	SC	67.4	20.02	10,913.60	9,390.40	16,013.80	4.1	0.53	0.82	17.1	25
AMER TELECOMMUN-GROWTH	TK	NO	32.1	49.55	11,609.70	9,350.60	☆	5.0	25.40	3.12	20.2	115
AMER TELECOMMUN-INCOME	S	NO	85.9	99.93	11,380.60	11,022.10	☆	7.1	1.46	7.18	10.7	6
AMERITRUST BALANCED	B	NO	7.1	10.38	10,734.20	9,980.80	☆	0.0	0.00	0.00	N/A	N/A
AMERITRUST US GOVT	FI	NO	5.8	10.72	10,458.50	10,613.90	☆	0.0	0.00	0.00	N/A	N/A
AMEV ADVNTGE: ASSET ALLOC	CA	SC	5.9	10.20	#10,210.20	☆	☆	0.0	0.00	0.00	N/A	N/A
AMEV ADVNTGE: CAP APP	SG	SC	2.7	11.34	#11,340.00	☆	☆	0.0	0.00	0.00	N/A	N/A
AMEV ADVNTGE: HIGH YLD	FI	SC	10.3	9.95	#10,475.30	☆	☆	0.0	0.00	0.52	N/A	N/A
AMEV CAPITAL FD	GI	SC	122.3	11.94	10,444.00	8,720.20	15,499.00	1.3	1.67	0.17	20.9	76
AMEV FIDUCIARY FD	CA	LO	33.2	18.69	10,649.40	8,509.70	16,526.10	0.2	0.64	0.03	21.2	79
AMEV GROWTH FD	CA	SC	202.1	15.35	10,930.80	8,351.90	14,310.80	0.5	1.40	0.08	27.0	80
AMEV SPECIAL FD	CA	NO	21.7	19.25	11,099.60	8,251.20	14,088.90	0.0	3.13	0.00	N/A	92
AMEV US GOVT FD	FI	SC	107.3	9.73	10,478.20	10,833.20	15,927.90	9.2	0.00	0.90	N/A	178
ANALYTIC OPTIONED EQU	OI	NO	98.3	12.29	11,026.00	10,245.40	16,610.50	2.6	2.19	0.35	N/A	84
API TRUST: GROWTH FD	CA	NO	28.9	11.10	12,211.20	9,676.10	☆	0.3	0.53	0.03	N/A	190
API TRUST: BAL FD	B	NO	0.4	20.03	#10,015.00	☆	☆	0.0	0.00	0.00	N/A	N/A
API TRUST: INV GRADE	FI	NO	0.4	14.98	#9,986.70	☆	☆	0.0	0.00	0.00	N/A	N/A
API TRUST: PREC RESOUR	S	NO	0.5	7.12	#10,171.40	☆	☆	0.0	0.00	0.00	N/A	N/A
API TRUST: US GOVT INTMDT	FI	NO	0.6	5.01	#10,020.00	☆	☆	0.0	0.00	0.00	N/A	N/A
ARIEL GROWTH	SG	LO	13.8	22.39	13,583.00	12,684.40	☆	0.3	0.74	0.07	N/A	60
ARMSTRONG ASSOCIATES	G	NO	10.4	7.17	11,399.00	9,215.40	11,790.70	1.7	1.80	0.14	N/A	51
ASSOCIATED PLANNERS GOVT	FI	SC	4.8	8.83	10,254.80	10,516.40	☆	9.2	0.16	0.81	N/A	148
ASSOCIATED PLANNERS STK	CA	SC	11.4	13.71	10,727.70	9,350.50	☆	0.0	1.45	0.00	N/A	254
AXE-HOUGHTON FUND B	B	NO	165.0	8.04	10,615.40	9,030.10	17,258.40	5.4	1.68	0.48	22.5	324
AXE-HOUGHTON INCOME	FI	NO	58.4	5.21	10,525.00	10,621.90	18,440.70	9.6	0.00	0.50	N/A	269

PERFORMANCE OF MUTUAL FUNDS *(continued)*

FUND NAME	OBJ.	LOAD	TOTAL NET ASTS (MIL) 6/30/88	NAV 6/30/88	PERFORMANCE (RETURN ON INITIAL $10,000 INVESTMENT) 12/31/87-6/30/88	6/30/87-6/30/88	6/30/83-6/30/88	YIELD % 6/30/88	PER SHARE LATEST 12 MONTHS CAP GAINS	INC DIVS	LATEST AVAILABLE PRICE/EARNINGS	ANNUAL % TURNOVER
AXE-HOUGHTON STOCK	G	NO	66.3	5.89	10,651.00	7,433.80	10,604.90	0.6	1.57	0.04	23.3	306
AYCO RISK	CA	NO	9.7	11.35	11,522.80	9,343.70	13,596.10	2.7	0.00	0.31	N/A	N/A
AYCO ROLLOVER	FI	NO	13.4	11.06	10,513.30	10,722.80	13,149.00	8.5	0.00	0.94	N/A	N/A
BABSON BOND TRUST	FI	NO	64.8	1.54	10,417.90	10,668.90	17,045.80	11.2	0.00	0.17	N/A	72
BABSON ENTERPRISE	SG	NO	51.5	12.07	13,091.10	9,942.60	☆	0.3	1.66	0.03	18.6	24
DAVID L BABSON GROWTH	G	NO	209.1	11.66	11,505.50	9,377.30	17,910.80	3.3	3.03	0.44	14.6	14
BABSON-STEWART IVORY INL	IF	NO	2.1	9.65	9,650.00	☆	☆	0.0	0.00	0.00	N/A	N/A
BABSON VALUE	GI	NO	12.0	17.11	11,898.50	9,631.00	☆	3.9	0.04	0.66	N/A	52
BAIRD BLUE CHIP	GI	LO	19.2	11.58	10,792.20	9,390.50	☆	0.2	0.04	0.02	N/A	9
BAIRD CAP DEVELOPMENT	G	LO	20.2	15.65	12,440.40	9,436.40	☆	0.0	1.12	0.00	N/A	80
BAKER EQUITY	CA	NO	1.3	15.64	10,064.40	9,806.50	☆	0.4	0.10	0.06	N/A	N/A
BAKER US GOVT	FI	NO	17.2	15.15	10,339.20	10,664.20	☆	7.2	0.00	1.08	N/A	98
BANKERS GRANIT FIX INC	FI	NO	2.0	9.81	10,419.50	10,657.00	☆	7.3	0.00	0.71	N/A	6
BANKERS GRANIT GOVT	FI	NO	5.4	9.99	10,390.70	10,721.60	☆	7.1	0.00	0.70	N/A	3
BANKERS GRANIT GR STK	G	NO	9.7	16.69	10,958.60	9,368.80	☆	0.0	0.38	0.00	N/A	64
BANKERS GRANIT STOCK	GI	NO	2.9	11.74	10,442.40	9,108.30	☆	0.6	0.59	0.06	N/A	27
BARON ASSET	SG	NO	9.8	12.68	12,554.50	12,073.30	☆	0.2	0.17	0.02	N/A	85
BARTLETT BASIC VALUE	GI	NO	83.3	12.93	11,929.10	9,923.50	18,544.60	2.9	0.00	0.37	N/A	58
BARTLETT CORPORATE CASH	EI	NO	18.4	0.98	10,236.00	10,208.70	☆	8.3	0.00	0.08	N/A	169
BARTLETT FIXED INCOME	FI	NO	163.2	9.69	10,551.00	10,692.90	☆	8.5	0.00	0.82	N/A	192
BASCOM HILL BALANCED (R)	B	NO	7.6	20.88	10,484.10	10,546.20	☆	3.9	0.00	0.82	N/A	N/A
BASCOM HILL INVESTORS	GI	NO	8.0	14.69	10,614.20	9,601.10	15,955.30	2.0	0.39	0.30	N/A	75
BB&K DIVERSA	CA	NO	107.9	10.71	10,562.10	10,093.00	☆	4.6	0.13	0.50	N/A	66
BB&K INTERNATIONAL	IF	NO	55.9	5.50	10,128.90	9,370.60	31,797.70	0.0	13.32	0.00	N/A	N/A
BEACON HILL MUTUAL	G	NO	3.1	24.70	9,825.00	8,283.00	15,215.00	0.0	0.00	0.00	N/A	1
BENCH BLUE CHIP	G	LO	14.9	7.88	11,010.60	9,124.70	☆	1.6	4.48	0.20	N/A	N/A
BENCH TOTAL RETURN	GI	LO	3.7	9.42	11,763.60	9,612.70	☆	3.3	0.97	0.33	N/A	N/A
BENHAM GNMA	FI	NO	255.2	9.90	10,595.80	10,938.90	☆	8.9	0.06	0.88	N/A	566
BENHAM TARGET 1990	FI	NO	15.1	83.97	10,364.10	10,627.80	☆	0.0	0.00	0.00	N/A	88
BENHAM TARGET 1995	FI	NO	10.6	54.84	10,501.70	10,615.60	☆	0.0	0.00	0.00	N/A	86
BENHAM TARGET 2000	FI	NO	9.8	35.13	10,540.10	10,606.90	☆	0.0	0.00	0.00	N/A	73
BENHAM TARGET 2005	FI	NO	5.7	22.73	10,681.40	10,696.50	☆	0.0	0.00	0.00	N/A	68
BENHAM TARGET 2010	FI	NO	7.2	15.70	10,494.70	10,349.40	☆	0.0	0.00	0.00	N/A	84
BENHAM TARGET 2015	FI	NO	3.7	11.65	10,246.30	9,948.80	☆	0.0	0.00	0.00	N/A	509
BERWYN FUND (R)	GI	NO	11.1	13.34	12,294.90	9,514.10	☆	0.4	1.27	0.05	N/A	43
BERWYN INCOME	FI	NO	2.1	10.13	10,857.60	☆	☆	0.0	0.00	0.22	N/A	N/A
BLANCHARD STRATEGIC GRO	CA	NO	246.1	9.53	10,366.40	9,791.90	☆	2.1	0.25	0.20	N/A	70
BMI EQUITY FUND	CA	SC	2.4	31.52	12,012.20	9,925.70	13,198.40	0.0	3.92	0.00	N/A	164
BOND FUND OF AMERICA	FI	SC	909.0	13.44	10,716.70	10,828.40	18,205.70	9.4	0.00	1.26	N/A	93
BOND PORT FOR ENDOWMENTS	FI	NO	34.3	17.13	10,554.60	10,807.80	17,380.90	8.0	0.54	1.40	N/A	84
BOSTON CO CAPITAL APPREC	G	NO	491.9	30.11	11,606.80	9,874.50	20,780.80	1.8	5.20	0.59	16.1	46
BOSTON CO GNMA	FI	NO	12.9	11.79	10,400.40	10,599.80	☆	7.6	0.00	0.89	N/A	122
BOSTON CO MANAGED INCO	FI	NO	58.2	11.43	10,564.40	10,712.10	18,094.00	9.4	0.00	1.07	N/A	306
BOSTON CO SPECIAL GROWTH	G	NO	34.9	14.15	11,772.00	9,410.10	13,157.80	3.5	1.55	0.52	19.4	322
BOSTON FRGN GR & INC (R)	IF	NO	9.7	9.70	11,266.00	☆	☆	0.0	0.00	0.00	N/A	N/A
BOSTON FRGN PERFORM (R)	AU	NO	5.9	14.97	9,001.80	8,115.40	☆	1.3	0.41	0.19	N/A	N/A
BOSTON GROWTH & INCO (R)	GI	NO	26.7	11.88	11,567.70	9,594.90	☆	2.6	2.66	0.35	N/A	N/A
BOWSER GROWTH	G	NO	2.0	1.62	11,020.40	6,923.10	☆	0.0	0.00	0.00	N/A	59
BRANDYWINE FUND	G	NO	126.4	13.69	12,479.50	9,600.40	☆	0.0	0.88	0.00	N/A	147
BRUCE FUND	G	NO	4.6	93.04	11,912.90	9,496.80	18,176.20	3.8	8.63	3.65	N/A	11
BULL&BEAR CAPITAL GROWTH	G	NO	67.0	9.62	11,521.00	8,978.80	12,603.40	0.0	1.57	0.00	20.4	112
BULL&BEAR EQUITY-INCOME	EI	NO	14.0	11.35	11,630.20	9,872.70	17,950.40	3.8	0.21	0.44	N/A	91
BULL&BEAR GOLD INVESTORS	AU	NO	47.5	14.24	9,264.80	8,278.00	11,390.40	0.0	1.39	0.00	25.6	42
BULL&BEAR HIGH YIELD	FI	NO	124.2	10.84	10,276.90	9,409.20	☆	13.2	0.00	1.43	N/A	84

BULL&BEAR OVERSEAS FD	IF	NO	1.1	15.11	10,160.00	☆	☆	0.0	0.00	0.04	N/A	N/A
BULL&BEAR SPECIAL EQU	CA	NO	2.6	18.79	11,930.20	9,265.30	☆	0.0	0.00	0.00	N/A	751
BULL&BEAR US GOVT SEC	FI	NO	65.4	14.35	10,490.60	10,835.30	☆	10.4	0.00	1.49	N/A	195
CALAMOS CONV INCOME	CV	NO	24.8	10.80	11,070.30	9,627.10	☆	6.5	0.07	0.70	N/A	45
CALDWELL FUND	G	NO	1.3	12.18	10,304.60	9,404.10	☆	3.1	0.02	0.38	N/A	264
CALVERT EQUITY	G	NO	8.8	17.96	12,201.10	9,318.60	13,672.30	0.6	3.41	0.11	N/A	34
CALVERT INCOME	FI	SC	20.0	15.73	10,604.20	10,972.90	17,632.20	9.5	0.30	1.50	N/A	42
CALVERT SOCIAL INV: BOND	FI	LO	3.3	15.48	10,514.60	☆	☆	0.0	0.00	0.79	N/A	N/A
CALVERT SOCIAL INV: EQTY	G	LO	1.6	14.60	11,406.30	☆	☆	0.0	0.00	0.07	N/A	N/A
CALVERT SOCIAL INV: GRO	B	LO	168.3	24.95	10,942.60	10,057.40	17,286.50	4.2	0.51	1.06	N/A	14
CALVERT US GOVT	FI	SC	2.6	14.36	10,551.30	10,812.00	☆	8.5	0.00	1.21	N/A	115
CAPITAL INCOME BUILDER	EI	SC	111.9	22.30	10,852.70	☆	☆	0.0	0.00	1.36	11.3	N/A
CAPITAL PRES T NOTE TR	FI	NO	56.0	9.98	10,382.90	10,554.60	16,484.10	7.5	0.18	0.75	N/A	396
CAP SUPERVISORS HELIOS	G	NO	35.6	3044.52	10,901.30	8,901.90	☆	1.4	325.41	41.54	N/A	114
CAPITAL WORLD BOND	WI	SC	34.9	15.07	9,826.90	☆	☆	0.0	0.01	0.91	N/A	N/A
CAPSTONE: EQUITYGUARD (R)	CA	NO	10.8	9.96	11,662.80	10,338.50	☆	1.4	0.58	0.14	N/A	N/A
CARDINAL FUND	GI	SC	130.1	15.61	11,491.30	9,798.20	19,843.20	3.5	0.64	0.55	12.0	13
CARDINAL GOVT GUARTD	FI	SC	151.0	8.89	10,530.70	10,755.40	☆	9.7	0.00	0.85	N/A	N/A
CARNEGIE CAPPIELLO GROW	G	SC	44.3	14.49	12,428.90	10,074.30	☆	2.2	0.89	0.32	N/A	47
CARNEGIE HI YLD GOVT	FI	SC	56.2	9.53	10,425.50	10,704.90	16,883.20	7.5	0.14	0.72	N/A	128
CARNEGIE TOTAL RETURN	GI	SC	66.0	10.11	11,707.20	9,908.80	☆	6.6	0.37	0.68	N/A	32
CASHMAN FARRELL VALUE	CA	SC	9.0	10.77	11,945.90	10,790.20	☆	2.8	1.30	0.32	N/A	111
CENTURY SHARES TRUST	S	NO	115.8	16.25	11,172.60	9,553.40	19,609.60	2.9	1.61	0.50	13.3	2
CHAMPION HI YLD FD-USA	FI	SC	14.7	12.21	11,186.70	☆	☆	0.0	0.00	0.88	N/A	N/A
CHARTER FUND	GI	SC	70.7	5.34	10,289.00	8,920.40	14,925.80	2.0	1.40	0.12	14.9	225
CIGNA AGGRESSIVE GROWTH	SG	SC	15.9	12.20	12,373.20	9,641.70	☆	0.0	0.84	0.00	N/A	118
CIGNA GOVT	FI	SC	41.9	9.94	10,449.80	10,692.80	☆	8.5	0.00	0.84	N/A	35
CIGNA UTILITIES FUND	UT	SC	9.6	10.59	#10,910.40	☆	☆	0.0	0.00	0.30	N/A	N/A
CIGNA GROWTH	G	SC	203.9	12.17	11,023.60	9,039.50	15,665.10	1.5	1.99	0.20	17.7	78
CIGNA HIGH YIELD	FI	SC	264.2	10.10	11,072.80	10,922.10	18,648.40	11.7	0.00	1.18	N/A	81
CIGNA INCOME	FI	SC	234.0	7.67	10,576.20	10,720.60	17,440.50	8.2	0.00	0.63	N/A	195
CIGNA VALUE	GI	SC	61.2	13.41	11,691.40	10,320.80	☆	1.7	1.05	0.23	19.1	219
CITIBANK CIT BALANCED	B	NO	176.2	1.75	10,736.20	9,722.20	16,826.90	0.0	0.00	0.00	N/A	N/A
CITIBANK CIT EQUITY	G	NO	137.1	1.92	10,971.40	9,365.90	16,551.70	0.0	0.00	0.00	N/A	N/A
CITIBANK CIT INCOME	FI	NO	62.5	1.70	10,303.00	10,759.50	16,831.70	0.0	0.00	0.00	N/A	N/A
CLAREMONT—COMBINED	GI	SC	16.5	12.78	11,036.30	9,949.40	☆	0.0	0.87	0.00	N/A	198
CLAREMONT—GOVT BOND	FI	SC	7.7	10.20	10,314.40	10,471.40	☆	6.8	0.00	0.69	N/A	155
CLIPPER FUND	GI	NO	80.0	38.52	11,410.00	10,515.20	☆	4.7	5.27	1.94	13.4	140
COLONIAL ADV STR GOLD	AU	SC	100.8	24.22	9,942.50	9,373.40	☆	1.0	1.91	0.23	24.2	54
COLONIAL CORP CASH I	EI	LO	217.9	42.92	10,963.70	9,724.60	15,264.80	8.3	0.75	3.57	11.3	206
COLONIAL CORP CASH II	EI	LO	155.3	43.38	10,179.10	9,756.60	☆	7.8	0.09	3.39	11.4	71
COLONIAL DVSD INCOME	OI	SC	771.3	7.49	11,438.60	9,943.60	16,267.20	4.8	0.59	0.37	22.9	82
COLONIAL EQUITY INCOME	EI	SC	16.7	15.03	11,396.50	9,816.60	15,956.50	4.8	0.03	0.72	N/A	89
COLONIAL FUND	GI	SC	257.2	18.53	11,681.30	10,178.70	20,283.40	4.0	0.57	0.76	14.7	47
COLONIAL GOVT MORTGAGE	FI	SC	20.2	13.04	10,416.40	10,459.90	☆	7.8	0.00	1.01	N/A	210
COLONIAL GOVT SEC PLUS	FI	SC	3,261.8	11.12	10,385.20	10,572.10	☆	8.0	0.38	0.89	N/A	140
COLONIAL GROWTH SHARES	G	SC	91.7	12.45	12,076.10	9,967.00	17,454.40	1.8	0.79	0.23	17.3	37
COLONIAL HIGH YIELD	FI	SC	465.9	7.41	10,927.00	10,842.60	18,412.20	11.4	0.00	0.84	N/A	51
COLONIAL INCOME FUND	FI	SC	165.3	6.64	10,731.70	10,614.10	16,801.30	10.9	0.00	0.72	N/A	32
COLONIAL INCOME PLUS	OI	SC	144.7	9.14	10,958.50	9,297.50	☆	3.1	1.02	0.30	15.9	153
COLONIAL INTL EQ INDEX	IF	SC	7.9	16.48	10,687.40	9,918.40	☆	0.0	0.15	0.00	N/A	10
COLONIAL SMALL STK INDEX	SG	SC	44.6	12.94	13,324.00	9,782.40	☆	0.6	0.50	0.07	17.9	34
COLONIAL US EQUITY INDEX	G	SC	41.9	13.41	11,235.60	9,213.70	☆	2.5	0.27	0.33	16.5	29
COLONIAL US GOVT TRUST	FI	SC	36.5	7.33	10,544.20	☆	☆	0.0	0.00	0.51	N/A	N/A
COLONIAL VIP: AGGR GRO (R)	G	NO	1.2	10.51	#10,533.10	☆	☆	0.0	0.00	0.02	N/A	N/A
COLONIAL VIP: DVSD RETN (R)	GI	NO	2.5	10.11	#10,172.80	☆	☆	0.0	0.00	0.06	N/A	N/A
COLONIAL VIP: FED SEC (R)	FI	NO	4.1	9.94	#10,056.00	☆	☆	0.0	0.00	0.11	N/A	N/A

PERFORMANCE OF MUTUAL FUNDS *(continued)*

FUND NAME	OBJ.	LOAD	TOTAL NET ASTS (MIL) 6/30/88	NAV 6/30/88	PERFORMANCE (RETURN ON INITIAL $10,000 INVESTMENT) 12/31/87-6/30/88	6/30/87-6/30/88	6/30/83-6/30/88	YIELD % 6/30/88	PER SHARE LATEST 12 MONTHS CAP GAINS	INC DIVS	LATEST AVAILABLE PRICE/EARNINGS	ANNUAL % TURNOVER
COLONIAL VIP: HIGH INC (R)	FI	NO	14.2	9.96	#10,125.60	☆	☆	0.0	0.00	0.16	N/A	N/A
COLONIAL VIP: INFLN HDG (R)	S	NO	1.4	10.05	#10,072.60	☆	☆	0.0	0.00	0.02	N/A	N/A
COLUMBIA FIXED INCOME	FI	NO	104.1	12.32	10,500.70	10,741.70	16,945.40	8.4	0.00	1.02	N/A	114
COLUMBIA GROWTH	G	NO	219.8	22.45	11,119.40	9,893.00	16,144.90	1.5	4.69	0.36	21.5	197
COLUMBIA SPECIAL (R)	CA	NO	26.5	35.67	12,835.60	9,687.70	☆	0.0	0.00	0.00	N/A	333
COLUMBIA US GOVT	FI	NO	11.5	8.30	10,334.00	10,680.00	☆	6.7	0.00	0.55	N/A	147
COMMON SENSE GOVT	FI	SC	55.3	11.16	10,416.40	10,439.40	☆	7.9	0.00	0.87	N/A	N/A
COMMON SENSE GROWTH	CA	SC	429.4	10.88	11,286.30	9,202.00	☆	0.0	0.09	0.00	16.8	N/A
COMMON SENSE GRO & INC	GI	SC	146.3	10.35	10,702.50	8,961.00	☆	2.3	0.03	0.23	18.3	N/A
COMMONWEALTH A&B	GI	SC	9.8	1.42	11,190.00	10,026.80	17,236.60	5.4	0.12	0.08	N/A	64
COMMONWEALTH C	GI	SC	38.2	1.98	11,120.30	9,986.80	16,171.60	5.1	0.16	0.10	14.5	54
COMPANION FUND	G	NO	70.6	10.39	11,041.40	9,070.80	16,131.10	1.9	1.97	0.22	18.5	75
COMPOSITE BOND & STOCK	B	LO	76.6	10.05	11,176.60	10,268.80	16,658.40	5.6	0.17	0.57	13.4	83
COMPOSITE DEFERRED GRO	CA	NO	1.2	11.83	11,437.40	10,228.80	☆	3.5	0.00	0.41	N/A	N/A
COMPOSITE DEFERRED INC	I	NO	2.7	11.78	10,619.80	10,848.30	☆	10.9	0.00	1.28	N/A	N/A
COMPOSITE GROWTH FD	GI	LO	70.3	10.75	11,439.00	10,054.10	18,180.10	4.7	0.80	0.52	14.0	71
COMPOSITE INCOME FUND	FI	LO	164.7	8.98	10,512.00	10,766.50	17,060.40	10.6	0.00	0.95	N/A	99
COMPOSITE SEL HI YLD	FI	LO	3.1	11.30	11,135.80	11,015.50	☆	11.5	0.00	1.30	N/A	21
COMPOSITE SEL NORTHWEST	G	LO	7.6	14.98	12,290.30	9,701.70	☆	0.8	0.00	0.12	N/A	40
COMPOSITE SEL VALUE	SG	LO	5.5	11.04	11,921.20	8,690.30	☆	2.6	0.00	0.29	N/A	66
COMPOSITE US GOVT SEC	FI	LO	89.0	10.00	10,579.90	10,849.80	16,546.70	9.2	0.00	0.91	N/A	43
CONCORD FUND	G	NO	1.5	26.92	12,034.00	9,474.20	13,197.40	1.1	2.25	0.30	N/A	N/A
CONCORD INCOME-US GOVT	FI	LO	10.6	6.95	10,512.10	10,947.00	☆	8.4	0.00	0.58	N/A	52
CONCORDE VALUE FUND	GI	NO	7.5	12.17	12,418.40	☆	☆	0.0	0.00	0.00	N/A	N/A
CONNECTICUT MUT GOVT	FI	SC	32.6	10.34	10,575.50	10,844.10	☆	8.0	0.00	0.82	N/A	N/A
CONNECTICUT MUT GROWTH	CA	SC	26.0	10.89	11,176.80	9,088.30	☆	1.8	1.40	0.21	N/A	N/A
CONNECTICUT MUT INCOME	FI	SC	16.2	9.92	10,369.90	10,607.20	☆	8.0	0.00	0.79	N/A	N/A
CONNECTICUT MUT TOT RET	GI	SC	54.4	11.61	10,864.50	9,567.20	☆	3.7	0.84	0.44	N/A	N/A
CONSTELLATION GROWTH	CA	SC	102.2	7.80	12,283.50	9,226.40	14,157.00	0.0	4.06	0.00	23.7	135
CONTINENTAL EQUITY + (R)	G	LO	10.3	9.37	11,411.60	8,285.30	☆	2.9	0.03	0.27	N/A	71
CONTINENTAL GOVT INC	FI	LO	1.9	9.77	10,319.70	10,811.00	☆	8.8	0.00	0.85	N/A	1
CONTINENTAL OPT INC + (R)	OI	LO	53.5	8.99	11,213.60	9,740.10	☆	3.3	0.93	0.31	N/A	171
CONTINENTAL US GOVT + (R)	FI	LO	79.6	9.13	10,339.00	10,636.10	☆	9.2	0.00	0.84	N/A	276
CONVERTIBLE SEC & INCO	CV	LO	9.4	9.46	11,800.20	10,259.10	☆	7.6	0.05	0.72	N/A	24
COPLEY FUND	GI	NO	23.9	11.11	10,989.10	9,788.50	18,703.70	0.0	0.00	0.00	12.0	16
CORPORATE LEADERS TR-B (X)	GI	SC	77.1	13.04	11,097.90	9,085.90	21,186.00	0.0	1.10	0.00	N/A	N/A
CORPORATE PREFERRED FD	FI	LO	15.1	41.70	9,831.60	9,806.70	☆	7.7	0.00	3.21	N/A	90
COUNSELLORS CAP APPREC	G	NO	24.0	9.44	11,878.40	☆	☆	0.0	0.00	0.13	N/A	20
COUNSELLORS EMERGING GR	SG	NO	7.9	11.66	#11,697.00	☆	☆	0.0	0.00	0.03	N/A	N/A
COUNSELLORS FIXED INC	FI	NO	63.7	10.01	10,660.40	☆	☆	0.0	0.00	0.88	N/A	30
COUNTRY CAPITAL GROWTH	G	SC	68.4	15.06	10,810.80	9,331.50	15,327.60	3.8	2.59	0.59	23.3	41
COUNTRY CAPITAL INCOME	FI	SC	6.0	10.51	10,468.90	10,641.00	16,970.80	6.9	0.26	0.72	N/A	51
COWEN INCOME & GROWTH (R)	EI	NO	30.8	9.67	11,161.50	9,779.00	☆	4.6	0.26	0.45	N/A	26
COWEN FUNDS: OPPORTUNITY	TK	SC	10.1	9.83	#10,325.60	☆	☆	0.0	0.00	0.00	N/A	N/A
CRITERION COMMERCE INC	I	SC	71.6	8.95	10,481.10	9,662.00	15,881.60	5.1	1.49	0.49	19.6	138
CRITERION INV QUAL INT	FI	SC	127.4	9.11	10,420.10	10,597.70	17,230.10	9.7	0.01	0.88	N/A	150
CRITERION LTD TRM INSTL	FI	NO	7.8	9.61	10,419.80	10,888.40	☆	8.3	0.00	0.80	N/A	118
CRITERION PILOT FUND	CA	SC	57.4	7.87	10,168.00	8,668.50	11,954.60	0.3	2.44	0.03	24.4	205
CRITERION SPEC: BL CHIP (R)	G	NO	4.6	8.29	10,184.30	9,227.60	☆	0.0	3.43	0.00	N/A	N/A
CRITERION SPEC: CONVERT (R)	CV	NO	15.3	9.29	10,542.60	8,997.80	☆	4.6	0.00	0.42	N/A	290
CRITERION SPEC: EMRG GR (R)	SG	NO	2.4	10.75	12,105.90	☆	☆	0.0	0.00	0.00	N/A	N/A
CRITERION SPEC: GLO GR (R)	GL	NO	9.9	10.79	9,747.10	8,335.00	☆	0.0	0.80	0.00	N/A	230
CRITERION SPEC: GOV INC (R)	FI	NO	4.0	10.13	10,622.60	☆	☆	0.0	0.00	0.49	N/A	N/A
CRITERION SPEC: HI YLD (R)	FI	NO	9.6	9.84	10,442.10	☆	☆	0.0	0.00	0.78	N/A	N/A

CRITERION SPEC: NAT RES (R)	NR	NO	1.2	10.16	11,189.40	9,004.80	☆	0.3	2.35	0.03	N/A	N/A
CRITERION SUNBELT GRO	G	SC	42.8	17.02	10,738.50	8,859.50	12,225 90	1.0	2.68	0.18	27.3	112
CRITERION TECHNOLOGY	TK	SC	6.0	18.55	12,333.30	10,027.00	☆	0.0	0.00	0.00	N/A	272
CRITERION US GOVT HI YLD	FI	SC	1,397.8	8.67	10,373.60	10,581.80	☆	9.0	0.20	0.79	N/A	295
CRITERION US GOVT INSTL	FI	LO	224.3	8.73	10,370.00	10,461.80	☆	8.8	0.20	0.78	N/A	364
CUMBERLAND GROWTH	CA	NO	2.3	10.05	11,330.30	8,869.00	11,871.50	1.0	0.00	0.09	N/A	N/A
DEAN WITTER AMER VALUE (R)	G	NO	103.0	13.22	10,895.00	9,480.80	14,301.50	1.5	0.48	0.20	N/A	203
DEAN WITTER CONVERT (R)	CV	NO	1,218.9	9.05	10,753.90	8,449.00	☆	3.0	1.00	0.28	N/A	572
DEAN WITTER DEV GRO (R)	SG	NO	123.8	10.19	11,766.70	10,009.80	10,414.80	0.0	0.00	0.00	22.0	68
DEAN WITTER DIVID GRO (R)	GI	NO	1,780.7	19.39	11,325.80	9,654.80	19,800.20	3.7	0.20	0.73	16.5	7
DEAN WITTER GOVT PLUS (R)	FI	NO	2,217.7	9.12	10,338.40	10,437.20	☆	8.1	0.21	0.74	N/A	32
DEAN WITTER HIGH YIELD	FI	SC	2,111.8	12.27	10,765.90	10,117.10	16,295.40	14.7	0.00	1.80	N/A	176
DEAN WITTER NTRL RES (R)	NR	NO	165.3	9.76	11,444.20	9,641.70	13,285.00	2.0	0.07	0.20	18.3	26
DEAN WITTER OPT INC (R)	OI	NO	341.3	8.22	11,062.10	9,453.30	☆	1.9	0.84	0.16	14.7	157
DEAN WITTER TAX-ADV	FI	NO	130.9	9.25	10,150.50	9,920.10	☆	9.7	0.00	0.90	N/A	52
DEAN WITTER US GOVT (R)	FI	NO	10,711.3	9.70	10,453.30	10,734.90	☆	9.9	0.00	0.96	N/A	51
DEAN WITTER UTILITIES (R)	UT	NO	303.7	10.36	#10,360.00	☆	☆	0.0	0.00	0.00	N/A	N/A
DEAN WITTER VAL ADD: EQ (R)	GI	NO	36.7	12.34	11,558.10	☆	☆	0.0	0.00	0.08	N/A	N/A
DEAN WITTER WORLD WIDE (R)	GL	NO	342.9	14.26	10,622.90	9,597.90	☆	0.4	2.22	0.07	19.5	65
DECATUR I	EI	SC	1,535.5	16.47	11,460.00	9,655.80	21,173.20	5.4	1.75	0.93	17.8	56
DECATUR II	GI	SC	184.5	10.90	11,729.70	9,499.70	☆	4.1	0.00	0.45	N/A	39
DELAWARE FUND	GI	SC	323.4	14.44	11,374.30	8,709.80	14,748.50	1.9	4.09	0.32	17.4	205
DELAWARE GOVT INCOME	FI	SC	161.1	8.74	10,464.80	10,896.10	☆	9.4	0.00	0.82	N/A	210
DELAWARE GROUP VALUE	CA	SC	8.8	10.65	12,269.60	11,232.40	☆	0.4	0.00	0.04	N/A	N/A
DELAWARE TREAS: INVESTORS	FI	NO	161.6	9.79	10,357.20	10,669.40	☆	7.3	0.00	0.71	N/A	304
DELCAP FUND I	CA	SC	117.7	14.32	12,115.10	10,556.70	☆	3.0	0.26	0.43	N/A	127
DELCHESTER BOND FUND: I	FI	SC	561.1	7.75	10,957.70	10,897.40	18,428.00	12.2	0.00	0.94	N/A	149
DELCHESTER BOND FUND: II	FI	SC	32.2	7.75	10,941.10	☆	☆	0.0	0.00	0.48	N/A	N/A
DELTA TREND FUND	CA	SC	59.9	8.13	12,281.00	8,914.50	9,727.40	0.0	0.00	0.00	22.8	93
DEVONSHIRE FUND	S	LO	1.9	10.10	#9,970.40	☆	☆	0.0	0.00	0.00	N/A	N/A
DFA FIXED INCOME PORT	FI	NO	313.4	101.67	10,379.30	10,762.20	☆	6.9	0.00	7.06	N/A	162
DFA JAPAN SMALL CO	IF	NO	84.3	29.36	12,748.60	16,681.10	☆	0.1	4.21	0.03	N/A	N/A
DFA SMALL COMPANY	SG	NO	968.8	8.15	12,577.20	9,515.40	13,641.90	1.2	1.30	0.10	20.6	23
DFA UNITED KINGDOM SM CO	IF	NO	97.8	26.57	10,623.80	9,520.20	☆	2.4	0.66	0.64	N/A	10
DIT CAPITAL GROWTH	G	NO	13.0	13.13	10,806.60	8,977.40	14,465.60	1.0	1.49	0.13	N/A	96
DIT CURRENT INCOME	FI	NO	6.8	9.69	10,903.30	10,751.90	17,569.80	11.8	0.00	1.14	N/A	116
DIV/GROWTH DIVIDEND SR	EI	NO	3.7	22.51	10,320.00	8,812.40	14,527.90	3.2	1.19	0.73	N/A	34
DIV/GRO LASER & ADV TECH	TK	NO	0.1	7.29	11,608.30	7,133.10	☆	0.0	0.00	0.00	N/A	25
DODGE & COX BALANCED	B	NO	39.8	32.82	10,964.90	9,996.40	19,931.50	5.2	2.67	1.76	16.9	15
DODGE & COX STOCK	GI	NO	75.2	36.76	11,329.00	9,894.80	22,615.60	2.9	1.57	1.10	18.8	12
DOLPHIN FRIC CONVERTIBLE	CV	LO	8.8	9.51	11,628.30	9,919.20	☆	6.6	0.19	0.63	N/A	109
DR EQUITY	GI	NO	31.2	10.62	11,261.90	10,300.00	☆	3.9	0.43	0.42	N/A	119
DREMAN: CONTRARIAN PORT	G	LO	2.2	9.98	#9,980.00	☆	☆	0.0	0.00	0.00	N/A	N/A
DREMAN: HIGH RETURN PORT	EI	LO	2.0	10.68	#10,680.00	☆	☆	0.0	0.00	0.00	N/A	N/A
DREXEL BURNHAM FUND	GI	LO	204.1	20.60	10,763.60	9,791.60	19,583.10	4.1	2.25	0.89	13.6	121
DREXEL SR: BOND-DEB (R)	FI	NO	24.7	10.73	10,536.30	10,576.50	☆	8.0	0.00	0.86	N/A	92
DREXEL SR: CONVERTIBLE (R)	CV	NO	24.5	8.83	10,665.00	8,841.70	☆	5.0	0.13	0.44	N/A	141
DREXEL SR: EMERGING GRO (R)	SG	NO	15.1	11.72	11,161.90	7,488.80	☆	0.0	0.00	0.00	21.6	59
DREXEL SR: GOVT (R)	FI	NO	296.3	9.52	10,349.10	10,528.10	☆	7.4	0.06	0.70	N/A	58
DREXEL SR: GROWTH (R)	G	NO	32.8	12.37	11,556.70	9,765.30	☆	2.3	1.19	0.30	19.5	60
DREXEL SR: LTD GOVT (R)	FI	NO	14.8	9.71	10,196.50	☆	☆	0.0	0.02	0.48	N/A	N/A
DREXEL SR: OPTION INC (R)	OI	NO	34.3	9.41	10,993.20	9,747.70	☆	2.8	0.90	0.28	15.3	110
DREXEL SR: PRIORITY SEL (R)	CA	NO	19.0	10.55	10,727.20	☆	☆	0.0	0.00	0.07	N/A	N/A
DREYFUS A BONDS PLUS	FI	NO	260.8	13.58	10,531.10	10,641.60	16,937.00	8.9	0.00	1.20	N/A	79
DREYFUS CAPITAL VALUE	CA	SC	488.0	25.00	10,429.70	11,106.00	☆	1.2	0.81	0.30	N/A	102
DREYFUS CONVERTIBLE SEC	CV	NO	262.2	8.97	11,979.50	10,415.10	20,235.50	5.2	0.22	0.47	28.4	91
DREYFUS CORP CASH TRUST	FI	NO	12.5	12.50	10,278.40	10,560.50	☆	5.5	0.00	0.68	N/A	270

PERFORMANCE OF MUTUAL FUNDS (continued)

FUND NAME	OBJ.	LOAD	TOTAL NET ASTS (MIL) 6/30/88	NAV 6/30/88	PERFORMANCE (RETURN ON INITIAL $10,000 INVESTMENT) 12/31/87-6/30/88	6/30/87-6/30/88	6/30/83-6/30/88	YIELD % 6/30/88	PER SHARE—LATEST 12 MONTHS CAP GAINS	INC DIVS	LATEST AVAILABLE PRICE/EARNINGS	ANNUAL % TURNOVER
DREYFUS FRGN INV GNMA LP	FI	LO	2.0	14.83	10,750.00	☆	☆	0.0	0.00	1.26	N/A	110
DREYFUS FRGN INV GOVT LP	FI	LO	0.3	14.98	10,366.30	☆	☆	0.0	0.00	0.98	N/A	N/A
DREYFUS FUND	GI	SC	2,648.0	10.83	10,787.60	9,731.10	18,330.60	4.7	2.05	0.56	15.5	110
DREYFUS GNMA	FI	NO	1,963.8	14.80	10,523.50	10,767.00	☆	8.9	0.00	1.31	N/A	257
DREYFUS GRO OPPORTUNITY	G	NO	548.6	9.97	11,521.80	9,816.30	16,226.10	3.7	1.27	0.39	24.4	130
DREYFUS INDEX	G	NO	32.7	11.80	11,250.30	9,341.20	☆	2.4	0.00	0.28	N/A	N/A
DREYFUS LEVERAGE FUND	CA	LO	496.7	14.26	10,229.60	9,124.90	20,210.40	2.5	3.66	0.41	24.5	124
DREYFUS NEW LEADERS	SG	NO	120.0	24.17	12,614.80	9,635.60	☆	0.4	0.00	0.10	N/A	177
DREYFUS SHT-INTERM GOVT	FI	NO	6.2	11.28	10,348.80	10,746.40	☆	9.0	0.00	1.01	N/A	24
DREYFUS STRAT AGG INV LP	CA	LO	155.4	25.87	10,576.50	11,727.10	☆	0.0	0.00	0.00	N/A	432
DREYFUS STRATEGIC INCO	FI	LO	36.5	12.91	10,691.30	11,002.70	☆	9.4	0.37	1.22	N/A	76
DREYFUS STRATEGIC INVEST	CA	LO	116.8	16.19	9,619.70	9,666.90	☆	1.2	0.21	0.20	N/A	321
DREYFUS STRAT WORLD LP	GL	LO	16.1	19.13	11,089.90	12,153.70	☆	0.0	0.00	0.00	N/A	396
DREYFUS THIRD CENTURY	G	NO	156.2	5.93	11,447.90	9,621.50	15,696.80	5.6	1.27	0.35	18.4	33
DREYFUS US GOVT BD LP	FI	NO	8.3	12.83	10,411.20	10,561.70	☆	9.4	0.00	1.20	N/A	2
DREYFUS US GOVT INTER LP	FI	NO	67.3	12.58	10,407.60	10,745.50	☆	9.7	0.00	1.22	N/A	N/A
EAGLE GROWTH SHARES	G	SC	2.0	7.80	12,302.80	10,788.40	10,609.20	0.0	0.00	0.00	N/A	349
EATON & HOWARD STOCK	GI	SC	79.2	13.28	11,042.70	9,746.10	19,544.60	3.4	0.77	0.46	14.2	26
EATON VANCE DOLR HI INC	FI	SC	18.6	11.11	10,873.80	10,906.10	☆	11.8	0.00	1.30	N/A	3
EATON VANCE DOLR US GOVT	FI	SC	3.5	11.34	10,435.30	10,848.60	☆	8.9	0.00	1.00	N/A	N/A
EATON VANCE EQUITY INC (R)	EI	NO	2.0	9.87	9,939.60	☆	☆	0.0	0.00	0.08	N/A	N/A
EATON VANCE GOVT OBLIG	FI	SC	353.1	11.54	10,503.40	10,788.40	☆	10.0	0.04	1.16	N/A	36
EATON VANCE GROWTH	G	SC	88.6	7.13	11,017.20	9,445.40	17,510.10	0.8	1.23	0.06	17.9	57
EATON VANCE HIGH INC (R)	FI	NO	237.4	9.34	10,871.10	10,656.20	☆	12.1	0.00	1.12	N/A	47
EATON VANCE HIGH YIELD	FI	SC	34.1	5.02	10,916.20	10,699.20	18,566.20	12.0	0.00	0.60	N/A	69
EATON VANCE INC OF BOSTON	FI	SC	45.0	9.43	10,953.90	10,820.30	18,927.00	13.1	0.26	1.25	9.3	86
EATON VANCE INVESTORS	B	SC	211.4	7.15	10,792.20	9,960.10	17,499.20	4.8	0.81	0.36	16.5	75
EATON VANCE NTRL RES (R)	NR	NO	2.1	12.12	11,068.50	☆	☆	0.0	0.00	0.04	N/A	N/A
EATON VANCE SPL EQUITIES	G	SC	35.2	18.45	11,243.10	9,736.10	12,226.00	0.0	0.08	0.00	18.9	54
EATON VANCE TOTAL RETURN	GI	SC	515.5	7.98	10,856.30	8,821.90	20,744.10	9.2	0.34	0.75	9.8	190
ECLIPSE EQUITY	SG	NO	159.9	10.06	10,911.70	10,446.20	☆	4.7	0.00	0.47	N/A	14
EHRENKRANTZ EQUITIES	CA	NO	2.0	4.98	11,116.10	9,928.20	☆	1.6	0.00	0.08	N/A	22
EHRENKRANTZ GROWTH	G	NO	2.7	4.87	11,352.00	9,414.00	☆	1.6	0.00	0.08	N/A	33
ELFUN TRUSTS	G	NO	512.5	26.70	11,059.00	9,349.50	18,296.50	3.1	2.31	0.86	19.4	N/A
EMERGING MEDICAL TECH	H	SC	7.4	13.15	11,575.70	7,993.90	☆	0.0	0.00	0.00	N/A	N/A
ENDOWMENTS INC	GI	NO	38.2	16.83	11,009.50	9,988.40	18,895.90	5.1	1.80	0.85	11.5	13
ENERGY FUND	NR	NO	388.9	17.43	11,252.40	9,144.60	16,144.00	3.4	3.35	0.59	24.2	88
ENTERPRISE: AGGR GROWTH (R)	CA	NO	2.1	13.19	10,741.00	☆	☆	0.0	0.00	0.02	N/A	N/A
ENTERPRISE: CORP BOND (R)	FI	NO	2.3	12.07	10,360.50	☆	☆	0.0	0.00	0.41	N/A	N/A
ENTERPRISE: GNMA (R)	FI	NO	4.9	11.92	10,286.80	☆	☆	0.0	0.00	0.45	N/A	N/A
ENTERPRISE: GOVT SEC (R)	FI	NO	3.1	11.89	10,251.30	☆	☆	0.0	0.00	0.45	N/A	N/A
ENTERPRISE: GROWTH (R)	G	NO	38.7	7.02	11,661.10	10,156.80	16,389.30	0.6	1.56	0.05	16.1	64
ENTERPRISE: GRO & INC (R)	GI	NO	6.0	13.30	11,003.60	☆	☆	0.0	0.00	0.12	N/A	N/A
ENTERPRISE: HI YLD BOND (R)	FI	NO	7.5	12.52	10,746.10	☆	☆	0.0	0.00	0.70	N/A	N/A
ENTERPRISE: INTL GRO (R)	IF	NO	2.5	11.83	9,858.30	☆	☆	0.0	0.00	0.06	N/A	N/A
ENTERPRISE: PREC METAL (R)	AU	NO	2.3	11.66	9,708.60	☆	☆	0.0	0.47	0.00	N/A	N/A
EQUITABLE BAL FD (R)	B	NO	2.4	11.66	10,897.20	☆	☆	0.0	0.00	0.05	N/A	N/A
EQUITABLE GOVT SEC FD (R)	FI	NO	7.2	10.08	10,411.00	☆	☆	0.0	0.00	0.44	N/A	N/A
EQUITABLE GROWTH FD (R)	G	NO	2.2	13.60	12,318.80	☆	☆	0.0	0.00	0.00	N/A	N/A
EQUITEC SIEBEL: AGGRES (R)	CA	NO	43.6	12.49	11,238.70	9,555.80	☆	4.8	0.18	0.60	17.2	154
EQUITEC SIEBEL EQU PLUS	EI	SC	1.2	9.67	10,836.00	10,201.80	☆	5.6	0.00	0.54	N/A	N/A
EQUITEC SIEBEL: GLOBAL (R)	GL	NO	1.4	9.97	#9,989.90	☆	☆	0.0	0.00	0.02	N/A	N/A
EQUITEC SIEBEL: HI YLD (R)	FI	NO	25.1	8.90	10,525.10	10,433.90	☆	10.8	0.00	0.95	N/A	102
EQUITEC SIEBEL: PRE MTL (R)	S	NO	1.0	10.71	#10,719.90	☆	☆	0.0	0.00	0.01	N/A	N/A

EQUITEC SIEBEL: TOT RET (R)	GI	NO	151.9	13.48	10,959.60	9,891.70	☆	2.2	0.65	0.31	16.5	76
EQUITEC SIEBEL: US GOVT (R)	FI	NO	191.4	9.41	10,537.80	10,652.70	☆	9.7	0.00	0.90	N/A	120
EQUITY PORT: GROWTH	G	NO	46.6	12.48	11,470.60	9,664.20	☆	0.1	0.76	0.01	N/A	226
EQUITY PORT: INCOME	EI	NO	457.7	11.20	12,003.80	10,083.40	19,463.50	6.0	1.65	0.72	24.8	137
EQUITY STRATEGIES (X)	S	NO	51.5	17.37	12,232.40	8,808.30	☆	0.0	0.00	0.00	N/A	99
EUROPEAN FUND	IF	SC	1.3	9.22	10,262.10	8,513.20	☆	2.4	0.00	0.22	N/A	99
EUROPACIFIC GROWTH	IF	SC	193.1	24.67	11,185.50	9,894.50	☆	1.8	2.78	0.47	N/A	22
EVERGREEN AMER RETIREMNT	B	NO	6.1	10.28	#10,280.00	☆	☆	0.0	0.00	0.00	N/A	N/A
EVERGREEN FUND	G	NO	740.3	12.29	12,314.60	10,016.30	17,500.20	1.9	1.55	0.24	15.1	46
EVERGREEN TOTAL RETURN	EI	NO	1,381.1	17.58	11,403.40	9,756.30	20,291.40	4.5	0.45	0.80	13.0	44
EVERGREEN VALUE TIMING	CA	NO	23.4	11.19	11,929.60	10,188.30	☆	1.6	0.00	0.17	N/A	48
EXECUTIVE INVEST HI YLD	FI	LO	2.3	9.12	11,540.50	11,022.40	☆	14.7	0.00	1.34	N/A	27
EXPLORER FUND (X)	TK	NO	266.8	29.41	12,430.30	9,699.50	9,143.80	0.4	1.96	0.11	18.6	9
EXPLORER II	SG	NO	69.1	20.61	12,385.80	9,378.30	☆	0.2	1.44	0.05	20.9	51
FAIRFIELD FUND	SG	SC	44.0	8.00	11,851.90	9,368.60	11,643.40	1.6	1.54	0.12	24.2	189
FAIRMONT FUND	CA	NO	81.5	51.39	11,453.10	8,884.60	17,748.70	1.0	0.24	0.53	N/A	1
FAM VALUE (R)	GI	NO	1.7	10.11	12,420.10	9,168.00	☆	1.0	0.02	0.10	N/A	N/A
FBL SERIES: AGG GRO STK (R)	CA	NO	1.4	11.80	11,501.00	☆	☆	0.0	0.00	0.02	N/A	N/A
FBL SERIES: BLUE CHIP (R)	GI	NO	1.4	11.64	11,106.90	☆	☆	0.0	0.00	0.00	N/A	N/A
FBL SERIES: GNMA (R)	FI	NO	1.5	10.02	10,386.20	☆	☆	0.0	0.00	0.37	N/A	N/A
FBL SERIES: HI QUAL BD (R)	FI	NO	3.0	9.94	10,258.60	☆	☆	0.0	0.00	0.39	N/A	N/A
FBL SERIES: HI YLD BD (R)	FI	NO	2.7	9.89	10,235.10	☆	☆	0.0	0.00	0.39	N/A	N/A
FBL SERIES: MANAGED (R)	GI	NO	3.6	0.00	N/A	☆	☆	0.0	0.00	0.05	N/A	N/A
FBL SERIES: GRO COM STK (R)	GI	NO	49.4	10.34	10,861.30	8,850.90	12,688.50	9.4	3.23	0.97	12.3	262
FEDERATED BOND	FI	NO	13.8	8.96	10,386.00	10,471.50	☆	8.6	0.00	0.77	N/A	62
FEDERATED CORP CASH	FI	NO	50.3	9.49	9,536.90	9,407.40	☆	6.5	0.00	0.61	N/A	37
FEDERATED FLOATING RATE	FI	NO	79.6	9.47	10,375.40	10,492.10	☆	9.8	0.00	0.92	N/A	82
FEDERATED GNMA TRUST	FI	NO	1,915.3	10.85	10,564.50	10,862.40	17,395.90	9.5	0.00	1.02	N/A	45
FEDERATED GROWTH TRUST	G	NO	114.4	17.40	12,891.20	10,369.60	☆	1.2	1.20	0.21	13.3	66
FEDERATED HIGH INCOME	FI	LO	369.3	11.18	10,926.00	10,494.40	17,203.60	12.8	0.00	1.43	N/A	25
FEDERATED HI QUAL STK	GI	LO	27.9	12.14	11,188.80	9,481.40	☆	2.4	0.16	0.29	14.5	28
FEDERATED HIGH YIELD TR	FI	NO	238.9	10.06	10,997.40	10,633.20	☆	12.5	0.00	1.26	N/A	57
FEDERATED INCOME TRUST	FI	NO	1,356.3	10.23	10,492.30	10,840.50	16,947.00	9.6	0.00	0.98	N/A	92
FEDERATED INTMDT GOVT	FI	NO	1,413.7	9.66	10,359.00	10,713.80	16,437.90	8.4	0.00	0.81	N/A	70
FEDERATED SH-INTMDT GOVT	FI	NO	2,867.3	10.05	10,338.10	10,694.90	☆	8.2	0.00	0.82	N/A	99
FEDERATED STOCK & BOND	B	NO	94.8	15.57	10,723.50	10,270.70	18,756.30	5.1	0.12	0.80	13.9	110
FEDERATED STOCK TRUST	GI	NO	642.1	22.84	11,194.10	9,369.40	22,130.50	3.0	0.63	0.68	14.1	51
FEDERATED US GOVT	FI	NO	15.9	9.13	10,483.10	10,649.50	☆	8.1	0.00	0.74	N/A	228
FEDERATED UTILITY	UT	NO	9.8	8.94	10,786.10	10,278.00	☆	6.4	0.00	0.57	N/A	N/A
FEDERATED VAR RATE MORT	FI	NO	34.9	9.99	10,379.40	☆	☆	0.0	0.00	0.54	N/A	N/A
FENIMORE INTL (R)	IF	NO	62.9	10.27	10,699.40	8,444.90	☆	1.8	1.69	0.00	N/A	185
FFB EQUITY	CA	NO	1.7	9.44	10,850.60	8,840.70	☆	2.4	0.93	0.24	N/A	107
FIDELITY ADJUSTABLE RATE	FI	NO	153.7	9.48	9,683.70	9,753.20	☆	8.2	0.18	0.78	N/A	172
FIDELITY BALANCED	B	LO	126.7	10.61	11,232.70	10,530.20	☆	6.6	0.07	0.70	16.7	161
FIDELITY BLUE CHIP GRO (R)	G	LO	41.5	10.68	10,680.00	☆	☆	0.0	0.00	0.00	N/A	N/A
FIDELITY CAPITAL APREC (R)	CA	LO	1,444.4	13.53	12,910.30	11,074.20	☆	0.1	0.82	0.02	15.0	598
FIDELITY CONTRAFUND	G	NO	99.0	12.60	11,753.70	8,910.90	15,046.80	0.0	0.00	0.00	14.0	196
FIDELITY CONVERTIBLE	CV	NO	47.1	10.23	11,536.70	10,235.80	☆	5.9	0.00	0.60	N/A	233
FIDELITY DESTINY I	G	SC	1,440.3	12.44	11,927.10	9,855.40	20,071.70	3.1	2.99	0.39	18.4	91
FIDELITY DESTINY II	G	SC	77.8	18.26	12,279.80	9,982.10	☆	0.5	2.58	0.09	18.9	183
FIDELITY EQUITY-INCOME	EI	LO	4,105.2	25.50	11,956.20	10,146.70	19,549.60	5.5	2.10	1.47	24.5	120
FIDELITY EUROPE	IF	LO	79.1	12.36	9,959.70	8,431.10	☆	0.0	0.00	0.00	N/A	241
FIDELITY FLEXIBLE BOND	FI	NO	319.2	6.76	10,486.60	10,703.00	16,459.70	8.9	0.00	0.60	N/A	127
FIDELITY FREEDOM FUND	CA	NO	1,355.5	12.75	11,762.00	9,678.40	19,000.20	1.6	3.18	0.23	18.9	171
FIDELITY FUND	GI	NO	936.1	15.43	11,547.90	9,556.20	17,763.80	3.0	1.35	0.48	19.2	211
FIDELITY GNMA	FI	NO	725.2	10.13	10,509.50	10,710.00	☆	8.5	0.00	0.86	N/A	177
FIDELITY GLOBAL BOND	WI	NO	79.2	11.07	9,875.10	11,114.30	☆	3.5	0.00	0.38	N/A	297

PERFORMANCE OF MUTUAL FUNDS (continued)

FUND NAME	OBJ.	LOAD	TOTAL NET ASTS (MIL) 6/30/88	NAV 6/30/88	PERFORMANCE (RETURN ON INITIAL $10,000 INVESTMENT) 12/31/87-6/30/88	6/30/87-6/30/88	6/30/83-6/30/88	YIELD % 6/30/88	PER SHARE LATEST 12 MONTHS CAP GAINS	INC DIVS	LATEST AVAILABLE PRICE/EARNINGS	ANNUAL % TURNOVER
FIDELITY GOVT SECURITIES	FI	NO	639.9	9.47	10,403.60	10,626.70	16,214.90	9.2	0.00	0.87	N/A	253
FIDELITY GROWTH & INCO	GI	LO	1,203.1	14.57	11,791.70	9,923.40	☆	4.2	1.35	0.64	19.7	165
FIDELITY GROWTH CO FUND	G	LO	148.1	14.97	11,497.70	9,522.50	15,616.20	0.1	0.72	0.01	21.1	212
FIDELITY HIGH INCOME	FI	NO	1,639.4	8.73	10,833.30	10,503.90	19,040.40	11.6	0.20	1.02	N/A	116
FIDELITY INSTL: EQ INDEX	GI	NO	2.9	10.55	#10,550.00	☆	☆	0.0	0.00	0.00	N/A	N/A
FIDELITY INTL GR & INC (R)	IF	LO	33.1	11.33	10,539.50	9,305.00	☆	0.6	0.00	0.07	N/A	158
FIDELITY INTERMED BD	FI	NO	468.6	10.03	10,420.10	10,676.40	17,043.60	14.6	0.00	1.45	N/A	85
FIDELITY INV TR: CANADA (R)	IF	LO	11.7	12.70	11,792.00	☆	☆	0.0	0.00	0.00	N/A	N/A
FIDELITY INV TR: UK (R)	IF	LO	2.2	10.80	9,818.20	☆	☆	0.0	0.00	0.00	N/A	N/A
FIDELITY MAGELLAN FUND	G	LO	9,257.4	47.83	11,927.70	9,554.70	20,883.90	0.7	3.18	0.35	16.8	101
FIDELITY MORTGAGE	FI	NO	488.8	10.00	10,481.80	10,736.20	☆	8.7	0.00	0.87	N/A	160
FIDELITY OVERSEAS	IF	LO	1,315.3	24.58	10,275.90	9,218.80	☆	0.0	8.24	0.00	N/A	122
FIDELITY OTC	SG	LO	967.6	18.01	12,301.90	9,901.20	☆	0.1	1.93	0.02	22.8	191
FIDELITY PACIFIC BASIN	IF	LO	165.2	14.01	10,362.40	9,591.60	☆	1.0	0.00	0.14	N/A	324
FIDELITY PURITAN	EI	LO	4,302.1	12.80	11,463.10	10,051.20	20,742.60	7.3	0.77	0.94	17.9	63
FIDELITY QUALIFIED DVD	EI	NO	83.1	12.12	10,772.50	10,040.60	20,365.40	6.8	1.78	0.87	10.2	38
FIDELITY REAL ESTATE	S	LO	71.3	9.19	11,011.60	9,578.30	☆	7.5	0.00	0.69	23.9	89
FIDELITY SEL AIR TRANS (R)	S	LO	7.8	9.57	12,760.00	8,583.40	☆	0.2	1.04	0.02	N/A	611
FIDELITY SEL AMER GOLD (R)	AU	LO	208.8	16.03	9,786.30	9,540.40	☆	0.4	0.18	0.06	19.9	78
FIDELITY SEL AUTOMATION (R)	S	LO	5.1	10.25	12,159.00	8,818.60	☆	0.2	0.19	0.02	N/A	303
FIDELITY SEL AUTO (R)	S	LO	9.2	12.43	12,788.10	9,749.00	☆	0.0	0.00	0.00	N/A	284
FIDELITY SEL BIO TECH (R)	H	LO	45.2	10.45	10,773.20	7,844.00	☆	0.0	0.28	0.00	40.8	431
FIDELITY SEL BROADCAST (R)	S	LO	16.6	12.24	11,649.20	10,380.20	☆	0.1	1.20	0.01	N/A	224
FIDELITY SEL BROKERAGE (R)	S	LO	6.6	7.59	11,837.90	7,243.70	☆	0.5	1.15	0.04	N/A	603
FIDELITY SEL CAP GOODS (R)	S	LO	7.9	11.20	11,914.90	8,769.00	☆	0.0	0.23	0.00	N/A	514
FIDELITY SEL CHEMICAL (R)	TK	LO	158.2	22.52	12,553.00	10,601.90	☆	0.0	0.04	0.00	16.7	170
FIDELITY SEL COMPUTER (R)	TK	LO	29.5	12.60	11,361.60	8,020.30	☆	0.1	0.33	0.01	N/A	259
FIDELITY SEL DEFENSE (R)	S	LO	2.4	12.18	11,194.90	8,105.20	☆	0.0	0.46	0.00	11.2	264
FIDELITY SEL ELECTRONIC (R)	TK	LO	18.6	8.33	11,379.80	8,056.10	☆	0.0	0.00	0.00	N/A	511
FIDELITY SEL ELEC UTIL (R)	UT	LO	25.6	9.02	11,360.90	10,073.10	☆	0.9	0.33	0.08	N/A	258
FIDELITY SEL ENERGY (R)	NR	LO	88.0	12.81	11,634.90	8,989.10	14,106.10	0.2	0.27	0.03	26.5	226
FIDELITY SEL ENRGY SER (R)	NR	LO	23.5	8.10	10,728.50	6,303.50	☆	0.0	0.00	0.00	33.3	575
FIDELITY SEL FINANCIAL (R)	S	LO	32.1	28.26	11,501.80	9,048.60	19,431.00	0.4	1.54	0.12	20.6	40
FIDELITY SEL FOOD (R)	S	LO	9.5	16.83	11,551.10	9,508.10	☆	0.2	0.55	0.03	N/A	608
FIDELITY SEL HEALTH (R)	H	LO	203.5	34.38	10,872.90	8,156.00	16,598.30	0.0	0.92	0.00	26.0	213
FIDELITY SEL HOUSING (R)	S	LO	7.6	11.84	12,758.60	9,106.20	☆	0.0	0.13	0.00	N/A	590
FIDELITY SEL INDUS MAT (R)	S	LO	49.4	14.23	11,692.70	9,555.00	☆	0.1	0.01	0.02	N/A	414
FIDELITY SEL LEISURE (R)	S	LO	58.8	22.85	11,958.00	9,616.40	☆	0.0	2.48	0.00	24.1	148
FIDELITY SEL LIFE INS (R)	S	LO	0.9	8.54	11,263.30	8,664.10	☆	0.2	0.00	0.02	N/A	854
FIDELITY SEL MEDICAL (R)	H	LO	3.4	7.53	11,106.20	8,367.20	☆	0.3	0.36	0.02	N/A	221
FIDELITY SEL PAPER & FRS (R)	S	LO	19.2	12.78	11,220.40	8,975.10	☆	0.3	1.04	0.04	N/A	466
FIDELITY SEL PREC-MTLS (R)	AU	LO	226.2	12.68	8,375.20	7,772.50	9,020.60	0.4	0.12	0.05	10.3	84
FIDELITY SEL PROP&CAS (R)	S	LO	3.7	10.63	11,201.30	9,375.80	☆	0.0	0.14	0.00	N/A	718
FIDELITY SEL REGL BANK (R)	S	LO	12.1	9.74	12,099.40	10,437.00	☆	0.6	0.15	0.06	N/A	227
FIDELITY SEL RESTAURANT (R)	S	LO	1.2	10.13	11,724.50	9,409.10	☆	0.3	0.01	0.03	N/A	245
FIDELITY SEL RETAIL (R)	S	LO	8.7	12.23	13,094.20	9,343.00	☆	1.8	0.76	0.23	N/A	596
FIDELITY SEL S&L (R)	S	LO	7.2	9.10	11,432.20	9,549.80	☆	0.0	3.50	0.00	N/A	335
FIDELITY SEL SOFTWARE (R)	TK	LO	22.7	15.07	11,460.10	9,423.20	☆	0.0	0.68	0.00	N/A	220
FIDELITY SEL TECH (R)	TK	LO	142.5	19.35	11,342.30	7,861.90	7,750.00	0.0	0.80	0.00	23.8	73
FIDELITY SEL TELECOM (R)	TK	LO	35.7	17.60	11,908.00	10,711.50	☆	0.1	0.36	0.02	15.7	284
FIDELITY SEL TRANS (R)	S	LO	1.6	10.81	12,869.00	8,738.90	☆	0.0	0.00	0.00	N/A	218
FIDELITY SEL UTILITIES (R)	UT	LO	93.9	26.11	11,115.40	10,276.50	22,141.80	1.7	0.84	0.45	12.1	161
FIDELITY SHORT-TERM BOND	FI	NO	386.4	9.41	10,343.30	10,643.70	☆	8.9	0.00	0.83	N/A	149
FIDELITY SP SIT: INITIAL	CA	LO	226.5	15.71	11,983.20	9,904.90	☆	1.5	1.91	0.25	15.5	225

FIDELITY SP SIT: PLYMOUTH	CA	LO	214.7	15.61	11,989.20	9,877.20	☆	1.4	1.91	0.24	N/A	225
FIDELITY TREND	G	NO	766.9	39.01	12,423.60	9,744.40	17,084.90	1.1	5.38	0.44	19.8	128
FIDELITY UTIL INCOME	UT	NO	128.8	10.80	11,021.60	☆	☆	0.0	0.00	0.24	10.1	N/A
FIDELITY VALUE FUND	CA	NO	90.5	24.11	11,686.90	9,160.30	13,233.60	0.0	0.00	0.00	23.6	442
FIDUCIARY CAPITAL GROWTH	SG	NO	44.3	15.98	12,592.60	9,896.60	13,380.50	0.8	3.45	0.14	21.4	83
FIDUCIARY TOTAL RETURN	GI	NO	0.4	10.04	12,243.90	10,919.40	☆	0.0	2.94	0.00	N/A	170
FINANCIAL DYNAMICS	CA	NO	122.6	7.00	11,433.10	8,723.60	12,439.90	0.3	0.46	0.01	23.4	234
FINANCIAL HIGH YIELD BND	FI	NO	57.2	8.02	10,968.00	10,768.10	☆	11.6	0.00	0.93	N/A	89
FINANCIAL INDUST FUND	GI	NO	356.8	3.71	10,939.80	8,816.80	14,103.30	1.8	0.63	0.06	21.0	250
FINANCIAL INDUST INCOME	EI	NO	381.0	7.98	11,277.50	9,881.80	19,977.80	4.4	0.35	0.36	15.7	195
FINANCIAL PORT-ENERGY	NR	NO	7.1	9.25	11,239.40	8,318.50	☆	1.5	0.64	0.14	N/A	452
FINANCIAL PORT-EUROPEAN	IF	NO	5.5	8.45	10,168.50	8,435.80	☆	0.6	0.00	0.05	N/A	131
FINANCIAL PORT-FINANCIAL	S	NO	3.5	7.69	12,015.60	10,170.30	☆	0.9	0.12	0.07	N/A	284
FINANCIAL PORT-GOLD	AU	NO	30.2	5.67	9,072.00	7,156.90	☆	1.1	0.04	0.06	21.5	124
FINANCIAL PORT-HEALTH	H	NO	13.6	13.48	10,871.00	8,779.70	☆	0.0	0.92	0.00	N/A	364
FINANCIAL PORT-LEISURE	S	NO	5.9	11.51	12,389.70	10,214.50	☆	0.0	1.43	0.00	N/A	376
FINANCIAL PORT-PACIFIC	IF	NO	34.5	12.16	11,603.10	9,347.30	☆	0.5	3.11	0.07	N/A	155
FINANCIAL PORT-TECH	TK	NO	20.3	11.29	12,338.80	8,759.50	☆	0.0	0.00	0.00	N/A	556
FINANCIAL PORT-UTILITIES	UT	NO	26.7	8.46	11,064.90	10,156.30	☆	5.9	0.00	0.50	N/A	84
FINANCIAL SELECT INCOME	FI	NO	23.1	6.45	10,637.40	10,575.00	16,260.60	9.7	0.00	0.62	N/A	131
FINANCIAL US GOVT	FI	NO	8.0	6.97	10,369.50	10,143.90	☆	7.6	0.00	0.53	N/A	284
FINL INDEPEN: GOVT SEC	FI	LO	35.2	10.12	10,491.00	10,730.30	☆	8.2	0.00	0.82	N/A	93
FINL INDEPEN: GROWTH FUND	G	SC	17.7	12.31	9,816.60	8,091.20	15,493.10	0.0	1.06	0.00	N/A	61
FIRST EAGLE FD OF AMER (R)	CA	NO	52.1	11.43	11,771.40	10,759.20	☆	0.6	0.00	0.07	N/A	N/A
FIRST INV BOND APPREC	FI	SC	219.3	10.82	11,055.80	9,507.50	14,094.70	10.9	0.28	0.07	N/A	40
FIRST INV DISCOVERY	SG	SC	24.6	9.21	12,599.20	8,008.70	5,741.90	0.0	0.00	1.20	N/A	37
FIRST INV FD FOR GROWTH	G	SC	38.6	5.67	11,009.70	7,947.10	6,563.20	0.7	0.00	0.00	14.7	98
FIRST INV FD FOR INCOME	FI	SC	1,728.2	5.27	10,889.90	10,319.60	14,817.80	12.4	0.00	0.04	6.7	100
FIRST INV GOVT	FI	SC	301.1	10.98	10,626.20	10,801.60	☆	8.3	0.00	0.65	N/A	74
FIRST INV HIGH YIELD	FI	SC	905.3	13.50	10,995.20	10,508.00	☆	11.9	0.15	0.91	N/A	153
FIRST INV INTERNATIONAL	GL	SC	99.5	4.38	11,375.60	10,462.80	20,114.70	0.0	0.00	1.61	N/A	137
FIRST INV OPTION FD	OI	SC	166.8	4.26	11,146.60	9,100.40	13,384.60	3.1	0.40	0.00	N/A	125
FIRST INV QUAL DIV	FI	SC	18.2	0.87	10,455.20	10,296.70	☆	8.7	0.42	0.14	16.0	20
FIRST INV SPECIAL BOND	FI	SC	55.5	13.53	11,031.80	10,706.70	19,250.30	11.9	0.00	0.07	N/A	71
FIRST INV US GOVT PLUS-I	FI	SC	1.7	10.61	10,706.40	10,257.10	☆	8.8	0.00	1.61	N/A	11
FIRST INV VALUE FUND (S)	NR	SC	10.4	11.55	10,968.70	9,134.80	11,065.10	0.7	1.42	1.00	N/A	22
FIRST LAKESHORE DVRSFD	I	NO	5.1	10.70	11,303.60	10,359.40	☆	6.6	0.00	0.08	N/A	24
FIRST TRUST AMERICA LP	FI	SC	10.2	10.73	10,540.00	10,788.60	☆	8.6	0.07	0.70	N/A	2
FIRST TRUST US GOVT	FI	SC	252.8	10.15	10,516.60	10,791.70	☆	8.7	0.00	0.92	N/A	73
FIRST UNION: IRA EQUITY	GI	NO	66.9	13.40	11,375.20	9,564.60	☆	0.0	0.01	0.88	N/A	8
FIRST UNION: IRA INCOME	FI	NO	15.1	9.92	10,456.50	10,577.20	☆	4.7	0.00	0.00	N/A	N/A
FIRST UTILITY	UT	NO	5.5	10.20	11,074.70	10,466.50	☆	5.8	0.00	0.46	N/A	N/A
FLAG INTERNATIONAL	IF	LO	38.2	11.25	10,484.60	9,323.80	☆	1.4	0.00	0.58	N/A	72
FLAG INV CORP CASH	EI	NO	36.7	9.68	10,488.90	10,671.80	☆	8.7	0.55	0.16	N/A	336
FLAG INV TELEPHONE INC	I	NO	104.4	16.66	11,404.30	10,988.40	☆	5.0	0.00	0.84	N/A	4
FLAGSHIP BASIC VALUE	FI	NO	85.8	37.05	8,781.10	8,640.20	☆	9.5	0.10	0.84	N/A	316
FLAGSHIP PLUS	FI	LO	4.5	40.93	10,193.40	9,619.00	☆	11.9	0.00	3.50	N/A	64
FLEX FUND-BOND	FI	NO	13.0	18.89	10,211.40	10,076.90	☆	8.0	0.09	4.86	N/A	258
FLEX FUND-GROWTH	CA	NO	15.7	10.75	9,880.50	9,038.40	☆	1.9	0.00	1.51	N/A	326
FLEX FUND-INC & GROWTH	EI	NO	3.7	18.95	10,364.30	9,276.10	☆	5.9	0.19	0.21	N/A	259
FLEX FUND-RETIRMNT GRO	CA	NO	79.9	10.75	9,426.40	8,424.50	12,628.70	2.5	0.00	1.11	N/A	274
FLORIDA INDEX	G	NO	0.2	8.53	11,997.20	☆	☆	0.0	0.28	0.27	N/A	N/A
44 WALL STREET	CA	NO	6.7	2.12	10,495.00	5,564.30	1,366.40	0.0	0.00	0.00	N/A	104
44 WALL STREET EQUITY	CA	LO	4.1	4.09	12,245.50	5,672.70	4,583.50	0.0	0.00	0.00	N/A	98
FOUNDERS: BLUE CHIP	GI	NO	173.7	6.35	10,466.80	8,708.70	17,421.20	2.3	0.00	0.00	N/A	56
FOUNDERS: EQUITY INCOME	EI	NO	12.5	6.83	10,659.40	9,589.00	16,208.50	6.2	1.70	0.16	N/A	133

PERFORMANCE OF MUTUAL FUNDS *(continued)*

					PERFORMANCE (RETURN ON INITIAL $10,000 INVESTMENT)				PER SHARE LATEST 12 MONTHS		LATEST AVAILABLE	
FUND NAME	OBJ.	LOAD	TOTAL NET ASTS (MIL) 6/30/88	NAV 6/30/88	12/31/87- 6/30/88	6/30/87- 6/30/88	6/30/83- 6/30/88	YIELD % 6/30/88	CAP GAINS	INC DIVS	PRICE/ EARNINGS	ANNUAL % TURNOVER
FOUNDERS: FRONTIER	CA	NO	8.4	14.10	12,783.30	11,863.70	☆	0.0	0.57	0.00	N/A	588
FOUNDERS: GROWTH	G	NO	64.9	7.72	10,418.40	8,892.60	14,829.90	1.6	1.61	0.13	19.4	147
FOUNDERS: SPECIAL	CA	NO	76.7	5.68	11,050.60	9,274.70	11,871.20	0.5	0.71	0.03	24.6	210
FPA CAPITAL	G	SC	68.2	14.11	13,119.20	11,408.80	19,593.00	1.2	0.85	0.17	24.7	44
FPA NEW INCOME	FI	LO	10.3	9.83	10,732.40	11,206.60	18,174.50	6.4	0.01	0.63	N/A	103
FPA PARAMOUNT (X)	GI	SC	138.7	14.33	12,236.10	11,229.40	21,676.20	1.4	2.55	0.22	17.1	98
FPA PERENNIAL FUND	GI	SC	53.2	18.93	11,774.50	10,329.80	☆	3.4	0.45	0.65	13.2	75
FRANKLIN CORP CASH	EI	NO	36.7	8.20	9,743.60	9,761.10	☆	8.8	0.00	0.72	N/A	11
FRANKLIN DYNATECH	TK	LO	38.9	12.89	11,522.10	9,932.90	11,768.30	0.5	0.00	0.06	26.0	8
FRANKLIN EQUITY FUND	G	LO	341.7	6.67	12,554.80	9,967.80	21,678.40	1.7	0.81	0.11	11.9	45
FRANKLIN GOLD FUND	AU	LO	276.1	11.74	9,342.90	8,921.90	11,564.60	4.4	0.39	0.53	20.4	10
FRANKLIN GROWTH	G	LO	108.6	19.77	10,959.00	10,476.50	18,505.70	2.0	0.38	0.40	16.1	9
FRANKLIN INCOME	I	LO	651.9	2.15	10,723.70	10,450.90	18,997.60	10.2	0.02	0.22	9.2	18
FRANKLIN IS TR: ADJ MTGE	FI	LO	40.9	10.19	10,398.90	☆	☆	0.0	0.00	0.20	N/A	N/A
FRANKLIN IS TR: COVERT	CV	LO	17.7	9.72	11,300.20	10,332.80	☆	6.1	0.00	0.59	N/A	149
FRANKLIN IS TR: SH-INT US	FI	LO	28.5	10.26	10,349.70	10,684.40	☆	5.9	0.00	0.61	N/A	13
FRANKLIN MGD: CORP CASH	FI	LO	10.2	21.26	10,252.40	9,647.40	☆	8.8	0.00	1.88	N/A	149
FRANKLIN MGD: INV GRADE	I	LO	13.2	8.88	10,511.20	10,408.30	☆	9.3	0.00	0.82	N/A	101
FRANKLIN MGD: RISING DVD	GI	LO	33.6	10.05	11,727.30	10,327.10	☆	3.0	0.00	0.30	N/A	45
FRANKLIN OPTION	OI	LO	46.9	5.37	11,214.90	9,994.90	15,589.70	2.6	0.77	0.14	14.6	176
FRANKLIN PART: TX-ADV HY	FI	LO	10.4	9.43	10,797.50	10,613.90	☆	10.2	0.00	1.05	N/A	N/A
FRANKLIN PART: TX-ADV USG	FI	LO	26.9	10.16	10,586.50	10,971.90	☆	8.9	0.00	0.98	N/A	N/A
FRANKLIN PA: EQUITY PORT	CA	LO	0.4	11.38	12,485.70	10,238.40	☆	2.4	1.47	0.44	N/A	N/A
FRANKLIN PA: HIGH INCOME	I	LO	0.7	9.29	10,933.20	10,507.80	☆	14.0	0.00	1.30	N/A	N/A
FRANKLIN PA: US GOVT SEC	FI	LO	1.9	10.00	10,549.50	10,847.20	☆	9.4	0.00	0.93	N/A	N/A
FRANKLIN US GOVERNMENT	FI	LO	12,479.7	7.06	10,580.20	10,902.70	17,160.40	9.9	0.00	0.69	N/A	53
FRANKLIN UTILITIES	UT	LO	675.0	7.55	10,894.20	10,271.10	20,458.70	7.5	0.00	0.56	10.0	N/A
FREEDOM EQUITY VALUE (R)	G	NO	14.6	9.96	12,289.20	9,908.30	☆	0.9	0.14	0.08	N/A	40
FREEDOM GLOBAL (R)	GL	NO	42.1	10.73	10,561.00	8,784.50	☆	0.0	0.45	0.00	16.6	91
FREEDOM GLOBAL INCOME (R)	WI	NO	130.7	11.01	10,929.50	11,666.50	☆	8.5	0.35	0.96	N/A	140
FREEDOM GOLD & GOVT (R)	AU	NO	83.7	15.05	10,161.80	10,497.30	☆	4.8	0.40	0.73	28.6	161
FREEDOM GOVT PLUS (R)	FI	NO	165.6	9.61	10,426.20	10,687.50	☆	8.1	0.02	0.77	N/A	83
FREEDOM REGIONAL BANK (R)	S	NO	44.7	11.16	12,373.50	10,502.70	☆	1.1	1.27	0.13	16.0	58
FT INTERNATIONAL	IF	NO	69.8	15.95	10,711.90	9,442.20	☆	1.2	5.88	0.23	N/A	130
FUND FOR US GOVT SEC	FI	LO	1,157.0	8.32	10,512.50	10,821.30	16,618.70	9.4	0.00	0.78	N/A	135
FUND OF AMERICA	GI	SC	185.1	11.24	11,717.30	9,499.10	16,567.00	1.8	1.42	0.22	19.9	49
FUND OF SOUTHWEST	CA	SC	14.6	10.25	11,503.90	9,399.10	9,878.60	0.3	0.03	0.03	N/A	41
FUNDAMENTAL INVESTORS	GI	SC	666.7	15.09	11,473.80	9,384.50	20,803.50	2.6	0.78	0.40	16.4	12
FUNDTRUST AGGRESSIVE GR	CA	LO	28.7	12.09	11,112.10	9,362.90	☆	1.5	1.99	0.19	N/A	64
FUNDTRUST GROWTH FUND	G	LO	48.8	12.68	11,227.80	9,588.20	☆	2.7	1.22	0.36	N/A	65
FUNDTRUST GROWTH & INC	GI	LO	58.2	12.37	11,537.70	9,842.30	☆	5.5	0.73	0.70	N/A	20
FUNDTRUST INCOME FUND	I	LO	54.2	9.84	10,604.10	10,313.40	☆	9.1	0.0	0.90	N/A	27
FUND SOURCE: EQUITY TR	G	LO	3.4	9.74	11,900.00	9,113.10	☆	0.5	0.95	0.05	N/A	212
FUND SOURCE: GOVT SEC INC	FI	LO	62.2	6.81	10,278.10	10,551.00	13,024.90	8.5	0.16	0.58	N/A	85
FUND SOURCE: INTL EQ	IF	NO	31.0	14.77	10,924.60	9,624.40	☆	0.0	1.33	0.00	N/A	78
GABELLI ASSET (R)	G	NO	110.5	14.62	12,395.00	11,220.50	☆	0.9	0.69	0.14	23.3	90
GABELLI GROWTH (R)	CA	NO	6.2	12.40	13,240.90	11,616.30	☆	1.2	0.00	0.15	N/A	80
GAM GLOBAL	GL	NO	19.6	93.86	10,596.70	9,237.70	☆	1.2	12.59	1.22	N/A	N/A
GAM INTERNATIONAL	IF	NO	21.8	130.25	9,773.40	8,645.40	☆	0.6	45.49	0.86	N/A	N/A
GAM PACIFIC BASIN	IF	NO	6.2	98.98	12,004.90	9,692.50	☆	0.0	0.00	0.00	N/A	N/A
GAM TOKYO	IF	NO	2.1	98.94	10,421.20	10,196.90	☆	0.0	23.75	0.00	N/A	N/A
GARDNER FUND	S	LO	10.7	7.87	9,764.10	8,888.90	☆	4.9	0.33	0.39	N/A	361
GATEWAY: GROWTH PLUS	G	NO	3.9	10.27	10,311.20	8,680.20	☆	0.4	0.00	0.04	N/A	157

GATEWAY: GOVERNMENT BOND	FI	NO	4.3	10.14	#10,188.40	☆	☆	0.0	0.00	0.04	N/A	N/A
GATEWAY: OPTION INDEX FD	OI	NO	28.3	12.89	11,200.30	9,540.20	14,729.20	1.4	1.71	0.19	14.7	175
GEICO QUAL DIVIDEND	FI	NO	40.1	21.96	9,946.70	9,343.70	☆	7.1	0.00	1.67	N/A	120
GENERAL AGGRESSIVE GRO	CA	NO	44.6	21.64	11,982.30	9,887.00	☆	1.0	1.72	0.22	N/A	179
GENL ELEC LT INTEREST	FI	NO	985.7	11.08	10,477.40	10,782.90	18,042.00	8.7	0.00	0.96	N/A	N/A
GENL ELEC S&S PROGRAM	G	NO	835.7	30.24	11,122.70	9,130.00	17,233.90	3.8	5.00	1.23	18.3	N/A
GENERAL SECURITIES (R)	CA	NO	17.6	12.05	11,293.30	10,706.20	17,303.10	3.4	0.31	0.41	N/A	1
GIBRALTAR FUND	GI	NO	1.1	12.26	10,820.80	9,181.60	☆	2.7	1.43	0.34	N/A	N/A
GINTEL CAPITAL APPREC	CA	NO	23.1	12.12	12,120.00	10,113.20	☆	0.8	0.00	0.09	N/A	125
GINTEL ERISA	GI	NO	79.6	34.06	11,433.40	9,835.50	18,580.90	3.5	6.45	1.29	13.6	109
GINTEL FUND	G	NO	83.2	61.12	11,879.50	9,277.40	15,187.20	1.6	0.00	0.96	10.1	52
GIT A RATED INCOME	FI	NO	6.4	10.07	10,424.60	10,551.90	☆	8.1	0.46	0.83	N/A	31
GIT EQUITY INCOME	EI	NO	2.1	12.61	11,017.70	9,656.80	☆	4.5	0.00	0.56	N/A	23
GIT MAX INCOME	FI	NO	10.6	8.36	10,603.40	10,022.70	☆	10.8	0.00	0.90	N/A	127
GIT SELECT GROWTH	G	NO	3.4	14.78	11,142.70	9,432.10	☆	2.3	1.09	0.35	N/A	9
GIT SPECIAL GROWTH	SG	NO	16.1	15.74	12,335.20	10,535.20	☆	0.7	2.61	0.12	N/A	8
GNA INVESTORS: US GOVT (R)	FI	NO	21.0	9.71	10,508.90	10,803.90	☆	8.4	0.05	0.82	N/A	N/A
GOVAARS MORTGAGE	FI	NO	7.8	10.45	10,532.70	10,765.60	☆	6.9	0.09	0.72	N/A	976
GOVERNMENT INC SEC (R)	FI	SC	1,753.2	9.30	10,524.20	10,815.90	☆	9.5	0.00	0.88	N/A	208
GPM FUND	GI	NO	6.0	17.56	11,248.80	9,394.10	17,755.80	2.4	2.17	0.45	N/A	66
GRADISON ESTABLISHED GRO	G	NO	80.5	16.76	11,205.90	10,497.50	☆	4.0	0.80	0.68	13.1	76
GRADISON OPPORTUNITY GRO	SG	NO	18.5	13.02	12,253.70	10,159.00	☆	1.7	0.17	0.22	N/A	64
GREENFIELD FUND	GI	NO	1.1	12.23	10,502.40	9,526.50	14,135.70	4.5	0.17	0.55	N/A	50
GREENSPRING FUND	G	NO	20.8	13.44	11,303.60	10,850.20	☆	7.5	0.13	1.01	N/A	929
GROWTH FUND OF AMERICA	G	SC	1,128.7	18.47	11,870.20	10,219.30	17,762.30	1.5	1.10	0.29	29.6	20
GROWTH FD OF WASHINGTON	G	SC	51.4	11.80	11,072.50	9,745.40	☆	1.2	0.60	0.14	N/A	19
GROWTH INDUSTRY SHARES	G	NO	66.1	8.84	10,866.70	9,582.40	13,499.70	1.6	1.33	0.15	18.5	22
GT AMERICA GROWTH	G	SC	1.6	10.08	11,775.70	9,683.00	☆	0.0	0.00	0.00	N/A	505
GT EUROPE GROWTH	IF	SC	7.7	16.02	10,315.50	8,841.50	☆	0.0	3.56	0.00	N/A	193
GT INTERNATIONAL GRO	IF	SC	21.1	18.87	11,009.30	9,633.20	☆	0.0	1.55	0.00	N/A	198
GT JAPAN GROWTH	IF	SC	20.4	25.15	12,143.90	14,733.10	☆	0.0	6.61	0.00	N/A	319
GT PACIFIC GROWTH FD	IF	SC	51.2	17.12	11,806.90	10,334.50	26,935.10	0.0	7.19	0.00	N/A	215
GT WORLDWIDE GROWTH	GL	SC	8.5	9.88	11,051.50	9,518.30	☆	0.0	0.00	0.00	N/A	152
GUARDIAN BOND FUND	FI	NO	115.1	11.24	10,554.50	10,773.80	16,962.10	9.5	0.00	1.06	N/A	67
GUARDIAN MUTUAL	GI	NO	535.4	39.80	12,432.30	10,023.20	18,803.50	3.0	4.21	1.24	12.6	91
GUARDIAN PARK AVENUE	G	SC	185.0	22.07	12,067.30	10,257.10	21,605.70	2.5	2.18	0.57	16.3	50
GUARDIAN STOCK FUND	G	NO	179.0	19.42	12,013.50	10,085.00	21,203.80	2.2	0.49	0.44	18.5	37
J HANCOCK BOND	FI	SC	1,111.2	14.74	10,547.80	10,717.10	17,660.70	9.4	0.00	1.38	N/A	159
J HANCOCK GLOBAL	GL	SC	141.4	14.77	10,535.00	8,813.90	☆	0.3	1.20	0.05	20.8	86
J HANCOCK GROWTH	G	SC	110.0	13.79	11,175.00	9,375.00	16,139.60	1.6	2.00	0.23	18.2	68
J HANCOCK HI INC FEDERAL	FI	SC	72.3	9.53	10,315.50	10,549.50	☆	9.9	0.00	0.93	N/A	N/A
J HANCOCK HI INC FIX INC	FI	SC	67.4	9.30	10,821.20	10,746.40	☆	12.1	0.00	1.12	N/A	207
J HANCOCK SPEC EQUITY	SG	SC	13.2	5.27	12,458.60	8,467.60	☆	0.0	0.44	0.00	N/A	93
J HANCOCK US GOVT SEC	FI	SC	203.1	8.83	10,356.60	10,494.10	16,673.70	8.8	0.00	0.77	N/A	7
J HANCOCK US GUAR MORT	FI	SC	412.7	9.97	10,429.30	10,704.40	☆	8.7	0.00	0.86	N/A	193
J HANCOCK VAR SR AGG GRO	CA	NO	9.1	10.60	10,861.20	9,352.90	☆	3.1	0.20	0.33	N/A	N/A
J HANCOCK VAR SR BOND	FI	NO	241.7	9.28	10,488.60	10,373.40	☆	9.2	0.03	0.86	N/A	N/A
J HANCOCK VAR SR STOCK	G	NO	380.6	9.74	11,078.40	9,515.50	☆	3.6	0.69	0.36	N/A	N/A
J HANCOCK VAR SR TOT RTN	B	NO	117.1	10.60	10,701.40	10,056.60	☆	5.3	0.00	0.55	N/A	N/A
J HANCOCK WLD PACIFIC	IF	SC	4.5	10.35	11,436.50	☆	☆	0.0	0.00	0.02	N/A	N/A
J HANCOCK WLD/WLD FIX IN	WI	SC	4.7	9.67	10,005.50	☆	☆	0.0	0.00	0.60	N/A	N/A
HARBOR BOND FUND	FI	NO	10.4	10.05	10,384.50	☆	☆	0.0	0.00	0.33	N/A	N/A
HARBOR GROWTH FUND	G	NO	119.3	11.64	12,062.20	9,719.30	☆	0.8	0.79	0.09	N/A	56
HARBOR INTERNATIONAL FD	IF	NO	7.8	11.64	11,640.00	☆	☆	0.0	0.00	0.00	N/A	N/A
HARBOR US EQUITIES FD	GI	NO	46.1	11.63	11,549.20	☆	☆	0.0	0.00	0.00	N/A	N/A
HARBOR VALUE FUND	GI	NO	10.4	10.74	10,905.20	☆	☆	0.0	0.00	0.16	N/A	N/A
HARTWELL EMERGING GRO	CA	LO	28.5	12.28	12,926.30	9,324.80	10,683.00	0.0	6.58	0.00	35.3	224

PERFORMANCE OF MUTUAL FUNDS (continued)

FUND NAME	OBJ.	LOAD	TOTAL NET ASTS (MIL) 6/30/88	NAV 6/30/88	PERFORMANCE (RETURN ON INITIAL $10,000 INVESTMENT) 12/31/87-6/30/88	6/30/87-6/30/88	6/30/83-6/30/88	YIELD % 6/30/88	PER SHARE LATEST 12 MONTHS CAP GAINS	INC DIVS	LATEST AVAILABLE PRICE/EARNINGS	ANNUAL % TURNOVER
HARTWELL GROWTH FUND	CA	LO	18.9	15.30	10,662.00	9,392.30	14,400.10	0.0	0.00	0.00	N/A	100
HEARTLAND US GOVT	FI	SC	13.4	9.22	10,417.00	10,629.00	☆	8.0	0.00	0.73	N/A	64
HEARTLAND VALUE	CA	SC	31.6	14.78	12,589.40	9,430.40	☆	0.4	0.64	0.06	N/A	78
HERITAGE CAPITAL APPREC	CA	LO	45.1	10.97	11,286.00	9,714.20	☆	0.6	1.19	0.07	N/A	48
HERITAGE CONV INC-GRO	CV	SC	20.4	9.04	11,495.50	9,622.50	☆	4.7	0.00	0.42	N/A	91
HIDDEN STR: US GOVT HI YD	FI	SC	57.1	9.97	10,571.10	10,977.20	☆	10.0	0.00	0.99	N/A	N/A
HIDDEN STR: GROWTH	G	SC	33.0	10.19	12,306.80	9,559.10	☆	0.5	0.00	0.05	N/A	82
HIDDEN STR: CONSERVATIVE	FI	SC	4.1	8.64	10,507.60	10,649.30	☆	8.1	0.00	0.70	N/A	71
HIDDEN STR: MODERATE	B	SC	29.7	7.54	11,419.90	10,091.00	☆	4.0	0.00	0.30	N/A	61
HIGH YIELD SECURITIES	FI	SC	80.5	8.61	10,437.20	10,124.00	15,223.70	13.2	0.00	1.14	N/A	63
HOME GROUP: GOVT SEC FD	FI	SC	29.6	9.77	#10,094.80	☆	☆	0.0	0.00	0.32	N/A	N/A
HOME GROUP: GR & INCOME	GI	SC	32.7	10.76	#10,760.00	☆	☆	0.0	0.00	0.00	N/A	N/A
HOME GROUP: HI YLD BOND	FI	SC	20.5	9.86	#10,252.60	☆	☆	0.0	0.00	0.38	N/A	N/A
HOME INV GUAR INCOME (R)	FI	NO	184.2	10.06	10,520.60	10,697.30	16,328.00	8.2	0.00	0.82	N/A	26
HORIZON CAP GNMA EXTRA	FI	SC	0.6	9.64	10,543.90	☆	☆	0.0	0.00	0.52	N/A	N/A
HORIZON CAP TOTAL RETURN	CV	SC	0.2	9.17	11,326.90	☆	☆	0.0	0.00	0.32	N/A	N/A
HUDSON GROWTH	G	SC	1.9	9.61	11,634.40	9,524.30	☆	0.0	0.00	0.00	N/A	N/A
HUTTON INV: BASIC VAL (R)	G	NO	407.0	12.66	11,042.60	9,190.80	☆	2.1	0.01	0.27	N/A	30
HUTTON INV: BOND & INC (R)	FI	NO	627.8	10.56	10,426.40	10,521.40	17,711.50	9.4	0.00	0.99	N/A	79
HUTTON INV: EUROPEAN (R)	IF	NO	2.0	10.57	10,247.80	☆	☆	0.0	0.00	0.12	N/A	N/A
HUTTON INV: GLOBAL (R)	GL	NO	10.0	11.63	10,901.10	☆	☆	0.0	0.00	0.09	N/A	N/A
HUTTON INV: GOVT SEC (R)	FI	NO	3,393.7	8.99	10,526.90	10,220.80	☆	9.5	0.00	0.85	N/A	249
HUTTON INV: GROWTH (R)	G	NO	1,206.0	11.55	10,376.30	8,806.10	14,656.80	2.1	2.00	0.26	N/A	423
HUTTON INV: OPTION INC (R)	OI	NO	44.6	8.51	11,313.80	9,684.20	☆	4.0	0.55	0.34	N/A	298
HUTTON INV: PACIFIC (R)	IF	NO	3.1	12.11	11,290.70	☆	☆	0.0	0.00	0.02	N/A	N/A
HUTTON INV: PREC MET (R)	AU	NO	116.0	15.54	9,575.60	9,442.00	☆	2.1	1.77	0.34	N/A	93
HUTTON INV: UTILITY (R)	UT	NO	137.4	12.29	#10,304.30	☆	☆	0.0	0.00	0.07	N/A	N/A
HUTTON MSTR CONVERTIBLE	CV	LO	11.5	9.88	11,415.00	10,521.10	☆	4.5	0.11	0.44	N/A	131
HUTTON INV: SPECIAL EQU (R)	SG	NO	187.8	12.91	11,528.20	8,770.30	11,394.20	0.0	0.28	0.00	N/A	148
IAI APOLLO FUND	CA	NO	22.7	11.58	11,761.20	9,925.50	☆	0.9	0.94	0.10	N/A	86
IAI BOND FUND	FI	NO	44.8	9.55	10,425.00	10,672.50	16,933.90	9.8	0.03	0.93	N/A	35
IAI INTERNATIONAL FUND	IF	NO	12.7	9.86	10,625.00	9,772.10	☆	0.0	0.00	0.00	N/A	N/A
IAI REGIONAL FUND	G	NO	91.0	18.26	11,526.60	10,062.40	19,772.10	1.2	1.89	0.22	16.9	133
IAI RESERVE FUND	FI	NO	71.9	10.08	10,322.10	10,644.60	☆	7.3	0.00	0.73	N/A	30
IAI STOCK FUND	CA	NO	82.1	15.58	10,575.50	9,333.50	17,653.60	1.8	0.75	0.28	17.8	68
IDEX FUND (X)	G	SC	66.2	11.43	10,927.00	9,093.00	☆	1.8	1.37	0.22	N/A	185
IDEX FUND II (X)	G	SC	64.5	10.75	11,046.40	9,295.20	☆	1.4	1.10	0.16	N/A	168
IDEX FUND 3	G	SC	41.7	9.63	10,874.10	9,354.90	☆	1.5	0.00	0.14	N/A	260
IDEX TOTAL INCOME	FI	SC	14.7	9.79	10,324.80	10,650.10	☆	8.5	0.00	0.82	N/A	68
IDS BOND FUND	FI	LO	1,770.2	4.65	10,605.20	10,520.40	17,415.60	9.6	0.24	0.44	N/A	73
IDS DISCOVERY FUND	SG	SC	198.0	7.04	12,438.20	9,460.70	10,526.40	1.6	1.11	0.11	24.4	33
IDS EQUITY +	GI	SC	399.8	8.82	11,110.30	9,481.80	16,211.00	2.5	1.87	0.24	16.0	115
IDS EXTRA INCOME	FI	SC	1,167.2	4.70	10,842.60	10,502.90	☆	11.2	0.10	0.52	N/A	87
IDS FEDERAL INCOME	FI	SC	183.0	5.02	10,526.80	10,745.10	☆	7.3	0.00	0.36	N/A	36
IDS GROWTH FUND	G	SC	659.3	17.83	10,793.00	8,110.80	11,609.00	1.3	4.06	0.25	23.3	24
IDS INTERNATIONAL	IF	SC	245.4	8.27	10,494.90	8,596.90	☆	0.0	1.33	0.00	N/A	134
IDS LIFE CAPITAL RES	G	NO	471.3	15.75	10,678.30	9,989.80	☆	2.1	2.59	0.33	N/A	171
IDS LIFE EQUITY	G	NO	8.2	11.38	11,103.30	9,424.60	☆	1.3	0.13	0.15	N/A	57
IDS LIFE GOVT	FI	NO	2.4	9.03	10,415.30	10,463.00	☆	6.9	0.00	0.62	N/A	43
IDS LIFE INCOME	FI	NO	4.5	9.03	10,439.30	10,471.20	☆	7.7	0.00	0.69	N/A	38
IDS LIFE MANAGED	B	NO	22.9	10.41	10,343.40	9,504.50	☆	4.0	0.13	0.42	N/A	48
IDS LIFE SPEC INCOME	FI	NO	425.4	10.96	10,618.60	10,576.40	☆	9.5	0.26	1.04	N/A	101
IDS MANAGED RETIREMENT	GI	SC	754.8	7.88	10,690.80	9,139.80	☆	1.7	0.00	0.13	22.5	87
IDS MUTUAL	B	SC	1,451.6	11.93	10,961.90	10,233.20	20,685.50	6.4	1.33	0.76	10.9	52

IDS NEW DIMENSIONS	G	SC	681.1	8.37	10,856.00	9,663.50	17,256.00	2.2	2.16	0.19	20.1	113
IDS PAN PACIFIC GRO (R)	GL	NO	60.3	4.08	10,515.50	8,482.30	☆	0.0	0.00	0.00	N/A	N/A
IDS PRECIOUS METALS	AU	SC	118.9	7.25	9,349.90	9,059.70	☆	1.4	0.79	0.10	29.0	77
IDS PROGRESSIVE	CA	SC	190.4	6.49	11,630.80	9,344.20	16,720.10	4.1	1.29	0.26	24.1	99
IDS SELECTIVE	FI	SC	1,111.1	8.47	10,567.30	10,684.20	17,287.90	8.9	0.05	0.75	N/A	74
IDS STOCK	GI	SC	1,285.7	17.97	10,716.30	9,349.10	17,183.40	3.0	3.35	0.58	16.3	42
IDS STRATEGY AGGR EQ (R)	CA	NO	265.1	9.45	11,130.70	8,164.90	☆	0.0	0.40	0.00	22.7	43
IDS STRATEGY EQUITY (R)	GI	NO	191.1	7.85	11,939.40	10,392.00	☆	2.7	0.40	0.21	N/A	30
IDS STRATEGY INCOME (R)	FI	NO	158.2	5.67	10,610.30	10,580.70	☆	9.1	0.00	0.51	N/A	124
IMG BOND ACCUMULATION	FI	LO	14.0	10.65	10,384.90	10,664.60	☆	6.7	0.00	0.71	N/A	99
IMG STOCK ACCUMULATION	CA	SC	6.3	12.41	11,484.50	9,851.80	☆	2.3	0.89	0.29	N/A	123
IMPERIAL: HI GR CORP BD	FI	LO	4.1	14.21	#9,653.30	☆	☆	0.0	0.00	0.26	N/A	N/A
IMPERIAL: HIGH YIELD	FI	LO	1.1	14.88	#10,206.40	☆	☆	0.0	0.00	0.42	N/A	N/A
IMPERIAL: S&P 100 PORT	GI	LO	3.7	15.67	#10,446.70	☆	☆	0.0	0.00	0.00	N/A	N/A
IMPERIAL: US GOVERNMENT	FI	LO	1.7	15.15	#10,256.70	☆	☆	0.0	0.00	0.23	N/A	N/A
INCOME FUND OF AMERICA	EI	SC	921.7	11.67	11,080.90	10,209.30	19,737.60	7.4	0.38	0.88	13.5	39
INCOME PORT: LIMITED TERM	FI	NO	401.2	10.29	10,485.20	10,758.90	☆	9.3	0.00	0.95	N/A	92
INSIDER REPORTS	G	LO	2.6	10.99	11,666.70	8,800.50	☆	0.0	0.20	0.00	N/A	35
INTEGRATED CAP APPREC (R)	G	NO	214.4	13.06	12,402.70	9,563.50	☆	0.2	1.20	0.02	N/A	41
INTEGRATED CORP INVESTOR	FI	NO	6.1	20.38	9,878.30	9,645.60	☆	9.5	0.00	1.93	N/A	103
INTEGRATED EQ-AGGR GRO	SG	SC	19.1	14.79	15,138.20	11,447.40	☆	0.0	0.00	0.00	N/A	98
INTEGRATED EQ-GROWTH	G	SC	32.7	13.80	12,147.90	10,211.10	☆	0.5	0.00	0.06	N/A	201
INTEGRATED INC-CONVERT	CV	SC	34.1	10.74	11,792.10	9,590.60	☆	4.7	0.20	0.51	N/A	N/A
INTEGRATED INC-GOVT PLUS	FI	SC	29.6	10.78	10,508.20	10,675.10	☆	10.0	0.00	1.07	N/A	N/A
INTEGRATED INC-HI YIELD	FI	SC	20.5	10.76	11,049.60	10,746.50	☆	11.5	0.00	1.23	N/A	43
INTEGRATED INCOME PLUS (R)	FI	NO	25.6	8.97	10,957.50	10,616.50	☆	10.8	0.00	0.97	N/A	56
INTEGRATED MUL-AST: TOTRT	GI	SC	15.3	14.23	11,411.40	☆	☆	0.0	0.00	0.02	N/A	N/A
INTERACT: MNGD INC & APPR	S	SC	0.4	12.16	#10,193.50	☆	☆	0.0	0.00	0.07	N/A	N/A
INTERACT: MNGD RESOURCES	S	SC	0.3	11.93	#9,941.70	☆	☆	0.0	0.00	0.00	N/A	N/A
INTERACT: QUALITY BOND	FI	SC	0.2	11.96	#10,086.80	☆	☆	0.0	0.00	0.14	N/A	N/A
INTERACT: QLTY GRO FD	G	SC	0.3	12.82	#10,683.30	☆	☆	0.0	0.00	0.00	N/A	N/A
INTERACT: QLTY INT-BD	FI	SC	0.5	5.00	#10,114.40	☆	☆	0.0	0.00	0.05	N/A	N/A
INTL CASH-AUSTRALIAN CSH	WI	LO	1.1	13.72	11,350.40	☆	☆	0.0	0.06	0.61	N/A	N/A
INTL CASH-CANADIAN CSH	WI	LO	2.5	13.23	10,791.10	☆	☆	0.0	0.00	0.58	N/A	N/A
INTL CASH-D-MARK CSH	WI	LO	2.5	11.90	8,765.50	☆	☆	0.0	0.28	0.21	N/A	N/A
INTL CASH-GLOBAL CASH	WI	LO	114.8	13.71	9,510.30	10,937.20	☆	4.0	0.43	0.56	N/A	71
INTL CASH-STERLING CSH	WI	LO	2.9	12.85	9,560.80	☆	☆	0.0	0.14	0.66	N/A	N/A
INTL CASH-SWISS FRNC CSH	WI	LO	7.7	11.71	8,579.70	☆	☆	0.0	0.33	0.07	N/A	N/A
INTL CASH-YEN CSH	WI	LO	9.0	13.28	9,268.40	☆	☆	0.0	0.00	0.23	N/A	N/A
INTL FD FOR INSTITUTIONS	IF	NO	13.8	10.63	10,790.60	9,420.60	☆	0.6	6.61	0.09	N/A	77
INTL HERITAGE GOVT (R)	FI	SC	12.0	9.28	10,463.90	10,769.80	☆	9.4	0.00	0.87	N/A	4
INTL HERITAGE HI YLD (R)	FI	SC	47.4	8.84	10,975.70	10,531.30	☆	14.3	0.00	1.26	N/A	22
INTL HERITAGE OVSEA IN (R)	WI	SC	4.3	9.82	9,169.10	10,839.00	☆	6.0	0.25	0.59	N/A	171
INTERNATIONAL INVESTORS	AU	SC	845.4	12.68	8,424.30	7,921.00	10,939.10	3.3	0.53	0.43	21.3	1
INTERSTATE CAP GROWTH	CA	LO	10.3	6.81	10,861.20	9,089.50	6,688.20	0.4	0.00	0.03	N/A	105
INVESTMENT CO OF AMERICA	GI	SC	4,148.6	13.62	11,021.00	9,579.20	20,286.40	3.7	0.75	0.52	15.9	12
INVEST PORT-EQUITY (R)	G	NO	280.0	11.05	10,717.70	9,046.90	☆	0.7	1.39	0.08	19.0	156
INVEST PORT-GOVT PLUS (R)	FI	NO	6,382.6	7.67	10,298.50	10,559.10	☆	10.6	0.00	0.81	N/A	139
INVEST PORT-HIGH YLD (R)	FI	NO	462.6	9.52	10,931.30	10,956.80	☆	12.3	0.06	1.17	N/A	112
INVEST PORT-OPTION INC (R)	OI	NO	445.1	6.33	11,540.70	9,214.30	☆	15.2	0.00	0.96	15.2	211
INVEST PORT-TOTL RTN (R)	B	NO	531.3	9.37	10,967.40	9,311.50	☆	2.2	0.02	0.21	15.9	42
INVESTMENT TRUST BOSTON	GI	SC	59.6	10.64	10,786.30	9,127.60	14,425.50	3.1	0.30	0.34	17.1	25
INVESTORS INCOME FUND	FI	SC	24.6	5.22	10,869.20	10,942.00	18,165.70	10.2	0.00	0.53	N/A	102
INVESTORS RESEARCH	CA	SC	77.9	5.17	10,465.60	9,218.40	14,313.70	1.1	0.64	0.06	18.6	75
IRI STOCK FUND	G	SC	6.4	7.23	10,987.80	9,832.50	17,582.50	2.9	1.68	0.23	N/A	104
ISI GROWTH FUND	G	SC	11.8	7.45	11,604.40	9,586.70	14,175.90	0.8	0.06	0.05	N/A	33
ISI TRUST FUND	GI	SC	99.9	10.64	11,148.40	10,372.70	15,923.30	4.5	0.40	0.48	17.7	6

PERFORMANCE OF MUTUAL FUNDS *(continued)*

FUND NAME	OBJ.	LOAD	TOTAL NET ASTS (MIL) 6/30/88	NAV 6/30/88	PERFORMANCE (RETURN ON INITIAL $10,000 INVESTMENT) 12/31/87-6/30/88	6/30/87-6/30/88	6/30/83-6/30/88	YIELD % 6/30/88	PER SHARE LATEST 12 MONTHS CAP GAINS	INC DIVS	LATEST AVAILABLE PRICE/EARNINGS	ANNUAL % TURNOVER
ITB HIGH INCOME PLUS	FI	SC	15.3	11.87	10,308.20	9,784.30	☆	13.1	0.13	1.56	N/A	39
IVY GROWTH FUND (S)	G	NO	182.0	13.23	10,942.90	9,163.70	18,863.20	2.8	0.00	0.37	18.1	74
IVY INSTITUTIONAL (X)	G	NO	124.4	106.29	11,743.50	9,695.90	☆	4.2	24.20	4.95	15.9	69
IVY INTERNATIONAL	IF	NO	22.4	15.06	11,665.40	10,229.10	☆	0.3	1.60	0.05	N/A	47
IVY MGD US GOVT	FI	NO	2.3	11.28	10,326.10	10,539.10	☆	7.9	0.00	0.89	N/A	48
JANUS FLEXIBLE INC	FI	NO	7.0	9.79	10,310.80	☆	☆	0.0	0.00	0.83	N/A	130
JANUS FUND	CA	NO	385.6	11.34	10,914.30	9,806.10	14,942.50	2.6	1.61	0.31	24.4	214
JANUS VALUE	CA	NO	13.9	9.99	11,002.20	8,323.40	☆	3.8	1.18	0.40	N/A	202
JANUS VENTURE	SG	NO	33.6	28.36	11,551.90	10,007.40	☆	0.5	4.17	0.14	25.2	250
JAPAN FUND	IF	NO	401.9	17.56	10,631.30	11,383.50	39,044.30	0.6	7.81	0.13	N/A	34
JP GROWTH FUND	G	SC	24.9	12.71	10,928.30	9,283.40	16,149.50	2.4	1.54	0.33	N/A	80
JP INCOME FUND	FI	SC	17.8	9.32	10,444.80	10,666.00	18,078.20	8.9	0.00	0.83	N/A	6
KAUFMANN FUND (S)	SG	NO	2.7	1.02	14,571.40	8,695.00	☆	1.0	0.00	0.01	N/A	125
KEMPER BLUE CHIP FUND	GI	SC	19.6	9.04	9,994.20	☆	☆	0.0	0.00	0.07	N/A	N/A
KEMPER ENHANCED GOVT INC	FI	SC	58.9	8.79	10,246.70	☆	☆	0.0	0.00	0.59	N/A	N/A
KEMPER GOLD FUND	AU	SC	1.7	8.93	#9,922.20	☆	☆	0.0	0.00	0.00	N/A	N/A
KEMPER GROWTH FUND	G	SC	291.9	7.72	11,199.40	9,233.10	15,224.30	2.2	3.31	0.21	25.1	247
KEMPER HIGH YIELD	FI	SC	757.4	11.11	11,020.40	11,184.90	20,188.50	11.8	0.44	1.33	N/A	118
KEMPER INCOME & CAP PRES	FI	SC	295.6	8.46	10,607.60	10,782.00	17,806.40	11.1	0.00	0.93	N/A	34
KEMPER INTERNATIONAL FD	IF	SC	178.0	8.88	10,772.60	9,818.20	25,312.50	1.2	1.58	0.11	N/A	144
KEMPER OPTION INCOME	OI	SC	406.9	8.54	11,810.20	9,243.60	13,907.30	12.5	0.18	1.06	15.6	150
KEMPER SUMMIT FUND	SG	SC	275.6	3.81	11,238.90	9,225.60	14,011.50	2.9	1.50	0.13	25.6	115
KEMPER TECHNOLOGY FD	TK	SC	570.2	10.10	11,158.40	9,179.20	15,587.90	2.4	2.35	0.27	20.7	41
KEMPER TOTAL RETURN	B	SC	1,033.7	7.23	10,537.50	8,444.30	14,586.30	3.9	0.19	0.28	17.3	171
KEMPER US GOVT SEC	FI	SC	4,423.3	9.07	10,445.30	10,627.20	17,887.00	10.7	0.00	0.97	N/A	278
KEYSTONE AMER EQ INC (R)	EI	LO	22.1	9.50	10,879.90	9,690.90	☆	5.6	0.00	0.53	N/A	16
KEYSTONE AMER GOVT (R)	FI	LO	74.8	9.83	10,151.20	10,427.80	☆	8.4	0.00	0.83	N/A	60
KEYSTONE AMER HI YLD (R)	FI	LO	113.2	9.39	10,739.50	10,423.20	☆	11.5	0.00	1.08	N/A	N/A
KEYSTONE AMER INV GRO (R)	FI	LO	39.1	9.13	10,140.30	10,254.30	☆	9.1	0.00	0.83	N/A	N/A
KEYSTONE B-1 (R)	FI	NO	469.2	15.60	10,359.50	10,361.10	15,633.90	8.5	0.00	1.32	N/A	127
KEYSTONE B-2 (R)	FI	NO	885.1	17.94	10,691.80	10,520.60	15,644.90	10.3	0.04	1.85	N/A	74
KEYSTONE B-4 (X,R)	FI	NO	1,251.0	6.82	10,884.10	10,045.80	14,578.20	12.3	0.00	0.84	N/A	135
KEYSTONE INTERNATIONAL (R)	IF	NO	117.4	6.69	10,340.00	8,942.20	21,188.40	1.1	1.22	0.08	N/A	61
KEYSTONE K-1 (R)	I	NO	685.4	8.37	10,760.80	9,662.30	17,324.80	7.1	0.42	0.60	17.1	79
KEYSTONE K-2 (R)	G	NO	344.0	6.42	10,664.50	8,617.00	15,183.60	2.0	1.25	0.14	19.4	104
KEYSTONE PREC METALS (R)	AU	NO	257.6	17.81	9,285.70	8,827.50	11,018.80	1.0	1.22	0.19	25.3	62
KEYSTONE S-1 (R)	GI	NO	196.4	19.86	10,683.30	8,684.10	15,861.10	2.3	1.53	0.46	15.8	71
KEYSTONE S-3 (R)	G	NO	266.5	7.50	11,467.90	9,271.20	14,534.10	2.1	1.66	0.16	21.0	118
KEYSTONE S-4 (R)	G	NO	493.7	4.84	11,606.70	8,438.10	9,745.10	0.0	0.89	0.00	21.1	74
KIDDER PEABODY EQU INC (R)	EI	NO	73.3	16.87	10,156.20	9,141.50	☆	2.4	0.92	0.41	N/A	159
KIDDER PEABODY GOV INC (R)	FI	NO	130.6	14.45	10,519.00	10,799.90	☆	8.0	0.03	1.15	N/A	163
KIDDER PEABODY MKTGUARD	S	LO	49.8	14.41	10,342.30	10,218.10	☆	6.2	0.01	0.89	N/A	143
KIDDER PEABODY SPL GR (R)	G	NO	20.2	15.05	10,252.00	9,020.60	☆	0.2	0.00	0.02	N/A	204
KOTROZO OPTION INCOME	OI	SC	4.7	9.65	10,715.60	☆	☆	0.0	0.42	0.00	N/A	N/A
LANDMARK CAPITAL GROWTH	CA	NO	11.7	9.36	10,858.50	7,388.00	☆	0.7	0.40	0.07	N/A	56
LANDMARK GROWTH & INCOME	GI	NO	12.0	10.32	11,363.50	9,682.60	☆	4.1	0.34	0.42	N/A	56
LANDMARK US GOVT INC	FI	NO	33.1	9.20	10,474.10	10,730.10	☆	8.5	0.00	0.78	N/A	411
LAZARD FRERES EQUITY	CA	NO	15.3	9.87	11,305.80	9,684.00	☆	1.0	0.00	0.10	N/A	97
LAZARD SPECIAL EQUITY	CA	NO	72.5	13.34	12,537.60	10,438.20	☆	0.8	0.50	0.10	N/A	91
LEGG MASON SPECIAL INV	SG	NO	47.2	10.95	12,615.20	9,409.50	☆	0.7	0.89	0.07	12.8	77
LEGG MASON TOTAL RETURN	G	NO	34.8	9.37	11,994.10	9,515.70	☆	2.5	0.44	0.24	20.7	83
LEGG MASON VALUE TRUST	G	NO	707.3	26.08	12,337.30	9,655.50	20,234.30	1.8	1.53	0.49	17.1	43
LEHMAN CAPITAL FUND	CA	SC	85.5	18.37	11,079.60	9,062.70	15,084.60	0.0	0.00	0.00	26.8	395
LEHMAN INVESTORS	GI	SC	372.4	16.10	11,274.70	9,166.10	16,335.60	2.6	2.20	0.45	19.4	80

LEHMAN OPPORTUNITY	CA	NO	93.7	23.59	11,848.30	10,288.40	20,777.60	3.0	2.94	0.75	15.4	25
LEPERCQ-ISTEL AGGR GRO	CA	NO	1.1	9.70	12,034.70	8,866.50	☆	0.0	0.00	0.00	N/A	71
LEPERCQ-ISTEL FUND	GI	NO	21.9	12.86	10,515.10	8,983.70	12,980.80	3.2	0.69	0.42	N/A	67
LEPERCQ-ISTEL INTL	IF	NO	2.0	12.20	10,941.70	10,347.80	☆	0.0	0.00	0.00	N/A	285
LEVERAGE FUND OF BOSTON	CA	NO	21.0	6.43	11,885.40	8,655.40	12,418.90	0.0	1.50	0.00	N/A	115
LEXINGTON GLOBAL	GL	SC	32.2	10.99	11,156.70	10,891.60	☆	0.1	0.00	0.01	20.8	96
LEXINGTON GNMA INCOME	FI	NO	105.3	7.67	10,459.90	10,569.60	16,299.90	7.7	0.05	0.59	N/A	89
LEXINGTON GOLDFUND	AU	NO	98.1	5.77	9,321.50	9,370.80	14,352.30	0.0	0.34	0.00	25.4	14
LEXINGTON GROWTH	G	NO	28.7	9.06	11,325.00	8,916.90	13,112.00	0.0	2.43	0.00	16.9	83
LEXINGTON RESEARCH	GI	NO	116.5	14.60	10,838.20	9,003.70	15,715.00	1.6	2.61	0.25	13.5	95
LEXINGTON TECH STRATEGY	CA	SC	5.3	9.99	10,616.40	☆	☆	0.0	0.00	0.00	N/A	N/A
LIBERTY FUND	FI	NO	12.4	4.31	11,034.30	10,243.20	16,687.40	9.7	0.00	0.42	N/A	186
LIBERTY MUTUAL US GOVT	FI	LO	27.8	9.75	10,535.80	10,871.10	☆	9.4	0.00	0.92	N/A	N/A
LIFE OF VIRGINIA-BOND	FI	NO	4.0	10.62	10,535.70	10,675.50	☆	6.2	0.02	0.65	N/A	11
LIFE OF VIRGINIA-COM STK	G	NO	2.2	12.42	12,093.50	9,944.30	☆	1.9	0.65	0.24	N/A	105
LIFE OF VIRGINIA-TOT RTN	GI	NO	2.1	10.69	11,507.00	10,072.00	☆	2.9	0.26	0.31	N/A	82
LINDNER DIVIDEND (R)	EI	NO	61.5	21.51	11,554.70	10,745.60	19,710.60	8.4	1.22	1.87	10.7	56
LINDNER FUND (R)	G	NO	404.4	17.74	11,732.80	10,754.00	20,092.00	5.4	1.60	0.98	11.1	39
LMH FUND	GI	NO	40.1	18.82	11,090.20	9,789.70	☆	11.6	3.12	2.36	12.7	19
LOCH NESS OPTION FUND	OI	NO	0.6	8.76	10,309.70	☆	☆	0.0	0.00	0.39	N/A	N/A
LOOMIS-SAYLES CAPITAL (X)	G	NO	217.4	16.72	10,096.60	8,839.60	18,049.90	0.2	7.77	0.04	16.4	187
LOOMIS-SAYLES MUTUAL	B	NO	324.8	21.04	10,415.30	9,656.00	21,202.60	3.6	4.12	0.83	19.6	197
LORD ABBETT BOND-DEB	FI	SC	759.2	9.82	11,042.90	10,513.10	15,809.80	10.9	0.00	1.07	N/A	176
LORD ABBETT DEVEL GROWTH	SG	SC	192.4	7.42	11,141.10	9,253.10	9,012.50	0.0	1.28	0.00	29.8	15
LORD ABBETT FUNDMNTL VAL	GI	SC	23.6	10.41	11,229.80	9,821.00	☆	2.0	0.49	0.21	N/A	45
LORD ABBETT US GOVT	FI	SC	904.5	2.97	10,551.50	10,829.40	17,343.10	11.0	0.00	0.32	N/A	429
LORD ABBETT VALUE APPREC	G	SC	234.8	11.00	12,101.20	10,165.00	☆	2.5	0.71	0.28	16.6	44
LOWRY MARKET TIMING	CA	SC	28.6	9.14	10,652.70	10,348.40	☆	4.5	0.95	0.43	N/A	190
LUTHERAN BRO FUND	GI	SC	269.4	14.84	10,675.00	8,802.20	17,939.20	2.9	1.65	0.46	17.1	88
LUTHERAN BRO HI YLD	FI	SC	91.6	9.80	10,810.80	10,737.90	☆	11.6	0.00	1.13	N/A	67
LUTHERAN BRO INCOME	FI	SC	714.2	8.47	10,599.50	10,814.60	16,611.50	9.5	0.00	0.80	N/A	48
MACKAY-SHIELDS: CAP APR (R)	CA	NO	31.7	10.15	10,774.90	8,319.70	☆	0.0	0.00	0.00	N/A	16
MACKAY-SHIELDS: CONV (R)	CV	NO	31.0	9.16	10,945.10	9,578.90	☆	4.6	0.07	0.42	N/A	147
MACKAY-SHIELDS: GLOBAL (R)	GL	NO	17.6	9.64	10,263.30	9,823.50	☆	1.8	0.00	0.16	N/A	44
MACKAY-SHIELDS: GOLD (R)	AU	NO	6.0	9.57	9,512.90	☆	☆	0.0	0.00	0.00	N/A	N/A
MACKAY-SHIELDS: GOVT+ (R)	FI	NO	426.6	9.15	10,369.40	10,607.50	☆	10.3	0.00	0.94	N/A	594
MACKAY-SHIELDS: HI YLD (R)	FI	NO	104.5	9.06	10,941.00	10,698.80	☆	11.4	0.00	1.02	N/A	48
MACKAY-SHIELDS: TOT RET (R)	B	NO	9.4	10.44	10,446.00	☆	☆	0.0	0.00	0.05	N/A	N/A
MACKAY-SHIELDS: VALUE (R)	GI	NO	17.3	9.49	10,910.70	8,896.30	☆	0.6	0.04	0.05	N/A	41
MACKENZIE AMERICAN	G	SC	31.5	12.03	11,711.20	10,673.80	☆	1.5	0.27	0.18	N/A	16
MACKENZIE FIXED INCOME	FI	SC	5.0	9.99	10,689.20	11,630.40	☆	7.3	0.06	0.73	N/A	N/A
MACKENZIE GOVT PLUS	FI	SC	10.3	7.52	10,498.00	9,923.20	☆	8.4	0.00	0.63	N/A	208
MACKENZIE OPTION INCOME	OI	SC	299.2	7.32	10,720.50	9,063.80	☆	11.3	0.49	0.83	14.4	148
MAIN STREET FDS: CAP PRES	CA	LO	0.1	10.60	#11,083.10	☆	☆	0.0	0.00	0.04	N/A	N/A
MAIN STREET FDS: GOVT SEC	FI	LO	0.7	9.52	#10,060.00	☆	☆	0.0	0.00	0.13	N/A	N/A
MAIN STREET FDS: INC & GR	GI	LO	0.3	10.13	#10,593.60	☆	☆	0.0	0.00	0.04	N/A	N/A
MANHATTAN FUND	CA	NO	416.2	9.04	11,574.90	9,131.80	20,016.00	1.8	0.81	0.17	19.0	111
HORACE MANN BALANCED	B	NO	26.7	13.67	10,755.30	10,004.20	☆	0.0	2.05	0.00	N/A	85
HORACE MANN GROWTH	G	NO	88.3	17.46	10,912.50	9,222.60	15,286.70	2.5	6.02	0.51	N/A	87
HORACE MANN INCOME	I	NO	3.1	12.17	10,500.40	10,703.20	☆	0.0	2.27	0.00	N/A	53
MARINER EQUITY	CA	NO	4.4	10.82	11,365.50	9,135.10	☆	2.8	0.14	0.31	N/A	164
MARINER INTERM BOND	FI	NO	10.3	9.76	10,273.90	10,549.30	☆	7.4	0.00	0.72	N/A	999
MAS POOLED: EQUITY	G	NO	359.6	36.72	11,184.00	9,848.70	☆	2.2	2.00	0.84	N/A	N/A
MAS POOLED: FIXED INCOME	FI	NO	373.1	28.62	10,532.20	10,729.30	☆	7.0	0.00	2.01	N/A	N/A
MAS POOLED: QUANT GRO	G	NO	0.9	20.15	11,650.30	9,520.50	☆	5.3	6.04	1.22	N/A	N/A
MAS POOLED: SELECT EQTY	G	NO	19.3	27.81	#11,153.00	☆	☆	0.0	0.00	0.07	N/A	N/A
MAS POOLED: SELECT FIX INC	FI	NO	38.1	26.77	10,472.60	☆	☆	0.0	0.03	0.81	N/A	N/A

PERFORMANCE OF MUTUAL FUNDS (continued)

FUND NAME	OBJ.	LOAD	TOTAL NET ASTS (MIL) 6/30/88	NAV 6/30/88	PERFORMANCE (RETURN ON INITIAL $10,000 INVESTMENT) 12/31/87-6/30/88	6/30/87-6/30/88	6/30/83-6/30/88	YIELD % 6/30/88	PER SHARE LATEST 12 MONTHS CAP GAINS	INC DIVS	LATEST AVAILABLE PRICE/EARNINGS	ANNUAL % TURNOVER
MAS POOLED: SELECT VALUE	GI	NO	53.2	29.63	11,918.40	☆	☆	0.0	0.00	0.27	N/A	N/A
MAS POOLED: SMALL CAP	SG	NO	206.1	21.73	12,263.00	9,052.60	☆	1.6	0.79	0.34	N/A	N/A
MAS POOLED: VALUE	GI	NO	610.6	31.24	11,936.50	9,963.40	☆	3.6	4.33	1.21	N/A	N/A
MASS CAPITAL DEVELOPMENT	G	SC	840.9	11.60	10,818.60	8,841.20	12,709.20	1.7	0.46	0.20	24.4	40
MASS FINL BOND	FI	SC	310.5	13.17	10,606.80	10,793.80	17,622.00	8.6	0.00	1.13	N/A	334
MASS FINL DEVELOPMENT	GI	SC	241.5	10.41	11,031.40	9,044.40	14,889.60	1.9	2.31	0.20	22.4	101
MASS FINL EMERGING GRO	SG	SC	245.6	14.28	12,122.20	8,778.30	12,535.10	0.0	3.18	0.00	20.9	73
MASS FINL HIGH INCOME	FI	SC	948.1	6.12	10,772.60	10,230.30	16,112.50	13.4	0.04	0.82	23.0	46
MASS FINL INTL TR-BOND	WI	SC	164.5	11.62	9,789.40	11,258.70	21,263.00	15.2	0.18	1.78	N/A	378
MASS FINL SPECIAL	CA	SC	121.2	9.13	12,158.40	9,390.50	15,438.10	1.2	0.10	0.10	15.3	135
MASS FINL TOTAL RETURN	B	SC	505.6	10.37	11,095.30	10,085.90	20,221.80	5.8	0.66	0.60	14.8	58
MASS INVESTORS GROWTH	G	SC	829.0	9.07	10,703.70	8,849.20	14,325.70	1.7	1.26	0.16	23.2	66
MASS INVESTORS TRUST	GI	SC	1,207.7	11.98	10,812.90	9,034.10	17,619.90	3.1	1.38	0.39	17.0	23
MASSMUTUAL FDS: INV GRADE	FI	SC	109.7	10.34	10,501.90	10,681.20	16,751.90	12.0	0.00	1.24	N/A	N/A
MATHERS FUND	G	NO	190.6	16.37	11,320.90	11,528.30	19,740.90	2.5	4.15	0.46	15.6	202
MAXIM BOND	FI	NO	33.0	1.20	10,370.80	10,752.50	17,676.90	7.3	0.00	0.08	N/A	N/A
MAXIM GROWTH	G	NO	125.2	1.32	11,433.90	9,830.70	18,567.90	4.4	0.08	0.05	N/A	N/A
MBL GROWTH FUND	G	NO	38.4	14.14	12,120.10	10,033.90	18,905.70	3.3	0.50	0.48	N/A	19
MEDICAL RESEARCH INV	H	LO	2.9	11.00	10,597.30	7,891.60	☆	0.0	1.04	0.00	N/A	95
MEDICAL TECHNOLOGY FUND	H	NO	40.8	10.43	10,774.80	8,557.90	11,304.80	0.0	4.22	0.00	31.1	6
MEESCHAERT CAPITAL (R)	G	NO	37.2	24.98	9,811.50	8,233.90	13,838.80	0.8	0.00	0.21	17.5	1
MEESCHAERT INTL (R)	WI	NO	8.8	8.64	9,557.50	8,884.00	☆	5.8	0.17	0.51	N/A	3
MERIDIAN FUND	G	NO	10.6	13.65	11,859.30	9,700.70	☆	0.2	1.21	0.02	N/A	88
MERITOR GROWTH OPP	G	NO	6.4	10.98	10,892.90	8,646.60	☆	0.0	1.43	0.00	N/A	310
MERITOR US GOVERNMENT	FI	NO	10.7	12.00	10,374.90	10,669.40	☆	7.4	0.00	0.88	N/A	500
MERRILL LYN BASIC VALUE	GI	SC	1,079.3	18.60	11,809.50	10,189.50	21,662.00	3.3	1.33	0.62	14.7	23
MERRILL LYN CAPITAL	GI	SC	664.1	22.38	11,308.70	10,006.60	20,697.70	1.7	1.49	0.38	16.7	109
MERRILL LYN CORP DIV	EI	LO	155.9	9.76	10,140.80	10,030.50	☆	9.7	0.21	0.95	9.9	81
MERRILL LYN EQUI-BOND (R)	GI	LO	14.5	11.88	10,513.30	10,244.80	16,804.50	3.6	1.95	0.46	N/A	18
MERRILL LYN EUROFUND (R)	IF	NO	295.4	8.54	9,918.70	8,423.40	☆	8.1	0.09	0.69	N/A	157
MERRILL LYN FEDERAL	FI	SC	3,808.5	9.29	10,489.20	10,731.60	☆	8.8	0.00	0.81	N/A	205
MERRILL LYN FD TOMOROW (R)	G	NO	627.5	15.15	11,671.80	9,290.20	☆	0.7	0.71	0.11	19.9	23
MERRILL LYN GLBL CONV (R)	WI	NO	43.5	10.21	#10,210.00	☆	☆	0.0	0.00	0.00	N/A	N/A
MERRILL LYN HIGH INCOME	FI	LO	771.3	7.97	10,850.00	10,693.10	17,604.70	12.0	0.00	0.95	N/A	57
MERRILL LYN HIGH QUALITY	FI	LO	257.8	11.07	10,502.30	10,723.70	17,336.50	8.9	0.00	0.98	N/A	126
MERRILL LYN INST INTER	FI	NO	344.7	9.49	10,337.30	10,665.20	☆	8.3	0.00	0.78	N/A	407
MERRILL LYN INTL HLDGS	GL	SC	232.8	12.08	10,486.10	9,421.20	☆	2.4	1.09	0.30	18.6	89
MERRILL LYN INTERMEDIATE	FI	LO	100.0	11.05	10,482.80	10,703.70	17,030.20	8.6	0.00	0.95	N/A	153
MERRILL LYN NATRL RES (R)	NR	NO	744.9	13.74	10,095.50	8,817.30	☆	6.4	1.23	0.89	18.9	69
MERRILL LYN PACIFIC	IF	SC	292.1	17.30	11,414.70	9,313.80	39,922.70	2.9	18.76	0.77	N/A	29
MERRILL LYN PHOENIX	GI	SC	116.8	13.48	12,838.10	11,028.70	22,840.40	2.9	1.55	0.41	13.2	54
MERRILL LYN RET BENFT (R)	B	NO	2,536.1	11.12	10,570.30	9,595.30	☆	2.7	0.22	0.30	N/A	145
MERRILL LYN RET EQTY (R)	GI	NO	560.6	9.51	11,201.40	9,632.80	☆	2.0	0.00	0.18	22.8	9
MERRILL LYN RET GLOBAL (R)	WI	NO	314.2	10.06	9,701.60	11,074.00	☆	12.3	0.38	1.23	N/A	124
MERRILL LYN RET INC (R)	FI	NO	1,932.9	9.36	10,448.80	10,609.90	☆	8.1	0.00	0.75	18.0	194
MERRILL LYN SPEC VALUE	G	SC	109.7	12.35	11,967.10	8,874.50	10,816.10	0.9	0.42	0.11	20.0	51
MERRILL LYN STRTG DVD (R)	EI	NO	150.7	10.85	10,894.80	☆	☆	0.0	0.00	0.11	N/A	N/A
METLIFE CAPITAL APPREC	CA	SC	29.8	10.96	12,226.30	9,657.20	☆	0.7	0.42	0.08	18.7	201
METLIFE EQUITY INCOME	EI	SC	30.3	8.93	11,299.90	9,764.90	☆	7.2	0.47	0.65	15.5	74
METLIFE EQU INVESTMENTS	GI	SC	25.2	9.70	10,950.90	9,313.70	☆	2.2	0.70	0.21	N/A	119
METLIFE GOVT INCOME	FI	NO	1,699.9	11.64	10,454.20	10,704.80	☆	9.5	0.00	1.11	N/A	149
METLIFE GOVT SECS	FI	SC	26.1	6.81	10,425.70	10,518.60	☆	8.5	0.00	0.57	N/A	41
METLIFE HIGH INCOME	FI	SC	47.6	7.29	11,126.30	10,969.00	☆	11.7	0.00	0.85	N/A	40
METRO PORTFOLIO INV STK	CA	NO	4.3	13.06	11,171.90	8,987.20	☆	0.7	0.60	0.09	N/A	65

MFS GOVT GUARANTEED SEC	FI	SC	388.5	9.42	10,434.80	10,605.60	☆	9.3	0.00	0.87	N/A	191
MFS GOVT SEC HIGH YIELD	FI	SC	1,301.0	8.04	10,304.60	10,296.50	☆	10.7	0.27	0.88	N/A	212
MFS LIFETIME CAP GRO (R)	CA	NO	130.5	9.37	11,358.10	9,028.40	☆	0.9	0.00	0.08	N/A	139
MFS LIFETIME DIV PLUS (R)	GI	NO	145.1	8.63	10,886.70	9,375.90	☆	6.7	0.00	0.57	N/A	133
MFS LIFETIME EMER GRO (R)	SG	NO	79.7	6.85	11,913.00	8,573.20	☆	0.0	0.00	0.00	N/A	81
MFS LIFETIME GLOBAL EQ (R)	GL	NO	42.3	10.80	9,712.20	9,098.60	☆	0.0	0.00	0.00	N/A	272
MFS LIFETIME GOVT INC (R)	FI	NO	2,788.3	7.95	10,243.40	10,257.40	☆	8.4	0.34	0.68	N/A	82
MFS LIFETIME HI INC (R)	FI	NO	119.5	6.99	10,843.30	10,297.90	☆	9.7	0.00	0.68	N/A	26
MFS LIFETIME MGD SECTR (R)	S	NO	162.1	8.35	10,879.20	8,759.30	☆	0.7	0.00	0.05	N/A	163
MFS-MANAGED SECTOR TR	S	SC	180.1	10.53	10,764.40	8,584.60	☆	1.2	0.15	0.12	20.5	163
MIDAMERICA HIGH GROWTH	CA	SC	12.2	3.84	11,261.00	9,455.20	14,345.70	2.5	1.19	0.11	N/A	211
MIDAMERICA HIGH YIELD FD	FI	SC	14.7	10.00	10,653.20	10,728.30	☆	10.9	0.05	1.09	N/A	34
MIDAMERICA MUTUAL	G	SC	34.9	5.35	10,819.80	9,508.30	16,955.50	3.4	1.25	0.20	17.5	92
MIDAS GOLD SHS & BULLION	AU	SC	16.5	2.92	9,240.50	8,574.10	☆	1.8	0.33	0.05	N/A	27
MIDWEST INCOME TR/INTMDT	FI	LO	55.1	10.15	10,298.50	10,582.80	15,386.70	7.5	0.00	0.76	N/A	54
MIMLIC INVESTORS I	GI	SC	8.2	10.82	11,306.20	9,225.80	☆	2.4	0.58	0.26	N/A	27
MIMLIC MORTGAGE	FI	SC	14.3	9.97	10,536.70	10,841.70	☆	8.8	0.00	0.87	N/A	43
MONETTA FUND	GI	NO	2.4	11.58	11,962.80	10,478.90	☆	0.5	0.00	0.06	N/A	333
MONEY MARKET/OPTIONS	OG	NO	5.1	17.77	10,240.40	9,276.40	15,374.40	6.0	0.72	1.09	N/A	N/A
MONITREND: VALUE FUND	CA	LO	19.3	16.05	9,913.50	9,626.90	☆	1.9	1.56	0.31	N/A	241
MONITREND: GOVERNMENT FD	FI	LO	3.9	14.04	10,060.20	10,143.20	☆	5.3	0.00	0.92	N/A	N/A
WL MORGAN GROWTH	G	NO	690.9	11.42	12,311.80	9,992.80	16,560.40	1.6	2.59	0.20	17.8	43
MORGAN KEEGAN SOUTHERN	G	LO	13.4	11.09	11,327.90	9,405.00	☆	3.6	0.00	0.40	N/A	292
MORISON ASSET ALLOCATION	CA	SC	24.8	5.19	10,380.00	9,364.70	☆	3.1	0.01	0.16	N/A	18
MUTUAL BEACON FUND	GI	NO	204.9	23.44	12,298.70	11,034.20	18,868.10	2.2	1.51	0.54	23.6	73
MUTUAL BENEFIT FUND	GI	SC	19.7	14.15	12,263.60	9,894.20	18,973.10	2.3	0.87	0.33	14.6	21
MUTUAL OMAHA AMERICA	FI	NO	53.6	9.91	10,490.30	10,725.40	15,966.60	8.3	0.02	0.82	N/A	35
MUTUAL OMAHA GROWTH	G	SC	39.6	7.38	11,770.30	9,435.50	14,952.60	0.9	0.50	0.06	21.2	51
MUTUAL OMAHA INCOME	I	SC	158.3	9.00	10,800.50	10,533.50	17,889.90	8.2	0.12	0.74	16.5	115
MUTUAL QUALIFIED FUND	GI	NO	935.8	23.68	12,244.10	10,884.30	24,824.40	3.6	1.44	0.88	23.9	74
MUTUAL SHARES	GI	NO	2,221.7	71.07	12,310.80	10,934.70	24,143.50	3.5	4.09	2.52	24.1	78
NAESS & THOMAS SPECIAL	SG	NO	28.5	36.33	12,549.20	9,354.20	8,863.60	0.0	3.64	0.00	22.4	92
NATL AVIATION & TECH	TK	SC	70.7	10.38	11,793.30	8,494.80	12,384.10	1.1	0.50	0.12	13.7	14
NATIONAL BOND	FI	SC	894.1	2.48	10,431.60	9,823.20	14,337.50	17.4	0.00	0.43	N/A	288
NATIONAL FEDERAL SEC TR	FI	SC	837.4	9.25	10,230.90	10,176.20	☆	10.4	0.00	0.96	N/A	158
NATIONAL GROWTH	G	SC	58.4	10.80	11,710.10	8,971.60	10,420.10	2.5	0.00	0.27	20.3	169
NATIONAL INDUSTRIES (R)	GI	NO	28.9	12.29	11,496.70	9,579.20	13,787.50	0.8	1.15	0.10	15.1	68
NATIONAL PREFERRED	FI	SC	4.8	7.40	10,800.10	9,762.00	17,168.70	9.1	0.12	0.68	17.1	37
NATIONAL PREMIUM INC	OI	SC	20.7	10.94	11,563.60	9,691.10	☆	1.9	1.10	0.22	N/A	127
NATIONAL REAL ESTATE: INC	S	SC	13.3	10.28	11,629.40	10,305.10	☆	10.7	0.02	1.10	N/A	N/A
NATIONAL REAL ESTATE: STK	S	SC	21.0	8.66	11,797.10	9,651.40	☆	7.7	0.41	0.68	N/A	55
NATIONAL STOCK	GI	SC	222.1	7.72	11,728.20	9,522.40	17,913.50	4.6	0.01	0.35	N/A	142
NATIONAL STRATEGIC ALLOC	CA	SC	154.5	10.74	10,293.50	☆		0.0	0.00	0.17	N/A	62
NATL TELECOM & TECH	TK	SC	44.3	15.63	11,228.00	9,371.10	11,343.80	1.1	0.00	0.17	29.4	9
NATIONAL TOTAL INCOME	EI	SC	142.5	7.64	10,938.00	10,285.20	19,930.50	5.6	0.37	0.44	13.5	17
NATIONAL TOTAL RETURN	EI	SC	278.4	7.20	10,990.00	9,768.10	17,640.50	4.8	0.21	0.35	15.6	9
NATIONAL VALUE	CA	SC	2.0	9.85	11,040.60	8,381.00	☆	7.8	0.53	0.79	N/A	135
NATIONWIDE BOND	FI	SC	35.0	9.16	10,403.10	10,589.20	16,391.80	10.9	0.00	0.99	N/A	61
NATIONWIDE FUND	GI	SC	403.0	13.14	11,246.10	9,263.90	19,816.70	3.4	1.42	0.47	15.0	22
NATIONWIDE GROWTH	G	SC	229.2	8.42	11,676.10	9,801.00	20,755.90	4.4	1.07	0.39	18.8	70
NAUTILUS FUND	TK	SC	15.5	11.51	11,952.20	8,662.90	6,953.90	0.0	0.99	0.00	N/A	62
NEUBERGER & BERMAN LT BD	FI	NO	124.9	9.88	10,415.10	10,721.40	☆	7.1	0.00	0.70	N/A	158
NEUWIRTH FUND	G	NO	26.4	14.89	12,925.30	9,424.00	13,074.20	0.0	0.00	0.00	N/A	117
NEW ALTERNATIVES FUND	NR	SC	5.2	44.81	11,889.10	9,963.90	16,618.60	1.0	0.76	0.47	N/A	9
"NEW BEGINNING" GROWTH	SG	NO	48.1	27.91	11,466.70	9,156.00	16,439.80	0.1	2.95	0.03	N/A	81
"NEW BEGINNING" INC & GR	GI	NO	12.2	18.31	10,715.30	9,355.40	16,576.90	2.9	1.14	0.53	N/A	61
"NEW BEGINNING" INV RESV	FI	NO	10.9	9.96	10,316.70	10,664.80	☆	6.4	0.00	0.63	N/A	N/A

PERFORMANCE OF MUTUAL FUNDS (continued)

FUND NAME	OBJ.	LOAD	TOTAL NET ASTS (MIL) 6/30/88	NAV 6/30/88	PERFORMANCE (RETURN ON INITIAL $10,000 INVESTMENT) 12/31/87-6/30/88	6/30/87-6/30/88	6/30/83-6/30/88	YIELD % 6/30/88	PER SHARE LATEST 12 MONTHS CAP GAINS	INC DIVS	LATEST AVAILABLE PRICE/EARNINGS	ANNUAL % TURNOVER
"NEW BEGINNING" US GOVT	FI	NO	10.7	10.24	10,542.30	11,069.40	☆	8.8	0.00	0.89	N/A	N/A
"NEW BEGINNING" YIELD (X)	FI	NO	5.8	10.29	10,546.50	10,601.50	☆	9.6	0.00	0.98	N/A	197
NEW ECONOMY FUND	G	SC	744.1	21.10	11,254.70	9,747.30	☆	2.2	1.08	0.48	27.1	15
NEW ENG: BOND INCOME	FI	SC	64.4	11.04	10,499.20	10,715.00	16,572.40	8.2	0.00	0.90	N/A	307
NEW ENG: EQUITY INCOME	GI	SC	51.2	9.72	10,872.50	9,415.60	17,658.50	2.2	0.76	0.22	19.5	63
NEW ENG: GOVERNMENT SEC	FI	SC	188.1	12.15	10,437.40	10,690.50	☆	7.4	0.02	0.89	N/A	178
NEW ENG: GLOBAL GOVT FD	WI	SC	16.5	11.88	#9,593.60	☆	☆	0.0	0.00	0.11	N/A	N/A
NEW ENG: GROWTH FUND	G	SC	486.9	7.95	10,474.30	9,253.70	16,400.30	0.0	2.76	0.00	17.9	154
NEW ENG: RETIREMENT EQU	GI	SC	142.9	6.38	9,937.70	8,624.00	18,451.80	0.6	1.46	0.04	18.6	202
NEW ENG: ZENITH BOND INC	FI	NO	19.6	100.56	10,533.20	10,741.50	☆	8.6	0.00	8.67	N/A	331
NEW ENG: ZENITH CAP GRO	CA	NO	36.0	216.15	9,343.40	8,530.60	☆	0.3	19.59	0.66	N/A	368
NEW ENG: ZENITH MNGD SRS	GI	NO	9.6	101.97	10,553.70	10,073.10	☆	2.7	0.00	2.73	N/A	N/A
NEW ENG: ZENITH STK INDEX	G	NO	10.4	95.41	11,259.10	9,313.00	☆	2.3	0.41	2.23	N/A	N/A
NEW PERSPECTIVE FUND	GL	SC	1,005.6	10.47	10,687.60	9,652.30	21,710.80	2.3	1.14	0.25	18.6	17
NEW YORK VENTURE	G	SC	166.3	8.02	11,644.30	9,881.40	20,174.00	2.6	2.14	0.21	19.2	55
NEWPORT FAR EAST	IF	SC	2.9	16.63	11,020.50	8,515.00	☆	0.0	5.65	0.00	N/A	73
NEWPORT GLOBAL GROWTH	GL	SC	1.2	10.84	10,433.10	8,936.50	☆	0.0	0.00	0.00	N/A	80
NEWTON GROWTH FUND	G	NO	38.0	21.47	11,655.80	8,943.50	12,499.90	1.2	1.30	0.27	23.7	96
NEWTON INCOME FUND	FI	NO	16.0	8.01	10,403.90	10,612.10	15,106.00	7.1	0.07	0.57	N/A	15
NICHOLAS FUND	G	NO	1,147.9	33.42	11,756.30	10,100.70	17,882.30	3.1	1.85	1.07	16.0	27
NICHOLAS INCOME	FI	NO	75.4	3.83	10,772.30	10,738.60	17,406.90	9.7	0.00	0.37	N/A	48
NICHOLAS LIMITED EDITION	G	NO	27.5	11.25	12,295.10	11,195.30	☆	0.8	0.00	0.09	N/A	N/A
NICHOLAS II	SG	NO	396.0	18.47	11,771.80	10,060.30	☆	1.8	1.30	0.33	16.6	26
NODDINGS CONV STRATEGIES	CV	NO	7.9	8.66	10,771.40	9,989.00	☆	12.8	1.21	1.19	N/A	62
NOMURA PACIFIC BASIN	IF	NO	86.5	19.01	11,050.80	10,860.30	☆	0.3	7.78	0.08	N/A	46
NORTHEAST INV GROWTH	G	NO	20.3	18.10	10,748.20	8,322.80	17,397.20	1.5	0.39	0.27	N/A	36
NORTHEAST INV TRUST	FI	NO	380.6	12.15	10,908.70	10,502.00	18,835.00	15.9	0.00	1.93	N/A	52
NOVA FUND	TK	SC	14.2	14.54	10,597.70	8,746.40	13,295.20	0.0	1.50	0.00	N/A	59
NOVA-INCOME (R)	FI	SC	0.1	10.28	10,610.90	☆	☆	6.6	0.00	0.67	N/A	N/A
NOVA-TOTAL RETURN (R)	GI	SC	0.1	10.16	10,270.90	☆	☆	2.7	0.00	0.38	N/A	N/A
OBERWEIS EMERGING GRO (R)	SG	LO	21.9	11.63	12,738.20	9,057.60	☆	0.0	0.00	0.00	N/A	55
OHIO NATIONAL-BOND (R)	FI	NO	3.6	9.82	10,334.10	10,429.20	16,428.80	9.3	0.00	0.90	N/A	13
OHIO NATIONAL-EQUITY (R)	G	NO	35.3	18.85	11,379.80	9,845.00	18,912.10	5.1	0.00	0.95	N/A	7
OHIO NATIONAL-OMNI (R)	G	NO	27.3	12.22	11,141.40	10,001.40	☆	6.7	0.00	0.81	N/A	12
OLYMPIC TR-BALANCED INC	GI	NO	6.7	14.40	10,923.80	10,558.30	☆	4.9	0.75	0.72	N/A	84
OLYMPIC TR-EQ INCOME	EI	NO	29.3	11.60	11,647.30	☆	☆	4.2	0.00	0.49	N/A	N/A
OLYMPIC TR-SMALL CAP	CA	NO	8.2	18.05	11,836.10	9,405.80	☆	0.0	0.06	0.00	N/A	30
OMEGA FUND	CA	SC	35.3	13.69	11,332.80	9,478.00	16,376.70	0.0	1.88	0.00	22.8	106
OMNI INVESTMENT	CA	NO	8.8	119.05	11,833.10	10,271.40	☆	1.7	9.94	2.06	N/A	N/A
ONE HUNDRED FUND	G	NO	10.8	18.60	10,385.30	9,555.10	11,390.40	0.0	4.75	0.00	N/A	106
ONE HUNDRED & ONE FUND	GI	NO	2.3	12.97	10,568.60	8,806.30	14,656.00	3.1	1.58	0.43	N/A	241
OPPENHEIMER ASSET ALOCTN	B	SC	40.8	9.87	11,268.60	10,117.90	☆	4.1	0.00	0.40	19.0	121
OPPENHEIMER BLUE CHIP	GI	SC	18.2	13.22	11,291.30	9,281.70	☆	3.4	0.46	0.45	N/A	203
OPPENHEIMER DIRECTORS	CA	SC	162.9	20.60	12,068.00	9,615.70	10,374.90	2.6	2.89	0.57	19.5	84
OPPENHEIMER EQUITY INCO	EI	SC	806.9	8.51	11,154.60	10,199.90	18,679.20	6.9	0.87	0.60	20.7	95
OPPENHEIMER FUND	G	SC	213.3	8.36	11,210.60	8,769.60	11,729.20	2.0	2.36	0.17	21.6	59
OPPENHEIMER GNMA	FI	SC	62.1	13.57	10,493.80	10,917.70	☆	8.8	0.00	1.19	N/A	186
OPPENHEIMER GLD & SP MIN	AU	SC	107.3	12.82	11,118.80	13,334.70	☆	2.6	2.57	0.35	17.1	192
OPPENHEIMER GLO BIO-TECH	H	SC	1.8	10.95	#10,408.70	☆	☆	0.0	0.00	0.00	N/A	N/A
OPPENHEIMER GLOBAL FUND	GL	SC	411.4	24.08	11,543.60	8,965.10	17,428.80	0.3	5.62	0.07	32.4	37
OPPENHEIMER HIGH YIELD	FI	SC	857.8	16.00	10,831.60	10,674.40	16,108.30	13.3	0.00	2.12	N/A	46
OPPENHEIMER NINETY-TEN	OG	SC	29.8	14.63	9,601.80	14,154.80	☆	2.7	2.05	0.42	N/A	N/A
OPPENHEIMER OTC	SG	SC	35.7	17.64	11,674.40	10,063.10	☆	0.3	1.97	0.05	24.3	145
OPPENHEIMER PREMIUM INC	OI	SC	323.4	22.07	10,059.80	11,799.50	18,726.20	1.8	2.58	0.42	20.0	379
OPPENHEIMER REGENCY	CA	SC	145.7	12.82	11,325.90	9,462.80	11,822.90	0.9	1.86	0.13	20.6	143
OPPENHEIMER SPECIAL	G	SC	552.9	17.13	11,740.90	9,896.80	13,579.90	7.4	1.75	1.26	14.6	371
OPPENHEIMER TARGET	CA	SC	72.8	15.82	12,851.50	9,149.90	10,663.60	1.1	4.19	0.19	18.0	95

OPPENHEIMER TIME	CA	SC	318.3	15.50	11,413.80	9,721.00	15,875.80	1.6	4.13	0.26	22.3	47
OPPENHEIMER TOTAL RETURN	GI	SC	311.5	6.59	11,301.50	10,407.50	17,434.90	4.1	1.28	0.29	19.6	173
OPPENHEIMER US GOVT TR	FI	SC	203.8	9.59	10,450.50	10,818.00	15,174.80	9.8	0.00	0.94	N/A	263
OTC 100 FUND	G	NO	117.0	13.59	11,870.00	9,313.10	☆	0.7	0.68	0.09	21.2	46
OVERLAND FDS: ASSET ALLOC	B	LO	9.3	10.24	#10,240.00	☆	☆	0.0	0.00	0.00	N/A	N/A
OVERLAND FDS: SPEC INCOME	FI	LO	1.4	10.08	#10,107.30	☆	☆	0.0	0.00	0.02	N/A	N/A
OVER-THE-COUNTER SEC	SG	SC	287.2	16.55	12,547.40	9,365.60	14,728.10	0.6	1.06	0.10	19.3	49
PACIFIC HORIZON AGG GRO	CA	SC	126.8	14.09	10,617.90	8,704.70	☆	0.7	0.86	0.10	30.3	250
PACIFIC HORIZON HI YLD	FI	SC	24.3	14.93	10,749.50	10,501.60	☆	12.1	0.00	1.81	N/A	131
PACIFIC INV INST GROWTH	CA	NO	4.9	9.07	11,368.80	9,340.50	☆	2.0	0.00	0.17	N/A	N/A
PACIFIC INV INST LOW DUR	FI	NO	137.9	9.93	10,462.80	10,825.70	☆	8.6	0.00	0.85	N/A	N/A
PACIFIC INV INST TOT RET	FI	NO	70.0	9.99	10,574.80	10,846.30	☆	7.4	0.00	0.74	N/A	N/A
PAINEWEBBER AMERICA	GI	SC	67.6	13.53	11,347.60	9,524.80	☆	5.4	2.10	0.73	17.7	132
PAINEWEBBER ASSET ALLOC (R)	GI	NO	674.7	9.86	10,851.90	10,740.30	☆	5.4	0.16	0.53	18.1	129
PAINEWEBBER ATLAS	GL	SC	214.1	14.06	10,941.60	9,106.80	☆	3.9	3.35	0.61	28.9	82
PAINEWEBBER GNMA	FI	LO	1,519.7	9.38	10,496.60	10,668.10	☆	9.0	0.00	0.84	N/A	98
PAINEWEBBER HIGH YIELD	FI	LO	621.5	8.99	10,825.60	10,141.90	☆	13.4	0.00	1.20	N/A	145
PAINEWEBBER INV GRADE	FI	LO	403.0	9.60	10,494.00	10,585.20	☆	9.4	0.00	0.90	N/A	88
PAINEWEBBER MSTR ENERGY (R)	S	NO	17.2	10.14	11,148.10	☆	☆	0.0	0.00	0.25	N/A	N/A
PAINEWEBBER MSTR GLOBAL (R)	WI	NO	1,096.7	11.14	10,513.10	11,993.70	☆	7.5	0.18	0.84	N/A	53
PAINEWEBBER MSTR GRO (R)	G	NO	90.6	10.74	11,610.80	9,450.10	☆	0.0	0.00	0.00	23.7	96
PAINEWEBBER MSTR INC (R)	FI	NO	307.0	9.04	10,486.50	10,507.60	☆	7.9	0.00	0.71	N/A	118
PAINEWEBBER OLYMPUS	G	SC	80.1	11.61	11,822.80	9,251.10	☆	0.7	1.40	0.08	26.5	66
PARIBAS QUANTUS EQ (R)	G	NO	11.9	10.17	10,912.00	8,906.70	☆	1.6	0.00	0.15	N/A	128
PARNASSUS FUND	G	LO	8.0	22.47	13,904.70	9,795.10	☆	0.0	0.00	0.00	N/A	32
PARTNERS FUND	G	NO	718.8	16.84	11,181.90	9,726.80	19,641.60	4.1	2.79	0.70	13.7	169
PASADENA INV: GROWTH FD	SG	SC	14.8	15.79	12,764.80	9,675.20	☆	0.0	0.00	0.00	N/A	115
PATRIOT CORP CASH	FI	LO	76.4	48.39	10,169.10	10,292.10	☆	6.3	0.00	3.02	N/A	264
PAX WORLD FUND	B	NO	72.2	12.55	10,837.70	9,688.70	16,908.20	4.2	0.41	0.53	13.5	124
PBHG GROWTH	CA	SC	31.2	11.18	11,338.70	9,499.10	☆	0.0	1.55	0.00	26.7	214
PDC&J PERFORMANCE	CA	NO	7.0	12.64	11,275.60	8,940.50	☆	0.8	0.03	0.09	N/A	51
PDC&J PRESERVATION	FI	NO	12.7	11.07	10,316.90	10,647.50	☆	4.6	0.00	0.50	N/A	4
PENN SQUARE MUTUAL	GI	NO	195.1	9.15	10,960.90	9,197.90	17,306.10	3.6	0.79	0.34	16.9	15
PENNSYLVANIA MUTUAL	SG	NO	358.4	6.67	12,193.80	10,655.90	18,249.60	2.6	1.20	0.19	18.7	23
PERMANENT PORTFOLIO	S	NO	103.2	15.16	10,250.20	10,163.90	12,298.10	0.0	0.12	0.00	22.3	22
PERRITT CAPITAL GROWTH	SG	NO	1.6	10.27	#10,270.00	☆	☆	0.0	0.00	0.00	N/A	N/A
PHILADELPHIA FUND	GI	SC	96.8	5.56	11,089.50	9,631.00	14,326.70	1.8	1.76	0.11	30.8	152
PHOENIX BALANCED	B	SC	421.6	12.11	10,097.30	9,577.30	20,506.50	4.8	0.97	0.60	16.1	171
PHOENIX CONVERTIBLE	CV	SC	165.0	15.81	10,373.40	9,831.50	18,036.60	6.5	2.56	1.10	14.9	299
PHOENIX GROWTH	G	SC	587.4	15.72	10,455.70	9,584.60	20,859.90	4.9	2.43	0.83	20.5	185
PHOENIX HIGH QUAL BOND	FI	SC	19.3	9.01	10,535.20	10,690.50	15,818.50	8.2	0.39	0.75	N/A	325
PHOENIX HIGH YIELD	FI	SC	154.6	8.86	10,793.80	10,579.60	17,228.00	11.6	0.00	1.03	N/A	97
PHOENIX SR: US GOVT BOND	FI	SC	7.7	9.16	10,474.30	10,638.00	☆	8.5	0.00	0.78	N/A	N/A
PHOENIX STOCK	CA	SC	131.0	11.48	10,820.80	9,711.70	19,614.00	4.0	3.00	0.51	24.3	152
PHOENIX TOTAL RETURN	G	SC	35.7	12.77	10,289.00	9,568.10	14,998.00	3.2	0.99	0.41	17.9	323
PIERPONT CAP APPREC	G	NO	0.0	0.00	N/A	N/A	☆	0.0	0.00	0.00	N/A	79
PIERPONT EQUITY	GI	NO	0.0	0.00	N/A	N/A	☆	0.0	0.00	0.00	N/A	32
PILGRIM ADJUSTABLE RATE	FI	LO	320.8	18.65	9,722.70	9,333.90	12,727.60	9.4	0.00	1.74	N/A	71
PILGRIM CORP CASH	FI	NO	31.1	10.00	10,264.80	10,526.60	☆	5.1	0.00	0.51	N/A	232
PILGRIM FORGN GOVT	FI	LO	16.8	9.57	10,546.50	10,765.70	☆	8.8	0.00	0.84	N/A	46
PILGRIM FORGN HI INC	FI	LO	13.4	9.01	10,928.00	10,285.70	☆	10.9	0.00	0.98	N/A	53
PILGRIM FORGN INTL BOND	WI	LO	12.8	10.98	9,797.90	11,356.00	☆	7.4	0.00	0.81	N/A	120
PILGRIM GNMA	FI	SC	184.7	14.22	10,610.50	10,785.10	☆	9.6	0.00	1.36	N/A	433
PILGRIM HIGH YIELD	FI	SC	46.1	7.37	10,857.40	10,466.20	16,010.30	12.3	0.00	0.90	N/A	114
PILGRIM MAGNACAP	G	SC	211.5	9.14	11,076.10	9,356.70	21,241.60	1.3	1.73	0.12	15.0	127
PILGRIM PREFERRED	FI	LO	153.5	21.04	11,159.90	9,805.10	☆	14.0	0.00	2.94	N/A	81
PILGRIM RISING PROFIT	CA	SC	7.9	8.79	10,838.50	8,542.30	☆	0.0	0.00	0.00	N/A	179
PINE STREET FUND	GI	NO	55.4	11.64	11,231.00	8,986.50	16,479.40	3.4	0.93	0.41	17.2	48
PINNACLE FUND	CA	NO	4.2	30.13	10,741.50	10,021.30	☆	1.2	1.10	0.35	N/A	86
PIONEER BOND FUND	FI	SC	53.3	9.04	10,442.50	10,712.60	16,338.90	8.9	0.00	0.80	N/A	19

PERFORMANCE OF MUTUAL FUNDS (continued)

FUND NAME	OBJ.	LOAD	TOTAL NET ASTS (MIL) 6/30/88	NAV 6/30/88	PERFORMANCE (RETURN ON INITIAL $10,000 INVESTMENT) 12/31/87-6/30/88	6/30/87-6/30/88	6/30/83-6/30/88	YIELD % 6/30/88	PER SHARE LATEST 12 MONTHS CAP GAINS	INC DIVS	LATEST AVAILABLE PRICE/EARNINGS	ANNUAL % TURNOVER
PIONEER FUND	GI	SC	1,438.6	21.31	11,688.70	9,927.00	17,392.70	2.9	1.53	0.63	16.7	14
PIONEER II	GI	SC	3,807.0	18.32	11,867.60	9,577.70	17,237.80	2.5	2.00	0.48	15.4	26
PIONEER THREE	GI	SC	631.4	15.09	12,588.00	9,794.30	16,996.80	2.6	1.41	0.41	15.7	23
PIPER JAFFRAY BALANCED	B	LO	13.3	9.09	10,578.80	9,818.50	☆	5.7	0.00	0.51	N/A	N/A
PIPER JAFFRAY GOVT INC	FI	LO	66.9	9.48	10,483.80	10,707.90	☆	8.6	0.00	0.81	N/A	N/A
PIPER JAFFRAY SECTOR	S	LO	25.5	8.97	11,290.10	9,085.00	☆	1.5	0.00	0.13	N/A	N/A
PIPER JAFFRAY VALUE	G	LO	19.1	9.65	11,382.60	9,527.00	☆	1.8	0.00	0.17	N/A	N/A
PLYMOUTH AGGRESSIVE INC	FI	LO	11.3	9.93	11,217.40	11,064.10	☆	11.5	0.00	1.14	N/A	166
PLYMOUTH FD: GROWTH OPP	G	LO	4.6	14.13	13,132.00	☆	☆	0.0	0.00	0.00	N/A	N/A
PLYMOUTH GOVERNMENT	FI	LO	6.2	9.25	10,443.60	10,698.50	☆	8.4	0.00	0.77	N/A	N/A
PLYMOUTH INC & GROWTH	GI	SC	37.7	10.93	11,760.70	10,445.40	☆	4.5	0.00	0.49	N/A	206
PLYMOUTH SHORT-TERM BOND	FI	LO	12.1	9.99	10,372.80	☆	☆	0.0	0.00	0.64	N/A	119
PLYMOUTH SR: GLOB NAT RES	NR	LO	0.8	11.64	11,640.00	☆	☆	0.0	0.00	0.00	N/A	N/A
PORT WASHINGTON FUND	CA	NO	0.2	9.59	11,059.80	10,806.10	☆	8.9	0.00	0.85	N/A	N/A
PPT: AGGRESSIVE GROWTH FD	CA	NO	0.3	10.34	#10,340.00	☆	☆	0.0	0.00	0.00	N/A	N/A
PPT: GOVT SEC FD	FI	NO	0.2	10.02	#10,020.00	☆	☆	0.0	0.00	0.00	N/A	N/A
PPT: HIGH YIELD FUND	FI	NO	0.5	10.11	#10,110.00	☆	☆	0.0	0.00	0.00	N/A	N/A
PPT: INTERNATIONAL FD	IF	NO	0.2	9.76	#9,760.00	☆	☆	0.0	0.00	0.00	N/A	N/A
PPT: TIMED EQUITY FD	CA	NO	0.2	10.57	#10,570.00	☆	☆	0.0	0.00	0.00	N/A	N/A
PPT: TOTAL RETURN FD	GI	NO	0.2	10.26	#10,260.00	☆	☆	0.0	0.00	0.00	N/A	N/A
PREMIER GNMA	FI	LO	10.0	14.44	10,915.00	11,234.40	☆	9.7	0.00	1.39	N/A	64
PREMIER INCOME	FI	LO	3.1	11.21	10,480.80	10,850.60	☆	10.0	0.00	1.12	N/A	74
T ROWE PRICE CAP APPREC	CA	NO	87.8	10.62	11,694.80	11,006.20	☆	3.1	1.55	0.35	N/A	291
T ROWE PRICE EQUITY INC	EI	NO	331.1	13.40	11,969.70	10,720.60	☆	4.4	1.11	0.61	N/A	80
T ROWE PRICE GNMA	FI	NO	377.3	9.35	10,466.50	10,635.50	☆	10.1	0.00	0.94	N/A	226
T ROWE PRICE GROWTH & INC	GI	NO	425.8	12.55	11,903.20	9,694.10	15,459.00	4.5	0.79	0.58	15.5	114
T ROWE PRICE GROWTH STK	G	NO	1,424.4	15.33	10,742.80	9,163.60	17,253.00	2.1	2.20	0.34	16.5	51
T ROWE PRICE HIGH YIELD	FI	NO	963.4	10.33	11,173.30	10,884.70	☆	12.1	0.00	1.25	N/A	166
T ROWE PRICE INTL BOND	WI	NO	420.4	10.07	9,301.00	10,956.50	☆	9.7	0.26	0.98	N/A	284
T ROWE PRICE INTL FUND	IF	NO	654.3	9.24	10,819.70	9,577.50	29,245.50	1.2	4.66	0.14	N/A	77
T ROWE PRICE NEW AMER GR	G	NO	71.3	12.56	12,019.10	9,603.90	☆	0.0	1.10	0.00	24.4	72
T ROWE PRICE NEW ERA	NR	NO	857.2	20.34	11,250.00	10,232.80	19,881.20	2.9	1.22	0.61	20.7	30
T ROWE PRICE NEW HORIZON	SG	NO	1,004.9	11.50	12,092.50	9,355.40	10,862.20	0.3	1.63	0.04	21.0	50
T ROWE PRICE NEW INCOME	FI	NO	823.9	8.54	10,452.70	10,828.00	16,499.80	9.3	0.00	0.79	N/A	126
T ROWE PRICE SCI & TECH	TK	NO	13.6	9.40	11,720.70	☆	☆	0.0	0.00	0.04	N/A	22
T ROWE PRICE SH-TERM BD	FI	NO	289.3	5.01	10,298.60	10,708.10	☆	8.1	0.00	0.40	N/A	7
PRIMARY TREND	GI	NO	45.9	11.82	11,796.40	10,564.10	☆	3.2	0.04	0.37	N/A	20
PRIMECAP	G	NO	197.8	47.79	11,923.70	9,405.60	☆	0.8	1.11	0.40	19.5	19
PRINCIPAL EQUITY	G	SC	0.4	0.00	N/A	N/A	N/A	0.0	0.85	0.00	N/A	119
PRINCIPAL PRES DV ACHEVR	G	SC	7.2	9.85	11,104.60	9,671.10	☆	2.8	0.00	0.28	N/A	11
PRINCIPAL PRES GOVT	FI	SC	31.8	8.98	10,264.50	10,588.90	☆	8.2	0.18	0.74	N/A	80
PRINCIPAL PRES RETIREMT	GI	SC	5.0	9.54	10,885.30	10,223.10	☆	4.9	0.00	0.47	N/A	3
PRINCIPAL PRES S&P 100	GI	SC	17.1	10.71	11,284.50	9,260.20	☆	2.7	0.94	0.30	N/A	54
PRINCIPAL WORLD	GL	SC	3.1	0.00	N/A	N/A	N/A	0.0	3.73	0.00	N/A	166
PRINCOR AGGR GROWTH FD	CA	SC	5.7	13.18	#11,895.30	☆	☆	0.0	0.00	0.00	N/A	N/A
PRINCOR BOND FUND	FI	SC	9.6	10.26	#10,536.70	☆	☆	0.0	0.00	0.37	N/A	N/A
PRINCOR CAPITAL ACCUM	CA	SC	97.1	18.82	11,675.90	9,767.90	21,954.30	2.2	1.81	0.41	23.0	28
PRINCOR GOVT SEC INCOME	FI	SC	59.9	10.33	10,606.50	10,859.00	☆	8.5	0.02	0.88	N/A	18
PRINCOR GROWTH FUND	G	SC	34.3	19.84	11,395.70	9,280.20	16,444.30	1.1	1.38	0.22	20.7	7
PRINCOR HIGH YIELD FUND	FI	SC	8.3	10.55	#10,945.40	☆	☆	0.0	0.00	0.45	N/A	N/A
PRINCOR MANAGED FUND	GI	SC	15.6	11.46	#11,208.00	☆	☆	0.0	0.00	0.07	N/A	N/A
PROGRESSIVE INCOME EQ	GI	NO	50.8	8.95	10,918.70	10,244.60	☆	8.3	0.00	0.74	10.5	N/A
PROVIDENT FD FOR INCOME	EI	SC	99.8	4.20	11,103.10	9,403.10	16,384.20	6.8	0.36	0.30	18.5	90
PRU-BACHE CORPORATE DVD	FI	NO	99.8	18.79	9,144.50	9,038.50	☆	12.3	0.00	2.30	N/A	252

PRU-BACHE EQUITY (R)	G	NO	556.6	9.51	11,611.70	9,332.20	19,149.4■	1.0	0.56	0.10	N/A	90
PRU-BACHE EQUITY INC (R)	EI	NO	63.8	9.38	11,686.70	9,648.70	☆	2.6	0.33	0.25	N/A	71
PRU-BACHE FLEX/AGGRES (R)	GI	NO	55.3	9.64	11,027.50	☆	☆	0.0	0.00	0.18	N/A	N/A
PRU-BACHE FLEX/CONSER (R)	GI	NO	149.2	9.49	10,589.40	☆	☆	0.0	0.01	0.25	N/A	N/A
PRU-BACHE GLOBAL (R)	GL	NO	560.4	9.83	10,347.40	8,892.20	☆	0.7	0.98	0.07	N/A	135
PRU-BACHE GLBL GENESIS (R)	SG	NO	11.1	10.98	#10,980.00	☆	☆	0.0	0.00	0.00	N/A	N/A
PRU-BACHE GLB NAT RES (R)	GL	NO	52.0	9.55	11,261.80	☆	☆	0.0	0.00	0.01	N/A	N/A
PRU-BACHE GNMA (R)	FI	NO	253.4	14.85	10,450.60	10,614.70	16,082.8■	7.7	0.02	1.14	N/A	331
PRU-BACHE GOVT INTMDT	FI	NO	529.0	10.13	10,392.70	10,712.70	16,662.9■	9.1	0.00	0.92	N/A	59
PRU-BACHE GOVT PLUS (R)	FI	NO	4,072.3	9.44	10,350.20	10,588.50	☆	7.1	0.37	0.67	N/A	266
PRU-BACHE GOVT PLUS II (R)	FI	LO	182.3	8.94	10,264.10	10,447.90	☆	7.5	0.11	0.67	N/A	N/A
PRU-BACHE GROWTH OPP (R)	G	NO	148.5	11.44	12,657.50	9,436.20	12,505.4■	0.4	1.23	0.05	18.9	113
PRU-BACHE HIGH YIELD (R)	FI	NO	2,419.2	10.01	10,900.40	10,567.20	17,754.6■	10.8	0.00	1.08	N/A	49
PRU-BACHE INCOMVRTIBLE (R)	S	NO	503.3	10.43	11,148.60	10,184.60	☆	5.9	0.93	0.64	N/A	138
PRU-BACHE OPTION GRO (R)	OG	NO	73.6	8.04	10,979.30	9,555.00	16,398.6■	1.8	0.65	0.15	16.9	117
PRU-BACHE RESEARCH (R)	G	NO	417.8	12.98	10,940.10	9,156.60	16,282.1■	1.7	0.52	0.22	N/A	109
PRU-BACHE UTILITY (R)	UT	NO	1,464.7	13.90	11,422.10	10,433.10	27,058.3■	4.7	0.33	0.66	14.7	65
PUTNAM CAPITAL (X)	SG	NO	10.4	5.82	12,462.50	10,039.10	17,097.1■	0.0	2.16	0.00	N/A	126
PUTNAM CONV INC-GRO TR	CV	SC	1,036.4	14.58	11,070.10	9,200.20	15,786.8■	6.4	0.61	0.96	20.0	87
PUTNAM CORP CASH ARP	FI	LO	290.5	40.83	9,798.10	9,691.30	☆	9.8	0.00	3.99	N/A	83
PUTNAM CORP CASH DSP	EI	LO	236.1	41.61	10,412.40	9,826.00	☆	10.4	0.00	4.34	N/A	175
PUTNAM ENERGY RESOURCES	NR	SC	108.3	13.69	11,759.10	9,691.50	13,359.5■	3.0	0.04	0.41	23.2	180
GEORGE PUTNAM FD BOSTON	B	SC	402.6	12.73	10,964.90	9,789.80	17,183.5■	5.5	0.85	0.72	14.9	143
PUTNAM GLOBAL GOVT INC	WI	SC	129.4	16.01	10,814.30	12,519.60	☆	9.7	0.00	1.56	N/A	35
PUTNAM GNMA PLUS	FI	SC	1,517.2	9.99	10,419.60	10,576.30	☆	10.3	0.00	1.03	N/A	130
PUTNAM GROWTH & INCOME	GI	SC	1,646.9	11.11	11,429.70	9,784.80	19,756.8■	6.1	1.47	0.72	17.4	143
PUTNAM HEALTH SCIENCE	H	SC	255.4	18.87	10,996.50	8,927.60	14,640.9■	0.6	1.30	0.12	22.0	33
PUTNAM HIGH INCOME GOVT	FI	SC	10,200.4	10.49	10,319.70	10,485.60	☆	8.7	0.42	0.93	N/A	99
PUTNAM HIGH YIELD	FI	SC	2,356.2	14.71	10,845.30	10,798.10	16,860.1■	12.6	0.00	1.86	N/A	93
PUTNAM HIGH YIELD II	FI	SC	379.6	11.36	10,961.50	11,063.90	☆	11.6	0.00	1.32	N/A	121
PUTNAM INCOME	FI	SC	346.0	6.83	10,642.50	10,915.60	17,401.0■	10.9	0.00	0.74	N/A	203
PUTNAM INFO SCIENCE	TK	SC	108.0	16.40	10,962.60	8,989.80	☆	0.0	0.78	0.00	23.4	115
PUTNAM INTL EQUITIES	GL	SC	506.4	25.18	10,379.20	9,114.70	27,669.6■	1.3	3.75	0.35	18.1	113
PUTNAM INVESTORS	G	SC	723.4	7.04	10,820.20	9,000.20	15,471.1■	3.3	1.70	0.26	19.6	84
PUTNAM OPTION INCOME	OI	SC	1,063.4	8.73	11,884.10	9,248.00	15,572.8■	4.3	1.61	0.41	18.2	225
PUTNAM OPTION INCOME II	OI	SC	1,487.3	9.33	11,581.60	9,643.30	☆	1.8	1.38	0.18	16.1	215
PUTNAM OTC EMERGING GRO	SG	SC	153.6	27.12	12,064.10	9,846.60	20,037.1■	0.0	2.53	0.00	25.3	93
PUTNAM US GOVERNMENT	FI	SC	1,360.1	13.98	10,544.40	10,840.70	☆	9.9	0.00	1.38	N/A	43
PUTNAM VISTA BASIC VALUE	CA	SC	253.6	17.74	11,315.30	8,395.20	15,897.4■	3.2	2.29	0.57	17.4	117
PUTNAM VOYAGER	CA	SC	589.9	20.37	11,180.00	9,687.30	16,905.4■	0.5	3.94	0.10	21.9	79
QUANTUM FUND	CA	SC	0.3	9.02	11,744.80	8,582.30	☆	0.0	0.00	0.00	N/A	115
QUASAR ASSOCIATES	SG	SC	100.1	18.10	12,818.70	10,069.60	15,997.8■	0.0	4.70	0.00	24.5	76
QUEST FOR VALUE FUND	CA	NO	87.4	26.54	11,717.40	9,928.80	17,843.5■	0.6	1.12	0.15	18.1	34
RAINBOW FUND	CA	NO	2.0	5.12	11,277.50	9,025.80	14,112.2■	4.1	0.61	0.20	N/A	113
RCS EMERGING GROWTH (R)	SG	NO	9.0	9.61	12,057.70	☆	☆	0.0	0.00	0.00	N/A	N/A
REA-GRAHAM FUND	B	SC	50.0	14.33	10,872.50	10,541.50	16,871.6■	3.8	0.16	0.55	N/A	111
REICH & TANG EQUITY	G	NO	110.5	15.16	11,721.40	10,303.70	☆	2.3	1.68	0.36	15.2	43
REICH & TANG GNMA INC	FI	NO	6.5	0.00	N/A	N/A	☆	0.0	0.00	0.06	N/A	604
RESERVE EQUITY CONTRARIAN	GI	NO	8.0	13.74	10,494.60	7,858.10	☆	2.2	1.33	0.30	N/A	25
RESERVE EQUITY GROWTH	G	NO	1.3	11.45	10,387.00	7,775.70	☆	2.2	2.47	0.24	N/A	12
RETIREMENT PLAN AM: BOND	FI	NO	71.8	7.13	10,395.60	10,641.80	15,437.2■	11.2	0.00	0.79	N/A	20
RETIREMENT PLAN AM: EQU	G	NO	16.7	19.49	11,431.10	9,466.60	19,072.7■	0.5	2.83	0.10	N/A	57
RIGHTIME BLUE CHIP	GI	SC	59.0	26.94	10,793.30	☆	☆	0.0	0.00	0.13	16.8	N/A
RIGHTIME FUND	GI	NO	250.4	32.63	10,536.00	10,872.40	☆	1.9	3.97	0.67	N/A	166
RIGHTIME GOVT	FI	SC	12.0	13.87	10,684.00	10,658.80	☆	8.1	0.00	1.12	N/A	111
RNC CONVERTIBLE	CV	SC	35.9	9.51	11,227.60	9,653.50	☆	4.5	0.36	0.43	N/A	91
RNC CORP CASH	FI	SC	3.5	8.27	10,679.70	9,767.40	☆	6.8	0.00	0.56	N/A	50

PERFORMANCE OF MUTUAL FUNCS *(continued)*

FUND NAME	OBJ.	LOAD	TOTAL NET ASTS (MIL) 6/30/88	NAV 6/30/88	PERFORMANCE (RETURN ON INITIAL $10,000 INVESTMENT) 12/31/87-6/30/88	6/30/87-6/30/88	6/30/83-6/30/88	YIELD % 6/30/88	PER SHARE LATEST 12 MONTHS CAP GAINS	INC DIVS	LATEST AVAILABLE PRICE/EARNINGS	ANNUAL % TURNOVER
RNC INCOME	I	SC	13.5	9.54	10,839.60	10,384.00	☆	8.0	0.00	0.75	N/A	31
RNC REGENCY FUND	G	SC	17.7	12.24	10,940.10	8,760.90	☆	3.0	0.11	0.36	N/A	38
RNC WESTWIND	B	SC	11.2	9.58	10,848.40	9,268.80	☆	3.3	0.00	0.31	N/A	7
ROCHESTER CONVERT GRO	CV	LO	6.3	9.71	11,736.40	9,349.00	☆	5.7	0.08	0.55	N/A	108
ROCHESTER CONVERT INC	CV	LO	6.4	7.20	11,397.00	9,487.20	☆	11.9	0.00	0.85	N/A	85
ROCHESTER GROWTH FUND	G	SC	2.3	7.64	12,050.50	8,872.10	9,603.50	0.0	1.61	0.00	N/A	127
ROCHESTER TAX-MGD	G	SC	16.3	11.60	12,133.90	10,078.20	12,125.00	0.0	0.00	0.00	N/A	43
ROCKWOOD GROWTH	CA	NO	0.6	12.85	12,610.40	10,271.30	☆	1.5	0.00	0.19	N/A	31
RODNEY SQUARE: GROWTH	GI	NO	28.0	9.89	11,853.30	9,598.90	☆	0.7	0.00	0.06	N/A	62
RODNEY SQUARE: INTL EQU	IF	NO	45.5	10.92	10,716.40	☆	☆	0.0	0.00	0.03	N/A	N/A
RODNEY SQUARE: TOTL RETN	CA	NO	19.0	9.09	10,826.10	9,278.70	☆	2.4	0.00	0.22	N/A	121
RODNEY SQUARE: VALUE	CA	NO	3.4	11.24	11,123.40	☆	☆	0.0	0.00	0.30	N/A	N/A
ROYCE INCOME (R)	FI	NO	15.6	8.82	10,975.10	10,589.80	☆	12.5	0.00	1.09	N/A	40
ROYCE TOTAL RETURN (R)	EI	NO	6.8	5.23	12,394.20	10,449.80	☆	5.7	0.08	0.30	0.00	87
ROYCE VALUE (R)	SG	NO	165.5	8.30	12,188.00	10,347.80	17,555.20	1.3	1.28	0.12	17.6	41
RUSHMORE OTC	G	NO	12.7	13.06	11,700.10	9,367.30	☆	0.9	0.00	0.11	N/A	42
RUSHMORE STK MKT	GI	NO	12.7	12.31	10,799.50	9,186.80	☆	4.3	0.48	0.53	N/A	188
RUSHMORE USG INT TERM	FI	NO	12.5	9.75	10,411.00	10,650.80	☆	8.0	0.00	0.77	N/A	87
RUSHMORE USG LONG TERM	FI	NO	7.6	9.31	10,442.10	10,687.20	☆	8.1	0.09	0.75	N/A	226
RXR DYNAMIC GOVT	FI	LO	16.1	11.45	10,200.60	10,590.20	☆	11.4	0.00	1.30	N/A	120
SAFECO EQUITY FUND	GI	NO	46.6	8.42	12,010.20	9,125.10	17,636.50	2.6	1.78	0.23	21.2	85
SAFECO GROWTH FUND	G	NO	75.8	15.42	11,662.70	10,141.80	14,610.20	2.3	1.25	0.37	16.1	24
SAFECO INCOME FUND	EI	NO	240.1	14.33	11,651.40	9,667.30	20,341.30	6.7	0.83	0.99	18.6	33
SAFECO US GOVT	FI	NO	27.7	9.13	10,393.80	10,571.80	☆	9.3	0.00	0.85	N/A	101
SALEM FUNDS	G	NO	21.4	13.25	11,188.80	9,399.00	☆	2.0	0.27	0.27	N/A	20
SBSF GROWTH FUND	G	NO	81.7	12.69	11,222.40	9,577.60	☆	3.5	0.40	0.45	N/A	66
SCHIELD PORT SR: AGG GRO	CA	LO	4.1	11.52	10,686.50	9,465.90	☆	0.0	0.00	0.00	N/A	57
SCHIELD PORT SR: HI YLD	FI	LO	1.9	10.11	11,185.80	11,048.50	☆	11.1	0.02	1.20	N/A	N/A
SCHIELD PORT SR: VALUE	G	LO	5.8	12.13	10,412.00	9,939.00	☆	0.3	0.29	0.04	N/A	90
SCHRODER CAPITAL-US EQU	G	NO	27.1	7.58	11,148.40	8,836.00	13,616.20	1.9	2.92	0.17	N/A	43
SCI/TECH HOLDINGS	TK	SC	71.8	10.49	10,596.00	9,713.20	15,301.50	0.0	1.30	0.00	26.0	92
SCUDDER CAPITAL GROWTH	G	NO	499.8	15.88	12,279.70	9,960.10	18,975.10	2.6	2.13	0.43	23.9	58
SCUDDER DEVELOPMENT	SG	NO	356.9	22.00	11,771.00	9,471.90	12,286.50	0.0	1.89	0.00	21.9	24
SCUDDER EQUITY INCOME	EI	NO	14.0	11.04	10,868.10	9,315.50	☆	3.8	0.00	0.41	N/A	N/A
SCUDDER GLOBAL	GL	NO	80.7	14.46	11,531.10	9,561.50	☆	0.4	0.24	0.06	16.0	32
SCUDDER GNMA	FI	NO	252.7	14.48	10,503.10	10,719.70	☆	9.1	0.00	1.31	N/A	59
SCUDDER GROWTH & INCOME	GI	NO	408.5	13.13	10,790.30	9,508.40	16,240.10	3.5	2.36	0.49	18.3	60
SCUDDER INCOME	FI	NO	241.2	12.71	10,468.10	10,618.10	16,988.90	6.4	0.00	0.81	8.7	34
SCUDDER INTERNATIONAL	IF	NO	551.1	33.10	11,038.50	9,412.60	26,793.90	2.0	5.13	0.72	N/A	67
SCUDDER TARGET GENL 1990	FI	NO	15.4	10.30	10,409.60	10,648.80	16,121.40	5.6	0.11	0.57	N/A	41
SCUDDER TARGET GENL 1994	FI	NO	10.2	11.33	10,402.70	10,478.80	☆	6.5	0.07	0.73	N/A	29
SCUDDER TARGET USGT 1990	FI	NO	6.8	9.87	10,318.70	10,667.60	15,865.50	4.9	0.00	0.48	N/A	75
SCUDDER TREAS AUCTN RATE	FI	NO	2.2	10.00	10,284.70	10,549.50	☆	5.4	0.0	0.53	N/A	N/A
SCUDDER TREAS LIQ PLUS	FI	NO	1.9	10.01	10,366.10	10,754.90	☆	6.8	0.03	0.68	N/A	N/A
SCUDDER TREAS DIV INC	EI	NO	1.2	8.54	9,868.80	9,783.30	☆	15.0	0.00	1.28	N/A	N/A
SCUDDER ZERO TARGT 1990	FI	NO	1.9	11.01	10,416.30	10,633.50	☆	6.3	0.00	0.69	N/A	19
SCUDDER ZERO TARGT 1995	FI	NO	3.2	11.14	10,569.30	10,570.80	☆	5.2	0.00	0.58	N/A	55
SCUDDER ZERO TARGT 2000	FI	NO	2.9	11.03	10,667.30	10,484.40	☆	6.1	0.00	0.66	N/A	37
SECURAL: GOVERNMENT BOND	FI	LO	0.3	10.00	10,032.60	☆	☆	0.0	0.00	0.03	N/A	N/A
SECURAL: SPECIAL EQUITY	CA	LO	0.5	11.56	11,693.70	☆	☆	0.0	0.00	0.13	N/A	N/A
SECURAL: STOCK FUND	GI	LO	0.2	10.43	10,536.10	☆	☆	0.0	0.00	0.10	N/A	N/A
SECURITY ACTION FUND	G	SC	145.8	8.90	11,528.50	9,238.40	13,447.60	1.7	0.59	0.16	16.7	159
SECURITY EQUITY FUND	G	SC	229.8	4.56	11,068.00	9,263.10	14,228.90	4.5	1.07	0.23	20.5	151
SECURITY INC-CORP BOND	FI	SC	51.4	7.61	10,297.60	10,497.90	16,617.50	10.8	0.00	0.82	N/A	127

SECURITY INC-HIGH YIELD	FI	SC	10.9	7.60	10,640.90	10,191.70	☆	13.1	0.00	0.99	N/A	138
SECURITY INC-US GOVT	FI	SC	4.6	4.96	10,406.80	10,657.50	☆	9.3	0.00	0.46	N/A	166
SECURITY INVESTMENT FUND	GI	SC	87.4	8.57	10,921.60	9,265.10	12,541.40	6.1	0.45	0.54	20.7	32
SECURITY OMNI	CA	SC	19.3	2.62	12,780.50	8,361.70	☆	1.9	0.05	0.05	N/A	175
SECURITY ULTRA FUND	CA	SC	77.0	6.61	12,401.50	8,564.90	11,917.00	2.4	0.00	0.16	18.2	301
SELECTED AMERICAN SHARES	GI	NO	280.1	13.05	11,553.70	9,659.50	22,559.60	3.2	0.45	0.43	19.0	45
SELECTED CAP PRES: GOVT	FI	NO	13.4	9.76	10,221.30	☆	☆	0.0	0.12	0.40	N/A	N/A
SELECTED SPECIAL SHARES	G	NO	37.2	19.13	12,023.90	9,512.40	15,117.10	4.7	0.65	0.91	15.1	89
SELIGMAN CAPITAL	CA	SC	140.5	11.82	10,726.00	8,379.60	11,895.30	0.0	1.25	0.00	19.3	73
SELIGMAN COMM & INFORMTN	TK	SC	43.7	11.22	11,000.00	9,698.80	☆	0.0	2.83	0.00	20.7	87
SELIGMAN COMMON STOCK	GI	SC	549.9	12.02	11,049.70	9,275.90	18,591.40	3.4	1.60	0.43	19.3	61
SELIGMAN GROWTH	G	SC	550.6	4.57	10,874.90	9,030.50	14,444.10	1.6	1.10	0.08	20.8	90
SELIGMAN HIGH YIELD	FI	SC	63.5	7.20	10,708.90	10,848.00	☆	11.2	0.00	0.80	N/A	103
SELIGMAN INCOME FUND	I	SC	173.0	12.39	10,904.10	10,409.40	18,019.00	7.9	0.10	0.98	11.7	80
SELIGMAN SECURED MORT	FI	SC	54.8	6.81	10,556.10	10,905.20	☆	10.1	0.00	0.68	N/A	399
SELIGMAN US GOVT	FI	SC	117.1	7.20	10,531.00	10,827.80	☆	8.9	0.00	0.63	N/A	283
SENTINEL BALANCED FUND	B	SC	67.1	12.17	10,693.50	9,624.40	19,654.80	5.9	0.00	0.72	16.8	32
SENTINEL BOND FUND	FI	SC	26.5	6.07	10,500.00	10,614.50	16,775.80	9.2	0.00	0.56	N/A	139
SENTINEL COMMON STOCK	GI	SC	500.4	22.70	10,870.90	8,990.40	20,610.10	3.6	1.54	0.83	18.7	9
SENTINEL GOVT	FI	SC	28.4	9.40	10,454.70	10,718.00	☆	8.5	0.00	0.80	N/A	57
SENTINEL GROWTH FUND	G	SC	53.0	11.84	10,487.20	8,702.40	14,680.80	1.8	3.18	0.24	17.1	98
SENTRY FUND	G	SC	43.1	11.83	11,718.50	9,043.50	14,888.90	1.8	1.47	0.23	16.7	35
SEQUOIA FUND (X)	G	NO	726.7	38.80	10,709.90	9,816.90	21,942.20	3.5	3.58	1.43	16.4	43
SFT: DIRECTIONS SERIES	CA	SC	0.1	11.06	10,543.40	8,246.90	☆	1.9	0.00	0.21	N/A	N/A
SFT: EQUITY SERIES	CA	SC	0.3	12.33	10,081.80	9,318.40	8,810.50	1.9	0.00	0.24	N/A	N/A
SFT: ODD LOT FUND	S	NO	0.1	30.33	#15,165.00	☆	☆	0.0	0.00	0.00	N/A	N/A
SFT: GOVERNMENT SERIES	FI	SC	9.4	6.65	10,553.80	11,071.90	☆	10.8	0.00	0.72	N/A	N/A
SHADOW STOCK	SG	NO	16.1	8.67	12,124.90	☆	☆	0.0	0.00	0.08	N/A	N/A
SHEARSON AGGRESSIVE GRO	CA	SC	95.3	15.38	11,625.10	9,536.90	☆	0.0	2.47	0.00	39.4	25
SHEARSON APPRECIATION	G	SC	453.2	28.53	10,998.50	9,480.10	19,391.60	2.1	1.01	0.62	18.2	26
SHEARSON FUNDAMENTAL VAL	G	SC	84.4	6.12	11,814.70	9,566.80	17,318.90	3.9	1.03	0.25	18.8	66
SHEARSON HIGH YIELD	FI	SC	520.7	17.95	10,760.50	10,670.60	17,071.40	12.5	0.03	2.23	N/A	32
SHEARSON LEHMAN CONV (R)	CV	NO	176.9	13.14	11,414.10	10,364.20	☆	6.4	0.27	0.84	N/A	21
SHEARSON LEHMAN GLB BD (R)	WI	NO	164.6	16.70	9,824.90	10,996.10	☆	3.6	0.70	0.62	N/A	112
SHEARSON LEHMAN GLBL OPP	GL	SC	139.5	23.67	10,548.10	8,553.60	☆	0.7	5.99	0.17	15.2	127
SHEARSON LEHMAN HI INC (R)	FI	NO	408.7	14.03	10,895.30	10,842.60	☆	10.9	0.04	1.53	N/A	19
SHEARSON LEHMAN INTL (R)	IF	NO	97.2	15.62	10,378.70	8,515.50	☆	0.0	3.06	0.00	N/A	111
SHEARSON LEHMAN INTMDT (R)	FI	NO	46.5	11.25	10,273.10	10,543.70	☆	6.0	0.00	0.66	N/A	254
SHEARSON LEHMAN LG GVT (R)	FI	NO	1,119.1	8.33	10,335.20	10,408.10	☆	7.4	0.02	0.61	N/A	170
SHEARSON LEHMAN MORT (R)	FI	NO	78.0	10.90	10,319.80	10,451.70	☆	8.5	0.00	0.92	N/A	445
SHEARSON LEHMAN MLT OP (R)	CA	NO	440.2	54.12	10,618.00	10,924.50	☆	0.0	0.00	0.00	N/A	110
SHEARSON LEHMAN OPT INC (R)	OI	NO	596.5	12.85	11,979.50	10,183.70	☆	1.5	1.28	0.20	12.5	297
SHEARSON LEHMAN PR MET (R)	AU	SC	60.1	18.78	9,465.70	8,835.80	☆	0.0	0.90	0.00	28.1	22
SHEARSON LEHMAN SM CAP	SG	SC	13.9	15.74	13,941.50	☆	☆	0.0	0.00	0.00	N/A	N/A
SHEARSON LEHMAN SP EQ (R)	CA	NO	23.9	14.38	11,401.30	8,989.30	☆	3.5	0.22	0.50	N/A	280
SHEARSON LEHMAN SP GRO (R)	G	NO	142.8	14.42	11,607.10	10,235.40	☆	2.1	1.00	0.32	18.2	38
SHEARSON LEHMAN SP SEC (R)	CA	NO	645.5	11.08	9,287.50	☆	☆	0.0	0.22	0.14	N/A	N/A
SHEARSON LEHMAN STRGIC (R)	GI	NO	146.2	14.17	11,276.00	10,149.70	☆	3.1	0.06	0.44	19.4	56
SHEARSON MANAGED GOVT	FI	SC	918.0	12.21	10,350.00	10,538.80	☆	9.1	0.01	1.10	N/A	241
SHERMAN, DEAN FUND	CA	NO	2.7	6.93	13,200.00	7,839.40	7,582.30	0.0	0.00	0.00	N/A	N/A
SIEBEL CAPITAL PARTNERS	CA	NO	22.8	8.14	10,753.00	9,902.70	☆	16.4	3.07	1.59	N/A	95
SIGMA CAPITAL SHARES	CA	SC	92.3	9.12	11,428.60	9,518.20	17,705.10	2.2	0.37	0.20	16.7	11
SIGMA INCOME SHARES	FI	SC	35.1	8.55	10,742.60	10,493.40	17,712.60	7.3	0.00	0.62	N/A	60
SIGMA INVESTMENT SHARES	GI	SC	91.9	10.28	10,883.60	9,483.90	20,053.00	2.8	0.34	0.29	15.6	19
SIGMA SPECIAL FUND	G	SC	18.9	9.30	11,383.10	9,153.90	17,314.20	1.3	1.33	0.12	N/A	16
SIGMA TRUST SHARES	B	SC	46.4	13.70	11,125.60	10,063.60	18,778.30	5.1	0.06	0.69	13.7	7
SIGMA US GOVT FUND	I	SC	5.1	3.17	10,653.60	10,726.60	12,787.50	7.8	0.00	0.24	N/A	45

PERFORMANCE OF MUTUAL FUNDS *(continued)*

FUND NAME	OBJ.	LOAD	TOTAL NET ASTS (MIL) 6/30/88	NAV 6/30/88	PERFORMANCE (RETURN ON INITIAL $10,000 INVESTMENT) 12/31/87-6/30/88	6/30/87-6/30/88	6/30/83-6/30/88	YIELD % 6/30/88	PER SHARE LATEST 12 MONTHS CAP GAINS	INC DIVS	LATEST AVAILABLE PRICE/EARNINGS	ANNUAL % TURNOVER
SIGMA VALUE SHARES	CA	SC	12.6	8.89	11,168.30	8,735.90	12,109.10	1.6	1.41	0.15	N/A	58
SIGMA VENTURE SHARES	SG	SC	59.6	8.99	10,976.80	7,998.60	10,633.70	0.0	1.53	0.00	17.7	10
SIGMA WORLD	IF	SC	7.8	14.33	11,256.90	9,494.60	☆	0.2	3.17	0.03	N/A	39
SIMMS GLOBAL	GL	SC	8.8	9.78	10,723.70	9,080.70	☆	0.5	0.00	0.05	N/A	220
SKYLINE BALANCED	B	LO	11.1	9.60	10,816.30	10,037.60	☆	2.8	0.02	0.26	N/A	38
SKYLINE SPECIAL EQUITIES	SG	LO	8.9	10.34	12,941.20	10,360.70	☆	0.0	0.00	0.00	N/A	173
SMITH BARNEY EQUITY	G	LO	82.9	13.09	10,241.10	9,264.50	16,353.30	3.4	2.17	0.48	20.0	38
SMITH BARNEY INC & GR	GI	SC	565.3	11.21	11,463.90	9,754.20	19,114.40	5.8	0.16	0.65	22.4	51
SMITH BARNEY US GOVT	FI	LO	348.6	12.84	10,605.10	10,946.90	☆	9.3	0.00	1.20	N/A	108
SOGEN INTERNATIONAL	G	LO	105.9	17.59	11,007.50	10,330.70	21,918.40	4.4	3.33	0.84	19.5	41
SOUND SHORE	G	NO	27.0	13.00	11,278.50	9,563.60	☆	1.4	0.37	0.19	N/A	91
SOUTHEASTERN GROWTH (R)	G	NO	105.2	13.24	11,853.20	9,272.70	☆	0.0	0.10	0.00	N/A	34
SOUTHEASTERN AST MGT VAL	G	NO	30.8	10.49	12,169.40	10,159.50	☆	0.8	0.00	0.07	N/A	N/A
SOVEREIGN INVESTORS	GI	SC	44.3	11.50	10,765.60	9,498.30	20,358.80	5.0	0.90	0.60	14.3	59
STATE BOND COMMON STOCK	G	SC	29.1	6.25	10,534.50	8,661.20	14,338.90	1.8	0.64	0.12	17.0	8
STATE BOND DIVERSIFIED	GI	SC	19.0	7.47	11,157.30	9,680.40	19,152.40	3.5	0.59	0.27	N/A	14
STATE BOND PROGRESS	G	SC	7.3	10.06	10,905.40	8,833.70	11,722.60	1.8	0.71	0.19	N/A	10
STATE BOND US GOVT SEC	FI	SC	11.4	4.84	10,442.50	10,824.90	☆	8.3	0.00	0.40	N/A	35
STATE FARM BALANCED	B	NO	60.7	18.59	10,830.00	10,204.00	18,465.90	4.3	0.33	0.80	21.1	12
STATE FARM GROWTH	G	NO	294.6	13.30	10,910.40	9,712.80	16,514.10	2.7	0.27	0.36	21.7	12
STATE FARM INTERIM	FI	NO	27.7	9.99	10,381.00	10,694.50	16,267.50	7.8	0.00	0.77	N/A	12
STATE STREET INVESTMENT (R)	GI	LO	518.4	78.65	10,891.50	9,018.80	16,299.40	2.8	5.55	2.30	17.2	34
STEADMAN AMER INDUSTRY	CA	NO	4.8	2.24	9,572.60	7,491.60	5,476.80	0.0	0.00	0.00	N/A	228
STEADMAN ASSOCIATED FUND	EI	NO	14.4	0.63	10,481.00	7,676.70	8,520.20	10.3	0.00	0.06	N/A	302
STEADMAN INVESTMENT	G	NO	5.5	1.35	10,337.90	7,376.20	7,901.70	1.1	0.00	0.01	N/A	96
STEADMAN OCEANOGRAPHIC	G	NO	2.8	3.75	9,146.30	5,805.00	4,681.60	0.0	0.00	0.00	N/A	196
STEINROE CAPITAL OPP	G	NO	235.8	23.09	10,876.10	8,747.20	11,179.00	0.2	6.55	0.04	30.2	133
STEINROE DISCOVERY	SG	NO	49.9	9.91	12,189.40	9,481.00	☆	0.2	2.56	0.02	26.7	207
STEINROE EQUITY: INTL GR	IF	NO	14.0	2.13	10,339.80	☆	☆	0.0	0.00	0.00	N/A	N/A
STEINROE GOVT PLUS	FI	NO	26.9	9.59	10,495.10	10,629.90	☆	7.6	0.05	0.73	N/A	205
STEINROE GROWTH & INCOME	GI	NO	13.9	9.06	10,768.20	☆	☆	0.0	0.03	0.12	N/A	N/A
STEINROE HIGH YLD BOND	FI	NO	96.6	9.60	10,760.70	10,930.10	☆	9.9	0.00	0.95	N/A	153
STEINROE MANAGED BONDS	FI	NO	162.3	8.51	10,464.30	10,680.40	17,076.30	7.9	0.13	0.68	N/A	230
STEINROE PRIME EQUITIES	G	NO	24.8	8.90	10,759.50	8,883.50	☆	1.6	0.00	0.14	21.6	32
STEINROE SPECIAL FUND	CA	NO	240.0	14.96	11,669.10	9,948.80	17,957.00	1.4	3.17	0.23	25.0	103
STEINROE STOCK	G	NO	213.3	15.14	10,383.80	8,338.20	12,200.60	1.4	2.42	0.23	21.3	143
STEINROE TOTAL RETURN	B	NO	138.7	22.93	10,636.10	9,621.70	16,061.20	5.7	1.01	1.33	15.8	86
STEINROE UNIVERSE FUND	CA	NO	27.1	13.98	11,095.20	8,879.80	11,106.00	1.9	5.48	0.27	20.6	242
STOVALL/21 CONSISTNT RET	CA	SC	7.2	8.51	10,179.40	9,418.50	☆	0.9	0.07	0.08	N/A	223
STRATEGIC CAPITAL GAINS	CA	SC	3.7	5.67	12,945.20	10,035.40	6,766.10	0.0	0.00	0.00	N/A	35
STRATEGIC INVESTMENTS	AU	SC	56.1	3.45	6,546.50	6,029.60	4,229.10	8.7	0.00	0.30	N/A	19
STRATEGIC SILVER	S	SC	31.0	4.52	9,847.50	8,263.30	☆	0.0	0.00	0.00	N/A	52
STRATTON GROWTH FUND	GI	NO	17.7	20.40	11,839.80	9,966.90	14,916.80	3.4	1.53	0.70	N/A	23
STRATTON MONTHLY DIV	UT	NO	35.9	25.23	11,189.80	9,809.70	19,232.00	7.5	0.32	1.91	10.2	27
STRONG DISCOVERY FUND	CA	LO	9.6	12.28	12,368.20	☆	☆	0.0	0.00	0.08	N/A	N/A
STRONG GOVT	FI	NO	12.4	10.00	10,576.40	11,684.80	☆	6.0	0.00	0.59	N/A	715
STRONG INCOME	FI	NO	167.2	12.01	10,812.90	10,836.70	☆	9.7	0.00	1.16	N/A	245
STRONG INVESTMENT	B	LO	268.9	17.87	10,434.50	9,961.90	16,521.60	5.3	0.88	0.96	N/A	337
STRONG OPPORTUNITY	CA	LO	173.7	17.62	11,285.20	9,737.60	☆	2.3	1.65	0.43	N/A	371
STRONG SHORT-TERM BOND	FI	NO	46.9	10.20	10,597.30	☆	☆	0.0	0.01	0.69	N/A	N/A
STRONG TOTAL RETURN	GI	LO	956.2	19.74	11,047.80	9,901.40	19,776.00	5.0	1.35	1.02	N/A	224
SUMMIT INVESTORS FD	G	SC	146.0	6.82	11,964.90	8,967.70	13,788.10	0.8	0.57	0.06	15.3	82
SURVEYOR FUND	G	SC	93.9	11.52	12,631.60	9,924.30	13,667.90	0.0	1.78	0.00	26.4	98
TECUMSEH: EQUITY PORT	GI	SC	37.2	9.85	#9,986.90	☆	☆	0.0	0.00	0.13	N/A	N/A

TECUMSEH: INCOME PORT	FI	SC	35.0	9.97	#10,355.60	☆	☆	0.0	0.00	0.38	N/A	N/A
TEMPLETON FOREIGN	IF	SC	297.0	19.52	11,250.70	10,380.70	25,285.70	2.9	1.23	0.58	N/A	15
TEMPLETON GLOBAL I (X)	GL	SC	277.6	40.92	12,525.30	9,394.80	18,159.30	2.7	2.24	1.14	12.8	13
TEMPLETON GLOBAL II	GL	SC	492.0	12.66	12,126.40	9,465.60	☆	2.9	0.63	0.38	18.3	17
TEMPLETON GROWTH	GL	SC	1,506.3	13.67	11,653.90	9,980.40	20,073.80	3.1	1.08	0.44	11.0	18
TEMPLETON INCOME	WI	SC	129.1	10.07	10,286.40	10,521.50	☆	8.4	0.02	0.85	N/A	105
TEMPLETON WORLD	GL	SC	3,858.4	14.52	11,469.20	10,003.10	20,468.20	3.9	1.95	0.61	13.5	23
THOMSON MCKINNON: CNVRT (R)	CV	NO	46.5	10.23	#10,230.00	☆	☆	0.0	0.00	0.00	N/A	N/A
THOMSON MCKINNON: GLOBL (R)	GL	NO	67.4	10.38	10,857.70	9,428.50	☆	0.0	0.86	0.00	N/A	134
THOMSON MCKINNON: GOVT (R)	FI	NO	764.0	9.49	10,396.10	10,535.60	☆	9.5	0.00	0.90	N/A	332
THOMSON MCKINNON: GRO (R)	G	NO	357.9	14.36	11,140.40	9,283.50	☆	0.6	1.13	0.09	N/A	128
THOMSON MCKINNON: INC (R)	I	NO	513.6	9.78	10,624.20	10,709.80	☆	10.2	0.00	0.99	N/A	82
THOMSON MCKINNON: OPPTY (R)	CA	NO	53.3	12.37	12,044.80	10,327.80	☆	0.2	2.55	0.02	N/A	189
THOMPSON UNGER & PLUMB	B	NO	5.7	10.21	11,420.60	10,086.10	☆	0.9	0.00	0.09	N/A	114
THORNBURG TR: LTD TERM US	FI	LO	14.5	12.14	10,405.50	☆	☆	0.0	0.00	0.64	N/A	N/A
THOROUGHBRED BOND	FI	NO	11.3	9.61	10,413.00	10,689.50	☆	7.3	0.00	0.70	N/A	16
THOROUGHBRED STOCK	GI	NO	6.8	9.68	10,745.20	8,990.70	☆	8.0	0.52	0.79	N/A	117
TOCQUEVILLE FUND	CA	LO	15.6	10.25	12,144.50	9,643.30	☆	0.2	0.38	0.02	N/A	73
TOWER SRS: BOND	FI	SC	5.7	7.64	9,909.20	☆	☆	0.0	0.00	0.00	N/A	N/A
TOWER SRS: EQUITY INCOME	EI	SC	1.2	5.15	11,171.40	☆	☆	0.0	0.00	0.00	N/A	N/A
TRANSATLANTIC GRO FD	IF	NO	56.9	13.99	10,911.60	9,684.50	25,954.80	0.0	11.11	0.00	N/A	59
TRANSATLANTIC INCOME	WI	NO	8.4	10.73	9,273.60	10,908.00	☆	7.8	0.00	0.84	N/A	36
TREASURY FIRST	FI	NO	41.2	9.76	10,164.90	10,800.80	☆	8.5	0.05	0.82	N/A	307
TRIFLEX FUND	B	SC	14.6	14.98	10,852.40	11,098.60	16,921.50	7.4	0.00	1.10	N/A	27
TRINITY TAX-ADVANTAGED	FI	NO	3.2	9.48	10,009.80	10,123.30	☆	6.3	0.00	0.59	N/A	N/A
TRUSTEES COMMINGLED INTL	IF	NO	602.2	30.61	11,117.60	10,632.40	30,875.40	2.7	18.77	1.09	N/A	N/A
TRUSTEES COMMINGLED US	GI	NO	120.8	27.22	12,237.30	9,623.60	17,340.90	2.8	5.45	0.84	17.1	N/A
TUDOR FUND	CA	NO	178.1	21.74	11,553.40	8,996.20	14,015.40	0.0	0.82	0.01	23.4	113
TWENTIETH CENTURY GIFT (R)	G	NO	14.4	7.76	11,993.30	10,068.10	☆	0.0	0.85	0.00	N/A	130
TWENTIETH CENTURY GROWTH	CA	NO	1,357.6	13.29	10,804.90	8,864.10	15,759.60	0.3	3.46	0.04	23.5	114
TWENTIETH CENTURY HERIT (R)	G	NO	41.5	6.34	11,740.70	☆	☆	0.0	0.00	0.01	N/A	N/A
TWENTIETH CENT LNG TM BD	FI	NO	20.9	91.78	10,479.90	10,664.90	☆	8.9	0.00	8.17	N/A	146
TWENTIETH CENTURY SELECT	G	NO	2,552.9	28.51	10,873.40	9,037.20	15,915.30	1.5	6.36	0.48	17.1	123
TWENTIETH CENTRY ULTRA (R)	CA	NO	296.8	7.59	12,183.00	9,598.00	11,893.70	0.0	3.25	0.00	35.1	137
TWENTIETH CENTURY US GOV	FI	NO	422.1	94.78	10,359.60	10,685.40	15,551.40	8.6	0.00	8.09	N/A	468
TWENTIETH CENTURY VISTA (R)	CA	NO	241.4	6.68	11,438.40	9,180.30	☆	0.0	0.46	0.00	31.0	123
UNIFIED GROWTH FUND	G	NO	19.2	18.85	11,358.10	8,793.80	14,305.10	1.4	1.83	0.27	N/A	61
UNIFIED INCOME FUND	I	NO	10.4	11.13	11,060.20	9,293.50	12,985.40	6.9	0.00	0.77	N/A	75
UNIFIED MUTUAL SHARES	GI	NO	17.6	14.37	10,969.50	9,490.60	17,143.90	3.8	3.19	0.56	N/A	49
UNITED ACCUMULATIVE	G	SC	743.3	6.33	11,217.00	9,746.90	18,354.30	4.6	1.27	0.32	22.4	317
UNITED BOND FUND	FI	SC	331.9	6.13	10,483.50	10,903.20	18,137.00	9.0	0.03	0.55	N/A	233
UNITED CONTL INCOME	B	SC	320.1	15.02	10,904.10	9,064.40	18,401.10	5.4	1.30	0.85	17.3	240
UNITED GOLD & GOVT	AU	SC	116.7	8.03	10,230.60	9,199.40	☆	2.4	0.80	0.20	28.0	107
UNITED GOVERNMENT	FI	LO	137.9	4.82	10,317.10	10,480.90	☆	8.0	0.00	0.38	N/A	240
UNITED HIGH INCOME (X)	FI	SC	1,251.1	12.04	10,667.00	10,226.60	17,112.40	13.1	0.06	1.58	N/A	118
UNITED HIGH INCOME II	FI	SC	239.3	4.68	10,942.50	10,667.50	☆	11.5	0.00	0.53	N/A	178
UNITED INCOME	EI	SC	1,107.0	16.93	11,448.90	10,350.60	22,428.40	4.0	2.23	0.72	14.0	58
UNITED INTL GROWTH	IF	SC	289.8	6.60	10,759.80	9,868.10	23,656.80	1.7	2.06	0.13	10.7	217
UNITED MISSOURI BK BOND	FI	NO	29.6	10.85	10,412.70	10,720.40	16,269.40	7.9	0.01	0.86	N/A	12
UNITED MISSOURI QUAL DVD	FI	NO	5.4	9.24	9,692.50	9,881.00	☆	7.3	0.01	0.67	N/A	14
UNITED MISSOURI BK STOCK	GI	NO	43.4	13.07	11,011.00	9,583.60	17,363.70	4.4	0.97	0.57	N/A	50
UNITED NEW CONCEPTS	SG	SC	98.8	5.76	11,803.30	9,413.60	15,043.10	1.0	0.11	0.06	25.5	183
UNITED RETIREMENT SHARES	GI	SC	103.8	5.39	11,370.40	9,826.70	15,380.90	5.2	0.74	0.30	13.6	161
UNITED SCIENCE & ENERGY	TK	SC	227.2	10.09	10,971.20	9,538.00	17,008.70	2.4	1.59	0.26	22.8	85
UNITED VANGUARD FUND	G	SC	682.9	6.01	11,541.80	10,256.60	16,075.60	2.7	1.37	0.18	21.5	161
US GOLD SHARES	AU	NO	237.9	3.74	6,867.10	6,354.60	5,769.20	10.7	0.00	0.40	7.8	24
US GOOD & BAD TIMES	GI	NO	16.8	16.44	10,196.50	8,454.10	14,374.30	4.5	0.00	0.74	N/A	58

PERFORMANCE OF MUTUAL FUNDS (continued)

FUND NAME	OBJ.	LOAD	TOTAL NET ASTS (MIL) 6/30/88	NAV 6/30/88	PERFORMANCE (RETURN ON INITIAL $10,000 INVESTMENT) 12/31/87-6/30/88	6/30/87-6/30/88	6/30/83-6/30/88	YIELD % 6/30/88	PER SHARE LATEST 12 MONTHS CAP GAINS	INC DIVS	LATEST AVAILABLE PRICE/EARNINGS	ANNUAL % TURNOVER
US GOVT GUARANTEED SEC	FI	SC	406.0	13.77	10,493.40	10,713.90	☆	9.6	0.00	1.32	N/A	68
US GOVT SEC FUND	FI	NO	10.0	9.64	10,554.50	10,669.80	☆	8.3	0.00	0.80	N/A	115
US GNMA	FI	NO	6.8	9.31	10,687.20	10,902.20	☆	10.0	0.00	0.93	N/A	107
US GROWTH FUND	CA	NO	6.3	7.13	11,513.50	8,918.30	☆	1.4	1.55	0.11	N/A	64
US INCOME FUND	I	NO	4.5	9.64	10,998.30	10,313.60	☆	7.7	0.35	0.76	N/A	174
US LOCAP FUND (R)	SG	NO	2.6	6.75	11,382.80	8,045.30	☆	0.0	0.00	0.00	N/A	52
US NEW PROSPECTOR (R)	AU	NO	104.1	1.40	9,396.00	7,870.20	☆	1.3	0.21	0.02	28.6	44
US PROSPECTOR FUND (X,R)	AU	NO	45.1	0.77	9,390.20	7,597.30	☆	0.0	0.07	0.00	26.1	8
US REAL ESTATE	S	NO	3.2	9.29	12,004.90	☆	☆	0.0	0.00	0.38	N/A	N/A
US TREND FUND	G	SC	90.7	11.79	10,861.70	9,266.00	14,294.70	2.6	0.29	0.31	N/A	56
USAA CORNERSTONE	S	NO	588.7	17.10	10,775.00	9,426.00	☆	2.1	0.02	0.36	25.0	15
USAA GOLD	AU	NO	188.5	9.18	9,125.20	7,074.40	☆	0.5	0.51	0.05	37.1	54
USAA GROWTH FUND	G	NO	218.0	11.99	10,591.90	8,834.70	12,069.60	2.7	3.88	0.37	13.2	124
USAA INCOME FUND	FI	NO	272.4	11.17	10,581.00	10,847.20	17,588.70	9.2	0.26	1.04	N/A	36
USAA INCOME STOCK	EI	NO	29.6	10.17	11,439.60	10,153.90	☆	3.3	0.02	0.34	N/A	7
USAA SUNBELT ERA	SG	NO	145.2	17.52	11,798.00	9,238.70	10,569.80	0.7	1.86	0.12	21.8	35
UST MASTER EQUITY	CA	NO	14.4	11.86	11,615.20	9,057.60	☆	1.1	0.15	0.13	N/A	86
UST MASTER INC & GROWTH	GI	NO	7.2	8.14	11,675.50	9,559.00	☆	5.0	0.06	0.40	N/A	7
UST MASTER INTERNATIONAL	GL	NO	10.8	7.69	10,420.10	☆	☆	0.0	0.01	0.02	N/A	N/A
UST MASTER MGD INC	FI	NO	13.4	8.63	10,523.30	11,042.50	☆	7.5	0.00	0.64	N/A	751
VALLEY FORGE FUND (R)	G	NO	9.3	10.17	10,560.70	10,403.50	14,599.60	6.4	0.13	0.66	N/A	56
VALUE LINE AGGRES INC	FI	NO	51.8	8.18	10,327.80	9,542.00	☆	12.9	0.00	1.05	N/A	134
VALUE LINE CENTURION	G	NO	189.1	12.52	11,218.60	8,914.00	☆	0.7	0.00	0.09	19.4	N/A
VALUE LINE CONVERTIBLE	CV	NO	66.5	10.75	11,288.20	9,723.90	☆	6.3	0.48	0.67	21.2	234
VALUE LINE FUND	GI	NO	214.9	13.78	11,113.50	9,618.10	13,495.10	1.8	2.46	0.26	17.6	118
VALUE LINE INCOME	EI	NO	141.9	5.82	10,887.10	9,524.00	14,825.70	8.7	0.52	0.53	12.5	96
VALUE LINE LVGE GROWTH	CA	NO	291.1	19.81	10,914.60	9,037.40	14,345.50	1.4	4.70	0.30	17.3	148
VALUE LINE SPECIAL SIT	G	NO	135.1	12.23	11,128.30	8,445.90	8,374.30	0.4	2.28	0.05	23.4	41
VALUE LINE US GOVT SEC	FI	NO	263.2	11.88	10,596.10	10,886.10	17,278.20	11.6	0.00	1.38	N/A	48
VANCE, SANDERS SPECIAL	G	SC	61.6	10.97	11,215.70	8,837.70	9,690.80	0.5	0.09	0.05	26.2	126
VAN ECK GOLD/RESOURCES	AU	SC	252.2	5.25	9,178.30	8,177.30	☆	0.4	0.00	0.02	29.4	2
VAN ECK WORLD INCOME	WI	SC	32.7	9.62	10,811.20	11,361.20	☆	6.1	0.28	0.60	N/A	N/A
VAN ECK WORLD TRENDS	GL	SC	78.9	13.42	10,205.30	9,471.90	☆	2.0	0.85	0.28	23.1	50
VANGUARD ADJ RATE PREF	FI	NO	76.1	19.96	9,544.30	9,516.80	☆	7.6	0.00	1.50	N/A	33
VANGUARD BOND MARKET	FI	NO	54.2	9.22	10,428.30	10,698.80	☆	8.9	0.00	0.82	N/A	N/A
VANGUARD CONVERTIBLE	CV	NO	76.1	8.90	11,423.80	9,555.60	☆	6.3	0.12	0.56	N/A	45
VANGUARD EQUITY INCOME	EI	NO	16.8	10.35	#10,470.20	☆	☆	0.0	0.00	0.12	N/A	N/A
VANGUARD FI: GNMA PORT	FI	NO	1,884.5	9.48	10,619.70	10,904.10	17,536.30	9.4	0.00	0.88	N/A	22
VANGUARD FI: HIGH YIELD	FI	NO	1,100.1	8.55	10,897.60	10,763.40	18,016.00	11.8	0.00	1.01	N/A	82
VANGUARD FI: INV GRADE	FI	NO	646.4	7.87	10,517.10	10,656.10	16,958.50	9.6	0.00	0.75	N/A	63
VANGUARD FI: SHT TERM BD	FI	NO	513.5	10.34	10,404.80	10,729.10	16,517.10	7.6	0.00	0.79	N/A	258
VANGUARD FI: SHT TERM GOV	FI	NO	60.6	9.92	#10,303.60	☆	☆	0.0	0.00	0.38	N/A	N/A
VANGUARD FI: US TREAS BD	FI	NO	99.9	9.18	10,479.70	10,612.60	☆	8.4	0.00	0.77	N/A	162
VANGUARD HIGH YIELD STK	EI	NO	160.9	14.19	12,174.90	10,304.60	25,105.10	9.6	2.82	1.49	N/A	53
VANGUARD INDEX: EXTND MKT	SG	NO	26.2	11.94	11,962.50	☆	☆	0.0	0.00	0.01	N/A	N/A
VANGUARD INDEX: 500 PORT	GI	NO	957.1	27.15	11,247.70	9,254.80	19,366.20	3.2	0.17	0.88	16.5	15
VANGUARD PREFERRED STK	FI	NO	83.4	7.75	10,377.10	9,758.80	16,615.50	11.5	0.12	0.89	N/A	67
VANGUARD QUANTITATIVE	GI	NO	154.1	11.06	11,407.90	9,383.10	☆	3.0	0.06	0.33	14.5	73
VANGUARD SPECIAL-ENERGY (R)	NR	NO	40.8	11.38	11,744.10	9,184.10	☆	4.9	1.29	0.59	23.4	34
VANGUARD SPECIAL-GOLD (R)	AU	NO	136.0	10.16	9,195.80	8,641.70	☆	3.1	0.99	0.33	19.5	32
VANGUARD SPECIAL-HEALTH (R)	H	NO	60.2	18.41	12,389.60	9,625.00	☆	1.8	1.87	0.35	20.3	27
VANGUARD SPECIAL-SERV (R)	S	NO	23.3	14.69	11,473.80	8,251.60	☆	3.5	0.76	0.53	N/A	96
VANGUARD SPECIAL-TECH (R)	TK	NO	19.7	11.78	11,863.00	8,685.90	☆	1.1	0.15	0.13	N/A	108
VANGUARD STAR	B	NO	651.9	11.18	11,413.10	10,308.10	☆	5.8	0.66	0.67	N/A	N/A

VANGUARD WORLD-INTL GRO	IF	NO	499.0	10.83	10,473.90	10,157.20	31,527.60	1.1	2.43	0.13	N/A	77
VANGUARD WORLD-US GRO	G	NO	141.1	7.60	10,919.50	8,690.30	14,533.90	3.4	3.26	0.31	16.7	142
VAN KAMPEN MERRITT-GOVT	FI	SC	4,622.5	15.02	10,452.00	10,748.30	☆	9.8	0.10	1.47	N/A	124
VAN KAMPEN MERRITT GR&IN	GI	SC	37.5	15.23	11,518.90	9,603.30	☆	3.8	0.22	0.58	N/A	1
VAN KAMPEN MERRITT HI YD	FI	SC	246.1	13.65	10,770.60	10,621.80	☆	12.3	0.07	1.68	N/A	135
VARIABLE STOCK FUND	G	NO	8.4	8.27	10,455.10	8,584.40	13,783.40	2.4	0.44	0.20	14.2	151
VENTURE INCOME (+) PLUS	FI	SC	64.1	8.60	10,602.80	9,918.10	15,830.00	13.9	0.10	1.20	N/A	167
VOLUMETRIC FUND	G	NO	3.3	13.17	12,056.90	9,708.80	☆	0.9	0.00	0.12	N/A	179
VOYAGEUR US GOVT SEC FD	FI	LO	10.0	9.98	10,394.00	☆	☆	0.0	0.00	0.58	N/A	N/A
WADE FUND	G	NO	0.5	36.98	9,803.80	8,739.90	14,666.00	1.1	1.82	0.43	N/A	5
WALL STREET FUND	G	SC	12.9	6.72	12,151.90	9,302.90	14,645.30	0.3	1.68	0.02	N/A	166
WASATCH AGGRES EQU	SG	NO	0.9	9.64	11,421.80	8,939.80	☆	0.1	1.04	0.01	N/A	N/A
WASATCH GROWTH	G	NO	2.2	9.79	11,188.60	9,176.20	☆	0.2	0.39	0.02	N/A	N/A
WASATCH INCOME	FI	NO	0.9	10.32	10,403.20	10,911.30	☆	5.9	0.00	0.61	N/A	N/A
WASHINGTON AREA GRO (R)	G	NO	19.9	18.23	12,017.10	9,573.40	☆	0.0	1.65	0.00	N/A	23
WASHINGTON MUTUAL INV	GI	SC	2,725.7	12.57	11,443.20	9,653.00	21,230.20	5.2	0.24	0.67	14.7	12
WAYNE HUMMER GROWTH FUND	G	NO	21.8	14.19	10,801.30	9,438.10	☆	1.4	0.51	0.20	N/A	28
WEALTH MONITORS	CA	SC	4.1	7.11	11,780.50	7,442.20	☆	0.9	0.00	0.06	N/A	119
WEINGARTEN EQUITY	G	SC	312.3	9.36	11,196.20	9,450.60	17,245.00	0.1	0.77	0.01	18.8	108
WEITZ VALUE	GI	NO	10.4	10.90	11,327.60	10,806.40	☆	3.1	0.00	0.33	N/A	55
WELLESLEY INCOME	I	NO	539.5	15.11	10,909.30	10,571.80	19,705.90	8.1	0.38	1.24	13.1	31
WELLINGTON FUND	B	NO	1,494.1	16.67	11,252.10	9,889.90	20,213.00	5.9	0.14	0.98	17.1	12
WESTWOOD FUND	CA	LO	33.5	12.27	11,277.60	9,769.20	☆	2.3	1.07	0.30	N/A	221
WILLIAM PENN QUALITY INC	FI	LO	1.0	9.99	10,355.90	☆	☆	0.0	0.00	0.55	N/A	N/A
WILLIAM PENN US GOVT	FI	LO	1.0	10.12	10,439.00	☆	☆	0.0	0.00	0.50	N/A	N/A
WINDSOR FUND (X)	GI	NO	5,688.6	13.53	12,479.10	10,232.80	24,417.70	5.9	2.21	0.87	15.0	37
WINDSOR II	GI	NO	1,401.6	12.36	11,695.20	9,625.10	☆	4.8	0.80	0.61	14.3	46
WINTHROP FOCUS FIX INC (R)	FI	NO	4.9	9.47	10,511.10	10,748.70	☆	7.4	0.00	0.70	N/A	51
WINTHROP FOCUS GROWTH (R)	G	NO	54.4	10.30	11,123.10	9,125.90	☆	0.5	0.20	0.05	N/A	91
WPG FUND	CA	NO	40.8	20.99	11,179.60	9,429.90	16,046.10	0.9	2.83	0.19	23.2	84
WPG FUNDS TR: DVD INCOME	EI	NO	3.4	11.03	#11,050.80	☆	☆	0.0	0.00	0.02	N/A	N/A
WPG FUNDS TR: GOVT SEC	FI	NO	78.8	9.88	10,509.20	10,764.70	☆	7.6	0.00	0.75	N/A	108
WPG GROWTH	SG	NO	134.5	96.60	11,491.40	8,680.70	☆	0.0	12.30	0.00	N/A	94

How to read the *Barron's*/Lipper gauge. These tables show the return on a $10,000 investment over three periods: second quarter, one year and five years.

FUND NAME-Mutual fund name, occasionally shortened, appearing in alphabetical order; municipal bond funds appear after debt and equity funds. The majority of open-end funds registered with the Securities and Exchange Commission are included with the exception of money market funds.

OBJ.-Investment objective of the fund as determined by both the language in the prospectus and a review of the funds' investment characteristics, such as yield, turnover, etc.

INVESTMENT OBJECTIVE DEFINITIONS:

AU-GOLD ORIENTED FUND-A fund which has at least 65% of its assets in shares of gold mines, gold-oriented mining finance houses, gold coins or bullion.

B-BALANCED FUND-A fund whose primary objective is stability of net asset value, achieved by maintaining a balanced portfolio of both stocks and bonds. Typically, the stock/bond ratio ranges around 60%/40%.

CA-CAPITAL APPRECIATION FUND-Any fund which meets at least two of the following criteria: (1) The investment objective shown in the prospectus is capital appreciation or similar wording. (2) A turnover rate of 100% or more is either expected or realized. (3) The fund is permitted to borrow more than 10% of the value of its portfolio. (4) The prospectus permits short selling, the purchase of options, or investing in common stocks or unregistered securities.

CV-CONVERTIBLE SECURITIES FUND-A fund that invests primarily in convertible bonds and convertible preferred shares.

EI-EQUITY INCOME FUND-A fund which normally has 60% or more of its assets in equities and has an above average yield.

FI-FIXED INCOME FUND-A fund which typically has more than 75% of its assets in fixed income issues, such as money market instruments, bonds and preferred stocks.

G-GROWTH FUND-A fund which normally invests in companies whose long-term earnings are expected to grow significantly faster than the earnings of the stocks represented in the major unmanaged stock averages.

GI-GROWTH & INCOME FUND-A fund which combines a growth of earnings objective and an income requirement for level and/or rising dividends.

GL-GLOBAL FUND-A fund which invests at least 25% of its portfolio in securities traded outside of the United States and may own U.S. securities as well.

H-HEALTH FUND-A fund which invests 65% of its equity portfolio in health and medical company shares.

I-INCOME FUND-A fund which normally invests less than 75% in fixed income issues and less than 50% in equities, and whose principal aim is the generation of income.

IF-INTERNATIONAL FUND-A fund which invests more than 50% of its assets in securities whose primary trading markets are outside of the United States.

OG-OPTION GROWTH FUND-A fund which attempts to increase its net asset value by investing at least 5% of its portfolio in options.

(Footnotes continued on following page.)

PERFORMANCE OF MUTUAL FUNDS *(concluded)*

OI-OPTION INCOME FUND-A fund which writes covered options on at least 50% of its portfolio.
NR-NATURAL RESOURCE FUND-A fund which typically invests more than 65% of its equity commitment in natural resource stocks.
S-SPECIALTY FUND-A fund which, by prospectus, limits its investments to a well-defined specialty, such as banks and utilities.
SG-SMALL COMPANY GROWTH FUND-A fund whose prospectus language and portfolio practice limits its investment to companies on the basis of the size of the company. (Those funds that use smaller companies some of the time or in conjunction with larger companies will not be considered a Small Company Growth Fund.)
TK-SCIENCE & TECHNOLOGY FUND-A fund which invests 65% of its equity portfolio in science and technology stocks.
UT-UTILITY FUND-A fund which invests 65% of its equity portfolio in utility shares.
WI-WORLD INCOME FUND-A fund that invests primarily in U.S. dollar and non-U.S. dollar debt instruments. The fund also may invest in common and preferred stocks.
LOAD-This tells whether a fund has a sales charge known as a load. Load definitions are:
SC-Sales charge-The fund is a load fund up to a maximum 8½% load.
LO-Low-load fund. A fund which charges a load up to 4½%.
NO-No-load fund. A fund which has no sales charge.
TOTAL NET ASSETS-Fund assets minus liabilities, fund expenses, advisory fees and commissions.
NAV (Net Asset Value)-Total net assets divided by the number of shares outstanding.
PERFORMANCE-The theoretical ending value of a $10,000 investment for the period analyzed. For complete comparability and regardless of a fund's stated policy, calculations include all capital gains distributions and income dividends, reinvested on the ex-dividend date at ex-date net asset value. Any fund charges not reflected in net asset value or gross income and any tax consequences incurred by the shareholder aren't taken into consideration.
YIELD-The latest 12 months' worth of income dividends divided by the adjusted ending net asset value. The ending net asset value is adjusted periodically for the impact of capital gains paid during the previous 12 months.
PER SHARE-LATEST 12 MONTHS CAP GAINS-Total amount of capital gains per share paid during the last 12 months.
PER SHARE-LATEST 12 MONTHS INC DIVS-Total amount of income dividends per share paid during the last 12 months.
LATEST AVAILABLE-PRICE/EARNINGS-The weighted, average reported price/earnings per share ratio of the underlying equities in the portfolio, based on latest 12 months earnings reported in the latest issue of the "Lipper-Equity Analysis Report on the Weighted Average Holdings of Large Investment Companies."
LATEST AVAILABLE—ANNUAL TURNOVER-The ratio of the smaller of purchases and sales divided by average total net assets expressed as a percentage. The turnover shown is for either the current fiscal year or the one preceding it.
☆-Fund not in existence for full time period covered.
#-Fund's first public offering occurred during the present calendar year.
N/A-Not available due either to size or availability of data.

(R)-Fund charges ½ of 1% each on sales and redemption. (X)-Fund closed to new accounts. (S) Significant events affecting performance: AMERICAN HERITAGE FUND, 12/27/85 new advisor; FIRST INVESTORS VALUE FUNDS, formerly First Investors 90/10 Fund; INDUSTRY FUND OF AMERICA, 12/27/85 new advisor; IVY GROWTH FUND, 4/01/85 new advisor; KAUFMANN FUND, inactive between 1/1/79-2/21/86. CAPSTONE EQUITYGUARD STOCK FUND, converted to open end effective 5/21/88; DELAWARE U.S. GOVERNMENT, merged into Delaware GNMA; MASS MUTUAL INCOME INVESTORS, became open end effective 4/15/88; NATIONAL BALANCED, merged into National Total Return as of 2/16/88; PARIBAS MCU-450, fund is being restructured; PROGRESSIVE INCOME EQUITY FUND, converted to open end effective 5/27/88; SCHRODER CAPITAL-U.S. EQUITY FUND, no longer exclusively available for foreign investors; STOCK MARKETAMERICA, merged into Colonial U.S. Equity Index Trust; WORLD OF TECHNOLOGY FUND, merged into Financial Port: Technology.
BOND PORTFOLIO FOR ENDOWMENTS, INC. and ENDOWMENTS, INC. FUNDS.-Shares are available only to institutions exempt from federal taxation under Section 501 (c) (1) of the Internal Revenue Code.
CITIBANK FUNDS-Availability limited to Individual Retirement Accounts established with Citibank, N.A. as trustee.
DFA JAPANESE SMALL COMPANY PORTFOLIO and DFA UNITED KINGDOM SMALL COMPANY PORTFOLIO—Purchase of shares must be made in yen and British pounds, respectively. For purposes of comparison, in this report, these funds convert their net asset values from local currency into U.S. dollars.
EATON VANCE TOTAL RETURN-The performance reflects the impact of a reversal of a tax reserve of $2.14 per share on Dec. 31, 1985 when the fund became a regulated investment company under Sub Chapter M of the IRS code.
ELFUN TRUSTS-Available to certain employees of the General Electric Co., regular and senior members of the Elfun Society.
EQUITY STRATEGIES FUND—The Fund commenced its operations as a closed-end Fund on 2/25/82 and was reclassified as an open-end fund under new management, effecte 7/2/86.
FIRST UNION FUNDS—Availability limited to Individual Retirement Accounts established with First Union National Bank of N.C. as trustee.
GENERAL ELECTRIC S&S PROGRAM: GENERAL ELECTRIC LONG TERM INTEREST-Available to General Electric employees.
HARTWELL GROWTH FUND-On Feb. 6, 1984, the net asset value for Hartwell Growth Fund was increased by $0.79 per share to reflect the receipt of payment in settlement of a class action lawsuit against Viatron Computer Systems.
PRUDENTIAL BACHE UTILITY-For periods which include Aug. 24, 1984, the dividend, and therefore the performance: includes a reversal of a reserve for taxes of $2.95 per share when the company became a regulated investment company under Sub Chapter M under the IRS code. On that date the net asset value was $20.35.
SCUDDER GROWTH & INCOME FUND-On Nov. 13, 1984 this Fund adopted its present name and objective. Prior performance is attributed to Scudder Common Stock Fund which had an objective of long-term capital growth.
SECURITY ACTION FUND—Sold only in a contractual plan.

Source: Lipper Analytical Services, Inc. Reprinted by courtesy of *Barron's National Business and Financial Weekly*, August 18, 1988.

Selected Mutual Funds Which Invest Abroad

Foreign investments provide a possible opportunity for increased returns and portfolio diversification. Since most investors lack the time, background and information, the only practical way for them to participate is through the purchase of U.S. based mutual funds which invest abroad. A number of these funds are listed below. In general, these mutual funds are divided into three categories: **global funds** which invest in both U.S. and foreign stocks, **international funds** which invest in foreign stocks, and **regional funds** which invest in the equities of a specific country or region. Here we have combined the first two categories.

Global/International Funds	Telephone in State	Out-of-State
Alliance International	(800) 523-5695 (NY)	(800) 221-5672
World of Technology[1] (Financial Programs)	(303) 779-1233	(800) 525-8085
Fidelity Overseas	(617) 523-1919	(800) 544-6666
First Investors International	(212) 208-6000	(800) 423-4026
Kemper International Fund	(312) 332-6472	(800) 537-3863
Keystone International	(617) 338-3395	(800) 225-2618
Merrill/Lynch International Holdings	(609) 282-2042	(212) 282-2042
Merrill Lynch Retirement Global		(800) 637-7455
Prudential Bache Global	(212) 214-2271	(212) 214-2271
Putnam International Equities	(617) 292-1000	(800) 225-1581
Scudder International[1]	(800) 225-2470 (MA)	(800) 453-3305
Shearson Lehman Spl. Inc.—Global Bond	(212) 528-2744	(212) 528-2744
Templeton Foreign/Global/World Funds	(800) 282-0106 (FL)	(800) 237-0738
T. Rowe Price International[1]	(301) 547-2308	(800) 638-5660
United International Growth	(800) 892-5811 (MO)	(800) 821-5664
Vanguard World Fund[1]	(215) 648-6000 (PA)	(800) 662-7447

[1] no-load

Regional Funds	Telephone in State	Out-of-State
Alliance Canadian	(800) 221-5672 (NY)	(800) 221-5672
Fidelity Europe[2]	(617) 523-1919	(800) 544-6666
Fidelity Pacific Basin[2]	(617) 523-1919	
GT Pacific	(800) 824-8361	(800) 824-1580
Merrill Lynch Pacific	(212) 692-2049	(212) 692-2049
Japan Fund (Closed end, NYSE)	(800) 225-2470	(800) 225-2470
Korean Fund	(Closed end, NYSE)	
Mexico Fund	(Closed end, NYSE)	
Nomura Pacific Basin[1]	(800) 833-0018	(800) 833-0018
Taiwan	(Closed end, AMEX)	

[1] no-load
[2] low-load

Selected Mutual Funds Investing in Gold and Precious Metals

Fidelity Select Precious Metals[2]
Fidelity Distributors Corp.
82 Devonshire Street
Boston, MA 02109
Telephone: (800) 544-6666
(617) 523-1919

Financial Programs—Gold[2]
Financial Programs, Inc.
P.O. Box 2040
Denver, CO 80201
Telephone: (800) 525-8085
(303) 779-1233 (CO)

Franklin Gold Fund[2]
Franklin Distributors, Inc.
777 Mariner's Island Boulevard
San Mateo, CA 94404
Telephone: (800) 632-2350

Gold Investors Ltd[1]
Bull & Bear Service Center, Inc.
11 Hanover Square
New York, NY 10005
Telephone: (800) 847-4200
(212) 363-1100

Keystone Precious Metals Holdings[2]
Keystone Distributors, Inc.
99 High Street
Boston MA 02110
Telephone: (800) 633-4900
(617) 338-3400

Lexington Goldfund[1]
Lexington Management Corp.
P.O. Box 1515
Saddlebrook, NJ 07662
Telephone: (800) 526-0056/7
(201) 845-7300

Strategic Investments
Strategic Distributors, Inc.
2030 Royal Lane
Dallas, TX 75229
Telephone: (800) 527-5027
(214) 484-1326

USSA Gold Fund
USSA Investment Management Co.
USSA Building
San Antonio, TX 78288
Telephone: (800) 531-8000
(512) 498-8000

United Services Gold Shares[1]
United Services Funds, Inc.
P.O. Box 29467
San Antonio, TX 78229
Telephone: (800) 824-4653
(512) 696-1234

Vanguard Gold and Precious Metals[2]
Vanguard Group, Inc.
P.O. Box 2600
Valley Forge, PA 19496
Telephone: (800) 662-SHIP

[1] No-load fund
[2] Low-load fund

Selected No Load/Low Load Mutual Fund Families with Switching Privileges

No load funds do not charge an initial sales fee while low load funds apply an initial sales fee of 1% to 3%. In comparison load funds charge a sales fee of about 8½%. With no load funds all of your investment is put to work immediately. The performance of no load funds is comparable to that of load funds.

The fund families listed below permit switching (exchanges) between other members of the fund family (including money market funds). Thus, investors who expect a marked decline have the option of switching into a money market fund while investors who expect a bull market may choose to switch into a growth oriented fund. Switching may be done by mail or by phone. For income tax purposes any exchange of shares is treated both as a new purchase and a new sale.

Since the performance of funds is quite variable, it is probably best for investors to diversify among three or four fund families.

Investors should study the fund prospectus carefully prior to investing, paying particular attention to average rates of return over the last five and ten year periods, and to risk level (fluctuations in the net asset value). Investors should also familiarize themselves with the switching procedures and restrictions; some funds charge per switch and limit the number of switches per year, others do not. The information can be obtained by phoning the fund.

Fund objectives vary and it is important to select the fund with objectives similar to yours. A detailed listing of funds by objective, performance record, and much more is given in Donoghues's *Mutual Fund Almanac* (Box 540, Holliston, MA 01746).

American Funds Distributors, Inc.
333 S. Hope Street
Los Angeles, CA 90071
(800) 421-9900
(213) 486-9651

Bull & Bear Management Corporation
11 Hanover Square
New York, NY 10005
(800) 847-4200
(212) 363-1100

Columbia Management Company
P.O. Box 1350
Portland, OR 97207
(800) 547-1037
(503) 222-3600

Dean Witter Reynolds
One World Trade Center
New York, NY 10048
(800) 221-2685
(212) 938-4553

Dreyfus Service Corporation
666 Old Country Road
Garden City, NY 11530
(718) 895-1206 (general information)
(800) 242-8671

Fidelity Investments Corporation
82 Devonshire Street
Boston, MA 02109
(800) 544-6666
(617) 523-1919

Financial Programs Inc.
P.O. Box 2040
Denver, CO 80201
(800) 525-9831
(303) 779-1233 (Denver)
(800) 332-9145 (Colorado)

Jones and Babson, Inc.
2440 Pershing Road
Kansas City, MO 64108
(800) 821-5591
(816) 471-5200

Kemper Financial Services, Inc.
120 South LaSalle Street
Chicago, IL 60603
(800) 621-1048
(312) 781-1121

Lehman Management Co.
55 Water Street
New York, NY 10041
(800) 221-5350
(212) 668-4308

Lexington Management Corp.
P.O. Box 1515
Saddle Brook, NJ 07662
(800) 526-0056/7

Neuberger & Berman Management Inc.
342 Madison Avenue
New York, NY 10017
(800) 367-0776
(212) 850-8300

Prudential-Bache Securities Inc.
One Seaport Plaza
New York, NY 10292
(800) 872-7787

Putnam Financial Services, Inc.
One Post Office Square
Boston, MA 02109
(800) 225-1581
(617) 292-1470

Scudder Fund Distributors, Inc.
175 Federal Street
Boston, MA 02110
(800) 225-2470
(617) 426-8300

Shearson Lehman Brothers, Inc.
Two World Trade Center
New York, NY 10048
(212) 825-3890

Stein Roe & Farnham Inc.
P.O. Box 1131
Chicago, IL 60690
(800) 621-0320
(312) 368-7700

T. Rowe Price Investor Services, Inc.
100 E. Pratt Street
Baltimore, MD 21202
(800) 638-5660
(301) 547-2008

Twentieth Century Investors, Inc.
P.O. Box 419200
Kansas City, MO 64112
(800) 345-2021
(816) 531-5575

USAA Investment Management Co.
USAA Buildup
San Antonio, TX 78288
(800) 531-8000
(512) 498-8000

Value Line Securities, Inc.
711 Third Avenue
New York, NY 10017
(800) 223-0818
(212) 687-3965

Vanguard Group, Inc.
P.O. Box 2600
Valley Forge, PA 19496
(800) 662-SHIP
(800) 662-2739

Foreign Securities Investments

This section provides data on the performance of major foreign securities markets and also listings of foreign stocks traded on the New York and American Exchanges. Over 200 foreign stocks and ADRs are also traded on the Over-The-Counter (OTC) market. A complete listing of foreign OTC stocks is available from the National Association of Securities Dealers, 1735 K Street, Washington, DC 20006.

Foreign securities not traded on the above exchanges may generally be purchased through stock brokers or major foreign banks in the country of interest. Most of these banks, which have U.S. branches in New York and other major cities, provide details concerning opening a foreign brokerage account.

A difficulty associated with foreign stock selection is that of obtaining timely information. The following general information sources may be helpful in this regard.

The Wall Street Journal
The Asian Wall Street Journal
Dow Jones & Company
22 Cortlandt Street
New York, NY 10007

The Asian Wall Street Journal, a weekly, is particularly helpful for the Asian region, including stock market coverage.

Barron's
World Financial Center
200 Liberty Street
New York, NY 10281

The weekly *International Trader* section is of special interest.

Capital International Perspectives
3 Place Des Bergues
1201 Geneva, Switzerland

Capital International Perspectives is a leading monthly publication dealing with international investments.

The Financial Times
Bracken House
10 Cannon Street
London EC4P 4BY, England

The Financial Times provides comprehensive coverage of European businesses and securities markets and is published daily.

Moody's Investor Services, International Manual
Moody's Investor Services
99 Church Street
New York, NY 10007

The International Manual provides financial information on about 3,000 major foreign corporations.

Disclosure
5161 River Road
Bethesda, MD 20816

This service also provides annual reports and filings on foreign firms.

A listing of mutual funds investing in foreign securities is given on page 365.

RETURN ON WORLD STOCK MARKETS (as of end March 1988)

	Market Value	Return in each Currency %				Currency Valuation %				Return in U. S. Dollars %				β
	Billion Dollars	3m	1yr	5yr	σⒶ	3m	1yr	5yr	σⒷ	3m	1yr	5yr	σⒸ	
New York	2327.4	4.8	-11.2	11.1	5.2	0.0	0.0	0.0	0.0	4.8	-11.2	11.1	5.2	0.98
Tokyo	3503.8	24.5	14.8	28.3	5.2	-2.7	20.5	14.0	3.4	21.1	38.4	46.2	6.4	1.09
London	656.1	1.0	-12.1	16.2	6.1	-0.1	17.3	4.9	4.0	0.9	3.1	21.9	7.0	1.16
Toronto	215.4	4.9	-11.4	9.0	4.9	5.2	5.7	0.0	1.2	10.3	-6.3	9.0	5.4	0.88
Frankfurt	216.0	6.0	-22.6	8.7	6.8	-5.3	9.1	7.9	3.9	0.4	-15.6	17.3	7.4	0.90
Sydney	88.5	9.9	-16.2	22.5	7.8	2.6	5.1	-3.0	3.7	12.8	-11.9	18.8	9.5	1.03
Paris	148.6	2.9	-34.0	18.8	6.9	-5.3	7.1	5.3	3.6	-2.5	-29.3	25.1	7.6	1.16
Zurich	137.5	7.7	-13.2	10.2	5.5	-7.1	10.5	8.8	4.2	0.1	-4.1	19.9	5.9	0.91
Hong Kong	61.1	10.5	-6.3	20.6	10.0	-0.5	0.1	-2.9	1.3	10.0	-6.2	17.1	10.5	0.81
Milano	119.6	5.1	-27.8	19.2	8.5	-5.6	4.9	3.3	3.5	-0.8	-24.3	23.1	8.7	0.92
Amsterdam	85.9	24.7	-20.9	13.0	6.6	-5.1	9.7	8.0	3.9	18.4	-13.2	22.0	6.8	0.92
Singapore	37.0	12.4	-12.4	1.3	8.3	-0.5	6.7	0.8	1.3	11.9	-6.5	2.2	8.3	0.88
Total	**7597.4**									**11.9**	**11.3**	**26.2**	**4.4**	

Source: *Tokyo Stock Market Quarterly Review,* 1988 Vol. 2. March 31, 1988. A publication of Daiwa Securities Co. Ltd. Available through Daiwa Securities America, Inc. One World Financial Center, New York, NY 10281.

NOTES

Market Value Estimate for the end of March, 1988.

Return in each currency Return derived solely based upon each market's Stock Price Index (dividends are not included) for the periods ending on the last trading date of the latest quarter. Five-years data are shown in the annual compound rate. Stock price indices referred to are; S & P500, TOPIX, FT industrial, Toronto composite, Commerzbank general index, Sydney Stock Exchange all ordinaries, CAC industrial, Swiss Bank Corporation general index, Hang Seng Bank index, Banca Commerciale Italiana index, ANP-CBS industrial, and Straits Times industrial.

Currency valuation Rate of change of each currency's value in U.S. dollar terms (NY market) for the corresponding periods. Five-years data are shown in the annual compound rate.

Return in U.S. Dollar Return of each market in U.S. $ terms. Five-years data are shown in the annual compound rate.

PERFORMANCES OF FOREIGN SECURITIES MARKETS

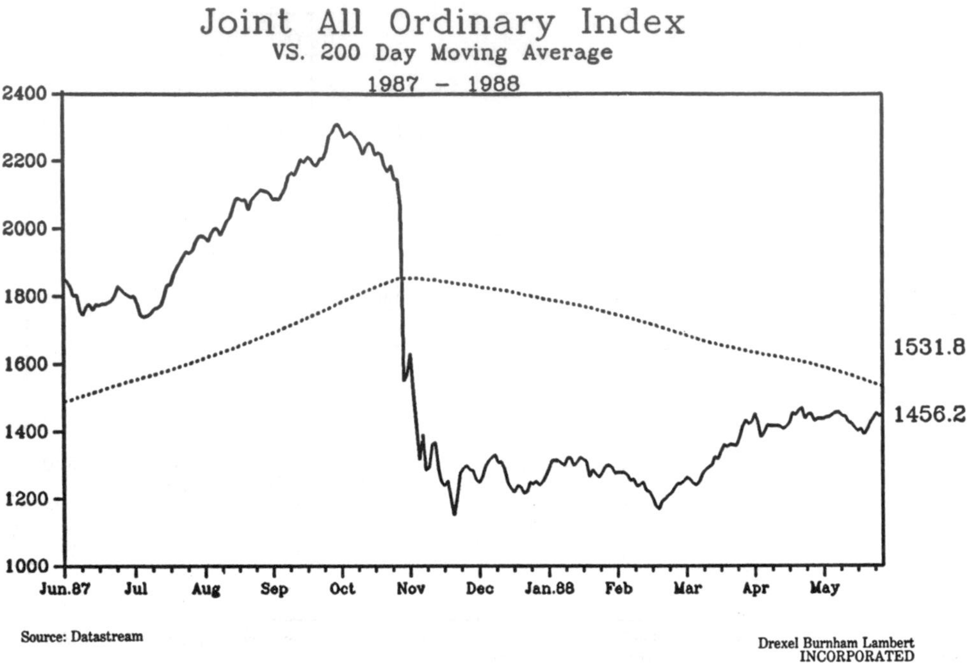

CANADA

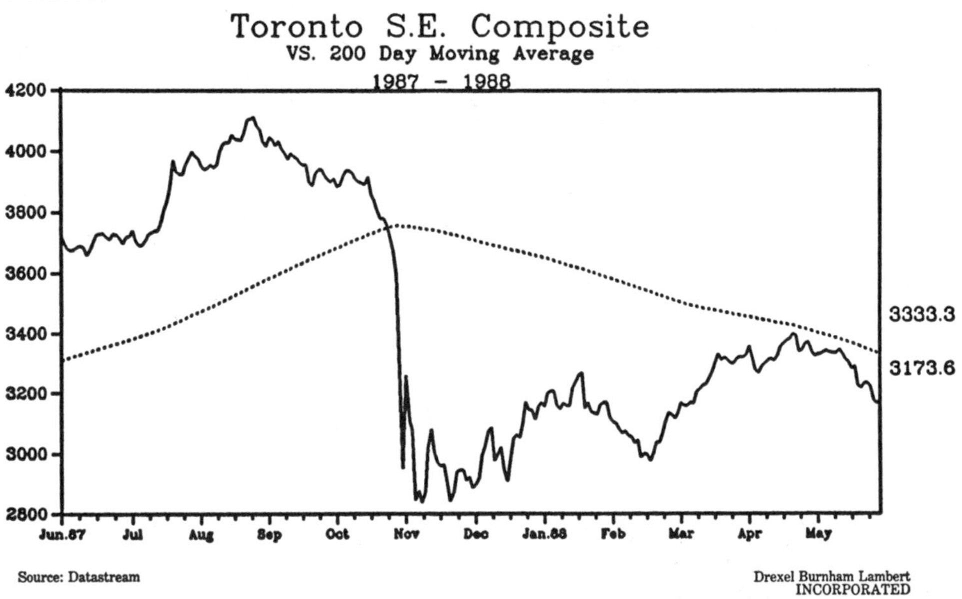

Source: *International Investment Monthly*, Drexel Burnham Lambert Incorporated, International Research Department.

PERFORMANCES OF FOREIGN SECURITIES MARKETS *(continued)*

FRANCE

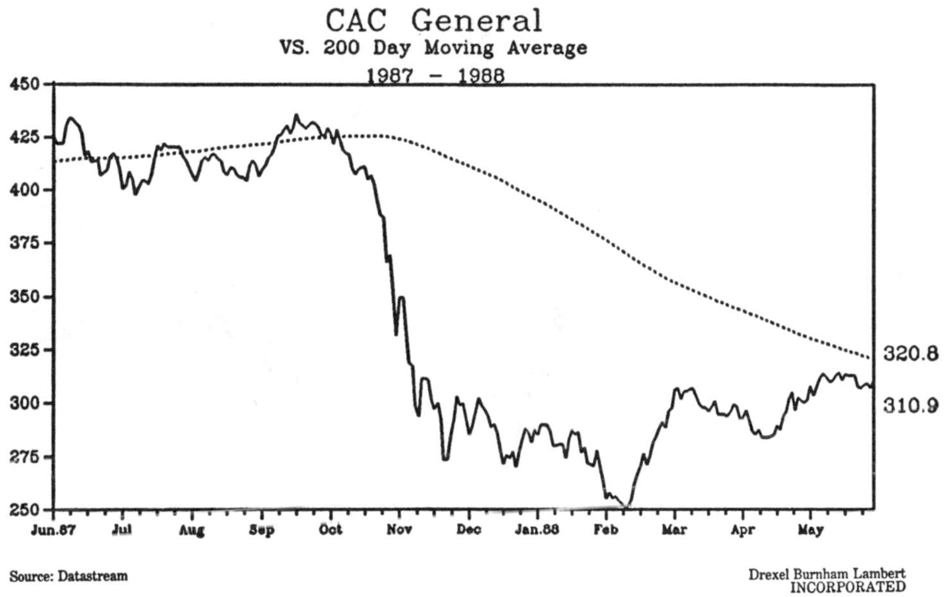

GERMANY

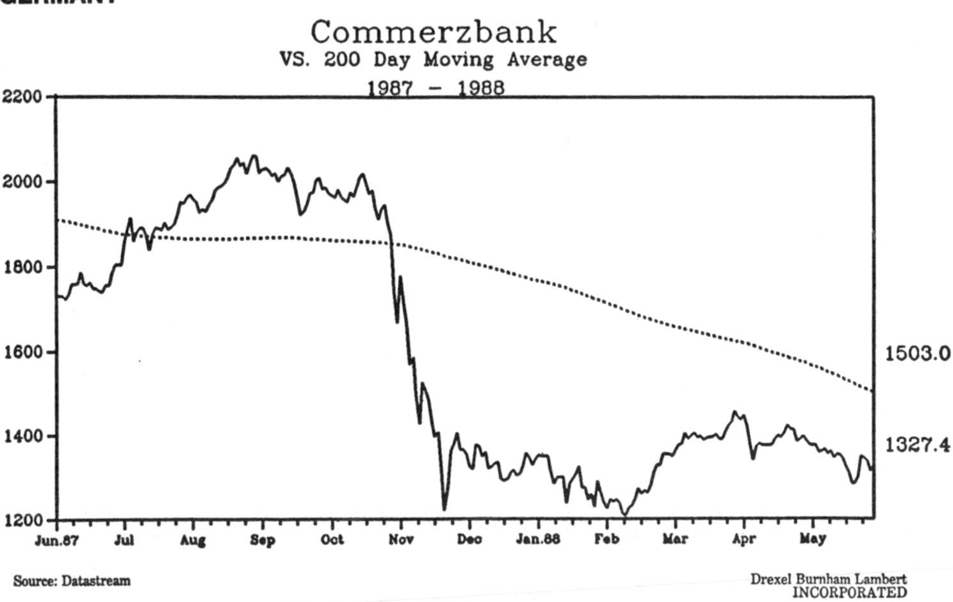

PERFORMANCES OF FOREIGN SECURITIES MARKETS *(continued)*

HOLLAND

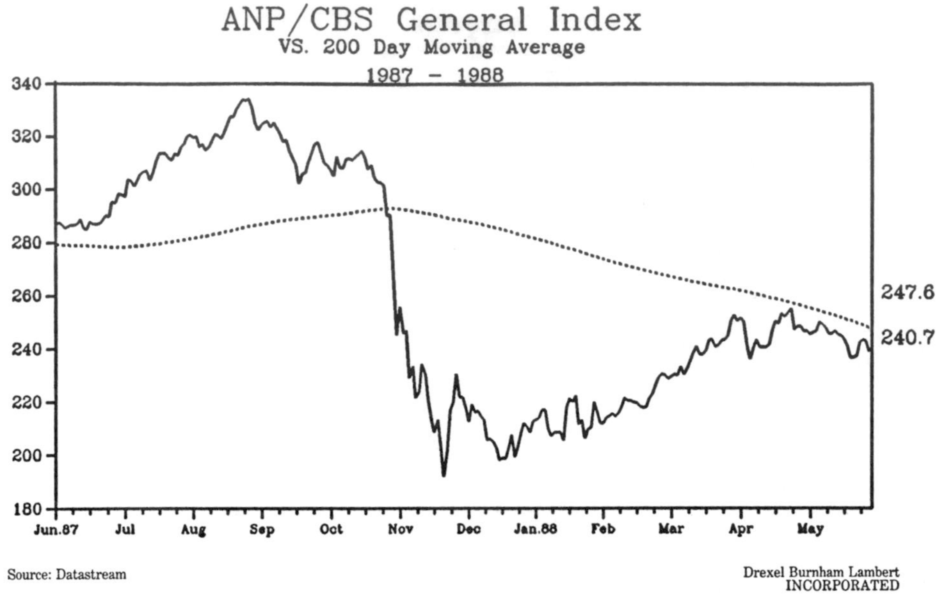

HONG KONG

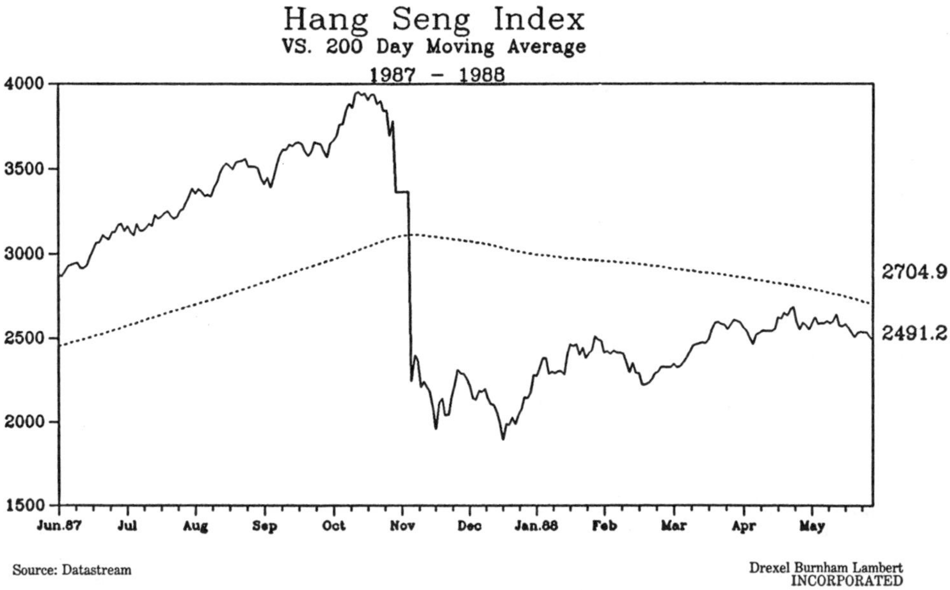

PERFORMANCES OF FOREIGN SECURITIES MARKETS *(continued)*

ITALY

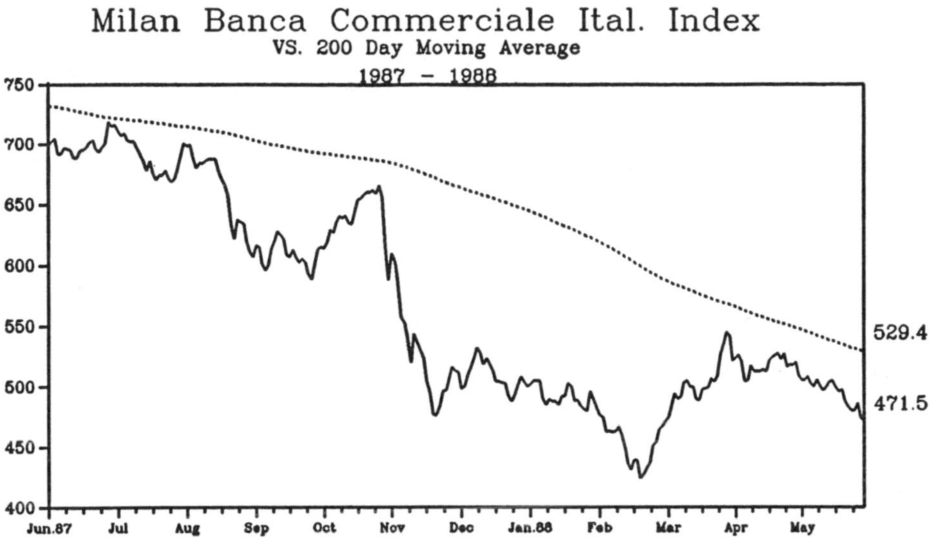

Source: Datastream

Drexel Burnham Lambert INCORPORATED

JAPAN

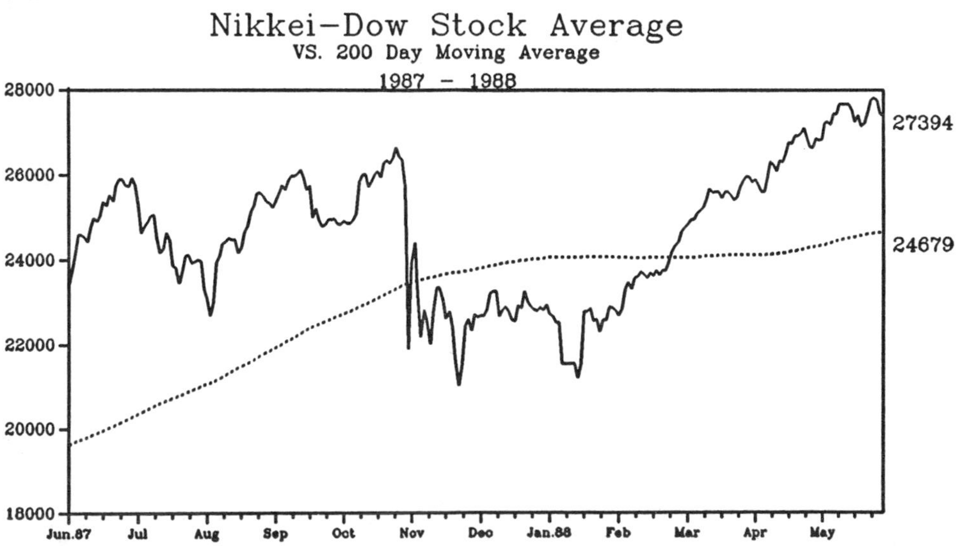

Source: Datastream

Drexel Burnham Lambert INCORPORATED

PERFORMANCES OF FOREIGN SECURITIES MARKETS *(continued)*

SINGAPORE

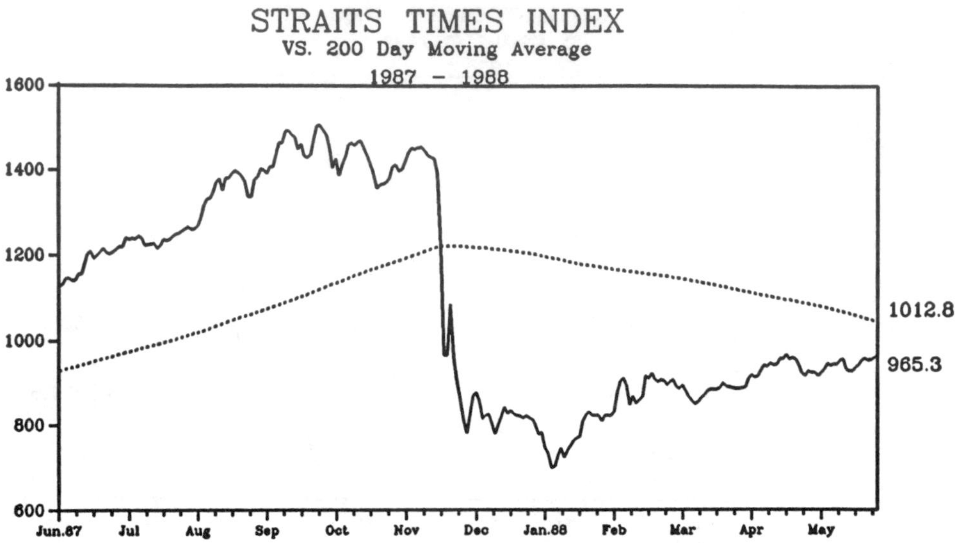

Source: Datastream

Drexel Burnham Lambert INCORPORATED

SWITZERLAND

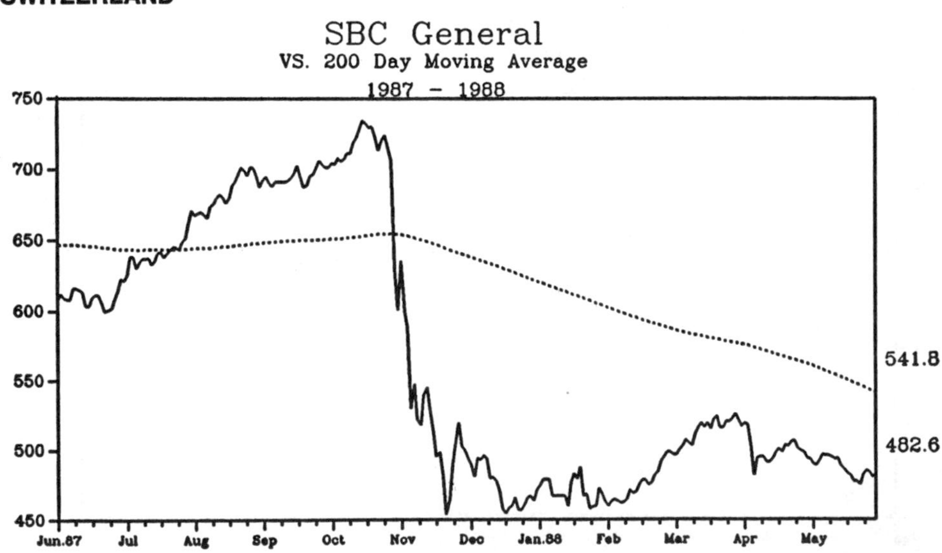

Source: Datastream

Drexel Burnham Lambert INCORPORATED

PERFORMANCES OF FOREIGN SECURITIES MARKETS
(concluded)

UNITED KINGDOM

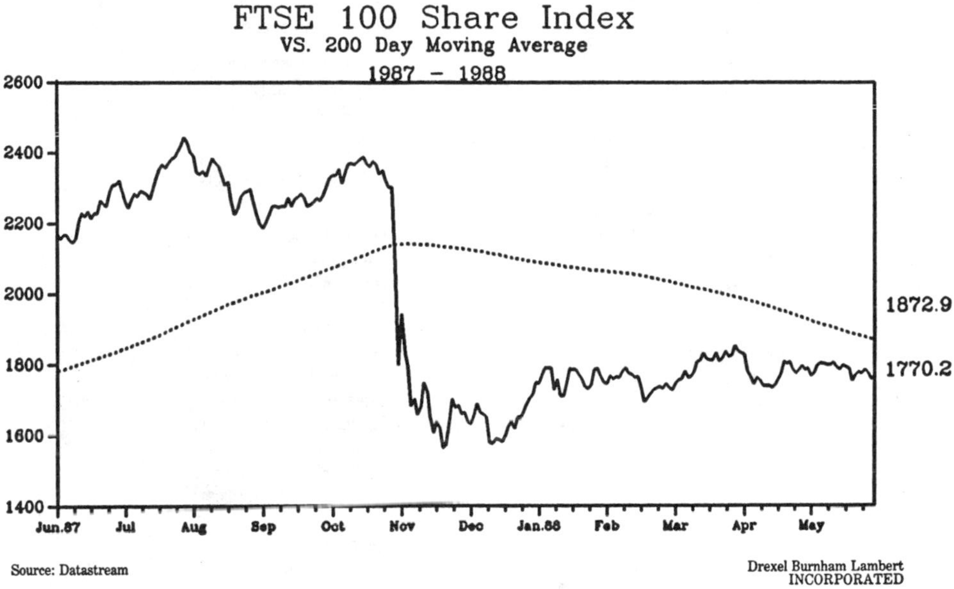

Source: *International Investment Monthly*, Drexel Burnham Lambert Incorporated, International Research Department.

Foreign Stocks Listed on the New York Stock Exchange, December 31, 1987

Country	Company	Industry
Australia	Broken Hill Proprietary Co. Ltd.*	Petroleum; minerals; steel
	News Corporation Ltd*	Publishing; broadcasting
British W.I.	Club Med, Inc.	Hotel, resort operator
Canada	Abitibi-Price Inc.	Newsprint, uncoated papers
	Alcan-Aluminium Ltd.	Aluminum producer
	AMCA International Limited	Industrial prods.; construct. services
	American Barrick Resources Corporation	Gold mining
	Bell Canada Enterprises Inc.	Holding co. - telecommunications services
	Campbell Resources Inc.	Holding co. - diversified natural resources
	Canadian Pacific Limited	Transportation; telecom.; oil; mining
	Cineplex Odeon Corporation	Motion pictures theatres operator
	Domtar Inc.	Pulp, paper, packaging; construction prods.
	Inco Ltd.	Nickel, copper producer
	LAC Minerals Ltd.	Gold mining
	McIntyre Mines Ltd.	Coal mining
	Mitel Corporation	Telecommunications equip. manufacturer
	Moore Corporation Ltd.	Business forms manufacturer
	Northern Telecom Ltd.	Telecommunications equip. manufacturer
	Northgate Exploration Limited	Holding co. - metal producer
	Placer Dome Inc.	Gold, silver, copper mining
	Ranger Oil Limited	Oil & gas exploration, production
	Seagram Co. Ltd.	Distilled spirits producer
	TransCanada PipeLines Ltd.	Natural gas transmission
	Varity Corporation (2 issues)	Farm equipment producer
	Westcoast Transmission Co., Ltd.	Natural gas distributor
Denmark	Novo Industri A/S*	Industrial enzymes; pharmaceuticals
England	Barclays PLC*	Holding company - bank
	BET Public Limited Company*	Industrial; transport.; construction servs.
	British Airways Plc*	Passenger airline
	British Gas PLC*	Natural gas distributor
	British Petroleum Company Ltd.* (2 issues)	Holding co. - integrated int'l oil co.
	British Telecommunications PLC*	Telecommunications services & products
	Dee Corporation plc*	Food; sporting goods retailer
	Dixons Group plc*	Consumer electronics, appliances retailer
	Glaxo Holdings p.l.c.*	Pharmaceuticals
	Hanson Trust PLC*	Consumer goods; building products
	Imperial Chemical Industries PLC*	Diversified chemical producer
	National Westminster Bank PLC*	Holding company - bank
	Plessey Company Ltd.*	Telecommunications & electronic equipment
	Saatchi & Saatchi Company PLC*	Advertising; consulting
	"Shell" Transport and Trading Co., PLC*	Holding co., - integrated int'l oil co.
	Tricentrol PLC*	Oil & gas production, oil trading
	Unilever PLC*	Holding co. - branded foods
Hong Kong	Universal Matchbox Group Ltd. Inc.	Designs and manufactures toys
Israel	Elscint Ltd.	Diagnostic medical imaging equipment
Italy	Montedison S.p.A.* (2 issues)	Diversified chemicals
Japan	Hitachi, Ltd.*	Electronic eq.; machinery; consumer products
	Honda Motor Co., Ltd.*	Motor vehicle manufacturer
	Kubota, Ltd.*	Agricultural equipment; pipe manufacturer
	Kyocera Corp.*	Ceramic products; electronic equipment
	Matsushita Electric Industrial Co., Ltd.*	Consumer electronic manufacturer
	Pioneer Electronic Corporation*	Consumer electronic manufacturer
	Sony Corporation*	Consumer electronic manufacturer
	TDK Corporation*	Electronic comp.; magnetic tape producer

Source: New York Stock Exchange *1988 Fact Book.*

Foreign Stocks listed on the New York Stock Exchange *(concluded)*

Country	Company	Industry
Netherlands	**Ausimont N.V.**	Chemicals
	KLM Royal Dutch Airlines**	Air transportation
	Philips N.V.**	Electronics, appliances; professional prods.
	Royal Dutch Petroleum Co.**	Holding co. - integrated int'l oil co.
	Unilever N.V.**	Holding co. - branded foods
Netherlands Antilles	**Erbamont N.V.**	Pharmaceuticals
	Schlumberger Limited	Oilfield services; electronics
Norway	**Norsk Hydro a.s.***	Agriculture; oil & gas
Philippines	**Benguet Corporation**	Mining; industrial construction
South Africa	**ASA Limited**	Closed-end inv. co. - gold mining
Spain	**Banco Central, S.A.***	Holding company - bank
	Banco de Santander, Sociedad Anonima de Credito*	Banking, financial services
	Compania Telefonica Nacional de Espana, S.A.*	Telephone service - Spain

*American depository receipts/shares.
**N.Y. shares and/or guilder shares.

Tokyo Stock Price Index (TOPIX)

(Jan.4,1968=100)

	Year-end	High		Low	
		Index	Date	Index	Date
1949	12.85	22.06	May 16	11.95	Dec. 14
1950	11.57	13.24	Aug. 21	9.59	July 3
1951	16.94	17.11	Oct. 20	11.58	Jan. 4
1952	33.35	33.55	Nov. 22	17.07	Jan. 8
1953	33.30	42.18	Feb. 4	28.46	Apr. 1
1954	30.27	33.22	Jan. 11	26.79	Nov. 13
1955	39.06	39.06	Dec. 28	30.00	Mar. 28
1956	51.21	52.95	Dec. 6	38.81	Jan. 25
1957	43.40	54.82	Jan. 21	43.18	Dec. 27
1958	60.95	60.95	Dec. 27	43.48	Jan. 4
1959	80.00	90.14	Nov. 30	61.11	Jan. 9
1960	109.18	112.53	Nov. 15	79.46	Jan. 4
1961	101.66	126.59	July 14	90.86	Dec. 19
1962	99.67	111.45	Feb. 14	83.39	Oct. 30
1963	92.87	122.96	May 10	91.21	Dec. 18
1964	90.68	103.77	July 3	87.94	Nov. 11
1965	105.68	105.68	Dec. 28	81.29	July 15
1966	111.41	114.51	Mar. 24	105.21	Jan. 19
1967	100.89	117.60	May 31	99.17	Dec. 11
1968	131.31	142.95	Oct. 2	100.00	Jan. 4
1969	179.30	179.30	Dec. 27	132.62	Jan. 4
1970	148.35	185.70	Apr. 8	147.08	Dec. 9
1971	199.45	209.00	Aug. 14	148.05	Jan. 6
1972	401.70	401.70	Dec. 28	199.93	Jan. 4
1973	306.44	422.48	Jan. 24	284.69	Dec. 18
1974	278.34	342.47	June 5	251.96	Oct. 9
1975	323.43	333.11	July 2	268.24	Jan. 10
1976	383.88	383.88	Dec. 28	326.28	Jan. 5
1977	364.08	390.93	Sept. 29	350.49	Nov. 24
1978	449.55	452.60	Dec. 13	364.04	Jan. 4
1979	459.61	465.24	Sept. 29	435.13	July 13
1980	494.10	497.96	Oct. 20	449.01	Mar. 10
1981	570.31	603.92	Aug. 17	495.79	Jan. 5
1982	593.72	593.72	Dec. 28	511.52	Aug. 17
1983	731.82	731.82	Dec. 28	574.51	Jan. 25
1984	913.37	913.37	Dec. 28	735.45	Jan. 4
1985	1,049.40	1,058.35	July 27	916.93	Jan. 4
1986	1,556.37	1,583.35	Aug. 20	1,025.85	Jan. 21
1987	1,725.83	2,258.56	June 11	1,557.46	Jan. 13

Source: *Tokyo Stock Exchange Fact Book 1988,* International Department, Tokyo Stock Exchange, Tokyo, Japan.

Tokyo Exchange: Stock Yields and Dividends

	All 1st Section Stocks	1st Section Dividend-Paying Stocks		
	Weighted Average Yields (%)	Average Dividend per Share (¥)	Total Amount of Dividends (¥ mil.)	Simple Average Yields (%)
1949	...	6.09	1,869	6.77
1950	...	6.97	11,525	9.53
1951	...	10.69	28,264	11.91
1952	...	12.88	41,311	9.85
1953	...	11.17	52,414	7.44
1954	...	9.89	60,499	9.44
1955	...	8.70	69,734	7.96
1956	...	8.27	85,109	6.68
1957	...	7.71	113,006	7.14
1958	...	7.14	122,938	6.66
1959	4.68	6.76	138,102	4.54
1960	4.27	6.71	174,225	3.93
1961	4.47	6.63	230,781	3.24
1962	5.82	6.47	307,253	3.86
1963	5.08	6.26	348,900	4.24
1964	6.01	6.26	391,501	5.69
1965	6.01	6.08	409,041	5.92
1966	4.76	5.92	407,890	4.44
1967	4.96	5.97	456,892	4.74
1968	5.00	6.09	506,603	4.36
1969	4.19	6.28	569,413	3.34
1970	4.30	6.55	647,271	3.47
1971	4.01	6.65	710,819	3.41
1972	2.42	6.55	717,714	2.24
1973	2.02	6.75	849,748	2.09
1974	2.55	6.88	912,452	2.53
1975	2.54	6.51	881,019	2.31
1976	2.27	6.25	995,343	1.91
1977	2.16	6.34	1,040,454	1.82
1978	2.00	6.45	1,090,007	1.60
1979	1.87	6.49	1,191,842	1.57
1980	1.79	6.58	1,200,537	1.63
1981	1.65	6.69	1,498,879	1.55
1982	1.80	6.80	1,525,765	1.68
1983	1.55	6.88	1,594,659	1.39
1984	1.24	7.11	1,709,559	1.09
1985	1.05	7.25	1,829,277	0.99
1986	0.83	7.33	1,850,248	0.78
1987	0.56	7.36	2,042,359	0.63

Source: *Tokyo Stock Exchange Fact Book 1988,* International Department, Tokyo Stock Exchange, Tokyo, Japan.

The International Stock Exchange (UK): Price/Volume Shares

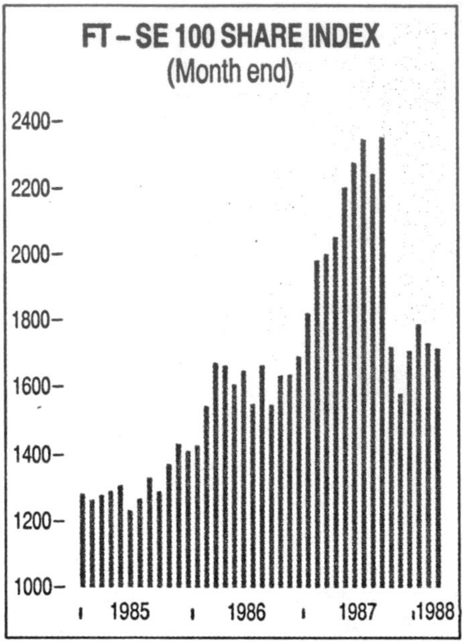

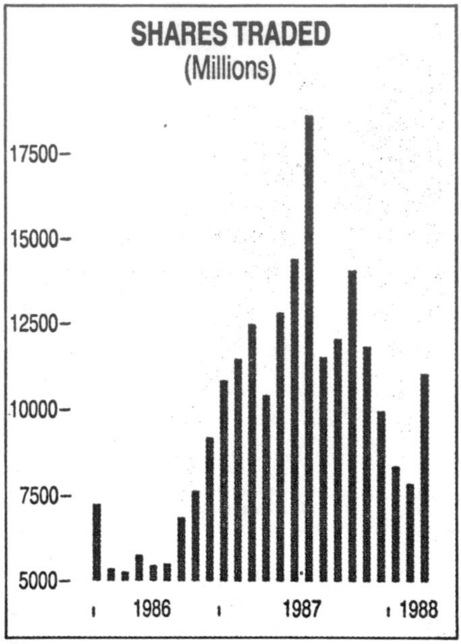

Source: *The International Stock Exchange Report and Accounts, 1988.* The International Stock Exchange of the United Kingdom and the Republic of Ireland Limited. The Stock Exchange, London, England.

The International Stock Exchange (UK): Classification of Shares

Full Listing

The Listed market is the principal and oldest market for domestic equities. It exists for well-established companies which must comply with stringent criteria relating to all aspects of their operations. They must submit themselves to extensive scrutiny and undertake to keep both actual and potential shareholders properly informed about the company's progress and prospects. They require at least 5 years trading record, and a minimum of 25% of their shares must be in public hands.

There are over 2000 Listed British companies.

The Unlisted Securities Market

Companies are required to provide a 3 year trading history and a minimum of 10% of their shares must be in public hands after flotation.

Disclosure requirements are less stringent than is the case of the List and the costs of joining the market are considerably lower. Over 550 companies have made use of the USM. The equities of some 400 are trading at present. The very large majority of the balance have transferred to the List or been acquired by other companies.

The Third Market

Smaller companies with short, or even no, trading record, and those without a broad spread of shareholders may obtain access to equity capital and effective regulation on the Third Market. It also caters for certain stocks previously traded off-market.

By means of these complementary subdivisions of the UK equity market, the facilities of the Exchange are offered to the greatest possible range of companies, while investors can, at a glance, appreciate the minimum level of experience of the company and the disclosure which it has made, and hence the likely risk inherent in making the investment.

Alpha, Beta, Gamma or Delta?

Whether a security is Listed or traded on the USM or Third Market, it is accorded a further classification according to the level of investor interest in the stock and hence the level of information which is required to be displayed on the SEAQ* system to serve the needs of the market. This classification is not a reflection of the quality of the company as an enterprise or as an investment, but simply the degree of interest it arouses among investors. As investor interest changes, so securities' SEAQ classifications may change.

ALPHA securities are the largest and most liquid stocks in the market. Many market makers are prepared to make markets in these stocks, which have high market capitalisation.

All the stocks in the Financial Times-Stock Exchange 100 Share Index are classified as alpha securities, as are an increasing number of UK shares with an international following.

Prices shown on SEAQ in these securities are firm in the size displayed to all other Member Firms. Transactions are reported to the Exchange within five minutes of their taking place and details are displayed both on a real-time basis on TOPIC and the next day in the Exchange's Daily Official List under the heading "Business Done."

BETA securities are not as highly capitalised as alphas but are still actively traded. They have fewer market makers. The price display and trade reporting obligations for Member Firms are the same as for alpha securities but trade details are not published in real-time on SEAQ. They are, however, shown the next day in the Daily Official List. There are some 550 beta securities.

GAMMA securities are those of smaller companies. They are less actively traded stocks in which fewer firms have registered to make markets. Prices on SEAQ may be firm *or* indicative. The market makers indicate their intentions in this respect on the screen display. There are 1500 gamma stocks. Most Third Market stocks fall into this category.

DELTA securities are largely illiquid stocks with very few market makers. An index is maintained on TOPIC to allow firms to identify market makers prepared to deal in them, and indicative mid-prices are displayed.

Which Sector?

Professional and personal investors alike need to balance their portfolios on the basis of sector analysis—the areas of business of the companies whose securities they hold. To assist in this, companies in the UK equity market are classified in newspapers and other publications according to the FT Actuaries Investment Index. The groupings are as follows:

THE FINANCIAL TIMES ACTUARIES INVESTMENT INDEX

CAPITAL GOODS	Building Materials	OTHER GROUPS	Agencies
	Contracting & Construction		Chemicals
	Electricals		Conglomerates
	Electronics		Shipping & Transport
	Mechanical Engineering		Telephone Networks
	Metals & Metal Forming		Miscellaneous
	Motors		
	Other Industrial Materials	OIL & GAS	
		FINANCIAL GROUP	Banks
			Insurance (Life)
CONSUMER GROUP	Brewers & Distillers		Insurance (Composite)
	Food Manufacturing		Insurance (Brokers)
	Food Retailing		Merchant Banks
	Health & Household Products		Property
	Leisure		Other Financial
	Packaging & Paper		
	Publishing & Printing	INVESTMENT TRUSTS	
	Stores	MINING FINANCE	
	Textiles	OVERSEAS TRADERS	

* The Stock Exchange Automated Quotations (SEAQ) system is an electronic information system at the centre of the Exchange's collection and display of equity market trading information for its UK Equity and International Equity Markets.

Source: *The UK Equity Market*, The International Stock Exchange of the United Kingdom and the Republic of Ireland Limited, The Stock Exchange, London, England.

STOCK EXCHANGES IN THE WORLD: Market Size

(During or End of 1986)

Stock Exchange			Tokyo	New York	Toronto	U.K.	Frankfurt	Paris	Zurich
No. of Stock-Listed Companies		[Domestic]	1,499	1,516	1,034	2,101	223	482	145
		[Foreign]	52	59	51	584	181	195	194
No. of Listed Issues	[Stocks]	[Domestic]	1,504	2,194	1,514	1,781	261	552	254
		[Foreign]	52	63	56	490	192	248	200
	[Bonds]	[Domestic]	742	3,384	—	2,917	5,293	2,195	1,425
		[Foreign]	231	222	—	1,556	692	191	870
Total Market Value ($ mil.)		[Stocks]	1,794,290	2,128,511	185,254	471,575	233,918	153,304	128,926
		[Bonds]	772,062	1,457,603	—	436,875	N.A.	289,571	118,947
Trading Value ($ mil.)		[Stocks]	955,305	1,374,350	45,816	133,244	65,098	55,470	310,129
		[Bonds]	821,352	10,464	—	286,103	81,693	241,488	
No. of Member Firms			93	611	72	357	107	45	25

Stock Exchange			Amsterdam	Milan	Australia	Hong Kong	Singapore	Taiwan	Korea
No. of Stock-Listed Companies		[Domestic]	267	184	1,363	247	122	130	355
		[Foreign]	242	—	25	6	195	—	—
No. of Listed Issues	[Stocks]	[Domestic]	272	286	2,137	261	123	133	485
		[Foreign]	300	—	45	6	199	—	—
	[Bonds]	[Domestic]	1,254	1,214	2,205	5	23	125	4,408
		[Foreign]	163	25	—	2	116	—	—
Total Market Value ($ mil.)		[Stocks]	83,786	140,241	122,090	53,844	16,582	15,501	13,924
		[Bonds]	103,689	274,252	30,097	450	83,646	13,493	19,866
Trading Value ($ mil.)		[Stocks]	30,312	44,715	40,603	15,300	3,670	19,097	10,889
		[Bonds]	21,215	4,487	35,138	44	43	20	3,593
No. of Member Firms			149	108	113	839	28	38	25

Source: *Tokyo Stock Exchange Fact Book 1988*, International Department, Tokyo Stock Exchange, Tokyo, Japan.

Securities Markets: Notable Dates

1792 Original brokers' agreement subscribed to by 24 brokers (May 17).

1817 Constitution and the name "New York Stock Exchange Board" adopted (March 8).

1830 Dullest day in history of exchange—31 shares traded (March 16).

1840s Outdoor trading in unlisted securities begins at Wall and Hanover Streets, moves to Wall and Broad, then shifts south along Broad Street.*

1863 Name changed to "New York Stock Exchange" (NYSE) (January 29).

1867 Stock tickers first introduced (November 15).

1868 Membership made salable (October 23).

1869 Gold speculation resulted in "Black Friday" (September 24).

1871 Continuous markets in stocks established.

1873 NYSE closed September 18–29.
Failure of Jay Cooke & Co. and others (September 18).

---

* Refers to American Exchange (AMEX).

† Applies to both the New York Stock Exchange and the American Exchange.

Sources: New York Stock Exchange *1988 Fact Book* and American Stock Exchange *Data Book* and *The Wall Street Journal*

Trading hours set at 10 A.M. to 3 P.M.; Saturdays, 10 A.M. to noon (December 1).
1878 First telephones introduced in the exchange (November 13).
1881 Annunciator board installed for paging members (January 29).
1885 Unlisted Securities Department established (March 25).
1886 First million-share day—1,200,000 shares traded (December 15).
1908 E. S. Mendels forms New York Curb Agency in first departure from informal trading.*
1910 Unlisted Securities Department abolished (March 31).
1911 Trading rules established with formation of New York Curb Market Association.*
1914 Exchange closed from July 31 through December 11—World War I.
1915 Stock prices quoted in dollars as against percent of par value (October 13).
1919 Separate ticker system installed for bonds (January 2).
1920 Stock Clearing Corporation established (April 26).
1921 New York Curb Market association moves indoors at 86 Trinity Place; name shortened to New York Curb Market and ticker service initiated (June 21).*
1927 Start of ten-share unit of trading for inactive stocks (January 3).
1929 Stock market crash; 16,410,000 shares traded (October 29).
New York Curb Market modifies its name to New York Curb Exchange.*
1930 Faster ticker—500 characters per minute—installed (September 2).
1931 Exchange building expanded; Telephone Quotation Department formed to send stock quotes to member firm offices.*
1933 New York Stock Exchange closed for bank holiday, March 4–14.
1934 Enactment of Securities Exchange Act of 1934 (June 6).
1938 First salaried president elected—Wm. McC. Martin, Jr. (June 30).
1946 Listed stocks outnumber unlisted stocks for first time since the 1934 act imposed restrictions on unlisted trading.*
1952 Trading hours changed: weekdays, 10 A.M. to 3:30 P.M. Closed Saturdays (September 29).*
1953 Name of New York Curb Exchange changed to American Stock Exchange.*
1958 First member corporation—Woodcock, Hess & Co. (June 4).
Mary C. Roebling becomes first woman governor.*
1962 Committee system of administration replaced by expanded paid staff reporting to president. Specialist system strengthened, surveillance of trading increased, listing and delisting standards introduced, and board restructured to give greater representation to commission and out-of-town brokers.*
1964 New member classification—Registered Trader (August 3).
New ticker—900 characters per minute—put into service (December 1).†
Am-Quote computerized telephone-quotation service was completed as first step in major automation program.*
1965 Fully automated quotation service introduced (March 8).
Electronic Systems Center created (October 15).
First women, Phyllis S. Peterson and Julia Montgomery Walsh, elected to regular membership.*
1966 New NYSE Stock Price Index inaugurated (July 14).
AMEX Price Change Index System introduced; computer complex installed for ticker, surveillance, and compared-clearance operations.*
1967 First woman member admitted—Muriel F. Siebert (December 28).
1968 Ticker speed increased to maximum 900 characters per minute; transmission begun to six European countries. Trading floor modernized; line capacity for communications doubled. Visitors gallery expanded.*
1969 Central Certificate Service fully activated (February 26).
1970 Public ownership of member firms approved (March 26).
Securities Investor Protection Corporation Act signed (December 30).
1971 First negotiated commission rates effective (April 5).
First member organization listed—Merrill Lynch (July 27).
AMEX incorporates and marks 50th anniversary of move indoors; Listed Company Advisory Committee formed, composed of nine chief executives of AMEX-listed companies.
1972 NYSE reorganization, based on Martin Report, approved (January 20).
Board of Directors, with ten public members, replaced Board of Governors (July 13).

Securities Industry Automation Corporation established with AMEX to consolidate facilities of both exchanges (July 17).*
First salaried chairman took office—James J. Needham (August 28).
Board of Governors reorganized to include ten public and ten industry representatives plus full-time salaried chairman as chief executive officer.*

1973 Depository Trust Company succeeded Central Certificate Service (May 11).
Chicago Board of Options Exchange opened with trading in 16 classes of call options (April 26).
AMEX formally adopts affirmative action employment plan; Market Value Index System introduced to replace Price Change Index.

1974 Trading hours extended to 4 P.M. (October 1).
Consolidated tape begun; 15 stocks reported (October 18).

1975 Fixed commission system abolished (April 30).
Full consolidated tape begun (June 16).
AMEX trades call options.
Trading begins in call options and odd lots of U.S. government instruments.*

1976 New data line installed, handling 36,000 characters per minute (January 19).
Specialists began handling odd lots in their stocks (May 24).
Varo, Inc.—first stock traded on both NYSE and AMEX (August 23).
Competition between specialists begun (October 11).

1977 Independent audit committee on listed companies' boards required (January 6).
Competitive Trader category for members approved (January 19).
National Securities Clearing Corporation (NSCC) began merging the clearing operations of the Stock Clearing Corporation of NYSE with American Stock Exchange Clearing Corporation and National Clearing Corporation of the NASD (January 20).
Foreign broker/dealers permitted to obtain membership (February 3).
Full Automated Bond System in effect (July 27).

1978 First 60 million share day in history (63,493,000 shares) (April 17).
Intermarket Trading System (ITS) began.
Registered Competitive Market-Maker category for members approved (May 2).
First 65 million share day in history (66,370,000 shares) (August 3).
Trading in Ginnie Maes inaugurated on the AMEX Commodities Exchange (ACE) (September 12).
AMEX reached an index high of 176.87 (September 13).

1979 Trading began at pilot post on the exchange floor. First stage in a $12-million upgrading of exchange facilities (January 29).
Board of Directors of NYSE approved plan for the creation of the New York Futures Exchange, a wholly owned subsidiary of NYSE. Futures contracts in seven financial instruments will be traded on the NYSE (March 1).
New York Commodities Exchange and NYSE terminated merger talks (March 15).
81,619,000 shares were traded on the NYSE, making it the heaviest trade day in exchange history (October 10).

1980 American Stock Exchange reached an all-time daily stock volume record of 14,980,680 shares sold (January 15).
NYSE volume of 67,752,000 shares traded was second largest volume on record to date (January 16).
NYSE Futures Exchange opened (August 7).
Option seat on the American Stock Exchange sold at an all-time high of $160,000 (December 24).
NYSE index reached an all time high of 81.02 (November 28).

1981 First 90 million share day in the history of the Exchange, 92,881,000 (January 7).
The New York Stock Exchange subsidiary, the New York Futures Exchange, started trading futures in Domestic Bank Certificates of Deposit.

1982 A new AMEX subsidiary, The American Gold Coin Exchange (AGCE), began trading in the Canadian Maple Leaf (January 21).
Trading in NYSE Common Stock Index Futures began on the New York Futures Exchange (May 6).
Trading started through experimental linkage between ITS operated by NYSE and six other exchanges and Computer Assisted Execution Service (CAES) operated by NASD, in 30 stocks exempted from exchange

off-board trading rules under SEC Rule 19c-3. (May 17).
Record advance of 38.81 points reached in NYSE trading as measured by Dow Jones Industrial Average (August 17).
First 100 million share day (132,681,120 shares. (August 18).
Trading in Interest Rate Options on U.S. Treasury Bills & Notes started in May on the AMEX.
Trading soared to an all time high of 147,081,070 shares on the NYSE (October 7).
All time options high of 340,550 contracts were traded on the AMEX (October 7).
Dow Jones Industrial Average plunged 36.33 points, the largest one-day loss since the record plunge of 38.33 points on October 28, 1929 (October 25).

1983 Trading in options on NYSE Common Stock Index Futures started on New York Futures Exchange (January 28).
NYSE started trading options on the NYSE Common Stock Index (September 23).
Dow Jones Industrial Average reached an all time high of 1260.77 (September 26).
New shares of common stocks of seven regional telephone companies and shares of the "new" AT&T began trading on a "when issued" basis. Divestiture of AT&T effective January 1, 1984 (November 21).
AMEX stock trading went over the two billion share mark for the first time.
The AMEX list of stock options increased by four index options, two on specific industry groups, one on the AMEX Market Value Index.

1984 Largest NYSE trading day of 159,999,031 shares traded (January 5).
CBOT (Chicago Board of Trade) began trading a futures contract on the Major Market Index (July 23).*
Trading began in NYSE Double Index Options (July 23).
NYSE volume soared to a record 236,565,110 shares traded (August 3).
Super DOT 250 (electronic order-routing system) launched on NYSE (November 16).

1985 For the first time the NYSE index went over 100, closing at 101.12 (January 21).
19,091,950 shares were traded on the AMEX, the highest single day volume ever (February 6).
Ronald Reagan visited the NYSE, the first President to do so while in office (March 28).
Trading in options on gold bullion started on AMEX (April 26).
50 billionth share listed in NYSE (May 30).
NYSE began trading options in three over-the-counter stocks (June 3).
NYSE reached an all time index high of 113.49 (July 17).
Amex and Toronto Stock Exchange linked together as part of the first two-way electronic hookup between primary equity markets in different countries (September 24).
Instinet Corporation and the AMEX reached an agreement enabling European institutional investors to have access to the AMEX options market via Reuter's electronic terminals.
The opening trading time on both the NYSE and AMEX went from 10:00 A.M. to 9:30 A.M. (September 30).
The Dow Jones Industrial Average reached an all-time high of 1368.50 (October 16).
Options traded on two listed stocks on the NYSE (October 21).
Tokyo Stock Exchange admitted its first foreign member firms (December 1).
A daily record of 119,969 contracts traded on the AMEX Major Markets Index Option (December 13).

1986 The Dow Jones Industrial Average for the first time closed above 1600 at 1600.69 (February 6).
The Dow Jones Industrial Average for the first time closed above 1700 at 1713.99. (February 27).
The Dow Jones Industrial Average for the first time closed above 1800 at 1804.24 (March 20).
NYSE began trading the NYSE Beta Index Option (May 22).
NYSE Board of Directors expanded to 24 outside directors: 12 public members and 12 industry members (June 5).
New York Futures Exchange (NYFE) began trading the Commodity Research Bureau (CRB) index futures contract (June 12).
The Dow Jones Industrial Average for the first time closed above 1900 at 1903.54 (July 1).
The Directors of the NYSE voted to abandon the one-share-one-vote

rule which gives common shareholders equal voting rights (July 3).

The Dow Jones Industrials nose-dived a record 86.61 points on a record volume of 237,600,000 shares traded (September 11).

$600,000.00 (the highest price ever) was paid for membership in the NYSE (December 1).

1987 The Dow Jones industrials passed the 2000 mark, closing at 2000.25 (January 8).

The Dow Jones Industrials closed above 2300 for the first time, up 33.95 points to 2333.52 (March 20).

The Dow Jones Industrials climbed above 2400 for the first time to close at 2405.54 (April 7).

Foreign currency warrants began trading (June 11).

The Chicago Board of Trade and the Chicago Board Options Exchange agreed to permit members of both exchanges to trade financial futures and options contracts side by side (June 25).

For the first time the Dow Jones Industrials closed over 2500 at 2510.04 (July 16).

AMEX Market Value closed at the all-time high of 365.0 (August 13).

A gain of 15.14 points brought the Dow Jones Industrials above 2700 points for the first time with the market closing at 2700.52 (August 17).

New York Futures Exchange began to trade the Russell 2000 and Russell 3000® Stock Index futures contracts (September 10).

A price of $1,150,000 was paid for a member of the NYSE, the highest ever (September 21).

The stock market 'crashed' with the Dow Jones Industrials down 508.00 points or 22% to close at 1738.74 on a record volume of 604.3 shares. Other record declines were: Dow Jones transportations off 164.78; utilities off 29.16; the S & P 500 stock index off 57.86; the AMEX index down 41.05, the NYSE down 30.51, and the NASDAQ composite of over-the-counter stocks off 46.12 (October 19).

A record volume of 608,148,710 shares traded on the NYSE and 43,432,760 on the AMEX (October 20).

The Dow Jones Industrials rocketed 186.84 points, the highest ever, on a volume of 449,350,000 shares (October 21).

Thc AMEX Market Value Index registered its largest increase ever, 23.81 (October 21).

1988 343,949,330 shares were traded on the NYSE, making it the highest volume day to date since the 'crash' of 1987. (June 17).

Investment and Financial Terms

Abandonment value The amount that can be realized by liquidating a project before its economic life has ended.*

Accelerated depreciation Depreciation methods that write off the cost of an asset at a faster rate than the write-off under the straight-line method. The three principal methods of accelerated depreciation are: (1) sum-of-the-years'-digits, (2) double-declining balance, and (3) units-of-production.*

Accountant's Opinion (See: *Auditor's Report.*)

Accruals Accruals Continuing recurring short-term liabilities. Examples are accrued wages, accrued taxes, and accrued interest.*

Accrued interest Interest accrued on a bond since the last interest payment was made. The buyer of the bond pays the market price plus accrued interest. Exceptions include bonds that are in default and income bonds. (See: *Flat income bond.*)†

Acquisition The acquiring of control of one corporation by another. In "unfriendly" takeover attempts, the potential buying company may offer a price well above current market values, new securities and other inducements to stockholders. The management of the subject company might ask for a better price or

---

* Entries from *Managerial Finance*, 6th edition, by J. Fred Weston and Eugene F. Brigham.

† Entries from *The Language of Investing Glossary.*

** Entries from *Tax-Exempt Securities & the Investor.*

†† Entries from the *Glossary.*

¶ Entries from the Federal Reserve *Glossary.*

Source: Form of credit Excerpted selection from MANAGERIAL FINANCE, 6/e, by J. Fred Weston and Eugene F. Brigham, copyright © 1978 by The Dryden Press, a division of Holt, Rinehart and Winston, Inc., copyright © 1975 by Holt, Rinehart and Winston, Inc, reprinted by permission of the publisher.

The *Language of Investing Glossary* published by the New York Stock Exchange, Inc.

The *Glossary* published by the New York Stock Exchange.

Tax-Exempt Securities & the Investor published by the Securities Industry Association.

The *Glossary* published by the Board of Governors of the Federal Reserve System.

try to join up with a third company. (See: *Merger, Proxy.*)††

Ad valorem tax A tax based on the value (or assessed value) of property.**

Aging schedule A report showing how long accounts receivable have been outstanding. It gives the percent of receivables not past due and the percent past due by, for example, one month, two months, or other periods.*

American Depository Receipt (ADR) Issued by American banks, an ADR is a certificate which serves as a proxy for a foreign stock deposited in a foreign bank. For all practical purposes, trading an ADR is equivalent to trading the foreign stock. Hundreds of ADRs are traded on U.S. stock exchange.

Amortization Accounting for expenses or charges as applicable rather than as paid. Includes such practices as depreciation, depletion, write-off of intangibles, prepaid expenses, and deferred charges.†

Amortize To liquidate on an installment basis; an amortized loan is one in which the principal amount of the loan is repaid in installments during the life of the loan.*

Annual report The formal financial statement issued yearly by a corporation. The annual report shows assets, liabilities, earnings—how the company stood at the close of the business year, how it fared profit-wise during the year and other information of interest to shareowners.†

Annuity A series of payments of a fixed amount for a specified number of years.*

Arbitrage A technique employed to take advantage of differences in price. If, for example, ABC stock can be bought in New York for $10 a share and sold in London at $10.50, an arbitrageur may simultaneously purchase ABC stock here and sell the same amount in London, making a profit of 50 cents a share, less expenses. Arbitrage may also involve the purchase of rights to subscribe to a security, or the purchase of a convertible security—and the sale at or about the same time of the security obtainable through exercise of the rights or of the security obtainable through conversion. (See: *Convertible, Rights.*)††

Arrearage Overdue payment; frequently omitted dividend on preferred stock.

Assessed valuation The valuation placed on property for purposes of taxation.**

Assets Everything a corporation owns or due to it: Cash, investments, money due it, materials and inventories, which are called current assets; buildings and machinery, which are known as fixed assets; and patents and good will, called intangible assets. (See: *Liabilities.*)†

Assignment A relatively inexpensive way of liquidating a failing firm that does not involve going through the courts.*

Assignment Notice to an option writer that an option holder has exercised the option and that the writer will now be required to deliver (receive) under the terms of the contract.††

Ask (See: *Bid and asked.*)†

Auction market The system of trading securities through brokers or agents on an exchange such as the New York Stock Exchange. Buyers compete with other buyers while sellers compete with other sellers for the most advantageous price.††

Auditor's report Often called the accountant's opinion, it is the statement of the accounting firm's work and its opinion of the corporation's financial statements, especially if they conform to the normal and generally accepted practices of accountancy.††

Averages Various ways of measuring the trend of securities prices, one of the most popular of which is the Dow-Jones average of 30 industrial stocks listed on the New York Stock Exchange. The prices of the 30 stocks are totaled and then divided by a divisor which is intended to compensate for past stock splits and stock dividends and which is changed from time to time. As a result point changes in the average have only the vaguest relationship to dollar price changes in stocks included in the average. (See: *NYSE composite index.*)††

Balance sheet A condensed financial statement showing the nature and amount of a company's assets, liabilities and capital on a given date. In dollar amounts the balance sheet shows what the company owned, what it owed, and the ownership interest in the company of its stockholders. (See: *Assets, Earnings report.*)†

Balloon payment When a debt is not fully amortized, the final payment is larger than the preceding payments and is called a *balloon* payment.*

Bankers acceptance Bankers acceptances are negotiable time drafts, or bills of exchange, that have been accepted by a bank which, by accepting, assumes the obligation to pay the holder of the draft the face amount of the instrument on the maturity date specified. They are used primarily to finance the export, import, shipment, or storage of goods.¶

Bankruptcy A legal procedure for formally liquidating a business, carried out under the jurisdiction of courts of law.*

Basis book A book of mathematical tables used to convert yields to equivalent dollar prices.**

Basis point One gradation on a 100-point scale representing one percent; used especially in expressing variations in the yields of bonds. Fixed income yields vary often and slightly within one percent and the basis point scale easily expresses these changes in hundredths of one percent. For example, the difference between 12.83% and 12.88% is 5 basis points.††

Basis price The price expressed in yield or percentage of return on the investment.**

Bear market A declining market. (See: *Bull market.*)†

Bearer bond A bond which does not have the owner's name registered on the books of the issuer and which is payable to the holder. (See: *Coupon bond, Registered bond.*)†

Bearer security A security that has no identification as to owner. It is presumed to be owned, therefore, by the bearer or the person who holds it. Bearer securities are freely and easily negotiable since ownership can be quickly transferred from seller to buyer.**

Beta coefficient Measures the extent to which the returns on a given stock move with "the stock market."*

Bid and asked Often referred to as a quotation or quote. The bid is the highest price anyone has declared that he wants to pay for a security at a given time, the asked is the lowest price anyone will take at the same time. (See: *Quote.*)†

Block A large holding or transaction of stock—popularly considered to be 10,000 shares or more.†

Blue chip A company known nationally for the quality and wide acceptance of its products or services, and for its ability to make money and pay dividends.†

Blue-sky laws A popular name for laws various states have enacted to protect the public against securities frauds. The term is believed to have originated when a judge ruled that a particular stock had about the same value as a patch of blue sky.†

Board room A room for registered representatives and customers in a broker's office where opening, high, low, and last prices of leading stocks used to be posted on a board throughout the market day. Today such price displays are normally electronically controlled although most board rooms have replaced the board with the ticker and/or individual quotation machines.†

Bond Basically an IOU or promissory note of a corporation, usually issued in multiples of $1,000 or $5,000, although $100 and $500 denominations are not unknown. A bond is evidence of a debt on which the issuing company usually promises to pay the bondholders a specified amount of interest for a specified length of time, and to repay the loan on the expiration date. In every case a bond represents debt—its holder is a creditor of the corporation and not a part owner as is the shareholder. (See: *Collateral, Convertible, Debenture, General Mortgage Bond, Income Bond.*)††

Bond funds Registered investment companies whose assets are invested in diversified portfolios of bonds.*

Book A notebook the specialist in a stock uses to keep a record of the buy and sell orders at specified prices, in sequence of receipt, which are left with him by other brokers. (See *Specialist.*)†

Book value The accounting value of an asset. The book value of a share of common stock is equal to the net worth (common stock plus retained earnings) of the corporation divided by the number of shares of stock outstanding.*

Break-even analysis An analytical technique for studying the relation between fixed cost, variable cost, and profits. A break-even *chart* graphically depicts the nature of break-even analysis. The break-even *point* represents the volume of sales at which total costs equal total revenues (that is, profits equal zero).*

Broker An agent, who handles the public's orders to buy and sell securities, commodities, or other property. For this service a commission is charged. (See: *Commission broker, dealer.*)†

Brokers' loans Money borrowed by brokers from banks or other brokers for a variety of uses. It may be used by specialists and to help finance inventories of stock they deal in; by brokerage firms to finance the underwriting of new issues of corporate and municipal securities; to help finance a firm's own investments; and to help finance the purchase of securities for customers who prefer to use the broker's credit when they buy securities. (See: *Margin.*)†

Bull market An advancing market. (See: *Bear market.*)†

Business risk The basic risk inherent in a firm's operations. Business risk plus financial risk resulting from the use of debt equals total corporate risk.*

Call (1) An option to buy (or "call") a share of stock at a specified price within a specified period. (2) The process of redeeming a bond or preferred stock issue before its normal maturity. (See: *Options.*)*

Call premium The amount in excess of par value that a company must pay when it calls a security.*

Call price The price that must be paid when a security is called. The call price is equal to the par value plus the call premium.*

Call privilege A provision incorporated into a bond or a share of preferred stock that gives the issuer the right to redeem (call) the security at a specified price.*

Callable A bond issue, all or part of which may be redeemed by the issuing corporation under definite conditions before maturity. The term also applies to preferred shares which may be redeemed by the issuing corporation.†

Capital asset An asset with a life of more than one year that is not bought and sold in the ordinary course of business.*

Capital budgeting The process of planning expenditures on assets whose returns are expected to extend beyond one year.*

Capital gain or capital loss Profit or loss from the sale of a capital asset. A capital gain, under current federal income tax laws, may be either short-term (12 months or less) or long-term (more than 12 months). A short-term capital gain is taxed at the reporting individual's full income tax rate. A long-term capital gain is subject to a lower tax. The capital gains provisions of the tax law are complicated. You should consult your tax advisor for specific information.†

Capital market line A graphical representation of the relationship between risk and the required rate of return on an efficient portfolio.*

Capital markets Financial transactions involving instruments with maturities greater than one year.*

Capital rationing A situation where a constraint is placed on the total size of the capital investment during a particular period.*

Capital stock All shares representing ownership of a business, including preferred and common. (See: *Common stock, Preferred stock.*)†

Capital structure The permanent long-term financing of the firm represented by long-term debt, preferred stock, and net worth (net worth consists of capital, capital surplus, and retained earnings). Capital structure is distinguished from *financial structure,* which includes short-term debt plus all reserve accounts.*

Capitalization Total amount of the various securities issued by a corporation. Capitalization may include bonds, debentures, preferred and common stock, and surplus. Bonds and debentures are usually carried on the books of the issuing company in terms of their par or face value. Preferred and common shares may be carried in terms of par or stated value. Stated value may be an arbitrary figure decided upon by the directors or may represent the amount received by the company from the sale of the securities at the time of issuance. (See: *Par.*)†

Capitalization rate A discount rate used to find the present value of a series of future cash receipts; sometimes called *discount rate.**

Carry-back; carry forward For income tax purposes, losses that can be carried backward or forward to reduce federal income taxes.*

Cash budget A schedule showing cash flows (receipts, disbursements, and net cash) for a firm over a specified period.*

Cash cycle The length of time between the purchase of raw materials and the collection of accounts receivable generated in the sale of the final product.*

Cash flow Reported net income of a corporation *plus* amounts charged off for depreciation, depletion, amortization, extraordinary charges to reserves, which are bookkeeping deductions and not paid out in actual dollars and cents. (See: *Amortization, Depreciation.*)††

Cash sale A transaction on the floor of the Stock Exchange which calls for delivery of the securities the same day. In "regular way" trades, the seller is to deliver on the fifth business day except for bonds, which is the next day. (See: *Regular way delivery.*)†

Certainty equivalents The amount of cash (or rate of return) that someone would require *with certainty* to make him indifferent between this certain sum (or *rate of return*) and a particular uncertain, risky sum (or rate of return).*

Certificate The actual piece of paper which is evidence of ownership of stock in a corporation. Watermarked paper is finely engraved with delicate etchings to discourage forgery.††

Certificate of Deposit (CD) A money market instrument issued by banks. The time CD is characterized by its set date of maturity and interest rate and its wide acceptance among investors, companies and institutions as a highly negotiable short-term investment vehicle.††

CFTC The Commodity Futures Trading Commission, created by Congress in 1974 to regulate exchange trading in futures.††

Characteristic line A linear least-squares regression line that shows the relationship between an individual security's return and returns on "the market." The slope of the characteristic line is the beta coefficient.*

Chattel mortgage A mortgage on personal property (not real estate). A mortgage on equipment would be a chattel mortgage.*

Closed-end investment company (See: *Investment company.*)

Coefficient of variation Standard deviation divided by the mean: CV.*

Collateral Assets that are used to secure a loan.*

Collateral trust bond A bond secured by collateral deposited with a trustee. The collateral is often the stocks or bonds of companies controlled by the issuing company but may be other securities.†

Commercial paper Unsecured, short-term promissory notes of large firms, usually issued in denominations of $1 million or more. The rate of interest on commercial paper is typically somewhat below the prime rate of interest.*

Commission The broker's basic fee for purchasing or selling securities or property as an agent.†

Commission broker An agent who executes the public's orders for the purchase or sale of securities or commodities.†

Commitment fee The fee paid to a lender for a formal line of credit.*

Commodities (See: *Futures.*)

Common stock Securities which represent an ownership interest in a corporation. If the company has also issued preferred stock, both common and preferred have ownership rights. Common stockholders assume the greater risk, but generally exercise the greater control and may gain the greater reward in the form of dividends and capital appreciation. The terms of common stock and capital stock are often used interchangeably when the company has no preferred stock.†

Compensating balance A required minimum checking account balance that a firm must maintain with a commercial bank. The required balance is generally equal to 15 to 20 percent of the amount of loans outstanding. Compensating balances can raise the effective rate of interest on bank loans.*

Competitive trader A member of the Exchange who trades in stocks on the Floor for an account in which he has an interest. Also known as a Registered Trader.†

Composite cost of capital A weighted average of the component costs of debt, preferred stock, and common equity. Also called the *weighted-average cost of capital,* but it reflects the cost of each additional dollar raised, not the average cost of all capital the firm has raised throughout its history.*

Composition An informal method of reorganization that voluntarily reduces creditors' claims on the debtor firm.*

Compound interest An interest rate that is applicable when interest in succeeding periods is earned not only on the initial principal but also on the accumulated interest of prior periods. Compound interest is contrasted to *simple interest,* in which returns are not earned on interest received.*

Compounding The arithmetic process of determining the final value of a payment or series of payments when compound interest is applied.*

Conditional sales contract A method of financing new equipment by paying it off in installments over a one-to-five-year period. The seller retains title to the equipment until payment has been completed.*

Conglomerate A corporation that has diversified its operations, usually by acquiring enterprises in widely varied industries.†

Consolidated balance sheet A balance sheet showing the financial condition of a corporation and its subsidiaries. (See: *Balance sheet.*)†

Consolidated tape The ticket tape reporting transactions in NYSE listed securities that take place on the NYSE or any of the participating regional stock exchanges and other markets. Similarly, transactions in AMEX-listed securities, and certain other securities listed on regional stock exchanges, are reported and identified on a separate tape.††

Consolidated tax return An income tax return that combines the income statement of several affiliated firms.*

Continuous compounding (discounting) As opposed to discrete compounding, interest is added continuously rather than at discrete points in time.*

Conversion price The effective price paid for common stock when the stock is obtained by converting either convertible preferred stocks or convertible bonds. For example, if a $1,000 bond is convertible into 20 shares of stock, the conversion price is $50 ($1,000/20).*

Conversion ratio or conversion rate The number of shares of common stock that may be obtained by converting a convertible bond or share of convertible preferred stock.*

Convertibles Securities (generally bonds or preferred stocks) that are exchangeable at the option of the holder for common stock of the issuing firm.*

Correlation coefficient Measures the degree of relationship between two variables.*

Correspondent A securities firm, bank, or other financial organization which regularly performs services for another in a place or market to which the other does not have direct access. Securities firms may have correspondents in foreign countries or on exchanges of which they are not members. Correspondents are frequently linked by private wires. Member organizations of the N.Y.S.E. with offices in New York City may also act as correspondents for out-of-town member organizations which do not maintain New York City offices.†

Cost of capital The discount rate that should be used in the capital budgeting process.*

Coupon bond Bond with interest coupons attached. The coupons are clipped as they come due and are presented by the holder for payment of interest. (See: *Bearer bond, Registered bond.*)†

Coupon rate The stated rate of interest on a bond.*

Covariance The correlation between two variables multiplied by the standard deviation of each variable:

$$\text{Cov} = r_{xy}\sigma_x\sigma_y.*$$

Covenant Detailed clauses contained in loan agreements. Covenants are designed to protect the lender and include such items as limits on total indebtedness, restrictions on dividends, minimum current ratio, and similar provisions.*

Coverage A term usually connected with revenue bonds. It is a ratio of net revenues pledged to principal and interest payments to debt service requirements. It is one of the factors used in evaluating the quality of an issue.**

Covered option An option position that is offset by an equal and opposite position in the underlying security.††

Covering Buying a security previously sold short. (See: *Short sale, Short covering.*)†

Cumulative dividends A protective feature on preferred stock that requires all past preferred dividends to be paid before any common dividends are paid.*

Cumulative preferred A stock having a provision that if one or more dividends are omitted, the omitted dividends must be paid before dividends may be paid on the company's common stock.†

Cumulative voting A method of voting for corporate directors which enables the shareholder to multiply the number of his shares by the number of directorships being voted on and cast the total for one director or a selected group of directors. A 10-share holder normally casts 10 votes for each of, say 12 nominees to the board of directors. He thus has 120 votes. Under the cumulative voting principle he may do that or he may cast 120 (10 × 12) votes for only one nominee, 60 for two, 40 for three, or any other distribution he chooses. Cumulative voting is required under the corporate laws of some states, is permitted in most others.†

Current assets Those assets of a company which are reasonably expected to be realized in cash, or sold, or consumed during the normal operating cycle of the business. These include cash, U.S. government bonds, receivables and money due usually within one year, and inventories.†

Current liabilities Money owed and payable by a company, usually within one year.†

Current return (See: *Yield.*)

Current yield A relation stated as a percent of the annual interest to the actual market price of the bond.**

Cut-off point In the capital budgeting process, the minimum rate of return on acceptable investment opportunities.*

Day order An order to buy or sell which, if not executed expires at the end of the trading day on which it was entered.†

Dealer An individual or firm in the securities business who buys and sells stocks and bonds as a principal rather than as an agent. The dealer's profit or loss is the difference between the price paid and the price received for the same security. The dealer's confirmation must disclose to the customer that the principal has been acted upon. The same individual or firm may function, at different times, either as broker or dealer. (See: *NASD, Specialist.*)††

Debenture A long-term debt instrument that is not secured by a mortgage on specific property.*

Debit balance In a customer's margin account that portion of purchase price of stock, bonds, or commodities covered by credit extended by the broker to the margin customer.†

Debt limit The statutory or constitutional maximum debt that a municipality can legally incur.**

Debt ratio Total debt divided by total assets.*

Debt service Refers to the payments required for interest and retirement of the principal amount of a debt.**

Default The failure to fulfill a contract. Generally, default refers to the failure to pay interest or principal on debt obligations.*

Degree of leverage The percentage increase in profits resulting from a given percentage increase in sales. The degree of leverage may be calculated for financial leverage, operating leverage, or both combined.*

Denomination The face amount or par value of a security which the issuer promises to pay on the maturity date. Most municipal bonds are issued with a minimum denomination of $5,000, although a few older issues are available in $1,000 denominations.**

Depletion accounting Natural resources, such as metals, oil and gas, and timber, which conceivably can be reduced to zero over the years, present a special problem in capital management. Depletion is an accounting practice consisting of charges against earnings based upon the amount of the asset taken out of the total reserves in the period for which accounting is made. A bookkeeping entry, it does not represent any cash outlay nor are any funds earmarked for the purpose.†

Depository trust company (DTC) A central securities certificate depository through which members effect security deliveries between each other via computerized bookkeeping entries thereby reducing the physical movement of stock certificates.†

Depreciation Normally, charges against earnings to write off the cost, less salvage value, of an asset over its estimated useful life. It is a bookkeeping entry and does not represent any cash outlay nor are any funds earmarked for the purpose.†

Devaluation The process of reducing the value of a country's currency stated in terms of other currencies; for example, the British pound might be devalued from $2.30 for one pound to $2.00 for one pound.*

Director Person elected by shareholders to establish company policies. The directors appoint the president, vice presidents, and all other operating officers. Directors decide, among other matters, if and when dividends shall be paid. (See: *Management, Proxy.*)†

Discount The amount by which a preferred stock or bond may sell below its par value. Also used as a verb to mean "takes into account" as the price of the stock has discounted the expected dividend cut. (See: *Premium.*)†

Discount rate [1]The interest rate used in the discounting process; sometimes called *capitalization rate.**

[2]The interest rate at which eligible depository institutions may borrow funds, usually for short periods, directly from the Federal Reserve Banks. The law requires the board of directors of each Reserve Bank to establish the discount rate every 14 days subject to the approval of the Board of Governors.¶

Discounted cash flow techniques Methods of ranking investment proposals. Included are (1) internal rate of return method, (2) net present value method, and (3) profitability index or benefit/cost ratio.*

Discounting The process of finding the present value of a series of future cash flows. Discounting is the reverse of compounding.*

Discounting of accounts receivable Short-term financing where accounts receivable are used to secure the loan. The lender does not *buy* the accounts receivable but simply uses them as collateral for the loan. Also called *assigning accounts receivable.**

Discretionary account An account in which the customer gives the broker or someone else discretion, which may be complete or within specific limits, either to the purchases, or sale of securities or commodities including selection, timing, amount, and price to be paid or received.†

Diversification Spreading investments among different companies in different fields. Another type of diversification is also offered by the securities of many individual companies because of the wide range of their activities. (See: *Investment trust.*)†

Dividend The payment designed by the board of directors to be distributed pro rata among the shares outstanding. On preferred shares, it is generally a fixed amount. On common shares, the dividend varies with the fortunes of the company and the amount of cash on hand, and may be omitted if business is poor or the directors determine to withhold earnings to invest in plant and equipment. Sometimes a company will pay a dividend out of past earnings even if it is not currently operating at a profit.†

Dividend yield The ratio of the current dividend to the current price of a share of stock.*

Dollar bond A bond that is quoted and traded in dollars rather than in terms of yield.**

Dollar cost averaging A system of buying securities at regular intervals with a fixed dollar amount. Under this system the investor buys by the dollars' worth rather than by the number of shares. If each investment is of the same number of dollars, payments buy more when the price is low and fewer when it rises. Thus temporary downswings in price benefit the investor if he continues periodic purchases in both good times and bad and the price at which the shares are sold is more than their average cost. (See: *Formula investing.*)†

Double-barrelled bond A bond secured by the pledge of two or more sources of repayment, e.g., secured by taxes as well as revenues.**

Double exemption Refers to securities that are exempt from state as well as Federal income taxes.**

Double taxation Short for *double taxation of dividends*. The federal government taxes corporate profits once as corporate income; any part of the remaining profits distributed as dividends to stockholders may be taxed again as income to the recipient stockholder.†

Dow theory A theory of market analysis based upon the performance of the Dow-Jones industrial and transportation stock price averages. The theory says that the market is in a basic upward trend if one of these averages advances above a previous important high, accompanied or followed by a similar advance in the other. When the averages both dip below previous important lows, this is regarded as confirmation of a basic downward trend. The theory does not attempt to predict how long either trend will continue, although it is widely misinterpreted as a method of forecasting future action.†

Down tick (See: *Up tick.*)

Dow theory A theory of market analysis based upon the performance of the Dow Jones industrial and transportation stock price averages. The Theory says that the market is in a basic upward trend if one of these averages advances above a previous important high, accompanied or followed by a similar advance in the other. When the averages both dip below previous important lows, this is regarded as confirmation of a downward trend. The Dow Jones is one type of market index. (See: *NYSE Composite Index.*)††

Earnings report A statement—also called an *income statement*—issued by a company showing its earnings or losses over a given period. The earnings report lists the income earned, expenses, and the net result. (See: *Balance sheet.*)†

EBIT Acronym for *earnings before interest and taxes.**

Economical ordering quantity (EOQ) The optimum (least cost) quantity of merchandise which should be ordered.*

EPS Acronym for *earnings per share.**

Equipment trust certificate A type of security, generally issued by a railroad, to pay for new equipment. Title to the equipment, such as a locomotive, is held by a trustee until the notes are paid off. An equipment trust certificate is usually secured by a first claim on the equipment.†

Equity The net worth of a business, consisting of capital stock, capital (or paid-in) surplus, earned surplus (or retained earnings), and occasionally, certain net worth reserves. *Common equity* is that part of the total net worth belonging to the common stockholders. *Total equity* would include preferred stockholders. The terms *common stock, net worth,* and *common equity* are frequently used interchangeably.†

Exchange acquisition A method of filling an order to buy a large block of stock on the floor of the exchange. Under certain circumstances, a member-broker can facilitate the purpose of a block by soliciting orders to sell. All orders to sell the security are lumped together and crossed with the buy order in the regular action market. The price to the buyer may be on a net basis or on a commission basis.†

Exchange distribution A method of selling large blocks of stock on the floor of the exchange. Under certain circumstances, a member-broker can facilitate the sale of a block of stock by soliciting and getting other member-brokers to solicit orders to buy. Individual buy orders are lumped together and crossed with the sell order in the regular auction market. A special commission is usually paid by the seller; ordinarily the buyer pays no commission.†

Exchange rate The rate at which one currency can be exchanged for another; for example, $2.30 can be exchanged for one British pound.*

Excise tax A tax on the manufacture, sale, or consumption of specified commodities.*

Ex-dividend A synonym for "without dividend." The buyer of a stock selling ex-dividend does not receive the recently declared dividend. Every dividend is payable on a fixed date to all shareholders recorded on the books of the company as of a previous date of record. For example, a dividend may be declared as payable to holders of record on the books of the company on a given Friday. Since five business days are allowed for delivery of stock in a "regular way" transaction on the New York Stock Exchange, the Exchange would declare the stock "ex-dividend" as of the opening of the market on the preceding Monday. That means anyone who bought it on and after Monday would not be entitled to that dividend. When stocks go ex-dividend, the stock tables include the symbol "x" following the name. (See: *Cash sale, Net change, Transfer.*)†

Ex-dividend date The date on which the right to the current dividend no longer accompanies a stock. (For listed stock, the ex-dividend date is four working days prior to the date of record.)*

Exercise Action taken by an option holder that requires the writer to perform the terms of the contract.††

Exercise price The price that must be paid for a share of common stock when it is bought by exercising a warrant.*

Expected return The rate of return a firm expects to realize from an investment. The expected return is the mean value of the probability distribution of possible returns.*

Expiration date The date the option contract expires.††

Ex-rights the date on which stock purchase rights are no longer transferred to the purchaser of the stock.*

Extension An informal method of reorganization in which the creditors voluntarily postpone the date of required payment on past-due obligations.*

External funds Funds acquired through borrowing or by selling new common or preferred stock.

Extra The short form of *extra dividend.* A dividend in the form of stock or cash in addition to the regular or usual dividend the company has been paying.†

Face value The value of a bond that appears on the face of the bond, unless the value is otherwise specified by the issuing company. Face value is ordinarily the amount the issuing company promises to pay at maturity. Face value is not an indication of market value. Sometimes referred to as par value. (See: *Par.*)†

Factoring A method of financing accounts receivable under which a firm sells its accounts receivable (generally without recourse) to a financial institution (the *factor*).*

Federal funds Reserve balances that depository institutions lend each other, usually on an overnight basis. In addition, Federal funds include certain other kinds of borrowings by depository institutions from each other and from federal agencies.¶

Field warehousing A method of financing inventories in which a "warehouse" is established at the place of business of the borrowing firm.*

Financial accounting standards board (FASB) A private (nongovernment) agency which functions as an accounting standards-setting body.*

Financial intermediation Financial transactions which bring savings surplus units together with savings deficit units so that savings can be redistributed into their most productive uses.*

Financial lease A lease that does not provide for maintenance services, is not cancellable, and is fully amortized over the life of the lease.*

Financial leverage The ratio of total debt to total assets. There are other measures of financial leverage, especially ones that relate cash inflows to required cash outflows.*

Financial markets Transactions in which the creation and transfer of financial assets and financial liabilities take place.*

Financial risk That portion of total corporate risk, over and above basic business risk, that results from using debt.*

Fiscal year A corporation's accounting year. Due to the nature of their particular business, some companies do not use the calendar year for their bookkeeping. A typical example is the department store which finds December 31 too early a date to close its books after the Christmas rush. For that reason many stores wind up their accounting year January 31. Their fiscal year, therefore, runs from February 1 of one year through January 31 of the next. The fiscal year of other companies may run from July 1 through the following June 30. Most companies, though, operate on a calendar year basis.†

Fixed charges Costs that do not vary with the level of output, especially fixed financial costs such as interest, lease payments, and sinking fund payments.*

Flat income bond This term means that the price at which a bond is traded includes consideration for all unpaid accruals of interest. Bonds which are in default of interest or principal are traded flat. Income bonds, which pay interest only to the extent earned are usually traded flat. All other bonds are usually dealt in "and interest," which means that the buyer pays to the seller the market price plus interest accrued since the last payment date.†

Float The amount of funds tied up in checks that have been written but are still in process and have not yet been collected.*

Floating exchange rates Exchange rates may be fixed by government policy *(pegged)* or allowed to *float* up or down in accordance with supply and demand. When market forces are allowed to function, exchange rates are said to be floating.*

Floor The huge trading area—about two-thirds the size of a football field—where stocks and bonds are bought and sold on the New York Stock Exchange.†

Floor broker A member of the Stock Exchange who executes orders on the floor of the exchange to buy or sell any listed securities. (See: *Commission broker, Two-dollar broker.*)†

Flotation cost The cost of issuing new stocks or bonds.*

Formula investing An investment technique. One formula calls for the shifting of funds from common shares to preferred shares or bonds as the market, on average, rises above a certain predetermined point—and the return of funds to common share investments as the market average declines. (See: *Dollar cost averaging.*)†

Free and open market A market in which supply and demand are freely expressed in terms of price. Contrasts with a controlled market in which supply, demand, and price may all be regulated.†

Fundamental research Analysis of industries and companies based on factors such as sales, assets, earnings, products or services, markets, and management. As supplied to the economy, fundamental research includes consideration of gross national product, interest rates, unemployment, inventories, savings, and so on. (See: *Technical research.*)†

Funded debt Usually long-term, interest-bearing bonds or debentures of a company. Could include long-term bank loans. Does *not* include short-term loans, preferred, or common stock.†

Funding The process of replacing short-term debt with long-term securities (stocks or bonds).*

General mortgage bond A bond which is secured by a blanket mortgage on the company's property, but which may be outranked by one or more other mortgages.†

General obligation bond A bond secured by the pledge of the issuer's full faith, credit and taxing power.**

General purchasing power reporting A proposal by the FASB that the current values of nonmonetary items in financial statements be adjusted by a general price index.*

Gilt-edged High-grade bond issued by a company which has demonstrated its ability to earn a comfortable profit over a period of years and pay its bondholders their interest without interruption.†

Give up A term with many different meanings. For one, a member of the exchange on the floor may act for a second member by executing an order for him with a third member. The first member tells the third member that he is acting on behalf of the second member and "gives up" the second member's name rather than his own.††

Gold fix The setting of the price of gold by dealers (especially in an twice-daily London meeting at the central bank); the fix is the fundamental worldwide price for setting prices of gold bullion and gold-related contracts and products.††

Good delivery Certain basic qualifications must be met before a security sold on the exchange may be delivered. The security must be in proper form to comply with the contract of sale and to transfer title to the purchaser.†

Good 'til cancelled order (GTC) or open order An order to buy or sell which remains in effect until it is either executed or cancelled.†

Goodwill Intangible assets of a firm established by the excess of the price paid for the going concern over its book value.*

Government bonds Obligations of the U.S. government, regarded as the highest grade issues in existence.†

Growth stock Stock of a company with a record of growth in earnings at a relatively rapid rate.†

Guaranteed bond A bond which has interest or principal, or both, guaranteed by a company other than the issuer. Usually found in the railroad industry when large roads, leasing sections of trackage owned by small railroads, may guarantee the bonds of the smaller road.†

Guaranteed stock Usually preferred stock on which dividends are guaranteed by another company; under much the same circumstances as a bond is guaranteed.†

Hedge (See: *Arbitrage, Options, Short sale.*)

Hedging The purchase or sale of a derivative security (such as options or futures) in order to reduce or neutralize all or some portion of the risk of holding another security.††

Holding company A corporation which owns the securities of another, in most cases with voting control.†

Hurdle rate In capital budgeting, the minimum acceptable rate of return on a project. If the expected rate of return is below the hurdle rate, the project is not accepted. The hurdle rate should be the marginal cost of capital.*

Hypothecation The pledging of securities as collateral—for example, to secure the debit balance in a margin account.†

Improper accumulation Earnings retained by a business for the purpose of enabling stockholders to avoid personal income taxes.*

Inactive stock An issue traded on an exchange or in the over-the-counter market in which there is a relatively low volume of transactions. Volume may be no more than a few hundred shares a week or even less. On the New York Stock Exchange many inactive stocks are traded in 10-share units rather than the customary 100. (See: *Round lot.*)†

In-and-out Purchase and sale of the same security within a short period—a day, a week, even a month. An in-and-out trader is generally more interested in day-to-day price fluctuations than dividends or long-term growth.†

Income bond Generally income bonds promise to repay principal but to pay interest only when earned. In some cases unpaid interest on an income bond may accumulate as a claim against the corporation when the bond becomes due. An income bond may also be issued in lieu of preferred stock.†

Incremental cash flow Net cash flow attributable to an investment project.*

Incremental cost of capital The average cost of the increment of capital raised during a given year.*

Indenture A written agreement under which bonds and debentures are issued, setting forth maturity date, interest rate, and other terms.†

Independent broker Members on the floor of the NYSE who execute orders for other brokers having more business at that time than they can handle themselves, or for firms who do not have their Exchange member on the floor. Formerly known as *two-dollar brokers* from the time when these independent brokers received $2 per hundred shares for executing such orders. Their fees are paid by the commission brokers. (See: *Commission broker.*)†

Index A statistical yardstick expressed in terms of percentages of a base year or years. For instance, the Federal Reserve Board's index of industrial production is based on 1967 as 100. An index is not an average. (See: *Averages, NYSE common stock index.*)†

Industrial revenue bond A security backed by private enterprises that have been financed by a municipal issue.**

Insolvency The inability to meet maturing debt obligations.*

Institutional Investor An organization whose primary purpose is to invest its own assets or those held in trust by it for others. Includes pension funds, investment companies, insurance companies, universities, and banks.†

Interest Payments a borrower pays a lender for the use of his money. A corporation pays interest on its bonds to its bondholders. (See: *Bond, dividend.*)†

Intermarket Trading System (ITS) An electronic communications network now linking the trading floor of seven registered exchanges to foster competition among them in stocks listed on either the NYSE or AMEX and one or more regional exchanges. Through ITS, any broker or market-maker on the floor of any participating market can reach out to other participants for an execution whenever the nationwide quote shows a better price is available.††

Internal financing Funds made available for capital budgeting and working-capital expansion through the normal operations of the firm; internal financing is approximately equal to retained earnings plus depreciation.*

Internal rate of return (IRR) The rate of return on an asset investment. The internal rate of return is calculated by finding the discount rate that equates the present value of future cash flows to the cost of the investment.*

Intrinsic value [1]That value which, in the mind of the analyst, is justified by the facts. It is often used to distinguish between the *true value* of an asset (the intrinsic value) and the asset's current market price.*

[2]The dollar amount of the difference between the exercise price of an option and the current cash value of the underlying security. Intrinsic value and time value are the two components of an option premium, or price.††

Investment The use of money for the purpose of making more money, to gain income or increase capital, or both.††

Investment banker Also known as an *underwriter*. The middleman between the corporation issuing new securities and the public. The usual practice is for one or more investment bankers to buy outright from a corporation a new issue of stocks or bonds. The group forms a syndicate to sell the securities to individuals and institutions. Investment bankers also distribute very large blocks of stocks or bonds—perhaps held by an estate. (See: *Primary Distribution, Syndicate.*)††

Investment company A company or trust which uses its capital to invest in other companies. There are two principal types: the closed-end and the open-end, or mutual fund. Shares in closed-end investment companies, some of which are listed on the New York Stock Exchange, are readily transferable in the open market and are bought and sold like other shares. Capitalization of these companies remains the same unless action is taken to change, which is seldom. Open-end funds sell their own new shares to investors, stand ready to buy back their old shares, and are not listed. Open-end funds are so called because their capitalization is not fixed; they issue more shares as people want them.†

Investment counsel One whose principal business consists of acting as investment adviser and a substantial part of his business consists of rendering investment supervisory services.†

Investment tax credit Business firms can deduct as a credit against their income taxes a specified percentage of the dollar amount of new investments in each of certain categories of assets.*

IRA Individual Retirement Account. A pension plan with major tax advantages. Any worker can begin an IRA and obtain a tax deduction for cash contributions up to $2,000 annually. IRA permits investment through intermediaries like mutual funds, insurance companies and banks or directly in stocks and bonds through stockbrokers. (See: *Keogh Plan.*)††

Issue Any of a company's securities, or the act of distributing such securities.†

Issuer A municipal unit that borrows money through the sale of bonds or notes.**

Keogh Plan Tax advantaged personal retirement program that can be established by a self-employed individual. Currently, annual contributions to a plan can be up to $15,000. Such contributions and reinvestments are not taxed as they accumulate but will be when withdrawn (presumably at retirement when taxable income may be less). (See: *IRA.*)††

Legal list A list of investments selected by various states in which certain institutions and fiduciaries, such as insurance companies and banks, may invest. Legal lists are often restricted to high quality securities meeting certain specifications. (See: *Prudent Man Rule.*)††

Legal opinion An opinion concerning the legality of a bond issue usually written by a recognized law firm specializing in public borrowings.**

Leverage The effect on a company when the company has bonds, preferred stock, or both outstanding. Example: If the earnings of a company with 1,000,000 common shares increases from $1,000,000 to $1,500,000—earnings per share would go from $1 to $1.50, or an increase of 50 percent. But if earnings of a company that had to pay $500,000 in bond interest increased that much—earnings per common share would jump from 50 cents to $1 a share, or 100 percent.††

Leverage factor The ratio of debt to total assets.*

Liabilities All the claims against a corporation. Liabilities include accounts and wages and salaries payable, dividends declared payable, accrued taxes payable, fixed or long-term liabilities such as mortgage bonds, debentures, and bank loans. (See: *Assets, balance sheet.*)†

Lien A lender's claim on assets that are pledged for a loan.*

Limit, limited order, or limited price order An order to buy or sell a stated amount of a security at a specified price, or at a better price, if obtainable after the order is represented in the Trading Crowd.†

Limited tax bond A bond secured by a pledge of a tax or group of taxes limited as to rate or amount.**

Line of credit An arrangement whereby a financial institution (bank or insurance company) commits itself to lend up to a specified maximum amount of funds during a specified period. Sometimes the interest rate on the loan is specified, at other times, it is not. Sometimes a commitment fee is imposed for obtaining the line of credit.*

Liquidation The process of converting securities or other property into cash. The dissolution of a company, with cash remaining after sale of its assets and payment of all indebtedness being distributed to the shareholders.†

Liquidity [1]Refers to a firm's cash position and its ability to meet maturing obligations.*

[2]The ability of the market in a particular security to absorb a reasonable amount of buying or selling at reasonable price changes. Liquidity is one of the most important characteristics of a good market.†

Listed stock The stock of a company which is traded on a securities exchange. The various stock exchanges have different standards for listing. Some of the guides used by the New York Stock Exchange for an original listing are national interest in the company, a minimum of 1.1-million shares publicly held among not less than 2,000 round-lot stockholders. The publicly held common shares should have a minimum aggregate market value of $18 million. The company should have net income in the latest year of over $2.5-million before federal income tax and $2-million in each of the preceding two years.††

Load The portion of the offering price of shares of open-end investment companies in excess of the value of the underlying assets which cover sales commissions and all other costs of distribution. The load is usually incurred only on purchase, there being, in most cases, no charge when the shares are sold (redeemed).†

Lock-box plan A procedure used to speed up collections and to reduce float.*

Locked in An investor is said to be locked in when he had a profit on a security he owns but does not sell because his profit would immediately become subject to the capital gains tax. (See: *Capital gain.*)†

Long Signifies ownership of securities: "I am long 100 U.S. Steel" means the speaker owns 100 shares. (See: *Short position, short sale.*)†

Management The board of directors, elected by the stockholders, and the officers of the corporation, appointed by the board of directors.†

Manipulation An illegal operation. Buying or selling a security for the purpose of creating a false or misleading appearance of active trading or for the purpose of raising or depressing the price to induce purchase or sale by others.†

Margin The amount paid by the customer when using a broker's credit to buy or sell a security. Under Federal Reserve regulations, the initial margin required since 1945 has ranged from the current rate 50 percent of the purchase price up to 100 percent. (See: *Brokers' loans, Equity, Margin call.*)††

Margin call A demand upon a customer to put up money or securities with the broker. The call is made when a purchase is made; also if a customer's equity in a margin account declines below a minimum standard set by the exchange or by the firm. (See: *Margin.*)†

Margin—profit on sales The *profit margin* is the percentage of profit after tax to sales.*

Marginal cost The cost of an additional unit. The marginal cost of capital is the cost of an additional dollar of new funds.*

Marginal efficiency of capital A schedule showing the internal rate of return on investment opportunities.*

Marginal revenue The additional gross revenue produced by selling one additional unit of output.*

Marketability The measure of the ease with which a security can be sold in the secondary market.**

Market order An order to buy or sell a stated amount of a security at the most advantageous price obtainable after the order is represented in the trading crowd. (See: *Good 'til cancelled order, Limit order, Stop order.*)††

Market price In the case of a security, market price is usually considered the last reported price at which the stock or bond sold.†

Maturity The date on which a loan or a bond or debenture comes due and is to be paid off.†

Member corporation A securities brokerage firm, organized as a corporation, with at least one member of the New York Stock Exchange, who is an officer or an employee of the corporation.††

Member firm A securities brokerage firm organized as a partnership and having at least one general partner who is a member of the New York Stock Exchange, Inc. (See: *Member corporation.*)†

Member organization This term includes New York Stock Exchange Member Firm *and* Member Corporation. (See: *Member corporation, Member firm.*)†

Merger Any combination that forms one company from two or more previously existing companies.*

Money market Financial markets in which funds are borrowed or lent for short periods (i.e., less than one year). (The money market is distinguished from the capital market, which is the market for long-term funds.)*

Mortgage A pledge of designated property as security for a loan.*

Mortgage bond A bond secured by a mortgage on a property. The value of the property may or may not equal the value of the bonds issued against it. (See: *Bond, Debenture.*)††

Municipal bond A bond issued by a state or a political subdivision, such as county, city, town, or village. The term also designates bonds issued by state agencies and authorities. In general, interest paid on municipal bonds is exempt from federal income taxes and state and local income taxes within the state of issue.†

Mutual fund (See: *Investment company.*)

Naked option An option position that is *not* offset by an equal and opposite position in the underlying security.††

NASD The National Association of Securities Dealers, Inc. An association of brokers and dealers in the over-the-counter securities business.††

NASDAQ An automated information network which provides brokers and dealers with price quotations on securities traded over-the-counter. NASDAQ is an acronym for National Association of Securities Dealers Automated Quotations.†

Negotiable Refers to a security, title to which is transferable by delivery. (See: *Good delivery.*)†

Negotiable Order of Withdrawal account An interest earning account on which checks may be drawn. Withdrawals from NOW accounts may be subject to a 14-day or more notice requirement although such is rarely imposed. NOW accounts may be offered by commercial banks, mutual savings banks, and savings and loan associations and may be owned only by individuals and certain nonprofit organizations and governmental units.¶

Net asset value Usually used in connection with investment companies to mean net asset value per share. An investment company computes its assets daily, or even twice daily, by totaling the market value of all securities owned. All liabilities are deducted, and the balance divided by the number of shares outstanding. The resulting figure is the net asset value per share. (See: *Assets, Investment Company.*)††

Net change The change in the price of a security from the closing price on one day and the closing price on the following day on which the stock is traded. The net change is ordinarily the last figure on the stock price list. The mark + 1⅛ means up $1.125 a share from the last sale on the previous day the stock traded.†

Net debt Gross debt less sinking fund accumulations and all self-supporting debt.**

Net present value (NPV) method A method of ranking investment proposals. The NPV is equal to the present value of future returns, discounted at the marginal cost of capital, minus the present value of the cost of the investment.*

Net worth The capital and surplus of a firm—capital stock, capital surplus (paid-in capital), earned surplus (retained earnings), and, occasionally, certain reserves. For some purposes, preferred stock is included; generally, net worth refers only to the common stockholders' position.*

New housing authority bonds A bond issued by a local public housing authority to finance public housing. It is backed by Federal funds and the solemn pledge of the U.S. Government that payment will be made in full.**

New issue A stock or bond sold by a corporation for the first time. Proceeds may be issued to retire outstanding securities of the company, for new plant or equipment, or for additional working capital, or to acquire a public ownership interest in the company for private owners.††

New York Futures Exchange (NYFE) A subsidiary of the New York Stock Exchange devoted to the trading of futures products.††

New York Stock Exchange (NYSE) The largest organized securities market in the United States, founded in 1792. The Exchange itself does not buy, sell, own, or set the prices of securities traded there. The prices are determined by public supply and demand. The Exchange is a not-for-profit corporation of 1,366 individual members, governed by a Board of Directors consisting of 10 public representatives, 10 Exchange members or allied members and a full-time chairman, executive vice chairman and president.††

New issue market Market for new issues of municipal bonds and notes.**

Nominal interest rate The contracted or stated interest rate, undeflated for price-level changes.*

Noncumulative A type of preferred stock on which unpaid dividends do not accrue. Omitted dividends are, as a rule, gone forever. (See: *Cumulative preferred.*)††

Normal probability distribution A symmetrical, bell-shaped probability function.*

Notes Short-term unsecured promises to pay specified amounts of money. For municipal notes maturities generally range from six to twelve months.**

NYSE composite index A composite index covering price movements of all common stocks listed on the "Big Board." It is based on the close of the market December 31, 1965 as 50.00 and is weighted according to the number of shares listed for each issue. The index is computed continuously and printed on the ticker tape each half hour. Point changes in the index are converted to dollars and cents so as to provide a meaningful measure of changes in the average price of listed stocks. The composite index is supplemented by separate indexes for four industry groups: industries, transportation, utilities, and finances. (See: *Averages.*)††

Odd lot An amount of stock less than the established 100-share unit. (See: *Round lot.*)††

Off-board This term may refer to transactions over-the-counter in unlisted securities, or to a transaction involving listed shares that is not executed on a national securities exchange.††

Offer The price at which a person is ready to sell. Opposed to bid, the price at which one is ready to buy. (See: *Bid and asked.*)†

Official statement Document prepared by or for the issuer that gives in detail the security and financial information about the issue.**

Open interest In options and futures trading, the number of outstanding option contracts, at a given point in time, which have not been exercised and have not yet reached expiration.††

Open order (See: *Good 'til cancelled order.*)

Open-end investment company (See: *Investment company.*)

Operating leverage The extent to which fixed costs are used in a firm's operation.

Break-even analysis is used to measure the extent to which operating leverage is employed.*

Opportunity cost The rate of return on the best *alternative* investment that is available. It is the highest return that will *not* be earned if the funds are invested in a particular project. For example, the opportunity cost of *not* investing in bond A yielding 8 percent might be 7.99 percent, which could be earned on bond B.*

Option A right to buy (call) or sell (put) a fixed amount of a given stock at a specified price within a limited period of time. The purchaser hopes that the stock's price will go up (a call) or down (a put) by an amount sufficient to provide a profit when the stock is sold. If the stock price holds steady or moves in the opposite direction, the price paid for the option is lost entirely. There are several other types of options available to the public but these are basically combinations of puts and calls. Individuals may write (sell) as well as purchase options. Options are also traded on stock indexes, futures, and debt instruments.††

Orders good until a specified time A market or limited price order which is to be represented in the Trading Crowd until a specified time, after which such order or the portion thereof not executed is to be treated as cancelled.†

Ordinary income Income from the normal operations of a firm. Operating income specifically excludes income from the sale of capital assets.*

Organized security exchanges Formal organizations having tangible, physical locations. Organized exchanges conduct an auction market in designated ("listed") investment securities. For example, the New York Stock Exchange is an organized exchange.*

Overbought An opinion as to price levels. May refer to a security which has had a sharp rise or to the market as a whole after a period of vigorous buying, which it may be argued, has left prices "too high."†

Overdraft system A system where a depositor may write checks in excess of his balance, with his bank automatically extending a loan to cover the shortage.*

Oversold The reverse of overbought. A single security or a market which, it is believed, has declined to an unreasonable level.††

Over-the-counter A market for securities made up of securities dealers who may or may not be members of a securities exchange. The over-the-counter market is conducted over the telephone and deals mainly with stocks of companies without sufficient shares, stockholders, or earnings to warrant listing on an exchange. Over-the-counter dealers may act either as principals or as brokers for customers. The over-the-counter market is the principal market for bonds of all types. (See: *NASD, NASDAQ.*)††

Paper profit (LOSS) An unrealized profit or loss on a security still held. Paper profits and losses become realized profits only when the security is sold. (See: *Profit taking.*)††

Par In the case of a common share, par means a dollar amount assigned to the share by the company's charter. Par value may also be used to compute the dollar amount of the common shares on the balance sheet. Par value has little relationship to the market value of common stock. Many companies issue no-par stock but give a stated per share value on the balance sheet. In the case of preferred stocks, it signifies the dollar value upon which dividends are figured. With bonds, par value is the face amount, usually $1,000.††

Par value The nominal or face value of stock or bond.*

Participating preferred A preferred stock which is entitled to its stated dividend and, also, to additional dividends on a specified basis upon payment of dividends on the common stock.†

Passed dividend Omission of a regular or scheduled dividend.†

Payback period The length of time required for the net revenues of an investment to return the cost of the investment.*

Paying agent Place where principal and interest is payable. Usually a designated bank or the treasurer's office of the issuer.**

Payout ratio The percentage of earnings paid out in the form of dividends.*

Pegging A market stabilization action taken by the manager of an underwriting group during the offering of new securities. He does this by continually placing order to buy at a specified price in the market.*

Penny stocks Low-priced issues often highly speculative, selling at less than $1 a share. Frequently used as a term of disparagement, although a few penny stocks have developed into investment-caliber issues.†

Perpetuity A stream of equal future payments expected to continue forever.*

Pledging of accounts receivable Short-term borrowing from financial institutions where the loan is secured by accounts receivable. The lender may physically take the accounts receivable but typically has recourse to the borrower; also called *discounting of accounts receivable.**

Point In the case of shares of stock, a point means $1. If ABC shares rises 3 points, each share has risen $3. In the case of bonds a point means $10, since a bond is quoted as a percentage of $1,000. A bond which rises 3 points gains 3 percent of $1,000, or $30 in value. An advance from 87 to 90 would mean an advance in dollar value from $870 to $900. In the case of market averages, the word point means merely that and no more. If, for example, the NYSE Composite Index rises from 90.25 to 91.25, it has risen a point. A point in this average, however, is not equivalent to $1. (See: *Indexes*.)††

Pooling of interest An accounting method for combining the financial statements of firms that merge. Under the pooling-of-interest procedure, the assets of the merged firms are simply added to form the balance sheet of the surviving corporation. This method is different from the "purchase" method, where goodwill is put on the balance sheet to reflect a premium (or discount) paid in excess of book value.*

Portfolio Holdings of securities by an individual or institution. A portfolio may contain bonds, preferred stocks, common stocks and other securities.††

Portfolio effect The extent to which the variation in returns on a combination of assets (a "portfolio") is less than the sum of the variations of the individual assets.*

Portfolio theory Deals with the selection of optimal portfolios; that is, portfolios that provide the highest possible return for any specified degree of risk.*

Preemptive right A provision contained in the corporate charter and by laws that gives holders of common stock the right to purchase on a pro rata basis new issues of common stock (or securities convertible into common stock.)*

Preferred stock A class of stock with a claim on the company's earnings before payment may be made on the common stock and usually entitled to priority over common stock if the company liquidates. Usually entitled to dividends at a specified rate—when declared by the board of directors and before payment of a dividend on the common stock—depending upon the terms of the issue. (See: *Cumulative preferred, Participating preferred*.)†

Premium The amount by which a bond or preferred stock, may sell above its par value. For options, the price that the buyer pays the writer for an option contract ("option premium") is synonymous with "the price of an option." (See: *Discount*.)††

Present value (PV) The value today of a future payment, or stream of payments, discounted at the appropriate discount rate.*

Price-earnings ratio A popular way to compare stocks selling at various price levels. The PE ratio is the price of a share of stock divided by earnings per share for a twelve-month period. For example, a stock selling for $50 a share and earning $5 a share is said to be selling at a price-earnings ratio of 10.††

Primary distribution Also called primary offering. The original sale of a company's securities. (See: *Investment banker*.)††

Primary market Market for new issues of securities.

Prime rate The lowest interest rate charged by commercial banks to their most creditworthy and largest corporate customers; other interest rates, such as personal, automobile, commercial and financing loans are often pegged to the prime.††

Principal The person for whom a broker executes an order, or dealers buying or selling for their own accounts. The term *principal* may also refer to a person's capital or to the face amount of a bond.††

Productivity The amount of physical output for each unit of productive input.¶

Pro forma A projection. A *pro forma* financial statement is one that shows how the actual statement will look if certain specified assumptions are realized. *Pro forma* statements may be either future or past projections. An example of a backward *pro forma* statement occurs when two firms are planning to merge and shows what their consolidated financial statements would have looked like if they had been merged in preceding years.*

Profit center A unit of a large, decentralized firm that has its own investments and for which a rate of return on investment can be calculated.*

Profit margin The ratio of profits after taxes to sales.*

Profitability index (PI) The present value of future returns divided by the present value of the investment outlay.*

Profit-taking Selling stock which has appreciated in value since purchase, in order to realize the profit. The term is often used to explain a downturn in the market following a period of rising prices. (See: *Paper profit*.)††

Progressive tax A tax that requires a higher percentage payment on higher incomes. The personal income tax in the United States, which is at a rate of 14 percent on the lowest increments of income to 70 percent on the highest increments, is progressive.*

Prospectus The official selling circular that must be given to purchasers of new securities registered with the Securities and Exchange Commission. It highlights the much longer Registration Statement filed with the commission.††

Proxy Written authorization given by a shareholder to someone else to represent him and vote his shares at a shareholders' meeting.††

Proxy statement Information given to stockholders in conjunction with the solicitation of proxies.††

Prudent man rule An investment standard. In some states, the law requires that a fiduciary, such as a trustee, may invest the fund's money only in a list of securities designated by the state—the so-called legal list. In other states, the trustee may invest in a security if it is one that would be bought by a prudent man of discretion and intelligence, who is seeking a reasonable income and preservation of capital.††

Public Offering (See: *Primary Distribution.*)

Pure (or primitive) security A security that pays off $1 if one particular state of the world occurs and pays off nothing if any other state of the world occurs.*

Put An option to sell a specific security at a specified price within a designated period.*

Puts and calls (See: *Option.*)

Quote The highest bid to buy and the lowest offer to sell a security in a given market at a given time. If you ask your broker for a "quote" on a stock, he may come back with something like "45¼ to 45½." This means that $45.25 is the highest price any buyer wanted to pay at the time the quote was given on the floor of the exchange and that $45.50 was the lowest price which any seller would take at the same time. (See: *Bid and asked.*)††

Rally A brisk rise following a decline in the general price level of the market, or in an individual stock.†

Rate of return The internal rate of return on an investment.*

Ratings Designations used by investors' services to give relative indications of quality.**

Record date The date on which you must be registered as a shareholder of a company in order to receive a declared dividend or, among other things, to vote on company affairs. (See: *Ex dividend, Transfer.*)††

Recourse arrangement A term used in connection with accounts-receivable financing. If a firm sells its accounts receivable to a financial institution under a recourse agreement, then, if the accounts receivable cannot be collected, the selling firm must repurchase the account from the financial institution.*

Redemption price The price at which a bond may be redeemed before maturity, at the option of the issuing company. Redemption value also applies to the price of the company must pay to call in certain types of preferred stock. (See: *Callable.*)†

Red Herring (See: *Prospectus.*)

Rediscount rate The rate of interest at which a bank may borrow from a Federal Reserve Bank.*

Refinancing Same as refunding. New securities are sold by a company and the money is used to retire existing securities. Object may be to save interest costs, extend the maturity of the loan, or both.*

Refunding Sale of new debt securities to replace an old debt issue.*

Registered bond A bond which is registered on the books of the issuing company in the name of the owner. It can be transferred only when endorsed by the registered owner. (See: *Bearer bond, Coupon bond.*)†

Registered representative The man or woman who serves the investor customers of a broker/dealer. In a New York Stock Exchange Member Organization, a Registered Representative must meet the requirements of the exchange as to background and knowledge of the securities business. Also known as an Account Executive or Customer's broker.††

Registrar Usually a trust company or bank charged with the responsibility of keeping a record of the owners of corporation's securities and preventing the issuance of more than the authorized amount. (See: *Transfer.*)††

Registration Before a public offering may be made of new securities by a company, or of outstanding securities by controlling stockholders—through the mails or in interstate commerce—the securities must be registered under the Securities Act of 1933. A statement is filed with the SEC by the issuer. It must disclose pertinent information relating to the company's operations, securities, management and purpose of the public offering.

Before a security may be admitted to dealings on a national securities exchange, it must be registered under the Securities Exchange Act of 1934. The application for registration must be filed with the exchange and the SEC by the company issuing the securities.††

Regression analysis A statistical procedure for predicting the value of one variable (dependent variable) on the basis of knowledge about one or more other variables (independent variables).*

Regulation T The federal regulation governing the amount of credit which may be advanced by brokers and dealers to customers for the purchase of securities. (See: *Margin.*)†

Regulation U The federal regulation governing the amount of credit which may be advanced by a bank to its customers for the purchase of listed stocks. (See: *Margin.*)†

Reinvestment rate The rate of return at which cash flows from an investment are reinvested. The reinvestment rate may or may not be constant from year to year.*

REIT Real Estate Investment Trust, an organization similar to an investment company in some respects but concentrating its holdings in real estate investments. The yield is generally liberal since REIT's are required to distribute as much as 90 percent of their income. (See: *Investment company.*)†

Reorganization When a financially troubled firm goes through reorganization, its assets are restated to reflect their current market value, and its financial structure is restated to reflect any changes on the asset side of the statement. Under a reorganizations the firm continues in existence; this is contrasted to bankruptcy, where the firm is liquidated and ceases to exist.*

Replacement-cost accounting A requirement under SEC release no. 190 (1976) that large companies disclose the replacement costs of inventory items and depreciable plant.*

Repurchase agreements When the Federal Reserve makes a repurchase agreement with a government securities dealer, it buys a security for immediate delivery with an agreement to sell the security back at the same price by a specific date (usually within 15 days) and receives interest at a specific rate. This arrangement allows the Federal Reserve to inject reserves into the banking system on a temporary basis to meet a temporary need and to withdraw these reserves as soon as that need has passed.¶

Required rate of return The rate of return that stockholders expect to receive on common stock investments.*

Residual value The value of leased property at the end of the lease term.*

Retained earnings That portion of earnings not paid out in dividends. The figure that appears on the balance sheet is the sum of the retained earnings for each year throughout the company's history.*

Return (See: *Yield.*)

Revenue bond A bond payable from revenues derived from tolls, charges, or rents paid by users of the facility constructed from the proceeds of the bond issue.**

Rights When a company wants to raise more funds by issuing additional securities, it may give its stockholders the opportunity, ahead of others, to buy the new securities in proportion to the number of shares each owns. The piece of paper evidencing this privilege is called a right. Because the additional stock is usually offered to stockholders below the current market price, rights ordinarily have a market value of their own and are actively traded. In most cases they must be exercised within a relatively short period. Failure to exercise or sell rights may result in actual loss to the holder. (See: *Warrant.*)†

Rights offering A securities flotation offered to existing stockholders.*

Risk The probability that actual future returns will be below expected returns. It is measured by standard deviation or coefficient of variation of expected returns.*

Risk-adjusted discount rates The discount rate applicable for a particular risky (uncertain) stream of income: the riskless rate of interest plus a risk premium appropriate to the level of risk attached to the particular income stream.*

Risk premium The difference between the required rate of return on a particular risky asset and the rate of return on a riskless asset with the same expected life.*

Risk-return trade-off function (See *Security market line.*)

Round lot A unit of trading or a multiple thereof. On the NYSE the unit of trading is generally 100 shares in stocks and $1,000 or $5,000 par value in the case of bonds. In some inactive stocks, the unit of trading is ten shares. (See: *Odd Lot.*)††

Sale and leaseback An operation whereby a firm sells land, buildings, or equipment to a financial institution and simultaneously executes an agreement to lease the property back for a specified period under specific terms.*

Salvage value The value of a capital asset at the end of a specified period. It is the current market price of an asset being considered for replacement in a capital budgeting problem.*

Scale order An order to buy (or sell) a security which specifies the total amount to be bought (or sold) and the amount to be bought (or sold) at specified price variations.†

Seat A traditional figure-of-speech for a membership on an exchange.††

SEC The Securities and Exchange Commission, established by Congress to help protect investors. The SEC administers the Securities Act of 1933, the Securities Exchange Act of 1934, the Securities Act Amendments of 1975, the Trust Indenture Act, the Investment Company Act, the Investment Advisers Act, and the Public Utility Holding Company Act.†

Secondary distribution Also known as a secondary offering. The redistribution of a block of stock, sometimes after it has been sold by the issuing company. The sale is handled off the NYSE by a securities firm or group of firms and the shares are usually offered at a fixed price related to the current market price of the stock. Usually the block is a large one, such as might be involved in the settlement of an estate. The security may be listed or unlisted. (See: *Investment banker, Primary distribution.*)††

Secondary market Market for issues previously offered or sold.**

Securities and Exchange Commission (See *SEC.*)

Securities, junior Securities that have lower priority in claims on assets and income than other securities *(senior securities)*. For example, preferred stock is junior to debentures, but debentures are junior to mortgage bonds. Common stock is the most junior of all corporate securities.*

Securities, senior Securities having claims on income and assets that rank higher than certain other securities *(junior securities)*. For example, mortgage bonds are senior debentures, but debentures are senior to common stock.*

Security market line A graphic representation of the relation between the required return on a security and the product of its risk times a normalized market measure of risk. Risk-return relationships for individual securities or investments.*

Self-supporting debt Debt incurred for a project or enterprise requiring no tax support other than the specific tax or revenue earmarked for that purpose.*

Seller's option A special transaction on the NYSE which gives the seller the right to deliver the stock or bond at any time within a specified period, ranging from not less than 6 business days to not more than 60 days.††

Selling group A group of stock brokerage firms formed for the purpose of distributing a new issue of securities; part of the investment banking process.*

Sensitivity analysis Simulation analysis in which key variables are changed and the resulting change in the rate of return is observed. Typically, the rate of return will be more sensitive to changes in some variables than it will in others.*

Serial bond An issue which matures in part at periodic stated intervals.†

Service lease A lease under which the lessor maintains and services the asset.*

Settlement Conclusion of a securities transaction when a customer pays a broker/dealer for securities purchased or delivers securities sold and receives from the broker the proceeds of a sale. (See: *Regular Way Delivery, Cash Sale.*)††

Short covering Buying stock to return stock previously borrowed to make delivery on a short sale.†

Short position Stocks, options, or futures sold short and not covered as of a particular date. On the NYSE, a tabulation is issued once a month listing all issues on the Exchange in which there was a short position of 5,000 or more shares and issues in which the short position had changed by 2,000 or more shares in the preceding month. Short position also means the total amount of stock an individual has sold short and has not covered, as of a particular date.††

Short sale A transaction by a person who believes a security will decline and sells it, though the person does not own any. For instance: You instruct your broker to sell short 100 shares of XYZ. Your broker borrows the stock so delivery of the 100 shares can be made to the buyer. The money value of the shares borrowed is deposited by your broker with the lender. Sooner or later you must cover your short sale by buying the same amount of stock you borrowed for return to the lender. If you are able to buy XYZ at a lower price than you sold it for, your profit is the difference between the two prices—not counting commissions and taxes. But if you have to pay more for the stock than the price you received, that is the amount of your loss. Stock exchange and federal regulations govern and limit the conditions under which a short sale may be made on a national securities exchange. Sometimes people will sell short a stock they already own in order to protect a paper profit. This is known as selling short against the box.††

Sinking fund Money regularly set aside by a company to redeem its bonds, debentures or preferred stock from time to time as specified in the indenture or charter.††

SIPC Securities Investor Protection Corporation, which provides funds for use, if necessary, to protect customers' cash and securities which may be on deposit with a SIPC member firm in the event the firm fails and is liquidated under the provisions of the SIPC Act. SIPC is not a government agency. It is a nonprofit membership corporation created, however, by an act of Congress.†

Special bid A method of filling an order to buy a large block of stock on the floor of the New York Stock Exchange. In a special bid, the bidder for the block of stock—a pension fund, for instance, will pay a special commission to the broker who represents him in making the purchase. The seller does not pay a commission. The special bid is made on the floor of the exchange at a fixed price which may not be below the last sale of the security or the current bid in the regular market, whichever is higher. Member firms may sell this stock for customers directly to the buyer's broker during trading hours.†

Special offering Opposite of special bid. A notice is printed on the ticker tape announcing the stock sale at a fixed price usually based on the last transaction in the regular auction market. If there are more buyers than stock, allotments are made. Only the seller pays the commission. (See: *Secondary distribution.*)†

Special tax bond A bond secured by a special tax, such as a gasoline tax.**

Specialist A member of the New York Stock Exchange, Inc., who has two functions: First, to maintain an orderly market in the securities registered to the specialist. In order to maintain an orderly market, the Exchange expects specialists to buy or sell for the own account, to a reasonable degree, when there is a temporary disparity between supply and demand. Second, the specialist acts as a broker's broker. When a commission broker on the Exchange floor receives a limit order, say, to buy at $50 a stock then selling at $60—he cannot wait at the post where the stock is traded to see if the price reaches the specified level. So he leaves the order with the specialist, who will try to execute it in the market if and when the stock declines to the specified price. At all times the specialist must put his customers' interests above his own. There are about 400 specialists on the NYSE. (See: *Limited Order.*)††

Speculation The employment of funds by a speculator. Safety of principal is a secondary factor. (See: *Investment.*)†

Speculator One who is willing to assume a relatively large risk in the hope of gain.††

Spin off The separation of a subsidiary or division of a corporation from its parent by issuing shares in a new corporate entity. Shareowners in the parent receive shares in the new company in proportion to their original holding and the total value remains approximately the same.††

Split The division of the outstanding shares of a corporation into a larger number of shares. A 3-for-1 split by a company with 1 million shares outstanding results in 3 million shares outstanding. Each holder of 100 shares before the 3-for-1 split would have 300 shares, although his proportionate equity in the company would remain the same; 100 parts of 1 million are the equivalent of 300 parts of 3 million. Ordinarily splits must be voted by directors and approved by shareholders. (See: *Stock dividends.*)

Standard deviation A statistical term that measures the variability of a set of observations from the mean of the distribution (σ.)*

State-preference model A framework in which decisions are based on probabilities of payoffs under alternative states of the world.*

Stock ahead Sometimes an investor who has entered an order to buy or sell a stock at a certain price will see transactions at that price reported on the ticker tape while his own order has not been executed. The reason is that other buy and sell orders at the same price came in to the specialist ahead of his and had priority. (See: *Book, Specialist.*)†

Stock dividend A dividend paid in securities rather than cash. The dividend may be additional shares of the issuing company, or shares of another company (usually a subsidiary) held by the company.††

Stock split An accounting action to increase the number of shares outstanding; for example, in a 3-for-1 split, shares outstanding would be tripled and each stockholder would be tripled and each stockholder would receive three new shares for each one formerly held. Stock splits involve no transfer from surplus to the capital account.*

Stockholder of record A stockholder whose name is registered on the books of the issuing corporation.†

Stock Index Futures Futures contracts based on market indexes, e.g., NYSE Composite Index Futures Contracts.††

Stop limit order A stop order which becomes a limit order after the specified stop price has been reached. (See: *Limit order, Stop order.*)†

Stop order An order to buy at a price above or sell at a price below the current market. Stop buy orders are generally used to limit loss or protect unrealized profits on a short sale. Stop sell orders are generally used to protect unrealized profits or limit loss on a holding. A stop order becomes a market order when the stock sells at or beyond the specified price and, thus, may not necessarily be executed at that price.†

Stopped stock A service performed—in most cases by the specialist—for an order given him by a commission broker. Let's say XYZ just sold at $50 a share. Broker A comes along with an order to buy 100 shares at the market. The lowest offer is $50.50. Broker A believes he can do better for his client than $50.50, perhaps might get the stock at $50.25. But he doesn't want to take a chance that he'll miss the market—that is, the next sale might be $50.50 and the following one even higher. So he asks the specialist if he will stop 100 at ½ ($50.50). The specialist agrees. The specialist guarantees Broker A he will get 100 shares at 50½ if the stock sells at that price. In the meantime, if the specialist or broker A succeeds in executing the order at $50.25, the stop is called off. (See: *Specialist.*)†

Street name Securities held in the name of a broker instead of his customer's name are said to be carried in a *street name*. This occurs when the securities have been bought on margin or when the customer wishes the security to be held by the broker.†

Subdivision Any legal and authorized political entity under a state's jurisdiction (county, city, water district, school district, etc.).**

Subjective probability distributions Probability distributions determined through subjective procedures without the use of statistics.*

Subordinated debenture A bond having a claim on assets only after the senior debt has been paid off in the event of liquidation.*

Subscription price The price at which a security may be purchased in a rights offering.*

Switch order or contingent order An order for the purchase (sale) of one stock and the sale (purchase) of another stock at a stipulated price difference.†

Swapping Selling one security and buying a similar one almost at the same time to take a loss, usually for tax purposes.††

Switching Selling one security and buying another.†

Syndicate A group of investment bankers who together underwrite and distribute a new issue of securities or a large block of an outstanding issue.†

Synergy A situation where "the whole is greater than the sum of its parts"; in a synergistic merger, the postmerger earnings exceed the sum of the separate companies' premerger earnings.*

Systematic risk That part of a security's risk that cannot be eliminated by diversification.*

Take-over The acquiring of one corporation by another—usually in a friendly merger but sometimes marked by a "proxy fight." In "unfriendly" take-over attempts, the potential buying company may offer a price well above current market values, new securities, and other inducements to stockholders. The management of the subject company might ask for a better price or fight the take-over or merger with another company. (See: *Proxy.*)†

Tangible assets Physical assets as opposed to intangible assets such as goodwill and the stated value of patents.*

Tax base The total resources available for taxation.**

Tax-exempt bond Another name for a municipal bond. The interest on a municipal bond is presently exempt from Federal income tax.**

Tax shelter A medium or process intended to reduce or eliminate the tax burden of an individual. They range from such conventional ones as tax-exempt municipal securities and interest or dividend exclusion to sophisticated limited partnerships in real estate, cattle raising, equipment leasing, oil drilling, research and development activities and motion picture production.††

Technical research Analysis of the market and stocks based on supply and demand. The technician studies price movements, volume, and trends and patterns which are revealed by charting these factors, and attempts to assess the possible effect of current market action on future supply and demand for securities and individual issues. (See: *Fundamental research.*)†

Tender offer A public offer to buy shares from existing stockholders of one public corporation by another company or other organization under specified terms good for a certain time period. Stockholders are asked to "tender" (surrender) their holdings for stated value, usually at a premium above current market price, subject to the tendering of a minimum and maximum number of shares.††

Term issue An issue that has a single maturity.**

Term loan A loan generally obtained from a bank or an insurance company with a maturity greater than one year. Term loans are generally amortized.*

Thin market A market in which there are comparatively few bids to buy or offers to sell, or both. The phrase may apply to a single security or to the entire stock market. In a thin market, price fluctuations between transactions are usually larger than when the market is liquid. A thin market in a particular stock may reflect lack of interest in that issue or a limited supply of or demand for stock in the market. (See: *Bid and asked, Liquidity, Offer.*)†

Third market Trading of stock exchange listed securities in the over-the-counter market by non-exchange-member brokers.††

Time order An order which becomes a market or limited price order at a specified time.†

Time value The part of an option premium that is in excess of the intrinsic value.††

Tips Supposedly "inside" information on corporation affairs.†

Trader Individuals who buy and sell for their own accounts for short-term profit. Also, an employee of a broker/dealer or financial institution who specializes in handling purchases and sales of securities for the firm and/or its clients. (See: *Investor, Speculator.*)††

Trading floor (See: *Floor.*)

Trading market The secondary market for outstanding securities.**

Trading post One of 23 trading locations on the floor of the New York Stock Exchange at which stocks assigned to that location are bought and sold. About 75 stocks are traded at each post.†

Transfer This term may refer to two different operations. For one, the delivery of a stock certificate from the seller's broker to the buyer's broker and legal change of ownership, normally accomplished within a few days. For another, to record the change of ownership on the books of the corporation by the transfer agent. When the purchaser's name is recorded, dividends, notices of meetings, proxies, financial reports, and all pertinent literature sent by the issuer to its securities holders are mailed direct to the new owner. (See: *Registrar, Street name.*)††

Transfer agent A transfer agent keeps a record of the name of each registered shareowner, his or her address, the number of shares owned, and sees that certificates presented for transfer are properly cancelled and new certificates issued in the name of the new owner. (See: *Registrar.*)††

Treasury bills Short-term U.S. Treasury securities issued in minimum denominations of $10,000 and usually having original maturities of 3, 6, or 12 months. Investors purchase bills at prices lower than the face value of the bills; the return to the investors is the difference between the price paid for the bills and the amount received when the bills are sold or when they mature. Treasury bills are the type of security used most frequently in open market operations.¶

Treasury bonds Long-term U.S. Treasury securities usually having initial maturities of more than 10 years and issued in denominations of $1,000 or more, depending on the specific issue. Bonds pay interest semiannually, with principal payable at maturity.¶

Treasury notes Intermediate-term coupon-bearing U.S. Treasury securities having initial maturities from 1 to 10 years and issued in denominations of $1,000 or more, depending on the maturity of the issue. Notes pay interest semiannually, and the principal is payable at maturity.¶

Treasury stock Stock issued by a company, but later reacquired. It may be held in the company's treasury indefinitely, reissued to the public, or retired. Treasury stock receives no dividends, and has no vote while held by the company.††

Trust receipt An instrument acknowledging that the borrower holds certain goods in trust for the lender. Trust receipt financing is used in connection with the financing of inventories for automobile dealers, construction equipment dealers, appliance dealers, and other dealers in expensive durable goods.*

Trustee The representative of bondholders who acts in their interest and facilitates communication between them and the issuer. Typically these duties are handled by a department of a commercial bank.*

Turnover rate The volume of shares traded in a year as a percentage of total shares listed on an exchange, outstanding for an individual issue, or held in an institutional portfolio.††

Underwriter (See: *Investment banker.*)

Underwriting (1) The entire process of issuing new corporate securities. (2) The insurance function of bearing the risk of adverse price fluctuations during the period in which a new issue of stock or bonds is being distributed.*

Underwriting syndicate A syndicate of investment firms formed to spread the risk associated with the purchase and distribution of a new issue of securities. The larger the issue, the more firms typically are involved in the syndicate.*

Unlimited tax bond A bond secured by pledge of taxes that are not limited by rate or amount.**

Unlisted A security not listed on a stock exchange. (See: *Over-the-counter.*)†

Unsystematic risk That part of a security's risk associated with random events; unsystematic risk can be eliminated by proper diversification.*

Up tick A term used to designate a transaction made at a price higher than the preceding transaction. Also called a *plus-tick.* A *zero-plus* tick is a term used for a transaction at the same price as the preceding trade but higher than the preceding different price.

Conversely, a *down tick,* or *minus* tick, is a term used to designate a transaction made at a price lower than the preceding trade.

A plus sign, or a minus sign, is displayed throughout the day next to the last price of each company's stock traded at each trading post on the floor of the New York Stock Exchange. (See: *Short sale.*)†

Utility theory A body of theory dealing with the relationships among money income, utility (or "happiness"), and the willingness to accept risk.*

Value additivity principle Neither fragmenting cash flows or recombining them will affect the resulting values of the cash flows.*

Variable annuity A life insurance policy where the annuity premium (a set amount of dollars) is immediately turned into units of a portfolio of stocks. Upon retirement, the policyholder is paid according to accumulated units, the dollar value of which varies according to the performance of the stock portfolio. Its objective is to preserve, through stock investment, the purchasing value of the annuity which otherwise is subject to erosion through inflation.††

Volume The number of shares traded in a security or an entire market during a given period. Volume is usually considered on a daily basis and a daily average is computed for longer periods.†

Voting right The common stockholder's right to vote their stock in the affairs of a company. Preferred stock usually has the right to vote when preferred dividends are in default for a specified period. The right to vote may be delegated by the stockholder to another person. (See: *Cumulative voting, Proxy.*)††

Warrant A certificate giving the holder the right to purchase securities at a stipulated price within a specified time limit or perpetually. Sometimes a warrant is offered with securities as an inducement to buy. (See: *Rights.*)††

Weighted cost of capital A weighted average of the component costs of debt, preferred stock, and common equity. Also called the *composite cost of capital.**

When issued A short form of "when, as, and if issued." The term indicates a conditional transaction in a security authorized for issuance but not as yet actually issued. All "when issued" transactions are on an "if" basis, to be settled if and when the actual security is issued and the exchange or National Association of Securities Dealers rules the transactions are to be settled.†

Wire house A member firm of an exchange maintaining a communications network linking either its own branch offices, offices of correspondent firms, or a combination of such offices.†

Working capital Refers to a firm's investment in short-term assets—cash, short-term securities, accounts receivable, and inventories. *Gross working capital* is defined as a firm's total current assets. *Net working capital* is defined as current assets minus current liabilities. If the term *working capital* is used without further qualification, it generally refers to gross working capital.*

Working control Theoretically, ownership of 51 percent of a company's voting stock is necessary to exercise control. In practice—and this is particularly true in the case of a large corporation—effective control sometimes can be exerted through ownership, individually or by a group acting in concert, of less than 50 percent.†

Yield Also known as return. The dividends or interest paid by a company expressed as a percentage of the current price. A stock with a current market value of $3.20 is said to return 8 percent ($3.20 ÷ $40.00). The current yield on a bond is figured the same way.††

Yield to maturity The yield of a bond to maturity takes into account the price discount from or premium over the face amount. It is greater than the current yield when the bond is selling at a discount and less than the current yield when the bond is selling at a premium.†

Zero coupon bonds Bonds which do not convey a coupon (i.e., do not pay interest) but which are offered at a substantial discount from par value and appreciate to their full value (usually $1,000) at maturity. However, under U.S. tax law, the imputed interest is taxed as it accrues. The appeal of Zero coupon bonds is primarily for IRA and other tax sheltered retirement accounts.

Acquisition Takeover Glossary

Asset Play[1] A firm whose underlying assets are worth substantially more (after paying off the firm's liabilities) than the market value of its stock.

Bear hug An unnegotiated offer, in the form of a letter made directly to the board of directors of the target company. The price and terms are sufficiently detailed so that the di-

[1]Source: From the *AAII Journal*, American Association of *Individual Investors*, 612 North Michigan Avenue, Chicago, IL 60611. Excerpted from Ben Branch "White Knight Rescues Investors From Terminology."

rectors are obliged to make the offer public. The offer states a time limit for a response and may threaten a tender offer or other action if it is not accepted.

Breakup value[1] The sum of the values of the firm's assets if sold off separately.

Crown jewel option[1] The strategem of selling off or spinning off the asset that makes the firm an attractive takeover candidate.

Four-nine position[1] A holding of approximately 4.9% of the outstanding shares of a company. At 5%, the holder must file a form [13d] with the SEC, revealing his position. Thus, a four-nine position is about the largest position that one can quietly hold.

Black knight[1] A potential acquirer that management opposes and would prefer to find an alternative to (i.e. a *white knight*).

Going private[1] The process of buying back the publicly held stock so that what was heretofore a public firm becomes private.

Golden handcuffs[1] Employment agreement that makes the departure of upper level managers very costly to them. For instance, such managers may lose very attractive stock option rights by leaving prior to their normal retirement age.

Golden handshake[1] A provision in a preliminary agreement to be acquired in which the target firm gives the acquiring firm an option to purchase its shares or assets at attractive prices or to receive a substantial bonus if the proposed takeover does not occur.

Golden parachute[1] Extremely generous separation payments for upper level executives that are required to be fulfilled if the firm's control shifts.

Greenmail[1] Incentive payments to dissuade the interest of outsiders who may otherwise seek control of a firm. The payment frequently takes the form of a premium price for the outsiders' shares, coupled with an agreement from them to avoid buying more stock for a set period of time.

The firm bears the cost of the payment. The stock price generally falls after the payment and the removal of the outside threat.

In play[1] The status of being a recognized takeover candidate.

Junk bonds[1] High-risk, high-yield bonds that are often used to finance takeovers.

LBO[1] A leveraged buyout. A purchase of a company financed largely by debt that is backed by the firm's own assets.

Loaded laggard[1] A stock of a company whose assets, particularly its liquid assets, have high values relative to the stock's price.

Lockup agreement[1] An agreement between an acquirer and target that makes the target very unattractive to any other acquirer; similar to a *golden handshake.*

Mezzanine financing Debt financing subordinate to the claims of the senior debt. This financing often has equity participation in the form of stock options, warrants or conversion to cheap stock.

Nibble strategy A takeover approach involving the purchase in the public market of minority stock position in the target company and a subsequent tender offer for the rest of the target stock.

PacMan defense[1] The tactic of seeking to acquire the firm that has targeted your own firm as a takeover prospect.

Poison pill[1] A provision in the corporate bylaws or other governance documents providing for a very disadvantageous result for a potential acquirer should its ownership position be allowed to exceed some preassigned threshold. For example, if anyone acquires more than 20% of Company A's stock, the acquirer might then have to sell $100 worth of its own stock to other shareholders at $50.

Raider A hostile outside party that seeks to take over other companies.

Saturday night special A seven day cash tender offer for all of the target firm's stock. It is usually launched on a Saturday on the assumption that the target company will have difficulty mobilizing its key advisors in reaction to the offer.

Scorched earth defense[1] A tactic in which the defending company's management engages in practices that reduce their company's value to such a degree that it is no longer attractive to the potential acquirer. This approach is more often threatened than actually employed.

Senior debt financing The issuance of debt instruments having first claim on a firm's assets (secured debt) or cash flow (unsecured debt).

Shark repellant[1] Anti-takeover provisions such as the poison pill.

Short swing profit[1] A gain made by an insider (including anyone with more than 10% of the stock) who holds stock for less than six months. Such gains must be paid back to the company whose shares were sold.

Standstill agreement[1] A reciprocal understanding between a company's management and an outside party that usually owns a significant minority position. Each party gives up certain rights in exchange for corresponding concessions by the other party. For example, the outside group may agree to limit its stock purchases to keep its ownership percentage below some level (for instance, 20%).

In exchange, management may agree to a minority board representation by the outsider.

Swipe An unnegotiated offer to purchase the shares of a target company's stock made after the target's board has announced its intention to sell the company (usually in a leverage buyout to management). The swipe price is higher than that initially proposed by the board of directors.

Tender offer An offer by a firm to buy the stock of another firm (target) by going directly to the stockholders of the target. The offer is often made over the opposition of the management of the target firm.

13d[1] A form that must be filed with the SEC when a single investor or an associated group owns 5% or more of a company's stock. The form reveals the size of the holding and the investor's intentions.

Two-tier offer[1] A takeover device in which a relatively high per share price is paid for controlling interest in a target and a lesser per share price is paid for the remainder.

White knight defense[1] Finding an alternative and presumably more friendly acquirer than the present takeover threat.

White squire defense[1] Finding an important ally to purchase a strong minority position (for example, 25%) of the potential acquisition's stock. Presumably this ally (the "white squire") will oppose and hopefully block the efforts of any hostile firm seeking to acquire the vulnerable firm.

Securities and Exchange Commission

JUDICIARY PLAZA
450 FIFTH STREET, NW
WASHINGTON, DC 20549
INFORMATION: 202-272-2650
FREEDOM OF INFORMATION ACT:
202-272-7450
FILINGS BY REGISTERED COMPANIES:
202-272-2624

FULL AND FAIR DISCLOSURE

The Securities Act of 1933 requires issuers of securities making public offerings of securities in interstate commerce or through the mails, directly or by others on their behalf, to file registration statements containing financial and other pertinent data about the issuer and the securities being offered. A similar requirement applies to such offerings on behalf of a controlling person of the issuer. Unless a registration statement is in effect with respect to such securities, it is unlawful to sell the securities in interstate commerce or through the mails. (There are certain limited exemptions, such as government securities, nonpublic offerings, and intrastate offerings, as well as offerings not exceeding $1,500,000 in amount, which comply with the commission's Regulation A.) The effectiveness of a registration statement may be refused or suspended after a public hearing, if the statement contains material misstatements or omissions, thus barring sale of the securities until it is appropriately amended. Registration of securities does not imply approval of the issue by the commission or that the commission has found the registration disclosures to be accurate. It does not insure investors against loss in their purchase but serves rather to provide information upon which investors may make an informed and realistic evaluation of the worth of the securities.

Persons responsible for filing false information with the commission subject themselves to the risk of fine or imprisonment or both; and persons connected with the public offering may be liable in damages to purchasers of the securities if the disclosures in the registration statement and prospectus are materially defective. Also, the above act contains antifraud provisions which apply generally to the sale of securities, whether or not registered (48 Stat. 74; 15 U.S.C. 77a et seq.).

REGULATION OF SECURITIES MARKETS AND PERSONS CONDUCTING A SECURITIES BUSINESS

The Securities Exchange Act of 1934 assigns to the commission board regulatory responsibilities over the securities markets, the self-regulatory organizations within the securities industry, and persons conducting a business in securities. Persons who execute transactions in securities generally are required to register with the Commission as broker-dealers. The commission is directed to facilitate the establishment of a national market system for securities and a national system for the clearance and settlement of securities transactions. Securities exchanges and certain clearing agencies are required to register with the commission, and associations of brokers or dealers are permitted to register with the commission. The securities Exchange Act also provides for the establishment of the Municipal Securities Rulemaking Board to formulate rules for the municipal

Source: This material was abstracted from the United States Government Manual.

securities industry. The commission oversees the self-regulatory activities of the national securities exchanges and associations, registered clearing agencies, and the Municipal Securities Rulemaking Board. In addition, the commission regulates industry professionals, such as securities brokers and dealers, certain municipal securities professionals, and transfer agents.

The Securities Exchange Act authorizes national securities exchanges, national securities associations, clearing agencies, and the Municipal Securities Rulemaking Board to adopt rules that are designed, among other things to promote just and equitable principles of trade and to protect investors. The commission is required to approve or disapprove most proposed rules of these self-regulatory organizations and has the power to abrogate or amend existing rules of the national securities exchanges, national securities associations, and the Municipal Securities Rulemaking Board.

In addition, the commission has broad rulemaking authority over the activities of brokers, dealers, municipal securities dealers, securities information processors, and transfer agents. The commission may regulate such securities trading practices as short sales and stabilizing transactions. It may regulate the trading of options on national securities exchanges and the activities of members of exchanges who trade on the trading floors and may adopt rules governing broker-dealer sales practices in dealing with investors. The commission also is authorized to adopt rules concerning the financial responsibility of brokers and dealers and reports to be made by brokers and dealers. The Securities Exchange Act also empowers the Board of Governors of the Federal Reserve System to prescribe rules relating to the extension of credit by brokers and dealers for securities transactions. Such rules include the establishment of minimum margin requirements with respect to securities registered on national securities exchanges and certain securities traded over-the-counter (48 Stat. 881; U.S.C. 78a et seq.).

The Securities Exchange Act also requires the filing of registration applications and annual and other reports with national securities exchanges and the commission by companies whose securities are listed upon the exchanges, by companies that have assets of $3 million or more and 500 or more shareholders of record, and by companies that distributed securities pursuant to a registration statement declared effective by the commission under the Securities Act of 1933. Such applications and reports must contain financial and other data prescribed by the commission as necessary or appropriate for the protection of investors and to issue fair dealing. In addition, the solicitation of proxies, authorizations, or consents from holders of such registered securities must be made in accordance with rules and regulations prescribed by the commission. These rules provide for disclosures to securities holders of information relevant to the subject matter of the solicitation.

Disclosure of the holdings and transactions by officers, directors, and large (10 percent) holders of equity securities of companies is also required, and any and all persons who acquire more than 5 percent of certain equity securities are required to file detailed information with the commission and any exchange upon which such securities may be traded. Moreover, any person making a tender offer for certain classes of equity securities is required to file reports with the commission, if as a result of the tender offer such person would own more than 5 percent of the outstanding shares of the particular class of equity involved. The commission also is authorized to promulgate rules governing the repurchase by a corporate issuer of its own securities.

REGULATION OF MUTUAL FUNDS AND OTHER INVESTMENT COMPANIES

The Investment Company Act of 1940 (54 Stat. 847; 15 U.S.C. 80a–51) requires investment companies to register with the Commission and regulates their activities to protect investors. The regulation covers sales and management fees, composition of boards of directors, and capital structure. Additionally, the act prohibits investment companies from engaging in various transactions, including transactions with affiliated persons unless the commission first determines that such transactions are fair. Under the act, the commission may institute court action to enjoin the consummation of mergers and other plans for reorganization of investment companies if such plans are unfair to security holders. It also may impose sanctions by administrative proceedings against investment company managements for violations of the act and other federal securities laws, and file court actions to enjoin acts and practices of management officials involving breaches of fiduciary duty involving personal misconduct and to disqualify such officials from office (54 Stat. 789; 15 U.S.C. 80a–1—80a–52).

REGULATION OF COMPANIES CONTROLLING ELECTRIC OR GAS UTILITIES

The Public Utility Holding Company Act of 1935 (49 Stat. 838; 15 U.S.C. 79 et seq.) provides for regulation by the commission of the purchase and sale of securities and assets by companies in electric and gas utility holding company systems, their intra-system transactions and service and management arrangements. It limits holding companies to a single coordinated utility system and requires simplification of complex corporate and capital structures and elimination of unfair distribution of voting power among holders of system securities.

The issuance and sale of securities by holding companies and their subsidiaries, unless exempt (subject to conditions and terms which the commission is empowered to impose) as an issue expressly authorized by the state commission in the state in which the issuer is incorporated, must be found by the commission to meet statutory standards, namely: that the new security is reasonably adapted to the security structure and earning power of the issuer; that the proposed financing is necessary and appropriate to the economical and efficient operation of the company's business; that the consideration received, and fees, commissions, and other remuneration paid, are fair; and that the terms and conditions of the sale are not detrimental to investors, consumers, or the public.

The purchase and sale of utility properties and other assets may not be made in contravention of rules, regulations, or orders of the commission regarding the consideration to be received, maintenance of competitive conditions, fees and commissions, accounts, disclosure of interest, and similar matters. In passing upon proposals for reorganization, merger, or consolidation, the commission must be satisfied that the objectives of the act generally are complied with and that the terms of the proposal are fair and equitable to all classes of security holders affected (49 Stat. 803; 15 U.S.C 79–92z–6).

REGULATION OF INVESTMENT COUNSELORS AND ADVISERS

The Investment Advisers Act of 1940 (54 Stat. 857; 15 U.S.C. 80b–20) provides that persons who, for compensation, engage in the business of advising others with respect to their security transactions must register with the commission. The act prohibits certain types of fee arrangements, makes unlawful practices of investment advisers involving fraud or deceit, and requires, among other things, disclosure of any adverse interests the advisers may have in transactions executed for clients. The act authorizes the commission to issue rules proscribing acts and practices that may operate as a fraud or deceit upon investors (54 Stat. 847; 15 U.S.C. 80b–1—80b–21).

REHABILITATION OF FAILING CORPORATIONS

Chapter 11, section 1109(a), of the Bankruptcy Code (92 Stat. 2629; 11 U.S.C. 1109) provides for Commission participation as a statutory party in corporate reorganization proceedings administered in Federal courts. The principal functions of the Commission are to protect the interests of public investors involved in such cases through efforts to ensure their adequate representation and to participate on legal and policy issues which are of concern to public investors generally.

INDEPENDENT REPRESENTATION OF THE INTERESTS OF HOLDERS OF DEBT SECURITIES

The interests of purchasers of publicly offered debt securities issued pursuant to trust indentures are safeguarded under the provisions of the Trust Indenture Act of 1939 (15 U.S.C. 77aaa). This act, among other things, requires the exclusion from such indentures of certain types of exculpatory clauses and the inclusion of certain protective provisions. The independence of the indenture trustee, who is a representative of the debt holder, is assured by proscribing certain relationships that might conflict with the proper exercise of his duties (53 Stat. 1149; 15 U.S.C. 77aaa–77bbbb).

ENFORCEMENT ACTIVITIES

The commission's enforcement activities are designed to secure compliance with the federal securities laws administered by the commission and the rules and regulations adopted thereunder. These activities include measures to compel obedience to the disclosure requirements of the registration and other provisions of the acts; to prevent fraud and deception in the purchase and sale of securities; to obtain court orders enjoining acts and practices that operate as a fraud upon investors or otherwise violate the laws; to suspend or revoke the registrations of brokers, dealers, investment companies and investment advisers who willfully engage in such acts and practices; to suspend or bar from association persons associated with brokers, dealers, investment companies and investment advisers who have violated any provision of the federal securities laws; and to prosecute persons who have engaged in fraudulent activities, or other willful violations of those laws. In addition, attorneys, accountants, and other professionals who violate the securities laws face possible loss of their privilege to practice before the commission. To this end, private investigations are conducted into complaints or other evidences of securities violations. Evidence thus established of law violations is used in appropriate administrative proceedings to revoke registration or in actions instituted in federal courts to restrain or enjoin such activities. Where the evidence tends to establish fraud or other willful violation of the securities laws, the facts are referred to the Attorney General for criminal prosecution of the offenders. The commission may assist in such prosecutions.

INVESTOR INFORMATION AND PROTECTION

Complaints and inquiries may be directed to the home office or to any regional office. Registration statements and other public documents filed with the commission are available for public inspection in the public reference room at the home office. Much of the information also is available in its New York, Chicago, and Los Angeles regional offices, and to a lesser extent in the other regional offices of the commission. Reproduction of the public material may be purchased from the commission as prescribed rates.

Small Business Activities Information on security laws which pertain to small businesses in relation to securities offerings may be obtained from the Commission. Phone, 202-272-2644.

Consumer Activities Publications detailing the Commission's activities, which include material of assistance to the potential investor, are available from the Publications Unit. In addition, the Office of Consumer Affairs and Information Services answers questions from investors, assists investors with specific problems regarding their relations with broker-dealers and companies, and advises the Commission and other offices and divisions regarding problems frequently encountered by investors and possible regulatory solutions to such problems. Phone, 202-272-7440.

Reading Rooms The Commission maintains a public reference room (phone, 202-272-7450) and also a library (phone, 202-272-2618) where additional information may be obtained.

REGIONAL OFFICES (Securities and Exchange Commission)

Region	Address
1. New York, New Jersey	26 Federal Plaza, New York, NY 10078 Phone: 212-264-1636
2. Maine, Vermont, New Hampshire, Massachusetts, Connecticut, Rhode Island	150 Causeway Street, Boston, MA 02114 Phone: 617-223-2721
3. Tennessee, North Carolina, South Carolina, Mississippi, Alabama, Georgia, Florida, Louisiana (southeastern portion only)	1375 Peachtree Street NE, Atlanta, GA 30367 Phone: 404-881-4768
4. Minnesota, Wisconsin, Michigan, Iowa, Missouri, Illinois, Indiana, Ohio, Kentucky	219 S. Dearborn Street, Chicago, IL 60604 Phone: 312-353-7390
5. Kansas, Oklahoma, Texas, Arkansas, Louisiana (except southeastern portion)	411 W. 7th Street, Fort Worth, TX 76102 Phone: 817-334-3821
6. North Dakota, South Dakota, Colorado, Kansas, Utah, Wyoming, New Mexico	410 17th Street, Denver, CO 80202 Phone: 303-837-2071
7. California, Nevada, Arizona, Hawaii, Guam	5757 Wilshire Boulevard, Los Angeles, CA 90036 Phone: 213-468-3098
8. Washington, Oregon, Alaska, Montana, Idaho	915 Second Avenue, Seattle, WA 98174 Phone: 206-442-7990
9. Pennsylvania, West Virginia, Virginia, Maryland, Delaware, Washington, D.C.	600 Arch St., Philadelphia, PA 19106 Phone: 215-597-3100

Tracing Obsolete Securities*

The following is a list of some of the available sources of information on tracing obsolete securities. This list should be useful to those who wonder whether their old securities have any value, to researchers, and to collectors. All of the books listed below should be available in large public libraries or in larger business libraries.

To trace a security, you need to know the name of the company, the date of issue and the state in which the company was incorporated; all three pieces of information should appear on the security. Start with volumes appropriate to the issue date of the security and continue through to the present, if necessary. If the security can not be found, contact the department that registers corporations in the state in which the company was incorporated. In most states this will be the office of the Secretary of State. They maintain records of name changes and bankruptcies and can usually answer your inquiry quickly; some charge a nominal fee for the service. Call the department to see what their procedures and costs are. You may need to send a copy of the certificate. Do not send the original certificate.

For an introduction to searching obsolete securities, the best guide, now out-of-print, is:

Cargiulo, Albert F. and Rocco Carlucci.
The Questioned Stock Manual: A Guide to Determining the True Worth of Old and Collectible Securities. New York: McGraw-Hill, 1979, xiv, 193 p.: ill. tables.
Chapters 3 and 4 deal with locating sources of information on securities. Chapter 6 covers the detection and recognition of fraudulent securities and a description of how securities are printed. The appendix contains a table of the top 100 firms, 1917–1977.

For historical data, beginning with colonial times, the Fisher, Scudder, and Smythe manuals are classics. The manuals are still published and the Smythe firm continues to do research into obsolete securities, charging a fee of $25 for each company. They also serve as dealers and appraisers of obsolete securities for collectors. You can contact them at:

R. M. Smythe & Co.
26 Broadway
New York, NY 10004
(212) 943–1880

* Frederick N. Nesta, Director, Library Associates, NY; Director, Marymount Manhattan College Library.

Robert D. Fisher
Manual of Valuable & Worthless Securities: Showing Companies That Have Been Reorganized, Merged, Liquidated or Dissolved, Little Known Companies and Oil Leases. New York: R. M. Smythe, 1926–. 15 v.
First published in 1926 as the *Marvyn Scudder Manual . . .*, the series was taken over by Robert D. Fisher with vol. 5 in 1937. It has been published by the R. M. Smythe firm since 1971 under the editorship of Robert D. Fisher, Jr. With vol. 6 the series limited itself to securities and the date on which they became worthless. The earlier volumes present brief corporate obituaries. Volume 15, 1984, includes a price guide for collectors of obsolete certificates.

Smythe, Roland M.
Valuable Extinct Securities: the Secret of the Obsolete Security Business. Unclaimed Money and How to Collect It, With a List of . . . Extinct Securities of Good Value From the Records of the Four Principal Dealers. . . . New York: R. M. Smythe, 1929. v, 398 p.
By the author and publisher of *Obsolete American Securities and Corporations*, later the *Robert D. Fisher Manual of Valuable and Worthless Securities.* This list of over 1,500 securities gives due and foreclosure dates and the dates of sale or merger.

Smythe, Roland M.
Obsolete American Securities and Corporations. New York: R. M. Smythe, 1911. liv, 1166 p.: ill.
(*Obsolete American Securities and Corporations:* vol. 2). Pages 1–28 discuss Continental and other early U.S. state and foreign notes and bonds. Twenty plates illustrate some of the bonds discussed. Volume 1 was published in 1904.
Valuable Extinct Securities Guide. 1939 ed. New York: R. M. Smythe, Inc., 1938. 127 p. The first edition was published in 1929 and was the sequel to *Obsolete American Securities and Corporations.*

The books below can be consulted to trace more recent corporate reorganizations:

Capital Changes Reporter for Federal Income Tax Purposes. Clark, NJ: Commerce Clearing House (NJ), 1949–. 6 v., looseleaf. Securities distributions, taxability of disbursements, splits, offers, rights, etc.

The National Monthly Stock Summary. Jer-

sey City, NJ: National Quotation Bureau, 1926–.
Summary data from the daily service, supplied either from the service or from dealers' lists. Name, par value, exchange, closing price, bids and offerings. May also include shares outstanding, control, reorganization, dividend or other information. Monthly, with bound cumulative volumes issued twice yearly.

Capital Adjustments, Reorganizations and Exchanges, Stock Dividends. Rights and Splits. Englewood Cliffs, NJ: Prentice-Hall, 1980–. 2 v. in 3, looseleaf.
Current changes, disbursements, etc. Includes notes on taxability. Supplements the bound volumes below.

Capital Adjustments: Stock Dividends, Stock Rights, Reorganizations. Englewood Cliffs, NJ: Prentice-Hall, 1962–.
The earlier volumes cover corporate and government securities from early in the century. Updated by looseleaf supplements. Includes name changes, incorporation dates, mergers.

Bank & Quotation Record. Arlington, MA: National News Services, 1928–.
"A publication of the Commercial and Financial Chronicle." Monthly opening and closing prices, highs, lows, etc. Includes equipment trusts, public utility bonds, Chicago Board Options Exchange, foreign exchange rates for the month, CDs, Federal funds, prime banker acceptance rates, commercial paper statistics. Published continuously for over sixty years, it is a fascinating document of American financial history.

FOREIGN CORPORATIONS

Canada

Canadian Mines Register of Dormant and Defunct Companies: Third Supplement. Toronto: Northern Miner Press Limited, 1976. 108 p. Originally published in 1960.

Survey of Predecessor and Defunct Companies. 3rd ed. Toronto: The Financial Post Corporation Service Group, 1985. 208 p.
Covers over 12,000 companies and spans over 50 years. Lists name changes, removals, the exchange basis for new shares, along with the addresses and telephone numbers of Canadian Federal and Provincial corporate registry offices.

United Kingdom

The Stock Exchange Official Year-Book. London: Macmillan, 1934–.
Contains substantial information on the London Stock Exchange, foreign securities, municipal securities, regulations and statistics and a directory of International exchanges. The main body lists each company with parent/subsidiary note, background, financial data, stock history, voting, dividends. Includes the *Register of Defunct and Other Companies Removed from the Stock Exchange Official Year-Book,* a listing of over 23,000 companies removed from the Official Year-Book since 1875, along with a list of Commonwealth Government and Provincial stocks redeemed or converted since 1940. The Register was published separately until 1980.

Australia

Register of Companies Removed from the Stock Exchanges Official Lists. Sydney: Stock Exchange Research Pty., 1984? 104 p.
Lists companies that were traded on one or more Australian exchanges. Historical data, with delistings going back to the early 1930s.

Bonds and Money Market Instruments

INTEREST RATES AND BOND YIELDS

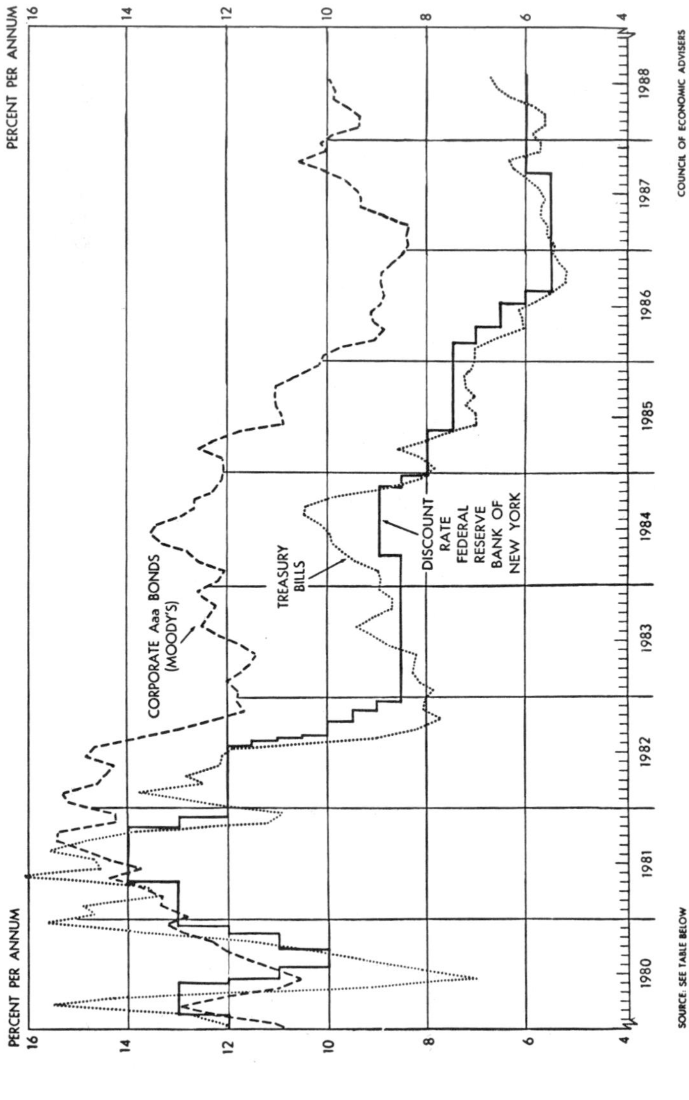

[Percent per annum]

Period	U.S. Treasury security yields: 3-month bills (new issues) [1]	U.S. Treasury security yields: Constant maturities [2]: 3-year	Constant maturities [2]: 10-year	High-grade municipal bonds (Standard & Poor's) [3]	Corporate Aaa bonds (Moody's) [4]	Prime commercial paper, 6 months [1]	Discount rate (N.Y. F.R. Bank) [5]	Prime rate charged by banks [5]	New-home mortgage yields (FHLBB) [6]
1981	14.029	14.44	13.91	11.23	14.17	14.76	13.41	18.87	14.70
1982	10.686	12.92	13.00	11.57	13.79	11.89	11.02	14.86	15.14
1983	8.63	10.45	11.10	9.47	12.04	8.89	8.50	10.79	12.57
1984	9.58	11.89	12.44	10.15	12.71	10.16	8.80	12.04	12.38
1985	7.48	9.64	10.62	9.18	11.37	8.01	7.69	9.93	11.55
1986	5.98	7.06	7.68	7.38	9.02	6.39	6.33	8.33	10.17
1987	5.82	7.68	8.39	7.73	9.38	6.85	5.66	8.22	9.31
1987: July	5.78	7.74	8.45	7.83	9.42	6.72	5.50–5.50	8.25–8.25	9.41
Aug	6.00	8.03	8.76	7.90	9.67	6.81	5.50–5.50	8.25–8.25	9.38
Sept	6.32	8.67	9.42	8.36	10.18	7.55	5.50–6.00	8.25–8.75	9.37
Oct	6.40	8.75	9.52	8.84	10.52	7.96	6.00–6.00	8.75–9.00	9.25
Nov	5.81	7.99	8.86	8.09	10.01	7.17	6.00–6.00	9.00–8.75	9.30
Dec	5.80	8.13	8.99	8.07	10.11	7.49	6.00–6.00	8.75–8.75	9.15
1988: Jan	5.90	7.87	8.67	7.81	9.88	6.92	6.00–6.00	8.75–8.75	9.10
Feb	5.69	7.38	8.21	7.55	9.40	6.58	6.00–6.00	8.75–8.50	9.12
Mar	5.69	7.50	8.37	7.80	9.39	6.64	6.00–6.00	8.50–8.50	9.15
Apr	5.92	7.83	8.72	7.91	9.67	6.92	6.00–6.00	8.50–8.50	9.13
May	6.27	8.24	9.09	8.01	9.90	7.31	6.00–6.00	8.50–9.00	8.95
June	6.50	8.22	8.92	7.86	9.86	7.53	6.00–6.00	9.00–9.00	9.07
July	6.73	8.44	9.06	7.87	9.96	7.90	6.00–6.00	9.00–9.50	....
Week ended:									
1988: July 9	6.57	8.27	8.93	7.84	9.84	7.67	6.00–6.00	9.00–9.00	....
16	6.72	8.45	9.08	7.86	9.95	7.88	6.00–6.00	9.00–9.50	....
23	6.76	8.51	9.13	7.89	10.03	8.01	6.00–6.00	9.50–9.50	....
30	6.88	8.56	9.12	7.87	10.03	8.07	6.00–6.00	9.50–9.50	....
Aug 6	6.89	....	....	....	....	....	6.00–	9.50–	....

[1] Bank-discount basis.
[2] Yields on the more actively traded issues adjusted to constant maturities by the Treasury Department.
[3] Weekly data are Wednesday figures.
[4] Series excludes public utility issues for January 17, 1984 through October 11, 1984 due to lack of appropriate issues.
[5] Average effective rate for year; opening and closing rate for month and week.
[6] Effective rate (in the primary market) on conventional mortgages, reflecting fees and charges as well as contract rate and assumed, on the average, repayment at end of 10 years.

Sources: Department of the Treasury, Board of Governors of the Federal Reserve System, Federal Home Loan Bank Board, Moody's Investors Service, and Standard & Poor's Corporation.

Source: *Economic Indicators*, Council of Economic Advisers.

PRIME RATE CHARGED BY BANKS on Short-Term Business Loans (percent per year)

Effective date	Rate	Effective Date	Rate	Month	Average rate	Month	Average rate
1985—Jan. 15	10.50	1987—Apr. 1	7.75	1985—Jan.	10.61	1986—Sept.	7.50
May 20	10.00	May 1	8.00	Feb.	10.50	Oct.	7.50
June 18	9.50	15	8.25	Mar.	10.50	Nov.	7.50
		Sept. 4	8.75	Apr.	10.50	Dec.	7.50
1986—Mar. 7	9.00	Oct. 7	9.25	May	10.31		
Apr. 21	8.50	22	9.00	June	9.78	1987—Jan.	7.50
July 11	8.00	Nov. 5	8.75	July	9.50	Feb.	7.50
Aug. 26	7.50			Aug.	9.50	Mar.	7.50
		1988—Feb. 2	8.50	Sept.	9.50	Apr.	7.75
				Oct.	9.50	May	8.14
				Nov.	9.50	June	8.25
				Dec.	9.50	July	8.25
						Aug.	8.25
				1986—Jan.	9.50	Sept.	8.70
				Feb.	9.50	Oct.	9.07
				Mar.	9.10	Nov.	8.78
				Apr.	8.83	Dec.	8.75
				May	8.50		
				June	8.50	1988—Jan.	8.75
				July	8.16	Feb.	8.51
				Aug.	7.90	Mar.	8.50
						Apr.	8.50

NOTE. These data also appear in the Board's H.15 (519) release.

Source: *Federal Reserve Bulletin,* Board of Governors of the Federal Reserve System.

INTEREST RATES Money and Capital Markets

Averages, percent per year; weekly and monthly figures are averages of business day data unless otherwise noted.

Instrument	1985	1986	1987	1988				1988, week ending				
				Jan.	Feb.	Mar.	Apr.	Apr. 1	Apr. 8	Apr. 15	Apr. 22	Apr. 29
MONEY MARKET RATES												
1 Federal funds[1,2]	8.10	6.80	6.66	6.83	6.58	6.58	6.87	6.62	6.82	6.81	6.93	6.85
2 Discount window borrowing[1,2,3]	7.69	6.32	5.66	6.00	6.00	6.00	6.00	6.00	6.00	6.00	6.00	6.00
Commercial paper[4,5]												
3 1-month	7.93	6.61	6.74	6.76	6.55	6.57	6.80	6.63	6.73	6.76	6.85	6.85
4 3-month	7.95	6.49	6.82	6.87	6.58	6.62	6.86	6.68	6.78	6.81	6.92	6.93
5 6-month	8.00	6.39	6.85	6.92	6.58	6.64	6.92	6.70	6.83	6.86	6.99	7.01
Finance paper, directly placed[4,5]												
6 1-month	7.90	6.57	6.61	6.65	6.45	6.44	6.71	6.52	6.64	6.68	6.78	6.76
7 3-month	7.77	6.38	6.54	6.62	6.39	6.38	6.67	6.45	6.58	6.63	6.73	6.75
8 6-month	7.74	6.31	6.37	6.53	6.27	6.23	6.51	6.29	6.47	6.48	6.54	6.57
Bankers acceptances[5,6]												
9 3-month	7.91	6.38	6.75	6.77	6.49	6.51	6.79	6.55	6.70	6.74	6.85	6.85
10 6-month	7.95	6.28	6.78	6.83	6.49	6.55	6.86	6.63	6.78	6.78	6.93	6.95
Certificates of deposit, secondary market[7]												
11 1-month	7.96	6.61	6.75	6.78	6.55	6.56	6.80	6.60	6.72	6.77	6.87	6.84
12 3-month	8.04	6.51	6.87	6.92	6.60	6.63	6.92	6.67	6.82	6.87	7.01	6.99
13 6-month	8.24	6.50	7.01	7.10	6.69	6.78	7.14	6.86	7.04	7.06	7.24	7.23

	U.S. Treasury bills[5]												
	Secondary market[9]												
15	3-month	7.47	5.97	5.78	5.81	5.66	5.70	5.91	5.74	5.99	5.89	5.83	5.91
16	6-month	7.65	6.02	6.03	6.25	5.93	5.91	6.21	6.04	6.20	6.14	6.22	6.28
17	1-year	7.81	6.07	6.33	6.52	6.21	6.28	6.56	6.36	6.55	6.49	6.58	6.60
	Auction average[10]												
18	3-month	7.47	5.98	5.82	5.90	5.69	5.69	5.92	5.69	5.98	5.98	5.78	5.92
19	6-month	7.64	6.03	6.05	6.31	5.96	5.91	6.21	6.00	6.21	6.19	6.14	6.28
20	1-year	7.80	6.18	6.33	6.67	6.18	6.30	6.57	......	......	6.57	......	......
	CAPITAL MARKET RATES												
	U.S. Treasury notes and bonds[11]												
	Constant maturities[12]												
21	1-year	8.42	6.45	6.77	6.99	6.64	6.71	7.01	6.78	7.01	6.92	7.03	7.07
22	2-year	9.27	6.86	7.42	7.63	7.18	7.27	7.59	7.42	7.55	7.52	7.62	7.67
23	3-year	9.64	7.06	7.68	7.87	7.38	7.50	7.83	7.66	7.78	7.75	7.88	7.92
24	5-year	10.12	7.30	7.94	8.18	7.71	7.83	8.19	8.03	8.13	8.12	8.25	8.27
25	7-year	10.50	7.54	8.23	8.48	8.02	8.19	8.52	8.40	8.47	8.44	8.59	8.60
26	10-year	10.62	7.67	8.39	8.67	8.21	8.37	8.72	8.57	8.62	8.63	8.81	8.82
27	20-year	10.97	7.85	......	......	......	......	......	......	......	......	......	......
28	30-year	10.79	7.78	8.59	8.83	8.43	8.63	8.95	8.82	8.84	8.85	9.05	9.07
	Composite[13]												
29	Over 10 years (long-term)	10.75	8.14	8.64	8.82	8.41	8.61	8.91	8.80	8.80	8.82	9.01	9.02
	State and local notes and bonds												
	Moody's series[14]												
30	Aaa	8.60	6.95	7.14	7.29	7.05	7.20	7.33	n.a.	7.40	7.30	7.30	7.30
31	Baa	9.58	7.76	8.17	8.12	7.62	7.80	7.82	n.a.	7.90	7.80	7.80	7.78
32	*Bond Buyer* series[15]	9.11	7.32	7.64	7.70	7.49	7.74	7.81	n.a.	7.80	7.81	7.87	7.77
	Corporate bonds												
	Seasoned issues[16]												
33	All industries	12.05	9.71	9.91	10.37	9.89	9.86	10.15	10.01	10.08	10.11	10.22	10.20
34	Aaa	11.37	9.02	9.38	9.88	9.40	9.39	9.67	9.53	9.61	9.61	9.73	9.73
35	Aa	11.82	9.47	9.68	10.09	9.60	9.59	9.86	9.75	9.79	9.81	9.90	9.92
36	A	12.28	9.95	9.99	10.43	9.94	9.89	10.17	10.04	10.09	10.13	10.25	10.22
37	Baa	12.72	10.39	10.58	11.07	10.62	10.57	10.90	10.73	10.83	10.86	10.98	10.92
38	A-rated, recently-offered utility bonds[17]	12.06	9.61	9.95	10.05	9.75	9.91	10.23	10.09	10.02	10.26	10.37	10.46
	MEMO: Dividend/price ratio[18]												
39	Preferred stocks	10.49	8.76	8.37	9.04	9.02	9.07	9.19	9.10	9.14	9.21	9.20	9.22
40	Common stocks	4.25	3.48	3.08	3.66	3.56	3.48	3.57	3.60	3.51	3.46	3.70	3.61

1. Weekly and monthly figures are averages of all calendar days, where the rate for a weekend or holiday is taken to be the rate prevailing on the preceding business day. The daily rate is the average of the rates on a given day weighted by the volume of transactions at these rates.
2. Weekly figures are averages for statement week ending Wednesday.
3. Rate for the Federal Reserve Bank of New York.
4. Unweighted average of offering rates quoted by at least five dealers (in the case of commercial paper), or finance companies (in the case of finance paper). Before November 1979, maturities for data shown are 30–59 days, 90–119 days, and 120–179 days for commercial paper; and 30–59 days, 90–119 days, and 150–179 days for finance paper.
5. Yields are quoted on a bank-discount basis, rather than in an investment yield basis (which would give a higher figure).
6. Dealer closing offered rates for top-rated banks. Most representative rate (which may be, but need not be, the average of the rates quoted by the dealers).
7. Unweighted average of offered rates quoted by at least five dealers early in the day.
8. Calendar week average. For indication purposes only.
9. Unweighted average of closing bid rates quoted by at least five dealers.
10. Rates are recorded in the week in which bills are issued. Beginning with the Treasury bill auction held on Apr. 18, 1983, bidders were required to state the percentage yield (on a bank discount basis) that they would accept to two decimal places. Thus, average issuing rates in bili auctions will be reported using two rather than three decimal places.
11. Yields are based on closing bid prices quoted by at least five dealers.
12. Yields adjusted to constant maturities by the U.S. Treasury. That is, yields are read from a yield curve at fixed maturities. Based on only recently issued, actively traded securities.
13. Averages (to maturity or call) for all outstanding bonds neither due nor callable in less than 10 years, including one very low yielding "flower" bond.
14. General obligations based on Thursday figures; Moody's Investors Service.
15. General obligations only, with 20 years to maturity, issued by 20 state and local governmental units of mixed quality. Based on figures for Thursday.
16. Daily figures from Moody's Investors Service. Based on yields to maturity on selected long-term bonds.
17. Compilation of the Federal Reserve. This series is an estimate of the yield on recently-offered, A-rated utility bonds with a 30-year maturity and 5 years of call protection. Weekly data are based on Friday quotations.
18. Standard and Poor's corporate series. Preferred stock ratio based on a sample of ten issues: four public utilities, four industrials, one financial, and one transportation. Common stock ratios on the 500 stocks in the price index.

NOTE. These data also appear in the Board's H.15 (519) and G.13 (415) releases.

Source: *Federal Reserve Bulletin*, Board of Governors of the Federal Reserve System.

NYSE bond volume

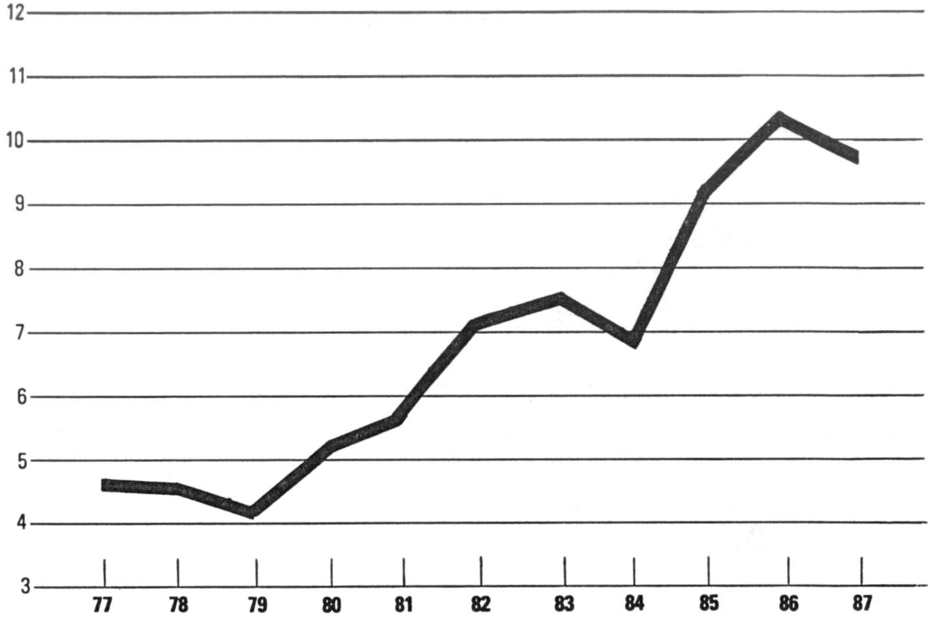

Source: The New York Stock Exchange *Fact Book, 1988.*

Reported bond volume and trades on NYSE, 1987 (par value in thousands)

	Par value		No. of	Avg. daily	Avg. trade size
	For month	Avg. daily	trades	trades	(No. of bonds)
January	$ 880,827	$41,944	58,092	2,766	15.16
February	$ 766,662	$40,351	50,742	2,671	15.11
March	$ 854,646	$38,848	56,068	2,549	15.24
April	$ 932,163	$44,389	63,186	3,009	14.75
May	$ 780,023	$39,001	52,570	2,629	14.84
June	$ 790,991	$35,954	54,474	2,476	14.52
July	$ 793,379	$36,063	54,246	2,466	14.63
August	$ 720,532	$34,311	48,986	2,333	14.71
September	$ 873,494	$41,595	56,247	2,678	15.53
October	$ 962,463	$43,748	64,162	2,916	15.00
November	$ 642,174	$32,109	46,810	2,341	13.72
December	$ 729,766	$33,171	53,648	2,439	13.60
Total	**$9,727,120**	**$38,447**	**659,231**	**2,606**	**14.76★**

	Par value	
High Day	$62,261	Oct. 19
Low Day	$20,082	Nov. 27
High Month	$962,463	October
Low Month	$642,174	November

★ Record High

Source: The New York Stock Exchange *Fact Book, 1988.*

Most active bonds on NYSE, 1987

Issue		Par value of reported volume (thousands)
International Business Machines	cv 7 7/8s '04	$149,988
Public Service Company of New Hampshire	17 1/2s '04	135,660
Bethlehem Steel Corporation	8.45s '05	134,792
Merrill Lynch	cv zero coupon '06	128,527
Occidental Petroleum	9.65s '94	110,289
National Gypsum Company	zero coupon '94	88,486
Marathon Oil Company	9 1/2s '94	73,623
Pan American World Airways	15s '94	72,210
Texaco Capital Incorporated	13s '91	71,537
American Telephone & Telegraph	8 3/4s '00	70,092
Marathon Oil Company	12 1/2s '94	66,039
Bethlehem Steel Corporation	8 3/8s '01	65,576
Texaco Capital Incorporated	11s '89	62,733
Texaco Capital Incorporated	13 5/8s '94	57,979
American Telephone & Telegraph	8.8s' 05	54,964
Republic Steel	12 1/8s '03	49,476
Occidental Petroleum	10s '91	48,774
McLean Industries Incorporated	14 1/4s '94	48,264
Pan American World Airways	13 1/2s '03	48,126
Storage Technology Corporation	cv 9s '01	48,085
Texaco Capital Incorporated	9s '88	47,363
LTV Corporation	14s '04	44,199
Bethlehem Steel Corporation	4 1/2s '90	43,876
McLean Industries Incorporated	12s '03	40,582
Occidental Petroleum	11 3/4s '11	40,350
National Medical Enterprises	cv zero coupon '04	39,844
Pan American World Airways	cv 9s '10	35,972
Valero Energy Corporation	16 1/4s '01	35,293
Public Service Co. of New Hampshire	13 3/4s '96	35,063
American Telephone & Telegraph	8 5/8s '07	34,769
Lomas & Nettleton	cv zero coupon '01	33,004
BankAmerica	zero coupon '92	31,998
du Pont de Nemours	6s '01	31,950
American Telephone & Telegraph	7s '01	31,038
Public Service Co. of New Hampshire	15s '03	30,471
G. Heileman Brewing Company	cv zero coupon '03	29,664
Storage Technology Corporation	11 5/8s '93	29,474
Occidental Petroleum	10 7/8s '96	27,846
General Motors Acceptance Corporation	6s '11	27,479
USC Corporation	9s '92	27,048
Texaco Incorporated	7 3/4s '01	26,857
Western Union Telegraph Company	16s '91	26,571
Philips Petroleum Company	14 3/4s '00	26,506
Mobil Corporation	8 1/2s '01	26,262
Beverly Enterprise	cv zero coupon '03	26,206
General Motors Acceptance Corporation	7 1/8s '92	26,163
Bethlehem Steel Corporation	9s '00	25,999
Waste Management	cv zero coupon '01	25,850
Tenneco Incorporated	6s '11	25,329
Internorth Incorporated	10 1/2s '08	25,273

Source: The New York Stock Exchange *Fact Book, 1988.*

Credit Ratings of Fixed Income and Money Market Securities

KEY TO STANDARD & POOR'S CORPORATE AND MUNICIPAL BOND RATING DEFINITIONS

A Standard & Poor's corporate or municipal debt rating is a current assessment of the creditworthiness of an obligor with respect to a specific debt obligation. This assessment may take into consideration obligors such as guarantors, insurers, or lessees.

The debt rating is not a recommendation to purchase, sell or hold a security, inasmuch as it does not comment as to market price or suitability for a particular investor.

The ratings are based on current information furnished by the issuer or obtained by Standard & Poor's from other sources it considers reliable. Standard & Poor's does not perform an audit in connection with any rating and may, on occasion, rely on unaudited financial information. The ratings may be changed, suspended or withdrawn as a result of changes in, or unavailability of, such information, or for other circumstances.

The ratings are based, in varying degrees, on the following considerations:

I. Likelihood of default—capacity and willingness of the obligor as to the timely payment of interest and repayment of principal in accordance with the terms of the obligation;
II. Nature of and provisions of the obligation;
III. Protection afforded by, and relative position of, the obligation in the event of bankruptcy, reorganization or other arrangement under the laws of bankruptcy and other laws affecting creditor's rights.

AAA

Debt rated **AAA** have the highest rating assigned by Standard & Poor's to a debt obligation. Capacity to pay interest and repay principal is extremely strong.

AA

Debt rated **AA** have a very strong capacity to pay interest and repay principal and differ from the highest rated issues only in a small degree.

A

Debt rated **A** have a strong capacity to pay interest and repay principal although they are somewhat more susceptible to the adverse effects of changes in circumstances and economic conditions than debts in higher rated categories.

BBB

Debt rated **BBB** are regarded as having an adequate capacity to pay interest and repay principal. Whereas they normally exhibit adequate protection parameters, adverse economic conditions or changing circumstances are more likely to lead to a weakened capacity to pay interest and repay principal for debts in this category than for debts in higher rated categories.

BB, B, CCC, CC

Debt rated **BB**, **B**, **CCC**, and **CC** are regarded, on balance, as predominantly speculative with respect to capacity to pay interest and repay principal in accordance with the terms of the obligation. **BB** indicates the lowest degree of speculation and **CC** the highest degree of speculation. While such debts will likely have some quality and protective characteristics, these are outweighed by large uncertainties or major risk exposures to adverse conditions.

C

The rating **C** is reserved for income bonds on which no interest is being paid.

D

Debt rated **D** are in default, and payment of interest and/or repayment of principal is in arrears.

Plus (+) or minus (−)

The ratings from **AA** to **B** may be modified by the addition of a plus or minus sign to show relative standing within the major rating categories.

Provisional ratings

The letter *p* indicates that the rating is provisional. A provisional rating assumes the successful completion of the project being financed by the debts being rated and indicates that payment of debt service requirements is largely or entirely dependent upon the successful and timely completion of the project. This rating, however, while addressing credit quality subsequent to completion of the proj-

Source: From Standard & Poor's Debt Rating Division.

* Continuance of the rating is contingent upon S&P's receipt of an executed copy of the escrow agreement or closing documentation confirming investments and the cash flows.

ect, makes no comment on the likelihood of, or the risk of default upon failure of, such completion. The investor should exercise his own judgment with respect to such likelihood and risk.

L*

The letter "L" indicates that the rating pertains to the principal amount of those bonds where the underlying deposit collateral is fully insured by the Federal Savings & Loan Insurance Corp. or the Federal Deposit Insurance Corp.

NR

Indicates that no rating has been requested, that there is insufficient information on which to base a rating or that S&P does not rate a particular type of obligation as a matter of policy.

Debt Obligations

Debt Obligations of issuers outside the United States and its territories are rated on the same basis as domestic corporate and municipal issues. The ratings measure the creditworthiness of the obligor but do not take into account currency exchange and other uncertainties.

Bond Investment Quality Standards

Under present commercial bank regulations issued by the Comptroller of the Currency, bonds rated in the top four categories (**AAA, AA, A, BBB,** commonly known as "Investment Grade" ratings) are generally regarded as eligible for bank investment. In addition, the Legal Investment Laws of various states impose certain rating or other standards for obligations eligible for investment by savings banks, trust companies, insurance companies and fiduciaries generally.

KEY TO STANDARD & POOR'S PREFERRED STOCK RATING DEFINITIONS

A Standard & Poor's preferred stock rating is an assessment of the capacity and willingness of an issuer to pay preferred stock dividends and any applicable sinking fund obligations. A preferred stock rating differs from a bond rating inasmuch as it is assigned to an equity issue, which issue is intrinsically different from, and subordinated to, a debt issue. Therefore, to reflect this difference, the preferred stock rating symbol will normally not be higher than the bond rating symbol assigned to, or that would be assigned to, the senior debt of the same issuer.

The preferred stock ratings are based on the following considerations.

I. Likelihood of payment—capacity and willingness of the issuer to meet the timely payment of preferred stock dividends and any applicable sinking fund requirements in accordance with the terms of the obligation.
II. Nature of, and provisions of, the issue.
III. Relative position of the issue in the event of bankruptcy, reorganization, or other arrangements affecting creditors' rights.

AAA

This is the highest rating that may be assigned by Standard & Poor's to a preferred stock issue and indicates in extremely strong capacity to pay the preferred stock obligations.

AA

A preferred stock issue rated **AA** also qualifies as a high-quality fixed income security. The capacity to pay preferred stock obligations is very strong, although not as overwhelming as for issues rated **AAA.**

A

An issue rated **A** is backed by a sound capacity to pay the preferred stock obligations, although it is somewhat more susceptible to the adverse effects of changes in circumstances and economic conditions.

BBB

An issue rated **BBB** is regarded as backed by an adequate capacity to pay the preferred stock obligations. Whereas it normally exhibits adequate protection parameters, adverse economic conditions or changing circumstances are more likely to lead to a weakened capacity to make payments for a preferred stock in this category than for issues in the **A** category.

BB, B, CCC

Preferred stock rated **BB, B,** and **CCC** are regarded, on balance, as predominately speculative with respect to the issuer's capacity to pay preferred stock obligations. **BB** indicates the lowest degree of speculation and **CCC** the highest degree of speculation. While such issues will likely have some quality and protective characteristics, these are outweighed by large uncertainties or major risk exposures to adverse conditions.

CC

The rating **CC** is reserved for a preferred stock issue in arrears on dividends or sinking fund payments but that is currently paying.

C

A preferred stock rated **C** is a non-paying issue.

D

A preferred stock rated **D** is a non-paying issue with the issuer in default on debt instruments.

NR

NR indicates that no rating has been requested, that there is insufficient information on which to base a rating, or that S&P does not rate a particular type of obligation as a matter or policy.

Plus (+) or Minus (−) To provide more detailed indications of preferred stock quality, the ratings from **AA** to **B** may be modified by the addition of a plus or minus sign to show relative standing within the major rating categories.

The preferred stock rating is not a recommendation to purchase or sell a security, inasmuch as market price is not considered in arriving at the rating. Preferred stock *ratings* are wholly unrelated to Standard & Poor's earnings and dividend *rankings* for common stocks.

MUNICIPAL NOTES

A Standard & Poor's role rating reflects the liquidity concerns and market access risks unique to notes. Notes due in 3 years or less will likely receive a long-term debt rating. The following criteria will be used in making that assessment.

—Amortization schedule (the larger the final maturity relative to other maturities the more likely it will be treated as a note).

—Source of Payment (the more dependent the issue is on the market for its refinancing, the more likely it will be treated as a note).

Note rating symbols are as follows:

SP-1 Very strong or strong capacity to pay principal and interest. Those issues determined to possess overwhelming safety characteristics will be given a plus (+) designation.

SP-2 Satisfactory capacity to pay principal and interest.

SP-3 Speculative capacity to pay principal and interest.

TAX-EXEMPT DEMAND BONDS

Standard & Poor's assigns "dual" ratings to all long-term debt issues that have as part of their provisions a demand or double feature.

The first rating addresses the likelihood of repayment of principal and interest as due, and the second rating addresses only the demand feature. The long-term debt rating symbols are used for bonds to denote the long-term maturity and the commercial paper rating symbols are used to denote the put option (for example, "AAA/A-1+"). For the newer "demand notes," S&P's note rating symbols, combined with the commercial paper symbols, are used (for example, "SP-1+/A-1+").

KEY TO STANDARD & POOR'S COMMERCIAL PAPER RATING DEFINITIONS

A Standard & Poor's Commercial Paper Rating is a current assessment of the likelihood of timely payment of debt having an original maturity of no more than 365 days.

Ratings are graded into four categories, ranging from **A** for the highest quality obligations to **D** for the lowest. The four categories are as follows:

A

Issues assigned this highest rating are regarded as having the greatest capacity for timely payment. Issues in this category are further refined with the designations 1, 2, and 3 to indicate the relative degree of safety.

A-1 This designation indicates that the degree of safety regarding timely payment is very strong.

A-2 Capacity for timely payment on issues with this designation is strong. However, the relative degree of safety is not as overwhelming as for issues designated **A-1.**

A-3 Issues carrying this designation have a satisfactory capacity for timely payment. They are, however, somewhat more vulnerable to the adverse effects of changes in circumstances than obligations carrying the higher designations.

B

Issues rated **B** are regarded as having only an adequate capacity for timely payment. However, such capacity may be damaged by changing conditions for short-term adversities.

C

This rating is assigned to short-term obligations with a doubtful capacity for payment.

D

This rating indicates that the issue is either a default or is expected to be in default upon maturity.

The Commercial paper Rating is not a recommendation to purchase or sell a security. The ratings are based on current information furnished to Standard & Poor's by the issuer or obtained from other sources it considers reliable. The ratings may be changed, suspended, or withdrawn as a result of changes in, or unavailability of, such information.

KEY TO MOODY'S MUNICIPAL RATINGS*

Aaa

Bonds which are rated **Aaa** are judged to be of the best quality. They carry the smallest degree of investment risk and are generally referred to as "gilt edge." Interest payments are protected by a large or by an exceptionally stable margin and principal is secure. While the various protective elements are likely to change, such changes as can be visualized are most unlikely to impair the fundamentally strong position of such issues.

Aa

Bonds which are rated **Aa** are judged to be of high quality by all standards. Together with the **Aaa** group they comprise what are generally known as high grade bonds. They are rated lower than the best bonds because margins of protection may not be as large as in **Aaa** securities or fluctuation of protective elements may be of greater amplitude or there may be other elements present which make the long term risks appear somewhat larger than in **Aaa** securities.

A

Bonds which are rated **A** possess many favorable instrument attributes and are to be considered as upper medium grade obligations. Factors giving security to principal and interest are considered adequate, but elements may be present which suggest a susceptibility to impairment sometime in the future.

Baa

Bonds which are rated **Baa** are considered as medium grade obligations; i.e., they are neither highly protected nor poorly secured. Interest payments and principal security appear adequate for the present but certain protective elements may be lacking or may be characteristically unreliable over any great length of time. Such bonds lack outstanding investment characteristics and in fact have speculative characteristics as well.

Ba

Bonds which are rated **Ba** are judged to have speculative elements; their future cannot be considered as well assured. Often the protection of interest and principal payments may be very moderate, and thereby not well safeguarded during both good and bad times over the future. Uncertainty of position characterizes bonds in this case.

B

Bonds which are rated **B** generally lack characteristics of the desirable investment. Assurance of interest and principal payments or of maintenance of other terms of the contract over any long period of time may be small.

Caa

Bonds which are rated **Caa** are of poor standing. Such issues may be in default or there may be present elements of danger with respect to principal or interest.

Ca

Bonds which are rated **Ca** represent obligations which are speculative in a high degree. Such issues are often in default or have other marked shortcomings.

C

Bonds which are rated **C** are the lowest rated class of bonds, and issues so rated can be regarded as having extremely poor prospects of ever attaining any real investment standing.

Con.(—)

Bonds for which the security depends upon the completion of some act or the fulfillment of some condition are rated conditionally. These are bonds secured by (a) earnings of projects under construction, (b) earnings of projects unseasoned in operation experience, (c) rentals which begin when facilities are completed, or (d) payments to which some other limiting condition attaches. Parenthetical rating denotes probable credit stature upon completion of construction or elimination of basis of condition.

* **Note:** Those bonds in the **Aa, A, Baa, Ba** and **B** groups which Moody's believes possess the strongest investment attributes are designated by the symbols **Aa 1, A 1, Baa 1, Ba 1** and **B 1.**

Source: Moody's Investors Service, Inc.

KEY TO MOODY'S CORPORATE RATINGS*

Aaa

Bonds which are rated **Aaa** are judged to be of the best quality. They carry the smallest degree of investment risk and are generally referred to as "gilt edge." Interest payments

* ***Note:*** Moody's applies numerical modifiers, **1, 2** and **3** in each generic rating classification from **Aa** through **B** in its corporate bond rating system. The modifier **1** indicates that the security ranks in the higher end of its generic rating category; the modifier **2** indicates a mid-range ranking; and the modifier **3** indicates that the issue ranks in the lower end of its generic rating category.

are protected by a large or by an exceptionally stable margin and principal is secure. While the various protective elements are likely to change, such changes as can be visualized are most unlikely to impair the fundamentally strong position of such issues.

Aa

Bonds which are rated **Aa** are judged to be of high quality by all standards. Together with the **Aaa** group they comprise what are generally known as high grade bonds. They are rated lower than the best bonds because margins of protection may not be as large as in **Aaa** securities or fluctuation of protective elements may be of greater amplitude or there may be other elements present which make the long term risks appear somewhat larger than in **Aaa** securities.

A

Bonds which are rated **A** possess many favorable investment attributes and are to be considered as upper medium grade obligations. Factors giving security to principal and interest are considered adequate but elements may be present which suggest a susceptibility to impairment sometime in the future.

Baa

Bonds which are rated **Baa** are considered as medium grade obligations, i.e., they are neither highly protected nor poorly secured. Interest payments and principal security appear adequate for the present but certain protective elements may be lacking or may be characteristically unreliable over any great length of time. Such bonds lack outstanding investment characteristics and in fact have speculative characteristics as well.

Ba

Bonds which are rated **Ba** are judged to have speculative elements; their future cannot be considered as well assured. Often the protection of interest and principal payments may be very moderate and thereby not well safeguarded during both good and bad times over the future. Uncertainty of position characterizes bonds in this class.

B

Bonds which are rated **B** generally lack characteristics of the desirable investment. Assurance of interest and principal payments or of maintenance of other terms of the contract over any long period of time may be small.

Caa

Bonds which are rated **Caa** are of poor standing. Such issues may be in default or there may be present elements of danger with respect to principal or interest.

Ca

Bonds which are rated **Ca** represent obligations which are speculative in a high degree. Such issues are often in default or have other marked shortcomings.

C

Bonds which are rated **C** are the lowest rated class of bonds and issues so rated can be regarded as having extremely poor prospects of ever attaining any real investment standing.

KEY TO MOODY'S COMMERCIAL PAPER RATINGS

The term "Commercial Paper" as used by Moody's means promissory obligations not having an original maturity in excess of nine months. Moody's makes no representation as to whether such Commercial Paper is by any other definition "Commercial Paper" or is exempt from registration under the Securities Act of 1933, as amended.

Moody's Commercial Paper ratings are opinions of the ability of issuers to repay punctually promissory obligations not having an original maturity in excess of nine months. Moody's makes no representation that such obligations are exempt from registration under the Securities Act of 1933, nor does it represent that any specific note is a valid obligation of a rated issuer or issued in conformity with any applicable law. Moody's employs the following three designations, all judged to be investment grade, to indicate the relative repayment capacity of rated issuers:

Issuers rated **Prime-1** (or related supporting institutions) have a superior capacity for repayment of short-term promissory obligations. Prime-1 repayment capacity will normally be evidenced by the following characteristics:

- Leading market positions in well established industries.
- High rates of return on funds employed.
- Conservative capitalization structures with moderate reliance on debt and ample asset protection.
- Broad margins in earnings coverage of fixed financial charges and high internal cash generation.
- Well established access to a range of financial markets and assured sources of alternate liquidity.

Issuers rated **Prime-2** (or related supporting institutions) have a strong capacity for short-term promissory obligations. This will normally be evidenced by many of the characteristics cited above but to a lesser degree. Earnings trends and coverage ratios, while sound, will be more sub-

Source: Moody's Investors Service, Inc.

ject to variation. Capitalization characteristics, while still appropriate, may be more affected by external conditions. Ample alternate liquidity is maintained.

Issuers rated **Prime-3** (or related supporting institutions) have an acceptable capacity for repayment of short-term promissory obligations. The effect of industry characteristics and market composition may be more pronounced. Variability in earnings and profitability may result in changes in the level of debt protection measurements and the requirement for relatively high financial leverage. Adequate liquidity is maintained.

Issuers rated **Not Prime** do not fall within any of the Prime rating categories.

If an issuer represents to Moody's that its Commercial Paper obligations are supported by the credit of another entity or entities, the name or names of such supporting entity or entities are listed within parenthesis beneath the name of the issuer. In assigning ratings to such issuers, Moody's evaluates the financial strength of the indicated affiliated corporations, commercial banks, insurance companies, foreign governments or other entities, but only as one factor in the total rating assessment. Moody's makes no representation and gives no opinion on the legal validity or enforceability of any support arrangement. You are cautioned to review with your counsel any questions regarding particular support arrangements.

KEY TO MOODY'S PREFERRED STOCK RATINGS*

Moody's Rating Policy Review Board Extended its rating services to include quality designations on preferred stocks on October 1, 1973. The decision to rate preferred stocks, which Moody's had done prior to 1935, was prompted by evidence of investor interest. Moody's believes that its rating of preferred stocks is especially appropriate in view of the ever-increasing amount of these securities outstanding, and the fact that continuing inflation and its ramifications have resulted generally in the dilution of some of the protection afforded them as well as other fixed-income securities.

Because of the fundamental differences between preferred stocks and bonds, a variation of our familiar bond rating symbols is being used in the quality ranking of preferred stocks. The symbols, presented below, are designed to avoid comparison with bond quality in absolute terms. It should always be borne in mind that preferred stocks occupy a junior position to bonds within a particular capital structure.

Preferred stock rating symbols and their definitions are as follows:

aaa

An issue which is rated **aaa** is considered to be a top-quality preferred stock. This rating indicates good asset protection and the least risk of dividend impairment within the universe of preferred stocks.

aa

An issue which is rated **aa** is considered a high-grade preferred stock. This rating indicates that there is reasonable assurance that earnings and asset protection will remain relatively well maintained in the foreseeable future.

a

An issue which is rated **a** is considered to be an upper-medium grade preferred stock. While risks are judged to be somewhat greater than in the "**aaa**" and "**aa**" classifications, earnings and asset protection are, nevertheless, expected to be maintained at adequate levels.

baa

An issue which is rated **baa** is considered to be medium grade, neither highly protected nor poorly secured. Earnings and asset protection appear adequate at present but may be questionable over any great length of time.

ba

An issue which is rated **ba** is considered to have speculative elements and its future cannot be considered well assured. Earnings and asset protection may be very moderate and not well safeguarded during adverse periods. Uncertainty of position characterized preferred stocks in this class.

b

An issue which is rated **b** generally lacks the characteristics of a desirable investment. Assurance of dividend payments and maintenance of other terms of the issue over any long period of time may be small.

caa

An issue which is rated **caa** is likely to be in arrears on dividend payments. This rating designation does not purport to indicate the future status of payments.

"ca"

An issue which is rated **"ca"** is speculative in a high degree and is likely to be in arrears on dividends with little likelihood of eventual payment.

*Note: Moody's applies numerical modifiers 1, 2 and 3 in each rating classification from 1 indicates that the security ranks in the higher end of its generic rating category; the modifier 2 indicates a mid-range ranking; and the modifier 3 indicates that the issue ranks in the lower end of its generic rating category.

Source: Moody's Investors Service, Inc.

"c"

This is the lowest rated class of preferred or preference stock. Issues so rated can be regarded as having extremely poor prospects of ever attaining any real investment standing.

KEY TO SHORT-TERM LOAN RATINGS

MIG 1/VMIG 1

This designation denotes best quality. There is present strong protection by established cash flows, superior liquidity support or demonstrated broadbased access to the market for refinancing.

MIG 2/VMIG 2

This designation denotes high quality. Margins of protection are ample although not so large as in the preceding group.

MIG 3/VMIG 3

This designation denotes favorable quality. All security elements are accounted for but there is lacking the undeniable strength of the preceding grades. Liquidity and cash flow protection may be narrow and market access for refinancing is likely to be less well established.

MIG 4/VMIG 4

This designation denotes adequate quality. Protection commonly regarded as required of an investment security is present and although not distinctly or predominantly speculative, there is specific risk.

Issues or the features associated with **MIG** or **VMIG** ratings are identified by date of issue, date of maturity or maturities or rating expiration date and description to distinguish each rating from other ratings. Each rating designation is unique with no implication as to any other similar issue of the same obligor. **MIG** ratings terminate at the retirement of the obligation while **VMIG** rating expiration will be a function of each issue's specific structural or credit features.

MAJOR MONEY MARKET AND FIXED INCOME SECURITIES

Type	Interest: When Paid	Marketability	Minimum Amount of Issue	Maturity
A. Interest Fully Taxable				
Corporate Bonds and Notes	S[1]	Very good to poor depending on quality	$1,000	1 to 50 years
Corporate Preferred Stock (Pays dividends as a fixed percentage of face value. Dividends not obligatory, but if declared must be paid before that of the common stock. Dividends fully taxable for individuals, but 85% exempt from federal tax for corporations)	Generally quarterly	Good to poor depending on quality	$100 or less	No maturity
Federal Home Loan Mortgage Corporate Bonds	S	Fair	$25,000	Up to 25 years
Federal Home Loan Mortgage Certificates	S	Fair	$100,000	Up to 3 years
Farmers' Home Administration Notes and Certificates	Annual	Fair	$25,000	1 to 25 years
Federal Housing Administration Debentures (Guaranteed by the U.S. Government)	S	Very good	$50	1 to 40 years
Federal National Mortgage Association Bonds	S	Fair	$25,000	2 to 25 years
Government National Mortgage Modified Pass through Certificates (interest plus some repayment of principal, guaranteed by U.S. Government)	Monthly	Good	$25,000	30 years; average life 12 years
Federal Home Loan Bank Bonds and Notes	S	Good	$10,000	1 to 20 years
Export-Import Bank Debentures and Certificates	S	Good	$5,000	3 to 7 years

MAJOR MONEY MARKET AND FIXED INCOME SECURITIES *(continued)*

Type	Interest: When Paid	Marketability	Minimum Amount of Issue	Maturity
International Bank for Reconstruction Development (World Bank), Inter-American Development Bank, Asia Development Bank	S	Fair to poor	$1,000	3 to 25 years
Foreign and Eurodollar Bonds and Notes	May be Annual or S	Poor	$1,000 (amounts vary in foreign currencies)	1 to 30 years
Bankers Acceptances (short-term debt obligations (resulting from international trade and guaranteed by a major bank)	Discounted[2] on a 360-day year basis	Fair	$5,000	1 to 270 days
Commercial Paper (short-term debt issued by a major corporation)	Discounted on a 360-day year basis	No secondary market	$100,000 (occasionally smaller)	1 to 270 days
Negotiable Certificates of Deposit (short-term debt issued by banks and which can be sold on the open market)	Interest paid on maturity; 360-day year basis	Fair	$100,000 (occasionally smaller)	30 days to 1 year
Non-negotiable Certificate of Deposit (savings certificates)	Interest paid on maturity; 360-day year basis	Non-negotiable	$500 $10,000	30 months 6 months
Collateralized Mortgage Obligations (CMO)	S or monthly	Good	$1,000	typically 2 to 20 years
Repurchase Agreements (generally short term loans by large investors, secured by U.S. Government or other high quality issues)[3]	Interest paid on maturity; 360-day year basis	No secondary market	$100,000	1 to 30 days (sometimes more)
Zero Coupon Bonds (Bonds stripped of coupons)	Bonds issued at deep discount. Full yield realized at maturity	Good	$1,000 on maturity	1 to 30 years
B. Interest Exempt from State and Local Income Taxes				
U.S. Treasury Bonds and Notes	S	Very good	$1,000	1 to 20 years
U.S. Treasury Bills	Discounted on a 360-day basis	Very good	$10,000	90 days to 1 year
U.S. Series EE Savings Bonds[4]	Issued at discount, full interest, paid on maturity	No secondary market: available for resale	$50 minimum $15,000 maximum	11 years (can be redeemed before maturity at reduced yields
U.S. Series HH Savings Bonds	S	No secondary market	$500 $15,000 maximum	10 years
Federal Land Bank Bonds	S	Good	$1,000	1 to 10 years
Federal Financing Bank Notes and Bonds	S	Good	$1,000	1 to 20 years
Tennessee Valley Authority Notes and Bonds	S	Fair	$1,000	5 to 25 years
Banks for Cooperatives Bonds	Interest: 360-day year basis	Good	$5,000	180 days
Federal Intermediate Credit Bank Bonds	Interest: 360-day year basis	Good	$5,000.	270 days
Federal Home Loan Bank Notes and Bonds	Discounted: 360-day year basis	Good	$10,000.	30 to 360-day year basis (some more)

MAJOR MONEY MARKET AND FIXED INCOME SECURITIES *(concluded)*

Type	Interest: When Paid	Marketability	Minimum Amount of Issue	Maturity
Farm Credit Bank Notes and Bonds	Interest: 360-day year basis	Good	$50,000.	270 days (some more)
C. Interest Exempt from Federal Income Tax				
State and Local Notes and Bonds (in-State issues, usually exempt from State and local income taxes)	S	Good to fair depending on rating	$5,000.	1 to 50 years
Housing Authority Bonds (in-State issues usually exempt from State and local income taxes)	S	Good to fair	$5,000.	1 to 40 years

[1] S means semiannually.

[2] A discount means interest paid in advance, thus a 10% discounted security maturing at $10,000 would cost $9,000 to purchase.

[3] Recently some banks have issued repurchase agreements for smaller amounts of money, i.e., several thousands of dollars.

[4] Since November 1982, U.S. Savings Bonds pay variable interest equal to 85% of the 5 year Treasury securities' rate adjusted semi-annually and have a minimum guaranteed rate which is adjustable.

U.S. Treasury Bonds, Notes, and Bills: Terms Defined*

U.S. Treasury bonds, notes and bills are interest paying securities representing a debt on the part of the U.S. Government. Treasury bonds have a maturity of over 5 years, while notes mature within 5 to 7 years. Bills are discussed below. Both Treasury bonds and notes are generally issued in minimum denominations of $1,000 and pay interest semiannually. The amount of semiannual interest paid is determined by the coupon rate specified on the bond and is calculated on a 365-day year basis. For a $1,000 face value† bond the interest is given by:

$$\text{semiannual interest} = 1/2\,(\$1{,}000 \times \text{coupon rate})$$

Bonds may be priced higher (at a premium) or lower (at a discount) than the face value (par) depending on current interest rates. The *current yield* is the rate the investor receives based on the prices actually paid for a bond. The price is given by:

$$\text{current yield} = \frac{\$1{,}000 \times \text{coupon rate}}{\text{purchase price}}$$

Thus, a $1,000 face value bond with an 8% coupon rate purchased at $850 has a current yield by:

$$\text{current yield} = \frac{\$1{,}000 \times 8\%}{\$850} = 9.41\%$$

The *yield to maturity* (YTM) is the yield obtained on taking into account the years remaining to maturity, annual interest payments, and the capital gain (or loss) realized at maturity. It is obtained from special tables.

However, the yield to maturity (YTM) may be found approximately from the formula

$$\text{YTM} = \frac{I + A}{B}$$

$$I = \text{annual interest rate}$$

$$A = \frac{\$1{,}000 - M}{N}$$

$$B = \frac{\$1{,}000 + M}{2}$$

where M = current market price of the bond
N = years remaining to maturity

As an example, a bond ($1,000 face value) has a 10% coupon and is currently priced at $1,100 with 10 years remaining to maturity. What is the approximate YTM?

$$I = \$1{,}000 \times .1 = \$100 \text{ interest per year}$$

$$A = \frac{\$1{,}000 - \$1{,}100}{10} = \$-10$$

$$B = \frac{\$1{,}000 + \$1{,}100}{2} = \$1{,}050$$

$$\text{YTM} = \frac{\$100 - \$10}{\$1{,}050} = .0857 = 8.57\%$$

U.S. Treasury bills (T-bills) are U.S. Government debt obligations which mature within one year. They are offered by the Federal Reserve Bank with maturities of 90 days (3 month bills) and 182 days (six month bills). Nine-month bills and one-year bills are also available. Treasury bills are sold in a minimum denomination of $10,000. Interest is paid by the discount method based on a 360-day year. With the discount method, interest is, in effect, paid at the time the bill is purchased. Thus a 91-day $10,000 bill (face value) with an 8% discount interest rate

* The terms *current yield, yield to maturity*, etc. defined in this section are generally applicable to all fixed incomes.

† Face value is the amount of the bond or note payable upon maturity.

would provide the buyer with $202.22 ($10,000 × .08 × $^{91}/_{360}$) interest at the time of purchase. This amount is deducted from the face value of the bill at the time of purchase so the buyer actually pays a net amount of $9,797.78 ($10,000 − $202.22). When the bill matures, the buyer receives $10,000 on redemption.

Since T-bills pay interest at the time of purchase (discount basis) on a 360-day year basis, while bonds (and notes) pay interest semiannually on a 365-day year basis, the two rates cannot be compared directly. To compare the two rates, the discount rate must be converted to the so-called *bond equivalent yield*, given by

$$\text{bond equivalent yield} = \frac{365 \times \text{discount rate}}{360 - (\text{discount rate} \times \text{days to maturity})}$$

As an example, a newly issued 91-day note with a discount rate of 12% has a

$$\text{bond equivalent yield} = \frac{365 \times (.12)}{360 - (.12 \times 91)} = 12.55\%$$

Interest from U.S. Treasury bonds, notes, and bills are subject to federal income tax, but are exempt from state and local income taxes.

How to Read U.S. Government Bond and Note Quotations

TREASURY BONDS AND NOTES

(1) Rate	(2) Mat.	(3) Date	(4) Bid	(5) Asked	(6) Bid Chg.	(7) Yld.
6¾s,	1981	Jun n ...	99.3	99.7	+ .1	16.51
9⅛s,	1981	Jun n ...	99.12	99.16	+ .2	15.10
9⅜s,	1981	Jul n	98.21	98.25	+ .3	16.54
7s,	1981	Aug	97.26	98.10	+ .2	15.19
7⅝s,	1981	Aug n ...	97.30	98.2	+ .6	17.66
8⅜s,	1981	Aug n ...	98.2	98.6	+ .2	17.15
9⅝s,	1981	Aug n ...	98.5	98.9	+ .4	16.53
6¾s,	1981	Sep n ...	96.29	97.1	+ .5	16.10
10⅛s,	1981	Sep n ...	97.28	98	+ .4	16.28
12⅝s,	1981	Oct n ...	98.14	98.18	+ .4	16.18
7s,	1981	Nov n ...	96.4	96.8	+ .10	15.86
7¾s,	1981	Nov n ...	96.18	96.22	+ .13	15.55
12⅛s,	1981	Nov n ...	98.1	98.5	+ .3	16.14
7¼s,	1981	Dec n ...	95.12	95.16	+ .10	15.14

Source: Reprinted by permission of *The Wall Street Journal*, Dow Jones & Co., Inc., 1981.

The above exhibit is an example of U.S. Government bond and note quotations as it appears in *The Wall Street Journal*.

(1) Indicates the coupon rate of interest which is designated by *s*. Rates are quoted to ⅛ of a percent. Thus 8⅜ means 8.375%. The semiannual interest payments are calculated, as described elsewhere, using this rate.

(2) Indicates the year of maturity.

(3) Indicates the month (of the above year) in which the bond or note matures. The letter *n* means the security is a note. Otherwise a bond is implied.

(4) The *bid price* per bond or note (the price at which the bond can be sold to the dealer), expressed as a percentage of the face value ($1,000) of the bond. Prices are quoted in terms of $\frac{1}{32}$ of a percent. Thus 98.5 means $98\frac{5}{32}$. To find the dollar value of the price, convert $98\frac{5}{32}$ to a decimal ($98\frac{5}{32}$ = .98156) and multiply by the face value of the bond to give $981.56 (.98156 × $1,000).

(5) The *ask price* per bond or note (the price at which the dealer will sell the bond). The dollar value is found as indicated above.

(6) The change in the bid price from the closing price of the previous day.

(7) The yield if the bond is held to maturity, based on the ask price.

Some U.S. Treasury bonds can be called back for redemption prior to maturity. These are shown with two dates (under item 2 for example)—*1993–98* indicating that the bonds mature in 1998, but may be called back and redeemed any time after 1993.

Some newspapers (such as *The New York Times*) use a slight modification of the above arrangement, though the various terms have the same meaning as defined above. Thus, a bond maturing in June of 1985 and bearing a 10⅜% coupon is indicated by *May '85 10⅜*.

How to Read U.S. Treasury Bill Quotations

(1) U.S. Treas. Mat. date	(2) Bills Bid	(3) Asked Discount	(4) Yield
-1981-			
6–18	17.62	17.44	17.69
6–25	17.15	17.03	17.33
7– 2	15.39	15.01	15.31
7– 9	15.18	15.04	15.39
7–16	15.02	14.78	15.17
7–23	14.83	14.67	15.10
7–30	14.72	14.42	14.88
8– 6	14.11	13.89	14.36
8–13	13.94	13.72	14.22
8–20	13.94	13.72	14.26
8–27	13.92	13.70	14.28
9– 3	13.97	13.63	14.24
9–10	13.72	13.64	14.29
9–17	13.52	13.34	14.00
9–24	13.63	13.43	14.14
10– 1	13.74	13.54	14.30

Source: Reprinted by permission of *The Wall Street Journal*, Dow Jones & Co., Inc. 1981.

The above exhibit is an example of Treasury bill quotations as it appears in *The Wall Street Journal*.

(1) The date of maturity, i.e., 6–18 means June 18, 1981.

(2) The bid price at market close quoted as a *discount* rate in percent. This bid price is the price at which the dealer will buy the bill. To convert the discount rate to a dollar price use the formula

$$\text{dollar price} = \$10{,}000 - (\text{discount rate} \times \text{days to maturity} \times .2778)$$

In the above, the discount must be expressed in percent. For example, if the dealer bids 16.18% discount for a bill which will mature in 110 days, the dollar price is given by

$$\text{dollar price} = \$10{,}000 - (16.18 \times 110 \times .2778) = \$9{,}505.57 \text{ per bill}$$

(3) The asked price at market close expressed as a discount rate in percent. The asked price is the price at which the dealer will sell a bill to a buyer. To convert to a dollar price use the above formula.

(4) The bond equivalent yield expressed in percent. This is calculated (as explained elsewhere) from the asked price expressed as a discount rate. This rate is used to compare T-bill yields to that of bonds, notes and certificates of deposit.

Some newspapers (e.g., *The New York Times*) use a somewhat different arrangement, though the meaning of the terms is the same as defined above. Thus, a bill maturing on June 4, 1981, is indicated as such. Also included in some newspapers is the change in bid price expressed as a discount rate.

How to Read Corporate Bond Quotations*

Corporate bonds are debt securities issued by private corporations. They generally have a face value (the amount due on maturity) of $1,000 and a specified interest rate (coupon rate) paid semiannually. Many corporate bonds have a *call* provision which permits the company to recall and redeem the bond after a specified date. Call privileges are usually exercised when interest rates fall sufficiently. Investors, therefore, cannot count on *locking in* high interest rates with corporate bonds. Bond quality designations used by Moody's and Standard & Poor's are given elsewhere in the Almanac (pp. 422–428).

* Yield terms are the same as those defined in the section on U.S. Treasury Bonds, Notes and Bills, p. 430.

The following is an example of price quotations for bonds traded on The New York Stock Exchange as they appear in *The Wall Street Journal.*

CORPORATION BONDS

VOLUME, $18,990,000

(1) Bonds		(2) Cur YID	(3) Vol	(4) High	(5) Low	(6) Close	(7) Net Chg.
AlaP	9s2000	14.	6	63	62	63	2
AlaP	8½s01	15.	10	57½	57½	57½	...
AlaP	8⅞s03	15.	25	60	59½	60	+ ½
AlaP	10⅞05	15.	3	72	72	72	− 2¼
AlaP	10½05	15.	12	70½	70½	70½	− 1
AlaP	12⅝10	16.	7	81¼	81⅛	81⅛	− 1⅝
AlaP	15¼10	16.	111	94⅝	93⅝	94	...
AlaP	14¾91	15.	31	97	96½	96½	...
AlaP	17⅜11	17.	99	104	103½	103¾	− ¼
Alexn	5½96	cv	34	61¾	61⅝	61¾	+ ¾
Allgl	10¾99	15.	2	70½	70½	70½	...
AllstF	8⅛87	11.	2	76⅜	76⅜	76⅜	+ 1⅞
AllstF	9⅝86	12.	10	83⅛	83	83	+ 1⅞

Source: Reprinted by permission of *The Wall Street Journal,* Dow Jones and Company, Inc. 1981.

(1) The name of the issue in abbreviated form, followed by the coupon rate of interest in percent (designated by the letter *s*), and the year in which the bond matures. The coupon rate is stated in terms of ⅛ of a percent; 9⅜ means 9.375%.

(2) This is the current yield which is calculated as stated elsewhere. (See U.S. Treasury Bonds, Notes, and Bills, p. 430.)

(3) This item is the number of bonds sold that day.

(4) This is the highest price quoted for the bond sold on that day, expressed as a percentage of face value ($1,000). To convert to dollars, express the price as a decimal and multiply by the face value of the bond. As an example:

$$58\tfrac{1}{2} = (.5850 \times \$1{,}000.) = \$585$$

(5) This is the lowest price quoted that day. It is converted into dollars as described above.

(6) This is the price at the close of the market that day.

(7) This is the change in the closing price from that of the previous day. To convert to dollars, express as a decimal and multiply by $1,000. Thus, −1⅞ means a decrease per bond of $18.75 (.01875 × $1,000) from that of the previous day.

TAX EXEMPT VERSUS TAXABLE YIELDS

tax bracket	To equal a tax-free yield of:											
	5½%	6%	6½%	7%	7½%	8%	8½%	9%	9½%	10%	10½%	11%
	a taxable investment has to earn:											
28%	7.64%	8.33%	9.03%	9.72%	10.42%	11.11%	11.81%	12.50%	13.19%	13.89%	14.58%	15.28%
30	7.86	8.57	9.29	10.00	10.71	11.43	12.14	12.86	13.57	14.29	15.00	15.71
31	7.97	8.70	9.42	10.14	10.87	11.59	12.32	13.04	13.77	14.49	15.22	15.94
32	8.09	8.82	9.56	10.29	11.03	11.76	12.50	13.24	13.97	14.71	15.44	16.18
34	8.33	9.09	9.85	10.61	11.36	12.12	12.88	13.64	14.39	15.15	15.91	16.67
36	8.59	9.38	10.16	10.94	11.72	12.50	13.28	14.06	14.84	15.63	16.41	17.19
37	8.73	9.52	10.32	11.11	11.90	12.70	13.49	14.29	15.08	15.87	16.67	17.47
39	9.02	9.84	10.66	11.48	12.30	13.11	13.93	14.75	15.57	16.39	17.21	18.03
42	9.48	10.34	11.21	12.07	12.93	13.79	14.66	15.52	16.38	17.24	18.10	18.97
43	9.65	10.53	11.40	12.28	13.16	14.04	14.91	15.79	16.67	17.54	18.42	19.30
44	9.82	10.71	11.61	12.50	13.39	14.29	15.18	16.07	16.96	17.86	18.75	19.64
46	10.19	11.11	12.03	12.96	13.89	14.81	15.74	16.67	17.59	18.52	19.44	20.37
49	10.78	11.76	12.75	13.73	14.71	15.69	16.67	17.65	18.63	19.61	20.59	21.57
54	11.96	13.04	14.13	15.22	16.30	17.39	18.48	19.57	20.65	21.74	22.83	23.91
55	12.22	13.33	14.44	15.56	16.67	17.78	18.89	20.00	21.11	22.22	23.33	24.44
59	13.41	14.63	15.85	17.07	18.29	19.51	20.73	21.95	23.17	24.39	25.61	26.83
63	14.86	16.22	17.57	18.92	20.27	21.62	22.97	24.32	25.68	27.03	28.38	29.73
64	15.28	16.67	18.06	19.44	20.83	22.22	23.61	25.00	26.39	27.78	29.17	30.56
68	17.19	18.75	20.31	21.88	23.44	25.00	26.56	28.13	29.69	31.25	32.81	34.38
70	18.33	20.00	21.67	23.33	25.00	26.67	28.33	30.00	31.67	33.33	35.00	36.67

Tax-Exempt Bonds

Tax exempt (municipal) bonds are issued by state and local governments and are free from federal income tax on interest payments. The bonds are often issued in $5,000 denominations and pay interest semiannually. Capital gains are taxable. In addition, holders of out-of-state bonds may be subject to state and local income taxes of the state in which they reside. For example, a New York City resident holding Los Angeles municipal bonds would be subject to New York State and City income taxes on the interest.

The taxable equivalent yield of a tax exempt bond is obtained by means of the expression

$$\text{taxable equivalent yield} = \frac{\text{tax exempt yield}}{1-(F+S+L)}$$

where

F is the federal tax bracket of the investor
S is the state tax bracket of the investor
L is the local tax bracket of the investor

Thus, an investor in the 50% federal bracket, 10% state bracket and 3% local bracket who holds a bond with a current yield of 6% which is exempt from all income taxes would enjoy a taxable equivalent yield (TEY) given by

$$\text{TEY} = \frac{6\%}{1-(.5+.1+.03)} = 16.21\%$$

A taxable yield of 16.21% would be necessary to provide the same yield as the 6% current yield on the tax exempt security.

TYPES OF TAX EXEMPT BONDS AND NOTES

General Obligation bonds, also known as GO's, are backed by a pledge of a city's or state's full faith and credit for the prompt repayment of both principal and interest. Most city, county and school district bonds are secured by a pledge of unlimited property taxes. Since general obligation bonds depend on tax resources, they are normally analyzed in terms of the size of the resources being taxed.

Revenue bonds are payable from the earnings of a revenue-producing enterprise such as a sewer, water, gas or electric system, airport, toll bridge, college dormitory, lease payments from property rented to industrial companies, and other income-producing facilities. Revenue bonds are analyzed in terms of their earnings.

Limited and Special Tax bonds are payable from the pledge of the proceeds derived by the issuer from a specific tax such as a property tax levied at a fixed rate, a special assessment, or a tax on gasoline.

Municipal notes are short term obligations maturing from 30 days to a year and are issued in anticipation of revenues coming from the sales of bonds (BANS), taxes (TANS), or other revenues (RANS).

Project notes, issued by local housing and urban renewal agencies, are backed by a U.S. Government guarantee and are also tax exempt.

How to Understand Tax-Exempt Bond Quotations

Generally the prices of municipal bonds are quoted in terms of the yield to maturity (defined elsewhere) rather than in percentage of face value, as with other bonds. The yield to maturity can be converted to a dollar price if the years remaining to maturity and the rate of interest due are known. Certain tables used for this purpose are given in the *Basis Book* (published by the Financial Publishing Company, 82 Brookline Avenue, Boston, Massachusetts). The books list the dollar price (per $1,000 face value of the bond) corresponding to a given coupon rate, yield, and years to maturity.

Some municipal bonds, however, are quoted directly in terms of percentage of face value. Thus, a bid price (the price at which the dealer will buy the bonds from the investor) of 98⅝ for a $5,000 face value bond can be converted to a dollar price by first converting the bid to a decimal expression (.98625) and then multiplying by the face value of the bond. The result in this case is $4,931.25 (.98625 × $5,000). The same calculation applies to the ask price (the price at which the dealer will sell the bond to the investor).

Prices of tax exempt bonds are not quoted in the daily press. They can be obtained by calling municipal bond dealers. Extensive quotations are given in some relatively expensive publications:

The Blue List
Standard & Poor's
25 Broadway
New York, New York 10004
(212) 208-8471

The Daily Bond Buyer
and
The Weekly Bond Buyer
The Bond Buyer
1 State Street Plaza
New York, New York 10004
(212) 943-8200

Bond Week (Formerly Money Manager)
Institutional Investor
488 Madison Avenue
New York, New York 10022
(212) 303-3300

Government National Mortgage Association (GNMA) Modified Pass Through Certificates

A GNMA Mortgage-Backed Security is a government-guaranteed security which is collateralized by a pool of federally-underwritten residential mortgages. The investor receives a monthly check for a proportionate share of the principal and interest on a pool of mortgages whether or not the payments have actually been collected from the borrowers.

The GNMA Mortgage-Backed Security offers the highest yield of any federally-guaranteed security. In addition, the GNMA security offers a very competitive return in comparison to private corporation debt issues. Moreover, the investor receives a monthly return on the GNMA guaranteed investment, rather than semi-annual payments as on most bonds. This monthly payment represents a cash flow available for reinvestment and has the effect of increasing the yield on GNMAs by 10 to 18 basis points (a basis point is 0.1%) when compared to the yield equivalent received on a bond investment with the same "coupon" rate but paying interest semi-annually.

On single-family securities (the most popular form) the maturity is typically 30 years. However, statistical studies have determined that the average life of a single-family security is approximately 12 years, due to prepayments of principal. Nevertheless, some of the mortgages in any pool are likely to remain outstanding for the full 30-year period.

The minimum size of original individual certificates is $25,000 with increments of $5,000 above that amount.

Due to the uncertainties in the maturity of the above mentioned pass-through certificates, collateralized mortgage obligations (CMOs) have been introduced. CMOs are bonds backed by Ginnie Maes, Freddie Macs, and other mortgage instruments providing investors with a wide choice of maturities ranging from 2 to 20 years. Essentially, the monthly payments from the underlying mortgage instruments are initially allocated to the nearest maturity CMO and subsequently to CMO maturities of successively longer duration. CMO interest payments are made semiannually or monthly.

How to Understand Convertible Securities

The term "Convertible Securities" refers to securities that can be exchanged for another type of security, usually the common stock of the company issuing the convertible.

Source: Reprinted, with permission, from *Understanding Convertible Securities*, © New York Stock Exchange, Inc., 1982. Further reprinting is prohibited without express written approval of New York Stock Exchange, Inc.

The two basic types of convertible securities are debentures (commonly known as bonds) and preferred stock. These securities have intrinsic value. Bonds represent a debt of the issuing company. Preferred stock represents an ownership interest. Intrinsic value may be enhanced by the convertible feature.

There are other certificates or contracts which are sometimes considered to be convertible securities but which have no intrinsic value based on ownership interest or debt. Their value is derived solely from their ability to be converted into another type of security. To do so requires a payment in addition to the surrender of the security. These are rights, warrants and options. To many investors these securities may offer certain advantages. However, our emphasis here will be on convertible securities—bonds and preferred stock—which have broader application as investment vehicles.

CONVERTIBLE BONDS

Convertible debt securities are almost always issued in the form of debentures. That is, there is no specific collateral pledged by the issuing corporation in the indenture which states the terms under which the security is issued. Rather, the promise to pay interest on stated dates and the principal amount at maturity is backed by the full faith and credit of the corporation. However, even the most sophisticated investors and those in the securities industry commonly refer to this type of security as a convertible bond.

Convertible bonds have been extolled as the ultimate investment medium offering the desirable features of other securities without the normal risks. If this were so, it would not be for long. Demand for such a security would be so great that the price would be driven up to the point where the element of risk would be very evident. Convertible bonds like all other securities have both advantages and disadvantages and the informed investor can measure these against his own objectives.

Here are the three most important characteristics:

1. Convertible bonds pay interest—which, as a general rule yields more than the dividends on common stock of comparable quality and less than the interest on straight (non-convertible) bonds of equivalent quality and maturity.

   The issuing company's obligation to pay this interest comes before dividends on preferred and common stock.
2. Convertible bonds offer appreciable possibilities linked to the earnings and growth of the company. As the common stock rises in value to reflect this growth, the price

of the convertible bond should also increase. Conversely, as the common stock declines in value, so should the convertible bond decline.

3. Convertible bonds enjoy some of the stability and relative safety associated with straight bonds and preferred stock. For each outstanding convertible bond, it is possible to estimate an investment value. This is the price below which the convertible bond is not expected to fall, if interest rates remain constant, even if the common stock price falls to such an extent as to render the convertible feature virtually valueless. Investment value is arrived at by estimating a price that would produce a yield comparable to straight bonds of equivalent quality. Investment value, it should be stressed, is only an estimate and subject to change from many influences such as fluctuating interest rates, economic and business conditions, ratings given by investment advisory services and the general well-being of the issuing company.

These characteristics can perhaps best be understood by examining how convertible bonds come into existence and how they behave in various circumstances.

XYZ COMPANY ISSUES CONVERTIBLE BONDS

Let's assume that the XYZ Company wants to raise more capital to expand its business. Interest rates are high and XYZ does not want to pay 12% or more to borrow money in the conventional bond market. XYZ is also reluctant at this time to issue additional common stock as a means of raising additional capital. This could be due to a number of reasons, one of which might be unwillingness to dilute the equity interest of its present stockholders. For example, if there are presently ten million shares outstanding and an additional million are issued, earnings per share will normally be reduced by ten percent at the moment of issue, and the market price of the common stock probably would fall proportionately unless it could support the higher price earnings ratio. (The dilution problem is not quite the same when additional stock is issued to acquire an interest in or control of another company. The acquired company will presumably have its own earnings to contribute to earnings per share.) The XYZ Company is also mindful of the fact that dividends on stock are paid after federal income taxes, whereas interest on debt securities, like bonds, is a deduction before taxes.

Accordingly, the management of the XYZ Company decides to issue convertible bonds. In conjunction with the underwriting firm, the interest is set at 10% and the bonds are priced at par—an even $1,000 per $1,000 face amount bond. Bond prices are commonly stated as a percentage of par which, in this case, would be 100. It is further stipulated that each $1,000 bond can be converted into 25 shares of XYZ common stock. At the time that the bonds are marketed, the common stocks is trading at $32 per share.

DEFINITION OF TERMS

In any discussion of convertible bonds, various terms, related to the above figures, are widely used. Before proceeding, these should be defined.

Market Price Price at which a convertible bond can be bought or sold at a given point in time. Market price is stated as a percentage of par, usually $1,000. 100 means $1,000, 90 means $900, 110 means $1,100, etc.

Conversion Ratio Number of shares of common stock obtainable through conversion of one bond. In the case of XYZ, conversion ratio is 25.

Conversion Price The reciprocal of conversion ratio or the price of the stock when the number of shares obtainable through conversion of one $1,000 bond equals exactly $1,000. Conversion price is $40 when conversion ratio is 25.

Conversion Value Current value of total shares into which a bond can be converted. Conversion value of XYZ $1,000 bond with conversion ratio of 25 shares is $800 when XYZ common stock is trading at $32 per share.

Conversion Premium Percentage difference between conversion value and market value of bond. When conversion value is $800 and market value is $1,000, conversion premium is 25% since difference between conversion and market values ($1,000 − $800 = $200) is 25% of conversion value ($800). This figure represents the judgment of investors, as expressed in the marketplace, with respect to the worth of the three characteristics of convertible securities discussed above. These were yield, appreciation potential and relative safety. With some issues, supply and demand is also a factor in the premium.

Investment Value Estimated price, usually set by investment advisory services, at which bond would be selling if it had no convertible feature. Investment value is arrived at by estimating the price at which the convertible bond would have to sell to provide a percentage yield comparable to percentage yield on a non-convertible bond of equivalent quality and maturity. Investment value, like market price, is normally stated as a percentage of $1,000. For the XYZ Bonds, investment value will be assumed to be 75 providing a current yield of 13.33%.

Premium Over Investment Value Percentage difference between estimated investment value and market price of bond. When market price is 100 and investment value is estimated at 75, the difference is 25 which is 33% of 75. Thus, the premium over investment value is 33%. This figure can be considered a measurement of the worth of the conversion privilege as well as an indication of the proportion of the price that is subject to the risks associated with common stock.

To summarize, the position of XYZ Convertible Bonds, and the related stock at the time the bonds are marketed, is as follows:

Market Price of Bond............100	($1,000)
Yield............10%	
Conversion Ratio............25	
Conversion Price............$40	$\left(\frac{\$1{,}000}{25}\right)$
Market Price of Stock............$32	
Conversion Value............$800	(25 × $32)
Conversion Premium...25%	$\left(\frac{\$1{,}000 - \$800}{\$800}\right)$
Investment Value.........75	($750)
Premium Over Investment Value 33%	$\left(\frac{\$1{,}000 - \$750}{\$750}\right)$

Obviously, no owners of the bonds would convert them into the common stock at this time, since they would be exchanging $1,000 for $800. However, it is not necessary to convert a convertible bond into stock in order to enjoy its advantages. Bonds are frequently sold many times before they are finally converted into stock and many investors have actively participated in the convertible bond market without ever exercising the conversion privilege. Let's now explore what could happen to the XYZ Convertible Bonds under various circumstances.

IF THE STOCK GOES UP

If the XYZ Company prospers and is considered to have appreciation potential, the price of the common stock should go up. By the same token, the price of the XYZ Convertible Bond should also rise. Let's assume the stock goes up by 25% to $40 per share. Normally, the bond will also go up but not necessarily at the same rate as the stock. There is a good reason for this. As the bond price increases, it acts more like a stock and less like a bond. Investment value is left further behind. The risk increases. Yield diminishes too. Accordingly, even though the appreciation potential of the stock may not have changed, the other factors (greater risk and lower yield) will tend to hold back the price of the bond. Therefore, a rise in the XYZ stock of 25% from $32 to $40 might be reflected in a rise in the bond of 20% from 100 to 120. The most significant figures are now as follows:

Market Price of Bond............120	($1,200)
Current Yield..........8.33%	$\left(\frac{\$100}{\$1{,}200}\right)$
Market Price of Stock............$40	
Conversion Value..........$1,000	(25 × $40)
Conversion Premium..20%	$\left(\frac{\$1{,}200 - \$1{,}000}{\$1{,}000}\right)$
Premium Over Investment Value 60%	$\left(\frac{\$1{,}200 - \$750}{\$750}\right)$

Conversion is still unrealistic. But bondholders who bought at the offering may want to take profits by selling their bonds to other investors who believe the stock will continue to go up but are not quite certain enough in their belief to buy the stock itself. Let's assume now that XYZ common stock goes up to $60 per share, an increase of 87½% since the bonds were issued. What is likely to happen to the XYZ bonds? The bond price may now rise to the level where virtually all of the bond-like characteristics are lost and, from the standpoint of risk, the bond is interchangeable with the stock. If we assume this is so, the bond's conversion value should be approximately the same as its market value and conversion premium will disappear. The picture would now look like this:

Market Price of Bond	150	($1,500)
Current Yield	6.67%	($100 / $1,500)
Market Price of Stock	$60	
Conversion Value	$1,500	(25 × $60)
Conversion Premium	0	($1,500 - $1,500 / $1,500)
Premium Over Investment Value	100%	

Now the owner of the bond will think very seriously about converting. His decision may depend to some extent on the comparative yields of the bond and the stock. Interest on the bond is $100 per year. If the dividend on the stock is less than $4.00 per share, conversion would result in less income. If, on the other hand, the dividend is $4.20 (a yield of 7%) conversion would result in more current income.

In the meantime, while the stock has been rising from $32 to $60 per share, the company has presumably been using the money received from the sale of the convertible bonds to expand its business and improve its earnings. This should have put it in a better position to absorb the dilution that conversion into common stock entails.

When a convertible bond's conversion value and market price become the same, the stock and the bond should move up and down together within a limited range to maintain this relationship. It is virtually impossible for a convertible bond to sell with a negative conversion premium (below its conversion value) for any length of time. If this should happen, professional traders will quickly move in and employ a device known as arbitrage to make a small but rapid profit. They will buy the bonds and simultaneously sell the stock short. Converting the bonds enables them to replace the stock borrowed for the short sale. If, for example, XYZ convertibles are selling at $1,450 while the conversion value is $1,500, the trader can buy ten bonds for $14,500. By selling short 250 shares, he receives $15,000 for an immediate gross profit of $500. This activity will tend to drive the price of the bond back up to or above conversion value.

IF THE STOCK GOES DOWN

Let us now consider what might happen to the XYZ convertible bonds if the common stock took an opposite course and declined from the price of $32 per share which it was enjoying at the time that the convertible bonds were issued. As the price falls the convertible bond's price will also fall. However, the bond's downside potential is less than that of the stock, since the bond should not decline below its investment value which is the estimated value of the bond when we disregard the conversion feature. We have assumed this to be a price of 75 which is 25% below par. Therefore, while the stock is falling from $32 to an unknown level, the bond should only travel from 100 to 75. This factor serves as a brake on the bond and is the reason why convertible bonds are generally considered to be a more conservative investment than the stock of the same issuing company. In reality, conditions which would cause a stock to decline drastically would probably produce a re-adjustment in the investment value of the convertible bond. Investment value is also subject to adjustment when money rates change.

To see how the convertible bond might be affected by a decline in the common stock of the XYZ Company, let's assume that the market price of the stock sags from its original price of $32 all the way down to $16 per share. It has lost half its value. If we estimated correctly the investment value of the convertible bond, and if other factors are the same, it will be selling in the area of $750. Thus, a drop of 50% in the price of the stock produces a drop of 25% in the price of the bond. The table of values will now be as follows:

Market Price of Bond	75	($750)
Current Yield	13.33%	($100 / $750)
Market Price of Stock	$16	
Conversion Value	$400	(25 × $16)
Conversion Premium	87½%	($750 - $400 / $400)
Premium Over Investment Value	0	

Thus, we have seen in this example that the price of a convertible bond is controlled primarily by the price of the stock into which it is convertible. However, when the stock goes up, the bond's rise should be held back somewhat as risk increases and yield decreases. Conversely, when the stock goes down, the bond's decline is cushioned as yield increases and investment value is approached. This is an oversimplification which disregards other influences but, hopefully, it provides a basic understanding of how convertible bonds behave. Prices, yields and ratios were chosen in order to illustrate the example and simplify the arithmetic. They are not intended to reflect actual market conditions at any time.

HEDGING

We have seen that convertible bonds offer an investor opportunities to participate in the stock market with somewhat less risk (and less profit potential) than is normally encountered with direct investment in common stocks. This opportunity can be pursued even further by employing hedges. Although extremely complex in practice, the basic principles of hedging are actually quite simple.

Typically, a hedge is established when an investor buys convertible bonds and, at the same time, sells short the stock into which the bond is convertible. If the stock goes up, there should be a profit in the bonds and a loss in the stock. If the stock goes down, there should be a profit in the stock and a loss in the bonds. Obviously, there is no advantage in a hedge unless the profit exceeds the loss and expenses. There is no way to assure a profit but the skillful and judicious use of hedges can greatly reduce the risk of loss and enhance the possibility of profit. An essential feature is the ability to sell stock short without margin when the corresponding convertible security is held.

Convertible hedges are a highly sophisticated investment technique and should not be attempted without a complete understanding of all of their ramifications.

CALLABILITY AND OTHER LIMITATIONS

An important factor to consider with convertible bonds is the call feature. This is the right of the issuing company to redeem the bonds before maturity at a stated price slightly above par. Usually the original purchasers of a bond are given some protection against this privilege of the company through an initial period during which the bond is non-callable. If a bond has been on the market for four years and commands a price of 130, this price may be short lived if the bond can be called at 105 after five years. When a convertible bond issue listed on the New York Stock Exchange is called for redemption some notice is always given in a newspaper of general circulation to permit the holders to exercise their conversion privilege or sell the bond to someone else who may convert it. Holders of record of registered bonds are notified directly. If, for some reason, the bond is not converted before expiration date for conversion, which may be the same or a few days before the redemption date, it is then worth no more nor less than the call price. It is, therefore, most important for holders of convertible bonds to know what the call features are and to be sure that they will receive information about calls when and if they occur. Obviously, the best way to do this is to hold registered bonds.

Most convertible bonds are convertible into stock at a fixed rate during the entire life of the bond. However, this rate may change because of a stock split, stock dividend, merger or other circumstances. The conversion privilege may expire before the bond matures or it may not be effective until some time after the bond is issued. Sometimes the conversion rate declines at regular intervals. A bond that is convertible into 25 shares of common stock when first issued may become convertible into only 20 shares after five years, 15 shares after ten years, etc. Although the typical convertible bond is exchangeable for the common stock of the issuing company, this is also subject to variation. Conversion may be made into a combination of common and preferred stock. Or a bond of one company may be convertible into the stock of a parent company.

All of these possible limitations should be checked by investors when investigating convertible securities. A member firm of the New York Stock Exchange, Inc. can usually supply the essential information.

MARGIN AND COMMISSION

Two other features of convertible bonds have traditionally appealed to investors—margin requirements and commission rates. Although the current margin requirement for the purchase of common stock or convertible bonds is the same—50%, the convertible bond rate has usually been significantly less. In 1973, for instance, an investor with $6,500 available in cash could have bought $10,000 worth of common stock or $13,000 of convertible bonds. (Margin requirements are subject to change by the Federal Reserve Board).

The commission paid to a member firm broker for the purchase or sale of listed stocks is one of the lowest fees paid for the transfer of property of any kind. However, in most cases, the commission paid for the purchase or sale of bonds is even lower on a given dollar investment.

CONVERTIBLE PREFERRED STOCK

Convertible preferred stock possesses many of the basic characteristics of convertible bonds and will normally perform in approximately the same manner when subject to the same conditions and influences. However, there are also basic differences which should be pointed out.

Convertible preferred stock represents an equity interest and is, therefore, junior to all debt securities including convertible bonds and would not—all else being equal—have as high a degree of relative safety as convertible bonds. However, all else is rarely equal and the convertible preferred stock of Company A could have more relative safety than the convertible bonds of Company B. Convertible preferred stocks do not have maturity dates as do bonds but are usually subject to redemption.

Convertible preferreds, like common stock, require 50% margin currently, and are subject to the same commission structure.

FOREIGN TREASURY BILL RATES (bond-equivalent yields, at or near end of month)

	1984	1985	1986	1987			1988				
	Dec	*Dec*	*Dec*	*Oct*	*Nov*	*Dec*	*Jan*	*Feb*	*Mar*	*Apr*	*May*
United States	8.12	7.28	5.83	5.41	5.79	5.84	5.80	5.78	5.87	6.15	6.67
Canada	9.84	9.24	8.24	7.84	8.31	8.41	8.37	8.32	8.53	8.87	8.92
Belgium	10.90	9.89	7.50	7.25	6.95	6.84	6.44	6.24	6.18	6.18	6.18
Ireland	15.10	11.15	13.60	8.80	9.10	8.69	8.34	8.76	8.33	7.83	7.17
Italy	14.69	13.10	10.00	11.98	12.06	11.66	11.37	10.78	10.78	10.81	10.82
Netherlands	5.88	5.69	6.37	5.50	5.25	4.95	4.75	4.25	4.12	4.38	4.25
Spain	12.27	9.52	8.37	8.23	6.78	6.67	5.56	5.83	10.17	n.a.	10.25
Sweden	11.83	12.49	9.20	9.49	9.20	9.05	9.20	9.32	9.58	10.70	10.29
United Kingdom	9.33	11.49	10.79	9.07	8.67	8.38	8.38	9.01	8.26	7.98	7.28
Australia	12.27	19.40	14.91	10.47	10.34	10.06	9.92	10.44	9.83	10.40	11.60
Japan	4.91	4.91	2.89	2.38	2.38	2.38	2.38	2.38	2.38	2.38	2.38
New Zealand	13.50	17.62	19.69	n.a.	n.a.	n.a.	n.a.	n.a.	n.a.	n.a.	n.a.
South Africa	21.94	12.99	8.84	8.68	8.64	8.85	9.49	9.55	10.51	10.97	11.61
Brazil	273.03	379.77	149.00	n.a.	n.a.	n.a.	n.a.	n.a.	n.a.	n.a.	n.a.
Mexico	48.67	72.98	104.03	96.43	110.67	133.04	155.67	153.86	75.16	54.51	50.04
Philippines	47.14	16.45	9.55	12.97	13.18	n.a.	n.a.	n.a.	n.a.	n.a.	n.a.
Singapore	2.91	2.94	2.10	3.57	3.69	3.23	2.92	2.97	2.97	3.02	n.a.

Source: *World Financial Markets*, a publication of Morgan Guaranty Trust Company of New York.

FOREIGN MONEY-MARKET RATES (bond-equivalent yields on major short-term (mostly 3–4-month) money-market instruments other than Treasury bills, at or near end of month)

	1984	1985	1986	1987			1988				
	Dec	*Dec*	*Dec*	*Oct*	*Nov*	*Dec*	*Jan*	*Feb*	*Mar*	*Apr*	*May*
United States	8.49	8.02	6.64	7.58	7.80	7.21	6.90	6.77	6.90	7.20	7.75
Canada	10.00	9.40	8.35	8.50	8.70	8.90	8.65	8.55	8.65	8.94	9.32
Belgium	10.85	9.89	7.60	7.35	7.15	6.95	6.54	6.34	6.24	6.24	6.24
France	10.69	9.12	8.37	8.25	8.62	8.56	8.06	7.44	8.25	7.88	n.a.
Germany	5.75	4.80	4.85	4.10	3.80	3.65	3.23	3.28	3.40	3.55	3.60
Ireland	15.13	12.00	14.06	9.25	9.19	8.81	8.62	8.94	8.38	8.13	7.38
Italy	16.88	15.13	11.37	12.00	11.62	11.50	10.75	11.13	11.13	10.38	11.00
Netherlands	5.75	5.75	6.19	5.25	4.94	4.56	4.32	4.06	4.06	4.13	4.19
Portugal	24.57	20.71	16 07	14.66	14.30	14.34	13.97	13.43	13.03	n.a.	n.a.
Spain	12.21	10.51	11.79	15.84	14.44	13.59	12.30	12.01	11.06	10.90	11.11
Switzerland	5.00	4.75	4.50	4.06	4.06	3.56	1.69	1.81	1.88	2.13	2.75
United Kingdom	9.88	12.75	11.25	9.19	8.87	8.94	8.31	9.38	8.56	8.31	7.81
Australia	12.90	19.75	15.10	13.55	12.15	11.25	10.85	10.90	11.50	11.55	12.87
Japan	6.33	7.03	4.34	3.88	3.90	3.90	3.85	3.80	3.80	3.75	3.80
New Zealand	15.00	20.00	24.25	20.30	16.90	17.70	17.00	17.35	n.a.	17.20	15.75
South Africa	22.78	13.35	8.55	8.90	8.50	8.90	9.60	10.25	10.90	11.85	12.65
Chile	20.68	22.42	19.56	31.37	34.49	15.25	11.35	10.69	21.41	20.84	11.09
Hong Kong	8.25	6.50	4.62	6.19	4.06	1.50	3.00	3.87	4.12	5.13	7.31
Indonesia	19.00	15.00	19.50	17.37	17.50	17.50	17.00	18.50	22.50	18.50	19.00
Korea	8.00	8.00	8.00	7.50	7.50	7.50	n.a.	n.a.	n.a.	n.a.	n.a.
Malaysia	10.30	8.20	6.00	n.a.	n.a.	n.a.	n.a.	n.a.	n.a.	3.70	3.85
Philippines	33.21	14.61	8.31	11.81	n.a.	10.55	13 80	n.a.	n.a.	n.a.	n.a.
Singapore	7.00	5.88	3.94	4.50	4.00	3.25	3.13	3.13	3.19	n.a.	n.a.
Taiwan	7.85	4.10	3.87	3.23	3.13	3.09	4.12	4.47	4.23	4.48	n.a.

Source: *World Financial Markets*, a publication of Morgan Guaranty Trust Company of New York.

FOREIGN GOVERNMENT BOND YIELDS (long-term issues, at or near end of month)

	1984	1985	1986	1987			1988				
	Dec	*Dec*	*Dec*	*Oct*	*Nov*	*Dec*	*Jan*	*Feb*	*Mar*	*Apr*	*May*
United States	11.61	9.49	7.79	9.04	9.10	8.95	8.42	8.39	8.82	9.07	9.31
Canada	11.66	10.04	9.23	10.21	10.50	10.34	9.74	9.61	10.13	10.36	10.38
Austria	8.03	7.61	7.33	7.26	7.13	6.89	6.83	6.80	6.71	6.62	6.61
Belgium	11.56	9.60	7.70	8.32	7.98	8.04	7.58	7.38	7.65	7.62	7.89
Denmark	14.60	9.67	11.70	12.56	11.84	12.05	11.18	10.91	11.22	11.44	n.a.
Finland	10.73	10.58	7.80	7.77	7.64	7.67	7.40	7.40	7.41	7.41	n.a.
France	12.70	11.33	9.89	10.95	10.46	10.57	9.73	9.33	9.61	9.42	9.38
Germany	7.17	6.57	6.25	6.62	6.46	6.51	6.50	6.28	6.30	6.47	6.68
Ireland	14.90	11.84	12.97	11.05	10.23	10.45	10.61	10.41	10.12	9.74	9.80
Italy	14.52	13.66	10 05	11.41	11.25	10.50	10.29	10.30	10.29	10.39	10.49
Netherlands	7.72	6.96	6 40	7.05	6.37	6.32	6.17	5.99	6.01	6.21	6.36
Norway	12.00	13 00	13.24	13.10	13.26	13.29	13.35	13.16	13.24	13.24	n.a.
Portugal	22.23	16.64	14.49	15.30	15.60	14.80	14.70	14.50	n.a.	n.a.	n.a.
Spain	13.93	12 52	10.36	14.24	13.34	13.14	12.48	11.91	11.82	11.35	11.63
Sweden	12.04	12.11	10.66	11.42	11.51	11.39	11.30	10.96	11.05	11.41	11.21
Switzerland	4.60	4.42	4 05	4.12	3.86	3.95	3.94	3.93	3.92	3.77	3.98
United Kingdom	10.25	10.35	10.17	9.22	9.23	9.47	9.26	9.10	8.96	9.14	9.17
Australia	13.50	14.85	13.40	13.65	13.30	12.85	12.40	12.30	11.90	11.50	12.30
Japan	6.47	5.92	4.61	4.58	5.00	4.88	4.23	4.36	4.43	4.45	4.60
New Zealand	16.90	17.00	16.00	15.70	14.90	14.30	14.00	13.30	13.08	13.15	13.05
South Africa	16.55	18.09	15.06	15.44	15.30	15.70	16.80	16.52	16.60	16.48	16.40
Philippines	18.54	n.t.	n.t.	n.t.	n.t.	n.t.	n.t.	n.t.	n.t.	n.t.	n.t.
Venezuela	14.00	12.00	12.00	12.50	12.50	12.50	n.a.	n.a.	n.a.	n.a.	n.a.

Source: *World Financial Markets*, a publication of Morgan Guaranty Trust Company of New York.

FOREIGN CORPORATE BOND YIELDS (long-term issues, at or near end of month)

	1984	1985	1986	1987			1988				
	Dec	*Dec*	*Dec*	*Oct*	*Nov*	*Dec*	*Jan*	*Feb*	*Mar*	*Apr*	*May*
United States	12.25	10.15	8.88	10.25	10.30	9.90	9.38	9.45	9.85	10.25	10.38
Canada	12.42	10.74	10.18	11.22	11.32	10.95	10.37	9.96	n.a.	10.97	10.86
France	12.94	11.76	10.18	11.28	10.96	10.92	10.38	9.91	10.03	9.78	9.77
Germany	7.20	6.90	6.50	7.00	6.70	6.70	6.70	6.70	6.60	6.60	6.80
Netherlands	7.51	n.t.	n.t.	n.t.	n.t.	n.t.	n.t.	n.t.	n.t.	n.t.	n.t.
Spain	18.32	14.92	13.40	17 39	17.08	16.15	15.79	14.68	14.78	12.89	12.89
Sweden	12.33	13.25	11.99	12.78	12.36	12.31	12.20	11.83	11.94	12.20	12.15
Switzerland	5.09	4.93	4.72	4.87	4.65	4.60	4.50	4.39	4.39	4.29	4.36
United Kingdom	11.64	11.47	11.71	10.75	10.59	11.11	10.76	10.82	10.66	10.55	10.69
Japan	7.10	6.79	5.93	5.95	5.59	5.32	5.06	5.03	4.99	4.93	4.95
Korea	15.00	13.60	12.80	12 50	12.90	12.80	12.80	13.20	13.70	13.90	n.a.
Venezuela	18.00	17.00	17.00	18.00	18.00	18.00	n.a.	n.a.	n.a.	n.a.	n.a.

Source: *World Financial Markets*, a publication of Morgan Guaranty Trust Company of New York.

Composition of Dow Jones 20 Bonds Averages

Components—Dow Jones 20 Bond Average

The Dow Jones Bond Averages are a simple arithmetic average compiled daily by using the New York Exchange closing bond prices. A list of the bonds on which these averages are based follows:

10 Public Utilities

Name	Coupon	Age
Alabama Pwr	9¾%	2004
Amer T&T	8.8%	2005
Comwlth Ed	8¾%	2005
Cons Ed	7.9%	2001
Cons Pwr	9¾%	2006
Detroit Edison	9%	1999
Mich Bell	7%	2012
Pac G&E	7¾%	2005
Phil Elec	7⅜%	2001
Pub Svc Ind	9.6%	2005

10 Industrials

Name	Coupon	Age
BankAm	7⅞%	2003
Beth Steel	6⅞%	1999
Eastman	8⅝%	2016
Exxon	6%	1997
Ford Mtr	8⅛%	1990
General Elec	8½%	2004
GM Accept	12%	2005
Pfizer	9¼%	2000
Socony	4¼%	1993
Weyerhaeusr	5.20%	1991

Source: Reprinted by courtesy of Barron's *Business and Financial Weekly*, July 7, 1988.

Components—Barron's Confidence Index

Barron's Confidence Index is the ratio of the average yield to maturity on best grade corporate bonds to the intermediate grade corporate bonds average yield to maturity. A list of the bonds on which the confidence index is based follows:

Best Grade Bonds

Name	Coupon	Age
AT&T	8¾%	2000
Balt G&E	8⅜%	2006
Exxon Pipeline	8¼%	2001
Gen. Elec.	8½%	2004
GMAC	8¼%	2006
IBM	9⅜%	2004
Ill. Bell T	7⅝%	2006
Pfizer	9¼%	2000
Proc. & G.	8¼%	2005
Sears Roe	7⅞%	2007

Intermediate Grade Bonds

Name	Coupon	Age
Ala Power	9¾%	2004
Beneficial	9%	2005
Cater Trac	8%	2001
Comwlth Ed	9⅛%	2008
Crown Zell	9¼%	2005
Firestone	9¼%	2004
GTE	9⅜%	1999
Union Carbide	8½%	2005
USX Corp	7¾%	2001
Woolworth	9%	1999

Source: Reprinted by courtesy of *Barron's National Business and Financial Weekly, July 7, 1988.*

Monetary Aggregates Defined

Money supply data has been revised and expanded to reflect the Federal Reserve's redefinition of the monetary aggregates. The redefinition was prompted by the emergence in recent years of new monetary assets—for example, negotiable order of withdrawal (NOW) accounts and money-market mutual fund shares—and alterations in the basic character of established monetary assets—for example, the growing similarity of and substitution between the deposits of thrift institutions and those of commercial banks.

M1-A has been discontinued with M1-B now designated as "M-1." M-1 is currency in circulation plus all checking accounts including those which pay interest, such as NOW accounts. M-1 excludes deposits due to foreign commercial banks and official institutions.

M-2 as redefined adds to M1-B overnight repurchase agreements (RPs) issued by commercial banks and certain overnight Eurodollars (those issued by Carribbean branches of member banks) held by U.S. nonbank residents, money-market mutual fund shares, and savings and small-denomination time deposits (those issued in denominations of less than $100,000) at all depository institutions. Depository institutions are commercial banks (including U.S. agencies and branches of foreign banks, Edge Act Corporations, and foreign investment companies), mutual savings banks, savings and loan associations, and credit unions.

M-3 as redefined is equal to new M-2 plus large-denomination time deposits (those issued as in denominations of $100,000 or more) at all depository institutions (including negotiable CDs) plus term RPs issued by commercial banks and savings and loan associations.

L, the very broad measure of liquid assets, equals new M-3 plus other liquid assets consisting of other Eurodollar holdings of U.S. nonbank residents, bankers acceptances, commercial paper, savings bonds, and marketable liquid Treasury obligations.

Federal Reserve Banks

Federal Reserve Bank of	
BOSTON	600 Atlantic Avenue, Boston, Massachusetts 02106—(617) 973-3462
NEW YORK	33 Liberty Street (Federal Reserve P.O. Station). New York, New York 10045—(212) 791-5823 (Telephone 24 hours a day, including Saturday & Sunday)
Buffalo Branch	160 Delaware Avenue (P.O. Box 961), Buffalo, New York 14240—(716) 849-5046
PHILADELPHIA	100 North Sixth Street (P.O. Box 90), Philadelphia, Pennsylvania 19105—(215)574-6580
CLEVELAND	1455 East Sixth Street (P.O. Box 6387), Cleveland, Ohio 44101—(216) 241-2800
Cincinnati Branch	150 East Fourth Street (P.O. Box 999), Cincinnati, Ohio 45201—(513) 721-4787 ext 333
Pittsburgh Branch	717 Grant Street (P.O. Box 867), Pittsburgh, Pennsylvania 15230—(412) 261-7864
RICHMOND	701 East Byrd Street (P.O. Box 27622), Richmond, Virginia 23261— (804) 643-1250
Baltimore Branch	502 South Sharp Street, Baltimore, Maryland 21201 (P.O. Box 1378), Baltimore, Maryland 21203—(301) 576-3300
Charlotte Branch	401 South Tyron Street (P.O. Box 300), Charlotte, North Carolina 28230—(704) 373-0200
ATLANTA	104 Marietta Street, N.W., (P.O. Box 1731) Atlanta, Georgia 30301—(404) 586-8657
Birmingham Branch	1801 Fifth Avenue, North (P.O. Box 10447), Birmingham, Alabama 35202—(205) 252-3141 ext. 215
Jacksonville Branch	515 Julia Street, Jacksonville, Florida 32231—(904) 632-4245
Miami Branch	9100 N.W. Thirty-sixth Street Extension, Miami, Florida 33178 (P.O. Box 520847), Miami, Florida 33153—(305) 591-2065
Nashville Branch	301 Eighth Avenue, North, Nashville, Tennessee 37203—(615) 259-4006
New Orleans Branch	525 St. Charles Avenue (P.O. Box 61630), New Orleans, Louisiana 70161 (540) 586-1505 ext. 230, 240, 242
CHICAGO	230 South LaSalle Street (P.O. Box 834), Chicago, Illinois 60690—(312) 786-1110 (Telephone 24 hours a day, including Saturday & Sunday)
Detroit Branch	160 Fort Street, West (P.O. Box 1059), Detroit, Michigan 48231—(313) 961-6880 ext. 372, 373
ST. LOUIS	411 Locust Street (P.O. Box 442), St. Louis, Missouri 63166—(314) 444-8444
Little Rock Branch	325 West Capitol Avenue (P.O. Box 1261), Little Rock, Arkansas 72203—(501) 372-5451 ext. 270
Louisville Branch	410 South Fifth Street (P.O. Box 32710), Louisville, Kentucky 40232 (502) 587-7351 ext. 237, 301
Memphis Branch	200 North Main Street (P.O. Box 407), Memphis, Tennessee 38101—(800) 238-5293 ext. 225
MINNEAPOLIS	250 Marquette Avenue, Minneapolis, Minnesota 55480—(612) 340-2051
Helena Branch	400 North Park Avenue, Helena, Montana 59601—(406) 442-3860
KANSAS CITY	925 Grand Avenue (Federal Reserve Station), Kansas City, Missouri 64198—(816) 881-2783
Denver Branch	1020 16th Street (P.O. Box 5228, Terminal Annex), Denver, Colorado 80217 (303) 292-4020
Oklahoma City Branch	226 Northwest Third Street (P.O. Box 25129), Oklahoma City, Oklahoma 73125—(405) 235-1721 ext. 182
Omaha Branch	102 South Seventeenth Street, Omaha, Nebraska 68102—(402) 341-3610 ext. 242

DALLAS	400 South Akard Street (Station K), Dallas, Texas 75222—(214) 651-6177
El Paso Branch	301 East Main Street (P.O. Box 100), El Paso, Texas 79999—(915) 544-4730 ext. 57
Houston Branch	1701 San Jacinto Street (P.O. Box 2578), Houston, Texas 77001—(713) 659-4433 ext 19, 74, 75, 76
San Antonio Branch	126 East Nueva Street (P.O. Box 1417), San Antonio, Texas 78295—(512) 224-2141 ext 61, 66
SAN FRANCISCO	101 Market Street (P.O. Box 7702), San Francisco, California 94120—(415) 392-6639
Los Angeles Branch	409 West Olympic Boulevard (P.O. Box 2077, Terminal Annex), Los Angeles, California 90051 (213) 683-8563
Portland Branch	915 S.W. Stark Street (P.O. Box 3436), Portland, Oregon 97208—(503) 228-7584
Salt Lake City Branch	120 South State Street (P.O. Box 30780), Salt Lake City, Utah 84130—(801) 355-3131
Seattle Branch	1015 Second Avenue (P.O. Box 3567), Seattle, Washington 98124—(206) 442-1650
TREASURY	**General information concerning Treasury Securities and requests for forms:** Bureau of the Public Debt, Dept. F Washington, D.C. 20226 Telephone: (202) 287-4113 **Specific questions concerning Bills:** Bureau of the Public Debt, Dept. X Washington, D.C. 20226 Telephone: (202) 287-4113 **Specific questions concerning registered Notes or Bonds:** Bureau of the Public Debt, Dept. A Washington, D.C. 20226 Telephone: (202) 287-4113

Options and Futures

What Are Stock Options?

There are two types of stock options—call and put. A call option is the right to buy a specified number of shares of a stock at a given price before a specific date. A put option is the right to sell a specific number of shares of a stock at a given price before a specific date. Options, unlike a futures contract, are a right *not an obligation* to buy or sell stock. The price at which the stock may be bought or sold is referred to as the exercise (or striking) price. The date at which the option expires is the *expiration* date. The term "in-the-money" option refers to either a call option with an exercise price less than that of the market price of the stock, or a put option with an exercise price above the market price of the stock.

Expiration months are set at intervals of three months for the cycles: the January–April–July–October cycle, February–May–August–November cycle, and the March–June–September–December cycle. Options expire at 11:59 P.M. Eastern Standard Time on the Saturday immediately following the third Friday of the expiration month.

The exercise prices are set at 5 point (dollar) intervals for stocks trading below $50, 10 point intervals for stocks trading between $50 to $200, and 20 point intervals for securities trading above $200. Initial exercise prices are set above and below the price of the security. Thus, if a security is priced at 32½ on the New York Stock Exchange at the time new options are opened, the opening exercise prices would be set at 30 and 40. If the price of the security is close to a standard exercise price, three prices are set: at the standard price, as well as above and below the latter.

Standard option contracts are written for 100 shares of stock of the underlying security. The price at which the seller (writer) agrees to sell an option to the buyer is called the *premium*. The premium is quoted *per share* of the underlying stock so that the price per contract is 100 times the quote.

After the option is issued, the premium will fluctuate with the price of the stocks. With call options the premium will increase with an increase in the price of stock. With put options the premium will increase when the stock price declines. The reason should be clear from the following examples. Assume that in January a July call option is written at the exercise price of 50 ($50 per share) on the XYZ Corporation stock. We assume that the stock is selling at $51. The call option writer (seller) asks and receives a premium of $2 ($200 per option contract). After brokerage commission on the sale (say $25 per contract) the option writer nets a profit of $175 per contract. The call option buyer pays $200 for the contract plus the commission or $225. Assume that the stock increases to 60 per share. The option holder (buyer) can, in principle, purchase the stock at 50 (the Exercise price) and sell it at 60 netting a profit on transaction of $10 per share (neglecting commissions). Clearly the call option has acquired increased value which will be reflected in the premium (option price). Let us assume that the premium increases from 2 to 10 ($200 to $1,000 per contract). If the option holder now sells the option, he will make a profit (after commissions) of $750 on a $250 investment ($200 premium and $50 commission).

Alternatively, the option holder may elect to exercise the option and acquire the shares at 50 (the exercise price). The option writer must then deliver 100 shares of XYZ Corporation at $50 per share.

If the stock price drops below the exercise price and remains so until expiration of the option, the call option buyer can lose his entire investment. Sometimes the loss may be reduced if the option is sold before it matures. The holder then is said to have *closed out* his position.

Similar arguments apply to put options. In this case the option holder benefits if the price of the stock decreases below the exercise price. Assume that the above stock drops to 40. The put holder could, in principle, buy the stock at 40 and sell it at 50 (the exercise price) to the put writer. The put holder would make a profit of $10 per share (neglecting commissions). The put premium would reflect this situation and, as a result, increase.

Instead of selling the option and taking a profit, the put holder may elect to exercise the option and sell 100 shares to the put writer who must purchase these shares at the 50 exercise price.

If the market price of the stock is greater than the exercise price when the put option expires, the holder will lose his investment.

Options are traded on the Chicago Board of Options Exchange, the American Stock Exchange, the Pacific Stock Exchange and the Philadelphia Stock Exchange.

How to Read Option Quotations

(1) Option & NY Close	(2) Strike Price	(3) Calls—Last Aug	Nov	Feb	(4) Puts—Last Aug	Nov	Feb
Slb							
94¾	100	2½	7	9½	5⅞	7¾	a
94¾	110	⅝	3⅜	5½	a	16	a
94¾	120	⅛	1⅛	b	a	a	b
94¾	130	1/16	b	b	a	b	b
Skylin	15	3⅜	4	a	a	⅝	a
17⅝	20	⅝	1 11/16	2¼	a	a	a
Southn	10	a	2⅜	2 7/16	b	b	b

Source: Reprinted by permission of *The Wall Street Journal* © Dow Jones and Company, Inc., 1981. All rights reserved.

(1) The name of the company in abbreviated form. Below the company name is the New York or American Exchange closing price of the stock in terms of ⅛ of a dollar.
(2) The striking (exercise) price of the option.
(3) The expiration month of the call option, beneath which is the option's premium (price) per share of stock. Contracts are for 100 shares of stock so that, for example, the price of a contract quoted as 2⅛ ($2.125 per share) is $212.50. Options expire on the Saturday following the third Friday of the expiration month. The premium does not include commissions.
(4) The same as item 3, but for a put option. The letter *a* means the option was not traded that day, and *b* means the option is not offered.

Stock Market Futures*

Standard & Poor's 500 Stock Index futures† combine the unique aspects of the futures market with the opportunities of stock ownership and stock options by helping many investors manage their inherent stock market risks, and at the same time allowing others to participate in broad market moves. S&P 500 Index futures can play an important role in an individual's or institution's overall market strategy.

Stock ownership is subject to several risks. Lower earnings reports or changes in industry fundamentals can cause severe declines in individual issues. Or, a promising industry or company might drop because the entire market is heading down. A myriad of decisions go into individual stock selection—but the first question is usually what is the state and direction of the entire market.

The introduction of the Standard & Poor's 500 Stock Index contract allows investors to hedge, and therefore, virtually eliminate their portfolio exposure in a declining market without disturbing their holdings. At the same time, others can purchase or sell the contract according to their expectations of future market activity. This simultaneous ability to hedge the risks of stock ownership and to take advantage of broad market moves creates opportunities for everyone with positions in or opinions about the stock market.

A NEW MARKET FOR TODAY'S INVESTOR

S&P 500 Index futures are traded on the Index and Option Market division of the Chicago Mercantile Exchange. One of the largest commodity exchanges in the world, the CME introduced financial futures trading in 1972 when it formed the International Monetary Market to trade contracts in foreign currencies. Later, the IMM added futures contracts in Gold, 90-Day Treasury Bills, Three-Month Domestic Certificates of Deposit, and Three-Month Eurodollar Time Deposits.

THE S&P 500 INDEX

The Standard & Poor's Stock Price Index has been the standard by which professional portfolio managers and individuals have measured their performance for 65 years. Begun in 1917 as an index based on 200 stocks, the list was expanded to 500 issues in 1957.

Currently, the Index is one of the U.S. Commerce Department's 12 leading economic indicators.

The S&P 500 Index is made up of 400 industrial, 40 public utilities, 20 transportation, and 40 financial companies and represents approximately 80% of the value of all issues traded on the New York Stock Exchange.

The S&P 500 Index is calculated by giving more "weight" to companies with more stock issued and outstanding in the market. Basically, each stock's price is multiplied by its number of shares outstanding. This assures that each

* Although every attempt has been made to ensure the accuracy of the information in this section, the Chicago Mercantile Exchange assumes no responsibility for any errors or omissions. All matters pertaining to rules and specifications herein are made subject to and are superseded by official Exchange rules.

† Editor's Note: Futures based on the Value Line (Kansas City Exchange) and the New York Stock Exchange (New York Futures Exchange) indices are also traded. The principles are the same as with the S&P 500 futures.

Source: *Opportunities in Stock Futures*, Index and Option Market, Chicago Mercantile Exchange, 444 West Jackson Street, Chicago, IL 60606.

stock influences the Index with the same importance that it carries in the actual stock market.

The Index is calculated by multiplying the shares outstanding of each of the 500 stocks by its market price. These amounts are then totaled and compared to a 1941–43 base period.

Calculations are performed continually while the market is open for each of the 500 stocks in the Index. The resulting Index is available minute-by-minute via quote machines throughout the world.

WHAT IS FUTURES TRADING?

The practice of buying or selling goods at prices agreed upon today, but with actual delivery made in the future, dates back to the 12th century. In the United States, organized futures exchanges were active as early as the 1840s. Today, the markets offer futures in grains, meats, lumber, metals, poultry products, currencies and interest-bearing securities.

The ability to contract today at a fixed price for future delivery performs two vital economic functions: risk transfer and price discovery.

For example, suppose a producer of cattle sees that someone is willing to buy his animals for delivery six months hence at a price that insures him an adequate profit. He decides to sell his production, with delivery after the animal matures, at the contracted price. In the process, he has locked in a price that is satisfactory to him and has insulated himself against the risk that the price may fall. In other words, he has transferred the risk of lower prices to someone else. Conversely, the purchaser of his animals has locked in his price and is assured that he will not have to pay a higher price in the future. This transaction could take place directly between the two men, or could be accomplished through futures trading at the CME—without the need for buyer and seller to actually meet. The open public trading system at the CME makes it easy to discover what the market currently considers to be a fair price for future delivery.

If the sale takes place on the Chicago Mercantile Exchange, the Exchange guarantees that both parties adhere to their agreement by placing itself and its resources between them. The Exchange thus becomes the buyer and the seller of the contract. This assures both parties that the contract will be carried out because the Exchange stands behind both parts of the agreement.

When delivery day arrives, the product is delivered to designated delivery points and inspected to make sure it is of the quality stipulated by the contract. The seller receives payment at the agreed price and buyer receives the produce.

Since full payment does not occur until the delivery day, the performance of both parties to the contract requires a good faith deposit or performance bond—known as the margin—when the contract is entered. Margins usually amount to a small percentage of the contract's total face value.

This payment differs from margin for stock purchases in that it is not a partial payment. It serves as a guarantee for both buyer and seller that there are sufficient funds on either side to cover adverse price movements that might otherwise bring the ability to meet contract terms into question.

At the close of business each day, each futures position is revalued at the contract's current closing price. This price is compared to the previous day's close (or if an initial position, the purchase or sale price) and the net gain or loss is calculated. Gains and losses are taken or made from the margin account each day in cash. There are no paper gains or losses in futures trading. If a margin account falls below a specified level, futures traders are required to deposit more money to maintain their positions.

All futures market participants should understand the operation of futures markets and consult with a Registered Commodity Representative before opening a futures trading account.

The S&P 500 Index futures contract is quoted in terms of the actual Index, but carries a face value of 500 times the Index. The contract does not move point-for-point with the actual Index, but it says close enough to act as an effective proxy for the Index, and by extension, for the stock market as a whole.

If, for example, the futures price is quoted at 108.75, then the face value of the contract would be $54,375 (500 × 108.75). Minimum futures price increments, or movements, are .05 of the Index or $25. So if the futures quote is at 108.75, trades can continue to take place at that level, or move to 108.80 or to 108.70, with each .05 move equal to $25.

Trading opens at 9:00 A.M. and closes at 3:15 P.M. (Chicago time) with contracts trading for settlement in March, June, September and December. The final settlement day is the third Thursday of the contract month. At the close of business on that day all open positions have one final mark-to-market calculation—only on this day the expiration of the contract is marked to the actual closing level of the S&P 500 Index itself. Unlike traditional commodities, there is no physical delivery of the underlying commodity or resulting payment for the commodity in S&P 500 futures.

It is this unique cash settlement feature of the S&P 500 futures contract that eliminates the prohibitively expensive costs of delivering 500 individual issues in varying amounts. Since there are little or no delivery costs, investors are assured that there will be no institutional factors to influence the futures contract's price. Thus, the price of the futures contract will reflect the current expectations about the direction of future stock prices. The International Monetary Market division of the CME pioneered this innovative concept in 1981, when its Eurodollar Time Deposit contract became the first cash settlement futures contract ever traded.

The S&P 500 futures contract should be viewed as a complement to equity ownership, not a substitute for it. Among the many benefits of S&P futures is the hedging ability that holders of stock can employ to provide an effective, cost efficient means of protecting security holdings against temporary market declines rather than selling and disturbing stock holdings. In addition, investors find the futures market equally as liquid for both buyers and sellers. Unlike the stock exchanges, short sellers do not require an up-tic before a trade can take place and there are no additional margin requirements.

SITUATIONS & STRATEGIES

Outright positions, either long or short, spreading and hedging are all uses for S&P futures. The contract also offers an unusually large number of hedging strategies when combined with equity portfolios and options. The following examples will show some of these uses in more detail.

LONG POSITION

Situation: An individual sees that interest rates are declining, the economy is firming and believes the entire market is undervalued. He notes that the S&P 500 futures contract for September delivery is at 108.85 and the actual S&P 500 Index is at 108.70.

It is apparent that most futures market participants also believe a move up is imminent. As supply and demand factors are balanced in an open marketplace, the intrinsic value of the September contract is established. The market is willing to pay a slight premium (.15) for the futures contract over the actual Index.

He calls his Registered Commodity Representative, enters an order to buy one September S&P 500 futures contract at the market and makes a good faith deposit to his account to guarantee his ability to meet his contractual commitment. For purposes of the following example, a margin account balance of $5,000 will be used. Margin requirements for actual positions vary. Individuals should contact their Registered Commodity Representatives for current information.

Day	Position	Cost	S&P Future Closing Price	Gain or (Loss) Points X $5 (.01 equals 1 point)		Account Balance	Cumulative Gain or (Loss)
1	Long one contract	108.85	108.90	.05	$ 25	$5,025	$ 25
2	same	108.85	108.60	(.30)	(150)	4,875	(125)
3	same	108.85	108.40	(.20)	(100)	4,775	(225)
4	same	108.85	107.00	(1.40)	(700)	4,075	(925)
5	same	108.85	108.00	1.00	500	4,575	(425)
6	same	108.85	108.70	.70	350	4,925	(75)
7	same	108.85	109.50	.80	400	5,325	325
Sub Total Period one		108 85	109 50	65	$325	$5 325	$325

Period one: Our investor was a little off on his timing and his margin account was debited each day that losses occurred If his margin balance had fallen to the maintenance minimum ($2 000 per contract) in this example he would have been required to make an additional payment to bring his balance back to the initial margin level ($5 000) As it is he ended the period with a credit of $325 in cash

Period two: With minor backing and filling the trend is up and the S&P futures price closes period two at a level of 115 65

	Position	Cost	S&P Future Closing Price	Gain or (Loss) Points X $5 (.01 equals 1 point)		Account Balance	Cumulative Gain or (Loss)
Sub Total Period Two	Long one contract	108.85	115.65	6.80	$3.400	$8.400	$3.400

Observations: During the first two weeks our investor's judgment of the market was correct and the S&P futures price advanced 680 index points or 6 25% This translated into a gain of $3.400 on his initial investment of $5.000. or a gain of 68%

At this point our investor believes that the market is due for a correction and decides to lock in his profit He calls his RCR and instructs him to "cover" his September long position His broker will then enter a sell order After the close of business. the Exchange Clearing House will match the investor's previous long position and his new short position for a net zero position. All margins will be returned with cash credited to the investor's account with his broker the next day Brokerage commissions have not been included in this example. but they are usually extremely reasonable and generally are quoted to include *both* the purchase and sale of the contract

SHORT POSITION

If, instead of a rising market our investor believed that tight money would increase interest rates and the economy was weakening, he might have concluded that the S&P 500 Index futures price of 108.85 was an overvaluation and that the price was vulnerable to a decline.

He decides to call his Registered Commodity Representative and enter a sell order for one September S&P 500 Stock Index future. Selling is just as easy as buying in an open outcry market. All bids to buy and offers to sell must be made publicly in the trading arena and are subject to immediate acceptance by any member. This differs greatly from stock exchanges where specialists or market makers require an up-tic from the previous sale to transact a short sale.

Let's again assume the initial margin required is $5,000. The above table shows the status of the short position over the course of seven trading days.

Day	Position	Cost	S&P Future Closing Price	Gain or (Loss) Points X $5 (.01 equals 1 point)		Account Balance	Cumulative Gain or (Loss)
	Short one						
1	contract	108.85	110.05	(1.20)	$ 600	$4,400	($ 600)
2	same	108.85	112.50	(2.45)	(1,225)	3,175	(1,825)
3	same	108.85	112.00	.50)	(250)	3,425	(1,575)
4	same	108.85	109.50	(2.50)	(1,250)	4,675	(325)
5	same	108.85	108.75	.75	375	5,050	50
6	same	108.85	107.40	1.35	675	5,725	725
7	same	108.85	107.05	.35	175	5,900	900
Sub Total		108.85	107.05	1.80	$ 900	$5,900	$ 900

In our hypothetical example, the short position eventually worked. If the price had gone to a closing level of 114.85, the investor's account balance would have dropped to the maintenance margin level of $2,000 and he would have been required to add additional funds to bring his balance back to $5,000.

Our investor decides at this point that he wants to cover his short position and lock in his profit. The next morning before the opening of trading, he enters an order to buy one September S&P Index contract to cover his short at the opening.

The opening is down on news that industrial production was weak and his position is covered at 106.55. His gain on his short then amounts to 2.30 at $25 per .05 or $1,150. The money is credited to his account the following day.

REDUCING THE VOLATILITY OF A STOCK PORTFOLIO

One reason for equity ownership is to take advantage of the long-term growth prospects of the company in which stock is purchased. Over time, higher earnings per share might be translated into a higher dividend payout. In the case of a company with a high return on investment and profits that are reinvested in the company's own growth, the expectation is that the growth will be reflected in higher share prices. However carefully constructed and diversified a portfolio may be, it is still subject in varying degrees to the risk that the market will decline. In order to protect principal values in a declining market, investors have traditionally sold stock to raise cash or shifted to more defensive issues with less volatility. These tactics very often are short-run solutions that disturb carefully tailored long-run objectives. S&P 500 Index futures can be used to add protection against a market downturn and allow an investor to maintain his equity holdings based on the prospects of the companies rather than the direction of the market.

SHORT HEDGE AGAINST A DIVERSIFIED PORTFOLIO

Situation: An investor owns a well-diversified portfolio with a current market value of $110,000. The S&P 500 futures contract is at 108.85. The market appears weak and the investor believes that there is substantial downside risk during the next three months. He decides to short S&P 500 futures to protect his portfolio.

Action: The S&P 500 futures contract at 108.85 represents a contract value of $54,425 (500 × 108.85). In order to protect his portfolio, he sells two contracts ($110,000 divided by $54,425 equals 2.02).

This hypothetical example assumed that the volatility of the portfolio very closely matched that of the market as measured by the S&P 500 futures contract prices. In reality, portfolios may be more or less sensitive to market moves. Statistical regression analysis for individual issues and entire portfolios can be calculated to measure past price volatility relative to the market. Expressed as "beta," it is a statistical measure of past movements which may change in the future. However, it is useful when hedging market risk in portfolios that are more volatile than the market.

Day	Position Short 2 Contracts	Closing Price S&P Contract	Gain or (Loss) Contract Points X $5 X 2 Contracts (.01 equals 1 point)		Value of Stock Portfolio	Portfolio Gain or (Loss)
1	108.85	110.05	(1.20)	($1.200)	$111.213	$1.213
18	108.85	109.50	(.65)	(650)	110.657	657
36	108.85	107.40	1.45	1.450	108.535	(1.465)
54	108.85	106.05	2.80	2.800	107.171	(2.829)
72	108.85	103.10	5.75	5.750	104.190	(5.810)
90	108.85	100.65	8.20	8.200	101.714	(8.286)
Position Closed	108.85	100.65	8.20	$8.200	$101.714	($8.286)

Observations: The market dropped and our investor hedged the cash decline in his portfolio with an offsetting gain in his futures position. Of course, if he were wrong about the direction of the market and it went up, he would have had losses in his futures positions but his stocks may have participated in the advance. The investor, throughout this period, did not have to disturb his holdings and continued to receive his dividend payments.

Let us assume that the S&P 500 has a beta of 1.00, (that is, a given percentage move in the market gives rise to the same percentage move in the S&P 500) and our hypothetical portfolio has a beta of 1.50. Our portfolio's past market action relative to moves in the market was 50% greater than a given move in the general market. To compensate for this greater volatility, our hedger would require more S&P contracts to offset a greater decline in the value of his portfolio. Known as a hedge ratio, the dollar value of the portfolio is divided by the dollar value of the S&P 500 futures contract, the resulting figure is multiplied by the beta of the portfolio. Using our investor's portfolio and having calculated a beta of 1.5, we arrive at three contracts instead of two when the beta was 1.00:

$$\frac{\$110{,}000}{54{,}425} \times 1.5 = 3.03 \text{ contracts}$$

Thus, our investor would have sold three contracts to offset the portfolio's greater volatility to the market.

The concept of volatility and hedge ratios also may be applied to industry groupings and individual stocks. However, as the number of individual stock holdings that are being hedged decreases, then the greater is the chance that factors affecting that smaller group will make their prices react differently relative to the market than they have in the past.

ADDITIONAL USES OF THE S&P 500 FUTURES CONTRACT

Spreads: The simultaneous purchase and sale of different contract months to take advantage of perceived price discrepancies is called "spreading." The technique is considered by many to be less volatile than an outright long or short position, and as such, spreads generally carry lower margin requirements.

A characteristic of the futures market is that the closest contract date behaves more like the cash market. (In the S&P 500 futures contract, the cash market is the actual S&P 500 Index.) More distant months or back months have a greater component of their price determined by the expectations of what the price will be in the future.

These changing expectations of price levels of the S&P 500 contract into the future creates spreading opportunities. Options strategists will use the S&P 500 futures contract to reduce market risk when writing uncovered puts and calls. Block traders, investment bankers, stock specialists, options principals and anyone with the risk of stock market volatility, now have a vehicle and a well-capitalized liquid market to buy and sell market risk—the Standard & Poor's 500 Stock Index futures contract.

CONTRACT TERMS SUMMARY

Size	500 times the value of the S&P 500 Index
Delivery	Mark-to-market at closing value of the actual S&P 500 Index on Settlement Date
Hours	9:00 am to 3:15 pm Central Time
Months Traded	March, June, September, December
Clearing House Symbol	SP
Ticker Symbol	SP
Prices	Contract quoted in terms of S&P 500 Index
Minimum Fluctuation in Price	.05 ($25)
Limit Move	3.00 ($1,500)
Last Day of Trading	3rd Thursday of Contract Month
Settlement Date	Last Day of Trading

Understanding the Commodities Market

COMMODITY EXCHANGES

A Commodity Exchange is an organized market of buyers and sellers of various types of commodities. It is public to the extent that anyone can trade through member firms. It provides a trading place for commodities, regulates the trading practices of the members, gathers and transmits price information, inspects and governs commodities traded on the Exchange, supervises warehouses that store the commodity, and provides means for settling disputes between members. All transactions must be conducted in a pit on the Exchange floor within certain hours.

FUTURES CONTRACT

A futures contract is a contract between two parties where the buyer agrees to accept delivery at a specified price from the seller of a particular commodity, in a designated month in the future, if it is not liquidated before the contract reaches maturity. A futures contract is not an option; nothing in it is conditional. Each contract calls for a specified amount, and grade of product. For example: *A person buying a February Pork Belly contract at 52.40 in effect is making a legal obligation, now, to accept delivery of 38,000 pounds of frozen Pork Bellies, to be delivered during the month of February, for which the buyer will pay 52.40 per pound.*

The average trader does not take delivery of a futures contract, since he normally will close out his position before the futures contract matures. As a matter of fact, a survey conducted by a leading exchange has estimated that less than 3% of the contracts traded are settled by actual delivery.

Editor's Note: The scope of the commodities market has been broadened in recent years to include contracts on financial (debt) instruments (T-bills, bonds, etc.) and composite stock market indices such as Value Line, S&P 500, and the New York Stock Exchange. With the stock market index futures, settlement is made in cash in amount based on the underlying index. Cash, not the securities, is used to offset the long and short positions. The cash value of the contract is defined as the index quotation × 500.

THE HEDGER AND SPECULATOR

A hedger buys or sells a futures contract in order to reduce the risk of loss through price variation. A short hedger sells a futures contract to protect the possible decline in the actual commodity owned by him. A long hedger purchases a futures contract to protect the possible advance in the value of an actual commodity needed to be purchased in the future.

The speculator is an important factor in the volume of future trading today. He, in effect, voluntarily assumes the risk, which the hedger tries to avoid, with the expectations of making a profit. He is somewhat of an insurance underwriter. The largest number of traders on any commodity exchange is the speculator. In order for the hedger to participate, he must have continuous trading interests and activity in the market. This trading activity stems from the role of the speculator, because he involves himself in buying or selling of futures contracts with the idea of making a profit on the advance or decline of prices. The speculator tries to forecast prices in advance of delivery and is willing to buy or sell on this basis. A speculator involves himself in an inescapable risk.

CAN YOU BE A SPECULATOR?

Now, can you be a speculator? Before considering entering into the futures market as a speculator, there are several facts which you should understand about the market and also about yourself. In order to enter into the futures market, you must understand that you are dealing with a margin account. Margins are as low as 5 to 10% of the total value of the futures contract, so you are obtaining a greater leverage on your capital.

Fluctuations in price are rapid, volatile, and wide. It is possible to make a very large profit in a short period of time, but also, it is possible to take a substantial loss. In fact, surveys taken by the Agricultural Department have shown that up to 75% of the individuals speculating in commodity markets have lost money. This does not mean that some of their trades were not profitable, but after a period of time with a given sum of money they ended up being a loser.

Now taking you as an individual, let us see whether you have the characteristics to become a commodity trader. Number one and the most important is that you do not take money that you have set aside for your future, or money you need daily to support your family or yourself. Number two, and almost equally important, is that you must be willing to assume losses and be willing to assume these losses with such a temperament that it is not going to affect your everyday life. Money used in the futures market should be money that has been set aside for strictly risk purposes, and if this money is not risk capital, your methods of trading could be seriously affected, because you cannot afford to be a loser.

Source: Commodity Educational Services, Division of Commodity Cassettes, Inc., 778 Frontage Road, Northfield, IL 60093.

Another very important factor is that you must not feel that you are going to take a thousand, two thousand, five or ten thousand dollars and place this with a brokerage firm and not follow the daily happenings of the market. Price fluctuations are fast, and as stated before, wide, so you must not only be in contact with your Account Executive daily, but know and study the technical facts that may be affecting the particular market in which you are speculating.

The individual who makes his first trade by buying a contract on Monday and selling this contract on the following Wednesday, making six hundred dollars on a $1,000 investment, in a period of two days, suddenly says to himself, "*Where has this market been all my life? Why am I working? Why not just concentrate on this market, if every two days or so I can make six hundred dollars?*" This is a fallacy, since this is an individual that is going to destroy himself and most likely his family. The next trade he will feel confident that because of his first profitable trade the market will always go his way even though he is now showing a loss in his position. He still feels that the market will turn around in his direction. If you become married to a particular commodity futures contract and constantly feel that the losses you are taking at the present time will reverse into profits, you are really fighting the market and in most cases fighting a losing battle. This could lead to disaster. There is a saying that you let your profits ride, but liquidate your losses fast.

In any way that you are uneasy with a position that you are holding, it is better to liquidate it. If, prior to the time of buying or selling a contract, you are not sure that this is the right step to take, do not take it. To protect yourself against this hazard you should pre-decide on every trade and exactly how much you intend to lose.

Another important point is not to involve yourself in too many markets. It is difficult to know all the technical facts and be able to follow numerous markets. In addition, if you are in a winning position, be conservative as to how you add additional contracts or pyramid your position. Being conservative will sometimes cause you to miss certain moves in certain markets and you may feel this to be wrong, but over a long period of time, this conservatism will be profitable to you.

If at this point you feel that you are ready, both financially and mentally to trade commodities, the next step is to begin the actual mechanics of trading a futures contract.

OPENING AN ACCOUNT

The first important factor is to decide which brokerage firm will afford you the best service. To accomplish this, you should do a little research by checking with the various exchanges about different brokerage firms. You should study their advertising, market letters, and other information. These should all be presented in a business-like manner and have no unwarranted claims, such as a guarantee of profit without indicating the possibility of loss.

The brokerage firm must be able to handle orders on all commodity exchanges. Do not pick just any Account Executive in a firm, but one you feel confident to help you make market decisions. Become acquainted with the Account Executive through phone or personal conversations. His knowledge of the factors entering into the market and the understanding of current market trends are important in your final choice.

After making a decision on the brokerage firm and the Account Executive that would be best for you, contact him and have him send you the literature concerning different contracts, and also, any additional information as to his organization. He will then send you the necessary signature cards required by the firm to open an account, and ask you for a deposit of margin money.

You will be trading in regulated commodities, and margin money will be deposited in a segregated fund at the brokerage firm's bank. A segregated account means that the money will only be used for margin and not for expenses of the brokerage firm.

Now you decide to enter into your first trade. Your Account Executive and you decide to enter into a December Live Cattle contract on the Chicago Mercantile Exchange. Your order will be executed as follows: Your Account Executive will place this order with his order desk who will then transmit the order to the floor of the Chicago Mercantile Exchange. There your order will be executed on the trading floor, in the pit. All technical details connected with the transaction will be handled by the brokerage firm.

Upon filling of your order, the filled order will be transmitted back to your Account Executive, who will then contact you, advising you that you have purchased one December Live Cattle contract at a given price. You will also receive a written confirmation on this transaction. You will now show an open position in December Live Cattle on the books of the brokerage firm.

MECHANICS OF A TRADE

Let us go back one step to explain in detail just how your order to buy one December Cattle was handled on the floor of the exchange. All buying and selling in the pit is done by open out-cry, and every price change is reported on the exchange ticker system. Each firm has brokers in the different pits, a pit meaning a trading area for the purpose of buying and selling contracts.

When your order was received on the exchange floor, it was time stamped and then given to a runner. This is a person who takes the order from the desk on the exchange floor and gives it to one of the brokers in the December Cattle trading pit. He is then responsible to the brokerage firm to fill that order, if possible, at the stated price. After filling the order, he then has the runner return it to the desk where it is time stamped and transmitted back to the order desk at the brokerage house, and the filled order is reported to you.

MARGIN

Futures trading requires the trader to place margin with his brokerage firm. Initial margin is required and this amount varies with each commodity. The minimum margin is established by each commodity exchange. Additional funds are needed when the equity of your account falls below this level. This is known as a maintenance margin call.

All margin calls must be met immediately. Normally you will be given a reasonable amount of time to comply with this request. If you do not comply, the firm has the right to liquidate your trades or a sufficient number of trades to restore your account to margin requirements.

The brokerage firm has the right to raise margin requirements to the customer at any time. This is normally done if the price of the commodity is changing sharply or if it is the brokerage firm's opinion that due to the volatility of the market the margin requirement is not sufficient at that particular time.

Most commodity contracts have a minimum fluctuation and also a maximum fluctuation for any one particular day. For example, if you are trading frozen Pork Bellies on the Chicago Mercantile Exchange the fluctuation is considered in points. A point equals three dollars and eighty cents. This means that if you buy a contract at 52.40 and the next price tick is 52.45, you have made a paper profit of five points or nineteen dollars. The maximum fluctuation on a belly contract is 200 points, so your profit or loss cannot exceed in one day more than 200 points from the previous day's settlement. There are exceptions in some commodity contracts, where the spot month has no limit.

Let us assume that you had originally placed in the hands of your brokerage firm two thousand dollars margin money, and that you and your Account Executive decide to purchase a December Live Cattle contract whose initial margin is $1200 with maintenance of $900.00. After the purchase of the contract your account would show initial margin required $1200 dollars with excess funds of eight hundred dollars. At the end of each day the settlement price of December Cattle would be applied to your purchase price and your account would be adjusted to either an increase due to profit or decrease due to loss in your contract.

Further, assume that in a period of two or three days there is a decline in the price of the December Cattle contract and your account now shows a loss of three hundred dollars. Since maintenance margin is only nine hundred dollars on this contract, you will still show an excess of eight hundred dollars over and above maintenance margin. But, in the next four days suppose there is an additional loss of nine hundred dollars. Your account will now need one hundred dollars to maintain the maintenance margin and four hundred dollars additional in order to bring your account up to initial margin. Your Account Executive, or a man from the margin department of the brokerage firm will then contact you, stating that you must place additional money with the firm in order to maintain the December Cattle contract.

At this point, you must decide whether you should continue with the contract, feeling that it may be profitable in the next few days, and thus sending the brokerage firm the required four hundred dollars to maintain your position, or whether to assume your loss and sell the contract.

Let us assume that you decide to sell your December contract at this point and that the selling price causes a loss of four hundred dollars. Added to this loss would be the commission of forty dollars, so your total loss on the transaction would be four hundred forty dollars. A confirmation and purchase and sales statement will be sent to you, showing the original price paid for the contract, the price for which it was sold, the gross loss of four hundred dollars plus the commission of forty dollars making the total loss four hundred forty dollars, and your new ledger balance on deposit with the firm as fifteen hundred sixty dollars.

As shown in our example, commission was charged only when the contract was closed out. A single commission is charged for each round-turn transaction consisting of the creation and liquidation of a single contract.

CONTROLLED, DISCRETIONARY, AND MANAGED ACCOUNTS

There are two methods of trading your account. The first is the professional approach where you and your Account Executive decide on each trade with no discretion being given directly to your Account Executive. This method was illustrated in the discussion about margins. The second method is called a controlled discretionary or managed account. Under this method, you are giving your Account Executive authorization to trade your account at his discretion at any time and as many times that he considers that a trade should be made. The Chicago Mercantile Exchange, and the Board of Trade have rules governing this type of relationship. The following is an excerpt from the C.M.E. rule regarding controlled, discretionary and managed accounts.

REQUIREMENTS

No clearing member shall accept or carry an account over which any individual or organization, other than the person in whose name the account is carried, exercises trading authority or control, hereinafter referred to as controlled accounts, unless:

> The account is initiated with a minimum of $5000*, and maintained at a minimum equity of $3,750*, regardless of lesser applicable margin requirements. In determining equity the accounts or ledger balances and positions in all commodities traded at the clearing member shall be included. Whenever at the close of any business day the equity, calculated with all open positions figured to the settling price, in any such account is below the required minimum, the clearing member shall immediately notify the customer in person, by telephone or telegraph and by written confirmation of such notice mailed directly to the customer, not later than the close of the following business day. Such notice shall advise the customer that unless additional funds are promptly received to restore the customer's controlled account to no less than $5,000*, the clearing member shall liquidate all of the customer's open futures positions at the Exchange.
>
> In the event the call for additional equity is not met within a reasonable time, the customer's entire open position shall be liquidated. No period of time in excess of five business days shall be considered reasonable unless such longer period is approved in writing by an officer or partner of the clearing member upon good cause shown.

REVIEWING YOUR CONFIRMATIONS AND STATEMENTS

An important factor in trading is that you must be sure that no errors occur in your account. For every trade made you should receive a confirmation, and for every close-out a profit and loss statement known as a Purchase-and-Sale, showing the financial results of each transaction closed out in your account. In addition, a monthly statement showing your ledger balance, your open position, the net profit or loss in all contracts liquidated since the date of your last previous statement, and the net unrealized profit and loss on all open contracts figured to the market should be sent to you.

You should carefully review these statements. Upon receiving a confirmation of a trade you should immediately check its accuracy as far as type of commodity, month, trading price and quantity of contracts. If this does not agree with your original order, it should be immediately reported to the main office of your brokerage firm, and any differences should be explained and adjustments should be made.

If you do not receive a confirmation on a trade after it was orally reported to you by your Account Executive, be sure to contact him and the main office so that if an error was made it can be corrected immediately. You should receive written confirmation when you deposit money with your brokerage firm. If within a few days, you have not received this confirmation, report it immediately to the main office of your brokerage firm.

Never assume that an order has been filled until you receive an oral confirmation from your broker. A ticker or a board that you may be observing can be running several minutes behind and is not the determining factor as to whether your trade was executed or not. Until you receive this oral confirmation, never re-enter an order to buy or sell, against that position.

If you receive a confirmation in the mail showing a trade not belonging to you, immediately notify the main office of your brokerage firm and have them explain why this is on a confirmation with your account number. If it is an error, be sure that it is adjusted immediately and a written confirmation sent to you showing the adjustment of the error. If an error is made and it is profitable to you do not consider this any differently than if it was not profitable. Regardless of whether there is a profit or loss, all errors should be immediately reported to the brokerage firm.

Be sure that when you request funds to be mailed from your account that they are received within a few days from the time of your request. If not, contact the accounting department of the brokerage firm to see what is the cause of the delay.

Never make a check out to an individual. Always make your check out to the brokerage firm.

DAY TRADING

Day trading is where there is a buy and sell made during the trading hours on one particular day. Day trading is not considered to be a sound practice for the new speculator and inexperienced trader. Day trading is something that should be executed only by a sophisticated trader who is in frequent communication with the floor, and even then, on a limited basis.

* Minimums can be changed by each exchange, so consult your Account Executive for current regulations.

ORDERS

In order to trade effectively in the commodity market there are several basic types of orders. The most common order is a market order. A market order is one which you authorize your Account Executive to buy or sell at the existing price. This is definitely not a predetermined price, but is executed at a bid or offer at that particular moment.

> *Example: Buy 5 Feb Pork Bellies at the market.*

LIMITED OR PRICE ORDERS AND "OB" DESIGNATION

This type of order to buy or sell commodities at a fixed or "limited" price and the ordinary "market" order are the most common types of orders.

> *Example: Buy Three Jan Silver 463.10.* This limit order instructs the floor broker to buy three contracts of January Silver futures at 463.10. Even with this simple order, however, one presumption is necessary—that the market price prevailing when the order enters the pit is 463.10 or higher. If the price is below 463.10, the broker could challenge on the basis that the client may have meant *"Buy Three Jan Silver 463.10 stop."* Therefore, while it is always assumed that a "limit: order means 'or better,'" if possible, it saves confusion and challenges if the "OB" designation is added to the limit price. This is particularly true on orders near the market, or on pre-opening orders with the limit price based on the previous close, because no one knows whether the opening will be higher or lower than the close, *i.e., Buy Three Jan Silver 463.10 OB.*

STOP ORDERS *(Orders having the effect of market orders)*

Buy Stop Buy stop orders must be written at a price higher than the price prevailing at the time of entry. If the prevailing price for December Wheat is 456 per bushel, a buy stop order must designate a price above 456.

> *Example: "Buy 20 Dec Wht 456½ Day Stop."* The effect of this order is that if December Wheat touches 456½ the order to buy 20 December Wheat becomes a market order. From that point, 456½ on, all the above discussion regarding market orders applies.

Sell Stop Sell stop orders must be written at a price lower than the price prevailing at the time of entry in the trading pit. If the prevailing price of December Wheat is 456 per bushel, a sell stop order must designate a price below 456.

> *Example: "Sell 20 Dec Wht 455 Day Stop."* If this order enters the trading pit with the above price of 456 prevailing, the order to sell 20 December Wheat becomes a market order. From that point 455 on, all the above discussion regarding market orders applies.

Buy stop orders have several specific uses. If you are short a December Wheat at 456, and wish to limit your loss to ½ cent per bushel, the above buy stop order at 456½ would serve this purpose. However, it is important to realize that such *"stop loss"* orders do not actually limit the loss to exactly ½ cent when *"elected"* or *"touched off"* because they become market orders and must be executed at whatever price the market conditions dictate.

Another use is when you are without a position and believe that, because of chart analysis or for other reasons, a buy of December Wheat at 456½ would signal the beginning of an important uptrend in Wheat prices. Thus, the same order to *"Buy 20 Dec Wheat 456½ Day Stop"* would serve this purpose.

Sell stop orders have the same uses in reverse. That is, if you are long 20 December Wheat at 456 and wish to limit this loss to 1 cent per bushel, the above sell stop order at 455 would serve this purpose, within the limitations of the market order possibilities. Similarly, if you are without a position and believe that a sale of December Wheat at 455 would signal a downtrend in wheat prices, and you wish to be short the market, you could use the order to *"Sell 20 December Wheat 455 Day Stop"* for this purpose.

STOP LIMIT ORDERS *(Variations of stop orders)*

Stop limit orders should be used by you when you wish to give the floor broker a limit beyond which he cannot go in executing the order which results when a stop price is *"elected."*

> *Example: "Buy 20 Dec Wheat 456½ Day Stop Limit."* This instructs the broker that when the price of 456½ is reached and *"elects"* this stop order, instead of making it a market order, it becomes a limited order to be executed at 456½ *(or lower)*, but no higher than 456½. Another possibility:

> *Example: "Buy One February Pork Belly 58.10 Day Stop Limit 58.25 (or any other price above 58.10)."* This instructs the broker that when the price of 58.10 *"elects"* the stop order instead of making it a market order, it becomes a limited order to buy at 58.25 *(or lower)*, but no higher as with any limit order.

Stop limit orders are particularly useful to you when you have no position and wish to enter a market via the stop order, but want to put some reasonable limit as to what you will pay. On the other hand, stop limit orders are not useful to you when you have an open position and wish to prevent a loss beyond a certain point. The reason is that by limiting the broker to a certain price after a *"stop loss"* order is elected, **you also run the risk that the market may exceed the limit too fast for the broker to execute.** This would leave you with your original position because the broker would have to wait for the return to the limit before executing. With a straight stop *(no limit)* order, the broker must execute *"at the market."*

Example: "Buy One February Pork Belly 58.10 Day Stop Limit 58.25." Suppose the market moves to 58.10 but then only 20 February Pork Bellies are offered at that price. Your broker bids for one at 58.10 but another broker in the pit catches the seller's eye first and buys 20 and your broker misses the sale. Your broker then bids 58.20 but the best offer is 58.30. He bids 58.25, but the offer at 58.30 remains unchanged. Then another broker bids for and buys February Pork Bellies at 58.30 and the market moves on up. Your broker is left with no execution to your order unless the market later declines to your limit making a fill possible.

If you did not have a position you might be disappointed, but you would be unhurt financially. However, if you had a position and were trying to limit your loss you would have defeated your purpose with the stop limit order, if you truly wanted *"out"* after the stop was elected.

Stop limit orders on the sell side have exactly the same uses, advantages and disadvantages as discussed above, but in reverse:

Example: "Sell 20 December Wheat 455 Day Stop Limit." This means that when the market declines to 455 per bushel, the broker may sell at 455 *(or higher)*, but no lower.

Another Example: "Sell One February Pork Belly 58.25 Stop Limit 58.10." This instructs the broker to sell a belly after the stop price of 58.25 is reached and *"elects"* the stop order, but no lower than 58.10.

M.I.T. ORDERS *(Market-if-touched)*

By adding MIT *(Market-If-Touched)* to a limit order, the limit order will have the effect of a market order when the limit price is reached or touched. This type of order is useful to you, when you have an open position and if a certain limit price is reached.

Example: "Sell One September Sugar 950 MIT." The floor broker is told that if and when the price of September Sugar rises to 9½¢ per pound, he is to sell one contract at the market. At this price of 9½¢ all prior discussion on market orders applies.

Under certain market conditions, not enough contracts are bid at 9½ cents to fill all offers to sell. Thus, you may see your straight limit price appear on the ticker, but your broker fails to make the sale.

But by adding MIT to the limit price, you will receive an execution, because the order becomes a market order, if the price is touched. However, the price will not necessarily be a good one in your eyes, since it became a market order when touched.

The same reasoning is true on the buy side of MIT orders but in reverse. Assume you are short one contract of September Sugar, with the prevailing price at 9½¢ per pound and you want to cover or liquidate your short at 9¢.

Example: "Buy One September Sugar 9¢ MIT." If and when the price of September sugar declines to 9¢ per pound, the floor broker must buy one contract at the market. Aside from the disadvantages of any market order, the MIT designation on the buy order prevents the disappointment which might arise if a straight limit buy at 9¢ were entered without the MIT added.

SPREAD ORDERS

As explained in the Glossary, a spread is a simultaneous long or short position in the same or related commodity. Thus a spread order would be to buy one month of a certain commodity and sell another month of the same commodity, or buy one month of one commodity and sell the same or another month of a related commodity.

Example: "Buy 5 July Beans Market and Sell 5 May Beans Market" or "Buy 10 Kansas City Dec Wheat Market and Sell 10 Chicago May Wheat Market."

Another Example: "Buy 5 May Corn Market and Sell 5 May Wheat Market."

In the example of the related commodity spread, normally the reason you would use such a spread, is that you expect to make a profit out of an expected tightness in the Corn Market, in the hope the corn contract will gain in value faster than wheat.

There may be a situation where you have a position either long or short in a commodity and want to change to a nearer or more distant option of the same commodity. For example you are long 5,000 bushels of May Soybeans on May 20 and want to avoid a delivery notice by moving your position forward into the July option. The basic spread order would be:

"Buy 5 July Beans Market and Sell 5 May Beans Market."

Sometimes you may prefer not to use market orders, in which case you use the difference spread.

> *Example: "Buy 5 July Beans and Sell 5 May Beans July 2¢ Over."* Even though the prices of the two options are not specified, the broker is allowed to execute at any time he can do so with July selling at 2¢ or less above May. Over or under designations are a necessity for clarity to the floor broker. Omitting either is like omitting the price.

All orders, except market orders, can be cancelled, prior to execution. Naturally, a market order is executed immediately upon reaching the pit, so its cancellation is almost impossible.

There are other variations of orders, but for you the new speculator, the types mentioned are sufficient for your trading.

Options on Stock Market Indices, Bond Futures, and Gold Futures

STOCK MARKET INDEX OPTIONS

Stock market index related options are options whose prices are determined by the value of a stock market average such as the Standard and Poor (S&P) 500 Index or the New York Stock Exchange Composite Index, among others. Two types of such options are currently traded; index options and index futures options. The former are settled in cash while the latter are settled by delivery of the appropriate index futures contract.

Both types of options move in the same way in response to the underlying market index, thereby providing investors the opportunity to speculate on the market averages. The buyer of a call index option is betting that the underlying market index value will increase significantly above the strike price (before the option expires) so as to provide a profit when the option is sold. On the other hand, the buyer of a put option is speculating that the market index value will fall sufficiently below the strike price before the option expires so as to provide a profit when the put option is sold. Options writers (sellers), on the other hand, assume an opposite position.

While index futures (page 449) also permit speculation on the market averages, index option tend to be less risky since option *buyers* are not subject to margin calls and losses are limited to the price (premium) paid for the option. However, index option writers (sellers), in return for the premium received, are subject to margin calls and are exposed to losses of indeterminate magnitude. However, writers of call options on index *futures* can protect themselves by holding the underlying futures contract.

Index Options

A number of index options based on the broad market averages are now traded:

- S&P 100 Index [Chicago Board of Options Exchange (CBOE)]
- S&P 500 Index (Chicago Board of Options Exchange)
- Major Market Index [American Exchange (Amex)]
- Institutional Index (American Exchange)
- NYSE Options Index (New York Stock Exchange)
- Value Line Index (Philadelphia Exchange)
- National OTC Index (Philadelphia Exchange)

A brief description of some of the more important indices follows.

The S&P 100 Index is a so-called weighted index obtained by multiplying the current price of each of the 100 stocks by the number of shares outstanding and then adding all of the products to obtain the weighted sum. The weighted sum is then multiplied by a scaling factor to provide an index of a convenient magnitude. The S&P 500 Index is calculated similarly except that all of the S&P 500 stocks are included.

The NYSE Index is based on the weighted sum of all of the stocks traded on the New York Exchange while the AMEX Index is based on the weighted sum of all of the issues traded on the American Exchange. The Institutional Index consists of 75 stocks most widely held by institutional investors.

The Major Market Index differs from the above in that it is just the simple (unweighted) sum of 20 blue chip stocks multiplied by a factor of one tenth. This index behaves very similarly to the Dow Jones Index.

Generally index options expire on the Saturday following the third Friday of the expiration month. Hence the last trading day is on the third Friday of the expiration month. The price of an index option contract is $100 times the premium as quoted in the financial press.

Example: The July 120 (an option with a strike price of 120 expiring in July) Major Market Index call option is quoted (Exhibit 1, see page 460) at 3.00. The cost of an option contract is $300 ($100 × 3).

Option premiums consist of the sum of two components; the intrinsic value and the time value. The intrinsic value of a *call* option is $100 times the difference obtained by subtracting the strike price from the current value of the index. The instrinsic value of a *put* option is $100 times the difference ob-

EXHIBIT 1 INDEX OPTIONS QUOTATIONS

CHICAGO BOARD

CBOE 100 INDEX

Strike Price	Calls—Last June	Calls—Last Sept	Calls—Last Dec	Puts—Last June	Puts—Last Sept	Puts—Last Dec
145	15¼	....	....	1/16	1	....
150	13¾	....	....	⅛	1¾	....
155	9⅛	10	....	7/16	3⅛	....
160	5⅛	9¼	....	17/16	4⅝	8¼
165	2⅛	6½	8⅝	3⅞	7¼	10½
170	11/16	3¾	6	7⅝	12	13½

Total call volume 20846. Total call open int. 62006.
Total put volume 25167. Total put open int. 103733.
The index closed at 163.55, +1.91.

AMERICAN EXCHANGE

MAJOR MARKET INDEX

Strike Price	Calls—Last Jul	Calls—Last Oct	Calls—Last Jan	Puts—Last Jul	Puts—Last Oct	Puts—Last Jan
115	5¾	8⅝	10	1⅞	3¾	5½
120	3	5¾	7	4	5⅞	7½
125	1⅛	3¼	....	7⅜	....	....
130	7/16	2¼	3⅝	....	....	

Total call volume 2351. Total call open int. 14572.
Total put volume 5276. Total put open int. 9593.
The index closed at 118.69, +1.00.

Source: Reprinted by permission of *The Wall Street Journal*, Dow Jones & Co., Inc.

tained by subtracting the current value of the index from the strike price. The time value is the money which an option buyer is willing to pay in the expectation that the option will become more valuable (*increase its intrinsic value*) before it expires. Obviously the time value decreases as the time to expiration decreases.

It should be noted that there is a distinction between exercising an index option and selling an index option to close out a position. Exercising an option gives the holder the right to a cash amount equal to the *intrinsic* value of the option. Hence, the time value of the option is lost. When an option is sold to close out a position, the option holder receives a cash amount equal to the *premium* which contains both the intrinsic value and the time value of the option. Thus, in most cases it is more profitable to sell the option. The profit realized (before commissions and taxes) on the *sale* of an option contract is equal to $100 times the difference obtained by subtracting the premium paid when the option was purchased from the premium received when the option was sold.

Example: On May 24 the CBOE 100 Index was 163.55. In anticipation of a market decline, an investor buys a September 165-put option quoted at 7¼ for a total premium of $725 (7.25 × 100) per option. Assume that on August 10 the puts were selling at a total premium of $850 due to a decline in the CBOE 100 Index to 160.10. If the investor sells the put option he will realize a profit, before commissions and taxes, of $125 (850 − 725). If the market moves in a contrary direction he could lose his entire investment.

Index Futures Options

Index futures options (also called futures options) are the right to buy (call) or sell (put) the underlying index futures contracts (see page 449). Futures options are currently traded on the New York Futures Exchange and the Chicago Mercantile Exchange. The dollar value of the underlying contract for the New York Futures Exchange option is equal to the New York Stock Exchange Composite Index multiplied by 500 while that for the Chicago Mercantile Exchange option is equal to the S&P 500 Index multiplied by 500. Quotations for futures options as they appear in *The Wall Street Journal* are shown in Exhibit 2. The total futures option premium per option is equal to the quoted value multiplied by 500. Gains and losses are calculated in the same way as index options.

The expiration day of the S&P 500 futures option is on the third Thursday of the expiration month while that for the NYSE futures option is the business day prior to the last business day of the expiration month.

Example: On May 24, 1983, the New York Composite Index is 94.39. An investor expects the Index to increase during the next six months and buys a September 96 futures call option at a total premium of $1750 (3.50 × 500), as indicated in Exhibit 2. Assume that by August 10 the Index is at 100 and that the September call premium is quoted at 8.00 corresponding to a total premium per option of $4000 (8.00 × 500). By selling the option at the current value the investor can realize a profit of $2250 (4000 − 1750) before commissions and taxes.

Example: Assume that on May 24, 1983 when the S&P 500 Index is at 163.43, an investor expects a market decline within six months. He purchases a September 155 S&P put option at a total premium per option of $1150 (2.30 × 500), as indicated in the quotations shown in Exhibit 2. Assume that the Index declines to 150 on August 10 and that the quoted put premium is 6.50 corresponding to a total premium per option of $3250 (6.50 × 500). By selling the option at the current value the investor can realize a profit of $2100 (3250 − 1150), before commissions and taxes.

While a number of the same basic concepts apply to both index options and future options, there are differences between the two because the futures options have underlying index futures contracts which are traded on the open market. This makes possible a

EXHIBIT 2 FUTURES OPTIONS

CHICAGO MERCANTILE EXCHANGE

S&P 500 STOCK INDEX – Price = $500 times premium.

Strike Price	Calls—Settle Jun	Calls—Settle Sep	Calls—Settle Dec	Puts—Settle Jun	Puts—Settle Sep	Puts—Settle Dec
135	....	....	....	.05	....	....
140	23.90	24.25	....	.05	.45	....
145	18.90	20.20	....	.05	.90	....
150	13.95	15.25	....	.10	1.25	....
155	9.20	11.50	....	.30	2.30	4.50
160	4.95	8.60	....	1.05	3.60	....
165	1.90	5.50	8.75	3.00	5.75	7.80
170	.45	3.50	....	6.50	9.50	....
175	.10	1.80	....	11.15	14.00	....

Estimated total vol. 1,440
Calls: Fri. vol. 766; open int. 6,216
Puts: Fri. vol 532; open int. 6,552

N.Y. FUTURES EXCHANGE

NYSE COMPOSITE INDEX – Price = $500 times premium.

Strike Price	Calls—Settle Jun	Calls—Settle Sep	Calls—Settle Dec	Puts—Settle Jun	Puts—Settle Sep	Puts—Settle Dec
84	10.90	11.70	....	.05	.40	.75
86	8.90	10.00	11.00	.05	.70	1.50
88	5.95	8.50	9.70	.05	1.00	1.75
90	5.15	7.00	8.30	.25	1.50	2.30
92	3.35	5.50	7.00	.50	2.00	2.95
94	1.95	4.50	6.00	1.15	3.00	3.75
96	.95	3.50	5.00	2.10	3.90	4.95
98	.40	2.75	3.95	3.50	5.25	6.05
100	.15	1.75	3.25	....	6.25	7.00

Estimated total vol. 1,405
Calls: Fri. vol. 844; open int. 4,836
Puts: Fri. vol. 549; open int. 4,801
S&P 500 Index 163.43
New York Composite Index = 94.39

Source: Reprinted by permission of *The Wall Street Journal*, Dow Jones & Co., Inc. All rights reserved.

number of trading strategies with futures options which are not available with index options; for example, simultaneously buying an index futures contract and writing a corresponding call option. Also, for the reason given above, there is a distinction between selling a futures option, the usual procedure, and exercising the option. When a futures option is exercised, the option is exchanged for a position in the index futures market which may result in a loss in the time value of the option.

Investors planning to trade options should read two free booklets available from any of the options exchanges:

Understanding the Risks and Uses of Options

Listed Options On Stock Indices

Subindex Options

Subindex options are based on an index made up of leading publicly traded companies within a specific industry. These options permit speculation on an industry without the necessity of selecting specific stocks within the industry. As with all stock index options they are settled in cash.

Subindex options currently traded are:

American Stock Exchange (AMEX)
- Computer Technology Index Option
- Oil and Gas Index Option
- Transportation Index Option

Pacific Stock Exchange
- Technology Index Option

Philadelphia Stock Exchange
- Gold/Silver Index Option

U.S. TREASURY BOND FUTURES OPTIONS

Options on U.S. Treasury Bonds (T-Bonds), traded on the Chicago Board of Trade, are the right to buy (call) or sell (put) a T-Bond futures contract. The T-Bond futures contract underlying the option is for $100,000 of Treasury Bonds, bearing an 8% or equivalent coupon, which do not mature (and are non-callable) for at least 15 years. When long term interest rates decline, the value of the futures contract and the call option increases while the value of a put option decreases. The reverse is true when long term rates increase.

Premiums for T-bond futures *options* are quoted in $1/64$ of 1% (point): Hence each $1/64$ of a point is equal to $15.63 ($100,000 × .01 × $1/64$) per option. Thus a premium quote of 2–16 means 2 $16/64$ or (2 × 64 + 16) × $15.63 or $2250.72 per option. It should be noted that prices of T-bond *futures* are quoted in $1/32$ (of a point) worth $31.25 per futures contract.

As with options trades in general, the profit (before taxes and commissions) is the premium received (per option) when the option is sold minus the premium paid when the option was purchased.

The last trading day for the options is the first Friday, preceded by at least five business days, in the month *prior* to the month in which the underlying futures contract expires. For example, in 1983 a December option stops trading on November 18, 1983.

GOLD FUTURES OPTIONS

The most widely traded gold futures option is on the New York Comex Exchange. The option is the right to buy (call) or sell (put) a gold futures contract for 100 Troy ounces of pure gold. Both the futures contract and the corresponding call option increase or decrease with the price of gold. Put option premiums move in the opposite direction to the price of gold.

Option premiums are in dollars per ounce

of gold. Thus a quoted premium of 2.50 corresponds to total premium of $2500 (2.50 × 100) per option.

The profit (before commissions and taxes) to an option buyer is simply the premium received when the option is sold less the premium paid when the option was purchased.

The last trading day for gold futures options is the second Friday in the month *prior* to the expiration date of the underlying gold futures contract. Thus in 1983 a December option expires on Friday November 11, 1983. Example: In August an investor buys a December 400 (an option with a strike price of 400 on a December gold futures contract) Comex call option quoted at 25.00. The total price per option is $2500 (25.00 × 100).

On November 5, the price of gold has increased and the investor sells the option at a quoted premium of 50.00 or $5000.00 (50 × 100) per option. His profit is $2500 (5000 − 2500).

The Commodities Glossary

Acreage allotment The portion of a farmer's total acreage that he can harvest and still qualify for government price supports, low interest crop loans and other programs. It currently applies to specialty crops—tobacco, peanuts and extra long staple cotton—for which complex federal marketing orders have been written to control production closely. Before the 1977 farm bill was passed, the same term also applied more loosely to the portion of a farmer's wheat or feed grain acreage for which government payments would be made. A farmer could harvest 100 acres of wheat, for instance, but he'd receive price support payments only for 70 acres if that was his allotment. The allotment in this sense is called "program acreage" in the new farm bill.

Arbitrage The simultaneous buying and selling of futures contracts to profit from what the trader perceives as a discrepancy in prices. Usually this is done in futures in the same commodity traded on different exchanges, such as cocoa in New York and cocoa in London or silver in New York and silver in Chicago. Some arbitrage occurs between cash markets and futures markets.

Asking price The price offered by one wishing to sell a physical commodity or a futures contract. Sometimes a futures market will close with an asking price when no buyers are around.

Backwardation An expression peculiar to New York markets. It means "nearby" contracts are trading at a higher price, or "premium," to the deferreds. See also *Inverted market.*

Basis A couple of meanings: (1) The difference between the price of the physical commodity (the cash price) and the futures price of that commodity. (2) A geographic reference point for a cash price; for example, the price of a beef carcass is quoted "basis Midwest packing plants."

Bear A trader who thinks prices will decline. "Bearish" is often used to describe news or developments that have, or are expected to have, a downward influence on prices. A bear market is one in which the predominant price trend is down. Some think this term originated with an old axiom about "selling the skin before you've caught the bear."

Bid The price offered by one who wishes to purchase a physical commodity or a futures contract. Sometimes a futures market will close with a bid price when no sellers are around.

Broker An agent who buys and sells futures on behalf of a client for a fee. They work for brokerage firms, some of which have extensive research and analysis departments that occasionally issue trading advice. A few firms have so many customers who follow such advisories that recommendations to buy or sell can influence market prices materially.

Bull A trader who thinks prices will go up. "Bullish" describes developments that have, or are expected to have, an upward influence on prices. A bull market is one in which the predominant price trend is up. Some theorize this term originally related to a bull's habit of tossing its head upward.

Butterfly An unusual sort of spread involving three contract months rather than two. Often used to move profits or losses from one year to the next for tax purposes.

Cash The price at which dealings in the physical commodity take place. Used more sweepingly, it can mean simply the physical commodity itself (as in "cash corn" or "cash lumber"), or refer to a market. For example, the cash hog market is a terminal (or, collectively, all terminals) where live hogs are sold by farmers and bought by meat packers.

Chart A graph of futures prices (and sometimes other statistical trading information) plotted in such a way that the charter believes gives insight into future price movements. Several futures markets regularly are influenced by buying or selling based on traders' price-chart indications.

Clearing house The part of all futures exchanges (usually a separate corporation with its

Source: The *Dow Jones Commodities Handbook*, edited by Dan Ruck, Dow Jones Books, Dow Jones Company, Inc. 1979.

own members, fees, etc.) which clears all trades made on the exchange during the day. It matches the buy transactions with the equal number of sell transactions to provide orderly control over who owns what and who owes what to whom. Although futures traders theoretically trade contracts among themselves, the clearing house technically is in the middle of each transaction—being the buyer to every seller and the seller to every buyer. That's how it keeps track of what is going on.

Close The end of the trading session. On some exchanges, the "close" lasts for several minutes to accommodate customers who have entered buy or sell orders to be consummated "at the close." On those exchanges, the closing price may be a range encompassing the highest and lowest prices of trades consummated at the close. Other exchanges officially use settlement prices as the closing prices.

Cold storage Refrigerated warehouses where perishable commodities are stored. In effect. the warehouses are secondary sources of commodities that aren't immediately available from the producers. The Agriculture Department periodically reports the quantities of various commodities stored in warehouses. Futures traders watch these reports to see if the supplies are building or dwindling abnormally fast, which indicates how closely supply and demand are balanced.

Commission The fee charged by a broker for making a trade on behalf of customers.

Contract In the case of futures, an agreement between two parties to make and in turn accept delivery of a specified quantity and quality of a commodity (or whatever is being traded) at a certain place (the delivery point) by a specified time (indicated by the month and year of the contract).

Country Refers to a place relatively close to a farmer where he can sell or deliver his crop or animals. For instance, a country elevator typically is located in a small town and accepts grain from farmers in the immediate vicinity. A country shipping point is a place where farmers in an area combine their marketings for shipment. A country price is the one these elevators, shipping points or whatever pay for the farmers' goods; it's based on the terminal-market prices, less transportation and handling costs.

Covering Buying futures contracts to offset those previously sold. "Short covering" often causes prices to rise even though the overall market trend may be down.

Crop report Estimates issued periodically by the Department of Agriculture on estimated size and condition of major U.S. crops. Similar reports are made on livestock.

Crush The process of reducing the raw, unusable soybean into its two major components, oil and meal. A "crush spread" is a futures spreading position in which a trader attempts to profit from what he believes to be discrepancies in the price relationships between soybeans and the two products. The "crush margin" is the gross profit that a processor makes from selling oil and meal minus the cost of buying the soybeans.

Deferred contracts In futures, those delivery months that are due to expire sometime beyond the next two or three months.

Delivery The tendering of the physical commodity to fulfill a short position in futures. This takes place only during the delivery month and normally takes the form of a warehouse receipt (from an exchange-accredited warehouse, elevator or whatever) that shows where the cash commodity is.

Delivery point The place(s) at which the cash commodity may be delivered to fulfill an expiring futures contract.

Discretionary accounts A futures trading account in which the customer puts up the money but the trading decisions are made at the discretion of the broker or some other person, or maybe a computer. Also known as "managed accounts."

Evening up Liquidating a futures position in advance of a significant crop report or some other scheduled development so as not to be caught on the wrong side of a surprise. In concentrated doses, evening up can cause a bull market to retreat somewhat and a bear market to rebound somewhat.

First notice day The first day of a delivery period when holders of short futures positions can give notice of their intention to deliver the cash commodity to holders of long positions. The number of contracts circulated on first notice day and how they are accepted or not accepted by the longs is often interpreted as an indication of future supply-demand expectations and thus often influence prices of all futures being traded, not just the delivery-month price. This effect also sometimes occurs on subsequent notice days. Rules concerning notices to deliver vary from contract to contract.

F.O.B. Free on Board, meaning that the commodity will be placed aboard the shipping vehicle at no cost to the purchaser, but thereafter the purchaser must bear all shipping costs.

Forward Contract A commercial agreement for the merchandising of commodities in which actual delivery is contemplated but is deferred for purposes of commercial convenience or necessity. Such agreements normally specify the quality and quantity of goods to be delivered at the particular future date. The forward contract may specify the price at which the commodity will be exchanged, or the agreement may stipulate that the price will be determined at some time prior to delivery.

Fundamentalist A trader who bases his buy-sell decisions on supply and demand trends or developments rather than on technical or chart considerations.

Futures Contracts traded on an exchange that call for a cash commodity to be delivered and received at a specified future time, at a specified place and at a specified price. Similar arrangements made directly between buyer and seller are called "forward contracts." They aren't traded on an exchange.

Hedge Using the futures market to reduce the risks of unforeseen price changes that are inherent in buying and selling cash commodities. For example, as an elevator operator buys cash grain from farmer, he can "hedge" his purchases by selling futures contracts; when he sells the cash commodity, he purchases an offsetting number of futures contracts to liquidate his position. If prices rise while he owns the cash grain, he sells the cash grain at a profit and closes out his futures at a loss, which almost always is no greater than his profit in the cash transaction. If prices fall while he owns the cash grain, he sells the cash grain at a loss but recoups all or almost all of the loss by buying back futures contracts at a price correspondingly lower than at which he first sold them. Some users of commodities assure themselves of supplies of their raw materials at a set price by buying futures, which is another form of hedging. When the time comes to acquire inventories, they can either take delivery on their futures contracts or, more likely, simply buy their supplies in the cash market. Futures-contract prices tend to match cash prices at the time the futures expire, so if cash prices have risen the users' higher costs are offset by profits on their futures contracts.

Hedger The Commodity Futures Trading Commission says a hedger in a general sense is someone who uses futures trading as a temporary, risk-reducing substitute for a cash transaction planned later in his main line of business. All other futures traders are classified as speculators. There are more legally specific definitions of hedging and hedgers in such markets as grains, soybeans, potatoes and cotton, where limits are placed on the number of contracts speculators may trade or own. The Commission has broadened these limits to allow hedging in closely related, rather than exactly matching, commodities. A sorghum producer, for instance, can use corn futures as a hedging tool where he couldn't before this rule-broadening. The more general distinction between hedgers and speculators may be important to potential traders. Some may want to use a market like interest rate futures to offset some expected heavy borrowing. The government hasn't set any speculative trading limits in those markets, but lenders or company directors are more apt to back a plan to trade futures for hedging purposes rather than speculation.

Inverted market A futures market where prices for deferred contracts are lower than those for nearby-delivery contracts because of great near-term demand for the cash commodity. Normally, prices of deferred contracts are higher, in part reflecting storage costs.

Last trading day The day when trading in an expiring contract ceases, and traders must either liquidate their positions or prepare to make or accept delivery of the cash commodity. After that, there is no more futures trading for that particular contract month and year.

Life of contract The period of time during which futures trading in a particular contract month and year may take place. This is usually less than a year, but sometimes up to 18 months.

Limit move The maximum that a futures price can rise or fall from the previous session's settlement price. This limit, set by each exchange, varies from commodity to commodity. Some exchanges have variable limits, whereby the limit is expanded automatically if the market moves by the limit for a certain number of consecutive trading sessions. When prices fail to move the expanded limit, or after a specified period of time, the limits revert to normal.

Liquidation Closing out a previous position by taking an opposite position in the same contract. Thus, a previous buyer liquidates by selling, and a previous seller liquidates by buying.

Long A trader who has bought futures, speculating the prices will rise. He is "long" until he liquidates by selling or fulfills his contracts by making delivery.

Margin The amount of "good faith" money that commodity traders must put in order to trade futures. The margins, set by each exchange, usually amount to 5% to 10% of the total value of the commodity contract. The "initial margin" is the amount of money that must be put up to establish a position in a futures market. Exchanges establish this margin, too, but brokerage firms often require even larger amounts to protect their own financial interests. "Maintenance margin" is the money that traders must put up to retain their position in the futures markets.

Margin call A request by a brokerage firm that a customer put up more money. That means the market price has gone against the customer's position and the brokerage firm wants the customer to cover his paper loss, which would become a real loss if the position were liquidated.

Nearby contracts The futures that expire the soonest. Those that expire later are called deferred contracts.

New crop The supply of a commodity that will be available after harvest. The term also is sometimes used in connection with pigs and hogs because the major farrowing periods in the spring and fall are referred to as "crops." There sometimes are substantial price differences between futures contracts related to new-crop supplies and those related to old-crop supplies.

Nominal price An artificial price—usually the midpoint between a bid and an asked price—that gives an indication of the market price level even though no actual transactions may have taken place at that price.

Old crop The supply from previous harvests.

Open The period each session when futures trading commences. Sometimes the open lasts several minutes to accommodate customers who have placed orders to buy or sell contracts "on the open." On these exchanges, opening prices often are reported by the exchange as a range, although these seldom are widely disseminated because of space restrictions in newspapers and periodicals; they are carried on tickers and display panels during that trading day, however.

Open interest Outstanding futures contracts that haven't been liquidated by purchase or sale of offsetting contracts, or by delivery or acceptance of the physical commodity.

Option The right to buy or sell a futures contract over a specified period of time at a set price.

Overbought A term used to express the opinion that prices have risen too high too fast and so will decline as traders liquidate their positions.

Oversold Like "overbought," except the opinion is that prices have fallen too far too fast and so probably will rebound.

Pit The areas on exchange floors where futures trading takes place. Pits usually have three or more levels and can accommodate a large number of traders. On several New York exchanges the trading areas are called rings and consist of open-center, circular tables around which traders sit or stand.

Position A trader's holdings, either long or short. A position limit is the maximum number of contracts a speculator can hold under law; it doesn't apply to bona-fide hedgers, although there really isn't any objective way of telling whether a person in position to hedge actually is hedging or is speculating instead.

Profit taking A trader holding a long position turns paper profits into real ones by selling his contracts. A trader holding a short position takes profits by buying back contracts.

Reaction A decline in prices following a substantial advance.

Recovery An increase in prices following a substantial decline.

Settlement price The single closing price, determined by each exchange's price committee of directors. It is used primarily by the exchange clearing house to determine the need for margin capital to be put up by brokerage-firm members to protect the net position of that firm's total accounts. It's also issued by some exchanges as the official closing price, and it is used to determine the price limits and net price changes on the following trading day. (See also: *Close.*)

Set-aside Acreage withdrawn from crop production for a season and used for soil conservation under a production-control program. Wheat farmers this year must set aside two acres of land for each 10 acres they plant to wheat in order to get any federal price support or disaster aid. The Agriculture Department has also said corn, sorghum and barley producers similarly may be required to set aside some of their acreage if it appears that surpluses will grow too much otherwise.

Short A trader who has sold futures, speculating that prices will decline. He is "short" until he liquidates by buying back contracts or fulfills his contracts by taking delivery.

Short squeeze A situation in which "short" futures traders are unable to buy the cash commodity to deliver against their positions and so are forced to buy offsetting futures at prices much higher than they'd ordinarily be willing to pay.

Speculation Buying or selling in hopes of making a profit. The word connotes a high degree of risk.

Spot The same as cash commodities. Literally, delivery "on the spot" rather than in the future.

Spreads and straddles Terms for the simultaneous buying of futures in one delivery month and selling of futures in another delivery month (or even the simultaneous buying of futures in one commodity and selling of futures in a different but related commodity). One purpose is to profit from perceived discrepancies in price relationships. Another purpose is to transfer current trading profits to some future time to avoid immediate tax liability.

Stop-loss order An open order given to a brokerage firm to liquidate a position when the market reaches a certain price so as to prevent losses from mounting or profits from eroding. Sometimes market price trends are accelerated when concentrations of stop-loss orders are touched off.

Support price A level below which the government tries to keep the agricultural-commodity prices that farmers receive from falling. They're set basically by Congress when farm legislation is passed and adjusted from time to time by the President or Agriculture Secretary. Subsidy payments, commodity purchases, production controls or commodity-secured loans are among the devices used to make up the difference when market prices dip below the support level. Futures and cash prices often tend to remain near the support level when there are large crop surpluses because lower prices keep commodities off the market and higher ones quickly draw willing sellers.

Switch A trading maneuver in which a trader liquidates his position in one futures delivery and takes the position in another delivery month in expectation that prices will change more rapidly in the second contract than in the first. Thus, a trader might switch out of a position in an October silver futures contract into a position in a December silver futures contract. Warning: Some people use the word "switch" when they mean "spread" or "straddle." Feel free to correct them.

Technical factors Futures prices often are affected by influences related to the market itself, rather than to supply-demand fundamentals of the commodity with which the market is concerned. For example, if a market moves up or down the limit several days in succession there frequently is a subsequent "technical reaction" caused in part by the liquidation of contracts held by traders on the wrong side of the price move.

Terminal Refers to an elevator or livestock market at key distribution points to which commodities are sent from a wide area.

Trading range The amount that futures prices can fluctuate during one trading session—essentially, the price "distance" between limit up and limit down. If, for instance, the soybean futures price can advance or fall by a maximum of 20 cents per bushel in one day, the trading range is double that, or 40 cents per bushel. In one market, cocoa, price movements are restricted to a daily range of six cents a pound.

Visible supply The amount of a commodity that can be accounted for and computed accurately, usually because it is being kept in major known storage places.

Warehouse or elevator receipt The negotiable slip of paper that a short can hand over to fulfill an expiring futures contract's delivery requirement. The receipt shows how much of the commodity is in storage.

Dow Jones Futures and Spot Commodity Indexes

The method for arriving at the Dow Jones Futures and Spot Commodity Indexes differs from some others in the order in which the computations are made. Instead of first weighting each price, then adding them up and finally calculating the percentage or index, this method first turns each price into an index or percentage of its base-year price, then weights each individual index, and finally adds them up. Stated mathematically, the more usual method calculates the percentage relation of one average to another, while the Dow Jones Commodity Index method calculates the average of a set of percentage changes. These two methods do not result in exactly the same figures. However, they are equally valid when used consistently, and the indexes they produce are of the same general magnitude.

The Dow Jones Commodity Index method has two advantages. One is that it saves computation, because the factors or multipliers perform two computations at once. They calculate the individual percentages and weight them at one stroke. The other advantage is that if you have yesterday's index, you can apply the multipliers to today's individual price changes. Then all you do is add the resulting figures to yesterday's index, or subtract them from it, depending on whether they're up or down. That gives today's index. No need to recalculate the whole thing each day.

As for the weights, they were obtained by the usual mathematical methods. Basically, the weight of each commodity is the percentage of its commercial production value to the total commercial production value of all commodities in the index, in this case for the years 1927–31. In calculating the weights, consideration also was given to the relation between volume of trading in each commodity and its commercial production.

A further refinement was necessary because price changes of the various commodities are quoted in different units. Grain prices change in eighths of a cent, wool prices change in tenths of a cent, and all the other staples in the Dow Jones index move in hundredths of a cent. This adjustment merely required appropriate treatment in each case of the multiplier, so that it would give the right figure for any price change. In the case of grains it meant an adjustment of 20%, since one-tenth is that much smaller than one-eighth. In other cases a mere adjustment of decimal points was sufficient.

The twelve commodities, with the weight of each and the multiplier applied to the price changes of each, are:

Source: The *Dow Jones Commodities Handbook*, edited by Dan Ruck, Dow Jones Books, Dow Jones & Company, Inc.

	Weight	Multiplier
Wheat	19.5	16
Corn	8	11
Oats	5	13
Rye	4	5
Wool Tops	5.5	4
Cotton	23	10
Cottonseed Oil	4.5	4
Coffee	7	3
Sugar	8.5	27
Cocoa	5	5
Rubber	6	3
Hides	4	3

These are the essentials for calculating the spot index. However, the futures index requires one more set of unusual steps. That's because several times a year an actual quoted "future" disappears. For instance, while early in the year it is possible to buy wheat to be delivered in December, when the month of December actually arrives that "delivery" expires and is no longer quoted.

The result is that futures prices are affected not only by market conditions but also by how close the delivery date looms. Interest charges and other such factors influence them. On July 1, the December delivery is just five months off, but a month later it is only four months away, and a five-month delivery should not, in a precise index, be compared with a four-month delivery.

This problem is overcome by the use of two futures quotations for each commodity. They are combined to produce on each market day the calculated price that would apply to a delivery exactly five months off.

On the first day of July, only the December delivery is used, since it is just five months away and thus no adjustment need be made. On the second day, the two quotations used are those for the same December delivery and the one for May of the following year. The quoted price for December is adjusted by one day's proportion of the difference between it and May's quoted price. Since there are 151 days between December and May (except in leap years) the figure for one day's proportion is 1/151 of the price difference between the two. The resulting fraction is added to December's price, or subtracted from it, depending on whether May is quoted above or below December.

The following day 2/151 of the difference are added or subtracted, the third day 3/151 and so on until December 1, on which day only the May contract's price is used. On December 2, the combination used is May and July, and so on around the year.

To facilitate the work of calculating the futures index every hour of each business day and the spot index once a day, tables have been prepared—resembling somewhat tables of logarithms or bond yields—which give the figures arrived at by multiplying the various quotational units of each commodity by its factor or multiplier. For instance, the tables show the proper multiples for one-eighth, one-quarter, three-eighths, etc., when each is multiplied by each grain's factor or multiplier.

The commodity futures index is published once an hour and as of the close of commodity markets each day on the Dow Jones News Service, where also the spot index is published once daily. Both are published likewise in *The Wall Street Journal*.

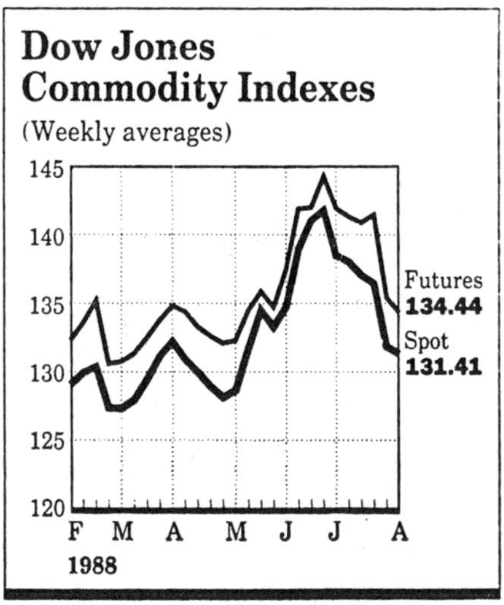

	Close		Net Chg.	Yr. Ago
Dow Jones Futures	135.39	+	.20	128.02
Dow Jones Spot	131.67	+	.08	128.19
Reuter United Kingdom	1880.9	+	8.6	1637.0
C R B Futures*	251.04	+	.87	222.49

*Division of Knight-Ridder.

On What Exchanges Futures and Options Are Traded

U.S. Futures Contracts

Chicago Board of Trade

Corn; Oats; Soybeans; Soybean Meal; Soybean Oil; Wheat (Soft winter); GNMA CDR; GNMA (Cash-settled); U.S. Treasury Bonds; U.S. Treasury Notes (6½–10 yr.); Municipal Bond Index; Major market Index-Maxi; Institutional Index; Gold; Silver

Chicago Mercantile Exchange

Cattle, Feeder; Cattle, Live; Eggs, Fresh White (Inactive); Hogs, Live; Pork Bellies; Lumber (Random-length)

Chicago Mercantile Exchange International Monetary Market Division

Deutsche Mark; Canadian Dollar; French Franc; Swiss Franc; British Pound; Mexican Peso (Inactive); Japanese Yen; Australian Dollar; European Currency Unit (ECU); Treasury Bills (90-day); Domestic Certificates of Deposit (3-month); Eurodollar Time Deposit (3-month); Gold

Chicago Mercantile Exchange Index and Option Market Division

Standard & Poor's 500 Stock Index; Standard & Poor's 100 Stock Index; Standard & Poor's Over-The-Counter Index (250 stocks)

Chicago Rice and Cotton Exchange

Rough Rice

Coffee, Sugar & Cocoa Exchange Inc.

Cocoa; Coffee "C"; Sugar No. 11 (World); Sugar No. 14; Sugar (White); Inflation Rate; Consumer Price Index (CPI-W)

Commodity Exchange Inc. (COMEX)

Aluminum; Copper; Silver; Gold (Linked to Sydney Futures Exchange)

Kansas City Board of Trade

Wheat (Hard red winter); Value Line Stock Index; Mini Value Line Stock Index

MidAmerica Commodity Exchange

Cattle, Live; Hogs, Live; Corn; Oats, Soybeans; Soybean Meal; Wheat (Soft winer); New York Gold; New York Silver; Platinum; U.S. Treasury Bonds; U.S. Treasury Bills (90-day); British Pound; Canadian Dollar; Deutsche Mark; Japanes Yen; Swiss Franc

Minneapolis Grain Exchange

Wheat (Hard red spring); High Fructose Corn Syrup

New York Cotton Exchange

Cotton No. 2

Citrus Associates of the New York Cotton Exchange Inc.

Orange Juice

Financial Instrument Exchange (FINEX)

U.S. Dollar Index; European Currency Unit (EUC); Five-Year U.S. Treasury Note (FYTR)

New York Futures Exchange

NYSE Composite Stock Index; CRB Futures Price Index; Russell 2000 Index; Russell 3000 Index

New York Merchantile Exchange

Palladium; Platinum; No. 2 Heating Oil (New York); Unleaded Gasoline; Crude Oil (Light sweet); Propane

Philadelphia Board of Trade

National Over-The-Counter Index; British Pound; Canadian Dollar; Deutsche Mark; Swiss Franc; French Franc; Japanese Yen; European Currency Unit (ECU); Australian Dollar

Canadian Futures Contracts

Toronto Futures Exchange

Canadian Bonds (15-year); Canadian T-Bills (13-week); Toronto Stock Exchange (TSE) 300 Index; TSE 300 Spot Contract; TSE Oil and Gas Index; U.S. Dollar; Toronto 35 Index

The Winnipeg Commodity Exchange

Domestic Feed Barley; Alberta Domestic Feed Barley; Flaxseed; Domestic Feed Oats; Canola/Rapeseed; Rye; Domestic Feed Wheat; Gold; Silver

Options on Futures

Chicago Board of Trade

U.S. Treasury Bonds; T-Notes; Municipal Bond Index; What (Soft winter); Soybeans; Soybean Meal; Soybean Oil; Corn; Silver

Chicago Mercantile Exchange Index and Option Markt

S&P 500 Stock Index; Deutsche Mark; Eurodollar Time Deposit (Three-month); Swiss Franc; British Pound; Cattle, Live; Cattle, Feeder; Hogs, Live; Pork Bellies; Lumber (Random-length)

Coffee, Sugar and Cocoa Exchange

Cocoa; Sugar No. 11; Coffee "C"

Commodity Exchange Inc. (COMEX)

Copper; Gold; Silver

Kansas City Board of Trade

Wheat (Hard red winter)

MidAmerica Commodity Exchange

Gold; What (Soft winter); Soybeans

Minneapolis Grain Exchange

Wheat (Spring)

New York Cotton Exchange

Cotton No. 2

Citrus Associates of the New York Cotton Exchange Inc.

Orange Juice

Financial Instrument Exchange (FINEX)*

U.S. Dollar Index

New York Futures Exchange

NYSE Composite Stock Index

New York Mercantile Exchange

Crude Oil (Light Sweet); Heating Oil

Winnipeg Commodity Exchange

Gold (Calls only)

Options on Actuals

American Stock Exchange (AMEX)

Major Market Index (XMI) (20 stocks); Institutional Index (European-style) (75 stocks); Computer Technology Index; Oil Index; U.S. Treasury Bills (90-day) (European-style); U.S. Treasury Notes (10-year)

Chicago Board Options Exchange (CBOE)

S&P 100 Stock Index; S&P 500 Stock Index; U.S. 30-Year Treasury Bonds (7¼%, 9¼%, 9⅞%); U.S. Five-Year Treasury Notes (7½%, 8⅛, 9⅛%)

Coffee, Sugar & Cocoa Exchange Inc.

Inflation Rate

New York Stock Exchange

New York Stock Exchange Composite Index; NYSE Beta Index

Pacific Stock Exchange

PSE Technology Index; Financial News Composite Index (FNCI)

Philadelphia Board of Trade

Eurodollar

Philadelphia Stock Exchange (PHLX)

Deutsche Mark; European Currency Unit (ECU); Swiss Franc; Canadian Dollar; British Pound; Japanese Yen; French Franc; Australian Dollar; Value Line Index; Value Line Index (European-style); Utility Index; Gold/Silver Stock Index; National Over-The-Counter Index

The Montreal Exchange

Canadian Bonds; ME T-Bill Index

Toronto Futures Exchange

Silver; Canadian Bonds (11¾%, 9% maturing Feb. 1, 2003; 8¾% maturing June 1, 1996)

Toronto Stock Exchange

TSE 300 Index; Toronto 35 Index

* Division of the New York Cotton Exchange, Inc.

Commodity Futures Trading Commission

Federal laws regulating commodity futures trading are enforced by the Commodity Futures Trading Commission. For information on commodity brokers call (202) 254-8630.

National Office

Commodity Futures Trading Commission
2033 K Street, NW
Washington, DC 20581
Telephone: (202) 254-6387

Regional Offices

Eastern Region
1 World Trade Center
New York, NY 10048
Telephone: (212) 466-2061

Central Region
233 S. Wacker Drive
Chicago, IL 60606
Telephone: (312) 353-5990

Southwestern Region
4901 Main Street
Kansas City, MO 64112
Telephone: (816) 374-2994

510 Grain Exchange Building
Minneapolis, MN 55415
Telephone: (612) 349-3255

Source: U.S. Government Manual.

Western Region
10880 Wilshire Boulevard
Los Angeles, CA 90024
Telephone: (213) 209-6783

The Commodity Futures Trading Commission (CFTC), the Federal regulatory agency for futures trading, was established by the Commodity Futures Trading Commission Act of 1974 (88 Stat. 1389; 7 U.S.C. 4a), approved October 23, 1974. The Commission began operation in April 1975, and its authority to regulate futures trading was renewed by Congress in 1978 and in 1982.

The CFTC consists of five Commissioners who are appointed by the President with the advice and consent of the Senate. One Commissioner is designated by the President to serve as Chairman. The Commissioners serve staggered 5-year terms, and by law no more than three Commissioners can belong to the same political party.

FUNCTIONS AND ACTIVITIES

The Commission consists of five major operating components: the divisions of enforcement, economics and education, trading and markets, and the offices of the executive director and the general counsel.

The Commission regulates trading on the 11 U.S. futures exchanges, which offer active futures and options contracts. It also regulates the activities of numerous commodity exchange members, public brokerage houses (futures Commission merchants), Commission-registered futures industry salespeople and associated persons, and 4,100 commodity trading advisers, and commodity pool operators. Some off-exchange transactions involving instruments similar in nature to futures contracts also fall under CFTC jurisdiction.

The Commission's regulatory and enforcement efforts are designed to ensure that the futures trading process is fair and that it protects both the rights of customers and the financial integrity of the marketplace. The CFTC approves the rules under which an exchange proposes to operate and monitors exchange enforcement of those rules. It reviews the terms of proposed futures contracts, and registers companies and individuals who handle customer funds or give trading advice. The Commission also protects the public by enforcing rules that require that customer funds be kept in bank accounts separate from accounts maintained by firms for their own use, and that such customer accounts be marked to present market value at the close of trading each day.

Futures contracts for agricultural commodities were traded in the United States for more than 100 years before futures trading was diversified to include trading in contracts for precious metals, raw materials, foreign currencies, commercial interest rates, and U.S. Government and mortgage securities. Contract diversification has grown in exchange trading volume, a growth not limited to the newer commodities.

Futures and Options Exchanges: Addresses

UNITED STATES

American Stock Exchange (AMEX)
86 Trinity Place
New York, NY 10006
(212) 306-1000

AMEX Commodity Corporation (ACC)
86 Trinity Place
New York, NY 10006
(212) 306-1000

Chicago Board of Trade (CBT)
141 West Jackson Boulevard
Chicago, IL 60604
(312) 435-3500

Chicago Board Options Exchange (CBOE)
400 South LaSalle
Chicago, IL 60605
(312) 786-5600

Chicago Mercantile Exchange (CME) and International Monetary Market (IMM)
30 South Wacker Drive
Chicago, IL 60606
(312) 930-8200

Chicago Rice & Cotton Exchange (CRCE)
444 W. Jackson Boulevard
Chicago, IL 60606
(312) 341-3078

Coffee, Sugar & Cocoa Exchange (CSCE)
4 World Trade Center
New York, NY 10048
(212) 938-2800

Commodity Exchange, Inc. (COMEX)
4 World Trade Center
New York, NY 10048
(212) 938-2900

International Monetary Market [IMM] (see Chicago Merchantile Exchange [CME]

Kansas City Board of Trade (KCBT)
4800 Main Street
Kansas City, MO 64112
(816) 753-7500

Midamerica Commodity Exchange (MCE)
444 West Jackson Boulevard
Chicago, IL 60606
(312) 341-3000

Minneapolis Grain Exchange (MGE)
150 Grain Exchange Building
400 S. Fourth Street
Minneapolis, MN 55415
(612) 338-6212

New York Cotton Exchange & Associates (NYCE)
4 World Trade Center
New York, NY 10048
(212) 938-2650

New York Futures Exchange (NYFE)
20 Broad Street
New York, NY 10005
(212) 623-4949
(800) 221-7722

New York Mercantile Exchange (NYME)
4 World Trade Center
New York, NY 10048
(212) 938-2222

New York Stock Exchange
11 Wall St.
New York, NY 10005
(800) 656-8533

Pacific Stock Exchange
301 Pine St.
San Francisco, CA 94104
(415) 393-4000

Philadelphia Board of Trade
1900 Market St.
Philadelphia, PA 19103
(215) 496-5025

Philadelphia Stock Exchange
1900 Market St.
Philadelphia, PA 19103
(215) 496-5000

CANADIAN

Montreal Stock Exchange
800 Victoria Square
Montreal, Quebec, Canada H4Z 1A9
(514) 871-2424

Toronto Futures Exchange
2 First Canadian Place
Exchange Tower
Toronto, Ontario, Canada M5X 1J2
(416) 947-4700

Toronto Stock Exchange
2 First Canadian Place
Exchange Tower
Toronto, Ontario, Canada M5X 1J2
(416) 947-4700

Vancouver Stock Exchange
609 Granville
Vancouver, British Columbia
Canada V7Y 1H1
(604) 689-3334

The Winnipeg Commodity Exchange
500 Commodity Exchange Tower
360 Main Street
Winnipeg, Manitoba
Canada R3C 3Z4
(204) 949-0495

SELECTED FOREIGN EXCHANGES

London Commodity Exchange Co. Ltd.
Cereal House, 58 Mark Lane
London, England EC3R 7NE
01-481-2080

The London International Financial Futures Exchange Ltd. (LIFFE)
Royal Exchange
London, England EC3
01-623-0444

The Hong Kong Futures Exchange Ltd.
Hutchison House, Second Floor
Harcourt Road
Hong Kong
5-251005

European Options Exchange (EOE)
DAM 21
1012 JS Amsterdam
The Netherlands
20-26 27 21

Paris Commodity Exchange
Bourse de Commerce
2, rue de Viarmes B.P. 53/01
75040 Paris, Cedex 01 France
1-508-82-50
(212) 751-9050-New York

The Singapore International Monetary Exchange Ltd.
24 Raffles Place
29-04 Clifford Centre
Singapore 0104

Sydney Futures Exchange Ltd.
13-15 O'Connell St.
Sydney, NSW, Australia 2000
02-233-7633

Futures and Securities Organizations

Futures Industry Association, Inc. (FIA)
1825 I Street, NW
Washington, DC 20006
(202) 466–5460

National Association of Futures Trading Advisors (NAFTA)
111 East Wacker Drive
Chicago, IL 60601
(312) 644–6610

National Association of Securities Dealers (NASD)
1735 K Street, NW
Washington, DC 20006
(202) 728-8000

National Futures Association (NFA)
200 West Madison
Chicago, IL 60606
(312) 781–1300

North American Securities Administrators Association, Inc. (NASAA)
425 13th Street, NW
Washington, DC 20004
(202) 783-2303

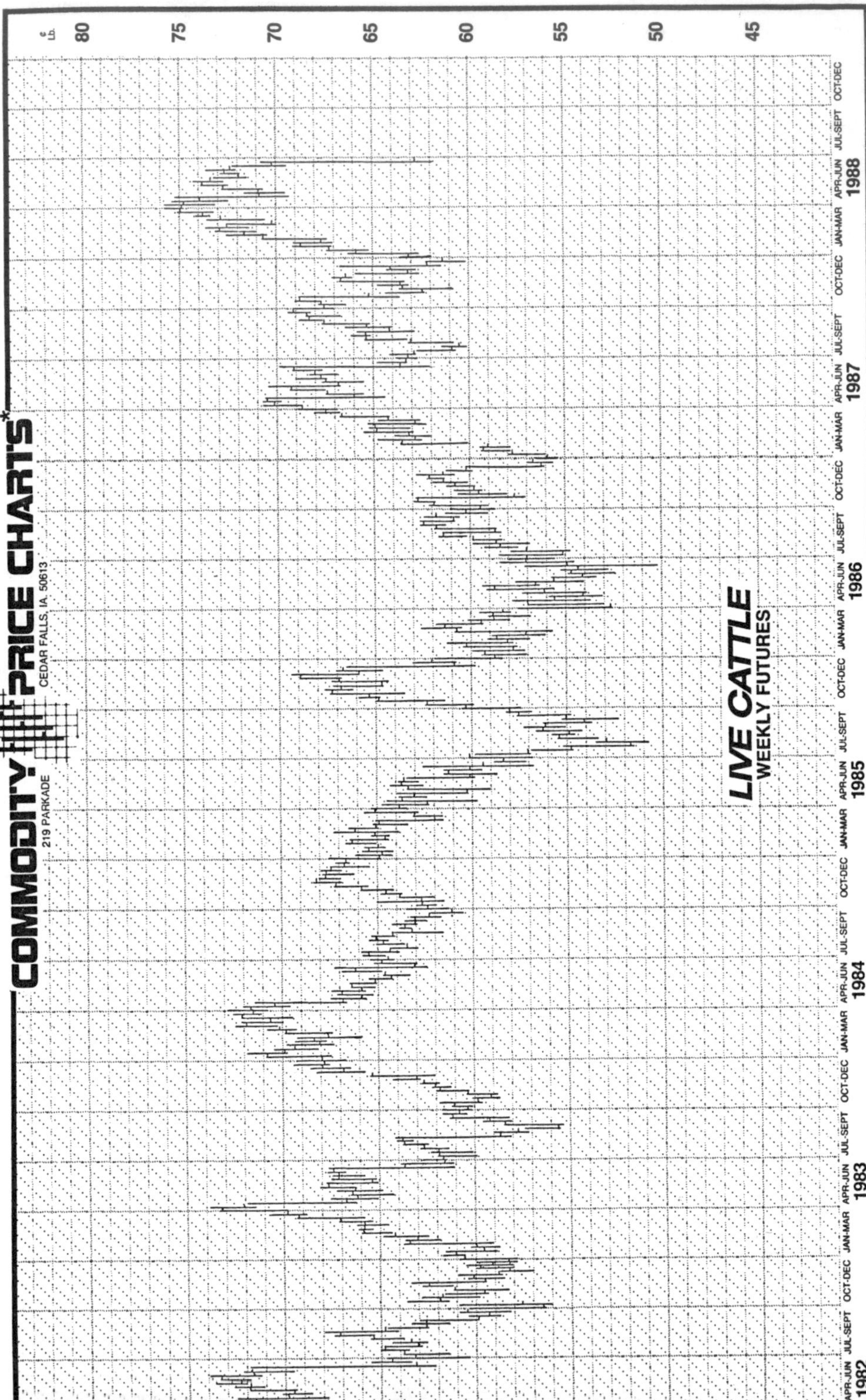

Source: Courtesy of *Commodity Price Charts*, 219 Parkade, Cedar Falls, Iowa 50613.
* See page 520 for data used in plotting.

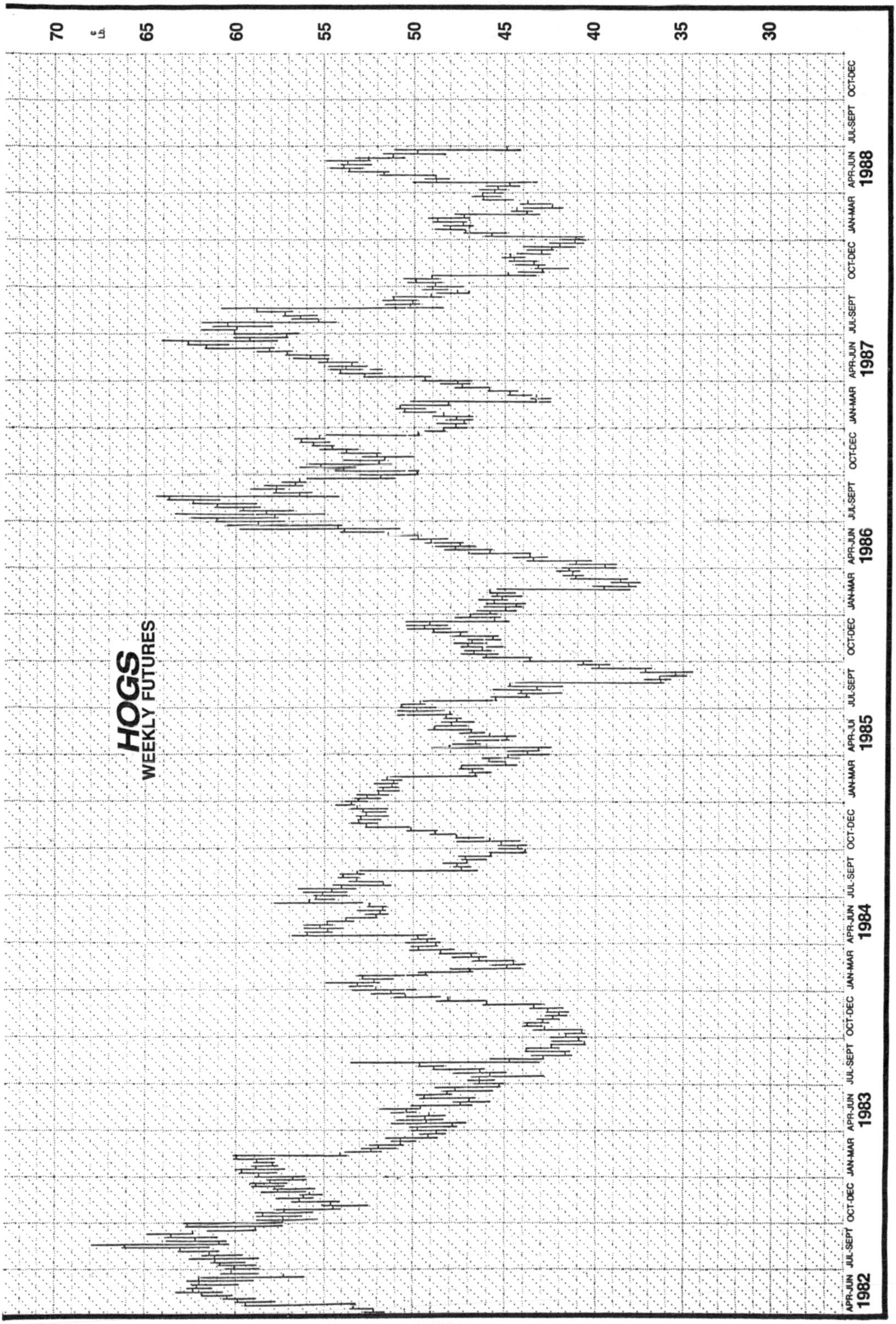
HOGS
WEEKLY FUTURES
¢
LB.
70
65
60
55
50
45
40
35
30
APR-JUN
JUL-SEPT
OCT-DEC
JAN-MAR
1982
1983
1984
1985
1986
1987
1988

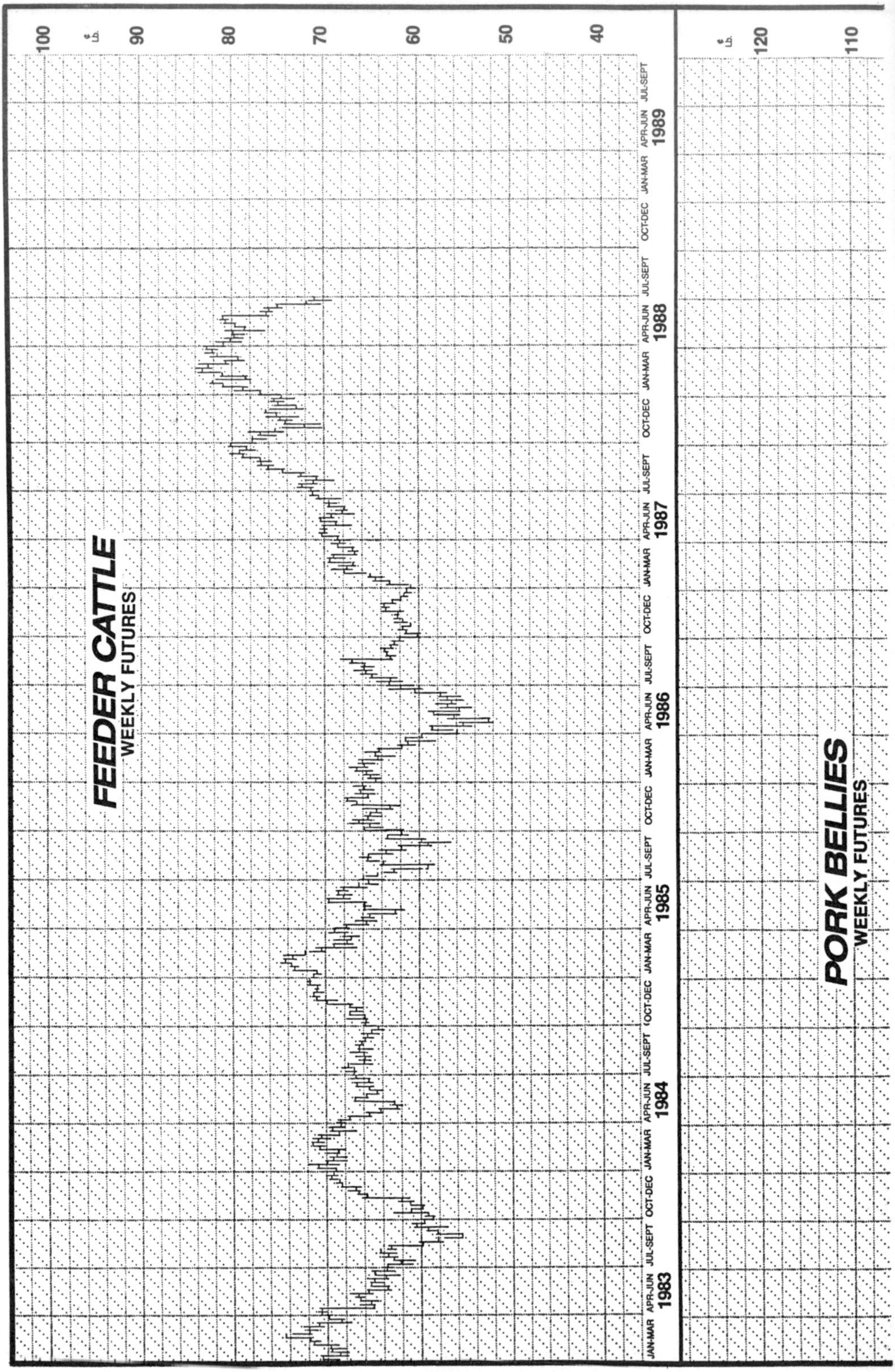
FEEDER CATTLE
WEEKLY FUTURES
100
¢/lb.
90
80
70
60
50
40
JAN-MAR APR-JUN JUL-SEPT OCT-DEC
1983
1984
1985
1986
1987
1988
1989
PORK BELLIES
WEEKLY FUTURES
¢/lb.
120
110

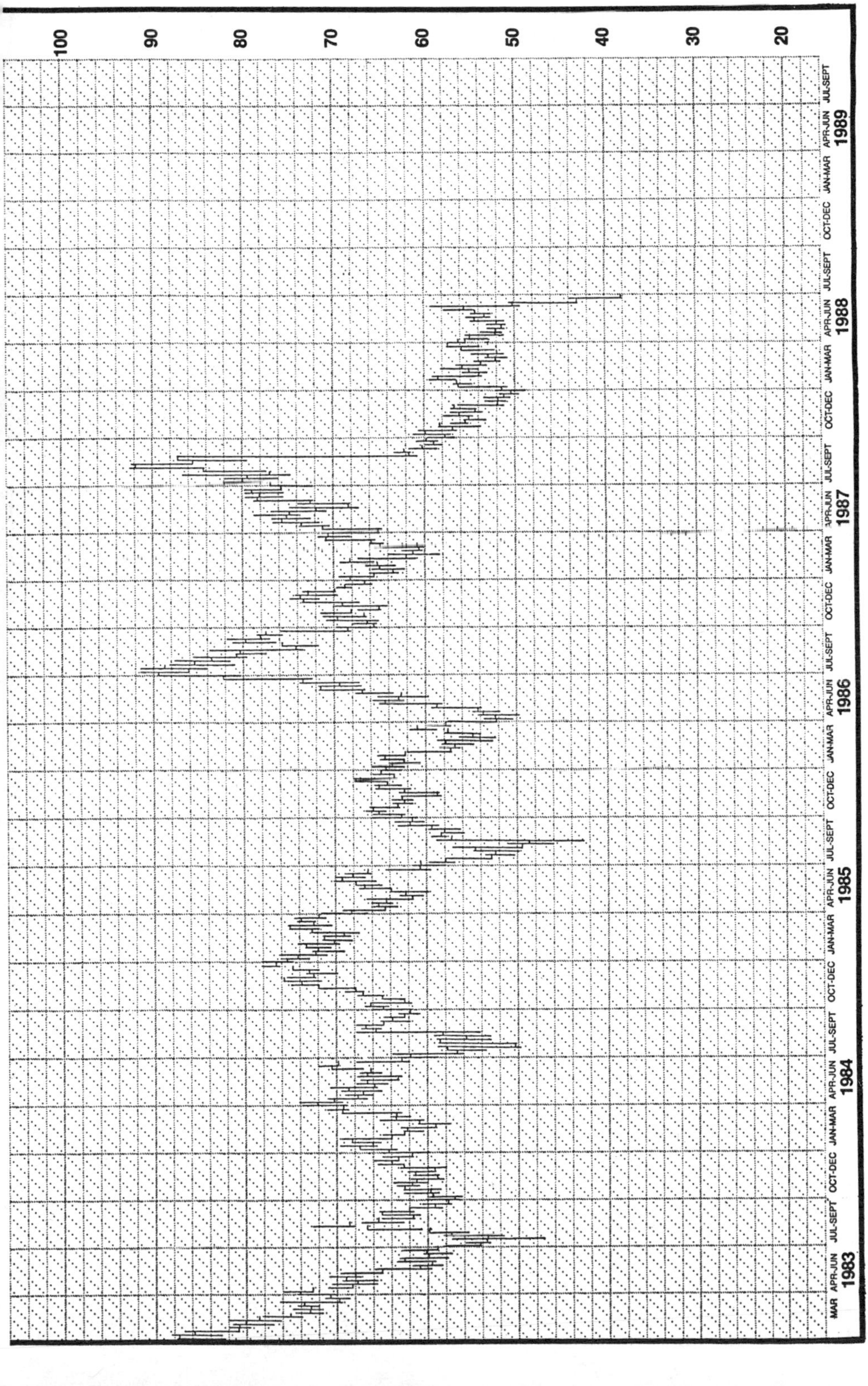
100
90
80
70
60
50
40
30
20
MAR
APR-JUN
1983
JUL-SEPT
OCT-DEC
JAN-MAR
APR-JUN
1984
JUL-SEPT
OCT-DEC
JAN-MAR
APR-JUN
1985
JUL-SEPT
OCT-DEC
JAN-MAR
APR-JUN
1986
JUL-SEPT
OCT-DEC
JAN-MAR
APR-JUN
1987
JUL-SEPT
OCT-DEC
JAN-MAR
APR-JUN
1988
JUL-SEPT
OCT-DEC
JAN-MAR
APR-JUN
1989
JUL-SEPT

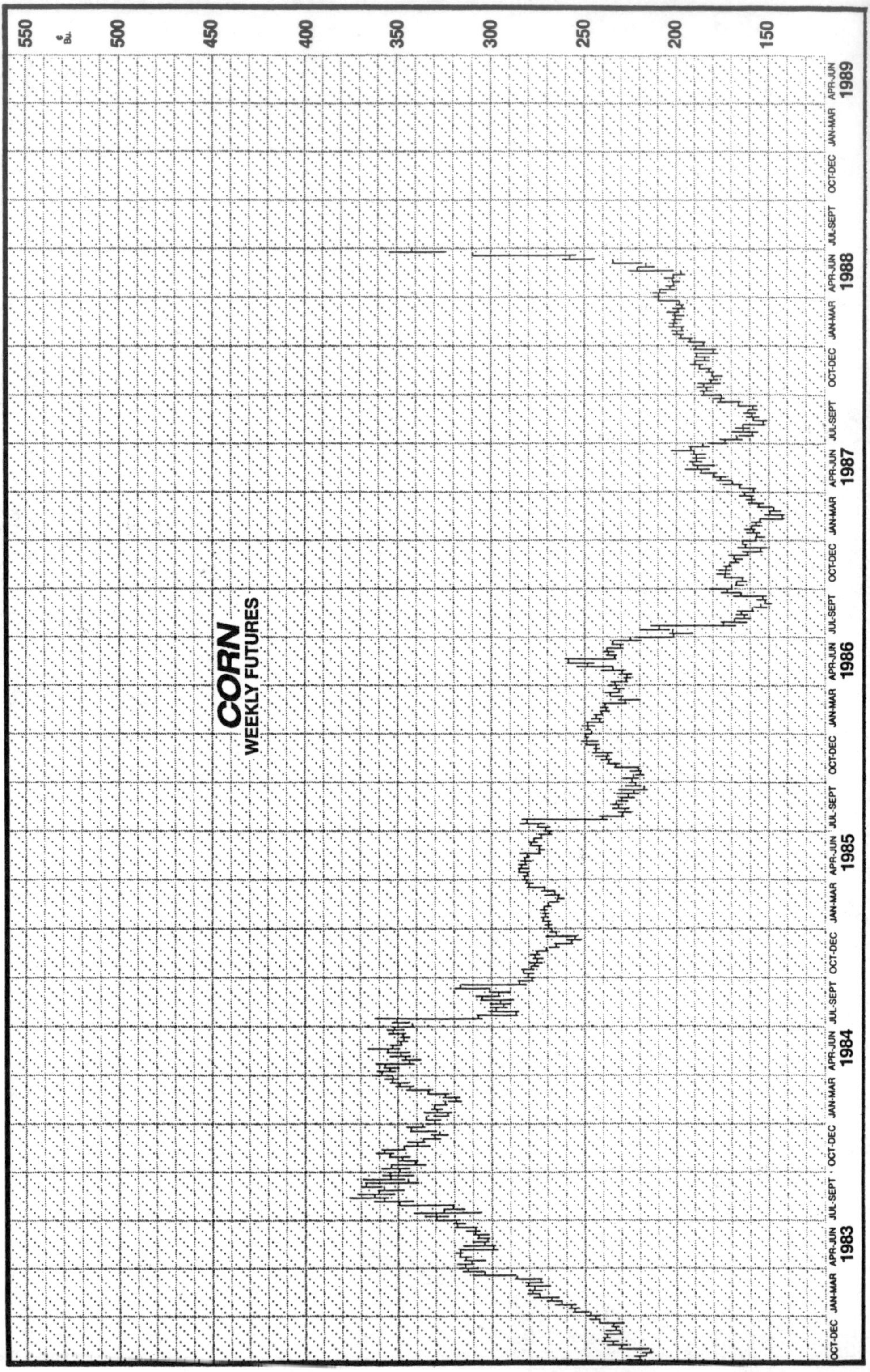
CORN
WEEKLY FUTURES
¢ Bu.
550
500
450
400
350
300
250
200
150
OCT-DEC
JAN-MAR
APR-JUN
JUL-SEPT
1983
1984
1985
1986
1987
1988
1989

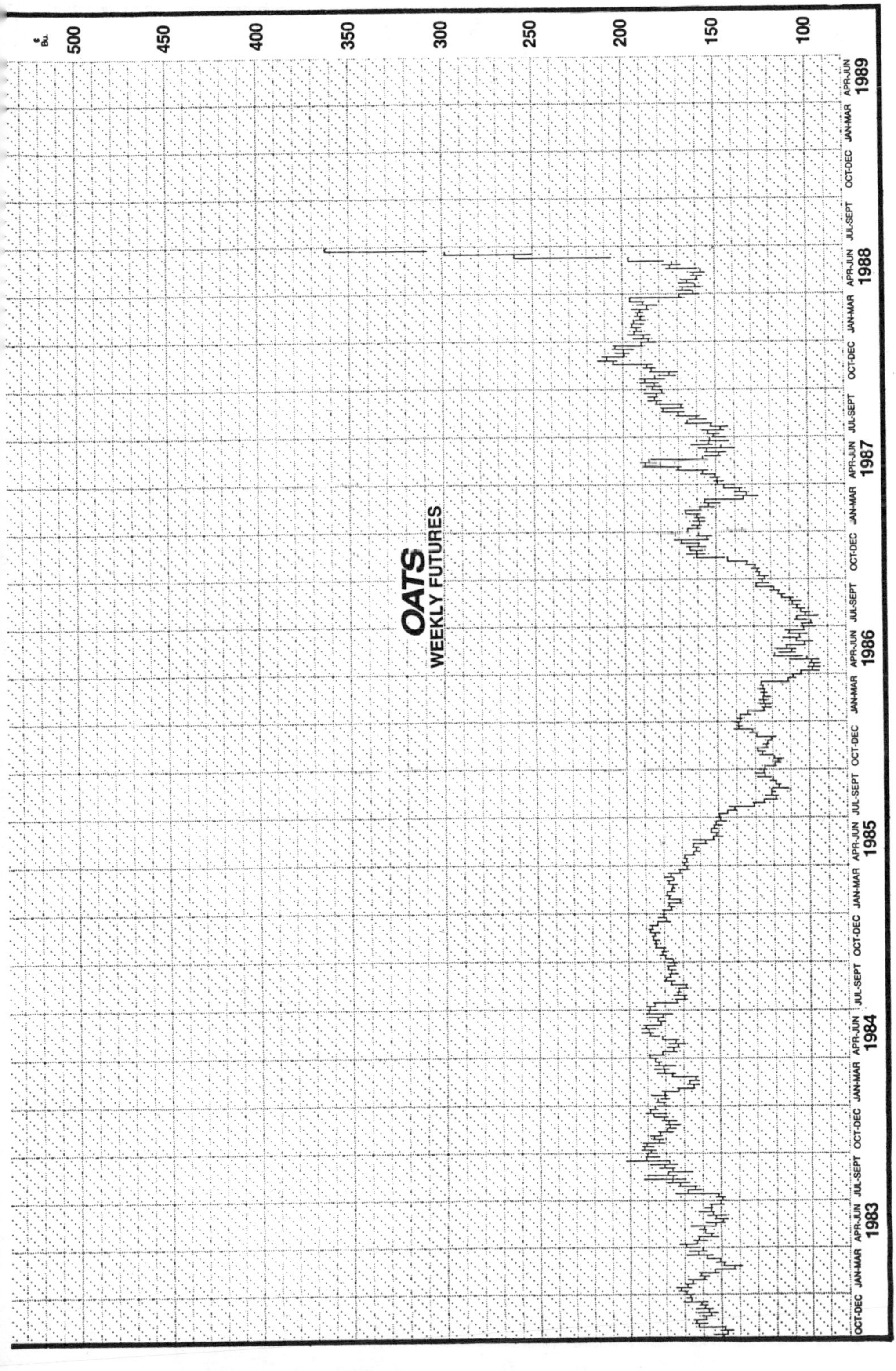
OATS
WEEKLY FUTURES
¢ Bu.
500
450
400
350
300
250
200
150
100
OCT-DEC JAN-MAR APR-JUN JUL-SEPT OCT-DEC JAN-MAR APR-JUN JUL-SEPT OCT-DEC JAN-MAR APR-JUN JUL-SEPT OCT-DEC JAN-MAR APR-JUN JUL-SEPT OCT-DEC JAN-MAR APR-JUN JUL-SEPT OCT-DEC JAN-MAR APR-JUN
1983
1984
1985
1986
1987
1988
1989

SOYBEANS
WEEKLY FUTURES
¢ Bu.
1350
1300
1250
1200
1150
1100
1050
1000
950
900

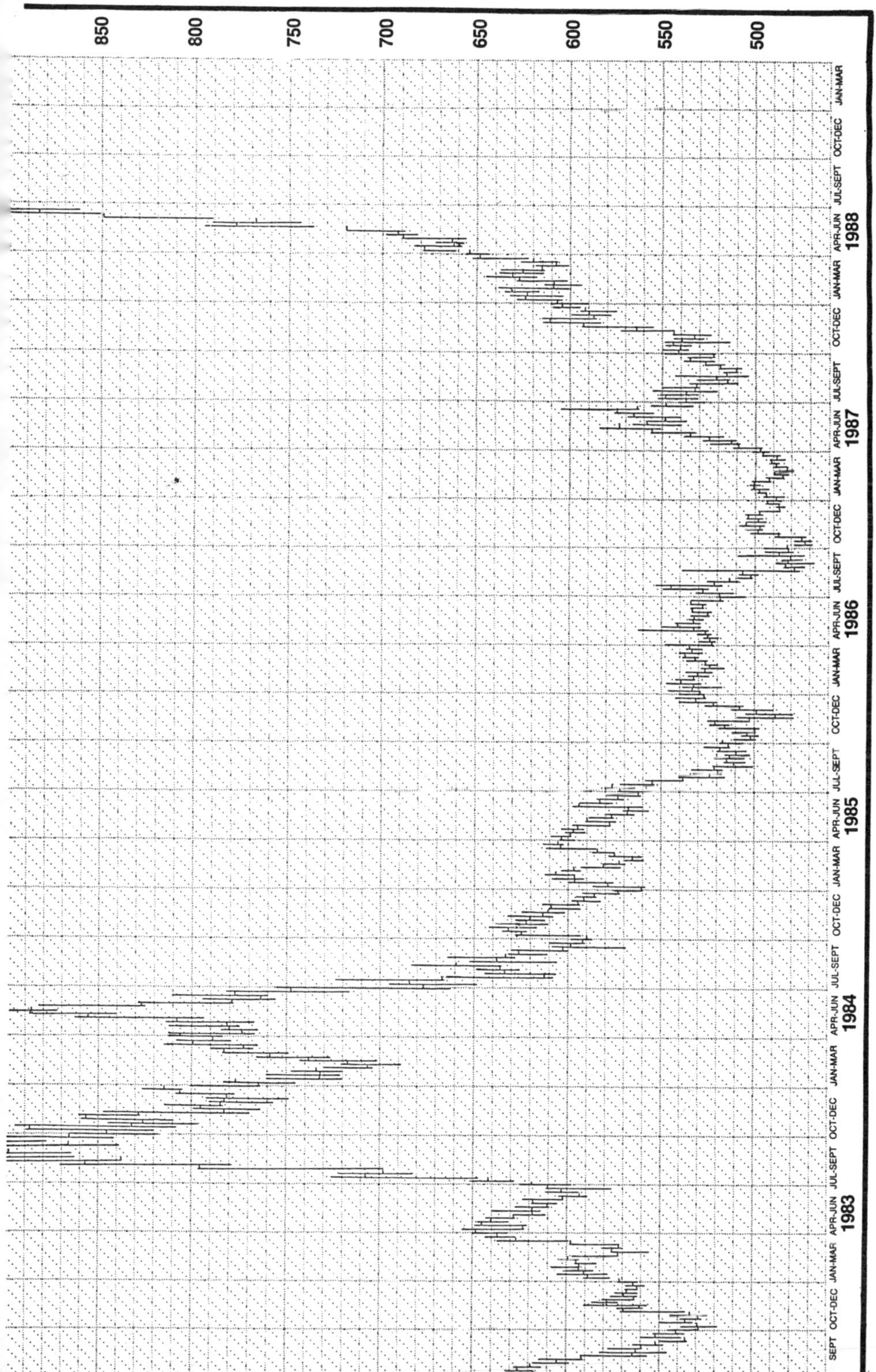
850
800
750
700
650
600
550
500
SEPT
OCT-DEC
JAN-MAR
APR-JUN
1983
JUL-SEPT
OCT-DEC
JAN-MAR
APR-JUN
1984
JUL-SEPT
OCT-DEC
JAN-MAR
APR-JUN
1985
JUL-SEPT
OCT-DEC
JAN-MAR
APR-JUN
1986
JUL-SEPT
OCT-DEC
JAN-MAR
APR-JUN
1987
JUL-SEPT
OCT-DEC
JAN-MAR
APR-JUN
1988
JUL-SEPT
OCT-DEC
JAN-MAR

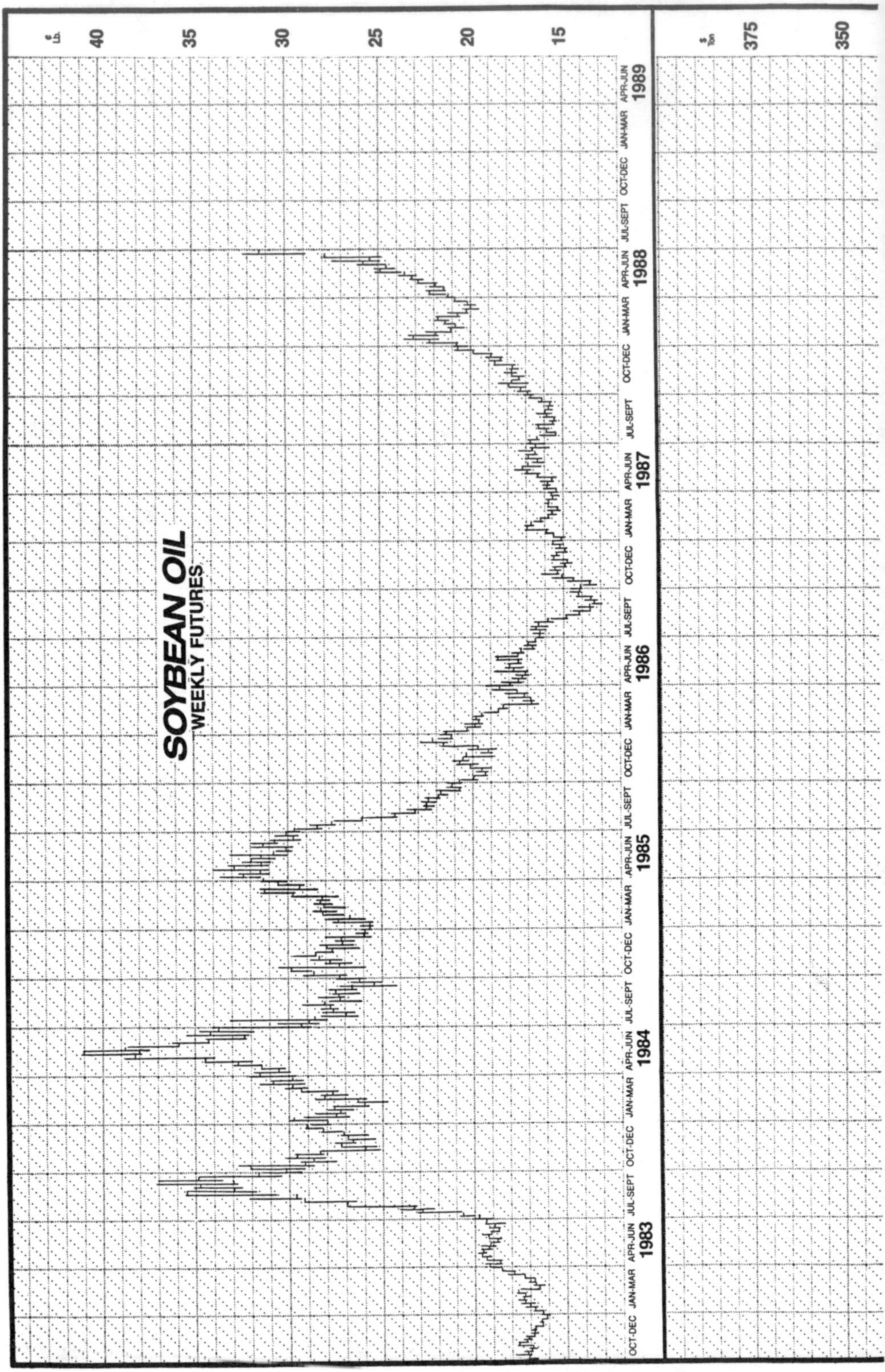
SOYBEAN OIL
WEEKLY FUTURES
¢/Lb.
40
35
30
25
20
15
$/Ton
375
350
OCT-DEC JAN-MAR APR-JUN 1983 JUL-SEPT OCT-DEC JAN-MAR APR-JUN 1984 JUL-SEPT OCT-DEC JAN-MAR APR-JUN 1985 JUL-SEPT OCT-DEC JAN-MAR APR-JUN 1986 JUL-SEPT OCT-DEC JAN-MAR APR-JUN 1987 JUL-SEPT OCT-DEC JAN-MAR APR-JUN 1988 JUL-SEPT OCT-DEC JAN-MAR APR-JUN 1989

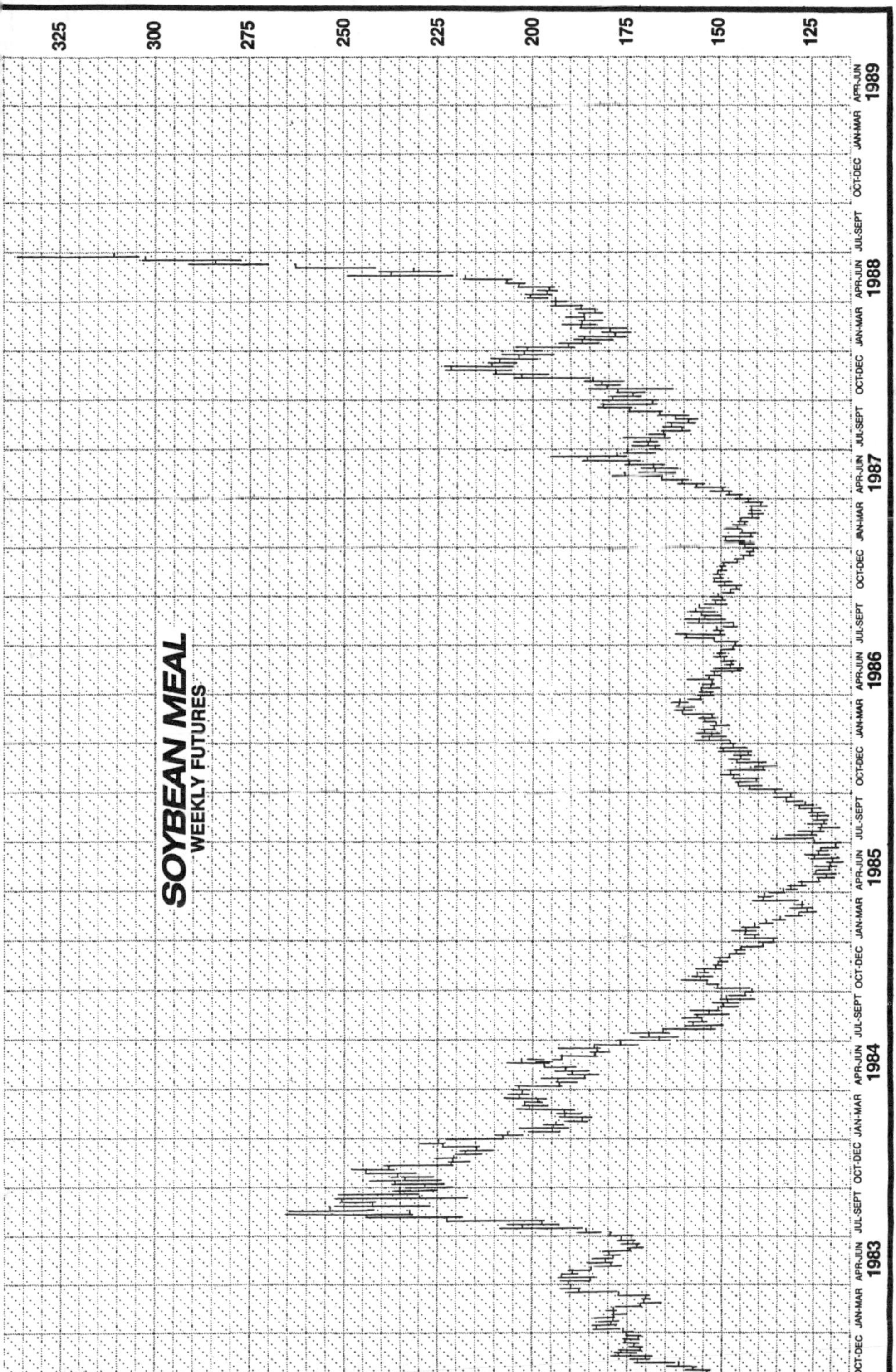

SOYBEAN MEAL
WEEKLY FUTURES
325
300
275
250
225
200
175
150
125
OCT-DEC JAN-MAR APR-JUN JUL-SEPT
1983
1984
1985
1986
1987
1988
1989

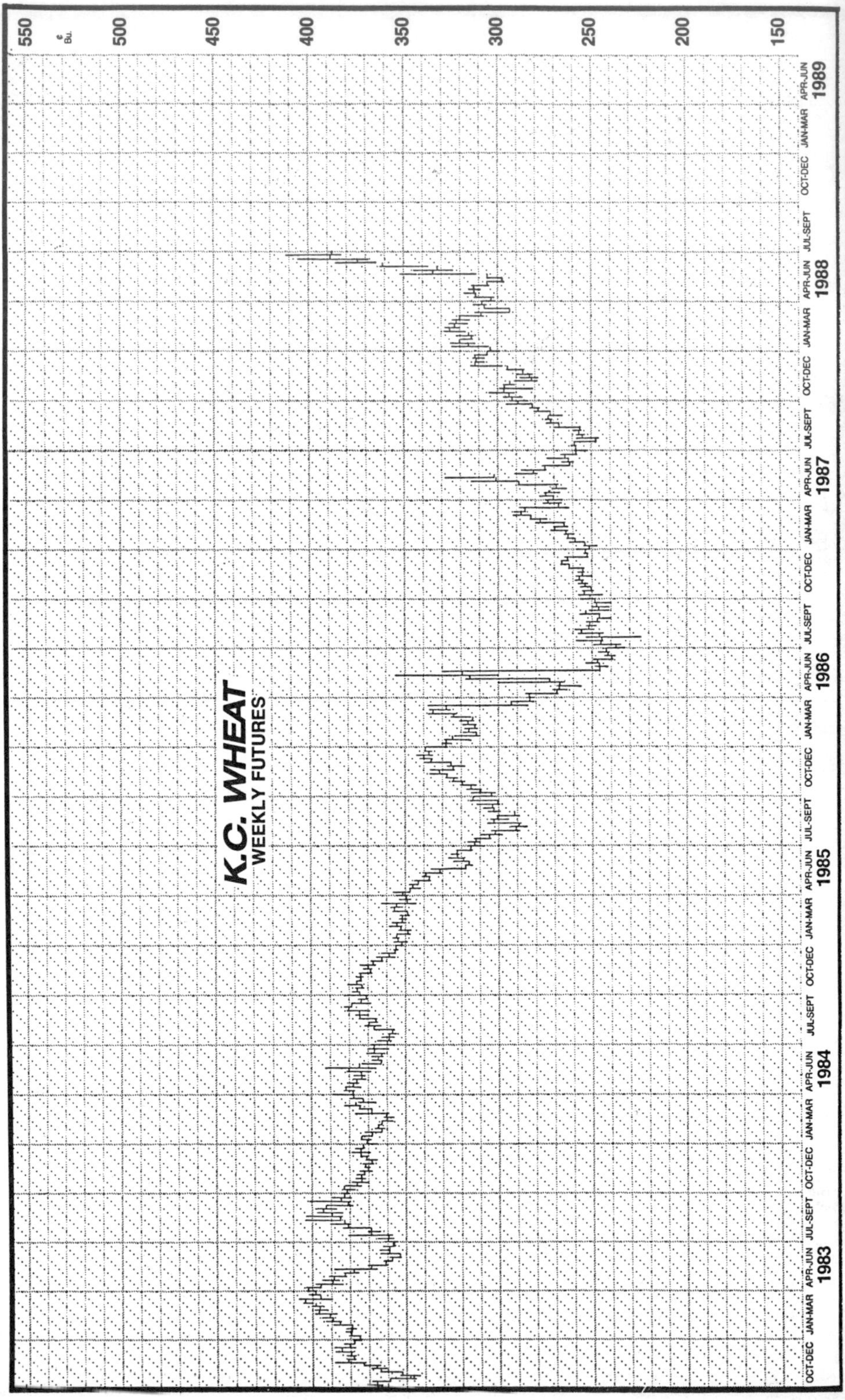
K.C. WHEAT
WEEKLY FUTURES
¢ Bu.
550
500
450
400
350
300
250
200
150
OCT-DEC JAN-MAR APR-JUN JUL-SEPT OCT-DEC JAN-MAR APR-JUN JUL-SEPT OCT-DEC JAN-MAR APR-JUN JUL-SEPT OCT-DEC JAN-MAR APR-JUN JUL-SEPT OCT-DEC JAN-MAR APR-JUN JUL-SEPT OCT-DEC JAN-MAR APR-JUN JUL-SEPT OCT-DEC JAN-MAR APR-JUN
1983
1984
1985
1986
1987
1988
1989

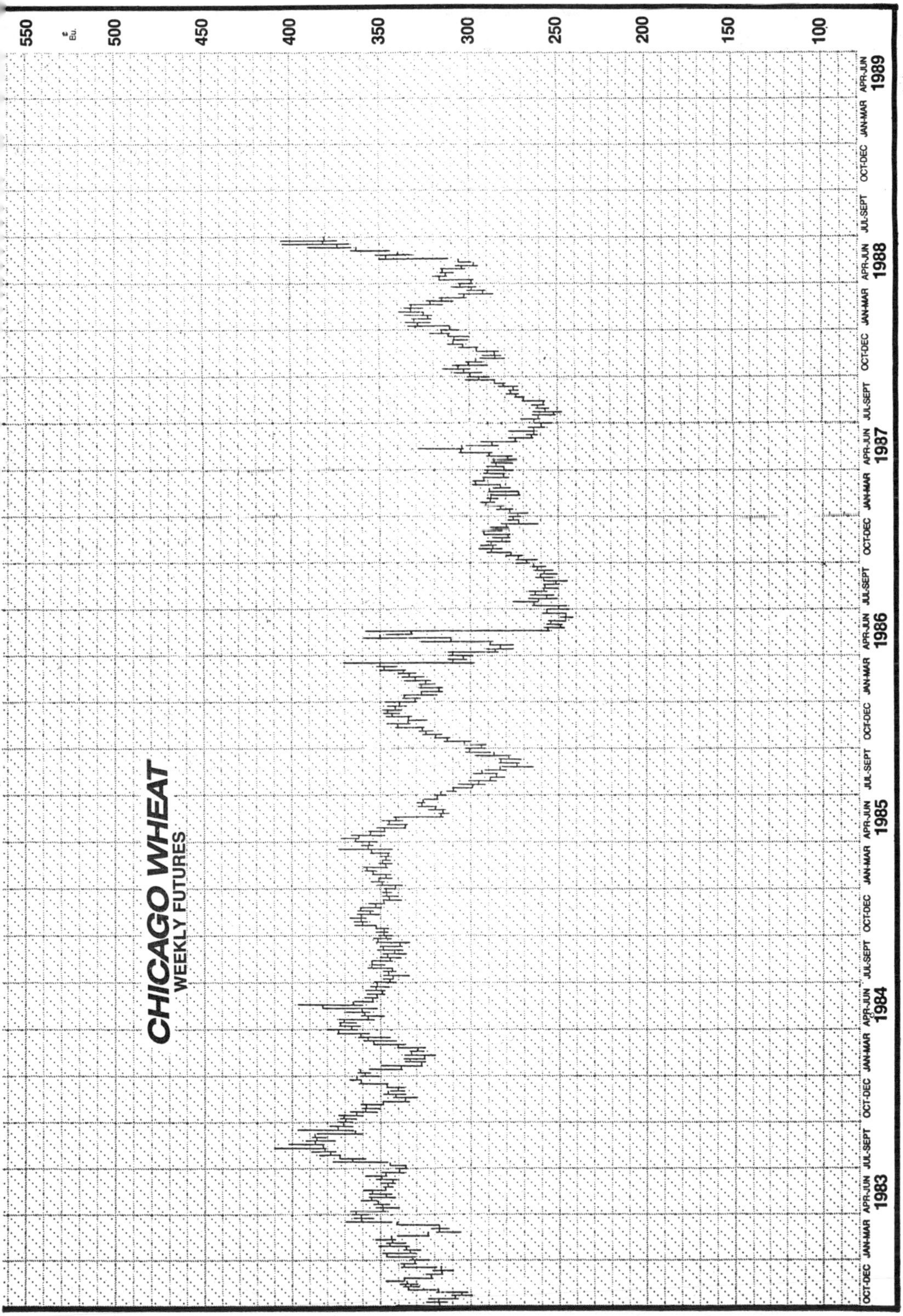
CHICAGO WHEAT
WEEKLY FUTURES
¢ Bu.
550
500
450
400
350
300
250
200
150
100
OCT-DEC JAN-MAR APR-JUN JUL-SEPT
1983
1984
1985
1986
1987
1988
1989

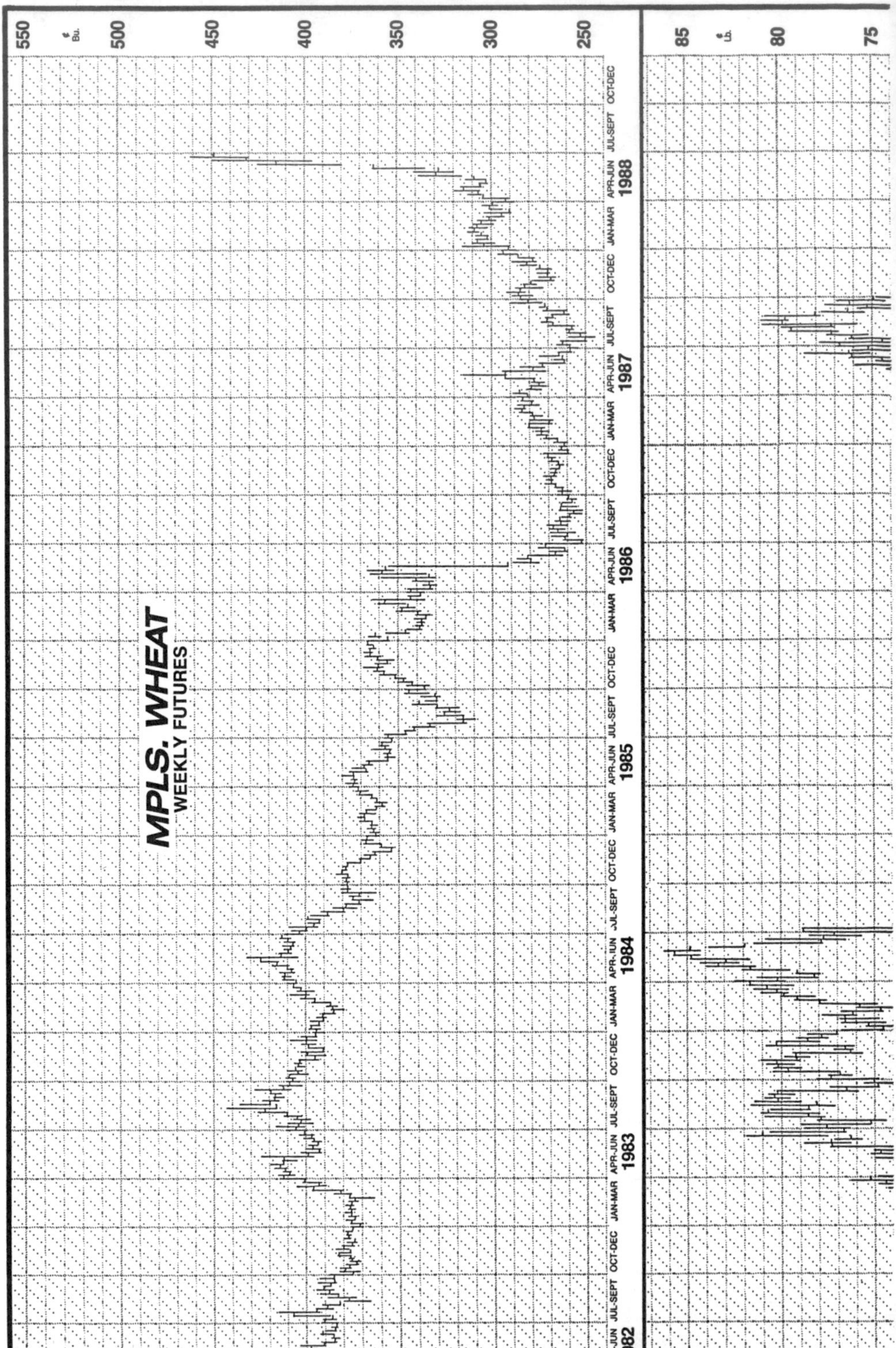
MPLS. WHEAT
WEEKLY FUTURES
550
¢ Bu.
500
450
400
350
300
250
85
¢ Lb.
80
75
APR-JUN JUL-SEPT OCT-DEC JAN-MAR
1982
1983
1984
1985
1986
1987
1988

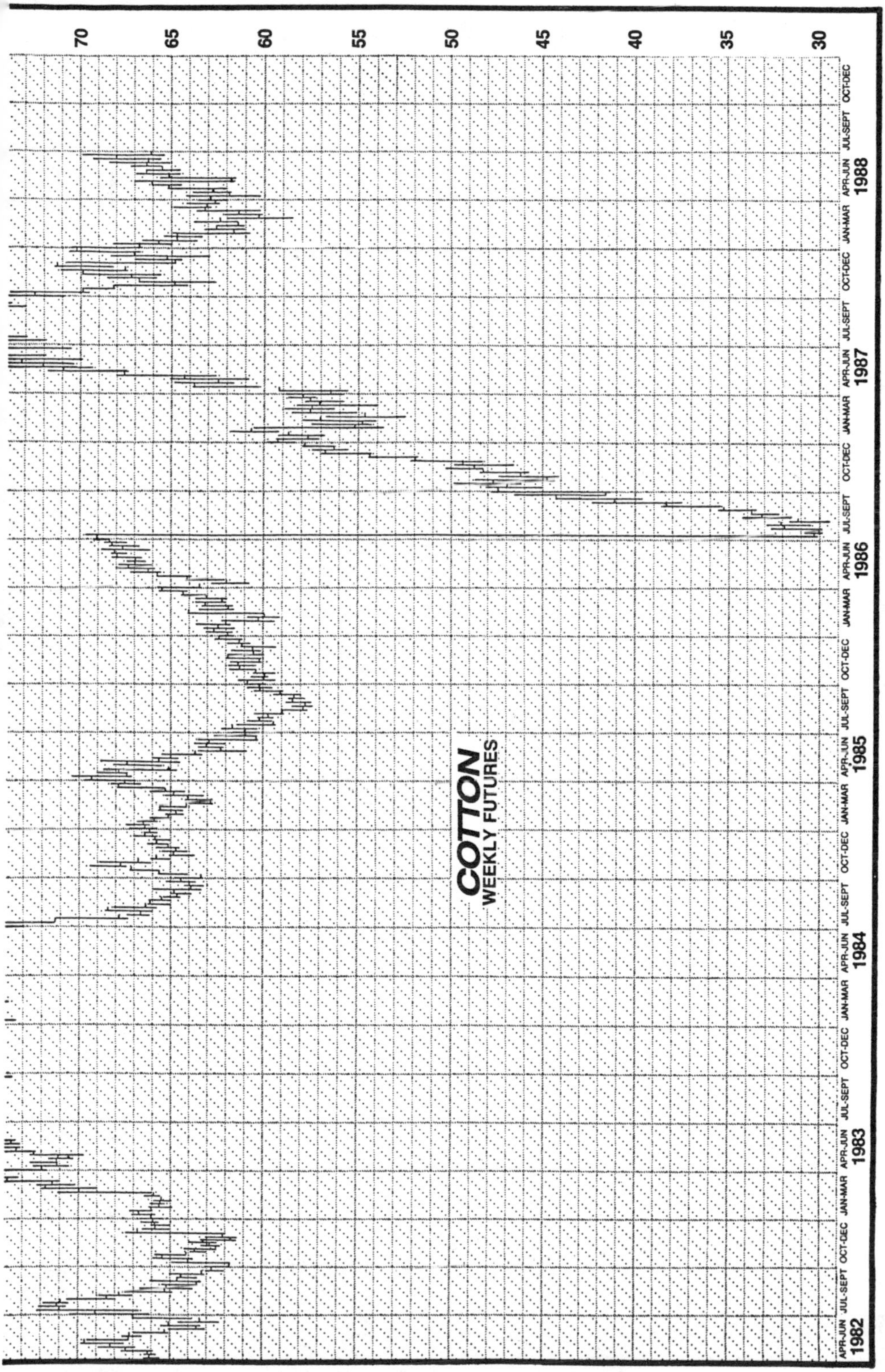
COTTON
WEEKLY FUTURES
70
65
60
55
50
45
40
35
30
APR-JUN JUL-SEPT OCT-DEC
1982
JAN-MAR APR-JUN JUL-SEPT OCT-DEC
1983
JAN-MAR APR-JUN JUL-SEPT OCT-DEC
1984
JAN-MAR APR-JUN JUL-SEPT OCT-DEC
1985
JAN-MAR APR-JUN JUL-SEPT OCT-DEC
1986
JAN-MAR APR-JUN JUL-SEPT OCT-DEC
1987
JAN-MAR APR-JUN JUL-SEPT OCT-DEC
1988

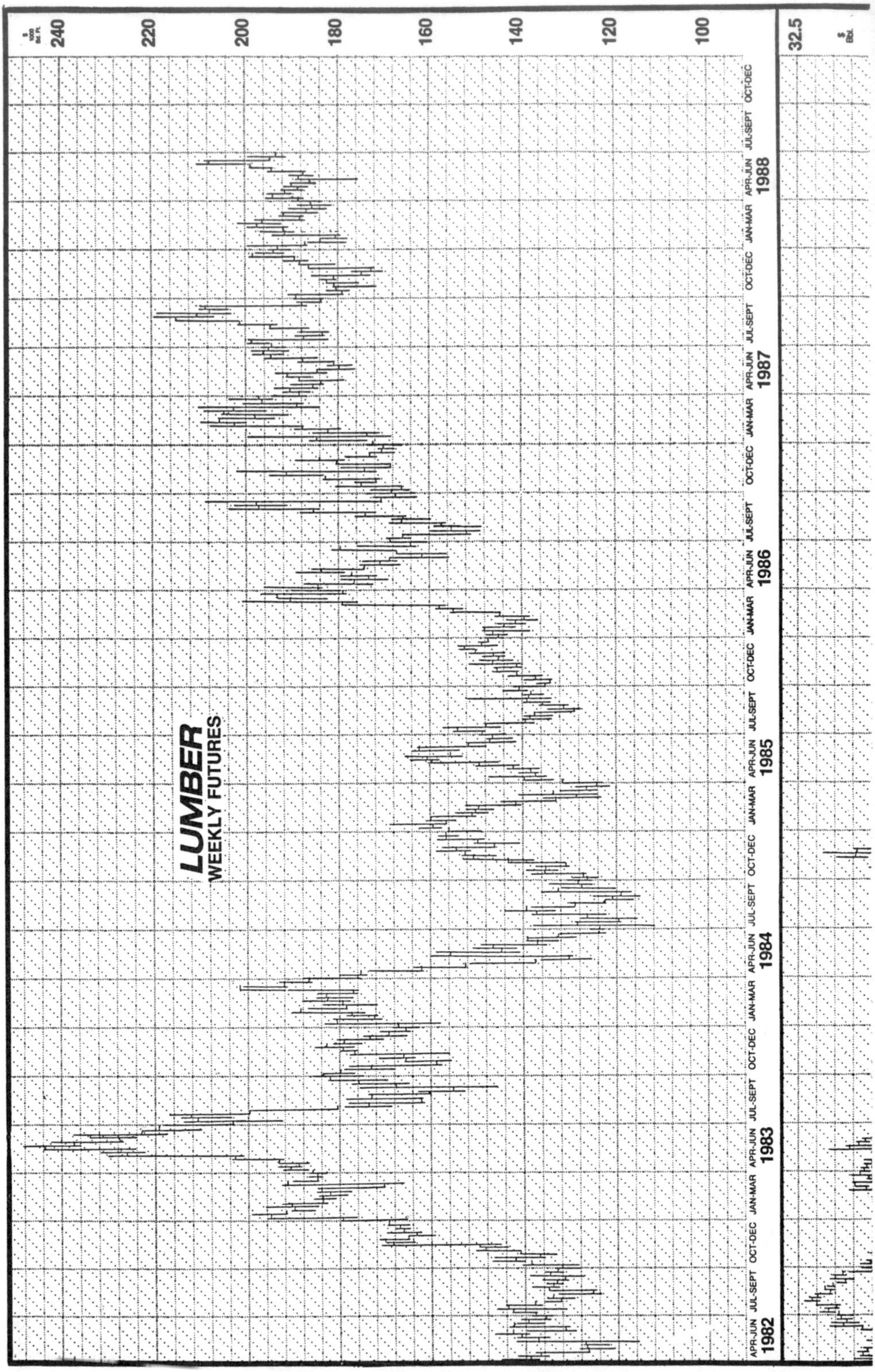
LUMBER
WEEKLY FUTURES
240
220
200
180
160
140
120
100
32.5
APR-JUN JUL-SEPT OCT-DEC JAN-MAR
1982
1983
1984
1985
1986
1987
1988

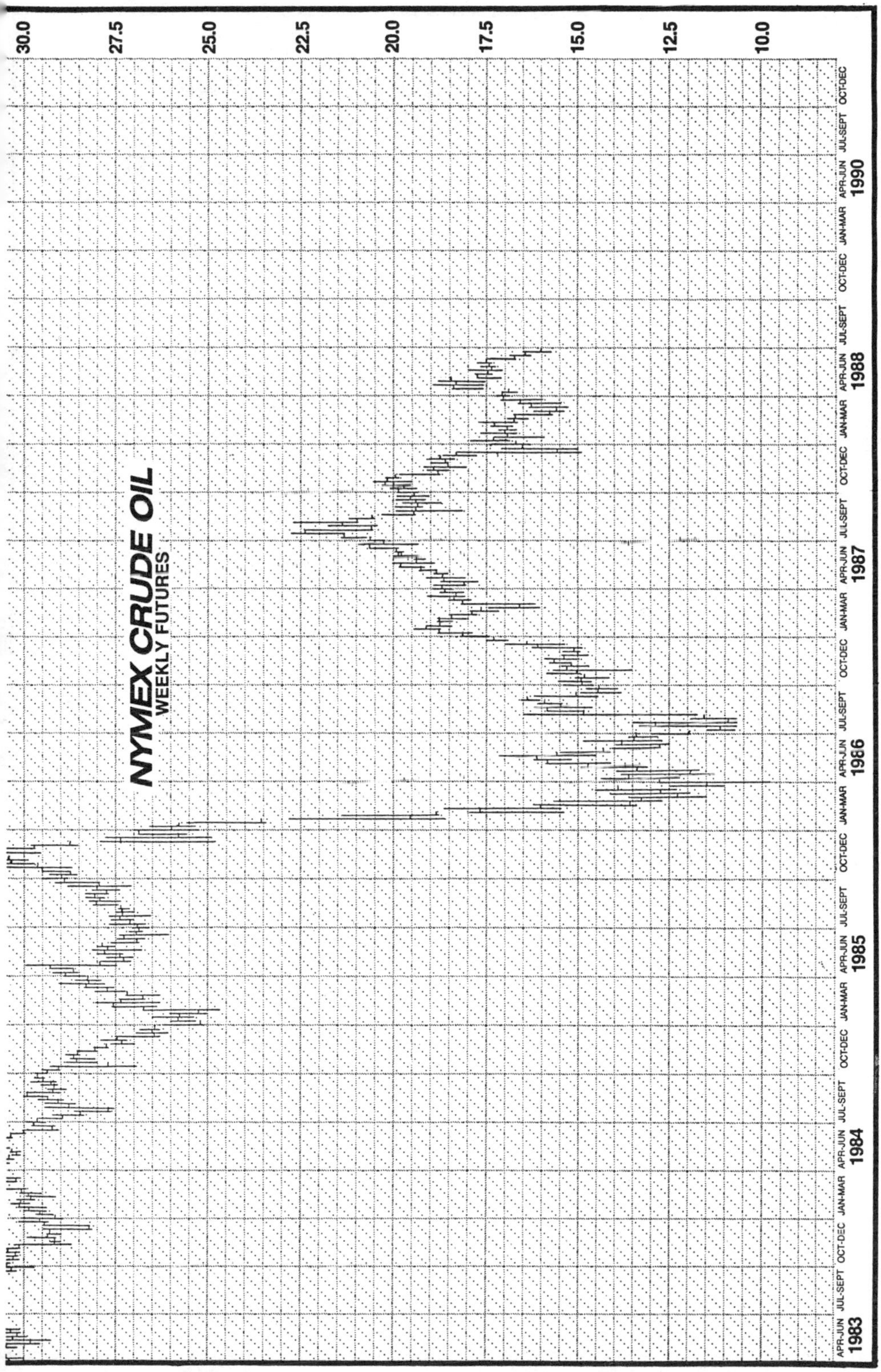
NYMEX CRUDE OIL
WEEKLY FUTURES
30.0
27.5
25.0
22.5
20.0
17.5
15.0
12.5
10.0
APR-JUN JUL-SEPT OCT-DEC
1983
JAN-MAR APR-JUN JUL-SEPT OCT-DEC
1984
JAN-MAR APR-JUN JUL-SEPT OCT-DEC
1985
JAN-MAR APR-JUN JUL-SEPT OCT-DEC
1986
JAN-MAR APR-JUN JUL-SEPT OCT-DEC
1987
JAN-MAR APR-JUN JUL-SEPT OCT-DEC
1988
JAN-MAR APR-JUN JUL-SEPT OCT-DEC
1990

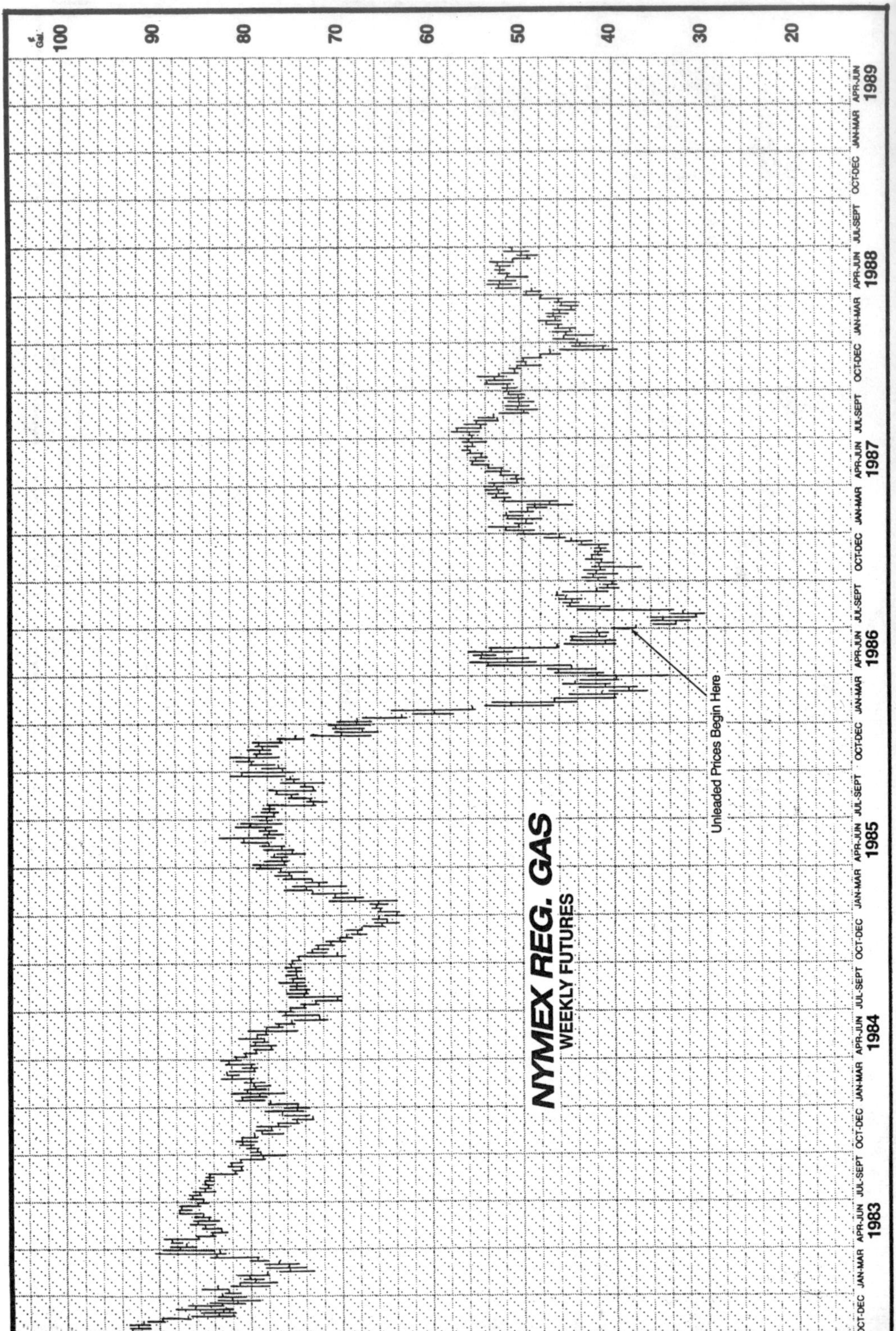
NYMEX REG. GAS
WEEKLY FUTURES
Unleaded Prices Begin Here
¢ Gal.
100
90
80
70
60
50
40
30
20
OCT-DEC JAN-MAR APR-JUN JUL-SEPT OCT-DEC JAN-MAR APR-JUN JUL-SEPT OCT-DEC JAN-MAR APR-JUN JUL-SEPT OCT-DEC JAN-MAR APR-JUN JUL-SEPT OCT-DEC JAN-MAR APR-JUN JUL-SEPT OCT-DEC JAN-MAR APR-JUN JUL-SEPT OCT-DEC JAN-MAR APR-JUN
1983
1984
1985
1986
1987
1988
1989

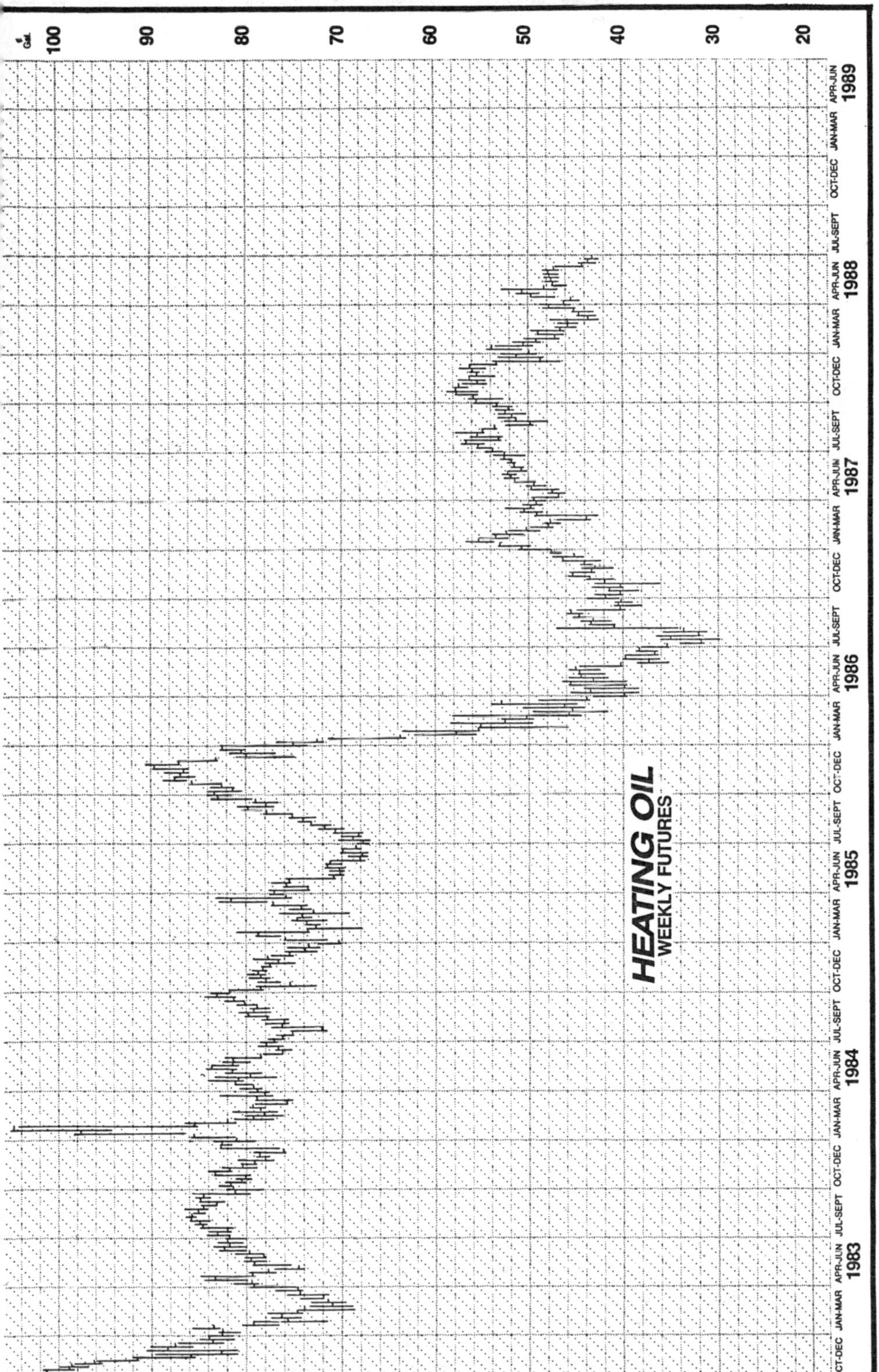
HEATING OIL
WEEKLY FUTURES
¢ Gal.
100
90
80
70
60
50
40
30
20
OCT-DEC
JAN-MAR
APR-JUN
JUL-SEPT
1983
1984
1985
1986
1987
1988
1989

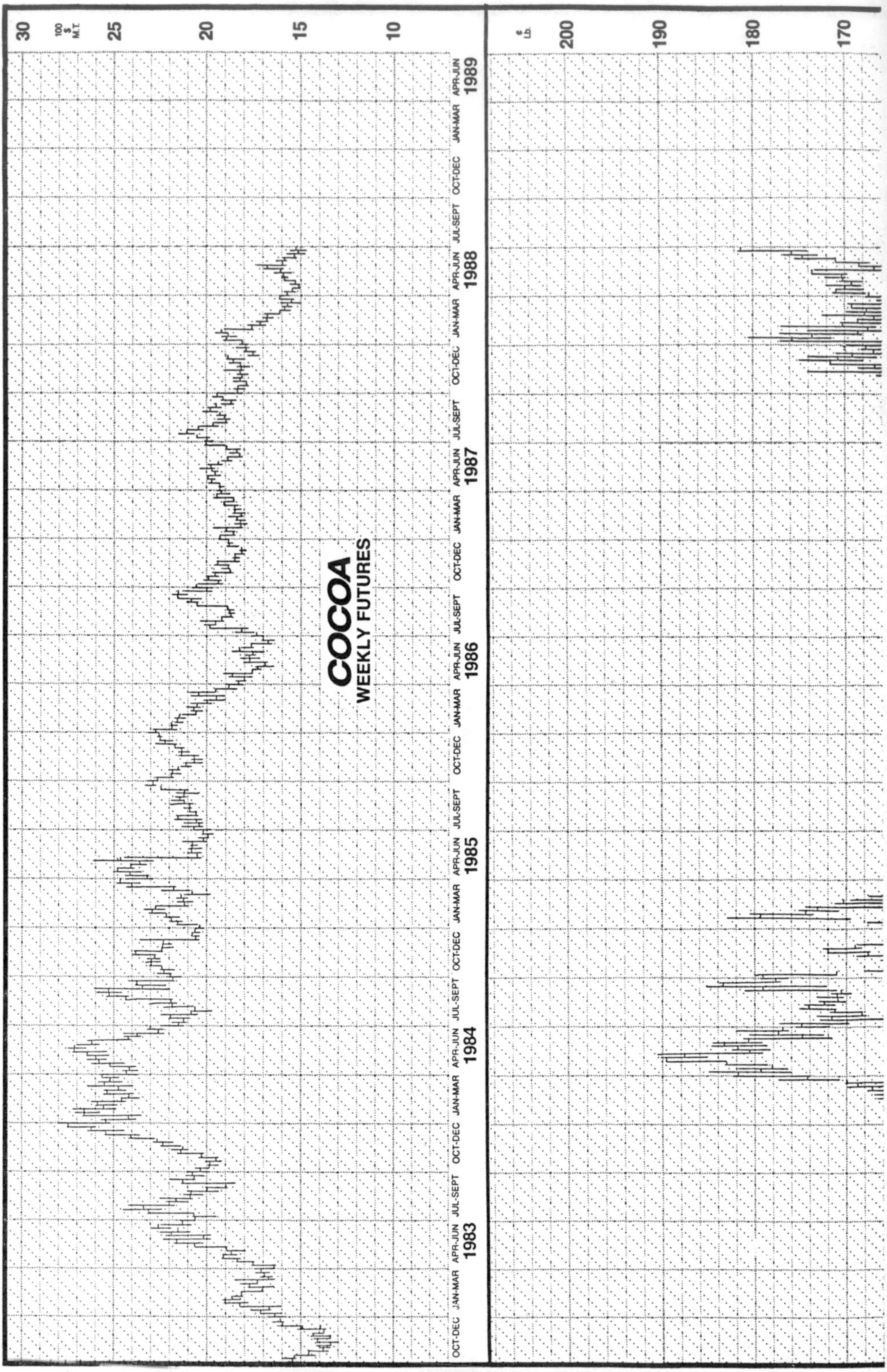
COCOA
WEEKLY FUTURES
100 $ M.T.
30
25
20
15
10
¢ LB.
200
190
180
170
OCT-DEC
JAN-MAR
APR-JUN
JUL-SEPT
1983
1984
1985
1986
1987
1988
1989

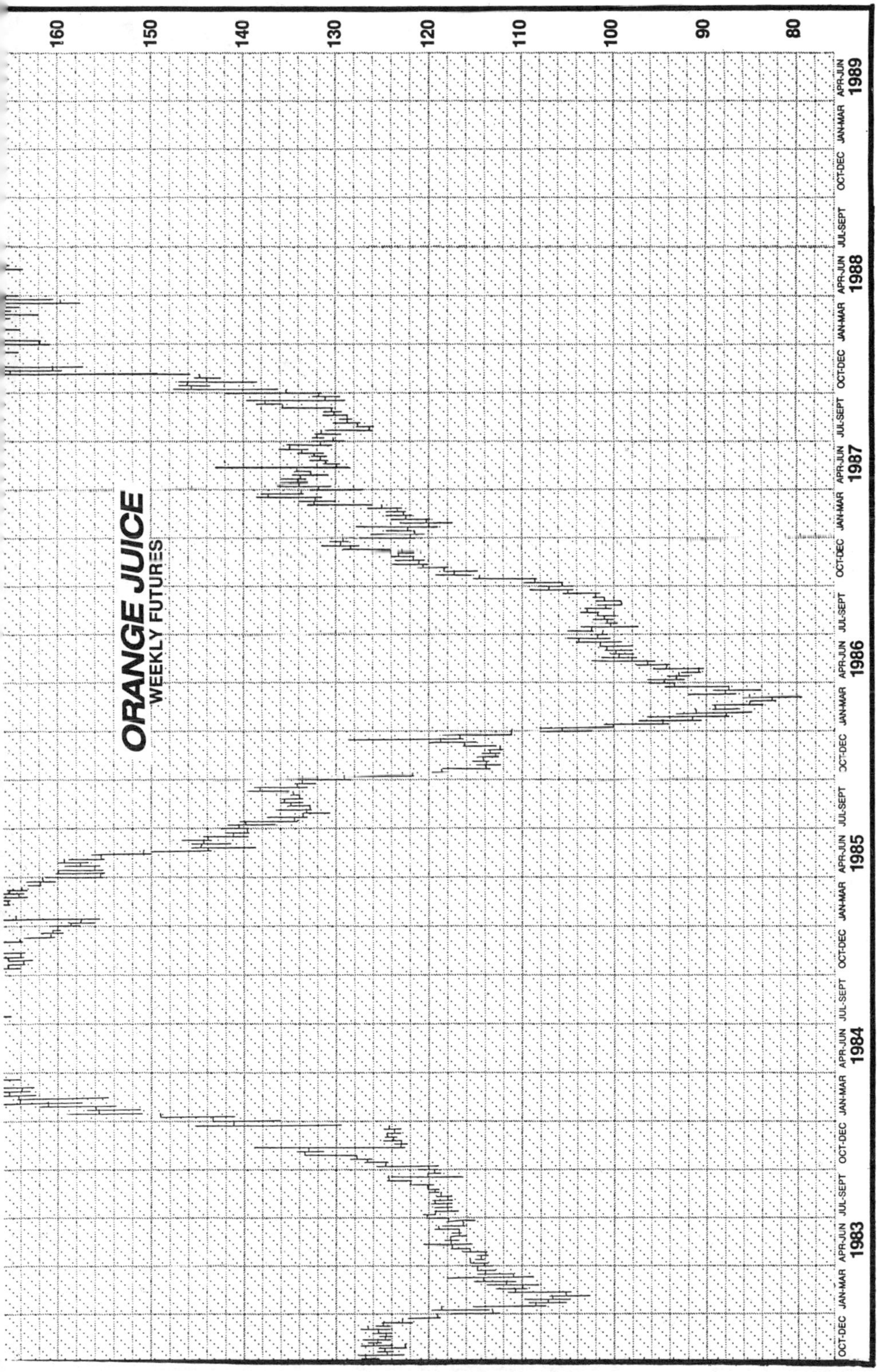
ORANGE JUICE
WEEKLY FUTURES
160
150
140
130
120
110
100
90
80
OCT-DEC
JAN-MAR
APR-JUN
1983
JUL-SEPT
OCT-DEC
JAN-MAR
APR-JUN
1984
JUL-SEPT
OCT-DEC
JAN-MAR
APR-JUN
1985
JUL-SEPT
OCT-DEC
JAN-MAR
APR-JUN
1986
JUL-SEPT
OCT-DEC
JAN-MAR
APR-JUN
1987
JUL-SEPT
OCT-DEC
JAN-MAR
APR-JUN
1988
JUL-SEPT
OCT-DEC
JAN-MAR
APR-JUN
1989

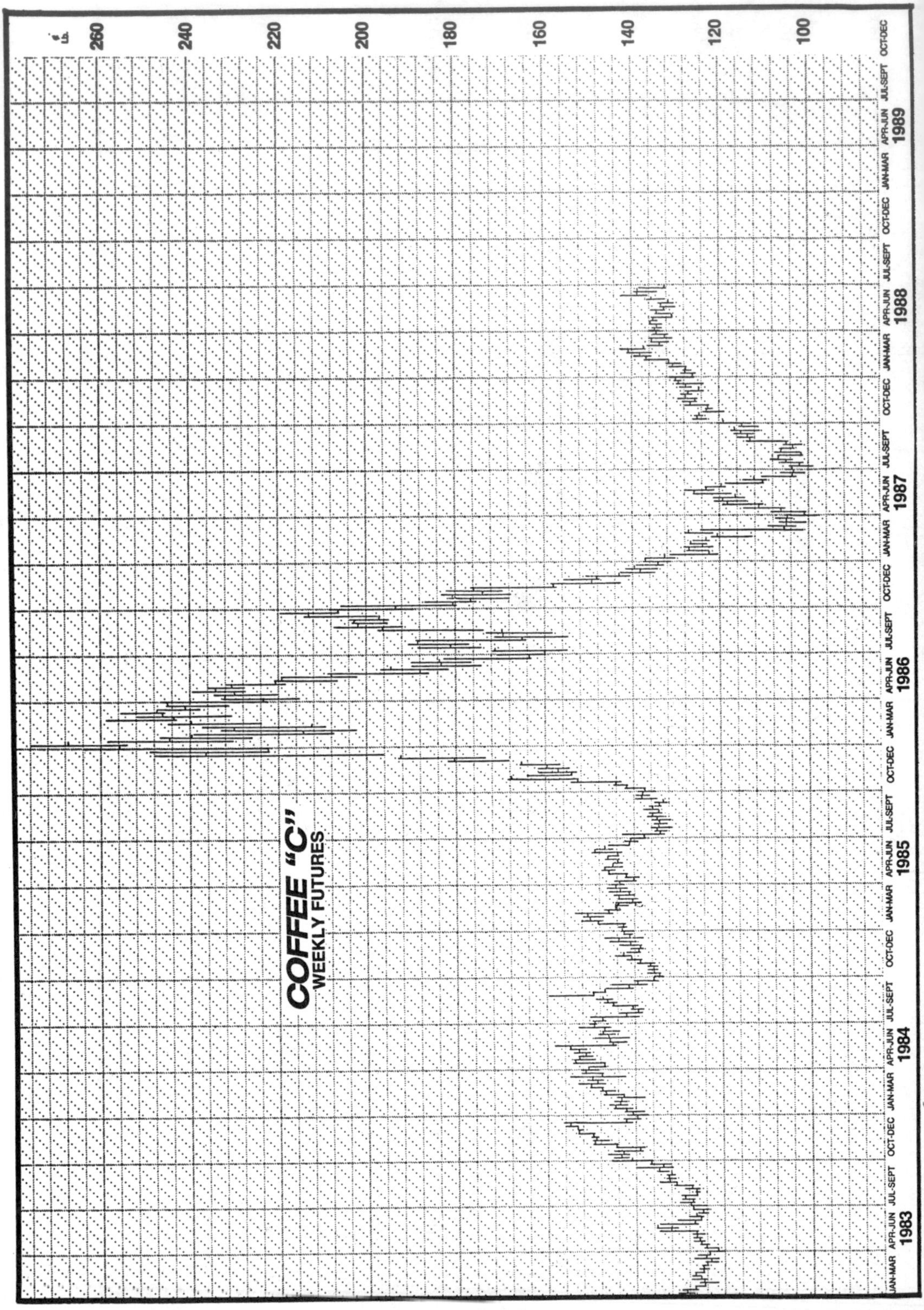
COFFEE "C"
WEEKLY FUTURES
¢ Lb.
260
240
220
200
180
160
140
120
100
JAN-MAR APR-JUN JUL-SEPT OCT-DEC
1983
1984
1985
1986
1987
1988
1989

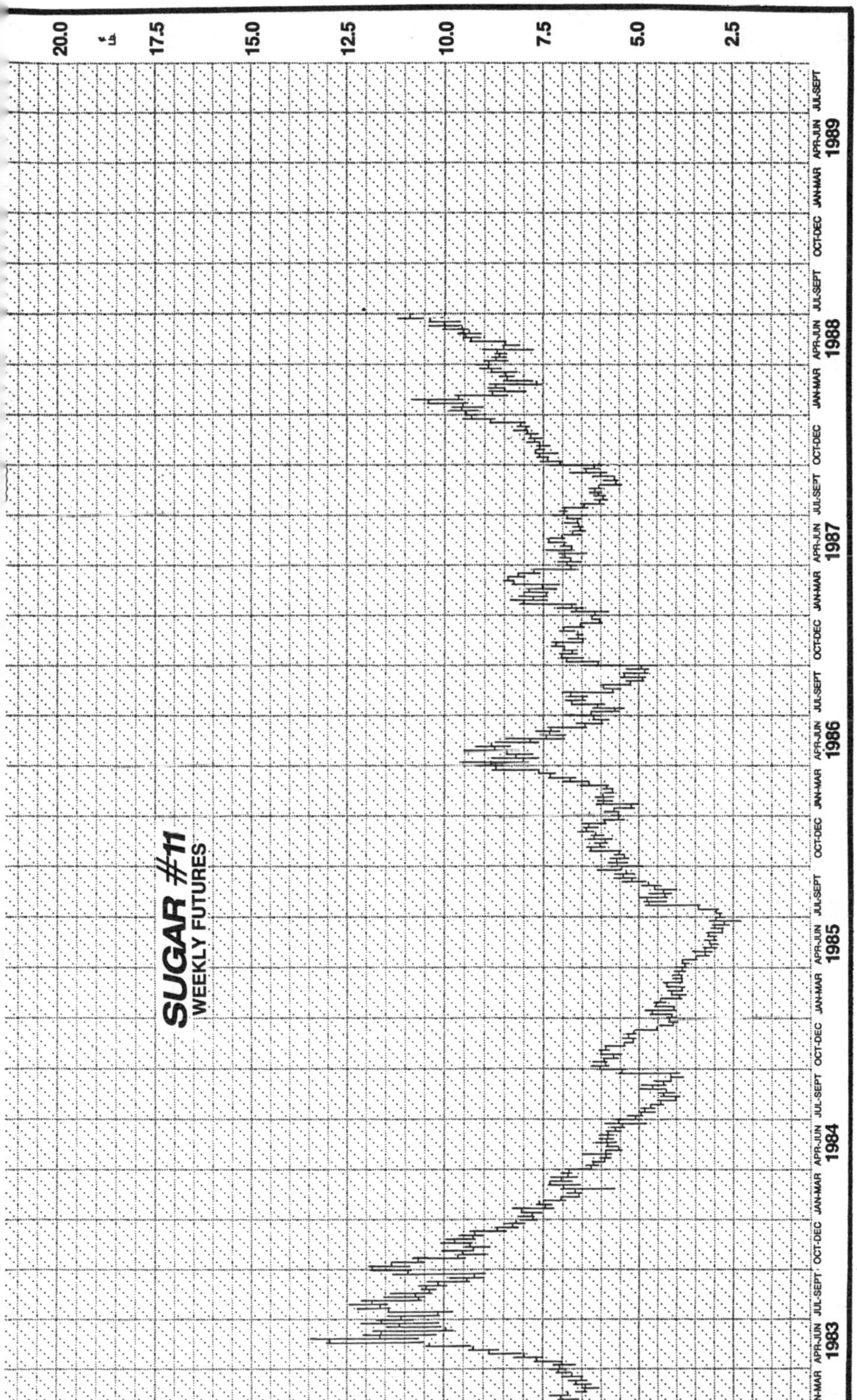
SUGAR #11
WEEKLY FUTURES
20.0
17.5
15.0
12.5
10.0
7.5
5.0
2.5
JAN-MAR APR-JUN JUL-SEPT OCT-DEC
1983
1984
1985
1986
1987
1988
1989

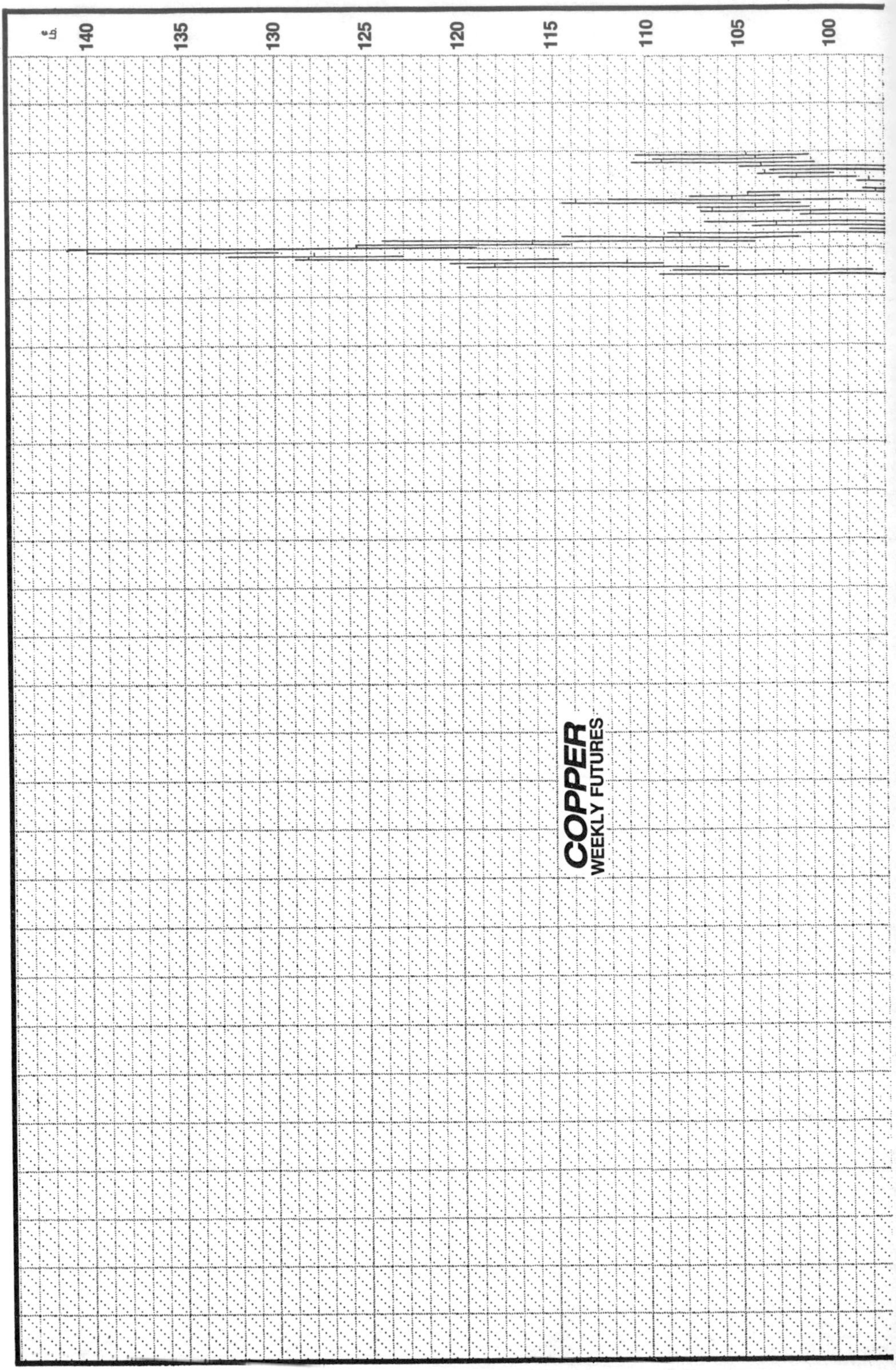
¢ Lb.
140
135
130
125
120
115
110
105
100
COPPER
WEEKLY FUTURES

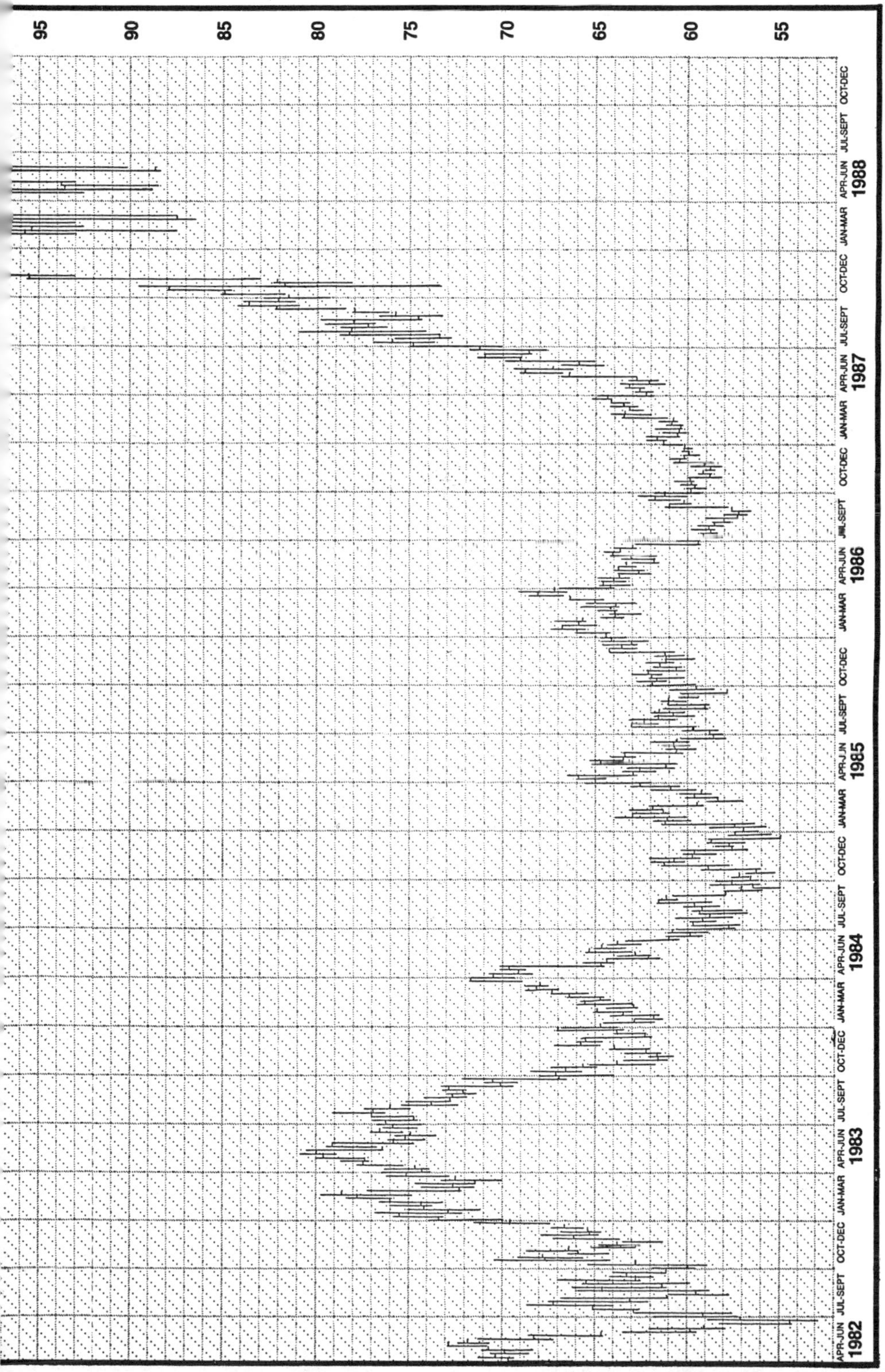
95
90
85
80
75
70
65
60
55
APR-JUN JUL-SEPT OCT-DEC
1982
JAN-MAR APR-JUN JUL-SEPT OCT-DEC
1983
JAN-MAR APR-JUN JUL-SEPT OCT-DEC
1984
JAN-MAR APR-JUN JUL-SEPT OCT-DEC
1985
JAN-MAR APR-JUN JUL-SEPT OCT-DEC
1986
JAN-MAR APR-JUN JUL-SEPT OCT-DEC
1987
JAN-MAR APR-JUN JUL-SEPT OCT-DEC
1988

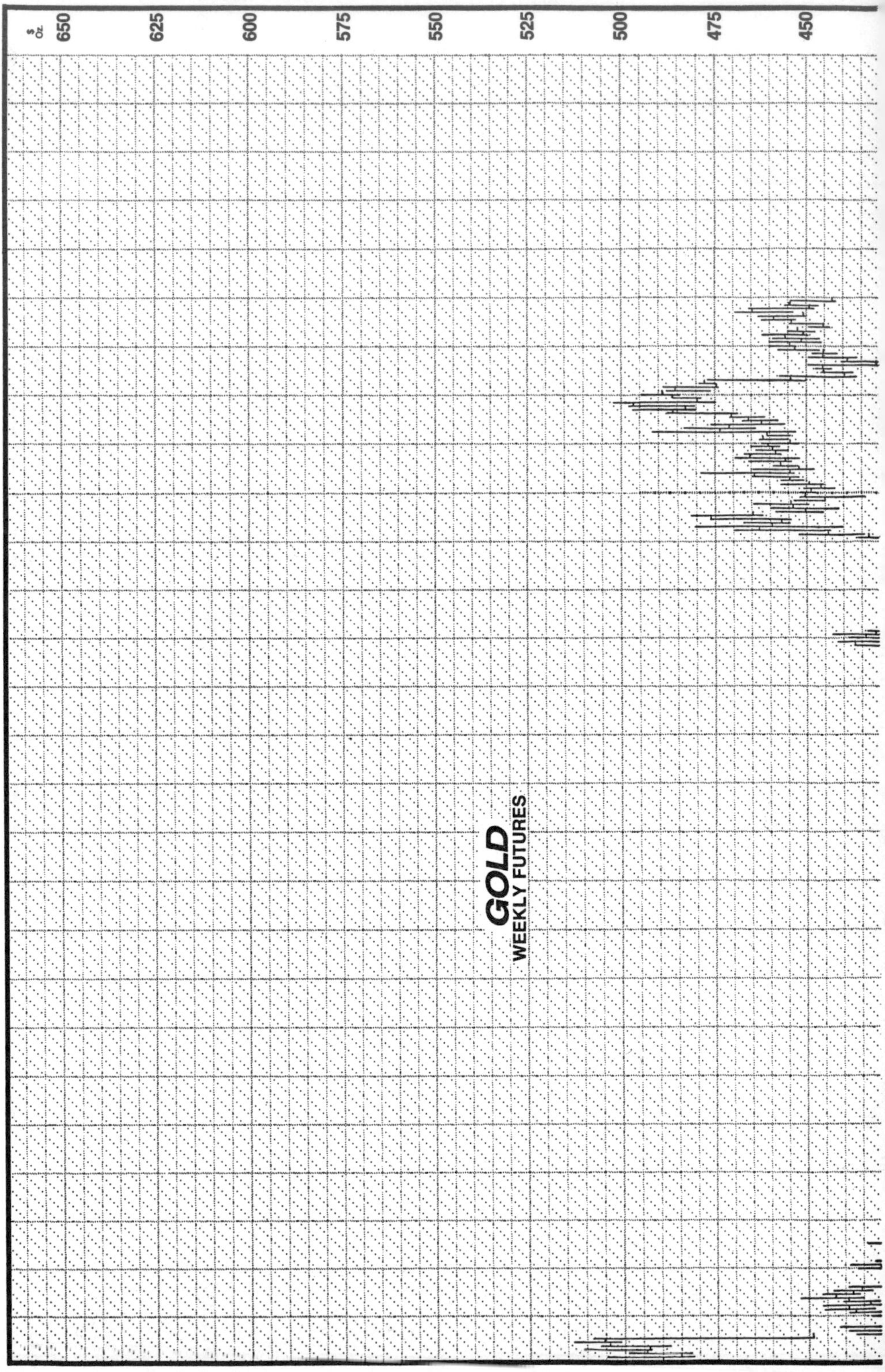
$ Oz.
650
625
600
575
550
525
500
475
450
GOLD
WEEKLY FUTURES

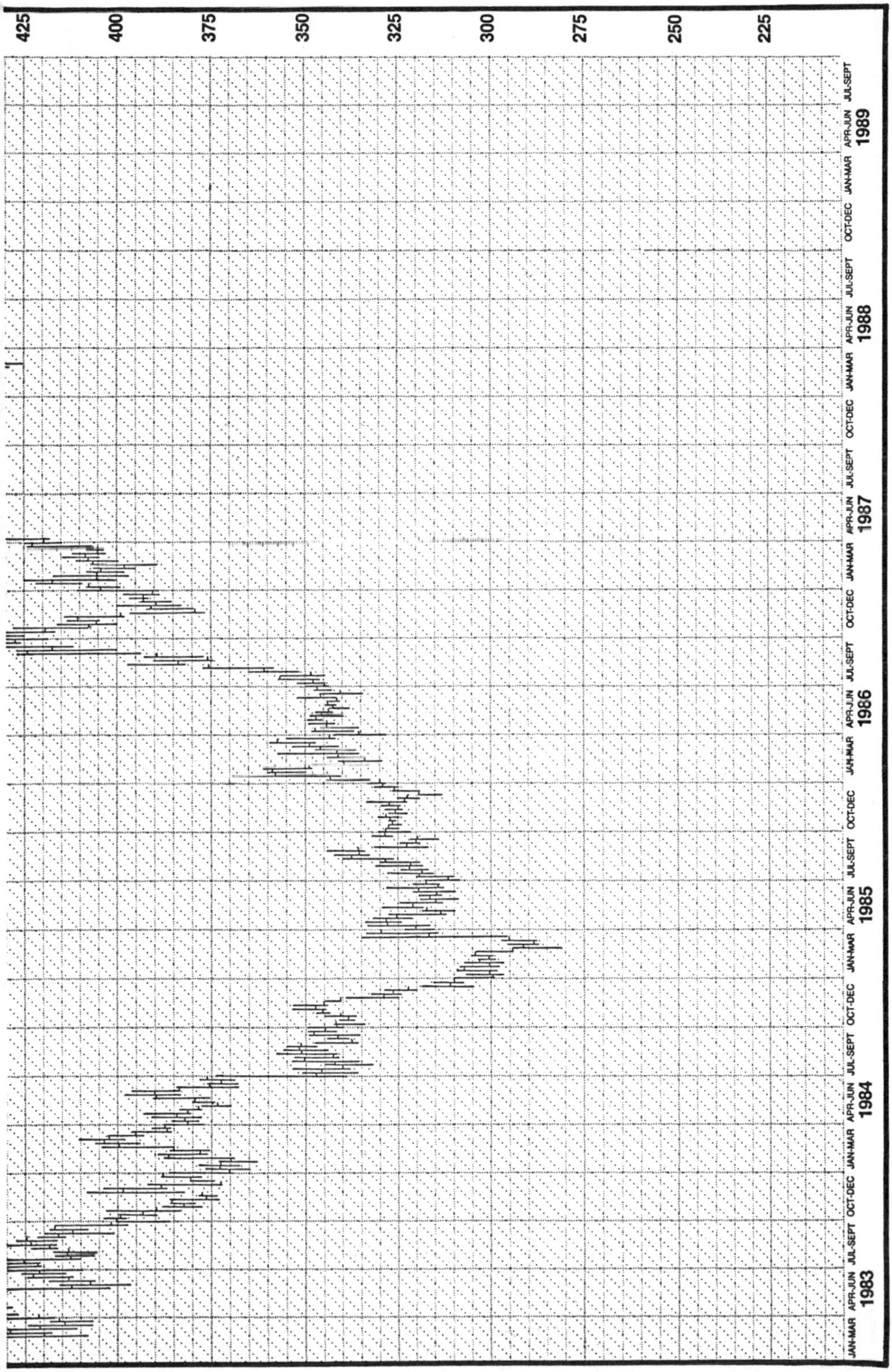

425
400
375
350
325
300
275
250
225
JAN-MAR APR-JUN JUL-SEPT OCT-DEC
1983
1984
1985
1986
1987
1988
1989

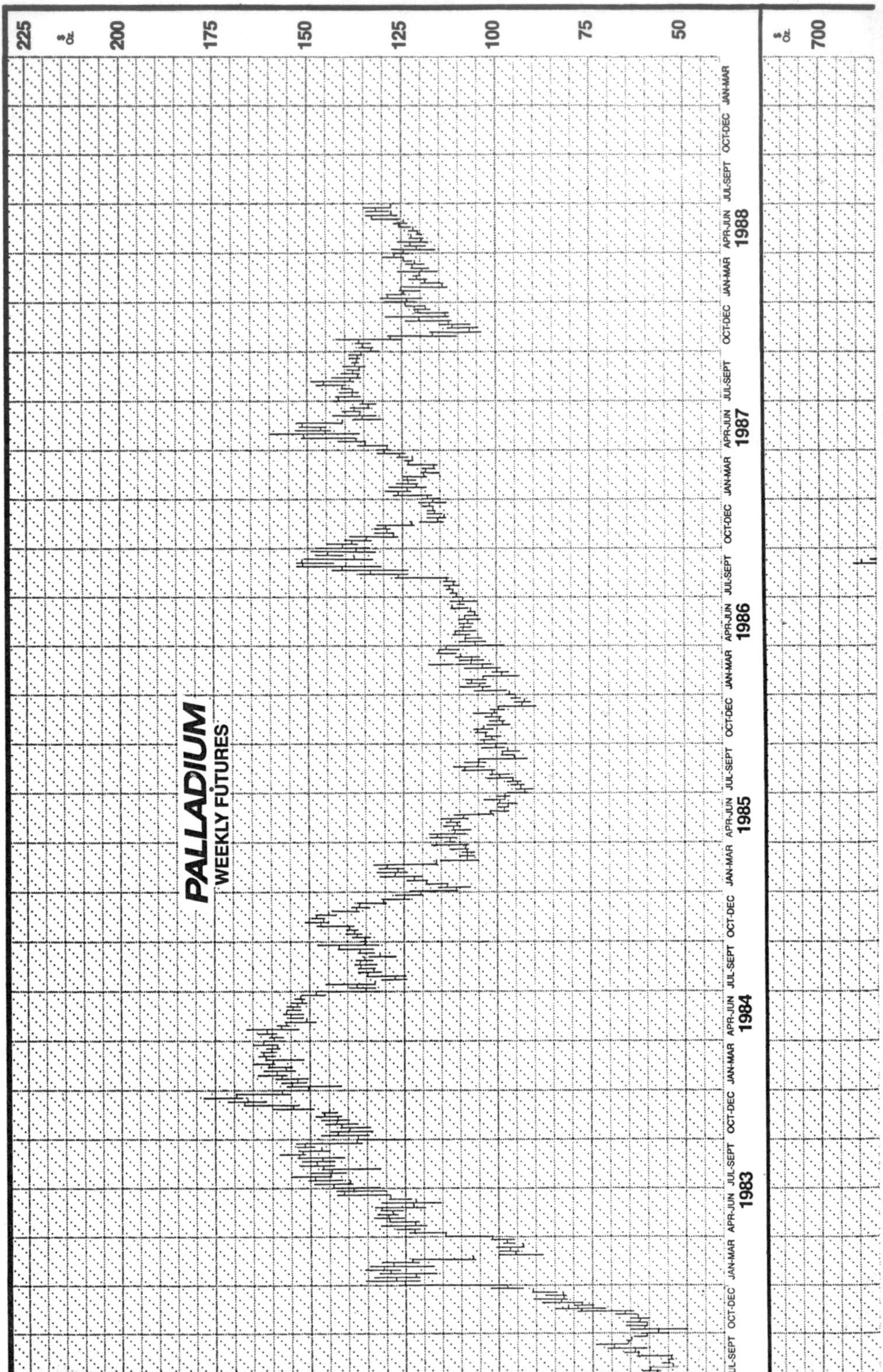
PALLADIUM
WEEKLY FUTURES
225
$ Oz
200
175
150
125
100
75
50
$ Oz
700
JUL-SEPT OCT-DEC JAN-MAR APR-JUN JUL-SEPT OCT-DEC JAN-MAR APR-JUN JUL-SEPT OCT-DEC JAN-MAR APR-JUN JUL-SEPT OCT-DEC JAN-MAR APR-JUN JUL-SEPT OCT-DEC JAN-MAR APR-JUN JUL-SEPT OCT-DEC JAN-MAR APR-JUN JUL-SEPT OCT-DEC JAN-MAR
1983
1984
1985
1986
1987
1988

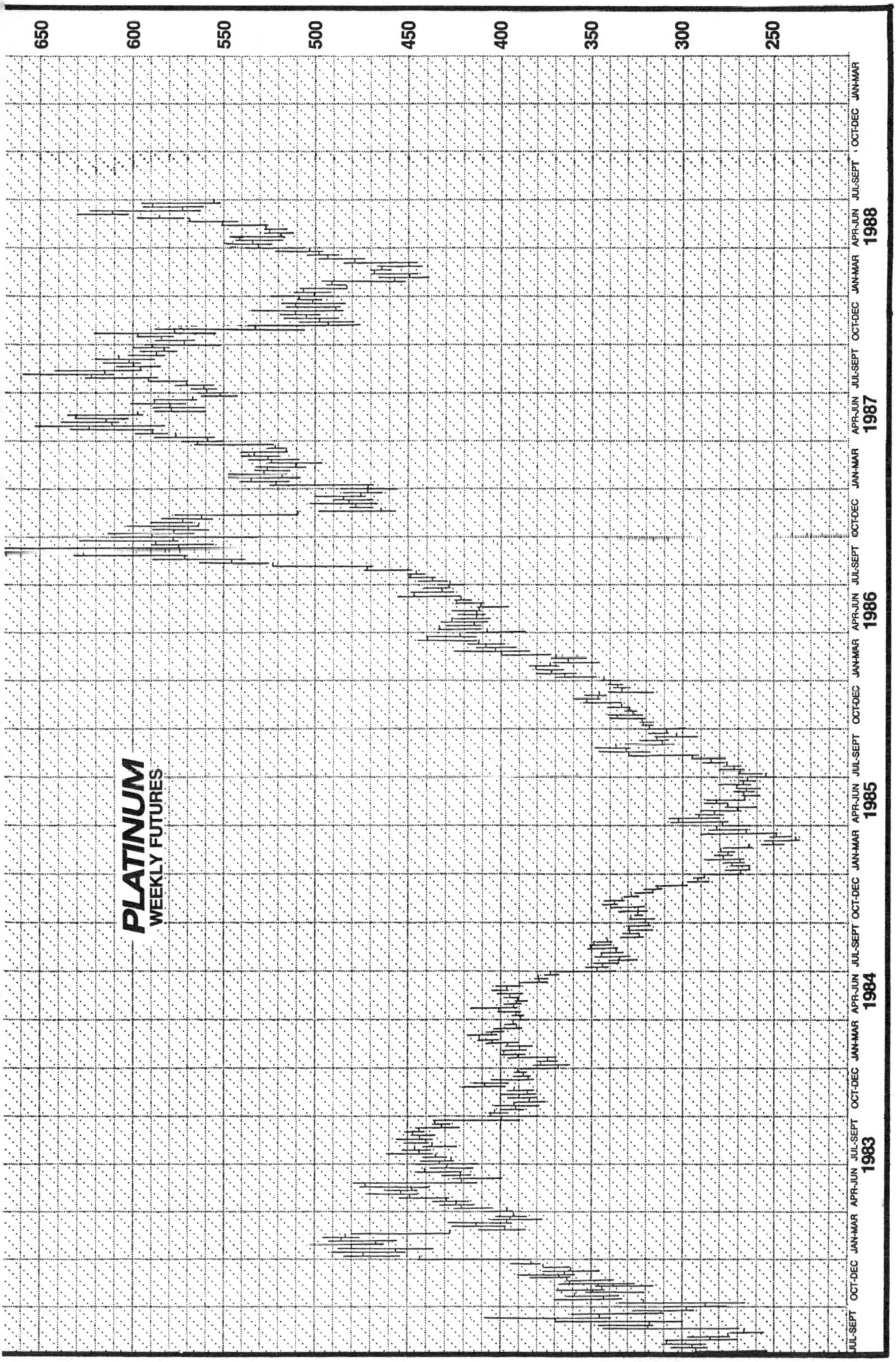
PLATINUM
WEEKLY FUTURES
650
600
550
500
450
400
350
300
250
JUL-SEPT
OCT-DEC
JAN-MAR
APR-JUN
1983
1984
1985
1986
1987
1988

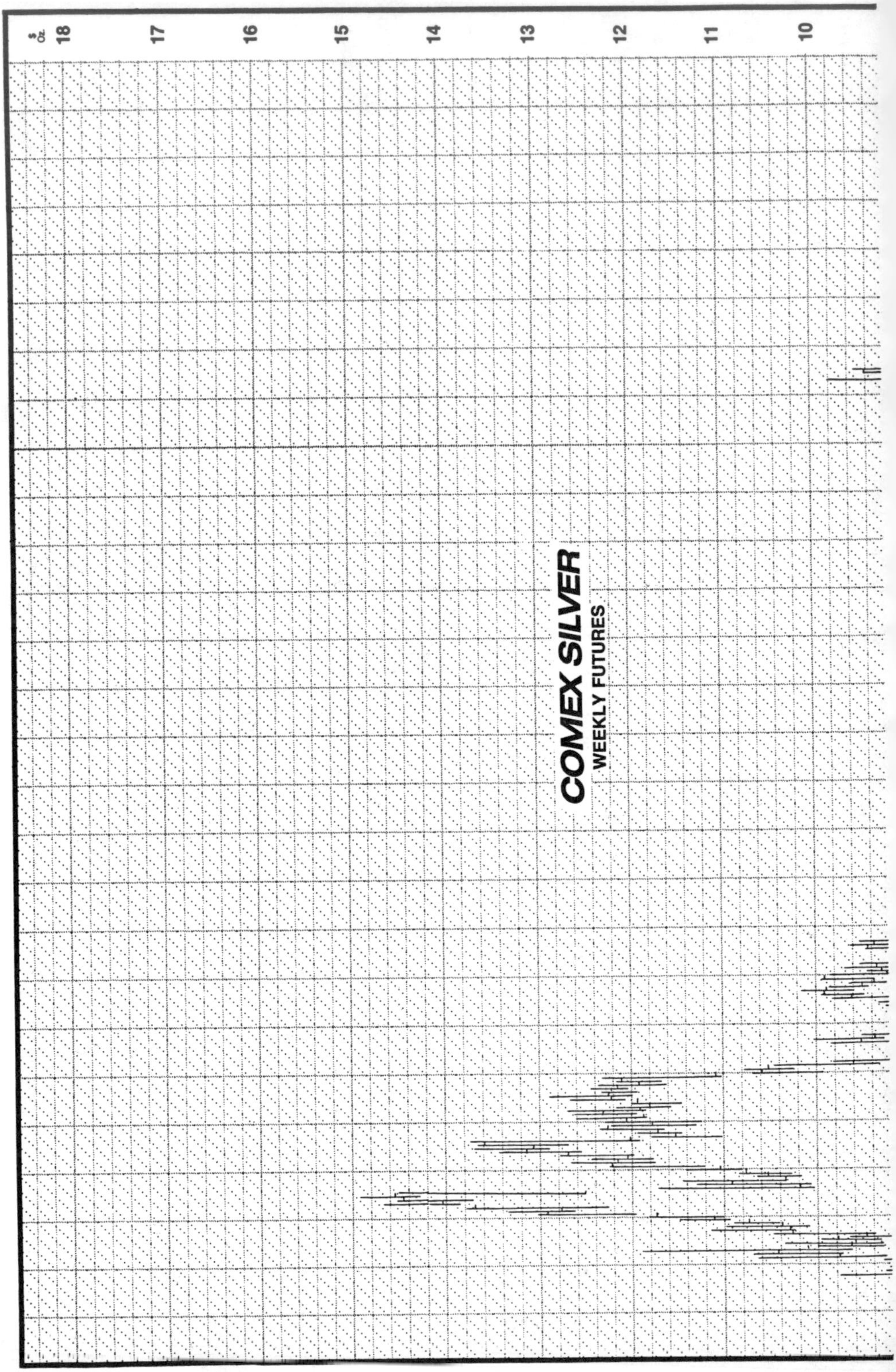
$ Oz.
18
17
16
15
14
13
12
11
10
COMEX SILVER
WEEKLY FUTURES

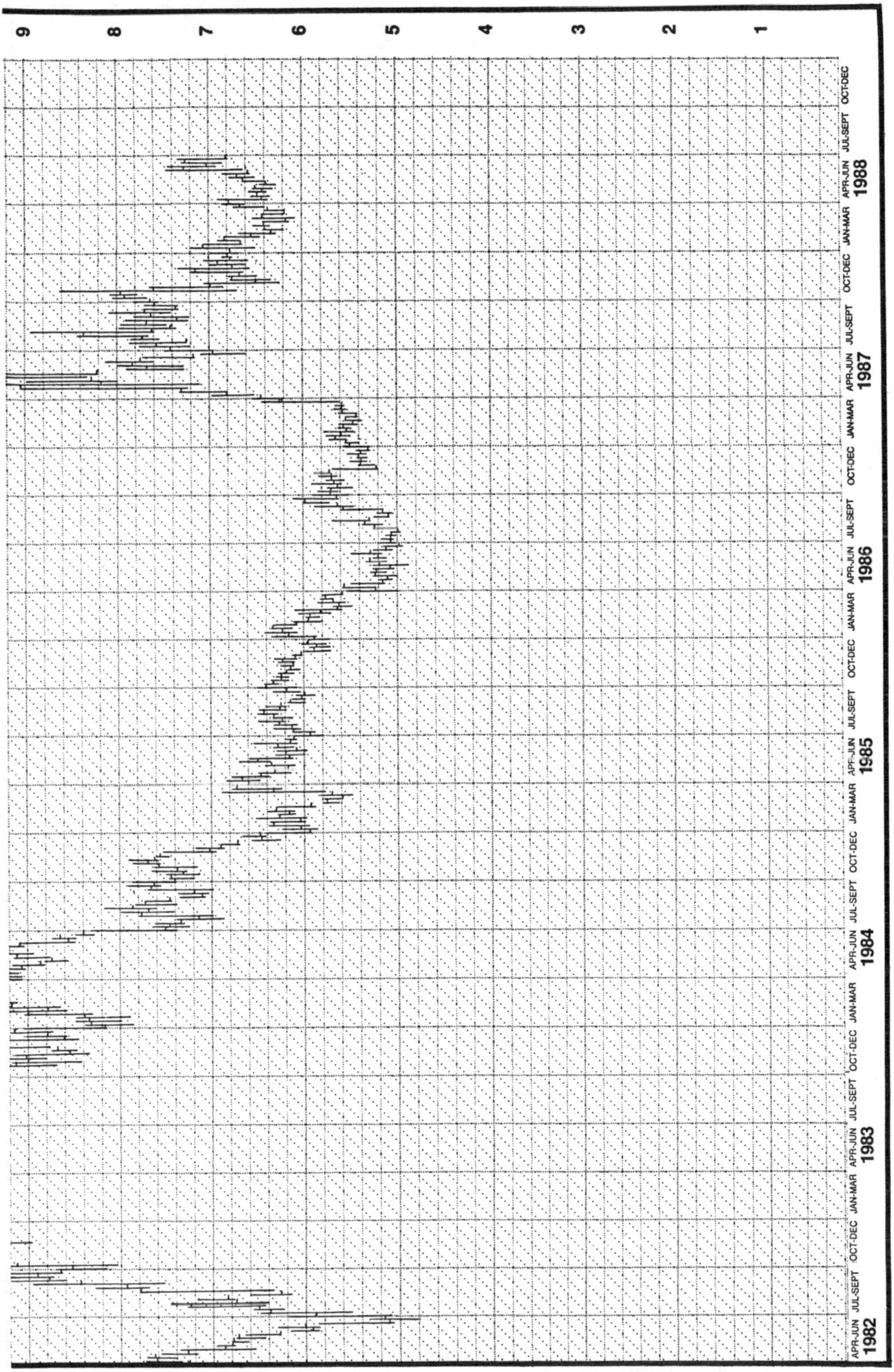
9
8
7
6
5
4
3
2
1
APR-JUN
JUL-SEPT
OCT-DEC
JAN-MAR
1982
1983
1984
1985
1986
1987
1988

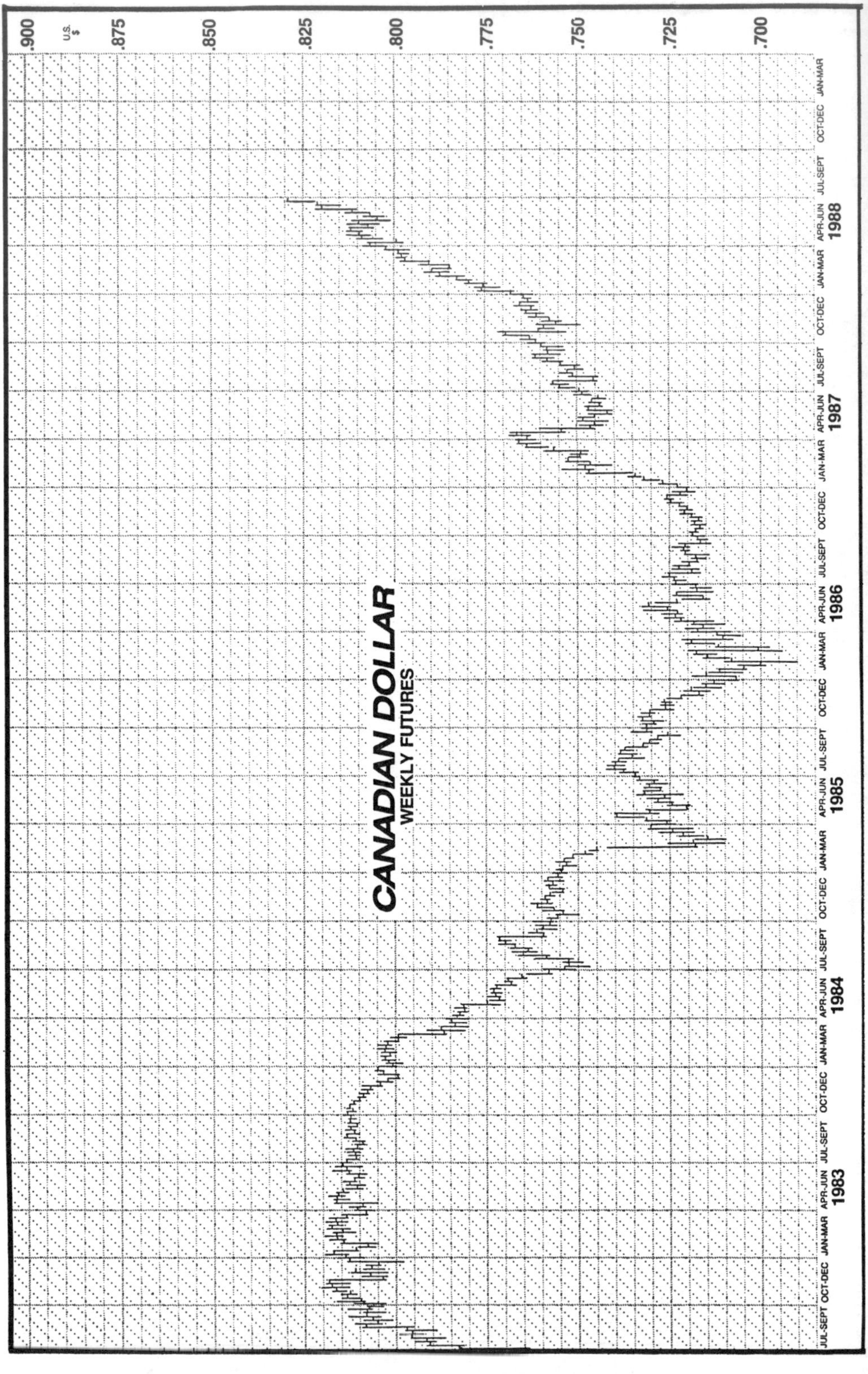
CANADIAN DOLLAR
WEEKLY FUTURES
U.S. $
.900
.875
.850
.825
.800
.775
.750
.725
.700
JUL-SEPT OCT-DEC JAN-MAR APR-JUN JUL-SEPT OCT-DEC JAN-MAR APR-JUN JUL-SEPT OCT-DEC JAN-MAR APR-JUN JUL-SEPT OCT-DEC JAN-MAR APR-JUN JUL-SEPT OCT-DEC JAN-MAR APR-JUN JUL-SEPT OCT-DEC JAN-MAR APR-JUN JUL-SEPT OCT-DEC JAN-MAR
1983
1984
1985
1986
1987
1988

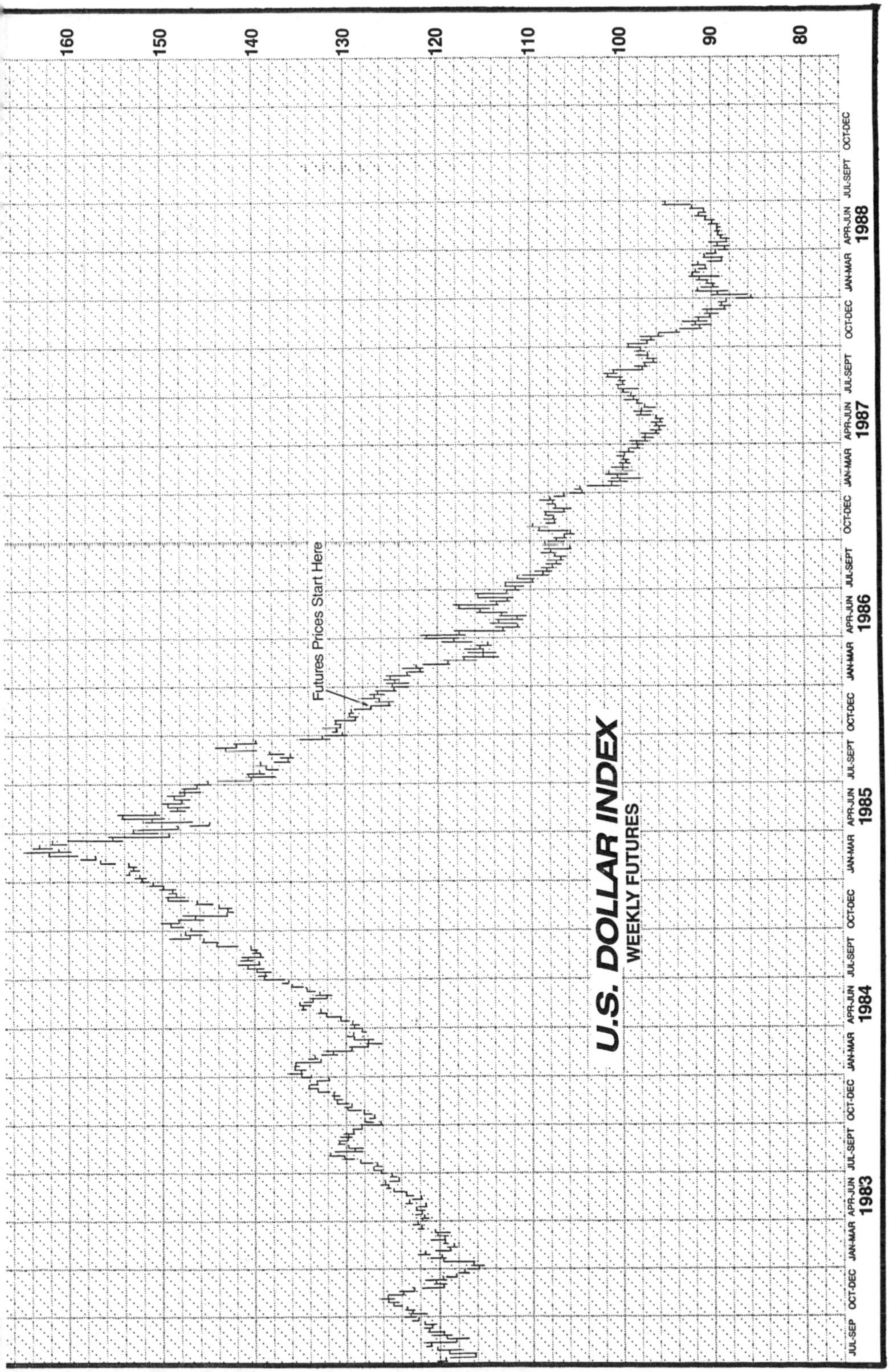
U.S. DOLLAR INDEX
WEEKLY FUTURES
Futures Prices Start Here
160
150
140
130
120
110
100
90
80
JUL-SEP OCT-DEC
JAN-MAR APR-JUN JUL-SEPT OCT-DEC
1983
JAN-MAR APR-JUN JUL-SEPT OCT-DEC
1984
JAN-MAR APR-JUN JUL-SEPT OCT-DEC
1985
JAN-MAR APR-JUN JUL-SEPT OCT-DEC
1986
JAN-MAR APR-JUN JUL-SEPT OCT-DEC
1987
JAN-MAR APR-JUN JUL-SEPT OCT-DEC
1988

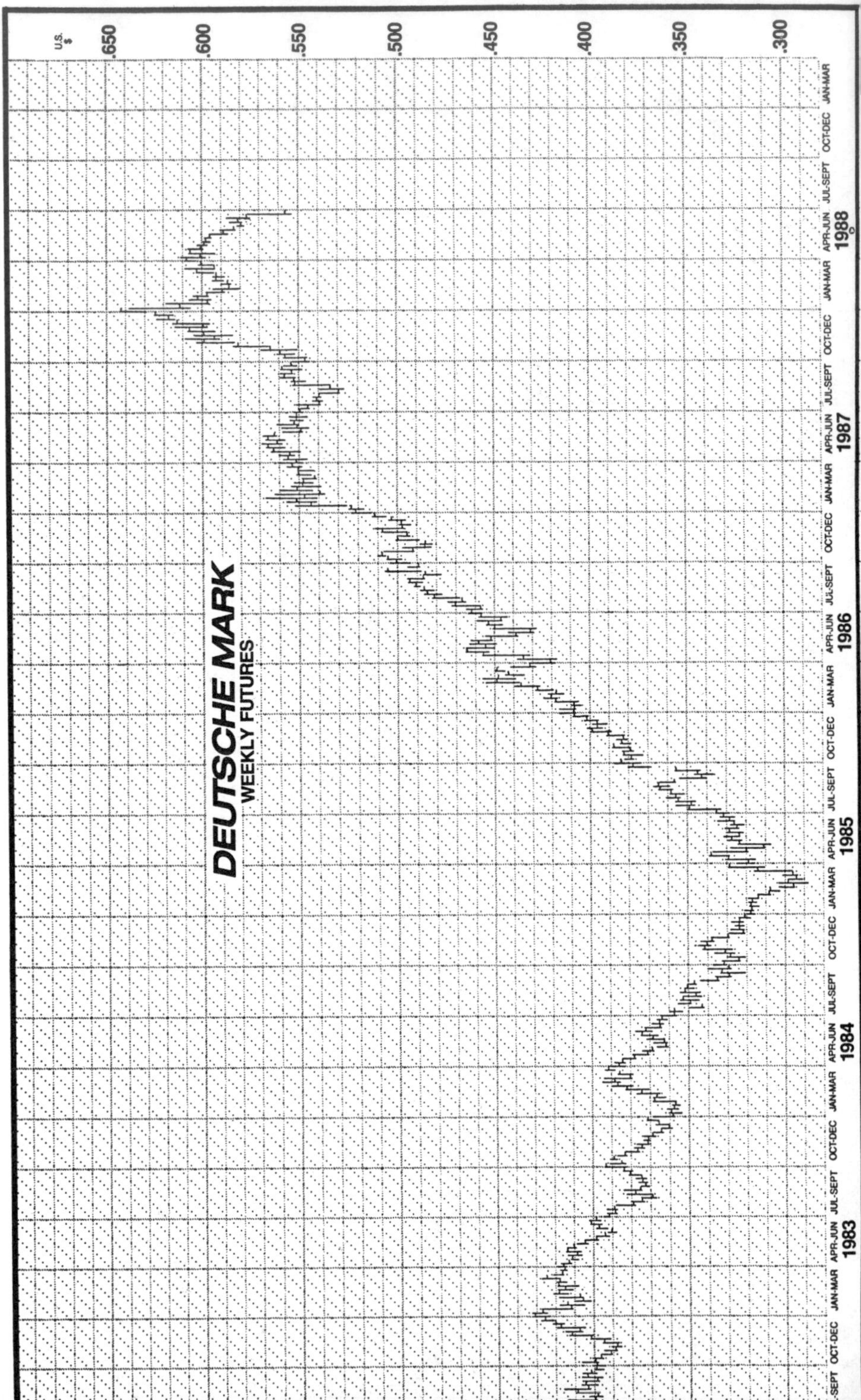
DEUTSCHE MARK
WEEKLY FUTURES
U.S. $
.650
.600
.550
.500
.450
.400
.350
.300
JUL-SEPT
OCT-DEC
JAN-MAR
APR-JUN
1983
1984
1985
1986
1987
1988

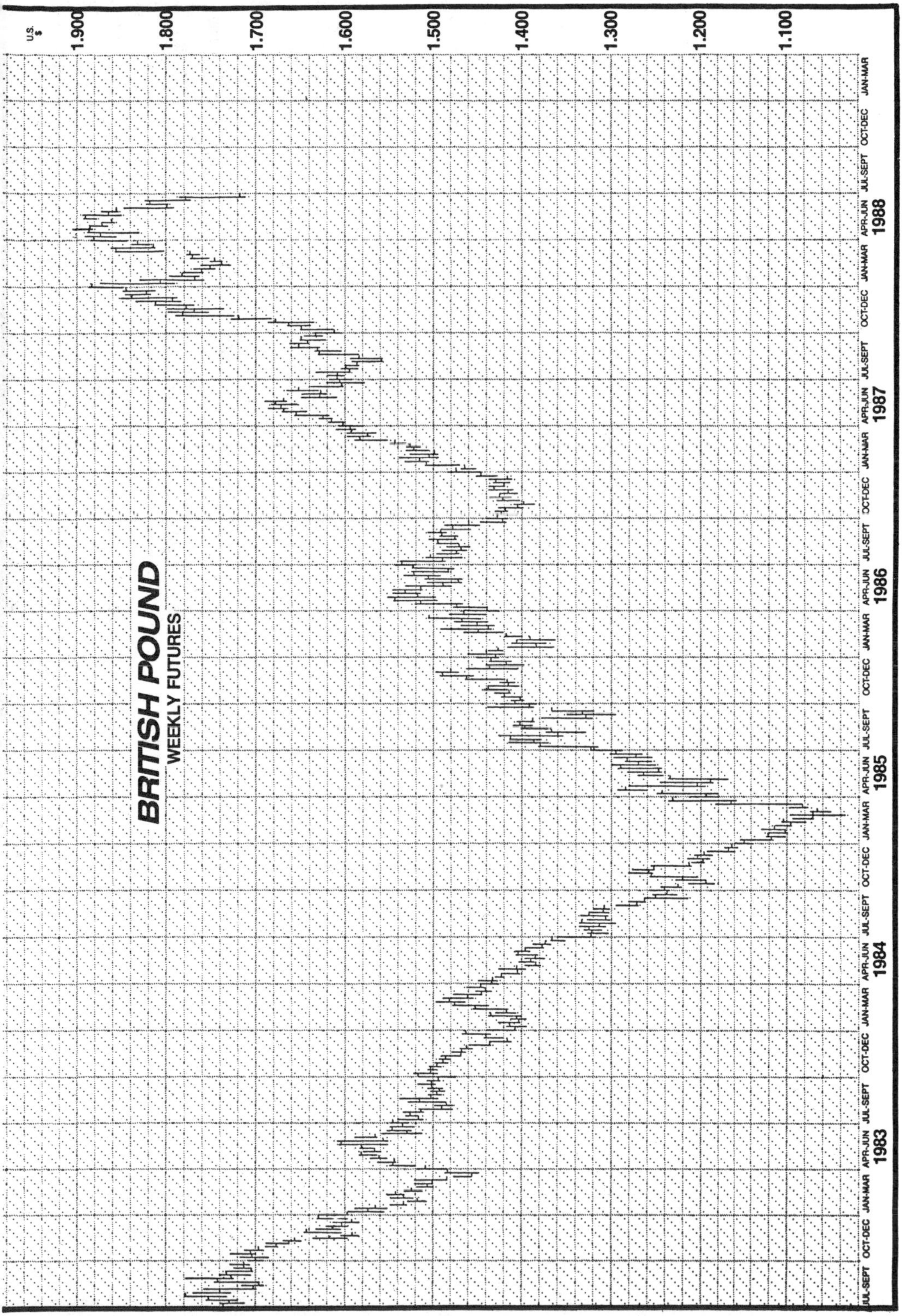
BRITISH POUND
WEEKLY FUTURES
U.S. $
1.900
1.800
1.700
1.600
1.500
1.400
1.300
1.200
1.100
JUL-SEPT OCT-DEC JAN-MAR APR-JUN JUL-SEPT OCT-DEC JAN-MAR APR-JUN JUL-SEPT OCT-DEC JAN-MAR APR-JUN JUL-SEPT OCT-DEC JAN-MAR APR-JUN JUL-SEPT OCT-DEC JAN-MAR APR-JUN JUL-SEPT OCT-DEC JAN-MAR APR-JUN JUL-SEPT OCT-DEC JAN-MAR
1983
1984
1985
1986
1987
1988

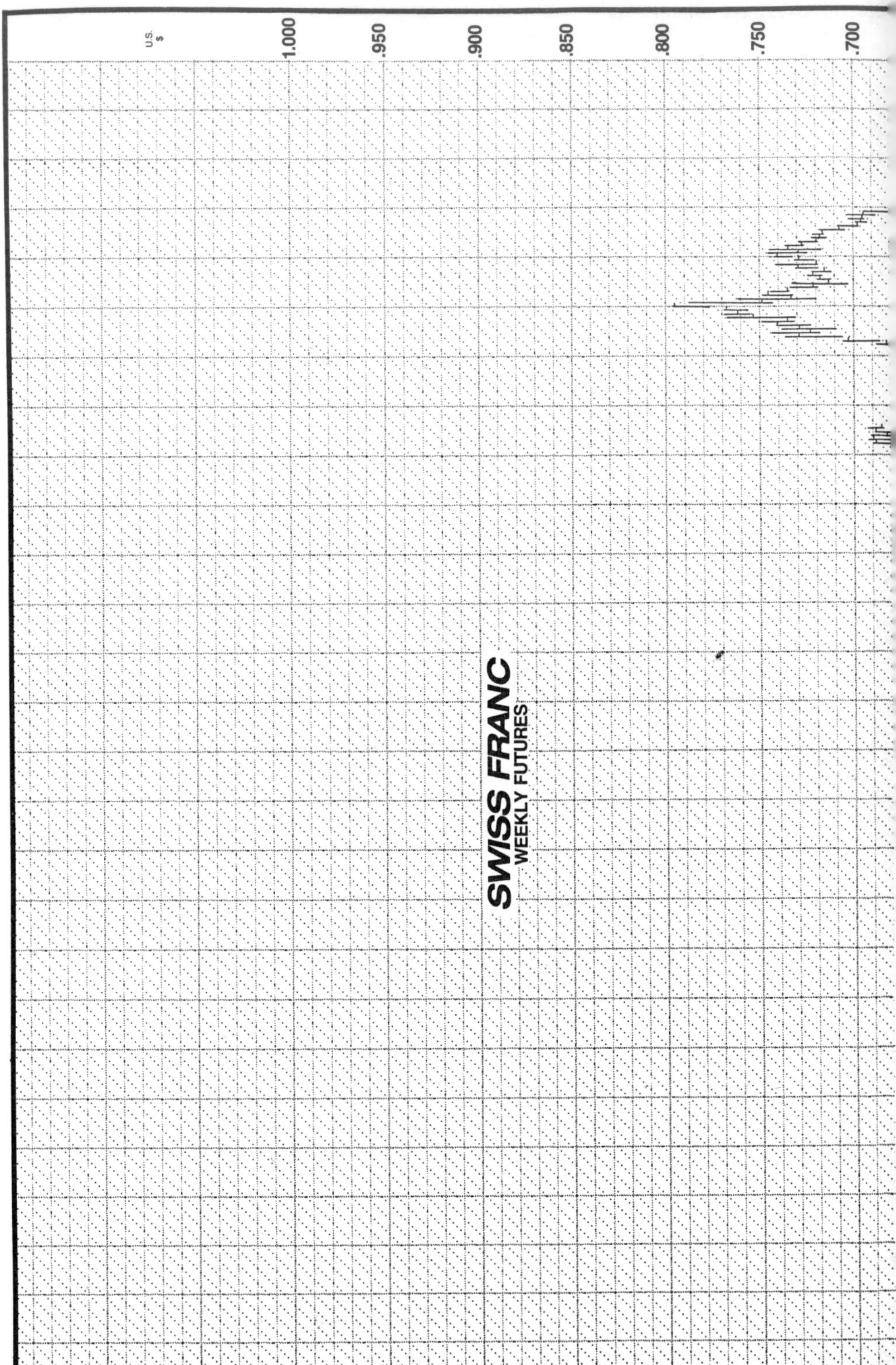
SWISS FRANC
WEEKLY FUTURES
U.S. $
1.000
.950
.900
.850
.800
.750
.700

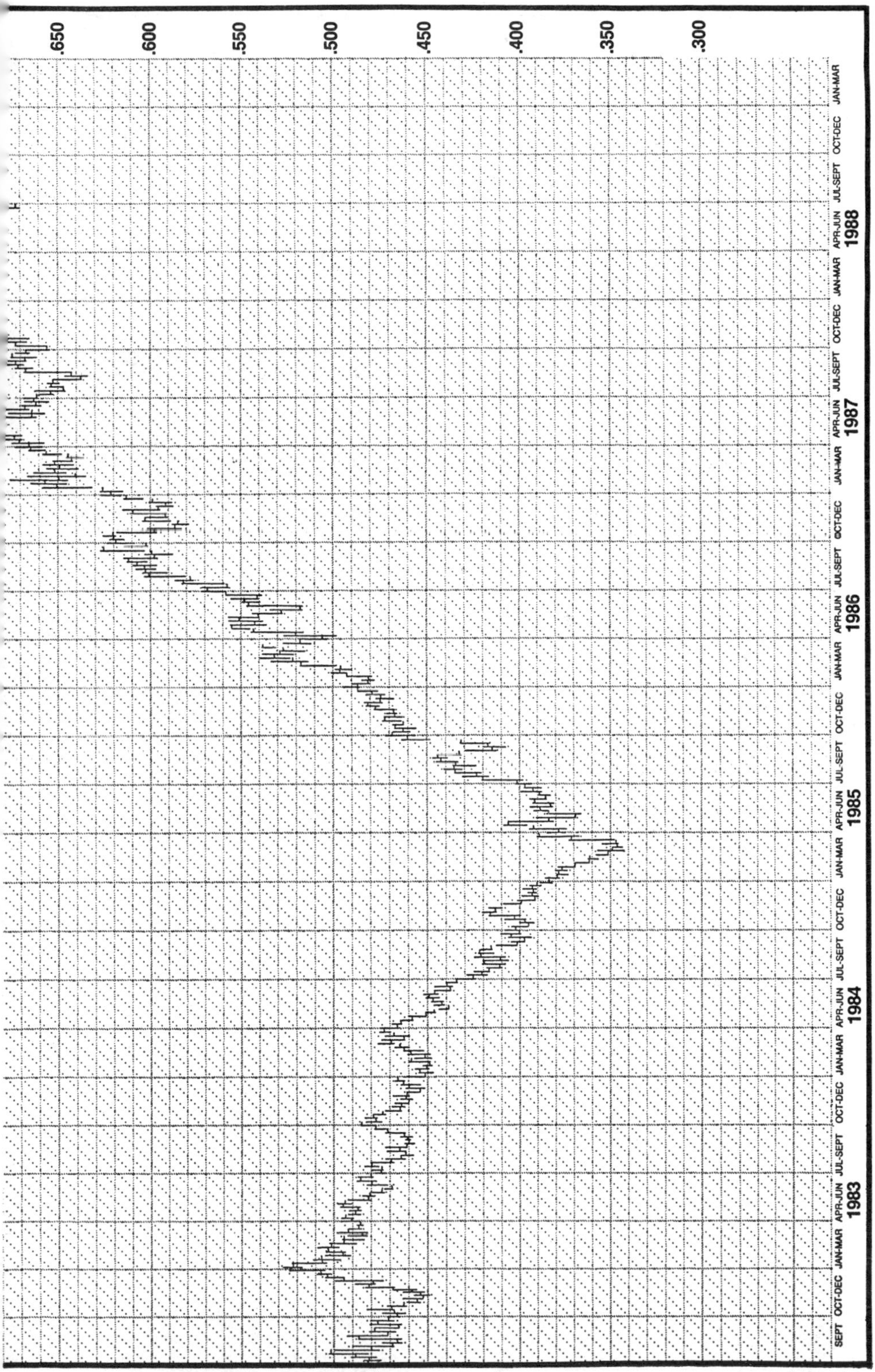
.650
.600
.550
.500
.450
.400
.350
.300
SEPT
OCT-DEC
JAN-MAR
APR-JUN
1983
JUL-SEPT
OCT-DEC
JAN-MAR
APR-JUN
1984
JUL-SEPT
OCT-DEC
JAN-MAR
APR-JUN
1985
JUL-SEPT
OCT-DEC
JAN-MAR
APR-JUN
1986
JUL-SEPT
OCT-DEC
JAN-MAR
APR-JUN
1987
JUL-SEPT
OCT-DEC
JAN-MAR
APR-JUN
1988
JUL-SEPT
OCT-DEC
JAN-MAR

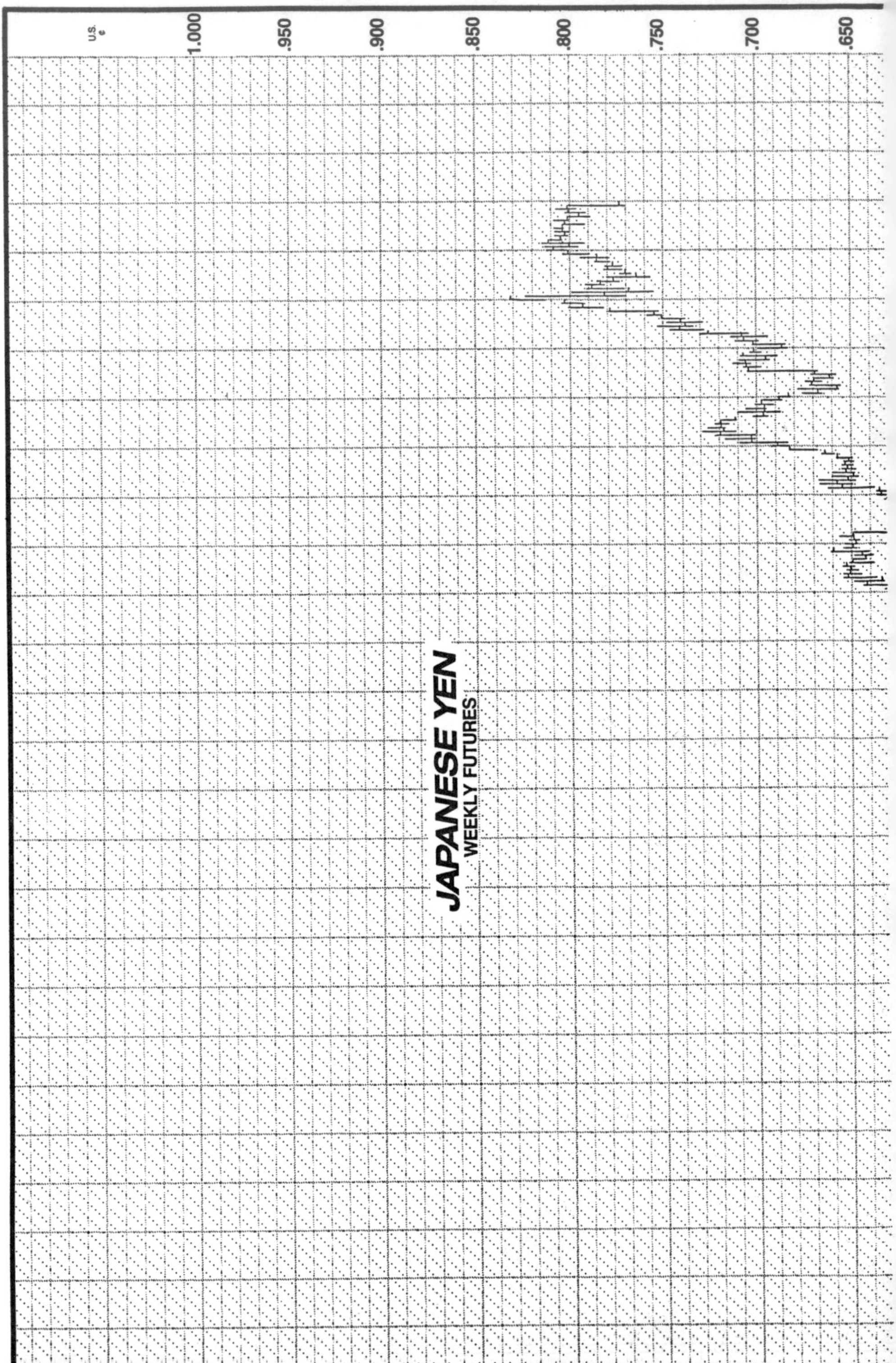
JAPANESE YEN
WEEKLY FUTURES
U.S. ¢
1.000
.950
.900
.850
.800
.750
.700
.650

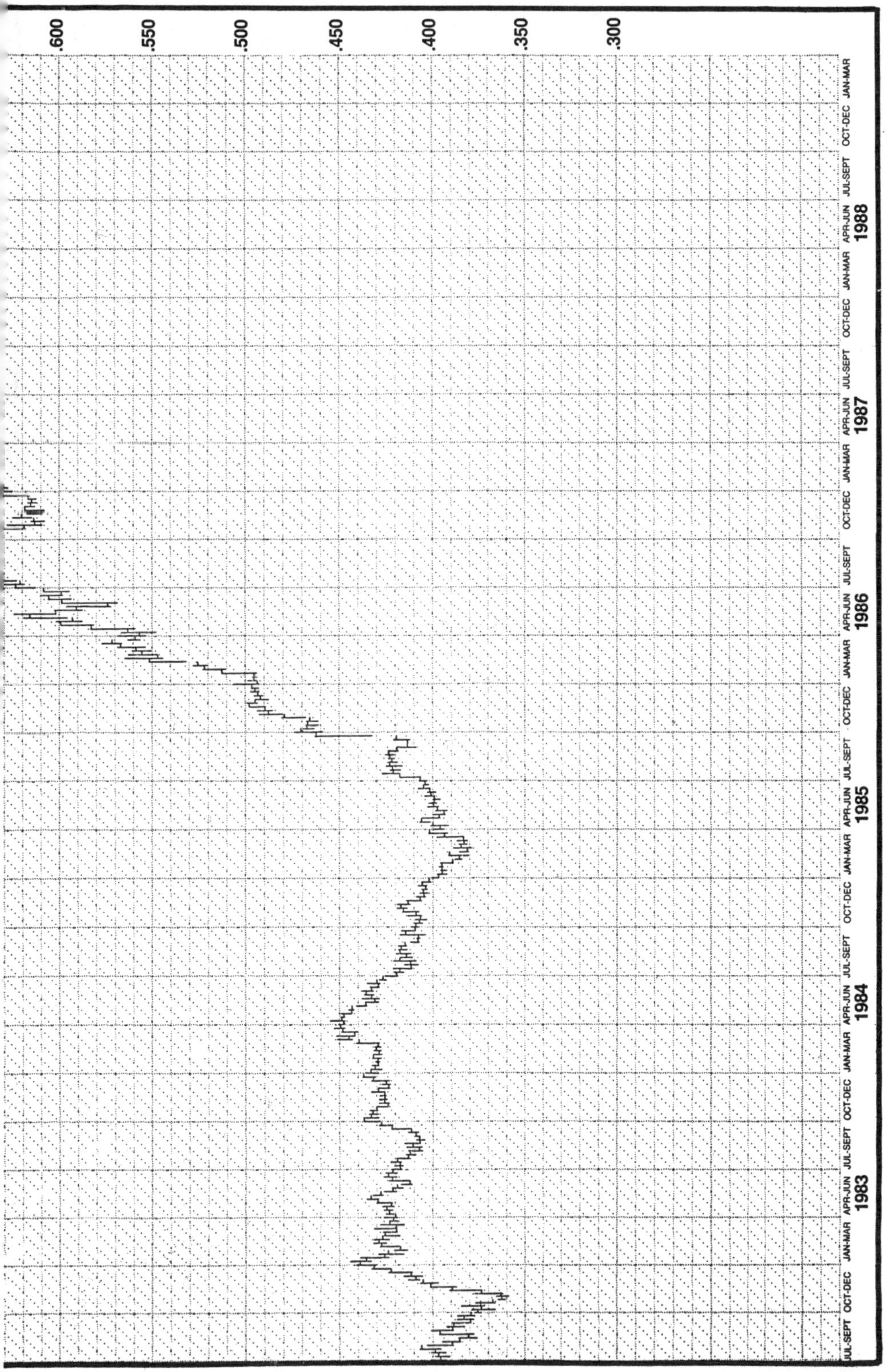
.600
.550
.500
.450
.400
.350
.300
JUL-SEPT
OCT-DEC
JAN-MAR
APR-JUN
1983
JUL-SEPT
OCT-DEC
JAN-MAR
APR-JUN
1984
JUL-SEPT
OCT-DEC
JAN-MAR
APR-JUN
1985
JUL-SEPT
OCT-DEC
JAN-MAR
APR-JUN
1986
JUL-SEPT
OCT-DEC
JAN-MAR
APR-JUN
1987
JUL-SEPT
OCT-DEC
JAN-MAR
APR-JUN
1988
JUL-SEPT
OCT-DEC
JAN-MAR

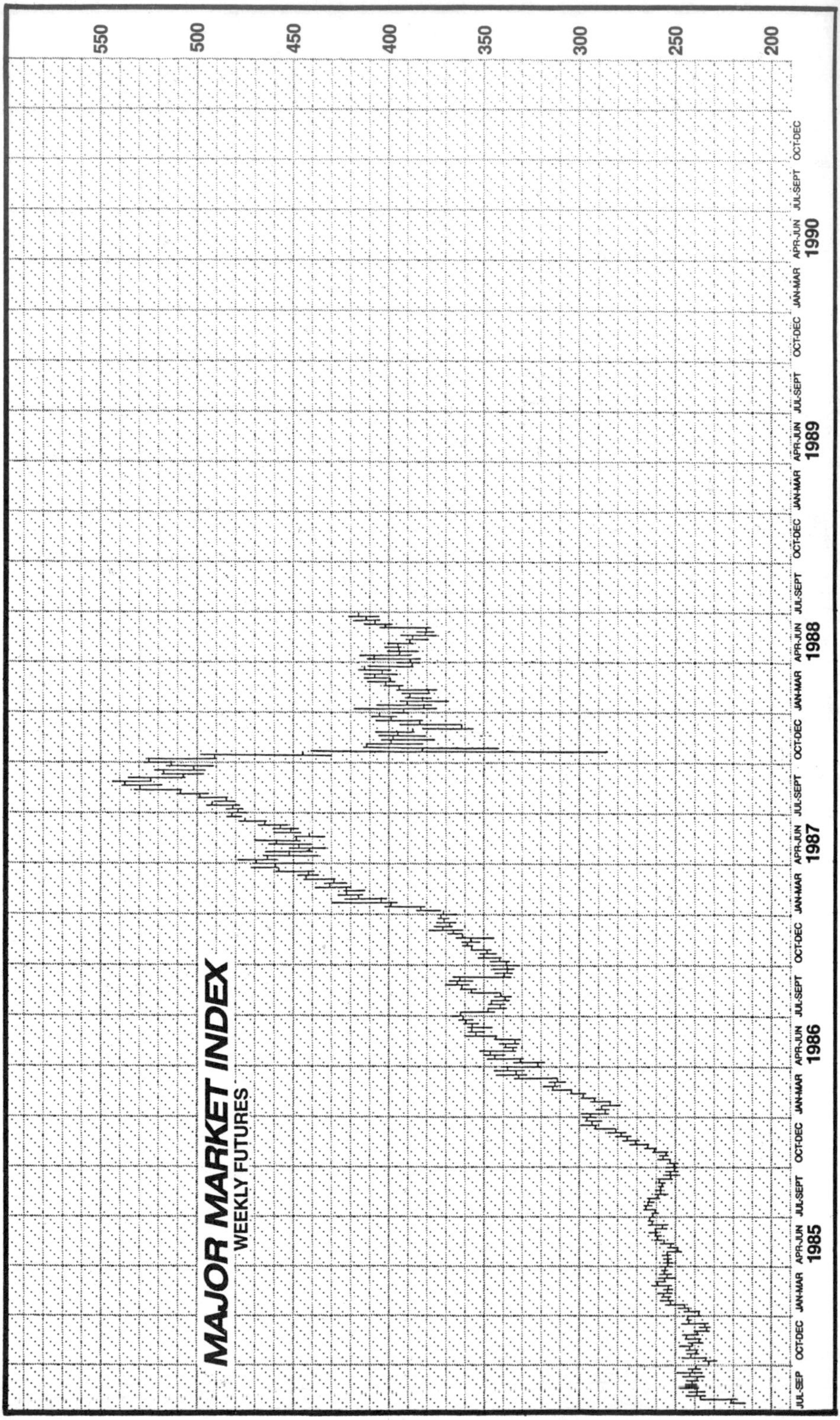
MAJOR MARKET INDEX
WEEKLY FUTURES
550
500
450
400
350
300
250
200
JUL-SEP
OCT-DEC
JAN-MAR
APR-JUN
JUL-SEPT
OCT-DEC
1985
1986
1987
1988
1989
1990

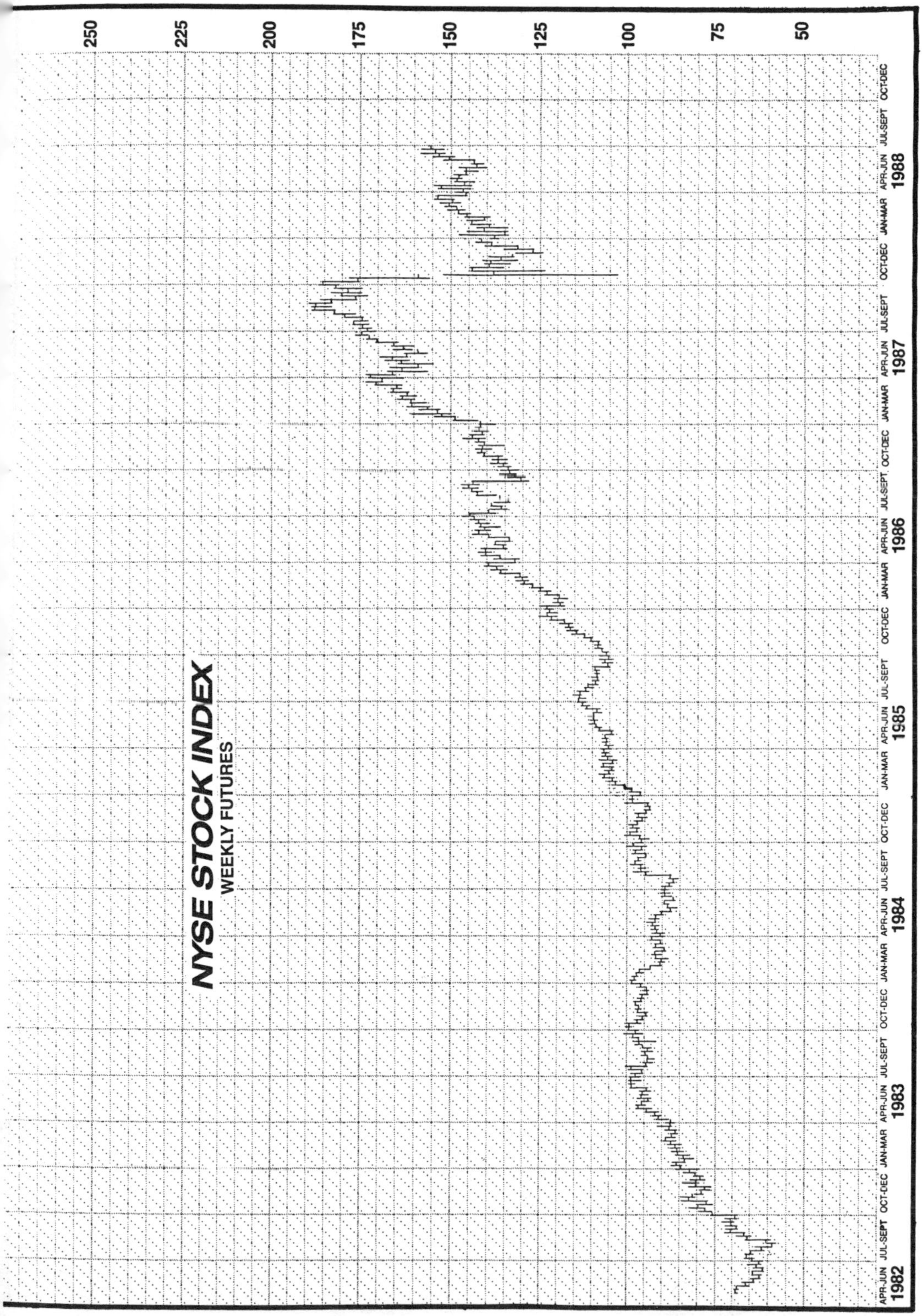
NYSE STOCK INDEX
WEEKLY FUTURES
250
225
200
175
150
125
100
75
50
APR-JUN JUL-SEPT OCT-DEC JAN-MAR APR-JUN JUL-SEPT OCT-DEC JAN-MAR APR-JUN JUL-SEPT OCT-DEC JAN-MAR APR-JUN JUL-SEPT OCT-DEC JAN-MAR APR-JUN JUL-SEPT OCT-DEC JAN-MAR APR-JUN JUL-SEPT OCT-DEC JAN-MAR APR-JUN JUL-SEPT OCT-DEC
1982
1983
1984
1985
1986
1987
1988

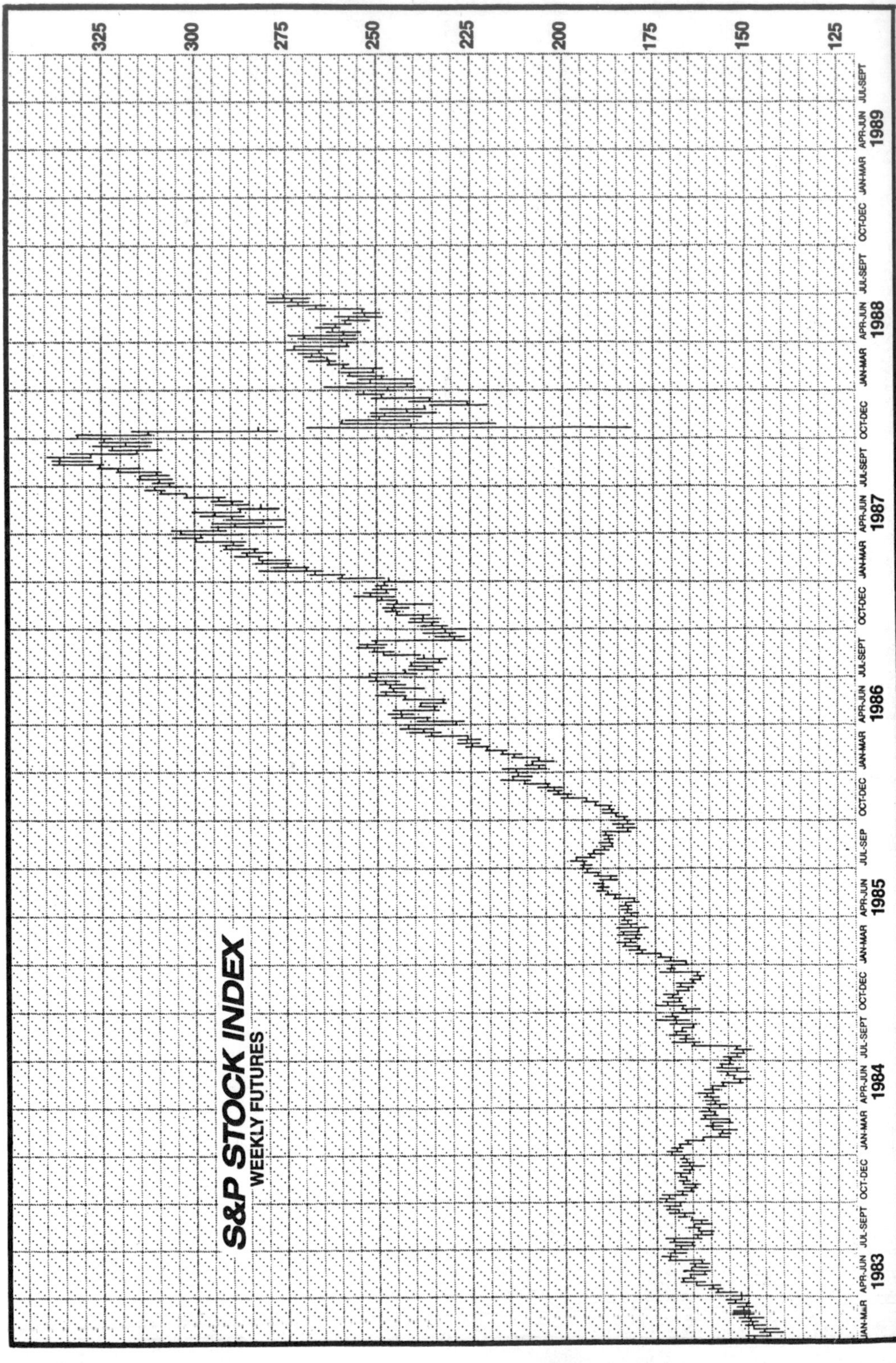
S&P STOCK INDEX
WEEKLY FUTURES
325
300
275
250
225
200
175
150
125
JAN-MAR APR-JUN JUL-SEPT OCT-DEC
1983
JAN-MAR APR-JUN JUL-SEPT OCT-DEC
1984
JAN-MAR APR-JUN JUL-SEP OCT-DEC
1985
JAN-MAR APR-JUN JUL-SEPT OCT-DEC
1986
JAN-MAR APR-JUN JUL-SEPT OCT-DEC
1987
JAN-MAR APR-JUN JUL-SEPT OCT-DEC
1988
JAN-MAR APR-JUN JUL-SEPT
1989

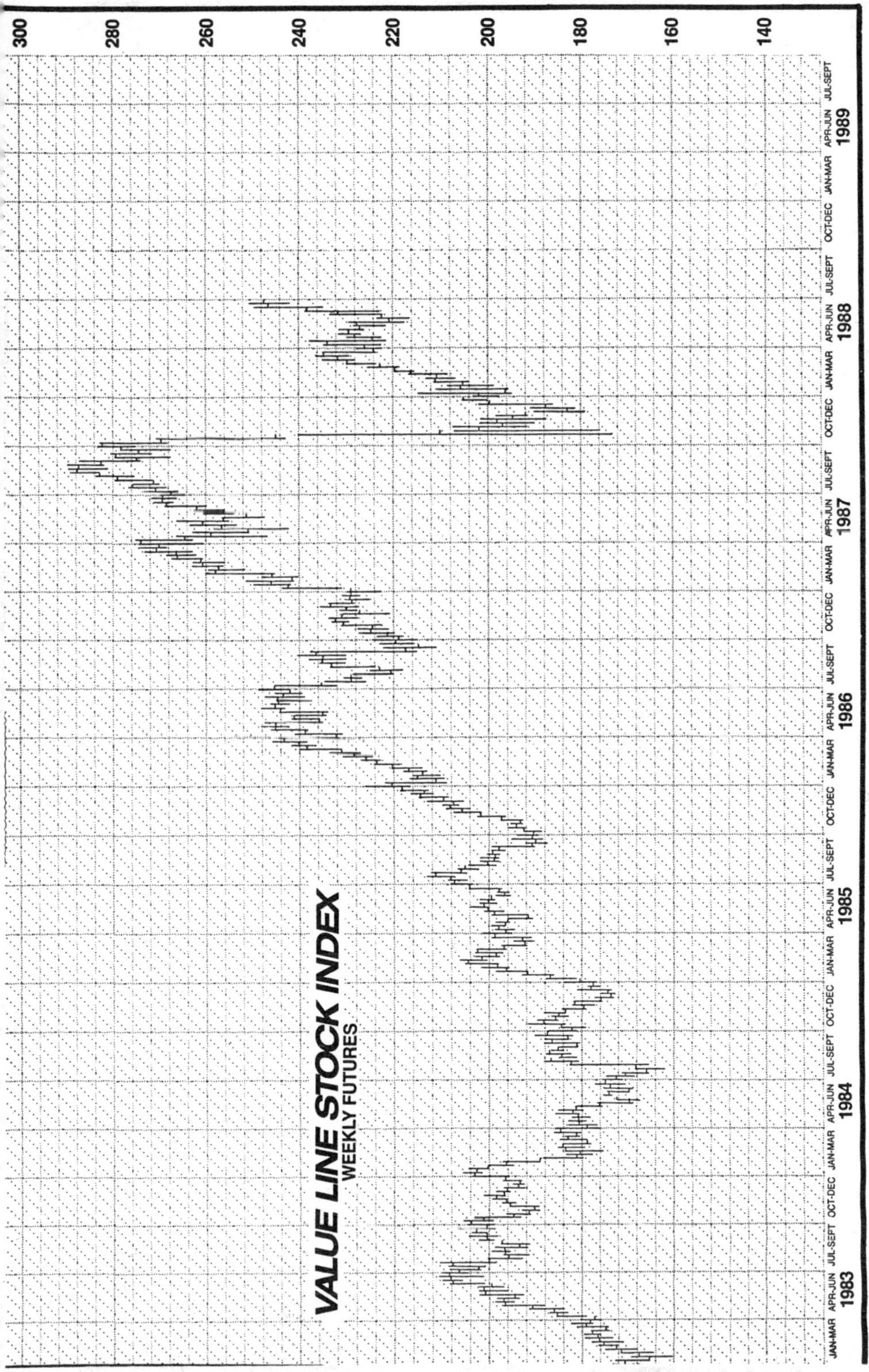
VALUE LINE STOCK INDEX
WEEKLY FUTURES
300
280
260
240
220
200
180
160
140
JAN-MAR APR-JUN JUL-SEPT OCT-DEC
1983
1984
1985
1986
1987
1988
1989

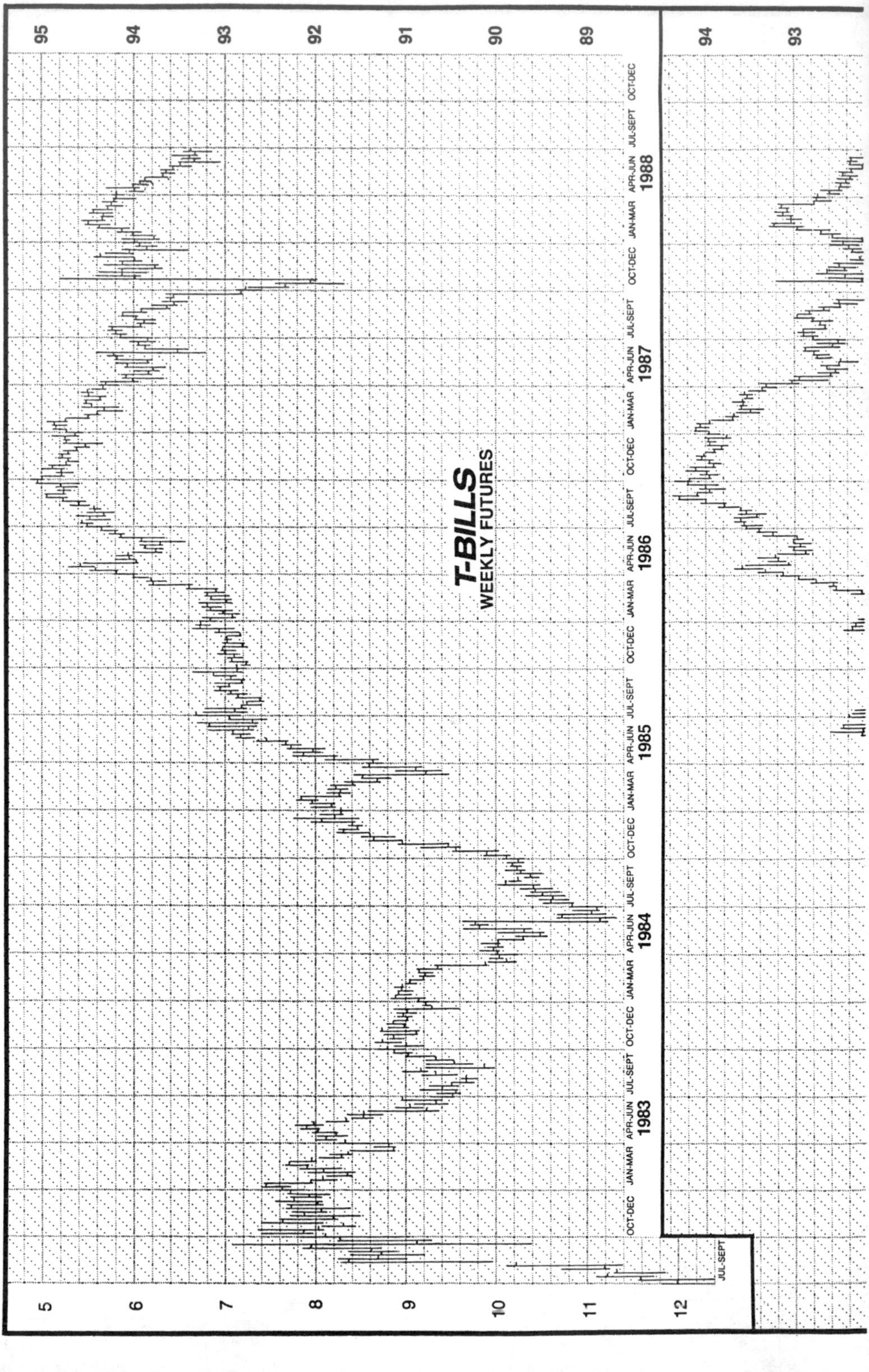
T-BILLS
WEEKLY FUTURES
95
94
93
92
91
90
89
5
6
7
8
9
10
11
12
JUL-SEPT
OCT-DEC
JAN-MAR
APR-JUN
1983
1984
1985
1986
1987
1988

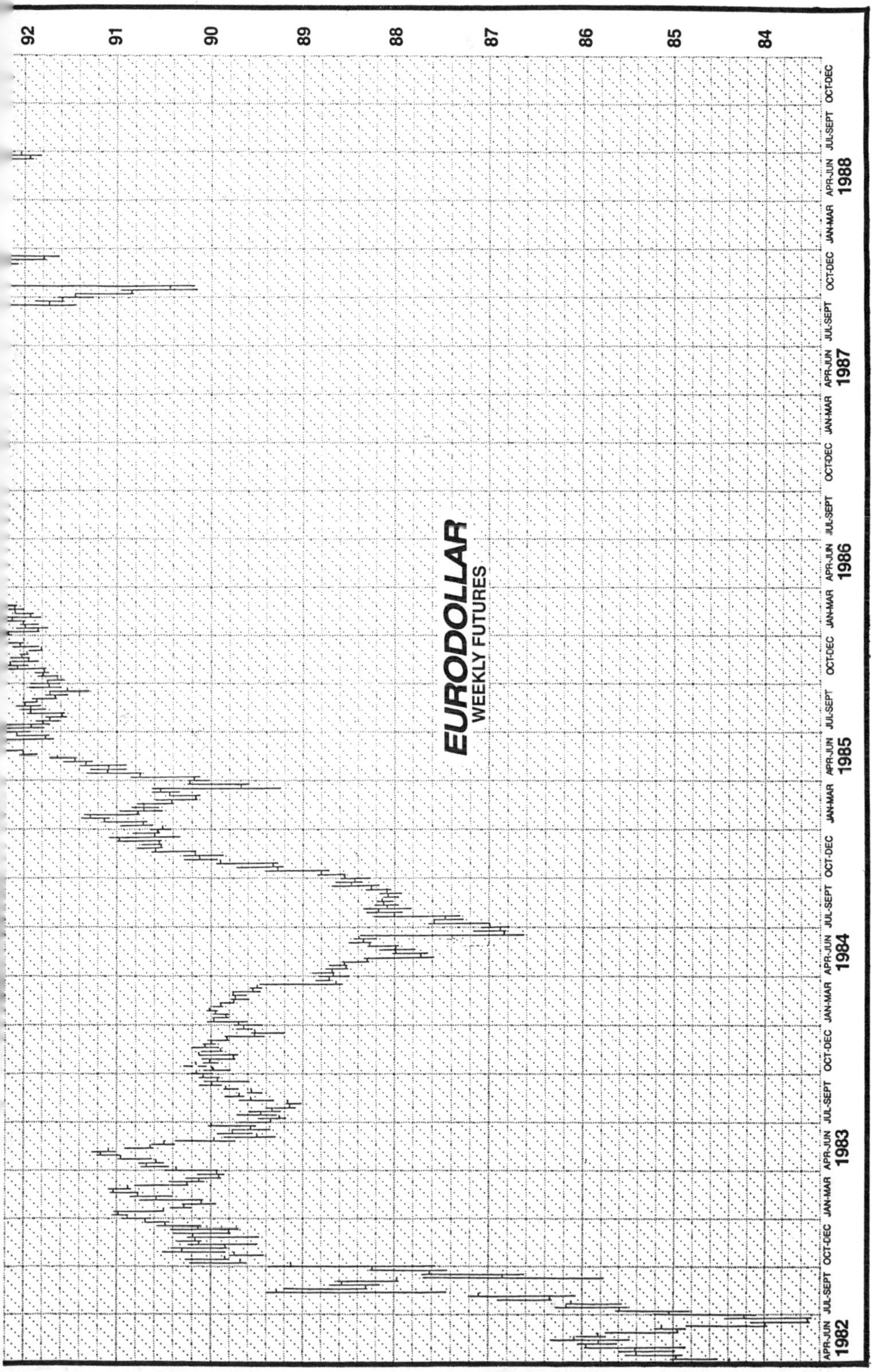
EURODOLLAR
WEEKLY FUTURES
92
91
90
89
88
87
86
85
84
APR-JUN JUL-SEPT OCT-DEC
1982
JAN-MAR APR-JUN JUL-SEPT OCT-DEC
1983
JAN-MAR APR-JUN JUL-SEPT OCT-DEC
1984
JAN-MAR APR-JUN JUL-SEPT OCT-DEC
1985
JAN-MAR APR-JUN JUL-SEPT OCT-DEC
1986
JAN-MAR APR-JUN JUL-SEPT OCT-DEC
1987
JAN-MAR APR-JUN JUL-SEPT OCT-DEC
1988

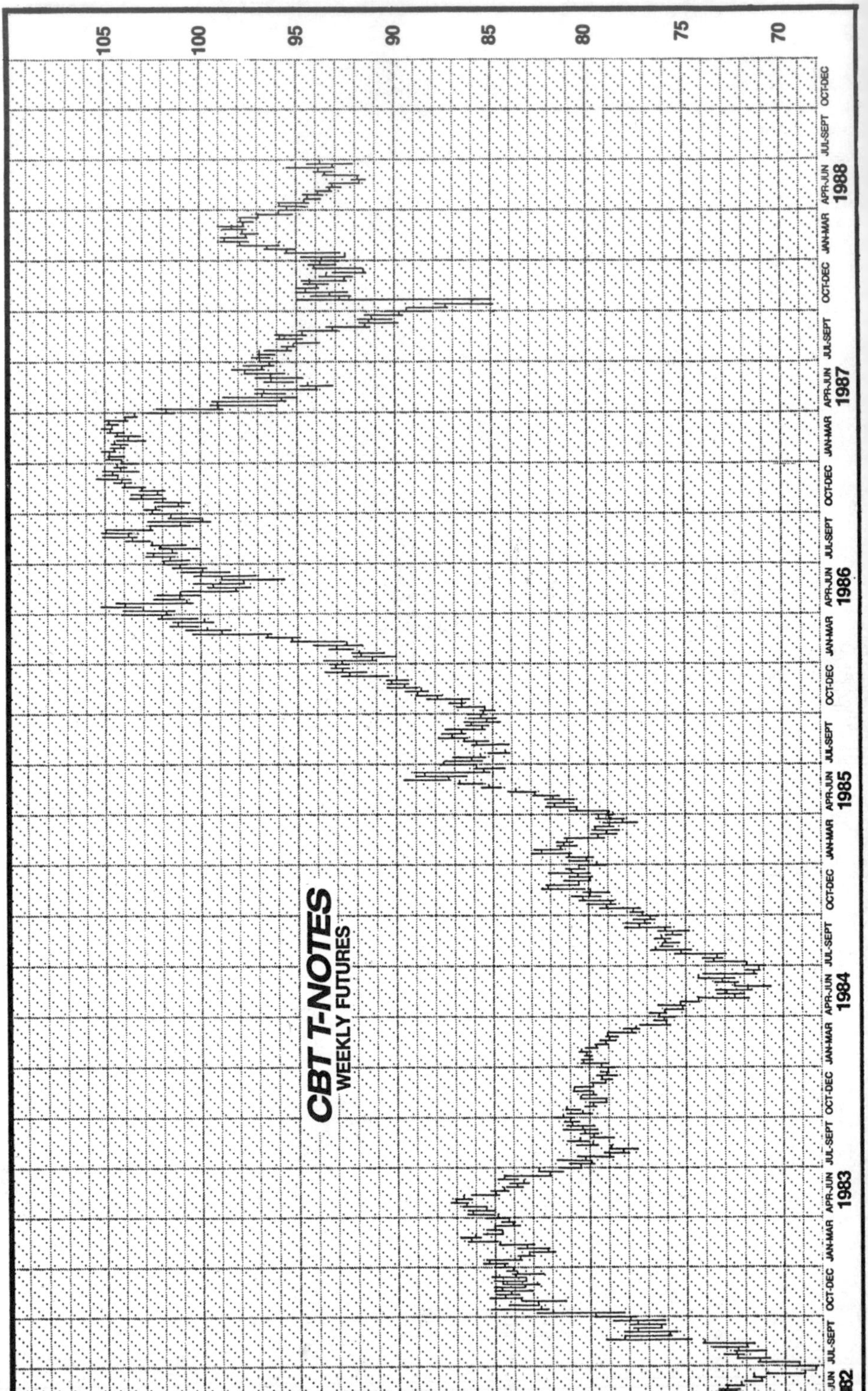
CBT T-NOTES
WEEKLY FUTURES
105
100
95
90
85
80
75
70
APR-JUN JUL-SEPT OCT-DEC JAN-MAR APR-JUN JUL-SEPT OCT-DEC JAN-MAR APR-JUN JUL-SEPT OCT-DEC JAN-MAR APR-JUN JUL-SEPT OCT-DEC JAN-MAR APR-JUN JUL-SEPT OCT-DEC JAN-MAR APR-JUN JUL-SEPT OCT-DEC JAN-MAR APR-JUN JUL-SEPT OCT-DEC
1982
1983
1984
1985
1986
1987
1988

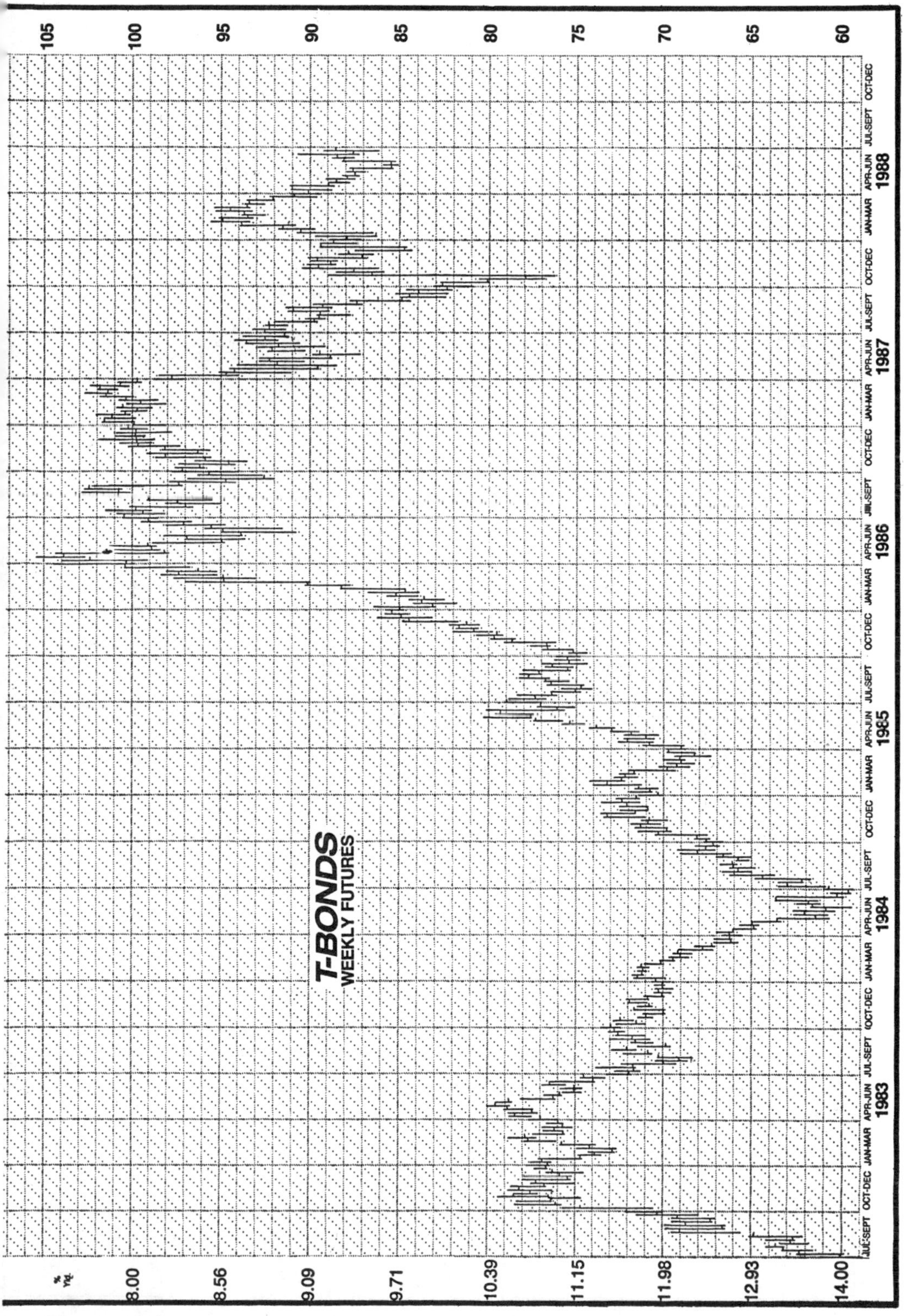
T-BONDS
WEEKLY FUTURES
105
100
95
90
85
80
75
70
65
60
% Yld.
8.00
8.56
9.09
9.71
10.39
11.15
11.98
12.93
14.00
1983
1984
1985
1986
1987
1988

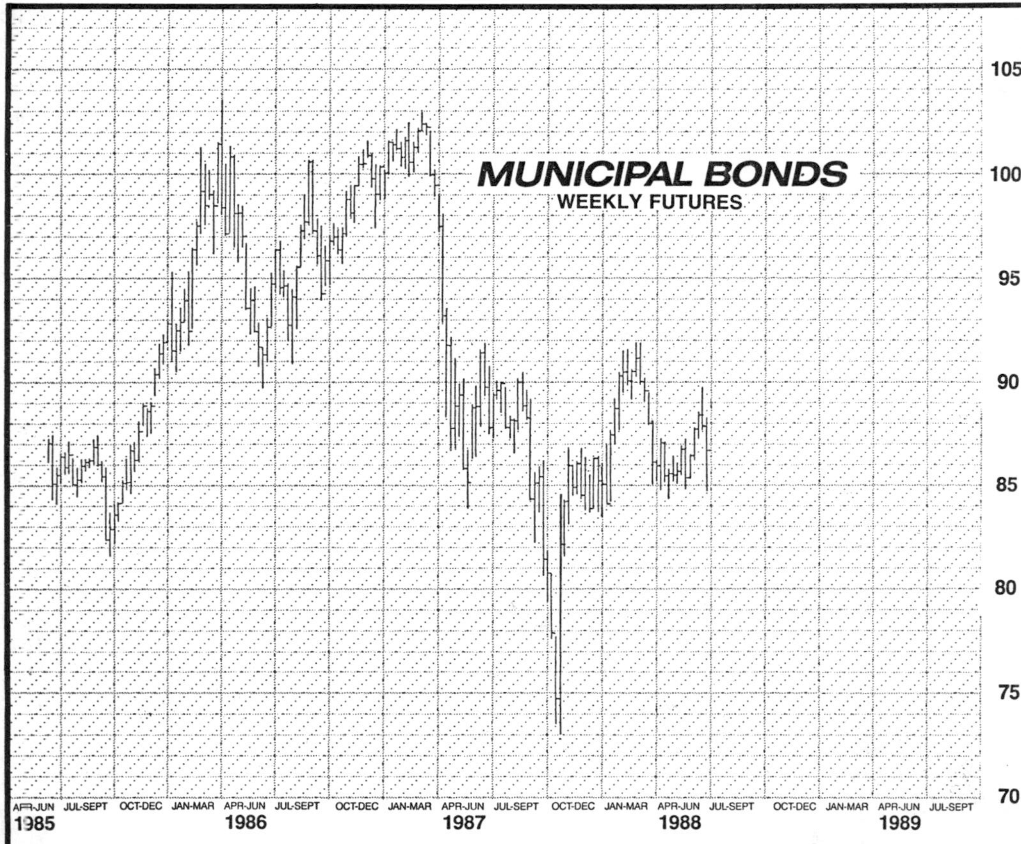

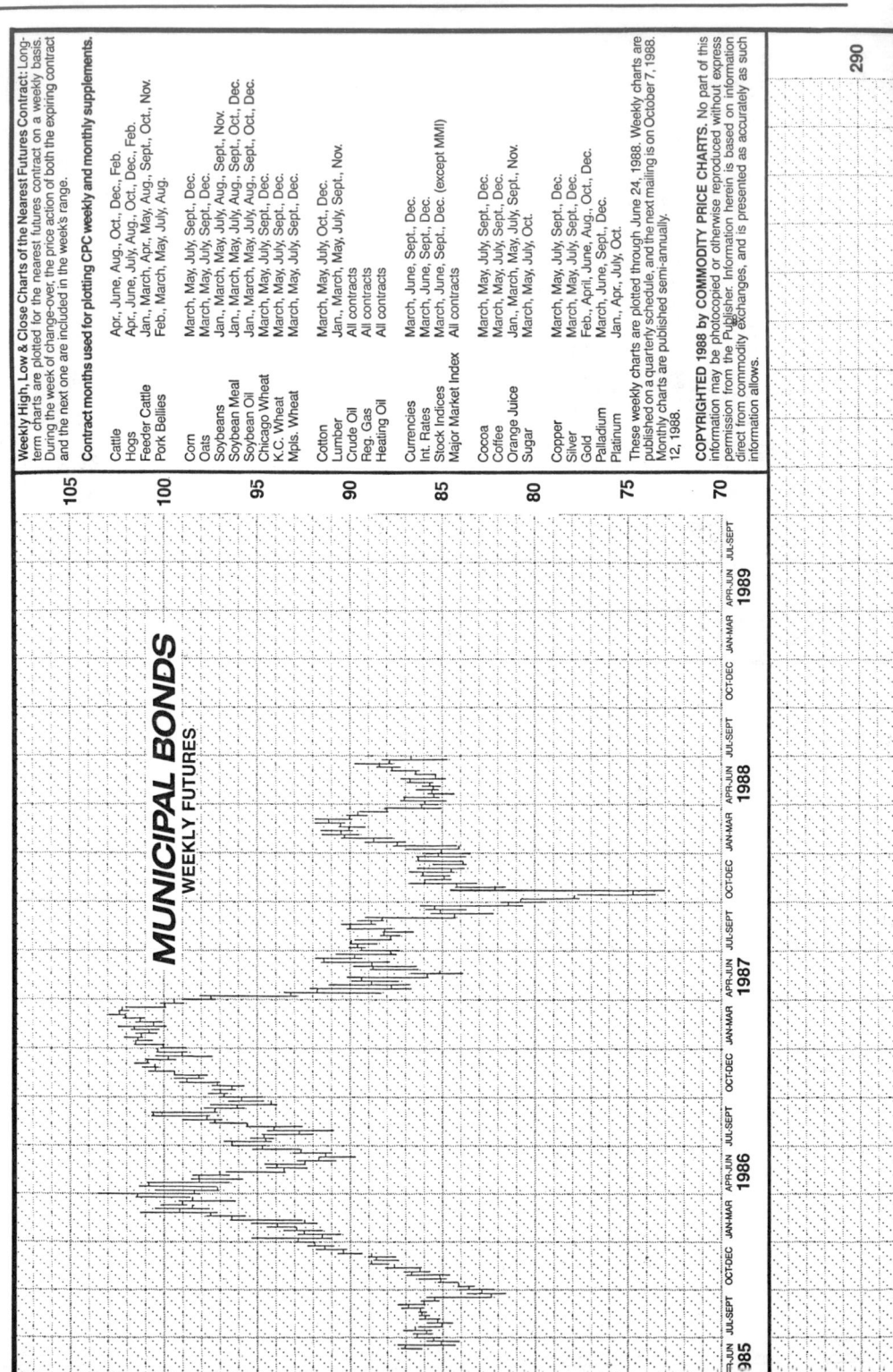

Weekly High, Low & Close Charts of the Nearest Futures Contract: Long-term charts are plotted for the nearest futures contract on a weekly basis. During the week of change-over, the price action of both the expiring contract and the next one are included in the week's range.

Contract months used for plotting CPC weekly and monthly supplements.

Cattle	Apr., June, Aug., Oct., Dec., Feb.
Hogs	Apr., June, July, Aug., Oct., Dec., Feb.
Feeder Cattle	Jan., March, Apr., May, Aug., Sept., Oct., Nov.
Pork Bellies	Feb., March, May, July, Aug.
Corn	March, May, July, Sept., Dec.
Oats	March, May, July, Sept., Dec.
Soybeans	Jan., March, May, July, Aug., Sept., Nov.
Soybean Meal	Jan., March, May, July, Aug., Sept., Oct., Dec.
Soybean Oil	Jan., March, May, July, Aug., Sept., Oct., Dec.
Chicago Wheat	March, May, July, Sept., Dec.
K.C. Wheat	March, May, July, Sept., Dec.
Mpls. Wheat	March, May, July, Sept., Dec.
Cotton	March, May, July, Oct., Dec.
Lumber	Jan., March, May, July, Sept., Nov.
Crude Oil	All contracts
Reg. Gas	All contracts
Heating Oil	All contracts
Currencies	March, June, Sept., Dec.
Int. Rates	March, June, Sept., Dec.
Stock Indices	March, June, Sept., Dec. (except MMI)
Major Market Index	All contracts
Cocoa	March, May, July, Sept., Dec.
Coffee	March, May, July, Sept., Dec.
Orange Juice	Jan., March, May, July, Sept., Nov.
Sugar	March, May, July, Oct.
Copper	March, May, July, Sept., Dec.
Silver	March, May, July, Sept., Dec.
Gold	Feb., April, June, Aug., Oct., Dec.
Palladium	March, June, Sept., Dec.
Platinum	Jan., Apr., July, Oct.

These weekly charts are plotted through June 24, 1988. Weekly charts are published on a quarterly schedule, and the next mailing is on October 7, 1988. Monthly charts are published semi-annually.
12, 1988.

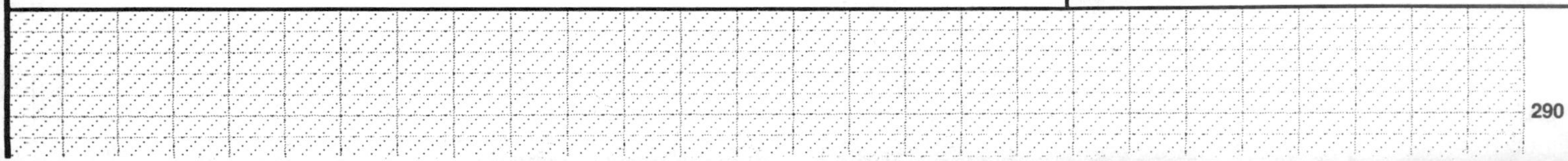

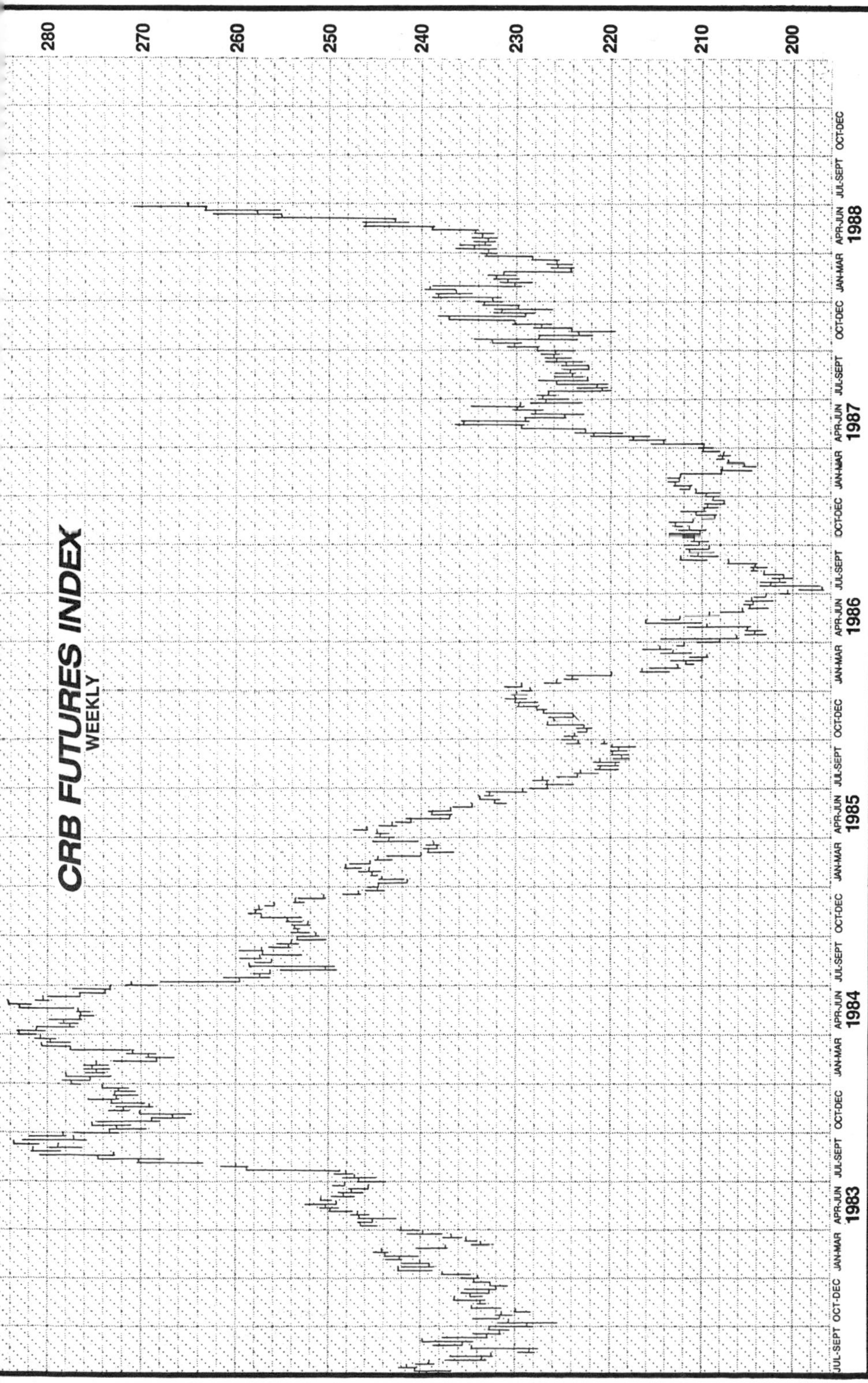

Source: Courtesy of *Commodity Price Charts*, 219 Parkade, Cedar Falls, Iowa 50613.

Taxes

UNDER THE 1986 LAW

Individual Taxation

Basic Rate Structure

The Act replaces the current 14-bracket rate structure, which has rates ranging from 11 to 50 percent, with a five-bracket structure for 1987 and a two-bracket structure for 1988 and later years.

Joint Returns—1987:

Taxable Income	Marginal Tax Rate
0–$ 3,000	11%
$ 3,000– 28,000	15
28,000– 45,000	28
45,000– 90,000	35
90,000 and over	38.5

Joint Returns—1988:

Taxable Income	Marginal Tax Rate
0–$29,750	15%
$29,750 and over	28

Single Returns—1987:

Taxable Income	Marginal Tax Rate
0–$ 1,800	11%
$ 1,800– 16,800	15
16,800– 27,000	28
27,000– 54,000	35
54,000 and over	38.5

Single Returns—1988:

Taxable Income	Marginal Tax Rate
0–$17,850	15%
$17,850 and over	28

For 1988 and later years, the benefit of the 15 percent tax bracket is phased out for higher income individuals and families. The phase out is accomplished by imposing a 5 percent surcharge on taxable income between $71,900 and $149,250 for joint returns and between $43,150 and $89,560 for single individuals. *The surcharge produces the effective marginal tax rate of 33 percent.* For 1987, there is no phase out of the benefits of the lower tax brackets.

For joint returns, the 15 percent tax bracket on the first $29,750 of taxable income saves $3,867.50 in taxes, compared with imposing a 28 percent rate on that income. A 5 percent surcharge on the $77,350 of taxable income between $71,900 and $149,250 will just recapture the $3,867.50. Thus, a taxpayer with $149,250 of taxable income will pay $41,790 in tax, 28 percent of $149,250.

The drop in marginal rates between 1986 and 1987 and between 1987 and 1988 will increase the advantage of deferring income and accelerating deductible expenses. Taxpayers will want to be careful that plans for income deferral do not push the taxpayer into the alternative minimum tax or the limit on investment interest.

Standard Deduction

Under the Act, the zero bracket amount (ZBA) is replaced by a standard deduction. For 1987 and 1988, the standard deduction is as follows:

Filing Status	Standard Deduction 1987	1988
Joint returns	$3,760	$5,000
Heads of households	2,540	4,400
Single individuals	2,540	3,000
Married individuals filing separately	1,880	2,500

Note: The elderly and blind may apply the 1988 standard deductions in 1987.

For those age 65 or over or blind, an extra standard deduction of $600 is allowed an individual if married, or $750 if single. The amounts are indexed for inflation beginning in 1989. These deductions replace the extra personal exemptions which are repealed. For those both elderly and blind, two extra standard deductions are allowed.

Personal Exemption

The Act increases the personal exemption for individuals, spouses, and dependents from its 1986 level of $1,080 to $1,900 for 1987, $1,950 for 1988, and $2,000 for 1989. The $2,000 personal exemption will be indexed for inflation beginning in 1990. The personal exemption is phased out for higher income individuals and families by imposing a 5 percent surcharge on taxable income above specified levels. The phase out begins at taxable income of $149,250 for joint returns, $123,790 for heads of household, $89,560 for single individuals, and $113,300 for married individuals filing separately. The phase out range is $10,920 per exemption in 1988 and $11,200 per exemption in 1989. For a four-person family, the phase out in 1988 ends at $192,930 of taxable income. *During the phase out of personal exemptions, the effective marginal tax rate is 33 percent on additional dollars of income. After personal exemptions are phased out, the marginal tax rate falls to 28 percent.*

In addition, an individual who is eligible to be claimed as a dependent on another taxpayer's return is not permitted a personal exemption. To reduce the number of dependents required to file tax returns and pay tax on small amounts of income, dependents may use up to $500 (reduced first by any earned income) of their standard deduction to offset unearned income.

Chart 1 compares the marginal rate schedules for joint returns for 1986, 1987 and 1988.

The personal exemption and the standard deduction together define the minimum income that an individual may receive without owing federal income tax, as shown in Table 1.

Source: *The Tax Revolution: A New Era Begins* © Deloitte Haskins & Sells, 114 Avenue of the Americas, New York, New York 10036.

Editor's note: Because of changes and modifications in the tax law consult your tax adviser.

PERSONAL INCOME TAXES – MARRIED COUPLES

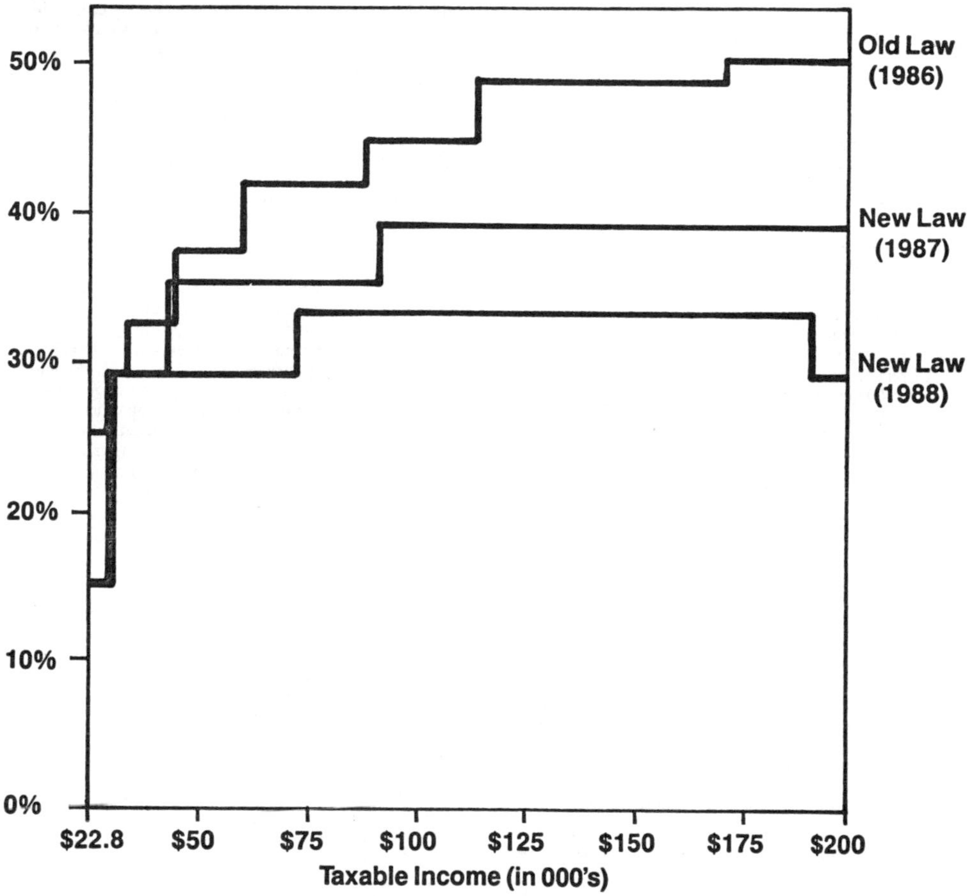

Notes: The rate schedule for 1986 has been adjusted to convert the zero bracket amount into a standard deduction. Also, for 1988, a four-person family is assumed.

Table 1. Income Tax Thresholds in 1987 and 1988

	Prior Law[a]	New Law
1987		
Single, No Dependents	$3,650	$ 4,440
Head of Household, 1 Dependent[b]	4,760	6,340
Married Couple	5,980	7,560
Married Couple, 2 Dependents[b]	8,200	11,360
1988		
Single, No Dependents	$3,700	$ 4,950
Head of Household, 1 Dependent[b]	4,820	8,300
Married Couple	6,060	8,900
Married Couple, 2 Dependents[b]	8,300	12,800

[a]Assumes inflation adjustment of 2.5 percent in 1987 and 4 percent in 1988.
[b]Excludes the effect of the earned income credit.

The dramatic increase in the income tax thresholds will remove 6 million low-income families and individuals from the income tax rolls.

Two-Earner Deduction; Income Averaging

Both the two-earner deduction and income averaging are repealed. *The flatter rate schedule and wider tax brackets reduce the marriage penalty for most two-earner couples and the need for averaging. Because of the phase-outs of the 15 percent tax bracket and personal exemptions, however, some higher-income two-earner families will have a marriage penalty greater than under prior law.*

Individual Capital Gains

The Act repeals the capital gains exclusion for individuals. Capital gains will be taxed at the same rates as other income, but in 1987, the top capital gains rate will be limited to 28 percent by means of an alternative tax computation like the old 25 percent alternative tax repealed in 1978. The Act does not provide for indexing the basis of capital assets.

As full taxation of capital gains does not begin until 1987, taxpayers may want to accelerate into 1986 the realization of long-term gains that otherwise might be realized in 1988 or 1989. But taxpayers probably should not accelerate the realization of gains that otherwise would not be realized for a number of years because the deferral of tax can be more valuable than the lower rate. Also, Congress could once again lower the tax rate on capital gains. If the taxpayer wants to continue to hold an investment, a wash sale to trigger gain in 1986 may still be advisable if the benefit of a lower tax on built-in gain exceeds the income potential for the amount of tax liability triggered in 1986. Brokerage commissions on such wash sales may be lower than on other types of sales.

As with ordinary income, the top marginal rate on capital gains can be as high as 33 percent if the taxpayer is in the 5 percent surcharge range or as high as 49.5 percent if the taxpayer also has real estate losses that are being phased out between $100,000 and $150,000 of income.

The Act does not repeal the concept of capital gains; rather it applies the same rates to capital gains that apply to ordinary income. The present law $3,000 limitation on the deduction of net capital losses is retained, but under the new law, a dollar of capital loss will be able to offset a full dollar of ordinary income up to the $3,000 limit.

The new law applies to gains realized before the effective date but reported on the installment method after the effective date.

Incentive Stock Options
Repeal of the capital gains exclusion will reduce the relative attractiveness of incentive stock options as a compensation technique since gain recognized upon disposition of stock acquired under the options will be taxed at ordinary rates. Nonetheless, the Act limits the granting of ISOs to grants of no more than $100,000 first exercisable in any given year. Restrictions on the order in which ISOs may be exercised are repealed. Given repeal of capital gains, no incentive exists to hold stock after exercise. Taxpayers will want to delay exercise until close to expiration or the time they wish to sell.

Exclusions from Income

The Act modifies a variety of the exclusions from income provided under prior law. Under the Act, unemployment compensation is fully taxed, the $100/$200 dividend exclusion is repealed, awards for artistic, scientific and charitable achievement are taxed unless assigned to a charity, and employee productivity awards are treated as compensation. The exclusion for scholarships is limited to the amount of tuition and course-required fees, books and supplies awarded to degree candidates (effective for taxable years beginning on or after January 1, 1987 for awards granted on or after August 16, 1986). The employee educational assistance exclusion is extended through 1987 and the limit is increased to $5,250. The dependent care assistance exclusion is limited to $5,000 ($2,500 for married filing separately). Finally, the pre-paid legal services exclusion is extended through 1987.

Itemized and Other Deductions

Medical Expenses and Health Insurance
The floor under the medical expense deduction is increased from 5 to 7.5 percent of the taxpayer's adjusted gross income. The Act permits self-employed individuals to deduct 25 percent of the amounts paid for health insurance on behalf of the self-employed individuals (but not in excess of self-employment income) and dependents, if such individuals are not eligible to participate in an employer-subsidized health plan. The provision is effective for taxable years beginning in 1987, 1988, and 1989.

State and Local Taxes
The itemized deduction for state and local sales taxes is repealed. *Taxpayers will want to consider accelerating planned major purchases into 1986 so as to preserve the sales tax deduction.* However, sales taxes (and other nonfederal taxes) which are not allowed as an itemized deduction and which are attributable to the purchase of property are added to the basis of such property. The deduction for state and local income and property taxes is unchanged.

Interest Expense
The Act disallows any deduction for personal interest (such as interest on credit card debt for personal expenses, automobile loans, and tax deficiencies). Mortgage interest on the taxpayer's principal and one other residence is deductible to the extent the mortgage does not exceed the cost of the home plus improvements. Interest on additional mortgage indebtedness (up to fair market value) incurred for qualified educational or medical expenses can also be deducted. In addition, investment interest may be deducted only to the extent of investment income. This latter limitation is discussed below in the section on "Tax Shelters and Real Estate."

These interest limitation rules will place a premium on the characterization of interest expenses. For example, taxpayers in the past may have treated interest used to fund investments or to buy into a business venture as personal interest. Under the new law, care should be taken to create a record establishing the link between a business or investment and related debt. For example, business expenses could be financed through credit card debt while the charges on a separate card used for personal purposes are paid currently.

Taxpayers who have outstanding disputes with the IRS will want to consider their options either to settle the case or to pay tax and sue for a refund before the interest with respect to the disputed liability becomes nondeductible.

Special effective date. — The disallowance of personal interest is phased in over five years starting in 1987. In 1987, 35 percent of previously deductible interest is non-deductible. Interest on mortgage debt incurred prior to August 17, 1986, is not subject to the limitation relating to purchase price plus improvements. The disallowance increases to 60 percent in 1988, 80 percent in 1989, 90 percent in 1990, and 100 percent in later years. *The limitations on mortgage interest to an amount not exceeding the interest on the purchase price and cost of improvements may adversely affect .axpayers who refinanced homes to pull out post-acquisition appreciation after August 16, 1986.*

Charitable Deduction
For taxpayers who itemize, the deduction for charitable contributions is unchanged except the cost of certain charitable travel is no longer deductible. Also, untaxed appreciation on charitable gifts is included in the base of the alternative minimum tax. The charitable deduction for non-itemizers is allowed to expire after 1986, as was scheduled under prior law. *Many charities are concerned that the steep decline in rates and the attendant increase in the tax cost of philanthropy will reduce charitable giving.*

Casualty and Theft Losses
The Act retains the prior law treatment for casualty and theft losses except under the new law taxpayers must file timely insurance claims. *Thus, if a taxpayer fails to pursue a claim for fear of a rate increase, no deduction is allowed.*

Treatment of Losses on Deposits in Insolvent Financial Institution
The Act permits individuals to deduct losses on deposits in qualified bankrupt or insolvent financial institutions as a

casualty loss in the year in which the loss can reasonably be estimated.

Special effective date. — Taxable years beginning after 1982. *Taxpayers who experienced qualified losses in prior years should consider filing amended returns.*

Employee Business Expenses and Miscellaneous Deductions
Under the Act, employee business expenses (other than those that are reimbursed) are permitted only as itemized deductions. Furthermore, the itemized deductions for unreimbursed business expenses and miscellaneous deductions are allowed only to the extent they exceed 2 percent of adjusted gross income.

Some employee business expenses and miscellaneous deductions are deductible as itemized deductions but not subject to the 2 percent floor: (1) moving expenses, (2) certain work expenses incurred by handicapped employees, (3) estate taxes incurred as a result of a decedent's income, (4) amortizable bond premiums, (5) interest expenses of short sales, (6) certain expenses incurred by cooperative housing corporations, (7) amounts included in the prior year's gross income because taxpayer was deemed to have unrestricted rights, (8) certain terminated annuity payments, and (9) gambling losses to the extent of gambling winnings.

Expenses for Travel and Entertainment
Deductions for meal and entertainment expenses are limited to 80 percent of the amount incurred. Those expenses not subject to the 80 percent limit on deductibility include items taxed as compensation to the recipient; expenditures for which the taxpayer receives reimbursement (the 80 percent limit is applied to the party reimbursing the taxpayer); recreational expenses paid on behalf of the employees; items made available to the general public; or banquet expenses in 1987 and 1988 with respect to a legitimate business purpose.

Meals
The Act increased the requirements for the deductibility of business meals to conform with current rules for the deductibility of entertainment expenses. Under these rules, business meals are deductible only if (1) business is discussed before, during, or after the meal (except for an individual eating alone), and (2) the meal has a clear business purpose directly related to the active conduct of the taxpayer's trade or business.

Entertainment
The Act imposes special restrictions on certain entertainment expenses. Specifically, the deduction for ticket cost is limited to 80 percent of face value. However, a premium added to the cost of sports tickets for charitable fundraising events is deductible.

Deductions for the rental or use of a luxury skybox at a sports arena, if used by the taxpayer for more than one event, are also limited to 80 percent of the cost of regular tickets. The disallowance of the skybox deduction is phased in during taxable years beginning in 1987 and 1988 with one-third disallowed in 1987 and two-thirds disallowed in 1988. In addition, deductions for luxury water transportation are limited to twice the highest Federal per diem for U.S. travel, times the number of days in transit.

Travel
The Act eliminates deductions for expenses incurred for (1) travel as a form of education, (2) charitable travel that serves personal, recreational, or vacation purposes, or (3) the expenses of attending a convention or seminar for investment purposes.

Two Percent Floor
Otherwise allowable travel, meals, and entertainment expenses will be aggregated with miscellaneous deductions and subject to the 2 percent of AGI floor. As a result, the taxpayer may not be able to fully utilize the 80 percent deduction for meals and entertainment expenses.

Other Individual Changes
The Act also

- repeals the deduction for certain adoption expenses
- repeals the credit for political contributions
- allows ministers and military personnel a full deduction for mortgage interest and real property taxes
- makes permanent the special filing status rule for spouses of MIAs
- increases the earned income credit
- tightens the hobby loss and home office deduction rules.

Individual Income Tax Effective Dates

Except where otherwise explicitly noted, the changes made to the individual income tax are effective for taxable years beginning after 1986.

Income Shifting and Trusts and Estates

Income Shifting
The Act substantially restricts a parent's ability to lower the effective tax rate on investment income by transferring assets to a child. Specifically, the net unearned income of a child under age 14 is taxed to the child as if it were the parent's income. The tax is calculated by determining what the parent's tax would have been if the child's net unearned income were added to the parent's taxable income. As a result, the child's income may be subject to the 5 percent surcharge effecting a phase out of lower bracket and personal exemption benefits. An exception is provided for the first \$500 of taxable, unearned income. A dependent is also allowed to use the greater of \$500 of the standard deduction or the amount of allowable deductions which are directly connected with the production of the unearned income to offset unearned income. *Thus, effectively, a child may have up to \$1,000 or more if allowable deductions exceed \$500 of unearned income before tax is imposed at the parent's rates.* The child's earned income and the first \$500 of taxable, unearned income are taxed to the child at the child's marginal tax rate.

Effective date. — Taxable years beginning after date of enactment. No relief is provided for income attributable to assets previously transferred to children.

Trusts
The rate structure for non-grantor trusts is revised to reduce the benefits derived from income-splitting. Specifically, the first \$5,000 of taxable income of the trust is taxed at 15 percent. Any excess is taxed at 28 percent. In addition, the benefit of the 15 percent rate is phased out between \$13,000 and \$26,000 of such income.

Prior law provided a rather complex set of rules requiring the person who created a trust to pay tax on the income of that trust (commonly referred to as the grantor trust rules). The Act amends existing rules to classify as grantor trusts two special trusts which previously escaped these provisions — the Clifford Trust and the Spousal Remainder Trust. A Clifford Trust or Spousal Remainder Trust allowed the shifting of income to the trust or a beneficiary. After the trust terminated, the trust property was returned to the grantor or the grantor's spouse. The Act provides that income from transfers after March 1, 1986, which will revert to either the grantor or his spouse will be taxed at the grantor's tax rates if, as of the inception of the trust, the revisionary interest exceeds 5 percent of the value of such trust. Thus, the Clifford Trust and Spousal Remainder Trust will cease to be viable income shifting techniques.

All trusts, other than tax exempt trusts and wholly charitable trusts, must adopt a calendar year as their taxable year. In addition, trusts are now required to pay estimated taxes in the same manner as individuals.

Estates
Under the Act, the undistributed income of estates is taxed at the same rates as are applicable to trusts. In addition, the Act now requires estates to make estimated income tax payments. However, there is an exception which provides that estates are not required to pay estimated taxes for their first two taxable years. Any amount not paid as estimated taxes may no longer be paid in four quarterly installments, but must be paid in full on the due date of the estate's income tax return.

Effective dates. – The rate changes are effective on July 1, 1987. 1987 returns will use a schedule that blends the old and new rates. The changes in grantor trust rules are generally effective for transfers in trust made after March 1, 1986. The change in taxable year rules is effective beginning after December 31, 1986. Net income distributed to beneficiaries in a short taxable year is included in the beneficiary's income over a four-year period. The requirement that trusts and estates pay estimated taxes is effective after December 31, 1986.

Generation-Skipping Transfer Tax
The Act imposes a simplified, flat rate tax on generation-skipping transfers, including direct generation-skipping transfers. However, a skip to a grandchild whose parent was a direct descendant of the transferor, but is deceased at the time of transfer, is not treated as a generation-skipping transfer. The new rate is equal to the maximum estate and gift tax rate. The present credit and grandchild exclusion are replaced by a $1 million exemption per transferor. Additional exemptions are provided for aggregate transfers of up to $2 million per grandchild for direct skips prior to January 1, 1990. In addition, a credit equal to 5 percent of state taxes on generation-skipping transfers is permitted against the generation-skipping transfer tax.

Effective date. – Testamentary transfers occurring after enactment and inter vivos transfers after September 25, 1985. The present generation-skipping transfer tax is repealed retroactively to June 11, 1976.

Compliance and Tax Administration

Information Reporting
The Act imposes new reporting requirements on real estate transactions, awards of federal contracts, and royalty payments beginning in 1987. For real estate transactions, gross proceeds and other information generally must be reported by the person responsible for closing the transaction, such as the attorney. For federal contracts, the executive agency awarding the contract must report the award.

Individuals filing returns must report the social security number of claimed dependents who are at least 5 years old (beginning in 1987) and the amount of tax-exempt interest received (beginning in 1988).

Penalties Relating to Information Returns. – The maximum penalty for failure to file information returns or supply copies is raised from $50,000 to $100,000 for each category of failure. In addition, the Act imposes a new $5 penalty per return for failure to include correct information on an information return or copy required after 1986. The maximum penalty is $20,000 in any calendar year, except for cases of intentional disregard.

Penalties

Fraud and Negligence. – The Act expands the scope of the negligence penalty by making it applicable to all Internal Revenue taxes and to any failures to properly report an amount shown on an information return. The negligence penalty applies to the entire amount of the underpayment, not just the portion of the underpayment attributable to negligence. The component which bears interest is not changed.

The fraud penalty is increased from 50 to 75 percent and restricted to the amount of underpayment attributable to fraud. The component of the fraud penalty which bears interest is not altered.

Beginning in 1987, various other penalties are increased as follows:

- from 1/2 a percent a month to 1 percent a month per month after notice of levy for failure to pay
- from 10 to 20 percent for substantial understatements
- from $50 to $250 for failure to report tax shelter ID numbers
- to 1 percent of amounts invested for failure to register a shelter.

Interest Rates

For periods after December 31, 1986, the new law provides that the interest rate that Treasury pays to taxpayers on overpayments is the federal short-term rate plus two percentage points. The interest rate that the taxpayers pay to Treasury is the federal short-term rate plus three percentage points.

The special higher interest rate on tax shelter deficiencies (120 percent of the otherwise applicable rate) is extended to tax motivated shams or fraudulent transactions.

Interest is imposed on the accumulated earnings tax from the due date (without regard to extensions) of the income tax return for the year the tax is initially imposed.

Estimated Tax Payments by Individuals
For taxable years beginning after 1986, the individual estimated tax payment requirement is increased from 80 percent to 90 percent of the portion of the current year's tax liability. The alternative test of 100 percent of the preceding year's liability remains unchanged. Under the new law, quarterly estimated payments must be made for the unrelated business income tax and the excise tax on private foundations.

Under the Act, authority is granted to the IRS to suspend various administrative actions and abate interest in specific cases.

Tax Shelters and Real Estate

The new law severely restricts the benefits of tax shelters by imposing new limitations on the utilization of passive losses to shelter non-passive income, by tightening the limitations on the deductibility of investment interest expense, and by cutting back on the deductions and credits that give rise to tax shelters. For taxpayers with significant investments in tax shelters, timely planning for the new system of income taxation will be especially critical.

Passive Loss Limitations

The most significant attempt to eliminate investments in tax shelters is a provision of the Act limiting the ability of individuals to offset losses or credits from "passive" trade or business activities against "active" or "portfolio" income under both the regular tax and the minimum tax. Items of income or loss are assigned to the "passive," "active" or "portfolio" categories by reference to the nature of the activity the taxpayer engaged in to generate the particular item.

Limitation of Passive Losses and Credits
The passive loss limitation does not disallow losses and credits from passive activities but, rather, determines how and when the losses and credits can be claimed by a taxpayer. Losses from a passive activity are deductible only against income from that or another passive activity. Unused or "suspended" losses can be carried forward (but not back) indefinitely and can be used to offset passive income realized by the taxpayer in subsequent years. Taxpayers are allowed to apply prior-year suspended passive losses against current year passive income prior to the application of net operating loss carryovers or other losses from non-passive activities.

The determination of whether a loss is suspended under the passive loss limitation is made after the application of the at-risk rules and most other provisions relating to the measurement of taxable income.

Any interest expense and income attributable to a passive activity will generally be subject to the passive loss limitation and will not be subject to the limitation on investment interest. Interest on debt secured by a taxpayer's principal or second residence will not be subject to the passive loss limitation.

Credits generated by passive activities are generally treated in the same manner as losses and can only be used against the tax attributable to such activities. Credits, like losses, can be carried forward indefinitely. However, once a credit becomes allowable under the passive loss rule it is aggregated with other credits for purposes of determining whether it is subject to other limitations (e.g., the 75 percent tax liability limitation).

A taxable disposition by a taxpayer of the entire interest in a passive activity will trigger the recognition of any suspended losses attributable to that activity. The Act provides an election for property used in the activity if the basis thereof was reduced by a tax credit. Upon final disposition, the taxpayer may elect to increase the basis of the credit property (by an amount not exceeding the original basis reduction) to the extent the credit has yet to be allowed under the passive loss rules. Exchanges of a taxpayer's entire interest in an activity in a nonrecognition transaction will not trigger suspended losses.

The passive loss limitation applies to individuals, estates, trusts, and most personal service corporations. A modified form of the rule also applies to closely held corporations. Although these corporations may offset passive losses and credits against active trade or business income, the losses may not be offset against portfolio income earned by the corporation. If an affiliated group of closely held corporations files a consolidated return, the passive loss rules will be applied on a consolidated basis whereby the passive losses of one group member may be offset against the passive income of another member. The limitation is applied at the shareholder level of S corporations and will focus upon the participation of the shareholders in the business activity of the S corporation.

Definition of Passive Activity
A passive activity generally involves the conduct of a trade or business. If the taxpayer investing in that trade or business does not materially participate in the conduct of the activity, the investment is "passive." Whether an activity constitutes a passive activity must be determined separately for each taxpayer holding an interest in the activity and for each separate activity in which a taxpayer holds an interest.

Generally, rental activities with respect to real or personal property will be treated as passive activities without regard to whether the taxpayer materially participates in the activity. However, activities in which substantial services are provided, such as operating a hotel or other transient lodging facility or daily equipment rentals, do not come within this presumption that an activity is passive. In addition, the activities of a dealer in real estate are not generally treated as a rental activity.

The Act establishes a conclusive presumption that a taxpayer holding a limited partnership interest in an activity does not materially participate in that activity. Thus, income and losses attributable to a limited partnership interest will be classified as passive (with an exception for oil and gas working interests).

The new passive loss provisions should increase the number of real estate syndications structured to produce passive activity income. The real estate in these limited partnerships will be purchased with little or no debt. Taxpayers should determine what their present passive income or loss position will be for 1987 and subsequent years before making any investment decisions as to purchases or sales of limited partnership interests or interests in real estate.

Active Income or Loss
Salaries and income or loss from the conduct of a trade or business in which the taxpayer materially participates are classified as "active" under the Act. The material participation of a taxpayer in an activity is determined separately for each year the taxpayer holds an interest in the trade or business. When determining whether an activity (other than a rental activity) conducted by a closely held consolidated group is active, the material participation test is applied on a group basis and will take into account material participation by shareholders. A taxpayer must be involved in the operations of the activity on a regular, continuous, and substantial basis to be a material participant therein. In determining material participation, the performance of management functions is treated no differently than the rendering of physical labor or other types of services. Providing legal, tax, or accounting services to an activity that does not involve the providing of such services, by itself, generally will not be viewed as a material participation in such activity.

Portfolio Income and Expense
The Act provides that portfolio income is not passive income and thus may not be sheltered by passive losses and credits. Dividends on stock, REIT dividends, interest, royalties, income from annuities, RICs and REMICs (explained below), and gain or loss realized on the sale of properties providing such income are portfolio income or loss. However, income

attributable to the business of a partnership, or an S corporation, or to a lease of property is not treated as portfolio income. Any portfolio income earned by a passive activity must be accounted for separately from the other items of income or expense relating to the activity. Consequently, dividends and interest earned by a limited partnership will be separately stated and represent portfolio income of the partners.

Portfolio income is reduced by the deductible expenses (other than interest) that are clearly and directly allocable to such income. Interest expenses that are properly allocable to portfolio income will also reduce the amount thereof. Such deductions will not be attributed to a passive activity.

The legislative history states that the gain from the disposition of a passive activity is passive activity income. Conference language does not state whether the interest income received on an installment sale of a passive activity will be treated as portfolio income or passive activity income. This determination will be extremely important to holders of installment notes from current or prior years' sales of passive activities, partners in partnerships that hold installment notes, or taxpayers who own real estate directly or indirectly through limited partnerships.

Rental Real Estate Activity

As previously indicated, rental activities are treated as passive without regard to whether the taxpayer materially participates in the activity. However, the Act provides some relief by allowing individuals to offset up to $25,000 of nonpassive income with losses from rental real estate activities in which the taxpayer "actively participates." The $25,000 allowance is applied by first netting income and loss from all of the rental real estate activities the taxpayer actively participates in. This relief provision will apply only if the individual does not have adequate net passive income from other sources against which the losses and credits from the rental real estate activity can be fully offset.

The $25,000 allowance is reduced by 50 percent of the amount by which the taxpayer's adjusted gross income for the year (exclusive of passive losses, IRA contributions and taxable social security benefits) exceeds $100,000. Thus, the $25,000 allowance is eliminated for taxpayers with at least $150,000 of adjusted gross income. For a married taxpayer filing separately, the allowance is $12,500 and is reduced by 50 percent of adjusted gross income in excess of $50,000. However, if married individuals live together at any time during the taxable year and file separately, the $25,000 allowance is not available.

A taxpayer will not be considered an active participant in an activity unless the taxpayer and the taxpayer's spouse own at least 10 percent (by value) of all interest in such activity. In addition, the taxpayer must actively participate in the management of the real estate by making management decisions or arranging for others to provide services (such as repairs) in a significant sense. Relevant management decisions would include approving new tenants, determining rental terms, approving capital or repair expenditures, and other similar decisions. The standard of "actively participates" is not as tough to meet as "materially participates." Nevertheless, a limited partner in such an activity will generally not be treated as meeting the active participation standard.

The Act also contains an exception for rehabilitation and low income housing credits regardless of the taxpayer's level of participation in the passive activity. These credits can be offset against the tax on up to $25,000 of non-passive income.

This exception is phased out as a taxpayer's adjusted gross income (exclusive of passive losses, IRA contributions and taxable social security benefits) increases from $200,000 to $250,000. This exception is available only to the extent nonpassive income has not been offset with $25,000 of losses from rentals of real estate in which the taxpayer actively participated.

Working Interest in Oil and Gas Property

The passive loss limitation does not apply to a working interest in an oil and gas property.

Effective Date. – The passive loss limitation is effective for tax years beginning after 1986. The rule applies to all losses incurred on or after that date (without regard to when the activity was entered into) and to passive activity credits for property placed in service on or after that date. The Act does, however, contain a specific phase-in rule for passive activities that were entered into prior to the date of enactment of the Act or acquired pursuant to a contract to purchase that was binding on that date. Losses and credits attributable to those activities will be allowed against non-passive income in accordance with the following percentages:

Taxable Years Beginning In:	Percentage Allowed
1987	65%
1988	40
1989	20
1990	10
1991	0

Passive losses that are disallowed during the transitional period must be carried forward to the succeeding year. However, once carried forward, a passive loss is no longer eligible to be deducted under the transitional rule and can be offset only against net passive income during the succeeding years. The phase-in rules do not apply to application of the passive loss limitations for minimum tax purposes.

The Act also contains a specific transitional rule for investments in low-income housing that were made after 1983. Losses from that activity may be exempted from the passive loss limitation for a period up to seven years from the original investment in the low income housing.

Investment Interest Limitations

The Act generally limits the amount of nonbusiness interest a taxpayer can deduct. The disallowance of personal interest deductions and the limitations on mortgage interest deductions are discussed above under individual taxation.

The deduction for investment interest is limited to the amount of net investment income. Any disallowed investment interest expense may be carried forward indefinitely. Investment interest includes all interest (other than consumer interest and mortgage interest on the taxpayer's principal or second home) on debt not incurred in connection with the taxpayer's trade or business.

Net investment income is the excess of investment income over investment expense. The current definition of net investment income is expanded to include gain or loss from the disposition of investment property, and from a limited business interest. Investment expense is determined by using the amount of depreciation and depletion the taxpayer actually utilizes. Interest (and income) from any activity that is subject to the passive loss rules is not treated as investment interest (or investment income). However, to the extent that passive losses are allowed as a deduction under the passive loss phase-in rule, they must be subtracted from net investment income.

Effective Date. – Interest paid or incurred after 1986 regardless of when the debt arose. The new interest expense limitations are phased in over a five-year period. The phase-in generally applies to interest that would not have been disallowed under prior law, whereupon the taxpayer is allowed to deduct a portion of the newly disallowed interest. The percentages for the phase-in period are the same as those used for the phase-in of the passive loss limitation (see previous discussion).

Vacation Homes

Section 280A limits the amount an individual may deduct for expenses attributable to the rental of a vacation home whenever the personal use thereof exceeds the greater of 14 days or 10 percent of the number of days during the year for which the dwelling is rented at a fair rental. Under the limitation, deductions attributable to the rental of a vacation home cannot exceed rental income. Section 280A, however, does not limit deductions for interest or taxes. Disallowed expenses cannot be carried forward for use in future years but are instead lost forever.

The Act provides that rental activities, including the rental of a vacation home, by an individual are subject to the passive loss limitations. It also provides that all qualified interest on first and second residences is fully deductible without limitation. For a vacation home to qualify as a residence, the taxpayer's personal use of the dwelling must be extensive enough to cause the section 280A limitation to apply. Whether a taxpayer should cause a vacation home to be a second residence will require careful analysis.

If the taxpayer is not concerned with the passive loss rules because of high passive income or eligibility for the $25,000 loss exception, vacation home classification will never provide an advantage. If the passive loss rules limit a taxpayer's deductions, deliberately falling into the vacation home rules may be advantageous because all of the interest can be deducted under the second residence mortgage exception as well as those taxes allocable to personal use. However, this advantage must be offset by the permanent loss, rather than suspension, of certain deductible expenses such as those incurred for insurance, utilities, maintenance and repairs.

At-Risk Rules

The Act extends the at-risk rules of prior law to real estate activities but provides exceptions for qualified nonrecourse financing. These rules will be significant, notwithstanding the passive activity loss rules, since the at-risk rules apply first. If the at-risk rules limit a loss, it will not be available even though the taxpayer has excess passive income.

Effective date. – Property placed in service after December 31, 1986, and losses attributable to an interest in a partnership or S corporation or other pass-through entity acquired after that date.

Tax Credit for Rehabilitation Expenditures

The Act reduces the credit for rehabilitating certified historic structures from 25 percent to 20 percent and requires a full basis adjustment for the amount of the credit. For non-historic structures, a single 10 percent credit is provided for rehabilitation of structures originally placed in service before 1936. *Although historic rehabilitations will now be one of the few clear tax shelter opportunities, application of the passive loss limitations and the minimum tax will adversely affect many of these projects.*

Effective dates. – Property placed in service after 1986.

Real Estate Investment Trusts

The Act liberalizes the rules relating to REITs to provide greater flexibility in their use. In general, entities may elect REIT status, even though they failed to qualify in an earlier year, provided they have been treated as a REIT for all taxable years beginning after February 28, 1986, or have no accumulated earnings and profits for pre-REIT years. REITs may now have wholly owned subsidiaries and treat the assets, liabilities, deductions and income of a subsidiary as belonging to the REIT. The definition of "rents from real property and interest" is expanded to allow the REIT to provide services in connection with rentals, and the minimum distribution requirements are liberalized for accrued and unpaid original issue discount. The Act also provides more generous safe harbors under the prohibited transaction rules.

Effective date. – Taxable years beginning after 1986.

Cooperative Housing Corporations

Under the Act, individuals, corporations, trusts, and other taxpayers may be treated as tenant-stockholders in cooperative housing corporations. The Act provides that maintenance and lease expenses are disallowed if payments by tenant stockholders are allocated to amounts properly chargeable to the capital account of the cooperative. Separately allocated amounts of interest and taxes are deductible by the tenant-stockholders when made on a reasonable basis.

Effective date. – Taxable years beginning after 1986.

Multi-Family Residential Rental

The Act replaces prior law incentives for low income housing (preferential depreciation, amortization of rehabilitation expenditures, and special treatment of construction period interest and taxes) with a new tax credit. The Act provides two separate credits that are claimed annually for 10 years. These credits are designed to produce a credit, on a present value basis, of either 70 percent or 30 percent of qualifying expenditures. The 70 percent credit applies to non-subsidized qualifying expenditures for new construction or rehabilitation. The 30 percent credit applies to expenditures for the construction and rehabilitation of low income units financed with tax-exempt bonds and similar federal subsidies or the acquisition and rehabilitation of existing low income housing units.

The new credits are generally effective for property placed in service after December 31, 1986, and before January 1, 1990.

Real Estate Mortgage Investment Conduits

The Act creates a new tax vehicle called a real estate mortgage investment conduit (REMIC) that is intended to facilitate the issuance of mortgage-backed securities. A REMIC is an entity that holds a fixed pool of mortgages and issues multiple classes of interests in itself. A corporation, association, trust or partnership may qualify as a REMIC, if it meets certain requirements and makes a proper election to be treated as such. The assets a REMIC is allowed to hold are generally limited to mortgages secured by real property.

Investments in a REMIC consist of "regular" and "residual" interests. A regular interest entitles the holder to the receipt of a specific sum of money, the timing of which may depend upon prepayment of the mortgages held by the REMIC. A residual interest is any interest other than a regular interest. It involves payments that are contingent upon several factors and more closely resembles an equity interest. A REMIC can only have one class of residual interest and all distributions from that class must be made on a pro rata basis.

Effective date. – Taxable years beginning after December 31, 1986.

Business Income

Corporate Tax Rates

The Act reduces the top corporate tax rate from 46 percent to 34 percent. The graduated rate structure for small companies is also modified so that taxable income of $50,000 and below is taxed at a 15 percent rate and taxable income from $50,000 to $75,000 is taxed at a 25 percent rate. The benefits of the graduated rate structure are phased out as taxable income increases from $100,000 to $335,000 with an effective marginal tax rate of 39 percent in this income range. Corporations with income in excess of $335,000, in effect, will pay a flat tax at a 34-percent rate. The revised corporate rates are fully effective for taxable years beginning on or after July 1, 1987. However, income in taxable years that include July 1, 1987, will be subject to blended rates. A calendar year corporation will have a top rate of 40 percent for 1987, for example. Public utilities must normalize any excess deferred tax reserve resulting from lower corporate tax rates.

Capital Gains
The Act increases the alternative tax on capital gains recognized after 1986 from 28 to 34 percent, which is the same rate that applies to ordinary income after July 1, 1987.

Gain on Disposition
The Act eliminates the recapture of depreciation on the sale of both residential and nonresidential real property. *This will have little significance, as net capital gains will be subject to the 34 percent rate applicable to ordinary income.*

Effective date. – Gains recognized after December 31, 1986.

Investment Tax Credit

The Act repeals the regular investment tax credit (ITC) for property placed in service after December 31, 1985 except for certain transition property (see effective date discussion below). Moreover, for years beginning after December 31, 1986, any ITC allowable either as a credit for transition property or as a carryover credit is reduced by 17 1/2 percent in 1987 and by 35 percent in 1988 and later years. *Taxpayers with an NOL for 1986 may wish to carry the NOL forward rather than back if the result of a carryback would be to create excess credits from prior years which would be cut back when carried forward to subsequent years.*

In addition, the basis of transition property in which an ITC is earned must be adjusted for the entire ITC without regard to the 35 percent reduction in current and carryover credits or any election to claim a reduced credit. The Act continues to apply normalization rules to the unamortized portion of ITCs allowed to public utilities.

Capital Cost Provisions

Capital Cost Recovery Classes
The Act modifies the ACRS system for property placed in service after 1986. Two new ACRS classes are provided and depreciable property is reclassified based generally on the asset depreciation range (ADR) system of pre-1981. The recovery method is double declining balance with switch to straight line for most machinery and equipment.

The new recovery system has eight classes of property as follows:

Recovery Period	Recovery Method	Assets
3-year	Double declining balance	ADR midpoint life of 4 years and less excluding cars and light trucks
5-year	Double declining balance	ADR midpoint life of more than 4 years and less than 10 years plus: cars and light trucks, qualified technological equipment, certain renewable resource property, R&D property
7-year	Double declining balance	ADR midpoint life of 10 years and less than 16 years plus: property without an ADR life
10-year	Double declining balance	ADR midpoint life of 16 years and less than 20 years
15-year	150 percent declining balance	ADR midpoint life of 20 years and less than 25 years plus: sewage plants
20-year	150 percent declining balance	ADR midpoint life of 25 years or more, other than real property with an ADR life of 27.5 or longer
27.5-year	Straight line	Residential rental real estate, elevators, and escalators
31.5-year	Straight line	Other real property

Certain assets are assigned new ADR lives by the Act.

Asset	ADR Life
Semi-conductor manufacturing equipment	5 years
Computer based central office switching equipment	9.5 years
Railroad track	10 years
Single purpose agricultural and horticultural structures	15 years

Asset	ADR Life
Telephone distribution plant and comparable two-way communication equipment	24 years
Municipal waste-water treatment plants	25 years
Sewer pipes	50 years

Generally, the Act permits Treasury to adjust the class lives of assets (other than real estate) based on experience, under factors outlined in the conference agreement. Treasury is prohibited from extending class lives of assets placed in service before 1992. Thereafter, Congress must be notified of any changes.

The Act requires lessees to recover the cost of leasehold improvements over the general recovery periods, without regard to the lease term. For purposes of amortizing leasehold acquisition costs, the lease term includes all renewable options and any reasonably expected renewals.

Conventions. —The Act generally continues the mid-year convention for determining when personal property is placed in service or disposed of and the mid-month convention for real property. In addition, a mid-quarter convention applies if more than 40 percent of all property is placed in service during the last quarter of the taxable year.

Alternative Recovery System

Under the Act, an alternative cost recovery system is prescribed for purposes of applying the minimum tax provisions, computing earnings and profits of a domestic corporation, and computing the depreciation deduction for foreign use and tax-exempt property and property financed through tax-exempt bonds. Satellites launched from the U.S. and used by U.S. persons are not foreign use property. Generally, the applicable depreciation method is straight line, using the asset's ADR midpoint life. However, for purposes of computing the minimum tax, 150 percent declining balance depreciation over ADR midpoint life is used to measure the tax preference on personal property.

For purposes of computing regular depreciation on property otherwise eligible for ACRS, taxpayers may elect either the alternative depreciation system described above or the straight-line method over the ACRS recovery period on a class-by-class, year-by-year basis. The Act grants the President authority to deny a taxpayer the right to use the accelerated depreciation method on property produced abroad. This authority is limited to assets that have not yet been ordered.

Expensing

Taxpayers may elect to expense up to $10,000 of the cost of personal property used in a trade or business provided that the amount expensed does not exceed the income derived from any active trade or business. The $10,000 ceiling is reduced dollar for dollar for taxpayers whose total investment in tangible personal property is greater than $200,000. Furthermore, if the property is converted to non-business use prior to the end of the property's recovery period, the difference between expensing and the allowable ACRS deductions is recaptured.

Effective Dates for Depreciation and ITC

The new depreciation rules are generally effective for assets placed in service after December 31, 1986. A special election is provided to apply the modified depreciation rules to property placed in service after July 31, 1986. In addition, the Act provides anti-churning rules to prevent the use of post-effective-date transactions among related parties to depreciate property placed in service prior to January 1, 1987 under the new depreciation system.

As noted above, the repeal of the *ITC* is generally effective for property placed in service after December 31, 1985.

The Act provides that ACRS will continue to apply and the investment credit will be available for qualifying "transition property." Transition property generally is property which was subject to a binding contract or under construction before 1986 in the case of ITC and before March 1986 in the case of recovery property.

To qualify for transition relief under the Act, transition property must actually be placed in service before specific deadlines which differ for cost recovery and ITC purposes as follows:

ADR Midpoint	Recovery Property	ITC Property
under 5	N/A	July 1, 1986
under 7	N/A	January 1, 1987
under 20	January 1, 1989	January 1, 1989
20 or more	January 1, 1991	January 1, 1991
residential rental	January 1, 1991	N/A
other real property	January 1, 1991	N/A

Limitation on Business Tax Credits

The Act reduces the amount of tax liability (in excess of $25,000) which may be offset by business tax credits from 85 percent to 75 percent. *However, the imposition of a minimum tax, in many instances, will prevent a taxpayer from fully utilizing the available business credit.*

Effective Date. —Taxable years beginning after 1985. *The early effective date of this change will frustrate taxpayers seeking to maximize current use of ITC carryovers before the 35 percent cutback takes effect.*

Treatment of Corporate Distributions

Appreciated Property

The Act generally repeals the limited exceptions to gain recognition on distributions of appreciated property to shareholders in nonliquidating distributions. Thus, the exceptions to gain recognition for certain distributions of appreciated property to 10 percent noncorporate shareholders and distributions in connection with the payment of estate taxes are repealed. The Act also provides that no losses can be recognized on nonliquidating distributions.

Effective date. —Distributions of ordinary income or short-term capital gain property after December 31, 1986 and distributions of other property after December 31, 1988.

Dividends Received Deduction

Under the Act, the 85 percent dividends received deduction is reduced to 80 percent. *Under present law the combination of the 46 percent rate and the 85 percent exclusion produces an effective tax of 6.9 percent on dividends received by corporations. The new rate structure and 80 percent exclusion will yield a 6.8 percent tax.* The 100 percent deduction for qualifying dividends received from affiliates is not affected.

Effective date. —Dividends received after 1986.

Extraordinary Dividends

The Act extends the 1984 Act rules requiring a basis adjustment for the non-taxed portion of extraordinary dividends received by a corporation. The rule now applies to dividends announced or agreed to within two years of acquisition of the stock rather than only those paid within one year of the acquisition. The Act extends the definition of extraordinary dividends to include all non-pro-rata redemptions of stock and distributions in partial liquidation regardless of holding period or size of the distribution. Except as provided in regulations, the extraordinary dividend rules will not apply to distributions between members of an affiliated group filing a consolidated return.

Effective date. —Dividends announced after July 18, 1986, except date of enactment for non-pro-rata redemptions and partial liquidations.

Greenmail Payments

No deduction is allowed for any amount paid or incurred by a corporation in connection with the redemption of its stock.

This rule applies to so-called "greenmail payments." *Any such amounts paid to a selling shareholder in connection with the redemption of stock will not be deductible if paid by the corporation or a related party.*

Effective date. – Payments on or after March 1, 1986.

Liquidating Distributions
The Act generally requires corporate liquidations to be taxed at both the corporate and shareholder levels. A liquidating corporation is required to recognize gain or loss as if its assets were sold at their fair market value. This rule also requires a corporation to recognize full gain on the deemed sale of its assets if an election under section 338 is made to step up the basis of its assets following the purchase of its stock.

The Act prohibits loss recognition on non-pro-rata distributions of property to related persons if the property was acquired as a contribution to capital within five years of the liquidation. Also, a pre-contribution built-in loss may not be recognized on liquidating distribution if the property distributed was acquired as a contribution to capital within two years of the adoption of the plan of liquidation, unless no tax avoidance motive for the contribution can be shown.

The Act furthers the repeal of the "General Utilities Doctrine" begun in the 1982 and 1984 Acts. Basically, the General Utilities Doctrine permitted a corporation non-recognition treatment on distributions to shareholders. As a result of the changes in the Act, the tax cost will rarely make asset acquisitions practical unless the acquisition can qualify under the tax-free reorganization provisions of the Code. Under prior law, the total tax on the liquidation would have been the 20 percent individual tax on the capital gain plus any corporate level recapture tax. Under the Act, the total tax will rise to 52.5 percent – 34 percent at the corporate level plus 18.5 percent (28 percent of 66 percent) at the individual level.

Transition rules preserve corporate level non-recognition treatment for the following transactions involving liquidating distributions:

1. All liquidations completed before January 1, 1987. *This transition rule also includes deemed sales under section 338 even if the election is made in 1987, if the stock purchase occurred prior to January 1, 1987.*
2. Liquidating distributions pursuant to a plan of liquidation adopted before August 1, 1986 if the liquidation is completed prior to January 1, 1988.
3. Liquidating distributions and liquidating sales where there was a binding contract entered into prior to August 1, 1986 to acquire a majority of the liquidating corporation's voting stock or substantially all of its assets, if the liquidation is completed on or before December 31, 1987.
4. Deemed liquidating sales under section 338 relating to stock acquisitions occurring on or after August 1, 1986 and before January 1, 1988 when a binding contract to acquire the stock existed prior to August 1, 1986.
5. Liquidations of closely held companies valued at less than $5 million (with no more than 10 individuals owning more than 50 percent of the stock) completed before January 1, 1989 are provided relief from recognition of gain on long-term capital gain property. There is also partial relief for closely held companies valued between $5 million and $10 million.
6. Liquidations completed before January 1, 1988 in which the company had taken significant action by November 20, 1985 (e.g., the board of directors approved a plan of liquidation or entered into a binding contract to sell substantially all of its assets).

The Act generally retains present law non-recognition treatment for liquidations of a subsidiary corporation into its parent corporation. Gain on distributions of appreciated property to minority shareholders is treated as under the rules for nonliquidating distributions.

The Act provides that if a subchapter S corporation liquidates within 10 years of converting from a subchapter C corporation, it must recognize its aggregate net unrealized gains at the date of the conversion.

Effective date. – Generally, liquidating sales and distributions after July 31, 1986.

Allocation of Purchase Price in Certain Sales of Assets
The Act requires both the buyer and the seller to allocate the purchase price in asset acquisitions using the residual method. Under the residual method, the purchase price is first allocated to the fair market value of tangible and intangible assets and then allocated to the value of goodwill and going concern. In addition, the Act authorizes the Treasury Department to require further information from the parties pertaining to the allocation.

Effective date. – Transactions after May 6, 1986.

Special Limitations on Net Operating Loss (NOL) Carryovers

The NOL carryover limitations adopted in 1976 that would have become effective January 1, 1986 are repealed retroactively. Thus, the NOL rules without the 1976 changes continue to apply for 1986. Starting in 1987, the Act provides that if there is greater than 50 percent ownership change in a loss corporation within a three year period, an annual limit on the use of NOLs will be imposed. The amount of an NOL that may be used to offset earnings is limited to the value of the loss corporation at the date of ownership change multiplied by the highest federal tax-exempt long term bond rate as adjusted for differences between rates on long term taxable and tax exempt obligations in effect during the three-month period ending with the month of ownership change.

The value of a loss corporation is reduced by capital contributions motivated by tax avoidance. Except as specified by regulation, capital contributions made within the two years preceding to the ownership change are presumed to have a tax avoidance motive.

In addition, a loss corporation may not utilize NOL carryovers following taxable purchases and tax-free reorganizations unless it continues substantially the same business for two years after the change in ownership.

Exceptions to the limitations on NOL carryovers are provided for stock acquired by gift, separation, divorce or death. In addition, exceptions are generally provided for acquisitions by ESOPs or ESOP participants if the ESOP owns at least 50 percent of the stock immediately after the transfer.

If the unrealized built-in gains or losses exceed 25 percent of the value of the corporation's assets before the ownership change, then special rules apply. Under these rules, built-in gains recognized within five years of the change may be fully sheltered by carryover NOLs, and built-in losses recognized during this period are treated as pre-change losses. Furthermore, the income against which NOL carryovers can be applied is reduced, if at least one-third of the loss corporation's assets are passive. An exception is provided for both RICs and REITs.

Bankruptcy Proceedings and Stock-for-Debt Exchanges
Special rules apply to NOL carryovers following bankruptcy reorganizations. The Act provides that if the shareholders and creditors of the loss corporation own at least 50 percent of the stock of the loss corporation after bankruptcy proceedings, the change in ownership limitations will not apply. This special rule requires that the debt exchanged for stock be held for an 18-month period prior to filing for bankruptcy

or be incurred in the corporation's ordinary course of business. In any event, the NOL carryover must be reduced by 50 percent of the amount by which the discharged debt exceeds the value of the stock received by the former creditors. A modified version of the bankruptcy exception applies to certain ownership changes of thrift institutions.

Effective Date. – Generally, applies to purchases made after December 31, 1986, and reorganizations pursuant to plans adopted after December 31, 1986.

For purposes of determining if a greater than 50 percent ownership change has occurred under the new rules, less than 50 percent changes in ownership occurring after May 5, 1986, and before January 1, 1987, must be aggregated with post-1986 changes.

Research and Development

The tax credit for eligible research and development expenses is extended through December 31, 1988; however, the present 25 percent tax credit is reduced to 20 percent. In addition, the general limitation on business credits is made applicable to the research credit. The Act modifies the definition of qualified research to target research that is aimed at technical discoveries. The augmented charitable deduction for the donation of newly manufactured scientific equipment to a college is extended to comparable donations to certain tax-exempt scientific research organizations.

The Act also reduces the credit for university basic research from 75 percent of corporate expenditures to 20 percent of the excess of (1) all corporate expenditures for university basic research over (2) the sum of a fixed research floor plus any decrease in nonresearch giving.

The credit for orphan drug clinical testing is extended through 1990.

Effective date. – The research credit is extended for taxable years ending after 1985. The other provisions are effective for taxable years beginning after 1985, except that modifications to the university basic research credit are effective beginning after 1986.

Other Business Changes

The Act also:

- permanently extends the elective deduction for removal of architectural barriers
- repeals elective amortization of trademarks and tradenames, and railroad gradings and tunnel bores
- reduces the depreciation limits on luxury cars to $2,560 for the first year, $4,100 for the second year, $2,450 for the third year, and $1,475 for each succeeding taxable year in the recovery period
- generally treats amortized bond premium as interest expense for all tax purposes
- repeals the exclusion for discharge of indebtedness income of solvent taxpayers which was permitted if an appropriate basis adjustment was made
- expands the definition of related party for purposes of the limits on installment sales reporting on sale of depreciable assets between related parties (effective August 14, 1986, except for binding contracts)
- provides a new simplified LIFO inventory method for taxpayers with less than $5 million in annual gross receipts
- limits the deduction for accrued vacation pay to amounts expected to be paid within 8 1/2 months of year-end
- repeals the special deduction for costs of redeeming "qualified" discount coupons
- retroactively excludes from the definitions of personal holding company income and foreign personal holding company income certain computer software royalties
- repeals the statutory finance lease rules
- generally, the Act scales back the targeted job credit and extends it for three years.

Accounting Methods

Long-Term Contracts

Under the Act, all long-term contracts other than those reported on the percentage of completion method, are subject to a modified form of the rules currently governing extended period long-term contracts. Amounts which must be capitalized include certain interest expense incurred, and costs identified by the taxpayer as being attributable to the contract. For example, general and administrative expenses identified pursuant to a cost-plus contract or pursuant to a contract with a federal agency in which costs are certified under federal statute or regulations must be capitalized regardless of whether such costs may be treated as period costs under existing regulations. However, independent research and development costs are generally not capitalized.

The prior-law completed contract method prescribed by regulations is replaced by a new "percentage of completion – capitalized cost method," which applies to any long-term contracts except certain real property construction contracts discussed below. Under this new method, the taxpayer must take into account 40 percent of the items with respect to the contract under the percentage of completion method; the remaining 60 percent of the items will be taken into account under the taxpayer's normal method of accounting.

Current rules are retained for real property construction contracts not requiring more than two years to complete and performed by a taxpayer with average annual gross receipts of $10 million or less.

Effective date. – Contracts entered into on or after March 1, 1986.

Capitalization Rules for Inventory, Construction, and Development Costs

The Act provides uniform capitalization rules for costs incurred in manufacturing property, constructing property (whether for use in a trade or business or sale to others), or purchasing and holding property for resale. The rules are patterned after the rules applicable to the extended period long-term contracts as set forth in final regulations recently issued by the Internal Revenue Service. Included are all "financial conformity" costs, all tax depreciation, current pension and fringe benefit costs, and a portion of general and administrative expenses.

Costs subject to capitalization for wholesalers and retailers include costs incident to purchasing inventories (e.g., wages of employees responsible for purchasing, repackaging and assembly), costs incurred in processing the goods while the taxpayer is in possession, costs of storing goods (only the *offsite* storage costs of retailers), and the portion of general and administrative costs allocable to these functions.

The Treasury Department is directed to provide a simplified method for applying the uniform capitalization rules to wholesalers and retailers.

In the case of property acquired by a taxpayer for resale, the uniform capitalization rules apply only if the taxpayer's average annual gross receipts for the three preceding taxable years were more than $10 million.

The new capitalization rules do not apply to research and experimental expenditures, to property produced under a long-term contract, or to property produced in a farming business.

The new rules require the capitalization of interest on debt incurred or continued to finance the construction or production of real property, long-lived personal property (a 20-year class life or longer) or other tangible property requiring two or more years to produce or construct (one year for property costing more than $1 million).

Effective date. —The new capitalization rules with respect to self-constructed property and noninventory property produced for resale will apply to costs incurred after December 31, 1986, unless incurred with respect to property on which substantial construction occurred before March 1, 1986. The same rule applies for interest. In the case of capitalized costs for inventory, the new rules take effect for taxable years beginning after December 31, 1986, and will be treated as a change in accounting method initiated by the taxpayer. The adjustment necessary to effect the change will be included in income ratably over a period of not more than four years.

The uniform capitalization rules will require taxpayers to identify certain period costs that will continue to be expensed for books but must now be capitalized for tax reporting purposes.

Installment Sales

One of the more important accounting provisions of the Act is the change made to installment sales reporting. Under the provision, the use of the installment method is completely eliminated for sales made pursuant to a revolving credit plan and for sales of certain publicly traded property. This provision is effective for sales of property after December 31, 1986. Taxpayers who will no longer be able to use the installment method for sales made under a revolving credit plan may include the resulting adjustment in income over a period not exceeding four years, taking 15 percent into account in the first year, 25 percent in the second year, and 30 percent in each of the succeeding two taxable years.

The provision effectively denies the use of the installment method for a portion of the sale made by dealers selling under the installment plan (rather than a revolving credit plan) and non-dealers selling business or rental property, the selling price of which exceeds $150,000. This denial is achieved by determining the taxpayer's "allocable installment indebtedness" (AII) for each taxable year and treating such amount as a payment immediately before the close of the taxable year on "applicable installment obligations" (AIO) which arose during the year and are still outstanding as of year end. The AII is determined by dividing (1) the AIO outstanding at year end by (2) the sum of (a) the face amount of all installment obligations and (b) the adjusted basis of all other assets. The result is then multiplied by the average quarterly indebtedness (annual basis for taxpayers who have no AIOs that arose from the sale on the installment method of either personal property by a person who regularly sells property of the same type on the installment method, or real property that was held for sale to customers in the ordinary course of a trade or business). Finally any AII that is attributable to AIOs in prior years is subtracted. In computing the AIO, installment obligations arising from the sale of personal use property by an individual and property used or produced in the trade or business of farming are omitted.

A special election is available for sales of "time shares" or unimproved land by a dealer to an individual. If the election is made, the proportionate disallowance rules will not apply to such installment obligations provided interest is paid on the deferral of the tax liability attributable to the use of the installment method.

An exception is provided for installment sales by a manufacturer to a dealer if (1) the terms are dependent upon when the property is disposed of by the dealer, (2) the manufacturer has the right to repurchase the property from the dealer if it is not disposed of within a specified period, (3) and the amount of these installment obligations exceeds 50 percent of the total sales to dealers giving rise to such obligations.

Generally, the limitation on the use of the installment method based on the proportionate disallowance rule is effective for taxable years ending after December 31, 1986, with respect to sales of property after February 28, 1986. Special transitional rules are provided for, depending on the type of property sold and the activity of the seller.

Limitations on the Use of Cash Method of Accounting

The Act prohibits the use of the cash method of accounting by any C corporation, partnership that has a C corporation as a partner, tax exempt trust with unrelated business income, or tax shelter. An exception from this prohibition is provided for certain entities (other than tax shelters), including farming and timber businesses, entities with average annual gross receipts of $5 million or less (based on the average of the prior three taxable years), and qualified personal service corporations.

A qualified personal service corporation is one that performs substantially all of its activities in certain fields and is substantially employee-owned (i.e., at least 95 percent). The specified fields include: (1) health, (2) law, (3) engineering, (4) architecture, (5) accounting, (6) actuarial science, (7) performing arts, and (8) consulting. Employee ownership includes: (1) present or retired employees who perform or had performed service for such corporation in connection with the qualified services performed by the company, (2) the estate of such present or retired employees, and (3) persons who acquired an ownership interest as a result of the death of a present or retired employee within a two-year period beginning with the death of such employee. Stock held by any plan described in section 401(a) of the Code that is exempt from tax under section 501(a) is treated as held by the employees of the entity. At the election of the common parent of an affiliated group, all members of such affiliated group may be treated as a single entity for the purposes of applying the ownership test if substantially all of the activities of such members involve the performance of services in the same qualified field.

In addition, payments made by a personal service corporation to employee-owners will not be deductible prior to the time that such employee-owners would include the payment in gross income.

Effective date. —The provision is effective for taxable years beginning after December 31, 1986, with any adjustment required to be taken into income over a period not to exceed four years.

Taxable Years of Partnerships, S Corporations, and Personal Service Corporations

The Act significantly changes the current rules regarding the adoption of or change in the taxable year of partnerships, S corporations, and personal service corporations.

A partnership must use the same year end as that of the partners owning the majority interest in the profits and capital. If such a majority does not have the same taxable year, the partnership is then required to adopt the taxable year of all of its principal partners. If neither of these first two situations applies, the partnership must adopt a calendar year.

S corporations and personal service corporations do not have the same flexibility as partnerships do, and must use a calendar year end. However, as under current IRS procedures, a partnership, S corporation, or personal service corporation may adopt or change to a different taxable year than that prescribed above, if it establishes to the satisfaction of the Secretary of the Treasury a business reason for doing so, such as a "natural business year." The Act repeals the present rule that accepts a year end which results in a three months' or less deferral to the partners or shareholders as being an adequate business reason.

Any partnership that received IRS permission under Rev. Proc. 74-33 to use a fiscal year on the basis that it had a natural business year rather than under the automatic rules permitting deferrals of three months or less is allowed to retain such year. The same is true for S corporations that received permission after the effective date of Rev. Proc. 74-33 to use a fiscal year end (other than a year end that resulted in a three month or less deferral).

Effective date. — Taxable years beginning after December 31, 1986. A partner in a partnership or a shareholder in an S corporation that would otherwise be required by this provision to include more than 12 months of income in a single taxable year may include such excess (income minus expenses for the short year required to effect the changes) in income ratably over a period of four taxable years. The rule applies to income from an S corporation only if such corporation was an S corporation for a taxable year beginning in 1986.

Income realized during the adjustment period will be spread over the years 1987 through 1990 in the case of partnerships and subchapter S corporations. By accelerating 1988 income into the adjustment period, taxpayers will be able to defer half of this income to 1989 and 1990, but one-quarter of the income will be accelerated into 1987.

Reserve Method for Bad Debts

The use of the reserve method for deducting bad debts and for losses on debts guaranteed by a dealer is repealed. An exception is provided for thrift institutions and "small" banks. (See below for a discussion of financial institutions changes.) Taxpayers affected by this change will be required to switch to the specific charge-off method allowed under current law. The switch to the specific charge-off method is a change in accounting method whereby the reserve balance is to be restored to income over a four-year period. *Taxpayers will want to carefully evaluate reserve additions for the last year under the reserve method.*

Under the specific charge-off method, a deduction for a partially worthless debt can be taken only in the year the debt is charged off on the books. No such rule applies to wholly worthless debts.

Effective date. — Taxable years beginnning after December 31, 1986.

Utilities Using Accrual Accounting

Under prior law, many utilities did not include services provided to customers after the last meter reading or billing for the year (unbilled revenue) in current income. The Act requires providers of utility services who use the accrual basis of accounting to recognize income attributable to the furnishing or sale of utility services to customers not later than the taxable year in which such services are provided. The adjustment to income resulting from the change in accounting method is recognized ratably over four years.

Effective date. — Taxable years beginning after December 31, 1986.

Contributions in Aid of Construction

Prior tax law permitted regulated public utility providers of electric, gas, water or sewer services to treat contributions in aid of construction (CIAC) as non-taxable contributions to capital. Property purchased with such contributions could not be depreciated for tax purposes.

The Act repeals the special provisions pertaining to contributions in aid of construction, thus taxing CIAC as ordinary income in the year received. Property purchased with these funds may be depreciated for tax purposes under ACRS or any other applicable depreciation method. (No ITC will be available under the new tax bill.)

Effective date. — Contributions received after December 31, 1986.

Financial Accounting Implications

The Act has important implications for financial reporting: When should the effects of the Act be recognized in financial statements? How will deferred taxes be adjusted? How will the 35 percent reduction in carryover investment tax credits be treated?

Timing
The effects of the new legislation *must* be recognized in year end and interim financial statements issued for periods ending on or after the date of enactment, that is, the date the President signs the legislation into law. Year end and interim financial statements for periods ending before the date of enactment, but issued after that date, cannot recognize the effects of the new legislation under the Financial Accounting Standards Board's proposals for implementing the accounting aspects of the Act. These proposals may change before final adoption.

Deferred Taxes
Many companies have set up deferred taxes at a 46 percent rate. Should these deferred taxes be adjusted to reflect the lower corporate tax rate? Under current rules, the reductions

in corporate rates are reflected in financial statements only when the timing differences that caused them reverse. However, the Financial Accounting Standards Board (FASB) has proposed to replace the current method of accounting for deferred taxes with the "liability" method. If the FASB adopts this method for deferred taxes (expected in 1987), companies will make a one-time adjustment in their deferred taxes to reflect the reduction in corporate rates. This will boost shareholder equity.

Investment Tax Credit
Companies with ITC carryovers often are able to book them for financial accounting purposes. If the allowable carryovers are reduced by 35 percent, must this change be reflected in financial statements? Current accounting standards do not permit companies to make an adjustment. If the FASB adopts the liability method for deferred taxes, the reduction in the ITC carryover probably would be netted against the deferred tax adjustment.

Minimum Tax

Under prior law, minimum taxes were imposed on individuals and corporations as a back-stop to the regular tax. Congress was concerned that wealthy individuals and profitable corporations should pay at least some tax. Under the Act, the minimum tax is elevated from its back-stop role to a central position in the tax system. Congressional policy is now that all high income individuals and corporations should pay a substantial tax.

Basic Structure

Taxpayers must pay the higher of their regular tax liability or their minimum tax liability. The minimum tax liability is 21 percent (20 percent in the case of corporations) of the taxpayer's alternative minimum taxable income reduced by the allowable exemption amount. The exemption amount is $40,000 for corporations and married taxpayers filing a joint return, and $30,000 for single taxpayers. The exemption amount is reduced 25 cents for each dollar by which AMTI exceeds $150,000 ($112,500 for single taxpayers). For married taxpayers filing a separate return, the exemption amount is $20,000 and phases out above $75,000 of AMTI.

The impact of the minimum tax will be expanded dramatically simply by reason of the narrowing of the gap between the minimum tax rates and the regular tax rates. Under prior law, the individual minimum tax rate was only 40 percent of the top regular individual tax rate; now the individual minimum tax rate (21 percent) is 75 percent of the top regular individual tax rate (28 percent). If an individual is in the midst of the phase out of the exemption amount, an additional dollar of income will be taxed at an effective marginal rate of 26.25 percent under the minimum tax.

The alternative minimum tax may be reduced by foreign tax credits (up to 90 percent of liability). For corporations, ITC on transition property or ITC carried over from prior years may reduce regular tax liability down to 75 percent of minimum tax liability, or if minimum tax exceeds regular tax, these credits may offset up to 25 percent of minimum tax liability. The 35 percent reduction in ITC under the regular tax also applies for minimum tax purposes.

The prohibition on offsetting more than 90 percent of minimum tax liability with foreign tax credits expands the traditional reach of U.S. taxation. A U.S. taxpayer who has only foreign source income taxed at a rate higher than the U.S. rate has, in the past, paid only the foreign tax on that income. Now, the U.S. will impose an effective tax of 2 percent on that income (2.1% in the case of individuals).

Computation of AMTI
The computation of income for minimum tax purposes differs substantially from the computation of income for purposes of the regular tax. The Act prescribes specific adjustments to the regular tax and specific preference amounts that must be taken into account in determining AMTI. These are described below.

Adjustments and Preferences

Adjustments and Preferences for Both Individuals and Corporations
Depreciation. – For minimum tax purposes, depreciation on personal property is computed using the 150 percent declining balance method over an asset's ADR midpoint life for assets (other than transition property) placed in service after 1986. Real estate (other than transition property) placed in service after 1986 is depreciated using the straight line method over 40 years. This adjustment effectively treats accelerated depreciation on real and personal property as a tax preference. Since depreciation is a substantial portion of many taxpayers' tax calculation, this provision will subject many taxpayers to the minimum tax.

For property placed in service before 1987, or under the transition rules of the Act, accelerated depreciation is a preference only to the extent provided under prior law.

When property acquired after 1986 (other than transition property) is disposed of, gain or loss for minimum tax purposes will be computed by reference to basis as adjusted for depreciation allowed under the minimum tax.

Tax-exempt interest. – Generally, tax-exempt interest on private activity bonds issued after August 7, 1986, is included in income for minimum tax purposes.

Untaxed appreciation on charitable contributions. – The charitable deduction for contributions of appreciated property is computed by limiting the value of the contribution to its adjusted basis.

Accounting methods. – The percentage of completion method of accounting must be used with respect to long-term contracts entered into after February 1, 1986 and installment sales treatment is not available for almost all installment sales made after March 1, 1986.

Intangible drilling costs. – Excess IDC deductions (but only to the extent that amount is in excess of 65 percent of net income from oil, gas and geothermal properties) are added to income as a tax preference.

Mining exploration and development costs. – Exploration and development costs incurred after 1986 and expensed for purposes of the regular tax must be amortized over 10 years for purposes of the minimum tax. As with depreciation, separate basis adjustments will be made for regular tax and minimum tax.

Net operating loss. – For minimum tax purposes, a separate net operating loss must be computed in a manner consistent with the adjustments and preferences defined by the minimum tax. Pre-1987 NOLs do not have to be recomputed. NOLs cannot offset more than 90 percent of AMTI.

Preferences from prior law. – The Act continues to treat as preferences: (1) excess amortization on pollution control facilities, (2) percentage depletion in excess of basis, and (3) expensing of mining exploration and development costs.

Adjustments and Preferences for Individuals Only
Passive losses. – No deduction for passive farm losses is allowed, and the limitations on passive activity losses are applied without a phase in. As with the regular tax, disallowed losses may be carried forward. The loss limitations apply to passive activity income or loss as computed for minimum tax purposes. Thus, a taxpayer who has a suspended loss for regular tax purposes may not have any loss for minimum tax purposes.

Interest expense. – The limitations on investment interest and personal interest apply (with necessary conforming modifications) under the minimum tax.

Prior law adjustments and preferences. – The Act continues the prior law minimum tax treatment of (1) circulation expenses, (2) research and experimentation expenditures, (3) itemized deductions, and (4) incentive stock options.

Adjustments and Preferences for Corporations Only
Merchant Marine Capital Construction Funds. – No deduction is allowed for amounts contributed to a capital construction fund of a shipping company and any tax free earnings after 1986 are included in income.

Bad debts. – The excess of bad debt deductions over deductions computed on the basis of actual experience is added to income of thrifts and small banks still permitted to use reserves.

Book income. – The Act requires an increase in AMTI for one-half of any excess of pre-tax book income over AMTI. Book income is the income of a corporation as reported on its financial statements. When more than one statement exists, the following priority is established: (1) SEC statements, (2) audited financials used for credit purposes or other substantial non-tax purposes, (3) regulatory filings, and (4) other non-audited statements used for credit or other substantial non-tax purposes.

The adoption of a book income preference is a novel and controversial approach to the publicity that surrounds the payment of low taxes by profitable companies. The provision necessarily removes from the government any ability to define this element of the tax base because the government, as a practical matter, will not be able to prescribe accounting rules. Given the variety of choices in accounting methods, the provision will treat similarly situated taxpayers differently. For example, taxpayers using full cost accounting and successful efforts accounting in the oil and gas industry will show different annual results for the same activity.

Similarly, a taxpayer facing the minimum tax may establish a larger reserve for a future liability than one facing the regular tax. Book income is computed using special consolidation rules designed to restate book income on a basis comparable to the basis upon which the taxpayer consolidates for income tax purposes.

The book income preference will typically tend to create tax liability in four cases: (1) when a taxpayer has significant exempt income, (2) when a taxpayer books a large liability in one year, but cannot recognize it for tax purposes until a later year, (3) when reserves established for book purposes, but never deducted for tax purposes, are released with resulting book income, and (4) when depreciable lives on major assets are significantly longer for book purposes than for minimum tax purposes.

The Act provides for a switch from the preference based on book income to one based on current earnings and profits after 1989. *The use of earnings and profits would return control of the preference to the government. Thus, reserves would no longer reduce the preference and accounting methods would be those used for tax purposes. The scheduled shift to an earnings and profits preference is likely to be the subject of controversy and legislation in future years.* The transition rules would have to be very complex because of the timing differences between book income and earnings and profits.

Minimum Tax Credit

If, in any post-1986 year, a taxpayer pays minimum tax in excess of its regular tax liability, then the excess (except to the extent attributable to exclusion preferences such as tax exempt interest) may be carried forward as a credit against any subsequent-year regular tax in excess of minimum tax. The amount of this credit is not affected by any investment credit used to reduce the minimum tax liability. The minimum tax credit provides some relief from the minimum tax resulting from timing differences between the regular and minimum taxes. *As there is no carryback for the minimum tax credit, the relief is inadequate when a company books a large liability before it is recognized for tax purposes.*

Estimated Tax Payments

Corporations must now make estimated tax payments with respect to minimum tax liability.

Retirement Savings and Qualified Plans

In General
The Act makes numerous direct changes to the rules governing tax-qualified plans, executive compensation and employee benefit plans. Moreover, other changes to the Internal Revenue Code discussed in this book have an indirect but profound influence on these compensation issues. For example, lower individual tax rates (an indirect change) and the $7,000 cap on 401(k) deferrals (a direct change) may combine to favor cash compensation. With corporate tax rates (34 percent) that exceed individual rates (28 percent or 33 percent), the tax efficiency of current compensation has increased.

Individuals and employers, however, must still provide funds for retirement needs. The changes to IRAs, qualified retirement plans, and employee-benefit plans will restrict the ability of those with higher income to take advantage of these plans. For example, the new 15 percent excise tax on excess retirement income and the new 10 percent excise taxes on excess contributions and early withdrawals may severely limit the attractiveness of these plans (including IRAs) to some people. These new restrictions on qualified plans may mean that, in some circumstances, an individual's retirement needs cannot be satisfied wholly from qualified plans and social security. Here, employers will need to re-evaluate whether and how much of the short-fall should come from non-qualified arrangements and/or from the retiree's personal savings.

Other direct changes, such as the new vesting and integra-

tion rules, may result in a greater proportion of plan costs flowing to lower compensated employees (a clear congressional intention behind the changes). Here, employers will face the issue of cost containment: should costs be increased to continue present levels of benefits, or should the benefit formula be adjusted to contain costs?

Many employers may conclude that the combination of these factors justifies a fresh look at all compensation techniques—tax qualified plans, executive compensation, and employee benefits.

Tax Qualified Plans—Retirement Savings

Individual Retirement Accounts
The Act phases out the deduction for IRA contributions by any moderate and high income taxpayer who is covered by a qualified plan, or whose spouse is covered by a plan. This phase out applies to taxpayers with adjusted gross income between $40,000 and $50,000 on a joint return or $25,000 and $35,000 on a single return. *During this phase out, taxpayers who would otherwise pay at a 15 or 28 percent tax rate will experience effective marginal rates of 18, 21, 33.6, or even 39.2 percent.*

To the extent the IRA deduction is reduced or eliminated by the phase out rule, a taxpayer may elect to make non-deductible IRA contributions. Earnings on the IRA would not be taxed until withdrawn. Total combined contributions to both types of IRAs may not exceed the $2,000 ($2,250 spousal) limitation on IRA contributions. As before, the regular income tax plus a 10 percent excise tax is applied if withdrawals are made before age 59 1/2, death, or disability, unless received in the form of an annuity payable over one's life expectancy. Withdrawals to the extent made from non-deductible contributions are free from income and excise taxes. IRAs may be invested in U.S. gold or silver coins. Rollovers to IRAs are not changed.

Taxpayers subject to the new IRA limits and their employers should carefully review other retirement savings options. Frequently, IRAs have been used where 401(k) plans, Keogh plans, and simplified employee pensions could now be substituted.

Effective date.—These changes are effective in 1987.

Cash or Deferred Arrangements (Section 401(k) Plans)
Beginning in 1987, pre-tax salary deferrals are limited to $7,000 per year. The limit is indexed to inflation. As before, employers may contribute up to the lesser of 25 percent of taxable compensation or $30,000, less the amount of salary deferral. For example, at a salary of $57,000, the employee can defer $7,000 and the employer may contribute $5,500, totaling $12,500 which is 25 percent of $50,000 ($57,000 less the $7,000 salary deferral.)

CHART
401(k) Plan Deferral Test

Non-Highly Compensated Employees' Deferral Percentage				Highly Compensated* Employees' Deferrals
OLD LAW:				
0% to 2%	×	2.5	=	0% to 5%
2% to 6%	+	3%	=	5% to 9%
6% to 10%	×	1.5	=	9% to 15%
NEW LAW:				
0% to 2%	×	2	=	0% to 4%
2% to 8%	+	2%	=	4% to 10%
8% to 12%	×	1.25	=	10% to 15%

*Top 1/3 under old law, and now newly defined by the Act.

The qualification rules, beginning in 1987, will further limit pre-tax deferrals of 401(k) plans (see chart) by members of a newly defined "highly compensated" group of employees. Excess contributions will not be excluded from income and must be returned to employees to avoid a 10 percent excise tax and eventual disqualification of the cash or deferred arrangement.

As before, withdrawals of pre-tax deferrals are prohibited before age 59-1/2, death, disability, severance of employment or hardship. A new exception permits total withdrawals upon plan termination, the sale of a subsidiary or the sale of substantially all of the assets used in a trade or business after 1984.

Beginning in 1989, hardship withdrawals will be limited to the amount of pre-tax deferrals (excluding earnings thereon), and plans cannot require participants to have more than one year of service to enter the plan.

These plans may not now be established by tax-exempt or public-sector employers.

Matching Contributions
New rules apply to all qualified plans in 1987 to limit employer matching and employee after-tax contributions in a manner similar to pre-tax deferrals in a 401(k) plan. *Consequently, highly compensated employees may experience lower employer matches and reduced after-tax contributions.* Excess matching contributions must be distributed to avoid a 10 percent excise tax and eventual plan disqualification.

Simplified Employee Plans (SEPs)
The Act modifies the SEP to permit salary deferrals up to $7,000 under rules similar to 401(k) plans. The new SEP is available to employers with 25 or fewer employees.

Tax Deferred [403(b)] Annuities

In general, the treatment of tax deferred annuity plans offered by charitable organizations or public schools, colleges, and universities will be brought more closely into conformity with qualified plans with respect to coverage, nondiscrimination, minimum distributions, early withdrawals and benefit commencement issues. Effective in 1987, the amount that an employee can defer under all taxed deferred annuities is limited to the greater of $9,500 or the indexed limit on elective deferrals to 401(k) plans. A special catch-up election will be available.

Contribution and Benefit Limits
The Act retains the current limit on annual additions to a defined contribution plan, which is the lesser of 25 percent of compensation or $30,000; and it retains the limit on annual benefits from a defined benefit plan, which is the lesser of 100 percent of compensation or $90,000. The $90,000 limit will be indexed for inflation after 1987; however, the $30,000 annual addition limit will not be indexed until the $90,000 limit reaches $120,000.

Currently, employee after-tax contributions are included in annual additions only to the extent they exceed the lesser of the excess over 6 percent of compensation or one-half of the employee's contribution. For years beginning after 1986, all employee contributions will be treated as annual additions. *Therefore, employees will be precluded from making after-tax contributions if the employer contributes the maximum.*

After 1986, early retirement benefits from defined benefit plans will be limited to the actuarial equivalent of the maximum dollar benefit at normal retirement age (currently age 65). Although former law required actuarial reduction for early retirement benefits, the reduced maximum benefit was $90,000 at age 62 and $75,000 at age 55. The new law produces significantly lower maximum early retirement benefits:

Age	Actuarial Equivalent of $90,000 Limit* Current Law	New Law
65	90,000	90,000
62	90,000	72,000
55	75,000	37,404
50	51,200	25,800

*Assume: 5 percent interest compounded annually and UP-1984 Mortality Table.

An important exception is provided for benefits already accrued. Anyone planning early retirement should examine the consequences of the new actuarial reduction rules.

Sponsors of defined contribution plans may wish to revise their plans to limit employee contributions so that the annual addition limit cannot be exceeded when all employee contributions are treated as annual additions. Sponsors of defined benefit plans in which early retirements are prevalent, particularly among key employees, should consider a redesign of their benefit formula. The early retirement benefits of non-highly-compensated employees may be disproportionately high when compared with similar benefits of highly-compensated employees. The new provisions with regard to includable compensation (discussed elsewhere) may restrict the sponsor's ability to redesign the benefit formula.

Qualification and Nondiscrimination

Definition of Highly Compensated Employee

The Act adopts a uniform definition of "highly compensated employee" to replace the prior law "prohibited group" for purposes of satisfying the nondiscrimination rules for qualified plans (including 401(k) plans) and other employee welfare benefit plans, including group term insurance and insured and self insured health plans. An employee is treated as highly compensated if, at any time during the current or preceding year, the employee (1) was a 5 percent owner, (2) earned more than $75,000 (to be indexed), (3) earned more than $50,000 (to be indexed) and was among the top 20 percent of employees by pay, or (4) was an officer earning more than $45,000 (to be indexed). Individuals coming into the highly compensated group under the second through fourth criteria for the current year must also be among the highest paid 100 employees. The determination of who is highly compensated is to be determined on a controlled group basis.

Effective date. — The definition of highly compensated employee is effective for qualified plans in years beginning after December 31, 1988, and for the special nondiscrimination tests applicable to 401(k) plans in years beginning after December 31, 1986. For employee welfare benefit plans, the rules may apply for post-1987 plan years, depending upon when regulations are issued by Treasury.

Plan Coverage

The Act modifies the coverage rules by requiring all qualified plans to meet one of three coverage tests that are more objective than the prior law. These tests are:

1. Percentage Test. — Seventy percent of all non-highly-compensated employees must be covered; or
2. Ratio Test. — The percentage of non-highly-compensated employees covered by the plan must be at least 70 percent of the percentage of highly compensated employees covered; or
3. Average Benefits Test. — The prior law classification test must be met and the average benefit for non-highly-compensated employees must be at least 70 percent of the average benefit for highly compensated employees (as a percentage of compensation).

The new coverage tests may be met with respect to a separate line of business. A transition rule is provided for certain dispositions or acquisitions.

Minimum Participation

The Act also requires a qualified plan to benefit at least the lesser of 50 employees or 40 percent of all employees. Plans not meeting this test must be merged or terminated by the end of the first plan year in which this rule takes effect. *This rule will require many professional organizations and closely held companies to merge or terminate plans established separately for partners or officers.*

Effective date. — The provisions are effective for plan years beginning after December 31, 1988. A special effective date applies to plans maintained pursuant to a collective bargaining agreement.

Vesting

The Act accelerates the vesting requirements for qualified plans (other than multi-employer plans) to require either 100 percent vesting after 5 years of service, or a graded schedule whereby a participant must be 20 percent vested after 3 years, increasing to 100 percent after 7 years. Under the Act, participants with at least 3 years of service may elect to remain under the plan's current vesting schedule.

Effective date. — The vesting provisions are effective for plan years beginning after December 31, 1988, with respect to all employees who have at least one hour of service in a plan year to which the provisions apply. As a result, benefits earned prior to 1986 under a slower vesting formula will vest in plan years beginning in 1988. A special effective date applies to plans maintained pursuant to a collective bargaining agreement.

Integration with Social Security

The Act significantly changes the social security integration rules and requires a minimum contribution or benefit with respect to earnings below the social security wage base. Conceptually, these rules limit the integrated benefit to no less than one-half of the non-integrated benefit.

Effective date. — The provisions are effective for plan years beginning after December 31, 1988. A special effective date applies to plans maintained pursuant to a collective bargaining agreement.

Distributions and Loans

Lump Sums

After December 31, 1986, 10-year averaging is replaced by a one-time-only 5-year averaging election for lump sum distributions received after the individual attains age 59 1/2. Beginning in 1987, capital gain treatment of the pre-1974 portion of a lump sum distribution is phased out over a six-year period as follows:

Year	Percentage of Pre-1974 Portion Treated as Capital Gain
1987	100%
1988	95%
1989	75%
1990	50%
1991	25%
1992	NONE

Individuals age 50 as of January 1, 1986 may elect 10-year averaging at present rates or 5-year averaging at new rates and to treat the entire pre-1974 amount as capital gain taxed at a rate of 20 percent. One transition election is permitted either before or after attaining age 59-1/2.

Basis Recovery

For distributions with an annuity starting date after July 1, 1986, the special 3-year basis recovery rule is repealed. *This repeal was expected to be the subject of a closely-fought floor fight in the House and may not have survived to final enactment.* For post-1986 distributions received prior to the annuity starting date a pro rata recovery of employee contributions and earnings will apply. Pre-1987 employee contributions are not subject to the pro rata recovery rule.

Minimum Distributions

Beginning January 1, 1989, the benefit commencement date and minimum distribution rules that apply to qualified plans and tax deferred annuities will be conformed to match the rules that currently apply to IRAs. Non-5-percent owners who attain age 70-1/2 by January 1, 1988 can continue to defer distribution to actual retirement. Individuals will be subject to a 50 percent excise tax on the amount which is not distributed.

Early Withdrawals

Subject to numerous exceptions, the 10 percent excise tax that currently applies to premature withdrawals from IRAs will apply to distributions from qualified plans and tax sheltered annuities if made prior to age 59 1/2. The new uniform early withdrawal rules generally are effective for distributions after 1986.

Excess Retirement Distributions

A new 15 percent excise tax will apply to an individual's aggregate distributions in excess of $112,500 received in a year from all qualified plans, tax deferred annuities and IRAs. As the defined benefit limit of $90,000 is indexed upward after 1987, the aggregate annual distribution limit (initially $112,500) will be increased to 125 percent of the indexed annual benefit limit. If an individual elects capital gain or 5-year averaging for a lump sum distribution, the aggregate annual distribution limit will be the lesser of the portion of the distribution to which capital gain or 5-year averaging applies or an amount that is five times the otherwise applicable aggregate annual distribution limit for the year. While the new limitation generally applies to distributions received after 1986, individuals with excess benefits accrued prior to August 1, 1986 will be allowed an election to exempt such pre-August 1, 1986 benefits or to use an alternative limitation.

Plan Loans

The $50,000 limit on plan loans is reduced by the participant's highest outstanding loan balance during the prior 12 months. The exception to the 5-year repayment period is more narrowly limited to loans applied to purchase the participant's principal residence. The interest deduction is denied for loans to key employees and for loans secured by elective deferrals under a qualified cash or deferred arrangement or tax sheltered annuity. The new loan limitations are effective for loan proceeds received after December 31, 1986.

Deductions and Funding

Defined Contribution Plans

Beginning in 1987, excess contributions to qualified plans are subject to a 10 percent excise tax. The Act eliminates the ability to make up for profit sharing and stock bonus contributions of less than 15 percent in a future year by repealing the credit-limit carryforward. Pre-1987 unused credit limits may still be carried forward. Furthermore, for deductions and most other plan purposes, "compensation" is limited to $200,000 per year (indexed for inflation after 1987). The $200,000 includable compensation change is effective after 1988.

The Act modifies the deduction limits for combinations of plans that include a money purchase pension plan (MPPP) for taxable years beginning in 1987. The combined limit for a defined benefit plan and an MPPP (or any other defined contribution plan) is 25 percent of compensation, or the required minimum funding requirement for the defined benefit plan, if greater.

Beginning in 1986, an an employer's contribution to a profit-sharing plan is not limited to current or accumulated profits. This will permit employers to amend plans now to take advantage of this rule change in 1986.

Defined Benefit Plans

After enactment, a new tax penalty is imposed on certain excess deductions due to the overvaluation of pension liabilities if the deductions result in an income tax underpayment.

As to pension plan terminations in 1986 and later, any assets reverting to the employer are subject to a 10 percent excise tax. For plans terminated prior to 1989 an exception is provided for transfers to an ESOP. Tax exempt employers are not subject to this new excise tax.

Employee Stock Ownership Plans

The numerous provisions favoring the use of ESOPs basically are retained and, in a few instances, enhanced by this Act.

The payroll-based tax credit is repealed for compensation paid after December 31, 1986. Distribution of employer securities from a terminated tax credit ESOP is permitted after 1984 without regard to the 84-month rule. ESOPs will be subject to new coverage and nondiscrimination requirements, more rapid vesting schedules, and includable compensation limits described elsewhere.

Beginning in 1987, a new diversification provision requires that older ESOP participants must be allowed annually to direct diversification of a portion of their account balance.

New distribution rules are added that will accelerate distributions from ESOPs. Payments upon the exercise of a put option for stock distributed from an ESOP must be made over five years. The new option payment rules apply to stock acquired after the date of enactment.

Incentives for ESOP financing include (1) a deduction for dividends used to repay the ESOP loan (tax years beginning after enactment), (2) extension of the 50 percent interest income exclusion to loans to the employer if securities are transferred to the ESOP within 30 days (loans after enactment), and (3) an estate tax exclusion for 50 percent of the proceeds from the qualified sale of employer securities to an ESOP (sales after enactment and before January 1, 1992).

International Taxation

The Act radically changes the taxation of U.S. companies doing business abroad, in part by reducing foreign tax credits available to offset their U.S. income tax liabilities. *By reducing the availability of foreign tax credits, the Act is likely to force many U.S. companies into an excess foreign tax credit position. Thus, the Act places a premium on U.S. corporations reducing foreign taxes imposed on their overseas earnings.*

Foreign Tax Credits

Separate Limitation Categories
Under the prior foreign tax credit (FTC) limitation, a taxpayer could generally average high-taxed foreign source income with low-taxed foreign source income, and thus increase the amount of foreign taxes available for credit in a year. To reduce the credit, the Act generally prevents averaging by creating separate categories of low-taxed foreign source income to which the FTC limitation is applied separately. These new categories are:

- income from the active conduct of a banking or financing business and offshore insurance income (referred to as "financial services income");
- shipping income from vessels or aircraft in foreign commerce;
- interest income subjected to a foreign withholding tax of at least five percent (referred to as "high withholding tax interest");
- dividends from non-controlled foreign corporations (non-CFCs) for which an indirect foreign tax credit can be claimed;
- passive income which includes dividends, interest, annuities, net gains from sales of non-inventory assets, certain foreign currency gains, rents and royalties other than those received from unrelated parties in the conduct of an active rental or leasing business, and other items.

Passive income does not include income on which the effective foreign tax rate exceeds 34 percent for corporations and 28 percent for individuals.

Subpart F income realized by a U.S. shareholder of a controlled foreign corporation (CFC) will be allocated to the above categories to the same extent the CFC's income was attributable to those categories. Generally, a similar look-through rule is applied to dividends, interest, rents, and royalties received by a U.S. shareholder from its CFC and similar controlled entities. Passive rents and royalties and all interest received by U.S. shareholders from foreign corporations that are not CFCs is now treated as passive income, whether or not the shareholder owns 10 percent of the CFC's voting stock.

Foreign Loss Recapture Provisions
The allowable foreign tax credit is further reduced by the manner in which losses are allocated to each separate limitation category. Specifically, a foreign-source loss occurring in one category is applied to reduce income in the other categories in proportion to the net foreign-source income in each category. Any remaining unallocated loss reduces U.S. source income. U.S. source losses are allocated on a similar basis to each of the separate foreign limitation categories. Foreign-source income realized in a later year in the separate limitation category producing the original loss is reallocated to the separate categories to which the prior loss was originally allocated.

Foreign Tax Credit for Alternative Minimum Tax Purposes
The Act imposes an alternative minimum tax (AMT) on corporations but limits the allowable foreign tax credit used to offset that tax to no more than 90 percent of the AMT.

Indirect Foreign Tax Credit
In computing the indirect foreign tax credit for actual dividends paid by a foreign corporation as well as for deemed dividends under subpart F, the annual concept of accumulated earnings and profits is repealed for years after 1986. Thus, the indirect foreign tax credit formula is as follows:

$$\text{Foreign income taxes for post-1986 years} \quad \times \quad \frac{\text{Dividends}}{\text{Earnings and profits for post-1986 years}}$$

In the case of actual dividends, earnings and profits are to be computed in this formula using the same rules as earnings and profits for deemed dividends under the subpart F provisions.

Carrybacks and Carryovers of Unused Foreign Tax Credits
Unused foreign tax credits generated on low-taxed foreign source income after the effective date of the Act can be carried back to offset U.S. income tax on high-taxed foreign source income earned in pre-Act years. However, in determining the amount of the carryback allowable, the foreign tax credit limitation for the carryback year is computed for this purpose using the appropriate U.S. tax rates in effect in the year the carryback arises.

By contrast, unused foreign tax credits arising in years prior to the effective date of the Act can be carried over to post-Act years. However, these credits can generally only offset U.S. taxes imposed on the same categories of income on which the carryover taxes were imposed.

Source Rules

The Act also reduces the allowable foreign tax credit by treating many items of income that would be foreign source under prior law as U.S. source in whole or in part.

Sources of Specific Items of Income
Under prior law income from the sale of personal property is generally sourced at the location where title to the property passes. However, the Act eliminates this title test in part by providing that income from sales of personal property (a) is U.S. source if the seller is a U.S. resident, and (b) is foreign source if the seller is a foreign resident, with the following exceptions:

- payments of income from the sale of intangibles that are contingent on productivity, use or disposition are generally sourced where the intangible is used.
- income from the sale of stock of a foreign corporate affiliate conducting an active business is foreign source if sold by a U.S. affiliate corporation in the foreign country where the foreign affiliate derived 50 percent of its gross income for the prior three years.
- income from sales by a U.S. resident of personal property (other than inventory, depreciable property, stock of a foreign affiliate, and intangibles contingent on productivity or use) is foreign source if attributable to a foreign office of the seller, and provided such income is subjected to a foreign income tax of at least 10 percent.
- income from the sale of both inventory property not manufactured by the seller and inventory property manufactured by the seller continues to be sourced under current law rules with exceptions for nonresidents.
- income (other than subpart F income) from the sale of all personal property by a nonresident (NR) will be U.S. source rather than foreign source (except for foreign tax credit

purposes) if the income is attributable to an office maintained by the NR in the U.S. and if the sale did not involve inventory property sold for use outside the United States in which a foreign office of the seller materially participated.

- income from the sale of depreciable property is sourced where the depreciation deductions on that property were sourced, and income in excess of those deductions is sourced where title passes.

For purposes of the Act, the seller is a resident of the country in which his tax home is located, except that a U.S. citizen or resident alien will not be treated as a nonresident of the U.S. on any income from the sale of personal property, unless foreign income tax of at least 10 percent was paid.

The new sourcing rules appear to override income tax treaties to the extent of any inconsistencies and apply to all sales by foreign persons (other than controlled foreign corporations) after March 18, 1986.

Transportation and Other Income From Offshore and Space Activities

The Act treats as U.S. source income 50 percent of all income realized by U.S. or foreign persons from transportation by vessel or aircraft which begins or ends in the U.S. The other 50 percent is foreign source.

The Act modifies prior law by providing that earnings of a nonresident alien or foreign corporation from the operation of a ship or aircraft will only be exempt from U.S. income tax if the foreign country of residence or incorporation (rather than the country where the vessel or aircraft is registered) grants an equivalent exemption to U.S. citizens and corporations. Foreign corporations claiming this exemption are subject to a look-through rule regarding their benefical owners. Income from leasing vessels on a bareboat charter basis is treated as "earnings from the operation of a ship," thus reversing the result in Rev. Rul. 74-170.

The Act also levies a four percent tax on non-effectively connected, U.S. source, gross transportation income earned by foreign persons unless exempted by a treaty or the reciprocal exemption. A special definition of effectively connected income is provided for this purpose.

Income derived from space or ocean activities (including those in Antarctica) will be U.S. source if realized by a U.S. person and foreign source if realized by a foreign person, with exceptions for income from transportation, international communications, and mineral deposits including oil and gas.

Sourcing Rules for 80/20 Companies

Prior law treats all interest and dividend payments as foreign source income when paid by a U.S. corporation (an 80/20 company) that has realized more than 80 percent of its income from foreign sources for the three preceding years. The Act repeals this provision. Thus, the above payments when made to foreign persons are no longer exempt from U.S. withholding tax, except generally for (a) interest payments to unrelated parties from an 80/20 company deriving more than 80 percent of its income from an active business in a foreign country, (b) interest payments on any debt outstanding on December 31, 1985, (c) dividend payments made by an 80/20 company that is a possessions corporation, and (d) interest payments to related parties and dividend payments to the extent attributable to foreign-source gross income of an 80/20 company that derives at least 80 percent of its income from an active business in a foreign country.

Allocation and Apportionment of Expenses

The Act allocates and apportions additional expenses to foreign source taxable income in the foreign tax credit limitation formula. This has the effect of further reducing allowable foreign tax credits in any taxable year.

To reach this result, the Act (a) requires interest and all other expenses (except research and development expenses) incurred by members of a consolidated group to be allocated and apportioned to foreign source taxable income on a consolidated basis instead of a separate company basis, (b) requires interest expense to be allocated and apportioned in the same percentage that the tax basis of the group's foreign assets bears to all assets, thus eliminating the gross income apportionment methods permitted by current law, (c) requires generally that the tax basis of any such asset which is stock of a 10-percent-owned foreign corporation be adjusted for earnings and profits or deficits accumulated during the period the taxpayer held the stock, and (d) requires that tax exempt assets and intragroup debt, equity, interest payments and other expenses be eliminated for allocation and apportionment purposes, subject to certain transition rules.

The Act *does not renew* Congress's moratorium barring the IRS from apportioning U.S. based research and development expenditures to foreign source taxable income under the existing IRS regulations. Instead, the Act says that for taxable years commencing after August 1, 1986 and before August 2, 1987, any part of these expenses (other than for FSC and DISC purposes) incurred to meet legal requirements imposed by a political entity are generally apportioned to income realized in the geographic area governed by that entity. One-half of the remaining expenses are apportioned to U.S. source income, and the other half is apportioned to U.S. or foreign source income in an amount equal to the percentage that sales or gross income from foreign or U.S. sources, respectively, bears to total sales or gross income. Congress will decide later what rules will apply for taxable years beginning after August 1, 1987.

Taxation of U.S. Shareholders of Foreign Corporations

Definition of Controlled Foreign Corporation

The Act treats all foreign corporations as controlled foreign corporations (CFCs) where more than 50 percent of either their voting stock or the value of all their stock is directly or constructively owned by U.S. shareholders, each of whom owns at least 10 percent of the voting stock. If a foreign corporation is a CFC, any tax-haven income earned by it is taxed currently to its U.S. shareholders. Similar ownership rules are adopted for foreign personal holding companies (FPHC). Also, previously exempted corporations organized in U.S. possessions are now treated as CFCs if the above ownership requirements are met.

Subpart F Income Exclusions and Limitations

The prior subjective test for determining whether a CFC was availed of to reduce tax on certain tax-haven income is replaced by an objective test under the Act. This new test requires that the effective rate of foreign tax paid by the CFC on certain tax-haven income (including certain insurance income) must be greater than 90 percent of the U.S. corporate rate. *Thus, if the effective foreign tax rate is greater than 30.6 percent (90% of 34%) on this income, U.S. shareholders of a CFC are not currently taxed on their pro rata share of this income.*

The Act reduces the CFC's income threshold for determining when a U.S. shareholder is currently taxable on the CFC's tax-haven income. Specifically, if the CFC's foreign base company income (i.e., a component of tax-haven income) does not exceed the lesser of 5 percent of the CFC's total gross income or $1 million, then none of the CFC's tax-haven income is taxed currently to the U.S. shareholder. However, if foreign base company income exceeds either 5 percent of the CFC's total gross income or $1 million, the U.S. shareholder is currently taxed on this income.

Under prior law, prior years' deficits in earnings and profits (or current year's deficits from a chain of foreign subsidiaries) reduce the CFC's tax haven income currently taxable to its U.S. shareholders. The Act no longer permits current year's deficits from a chain of foreign subsidiaries to be used for this purpose. In addition, the use of prior years' deficits of a

CFC to reduce its current year tax haven income have been eliminated except for deficits attributable to certain shipping, oil-related, insurance and banking income.

Controlled Partnerships as Related Parties
The Act treats a partnership or trust (which is controlled by a CFC or the CFC's controlling shareholders) as a related person for purposes of the subpart F provisions of the Code. *Thus, tax haven income received by the CFC from a controlled partnership or trust will now be taxable to the U.S. shareholders of the CFC.*

Types of Includable Tax-Haven Income
The Act expands the type of tax haven income earned by a CFC that is currently taxable to its U.S. shareholders. Specifically, under prior law foreign personal holding company (FPHC) income, a type of tax haven income, includes passive income such as dividends, interest, rents, royalties, and annuities. FPHC income is now expanded to include:

- net gains from sales of non-inventory assets which generate passive income or no current income;
- net income from certain non-hedging transactions in commodities but not including income from the active conduct of a commodities business;
- foreign currency net gains from transactions in a nonfunctional currency;
- passive leasing or licensing income;
- income equivalent to interest, such as loan commitment fees;
- interest, rent or royalty payments received by a CFC from a related person (payor) operating in the same foreign country as the CFC that reduces the payor's tax haven income.

In addition, the Act repeals the exceptions from FPHC income for gains from stock or securities, dividends, and interest (except interest in connection with certain export financing) received by a CFC that is a bank or financial institution.

Tax haven insurance income of a CFC is expanded to include income from foreign risks located outside the CFC's country of incorporation. In addition, generally if a foreign insurance company that is not publicly traded (typically a captive) is (1) owned 25 percent or more by U.S. shareholders, whether or not they own 10 percent of the CFC's voting stock, and (2) earns income from insuring risks of its shareholders or related parties, such income will be currently taxable to those shareholders. However, this result can be avoided if the foreign insurance company elects to treat this related person insurance income as effectively connected with the conduct of a U.S. trade or business.

Tax-haven income from shipping operations realized by a CFC is likewise expanded to include any income derived from space and ocean activities (including Antarctica) conducted outside the jurisdiction of any country. Also, the Act repeals the provision that says that tax haven shipping income of a CFC reinvested in certain shipping operations is not currently taxable to the U.S. shareholders.

Taxation of Possession and Other Foreign Income

Possessions Corporations Credit
U.S. companies (possessions corporations) can currently elect to claim a credit equal to the U.S. taxes imposed on certain taxable income derived in most U.S. possessions. This privilege is now extended to such corporations doing business in the Virgin Islands. The Act increases the amount of active business income from a possession that must be earned by these corporations to qualify for the credit from 65 to 75 percent of their gross income. In addition, the Act effectively increases the intercompany price for intangibles that possessions corporations must pay their U.S. affiliates by increasing their cost sharing payment to U.S. affiliates or the amount of allocable product area research expenditures in determining the combined taxable income. *The effect of this change is to reduce the income of possessions corporations eligible for the credit and correspondingly to increase the taxable income of U.S. affiliates.*

Virgin Islands
The Act repeals for open years (i.e., the statute of limitations has not expired) the rules which had permitted U.S. citizens and corporations to qualify as permanent inhabitants of the Virgin Islands (V.I.) and thus to pay income tax on their worldwide income only to the V.I. and not the U.S.

Special Tax Provisions for Americans Working or Living Abroad
The Act reduces the prior exclusion from U.S. income tax for foreign compensation earned by American taxpayers working overseas from $80,000 to $70,000. Additionally, any individual who applies for a U.S. passport (or renewal thereof) is required to file an IRS information return disclosing his taxpayer information number and his foreign residence, if any.

The Act also imposes withholding on all pension payments to U.S. persons living outside the United States.

Transfers of Intangibles to Related Parties Outside the U.S.
Prior law required that a U.S. person who transfers or licenses intangibles to foreign related parties must receive an "arm's-length" payment for their use. The Act now requires that these payments must be commensurate with the income attributable to using the intangible. *Thus, U.S. companies which transfer or license their intangibles offshore after November 16, 1985, may have to adjust annually the payment for any significant changes in the income attributable to the intangible realized by the related party.*

Taxation of Foreign Taxpayers

Branch-Profits Tax and Other Income Subject to U.S. Withholding Taxes
Prior law did not require a foreign corporation (FC) doing business through a branch in the United States to pay U.S. withholding tax when its branch profits are remitted to the home office overseas. The Act now levies a 30 percent withholding tax on an FC's branch profits (earnings and profits effectively connected with the conduct of a U.S. business) whether or not remitted. If effectively connected income is not attributable to a permanent establishment under a treaty, no branch tax will generally be imposed on that income. Also, a tax treaty may reduce the 30 percent tax rate (except in treaty shopping cases) to the treaty branch-profits tax rate, or if none, then the treaty dividend rate. No foreign tax credits can be claimed against the branch-profits tax.

If a treaty bars the U.S. from imposing a branch-profits tax on an FC, none will be imposed except in treaty shopping cases and then only if the treaty prevents U.S. withholding tax from being imposed on dividends paid by the FC.

The Act reduces the threshold for when U.S. withholding tax is imposed on dividends paid by an FC to only those cases in which 25 percent or more of the FC's gross income for the three preceding years was effectively connected with the conduct of its U.S. business. However, if the branch profits tax is payable, no withholding tax will be imposed on dividends paid by the FC.

The Act modifies prior law treatment of U.S. withholding tax on interest paid by a foreign corporation (FC) with a branch in the U.S. Specifically, the Act levies a 30 percent withholding tax (reduced by applicable treaty) on, in effect, the greater of the interest paid or deductible by the branch. If an FC is found to be treaty shopping, the withholding tax rate is not reduced by an applicable treaty unless the recipient of the interest is protected by another treaty.

Withholding on Foreign Investors in Partnerships
The Act levies a 20% withholding tax on that part of any distribution made to a foreign partner by a partnership attributable to income effectively connected (ECI) with the partnership's conduct of a U.S. business. Moreover, the tax will be levied on the entire distribution if ECI is, at least, 80 percent of the partnership's total gross income. This provision is effective for distributions after December 31, 1987, unless regulations are issued before that date.

Income of Foreign Governments
Effective July 1, 1986, the Act taxes a foreign government on any income derived directly or indirectly from engaging in commercial activity in the U.S. (including athletic and cultural group activities). *Additionally, if a controlled entity is itself engaged in commercial activity anywhere in the world, its income is treated like income of a privately owned entity.*

Transfer Prices for Imports
For U.S. income tax purposes the Act requires that transfer prices on import transactions between related persons after March 18, 1986 not exceed those used for U.S. customs purposes.

Dual Resident Companies
The Act denies a U.S. corporation managed and controlled in the U.K. or Australia (a dual resident) the right to deduct any expenses in excess of its income in a U.S. consolidated return with its subsidiaries to the extent those expenses have been deducted by a related foreign corporation for U.K. or Australian tax purposes. However, those excess expenses can be used for U.S. tax purposes by the dual resident in future years when it generates sufficient income to absorb them. In addition, net operating losses incurred by a dual resident prior to the effective date of the Act and deducted by a related foreign corporation can still be deducted in the dual resident's U.S. consolidated return for taxable years after the effective date of the Act.

Foreign Exchange Gains and Losses

The Act adopts uniform rules for the tax treatment of foreign currency.

Functional Currency of an Entity
The Act requires that all income or expenses of a taxpayer must be computed in its "functional currency." In general, a taxpayer's functional currency is the currency in which it keeps its books and records and in which a significant part of its activities are conducted. Thus, the functional currency of most U.S. taxpayers operating in the United States would be the U.S. dollar.

The functional currency of most foreign persons operating in a foreign country would be foreign currency of that country, with exceptions. However, if either the activities of the foreign person are conducted primarily in U.S. dollars, or the foreign person keeps its books and records in U.S. dollars and elects the dollar as its functional currency, then the U.S. dollar is the functional currency.

It is possible for a U.S. taxpayer or a foreign person to have more than one functional currency, provided it has a qualified business unit, the unit maintains separate books and records in a different currency, and other requirements are met. For this purpose, a "qualified business unit" (QBU) is any separate and clearly identified unit of a business conducted by the taxpayer that "is capable of producing income independently." Thus, a QBU includes foreign branches as well as foreign subsidiaries of a U.S. corporation.

Foreign Branch
A foreign branch is required to compute its profit (or loss) in its functional currency and then translate it into U.S. dollars at the weighted average exchange rate for the taxable year. This amount is then included in the taxpayer's income without reduction for remittances from the branch during the year. Only realized exchange gains and losses from foreign currency transactions are reflected in the U.S. taxpayer's income. *Thus, taxpayers are no longer permitted to accelerate the recognition of unrealized foreign exchange gains or losses by use of the net worth method for measuring the U.S. tax results of branch operations.*

Translated branch losses are deductible in computing the taxpayer's taxable income only to the extent of the taxpayer's dollar basis in the branch. That basis initially is equal to the translated value of net assets contributed to the branch and by unremitted branch profits. All contributions to the branch are translated for this purpose at the exchange rate on the date they are made. Similarly, the taxpayer's basis is reduced for branch losses deducted and for remittances to the head office in the U.S.

All branch remittances are treated as paid first out of its post-1986 accumulated earnings. Exchange gains or losses on branch remittances are treated as foreign source income if the remittances are foreign source.

For foreign tax credit purposes foreign income taxes paid by the branch including any refund or credit thereof are translated into U.S. dollars on the date the tax is paid.

Foreign Corporation
In determining the U.S. tax of any shareholder of a foreign corporation (FC), the FC's earnings and profits are computed annually in its functional currency and are *not* translated into U.S. dollars, until distributed to the shareholder. When actual dividend distributions (including deemed dividends under section 1248) are made, both the dividends and the FC's earnings and profits are translated into U.S. dollars at the exchange rate on the date of distribution (or deemed distribution). Thus, no exchange gains and losses are recognized for exchange rate fluctuations between the time the FC's earnings and profits are realized and the time they are distributed.

If an FC's earnings and profits are deemed distributed to U.S. shareholders because of subpart F, an investment in U.S. property, or the foreign personal holding company provisions, they are translated at the weighted average exchange rate for the FC's taxable year.

Although generally no income is realized by U.S. shareholders upon the actual distribution of previously taxed subpart F income (PTI), gain or loss caused by fluctuating exchange rates between the time of the deemed and actual distributions is recognized and treated as foreign source if the PTI was foreign source.

For indirect foreign tax credit purposes, foreign income taxes paid by FCs (including any refund or credit thereof) is translated into U.S. dollars on the date the tax is paid. Thus, the Act repeals the *Bon Ami* rule which had required taxes to be translated at the exchange rate on the date dividends were distributed.

Foreign Currency Transactions
Transactions denominated in nonfunctional currencies generally produce exchange gains and losses. Exchange gains or losses arise when taxpayers

- accrue income or expenses (payables or receivables) in non-functional currency,
- borrow or lend in such currency (notes payable or receivables),
- or dispose of non-functional currency, coins, currency-denominated demand or time deposits issued by a bank, or forward contracts, futures contracts or options not marked to market,

when the exchange rate fluctuates between the date these items are booked and their disposition. These exchange gains or losses are classified as ordinary income or losses, and are generally sourced (or the losses are allocated) by the residence of the taxpayer on whose books the underlying assets (or liabilities) are reflected. Treasury is to issue regulations prescribing when the above exchange gains or losses are treated as interest income or expense.

Foreign Exchange Hedging Contracts
The Treasury is to issue special rules for hedging transactions.

Taxpayers Using U.S. Dollar as Functional Currency
The Act generally does not change current law for a taxpayer or qualified business unit using the U.S. dollar as its functional currency.

Revocation of Contiguous Country Corporation Elections To Be Included in U.S. Consolidated Return
The Act requires Treasury to issue regulations allowing a U.S. parent corporation to revoke its election to include wholly-owned contiguous country corporations (Canada or Mexico) in its consolidated U.S. tax return. This is being done because these contiguous corporations can no longer recognize unrealized exchange gains or losses in computing their taxable income for U.S. purposes.

Effective Dates for International Provisions

The effective dates for most provisions affect taxable years beginning after December 31, 1986, or transactions occurring after that date. Where different effective dates are imposed for certain provisions of the Act, an attempt has been made to describe those. Various transitional rules and grandfather rules have been omitted from this explanation.

Rate Structure as of 1987: Summary

For taxable years beginning in 1987, five-bracket rate schedules are provided, as shown in the table below.

For married individuals filing separate returns, the taxable income bracket amounts for 1987 begin at one-half the amounts for joint returns.

Tax rate	Taxable income brackets		
	Married, filing joint returns	Heads of household	Singles
11%	0–$3,000	0–$2,500	0–$1,800
15%	3,000–28,000	2,500–23,000	1,800–16,800
28%	28,000–45,000	23,000–38,000	16,800–27,000
35%	45,000–90,000	38,000–80,000	27,000–54,000
38.5%	Above 90,000	Above 80,000	Above 54,000

Source: Joint Committee on Taxation, *Summary of Conference Agreement on H.R. 3838* (Tax Reform Act of 1986 (JCS–16–86), August 29, 1986.

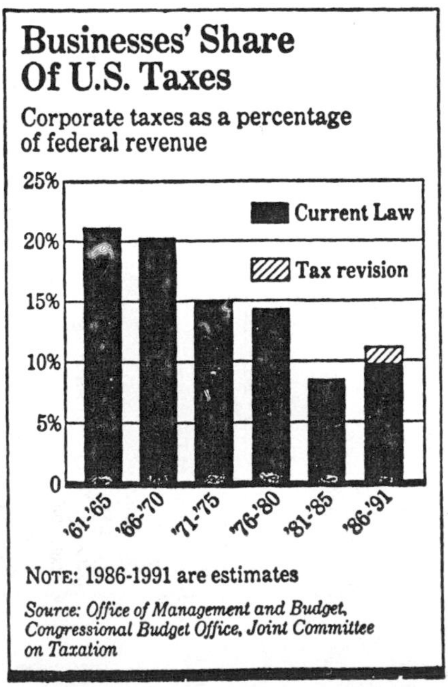

Source: "Reprinted by permission of *The Wall Street Journal*, © Dow Jones & Company, Inc., 1986. ALL RIGHTS RESERVED."

Federal Revenue Impact of Major Enacted Tax Legislation, Fiscal Years 1964–1990
Individual, Corporate, and Total Impact and Percentage of GNP (a)
Budget Effect in Billions of Dollars (c)

	1964	1965	1966	1967	1968	1969	1970	1971	1972	1973	1974	1975	1976	1977	1978	1979	1980
Revenue Act of 1964	-2.4	-10.2	-15.3	-17.3	-18.3												
Individual	-2.4	-8.7	-12.4	-14.1	-15.5												
Corporate		-1.5	-2.9	-3.2	-3.2												
Total as a percent of GNP	-0.38%	-1.52%	-2.07%	-2.18%	-2.15%												
Revenue and Expenditure Control Act of 1968						16.0	4.7										
Individual						8.4	0.8										
Corporate						3.8	1.5										
Total as a percent of GNP						1.72%	0.47%										
Tax Reform Act of 1969							1.2	0.2	-1.1	-3.8	-5.4						
Total as a percent of GNP							0.12%	0.02%	-0.10%	-0.28%	-0.37%						
Revenue Act of 1971									-4.4	-6.9							
Individual									-1.9	-2.9							
Corporate									(b)	-1.7							
Total as a percent of GNP									-0.38%	-0.54%							
Tax Reduction Act of 1975												-10.2	-10.8	0.4	2.8	3.2	3.4
Individual												-9.4	-8.7	-0.6	-0.2	-0.1	-0.1
Corporate												-0.8	-2.0	1.0	2.9	3.3	3.6
Total as a percent of GNP												-0.67%	-0.64%	0.02%	0.13%	0.13%	0.13%
Tax Reform Act of 1976														-14.4	-13.2	-7.4	-8.0
Individual														-13.2	-8.7	-3.8	-3.9
Corporate														-2.6	-3.5	-2.4	-2.5
Total as a percent of GNP														-0.74%	-0.61%	-0.30%	-0.30%
Tax Reduction and Simplification Act of 1977														-2.6	-17.8	-13.7	-5.8
Individual														-2.1	-15.3	-11.3	-5.6
Corporate														-0.6	-2.5	-2.3	-0.2
Total as a percent of GNP														-0.13%	-0.82%	-0.56%	-0.22%

	1979	1980	1981	1982	1983	1984	1985	1986	1987	1988[d]	1989[d]	1990[d]
Revenue Act of 1978	-4.4	-21.7	-25.1	-29.0	-33.1							
Individual	-3.4	-15.3	-17.7									
Corporate	-1.0	-6.3	-7.3									
Total as a percent of GNP	-0.18%	-0.81%	-0.84%	-0.92%	-1.00%							
Crude Oil Windfall Profits Tax of 1980		3.9	13.0	18.4	18.8	21.0						
Total as a percent of GNP		0.15%	0.44%	0.59%	0.57%	0.57%						
Economic Recovery Tax Act of 1981			-0.2	-35.6	-91.1	-136.8	-170.3	-209.8	-238.5	-253.7	-282.0	-309.4
Individual			-0.2	-25.2	-67.0	-101.3	-120.3	-142.2	-162.1	-179.6	-201.7	
Corporate			(b)	-9.5	-14.9	-22.4	-32.0	-43.9	-50.3	-51.8	-52.2	
Total as a percent of GNP			-0.01%	-1.13%	-2.74%	-3.71%	-4.32%	-5.08%	-5.40%	-5.47%	-5.56%	-5.69%
Tax Equity and Fiscal Responsibility Act of 1982					16.6	36.0	39.2	46.7	56.8	58.8	58.2	59.9
Individual					3.4	10.9	12.9	13.4	14.9	15.8	16.6	
Corporate					7.6	16.9	19.2	28.8	38.1	40.9	40.2	
Total as a percent of GNP					0.50%	0.98%	0.99%	1.13%	1.29%	1.24%	1.15%	1.10%
Social Security Admendments of 1983						5.7	8.7	10.2	12.1	24.6	31.0	23.8
Total as a percent of GNP						0.15%	0.22%	0.25%	0.27%	0.52%	0.61%	0.44%
Deficit Reduction Act of 1984						0.9	9.3	16.1	22.0	25.3	27.7	31.1
Individual						0.7	5.6	8.0	10.2	13.1	16.0	
Corporate						0.5	3.3	5.8	8.1	9.7	10.6	
Total as a percent of GNP						0.02%	0.24%	0.39%	0.50%	0.53%	0.55%	0.57%
Tax Reform Act of 1986									18.6	0.9	-11.7	-9.0
Individual									-10.6	-27.4	-38.8	-38.5
Corporate									28.2	25.0	23.5	25.4
Total as a percent of GNP									0.42%	0.02%	-0.23%	-0.17%
EXHIBIT												
Net budget effect of all major acts: 1981-1986								-132.4	-117.5	-136.4	-164.4	-193.1
Individual								-134.4	-157.0	-186.2	-216.9	-238.6
Corporate								-14.8	18.5	19.7	20.6	24.2
Total net 1981-1986 as a percent of GNP								-3.20%	-2.70%	-2.90%	-3.20%	-3.60%

(a) Totals include all taxes and miscellaneous receipts.

(b) Less than $50 million.

(c) Budget effect revenue estimates are prepared by the Office of Management and Budget for purposes of the budget presentation. They measure only the direct effect of tax legislative changes on receipts with "feedback" effect limited to the overall income forecast and its impact on receipts by major source. Budget estimates reflect actual economic experience or revisions in the economic forecast; the original legislative intent estimates do not.

(d) Revenue and GNP projections from the Fiscal Year 1988 Budget of the United States Government (Supplement), February 1987.

Source: Office of Management and Budget, Budget of the United States Government for fiscal years 1984 through 1988.

Source: Tax Foundation, One Thomas Circle, N.W., Washington, DC 20005.

Property Tax Collections by State, Per Capita and Per $1,000 of Personal Income

Fiscal Years 1976 and 1986

State	Per Capita Property Tax: Amount 1976	Per Capita Property Tax: Amount 1986	Per Capita Property Tax: Percent Change	Per Capita Property Tax: Rank 1986	Property Tax Per $1,000 of Personal Income: Amount 1976	Property Tax Per $1,000 of Personal Income: Amount 1986	Property Tax Per $1,000 of Personal Income: Percent Change	Property Tax Per $1,000 of Personal Income: Rank 1986
Total	$ 266	$ 463	74.1%	—	$ 45	$ 34	-24.4%	—
Alabama	57	118	107.0	51	13	11	-15.4	51
Alaska	1,048	1,084	3.4	2	120	61	-49.2	2
Arizona	282	422	49.6	27	54	34	-37.0	25
Arkansas	101	182	80.2	49	22	17	-22.7	47
California	415	451	8.7	24	64	29	-54.7	32
Colorado	271	521	92.3	20	46	36	-21.7	23
Connecticut	369	731	98.1	7	53	41	-22.6	16
Delaware	130	223	71.5	44	19	16	-15.8	49
Florida	191	411	115.2	28	34	31	-8.8	28
Georgia	178	329	84.8	36	35	27	-22.9	36
Hawaii	174	314	80.5	37	27	23	-14.8	41
Idaho	190	299	57.4	38	37	27	-27.0	35
Illinois	284	539	89.8	17	42	37	-11.9	22
Indiana	226	393	73.9	31	40	32	-20.0	27
Iowa	278	544	95.7	16	46	43	-6.5	14
Kansas	274	533	94.5	18	46	39	-15.2	19
Kentucky	105	195	85.7	47	22	18	-18.2	46
Louisiana	90	189	110.0	48	19	17	-10.5	48
Maine	297	478	60.9	22	63	41	-34.9	17
Maryland	239	438	83.3	26	37	28	-24.3	33
Massachusetts	431	601	39.4	12	70	37	-47.1	21
Michigan	324	650	100.6	10	52	48	-7.7	6

Minnesota	254	529	108.3	19	44	38	-13.6	20
Mississippi	110	221	100.9	45	27	24	-11.1	38
Missouri	195	243	24.6	41	35	19	-45.7	45
Montana	350	650	85.7	9	65	59	-9.2	3
Nebraska	319	579	81.5	14	53	43	-18.9	12
Nevada	272	340	25.0	35	42	24	-42.9	39
New Hampshire	348	738	112.1	6	66	51	-22.7	5
New Jersey	446	757	69.7	4	67	44	-34.3	11
New Mexico	103	143	38.8	50	22	13	-40.9	50
New York	412	748	81.6	5	63	47	-25.4	7
North Carolina	130	265	103.8	39	26	23	-11.5	40
North Dakota	212	364	71.7	34	37	30	-18.9	29
Ohio	224	394	75.9	30	38	30	-21.1	30
Oklahoma	124	234	88.7	43	24	19	-20.8	44
Oregon	333	651	95.5	8	59	52	-11.9	4
Pennsylvania	176	388	120.5	32	30	29	-3.3	31
Rhode Island	294	624	112.2	11	50	45	-10.0	10
South Carolina	116	260	124.1	40	25	25	0.0	37
South Dakota	288	477	65.6	23	59	43	-27.1	13
Tennessee	129	235	82.2	42	27	21	-22.2	42
Texas	213	517	142.7	21	39	39	0.0	18
Utah	172	366	112.8	33	36	35	-2.8	24
Vermont	308	556	80.5	15	63	46	-27.0	8
Virginia	173	396	128.9	29	30	28	-6.7	34
Washington	236	442	87.3	25	38	32	-15.8	26
West Virginia	106	203	91.5	46	22	20	-9.1	43
Wisconsin	289	600	107.6	13	51	46	-9.8	9
Wyoming	352	1,173	233.2	1	60	88	46.7	1
District of Columbia	210	773	268.1	3	27	43	59.3	15

Source: Department of Commerce, Bureau of the Census; and Tax Foundation computations.

Source: Tax Foundation, One Thomas Circle, N.W., Washington, DC 20005

Estimated Federal Total and Per Capita Tax Burden by State

Fiscal Years 1987-1989

($Millions)

State	Federal Total Tax Burden			Federal Funds Tax Burden			Per Capita Burden (Dollars)			State Rank 1988	
	1987	1988	1989	1987	1988	1989	1987	1988	1989	Total	Per Capita
U.S.Total	$ 830,536	$ 885,116	$ 940,290	$ 514,478	$ 538,872	$ 570,568	$ 3,414	$ 3,603	$ 3,790	—	—
Alabama	10,209	10,893	11,568	6,072	6,357	6,727	2,505	2,656	2,802	25	43
Alaska	2,419	2,560	2,713	1,464	1,519	1,605	4,358	4,430	4,506	46	5
Arizona	10,209	10,915	11,608	6,368	6,668	7,086	2,991	3,108	3,213	24	33
Arkansas	5,633	6,042	6,421	3,241	3,418	3,623	2,371	2,536	2,690	32	48
California	104,606	111,631	118,703	65,052	68,193	72,221	3,806	3,985	4,158	1	11
Colorado	11,322	12,081	12,843	7,040	7,382	7,818	3,406	3,570	3,728	23	19
Connecticut	16,402	17,398	18,481	10,815	11,261	11,910	5,124	5,410	5,720	16	1
Delaware	2,486	2,648	2,813	1,472	1,538	1,628	3,890	4,106	4,321	44	8
Flordia	40,820	43,585	46,379	27,638	29,054	30,804	3,409	3,547	3,678	5	21
Georgia	18,782	20,023	21,270	11,522	12,042	12,741	3,029	3,177	3,320	12	29
Hawaii	3,449	3,688	3,924	2,057	2,161	2,288	3,206	3,378	3,544	40	24
Idaho	2,455	2,632	2,796	1,369	1,448	1,535	2,428	2,581	2,717	45	47
Illinois	43,850	46,638	49,511	27,231	28,501	30,174	3,789	4,020	4,257	4	10
Indiana	16,590	17,712	18,830	10,305	10,794	11,428	3,012	3,212	3,409	15	27
Iowa	8,208	8,797	9,351	4,862	5,144	5,459	2,887	3,100	3,302	30	34
Kansas	8,285	8,851	9,409	5,089	5,345	5,664	3,349	3,555	3,753	29	20
Kentucky	9,108	9,724	10,325	5,484	5,761	6,101	2,435	2,591	2,742	27	46
Louisiana	11,560	12,315	13,067	7,064	7,402	7,836	2,564	2,726	2,886	22	41
Maine	3,268	3,494	3,712	1,967	2,069	2,192	2,769	2,941	3,104	42	37
Maryland	18,351	19,533	20,757	11,454	11,959	12,654	4,079	4,303	4,533	13	7
Massachusetts	24,874	26,456	28,114	15,991	16,704	17,678	4,254	4,510	4,777	10	4
Michigan	32,959	34,996	37,100	19,793	20,692	21,897	3,609	3,835	4,069	9	12

Minnesota	14,450	15,457	16,434	8,425	8,859	9,387	3,412	3,629	3,838	20	17
Mississippi	5,345	5,723	6,080	3,109	3,269	3,461	2,024	2,153	2,273	33	51
Missouri	16,292	17,397	18,489	10,104	10,609	11,240	3,202	3,401	3,596	17	23
Montana	2,160	2,316	2,460	1,258	1,330	1,412	2,621	2,793	2,946	47	40
Nebraska	4,774	5,126	5,457	2,842	2,999	3,181	2,980	3,188	3,383	34	28
Nevada	3,580	3,794	4,023	2,379	2,481	2,624	3,624	3,738	3,861	39	13
New Hampshire	4,056	4,315	4,588	2,656	2,770	2,930	3,888	4,071	4,260	36	9
New Jersey	36,840	39,083	41,474	23,504	24,525	29,951	4,811	5,075	5,356	7	2
New Mexico	3,822	4,087	4,342	2,291	2,406	2,549	2,538	2,664	2,780	38	42
New York	72,710	77,480	82,374	45,368	47,499	50,300	4,083	4,339	4,601	2	6
North Carolina	17,920	19,124	20,314	10,630	11,129	11,778	2,800	2,955	3,104	14	36
North Dakota	1,887	2,019	2,145	1,151	1,213	1,286	2,763	2,939	3,099	48	38
Ohio	35,304	37,644	39,977	20,994	22,001	23,295	3,284	3,500	3,716	8	22
Oklahoma	9,548	10,173	10,800	5,895	6,166	6,526	2,853	3,000	3,143	26	35
Oregon	8,074	8,635	9,170	4,680	4,935	5,234	2,982	3,175	3,557	31	30
Pennsylvania	40,029	42,622	45,225	24,108	25,287	26,781	3,365	3,579	3,792	6	18
Rhode Island	3,434	3,660	3,886	2,013	2,112	2,237	3,508	3,720	3,929	41	14
South Carolina	8,440	9,019	9,582	4,975	5,214	5,518	2,472	2,610	2,740	28	45
South Dakota	1,737	1,872	1,993	1,014	1,074	1,140	2,443	2,621	2,780	49	44
Tennessee	13,315	14,201	15,086	8,098	8,465	8,955	2,754	2,916	3,076	21	39
Texas	55,196	58,648	62,260	35,515	37,031	39,164	3,235	3,360	3,486	3	25
Utah	3,940	4,217	4,481	2,271	2,386	2,526	2,323	2,440	2,543	37	50
Vermont	1,603	1,710	1,814	972	1,023	1,084	2,942	3,109	3,268	50	32
Virginia	20,565	21,928	23,318	13,081	13,682	14,482	3,514	3,702	3,891	11	15
Washington	15,607	16,610	17,624	9,555	10,018	10,610	3,460	3,639	3,817	18	16
West Virginia	4,459	4,755	5,043	2,655	2,788	2,952	2,330	2,487	2,642	35	49
Wisconsin	15,080	16,086	17,064	8,770	9,232	9,785	3,144	3,342	3,534	19	26
Wyoming	1,543	1,642	1,739	953	998	1,057	3,014	3,169	3,319	51	31
Dist. of Columbia	2,973	3,155	3,350	1,856	1,935	2,047	4,757	5,057	5,376	43	3

Source: Total U.S. taxes as shown in the Fiscal Year 1989 Budget of the U.S. Government.
Computations of total and per capita tax burden by state were made by Tax Foundation.

Source: Tax Foundation, One Thomas Circle, N.W., Washington, DC 20005.

Federal and State/Local Corporate Income Taxes and Corporate Payroll Taxes National Income Accounts Series (1970–1987)

(Dollar Figures in Billions)

Year	A Corporate Profits Net of Federal Reserve Earnings	B Federal Corporate Income Tax Accruals	C Effective Rate of Federal Tax (B/A)	D State/Local Corporate Income Tax Accruals	E Effective Rate of Federal and State/Local Tax (B+D/A)	F Corporate Payroll Taxes[1]	G Income and Payroll Taxes as % of Corp. Profits (B+D+F/A)
1970[2]	$ 72.4	$ 27.1	37.4%	$ 3.7	42.5%	—	—
1971	84.0	30.1	35.8	4.3	41.0	—	—
1972	98.1	33.4	34.0	5.3	39.4	$ 22.7	62.6%
1973	122.7	39.0	31.8	6.0	36.7	29.5	60.7
1974	133.2	39.5	29.7	6.7	34.7	33.2	59.6
1975	129.1	38.2	29.6	7.3	35.2	33.6	61.3
1976	164.3	48.7	29.6	9.6	35.5	39.8	59.7
1977	194.2	55.7	28.7	11.4	34.6	45.4	57.9
1978	225.8	64.4	28.5	12.1	33.9	53.7	57.7
1979	247.6	65.1	26.3	13.6	31.8	62.2	56.9
1980	225.2	58.6	26.0	14.5	32.5	66.6	62.0
1981	212.0	51.7	24.4	15.4	31.7	77.6	68.3
1982	154.2	33.8	21.9	14.0	31.0	81.7	84.0
1983	192.8	47.1	24.4	15.9	32.7	89.0	78.8
1984	223.3	59.1	26.5	18.7	34.8	104.4	81.6
1985	208.0	58.3	28.0	20.6	37.9	110.4	91.0
1986	215.9	65.9	30.5	21.3	40.4	115.6	93.9
1987(e)	259.7	93.8	36.1	27.2	46.6	121.8	93.5

[1] Includes corporate employer share of OASDHI, state unemployment insurance tax, federal unemployment tax, railroad unemployment insurance and retirement, and workers' compensation.

[2] Includes some effect from Vietnam period surcharge.

Sources: Economic Reports of the President, various years, and unpublished statistics of the Department of Commerce, Bureau of Economic Analysis.

Source *Federal Tax Policy Memo*, 1988, Tax Foundation, One Thomas Circle, N.W., Washington, D.C. 20005.

MAJOR STATE TAXES AND RATES*

State	Income Taxes: Corporate	Income Taxes: Individual	General Sales and Use Tax	Gasoline Tax (per gallon)	Cigarette Tax (per pack of 20)	Property Tax
Alabama	5%(F)	2 to 5%(F)	4%(a)	11 cents	16.5 cents	X
Arizona	2.5 to 10.5(F)	2 to 8(F)	5(a)	16	15	X
Arkansas	1 to 6	1 to 7	4(a)	13.5	21	X
California	9.3(q)	1 to 9.3(q)	4.75(a)	9	10	X
Colorado	5.5 to 6(b)	5(q)	3(a)	18(b)	20	X
Connecticut	11.5(c)	1 to 12(d)	7.5	19(e)	26	X
Georgia	6	1 to 6	3(a)	7.5 + 3% of retail	12	X
Hawaii	4.4 to 6.4	2.25 to 10(b)	4	15 to 22.5	40% wholesale	
Idaho	8	2 to 8.2	5	18	18	X
Illinois	4(p)	2.5	5(a)	13	20	X
Indiana	3.4(f)	3.4	5	15	15.5	X
Iowa	6 to 12(F,h,q)	.5 to 13(F)(q)	4(a)	18(e)	34(b)	
Kansas	4.5(g)	2 to 9(F)	4(a)	11	24	X
Kentucky	3 to 7.25	2 to 6(F,r)	5(a)	15(i,l)	3.001	X
Louisiana	4 to 8(F)	2 to 6(F)	4(a)	16	16	
Maine	3.5 to 8.93(q)	1 to 10	5	14	28	X
Maryland	7	2 to 5	5	18.5	13	X
Massachusetts	8.33(j)	5(k)	5	11	26	X
Michigan	2.35	4.6	4	15	25	X
Minnesota	9.5(q)	6 to 8(o,q)	6(a)	17	38	X
Mississippi	3 to 5	3 to 5	6	17(e)	18	X
Missouri	5(F)	1.5 to 6(F)	4.225(a,b)	11	13	X
Nebraska	4.75 to 6.65	2 to 5.9	4(a)	17.3(l)	27	
New Jersey	9(g)	2 to 3.5	6	8(e)	27	X
New Mexico	4.8 to 7.6	1.8 to 8.5	4.75(a)	14	15	X
New York	9(c)	3 to 8.375(b,s)	4(a)	8	21	
North Carolina	7	3 to 7	3(a)	15.8(l)	2	X
North Dakota	3 to 10.5(F)	2.67 to 12(F,m)	5.5(b)	17	27	X
Ohio	5.1 to 8.9(c)	.743 to 6.9	5(a)	14.7(l)	18	X
Oklahoma	5	.5 to 6(F,r)	4(a)	16	23	
Pennsylvania	8.5	2.1	6	12	18	X
Rhode Island	8(c)	22.96% of Federal income tax	6	15(i,l)	25	X
South Carolina	5.5(b)	3 to 7	5	15(e)	7	X
Tennessee	6	6(d)	5.5(a)	17	13	
Utah	5	2.75 to 7.75	5.094(a,b)	19	23	X
Vermont	5.5 to 8.25	25% of Federal income tax	4	13	17	X
Virginia	6	2 to 5.75	3.5(a)	17.5	2.5	X
West Virginia	9.75(b)	3 to 6.5(q)	5	10.5	17	
Wisconsin	7.9	4.9 to 6.93(q)	5(a)	20.9(l)	30	X
Florida	5.5(q)		6(a)	4	24	X
Nevada	These 5 states	These 7 states	5.75(a)	14.25(e)	20(b)	X
South Dakota	have no	have no	4(a)	18	23	
Texas	corporate income tax	individual income tax	6(a)	15	26	
Washington			6.5(a)	18	31	X
Wyoming			3(a)	8	8	X
Alaska	1 to 9.4(q)		These	8	16	X
Delaware	8.7	3.2 to 7.7(F,h)	5 states	16	14	
Montana	6.75(g,t)	2 to 11(F,n)	have no	20	16	X
New Hampshire	8	5(d)	general	14	17	X
Oregon	6.6	5 to 9(F,h)	sales tax	14(e)	27	X

(X) Indicates state levies a property tax.
(F) Allows Federal income tax as a deduction.

(a) Local taxes are additional.
(b) Future reduction scheduled under current law.
(c) Alternative methods of calculation may be required.
(d) In Connecticut, New Hampshire, and Tennessee, tax applies to income from intangibles only, at various rates according to type. In Connecticut, capital gains are taxed at 7%.
(e) Future increases scheduled under current law.
(f) A supplemental net income tax is imposed at 4.5%.
(g) Corporate surtax imposed: Kansas, 2.25%; Montana, 4%; New Jersey's rate is computed annually.
(h) Deductions limited.
(i) Tax imposed at percent of wholesale value.
(j) A 14% surtax is imposed on the sum of the income tax and a tax on net worth or tangible property not taxed locally.
(k) Tax of 10% on income derived from intangibles, and 5% on all other income.
(l) Tax rate is periodically adjusted administratively.
(m) Optional tax of 14% of taxpayer's adjusted Federal income tax liability.
(n) Additional 10% surtax is imposed for 1987.
(o) Plus 10% of Federal 15% rate and personal exemption phaseout for taxpayers above certain income levels.
(p) Additional 2.5% personal property replacement tax.
(q) Alternative minimum tax is imposed.
(r) Qualified taxpayers may elect to pay alternative taxes at varying rates.
(s) Separate tax is imposed on unearned income through 1988.
(t) 7% rate for corporations using water's edge apportionment.

Source: Compiled by Tax Foundation from data reported by Commerce Clearing House.

* As reported through April 1, 1988.

Source: Tax Foundation, One Thomas Circle, N.W., Washington, D.C. 20005.

FEDERAL INCOME TAXES PAID BY HIGH- AND LOW-INCOME TAXPAYERS 1979 AND 1986[a]

Adjusted Gross Income Class	Income Level 1979	Income Level 1986	Percent of Tax Paid 1979	Percent of Tax Paid 1986	Average Tax 1979	Average Tax 1986
Highest 5%	$ 39,900 or more	$ 67,000 or more	37.6%	42.9%	$ 17,407	$ 31,309
Highest 10%	32,710 or more	48,980 or more	49.5	55.5	11,456	20,248
Highest 25%	21,760 or more	32,420 or more	73.1	76.2	6,769	11,132
Highest 50%	11,870 or more	17,148 or more	93.2	93.8	4,315	6,845
Lowest 50%	11,869 or less	17,147 or less	6.8	6.2	313	455
Lowest 25%	5,565 or less	7,806 or less	0.5	0.6	46	90
Lowest 10%	2,212 or less	3,123 or less	b	b	9	27

1986 Income and Tax Data

Adjusted Gross Income Class	Total Individual Returns (thousands)	Total Adjusted Gross Income ($billions)	Percentage of Adjusted Gross Income	Average Tax Rate
Highest 5%	5,165	$ 613.7	24.3%	26.3%
Highest 10%	10,330	909.2	36.0	23.0
Highest 25%	25,825	1,512.7	60.0	19.0
Highest 50%	51,650	2,139.6	84.8	16.5
Lowest 50%	51,650	383.0	15.2	6.1
Lowest 25%	25,825	68.0	2.7	3.4
Lowest 10%	10,330	-16.2	—	—

[a] Data for 1986 are preliminary.
[b] Less than .07 percent.
Source: Tax Foundation computations based on Statistics of Income, Internal Revenue Service, U.S. Department of the Treasury.

Source: Tax Foundation, One Thomas Circle, N.W., Washington, DC 20005.

MEDIAN FAMILY INCOME BEFORE AND AFTER DIRECT FEDERAL TAXES AND INFLATION 1980–1988

Year	Two-Earner Median Family Income[a]	Direct Federal Taxes: Income Tax[b]	Direct Federal Taxes: Social Security	Direct Federal Taxes: Total	After-Tax Income: Current Dollars	After-Tax Income: 1988 Dollars[c]
1980	$29,627	$4,050	$1,816	$5,866	$23,761	$33,993
1981	32,224	4,386	2,143	6,529	25,695	33,327
1982	34,515	4,450	2,313	6,763	27,752	33,927
1983	36,106	4,300	2,419	6,719	29,387	34,778
1984	38,713	4,634	2,710	7,344	31,369	35,606
1985	40,593	4,787	2,862	7,649	32,944	36,083
1986	42,492	5,158	3,038	8,196	34,296	36,877
1987[d]	44,617	5,319	3,190	8,509	36,108	37,456
1988[d]	46,848	5,623	3,518	9,141	37,707	37,707

[a] Median income for household with two earners employed full-time, year round.
[b] Married couple filing joint return, two dependent children.
[c] Adjusted by Consumer Price Index, assumes 3.8% inflation in 1988.
[d] Estimated by Tax Foundation.
Source: U.S. Department of Commerce, Bureau of the Census; U.S. Department of Labor, Bureau of Labor Statistics; Treasury Department, Internal Revenue Service.

Source: Tax Foundation, One Thomas Circle, N.W., Washington, DC 20005.

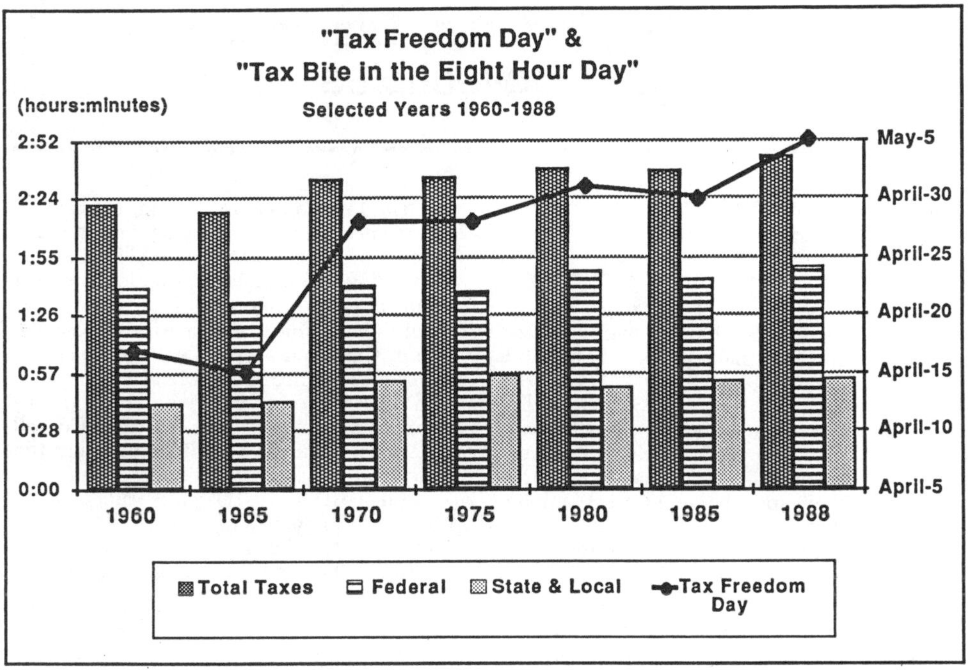

Source: Tax Foundation, One Thomas Circle, N.W., Washington, D.C. 20005-5802.

Investing in Gold, Diamonds and Collectibles

Investing in Gold

Gold has been one of the more widely promoted investment vehicles over the last several years. Prices moved from about $140 per ounce in early 1977 to over $800 in early 1980. However, by August 1985 prices declined to $291 an ounce but climbed to over $450.00 by August 1987. Because of such large fluctuations, the metal has stimulated a great deal of speculative interest among many investors.

Investment in gold can be made in a variety of ways:

Gold bullion (bars and wafers) This can be purchased through many stock brokers, bullion currency dealers, and some investment (mutual fund) companies. The purity of gold is indicated by the fineness. Pure gold has a fineness of 1.000 and corresponds to 24 karats.* Each bar is stamped with the fineness as determined by an assay, the refiner's number, a bar identification number and the weight. A bar fineness of .995 or better is acceptable.

Individuals who accept delivery of gold bars and who subsequently wish to resell must have the bar reassayed prior to sale because of the possibility of adulteration with cheaper metals. Because of the latter possibility, individuals should always buy from reputable dealers, and the bar should bear the stamp of well recognized refiners or assayers. Individuals taking physical possession of the metal also have sales taxes, storage, and insurance costs.

The purchaser may arrange to have the dealer (or agent) retain physical possession of the bullion. In this case, evidence of ownership is provided by a *gold deposit certificate* (receipt) issued by the dealer. Since gold certificates are generally nonnegotiable or assignable, there is no loss if it is stolen. The gold deposit certificate method of buying bullion eliminates sales taxes, storage risks (though the dealer will charge a modest storage fee) and the need for assay on resale. It is probably the most convenient way of purchasing gold.

* This "karats" is not to be confused with the "carats" that apply to diamonds.

Gold bullion coins Bullion coins are issued in large number by several governments which guarantee their gold content. They have no numismatic value. The best known gold bullion coins are the U.S. Gold One Ounce, South African Krugerrand, Canadian Maple Leaf, Austrian 100 Corona and the Gold Mexican 50 peso. The first three coins have a pure gold content of one ounce. The Austrian Corona has a gold content of .9802 ounce and the Mexican peso 1.2057 ounces. The premium (cost above the gold value) varies from dealer to dealer. For those who do not want to take physical possession, deposit certificates are available for the coins.

One of the largest bullion dealers is Deak International (212-757-0100) headquartered in New York City. Gold coins can also be purchased at banks where there is generally a very low premium over the gold content value.

Gold stocks The stocks of a number of Canadian and U.S. gold mining companies are traded on the New York (N), American (A) and Over-The-Counter (O) exchanges. Of course, with stocks, the investor is not just buying into gold, but also into the many special problems associated with running a company—production costs, quality of the ore, lifetime of the deposit, etc. However, many gold stocks pay dividends, whereas other gold investments do not pay any return during the holding period.

Some listed stocks are given below:

Agnico-Eagle Mines (O)
Campbell Red Lake Mines (N)
Dome Mines (N)
Sunshine Mining (N)
Homestake Mining Company (N)

A publicly-held New York Stock Exchange closed-end gold fund is ASA Limited. Several mutual funds which invest in gold are given in the mutual fund section of the Almanac (page 366).

South African gold mines are traded on the Over-The-Counter Market by means of ADR (American Depository Receipt). ADR is a claim on foreign stocks (South African gold shares, in this case) held by the foreign branches of large U.S. banks. Holders of ADRs are entitled to dividends which, in the case of South African gold shares, may be substantial. The ADRs of these companies are listed in *The Wall Street Journal* under the Foreign Securities section, which follows the OTC quotations.

Some major South African gold mining companies are:

Blyvooruitzicht
Buffelsfontein
East Driefontein
Kloof
President Brand
President Steyn
Randfontein
West Dreifontein
Western Deep Levels
Western Holdings

Mutual funds specializing in gold and precious metals A number of mutual funds (see page 366) specialize in gold and precious metals stocks. These funds provide diversification among a number of issues thereby reducing risk associated with any particular stock.

Options on gold stocks Put and call options are available on Homestake Mining (Chicago Options Exchange) and on ASA Limited (American Options Exchange). These options may be used for leveraged speculation or for hedging existing gold holdings. Holders of call options gain if the gold shares increase, while holders of put options benefit if prices decline.

The Philadelphia Stock Exchange trades a gold/silver option based on an index of seven different stocks in the industry.

Options on gold bullion Put and call options on gold bullion are traded on the International Options Market (IOM) of the Montreal Stock Exchange. IOM options are on 10 ounces of gold. Contract months are Feb/May/Aug/Nov.

Monex (Newport Beach, CA) provides put and call options on 32.15 ounces of gold. The Monex options are not tradeable but can be exercized during the option period. Expiration periods are 30, 60, 90, and 185 days. Mocatta Metals (New York) also offers futures contracts.

Since options are paid in full, they are not subject to margin calls or forced liquidation as is the case with futures contracts. At this time, quotations on bullion options are not available in the daily press.

Gold futures contract Gold futures contracts are obligations to buy or sell 100 ounces of gold on or before a specified date at a specified price. Futures contracts must be exercised if held to maturity, while options contracts need not be exercised if held to maturity. Futures contracts are purchased on margin, and hence, are subject to margin call and possible forced liquidation. They are widely quoted in the financial press, and the market is highly organized.

As with options, futures contracts may be used for leveraged speculation or for hedging. Speculators will buy contracts if they anticipate a price increase or sell contracts in anticipation of a price decrease.

Gold futures are traded on the N.Y. Commodity Exchange, the International Monetary Market of the Chicago Mercantile Exchange, and other markets.

Options on Gold Futures Contracts Options on Gold Futures contracts (the right to buy and sell a gold futures contract rather than the metal) are actively traded on the New York Comex. The futures contract underlying the options is for 100 ounces of gold. Contract months are April/Aug./Dec. Gold futures options premiums are reported daily in the *Wall Street Journal*.

Investing in Diamonds

Diamond prices are very volative. For example, they have appreciated on the average of about 12.6% over the ten-year period 1969–1979 (compared to a consumer price index of 6.1% during the same period of time). There have been periods (the recession of 1973—1974 and in 1981) when the price of investment quality diamonds slipped as much as 40%. A major factor stabilizing the market is DeBeers, a South African diamond company which handles as much as 80% of the world's diamonds. While the appreciation of diamonds has been impressive, potential buyers should be aware that prices are not quoted in the daily newspapers; therefore, selling the stones at a profit may be difficult. Quotes are available in the *Rappaport Diamond Report*, 15 West 47 Street, New York, NY 10036, (212) 354-0575. Another good source of information on the diamond industry is the Diamond Registry, 30 West 47 Street, New York, NY 10036, (212) 575-0444. The registry publishes a monthly newsletter which includes price ranges, trends, and forecasts as well as other pertinent material.

To locate reputable gem dealers check with the Diamond Registry (address above) or the

American Gem Society
5901 West 3rd Street
Los Angeles, CA 90036-2898
(213) 936-4367

American Diamond Industry Association
71 West 47 Street
New York, NY 10036
(212) 575-0525

Buyers should only deal with reputable firms, and the stones should be certified by an independent laboratory such as the Gemological Institute of America and International Gemological Institute with offices in New York City.

Diamonds are ranked in terms of the 4 C's—carat (one carat equals 1/142 ounces weight), color, clarity, and cut.

Carat For investment purposes the diamond should be more than .5 carat. However, diamonds of more than 2 carats may be difficult to sell.

Color There are six main categories, each with subdivisions:

D,E,F—Colorless
G,H,I,J—Near colorless
K,L,M—Faint yellow
N,O,P,Q,R—Very light yellow
S,T,U,V,W,X,Y,Z—Light yellow
Fancy yellow stone

Color should be in the range from D to H. However, Fancy Yellow Stones often command very high prices because of their scarcity.

Clarity Although bubbles, lines, and specks (inclusions) are natural to diamonds, they may interfere with the passage of light through the diamond. With a 10X magnification, a professional appraiser can grade the diamond according to the ten clarity grades:

FL—Flawless
IF—Internally flawless
VVS-1, VVS-2—Very, very slight inclusions
VS-1, VS-2—Very slight inclusions
SI-1, SI-2—Slight inclusions
I-1, I-2, I-3—Imperfect

Investment grade stones should be in the range FL to VS-2.

Cut There are several types of cuts—oval, marquise, pear shaped, round brilliant and emerald. Round brilliant stones are preferred for investment purposes. Proportions are important, and the preferred values are:

Depth % (total depth divided by girdle diameter): 57% to 63%.
Table (table diameter divided by girdle diameter): 57% to 66%.
Girdle thickness should be neither very thick nor very thin.

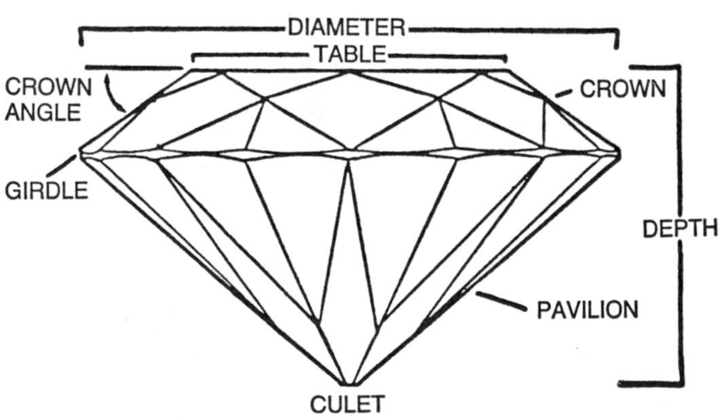

THE ROUND BRILLIANT DIAMOND

Investing in Collectibles

Sotheby's Art Market Trends

Index sectors	May 1988	One month ago	One year ago	Two years ago	Five years ago	One month % change	One year % change	Two year % change	Five years % change	Five years Average annual % change
Old Master paintings	373	373	329	303	212	nil	+13.4	+23.1	+75.9	+12.0
19th-century European paintings	347	333	303	249	185	+ 4.2	+14.5	+39.4	+87.6	+13.4
Impressionist & Post-impressionist art	1,091	723	521	380	267	+50.90	+109.4	+187.1	+308.6	+32.5
Modern paintings (1900-1950)	1,090	757	544	364	245	+44.0	+100.4	+199.5	+344.9	+34.8
Contemporary art (1945 onward)	728	609	597	524	366	+19.5	+21.9	+38.9	+98.9	+14.7
American paintings (1800–pre-WWII)	958	871	698	667	452	+10.0	+37.2	+43.6	+111.9	+16.2
Continental ceramics	407	407	320	284	263	nil	+27.2	+43.3	+54.8	+ 9.1
Chinese ceramics	684	581	550	493	445	+17.7	+24.4	+38.7	+53.7	+ 9.0
English silver	388	388	343	314	209	nil	+13.1	+23.6	+85.6	+13.2
Continental silver	260	220	201	190	156	+18.2	+29.4	+36.8	+66.7	+10.8
American furniture	469	469	451	333	239	nil	+ 4.0	+40.8	+96.2	+14.4
French & Continental furniture	355	324	299	285	249	+9.6	+18.7	+24.6	+42.6	+ 7.4
English furniture	720	657	594	447	282	+ 9.6	+21.2	+61.1	+155.3	+20.6
Aggregate index*	650	517	430	351	259	+25.7	+51.2	+85.2	+151.0	+20.2

Basis: 1975 = 100 ($).

*Contemporary art was added to the Art Index in September 1987. The aggregate index excludes this category prior to that date.

Sotheby's Art Market Trends reflect subjective analyses and opinions of Sotheby's art experts, based on auction sales and other information deemed relevant. Nothing in Sotheby's Art Market Trends is intended as investment advice or as a prediction or guarantee of future performance or otherwise.

Source: *Forbes*, July 11, 1988.

MEDIAN SALES PRICE OF EXISTING SINGLE-FAMILY HOMES FOR METROPOLITAN AREAS* (not seasonally adjusted in thousands of dollars)

	Years			Quarters				
				1987[r]				1988[p]
Metropolitan Area	1985	1986	1987	I	II	III	IV	I
Akron	$ 52.7	$ 56.2	$ 57.1	$ 54.7	$ 56.9	$ 57.8	$ 58.1	$57.1
Albany/Schenectady/Troy	60.3	72.7	86.4	80.1	86.5	88.6	90.3	82.8
Albuquerque	76.8	81.6	82.6	83.1	82.5	84.4	79.8	79.7
Orange County(Anaheim/Santa Ana MSA)**	136.2	147.7	166.9	156.1	167.3	167.7	174.5	183.8
Baltimore	72.6	74.0	81.1	81.0	76.8	81.9	84.3	83.6
Baton Rouge	74.6	70.9	67.8	68.3	68.1	69.2	65.5	65.7
Birmingham	64.5	68.3	71.6	67.5	72.7	71.6	73.9	73.1
Boston	134.2	159.2	177.2	170.0	176.2	182.2	177.5	176.9
Buffalo/Niagara Falls	46.7	52.4	56.7	55.6	56.8	56.6	59.2	64.1
Charleston	64.8	n/a	72.7	71.9	72.1	74.6	73.2	72.6
Chattanooga	52.3	55.3	59.0	57.5	58.9	58.8	60.3	61.2
Chicago	81.1	86.1	90.8	85.7	90.9	91.2	91.5	92.8
Cincinnati	60.2	n/a	66.1	63.8	65.9	66.9	69.1	67.0
Cleveland	64.4	66.9	68.1	62.9	68.8	68.5	67.6	65.3
Columbus	62.2	65.5	68.7	66.9	67.2	72.7	69.3	66.2
Dallas/Ft. Worth	87.7	92.8	89.2	91.2	90.0	89.3	85.8	85.9
Denver	84.3	86.4	88.9	89.9	88.2	91.0	86.5	83.7
Des Moines	52.5	55.9	55.6	55.9	56.8	56.2	52.1	54.5
Detroit	51.7	58.1	65.6	64.3	66.2	65.9	66.3	71.5
El Paso	57.6	59.0	59.2	58.0	58.0	62.6	58.6	57.8
Ft.Lauderdale/Hollywood/PompanoBeach	74.6	77.7	79.6	76.6	79.7	80.8	80.6	78.6
Grand Rapids	46.7	50.4	53.5	51.7	53.4	54.0	55.7	55.4
Hartford	99.6	129.0	157.4	136.6	157.0	165.4	163.9	166.4
Honolulu	162.1	172.0	186.0	174.0	182.9	190.6	193.3	198.4
Houston	78.6	69.9	65.9	64.7	67.4	67.3	62.8	60.2
Indianapolis	55.0	59.0	62.5	61.6	63.8	62.8	60.7	61.8
Jacksonville	58.4	62.8	65.1	62.7	65.8	66.3	65.2	68.9
Kansas City	61.4	65.4	69.8	72.9	71.1	69.2	68.5	70.9
Knoxville	58.2	60.3	65.4	63.2	66.2	66.1	65.6	66.3
Lansing	50.3	52.4	54.5	53.2	56.0	56.3	53.6	53.4

Las Vegas	75.1	77.5	77.0	76.1	77.9	76.7	76.7	75.7
Los Angeles Area**	n/a	128.8	139.5	130.1	139.6	145.4	145.2	159.9
Louisville	50.6	51.7	51.7	52.1	53.4	53.3	51.5	51.1
Memphis	64.6	70.6	75.0	70.6	76.9	75.2	76.3	77.5
Miami/Hialeah	80.5	81.1	81.1	74.7	84.4	83.5	80.4	78.0
Milwaukee	67.5	69.9	70.5	67.8	71.7	70.9	70.8	72.6
Minneapolis/St Paul	75.2	77.9	80.5	80.4	80.2	80.9	80.6	84.4
Nashville/Davidson	66.1	70.8	75.5	73.4	75.6	75.7	77.2	77.6
New Orleans	n/a	n/a	n/a	n/a	n/a	n/a	74.1	73.0
New York/Northern New Jersey/Long Island	134.0	160.6	183.5	169.4	183.0	190.3	185.1	186.6
Oklahoma City	64.7	63.0	62.3	62.4	65.2	61.4	59.5	56.5
Omaha	58.3	58.8	59.0	57.8	60.0	59.7	57.5	58.3
Orlando	70.3	72.5	76.2	73.6	76.4	72.9	78.7	81.4
Philadelphia	70.8	74.5	81.5	79.8	84.6	84.5	76.9	73.9
Phoenix	74.7	78.4	80.9	78.4	81.4	82.7	80.4	79.0
Pittsburgh	n/a	n/.a	n/.a	n/a	n/a	n/a	n/a	60.9
Portland	61.5	62.6	64.2	62.7	64.3	64.0	66.3	62.8
Providence	67.5	87.6	121.4	102.8	119.7	126.6	127.6	123.3
Riverside/San Bernadino**	87.3	94.5	98.7	91.9	98.3	100.7	101.2	95.5
Rochester	64.2	68.3	72.5	69.5	72.3	74.1	72.8	73.2
St. Louis	65.7	70.9	74.3	71.9	74.7	75.7	73.3	74.1
Salt Lake City/Ogden	66.7	68.5	69.4	68.1	69.5	71.1	67.9	65.3
San Antonio	67.7	69.2	70.2	67.6	72.6	72.1	67.6	63.4
San Diego**	106.4	118.2	128.8	121.1	127.1	131.7	131.8	134.4
San Francisco Bay Area**	n/a	n/a	171.4	161.3	169.9	175.9	176.0	178.8
Seattle/Tacoma	n/a	n/a	82.6	79.0	84.2	82.6	84.2	85.1
Syracuse	58.8	64.3	68.9	65.2	68.1	71.3	70.0	68.1
Tampa/St.Petersburg/Clearwater	58.4	61.1	63.8	59.8	64.9	65.0	63.4	60.2
Toledo	51.9	56.0	56.3	53.4	58.2	56.9	54.7	56.5
Tulsa	66.7	65.5	65.7	64.1	67.4	66.7	63.1	63.5
Washington, DC	97.1	101.6	114.2	106.2	115.0	117.7	121.5	132.4
West Palm Beach/Boca Raton/Delray Beach	88.3	92.6	102.6	96.9	108.8	99.1	102.4	94.5

n/a Not Available p Preliminary r Revised

* All areas are metropolitan statistical areas (MSA) as defined by the US Office of Management and Budget. They include the named central city and surrounding areas. **Provided by the California Association of REALTORS®.

Source: National Association of REALTORS®, Economics and Research Division, 777 14th Street, N.W., Washington, D.C. 20005.

MEDIAN SALES PRICE OF APARTMENT CONDOS AND CO-OPS, QUARTERLY (not seasonally adjusted)

Year		United States	Northeast	Midwest	South	West
1983		$64,000	$ 61,300	$55,200	$62,000	$ 97,300
1984		65,100	64,700	55,600	63,300	94,600
1985		67,600	73,600	56,100	62,300	91,100
1986		72,600	84,900	58,700	64,600	90,800
1987		77,800	98,300	61,700	64,100	97,200
1987	I	$71,600	$ 85,600	$59,300	$61,500	$ 89,000
	II	77,700	97,400	59,300	69,000	95,800
	III	80,300	100,000	65,800	62,900	101,500
	IV	78,300	108,800	58,700	59,100	99,300
1988	I[p]	$81,500	$111,100	$57,600	$65,300	$105,100

p preliminary

Source: National Association of REALTORS®, Economics and Research Division, 777 14th Street, N.W., Washington, D.C. 20005.

HOUSING AFFORDABILITY

Year	Median-Priced Existing Single-Family Home	Mortgage Rate*	Monthly P & I Payment	Payment as % Income	Median Family Income	Qualifying Income**	Affordability Indexes Composite	Affordability Indexes Fixed	Affordability Indexes ARM
1982	$67,800	15.38%	$702	35.9%	$23,433	$33,713	69.5	69.4	69.7
1983	70,300	12.85	616	30.1	24,580	29,546	83.2	81.7	85.2
1984	72,400	12.49	618	28.2	26,433	29,650	89.1	84.6	92.1
1985	75,500	11.74	609	26.2	27,735	29,243	94.8	89.6	100.6
1986	80,300	10.25	563	23.0	29,458	27,047	108.9	105.7	116.3
1987	85,600	9.28	565	21.8	31,100	27,101	114.8	108.0	123.0
1987									
Mar	$85,200	9.09%	$553	22.2%	$29,868	$26,537	112.6	110.3	120.1
Apr	86,000	9.09	558	22.3	30,005	26,786	112.0	110.1	119.8
May	86,000	9.27	567	22.6	30,142	27,216	110.8	108.0	118.9
Jun	85,900	9.38	572	22.7	30,279	27,448	110.3	104.6	120.9
Jul	88,300	9.41	589	23.3	30,416	28,289	107.5	99.4	116.7
Aug	86,500	9.40	577	22.7	30,553	27,688	110.3	102.1	119.3
Sep	85,500	9.25	563	22.0	30,689	27,010	113.6	104.2	122.2
Oct	84,600	9.22	555	21.6	30,827	26,655	115.7	104.4	124.0
Nov	85,000	9.25	559	21.7	30,963	26,852	115.3	103.8	122.4
Dec	85,400	9.20	560	21.6	31,100	26,860	115.8	104.6	121.4
1988									
Jan	$87,400	9.24%	$575	22.1%	$31,242	$27,586	113.3	102.4	120.1
Feb[r]	88,100	9.16	575	22.0	31,384	27,611	113.7	103.5	120.5
Mar[p]	88,700	9.08	575	21.9	31,526	27,602	114.2	105.1	121.8

r Revised
p Preliminary
* Effective rate on loans closed on existing homes-Federal Home Loan Bank Board.
** Based on current lending requirements of the Federal National Mortgage Association using a 20 percent down payment.

Source: National Association of REALTORS®, Economics and Research Division, 777 14th Street, N.W., Washington, D.C. 20005.

AVERAGE VALUE PER ACRE OF FARMLAND AND BUILDINGS, BY STATE, 1982–88[1]

State	As of April 1				As of February 1			Percent change
	1982	1983	1984	1985	1986	1987	1988	1987–88
				Dollars				Percent
Northeast	1,364	1,343	1,414	1,392	1,416	1,607	1,747	9
Maine	680	708	750	856	993	1,082	1,236	14
New Hampshire	1,136	1,174	1,244	1,419	1,646	1,794	2,037	14
Vermont	815	842	893	1,017	1,180	1,286	1,345	5
Massachusetts	1,874	1,963	2,081	2,372	2,752	2,999	3,534	18
Rhode Island	2,729	2,760	2,926	3,335	3,869	4,217	6,240	48
Connecticut	2,610	2,655	2,814	3,208	3,721	4,056	4,914	21
New York	821	817	842	808	824	931	956	3
New Jersey	3,181	3,140	3,234	3,525	3,913	5,321	6,189	16
Pennsylvania	1,513	1,520	1,642	1,510	1,450	1,725	1,819	5
Delaware	1,787	1,829	1,866	1,642	1,757	1,775	1,895	7
Maryland	2,376	2,121	2,185	2,097	1,887	1,831	2,014	10
Lake States	1,234	1,160	1,099	874	702	598	639	7
Michigan	1,278	1,223	1,223	1,052	936	833	853	2
Wisconsin	1,144	1,113	1,046	847	711	626	630	1
Minnesota	1,272	1,165	1,083	823	609	493	563	14
Corn Belt	1,642	1,482	1,414	1,055	903	815	888	9
Ohio	1,629	1,504	1,444	1,126	1,013	942	991	5
Indiana	1,804	1,610	1,594	1,259	1,058	931	983	6
Illinois	2,023	1,837	1,800	1,314	1,143	1,040	1,114	7
Iowa	1,889	1,684	1,499	1,064	841	748	890	19
Missouri	945	856	856	659	606	552	572	4
Northern Plains	547	528	499	383	323	286	306	7
North Dakota	455	439	439	360	317	282	292	4
South Dakota	349	348	338	250	215	178	187	5
Nebraska	730	701	617	444	364	335	366	9
Kansas	628	601	583	466	387	340	368	8
Appalachia	1,083	1,082	1,090	1,005	983	951	972	2
Virginia	1,096	1,125	1,114	1,091	1,146	1,111	1,143	3
West Virginia	723	688	667	554	537	527	542	3
North Carolina	1,297	1,314	1,380	1,242	1,130	1,096	1,062	-3
Kentucky	1,058	1,049	1,007	906	870	791	786	-1
Tennessee	1,040	1,014	1,044	982	992	1,012	1,104	9
Southeast	1,095	1,095	1,094	1,042	999	1,000	1,056	6
South Carolina	980	946	927	899	872	794	874	10
Georgia	926	929	910	865	822	846	865	2
Florida	1,518	1,576	1,608	1,527	1,435	1,464	1,596	9
Alabama	885	826	809	769	761	731	731	0
Delta States	1,135	1,039	1,040	946	797	666	665	0
Mississippi	981	894	939	835	752	654	658	1
Arkansas	1,096	972	933	849	705	634	645	2
Louisiana	1,414	1,351	1,351	1,256	1,005	734	708	-4
Southern Plains	576	574	614	635	529	471	457	-3
Oklahoma	725	699	699	566	481	428	421	-2
Texas	539	544	593	652	541	482	466	-3
Mountain States	325	314	319	286	247	233	227	-2
Montana	271	259	264	222	204	167	164	-2
Idaho	839	814	814	749	644	567	592	4
Wyoming	193	193	197	177	154	151	140	-7
Colorado	451	454	468	435	357	364	364	0
New Mexico	195	178	182	163	134	122	132	8
Arizona	302	289	295	265	231	242	214	-12
Utah	589	560	571	514	478	454	428	-6
Nevada	268	249	254	229	199	211	193	-9
Pacific States	1,346	1,357	1,361	1,225	1,107	974	951	-2
Washington	922	933	961	923	812	723	699	-3
Oregon	705	705	698	579	521	479	466	-3
California	1,900	1,918	1,918	1,726	1,571	1,366	1,341	-2
48 States	823	788	782	679	595	547	564	3
Alaska					1,902	1,437	1,322	-8

1/ Current dollars.

Source: *Agriculture Land Values*, Economics Research Service, U.S. Department of Agriculture.

Industrial Real Estate Market: Selected Cities*

DEMOGRAPHICS

POPULATION: 2,560,500
POPULATION GROWTH RATE: 19.8%
EMPLOYMENT GROWTH RATE: 4.9%
UNEMPLOYMENT RATE: 4.7%
PER CAPITA INCOME: $12,806

MARKET DATA

TOTAL INVENTORY
Central City: 27,550,000 sq.ft.
Suburban: 190,403,000 sq.ft.

VACANT INVENTORY
Central City: 3,830,000 sq.ft.(13.9%)
Suburban: 25,662,000 sq.ft.(13.4%)

NET ABSORPTION
Central City: 1,563,000 sq.ft.
Suburban: 5,141,988 sq.ft.

CURRENT CONSTRUCTION
Central City: 102,245 sq.ft.
Suburban: 7,381,000 sq.ft.

MORTGAGE MONEY SUPPLY
Ample

PRIME SOURCE OF FINANCING
Insurance Companies

ATLANTA: INDUSTRIAL

Market Area: Atlanta Metropolitan Area

1987 REVIEW

Atlanta's economy is fueled by growth in service industries, wholesale trade, and retail trade. The manufacturing sector accounts for only 14 percent of jobs in the Atlanta area which is low compared to other major cities.

Warehouse and distribution space accounted for 70 percent of the absorption of industrial space in 1987. Construction of warehouse and distribution properties is up 11 to 15 percent compared to a year ago. Despite a substantial oversupply of prime industrial space in nearly every SIOR building-size category, SIOR panellsts in the Atlanta area report that demand for most types of industrial properties remains strong.

1988 FORECAST

The overall economic climate in Atlanta is healthy and unless the national economy falters, the Atlanta market should continue to sustain moderate growth. Construction and absorption of warehouse and distribution space will increase between 11 and 15 percent in 1988.

OUTLOOK

SALES PRICES
Manufacturing: Same
Warehouse/Distribution: Up 1-5%
High Tech/R & D: Down 11-15%

LEASE PRICES
Manufacturing: Same
Warehouse/Distribution: Up 11-15%
High Tech/R & D: Down 1-5%

ABSORPTION
Manufacturing: Same
Warehouse/Distribution: Up 11-15%
High Tech/R & D: Same

CONSTRUCTION
Manufacturing: Same
Warehouse/Distribution: Up 11-15%
High Tech/R & D: Down 11-15%

DOLLAR VOLUME
Sales: Same
Leases : Up 6-10%

PROFILE OF BUILDINGS BY TYPE

	WAREHOUSING & DISTRIBUTION	MANUFACTURING	HIGH TECH/ R & D
COMPOSITION OF ABSORPTION	70%	10%	20%
RATE OF NEW CONSTRUCTION ••	Up 11-15%	Same	Down 11-15%
DOLLAR VOLUME - SALES ••	Same	Same	Up 11-15%
DOLLAR VOLUME - LEASES ••	Up 11-15%	Same	Down 11-15%

•• Compared to A Year Ago

SITE PRICES

(Dollars Per Square Foot)

	IMPROVED SITES				UNIMPROVED SITES		
LOCATION	LESS THAN 2 ACRES	2 TO 5 ACRES	5 TO 10 ACRES	MORE THAN 10 ACRES	LESS THAN 10 ACRES	10 TO 100 ACRES	MORE THAN 100 ACRES
SUBURBAN	$2.50	$2.00	$1.75	$1.50	$2.00	$1.75	$1.50
CENTRAL CITY	$3.00	$2.50	$1.75	$1.50	$1.75	$1.00	$0.75

PROFILE OF BUILDINGS BY SIZE

(All prices are per square foot. Lease prices in this market area are ***GROSS*** prices.)

SIZE	SALES PRICES CENTRAL CITY	SALES PRICES SUBURBAN	LEASE PRICES CENTRAL CITY	LEASE PRICES SUBURBAN	CONSTRUCTION COSTS	VACANCY SITUATION
Less Than 5000	$27.00	$37.00	$5.00	$5.00	$42.00	Balanced Market
5,000 to 19,999	$25.00	$32.00	$4.75	$4.50	$32.00	Substantial Oversupply
20,000 to 39,999	$20.00	$29.00	$4.50	$4.00	$27.00	Substantial Oversupply
40,000 to 59,999	$23.00	$25.00	$3.50	$3.50	$24.00	Substantial Oversupply
60,000 to 99,999	$21.00	$23.00	$3.25	$3.25	$19.00	Substantial Oversupply
More Than 100,000	$18.00	$22.00	$2.75	$2.75	$16.00	Substantial Oversupply
High Tech/R & D	$50.00	$60.00	$9.00	$6.00	$47.00	Substantial Oversupply

Source: *1988 GUIDE TO INDUSTRIAL AND OFFICE REAL ESTATE MARKETS.* Society of Industrial and Office REALTORS® & the Economics and Research Division of the National Association of REALTORS®, 777 14th Street, NW, Suite 400, Washington, DC 20005-3271.

* See Glossary of Terms on page 595.

DEMOGRAPHICS

POPULATION: 6,188,000
POPULATION GROWTH RATE: 0.4%
EMPLOYMENT GROWTH RATE: 1.2%
UNEMPLOYMENT RATE: 5.8%
PER CAPITA INCOME: $13,555

MARKET DATA

TOTAL INVENTORY
Central City: 175,000,000 sq.ft.
Suburban: 510,000,000 sq.ft.

VACANT INVENTORY
Cent.City: 12,125,415 sq.ft.(14.4%)
Suburban: 38,627,112 sq.ft.(13.2%)

NET ABSORPTION
Central City: n/a
Suburban: n/a

CURRENT CONSTRUCTION
Central City: n/a
Suburban: n/a

MORTGAGE MONEY SUPPLY
Ample

PRIME SOURCE OF FINANCING
Insurance Companies

CHICAGO: INDUSTRIAL

Market Area: Chicago Metropolitan Area

1987 REVIEW

Chicago's strategic location within the country, its highway and rail networks, abundant labor supply, and access to water transportation all make the metro area an attractive location for manufacturing, warehousing/distribution, and high technology business operations.

In 1987, 68 percent of absorption was for use in warehousing and distribution. Construction of warehouse and distribution space was up 11 to 15 percent from a year earlier. There are currently substantial shortages of buildings with less than 20,000 square feet and large structures with more than 100,000 square feet.

1988 FORECAST

SIOR panelists in Chicago suggest that the Chicago area stands to benefit more than most cities from improvement in the trade deficit. Chicago's enormous manufacturing base would benefit from increased exports of locally produced goods.

OUTLOOK

SALES PRICES
Manufacturing: Up 1-5%
Warehouse/Distribution: Up 6-10%
High Tech/R & D: Same

LEASE PRICES
Manufacturing: Up 6-10%
Warehouse/Distribution: Up 6-10%
High Tech/R & D: Same

ABSORPTION
Manufacturing: Up 1-5%
Warehouse/Distribution: Up 6-10%
High Tech/R & D: Same

CONSTRUCTION
Manufacturing: Up 1-5%
Warehouse/Distribution: Up 1-5%
High Tech/R & D: Up 1-5%

DOLLAR VOLUME
Sales: Up 6-10%
Leases : Up 6-10%

PROFILE OF BUILDINGS BY TYPE

	WAREHOUSING & DISTRIBUTION	MANUFACTURING	HIGH TECH/ R & D
COMPOSITION OF ABSORPTION	68%	24%	8%
RATE OF NEW CONSTRUCTION ••	Up 11-15%	Up 1-5%	Up 1-5%
DOLLAR VOLUME - SALES ••	Up 11-15%	n/a	n/a
DOLLAR VOLUME - LEASES ••	Up 11-15%	Up 1-5%	Up 1-5%

•• Compared to A Year Ago

SITE PRICES

(Dollars Per Square Foot)

LOCATION	IMPROVED SITES: LESS THAN 2 ACRES	IMPROVED SITES: 2 TO 5 ACRES	IMPROVED SITES: 5 TO 10 ACRES	IMPROVED SITES: MORE THAN 10 ACRES	UNIMPROVED SITES: LESS THAN 10 ACRES	UNIMPROVED SITES: 10 TO 100 ACRES	UNIMPROVED SITES: MORE THAN 100 ACRES
SUBURBAN	$1.50-$5.00	$1.50-$4.50	$1.50-$4.50	$1.25-$4.50	$1.25	$1.00	$0.75
CENTRAL CITY	$1.50-$5.00	$1.50-$4.00	$1.00-$3.00	$1.00-$3.00	n/a	n/a	n/a

PROFILE OF BUILDINGS BY SIZE

(All prices are per square foot. Lease prices in this market area are *NET* prices.)

SIZE	SALES PRICES CENTRAL CITY	SALES PRICES SUBURBAN	LEASE PRICES CENTRAL CITY	LEASE PRICES SUBURBAN	CONSTRUCTION COSTS	VACANCY SITUATION
Less Than 5000	$35.00	$49.00	$4.75	$6.00	$39.00	Substantial Shortage
5,000 to 19,999	$30.00	$41.00	$4.25	$5.50	$34.00	Substantial Shortage
20,000 to 39,999	$26.00	$34.00	$3.75	$5.00	$27.00	Moderate Shortage
40,000 to 59,999	$23.00	$30.00	$3.50	$4.75	$25.00	Balanced Market
60,000 to 99,999	$19.00	$25.00	$3.25	$4.50	$22.00	Moderate Shortage
More Than 100,000	$16.00	$23.00	$2.75	$4.25	$20.00	Substantial Shortage
High Tech/R & D	n/a	$60.00	n/a	$14.00	$57.00	n/a

DEMOGRAPHICS

POPULATION: 3,222,000
POPULATION GROWTH RATE: 3.1%
EMPLOYMENT GROWTH RATE: 4.1%
UNEMPLOYMENT RATE: 8.0%
PER CAPITA INCOME: $13,428

MARKET DATA

TOTAL INVENTORY
Central City: 85,000,000 sq.ft.
Suburban: 125,000,000 sq.ft.

VACANT INVENTORY
Central City: 14,450,000 sq.ft.(17%)
Suburban: 25,000,000 sq.ft.(20%)

NET ABSORPTION
Central City: -4,000,000 sq.ft.
Suburban: 3,000,000 sq.ft.

CURRENT CONSTRUCTION
Central City: 0 sq.ft.
Suburban: 0 sq.ft.

MORTGAGE MONEY SUPPLY
Tight

PRIME SOURCE OF FINANCING
Owner Financing

HOUSTON: INDUSTRIAL

Market Area: Houston and Harris County

1987 REVIEW

Houston's economy has not bounced back from the slump that propelled it into the national limelight. There are signs that the area's economy is improving but it still has a long way to go. There are some promising growth sectors that will improve conditions in 1988 such as computer equipment manufacturing. Compaq Computer Corp. is one of the fastest growing high-tech companies in the U.S.

The industrial market is mired in overcapacity. Nearly 19 percent of the 210 million square foot inventory is currently vacant. Every SIOR building category is reported to be oversupplied. Rental rates and purchase prices are very attractive to potential investors.

1988 FORECAST

The worst is over and 1988 is expected to be a year of recovery. Absorption of manufacturing and high tech space will be up 11 to 15 percent. Sales and lease prices will increase in all building categories.

OUTLOOK

SALES PRICES
Manufacturing: Up 11-15%
Warehouse/Distribution: Up 6-10%
High Tech/R & D: Up 6-10%

LEASE PRICES
Manufacturing: Up 6-10%
Warehouse/Distribution: Up 11-15%
High Tech/R & D: Up 6-10%

ABSORPTION
Manufacturing: Up 11-15%
Warehouse/Distribution: Up 6-10%
High Tech/R & D: Up 11-15%

CONSTRUCTION
Manufacturing: up 1-5%
Warehouse/Distribution: Same
High Tech/R & D: Same

DOLLAR VOLUME
Sales: n/a
Leases: n/a

PROFILE OF BUILDINGS BY TYPE

	WAREHOUSING & DISTRIBUTION	MANUFACTURING	HIGH TECH/ R & D
COMPOSITION OF ABSORPTION	75%	15%	10%
RATE OF NEW CONSTRUCTION **	Down 6-10%	Down 11-15%	Down 11-15%
DOLLAR VOLUME - SALES **	Down 11-15%	Down 11-15%	Down 11-15%
DOLLAR VOLUME - LEASES **	Down 6-10%	Down 6-10%	Down 11-15%

** Compared to A Year Ago

SITE PRICES

(Dollars Per Square Foot)

	IMPROVED SITES				UNIMPROVED SITES		
LOCATION	LESS THAN 2 ACRES	2 TO 5 ACRES	5 TO 10 ACRES	MORE THAN 10 ACRES	LESS THAN 10 ACRES	10 TO 100 ACRES	MORE THAN 100 ACRES
SUBURBAN	$2.00-$5.00	$2.00-$5.00	$1.00-$4.00	$1.00-$4.00	$0.50-$2.50	$0.30-$2.00	$0.10-$1.00
CENTRAL CITY	$3.00-$6.00	$2.50-$6.00	$2.00-$5.00	$1.50-$5.00	$2.00-$5.00	n/a	n/a

PROFILE OF BUILDINGS BY SIZE

(All prices are per square foot. Lease prices in this market area are ***GROSS*** prices.)

SIZE	SALES PRICES CENTRAL CITY	SALES PRICES SUBURBAN	LEASE PRICES CENTRAL CITY	LEASE PRICES SUBURBAN	CONSTRUCTION COSTS	VACANCY SITUATION
Less Than 5000	$30.00-$40.00	$15.00-$45.00	$2.00-$4.00	$2.00-$4.00	$29.00-$30.00	Moderate Oversupply
5,000 to 19,999	$25.00-$35.00	$20.00-$30.00	$2.20-$4.00	$2.20-$4.00	$27.00-$28.00	Substantial Oversupply
20,000 to 39,999	$20.00-$30.00	$15.00-$35.00	$2.00-$3.25	$2.00-$3.25	$19.00-$21.00	Substantial Oversupply
40,000 to 59,999	$15.00-$30.00	$15.00-$30.00	$1.50-$3.00	$1.50-$3.00	$17.00-$18.00	Moderate Oversupply
60,000 to 99,999	$10.00-$22.00	$15.00-$25.00	$1.25-$2.50	$1.50-$2.50	$17.00-$18.00	Moderate Oversupply
More Than 100,000	$10.00-$15.00	$12.00-$20.00	$1.00-$2.00	$1.85-$2.00	$14.00-$16.00	Moderate Oversupply
High Tech/R & D	$10.00-$25.00	$25.00-$50.00	$3.50-$7.50	$3.50-$7.50	$25.00-$35.00	Moderate Oversupply

DEMOGRAPHICS

POPULATION
Los Angeles-Anaheim-Riverside: 12,738,000
Anaheim-Santa Ana: 2,123,000
Los Angeles-Long Beach: 8,109,000
Oxnard-Ventura: 600,000
Riverside-San Bernadino: 1,907,000

POPULATION GROWTH RATE
Los Angeles-Anaheim-Riverside: 2.0%
Anaheim-Santa Ana: 1.8%
Los Angeles-Long Beach: 2.4%
Oxnard-Ventura: 5.0%
Riverside-San Bernadino: 4.5%

EMPLOYMENT GROWTH RATE
Los Angeles-Long Beach: 2.4%
Oxnard-Ventura: 5.0%
Riverside-San Bernadino: 4.5%

UNEMPLOYMENT RATE
Anaheim-Santa Ana: 3.0%
Los Angeles-Long Beach: 4.5%
Oxnard-Ventura: 5.5%
Riverside-San Bernadino: 5.5%

PER CAPITA INCOME
Los Angeles-Long Beach: $13,436
Oxnard-Ventura: $13,260
Riverside-San Bernadino: $11,409

LOS ANGELES METROPOLITAN AREA

Los Angeles Industrial Markets

The Los Angeles market area almost defies description. It encompasses an enormous area of Southern California and is currently in a period of remarkable change.

The area's populaton is approximately 12.7 million and growing at an average annual rate of two percent. The pace of growth has made the area famous for traffic congestion and its cost of housing. Still, Los Angeles has such a rich diversity of social and cultural resources to go along with its appealing climate that it remains an attractive place to live.

The Los Angeles economy is naturally quite diverse with a significant manufacturing employment base in defense-related industries and durable goods manufacturing. Non-manufacturing employment is high in wholesale and retail trade, business services, and financial services.

High growth sectors of the economy are tied into the role the city plays in U.S. trade with the Pacific Basin. Trade impacts the area in several ways. Clearly, goods passing through the area create the need for warehouse and distribution space. But, also a significant amount of activity related to finance, banking, real estate, insurance, legal affairs, and consulting is centered in Los Angeles.

SIOR panelists have divided the Los Angeles Metropolitan Area into seven separate market areas to more accurately reflect the diversity of market characteristics. On the followng pages are reports from seven market areas in and around the Los Angeles Metropolitan Area. They are

Los Angeles–City of Industry,
Los Angeles–East,
Los Angeles–Orange County,
Los Angeles–San Bernadino/Riverside,
Los Angeles–San Fernando Valley,
Los Angeles–South Bay,
and Los Angeles–West.

MARKET DATA

TOTAL INVENTORY
Central City: n/a
Suburban: 35,000,000 sq.ft.

VACANT INVENTORY
Central City: n/a
Suburban: 6,000,000 sq.ft.(17.0%)

NET ABSORPTION
Central City: n/a
Suburban: 4,000,000 sq.ft.

CURRENT CONSTRUCTION
Central City: n/a
Suburban: n/a

MORTGAGE MONEY SUPPLY
Ample

PRIME SOURCE OF FINANCING
Commercial Banks
Insurance Companies
Savings and Loans

LOS ANGELES–CITY OF INDUSTRY: INDUSTRIAL

Market Area: Los Angeles, Eastern Los Angeles County, San Gabriel Valley

1987 REVIEW

The City of Industry market area is located in the eastern part of Los Angeles County but to the north of the Los Angeles--East market area. Sales, lease, and site prices are generally higher than in the southern part of Los Angeles County.

The City of Industry area has an inventory of approximately 35 million square feet. Six million square feet are currently vacant but net absorption in 1987 totalled four million square feet. Seventy percent of total absorption was for use in warehousing and distribution.

SIOR panelists report that high-tech space and properties with more than 60,000 square feet are currently oversupplied.

1988 FORECAST

In 1988, the City of Industry market area will realize six to 10 percent increases in construction and absorption. Sales, lease, and site prices for all types of industrial properties will also increase six to 10 percent.

OUTLOOK

SALES PRICES
Manufacturing: Up 6-10%
Warehouse/Distribution: Up 6-10%
High Tech/R & D: Up 6-10%

LEASE PRICES
Manufacturing: Up 6-10%
Warehouse/Distribution: Up 6-10%
High Tech/R & D: Up 6-10%

ABSORPTION
Manufacturing: Up 6-10%
Warehouse/Distribution: Up 6-10%
High Tech/R & D: Up 6-10%

CONSTRUCTION
Manufacturing: Up 6-10%
Warehouse/Distribution: Up 6-10%
High Tech/R & D: Up 6-10%

DOLLAR VOLUME
Sales: Up 6-10%
Leases: Up 6-10%

PROFILE OF BUILDINGS BY TYPE

	WAREHOUSING & DISTRIBUTION	MANUFACTURING	HIGH TECH/ R & D
COMPOSITION OF ABSORPTION	70%	15%	15%
RATE OF NEW CONSTRUCTION ••	Up 6-10%	Down 6-10%	n/a
DOLLAR VOLUME - SALES ••	Up 6-10%	Up 6-10%	Up 6-10%
DOLLAR VOLUME - LEASES ••	Up 6-10%	Up 6-10%	Up 6-10%

•• Compared to A Year Ago

SITE PRICES
(Dollars Per Square Foot)

	IMPROVED SITES				UNIMPROVED SITES		
LOCATION	LESS THAN 2 ACRES	2 TO 5 ACRES	5 TO 10 ACRES	MORE THAN 10 ACRES	LESS THAN 10 ACRES	10 TO 100 ACRES	MORE THAN 100 ACRES
SUBURBAN	$6.50	$6.00	$5.75-$6.00	$5.75	$5.00	n/a	n/a
CENTRAL CITY	n/a	n/a	n/a	n/a	n/a	n/a	n/a

PROFILE OF BUILDINGS BY SIZE
(All prices are per square foot. Lease prices in this market area are *NET* prices.)

SIZE	SALES PRICES CENTRAL CITY	SALES PRICES SUBURBAN	LEASE PRICES CENTRAL CITY	LEASE PRICES SUBURBAN	CONSTRUCTION COSTS	VACANCY SITUATION
Less Than 5000	n/a	$57.00	n/a	$5.04	$32.00	Balanced Market
5,000 to 19,999	n/a	$49.00	n/a	$4.56	$33.00	Moderate Oversupply
20,000 to 39,999	n/a	$40.00	n/a	$4.08	$26.00	Balanced Market
40,000 to 59,999	n/a	$35.00-$38.00	n/a	$3.60	$18.00	Moderate Oversupply
60,000 to 99,999	n/a	$34.00	n/a	$3.36-$3.84	$14.00	Substantial Oversupply
More Than 100,000	n/a	$32.00-$34.00	n/a	$2.88-$3.48	$13.00	Substantial Market
High Tech/R & D	n/a	n/a	n/a	n/a	n/a	Substantial Oversupply

LOS ANGELES–EAST: INDUSTRIAL

Market Area: Santa Fe Springs, La Mirada, Cerritos, Buena Park

MARKET DATA

TOTAL INVENTORY
Central City: 67,000,000 sq.ft.
Suburban: n/a

VACANT INVENTORY
Central City: 2,500,000 sq.ft.(3.7%)
Suburban: n/a

NET ABSORPTION
Central City: 2,600,000 sq.ft.
Suburban: n/a

CURRENT CONSTRUCTION
Central City: 1,080,000 sq.ft.
Suburban: n/a

MORTGAGE MONEY SUPPLY
Ample

PRIME SOURCE OF FINANCING
Insurance Companies

1987 REVIEW

The Los Angeles-East industrial market is excellent, experiencing another year of solid gains in 1987. There is a moderate shortage of properties with less than 20,000 square feet. SIOR panelists report that demand is particularly strong in Santa Fe Springs resulting in rising land prices.

Vacancy rates were low, ranging from 3.7 percent in the central city locations to five percent in suburban areas. High-tech construction is off six to 10 percent as this segment of the market is still moderately oversupplied. A total of 80 percent of all absorption activity in 1987 was for use in warehousing and distribution.

1988 FORECAST

Market conditions will remain strong in 1988. Warehouse/distribution construction, absorption, and lease prices will be up one to five percent. Sales prices will rise sharply by six to 10 percent. Manufacturing sales prices and site prices will also increase six to 10 percent.

OUTLOOK

SALES PRICES
Manufacturing: Up 6-10%
Warehouse/Distribution: Up 6-10%
High Tech/R & D: Same

LEASE PRICES
Manufacturing: Up 1-5%
Warehouse/Distribution: Up 1-5%
High Tech/R & D: Same

ABSORPTION
Manufacturing: Up 1-5%
Warehouse/Distribution: Up 1-5%
High Tech/R & D: Down 1-5%

CONSTRUCTION
Manufacturing: Same
Warehouse/Distribution: Up 1-5%
High Tech/R & D: Down 1-5%

DOLLAR VOLUME
Sales: Same
Leases: Same

PROFILE OF BUILDINGS BY TYPE

	WAREHOUSING & DISTRIBUTION	MANUFACTURING	HIGH TECH/ R & D
COMPOSITION OF ABSORPTION	80%	15%	5%
RATE OF NEW CONSTRUCTION **	Down 1-5%	Down 1-5%	Down 6-10%
DOLLAR VOLUME - SALES **	Up 11-15%	Up 11-15%	Up 1-5%
DOLLAR VOLUME - LEASES **	Up 11-15%	Up 11-15%	Up 1-5%

** Compared to A Year Ago

SITE PRICES
(Dollars Per Square Foot)

	IMPROVED SITES				UNIMPROVED SITES		
LOCATION	LESS THAN 2 ACRES	2 TO 5 ACRES	5 TO 10 ACRES	MORE THAN 10 ACRES	LESS THAN 10 ACRES	10 TO 100 ACRES	MORE THAN 100 ACRES
SUBURBAN	n/a	n/a	n/a	n/a	n/a	n/a	n/a
CENTRAL CITY	$12.00	$11.00	$10.00	$10.00	$8.00	$7.00	$6.00

PROFILE OF BUILDINGS BY SIZE
(All prices are per square foot. Lease prices in this market area are *NET* prices.)

SIZE	SALES PRICES CENTRAL CITY	SALES PRICES SUBURBAN	LEASE PRICES CENTRAL CITY	LEASE PRICES SUBURBAN	CONSTRUCTION COSTS	VACANCY SITUATION
Less Than 5000	$70.00	n/a	$6.00	n/a	$28.00	Moderate Shortage
5,000 to 19,999	$65.00	n/a	$5.40	n/a	$25.00	Moderate Shortage
20,000 to 39,999	$55.00	n/a	$4.80	n/a	$22.00	Balanced Market
40,000 to 59,999	$53.00	n/a	$4.50	n/a	$21.00	Moderate Oversupply
60,000 to 99,999	$48.00	n/a	$4.00	n/a	$17.00	Balanced Market
More Than 100,000	$46.00	n/a	$3.85	n/a	$16.00	Balanced Market
High Tech/R & D	$55.00	n/a	$5.00	n/a	$40.00	Moderate Oversupply

MARKET DATA

TOTAL INVENTORY
Central City: n/a
Suburban: 124,317,112 sq.ft.

VACANT INVENTORY
Central City: n/a
Suburban: 17,456,108 sq.ft.(14.0%)

NET ABSORPTION
Central City: n/a
Suburban: 3,540,372 sq.ft.

CURRENT CONSTRUCTION
Central City: n/a
Suburban: 1,860,694 sq.ft.

MORTGAGE MONEY SUPPLY
Ample

PRIME SOURCE OF FINANCING
Insurance Companies

LOS ANGELES–ORANGE COUNTY: INDUSTRIAL

Market Area: Orange County

1987 REVIEW

Los Angeles-Orange County's industrial market was very active in 1987. Fifty percent of all absorption occurred in the warehouse/distribution sector. Heavy manufacturing has been moving east into Riverside and San Bernardino County. Research and Development activity has also increased.

In 1987, Orange County's industrial vacancy rate hovered around 14 percent. However, more than 3.5 million square feet were absorbed. Currently, 1,860,694 square feet are under construction. Warehouse and distribution construction was down six to 10 percent from 1986. Manufacturing and high-tech/R & D construction as off 11 to 15 percent.

1988 FORECAST

Leasing of industrial warehouse/distribution and light manufacturing will remain strong in 1988. Construction and absorption of high-tech properties will increase one to five percent. Site prices and high-tech sales and lease prices will increase six to 10 percent.

OUTLOOK

SALES PRICES
Manufacturing: Up 6-10%
Warehouse/Distribution: Up 6-10%
High Tech/R & D: Up 6-10%

LEASE PRICES
Manufacturing: Up 6-10%
Warehouse/Distribution: Up 6-10%
High Tech/R & D: Up 6-10%

ABSORPTION
Manufacturing: Down 1-5%
Warehouse/Distribution: Same
High Tech/R & D: Up 1-5%

CONSTRUCTION
Manufacturing: Down 1-5%
Warehouse/Distribution: Same
High Tech/R & D: Up 1-5%

DOLLAR VOLUME
Sales: Same
Leases: Down 1-5%

PROFILE OF BUILDINGS BY TYPE

	WAREHOUSING & DISTRIBUTION	MANUFACTURING	HIGH TECH/ R & D
COMPOSITION OF ABSORPTION	50%	20%	30%
RATE OF NEW CONSTRUCTION ••	Down 6-10%	Down 11-15%	Down 11-15%
DOLLAR VOLUME - SALES ••	Up 6-10%	Down 6-10%	Same
DOLLAR VOLUME - LEASES ••	Up 6-10%	Down 6-10%	Up 6-10%

•• Compared to A Year Ago

SITE PRICES

(Dollars Per Square Foot)

	IMPROVED SITES				UNIMPROVED SITES		
LOCATION	LESS THAN 2 ACRES	2 TO 5 ACRES	5 TO 10 ACRES	MORE THAN 10 ACRES	LESS THAN 10 ACRES	10 TO 100 ACRES	MORE THAN 100 ACRES
SUBURBAN	$12.00-$23.00	$12.00-$20.00	$9.00-$13.00	$8.00-$12.50	$9.00-$10.00	$7.00-$11.00	n/a
CENTRAL CITY	n/a	n/a	n/a	n/a	n/a	n/a	n/a

PROFILE OF BUILDINGS BY SIZE

(All prices are per square foot. Lease prices in this market area are *NET* prices.)

SIZE	SALES PRICES CENTRAL CITY	SALES PRICES SUBURBAN	LEASE PRICES CENTRAL CITY	LEASE PRICES SUBURBAN	CONSTRUCTION COSTS	VACANCY SITUATION
Less Than 5000	n/a	$70.00-$84.00	n/a	$6.84-$8.40	$28.00	Balanced Market
5,000 to 19,999	n/a	$62.00-$68.00	n/a	$5.04-$5.76	$25.00	Moderate Oversupply
20,000 to 39,999	n/a	$50.00-$56.00	n/a	$5.04-$5.52	$20.00	Balanced Market
40,000 to 59,999	n/a	$48.00-$54.00	n/a	$4.32-$4.80	$18.00	Moderate Shortage
60,000 to 99,999	n/a	$45.00-$50.00	n/a	$4.08-$4.56	$15.00-$16.00	Balanced Market
More Than 100,000	n/a	$40.00-$45.00	n/a	$3.80-$4.56	$14.00	Moderate Shortage
High Tech/R & D	n/a	$60.00-$120.00	n/a	$7.80-$13.80	$35.00	Substantial Oversupply

MARKET DATA

TOTAL INVENTORY
Central City: n/a
Suburban: 21,850,000 sq.ft.

VACANT INVENTORY
Central City: n/a
Suburban: 3,700,000 sq.ft.(16.9%)

NET ABSORPTION
Central City: n/a
Suburban: n/a

CURRENT CONSTRUCTION
Central City: n/a
Suburban: 7,500,000 sq.ft.

MORTGAGE MONEY SUPPLY
Ample

PRIME SOURCE OF FINANCING
Insurance Companies

LOS ANGELES –SAN BERNADINO/RIVERSIDE: INDUSTRIAL

Market Area: The Inland Empire Area, San Bernadino and Riverside Counties

1987 REVIEW

The San Bernadino/Riverside industrial market area has experienced very rapid growth in recent years. Absorption has increased from less than 250,000 square feet in 1981 to more than seven million square feet in 1986. Construction has surged, too, with approximately 7.5 million square feet currently under construction.

Such rapid change has led to a comparatively high vacancy rate, but that is only because the market is so young that the industrial base is not yet very large. Currently, moderate oversupplies are reported for most SIOR building categories. The area has very little high-tech space.

1988 FORECAST

SIOR panelists in the San Bernadino/Riverside area expect construction and absorption to stabilize at 1987 levels. The excess supply of space will force slight declines in rental rates. Site prices will be up six to 10 percent.

OUTLOOK

SALES PRICES
Manufacturing: Same
Warehouse/Distribution: Same
High Tech/R & D: n/a

LEASE PRICES
Manufacturing: Same
Warehouse/Distribution: Same
High Tech/R & D: n/a

ABSORPTION
Manufacturing: Same
Warehouse/Distribution: Same
High Tech/R & D: n/a

CONSTRUCTION
Manufacturing: Same
Warehouse/Distribution: Same
High Tech/R & D: n/a

DOLLAR VOLUME
Sales: Up 1-5%
Leases: Down 1-5%

PROFILE OF BUILDINGS BY TYPE

	WAREHOUSING & DISTRIBUTION	MANUFACTURING	HIGH TECH/ R & D
COMPOSITION OF ABSORPTION	n/a	n/a	n/a
RATE OF NEW CONSTRUCTION ••	Up 20%	Same	n/a
DOLLAR VOLUME - SALES ••	Up 25%	Same	n/a
DOLLAR VOLUME - LEASES ••	Up 25%	Same	n/a

•• Compared to A Year Ago

SITE PRICES
(Dollars Per Square Foot)

	IMPROVED SITES				UNIMPROVED SITES		
LOCATION	LESS THAN 2 ACRES	2 TO 5 ACRES	5 TO 10 ACRES	MORE THAN 10 ACRES	LESS THAN 10 ACRES	10 TO 100 ACRES	MORE THAN 100 ACRES
SUBURBAN	n/a	n/a	n/a	n/a	n/a	n/a	n/a
CENTRAL CITY	n/a	n/a	n/a	n/a	n/a	n/a	n/a

PROFILE OF BUILDINGS BY SIZE
(All prices are per square foot.)

SIZE	SALES PRICES CENTRAL CITY	SALES PRICES SUBURBAN	LEASE PRICES CENTRAL CITY	LEASE PRICES SUBURBAN	CONSTRUCTION COSTS	VACANCY SITUATION
Less Than 5000	n/a	n/a	n/a	n/a	$20.00-$25.00	Moderate Oversupply
5,000 to 19,999	n/a	n/a	n/a	n/a	$16.00-$25.00	Moderate Oversupply
20,000 to 39,999	n/a	n/a	n/a	n/a	$12.00-$17.00	Moderate Oversupply
40,000 to 59,999	n/a	n/a	n/a	n/a	$11.00-$16.00	Moderate Oversupply
60,000 to 99,999	n/a	n/a	n/a	n/a	$10.00-$15.00	Moderate Oversupply
More Than 100,000	n/a	n/a	n/a	n/a	$10.00-$15.00	Balanced Market
High Tech/R & D	n/a	n/a	n/a	n/a	n/a	n/a

LOS ANGELES–SAN FERNANDO VALLEY: INDUSTRIAL

Market Area: Ventura County, San Fernando Valley

MARKET DATA

TOTAL INVENTORY

Central City: 50,000,000 sq.ft.
Suburban: 15,000,000 sq.ft.

VACANT INVENTORY

Cent. City: 11,320,940 sq.ft.(23.0%)
Suburban: 5,000,000 sq.ft.(33.0%)

NET ABSORPTION

Central City: 3,000,000 sq.ft.
Suburban: 200,000 sq.ft.

CURRENT CONSTRUCTION

Central City: 1,327,250 sq.ft.
Suburban: 877,270 sq.ft.

MORTGAGE MONEY SUPPLY

Ample

PRIME SOURCE OF FINANCING

Insurance Companies
Commercial Banks

1987 REVIEW

The Los Angeles-San Fernando market area is a rapidly growing industrial market. There is currently a considerable amount of construction activity. Presently 1,327,250 square feet of industrial space is under construction in central city areas and another 877,270 square feet is under construction in the suburban areas.

Substantial shortages are reported for small properties with less than 5,000 square feet and for large properties with more than 60,000 square feet. High-tech space and buildings with between 20,000 and 40,000 square feet are substantially oversupplied.

1988 FORECAST

In 1988, the Los Angeles-San Fernando market will experience an increase in construction and absorption. Sales and lease prices of manufacturing and warehouse/distribution properties will increase six to 10 percent. The high-tech sector will remain relatively weak.

OUTLOOK

SALES PRICES

Manufacturing: Up 6-10%
Warehouse/Distribution: Up 6-10%
High Tech/R & D: Down 6-10%

LEASE PRICES

Manufacturing: Up 1-5%
Warehouse/Distribution: Up 6-10%
High Tech/R & D: Down 6-10%

ABSORPTION

Manufacturing: Up 6-10%
Warehouse/Distribution: Up 6-10%
High Tech/R & D: Down 6-10%

CONSTRUCTION

Manufacturing: Up 1-5%
Warehouse/Distribution: Up 1-5%
High Tech/R & D: Down 11-15%

DOLLAR VOLUME

Sales: Up 6-10%
Leases: Up 6-10%

PROFILE OF BUILDINGS BY TYPE

	WAREHOUSING & DISTRIBUTION	MANUFACTURING	HIGH TECH/ R & D
COMPOSITION OF ABSORPTION	n/a	n/a	n/a
RATE OF NEW CONSTRUCTION **	Up 6-10%	Up 1-5%	Up 6-10%
DOLLAR VOLUME - SALES **	Up 1-5%	Up 1-5%	Down 6-10%
DOLLAR VOLUME - LEASES **	Up 1-5%	Up 1-5%	Down 6-10%

** Compared to A Year Ago

SITE PRICES

(Dollars Per Square Foot)

	IMPROVED SITES				UNIMPROVED SITES		
LOCATION	LESS THAN 2 ACRES	2 TO 5 ACRES	5 TO 10 ACRES	MORE THAN 10 ACRES	LESS THAN 10 ACRES	10 TO 100 ACRES	MORE THAN 100 ACRES
SUBURBAN	$7.00	n/a	$6.00	$6.00	$5.50	$6.00	$3.00
CENTRAL CITY	$22.00	$15.00	n/a	n/a	n/a	n/a	n/a

PROFILE OF BUILDINGS BY SIZE

(All prices are per square foot. Lease prices in this market area are ***GROSS*** prices.)

SIZE	SALES PRICES CENTRAL CITY	SALES PRICES SUBURBAN	LEASE PRICES CENTRAL CITY	LEASE PRICES SUBURBAN	CONSTRUCTION COSTS	VACANCY SITUATION
Less Than 5000	$65.00-$85.00	$60.00-$70.00	$7.80	$6.60	$30.00	Substantial Shortage
5,000 to 19,999	$55.00-$65.00	$45.00-$55.00	$6.00	$5.40	$28.00	Balanced Market
20,000 to 39,999	$50.00-$55.00	$45.00-$50.00	$6.00	$5.40	$28.00	Substantial Oversupply
40,000 to 59,999	$50.00	$43.00	$4.80-$5.40	$4.80-$5.40	$26.00	Balanced Market
60,000 to 99,999	$45.00-$50.00	$40.00	$5.40-$6.60	$4.80-$5.40	$25.00	Substantial Shortage
More Than 100,000	$45.00-$50.00	$35.00	$5.04	$4.20	$20.00	Substantial Shortage
High Tech/R & D	$80.00	$68.00	$10.20	$7.80	$48.00-$60.00	Substantial Oversupply

MARKET DATA

TOTAL INVENTORY
Central City: n/a
Suburban: 160,000,000 sq.ft.

VACANT INVENTORY
Central City: n/a
Suburban: 10,000,000 sq.ft.(6.3%)

NET ABSORPTION
Central City: n/a
Suburban: n/a

CURRENT CONSTRUCTION
Central City: n/a
Suburban: 1,500,000 sq.ft.

MORTGAGE MONEY SUPPLY
Ample

PRIME SOURCE OF FINANCING
Savings & Loans
Insurance Companies

LOS ANGELES–SOUTH BAY: INDUSTRIAL

Market Area: Torrance, Manchester Boulevard on the North to Orange County line on the South

1987 REVIEW

The Los Angeles-South Bay industrial market area benefited from the high volume of goods moving through the area's ports. Overall industrial vacancies are 6.3 percent. The area has an industrial inventory of approximately 160 million square feet. An additional 1.5 million square feet is currently under construction. The rate of construction, however, is down compared to 1986.

Market demand for vacant space varies considerably according to the property size and type. SIOR panelists report a moderate shortage for properties with 5,000 to 19,999 square feet and 60,000 to 99,999 square feet. High-tech properties are still substantially oversupplied.

1988 FORECAST

In 1988, overall construction activity will decline. Warehouse/distribution absorption, and sales and lease prices will increase by as much as 10 percent. Site prices will continue to increase rapidly, up six to 10 percent in 1988.

OUTLOOK

SALES PRICES
Manufacturing: Up 1-5%
Warehouse/Distribution: Up 6-10%
High Tech/R & D: Same

LEASE PRICES
Manufacturing: Up 1-5%
Warehouse/Distribution: Up 6-10%
High Tech/R & D: Same

ABSORPTION
Manufacturing: Same
Warehouse/Distribution: Up 1-5%
High Tech/R & D: Same

CONSTRUCTION
Manufacturing: Same
Warehouse/Distribution: Down 1-5%
High Tech/R & D: Down 6-10%

DOLLAR VOLUME
Sales: Up 6-10%
Leases: Same

PROFILE OF BUILDINGS BY TYPE

	WAREHOUSING & DISTRIBUTION	MANUFACTURING	HIGH TECH/ R & D
COMPOSITION OF ABSORPTION	85%	10%	5%
RATE OF NEW CONSTRUCTION ••	Down 1-5%	Substantial Decrease	Down 6-10%
DOLLAR VOLUME - SALES ••	Up 11-15%	Down 6-10%	Same
DOLLAR VOLUME - LEASES ••	Down 6-10%	Same	Down 1-5%

•• Compared to A Year Ago

SITE PRICES

(Dollars Per Square Foot)

	IMPROVED SITES				UNIMPROVED SITES		
LOCATION	LESS THAN 2 ACRES	2 TO 5 ACRES	5 TO 10 ACRES	MORE THAN 10 ACRES	LESS THAN 10 ACRES	10 TO 100 ACRES	MORE THAN 100 ACRES
SUBURBAN	$13.00-$15.00	$13.00-$25.00	$13.00-$20.00	$13.00-$18.00	$9.00-$16.00	$9.00-$15.00	n/a
CENTRAL CITY	n/a	n/a	n/a	n/a	n/a	n/a	n/a

PROFILE OF BUILDINGS BY SIZE

(All prices are per square foot. Lease prices in this market area are *GROSS* prices.)

SIZE	SALES PRICES CENTRAL CITY	SALES PRICES SUBURBAN	LEASE PRICES CENTRAL CITY	LEASE PRICES SUBURBAN	CONSTRUCTION COSTS	VACANCY SITUATION
Less Than 5000	n/a	$54.00-$70.00	n/a	$6.00-$9.00	$34.75	Moderate Oversupply
5,000 to 19,999	n/a	$48.00-$65.00	n/a	$5.40-$7.80	$30.00	Moderate Shortage
20,000 to 39,999	n/a	$39.00-$59.00	n/a	$4.70-$5.90	$26.00	Moderate Oversupply
40,000 to 59,999	n/a	$39.00-$59.00	n/a	$4.20-$5.40	$20.75	Balanced Market
60,000 to 99,999	n/a	$39.00-$59.00	n/a	$4.00-$5.40	$17.95	Moderate Shortage
More Than 100,000	n/a	$37.00-$48.00	n/a	$3.80-$5.00	$15.35	Balanced Market
High Tech/R & D	n/a	$70.00-$80.00	n/a	$7.80-$13.20	$55.00	Substantial Oversupply

MARKET DATA

TOTAL INVENTORY
Central City: n/a
Suburban: n/a

VACANT INVENTORY
Central City: n/a
Suburban: n/a

NET ABSORPTION
Central City: n/a
Suburban: n/a

CURRENT CONSTRUCTION
Central City: n/a
Suburban: n/a

MORTGAGE MONEY SUPPLY
Ample

PRIME SOURCE OF FINANCING
Pension Funds
Insurance Companies

LOS ANGELES–WEST: INDUSTRIAL

Market Area: Los Angeles–West Metropolitan Area

1987 REVIEW

The West Los Angeles, Santa Monica, Marina, Culver City, and LAX market caters to higher end industrial users. The LAX market for airport-related uses, including dock high loading with yard area for large tractor/trailors, is the highest price per square foot industrial real estate in the area. Prices range from $0.80 to $1.05 net per square foot per month.

Older, brick manufacturing buildings with low truss and inadequate loading and/or parking lease at a minimum of $0.45 net per square foot per month. Industrial space in all SIOR building categories except high-tech are reported to be in short supply.

1988 FORECAST

SIOR panelists expect construction of industrial space to decline six to 10 percent in 1988. Absorption will be off by one to five percent. Sales and site prices will increase sharply and lease prices will be up one to five percent.

OUTLOOK

SALES PRICES
Manufacturing: Up 6-10%
Warehouse/Distribution: Up 6-10%
High Tech/R & D: Up 6-10%

LEASE PRICES
Manufacturing: Up 1-5%
Warehouse/Distribution: Up 1-5%
High Tech/R & D: Up 1-5%

ABSORPTION
Manufacturing: Down 1-5%
Warehouse/Distribution: Down 1-5%
High Tech/R & D: Down 1-5%

CONSTRUCTION
Manufacturing: Down 6-10%
Warehouse/Distribution: Down 6-10%
High Tech/R & D: Down 6-10%

DOLLAR VOLUME
Sales: Up 6-10%
Leases: Up 6-10%

PROFILE OF BUILDINGS BY TYPE

	WAREHOUSING & DISTRIBUTION	MANUFACTURING	HIGH TECH/ R & D
COMPOSITION OF ABSORPTION	35%	30%	35%
RATE OF NEW CONSTRUCTION ••	Down 1-5%	Down 1-5%	Down 1-5%
DOLLAR VOLUME - SALES ••	Same	Same	Same
DOLLAR VOLUME - LEASES ••	Up 6-10%	Up 6-10%	Up 6-10%

•• Compared to A Year Ago

SITE PRICES
(Dollars Per Square Foot)

	IMPROVED SITES				UNIMPROVED SITES		
LOCATION	LESS THAN 2 ACRES	2 TO 5 ACRES	5 TO 10 ACRES	MORE THAN 10 ACRES	LESS THAN 10 ACRES	10 TO 100 ACRES	MORE THAN 100 ACRES
SUBURBAN	n/a	n/a	n/a	n/a	n/a	n/a	n/a
CENTRAL CITY	$20.00-$65.00	$20.00-$60.00	$20.00-$50.00	$20.00-$50.00	$20.00-$65.00	$20.00-$50.00	n/a

PROFILE OF BUILDINGS BY SIZE
(All prices are per square foot. Lease prices in this market area are *NET* prices.)

SIZE	SALES PRICES CENTRAL CITY	SALES PRICES SUBURBAN	LEASE PRICES CENTRAL CITY	LEASE PRICES SUBURBAN	CONSTRUCTION COSTS	VACANCY SITUATION
Less Than 5000	$100.00	n/a	$9.60	n/a	$35.00	Substantial Shortage
5,000 to 19,999	$90.00	n/a	$9.00	n/a	$35.00	Moderate Shortage
20,000 to 39,999	$80.00	n/a	$8.40	n/a	$30.00	Moderate Shortage
40,000 to 59,999	$70.00	n/a	$8.40	n/a	$25.00	Moderate Shortage
60,000 to 99,999	$60.00	n/a	$7.20	n/a	$19.00	Moderate Shortage
More Than 100,000	$55.00	n/a	$7.20	n/a	$16.00	Moderate Shortage
High Tech/R & D	$75.00	n/a	$14.00	n/a	$30.00	Moderate Oversupply

DEMOGRAPHICS

POPULATION
New York-Northern New Jersey-Long Island: 17,931,000
Bergen-Passaic, NJ: 1,301,000
Middlesex-Somerset-Hunterdon, NJ: 930,000
Nassau-Suffolk, NY: 2,645,000
New York, NY: 8,466,000
Newark, NJ: 1,882,000

POPULATION GROWTH RATE
New York-Northern New Jersey-Long Island: 0.4%
Bergen-Passaic, NJ: 0.1%
Middlesex-Somerset-Hunterdon, NJ: 0.9%
Nassau-Suffolk, NY: 0.3%
New York, NY: 0.4%
Newark, NJ: 0%

EMPLOYMENT GROWTH RATE
Bergen-Passaic, NJ: 2.1%
Middlesex-Somerset-Hunterdon, NJ: 4.0%
Nassau-Suffolk, NY: 3.1%
New York, NY: 0.8%
Newark, NJ: 2.0%

UNEMPLOYMENT RATE
Bergen-Passaic, NJ: 2.7%
Middlesex-Somerset-Hunterdon, NJ: 2.3%
Nassau-Suffolk, NY: 3.0%
New York, NY: 5.9%
Newark, NJ: 3.4%

PER CAPITA INCOME
Bergen-Passaic, NJ: $16,399
Middlesex-Somerset-Hunterdon, NJ: $15,628
Nassau-Suffolk, NY: $16,239
New York, NY: $13,946
Newark, NJ: $15,053

NEW YORK METROPOLITAN AREA

New York Industrial Markets

The New York-Northern New Jersey-Long Island consolidated metropolitan statistical area has a population of approximately 17.9 million. Over eight million people live in New York City alone. No other city has such a high concentration of banking and financial services, but nearly every industry maintains a presence in the New York area.

The limited supply and high cost of land has reinforced the movement of business and residence to more outlying areas in Northern New Jersey, Connecticut, and New York state. Manufacturing employment declined at an average annual rate of 2.2 percent between 1975 and 1985 as numerous firms relocated to areas with lower costs and warmer climates. The area's economic restructuring was accompanied by nonmanufacturing employment growth over the same period. The financial and business services industries have experienced incredible growth, riding Wall Street's bull market since 1982.

The events of October 19, 1987 probably signaled the end to continuing employment growth from the financial sector of New York's economy. Despite the central role of New York's financial district in its overall economy, this market area is deep and wide. It's too early to forecast the demise of New York's popularity as a business address.

SIOR panelists have divided the New York area into five separate industrial markets to more accurately reflect the diversity of market characteristics. On the following pages are reports from five market areas in and around the New York Metropolitan Area. They are

New Jersey–Northern,*
New York City,
New York City–Brooklyn/Queens,
New York–Nassau/Suffolk Counties,
and New York–Rockland/Westchester Counties.

* See page 706.

MARKET DATA

TOTAL INVENTORY
Central City: 400,000,000 sq.ft.
Suburban: n/a

VACANT INVENTORY
Central City: n/a
Suburban: n/a

NET ABSORPTION
Central City: n/a
Suburban: n/a

CURRENT CONSTRUCTION
Central City: n/a
Suburban: n/a

MORTGAGE MONEY SUPPLY
Moderate

PRIME SOURCE OF FINANCING
Owner Financing
Commercial Banks

NEW YORK CITY: INDUSTRIAL

Market Area: Manhattan, Brooklyn, Queens, Bronx

1987 REVIEW

The New York City industrial real estate market is varied and unusual. There are excellent one-story industrial buildings five to 20 years old in demand in Brooklyn, Queens, and the Bronx. The Manhattan market is generally loft-type, multi-floor buildings used for light assembly and manufacturing.

New York's industrial real estate prices are exceptionally high, reaching $250 per square foot for site with less than two acres. The market is fairly balanced with a moderate shortage of properties with less than 20,000 square feet. Properties with more than 60,000 square feet are moderately oversupplied.

1988 FORECAST

For 1988, SIOR panelists expect a six to 10 percent increase in manufacturing and warehouse/distribution sales and lease prices. Also, they project an 11 to 15 percent increase in site prices and dollar volumes of sales and leases.

OUTLOOK

SALES PRICES
Manufacturing: Up 6-10%
Warehouse/Distribution: Up 6-10%
High Tech/R & D: Same

LEASE PRICES
Manufacturing: Up 6-10%
Warehouse/Distribution: Up 6-10%
High Tech/R & D: Same

ABSORPTION
Manufacturing: Same
Warehouse/Distribution: Same
High Tech/R & D: Same

CONSTRUCTION
Manufacturing: Same
Warehouse/Distribution: Same
High Tech/R & D: Same

DOLLAR VOLUME
Sales: Up 11-15%
Leases: Up 11-15%

PROFILE OF BUILDINGS BY TYPE

	WAREHOUSING & DISTRIBUTION	MANUFACTURING	HIGH TECH/ R & D
COMPOSITION OF ABSORPTION	n/a	n/a	n/a
RATE OF NEW CONSTRUCTION **	Same	Same	Same
DOLLAR VOLUME - SALES **	Up 6-10%	Up 6-10%	Same
DOLLAR VOLUME - LEASES **	Up 6-10%	Up 6-10%	Up 6-10%

** Compared to A Year Ago

SITE PRICES

(Dollars Per Square Foot)

	IMPROVED SITES				UNIMPROVED SITES		
LOCATION	LESS THAN 2 ACRES	2 TO 5 ACRES	5 TO 10 ACRES	MORE THAN 10 ACRES	LESS THAN 10 ACRES	10 TO 100 ACRES	MORE THAN 100 ACRES
SUBURBAN	n/a	n/a	n/a	n/a	n/a	n/a	n/a
CENTRAL CITY	$10.00-$250.00	$8.00-$50.00	$8.00-$40.00	n/a	n/a	n/a	n/a

PROFILE OF BUILDINGS BY SIZE

(All prices are per square foot. Lease prices in this market area are *NET* prices.)

SIZE	SALES PRICES CENTRAL CITY	SALES PRICES SUBURBAN	LEASE PRICES CENTRAL CITY	LEASE PRICES SUBURBAN	CONSTRUCTION COSTS	VACANCY SITUATION
Less Than 5000	$40.00-$150.00	n/a	$6.00-$15.00	n/a	$45.00-$75.00	Moderate Shortage
5,000 to 19,999	$35.00-$75.00	n/a	$4.00-$12.00	n/a	$45.00-$60.00	Moderate Shortage
20,000 to 39,999	$35.00-$75.00	n/a	$4.00-$10.00	n/a	$45.00-$60.00	Balanced Market
40,000 to 59,999	$32.00-$60.00	n/a	$5.00-$10.00	n/a	$45.00-$60.00	Balanced Market
60,000 to 99,999	$30.00-$60.00	n/a	$5.00-$10.00	n/a	$45.00-$60.00	Moderate Oversupply
More Than 100,000	$30.00-$50.00	n/a	$3.75-$6.50	n/a	$50.00	Moderate Oversupply
High Tech/R & D	n/a	n/a	n/a	n/a	n/a	n/a

MARKET DATA

TOTAL INVENTORY
Central City: 330,000,000 sq.ft.
Suburban: n/a

VACANT INVENTORY
Cent. City: 38,000,000 sq.ft.(11.5%)
Suburban: n/a

NET ABSORPTION
Central City: 10,000,000 sq.ft.
Suburban: n/a

CURRENT CONSTRUCTION
Central City: n/a
Suburban: n/a

MORTGAGE MONEY SUPPLY
Ample

PRIME SOURCE OF FINANCING
Commercial Banks

NEW YORK CITY–BROOKLYN/QUEENS: INDUSTRIAL

Market Area: Brooklyn and Queens

1987 REVIEW

In 1987, absorption in the Brooklyn/Queens industrial market area was particularly strong in the warehouse and distribution sector, which accounted for 60 percent of the 10 million square feet of absorption. Another 35 percent of absorption was for use by manufacturing firms. The area maintained an 11.5 percent vacancy rate.

SIOR panelists report that the market continued to be strong with primary activity in buildings under 20,000 square feet. The shelf-life of space is increasing and the rate of absorption is decreasing causing vacancy rates to rise.

1988 FORECAST

In 1988, high-tech construction and absorption will decline six to 10 percent. Manufacturing construction and absorption, as well as warehouse/distribution absorption, will be down one to five percent. Site prices will increase one to five percent.

OUTLOOK

SALES PRICES
Manufacturing: Same
Warehouse/Distribution: Same
High Tech/R & D: Same

LEASE PRICES
Manufacturing: Same
Warehouse/Distribution: Same
High Tech/R & D: Same

ABSORPTION
Manufacturing: Down 1-5%
Warehouse/Distribution: Down 1-5%
High Tech/R & D: Down 6-10%

CONSTRUCTION
Manufacturing: Down 1-5%
Warehouse/Distribution: Same
High Tech/R & D: Down 6-10%

DOLLAR VOLUME
Sales: Up 1-5%
Leases: Up 1-5%

PROFILE OF BUILDINGS BY TYPE

	WAREHOUSING & DISTRIBUTION	MANUFACTURING	HIGH TECH/ R & D
COMPOSITION OF ABSORPTION	60%	35%	5%
RATE OF NEW CONSTRUCTION ••	Same	Down 11-15%	Down 50%
DOLLAR VOLUME - SALES ••	Same	Same	Same
DOLLAR VOLUME - LEASES ••	Down 1-5%	Down 6-10%	Down 30%

•• Compared to A Year Ago

SITE PRICES
(Dollars Per Square Foot)

	IMPROVED SITES				UNIMPROVED SITES		
LOCATION	LESS THAN 2 ACRES	2 TO 5 ACRES	5 TO 10 ACRES	MORE THAN 10 ACRES	LESS THAN 10 ACRES	10 TO 100 ACRES	MORE THAN 100 ACRES
SUBURBAN	n/a	n/a	n/a	n/a	n/a	n/a	n/a
CENTRAL CITY	$20.00-$45.00	$12.00-$20.00	$8.00-$15.00	$4.50-$10.00	n/a	n/a	n/a

PROFILE OF BUILDINGS BY SIZE
(All prices are per square foot. Lease prices in this market area are *NET* prices.)

SIZE	SALES PRICES CENTRAL CITY	SALES PRICES SUBURBAN	LEASE PRICES CENTRAL CITY	LEASE PRICES SUBURBAN	CONSTRUCTION COSTS	VACANCY SITUATION
Less Than 5000	$80.00-$100.00	n/a	$7.50-$8.50	n/a	$60.00	Substantial Shortage
5,000 to 19,999	$70.00-$100.00	n/a	$7.00-$8.00	n/a	$60.00	Moderate Shortage
20,000 to 39,999	$60.00-$85.00	n/a	$6.50-$8.00	n/a	$55.00	Balanced Market
40,000 to 59,999	$45.00-$65.00	n/a	$6.00-$8.00	n/a	$55.00	Moderate Oversupply
60,000 to 99,999	$35.00-$60.00	n/a	$5.00-$7.50	n/a	$50.00	Moderate Oversupply
More Than 100,000	$40.00-$60.00	n/a	$4.50-$6.00	n/a	$50.00	Balanced Market
High Tech/R & D	$80.00-$120.00	n/a	$9.00-$12.00	n/a	$100.00-$150.00	Balanced Market

MARKET DATA

TOTAL INVENTORY
Central City: n/a
Suburban: 210,000,000 sq.ft.

VACANT INVENTORY
Central City: n/a
Suburban: 19,000,000 sq.ft. (9.0%)

NET ABSORPTION
Central City: n/a
Suburban: 9,000,000 sq.ft.

CURRENT CONSTRUCTION
Central City: n/a
Suburban: 800,000 sq.ft.

MORTGAGE MONEY SUPPLY
Ample

PRIME SOURCE OF FINANCING
Commercial Banks

NEW YORK–NASSAU/SUFFOLK COUNTIES: INDUSTRIAL

Market Area: New York City Suburbs–Nassau and Suffolk Counties

1987 REVIEW

There is a trend toward the conversion of large, older industrial buildings to discount retail space in the Nassau/Suffolk area. Also, high quality manufacturing space is being converted to high-tech space.

Vacancy rates remained at nine percent during 1987. Construction increased one to five percent for warehouse/distribution properties and six to 10 percent for manufacturing properties. Presently 800,000 square feet are under construction. Net absorption in 1987 was 9,000,000 square feet.

1988 FORECAST

SIOR panelists expect a one to five percent increase in sales and site prices in 1988. Construction of manufacturing and warehouse/distribution properties will decrease one to five percent. High-tech construction and absorption will decrease 11 to 15 percent.

OUTLOOK

SALES PRICES
Manufacturing: Up 1-5%
Warehouse/Distribution: Same
High Tech/R & D: Same

LEASE PRICES
Manufacturing: Same
Warehouse/Distribution: Same
High Tech/R & D: Same

ABSORPTION
Manufacturing: Down 1-5%
Warehouse/Distribution: Down 6-10%
High Tech/R & D: Down 11-15%

CONSTRUCTION
Manufacturing: Down 1-5%
Warehouse/Distribution: Down 1-5%
High Tech/R & D: Down 11-15%

DOLLAR VOLUME
Sales: Same
Leases: Same

PROFILE OF BUILDINGS BY TYPE

	WAREHOUSING & DISTRIBUTION	MANUFACTURING	HIGH TECH/ R & D
COMPOSITION OF ABSORPTION	30%	40%	30%
RATE OF NEW CONSTRUCTION ••	Up 1-5%	Up 6-10%	Same
DOLLAR VOLUME - SALES ••	Up 1-5%	Up 6-10%	Same
DOLLAR VOLUME - LEASES ••	Down 6-10%	Down 1-5%	Down 11-15%

•• Compared to A Year Ago

SITE PRICES

(Dollars Per Square Foot)

	IMPROVED SITES				UNIMPROVED SITES		
LOCATION	LESS THAN 2 ACRES	2 TO 5 ACRES	5 TO 10 ACRES	MORE THAN 10 ACRES	LESS THAN 10 ACRES	10 TO 100 ACRES	MORE THAN 100 ACRES
SUBURBAN	$7.00-$15.00	$5.00-$9.00	$5.00-$9.00	$4.00-$6.00	n/a	n/a	n/a
CENTRAL CITY	n/a	n/a	n/a	n/a	n/a	n/a	n/a

PROFILE OF BUILDINGS BY SIZE

(All prices are per square foot. Lease prices in this market area are *NET* prices.)

SIZE	SALES PRICES CENTRAL CITY	SALES PRICES SUBURBAN	LEASE PRICES CENTRAL CITY	LEASE PRICES SUBURBAN	CONSTRUCTION COSTS	VACANCY SITUATION
Less Than 5000	n/a	$85.00-$100.00	n/a	$7.50-$9.50	$75.00-$85.00	Moderate Shortage
5,000 to 19,999	n/a	$75.00-$80.00	n/a	$6.50-$7.50	$60.00-$70.00	Moderate Shortage
20,000 to 39,999	n/a	$55.00-$60.00	n/a	$6.00-$7.00	$50.00-$60.00	Balanced Market
40,000 to 59,999	n/a	$50.00-$55.00	n/a	$5.50-$6.50	$50.00-$60.00	Balanced Market
60,000 to 99,999	n/a	$50.00	n/a	$5.50-$6.50	$50.00-$55.00	Moderate Oversupply
More Than 100,000	n/a	$45.00-$50.00	n/a	$5.00-$6.00	$50.00-$55.00	Moderate Oversupply
High Tech/R & D	n/a	$85.00-$150.00	n/a	$8.00-$12.00	$75.00-$150.00	Moderate Shortage

MARKET DATA

TOTAL INVENTORY
Central City: n/a
Suburban: 33,300,000 sq.ft.

VACANT INVENTORY
Central City: n/a
Suburban: 1,665,000 sq.ft.(5.0%)

NET ABSORPTION
Central City: n/a
Suburban: 435,000 sq.ft.

CURRENT CONSTRUCTION
Central City: n/a
Suburban: 500,000 sq.ft.

MORTGAGE MONEY SUPPLY
Ample

PRIME SOURCE OF FINANCING
Commercial Banks

NEW YORK– ROCKLAND/WESTCHESTER COUNTIES: INDUSTRIAL

Market Area: New York City Suburbs–Rockland and Westchester Counties

1987 REVIEW

The Rockland/Westchester industrial economy was healthy, but not booming in 1987. Vacancies hovered around five percent and net absorption totalled 435,000 square feet. Currently 500,000 square feet are under construction. There has been a noticable shift in construction volume away from office to industrial projects.

There was a great demand for properties for sale and a substantial shortage of properties of all sizes available for sale. Also, there was a good deal of prime space available for lease, but at prices which discourage rapid absorption.

1988 FORECAST

SIOR panelists expect a one to five percent increase in manufacturing and warehouse/distribution sales and lease prices. Site prices will also increase one to five percent. High-tech construction will decline six to 10 percent in response to lagging activity for this type of property.

OUTLOOK

SALES PRICES
Manufacturing: Up 1-5%
Warehouse/Distribution: Up 1-5%
High Tech/R & D: Same

LEASE PRICES
Manufacturing: Up 1-5%
Warehouse/Distribution: Up 1-5%
High Tech/R & D: Same

ABSORPTION
Manufacturing: Same
Warehouse/Distribution: Same
High Tech/R & D: Same

CONSTRUCTION
Manufacturing: Same
Warehouse/Distribution: Same
High Tech/R & D: Down 6-10%

DOLLAR VOLUME
Sales: Same
Leases: Same

PROFILE OF BUILDINGS BY TYPE

	WAREHOUSING & DISTRIBUTION	MANUFACTURING	HIGH TECH/ R & D
COMPOSITION OF ABSORPTION	80%	17%	3%
RATE OF NEW CONSTRUCTION ••	Down 1-5%	Same	Up 1-5%
DOLLAR VOLUME - SALES ••	Down 11-15%	Down 11-15%	Down 11-15%
DOLLAR VOLUME - LEASES ••	Down 11-15%	Down 11-15%	Down 11-15%

•• Compared to A Year Ago

SITE PRICES
(Dollars Per Square Foot)

	IMPROVED SITES				UNIMPROVED SITES		
LOCATION	LESS THAN 2 ACRES	2 TO 5 ACRES	5 TO 10 ACRES	MORE THAN 10 ACRES	LESS THAN 10 ACRES	10 TO 100 ACRES	MORE THAN 100 ACRES
SUBURBAN	n/a	n/a	n/a	n/a	$4.00-$10.00	$3.00-$8.00	n/a
CENTRAL CITY	n/a	n/a	n/a	n/a	n/a	n/a	n/a

PROFILE OF BUILDINGS BY SIZE
(All prices are per square foot. Lease prices in this market area are ***GROSS*** prices.)

SIZE	SALES PRICES CENTRAL CITY	SALES PRICES SUBURBAN	LEASE PRICES CENTRAL CITY	LEASE PRICES SUBURBAN	CONSTRUCTION COSTS	VACANCY SITUATION
Less Than 5000	n/a	$100.00	n/a	$10.00	$65.00	Substantial Shortage
5,000 to 19,999	n/a	$80.00	n/a	$8.00	$60.00	Moderate Shortage
20,000 to 39,999	n/a	$75.00	n/a	$7.50	$55.00	Moderate Shortage
40,000 to 59,999	n/a	$70.00	n/a	$7.00	$50.00	Moderate Shortage
60,000 to 99,999	n/a	$67.00	n/a	$6.75	$45.00	Moderate Shortage
More Than 100,000	n/a	$65.00	n/a	$6.50	$40.00	Substantial Shortage
High Tech/R & D	n/a	$100.00	n/a	$14.00	$90.00	Moderate Oversupply

Office Real Estate Market: Selected Cities*

DEMOGRAPHICS

POPULATION: 2,560,500
POPULATION GROWTH RATE: 2.8%
EMPLOYMENT GROWTH RATE: 4.9%
UNEMPLOYMENT RATE: 4.7%
PER CAPITA INCOME: $12,806

MARKET DATA

TOTAL INVENTORY
Class A/CBD: 8,500,000 sq.ft.
Class A/OutCBD: 35,000,000 sq.ft.
Class B/CBD: 3,200,000 sq.ft.
Class B/OutCBD: 21,000,000 sq.ft.

VACANT INVENTORY
Class A/CBD: 1,500,000 sq.ft.
Class A/OutCBD: 8,800,000 sq.ft.
Class B/CBD: 400,000 sq.ft.
Class B/OutCBD: 4,500,000 sq.ft.

VACANCY RATES
Class A/CBD: 17.6%
Class A/OutCBD: 25.1%
Class B/CBD: 12.5%
Class B/OutCBD: 21.4%

SUBLEASE INVENTORY
Class A: 1,000,000 sq.ft.
Class B: 1,500,000 sq.ft.

CURRENT CONSTRUCTION
Class A/CBD: 428,000 sq.ft.
Class A/OutCBD: 5,000,000 sq.ft.
Class B/CBD: 0 sq.ft.
Class B/OutCBD: 600,000 sq.ft.

NET ABSORPTION
Class A/CBD: 240,000 sq.ft.
Class A/OutCBD: 3,900,000 sq.ft.
Class B/CBD: 50,000 sq.ft.
Class B/OutCBD: 1,200,000 sq.ft.

STANDARD WORK LETTER
Typically based on dollars per square foot. Approximate dollar value: $14

TYPICAL PARKING RATIO
CBD: 1 per 2000 sq.ft.
OutCBD: 1 per 400 sq. ft.

AVERAGE UTILITY RATES
CBD: $1.50 per sq.ft.
OutCBD: $1.25 per sq.ft.
Space for lease is typically not separately metered.

OPERATING COST ESCALATION
Base Year and Stop: Typically $5.00 per sq.ft.

MAJOR DEVELOPERS
Hines
Vantage
Trammel Crow
Lincoln
Taylor & Mathis
The Landmarks Group

OUTLOOK

ABSORPTION: Down 6-10%
CONSTRUCTION: Down 11-15%
VACANCIES: Down 1-5%
RENTAL RATES: Up 1-5%
LANDLORD CONCESSIONS: Same

ATLANTA: OFFICE

Market Area: Atlanta Metropolitan Area

1987 REVIEW

Atlanta's office market is soft due to very aggressive development in recent years. Vacancy rates are particularly high in areas outside the central business district where over 80 percent of the total office inventory is located. Absorption has been good, however, approaching 4.5 million square feet annually for the past three years.

Class A rental rates vary from $20 to $25 per square foot in the CBD and $16 to $22 per square foot in areas outside the CBD. Landlord concessions are widespread and typically lead to a discount factor of between 16 and 20 percent.

1988 REVIEW

Absorption will be off six to 10 percent in 1988. Construction will decline 11 to 15 percent so that the net result will be a slight improvement in vacancy rates. Rental rates will edge up by one to five percent.

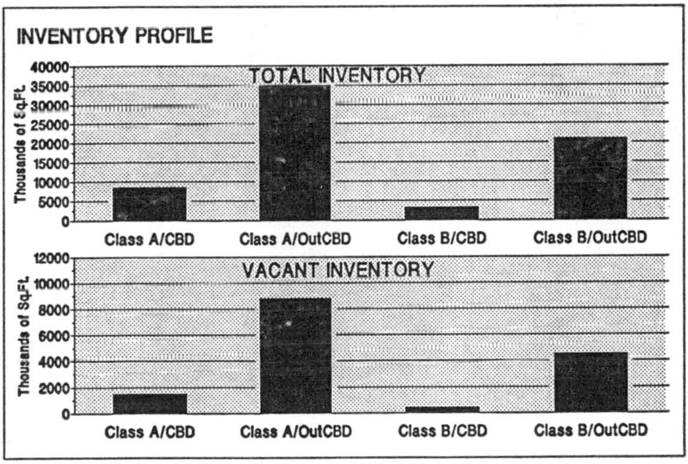

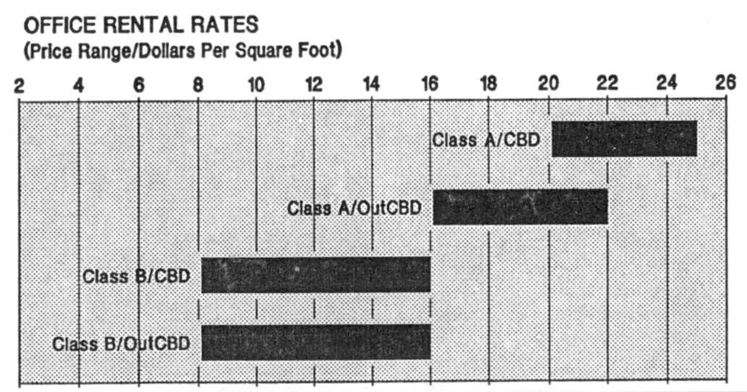

TYPICAL CONCESSIONS:
Parking
Rental Abatement
Lease Assumptions
Moving Allowance
Additional Interior Improvements
Club Memberships

RENTAL RATE DISCOUNT FACTOR: 16-20%

* See Glossary of Terms on page 595.

DEMOGRAPHICS

POPULATION: 6,188,000
POPULATION GROWTH RATE: 0.4%
EMPLOYMENT GROWTH RATE: 1.2%
UNEMPLOYMENT RATE: 5.8%
PER CAPITA INCOME: $13,555

MARKET DATA

TOTAL INVENTORY

Class A/CBD: 40,454,120 sq.ft.
Class B/CBD: 42,763,021 sq.ft.
Class A & B/OutCBD: 53,202,650 sq.ft.

VACANT INVENTORY

Class A/CBD: 5,563,609 sq.ft.
Class B/CBD:5,537,907 sq.ft.
Class A & B/OutCBD: 11,612,456 sq.ft.

VACANCY RATES

Class A/CBD: 13.8%
Class B/CBD: 12.9%
Class A & B/OutCBD: 21.8%

SUBLEASE INVENTORY

Class A: n/a
Class B: n/a

CURRENT CONSTRUCTION

Class A/CBD: 7,898,000 sq.ft.
Class A/OutCBD: 1,915,682 sq.ft.
Class B/CBD: 0 sq.ft.
Class B/OutCBD: 0 sq.ft.

NET ABSORPTION

Class A/CBD: n/a
Class A/OutCBD: n/a
Class B/CBD: n/a
Class B/OutCBD: n/a

STANDARD WORK LETTER

Typically based on dollars per square foot. Approximate dollar value: Varies Considerably

TYPICAL PARKING RATIO

CBD: None
OutCBD: 1 per 250 sq. ft.

AVERAGE UTILITY RATES

CBD: $1.35 per sq.ft.
OutCBD: $1.25 per sq.ft.
Space for lease is typically separately metered.

OPERATING COST ESCALATION

Net

MAJOR DEVELOPERS

Vantage
Trammel Crow
Lincoln
Fifield Development
John Buck Co.
Metropolitan Structures
Hawthorn Realty
Stein & Co.

OUTLOOK

ABSORPTION: n/a
CONSTRUCTION: Same
VACANCIES: Down 1-5%
RENTAL RATES: Up 1-5%
LANDLORD CONCESSIONS: Down 1-5%

CHICAGO: OFFICE

Market Area: Chicago Metropolitan Area

1987 REVIEW

According to a recent Salomon Brothers report, *Chicago Real Estate Market,* Chicago's employment base is 60 percent more office-intensive than is typical nationwide. Between 1983 and 1986 office employment in Chicago increased 5.6 percent annually.

The Chicago metro area has approximately 136 million square feet of rentable office space (not including owner-occupied space). Over 9.8 million square feet of new office space is presently under construction with 80 percent of it located in the CBD.

1988 FORECAST

SIOR panelists in Chicago expect rental rates to increase moderately in 1988. Landlord concessions will decrease, reducing the spread between gross and effective rates. Absorption will be strong enough to reduce vacancies by one to five percent.

INVENTORY PROFILE

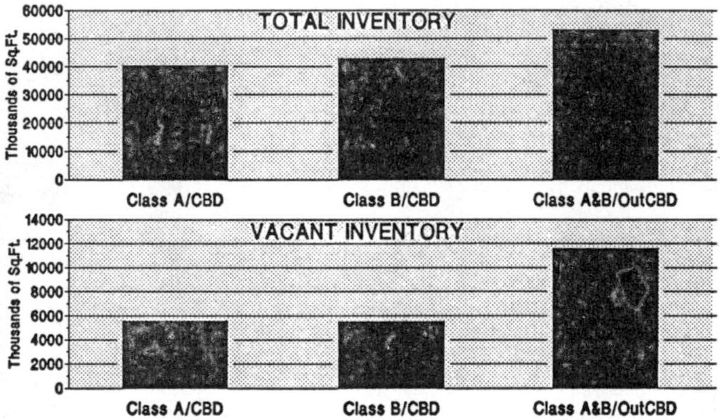

OFFICE RENTAL RATES
(Price Range/Dollars Per Square Foot)

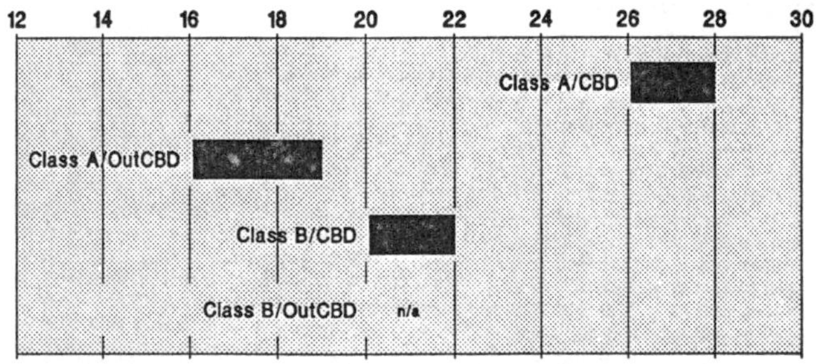

TYPICAL CONCESSIONS:

Parking
Rental Abatement
Lease Assumptions
Moving Allowance
Additional Interior Improvements

RENTAL RATE DISCOUNT FACTOR: n/a

DEMOGRAPHICS

POPULATION: 3,222,000
POPULATION GROWTH RATE: 3.1%
EMPLOYMENT GROWTH RATE: 4.1%
UNEMPLOYMENT RATE: 8.0%
PER CAPITA INCOME: $13,428

MARKET DATA

TOTAL INVENTORY

Class A/CBD: 26,000,000 sq.ft.
Class A/OutCBD: 34,000,000 sq.ft.
Class B/CBD: 10,000,000 sq.ft.
Class B/OutCBD: 49,000,000 sq.ft.

VACANT INVENTORY

Class A/CBD: 5,900,000 sq.ft.
Class A/OutCBD: 8,500,000 sq.ft.
Class B/CBD: 2,700,000 sq.ft.
Class B/OutCBD: 18,500,000 sq.ft.

VACANCY RATES

Class A/CBD: 22.7%
Class A/OutCBD: 25.0%
Class B/CBD: 27.0%
Class B/OutCBD: 37.8%

SUBLEASE INVENTORY

Class A: 3,000,000 sq.ft.
Class B: 1,000,000 sq.ft.

CURRENT CONSTRUCTION

Class A/CBD: 0 sq.ft.
Class A/OutCBD: 0 sq.ft.
Class B/CBD: 0 sq.ft.
Class B/OutCBD: 0 sq.ft.

NET ABSORPTION

Class A/CBD: -50,000 sq.ft.
Class A/OutCBD: 1,200,000 sq.ft.
Class B/CBD: -200,000 sq.ft.
Class B/OutCBD: -500,000 sq.ft.

STANDARD WORK LETTER

Typically based on dollars per square foot. Approximate dollar value: $12

TYPICAL PARKING RATIO

CBD: 1 per 1500 sq.ft.
OutCBD: 1 per 300 sq. ft.

AVERAGE UTILITY RATES

CBD: $1.60 per sq.ft.
OutCBD: $1.60 per sq.ft.
Space for lease is typically not separately metered.

OPERATING COST ESCALATION

Base year

MAJOR DEVELOPERS

Hines
Vantage
Trammel Crow
Paragon
Friendswood
Homart
Century

OUTLOOK

ABSORPTION: Up 1-5%
CONSTRUCTION: Same
VACANCIES: Same
RENTAL RATES: Up 1-5%
LANDLORD CONCESSIONS: Same

HOUSTON: OFFICE

Market Area: Houston and Harris County

1987 REVIEW

Houston is the headquarters for 13 Fortune 500 companies and a primary location for 45 of the world's largest non-U.S. based companies. It also has a significant high technology base with firms concentrated in the computer and aerospace industries. But, of course, the oil industry is still crucially important to Houston's economic prosperity.

Office vacancy rates currently range from 22.7 percent for Class A space in the CBD to 37.8 percent for Class B space in areas outside the CBD. Construction has come to a virtual halt. In 1987 the only segment of the market to experience positive net absorption was suburban Class A space where 1.2 million square feet was absorbed.

1988 FORECAST

SIOR panelists in Houston expect some improvement in conditions during 1988. Absorption will rise moderately allowing for some marginal improvement in rental rates. There will be little or no new construction again in 1988.

INVENTORY PROFILE

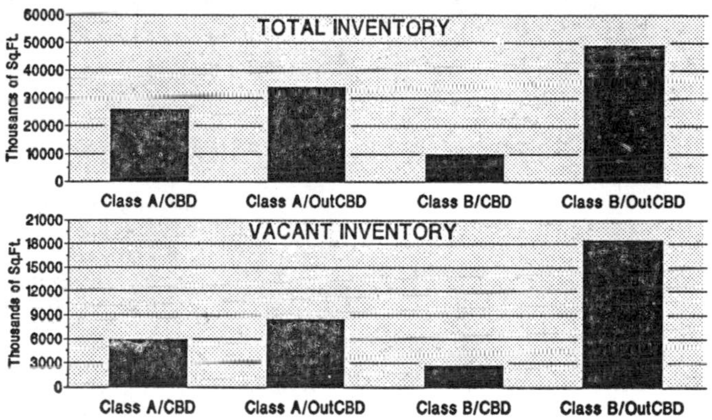

OFFICE RENTAL RATES
(Price Range/Dollars Per Square Foot)

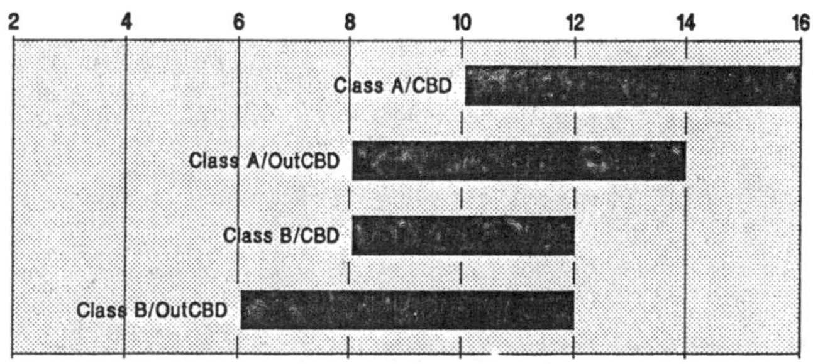

TYPICAL CONCESSIONS:

Parking
Lease Assumptions
Moving Allowance
Additional Interior Improvements
Club Memberships

RENTAL RATE DISCOUNT FACTOR: 16-20%

DEMOGRAPHICS

POPULATION
Los Angeles-Anaheim-Riverside: 12,738,000
Anaheim-Santa Ana: 2,123,000
Los Angeles-Long Beach: 8,109,000
Oxnard-Ventura: 600,000
Riverside-San Bernadino: 1,907,000

POPULATION GROWTH RATE
Los Angeles-Anaheim-Riverside: 2.0%
Anaheim-Santa Ana: 1.8%
Los Angeles-Long Beach: 2.4%
Oxnard-Ventura: 5.0%
Riverside-San Bernadino: 4.5%

EMPLOYMENT GROWTH RATE
Los Angeles-Long Beach: 2.4%
Oxnard-Ventura: 5.0%
Riverside-San Bernadino: 4.5%

UNEMPLOYMENT RATE
Anaheim-Santa Ana: 3.0%
Los Angeles-Long Beach: 4.5%
Oxnard-Ventura: 5.5%
Riverside-San Bernadino: 5.5%

PER CAPITA INCOME
Los Angeles-Long Beach: $13,436
Oxnard-Ventura: $13,260
Riverside-San Bernadino: $11,409

LOS ANGELES METROPOLITAN AREA

Los Angeles Office Markets

The Los Angeles market area almost defies description. It encompasses an enormous area of Southern California and is currently in a period of remarkable change.

The area's populaton is approximately 12.7 million and growing at an average annual rate of two percent. The pace of growth has made the area famous for traffic congestion and its cost of housing. Still, Los Angeles has such a rich diversity of social and cultural resources to go along with its appealing climate that it remains an attractive place to live.

The Los Angeles economy is naturally quite diverse with a significant manufacturing employment base in defense-related industries and durable goods manufacturing. Non-manufacturing employment is high in wholesale and retail trade, business services, and financial services.

High growth sectors of the economy are tied into the role the city plays in U.S. trade with the Pacific Basin. Trade impacts the area in several ways. Clearly, goods passing through the area create the need for warehouse and distribution space. But, also a significant amount of activity related to finance, banking, real estate, insurance, legal affairs, and consulting is centered in Los Angeles.

SIOR panelists have divided the Los Angeles Metropolitan Area into five separate market areas to more accurately reflect the diversity of market characteristics. On the followng pages are reports from five market areas in and around the Los Angeles Metropolitan Area. They are

Los Angeles–Central,
Los Angeles–Orange County,
Los Angeles–San Fernando Valley,
Los Angeles–South Bay,
and Los Angeles–West.

MARKET DATA

TOTAL INVENTORY

Class A/CBD: 24,662,360 sq.ft.
Class A/OutCBD: 157,381,037 sq.ft.
Class B/CBD: n/a
Class B/OutCBD: n/a

VACANT INVENTORY

Class A/CBD: 4,100,000 sq.ft.
Class A/OutCBD: 23,607,154 sq.ft.
Class B/CBD: n/a
Class B/OutCBD: n/a

VACANCY RATES

Class A/CBD: 17.0%
Class A/OutCBD: 15.0%
Class B/CBD: n/a
Class B/OutCBD: n/a

SUBLEASE INVENTORY

Class A: 720,000 sq.ft.
Class B: n/a

CURRENT CONSTRUCTION

Class A/CBD: 2,186,135 sq.ft.
Class A/OutCBD: 15,017,630 sq.ft.
Class B/CBD: n/a
Class B/OutCBD: n/a

NET ABSORPTION

Class A/CBD: 1,200,000 sq.ft.
Class A/OutCBD: 7,900,000 sq.ft.
Class B/CBD: n/a
Class B/OutCBD: n/a

STANDARD WORK LETTER

Approximate dollar value: $30

TYPICAL PARKING RATIO

CBD: 1 per 1000 sq.ft.
OutCBD: 1 per 400 sq.ft.

AVERAGE UTILITY RATES

CBD: $5.00 per sq.ft.
OutCBD: $5.50-$7.00 per sq.ft.
Space for lease is typically not separately metered.

OPERATING COST ESCALATION

Base year

MAJOR DEVELOPERS

Hines
Lincoln
Oxford
Maguire Thomas Partners
Manufactures Real Estate
Raffi Cohen (RCI)
Metropolitan Structures

OUTLOOK

ABSORPTION: Up 6-10%
CONSTRUCTION: Up 1-5%
VACANCIES: Down 1-5%
RENTAL RATES: Up 1-5%
LANDLORD CONCESSIONS: Down 1-5%

LOS ANGELES–CENTRAL: OFFICE

Market Area: Downtown Los Angeles and Los Angeles County

1987 REVIEW

The Los Angeles--Central market area continues to experience remarkable growth. Vacancy rates range from 15 percent outside the CBD to 17 percent inside the CBD. Absorption totalled 9,100,000 square feet in 1987. Over 17 million square feet of space is presently under construction, primarily outside of the CBD.

Gross rental rates range from $17 to $31 per square foot. SIOR panelists report that landlord concessions result in an 11 to 15 percent rental rate discount factor.

1988 FORECAST

The Los Angeles-Central office market continues to tighten for users of 25,000 square feet or more. Between 1988 and 1993 an additional 9,000,000 square feet will be developed. Construction and rental rates will increase one to five percent in 1988. Absorption will increase six to 10 percent allowing vacancies and concessions to decline moderately.

INVENTORY PROFILE

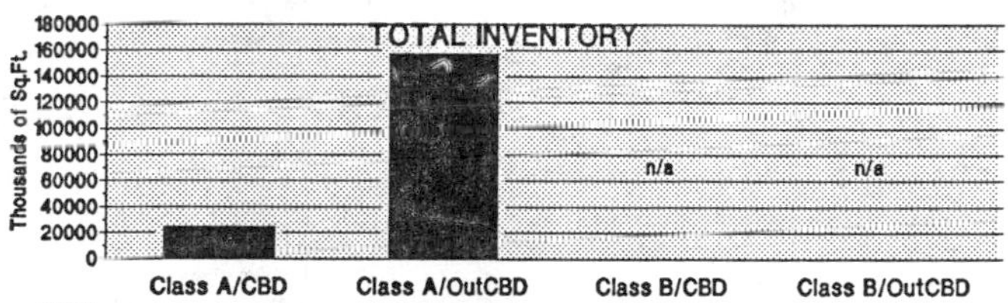

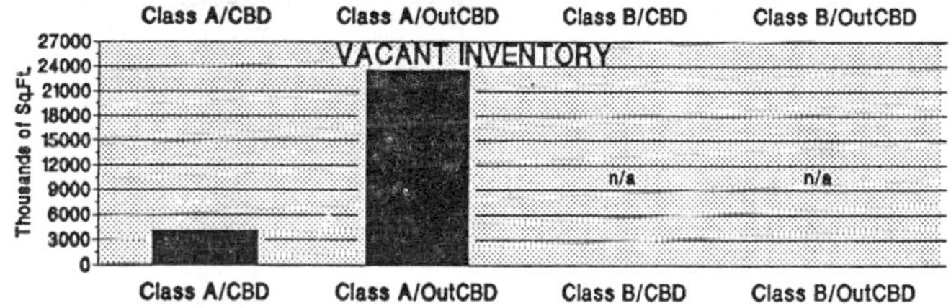

OFFICE RENTAL RATES
(Price Range/Dollars Per Square Foot)

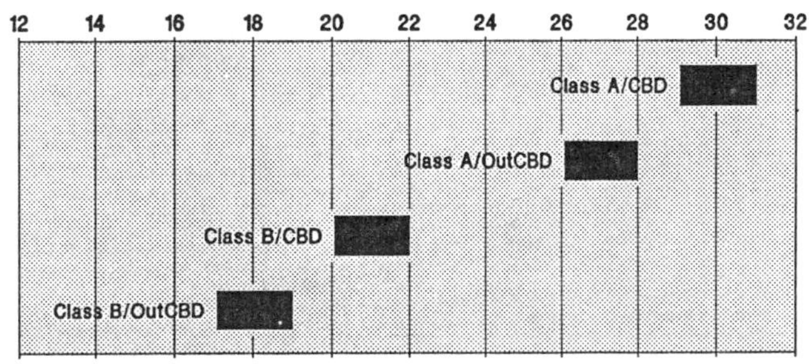

TYPICAL CONCESSIONS:

Rental Abatement
Lease Assumptions
Moving Allowance
Additional Interior Improvements
Signing Bonuses

RENTAL RATE DISCOUNT FACTOR: 11-15%

MARKET DATA

TOTAL INVENTORY
Class A/CBD: 36,231,309 sq.ft.
Class A/OutCBD: n/a
Class B/CBD: n/a
Class B/OutCBD: n/a

VACANT INVENTORY
Class A/CBD: 8,221,690 sq.ft.
Class A/OutCBD: n/a
Class B/CBD: n/a
Class B/OutCBD: n/a

VACANCY RATES
Class A/CBD: 22.7%
Class A/OutCBD: n/a
Class B/CBD: n/a
Class B/OutCBD: n/a

SUBLEASE INVENTORY
Class A: 339,916 sq.ft.
Class B: n/a

CURRENT CONSTRUCTION
Class A/CBD: 7,191,531 sq.ft.
Class A/OutCBD: n/a
Class B/CBD: n/a
Class B/OutCBD: n/a

NET ABSORPTION
Class A/CBD: 2,546,419 sq.ft.
Class A/OutCBD: n/a
Class B/CBD: n/a
Class B/OutCBD: n/a

STANDARD WORK LETTER
Typically based on dollars per square foot. Approximate dollar value: $18-$25

TYPICAL PARKING RATIO
CBD: 1 per 250 sq.ft.
OutCBD: 1 per 250 sq.ft.

AVERAGE UTILITY RATES
CBD: $1.80 per sq.ft.
OutCBD: $1.80 per sq.ft.

OPERATING COST ESCALATION
Base year

MAJOR DEVELOPERS
Irvine Company
Koll Company
Trammel Crow
Lincoln
Birtcher Development
Seagerstrom Family
Transpacific Development
Nexus USA

OUTLOOK

ABSORPTION: Up 6-10%
CONSTRUCTION: Down 11-15%
VACANCIES: Same
RENTAL RATES: Same
LANDLORD CONCESSIONS:Up 6-10%

LOS ANGELES–ORANGE COUNTY: OFFICE

Market Area: Orange County

1987 REVIEW

The Los Angeles-Orange County office market area has approximately 36.2 million square feet of office space. In 1987, the office market vacancy rate was 22.7 percent and absorption totalled more than 2.5 million square feet. Presently 7,191,531 square feet are under construction.

Class A rental rates vary from $20 to $25 per square foot. SIOR panelists state that landlord concessions, including parking, rental abatement, lease assumptions, moving allowance, and additional interior improvements typically result in a rental rate discount factor of 16 to 20 percent.

1988 FORECAST

In 1988, Orange County's office market will experience a six to 10 percent increase in absorption. Construction, however, will decrease by 11 to 15 percent. Rental rates will remain at 1987 levels but landlord concessions and work letters will become more generous.

INVENTORY PROFILE

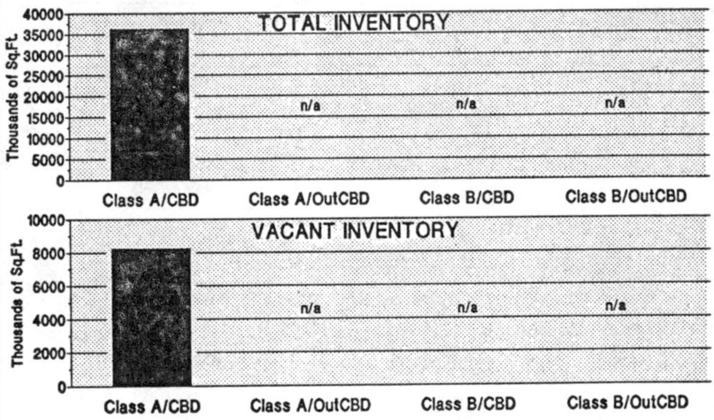

OFFICE RENTAL RATES
(Price Range/Dollars Per Square Foot)

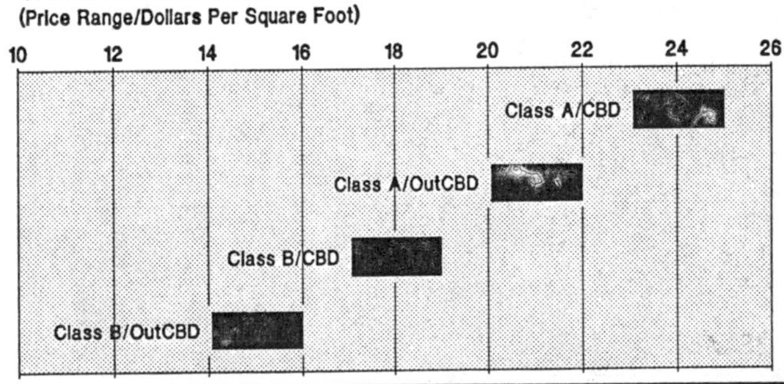

TYPICAL CONCESSIONS:
Parking
Rental Abatement
Lease Assumptions
Moving Allowance
Additional Interior Improvements

RENTAL RATE DISCOUNT FACTOR: 16-20%

MARKET DATA

TOTAL INVENTORY

Class A/CBD: n/a
Class B/CBD: n/a
Class A & B/OutCBD: 19,510,700 sq.ft.

VACANT INVENTORY

Class A/CBD: n/a
Class B/CBD: n/a
Class A & B/OutCBD: 6,467,206 sq.ft.

VACANCY RATES

Class A/CBD: n/a
Class B/CBD: n/a
Class A & B/OutCBD: 33.0%

SUBLEASE INVENTORY

Class A & B: 160,000 sq.ft.

CURRENT CONSTRUCTION

Class A/CBD: n/a
Class B/CBD: n/a
Class A & B/OutCBD: 2,350,420 sq.ft.

NET ABSORPTION

Class A/CBD: n/a
Class A/OutCBD: 400,000 sq.ft.
Class B/CBD: n/a
Class B/OutCBD: 200,000 sq.ft.

STANDARD WORK LETTER

Typically based on dollars per square foot. Approximate dollar value: $18

TYPICAL PARKING RATIO

CBD: n/a
OutCBD: 3 per 1000 sq.ft.

AVERAGE UTILITY RATES

CBD: n/a
OutCBD: $1.20 per sq.ft.
Space for lease is typically not separately metered.

OPERATING COST ESCALATION

Base year

MAJOR DEVELOPERS

Trammel Crow
Lincoln
Cabot, Cabot, & Forbes
Voit Companies

OUTLOOK

ABSORPTION: Same
CONSTRUCTION: Down 6-10%
VACANCIES: Down 6-10%
RENTAL RATES: Up 6-10%
LANDLORD CONCESSIONS: Same

LOS ANGELES–SAN FERNANDO VALLEY: OFFICE

Market Area: San Fernando Valley

1987 REVIEW

The Los Angeles-San Fernando market area has a good mix of general office-intensive service industries including insurance companies, law firms, financial services, and high-tech/research and development companies. In 1987, a total of 600,000 square feet were absorbed in the market area. Approximately 2,350,420 square feet are presently under construction.

Gross rental rates range from $20 to $28 per square foot. SIOR panelists report that landlord lease concessions typically result in an 11 to 15 percent discount factor.

1988 FORECAST

Rental rates will increase by six to 10 percent in 1988, while construction, vacancies, and landlord concessions decrease by six to 10 percent. Los Angeles City's slow growth policies may hamper future absorption rates and new development. Expanding tenants may have to look to more outlying areas in the future.

INVENTORY PROFILE

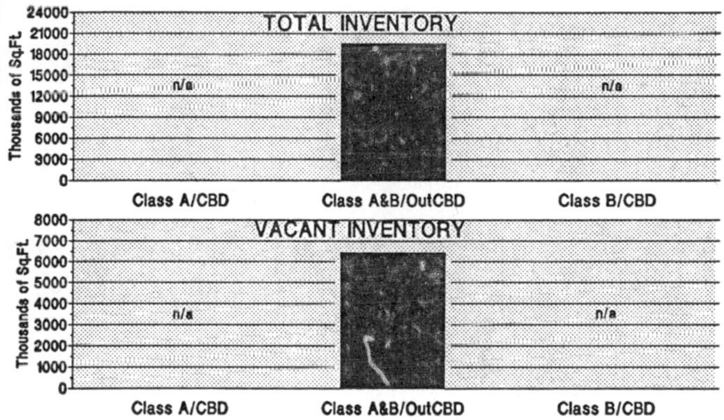

OFFICE RENTAL RATES
(Price Range/Dollars Per Square Foot)

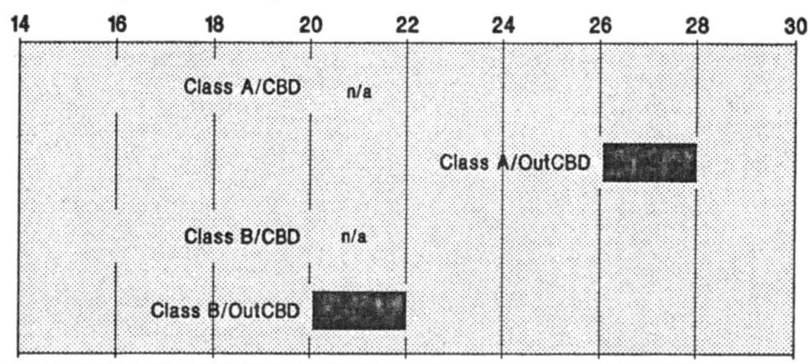

TYPICAL CONCESSIONS:

Rental Abatement
Additional Interior Improvements

RENTAL RATE DISCOUNT FACTOR: 11-15%

LOS ANGELES–SOUTH BAY: OFFICE

Market Area: Torrance, Manchester Boulevard on the North to Orange County Line on the South

MARKET DATA

TOTAL INVENTORY
Class A/CBD: n/a
Class A/OutCBD: 16,893,000 sq.ft.
Class B/CBD: n/a
Class B/OutCBD: 9,131,000 sq.ft.

VACANT INVENTORY
Class A/CBD: n/a
Class A/OutCBD: 4,230,000 sq.ft.
Class B/CBD: n/a
Class B/OutCBD: 1,740,000 sq.ft.

VACANCY RATES
Class A/CBD: n/a
Class A/OutCBD: 25.0%
Class B/CBD: n/a
Class B/OutCBD: 19.1%

SUBLEASE INVENTORY
Class A: 316,000 sq.ft.
Class B: 82,000 sq.ft.

CURRENT CONSTRUCTION
Class A/CBD: n/a
Class A/OutCBD: 1,729,000 sq.ft.
Class B/CBD: n/a
Class B/OutCBD: 256,000 sq.ft.

NET ABSORPTION
Class A & B/CBD: n/a
Class A & B/OutCBD: -649,000 sq.ft

STANDARD WORK LETTER
Typically based on dollars per square foot. Approximate dollar value: $25

TYPICAL PARKING RATIO
CBD: n/a
OutCBD: 1 per 250 sq.ft.

AVERAGE UTILITY RATES
CBD: n/a
OutCBD: $1.75 per sq.ft.
Space for lease is typically not separately metered.

OPERATING COST ESCALATION
Stop: $4.50-$5.50 per sq.ft.

MAJOR DEVELOPERS
Oxford
Koll
Kilroy
Transpacific Development Co.
IDM
Watt Investment Properties

OUTLOOK

ABSORPTION: Same
CONSTRUCTION: Down 50%
VACANCIES: Up 1-5%
RENTAL RATES: Down 1-5%
LANDLORD CONCESSIONS:Up 6-10%

1987 REVIEW

In 1987, the Los Angeles-South Bay office market was heavily impacted by reduced needs in the aerospace defense industry. The area has an estimatd 26 million square feet of office space, primarily Class A space. Approximately 25 percent of the Class A inventory is vacant. Net absorption was a negative 649,000 square feet in 1987.

Class A gross rental rates range from $20 to $29 per square foot. Landlord concessions, including parking, rental abatement, lease assumptions, moving allowances, and interior improvements, typically result in a rental rate discount factor of 16 to 20 percent

1988 FORECAST

SIOR panelists in the South Bay market area report that 1988 may prove to be another soft year for office leasing. Several major new developments have been delayed due to the uncertainty surrounding growth in the area. Rental rates will decline one to five percent and landlord concessions will increase.

INVENTORY PROFILE

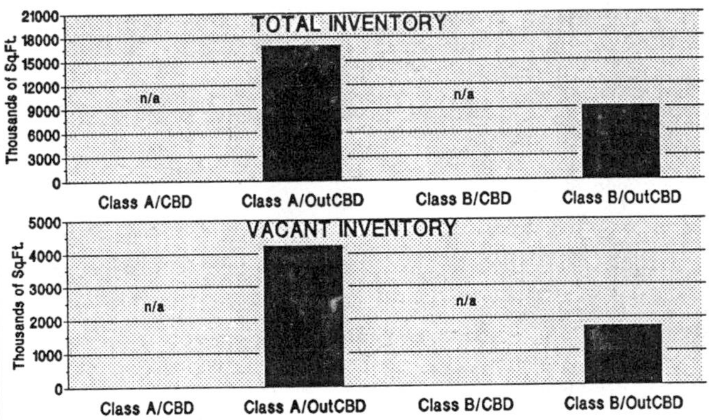

OFFICE RENTAL RATES
(Price Range/Dollars Per Square Foot)

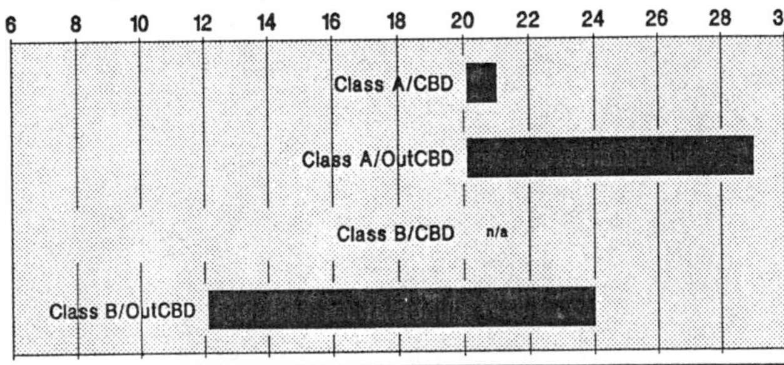

TYPICAL CONCESSIONS:
Rental Abatement
Lease Assumptions
Moving Allowance
Additional Interior Improvements
Parking

RENTAL RATE DISCOUNT FACTOR: 16-20%

MARKET DATA

TOTAL INVENTORY
Class A/CBD: 8,148,401 sq.ft.
Class A/OutCBD: 4,662,074 sq.ft.
Class B/CBD: 15,085,861 sq.ft.
Class B/OutCBD: 9,085,807 sq.ft.

VACANT INVENTORY
Class A/CBD: 1,888,102 sq.ft.
Class A/OutCBD: 1,000,205 sq.ft.
Class B/CBD: 1,608,170 sq.ft.
Class B/OutCBD: 1,221,980 sq.ft.

VACANCY RATES
Class A/CBD: 23.2%
Class A/OutCBD: 21.5%
Class B/CBD: 10.7%
Class B/OutCBD: 13.4%

SUBLEASE INVENTORY
Class A: 404,510 sq.ft.
Class B: 521,189 sq.ft.

CURRENT CONSTRUCTION
Class A/CBD: 1,158,761 sq.ft.
Class A/OutCBD: 755,600 sq.ft.
Class B/CBD: 75,000 sq.ft.
Class B/OutCBD: 65,000 sq.ft.

NET ABSORPTION
Class A/CBD: 1,492,076 sq.ft.
Class A/OutCBD: 322,516 sq.ft.
Class B/CBD: 49,801 sq.ft.
Class B/OutCBD: 189,212 sq.ft.

STANDARD WORK LETTER
Typically based on dollars per square foot. Approximate dollar value: $15-$20

TYPICAL PARKING RATIO
CBD: 2.7 per 1000 sq.ft.
OutCBD: 3 per 1000 sq.ft.

AVERAGE UTILITY RATES
CBD: $12-$15 per sq.ft.
OutCBD: $12-$15 per sq.ft.
Space for lease is typically not separately metered.

OPERATING COST ESCALATION
Stop: $5.25-$7.50 per sq.ft.

MAJOR DEVELOPERS
Koll
Bren
Homart
Tishman West
Bramalea

OUTLOOK

ABSORPTION: Up 6-10%
CONSTRUCTION: Same
VACANCIES: Down 1-5%
RENTAL RATES: Same
LANDLORD CONCESSIONS: Down 1-5%

LOS ANGELES-WEST: OFFICE

Market Area: Los Angeles-West Metropolitan Area

1987 REVIEW

The Los Angeles-West office market has approximately 37 million square feet of rentable office space. The market absorbed over two million square feet in 1987. Currently, 2,054,361 square feet are under construction and will be available for lease by the end of 1988. Class A vacancy rates range from 21.5 percent in areas outside the CBD to 23.2 percent in the CBD.

Gross rental rates range from $18 to $27 per square foot for Class B space and $24 to $42.60 per square foot for Class A space. SIOR panelists report that rental abatement, lease assumptions and additional interior improvements typically result in an 11 to 15 percent rental rate discount factor.

1988 FORECAST

Absorption is expected to increase sharply in 1988 increasing six to 10 percent. The rate of construction will remain unchanged allowing vacancies to decline moderately.

INVENTORY PROFILE

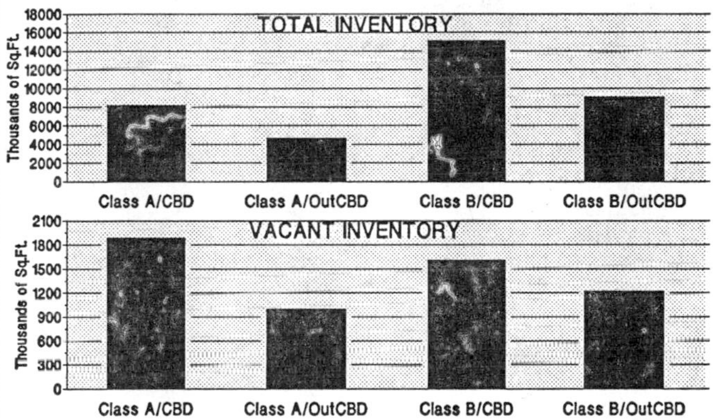

OFFICE RENTAL RATES
(Price Range/Dollars Per Square Foot)

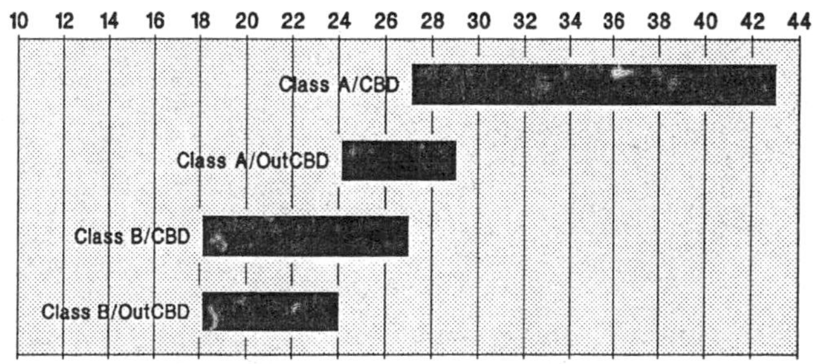

TYPICAL CONCESSIONS:
Rental Abatement
Lease Assumptions
Additional Interior Improvements

RENTAL RATE DISCOUNT FACTOR: 11-15%

DEMOGRAPHICS

POPULATION
New York-Northern New Jersey-Long Island: 17,931,000
Bergen-Passaic, NJ: 1,301,000
Middlesex-Somerset-Hunterdon, NJ: 930,000
Nassau-Suffolk, NY: 2,645,000
New York, NY: 8,466,000
Newark, NJ: 1,882,000

POPULATION GROWTH RATE
New York-Northern New Jersey-Long Island: 0.4%
Bergen-Passaic, NJ: 0.1%
Middlesex-Somerset-Hunterdon, NJ: 0.9%
Nassau-Suffolk, NY: 0.3%
New York, NY: 0.4%
Newark, NJ: 0%

EMPLOYMENT GROWTH RATE
Bergen-Passaic, NJ: 2.1%
Middlesex-Somerset-Hunterdon, NJ: 4.0%
Nassau-Suffolk, NY: 3.1%
New York, NY: 0.8%
Newark, NJ: 2.0%

UNEMPLOYMENT RATE
Bergen-Passaic, NJ: 2.7%
Middlesex-Somerset-Hunterdon, NJ: 2.3%
Nassau-Suffolk, NY: 3.0%
New York, NY: 5.9%
Newark, NJ: 3.4%

PER CAPITA INCOME
Bergen-Passaic, NJ: $16,399
Middlesex-Somerset-Hunterdon, NJ: $15,628
Nassau-Suffolk, NY: $16,239
New York, NY: $13,946
Newark, NJ: $15,053

NEW YORK METROPOLITAN AREA

New York Office Markets

The New York-Northern New Jersey-Long Island consolidated metropolitan statistical area has a population of approximately 17.9 million. Over eight million people live in New York City alone. No other city has such a high concentration of banking and financial services, but nearly every industry maintains a presence in the New York area.

The limited supply and high cost of land has reinforced the movement of business and residence to more outlying areas in Northern New Jersey, Connecticut, and New York state. Manufacturing employment declined at an average annual rate of 2.2 percent between 1975 and 1985 as numerous firms relocated to areas with lower costs and warmer climates. The area's economic restructuring was accompanied by non-manufacturing employment growth over the same period. The financial and business services industries have experienced incredible growth, riding Wall Street's bull market since 1982.

The events of October 19, 1987 probably signaled the end to continuing employment growth from the financial sector of New York's economy. Despite the central role of New York's financial district in its overall economy, this market area is deep and wide. It's too early to forecast the demise of New York's popularity as a business address.

SIOR panelists have divided the New York area into five separate office markets to more accurately reflect the diversity of market characteristics. On the following pages are reports from five market areas in and around the New York Metropolitan Area. They are

New Jersey–Northern,*
New York City,
New York City–Brooklyn/Queens,
New York–Nassau/Suffolk Counties,
and New York–White Plains and Westchester County.

---

* See page 707.

MARKET DATA

TOTAL INVENTORY
Class A/CBD: 233,017,941 sq.ft.
Class A/OutCBD: n/a
Class B/CBD: 94,051,890 sq.ft.
Class B/OutCBD: n/a

VACANT INVENTORY
Class A/CBD: 24,714,338 sq.ft.
Class A/OutCBD: 11,975,253 sq.ft.
Class B/CBD: n/a
Class B/OutCBD: n/a

VACANCY RATES
Class A/CBD: 10.6%
Class A/OutCBD: n/a
Class B/CBD: 12.7%
Class B/OutCBD: n/a

SUBLEASE INVENTORY
Class A: 6,840,345 sq.ft.
Class B: 1,508,727 sq.ft.

CURRENT CONSTRUCTION
Class A/CBD: 9,345,721 sq.ft.
Class A/OutCBD: n/a
Class B/CBD: 0 sq.ft.
Class B/OutCBD: n/a

NET ABSORPTION
Class A/CBD: n/a
Class A/OutCBD: n/a
Class B/CBD: n/a
Class B/OutCBD: n/a

STANDARD WORK LETTER
Typically based on dollars per square foot. Approximate dollar value: $20-$25

TYPICAL PARKING RATIO
CBD: n/a
OutCBD: n/a

AVERAGE UTILITY RATES
CBD: $3.00 per sq.ft.
OutCBD: n/a

OPERATING COST ESCALATION
n/a

MAJOR DEVELOPERS
Hines
Olympia & York
William Zeckendorf, Jr.
Silverstein
Rudin
Resnick
George Klein
Gladstone
Boston Properties
Macklowe
Eicher
Durst
Trump
Prudential

OUTLOOK

ABSORPTION: Down 6-10%
CONSTRUCTION: Down 1-5%
VACANCIES: Up 1-5%
RENTAL RATES: Same
LANDLORD CONCESSIONS: Same

NEW YORK CITY: OFFICE

Market Area: Manhattan

1987 REVIEW

The Manhattan office market is said to be the most active office leasing market in the world. The inventory of Class A space totals a staggering 233 million square feet. Vacancy rates for Class A space were 10.6 percent at the end of 1987. Presently, 9,345,721 square feet are under construction.

Gross rental rates are some of the highest nationwide, at $30 to $60 per square foot for Class A space and $18 to $32 per square foot for Class B space. SIOR panelists state that landlord concessions had little effect, if any, on gross rental rates.

1988 FORECAST

SIOR panelists expect a decrease in absorption of six to 10 percent in 1988. Much has been written about the possible fallout from October's market crash. Very large blocks of space could be put on the market if financial services firms scale back their space requirements like some analysts have suggested. At this point, however, only a small change in market conditions is apparent.

INVENTORY PROFILE

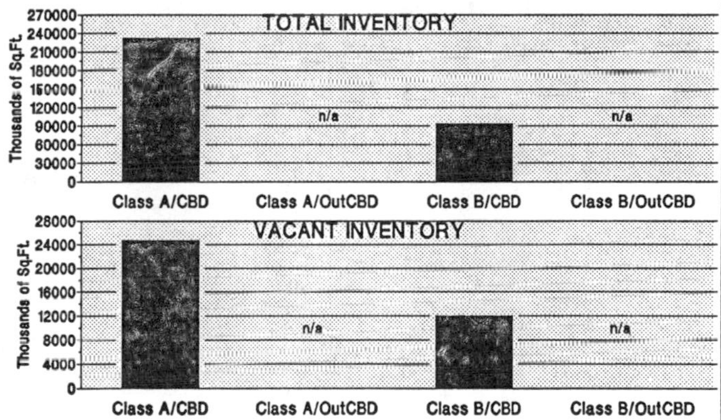

OFFICE RENTAL RATES
(Price Range/Dollars Per Square Foot)

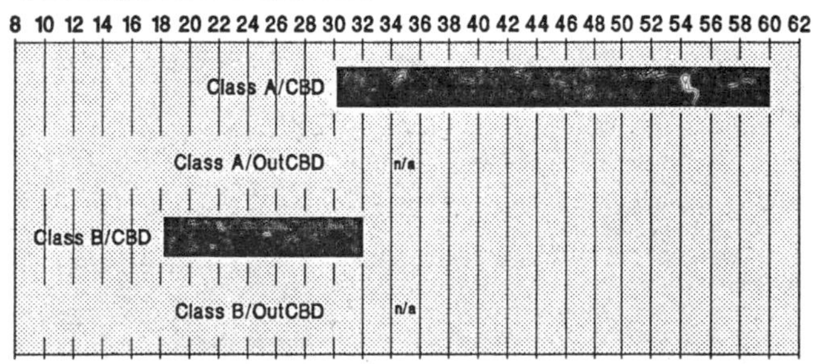

TYPICAL CONCESSIONS:

Some developers will negotiate for concessions including rental abatement, lease assumptions, and additional interior improvements to attract a major tenant for substantial space in new buildings.

RENTAL RATE DISCOUNT FACTOR: 0-5%

MARKET DATA

TOTAL INVENTORY

Class A/CBD: n/a
Class A/OutCBD: 15,000,000 sq.ft.
Class B/CBD: n/a
Class B/OutCBD: n/a

VACANT INVENTORY

Class A/CBD: n/a
Class A/OutCBD: 2,000,000 sq.ft.
Class B/CBD: n/a
Class B/OutCBD: n/a

VACANCY RATES

Class A/CBD: n/a
Class A/OutCBD: 13.3%
Class B/CBD: n/a
Class B/OutCBD: n/a

SUBLEASE INVENTORY

Class A: 100,000 sq.ft.
Class B: n/a

CURRENT CONSTRUCTION

Class A/CBD: n/a
Class A/OutCBD: 1,500,000 sq.ft.
Class B/CBD: n/a
Class B/OutCBD: n/a

NET ABSORPTION

Class A/CBD: n/a
Class A/OutCBD: 500,000 sq.ft.
Class B/CBD: n/a
Class B/OutCBD: n/a

STANDARD WORK LETTER

Approximate dollar value: $12-$20

TYPICAL PARKING RATIO

CBD: n/a
OutCBD: n/a

AVERAGE UTILITY RATES

CBD: n/a
OutCBD: $2.50 per sq.ft.

OPERATING COST ESCALATION

Base year

MAJOR DEVELOPERS

Edward Blumenfeld
George Phohl
Richard Zirinsky
Gertz Associates
Rose Associates
George Klein

OUTLOOK

ABSORPTION: Down 6-10%
CONSTRUCTION: Up 1-5%
VACANCIES: Up 6-10%
RENTAL RATES: Up 1-5%
LANDLORD CONCESSIONS: Up 11-15%

NEW YORK CITY–BROOKLYN/QUEENS: OFFICE

Market Area: Brooklyn and Queens

1987 REVIEW

In 1987, the Brooklyn/Queens area had 15 million square feet of rentable office space. Another 1.5 million square feet is presently under construction. Net absorption in the office market during 1987 totalled 500,000 square feet.

There is a considerable amount of variance in gross rental rates for both Class A and Class B space. Class A rates range from $12 to $28 per square foot and Class B space ranged from $14 to $22 per square foot. Typical concessions in this market area include rental abatement, lease assumptions, moving allowance, additional interior improvements and signing bonuses

1988 FORECAST

SIOR panelists expect a stronger market in 1988. The uncertainty about New York's high concentration of financial services firms spills over to the Brooklyn/Queens market area. Vacancies are expected to increase six to 10 percent in 1988.

INVENTORY PROFILE

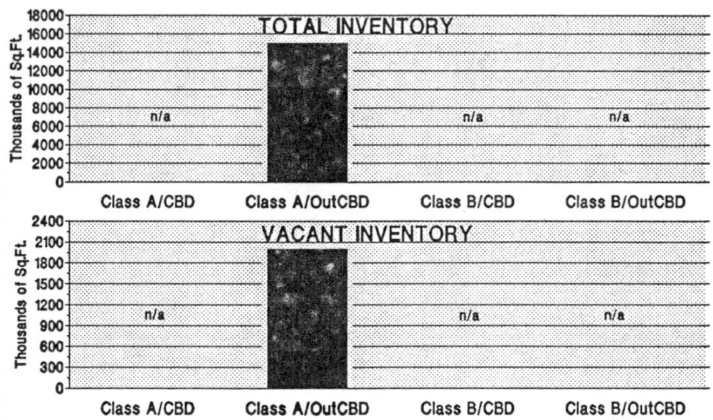

OFFICE RENTAL RATES
(Price Range/Dollars Per Square Foot)

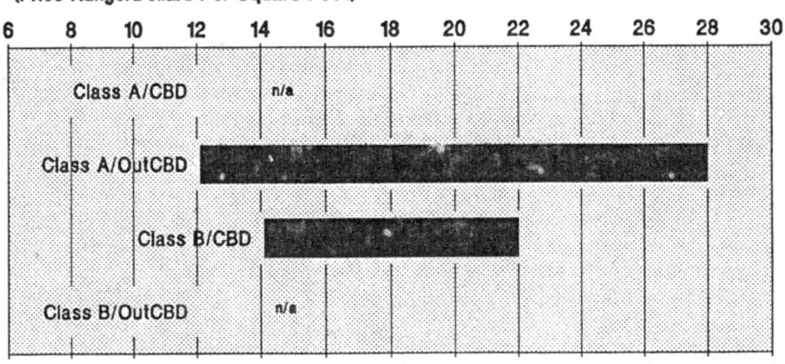

TYPICAL CONCESSIONS:

Rental Abatement
Lease Assumptions
Moving Allowance
Additional Interior Improvements
Signing Bonuses

RENTAL RATE DISCOUNT FACTOR: 6-10%

MARKET DATA

TOTAL INVENTORY
Class A/CBD: n/a
Class A/OutCBD: 11,520,833 sq.ft.
Class B/CBD: n/a
Class B/OutCBD: 8,582,494 sq.ft.

VACANT INVENTORY
Class A/CBD: n/a
Class A/OutCBD: 1,211,414 sq.ft.
Class B/CBD: n/a
Class B/OutCBD: 1,071,731 sq.ft.

VACANCY RATES
Class A/CBD: n/a
Class A/OutCBD: 10.5%
Class B/CBD: n/a
Class B/OutCBD: 12.5%

SUBLEASE INVENTORY
Class A & B: 324,647 sq.ft.

CURRENT CONSTRUCTION
Class A/CBD: n/a
Class A/OutCBD: 2,210,277 sq.ft.
Class B/CBD: n/a
Class B/OutCBD: 492,525 sq.ft.

NET ABSORPTION
Class A/CBD: n/a
Class A/OutCBD: 1,400,000 sq.ft.
Class B/CBD: n/a
Class B/OutCBD: n/a

STANDARD WORK LETTER
Typically based on quantity of materials. Approximate dollar value: $15

TYPICAL PARKING RATIO
CBD: n/a
OutCBD: 1 per 200 sq.ft.

AVERAGE UTILITY RATES
CBD: n/a
OutCBD: $2.00 per sq.ft.

OPERATING COST ESCALATION
Base year

MAJOR DEVELOPERS
Reckson Associates
Gilbert Tilles Projects
DeMatteis Organization
Chasanoff Properties
WE'RE Associates
Feldman Properties

OUTLOOK

ABSORPTION: Same
CONSTRUCTION: Up 6-10%
VACANCIES: Up 6-10%
RENTAL RATES: Up 1-5%
LANDLORD CONCESSIONS: Up 1-5%

NEW YORK–NASSAU/SUFFOLK COUNTIES: OFFICE

Market Area: New York City Suburbs–Nassau and Suffolk Counties, and Long Island

1987 REVIEW

Nassau and Suffolk Counties have remained among the strongest office markets in the country. In 1987, vacancy rates ranged from 10.5 percent for Class A space to 12.5 percent for Class B space. Net absorption totalled 1,400,000 square feet. Currently, another 2,702,802 square feet are under construction.

Rental rates for Class A space ranged from $23 to $25 per square foot. Landlord concessions such as parking, rental abatement and additional interior improvements result in a rental rate discount factor of less than 10 percent.

1988 FORECAST

SIOR panelists expect 1988 to be another strong year. Construction will be up six to 10 percent, temporarily boosting vacancies. Rental rates and landlord concessions are expected to increase one to five percent. Absorption will remain at 1987 levels.

INVENTORY PROFILE

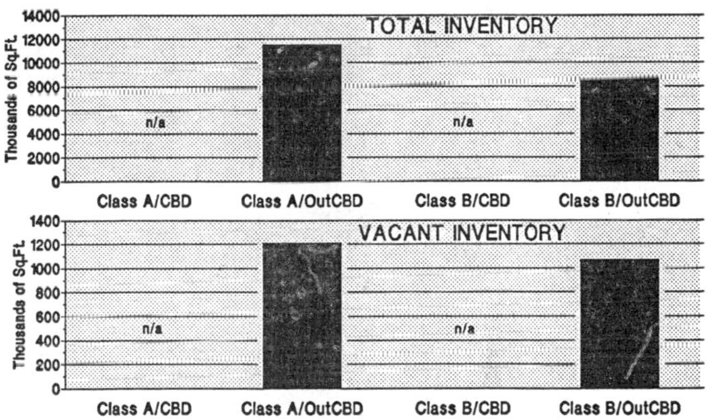

OFFICE RENTAL RATES
(Price Range/Dollars Per Square Foot)

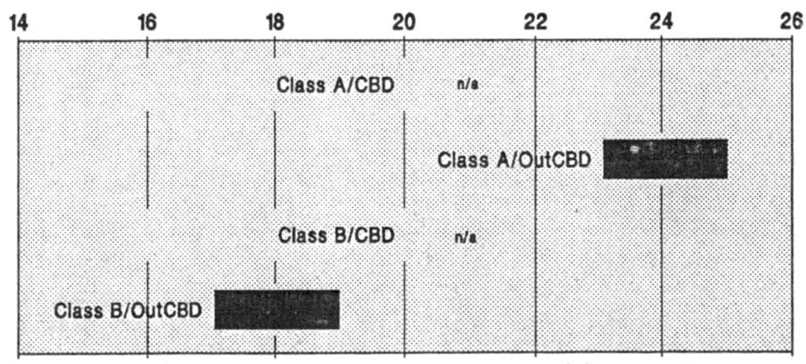

TYPICAL CONCESSIONS:
Parking
Rental Abatement
Additional Interior Improvements
Interior Plans and Drawings

RENTAL RATE DISCOUNT FACTOR: 0-10%

MARKET DATA

TOTAL INVENTORY

Class A/CBD: 3,700,000 sq.ft.
Class A/OutCBD: 20,100,000 sq.ft.
Class B/CBD: 1,200,000 sq.ft.
Class B/OutCBD: 5,800,000 sq.ft.

VACANT INVENTORY

Class A/CBD: 450,000 sq.ft.
Class A/OutCBD: 3,100,000 sq.ft.
Class B/CBD: 85,000 sq.ft.
Class B/OutCBD: 1,300,000 sq.ft.

VACANCY RATES

Class A/CBD: 12.2%
Class A/OutCBD: 15.4%
Class B/CBD: 7.0%
Class B/OutCBD: 22.4%

SUBLEASE INVENTORY

Class A: 120,000 sq.ft.
Class B: 45,000 sq.ft.

CURRENT CONSTRUCTION

Class A/CBD: 0 sq.ft.
Class A/OutCBD: 0 sq.ft.
Class B/CBD: 0 sq.ft.
Class B/OutCBD: 30,000 sq.ft.

NET ABSORPTION

Class A/CBD: 400,000 sq.ft.
Class A/OutCBD: 400,000 sq.ft.
Class B/CBD: 60,000 sq.ft.
Class B/OutCBD: 140,000 sq.ft.

STANDARD WORK LETTER

Typically based on dollars per square foot. Approximate dollar value: $14

TYPICAL PARKING RATIO

CBD: 1 per 700 sq.ft.
OutCBD: 1 per 285 sq.ft.

AVERAGE UTILITY RATES

CBD: $2.00 per sq.ft.
OutCBD: $2.25 per sq.ft.
Space for lease is typically not separately metered.

OPERATING COST ESCALATION

Base year

MAJOR DEVELOPERS

Robert Martin
Schulman Realty
Halpern Enterprises
London & Leeds

OUTLOOK

ABSORPTION: Down 6-10%
CONSTRUCTION: Same
VACANCIES: Up 6-10%
RENTAL RATES: Same
LANDLORD CONCESSIONS: Up 6-10%

NEW YORK–WHITE PLAINS AND WESTCHESTER COUNTY: OFFICE

Market Area: New York City Suburbs–White Plains and Westchester County

1987 REVIEW

The White Plains/Westchester market has approximately 31 million square feet of office space. Class A vacancy rates ranged from 12.2 percent inside the CBD to 15.4 percent in areas outside the CBD. During the year one million square feet was absorbed. Presently, only 30,000 square feet are under construction.

Rental rates range from $14 to $19 per square foot for Class B space and $23 to $28 per square foot for Class A space. Landlord concessions include rental abatement, lease assumptions, moving allowances, and additional interior improvements.

1988 FORECAST

SIOR panelists report that in 1988, the area's office market will depend on the strength of the New York City office market even more than in the past. Vacancies and landlord concessions will increase six to 10 percent. Absorption will decline six to 10 percent.

INVENTORY PROFILE

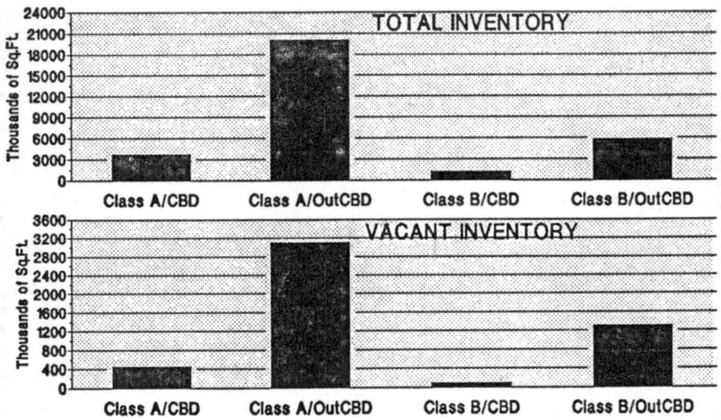

OFFICE RENTAL RATES
(Price Range/Dollars Per Square Foot)

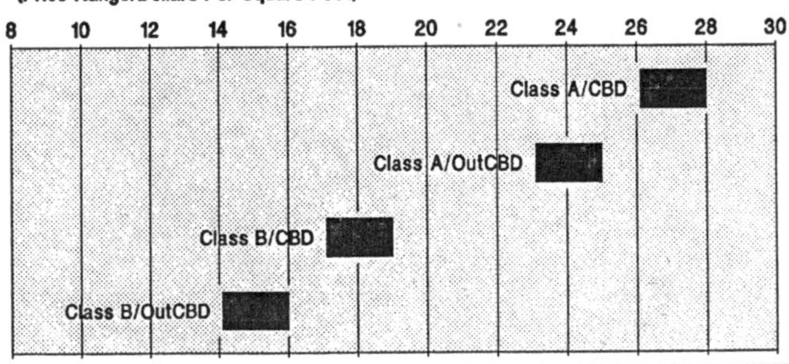

TYPICAL CONCESSIONS:

Rental Abatement
Lease Assumptions
Moving Allowance
Additional Interior Improvements

RENTAL RATE DISCOUNT FACTOR: 6-10%

Glossary of Terms

Demographics

Population. Figures are for 1985 and are based on information from Primary or Consolidated metropolitan statistical areas chosen to most closely match SIOR market areas.

Population Growth Rate. This is the average annual percent change in populations between 1980 and 1985. Figures are based on U.S. Bureau of Census Data.

Employment Growth Rate. This is the average annual percent change in employment between 1975 and 1985. Figures are based on data from the Data Resources Regional Information Service.

Unemployment Rate. Figures are for November 1987 and are based on data from the Bureau of Labor Statistics.

Per Capital Income. Figures are real (1982 dollars) income per capita for 1984 and are based on data from the Data Resources Regional Information Service.

Industrial Markets

Central City versus Suburbs. Since the definition of urban and suburban varies widely from city to city, it is the responsibility of the individual market survey panelist to reflect his or her area's particular characteristics.

Construction Costs. Construction costs should reflect only hard construction costs such as general contractor, overhead, and profit, but exclude architectural and engineering fees, financing fees, and mortgage/brokerage fees for both construction and permanent financing.

Lease Prices. A gross lease is one in which the tenant's rent includes real estate taxes, fire and extended coverage insurance, as well as maintenance of the roof structure and outside walls. A net lease is one in which the tenant assumes the operating expenses of the leased premises.

Improved Sites. These sites are in the top 25 percent of overall desirability of the existing inventory. Such sites are in a "ready-to-build" condition and are essentially level and graded and serviced with all necessary utilities. Rail service may or may not be available.

Unimproved Sites. These sites are also in the top 25 percent of overall desirability of the existing inventory and zoned for industrial use. Streets and utilities may not yet be installed, but are reasonably close and available. Rail service may or may not be available

Prime High-Technology Building. Generally, high-technology buildings are 30 percent or more office, fully air-conditioned, 12-18' clear, have extensive landscaping and parking, and are architecturally impressive. In some areas of the country where high-tech industries are not prevalent, this building could be used as a showroom or as pure office.

Prime Industrial Building. A prime industrial building is in the top 25 percent of overall desirability of the existing inventory. Such buildings are considered to be for general purpose uses such as industrial, research, warehouse and/or manufacturing. (Special purpose buildings are not to be considered in this category.)

Vacancy. Only completed buildings should be included in the available space inventory.

Office Markets

CBD. Central Business District space located near the historical urban core commonly associated with traditional government and financial districts in most cities.

OutCBD. Outside the CBD includes both suburban areas and "urban clusters" with areas of high office space concentrations which often rival nearby CBD's.

Class A. Excellent location, high quality tenants, high quality finish, well-maintained, professionally managed, and usually new, or old buildings that are competitive with new buildings.

Class B. Good location, professionally managed, fairly high quality construction and tenancy. Class B buildings generally show very little functional obsolescence and deterioration.

Current Construction. Total square footage presently under construction. Includes any space that will be available for occupancy before the end of 1988.

Net Absorption. Net absorption refers to the net change in occupied stock.

Standard Work Letter. Sometimes called a construction rider, this refers to the work that is to be done for the tenant by the landlord.

Typical Parking Ratio. The ratio refers to the availability of parking spaces per number of square feet leased by a tenant.

Average Utility Rates. Figures presented are dollars per square foot per year.

Operating Cost Escalation. Operating cost escalation refers to the procedure used to adjust rents over the term of a lease.

Rental Rate Discount Factor. The rental rate discount factor is the cumulative effect of landlord lease concessions on gross rental rates.

Source: *1988 GUIDE TO INDUSTRIAL AND OFFICE REAL ESTATE MARKETS.* Society of Industrial and Office REALTORS® & the Economics and Research Division of the National Association of Realtors®, 777 14th Street, NW, Suite 400, Washington, DC 20005-3271.

Glossary of Real Estate and REIT Terms

This glossary of terminology used in conjunction with discussions of real estate investment trusts has been prepared by the Research Department of the National Association of Real Estate Investment Trusts. Credit should be given to Realty Income Trust, a NAREIT member, which produced a glossary of terms upon which NAREIT drew heavily.

Acceleration clause A condition in a loan contract or mortgage note which permits the lender to demand immediate repayment of the entire balance if the contract is breached or conditions for repayment occur, such as sale or demolition.

Accrued interest or rent An amount of interest or rent which has been earned but which may not have been received in the same period as earned. On many short-term first mortgages, accrued interest is not received in cash until permanent financing is obtained.

Acquisition loan See C&D loan.

Advisor A REIT's investment advisor (usually pursuant to a renewable one-year contract) provides analysis of proposed investments, servicing of the portfolio, and other advisory services. Fee limits for advisory services are prescribed by many state securities regulators. Also spelled "adviser."

Amortization The process of retiring debt or recovering a capital investment through scheduled, systematic repayments of principal; that portion of fixed mortgage payment applied to reduction of the principal amount owed.

Anchor Tenant An important tenant, usually with an excellent credit rating (also known as a triple-A tenant), which takes a large amount of space in a shopping center or office building and is usually one of the first tenants to commit to lease. The anchor tenant usually is given lower rent because of the desirability of having that tenant at the property, both because of its credit rating and its ability to generate traffic.

Appraisal An opinion by an expert of the value of a property as of a specified date, supported by the presentation and analysis of relevant data. The appraisal may be arrived at by any or all of three methods: the cost approach (cost to reproduce), the market approach (comparison with other similar properties), or the income approach (capitalization of actual or projected income figures).

Assessed value The value of a property which is assigned to it by a taxing authority for purposes of assessing property taxes; often assessed value bears a fixed relationship by local statute to market value.

Asset swaps See swap program.

Assets Anything of value owned by the company. Assets are either financial, as cash or bonds; or physical, as real or personal property. For REIT tax purposes, more than 75% of the trust's assets must be property owned or securities backed by real estate.

Assumption of mortgage When the responsibility for repaying existing indebtedness secured by property is "assumed" by the second purchaser. In most jurisdictions, this relieves the first owner of the original obligations, at least to the extent that can be satisfied by sale of this asset after foreclosure.

Attribution More than 50% of a REIT's shares cannot be held by fewer than six people (otherwise it becomes a personal holding company for tax purposes). When someone has indirect control over someone else's shares (such as a trustee over shares held for the benefit of another) then "control" for personal holding company purposes may be "attributed." This complicated legal topic of "attribution" arises, however, only when the REIT's shares are held by a few.

Audit An examination of the financial status and operations of an enterprise, based mostly on the books of account, and undertaken to assure conformity to generally accepted accounting principles and to secure information for, or to check the accuracy of, the enterprise's balance sheet, income statement, and/or cash flow statement.

Balloon mortgage A mortgage loan which provides for periodic payments, which may include both interest and principal, but which leaves the loan less than fully ammortized at maturity, requiring a final large payment which is the "balloon." Usually the term does not apply to an "interest only" loan whose full principal is due upon maturity or upon call during its life.

Bankrupt When liabilities exceed assets, Federal laws enable the entity to dissolve in an orderly fashion (Chapter VII), or permit a court officer to restructure the company into a survivor "going business" (Chapter X), or permit existing management to do the same under court supervision (Chapter XI), or to do so despite the preferred position of secured creditors if real property is the only asset of the business (Chapter XII).

Beneficial owner The person who ultimately benefits from ownership of shares or other securities—in contrast to "nominees" (often pseudonyms for control of investment professionals so as to facilitate security transactions without having to track down beneficial owners to participate in each step of the procedures).

Source: National Association of Real Estate Trusts, 1101 Seventeenth Street, N.W., Washington, D.C. 20036.

Blue sky laws State laws regulating conditions of sale of securities of companies, (particularly those just starting out of the "clear blue sky") for the protection of the investing public. National stock exchange rules usually supercede state laws pursuant to a "blue chip" exemption contained in such state laws. The federal securities laws dovetail with state laws and pertain to publicly held companies, primarily as to accounting and disclosure practices.

Bond A debt certificate which (a) represents a loan to a trust, (b) bears interest, and (c) matures on a stated future date. Short term bonds (generally with a maturity of five years or less from the date of issuance) are often called notes. See debentures.

Book value per share Shareholder equity as adjusted to tangible net worth (assets minus liabilities plus paid-in capital) per share outstanding.

Borrower A person or entity who received something of value, ordinarily money, and is obligated to pay it back, as the debtor to the creditor, usually pursuant to a note or "IOU" containing terms and conditions.

Broker A person who is paid to act as an intermediary in connection with a transaction, in contrast to a dealer or principal who buys or sells for his own account. In the REIT world, the term "broker" usually refers to a real estate salesman, although the term is also used for "stockbrokers" too.

Building lien An encumbrance upon the property by the contractor or subcontractors. Also known as a "mechanic's" or "materialman's" lien.

Building permit Written permission by the local municipality (usually through the building inspector or other agent) allowing construction work on a piece of property in accordance with plans which were submitted and conforming to local building codes and regulations.

Business trust An unincorporated business in which assets are given to trustees for management to hold or to sell, as investments. The business trust form was first fully developed in Massachusetts, under common law, and the term "Massachusetts business trust" is sometimes used to describe entities formed in other states. It is a form of business through a trustee or trustees who hold legal title to the property of the business. Capital contributions are made to the trustees by the beneficiaries whose equitable title and interest in the property of the trust are evidenced by trust certificates, usually called shares of beneficial interest. The earnings of the trust are paid to them, as dividends are paid to stockholders. The beneficiaries generally enjoy limited liability, as the control and management of the trust rests solely with the trustees, but the trust form or organization can be distinguished from a corporation. Early REIT tax laws relied on this distinction to define eligible real estate operations.

Capital gain The amount by which the net proceeds from resale of a capital item exceed the adjusted cost (or "book value") of the asset. If a capital asset is held for more than twelve months before disposition it is taxed on a more favorable basis than a gain after a shorter period of time.

Capitalization rate The rate of return utilized to value a given cash flow, the sum of a Discount Rate and a Capital Recapture Rate. It is applied to any income stream with a finite term over which the invested principal is to be returned to the investor or lender.

Cash flow The revenue remaining after all cash expenses are paid, i.e., non-cash charges such as depreciation are not included in the calculation.

Cash flow per share. Cash flow divided by the common shares outstanding. Shareholders must make this computation themselves since the SEC has prohibited companies from stating this calculation.

Net cash flow. Generally determined by net income plus depreciation less principal payments on long-term mortgages.

Cash on cash return The "cash flow" from a property expressed as a percentage of the cash "equity" invested in a property.

Chapter X See bankrupt.

Collateral An item of value, such as real estate or securities, which a borrower pledges as security. A mortgage gives the creditor the right to seize the real estate collateral after non-performance of the debtor.

Commitment A promise to make an investment at some time in the future if certain specified conditions are met. A REIT may charge a fee to the borrower at the time of making the commitment. A REIT's level of commitments minus expected repayments can be regarded as an indication of future funding requirements.

"Take-out" commitment is one provided by the anticipated long-term lender, usually with complicated terms and conditions that must be met before the "take out" becomes effective.

"Gap" commitment is an anticipated short-term loan to cover part of the final "take-out" that the long-term lender refuses to advance until certain conditions are met (like 90% rent-up of an apartment after construction is completed). The amount above the "floor" or basic part of the loan is the "gap," and the gap commitment is issued to enable the construction lender to make a construction loan commitment for the full amount of the takeout loan instead of only for the "floor" amount.

"Standby" commitment is one that the lender and borrower doubt will be used. It exists as reassurance to a short-term construction lender that if, after completion of a building, the borrower cannot find adequate long-term "take-out" financing, the construction lender will be repaid.

Compensating balances Money which is sometimes required by banks to be held in checking accounts by borrowers, as part of their loan agreement.

Condominium A form of fee ownership of whole units or separate portions of multi-unit buildings which facilitates the formal filing, recording and financing of a divided interest in real property. The condominium concept may be used for apartments, offices and other professional uses. See cooperatives.

Conduit tax treatment So long as most (if not all) earnings are passed along by an entity, then federal taxation is avoided at the entity's level. REITs, mutual funds, and certain kinds of holding companies are elibible for "conduit tax treatment" under certain conditions.

Constant The agreed-upon periodic (usually monthly) payment to pay the face interest rate, with any residual amount going to amortize the loan.

Construction and development loan (C&D) A short-term loan for the purpose of constructing a building, shopping center, or other improvement upon real estate, or developing a site in preparation for construction. A C&D loan is normally disbursed in increments (called *draws* or *draw-downs*) as building proceeds, rather than in a single disbursement, and is conditioned upon compliance with a variety of factors. It is usually repaid with the proceeds of the permanent loan. A land loan or purchase and development loan is sometimes made for the purpose of acquiring unimproved vacant land, usually as a future building site and for financing improvements to such land (street, sewers, etc.) as a prerequisite to construction of a building upon the site.

Contingent Interest Interest on a loan that is payable only if certain conditions occur, in contrast to interest that becomes an accrued liability (whether or not paid) at a specific time.

Cooperative A form of ownership whereby a structure is owned by a corporation or trust with each individual owner holding stock in the corporation representative of the value of his apartment. Title to the apartment is evidenced by a proprietary lease which often does not qualify as adequate collateral for some lenders.

Cost-to-carry The concept specified by the accounting profession to be used by REITs in computing anticipated interest cost on debt needed to "carry" non-earning or partially-earning assets until they're restored to earning status or sold.

Current Liabilities Money owed and due to be paid within one year.

Dealer Someone who buys property with the purpose of selling it at a profit rather than holding it as an investment. A dealer's profits are taxed at the ordinary income rate rather than the capital gains rate regardless of how long the property is held for resale (in contrast to the investor who sells a property after a year and pays at the capital gains rate). A REIT is not permitted to be a dealer unless it is willing to pay a 100% tax on gains from such sales in the year in which it is deemed to be a dealer; sales of foreclosed property do not fall within this definition. See principal.

Debenture An obligation which is secured only by the general credit of the issuing trust, as opposed to being secured by a direct lien on its assets, real estate or otherwise. A debenture is a form of a bond.

Declaration of Trust Similar to articles of incorporation for a corporation, this document contains rules for operation of the trust, selection of its governing trustees, etc., and is the keystone of a REIT.

Deed A legal instrument which conveys title from one to another. It must be (a) made between competent parties (b) have legally sound subject matter (c) correctly state what is being conveyed (d) contain good and valuable consideration (e) be properly executed by the parties involved and (f) be delivered to be valid.

Deed in lieu of foreclosure The device by which title to property is conveyed from the mortgagor (borrower) to the mortgagee (lender) as an alternative to foreclosure. While this procedure can transfer effective control more quickly, many lenders eschew it because undiscovered prior liens (from a workman who was never paid but hadn't gotten around to filing his valid, but late, claim for example) remain enforceable in contrast to the more formal foreclosure procedures which wipe out prior claims after due notice.

Deferred maintenance the amount of repairs that should have been made to keep a property in good running condition, but which have been put off. The term contemplates the desirability of immediate expenditures, although it does not necessarily denote inadequate maintenance in the past.

Deficiency dividend The process of paying an "extra" dividend after the close of the fiscal year so as to comply with REIT tax requirements to pay out more than 90% of income. See dividend.

Depreciation The loss in value of a capital asset, due to wear and tear which cannot be compensated for by ordinary repairs, or an allowance made to allow for the fact that the asset may become obsolete before it wears out. The purpose of a depreciation charge is to write off the original cost of an asset by equitably distributing charges against its operation over its useful life, matching "cost" to the period in which it was used to generate earnings. Depreciation is an optional noncash expense recognizable for tax purposes. If the REIT pays out more than its taxable earnings, then it is distributing a "return of capital" or—as is commonly stated in the industry—"paying out depreciation."

Development loans See Construction and development loan.

Dilution The situation which results when an increase occurs in a company's outstanding securities without a corresponding increase in the company's assets and/or income.

Discount rate An interest rate used to convert a future stream of payments into a single present value. See capitalization rate.

Dividend or distribution The distribution of cash or stock to shareholders of a company which is made periodically as a means of distributing all or a portion of net income or cash flow. Technically, a dividend can be paid only from net taxable income, so many REITs distribute cash and later characterize their distributions as capital gains or a tax-free return of capital if net taxable income is less than the cash paid out.

Dividend or distribution yield The annual dividend or distribution rate for a security expressed as a percent of its market price. For most REITs, the "annualized" rate is the previous quarter's distribution times four, regardless of how the distribution is characterized.

Draw A request from a borrower to obtain partial payment from the lender pursuant to a loan commitment. The lender reassures himself that the borrower has completed the required steps (such as putting in the concrete properly) before advancing money. Often, the borrower submits bills from subcontractors, which are then "paid" by the lender after inspecting the subcontractor's work. In such cases, the check is usually made out to the subcontractor but must be signed by the borrower, too, so that the lender ends up only with one borrower. See construction and development loan.

Effective Borrowing Costs The cost of borrowing after adjustment for compensating balances or fees in lieu of compensating balances, and selling expenses in the case of publicly sold debt.

Encumbrance A legal right or interest in real estate which diminishes its value. Encumbrances can take a number of forms, such as easements, zoning restrictions, mortgages, etc.

Entrepreneur An individual who is responsible for a commercial or real estate activity who takes a certain risk of loss in a transaction for the right to enjoy any profit which may result.

Equity The interest of the shareholders in a company as measured by their paid-in capital and undistributed income. The term is also used to describe (i) the difference between the current market value of a property and the liens or mortgages which encumber it or (ii) the cash which makes up the difference between the mortgage(s) and the construction or sale price.

Equity leveraging The process by which shares are sold at a premium above book value (in anticipation of greater earnings).

Equity participation Usually, the right of an investor to participate to some extent in the increased value of a project by receiving a percentage of the increased income from the project. If a REIT were to participate in a percentage of the net income of a venture (such as the shopping center's owner/lessor), then it could be deemed to be a partner in an active business. Thus, most REIT leases spell out the "equity participation" as a percentage of gross receipts or sales (which is a more stable measure of sales activity, anyway, and one readily identifiable from the lessor's federal income tax statement).

Escrow A deposit of "good faith" money which is entrusted to a third party (often a bank) until fulfillment of certain conditions and agreements, when the escrow may be released or applied as payment for the purchase of property or for services rendered.

Estoppel certificate An instrument used when a mortgage or lease is assigned to another. The certificate sets forth the exact remaining balance of the lease or mortgage as of a certain date and verifies any promises to tenants that may have been made by the first owner for which the second owner may be held accountable.

Exculpatory clause A clause which relieves one of liability for injuries or damages to another. Exculpatory clauses are placed in REIT documents with the intention of eliminating personal liability of its trustees, shareholders and officers.

Expenses The costs which are charges against current operations or earnings of a building, company or other reporting entity. They may have been "paid out" in cash, or accrued to be paid later, or charged as a bookkeeping procedure to reflect the "using up" of assets (as in depreciation) utilized in the production of income during the period of current operations.

Face value The value which is shown on the face of an instrument such as a bond, debenture or stock certificate. The "face rate" of a debt instrument is often known as its "coupon rate."

Fair market value See Market value.

Fee or fee simple Title to a property which is absolute, good and marketable; ownership without condition.

Fiduciary A relationship of trust and confidence between a person charged with the duty of acting for the benefit of another and the person to whom such duty is owed, as in the case of guardian and ward, trustee and beneficiary, executor and heir.

First mortgage That mortgage which has a prior claim over all other liens against real estate. In some jurisdictions, real estate taxes, mechanics liens, court costs, and other involuntary liens may take priority over such a contractual lien: title companies "clear" properties so as to reassure first mortgage lenders (and owners) of their uncontested position and to guarantee them of that position under certain conditions.

Fiscal year The 12-month period selected as a basis for computing and accounting for a business. A fiscal year need not coincide with the calendar year, except for all REITs initially qualifying for special tax treatment after 1976.

Fixed assets Assets, such as land, buildings and machinery, which cannot be quickly converted into cash. For REITs, most "fixed assets" are real property although some (like furniture in an apartment lobby) may be personal property.

Fixed charges Those interest charges, insurance costs, taxes and other expenses which remain relatively constant regardless of revenue. See net lease.

Floating rate A variable interest rate charged for the use of borrowed money. It is determined by charging a specific percentage above a fluctuating base rate, usually the prime rate as announced by a major commercial bank.

Floor loan A portion or portions of a mortgage loan commitment which is less than the full amount of the commitment and which may be funded upon conditions less stringent than those required for funding the full amount, or the "ceiling" of the loan. For example, the floor loan, equal to perhaps 80% of the full amount of the loan, may be funded upon completion of construction without any occupancy requirements, but substantial occupancy of the building may be required for funding the full amount of the loan, which is referred to as the "ceiling." See commitment, gap.

Foreclosure The legal process of enforcing payment of a debt by taking the properties which secure the debt, once the terms of the obligation are not followed. Upon foreclosure, the entire debt might not be fully discharged by transfer and disposition of the property (as determined by the courts). If so, a "deficiency judgment" may be obtained, at which point the lender is like any other creditor in attempting to get the debtor to pay the deficiency. Collection of the deficiency judgment in major real estate transactions is rare, but it becomes a major factor in negotiations if the borrower decides to return to the real estate business in the future.

Fully diluted earnings The hypothetical earnings per share of a company, computed after giving effect to the number of shares which would be outstanding if all convertible debt and warrants were exercised, and also to any reduction in interest payments resulting from such exercise.

Gap commitment See commitment, gap. Also see floor loan.

General lien A lien against the property of an individual or other entity generally, rather than against specific items of realty or personal property.

Ground lease See sale-leaseback.

Holding company A corporation that owns or controls the operations of various other companies. Many REITs were sponsored by bank or insurance holding companies whose subsidiary companies advise and manage REITs, pursuant to contracts with the REIT's trustees.

Independent contractor A firm hired to actively manage property investments. A tax-qualified REIT must hire an independent contractor to manage and operate its property, so as to distinguish itself as an investor rather than an active manager.

Income property Developed real estate, such as office buildings, shopping centers, apartments, hotels and motels, warehouses and some kinds of agricultural or industrial property, which produce a flow of income—in contrast to non-income generating real estate like raw land which would be bought and held for a speculative profit upon resale or development.

Indenture The legal document prepared in connection with, for example, a bond issue, setting forth the terms of the issue, its specific security, remedies in case of default, etc. It may also be called the "deed of trust."

Indentured trustee A trustee, generally the trust department of a major bank, which represents the interest of bondholders under a publicly offered issue.

Insider A person close to a trust who has intimate knowledge of financial developments before they become public knowledge.

Interest rate The percentage rate which an individual pays for the use of borrowed money for a given period of time.

Intermediate-term loan A loan for a term of three to ten years which is usually not fully amortized at maturity. Often, developers will seek interim loans by which to pay off construction financing, in anticipation of obtaining long-term financing at a later date on more favorable terms, either because long-term rates decline generally or because the project can show an established, stable earnings history.

Interim loan A type of loan which is to be repaid out of the proceeds of another loan. Ordinarily, not self-liquidating (amortized), the lender evaluates the risk of obtaining refinancing as much as the period risk. See C&D loans.

Investment advisor See advisor.

Joint venture The entity which is created when two or more persons or corporate entities join together to carry out a specific business transaction of real estate development. A joint venture is usually of limited duration and usually for a specific property; it can be treated as a partnership for tax purposes. The parties have reciprocal and paralleling rights and obligations.

Junior mortgage loan Any mortgage loan in which the lien and the right of repayment is subordinate to that of another mortgage loan or loans. A "second mortgage" is a junior mortgage. "Third, fourth," etc. mortgages are always deemed to be secondary.

Land loan See Construction and development loan.

Land-purchase leaseback See sale-leaseback.

Late charge The charge which is levied against a borrower for a payment which was not made in a timely manner.

Lease A contract between the owner of property (lessor) and a tenant (lessee) setting forth the terms, conditions and consideration for the use of the property for a specified period of time at a specified rental. See sale-leaseback and net lease.

Leasehold improvements The cost of improvements or betterments to property leased for a period of years, often paid for by the tenant. Such improvements ordinarily become the property of the lessor (owner) on expiration of the lease; consequently their cost is normally amortized over the life of the lease if the lessor pays for them.

Leverage The process of borrowing upon one's capital base with the expectation of generating a profit above the cost of borrowing.

Liability management The aspect of the management of a company concerned with the planning and procurement of funds for investment through the sale of equity, public debt and bank borrowings. In the REIT industry, the phrase contrasts to "asset management" or the real estate side of the business.

Line of credit Usually, an agreement between a commercial bank and a borrower under which the bank agrees to provide unsecured credit to the borrower upon certain terms and conditions. Normally, the borrower may draw on all or any part of the credit from time to time.

Limited partnership A partnership which limits certain of the partners' (the limited partners) liability to the amount of their investment. At least one partner (the "general partner") is fully liable for the obligations of the partnership and its operations, usually with the limited partners participating as investors only.

Loan loss reserve A reserve set up to offset asset values in anticipation of losses that are reasonably expected. Initially, REITs had insufficient operating experience to anticipate losses in any one class of investments or for a portfolio as a whole, so tax authorities would not permit substantial contributions toward a reserve as an allowable period expense. When difficulties arose, the conversion of short-term loans to longer-term property holdings required some form of recognition of likely losses in the financial statements. A novel procedure for REITs was devised by requiring, for book purposes, computation of additions to the reserve based in part on the probable cost of sustaining the troubled assets over the longer period of time necessary to "cure" the problem. Also known as "allowance for losses."

Loan run-off The rate at which an existing mortgage portfolio will reduce (or "run-off") to zero if no new loans are added to the portfolio.

Loan swaps See asset swaps.

Long-term mortgage Any financing, whether in the form of a first or junior mortgage, the term of which is ten years or more. It is generally fully amortized.

Loss carry forwards The net operating loss (NOL) incurred in prior years, which may be applied for tax purposes against future earnings, thereby reducing taxable income. For REITs (which must pay out most of their taxable income), NOLs can be carried forward eight years; for non-REIT-taxed companies, NOL can be carried forward for only seven years.

Market value The highest price in terms of money which a property will bring in a competitive and open market under all conditions requisite to a fair sale—the buyer and the seller each acting prudently, knowledgeably, and at arm's length. See appraisal.

Moratorium A period in which payments of debts or other performance of a legal obligation is suspended temporarily, usually because of unforeseen circumstances which make timely payment or performance difficult or impossible. This forebearance can be whole or partial.

Mortgage A publicly recorded lien by which the property is pledged as security for the payment of a debt valid even beyond death ("mort" is death in French). In some states a mortgage is an actual conveyance of the property to the creditor until the terms of the mortgage are satisfied. While there is always a "note" secured by a mortgage document, both the note and mortgage instrument are commonly called "the mortgage." For types, see: first, junior, short-term, long-term, wrap-around and construction and development mortgage definitions.

Mortgage banker A non-depository lender who makes loans secured by real estate and then usually packages and sells those loans in large groups to institutional investors, pursuant to a "long-term commitment" he has negotiated with the life insurance company or other institutional investor. Mortgage bankers frequently arrange to service these mortgages for the out-of-town institutions, collecting regular payments, keeping the lender up to date on the progress of the loan, escrowing payments for taxes and insurance premiums, and, if necessary, administering foreclosure proceedings. Many REITs were sponsored by mortgage bankers.

Mortgage constant The total annual payments of principal and interest (annual debt service) on a mortgage with level-payment amortization schedule, expressed as a percentage of the initial principal amount of the loan.

Mortgagee in possession A lender or one who holds a mortgage who has taken possession of a property in order to protect an interest in the property. Usually, this is done with commercial properties as to which rents, management fees and other disbursements continue even if the mortgage is in default. The possession must be taken with the consent of the mortgagor (or a court, in cases of foreclosure) and the mortgagee must be careful to do only those things to the property that the mortgagor (or court) will agree to accept, should it resume its role as a credit-worthy owner.

Net Income The dollar amount that remains after all expenses, including taxes, are deducted from gross income. For regular companies, it is also called after-tax profit, the "bottom line" figure of how a company has performed with its investors' money. For REITs, it is net taxable income which, if fully distributed, is not taxed.

Net lease A lease, sometimes called a net-net (insurance and taxes) or even a net-net-net lease (insurance, taxes, and maintenance) in which the tenant pays all costs, including insurance, taxes, repairs, upkeep and other expenses, and the rental payments are "net" of all these expenses. See lease and fixed charges.

Net worth The remaining asset value of a property company or other entity after deduction of all liabilities against it.

Non-accrual loans See non-earning investments.

Non-earning investments The category of loans or investments which are not earning the originally anticipated rate of return. Some may be characterized as "partially earning." When interest is recorded as earned rather than as received (accrued interest), "non-accrual investments" are those which management expects not to receive interest as originally contemplated. In the vernacular, nonearning investments are "problem loans" or "troubled properties."

Non-qualified REIT A REIT that was formerly qualified, or conducts its affairs as if it is qualified, but that has elected for the tax year in question to be treated like a normal business corporation for tax purposes. Thus, some restraints (primarily against active management and holding property for sale) are lifted, while REIT conduit tax treatment is lost.

Occupancy rate The amount of space or number of apartments or offices or hotel rooms which are rented as compared with the total amount or number available. The rate is usually expressed as a percentage.

Operating expenses Expenses arising out of or relating to business activity such as interest expense, professional fees, salaries, etc.

Operating income Income received directly from business activity in the normal course, as contrasted with capital gains income, or other extraordinary income.

Option A right to buy or lease property at a certain specified price for specified terms. Consideration is typically given for the option, which is exercisable over a limited time span. If the option is not exercised, the consideration is forfeited. A loan to a developer secured by his option to obtain real estate is considered a "qualified" REIT asset.

Origination The process by which a loan is created, including the search for (or receipt of) the initial plans, the analysis and structuring of the proposed financing, and the review and acceptance procedures by which the commitment to make the investment is finally issued.

Overage income Rental income above a guaranteed minimum depending on a particular level of profit or retail sales volume by the tenant, payable under the terms of a lease.

Participations A lender often "participates out" or sells a portion of his loan to another lender while retaining a portion and managing the investment. REITs buy real estate secured participations as well as originating them.

Par Value The face value assigned to a security when it is issued. The stated par value of a security generally has nothing to do with its market or book value.

Passivity The state of owning investments but not actively managing them (as a property management firm does for the investor) or engaging in trading the securities (like a broker or dealer). This "passivity" test is implicit behind several of the REIT tax requirements.

Pension funds Money which is accumulated in trust to fund pensions for companies or unions and which is frequently invested in part in real estate. A co-mingled real estate pension fund account is managed, usually under contract to a financial institution, much like a REIT except that its shares are not publicly traded but instead sold to other pension funds.

Permanent financing See long-term loan.

Point An amount which represents 1% of the maximum principal amount of an investment. Used in connection with a discount from, or a share of, a principal amount deducted at the time funds are advanced, it represents additional compensation to the lender.

Portfolio The investments of a company, including investments in mortgages and/or ownership of real property. REIT portfolios usually consist of equity in property, short-term mortgages, long-term mortgages and/or subordinated land sale-lease-backs.

Portfolio turnover The average length of time from the funding of investments until they are paid off or sold.

Preferred shares Stocks which have prior claim on distributions (and/or assets in the event of dissolution) up to a certain definite amount before the shares of beneficial interest are entitled to anything. As a form of ownership, preferred shares stand behind senior subordinated and secured debtholders in dissolution, as well as other creditors.

Prepayment penalty The penalty which is imposed on the borrower for payment of the mortgage before it is due. Often a mortgage contains a clause specifying that there is to be no prepayment penalty, or limits the prepayment penalty to only the first few years of the mortgage term.

Price earning ratio A ratio which consists of the market price divided by current annualized earnings per share. Such a computation is now found in most daily stock listings. For REITs, annualization of quarterly earnings is computed by multiplying the most recent distribution by four, regardless of the distribution's later characterization as a dividend, return-of-capital, or capital gains.

Prime lending rate The rate at which commercial banks will lend money from time to time to their most credit-worthy customers, used as a base for most loans to financial intermediaries such as REITs.

Principal The buyer or seller in a real estate transaction as distinguished from an agent.

Principal The sum of money loaned. The amount of money to be repaid on a loan excluding interest charges.

Prior lien A lien or mortgage ranking ahead of some other lien. A prior lien need not itself be a first mortgage.

Pro forma Projected or hypothetical as opposed to actual as related, for example, to a balance sheet or income statement.

Problem investments See nonearning investments.

Prospectus A document describing an investment opportunity; the detailed description of new securities which must be supplied to prospective interstate purchasers under the Securities Act of 1933.

Provision for loan losses Periodic allocation of funds to loan loss reserves in recognition of a decline in the value of a loan or loans in a trust's portfolio due to a default on the part of the borrowers.

Proxy An authorization given by a registered security holder to vote stock at the annual meeting or at a special meeting of security holders.

Purchase and leaseback See sale-leaseback.

Pyramiding In stock market transactions, this term refers to the practice of borrowing against unrealized "paper" profits in securities to make additional purchases. In corporate finance, it refers to the practice of creating a speculative capital structure by a series of holding companies, whereby a relatively small amount of voting stock in the parent company controls a large corporate system. In real estate, it refers to the practice of financing 100% or more of the value of the property.

Qualified assets Assets which meet tax requirements for special REIT tax treatment, i.e. real property. In any tax year, 75% of a REIT's assets must be invested in real property, either through ownership or by securities secured by real estate. A "partially qualified" asset is one that qualifies under the 90% test of being a passive investment in a security, but not under the 75% real estate test.

Qualified income That portion of income which is classified as interest, rents, or other gain from real property, as spelled out in the REIT tax laws.

Raw land Land which has not been developed or improved.

RCA See revolving credit agreement.

Real estate investment trust (REIT, pronounced "reet") A trust established for the benefit of a group of investors which is managed by one or more trustees who hold title to the assets for the trust and control its acquisitions and investments, at least 75% of which are real estate related. A major advantage of a REIT is that no federal income tax need be paid by the trust if certain qualifications are met. Congress enacted these special tax provisions to encourage an assembly method, which is essentially designed to provide for investment in real estate what the mutual provided for investment in securities. The REIT provides the small investor with a means of combining his funds with those of others, and protects him from the double taxation that would be levied against an ordinary corporation or trust.

Revolving credit agreement (or "revolver") A formal credit agreement between a group of banks and a REIT, the terms of which are reviewed periodically when it is "rolled over" or "revolved" or refinanced by a similar agreement. For many trusts, "revolvers" have replaced informal lines of credit extended by individual banks to REITs, thereby providing a uniform (and usually restrictive) approach by all creditors, reassuring each bank that others in the RCA would not be paid off preferentially.

Registration statement The forms filed by a company with the Securities and Exchange Commission in connection with an offering of new securities or the listing of outstanding securities on a national exchange.

Reserves for loss See loan loss reserve.

Return of capital A distribution to shareholders in excess of the trust's earnings and profits, usually consisting of either depreciation or repayment of principal from properties or mortgages held by the trust. Each shareholder receiving such a distribution is required to reduce the tax basis of his shares by the amount of such distribution. For financial accounting purposes, what constitutes a return of capital may differ from that determined under Federal income tax requirements.

Return on equity A figure which consists of net income for the period divided by equity and which is normally expressed as a percentage.

Right of first refusal The right or option granted by a seller to a buyer, to have the first opportunity of acquiring a property.

Rights offering The privilege extended to a shareholder of subscribing to additional stock of the same or another class or to bonds, usually at a price below the market and in an amount proportional to the number of shares already held. Rights must be exercised within a time limit and often may be sold if the holder does not wish to purchase additional shares.

Sale-leaseback A common real estate transaction whereby the investor buys property from and simultaneously leases it back to, the seller. This enables the previous owner (often a developer) to "cash out" on an older property while retaining control.

Land sale-leaseback—this procedure, made common by several REITs that specialize in the transaction, affects only the land under income—producing improvements (such as shopping centers, etc.)—leaving the depreciable improvements in the hands of those who might benefit from the tax consequences. Since the improvements were probably financed with the proceeds of a first mortgage which remains in effect, the rights of the new investor are made second, or junior, to those of the first mortgage holder. Hence the common phrase "subordinated land sale-leaseback." In return for accepting a less secure position, the new investor usually obtains an "overage" clause whereby additional rent is paid anytime gross income of the shopping center (or whatever) exceeds a pre-determined floor.

Seasoned issues Securities of large, established companies which have been known to the investment public for a period of years, covering good times and bad.

Second mortgages See junior mortgage loan.

Secured debt For REITs, senior mortgage debt secured by specific properties. In case of default on "nonrecourse" debt, the lender may assume property ownership but may not pursue other assets of the lender.

Senior mortgage A mortgage which has first priority.

Senior unsecured debt Funds borrowed under open lines without security. Most bank lines to REITs were unsecured.

Shares of beneficial interest Tradable shares in a REIT. Analogous to common stock in a corporation.

Shareholders' equity Primarily money invested by shareholders through purchase of shares, plus the accumulation of that portion of net income that has been reinvested in the business since the commencement of operations.

Short-term mortgage A loan upon real estate for a term of three years or less, bearing interest payable periodically, with principal usually payable in full at maturity.

Sinking fund An arrangement under which a portion of a bond or preferred stock issue is retired periodically, in advance of its fixed maturity. The company may either purchase a stipulated quantity of the issue itself, or supply funds to a trustee or agent for that purpose. Retirement may be made by call at a fixed price, or by inviting tenders, or by purchase in the open market.

Sponsor The entity which initiated the formation of a REIT and usually acts (often via a subsidiary) as investment advisor to the trust thereafter. The sponsor puts the reputation of its institution on the line for the REIT and usually arranges lines of credit, provides support services and, occasionally, compensating balances.

Spread Difference between percentage return on an investment and cost of funds to support the investment.

Standby commitment See commitment, standby.

Standing loan Usually not amortized, the loan is secured by completed property that has not yet been refinanced with a "permanent" long-term mortgage.

Subordinated debt Debt which is junior to secured and unsecured senior debt, it may be convertible into shares of beneficial interest for

REITs. Senior subordinated debt is senior to other subordinated debt.

Subordinated ground lease See sale-leaseback.

Swap Program A procedure for reducing debt (by a troubled REIT) by trading an asset to the creditor in return for cancellation of part of a loan to the REIT. Often a cash premium payment is made in addition to reduction of the debt. The premium may then be distributed to the other creditors pro rata. The amount of the cash premium, or the ratio of cash-to-debt reduction to be applied against the value of the asset, is sometimes determined by a sealed-bid "auction" process as set forth in the "revolving credit agreement" between the creditors and the REIT. See RCA.

Syndicate A group of investors who transact business for a limited period of time and sometimes with a single purpose. It is a short-term partnership.

Take-out commitment See commitment.

Tax shelter The various aspects of an investment which offer relief from income taxes or opportunities to claim deductions from taxable income. Although tax shelters are an important facet of real estate investment, they do not have a direct influence on REIT investment choices because qualified trusts are exempt from income taxes.

Usury The charging of interest rates for the use of money higher than what's allowed by local law.

Warrants Stock purchase warrants or options give the holder rights to purchase shares of stock, generally running for a longer period of time than ordinary subscription rights given shareholders. Warrants are often attached to other securities, but they may be issued separately or detached after issuance.

Working capital Determined by subtracting current liabilities from current assets. It represents the amount available to carry on the day-to-day operation of the business.

Work-out When a borrower has problems, the process undertaken by the lender to help the borrower "work out" of the problems becomes known itself as a "work out." The presumption during a "work out" is that the borrower will eventually resume a more normal debtor's position once problems are solved within (presumably) a reasonably short time.

Wrap-around mortgage A type of junior mortgage used to refinance properties on which there is an existing first mortgage loan. The face amount of the wrap-around loan is equivalent to the unpaid balance on the existing mortgage plus cash advanced to the property owner upon funding. Such loans carry a higher interest rate than the existing mortgage. The wrap-around lender assumes the obligation to maintain payments of principal and interest on the existing mortgage so as to enhance his right to make claim from his secondary position.

Yield In the stock market, the rate of annual distribution or dividend expressed as a percentage of price. Current yield is found by dividing the market price into the distribution rate in dollars. In real estate, the term refers to the effective annual amount of income which is being accrued on an investment expressed as a percentage of its value.

Selected On-Line Business/Financial Data Bases

On-line data bases are collections of computer stored data which are retrievable by remote terminals. The data bases are collected and organized by a so-called *producer*. The latter provides the data base to a *vendor* who distributes the data by means of a telecommunication network to the user. Often a vendor will offer a large number of different data bases. In some instances the producer and vendor are the same.

Using an on-line data base requires: (1) a *terminal* (a typewriter-like device usually equipped with a video display) to receive data and send commands to the vendor's computers, and (2) a *modem* for coupling the terminal to a telephone line. Printouts (hard copy) of the desired information can be obtained with the aid of electronic printers located at the user's terminal or, alternatively, ordered from the vendor.

The user accesses the data base by dialing a telephone number and then typing (on the terminal keyboard) a password provided by the vendor. Searching the data base is done with special commands and procedures peculiar to each base.

The contents of data bases vary. Some provide statistical data only—usually in the form of time series. Other bases provide bibliographic references and, in some instances, abstracts or the full text of articles.

Specifics concerning data base contents, instructions, and prices are available from vendors. Listed below are some major business data bases and vendors. More complete information concerning data bases is available from the sources given below.

ABI Inform
Provides references on all areas of business management with emphasis on "how-to" information.
Producer: Data Courier Inc. (Louisville, KY)
Vendors: BRS, DIALOG, SDC

Accountants Index
Contains reference information on accounting, auditing taxation, management and securities.
Producer: American Institute of Certified Public Accountants (New York, NY)
Vendors: SDC

American Profile
Provides statistical information on U.S. households including population, income, dependents, and also data on types of businesses in an area.
Producer: Donnelley Marketing (Stamford, CT)
Vendors: Business Information Service

Business Credit Service
Provides business credit and financial information.
Producer: TRW, Inc. (Orange, CA)
Vendors: TRW

Canadian Business and Current Affairs
English language business and popular periodicals
Producer: Micromedia Limited (Toronto, Ontario)
Vendor: DIALOG, CISTI

CIS Index
Contains references and abstracts from nearly every publication resulting from Senate and House Committee meetings since 1970.
Producer: Congressional Information Services, Inc. (Washington, DC)
Vendors: Dialog, SDC

Commodities
Contains over 41,000 times series of current commodity prices for the U.S., Canada, U.K., and France.
Producer: Wolff Research (London, U.K.)
Vendor: I. P. Sharp

Compendex (Computerized Engineering Index)
Contains over 1 million citations and abstracts to the world wide engineering literature.
Producer: Engineering Information Inc. (New York)
Vendor: BRS, D-STAR, DIALOG.

CompuServe, Inc.
Provides reference, statistical and full text retrieval of information of personal interest including health, recipes, gardening, financial and investment data in-

cluding the Compustat and Value Line data bases.

Producer: CompuServe, Inc. (Columbus, OH)

Vendor: CompuServe

Compustat

Provides very extensive financial data on companies.

Producer: Standard And Poor's Compustat Service, Inc. (Englewood, CO)

Vendors: ADP, Business Information Services, CompuServe, Data Resources, Chase Econometrics/Interactive Data Corp.

Disclosure II

Provides extracts of 10K and other reports filed with the Securities and Exchange Commission.

Producer: Disclosure Inc. (Bethesda, Maryland)

Vendors: Business Information Services (Control Data). Dialog, Dow Jones, New York Times Information Services, Mead Data Central.

Dow Jones News/Retrieval Service and Stock Quote Reporters

Contains text of articles appearing in major financial publications including the *Wall Street Journal* and *Barrons*. Quote Service provides quotes on stocks, bonds, mutual funds.

Producer: Dow Jones & Company (New York, NY)

Vendors: BRS, Dow Jones & Company

DRI Capsule/EEI Capsule

Provides over 3700 U.S. social and economic statistical time series such as population, income, money supply data, etc.

Producers: Data Resources, Inc. (Lexington, MA) and Evans Economics Inc. (Washington, DC)

Vendors: Business Information Services, United Telecom Group, I. P. Sharp

Federal Register Abstracts

Provides coverage of federal regulatory agencies as published in the Federal Register.

Producer: Capitol Services (Washington, DC)

Vendors: DIALOG, SDC

GTE Financial System One Quotation Service

Provides current U.S. and Canadian quotations and statistical data on stocks, bonds, options, commodities and other market data.

Producer: GTE Information Systems (Reston, VA)

Vendor: GTE Information Systems, Inc.

The Information Bank

Provides an extensive current affairs data source consisting of abstracts from numerous English language publications.

Producer: The New York Times Information Service

Vendor: The New York Times Information Service

LEXIS

Contains full text references to a wide range of legal information including court decisions, regulations, government statutes.

Producer: Mead Data Central (New York, NY)

Vendor: Mead Data Central

NEXIS

Provides full text business and general news including management, technology, finance, science, politics, religion.

Producer: Mead Data Central (New York, NY)

Vendor: Mead Data Central

PTS Marketing and Advertising Reference Service

Provides citations with abstracts & articles on the marketing and advertising of consumer goods and services.

Producer: Predicast, Inc. (Cleveland, OH)

Vendors: DIALOG, BRS, DATA-STAR

PTS Prompt

Covers world wide business news on new products, market data, etc.

Producer: Predicast, Inc. (Cleveland, OH)

Vendors: ADP, BRS, DIALOG

Quick Quote

Provides current quotations, volume, high-low data for securities of U.S. public corporations.

Producer: CompuServe Inc.

Vendor: CompuServe

Quotron 800

Provides up to the minute quotation and statistics on a broad range of securities such as stocks, bonds, options, commodities.

Producer: Quotron Systems Inc. (Los Angeles, CA)

Vendor: Quotron Systems Inc.

The Source

Covers a broad variety of consumer services business and financial information including travel information, reservations, restaurant reviews etc.

Producer: Source Telecomputing (McLean, VA)

Vendor: Source Telecomputing Corp.

Trinet Company Data Base

Provides data on about 250,000 companies in the U.S.

Producer: Trinet, Inc. (Parsippany, NJ)

Vendors: DRI, DIALOG, Mead Data Central

Value Line II

Provides extensive financial data from the Value Line Investment Survey covering over 1600 major companies.

Producer: Arnold Bernhard & Co. (New York, NY)

Vendors: ADP Service, Chase Econometrics/Interactive Data Corp., CompuServe Data Resources, Inc.

For further information:

A. T. Kruzas and J. Schmittroth, *Encyclopedia of Information Systems*, Gale Research (Book Tower, Detroit, MI 48226) revised periodically.

The North American On Line Directory 1985, R. R. Bowker (New York, NY 10017) annual.

On Line Data Base Services Directory; Gale Research (address above) revised periodically.

The Federal Data Base Finder. A guide to more than 3,000 free and fee based data bases provided by the US Government. Available from Information USA, 1200 Beall Mt. Road, Potomac, MD 20854.

Guidance on Software Maintenance. Superintendent of Documents, Government Printing Office, Washington, DC 20402. Offers advice on maintaining software and suggestions on how to streamline your system.

Introduction to Software Packages. Superintendent of Documents (address given above). Sources of information on available software packages.

Databasics: Your Guide to On Line Business Information, Garland Publishing Co. (New York, NY 10016).

Directory On Line Data Bases, Cuadra/Elsevier Associates, 25 Vanderbilt Avenue, New York, NY 10017. A comprehensive standard reference.

Wall Street Computer Review, 150 Broadway, New York, NY 10038. This periodical covers current developments and contains informative articles.

Data Base Vendors

ADP Network Services, Inc.
175 Jackson Plaza
Ann Arbor, MI 48106
313-769-6800

BRS, Inc.
1200 Route 7
Latham, NY 12110
518-783-1161
800-833-4707

Business Information Services
Control Data Corporation
500 West Putnam Avenue
Greenwich, CT 06830
203-622-2000

Chase Econometrics/Interactive Data Corporation
95 Hayden Avenue
Lexington, MA 02173
617-890-8100

CompuServe, Inc.
5000 Arlington Centre Boulevard
Columbus, OH 43220
614-457-8600
800-848-8990

Data Resources, Inc. (DRI)
1750 K Street NW
Washington, DC 20006
202-663-7720

DIALOG Information Services, Inc.
3460 Hillview Avenue
Palo Alto, CA 94304
415-858-3810
800-334-2564

Dow Jones & Company, Inc.
P.O. Box 300
Princeton, NJ 08540
609-452-2000
800-257-5114

General Electric Information Services Company
401 North Washington Street
Rockville, MD 20850
301-294-5405

GTE Information Systems, Inc.
12490 Sunrise Valley
Reston, VA 22046
800-638-4215

Mead Data Central
P.O. Box 933
Dayton, OH 45401
800-227-4908

The New York Times Information Services, Inc.
229 West 43 Street
New York, NY 10036
800-543-6862

Quotron Systems, Inc.
5454 Beethoven Street
Los Angeles, CA 90066
213-398-2761

SDC Search Service/Orbit
1340 Old Chain Bridge Road
McLean, VA 22101
703-442-0000
800-334-7575

I. P. Sharp Associates
Exchange Tower
Toronto, Ontario, Canada M5X IE3
416-364-5361
800-387-1588

Source Telecomputing Corporation
1616 Anderson Road
McLean, VA 22102
703-734-7500X546
800-336-3366

TRW Information Services Division
505 City Parkway West
Orange, CA 92668
714-937-2000

Business Information Directory

General Reference Sources

The *United States Government Manual* is an annual publication. It describes the organization, purposes, and programs of most government agencies and lists top personnel. Available from the Superintendent of Documents, Government Printing Office, Washington, DC 20402.

Washington Information Directory is an annual publication listing, by topic, organizations and publications which provide information on a wide range of subjects. It also lists congressional committee assignments, regional federal offices, embassies, and state and local officials. Published by the Congressional Quarterly, Inc., 1414 22nd Street NW, Washington, DC 20037.

Statistical Abstracts of the United States, published annually by the Bureau of the Census, is the standard summary on the social, political, and economic statistics of the United States. It includes data from both government and private sources. Appendix II gives a comprehensive list of sources. (Available from the Superintendent of Documents, Government Printing Office, Washington, DC 20402.)

Business Information Sources by Lorna M. Daniells ranks among the best general guides to business publications. It contains extensive references to U.S. business and economic data, including statistics, U.S. and foreign investment. Published by the University of California Press, Berkeley, CA.

Researcher's Guide to Washington Experts, Washington Researchers, 2612 P Street NW, Washington, DC 20007.

Population information on all aspects of national and world population is provided by the Population Reference Bureau, Inc., 777 14th Street NW, Washington, DC, or call 202–689–8040.

The Washington Information Research Service provides reports and guidance to information on a fee basis. Write Washington Researchers, 2612 P Street NW, Washington, DC 20007, or call 202–333–3499.

Information USA is a reference book with leads about how to tap the information mine of the federal government. Published by Penguin Books, 624 Madison Avenue, New York, NY 10022.

FEDfind which explains how to get services and publications from the U.S. Government is published by ICUC Press, P.O. Box 1447-NR, Springfield, VA 22151.

Standard Rate and Data Service provides information on periodical circulation and advertising rates. Published by Standard Rates and Data Service, Inc., 5201 Old Orchard Road, Skokie, IL 60077–1021.

Encyclopedia of Information Systems and Services. Descriptions of U.S. organizations (and some foreign) that produce, process, store, and use bibliographic and non-bibliographic information. About 1500 data bases covered. Published by Gale Research Co., Book Tower, Detroit, MI 48226.

National Directory of Addresses and Telephone Numbers. A national business directory that lists all SEC registered companies, major accounting and law firms, banks, and financial institutions, associations, unions, etc. Available from General Information, Inc., 401 Parkplace, Kirkland, WA 98033.

Encyclopedia of Business Information, a comprehensive single-volume source, is updated periodically. Available from Gale Research Co., Book Tower, Detroit, MI 48226.

Business Publications Index and Abstracts is a two volume set listing books, transaction proceedings, etc. with abstracts of each entry. Published by Gale Research Co., Book Tower, Detroit, MI 48226.

Professional and trade organizations and publications are a major source of contacts and information. Key directories to these sources are listed below:

Encyclopedia of Associations, published by Gale Research Co., Book Tower, Detroit, MI 48226.

The World Guide to Trade Associations gives a comprehensive national and international listing of associations. Published by R. R. Bowker Co., 205 East 42 Street, New York, NY 10017.

Ulrich's International Periodical Directory covers both domestic and foreign periodicals. Published by R. R. Bowker Co., 205 East 42 Street, New York, NY 10017.

Standard Periodical Directory covers U.S. and Canadian periodicals. Published by Oxbridge Communications, Inc., 150 Fifth Avenue, New York, NY 10011.

The 1988 IMS Directory of Publications provides titles of trade newspapers and periodicals. Published by IMS Press, 426 Pennsylvania Avenue, Fort Washington, PA 19034.

Trade Directories of the World is published annually (with monthly updates) by Croner Publications, 211–05 Jamaica Avenue, Queens Village, New York 11428.

National Trade and Professional Associations of the United States. A comprehensive listing of professional trade and labor associations, including addresses, membership size, publications by the associations, and convention schedules. An annual published by Columbia Books, 777 14th Street NW, Washington, DC 20005.

Encyclopedia of Banking and Finance, is a comprehensive source on subjects indicated in title. Bankers Publishing Co., Boston, MA.

Guide to American Directories, published by B. Klein Publications, Inc., P.O. Box 8503, Coral Springs, FL 33065.

Directory of Directories, distributed by Gale Research Co., Book Tower, Detroit, MI 48226.

Directory of Marketing Research Houses and Services is an annual available from the American Marketing Association, 420 Lexington Avenue, New York, NY 10022.

BUSINESS AND ECONOMICS INFORMATION

Government publications referred to below may be obtained from the Government Printing Office (GPO), Washington, DC, 20402, unless otherwise indicated.

Census Catalog and Guide is an annual one-step guide to Census Bureau resources. Includes explanations of the censuses and surveys of business, manufacturing, and population, names and phone numbers of over 1,600 sources of assistance—Census Bureau specialists, State and local agencies, and private companies.

Business and economic information is provided by the following key references.

Survey of Current Business is a major publication which is supplemented on a weekly basis with *Current Statistics.* The publication contains articles as well as comprehensive statistics on all aspects of the economy, including data on the GNP, employment, wages, prices, finance, foreign trade, and production by industrial sector. (GPO)

Business Conditions Digest is a monthly with an extensive collection of charts and tables on the national income and products, leading coincident and lagging cyclical indicators, foreign trade, prices, wages, analytical ratios, and international production and stock prices. (GPO)

Economic Indicators is a monthly summary-type publication prepared by the Council of Economic Advisers. It contains charts and tables on natural output, income, spending, employment, unemployment, wages, industrial production, construction, prices, money, credit, federal finance, and international statistics. (GPO)

Federal Reserve Bulletin is a monthly issued by the Federal Reserve System, containing articles and very extensive tabulated data on all aspects of the monetary situation, credit, mortgage markets, interest rates, and stock and bond yields. A monthly *Chart Book* is available which contains charts of financial and monetary data. Both are available from the Board of Governors, Federal Reserve System, Washington, DC 20551.

Monthly Labor Review. This monthly publication provides articles and statistics on employment, productivity, wages, earnings, prices, wage settlements, and work stoppages. (GPO)

U.S. Industrial Outlook is an annual providing evaluations and projections of all major industrial and commercial segments of the domestic economy. (GPO)

Quarterly Financial Report for Manufacturing, Mining, and Trade Corporations is issued by the Bureau of the Census of the U.S. Department of Commerce. It covers corporate financial statistics including sales, profits, assets, and financial ratios, classified by industry group and size. (GPO)

Current Industrial Reports are a series of over 100 monthly, quarterly, semiannual, and annual reports on major products manufactured in the United States. For subscription, contact the Bureau of the Census, U.S. Department of Commerce, Washington, DC 20233. (GPO)

Annual Survey of Manufacturers. General statistics of manufacturing activity for industry groups, individual industries, states, and geographical regions are provided. (GPO)

County Business Patterns is an annual publication on employment and payrolls, which include a separate paperbound report for each state. (GPO)

Foreign Trade is a Bureau of the Census publication giving monthly reports on U.S. foreign trade. (GPO)

Population: Current Report is a series of monthly and annual reports covering population changes and socioeconomic characteristics of the population. (GPO)

Retail Sales: Current Business Report is a weekly report which provides retail statistics. (GPO)

Wholesale Trade, Sales and Inventories: Current Business Report provides a monthly report on wholesale trade. (GPO)

Key Economic Data Service Package provides access to the Department of Commerce Electronic Bulletin Board. The Bulletin Board includes same day postings of data provided by both the Bureau of Labor Statistics and the Bureau of Economic Analysis. Twice a month there are updates from the Bureau of the Census on the principal indicators, monetary statistics and foreign trade. Also provided is the most current *SIC Manual.* Available from the National Technical Information Service, 5285 Port Royal Road, Springfield, VA 22161.

CORPORATE INFORMATION

The major sources of information on publicly held corporations (as well as government and municipal issues) are: *Moody's Investor Services, Inc.*, owned by Dun & Bradstreet, 99 Church Street, New York, NY 10007, and *Standard & Poor's Corp.*, owned by McGraw-Hill, 25 Broadway, New York, NY 10004.

Standard & Poor's *Corporate Records* and Moody's *Manuals* are large multivolume works published annually and kept up to date with daily (for Standard & Poor's) or semiweekly (for Moody's) reports. The services provide extensive coverage of industrials, public utilities, transportation, banks, and financial companies. Also included are municipal and government issues.

In addition, the above corporations provide computerized data services and magnetic tapes. Compustat tapes, containing major corporate financial data, are available from Investor's Management Services, Inc., Denver, CO, a subsidiary of Standard & Poor's. Time-sharing access to Compustat and other financial data bases is available through Interactive Data Corporation, Waltham, MA (617) 890–1234.

DISCLOSURE II, available from Disclosure, Inc., (5161 River Road, Bethesda, MD 20816) provides an on line data base of corporate information for some 10,000 companies. Disclosure II can be used via the Dow Jones Retrieval Service, New York Times Information Service, Lockheed's DIALOG Information Services, Inc., ADP, CompuServe, among others.

Also available from Disclosure is MICRO/SCAN: Disclosure II, a monthly diskette service which provides information on dividends per share, 4-year growth rate in earnings per share, price/book value, etc. For information call 800–638–8076.

The 10-K and other corporate reports are filed with the Securities and Exchange Commission and are available at local SEC offices, investor relations departments of publicly traded companies, as well as various private services, such as Disclosure Inc. which provides a complete microfiche service. *The SEC News Digest*, formerly published by the government, is now available from Disclosure, Inc. (address above). Included in the *Digest* is a daily listing of 8K reports, a daily Acquisitions of Securities Report, as well as information about what's happening inside the SEC.

Disclosure Inc. has two additional services helpful for researching a corporation. Through the *SEC Watch Service* any report filed by a company with the SEC can be retrieved while corporate information such as prospective supplements and tender offers can be retrieved through the *SEC Research Service.*

Betchel Information Service located at 15740 Shady Grove Road, Gaithersburg, MD 20877 is another SEC document retrieval service. The Index of financial documents is updated several times a day.

Major trade directories include the annual *Thomas Register of American Manufacturers* (published by Thomas Publishing Company, 1 Pennsylvania Plaza, New York, NY 10005) and Dun & Bradstreet's *Reference Book of Manufacturers.*

Thomas Register includes in one volume an alphabetical listing of manufacturers, giving address, phone number, product, subsidiaries, plant location, and an indication of assets. Dun & Bradstreet's *Reference Book* covers similar information, including sales and credit. Dun & Bradstreet's *Million Dollar Directory* series provides data on U.S. companies whose net worth is $1,000,000 and up, including information on privately held corporations; also published is a companion volume the *Billion Dollar Directory* which tracks America's corporate families.

Directory of Wall Street Research, an annual published by Nelson Publishing, Rye, NY lists security analysts with a subject specialty, top corporate officers, and brokerage firms researching a given company.

Register of Corporations is published by Standard and Poor's Corp., 345 Hudson Street, New York, NY 10014.

Directory of Corporate Affiliations and International Directory of Corporate Affiliations are references to the structure of major domestic and international corporations. Published by NRPC, 3004 Glen View Road, Wilmette, IL 60091.

Sources of State Information on Corporations, provides information filed by companies with the state governments and also business related data collected by the states. Washington Researchers Publishing, 2612 P Street NW, Washington, DC 20007.

How to Find Information About Companies: The Corporate Intelligence Sourcebook provides information on sources helpful in researching either private or public companies. Available from Washington Researchers Publishing. (See above for the address.)

Ward's Directory of Private Companies supplies data on private companies (and their subsidiaries) with annual sales volume of one half to $11 million that are not publically traded. Available from Ward's Business Directory, 11 Davis Drive, Belmont, CA 94002.

Zacks Investment Research, Inc., 2 North Riverside Plaza, Chicago, IL 60606 (312-559-9405) also provides future earnings projections.

Future earnings projections of listed companies based on surveys by securities analysts are provided by Lynch, Jones, and Ryan, 345 Hudson Street, New York, NY 10013 (212-243-3137).

Information on foreign corporations is provided in *World Trade Data Reports*, distributed by the District Offices of the U.S. Department of Commerce.

TRACKING FEDERAL GOVERNMENT DEVELOPMENTS

Commerce Business Daily (*CB*). This daily provides information on contract awards and subcontract opportunities, Defense Department awards, and surplus sales. *CB* is available on-line from: United Communications Group, 8701 Georgia Avenue, Silver Springs, MD 20910; DIALOG Information Services, 3460 Hillview Avenue, Palo Alto, CA 94304; or Data Resources, Inc., 2400 Hartwell Avenue, Lexington, ME 02173. (GPO)*

Federal Register. This daily provides information on federal agency regulations and other legal documents (GPO).*

CQ Weekly Report. This major service follows every important piece of legislation through both houses of Congress and reports on the political and lobbying pressures being applied. Available from the Congressional Quarterly Service, 1414 22nd Street, Washington, DC 20037.

Daily Report for Executives. A daily series of reports giving Washington developments that affect all aspects of business operations. Available from the Bureau of National Affairs, Inc., 1231 25th Street NW, Washington, DC 20037. Call: 301-258-1033.

Two major services, the *Bureau of National Affairs, Inc.* (address above) and the *Commerce Clearing House, Inc.* (4025 West Peterson Avenue, Chicago, IL 60646), publish a large number of valuable weekly looseleaf reports covering developments in all aspects of law, government regulations, and taxation.

INDEX PUBLICATIONS

Indexes of a wide variety of articles appearing in periodicals, trade presses, and financial services dealing with corporations, industry, and finance are given in the following:

Business Periodicals Index published by H. W. Wilson Co., 950 University Avenue, Bronx, NY.

Funk and Scott Index of Corporations and Industries, published by Predicast, Inc., 11001 Cedar Street, Cleveland, OH 44141.

Major newspaper indexes are:

Wall Street Journal Index published by Dow Jones & Co. Inc., 22 Cortlandt Street, New York, NY 10007 (monthly).

New York Times Index published by the New York Times Company, 229 W. 43rd Street, New York, NY 10036 (semimonthly, cumulates annually).

TRACKING ECONOMIC INDICATORS

Composite Index of Leading Economic Indicators: Each month the Bureau of Economic Analysis compiles this data from the 12 leading economic indicators. This material appears each month in the *Bureau's Business Conditions Digest* (BCD) available by subscription from:

Superintendent of Documents
Government Printing Office
Washington, DC 20402

Index values are available towards the very end of each month by calling: 202-523-0541.

Consumer Price Index (*CPI*) (changes in cost of goods to customers): For these monthly reports prepared by the Bureau of Labor Statistics write:

Bureau of Labor Statistics
Department of Labor
441 G Street NW
Washington, DC 20212

CPI 24 hour hotline: 202-523-1239.

Producer Price Index (*PPI*) (measures changes in prices received in primary markets by producers). For monthly reports write:

Bureau of Labor Statistics
Department of Labor
441 G Street NW
Washington, DC 20212

PPI 24 hour hotline: 202-523-1765.

Available from the Bureau of Labor Statistics (BLS) are press releases on *State and Metropolitan Area Unemployment* (issued monthly), the *Employment Cost Index* (issued quarterly, and the *Employment Situation Study* (released monthly). For a sample copy call 202-523-1221. To subscribe write:

Bureau of Labor Statistics
Department of Labor
Washington, DC 20230

BLS hotline: 202-523-1239
Major BLS Statistics: 523-9658

* Available from the Superintendent of Documents, Government Printing Office, Washington, DC 20402.

Unemployment Insurance Claims Weekly may be obtained by calling or by writing:

Employment and Training Administration
Department of Labor
601 D Street, NW
Washington, DC 20213

Releases on the *Money Supply* (Report H-6, issued weekly) and on *Consumer Credit* (Report G-19, issued monthly) may be obtained from the

Publications Services
Federal Reserve Board
Washington, DC 20551
202-452-3244

Personal Consumption Expenditure Deflator is prepared monthly by the Bureau of Economic Analysis of the Department of Commerce. This information appears in a press release *Personal Income and Outlays* and can be obtained in writing from the

Current Business Analysis
Bureau of Economic Analysis
Department of Commerce
Washington, DC 20230

For information call 202-523-0777.

Monthly Trade Report (index of retail sales and accounts receivable) is compiled by the Bureau of the Census and published in *Current Business Reports* as part of what is known as the BR series. Also available are *Current Business Reports Wholesale Trade* and *Current Business Reports Selected Services.* To subscribe contact the Superintendent of Documents (Address given above). For a sample copy call: 301-763-4100.

Value of New Construction Put in Place is a Census Bureau monthly report (part of the C-30 Series) which charts the dollar amount of new construction. It is available on an annual subscription basis from the Superintendent of Documents, Government Printing Office, Washington, DC 20402. For a sample copy call: 301-763-5717.

Joint Economic Committee of Congress Reports

Reports on the economic issues studied by the Joint Economic Committee are available free of charge from:

Joint Economic Committee of Congress
Dirksen Senate Office Building
Washington, DC 20510
202–224–5321

TRACKING CONGRESSIONAL ACTION

Congressional action information can be obtained from several sources. The Legis Office will provide information on whether legislation has been introduced, who sponsored it, and its current status. For House or Senate action, call 202–225–1772.

Cloakrooms of both houses will provide details on what is happening on the floor of the chamber. House cloakrooms: Democrat 202–225–7330; Republican 202–225–7350. Senate cloakrooms: Democrat 202–224–4691; Republican 202–224–6391.

ASSISTANCE FROM U.S. GOVERNMENT AGENCIES

The **Office of Business Liaison (OBL)** serves as the focal point for contact between the Department of Commerce and the business community. Through the *Business Assistance Program* individuals and firms are guided through the entire government complex. Other services include dissemination of information and reports such as *Outlook.* Write Office of Business Liaison, U.S. Department of Commerce, Washington, DC 20230. This office is also a focal point for handling inquiries for domestic business information.

OBL telephone numbers:

Office of the Director	(202) 377-3942
Outreach Program	377-1360
Business Assistance Program	3176

Industry experts in the International Trade Administration can provide specifics about an industry.

Country experts in the Department of State provide up to date economic and political information on countries throughout the world, as well as background reports on specific countries. For information contact:

Country Desk Officers
U.S. Department of State
2201 C Street NW
Washington, DC 20520
Telephone: 202–647–4000

Major Bureau of Labor Statistics Indicators are available daily from a recorded message at 202–523-9658.

Economic news and highlights of the day are provided by phone from the Department of Commerce. For economic news call 202–393–4100. For news highlights call 202–393–1847.

The Energy Information Center will provide free information on energy and related matters. Write National Energy Information Center, Forrestal Building, 1000 Independence Avenue SW, Washington, DC 20585. Call 202–586–5000.

Technical and scientific information is provided by the **National Technical Information Service** of the Department of Commerce, 5285 Port Royal, Springfield, VA 22161, which handles requests about government-sponsored research of all kinds. The basic charge to research a subject is $125. For information call 703–487–4600. For orders call 703–487–4650. For rush orders within the local calling area call 703–487–4700. For rush order outside the local calling area call 800–336–4700.

The **Census Bureau** produces detailed statistical information for the U.S. Information is available on population, housing, agriculture, manufacturing, retail trade, service industries, wholesale trade, foreign trade, mining, transportation, construction, and the revenues and expenditures of state and local governments. The Bureau also produces statistical studies of many foreign countries.

Information Sources in the Bureau of the Census

User Services

Product Information ....(301) 763-4100
Guides, Catalogs and Directories..... 763-1584
Data User Training 763-1510

Government, Commerce and Industry Subjects

Agriculture Data.......................... (301) 763-1113
Business Data (Retail, Wholesale, Services)...763-7564
Construction Statistics........................ 763-7163
Foreign Trade Data............................. 763-5140
State Exports 763-5708
Government Data................................ 763-7366
Industry Data 763-7800
Manufactures Data 763-7666

Population, Housing and Income Subjects

Housing Data .... (301) 763-2881
International Statistics 763-2870
Neighborhood Statistics 763-2358
Population Data 763-5020
Special Demographic Studies............. 763-7720

Government, Commerce and Civic Relations..763-2436

Regional Assistance

Atlanta, Georgia.......................... (404) 257-2271
Boston, Massachusetts ....(617) 565-7104
Charlotte, North Carolina .... (704) 672-6142
Chicago, Illinois ....(312) 353-6251
Dallas, Texas............................... (214) 767-0625
Denver, Colorado .... (303) 236-2200
Detroit, Michigan......................... (313) 226-7742
Kansas City, Kansas .... (913) 236-3728
Los Angeles, California...............(213) 209-6616
New York, New York .... (212) 264-3860
Philadelphia, Pennsylvania.........(215) 597-4920
Seattle, Washington ....(206) 399-7800

For a detailed telephone contact list...(301) 763-2436

Source: *Business Services Directory*, U.S. Department of Commerce, Office of Business Liaison.

Information Sources in the U.S. Department of Commerce: Quick Reference List

Aeronautical Chart Sales........... (301) 436-6990
Business Assistance...................(202) 377-3176
Commerce Speakers..................(202) 377-1360
Copyright Information*.............. (202) 479-0700
Consumer Affairs........................(202) 377-5001
District Export Councils............. (202) 377-2975
Energy Related Inventions-
Evaluation................................(301) 975-5500

EXPORT
Counseling.............................. (202) 377-3181
Export Trading Company........(202) 377-5131
License/Application
(STELA)................................(202) 377-2752
Fish Exports/Imports................. (202) 673-5335
Fishery Management Plans........ (202) 673-5268
Foreign Trade Zones.................. (202) 377-2862
Franchising................................ (202) 377-0342
Freight Rates** ....(202) 366-2271
Industry/Products Infor-
mation.................................... (202) 377-1461
Joint Ventures (National)............(202) 377-1093
Leading Economic Indicators.....(202) 523-0777
Metric Information .... (202) 377-3036
Minority Owned Business...........(202) 377-2414
Nautical Chart Sales .... (301) 436-6990
NTIS Sales Desk.........................(703) 487-4650
Overseas Customer Lists........... (202) 377-3181
Overseas Marketing ....(202) 377-3022
Overseas Trade Fairs................. (202) 377-1209
Patent Information..................... (703) 557-5168
Productivity Enhancement
Information..............................(202) 377-0940

PROCUREMENT
Bidder's List............................ (202) 377-3387
Federal Procurement
Conferences....................... (202) 377-2975
MBDA Profile System............ (202) 377-3163
NOAA Opportunities...............(202) 377-1537
Small Business........................(202) 377-1472
Women Owned Business........(202) 377-3387

PUBLICATIONS
"Business America" Maga-
zine.....................................(202) 377-3251
Commerce Business Daily...... (202) 377-0632
NBS Reference Materials....... (301) 975-2012
Survey of Current Business....(202) 523-0777

Quality Award ....(301) 975-2036
Sea Grant Research...................(301) 443-8923

SMALL BUSINESS
Assistance..............................(202) 377-3176
Procurement/Set Asides........ (202) 377-3387
Technology (OPTI) ....(202) 377-8111
Standards & Codes for
Products............................ (301) 975-4036

STATISTICS
Business Cycles...................... (202) 523-0908
Capital Investment.................. (202) 523-0874
Gross National Product.......... (202) 523-0669
Foreign Travelers to U.S. .... (202) 377-4028
Housing Starts........................ (301) 763-5731
Income Data .... (301) 763-8203
International Trade
Balance...............................(202) 523-0620
Personal Income by
County............................... (202) 523-0966
Population.............................. (301) 763-5020
Price Indexes.......................... (202) 523-0828
Retail Trade Data .... (301) 763-5294
Trade Statistics....................... (202) 377-2185
Time of Day................................(303) 499-7111
Trademark Information............. (703) 557-3281

WEATHER
Climate for Farming ....(301) 427-7677
Forecast—U.S. Eastern
Cities..................................(301) 899-3244
Forecast—U.S. Western
Cities..................................(301) 899-3244
Historic Weather Conditions
with certified copies............(704) 259-0682
Tide Predictions......................(301) 443-8060

*Handled by the Library of Congress
**Handled by Maritime Commission

Source: *Business Services Directory*, U.S. Department of Commerce, Office of Business Liaison.

COMMODITIES: SOURCES OF GOVERNMENT INFORMATION

Information on various commodities may be obtained by calling the following:

Office of Industries
International Trade Commission
Telephone: 292–523–0146

Bureau of Mines
The Bureau uses three basic classifications:
Ferrous Metals
Telephone: 202–634–1010
Nonferrous Metals
Telephone: 202–634–1055
Industrial Minerals
Telephone: 202–634–1202

Crops Branch
Department of Agriculture
Telephone: 202–786–1840

Metals, Minerals and Commodities
Trade Development
Telephone: 202–377–0575

Minerals Industries
Bureau of the Census
Telephone: 202–763–5938

Industry and Commodity Classification
Bureau of the Census
Telephone: 202–763–1935

Available through the Government Printing Office (202–783–3238) are the Bureau of the Census Publications, *U.S. Imports, U.S.A. Commodities by Country* and *U.S. Exports Schedule 13, Commodities by Country*.

DOING BUSINESS WITH THE FEDERAL GOVERNMENT

Publications

Doing Business with the Federal Government contains helpful material for marketing products or services to the Government, i.e., how to make products known, how and where to obtain the necessary forms and papers to get started, and how to bid on Government contracts. It also provides a geographical listing of Business Service Centers that have information about contract opportunities, as well as whom to contact and where to go for the information needed to sell to individual Government agencies. A list of Business Service Centers is given below.

The *Commerce Business Daily* tells, for example, what products and services the Government is buying, which agencies are buying, due dates for bids, how to get complete specifications. Each weekday, the *Commerce Business Daily* gives a complete listing of products and services wanted by the U.S. Government. Each listing includes product or service, along with a short description, name and address of agency, deadline for proposals or bids, phone number to request specifications, and solicitation numbers of product or service needed. Issued Monday through Friday.

The *Federal Acquisition Regulation* (FAR) is the primary source of procurement regulations used by all Federal agencies in their acquisition of supplies and services. It sets forth all the provisions and clauses that are used in Government contracting. Because the clauses in a specific solicitation for bids refer to a numbered provision of FAR rather than providing the full text, the FAR is necessary to understand the solicitation. Subscription service consists of a basic manual and supplementary material for an indeterminate period.

The *United States Government Purchasing and Sales Directory* contains an alphabetical listing of the products and services bought by all military departments and a separate listing for civilian agencies. It also includes an explanation of the ways in which the Small Business Administration can help a business obtain Government prime contracts and subcontracts, data on Government sales of surplus property, and comprehensive descriptions of the scope of the Government market for research and development.

The *Small Business Subcontracting Directory* is designed to aid small business professionals interested in subcontracting opportunities within the Department of Defense (DOD). The guide is arranged alphabetically by state and includes the name and address of each current DOD prime contractor as well as the product or service being provided to DOD. It also includes the name and telephone number for each DOD Small Business Liaison Officer who knows what the subcontracted products and services are, what the prime contracting firm has purchased in the past, what it is presently purchasing, and what it may be planning to purchase in the future.

The *Federal Register* provides the official version of public regulations issued by the Federal agencies. It also includes announcements of grants and other funding information, as well as data on the availability of Government contracts.

U.S. GENERAL SERVICES ADMINISTRATION: BUSINESS SERVICE CENTERS

The Business Service Centers are a one stop, one point of contact for information on General Services Administration and other Government contract programs. The primary function is to provide advice on doing business with the Federal Government. The Centers provide information, assistance, and counseling and sponsor business clinics, procurement conferences, and business opportunity meetings.

Business representatives interested in selling products and services to the Government should contact the nearest Business Service Center given below.

Mailing Address and Telephone	Area of Service
Business Service Center General Services Administration John W. McCormack Post Office and Courthouse Boston, MA 02109 (617) 223–2868	Connecticut, Maine, Massachusetts, New Hampshire, Rhode Island, and Vermont

Mailing Address and Telephone	Area of Service
Business Service Center General Services Administration 26 Federal Plaza New York, NY 10007 (212) 264–1234	New Jersey, New York, Puerto Rico, and Virgin Islands
Business Service Center General Services Administration 7th and D Streets, SW., RM. 1050 Washington, DC 20407 (202) 472–1804	District of Columbia, nearby Maryland, Virginia
Business Service Center General Services Administration 9th and Market Streets Room 1300 Philadelphia, PA 19107 (215) 597–9613	Delaware, Pennsylvania, West Virginia, Maryland, Virginia
Business Service Center General Services Administration Richard B. Russell Federal Building and Court House 75 Spring Street Atlanta, GA 30303 (404) 221–5103	Alabama, Florida, Georgia, Kentucky, Mississippi, North Carolina, South Carolina, and Tennessee
Business Service Center General Services Administration 230 South Dearborn Street Chicago, IL 60604 (312) 353–5383	Illinois, Indiana, Ohio, Michigan, Minnesota, and Wisconsin
Business Service Center General Services Administration 1500 East Bannister Road Kansas City, MO 64131 (816) 926–7203	Iowa, Kansas, Missouri, and Nebraska
Business Service Center General Services Administration 819 Taylor Street Fort Worth, TX 76102 (817) 334–3284	Arkansas, Louisiana, New Mexico, Oklahoma, and Texas
Business Service Center General Services Administration Building 41, Denver Federal Center Denver, CO 80225 (303) 236–7409	Colorado, Montana, North Dakota, South Dakota, Utah, and Wyoming
Business Service Center General Services Administration 525 Market Street San Francisco, CA 94105 (415) 454–9000	California (northern), Hawaii, and Nevada (except Clark County)
Business Service Center General Services Administration 300 North Los Angeles Street Los Angeles, CA 90012 (213) 688–3210	Arizona, Los Angeles, California (southern), and Nevada (Clark County only)
Business Service Center General Services Administration 440 Federal Building 915 Second Avenue Seattle, WA 98174 (206) 442–5556	Alaska, Idaho, Oregon, and Washington

FEDERAL AND STATE GOVERNMENT ASSISTANCE AVAILABLE TO U.S. BUSINESSES: CENTER FOR THE UTILIZATION OF FEDERAL TECHNOLOGY

Government support of technical innovation is growing rapidly both at the Federal and State levels. A helpful source for information regarding the transfer of Federal technology to the U.S. economy is the **Center for the Utilization of Federal Technology (CUFT),** which is part of the National Technical Information Service (NTIS) of the U.S. Department of Commerce, (703) 487-4805. One of its major roles is to link U.S. businesses with federally developed technologies and resources having commercial or practical application. By working directly with U.S. Government agencies, CUFT has prepared a number of directories and catalogs to alert companies to these valuable Government resources.

Its most recent directory, *Directory of Federal and State Business Assistance–A Guide for New and Growing Companies,* presents full descriptions to financial, management, innovation, and information programs and services established to help both large and small firms in their day-to-day operations. A listing of state services is given on page 621.

A companion directory, *Directory of Federal Laboratory and Technical Resources–A Guide to Services, Facilities, and Expertise,* provides detailed descriptions of technology-oriented Federal resources. Especially notable are the entries describing the technical information centers offering information assistance in focused technology areas.

Also available are the *Federal Technology Catalogs–Guides to New and Practical Technologies* which annually offer full descriptions to more than 1,200 new technologies and R&D developments. Another annual catalog series, *Catalog of Government Inventions Available for Licensing.* The *Catalog* contains information on licensing and marketing government-owned-inventions, frequently with the benefit of exclusive licensing and/or with the protection of foreign patent rights. To order write the National Technical Information Service, 5285 Port Royal Road, Springfield, VA 22161 or call 703-487-4650.

BUSINESS ASSISTANCE PROGRAM: COMMERCE DEPARTMENT

The Business Assistance program is designed to shorten the time it takes a businessperson to track down information within the labyrinth of government bureaus and agencies. Business Assistance Program staffers can provide information or direct inquiries to the proper authority on such subjects as regulatory changes, government programs, services, policies, and even relevant government publications for the business community. For information call 202–377–3176 or write: Business Assistance Program Business Liason Office, Rm 5898-C, Department of Commerce, Washington, DC 20230.

FEDERAL INFORMATION CENTERS (FICs)

FICs located in key cities throughout the country are a joint venture of the U.S. General Services Administration and the U.S. Civil Services. Each center is a focal point for obtaining information about the federal government and often about state and local governments. A member of the center's staff can either provide information or direct inquiries to an expert who can. Some centers have specialists who speak foreign languages. The coordinator of the FICs is located at 18th and F Streets, NW, Washington, DC 20405. For a list of FICs write to: Consumer Information Center, Pueblo, CO 81009.

Alabama
Birmingham (205) 322-8591
Mobile (205) 438-1421

Alaska
Anchorage (907) 271-3650

Arizona
Phoenix (602) 261-3313

Arkansas
Little Rock (501) 378-6177

California
Los Angeles (213) 894-3800
Sacramento (916) 551-2380
San Diego (619) 557-6030
San Francisco (415) 556-6600
Santa Ana (714) 836-2386

Colorado
Colorado Springs (303) 471-9491
Denver (303) 844-6575
Pueblo (303) 544-9523

Connecticut
Hartford (203) 527-2617
New Haven (203) 624-4720

Florida
Ft. Lauderdale (305) 522-8531
Jacksonville (904) 354-4756
Miami (305) 536-4155
Orlando (305) 422-1800
St. Petersburg (813) 893-3495
Tampa (813) 229-7911
West Palm Beach (305) 833-7566

Georgia
Atlanta (404) 331-6891

Hawaii
Honolulu (808) 551-1365

Illinois
Chicago (312) 353-4242

Indiana
Gary (219) 883-4110
Indianapolis (317) 269-7373

Iowa
{From all points in Iowa} (800) 532-1556

Kansas
{From all points in Kansas} (800) 432-2934

Kentucky
Louisville (502) 582-6261

Louisiana
New Orleans (504) 589-6696

Maryland
Baltimore (301) 962-4980

Massachusetts
Boston (617) 565-8121

Michigan
Detroit (313) 226-7016
Grand Rapids (616) 451-2628

Minnesota
Minneapolis (612) 370-3333

Missouri
St. Louis (314) 425-4106
{From elsewhere in Missouri}
(800) 392-7711

Nebraska
Omaha (402) 221-3353
{From elsewhere in Nebraska}
(800) 642-8383

New Jersey
Newark (201) 645-3600
Trenton (609) 396-4400

New Mexico
Albuquerque (505) 766-3091

New York
Albany (518) 463-4421
Buffalo (716) 846-4010
New York (212) 264-4464
Rochester (716) 546-5075
Syracuse (315) 476-8545

North Carolina
Charlotte (704) 376-3600

Ohio
Akron (216) 375-5638
Cincinnati (513) 684-2801
Cleveland (216) 522-4040
Columbus (614) 221-1014
Dayton (513) 223-7377
Toledo (419) 241-3223

Oklahoma
Oklahoma City (405) 231-4868
Tulsa (918) 584-4193

Oregon
Portland (503) 221-2222

Pennsylvania
Philadelphia (215) 597-7042
Pittsburgh (412) 644-3456

Rhode Island
Providence (401) 331-5565

Tennessee
Chattanooga (615) 265-8231
Memphis (901) 521-3285
Nashville (615) 242-5056

Texas
Austin (512) 472-5494
Dallas (214) 767-8585
Fort Worth (817) 334-3624
Houston (713) 229-2552
San Antonio (512) 224-4471

Utah
Salt Lake City (801) 524-5353

Virginia
Norfolk (804) 441-3101
Richmond (804) 643-4928
Roanoke (703) 982-8591

Washington
Seattle (206) 442-0570
Tacoma (206) 383-5230

Wisconsin
Milwaukee (414) 271-2273

State Information Guide

Regional Directories

Central Atlantic States Manufacturing Directory, T. K. Sanderson Organization, 1115 E. 30 Street, Baltimore, MD 21218

Daltons' Greater Philadelphia Industrial Directory, Dalton Corp., 2925 N. Broad Street, Philadelphia, PA 19132

Directory of Central Atlantic States Manufacturers, Manufacturers' News, Inc., 4 E. Huron Street, Chicago, IL 60611; George D. Hall Company, 20 Kilby Street, Boston, MA 02109

Directory of New England Manufacturers, The, George D. Hall Company, 20 Kilby Street, Boston, MA 02109

Eastern Manufacturers' and Industrial Directory, Bell Directory Publishers, Inc., 1995 Broadway, New York, NY 10023

MacRae's Blue Book, The National Industrial Directory, 87 Terminal Drive, Plainview, NY 11803

Midwest Manufacturers' and Industrial Directory, Industrial Directory Publishers, 1002 Park Avenue Building, Detroit, MI 48226

New England Apparel Directory, Register Publication, Inc., 99 Chauncey Street, Boston, MA 02111

New England Industrial Service Directory, George D. Hall Company, 20 Kilby Street, Boston, MA 02109

New England Manufacturers Directory, Manufacturers' News, Inc., 3 E. Huron Street, Chicago, IL 60611

State Executive Directory, Carroll Publishing Company, 1058 Thomas Jefferson NW, Washington, DC 20007

State Sales Guides, Dun & Bradstreet, Inc., 99 Church Street, New York, NY 10007

Survey of Industries in Texarkana (Arkansas-Texas), Texarkana Chamber of Commerce, Box 1468, Texarkana, AK 75501

State Business Assistance Publications

Directory of Incentives for Business Investment and Development in the U.S., The Urban Institute Press, available from UPA, 4720 Boston Way, Lanlam, MD 20706. State by state guide to economic business incentives. Included are descriptions of state assistance and financial assistance programs.

Monthly Checklist of State Publications, Superintendent of Documents. Washington, DC 20402. A monthly list of documents and publications received from the States.

State Administrative Officials Classified by Function, Council of State Governments, Iron Works Pike, P.O. Box 1190, Lexington, KY 40578. Names, titles, telephone numbers and addresses of state officials and administrators.

Business Assistance Centers by State*

These centers offer assistance in business related matters. Entries were chosen and edited to reflect their assistance to technology-oriented companies. Such assistance includes information gathering, location of expert help, and guidance on new technologies. Most of these centers also are able to offer other types of assistance, such as market feasibility, or at least link businesses with appropriate contacts.

Alabama (AL)

Alabama Development Office, c/o State Capital, Montgomery 36130. Contact Ms. Ellen McNair at (205) 263-0048. *Assistance:* Business planning/Financial/Information/Networking/Technical

Alabama High Technology Assistance Center, University of Alabama in Huntsville, 336 Morton Hall, Huntsville 35899. Contact (205) 895-6409. *Assistance:* Technology transfer/Patent information/Business planning / Information / Networking / Technical. *Eligibility:* Smaller businesses

Alabama International Trade Center, P.O. Box 1996, Martha Tarham West, Tuscaloosa 35487. Contact (205) 348-7621. *Assistance:* Importing/exporting counseling/Business planning/Information/Networking/Technical. *Eligibility:* Smaller businesses

Alabama Small Business Development Consortium, Medical Towers Building, 1717 11th Avenue South, Birmingham 35294. Contact Dr. Jeff D. Gibbs at (205) 934-7260. *Assistance:* Business planning/Financial/In-

* Source: *Directory of Federal and State Business Assistance: A Guide for New and Growing Companies,* National Technical Information Service, Center for the Utilization of Federal Technology, U.S. Department of Commerce. For detailed information on any entry call 703-487-4650.

formation/Management/Networking/Technical. *Eligibility:* Smaller businesses

Alabama State Department of Revenue, Research and Information Division, Folsom Administrative Building, 64 North Union Street, Montgomery 36130. Contact Mr. William E. Crawford at (205) 261-3094 or 261-3366. *Assistance:* Information

Auburn Technical Assistance Center, 111 Drake Center, Auburn University 36849-5350. Contact Mr. Henry Burdg at (205) 826-4659. *Assistance:* Management/Technical

Center for Business and Economic Services, Sorrell College of Business, Troy State University, Troy, 36082-0001. Contact Mr. Joseph W. Creek at (205) 566-3000 Ext: 144. *Assistance:* Research/Information/Management/Technical

Center for Economic Development & Business Research, Jacksonville State University, College of Commerce and Business Administration, 114 Merrill Hall, Jacksonville 36265. Contact Mr. Pat W. Shaddix at (205) 231-5324. *Assistance:* Business planning/Financial/Information/Management/Networking/Technical

Department of Agriculture and Industries, Post Office Box 3336, Montgomery 36193. Contact (205) 261-2650. *Assistance:* Information/Technical

Department of Economic and Community Affairs, Science Technology and Energy Division, 3465 Norman Bridge Road, P.O. Box 2939, Montgomery 36105-0939. Contact Mr. Fred Braswell at (205) 284-8952. *Assistance:* Financial/Information/Networking/Technical

Department of Environmental Management, 1751 Federal Drive, Montgomery 36130. Contact Ms. Marilyn Elliott at (205) 271-7715. *Assistance:* Information/Networking

Management Development Center, Jacksonville State University, Merrill Bldg., Jacksonville 36265. Contact Mr. David R. Copeland at (205) 231-5342 ext: 5342. *Assistance:* Business planning/Management

Planning and Economic Development, Alabama Department of Economic & Community Affairs, 3465 Norman Bridge Road, P.O. Box 2939, Montgomery 36105-0939. Contact Dr. Don Hines at (205) 261-3572. *Assistance:* Economic development/Business planning/Information/Networking/Technical

Alaska (AK)

Agricultural Loan Fund, Alaska Department of Natural Resources, Division of Agriculture, P.O. Box 949, Palmer 99645-0949. Contact Mr. Mark Weaver at (907) 745-7200. *Assistance:* Financial

Alaska Industrial Development Authority, 1577 C Street, Suite 304, Anchorage 99501-5177. Contact (907) 274-1651. *Assistance:* Financial/Networking

Economic Development Center, School of Business and Public Administration, University of Alaska-Juneau, 1108 F Street, Juneau 99801. Contact Dr. Al Borrego at (907) 789-4402. *Assistance:* Business planning/Technical

Loan Fund Programs, Department of Commerce and Economic Development, Division of Investments, Pouch DI, Juneau 99811. Contact (907) 465-2510. *Assistance:* Financial

Arizona (AZ)

Arizona Department of Commerce, 1700 West Washington, 4th Floor, Phoenix 85007. Contact (602) 255-5371. *Assistance:* Business planning/Financial/Information/Technical

Business Development and Trade Division, Arizona Department of Commerce, 1700 West Washington, 4th Floor, Phoenix 85007. Contact Mr. William H. Maxwell at (602) 255-5371. *Assistance:* Business planning/Information/Networking/Technical

Development Finance Program, Arizona Department of Commerce, 1700 West Washington, 4th Floor, Phoenix 85007. Contact Mr John Lopach at (602) 255-5371. *Assistance:* Business planning/Financial/Information/Technical

Arkansas (AR)

Arkansas Capital Corporation, 800 Pyramid Place, 221 West Second Street, Little Rock 72201. Contact Mr. George Egan at (501) 374-9247.

Arkansas Development Finance Authority, 100 Main Street, 2nd Floor, Little Rock 72203. Contact (501) 371-3545. *Assistance:* Financial

Arkansas Industry Training Program, Education Building-West, #3 Capitol Mall, Little Rock 72201. Contact Mr. Richard Cochran at (501) 682-1302. *Assistance:* Training

Arkansas Science and Technology Authority, 100 Main Street, Suite 450, Little Rock 72201. Contact Dr. John Ahlen at (501) 371-3554. *Assistance:* Financial/Information/Networking/Technical

Business Development Services, Technology Center at Little Rock, 5th Floor, Library Building, 100 South Main, Suite 401, Little Rock 72201. Contact Mr. Paul McGinnis at (501) 371-5381. *Assistance:* Business education workshop/Business planning/Financial/Information/Networking/Technical

Business Information Clearinghouse, One State Capitol Mall, Little Rock, 72201. Contact (501) 682-3358. *Assistance:* Information

Center for Technology Transfer–University of Arkansas at Fayetteville, College of Engineering, Room 49, Engineering Research Center, Fayetteville 72701. Contact Mr. W. H. (Bill) Rader at (501) 575-3747. *Assistance:* Information/Networking/Technical

East Arkansas Business Incubator System, Inc., 5501 Krueger Drive, Jonesboro 72401. Contact Mr. Guy Enchelmayer at (501) 935-8365. *Assistance:* Marketing/Information/Management/Networking/Technical

Energy Division–Arkansas Industrial Development Commission, One State Capitol Mall, Little Rock 72201. Contact Ms. Cherry Duckett at (501) 682-1370. *Assistance:* Information/Networking/Technical

Entrepreneurial Service Center, Bureau of Business and Economic Research, College of Business Administration, University of Arkansas, Fayetteville 72701. Contact Dr. Phillip Taylor at (510) 575-4151. *Assistance:* Business Planning/Information/Management

Finance Division–Arkansas Industrial Development Commission, One State Capitol Mall, Little Rock 72201. Contact Mr. Larry Patrick at (501) 682-1151. *Assistance:* Financial/Information/Networking/Technical

Institute for Economic Development, Pittsburg State University, Pittsburg, KS 66762. Contact (316) 231-7000 Ext. 4920. *Assistance:* Business planning/Financial/Information/Management/Technical

Marketing Division–Arkansas Industrial Development Commission, One State Capitol Mall, Little Rock 72201. Contact Ms. Maria Luisa Haley at (501) 682-7678. *Assistance:* Information/Networking/Technical

Minority Business Division–Arkansas Industrial Development Commission, One State Capitol Mall, Little Rock 72201. Contact Mr. James Hall or Ms. Berthenia Gill at (501) 682-1060. *Assistance:* Financial/Information. *Eligibility:* Minority-owned businesses

California (CA)

Business Development Office, Department of Commerce, 1121 L Street, Sacramento 95814. Contact (916) 322-5665. *Assistance:* Information

Economic Adjustment Unit, Department of Commerce, 1121 L Street, Sacramento 95814. Contact (916) 322-1515. *Assistance:* Training/Business planning/Information/Technical

Economic Research Office, Department of Commerce, 1121 L Street, Sacramento 95814. Contact (916) 322-5853. *Assistance:* Information

Enterprise Zone Unit, Department of Commerce, 1121 L Street, Sacramento 95814. Contact (916) 324-8211. *Assistance:* Information

Small Business Office, Department of Commerce, 1121 L Street, Sacramento 95814. Contact (916) 445-6545. *Assistance:* Business planning/Financial/Information/Technical. *Eligibility:* Smaller businesses

Urban University Center, Western Research Application Center, University of Southern California, 3716 South Hope Street, Los Angeles 90007-4344. Contact (213) 743-2371. *Assistance:* Business planning/Information/Management/Networking/Technical. *Eligibility:* Smaller businesses

Colorado (CO)

Business Information Center, Office of Regulatory Reform, 1525 Sherman Street, Denver 80203. Contact (303) 866-3933. *Assistance:* Small business advocacy/ombudsman/Information

Colorado Housing and Finance Authority, Commercial Programs, 777 Pearl Street, Denver 80203. Contact (303) 861-8962. *Assistance:* Business planning/Financial/Information/Management/Networking/Technical. *Eligibility:* Smaller businesses and minority-owned businesses

Colorado Small Business Office, 1625 Broadway, Suite 1710, Denver 80202. Contact (303) 892-3840. *Assistance:* Information/Networking/Technical

CU Business Advancement Centers, 1690 38th Street, #101, Boulder 80301. Contact (800) 521-1243 (in state) or (303) 444-5723. *Assistance:* Procurement/Business planning/Information/Technical

Small Business Hotline, 1625 Broadway, Suite 1710, Denver 80202. Contact Mr. Bradley Green at 1 (800) 323-7798 (in state), 534-2525 (Denver metro area), or (303) 892-3825. *Assistance:* Information

Connecticut (CT)

Business Services, Connecticut Department of Economic Development, 210 Washington Street, Hartford 06106. Contact Mr. John J. Carson at (203) 566-3787. *Assistance:* Site selection assistance/Business planning/Information/Networking/Technical

Connecticut Department of Economic Development, 210 Washington Street, Hartford

06106. Contact Mr. John J. Carson at (203) 566-3787. *Assistance:* Site selection assistance/Business planning/Financial/Information/Management/Networking/Technical

Connecticut Development Authority, 217 Washington Street, Hartford 06106. Contact Mr. Richard L. Higgins at (203) 522-3730. *Assistance:* Financial

Connecticut Product Development Corporation, 93 Oak Street, Hartford 06106. Contact Mr. Jack Frazier at (203) 566-2920. *Assistance:* Financial

Connecticut State Small Business Office, Connecticut Department of Economic Development, 210 Washington Street, Hartford 06106. Contact Mr. Frank Silva at (203) 566-4051. *Assistance:* Procurement/Business planning/Financial/Information/Management/Technical

Connecticut Technology Assistance Center, Connecticut Department of Economic Development, 210 Washington Street, Hartford 06106. Contact Mr. Eric Ott at (203) 566-4587 or 556-5022. *Assistance:* Training/Business planning/Financial/Information/Networking/Technical

Technical Assistance, Connecticut Department of Economic Development, 210 Washington Street, Hartford 06106. Contact Mr. Graham Waldron at (203) 566-3887. *Assistance:* Site selection assistance/Business planning/Financial/Information/Technical

Delaware (DE)

Small Business Advocate, Delaware Development Office, 99 Kings Highway, P.O. Box 1401, Dover 19903. Contact Mr. Gary Smith at (302) 736-4271. *Assistance:* Financial/Information/Networking

Small Business Development Center, Suite 005 Purnell Hall, University of Delaware, Newark 19716. Contact Ms. Helene R. Butler at (302) 451-2747. *Assistance:* Business planning/Financial/Information/Management/Networking/Technical

District of Columbia (DC)

District of Columbia Department of Employment Services, 500 C Street, N.W., Washington 20001. Contact Mr. Larry Brown at (202) 639-1000. *Assistance:* Training/Job placement/Information/Networking/Technical

Economic Development Finance Corporation, 1660 L Street, N.W., Washington 20036. Contact (202) 775-8815. *Assistance:* This quasi-public, non-profit corporation assists District-based businesses or entrepreneurs particularly those owned by women and minorities.

Financial Services Division, Office of Business and Economic Development, 1111 E Street, N.W., Suite 700, Washington 20004. Contact Ms. Pamela Vaughn Cooke Henry at (202) 727-6600. *Assistance:* Financial. *Eligibility:* Smaller businesses

Minority Business Opportunity Commission, 2000 14th Street, N.W., Washington 20009. Contact Ms. Maudine R. Cooper at (202) 939-8780. *Assistance:* Certification/Business planning/Information/Networking

Technical Services Division, Office of Business and Economic Development, 1111 E Street, N.W., Washington DC 20004. Contact Mr. Raymond Skinner at (202) 727-6600. *Assistance:* Financial/Information/Networking/Technical

Florida (FL)

Business Service Program, Bureau of Business Assistance, Florida Department of Commerce, 107 West Gaines Street, Tallahassee 32399-2000. Contact Mr. James Hosler at 1 (800) 342-0771 (in state) or (904) 488-9357. *Assistance:* Information/Networking.

Entrepreneurship Program, Bureau of Business Development, Florida Department of Commerce, 107 West Gaines Street, Tallahassee 32399-2000. Contact Mr. James Hosler at (904) 488-9357. *Assistance:* Information/Networking

Financial Service, Bureau of Business Assistance, Florida Department of Commerce, 107 West Gaines Street, Tallahassee 32399-2000. Contact Mr. James Hosler at (904) 488-9357. *Assistance:* Financial/Information/Networking

Florida Economic Development Center, 335 College of Business, Florida State University, Tallahassee 32306-1007. Contact Mr. Roy Thompson at (904) 644-1044. *Assistance:* Business planning/Financial/Information/Networking/Technical

Florida Entrepreneurial Network, Florida State University, Florida Economic Development Center, College of Business, Room 335, Tallahassee 32306-1007. Contact Mr. Roy Thompson at (904) 644-1044. *Assistance:* Information/Networking/Technical

Florida Small Business Development Centers, University of West Florida, Pensacola 32514. Contact Mr. Gregory Higgins at (904) 474-3016. *Assistance:* Business planning/Information/Management/Networking/Technical. *Eligibility:* Smaller businesses

NASA/Southern Technology Applications Center, University of Florida, One Progress Boulevard, Box 24, Alachua 32615. Contact Mr. J. Ronald Thornton at (904)

392-0854. *Assistance:* Information/Networking/Technical

Product Innovation Center, The Progress Center, One Progress Boulevard, Box 7, Alachua, 32615. Contact Ms. Pamela H. Riddle at (904) 462-3942. *Assistance:* Legal/Business planning/Financial/Information/Management/Networking/Technical. *Eligibility:* Smaller businesses

Georgia (GA)

Advanced Technology Development Center, 430 Tenth Street, N.W., Suite N-116, Atlanta 30318. Contact (404) 894-3575. *Assistance:* Information/Networking/Technical

Economic Development Division, Economic Development Laboratory, Georgia Tech Research Institute, Atlanta 30332. Contact Mr. Arthur Brown at (404) 894-6121. *Assistance:* Business planning/Information/Technical

Georgia Department of Community Affairs, 1200 Equitable Building, 100 Peachtree Street, Small Business Revitalization Program, Atlanta 30303. Contact Mr. Steve Storey at (404) 656-6200. *Assistance:* Financial/Information/Networking/Technical

Georgia Productivity Center, Georgia Institute of Technology, Atlanta 30332. Contact (404) 894-6101. *Assistance:* Business planning/Information/Networking/Technical

Technical Assistance Center, Atlanta University, Inc., 223 James P. Brawley Drive, Atlanta 30314. Contact Mr. LeRoy Rankin at (404) 653-8444. *Assistance:* Business planning/Technical. *Eligibility:* Minority-owned businesses

The Small Business Development Center, College of Business Administration, Brooks Hall, The University of Georgia, Athens, GA 30601. Contact Mr. Frank Hoy at (404) 542-5760. *Assistance:* Business planning/Information/Networking/Technical

Hawaii (HI)

Department of Agriculture, State of Hawaii, 1428 South King Street, Honolulu 96814. Contact (808) 548-7106. *Assistance:* Financial/Information/Networking/Technical

Deputy Attorney General, State of Hawaii, 335 Merchant Street, Room 241A, Honolulu 96813. Contact (808) 548-6744. *Assistance:* Information/Technical

Financial Assistance Branch, Department of Business and Economic Development, 250 South King Street, Honolulu 96813. Contact (808) 548-4617. *Assistance:* Financial/Information/Networking. *Eligibility:* Smaller businesses

Industry and Product Promotion, Business Development Branch, Department of Business and Economic Development, P.O. Box 2359, Honolulu 96804. Contact (808) 548-4613. *Assistance:* Business planning/Information/Networking

International Services Branch, Department of Business and Economic Development, P.O. Box 2359, Honolulu 96804. Contact (808) 548-3048. *Assistance:* Business planning/Information/Networking

Pacific Business Center Program, College of Business Administration, 2404 Maile Way, Honolulu 96822. Contact (808) 948-6286. *Assistance:* Business planning/Management/Technical. *Eligibility:* Smaller businesses

Small Business Information Service, Department of Planning and Economic Development, 250 South King Street, Room 724, Honolulu 96813. Contact (808) 548-7645. *Assistance:* Business planning/Information/Networking

Idaho (ID)

Idaho Business and Economic Development Center, 1910 University Drive, Boise State University, Boise 83725. Contact Mr. Ronald R. Hall at (208) 385-3857. *Assistance:* Business planning/Information/Management/Networking/Technical

Idaho Department of Commerce, Hall of Mayors, 2nd Floor, 700 West State Street, Boise 83720. Contact (208) 334-2470. *Assistance:* Business planning/Financial/Information/Networking/Technical

Idaho Small Business Development Center, 1910 University Drive, Boise State University, Boise 83725. Contact (208) 385-1640. *Assistance:* Business planning/Information/Management/Networking/Technical. *Eligibility:* Smaller businesses

Region District Associations, Idaho Department of Commerce, Statehouse, Boise 83720. Contact Mr. Gordon Thompson at (208) 334-2470. *Assistance:* Business planning / Financial / Information / Networking/Technical

Illinois (IL)

Advocacy Division, Illinois Department of Commerce and Community Affairs, 100 West Randolph Street, Chicago 60601. Contact Mr. Paul Gibson at (312) 917-3982. *Assistance:* Financial/Information/Management/Networking/Technical. *Eligibility:* Minority-owned businesses

Bond Programs, Illinois Development Finance Authority, 2 North Vascant Street, Chicago 60602. Contact (217) 782-6861. *Assistance:* Financial

Business Expansion Assistance, Division of Marketing, Illinois Department of Commerce and Community Affairs, 620 East Adams Street, Springfield 62701. Contact (217) 782-6861. For the Chicago area, contact State of Illinois Center, 100 West Randolph Street, (312) 917-3133. *Assistance:* Information/Networking

Center for Urban Economic Development, School of Urban Planning and Policy, The University of Illinois at Chicago, Box 4348, Chicago 60680. Contact (312) 996-2178. *Assistance:* Business planning/Information/Technical

Export Assistance, Illinois Department of Commerce and Community Affairs, 620 East Adams Street, Springfield 62701. Contact Mr. Charlie Reed at (312) 917-2088. For the Chicago area, contact State of Illinois Center, 100 West Randolph Street, (312) 917-3133. *Assistance:* Information/Networking/Technical

Export Council, 321 North Clark Street, 5th Floor, Chicago, 60610. Contact Mr. Robert H. Newtson at (312) 917-5220. *Assistance:* Information/Networking/Technical

Export Development Authority, 321 North Clark Street, 5th Floor, Chicago 60610. Contact Mr. John Kerwitz at (312) 917-3401. *Assistance:* Financial/Information

Export Financing, Illinois Export Development, 321 North Clark, Chicago 60610-4714. Contact Mr. John Kerwitz at (312) 793-4982. *Assistance:* Financial/Technical

I-TEC Program, Illinois Department of Commerce and Community Affairs, 100 West Randolph Street, Chicago 60601. Contact Ms. Barbara Campbell at (312) 917-3982. *Assistance:* Information/Networking/Technical

Illinois Enterprise Zone Program, Illinois Department of Commerce and Community Affairs, 620 East Adams Street, Springfield 62701. Contact Mr. Jeff Johnson at (217) 785-6148. For the Chicago area, contact State of Illinois Center, 100 West Randolph Street, (312) 917-3133. *Assistance:* Information/Management/Networking/Technical

Illinois Resource Network, Illinois Department of Commerce and Community Affairs, 100 West Randolph Street, Chicago, 60601. Contact Ms. Barb Campbell at (217) 785-6130. *Assistance:* Information/Networking

Illinois Software Association, 20 N. Wacker Drive, Suite 1929, Chicago 60606. Contact Ms. Sheridan Turner at (312) 641-0311. *Assistance:* Training/Information/Networking

Industrial Health and Safety Consultation, Illinois Department of Commerce and Community Affairs, 620 East Adams Street, Springfield 62701. Contact (217) 782-6861. For the Chicago area, contact State of Illinois Center, 100 West Randolph Street; (312) 917-3133. *Assistance:* Technical

Inventor's Council, 53 West Jackson, Chicago 60604. Contact Mr. Donald Moyer at (312) 939-3329. *Assistance:* Networking/Technical

Job Training Program, Illinois Department of Commerce and Community Affairs, 620 East Adams Street, Springfield 62701. Contact Mr. Jerry Burger at (217) 785-6006. For the Chicago Area, contact State of Illinois Center, 100 West Randolph Street, (312) 917-3133. *Assistance:* Training/Financial

Large Business Development Program, Illinois Department of Commerce and Community Affairs, 620 East Adams Street, Springfield 62701. Contact (217) 782-6861. For the Chicago area, contact State of Illinois Center, 100 West Randolph Street; (312) 917-3133. *Assistance:* Financial

One-Stop Permit Center, Illinois Department of Commerce and Community Affairs, 620 East Adams Street, Springfield 62701. Contact 1 (800) 252-2923 (in state) or (217) 785-7546. For the Chicago area, contact State of Illinois Center, 100 West Randolph Street; (312) 917-3133. *Assistance:* Information

Procurement Assistance Program, Illinois Department of Commerce and Community Affairs, 620 East Adams Street, Springfield 62701. Contact Mr. Mark Petrilli or Mr. Pete Ramirez at (217) 785-6165. *Assistance:* Information/Technical

Program Development Division, Illinois Department of Commerce and Community Affairs, 620 East Adams Street, Springfield 62701. Contact (217) 785-6130. For the Chicago area, contact State of Illinois Center, 100 West Randolph Street; (312) 917-3133. *Assistance:* Information/Networking/Technical

Sites, Buildings, and Community Profile Program, Illinois Department of Commerce and Community Affairs, 620 East Adams Street, Springfield 62701. Contact Mr. Tom Hamrick at (217) 785-6167. For the Chicago area, contact State of Illinois Center, 100 West Randolph Street; (312) 917-3133. *Assistance:* Information

Small Business Development Centers, Illinois Department of Commerce and Community Affairs, 620 East Adams Street, Springfield 62701. Contact Mr. Pete Ramerez or Mr. Mark Grant at (217) 785-7549. For the Chicago area, contact State of Illinois Center, 100 West Randolph Street; (312) 917-3133. *Assistance:* Business planning/Information/Networking/Technical. *Eligibility:* Smaller businesses

Small Business Development Program, Illinois Department of Commerce and Community Affairs, 620 East Adams Street, Springfield 62701. Contact (217) 782-3891. For the Chicago area, contact State of Illinois Center, 100 West Randolph Street; (312) 917-3133. *Assistance:* Financial. *Eligibility:* Smaller businesses

Small Business Energy Assistance Program, Illinois Department of Commerce and Community Affairs, 620 East Adams Street, Springfield 62701. Contact Mr. Mark Enstrom at (217) 785-2428. For the Chicago area, contact State of Illinois Center, 100 West Randolph Street (312) 917-3133. *Assistance:* Financial/Information/Technical. *Eligibility:* Smaller businesses

Small Business Financing Funds, Illinois Department of Commerce and Community Affairs, 620 East Adams Street, Springfield 62701. Contact (217) 782-3891. For the Chicago area, contact State of Illinois Center, 100 West Randolph Street; (312) 917-3133. *Assistance:* Financial. *Eligibility:* Smaller businesses

Small Business Hotline, Illinois Department of Commerce and Community Affairs, 620 East Adams Street, Springfield 62701. Contact Ms. Carolene Leslie at (800) 252-2923 or (217) 785-6130. *Assistance:* Information

Small Business Investment Companies, Illinois Department of Commerce and Community Affairs, 620 East Adams Street, Springfield 62701. Contact (217) 782-6861. For the Chicago area, contact State of Illinois Center, 100 West Randolph Street; (312) 917-3133. *Assistance:* Financial. *Eligibility:* Smaller businesses

Venture Capital and Direct Loan Programs, Illinois Development Finance Authority, 2 North Vasant Street, Chicago 60602. Contact (217) 782-6861. *Assistance:* Financial

Indiana (IN)

Agricultural Development Corporation, Division of Business and Financial Services, Indiana Department of Commerce, One North Capitol, Indianapolis 46204. Contact Mr. Jeffery S. Dorman at (317) 232-8782. *Assistance:* Financial

Basic Industries Retraining Program, Division of Business and Financial Services, Indiana Department of Commerce, One North Capitol, Indianapolis 46204. Contact (317) 232-8782. *Assistance:* Financial

Business and Industrial Development Center, Purdue University, Engineering Administration Building, West Lafayette, IN 47907. Contact (800) 821-8261. *Assistance:* Financial/Information/Networking/Technical

Business Ombudsman Office, Division of Business Expansion, Indiana Department of Commerce, One North Capitol, Indianapolis, IN 46204. Contact (800) 824-2476 (in state) or (317) 232-7304. *Assistance:* Technical

Center for Entrepreneurial Resources Research, Carmichael Hall, Ball State University, Muncie 47306. Contact Dr. B. J. Bischoff Whittaker at (800) 541-9313 (in state) or (317) 285-1588. *Assistance:* Training/Consulting/Business planning/Information/Management/Networking/Technical

Center for Research and Management Services, Indiana State University, School of Business, Terre Haute 47809. Contact (812) 232-3232. *Assistance:* Business planning/Information/Management/Technical

Commercial/Industrial Liaison, Indiana University-Purdue University Indianapolis, 355 North Lansing, Indianapolis 46202. Contact (317) 264-8285. *Assistance:* Networking

Commissioner of Agriculture, Indiana Department of Commerce, One North Capitol, Indianapolis 46204. Contact (317) 232-8770. *Assistance:* Information/Technical

Disadvantaged Business Enterprise Program, Equal Employment Opportunity Section, Indiana Department of Highways, State Office Building, Indianapolis, IN 46204. Contact (317) 232-5093. *Assistance:* DBE Certification/Technical. *Eligibility:* Minority-owned businesses

Division of Continuing Studies and Community Services, Indiana University East, 2325 Chester Blvd., Richmond 47374. Contact (317) 966-8261. *Assistance:* Training/Management

Division of Economic Analysis, Indiana Department of Commerce, One North Capitol, Indianapolis 46204. Contact Mr. Charles Sim at (317) 232-8959. *Assistance:* Information

Division of Energy Policy, Indiana Department of Commerce, One North Capitol, Indianapolis 46204. Contact (317) 232-8987. *Assistance:* Financial/Information/Technical

Division of Industrial Development, Indiana Department of Commerce, One North Capitol, Indianapolis 46204. Contact (317) 232-8888. *Assistance:* Information/Networking

Economic Development Administration University Center at IUPUI, 611 North Capitol Avenue, Indianapolis, IN 46204. Contact Ms. Lucinda Pile at (317) 262-5083. *Assistance:* Information/Networking/Technical

Enterprise Zone Program, Division of Economic Development, Indiana Department of Commerce, One North Capitol, Indianapolis 46204-2288. Contact (317) 232-8913. *Assistance:* Financial

Entrepreneur in Residence, School of Business, Indiana University, Bloomington 47405. Contact (812) 335-9200. *Assistance:* Business planning/Management/Networking. *Eligibility:* Smaller businesses

Indiana Business Research Center, Graduate School of Business, Indiana University, Bloomington, 47405. Contact (812) 335-5507. *Assistance:* Information

Indiana Employment Development Commission, Division of Business and Financial Services, Indiana Department of Commerce, One North Capitol, Indianapolis 46204. Contact Mr. Jeffrey Dorman at (317) 232-8782. *Assistance:* Issue bonds IRB's/Business planning/Financial/Information/Technical

Indiana Institute for New Business Ventures, Inc., One North Capitol, Indianapolis, 46204. Contact Mr. John E. Ridder at (317) 634-8418. *Assistance:* Information

Indiana Regional Minority Suppliers Development Council, 300 E. Fall Creek Parkway, N.D., Box 44801, Indianapolis 46224-0801. Contact (317) 923-2110. *Assistance:* Information/Networking. *Eligibility:* Minority-owned businesses

Industrial Training and Development Office, Indiana Vocational Technical College, One West 26th Street, P.O. Box 1763, Indianapolis 46206. Contact (317) 921-4772. *Assistance:* Training/Technical

Innovators Forum, Rose-Hulman Institute of Technology, 5500 Wabash Avenue, Terre Haute 47803. Contact Mr. Russell Holcomb at (812) 877-1511. *Assistance:* Networking/Technical

Institute for Molecular and Cellular Biology, Indiana University, Jordan Hall, Bloomington, 47405. Contact (812) 335-4183. *Assistance:* Technical

Institute of Transnational Business, College of Business, Ball State University, Muncie 47306. Contact (317) 285-5207. *Assistance:* Information/Technical. *Eligibility:* Smaller businesses

International Trade Division, Division of Business Expansion, Indiana Department of Commerce, One North Capitol, Indianapolis 46204. Contact (317) 232-8845. *Assistance:* Information

Inventors and Entrepreneurs Society of Indiana, Purdue University Calumet, Hammond 46323. Contact Mr. Daniel Yovich at (219) 989-2354. *Assistance:* Information/Networking

Investment Incentive Program, Division of Business and Financial Services, Indiana Department of Commerce, One North Capitol, Indianapolis 46204. Contact (317) 232-8782. *Assistance:* Financial

Materials Research Institute, Indiana University, Bloomington 47405. Contact (812) 335-9127. *Assistance:* Technical

McMillen Productivity and Design Center, Indiana Institute of Technology, 1600 East Washington Blvd., Fort Wayne 46803. Contact (219) 422-5561. *Assistance:* Technical

Minority and Women Business Development, Division of Business Expansion, Indiana Department of Commerce, One North Capitol, Indianapolis 46204-2288. Contact (317) 232-8820. *Assistance:* Certification/Business planning/Financial/Information/Management/Technical. *Eligibility:* Minority-owned businesses

Research and Graduate Development Office, Indiana University, Bryan Hall, Bloomington 47405. Contact Mr. Jeremy Dunning at (812) 335-6294. *Assistance:* Networking/Technical

SBIR Proposal Assistance, Office of Research, Ball State University, 1825 Riverside Avenue, Muncie 47306. Contact (317) 285-1600. *Assistance:* Information/Networking/Technical. *Eligibility:* Smaller businesses

Small Business Development Centers, Indiana Economic Development Council, One North Capitol Street, Indianapolis, 46204. Contact (317) 634-1690. *Assistance:* Business planning/Information/Technical. *Eligibility:* Smaller businesses

Tech Net, EDA University Center at IUPUI, 611 North Capital Avenue, Indianapolis 46204. Contact (800) 641-4434 (in state) or (317) 262-5003. *Assistance:* Information/Networking/Technical

Technical Assistance Program, Purdue University, West Lafayette 47907. Contact (317) 494-6258. *Assistance:* Business planning/Management/Technical

Technical Information Service, Purdue University, West Lafayette, 47907. Contact (317) 494-9876. *Assistance:* Information

Iowa (IA)

Business and Engineering Extension, Iowa State University of Science and Technology, Scheman Building, Ames 50011. Contact (515) 294-8815. *Assistance:* Seminars and conferences/Information/Management/Networking/Technical

Center for Industrial Research and Service, Iowa State University of Science and Technology, Ames 50011. Contact (515) 294-3420. *Assistance:* Information/Management/Networking/Technical

Community Economic Betterment Account, Department of Economic Development, 200 East Grand Avenue, Des Moines 50309. Contact (515) 281-3746. *Assistance:* Information/Networking/Technical

Economic Development Set-Aside Program, Department of Economic Development, 200 East Grand Avenue, Des Moines 50309. Contact (515) 281-3746. *Assistance:* Financial/Information/Networking/Technical

Financial Rural Economic Development, Department of Economic Development, 200 East Grand Avenue, Des Moines 50309. Contact (515) 281-2746. *Assistance:* Information/Networking/Technical. *Eligibility:* Smaller businesses

Golden Circle Loan Guaranty Fund, Small Business Development Center, Drake University, 210 Aliber Hall, Des Moines 50311. Contact (515) 271-2655. *Assistance:* Marketing/Financial/Information/Management/Technical. *Eligibility:* Smaller businesses

Industrial New Jobs Training Program, Department of Economic Development, 200 East Grand Avenue, Des Moines 50309. Contact Ms. Dory L. Briles at (515) 281-3600. *Assistance:* Training

Iowa High Technology Council, Department of Economic Development, 200 East Grand Avenue, Des Moines 50309. Contact (515) 281-3036. *Assistance:* Financial/Information/Technical

Iowa Procurement Outreach Center, Kirkwood Community College, 6301 Kirkwood Boulevard, S.W., Cedar Rapids 52406. Contact Ms. Kim Hanks at (319) 398-5666. *Assistance:* Procurement. *Eligibility:* Smaller businesses

Iowa Product Development Corporation, Department of Economic Development, 200 East Grand Avenue, Des Moines 50309. Contact Mr. Doug Dittemore at (515) 281-5451. *Assistance:* Financial

Self-Employment Loan Program, Department of Economic Development, 200 East Grand Avenue, Des Moines 50309. Contact (515) 281-4219. *Assistance:* Information/Networking/Technical

Small Business Development Center, 137 Lynn Avenue, Ames 50010. Contact Mr. Ronald A. Manning at (515) 292-6351. *Assistance:* Marketing/Innovation/Procurement/Business planning/Financial/Information/Management/Networking/Technical. *Eligibility:* Smaller businesses

Small Business Loan Program, Iowa Finance Authority, 200 East Grand Avenue, Des Moines 50309. Contact (515) 281-4058. *Assistance:* Financial

Targeted Small Business Loan and Equity Grant Program, Department of Economic Development, 200 East Grand Avenue, Des Moines 50309. Contact (515) 281-3746. *Assistance:* Information/Networking/Technical. *Eligibility:* Smaller businesses

Kansas (KS)

Center for Entrepreneurship, 008 Clinton Hall, Box 147, Wichita State University, Wichita 67208. Contact Prof. Fran Jabarra at (316) 689-3000. *Assistance:* Academic programs/Business planning/Information/Networking

Center for Productivity Enhancement, Wichita State University, Engineering, Wichita 67208-1595. Contact Dr. Richard Graham at (316) 689-3525. *Assistance:* Information/Management/Networking/Technical

Engineering Extension, Ward Hall 133, Kansas State University, Manhattan 66506. Contact (913) 532-6026. *Assistance:* Information/Technical

Institute for Economic Development, Pittsburg State University, Pittsburg 66762. Contact (316) 231-7000 Ext. 4920. *Assistance:* Business planning/Financial/Information/Management/Technical

Kansas Technology Enterprise Corporation, 400 S.W. 8th Street, Topeka 66603. Contact Dr. William G. Brundage at (913) 296-5272. *Assistance:* Financial/Information/Networking

Small Business Development Centers, Clinton Hall, Room 021, Box 148, Wichita State University, Wichita 67208. Contact Ms. Cynthia Friend at (316) 689-3193. *Assistance:* Business planning/Information/Management/Networking/Technical. *Eligibility:* Smaller businesses

Kentucky (KY)

Business and Technology Office, Kentucky Commerce Cabinet, Capital Plaza Tower, Frankfort 40601. Contact Dr. D. M. Stein at (502) 564-7670. *Assistance:* Information/Networking

Business Development Center, College of Business and Economics, University of Kentucky, Lexington 40506-0205. Contact Mr. James G. Owen at (606) 257-7668. *Assistance:* Business planning

Business Information Clearinghouse, Kentucky Commerce Cabinet, Department of Economic Development, Capital Plaza Tower, Frankfort 40601. Contact (502) 564-4252. *Assistance:* Information

Development Finance Authority, Kentucky Commerce Cabinet, Capital Plaza Tower, Frankfort 40601. Contact (502) 564-4554. *Assistance:* Financial

Industrial Development and Marketing Division, Kentucky Commerce Cabinet, Department of Economic Development, Capital Plaza Tower, Frankfort 40601. Contact (502) 564-7140. *Assistance:* Site selection assistance/Information

International Marketing Office, Kentucky Commerce Cabinet, Capital Plaza Tower, Frankfort 40601. Contact (502) 564-2170. *Assistance:* Foreign investment

Kentucky Small Business Development Center, University of Kentucky, 18 Porter Building, Lexington 40506-0205. Contact Mr. James G. Owen at (606) 257-7668. *Assistance:* Business planning/Information/Technical. *Eligibility:* Smaller businesses

Minority Business Division, Kentucky Commerce Cabinet, Department of Economic Development, Capital Plaza Tower, Frankfort 40601. Contact (502) 564-2064. *Assistance:* Information

NASA/University of Kentucky Technology Applications Program, University of Kentucky, 109 Kinkead Hall, Lexington 40506-0057. Contact Ms. Sally Crouch at (606) 257-6322. *Assistance:* Information

Small Business Division, Kentucky Commerce Cabinet, Department of Economic Development, Capital Plaza Tower, Frankfort 40601. Contact (502) 564-4252. *Assistance:* Information

Louisiana (LA)

Department of Commerce, P.O. Box 94185, Baton Rouge, 70804-9185. Contact (504) 342-5361. *Assistance:* Site selection assistance/Financial/Information/Networking

Economic Development Center, College of Business Administration, University of New Orleans, New Orleans 70122. Contact Dr. Ivan J. Miestchovich (504) 286-6663 or 286-6978. *Assistance:* Business planning/Information/Management/Networking/Technical

Louisiana Minority Business Development Authority, Department of Commerce, P.O. Box 94185, Baton Rouge 70804-9185. Contact (504) 342-5363. *Assistance:* Financial/Information/Management/Networking

Louisiana Small Business Development Center, Northeast Louisiana University, College of Business Administration, Monroe, 71209. Contact Dr. John Baker at (318) 342-2464. *Assistance:* Business planning/Information/Management/Technical

Louisiana Small Business Equity Corporation, Department of Commerce, 4521 Jamestown Avenue, Baton Rouge 70808. Contact (504) 925-4112. *Assistance:* Financial

Xavier University Economic Development Center, 7325 Palmetto Street, New Orleans 70125. Contact (504) 483-7675. *Assistance:* Business planning/Management/Technical

Maine (ME)

Business Answers Program, Office of Business Development, Department of Economic and Community Development, State House Station 59, Augusta, 04333. Contact (800) 872-3838 (in state) or (207) 289-2658. *Assistance:* Information

Economic and Community Development Department, 193 State Street, State House Station 59, Augusta 04333. Contact (207) 289-2656. *Assistance:* Business planning/Financial/Information/Networking

Maine Development Foundation, One Memorial Circle, Augusta 04330. Contact (207) 622-6345. *Assistance:* Business planning/Information/Networking/Technical

Small Business Development Center, Center for Research and Advanced Study, University of Southern Maine, 246 Deering Avenue, Portland 04102. Contact Mr. Robert H. Hird at (207) 780-4420. *Assistance:* Business planning/Financial/Information/Management/Networking/Technical

The New Enterprise Institute, Center for Research and Advanced Study, University of Southern Maine, 246 Deering Avenue, Portland 04102. Contact Dr. Richard J. Clarey at (207) 780-4420. *Assistance:* Business planning/Information/Management/Networking/Technical

Maryland (MD)

Development Credit Corporation of Maryland, Maryland Department of Economic and Employment Development, 217 East Redwood Street, Baltimore 21202. Contact 1 (800) 654-7336 (in state) or (301) 269-3514. *Assistance:* Financial

Development Credit Fund, Inc., 1925 Eutaw Place, Baltimore 21217. Contact Mr. Ackneil Muldraw at (301) 223-6400. *Assistance:* Financial. *Eligibility:* Minority-owned businesses.

Maryland Business Assistance Center, Maryland Department of Economic and Employment Development, 45 Calvert Street, Annapolis 21401. Contact 1 (800) 654-7336 (in state) or (301) 974-2945. *Assistance:* Financial/Information/Networking/Technical

Maryland Economic Development Corporation, 36 S. Charles Street, Suite 1911, Baltimore 21201. Contact Mr. Hans F. Mayer at (301) 625-0051. *Assistance:* Marketing/Financial/Information/Networking

Maryland Energy Financing Administration, Maryland Department of Economic and

Employment Development, 217 East Redwood Street, Baltimore 21202. Contact 1 (800) 654-7336 (in state) or (301) 333-6985. *Assistance:* Financial

Maryland Industrial Development Financing Authority, Maryland Department of Economic and Employment Development, 217 East Redwood Street, Baltimore 21202. Contact 1 (800) 654-7336 (in state) or (301) 333-6985. *Assistance:* Financial

Maryland Industrial Training Program, Maryland Department of Economic and Employment Development, 217 East Redwood Street, Baltimore 21202. Contact 1 (800) 654-7336 (in state) or (301) 333-6985. *Assistance:* Technical

Maryland Office of Business and Industrial Development, Maryland Department of Economic and Employment Development, 217 East Redwood Street, Baltimore 21202. Contact 1 (800) 654-7336 (in state) or (301) 333-6985. *Assistance:* Financial/Information/Technical

Maryland Small Business Development Financing Authority, Maryland Department of Economic and Employment Development, 217 East Redwood Street, Baltimore 21202. Contact 1 (800) 654-7336 (in state) or (301) 333-6985. *Assistance:* Financial. *Eligibility:* Smaller businesses

Technology Extension Service, University of Maryland, Engineering Research Center, College Park 20742-3261. Contact Mr. W. Travis Walton at (301) 454-7941. *Assistance:* Productivity audits/Information/Networking/Technical

Massachusetts (MA)

Business Information Line, Massachusetts Office of Business Development, 100 Cambridge Street, Boston, MA 02202. Contact Mr. Robert P. Higgins at 1 (800) 632-8181 (in state) or (617) 727-3207. *Assistance:* State Regulations/Business planning/Financial/Information/Networking/Technical

Community Development Finance Corporation, 131 State Street, Suite 600, Boston 02109. Contact (617) 742-0366. *Assistance:* Financial. *Eligibility:* Smaller businesses

Economic Development Center, 203 Hampshire House, University of Massachusetts, Amherst 01003. Contact (413) 549-4930. *Assistance:* Business planning/Information/Networking/Technical

Employment Security Division, Charles F. Hurley Building, Government Center, Boston 02114. Contact Ms. Marlene B. Seltzer at (617) 727-6600. *Assistance:* Training/Business planning/Financial/Information/Management/Networking/Technical

Financial Development Office, Massachusetts Office of Business Development, 100 Cambridge Street, Boston 02202. Contact Mr. David Sheahan at (617) 727-3211. *Assistance:* Information/Networking

Massachusetts Business Development Corporation, One Liberty Square, Boston 02109. Contact Mr. Kenneth J. Smith at (617) 350-8877. *Assistance:* Financial

Massachusetts Industrial Finance Agency, 400 Atlantic Avenue, Boston 02110. Contact (617) 451-2477. *Assistance:* Financial

Massachusetts Technology Development Corporation, 84 State Street, Suite 500, Boston 02109. Contact Mr. John F. Hodgman at (617) 723-4920. *Assistance:* Financial. *Eligibility:* Smaller businesses

Massport Trade Development Unit, Boston World Trade Center, Boston 02210. Contact Ms. Susan Rowan at (617) 439-5560. *Assistance:* Marketing/Business planning/Information/Networking/Technical

Minority and Women Business Assistance Office, Massachusetts Office of Economic Affairs, 100 Cambridge Street, Room 1300, Boston 02202. Contact (617) 727-8692. *Assistance:* Information/Networking/Technical. *Eligibility:* Minority-owned businesses

Site Inventory Tracking Exchange, Massachusetts Office of Business Development, 100 Cambridge Street, Boston 02202. Contact (617) 727-3215. *Assistance:* Real estate locations/Information

Small Business Assistance Division, Massachusetts Office of Business Development, 100 Cambridge Street, Boston 02202. Contact (617) 727-4005. *Assistance:* Business planning/Financial/Information/Networking. *Eligibility:* Smaller businesses

Michigan (MI)

Environmental Research Institute of Michigan, P.O. Box 8618, Ann Arbor 48107. Contact Mr. George Peace at (313) 994-1200. *Assistance:* Technical

Food Industry Institute, 201 Food Science Building, Michigan State University, East Lansing 48824. Contact Dr. William Hailles at (517) 355-8295. *Assistance:* Business planning/Information/Management/Technical

Industrial Development Institute, Michigan State University, D130 West Fee, East Lansing 48824. Contact Mr. Michael Martin at (517) 355-0143. *Assistance:* Business planning/Information/Networking/Technical

Industrial Technology Institute, P.O. Box 1485, Ann Arbor 48106. Contact Mr. John G. Sulewski at (313) 769-4000. *Assistance:* Information/Management/Technical

Institute of Science and Technology, The University of Michigan, 2200 Bonisteel Boulevard, Ann Arbor 48109. Contact Mr. Larry R. Crockett at (313) 763-9000. *Assistance:* Business planning/Financial/Information/Management/Networking/Technical

Manufacturing Development Group, P.O. Box 30225, Lansing 48909. Contact (517) 373-8495. *Assistance:* Financial/Information/Technical

Metropolitan Center for High Technology, 2727 Second Avenue, Detroit 48201. Contact Mr. Charles Henderson at (313) 963-0616. *Assistance:* Incubation/Business planning/Information/Networking/Technical. *Eligibility:* Smaller businesses

Michigan Biotechnology Institute, P.O. Box 27609, Lansing 48909. Contact Dr. Jack H. Pincus at (517) 355-2277. *Assistance:* Business planning/Information/Networking/Technical

Michigan Energy and Resource Research Association, 328 Executive Plaza, 1200 Sixth Street, Detroit 48226. Contact Mr. Todd Anuskiewicz at (313) 964-5030. *Assistance:* Information/Networking/Technical

Michigan Molecular Institute, 1910 West St. Andrews Road, Midland 48640. Contact Mr. Robert Kotchkiss at (517) 832-5587. *Assistance:* Technical

Michigan Strategic Fund, Michigan Department of Commerce, P.O. Box 30234, Lansing 48909. Contact (517) 373-7550. *Assistance:* Financial

Michigan Technology Deployment Service, Michigan Modernization Service, Michigan Department of Commerce, 2901 Hubbard, Ann Arbor 48109. Contact (313) 769-4664. *Assistance:* Financial/Information/Networking/Technical

New Enterprise Services Office, Michigan Modernization Service, Michigan Department of Commerce, 2901 Hubbard, Ann Arbor 48109 Contact (313) 769-4664. *Assistance:* Financial/Information/Networking

Research on Integrated Manufacturing Center, University of Michigan College of Engineering, 170 Advanced Technology Laboratory, Ann Arbor 48109-2110. Contact Mr. Robert W. Schneider at (313) 763-5630. *Assistance:* Technical

Small Business Development Center, 1107 Hazeltine Boulevard, Chaska 55318. Contact (612) 448-8810. *Assistance:* Training/Business planning/Information. *Eligibility:* Smaller businesses

Technology Transfer Network, Michigan Department of Commerce, P.O. Box 30225, Lansing, 48909. Contact Ms. Sharon Woollard at (517) 335-2139. *Assistance:* Business planning/Financial/Information/Networking/Technical

Workforce Development Group, Governor's Office for Job Training, 222 Hollister Building, Lansing 48933. Contact (313) 769-4664 (Ms. Sharon English) or (517) 373-6227 (Ms. Phyllis Grummon). *Assistance:* Training

Minnesota (MN)

College of St. Thomas Entrepreneurial Enterprise Center, 1107 Hazeltine Boulevard, Chaska 55318. Contact (612) 448-8800. *Assistance:* Business planning/Information/Networking/Technical. *Eligibility:* Smaller businesses

Community Development Division, Department of Trade and Economic Development, 900 American Center Building, 150 East Kellogg Boulevard, St. Paul 55101. Contact Mr. Bob Benner at (612) 296-5005. *Assistance:* Financial

Department of Trade and Economic Development, 900 American Center Building, 150 East Kellogg Boulevard, St. Paul 55101. Contact Mr. David Speer at (612) 296-6424. *Assistance:* Business planning/Information/Networking/Technical

Development Resources Program, Department of Trade and Economic Development, 900 American Center Building, 150 East Kellogg Boulevard, St. Paul 55101. Contact Mr. Harry Rosefelt at (612) 296-5010. *Assistance:* Financial/Information/Networking/Technical

Inno-Media, 230 Tenth Avenue South, Minneapolis 55415. Contact Mr. Sam Koutavas at (612) 342-4311. *Assistance:* Product development/Business planning/Information/Networking/Technical

Job Training Office, Department of Jobs and Training, 690 American Center Building, 150 East Kellogg Boulevard, St. Paul 55101. Contact 1 (800) 652-9747 (in state) or (612) 296-8004. *Assistance:* Information

Jobs Services, Department of Jobs and Training, 390 North Robert Street, St. Paul 55101. Contact 1 (800) 652-9747 (in state) or (612) 296-3625. *Assistance:* Information

Minnesota Cooperation Office, 1005 Southgate Office Plaza, 5001 West 80th Street, Bloomington 55437. Contact Mr. Theodore A. Johnson at (612) 830-1230. *Assistance:* Business planning/Information/Networking/Technical. *Eligibility:* Smaller businesses

Minnesota Project Innovation, Inc., 1107 Hazeltine Boulevard, Chasta 55318. Contact Mr. James W. Swiderski at (612) 448-8826. *Assistance:* Proposal preparation/Business planning/Financial/Information/Networking/Technical. *Eligibility:* Smaller businesses

Minnesota Trade Office, Department of Trade and Economic Development, 1000 World Trade Center, 30 East 7th Street, St. Paul 55101-4902. Contact Mr. Michael A. Olson at (612) 297-4222. *Assistance:* Information/Networking

Science and Technologies Office, 900 American Center Building, 150 East Kellogg Boulevard, St. Paul 55101. Contact (612) 297-1554. *Assistance:* Business planning/Financial/Information/Networking/Technical

Small Business Assistance Office, Department of Trade and Economic Development, 900 American Center Building, 150 East Kellogg Boulevard, St. Paul 55101. Contact (612) 296-3871. *Assistance:* Business planning/Information

University Research Consortium, Minneapolis Business and Technology Center, 511 11th Avenue South, Minneapolis 55415. Contract Dr. Ellen Fitzgerald at (612) 341-0122. *Assistance:* Business planning/Information/Management/Networking/Technical

Mississippi (MS)

Finance Division Department of Economic Development, P.O. Box 849, Jackson 39205. Contact Mr. E. F. Mitcham at (601) 359-3437. *Assistance:* Financial

Industrial Division Department of Economic Development, P.O. Box 849, Jackson 39205. Contact Mr. Roy Braswell at (601) 359-3439. *Assistance:* Information/Networking

Institute for Technology Development, 700 North State Street, Suite 500, Jackson 39202. Contact Neil Yawn at (601) 960-3615. *Assistance:* Information/Networking/Technical

Marketing Division Department of Economic Development, P.O. Box 849, Jackson 39205. Contact Mr. Bill McGinnis at (601) 359-3444. *Assistance:* Information/Technical

Mississippi Research and Development Center, 3825 Ridgewood Rd., Jackson 39211-6453. Contact Ms. Joyce Lewis at (601) 982-6231. *Assistance:* Business planning/Management/Networking/Technical

Missouri (MO)

Business and Industry Extension Service, 821 Clark Hall, University of Missouri-Columbia, Columbia 65211. Contact Dr. Tom Henderson at (314) 882-4321. *Assistance:* Business planning/Information/Networking/Technical

Enterprise Zones Program, Missouri Department of Economic Development, P.O. Box 118, Jefferson City 65102. Contact Mr. Bob Simonds at (314) 751-4241. *Assistance:* Financial/Technical

Financial Programs, Missouri Department of Economic Development, P.O. Box 118, Jefferson City 65102. Contact Mr. Mike Downing at (314) 751-4241. *Assistance:* Financial

High Technology Program, Missouri Department of Economic Development, P.O. Box 118, Jefferson City 65102. Contact Mr. John S. Johnson at (314) 751-4241. *Assistance:* Information/Networking/Technical

Industrial Development Time Deposit Program, Missouri Department of Economic Development, P.O. Box 118, Jefferson City 65102. Contact Mr. Mike Downing at (314) 751-4241. *Assistance:* Financial

Institute for Economic Development, Pittsburg State University, Pittsburg, KS 66762. Contact (316) 231-7000 Ext. 4920. *Assistance:* Business planning/Financial/Information/Management/Technical

Missouri Corporation for Science and Technology, Missouri Department of Economic Development, P.O. Box 118, Jefferson City 65102. Contact Mr. John Johnson at (314) 751-3906. *Assistance:* Business planning/Financial/Information/Networking/Technical

On-The-Job Training, Division of Employment Security, P.O. Box 59, Jefferson City 65104. Contact Mr. Bruce Carnet at (314) 751-3215. *Assistance:* Training

Small Business Development Office, Missouri Department of Economic Development, P.O. Box 118, Jefferson City 65102. Contact Mr. Phillip L. Gaffke at (314) 751-4982. *Assistance:* Financial/Information/Technical

Montana (MT)

Agriculture Marketing Assistance, Department of Agriculture, Sixth & Roberts, Helena 59620. Contact Mr. Moe Wosepka at (406) 444-2402. *Assistance:* Information/Technical

Business Assistance Division, Department of Commerce, 1424 Ninth Avenue, Helena 59620. Contact Ms. Carol Daly at (406) 444-3923. *Assistance:* Rural development/Marketing/Business planning/Financial/Information/Management/Networking/Technical.

Development Finance Technical Assistance, Business Assistance Division, Department of Commerce, 1424 Ninth Avenue, Helena 59620. Contact Mr. Barry Roose or Ms. Delrene Rasmussen at (406) 444-3923. *As-*

sistance: Business planning/Financial/Information/Networking/Technical

Disadvantaged Business Enterprise and Women Business Enterprise, Department of Highways, Capital Station, Helena 59620. Contact Mr. Raymond D. Brown at (406) 444-6333. *Assistance:* Business planning / Information / Management / Networking/Technical

Economic Development Center, North Dakota State University, Fargo, ND 58102. Contact Dr. Robert L. Sullivan at (701) 237-8873. *Assistance:* Business planning/Financial/Information/Management/Networking/Technical

Entrepreneurship Center, 412 Reid Hall, Montana State University, Bozeman 59717. Contact (406) 994-4423. *Assistance:* Business planning/Financial/Information/Management/Technical. *Eligibility:* Smaller businesses

International Export Assistance, Business Assistance Division, Department of Commerce, 1424 Ninth Avenue, Helena 59620. Contact Mr. John J. Maloney at (406) 444-4380. *Assistance:* Information/Technical.

Montana Science and Technology Alliance, Department of Commerce, 46 North Last Chance Gulch, Suite 2B, Helena 59620. Contact Mr. Frank Culver at (406) 449-2778. *Assistance:* Financial/Information/Networking/Technical

Product Marketing Assistance, Business Assistance Division, Department of Commerce, 1424 Ninth Avenue, Helena 59620. Contact Mr. Gene Marcille at (406) 444-4392. *Assistance:* Information/Networking

Renewable Energy and Conservation Program, Grant & Loan Section, Department of Natural Resources & Conservation, 1520 East Sixth Avenue, Helena 59620. Contact Mr. Greg Mills at (406) 444-6774. *Assistance:* Financial/Information/Technical

Small Business Advocate and Business Licensing Center, Business Assistance Division, Department of Commerce, 1424 Ninth Avenue, Helena 59620. Contact Ms. Rebecca R. Baumann at 1 (800) 221-8015 (in state) or (406) 444-3923. *Assistance:* Information

Nebraska (NE)

Food Processing Center, University of Nebraska-Lincoln, 134 Filley Hall, East Campus, Lincoln 68583-0919. Contact Dr. Steve Taylor at (402) 472-2831. *Assistance:* Marketing/Information/Networking/Technical

Nebraska Development Business Centers, University of Nebraska-Omaha, College of Business Administration, Omaha 68182. Contact Mr. Bob Bernier at (402) 554-2521. *Assistance:* Marketing/Business planning/Information/Management

Nebraska Technical Assistance Center, University of Nebraska-Lincoln, W191 Nebraska Hall, Lincoln 68588-0535. Contact Mr. Herbert Hoover at (402) 472-5600. *Assistance:* Patent/Information/Networking/Technical

One-Stop Business Assistance Center, Department of Economic Development, P.O. Box 94666, 301 Centennial Mall South, Lincoln 68509-4666. Contact Mr. Steve Williams at (402) 471-3782 or (800) 425-6505. *Assistance:* Business planning/Financial/Information/Management/Networking/Technical

Small Business Division, Department of Economic Development, P.O. Box 9466, 301 Centennial Mall South, Lincoln 68509-4666. Contact Mr. Gary Targoff at (800) 426-6505 or (402) 471-3742. *Assistance:* Procurement/Business planning/Financial/Information / Management / Networking / Technical

Nevada (NV)

City of Las Vegas Loan Program, 400 E. Stewart, Las Vegas 89101. Contact Mr. Jack Thomason at (702) 386-6551. *Assistance:* Site selection assistance/Financial/Information/Technical

Commission on Economic Development, Capitol Complex, 600 E. William, Suite 203, Carson City 89710. Contact Mr. Andrew P. Grose at (702) 885-4325. *Assistance:* Financial

Nevada Small Business Development Center, University of Nevada-Reno, College of Business Administration, Business Building, Room 411, Reno 89557-0100. Contact Mr. Sam Males at (702) 784-1717. *Assistance:* Business planning/Information/Management/Technical. *Eligibility:* Smaller businesses

State Office of Community Services, Capitol Complex, Carson City 89710. Contact (702) 885-5978. *Assistance:* Financial/Information/Technical

White Pine Country Loan Programs, P.O. Box 1002, Ely 89301. Contact Ms. Karen Rajala at (702) 289-8841 or 289-8877. *Assistance:* Business planning/Financial/Information/Technical. *Eligibility:* Smaller businesses

New Hampshire (NH)

Industrial Development Office, Department of Resources and Economic Development, P.O. Box 856, Concord 03301. Contact Mr. Paul H. Guilderson at (603) 271-2591. *As-*

sistance: Business planning/Financial/Information /Networking/Technical

Industrial Development–Export Assistance Program, Department of Resources and Economic Development, P.O. Box 856, Concord 03301. Contact Mr. Paul H. Guilderson at (603) 271-2591. *Assistance:* Business planning/Information/Networking/Technical

Small Business Development Center, University Center, Room 311, 400 Commercial Street, Manchester 03101. Contact Mr. James E. Bean at 1 (800) 322-0390 or (603) 625-4522. *Assistance:* Business planning/ Financial / Information / Management / Networking/Technical. *Eligibility:* Smaller businesses

New Jersey (NJ)

Business Advocacy Office, Department of Commerce, Energy, and Economic Development, 20 West State Street, Trenton 08625. Contact Mr. Paul Krane at (609) 292-0700. *Assistance:* Information/Networking/ Technical

Business Development Office, Department of Commerce, Energy, and Economic Development, CN 823, Trenton 08625. Contact Mr. Jsoeph R. Ridolfi at (609) 292-2462. *Assistance:* Site selection assistance/Business planning/Financial/Information/Networking/Technical

Commission on Science and Technology, 122 West State Street, CN 832, Trenton 08625. Contact Mr. Edward Cohen at (609) 984-1671. *Assistance:* Financial. *Eligibility:* Smaller businesses

Economic Development Authority, 200 South Warren Street, Capital Place One, CN 990, Trenton 08625. Contact Ms. Rose Smith at (609) 292-1800. *Assistance:* Business real estate development/Financial/Technical

Hispanic Enterprise Bureau, Division of Development for Small Businesses and Women and Minority Businesses, Department of Commerce, Energy, and Economic Development, 20 West State Street, CN 835, Trenton 08625. Contact Mr. Roland A. Alum at (609) 984-9668. *Assistance:* Business planning/Financial/Information/ Management/Networking/Technical

International Trade Division, Department of Commerce and Economic Development, 744 Broad Street, Newark 07102. Contact (201) 648-3518. *Assistance:* Exporting

Minority Business Enterprise Office, Division of Development for Small Businesses and Women and Minority Businesses, Department of Commerce, Energy, and Economic Development, 20 West State Street, CN 835 Trenton 08625. Contact Mr. Lee L. Davis at (609) 292-0500. *Assistance:* Procurement/Business planning/Financial/Information/Networking/Technical

Rutgers University Technical Assistance Program, Rutgers University, 180 University Avenue, Newark 07102. Contact Ms. Patricia Johnson at (201) 648-5891. *Assistance:* Business planning/Technical. *Eligibility:* Smaller businesses

Set-Aside and Certification Office, Division of Development for Small Businesses and Women and Minority Businesses, Department of Commerce, Energy, and Economic Development, 20 West State Street, CN 835, Trenton 08625. Contact Mr. Anthony Vergara at (609) 984-9835. *Assistance:* Procurement. *Eligibility:* Smaller businesses

Small Business Assistance Office, Division of Development for Small Businesses and Women and Minority Businesses, Department of Commerce, Energy, and Economic Development, 20 West State Street, CN 835, Trenton 08625. Contact Mr. Lois G. Rand at (609) 984-4442. *Assistance:* Business planning/Financial/Information/Management/Networking/Technical. *Eligibility:* Smaller businesses and minority-owned businesses

The Port Authority of New York and New Jersey (Industrial Parks), World Trade and Economic Development Department, One World Trade Center-74 South, New York, NY 10048. Contact Mr. Roy Perez Daple at (800) 221-5468 or (212) 466-8848. *Assistance:* Site selection assistance/Financial

Women Business Enterprise Office, Division of Development for Small Businesses and Women and Minority Businesses, Department of Commerce, Energy, and Economic Development, 20 West State Street, CN 835, Trenton 08625. Contact Ms. Norma Chandler Brown at (609) 292-3862. *Assistance:* Procurement/Business planning/ Financial / Information / Management / Networking/Technical

New Mexico (NM)

Agricultural Marketing Development Office, New Mexico Department of Agriculture, New Mexico State University, P.O. Box 30005/Dept. 5600, Las Cruces 88003. Contact (505) 646-4929. *Assistance:* Information/Technical

Business Assistance and Resource Center, 1920 Lomas, N.E., Albuquerque 87131. Contact Mr. James T. Ray at (505) 277-3541. *Assistance:* Specialized NASA searches/Business planning/Financial/Information/Management/Technical

Center for Business Research and Services, New Mexico State University, Box 3CR,

Las Cruces 88003. Contact (505) 646-1434. *Assistance:* Business planning/Information/Technical

Development Training Programs, Economic Development and Tourism Department, Joseph Montoya Building, 1100 St. Francis Drive, Santa Fe 87503. Contact Mr. David Henkel at (505) 827-0300. *Assistance:* Training

New Mexico Industry Development Corporation, 300 San Mateo, N.E., Suite 200, Albuquerque 87108. Contact (505) 262-2247. *Assistance:* Financial/Technical. *Eligibility:* Smaller businesses

Research and Development Institute, 1220 South Francis Drive #358, Santa Fe 87501. Contact Dr. Larry Iceman at (505) 827-5886. *Assistance:* Financial

Technological Innovation Program, Anderson School of Management, University of New Mexico, Albuquerque 87131. Contact (505) 277-5934. *Assistance:* Business planning/Financial/Information/Management/Networking/Technical

The Economic Incentive Loan Program, Economic Development and Tourism Department, Joseph M. Montoya Building, 1100 St. Francis Drive, Sante Fe 87503. Contact (505) 827-0272. *Assistance:* Financial

New York (NY)

Business Permits and Regulatory Assistance Office, Alfred E. Smith Office Building, 17th Floor, Albany 12225. Contact (800) 342-3464 (in state) or (518) 474-8275. *Assistance:* Permit assistance

Business Services Ombudsman Program, Division for Small Business, New York State Department of Economic Development, 230 Park Avenue, New York 10169. Contact (212) 309-0462. *Assistance:* Business Planning/Financial/Information/Networking/Technical

Centers for Advanced Technology Program, New York State Science and Technology Foundation, 99 Washington Avenue, Albany 12210. Contact Mr. Vernon Ozarow at (518) 474-4347. *Assistance:* Collaborative research/Information/Networking/Technical

Corporation for Innovation Development Program, New York State Science and Technology Foundation, 99 Washington Avenue, Suite 1730, Albany 12210. Contact (518) 473-9741. *Assistance:* Business planning/Financial

Direct Loan Program, New York Job Development Authority, 605 Third Avenue, New York 10158. Contact (212) 818-1700. *Assistance:* Financial

Economic Development and Technical Assistance Center, State University of New York, Plattsburg 12901. Contact Mr. Stephen Hyde at (518) 564-2214. *Assistance:* Business planning/Information

Foreign Marketing/Export Assistance, New York State Department of Commerce, International division, 230 Park Avenue, New York 10169. Contact (212) 309-0503. *Assistance:* Exporting

Industrial Innovation Extension Service, New York State Science and Technology Foundation, 99 Washington Avenue, Suite 1730, Albany 12210. Contact Mr. Tab Wilkins at (518) 474-4349. *Assistance:* Worker training referral/Information/Networking/Technical

Industrial Materials Recycling Program, New York State Environmental Facilities Corporation, Director of Hazardous Waste Programs, 50 Wolf Road, Albany 12205. Contact (518) 457-4138.

Procurement Assistance Program, Division for Small Business, New York State Department of Economic Development, One Commerce Plaza, Albany 12245. Contact (518) 474-7756. *Assistance:* Procurement

Project STAMP (State Training and Manpower Program), Division of Small Business, New York State Department of Economic Development, 50 Court Street, Brooklyn 11201. Contact (718) 596-4120. *Assistance:* Financial

Regional Technology Development Organization, New York State Science and Technology Foundation, 99 Washington Avenue, Albany 12210. Contact Mr. Mark Tebbano at (518) 474-4349. *Assistance:* Financial/Information/Networking

Site and Building Selection Assistance, New York State Department of Commerce, Regional Technical Services Unit, One Commerce Plaza, Albany 12245. Contact (518) 473-1325. *Assistance:* Site selection assistance

Small Business Development Center, State University of New York, State University Plaza, Albany 12246. Contact Mr. James L. King at (518) 443-5398. *Assistance:* Counseling/Training/Research/Business planning/Information/Management/Technical

Small Business Innovation Research (SBIR) Promotion Program, 99 Washington Avenue, Suite 1730, Albany 12210. Contact Mr. Tab Wilkins at (518) 474-4349. *Assistance:* Research support/Business planning/Financial/Information. *Eligibility:* Smaller businesses

Small- and Medium-Sized Business Assistance, New York State Urban Development Corporation, 1515 Broadway, New York

10036. Contact (212) 930-0285. *Assistance:* Financial

The Port Authority of New York and New Jersey (Industrial Parks), World Trade and Economic Development Department, One World Trade Center—74 South, New York 10048. Contact Mr. Roy Perez Daple at (800) 221-5468 or (212) 466-8848. *Assistance:* Site selection assistance/Financial

Workshops and Seminars Unit, Division of Small Business, New York State Department of Economic Development, 230 Park Avenue, New York 10169. Contact (212) 309-0465. *Assistance:* Seminars. *Eligibility:* Smaller businesses

North Carolina (NC)

Business Information Referral Center, North Carolina Department of Commerce, 430 North Salisbury Street, Raleigh 27611. Contact (919) 733-9013. *Assistance:* Referral assistance

Business/Industry Development Division, North Carolina Department of Commerce, 430 North Salisbury Street, Raleigh 27611. Contact Mr. Robert G. Brinkley at (919) 733-4151. *Assistance:* Site selection assistance/Information/Networking/Technical

Center for Applied Technology, East Carolina University, Greenville 27834. Contact (919) 757-6708. *Assistance:* Business planning/Information/Management/Technical

Improving Mountain Living Center, Western Carolina University, Cullowhee 28723. Contact Mr. Tom McClure at (704) 227-7492. *Assistance:* Business planning/Information/Management/Technical.

Industrial Extension Service, North Carolina State University, Box 7902, Raleigh, NC 27695. Contact (919) 737-2358. *Assistance:* Information/Management/Technical

Minority Business Development Agency, North Carolina Department of Commerce, 430 North Salisbury Street, Raleigh 27611. Contact Mr. Julian Brown at (919) 733-2712. *Assistance:* Business planning/Information/Networking/Technical. *Eligibility:* Minority-owned businesses

Northeastern North Carolina Tomorrow, Elizabeth City State University, Elizabeth City 27909. Contact (919) 335-3491. *Assistance:* Financial/Management

Science and Technology Research Center, P.O. Box 12235, Research Triangle Park 27709-0671. *Assistance:* Information/Technical

Small Business and Technology Development Center, 820 Clay Street, Raleigh 27605. Contact 1 (800) 258-0862 (in state) or (919) 733-4643. *Assistance:* Business planning/Financial/Management/Technical. *Eligibility:* Smaller businesses

Small Business Centers, North Carolina Department of Community Colleges, 116 West Edenton Street, Raleigh 27603-1712. Contact (919) 733-6385. *Assistance:* Training/Counseling/Information. *Eligibility:* Smaller businesses

Small Business Development Centers, North Carolina Department of Community College, 200 West Jones Street, Caswell Building, Raleigh 27603-1337. Contact Dr. Jean Overton at (919) 733-7051. *Assistance:* Business planning/Information/Networking/Technical. *Eligibility:* Smaller businesses

Small Business Development Division, North Carolina Department of Commerce, 430 North Salisbury Street, Raleigh 27611. Contact Mr. Lewis Myers at (919) 733-7980. *Assistance:* Business planning/Financial/Information/Networking. *Eligibility:* Smaller businesses

Technological Development Authority, North Carolina Department of Commerce, 430 North Salisbury Street, Raleigh 27611. Contact Mr. Brent Lane at (919) 733-7022. *Assistance:* Financial/Information. *Eligibility:* Smaller businesses

North Dakota (ND)

Bank of North Dakota, 700 East Main Avenue, Bismarck 58501. Contact Mr. Joe Lamb at (701) 224-5690. *Assistance:* Financial

Economic Development Center, North Dakota State University, Fargo 58102. Contact Dr. Robert L. Sullivan at (701) 237-8873. *Assistance:* Business planning/Financial/Information/Management/Networking/Technical

Economic Development Commission, Liberty Memorial Building, Bismarck 58505. Contact (701) 224-2810. *Assistance:* Financial/Information/Networking/Technical

Innovation and Business Development Center, University of North Dakota, Box 8103, University Station, Grand Forks 58202. Contact Mr. Bruce Gjovig at (701) 777-3132. *Assistance:* NASA Industrial Applications Center/Business planning/Information/Networking/Technical. *Eligibility:* Smaller businesses

Small Business Development Center, Liberty Memorial Building, Bismarck 58505. Contact Mr. Terry Stallman at (701) 224-2808. *Assistance:* Marketing/Information

Small Business Loan Services, P.O. Box 2443, Fargo 58108. Contact Mr. Toby Sticka at (701) 237-6132. *Assistance:* Financial

Ohio (OH)

Industrial Training Program, P.O. Box 1001, Columbus 43266-0101. Contact (614) 466-4155. *Assistance:* Training/Financial

Minority Business Development, Ohio Department of Development, P.O. Box 1001, Columbus 43266-0101. Contact (614) 462-7708. *Assistance:* Financial

Ohio Technology Transfer Organization (OTTO), 1712 Neil Avenue, Columbus 43210. Contact Dr. Robert E. Bailey at (614) 292-5485. FAX (614) 292-4315, TELEX 857233. *Assistance:* Business planning/Information/Networking/Technical

Technology Information Exchange–Innovation Network (TIE-IN), Department of Development, Ohio Data Users Center, P.O. Box 1001, Columbus 43266-0413. Contact Mr. Keith Ewald at (614) 466-2115. *Assistance:* Marketing/Information

The Thomas Edison Program, 65 East State Street, Suite 200, Columbus 43266-0330. Contact Mr. Christopher Coburn at (614) 466-3086. *Assistance:* Advanced research/Workforce training/Financial/Information

Urban Economic Development Program, Cleveland State University, Cleveland 44115. Contact Mr. Donald Iannone at (216) 687-6947. *Assistance:* Business planning/Management/Networking/Technical

Oklahoma (OK)

Association of Central Oklahoma Governments, 6600 North Harvey Place, Suite 200, Oklahoma City 73116. Contact (405) 848-8961. *Assistance:* Information/Networking/Technical

Capital Resources Network, Department of Commerce, 6601 Broadway Extension, Oklahoma City 73116. Contact (405) 843-9770. *Assistance:* Financial

Central Industrial Applications Center, Southeastern Oklahoma State University, Sta. A, Box 2584, Durant 74701-2584. Contact Dr. Dickie Deel at (405) 924-6822. *Assistance:* Information/Technical

Central Oklahoma Economic Development District, 400 N. Bell, Shawnee 74801. Contact (405) 273-6410. *Assistance:* Business planning/Financial/Information/Technical

Institute for Economic Development, Pittsburg State University, Pittsburg, KS 66762. Contact (316) 231-7000 ext. 4920. *Assistance:* Business planning/Financial/Information/Management/Technical

Oklahoma Industrial Finance Authority, Two Broadway Executive Park, 205 N.W. 63rd Street, Oklahoma City 73116-8209. Contact Mr. John G. Umdenstock at (405) 521-2182. *Assistance:* Financial

Oklahoma International Export Services, 440 South Houston, Room 505, Tulsa 74127. Contact (918) 521-2865 and 581-2806. *Assistance:* Information/Networking/Technical

Rural Enterprises, 10 Waldron Drive, P.O. Box 1335, Durant 74702-1335. Contact Ms. Jackie Meeks at (405) 924-5094. *Assistance:* Marketing/Business planning/Financial/Information/Networking/Technical

Small Business Development Center, 517 West University Boulevard, Durant 74701. Contact Mr. Lloyd Miller at (405) 924-0277. *Assistance:* Business planning/Financial/Information/Networking/Technical. *Eligibility:* Smaller businesses

South Western Oklahoma Development Authority, P.O. Box 569, Building 400, Clinton-Sherman Industrial Air Park, Burns Flats 73624. Contact (405) 562-4884. *Assistance:* Business planning/Financial/Information/Networking/Technical

Technology Transfer Center, OSU District Office, P.O. Box 1378, Ada 74820. Contact (405) 332-4100. *Assistance:* Information/Networking

Training for Industry Program, State Vo-Tech Department, 1500 West 7th Street, Stillwater 74074. Contact (405) 377-2000 ext. 337. *Assistance:* Training

University Business Assistance Center of Oklahoma, East Central University, Ada 74820. Contact Mr. Thomas Beebe at (405) 436-2422. *Assistance:* Business planning/Financial/Information/Management/Technical

Oregon (OR)

Business Development Division, Oregon Economic Development Department, 595 Cottage Street, N.E., Salem 97310. Contact (503) 373-1200. *Assistance:* Financial/Information

International Trade Division, Oregon Economic Development Department, 1500 S.W. 1st Avenue, Portland 97201. Contact (503) 229-5625. *Assistance:* Business planning/Information/Technical

Oregon Small Business Development Network, 1059 Willamette Street, Eugene 97401. Contact Ms. Barbara Cardwell at (503) 726-2250. *Assistance:* Business planning / Information / Networking / Technical. *Eligibility:* Smaller businesses

The Oregon Productivity and Technology Center, School of Industrial and General Engineering, Oregon State University, Corvallis 97331. Contact Dr. James Riggs at (503) 754-3249. *Assistance:* Business planning/Information/Technical

Pennsylvania (PA)

Appalachian Regional Commission Program, Department of Commerce, Office of Enterprise Development, 402 Forum Bldg., Harrisburg 17120. Contact Ms. Katherine Wilson at (717) 787-4791. *Assistance:* Financial/Technical

Business Infrastructure Development Program, Department of Commerce, Bureau of Financing, 494 Forum Building, Harrisburg 17120. Contact Mr. William Logan at (717) 787-7120. *Assistance:* Infrastructure improvements/Financial

Business Resource Network, Department of Commerce, 406 Forum Building, Harrisburg 17120. Contact (717) 783-5700. *Assistance:* Business planning/Information/Networking/Technical

Challenge Grants/Advanced Technology Centers, Ben Franklin Partnership, Department of Commerce, 463 Forum Building, Harrisburg 17120. Contact Mr. Jacques Koppel at (717) 787-4147. *Assistance:* Business planning/Financial/Information/Networking/Technical

Customized Job Training Program, Department of Education, Bureau of Vocational and Adult Education, 333 Market Street, Harrisburg 17126-0333. Contact Mr. Bill Krash at (717) 787-5293. *Assistance:* Financial/Technical

Employee Ownership Assistance Program, Department of Commerce, Bureau of Business Financing, 494 Forum Building, Harrisburg 17120. Contact Mr. James N. Graham at (717) 783-1768. *Assistance:* Financial/Technical

Energy Development Authority, Department of Energy, P.O. Box 8040, Harrisburg 17105. Contact Dr. Dane C. Bickley at (717) 783-9981. *Assistance:* Financial

Industrial Development Authority, Department of Commerce, Bureau of Bond and Loan Programs, 479 Forum Building, Harrisburg 17120. Contact Mr. Gerald W. Kapp, Jr. at (717) 787-6245. *Assistance:* Financial

International Investment and Trade, Department of Commerce, Forum Building, Harrisburg 17120. Contact (717) 787-7190. *Assistance:* Management/Technical

Minority and Women Business Enterprise Office, Department of General Services, 400 North Office Building, Harrisburg 17120. Contact Mr. George Fields at (717) 787-7380. *Assistance:* Business planning/Financial/Information/Networking. *Eligibility:* Minority-owned businesses

Minority Business Development Authority, Department of Commerce, Forum Building, Harrisburg 17120. Contact Mr. William Peterson at (717) 783-1127. *Assistance:* Business planning/Financial/Technical. *Eligibility:* Minority-owned businesses

NASA Industrial Applications Center, University of Pittsburgh, 823 William Pitt Union, Pittsburgh 15260. Contact Dr. Paul A. McWilliams at (412) 648-7000. *Assistance:* Marketing/Information/Technical

Pennsylvania Capital Loan Fund, Department of Commerce, Bureau of Business Financing, 494 Forum Building, Harrisburg 17120. Contact: Mr. James N. Graham at (717) 783-1768. *Assistance:* Financial. *Eligibility:* Smaller businesses

Pennsylvania Technical Assistance Program (PENNTAP), The Pennsylvania State University, 501 J Orvis Keller Building, University Park 16802. Contact Mr. Roy Marlow at (814) 865-0427. *Assistance:* Information/Technical

Research "Seed" Grants, Ben Franklin Partnership, Department of Commerce, 463 Forum Building, Harrisburg 17120. Contact Mr. William J. Cook at (717) 787-4147. *Assistance:* Financial *Eligibility:* Smaller businesses

Revenue Bond and Mortgage Program, Department of Commerce, Bureau of Economic Assistance, Forum Building, Harrisburg 17120. Contact (717) 783-1108. *Assistance:* Financial

Seed "Venture" Capital Fund, Ben Franklin Partnership, Department of Commerce, Forum Building, Harrisburg 17120. Contact Mr. Jacques Koppel at (717) 787-4147. *Assistance:* Financial. *Eligibility:* Smaller businesses

Small Business Incubator Loan Program, Ben Franklin Partnership, Department of Commerce, Forum Building, Harrisburg 17120. Contact Ms. Molly McLaughlin at (717) 787-4147. *Assistance:* Business planning/Financial/Information/Networking/Technical. *Eligibility:* Smaller businesses

Puerto Rico (PR)

Economic Development Administration, P.O. Box 2305, San Juan 00936. Contact Mr. Antonio J. Colorado at (809) 758-4747 San Juan or (212) 245-1200 New York. In New York 1290 Avenue of the Americas, New York, NY 10104-0092 (Mr. Hector Melendez). *Assistance:* Business planning/Financial/Information/Management/Networking/Technical

Scientific Community Council, Inc., P.O. Box 2284, Rato Rey 00918. Contact (809) 751-1815.

Rhode Island (RI)

Brown Venture Forum, Box 1949, Providence, RI 02912. Contact Mr. William Jackson at (401) 863-3528. *Assistance:* Business planning/Information/Networking

Business Action Center, Rhode Island Department of Economic Development, 7 Jackson Walkway, Providence, RI 02903. Contact (401) 277-2832. *Assistance:* Information

Business Development Company of Rhode Island, 30 Exchange Terrace, Providence, 02903. Contact Mr. Lester B. Stevens at (401) 351-3036. *Assistance:* Financial

Federal Procurement Program, Rhode Island Department of Economic Development, 7 Jackson Walkway, Providence 02903. Contact (401) 277-2601. *Assistance:* Information/Technical

Financing Program, Rhode Island Department of Economic Development, 7 Jackson Walkway, Providence 02903. Contact (401) 277-2601. *Assistance:* Financial

International Trade Program, Rhode Island Department of Economic Development, 7 Jackson Walkway, Providence 02903. Contact Ms. Christine M. B. Smith at (401) 277-2601. *Assistance:* Information/Networking/Technical

Job Development and Training Division, Rhode Island Department of Economic Development, 555 Valley Street, Providence 02908. Contact (401) 277-2090. *Assistance:* Training

Marketing Division, Rhode Island Department of Economic Development, 7 Jackson Walkway, Providence 02903. Contact (401) 277-2601. *Assistance:* Information/Technical

Minority Business Program, Rhode Island Department of Economic Development, 7 Jackson Walkway, Providence 02903. Contact (401) 277-2601. *Assistance:* Procurement/Business planning/Information/Management/Networking/Technical

Opportunities Industrialization Center, 1 Hilton Street, Providence 02905. Contact Mr. Rufus W. Whitmore, Jr. at (401) 272-4400. *Assistance:* Financial/Information/Technical

Rhode Island Department of Environmental Management, 9 Hayes Street, Providence 02908. Contact (401) 277-2781. *Assistance:* Information

Rhode Island Partnership for Science and Technology, Rhode Island Department of Economic Development, 7 Jackson Walkway, Providence 02903. Contact Mr. Bruce R. Lang at (401) 277-2601. *Assistance:* Financial

Rhode Island Small Business Development Center, Bryant College, Smithfield 02917. Contact (401) 232-6111. *Assistance:* Business planning/Information/Technical. *Eligibility:* Smaller businesses

University of Rhode Island Business Assistance Programs, University of Rhode Island, Kingston 02881. Contact Mr. Robert Comerford at (401) 792-2337. *Assistance:* Information/Technical

South Carolina (SC)

Agriculture Marketing Division, Fruit and Vegetable Market News, Department of Agriculture, P.O. Box 13531, Columbia 29201-0531. Contact Ms. Wanda Amick at (803) 253-4044. *Assistance:* Information

Business Development and Assistance Division, State Development Board, 1301 Gervais Street, P.O. Box 927, Columbia 29202. Contact (800) 922-6684 (in state) or (803) 737-0400. *Assistance:* Financial/Information/Networking/Technical

Economic Development and Technical Assistance Center, Benedict College, Harden & Blanding Streets, Columbia 29204. Contact Ms. Mattie R. Harris at (800) 922-2820 (in state) or (803) 253-5315. *Assistance:* Business planning/Information/Technical. *Eligibility:* Smaller businesses and minority-owned businesses

Job Creation Network–Incubators, South Carolina State Development Board, Business Development and Assistance Division, P.O. Box 927, Columbia 29202. Contact 1 (800) 922-6684 (in-state) or (803) 758-3046. *Assistance:* Business planning/Financial/Information/Networking/Technical

Minority Business Development Centers, Columbia Center, P.O. Box 5915, Columbia 29250. Contact (803) 256-0528 for Columbia; (803) 723-2771 for Charleston; (803) 271-8753 for Greenville. *Assistance:* Marketing/Management/Technical

National Minority Suppliers Development Council, Carolina Association Minority Suppliers Development Council, P.O. Box 9156, Charlotte 28299. Contact (704) 372-8732. *Assistance:* Business planning/Information/Networking/Technical. *Eligibility:* Minority-owned businesses

Office of Small and Minority Business Assistance, 1205 Pendleton Street, Columbia 29201. Contact (803) 734-0562. *Assistance:* Business planning/Information/Networking/Technical

Research and Information Resources Division, South Carolina State Development Board, P.O. Box 927, Columbia 29202. Contact Ms. Sena H. Black at (803) 737-

0400. *Assistance:* Business planning/Financial/Information/Networking/Technical

Small Business Development Center, College of Business Administration, University of South Carolina, Columbia 29208. Contact Mr. William F. Littlejohn at (803) 777-4907. *Assistance:* Business planning/Information/Networking/Technical. *Eligibility:* Smaller businesses

The South Carolina Jobs Economic Development Authority, 1201 Main Street, Suite 1750, Columbia 29201. Contact Mr. Elliott Franks at (803) 737-0079. *Assistance:* Financial/Technical

South Dakota (SD)

Division of Export Development and Product Promotion, Capitol Lake Plaza, Pierre 57501. Contact Mr. Troy Jones at (605) 773-5032. *Assistance:* Information/Networking/Technical

Economic Development Center, North Dakota State University, Fargo 58102. Contact Dr. Robert L. Sullivan at (701) 237-8873. *Assistance:* Business planning/Financial/Information/Management/Networking/Technical

Financial Assistance Program, Office of Economic Development, Capitol Lake Plaza, Pierre 57501. Contact (605) 773-5032. *Assistance:* Business planning/Financial/Information/Technical. *Eligibility:* Smaller businesses

Procurement Assistance Program, Department of State Development, Capitol Lake Plaza, Pierre 57501. Contact (605) 773-5032. *Assistance:* Business planning/Financial/Information/Networking/Technical

Revolving Economic Development and Initiative Fund (REDI Fund), Office of Economic Development, Capitol Lake Plaza, Pierre 57501. Contact (800) 952-3625 (in state) or (800) 843-8000 (out of state). *Assistance:* Financial

Tennessee (TN)

Export Office, Department of Economic and Community Development, Rachel Jackson Building, 320 Sixth Avenue, North, Nashville 37219-5308. Contact (615) 741-5870. *Assistance:* Exporting assistance

Office of Minority Business Enterprise, 7th Floor, 320 6th Avenue North, Nashville 37219-5305. Contact (615) 741-2545. *Assistance:* Business planning/Financial/Information/Technical. *Eligibility:* Minority-owned businesses

Regional Economic Development Center, 226 Johnson Hall, Memphis State University, Memphis 38152. Contact Ms. Luchy S. Burrell at (901) 454-2056. *Assistance:* Business planning/Information/Technical

Small Business Office, Department of Economic and Community Development, Rachel Jackson Building, 320 6th Avenue North, Nashville 37219-5308. Contact Mr. David Webber at (615) 741-2626. *Assistance:* Financial/Information/Networking

Tennessee Technology Foundation, P.O. Box 23184, Knoxville 37933. Contact Dr. David A. Patterson at (615) 694-6772. *Assistance:* Business planning/Financial/Information/Networking/Technical

The University of Tennessee Center for Industrial Services, 226 Capitol Boulevard Building, Suite 401, Nashville 37219-1804. Contact Mr. T. C. Parsons at (615) 242-2456. *Assistance:* Business planning/Financial/Technical

Texas (TX)

Business Expansion Services, Texas Economic Development Commission, 816 Congress, Suite 1200, P.O. Box 12728, Capitol Station, Austin 78711. Contact (512) 472-5059. *Assistance:* Financial

Center for Technology Development and Transfer, ECJ 2.516, University of Texas, Austin 78712 Contact (512) 471-1653. *Assistance:* Licensing inventions

Economic Development Center, Texas Southern University, School of Business, 3100 Cleburne Avenue, Houston 77004. Contact (713) 527-7785. *Assistance:* Business planning/Information/Networking/Technical

Economic Development Centers, University of Texas at San Antonio, College of Business, San Antonio 78285. Contact (512) 224-1945. *Assistance:* Business planning/Information/Management/Technical

Small Business Loan Programs, Texas Economic Development Commission, 816 Congress, Suite 1200, P.O. Box 12728, Capitol Station, Austin 78711. Contact (512) 472-5059. *Assistance:* Financial. *Eligibility:* Smaller businesses

Technology Business Development, Small Business Technical Development Center, Texas Engineering Experiment Station, The Texas A&M University, W. Engineering Research Center, Room 310, College Station 77843-3369. Contact Ms. Christine M. Hafernick at (409) 845-8717. *Assistance:* Business planning/Information/Networking/Technical. *Eligibility:* Smaller businesses and minority-owned businesses

Texas Research and Technology Foundation, Suite 345, 8207 Callaghan Road, San Antonio 78230. Contact (512) 342-6063. *Assistance:* R&D programming/Business planning/Financial/Information/Networking/ Technical

Utah (UT)

Business Development Program, Department of Community and Economic Development, 6290 State Office Building, Salt Lake City 84114. Contact (801) 533-5325. *Assistance:* Financial/Information/Networking/ Technical. *Eligibility:* Smaller businesses

IMPACT: Minority Business Program, U.S. Department of Commerce, 350 East 500 South, Salt Lake City 84111. Contact (801) 328-8181. *Assistance:* Information

Small Business Development Centers, University of Utah, 600 South 2nd East No. 418, Salt Lake City 84111. Contact Mr. James Bean at (801) 581-7905. *Assistance:* Business planning/Financial/Information/ Technical

Utah Innovation Center, 419 Wakara Way, Research Park, Salt Lake City 84108. Contact Dr. Gerald L. Davey at (801) 584-2500. *Assistance:* Business planning/Financial/Information/Management/Networking/Technical

Utah Technology Finance Corporation, 419 Wakara Way, Salt Lake City 84108. Contact Mr. Grant Cannon at (801) 583-8832. *Assistance:* Financial. *Eligibility:* Smaller businesses

Vermont (VT)

Entrepreneurship Program, Division of Economic Development, Pavilion Building, 109 State Street, Montpelier 05602. Contact Mr. Curt Carter at (802) 828-3221. *Assistance:* Business planning/Information/ Networking/Technical

Export Development Program, Division of Economic Development, Pavilion Building, 109 State Street, Montpelier 05602. Contact Mr. Graeme Freeman at (802) 828-3221. *Assistance:* Business planning/Financial/Information/Networking/ Technical

Site Selection Office, Division of Economic Development, Pavilion Building, 109 State Street, Montpelier 05602. Contact Mr. Fred Newhall at (802) 828-3221. *Assistance:* Information

Small Business Resource and Referral Service, Division of Economic Development, Pavilion Building, 109 State Street, Montpelier 05602. Contact Ms. Lanora Preedom at (802) 828-3221. *Assistance:* Information/ Networking. *Eligibility:* Smaller businesses

Vermont Business Expansion Program, Division of Economic Development, Pavilion Building, 109 State Street, Montpelier 05602. Contact (802) 828-3221. *Assistance:* Business planning/Financial/Information/ Networking/Technical

Vermont Trading Program, Division of Economic Development, Pavilion Building, 109 State Street, Montpelier 05602. Contact Mr. Phil Fagan at (802) 828-3221. *Assistance:* Training. *Eligibility:* Smaller businesses

Virginia (VA)

Center for Innovative Technology, The Hallmark Building, 13873 Park Center Road, Herndon 22071. Contact (703) 689-3000. *Assistance:* Marketing/Business planning/ Financial/Information/Networking

Central Virginia Community College, 3406 Wards Road, Lynchburg 24502. Contact Mr. Homer Hammett at (804) 386-4571. *Assistance:* Business planning/Management/Networking/Technical

Employment Commission, Economic Information Services, 703 East Main Street, P.O. Box 1358, Richmond 23233. Contact (804) 786-8223. *Assistance:* Information/ Technical

Energy Division, Department of Mines, Minerals, and Energy, 2201 West Broad Street, Richmond 23220. Contact (804) 357-0330. *Assistance:* Information

Export Development–International Marketing Division, Virginia Department of Economic Development, 1000 Washington Building, Richmond 23219. Contact (804) 786-3791. *Assistance:* Information/Technical

George Mason Entrepreneur Center, George Mason University, 4400 University Drive, Fairfax 22030. Contact (703) 323-2568. *Assistance:* Business planning/Management/ Networking/Financial

Halifax County/South Boston Continuing Education Center, Highway 129, P.O. Box 1117, South Boston 24592. Contact Ms. Sandra Feagan at (804) 575-0292. *Assistance:* Business planning/Management/ Networking/Technical

Hampton University Business Assistance Center, P.O. Box 6148, Hampton 23668. Contact (804) 727-5570. *Assistance:* Business planning/Information/Management/ Technical

Lynchburg Community Action Group, Inc., Planning and Community Services, 901 Main Street, Level B, Lynchburg 24504. Contact Ms. Junius Haskins at (804) 846-2778. *Assistance:* Marketing/Business planning/ Financial/ Information/ Management/ Networking/Technical. *Eligibility:* Minority-owned businesses

Minority Business Enterprise, 200–202 North 9th Street, 11th Floor, Richmond 23219. Contact (804) 786-5560. *Assistance:* Marketing/Business planning/Financial/Information/Management/Networking/Technical

New River Community College, P.O. Drawer 1127, Dublin 24084. Contact Mr. James Stewart at (703) 674-3643. *Assistance:* Business planning/Management/Networking/Technical

Northern Virginia Community College, Center for Business and Government Services, 4001 Wakefield Chapel Road, Annandale 22003. Contact Mr. John Jerke at (703) 323-4293. *Assistance:* Business planning/Management/Networking/Technical.

Small Business and Financial Services Office. Virginia Department of Economic Development, 1000 Washington Building, Richmond 23219. Contact Small Business Coordinator at (804) 786-3791. *Assistance:* Financial/Information/Management/Networking/Technical

Southwest Virginia Community College, P.O. Box SVCC, Richlands, 24640. Contact Mr. John Curran at (703) 964-2555. *Assistance:* Business planning/Management/Networking/Technical

The Metropolitan Business League, 121 East Marshall Street, P.O. Box 26751, Richmond 23261. Contact (804) 649-7473. *Assistance:* Business planning/Management/Networking/Technical

Thomas Nelson Community College, P.O. Box 9407, Hampton 23670. Contact Mr. Stephen Cooper at (804) 825-2739. *Assistance:* Business planning/Management/Networking/Technical

Tidewater Community College, 1428 Cedar Road, Chesapeake 23320. Contact Mr. Robert Harrell at (804) 547-9271 Ext. 272. *Assistance:* Business planning/Management/Networking/Technical

Tidewater Regional Minority Purchasing Council, Inc., 142 West York Street, Suite 611, Norfolk 23510. Contact Mr. Bernard Big at (804) 627-8471. *Assistance:* Information/Networking/Technical

Virginia Port Authority, 600 World Trade Center, Norfolk 23510. Contact (804) 623-8000. *Assistance:* Information/Technical

Virginia Regional Minority Supplier Development Council, 2025 East Main Street, Room 203, Richmond 23223. Contact Mr. Gustave R. Thomas at (804) 780-2322. *Assistance:* Technical. *Eligibility:* Minority-owned businesses

Virginia Weston Community College, P.O. Box 14045, Roanoke, 24038. Contact Mr. Gary Atkinson at (703) 982-7311. *Assistance:* Business planning/Management/Networking/Technical

Wytheville Community College, 1000 East Main Street, Wytheville, 24382. Contact Mr. Dan Mills at (703) 228-5541. *Assistance:* Business planning/Management/Networking/Technical

Washington (WA)

Business Assistance Center, Department of Trade and Economic Development, 919 Lakeridge Way, S.W. Olympia 98504. Contact Ms. Sandra Granger at 1 (800) 237-1233 (in state) or (206) 753-5614. *Assistance:* Information/Networking

Community Development Finance Program, Department of Community Development, 9th & Columbia Bldg., Olympia 98504. Contact Ms. Christine Gowdey at 1 (800) 562-5677 or (206) 753-4900. *Assistance:* Financial/Information

Department of Revenue, Department of Revenue, General Administration Building, Olympia 98504. Contact (206) 753-5540. *Assistance:* Financial/Information

Development Loan Fund, Department of Community Development, 9th & Columbia Bldg., Olympia 98504. Contact Ms. Joan Machlis at (206) 754-8976. *Assistance:* Financial

Domestic and International Trade Division, Department of Trade and Economic Development, 312 First Avenue North, Seattle 98109. Contact Mr. Don Lorentz at (206) 464-6283. *Assistance:* Information/Networking/Technical

Job Skills Program, Commission for Vocational Education, Building 17, Industrial Park, Olympia 98504. Contact Mr. Ken Lisk or Mr. John Knold at 1 (800) 233-6267 (in state) or (206) 753-0838. *Assistance:* Training

License Information Service, Business License Center, 405 Black Lake Boulevard, S.W., Olympia 98504. Contact 1 (800) 562-8203 (in state) or (206) 586-2784 or 586-2786. *Assistance:* Information

Office of Minority and Women's Business Enterprises, FK-11, 406 South Water, Olympia 98504. Contact (206) 753-9693. *Assistance:* Information. *Eligibility:* Smaller businesses and minority-owned businesses

Small Business Assistance Program, State Board for Community College Education, 319 East Seventh Avenue, FF-11, Olympia 98504-3111. Contact Mr. Ronald Crossland at (206) 753-3674. *Assistance:* Training. *Eligibility:* Smaller businesses

Small Business Development Center, College of Business and Economics, Washington State University Pullman 99164-4740. Contact Mr. Frank Hoy at (509) 542-5760. *Assistance:* Business planning/Information/Networking/Technical

Small Business Export Finance Assistance Center, 2001 6th Avenue, Suite 1700, Seattle 98121. Contact Mr. Robert Sebastian at (206) 464-7123. *Assistance:* Business planning/Financial/Networking

Washington Business Assistance Center, Department of Trade & Economic Development, 919 Lakeridge Way, S.W., Olympia 98502. Contact 1 (800) 237-1233 or (206) 753-5632. *Assistance:* Business planning/ Financial / Information / Management / Networking/Technical

Washington State Business Resource Network, Department of Employment Security, 212 Maple Park, Olympia 98504. Contact Mr. Gary Gallwas at 1 (800) 233-6267 (in state) or (206) 753-5211. *Assistance:* Training/Business planning/Financial/Information/Networking/Technical

West Virginia (WV)

Center for Education and Research with Industry, Marshall Univeristy, Huntington 25755-2130. Contact Mr. William Edwards at (304) 696-3368. *Assistance:* Financial/ Information / Management / Networking / Technical

Center for Regional Progress, Marshall University, Huntington 25755. Contact Dr. John R. Spears at (304) 696-6797. *Assistance:* Research and reporting/Business planning / Financial / Information / Management/Technical

Economic Development, Governor's Office of Community and Industrial Development, Capital Complex, Charleston 25305. Contact (304) 348-0400. *Assistance:* Business planning/Financial/Management

Higher Education, Governor's Office of Community and Industrial Development, Center for Education and Research with Industry, Marshall University, Huntington 25701. Contact (304) 696-3367. *Assistance:* Information

Small Business Development Center, Marshall University, Huntington 25755-2126. Contact (304) 696-6798. *Assistance:* Business planning/Information/Management/ Networking/Technical

West Virginia Division of Small Business, Governor's Office of Community and Industrial Development, State Capitol Complex, Charleston 25305. Contact Ms. Eloise Jack at (304) 348-2960. *Assistance:* Business planning / Financial / Information / Networking/Technical. *Eligibility:* Smaller businesses

Wisconsin (WI)

Bureau of Business Development Services, Department of Development, 123 West Washington Ave., P.O. Box 7970, Madison 53707. Contact Mr. Robert Fleming at (608) 266-0165. *Assistance:* Business planning/ Information/Networking/Technical

Business Development Bond Program, Wisconsin Housing and Economic Development Authority, P.O. Box 1728, Madison 53701-1728. Contact Mr. Richard Longabough at (608) 266-7884. *Assistance:* Financial

Development Financing Bureau, Wisconsin Department of Development, P.O. Box 7970, Madison 53707. Contact Mr. Jim Gruentzel at (608) 266-7099. *Assistance:* Financial

Innovation Network Foundation, P.O. Box 71, Madison 53701, Contact Ms. Diane Crutz at (608) 256-8348. *Assistance:* Information

Innovation Service Center, University of Wisconsin-Whitewater, 402 McCutchan Hall, Whitewater 53190. Contact Ms. Debra Knox-Malewicki at (414) 472-1365. *Assistance:* Information/Management/Technical

International Development Bureau, Wisconsin Department of Development, P.O. Box 7970, Madison 53707. Contact Mr. Ralph Graner at (608) 266-1480. *Assistance:* Marketing/Information

Marketing Division, Department of Agriculture, Trade, and Consumer Protection, 801 West Badge Road, Madison 53713. Contact Mr. James Smith at (606) 266-7170. *Assistance:* Marketing/Information/Technical

Minority Business Development Program, Wisconsin Department of Development, P.O. Box 7970, Madison 53707. Contact Mr. Robert Wynn at (608) 266-8380. *Assistance:* Information/Management/Technical

Permit Information Center, Department of Development, 123 West Washington Ave., P.O. Box 7970, Madison 53707. Contact Mr. Phillip Albert at 1(800) 435-7287 (in state) or (608) 266-9869. *Assistance:* Information/Networking

Small Business Development Center, University of Wisconsin, 602 State Street, Madison 53703. Contact (608) 263-7766. *Assistance:* Marketing/Information/Management

Small Business Ombudsman, Wisconsin Department of Development, P.O. Box 7970, Madison 53707. Contact Ms. Sara Burr at (608) 266-0562. *Assistance:* Information/ Management

Wisconsin Business Development Finance Corporation, P.O. Box 2717, Madison 53701-8830. Contact Mr. John Geigel at (608) 258-8830. *Assistance:* Financial

Wyoming (WY)

Economic Development and Stabilization Board, Herschler Building, Third Floor, Cheyenne 82002. Contact (307) 777-7284. *Assistance:* Financial/Information/Networking/Technical

Job Training Administration, Barrett Building, 3rd Floor, Cheyenne 82002. Contact Mr. David Griffin at (307) 777-7671. *Assistance:* Training/Financial/Technical

Wyoming Community Development Authority, P.O. Box 634, Casper 82602. Contact Mr. George Axlund at (307) 265-0603. *Assistance:* Financial/Networking/Technical

Wyoming Small Business Development Center Network, 130 N. Ash, Suite A, Casper 82601. Contact Mr. Mac Bryant at (307) 235-4825. *Assistance:* Business planning/Information/Management/Networking. *Eligibility:* Smaller businesses

State Data Center Program of the Bureau of the Census

Access to the many statistical products available from the Bureau of the Census is provided through the services of the joint federal-state cooperative State Data Center Program. Through the Program, the Bureau furnishes statistical products, training in the data access and use, technical assistance, and consultation to states which, in turn, disseminate the products and provide assistance in their use.

Additional information on the State Data Program and a list of the State Data Centers can be obtained by contacting the User Services staff in any of the Bureau's regional offices or by calling the Data User Services Division of the Bureau of the Census at 301-763-1580.

State Information Offices

Alabama*

State Capitol, Montgomery, AL 36130
(205) 261-2500

INFORMATION OFFICES

Commerce/Economic Development
Alabama Development Office
135 S. Union Street
Montgomery, AL 36130

* For Small Business Administration offices, see page 254.

Department of Economic & Community Affairs
3465 Norman Bridge Road
Montgomery, AL 36105

Corporate
Secretary of State
State Office Building
Montgomery, AL 36130

Taxation
Department of Revenue
Administrative Building
64 N. Union Street
Montgomery, AL 36130

State Chamber of Commerce
Alabama Chamber of Commerce
468 S. Perry Street
P.O. Box 76
Montgomery, AL 36101

International Commerce
Department of International Trade
Alabama Development Office
135 South Union
Montgomery, AL 36130

Banking
State Banking Department
166 Commerce
Montgomery, AL 36130

Securities
Alabama Securities Exchange Commission
100 Commerce Street
First Southern Towers
Montgomery, AL 36130

Labor and Industrial Relations
Department of Industrial Relations
649 Monroe Street
Montgomery, AL 36130

Alabama Department of Labor
Administrative Building
64 N. Union Street
Montgomery, AL 36130

Insurance
Department of Insurance
135 S. Union Street
Montgomery, AL 36130

Uniform Industrial Code
Alabama Development Office
State Capitol
Montgomery, AL 36130

INDUSTRIAL AND BUSINESS DIRECTORIES

Alabama Directory of Mining and Manufacturing, Alabama Development Office, State Capitol, Montgomery, AL 36130

Alabama Industrial Directory, Manufacturers' News, Inc., 3 E. Huron Street, Chicago, IL 60611; State Industrial Directories Corp., 2 Penn Plaza, New York, NY 10001

Alabama International Trade Directory, Office of State Planning and Federal Programs, State Capitol, Montgomery, AL 36130

Alabama Metalworking Directory, Office of State Planning and Federal Programs, 3465 Norman Bridge Road, Montgomery, AL 36105

Birmingham Industrial Directory, Birmingham Chamber of Commerce, 1914 6th Avenue, Birmingham, AL 35203

Alaska

STATE CAPITOL, JUNEAU, AK 99811
(907) 465-2111

INFORMATION OFFICES

Commerce/Economic Development
Department of Commerce & Economic Development
P.O. Box D
Juneau, AK 99811

Corporate
Department of Commerce & Economic Development
Corporation Section
P.O. Box D
Juneau, AK 99811

Taxation
Department of Revenue
P.O. Box S
Juneau, AK 99811

State Chamber of Commerce
Alaska State Chamber of Commerce
310 2nd Street
Juneau, AK 99801

International Commerce
Office of the Governor
Department of Commerce & Economic Development
3601 C Street
Anchorage, AK 99503

Banking
Division of Banking
Department of Commerce & Economic Development
P.O. Box D
Juneau, AK 99811

Securities
Division of Securities and Corporations
Department of Commerce and Economic Development
P.O. Box D
Juneau, AK 99811

Labor and Industrial Relations
Department of Labor
1111 W. 8th Street
Juneau, AK 99801

Insurance
Division of Insurance
Department of Commerce and Economic Development
P.O. Box D
Juneau, AK 99811

Uniform Industrial Code
Department of Natural Resources
Uniform Commercial Code
3601 C Street
Anchorage, AK 99503

INDUSTRIAL AND BUSINESS DIRECTORIES

Alaska Directory of Commercial Establishments, Manufacturers' News, Inc., 4 E. Huron Street, Chicago, IL 60611; State Industrial Directories Corp., 2 Penn Plaza, New York, NY 10001

Alaska Petroleum and Industrial Directory, 409 W. Northern Lights Boulevard, Anchorage, AK 99603

Arizona

STATE CAPITOL, PHOENIX, AZ 85007
(602) 255-4900

INFORMATION OFFICES

Commerce/Economic Development
Department of Commerce
1700 W. Washington Avenue
Phoenix, AZ 85007

Corporate
Arizona Corporation Commission
P.O. Box 6019
Phoenix, AZ 85005

Taxation
Department of Revenue
1600 W. Monroe
Phoenix, AZ 85007

State Chamber of Commerce
Arizona State Chamber of Commerce
1366 E. Thomas Road
Phoenix, AZ 85014

Banking
Banking Department
3225 N. Central
Phoenix, AZ 85012

Insurance
Insurance Department
801 E. Jefferson
Phoenix, AZ 85034

Securities
Arizona Corporation Commission
1200 W. Washington Avenue
Phoenix, AZ 85007

International Commerce
Department of Commerce
1700 W. Washington Avenue
Phoenix, AZ 85007

Labor and Industrial Relations
Industrial Commission
800 W. Washington Street
P.O. Box 19070
Phoenix, AZ 85005

INDUSTRIAL AND BUSINESS DIRECTORIES

Arizona Directory of Industries, Manufacturers' News, 3 E. Huron Street, Chicago, IL 60611

Arizona Directory of Manufacturers, Manufacturers' News, Inc., 3 E. Huron Street, Chicago, IL 60611; State Industrial Directories Corp., 2 Penn Plaza, New York, NY 10001

Arizona USA International Trade Directory, Arizona State Department of Commerce, 1700 W. Monroe Avenue, Phoenix, AZ 85007

Directory of Arizona Manufacturers, Phoenix Chamber of Commerce, 34 W. Monroe, Phoenix, AZ 85003

Arkansas

STATE CAPITOL, LITTLE ROCK, AR 72201
(501) 371-1010

INFORMATION OFFICES

Commerce/Economic Development
Industrial Development Commission
Big Mac Building
One State Capitol Mall
Little Rock, AR 72201

Corporate
Secretary of State
Corporation Department
State Capitol
Little Rock, AR 72201

Taxation
Division of Revenue Services
Department of Finance and Administration
Joel Y. Ledbetter Building
7th and Wolfe Streets
Little Rock, AR 72201

State Chamber of Commerce
Arkansas State Chamber of Commerce
911 Wallace Building
Little Rock, AR 72201

International Commerce
Industrial Development Commission
Big Mac Building
One State Capitol Mall
Little Rock, AR 72201

Banking
Bank Department
323 Center Street
Little Rock, AR 72201

Securities
Securities Department
Heritage West Building
201 East Markham
Little Rock, AR 72201

Labor and Industrial Relations
Arkansas Department of Labor
1022 High Street
Little Rock, AR 72202

Insurance
Insurance Division
University Towers Building
Little Rock, AR 72204

Ombudsman
State Claims Commission
State Capitol
Little Rock, AR 72201

INDUSTRIAL AND BUSINESS DIRECTORIES

Arkansas Directory of Industries, Manufacturers' News, 3 E. Huron Street, Chicago, IL 60611

Directory of Arkansas Manufacturers, Arkansas Industrial Development Foundation, P.O. Box 1784, Little Rock, AR 72203; State Industrial Directories Corp., 2 Penn Plaza, New York, NY 10001

State and County Economic Data (annual), University of Arkansas Industrial Research Center, University of Arkansas, Little Rock College of Business Administration, 33rd and University Avenue, Little Rock, AR 72204

California

STATE CAPITOL, SACRAMENTO, CA 95814
(916) 332-9900

INFORMATION OFFICES

Commerce/Economic Development
Department of Commerce
1121 L Street
Sacramento, CA 95814

Corporate
Secretary of State
1230 "J" Street
Sacramento, CA 95814

Taxation
Board of Equalization
1020 N Street
Sacramento, CA 95814

State Chamber of Commerce
California Chamber of Commerce
1027 10th Street
P.O. Box 1736
Sacramento, CA 95814

International Commerce
California State World Trade Commission
1121 L Street
Sacramento, CA 95814

Banking
State Banking Department
11 Pine Street
San Francisco, CA 94111-5613

Securities
Department of Corporations
1025 P Street
Sacramento, CA 95814

Labor and Industrial Relations
Department of Industrial Relations
525 Golden Gate Avenue
P.O. Box 603
San Francisco, CA 94101
or
1121 L Street
Sacramento, CA 95814
Insurance
Department of Insurance
600 S. Commonwealth Avenue
Los Angeles, CA 90005
or
100 Van Ness Avenue
San Francisco, CA 94102

INDUSTRIAL AND BUSINESS DIRECTORIES

California Handbook, Center for California Public Affairs, 226 W. Foothill Boulevard, Claremont, CA 91711
California International Business Directory, Center for International Business, 333 S. Flower Street, Los Angeles, CA 90071
California Manufacturers Register, Time-Mirror Press, 1115 S. Boyle Avenue, Los Angeles, CA 90023; Manufacturers' News, Inc., 4 E. Huron Street, Chicago, IL 60611; State Industrial Directories Corp., 2 Penn Plaza, New York, NY 10001
Los Angeles Area Chamber of Commerce Southern California Business Directory and Buyers Guide, Los Angeles Chamber of Commerce, 404 S. Bixel Street, Los Angeles, CA 95113
San Francisco Manufacturers Directory, San Francisco Chamber of Commerce, 333 Pine Street, San Francisco, CA 94577

Colorado

State Capitol, Denver, CO 80203
(303) 866-5000

INFORMATION OFFICES

Commerce/Economic Development
Office of Economic Development
Business Development
1625 Broadway
Denver, CO 80202
Corporate
Secretary of State
Corporation Division
1560 Broadway
Denver, CO 80202
Taxation
Administrative Division
Department of Revenue
1375 Sherman Street
Denver, CO 80261
State Chamber of Commerce
Colorado Association of Commerce and Industry
1860 Lincoln Street
Denver, CO 80295
International Commerce
Office of Economic Development
International Trade Office
1625 Broadway
Denver, CO 80202
Banking
Division of Banking
1525 Sherman
State Services Building
Denver, CO 80203
Securities
Division of Securities
1560 Broadway
Denver, CO 80202
Labor and Industrial Relations
Division of Labor
1313 Sherman Street
Denver, CO 80203
Insurance
Division of Insurance
303 W. Colfax Street
Denver, CO 80204
Uniform Industrial Code
Commercial Recordings Division
1560 Broadway
Denver, CO 80202
Business Ombudsman
Business Information Center
1525 Sherman Street
Denver, CO 80202

INDUSTRIAL AND BUSINESS DIRECTORIES

Directory of Colorado Manufacturers, Business Research Division, Graduate School of Business Administration, Campus Box 420, University of Colorado, Boulder, CO 80309

Connecticut

State Capitol, Hartford, CT 06106
(203) 566-4200

INFORMATION OFFICES

Commerce/Economic Development
Department of Economic Development
210 Washington Street
Hartford, CT 06106
Corporate
Secretary of State
Corporations Division
30 Trinity Street
Hartford, CT 06106

Taxation
Department of Revenue Services
92 Farmington Avenue
Hartford, CT 06106

State Chamber of Commerce
Connecticut Business and Industry Association
370 Asylum Street
Hartford, CT 06103

International Commerce
Department of Economic Development
210 Washington Street
Hartford, CT 06106

Banking
Department of Banking
44 Capitol Avenue
Hartford, CT 06106

Securities
Divisions of Securities & Business Investments
Department of Banking
44 Capitol Avenue
Hartford, CT 06106

Labor and Industrial Relations
Department of Labor
200 Folly Brook Boulevard
Wethersfield, CT 06109

Insurance
Department of Insurance
165 Capitol Avenue
Hartford, CT 06106

Uniform Industrial Code
Department of Economic Development
210 Washington Street
Hartford, CT 06106

Business Ombudsman
Department of Economic Development
210 Washington Street
Hartford, CT 06106

INDUSTRIAL AND BUSINESS DIRECTORIES

Classified Business Directory—State of Connecticut, Connecticut Directory Co., Inc., 322 Main Street, Stamford, CT 06901

Connecticut Classified Business Directory, Connecticut Directory Co., Inc., 322 Main Street, Stamford, CT 06901

Connecticut State Industrial Directory, Manufacturers' News, 3 E. Huron Street, Chicago, IL 60611; State Industrial Directories Corp., 2 Penn Plaza, New York, NY 10001

Directory of Connecticut Manufacturing Establishments, Connecticut Department of Labor, 200 Folly Brook Boulevard, Wethersfield, CT 06109

Delaware

Legislative Hall, Dover, DE 19901
(302) 736-4101

INFORMATION OFFICES

Commerce/Economic Development
Delaware Development Office
99 Kings Highway
P.O. Box 1401
Dover, DE 19903

Corporate
Secretary of State
Corporations Department
Townsend Building
P.O. Box 898
Dover, DE 19903

Taxation
Department of Finance
Division of Revenue
Carvel State Office Building
820 N. French Street
Wilmington, DE 19801

International Commerce
Delaware Development Office
99 Kings Highway
P.O. Box 1401
Dover, DE 19903

State Chamber of Commerce
Delaware State Chamber of Commerce, Inc.
One Commerce Center
Wilmington, DE 19801

Banking
State Bank Commission
Department of State
Thomas Collins Building
P.O. Box 1401
Dover, DE 19903

Labor and Industrial Relations
Division of Industrial Affairs
Department of Labor
Carvel State Office Building
820 N. French Street
Wilmington, DE 19801

Insurance
State Insurance Commission
841 Silver Lake Boulevard
Rodney Building
Dover, DE 19901

INDUSTRIAL AND BUSINESS DIRECTORIES

Delaware Directory of Commerce and Industry, Delaware State Chamber of Commerce, One Commerce Center, Wilmington, DE 19801

Delaware State Industrial Directory, State Industrial Directories Corp., 2 Penn Plaza, New York, NY 10001

Florida

State Capitol, Tallahassee, FL 32301
(904) 488-1234

INFORMATION OFFICES

Commerce/Economic Development
Department of Commerce
Collins Building
107 W. Gaines Street
Tallahassee, FL 32301

Division of Economic Development
Department of Commerce
Collins Building
Tallahassee, FL 32301

Corporate
Secretary of State
Division of Corporations
Capitol Building
Tallahassee, FL 32304

Taxation
Department of Revenue
Carlton Building
Tallahassee, FL 32301

State Chamber of Commerce
Florida State Chamber of Commerce
P.O. Box 11309
Tallahassee, FL 32302

International Commerce
Florida Department of Commerce
Bureau of International Trade
Collins Building
Tallahassee, FL 32301

Banking
Florida Department of Banking & Finance
The Capitol
Tallahassee, FL 32301

Securities
Florida Department of Banking & Finance
Division of Securities
1402 Capitol
Tallahassee, FL 32301

Labor and Industrial Relations
Florida Department of Labor and Employment Security
Atkins Building
1320 Executive Center Drive, East
Tallahassee, FL 32301

Insurance
Florida Department of Insurance
The Capitol
Tallahassee, FL 32301

Uniform Commercial Code
Florida Department of State
Bureau of Uniform Commercial Code
P.O. Box 5588
Tallahassee, FL 32314

Business Ombudsman
Florida Department of Commerce
Bureau of Business and Community Development
Collins Building
Tallahassee, FL 32301

INDUSTRIAL AND BUSINESS DIRECTORIES

Directory of Florida Industries, Manufacturers' News, Inc., 4 E. Huron Street, Chicago, IL 60611; Florida State Chamber of Commerce, P.O. Box 11309, Tallahassee, FL 32302; State Industrial Directories Corp., 2 Penn Plaza, New York, NY 10001

Florida Industries Guide, McHenry Publishing Co., Inc., Box 935, Orlando, FL 32802

Georgia

State Capitol, Atlanta, GA 30334
(404) 656-2000

INFORMATION OFFICES

Commerce/Economic Development
Department of Industry and Trade
230 Peachtree Street NW
Atlanta, GA 30303

Corporate
Corporations Division
Secretary of State
2 Martin Luther King Jr. Drive, SE
Atlanta, GA 30334

Taxation
Department of Revenue
270 Washington Street, SW
Atlanta, GA 30334

State Chamber of Commerce
Business Council of Georgia
1280 CNN Center
Atlanta, GA 30303-2705

International Commerce
Department of Industry and Trade
230 Peachtree Street, NW
Atlanta, GA 30303

Banking
Department of Banking and Finance
2990 Brandywine Road
Atlanta, GA 30341

Securities
Securities Division
Secretary of State
2 Martin Luther King Jr. Drive, SE
Atlanta, GA 30334

Labor and Industrial Relations
Department of Labor
148 International Boulevard
Atlanta, GA 30303

Insurance
Office of Commissioner of Insurance
2 Martin Luther King Jr. Drive, SE
Atlanta, GA 30334

INDUSTRIAL AND BUSINESS DIRECTORIES

Georgia Manufacturing Directory, Department of Industry and Trade, 230 Peachtree Street, NW, Atlanta, GA 30303

Georgia World Trade Directory, Business Council of Georgia, 575 CNN Center, Atlanta, GA 30303-2705

Industrial Sites in Georgia, Georgia Power Company, Box 4545DJ, Atlanta, GA 30303

Georgia International Trade Directory, Department of Industry and Trade, 230 Peachtree Street NE, Atlanta, GA 30303
Georgia Directory of International Services, World Congress Institute, 1 Park Place S, Fulton Federal Building, Atlanta, GA 30303
International Companies with Facilities in Georgia. Department of Industry and Trade, 230 Peachtree Street, NW, Atlanta, GA 30303

Hawaii

STATE CAPITOL, HONOLULU, HI 96813
(808) 548-6222

INFORMATION OFFICES

Commerce/Economic Development
Department of Planning and Economic Development
250 S. King Street
Honolulu, HI 96813

Department of Commerce and Consumer Affairs
1010 Richards Street
Honolulu, HI 96813

Corporate
Department of Commerce and Consumer Affairs
Business Registration Division
P.O. Box 40
Honolulu, HI 96810

Taxation
Department of Taxation
830 Punchbowl Street
Honolulu, HI 96813

State Chamber of Commerce
Chamber of Commerce of Hawaii
735 Bishop Street
Honolulu, HI 96813

International Commerce
International Services Branch
State Department of Planning and Economic Development
P.O. Box 2359
Honolulu, HI 96804

Hawaii Foreign-Trade Zone No. 9, Pier 2
Honolulu, HI 96804

Banking
Division of Financial Institutions
State Department of Commerce and Consumer Affairs
1010 Richards Street
Honolulu, HI 96813

Securities
Division of Financial Institutions
State Department of Commerce and Consumer Affairs
1010 Richards Street
Honolulu, HI 96813

Labor and Industrial Relations
State Department of Labor and Industrial Relations
830 Punchbowl Street
Honolulu, HI 96813

Insurance
Insurance Division
State Department of Commerce and Consumer Affairs
1010 Richards Street
Honolulu, HI 96813

Business Ombudsman
Office of the Ombudsman
465 S. King Street
Honolulu, HI 96813

INDUSTRIAL AND BUSINESS DIRECTORIES

Directory of Manufacturers, State of Hawaii, Chamber of Commerce of Hawaii, Dillingham Building, 735 Bishop Street, Honolulu, HI 96813
Hawaii Business Directory, Hawaii Business Directory, Inc., 1164 Bishop Street, Honolulu, HI 96813
Hawaii Directory of Manufacturers, Manufacturers' News, Inc., 4 E. Huron Street, Chicago, IL 60611; State Industrial Directories Corp., 2 Penn Plaza, New York, NY 10001

Idaho

STATE CAPITOL, BOISE, ID 83720
(208) 334-2411

INFORMATION OFFICES

Mailing address for all state offices is:
Statehouse
Boise, ID 83720

Commerce/Economic Development
Department of Commerce
700 W. State Street
Boise, ID 83720

Corporate
Secretary of State
State Capitol
Boise, ID 83720

Taxation
Department of Revenue and Taxation
700 W. State Street
Boise, ID 83720

State Chamber of Commerce
Idaho Association of Commerce and Industry
805 West Idaho
Boise, ID 83702

International Commerce
Department of Commerce
700 W. State Street
Boise, ID 83720

Banking
Department of Finance
700 W. State Street
Boise, ID 83720
Securities
Department of Finance
700 W. State Street
Boise, ID 83720
Labor and Industrial Relations
Department of Labor and Industrial Services
277 N. 6th Street
Boise, ID 83720
Insurance
Department of Insurance
500 S. 10th Street
Boise, ID 83720
Uniform Industrial Code
Department of Labor and Industrial Services
277 N. 6th Street
Boise, ID 83720
Business Ombudsman
Department of Commerce
700 W. State Street
Boise, ID 83720

INDUSTRIAL AND BUSINESS DIRECTORIES

Manufacturing Directory of Idaho, Center for Business and Research, University of Idaho, Moscow, ID 83843
Idaho Opportunities, Department of Commerce, 700 W. State Street, Boise, ID 83720

Illinois

State House, Springfield, IL 62706
(217) 782-2000

INFORMATION OFFICES

Commerce/Economic Development
Department of Commerce and Community Affairs
620 E. Adams Street
Springfield, IL 62701
Corporate
Corporate Division
Centennial Building
Springfield, IL 62756
Taxation
Department of Revenue
101 W. Jefferson Street
Springfield, IL 62708
State Chamber of Commerce
Illinois State Chamber of Commerce
20 N. Wacker Drive
Chicago, IL 60606
International Commerce
Department of Commerce & Community Affairs
State of Illinois Center
100 W. Randolph Street
Chicago, IL 60601
Banking
Department of Financial Institutions
100 W. Randolph Street
Chicago, IL 60601
Securities
Secretary of State
840 S. Spring Street
Springfield, IL 62704
Labor and Industrial Relations
Department of Labor
100 N. 1st, Alzina Building
Springfield, IL 62706
Department of Commerce & Community Affairs
620 E. Adams Street
Springfield, IL 62701
Insurance
Department of Insurance
320 W. Washington Street
Springfield, IL 62767
Uniform Industrial Code
Department of Commerce & Community Affairs
620 E. Adams Street
Springfield, IL 62701
Business Ombudsman
Department of Commerce & Community Affairs
620 E. Adams Street
Springfield, IL 62701

INDUSTRIAL AND BUSINESS DIRECTORIES

Chicago Buyers' Guide, Chicago Association of Commerce and Industry, 130 S. Michigan Avenue, Chicago, IL 60603
Chicago Cook County and Illinois Industrial Directory, National Publishing Corp., 3150 Des Plaines Avenue, Des Plaines, IL 60018
Chicago Geographic Edition, Manufacturers' News, Inc., 4 E. Huron Street, Chicago, IL 60611; State Industrial Directories Corp., 2 Penn Plaza, New York, NY 10001
Illinois Industrial Directory, Illinois Industrial Directories National Publishing Corp., 3150 Des Plaines Avenue, Des Plaines, IL 60018
Illinois Manufacturers Directory, Manufacturers' News, Inc., 3 E. Huron Street, Chicago, IL 60611; State Industrial Directories Corp., 2 Penn Plaza, New York, NY 10001
Illinois Services Directory, Manufacturers' News, Inc., 3 E. Huron Street, Chicago, IL 60611
Business Financing Programs, Department

of Commerce and Community Affairs, 620 E. Adams, Springfield, IL 62701

Indiana

STATE HOUSE, INDIANAPOLIS, IN 46204
(317) 232-3140

INFORMATION OFFICES

Commerce/Economic Development
Department of Commerce
1 N. Capitol Avenue
Indianapolis, IN 46204
Corporate
Secretary of State
Corporation Division
State House
Indianapolis, IN 46204
Taxation
Department of Revenue
State Office Building
100 N. Senate Avenue
Indianapolis, IN 46204
State Board of Tax Commissioners
201 State Office Building
100 N. Senate Avenue
Indianapolis, IN 46204
State Chamber of Commerce
Indiana State Chamber of Commerce, Inc.
1 N. Capitol Avenue, Ste 200
Indianapolis, IN 46204
International Commerce
International Trade Division
Indiana Department of Commerce
1 N. Capitol Avenue
Indianapolis, IN 46204
Banking
Department of Financial Institutions
State Office Building
100 N. Senate Avenue
Indianapolis, IN 46204
Securities
Secretary of State
Securities Commission
1 N. Capitol Avenue
Indianapolis, IN 46204
Labor and Industrial Relations
Indiana Industrial Board
State Office Building
100 N. Senate Avenue
Indianapolis, IN 46204
Insurance
Indiana Department of Insurance
311 W. Washington Street
Indianapolis, IN 46204
Uniform Industrial Code
Uniform Commercial Code Division
Secretary of State Office
State House
Indianapolis, IN 46204
Business Ombudsman
Business Ombudsman Office
Department of Commerce
1 N. Capitol Avenue
Indianapolis, IN 46204

INDUSTRIAL AND BUSINESS DIRECTORIES

Indiana Industrial Directory, Harris Publishing Co., 2057–2 Aurora Rd., Twinsburg, OH 44087 Indiana State Chamber of Commerce, 1 N. Capitol Avenue, Ste 200, Indianapolis, IN 46204

Iowa

STATE CAPITOL, DES MOINES, IA 50319
(515) 281-5011

INFORMATION OFFICES

Commerce/Economic Development
Department of Economic Development
200 E. Grand
Des Moines, IA 50309
Corporate
Secretary of State
Corporation Division
Hoover Building
Des Moines, IA 50319
Taxation
Department of Revenue
Hoover Building
Des Moines, IA 50319
International Commerce
Department of Economic Development
200 E. Grand
Des Moines, IA 50309
Banking
Department of Commerce
Banking Division
200 E. Grant
Des Moines, IA 50309
Iowa Housing Finance Authority
200 E. Grant
Des Moines, IA 50309
Securities
Department of Commerce
Insurance Division
Securities Bureau
Lucas Building
Des Moines, IA 50319
Labor
Department of Employment Service
Division of Industrial Services
1000 E. Grand
Des Moines, IA 50319
Bureau of Labor
100 E. Grand
Des Moines, IA 50319
Insurance
Department of Commerce
Insurance Division
Lucas Building
Des Moines, IA 50319

INDUSTRIAL AND BUSINESS DIRECTORIES

Directory of Iowa Manufacturers, Iowa Department of Economic Development, 200 E. Grand, Des Moines, IA 50309

Doing Business in Iowa, Iowa Department of Economic Development, 200 E. Grand, Des Moines, IA 50309

Kansas

STATE HOUSE, TOPEKA, KS 66612
(913) 296-0111

INFORMATION OFFICES

Commerce/Economic Development
Department of Economic Development
400 S.W. 8th Street
Topeka, KS 66612

Corporate
Secretary of State
State House
Corporation Department
Topeka, KS 66612

Taxation
Department of Revenue
State Office Building
915 Harrison Street
Topeka, KS 66612

State Chamber of Commerce
Kansas Chamber of Commerce and Industry
500 Bank IV Tower
534 Kansas
Topeka, KS 66603-3460

International Commerce
Department of Economic Development
400 S.W. 8th Street
Topeka, KS 66612

Banking
Banking Department
700 Jackson Street
Topeka, KS 66603

Securities
Securities Commissioner of Kansas
900 S.W. Jackson Street
Topeka, KS 66612

Labor and Industrial Relations
Department of Human Resources
401 Topeka
Topeka, KS 66603

Insurance
Insurance Department
420 W. 9th Street
Topeka, KS 66612

Business Ombudsman
Department of Economic Development
400 W. 8th Street
Topeka, KS 66612

INDUSTRIAL AND BUSINESS DIRECTORIES

Directory of Kansas Manufacturers and Products, Kansas Department of Economic Development, 400 W. 8th Street, Topeka, KS 66603-3957; State Industrial Directories Corp., 2 Penn Plaza, New York, NY 10001

Directory of Manufacturers, Wichita, Kansas, Wichita Area Chamber of Commerce, 350 West Douglas, Wichita, KS 67202

Kansas Fortune 500 Companies, Kansas Department of Economic Development, 400 W. 8th Street, Topeka, KS 66603-3957

Kansas Manufacturing Firms in Export, Kansas Department of Economic Development, 400 W. 8th Street, Topeka, KS 66603-3957

Kansas Association Directory, Kansas Department of Economic Development, 400 W. 8th Street, Topeka, KS 66603-3957

Kentucky

STATE CAPITOL, FRANKFORT, KY 40601
(502) 564-3130

INFORMATION OFFICES

Commerce/Economic Development
Department of Business Development
Capital Plaza Office Tower
Frankfort, KY 40601

Corporate
Office of Secretary of State
Corporation Division
Capitol Building
Frankfort, KY 40601

Taxation
Revenue Cabinet
Capitol Annex
Frankfort, KY 40601

State Chamber of Commerce
Kentucky Chamber of Commerce
Versailles Road
P.O. Box 817
Frankfort, KY 40602

International Commerce
Kentucky Economic Development Cabinet
Office of International Marketing
Capitol Plaza Tower
Frankfort, KY 40601

Banking
Kentucky Department of Financial Institutions
Division of Banking and Thrift Institutions
911 Leawood Drive
Frankfort, KY 40601-3392

Securities
Kentucky Department of Financial Institutions
Division of Securities
911 Leawood Drive
Frankfort, KY 40601

Labor Industrial Relations
Kentucky Labor Cabinet
The 127 Building
Frankfort, KY 40601

Insurance
Kentucky Department of Insurance
P.O. Box 517
Frankfort, KY 40602

Uniform Industrial Code
Kentucky Department of Housing, Buildings, and Construction
The 127 Building
Frankfort, KY 40601

Business Ombudsman
Kentucky Department of Business Development
Capitol Plaza Tower
Frankfort, KY 40601

INDUSTRIAL AND BUSINESS DIRECTORIES

Kentucky International Trade, Kentucky Commerce Cabinet, Capitol Plaza Tower, Frankfort, KY 40601

Kentucky Directory of Manufacturers, Department of Business Development, Capitol Plaza Tower, Frankfort, KY 40601; and from Manufacturers' News, 4 E. Huron Street, Chicago, IL 60611; State Industrial Directories Corp., 2 Penn Plaza, New York, NY 10001; Harris Publishing Co., 20572 Aurora Road, Twinsburg, OH 44087

Louisiana

State Capitol, Baton Rouge, LA 70804
(504) 342-7015

INFORMATION OFFICES

Commerce/Economic Development
Department of Commerce
P.O. Box 94185
Baton Rouge, LA 70804-9185

Corporate
Secretary of State
Division of Corporation
P.O. Box 94125
Baton Rouge, LA 70804-9125

Taxation
Department of Revenue
P.O. Box 3440
Baton Rouge, LA 70823

State Chamber of Commerce
Louisiana Association of Business and Industry
P.O. Box 80258
Baton Rouge, LA 70898

International Commerce
Department of Commerce
Office of International Trade, Finance and Development
P.O. Box 94185
Baton Rouge, LA 70804-9185

Banking
Department of Commerce
Office of Financial Institutions
P.O. Box 94095
Baton Rouge, LA 70804

Securities
Louisiana Securities Commission
315 Louisiana State Office Building
325 Loyola Avenue
New Orleans, LA 70112

Labor and Industrial Relations
Department of Labor
P.O. Box 94094
Baton Rouge, LA 70804-9094

Insurance
Office of Insurance Rating Commission
P.O. Box 94157
Baton Rouge, LA 70804

Uniform Industrial Code
Department of Commerce
P.O. Box 94185
Baton Rouge, LA 70804-9185

Department of Labor
P.O. Box 94094
Baton Rouge, LA 70804-9094

Business Ombudsman
Department of Commerce
P.O. Box 94185
Baton Rouge, LA 70804-9185

INDUSTRIAL AND BUSINESS DIRECTORIES

Louisiana Directory of Manufacturers, Department of Commerce, 101 France Street, Baton Rouge, LA 70802; and from Manufacturers' News, Inc., 4 E. Huron Street, Chicago, IL 60611; State Industrial Directories Corp., 2 Penn Plaza, New York, NY 10001

Louisiana International Trade Directory, World Trade Center, 2 Canal Street, New Orleans, LA 70130

Maine

State House, Augusta, ME 04333
(207) 289-1110

INFORMATION OFFICES

Commerce/Economic Development
Department of Economic and Community Development
193 State Street
State House Station #59
Augusta, ME 04333

Corporate
Department of State
Division of Corporations
Statehouse Station #101
Augusta, ME 04333

Private Development Associations
Maine Development Foundation
1 Memorial Circle
Augusta, ME 04330

Taxation
Bureau of Taxation
Department of Finance
State House Station #24
Augusta, ME 04333

State Chamber of Commerce
Maine State Chamber of Commerce and Industry
126 Sewall Street
Augusta, ME 04330

International Commerce
Department of Economic and Community Development
193 State Street
State House Station #59
Augusta, ME 04333

Banking
Bureau of Banking
Hallowell Annex
Correspondence to:
State House Station #36
Hallowell, ME 04347

Securities
Bureau of Banking
Securities Division
State House Station #121
Augusta, ME 04333

Labor and Industrial Relations
Department of Labor
20 Union Street
P.O. Box 309
Augusta, ME 04330

Insurance
Bureau of Insurance
Hallowell Annex
Hallowell, ME 04347
Correspondence to:
State House #34
Augusta, ME 04333

INDUSTRIAL AND BUSINESS DIRECTORIES

Maine Marketing Directory, Department of Economic and Community Development, State House Station #59, Augusta, ME 04333

Maine Register, Tower Publishing Company, 34 Diamond Street, Portland, ME 04101

Maryland

State House, Annapolis, MD 21404
(301) 974-2000

INFORMATION OFFICES

Commerce/Economic Development
Department of Economic and Community Development
45 Calvert Street
Annapolis, MD 21401

Corporate
State Department of Assessments and Taxation
301 W. Preston Street
Baltimore, MD 21201

Taxation
Comptroller of the Treasury
Louis L. Goldstein Treasury Building
P.O. Box 466
Annapolis, MD 21404

State Chamber of Commerce
Maryland State Chamber of Commerce
60 West Street
Annapolis, MD 21401

International Commerce
Department of Economic and Community Development
Office of International Trade
World Trade Center
401 East Pratt Street
Baltimore, MD 21202

Maryland Port Administrator
Office of Port Administration
World Trade Center
Baltimore, MD 21202

Banking
State Banking Commission
34 Market Place
Baltimore, MD 21202

Securities
Division of Securities
Office of the Attorney General
7 N. Calvert Street
Baltimore, MD 21202

Labor and Industrial Relations
Division of Labor and Industry
Department of Licensing and Regulations
501 St. Paul Place
Baltimore, MD 21202

Insurance
State Insurance Division
Department of Licensing and Regulation
501 St. Paul Place
Baltimore, MD 21202

Business Ombudsman
Department of Economic and Community Development
Maryland Business Assistance Center
45 Calvert Street
Annapolis, MD 21401

INDUSTRIAL AND BUSINESS DIRECTORIES

Directory of Maryland Manufacturers, Maryland Department of Economic and Community Development, 45 Calvert Street, Annapolis, MD 21401

Maryland State Industrial Directory, State Industrial Directories Corp., 2 Penn Plaza, New York, NY 10001

Maryland High-Tech Directory, Maryland Department of Economic and Community Development, 45 Calvert Street, Annapolis, MD 21401

Massachusetts

STATE HOUSE, BOSTON, MA 02133
(617) 727-2121

INFORMATION OFFICES

Commerce/Economic Development
Governor's Office of Economic Development
Room 109
State House
Boston, MA 02133

Massachusetts Department of Commerce and Development
Division of Economic Development
100 Cambridge Street
Boston, MA 02202

Executive Office of Economic Affairs
2101 McCormack Building
1 Ashburton Place
Boston, MA 02108

Department of Commerce and Development
Leverett Saltonstall Building
100 Cambridge Street
Boston, MA 02202

Corporate
Secretary of State
1 Ashburton Place
Boston, MA 02108

Taxation
Accounting Bureau
Leverett Saltonstall Building
100 Cambridge Street
Boston, MA 02202

International Commerce
Office of International Trade and Investment
Executive Office of Economic Affairs
1 Ashburton Place
Boston, MA 02208

Banking
Division of Banks and Loan Agencies
100 Cambridge Street
Boston, MA 02202

Securities
Secretary of State
Securities Division
1 Ashburton Place
Boston, MA 02108

Labor and Industrial Relations
Executive Office of Labor
1 Ashburton Place
Boston, MA 02108

Department of Labor and Industries
Executive Office of Economic Affairs
100 Cambridge Street
Boston, MA 02202

Insurance
Division of Insurance
100 Cambridge Street
Boston, MA 02202

INDUSTRIAL AND BUSINESS DIRECTORIES

Directory of Directors in the City of Boston and Vicinity, Bankers Service Co., 14 Beacon Street, Boston, MA 02108

Directory of Massachusetts Manufacturers, George D. Hall Company, 20 Kilby Street, Boston, MA 02109

Massachusetts Directory of Manufacturers, Manufacturers' News, Inc., 4 E. Huron Street, Chicago, IL 60611

Massachusetts State Industrial Directory, State Industrial Directories Corp., 2 Penn Plaza, New York, NY 10001

Michigan

STATE CAPITOL, LANSING, MI 48913
(517) 373-1837

INFORMATION OFFICES

Commerce/Economic Development
Department of Commerce
525 W. Ottawa Street
P.O. Box 30225
Lansing, MI 48909

Corporate
Corporation and Securities Bureau
6546 Mercantile Way
P.O. Box 30054
Lansing, MI 48909

Taxation
Bureau of Collection
Department of Treasury
Treasury Building
Lansing, MI 48922

State Chamber of Commerce
Michigan State Chamber of Commerce
200 N. Washington Square
Lansing, MI 48933

International Commerce
Office of International Development
Department of Commerce
P.O. Box 30105
Lansing, MI 48909

Banking
Financial Institutions Bureau
Department of Commerce
Law Building
P.O. Box 30224
Lansing, MI 48909

Securities
Corporation and Securities Bureau
Department of Commerce

6546 Mercantile Way
P.O. Box 30222
Lansing, MI 48909

Labor and Industrial Relations
Bureau of Labor Relations
Department of Labor
State of Michigan Plaza Building
1200 Sixth Street
Detroit, MI 48226

Department of Labor
Lansing Plaza
309 North Washington
P.O. Box 30015
Lansing, MI 48909

Insurance
Insurance Bureau
Department of Licensing and Regulation
611 West Ottawa
North Ottawa Tower
P.O. Box 30220
Lansing, MI 48909

INDUSTRIAL AND BUSINESS DIRECTORIES

Directory of Michigan Manufacturers, Manufacturers' News, Inc., 4 E. Huron Street, Chicago, IL 60611; Manufacturers Publishing Co., 8543 Puritan Avenue, Detroit, MI 48238

Harris Michigan Marketers Industrial Directory, Harris Publishing Company, 33140 Aurora Road, Cleveland, OH 44139

Michigan State Industrial Directory, State Industrial Directories Corp., 2 Penn Plaza, New York, NY 10001

MacRae's Michigan State Industrial Directory, MacRae Publishing, 817 Broadway, New York, NY 10003

Economic Development Corporations Directory for the State of Michigan, Department of Commerce, Office of Business and Community Development, Lansing, MI 48909

Minnesota

State Capitol, St. Paul, MN 55155
(612) 296-6013

INFORMATION OFFICES

Commerce/Economic Development
Department of Trade and Economic Development
900 American Center Building
St. Paul, MN 55101

Minnesota Department of Commerce
Metro Square Building
7th and Robert Streets
St. Paul, MN 55101

Corporate
Corporation Division
180 State Office Building
St. Paul, MN 55155

Taxation
Department of Revenue
Centennial Office Building
St. Paul, MN 55145

State Chamber of Commerce
Minnesota Association of Commerce and Industry
Hanover Building
480 Cedar Street
St. Paul, MN 55101

International Commerce
Minnesota Trade Office
1000 World Trade Center
St. Paul, MN 55101

Banking
Minnesota Department of Commerce
Banking Division
Metro Square Building
7th & Robert Streets
St. Paul, MN 55101

Securities
Minnesota Department of Commerce
Registration Unit
Metro Square Building
7th & Robert Streets
St. Paul, MN 55101

Labor and Industrial Relations
Minnesota Department of Labor and Industry
444 Lafayette Road
St. Paul, MN 55101

Insurance
Minnesota Department of Commerce
Policy Analysis Division
Metro Square Building
7th & Robert Streets
St. Paul, MN 55101

Business Ombudsman
Department of Trade and Economic Development
Small Business Assistance Office
900 American Center Building
St. Paul, MN 55101

INDUSTRIAL AND BUSINESS DIRECTORIES

Minnesota Directory of Manufacturers, Manufacturers' News, Inc., 4 E. Huron Street, Chicago, IL 60611; State Industrial Directories Corp., 2 Penn Plaza, New York, NY 10001

Mississippi

New Capitol, Jackson, MS 39205
(601) 359-3100

INFORMATION OFFICES

Commerce/Economic Development
Mississippi Department of Economic Development

P.O. Box 849
Jackson, MS 39205

Department of Agriculture and Commerce
1604 Sillers Building
Jackson, MS 39205

Corporate
Secretary of State
Corporation Division
P.O. Box 136
Jackson, MS 39205

Taxation
Tax Commission
102 Woolfolk Building
Jackson, MS 39201

State Chamber of Commerce
P.O. Box 1849
Jackson, MS 39205-1849

Banking
Department of Banking and Consumer Finance
1206 Woolfolk State Office Building
Jackson, MS 39205

Securities
Department of State
Securities Division
P.O. Box 136
Jackson, MS 39205

Labor and Industrial Relations
1520 W. Capitol Street
Jackson, MS 39205

Insurance
Department of Insurance
1804 Sillers Building
Jackson, MS 39205

INDUSTRIAL AND BUSINESS DIRECTORIES

Mississippi International Trade Directory, Mississippi Marketing Council, Box 849, Sillers State Office Building, Jackson, MS 39205

Mississippi Manufacturers' Directory, Manufacturers' News, Inc., 4 E. Huron Street, Chicago, IL 60611; Public Information Office, Mississippi Research and Development Center, Jackson, MS 39205; State Industrial Directories Corp., 2 Penn Plaza, New York, NY 10001

Missouri

State Capitol, Jefferson City, MO 65101 (314) 751-2151

INFORMATION OFFICES

Commerce/Economic Development
Department of Economic Development
Economic Development Programs
P.O. Box 118
Jefferson City, MO 65102

Corporate
Secretary of State
Corporations Division
P.O. Box 778
Jefferson City, MO 65102

Taxation
Department of Revenue
Division of Taxation
Truman State Office Building
P.O. Box 629
Jefferson City, MO 65105

State Chamber of Commerce
Missouri Chamber of Commerce
428 East Capitol Avenue
P.O. Box 149
Jefferson City, MO 65102

International Commerce
International Business Development
Economic Development Program
Truman State Office Building
P.O. Box 1157
Jefferson City, MO 65102

Banking
Missouri Division of Finance
Truman State Office Building
P.O. Box 716
Jefferson City, MO 65102

Securities
Office of the Secretary of State
Securities Division
Truman State Office Building
P.O. Box 778
Jefferson City, MO 65102

Labor and Industrial Relations
Missouri Dept. of Labor & Industrial Relations
421 E. Dunklin
Jefferson City, MO 65102

Insurance
Missouri Division of Insurance
Truman State Office Building
P.O. Box 690
Jefferson City, MO 65102

Uniform Industrial Code
Missouri Division of Labor Standards
P.O. Box 449
Jefferson City, MO 65102

Business Ombudsman
Office of the Lieutenant Governor
Missouri State Capitol
P.O. Box 563
Jefferson City, MO 65102

INDUSTRIAL AND BUSINESS DIRECTORY

Contacts Influential: Commerce and Industrial Directory (for Kansas City Area), Contacts Influential, Inc., 6347 Brookside Boulevard, Suite 204, Kansas City, MO 64113

Missouri Directory of Manufacturing and Mining (annual), Informative Data Co., 3546 Watson Road, St. Louis, MO 63139

Montana

State Capitol, Helena, MT 59620
(406) 444-3111

INFORMATION OFFICES

Commerce/Economic Development
Department of Commerce
1424 9th Avenue
Helena, MT 59620

Economic Development and Research
Department of Commerce
1429 9th Avenue
Helena, MT 59620

Census and Economic Information Center
Department of Commerce
1429 9th Avenue
Helena, MT 59620

Corporate
Secretary of State
Corporation Bureau
State Capitol Building
Helena, MT 59620

State Chamber of Commerce
Montana Chamber of Commerce
P.O. Box 1730
Helena, MT 59601

International Commerce
International Export Officer
Montana Department of Commerce
1424 9th Avenue
Helena, MT 59620

Banking
Commissioner of Financial Institutions
Montana Department of Commerce
1424 9th Avenue
Helena, MT 59620

Securities
Securities Division
State Auditor's Office
Sam Mitchell Building
Helena, MT 59620

Labor & Industrial Relations
Commissioner's Office
Montana Department of Labor & Industry
Lockey and Roberts
Helena, MT 59620

Insurance
Insurance Division
State Auditor's Office
Sam Mitchell Building
Helena, MT 59620

Uniform Commercial Code
Secretary of State
Uniform Commercial Code Bureau
State Capitol Building
Capitol Station
Helena, MT 59620

Business Ombudsman
Small Business Advocate
Montana Department of Commerce
1424 9th Avenue
Helena, MT 59620

INDUSTRIAL AND BUSINESS DIRECTORIES

Montana Manufacturers and Products Directory, Department of Commerce, 1424 9th Avenue, Helena, MT 59620

Montana Business & Industrial Location Guide, Department of Commerce, 1424 9th Avenue, Helena, MT 59620

Nebraska

State Capitol, Lincoln, NE 68509
(402) 471-2311

INFORMATION OFFICES

Commerce/Economic Development
Department of Economic Development
301 Centennial Mall South
P.O. Box 94666
Lincoln, NE 68509-4666

Corporate
Secretary of State
Corporation Division
P.O. Box 94608
Lincoln, NE 68509-4608

Taxation
Department of Revenue
301 Centennial Mall South
P.O. Box 94818
Lincoln, NE 68509-4818

State Chamber of Commerce
Nebraska Chamber of Commerce and Industry
1320 Lincoln Mall
P.O. Box 95128
Lincoln, NE 68501

International Commerce
Nebraska Department of Economic Development
Small Business Division
P.O. Box 94666
Lincoln, NE 68509-4666

Banking
Department of Banking and Finance
301 Centennial Mall South
P.O. Box 95006
Lincoln, NE 68509-5006

Securities
Department of Banking and Finance
301 Centennial Mall South
P.O. Box 95006
Lincoln, NE 68509-5006

Labor and Industrial Relations
Nebraska Department of Labor
550 South 16th Street
P.O. Box 94600
Lincoln, NE 68509-4600

Insurance
Department of Insurance
The Terminal Building
941 O Street
Lincoln, NE 68508

Uniform Industrial Code
Uniform Commercial Code Division
301 Centennial Mall South
P.O. Box 5104
Lincoln, NE 68509-5104

Business Ombudsman
One-Stop Center
Department of Economic Development
P.O. Box 94666
Lincoln, NE 68509-4666

INDUSTRIAL AND BUSINESS DIRECTORIES

Directory of Nebraska Manufacturers and Their Products, Manufacturers' News, Inc., 4 E. Huron Street, Chicago, IL 60611

Directory of Nebraska Manufacturers and Their Products, Nebraska State Department of Economic Development, P.O. Box 94666, Lincoln, NE 68509-4666

Manufacturers Directory, Lincoln Chamber of Commerce, 1221 N Street, Lincoln, NE 68508

Directory of Manufacturers for the Omaha Metropolitan Area, Omaha Economic Development Council, 1301 Harney, Omaha, NE 68102.

Directory of Major Employers for the Omaha Area, Omaha Economic Development Council, 1301 Harney, Omaha, NE 68102.

Nevada

State Capitol, Carson City, NV 89710
(702) 885-5627

INFORMATION OFFICES

Commerce/Economic Development
Department of Commerce
201 S. Fall Street
Carson City, NV 89710

Commission on Economic Development
600 E. William Street
Capitol Complex
Carson City, NV 89710

Corporate
Secretary of State
Capitol Complex
Carson City, NV 89710

Taxation
Department of Taxation
1340 S. Curry Street
Carson City, NV 89710

State Chamber of Commerce
Nevada Chamber of Commerce Association
P.O. Box 2806
Reno, NV 89505

International Commerce
Department of Commerce
201 S. Fall Street
Carson City, NV 89710

Banking
Financial Institutions Division
Department of Commerce
406 E. Second Street
Carson City, NV 89710

Securities
Secretary of State
Capitol Complex
Carson City, NV 89710

Labor and Industrial Relations
Labor Commission
505 E. King Street
Carson City, NV 89710

Department of Industrial Relations
1390 S. Curry Street
Carson City, NV 89710

Insurance
Insurance Division
Department of Commerce
201 S. Fall Street
Carson City, NV 89710

INDUSTRIAL AND BUSINESS DIRECTORIES

Nevada Economic Development Handbook, Commission on Economic Development, 600 E. William Street, Capitol Complex, Carson City, NV 89710

Nevada Industrial Directory, Gold Hill Publishings Co., Inc., P.O. Drawer F, Virginia City, NV 89440

Nevada Directory of Business, Manufacturers' News, Inc., 4 E. Huron Street, Chicago, IL 60611

Directory of Nevada Mine Operations, Division of Mine Inspection Department of Industrial Relations, 1380 S. Curry Street, Carson City, NV 89710

New Hampshire

State House, Concord, NH 03301
(603) 271-1110

INFORMATION OFFICES

Commerce/Economic Development
Department of Resources and Economic Development
Division of Economic Development
105 Loudon Road, Building #2
Prescott Park
Concord, NH 03301

Corporate
Secretary of State
Corporations Division
State House Annex
Concord, NH 03301

Taxation
Board of Taxation
61 S. Spring Street
Concord, NH 03301

Department of Revenue Administration
61 S. Spring Street
Concord, NH 03301

State Chamber of Commerce
Business and Industry Association of New Hampshire
23 School Street
Concord, NH 03301

International Commerce
Department of Resources & Economic Development
Division of Economic Development
105 Loudon Road, Building #2
Prescott Park—Concord, NH 03301

Banking
Banking Department
State of New Hampshire
47 N. Main Street
Concord, NH 03301

New Hampshire Banking Association
125 N. Main Street
Concord, NH 03301

Securities
Insurance Department, Securities Division
State of New Hampshire
169 Manchester Street
Concord, NH 03301

Labor and Industrial Relations
Department of Employment Security
State of New Hampshire
32 S. Main Street
Concord, NH 03301

Department of Labor
19 Pillsbury Street
Concord, NH 03301

Insurance
Insurance Department
State of New Hampshire
169 Manchester Street
Concord, NH 03301

Standard Industrial Code
Department of Employment Security
State of New Hampshire
32 S. Main Street
Concord, NH 03301

INDUSTRIAL AND BUSINESS DIRECTORIES

Made in New Hampshire, New Hampshire Office of Industrial Development, Department of Resources, Concord, NH 03301

New Hampshire Register, Tower Publishing Company, 163 Middle Street, Portland, ME 04111

New Jersey

State House, Trenton, NJ 08625
(609) 292-2121

INFORMATION OFFICES

Commerce/Economic Development
Department of Commerce and Economic Development
CN 820, 1 W. State Street
Trenton, NJ 08625

Division of Travel and Tourism
CN 826, 1 West State Street
Trenton, NJ 08625

Economic Development Authority
CN 990, Capitol Place One
Trenton, NJ 08625

Corporate
Secretary of State
Division of Commercial Recreation
820 Bear Tavern Road
W. Trenton, NJ 08625

Taxation
Department of Treasury
Division of Taxation
CN 240, 50 Barrack Street
Trenton, NJ 08625

State Chamber of Commerce
New Jersey State Chamber of Commerce
240 W. State Street
Trenton, NJ 08625

International Commerce
Division of International Trade
744 Broad Street
Newark, NJ 07102

Banking
Department of Banking
CN 040, 20 W. State Street
Trenton, NJ 08625

Securities
Bureau of Securities
80 Mulberry Street
Newark, NJ 07102

Labor and Labor Relations
Department of Labor and Industry
John Fitch Plaza
Trenton, NJ 08625

Insurance
Department of Insurance
CN 325, 20 W. State Street
Trenton, NJ 08625

Business Ombudsman
Department of Public Advocate
CN 850
Trenton, NJ 08625

INDUSTRIAL AND BUSINESS DIRECTORIES

New Jersey State Industrial Directory, Manufacturers' News, Inc., 4 E. Huron Street, Chicago, IL 60611; State Industrial Directories Corp., 2 Penn Plaza, New York, NY 10001

New Mexico

STATE CAPITOL, SANTE FE, NM 87503
(505) 827-4011

INFORMATION OFFICES

Commerce/Economic Development
Economic Development and Tourism
Joseph M. Montoya Building
1100 St. Francis Drive
Sante Fe, NM 87503
Corporate
State Corporation Commission
P.O. Drawer 1269
Sante Fe, NM 87501
Taxation
Bureau of Revenue
Manuel Lujan Sr. Building
Santa Fe, NM 87501
State Chamber of Commerce
Association of Commerce and Industry of New Mexico
4001 Indian School NE
Albuquerque, NM 87108
International Commerce
Department of International Trade
Joseph M. Montoya Building
1100 St. Francis Drive
Sante Fe, NM 87503
Banking
Lew Wallace Building
Sante Fe, NM 87503
Securities
Bataan Memorial Building
Sante Fe, NM 87503
Labor and Industrial Commission
23 W Manhatten
Sante Fe, NM 87501
Insurance
State Corporation Commission
P.O. Box 1269
Sante Fe, NM 87501

INDUSTRIAL AND BUSINESS DIRECTORIES

New Mexico Directory of Manufacturing, Manufacturers' News, Inc., 4 E. Huron Street, Chicago, IL 60611; State Industrial Directories Corp., 2 Penn Plaza, New York, NY 10001

New York

STATE CAPITOL, ALBANY, NY 12224
(518) 474-2121

INFORMATION OFFICES

Commerce/Economic Development
Department of Economic Development
One Commerce Plaza
Albany, NY 12245
Division of Regional Economic Development
One Commerce Plaza
Albany, NY 12245
Corporate
Secretary of State
162 Washington Avenue
Albany, NY 12231
Taxation
Department of Taxation and Finance
State Campus Building #9
Albany, NY 12227
State Chamber of Commerce
Business Council of New York State
152 Washington Avenue
Albany, NY 12210
Small Business Advisory Board
Division for Small Business
1515 Broadway
New York, NY 10036
International Commerce
Department of Economic Development
1515 Broadway
New York, NY 10036
Banking
Department of Banking
194 Washington Avenue
New York, NY 12210
Labor and Industrial Relations
Department of Labor
State Campus
Albany, NY 12240
Insurance
Department of Insurance
Empire State Plaza
Agency Building #1
Albany, NY 12257
Business Ombudsman
Department of Economic Development
Division for Small Business
1515 Broadway
New York, NY 10036

INDUSTRIAL AND BUSINESS DIRECTORIES

New York and Surrounding Territory Classified Business Directory, New York Directory Co., Inc., 358 New York Avenue, Huntington, NY 11743
New York Classified Business Directory, New York Directory Co., Inc., 1440 Broadway, New York, NY 10018
MacRae's New York State Industrial Directory, Business Research, Inc., 817 Broadway, New York, NY 10003
Directory of Certified Minority and Women-Owned Business Enterprises, Minority and Women's Business Division, New York State Department of Economic Development, 515 Broadway, New York, NY 10036

North Carolina

State Legislative Building, Raleigh, NC 27611
(919) 733-1110

INFORMATION OFFICES

Commerce/Economic Development
Department of Commerce
430 N. Salisbury Street
Raleigh, NC 27611

Corporate
Secretary of State
Corporation Division
300 N. Salisbury Street
Raleigh, NC 27611

Taxation
Department of Revenue
2 S. Salisbury Street
Raleigh, NC 27602

State Chamber of Commerce
North Carolina Citizens for Business and Industry
P.O. Box 2508
Raleigh, NC 27602

International Commerce
International Development
Department of Commerce
430 N. Salisbury Street
Raleigh, NC 27611

Banking
Banking Commission
Department of Commerce
430 N. Salisbury Street
Raleigh, NC 27611

Securities
Secretary of State
Securities Division
300 N. Salisbury Street
Raleigh, NC 27611

Labor and Industrial Relations
Department of Labor
4 W. Edenton Street
Raleigh, NC 27611

Insurance
Department of Insurance
430 N. Salisbury Street
Raleigh, NC 27611

Business Ombudsman
Business Assistance
Department of Commerce
430 N. Salisbury Street
Raleigh, NC 27611

INDUSTRIAL AND BUSINESS DIRECTORIES

Directory of North Carolina Manufacturing Firms, North Carolina Department of Commerce, Raleigh, NC 27611; State Industrial Directories Corp., 2 Penn Plaza, New York, NY 10001; Manufacturers' News, Inc., 4 E. Huron Street, Chicago, IL 60611

North Dakota

State Capitol, Bismarck, ND 58505
(701) 224-2000

INFORMATION OFFICES

Commerce/Economic Development
Economic Development Commission
Liberty Memorial Building
Bismarck, ND 58505

Corporate
Corporation Department
Office of the Secretary of State
Bismarck, ND 58505

Taxation
Tax Department
State Capitol
Bismarck, ND 58505

State Chamber of Commerce
Greater North Dakota Association—State Chamber of Commerce
P.O. Box 2467
Fargo, ND 58102

International Commerce
International Trade Department
Economic Development Commission
Liberty Memorial Building
Bismarck, ND 58505

Banking
State Banking Commission
State Capitol
Bismarck, ND 58505

Securities
Securities Commissioner
State Capitol
Bismarck, ND 58505

Labor and Industrial Relations
State Commissioner of Labor
State Capitol
Bismarck, ND 58505

Insurance
Insurance Commissioner
State Capitol
Bismarck, ND 58505

Uniform Industrial Code
Secretary of State
State Capitol
Bismarck, ND 58505

Business Ombudsman
Economic Development Commission
Liberty Memorial Building
Bismarck, ND 58505

INDUSTRIAL AND BUSINESS DIRECTORIES

North Dakota Manufacturers Directory, Economic Development Commission, Liberty Memorial Building, Bismarck, ND

58505; Manufacturers' News, Inc., 4 E. Huron Street, Chicago, IL 60611; State Industrial Directories Corp., 2 Penn Plaza, New York, NY 10001

Strictly Business, Frontier Directory Co., Inc., 515 E. Main Street, Bismarck, ND 58501

Ohio

State House, Columbus, OH 43215
(614) 466-3455
State Operator: (614) 466-2000

INFORMATION OFFICES

Commerce/Economic Development
Ohio Department of Development
30 E. Broad Street
Columbus, OH 43266

Corporate
Secretary of State
Corporation Section
30 East Broad Street
Columbus, OH 43266

Taxation
Department of Taxation
30 E. Broad Street
Columbus, OH 43266

State Chamber of Commerce
Ohio Chamber of Commerce
35 E. Gay Street
Columbus, OH 43215

International Commerce
Ohio Department of Development
International Trade Division
30 E. Broad Street
P.O. Box 1001
Columbus, OH 43266

Banking
Ohio Department of Commerce
Division of Banks
Two Nationwide Plaza
Columbus, OH 43266

Securities
Ohio Department of Commerce
Division of Securities
Two Nationwide Plaza
Columbus, OH 43266

Labor and Industrial Relations
Ohio Department of Industrial Relations
2323 W. Fifth Avenue
P.O. Box 825
Columbus, OH 43266

Office of Collective Bargaining

Insurance
Ohio Department of Insurance
2100 Stella Court
Columbus, OH 43266

Uniform Industrial Code
Industrial Commission of Ohio
Division of Safety and Hygiene
246 N. High Street
Columbus, OH 43266

Business Ombudsman
Ohio Department of Development
Small and Developing Business Division
Minority Business Development Division
P.O. Box 1001
Columbus, OH 43266

INDUSTRIAL AND BUSINESS DIRECTORIES

Akron, Ohio Membership Directory and Buyers Guide, Akron Area Chamber of Commerce, P.O. Box 436, Crystal Lake, IL 60014

Directory of Manufacturers in the Toledo Area, Toledo Area Chamber of Commerce, 218 Huron Street, Toledo, OH 43604

Directory of Ohio Manufacturers, Harris Publishing Co., 2057–2 Aurora Road, Twinsburg, OH 44087; Manufacturers' News, Inc., 4 E. Huron Street, Chicago, IL 60611

Manufacturers Directory, Columbus Area Chamber of Commerce, 37 North High Street, Columbus, OH 43215

Ohio and International Trade, Division of International Trade, Department of Development, P.O. Box 1001, Columbus, OH 43266

Oklahoma

State Capitol, Oklahoma City, OK 73105
(405) 521-1601

INFORMATION OFFICES

Commerce/Economic Development
Department of Commerce
6601 Broadway Extension
Oklahoma City, OK 73116

Corporate
Secretary of State
State Capitol
Oklahoma City, OK 73105

Taxation
Tax Commission
M. C. Connors Building
Oklahoma City, OK 73105

State Chamber of Commerce
Oklahoma State Chamber of Commerce & Industry
4020 North Lincoln
Oklahoma City, OK 73105

International Commerce
International Trade Division
Department of Commerce
6601 Broadway Extension
Oklahoma City, OK 73116

Banking
Oklahoma Banking Department
4100 Lincoln Boulevard
Oklahoma City, OK 73105

Securities
Oklahoma Securities Commission
2915 Lincoln Boulevard
Oklahoma City, OK 73152
Labor and Industrial Relations
Oklahoma Labor Department
1315 Broadway Place
Oklahoma City, OK 73103
Insurance
Insurance Commission
1901 N. Walnut Street
P.O. Box 53408
Oklahoma City, OK 73152
Uniform Industrial Code
Universal Commercial Code Division
County Clerk's Office
County Court House
Oklahoma City, OK 73102

INDUSTRIAL AND BUSINESS DIRECTORIES

Oklahoma Directory of Manufacturers and Products, Media/Marketing & Advertising, Department of Commerce, 6601 Broadway Extension, Oklahoma City, OK 73116

Oregon

State Capitol, Salem, OR 97310
(503) 378-3131

INFORMATION OFFICES

Commerce/Economic Development
Economic Development Department
595 Cottage Street N.E.
Salem, OR 97310
Corporate
Corporation Division
Office of Secretary of State
Commerce Building
158 12th Street N.E.
Salem, OR 97310
Taxation
Department of Revenue
Revenue Building
955 Center Street
Salem, OR 97310
International Commerce
International Trade Division
Economic Development Department
620 Crown Plaza
1500 S.W. 1st Avenue
Portland, OR 97201
Banking
Finance Section
Division of Finance and Corporate Securities
Department of Insurance and Finance
21 Labor and Industries Building
Salem, OR 97310
Securities
Corporate Securities Section
Division of Finance and Corporate Securities
Department of Insurance and Finance
21 Labor and Industries Building
Salem, OR 97310
Labor and Industry
Bureau of Labor and Industries
1400 S.W. 5th Avenue
Portland, OR 97201
Insurance
Insurance Division
Department of Insurance and Finance
21 Labor and Industries Building
Salem, OR 97310
Uniform Industrial Code
Building Codes Agency
401 Labor and Industries Building
Salem, OR 97310

INDUSTRIAL AND BUSINESS DIRECTORIES

Directory of Oregon Manufacturers, Economic Development Department, 595 Cottage Street N.E., Salem, OR 97310; Manufacturers' News, Inc., 4 E. Huron Street, Chicago, IL 60611

Pennsylvania

Main Capitol Building, Harrisburg, PA 17120
(717) 787-2121

INFORMATION OFFICES

Department of Commerce
Department of Commerce
433 Forum Building
Harrisburg, PA 17120

Bureau of Domestic Commerce
Department of Commerce
453 Forum Building
Harrisburg, PA 17120

Bureau of International Commerce
Department of Commerce
450 Forum Building
Harrisburg, PA 17120

Office of Program Management
Department of Commerce
480 Forum Building
Harrisburg, PA 17120

Business Resource Network
Department of Commerce
404 Forum Building
Harrisburg, PA 17120
Corporate
Department of State
Bureau of Corporations
North Office Building
Harrisburg, PA 17120

Taxation
Department of Revenue
Strawberry Square
Harrisburg, PA 17127
State Chamber of Commerce
Pennsylvania Chamber of Commerce
222 N. Third Street
Harrisburg, PA 17101
Banking
Banking
333 Market Street
Harristown II
Harrisburg, PA 17101-2290
Securities
Securities Commission
333 Market Street, Harristown II,
Harrisburg, PA 17101
Labor and Industrial Relations
Department of Labor & Industry
Labor & Industry Building
7th & Forster Streets
Harrisburg, PA 17120
Insurance
Insurance
Strawberry Square
Harrisburg, PA 17120

INDUSTRIAL AND BUSINESS DIRECTORIES

Industrial Directory of the Commonwealth of Pennsylvania, Department of General Services, Harris Publishing Company, 2057-2 Aurora Road, Twinsburg, OH 44087

Rhode Island

State House, Providence, RI 02903
(401) 277-2000

INFORMATION OFFICES

Commerce/Economic Development
Department of Economic Development
7 Jackson Walkway
Providence, RI 02903
Taxation
Division of Taxation
Department of Administration
289 Promenade Street
CIC Complex
Providence, RI 02908
Corporate
Secretary of State
Corporation Department
270 Westminster Street
Providence, RI 02903
State Chamber of Commerce
Rhode Island Chamber of Commerce
91 Park Street
Providence, RI 02908
International Commerce
Rhode Island Department of Economic Development
European Office
Meir 24
2000 Antwerp
Belgium
Banking
Department of Business Regulation
Banking Division
100 N. Main Street
Providence, RI 02903
Securities
Department of Business Regulation
Banking Division
100 N. Main Street
Providence, RI 02903
Labor and Industrial Relations
Department of Labor
220 Elmwood Avenue
Providence, RI 02907
Insurance
Department of Business Regulation
Insurance Division
100 N. Main Street
Providence, RI 02903
Uniform Industrial Code
Department of Labor
220 Elmwood Avenue
Providence, RI 02907
Business Ombudsman
Business Action Center
Department of Economic Development
7 Jackson Walkway
Providence, RI 02903

INDUSTRIAL AND BUSINESS DIRECTORIES

Rhode Island Directory of Manufacturers, Department of Economic Development, 7 Jackson Walkway, Providence, RI 02903
Rhode Island State Industrial Directory, State Industrial Directories Corp., 2 Penn Plaza, New York, NY 10001

South Carolina

State House, Columbia, SC 29211
(803) 734-9818

INFORMATION OFFICES

Commerce/Economic Development
South Carolina State Development Board
P.O. Box 927
1301 Gervais Street
Columbia, SC 29202
Taxation
Tax Commission
P.O. Box 125
Columbia Mill Building
Columbia, SC 29201
Corporate
Secretary of State
P.O. Box 11350
Columbia, SC 29211

State Chamber of Commerce
South Carolina Chamber of Commerce
1301 Gervais Street
Columbia, SC 29202
International Commerce
South Carolina State Development Board
1301 Gervais Street
P.O. Box 927
Columbia, SC 29202
Labor and Industrial Relations
South Carolina Labor Department
Landmark Center, 3600 Forest Drive
P.O. Box 11329
Columbia, SC 29211
Insurance
South Carolina Department of Insurance
1612 Marion Street
P.O. Box 100105
Columbia, SC 29202-3105
Business Ombudsman
South Carolina State Development Board
1301 Gervais Street
P.O. Box 927
Columbia, SC 29202

INDUSTRIAL AND BUSINESS DIRECTORIES

Industrial Directory of South Carolina, South Carolina State Development Board, P.O. Box 927, 1301 Gervais Street, Columbia, SC 29202

South Dakota

State Capitol, Pierre, SD 57501
(605) 773-3011

INFORMATION OFFICES

Commerce/Economic Development
Governor's Office of Economic Development
711 Wells Avenue
Capitol Lake Plaza
Pierre, SD 57501

Department of Commerce and Regulation
910 E. Sioux
Pierre, SD 57501
Corporate
Secretary of State
Corporation Division
Capitol Building
Pierre, SD 57501
Taxation
Department of Revenue
Kneip Building
Pierre, SD 57501
State Chamber of Commerce
Industry & Commerce Association of South Dakota
300 S. Highland
P.O. Box 548
Pierre, SD 57501
International Commerce
Governor's Office of Economic Development
711 Wells
Capitol Lake Plaza
Pierre, SD 57501
Banking
Department of Commerce and Regulation
Division of Banking
105 S. Euclid
Pierre, SD 57501
Securities
Department of Commerce and Regulation
Division of Securities
910 E. Sioux
Pierre, SD 57501
Labor and Industrial Relations
Department of Labor
Division of Labor and Management
Kneip Building
Pierre, SD 57501
Insurance
Department of Commerce and Regulation
Division of Insurance
910 E. Sioux
Pierre, SD 57501

INDUSTRIAL AND BUSINESS DIRECTORIES

Directory of South Dakota Industries, Manufacturers' News, Inc., 4 E. Huron Street, Chicago, IL 60611
South Dakota Manufacturers and Processors Directory, Governor's Office of Economic Development, 711 Well Avenue, Capitol Lake Plaza, Pierre, SD 57501; State Industrial Directories Corp., 2 Penn Plaza, New York, NY 10001
South Dakota Export Directory, Governor's Office of Economic Development, 711 Well Avenue, Capitol Lake Plaza, Pierre, SD 57501

Tennessee

State Capitol, Nashville, TN 37219
(615) 741-2001

INFORMATION OFFICES

Commerce/Economic Development
Department of Economic and Community Development
Rachel Jackson Building
320 6th Avenue North
Nashville, TN 37219
Corporate
Secretary of State
Records Division
James K. Polk Building
Nashville, TN 37219

Taxation
Department of Revenue
927 Andrew Jackson Building
500 Deaderick Street
Nashville, TN 37242

State Chamber of Commerce
State Chamber Division of the Tennessee Taxpayers Association
242 Doctors Building
Nashville, TN 37203

International Commerce
Department of Economic & Community Development
International Sales & Marketing
Rachel Jackson Building
320 6th Avenue North
Nashville, TN 37219

Banking
Department of Financial Institutions
James K. Polk State Office Building
505 Deaderick Street
Nashville, TN 37219

Securities
Department of Commerce & Insurance
Securities Division
614 Tennessee Building
Nashville, TN 37219

Labor and Industrial Relations
Department of Labor
501 Union Building
Nashville, TN 37219

Insurance
Department of Commerce & Insurance
Insurance Division
State Office Building
Nashville, TN 37219

Business Ombudsman
Department of Economic & Community Development
Business & Industry Services Division
Rachel Jackson Building
320 6th Avenue North
Nashville, TN 37219-5308

INDUSTRIAL AND BUSINESS DIRECTORIES

Directory of Tennessee Industries, Manufacturers' News, Inc., 4 E. Huron Street, Chicago, IL 60611; State Industrial Directories Corp., 2 Penn Plaza, New York, NY 10001

Texas

State Capitol, Austin, TX 78701
State Information: (512) 463-4630

INFORMATION OFFICES

Commerce/Economic Development
Texas Economic Development Commission
410 East 5th Street
Austin, TX 78711

Corporate
Secretary of State
P.O. Box 13601
Sam Houston Building
Austin, TX 78711

Taxation
Comptroller of Public Accounts
104 LBJ State Office Building
Austin, TX 78774

State Chamber of Commerce
Texas State Chamber of Commerce
206 W. 13th Street
Austin, TX 78752

Tourism Department
P.O. Box 12008
Austin, TX 78711

Lower Rio Grand Valley Chamber of Commerce
P.O. Box 1499
Weslaco, TX 78596

South Texas Chamber of Commerce
300 W. 15th Street
Austin, TX 78101

East Texas Chamber of Commerce
P.O. Box 1592
Longview, TX 75606

West Texas Chamber of Commerce
P.O. Box 1561
Abilene, TX 79604

International Commerce
International Division
Texas Economic Development Commission
P.O. Box 12728, Capitol Station
Austin, TX 78711

Banking
Texas Department of Banking
2601 North Lamar
Austin, TX 78705

Securities
Securities Board
P.O. Box 367, Capitol Station
1800 San Jacinto St.
Austin, TX 78711-3169

Labor and Industrial Relations
Texas Department of Labor and Standards
P.O. Box 12157, Capitol Station
Austin, TX 78711

Insurance
Texas State Board of Insurance
State Insurance Building
1110 San Jacinto
Austin, TX 78701-1998

Uniform Industrial Code
Uniform Commercial Code Section
Secretary of State's Office
P.O. Box 12887, Capitol Station
Austin, TX 78711

Business Ombudsman
Texas Economic Department Commission
410 E. 5th Street
P.O. Box 12728
Austin, TX 78711

INDUSTRIAL AND BUSINESS DIRECTORIES

Dallas Business Guide, Dallas Chamber of Commerce, Fidelity Tower, Dallas, TX 75201

Directory of Texas Manufacturers, Bureau of Business Research, University of Texas, Austin, TX 78712; State Industrial Directories Corp., 2 Penn Plaza, New York, NY 10001

Fort Worth Directory of Manufacturers, Fort Worth Area Chamber of Commerce, 700 Throckmorton Street, Fort Worth, TX 76102

Texas Exporter-Importer Directory, Gulf International Trades, Box 52717, Houston, TX 77052

Texas Manufacturers Directory, Manufacturers' News, Inc., 4 E. Huron Street, Chicago, IL 60611

Utah

State Capitol, Salt Lake City, UT 84114 (801) 533-4000

INFORMATION OFFICES

Commerce/Economic Development
Department of Business Regulation
160 East 300 South
Salt Lake City, UT 84145-0802

Department of Community and Economic Development
6290 State Office Building
Salt Lake City, UT 84114

Office of Planning & Budget
Data Resources Section
116 Capitol Building
Salt Lake City, UT 84114

Corporate
Division of Corporations and Commercial Code
Heber M. Wells Building
160 E. 300 South
Salt Lake City, UT 84145-0801

Taxation
Department of State Tax Commission
Heber M. Wells Building
160 E. 300 South
Salt Lake City, UT 84134-4000

International Commerce
International Business Development
Division of Economic & Business Development
6150 State Office Building
Salt Lake City, UT 84114

Banking
Department of Financial Institutions
Heber M. Wells Building
160 E. 300 South
P.O. Box 89
Salt Lake City, UT 84110-5802

Securities
Division of Securities
Heber M. Wells Building
160 E. 300 South
P.O. Box 89
Salt Lake City, UT 84110-5802

Labor and Industrial Relations
Industrial Commission of Utah
Heber M. Wells Building
160 E. 300 South
Salt Lake City, UT 84110-5800

Insurance
Department of Insurance
Heber M. Wells Building
160 E. 300 South
Salt Lake City, UT 84110-5803

Division of Occupational and Professional Licensing
160 East 300 South
P.O. Box 45802
Salt Lake City, UT 84145-0802

Uniform Industrial Code
Employment Security/Job Service
174 Social Hall Avenue
Salt Lake City, UT 84147

INDUSTRIAL AND BUSINESS DIRECTORIES

Directory of Utah Manufacturers, Manufacturers' News, Inc., 4 E. Huron Street, Chicago, IL 60611; Department of Employment Security, 1234 S. Main Street, Salt Lake City, UT 84147

Vermont

State House, Montpelier, VT 05602
(802) 828-3333 (Action Line)

INFORMATION OFFICES

Commerce/Economic Development
Agency of Development and Community Affairs
Department of Economic Development
109 State Street
Montpelier, VT 05602

Corporate
Secretary of State
Corporation Department
26 Terrace Street
Montpelier, VT 05602

Taxation
Department of Taxes
Agency of Administration
109 State Street
Montpelier, VT 05602

State Chamber of Commerce
Vermont State Chamber of Commerce
P.O. Box 37
Montpelier, VT 05602

Insurance
Department of Banking and Insurance
120 State Street
Montpelier, VT 05602

Banking
Department of Banking and Insurance
120 State Street
Montpelier, VT 05602
Securities
Department of Banking and Insurance
120 State Street
Montpelier, VT 05602
Labor and Industrial Relations
Department of Labor and Industry
120 State Street
Montpelier, VT 05602
Uniform Commercial Code
Department of Banking and Insurance
120 State Street
Montpelier, VT 05602
Business Ombudsman
Agency Development and Community Affair
Department of Economic Development
109 State Street
Montpelier, VT 05602

INDUSTRIAL AND BUSINESS DIRECTORIES

Vermont Directory of Manufacturers, Vermont Agency of Development and Community Affairs, Montpelier, VT 05602
Vermont State Industrial Directory, Manufacturers' News, Inc., 4 E. Huron Street, Chicago, IL 60611; State Industrial Directories Corp., 2 Penn Plaza, New York, NY 10001
Vermont Yearbook, The National Survey, Chester, VT 05143

Virginia

State Capitol, Richmond, VA 23219
(804) 786-0000

INFORMATION OFFICES

Commerce/Economic Development
Department of Economic Development
1000 Washington Building
Richmond, VA 23219

Department of Conservation and Historic Resources
1100 Washington Building
Richmond, VA 23219
Corporate
State Corporation Commission
1220 Bank Street
Richmond, VA 23209
Taxation
Department of Taxation
2200 W. Broad Street
P.O. Box 6-L
Richmond, VA 23282
State Chamber of Commerce
Virginia State Chamber of Commerce
611 E. Franklin Street
Richmond, VA 23219
International Commerce
Department of Economic Development
1000 Washington Building
Richmond, VA 23219
Banking
State Corporation Commission
Bureau of Financial Institutions
701 E. Byrd Street
P.O. Box 2AE
Richmond, VA 23205
Securities
State Corporation Commission
Division of Securities and Retail Franchising
11 S. 12th Street
Richmond, VA 23219
Labor and Industrial Relations
Department of Labor and Industry
205 N. 4th Street
P.O. Box 12064
Richmond, VA 23241
Insurance
State Corporation Commission
Bureau of Insurance
1220 Bank Street
Richmond, VA 23209
Uniform Industrial Code
Virginia Employment Commission
Research and Analysis Division
703 E. Main Street
Richmond, VA 23211
Business Ombudsman
Department of Agriculture and Consumer Services
Office of Consumer Affairs
1100 Bank Street
Richmond, VA 23219

INDUSTRIAL AND BUSINESS DIRECTORIES

Industrial Directory of Virginia, Chamber of Commerce, 611 E. Franklin Street, Richmond, VA 23219
Virginia Industrial Directory, Manufacturers' News, Inc., 4 E. Huron Street, Chicago, IL 60611; State Industrial Directories Corp., 2 Penn Plaza, New York, NY 10001

Washington

101 General Administration Building,
Olympia, WA 98504
(206) 753-5630

INFORMATION OFFICES

Commerce/Economic Development
Department of Trade and Economic Development
101 General Administration Building
Olympia, WA 98504

Corporate
Secretary of State
Corporate Division
505 E. Union
Olympia, WA 98504
Taxation
Department of Revenue
412 General Administration Building
Olympia, WA 98504
State Chamber of Commerce
Association of Washington Business
1414 S. Cherry Street
Olympia, WA 98501
International Commerce
Department of Trade & Economic Development
Domestic & International Trade Division
312 First Avenue North
Seattle, WA 98109
Banking
General Administration Building
Banking & Consumer Finance
219 General Administration Building
Olympia, WA 98504
Securities
Department of Licensing Building
Att: Securities Division
1300 Quince Street SE
Olympia, WA 98504
Labor and Industrial Relations
Department of Labor & Industries
Employment Standards—Apprenticeship
Crime Victims Division
925 Plum Street SE
Olympia, WA 98504
Insurance
Insurance Commissioner's Office
Insurance Building
Olympia, WA 98504
Uniform Commercial Code
Department of Licensing
Business License Centre
405 Black Lake Place
Olympia, WA 98502
Business Ombudsman
Department of Trade & Economic Development
Business Assistance Center
919 Lakeridge Way, S.W.
Olympia, WA 98504

INDUSTRIAL AND BUSINESS DIRECTORIES

1988 Directory of Advanced Technology Industries in Washington State, Economic Development Partnership for Washington State, 18000 Pacific Highway South, Seattle, WA 98188

Business Assistance in Washington State, Washington State International Trade Directory, Department of Trade and Economic Development, 101 General Administration Building, Olympia, WA 98504

Minority Women Business Enterprises, Office of Minority Women Business Enterprises, 406 S. Water Street, Olympia, WA 98504

Washington Manufacturers Register, Times Mirror Press, P.O. Box 7440, Newport Beach, CA 92658

Washington Forest Industry Mill Directory (1984), Department of Natural Resources, 1065 S. Capitol Way, Olympia, WA 98504

Directory of Washington Mining Operations, Department of Natural Resources, Division of Geology, Olympia, WA 98504

West Virginia

State Capitol, Charleston, WV 25305
(304) 348-3456

INFORMATION OFFICES

Commerce/Economic Development
Governor's Office of Community and Industrial Development
1900 Washington Street East
Building I
Charleston, WV 25305
Corporate
Secretary of State
Corporate Division
1900 Washington Street East
Building 1
Charleston, WV 25305
Taxation
Tax Department
1900 Washington Street East
Building 1
Charleston, WV 25305
State Chamber of Commerce
P.O. Box 2789
1101 Kanawha Valley Building
Charleston, WV 25330
International Commerce
Governor's Office of Community and Industrial Development
1900 Washington Street East
Building 6
Charleston, WV 25305
Banking
Department of Banking
1900 Washington Street East
Building 5
Charleston, WV 25305
Securities
Auditor's Office
1900 Washington Street East
Building 1
Charleston, WV 25305
Labor & Industrial Relations
Governor's Office of Community and Industrial Development
1900 Washington Street East
Building 6
Charleston, WV 25305

Insurance
Insurance Department
2100 Washington Street East
Charleston, WV 25305

Uniform Industrial Code
Governor's Office of the Secretary of State
1900 Washington Street East
Building 1
Charleston, WV 25305

Business Ombudsman
Governor's Office of Community and Industrial Development East
Building 6
Charleston, WV 25305

INDUSTRIAL AND BUSINESS DIRECTORIES

West Virginia Manufacturing Directory, Harris Publishing Company, Inc., 2057–2 Aurora Road, Twinsburg, OH 44087; State Industrial Directories Corp., 2 Penn Plaza, New York, NY 10001

Wisconsin

State Capitol, Madison, WI 53702
(608) 266-2211

INFORMATION OFFICES

Commerce/Economic Development
Department of Trade Development
123 W. Washington Avenue
Madison, WI 53702

Corporate
Secretary of State
Corporate Division
201 E. Washington Avenue
Madison, WI 53707

Taxation
Department of Revenue
125 S. Webster Avenue
P.O. Box 5933
Madison, WI 53708

State Chamber of Commerce
Wisconsin Association of Manufacturers and Commerce
111 E. Wisconsin Avenue
Milwaukee, WI 53202

International Commerce
International Business Services
Department of Development
123 W. Washington Avenue
Madison, WI 53702

Banking
Banking, Office of the Commissioner
123 West Washington Avenue
P.O. Box 7876
Madison, WI 53707

Securities
Securities—Office of the Commissioner
111 West Wilson Avenue
Madison, WI 53703

Labor and Industrial Relations
Department of Industry, Labor, and Human Relations
201 E. Washington Avenue
P.O. Box 7946
Madison, WI 53707

Insurance
Office of the Commissioner of Insurance
123 West Washington Avenue
Madison, WI 53702

Uniform Industrial Code
Department of Industry, Labor and Human Relations
201 E. Washington Avenue
Madison, WI 53702

Business Ombudsman
Small Business Ombudsman
Department of Development
123 W. Washington Avenue
Madison, WI 53702

INDUSTRIAL AND BUSINESS DIRECTORIES

Classified Directory of Wisconsin Manufacturers, Wisconsin Association of Manufacturers and Commerce, 111 E. Wisconsin Avenue, Milwaukee, WI 53202; State Industrial Directories Corp., 2 Penn Plaza, New York, NY 10001

Wisconsin Manufacturers Directory, Manufacturers' News, Inc., 4 E. Huron Street, Chicago, IL 60611

Wisconsin Local Development Organizations (annual), Wisconsin Department of Development, 123 W. Washington Avenue, Madison, WI 53702

Wyoming

State Capitol, Cheyenne, WY 82002
(307) 777-7011

INFORMATION OFFICES

Commerce/Economic Development
Economic Development and Stabilization Board
Herschler Building
Cheyenne, WY 82002

Wyoming Small Business Development Center
130 N. Ash
Casper, WY 82601

Corporate
Secretary of State
Corporate Division
State Capitol
Cheyenne, WY 82002

Taxation
Department of Revenue and Taxation
Herschler Building
Cheyenne, WY 82002

International Commerce
International Trade Office
State Planning Coordinator
Herschler Building
Cheyenne, WY 82002

Banking
State Examiner
Herschler Building
Cheyenne, WY 82002

Securities
Secretary of State
Securities Division
State Capitol
Cheyenne, WY 82002

Labor and Industrial Relations
Department of Labor and Statistics
Herschler Building
Cheyenne, WY 82002

Insurance
Insurance Commission
Herschler Building
Cheyenne, WY 82002

Uniform Industrial Code
Industrial Siting Administration
Barrett Building
2301 Central
Cheyenne, WY 82002

Industrial Development Division
Economic Planning Development and Stabilization Board
Herschler Building
Cheyenne, WY 82002

INDUSTRIAL AND BUSINESS DIRECTORIES

Wyoming Directory of Manufacturing and Mining, Manufacturers' News, Inc., 4 E. Huron Street, Chicago, IL 60611; Economic Development and Stabilization Board, Herschler Building, Cheyenne, WY 82002; State Industrial Directories Corp. 2 Penn Plaza, New York, NY 10001

Puerto Rico

Capitol, San Juan, PR 00901
(809) 724-6040 (House of Representatives)
(809) 724-2030 (Senate)

INFORMATION OFFICES

Commerce/Economic Development
Puerto Rico Department of Commerce
P.O. Box S 4275
San Juan, PR 00905

Puerto Rico Economic Development Administration
G.P.O. Box 2350
San Juan, PR 00936

Puerto Rico Planning Board
P.O. Box 41119
San Juan, PR 00940

Government Development Bank
P.O. Box 42001
Minillas Station
Santurce, PR 00940

Economic Development Bank
P.O. Box 5009
Hato Rey, PR 00929-5009

Taxation
Puerto Rico Department of Treasury
P.O. Box S-4515
San Juan, PR 00901

Office of Industrial Tax Exemption
P.O. Box 2121
Hato Rey, PR 00918-2121

Chamber of Commerce
Chamber of Commerce of Puerto Rico
P.O. Box 3789
San Juan, PR 00904

Puerto Rico Manufacturers Association
P.O. Box 2410
Hato Rey, PR 00919

Securities
Office of the Commissioner of Financial Institutions
P.O. Box 4515
San Juan, PR 00905

Labor and Industrial Relations
Puerto Rico Labor Relations Board
P.O. Box 4048
San Juan, PR 00905

National Labor Relations Board
Federal Building
Charlos E. Chardon Street
Hato Rey, PR 00918

Insurance
Office of the Insurance Commissioner
P.O. Box 8330, Fdez Juncos Station
Santurce, PR 00910

Puerto Rico Insurance Companies Association, Inc.
Housing Investment Building
San Juan, PR 00918

Uniform Industrial Code
Department of Labor and Human Resources
505 Muñoz Rivera Avenue
Prudencio Rivera Martínez Building
Hato Rey, PR 00918

Business Ombudsman
Ombudsman Office
1205 Ponce de León Avenue
Banco de San Juan
Santurce, PR 00907-3995

International Commerce
Puerto Rico Department of Commerce
External Trade Promotion Program
P.O. Box S 4275
San Juan, PR 00905

US Department of Commerce
International Trade Administration
Charlos E. Chardon Street

Federal Building
Hato Rey, PR 00918

Puerto Rico Chamber of Commerce
International Trade Division
P.O. Box 3789
San Juan, PR 00904

Banking

Puerto Rico Bankers Association
Banco Popular Center
Hato Rey, PR 00918

INDUSTRIAL AND BUSINESS DIRECTORIES

Puerto Rico Official Industrial and Trade Directory, Witcom Group, Inc., P.O. Box 2310, San Juan, PR 00902

The Businessman's Guide to Puerto Rico, Puerto Rico Almanacs, Inc., P.O. Box 9582, Santurce, Puerto Rico 00908

International Information Sources

Foreign Trade Information

Business people seeking information about foreign commercial opportunities or sources of business contacts have available a number of government and private services that are described in this and subsequent sections. The extensive nature of these services is not always fully appreciated by members of the business community. Some of the most helpful services are provided by the International Trade Administration (ITA) 202-377-3808 of the Department of Commerce, described below. This agency is particularly helpful in establishing initial contacts and in evaluating foreign markets.

Foreign credit information sources are provided at the end of this section.

DEPARTMENT OF COMMERCE

Address: Constitution and 14th Street NW, Washington, DC 20230. Information phone: 202-377-2000.

The central export information source within the Department of Commerce is the **International Trade Administration** (ITA), which promotes the growth of U.S. industry and commerce, both foreign and domestic. Office of Public Affairs: (202) 377-3808. The four units of ITA and the Bureau of Export Administration are discussed below.

- U.S. and Foreign Commercial Service (US&FCS)—the framework within which ITA gathers accurate and timely commercial information, distributes it through a worldwide network of trade specialists, and provides in-depth counseling, assistance, and support to the business community both in the U.S. and abroad (below)
- International Economic Policy (IEP)—the office organized on a country and regional basis which develops and implements policy concerning U.S. international trade, investment, and commercial relations with foreign businesses and governments, and which gives market-specific counsel to American business (page 677).
- Trade Development (TD)—the industry unit responsible for formulating trade policy and promotion activities (page 678).
- Import Administration (IA)—the office responsible for safeguarding the national interest through effective administration of U.S. trade laws (page 678).
- Bureau of Export Administration (BXA)—responsible for export licensing, technology and policy analysis, and foreign availability determinations (page 679).

Sources: Excerpted from *Business America, Business Services Directory, A Basic Guide to Exporting,* and other U.S. Department of Commerce sources.

U.S. and Foreign Commercial Service (US&FCS)

The U.S. and Foreign Commercial Service (US&FCS), the only federal agency with a global network of international trade professionals, is charged with the nuts-and-bolts work of improving the ability of U.S. business to compete overseas. US&FCS collects marketing information at overseas posts and makes it available to U.S. companies at district offices and branch offices.

The US&FCS emphasizes practical advice and information help U.S. exporters in very specific ways. A company can find out which countries have the best market potential for its products and can then find out who to contact overseas.

Through the US&FCS, U.S. firms have direct access to more than 95 percent of the global marketplace for goods and services. Such access can be a big advantage for American firms, particularly small- and medium-sized businesses that lack export departments and overseas representation.

District office trade specialists, drawing from a large commercial data base fed by overseas commercial officers, provide individualized marketing packages for U.S. companies on their specific products and services and offer one-on-one export counseling. Beginners and experienced exporters both are eligible.

The district offices arrange export seminars, conferences, and workshops. To multiply the effects of their efforts, they coordinate activities with state and local governments, trade associations, world trade clubs, banks, local chambers of commerce, small business development centers, and colleges and universities. More than 900 of these organizations are termed "associate offices"; they distribute information to areas where no US&FCS district offices are located. The district offices give U.S. companies direct contact with seasoned exporters through District Export Councils (DECs) comprised of experienced business people.

Commercial officers attached to U.S. embassies and consulates search for sales leads, qualified agents, and distributors; make appointments with key buyers and government officials; and counsel firms frustrated by trade barriers.

The US&FCS's new Commercial Information Management System (CIMS) makes it possible to transmit information electronically from overseas posts to the district offices. Thus, U.S. exporters have quick and easy access to information on:

Market statistics dealing with exports, imports, consumption, production or infrastructure;

Tariff and non-tariff trade barriers, import regulations, policies, and product standards;

Domestic and foreign competition, individual competitor firms and competitive factors;

Distribution practices;

End users; and

How to promote products in the market.

The US&FCS has several programs geared toward helping companies make contact with potential agents, distributors, buyers, or joint-venture partners, including:

Agent Distributor Service—This customized search for interested and qualified foreign representatives will identify up to six foreign prospects who have examined a company's product literature and have expressed interest in representing its product. For information contact your local ITA district office (page 681).

Commercial News USA—This monthly magazine will promote a company's product or service to more than 90,000 overseas agents, distributors, government officials, and end-users. A black-and-white photo and brief description will highlight a product or service and give a firm an opportunity to search for its best markets worldwide or to focus on a particular region.

In *Commerce Business Daily*, US&FCS publicizes proposed foreign government procurement actions and foreign trade leads, as well as information on U.S. Government procurement actions. For a sample, write US&FCS, U.S. Department of Commerce, Washington, D.C. 20230. To subscribe, call the Superintendent of Documents, U.S. Government Printing Office, Washington, D.C. 20402.

Commercial Information Management System (CIMS)—This service electronically links US&FCS posts and offices worldwide to provide timely, in-depth data. CIMS creates export information packages customized for special needs, including highly specific market research, trade contact lists and sales leads. Useful for situation and competitive assessment reports. For detailed information on CIMS, including cost, contact CIMS, U.S. & Foreign Commercial Service, U.S. Department of Commerce, Washington, D.C. 20230. Telephone: 202-377-1887

Foreign Buyer Program—Without the expense of traveling overseas, an exporter can meet qualified foreign buyers for his product or service at selected trade shows in the United States. The US&FCS promotes these shows worldwide to attract foreign buyer delegations, manages an International Business Center, counsels U.S. firms, and brings together buyer and seller.

Trade Opportunities Program—This program can provide a firm with current sales leads from overseas firms seeking to buy or represent its product or service. These leads are available electronically or printed. Trade opportunity information is available through the *Journal of Commerce*, 110 Wall Street, New York, NY 10005.

Trade events constitute another major type of US&FCS export assistance. A company can do as little as sending a product catalog overseas or as much as fully participating in trade missions or major international exhibitions. US&FCS programs include:

Catalog and Video-Catalog Shows—A firm can gain market exposure for its product or service without the cost of traveling overseas by participating in a catalog or video-catalog show. The firm provides its product literature or promotional video, and the US&FCS will send an industry expert to display this material to select foreign audiences in several countries.

Trade Missions—Participating in a trade mission will give an exporter an opportunity to confer directly, on-the-spot, with targeted foreign business and government representatives. US&FCS staff provides complete logistical and promotional support to the missions. They will identify and arrange a full schedule of appointments for an exporter in each country that he visits.

Trade Fairs—Trade fairs are one of the most popular ways of promoting goods and services overseas because they not only give the seller an opportunity to meet customers face-to-face but also to assess the competition. US&FCS supports U.S. participation in international trade fairs, making it easier for U.S. firms to exhibit and gain international recognition. US&FCS selects certain international trade fairs for special endorsement, called certification. As a result of this cooperation with private show organizers, U.S. exhibitors receive special services designed to enhance their market promotion efforts.

The best way for a U.S. exporter to make use of these services is to visit the closest US&FCS district office.

Useful US&FCS Telephone Numbers:

Headquarters	(202) 377-5777
Caribbean Basin Business Information Center	377-0703
Domestic Operations	377-4767
Export Counseling	377-5551
Export Promotion Services:	377-8220
Marketing Programs Division	377-4231
Trade Event Programs	377-8220
Foreign Operations	377-8300
Public Affairs	377-3808

International Economic Policy (IEP)

International Economic Policy (IEP) identifies and analyzes foreign commercial barriers and opportunities, offers a range of counseling services to U.S. businesses, and participates in bilateral and multilateral consultations and negotiations.

IEP is organized by region and country; it has four regional groups: Africa, the Near East, and South Asia; East Asia and the Pacific; Europe; and the Western Hemisphere. IEP's Office of Policy Coordination complements the individual efforts of the regional units by coordinating projects and initiatives affecting countries in more than one region.

The regional groups are staffed by country specialists who counsel U.S. businesses on foreign market conditions, business practices, and government regulations; develop specific information on promising commercial opportunities; identify foreign trade and investment barriers and devise strategies to remove them; and support the efforts of senior U.S. government policymakers to improve U.S. commercial opportunities worldwide. The unit's country specialists publish periodic reports on foreign market conditions and requirements (*Overseas Business Reports* and *Foreign Economic Trends*) and numerous special studies.

Overseas Business Reports (OBR) include current and detailed marketing information, trade outlooks, statistics, regulations, and market profiles. They are available from the Superintendent of Documents, U.S. Government Printing Office, Washington, DC 20402.

Foreign Economic Trends (FET) present current business and economic developments and the latest economic indicators in more than 100 countries. They are prepared on an annual or semiannual basis by the U.S. Foreign Service and U.S. Foreign Commerical Service. Available from the Superintendent of Documents, U.S. Government Printing Office, Washington, D.C. 20402.

Through its Office of Multilateral Affairs, IEP coordinates the Department's involvement in U.S. government efforts to strengthen the world trading system and improve U.S. commercial opportunities through multilateral agencies, such as the General Agreement on Tariffs and Trade (GATT).

The office also develops and coordinates departmental positions on several issue areas affecting multilateral trade policy. These include the U.S. Generalized System of Preferences (GSP) program and Section 301 of the Trade Act of 1974, which provides redress from unfair foreign trade practices.

IEP also works to ensure that foreign governments meet their obligations under existing multilateral agreements, such as the GATT non-tariff codes negotiated during the last major trade round.

Useful IEP Telephone Numbers

Headquarters	(202) 377-3022
GATT Division	377-3681
International Organizations	377-3227
U.S. Trade by Region	
Africa	377-2175
Canada	377-3101
Caribbean Basin & Mexico	377-5327
Eastern Europe	377-2645
European Community	377-5276
Israel Information Center	377-4652
Japan	377-4527
Near East	377-4441
Pacific Basin	377-4008
Peoples Republic of China and Hong Kong	377-3583
South America	377-2436
South Asia	377-2954
U.S.S.R.	377-4655
Western Europe	377-5341

Trade Development

Trade Development's analysis, policy development, and export promotion capability are designed to enhance the efforts of businesses of all sizes to increase market share at home and abroad.

Of TD's nine operating units, seven specialize in specific industrial sectors—Science and Electronics, Capital Goods and International Construction, Automotive Affairs and Consumer Goods, Textiles and Apparel, Aerospace, Services, and Basic Industries. An eighth unit is Trade Information and Analysis, which addresses international debt and currency questions and other issues that affect all sectors and coordinates TD policy recommendations on issues that cut across industry sectors. The ninth unit is Trade Adjustment Assistance, which provides technical assistance to firms and industries injured by import competition.

TD industry sector analysts monitor significant developments affecting their industries, especially those relating to efforts by foreign competitors. The Trade Information and Analysis unit follows important trends that affect overall U.S. industry and identify cross-cutting issues that, while of primary concern to one sector, have potential for affecting others.

Each year, TD publishes two major publications. *The U.S. Trade Performance and Outlook* analyzes the factors that influence the U.S. trade balance. The *U.S. Industrial Outlook* contains analyses and forecasts of domestic and international trends for more than 350 U.S. manufacturing and service industries.

TD conducts a two-part analytical program. The first measures overall U.S. and foreign competitive performance, using indicators such as productivity and growth rates, and assesses the effectiveness of various measures of competitiveness. The second produces a series of published *Competitive Assessments,* which include in-depth analyses of individual industries and detailed discussions of their specific position in the international arena.

TRADE PROMOTION

TD helps U.S. businesses in specific export efforts. Analysts identify industries with high export potential and work with the U.S. and Foreign Commercial Service to assist exporters.

Each year, TD organizes dozens of seminars to introduce U.S. producers to export markets. TD recruits companies for trade missions, helps participants in meetings with prospective customers and foreign officials, and assists with trade shows.

TD also organizes "Foreign Buyer" groups to visit U.S. trade shows; administers the Export Trading Company Act program to help companies pool their export efforts, and offers technical assistance to import-injured companies under the Trade Adjustment Assistance program.

Even firms in those U.S. industries unaffected by increased foreign competition need to redouble their efforts to secure their market position. The Trade Development unit can give them some good pointers.

Useful TD Telephone Numbers

Headquarters	202-377-1461
Foreign Trade Reference Room	377-2185
Major Projects Reference Room	377-4876
Science and Electronics	377-3548
Capital Goods and International Construction	377-5023
Automotive Affairs and Consumer Goods	377-0823
Textiles and Apparel	377-3737
Aerospace	377-8228
Services	377-5261
Basic Industries	377-0614
Trade Information and Analysis	377-1316
Trade Adjustment Assistance	377-0150
World Fairs and International Expositions	377-0530

Import Administration (IA)

Import Administration (IA) investigates allegations under the U.S. antidumping (AD) and countervailing duty (CVD) laws that foreign goods are being sold in the United States at less than fair value ("dumped") or being unfairly subsidized by foreign governments. The International Trade Commission, a separate independent agency, conducts a parallel review of injury (or threat of injury) to the domestic industry as a result of these unfairly traded imports. IA also conducts annual reviews of AD and CVD orders, which are imposed to offset findings of injurious dumping and subsidization, to update duty levels, as well as reviews of suspended AD and CVD investigations to monitor compliance with suspension agreements.

In addition, IA implements and enforces four monitoring programs involving bilateral trade agreements with foreign governments for steel, machine tools, semiconductors and softwood lumber. IA oversees the operations of U.S. foreign-trade zones, implements statutory import programs, including the watch quota program for insular possessions and the Florence agreement, and, in conjunction with the U.S. Customs Service, administers quotas covering imports of certain specialty steel products

Useful IA Telephone Numbers

Headquarters	202-377-1780
Compliance	377-2104
Foreign Trade Zones	377-2862
Industrial Resources	377-4506
Investigations	377-5497
Public Affairs	377-3808

Bureau of Export Administration (BXA)

Public Affairs: 202-377-2721

Established in 1987, the Bureau of Export Administration (BXA) is responsible for export licensing, technology and policy analysis, and foreign availability determinations. These responsibilities include reducing the processing time for granting export licenses, decontrolling those technologies that offer no real threat to U.S. security, and eliminating controls in areas where there is widespread foreign availability.

To reduce unnecessary burdens on U.S. industry through improvements in export control procedures, Commerce has:

- Reduced license processing times by one-half, to 15 days;
- Opened "ELAIN" (Electronic License Application and Information Network), information 202-377-4811 allowing exporters to send applications and receive export licenses from Commerce electronically
- Installed an audio response unit—STELA (System for Tracking Export License Applications)—which automatically handles requests for status checks on export license applications using synthesized voice technology (tel. 202-377-2752);
- Implemented general regulatory changes to reduce the licensing burdon on exporters, particularly on exports of certain low level technologies.
- Raised the processing data rate (PDR) levels of computers eligible for export under the distribution license program;
- Reached agreement with countries that are members of the Coordinating Committee for Multilateral Export Controls (COCOM) to improve license processing for the People's Republic of China;
- Reduced paperwork burden by authorizing a 24-month validity period for individual validated licenses; and
- Expanded its export control information program, both in the United States and abroad, through the Exporter Outreach Staff.

The Bureau of Export Administration issues the *Export Administration Regulations* to enforce U.S. export controls. These Regulations contain information on obtaining an export license, documentation requirements, special nuclear controls, reexports, technical data, special commodity and country policies, and other essential guidance on exporting.

SEMINAR PROGRAMS

In its effort to make applying for an export license less intimidating, BXA conducts seminars on export controls and licensing all over the nation as well as overseas.

Learning about export controls and licensing is a must for most U.S. businesses, particularly for high-technology firms most subject to national security controls. The BXA seminars are aimed at providing the knowledge that exporters must have.

Licensing officers and export administration specialists from the Commerce Department teach the courses that are usually cosponsored by District Export Councils and other not-for-profit trade organizations in conjunction with US&FCS district offices. For information call: 202-377-8731.

The basic program in the BXA seminars focuses on export control fundamentals. Attendees learn about general, special, and individual validated licenses, the Commodity Control List, how to fill out the 622P Application for an export license, and what documentation is needed, depending on commodity and country destination. They receive hands-on instruction in the use of the regulations. In the advanced seminar, attendees receive more in-depth explanations and analyses of the regulations, requirements of supporting documentation, the interagency review process, and distribution license control requirements.

ADDITIONAL BXA PROGRAMS AND SERVICES

To assist the exporter, the following programs are available:

Publication Program: For information on booklets/brochures for the business community call 202-377-8731. Recent publications include: *Export Licensing Information and Assistance* (telephone referral), *Introduction to the Export Administration Regulations, The Quick Reference Guide to the Export Administration Regulations,* and an updated copy of the *Denial Orders Currently Affecting Export Privileges.*

Technical Advisory Committees (TACs):

The TACs are a voluntary joint industry-government mechanism through which the concerns of various industries can be discussed. For information, call 202-377-2583.

Useful BXA Telephone Numbers

Press and Public Information	(202) 377-2721
Headquarters	(202) 377-5491
Exporter assistance staff	(202) 377-4811

STELA (System for Tracking Export License Applications) Answers the question most frequently asked by business: What is the status of my license application?

Information about STELA	(202) 377-2753

ELAIN (Export License Application and Information Network) . . . (202) 377-4811 Accepts export license applications ELECTRONICALLY for all freeworld destinations.

Emergency Licensing Requests	377-4811
Trade Fair Licenses	377-4811
General Regulations Information	377-4811
Export Seminar Program	377-8731

Dates and locations of export regulations courses

Major Offices Administering Export Controls:

Office of Export Licensing	(202) 377-4811
Special Licensing Division	377-3287
Office of Technology and Policy Analysis	377-4188
Capital Goods Technical Center	377-5695
Computer Systems Technical Center	377-2279
Telecommunications Technical Center	377-0730
Electronic Components and Instrumentation	377-1641
Foreign Availability	377-8074
Assessments	377-5953
Export Enforcement	377-1561

Major Offices Administering Export Enforcement:

Washington, D.C.	(202) 377-5282 (202) 377-8208

BXA Enforcement Field Offices

California—Los Angeles	(818) 904-6019
California—San Jose	(408) 291-4204
Florida—Miami	(305) 523-1401
Illinois—Chicago	(312) 353-6640
Massachusetts—Boston	(617) 565-6030
New York—New York	(212) 264-1365
Texas—Dallas	(214) 767-9294
Virginia—Springfield	(703) 487-4950
Office of Antiboycott Compliance	(202) 377-5914
Office of Export Intelligence	(202) 377-4255

SELECTED INTERNATIONAL TRADE ADMINISTRATION PUBLICATIONS AND SERVICES

In addition to the previously mentioned publications there are others to help exporters reach and expand foreign markets. The foremost of these is *Business America*, which is Commerce Department's principal periodical for domestic and international business news and covers a wide range of topics. Subscriptions are available from the Superintendent of Documents, General Printing Office, Washington, DC 20402. Other publications include:

A Basic Guide to Exporting: This publication takes a step-by-step approach to exporting especially designed for firms with little or no export experience. Assessment of export potential is treated first, along with sources of export counseling and education. Other topics include: selecting markets, export strategies, pricing, financing, shipment, methods of payment, export documentation, and government regulations. A glossary of export terms and list of export-assistance groups is provided. Available from the Superintendent of Documents, General Printing Office, Washington, DC 20402.

Expand Overseas Sales With Commerce Department Help describes the various types of assistance available from the Commerce Department for small businesses seeking foreign markets. Available from International Trade Administration.

The U.S. Department of Commerce has discontinued publication of the *Export Promotion Calendar* due to budget cutbacks. However, the same information (e.g., listings of Commerce Department supported trade events in the U.S. and overseas, etc.) that was in the printed publication is now on-line at Department of Commerce District Offices around the country.

Other services available to exporters include the following.

Custom Statistical Service (CSS) is a tailored set of tables of U.S. export or import statistics. The custom service allows an exporter to obtain data for specific products or countries of interest, or for ones which may not appear in the standard ESP country and product rankings. Data can be supplied in other formats such as quantity, unit quantity, unit value and percentages.

New Product Information Service (NPIS)

This program provides worldwide publicity for new U.S. products available for immediate export. Promotional descriptions are published in *Commercial News USA* magazine. Information on selected NPIS products is also broadcast overseas by the U.S. Information Agency's "Voice of America" radio shows. For an application, contact a Trade Specialist at the nearest ITA District Office or write the Director, New Product Information Service, US&FCS, Room 2106, U.S. Department of Commerce, Washington, D.C. 20230.

Industry-Organized Government-Approved (IOGA) Trade Missions

Trade missions of this type are export-oriented events planned and organized by non-federal government groups such as local and state governments, industry trade associations, and chambers of commerce. For information, contact: Export Promotion Services, US&FCS, U.S. Department of Commerce, Washington, D.C. 20230; telephone: 202-377-4231.

DEPARTMENT OF AGRICULTURE

The U.S. Department of Agriculture's (USDA) export promotion efforts are centered in the Foreign Agricultural Service (FAS), but other USDA agencies also offer services to the U.S. exporter of agricultural products. For information on the promotion of U.S. farm products in foreign markets, services of commodity and marketing specialists in Washington, D.C., trade fair exhibits, publications and information services, and financing programs contact the Director of Export Programs Division, FAS, U.S. Department of Agriculture, Washington, D.C. Telephone: (202) 477-6343.

Department of Commerce International Trade Administration District and Branch Offices

District Office Assistance

Alabama—Birmingham	(205) 731-1331
Alaska—Anchorage	(907) 271-5041
Arizona—Phoenix	(602) 261-3285
Arkansas—Little Rock	(501) 378-5794
California—Los Angeles	(213) 209-6707
*California—Santa Ana	(714) 836-2461
California—San Diego	(619) 557-5395
California—San Francisco	(415) 556-5860
Colorado—Denver	(303) 844-3246
Connecticut—Hartford	(203) 240-3530
D.C.—Washington	(202) 377-3181
Florida—Miami	(305) 536-5267
*Florida—Clearwater	(813) 461-0011
*Florida—Jacksonville	(904) 791-2796
*Florida—Orlando	(305) 425-1234
*Florida—Tallahassee	(904) 488-6469
Georgia—Atlanta	(404) 347-7000
Georgia—Savannah	(912) 944-4204
Hawaii—Honolulu	(808) 541-1782
*Idaho—Boise	(208) 334-2470
Illinois—Chicago	(312) 353-4450
*Illinois—Palantine	(312) 397-3000 Ext. 532
Illinois—Rockford	(815) 987-8123
Indiana—Indianapolis	(317) 269-6214
Iowa—Des Moines	(515) 284-4222
*Kansas—Wichita	(316) 269-6160
Kentucky—Louisville	(502) 582-5066
Louisiana—New Orleans	(504) 589-6546
*Maine—Augusta	(207) 622-8249
Maryland—Baltimore	(301) 962-3560
*Maryland—Rockville	(301) 251-2345
Massachusetts—Boston	(617) 565-8563
Michigan—Detroit	(313) 226-3650
*Michigan—Grand Rapids	(616) 456-2411
Minnesota—Minneapolis	(612) 348-1638
Mississippi—Jackson	(601) 965-4388
Missouri—Kansas City	(816) 374-3141
Missouri—St. Louis	(314) 425-3302
Nebraska—Omaha	(402) 221-3664
Nevada—Reno	(702) 784-5203
*New Jersey—Trenton	(609) 989-2100
New Mexico—Albuquerque	(505) 766-2386
New York—Buffalo	(716) 846-4191
New York—New York	(212) 264-0634
*New York—Rochester	(716) 263-6480
North Carolina—Greensboro	(919) 378-5345
Ohio—Cincinnati	(513) 684-2944
Ohio—Cleveland	(216) 522-4750
Oklahoma—Oklahoma City	(405) 231-5302
*Oklahoma—Tulsa	(918) 581-7650
Oregon—Portland	(503) 221-3001
Pennsylvania—Philadelphia	(215) 597-2850
Pennsylvania—Pittsburgh	(412) 644-2850
Puerto Rico—San Juan	(809) 753-4555
*Rhode Island—Providence	(401) 528-5104 Ext. 22
South Carolina—Columbia	(803) 765-5345
South Carolina—Charleston	(803) 724-4361
*Tennessee—Memphis	(901) 222-4137
Tennessee—Nashville	(615) 736-5161
*Texas—Austin	(512) 472-5059
Texas—Dallas	(214) 767-0542
Texas—Houston	(713) 229-2578
Utah—Salt Lake City	(801) 524-5116
Virginia—Richmond	(804) 771-2246
Washington—Seattle	(206) 442-5616
*Washington—Spokane	(509) 456-4557
West Virginia—Charleston	(304) 347-5123
Wisconsin—Milwaukee	(414) 291-3473

*Denotes Branch Office

Financing Exports*

Many sources of financial assistance are available to exporters. In addition to your own working capital or bank line of credit, the following are brief descriptions of some important sources of export financing assistance.

COMMERCIAL BANKS

A logical first step in choosing financing is to approach a local commercial bank for advice. If a company finds that its bank does not have an international department, then a good bank can be recommended by several sources:

- The US&FCS District Office.
- Eximbank or The Small Business Administration.
- The company's current bank.
- The company's freight forwarder.
- An experienced exporter referred by the local District Export Council or World Trade Club.

Most of these sources can also discuss financing needs and make helpful suggestions.

If a company is new to exporting or is a small or medium-sized business, it is important to select a bank that not only has an international department, but that also is sincerely interested in serving businesses of similar type or size. Of the many thousands of banks in the United States, several hundred have international departments, about half of which find it profitable to serve small- or medium-sized exporters.

When selecting a bank, the exporter should ask the following questions:

- How big is the bank's international department?
- Does it have foreign branches or correspondent banks? Where are they located?
- What are charges for confirming a letter of credit, processing drafts, and collecting payment?
- Can the bank provide buyer credit reports? Free or at what cost?
- Does it have experience with U.S. and State government financing programs that support small business export transactions? If not, is it willing to participate in these programs?
- What other services can it provide (trade leads, etc.)?

TYPES OF BANK FINANCING

The same type of commercial loans that finance domestic activities—including loans for working capital and revolving lines of credit—are available to finance export sales until payment is received. However, most banks do not usually extend credit solely on the basis of an order; thus these loans can tie up assets that must be used as collateral and can use up limited credit lines that may be needed for other transactions.

In many cases, Federal and State small business export finance programs can help reduce the need for collateral and extend the amount of credit available. There are also ways to avoid normal commercial loans altogether by requesting banker's acceptance financing.

If an export transaction is paid by using letters of credit or trade drafts, banker's acceptance financing can be used to provide immediate payment to the exporter. This follows even though the letter of credit or draft calls for payment from the buyer up to 180 days in the future.

When a letter of credit or draft is formally approved for payment (through endorsement by a bank or by the buyer), it is called an "acceptance." This document can either be kept by the exporter until the stated terms of credit have expired and then be presented for payment, or it can usually be sold immediately to a U.S. bank at a discount. In the case of an irrevocable letter of credit, payment is guaranteed by a foreign bank, and the U.S. bank will not require collateral or other proof of ability to pay from the exporter. With a trade draft, such proof may be required since the bank must come to the exporter for repayment if the buyer defaults.

The advantages of banker's acceptance financing, especially when a letter of credit is used, are the following:

- The exporter receives immediate payment in contrast to commerical loans where the cost of goods is financed but profit is not realized until payment is received.
- Less of the exporter's capital and credit line is tied up in financing (none if a letter of credit is used).
- The total interest charges and fees are usually lower—thus costs are lower for both buyer and seller.

As with any type of export financing, it should be noted that finance charges for banker's acceptances may be passed through to the buyer as part of the terms of sale (made

* Source: Excerpted from *A Basic Guide to Exporting*, U.S. Department of Commerce and other sources.

clear in the quotation and invoice as part of the price or an added charge). For more information on this type of financing, contact one of the sources of advice listed earlier in this chapter.

FEDERAL GOVERNMENT EXPORT FINANCING PROGRAMS

A bank with a good international department experienced with government export finance programs can often advise an exporter on the different programs available. Most of the programs described below—including State programs—are intended to work through a commercial bank. Banks that participate in these programs are the agents that apply on the exporter's behalf for program benefits. The exporter need not become an expert, yet knowing the existence of these financing opportunities can be quite valuable.

Even if a bank that is currently being used by an exporter has had no experience with government export financing programs, this bank may still be used if it is willing to follow program guidelines. If assistance is needed in locating a bank that uses any of these programs, contact the appropriate Federal or State agency. The descriptions below provide a basic overview. More information can be had from the government agency listed, from banks, and also from the Department of Commerce publication *A Guide to Financing Exports*, available from US&FCS District Offices. The Department of Commerce operates no financing programs but can help exporters choose among programs that exist: Contact a local US&FCS District Office or the Office of Trade Finance, International Trade Administration, in Washington, DC. Telephone: (202) 377-3277.

EXPORT-IMPORT BANK

Address: 811 Vermont Avenue NW, Washington, DC 20571. Phone: 202–566–8990. Public Affairs Phone: 202–566–8860

Small Business Advisory Hotline Service

800–424–5201

The Export-Import Bank (Eximbank) of the United States offers direct loans for large projects and equipment sales that usually require long-term financing; it guarantees loans made by cooperating U.S. and foreign commercial banks to U.S. exporters and to foreign buyers of U.S. products and services; and, through a private insurance association, the Foreign Credit Insurance Association (FCIA) (see below), it provides insurance to U.S. exporters enabling them to extend credit to their overseas buyers.

In all cases, Eximbank must find a "reasonable assurance of repayment" as a precondition of participating in the transaction. However, because the bank offers loan guarantees and credit insurance, a major effect of using Eximbank programs is to reduce the amount of collateral required to finance a loan and to generally make financing more available than would be the case without its support.

Among Eximbank's array of loan, guarantee, and insurance programs are four that are especially helpful to small companies and those that are new to exporting:

- Working Capital Guarantee Program.
- Export Credit Insurance.
- Commercial Bank Guarantees.
- Small Business Credit Program.

Details on these programs are available from Eximbank.

Eximbank and FCIA also provide other credit programs for medium and long-term financing. Long-term financing (5 years and longer) is generally for export of capital equipment and large-scale installations. This financing takes the form either of a direct credit to an overseas buyer or a financial guarantee assuring repayment of a private bank credit. Eximbank often blends these two forms of support into a single financing package. The chart on page 684 gives a brief guide to the use of different programs. In the chart, exports are divided into three categories, and for each category there are two or more program options.

For complete information on the above programs contact the Export-Import Bank at (202) 566-8860.

FOREIGN CREDIT INSURANCE ASSOCIATION (FCIA)

Address: 40 Rector Street, New York, NY 10006. Phone: 212–306–5000.

The export credit insurance offered by FCIA provides three basic incentives for American exporters when they do offer competitive terms to buyers. It enables them to (1) protect corporate assets as credit is extended; (2) maximize the rate of plant utilization as overseas competition is matched and orders won; and (3) improve corporate liquidity when insured foreign receivables are financed.

FCIA administers the U.S. export credit insurance program on behalf of its member insurance companies and the Export-Import Bank, an agency of the U.S. Government. The private insurers cover the normal commercial credit risks, primarily the insolvency of or protracted payment default by overseas buyers.

EXIMBANK/FCIA Program Selection Chart

Exports	Appropriate Programs
Short-Term (up to 180 days)	
Consumable	Export Credit Insurance
Small manufactured items	Working Capital Guarantee
Spare Parts	
Raw Materials	
Medium-Term (181 days to 5 years)	
Mining and refining equipment	Export Credit Insurance
Construction equipment	Commercial Bank Guarantees
Agricultural equipment	Small Business Credit Program
General aviation aircraft	Medium-Term Credit
Planning/feasibility studies	Working Capital Guarantee
Long-Term (5 years and longer)	
Power plants	Direct Loans
LPG & gas producing plants	Financial Guarantees
Other major projects	
Commercial jet aircraft or locomotives	
Other heavy capital goods	

U.S. SMALL BUSINESS ADMINISTRATION [SBA]

Answer desk: 800–368–5855

Through financial assistance programs, the SBA can promote small business participation in international trade by making funds available for export-oriented activities.

Funds may be used to purchase machinery, equipment, facilities, supplies, or materials needed to manufacture or sell products overseas, as well as for working capital. Working capital loans may be used to defray the costs of developing or penetrating foreign markets. Specifically, this can include costs for professional foreign marketing advice and services, foreign business travel, shipping sample merchandise abroad, shopping foreign markets, participating in overseas trade center shows and international fairs, foreign advertising and preparation of promotional materials, and other related purposes.

For information on the SBA financial assistance programs, policies and requirements, contact the nearest SBA field office (see page 254).

PRIVATE EXPORT FUNDING CORPORATION (PEFCO)

Address: 280 Park Avenue, New York, NY 10017. Telephone: 212–557–3100.

PEFCO, owned mostly by commercial banks, lends only to finance export of goods and services of U.S. manufacture and origin. PEFCO's loans generally have maturities in the medium-term area and all are unconditionally guaranteed by Eximbank as to payment of interest and repayment of principal. PEFCO's funds supplement the financing of U.S. exports available through commercial banks and Eximbank.

Before contacting PEFCO, the potential borrower (a foreign buyer) or the U.S. exporter should obtain an indication from Eximbank that its board will issue a Financial Guarantee for part of the required financing. Exporters or foreign buyers with no experience in using Eximbank or PEFCO funding should first approach an experienced commercial bank; the bank will then determine whether a PEFCO loan would be a reasonable supplement to the funds provided by other sources.

OVERSEAS PRIVATE INVESTMENT CORPORATION (OPIC)

Address: 1615M 20th Street NW, Washington, DC. 20527. Information phone: 800–424–OPIC; in DC: 202–457–7010.

OPIC, established in 1971, is an independent agency of the U.S. government with the mission of reducing or eliminating private investment risks in the developing countries. OPIC insures U.S. investors against political risks of expropriation, inconvertability of local currency holdings, and damage from war, revolution, or insurrection. The agency offers lenders protection by guaranteeing payment of principal, interest, and loans.

The corporation offers investment information and counseling to business and participates in the cost of locating and developing projects.

DEPARTMENT OF AGRICULTURE

The Foreign Agricultural Service (FAS) of the U.S. Department of Agriculture provides financial support for U.S. agricultural exports through the Food for Peace program and the Commodity Credit Corporation. Under the Food for Peace program, Title I of the Agricultural Trade Development and Assistance Act of 1954 (Public Law 480, as amended) authorizes U.S. Government financing of sales of U.S. agricultural commodities to friendly countries on concessional credit terms. Sales are made by private business firms usually by bids. FAS administers agreements under this program.

Through the Commodity Credit Corporation (CCC), FAS provides U.S. exporters with short-term, commercial export financing support under two programs: The Export Credit Guarantee Program and the Blended Credit Program.

For additional information contact: General Sales Manager, Export Credits, Foreign Agricultural Service, 14th Street and Independence Ave., S.W., Washington, DC 20250. Telephone: (202) 447-3224.

STATE AND LOCAL EXPORT FINANCE PROGRAMS

As of January 1, 1985, 15 State governments have authority to operate export financing programs. Some of these programs allow a State development agency to act as a delivery agent for Eximbank programs. Other programs include State funded loan guarantee programs. Exporters should contact the State's economic development agency for more information (see page 645).

U.S. FOREIGN-TRADE ZONES (FTZs)

Firms involved in certain operations subject to significant customs duties should consider using Foreign Trade Zones (FTZs), which are now available in more than 100 port of entry communities throughout the United States. Among the advantages of using an FTZ are the following:

1. Foreign and domestic merchandise may be moved into an FTZ for storage, exhibition, assembly, manufacture, or other processing free of duties and quotas;
2. Duties are payable and quotas are applied if and when the merchandise enters the U.S. market;
3. Domestic goods entering the FTZ for export are considered exported when they enter the zone.

Information on FTZs is available by calling 202-377-2862.

Export Trading Companies and Export Management Companies

Many export trading companies (ETC's) and export management companies (EMC's) can help finance export sales in addition to acting as export representatives. However, this is true mainly for larger companies. Large ETC's may of course be able to purchase goods for export on-the-spot and thus eliminate the need for financing and other risks. When this is not the case, trading companies in a few instances may provide short-term financing themselves, but more significantly, they are also offering established contacts to make it easier for their exporter clients to obtain credit and credit insurance. Moreover, several trading companies are large enough to arrange countertrade transactions, in which trading and financing would be inseparable.

EXPORT MANAGEMENT COMPANIES (EMCs)

Export management companies (EMCs) will not only act as your export representative but, in some cases, will carry the financing for your export sale, assuring you of immediate payment and removing from your firm any foreign credit risk. EMCs solicit and transact business in the name of the manufacturers they represent for a commission, salary, or retainer plus commission. Many EMCs will also carry the financing for export sales, ensuring immediate payment for the manufacturer's products.

An agreement with an EMC can be an especially advantageous arrangement for smaller firms that do not have the time, personnel, or money to develop foreign markets, but wish nonetheless to establish a corporate and product identity overseas. For a description of services rendered to exporters by EMCs (and suggestions for choosing an appropriate firm) request Commerce's pamphlet, *"The EMC—Your Export Department."* Commerce also publishes a *"U.S. Export Management Companies Directory"* listing the names, addresses, and industry specialties of more than 1,100 EMCs in the United States. A copy of the first publication may be requested from the Publications Sales Branch, International Trade Administration, U.S. Department of Commerce, Washington, D.C. 20230. The "EMC Directory" can be purchased from: Superintendent of Documents, U.S. Government Printing Office, Washington, D.C. 20402.

The Foreign Trade Market Place, edited by George J. Schults, contains a listing of export management companies with sections on export opportunities, trade shows, financing, etc. Published by Gale Research, Book Tower, Detroit, MI 48226.

Export Trading Companies

The Office of Export Trading Company Affairs (OETCA) promotes the formation of export trading companies and is responsible for administering the antitrust preclearance program set up by the Export Trading Company Act of 1982.

OETCA is also responsible for the Contact Facilitation Service, a clearinghouse for matching U.S. suppliers of exportable goods and services with firms that provide trade facilitation services. To register for this service, contact the nearest Commerce Department District Office. The *Contact Facilitation Service Directory,* giving the names of registered firms and their products and services.

The *Export Trading Company Guidebook,* published by the Department of Commerce, explains the Export Trading Company Act and the Certificate of Review program and offers guidance in setting up and operating various types of export trading companies.

For further information contact OETCA at 202-377-5131.

Other Private Sources of Financing

FACTORING HOUSES

Certain companies, known as "factoring houses" or simply "factors" will purchase your export receivables (i.e., your invoices to foreign buyers) for a somewhat discounted price, perhaps 2 to 4 percent less than their face value. The actual amount of the discount will depend on the factoring house, the kind of product(s) involved, the customer, and the country. Factors offer two important advantages: (1) They enable you to receive immediate payment for your goods, freeing cash that could otherwise be tied up for months. (2) They relieve you of the burden of collection.

Arrangements with factoring houses are made either with or without "recourse." Arrangements "with recourse" leave you, the exporter, ultimately liable for repaying the factor if the foreign buyer defaults or other problems prevent payment within a reasonable period. Arrangements "without recourse" free you from this responsibility. Naturally, factors that accept export receivables "without recourse" generally require a large discount.

CONFIRMING

Designed to help exporters and importers expand their markets, improve cash flow, and create greater profit leverage, "confirming" is a financial service in which an independent company confirms an export order in the vendor's own country and makes payment for the goods in the currency of that country. This service can pay for and finance on terms the following items: The goods themselves, transportation (ocean or air), inland transportation at both ends, forwarding fees, customs brokerage fees, duties, etc. For the U.S. exporter, this means that the entire export transaction, from factory to end-user, can be fully coordinated and paid for with terms. Though common in Europe, confirming is still in its infancy in the United States. There are, however, U.S. firms that will provide such assistance. For further information, contact: Director, Office of Export Marketing Assistance, International Trade Administration, U.S. Department of Commerce, Washington, D.C. 20230.

Foreign Sales Corporation (FSC)*

A Foreign Sales Corporation (FSC) is a foreign chartered corporation through which exports can be made. A portion of the foreign income thus generated is exempt from Federal taxation.

In order to qualify as a FSC certain criteria must be met with respect to the management of the FSC and the exports made through it. Among the requirements are:

- The FSC must be incorporated and have its main office in a qualified foreign country or U.S. possession.
- The FSC must not have more than 25 shareholders.
- A statement of election to be treated as a FSC must be filed with the Internal Revenue Service.
- A bank account must be maintained in a foreign bank and accounting records kept in a foreign office.

There are two exceptions for small exporters. (1) Small exporters may use the FSC without meeting some of the export activities test or (2) small exporters may maintain their DISC (Domestic International Sales Corporation) by paying an annual interest charge on the DISC deferred tax liability.

* Source: International Trade Administration, U.S. Department of Commerce.

Further information can be obtained by calling 202–377–4471.

Export Assistance from State Governments

State development agencies, departments of commerce, and other departments within State governments often provide valuable assistance to exporters within the State. These groups may provide assistance in marketing, market development, and in arranging for trade shows and trade missions. The agencies in each state responsible for international trade and export assistance to local firms are given under each state in the State Information Guide section of the *Almanac*, page 645. Information is also obtainable from the National Association of State Development Agencies (NASDA), 444 N. Capitol Street, Washington, DC 20001. Telephone: 202–624–5411.

Private and Government Information Sources: International Commerce*

ASEAN-U.S. Business Council (U.S. Section)[1]
Phone: (202) 463–5486

Academy of International Business
World Trade Education Center
Cleveland State University
Cleveland, OH 44115
Phone: (216) 687–6952

Advisory Council on Japan-U.S. Economic Relations (U.S. Section)[1]
Phone: (202) 463–5489

Affiliated Advertising Agencies International
World Headquarters
2280 South Xanadu Way
Aurora, CO 80014
Phone: (303) 671–8551

American Arbitration Association
140 West 51st Street
New York, NY 10020
Phone: (212) 484–4000

* Source: *Basic Guide to Exporting*, International Trade Administration, U.S. Department of Commerce.

[1] Address: Chamber of Commerce of the United States, International Division, 1615 H Street NW, Washington, DC 20062.

American Association of Exporters and Importers
30th Floor, 11 West 42nd Street
New York, NY 10036
Phone: (212) 944–2230

American Enterprise Institute for Public Policy Research
1150 17th Street, NW
Washington, DC 20036
Phone: (202) 862–5800

American Importers Association
11 West 42nd Street
New York, NY 10036
Phone: (212) 944–2230

American Institute of Marine Underwriters
14 Wall Street, 21st Floor
New York, NY 10005
Phone: (212) 233–0550

American Management Association
440 1st Street, NW.
Washington, DC 20001
Phone: (202) 347–3092

American National Metric Council
1010 Vermont Avenue, NW.
Washington, DC 20005
Phone: (202) 628–5757

American Society of International Executives
1777 Walton
Blue Bell, PA 19422
Phone: (215) 643–3040

American Society of International Law
2223 Massachusetts Avenue, NW.
Washington, DC 20008
Phone: (202) 265–4313

Bankers Association for Foreign Trade
1101 16th Street, NW.
Washington, DC 20036
Phone: (202) 833–3060

Brazil-U.S. Business Council (U.S. Section)[1]
Phone: (202) 463–5485

Brookings Institution (The)
1775 Massachusetts Avenue, NW.
Washington, DC 20036
Phone: (202) 797–6000

Bulgarian-U.S. Economic Council (U.S. Section)[1]
Phone: (202) 463–5482

Carribbean Central American Action
1211 Connecticut Avenue, NW.
Washington, DC 20036
Phone: (202) 466–7464

Chamber of Commerce of the United States
1615 H Street, NW.
Washington, DC 20062
Phone: (202) 659–6000

Coalition for Employment Through Exports, Inc.
1801 K Street, NW.
Washington, DC 20006
Phone: (202) 296–6107

Committee for Economic Development
1700 K Street, NW
Washington, DC 20006
Phone: (202) 296–5860

Committee on Canada-United States Relations (U.S. Section)[1]
Phone: (202) 463–5488

Conference Board (The)
845 Third Avenue
New York, NY 10022
Phone: (212) 759–0900

Council of the Americas
680 Park Avenue
New York, NY 10021
Phone: (212) 628–3200

Council on Foreign Relations, Inc.
58 East 68th Street
New York, NY 10021
Phone: (212) 734–0400

Customs and International Trade Bar Association
% Barnes, Richardson & Colburn
457 Park Avenue South
New York, NY 10016
Phone: (212) 725–0200

Czechoslovak-U.S. Economic Council (U.S. Section)[1]
Phone: (202) 463–5482

Egypt-U.S. Business Council (U.S. Section)[1]
Phone: (202) 463–5487

Emergency Committee for American Trade
1211 Connecticut Avenue, Suite 801
Washington, DC 20036
Phone: (202) 659–5147

Foreign Policy Association
205 Lexington Avenue
New York, NY 10016
Phone: (212) 481–8450

Fund for Multi-National Management Education (FMME)
680 Park Avenue
New York, NY 10021
Phone: (212) 535–9386

Hungarian-U.S. Economic Council (U.S. Section)[1]
Phone: (202) 463–5482

Ibero American Chamber of Commerce
2100 M Street, NW.
Washington, DC 20037
Phone: (202) 296–0335

India-U.S. Business Council (U.S. Section)[1]
Phone: (202) 463–5492

International Advertising Association
342 Madison Avenue
New York, NY 10017
Phone: (212) 557–1133

International Bank for Reconstruction and Development
1818 H Street, NW.
Washington, DC 20006
Phone: (202) 477–1234

International Cargo Gear Bureau
17 Battery Place
New York, NY 10004
Phone: (212) 425–2750

International Economic Policy Association
5428 MacArthur Boulevard, NW.
Washington, DC 20006
Phone: (202) 686–2020

International Finance Corporation
1818 H Street, NW.
Washington, DC 20433
Phone: (202) 477–1234

International Insurance Advisory Council (U.S. Section)[1]
Phone: (202) 463–5480

International Trade Council
750 13th Street, SE.
Washington, DC 20003
Phone: (202) 546–4770

National Association of Export Management Companies, Inc.
17 Battery Place
New York, NY 10004
Phone: (212) 809–8023

National Association of Manufacturers
1331 Pennsylvania Avenue, NW.
Washington, DC 20006
Phone: (202) 626–3000

National Association of State Development Agencies
444 North Capitol, NW.
Washington, DC 20001
Phone: (202) 624–5411

National Committee on International Trade Documentation (The)
350 Broadway
New York, NY 10013
Phone: (212) 925–1400

National Customs Brokers and Forwarders Association of America
Five World Trade Center
New York, NY 10048
Phone: (212) 432–0050

National Export Traffic League
234 Fifth Avenue
New York, NY 10001
Phone: (212) 697–5895

National Foreign Trade Council
100 East 42nd Street
New York, NY 10017
Phone: (212) 355–3600

National Industrial Council
1331 Pennsylvania Avenue, NW.
Washington, DC 20006
Phone: (202) 637–3000

Nigeria-U.S. Business Council
1701 K Street, NW.
Washington, DC 20006
Phone: (202) 775–5930

Organization of American States
19th & Constitution Avenue, NW.
Washington, DC 20006
Phone: (202) 458–3000

Overseas Development Council
1717 Massachusetts Avenue, NW.
Suite 501
Washington, DC 20036
Phone: (202) 234–8701

Pan American Development Fund
1889 F Street, NW.
Washington, DC 20006
Phone: (202) 458–3969

Partners of the Americas
1424 K Street, NW.
Washington, DC 20005
Phone: (202) 628–3300

Polish-U.S. Economic Council (U.S. Section)[1]
Phone: (202) 463–5482

Private Export Funding Corporation
280 Park Avenue
New York, NY 10017
Phone: (202) 557–3100

Romanian-U.S. Economic Council (U.S. Section)[1]
Phone: (202) 463–5482

Sudan-U.S. Business Council (U.S. Section)[1]
Washington, D.C. 20062
Phone: (202) 463–5487

Trade Relations Council of the United States, Inc.
1001 Connecticut Avenue, NW.
Washington, DC 20036
Phone: (202) 785–4185

U.S. China Business Council
1818 N Street, NW.
Washington, DC 20036
Phone: (202) 429-0340

The U.S.-U.S.S.R. Trade and Economic Council
805 Third Avenue
New York, NY 10022
Phone: (212) 644–4550

The U.S.-Yugoslav Economic Council, Inc.
818 18th Street, NW.
Washington, DC 20005
Phone: (202) 857–0170

The U.S.A.-Republic of China Economic Council
200 Main Street
Crystal Lake, IL 60014
Phone: (815) 459–5875

United States of America Business and Industry Advisory Committee
1212 Avenue of the Americas
New York, NY 10036
Phone: (212) 354–4480

World Trade Institute
1 World Trade Center
New York, NY 10048
Phone: (212) 466–4044

DUN & BRADSTREET

Address: 299 Park Avenue, New York, NY. 10171 Phone: 212–593–6800.

Dun & Bradstreet provides a number of valuable services and publications in the area of international business, i.e., international credit reports on companies, international marketing guides and services, and directories of foreign firms. Dun & Bradstreet's Dun's Marketing Services in Parisipphany, NJ publishes the comprehensive annual, *Exporters Encyclopedia,* with monthly supplements. It details the rules and regulations in over 220 world markets and is arranged alphabetically by country and market area. *Principal International Businesses,* also published by Dun's Marketing Service, is a useful marketing publication providing addresses, lines of business, sales figures, and other information on nearly 50,000 foreign firms.

INTERNATIONAL REPORTS

Address: 200 Park Avenue South, New York, NY 10003 Phone: 888–1508

International Reports publishes reports on sources of worldwide export credit insurance, foreign investment guarantees, and export financing under the title of *Insurance in International Finance.*

It also publishes the monthly *International Commercial Finance Service,* containing extensive information and data on financing and interest rates, surveys of credit ratings, and foreign payment records of individual countries.

BUSINESS INTERNATIONAL

Address: One Dag Hammarskjold Plaza, New York, NY 10017. Phone: 212–750–6300.

Business International publishes a series of weekly reports: *Business International* (a global view of business); *Business Europe; Business Latin America; Business Asia; Eastern Europe Report; Business China* (People's Republic); *Business International Money Report; Investing, Licensing, Trading Report;* and *Financing Foreign Operations.* It publishes a multivolume series, *Doing Business with Eastern Europe.*

COMMERCE CLEARING HOUSE

Address: 4025 West Peterson Avenue, Chicago, IL 60646. Phone 312–583–8500.

Commerce Clearing House publishes a number of widely used looseleaf series updated on a weekly or monthly basis. In the international field these include: *Euromarket News; Doing Business in Europe; Balance of Payment Reports; Common Market Reports;* and *Income Taxes World Wide.* It also publishes a number of detailed tax and legal guides for specific countries, i.e., Canada, Mexico, Australia, England, and Germany.

U.S. DEPARTMENT OF STATE

Address: New State Building, 2201 C Street, NW, Washington, DC 20520.
Information: 202–647–4000.

Selected Publications

To order: Superintendent of Documents, Government Printing Office, Washington, DC 20402

Background Notes of the Countries of the World gives profiles of foreign countries.

Key Officers of Foreign Service Posts lists the addresses and phone numbers of all American embassies and consulates and their key personnel.

Department of State Bulletin is a monthly publication devoted to the latest developments in international politics and trade agreements.

For a list of State Department publications contact the Bureau of Public Affairs, Department of State, Washington, DC 20520.

THE LIBRARY OF CONGRESS

The Library of Congress's international divisions provide overseas free research assistance on social, economic, and political topics. Call:

African and Middle East Division	202–287–7937
Asian Division	202–287–5420
European Division	202–287–5413
Hispanic Division	202–287–5400

Write: Library of Congress, 10 First Street SE, Washington, DC 20540.

UNITED STATES GOVERNMENT INTERNATIONAL TRADE COMMISSION*

Address: 500 E Street SW, Washington, DC 20436. Information phone: 202–252–1000.

Formerly the U.S. Tariff Commission, the name was changed to the U.S. International Trade Commission in 1974.

> The commission is given broad powers of investigation relating to the customs laws of the United States and foreign countries, the volume of importation in comparison with domestic production and consumption, the conditions, causes, and effects relating to competition of foreign industries with those of the United States and all other factors affecting competition between articles of the United States and imported articles.

Businesspersons who believe they have been injured by unfair trade methods from abroad may file a complaint with this commission.

Summaries of trade and tariff information may be obtained directly from the commission.

Sources of International Credit Information

International Trade Administration, U.S. Department of Commerce, Washington, DC.

* Source: *U.S. Government Organization Manual.*

Dun & Bradstreet International, 1 World Trade Center, New York, NY 10048. Phone: 212–524–8200.

Major Commercial Banks

U.S. Department of Agriculture, U.S. Foreign Agriculture Service, Export Credit Sales Program, Washington, DC 20250.

International Organizations

UNITED NATIONS (UN)

Address: New York, NY 10017. Information phone: 212–963–7113.

The UN and its affiliated organizations publish a large number of reports and statistical tables covering all member nations. Publications may be obtained by writing: Sales Section, United Nations Publications, New York, NY 10017. For a catalog of publications call 212–963–8302.

PUBLICATIONS

Economic Survey of Europe.

Journal of Development Planning.

Guidelines for Contracting for Industrial Projects in Developing Countries.

World Economic Survey.

Annual Bulletin of Exports of Chemical Products.

Annual Bulletin of Coal Statistics for Europe.

Statistics of World Trade in Steel.

Annual Bulletin of Gas Statistics for Europe.

Annual Bulletin of Electric Energy Statistics for Europe.

Economic Bulletin for Europe.

Economic Bulletin for Asia and the Pacific.

Economic Bulletin for Africa.

Economic Bulletin for Latin America.

Quarterly Bulletin of Statistics for Asia and the Pacific.

Statistical Yearbook for Asia and the Pacific.

Demographic Yearbook.

Yearbook of International Trade Statistics Vol. I: Trade by Country; Vol. II: Trade by Commodity.

Monthly Bulletin of Statistics provides monthly statistics on a wide variety of subjects from more than 200 countries and territories together with special tables illustrating important economic developments. Quarterly data for significant world and regional aggregates are also prepared regularly for the bulletin.

Statistical Yearbook is a comprehensive compilation of international statistics relating to: population and manpower; agricultural, mineral, and manufacturing production; construction; energy; trade; transport; communications; consumption; balance of payments; wages and prices; national accounts; finance; development assistance; health; housing; education; science and technology; and culture.

Population and Vital Statistics Reports (quarterly).

Yearbook of National Accounts Statistics.

Yearbook of International Trade Statistics.

Yearbook of Construction Statistics.

Commodity Trade Statistics (quarterly).

World Trade Annual.

The Growth of World Industry: Vol. I General Industrial Statistics; Vol. II Commodities Production Data.

INTERNATIONAL MONETARY FUND (IMF)

Address: 19th and H Streets NW, Washington, DC 20431. Phone: 202–623–7061.

The IMF was organized in 1945 with the purpose of promoting international monetary cooperation and consultation. The fund also seeks to facilitate the expansion of international trade and currency exchange stability. The fund issues Special Drawing Rights (SDR), a form of reserve currency used by central banks for settling balance of payment obligations.

PUBLICATIONS

The IMF issues a broad range of publications (some in conjunction with the World Bank Group) of interest to the business community. A publication catalog is available from: IMF Publications Services 700 19th Street, NW, Washington, DC 20431. Phone: 202–623–7430.

Foreign Trade Statistics. Series A. This monthly bulletin provides a breakdown of overall trade by main commodity categories and available indices of foreign trade unit values and volumes. *Series B. Trade by Commodities. Analytical Abstracts* (quarterly). *Series C. Trade by Commodities. Market Summaries* (yearly).

Provisional Oil Statistics (quarterly).

The Annual Report of the Executive Board reviews the funds' activities, policies, organization, and administration and surveys the world economy, with special emphasis on international liquidity, payments problems, exchange rates, and world trade.

Annual Report on Exchange Arrangements and Exchange Restrictions reviews developments in exchange controls and restrictions and other measures that may have direct implications for the balance of payments of member countries.

International Financial Statistics (monthly) reports for most countries of the world current data needed for analyzing problems of international payments and inflation and deflation, i.e., data on exchange rates, international liquidity, money and banking, international trade, prices, production, government finance, interest rates, and other items. Information is presented in country tables for each country and in tables with area and world aggregates. Charts on each country page show recent changes in important series. There is also a yearbook issue.

Balance of Payments Yearbook presents statistics in a standard form, expressed in a common unit of account, for countries that report information to the fund on their balance of payments transactions. In the tables that are designated as "standard presentations," these transactions are classified in terms of objective criteria; in the tables designated as "analytic presentations," they are regrouped to facilitate further analysis and certain cumulative balances are drawn.

Direction of Trade Statistics is published jointly by the International Monetary Fund and the International Bank for Reconstruction and Development. The monthly issues provide the latest available information on each country's direction of trade, with comparative data for the corresponding period of the preceding year. A yearbook is usually published in July.

The *IMF Survey* is a topical report of the fund's activities (including all press releases, texts of communiques and major statements, SDR valuations, and exchange rates) presented in the broader context of developments in national economics and international finance.

ORGANIZATION FOR ECONOMIC COOPERATION AND DEVELOPMENT (OECD)

Address: 2001 L Street NW, Washington, DC, 20036. Phone: 202-785-6323.

The OECD, established in 1961, is an outgrowth of the Organization for European Economic Cooperation, set up under the Marshall Plan in 1948. It consists of 24 developed countries: Canada, United States, Japan, Australia, New Zealand, Austria, Belgium, Denmark, England, Finland, France, West Germany, Greece, Iceland, Italy, Luxembourg, Netherlands, Norway, Portugal, Spain, Sweden, Turkey, Switzerland, and Yugoslavia.

PUBLICATIONS

OECD Observer is intended for people who are interested in and concerned with economic and social planning in the broadest sense and who want to have relevant information in the most succinct form possible. It presents in readable fashion the entire range of OECD's work—in economic affairs, trade, manpower, social affairs, science and education, the environment, financial affairs, and development assistance. (Published bimonthly.)

The *OECD Economic Outlook* is a twice yearly, detailed survey of economic trends and prospects for the immediate future.

OECD Financial Statistics supplies complete, up-to-date, authoritative information on financial markets in European countries, the United States, Canada, and Japan. (Published yearly with bimonthly supplements.)

OECD Economic Surveys is an annual analysis of the economic policy of each OECD country as seen by the others.

Main Economic Indicators, a monthly publication, is an essential source of statistics for the student of the international business cycle.

Indicators of Industrial Activity is a quarterly publication that provides an overall view of short-term economic developments in different industries for all OECD member countries.

Monthly Statistics of Foreign Trade includes a detailed regional analysis of trade of the main country groupings in the OECD area. Series are shown non-adjusted and seasonally adjusted.

Foreign Trade by Commodities is an annual publication with matrix tables showing trade between OECD countries and partner countries of commodity groups defined at 1- and 2-digit levels of the Standard International Trade Classification. Separate volumes are published for exports and imports.

GENERAL AGREEMENT ON TRADE AND TARIFFS (GATT)

Address: Centre William Rappard, 154 Rue de Lausanne, Geneva, Switzerland.

GATT is a multilateral trade treaty (entered into force in 1948) among 83 countries providing for the reduction of tariffs and other trade barriers, standardization of trade procedures, and the resolution of trade disputes. GATT publishes *Compilations of Basic Information on Export Markets; Guide to Sources of Foreign Trade Information; Analytical Bibliography: A Compendium of Sources: International Trade Statistics;* and *World Directory of Industry and Trade Associations.*

Selected Bibliography[1]

A. Market Identification and Assessment

Addresses to AID Missions Overseas, Office of Small and Disadvantaged Business Utilization/Minority Business Center, Agency for International Development, Washington, DC 20523.

AID Commodity Eligibility Listing, Office of Small and Disadvantaged Business Utilization/Minority Resource Center, Agency for International Development, Washington, DC 20523, 1984 revised. Lists groups of commodities, presents the Agency for International Development (AID) commodity eligibility list, gives eligibility requirements for certain commodities and describes commodities that are not eligible for financing by the agency.

AID Regulation 1, Office of Small and Disadvantaged Business Utilization/Minority Resource Center, Agency for International Development, Washington, DC 20523. This tells what transactions are eligible for financing by the Agency for International Development (AID), and the responsibilities of importers, as well as the bid procedures.

AID Financed Export Opportunities, Office of Small and Disadvantaged Business Utilization/Minority Resource Center, Agency for International Development, Washington, DC 20523. Fact sheets also referred to as "Small Business Circulars", they present procurement data about proposed foreign purchases.

American Bulletin of International Technology Transfer, International Advancement, P.O. Box 75537, Los Angeles, CA 90057. Bimonthly. A comprehensive listing of product and service opportunities offered and wanted for licensing and joint ventures agreements in the United States and overseas.

Big Business Blunders: Mistakes in Multinational Marketing, 1982, David A. Ricks, Doug Jones-Irwin, Homewood, IL 60430. 200 pp. $13.95.

Source: Excerpted from *A Basic Guide to Exporting,* International Trade Administration, U.S. Department of Commerce, and other sources.

1. Prices are not given in this section.
2. To order: Superintendent of Documents, General Printing Office, Washington, DC 20402.
3. For information: U.S. Department of Agriculture, Foreign Agricultural Services, Washington, DC 20250. Telephone: 202–477–7937.
4. Contact Local U.S. & FC District Office, page 681.

Business America.[2] International Trade Administration, U.S. Department of Commerce. Principle Commerce Department publication for presenting domestic and international business news and news of the application of technology to business and industrial problems.

Catalogo de Publicaciones de la OPS, Pan American Health Organization/World Health Organization, 525 23rd Street, NW., Washington, DC 20037. A free guide of publications, many of which are in English. This catalog is published in Spanish.

Developments in International Trade Policy, International Monetary Fund, Publications Unit, 700 19th Street, NW., Washington, DC 20431. This paper focuses on the main current issues in trade policies of the major trading nations.

Direction of Trade Statistics, International Monetary Fund, Publications Unit, 700 19th Street, NW., Washington, DC 20431. This monthly publication provides data on the country and area distribution of countries' exports and imports as reported by themselves or their partners. A yearbook is published annually which gives seven years of data for 157 countries and two sets of world and area summaries.

Directory of Exporters and Importers, Journal of Commerce, Marshall Street, Phillipsburg, NJ 08865.

Directory of Leading U.S. Export Management Companies, 1984, Bergamo Book Co., 15 Ketchum Street, Westport, CT 06881.

Economic and Social Survey for Asia and the Pacific, UNIPUB, 4611-F Assembly Drive, Lanham, MD 20706–4391. Tel: (800) 521–8110. Analyzes recent economic and social developments in the region in the context of current trends. Examines agriculture, food, industry, transport, public finance, wages and prices, and external trade sectors.

Element of Export Marketing, John Stapleton, 1984, Woodhead-Faulkner, Dover, NH.

Entry Strategies for Foreign Markets—From Domestic to International Business, Franklin R. Root, American Management Association, 1977.

EXIM Bank Information Kit, Public Affairs Office, Export-Import Bank of the United States, 811 Vermont Avenue, NW., Washington, DC 20571. Includes the Bank's annual report, which provides information on interest rates and the Foreign Credit Insurance Association.

Export Development Strategies: U.S. Promotion Policy, Michael R. Czinkota and

George Tasar, Praeger, New York, NY, 1982.

Export Directory.[3] Describes the principle functions of the Foreign Agricultural Service and lists agricultural attaches.

Export-Import Bank: Financing for American Exports—Support for American Jobs, Export-Import Bank of the United States, 1980.

Export Strategies: Markets and Competition, Nigel Percy, 1982, Allen & Unwin, Winchester, MA 01890.

Exporter's Encyclopedia, annual with semimonthly updates, Dun's Marketing Service, 49 Old Bloomfield Avenue, Mt. Lakes, NJ 07046. Provides a comprehensive, country-by-country coverage of 150 world markets. It contains an examination of each country's communications and transportation facilities, customs and trade regulations, documentation, key contacts, and unusual conditions that may affect operations. Financing and Credit abroad are also examined.

Exporting from the U.S.A.: How to Develop Export Markets and Cope with Foreign Customs, A.B. Marring, 1981, Self-Counsel Press.

FAS Commodity Report.[3] These reports provide information on foreign agricultural production in 22 commodity areas.

FATUS: Foreign Agricultural Trade of the United States.[3] This report of trends in U.S. agricultural trade by commodity and country and of events affecting this trade is published six times a year with two supplements.

Findex: The Directory of Market Research Reports, Studies and Surveys, FIND/SVP, The Information Clearinghouse, 625 Sixth Avenue, New York, NY 10016. Over 10,000 listings.

Foreign Agriculture.[3] A monthly publication containing information on overseas markets and buying trends, new competitors and products, trade policy developments and overseas promotional activities.

Foreign Agriculture Circulars.[3] Individual circulars report on the supply and demand for commodities around the world. Products covered include: diary, livestock, poultry, grains, coffee, and wood products.

Foreign Commerce Handbook, Chamber of Commerce of the United States, 1615 H Street, NW., Washington, DC 20062. Lists organizations of assistance to U.S. exporters, as well as up-to-date published information on all important phases of international trade and investment.

Foreign Economic Trends (FET), Superintendent of Documents, U.S. Government Printing Office, Washington, DC 20402. Prepared by the U.S. and Foreign Commercial Service. Presents current business and economic developments and the latest economic indications in more than 100 countries. Available from ITA Publications Distribution, Rm. 1617D, U.S. Department of Commerce, Washington, DC 20230.

Foreign Market Entry Strategies, Franklin R. Root, 1982, AMACOM, New York, NY 10020.

Glossary of International Terms, International Trade Institute, Inc., 5055 N. Main Street, Dayton, OH 45415.

A Guide to Export Marketing, International Trade Institute, Inc., 5055 North Main Street, Dayton, OH 45415.

Handbook of International Trade and Development Statistics, UNIPUB, 4611-F Assembly Drive, Lanham, MD 20706-4391. Examines structural trends in developing and developed countries.

Highlights of U.S. Import and Export Trade.[2] Statistical book of U.S. imports and exports.

How to Build an Export Business: An International Marketing Guide for Minority-Owned Businesses.[2]

International Financial Statistics, International Monetary Fund, Publications Unit, 700 19th Street, NW., Washington, DC 20431. Monthly publication is a standard source of international statistics on all aspects of international and domestic finance.

International Marketing, 5th edition, 1983, Philip R. Cateora, Irwin, Homewood, IL 60430.

International Marketing, Raul Kahler, 1983, Southwestern Publishing Co., Cincinnati, OH 45227.

International Marketing, 3rd edition, Vern Terpstra, 1983, Dryden Press, Hinsdale, IL 60521.

International Marketing, Revised Edition, Hans Thorelli & Helmut Becker, eds., 1980, Pergamon Press, Elmsford, NY 10523.

International Marketing, 2nd edition, 1981, L. S. Walsh, International Ideas, Philadelphia, PA 19103.

International Marketing: An Annotated Bibliography, 1983, S. T. Cavusgil & John R. Nevin, eds., American Marketing Association.

International Marketing Handbook, 1985, 3 Vols., Frank S. Bair, ed., Gale Research Co., Detroit, MI 48226.

International Marketing Research, 1983, Susan P. Douglas & C. Samual Craig, Prentice-Hall, Englewood Cliffs, NJ 07632.

International Monetary Fund: Publications Catalog, International Monetary Fund, Publications Unit, 700 19th Street, NW., Washington, DC 20431.

International Trade Operations . . . A Managerial Approach, R. Duane Hall, Unz & Co., 190 Baldwin Ave., Jersey City, NJ 07303.

International Trade Reporter, Bureau of National Affairs, 1231 25th Street NW, Washington, DC 20037.

Local Chambers of Commerce Which Maintain Foreign Trade Services, 1983. International Division, Chamber of Commerce of the United States, 1615 H Street, NW., Washington, DC 20062. A list of chambers of commerce that have programs to aid exporters.

Market Shares Reports, National Technical Information Services, U.S. Department of Commerce, Box 1553, Springfield, VA 22161. These are reports for over 88 countries. They provide basic data needed by exporters to evaluate overall trends in the size of markets for manufacturers.

Marketing Aspects of International Business, 1983, Gerald M. Hampton & Aart Van Gent, Klewer-Nijhoff Publishing, Bingham, MA.

Marketing High-Technology, William L. Shanklin & John K. Ryans, Jr., DC Heath & Co., 125 Spring Street, Lexington, MA 02173.

Marketing in Europe, Economic Intelligence Unit, Ltd., 10 Rockefeller Plaza, New York, NY 10020, monthly. Journal provides detailed analysis of the European market for consumer goods. The issues are published in three subject groups: Food, drink and tobacco; clothing, furniture and consumer goods; and chemists' goods such as pharmaceuticals and toiletries.

Marketing in the Third World, Erdener Kaynak, Praeger, New York, NY 10175.

Metric Laws and Practices in International Trade—Handbook for U.S. Exporters, 1982.[2]

Monthly World Crop Production.[3] Report provides estimates on the projection of wheat, rice, coarse grains, oilseeds, and cotton in selected regions and countries around the world.

Multinational Marketing Management, 3rd edition, 1984, Warren J. Keegan, Prentice Hall, Englewood Cliffs, NJ 07632.

OECD Publications, OECD Publications and Information Center, Suite 1207, 1750 Pennsylvania Avenue, NW., Washington, DC 20006–4582.

Outlook for U.S. Agricultural Exports.[3] This report analyzes current developments and forecasts U.S. farm exports in coming months by commodity and region. Country and regional highlights discuss the reasons why sales of major commodities are likely to rise or fall in those areas.

Overseas Business Reports (OBR).[2] Reports include current-marketing information, trade forecasts, statistics, regulations, and marketing profiles. Available from ITA Publications, Rm. 1617D, U.S. Department of Commerce, Washington, DC 20230.

Profitable Export Marketing: A Strategy for U.S. Business, Maria Ortiz-Buonafina, Prentice-Hall, Englewood Cliffs, NJ 07632.

Reference Book for World Traders, Annual, Croner Publications, Inc., 211 Jamaica Avenue, Queens Village, NY 11428. A loose-leaf reference book for traders. Gives information about export documentation, steamship lines and airlines, free trade zones, credit and similar matters.

Source Book . . . The "How to" Guide for Exporters and Importers, Unz & Co., 190 Baldwin Avenue, Jersey City, NJ 07036.

Trade Directories of the World, Annual, Croner Publications, Inc., 211 Jamaica Avenue, Queens Village, NY 11428.

Trends in World Production and Trade, 1982, UNIPUB, P.O. Box 1222, Ann Arbor, MI 48106. 4611-F Assembly Drive, Lanham, MD 20706-4391. Report discusses the structural change in world output, industrial growth patterns since 1960, changes in the pattern of agricultural output, and changes in patterns in trade in goods and services. Product groups and commodity groups are defined according to SITC criteria.

United Nations Publications, United Nations and Information Center, 1889 F Street, NW., Washington, DC 20006. Free.

U.S. Export Sales.[3] A weekly report of agricultural export sales based on reports provided by private exporters.

U.S. Farmers Export Arm.[3] 1980.

Weekly Roundup of World Production and Trade.[3] Provides a summary of the week's important events in agricultural foreign trade and world production.

World Agriculture.[3] Provides production information, data and analyses by commodity and country, along with a review of recent economic conditions and changes in food and trade policies.

World Agriculture Regional Supplements.[3] Provides a look by region at agricultural developments during the previous year and the outlook for the year ahead.

The World Bank Catalog of Publications, World Bank Publications, P.O. Box 37525, Washington, DC 200013.

World Economic Outlook: A Survey by the Staff of the International Monetary Fund, International Monetary Fund, Publications Unit, 700 19th Street, NW., Washington, DC 20431. This yearly report provides a comprehensive picture of the international situation and prospects. Highlights the imbalances that persist in the world economy and their effects on inflation, unemployment, real rates of interest and exchange rates.

World Economic Survey, UNIPUB, 4611-F Assembly Drive, Lanham, MD 20706-4301. Assesses the world economy. It provides an overview of developments in global economics for the past year and provides an outlook for the future.

Yearbook of International Trade Statistics, UNIPUB, 4611-F Assembly Drive, Lanham, MD 20706-4391. Offers international coverage of foreign trade statistics. Tables are provided for overall trade by regions and countries. Vol. I: Trade by Commodity. Vol. II: Commodity Matrix Tables.

B. Selling & Sales Contacts

American Export Register, Thomas Publishing Co., 1 Penn Plaza, 250 N. 34th Street, New York, NY 10010, 1984. This book is designed for persons searching for U.S. suppliers, for foreign manufacturers seeking U.S. buyers or representatives for their products. Contains product lists in four languages, an advertiser's index, information about and a list of U.S. Chambers of Commerce abroad, and a list of banks with international services and shipping, financing and insurance information.

Background Notes.[2] Four to twelve page summaries on the economy, people, history, culture and government of about 160 countries.

Commercial News USA (CN), Monthly export promotion magazine circulated only overseas, listing specific products and services of U.S. firms. Applications for participation in the magazine are available from the District Offices of the U.S. and Foreign Commercial Service, U.S. Department of Commerce.

Directory of American Firms Operating in Foreign Countries, 11th Edition, (3 volumes) World Trade Academy Press, 50 E. 42nd Street, New York, NY 10017. Contains the most recent data on some 3000 American companies with more than 22,500 subsidiaries and affiliates in 122 foreign countries. Lists every American firm under the country in which it has subsidiaries or branches, together with their home office branch in the United States. Gives the names and addresses of their subsidiaries or branches, products manufactured or distributed. Foreign operations are grouped by country.

Directory of Foreign Firms Operating in the United States, 5th edition, World Trade Academy Press, 50 E. 42nd Street, New York, NY 10017. Directory is in three parts: (1) foreign firms grouped by country, (2) Alphabetical index of foreign firms, (3) alphabetical index of firms in the U.S.

Export Mailing List Service (EMLS).[4] Targeted mailing lists of prospective overseas customers from the Commerce Department's automated worldwide file of foreign firms. EMLs identify manufacturers, agents, retailers, service firms, government agencies and other one-to-one contacts. Information includes name and address, cable and telephone numbers, name and title of a key official, product/service interests, and additional date.

How to Get the Most from Overseas Exhibitions, International Trade Administration, Publications Distribution, Room 1617D, U.S. Department of Commerce, Washington, DC 20230.

Japan: Business Obstacles and Opportunities, 1983, McKinney & Co., John Wiley, NY.

Management of International Advertising: A Marketing Approach, 1984, Dean M. Peeples & John K. Ryans. Allyn & Bacon, Boston, MA 02159.

Service Industries and Economic Development: Case Studies in Technology Transfer. Praeger Publishers, New York, NY 10175. 1984.

Top Bulletin. Journal of Commerce, 445 Marshall Street, Phillipsburg, NJ 08865. Weekly publication of trade opportunities received each week from overseas embassies and consulates. Also available on computer tape.

World Traders Data Reports (WTDRs).[4] Service provides background reports on individual foreign firms. WTDRs are designed to help U.S. firms evaluate potential foreign customers before making a business commitment.

C. Financing Exports

Chase World Guide for Exporters, Export Credit Reports, Chase World Information

Corporation, One World Trade Center, Suite 4533, New York, NY 10048. The *Guide*, covering 180 countries, contains current export financing methods, collection experiences and charges, foreign import and exchange regulations and related subjects. Supplementary bulletins keep the guide up to date throughout the year. The *Reports*, issued quarterly, specify credit terms granted for shipment to all the principal world markets. The reports show the credit terms offered by the industry groups as a whole, thereby enabling the reader to determine whether his or her terms are more liberal or conservative than the average for specific commodity groups.

Financing and Insuring Exports: A User's Guide to Eximbank and FCIA Programs, Export-Import Bank of the United States, User's Guide, 811 Vermont Avenue, NW., Washington, DC 20571. A 350 page guide which covers Eximbank's working capital guarantees, credit risk protection (guarantees and insurance), medium-term and long-term lending programs. Includes free updates during calendar year in which the guide is purchased.

A Guide to Checking International Credit, International Trade Institute, Inc., 5055 North Main Street, Suite 270, Dayton, OH 45415.

A Guide to Financing Exports, U.S. and Foreign Commercial Service, International Trade Administration Publications Distribution, Room 1617D, U.S. Department of Commerce, Washington, DC 20230, 1985. Brochure.

A Guide to Understanding Drafts, International Trade Institute, Inc., 5055 N. Main Street, Dayton, OH 45415.

A Guide to Understanding Letters of Credit, International Trade Institute, Inc., 5055 N. Main Street, Dayton, OH 45415.

A Handbook on Financing U.S. Exports, Machinery and Allied Products Institute, 1200 18th Street, NW., Washington, DC 20036.

Official U.S. and International Financing Institutions: A Guide for Exporters and Investors, International Trade Administration, U.S. Department of Commerce. Available from the Superintendent of Documents, U.S. Government Printing Office, Washington, DC 20402.

Specifics on Commercial Letters of Credit and Bankers Acceptances, James A. Harrington, 1979 UNZ & Co., Division of Scott Printing Corp., 190 Baldwin Avenue, Jersey City, NJ 07036, 1979.

D. Laws and Regulations

Customs Regulations of the United States.[2]

Distribution License, 1985 Office of Export Administration, Room 1620, U.S. Department of Commerce, Washington, DC 20230

Export Administration Regulations.[2] Covers U.S. export control regulations and policies, with instructions, interpretations and explanatory material. Last revised Oct 1, 1984.

Export Marketing of Capital Goods to the Socialist Countries of Eastern Europe, 1978, M. R. Hill, Gower Publishing Company.

Manual for the Handling of Applications for Patents, Designs and Trademarks Throughout the World, Ocrooibureau Los En Stigter B.V., Amsterdam, the Netherlands.

Summary of U.S. Export Regulations, 1985, Office of Export Administration, Room 1620, Department of Commerce, Washington, DC 20230.

Technology and East-West Trade, 1983, Summarizes the major provisions of the Export Administration Act of 1979 and its implications in East-West trade, Office of Technology Assessment, U.S. Department of Commerce, Washington, DC 20230.

E. Shipping and Logistics

Export-Import Traffic Management and Forwarding, 6th edition, 1979. Alfred Murr, Cornell Maritime Press, Box 456, Centerville, MD 21617. Presents the diverse functions and varied services concerned with the entire range of ocean traffic management.

Export Shipping Manual, Indexed, looseleaf reference binder. Detailed current information on shipping and import regulations for all areas of the world. Bureau of National Affairs, 1231 25th Street, NW., Washington, DC 20037.

Guide to Canadian Documentation, International Trade Institute, Inc., 5055 N. Main Street, Dayton, OH 45415.

Guide to Documentary Credit Operations, ICC Publishing Corporation, New York, NY 1985.

Guide to Export Documentation, International Trade Institute, Inc., 5055 N. Main Street, Dayton, OH 45415.

Guide to International Ocean Freight Shipping, International Trade Institute, 5055 N. Main Street, Dayton, OH 45415.

Guide to Selecting the Freight Forwarder, International Trade Institute, Inc., 5055 North Main Street, Suite 270, Dayton, OH 45415.

Journal of Commerce Export Bulletin, 110 Wall Street, New York, NY 10005. A weekly newspaper that reports port and shipping developments. Lists products shipped from New York and ships and cargoes departing from 25 other U.S. ports. A "trade prospects" column lists merchandise offered and merchandise wanted.

Shipping Digest, Geyer-McAllister Publications, Inc., 51 Madison Avenue, New York, NY 10010. A weekly which contains cargo sailing schedules from every U.S. port to every foreign port, as well as international air and sea commerce news.

F. Licensing

Foreign Business Practices . . . Material on Practical Aspects of Exporting,[2] International Licensing and Investment, 1981.

American Bulletin of International Technology Transfer, International Advancement, P.O. Box 75537, Los Angeles, CA 90057, bimonthly. Comprehensive listing of product and service opportunities offered and sought for licensing and joint ventures agreements in the United States and overseas.

International Technology Licensing: Competition, Costs, and Negotiation, 1981, J. Farok Contractor, Lexington Books, Lexington, MA 02173.

Investing, Licensing, and Trading Conditions Abroad, Business International Corporation, base volume with monthly updates.

Sources for Market Research

Product/Industry Data Resources

Foreign Trade Report, FT 410.[2] Monthly FT 410 provides a statistical record of shipments of all merchandise from the United States to foreign countries, including both the quantity and dollar value of exports to each country during the month covered by the report. Also contains cumulative export statistics from the first of the calendar year. Report FT 410 (monthly and cumulative for U.S. Exports, Schedule E Commodity by Country) is available by subscription. The reports may also be available at US&FCS District Offices and many large libraries.

International Market Research (IMR).[4] These reports are in-depth analyses for those who want a more complete picture for one industry in one country. A report includes information such as market size and outlook, end-user analysis, distribution channels, cultural characteristics, business customs and practices, competitive situation, trade barriers, and trade contacts.

Comparison Shopping Service. Service provides a custom-tailored export market research survey on a U.S. client firm's specific product in a single country. The survey covers key marketing factors in the target country, including overall marketability, names of competitors, comparative prices, entry and distribution channels, and names of potential sales representatives or licensees. The survey is conducted on-site by U.S. commercial officers and is available for standard off-the-shelf products (no custom or specialty items) in selected countries.

Market Share Reports. Provides basic data to evaluate overall trends in the size of markets for exporters. Also measures changes in the import demand for specific products and compares the competitive position of U.S. and foreign exporters. Contact the National Technical Information Service, U.S. Department of Commerce, Box 1553, Springfield, VA 22161. Telephone: (202) 487–4630.

Export Information System (XIS) Data Reports. Available from the U.S. Small Business Administration (SBA) for approximately 1700 product categories, the XIS Data Reports provide to a small business a list of the 25 largest importing markets for its product, the 10 best markets for U.S. exporters of that product, the trends within those markets and the major sources of foreign competition, based on Department of Commerce and United Nations data. There is no charge to small businesses for this service. Contact the local SBA Field Office.

FINDEX: The Directory of Market Research Reports, Studies and Surveys. Publication contains over 10,000 listings of market research reports, studies, and surveys. Contact FIND/SVP The Information Clearinghouse, 625 Sixth Avenue, New York, NY 10016. Telephone: (212) 354–2424.

Country Data Resources:

Foreign Economic Trends (FET).[4] FET's present current business and economic developments and the latest economic indicators for more than 100 countries. FET's are prepared either annually or semiannually depending on the country.

Overseas Business Reports (OBR's).[2] Reports provide background statistics and information on specific countries useful to exporters. They present economic and commercial profiles, issue semiannual outlooks for U.S. trade, and publish selected statistical reports on the direction, volume, and nature of U.S. foreign trade with the country.

Background Notes.[2] This series surveys a country's people, geography, economy, government, and foreign policy. Prepared by the Department of State, it includes important national economic and trade information, including major trading partners.

U.S. Agency for International Development's Congressional Presentations. Provide country-by-country data on nations to which the agency will provide funds in the coming year. Also provide detailed information on past funding activities in each individual country. In addition, the publications list projects and their locations that the agency desires to fund in the upcoming year (i.e. a hydroelectrical project in Egypt). Since these projects require U.S. goods and services, the *Congressional Presentations* can give U.S. exporters an opportunity to plan ahead by allowing an early look at potential projects. For ordering information, contact the U.S. Agency for International Development (AID), Department of State, Washington, DC 20523. Telephone: (703) 235–1840.

Trade and Development Program's Congressional Presentation. This publication reports the dollar amount spent by the agency by industry in specific countries around the world for the past several years. For ordering information about Trade and Development's *Congressional Presentation,* contact Trade and Development Program, U.S. Department of State, Washington, DC 20523. Telephone: (703) 235–3663.

Exporters Encyclopedia. An extensive handbook on exporting, this publication contains market information on over 150 world markets, which are individually covered. Contact Dun's Marketing Services, 49 Old Bloomfield Avenue, Mt. Lakes, NJ 07046.

Doing Business in Foreign Countries.[2] A series on doing business in most foreign countries, these individual guides are often provided to clients or interested parties by some large or international accounting firms, banks, or other service firms. These publications provide information on specific countries and include demographic and cultural backgrounds, economic climates, restrictions and incentives to trade, duties, documentation requirements, tax structure, and other useful information.

Worldwide Background Data

Statistical Yearbook. This international trade information on products is provided by the United Nations. Information on importing countries and, to help assess competition, exports by country are included. Order by calling 800–521–8110.

World Population. The U.S. Bureau of the Census collects and analyzes worldwide demographic data that can assist exporters in identifying potential markets for their products. Information on each country—total population, fertility, mortality, urban population, growth rate, and life expectancy—is updated every 2 years. Also published are detailed demographic profiles (including analysis of labor force structure, infant mortality, etc.) of individual countries (price and availability varies). *World Population.* Contact the Center for International Research, Room 407, Scuderi Building, U.S. Bureau of the Census, Washington, DC 20233.

International Economic Indicators. These are quarterly reports providing basic data (for years and quarters) on the economies of the United States and seven principal industrial countries. Include statistics on gross national product, industrial production, trade, prices, finance, and labor; they also measure changes in key competitive indicators. Reports can provide an overall view of international trends or a basis for more detailed analyses of the economic situation. Annual subscription is available through: ITA Publications Sales Branch, Room 1617D, U.S. Department of Commerce, Washington, DC 20230.

International Financial Statistics. A monthly publication produced by the International Monetary Fund. It presents statistics on exchange rates, money and banking, production, government finance, interest rates, and other subjects. Available from the International Monetary Fund, Publications Unit, 700 19th Street, NW., Washington, DC 20431. Telephone: (202) 473–7430.

World Bank Atlas. Published by the World Bank, this publication presents population, gross domestic product, and average growth rates for every country. Available from World Bank Publications, P.O. Box 37525, Washington, DC 20013.

Other Publications

Europa Year Book is an annual two-volume work covering a wide range of commercial, economic, and political statistics and information about every country in the world. Volume I deals with international organizations and the countries of Europe, while Volume II covers Africa, the Americas, Asia, and Australia. It is published by Europe Publications, Ltd., 18 Bedford Square, London, England.

Jane's Major Companies of Europe is an annual providing extensive information about all major European companies. It is available from Jane's Yearbooks, 8 Shepherdess, London N1 7LW, England.

Foreign Commerce Handbook provides information on international trade and foreign markets. Included are addresses and phone numbers of organizations involved with foreign trade, a glossary of foreign commercial terms and a bibliography of indexes and periodicals. Available from the Chamber of Commerce of the United States, 1615 H Street NW, Washington, DC 20062.

International Directory of Marketing Research Houses and Services (the "Green Book") is a directory of marketing research organizations in some 50 countries and includes descriptions of services, contact people, phone numbers, and addresses. Available from: American Marketing Association, 420 Lexington Avenue, New York, NY 10170.

Lambert's World Government Directory identifies government officials in 168 countries as well as officials in Inter-Governmental organizations. Published by International Executive Reports, 115 Massachusetts Avenue NW, Washington, DC 20005.

Country Experts in the Federal Government is a guide to U.S. government analysts for almost all countries. Published by Washington Researchers, 2612 P Street, NW, Washington, DC 20007.

International Research Center Directory edited by Anthony F. Kruzas and Kay Gill identifies 15,000 university-related, independent and government research organizations throughout the world. Available from Gale Research Company, Book Tower, Detroit, MI 48226.

Croner's Reference Book for World Traders is a three volume work covering basic data and hard-to-locate information for international traders and market researchers. Available from Croner Publications, 211–05 Jamaica Avenue, Queens Village, New York, 11428.

Incoterms is a booklet providing a set of international rules for interpreting the main terms used in foreign trade contracts. Available from the U.S. Council of the International Chamber of Commerce, Inc. 1212 Avenue of the Americas, New York, NY 10036. Also publishes other useful material.

Revised American Foreign Trade Definitions, is a compilation from the National Council of Importers, the Chamber of Commerce of the U.S., and the National Foreign Trade Council. Available from the National Foreign Trade Council at 100 E. 42nd Street, New York, NY 10017.

European Markets: A Guide to Company and Industry Information Sources is a three volume resource for accessing information on European companies and markets. Available from Washington Researchers, 2612 P Street NW, Washington, DC 20007.

Exporters' Encyclopaedia, Dun's Marketing Service, 49 Old Bloomfield Avenue, Mt. Lakes, NJ 07046. Gives country by country coverage of 150 world markets.

International Information Available in the U.S. by Country

This section lists helpful addresses in the United States for those doing business with countries where business practices may present certain problems.

JAPAN

Exporters and importers generally find it essential to use the services of the Japanese trading companies, which offer a wide range of services including negotiation of overseas deals, transportation, storage, finance, and marketing. The largest trading companies are listed below. The small exporter will often do better using smaller trading companies that specialize in one or two types of products. Exporters seeking an appropriate trading company should contact a local JETRO Office (Japan External Trade Office):

Bank of America Tower
555 S. Flower Street
Los Angeles, CA 90071
Telephone: 213–626–5700

360 Post Street
San Francisco, CA 94108
Telephone: 415–392–1333

229 Peachtree Street, NE
Atlanta, GA 30303
Telephone: 404–681–0600

230 N. Michigan Avenue
Chicago, IL 60601
Telephone: 312–527–9000

1221 Avenue of the Americas
New York, NY 10020
Telephone: 212–997–0400

One World Trade Center
2100 Stemmons Freeway
Dallas, TX 75258
Telephone: 214–651–0839

One Houston Center
1221 McKinney Street
Houston, TX 77010
Telephone: 713–759–9595

P.O. Box 3356
Marina Station
Mayaguez, PR 00708
Telephone: Mayaquez 832–0861

When U.S. firms encounter difficulty doing business with Japanese companies because of Japanese regulations contact the Japan desk of the International Trade Administration at 202–377–4527.

MAJOR TRADING COMPANIES (NEW YORK OFFICES)

Mitsubishi International Corporation
520 Madison Avenue
New York, NY 10022

Mitsui & Company
200 Park Avenue
New York, NY 10017

Marubeni America Corporation
200 Park Avenue
New York, NY 10066

C. Itoh & Co. (America), Inc.
335 Madison Avenue
New York, NY 10017

Sumitomo Corporation of America
345 Park Avenue
New York, NY 10154

Toyo Menka (America), Inc.
One World Trade Center
New York, NY 10048

Kanematsu-Gosho (USA), Inc.
1133 Avenue of the Americas
New York, NY 10036

Nichimen America, Inc.
1185 Avenue of the Americas
New York, NY 10036

Nissho Iwai America
1211 Avenue of the Americas
New York, NY 10036

PUBLICATIONS ON TRADING WITH JAPAN

Country Market Profiles—Japan contains statistics on exports, information on some seven industries with export potential to Japan, developments in bilateral trade, and much more. This book is available from the Office of Japan, U.S. Department of Commerce, Washington, DC 20030.

Directory of Japanese Technical Resources provides information to assist U.S. business and industry to take full advantage of technical information emanating from Japan. Included are: translations of Japanese technical documents, commercial services which collect, abstract, translate and disseminate Japanese technical information, U.S. Government agencies, programs, or services involving Japanese technical information, libraries with extensive Japanese holdings, a comparison of technology transfer infrastructures that exist in the U.S. and Japan, and a private sector view on how the Government can work with industry to make Japanese scientific and technical information assessible in the United States. Available from: U.S. Department Commerce, National Technical Information Serivce, Springfield, VA 22161.

How to Find Information about Japanese Companies and Industries is an extensive guide to information sources both here and abroad helpful for doing business with Japan. Available from Washington Researchers Publishing, 2612 P Street NW, Washington, DC 20007.

Industrial Grouping in Japan, a guide to the Japanese industrial environment, surveys over 3000 leading companies. Includes information on: major product lines, annual sales, sources of loans, number of employees and degrees of affiliation with their respective groups. This publication also explains origins, structures, and methods of functioning of various groups, together with recent developments. Available from Taylor & Francis, 242 Cherry Street, Philadelphia, PA 19106.

THE PEOPLE'S REPUBLIC OF CHINA (PRC)

For information or advice on contacting the Chinese on commercial matters, call or write to:

U.S. Department of Commerce
International Trade Administration Office of PRC and Hong Kong
Washington, DC 20230
Telephone: 202–377–3583/4681

Commercial Office
Embassy of the People's Republic of China
2300 Connecticut Avenue, N.W.
Washington, DC 20008

For free publications on trade with China call 202–328–2520.

Doing Business with China, prepared by the International Trade Administration (Department of Commerce) is available from the:

Superintendent of Documents
Government Printing Office
Washington, D.C. 20402

THE NATIONAL COUNCIL FOR U.S.-CHINA TRADE

Address: 1818 N Street NW, Suite 500. Washington, DC 20220. Phone: 202–429–0340.

The Council, a nonprofit, private organization maintaining close liaison with the U.S. government, serves as a forum for the discussion of trade policy and issues. It also serves as a focal point for business contact and the dissemination of information on marketing in the PRC. The council maintains a business counseling service; it also publishes the *China Business Review* bimonthly. The council facilitates the reciprocal arrangements of trade missions and trade exhibitions in the United States and China.

USSR AND EASTERN EUROPE*

USSR

USSR Affairs Division, International Economic Policy (202–377–4655). This division collects, analyzes, and disseminates current information on economic, commercial, and other developments in the USSR and estimates their impact on the U.S. business community. The division develops policy guidance in our commercial relationship with the Soviet Union and provides staff support to and representation on the Joint Commercial Commission. It also maintains close contact with the U.S. Commercial Office in Moscow and with USSR commercial officials in the United States in order to initiate and pursue official representations on behalf of the American business community.

Within the U.S. Department of Commerce there are several helpful sources. Among them are:

U.S.S.R. Division: 202–377–4655
Export Administration: 202–377–5497
Export Counseling Center: 202–377–3181

It may be to the company's advantage to touch base with the following USSR commercial organizations in the United States to try to obtain some indication of Soviet interest and to identify contacts in the Soviet Union:

The Trade Representation of the USSR in the U.S.A., 2001 Connecticut Avenue NW, Washington, DC 20008, telephone: 202–232–5988.

The Amtorg Trading Corporation, 750 Third Avenue, New York, NY 10017, telephone: 212–972–1220.

The staffs of both Amtorg and the Trade Representation include representatives of individual foreign trade organizations (FTOs).

The USSR Consulate General, 2790 Green Street, San Francisco, CA 94123, telephone: 415–922–6642, may have information conveniently available for companies on the West Coast.

U.S.-U.S.S.R. Trade and Economic Council, 805 Third Avenue, New York, NY 10022, telephone: 212–644–4550.

For a list of U.S. business representatives, consultants and trading companies doing business with the U.S.S.R. call 202–377–4655.

EASTERN EUROPE

Commercial transactions with Bulgaria, Czechoslovakia, East Germany, Hungary, Poland, and Romania are similar to those with the USSR. Contracts are negotiated with the appropriate Foreign Trade Organization. For detailed information about trade shows, missions, export licenses, and FTOs, contact the Office of East-West Trade, Department of Commerce in Washington, or the Commerce Department Offices at the district level. Another key source of information is the U.S. East-West Trade Development Office in Vienna.

BULGARIA

Bulgarian Embassy
2100 16th Street NW
Washington, DC 20009

Bulgarian Commercial Counselor
121 E. 62nd Street
New York, NY 10021

CZECHOSLOVAKIA

Czechoslovakian Embassy
3900 Linnean Avenue NW
Washington, DC 20008

Office of the Czechoslovakian Commercial Counselor
292 Madison Avenue
New York, NY 10016

EAST GERMANY
(German Democratic Republic)

Embassy of the German Democratic Republic
1717 Massachusetts Avenue NW
Washington, DC 20036

German American Chamber of Commerce
666 Fifth Avenue
New York, NY 10009

HUNGARY

Embassy of Hungary to the United States
3910 Shoemaker Street NW
Washington, DC 20009

Office of the Commercial Counselor of the Embassy of Hungary
2401 Calvert Street
Washington, DC 20008

Hungarian Consulate
8 E. 75th Street
New York, NY 10021

* Source: Excerpted from Department of Commerce Overseas Reports, "Trading with the USSR" and other Department of Commerce sources.

POLAND

Embassy of the Polish People's Republic
2640 16th Street NW
Washington, DC 20008

Polish Consulate General
820 2nd Avenue
New York, NY 10009

Polish Commercial Counselor's Office
820 2nd Avenue
New York, NY 10009

Polish Chamber of Foreign Trade
44 Montgomery Street
San Francisco, CA 94104

U.S. banks with offices in Warsaw
First National Bank, Chicago

ROMANIA

Romanian Embassy
1607 23rd Street NW
Washington, DC 20008

Romanian Trade Commission
200 E. 38th Street
New York, NY 10016

U.S. Banks with offices in Bucharest
Manufacturer's Hanover Trust, New York, NY

NEAR EAST AND NORTH AFRICA*

The Office of the Near East (Telephone: 202–377–4441) within the International Trade Administration serves as the focal point for the U.S. Department of Commerce response to the changing economic situation and significant business opportunities in the Near East and North Africa. The group assembles, analyzes, and disseminates to the U.S. business community information on economic conditions and new opportunities in the area, provides counseling for and makes representations on behalf of U.S. exporters, and plans promotional programs to assist U.S. firms to take advantage of the expanded commercial potential.

For information on major projects call 202–377–4332.

ALGERIA

Embassy of Algeria
2118 Kalorama Road NW
Washington, DC 20008

BAHRAIN

Embassy of Bahrain
3502 International Drive NW
Washington, DC 20008

ARAB REPUBLIC OF EGYPT

Embassy of the Arab Republic of Egypt
2310 Decatur Place NW
Washington, DC 20008

Commercial and Economic Office
2232 Connecticut Avenue NW
Washington, DC 20008

Egypt American Chamber of Commerce
1 World Trade Center
New York, NY 10017

Permanent Economic Mission to the U.N.
36 East 67 Street
New York, NY 1010

Consulate of the Arab Republic of Egypt
1110 Second Avenue
New York, NY 10022

Consulate of the Arab Republic of Egypt
3001 Pacific Avenue
San Francisco, CA 94115

IRAQ

Indian Embassy
1801 P Street NW
Washington, DC 20008

ISRAEL

Embassy of Israel
3514 International Drive NW
Washington, DC 20008

Israel Consulates General
Atlanta, Boston, Chicago, Houston, Los Angeles, New York City, Philadelphia, and San Francisco

Investment Authority
350 Fifth Avenue
New York, NY 10001

Israel Trade Center
174 N. Michigan Avenue
Chicago, IL 60601

Israel Trade Center
350 Fifth Avenue
New York, NY 10001

Israel Supply Mission
350 Fifth Avenue
New York, NY 10001

6380 Wilshire Boulevard
Los Angeles, CA 90048

JORDAN (HASHEMITE KINGDOM OF)

Embassy of Jordan
3504 International Drive, NW
Washington, DC 20008

Consulate General
866 U.N. Plaza
New York, NY 10017

Consulates are also located in Houston, Chicago, Scottsdale, and Palm Beach.

* Source: *A Business Guide to the Near East & North Africa*, International Trade Administration, U.S. Department of Commerce.

STATE OF KUWAIT

Embassy of Kuwait
2940 Tilden Street NW
Washington, DC 20008

LEBANON

Embassy of Lebanon
2560 28th Street NW
Washington, DC 20008

Consulate General
9 E. 76th Street
New York, NY 10021

Consulate General
1300 Lafayette East
Detroit, Michigan 48207

MOROCCO

Embassy of Morocco
1601 21st Street NW
Washington, DC 20009

Consulate General
437 Fifth Avenue
New York, NY 10016

OMAN

Embassy of the Sultanate of Oman
2342 Massachusetts Avenue NW
Washington, DC 20008

Permanent Mission to the United Nations
866 U.N. Plaza
New York, NY 10017

QATAR

Embassy of Qatar
600 New Hampshire Avenue NW
Washington, DC 20037

SAUDI ARABIA

Saudi Arabian Embassy
1520 18th Street NW
Washington, DC 20036

Consulate General
866 United Nations Plaza
New York, NY 10017

Consulate
5433 West Heimer
Houston, Texas 77056

SYRIAN ARAB REPUBLIC

Embassy of the Syrian Arab Republic
2215 Wyoming Avenue NW
Washington, DC 20008

TUNISIA

Embassy of Tunisia
1515 Massachusetts Avenue NW
Washington, DC 20008

UNITED ARAB EMIRATES

Embassy of the United Arab Emirates
600 New Hampshire Avenue, N.W.
Washington, DC 20037

YEMEN ARAB REPUBLIC

Embassy of the Yemen Arab Republic
600 New Hampshire Avenue, NW
Washington, DC 20037

Yemen Arab Republic Mission to the U.N.
737 3rd Avenue
New York, NY 10017

FAST MATCH

A quick, easy way to match your international business requirements to the appropriate Government programs or services designed to satisfy those needs

IF YOU ARE SEEKING INFORMATION REGARDING ➡

USE ⬇

	Potential Markets	Market Research*	Direct Sales Leads	Agents/Distributors	Licenses	Credit Analysis	Financial Assistance	Risk Insurance	Tax Incentives
Foreign Trade Statistics (FT-410)	•								
Global Market Surveys	•	•							
Foreign Market Reports	•	•							
Market Share Reports	•	•							
Foreign Economic Trends	•	•							
Business America	•	•	•	•	•				
Commercial Exhibitions	**	**	•	•	•				
Overseas Business Reports (OBR)		•							
Overseas Private Investment Corp.		•					•	•	
Commerce Business Daily			•						
New Product Information Service			•	•	•				
Trade Opportunity Program (TOP)			•	•	•				
Industry Trade Lists			•	•	•				
Special Trade Lists			•	•	•				
Export Mailing List Service (EMLS)			•	•	•				
Agent/Distributor Service (ADS)				•					
World Traders Data Reports (WTDR)						•			
Export—Import Bank							•	•	
Foreign Credit Insurance Assoc. (FCIA)								•	
Domestic Int'l. Sales Corp. (DISC)							•		•

* Foreign Trade Outlook Market Profiles; Industry Trends; Distribution and Sales Channels; Transportation Facilities; Local Business Practices and Customs; Investment Criteria; Import Procedures and Trade Regulations; and Industrial Property Rights.

** Research material developed regarding a planned exhibition and released to support promotional activities.

Cost of services may be obtained from Commerce District Offices.

Source: Industry and Trade Administration, U.S. Department of Commerce.

MARKET DATA

TOTAL INVENTORY
Central City: 92,000,000 sq.ft.
Suburban: 1,460,000,000 sq.ft.

VACANT INVENTORY
Central City: 4,600,000 sq.ft.(5.0%)
Suburban: 8,000,000 sq.ft.(.5%)

NET ABSORPTION
Central City: n/a
Suburban: n/a

CURRENT CONSTRUCTION
Central City: 250,000 sq.ft.
Suburban: n/a

MORTGAGE MONEY SUPPLY
Moderate

PRIME SOURCE OF FINANCING
Insurance Companies

NEW JERSEY–NORTHERN: INDUSTRIAL

Market Area: Newark, Hackensack, Elizabeth, Jersey City and the Northern New Jersey Metropolitan Area

1987 REVIEW

The Northern New Jersey Industrial market currently has over 1.5 billion square feet of inventory. The market area has been hurt somewhat by very low levels of unemployment and very strict environmental laws. A scarcity of developable land has resulted in relatively little construction for the past three years. Consequently, the area has experienced escalating sales and lease prices.

Vacancy rates are very low and moderate shortages are reported in every SIOR building category except high-tech. Approximately 250,000 square feet of industrial space is currently under construction.

1988 FORECAST

Market activity in 1988 will be similar to 1987 and dominated by moves within the region with relatively little net absorption. Site prices will increase sharply by 11 to 15 percent. Sales prices will increase six to 10 percent reflecting strong investor enthusiasm for this market area.

OUTLOOK

SALES PRICES
Manufacturing: Up 6-10%
Warehouse/Distribution: Up 6-10%
High Tech/R & D: Up 6-10%

LEASE PRICES
Manufacturing: Up 1-5%
Warehouse/Distribution: Up 1-5%
High Tech/R & D: Up 1-5%

ABSORPTION
Manufacturing: Same
Warehouse/Distribution: Same
High Tech/R & D: Same

CONSTRUCTION
Manufacturing: Down 6-10%
Warehouse/Distribution: Down 6-10%
High Tech/R & D: Down 11-15%

DOLLAR VOLUME
Sales: Same
Leases: Same

PROFILE OF BUILDINGS BY TYPE

	WAREHOUSING & DISTRIBUTION	MANUFACTURING	HIGH TECH/ R & D
COMPOSITION OF ABSORPTION	40%	10%	50%
RATE OF NEW CONSTRUCTION ••	Same	Same	Down 11-15%
DOLLAR VOLUME - SALES ••	Same	Same	Same
DOLLAR VOLUME - LEASES ••	Same	Same	Same

•• Compared to A Year Ago

SITE PRICES

(Dollars Per Square Foot)

LOCATION	IMPROVED SITES: LESS THAN 2 ACRES	IMPROVED SITES: 2 TO 5 ACRES	IMPROVED SITES: 5 TO 10 ACRES	IMPROVED SITES: MORE THAN 10 ACRES	UNIMPROVED SITES: LESS THAN 10 ACRES	UNIMPROVED SITES: 10 TO 100 ACRES	UNIMPROVED SITES: MORE THAN 100 ACRES
SUBURBAN	$4.50	$3.75	$3.50	$3.50	$2.50	$2.00	$1.25
CENTRAL CITY	$4.50	$4.50	$4.00	n/a	n/a	n/a	n/a

PROFILE OF BUILDINGS BY SIZE

(All prices are per square foot. Lease prices in this market area are *NET* prices.)

SIZE	SALES PRICES CENTRAL CITY	SALES PRICES SUBURBAN	LEASE PRICES CENTRAL CITY	LEASE PRICES SUBURBAN	CONSTRUCTION COSTS	VACANCY SITUATION
Less Than 5000	$25.00	$70.00	$5.00	$7.00	$37.00	Moderate Shortage
5,000 to 19,999	$25.00	$60.00	$4.75	$5.50	$34.00	Moderate Shortage
20,000 to 39,999	$25.00	$50.00	$4.25	$5.50	$37.00	Moderate Shortage
40,000 to 59,999	$25.00	$42.00	$4.25	$5.50	$29.00	Moderate Shortage
60,000 to 99,999	$25.00	$42.00	$4.25	$5.50	$29.00	Moderate Shortage
More Than 100,000	$30.00	$40.00	$4.25	$5.00	$27.00	Moderate Shortage
High Tech/R & D	n/a	$66.00	n/a	$12.00	$55.00	Balanced Market

Source: *1988 GUIDE TO INDUSTRIAL AND OFFICE REAL ESTATE MARKETS.* Society of Industrial and Office REALTORS® & the Economics and Research Division of the National Association of REALTORS®, 777 14th Street, NW, Suite 400, Washington, DC 20005-3271.

NEW JERSEY–NORTHERN: OFFICE

Market Area: Bergen, Passaic, Hudson and Essex Counties

MARKET DATA

TOTAL INVENTORY

Class A/CBD: 6,000,000 sq.ft.
Class A/OutCBD: 8,325,000 sq.ft.
Class B/CBD: 18,300,000 sq.ft.
Class B/OutCBD: 24,975,000 sq.ft.

VACANT INVENTORY

Class A/CBD: 3,000,000 sq.ft.
Class A/OutCBD: 4,000,000 sq.ft.
Class B/CBD: 1,800,000 sq.ft.
Class B/OutCBD: 2,500,000 sq.ft.

VACANCY RATES

Class A/CBD: 50.0%
Class A/OutCBD: 48.0%
Class B/CBD: 9.8%
Class B/OutCBD: 10.0%

SUBLEASE INVENTORY

Class A: 600,000 sq.ft.
Class B: 3,000,000 sq.ft.

CURRENT CONSTRUCTION

Class A/CBD: 2,500,000 sq.ft.
Class A/OutCBD: 3,500,000 sq.ft.
Class B/CBD: 600,000 sq.ft.
Class B/OutCBD: 850,000 sq.ft.

NET ABSORPTION

Class A/CBD: 2,000,000 sq.ft.
Class A/OutCBD: 2,500,000 sq.ft.
Class B/CBD: 500,000 sq.ft.
Class B/OutCBD: 637,500 sq.ft.

STANDARD WORK LETTER

Typically based on dollars per square foot. Approximate dollar value: $10

TYPICAL PARKING RATIO

CBD: 1 per 2500 sq.ft.
OutCBD: 1 per 2500 sq.ft.

AVERAGE UTILITY RATES

CBD: $2.10 per sq.ft.
OutCBD: $1.90 per sq.ft.
Space for lease is typically not separately metered.

OPERATING COST ESCALATION

Base year

MAJOR DEVELOPERS

Vantage
Trammel Crow
Lincoln
Mack Construction Company
Poskanzer Tulp Company
Cali Associates
McBride Enterprises
Hartz Development Co.

OUTLOOK

ABSORPTION: Down 1-5%
CONSTRUCTION: Up 1-5%
VACANCIES: Up 1-5%
RENTAL RATES: Up 6-10%
LANDLORD CONCESSIONS: Same

1987 REVIEW

Northern New Jersey has been experiencing extremely high growth rates during the past year due to substantially lower costs as compared with surrounding New York and its suburbs. Construction activity is ahead of absorption causing comparatively high vacancy rates. Absorption totalled over 5.6 million square feet in 1987. Nearly 7.5 million square feet of space is under construction.

SIOR panelists in Northern New Jersey report that landlord concessions typically result in a 16 to 20 percent discount factor.

1988 FORECAST

A pending collapse in employment in the financial services industry could likely result in higher vacancy rates and lower absorption in 1988. SIOR panelists expect a one to five percent increase in both construction and vacancies and a six to 10 percent increase in rental rates. Absorption will decline one to five percent.

INVENTORY PROFILE

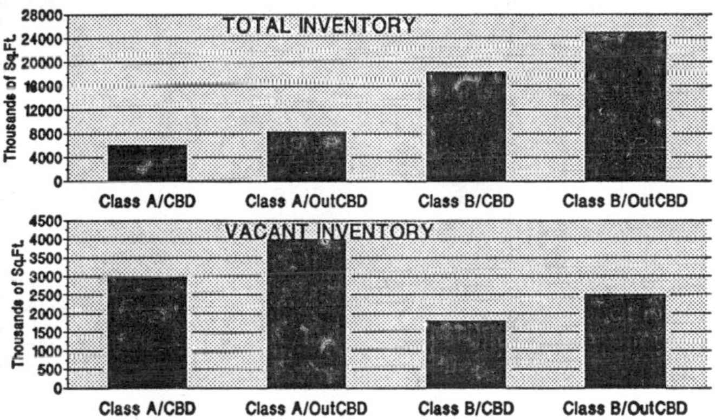

OFFICE RENTAL RATES
(Price Range/Dollars Per Square Foot)

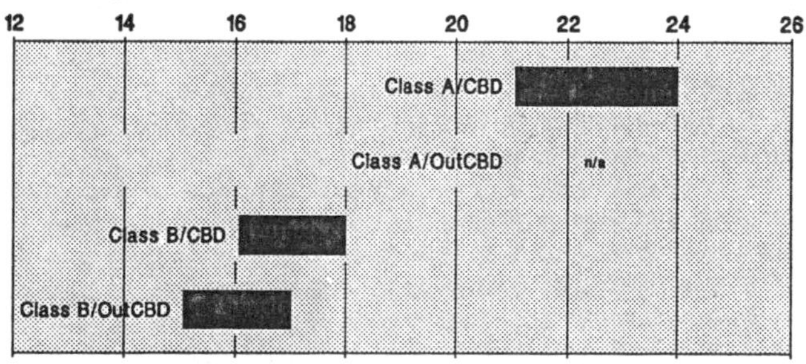

TYPICAL CONCESSIONS:

Rental Abatement
Lease Assumptions
Additional Interior Improvements

RENTAL RATE DISCOUNT FACTOR: 16-20%

Index

D

E

F

G